Current Law

Legislation Citator

STATUTE CITATOR 2008

STATUTORY INSTRUMENT CITATOR 2008

Current Law

Legislation Citator

STATUTE CITATOR 2008

STATUTORY INSTRUMENT CITATOR 2008

Sweet & Maxwell Editorial and Production Team

Shahnaila Aziz
Roger Greenwood
Lucy Naisbitt

SWEET & MAXWELL

Published and typeset in 2009 by Thomson Reuters (Legal) Limited
(Registered in England & Wales, Company No 1679046. Registered Office and address for service:
100 Avenue Road, London, NW3 3PF) trading as Sweet & Maxwell.

For further information on our products and services, visit:
www.sweetandmaxwell.co.uk

Printed in Germany by Bercker.

A CIP catalogue record for this book is available from The British Library

ISBN 978-1-84703-760-2

No forests were destroyed to make this product;
farmed timber was used and then replanted.

PREFACE

The Sweet & Maxwell Current Law Service

The Current Law Service began in 1947 and provides a comprehensive guide to developments in case law, primary legislation and secondary legislation in the UK and mainland Europe. The Current Law service presently consists of the Monthly Digests, the Year Book, Current Law Statutes, the Statute Citator, the Statutory Instrument Citator, the Case Citator, Current Law Week and European Current Law.

Also available on Current Legal Information which contains an archive of Year Books dating back to 1986 and the present year's cumulated Monthly Digests, as well as a range of other Sweet & Maxwell current awareness products such as the Current Law Case Citator, Current Law Statute Citator, the Legal Journals Index and the Financial Journals Index.

The Statute Citators and the Statutory Instrument Citators

The Current Law Statute Citators comprise six volumes covering the years 1947-1971, 1972-1988, 1989-1995, 1996-1999, 2000-2001 and 2002-2004. The Statutory Instrument Citators cover the years 1993-1995, 1996-1999, 2000-2001 and 2002-2004, 2005, 2006, 2007 and 2008.

Monthly updates to these Citators are available in Current Law Statutes. The Citators list all amendments, modifications, repeals, etc. to primary and secondary legislation made in the years indicated. This volume contains the Statute Citator 2008 and the Statutory Instrument Citator 2008.

The Statute Citator

The material within the Statute Citator is arranged in chronological order and the following information is provided:

(a) in respect of any Act passed between 1947 and 1959, where the Act is summarised in the Current Law Yearbook, and for any Act thereafter the sate of Royal Assent;

(b) in respect of any Act of any date, whether it has been repealed, amended or otherwise modified since 1947;

(c) in respect of any Act of any date, the cases in which it has been judicially considered since 1947;

(d) in respect of any Act of any date, the Statutory Instruments which have been made under its provisions; and

(e) in respect of any Act of any date, where it has been consolidated by an Act passed in 2008.

The Statutory Instrument Citator

The material within the Statutory Instrument Citator is arranged in chronological order and the following information is provided:

(a) in respect of any SI passed of any date, whether it has been repealed, amended or otherwise modified in 2008;
(b) in respect of any SI of any date, the cases in which it has been judicially considered in 2008;
(c) in respect of any SI of any date, the Statutory Instruments issued in 2008 which have been made under its provisions; and
(d) in respect of any SI of any date, where it has been consolidated by an Act passed in 2008.

HOW TO USE THIS WORK

The following fictional entries to the Statute and Statutory Instrument Citators indicate how to determine developments which hace occurred to the piece of legislation in which you are interested. Entries to the Citators are arranged chronologically.

Statute Citator	
12. Example Act 2001	—Chapter number, name of Act and year
Royal Assent May 5, 2001	—Date of Royal Assent
Commencement Orders: SI 2002/1234; SI 2003/78	—Commencement orders bringing provisions into force
s.1, enabling SI 2002/1234; SI 2003/78	—Statutory Instruments made under the powers of s.1 of the Act
s.2, see *R. v Brown* [2003] Crim.L.R. 43	—Case judicially considering s.2
s.3, amended: 2004 c.3 s.2	—s.3 amended by Act(s.2 of chapter 3 of 2004) and two SI's
s.3, enabling: SI 2001/82; S2004/70	
s.4, repealed: 2004 c.3 Sch. 4	—s.4 repealed by Schedule 4 of chapter 3 of 2004
s.4A added: SI 2002/42	—s.4A added by SI Number 42 of 2002
Sch. 8, C 2002 c. 1 s.89	—Schedule 8 considered by s.89 of chapter 1 of 2002
SI Citator	
1234 Example Regulation 2001.	—Number, name and year of SI
Reg. 2, amended: SI 2002/65 Art. 2	—reg. 2 amended by article 2 of SI number 65 of 2002
Reg. 3, revoked: 2002 c.23 Sch. 15	—reg. 3 revoked by Schedule 15 of chapter 23 of 2002
Reg. 4, see *R v. Smith* [2002] C.O.D. 54	—Case judicially considering reg. 4
Reg. 5, C. 2004 c.7 Sch 4	—reg. 5 consolidated by Schedule 4 of chapter 7 of 2004

CONTENTS

TABLE OF ABBREVIATIONS

Publishers name follows reports and journals.

(S&M = Sweet & Maxwell; ICLR = Incorporated Council of Law Reporting for England and Wales; LBC = Law Book Company of Australia; OUP = Oxford University Press; Kluwer = Kluwer Law International; Cass = Frank Cass & Co Ltd; CUP = Cambridge University Press; CLP = Central Law Publishing; TSO = The Stationery Office. LLP = Lloyd's of London Press Ltd.) All other names are in full.

A. & B. = Accounting & Business (*Association of Chartered Certified Accountants*)
A. & B.R. = Accounting and Business Research (*The Institute of Chartered Accountants in England & Wales*)
A. & O.P. & E.L.U. = Allen & Overy Pensions & Employment Law Update (*Allen & Overy*)
A. & S.L. = Air & Space Law (*Turpin Distribution Serv Ltd*)
A.A. & L. = Art Antiquity and Law (*Institute of Art and Law*)
A.B. = Advising Business (*XPL Publishing*)
A.B.T. Bull. = Association of Banking Teachers Bulletin (*Association of Banking Teachers Bulletin*)
A.C. = Law Reports Appeal Cases (*ICLR*)
A.C.D. = Administrative Court Digest (*S&M*)
A.C.L. Rev. = Asian Commercial Law Review (*S&M*)
A.D.R.L.J. = Arbitration and Dispute Resolution Law Journal (*Informa Publishing Group Ltd*)
A.D.R.L.N. = Arbitration & Dispute Resolution Law Newsletter (*Informa Publishing Group Ltd*)
A.E.L.N. = Alliance Environmental Law News (*Turpin Distribution Serv Ltd*)
A.F.I. = Asset Finance International (*Euromoney Institutional Investor Plc*)
A.I. & L. = Artificial Intelligence and Law (*Kluwer*)
A.I.A.J. = Asian International Arbitration Journal (*Kluwer*)
A.I.B. Review = Allied Irish Banks Review (*Allied Irish Banks Plc*)
A.I.I.J. = Australian Insurance Institute Journal (*Australian Insurance Institute*)
A.I.R. = Asia Insurance Review (*Ins Communications Pte Ltd*)
A.J.I.C.L. = African Journal of International and Comparative Law (*Edinburgh University Press Ltd*)
A.J.I.L. = Journal African De Droit International (*ISAL Publications*)
A.L.E.R. = American Law and Economic Review (*OUP*)
A.L.M. Brief. = Association of Lloyd's Members Briefing (*Association of Lloyd's Members*)
A.L.M. News = Association of Lloyd's Members News (*Association of Lloyd's Members*)
A.L.Q. = Arab Law Quarterly (*Brill Academic Publishers*)
A.P.J.E.L. = Asia Pacific Journal of Environmental Law (*Australian Centre for Environmental Law*)
A.P.J.H.R.L. = Asia-Pacific Journal on Human Rights and the Law (*Martinus Nijhoff Publishers*)
A.P.L.R. = Asia Pacific Law Review (*Butterworth Tolley Publishing*)
A.W. EC News. = Alsop Wilkinson EC Newsletter (*Alsop Wilkinson*)
AIDA P.I.B. = AIDA Pollution Insurance Bulletin (*Dr Carl Martin Roos*)
AVMA M. & L.J. = Action for Victims of Medical Accidents Medical & Legal Journal (*Action for Victims of Medical Accidents Services Ltd*)
Accountancy = Accountancy (*Institute of Chartered Accountants in England and Wales*)
Accountancy Irl. = Accountancy Ireland (*Institute of Chartered Accountants in Ireland*)
Accountant = Accountant (*Lafferty Publications Ltd*)
Acquisitions M. = Acquisitions Monthly (*Thomson Financial Services*)
Actuary = Actuary (*Institute of Actuaries*)
Ad. & Fos. = Adoption & Fostering (*British Agencies for Adoption & Fostering*)
Ad. & Mar. L. & P. = Advertising & Marketing Law & Practice (*Cass*)
Ad. & Mar. L.L. = Advertising & Marketing Law Letter (*Informa Publishing Group Ltd*)
Admin. L.R. = Administrative Law Reports (*Butterworth Tolley Publishing*)
Adviser = Adviser (*National Association of Citizens Advice Bureaux*)
Agri. Law = Agricultural Law (*XPL Publishing*)
All E.R. = All England Law Reports (*Butterworth Tolley Publishing*)
All E.R. (EC) = All England Law Reports European Cases (*Butterworth Tolley Publishing*)
All E.R. Rev. = All England Law Reports Annual Review (*Butterworth Tolley Publishing*)
All. E.R. (Comm) = All England Law Reports (Commercial Cases) (*Butterworth Tolley Publishing*)
Amex. B.R. = Amex Bank Review (*American Express Bank Ltd*)
Amicus Curiae = Amicus Curiae (*Institute of Advanced Legal Studies*)
Anglo-Am. L.R. = Anglo-American Law Review (*Vathek Publishing*)
App. Comp. & Comm. L. = Applied Computer & Communications Law (*Informa Publishing Group Ltd*)
Arb. L.M. = Arbitration Law Monthly (*Informa Publishing Group Ltd*)
Arbitration = Arbitration (*Chartered Institute of Arbitrators*)
Arbitration Int. = Arbitration International (*Turpin Distribution Serv Ltd*)
Arch. News = Archbold News (*S&M*)
Ass. = Assurances (*Assurances Publications Ltd*)
Astin Bull. = Astin Bulletin (*Ceuterick S.A.*)
Aviation I.R. = Aviation Insurance Report (*Informa Publishing Group Ltd*)
Axiom = Axiom (*Hammicks*)

B. & C. Int. = Benefits & Compensation International (*Pension Publications Ltd*)
B. & F.T. = Banking & Financial Training (*Armstrong Information Ltd*)

B. & M.E.B.L. = Baker & McKenzie Employee Benefits Law (*Baker & McKenzie*)
B. & M.E.L. = Baker & McKenzie Employment Law (*Baker & McKenzie*)
B. & M.P.L. = Baker & McKenzie Pensions Law (*Baker & McKenzie*)
B. & M.P.L. & E.B. = Baker & McKenzie Pensions Law & Employee Benefits (*Baker & McKenzie*)
B. & W.A. = Bacon & Woodrow Analysis (*Bacon & Woodrow*)
B. & W.P. = Bacon & Woodrow Primer (*Bacon & Woodrow*)
B. Ire. = Banking Ireland (*Institute of Bankers in Ireland*)
B. News = Business News (*HM Customs and Excise*)
B.A.J. = British Actuarial Journal (*Institute of Actuaries*)
B.B. & F.L.R. = Butterworths Banking & Financial Law Review (*Butterworth Tolley Publishing*)
B.C.C. = British Company Cases (*S&M*)
B.C.L.C. = Butterworths Company Law Cases (*Butterworth Tolley Publishing*)
B.E.Q.B. = Bank of England Quarterly Bulletin (*Bank of England*)
B.F.I.T. = Bulletin For International Taxation (*IBFD Publications BV*)
B.H. Eur. Bus. Brief = Boodle Hatfield European Business Brief (*Boodle Hatfield*)
B.H.R.C. = Butterworths Human Rights Cases (*Butterworth Tolley Publishing*)
B.I.F.D. = Bulletin for International Fiscal Documentation (*IBFD Publications BV*)
B.I.L.A.J. = British Insurance Law Association Journal (*British Insurance Law Association*)
B.J.I.B. & F.L. = Butterworths Journal of International Banking & Financial Law (*Butterworth Tolley Publishing*)
B.L.E. = Business Law Europe (*Financial Times Finance*)
B.L.G.R. = Butterworths Local Government Reports (*Butterworth Tolley Publishing*)
B.L.R. = Building Law Reports (*Informa Publishing Group Ltd*)
B.M. & I.A. = Brokers' Monthly & Insurance Adviser (*LLP*)
B.M.C.R. = Butterworths Merger Control Review (*Butterworth Tolley Publishing*)
B.M.L.R. = Butterworths Medico-Legal Reports (*Butterworth Tolley Publishing*)
B.O.F. = Back Office Focus (*Informa Publishing Group Ltd*)
B.P.I.L.S. = Butterworths Personal Injury Litigation Service (*Butterworth Tolley Publishing*)
B.P.I.R. = Bankruptcy and Personal Insolvency Reports (*Jordan & Sons Ltd*)
B.P.L. = British Pension Lawyer (*Keith Wallace Publishers*)
B.S. = Balance Sheet (*Risk Publications*)
B.S. EU Bull. = Beachcroft Stanleys EU Bulletin (*Beachcroft Stanleys*)
B.S.L.R. = BIO-Science Law Review (*Lawtext Publishing Ltd*)
B.T. = Banking Technology (*Banking Technology Ltd*)
B.T.C. = British Tax Cases (*Croner CCH Group Ltd*)
B.T.R. = British Tax Review (*S&M*)
B.V.C. = British Value Added Tax Reporter (*Croner CCH Group Ltd*)
B.W. = Banking World (*Headway, Home and Law Publishing Group Ltd*)
B.Y.B.I.L. = British Year Book of International Law (*OUP*)
BLG E.L.R. = Barlow Lyde & Gilbert Employment Law Review (*Barlow Lyde & Gilbert*)
BLG Ins. Law Q. = Barlow Lyde & Gilbert Insurance Law Quarterly (*Barlow Lyde & Gilbert*)
BLG P. & E.R.D. = Barlow Lyde & Gilbert Pollution & Environmental Risk Digest (*Barlow Lyde & Gilbert*)
Bank. L.R. = Banking Law Reports (*Informa Publishing Group Ltd*)
Bank. Law = Bankers' Law (*Guthrum House Ltd*)
Banker = Banker (*Financial Times Finance*)
Bankers Mag. = Bankers Magazine (*Warren, Gorham & Lamont*)
Bar Review = Bar Review (*Round Hall/S&M*)
Ben. File = Benefits File (*Wyatt Company (UK) Ltd*)
Bests Rev. L./H. = Best's Review Life/Health (*A.M. Best Co Inc*)
Bests Rev. P./C. = Best's Review Property/Casualty (*A.M. Best Co Inc*)
Bileta News. = Bileta Newsletter (*University of Warwick*)
Bracton L.J. = Bracton Law Journal (*Exeter University*)
Brit. J. Criminol. = British Journal of Criminology (*OUP*)
Broker = Broker (*LLP*)
Build. L.M. = Building Law Monthly (*Informa Publishing Group Ltd*)
Building = Building (*Tower Publishing Services Ltd*)
Bull. Med. E. = Bulletin of Medical Ethics (*Professional & Scientific Publications*)
Bus. Ins. = Business Insurance (*Crain Communications Inc.*)
Bus. L.B. = Business Law Bulletin (*S&M/W. Green*)
Bus. L.I. = Business Law International (*International Bar Association*)
Bus. L.R. = Business Law Review (*Turpin Distribution Serv Ltd*)
Bus. Risk = Business Risk (*Informa Publishing Group Ltd*)
Bus. T.P. = Business Tax Planning (*S&M*)
Busy P. = Busy Practitioner (*Tottel Publishing*)
Buyer = Buyer (*Informa Publishing Group Ltd*)

C. & C.C. = Consumer & Commercial Contracts (*CLT Publishing*)
C. & E.E.B.L.B. = Central and East European Business Law Bulletin (*Butterworth Tolley Publishing*)
C. & E.L. = Construction & Engineering Law (*XPL Publishing*)
C. & F.L. = Credit and Finance Law (*Informa Publishing Group Ltd*)
C. & F.L.U. = Child & Family Law Update (*SLS Legal Publications (NI)*)
C. Bank. = Central Banking (*Central Banking Publications Ltd*)
C. McK. Env. L.B. = CMS Cameron McKenna Environment Law Bulletin (*CMS Cameron McKenna & Co*)
C. Risk = Clinical Risk (*Royal Society of Medicine Press*)
C.A. = Certified Accountant (*Cork Publishing Ltd*)
C.A. Mag. = Chartered Accountant Magazine (*The Institute of Chartered Accountants of Scotland*)
C.B.S.I. Jour. = Chartered Building Societies Institute Journal (*Chartered Building Societies Institute Ltd*)
C.C. = Corporate Cover (*Corporate Cover Publications Ltd*)
C.C.A. = Cargo Claims Analysis (*Turpin Distribution Serv Ltd*)

TABLE OF ABBREVIATIONS

C.C.B. & E.B. = Clifford Chance Benefits and Employment Bulletin (*Clifford Chance*)
C.C.F. = Child Care Forum (*Child Care Forum Publishing Ltd*)
C.C.L. = Commercial Conflict of Laws (*Informa Publishing Group Ltd*)
C.C.L. Rep. = Community Care Law Reports (*Legal Action Group*)
C.C.L. Rev. = Carbon & Climate Law Review (*The Legal Publisher Lexxion*)
C.C.L.R. = Consumer Credit Law Reports (*S&M - published as part of the Encyclopaedia of Consumer Credit Law*)
C.C.M.L.R. = Clifford Chance Media Law Review (*Clifford Chance*)
C.C.R. = Chambers Client Report (*Chambers & Partners Publishing*)
C.D.F.N. = Clinical Disputes Forum Newsletter (*Clinical Disputes Forum*)
C.E. = Central European (*Euromoney Institutional Investor Plc*)
C.E.C. = European Community Cases (*S&M*)
C.F. = Corporate Finance (*Euromoney Institutional Investor Plc*)
C.F.I.L.R = Company Financial and Insolvency Law Review (*Informa Publishing Group Ltd*)
C.F.L.Q. = Child and Family Law Quarterly (*Jordan & Sons Ltd*)
C.G. = Corporate Governance (*Blackwell Publishers*)
C.G.T.B. = Capital Gains Tax Brief (*Tax and Financial Publishing*)
C.H.R.L.D. = Commonwealth Human Rights Law Digest (*Interights*)
C.I.C. Reps. = Captive Insurance Company Reports (*Risk Management Publications*)
C.I.C. Rev. = Captive Insurance Company Review (*Risk & Insurance Research Group Ltd*)
C.I.I. Jour. = Chartered Insurance Institute Journal (*Chartered Insurance Institute*)
C.I.L. = Contemporary Issues in Law (*Lawtext Publishing Limited*)
C.I.L.L. = Construction Industry Law Letter (*Informa Publishing Group Ltd*)
C.I.P.A.J. = Chartered Institute of Patent Agents Journal (*The Chartered Institute of Patent Agents*)
C.J. = Contract Journal (*Reed Business Information Ltd*)
C.J.Q. = Civil Justice Quarterly (*S&M*)
C.J.R.B. = Commercial Judicial Review Bulletin (*Chancery Law Publishing Ltd*)
C.L. & J. = Criminal Law & Justice Weekly (*Butterworth Tolley Publishing*)
C.L. & P. = Computer Law & Practice (*Butterworth Tolley Publishing*)
C.L. & P.R. = Charity Law and Practice Review (*Key Haven Publications Plc*)
C.L. Pract. = Commercial Law Practitioner (*Round Hall/S&M*)
C.L.B. = Commonwealth Law Bulletin (*Informa Publishing Group Ltd*)
C.L.C. = Commercial Law Cases (*S&M*)
C.L.D. = Company Lawyer (*S&M*)
C.L.E. = Commercial Law of Europe (*S&M*)
C.L.E.A. Newsletter = Commonwealth Legal Education Association Newsletter (*Commonwealth Legal Education Association*)
C.L.I. = Commodity Law International (*Business & Maritime Publications Ltd*)
C.L.J. = Cambridge Law Journal (*CUP*)
C.L.L. = Corporate Legal Letter (*Informa Publishing Group Ltd*)
C.L.L. Rev. = Commercial Liability Law Review (*Informa Publishing Group Ltd*)
C.L.M. = Company Law Monitor (*Informa Publishing Group Ltd*)
C.L.M.D. = Current Law Monthly Digest (*S&M/W. Green*)
C.L.N. = Construction Law Newsletter (*Informa Publishing Group Ltd*)
C.L.P. = Current Legal Problems (*OUP*)
C.L.S. = Current Law Statutes (*S&M/W. Green*)
C.L.S.R. = Computer Law & Security Report (*Elsevier Advanced Technology*)
C.L.W. = Current Law Week (*S&M*)
C.L.W.R. = Common Law World Review (*Portland Press Ltd*)
C.L.Y. = Current Law Year Book (*S&M*)
C.M. = Compliance Monitor (*Informa Publishing Group Ltd*)
C.M.I.R. = Continuous Mortality Investigation Reports (*The Alden Press*)
C.M.L. Rev. = Common Market Law Review (*Turpin Distribution Serv Ltd*)
C.M.L.J. = Capital Markets Law Journal (*OUP*)
C.M.L.N.U. = Council Mortgage Lenders News Update (*BSA CML Publications*)
C.M.L.R. = Common Market Law Reports (*S&M*)
C.M.L.R. (AR) = Common Markets Law Reports (*S&M*)
C.N. = Construction Newsletter (*Tottel Publishing*)
C.O.D. = Crown Office Digest (*S&M*)
C.P. Rep. = Civil Procedure Reports (*S&M*)
C.P. Rev. = Consumer Policy Review (*Consumers' Association Ltd*)
C.P.C.U. Jour. = Chartered Property and Casualty Underwriters Journal (*Society of Chartered Property and Law Casualty Underwriters*)
C.P.L.J. = Conveyancing and Property Law Journal (*Round Hall/S&M*)
C.P.L.R. = Civil Practice Law Reports (*XPL Publishing*)
C.P.N. = Civil Procedure News (*S&M*)
C.R. & I. = Corporate Rescue and Insolvency (*Butterworth Tolley Publishing*)
C.R.N.I. = Competition and Regulation in Network Industries (*Intersentia*)
C.S. = Corporate Solutions (*Financial Times Finance*)
C.S. Bull. = Credit Suisse Bulletin (*Credit Suisse*)
C.S.P. = Current Sentencing Practice (*S&M*)
C.S.R. = Company Secretary's Review (*Butterworth Tolley Publishing*)
C.S.R. & E.M. = Corporate Social Responsibility and Environmental Management (*John Wiley & Sons Ltd*)
C.S.W. = Chartered Surveyor Weekly (*Builder Group Ltd*)
C.T. & E.P.Q. = Capital Taxes and Estate Planning Quarterly (*S&M/Pearson Prof. Ltd*)
C.T. News & Reps. = Capital Taxes News & Reports (*S&M*)
C.T.L.R. = Computer and Telecommunications Law Review (*S&M/ESC Publishing*)
C.T.P. = Capital Tax Planning (*S&M*)
C.T.R. = Corporate Tax Review (*Key Haven Publications Plc*)
C.W. = Copyright World (*Informa Publishing Group Ltd*)
C.Y.E.L.S. = Cambridge Yearbook of European Legal Studies (*Hart Publishing Ltd*)
CJ Europe = Criminal Justice Europe (*OICJ Europe*)
CPD Papers = Criminal Law Week - CPD Extended Papers (*S&M*)

TABLE OF ABBREVIATIONS

Cambrian L.R. = Cambrian Law Review (*University College of Wales*)
Can. Ins. = Canadian Insurance (*Stone & Cox Ltd*)
Can. J.L.I. = Canadian Journal of Life Insurance (*Canadian Journal of Life Insurance Publications Ltd*)
Cap. Tax. = Capital Taxes (*S&M*)
Ch. = Law Reports Chancery Division (*ICLR*)
Charities M. = Charities Management (*Mitre House Publishing Ltd*)
Chart. I. = Charter-Party International (*S&M*)
Childright = Childright (*Children's Legal Centre Ltd*)
Civ. Lit. = Civil Litigation (*XPL Publishing*)
Civ. P.B. = Civil Practice Bulletin (*S&M/W. Green*)
Clarity = Clarity (*Cripps Harries Hall*)
Co. Acc. = Company Accountant (*Institute of Company Accountants*)
Co. L. Dig. = Company Law Digest (*Butterworth Tolley Publishing*)
Co. L.J. = Commercial Litigation Journal (*Legalease Ltd*)
Com. Jud. J. = Commonwealth Judicial Journal (*Commonwealth Magistrates & Judges Association*)
Com. L.L. = Commonwealth Law Librarian (*Legal Library Services*)
Com. Lawyer = The Commonwealth Lawyer (*Commonwealth Lawyers' Association*)
Comm. Int. = Communications International (*EMAP Communications*)
Comm. L.J. = Commercial Law Journal (*Legalease Ltd*)
Comm. Law. = Commercial Lawyer (*Chambers and Partners Publishing*)
Comm. Leases = Commercial Leases (*Informa Publishing Group Ltd*)
Comm. Prop. = Commercial Property (*XPL Publishing*)
Comms. L. = Communications Law (*Tottel Publishing*)
Comp. L. Rev. = Competition Law Review (*Competition Law Scholars Forum*)
Comp. L.I. = Competition Law Insight (*Informa Publishing Group Ltd*)
Comp. L.J. = Competition Law Journal (*Jordan Publishing Ltd*)
Comp. L.M. = Competition Law Monitor (*Informa Publishing Group Ltd*)
Comp. Law E.C. = Competition Law in the European Communities (*Fairford Press Ltd*)
Comp. Law. = Company Lawyer (*S&M*)
Comps. & Law = Computers & Law (*Society for Computers and Law*)
Con. L.D. = Construction Law Digest (*Blackwell Scientific Publications*)
Con. L.R. = Construction Law Reports (*Butterworth Tolley Publishing*)
Cons. & Mar. Law = Consumer and Marketing Law (*Informa Publishing Group Ltd*)
Cons. L. Today = Consumer Law Today (*Informa Publishing Group Ltd*)
Cons. Law = Construction Law (*Eclipse/Butterworth Tolley Publishing*)
Const. L.J. = Construction Law Journal (*S&M*)
Const. Ref. = Constitutional Reform (*Constitutional Reform Centre*)
Consum. L.J. = Consumer Law Journal (*CDC Publications*)
Consumer C. = Consumer Credit (*Consumer Credit Trade Association*)
Conv. = Conveyancer and Property Lawyer (*S&M*)
Corp. Brief. = Corporate Briefing (*Informa Publishing Group Ltd*)
Corp. C. = Corporate Counsel (*Commercial Lawyer*)
Costs L.R. = Costs Law Reports (*XPL Publishing*)
Counsel = Counsel (*Butterworth Tolley Publishing*)
Cov. L.J. = Coventry Law Journal (*Coventry University*)
Cr. App. R. = Criminal Appeal Reports (*S&M*)
Cr. App. R. (S.) = Criminal Appeal Reports (Sentencing) (*S&M*)
Crim. L.B. = Criminal Law Bulletin (*S&M/W. Green*)
Crim. L.F. = Criminal Law Forum (*Springer*)
Crim. L.R. = Criminal Law Review (*S&M*)
Crim. Law. = Criminal Lawyer (*Tottel Publishing*)
Criminal Law Week = Criminal Law Week (*S&M*)
Criminologist = Criminologist (*Butterworth Tolley Publishing*)

D. & P. = Development & Planning (*Policy Journals*)
D.C.J. = Defense Counsel Journal (*International Association of Defense Counsels*)
D.D. & R.M. = Due Diligence & Risk Management (*XPL Publishing*)
D.E. & E.S.L.R. = Digital Evidence and Electronic Signature Law Review (*Pario Communications Ltd*)
D.E.J. = Digital Evidence Journal (*Pario Communications Ltd*)
D.F.I. = Derivatives & Financial Instruments (*IBFD Publications BV*)
D.H.B. & W. F. & T. News. = Denton Hall Burgin & Warren Film & Television Newsletter (*Denton Hall*)
D.H.E.L. = Denton Hall Energy Law (*Denton Hall*)
D.H.E.N. = Denton Hall Employment Newsletter (*Denton Hall*)
D.H.I.T. News. = Denton Hall Information Technology Newsletter (*Denton Hall*)
D.H.P.N. = Denton Hall Pensions Newsletter (*Denton Hall*)
D.H.T.I. News. = Denton Hall The Interface Newsletter (*Denton Hall*)
D.I. Bank. & F.N. = Denton International Banking & Finance Newsletter (*Denton Hall*)
D.I. Comp. & EC N. = Denton International Competition and EC Newsletter (*Denton Hall*)
D.I. F.T. News. = Denton International Film & Television Newsletter (*Denton International*)
D.I.C.S. = Denton International Creative Spark (*Denton International*)
D.L. = Daily List (*TSO*)
D.L.B. Bus. Brief = Dibb Lupton Broomhead Business Brief (*Dibb Lupton Broomhead*)
D.L.R. = Discrimination Law Reports (*CLT Publishing*)
D.N.Q. = Domain Names Quarterly (*Informa Publishing Group Ltd*)
D.P. & P.P. = Data Protection and Privacy Practice (*Pinsent Masons*)
D.P.I. = Data Protection Ireland (*Privacy & Data Protection*)
D.P.L. & P. = Data Protection Law & Policy (*Cecile Park Publishing Ltd*)
D.P.Q. = Data Protection Quarterly (*Pinsent Masons*)
D.U.L.J. = Dublin University Law Journal (*Round Hall/S&M*)
DLi = DLi University College Galway Law Graduates Association Gazette (*Toevaro Investments Ltd*)
Data Base Reps. = Data Base Reports (*Insurance Information Institute*)
De Voil I.T.I. = De Voil Indirect Tax Intelligence (*Butterworth Tolley Publishing*)

Denning L.J. = Denning Law Journal (*University of Buckingham*)

E & S.L.J. = Entertainment and Sports Law Journal (*Warwick*)
E-Law Review = E-Law Review (*S&M/W. Green*)
E. & L. = Education and the Law (*Taylor & Francis Ltd*)
E. & P. = International Journal of Evidence & Proof (*Vathek Publishing*)
E. St. A.L. = European State Aid Law Quarterly (*Lexxion Verlagsgesellschaft mbH*)
E.A.F. = European Accounting Focus (*Informa Publishing Group Ltd*)
E.B. & F.L.J. = European Banking & Financial Law Journal (*Intersentia NV*)
E.B. Mag. = Environment Business Magazine (*Faversham House Group Ltd*)
E.B.J. = Employee Benefits Journal (*International Foundation of Employee Benefits Plans Inc*)
E.B.L. = Electronic Business Law (*Eclipse/Butterworth Tolley Publishing*)
E.B.L. Rev. = European Business Law Review (*Turpin Distribution Serv Ltd*)
E.B.L.R. = Electronic Business Law Reports (*Butterworth Tolley Publishing*)
E.B.M. = European Business Monitor (*Butterworth Tolley Publishing*)
E.B.O.R. = European Business Organization Law Review (*CUP*)
E.C. Law = European Company Law (*Kluwer*)
E.C.A. = Elderly Client Adviser (*Ark Publishing*)
E.C.C. = European Commercial Cases (*S&M*)
E.C.D.R. = European Copyright and Design Reports (*S&M*)
E.C.F.R. = European Company and Financial Law Review (*Rhenus Medien Logistik GmbH & Co*)
E.C.J. = Environmental Claims Journal (*Executive Enterprises Publications Co Inc*)
E.C.L. = European Corporate Lawyer (*Legalease Ltd*)
E.C.L. & P. = E-Commerce Law & Policy (*Cecile Park Publishing Ltd*)
E.C.L. Rep. = E-Commerce Law Reports (*Cecile Park Publishing Ltd*)
E.C.L. Rev. = Electronic Communications Law Review (*Turpin Distribution Serv Ltd*)
E.C.L. Review = European Constitutional Law Review (*CUP*)
E.C.L.R. = European Competition Law Review (*S&M/ESC Publishing*)
E.D.D. & R.M. = Environmental Due Diligence & Risk Management (*XPL Publishing*)
E.E.B.L. = East European Business Law (*Financial Times Finance*)
E.E.E.L.R. = European Energy and Environmental Law Review (*Turpin Distribution Serv Ltd*)
E.E.F.N. = Eastern European Forum Newsletter (*International Bar Association*)
E.E.I.R. = East European Insurance Report (*Financial Times Finance*)
E.E.L.R. = European Environmental Law Review (*Turpin Distribution Serv Ltd*)
E.F.A. Rev. = European Foreign Affairs Review (*Turpin Distribution Serv Ltd*)
E.F.F.L.R. = European Food and Feed Law Review (*Lexxion Verlagsgesellschaft mbH*)
E.F.P.L. & P. = E-Finance & Payments Law & Policy (*Cecile Park Publishing Ltd*)
E.F.S.L. = European Financial Services Law (*Turpin Distribution Serv Ltd*)
E.G. = Estates Gazette (*Estates Gazette Ltd*)
E.G.C.S. = Estates Gazette Case Summaries (*Estates Gazette Ltd*)
E.G.L.R. = Estates Gazette Law Reports (*Estates Gazette Ltd*)
E.H.L.R. = Environmental Health Law Reports (*S&M*)
E.H.R.L.R. = European Human Rights Law Review (*S&M*)
E.H.R.R. = European Human Rights Reports (*S&M*)
E.I.B. = Environment Information Bulletin (*Eclipse/Butterworth Tolley Publishing*)
E.I.M. = European Insurance Market (*Informa Publishing Group Ltd*)
E.I.P.R. = European Intellectual Property Review (*S&M/ESC Publishing*)
E.I.R.R. = European Industrial Relations Review (*Reed Business Information Ltd*)
E.I.S. = European Insurance Strategies (*Evandale Publishing Co Ltd*)
E.J.C. = European Journal of Criminology (*Sage Publications Ltd*)
E.J.C.L. = Electronic Journal of Comparative Law (*Electronic Journal of Comparative Law*)
E.J.E.L. & P. = European Journal for Education Law and Policy (*Turpin Distribution Serv Ltd*)
E.J.H.L. = European Journal of Health Law (*Martinus Nijhoff Publishers*)
E.J.I.L. = European Journal of International Law (*OUP*)
E.J.L.E. = European Journal of Legal Education (*Routledge Taylor & Francis Group*)
E.J.L.R. = European Journal of Law Reform (*Turpin Distribution Serv Ltd*)
E.J.M.L. = European Journal of Migration and Law (*Martinus Nijhoff Publishers*)
E.J.R.B. = Environmental Judicial Review Bulletin (*Chancery Law Publishing Ltd*)
E.J.S.S. = European Journal of Social Security (*Intersentia NV*)
E.L. = Equitable Lawyer (*Gostick Hall Publications*)
E.L. & P.D. = European Life & Pensions Digest (*European Business Digest Ltd*)
E.L. Rev. = European Law Review (*S&M*)
E.L.A. Briefing = Employment Lawyers Association Briefing (*Employment Lawyers Association*)
E.L.B. = Environment Law Brief (*Informa Publishing Group Ltd*)
E.L.F. = Elder Law and Finance (*Jordan & Sons Ltd*)
E.L.J. = European Law Journal (*Blackwell Publishers*)
E.L.L.R. = Environmental Liability Law Review (*Koninklijke Vermande BV*)
E.L.M. = Environmental Law & Management (*Lawtext Publishing Limited*)
E.L.R. = Education Law Reports (*Jordan & Sons Ltd*)
E.L.R.I. = Employment Law Review - Ireland (*First Law*)
E.M. = European Mergers (*Informa Publishing Group Ltd*)
E.M.I. = Emerging Markets Investor (*Chiltern Magazine Services*)
E.M.L.R. = Entertainment and Media Law Reports (*S&M/ESC Publishing*)
E.N.P.R. = European National Patent Reports (*S&M*)
E.O.R. = Equal Opportunities Review (*Michael Rubenstein Publishing*)
E.O.R. Dig. = Equal Opportunities Review and Discrimination Case Law Digest (*Eclipse/Butterworth Tolley Publishing*)

TABLE OF ABBREVIATIONS

E.P. & L. = Environmental Policy and Law (*IOS Press*)
E.P.E.F. = Economic Policy: A European Forum (*CUP*)
E.P.G. = Environmental Policy and Governance (*John Wiley & Sons Ltd*)
E.P.I.S. = EMIS Personal Injury Service (*XPL Publishing*)
E.P.L. = European Public Law (*Turpin Distribution Serv Ltd*)
E.P.L.I. = Education, Public Law and the Individual (*Education Law Association Ltd*)
E.P.O.R. = European Patent Office Reports (*S&M*)
E.P.P.P.L.R. = European Public Private Partnership Law Review (*Lexxion Verlagsgesellschaft mbH*)
E.P.S. = EMIS Property Service (*XPL Publishing*)
E.R.C.L. = European Review of Contract Law (*Walter de Gruyter GmbH & Co. KG*)
E.R.P.L. = European Review of Private Law (*Turpin Distribution Serv Ltd*)
E.S.L.J. = E-Signature Law Journal (*Pario Communications Ltd*)
E.T. = Estates Times (*Morgan Grampian Plc*)
E.T.M.R. = European Trade Marks Reports (*S&M*)
E.U. News = European Union News (*S&M*)
E.W.C.B. = European Works Councils Bulletin (*Eclipse/Butterworth Tolley Publishing*)
EC C.P.N. = European Commission Competition Policy Newsletter (*Commission of The European Communities*)
EC E.M. = EC Energy Monthly (*Financial Times Finance*)
EC F.L.M. = EC Food Law Monthly (*Agra Europe (London) Ltd*)
EC P.R. = EC Packaging Report (*Agra Europe (London) Ltd*)
EC T.J. = EC Tax Journal (*Key Haven Publications Plc*)
EC T.R. = EC Tax Review (*Turpin Distribution Serv Ltd*)
EDI L.R. = Electronic Data Interchange Law Review (*Turpin Distribution Serv Ltd*)
EMIS E.L.S. = EMIS E-Law Service (*XPL Publishing*)
ENDS = ENDS Report (*Environmental Data Services Ltd*)
EPLC Brief = European Pharma Law Centre Brief (*European Pharma Law Centre Ltd*)
EU Brief. Notes = EU Briefing Notes (*SJ Berwin & Co*)
EU Focus = EU Focus (*S&M*)
Eagle = Eagle (*Stratton Publishing Ltd*)
Ec. Aff. = Economic Affairs (*The Institute of Economic Affairs*)
Ec. Rev. = Economic Review (*Philip Allan Publishers Ltd*)
Ecc. L.J. = Ecclesiastical Law Journal (*CUP*)
Eco M. & A. = Eco-Management & Auditing (*John Wiley & Sons Ltd*)
Ed. C.R. = Education Case Reports (*S&M*)
Ed. L.M. = Education Law Monitor (*Informa Publishing Group Ltd*)
Ed. Law = Education Law Journal (*Jordan & Sons Ltd*)
Edin. L.R. = Edinburgh Law Review (*Edinburgh University Press Ltd*)
Emp. L. & L. = Employment Law & Litigation (*XPL Publishing*)
Emp. L. & L.U. = Employment Law and Litigation Updates (*XPL Publishing*)
Emp. L. Brief. = Employment Law Briefing (*S&M*)
Emp. L.B. = Employment Law Bulletin (*S&M/W. Green*)
Emp. L.J. = Employment Law Journal (*Legalease Ltd*)
Emp. L.N. = Employment Law Newsletter (*S&M*)
Emp. Law. = Employment Lawyer (*S&M*)
Emp. Lit. = Employment Litigation (*XPL Publishing*)
Employ. L. = Employer's Law (*Reed Business Information Ltd*)
Enc. C.S.P. = Encyclopedia of Current Sentencing Practice (*S&M*)
Enc. F.S.L. = Encyclopedia of Financial Services Law (*S&M*)
Enc. I.T.L. = Encyclopedia of Information Technology Law (*S&M*)
Enc. P.L. & P. = Encyclopedia of Planning Law & Practice (*S&M*)
Ent. L.R. = Entertainment Law Review (*S&M/ESC Publishing*)
Ent. Law = Entertainment Law (*Cass*)
Env. I.B. = Environment In Business (*Lexis Nexis*)
Env. L. Rev. = Environmental Law Review (*Vathek Publishing*)
Env. L.B. = Environmental Law Bulletin (*S&M/W. Green*)
Env. L.M. = Environmental Law Monthly (*Informa Publishing Group Ltd*)
Env. L.N. = Environmental Law Newsletter (*SJ Berwin & Co*)
Env. L.R. = Environmental Law Reports (*S&M*)
Env. Law = Environmental Law (*UKELA*)
Env. Liability = Environmental Liability (*Lawtext Publishing Ltd*)
Env. Man. = Environmental Manager (*Informa Publishing Group Ltd*)
Env. Risk = Environment Risk (*Euromoney Institutional Investor Plc*)
Eu. L.F. = European Legal Forum (*IPR Verlag GmbH*)
Eu. L.R. = European Law Reports (*Hart Publishing Ltd*)
Eur. Access = European Access (*Chadwyck Healey Ltd*)
Eur. Counsel = European Counsel (*Legal & Commercial Publishing*)
Eur. J. Crime Cr. L. Cr. J. = European Journal of Crime, Criminal Law and Criminal Justice (*Martinus Nijhoff Publishers*)
Eurlegal = Eurlegal (*Incorporated Law Society of Ireland*)
Euro. C.J. = European Competition Journal (*Hart Publishing Ltd*)
Euro. C.L. = European Current Law (*S&M*)
Euro. Env. = European Environment (*John Wiley & Sons Ltd*)
Euro. L.B. = European Legal Business (*Legalease Ltd*)
Euro. L.M. = European Law Monitor (*Informa Publishing Group Ltd*)
Euro. Law. = European Lawyer (*The European Lawyer Ltd*)
Euro. T.L. = European Transport Law (*Robert H Wijffels*)
Euro. T.S. = European Tax Service (*BNA International Inc*)
Euro. Tax. = European Taxation (*IBFD Publications BV*)
Euromoney = Euromoney (*Euromoney Institutional Investor Plc*)
Eurosafety = Eurosafety (*Butterworth Tolley Publishing*)
Exp. = Experiodica (*Swiss Reinsurance Company*)
Expert = Expert (*Bristish Academy of Experts*)

TABLE OF ABBREVIATIONS

F. & C.L. = Finance & Credit Law (*Informa Publishing Group Ltd*)
F. & D. = Finance & Development (*Finance & Development*)
F. & D.L.M. = Food & Drink Law Monthly (*Agra Europe*)
F. & D.L.R. = Futures & Derivatives Law Review (*Routledge-Cavendish*)
F.A. = Financial Adviser (*Financial Times Finance*)
F.C.R. = Family Court Reporter (*Butterworth Tolley Publishing*)
F.D. & D.I.B. = Food, Drinks & Drugs Industry Bulletin (*Informa Publishing Group Ltd*)
F.E. & P.I. = Freshfields Employment & Pensions Issues (*Freshfields*)
F.I. = Fraud Intelligence (*Informa Publishing Group Ltd*)
F.I.T.A.R. = Financial Instruments Tax & Accounting Review (*Informa Publishing Group Ltd*)
F.L.R. = Family Law Reports (*Jordan & Sons Ltd*)
F.L.T. = Family LawToday (*Informa Publishing Group Ltd*)
F.M. = Financial Management (*Chartered Institute Management Accountants*)
F.O.I. = Freedom of Information (*Privacy & Data Protection*)
F.P.B. = Four Pillars Bulletin (*Geneva Association*)
F.R. = Financial Regulator (*Central Banking Publications Ltd*)
F.R. & F.N. = Financial Reinsurance & Futures Newsletter (*Informa Publishing Group Ltd*)
F.R.B.N.Y.Q.R. = Federal Reserve Bank of New York Quarterly Review (*Federal Reserve Bank of New York*)
F.R.I. = Financial Regulation International (*Informa Publishing Group Ltd*)
F.R.N. = Financial Reinsurance Newsletter (*Informa Publishing Group Ltd*)
F.R.R. = Financial Regulation Report (*Informa Publishing Group Ltd*)
F.S. Bulletin = Financial Services Bulletin (*Informa Publishing Group Ltd*)
F.S.B. = Financial Services Brief (*S&M*)
F.S.L.J. = Financial Services Law Journal (*Round Hall/S&M*)
F.S.L.L. = Financial Services Law Letter (*Informa Publishing Group Ltd*)
F.S.R. = Fleet Street Reports (*S&M*)
F.T.I. = Financial Technology Insight (*Elsevier Advanced Technology*)
Fairplay = Fairplay (*Fairplay Publications Ltd*)
Fam. = Law Reports Family Division (*ICLR*)
Fam. L.B. = Family Law Bulletin (*S&M/W. Green*)
Fam. L.J. = Family Law Journal (*Legalease Ltd*)
Fam. L.R. = Family Law Reports (Greens) (*S&M/W. Green*)
Fam. Law = Family Law (*Jordan & Sons Ltd*)
Fam. Law B. = Family Law Bulletin (*S&M*)
Fam. M. = Family Matters (*S&M*)
Fam. Med. = Family Mediation (*National Association of Family Mediation & Conciliation Services*)
Farm Law = Farm Law (*Agra Europe*)
Farm T. & F. = Farm Tax & Finance (*Tax and Financial Publishing*)
Farm T.B. = Farm Tax Brief (*Informa Publishing Group Ltd*)
Fem. L.S. = Feminist Legal Studies (*Turpin Distribution Serv Ltd*)
Fin. Con. = Finance Confidential (*Fleet Street Publications Ltd*)
Focus = Focus (*Zurich International (UK) Ltd*)
Food & Drugs I.B. = Food & Drugs Industry Bulletin (*Informa Publishing Group Ltd*)
Food L.M. = Food Law Monthly (*Agra Europe*)
Foresight = Foresight (*Risk & Insurance Research Group Ltd*)

G.C. = Global Crime (*Routledge Taylor & Francis Group*)
G.C.L.R. = Global Competition Litigation Review (*S&M/ESC Publishing*)
G.C.R. = Global Competition Review (*Law Business Research Ltd*)
G.I.L.S.I. = Gazette Incorporated Law Society of Ireland (*The Law Society*)
G.L. & B. = Global Law & Business (*Global Law & Business Ltd*)
G.L.J. = Guernsey Law Journal (*Her Majesty's Greffier*)
G.L.S.I. = Gazette of the Law Society Ireland (*The Law Society*)
G.P.R.I.I.P. = Geneva Papers on Risk & Insurance Issues & Practice (*Geneva Association*)
G.P.R.I.T. = Geneva Papers on Risk & Insurance: Theory (*Geneva Association*)
G.R. = Global Reinsurance (*Southern Magazines Ltd*)
G.R.A. = Global Re Analysis (*Southern Magazines Ltd*)
G.T.B. = Global Telecoms Business (*Euromoney Institutional Investor Plc*)
G.W.D. = Greens Weekly Digest (*S&M/W. Green*)
Gen. Ins. = General Insurance (*Mitre House Publishing Ltd*)
Global Counsel = Global Counsel (*Legal & Commercial Publishing*)
Go. J.I.L. = Gottingen Journal of International Law (*Universitatsverlag Gottingen*)
Gov. = Governance (*Plaza Publishing*)
Guide = Guide (*S&M*)

H. & S.B. = Health and Safety Bulletin (*Butterworth Tolley Publishing*)
H. & S.L. = Health & Safety Law (*XPL Publishing*)
H. & S.M. = Health & Safety Monitor (*Silverdog Publishing*)
H. & S.W. = Health & Safety at Work (*Butterworth Tolley Publishing*)
H.A.L.L. = Health & Law Letter (*Business & Maritime Publications*)
H.C.L.M. = High Court Litigation Manual (*S&M*)
H.C.W.I.B. = House of Commons Weekly Information Bulletin (*TSO*)
H.K.L.J. = Hong Kong Law Journal (*Hong Kong Law Journal Ltd*)
H.L.J. = Hibernian Law Journal (*Law Society of Ireland*)
H.L.M. = Housing Law Monitor (*Informa Publishing Group Ltd*)
H.L.R. = Housing Law Reports (*S&M*)
H.R. = Human Rights (*Jordan & Sons Ltd*)
H.R. & I.L.D. = Human Rights & International Legal Discourse (*Intersentia*)
H.R. & UK P. = Human Rights & UK Practice (*XPL Publishing*)
H.R.C.D. = Human Rights Case Digest (*S&M*)
H.R.L. Rev. = Human Rights Law Review (*OUP*)
H.R.L.R. = Human Rights Law Reports (*S&M*)
H.S. = Hazardous Substances (*Informa Publishing Group Ltd*)
H.S. Brief. = Herbert Smith Briefing (*Herbert Smith*)
H.S. at W. = Health & Safety at Work (*Tottel Publishing*)
H.S.I. = Halsbury's Statutory Instruments (*Legal Library Services Ltd*)

H.S.I.B. = Health & Safety Information Bulletin (*Butterworth Tolley Publishing*)
Haldane S.E.L.B. = Haldane Society Employment Law Bulletin (*Haldane Society of Socialist Lawyers*)
Halsbury S. = Halsbury's Statutes (*Legal Library Services Ltd*)
Health Law = Health Law for Healthcare Professionals (*Informa Publishing Group Ltd*)
Hert. L.J. = Hertfordshire Law Journal (*University of Hertfordshire*)
Hold. L.R. = Holdsworth Law Review (*University of Birmingham*)
Hous. L.R. = Greens Housing Law Reports (*S&M/W. Green*)
Howard Journal = Howard Journal of Criminal Justice (*Blackwell Publishers*)
Hull C.A. = Hull Claims Analysis (*S&M*)

I. & C.T.L. = Information & Communications Technology Law (*Taylor & Francis Ltd*)
I. & N.L. & P. = Immigration & Nationality Law & Practice (*Butterworth Tolley Publishing*)
I. & P.E. = Investment & Pensions Europe (*IPE International Publishers Ltd*)
I. & R.L.B. = Insurance & Reinsurance Law Briefing (*S&M*)
I. Bull. = Interights Bulletin (*Interights*)
I. Prop. = Intellectual Property (*CLT Publishing*)
I.A.N.L. = Immigration, Asylum and Nationality Law (*Tottel Publishing*)
I.B.F.L. = International Banking and Financial Law (*S&M*)
I.B.L. = International Business Lawyer (*International Bar Association*)
I.B.L.J. = International Business Law Journal (*S&M*)
I.B.L.Q. = Irish Business Law Quarterly (*Clarus Press*)
I.B.R. = Irish Banking Review (*Irish Bankers' Federation*)
I.C. = Investors Chronicle (*Investors Chronicle Publications Ltd*)
I.C. Lit. = International Commercial Litigation (*Euromoney Institutional Investor Plc*)
I.C.C.L.J. = International and Comparative Corporate Law Journal (*Institute of Advanced Legal Studies*)
I.C.C.L.R. = International Company and Commercial Law Review (*S&M/ESC Publishing*)
I.C.L. = International Corporate Law (*Euromoney Institutional Investor Plc*)
I.C.L. Rev. = International Construction Law Review (*Informa Publishing Group Ltd*)
I.C.L.B. = International Corporate Law Bulletin (*Turpin Distribution Serv Ltd*)
I.C.L.J. = Irish Criminal Law Journal (*Round Hall/S&M*)
I.C.L.M.D. = Irish Current Law Monthly Digest (*Round Hall/S&M*)
I.C.L.Q. = International & Comparative Law Quarterly (*CUP*)
I.C.L.S.A. = Irish Current Law Statutes Annotated (*Round Hall/S&M*)
I.C.R. = Industrial Cases Reports (*ICLR*)
I.E.L.J. = Irish Employment Law Journal (*Round Hall/S&M*)
I.E.L.R. = International Energy Law Review (*S&M*)
I.E.L.T.R. = International Energy Law & Taxation Review (*S&M*)
I.F.L. = International Family Law (*Jordan & Sons Ltd*)
I.F.L. Rev. = International Financial Law Review (*Euromoney Institutional Investor Plc*)
I.H.L. = In-House Lawyer (*Legalease Ltd*)
I.H.R.R. = International Human Rights Reports (*University of Nottingham, School of Law*)
I.I.E.L. = Immigration and International Employment Law (*Eclipse/Butterworth Tolley Publishing*)
I.I.I. = Insurance Industry International (*Lafferty Publications Ltd*)
I.I.L. Rev. = International Internet Law Review (*Euromoney Institutional Investor Plc*)
I.I.L.R. = Irish Insurance Law Review (*Round Hall/S&M*)
I.I.P.R. = Irish Intellectual Property Review (*Round Hall/S&M*)
I.I.R. = International Insolvency Review (*John Wiley & Sons Ltd*)
I.I.U. = Insurance Issues Update (*Insurance Information Institute*)
I.J.B.L. = International Journal of Biosciences and the Law (*A B Academic Publishers*)
I.J.C.L. = International Journal of Constitutional Law (*OUP*)
I.J.C.L.E. = International Journal of Clinical Legal Education (*Northumbria Law Press*)
I.J.C.L.P. = International Journal of Communications Law and Policy (*Institute for Information, Telecommunications and Media Law*)
I.J.D.G. = International Journal of Disclosure and Governance (*Palgrave Macmillan*)
I.J.D.L. = International Journal of Discrimination and the Law (*A B Academic Publishers*)
I.J.E.C.L. = International Journal of Estuarine and Coastal Law (*Turpin Distribution Serv Ltd*)
I.J.E.C.L. & P. = International Journal of Electronic Commerce Law & Practice (*XPL Publishing*)
I.J.E.L. = Irish Journal of European Law (*Round Hall/S&M*)
I.J.F.D.L. = International Journal of Franchising and Distribution Law (*Richmond Law & Tax Ltd*)
I.J.F.L. = Irish Journal of Family Law (*Round Hall/S&M*)
I.J.H.R. = International Journal of Human Rights (*Taylor & Francis Ltd*)
I.J.I.L. = International Journal of Insurance Law (*Informa Publishing Group Ltd*)
I.J.L. & I.T. = International Journal of Law & Information Technology (*OUP*)
I.J.L.C.J. = International Journal of Law Crime and Justice (*Elsevier BV*)
I.J.L.P. = International Journal of the Legal Profession (*Taylor & Francis Ltd*)
I.J.M.C.L. = International Journal of Marine & Coastal Law (*Martinus Nijhoff Publishers*)
I.J.O.S.L. = International Journal Of Shipping Law (*Informa Publishing Group Ltd*)
I.J.R.L. = International Journal of Refugee Law (*OUP*)
I.J.R.L. & P. = International Journal of Regulatory Law & Practice (*Henry Stewart Publications*)
I.J.S.L. = International Journal for the Semiotics of Law (*Turpin Distribution Serv Ltd*)
I.J.T. = Irish Journal of Taxation (*University of Ulster*)
I.J.T.J. = International Journal of Transitional Justice (*OUP*)
I.L. & P. = Insolvency Law & Practice (*Butterworth Tolley Publishing*)
I.L. & S. = Islamic Law and Society (*Brill Academic Publishers*)
I.L. Pr. = International Litigation Procedure (*S&M*)
I.L.D. = Immigration Law Digest (*Immigration Advisory Service*)
I.L.F.M. = International Law Firm Management (*Euromoney Institutional Investor Plc*)

TABLE OF ABBREVIATIONS

I.L.J. = Industrial Law Journal (*OUP*)
I.L.P. = International Legal Practitioner (*International Bar Association*)
I.L.R.M. = Irish Law Reports Monthly (*Round Hall/S&M*)
I.L.T. = Irish Law Times (*Round Hall/S&M*)
I.M. & E. = Insurance: Mathematics & Economics (*Elsevier Science Publishers*)
I.M.L. = International Media Law (*S&M*)
I.N.L. = Internet Newsletter for Lawyers (*Delia Venables*)
I.N.L.R. = Immigration and Nationality Law Reports (*Jordan & Sons Ltd*)
I.O.L.R. = International Organizations Law Review (*Martinus Nijhoff Publishers*)
I.P. = International Peacekeeping (*Kluwer*)
I.P. & I.T. Law = Intellectual Property & Information Technology Law (*XPL Publishing*)
I.P. & I.T.L.U. = Intellectual Property & Information Technology Law Updates (*XPL Publishing*)
I.P. & T. = Intellectual Property and Technology (*Butterworth Tolley Publishing*)
I.P. Business = Intellectual Property Business (*OUP*)
I.P. Law. = Intellectual Property Lawyer (*S&M*)
I.P. News. = Intellectual Property Newsletter (*Informa Publishing Group Ltd*)
I.P.B. Rev. = Intellectual Property in Business Review (*Euromoney Institutional Investor Plc*)
I.P.B. Rev. Brief. = Intellectual Property in Business Briefing (*Euromoney Institutional Investor Plc*)
I.P.D. = Intellectual Property Decisions (*Informa Publishing Group Ltd*)
I.P.E.L.J. = Irish Planning and Environmental Law Journal (*Round Hall/S&M*)
I.P.L. = International Pension Lawyer (*International Association of Pension and Employee Benefits Lawyers*)
I.P.Q. = Intellectual Property Quarterly (*S&M*)
I.R.L.A. = Insurance & Reinsurance Law Alert (*Informa Publishing Group Ltd*)
I.R.L.B. = Industrial Relations Law Bulletin (*Reed Business Information Ltd*)
I.R.L.C.T. = International Review of Law Computers & Technology (*Taylor & Francis Ltd*)
I.R.L.I.B. = Industrial Relations Legal Information Bulletin (*Eclipse/Butterworth Tolley Publishing*)
I.R.L.N. = Insurance and Reinsurance Law Newsletter (*Informa Publishing Group Ltd*)
I.R.L.R. = Industrial Relations Law Reports (*Eclipse/Butterworth Tolley Publishing*)
I.R.R.R. = Industrial Relations Review and Report (*Eclipse/Butterworth Tolley Publishing*)
I.R.S.R. = Insurance & Reinsurance Solvency Report (*Informa Publishing Group Ltd*)
I.R.T.B. = Inland Revenue Tax Bulletin (*Inland Revenue*)
I.R.V. = International Review of Victimology (*A B Academic Publishers*)
I.S.B. = Insurance Systems Bulletin (*Chiltern Magazine Services*)
I.S.I. = Insurance Systems International (*Informa Publishing Group Ltd*)
I.S.L.J. = International Sports Law Journal (*TMC Asser Press*)
I.S.L.R. = International Sports Law Review (*S&M*)
I.S.L.Rev. = Irish Student Law Review (*The Honourable Society of Kings' Inn*)
I.S.R. = International Securitisation Report (*IFA Publishing Ltd*)
I.T. & C.L.J. = Information Technology & Communications Law Journal (*Legalease Ltd*)
I.T. Rep. = International Tax Report (*Informa Publishing Group Ltd*)
I.T. Rev. = International Tax Review (*Euromoney Institutional Investor Plc*)
I.T.E.L.R. = International Trust and Estate Law Reports (*Tottel Publishing*)
I.T.I. = Information Technology in Insurance (*Informa Publishing Group Ltd*)
I.T.L. Rep. = International Tax Law Reports (*Butterworth Tolley Publishing*)
I.T.L.J. = International Travel Law Journal (*The Travel Law Centre*)
I.T.L.Q. = International Trade Law Quarterly (*Informa Publishing Group Ltd*)
I.T.L.R. = International Technology Law Review (*Euromoney Institutional Investor Plc*)
I.T.P.J. = International Transfer Pricing Journal (*IBFD Publications BV*)
I.V.M. = International VAT Monitor (*IBFD Publications BV*)
I.Y.L.C.T. = International Yearbook of Law, Computers & Technology (*Taylor & Francis Ltd*)
IALS Bull. = Institute of Advanced Legal Studies Bulletin (*Institute of Advanced Legal Studies*)
IBIS Rep. = International Benefits Information Service Report (*Charles D. Spencer & Associates, Inc.*)
IBIS Review = International Benefits Information Service Review (*Charles D. Spencer & Associates Inc*)
IDS Brief = IDS Brief Employment Law & Practice (*S&M/IDS*)
IDS D.W. = IDS Diversity at Work (*S&M/IDS*)
IDS Emp. E. = IDS Employment Europe (*S&M/IDS*)
IDS Emp. L. Brief = IDS Employment Law Brief (*S&M/IDS*)
IDS Euro. R. = IDS European Report (*S&M/IDS*)
IDS P.B. = IDS Pensions Bulletin (*S&M/IDS*)
IDS P.L.R. = IDS Pensions Law Reports (*S&M/IDS*)
IDS P.S.B. = IDS Pensions Service Bulletin (*S&M/IDS*)
IFA Review = Independent Financial Adviser Review (*Mitre House Publishing Ltd*)
IIB Mag. = Institute of Insurance Brokers Magazine (*MSM International Ltd*)
IIC = International Review of Intellectual Property and Competition Law (*IPR Verlag GmbH*)
INSOL W. = INSOL World (*INSOL International*)
IP Scan = IP Scan (*Register.com, Corporate Services Division*)
IRS Emp. L.B. = IRS Employment Law Bulletin (*Reed Business Information Ltd*)
IRS Emp. Law = IRS Employment Law (*Reed Business Information Ltd*)
IRS Emp. Rev. = IRS Employment Review (*Reed Business Information Ltd*)
IRS Emp. Trends = IRS Employment Trends (*Butterworth Tolley Publishing*)
IRS Euro. Emp. Rev. = IRS European Employment Review (*Reed Business Information Ltd*)
ISBA L. & R.R. = ISBA Legislative & Regulatory Review (*The Incorporated Society of British Advertisers Ltd*)
IT & C.L.R. = IT & Communications Law Reports (*Legalease Ltd*)
IT & Comm. News. = Information Technology & Communications Newsletter (*Legalease Ltd*)
IT L.T. = IT Law Today (*Informa Publishing Group Ltd*)
Imm. A.R. = Immigration Appeal Reports (*TSO*)
In Comp. = In Competition (*S&M*)
In-House L. = In-House Lawyer (*Legalease Ltd*)
Ind. L.R. = Independent Law Review (*Clarus Press*)
Ind. Sol. = Independent Solicitor (*British Legal Association*)

Ind. T.R. = Industrial Tribunal Reports (*TSO*)
Info. T.L.R. = Information Technology Law Reports (*Lawtext Publishers*)
Ins. & Reins. Law Int. = Insurance & Reinsurance Law International (*Turpin Distribution Serv Ltd*)
Ins. Age = Insurance Age (*Maxwell Business Communications Ltd*)
Ins. Int. = Insurance International (*Mitre House Publishing Ltd*)
Ins. L. & C. = Insurance Law & Claims (*Mitre House Publishing Ltd*)
Ins. L. & P. = Insurance Law & Practice (*Butterworth Tolley Publishing*)
Ins. L.J. = Insurance Law Journal (*Butterworths Pty Ltd*)
Ins. L.M. = Insurance Law Monthly (*Informa Publishing Group Ltd*)
Insolv. B. = Insolvency Bulletin (*Informa Publishing Group Ltd*)
Insolv. Int. = Insolvency Intelligence (*S&M*)
Insolv. L. = Insolvency Lawyer (*S&M*)
Insolv. L. & P. = Insolvency Litigation & Practice (*CLT Publishing*)
Insolv. P. = Insolvency Practitioner (*Association of Business Recovery Professionals*)
Insolvency = Insolvency (*Griffin Multimedia*)
Int. A.L.R. = International Arbitration Law Review (*S&M*)
Int. Acc. = International Accountant (*Association of International Accountants*)
Int. Bank. L. = International Banking Law (*S&M*)
Int. Broker = International Broker (*Risk & Insurance Research Group Ltd*)
Int. C.L. Rev. = International Community Law Review (*Martinus Nijhoff Publishers*)
Int. C.L.R. = International Criminal Law Review (*Martinus Nijhoff Publishers*)
Int. C.R. = International Corporate Rescue (*Chase Cambria Co (Publishing) Ltd*)
Int. I.L.R. = International Insurance Law Review (*S&M/ESC Publishing*)
Int. I.R. = International Insurance Report (*Risk & Insurance Research Group Ltd*)
Int. J. Comp. L.L.I.R. = International Journal of Comparative Labour Law and Industrial Relations (*Turpin Distribution Serv Ltd*)
Int. J. Law & Fam. = International Journal of Law & the Family (*OUP*)
Int. J. Soc. L. = International Journal of the Sociology of Law (*Elsevier BV*)
Int. J.F.L. = International Journal of Franchising Law (*Claerhout Publishing Ltd*)
Int. J.L.C. = International Journal of Law in Context (*CUP*)
Int. J.L.P.F. = International Journal of Law, Policy and the Family (*OUP*)
Int. M.L. = International Maritime Law (*Lawtext Publishing Ltd*)
Int. Rel. = International Relations (*Sage Publications Ltd*)
Int. Rev. Law & Econ. = International Review of Law & Economics (*Butterworth Tolley Publishing*)
Int. T.L.R. = International Trade Law & Regulation (*S&M/ESC Publishing*)
Intertax = Intertax (*Turpin Distribution Serv Ltd*)
Inv. Man. = Investment Management (*Mitre House Publishing Ltd*)
Ir. B.L. = Irish Business Law (*Inns Quay Publishing*)
Ir. T.R. = Irish Tax Review (*Institute of Taxation in Ireland*)
Irish Jurist = Irish Jurist (*Round Hall/S&M*)
J. Civ. Lib. = Journal of Civil Liberties (*Northumbria Law Press*)
J. Com. Mar. St. = Journal of Common Market Studies (*Blackwell Publishers*)
J. Crim. L. = Journal of Criminal Law (*Portland Press Ltd*)
J. En. & Nat. Res. L. = Journal of Energy & Natural Resources Law (*Turpin Distribution Serv Ltd*)
J. Env. L. = Journal of Environmental Law (*OUP*)
J. Int. Arb. = Journal of International Arbitration (*Aspen Publishers*)
J. Int. P. = Journal of International Trust and Corporate Planning (*Jordan & Sons Ltd*)
J. Law & Soc. = Journal of Law and Society (*Blackwell Publishers*)
J. Leg. Hist. = Journal of Legal History (*Cass*)
J. Priv. Int. L. = Journal of Private International Law (*Hart Publishing Ltd*)
J. Prop. Fin. = Journal of Property Finance (*MCB University Press Ltd*)
J. Soc. Wel. & Fam. L. = Journal of Social Welfare and Family Law (*Taylor & Francis Ltd*)
J. Soc. Wel. L. = Journal of Social Welfare Law (*S&M*)
J.A.C.L. = Journal of Armed Conflict Law (*Nottingham University Press*)
J.A.L. = Journal of African Law (*CUP*)
J.A.M.N. = Journal of ADR, Mediation and Negotiation (*XPL Publishing*)
J.B.L. = Journal of Business Law (*S&M*)
J.B.R. = Journal of Banking Regulation (*Palgrave Macmillan*)
J.C. & S.L. = Journal of Conflict & Security Law (*OUP*)
J.C.L. = Journal of Child Law (*Butterworth Tolley Publishing*)
J.C.L. & E. = Journal of Competition Law & Economics (*OUP*)
J.C.L.L.E. = Journal of Commonwealth Law and Legal Education (*Taylor & Francis Ltd*)
J.C.L.P. = Journal of Competition Law & Policy (*OECD Publications Service (Databeuro Ltd)*)
J.C.L.S. = Journal of Corporate Law Studies (*Hart Publishing Ltd*)
J.C.P. = Journal of Consumer Policy (*Kluwer*)
J.C.P.P. = Journal of Civil Practice and Procedure (*Round Hall/S&M*)
J.E.C.L. & P. = Journal of Electronic Commerce Law & Practice (*Butterworth Tolley Publishing*)
J.E.E.P.L. = Journal for European Environmental & Planning Law (*Lexxion Verlagsgesellschaft mbH*)
J.E.L.P. = Journal of Employment Law & Practice (*Butterworth Tolley Publishing*)
J.E.L.S. = Journal of Empirical Legal Studies (*Blackwell Publishers*)
J.E.P.P. = Journal of European Public Policy (*Taylor & Francis Ltd*)
J.E.R.L. = Journal of Energy & Natural Resources Law (*International Bar Association*)
J.F.C. = Journal of Financial Crime (*Emerald Group Publishing Limited*)
J.F.R. & C. = Journal of Financial Regulation and Compliance (*Emerald Group Publishing Limited*)
J.F.S.M. = Journal of Financial Services Marketing (*Henry Stewart Publications*)
J.G.L.R. = Jersey and Guernsey Law Review (*The Jersey and Guernsey Law Review Ltd*)
J.H.L. = Journal of Housing Law (*S&M*)
J.I.A. = Journal of the Institute of Actuaries (*Institute of Actuaries*)
J.I.A.N.L. = Journal of Immigration Asylum and Nationality Law (*Tottel Publishing*)
J.I.B. Law = Journal of International Biotechnology Law (*Walter de Gruyter GmbH & Co. KG*)

J.I.B.L. = Journal of International Banking Law (*S&M/ESC Publishing*)
J.I.B.L.R. = Journal of International Banking Law and Regulation (*S&M/ESC Publishing*)
J.I.B.R. = Journal of International Banking Regulation (*Palgrave Macmillan*)
J.I.C.J. = Journal of International Criminal Justice (*OUP*)
J.I.C.L. = Journal of International Commercial Law (*Ashgate Publishing Ltd*)
J.I.C.M. = Journal of the Institute of Credit Management (*Institute of Credit Management*)
J.I.E.L. = Journal of International Economic Law (*OUP*)
J.I.F.D.L. = Journal of International Franchising & Distribution Law (*Butterworth Tolley Publishing*)
J.I.F.M. = Journal of International Financial Markets (*S&M*)
J.I.L. & C. = Journal of Islamic Law and Culture (*Taylor & Francis Ltd*)
J.I.L.T. = Journal of Information, Law & Technology (*CTI Law Technology Centre*)
J.I.M.F. = Journal of International Money and Finance (*Elsevier Science Publishers*)
J.I.M.L. = Journal of International Maritime Law (*Lawtext Publishers*)
J.I.P.L.P. = Journal of Intellectual Property Law & Practice (*OUP*)
J.I.T.L. & P. = Journal of International Trade Law & Policy (*Emerald Group Publishing Limited*)
J.J. = Justice Journal (*Justice*)
J.L.E. & O. = Journal of Law, Economics & Organization (*OUP*)
J.L.G.L. = Journal of Local Government Law (*S&M*)
J.L.M &. E. = Journal of Law, Medicine & Ethics (*Blackwell Publishers*)
J.L.S. = Journal of Legislative Studies (*Taylor & Francis Ltd*)
J.L.S.S. = Journal of the Law Society of Scotland (*The Law Society of Scotland*)
J.M.C.B. = Journal of Money, Credit and Banking (*Ohio State University Press*)
J.M.H.L. = Journal of Mental Health Law (*Northumbria Law Press*)
J.M.L. & P. = Journal of Media Law and Practice (*Butterworth Tolley Publishing*)
J.M.L.C. = Journal of Money Laundering Control (*Emerald Group Publishing Limited*)
J.N.I. = Journal of Network Industries (*Intersentia*)
J.O. & R. = Journal of Obligations and Remedies (*Northumbria Law Press*)
J.P. = Justice of the Peace & Local Government Law (*Butterworth Tolley Publishing*)
J.P.I. Law = Journal of Personal Injury Law (*S&M*)
J.P.I.L. = Journal of Personal Injury Litigation (*S&M*)
J.P.L. = Journal of Planning & Environment Law (*S&M*)
J.P.M. = Journal of Pensions Management (*Henry Stewart Publications*)
J.P.M. & M. = Journal of Pensions Management & Marketing (*Henry Stewart Publications*)
J.P.N. = Justice of the Peace & Local Government Law (*Butterworth Tolley Publishing*)
J.R. = Judicial Review (*Hart Publishing Ltd*)
J.R. & I. = Journal of Risk and Insurance (*American Risk & Insurance Association Inc*)
J.R.S. = Journal of Refugee Studies (*OUP*)
J.S.B.J. = Judicial Studies Board Journal (*OUP*)
J.S.F. = Journal of the Society of Fellows (*Chartered Insurance Institute*)
J.S.I.J. = Judicial Studies Instiutute Journal (*Judicial Studies Institute*)
J.S.S.L. = Journal of Social Security Law (*S&M*)
J.T.C.P. = Journal of International Trust & Corporate Planning (*Jordan & Sons Ltd*)
J.W.E.L. & B. = Journal of World Energy Law & Business (*OUP*)
J.W.I.P. = Journal of World Intellectual Property (*Blackwell Publishers*)
J.W.T. = Journal of World Trade (*Turpin Distribution Serv Ltd*)
J.W.T.L. = Journal of World Trade Law (*Werner Publishing Co Ltd*)
Jersey L.R. = Jersey Law Review (*The Jersey and Guernsey Law Review Ltd*)
Jour. G.M. = Journal of General Management (*Braybrooke Press Ltd*)
Jur. Rev. = Juridical Review (*S&M/W. Green*)

K.B. = Law Reports Kings Bench (*ICLR*)
K.C.L.J. = Kings College Law Journal (*Hart Publishing Ltd*)
K.H.R.P.L.R. = Kurdish Human Rights Project Legal Review (*Kurdish Human Rights Project*)
K.I.R. = Knights Industrial Reports (*Charles Knight Publishing*)
K.L.J. = King's Law Journal (*Hart Publishing Ltd*)
KIM Legal = Knowledge and Information Management (*Ark Group*)
KM Legal = KM Legal (*Ark Publishing*)
Kemp & Kemp = Kemp & Kemp The Quantum of Damages (*S&M*)
King's Counsel = King's Counsel (*King's College London*)
Kingston L.R. = Kingston Law Review (*Kingston Polytechnic*)

L & T.R. = Landlord and Tenant Reports (*S&M*)
L&P Comp. EC = Linklaters & Paines Competition EC (*Linklaters*)
L&P E. & B.L.N. = Linklaters & Paines Employment & Benefits Law Newsletter (*Linklaters*)
L&P E.C. Law = Linklaters & Paines European Community Law (*Linklaters*)
L&P F.S. News. = Linklaters & Paines Financial Services Newsfile (*Linklaters*)
L&P I.F. News. = Linklaters & Paines Investment Funds Newsfile (*Linklaters*)
L&P I.M. Rep. = Linklaters & Paines Internal Market Report (*Linklaters*)
L&P I.P.N. = Linklaters & Paines Intellectual Property News (*Linklaters*)
L&P P.L.N. = Linklaters & Paines Property Law Now (*Linklaters*)
L. & F.M.R. = Law & Financial Markets Review (*Hart Publishing Ltd*)
L. & H. = Law & Humanities (*Hart Publishing Ltd*)
L. & T. Review = Landlord & Tenant Review (*S&M*)
L. D'I. = Lettre D'Information (*Geneva Association*)
L. Ex. = Legal Executive (*ILEX Publishing & Advertising Services Ltd*)
L.A.L. = Local Authority Law (*S&M*)
L.B.E.B. = Lloyds Bank Economic Bulletin (*Lloyd's Bank Plc*)
L.C. & A.I. = Law, Computers & Artificial Intelligence (*Taylor & Francis Ltd*)
L.C. News = Law Centres News (*Law Centres Federation*)
L.D. = Legal Director (*Legal Week Global Media*)
L.E. = Lawyers' Europe (*The Journal of the Law Society's European Group*)
L.F. = Litigation Funding (*Law Society Publishing*)

TABLE OF ABBREVIATIONS

L.G. Rev. = Local Government Review (*Butterworth Tolley Publishing*)
L.G. and L. = Local Government and Law (*Informa Publishing Group Ltd*)
L.G.C. = Local Government Chronicle (*Local Government Chronicle Ltd*)
L.G.C. Law & Admin. = Local Government Chronicle Law & Administration (*Local Government Chronicle Ltd*)
L.G.D. = Law, Social Justice & Global Development (*Electronic Law Journals*)
L.G.I. = Law Gazette International (*Law Society Services Ltd*)
L.G.L.R. = Local Government Law Reports (*S&M*)
L.G.R. = Local Government Reports (*Charles Knight Publishing*)
L.G.R. Rep. = Local Government Review Reports (*Barry Rose Law Periodicals*)
L.I.E.I. = Legal Issues of European Integration (*Turpin Distribution Serv Ltd*)
L.I.I. = Life Insurance International (*L.L.P Ltd*)
L.I.M. = Legal Information Management (*CUP*)
L.J.I.L. = Leiden Journal of International Law (*CUP*)
L.L.I.D. = Lloyd's List Insurance Day (*Informa Publishing Group Ltd*)
L.L.R. = London Law Review (*London Law Review*)
L.M.C.L.Q. = Lloyd's Maritime and Commercial Law Quarterly (*Informa Publishing Group Ltd*)
L.M.E.L.R. = Land Management and Environmental Law Report (*Chancery Law Publishing Ltd*)
L.M.L.N. = Lloyd's Maritime Law Newsletter (*Informa Publishing Group Ltd*)
L.M.N. = London Market Newsletter (*Informa Publishing Group Ltd*)
L.P. & R. = Law, Probability & Risk (*OUP*)
L.P.I.C.T. = Law & Practice of International Courts and Tribunals (*Martinus Nijhoff Publishers*)
L.Q.R. = Law Quarterly Review (*S&M*)
L.R. = Licensing Review (*Benedict Books*)
L.R. & I. = Liability Risk & Insurance (*Informa Publishing Group Ltd*)
L.R.L.R. = Lloyd's Reinsurance Law Reports (*LLP*)
L.S. = Legal Studies (*Blackwell Publishers*)
L.S. & P. = Law, Science and Policy (*A B Academic Publishers*)
L.S.G. = Law Society's Gazette (*The Law Society's Hall*)
L.T.J. = Law Technology Journal (*CTI Law Technology Centre*)
L.W.D. EC News. = Lovell White Durrant EC Newsletter (*Lovell White Durrant*)
L.W.D. L.A.P. = Lovell White Durrant Legal Advice on Pensions (*Lovell White Durrant*)
Law = Law (*The Law*)
Law & Crit. = Law and Critique (*Kluwer*)
Law & Just. = Law & Justice (*Edmund Plowden Trust*)
Law & Pol. = Law & Policy (*Blackwell Publishers*)
Law & Tax R. = Law & Tax Review (*S&M*)
Law Lib. = Law Librarian (*S&M*)
Law Mag. = Law Magazine (*S&M*)
Law Teach. = Law Teacher (*S&M*)
Law for Bus. = Law for Business (*Wallace Publishing Ltd*)
Law. in Eur. = Lawyers in Europe (*Lawyers in Europe Ltd*)
Lawyer = Lawyer (*Centaur Communications Group*)
Lawyer 2B = Lawyer 2B (*Centaur Communications Group*)
Leg. = Legisprudence (*Hart Publishing Ltd*)
Legal Action = Legal Action (*Legal Action Group*)
Legal Bus. = Legal Business (*Legalease Ltd*)
Legal Ethics = Legal Ethics (*Hart Publishing Ltd*)
Legal I.E.I. = Legal Issues of Economic Integration (*Turpin Distribution Serv Ltd*)
Legal IT = Legal IT (*Legal Week Global Media*)
Legal M. = Legal Marketing (*Ark Publishing*)
Legal T.J. = Legal Technology Journal (*Legalease Ltd*)
Legal Times = Legal Times (*Legalease Ltd*)
Legal Week = Legal Week (*Legal Week Global Media*)
Link AWS = Link Association of Women Solicitors (*Association of Women Solicitors*)
Lit. = Litigation (*Butterworth Tolley Publishing*)
Lit. L. = Litigation Letter (*Informa Publishing Group Ltd*)
Litigator = Litigator (*S&M*)
Liverpool L.R. = Liverpool Law Review (*Kluwer*)
Ll. Ins. Int. = Lloyd's Insurance International (*Lloyd's of London Press Inc*)
Ll. Log = Lloyds Log (*Informa Publishing Group Ltd*)
Ll. News. = Lloyd's of London Newsletter (*Informa Publishing Group Ltd*)
Lloyd's List = Lloyd's List (*Informa Publishing Group Ltd*)
Lloyd's Rep. = Lloyd's Law Reports (*Informa Publishing Group Ltd*)
Lloyd's Rep. Bank. = Lloyd's Law Reports Banking (*Informa Publishing Group Ltd*)
Lloyd's Rep. I.R. = Lloyd's Law Reports Insurance & Reinsurance (*Informa Publishing Group Ltd*)
Lloyd's Rep. Med. = Lloyd's Law Reports Medical (*Informa Publishing Group Ltd*)
Lloyd's Rep. P.N. = Lloyd's Law Reports Professional Negligence (*Informa Publishing Group Ltd*)

M. & A. Ins. Rep. = Marine & Aviation Insurance Report (*Informa Publishing Group Ltd*)
M. Advice = Money Advice (*Money Advice Association*)
M. Advocate = Maritime Advocate (*Merlin Legal Publishing*)
M. Bulletin = Mercer Bulletin European Newsletter (*William M Mercer Ltd*)
M. Direct = Mercer Direct European Communication Newsletter (*William M Mercer Ltd*)
M. EC News. = Mercer European Community Newsletter (*William M Mercer Ltd*)
M. Euro. News = Mercer European News (*William M Mercer Ltd*)
M. Man. = Money Management (*Financial Times Finance*)
M. Prospect = Mercer Prospect Eastern European Newsletter (*William M Mercer Ltd*)
M. Review = Mercer Review (*William M Mercer Ltd*)
M. Transatlantic = Mercer Transatlantic (*William M Mercer Ltd*)
M. Update = Mercer Update (*William M Mercer Ltd*)
M. World = Media World (*Informa Publishing Group Ltd*)
M.A. = Management Accounting (*Chartered Institute Management Accountants*)
M.A.L.Q.R. = Model Arbitration Law Quarterly Reports (*Simmonds & Hill Publishing Ltd*)
M.C.P. = Magistrates' Courts Practice (*XPL Publishing*)
M.D.U. Jour. = Medical Defence Union Journal (*The Medical Defence Union*)

TABLE OF ABBREVIATIONS

M.E.C.L.R. = Middle East Commercial Law Review (*S&M/ESC Publishing*)

M.F.G. = Mortgage Finance Gazette (*Professional & Business Information Publishing*)

M.F.S. = Managing for Success (*Law Management Section/The Law Society*)

M.I.M. = Motor Insurance Market (*Informa Publishing Group Ltd*)

M.I.P. = Managing Intellectual Property (*Euromoney Institutional Investor Plc*)

M.J. = Municipal Journal (*Hemming Information Services*)

M.J.L.S. = Mountbatten Journal of Legal Studies (*Southampton Institute*)

M.L.B. = Manx Law Bulletin (*Attorney General's Chambers*)

M.L.J.I. = Medico-Legal Journal of Ireland (*Round Hall/S&M*)

M.L.N. = Media Lawyer Newsletter (*The Press Association*)

M.L.R. = Modern Law Review (*Blackwell Publishers*)

M.M. = Money Marketing (*Centaur Communications Group*)

M.R. = Media Review (*SJ Berwin & Co*)

M.R.D.B. = Monthly Report Deutsche Bundesbank (*Deutshe Bundesbank*)

M.R.I. = Maritime Risk International (*Informa Publishing Group Ltd*)

M.T. & F. = Matrimonial Tax & Finance (*Tax and Financial Publishing*)

M.W. = Money Week (*EMAP Communications*)

Maastricht J. = Maastricht Journal of European and Comparative Law (*Intersentia NV*)

Magistrate = Magistrate (*Magistrates Association*)

Man. L. = Managerial Law (*MCB University Press Ltd*)

Marine I.R. = Marine Insurance Report (*Informa Publishing Group Ltd*)

Masons C.L.R. = Masons Computer Law Reports (*Mason's Solicitor*)

McK. E.B.B. = McKenna Employment Benefits Bulletin (*McKenna & Co*)

McK. Env. L.B. = McKenna Environmental Law Bulletin (*Cameron McKenna & Co*)

McK. Euro. R. = McKenna European Review (*McKenna & Co*)

McK. Law Let. = McKenna Law Letter (*McKenna & Co*)

McK. P.B. = McKenna Pension Brief (*McKenna & Co*)

McK. P.L.B. = McKenna Pension Law Bulletin (*McKenna & Co*)

Med. L. Int. = Medical Law International (*A B Academic Publishers*)

Med. L. Mon. = Medical Law Monitor (*Informa Publishing Group Ltd*)

Med. L. Rev. = Medical Law Review (*OUP*)

Med. L.R. = Medical Law Reports (*Informa Publishing Group Ltd*)

Med. Leg. J. = Medico-Legal Journal (*XPL Publishing*)

Med. Lit. = Medical Litigation (*Medical Litigation Strategies*)

Med. Sci. Law = Medicine, Science & the Law (*Barnsbury Publishing*)

Money L.B. = Money Laundering Bulletin (*Informa Publishing Group Ltd*)

Mortgage M. = Mortgage Monthly (*BSA CML Publication*)

N.E.G.R.I.E. = Newsletter of the European Group of Risk and Insurance Economists (*Geneva Association*)

N.I.E.R. = National Institute of Economic Review (*The National Institute of Economic Review*)

N.I.L.Q. = Northern Ireland Legal Quarterly (*School of Law*)

N.I.L.R. = Northern Ireland Law Reports (*Butterworth Tolley Publishing*)

N.J.I.L. = Nordic Journal of International Law (*Martinus Nijoff Publishers*)

N.L.J. = New Law Journal (*Butterworths Tolley Publishing*)

N.L.T. = Northern Law Today (*Northern Law Today*)

N.N. EC News = Nabarro Nathanson EC News (*Nabarro Nathanson*)

N.N.P.D. = Nabarro Nathanson The Pension Dimension (*Nabarro Nathanson*)

N.N.R. = Nabarro Nathanson Resource (*Nabarro Nathanson*)

N.P.C. = New Property Cases (*New Property Cases Ltd*)

N.Q.H.R. = Netherlands Quarterly of Human Rights (*Intersentia NV*)

N.R. EC Init. = Norton Rose M5 Group EC Initiative (*Norton Rose M5 Group*)

N.R. EU Init. = Norton Rose M5 Group EU Initiative (*Norton Rose M5 Group*)

N.R.G.Q. = Netherlands Reinsurance Group Quarterly (*Nederlandse Reassurantie Groep nv*)

N.S.A.I.L. = Non-State Actors and International Law (*Martinus Nijhoff Publishers*)

N.W.B.Q.R. = National Westminster Bank Quarterly Review (*National Westminster Bank Plc*)

Natwest I.T.B. = National Westminster Bank International Trade Bulletin (*National Westminster Bank*)

Nott. L.J. = Nottingham Law Journal (*Nottingham Law School*)

O. & I.T. Rev. = Offshore & International Taxation Review (*Key Haven Publications Plc*)

O.D. and I.L. = Ocean Development and International Law (*Taylor & Francis Ltd*)

O.G.J.F.I. = Open Government: A Journal on Freedom of Information (*Liverpool John Moores University*)

O.G.L.T.R. = Oil & Gas Law & Taxation Review (*S&M/ESC Publishing*)

O.H.R. = Occupational Health Review (*Eclipse/Butterworth Tolley Publishing*)

O.J.L.S. = Oxford Journal of Legal Studies (*OUP*)

O.L.S. = One Lime Street (*Informa Publishing Group Ltd*)

O.N. = Oftel News (*Oftel Update*)

O.P.L.R. = Occupational Pensions Law Reports (*Eclipse/Butterworth Tolley Publishing*)

O.S.S. Bull. = Office for the Supervision of Solicitors Bulletin (*The Law Society's Gazette*)

O.T.P.R. = Offshore Tax Planning Review (*Key Haven Publications Plc*)

O.T.R. = Offshore Tax Planning Review (*Key Haven Publications Plc*)

O.U.C.L.J. = Oxford University Commonwealth Law Journal (*Hart Publishing Ltd*)

Observer = OECD Observer (*Databeuro Ltd*)

Occ. Pen. = Occupational Pensions (*Eclipse/Butterworth Tolley Publishing*)

Offshore Red = Offshore Red (*Campden Publishing*)

P & I Int. = P & I International (*Informa Publishing Group Ltd*)

P. & C.R. = Property, Planning and Compensation Reports (*S&M*)
P. & D.P. = Privacy & Data Protection (*Privacy & Data Protection*)
P. & E.B. = Pensions & Employee Benefits (*Butterworth Tolley Publishing*)
P. & M.I.L.L. = Personal and Medical Injuries Law Letter (*Informa Publishing Group Ltd*)
P. & P. = Practice and Procedure (*Round Hall/ S&M*)
P. & S. = Punishment & Society (*Sage Publications Ltd*)
P. Injury = Personal Injury (EMIS) (*XPL Publishing*)
P. Int. = Portfolio International (*MSM International*)
P. Treas. = Public Treasurer (*Local Government Chronicle Ltd*)
P. Week = Property Week (*CMP Information Ltd*)
P.A. = Product Adviser (*Financial Times Finance*)
P.A.B.B. = Pay And Benefits Bulletin (*Butterworth Tolley Publishing*)
P.A.D. = Planning Appeal Decisions (*S&M*)
P.B. = Professional Broking (*Timothy Benn Publishing Ltd*)
P.C. & L. = Psychology, Crime & Law (*Taylor & Francis Ltd*)
P.C.B. = Private Client Business (*S&M*)
P.C.L.B. = Practitioners' Child Law Bulletin (*S&M*)
P.C.P. = Private Client Practitioner (*Tru-Est Limited*)
P.E.B.L. = Perspectives on European Business Law (*European Perspectives Publicatons Ltd*)
P.E.L.B. = Planning and Environmental Law Bulletin (*S&M*)
P.F. = Property Finance (*Informa Publishing Group Ltd*)
P.F. & D. = Property Finance & Development (*Informa Publishing Group Ltd*)
P.H.B. = Parliament House Book (*S&M/W. Green*)
P.I. = Personal Injury (Wiley) (*John Wiley & Sons Ltd*)
P.I. Comp. = Personal Injury Compensation (*Informa Publishing Group Ltd*)
P.I.B.U.L.J. = Personal Injury Brief Update Law Journal (*Law Brief Publishing Ltd*)
P.I.C. = Palmer's In Company (*S&M*)
P.I.J. = Planning Inspectorate Journal (*The Planning Inspectorate*)
P.I.L.J. = Personal Injury Law Journal (*Legalease Ltd*)
P.I.L.M.R. = Personal Injury Law and Medical Review (*Butterworth Tolley Publishing*)
P.I.P. = Property in Practice (*Property Section/The Law Society*)
P.I.Q.R. = Personal Injuries and Quantum Reports (*S&M*)
P.L. = Public Law (*S&M*)
P.L. & B.I.N. = Privacy Laws & Business International Newsletter (*Privacy Laws & Business*)
P.L. & B.U.K.N. = Privacy Laws & Business United Kingdom Newsletter (*Privacy Laws & Business*)
P.L.B. = Property Law Bulletin (S&M) (*S&M*)
P.L.C. = Practical Law Companies (*Practical Law Company Ltd*)
P.L.C.R. = Planning Law Case Reports (*S&M*)
P.L.I. = Product Liability International (*Informa Publishing Group Ltd*)
P.L.J. = Property Law Journal (*Legalease Ltd*)
P.L.R. = Estates Gazette Planning Law Reports (*Estates Gazette*)
P.L.T. = Professional Liability Today (*Informa Publishing Group Ltd*)
P.L.U. = Pensions Law Update (*Ellison Westhorp Publications*)
P.M. = Pensions Management (*Financial Times Finance*)
P.N. = Professional Negligence (*Tottel Publishing*)
P.N. & L. = Professional Negligence & Liability (*CLT Publishing*)
P.N.L.R. = Professional Negligence and Liability Reports (*S&M*)
P.P. = Professional Pensions (*MSM International Ltd*)
P.P. & D. = Practical Planning & Development (*CLT Publishing*)
P.P.L. = Practical Planning Law (*CLT Publishing*)
P.P.L.R. = Public Procurement Law Review (*S&M*)
P.P.M. = Professional Practice Management (*Informa Publishing Group Ltd*)
P.R. = Property Review (*Eclipse/Butterworth Tolley Publishing*)
P.S. = Pensions Systems (*Mitre House Publishing Ltd*)
P.S.E.L.J. = Public Sector Employment Law Journal (*Legalease Ltd*)
P.S.P. = Police Station Practice (*XPL Publishing*)
P.S.T. = Pension Scheme Trustee (*Informa Publishing Group Ltd*)
P.T. = Pensions Today (*Informa Publishing Group Ltd*)
P.T.P.R. = Personal Tax Planning Review (*Key Haven Publications Plc*)
P.V. = Property Valuer (*Irish Auctioneers & Valuers Institute*)
P.W. = Patent World (*Informa Publishing Group Ltd*)
PS = Probate Section (*Probate Section/The Law Society*)
Paisner C.U. = Paisner Company Update (*Paisner & Co*)
Paisner E.B. = Paisner European Bulletin (*Paisner & Co*)
Paisner E.U. = Paisner Environment Update (*Paisner & Co*)
Paisner I.P.B. = Paisner Intellectual Property Briefing (*Paisner & Co*)
Palmer's C.L. = Palmer's Company Law (*S&M*)
Parl. Aff. = Parliamentary Affairs (*OUP*)
Pay Mag. = Pay Magazine (*Wolters Kluwer (UK) Ltd*)
Pen. = Pensions (*Palgrave Macmillan*)
Pen. L.R. = Pensions Law Reports (*Incomes Data Services Ltd*)
Pen. Law. = Pension Lawyer (*Association of Penion Lawyers*)
Pen. Week = Pensions Week (*Financial Times Finance*)
Pen. World = Pensions World (*Butterworth Tolley Publishing*)
Pers. Today = Personnel Today (*Reed Business Information Ltd*)
Pharm. L.I. = Pharmaceutical Law Insight (*Informa Publishing Group Ltd*)
Pl. Sav. = Planned Savings (*EMAP Media Ltd*)
Pol. J. = Police Journal (*Portland Press Ltd*)
Policing = Policing (*Police Review Publishing Co Ltd*)
Policing T. = Policing Today (*Police Review Publishing Co Ltd*)
Post Mag. = Post Magazine (*Incisive Media Plc*)
Pract. Today = Practice Today (*S&M*)
Pract. VAT = Practical VAT (*Butterworth Tolley Publishing*)
Press R. = Press Releases (*Centre Office of Information*)
Prison Serv. J. = Prison Service Journal (*Governor, H.M. Prison Leyhill*)
Probat. J. = Probation Journal (*Sage Publications Ltd*)
Prof. L. = Professional Lawyer (*Chancery Law Publishing Ltd*)

TABLE OF ABBREVIATIONS

Progres = Progres (*Geneva Association*)
Prop. L.B. = Property Law Bulletin (W Green) (*S&M/W. Green*)
Prop. S. = Property Service (*XPL Publishing*)
Prospect = Prospect (*Life Insurance Association*)
Pub. Law Bull. = Public Law Bulletin (*Manchester Metropolitan University*)
Public F. = Public Finance (*FSF Limited*)

Q.A. = Quarterly Account (*Institute of Money Advisers*)
Q.B. = Law Reports Queen's Bench (*ICLR*)
Q.R. = Quantum Reports (*S&M*)
Q.R.T.L. = Quarterly Review of Tort Law (*Clarus Press*)

R. & B.C.P. = Renton & Brown's Criminal Procedure (*S&M/W. Green*)
R. & B.C.P.L. = Renton & Brown's Criminal Procedure Legislation (*S&M/W.Green*)
R. & B.S.O. = Renton & Brown's Statutory Offences (*S&M/W. Green*)
R.A. = Rating Appeals (*Rating Publishers Ltd*)
R.A.D.I.C. = African Journal of International and Comparative Law (*African Society of International and Comparative Law*)
R.A.L.Q. = Receivers, Administrators and Liquidators Quarterly (*Key Haven Publications Plc*)
R.E.C.I.E.L. = Review of European Community and International Environmental Law (*Blackwell Publishers*)
R.L.R. = Restitution Law Review (*Marenex Productions*)
R.M.B. = Risk Management Bulletin (*Ark Publishing*)
R.M.R. = Reinsurance Market Report (*Informa Publishing Group Ltd*)
R.P.C. = Reports of Patent, Design and Trade Mark Cases (*S&M*)
R.P.R.M. = Research Programme on Risk Management (*Geneva Association*)
R.Q. = Reinsurance Quarterly (*Evandale Publishing Co Ltd*)
R.R.L.R. = Rent Review & Lease Renewal (*Informa Publishing Group Ltd*)
R.S.I. = Reinsurance Security Insider (*Evandale Publishing Co Ltd*)
R.T.I. = Road Traffic Indicator (*S&M*)
R.T.R. = Road Traffic Reports (*S&M*)
R.V.R. = Rating and Valuation Reporter (*Rating Publishers Ltd*)
R.W.B. = Rights Workers Bulletin (*NACAB*)
R.W.L.R. = Rights of Way Law Review (*Rights of Way Law Review*)
ROW Bulletin = Rights Of Women Bulletin (*Rights Of Women*)
Ratio Juris = Ratio Juris (*Blackwell Publishers*)
Re Re. = Re Report (*Evandale Publishing Co Ltd*)
Re. L.R. = Reinsurance Law Reports (*Informa Publishing Group Ltd*)
Reactions = Reactions (*Euromoney Institutional Investor Plc*)
Recovery = Recovery (*Association of Business Recovery Professionals*)
Regulator = Regulator & Professional Conduct Quarterly (*Butterworth Tolley Publishing*)
Reins. = Reinsurance (*Timothy Benn Publishing Ltd*)
Rep. B. = Reparation Bulletin (*S&M/W. Green*)
Rep. L.R. = Reparation Law Reports (*S&M/W. Green*)
Res Publica = Res Publica (*Kluwer*)
Res. B. = Home Office Research Bulletin (*Home Office Research & Statistics Department*)
Rev. = The Review (*Resolution*)
Rev. C.E.E. Law = Review of Central and East European Law (*Martinus Nijhoff Publishers*)
Revenue = Revenue (*S&M*)
Review = Review (*Informa Publishing Group Ltd*)
Risk M.R. = Risk Management Reports (*Seawrack Press, Inc.*)
Risk Man. = Risk Management (*Risk Management Society Publishing Inc*)
Risk Update = Risk Update (*Informa Publishing Group Ltd*)
Road L. = Road Law (*Butterworth Tolley Publishing*)
Road L.R. = Road Law Reports (*Butterworth Tolley Publishing*)
Road Law = Road Law and Road Law Reports (*Butterworth Tolley Publishing*)

S. & C.L. = Sports and Character Licensing (*Informa Publishing Group Ltd*)
S. & L.J. = Sport and the Law Journal (*British Association for Sport and Law*)
S. & L.S. = Social & Legal Studies (*Sage Publications Ltd*)
S. & T.I. = Shipping & Transport International (*Guthrum House Ltd*)
S. & T.L.I. = Shipping & Transport Lawyer International (*Guthrum House Ltd*)
S. News = Sentencing News (*S&M*)
S.B. = Scottish Banker (*The Chartered Institute of Bankers in Scotland*)
S.B.T. & F. = Small Business Tax & Finance (*Cyan Publishing Services*)
S.C. = Session Cases (*S&M/W. Green*)
S.C.A.L. & P. = Scottish Constitutional and Administrative Law & Practice (*XPL Publishing*)
S.C.C.R. = Scottish Criminal Case Reports (*The Law Society of Scotland*)
S.C.L. = Scottish Criminal Law (*S&M/W. Green*)
S.C.L. Rev. = Scottish Construction Law Review (*S&M/W. Green*)
S.C.L.R. = Scottish Civil Law Reports (*The Law Society of Scotland*)
S.C.P. = Supreme Court Practice, The (*S&M*)
S.C.P. News = Supreme Court Practice News (*S&M*)
S.E.G.J. = Law Society Solicitors' European Group Journal (*Butterworth Tolley Publishing*)
S.F.L.L. = Scottish Family Law Legislation (*S&M/W. Green*)
S.H.E. & P.G. = Stephenson Harwood Employment and Pensions Group (*Stephenson Harwood*)
S.H.R.J. = Scottish Human Rights Journal (*S&M/W. Green*)
S.I. = Statutory Instruments (*TSO*)
S.I.R. = Space Insurance Report (*Informa Publishing Group Ltd*)
S.J. = Solicitors Journal (*Waterlow Professional Publishing*)
S.J.L.B. = Solicitors Journal LawBrief (*Waterlow Professional Publishing*)
S.L. & F. = Sports Law & Finance (*Informa Publishing Group Ltd*)
S.L. Rev. = Student Law Review (*Routledge-Cavendish*)
S.L.A. & P. = Sports Law Administration & Practice (*Ivy House Sports Law Publications Ltd*)
S.L.B. = Sports Law Bulletin (*Anglia Sports Law Research Centre*)
S.L.C.R. = Scottish Land Court Reports (*The Law Society of Scotland*)

TABLE OF ABBREVIATIONS

S.L.G. = Scottish Law Gazette (*Scottish Law Agents Society*)
S.L.L.P. = Scottish Licensing Law and Practice (*Licensing Services Ltd*)
S.L.P.Q. = Scottish Law & Practice Quarterly (*Butterworth Tolley Publishing*)
S.L.T. = Scots Law Times (*S&M/W. Green*)
S.M.M. = Single Market Monitor (*Butterworth Tolley Publishing*)
S.P.C.L.R. = Scottish Private Client Law Review (*S&M/W. Green*)
S.P.E.L. = Scottish Planning and Environmental Law (*IDOX Information Services*)
S.P.L.P. = Scottish Planning Law & Practice (*IDOX Information Services*)
S.P.L.R. = Scottish Parliament Law Review (*S&M/W. Green*)
S.P.T.L. Reporter = Society of Public Teachers of Law Reporter (*OUP*)
S.T.C. = Simon's Tax Cases (*Butterworth Tolley Publishing*)
S.T.L. = Shipping and Trade Law (*Informa Publishing Group Ltd*)
S.W.T.I. = Simon's Weekly Tax Intelligence (*Butterworth Tolley Publishing*)
SCOLAG = SCOLAG (*Scottish Legal Action Group*)
SCRIPT-ed = SCRIPT-ed (*University of Edinburgh*)
STEP Journal = The STEP Journal (*Barker Brooks Media Ltd*)
Sigma = Sigma (*Swiss Reinsurance Company*)
Soc. L. = Socialist Lawyer (*Haldane Society of Socialist Lawyers*)
Sol. = Solutions (*Dispute Resolution Section/The Law Society*)
Stat. L.R. = Statute Law Review (*OUP*)
Sudebnik = Sudebnik (*Wildy & Sons Ltd*)

T. & E.P. = Trust & Estates Practitioner (*Tru-Est Limited*)
T. & E.T.J. = Trusts and Estates Tax Journal (*Legalease Ltd*)
T. & T. = Trusts & Trustees (*OUP*)
T.A.Q. = The Aviation Quarterly (*Informa Publishing Group Ltd*)
T.B. = Technical Bulletin (*Association of Business Recovery Professionals*)
T.B.S.P.I. = Technical Bulletin of the Society of Practitioners of Insolvency (*Association of Business Recovery Professionals*)
T.C. = Tax Cases (*TSO*)
T.C.L.R. = Technology and Construction Law Reports (*S&M*)
T.E.L. & P. = Tolley's Employment Law & Practice (*Butterworth Tolley Publishing*)
T.E.L. & T.J. = Trusts and Estates Law & Tax Journal (*Legalease Ltd*)
T.E.L.J. = Technology and Entertainment Law Journal (*Round Hall/S&M*)
T.E.L.L. = Tolley's Employment Law-Line (*Butterworth Tolley Publishing*)
T.F.A. = Transactions of the Faculty of Actuaries (*Faculty of Actuaries*)
T.I.A. = Troubled Insurer Alert (*Evandale Publishing Co Ltd*)
T.I.J.M.C.L. = The International Journal of Marine & Coastal Law (*Martinus Nijhoff Publishers*)
T.K.B.E.L.I.S. = Turner Kenneth Brown European Legal Information Service (*Turner Kenneth Brown*)
T.L. & P. = Trust Law & Practice (*Cass*)
T.L.J. = Travel Law Journal (*The Travel Law Centre*)
T.L.P. = Transport Law & Policy (*The Waterfront Partnership*)
T.L.T. = Telecoms Law Today (*Informa Publishing Group Ltd*)
T.M.I.F. = Tax Management International Forum (*BNA International Inc*)
T.N.I.B. = Tolley's National Insurance Brief (*Butterworth Tolley Publishing*)
T.O.C. = Transnational Organized Crime (*Cass*)
T.O.T.R. = Tolley's Overseas Tax Reporter (*Butterworth Tolley Publishing*)
T.P.A. & A. = Tolley's Practical Audit & Accounting (*Butterworth Tolley Publishing*)
T.P.H. = Towers Perrin Headlines (*Towers Perrin*)
T.P.I. e-commerce = Tax Planning International e-commerce (*BNA International Inc*)
T.P.I.A.P.F. = Tax Planning International Asia-Pacific Focus (*BNA International Inc*)
T.P.I.E.U.F. = Tax Planning International European Union Focus (*BNA International Inc*)
T.P.I.I.T. = Tax Planning International Indirect Taxes (*BNA International Inc*)
T.P.I.R. = Tax Planning International Review (*BNA International Inc*)
T.P.I.T.P. = Tax Planning International Transfer Pricing (*BNA International Inc*)
T.P.I.U. = Towers Perrin International Update (*Towers Perrin*)
T.P.N. = Tolley's Practical NIC (*Butterworth Tolley Publishing*)
T.P.N.N. = Tolley's Practical NIC Newsletter (*Butterworth Tolley Publishing*)
T.P.N.S. = Tolley's Practical NIC Service (*Butterworth Tolley Publishing*)
T.P.T. = Tolley's Practical Tax (*Butterworth Tolley Publishing*)
T.P.T.N. = Tolley's Practical Tax Newsletter (*Butterworth Tolley Publishing*)
T.P.T.S. = Tolley's Practical Tax Service (*Butterworth Tolley Publishing*)
T.P.U. = Towers Perrin Update (*Towers Perrin*)
T.P.V. = Tolley's Practical VAT (*Butterworth Tolley Publishing*)
T.P.V.N. = Tolley's Practical VAT Newsletter (*Butterworth Tolley Publishing*)
T.P.V.S. = Tolley's Practical VAT Service (*Butterworth Tolley Publishing*)
T.Q.R. = Trust Quarterly Review (*Barker Brooks Media Ltd*)
T.T.I. = Tolley's Tax Investigation (*Butterworth Tolley Publishing*)
T.W. = Trademark World (*Informa Publishing Group Ltd*)
TACT Review = The Association of Corporate Trustees Review (*The Association of Corporate Trustees*)
Tax & Inv. = Tax and Investment (*Tax & Financial Publishing*)
Tax A. = Tax Adviser (*Croner CCH Group Ltd*)
Tax B. = Tax Briefing (*Office of the Revenue Commissioners*)
Tax Bus. = Tax Business (*Legalease Ltd*)
Tax C. = Tax Commentary (*Incorporated Law Society of Ireland*)
Tax J. = Tax Journal (*Butterworth Tolley Publishing*)
Tax P.N. = Tax Practice Notes (*Incorporated Law Society of Ireland*)
Tax. = Taxation (*Butterworth Tolley Publishing*)
Tax. Int. = Taxation International (*Butterworth Tolley Publishing*)
Tax. P. = Taxation Practitioner (*The Chartered Institute of Taxation*)
Taxline = Taxline (*ICAEW*)
The Sentence = The Sentence (*Sentencing Guidelines Secretariat*)

TABLE OF ABBREVIATIONS

Theo. Crim. = Theoretical Criminology (*Sage Publications Ltd*)
Tort & Ins. L.J. = Tort and Insurance Law Journal (*Tort and Insurance Practice Section*)
Tr. & Est. = Trusts & Estates (*Informa Publishing Group Ltd*)
Tr. L.R. = Trading Law Reports (*Butterworth Tolley Publishing*)
Tr. Law = Trading Law & Trading Law Reports (*Butterworth Tolley Publishing*)
Trad. L. = Trading Law (*Barry Rose Law Periodicals*)
Trans. L. & P. = Transport Law & Policy (*The Waterfront Partnership*)
Trent L.J. = Trent Law Journal (*Nottingham Law School*)
Tribunals = Tribunals (*Judicial Studies Board*)
Tru. & E.L.J. = Trusts & Estates Law Journal (*Legalease Ltd*)
Tru. L.I. = Trust Law International (*Tottel Publishing*)
Trustee = Trustee (*MSM International Ltd*)

U.K. Ins. Broker = UK Insurance Broker (*Institute of Insurance Broker Publication Ltd*)
U.K.C.L.R. = UK Competition Law Reports (*Jordan & Sons Ltd*)
U.K.H.R.R. = United Kingdom Human Rights Reports (*Jordan & Sons Ltd*)
U.L.R. = Utilities Law Review (*Lawtext Publishing Limited*)
UCELNET = Universities and Colleges Education Law Network (*University of Stirling*)
UK Prac. Dir. = UK Practice Directions (*TSO*)
UK Pre. Pro. = UK Preaction Protocols (*TSO*)
Uniform L.R. = Uniform Law Review (*UNIDROIT*)

V. & D.R. = Value Added Tax and Duties Tribunals Reports (*TSO*)
V.A.T.T.R. = Value Added Tax Tribunal Reports (*TSO*)
VAT Dig. = VAT Digest (*Tottel Publishing*)
VAT Int. = VAT Intelligence (*Watchfield Publishing Ltd*)
VAT Plan. = VAT Planning (*Butterworth Tolley Publishing*)

W. Comp. = World Competition (*Turpin Distribution Serv Ltd*)
W.B. = Welfare Benefits (*XPL Publishing*)
W.C.R.R. = World Communications Regulation Report (*BNA International Inc*)
W.D.P.R. = World Data Protection Report (*BNA International Inc*)
W.E.C. & I.P.R. = World E-Commerce & IP Report (*BNA International Inc*)
W.F.S.B. = World Fire Statistics Bulletin (*Geneva Association*)
W.I. Rep. = World Insurance Report (*Financial Times Finance*)
W.I.C.R. = World Insurance Corporate Report (*Financial Times Finance*)
W.I.P.R. = World Intellectual Property Report (*BNA International Inc*)
W.L. = Water Law (*Lawtext Publishing Limited*)
W.L.L.R. = World Licensing Law Report (*BNA International Inc*)
W.L.R. = Weekly Law Reports (*ICLR*)
W.L.T.B. = Woodfall Landlord & Tenant Bulletin (*S&M*)
W.M. = Wastes Management (*IWM Business Services Ltd*)
W.O.G.L.R. = World Online Gambling Law Report (*Cecile Park Publishing Ltd*)
W.P.G. = World Policy Guide (*Financial Times Finance*)
W.Q. = Watsons Quarterly (*R. Watson & Sons*)
W.R.T.L.B. = Wilkinson's Road Traffic Law Bulletin (*S&M*)
W.S.L.R. = World Sport Law Report (*Cecile Park Publishing Ltd*)
W.T.L.R. = Wills & Trusts Law Reports (*Legalease Ltd*)
W.T.R. = World Tax Report (*Financial Times Finance*)
Watsons E.C. = Watsons Euro Comment (*R. Watson & Sons*)
Watsons I.R. = Watsons Insurance Review (*R. Watson & Sons*)
Watsons P.N. = Watsons Pensions News (*R. Watson & Sons*)
Watsons R.R. = Watsons Remuneration Review (*R. Watson & Sons*)
Watsons W.R. = Watsons Worldwide Review (*R. Watson & Sons*)
Web J.C.L.I. = Web Journal of Current Legal Issues (*OUP*)
Wel. & Fam. L. & P. = Welfare and Family: Law & Practice (*XPL Publishing*)
Welf. R. Bull. = Welfare Rights Bulletin (*Child Poverty Action Group Ltd*)
Woodfall = Woodfall: Landlord & Tenant (*S&M*)
World I.L.R. = World Internet Law Report (*BNA International Inc*)
World T.R. = World Trade Review (*CUP*)
Worldlaw Bus. = Worldlaw Business (*Euromoney Institutional Investor Plc*)
Writ = Writ (*Law Society of Northern Ireland*)

Y.C. & M.L. = Yearbook of Copyright & Media Law (*OUP*)
Y.E.L. = Yearbook of European Law (*OUP*)
Y.J. = Youth Justice (*Sage Publications Ltd*)
Y.L.C.T. = Yearbook of Law Computers & Technology (*Taylor & Francis Ltd*)
Y.M.E.L. = Yearbook of Media & Entertainment Law (*OUP*)
YSG Mag. = Young Solicitors Group Magazine (*Young Solicitors Group*)
Yb. Int'l Env. L. = Yearbook of International Environmental Law (*OUP*)

ALPHABETICAL TABLE OF STATUTES

This table lists all the statutes cited in the Statute Citator

Abolition of Bridge Tolls (Scotland) Act 2008 (asp 1)
Abolition of Feudal Tenure etc (Scotland) Act 2000 (asp 5)
Abortion Act 1967 (c.87)
Access to Justice Act 1999 (c.22)
Accommodation Agencies Act 1953 (c.23)
Acquisition of Land (Authorisation Procedure) (Scotland) Act 1947 (c.42)
Acquisition of Land Act 1981 (c.67)
Activity Centres (Young Persons Safety) Act 1995 (c.15)
Administration of Estates (Small Payments) Act 1965 (c.32)
Administration of Estates Act 1925 (c.23)
Administration of Justice (Miscellaneous Provisions) Act 1933 (c.36)
Administration of Justice (Scotland) Act 1933 (c.41)
Administration of Justice Act 1960 (c.65)
Administration of Justice Act 1969 (c.58)
Administration of Justice Act 1970 (c.31)
Administration of Justice Act 1982 (c.53)
Administration of Justice Act 1985 (c.61)
Admiralty Pensions Act 1921 (c.39)
Adoption (Scotland) Act 1978 (c.28)
Adoption Act 1976 (c.36)
Adoption and Children (Scotland) Act 2007 (asp 4)
Adoption and Children Act 2002 (c.38)
Adult Support and Protection (Scotland) Act 2007 (asp 10)
Adults with Incapacity (Scotland) Act 2000 (asp 4)
Age of Legal Capacity (Scotland) Act 1991 (c.50)
Agricultural Holdings (Scotland) Act 1991 (c.55)
Agricultural Holdings (Scotland) Act 2003 (asp 11)
Agricultural Holdings Act 1986 (c.5)
Agricultural Marketing Act 1983 (c.3)
Agricultural Produce (Grading and Marking) Act 1928 (c.19)
Agricultural Wages (Scotland) Act 1949 (c.30)
Agricultural Wages Act 1948 (c.47)
Agriculture (Miscellaneous Provisions) Act 1943 (c.16)
Agriculture (Miscellaneous Provisions) Act 1954 (c.39)
Agriculture (Miscellaneous Provisions) Act 1968 (c.34)
Agriculture (Miscellaneous Provisions) Act 1972 (c.62)
Agriculture (Miscellaneous Provisions) Act 1976 (c.55)
Agriculture Act 1947 (c.48)
Agriculture Act 1967 (c.22)
Agriculture Act 1970 (c.40)
Agriculture Act 1986 (c.49)
Agriculture Act 1993 (c.37)
Agriculture and Horticulture Act 1964 (c.28)
AIDS (Control) Act 1987 (c.33)
Air Force Act 1955 (c.19)
Aircraft and Shipbuilding Industries Act 1977 (c.3)
Airports Act 1986 (c.31)
Alcoholic Liquor Duties Act 1979 (c.4)
Ancient Monuments and Archaeological Areas Act 1979 (c.46)
Anglo-Portuguese Commercial Treaty Act 1914 (c.1)
Anglo-Portuguese Commercial Treaty Act 1916 (c.39)
Animal Boarding Establishments Act 1963 (c.43)
Animal Health Act 1981 (c.22)
Animal Health and Welfare Act 1984 (c.40)
Animal Welfare Act 2006 (c.45)
Animals (Scientific Procedures) Act 1986 (c.14)
Animals (Scotland) Act 1987 (c.9)
Animals Act 1971 (c.22)
Antarctic Act 1994 (c.15)
Anti-social Behaviour Act 2003 (c.38)
Antisocial Behaviour etc (Scotland) Act 2004 (asp 8)
Anti-terrorism, Crime and Security Act 2001 (c.24)
Appellate Jurisdiction Act 1876 (c.59)
Appropriation (No.2) Act 2006 (c.24)
Appropriation (No.2) Act 2007 (c.10)
Appropriation (No.2) Act 2008 (c.8)
Appropriation (No.3) Act 2008 (c.19)
Appropriation Act 2006 (c.6)
Appropriation Act 2008 (c.3)
Aquaculture and Fisheries (Scotland) Act 2007 (asp 12)
Arbitration Act 1979 (c.42)
Arbitration Act 1996 (c.23)
Architects Act 1997 (c.22)
Armed Forces (Pensions and Compensation) Act 2004 (c.32)
Armed Forces Act 1966 (c.45)
Armed Forces Act 1976 (c.52)
Armed Forces Act 2001 (c.19)
Armed Forces Act 2006 (c.52)
Army (Artillery &c.) Pensions Act 1833 (c.29)
Army Act 1881 (c.58)
Army Act 1955 (c.18)
Asylum and Immigration (Treatment of Claimants, etc.) Act 2004 (c.19)
Asylum and Immigration Act 1996 (c.49)
Atomic Energy Authority Act 1954 (c.32)
Attachment of Earnings Act 1971 (c.32)
Attempted Rape, etc., Act (Northern Ireland) 1960 (c.3)
Audit Commission Act 1998 (c.18)
Aviation and Maritime Security Act 1990 (c.31)
Aviation Security Act 1982 (c.36)
Aylesbury Gaol and Shire Hall Rate in Bucks Act 1736 (c.10)
Bail Act 1976 (c.63)
Bank of England Act 1998 (c.11)
Bankers Books Evidence Act 1879 (c.11)
Banking (Special Provisions) Act 2008 (c.2)
Banking and Financial Dealings Act 1971 (c.80)
Bankruptcy (Scotland) Act 1985 (c.66)
Bankruptcy Act 1914 (c.59)
Bankruptcy and Diligence etc (Scotland) Act 2007 (asp 3)
Barracks Act 1890 (c.25)
Bees Act 1980 (c.12)
Betting and Gaming Duties Act 1981 (c.63)
Bills of Exchange Act 1882 (c.61)
Bills of Sale Act (1878) Amendment Act 1882 (c.43)
Bills of Sale Act 1878 (c.31)
Biological Standards Act 1975 (c.4)
Biological Weapons Act 1974 (c.6)
Births and Deaths Registration Act 1926 (c.48)
Births and Deaths Registration Act 1953 (c.20)

East India Merchants and Land for Warehouses, etc Act 1796 (c.127)
East India Merchants and Purchase of Land in City, etc Act 1796 (c.119)
Education (Additional Support for Learning) (Scotland) Act 2004 (asp 4)
Education (Fees and Awards) Act 1983 (c.40)
Education (Graduate Endowment and Student Support) (Scotland) Act 2001 (asp 6)
Education (Schools) Act 1997 (c.59)
Education (Scotland) Act 1980 (c.44)
Education (Student Loans) Act 1990 (c.6)
Education Act 1962 (c.12)
Education Act 1973 (c.16)
Education Act 1994 (c.30)
Education Act 1996 (c.56)
Education Act 1997 (c.44)
Education Act 2002 (c.32)
Education Act 2005 (c.18)
Education and Inspections Act 2006 (c.40)
Education and Skills Act 2008 (c.25)
Education and Training (Scotland) Act 2000 (asp 8)
Education Reform Act 1988 (c.40)
Elected Authorities (Northern Ireland) Act 1989 (c.3)
Electoral Administration Act 2006 (c.22)
Electricity (Scotland) Act 1979 (c.11)
Electricity Act 1989 (c.29)
Electronic Communications Act 2000 (c.7)
Emergency Workers (Scotland) Act 2005 (asp 2)
Employers Liability (Compulsory Insurance) Act 1969 (c.57)
Employment Act 2002 (c.22)
Employment Act 2008 (c.24)
Employment Agencies Act 1973 (c.35)
Employment and Training (Northern Ireland) Act 1950 (c.29)
Employment and Training Act 1973 (c.50)
Employment and Training Act 1981 (c.57)
Employment of Children Act 1973 (c.24)
Employment Relations Act 1999 (c.26)
Employment Relations Act 2004 (c.24)
Employment Rights Act 1996 (c.18)
Employment Tribunals Act 1996 (c.17)
Energy Act 1976 (c.76)
Energy Act 2004 (c.20)
Energy Act 2008 (c.32)
Enterprise Act 2002 (c.40)
Enterprise and New Towns (Scotland) Act 1990 (c.35)
Environment Act 1995 (c.25)
Environment and Safety Information Act 1988 (c.30)
Environmental Assessment (Scotland) Act 2005 (asp 15)
Environmental Protection Act 1990 (c.43)
Equal Pay Act 1970 (c.41)
Equality Act 2006 (c.3)
Erskine Bridge Tolls Act 1968 (c.4)
Erskine Bridge Tolls Act 2001 (asp 12)
Essex Gaol Act 1772 (c.35)
Essex Roads Act 1702 (c.10)
Essex Roads Act 1725 (c.23)
Essex Roads Act 1746 (c.7)
Essex Roads Act 1793 (c.149)
Essex, Suffolk and Hertford Roads Act 1765 (c.60)
Estate Agents Act 1979 (c.38)
Ethical Standards in Public Life etc (Scotland) Act 2000 (asp 7)
European Communities (Finance) Act 2001 (c.22)
European Communities (Finance) Act 2008 (c.1)
European Communities Act 1972 (c.68)
European Parliament (Representation) Act 2003 (c.7)
European Parliamentary Elections Act 1978 (c.10)
European Parliamentary Elections Act 2002 (c.24)
European Union (Accessions) Act 2006 (c.2)
European Union (Amendment) Act 2008 (c.7)
Evidence (Proceedings in Other Jurisdictions) Act 1975 (c.34)
Exchequer and Audit Departments Act 1866 (c.39)
Excise Duties (Surcharges or Rebates) Act 1979 (c.8)
Execution of Diligence (Scotland) Act 1926 (c.16)
Explosive Substances Act 1883 (c.3)
Explosives (Age of Purchase &c.) Act 1976 (c.26)
Explosives Act 1875 (c.17)
Export Control Act 2002 (c.28)
Extradition Act 1989 (c.33)
Extradition Act 2003 (c.41)
Factories Act 1961 (c.34)
Fair Trading Act 1973 (c.41)
Family Law (Scotland) Act 1985 (c.37)
Family Law Act 1986 (c.55)
Family Law Act 1996 (c.27)
Family Law Reform Act 1969 (c.46)
Family Law Reform Act 1987 (c.42)
Farm and Garden Chemicals Act 1967 (c.50)
Farriers (Registration) Act 1975 (c.35)
Fatal Accidents Act 1846 (c.93)
Fatal Accidents Act 1976 (c.30)
Fatal Accidents and Sudden Deaths Inquiry (Scotland) Act 1976 (c.14)
Female Genital Mutilation Act 2003 (c.31)
Films Act 1985 (c.21)
Finance (No.2) Act 1939 (c.109)
Finance (No.2) Act 1987 (c.51)
Finance (No.2) Act 1992 (c.48)
Finance (No.2) Act 1997 (c.58)
Finance (No.2) Act 2005 (c.22)
Finance Act 1894 (c.30)
Finance Act 1901 (c.7)
Finance Act 1902 (c.7)
Finance Act 1911 (c.48)
Finance Act 1923 (c.14)
Finance Act 1932 (c.25)
Finance Act 1944 (c.23)
Finance Act 1945 (c.24)
Finance Act 1947 (c.35)
Finance Act 1948 (c.49)
Finance Act 1949 (c.47)
Finance Act 1952 (c.33)
Finance Act 1953 (c.34)
Finance Act 1958 (c.56)
Finance Act 1961 (c.36)
Finance Act 1962 (c.44)
Finance Act 1963 (c.25)
Finance Act 1964 (c.49)
Finance Act 1966 (c.18)
Finance Act 1968 (c.44)
Finance Act 1969 (c.32)
Finance Act 1973 (c.51)
Finance Act 1975 (c.7)
Finance Act 1976 (c.40)
Finance Act 1978 (c.42)
Finance Act 1980 (c.48)
Finance Act 1982 (c.39)
Finance Act 1983 (c.28)
Finance Act 1984 (c.43)
Finance Act 1985 (c.54)
Finance Act 1986 (c.41)
Finance Act 1987 (c.16)
Finance Act 1988 (c.39)
Finance Act 1989 (c.26)
Finance Act 1990 (c.29)
Finance Act 1991 (c.31)

ALPHABETICAL TABLE OF STATUTES

Housing Act 1996 (c.52)
Housing Act 2004 (c.34)
Housing and Planning Act 1986 (c.63)
Housing and Regeneration Act 2008 (c.17)
Housing Associations Act 1985 (c.69)
Housing Grants, Construction and Regeneration Act 1996 (c.53)
Hovercraft Act 1968 (c.59)
Human Fertilisation and Embryology (Deceased Fathers) Act 2003 (c.24)
Human Fertilisation and Embryology (Disclosure of Information) Act 1992 (c.54)
Human Fertilisation and Embryology Act 1990 (c.37)
Human Fertilisation and Embryology Act 2008 (c.22)
Human Reproductive Cloning Act 2001 (c.23)
Human Rights Act 1998 (c.42)
Human Tissue (Scotland) Act 2006 (asp 4)
Human Tissue Act 2004 (c.30)
Hydrocarbon Oil Duties Act 1979 (c.5)
Hypnotism Act 1952 (c.46)
Identity Cards Act 2006 (c.15)
Immigration Act 1971 (c.77)
Immigration Act 1988 (c.14)
Immigration and Asylum Act 1999 (c.33)
Immigration, Asylum and Nationality Act 2006 (c.13)
Import of Live Fish (England and Wales) Act 1980 (c.27)
Inclosure Act 1845 (c.118)
Inclosure Act 1846 (c.70)
Income and Corporation Taxes Act 1970 (c.10)
Income and Corporation Taxes Act 1988 (c.1)
Income Tax (Earnings and Pensions) Act 2003 (c.1)
Income Tax (Trading and Other Income) Act 2005 (c.5)
Income Tax Act 2007 (c.3)
Industrial and Provident Societies Act (Northern Ireland) 1969 (c.24)
Industrial and Provident Societies Act 1965 (c.12)
Industrial Development Act 1982 (c.52)
Industrial Diseases (Notification) Act 1981 (c.25)
Industrial Organisation and Development Act 1947 (c.40)
Industrial Training Act 1982 (c.10)
Industry Act 1980 (c.33)
Infanticide Act (Northern Ireland) 1939 (c.5)
Infectious Disease (Notification) Act 1889 (c.72)
Inheritance (Provision for Family and Dependants) Act 1975 (c.63)
Inheritance Tax Act 1984 (c.51)
Injuries in War (Compensation) Act 1914 (c.30)
Injuries in War Compensation Act 1914 (Session 2) 1914 (c.18)
Inquiries Act 2005 (c.12)
Inshore Fishing (Scotland) Act 1984 (c.26)
Insolvency Act 1986 (c.45)
Intelligence Services Act 1994 (c.13)
Interest on Damages (Scotland) Act 1958 (c.61)
International Carriage of Perishable Foodstuffs Act 1976 (c.58)
International Criminal Court Act 2001 (c.17)
International Development Act 2002 (c.1)
International Headquarters and Defence Organisations Act 1964 (c.5)
International Organisations Act 1968 (c.48)
Interpretation Act 1889 (c.63)
Interpretation Act 1978 (c.30)
Intoxicating Substances (Supply) Act 1985 (c.26)
Ipswich and Yaxley Roads Act 1793 (c.128)
Jobseekers Act 1995 (c.18)
Joint Stock Companies Act, 1856 (c.47)
Judgments Act 1838 (c.110)
Judicature (Northern Ireland) Act 1978 (c.23)
Judicial Committee Act 1833 (c.41)
Judicial Committee Act 1844 (c.69)
Judicial Factors (Scotland) Act 1880 (c.4)
Judicial Pensions Act 1981 (c.20)
Judicial Pensions and Retirement Act 1993 (c.8)
Judicial Trustees Act 1896 (c.35)
Judiciary and Courts (Scotland) Act 2008 (asp 6)
Juries Act 1974 (c.23)
Justice (Northern Ireland) Act 2002 (c.26)
Justice and Security (Northern Ireland) Act 2007 (c.6)
Knives Act 1997 (c.21)
Land Compensation (Scotland) Act 1963 (c.51)
Land Compensation Act 1961 (c.33)
Land Compensation Act 1973 (c.26)
Land Drainage Act 1991 (c.59)
Land Reform (Scotland) Act 2003 (asp 2)
Land Registration Act 1925 (c.21)
Land Registration Act 2002 (c.9)
Land Settlement (Scotland) Act 1919 (c.97)
Land Tenure Reform (Scotland) Act 1974 (c.38)
Landlord and Tenant (Covenants) Act 1995 (c.30)
Landlord and Tenant Act 1954 (c.56)
Landlord and Tenant Act 1985 (c.70)
Landlord and Tenant Act 1987 (c.31)
Lands Clauses Consolidation (Scotland) Act 1845 (c.19)
Lands Clauses Consolidation Act 1845 (c.18)
Lands Valuation (Scotland) Act 1854 (c.91)
Law of Libel Amendment Act 1888 (c.64)
Law of Property (Miscellaneous Provisions) Act 1989 (c.34)
Law of Property (Miscellaneous Provisions) Act 1994 (c.36)
Law of Property Act 1922 (c.16)
Law of Property Act 1925 (c.20)
Law Reform (Contributory Negligence) Act 1945 (c.28)
Law Reform (Miscellaneous Provisions) (Scotland) Act 1940 (c.42)
Law Reform (Miscellaneous Provisions) (Scotland) Act 1985 (c.73)
Law Reform (Miscellaneous Provisions) (Scotland) Act 1990 (c.40)
Learner Travel (Wales) Measure 2008 (m.02)
Learning and Skills Act 2000 (c.21)
Leasehold Reform Act 1967 (c.88)
Leasehold Reform, Housing and Urban Development Act 1993 (c.28)
Legal Aid (Scotland) Act 1986 (c.47)
Legal Profession and Legal Aid (Scotland) Act 2007 (asp 5)
Legal Services Act 2007 (c.29)
Legislative and Regulatory Reform Act 2006 (c.51)
Legitimacy Act 1976 (c.31)
Licensing (Alcohol Education and Research) Act 1981 (c.28)
Licensing (Scotland) Act 1976 (c.66)
Licensing (Scotland) Act 2005 (asp 16)
Licensing Act 2003 (c.17)
Limitation Act 1980 (c.58)
Limited Liability Partnerships Act 2000 (c.12)
Limited Partnerships Act 1907 (c.24)
Litigants in Person (Costs and Expenses) Act 1975 (c.47)
Litter Act 1983 (c.35)
Local Authorities (Goods and Services) Act 1970 (c.39)
Local Authority Social Services Act 1970 (c.42)
Local Electoral Administration and Registration Services (Scotland) Act 2006 (asp 14)
Local Governance (Scotland) Act 2004 (asp 9)

Local Government (Financial Provisions etc.) (Scotland) Act 1962 (c.9)
Local Government (Miscellaneous Provisions) (Scotland) Act 1981 (c.23)
Local Government (Miscellaneous Provisions) Act 1976 (c.57)
Local Government (Miscellaneous Provisions) Act 1982 (c.30)
Local Government (Overseas Assistance) Act 1993 (c.25)
Local Government (Scotland) Act 1947 (c.43)
Local Government (Scotland) Act 1966 (c.51)
Local Government (Scotland) Act 1973 (c.65)
Local Government (Scotland) Act 1975 (c.30)
Local Government (Wales) Act 1994 (c.19)
Local Government Act 1972 (c.70)
Local Government Act 1974 (c.7)
Local Government Act 1985 (c.51)
Local Government Act 1988 (c.9)
Local Government Act 1992 (c.19)
Local Government Act 1999 (c.27)
Local Government Act 2000 (c.22)
Local Government Act 2003 (c.26)
Local Government and Housing Act 1989 (c.42)
Local Government and Public Involvement in Health Act 2007 (c.28)
Local Government and Rating Act 1997 (c.29)
Local Government etc (Scotland) Act 1994 (c.39)
Local Government Finance (Publicity for Auditors Reports) Act 1991 (c.15)
Local Government Finance Act 1988 (c.41)
Local Government Finance Act 1992 (c.14)
Local Government in Scotland Act 2003 (asp 1)
Local Government, Planning and Land Act 1980 (c.65)
Local Land Charges Act 1975 (c.76)
Local Transport Act 2008 (c.26)
London Government Act 1963 (c.33)
London Local Authorities Act 2000 (c.vii)
London Olympic Games and Paralympic Games Act 2006 (c.12)
London Regional Transport (Amendment) Act 1985 (c.10)
London Regional Transport Act 1996 (c.21)
London to Harwich Roads Act 1695 (c.9)
London to Harwich Roads Act 1707 (c.47)
Lotteries and Amusements Act 1976 (c.32)
Lyon King of Arms Act 1867 (c.17)
Magistrates Courts Act 1980 (c.43)
Maintenance Orders (Facilities for Enforcement) Act 1920 (c.33)
Maintenance Orders (Reciprocal Enforcement) Act 1972 (c.18)
Maintenance Orders Act 1950 (c.37)
Maintenance Orders Act 1958 (c.39)
Malicious Communications Act 1988 (c.27)
Management of Offenders etc (Scotland) Act 2005 (asp 14)
Marine Insurance Act 1906 (c.41)
Marriage (Registrar General's Licence) Act 1970 (c.34)
Marriage Act 1949 (c.76)
Marriage with Foreigners Act 1906 (c.40)
Matrimonial and Family Proceedings Act 1984 (c.42)
Matrimonial Causes Act 1973 (c.18)
Matrimonial Homes (Family Protection) (Scotland) Act 1981 (c.59)
Matrimonial Proceedings and Property Act 1970 (c.45)
Medical Act 1983 (c.54)
Medicines Act 1968 (c.67)
Medicines Act 1971 (c.69)
Mental Capacity Act 2005 (c.9)
Mental Health (Care and Treatment) (Scotland) Act 2003 (asp 13)
Mental Health (Scotland) Act 1984 (c.36)
Mental Health Act 1959 (c.72)
Mental Health Act 1983 (c.20)
Mental Health Act 2007 (c.12)
Merchant Shipping (Liner Conferences) Act 1982 (c.37)
Merchant Shipping Act 1995 (c.21)
Metropolitan Commons Act 1866 (c.122)
Metropolitan Commons Act 1878 (c.71)
Metropolitan Commons Act 1898 (c.43)
Metropolitan Commons Amendment Act 1869 (c.107)
Metropolitan Public Carriage Act 1869 (c.115)
Middlesex Gaol Act 1786 (c.55)
Middlesex Sessions House Act 1778 (c.67)
Mines (Working Facilities and Support) Act 1923 (c.20)
Mines (Working Facilities and Support) Act 1966 (c.4)
Mines Act (Northern Ireland) 1969 (c.6)
Mines and Quarries (Tips) Act 1969 (c.10)
Mines and Quarries Act 1954 (c.70)
Ministerial and other Salaries Act 1975 (c.27)
Ministers of the Crown Act 1975 (c.26)
Ministry of Defence Police Act 1987 (c.4)
Misrepresentation Act 1967 (c.7)
Misuse of Drugs Act 1971 (c.38)
Mobile Homes Act 1983 (c.34)
Mock Auctions Act 1961 (c.47)
Mortgage Rights (Scotland) Act 2001 (asp 11)
Motor Cycle Noise Act 1987 (c.34)
Motor Vehicles (International Circulation) Act 1952 (c.39)
Museums and Galleries Act 1992 (c.44)
National Assistance Act 1948 (c.29)
National Audit Act 1983 (c.44)
National Debt Act 1972 (c.65)
National Health Service (Consequential Provisions) Act 2006 (c.43)
National Health Service (Scotland) Act 1972 (c.58)
National Health Service (Scotland) Act 1978 (c.29)
National Health Service (Wales) Act 2006 (c.42)
National Health Service Act 1977 (c.49)
National Health Service Act 2006 (c.41)
National Health Service and Community Care Act 1990 (c.19)
National Health Service Reform and Health Care Professions Act 2002 (c.17)
National Heritage Act 1983 (c.47)
National Insurance Act 1965 (c.51)
National Insurance Contributions Act 2008 (c.16)
National Insurance Contributions and Statutory Payments Act 2004 (c.3)
National Loans Act 1968 (c.13)
National Lottery etc Act 1993 (c.39)
National Minimum Wage (Enforcement Notices) Act 2003 (c.8)
National Minimum Wage Act 1998 (c.39)
National Parks (Scotland) Act 2000 (asp 10)
National Savings Bank Act 1971 (c.29)
Nationality, Immigration and Asylum Act 2002 (c.41)
Natural Environment and Rural Communities Act 2006 (c.16)
Natural Heritage (Scotland) Act 1991 (c.28)
Nature Conservation (Scotland) Act 2004 (asp 6)
Naval and Military War Pensions &c Act 1915 (c.83)
Naval and Military War Pensions etc (Administrative Expenses) Act 1917 (c.14)
Naval Discipline Act 1957 (c.53)

ALPHABETICAL TABLE OF STATUTES

Naval Medical Compassionate Fund Act 1915 (c.28)
New Roads and Street Works Act 1991 (c.22)
New Towns (Amendment) Act 1994 (c.5)
New Towns (Scotland) Act 1968 (c.16)
New Towns Act 1981 (c.64)
New Towns and Urban Development Corporations Act 1985 (c.5)
Newgate Gaol and Sessions House Act 1778 (c.48)
NHS Redress (Wales) Measure 2008 (m.01)
NHS Redress Act 2006 (c.44)
Noise Act 1996 (c.37)
Noise and Statutory Nuisance Act 1993 (c.40)
Non-parochial Registers Act 1840 (c.92)
Norfolk and Suffolk Broads Act 1988 (c.4)
Norfolk Roads Act 1770 (c.54)
Norfolk Roads Act 1792 (c.148)
Northern Ireland (Miscellaneous Provisions) Act 2006 (c.33)
Northern Ireland (Sentences) Act 1998 (c.35)
Northern Ireland Act 1998 (c.47)
Northern Ireland Act 2000 (c.1)
Northern Ireland Arms Decommissioning Act 1997 (c.7)
Northern Ireland Assembly Disqualification Act 1975 (c.25)
Norwich to Bixley Roads Act 1790 (c.85)
Nuclear Installations Act 1965 (c.57)
Nuclear Material (Offences) Act 1983 (c.18)
Obscene Publications Act 1959 (c.66)
Offences against the Person Act 1861 (c.100)
Offender Management Act 2007 (c.21)
Offices, Shops and Railway Premises Act 1963 (c.41)
Official Secrets Act 1911 (c.28)
Official Secrets Act 1920 (c.75)
Official Secrets Act 1939 (c.121)
Official Secrets Act 1989 (c.6)
Offshore Petroleum Development (Scotland) Act 1975 (c.8)
Offshore Safety Act 1992 (c.15)
Oil and Pipelines Act 1985 (c.62)
Oil Taxation Act 1975 (c.22)
Oil Taxation Act 1983 (c.56)
Olympic Symbol etc (Protection) Act 1995 (c.32)
Opencast Coal Act 1958 (c.69)
Opticians Act 1989 (c.44)
Osteopaths Act 1993 (c.21)
Parliamentary Commissioner Act 1967 (c.13)
Parliamentary Constituencies Act 1986 (c.56)
Partnership Act 1890 (c.39)
Party Wall etc Act 1996 (c.40)
Patents Act 1977 (c.37)
Pedlars Act 1871 (c.96)
Pembroke Gaol Act 1779 (c.46)
Pension Schemes (Northern Ireland) Act 1993 (c.49)
Pension Schemes Act 1993 (c.48)
Pensions (Increase) Act 1971 (c.56)
Pensions (Increase) Act 1974 (c.9)
Pensions Act 1995 (c.26)
Pensions Act 2004 (c.35)
Pensions Act 2007 (c.22)
Pensions Act 2008 (c.30)
Pensions Appeal Tribunals Act 1943 (c.39)
Performing Animals (Regulation) Act 1925 (c.38)
Perjury Act 1911 (c.6)
Personal Injuries (Emergency Provisions) Act 1939 (c.82)
Pests Act 1954 (c.68)
Pet Animals Act 1951 (c.35)
Petroleum (Consolidation) Act 1928 (c.32)
Petroleum (Production) Act 1934 (c.36)
Petroleum (Transfer of Licences) Act 1936 (c.27)
Petroleum Act 1987 (c.12)
Petroleum Act 1998 (c.17)
Petroleum Revenue Tax Act 1980 (c.1)
Pilotage Act 1987 (c.21)
Pipe-lines Act 1962 (c.58)
Places of Worship Registration Act 1855 (c.81)
Planning (Consequential Provisions) Act 1990 (c.11)
Planning (Hazardous Substances) (Scotland) Act 1997 (c.10)
Planning (Hazardous Substances) Act 1990 (c.10)
Planning (Listed Buildings and Conservation Areas) (Scotland) Act 1997 (c.9)
Planning (Listed Buildings and Conservation Areas) Act 1990 (c.9)
Planning Act 2008 (c.29)
Planning and Compensation Act 1991 (c.34)
Planning and Compulsory Purchase Act 2004 (c.5)
Planning and Energy Act 2008 (c.21)
Planning etc (Scotland) Act 2006 (asp 17)
Planning-gain Supplement (Preparations) Act 2007 (c.2)
Plant Health Act 1967 (c.8)
Plant Varieties Act 1997 (c.66)
Plant Varieties and Seeds Act 1964 (c.14)
Plymouth Poor Relief Act 1758 (c.59)
Plymouth Poor Relief Act 1786 (c.19)
Plymouth Workhouse Act 1707 (c.46)
Pneumoconiosis etc (Workers Compensation) Act 1979 (c.41)
Poisons Act 1972 (c.66)
Police (Insurance of Voluntary Assistants) Act 1997 (c.45)
Police (Northern Ireland) Act 1998 (c.32)
Police (Northern Ireland) Act 2000 (c.32)
Police (Scotland) Act 1967 (c.77)
Police Act 1964 (c.48)
Police Act 1996 (c.16)
Police Act 1997 (c.50)
Police and Criminal Evidence Act 1984 (c.60)
Police and Firemen (War Service) Act 1939 (c.103)
Police and Firemen (War Service) Act 1944 (c.22)
Police and Justice Act 2006 (c.48)
Police and Magistrates Courts Act 1994 (c.29)
Police Pensions Act 1976 (c.35)
Police Reform Act 2002 (c.30)
Police, Factories, & C (Miscellaneous Provisions) Act 1916 (c.31)
Police, Public Order and Criminal Justice (Scotland) Act 2006 (asp 10)
Polish Resettlement Act 1947 (c.19)
Political Parties, Elections and Referendums Act 2000 (c.41)
Pollution Prevention and Control Act 1999 (c.24)
Population (Statistics) Act 1938 (c.12)
Port of London Act 1968 (c.xxxii)
Port of Tyne (North Shields Fish Harbour) Act 1974 (c.xxxvi)
Ports (Finance) Act 1985 (c.30)
Ports Act 1991 (c.52)
Post Office Act 1969 (c.48)
Postal Services Act 2000 (c.26)
Powers of Criminal Courts (Sentencing) Act 2000 (c.6)
Prescription Act 1832 (c.71)
Prescription and Limitation (Scotland) Act 1973 (c.52)
Prevention of Corruption Act 1906 (c.34)
Prevention of Corruption Act 1916 (c.64)
Prevention of Damage by Pests Act 1949 (c.55)
Prevention of Oil Pollution Act 1971 (c.60)
Prevention of Terrorism Act 2005 (c.2)
Prices Act 1974 (c.24)
Prison Act 1952 (c.52)

Schools (Health Promotion and Nutrition) (Scotland) Act 2007 (asp 15)
Science and Technology Act 1965 (c.4)
Scotch Whisky Act 1988 (c.22)
Scotland Act 1998 (c.46)
Scottish Commission for Human Rights Act 2006 (asp 16)
Scottish Public Services Ombudsman Act 2002 (asp 11)
Scottish Register of Tartans Act 2008 (asp 7)
Scrap Metal Dealers Act 1964 (c.69)
Sea Fish (Conservation) Act 1967 (c.84)
Sea Fisheries (Shellfish) Act 1967 (c.83)
Sea Fisheries Act 1968 (c.77)
Sea Fisheries Regulation Act 1966 (c.38)
Seamen's and Soldiers False Characters Act 1906 (c.5)
Security Service Act 1989 (c.5)
Self-Governing Schools etc (Scotland) Act 1989 (c.39)
Senior Judiciary (Vacancies and Incapacity) (Scotland) Act 2006 (asp 9)
Serious Crime Act 2007 (c.27)
Serious Organised Crime and Police Act 2005 (c.15)
Servants Characters Act 1792 (c.56)
Sessions Houses, Westminster, etc Act 1804 (c.61)
Settled Land Act 1925 (c.18)
Severn Bridges Act 1992 (c.3)
Sewerage (Scotland) Act 1968 (c.47)
Sex Discrimination Act 1975 (c.65)
Sex Discrimination Act 1986 (c.59)
Sex Offenders Act 1997 (c.51)
Sexual Offences (Amendment) Act 1992 (c.34)
Sexual Offences (Conspiracy and Incitement) Act 1996 (c.29)
Sexual Offences Act 1956 (c.69)
Sexual Offences Act 2003 (c.42)
Sheriff Courts (Scotland) Act 1907 (c.51)
Sheriff Courts (Scotland) Act 1971 (c.58)
Sheriff Courts (Scotland) Extracts Act 1892 (c.17)
Sheriff Courts and Legal Officers (Scotland) Act 1927 (c.35)
Slaughter of Poultry Act 1967 (c.24)
Slaughterhouses Act 1974 (c.3)
Small Landholders (Scotland) Act 1911 (c.49)
Smoking, Health and Social Care (Scotland) Act 2005 (asp 13)
Social Security (Consequential Provisions) Act 1992 (c.6)
Social Security (Miscellaneous Provisions) Act 1977 (c.5)
Social Security (Recovery of Benefits) Act 1997 (c.27)
Social Security Act 1975 (c.14)
Social Security Act 1986 (c.50)
Social Security Act 1988 (c.7)
Social Security Act 1990 (c.27)
Social Security Act 1998 (c.14)
Social Security Administration (Northern Ireland) Act 1992 (c.8)
Social Security Administration Act 1992 (c.5)
Social Security Contributions (Transfer of Functions, etc.) Act 1999 (c.2)
Social Security Contributions and Benefits (Northern Ireland) Act 1992 (c.7)
Social Security Contributions and Benefits Act 1992 (c.4)
Social Security Fraud Act 2001 (c.11)
Social Security Pensions Act 1975 (c.60)
Social Work (Scotland) Act 1968 (c.49)
Solicitors (Scotland) Act 1980 (c.46)
Solicitors Act 1974 (c.47)
Somerset House Act 1984 (c.21)
Southwark Workhouse Act 1774 (c.75)
Special Educational Needs (Information) Act 2008 (c.11)
Special Educational Needs and Disability Act 2001 (c.10)
Special Immigration Appeals Commission Act 1997 (c.68)
Stafford Gaol Act 1787 (c.60)
Stamp Act 1891 (c.39)
State Immunity Act 1978 (c.33)
State Pension Credit Act 2002 (c.16)
Statistics and Registration Service Act 2007 (c.18)
Statistics of Trade Act 1947 (c.39)
Statute Law (Repeals) Act 1981 (c.19)
Statute Law (Repeals) Act 1993 (c.50)
Statute Law (Repeals) Act 1995 (c.44)
Statute Law (Repeals) Act 2008 (c.12)
Statute of Frauds Amendment Act 1828 (c.14)
Statutory Corporations (Financial Provisions) Act 1974 (c.8)
Statutory Instruments Act 1946 (c.36)
Statutory Water Companies Act 1991 (c.58)
Stock Transfer Act 1963 (c.18)
Suicide Act 1961 (c.60)
Sunday Trading Act 1994 (c.20)
Sunderland Poor Relief Act 1791 (c.87)
Superannuation (Miscellaneous Provisions) Act 1967 (c.28)
Superannuation Act 1972 (c.11)
Supplementary Benefits Act 1976 (c.71)
Supply of Goods (Implied Terms) Act 1973 (c.13)
Supply of Goods and Services Act 1982 (c.29)
Supreme Court Act 1981 (c.54)
Supreme Court of Judicature Act 1873 (c.66)
Surrey Gaol Act 1791 (c.22)
Surrogacy Arrangements Act 1985 (c.49)
Sussex Gaol Act 1787 (c.58)
Sustainable Communities Act 2007 (c.23)
Sustainable Energy Act 2003 (c.30)
Taking of Hostages Act 1982 (c.28)
Tax Credits Act 2002 (c.21)
Taxation of Chargeable Gains Act 1992 (c.12)
Taxes Management Act 1970 (c.9)
Teaching and Higher Education Act 1998 (c.30)
Teaching Council (Scotland) Act 1965 (c.19)
Telecommunications Act 1984 (c.12)
Tenures Abolition Act 1660 (c.24)
Territorial Waters Jurisdiction Act 1878 (c.73)
Terrorism Act 2000 (c.11)
Terrorism Act 2006 (c.11)
Thames Embankment Act 1766 (c.37)
Theatres Act 1968 (c.54)
Theatres Trust Act 1976 (c.27)
Theft Act 1968 (c.60)
Theft Act 1978 (c.31)
Third Parties (Rights against Insurers) Act 1930 (c.25)
Timeshare Act 1992 (c.35)
Tithe Act 1836 (c.71)
Title Conditions (Scotland) Act 2003 (asp 9)
Tobacco Advertising and Promotion Act 2002 (c.36)
Tobacco Products Duty Act 1979 (c.7)
Torts (Interference with Goods) Act 1977 (c.32)
Tourist Boards (Scotland) Act 2006 (asp 15)
Town and Country Amenities Act 1974 (c.32)
Town and Country Planning (Costs of Inquiries etc.) Act 1995 (c.49)
Town and Country Planning (Scotland) Act 1997 (c.8)
Town and Country Planning Act 1990 (c.8)
Town Police Clauses Act 1847 (c.89)
Towns Improvement (Ireland) Act 1854 (c.103)
Trade Descriptions Act 1968 (c.29)

ALPHABETICAL TABLE OF STATUTORY INSTRUMENTS

This table lists all the Statutory Instruments cited in the Statutory Instruments Citator.

A1 Motorway (North of Leeming to Scotch Corner Section and Connecting Roads) Scheme 1996 (S.I. 1830)
A1 Trunk Road (Lengths of A1 Carriageway between Catterick and Barton) (Detrunking) Order 1996 (S.I. 1831)
A26 and A27 Trunk Roads (Beddingham) (40 Miles Per Hour Speed Limit) Order 2004 (S.I. 2085)
A282 Trunk Road (Dartford-Thurrock Crossing Charging Scheme) Order 2002 (S.I. 1040)
A556 Trunk Road (Church Farm-Turnpike Wood, Over Tabley) Order 1996 (S.I. 1650)
A556 Trunk Road (Turnpike Wood, Over Tabley-A56 Bowdon Roundabout) (Detrunking) Order 1996 (S.I. 1651)
A556(M) Motorway (M6 to M56 Link) and Connecting Roads Scheme 1996 (S.I. 1648)
A556(M) Motorway (M6 to M56 Link) Supplementary Connecting Roads Scheme 1996 (S.I. 1649)
Abolition of the NHS Tribunal (Consequential Provisions) Regulations 2001 (S.I. 3744)
Abolition of the NHS Tribunal (Consequential Provisions) Regulations 2002 (S.I. 1920)
Abortion Regulations 1991 (S.I. 499)
ABRO Trading Fund Order 2002 (S.I. 719)
Absent Voting (Transitional Provisions) (Scotland) Regulations 2008 (S.I. 48)
Access to Justice (Northern Ireland) Order 2003 (S.I. 435)
Accession (Immigration and Worker Authorisation) Regulations 2006 (S.I. 3317)
Accession (Immigration and Worker Registration) Regulations 2004 (S.I. 1219)
Accounting Standards (Prescribed Body) Regulations 2005 (S.I. 697)
Accounts and Audit (Wales) Regulations 2005 (S.I. 368)
Accounts and Audit Regulations 2003 (S.I. 533)
Act of Adjournal (Criminal Procedure Rules Amendment No.3) (Vulnerable Witnesses (Scotland) Act 2004) 2005 (S.S.I. 188)
Act of Adjournal (Criminal Procedure Rules Amendment No.6) (Vulnerable Witnesses (Scotland) Act 2004) (Evidence on Commission) 2005 (S.S.I. 574)
Act of Adjournal (Criminal Procedure Rules Amendment) (Vulnerable Witnesses (Scotland) Act 2004) 2006 (S.S.I. 76)
Act of Adjournal (Criminal Procedure Rules) 1996 (S.I. 513)
Act of Sederunt (Child Care and Maintenance Rules) 1997 (S.I. 291)
Act of Sederunt (Child Support Rules) 1993 (S.I. 920)
Act of Sederunt (Consumer Credit Act 1974) 1985 (S.I. 705)
Act of Sederunt (Debt Arrangement and Attachment (Scotland) Act 2002) 2002 (S.S.I. 560)
Act of Sederunt (Fees of Messengers-at-Arms) (No.2) 2002 (S.S.I. 566)
Act of Sederunt (Fees of Sheriff Officers) (No.2) 2002 (S.S.I. 567)
Act of Sederunt (Fees of Solicitors in the Sheriff Court) (Amendment and Further Provisions) 1993 (S.I. 3080)
Act of Sederunt (Fees of Solicitors in the Sheriff Court) (Amendment) 2008 (S.S.I. 40)
Act of Sederunt (Fees of Witnesses and Shorthand Writers in the Sheriff Court) 1992 (S.I. 1878)
Act of Sederunt (Judicial Factors Rules) 1992 (S.I. 272)
Act of Sederunt (Ordinary Cause Rules, Sheriff Court) 1983 (S.I. 747)
Act of Sederunt (Proceedings in the Sheriff Court under the Debtors (Scotland) Act 1987) 1988 (S.I. 2013)
Act of Sederunt (Rules of the Court of Session 1994) 1994 (S.I. 1443)
Act of Sederunt (Sheriff Court Bankruptcy Rules) 1996 (S.I. 2507)
Act of Sederunt (Sheriff Court Company Insolvency Rules) 1986 (S.I. 2297)
Act of Sederunt (Sheriff Court Ordinary Cause Rules) 1993 (S.I. 1956)
Act of Sederunt (Small Claim Rules) 2002 (S.S.I. 133)
Act of Sederunt (Summary Applications, Statutory Applications and Appeals etc Rules) 1999 (S.I. 929)
Act of Sederunt (Summary Cause Rules) 2002 (S.S.I. 132)
Action Programme for Nitrate Vulnerable Zones (Amendment) (Wales) Regulations 2003 (S.I. 1852)
Action Programme for Nitrate Vulnerable Zones (England and Wales) Regulations 1998 (S.I. 1202)
Action Programme for Nitrate Vulnerable Zones (Scotland) Amendment Regulations 2003 (S.S.I. 169)
Action Programme for Nitrate Vulnerable Zones (Scotland) Regulations 2003 (S.S.I. 51)
Action Programme for Nitrate Vulnerable Zones (Scotland) Regulations 2008 (S.S.I. 298)
Activity Centres (Young Person's Safety) (Northern Ireland) Order 1998 (S.I. 1069)
Adjudicator to Her Majesty's Land Registry (Practice and Procedure) Rules 2003 (S.I. 2171)
Administration of the Rent Officer Service (England) Order 1999 (S.I. 2403)
Administrative Justice and Tribunals Council (Listed Tribunals) Order 2007 (S.I. 2951)
Adoption (Designation of Overseas Adoptions) Order 1973 (S.I. 19)
Adoption (Northern Ireland) Order 1987 (S.I. 2203)
Adoption Agencies (Scotland) Regulations 1996 (S.I. 3266)
Adoption Agencies (Wales) Regulations 2005 (S.I. 1313)
Adoption Agencies Regulations 1983 (S.I. 1964)
Adoption and Children Act 2002 (Consequential Amendments) Order 2005 (S.I. 3504)
Adoption Support Agencies (England) and Adoption Agencies (Miscellaneous Amendments) Regulations 2005 (S.I. 2720)
Adoption Support Agencies (Wales) Regulations 2005 (S.I. 1514)
Adoption Support Services (Local Authorities) (Wales) Regulations 2005 (S.I. 1512)

ALPHABETICAL TABLE OF STATUTORY INSTRUMENTS

ALPHABETICAL TABLE OF STATUTORY INSTRUMENTS

Borough of Congleton (Electoral Changes) Order 1998 (S.I. 2843)
Borough of Crewe and Nantwich (Electoral Changes) Order 1998 (S.I. 2845)
Borough of Macclesfield (Electoral Changes) Order 1998 (S.I. 2847)
Borough of Shrewsbury and Atcham (Electoral Changes) Order 2000 (S.I. 1725)
Boulby Mine (Storage Battery Locomotives) Special Regulations 1972 (S.I. 472)
Bovine Embryo (Collection, Production and Transfer) Regulations 1995 (S.I. 2478)
Bovine Products (Restriction on Placing on the Market) (England) (No.2) Regulations 2005 (S.I. 3068)
Bovine Products (Restriction on Placing on the Market) (Wales) (No.2) Regulations 2005 (S.I. 3296)
Bovine Semen (Scotland) Regulations 2007 (S.S.I. 330)
Bovine Spongiform Encephalopathy (BSE) Compensation (Wales) Regulations 2006 (S.I. 1512)
Bradford & Bingley plc Transfer of Securities and Property etc Order 2008 (S.I. 2546)
British Citizenship (Designated Service) Order 2006 (S.I. 1390)
British Dependent Territories Citizenship (Designated Service) Order 1982 (S.I. 1710)
British Wool Marketing Scheme (Approval) Order 1950 (S.I. 1326)
Bro Morgannwg National Health Service Trust (Establishment) Amendment Order 2000 (S.I. 1076)
Bro Morgannwg National Health Service Trust (Establishment) Order 1998 (S.I. 3319)
Broadcasting and Communications (Jersey) Order 2004 (S.I. 308)
Brucellosis (England) Order 2000 (S.I. 2055)
Building (Approved Inspectors etc.) Regulations 2000 (S.I. 2532)
Building (Fees) (Scotland) Regulations 2004 (S.S.I. 508)
Building (Procedure) (Scotland) Regulations 2004 (S.S.I. 428)
Building (Scotland) Regulations 2004 (S.S.I. 406)
Building Regulations 2000 (S.I. 2531)
Building Societies (Accounts and Related Provisions) Regulations 1998 (S.I. 504)
Burma (Sale, Supply, Export, Technical Assistance, Financing and Financial Assistance) (Penalties and Licences) Regulations 2006 (S.I. 2682)
Bus Lane Contraventions (Penalty Charges, Adjudication and Enforcement) (England) Regulations 2005 (S.I. 2757)
Bus Service Operators Grant (England) Regulations 2002 (S.I. 1015)
Bus Service Operators Grant (Scotland) Regulations 2002 (S.S.I. 289)
Bus Service Operators Grant (Wales) Regulations 2002 (S.I. 2022)
Business Advertisements (Disclosure) Order 1977 (S.I. 1918)
Business Improvement Districts (Scotland) Regulations 2007 (S.S.I. 202)
Cableway Installations Regulations 2004 (S.I. 129)
Cairngorms National Park Designation, Transitional and Consequential Provisions (Scotland) Order 2003 (S.S.I. 1)
Capital Allowances (Energy-saving Plant and Machinery) Order 2001 (S.I. 2541)
Capital Allowances (Environmentally Beneficial Plant and Machinery) Order 2003 (S.I. 2076)
Cardiothoracic Centre-Liverpool National Health Service Trust (Establishment) Order 1990 (S.I. 2404)
Care Homes (Adult Placements) (Amendment) Regulations 2003 (S.I. 1845)
Care Homes (Amendment No.2) Regulations 2003 (S.I. 1703)
Care Homes (Amendment) (Wales) Regulations 2003 (S.I. 947)
Care Homes (Amendment) Regulations 2003 (S.I. 534)
Care Homes (Wales) (Amendment No.2) Regulations 2003 (S.I. 1004)
Care Homes (Wales) (Amendment) Regulations 2004 (S.I. 1314)
Care Homes (Wales) Regulations 2002 (S.I. 324)
Care Homes Regulations 2001 (S.I. 3965)
Care Standards Act 2000 (Domiciliary Care Agencies and Nurses Agencies) (Amendment) (England) Regulations 2003 (S.I. 2323)
Care Standards Act 2000 (Establishments and Agencies) (Miscellaneous Amendments) Regulations 2002 (S.I. 865)
Care Standards Act 2000 (Establishments and Agencies) (Miscellaneous Amendments) Regulations 2004 (S.I. 1770)
Care Standards Act 2000 (Establishments and Agencies) (Miscellaneous Amendments) Regulations 2006 (S.I. 1493)
Care Standards Act 2000 (Extension of the Application of Part 2 to Adult Placement Schemes) (England) Regulations 2004 (S.I. 1972)
Care Standards Act 2000 and the Children Act 1989 (Abolition of Fees) (Wales) Regulations 2006 (S.I. 878)
Care Standards Act 2000 and the Children Act 1989 (Amendment of Miscellaneous Regulations) (Wales) Regulations 2004 (S.I. 2414)
Care Standards Act 2000 and the Children Act 1989 (Regulatory Reform and Complaints) (Wales) Regulations 2006 (S.I. 3251)
Carmarthenshire National Health Service Trust (Establishment) Order 1998 (S.I. 3316)
Carriage by Air Acts (Application of Provisions) Order 1967 (S.I. 480)
Carriage of Dangerous Goods by Rail Regulations 1996 (S.I. 2089)
Carriage of Dangerous Goods by Road Regulations 1996 (S.I. 2095)
Cash Ratio Deposits (Value Bands and Ratios) Order 2004 (S.I. 1270)
Cattle Identification Regulations 2007 (S.I. 529)
Cattle Plaque Order 1928 (S.I. 206)
Cayman Islands (Constitution) Order 1972 (S.I. 1101)
Central Institutions (Recognition) (Scotland) (No.2) Regulations 1990 (S.I. 2386)
Central Rating List (England) Regulations 2005 (S.I. 551)
Central Rating List (Wales) Regulations 2005 (S.I. 422)
Cereals Marketing Act (Application to Oilseeds) Order 1989 (S.I. 1200)
Cereals Marketing Act 1965 (Amendment) Regulations 1977 (S.I. 181)
Cereals Marketing Act 1965 (Amendment) Regulations 1979 (S.I. 26)
Ceredigion and Mid Wales National Health Service Trust (Establishment) Order 1992 (S.I. 2735)
Channel Tunnel (International Arrangements) Order 2005 (S.I. 3207)
Channel Tunnel (Security) Order 1994 (S.I. 570)
Channel Tunnel Rail Link (Nomination) Order 1999 (S.I. 391)
Charges for Residues Surveillance (Amendment) Regulations 2007 (S.I. 2439)

Common Agricultural Policy Single Payment and Support Schemes (Cross-compliance) (England) Regulations 2005 (S.I. 3459)
Common Agricultural Policy Single Payment and Support Schemes (Integrated Administration and Control System) Regulations 2005 (S.I. 218)
Common Agricultural Policy Single Payment and Support Schemes (Wales) Regulations 2005 (S.I. 360)
Common Agricultural Policy Single Payment and Support Schemes Regulations 2005 (S.I. 219)
Common Services Agency (Withdrawal and Amendment of Functions) (Scotland) Order 1991 (S.I. 900)
Commonhold (Land Registration) Rules 2004 (S.I. 1830)
Commons (Deregistration and Exchange Orders) (Interim Arrangements) (England) Regulations 2007 (S.I. 2585)
Commons (Registration of Town or Village Greens) (Interim Arrangements) (England) Regulations 2007 (S.I. 457)
Communications (Bailiwick of Guernsey) Order 2003 (S.I. 3195)
Communications (Bailiwick of Guernsey) Order 2004 (S.I. 307)
Communications (Isle of Man) Order 2003 (S.I. 3198)
Communications (Jersey) Order 2003 (S.I. 3197)
Communications (Television Licensing) Regulations 2004 (S.I. 692)
Community Benefit Societies (Restriction on Use of Assets) Regulations 2006 (S.I. 264)
Community Bus Regulations 1986 (S.I. 1245)
Community Care (Direct Payments) (Scotland) Regulations 2003 (S.S.I. 243)
Community Care (Personal Care and Nursing Care) (Scotland) Regulations 2002 (S.I. 303)
Community Care (Personal Care and Nursing Care) (Scotland) Regulations 2002 (S.S.I. 303)
Community Care, Services for Carers and Children's Services (Direct Payments) (England) Regulations 2003 (S.I. 762)
Community Care, Services for Carers and Children's Services (Direct Payments) (Wales) Regulations 2004 (S.I. 1748)
Community Charges (Deductions from Income Support) (No.2) Regulations 1990 (S.I. 545)
Community Charges (Deductions from Income Support) (Scotland) Regulations 1989 (S.I. 507)
Community Emissions Trading Scheme (Allocation of Allowances for Payment) Regulations 2008 (S.I. 1825)
Community Interest Company Regulations 2005 (S.I. 1788)
Community Investment Tax Relief (Accreditation of Community Development Finance Institutions) Regulations 2003 (S.I. 96)
Community Justice Authorities (Establishment, Constitution and Proceedings) (Scotland) Order 2006 (S.S.I. 182)
Community Legal Service (Financial) Regulations 2000 (S.I. 516)
Community Legal Service (Funding) (Counsel in Family Proceedings) Order 2001 (S.I. 1077)
Community Legal Service (Funding) Order 2000 (S.I. 627)
Community Legal Service (Funding) Order 2007 (S.I. 2441)
Community Trade Mark Regulations 2006 (S.I. 1027)
Companies (Cross-Border Mergers) Regulations 2007 (S.I. 2974)
Companies (Defective Accounts) (Authorised Person) Order (Northern Ireland) 1991 (S.I. 269)
Companies (Defective Accounts) (Authorised Person) Order 2005 (S.I. 699)
Companies (Disclosure of Auditor Remuneration and Liability Limitation Agreements) Regulations 2008 (S.I. 489)
Companies (Disclosure of Auditor Remuneration) Regulations 2005 (S.I. 2417)
Companies (Forms Amendment No.2 and Company's Type and Principal Business Activities) Regulations 1990 (S.I. 1766)
Companies (Forms) (Amendment) Regulations 1999 (S.I. 2356)
Companies (Forms) (Amendment) Regulations 2002 (S.I. 691)
Companies (Inspection and Copying of Registers, Indices and Documents) Regulations 1991 (S.I. 1998)
Companies (Late Filing Penalties) and Limited Liability Partnerships (Filing Periods and Late Filing Penalties) Regulations 2008 (S.I. 497)
Companies (No.2) (Northern Ireland) Order 1990 (S.I. 1504)
Companies (Northern Ireland) Order 1986 (S.I. 1032)
Companies (Northern Ireland) Order 1989 (S.I. 2404)
Companies (Northern Ireland) Order 1990 (S.I. 593)
Companies (Registrar, Languages and Trading Disclosures) Regulations 2006 (S.I. 3429)
Companies (Revision of Defective Accounts and Report) Regulations 1990 (S.I. 2570)
Companies (Summary Financial Statement) Regulations 1995 (S.I. 2092)
Companies (Summary Financial Statement) Regulations 2008 (S.I. 374)
Companies (Tables A to F) Regulations 1985 (S.I. 805)
Companies (Welsh Language Forms) (Amendment) Regulations 1999 (S.I. 2357)
Companies (Welsh Language Forms) (Amendment) Regulations 2000 (S.I. 2413)
Companies (Welsh Language Forms) Regulations 2003 (S.I. 62)
Companies Act 1989 (Delegation) Order 2005 (S.I. 2337)
Companies Act 1989 (Eligibility for Appointment as Company Auditor) (Consequential Amendments) Regulations 1991 (S.I. 1997)
Companies Act 2006 (Commencement No.1, Transitional Provisions and Savings) Order 2006 (S.I. 3428)
Companies Act 2006 (Commencement No.2, Consequential Amendments, Transitional Provisions and Savings) Order 2007 (S.I. 1093)
Companies Act 2006 (Commencement No.3, Consequential Amendments, Transitional Provisions and Savings) Order 2007 (S.I. 2194)
Companies Act 2006 (Commencement No.5, Transitional Provisions and Savings) Order 2007 (S.I. 3495)
Companies Act 2006 (Commencement No.6, Saving and Commencement Nos 3 and 5 (Amendment)) Order 2008 (S.I. 674)
Companies Act 2006 (Commencement No.7, Transitional Provisions and Savings) Order 2008 (S.I. 1886)
Company Directors Disqualification (Northern Ireland) Order 2002 (S.I. 3150)
Compensation (Claims Management Services) Regulations 2006 (S.I. 3322)
Competition Appeal Tribunal Rules 2003 (S.I. 1372)

ALPHABETICAL TABLE OF STATUTORY INSTRUMENTS

Education (Student Fees, Awards and Support) (Amendment) Regulations 2007 (S.I. 1336)
Education (Student Loans) (Amendment) (England and Wales) Regulations 2007 (S.I. 1630)
Education (Student Loans) (Northern Ireland) Order 1990 (S.I. 1506)
Education (Student Loans) (Repayment) (Amendment) Regulations 2001 (S.I. 971)
Education (Student Loans) (Repayment) Regulations 2000 (S.I. 944)
Education (Student Loans) (Scotland) Regulations 2007 (S.S.I. 154)
Education (Student Loans) Regulations 1998 (S.I. 211)
Education (Student Support) (Amendment) Regulations 2008 (S.I. 235)
Education (Student Support) (Dance and Drama) Regulations 1999 (S.I. 2263)
Education (Student Support) (European Institutions) (No.2) Regulations 2006 (S.I. 3156)
Education (Student Support) (No.2) Regulations 2002 (S.I. 3200)
Education (Student Support) (No.2) Regulations 2008 (S.I. 1582)
Education (Student Support) (Northern Ireland) Order 1998 (S.I. 1760)
Education (Student Support) Regulations 1998 (S.I. 2003)
Education (Student Support) Regulations 2005 (S.I. 52)
Education (Student Support) Regulations 2007 (S.I. 176)
Education (Student Support) Regulations 2008 (S.I. 529)
Education (Teacher Student Loans) (Repayment etc.) Regulations 2002 (S.I. 2086)
Education and Inspections Act 2006 (Commencement No.1 and Saving Provisions) Order 2006 (S.I. 2990)
Education and Inspections Act 2006 (Consequential Amendments) Regulations 2007 (S.I. 603)
Education and Libraries (Northern Ireland) Order 1986 (S.I. 594)
Education Maintenance Allowances (Scotland) Regulations 2007 (S.S.I. 156)
Eggs (Marketing Standards) (Enforcement) (Scotland) Regulations 2005 (S.S.I. 332)
Eggs (Marketing Standards) Regulations 1995 (S.I. 1544)
Eggs and Chicks (England) Regulations 2007 (S.I. 2245)
Eggs and Chicks (Scotland) Regulations 2008 (S.S.I. 129)
Election Petition Rules 1960 (S.I. 543)
Electoral Administration Act 2006 (Regulation of Loans etc Northern Ireland) Order 2008 (S.I. 1319)
Electoral Law (Northern Ireland) Order 1972 (S.I. 1264)
Electrically Assisted Pedal Cycles Regulations 1983 (S.I. 1168)
Electricity (Applications for Licences, Modifications of an Area and Extensions and Restrictions of Licences) Regulations 2007 (S.I. 1972)
Electricity (Northern Ireland) Order 1992 (S.I. 231)
Electricity and Gas (Energy Efficiency Obligations) Order 2001 (S.I. 4011)
Electricity and Gas (Energy Efficiency Obligations) Order 2004 (S.I. 3392)
Electricity at Work Regulations 1989 (S.I. 635)
Electricity Generating Stations and Overhead Lines (Inquiries Procedure) (England and Wales) Rules 2007 (S.I. 841)
Electricity Works (Environmental Impact Assessment) (Scotland) Regulations 2000 (S.S.I. 320)
Electro-medical Equipment (EEC Requirements) Regulations 1988 (S.I. 1586)
Employers Liability (Compulsory Insurance) Regulations 1998 (S.I. 2573)
Employers Liability (Defective Equipment and Compulsory Insurance) (Northern Ireland) Order 1972 (S.I. 963)
Employment Act 2002 (Dispute Resolution) Regulations 2004 (S.I. 752)
Employment and Support Allowance (Consequential Provisions) (No.2) Regulations 2008 (S.I. 1554)
Employment and Support Allowance (Consequential Provisions) Regulations 2008 (S.I. 1082)
Employment and Support Allowance (Transitional Provisions) Regulations 2008 (S.I. 795)
Employment and Support Allowance Regulations 2008 (S.I. 794)
Employment Appeal Tribunal Rules 1993 (S.I. 2854)
Employment Equality (Age) Regulations 2006 (S.I. 1031)
Employment Equality (Religion or Belief) Regulations 2003 (S.I. 1660)
Employment Equality (Sexual Orientation) Regulations 2003 (S.I. 1661)
Employment Protection (Offshore Employment) Order 1976 (S.I. 766)
Employment Protection (Recoupment of Jobseeker's Allowance and Income Support) Regulations 1996 (S.I. 2349)
Employment Rights (Increase of Limits) Order 2007 (S.I. 3570)
Employment Rights (Northern Ireland) Order 1996 (S.I. 1919)
Employment Tribunals (Constitution and Rules of Procedure) Regulations 2004 (S.I. 1861)
End-of-Life Vehicles Regulations 2003 (S.I. 2635)
Energy (Northern Ireland) Order 2003 (S.I. 419)
Energy Information (Combined Washer-driers) Regulations 1997 (S.I. 1624)
Energy Information (Dishwashers) Regulations 1999 (S.I. 1676)
Energy Information (Household Electric Ovens) Regulations 2003 (S.I. 751)
Energy Information (Household Refrigerators and Freezers) Regulations 2004 (S.I. 1468)
Energy Information (Lamps) Regulations 1999 (S.I. 1517)
Energy Information (Tumble Driers) Regulations 1996 (S.I. 601)
Energy Information (Washing Machines) Regulations 1996 (S.I. 600)
Energy Performance of Buildings (Certificates and Inspections) (England and Wales) Regulations 2007 (S.I. 991)
Energy Performance of Buildings (Scotland) Regulations 2008 (S.S.I. 309)
Enforcement of Road Traffic Debts Order 1993 (S.I. 2073)
Enterprise Act 2002 (Bodies Designated to make Super-complaints) Order 2004 (S.I. 1517)
Enterprise Act 2002 (Commencement No.4 and Transitional Provisions and Savings) Order 2003 (S.I. 2093)
Enterprise Act 2002 (Disqualification from Office General) Order 2006 (S.I. 1722)
Enterprise Act 2002 (Part 8 Community Infringements Specified UK Laws) Order 2003 (S.I. 1374)

Firefighters Compensation Scheme (Scotland) Order 2006 (S.S.I. 338)
Firefighters Compensation Scheme (Wales) Order 2007 (S.I. 1073)
Firefighters Pension Scheme (England) Order 2006 (S.I. 3432)
Firefighters Pension Scheme (Scotland) Order 2007 (S.S.I. 199)
Firefighters Pension Scheme (Wales) Order 2007 (S.I. 1072)
Firemen's Pension Scheme Order 1992 (S.I. 129)
First-tier Tribunal and Upper Tribunal (Chambers) Order 2008 (S.I. 2684)
Fisheries and Aquaculture Structures (Grants) (England) Regulations 2001 (S.I. 1117)
Fishery Products (Official Controls Charges) (Scotland) Regulations 2007 (S.S.I. 537)
Fishing Boats (Marking and Documentation) (Enforcement) Order 1993 (S.I. 2015)
Fixed-term Employees (Prevention of Less Favourable Treatment) Regulations 2002 (S.I. 2034)
Food Hygiene (Scotland) Regulations 2006 (S.S.I. 3)
Food Labelling (Amendment) (England) (No.2) (Amendment) Regulations 2005 (S.I. 2969)
Food Labelling (Amendment) (England) (No.2) Regulations 2004 (S.I. 2824)
Food Labelling (Amendment) (England) (No.2) Regulations 2005 (S.I. 2057)
Food Labelling (Amendment) (No.2) (Wales) Regulations 2004 (S.I. 3022)
Food Labelling (Amendment) (Wales) (No.2) (Amendment) Regulations 2005 (S.I. 3626)
Food Labelling (Amendment) (Wales) (No.2) Regulations 2005 (S.I. 2835)
Food Labelling (Declaration of Allergens) (England) Regulations 2007 (S.I. 3256)
Food Labelling (Declaration of Allergens) (Scotland) Regulations 2007 (S.S.I. 534)
Food Labelling (Declaration of Allergens) (Wales) Regulations 2007 (S.I. 3379)
Food Labelling Amendment (No.2) (Scotland) Regulations 2004 (S.S.I. 472)
Food Labelling Amendment (No.3) (Scotland) Regulations 2005 (S.S.I. 542)
Food Labelling Regulations 1996 (S.I. 1499)
Food Protection (Emergency Prohibitions) (Dounreay Nuclear Establishment) Order 1997 (S.I. 2622)
Food Protection (Emergency Prohibitions) (Radioactivity in Sheep) Order 1991 (S.I. 20)
Food Safety (Sampling and Qualifications) Regulations 1990 (S.I. 2463)
Food Standards Act 1999 (Transitional and Consequential Provisions and Savings) (England and Wales) Regulations 2000 (S.I. 656)
Foods for Special Medical Purposes (Scotland) Regulations 2000 (S.S.I. 130)
Foot-and-Mouth Disease (Scotland) Order 2006 (S.S.I. 44)
Footwear (Indication of Composition) Labelling Regulations 1995 (S.I. 2489)
Foreign Companies (Execution of Documents) Regulations 1994 (S.I. 950)
Foreign Fishing Boats (Stowage of Gear) Order 1970 (S.I. 318)
Foreign Limitation Periods (Northern Ireland) Order 1985 (S.I. 754)
Foreign Marriage Order 1970 (S.I. 1539)
Forest Reproductive Material (Great Britain) Regulations 2002 (S.I. 3026)
Forth Estuary Transport Authority Order 2002 (S.S.I. 178)
Fostering of Children (Scotland) Regulations 1996 (S.I. 3263)
Fostering Services (Amendment) Regulations 2008 (S.I. 640)
Fostering Services (Wales) (Amendment) Regulations 2003 (S.I. 896)
Fostering Services (Wales) Regulations 2003 (S.I. 237)
Fostering Services Regulations 2002 (S.I. 57)
Freedom of Information Act 2000 (Commencement No.3) Order 2003 (S.I. 2603)
Freight Containers (Safety Convention) Regulations 1984 (S.I. 1890)
Friendly Societies (Accounts and Related Provisions) Regulations 1994 (S.I. 1983)
Friendly Societies (Modification of the Corporation Tax Acts) Regulations 2005 (S.I. 2014)
Fuel-testing Pilot Projects (Biomix Project) Regulations 2007 (S.I. 314)
Gambling (Operating Licence and Single-Machine Permit Fees) Regulations 2006 (S.I. 3284)
Gambling Act 2005 (Advertising of Foreign Gambling) (Amendment) Regulations 2008 (S.I. 19)
Gambling Act 2005 (Advertising of Foreign Gambling) Regulations 2007 (S.I. 2329)
Gambling Act 2005 (Licensing Authority Policy Statement) (England and Wales) Regulations 2006 (S.I. 636)
Gambling Appeals Tribunal Fees Regulations 2006 (S.I. 3287)
Gaming Duty (Amendment) Regulations 2006 (S.I. 1999)
Gaming Duty Regulations 1997 (S.I. 2196)
Gangmasters (Licensing Conditions) (No.2) (Amendment) Rules 2007 (S.I. 401)
Gangmasters (Licensing Conditions) (No.2) Rules 2006 (S.I. 2373)
Gas (Applications for Licences and Extensions and Restrictions of Licences) Regulations 2007 (S.I. 1971)
Gas (Northern Ireland) Order 1996 (S.I. 275)
Gas (Standards of Performance) Regulations 2005 (S.I. 1135)
Gas Safety (Installation and Use) Regulations 1998 (S.I. 2451)
Gas Safety (Management) Regulations 1996 (S.I. 551)
Gender Recognition (Application Fees) Order 2006 (S.I. 758)
General and Special Commissioners (Amendment of Enactments) Regulations 1994 (S.I. 1813)
General and Specialist Medical Practice (Education, Training and Qualifications) Order 2003 (S.I. 1250)
General Chiropractic Council (Constitution and Procedure) Rules Order 1999 (S.I. 1537)
General Chiropractic Council (Election of Members and Chairman of Council) Rules Order 2002 (S.I. 1263)
General Commissioners (Jurisdiction and Procedure) (Amendment) Regulations 1999 (S.I. 3293)
General Commissioners (Jurisdiction and Procedure) (Amendment) Regulations 2005 (S.I. 340)
General Commissioners (Jurisdiction and Procedure) Regulations 1994 (S.I. 1812)
General Commissioners and Special Commissioners (Jurisdiction and Procedure) (Amendment) Regulations 2007 (S.I. 3612)
General Dental Council (Constitution) Order of Council 2006 (S.I. 1666)
General Medical Council (Constitution) (Amendment) Order 2007 (S.I. 616)

Local Authorities (Charges for Land Searches) Regulations 1994 (S.I. 1885)
Local Authorities (Code of Conduct) (Local Determination) Regulations 2003 (S.I. 1483)
Local Authorities (Conduct of Referendums) (Wales) Regulations 2004 (S.I. 870)
Local Authorities (Executive Arrangements) (Functions and Responsibilities) (Wales) Regulations 2007 (S.I. 399)
Local Authorities (Functions and Responsibilities) (England) (Amendment) Regulations 2008 (S.I. 516)
Local Authorities (Functions and Responsibilities) (England) Regulations 2000 (S.I. 2853)
Local Authorities (Members Allowances) (England) Regulations 2003 (S.I. 1021)
Local Authorities (Precepts) (Wales) Regulations 1995 (S.I. 2562)
Local Authorities (Referendums) (Petitions and Directions) (Wales) Regulations 2001 (S.I. 2292)
Local Authorities (Standing Orders) (England) Regulations 2001 (S.I. 3384)
Local Authorities (Standing Orders) Regulations 1993 (S.I. 202)
Local Authorities Traffic Orders (Procedure) (Scotland) Regulations 1999 (S.I. 614)
Local Authority (Overview and Scrutiny Committees Health Scrutiny Functions) Regulations 2002 (S.I. 3048)
Local Authority Adoption Service (Wales) Regulations 2005 (S.I. 3115)
Local Authority Targets (Well-Being of Young Children) Regulations 2007 (S.I. 1415)
Local Elections (Parishes and Communities) (England and Wales) Rules 2006 (S.I. 3305)
Local Elections (Parishes and Communities) Rules 1986 (S.I. 2215)
Local Governance (Scotland) Act 2004 (Remuneration) Regulations 2007 (S.S.I. 183)
Local Government (Allowances and Expenses) (Scotland) Regulations 2007 (S.S.I. 108)
Local Government (Best Value Performance Indicators) (Wales) Order 2005 (S.I. 665)
Local Government (Early Termination of Employment) (Discretionary Compensation) (England and Wales) Regulations 2006 (S.I. 2914)
Local Government (Parishes and Parish Councils) Regulations 1999 (S.I. 545)
Local Government (Politically Restricted Posts) (No.2) Regulations 1990 (S.I. 1447)
Local Government (Superannuation and Compensation for Premature Retirement) (Scotland) Amendment Regulations 1995 (S.I. 750)
Local Government (Superannuation and Compensation for Premature Retirement) (Scotland) Amendment Regulations 1996 (S.I. 1241)
Local Government (Superannuation and Compensation for Redundancy or Premature Retirement) (Scotland) Amendment Regulations 1995 (S.I. 3294)
Local Government and Public Involvement in Health Act 2007 (Commencement No.2 and Savings) Order 2008 (S.I. 172)
Local Government and Public Involvement in Health Act 2007 (Commencement No.3, Transitional and Saving Provisions and Commencement No.2 (Amendment)) Order 2008 (S.I. 337)
Local Government Area Changes Regulations 1976 (S.I. 246)
Local Government Changes for England (Education) (Miscellaneous Provisions) Regulations 1996 (S.I. 710)
Local Government Changes for England Regulations 1994 (S.I. 867)
Local Government Finance (New Parishes) Regulations 1998 (S.I. 119)
Local Government Finance (Scotland) Order 2007 (S.S.I. 65)
Local Government Finance (Scotland) Order 2008 (S.S.I. 33)
Local Government Pension Scheme (Administration) (Scotland) Regulations 2008 (S.S.I. 228)
Local Government Pension Scheme (Administration) Regulations 2008 (S.I. 239)
Local Government Pension Scheme (Amendment etc.) Regulations 1999 (S.I. 3438)
Local Government Pension Scheme (Amendment No.2) Regulations 2001 (S.I. 3401)
Local Government Pension Scheme (Amendment) (Environment Agency) Regulations 1998 (S.I. 568)
Local Government Pension Scheme (Amendment) (No.2) Regulations 2003 (S.I. 3004)
Local Government Pension Scheme (Amendment) (No.2) Regulations 2004 (S.I. 3372)
Local Government Pension Scheme (Amendment) (No.2) Regulations 2005 (S.I. 3199)
Local Government Pension Scheme (Amendment) (No.2) Regulations 2006 (S.I. 2008)
Local Government Pension Scheme (Amendment) (No.2) Regulations 2007 (S.I. 1488)
Local Government Pension Scheme (Amendment) (No.3) Regulations 2007 (S.I. 1561)
Local Government Pension Scheme (Amendment) Regulations 1998 (S.I. 530)
Local Government Pension Scheme (Amendment) Regulations 2000 (S.I. 1005)
Local Government Pension Scheme (Amendment) Regulations 2001 (S.I. 1481)
Local Government Pension Scheme (Amendment) Regulations 2002 (S.I. 206)
Local Government Pension Scheme (Amendment) Regulations 2003 (S.I. 2249)
Local Government Pension Scheme (Amendment) Regulations 2004 (S.I. 573)
Local Government Pension Scheme (Amendment) Regulations 2005 (S.I. 1903)
Local Government Pension Scheme (Amendment) Regulations 2006 (S.I. 966)
Local Government Pension Scheme (Amendment) Regulations 2007 (S.I. 228)
Local Government Pension Scheme (Benefits, Membership and Contributions) (Scotland) Regulations 2008 (S.S.I. 230)
Local Government Pension Scheme (Benefits, Membership and Contributions) Regulations 2007 (S.I. 1166)
Local Government Pension Scheme (Civil Partnership) (Amendment) (England and Wales) Regulations 2005 (S.I. 3069)
Local Government Pension Scheme (Greater London Authority etc.) Regulations 2000 (S.I. 1164)
Local Government Pension Scheme (Her Majesty's Chief Inspector of Schools in England) (Transfers) Regulations 2001 (S.I. 2866)
Local Government Pension Scheme (Management and Investment of Funds) (Scotland) Regulations 1998 (S.I. 2888)
Local Government Pension Scheme (Management and Investment of Funds) Regulations 1998 (S.I. 1831)
Local Government Pension Scheme (Merseyside Transport Limited) Regulations 2000 (S.I. 2826)
Local Government Pension Scheme (Miscellaneous Provisions) Regulations 1999 (S.I. 1212)
Local Government Pension Scheme (Miscellaneous) Regulations 2001 (S.I. 770)

Provision of School Lunches (Disapplication of the Requirement to Charge) (Scotland) Order 2007 (S.S.I. 451)
Public Bodies Land (Appropriate Ministers) Order 1981 (S.I. 15)
Public Contracts (Scotland) Regulations 2006 (S.S.I. 1)
Public Contracts Regulations 2006 (S.I. 5)
Public Gas Transporter Pipe-line Works (Environmental Impact Assessment) Regulations 1999 (S.I. 1672)
Public Health (Aircraft) (Scotland) Amendment Regulations 1974 (S.I. 1017)
Public Health (Aircraft) (Scotland) Amendment Regulations 1978 (S.I. 370)
Public Health (Aircraft) (Scotland) Regulations 1971 (S.I. 131)
Public Health (Notification of Infectious Diseases) (Scotland) Regulations 1988 (S.I. 1550)
Public Health (Ships) (Scotland) Amendment Regulations 1974 (S.I. 1008)
Public Health (Ships) (Scotland) Amendment Regulations 1978 (S.I. 369)
Public Health (Ships) (Scotland) Regulations 1971 (S.I. 132)
Public Interest Disclosure (Prescribed Persons) Order 1999 (S.I. 1549)
Public Lending Right Scheme 1982 (Commencement) Order 1982 (S.I. 719)
Public Order (Northern Ireland) Order 1987 (S.I. 463)
Public Path Orders Regulations 1993 (S.I. 11)
Public Service Vehicles (Conditions of Fitness, Equipment, Use and Certification) Regulations 1981 (S.I. 257)
Public Service Vehicles (Operators Licences) (Fees) Regulations 1995 (S.I. 2909)
Public Service Vehicles (Registration of Local Services) (Scotland) Regulations 2001 (S.S.I. 219)
Public Service Vehicles (Registration of Local Services) Regulations 1986 (S.I. 1671)
Public Service Vehicles (Traffic Commissioners Publication and Inquiries) Regulations 1986 (S.I. 1629)
Public Service Vehicles (Traffic Regulation Conditions) Regulations 1986 (S.I. 1030)
Public Service Vehicles Accessibility Regulations 2000 (S.I. 1970)
Public Services Contracts Regulations 1993 (S.I. 3228)
Public Transport Users Committee for Scotland Amendment Order 2008 (S.S.I. 186)
Public Transport Users Committee for Scotland Order 2006 (S.S.I. 250)
Public Trustee (Fees) (Amendment) Order 2002 (S.I. 2232)
Public Trustee (Fees) (Amendment) Order 2003 (S.I. 690)
Public Trustee (Fees) (Amendment) Order 2004 (S.I. 799)
Public Trustee (Fees) (Amendment) Order 2005 (S.I. 351)
Public Trustee (Fees) (Amendment) Order 2007 (S.I. 681)
Public Trustee (Fees) Order 1999 (S.I. 855)
Public Trustee Rules 1912 (S.I. 348)
Qualifications for Appointment of Members to the First-tier Tribunal and Upper Tribunal Order 2008 (S.I. 2692)
Qualifications, Curriculum and Assessment Authority for Wales (Transfer of Functions to the National Assembly for Wales and Abolition) Order 2005 (S.I. 3239)
Quarries Regulations 1999 (S.I. 2024)
Rabies (Importation of Dogs, Cats and Other Mammals) Order 1974 (S.I. 2211)
Race Relations Act 1976 (General Statutory Duty) Order 2001 (S.I. 3457)
Race Relations Act 1976 (General Statutory Duty) Order 2003 (S.I. 3007)
Race Relations Act 1976 (Statutory Duties) Order 2001 (S.I. 3458)
Race Relations Act 1976 (Statutory Duties) Order 2003 (S.I. 3006)
Radiation (Emergency Preparedness and Public Information) Regulations 2001 (S.I. 2975)
Radioactive Contaminated Land (Modification of Enactments) (England) (Amendment) Regulations 2007 (S.I. 3245)
Radioactive Contaminated Land (Modification of Enactments) (England) Regulations 2006 (S.I. 1379)
Radioactive Contaminated Land (Modification of Enactments) (Wales) (Amendment) Regulations 2007 (S.I. 3250)
Radioactive Contaminated Land (Modification of Enactments) (Wales) Regulations 2006 (S.I. 2988)
Rail Crossing Extinguishment and Diversion Orders Regulations 1993 (S.I. 9)
Rail Vehicle Accessibility Regulations 1998 (S.I. 2456)
Railways (Heathrow Express) (Exemptions) Order 1994 (S.I. 574)
Railways (Interoperability) Regulations 2006 (S.I. 397)
Rating Lists (Valuation Date) (England) Order 2003 (S.I. 329)
Receiving of Trans-shipped Sea Fish (Licensing) Order 1982 (S.I. 80)
Recovery of Duties and Taxes Etc Due in Other Member States (Corresponding UK Claims, Procedure and Supplementary) Regulations 2004 (S.I. 674)
Recovery of Taxes etc Due in Other Member States (Amendment of Section 134 of the Finance Act 2002) Regulations 2005 (S.I. 1479)
Redundancy Payments (Continuity of Employment in Local Government, etc.) (Modification) Order 1999 (S.I. 2277)
Referral Orders (Amendment of Referral Conditions) Regulations 2003 (S.I. 1605)
Refugee or Person in Need of International Protection (Qualification) Regulations 2006 (S.I. 2525)
Regional Transport Planning (Wales) Order 2006 (S.I. 2993)
Register of Patent Agents Rules 1990 (S.I. 1457)
Register of Trade Mark Agents Rules 1990 (S.I. 1458)
Registered Designs Rules 2006 (S.I. 1975)
Registered Homes (Northern Ireland) Order 1992 (S.I. 3204)
Registered Pension Schemes (Audited Accounts) (Specified Persons) Regulations 2005 (S.I. 3456)
Registered Pension Schemes (Enhanced Lifetime Allowance) Regulations 2006 (S.I. 131)
Registered Pension Schemes (Provision of Information) Regulations 2006 (S.I. 567)
Registered Pension Schemes (Transfer of Sums and Assets) Regulations 2006 (S.I. 499)
Registration of Fish Farming and Shellfish Farming Businesses Order 1985 (S.I. 1391)
Registration of Fish Sellers and Buyers and Designation of Auction Sites (Scotland) Regulations 2005 (S.S.I. 286)
Registration of Social Care and Independent Health Care (Wales) Regulations 2002 (S.I. 919)

Travellers Allowances Amendment Order 1995 (S.I. 3044)
Travellers Allowances Order 1994 (S.I. 955)
Treatment of Offenders (Northern Ireland) Order 1976 (S.I. 226)
Treatment of Offenders (Northern Ireland) Order 1989 (S.I. 1344)
Tribunal Procedure (First-tier Tribunal) (Social Entitlement Chamber) Rules 2008 (S.I. 2685)
Tribunal Procedure (First-tier Tribunal) (War Pensions and Armed Forces Compensation Chamber) Rules 2008 (S.I. 2686)
Tyne and Wear Passenger Transport Executive (Exclusion of Bus Operating Powers) Order 1986 (S.I. 1648)
Uncertificated Securities (Amendment) (Eligible Debt Securities) Regulations 2003 (S.I. 1633)
Undersized Bass Order 1989 (S.I. 1285)
Undersized Edible Crabs (Scotland) Order 2000 (S.S.I. 228)
Undersized Lobsters (Scotland) Order 2000 (S.S.I. 197)
Undersized Scallops (West Coast) Order 1984 (S.I. 1522)
Undersized Velvet Crabs Order 1989 (S.I. 919)
Unfair Terms in Consumer Contracts Regulations 1999 (S.I. 2083)
Unfitness to Stand Trial and Insanity (Army) Regulations 2005 (S.I. 1390)
Unfitness to Stand Trial and Insanity (Royal Air Force) Regulations 2005 (S.I. 1388)
Unfitness to Stand Trial and Insanity (Royal Navy) Regulations 2005 (S.I. 1389)
United Nations Arms Embargoes (Dependent Territories) Order 1995 (S.I. 1032)
United Nations Arms Embargoes (Liberia, Somalia and the Former Yugoslavia) Order 1993 (S.I. 1787)
Urban Development Corporations in England (Transfer of Property, Rights and Liabilities) (Commission for the New Towns) Order 1998 (S.I. 85)
Urban Waste Water Treatment (England and Wales) Regulations 1994 (S.I. 2841)
Urban Waste Water Treatment (Scotland) Regulations 1994 (S.I. 2842)
Utilities Contracts (Scotland) Regulations 2006 (S.S.I. 2)
Utilities Contracts Regulations 2006 (S.I. 6)
Valuation Appeal Committee (Procedure in Appeals under the Valuation Acts) (Scotland) Regulations 1995 (S.I. 572)
Valuation for Rating (Plant and Machinery) (England) Regulations 2000 (S.I. 540)
Valuation for Rating (Plant and Machinery) (Scotland) Regulations 2000 (S.S.I. 58)
Valuation Tribunals (Wales) Regulations 2005 (S.I. 3364)
Value Added Tax (Buildings and Land) Order 1994 (S.I. 3013)
Value Added Tax (Buildings and Land) Order 1995 (S.I. 279)
Value Added Tax (Buildings and Land) Order 1999 (S.I. 593)
Value Added Tax (Buildings and Land) Order 2002 (S.I. 1102)
Value Added Tax (Buildings and Land) Order 2004 (S.I. 778)
Value Added Tax (Disclosure of Avoidance Schemes) (Designations) Order 2004 (S.I. 1933)
Value Added Tax (Finance) Order 2008 (S.I. 1892)
Value Added Tax (Input Tax) (Specified Supplies) Order 1999 (S.I. 3121)
Value Added Tax (Reduced Rate) Order 2007 (S.I. 1601)
Value Added Tax (Refund of Tax to Museums and Galleries) Order 2001 (S.I. 2879)
Value Added Tax (Registered Social Landlords) (No.2) Order 1997 (S.I. 51)
Value Added Tax (Special Provisions) Order 1995 (S.I. 1268)
Value Added Tax (Tour Operators) Order 1987 (S.I. 1806)
Value Added Tax Regulations 1995 (S.I. 2518)
Value Added Tax Tribunals Rules 1986 (S.I. 590)
Vehicle Drivers (Certificates of Professional Competence) Regulations 2007 (S.I. 605)
Vehicle Excise Duty (Immobilisation, Removal and Disposal of Vehicles) Regulations 1997 (S.I. 2439)
Vehicles Crime (Registration of Registration Plate Suppliers) (England and Wales) (Amendment) Regulations 2003 (S.I. 228)
Vehicles Crime (Registration of Registration Plate Suppliers) (England and Wales) (Amendment) Regulations 2005 (S.I. 2981)
Vehicles Crime (Registration of Registration Plate Suppliers) (England and Wales) Regulations 2002 (S.I. 2977)
Venture Capital Trust (Winding up and Mergers) (Tax) Regulations 2004 (S.I. 2199)
Venture Capital Trust Regulations 1995 (S.I. 1979)
Veterinary Medicines Regulations 2007 (S.I. 2539)
Veterinary Medicines Regulations 2008 (S.I. 2297)
Veterinary Surgeons (Examination of Commonwealth and Foreign Candidates) Regulations Order of Council 2005 (S.I. 3240)
Veterinary Surgeons and Veterinary Practitioners (Registration) Regulations Order of Council 2005 (S.I. 3517)
Veterinary Surgeons Qualifications (European Recognition) Order 2007 (S.I. 1348)
Veterinary Surgeons&apos Qualifications (European Recognition) Order 2003 (S.I. 2919)
Veterinary Surgery (Blood Sampling) Order 1983 (S.I. 6)
Victims of Violent Intentional Crime (Arrangements for Compensation) (European Communities) Regulations 2005 (S.I. 3396)
Voluntary Adoption Agencies and the Adoption Agencies (Miscellaneous Amendments) Regulations 2003 (S.I. 367)
War Pensions (Commencing Dates of Past Awards) Order 1982 (S.I. 1046)
War Pensions (Mercantile Marine) Scheme 1964 (S.I. 2058)
Waste and Contaminated Land (Northern Ireland) Order 1997 (S.I. 2778)
Waste Management Licensing Regulations 1994 (S.I. 1056)
Water (Northern Ireland) Order 1999 (S.I. 662)
Water and Sewerage Services (Northern Ireland) Order 2006 (S.I. 3336)
Water Environment (Controlled Activities) (Scotland) Regulations 2005 (S.S.I. 348)
Water Environment (Relevant Enactments) Order 2006 (S.S.I. 554)
Water Environment (Water Framework Directive) (England and Wales) Regulations 2003 (S.I. 3242)
Water Environment (Water Framework Directive) (Northumbria River Basin District) Regulations 2003 (S.I. 3245)
Water Environment (Water Framework Directive) (Solway Tweed River Basin District) Regulations 2004 (S.I. 99)

STATUTE CITATOR 2008

The Current Law Statute Citator covers the period 2008 and is up to date to **March 1, 2009** (orders and Acts received). It covers both public and local statutes and comprises in a single table:

(i) Statutes passed during this period;
(ii) Statutes affected during this period by Statute or Statutory Instrument;
(iii) Statutes judicially considered during this period;
(iv) Statutes repealed and amended during this period;
(v) Statutes under which Statutory Instruments have been made during this period.

The material is arranged in numerical order under the relevant year.

Definitions of legislative effects:

"added" : new provisions are inserted by subsequent legislation
"amended" : text of legislation is modified by subsequent legislation
"applied" : brought to bear, or exercised by subsequent legislation
"consolidated" : used where previous Acts in the same subject area are brought together in subsequent legislation, with or without amendments
"disapplied" : an exception made to the application of an earlier enactment
"enabling" : giving power for the relevant SI to be made
"referred to" : direction from other legislation without specific effect or application
"repealed" : rescinded by subsequent legislation
"restored" : reinstated by subsequent legislation (where previously repealed/revoked)
"substituted" : text of provision is completely replaced by subsequent legislation
"varied" : provisions modified in relation to their application to specified areas or circumstances, however the text itself remains unchanged

ACTS OF THE SCOTTISH PARLIAMENT

CAP.

2000

asp 1. Public Finance and Accountability (Scotland) Act 2000
s.4, applied: 2008 asp 2 s.3, s.6
s.21, amended: SI 2008/948 Sch.1 para.27

asp 4. Adults with Incapacity (Scotland) Act 2000
applied: 2008 c.6 s.52, SI 2008/3109 Reg.12
Part 6, applied: SSI 2008/52 Sch.1
s.6, applied: 2008 asp 6 s.62, SSI 2008/52 Sch.1
s.7, enabling: SSI 2008/52, SSI 2008/56, SSI 2008/238
s.15, applied: SSI 2008/56 Reg.2, Reg.4
s.15, enabling: SSI 2008/56
s.16, applied: SSI 2008/56 Reg.2, Reg.4
s.16, enabling: SSI 2008/56
s.19, applied: SSI 2008/52 Sch.1
s.19A, added: SSI 2008/380 Art.2
s.20, applied: SSI 2008/52 Sch.1
s.22A, applied: SSI 2008/56 Reg.3, Reg.4
s.22A, enabling: SSI 2008/56

CAP.

2000–cont.

asp 4. Adults with Incapacity (Scotland) Act 2000–*cont.*
s.24C, applied: SSI 2008/52 Sch.1
s.24D, applied: SSI 2008/51 Reg.2, SSI 2008/52 Sch.1
s.24D, enabling: SSI 2008/51
s.25, applied: SSI 2008/49 Art.3, Art.4, SSI 2008/52 Sch.1
s.26, applied: SSI 2008/49 Art.3, Art.4
s.26B, applied: SSI 2008/52 Sch.1
s.26D, applied: SSI 2008/52 Sch.1
s.26E, applied: SSI 2008/52 Sch.1
s.26F, applied: SSI 2008/52 Sch.1
s.26G, applied: SSI 2008/52 Sch.1
s.27B, applied: SSI 2008/51 Reg.3
s.27B, enabling: SSI 2008/51
s.27E, applied: SSI 2008/51 Reg.4
s.27E, enabling: SSI 2008/51
s.31B, applied: SSI 2008/52 Sch.1
s.57, enabling: SSI 2008/55
s.60, enabling: SSI 2008/55
s.66, applied: SSI 2008/52 Sch.1

CAP.

2000–cont.

asp 4. Adults with Incapacity (Scotland) Act 2000–*cont.*
s.73, applied: SSI 2008/52 Sch.1
s.73, enabling: SSI 2008/53
s.84A, added: 2008 c.22 Sch.7 para.18
s.84B, added: 2008 c.22 Sch.7 para.18
s.86, enabling: SSI 2008/52, SSI 2008/55
Sch.2 para.1, applied: SSI 2008/52 Sch.1
Sch.2 para.3, applied: SSI 2008/52 Sch.1
Sch.2 para.6, applied: SSI 2008/52 Sch.1
Sch.2 para.7, applied: SSI 2008/52 Sch.1

asp 5. Abolition of Feudal Tenure etc (Scotland) Act 2000
Sch.12 Part 1 para.49, repealed: SI 2008/1277 Sch.4 Part 1

asp 7. Ethical Standards in Public Life etc (Scotland) Act 2000
s.19, applied: SI 2008/2252 Sch.1 para.19
Sch.3, amended: 2008 asp 6 Sch.1 para.19

asp 8. Education and Training (Scotland) Act 2000
s.1, enabling: SSI 2008/1, SSI 2008/204
s.2, enabling: SSI 2008/204
s.3, enabling: SSI 2008/1, SSI 2008/204

asp 10. National Parks (Scotland) Act 2000
referred to: SSI 2008/263 Sch.2
s.6, applied: SSI 2008/263 Sch.2

2001

asp 2. Transport (Scotland) Act 2001
Part 3, applied: 2008 c.26 s.119
s.49, amended: 2008 asp 1 Sch.1 para.2
s.61, applied: 2008 c.26 s.119
s.69, repealed (in part): 2008 asp 1 Sch.2 Part 1
s.72, enabling: SSI 2008/187, SSI 2008/247
s.81, enabling: SSI 2008/187, SSI 2008/247
s.82, referred to: SSI 2008/426 Reg.10

asp 6. Education (Graduate Endowment and Student Support) (Scotland) Act 2001
s.1, repealed: 2008 asp 3 s.1
s.2, repealed: 2008 asp 3 s.1

asp 7. Convention Rights (Compliance) (Scotland) Act 2001
see *Locke (John) v HM Advocate* [2008] HCJAC 6, 2008 S.L.T. 159 (HCJ), Lord Hamilton L.J.G.
Sch.1 para.29, see *Locke (John) v HM Advocate* [2008] HCJAC 6, 2008 S.L.T. 159 (HCJ), Lord Hamilton L.J.G.

asp 8. Regulation of Care (Scotland) Act 2001
Part 1, applied: SI 2008/976 Reg.5
s.2, referred to: 2008 c.14 s.145

asp 10. Housing (Scotland) Act 2001
s.14, applied: SSI 2008/324 Reg.2
s.36, applied: SSI 2008/324 Reg.2
s.91, enabling: SSI 2008/28

CAP.

2001–cont.

asp 10. Housing (Scotland) Act 2001–*cont.*
s.94, enabling: SSI 2008/28
s.109, enabling: SSI 2008/28
Sch.7 Part 2 para.6, amended: SI 2008/948 Sch.1 para.219
Sch.7 Part 2 para.9, amended: SI 2008/948 Sch.1 para.219
Sch.7 Part 2 para.10, amended: SI 2008/948 Sch.1 para.219

asp 11. Mortgage Rights (Scotland) Act 2001
s.4, applied: SSI 2008/324 Reg.2

asp 12. Erskine Bridge Tolls Act 2001
repealed: 2008 asp 1 Sch.2 Part 1

2002

asp 3. Water Industry (Scotland) Act 2002
referred to: SSI 2008/263 Sch.2
s.20, applied: SSI 2008/228 Sch.2
s.42, applied: 2008 asp 2 Sch.5

asp 5. Community Care and Health (Scotland) Act 2002
see *Argyll and Bute Council v Scottish Public Services Ombudsman* 2008 S.L.T. 168 (OH), Lord Macphail
s.1, see *Argyll and Bute Council v Scottish Public Services Ombudsman* 2008 S.C. 155 (OH), Lord Macphail
s.1, enabling: SSI 2008/78
s.2, enabling: SSI 2008/78
s.15, applied: SSI 2008/228 Reg.9
s.23, applied: SSI 2008/78
s.23, enabling: SSI 2008/78

asp 6. Protection of Wild Mammals (Scotland) Act 2002
see *Friend v Lord Advocate* [2007] UKHL 53, 2008 S.C. (H.L.) 107 (HL), Lord Bingham

asp 11. Scottish Public Services Ombudsman Act 2002
s.7, amended: 2008 c.27 Sch.1 para.34
Sch.2 Part 2 para.25A, added: 2008 asp 6 Sch.1 para.20
Sch.2 Part 2 para.91B, added: 2008 c.27 Sch.1 para.34

asp 13. Freedom of Information (Scotland) Act 2002
s.1, applied: SSI 2008/339
s.4, enabling: SSI 2008/297
s.26, applied: SSI 2008/339
s.29, disapplied: SSI 2008/399 Sch.1 para.9
s.30, disapplied: SSI 2008/399 Sch.1 para.9
s.38, see *Common Services Agency v Scottish Information Commissioner* [2008] UKHL 47, [2008] 1 W.L.R. 1550 (HL), Lord Hoffmann
s.64, enabling: SSI 2008/339
s.72, applied: SSI 2008/339
Sch.1 Part 2 para.7A, added: SSI 2008/297 Sch.1

CAP.

2002–cont.

asp 13. Freedom of Information (Scotland) Act 2002–*cont.*
Sch.1 Part 2 para.12A, added: SSI 2008/297 Sch.1
Sch.1 Part 2 para.18A, added: 2008 asp 6 Sch.3 para.18
Sch.1 Part 4 para.25, repealed: SSI 2008/297 Sch.2
Sch.1 Part 4 para.28, repealed: SSI 2008/297 Sch.2
Sch.1 Part 4 para.29, repealed: SSI 2008/297 Sch.2
Sch.1 Part 4 para.29A, added: SSI 2008/297 Sch.1
Sch.1 Part 4 para.32A, added: SSI 2008/297 Sch.1
Sch.1 Part 4 para.32B, added: SSI 2008/297 Sch.1
Sch.1 Part 4 para.32C, added: SSI 2008/297 Sch.1
Sch.1 Part 4 para.36, repealed: SSI 2008/297 Sch.2
Sch.1 Part 4 para.38, repealed: SSI 2008/297 Sch.2
Sch.1 Part 4 para.40, repealed: SSI 2008/297 Sch.2
Sch.1 Part 4 para.42, repealed: SSI 2008/297 Sch.2
Sch.1 Part 7 para.62ZA, added: SSI 2008/297 Sch.1
Sch.1 Part 7 para.66A, added: SSI 2008/297 Sch.1
Sch.1 Part 7 para.68A, added: 2008 asp 6 Sch.1 para.21
Sch.1 Part 7 para.75B, added: SSI 2008/297 Sch.1
Sch.1 Part 7 para.75C, added: SSI 2008/297 Sch.1
Sch.1 Part 7 para.79, repealed: SSI 2008/297 Sch.2
Sch.1 Part 7 para.88, repealed: SSI 2008/297 Sch.2
Sch.1 Part 7 para.92B, added: SSI 2008/297 Sch.1
Sch.1 Part 7 para.103, repealed: SSI 2008/297 Sch.2

asp 17. Debt Arrangement and Attachment (Scotland) Act 2002
s.4, applied: SSI 2008/119 Sch.1 para.12
s.9C, enabling: SSI 2008/121, SSI 2008/122
s.9F, enabling: SSI 2008/121, SSI 2008/122
s.9L, enabling: SSI 2008/121, SSI 2008/122
s.9M, enabling: SSI 2008/121, SSI 2008/122
s.9N, enabling: SSI 2008/121, SSI 2008/122
s.10, amended: 2008 c.6 Sch.7 para.5
s.10, referred to: SSI 2008/143 Reg.6
s.39, applied: 2008 c.9 s.128
Sch.3 Part 1 para.9, repealed: 2008 asp 5 Sch.3 Part 1

CAP.

2003

asp 1. Local Government in Scotland Act 2003
s.2, applied: SSI 2008/228 Reg.5
s.3, applied: SSI 2008/228 Reg.5
s.20, applied: SSI 2008/400
s.57, applied: SSI 2008/400
s.57, referred to: SSI 2008/400
s.57, enabling: SSI 2008/400

asp 2. Land Reform (Scotland) Act 2003
Part 1, applied: SSI 2008/159 Sch.2
Part 1, referred to: SSI 2008/100 Sch.2 Part 1
s.6, see *Snowie v Stirling Council* 2008 S.L.T. (Sh Ct) 61 (Sh Ct (Tayside)), Sheriff A Cubie
s.17, applied: SSI 2008/159 Sch.2
s.17, referred to: SSI 2008/100 Sch.2 Part 1
s.23, see *Snowie v Stirling Council* 2008 S.L.T. (Sh Ct) 61 (Sh Ct (Tayside)), Sheriff A Cubie
s.32, applied: SSI 2008/159 Sch.2
s.32, referred to: SSI 2008/100 Sch.2 Part 1

asp 3. Water Environment and Water Services (Scotland) Act 2003
Commencement Orders: SSI 2008/269 Art.2
applied: SSI 2008/159 Sch.3 Part 2, SSI 2008/170 Reg.6
Part 1, applied: SSI 2008/263 Art.3
s.2, applied: SSI 2008/263 Art.2
s.2, enabling: SSI 2008/263
s.20, enabling: SSI 2008/54
s.21, applied: SSI 2008/54
s.21, referred to: SSI 2008/54
s.36, enabling: SSI 2008/54
s.38, enabling: SSI 2008/269
Sch.2, enabling: SSI 2008/54

asp 4. Public Appointments and Public Bodies etc (Scotland) Act 2003
s.2, applied: 2008 asp 6 Sch.1 para.18
s.3, enabling: SSI 2008/348
s.18, applied: SSI 2008/348
Sch.2, amended: 2008 asp 6 Sch.1 para.18, SSI 2008/348 Art.2

asp 5. Protection of Children (Scotland) Act 2003
applied: SSI 2008/260
s.21, enabling: SSI 2008/260
Sch.2, referred to: SSI 2008/260 Art.2
Sch.2 para.2, amended: SSI 2008/260 Art.3
Sch.2 para.2A, added: SSI 2008/260 Art.4
Sch.2 para.2B, added: SSI 2008/260 Art.4
Sch.2 para.6, amended: SSI 2008/260 Art.5
Sch.2 para.12, amended: SSI 2008/260 Art.6
Sch.2 para.13, enabling: SSI 2008/260

asp 7. Criminal Justice (Scotland) Act 2003
s.16, amended: SSI 2008/185 Art.2
s.16, enabling: SSI 2008/185
s.56, applied: SSI 2008/117 Reg.12, Reg.13
s.88, applied: SSI 2008/185

CAP.

2003–cont.

asp 8. Building (Scotland) Act 2003
s.1, applied: SSI 2008/310
s.1, enabling: SSI 2008/310
s.8, applied: SSI 2008/159 Sch.2
s.8, enabling: SSI 2008/310
s.38, enabling: SSI 2008/397

asp 9. Title Conditions (Scotland) Act 2003
s.8, see *Barker v Lewis* 2008 S.L.T. (Sh Ct) 17 (Sh Pr), Sheriff Principal RA Dunlop Q.C.
s.38, referred to: SSI 2008/217
s.38, enabling: SSI 2008/217
s.43, referred to: SSI 2008/391
s.43, enabling: SSI 2008/391

asp 10. Homelessness etc (Scotland) Act 2003
Commencement Orders: SSI 2008/313 Art.2
s.11, applied: SSI 2008/324 Reg.2
s.11, enabling: SSI 2008/324
s.14, enabling: SSI 2008/313

asp 11. Agricultural Holdings (Scotland) Act 2003
applied: SSI 2008/100 Sch.4 Part 2

asp 13. Mental Health (Care and Treatment) (Scotland) Act 2003
applied: SSI 2008/356 Reg.5, Reg.8, Reg.11, Reg.13, Reg.16, Reg.19, Reg.22, Reg.25, Reg.33, SSI 2008/228 Reg.4
referred to: SSI 2008/356 Reg.28
s.14, applied: SSI 2008/356 Reg.32
s.21, enabling: SSI 2008/396
s.25, applied: SI 2008/794 Sch.8 para.56
s.66, referred to: SSI 2008/356 Reg.20
s.76, varied: SSI 2008/356 Reg.29
s.77, referred to: SSI 2008/356 Reg.33
s.78, referred to: SSI 2008/356 Reg.33
s.113, applied: SSI 2008/356 Reg.2
s.114, applied: SSI 2008/356 Reg.2
s.115, applied: SSI 2008/356 Reg.2
s.127, applied: SSI 2008/181 Reg.2
s.136, applied: SI 2008/794 Reg.160, Sch.5 Part 2
s.137, varied: SSI 2008/356 Reg.29
s.139, referred to: SSI 2008/356 Reg.33
s.140, referred to: SSI 2008/356 Reg.33
s.176, applied: SSI 2008/356 Reg.2
s.177, applied: SSI 2008/356 Reg.2
s.229, applied: SSI 2008/356 Reg.17, Reg.24, Reg.25
s.229, varied: SSI 2008/356 Reg.17
s.230, applied: SSI 2008/356 Reg.18
s.230, varied: SSI 2008/356 Reg.18
s.231, applied: SSI 2008/356 Reg.24
s.231, varied: SSI 2008/356 Reg.24
s.245, enabling: SSI 2008/316
s.246, enabling: SSI 2008/316
s.259, applied: SSI 2008/356 Reg.24
s.260, varied: SSI 2008/356 Reg.30
s.261, varied: SSI 2008/356 Reg.31

CAP.

2003–cont.

asp 13. Mental Health (Care and Treatment) (Scotland) Act 2003–*cont.*
s.289, applied: SI 2008/1184 Reg.16, SI 2008/2439 Reg.29
s.289, enabling: SSI 2008/356
s.290, applied: SI 2008/1184 Reg.15, SI 2008/2439 Reg.29
s.301, applied: SSI 2008/333 Reg.2, SSI 2008/356 Reg.12
s.301, disapplied: SSI 2008/333 Reg.4
s.301, varied: SSI 2008/333 Reg.3, SSI 2008/356 Reg.12
s.302, applied: SSI 2008/333 Reg.4
s.302, disapplied: SSI 2008/333 Reg.2
s.302, varied: SSI 2008/181 Reg.2, SSI 2008/333 Reg.5
s.303, applied: SSI 2008/333 Reg.6, SSI 2008/356 Reg.12
s.303, varied: SSI 2008/181 Reg.2, SSI 2008/333 Reg.7
s.309, enabling: SSI 2008/333
s.309A, enabling: SSI 2008/181
s.310, applied: SSI 2008/356 Reg.12
s.311, referred to: SI 2008/1062 Sch.1 para.1, Sch.1 para.2
s.313, referred to: SI 2008/1062 Sch.1 para.1, Sch.1 para.2
s.320, applied: SSI 2008/356 Reg.9
s.320, varied: SSI 2008/356 Reg.9
s.321, applied: SSI 2008/356 Reg.9
s.321, varied: SSI 2008/356 Reg.9
s.325, enabling: SSI 2008/316
s.326, applied: SSI 2008/181, SSI 2008/333, SSI 2008/356
s.326, enabling: SSI 2008/333, SSI 2008/356, SSI 2008/396
s.328, referred to: SSI 2008/356 Reg.14, Reg.28
Sch.2 Part 3 para.10, enabling: SSI 2008/396

asp 15. Salmon and Freshwater Fisheries (Consolidation) (Scotland) Act 2003
referred to: SSI 2008/263 Sch.2
s.37, enabling: SSI 2008/19
s.43, applied: SSI 2008/263 Sch.2
s.51A, enabling: SSI 2008/419
Sch.1 para.5, applied: SSI 2008/19
Sch.1 para.9A, applied: SSI 2008/419
Sch.1 para.10, applied: SSI 2008/19
Sch.1 para.11, applied: SSI 2008/19, SSI 2008/419
Sch.1 para.14, applied: SSI 2008/19

2004

asp 3. Vulnerable Witnesses (Scotland) Act 2004
Commencement Orders: SSI 2008/57 Art.2, Art.3
s.12, applied: SSI 2008/119 Sch.1 para.14
s.25, enabling: SSI 2008/57

CAP.

2004–cont.

asp 4. Education (Additional Support for Learning) (Scotland) Act 2004

see *D v Glasgow City Council* 2008 S.C. 117 (IH (1 Div)), Lord Hamilton L.P.

s.18, see *D v Glasgow City Council* 2008 S.C. 117 (IH (1 Div)), Lord Hamilton L.P.

s.19, see *C v Edinburgh City Council* [2008] CSOH 60, 2008 S.L.T. 522 (OH), Lord Wheatley; see *D v Glasgow City Council* 2008 S.C. 117 (IH (1 Div)), Lord Hamilton L.P.

Sch.2 para.2, see *D v Glasgow City Council* 2008 S.C. 117 (IH (1 Div)), Lord Hamilton L.P.

asp 6. Nature Conservation (Scotland) Act 2004

Commencement Orders: SSI 2008/193 Art.2

applied: SSI 2008/100 Sch.4 Part 2, SSI 2008/159 Sch.3 Part 2

referred to: SSI 2008/263 Sch.2

s.3, applied: SSI 2008/221 Reg.3, SSI 2008/432 Sch.5 para.2

s.3, disapplied: SSI 2008/221 Reg.3

s.5, applied: SSI 2008/221 Reg.3, Reg.5, Reg.6, SSI 2008/432 Sch.5 para.2

s.6, applied: SSI 2008/221 Reg.5

s.7, applied: SSI 2008/221 Reg.5

s.8, applied: SSI 2008/221 Reg.5

s.9, applied: SSI 2008/221 Reg.3, Reg.5, Reg.6

s.22, enabling: SSI 2008/221

s.53, enabling: SSI 2008/193, SSI 2008/221

s.59, enabling: SSI 2008/193

Sch.1 para.5, referred to: SSI 2008/221 Reg.6

Sch.1 para.10, applied: SSI 2008/221 Reg.5, Reg.6

Sch.1 para.15, applied: SSI 2008/221 Reg.5

Sch.5 para.12, applied: SSI 2008/221 Reg.4

asp 8. Antisocial Behaviour etc (Scotland) Act 2004

s.9, see *Gordon v Griffiths* 2008 J.C. 87 (HCJ Appeal), Lord Gill L.J.C.

s.83, enabling: SSI 2008/403

s.87, enabling: SSI 2008/403

s.99, enabling: SSI 2008/402

asp 9. Local Governance (Scotland) Act 2004

s.11, applied: SSI 2008/414, SSI 2008/415

s.11, enabling: SSI 2008/414, SSI 2008/415

s.16, enabling: SSI 2008/414, SSI 2008/415

2005

asp 2. Emergency Workers (Scotland) Act 2005

s.1, amended: SSI 2008/37 Art.2

s.2, repealed (in part): SSI 2008/37 Art.3

s.8, applied: SSI 2008/37

s.8, enabling: SSI 2008/37

CAP.

2005–cont.

asp 3. Water Services etc (Scotland) Act 2005

s.6, applied: SSI 2008/44 Art.3

s.14, enabling: SSI 2008/44

s.26, amended: 2008 asp 5 s.115

asp 5. Fire (Scotland) Act 2005

s.1, referred to: SI 2008/794 Reg.43

s.6, applied: SI 2008/2852 Sch.3 para.5

s.6, referred to: SSI 2008/228 Reg.9

s.61, amended: SI 2008/960 Sch.3

asp 6. Further and Higher Education (Scotland) Act 2005

s.7, applied: SSI 2008/241

s.7, enabling: SSI 2008/241, SSI 2008/412

s.34, applied: SSI 2008/241, SSI 2008/412

Sch.2, amended: SSI 2008/241 Art.2, SSI 2008/412 Art.2

Sch.3 para.10, repealed: 2008 asp 3 s.1

asp 10. Charities and Trustee Investment (Scotland) Act 2005

see *Jeanfield Swifts Football Club v Revenue and Customs Commissioners* [2008] B.V.C. 2490 (V&DTr (Edinburgh)), T Gordon Coutts Q.C. (Chairman)

s.7, disapplied: SSI 2008/268 Art.2

s.7, enabling: SSI 2008/268, SSI 2008/413

s.15, enabling: SSI 2008/59

s.19, enabling: SSI 2008/413

s.34, applied: SI 2008/2553 Art.5, SI 2008/2554 Art.5, SI 2008/2927 Reg.2, SI 2008/3047 Art.5, SI 2008/3148 Sch.1

s.46, amended: SI 2008/948 Sch.1 para.241

s.46, repealed (in part): SI 2008/948 Sch.1 para.241

s.102, enabling: SSI 2008/262

s.103, applied: SSI 2008/262, SSI 2008/268, SSI 2008/413

s.105, amended: SI 2008/948 Sch.1 para.241

asp 12. Transport (Scotland) Act 2005

Commencement Orders: SSI 2008/15 Art.2, Art.3, Sch.1, Sch.2; SSI 2008/90 Art.2; SSI 2008/15 Art.2, Art.3, Sch.1

s.1, applied: SSI 2008/228 Sch.2, SSI 2008/426 Reg.28

s.2, applied: SSI 2008/228 Sch.4 Part II

s.10, applied: SSI 2008/228 Sch.4 Part II

s.18, applied: SSI 2008/89 Reg.3

s.18, enabling: SSI 2008/89

s.19, applied: SSI 2008/15 Art.3

s.19, disapplied: SSI 2008/15 Art.3

s.19, referred to: SSI 2008/15 Art.3

s.22, referred to: SSI 2008/15 Art.3

s.41, enabling: SSI 2008/186, SSI 2008/248

s.52, enabling: SSI 2008/15, SSI 2008/90

s.54, enabling: SSI 2008/15, SSI 2008/90

asp 13. Smoking, Health and Social Care (Scotland) Act 2005

s.36, repealed: 2008 asp 5 Sch.3 Part 1

Sch.2 para.1, repealed: 2008 asp 5 Sch.3 Part 1

CAP.

2005–cont.

asp 14. Management of Offenders etc (Scotland) Act 2005
Commencement Orders: SSI 2008/21 Art.2; SSI 2008/149 Art.2
s.3, applied: SSI 2008/30, SSI 2008/30 Art.2
s.3, enabling: SSI 2008/30
s.4, applied: SSI 2008/30 Art.2
s.22, applied: SSI 2008/30
s.22, enabling: SSI 2008/30
s.24, enabling: SSI 2008/21, SSI 2008/149

asp 15. Environmental Assessment (Scotland) Act 2005
s.16, applied: SSI 2008/426 Reg.20

asp 16. Licensing (Scotland) Act 2005
Commencement Orders: SSI 2008/292 Art.2
s.132, enabling: SSI 2008/9
s.145, enabling: SSI 2008/194
s.146, enabling: SSI 2008/292
s.150, enabling: SSI 2008/292

2006

asp 1. Housing (Scotland) Act 2006
Commencement Orders: SSI 2008/308 Art.3, Art.4
Part 2, applied: SSI 2008/406 Reg.5
s.71, referred to: SSI 2008/406 Reg.3
s.73, applied: SSI 2008/406 Reg.3, Reg.4
s.73, enabling: SSI 2008/406
s.77, referred to: SSI 2008/406 Reg.4
s.77, enabling: SSI 2008/406
s.79, applied: SSI 2008/406 Reg.4
s.79, enabling: SSI 2008/406
s.98, applied: SSI 2008/76 Reg.4
s.98, disapplied: SSI 2008/308 Art.4
s.99, applied: SI 2008/1889 Art.3, SSI 2008/76 Reg.3, Reg.4
s.99, disapplied: SSI 2008/308 Art.4
s.99, enabling: SSI 2008/76
s.100, disapplied: SSI 2008/308 Art.4
s.101, applied: SSI 2008/76 Reg.4
s.101, disapplied: SSI 2008/308 Art.4
s.102, disapplied: SSI 2008/308 Art.4
s.103, disapplied: SSI 2008/308 Art.4
s.104, disapplied: SSI 2008/308 Art.4
s.104, enabling: SSI 2008/76
s.105, disapplied: SSI 2008/308 Art.4
s.105, enabling: SSI 2008/76
s.106, disapplied: SSI 2008/308 Art.4
s.107, disapplied: SSI 2008/308 Art.4
s.108, disapplied: SSI 2008/308 Art.4
s.109, disapplied: SSI 2008/308 Art.4
s.110, disapplied: SSI 2008/308 Art.4
s.111, disapplied: SSI 2008/308 Art.4
s.112, disapplied: SSI 2008/308 Art.4
s.113, disapplied: SSI 2008/308 Art.4
s.114, disapplied: SSI 2008/308 Art.4
s.115, disapplied: SSI 2008/308 Art.4
s.116, disapplied: SSI 2008/308 Art.4

CAP.

2006–cont.

asp 1. Housing (Scotland) Act 2006–*cont.*
s.117, disapplied: SSI 2008/308 Art.4
s.118, disapplied: SSI 2008/308 Art.4
s.173, repealed (in part): 2008 asp 5 Sch.3 Part 1
s.191, applied: SSI 2008/76, SSI 2008/406
s.191, enabling: SSI 2008/308
s.195, enabling: SSI 2008/308

asp 4. Human Tissue (Scotland) Act 2006
s.58, enabling: SSI 2008/259
s.59, applied: SSI 2008/259

asp 9. Senior Judiciary (Vacancies and Incapacity) (Scotland) Act 2006
repealed: 2008 asp 6 Sch.5 para.4

asp 10. Police, Public Order and Criminal Justice (Scotland) Act 2006
s.1, applied: SSI 2008/228 Sch.2
s.94, enabling: SSI 2008/232
Sch.3 Part 1 para.2, applied: SSI 2008/228 Sch.4 Part II

asp 14. Local Electoral Administration and Registration Services (Scotland) Act 2006
Commencement Orders: SSI 2008/405 Art.2
s.54, applied: SSI 2008/386 Reg.3, Sch.9
s.54, enabling: SSI 2008/386
s.55, applied: SSI 2008/386 Reg.4, Sch.9, Sch.10
s.55, enabling: SSI 2008/386
s.57, enabling: SSI 2008/358
s.60, applied: SSI 2008/358, SSI 2008/386
s.61, enabling: SSI 2008/386
s.63, enabling: SSI 2008/405

asp 15. Tourist Boards (Scotland) Act 2006
Sch.1 para.1, applied: SSI 2008/228 Sch.4 Part II

asp 16. Scottish Commission for Human Rights Act 2006
Commencement Orders: SSI 2008/112 Art.2
s.9, applied: SSI 2008/355, SSI 2008/355 Art.2
s.9, enabling: SSI 2008/355
s.14, enabling: SSI 2008/123, SSI 2008/223
s.22, enabling: SSI 2008/112

asp 17. Planning etc (Scotland) Act 2006
Commencement Orders: SSI 2008/164 Art.2, Sch.1; SSI 2008/191 Art.2; SSI 2008/411 Art.2
s.2, disapplied: SSI 2008/165 Art.2
s.46, enabling: SSI 2008/359
s.58, enabling: SSI 2008/165, SSI 2008/427
s.59, enabling: SSI 2008/164, SSI 2008/191, SSI 2008/411

2007

asp 3. Bankruptcy and Diligence etc (Scotland) Act 2007
Commencement Orders: SSI 2008/45 Art.2; SSI 2008/115 Art.3, Sch.1, Sch.2, Sch.3
s.221, amended: 2008 c.6 Sch.7 para.6

CAP.

2007–cont.

asp 3. Bankruptcy and Diligence etc (Scotland) Act 2007–*cont.*

s.224, enabling: SSI 2008/45, SSI 2008/115

s.225, enabling: SSI 2008/79, SSI 2008/82

s.227, enabling: SSI 2008/45, SSI 2008/115

asp 4. Adoption and Children (Scotland) Act 2007

Commencement Orders: SSI 2008/130 Art.2, Sch.1; SSI 2008/282 Art.2

s.30, amended: 2008 c.22 Sch.6 para.56

s.62, applied: SSI 2008/303 Reg.2

s.62, referred to: SSI 2008/304 Art.2, SSI 2008/305 Art.2

s.62, enabling: SSI 2008/304, SSI 2008/305

s.64, referred to: SSI 2008/303 Reg.2

s.64, enabling: SSI 2008/303

s.65, applied: SSI 2008/303 Reg.7

s.65, enabling: SSI 2008/303

s.117, enabling: SSI 2008/303

s.121, enabling: SSI 2008/130, SSI 2008/282

asp 5. Legal Profession and Legal Aid (Scotland) Act 2007

Commencement Orders: SSI 2008/311 Art.2

s.23, applied: SSI 2008/428 Art.2

s.23, enabling: SSI 2008/428

s.26, enabling: SSI 2008/352

s.27, applied: SSI 2008/428 Art.3

s.27, enabling: SSI 2008/428

s.28, applied: SSI 2008/428 Art.4

s.28, enabling: SSI 2008/428

s.78, enabling: SSI 2008/332

s.79, applied: SSI 2008/332

s.82, enabling: SSI 2008/311

Sch.1 para.16, varied: SI 2008/2341 Art.5, SSI 2008/332 Art.5

asp 6. Criminal Proceedings etc (Reform) (Scotland) Act 2007

Commencement Orders: SSI 2008/42 Art.3, Sch.1, Art.3; SSI 2008/192 Sch.1, Art.3; SSI 2008/329 Art.3, Sch.1; SSI 2008/330 Art.2; SSI 2008/362 Art.3; SSI 2008/42 Sch.1; SSI 2008/192 Art.3; SSI 2008/362 Sch.1

s.7, amended: SSI 2008/109 Art.3

s.7, referred to: SSI 2008/42 Art.4

s.12, referred to: SSI 2008/42 Art.5

s.45, disapplied: SI 2008/295 Reg.6, SI 2008/296 Reg.6, Reg.7

s.50, referred to: SSI 2008/42 Art.6

s.52, referred to: SSI 2008/42 Art.6

s.53, referred to: SSI 2008/42 Art.6

s.54, referred to: SSI 2008/42 Art.6

s.59, amended: 2008 asp 6 s.57

s.59, applied: SSI 2008/31, SSI 2008/93, SSI 2008/328, SSI 2008/363

s.59, repealed (in part): 2008 asp 6 s.57, Sch.5 para.5

s.59, enabling: SSI 2008/31, SSI 2008/93, SSI 2008/328, SSI 2008/363

s.60, repealed: 2008 asp 6 Sch.5 para.5

CAP.

2007–cont.

asp 6. Criminal Proceedings etc (Reform) (Scotland) Act 2007–*cont.*

s.61, substituted: 2008 asp 6 s.58

s.63, amended: 2008 asp 6 s.57

s.63, repealed (in part): 2008 asp 6 Sch.5 para.5

s.64, applied: SSI 2008/31, SSI 2008/93, SSI 2008/179 Art.1, SSI 2008/328, SSI 2008/363, SSI 2008/374

s.64, enabling: SSI 2008/31, SSI 2008/93, SSI 2008/179, SSI 2008/328, SSI 2008/363, SSI 2008/374, SSI 2008/416

s.65, applied: SSI 2008/31 Art.4, SSI 2008/93 Art.7, SSI 2008/328 Art.4, SSI 2008/363 Art.4

s.65, enabling: SSI 2008/31, SSI 2008/179, SSI 2008/328, SSI 2008/363, SSI 2008/374

s.66, applied: SSI 2008/93 Art.5, SSI 2008/363 Art.6

s.66, referred to: SSI 2008/328 Art.6

s.69, amended: 2008 asp 6 s.42

s.69, repealed (in part): 2008 asp 6 s.42

s.71, amended: 2008 asp 6 s.41

s.74, amended: 2008 asp 6 s.58

s.74, applied: SSI 2008/330 Art.2

s.74, enabling: SSI 2008/330

s.81, amended: 2008 asp 6 Sch.5 para.5

s.81, enabling: SSI 2008/31, SSI 2008/93, SSI 2008/328, SSI 2008/330, SSI 2008/363

s.82, enabling: SSI 2008/109, SSI 2008/328

s.84, enabling: SSI 2008/42, SSI 2008/192, SSI 2008/329, SSI 2008/362

asp 8. Transport and Works (Scotland) Act 2007

referred to: SSI 2008/263 Sch.1

s.1, applied: SSI 2008/199 Art.3, Art.4, Art.5, Art.14

s.6, applied: SSI 2008/200 Art.3, Art.4

s.18, enabling: SSI 2008/199, SSI 2008/200

s.28, applied: SSI 2008/199, SSI 2008/200

s.28, enabling: SSI 2008/199, SSI 2008/200

asp 9. Budget (Scotland) Act 2007

s.3, amended: SSI 2008/107 Art.2

s.6, repealed: 2008 asp 2 s.8

s.7, applied: SSI 2008/107

s.7, enabling: SSI 2008/107

Sch.1, amended: SSI 2008/107 Art.3

Sch.2 Part 1, amended: SSI 2008/107 Art.4

Sch.2 Part 2, amended: SSI 2008/107 Art.4

Sch.2 Part 3, amended: SSI 2008/107 Art.4

Sch.2 Part 7, amended: SSI 2008/107 Art.4

Sch.2 Part 8, amended: SSI 2008/107 Art.4

Sch.2 Part 10, amended: SSI 2008/107 Art.4

Sch.2 Part 12, amended: SSI 2008/107 Art.4

Sch.2 Part 13, amended: SSI 2008/107 Art.4

Sch.3, amended: SSI 2008/107 Art.5

Sch.4 Part 1, amended: SSI 2008/107 Art.6

Sch.5, amended: SSI 2008/107 Art.7

CAP.

2007–cont.

asp 10. Adult Support and Protection (Scotland) Act 2007
Commencement Orders: SSI 2008/49 Art.2; SSI 2008/116 Art.2; SSI 2008/314 Art.2, Art.3
referred to: SSI 2008/306 Art.2
s.7, applied: SSI 2008/306 Art.3
s.8, applied: SSI 2008/306 Art.3
s.9, applied: SSI 2008/306 Art.3
s.10, applied: SSI 2008/306 Art.3
s.21, enabling: SSI 2008/335
s.25, enabling: SSI 2008/335
s.26, enabling: SSI 2008/335, SSI 2008/375
s.27, enabling: SSI 2008/335, SSI 2008/375
s.52, enabling: SSI 2008/306
s.76, enabling: SSI 2008/50, SSI 2008/306
s.79, enabling: SSI 2008/49, SSI 2008/116, SSI 2008/314

asp 12. Aquaculture and Fisheries (Scotland) Act 2007
referred to: SSI 2008/263 Sch.1
s.1, enabling: SSI 2008/326
s.25, applied: SSI 2008/101 Art.2, Art.4
s.25, enabling: SSI 2008/101, SSI 2008/151
s.26, applied: SSI 2008/101 Art.3, Art.4
s.26, enabling: SSI 2008/101
s.27, applied: SSI 2008/101 Art.4, Art.5
s.27, enabling: SSI 2008/101
s.28, applied: SSI 2008/101 Art.4
s.29, applied: SSI 2008/101 Art.4, Art.6
s.29, enabling: SSI 2008/101
s.30, applied: SSI 2008/101 Art.4
s.31, applied: SSI 2008/101 Art.4
s.43, enabling: SSI 2008/101

asp 14. Protection of Vulnerable Groups (Scotland) Act 2007
applied: SI 2008/2553 Art.5, SI 2008/2554 Art.5, SI 2008/2927 Reg.2, SI 2008/3047 Art.5, SI 2008/3148 Sch.1

asp 15. Schools (Health Promotion and Nutrition) (Scotland) Act 2007
Commencement Orders: SSI 2008/171 Art.2
s.11, enabling: SSI 2008/171

CAP.

2008

asp 1. Abolition of Bridge Tolls (Scotland) Act 2008
Commencement Orders: SSI 2008/22 Art.2
Royal Assent, January 24, 2008
s.4, enabling: SSI 2008/22

asp 2. Budget (Scotland) Act 2008
Royal Assent, March 12, 2008
s.3, amended: SSI 2008/424 Art.2
s.7, applied: SSI 2008/424
s.7, enabling: SSI 2008/424
Sch.1, amended: SSI 2008/424 Art.3
Sch.2 Part 1, amended: SSI 2008/424 Art.4
Sch.2 Part 2, amended: SSI 2008/424 Art.4
Sch.2 Part 4, amended: SSI 2008/424 Art.4
Sch.2 Part 5, amended: SSI 2008/424 Art.4
Sch.2 Part 6, amended: SSI 2008/424 Art.4
Sch.2 Part 7, amended: SSI 2008/424 Art.4
Sch.2 Part 8, amended: SSI 2008/424 Art.4
Sch.2 Part 9, amended: SSI 2008/424 Art.4
Sch.3, amended: SSI 2008/424 Art.5
Sch.5, amended: SSI 2008/424 Art.6

asp 3. Graduate Endowment Abolition (Scotland) Act 2008
Royal Assent, April 04, 2008

asp 4. Glasgow Commonwealth Games Act 2008
Commencement Orders: SSI 2008/245 Art.2
Royal Assent, June 10, 2008
s.49, enabling: SSI 2008/245

asp 5. Public Health etc (Scotland) Act 2008
Royal Assent, July 16, 2008

asp 6. Judiciary and Courts (Scotland) Act 2008
Royal Assent, October 29, 2008

asp 7. Scottish Register of Tartans Act 2008
Royal Assent, November 13, 2008

ACTS OF THE NORTHERN IRELAND ASSEMBLY

CAP.

1969

24. Industrial and Provident Societies Act (Northern Ireland) 1969
referred to: SI 2008/565 Reg.14
s.38A, repealed (in part): SI 2008/565 Reg.15
s.48, applied: SI 2008/565 Reg.4

CAP.

1970

1. Harbours Act (Northern Ireland) 1970
s.30, amended: SI 2008/948 Sch.1 para.41

ACTS OF THE PARLIAMENT OF ENGLAND, WALES & THE UNITED KINGDOM

CAP.

12 Cha. 2 (1660)

24. Tenures Abolition Act 1660
s.1, see *Crown Estate Commissioners v Roberts* [2008] EWHC 1302 (Ch), [2008] 4 All E.R. 828 (Ch D), Lewison, J.
s.7, see *Crown Estate Commissioners v Roberts* [2008] EWHC 1302 (Ch), [2008] 4 All E.R. 828 (Ch D), Lewison, J.

7 & 8 Will. 3 (1695)

9. London to Harwich Roads Act 1695
repealed: 2008 c.12 Sch.1 Part 10

1700

21. Removal of Hertford Gaol Act 1700
repealed: 2008 c.12 Sch.1 Part 2

1702

10. Essex Roads Act 1702
repealed: 2008 c.12 Sch.1 Part 10

1707

46. Plymouth Workhouse Act 1707
repealed: 2008 c.12 Sch.1 Part 7

47. London to Harwich Roads Act 1707
repealed: 2008 c.12 Sch.1 Part 10

1725

23. Essex Roads Act 1725
repealed: 2008 c.12 Sch.1 Part 10

1736

10. Aylesbury Gaol and Shire Hall Rate in Bucks Act 1736
repealed: 2008 c.12 Sch.1 Part 2

20 Geo. 2 (1746)

7. Essex Roads Act 1746
repealed: 2008 c.12 Sch.1 Part 10

25 Geo. 2 (1751)

36. Disorderly Houses Act 1751
repealed: 2008 c.12 Sch.1 Part 3

1753

57. Debtors&apos Prison, Devonshire Act 1753
repealed: 2008 c.12 Sch.1 Part 2

CAP.

1758

59. Plymouth Poor Relief Act 1758
repealed: 2008 c.12 Sch.1 Part 7

5 Geo. 3 (1765)

60. Essex, Suffolk and Hertford Roads Act 1765
repealed: 2008 c.12 Sch.1 Part 10

1766

37. Thames Embankment Act 1766
s.4, repealed: 2008 c.12 Sch.1 Part 2
s.10, repealed: 2008 c.12 Sch.1 Part 2

1768

40. Coventry Gaol Act 1768
repealed: 2008 c.12 Sch.1 Part 2

1770

54. Norfolk Roads Act 1770
repealed: 2008 c.12 Sch.1 Part 10

79. Holborn Poor Relief Act 1770
repealed: 2008 c.12 Sch.1 Part 5

80. Holborn Poor Relief Act 1770
repealed: 2008 c.12 Sch.1 Part 5

12 Geo. 3 (1772)

35. Essex Gaol Act 1772
repealed: 2008 c.12 Sch.1 Part 2

14 Geo. 3 (1774)

75. Southwark Workhouse Act 1774
repealed: 2008 c.12 Sch.1 Part 5

1775

25. Hertford Prison Act 1775
repealed: 2008 c.12 Sch.1 Part 2

16 Geo. 3 (1776)

54. Westmorland Gaol, etc Act 1776
repealed: 2008 c.12 Sch.1 Part 2

18 Geo. 3 (1777)

58. Warwick Gaol Act 1777
repealed: 2008 c.12 Sch.1 Part 2

1778

48. Newgate Gaol and Sessions House Act 1778
repealed: 2008 c.12 Sch.1 Part 2

CAP.

1778–cont.

67. Middlesex Sessions House Act 1778
repealed: 2008 c.12 Sch.1 Part 5

72. Westminster Improvement Act 1778
repealed: 2008 c.12 Sch.1 Part 5

19 Geo. 3 (1779)

46. Pembroke Gaol Act 1779
repealed: 2008 c.12 Sch.1 Part 2

1781

74. Gloucester Gaol Act 1781
s.1, repealed: 2008 c.12 Sch.1 Part 2
s.40, repealed: 2008 c.12 Sch.1 Part 2
s.64, repealed: 2008 c.12 Sch.1 Part 2
s.75, repealed: 2008 c.12 Sch.1 Part 2
Sch, repealed: 2008 c.12 Sch.1 Part 2

1785

10. Gloucester Gaol Act 1785
repealed: 2008 c.12 Sch.1 Part 2

97. City of London Improvement Act 1785
repealed: 2008 c.12 Sch.1 Part 2

1786

19. Plymouth Poor Relief Act 1786
repealed: 2008 c.12 Sch.1 Part 7

55. Middlesex Gaol Act 1786
repealed: 2008 c.12 Sch.1 Part 2

27 Geo. 3 (1787)

58. Sussex Gaol Act 1787
repealed: 2008 c.12 Sch.1 Part 2

59. Devon Gaol Act 1787
repealed: 2008 c.12 Sch.1 Part 2

60. Stafford Gaol Act 1787
repealed: 2008 c.12 Sch.1 Part 2

1788

82. Chester Improvement Act 1788
repealed: 2008 c.12 Sch.1 Part 2

1790

85. Norwich to Bixley Roads Act 1790
repealed: 2008 c.12 Sch.1 Part 10

31 Geo. 3 (1791)

22. Surrey Gaol Act 1791
repealed: 2008 c.12 Sch.1 Part 2

87. Sunderland Poor Relief Act 1791
repealed: 2008 c.12 Sch.1 Part 7

32 Geo. 3 (1792)

56. Servants Characters Act 1792
repealed: 2008 c.12 Sch.1 Part 3

CAP.

32 Geo. 3 (1792)–cont.

148. Norfolk Roads Act 1792
repealed: 2008 c.12 Sch.1 Part 10

33 Geo. 3 (1793)

128. Ipswich and Yaxley Roads Act 1793
repealed: 2008 c.12 Sch.1 Part 10

149. Essex Roads Act 1793
repealed: 2008 c.12 Sch.1 Part 10

34 Geo. 3 (1794)

137. Chelmsford Roads Act 1794
repealed: 2008 c.12 Sch.1 Part 10

36 Geo. 3 (1796)

119. East India Merchants and Purchase of Land in City, etc Act 1796
repealed: 2008 c.12 Sch.1 Part 4

127. East India Merchants and Land for Warehouses, etc Act 1796
repealed: 2008 c.12 Sch.1 Part 4

1804

61. Sessions Houses, Westminster, etc Act 1804
s.3, repealed: 2008 c.12 Sch.1 Part 5

59 Geo. 3 (1819)

1. Unlawful Drilling Act 1819
repealed (in part): 2008 c.12 Sch.1 Part 3

8. Criminal Libel Act 1819
s.1, amended: 2008 c.4 s.79, Sch.28 Part 5
s.3, amended: 2008 c.4 s.79
s.4, amended: 2008 c.4 s.79

7 Geo. 4 (1826)

16. Chelsea and Kilmainham Hospitals Act 1826
s.3, repealed: 2008 c.12 Sch.1 Part 1
s.10, repealed: 2008 c.12 Sch.1 Part 1
s.11, repealed: 2008 c.12 Sch.1 Part 1
s.13, repealed: 2008 c.12 Sch.1 Part 1
s.23, repealed: 2008 c.12 Sch.1 Part 1
s.27, repealed: 2008 c.12 Sch.1 Part 1
s.31, repealed: 2008 c.12 Sch.1 Part 1
s.34, repealed: 2008 c.12 Sch.1 Part 1
s.46, amended: 2008 c.12 Sch.1 Part 1
s.47, repealed: 2008 c.12 Sch.1 Part 1
s.48, repealed: 2008 c.12 Sch.1 Part 1

9 Geo. 4 (1828)

14. Statute of Frauds Amendment Act 1828
s.6, see *Contex Drouzhba Ltd v Wiseman* [2007] EWCA Civ 1201, [2008] B.C.C. 301 (CA (Civ Div)), Waller, L.J. (V-P)

CAP.

1 & 2 Will. 4 (1831)

32. Game Act 1831
see *Crown Estate Commissioners v Roberts* [2008] EWHC 1302 (Ch), [2008] 4 All E.R. 828 (Ch D), Lewison, J.
applied: 2008 c.13 Sch.3
s.3, referred to: 2008 c.13 Sch.6
s.3A, referred to: 2008 c.13 Sch.6
s.24, referred to: 2008 c.13 Sch.6

2 & 3 Will. 4 (1832)

71. Prescription Act 1832
see *Housden v Conservators of Wimbledon and Putney Commons* [2008] EWCA Civ 200, [2008] 1 W.L.R. 1172 (CA (Civ Div)), Mummery, L.J.
s.2, see *Housden v Conservators of Wimbledon and Putney Commons* [2008] EWCA Civ 200, [2008] 1 W.L.R. 1172 (CA (Civ Div)), Mummery, L.J.
s.3, see *RHJ Ltd v FT Patten (Holdings) Ltd* [2008] EWCA Civ 151, [2008] Ch. 341 (CA (Civ Div)), Mummery, L.J.

3 & 4 Will. 4 (1833)

29. Army (Artillery &c.) Pensions Act 1833
repealed: 2008 c.12 Sch.1 Part 1

41. Judicial Committee Act 1833
s.4, applied: SI 2008/2846 Sch.1
s.24, enabling: SI 2008/300

6 & 7 Will. 4 (1836)

71. Tithe Act 1836
applied: SI 2008/2470 Sch.1 Part 1

7 Will. 4 & 1 Vict. (1837)

26. Wills Act 1837
s.9, see *Papillon (Deceased), Re* [2006] EWHC 3419 (Ch), [2008] W.T.L.R. 269 (Ch D), Guy Newey Q.C.

91. Punishment of Offences Act 1837
repealed: 2008 c.12 Sch.1 Part 3

1 & 2 Vict. (1837-38)

89. Drouly Fund Act 1838
repealed: 2008 c.12 Sch.1 Part 1

110. Judgments Act 1838
s.17, see *Gater Assets Ltd v Nak Naftogaz Ukrainiy* [2008] EWHC 1108 (Comm), [2008] 2 Lloyd's Rep. 295 (QBD (Comm)), Beatson, J.

2 & 3 Vict. (1839)

45. Highway (Railway Crossing) Act 1839
disapplied: 2008 c.18 Sch.11 para.1

CAP.

3 & 4 Vict. (1840)

92. Non-parochial Registers Act 1840
s.5, amended: SI 2008/678 Sch.2 para.1
s.5, applied: SI 2008/678 Sch.1 para.1

97. Railway Regulation Act 1840
s.16, varied: 2008 c.18 Sch.11 para.7

5 & 6 Vict. (1842)

55. Railway Regulation Act 1842
s.9, disapplied: 2008 c.18 Sch.11 para.2
s.17, varied: 2008 c.18 Sch.11 para.7

7 & 8 Vict. (1844)

69. Judicial Committee Act 1844
s.1, enabling: SI 2008/300

8 & 9 Vict. (1845)

18. Lands Clauses Consolidation Act 1845
applied: SI 2008/1961 Sch.4 para.8
disapplied: 2008 c.18 Sch.6 para.1
s.2, referred to: SI 2008/1961 Sch.4 para.8
s.68, see *Union Railways (North) Ltd v Kent CC* [2008] 2 P. & C.R. 22 (Lands Tr), George Bartlett Q.C. (President)
s.99, applied: SI 2008/1961 Sch.4 para.8
s.107, applied: SI 2008/1961 Sch.4 para.8

19. Lands Clauses Consolidation (Scotland) Act 1845
s.116, varied: 2008 c.29 s.125

20. Railways Clauses Consolidation Act 1845
applied: 2008 c.18 Sch.11 para.3
s.1, disapplied: 2008 c.18 Sch.11 para.3
s.2, varied: 2008 c.18 Sch.11 para.3
s.6, applied: 2008 c.18 Sch.2 para.7
s.6, varied: 2008 c.18 Sch.11 para.3
s.7, disapplied: 2008 c.18 Sch.11 para.3
s.8, disapplied: 2008 c.18 Sch.11 para.3
s.9, disapplied: 2008 c.18 Sch.11 para.3
s.11, disapplied: 2008 c.18 Sch.11 para.3
s.12, disapplied: 2008 c.18 Sch.11 para.3
s.13, disapplied: 2008 c.18 Sch.11 para.3
s.14, disapplied: 2008 c.18 Sch.11 para.3
s.15, disapplied: 2008 c.18 Sch.11 para.3
s.17, disapplied: 2008 c.18 Sch.11 para.3
s.18, varied: 2008 c.18 Sch.11 para.3
s.19, disapplied: 2008 c.18 Sch.11 para.3
s.20, disapplied: 2008 c.18 Sch.11 para.3
s.21, varied: 2008 c.18 Sch.11 para.3
s.22, disapplied: 2008 c.18 Sch.11 para.3
s.23, disapplied: 2008 c.18 Sch.11 para.3
s.24, applied: SI 2008/1261 Art.7
s.42, disapplied: 2008 c.18 Sch.11 para.3
s.46, amended: SI 2008/2512 Art.3
s.46, applied: SI 2008/1261 Art.7, SI 2008/2512 Art.3
s.46, disapplied: 2008 c.18 Sch.3 para.12
s.46, varied: SI 2008/1261 Art.7
s.47, applied: SI 2008/1261 Art.7

CAP.

8 & 9 Vict. (1845)–cont.

20. Railways Clauses Consolidation Act 1845–*cont.*

s.47, disapplied: 2008 c.18 Sch.11 para.3
s.48, disapplied: 2008 c.18 Sch.11 para.3
s.58, applied: SI 2008/1261 Art.7, SI 2008/2512 Art.3
s.58, varied: SI 2008/1261 Art.7
s.59, disapplied: 2008 c.18 Sch.11 para.3
s.60, disapplied: 2008 c.18 Sch.11 para.3
s.61, applied: SI 2008/1261 Art.7, SI 2008/2512 Art.3
s.61, disapplied: 2008 c.18 Sch.11 para.3
s.62, disapplied: 2008 c.18 Sch.11 para.3
s.68, applied: SI 2008/1261 Art.7, SI 2008/2512 Art.3
s.68, varied: 2008 c.18 Sch.11 para.3
s.71, applied: SI 2008/1261 Art.7, SI 2008/2512 Art.3
s.71, varied: SI 2008/1261 Art.7
s.72, applied: SI 2008/1261 Art.7, SI 2008/2512 Art.3
s.73, applied: SI 2008/1261 Art.7, SI 2008/2512 Art.3
s.74, disapplied: 2008 c.18 Sch.11 para.3
s.75, applied: SI 2008/1261 Art.7, SI 2008/2512 Art.3
s.75, disapplied: 2008 c.18 Sch.11 para.3
s.77, applied: SI 2008/1261 Art.7, SI 2008/2512 Art.3
s.77, disapplied: 2008 c.18 Sch.11 para.3
s.78, see *National Grid Gas Plc v Lafarge Aggregates Ltd Pt* [2006] EWHC 2559 (Ch), [2008] R.V.R. 126 (Ch D), Cooke, J.
s.78, applied: SI 2008/1261 Art.7, SI 2008/2512 Art.3
s.78, disapplied: 2008 c.18 Sch.11 para.3
s.78A, applied: SI 2008/1261 Art.7, SI 2008/2512 Art.3
s.78A, disapplied: 2008 c.18 Sch.11 para.3
s.79, applied: SI 2008/1261 Art.7, SI 2008/2512 Art.3
s.79, disapplied: 2008 c.18 Sch.11 para.3
s.79A, applied: SI 2008/1261 Art.7, SI 2008/2512 Art.3
s.79A, disapplied: 2008 c.18 Sch.11 para.3
s.79B, applied: SI 2008/1261 Art.7, SI 2008/2512 Art.3
s.79B, disapplied: 2008 c.18 Sch.11 para.3
s.80, applied: SI 2008/1261 Art.7, SI 2008/2512 Art.3
s.80, disapplied: 2008 c.18 Sch.11 para.3
s.81, see *National Grid Gas Plc v Lafarge Aggregates Ltd Pt* [2006] EWHC 2559 (Ch), [2008] R.V.R. 126 (Ch D), Cooke, J.
s.81, applied: SI 2008/1261 Art.7, SI 2008/2512 Art.3
s.81, disapplied: 2008 c.18 Sch.11 para.3
s.82, applied: SI 2008/1261 Art.7, SI 2008/2512 Art.3
s.82, disapplied: 2008 c.18 Sch.11 para.3

CAP.

8 & 9 Vict. (1845)–cont.

20. Railways Clauses Consolidation Act 1845–*cont.*

s.83, applied: SI 2008/1261 Art.7, SI 2008/2512 Art.3
s.83, disapplied: 2008 c.18 Sch.11 para.3
s.84, applied: SI 2008/1261 Art.7, SI 2008/2512 Art.3
s.84, disapplied: 2008 c.18 Sch.11 para.3
s.85, applied: SI 2008/1261 Art.7, SI 2008/2512 Art.3
s.85, disapplied: 2008 c.18 Sch.11 para.3
s.85A, applied: SI 2008/1261 Art.7, SI 2008/2512 Art.3
s.85B, applied: SI 2008/1261 Art.7, SI 2008/2512 Art.3
s.85C, applied: SI 2008/1261 Art.7, SI 2008/2512 Art.3
s.85D, applied: SI 2008/1261 Art.7, SI 2008/2512 Art.3
s.85E, applied: SI 2008/1261 Art.7, SI 2008/2512 Art.3
s.87, disapplied: 2008 c.18 Sch.11 para.3
s.88, disapplied: 2008 c.18 Sch.11 para.3
s.94, disapplied: 2008 c.18 Sch.11 para.3
s.95, disapplied: 2008 c.18 Sch.11 para.3
s.103, applied: SI 2008/2512 Art.3
s.104, applied: SI 2008/2512 Art.3
s.105, applied: SI 2008/1261 Art.7, SI 2008/2512 Art.3
s.112, disapplied: 2008 c.18 Sch.11 para.3
s.113, disapplied: 2008 c.18 Sch.11 para.3
s.114, disapplied: 2008 c.18 Sch.11 para.3
s.115, disapplied: 2008 c.18 Sch.11 para.3
s.116, disapplied: 2008 c.18 Sch.11 para.3
s.116, varied: 2008 c.18 Sch.3 para.13
s.117, disapplied: 2008 c.18 Sch.11 para.3
s.117, varied: 2008 c.18 Sch.3 para.13
s.118, disapplied: 2008 c.18 Sch.11 para.3
s.119, disapplied: 2008 c.18 Sch.11 para.3
s.120, disapplied: 2008 c.18 Sch.11 para.3
s.121, disapplied: 2008 c.18 Sch.11 para.3
s.122, disapplied: 2008 c.18 Sch.11 para.3
s.123, disapplied: 2008 c.18 Sch.11 para.3
s.124, disapplied: 2008 c.18 Sch.11 para.3
s.145, applied: SI 2008/1261 Art.7, SI 2008/2512 Art.3
s.154, applied: SI 2008/2512 Art.3
Sch.1, applied: SI 2008/1261 Art.7, SI 2008/2512 Art.3
Sch.2, applied: SI 2008/1261 Art.7, SI 2008/2512 Art.3
Sch.3, applied: SI 2008/1261 Art.7, SI 2008/2512 Art.3

33. Railways Clauses Consolidation (Scotland) Act 1845

s.60, see *Network Rail Infrastructure Ltd, Petitioner* 2008 S.L.T. 25 (OH), Lord Glennie
s.147, see *Network Rail Infrastructure Ltd, Petitioner* 2008 S.L.T. 25 (OH), Lord Glennie

CAP.

8 & 9 Vict. (1845)–cont.

33. Railways Clauses Consolidation (Scotland) Act 1845–*cont.*

s.150, see *Network Rail Infrastructure Ltd, Petitioner* 2008 S.L.T. 25 (OH), Lord Glennie

118. Inclosure Act 1845

s.147, applied: SI 2008/1961 Sch.4 para.8
s.149, applied: SI 2008/1961 Sch.4 para.8

9 & 10 Vict. (1846)

70. Inclosure Act 1846

s.11, applied: SI 2008/1961 Sch.4 para.8

93. Fatal Accidents Act 1846

see *Thompson v Arnold* [2007] EWHC 1875 (QB), [2008] P.I.Q.R. P1 (QBD), Langstaff, J.

10 & 11 Vict. (1847)

27. Harbours, Docks, and Piers Clauses Act 1847

applied: SSI 2008/182 Art.3
referred to: SI 2008/1261 Art.8
varied: SI 2008/1261 Art.3
applied: SI 2008/1261 Art.3, SSI 2008/189 Art.3, SSI 2008/190 Art.3, SSI 2008/361 Art.3
referred to: SI 2008/1261 Art.41
varied: SSI 2008/188 Art.3
applied: SI 2008/1261 Art.3, SSI 2008/189 Art.3, SSI 2008/190 Art.3, SSI 2008/361 Art.3
referred to: SI 2008/1261 Art.41
varied: SSI 2008/188 Art.3
s.1, applied: SI 2008/1261 Art.3, SSI 2008/189 Art.3, SSI 2008/190 Art.3, SSI 2008/361 Art.3
s.1, referred to: SI 2008/1261 Art.41
s.1, varied: SSI 2008/188 Art.3
s.5, disapplied: SSI 2008/189 Art.3, SSI 2008/190 Art.3
s.6, disapplied: SSI 2008/182 Art.3, SSI 2008/189 Art.3, SSI 2008/190 Art.3
s.7, disapplied: SSI 2008/182 Art.3, SSI 2008/189 Art.3, SSI 2008/190 Art.3
s.8, disapplied: SSI 2008/182 Art.3, SSI 2008/189 Art.3, SSI 2008/190 Art.3
s.9, disapplied: SSI 2008/182 Art.3, SSI 2008/189 Art.3, SSI 2008/190 Art.3
s.10, disapplied: SSI 2008/182 Art.3, SSI 2008/189 Art.3, SSI 2008/190 Art.3
s.11, disapplied: SSI 2008/182 Art.3, SSI 2008/189 Art.3, SSI 2008/190 Art.3
s.12, disapplied: SSI 2008/182 Art.3, SSI 2008/189 Art.3, SSI 2008/190 Art.3
s.13, disapplied: SSI 2008/182 Art.3, SSI 2008/189 Art.3, SSI 2008/190 Art.3
s.14, disapplied: SSI 2008/182 Art.3, SSI 2008/189 Art.3, SSI 2008/190 Art.3
s.15, disapplied: SSI 2008/182 Art.3, SSI 2008/189 Art.3, SSI 2008/190 Art.3

CAP.

10 & 11 Vict. (1847)–cont.

27. Harbours, Docks, and Piers Clauses Act 1847–*cont.*

s.16, disapplied: SSI 2008/182 Art.3, SSI 2008/189 Art.3, SSI 2008/190 Art.3
s.17, disapplied: SSI 2008/182 Art.3, SSI 2008/189 Art.3, SSI 2008/190 Art.3
s.18, disapplied: SSI 2008/182 Art.3, SSI 2008/189 Art.3, SSI 2008/190 Art.3
s.19, disapplied: SSI 2008/182 Art.3, SSI 2008/189 Art.3, SSI 2008/190 Art.3
s.20, applied: SSI 2008/189 Art.3, SSI 2008/190 Art.3
s.20, varied: SSI 2008/188 Art.3
s.21, applied: SSI 2008/189 Art.3, SSI 2008/190 Art.3
s.21, varied: SSI 2008/188 Art.3
s.22, disapplied: SSI 2008/182 Art.3, SSI 2008/189 Art.3, SSI 2008/190 Art.3
s.23, applied: SSI 2008/189 Art.3, SSI 2008/190 Art.3
s.23, disapplied: SSI 2008/182 Art.3
s.23, varied: SSI 2008/188 Art.3
s.24, applied: SI 2008/1261 Art.3
s.24, disapplied: SSI 2008/182 Art.3, SSI 2008/189 Art.3, SSI 2008/190 Art.3
s.24, referred to: SI 2008/1261 Art.41
s.25, disapplied: SSI 2008/182 Art.3, SSI 2008/189 Art.3, SSI 2008/190 Art.3
s.26, applied: SI 2008/1261 Art.3, SSI 2008/361 Art.3
s.26, disapplied: SSI 2008/182 Art.3, SSI 2008/189 Art.3, SSI 2008/190 Art.3
s.26, referred to: SI 2008/1261 Art.41
s.27, applied: SI 2008/1261 Art.3, SSI 2008/189 Art.3, SSI 2008/190 Art.3
s.27, referred to: SI 2008/1261 Art.41
s.27, varied: SSI 2008/188 Art.3
s.28, applied: SI 2008/1261 Art.3
s.28, disapplied: SSI 2008/182 Art.3, SSI 2008/189 Art.3, SSI 2008/190 Art.3
s.28, referred to: SI 2008/1261 Art.41
s.29, applied: SI 2008/1261 Art.3, SSI 2008/189 Art.3, SSI 2008/190 Art.3, SSI 2008/361 Art.3
s.29, referred to: SI 2008/1261 Art.41
s.29, varied: SSI 2008/188 Art.3
s.30, applied: SI 2008/1261 Art.3, SSI 2008/361 Art.3
s.30, disapplied: SSI 2008/189 Art.3, SSI 2008/190 Art.3
s.30, referred to: SI 2008/1261 Art.41
s.31, applied: SSI 2008/189 Art.3, SSI 2008/190 Art.3
s.31, varied: SSI 2008/188 Art.3
s.32, applied: SI 2008/1261 Art.3, SSI 2008/189 Art.3, SSI 2008/190 Art.3, SSI 2008/361 Art.3
s.32, referred to: SI 2008/1261 Art.41
s.32, varied: SSI 2008/188 Art.3
s.33, applied: SI 2008/1261 Art.3, SSI 2008/189 Art.3, SSI 2008/190 Art.3

CAP.

10 & 11 Vict. (1847)–cont.

27. **Harbours, Docks, and Piers Clauses Act 1847**–*cont.*

s.33, disapplied: SI 2008/1261 Art.42, SSI 2008/182 Art.3
s.33, referred to: SI 2008/1261 Art.41
s.33, varied: SSI 2008/188 Art.3
s.34, applied: SI 2008/1261 Art.3, SSI 2008/189 Art.3, SSI 2008/190 Art.3, SSI 2008/361 Art.3
s.34, referred to: SI 2008/1261 Art.41
s.34, varied: SSI 2008/188 Art.3
s.35, applied: SI 2008/1261 Art.3, SSI 2008/189 Art.3, SSI 2008/190 Art.3, SSI 2008/361 Art.3
s.35, referred to: SI 2008/1261 Art.41
s.35, varied: SSI 2008/188 Art.3
s.36, applied: SI 2008/1261 Art.3, SSI 2008/189 Art.3, SSI 2008/190 Art.3, SSI 2008/361 Art.3
s.36, referred to: SI 2008/1261 Art.41
s.36, varied: SSI 2008/188 Art.3
s.37, applied: SI 2008/1261 Art.3, SSI 2008/361 Art.3
s.37, disapplied: SSI 2008/189 Art.3, SSI 2008/190 Art.3
s.37, referred to: SI 2008/1261 Art.41
s.38, applied: SI 2008/1261 Art.3, SSI 2008/361 Art.3
s.38, disapplied: SSI 2008/189 Art.3, SSI 2008/190 Art.3
s.38, referred to: SI 2008/1261 Art.41
s.39, applied: SI 2008/1261 Art.3, SSI 2008/361 Art.3
s.39, disapplied: SSI 2008/189 Art.3, SSI 2008/190 Art.3
s.39, referred to: SI 2008/1261 Art.41
s.40, applied: SI 2008/1261 Art.3, SSI 2008/361 Art.3
s.40, disapplied: SSI 2008/189 Art.3, SSI 2008/190 Art.3
s.40, referred to: SI 2008/1261 Art.41
s.41, applied: SI 2008/1261 Art.3, SSI 2008/361 Art.3
s.41, disapplied: SSI 2008/189 Art.3, SSI 2008/190 Art.3
s.41, referred to: SI 2008/1261 Art.41
s.42, applied: SSI 2008/361 Art.3
s.42, disapplied: SSI 2008/189 Art.3, SSI 2008/190 Art.3
s.43, applied: SI 2008/1261 Art.3, SSI 2008/189 Art.3, SSI 2008/190 Art.3, SSI 2008/361 Art.3, Art.19
s.43, referred to: SI 2008/1261 Art.41
s.43, varied: SSI 2008/188 Art.3
s.44, applied: SI 2008/1261 Art.3, SSI 2008/361 Art.3, Art.19
s.44, disapplied: SSI 2008/190 Art.3
s.44, referred to: SI 2008/1261 Art.41
s.44, varied: SI 2008/1261 Art.37
s.45, applied: SSI 2008/361 Art.3, Art.19
s.45, disapplied: SSI 2008/190 Art.3

CAP.

10 & 11 Vict. (1847)–cont.

27. **Harbours, Docks, and Piers Clauses Act 1847**–*cont.*

s.46, applied: SI 2008/1261 Art.3, SSI 2008/361 Art.3, Art.19
s.46, disapplied: SSI 2008/190 Art.3
s.46, referred to: SI 2008/1261 Art.41
s.46, varied: SI 2008/1261 Art.40
s.47, applied: SI 2008/1261 Art.3, SSI 2008/188 Art.42, SSI 2008/361 Art.3, Art.19
s.47, disapplied: SSI 2008/190 Art.3
s.47, referred to: SI 2008/1261 Art.41
s.48, applied: SSI 2008/361 Art.3, Art.19
s.48, disapplied: SSI 2008/190 Art.3
s.49, disapplied: SSI 2008/182 Art.3, SSI 2008/190 Art.3
s.50, disapplied: SSI 2008/182 Art.3, SSI 2008/190 Art.3
s.51, applied: SI 2008/1261 Art.3, SSI 2008/361 Art.3
s.51, disapplied: SSI 2008/189 Art.3, SSI 2008/190 Art.3
s.51, referred to: SI 2008/1261 Art.41
s.52, applied: SI 2008/1261 Art.3, Sch.8 para.18, SSI 2008/189 Art.3, SSI 2008/190 Art.3
s.52, referred to: SI 2008/1261 Art.41
s.52, varied: SSI 2008/188 Art.3
s.53, applied: SI 2008/1261 Art.3, SSI 2008/189 Art.3, SSI 2008/190 Art.3
s.53, referred to: SI 2008/1261 Art.41
s.53, varied: SI 2008/1261 Art.3, SSI 2008/188 Art.3
s.54, applied: SI 2008/1261 Art.3, SSI 2008/189 Art.3, SSI 2008/190 Art.3, SSI 2008/361 Art.3
s.54, referred to: SI 2008/1261 Art.41
s.54, varied: SSI 2008/188 Art.3
s.55, applied: SI 2008/1261 Art.3, SSI 2008/189 Art.3, SSI 2008/190 Art.3, SSI 2008/361 Art.3
s.55, referred to: SI 2008/1261 Art.41
s.55, varied: SSI 2008/188 Art.3
s.56, applied: SI 2008/1261 Art.3, Sch.8 para.23, SSI 2008/189 Art.3, SSI 2008/190 Art.3, SSI 2008/361 Art.3
s.56, referred to: SI 2008/1261 Art.41
s.56, varied: SSI 2008/188 Art.3
s.57, applied: SI 2008/1261 Art.3, Sch.8 para.18, SSI 2008/189 Art.3, SSI 2008/190 Art.3, Art.4, SSI 2008/361 Art.3
s.57, referred to: SI 2008/1261 Art.41
s.57, varied: SSI 2008/188 Art.3
s.58, applied: SI 2008/1261 Art.3, SSI 2008/188 Art.15, SSI 2008/189 Art.3, Art.15, SSI 2008/190 Art.3, SSI 2008/361 Art.3
s.58, referred to: SI 2008/1261 Art.41
s.58, varied: SI 2008/1261 Art.42, SSI 2008/188 Art.3
s.59, applied: SI 2008/1261 Art.3, SSI 2008/189 Art.3, SSI 2008/190 Art.3, SSI 2008/361 Art.3

CAP.

10 & 11 Vict. (1847)–cont.

27. **Harbours, Docks, and Piers Clauses Act 1847**–*cont.*

s.59, referred to: SI 2008/1261 Art.41
s.59, varied: SSI 2008/188 Art.3
s.60, applied: SSI 2008/189 Art.3, SSI 2008/190 Art.3, SSI 2008/361 Art.3
s.60, disapplied: SSI 2008/182 Art.3
s.60, varied: SSI 2008/188 Art.3
s.61, applied: SSI 2008/189 Art.3, SSI 2008/190 Art.3, SSI 2008/361 Art.3
s.61, varied: SSI 2008/188 Art.3
s.62, applied: SSI 2008/189 Art.3, SSI 2008/190 Art.3, SSI 2008/361 Art.3
s.62, varied: SSI 2008/188 Art.3
s.63, applied: SSI 2008/189 Art.3, SSI 2008/190 Art.3, SSI 2008/361 Art.3
s.63, varied: SSI 2008/182 Art.3, SSI 2008/188 Art.3, SSI 2008/189 Art.3, SSI 2008/190 Art.3, SSI 2008/361 Art.3
s.64, applied: SI 2008/1261 Art.3, SSI 2008/189 Art.3, SSI 2008/190 Art.3, SSI 2008/361 Art.3
s.64, referred to: SI 2008/1261 Art.41
s.64, varied: SSI 2008/188 Art.3
s.65, applied: SI 2008/1261 Art.3, Sch.8 para.18, SSI 2008/189 Art.3, SSI 2008/190 Art.3, SSI 2008/361 Art.3
s.65, referred to: SI 2008/1261 Art.41
s.65, varied: SSI 2008/188 Art.3
s.66, applied: SSI 2008/189 Art.3, SSI 2008/190 Art.3, SSI 2008/361 Art.3
s.66, varied: SSI 2008/188 Art.3
s.67, disapplied: SSI 2008/182 Art.3, SSI 2008/189 Art.3, SSI 2008/190 Art.3
s.68, applied: SSI 2008/189 Art.3, SSI 2008/190 Art.3, SSI 2008/361 Art.3
s.68, varied: SSI 2008/188 Art.3
s.69, applied: SI 2008/1261 Art.3, Sch.8 para.18, SSI 2008/189 Art.3, SSI 2008/190 Art.3, SSI 2008/361 Art.3
s.69, disapplied: SSI 2008/182 Art.3
s.69, referred to: SI 2008/1261 Art.41
s.69, varied: SI 2008/1261 Art.3, SSI 2008/182 Art.3, SSI 2008/188 Art.3, SSI 2008/189 Art.3, SSI 2008/190 Art.3, SSI 2008/361 Art.3
s.70, applied: SI 2008/1261 Art.3, SSI 2008/189 Art.3, SSI 2008/190 Art.3, SSI 2008/361 Art.3
s.70, referred to: SI 2008/1261 Art.41
s.70, varied: SSI 2008/188 Art.3
s.71, applied: SI 2008/1261 Art.3, SSI 2008/189 Art.3, SSI 2008/190 Art.3, SSI 2008/361 Art.3
s.71, referred to: SI 2008/1261 Art.41
s.71, varied: SSI 2008/188 Art.3
s.72, applied: SI 2008/1261 Art.3, SSI 2008/361 Art.3
s.72, disapplied: SSI 2008/189 Art.3, SSI 2008/190 Art.3
s.72, referred to: SI 2008/1261 Art.41

CAP.

10 & 11 Vict. (1847)–cont.

27. **Harbours, Docks, and Piers Clauses Act 1847**–*cont.*

s.73, applied: SSI 2008/189 Art.3, SSI 2008/190 Art.3, SSI 2008/361 Art.3
s.73, varied: SSI 2008/182 Art.3, SSI 2008/188 Art.3, SSI 2008/189 Art.3, SSI 2008/190 Art.3
s.74, applied: SI 2008/1261 Art.3, SSI 2008/361 Art.3
s.74, disapplied: SSI 2008/189 Art.3, SSI 2008/190 Art.3
s.74, referred to: SI 2008/1261 Art.41
s.75, applied: SI 2008/1261 Art.3, SSI 2008/361 Art.3
s.75, disapplied: SSI 2008/189 Art.3, SSI 2008/190 Art.3
s.75, referred to: SI 2008/1261 Art.41
s.76, applied: SI 2008/1261 Art.3, SSI 2008/361 Art.3
s.76, disapplied: SSI 2008/189 Art.3, SSI 2008/190 Art.3
s.76, referred to: SI 2008/1261 Art.41
s.77, applied: SSI 2008/189 Art.3, SSI 2008/190 Art.3, SSI 2008/361 Art.3
s.77, varied: SSI 2008/188 Art.3
s.78, applied: SI 2008/1261 Art.3, SSI 2008/189 Art.3, SSI 2008/190 Art.3, SSI 2008/361 Art.3
s.78, referred to: SI 2008/1261 Art.41
s.78, varied: SSI 2008/188 Art.3
s.79, applied: SSI 2008/361 Art.3
s.79, disapplied: SSI 2008/182 Art.3, SSI 2008/189 Art.3, SSI 2008/190 Art.3
s.80, applied: SSI 2008/361 Art.3
s.80, disapplied: SSI 2008/182 Art.3, SSI 2008/189 Art.3, SSI 2008/190 Art.3
s.81, applied: SSI 2008/361 Art.3
s.81, disapplied: SSI 2008/182 Art.3, SSI 2008/189 Art.3, SSI 2008/190 Art.3
s.82, applied: SSI 2008/361 Art.3
s.82, disapplied: SSI 2008/182 Art.3, SSI 2008/189 Art.3, SSI 2008/190 Art.3
s.83, disapplied: SSI 2008/182 Art.3, SSI 2008/189 Art.3, SSI 2008/190 Art.3
s.83, referred to: SI 2008/230 Art.6
s.84, applied: SI 2008/1261 Art.3
s.84, disapplied: SSI 2008/182 Art.3, SSI 2008/189 Art.3, SSI 2008/190 Art.3
s.84, referred to: SI 2008/1261 Art.41
s.84, varied: SSI 2008/189 Art.3, SSI 2008/190 Art.3
s.85, applied: SI 2008/1261 Art.3
s.85, disapplied: SSI 2008/182 Art.3, SSI 2008/189 Art.3, SSI 2008/190 Art.3
s.85, referred to: SI 2008/1261 Art.41
s.85, varied: SI 2008/1261 Art.4
s.86, applied: SI 2008/1261 Art.3
s.86, disapplied: SSI 2008/182 Art.3, SSI 2008/189 Art.3, SSI 2008/190 Art.3
s.86, referred to: SI 2008/1261 Art.41
s.87, applied: SI 2008/1261 Art.3

CAP.

10 & 11 Vict. (1847)–cont.

27. Harbours, Docks, and Piers Clauses Act 1847–*cont.*
s.87, disapplied: SSI 2008/182 Art.3, SSI 2008/189 Art.3, SSI 2008/190 Art.3
s.87, referred to: SI 2008/1261 Art.41
s.88, applied: SI 2008/1261 Art.3
s.88, disapplied: SSI 2008/182 Art.3, SSI 2008/189 Art.3, SSI 2008/190 Art.3
s.88, referred to: SI 2008/1261 Art.41
s.89, applied: SI 2008/1261 Art.3
s.89, disapplied: SSI 2008/182 Art.3, SSI 2008/189 Art.3, SSI 2008/190 Art.3
s.89, referred to: SI 2008/1261 Art.41
s.90, applied: SI 2008/1261 Art.3
s.90, disapplied: SSI 2008/182 Art.3, SSI 2008/189 Art.3, SSI 2008/190 Art.3
s.90, referred to: SI 2008/1261 Art.41
s.91, applied: SI 2008/1261 Art.3, SSI 2008/361 Art.3
s.91, disapplied: SSI 2008/182 Art.3, SSI 2008/189 Art.3, SSI 2008/190 Art.3
s.91, referred to: SI 2008/1261 Art.41
s.92, applied: SI 2008/1261 Art.3, SSI 2008/189 Art.3, SSI 2008/190 Art.3
s.92, referred to: SI 2008/1261 Art.41
s.92, varied: SSI 2008/188 Art.3
s.93, applied: SI 2008/1261 Art.3, SSI 2008/361 Art.3
s.93, disapplied: SSI 2008/189 Art.3, SSI 2008/190 Art.3
s.93, referred to: SI 2008/1261 Art.41
s.94, applied: SI 2008/1261 Art.3, SSI 2008/189 Art.3, SSI 2008/190 Art.3, SSI 2008/361 Art.3
s.94, disapplied: SSI 2008/182 Art.3
s.94, referred to: SI 2008/1261 Art.41
s.94, varied: SSI 2008/188 Art.3
s.95, applied: SI 2008/1261 Art.3, SSI 2008/361 Art.3
s.95, disapplied: SSI 2008/182 Art.3, SSI 2008/189 Art.3, SSI 2008/190 Art.3
s.95, referred to: SI 2008/1261 Art.41
s.96, applied: SI 2008/1261 Art.3, SSI 2008/361 Art.3
s.96, disapplied: SSI 2008/182 Art.3, SSI 2008/189 Art.3, SSI 2008/190 Art.3
s.96, referred to: SI 2008/1261 Art.41
s.97, applied: SI 2008/1261 Art.3, SSI 2008/361 Art.3
s.97, disapplied: SSI 2008/182 Art.3, SSI 2008/189 Art.3, SSI 2008/190 Art.3
s.97, referred to: SI 2008/1261 Art.41
s.98, applied: SI 2008/1261 Art.3, SSI 2008/361 Art.3
s.98, disapplied: SSI 2008/182 Art.3, SSI 2008/189 Art.3, SSI 2008/190 Art.3
s.98, referred to: SI 2008/1261 Art.41
s.99, applied: SI 2008/1261 Art.3, SSI 2008/361 Art.3
s.99, disapplied: SSI 2008/182 Art.3, SSI 2008/189 Art.3, SSI 2008/190 Art.3

CAP.

10 & 11 Vict. (1847)–cont.

27. Harbours, Docks, and Piers Clauses Act 1847–*cont.*
s.99, referred to: SI 2008/1261 Art.41
s.100, applied: SI 2008/1261 Art.3, SSI 2008/361 Art.3
s.100, disapplied: SSI 2008/182 Art.3, SSI 2008/189 Art.3, SSI 2008/190 Art.3
s.100, referred to: SI 2008/1261 Art.41
s.101, applied: SI 2008/1261 Art.3
s.101, disapplied: SSI 2008/182 Art.3, SSI 2008/189 Art.3, SSI 2008/190 Art.3
s.101, referred to: SI 2008/1261 Art.41
s.102, applied: SI 2008/1261 Art.3, SSI 2008/361 Art.3
s.102, disapplied: SSI 2008/182 Art.3, SSI 2008/189 Art.3, SSI 2008/190 Art.3
s.102, referred to: SI 2008/1261 Art.41
s.103, applied: SI 2008/1261 Art.3, SSI 2008/361 Art.3
s.103, disapplied: SSI 2008/182 Art.3, SSI 2008/189 Art.3, SSI 2008/190 Art.3
s.103, referred to: SI 2008/1261 Art.41
s.104, applied: SI 2008/1261 Art.3, SSI 2008/361 Art.3
s.104, disapplied: SSI 2008/189 Art.3, SSI 2008/190 Art.3
s.104, referred to: SI 2008/1261 Art.41
s.109, applied: SI 2008/1261 Art.3, SSI 2008/361 Art.3
s.109, disapplied: SSI 2008/189 Art.3, SSI 2008/190 Art.3
s.109, referred to: SI 2008/1261 Art.41

89. Town Police Clauses Act 1847
see *Key Cabs Ltd (t/a Taxifast) v Plymouth City Council* [2007] EWHC 2837 (Admin), [2008] R.T.R.11 (QBD (Admin)), Mitting, J.
applied: 2008 c.13 Sch.3
s.28, amended: SI 2008/1769 Sch.1 para.2, Sch.3
s.37, see *Key Cabs Ltd (t/a Taxifast) v Plymouth City Council* [2007] EWHC 2837 (Admin), [2008] R.T.R.11 (QBD (Admin)), Mitting, J.
s.40, see *Key Cabs Ltd (t/a Taxifast) v Plymouth City Council* [2007] EWHC 2837 (Admin), [2008] R.T.R. 11 (QBD (Admin)), Mitting, J.
s.41, see *Key Cabs Ltd (t/a Taxifast) v Plymouth City Council* [2007] EWHC 2837 (Admin), [2008] R.T.R.11 (QBD (Admin)), Mitting, J.

14 & 15 Vict. (1851)

42. Crown Lands Act 1851
s.22, applied: 2008 c.18 s.43

17 & 18 Vict. (1854)

91. Lands Valuation (Scotland) Act 1854
s.42, enabling: SSI 2008/360

CAP.

17 & 18 Vict. (1854)–cont.

103. Towns Improvement (Ireland) Act 1854
s.72, amended: SI 2008/1769 Sch.1 para.3, Sch.3

18 & 19 Vict. (1855)

81. Places of Worship Registration Act 1855
s.7, amended: SI 2008/678 Sch.2 para.2
s.7, applied: SI 2008/678 Sch.1 para.2

19 & 20 Vict. (1856)

47. Joint Stock Companies Act, 1856
tableB, applied: SI 2008/2860 Sch.2 para.1

20 & 21 Vict. (1857)

44. Crown Suits (Scotland) Act 1857
applied: 2008 c.6 Sch.1 para.22

81. Burial Act 1857
applied: 2008 c.18 Sch.15 para.3
s.25, applied: 2008 c.18 Sch.15 para.1, Sch.15 para.5, Sch.15 para.7, SI 2008/2841 Reg.21
s.25, disapplied: 2008 c.17 Sch.3 para.25

24 & 25 Vict. (1861)

100. Offences against the Person Act 1861
see *Downs v Secretary of State for Environment, Food and Rural Affairs* [2008] EWHC 2666 (Admin), Times, December 1, 2008 (QBD (Admin)), Collins, J.
s.4, applied: 2008 c.28 Sch.2, SI 2008/1216 Sch.1 para.7, Sch.2 para.6
s.16, applied: SI 2008/1216 Sch.1 para.7, Sch.2 para.6
s.18, applied: SI 2008/1216 Sch.1 para.7, Sch.2 para.6
s.20, applied: SI 2008/1216 Sch.2 para.6
s.21, applied: SI 2008/1216 Sch.1 para.7, Sch.2 para.6
s.22, applied: SI 2008/1216 Sch.1 para.7, Sch.2 para.6
s.23, see *R. v Kennedy (Simon)* [2007] UKHL 38, [2008] 1 A.C. 269 (HL), Lord Bingham of Cornhill
s.23, applied: 2008 c.28 Sch.2, SI 2008/1216 Sch.1 para.7, Sch.2 para.6
s.27, applied: SI 2008/1216 Sch.2 para.6
s.28, applied: 2008 c.28 Sch.2, SI 2008/1216 Sch.1 para.7, Sch.2 para.6
s.29, applied: 2008 c.28 Sch.2, SI 2008/1216 Sch.1 para.7, Sch.2 para.6
s.30, applied: 2008 c.28 Sch.2, SI 2008/1216 Sch.1 para.7, Sch.2 para.6
s.31, see *R. v Cockburn (Nigel Philip)* [2008] EWCA Crim 316, [2008] Q.B. 882 (CA (Crim Div)), Sir Igor Judge (President, QB)
s.31, applied: SI 2008/1216 Sch.2 para.6

CAP.

24 & 25 Vict. (1861)–cont.

100. Offences against the Person Act 1861–*cont.*
s.32, applied: SI 2008/1216 Sch.1 para.7, Sch.2 para.6
s.35, applied: SI 2008/1216 Sch.2 para.6
s.37, applied: SI 2008/1216 Sch.2 para.6
s.47, applied: SI 2008/1216 Sch.2 para.7
s.48, repealed (in part): SI 2008/1769 Sch.1 para.4, Sch.3
s.52, applied: SI 2008/1216 Sch.1 para.7, Sch.2 para.2
s.52, repealed (in part): SI 2008/1769 Sch.1 para.4, Sch.3
s.53, applied: SI 2008/1216 Sch.1 para.7, Sch.2 para.2
s.53, repealed (in part): SI 2008/1769 Sch.1 para.4, Sch.3
s.54, applied: SI 2008/1216 Sch.1 para.7, Sch.2 para.2
s.54, repealed (in part): SI 2008/1769 Sch.1 para.4, Sch.3
s.55, applied: SI 2008/1216 Sch.2 para.2
s.55, repealed (in part): SI 2008/1769 Sch.1 para.4, Sch.3
s.64, applied: 2008 c.28 Sch.2

25 & 26 Vict. (1862)

37. Crown Private Estates Act 1862
s.1, applied: 2008 c.29 s.227

26 & 27 Vict. (1863)

92. Railways Clauses Act 1863
Part I, applied: 2008 c.18 Sch.11 para.4
s.5, applied: SI 2008/2512 Art.3
s.5, disapplied: 2008 c.18 Sch.11 para.4
s.6, disapplied: 2008 c.18 Sch.11 para.4
s.7, applied: SI 2008/2512 Art.3
s.7, disapplied: 2008 c.18 Sch.11 para.4
s.12, applied: SI 2008/2512 Art.3
s.13, disapplied: 2008 c.18 Sch.11 para.4
s.14, disapplied: 2008 c.18 Sch.11 para.4
s.15, disapplied: 2008 c.18 Sch.11 para.4
s.16, disapplied: 2008 c.18 Sch.11 para.4
s.17, disapplied: 2008 c.18 Sch.11 para.4
s.18, disapplied: 2008 c.18 Sch.11 para.4
s.19, disapplied: 2008 c.18 Sch.11 para.4

28 & 29 Vict. (1865)

56. Trespass (Scotland) Act 1865
s.3, applied: SSI 2008/103 Reg.7

63. Colonial Laws Validity Act 1865
see *R. (on the application of Bancoult) v Secretary of State for Foreign and Commonwealth Affairs* [2007] EWCA Civ 498, [2008] Q.B. 365 (CA (Civ Div)), Sir Anthony Clarke, M.R.; see *R. (on the application of Bancoult) v Secretary of State for Foreign and Commonwealth*

28 & 29 Vict. (1865)–cont.

63. Colonial Laws Validity Act 1865–*cont.*
see–*cont.*
Affairs [2008] UKHL 61, [2008] 3 W.L.R. 955 (HL), Lord Hoffmann

29 & 30 Vict. (1866)

39. Exchequer and Audit Departments Act 1866
s.15, applied: 2008 c.9 s.159

122. Metropolitan Commons Act 1866
applied: SI 2008/1961 Reg.47

30 & 31 Vict. (1867)

17. Lyon King of Arms Act 1867
Sch.B, amended: SI 2008/1166 Sch.1
Sch.B, repealed: SSI 2008/168 Art.3
Sch.B Part 1, added: SI 2008/1166 Sch.2
Sch.B Part 2, added: SSI 2008/168 Sch.1

133. Consecration of Churchyards Act 1867
applied: SI 2008/1969 Sch.2 para.1

31 & 32 Vict. (1868)

37. Documentary Evidence Act 1868
s.2, see *West Midlands Probation Board v French* [2008] EWHC 2631 (Admin), (2008) 172 J.P. 617 (DC), Scott Baker, L.J.

72. Promissory Oaths Act 1868
Sch.1 Part 2, amended: 2008 asp 6 s.27

32 & 33 Vict. (1869)

107. Metropolitan Commons Amendment Act 1869
applied: SI 2008/1961 Reg.47

115. Metropolitan Public Carriage Act 1869
s.4, see *Bugbugs Ltd v Transport for London* [2007] EWHC 2987 (QB), [2008] R.T.R. 21 (QBD), Swift, J.

33 & 34 Vict. (1870)

23. Forfeiture Act 1870
s.2, referred to: SI 2008/653 Reg.7

90. Foreign Enlistment Act 1870
s.3, repealed: 2008 c.12 Sch.1 Part 3

34 & 35 Vict. (1871)

cciv. Wimbledon and Putney Commons Act 1871
see *Housden v Conservators of Wimbledon and Putney Commons* [2008] EWCA Civ 200, [2008] 1 W.L.R. 1172 (CA (Civ Div)), Mummery, L.J.
s.35, see *Housden v Conservators of Wimbledon and Putney Commons* [2008] EWCA Civ 200, [2008] 1 W.L.R. 1172 (CA (Civ Div)), Mummery, L.J.

34 & 35 Vict. (1871)–cont.

56. Dogs Act 1871
s.2, see *R. (on the application of Chief Constable of North Wales) v Anglesey Justices* [2008] EWHC 309 (Admin), (2008) 172 J.P. 225 (DC), Maurice Kay, L.J.

96. Pedlars Act 1871
applied: 2008 c.13 Sch.3
s.4, referred to: 2008 c.13 Sch.6
s.12, referred to: 2008 c.13 Sch.6
s.14, referred to: 2008 c.13 Sch.6

36 & 37 Vict. (1873)

66. Supreme Court of Judicature Act 1873
see *Masri v Consolidated Contractors International Co SAL* [2008] EWCA Civ 303, [2008] 2 All E.R. (Comm) 1099 (CA (Civ Div)), Ward, L.J.

37 & 38 Vict. (1874)

81. Great Seal (Offices) Act 1874
s.9, enabling: SI 2008/1977

38 & 39 Vict. (1875)

17. Explosives Act 1875
applied: 2008 c.13 Sch.3, SI 2008/2852 Sch.2 para.3
s.30, referred to: 2008 c.13 Sch.6
s.31, referred to: 2008 c.13 Sch.6
s.32, referred to: 2008 c.13 Sch.6
s.40, applied: SI 2008/736 Sch.8 Part 3
s.40, varied: 2008 c.20 Sch.3 para.1
s.43, amended: 2008 c.20 Sch.3 para.1
s.43, referred to: 2008 c.13 Sch.6
s.73, referred to: 2008 c.13 Sch.6
s.80, referred to: 2008 c.13 Sch.6
s.103, amended: SI 2008/960 Sch.3

55. Public Health Act 1875
s.171, applied: SI 2008/2840 Art.3

86. Conspiracy, and Protection of Property Act 1875
repealed: 2008 c.12 Sch.1 Part 3

39 & 40 Vict. (1876)

36. Customs Consolidation Act 1876
s.42, amended: 2008 c.12 Sch.2 para.1
s.42, applied: SI 2008/1216 Sch.2 para.9

56. Commons Act 1876
applied: SI 2008/1961 Reg.47

59. Appellate Jurisdiction Act 1876
s.5, applied: SI 2008/1863 Art.43, Art.62

40 & 41 Vict. (1877)

13. Customs, Inland Revenue, and Savings Banks Act 1877
repealed (in part): 2008 c.12 Sch.1 Part 8

53. Prisons (Scotland) Act 1877
applied: SSI 2008/8 r.3, r.4, r.5, r.6

CAP.

41 & 42 Vict. (1878)

31. Bills of Sale Act 1878
applied: SI 2008/1053 Sch.1
s.15, applied: SI 2008/1053 Sch.1

71. Metropolitan Commons Act 1878
applied: SI 2008/1961 Reg.47

73. Territorial Waters Jurisdiction Act 1878
s.3, disapplied: 2008 c.32 s.14, s.28
s.3, referred to: 2008 c.30 s.96, s.97

42 & 43 Vict. (1879)

11. Bankers Books Evidence Act 1879
applied: SI 2008/570 Sch.1 para.12, SI 2008/700 Sch.1 para.13

21. Customs and Inland Revenue Act 1879
repealed: 2008 c.12 Sch.1 Part 8

43 & 44 Vict. (1880)

4. Judicial Factors (Scotland) Act 1880
s.5, enabling: SSI 2008/223

47. Ground Game Act 1880
applied: 2008 c.13 Sch.3
s.6, referred to: 2008 c.13 Sch.6

44 & 45 Vict. (1881)

Freedom of the Press Act (France) 1881
see *Lindon v France (21279/02)* (2008) 46 E.H.R.R. 35 (ECHR (Grand Chamber)), Judge Rozakis (President)

58. Army Act 1881
repealed: 2008 c.12 Sch.1 Part 1

45 & 46 Vict. (1882)

37. Corn Returns Act 1882
repealed: SI 2008/576 Sch.5 para.7

43. Bills of Sale Act (1878) Amendment Act 1882
applied: SI 2008/1053 Sch.1

61. Bills of Exchange Act 1882
s.27, see *Lomax Leisure Ltd (In Liquidation) v Miller* [2007] EWHC 2508 (Ch), [2008] 1 B.C.L.C. 262 (Ch D), Mark Cawson Q.C.

46 & 47 Vict. (1883)

3. Explosive Substances Act 1883
s.2, applied: 2008 c.28 Sch.2, SI 2008/1216 Sch.1 para.8, Sch.2 para.8
s.3, applied: 2008 c.28 Sch.2, SI 2008/1216 Sch.1 para.8, Sch.2 para.8
s.4, applied: 2008 c.28 Sch.2, SI 2008/1216 Sch.1 para.8, Sch.2 para.8
s.5, applied: 2008 c.28 Sch.2

32. Greenwich Hospital Act 1883
s.2, referred to: 2008 c.12 Sch.2 para.2
s.3, amended: 2008 c.12 Sch.1 Part 1

CAP.

47 & 48 Vict. (1884)

31. Colonial Prisoners Removal Act 1884
applied: SI 2008/794 Reg.160

48 & 49 Vict. (1885)

69. Criminal Law Amendment Act 1885
s.2, applied: SI 2008/1216 Sch.2 para.3
s.2, repealed (in part): SI 2008/1769 Sch.1 para.5, Sch.3
s.3, applied: SI 2008/1216 Sch.2 para.3
s.3, repealed (in part): SI 2008/1769 Sch.1 para.5, Sch.3
s.4, applied: SI 2008/1216 Sch.1 para.9, Sch.2 para.3
s.4, referred to: SI 2008/1062 Sch.1 para.1
s.4, repealed (in part): SI 2008/1769 Sch.1 para.5, Sch.3
s.5, applied: SI 2008/1216 Sch.2 para.3
s.5, repealed (in part): SI 2008/1769 Sch.1 para.5, Sch.3
s.6, repealed (in part): SI 2008/1769 Sch.1 para.5
s.7, applied: SI 2008/1216 Sch.2 para.3
s.7, repealed (in part): SI 2008/1769 Sch.1 para.5, Sch.3
s.8, applied: SI 2008/1216 Sch.2 para.3
s.8, repealed (in part): SI 2008/1769 Sch.1 para.5, Sch.3
s.13, applied: SI 2008/1769 Art.64
s.13, repealed (in part): SI 2008/1769 Sch.1 para.5, Sch.3
s.77, applied: SI 2008/1216 Sch.2 para.3
s.77, repealed (in part): SI 2008/1769 Sch.3

50 & 51 Vict. (1887)

37. Public Works Loans Act 1887
s.4, amended: 2008 asp 5 Sch.2 para.1

54. British Settlements Act 1887
enabling: SI 2008/2846

51 & 52 Vict. (1888)

64. Law of Libel Amendment Act 1888
s.3, amended: 2008 c.4 Sch.28 Part 5
s.4, amended: 2008 c.4 Sch.28 Part 5

52 & 53 Vict. (1889)

10. Commissioners for Oaths Act 1889
s.6, referred to: SI 2008/569 Reg.6

57. Regulation of Railways Act 1889
s.5, varied: 2008 c.18 Sch.11 para.7

63. Interpretation Act 1889
s.38, applied: 2008 c.14 Sch.13 para.6

72. Infectious Disease (Notification) Act 1889
repealed: 2008 asp 5 Sch.3 Part 1

CAP.

53 & 54 Vict. (1890)

25. Barracks Act 1890
repealed: 2008 c.12 Sch.1 Part 1

39. Partnership Act 1890
s.38, see *Hopper v Hopper* [2008] EWHC 228 (Ch), [2008] 1 F.C.R. 557 (Ch D), Briggs, J.
s.42, see *Hopper v Hopper* [2008] EWHC 228 (Ch), [2008] 1 F.C.R. 557 (Ch D), Briggs, J.

54 & 55 Vict. (1891)

39. Stamp Act 1891
referred to: 2008 c.18 Sch.13 para.32
s.12, applied: 2008 c.17 Sch.7 para.12, 2008 c.18 Sch.13 para.32
s.14, see *McGuane v Welch* [2008] EWCA Civ 785, [2008] 2 P. & C.R. 24 (CA (Civ Div)), Mummery, L.J.
s.14, applied: 2008 c.9 s.98, s.99, s.100
s.15B, see *De Nemethy v Revenue and Customs Commissioners* [2008] S.T.C. (S.C.D.) 136 (Sp Comm), Adrian Shipwright (Chairman)
s.25, repealed: 2008 c.12 Sch.1 Part 8
s.49, repealed: 2008 c.12 Sch.1 Part 8
s.111, repealed: 2008 c.12 Sch.1 Part 8
s.120, repealed: 2008 c.12 Sch.1 Part 8
s.122, amended: 2008 c.12 Sch.1 Part 8

55 & 56 Vict. (1892)

8. Hares Preservation Act 1892
s.2, referred to: 2008 c.13 Sch.6

17. Sheriff Courts (Scotland) Extracts Act 1892
s.7, varied: SSI 2008/104 Reg.2

23. Foreign Marriage Act 1892
applied: SI 2008/676 Art.3, Sch.1 Part VI

57 & 58 Vict. (1894)

30. Finance Act 1894
s.17, referred to: 2008 c.9 Sch.4 para.10

58 & 59 Vict. (1895)

14. Courts of Law Fees (Scotland) Act 1895
s.2, amended: 2008 asp 6 Sch.5 para.1
s.2, enabling: SSI 2008/236, SSI 2008/237, SSI 2008/239

59 & 60 Vict. (1896)

35. Judicial Trustees Act 1896
s.1, see *Thomas & Agnes Carvel Foundation v Carvel* [2007] EWHC 1314 (Ch), [2008] Ch. 395 (Ch D), Lewison, J.

CAP.

60 & 61 Vict. (1897)

31. Cleansing of Persons Act 1897
repealed: 2008 asp 5 Sch.3 Part 1

38. Public Health (Scotland) Act 1897
s.1, repealed: 2008 asp 5 Sch.3 Part 1
s.2, repealed: 2008 asp 5 Sch.3 Part 1
s.3, repealed: 2008 asp 5 Sch.3 Part 1
s.4, repealed: 2008 asp 5 Sch.3 Part 1
s.5, repealed: 2008 asp 5 Sch.3 Part 1
s.6, repealed: 2008 asp 5 Sch.3 Part 1
s.7, repealed: 2008 asp 5 Sch.3 Part 1
s.8, repealed: 2008 asp 5 Sch.3 Part 1
s.9, repealed: 2008 asp 5 Sch.3 Part 1
s.10, repealed: 2008 asp 5 Sch.3 Part 1
s.11, repealed: 2008 asp 5 Sch.3 Part 1
s.12, repealed: 2008 asp 5 Sch.3 Part 1
s.13, repealed: 2008 asp 5 Sch.3 Part 1
s.14, repealed: 2008 asp 5 Sch.3 Part 1
s.15, repealed: 2008 asp 5 Sch.3 Part 1
s.16, repealed: 2008 asp 5 Sch.3 Part 1
s.17, repealed: 2008 asp 5 Sch.3 Part 1
s.18, repealed: 2008 asp 5 Sch.3 Part 1
s.19, repealed: 2008 asp 5 Sch.3 Part 1
s.20, repealed: 2008 asp 5 Sch.3 Part 1
s.21, repealed: 2008 asp 5 Sch.3 Part 1
s.22, repealed: 2008 asp 5 Sch.3 Part 1
s.23, repealed: 2008 asp 5 Sch.3 Part 1
s.24, repealed: 2008 asp 5 Sch.3 Part 1
s.25, repealed: 2008 asp 5 Sch.3 Part 1
s.26, repealed: 2008 asp 5 Sch.3 Part 1
s.27, repealed: 2008 asp 5 Sch.3 Part 1
s.28, repealed: 2008 asp 5 Sch.3 Part 1
s.29, repealed: 2008 asp 5 Sch.3 Part 1
s.30, repealed: 2008 asp 5 Sch.3 Part 1
s.31, repealed: 2008 asp 5 Sch.3 Part 1
s.32, repealed: 2008 asp 5 Sch.3 Part 1
s.33, repealed: 2008 asp 5 Sch.3 Part 1
s.34, repealed: 2008 asp 5 Sch.3 Part 1
s.35, repealed: 2008 asp 5 Sch.3 Part 1
s.36, repealed: 2008 asp 5 Sch.3 Part 1
s.37, repealed: 2008 asp 5 Sch.3 Part 1
s.38, repealed: 2008 asp 5 Sch.3 Part 1
s.39, repealed: 2008 asp 5 Sch.3 Part 1
s.40, repealed: 2008 asp 5 Sch.3 Part 1
s.41, repealed: 2008 asp 5 Sch.3 Part 1
s.42, repealed: 2008 asp 5 Sch.3 Part 1
s.43, repealed: 2008 asp 5 Sch.3 Part 1
s.44, repealed: 2008 asp 5 Sch.3 Part 1
s.45, repealed: 2008 asp 5 Sch.3 Part 1
s.46, repealed: 2008 asp 5 Sch.3 Part 1
s.47, repealed: 2008 asp 5 Sch.3 Part 1
s.48, repealed: 2008 asp 5 Sch.3 Part 1
s.49, repealed: 2008 asp 5 Sch.3 Part 1
s.50, repealed: 2008 asp 5 Sch.3 Part 1
s.51, repealed: 2008 asp 5 Sch.3 Part 1
s.52, repealed: 2008 asp 5 Sch.3 Part 1
s.53, repealed: 2008 asp 5 Sch.3 Part 1
s.54, repealed: 2008 asp 5 Sch.3 Part 1
s.55, repealed: 2008 asp 5 Sch.3 Part 1
s.56, repealed: 2008 asp 5 Sch.3 Part 1
s.57, repealed: 2008 asp 5 Sch.3 Part 1

CAP.

60 & 61 Vict. (1897)–cont.

38. Public Health (Scotland) Act 1897– *cont.*

s.58, repealed: 2008 asp 5 Sch.3 Part 1
s.59, repealed: 2008 asp 5 Sch.3 Part 1
s.60, repealed: 2008 asp 5 Sch.3 Part 1
s.61, repealed: 2008 asp 5 Sch.3 Part 1
s.62, repealed: 2008 asp 5 Sch.3 Part 1
s.63, repealed: 2008 asp 5 Sch.3 Part 1
s.64, repealed: 2008 asp 5 Sch.3 Part 1
s.65, repealed: 2008 asp 5 Sch.3 Part 1
s.66, repealed: 2008 asp 5 Sch.3 Part 1
s.67, repealed: 2008 asp 5 Sch.3 Part 1
s.68, repealed: 2008 asp 5 Sch.3 Part 1
s.69, repealed: 2008 asp 5 Sch.3 Part 1
s.70, repealed: 2008 asp 5 Sch.3 Part 1
s.71, repealed: 2008 asp 5 Sch.3 Part 1
s.72, repealed: 2008 asp 5 Sch.3 Part 1
s.73, repealed: 2008 asp 5 Sch.3 Part 1
s.74, repealed: 2008 asp 5 Sch.3 Part 1
s.75, repealed: 2008 asp 5 Sch.3 Part 1
s.76, repealed: 2008 asp 5 Sch.3 Part 1
s.77, repealed: 2008 asp 5 Sch.3 Part 1
s.101, repealed: 2008 asp 5 Sch.3 Part 1
s.102, repealed: 2008 asp 5 Sch.3 Part 1
s.103, repealed: 2008 asp 5 Sch.3 Part 1
s.104, repealed: 2008 asp 5 Sch.3 Part 1
s.105, repealed: 2008 asp 5 Sch.3 Part 1
s.106, repealed: 2008 asp 5 Sch.3 Part 1
s.107, repealed: 2008 asp 5 Sch.3 Part 1
s.108, repealed: 2008 asp 5 Sch.3 Part 1
s.109, repealed: 2008 asp 5 Sch.3 Part 1
s.110, repealed: 2008 asp 5 Sch.3 Part 1
s.111, repealed: 2008 asp 5 Sch.3 Part 1
s.112, repealed: 2008 asp 5 Sch.3 Part 1
s.113, repealed: 2008 asp 5 Sch.3 Part 1
s.114, repealed: 2008 asp 5 Sch.3 Part 1
s.115, repealed: 2008 asp 5 Sch.3 Part 1
s.116, repealed: 2008 asp 5 Sch.3 Part 1
s.117, repealed: 2008 asp 5 Sch.3 Part 1
s.118, repealed: 2008 asp 5 Sch.3 Part 1
s.119, repealed: 2008 asp 5 Sch.3 Part 1
s.120, repealed: 2008 asp 5 Sch.3 Part 1
s.121, repealed: 2008 asp 5 Sch.3 Part 1
s.122, repealed: 2008 asp 5 Sch.3 Part 1
s.123, repealed: 2008 asp 5 Sch.3 Part 1
s.124, repealed: 2008 asp 5 Sch.3 Part 1
s.125, repealed: 2008 asp 5 Sch.3 Part 1
s.126, repealed: 2008 asp 5 Sch.3 Part 1
s.127, repealed: 2008 asp 5 Sch.3 Part 1
s.128, repealed: 2008 asp 5 Sch.3 Part 1
s.129, repealed: 2008 asp 5 Sch.3 Part 1
s.130, repealed: 2008 asp 5 Sch.3 Part 1
s.131, repealed: 2008 asp 5 Sch.3 Part 1
s.132, repealed: 2008 asp 5 Sch.3 Part 1
s.139, repealed: 2008 asp 5 Sch.3 Part 1
s.140, repealed: 2008 asp 5 Sch.3 Part 1
s.141, repealed: 2008 asp 5 Sch.3 Part 1
s.142, repealed: 2008 asp 5 Sch.3 Part 1
s.143, repealed: 2008 asp 5 Sch.3 Part 1
s.146, repealed: 2008 asp 5 Sch.3 Part 1

CAP.

60 & 61 Vict. (1897)–cont.

38. Public Health (Scotland) Act 1897– *cont.*

s.147, repealed: 2008 asp 5 Sch.3 Part 1
s.148, repealed: 2008 asp 5 Sch.3 Part 1
s.149, repealed: 2008 asp 5 Sch.3 Part 1
s.150, repealed: 2008 asp 5 Sch.3 Part 1
s.151, repealed: 2008 asp 5 Sch.3 Part 1
s.152, repealed: 2008 asp 5 Sch.3 Part 1
s.153, repealed: 2008 asp 5 Sch.3 Part 1
s.154, repealed: 2008 asp 5 Sch.3 Part 1
s.155, repealed: 2008 asp 5 Sch.3 Part 1
s.156, repealed: 2008 asp 5 Sch.3 Part 1
s.156A, repealed: 2008 asp 5 Sch.3 Part 1
s.156B, repealed: 2008 asp 5 Sch.3 Part 1
s.156C, repealed: 2008 asp 5 Sch.3 Part 1
s.156D, repealed: 2008 asp 5 Sch.3 Part 1
s.157, repealed: 2008 asp 5 Sch.3 Part 1
s.158, repealed: 2008 asp 5 Sch.3 Part 1
s.159, repealed: 2008 asp 5 Sch.3 Part 1
s.160, repealed: 2008 asp 5 Sch.3 Part 1
s.161, repealed: 2008 asp 5 Sch.3 Part 1
s.162, repealed: 2008 asp 5 Sch.3 Part 1
s.163, repealed: 2008 asp 5 Sch.3 Part 1
s.164, repealed: 2008 asp 5 Sch.3 Part 1
s.165, repealed: 2008 asp 5 Sch.3 Part 1
s.166, repealed: 2008 asp 5 Sch.3 Part 1
s.167, repealed: 2008 asp 5 Sch.3 Part 1
s.168, repealed: 2008 asp 5 Sch.3 Part 1
s.169, repealed: 2008 asp 5 Sch.3 Part 1
s.170, repealed: 2008 asp 5 Sch.3 Part 1
s.171, repealed: 2008 asp 5 Sch.3 Part 1
s.177, repealed: 2008 asp 5 Sch.3 Part 1
s.178, repealed: 2008 asp 5 Sch.3 Part 1
s.179, repealed: 2008 asp 5 Sch.3 Part 1
s.180, repealed: 2008 asp 5 Sch.3 Part 1
s.181, repealed: 2008 asp 5 Sch.3 Part 1
s.182, repealed: 2008 asp 5 Sch.3 Part 1
s.183, repealed: 2008 asp 5 Sch.3 Part 1
s.184, repealed: 2008 asp 5 Sch.3 Part 1
s.185, repealed: 2008 asp 5 Sch.3 Part 1
s.186, repealed: 2008 asp 5 Sch.3 Part 1
s.187, repealed: 2008 asp 5 Sch.3 Part 1
s.188, repealed: 2008 asp 5 Sch.3 Part 1
s.189, repealed: 2008 asp 5 Sch.3 Part 1
s.190, repealed: 2008 asp 5 Sch.3 Part 1
s.191, repealed: 2008 asp 5 Sch.3 Part 1
s.192, repealed: 2008 asp 5 Sch.3 Part 1
s.193, repealed: 2008 asp 5 Sch.3 Part 1
s.194, repealed: 2008 asp 5 Sch.3 Part 1
s.195, repealed: 2008 asp 5 Sch.3 Part 1
s.196, repealed: 2008 asp 5 Sch.3 Part 1

61 & 62 Vict. (1898)

36. Criminal Evidence Act 1898

see *R. v Lamaletie (Mervyn)* [2008] EWCA Crim 314, (2008) 172 J.P. 249 (CA (Crim Div)), Hooper, L.J.

39. Vagrancy Act 1898

s.1, applied: SI 2008/1216 Sch.2 para.4

CAP.

61 & 62 Vict. (1898)–cont.

43. Metropolitan Commons Act 1898
applied: SI 2008/1961 Reg.47

62 & 63 Vict. (1899)

30. Commons Act 1899
Part I, applied: SI 2008/1961 Reg.47
s.22, applied: SI 2008/1961 Sch.4 para.8

1 Edw. 7 (1901)

7. Finance Act 1901
s.10, amended: 2008 c.12 Sch.2 para.3

2 Edw. 7 (1902)

7. Finance Act 1902
repealed: 2008 c.12 Sch.1 Part 8

8. Cremation Act 1902
s.7, enabling: SI 2008/2841

6 Edw. 7 (1906)

5. Seamen's and Soldiers False Characters Act 1906
repealed: 2008 c.12 Sch.1 Part 1

32. Dogs Act 1906
applied: 2008 c.13 Sch.3

34. Prevention of Corruption Act 1906
applied: 2008 c.17 Sch.1 para.16

40. Marriage with Foreigners Act 1906
applied: SI 2008/676 Art.3

41. Marine Insurance Act 1906
s.53, see *Allianz Insurance Co Egypt v Aigaion Insurance Co SA* [2008] EWHC 1127 (Comm), [2008] 2 Lloyd's Rep. 595 (QBD (Comm)), Judge Chambers Q.C.

55. Public Trustee Act 1906
s.9, enabling: SI 2008/611
s.13, applied: SI 2008/611 Art.23

7 Edw. 7 (1907)

24. Limited Partnerships Act 1907
applied: SI 2008/1715 Reg.4, SSI 2008/143 Reg.4

30. Public Health (Scotland) Amendment Act 1907
repealed: 2008 asp 5 Sch.3 Part 1

51. Sheriff Courts (Scotland) Act 1907
Appendix 1, added: SSI 2008/121 Sch.1, SSI 2008/365 r.2
Appendix 1, amended: SSI 2008/223 Sch.1
Appendix 1, repealed: SSI 2008/121 r.2
s.40, enabling: SSI 2008/40, SSI 2008/72, SSI 2008/118, SSI 2008/430
s.50, see *Sinclair v Private Rented Housing Panel* 2008 S.L.T. (Sh Ct) 84 (Sh Ct (Grampian)), Sheriff Graeme Napier
s.50, applied: SSI 2008/188 Art.33, SSI 2008/189 Art.33, SSI 2008/190 Art.33

CAP.

7 Edw. 7 (1907)–cont.

51. Sheriff Courts (Scotland) Act 1907–*cont.*
Sch.1, see *Barr Roads & Contracting v Lusk Construction Ltd* 2008 S.C.L.R. 749 (Sh Ct (North Strathclyde) (Kilmarnock)), Sheriff Ireland
Sch.1 para.1, see *Barr Roads & Contracting v Lusk Construction Ltd* 2008 S.C.L.R. 749 (Sh Ct (North Strathclyde) (Kilmarnock)), Sheriff Ireland
Sch.1 Part 3 para.5, repealed: SSI 2008/121 r.5
Sch.1 Part 5 para.5, amended: SSI 2008/365 r.7
Sch.1 Part 5 para.6, amended: SSI 2008/121 r.5
Sch.1 Part 6 paraA.1, added: SSI 2008/121 r.5
Sch.1 Part 6 paraA.1, amended: SSI 2008/121 r.5
Sch.1 Part 6 para.1, amended: SSI 2008/121 r.5
Sch.1 Part 6 paraA.2, added: SSI 2008/121 r.5
Sch.1 Part 6 paraA.2, amended: SSI 2008/121 r.5
Sch.1 Part 6 para.2, amended: SSI 2008/121 r.5
Sch.1 Part 6 para.2, repealed: SSI 2008/121 r.5
Sch.1 Part 6 paraA.3, added: SSI 2008/121 r.5
Sch.1 Part 6 paraA.3, amended: SSI 2008/121 r.5
Sch.1 Part 6 para.3, amended: SSI 2008/121 r.5
Sch.1 Part 6 paraA.4, added: SSI 2008/121 r.5
Sch.1 Part 6 paraA.4, amended: SSI 2008/121 r.5
Sch.1 Part 6 paraA.5, added: SSI 2008/121 r.5
Sch.1 Part 6 paraA.5, amended: SSI 2008/121 r.5
Sch.1 Part 6 paraA.6, added: SSI 2008/121 r.5
Sch.1 Part 6 paraA.6, amended: SSI 2008/121 r.5
Sch.1 Part 6 paraA.7, added: SSI 2008/121 r.5
Sch.1 Part 6 paraA.7, amended: SSI 2008/121 r.5
Sch.1 Part 6 para.99, amended: SSI 2008/121 r.5
Sch.1 Part 6 para.100, amended: SSI 2008/121 r.5
Sch.1 Part 6 para.101, amended: SSI 2008/121 r.5
Sch.1 Part 6 para.102, amended: SSI 2008/121 r.5
Sch.1 Part 6 para.103, amended: SSI 2008/121 r.5
Sch.1 Part 6 para.104, amended: SSI 2008/121 r.5
Sch.1 Part 6 para.105, amended: SSI 2008/121 r.5
Sch.1 Part 6 para.106, amended: SSI 2008/121 r.5

CAP.

7 Edw. 7 (1907)–cont.

51. Sheriff Courts (Scotland) Act 1907– *cont.*

Sch.1 Part 6 para.107, amended: SSI 2008/121 r.5

Sch.1 Part 6 para.107A, amended: SSI 2008/121 r.5

Sch.1 Part 6 para.108, amended: SSI 2008/121 r.5

Sch.1 Part 6 para.109, amended: SSI 2008/121 r.5

Sch.1 Part 6 para.110, amended: SSI 2008/121 r.5

Sch.1 Part 6 para.111, amended: SSI 2008/121 r.5

Sch.1 Part 6 para.112, amended: SSI 2008/121 r.5

Sch.1 Part 6 para.113, amended: SSI 2008/121 r.5

Sch.1 Part 6 para.114, amended: SSI 2008/121 r.5

Sch.1 Part 6 para.115, amended: SSI 2008/121 r.5

Sch.1 Part 6 para.116, amended: SSI 2008/121 r.5

Sch.1 Part 6 para.117, amended: SSI 2008/121 r.5

Sch.1 Part 6 para.118, amended: SSI 2008/121 r.5

Sch.1 Part 6 para.119, amended: SSI 2008/121 r.5

Sch.1 Part 6 para.120, amended: SSI 2008/121 r.5

Sch.1 Part 6 para.121, amended: SSI 2008/121 r.5

Sch.1 Part 6 para.122, amended: SSI 2008/121 r.5

Sch.1 Part 6 para.123, amended: SSI 2008/121 r.5

Sch.1 Part 6 para.124, amended: SSI 2008/121 r.5

Sch.1 Part 6 para.125, amended: SSI 2008/121 r.5

Sch.1 Part 6 para.126, amended: SSI 2008/121 r.5

Sch.1 Part 6 para.127, amended: SSI 2008/121 r.5

Sch.1 Part 6 para.128, amended: SSI 2008/121 r.5

Sch.1 Part 6 para.129, amended: SSI 2008/121 r.5

Sch.1 Part 6 para.130, amended: SSI 2008/121 r.5

Sch.1 Part 6 para.131, amended: SSI 2008/121 r.5

Sch.1 Part 6 para.132, amended: SSI 2008/121 r.5

Sch.1 Part 6 para.132A, amended: SSI 2008/121 r.5

Sch.1 Part 6 para.132B, amended: SSI 2008/121 r.5

CAP.

7 Edw. 7 (1907)–cont.

51. Sheriff Courts (Scotland) Act 1907– *cont.*

Sch.1 Part 6 para.132C, amended: SSI 2008/121 r.5

Sch.1 Part 6 para.132D, amended: SSI 2008/121 r.5

Sch.1 Part 6 para.132E, amended: SSI 2008/121 r.5

Sch.1 Part 6 para.132F, amended: SSI 2008/121 r.5

Sch.1 Part 6 para.132G, amended: SSI 2008/121 r.5

Sch.1 Part 6 para.133, amended: SSI 2008/121 r.5

Sch.1 Part 6 para.134, amended: SSI 2008/121 r.5

Sch.1 Part 6 para.135, amended: SSI 2008/121 r.5

Sch.1 Part 6 para.136, amended: SSI 2008/121 r.5

Sch.1 Part 6 para.137, amended: SSI 2008/121 r.5

Sch.1 Part 6 para.138, amended: SSI 2008/121 r.5

Sch.1 Part 6 para.139, amended: SSI 2008/121 r.5

Sch.1 Part 6 para.140, amended: SSI 2008/121 r.5

Sch.1 Part 6 para.141, amended: SSI 2008/121 r.5

Sch.1 Part 6 para.142, amended: SSI 2008/121 r.5

Sch.1 Part 6 para.143, amended: SSI 2008/121 r.5

Sch.1 Part 13A para.1, added: SSI 2008/223 r.4

Sch.1 Part 13A para.2, added: SSI 2008/223 r.4

Sch.1 Part 13A para.3, added: SSI 2008/223 r.4

Sch.1 Part 13A para.4, added: SSI 2008/223 r.4

Sch.1 Part 13B para.1, added: SSI 2008/223 r.4

Sch.1 Part 13B para.2, added: SSI 2008/223 r.4

Sch.1 Part 13B para.3, added: SSI 2008/223 r.4

Sch.1 Part 13B para.4, added: SSI 2008/223 r.4

Sch.1 Part 28 para.10, amended: SSI 2008/223 r.11

Sch.1 Part 29 para.14, repealed (in part): SSI 2008/365 r.4

Sch.1 Part 31 para.2A, added: SSI 2008/365 r.3

Sch.1 Part 33A para.33A, added: SSI 2008/223 r.2

Sch.1 Part 33A para.48A, added: SSI 2008/223 r.3

CAP.

7 Edw. 7 (1907)–cont.

51. Sheriff Courts (Scotland) Act 1907– *cont.*
Sch.1 Part 33 para.33A, added: SSI 2008/223 r.2
Sch.1 Part 33 para.51A, added: SSI 2008/223 r.3
Sch.1 Part 34 para.1, repealed: SSI 2008/121 r.2
Sch.1 Part 34 para.2, repealed: SSI 2008/121 r.2
Sch.1 Part 34 para.3, repealed: SSI 2008/121 r.2
Sch.1 Part 34 para.4, repealed: SSI 2008/121 r.2
Sch.1 Part 44 para.1, amended: SSI 2008/223 r.4
Sch.1 Part 44 para.2, substituted: SSI 2008/223 r.4
Sch.1 Part 44 para.4, repealed: SSI 2008/223 r.4
Sch.1 Part 45, applied: SSI 2008/119 Sch.1 para.14

8 Edw. 7 (1908)

45. Punishment of Incest Act 1908
s.1, applied: SI 2008/1216 Sch.2 para.5
s.1, repealed (in part): SI 2008/1769 Sch.1 para.6, Sch.3
s.2, applied: SI 2008/1216 Sch.2 para.5
s.2, repealed (in part): SI 2008/1769 Sch.1 para.6, Sch.3

1 & 2 Geo. 5 (1911)

6. Perjury Act 1911
s.2, applied: SI 2008/1651 Reg.12
s.5, applied: SI 2008/1651 Reg.12, SI 2008/2852 Sch.6 para.14

27. Protection of Animals Act 1911
applied: 2008 c.13 Sch.3

28. Official Secrets Act 1911
applied: SI 2008/239 Reg.75, SI 2008/2852 Sch.6 para.4, SSI 2008/224 Reg.7, SSI 2008/228 Reg.69

34. Railway Companies (Accounts and Returns) Act 1911
applied: 2008 c.18 Sch.11 para.5

48. Finance Act 1911
repealed: 2008 c.12 Sch.1 Part 8

49. Small Landholders (Scotland) Act 1911
s.11, repealed: 2008 asp 5 Sch.3 Part 1

4 & 5 Geo. 5 (1914)

1. Anglo-Portuguese Commercial Treaty Act 1914
s.1, amended: SI 2008/1277 Sch.4 Part 1

18. Injuries in War Compensation Act 1914 (Session 2) 1914
repealed: 2008 c.12 Sch.1 Part 1

CAP.

4 & 5 Geo. 5 (1914)–cont.

30. Injuries in War (Compensation) Act 1914
repealed: 2008 c.12 Sch.1 Part 1

47. Deeds of Arrangement Act 1914
applied: SI 2008/386 Reg.4, SI 2008/2499 Reg.4

59. Bankruptcy Act 1914
see *Pannell v Official Receiver* [2008] EWHC 736 (Ch), [2008] B.P.I.R. 629 (Ch D (Bristol)), Judge Havelock-Allan Q.C.

5 & 6 Geo. 5 (1914-15)

28. Naval Medical Compassionate Fund Act 1915
s.1, enabling: SI 2008/1488, SI 2008/3129

83. Naval and Military War Pensions &c Act 1915
repealed: 2008 c.12 Sch.1 Part 1

6 & 7 Geo. 5 (1916)

31. Police, Factories, & C (Miscellaneous Provisions) Act 1916
applied: 2008 c.13 Sch.3

39. Anglo-Portuguese Commercial Treaty Act 1916
s.1, amended: SI 2008/1277 Sch.4 Part 1

60. Sailors and Soldiers (Gifts for Land Settlement) Act 1916
repealed: 2008 c.12 Sch.1 Part 1
s.1, referred to: 2008 c.12 Sch.2 para.4

64. Prevention of Corruption Act 1916
applied: 2008 c.17 Sch.1 para.16

7 & 8 Geo. 5 (1917)

14. Naval and Military War Pensions etc (Administrative Expenses) Act 1917
s.6A, added: 2008 c.12 Sch.2 para.5

9 & 10 Geo. 5 (1919)

53. War Pensions (Administrative Provisions) Act 1919
applied: SI 2008/2684 Art.4
s.1, repealed: 2008 c.12 Sch.1 Part 1
s.8, amended: SI 2008/2833 Sch.3 para.2
s.8, applied: SI 2008/2833 Sch.1
Sch.1 para.1, amended: SI 2008/2833 Sch.3 para.3

97. Land Settlement (Scotland) Act 1919
s.18, amended: 2008 asp 5 Sch.3 Part 1

10 & 11 Geo. 5 (1920)

33. Maintenance Orders (Facilities for Enforcement) Act 1920
applied: SI 2008/1202 Art.4
s.2, applied: SI 2008/1202 Art.4
s.3, applied: SI 2008/1202 Art.4
s.4, applied: SI 2008/1202 Art.4

CAP.

10 & 11 Geo. 5 (1920)–cont.

75. Official Secrets Act 1920
applied: SI 2008/239 Reg.75, SSI 2008/224 Reg.7, SSI 2008/228 Reg.69

11 & 12 Geo. 5 (1921)

35. Corn Sales Act 1921
s.2, repealed: SI 2008/576 Sch.5 para.7

39. Admiralty Pensions Act 1921
s.2, repealed (in part): 2008 c.12 Sch.1 Part 1

12 & 13 Geo. 5 (1922)

16. Law of Property Act 1922
see *Jasmine Trustees Ltd v Wells & Hind (A Firm)* [2007] EWHC 38 (Ch), [2008] Ch. 194 (Ch D), Mann, J.

35. Celluloid and Cinematograph Film Act 1922
applied: 2008 c.13 Sch.3

13 & 14 Geo. 5 (1923)

14. Finance Act 1923
repealed: 2008 c.12 Sch.1 Part 8

20. Mines (Working Facilities and Support) Act 1923
see *National Grid Gas Plc v Lafarge Aggregates Ltd Pt* [2006] EWHC 2559 (Ch), [2008] R.V.R. 126 (Ch D), Cooke, J.
s.15, applied: SI 2008/2512 Art.3
s.15, referred to: SI 2008/1261 Art.7

15 & 16 Geo. 5 (1925)

18. Settled Land Act 1925
applied: SI 2008/611 Art.17
s.39, disapplied: 2008 c.17 s.188

19. Trustee Act 1925
s.37, see *Jasmine Trustees Ltd v Wells & Hind (A Firm)* [2007] EWHC 38 (Ch), [2008] Ch. 194 (Ch D), Mann, J.
s.57, see *NBPF Pension Trustees Ltd v Warnock-Smith* [2008] EWHC 455 (Ch), [2008] 2 All E.R. (Comm) 740 (Ch D), Floyd, J

20. Law of Property Act 1925
see *Odey v Barber* [2006] EWHC 3109 (Ch), [2008] Ch. 175 (Ch D (Bristol)), Silber, J.
s.49, see *Aribisala v St James Homes (Grosvenor Dock) Ltd* [2008] EWHC 456 (Ch), [2008] 3 All E.R. 762 (Ch D), Floyd, J; see *Chinnock v Hocaoglu* [2007] EWHC 2933 (Ch), [2008] 29 E.G. 92 (Ch D), Blackburne, J.
s.53, see *Hanchett-Stamford v Attorney General* [2008] EWHC 330 (Ch), [2008] 4 All E.R. 323 (Ch D), Lewison, J.
s.54, see *Fitzkriston LLP v Panayi* [2008] EWCA Civ 283, [2008] L. & T.R. 26 (CA (Civ Div)), Laws, L.J.

CAP.

15 & 16 Geo. 5 (1925)–cont.

20. Law of Property Act 1925–*cont.*
s.78, see *Mohammadzadeh v Joseph* [2006] EWHC 1040 (Ch), [2008] 1 P. & C.R. 6 (Ch D), Etherton, J.
s.84, see *Winter v Traditional & Contemporary Contracts Ltd* [2007] EWCA Civ 1088, [2008] 3 E.G.180 (CA (Civ Div)), Ward, L.J.
s.101, see *Horsham Properties Group Ltd v Clark* [2008] EWHC 2327 (Ch), [2008] 47 E.G. 114 (Ch D), Briggs, J.
s.114, see *Meretz Investments NV v ACP Ltd* [2007] EWCA Civ 1303, [2008] Ch. 244 (CA (Civ Div)), Pill, L.J.
s.136, see *Midlands Co-operative Society Ltd v Revenue and Customs Commissioners* [2008] EWCA Civ 305, [2008] Bus. L.R. 1187 (CA (Civ Div)), Arden, L.J.
s.138, applied: SI 2008/611 Art.28
s.146, see *Greenwood Reversions Ltd v World Environment Foundation Ltd* [2008] EWCA Civ 47, [2008] H.L.R. 31 (CA (Civ Div)), Pill, L.J.; see *Metro Nominees (Wandsworth) (No.1) Ltd v Rayment* [2008] B.C.C. 40 (CC (Birmingham)), Judge Norris Q.C.
s.193, applied: SI 2008/1961 Reg.47

21. Land Registration Act 1925
see *JA Pye (Oxford) Ltd v United Kingdom (44302/02)* (2008) 46 E.H.R.R. 45 (ECHR (Grand Chamber)), Judge Costa (President)
applied: SI 2008/1919 r.6

23. Administration of Estates Act 1925
s.47A, enabling: SI 2008/3162

38. Performing Animals (Regulation) Act 1925
applied: 2008 c.13 Sch.3

86. Criminal Justice Act 1925
s.33, applied: 2008 c.14 s.92, 2008 c.25 s.136, 2008 c.28 Sch.7 para.37, 2008 c.30 s.47

16 & 17 Geo. 5 (1926)

16. Execution of Diligence (Scotland) Act 1926
s.1, varied: SSI 2008/104 Reg.3
s.2, varied: SSI 2008/104 Reg.3
s.6, enabling: SSI 2008/430, SSI 2008/431

48. Births and Deaths Registration Act 1926
s.9, amended: SI 2008/678 Sch.2 para.3
s.9, applied: SI 2008/678 Art.3, Sch.1 para.3
s.12, amended: SI 2008/678 Sch.2 para.3
s.12, applied: SI 2008/678 Sch.1 para.3

57. Prisons (Scotland) Act 1926
applied: SSI 2008/8 r.3, r.4

59. Coroners (Amendment) Act 1926
disapplied: SI 2008/239 Reg.9

CAP.

17 & 18 Geo. 5 (1927)

35. Sheriff Courts and Legal Officers (Scotland) Act 1927
s.1, amended: 2008 asp 6 Sch.4 para.2
s.2, amended: 2008 asp 6 Sch.4 para.2
s.3, amended: 2008 asp 6 Sch.4 para.2
s.4, amended: 2008 asp 6 Sch.4 para.2
s.5, amended: 2008 asp 6 Sch.4 para.2
s.8, amended: 2008 asp 6 Sch.4 para.2
s.9, amended: 2008 asp 6 Sch.4 para.2

18 & 19 Geo. 5 (1928)

13. Currency and Bank Notes Act 1928
s.3, amended: 2008 c.12 Sch.2 para.6

19. Agricultural Produce (Grading and Marking) Act 1928
applied: 2008 c.13 Sch.3
s.4, amended: SI 2008/1277 Sch.4 Part 1

32. Petroleum (Consolidation) Act 1928
applied: 2008 c.13 Sch.3
s.1, referred to: 2008 c.13 Sch.6
s.4, applied: SI 2008/736 Sch.8 Part 4
s.4, disapplied: SI 2008/736 Reg.10
s.5, referred to: 2008 c.13 Sch.6
s.18, referred to: 2008 c.13 Sch.6
s.19, applied: SI 2008/736 Sch.8 Part 4

20 & 21 Geo. 5 (1930)

25. Third Parties (Rights against Insurers) Act 1930
see *Junespear Ltd v Dear* 2008 S.L.T. (Sh Ct) 69 (Sh Pr), Sheriff Principal RA Dunlop Q.C.; see *Law Society v Shah* [2007] EWHC 2841 (Ch), [2008] 3 W.L.R. 1401 (Ch D), Floyd, J
s.1, see *Junespear Ltd v Dear* 2008 S.L.T. (Sh Ct) 69 (Sh Pr), Sheriff Principal RA Dunlop Q.C.

22 & 23 Geo. 5 (1931-32)

12. Destructive Imported Animals Act 1932
s.6, referred to: 2008 c.13 Sch.6

25. Finance Act 1932
repealed: 2008 c.12 Sch.1 Part 8

23 & 24 Geo. 5 (1932-33)

12. Children and Young Persons Act 1933
Part I, applied: 2008 c.13 Sch.3
Part II, applied: SI 2008/228 Sch.1 para.31
s.7, referred to: 2008 c.13 Sch.6
s.12A, added: 2008 c.4 s.143
s.12B, added: 2008 c.4 s.143
s.12C, added: 2008 c.4 s.143
s.12D, added: 2008 c.4 s.143
s.34, amended: 2008 c.4 Sch.4 para.2, Sch.28 Part 1

CAP.

23 & 24 Geo. 5 (1932-33)–cont.

12. Children and Young Persons Act 1933–*cont.*
s.39, see *Crawford v Crown Prosecution Service* [2008] EWHC 854 (Admin), (2008) 172 J.P. 273 (DC), Thomas, L.J.
s.44, amended: 2008 c.4 s.9
s.49, amended: 2008 c.4 Sch.4 para.3, Sch.4 para.100
s.49, repealed (in part): 2008 c.4 Sch.4 para.3, Sch.28 Part 1
s.102, amended: 2008 c.4 s.143
Sch.1, referred to: SI 2008/1185 Reg.4, Sch.1 para.44

36. Administration of Justice (Miscellaneous Provisions) Act 1933
s.1, see *R. v Clarke (Ronald Augustus)* [2008] UKHL 8, [2008] 1 W.L.R. 338 (HL), Lord Bingham of Cornhill
s.2, see *R. v Clarke (Ronald Augustus)* [2008] UKHL 8, [2008] 1 W.L.R. 338 (HL), Lord Bingham of Cornhill

41. Administration of Justice (Scotland) Act 1933
s.23, amended: 2008 asp 6 Sch.4 para.1
s.24, amended: 2008 asp 6 Sch.4 para.1
s.25, substituted: 2008 asp 6 Sch.4 para.1
s.27, amended: 2008 asp 6 Sch.4 para.1

24 & 25 Geo. 5 (1933-34)

36. Petroleum (Production) Act 1934
see *Bocardo SA v Star Energy UK Onshore Ltd* [2008] EWHC 1756 (Ch), [2008] 2 P. & C.R. 23 (Ch D), Peter Smith, J.
applied: 2008 c.32 s.77

26 Geo. 5 & Edw. 8 (1935-36)

27. Petroleum (Transfer of Licences) Act 1936
applied: 2008 c.13 Sch.3
s.1, applied: SI 2008/736 Sch.8 Part 4
s.1, disapplied: SI 2008/736 Reg.10

33. Widows Orphans and Old Age Contributory Pensions Act 1936
applied: 2008 c.30 s.140, s.141

49. Public Health Act 1936
applied: 2008 c.13 Sch.3
Part II, referred to: 2008 c.13 Sch.6
s.6, applied: SI 2008/622 Reg.2, SI 2008/781 Reg.2, SI 2008/1079 Reg.2, SI 2008/1080 Reg.2
s.87, amended: SI 2008/963 Reg.3
s.269, referred to: 2008 c.13 Sch.6
s.276, applied: 2008 c.29 s.170
s.288, referred to: 2008 c.13 Sch.6
s.289, applied: 2008 c.29 s.170
s.290, referred to: 2008 c.13 Sch.6
s.294, applied: 2008 c.29 s.170

CAP.

1 Edw. 8 & 1 Geo. 6 (1936-37)

33. Diseases of Fish Act 1937
referred to: 2008 c.13 Sch.6, SSI 2008/263 Sch.1

37. Children and Young Persons (Scotland) Act 1937
s.35, amended: 2008 asp 5 Sch.2 para.2
s.110, amended: 2008 c.22 Sch.6 para.41

39. Widows', Orphans and Old Age Contributory Pensions (voluntary Contributors) Act 1937
applied: 2008 c.30 s.140, s.141

43. Public Records (Scotland) Act 1937
s.7, amended: 2008 asp 7 s.15
s.8, applied: 2008 asp 7 s.3
s.9, applied: 2008 asp 7 s.3
s.10, applied: 2008 asp 7 s.3
s.11, applied: 2008 asp 7 s.3
s.11A, applied: 2008 asp 7 s.3
s.12, applied: 2008 asp 7 s.3
s.12A, referred to: 2008 asp 7 s.4

1 & 2 Geo. 6 (1937-38)

xciii. Green Belt (London and Home Counties) Act 1938
applied: 2008 c.29 Sch.5 para.9

12. Population (Statistics) Act 1938
s.2, amended: SI 2008/678 Sch.2 para.4
s.2, applied: SI 2008/678 Sch.1 para.4
s.6, amended: SI 2008/678 Sch.2 para.4
Sch.1, referred to: 2008 c.22 s.53
Sch.1 para.1, amended: 2008 c.22 Sch.6 para.1

22. Trade Marks Act 1938
see *West v Hudson* [2007] EWHC 1938 (Ch), (2008) 31(2) I.P.D. 31009 (Ch D), Sir Andrew Morritt (Chancellor)
applied: SI 2008/1797 r.58
s.38, see *West v Hudson* [2007] EWHC 1938 (Ch), (2008) 31 (2) I.P.D. 31009 (Ch D), Sir Andrew Morritt (Chancellor)
s.58A, see *R. v Rose (Costs)* [2008] 1 Costs L.R. 198 (Sup Ct Costs Office), Costs Judge Rogers

2 & 3 Geo. 6 (1938-39)

5. Infanticide Act (Northern Ireland) 1939
s..1, applied: SI 2008/1216 Sch.1 para.10, Sch.2 para.9

13. Cancer Act 1939
s.4, amended: SI 2008/2840 Art.2
s.4, applied: 2008 c.13 Sch.3
s.4, referred to: 2008 c.13 Sch.6
s.4, repealed (in part): SI 2008/2840 Art.2

44. House to House Collections Act 1939
applied: 2008 c.13 Sch.3

82. Personal Injuries (Emergency Provisions) Act 1939
s.1, enabling: SI 2008/592
s.2, enabling: SI 2008/592

CAP.

2 & 3 Geo. 6 (1938-39)–cont.

103. Police and Firemen (War Service) Act 1939
repealed: 2008 c.12 Sch.1 Part 6

109. Finance (No.2) Act 1939
repealed: 2008 c.12 Sch.1 Part 8

121. Official Secrets Act 1939
applied: SI 2008/239 Reg.75, SSI 2008/224 Reg.7, SSI 2008/228 Reg.69

3 & 4 Geo. 6 (1939-40)

42. Law Reform (Miscellaneous Provisions) (Scotland) Act 1940
s.3, see *Wright v Stoddard International Plc* 2008 Rep. L.R. 2 (OH), Lord Uist

5 & 6 Geo. 6 (1941-42)

35. Greenwich Hospital Act 1942
s.1, repealed (in part): 2008 c.12 Sch.1 Part 1

6 & 7 Geo. 6 (1942-43)

16. Agriculture (Miscellaneous Provisions) Act 1943
Sch.3, repealed: SI 2008/576 Sch.5 para.7

39. Pensions Appeal Tribunals Act 1943
applied: SI 2008/2684 Art.4, SI 2008/2686 r.21
s.1, amended: SI 2008/2833 Sch.3 para.5
s.2, amended: SI 2008/2833 Sch.3 para.6
s.3, amended: SI 2008/2833 Sch.3 para.7
s.4, amended: SI 2008/2833 Sch.3 para.8
s.5, amended: SI 2008/2833 Sch.3 para.9
s.5, applied: SI 2008/2684 Art.7, SI 2008/2686 r.21, SI 2008/2833 Art.7, Art.8
s.5A, amended: SI 2008/2833 Sch.3 para.10
s.5B, amended. SI 2008/2833 Sch.3 para.11
s.6, amended: SI 2008/2833 Sch.3 para.12
s.6A, amended: SI 2008/2833 Sch.3 para.13
s.6A, repealed (in part): SI 2008/2833 Sch.3 para.13
s.6A, substituted: SI 2008/2833 Sch.3 para.13
s.6B, amended: SI 2008/2833 Sch.3 para.14
s.6C, amended: SI 2008/2833 Sch.3 para.15
s.6D, amended: SI 2008/2833 Sch.3 para.16
s.6D, repealed (in part): SI 2008/2833 Sch.3 para.16
s.8, see *Secretary of State for Defence v Pensions Appeal Tribunal* [2007] EWHC 1177 (Admin), [2008] 1 All E.R. 287 (QBD (Admin)), Stanley Burnton, J.
s.8, amended: SI 2008/2833 Sch.3 para.17
s.9, see *Secretary of State for Defence v Pensions Appeal Tribunal* [2007] EWHC 1177 (Admin), [2008] 1 All E.R. 287 (QBD (Admin)), Stanley Burnton, J.
s.9, amended: SI 2008/2833 Sch.3 para.18
s.11A, repealed (in part): SI 2008/2833 Sch.3 para.19
s.12, amended: SI 2008/2833 Sch.3 para.20

CAP.

6 & 7 Geo. 6 (1942-43)–cont.

39. Pensions Appeal Tribunals Act 1943– *cont.*

Sch.1 para.1, amended: SI 2008/2833 Sch.3 para.21

Sch.1 para.1, applied: SI 2008/2684 Art.7, SI 2008/2833 Sch.1

Sch.1 para.1, repealed (in part): SI 2008/2833 Sch.3 para.21

Sch.1 para.2, amended: SI 2008/2833 Sch.3 para.21

Sch.1 para.2, repealed (in part): SI 2008/2833 Sch.3 para.21

Sch.1 para.2A, applied: SI 2008/2833 Sch.2

Sch.1 para.2B, amended: SI 2008/2833 Sch.3 para.21

Sch.1 para.2B, applied: SI 2008/2833 Sch.2

Sch.1 para.2B, repealed (in part): SI 2008/2833 Sch.3 para.21

Sch.1 para.3A, amended: SI 2008/2833 Sch.3 para.21

Sch.1 para.3B, amended: SI 2008/2833 Sch.3 para.21

Sch.1 para.3C, amended: SI 2008/2833 Sch.3 para.21

Sch.1 para.3C, repealed (in part): SI 2008/2833 Sch.3 para.21

Sch.1 para.5, amended: SI 2008/2833 Sch.3 para.21

Sch.1 para.5, repealed (in part): SI 2008/2833 Sch.3 para.21

Sch.1 para.6, amended: SI 2008/2833 Sch.3 para.21

Sch.1 para.6B, amended: SI 2008/2833 Sch.3 para.21

Sch.1 para.7, amended: SI 2008/2833 Sch.3 para.21

Sch.1 para.7B, repealed (in part): SI 2008/2833 Sch.3 para.21

7 & 8 Geo. 6 (1943-44)

10. Disabled Persons (Employment) Act 1944

applied: SI 2008/794 Sch.8 para.48, Sch.9 para.41

s.3, applied: SI 2008/794 Sch.9 para.42

22. Police and Firemen (War Service) Act 1944

repealed: 2008 c.12 Sch.1 Part 6

23. Finance Act 1944

s.32, repealed: 2008 c.12 Sch.1 Part 8

s.33, repealed: 2008 c.12 Sch.1 Part 8

s.34, repealed: 2008 c.12 Sch.1 Part 8

s.46, repealed: 2008 c.12 Sch.1 Part 1

s.49, repealed (in part): 2008 c.12 Sch.1 Part 8

8 & 9 Geo. 6 (1944-45)

7. British Settlements Act 1945

enabling: SI 2008/2846

15. Public Health (Scotland) Act 1945

repealed: 2008 asp 5 Sch.3 Part 1

CAP.

8 & 9 Geo. 6 (1944-45)–cont.

24. Finance Act 1945

repealed: 2008 c.12 Sch.1 Part 8

28. Law Reform (Contributory Negligence) Act 1945

see *Scottish & Southern Energy Plc v Lerwick Engineering & Fabrication Ltd* 2008 S.C.L.R. 317 (OH), Lady Clark of Calton

s.1, see *St George v Home Office* [2008] EWCA Civ 1068, [2008] 4 All E.R. 1039 (CA (Civ Div)), Ward, L.J.

9 & 10 Geo. 6 (1945-46)

36. Statutory Instruments Act 1946

applied: 2008 c.29 s.117, Sch.4 para.1, Sch.6 para.2, Sch.6 para.4

s.1, applied: SI 2008/1485 Art.4, SI 2008/1774 Art.7, SI 2008/3131 Art.6

s.5, applied: SI 2008/1216 Art.61, Art.100, SI 2008/1769 Art.80

45. United Nations Act 1946

see *A v HM Treasury* [2008] EWCA Civ 1187, Times, November 12, 2008 (CA (Civ Div)), Sir Anthony Clarke, M.R.

s.1, see *A v HM Treasury* [2008] EWHC 869 (Admin), [2008] 3 All E.R. 361 (QBD (Admin)), Collins, J.

s.1, applied: 2008 c.28 s.64

s.1, enabling: SI 2008/3123, SI 2008/3128

73. Hill Farming Act 1946

s.20, enabling: SI 2008/1081

10 & 11 Geo. 6 (1946-47)

5. Greenwich Hospital Act 1947

repealed: 2008 c.12 Sch.1 Part 1

s.2, referred to: 2008 c.12 Sch.2 para.2

Sch.1, referred to: 2008 c.12 Sch.2 para.2

19. Polish Resettlement Act 1947

s.1, amended: 2008 c.30 s.139

s.1, applied: 2008 c.30 s.139

s.3, applied: SI 2008/794 Reg.118, Sch.5 Part 1

s.7, repealed: 2008 c.12 Sch.1 Part 1

Sch.1 Part II, applied: SI 2008/794 Reg.118, Sch.5 Part 1

33. Foreign Marriage Act 1947

applied: SI 2008/676 Sch.1 Part VI

35. Finance Act 1947

s.63, repealed: 2008 c.12 Sch.1 Part 8

s.64, repealed: 2008 c.12 Sch.1 Part 8

s.74, repealed (in part): 2008 c.12 Sch.1 Part 8

39. Statistics of Trade Act 1947

s.1, applied: SI 2008/792 Art.4

s.2, applied: SI 2008/792 Art.4

s.3, applied: SI 2008/792 Art.4

s.6, applied: SI 2008/792 Art.4

s.7, applied: SI 2008/792 Art.4

s.8, applied: SI 2008/792 Art.4

s.9, applied: SI 2008/792 Art.6

s.9A, applied: SI 2008/792 Art.6

CAP.

10 & 11 Geo. 6 (1946-47)–cont.

39. Statistics of Trade Act 1947–*cont.*
s.17, applied: SI 2008/792 Art.4

40. Industrial Organisation and Development Act 1947
s.7, amended: SI 2008/948 Sch.1 para.1
s.9, applied: SI 2008/2932
s.9, enabling: SI 2008/2932

41. Fire Services Act 1947
s.26, enabling: SI 2008/214, SSI 2008/161

42. Acquisition of Land (Authorisation Procedure) (Scotland) Act 1947
applied: 2008 c.29 s.125
s.1, referred to: 2008 c.29 s.125
Sch.1 Part II para.7, varied: 2008 c.29 s.125
Sch.1 Part III para.8, varied: 2008 c.29 s.125
Sch.1 Part III para.9, varied: 2008 c.29 s.125
Sch.1 Part III para.10, varied: 2008 c.29 s.125
Sch.1 Part III para.10A, varied: 2008 c.29 s.125
Sch.1 Part III para.11, varied: 2008 c.29 s.125
Sch.1 Part III para.12, varied: 2008 c.29 s.125
Sch.1 Part III para.13, varied: 2008 c.29 s.125
Sch.1 Part III para.14, varied: 2008 c.29 s.125

43. Local Government (Scotland) Act 1947
s.377, repealed (in part): 2008 asp 5 Sch.3 Part 1

44. Crown Proceedings Act 1947
see *Roberts v Swangrove Estates Ltd* [2008] EWCA Civ 98, [2008] Ch. 439 (CA (Civ Div)), Mummery, L.J.
applied: 2008 c.6 Sch.1 para.22, 2008 c.9 Sch.36 para.38
s.2, see *Hinds v Liverpool County Court* [2008] EWHC 665 (QB), [2008] 2 F.L.R. 63 (QBD (Liverpool)), Akenhead, J.
s.21, see *Revenue and Customs Commissioners v Xicom Systems Ltd* [2008] EWHC 1945 (Ch), [2008] S.T.C. 3492 (Ch D), David Richards, J.
s.25, see *Revenue and Customs Commissioners v Xicom Systems Ltd* [2008] EWHC 1945 (Ch), [2008] S.T.C. 3492 (Ch D), David Richards, J.
s.35, see *Advocate General for Scotland v Montgomery* 2008 S.C.L.R. 1 (OH), Lady Paton
s.38, applied: 2008 c.14 s.96, s.122, 2008 c.28 Sch.7 para.43, SI 2008/2668 Art.13

48. Agriculture Act 1947
s.100, referred to: 2008 c.13 Sch.6

11 & 12 Geo. 6 (1947-48)

29. National Assistance Act 1948
see *R. (on the application of St Helens BC) v Manchester Primary Care Trust* [2008] EWCA Civ 931, (2008) 11 C.C.L. Rep. 774 (CA (Civ Div)), May, L.J.
referred to: 2008 c.14 Sch.13 para.6

CAP.

11 & 12 Geo. 6 (1947-48)–cont.

29. National Assistance Act 1948–*cont.*
Part III, applied: 2008 c.14 Sch.13 para.5, SI 2008/794 Sch.8 para.32, SSI 2008/228 Reg.4
Part III, referred to: SI 2008/794 Sch.8 para.56
s.21, see *L v Birmingham City Council* [2007] EWCA Civ 26, [2008] Q.B. 1 (CA (Civ Div)), Sir Anthony Clarke, M.R.; see *L v Birmingham City Council* [2007] UKHL 27, [2008] 1 A.C. 95 (HL), Lord Bingham of Cornhill; see *R. (on the application of M) v Slough BC* [2008] UKHL 52, [2008] 1 W.L.R. 1808 (HL), Lord Bingham of Cornhill; see *R. (on the application of St Helens BC) v Manchester Primary Care Trust* [2008] EWCA Civ 931, (2008) 11 C.C.L. Rep. 774 (CA (Civ Div)), May, L.J.; see *Westminster City Council v Boraliu* [2007] EWCA Civ 1339, [2008] 1 W.L.R. 2408 (CA (Civ Div)), Chadwick, L.J.
s.22, applied: SI 2008/743 Reg.2, SSI 2008/14 Reg.2
s.22, enabling: SI 2008/593, SI 2008/743, SSI 2008/13, SSI 2008/14
s.24, amended: 2008 c.14 s.148
s.26, see *L v Birmingham City Council* [2007] EWCA Civ 26, [2008] Q.B. 1 (CA (Civ Div)), Sir Anthony Clarke, M.R.; see *L v Birmingham City Council* [2007] UKHL 27, [2008] 1 A.C. 95 (HL), Lord Bingham of Cornhill
s.26, applied: SI 2008/794 Sch.8 para.29, Sch.8 para.34
s.29, see *Sandford v Waltham Forest LBC* [2008] EWHC 1106 (QB), [2008] B.L.G.R. 816 (QBD), Judge Richard Seymour Q.C.
s.29, amended: 2008 c.14 s.147
s.29, applied: SI 2008/794 Sch.6 para.19, SI 2008/1186 Reg.3
s.32, amended: 2008 c.14 s.148
s.42, repealed (in part): 2008 c.14 Sch.15 Part 5
s.43, applied: 2008 c.14 Sch.13 para.2
s.43, repealed (in part): 2008 c.14 s.147, Sch.15 Part 5
s.47, amended: 2008 c.14 s.147, Sch.15 Part 5
s.47, applied: 2008 c.14 Sch.13 para.2, Sch.13 para.3
s.48, amended: 2008 c.14 s.147, Sch.15 Part 5
s.48, applied: 2008 c.14 Sch.13 para.4
s.48, referred to: 2008 c.14 Sch.13 para.4
s.51, amended: 2008 c.14 s.147, Sch.15 Part 5
s.51, applied: 2008 c.14 Sch.13 para.5
s.56, amended: 2008 c.14 Sch.15 Part 5
Sch.6 para.19, amended: 2008 c.14 s.147, Sch.15 Part 5
Sch.6 para.19, disapplied: 2008 c.14 Sch.13 para.6
Sch.6 para.19, referred to: 2008 c.14 Sch.13 para.7

CAP.

11 & 12 Geo. 6 (1947-48)–cont.

29. National Assistance Act 1948–*cont.*
Sch.6 para.19, repealed (in part): 2008 c.14 s.147, Sch.15 Part 5

47. Agricultural Wages Act 1948
s.3A, amended: 2008 c.24 s.8, s.9

49. Finance Act 1948
s.47, repealed: 2008 c.12 Sch.1 Part 8
s.48, repealed: 2008 c.12 Sch.1 Part 8
s.49, repealed: 2008 c.12 Sch.1 Part 8
s.50, repealed: 2008 c.12 Sch.1 Part 8
s.51, repealed: 2008 c.12 Sch.1 Part 8
s.52, repealed: 2008 c.12 Sch.1 Part 8
s.53, repealed: 2008 c.12 Sch.1 Part 8
s.54, repealed: 2008 c.12 Sch.1 Part 8
s.55, repealed: 2008 c.12 Sch.1 Part 8
s.56, repealed: 2008 c.12 Sch.1 Part 8
s.57, repealed: 2008 c.12 Sch.1 Part 8
s.58, repealed: 2008 c.12 Sch.1 Part 8
s.59, repealed: 2008 c.12 Sch.1 Part 8
s.60, repealed: 2008 c.12 Sch.1 Part 8
s.61, repealed: 2008 c.12 Sch.1 Part 8
s.62, repealed: 2008 c.12 Sch.1 Part 8
s.63, repealed: 2008 c.12 Sch.1 Part 8
s.64, repealed: 2008 c.12 Sch.1 Part 8
s.65, repealed: 2008 c.12 Sch.1 Part 8
s.66, repealed: 2008 c.12 Sch.1 Part 8
s.67, repealed: 2008 c.12 Sch.1 Part 8
s.68, repealed: 2008 c.12 Sch.1 Part 8
s.72, repealed: 2008 c.12 Sch.1 Part 8
s.73, repealed: 2008 c.12 Sch.1 Part 8
s.74, repealed: 2008 c.12 Sch.1 Part 8
s.75, repealed: 2008 c.12 Sch.1 Part 8

56. British Nationality Act 1948
s.3, referred to: SI 2008/3133 Art.30

57. Public Registers and Records (Scotland) Act 1948
s.1, applied: 2008 asp 7 s.3

58. Criminal Justice Act 1948
s.69, repealed: 2008 c.12 Sch.1 Part 3
s.70, applied: SI 2008/653 Reg.7
s.78, repealed: 2008 c.12 Sch.1 Part 3
Sch.8 para.1, repealed: 2008 c.12 Sch.1 Part 3
Sch.8 para.2, repealed: 2008 c.12 Sch.1 Part 3
Sch.8 para.3, repealed: 2008 c.12 Sch.1 Part 3
Sch.8 para.4, repealed: 2008 c.12 Sch.1 Part 3
Sch.8 para.5, repealed: 2008 c.12 Sch.1 Part 3
Sch.8 para.6, repealed: 2008 c.12 Sch.1 Part 3
Sch.8 para.7, repealed: 2008 c.12 Sch.1 Part 3
Sch.8 para.8, repealed: 2008 c.12 Sch.1 Part 3
Sch.8 para.9, repealed: 2008 c.12 Sch.1 Part 3

12, 13 & 14 Geo. 6 (1948-49)

30. Agricultural Wages (Scotland) Act 1949
applied: 2008 c.24 s.8, s.9, s.10, s.11

47. Finance Act 1949
s.49, repealed: 2008 c.12 Sch.1 Part 8
s.51, amended: 2008 c.12 Sch.1 Part 8
s.51, repealed (in part): 2008 c.12 Sch.1 Part 8

CAP.

12, 13 & 14 Geo. 6 (1948-49)–cont.

55. Prevention of Damage by Pests Act 1949
applied: 2008 c.13 Sch.3
s.1, amended: 2008 asp 5 Sch.2 para.3
s.3, referred to: 2008 c.13 Sch.6
s.17, referred to: 2008 c.13 Sch.6
s.22, referred to: 2008 c.13 Sch.6

67. Civil Aviation Act 1949
s.8, enabling: SI 2008/3119, SI 2008/3125
s.41, enabling: SI 2008/3119, SI 2008/3125
s.57, enabling: SI 2008/3119, SI 2008/3125
s.58, enabling: SI 2008/3119, SI 2008/3125
s.59, enabling: SI 2008/3119, SI 2008/3125
s.61, enabling: SI 2008/3119, SI 2008/3125

74. Coast Protection Act 1949
applied: 2008 c.29 Sch.6 para.2, Sch.6 para.5
referred to: SSI 2008/263 Sch.1, Sch.2
Part I, applied: SSI 2008/188 Art.53
Part I, disapplied: SSI 2008/189 Art.53, SSI 2008/190 Art.53
s.18, referred to: 2008 c.13 Sch.6
s.34, applied: 2008 c.29 s.148, Sch.5 para.27
s.34, disapplied: 2008 c.18 Sch.14 para.5, SSI 2008/189 Art.53, SSI 2008/190 Art.53
s.36, disapplied: SSI 2008/189 Art.53, SSI 2008/190 Art.53
s.36, referred to: 2008 c.13 Sch.6
Sch.4 para.27, applied: 2008 c.29 Sch.4 para.1
Sch.4 para.28, applied: 2008 c.29 Sch.4 para.1
Sch.4 para.29, applied: 2008 c.29 Sch.4 para.1
Sch.4 para.30, applied: 2008 c.29 Sch.4 para.1

76. Marriage Act 1949
applied: SI 2008/1969 Sch.2 para.1
s.31, amended: SI 2008/678 Sch.2 para.5
s.31, applied: SI 2008/678 Sch.1 para.5
s.46A, amended: SI 2008/678 Sch.2 para.5
s.46A, applied: SI 2008/678 Sch.1 para.5
s.46B, amended: SI 2008/678 Sch.2 para.5
s.58, amended: SI 2008/678 Sch.2 para.5
s.58, applied: SI 2008/678 Sch.1 para.5
s.74, amended: SI 2008/678 Sch.2 para.5
s.74, applied: SI 2008/678 Sch.1 para.5

88. Registered Designs Act 1949
s.1B, see *Rolawn Ltd v Turfmech Machinery Ltd* [2008] EWHC 989 (Pat), [2008] E.C.D.R. 13 (Ch D (Patents Ct)), Mann, J.
s.7, see *Rolawn Ltd v Turfmech Machinery Ltd* [2008] EWHC 989 (Pat), [2008] E.C.D.R. 13 (Ch D (Patents Ct)), Mann, J.
s.24B, see *J Choo (Jersey) Ltd v Towerstone Ltd* [2008] EWHC 346 (Ch), [2008] E.C.C. 20 (Ch D), Floyd, J

CAP.

14 Geo. 6 (1950)

29. Employment and Training (Northern Ireland) Act 1950

s.1, applied: SI 2008/1909 Sch.1

37. Maintenance Orders Act 1950

applied: SI 2008/1054 Sch.1
s.4, amended: 2008 c.14 Sch.15 Part 5
s.4, repealed (in part): 2008 c.14 Sch.15 Part 5
s.9, amended: 2008 c.14 Sch.15 Part 5
s.9, repealed (in part): 2008 c.14 Sch.15 Part 5
s.16, amended: 2008 c.14 Sch.15 Part 5
s.16, repealed (in part): 2008 c.14 Sch.15 Part 5

14 & 15 Geo. 6 (1950-51)

33. Fraudulent Mediums Act 1951

repealed: SI 2008/1277 Sch.4 Part 1

35. Pet Animals Act 1951

applied: 2008 c.13 Sch.3
referred to: 2008 c.13 Sch.6

65. Reserve and Auxiliary Forces (Protection of Civil Interests) Act 1951

Part V, applied: SI 2008/239 Reg.45, SSI 2008/228 Reg.16, Reg.40
Sch.2 Part I, amended: SI 2008/912 Sch.1 para.1

15 & 16 Geo. 6 & 1 Eliz. 2 (1951-52)

33. Finance Act 1952

s.36, repealed: 2008 c.12 Sch.1 Part 8
s.37, repealed: 2008 c.12 Sch.1 Part 8
s.38, repealed: 2008 c.12 Sch.1 Part 8
s.39, repealed: 2008 c.12 Sch.1 Part 8
s.40, repealed: 2008 c.12 Sch.1 Part 8
s.41, repealed: 2008 c.12 Sch.1 Part 8
s.42, repealed: 2008 c.12 Sch.1 Part 8
s.43, repealed: 2008 c.12 Sch.1 Part 8
s.44, repealed: 2008 c.12 Sch.1 Part 8
s.45, repealed: 2008 c.12 Sch.1 Part 8
s.46, repealed: 2008 c.12 Sch.1 Part 8
s.47, repealed: 2008 c.12 Sch.1 Part 8
s.48, repealed: 2008 c.12 Sch.1 Part 8
s.49, repealed: 2008 c.12 Sch.1 Part 8
s.50, repealed: 2008 c.12 Sch.1 Part 8
s.51, repealed: 2008 c.12 Sch.1 Part 8
s.52, repealed: 2008 c.12 Sch.1 Part 8
s.53, repealed: 2008 c.12 Sch.1 Part 8
s.54, repealed: 2008 c.12 Sch.1 Part 8
s.55, repealed: 2008 c.12 Sch.1 Part 8
s.56, repealed: 2008 c.12 Sch.1 Part 8
s.57, repealed: 2008 c.12 Sch.1 Part 8
s.58, repealed: 2008 c.12 Sch.1 Part 8
s.59, repealed: 2008 c.12 Sch.1 Part 8
s.60, repealed: 2008 c.12 Sch.1 Part 8
s.61, repealed: 2008 c.12 Sch.1 Part 8
s.62, repealed: 2008 c.12 Sch.1 Part 8
s.63, repealed: 2008 c.12 Sch.1 Part 8
s.64, repealed: 2008 c.12 Sch.1 Part 8
s.65, repealed: 2008 c.12 Sch.1 Part 8
s.66, repealed: 2008 c.12 Sch.1 Part 8

CAP.

15 & 16 Geo. 6 & 1 Eliz. 2 (1951-52)–cont.

33. Finance Act 1952–*cont.*

s.69, repealed: 2008 c.12 Sch.1 Part 8
s.76, repealed (in part): 2008 c.12 Sch.1 Part 8

39. Motor Vehicles (International Circulation) Act 1952

s.1, applied: 2008 c.13 Sch.7

46. Hypnotism Act 1952

applied: 2008 c.13 Sch.3

52. Prison Act 1952

applied: SI 2008/794 Reg.156, SI 2008/1863 Art.33, SI 2008/2551 Reg.4
s.30, applied: SI 2008/794 Reg.112
s.43, amended: 2008 c.4 Sch.26 para.3
s.47, enabling: SI 2008/597, SI 2008/599
Sch.A1 para.2, amended: 2008 c.14 Sch.5 para.53, SI 2008/912 Sch.1 para.27
Sch.A1 para.2, repealed (in part): 2008 c.14 Sch.5 para.53, Sch.15 Part 1
Sch.A1 para.2, varied: SI 2008/2250 Art.3
Sch.A1 para.3, amended: 2008 c.14 Sch.5 para.53, SI 2008/912 Sch.1 para.26
Sch.A1 para.3, repealed (in part): 2008 c.14 Sch.5 para.53, Sch.15 Part 1
Sch.A1 para.3, varied: SI 2008/2250 Art.3
Sch.A1 para.4, amended: SI 2008/912 Sch.1 para.26
Sch.A1 para.5, amended: SI 2008/912 Sch.1 para.27

67. Visiting Forces Act 1952

s.1, enabling: SI 2008/299
s.2, applied: SI 2008/299 Art.4
s.3, applied: SI 2008/299 Art.4
s.4, applied: SI 2008/299 Art.4
s.5, applied: SI 2008/299 Art.4
s.6, applied: SI 2008/299 Art.4
s.7, applied: SI 2008/299 Art.4
s.8, applied: SI 2008/299 Art.4
s.9, applied: SI 2008/299 Art.4
s.10, applied: SI 2008/299 Art.4
s.11, applied: SI 2008/299 Art.4
s.12, applied: SI 2008/299 Art.4, SI 2008/2852 Sch.3 para.5, Sch.3 para.6
s.13, applied: SI 2008/299 Art.4
s.14, applied: SI 2008/299 Art.4
s.15, applied: SI 2008/299 Art.4
s.15, referred to: SI 2008/299 Art.5
s.15, enabling: SI 2008/299
s.16, applied: SI 2008/299 Art.4
s.17, applied: SI 2008/299 Art.4
s.18, applied: SI 2008/299 Art.4
s.19, applied: SI 2008/299 Art.4
Sch.1, applied: SI 2008/299 Art.4
Sch.1 para.1, amended: SI 2008/1769 Sch.1 para.10
Sch.1 para.1, repealed (in part): SI 2008/1769 Sch.1 para.10, Sch.3

CAP.

1 & 2 Eliz. 2 (1952-53)

20. Births and Deaths Registration Act 1953
applied: 2008 c.23 s.31
referred to: 2008 c.22 s.53
s.1, amended: 2008 c.22 Sch.6 para.2
s.2, substituted: 2008 c.22 Sch.6 para.3
s.9, amended: 2008 c.22 Sch.6 para.4
s.10, amended: 2008 c.22 Sch.6 para.5
s.10A, amended: 2008 c.22 Sch.6 para.7
s.10ZA, substituted: 2008 c.22 Sch.6 para.6
s.11, applied: SI 2008/2841 Reg.19, Reg.20
s.13, amended: 2008 c.22 Sch.6 para.8
s.14, amended: 2008 c.22 Sch.6 para.9
s.24, applied: SI 2008/2841 Reg.16, Reg.19
s.28, applied: SI 2008/678 Sch.1 para.6
s.29A, amended: 2008 c.22 Sch.6 para.10
s.30, applied: SI 2008/2841 Reg.16, Reg.19
s.31, applied: SI 2008/2841 Reg.16, Reg.19
s.32, applied: SI 2008/2841 Reg.16, Reg.19
s.39, applied: SI 2008/678 Sch.1 para.6
s.41, amended: SI 2008/678 Sch.2 para.6

23. Accommodation Agencies Act 1953
s.1, applied: 2008 c.13 Sch.3
s.1, referred to: 2008 c.13 Sch.6

34. Finance Act 1953
s.32, repealed: 2008 c.12 Sch.1 Part 8
s.35, repealed (in part): 2008 c.12 Sch.1 Part 8

37. Registration Service Act 1953
s.14, applied: SI 2008/239 Reg.9, SI 2008/678 Sch.1 para.7
s.20, applied: SI 2008/678 Sch.1 para.7
s.21, amended: SI 2008/678 Sch.2 para.7

49. Historic Buildings and Ancient Monuments Act 1953
s.4, referred to: 2008 c.12 Sch.2 para.7

2 & 3 Eliz. 2 (1953-54)

32. Atomic Energy Authority Act 1954
s.5, amended: 2008 asp 5 Sch.3 Part 1
s.6, applied: SI 2008/2852 Sch.6 para.4

39. Agriculture (Miscellaneous Provisions) Act 1954
s.9, applied: 2008 c.13 Sch.3

56. Landlord and Tenant Act 1954
Part II, see *Cameron Ltd v Rolls-Royce Plc* [2007] EWHC 546 (Ch), [2008] L. & T.R. 22 (Ch D), Mann, J.; see *Chiltern Railway Co Ltd v Patel* [2008] EWCA Civ 178, [2008] Bus. L.R. 1295 (CA (Civ Div)), Mummery, L.J.
s.24, see *Chiltern Railway Co Ltd v Patel* [2008] EWCA Civ 178, [2008] Bus. L.R. 1295 (CA (Civ Div)), Mummery, L.J.
s.28, see *Cameron Ltd v Rolls-Royce Plc* [2007] EWHC 546 (Ch), [2008] L. & T.R. 22 (Ch D), Mann, J.
s.30, applied: SI 2008/576 Sch.4 para.2
s.32, see *Picture Warehouse Ltd v Cornhill Investments Ltd* [2008] EWHC 45 (QB), [2008] 12 E.G. 98 (QBD), Jack, J.

CAP.

2 & 3 Eliz. 2 (1953-54)–cont.

56. Landlord and Tenant Act 1954–*cont.*
s.35, see *Picture Warehouse Ltd v Cornhill Investments Ltd* [2008] EWHC 45 (QB), [2008] 12 E.G. 98 (QBD), Jack, J.
s.38, see *Cameron Ltd v Rolls-Royce Plc* [2007] EWHC 546 (Ch), [2008] L. & T.R. 22 (Ch D), Mann, J.
s.38A, see *Chiltern Railway Co Ltd v Patel* [2008] EWCA Civ 178, [2008] Bus. L.R. 1295 (CA (Civ Div)), Mummery, L.J.
Sch.2 para.4, see *Chiltern Railway Co Ltd v Patel* [2008] EWCA Civ 178, [2008] Bus. L.R. 1295 (CA (Civ Div)), Mummery, L.J.
Sch.2 para.7, see *Chiltern Railway Co Ltd v Patel* [2008] EWCA Civ 178, [2008] Bus. L.R. 1295 (CA (Civ Div)), Mummery, L.J.

64. Transport Charges &c (Miscellaneous Provisions) Act 1954
s.6, enabling: SI 2008/2102

68. Pests Act 1954
applied: 2008 c.13 Sch.3, SSI 2008/100 Sch.2 Part 1
s.6, amended: 2008 asp 5 Sch.2 para.4
s.8, referred to: 2008 c.13 Sch.6
s.9, referred to: 2008 c.13 Sch.6
s.12, referred to: 2008 c.13 Sch.6

70. Mines and Quarries Act 1954
applied: 2008 c.13 Sch.3
s.83, disapplied: SI 2008/1597 Reg.27

3 & 4 Eliz. 2 (1954-55)

9. Rating and Valuation (Miscellaneous Provisions) Act 1955
repealed: 2008 c.12 Sch.1 Part 7

18. Army Act 1955
applied: 2008 c.28 Sch.6 para.11, SI 2008/635 Art.5
referred to: SI 2008/1780 Art.2
Part II, applied: SI 2008/635 Art.19
s.57, applied: SI 2008/635 Art.19
s.70, applied: 2008 c.4 s.98
s.70, referred to: SI 2008/1062 Sch.1 para.1, Sch.1 para.2
s.71A, applied: 2008 c.28 Sch.6 para.5
s.74, substituted: SI 2008/1694 Art.3
s.75F, amended: SI 2008/1694 Art.16
s.75F, repealed (in part): SI 2008/1694 Art.16
s.75K, referred to: 2008 c.28 Sch.6 para.7
s.83A, substituted: SI 2008/3294 Art.2
s.83A, varied: SI 2008/3294 Art.5
s.83B, amended: SI 2008/1694 Art.17
s.83B, applied: SI 2008/635 Art.2, Art.19, SI 2008/648 Sch.1
s.83BB, amended: SI 2008/1694 Art.18
s.83BB, applied: SI 2008/1694 Sch.1 para.2, Sch.1 para.3
s.83BB, repealed (in part): SI 2008/1694 Art.18
s.85A, applied: SI 2008/1694 Sch.1 para.2

CAP.

3 & 4 Eliz. 2 (1954-55)–cont.

18. Army Act 1955–*cont.*
s.85A, repealed (in part): SI 2008/1694 Art.19
s.94, see *Times Newspapers Ltd v R* [2008] EWCA Crim 2559, Times, October 31, 2008 (CMAC), Latham, L.J.
s.101, varied: 2008 c.15 s.8
s.103, enabling: SI 2008/1699
s.113AA, repealed (in part): SI 2008/1694 Art.33
s.118, amended: SI 2008/1694 Art.23
s.118, referred to: SI 2008/1694 Sch.1 para.13
s.118, repealed (in part): SI 2008/1694 Art.23
s.120, amended: SI 2008/1694 Art.24
s.120, applied: SI 2008/1694 Sch.1 para.3, Sch.1 para.4, Sch.1 para.5, Sch.1 para.6, Sch.1 para.7
s.120, repealed (in part): SI 2008/1694 Art.24
s.120, varied: SI 2008/1694 Sch.1 para.4
s.120A, applied: SI 2008/1694 Sch.1 para.13
s.120A, repealed: SI 2008/1694 Art.33
s.120ZA, added: SI 2008/1694 Art.25
s.120ZA, referred to: SI 2008/1694 Sch.1 para.7
s.120ZA, varied: SI 2008/1694 Sch.1 para.6
s.131, amended: SI 2008/1694 Art.5
s.131, applied: SI 2008/635 Art.5, Art.19
s.132, amended: SI 2008/1694 Art.6
s.135, applied: SI 2008/1650 Art.3
s.137, applied: SI 2008/1650 Art.3
s.209, amended: SI 2008/1694 Art.7
s.209, applied: SI 2008/635 Art.19
s.209, repealed (in part): SI 2008/1694 Art.7
s.225, amended: SI 2008/1694 Art.13

19. Air Force Act 1955
applied: 2008 c.28 Sch.6 para.11, SI 2008/635 Art.5, SI 2008/648 Sch.1
referred to: SI 2008/1780 Art.2
Part II, applied: SI 2008/635 Art.19
s.22, enabling: SI 2008/1585
s.23, enabling: SI 2008/1585
s.57, applied: SI 2008/635 Art.19
s.70, applied: 2008 c.4 s.98
s.70, referred to: SI 2008/1062 Sch.1 para.1, Sch.1 para.2
s.71A, applied: 2008 c.28 Sch.6 para.5
s.74, substituted: SI 2008/1694 Art.4
s.75F, amended: SI 2008/1694 Art.16
s.75F, repealed (in part): SI 2008/1694 Art.16
s.75K, referred to: 2008 c.28 Sch.6 para.7
s.83A, substituted: SI 2008/3294 Art.3
s.83A, varied: SI 2008/3294 Art.5
s.83B, amended: SI 2008/1694 Art.17
s.83B, applied: SI 2008/635 Art.2, Art.19, SI 2008/648 Sch.1
s.83BB, amended: SI 2008/1694 Art.18
s.83BB, applied: SI 2008/1694 Sch.1 para.2, Sch.1 para.3
s.83BB, repealed (in part): SI 2008/1694 Art.18

CAP.

3 & 4 Eliz. 2 (1954-55)–cont.

19. Air Force Act 1955–*cont.*
s.85A, applied: SI 2008/1694 Sch.1 para.2
s.85A, repealed (in part): SI 2008/1694 Art.19
s.101, varied: 2008 c.15 s.8
s.103, enabling: SI 2008/1699
s.113AA, repealed (in part): SI 2008/1694 Art.33
s.118, referred to: SI 2008/1694 Sch.1 para.13
s.118, repealed (in part): SI 2008/1694 Art.23
s.120, amended: SI 2008/1694 Art.24
s.120, applied: SI 2008/1694 Sch.1 para.3, Sch.1 para.4, Sch.1 para.5, Sch.1 para.6, Sch.1 para.7
s.120, repealed (in part): SI 2008/1694 Art.24
s.120, varied: SI 2008/1694 Sch.1 para.4
s.120A, applied: SI 2008/1694 Sch.1 para.13
s.120A, repealed: SI 2008/1694 Art.33
s.120ZA, added: SI 2008/1694 Art.25
s.120ZA, referred to: SI 2008/1694 Sch.1 para.7
s.120ZA, varied: SI 2008/1694 Sch.1 para.6
s.131, amended: SI 2008/1694 Art.5
s.131, applied: SI 2008/635 Art.5, Art.19
s.132, amended: SI 2008/1694 Art.6
s.135, applied: SI 2008/1650 Art.3
s.137, applied: SI 2008/1650 Art.3
s.209, amended: SI 2008/1694 Art.7
s.209, applied: SI 2008/635 Art.19
s.209, repealed (in part): SI 2008/1694 Art.7
s.223, amended: SI 2008/1694 Art.13

4 & 5 Eliz. 2 (1955-56)

60. Valuation and Rating (Scotland) Act 1956
s.6, see *Lothian Assessor v Belhaven Brewery Co Ltd* [2008] CSIH 60, 2008 S.L.T. 1126 (LVAC), The Lord Justice Clerk (Gill); see *Suburban Taverns (Glasgow) Ltd v Glasgow Assessor* [2008] CSIH 5, 2008 S.C. 298 (LVAC), Lord Gill L.J.C.
s.6, applied: SSI 2008/85 Reg.3
s.6A, enabling: SSI 2008/84
s.7B, applied: SSI 2008/85 Reg.3

69. Sexual Offences Act 1956
see *Assets Recovery Agency v Virtosu* [2008] EWHC 149 (QB), [2008] 3 All E.R. 637 (QBD), Tugendhat, J.
s.1, referred to: SI 2008/1062 Sch.1 para.1
s.5, referred to: SI 2008/1062 Sch.1 para.1
s.12, applied: SI 2008/1466 Art.3
s.35, amended: 2008 c.12 Sch.1 Part 3
s.52, repealed (in part): 2008 c.12 Sch.1 Part 3

5 & 6 Eliz. 2 (1957)

11. Homicide Act 1957
s.2, see *R. v Wood (Clive)* [2008] EWCA Crim 1305, [2008] 3 All E.R. 898 (CA (Crim Div)), Sir Igor Judge (President, QB)

CAP.

5 & 6 Eliz. 2 (1957)–cont.

12. Public Trustee (Fees) Act 1957
s.1, applied: SI 2008/611, SI 2008/611 Art.3

53. Naval Discipline Act 1957
applied: 2008 c.28 Sch.6 para.11, SI 2008/635 Art.5
referred to: SI 2008/1780 Art.2
Part I, applied: SI 2008/635 Art.19
Part II, applied: SI 2008/635 Art.19
s.38, applied: SI 2008/635 Art.19
s.42, applied: 2008 c.4 s.98
s.42, referred to: SI 2008/1062 Sch.1 para.1, Sch.1 para.2
s.43A, applied: 2008 c.28 Sch.6 para.5
s.45, amended: SI 2008/1694 Art.8
s.45, applied: SI 2008/1694 Sch.1 para.1
s.45A, added: SI 2008/1694 Art.9
s.47G, amended: SI 2008/1694 Art.16
s.47G, repealed (in part): SI 2008/1694 Art.16
s.47L, referred to: 2008 c.28 Sch.6 para.7
s.51, amended: SI 2008/1694 Art.10
s.51, applied: SI 2008/635 Art.5, Art.19, SI 2008/1694 Sch.1 para.1
s.52F, amended: SI 2008/1694 Art.28
s.52H, substituted: SI 2008/3294 Art.4
s.52H, varied: SI 2008/3294 Art.5
s.52I, amended: SI 2008/1694 Art.20
s.52I, applied: SI 2008/635 Art.2, Art.19, SI 2008/648 Sch.1
s.52II, amended: SI 2008/1694 Art.21
s.52II, applied: SI 2008/1694 Sch.1 para.2, Sch.1 para.3
s.52II, repealed (in part): SI 2008/1694 Art.21
s.58, enabling: SI 2008/1699
s.62ZA, applied: SI 2008/1694 Sch.1 para.2
s.62ZA, repealed (in part): SI 2008/1694 Art.22
s.65, varied: 2008 c.15 s.8
s.71, repealed (in part): SI 2008/1694 Art.34
s.81, amended: SI 2008/1694 Art.29
s.81, referred to: SI 2008/1694 Sch.1 para.9
s.85, referred to: SI 2008/1694 Sch.1 para.13
s.89A, applied: SI 2008/1694 Sch.1 para.13
s.89A, repealed: SI 2008/1694 Art.34
s.90, amended: SI 2008/1694 Art.30
s.90, applied: SI 2008/1694 Sch.1 para.11
s.91, applied: SI 2008/1694 Sch.1 para.3, Sch.1 para.12
s.91, referred to: SI 2008/1694 Sch.1 para.10
s.91, substituted: SI 2008/1694 Art.31
s.91B, applied: SI 2008/1694 Sch.1 para.11
s.91B, referred to: SI 2008/1694 Sch.1 para.10
s.92, amended: SI 2008/1694 Art.32
s.92, applied: SI 2008/1694 Sch.1 para.12
s.118, amended: SI 2008/1694 Art.11
s.118, applied: SI 2008/635 Art.19
s.135, amended: SI 2008/1694 Art.13
Sch.4 para.3, repealed: SI 2008/1694 Art.12

CAP.

5 & 6 Eliz. 2 (1957)–cont.

58. Registration of Births, Deaths and Marriages (Special Provisions) Act 1957
referred to: 2008 c.22 s.53
s.3A, amended: 2008 c.22 Sch.6 para.11
s.5, amended: 2008 c.22 Sch.6 para.12

6 & 7 Eliz. 2 (1957-58)

39. Maintenance Orders Act 1958
applied: SI 2008/1054 Sch.1
s.19, enabling: SI 2008/1203

49. Trading Representations (Disabled Persons) Act 1958
applied: 2008 c.13 Sch.3
repealed: SI 2008/1277 Sch.4 Part 1

51. Public Records Act 1958
Sch.1 Part 2, amended: 2008 c.6 Sch.1 para.24, 2008 c.13 Sch.1 para.16, 2008 c.14 Sch.5 para.54, Sch.10 para.2, Sch.15 Part 1, 2008 c.17 Sch.8 para.1, Sch.9 para.1, 2008 c.27 Sch.1 para.28, 2008 c.29 Sch.1 para.26, 2008 c.30 Sch.1 para.23
Sch.1 para.3, amended: 2008 c.29 Sch.1 para.26

56. Finance Act 1958
s.35, repealed: 2008 c.12 Sch.1 Part 8
s.40, repealed (in part): 2008 c.12 Sch.1 Part 8

61. Interest on Damages (Scotland) Act 1958
s.1, see *Wilson v Dunbar Bank Plc* [2008] CSIH 27, 2008 S.C. 457 (IH (Ex Div)), Lord Kingarth

69. Opencast Coal Act 1958
s.51, applied: SI 2008/1034 Art.5

7 & 8 Eliz. 2 (1958-59)

54. Weeds Act 1959
applied: 2008 c.13 Sch.3
s.2, referred to: 2008 c.13 Sch.6

66. Obscene Publications Act 1959
s.2, amended: 2008 c.4 s.71

72. Mental Health Act 1959
s.128, referred to: SI 2008/1062 Sch.1 para.1

8 & 9 Eliz. 2 (1959-60)

3. Attempted Rape, etc., Act (Northern Ireland) 1960
s.2, repealed: SI 2008/1769 Sch.1 para.11, Sch.3

58. Charities Act 1960
s.22, applied: SI 2008/629 Sch.1 para.3

62. Caravan Sites and Control of Development Act 1960
applied: 2008 c.13 Sch.3

65. Administration of Justice Act 1960
s.1, applied: SI 2008/1586 Sch.2 para.11
s.5, amended: 2008 c.4 Sch.8 para.26, SI 2008/1587 Art.4

CAP.

8 & 9 Eliz. 2 (1959-60)–cont.

65. Administration of Justice Act 1960– *cont.*

s.5, varied: SI 2008/1587 Art.4

s.5A, varied: SI 2008/1900 Sch.1 para.2

s.12, see *Medway Council v G* [2008] EWHC 1681 (Fam), [2008] 2 F.L.R. 1687 (Fam Div), Sir Mark Potter (President, Fam); see *X Council v B* [2008] EWHC 270 (Fam), [2008] 1 F.L.R. 1460 (Fam Div (Liverpool)), Munby, J.

s.12, amended: SI 2008/2833 Sch.3 para.22

s.13, see *Haw v Westminster Magistrates Court* [2007] EWHC 2960 (Admin), [2008] Q.B. 888 (DC), Thomas, L.J.

67. Public Bodies (Admission to Meetings) Act 1960

Sch.1 para.1, amended: 2008 c.14 Sch.5 para.55, Sch.10 para.3

Sch.1 para.1, repealed (in part): 2008 c.14 Sch.5 para.55, Sch.15 Part 1

Sch.1 para.2, amended: 2008 c.14 Sch.10 para.3

9 & 10 Eliz. 2 (1960-61)

33. Land Compensation Act 1961

see *Spirerose Ltd v Transport for London* [2008] R.V.R. 12 (Lands Tr), George Bartlett Q.C.

applied: 2008 c.17 Sch.2 para.7

varied: SI 2008/2512 Art.30, SI 2008/3163 Art.10

Part I, applied: 2008 c.18 s.8, Sch.2 para.7, Sch.2 para.9, Sch.2 para.10, Sch.3 para.3, Sch.5 para.1, Sch.5 para.3, Sch.5 para.4, Sch.5 para.5, SI 2008/1238 Art.8, SI 2008/1261 Art.22, Art.32, SI 2008/2512 Art.8, Art.10, Art.17, Art.18, Art.20, Art.21, Art.26, Art.27, Art.28, Art.32, Art.35, SI 2008/3163 Art.8, Art.12

s.2, applied: 2008 c.29 s.165, s.219

s.4, applied: 2008 c.29 s.165, s.219

s.5, see *Esso Petroleum Co Ltd v Secretary of State for Transport* [2008] R.V.R. 351 (Lands Tr), George Bartlett Q.C. (President); see *Greenweb Ltd v Wandsworth LBC* [2008] EWCA Civ 910, [2008] R.V.R. 294 (CA (Civ Div)), Buxton, L.J.; see *Lathar v Sandwell Metropolitan DC* [2008] R.V.R. 175 (Lands Tr), PR Francis FRICS; see *Port of London Authority v Transport for London* [2008] R.V.R. 93 (Lands Tr), PR Francis FRICS

s.9, see *Spirerose Ltd v Transport for London* [2008] R.V.R. 12 (Lands Tr), George Bartlett Q.C.

s.14, see *Greenweb Ltd v Wandsworth LBC* [2008] EWCA Civ 910, [2008] R.V.R. 294 (CA (Civ Div)), Buxton, L.J.; see *Spirerose Ltd v Transport for London* [2008] R.V.R. 12 (Lands Tr), George Bartlett Q.C.

CAP.

9 & 10 Eliz. 2 (1960-61)–cont.

33. Land Compensation Act 1961–*cont.*

s.15, see *Greenweb Ltd v Wandsworth LBC* [2008] EWCA Civ 910, [2008] R.V.R. 294 (CA (Civ Div)), Buxton, L.J.; see *Spirerose Ltd v Transport for London* [2008] R.V.R. 12 (Lands Tr), George Bartlett Q.C.

s.16, see *Spirerose Ltd v Transport for London* [2008] R.V.R. 12 (Lands Tr), George Bartlett Q.C.

s.17, see *Greenweb Ltd v Wandsworth LBC* [2008] EWCA Civ 910, [2008] R.V.R. 294 (CA (Civ Div)), Buxton, L.J.

s.23, amended: 2008 c.17 Sch.8 para.2

34. Factories Act 1961

applied: 2008 c.13 Sch.3

s.154A, amended: SSI 2008/339 Art.2

36. Finance Act 1961

s.32, repealed: 2008 c.12 Sch.1 Part 8

39. Criminal Justice Act 1961

s.38, amended: 2008 c.4 Sch.26 para.4

41. Flood Prevention (Scotland) Act 1961

referred to: SSI 2008/263 Sch.1, Sch.2

47. Mock Auctions Act 1961

applied: 2008 c.13 Sch.3, SI 2008/1277 Sch.3 para.9, Sch.3 para.11

repealed: SI 2008/1277 Sch.4 Part 1

55. Crown Estate Act 1961

s.3, disapplied: 2008 c.18 s.43

60. Suicide Act 1961

s.2, see *R. (on the application of Purdy) v DPP* [2008] EWHC 2565 (Admin), (2008) 104 B.M.L.R. 231 (DC), Scott Baker, L.J.

64. Public Health Act 1961

applied: 2008 c.13 Sch.3

Sch.4, amended: 2008 c.17 Sch.8 para.3

10 & 11 Eliz. 2 (1961-62)

9. Local Government (Financial Provisions etc.) (Scotland) Act 1962

s.4, applied: SSI 2008/85 Reg.3, Reg.5

12. Education Act 1962

applied: SI 2008/529 Reg.3, SI 2008/1273 Reg.3, SI 2008/1582 Reg.4, SI 2008/3170 Reg.3

s.1, applied: SI 2008/228 Sch.1 para.12, Sch.1 para.13

s.1, enabling: SI 2008/1477

s.2, applied: SI 2008/228 Sch.1 para.13

s.4, enabling: SI 2008/1477

19. West Indies Act 1962

s.5, enabling: SI 2008/3127

s.7, enabling: SI 2008/3127

44. Finance Act 1962

s.34, repealed (in part): 2008 c.12 Sch.1 Part 8

46. Transport Act 1962

referred to: SSI 2008/263 Sch.2

s.24, amended: SI 2008/948 Sch.1 para.1

s.50, disapplied: SI 2008/230 Art.5

Sch.9, disapplied: SI 2008/230 Art.5

CAP.

10 & 11 Eliz. 2 (1961-62)–cont.

58. Pipe-lines Act 1962
applied: 2008 c.29 s.21
s.1, amended: 2008 c.29 Sch.2 para.6
s.1, applied: 2008 c.29 s.21, s.33
s.10E, amended: 2008 c.32 s.79
s.10F, amended: 2008 c.32 s.79
s.10G, added: 2008 c.32 s.79
s.10H, added: 2008 c.32 s.79
s.54, amended: 2008 c.32 Sch.5 para.1
s.66, amended: 2008 c.29 Sch.2 para.7, 2008 c.32 s.78, Sch.6

1963

9. Purchase Tax Act 1963
see *Revenue and Customs Commissioners v Premier Foods (Holdings) Ltd* [2007] EWHC 3134 (Ch), [2008] S.T.C. 176 (Ch D), Sir Andrew Morritt (Chancellor)
18. Stock Transfer Act 1963
s.2, amended: SI 2008/948 Sch.1 para.37
25. Finance Act 1963
s.65, repealed (in part): 2008 c.12 Sch.1 Part 8
33. London Government Act 1963
applied: 2008 c.13 Sch.3
37. Children and Young Persons Act 1963
Part II, applied: 2008 c.13 Sch.3
s.40, referred to: 2008 c.13 Sch.6
41. Offices, Shops and Railway Premises Act 1963
applied: 2008 c.13 Sch.3
s.9, amended: 2008 asp 5 Sch.2 para.5, Sch.3 Part 1
s.59A, amended: SSI 2008/339 Art.3
43. Animal Boarding Establishments Act 1963
applied: 2008 c.13 Sch.3
s.1, referred to: 2008 c.13 Sch.6
51. Land Compensation (Scotland) Act 1963
s.9, varied: SSI 2008/199 Art.11, SSI 2008/200 Art.10
s.11, varied: SSI 2008/199 Art.11, SSI 2008/200 Art.10

1964

5. International Headquarters and Defence Organisations Act 1964
applied: SI 2008/2852 Sch.3 para.5, Sch.3 para.6
14. Plant Varieties and Seeds Act 1964
s.16, referred to: 2008 c.13 Sch.6
s.16, enabling: SI 2008/560, SI 2008/1063
s.25, referred to: 2008 c.13 Sch.6
24. Trade Union (Amalgamations, etc.) Act 1964
see *Unison v Allen* [2008] I.C.R. 114 (EAT), Elias, J (President)
28. Agriculture and Horticulture Act 1964
Part III, applied: 2008 c.13 Sch.3

CAP.

1964–cont.

28. Agriculture and Horticulture Act 1964–*cont.*
s.14, referred to: 2008 c.13 Sch.6
s.15, referred to: 2008 c.13 Sch.6
29. Continental Shelf Act 1964
s.1, applied: 2008 c.29 s.148, s.149, 2008 c.32 s.33, s.80
40. Harbours Act 1964
applied: SI 2008/1261 Art.2
s.14, amended: 2008 c.29 Sch.2 para.9
s.14, applied: 2008 c.29 s.33, s.145, SI 2008/230, SI 2008/1160, SI 2008/1817, SI 2008/2359, SSI 2008/182, SSI 2008/422
s.14, disapplied: 2008 c.29 s.120
s.14, referred to: SI 2008/230, SI 2008/1160, SI 2008/1817, SI 2008/2359, SSI 2008/182, SSI 2008/331, SSI 2008/361
s.14, enabling: SI 2008/230, SI 2008/1160, SI 2008/1817, SI 2008/2359, SSI 2008/182, SSI 2008/331, SSI 2008/361, SSI 2008/422
s.16, amended: 2008 c.29 Sch.2 para.10
s.16, applied: 2008 c.29 s.33, SI 2008/1261, SSI 2008/188 Art.54, SSI 2008/189 Art.54, SSI 2008/190 Art.54
s.16, disapplied: 2008 c.29 s.120
s.16, referred to: SSI 2008/188
s.16, enabling: SI 2008/1261, SSI 2008/188, SSI 2008/189, SSI 2008/190
s.26, applied: SI 2008/1261 Art.35
s.30, applied: SSI 2008/182 Art.46, SSI 2008/188 Art.39, SSI 2008/189 Art.39, SSI 2008/190 Art.39
s.30, disapplied: SSI 2008/182 Art.46, SSI 2008/188 Art.41, SSI 2008/189 Art.41, SSI 2008/190 Art.41
s.31, applied: SSI 2008/188 Art.39, SSI 2008/189 Art.39, SSI 2008/190 Art.39
s.31, referred to: SI 2008/1261 Art.41
s.42, amended: SI 2008/948 Sch.1 para.39
s.46, applied: SSI 2008/190 Art.42
s.48A, applied: SI 2008/1261 Sch.8 para.11
s.57, applied: SI 2008/230 Art.3, SSI 2008/182 Art.4, SSI 2008/188 Art.4, SSI 2008/189 Art.4
s.57, referred to: SSI 2008/188 Art.39, SSI 2008/189 Art.39, SSI 2008/190 Art.39
Sch.2, applied: 2008 c.29 s.145
Sch.2 para.9B, applied: SSI 2008/182 Art.53
Sch.2 para.9B, referred to: 2008 c.29 s.145, SSI 2008/422 Sch.2 para.15
Sch.3 Part I para.1, amended: SSI 2008/202 Reg.2
Sch.3 Part I para.4, applied: SSI 2008/331, SSI 2008/361
Sch.3 Part I para.8, applied: SSI 2008/331, SSI 2008/361
Sch.3 Part I para.10, applied: SSI 2008/331, SSI 2008/361, SSI 2008/422
Sch.3 Part I para.10A, applied: SSI 2008/361

CAP.

1964–cont.

40. Harbours Act 1964–*cont.*
Sch.3 Part I para.15, applied: SSI 2008/331, SSI 2008/361
Sch.3 Part I para.18, applied: SI 2008/1261
Sch.3 Part I para.19, applied: SSI 2008/361

48. Police Act 1964
see *Holmes v South Yorkshire Police Authority* [2008] EWCA Civ 51, [2008] H.L.R. 33 (CA (Civ Div)), Sedley, L.J.
s.33, see *Holmes v South Yorkshire Police Authority* [2008] EWCA Civ 51, [2008] H.L.R. 33 (CA (Civ Div)), Sedley, L.J.

49. Finance Act 1964
repealed: 2008 c.12 Sch.1 Part 8

53. Hire-Purchase Act 1964
Part III, applied: SI 2008/794 Sch.8 para.33

56. Housing Act 1964
s.46, applied: SSI 2008/189 Art.42

69. Scrap Metal Dealers Act 1964
applied: 2008 c.13 Sch.3
s.1, referred to: 2008 c.13 Sch.6
s.5, referred to: 2008 c.13 Sch.6

70. Riding Establishments Act 1964
applied: 2008 c.13 Sch.3

84. Criminal Procedure (Insanity) Act 1964
s.4A, see *R. v B* [2008] EWCA Crim 1997, Times, October 8, 2008 (CA (Crim Div)), Toulson, L.J.; see *R. v Chal (Amolak Singh)* [2007] EWCA Crim 2647, [2008] 1 Cr. App. R. 18 (CA (Crim Div)), Toulson, L.J.; see *R. v Chal (Amolak Singh)* [2007] EWCA Crim 2647, [2008] 1 Cr. App. R. 18 (CA (Crim Div)), Toulson, L.J.
Sch.1A Part 1 para.1, amended: SI 2008/912 Sch.1 para.2
Sch.1A Part 2 para.3, amended: SI 2008/912 Sch.1 para.2

89. Hairdressers (Registration) Act 1964
s.13, amended: SI 2008/948 Sch.1 para.1

1965

4. Science and Technology Act 1965
s.3, enabling: SI 2008/1405
s.5, applied: SI 2008/1405 Art.2

12. Industrial and Provident Societies Act 1965
see *Midlands Co-operative Society Ltd v Revenue and Customs Commissioners* [2008] EWCA Civ 305, [2008] Bus. L.R. 1187 (CA (Civ Div)), Arden, L.J.
applied: 2008 c.28 Sch.7 para.6, SI 2008/2361 Reg.17
disapplied: 2008 c.17 s.167
s.6, applied: 2008 c.28 Sch.7 para.6
s.7, applied: 2008 c.28 Sch.7 para.6
s.10, applied: 2008 c.17 s.212
s.39, applied: SI 2008/565 Reg.4
s.50, applied: 2008 c.17 s.157, s.163, s.255

CAP.

1965–cont.

12. Industrial and Provident Societies Act 1965–*cont.*
s.51, see *Midlands Co-operative Society Ltd v Revenue and Customs Commissioners* [2008] EWCA Civ 305, [2008] Bus. L.R. 1187 (CA (Civ Div)), Arden, L.J.
s.51, applied: 2008 c.17 s.157, s.163
s.52, applied: 2008 c.17 s.157, s.163
s.53, applied: 2008 c.17 s.161
s.55, applied: 2008 c.17 s.164, s.167
s.58, applied: 2008 c.17 s.165, SI 2008/653 Reg.15, Reg.16, SSI 2008/224 Reg.15
Sch.1 para.10, amended: SI 2008/948 Sch.1 para.4

14. Cereals Marketing Act 1965
applied: SI 2008/576 Sch.4 para.10
repealed: SI 2008/576 Sch.5 para.7
s.21, amended: SI 2008/948 Sch.1 para.1
s.22, disapplied: SI 2008/576 Sch.4 para.10

19. Teaching Council (Scotland) Act 1965
s.11, applied: SI 2008/1884 Reg.2
Sch.1 Part II para.13, amended: SI 2008/948 Sch.1 para.1

32. Administration of Estates (Small Payments) Act 1965
s.1, applied: SI 2008/653 Reg.21
s.1, referred to: SSI 2008/224 Reg.21
s.6, applied: SI 2008/239 Reg.52, SI 2008/653 Reg.21, SSI 2008/224 Reg.21, SSI 2008/228 Reg.48

36. Gas Act 1965
s.4, amended: 2008 c.29 Sch.2 para.12
s.4, applied: 2008 c.29 s.33
s.4, disapplied: 2008 c.29 s.120
s.5, amended: 2008 c.29 Sch.2 para.13
s.6, amended: 2008 c.29 Sch.2 para.14

49. Registration of Births, Deaths and Marriages (Scotland) Act 1965
applied: SSI 2008/27 Reg.7
Part II, referred to: 2008 c.22 s.53
s.5, applied: SSI 2008/228 Reg.7
s.7, applied: SSI 2008/228 Reg.7
s.14, amended: 2008 c.22 Sch.6 para.42
s.18B, added: 2008 c.22 Sch.6 para.44
s.18ZA, substituted: 2008 c.22 Sch.6 para.43
s.20, amended: 2008 c.22 Sch.6 para.45

51. National Insurance Act 1965
applied: 2008 c.30 s.141, SI 2008/794 Sch.1 para.10
s.36, amended: SI 2008/632 Art.12
s.36, applied: 2008 c.30 s.102
s.37, varied: SI 2008/632 Art.12

56. Compulsory Purchase Act 1965
applied: 2008 c.17 Sch.2 para.8, 2008 c.18 Sch.6 para.5, SI 2008/1961 Sch.4 para.8, SI 2008/2512 Art.31, Sch.6 para.3
referred to: SI 2008/1238 Art.5, Sch.1 para.3, SI 2008/1261 Art.30, SI 2008/3163 Art.5, Art.6

CAP.

1965–cont.

56. Compulsory Purchase Act 1965–*cont.*
varied: 2008 c.17 Sch.2 para.8, 2008 c.18 Sch.6 para.7
Part I, applied: 2008 c.17 Sch.2 para.9, Sch.2 para.17, 2008 c.18 s.6, s.7, Sch.6 para.6, Sch.6 para.14, Sch.6 para.18, 2008 c.29 s.125, SI 2008/1238 Art.4, Art.6, Sch.1 para.3, SI 2008/1261 Art.29, Art.33, SI 2008/2512 Art.23, Art.33, Sch.6 para.3, SI 2008/3163 Art.13
Part I, disapplied: SI 2008/1238 Art.9
Part I, referred to: SI 2008/1238 Art.6, Art.9
s.1, referred to: SI 2008/1961 Sch.4 para.8
s.1, varied: 2008 c.18 Sch.6 para.2, SI 2008/2512 Art.23, SI 2008/3163 Art.4
s.2, varied: 2008 c.18 Sch.6 para.2, SI 2008/2512 Art.23, SI 2008/3163 Art.4
s.3, varied: 2008 c.18 Sch.6 para.2, SI 2008/2512 Art.23, SI 2008/3163 Art.4
s.4, varied: 2008 c.18 Sch.6 para.2, Sch.6 para.3, 2008 c.29 s.125, SI 2008/1238 Art.4, SI 2008/1261 Art.29, SI 2008/2512 Art.23, SI 2008/3163 Art.4
s.5, see *Union Railways (North) Ltd v Kent CC* [2008] 2 P. & C.R. 22 (Lands Tr), George Bartlett Q.C. (President)
s.5, applied: 2008 c.18 s.47
s.5, referred to: 2008 c.29 s.44, s.52, s.57
s.5, varied: 2008 c.18 Sch.6 para.2, SI 2008/2512 Art.23, SI 2008/3163 Art.4
s.6, see *Union Railways (North) Ltd v Kent CC* [2008] 2 P. & C.R. 22 (Lands Tr), George Bartlett Q.C. (President)
s.6, varied: 2008 c.18 Sch.6 para.2, SI 2008/2512 Art.23, SI 2008/3163 Art.4
s.7, see *Esso Petroleum Co Ltd v Secretary of State for Transport* [2008] R.V.R. 351 (Lands Tr), George Bartlett Q.C. (President); see *Lall v Transport for London* [2008] R.V.R. 183 (Lands Tr), George Bartlett Q.C. (President)
s.7, applied: 2008 c.17 Sch.3 para.2, SI 2008/1238 Sch.1 para.2, SI 2008/2512 Sch.6 para.2
s.7, varied: 2008 c.17 Sch.2 para.10, 2008 c.18 Sch.6 para.2, Sch.6 para.7, SI 2008/1238 Sch.1 para.4, SI 2008/2512 Art.23, Sch.6 para.4, SI 2008/3163 Art.4
s.8, applied: SI 2008/1238 Art.5, Sch.1 para.2, SI 2008/2512 Sch.6 para.2, SI 2008/3163 Art.6
s.8, disapplied: 2008 c.18 Sch.6 para.11, Sch.6 para.14, SI 2008/2512 Art.31, SI 2008/3163 Art.11
s.8, varied: 2008 c.17 Sch.2 para.11, 2008 c.18 Sch.6 para.2, Sch.6 para.7, SI 2008/1238 Sch.1 para.5, SI 2008/2512 Art.23, Sch.6 para.5, SI 2008/3163 Art.4
s.9, varied: 2008 c.17 Sch.2 para.12, 2008 c.18 Sch.6 para.2, Sch.6 para.7, SI 2008/1238 Sch.1 para.6, SI 2008/2512 Art.23, Sch.6 para.6, SI 2008/3163 Art.4

CAP.

1965–cont.

56. Compulsory Purchase Act 1965–*cont.*
s.10, see *Moto Hospitality Ltd v Secretary of State for Transport* [2007] EWCA Civ 764, [2008] 1 W.L.R. 2822 (CA (Civ Div)), Lord Phillips, L.C.J.; see *Union Railways (North) Ltd v Kent CC* [2008] 2 P. & C.R. 22 (Lands Tr), George Bartlett Q.C. (President)
s.10, applied: 2008 c.17 Sch.3 para.2, 2008 c.18 Sch.2 para.7, Sch.5 para.1, Sch.5 para.4, 2008 c.29 s.152, SI 2008/1238 Art.6, SI 2008/2512 Art.20, Art.27, Art.28
s.10, varied: 2008 c.18 s.45, Sch.6 para.2, 2008 c.29 s.125, SI 2008/2512 Art.23, SI 2008/3163 Art.4
s.11, see *Welford v Transport for London* [2008] R.V.R. 178 (Lands Tr), George Bartlett Q.C. (President)
s.11, applied: 2008 c.18 s.8, s.47, SI 2008/1238 Art.8, SI 2008/1261 Art.32, Sch.7 para.4, SI 2008/2512 Art.32, Sch.10 para.4, SI 2008/3163 Art.12
s.11, varied: 2008 c.17 Sch.2 para.13, 2008 c.18 Sch.6 para.2, Sch.6 para.3, Sch.6 para.7, SI 2008/1238 Sch.1 para.7, SI 2008/1261 Art.29, SI 2008/2512 Art.23, Sch.6 para.7, SI 2008/3163 Art.4
s.12, varied: 2008 c.17 Sch.2 para.13, 2008 c.18 Sch.6 para.2, Sch.6 para.7, SI 2008/1238 Sch.1 para.7, SI 2008/2512 Art.23, Sch.6 para.7, SI 2008/3163 Art.4
s.13, applied: SI 2008/1238 Art.6, SI 2008/2512 Art.27, Art.28
s.13, varied: 2008 c.17 Sch.2 para.13, 2008 c.18 Sch.5 para.6, Sch.6 para.2, Sch.6 para.7, SI 2008/1238 Sch.1 para.7, SI 2008/2512 Art.23, Sch.6 para.7, SI 2008/3163 Art.4
s.14, varied: 2008 c.18 Sch.6 para.2, SI 2008/2512 Art.23, SI 2008/3163 Art.4
s.15, varied: 2008 c.18 Sch.6 para.2, SI 2008/2512 Art.23, SI 2008/3163 Art.4
s.16, varied: 2008 c.18 Sch.6 para.2, SI 2008/2512 Art.23, SI 2008/3163 Art.4
s.17, varied: 2008 c.18 Sch.6 para.2, SI 2008/2512 Art.23, SI 2008/3163 Art.4
s.18, varied: 2008 c.18 Sch.6 para.2, SI 2008/2512 Art.23, SI 2008/3163 Art.4
s.19, varied: 2008 c.18 Sch.6 para.2, SI 2008/2512 Art.23, SI 2008/3163 Art.4
s.20, varied: 2008 c.17 Sch.2 para.14, 2008 c.18 Sch.6 para.2, Sch.6 para.7, SI 2008/1238 Sch.1 para.8, SI 2008/2512 Art.23, Sch.6 para.8, SI 2008/3163 Art.4
s.21, applied: SI 2008/1961 Sch.4 para.8
s.21, varied: 2008 c.18 Sch.6 para.2, SI 2008/2512 Art.23, SI 2008/3163 Art.4
s.22, see *Union Railways (North) Ltd v Kent CC* [2008] 2 P. & C.R. 22 (Lands Tr), George Bartlett Q.C. (President)
s.22, varied: 2008 c.17 Sch.2 para.15, 2008 c.18 Sch.6 para.2, Sch.6 para.3, Sch.6 para.7, SI 2008/1238 Sch.1 para.9, SI

CAP.

1965–cont.

56. Compulsory Purchase Act 1965–*cont.*
s.22, varied:–*cont.*
2008/2512 Art.23, Sch.6 para.9, SI 2008/3163 Art.4
s.23, varied: 2008 c.18 Sch.6 para.2, SI 2008/2512 Art.23, SI 2008/3163 Art.4
s.24, varied: 2008 c.18 Sch.6 para.2, SI 2008/2512 Art.23, SI 2008/3163 Art.4
s.25, varied: 2008 c.18 Sch.6 para.2, SI 2008/2512 Art.23, SI 2008/3163 Art.4
s.26, varied: 2008 c.18 Sch.6 para.2, SI 2008/2512 Art.23, SI 2008/3163 Art.4
s.27, varied: 2008 c.18 Sch.6 para.2, SI 2008/2512 Art.23, SI 2008/3163 Art.4
s.28, varied: 2008 c.18 Sch.6 para.2, SI 2008/2512 Art.23, SI 2008/3163 Art.4
s.29, varied: 2008 c.18 Sch.6 para.2, SI 2008/2512 Art.23, SI 2008/3163 Art.4
s.30, varied: 2008 c.18 Sch.6 para.2, SI 2008/2512 Art.23, SI 2008/3163 Art.4
s.31, disapplied: 2008 c.17 Sch.2 para.17
s.31, varied: 2008 c.18 Sch.6 para.2, SI 2008/2512 Art.23, SI 2008/3163 Art.4
s.32, varied: 2008 c.18 Sch.6 para.2, SI 2008/2512 Art.23, SI 2008/3163 Art.4
Sch.1 para.10, varied: 2008 c.17 Sch.2 para.12, 2008 c.18 Sch.6 para.7, SI 2008/1238 Sch.1 para.6, SI 2008/2512 Sch.6 para.6
Sch.2 para.2, varied: 2008 c.17 Sch.2 para.12, 2008 c.18 Sch.6 para.7, SI 2008/1238 Sch.1 para.6, SI 2008/2512 Sch.6 para.6
Sch.3 para.3, varied: 2008 c.18 Sch.6 para.3, 2008 c.29 s.125, SI 2008/1238 Art.4, SI 2008/1261 Art.29, SI 2008/2512 Art.23
Sch.4, applied: SI 2008/1961 Sch.4 para.8
Sch.4 para.2, varied: 2008 c.17 Sch.2 para.12, 2008 c.18 Sch.6 para.7, SI 2008/1238 Sch.1 para.6, SI 2008/2512 Sch.6 para.6
Sch.4 para.7, varied: 2008 c.17 Sch.2 para.12, 2008 c.18 Sch.6 para.7, SI 2008/1238 Sch.1 para.6, SI 2008/2512 Sch.6 para.6

57. Nuclear Installations Act 1965
applied: 2008 c.29 s.151, 2008 c.32 s.59, SI 2008/3087 Sch.1 para.2, Sch.1 para.6
s.1, amended: 2008 c.32 s.65
s.1, applied: SI 2008/736 Sch.14
s.3, applied: SI 2008/736 Sch.14
s.24A, amended: SI 2008/960 Sch.3

64. Commons Registration Act 1965
applied: SI 2008/1961 Reg.6, Reg.14, Reg.40, Sch.4 para.14
s.1, disapplied: SI 2008/1961 Reg.10
s.2, applied: SI 2008/1961 Reg.5
s.2, disapplied: SI 2008/1961 Reg.10
s.3, disapplied: SI 2008/1961 Reg.10
s.4, disapplied: SI 2008/1961 Reg.10
s.5, disapplied: SI 2008/1961 Reg.10
s.6, applied: SI 2008/1960 Art.3
s.6, disapplied: SI 2008/1961 Reg.10
s.7, applied: SI 2008/1960 Art.3
s.7, disapplied: SI 2008/1961 Reg.10

CAP.

1965–cont.

64. Commons Registration Act 1965–*cont.*
s.8, disapplied: SI 2008/1961 Reg.10
s.9, disapplied: SI 2008/1961 Reg.10
s.10, disapplied: SI 2008/1961 Reg.10
s.11, applied: SI 2008/1961 Reg.10
s.13, see *Betterment Properties (Weymouth) Ltd v Dorset CC* [2008] EWCA Civ 22, [2008] 3 All E.R. 736 (CA (Civ Div)), Laws, L.J.
s.13, applied: SI 2008/1960 Art.3
s.14, see *Betterment Properties (Weymouth) Ltd v Dorset CC* [2008] EWCA Civ 22, [2008] 3 All E.R. 736 (CA (Civ Div)), Laws, L.J.
s.14, applied: SI 2008/1960 Art.3
s.19, applied: SI 2008/1960 Art.3
s.22, see *Betterment Properties (Weymouth) Ltd v Dorset CC* [2008] EWCA Civ 22, [2008] 3 All E.R. 736 (CA (Civ Div)), Laws, L.J.

69. Criminal Procedure (Attendance of Witnesses) Act 1965
s.2, see *R. v Popat (Harish)* [2008] EWCA Crim 1921, Times, September 10, 2008 (CA (Crim Div)), Hughes, L.J.
s.3, see *R. v Popat (Harish)* [2008] EWCA Crim 1921, Times, September 10, 2008 (CA (Crim Div)), Hughes, L.J.

1966

4. Mines (Working Facilities and Support) Act 1966
s.8, see *Bocardo SA v Star Energy UK Onshore Ltd* [2008] EWHC1756 (Ch), [2008] 2 P. & C.R. 23 (Ch D), Peter Smith, J.

13. Universities (Scotland) Act 1966
s.12, amended: SI 2008/948 Sch.1 para 1

18. Finance Act 1966
s.27, repealed: 2008 c.12 Sch.1 Part 8
Sch.6 para.1, repealed: 2008 c.12 Sch.1 Part 8
Sch.6 para.2, repealed: 2008 c.12 Sch.1 Part 8
Sch.6 para.3, repealed: 2008 c.12 Sch.1 Part 8
Sch.6 para.4, repealed: 2008 c.12 Sch.1 Part 8
Sch.6 para.5, repealed: 2008 c.12 Sch.1 Part 8
Sch.6 para.6, repealed: 2008 c.12 Sch.1 Part 8
Sch.6 para.7, repealed: 2008 c.12 Sch.1 Part 8
Sch.6 para.8, repealed: 2008 c.12 Sch.1 Part 8
Sch.6 para.9, repealed: 2008 c.12 Sch.1 Part 8
Sch.6 para.10, repealed: 2008 c.12 Sch.1 Part 8
Sch.6 para.11, repealed: 2008 c.12 Sch.1 Part 8
Sch.6 para.12, repealed: 2008 c.12 Sch.1 Part 8
Sch.6 para.13, repealed: 2008 c.12 Sch.1 Part 8
Sch.6 para.14, repealed: 2008 c.12 Sch.1 Part 8
Sch.6 para.15, repealed: 2008 c.12 Sch.1 Part 8

CAP.

1966–cont.

18. Finance Act 1966–*cont.*
Sch.6 para.16, repealed: 2008 c.12 Sch.1 Part 8
Sch.6 para.17, repealed: 2008 c.12 Sch.1 Part 8
Sch.6 para.18, repealed: 2008 c.12 Sch.1 Part 8
Sch.6 para.19, repealed: 2008 c.12 Sch.1 Part 8
Sch.6 para.20, repealed: 2008 c.12 Sch.1 Part 8
Sch.6 para.21, repealed: 2008 c.12 Sch.1 Part 8
Sch.6 para.22, repealed: 2008 c.12 Sch.1 Part 8
Sch.6 para.23, repealed: 2008 c.12 Sch.1 Part 8
Sch.6 para.24, repealed: 2008 c.12 Sch.1 Part 8
Sch.6 para.25, repealed: 2008 c.12 Sch.1 Part 8
Sch.6 para.26, repealed: 2008 c.12 Sch.1 Part 8
Sch.6 para.27, repealed: 2008 c.12 Sch.1 Part 8

36. Veterinary Surgeons Act 1966
applied: 2008 c.13 Sch.3, SI 2008/2692 Art.2
referred to: 2008 c.13 Sch.6
s.1A, added: SI 2008/1824 Sch.1 para.1
s.2, amended: SI 2008/1824 Sch.1 para.2
s.3, amended: SI 2008/1824 Sch.1 para.3
s.4, amended: SI 2008/1824 Sch.1 para.4
s.5, amended: SI 2008/1824 Sch.1 para.5
s.5A, substituted: SI 2008/1824 Sch.1 para.6
s.5B, substituted: SI 2008/1824 Sch.1 para.7
s.5C, substituted: SI 2008/1824 Sch.1 para.8
s.5D, amended: SI 2008/1824 Sch.1 para.9
s.6, amended: SI 2008/1824 Sch.1 para.10
s.6, applied: SI 2008/2501 Sch.1
s.6, enabling: SI 2008/2501
s.7A, added: SI 2008/1824 Sch.1 para.11
s.10, amended: SI 2008/1824 Sch.1 para.12
s.11, amended: SI 2008/1824 Sch.1 para.13
s.11, enabling: SI 2008/2933
s.16, amended: SI 2008/1824 Sch.1 para.14
s.25, applied: SI 2008/2501, SI 2008/2933
s.27, amended: SI 2008/1824 Sch.1 para.15
Sch.1A, substituted: SI 2008/1824 Sch.1 para.16
Sch.1A para.1, substituted: SI 2008/1824 Sch.1 para.16
Sch.1A para.2, substituted: SI 2008/1824 Sch.1 para.16
Sch.1A para.3, substituted: SI 2008/1824 Sch.1 para.16
Sch.1A para.4, substituted: SI 2008/1824 Sch.1 para.16
Sch.1A para.5, substituted: SI 2008/1824 Sch.1 para.16

CAP.

1966–cont.

36. Veterinary Surgeons Act 1966–*cont.*
Sch.1A para.6, substituted: SI 2008/1824 Sch.1 para.16
Sch.1B para.1, added: SI 2008/1824 Sch.1 para.17
Sch.1B para.2, added: SI 2008/1824 Sch.1 para.17
Sch.1B para.3, added: SI 2008/1824 Sch.1 para.17
Sch.1B para.4, added: SI 2008/1824 Sch.1 para.17
Sch.1B para.5, added: SI 2008/1824 Sch.1 para.17
Sch.1B para.6, added: SI 2008/1824 Sch.1 para.17
Sch.1B para.7, added: SI 2008/1824 Sch.1 para.17
Sch.1B para.8, added: SI 2008/1824 Sch.1 para.17
Sch.3 Part 1 para.6, amended: SI 2008/1824 Sch.1 para.18

38. Sea Fisheries Regulation Act 1966
applied: 2008 c.13 Sch.3
referred to: 2008 c.13 Sch.6
s.5, applied: 2008 c.13 Sch.7

45. Armed Forces Act 1966
s.2, enabling: SI 2008/1849

51. Local Government (Scotland) Act 1966
s.24, applied: SSI 2008/85 Reg.3
s.24, enabling: SSI 2008/83
s.24A, applied: SSI 2008/85 Reg.3
s.24A, enabling: SSI 2008/83
s.25A, applied: SSI 2008/85 Reg.5

1967

7. Misrepresentation Act 1967
see *Trident Turboprop (Dublin) Ltd v First Flight Couriers Ltd* [2008] EWHC 1686 (Comm), [2008] 2 Lloyd's Rep. 581 (QBD (Comm)), Aikens, J.
s.3, see *Trident Turboprop (Dublin) Ltd v First Flight Couriers Ltd* [2008] EWHC 1686 (Comm), [2008] 2 Lloyd's Rep. 581 (QBD (Comm)), Aikens, J.

8. Plant Health Act 1967
applied: 2008 c.13 Sch.3
s.2, enabling: SI 2008/644, SI 2008/2411, SI 2008/2765, SI 2008/2781, SI 2008/2913, SSI 2008/299, SSI 2008/300, SSI 2008/350
s.3, applied: 2008 c.13 Sch.7
s.3, enabling: SI 2008/644, SI 2008/2411, SI 2008/2765, SI 2008/2781, SI 2008/2913, SSI 2008/299, SSI 2008/300, SSI 2008/350
s.4, enabling: SSI 2008/299, SSI 2008/300, SSI 2008/350

9. General Rate Act 1967
s.48, applied: SI 2008/794 Sch.6 para.7

CAP.

1967–cont.

9. General Rate Act 1967–*cont.*
Sch.1, applied: SI 2008/386 Reg.6, SI 2008/2499 Reg.6

10. Forestry Act 1967
referred to: SSI 2008/263 Sch.2
s.1, applied: SSI 2008/263 Sch.2
s.15, amended: 2008 c.29 Sch.8 para.2
s.18, amended: 2008 c.29 Sch.8 para.3
s.21, amended: 2008 c.29 Sch.8 para.4
s.35, amended: 2008 c.29 Sch.8 para.5
Sch.3 para.2, amended: 2008 c.29 Sch.8 para.6, Sch.13
Sch.3 para.2A, added: 2008 c.29 Sch.8 para.6
Sch.3 para.3, amended: 2008 c.29 Sch.8 para.6
Sch.3 para.3A, added: 2008 c.29 Sch.8 para.6

13. Parliamentary Commissioner Act 1967
see *R. (on the application of Bradley) v Secretary of State for Work and Pensions* [2008] EWCA Civ 36, [2008] 3 W.L.R. 1059 (CA (Civ Div)), Wall, L.J.
s.4, enabling: SI 2008/3115
s.5, see *R. (on the application of Bradley) v Secretary of State for Work and Pensions* [2008] EWCA Civ 36, [2008] 3 W.L.R. 1059 (CA (Civ Div)), Wall, L.J.
s.5, enabling: SI 2008/3115
s.11B, repealed (in part): SI 2008/2833 Sch.3 para.24
Sch.2, amended: 2008 c.6 Sch.1 para.25, 2008 c.13 Sch.1 para.18, 2008 c.14 Sch.5 para.56, Sch.14 para.2, Sch.15 Part 1, Sch.15 Part 6, Sch.15 Part 7, 2008 c.17 Sch.8 para.4, Sch.9 para.2, Sch.16, 2008 c.27 Sch.1 para.29, 2008 c.29 Sch.1 para.24, SI 2008/576 Sch.5 para.1, Sch.5 para.7, SI 2008/960 Sch.3
Sch.2, substituted: SI 2008/3115 Sch.1
Sch.3 para.6C, repealed: SI 2008/2833 Sch.3 para.25
Sch.3 para.8, amended: SI 2008/3115 Art.3, Art.4
Sch.4, amended: SI 2008/2833 Sch.3 para.26, SI 2008/3115 Art.5

18. Criminal Law Act (Northern Ireland) 1967
s.3, referred to: 2008 c.4 s.76
s.4, amended: SI 2008/1769 Art.79

22. Agriculture Act 1967
applied: 2008 c.13 Sch.3
s.1, repealed: SI 2008/576 Sch.5 para.7
s.1A, repealed: SI 2008/576 Sch.5 para.7
s.2, repealed: SI 2008/576 Sch.5 para.7
s.3, repealed: SI 2008/576 Sch.5 para.7
s.4, repealed: SI 2008/576 Sch.5 para.7
s.5, repealed: SI 2008/576 Sch.5 para.7
s.6, repealed: SI 2008/576 Sch.5 para.7
s.7, repealed: SI 2008/576 Sch.5 para.7
s.8, repealed: SI 2008/576 Sch.5 para.7

CAP.

1967–cont.

22. Agriculture Act 1967–*cont.*
s.9, repealed: SI 2008/576 Sch.5 para.7
s.10, repealed: SI 2008/576 Sch.5 para.7
s.11, repealed: SI 2008/576 Sch.5 para.7
s.12, repealed: SI 2008/576 Sch.5 para.7
s.13, repealed: SI 2008/576 Sch.5 para.7
s.14, referred to: 2008 c.13 Sch.6
s.14, repealed: SI 2008/576 Sch.5 para.7
s.15, repealed: SI 2008/576 Sch.5 para.7
s.16, repealed: SI 2008/576 Sch.5 para.7
s.17, repealed: SI 2008/576 Sch.5 para.7
s.18, repealed: SI 2008/576 Sch.5 para.7
s.19, amended: SI 2008/948 Sch.1 para.1
s.19, repealed: SI 2008/576 Sch.5 para.7
s.20, repealed: SI 2008/576 Sch.5 para.7
s.21, repealed: SI 2008/576 Sch.5 para.7
s.22, repealed: SI 2008/576 Sch.5 para.7
s.23, repealed: SI 2008/576 Sch.5 para.7
s.24, repealed: SI 2008/576 Sch.5 para.7
s.25, repealed: SI 2008/576 Sch.5 para.7
Sch.1 Part I para.1, repealed: SI 2008/576 Sch.5 para.7
Sch.1 Part I para.2, repealed: SI 2008/576 Sch.5 para.7
Sch.1 Part I para.3, repealed: SI 2008/576 Sch.5 para.7
Sch.1 Part I para.4, repealed: SI 2008/576 Sch.5 para.7
Sch.1 Part I para.5, repealed: SI 2008/576 Sch.5 para.7
Sch.1 Part I para.6, repealed: SI 2008/576 Sch.5 para.7
Sch.1 Part I para.7, repealed: SI 2008/576 Sch.5 para.7
Sch.1 Part I para.8, repealed: SI 2008/576 Sch.5 para.7
Sch.1 Part I para.9, repealed: SI 2008/576 Sch.5 para.7
Sch.1 Part I para.10, repealed: SI 2008/576 Sch.5 para.7
Sch.1 Part I para.10A, repealed: SI 2008/576 Sch.5 para.7
Sch.1 Part I para.10B, repealed: SI 2008/576 Sch.5 para.7
Sch.1 Part I para.11, repealed: SI 2008/576 Sch.5 para.7
Sch.1 Part I para.12, repealed: SI 2008/576 Sch.5 para.7
Sch.1 Part I para.13, repealed: SI 2008/576 Sch.5 para.7
Sch.1 Part I para.14, repealed: SI 2008/576 Sch.5 para.7
Sch.1 Part I para.15, repealed: SI 2008/576 Sch.5 para.7
Sch.1 Part I para.16, repealed: SI 2008/576 Sch.5 para.7
Sch.1 Part I para.17, repealed: SI 2008/576 Sch.5 para.7
Sch.1 Part I para.18, repealed: SI 2008/576 Sch.5 para.7

CAP.

1967–cont.

22. Agriculture Act 1967–*cont.*
Sch.1 Part I para.19, repealed: SI 2008/576 Sch.5 para.7
Sch.1 Part I para.20, repealed: SI 2008/576 Sch.5 para.7
Sch.1 Part I para.21, repealed: SI 2008/576 Sch.5 para.7
Sch.1 Part I para.22, repealed: SI 2008/576 Sch.5 para.7
Sch.1 Part II para.1, repealed: SI 2008/576 Sch.5 para.7
Sch.1 Part II para.2, repealed: SI 2008/576 Sch.5 para.7
Sch.1 Part II para.3, repealed: SI 2008/576 Sch.5 para.7
Sch.1 Part II para.4, repealed: SI 2008/576 Sch.5 para.7
Sch.1 Part II para.5, repealed: SI 2008/576 Sch.5 para.7
Sch.1 Part II para.6, repealed: SI 2008/576 Sch.5 para.7
Sch.1 Part II para.7, repealed: SI 2008/576 Sch.5 para.7
Sch.1 Part II para.8, repealed: SI 2008/576 Sch.5 para.7
Sch.1 Part II para.9, repealed: SI 2008/576 Sch.5 para.7
Sch.1 Part IIA, repealed: SI 2008/576 Sch.5 para.7
Sch.1 Part II para.10, repealed: SI 2008/576 Sch.5 para.7
Sch.1 Part III para.1, repealed: SI 2008/576 Sch.5 para.7
Sch.1 Part III para.2, repealed: SI 2008/576 Sch.5 para.7
Sch.1 Part III para.3, repealed: SI 2008/576 Sch.5 para.7
Sch.2 para.1, repealed: SI 2008/576 Sch.5 para.7
Sch.2 para.2, repealed: SI 2008/576 Sch.5 para.7
Sch.2 para.3, repealed: SI 2008/576 Sch.5 para.7
Sch.2 para.4, repealed: SI 2008/576 Sch.5 para.7
Sch.2 para.5, repealed: SI 2008/576 Sch.5 para.7
Sch.2 para.6, repealed: SI 2008/576 Sch.5 para.7
Sch.2 para.7, repealed: SI 2008/576 Sch.5 para.7
Sch.2 para.8, repealed: SI 2008/576 Sch.5 para.7

24. Slaughter of Poultry Act 1967
applied: 2008 c.13 Sch.3

28. Superannuation (Miscellaneous Provisions) Act 1967
s.7, applied: SSI 2008/224 Reg.1

50. Farm and Garden Chemicals Act 1967
applied: 2008 c.13 Sch.3

CAP.

1967–cont.

58. Criminal Law Act 1967
s.3, referred to: 2008 c.4 s.76
s.4, see *R. v Khatab (Amar)* [2008] EWCA Crim 541, [2008] 2 Cr. App. R. (S.) 94 (CA (Crim Div)), Dyson, L.J.
s.6, see *R. v James (Liam Martin)* [2007] EWCA Crim 1906, [2008] 1 Cr. App. R. (S.) 44 (CA (Crim Div)), Longmore, L.J.
s.10, applied: SI 2008/648 Sch.1

69. Civic Amenities Act 1967
s.15, repealed: 2008 c.12 Sch.1 Part 9
s.30, repealed (in part): 2008 c.12 Sch.1 Part 9
s.32, repealed (in part): 2008 c.12 Sch.1 Part 9

74. Greenwich Hospital Act 1967
s.1, repealed (in part): 2008 c.12 Sch.1 Part 1
s.2, repealed: 2008 c.12 Sch.1 Part 1

76. Road Traffic Regulation Act 1967
s.12, see *DPP v Wells* [2007] EWHC 3259 (Admin), [2008] R.T.R. 23 (DC), Maurice Kay, L.J.
s.78A, see *DPP v Wells* [2007] EWHC 3259 (Admin), [2008] R.T.R. 23 (DC), Maurice Kay, L.J.

77. Police (Scotland) Act 1967
s.3, enabling: SSI 2008/117
s.7, enabling: SSI 2008/117
s.13, applied: 2008 c.28 s.88
s.16, applied: SSI 2008/117 Reg.7
s.16, enabling: SSI 2008/117
s.26, applied: SSI 2008/117, SSI 2008/117 Reg.15
s.26, enabling: SSI 2008/117
s.32, enabling: SSI 2008/20, SSI 2008/46
s.41, see *McDonagh v Pattison* 2008 J.C. 125 (HCJ), Lord Osborne
s.48, enabling: SSI 2008/117

80. Criminal Justice Act 1967
s.67, applied: 2008 c.4 Sch.6 para.1
s.92, repealed (in part): 2008 asp 5 Sch.3 Part 1

83. Sea Fisheries (Shellfish) Act 1967
referred to: 2008 c.13 Sch.6
s.1, enabling: SI 2008/1472
s.3, applied: SI 2008/1472 Art.4, Sch.1 para.3, Sch.1 para.5
s.3, enabling: SI 2008/1472, SSI 2008/10
s.4, applied: SI 2008/1472 Sch.2
s.4, enabling: SI 2008/1472
s.14, applied: SSI 2008/101 Sch.1 Part 1
s.17, applied: SSI 2008/101 Sch.1 Part 1
Sch.1, enabling: SI 2008/1472
Sch.1 para.1, applied: SI 2008/1472
Sch.1 para.2, applied: SI 2008/1472
Sch.1 para.3, applied: SI 2008/1472
Sch.1 para.4, applied: SI 2008/1472

84. Sea Fish (Conservation) Act 1967
referred to: 2008 c.13 Sch.6
s.1, applied: SSI 2008/101 Sch.1 Part 1
s.3, applied: SI 2008/1811 Art.4, SSI 2008/101 Sch.1 Part 1

CAP.

1967–cont.

84. Sea Fish (Conservation) Act 1967– *cont.*

s.3, enabling: SI 2008/1811, SI 2008/3144, SSI 2008/10
s.4, applied: SSI 2008/101 Sch.1 Part 1
s.4A, applied: SSI 2008/101 Sch.1 Part 1
s.5, applied: SI 2008/691 Art.6, SI 2008/1438 Art.6, SSI 2008/29 Art.4, SSI 2008/101 Sch.1 Part 1
s.5, enabling: SI 2008/691, SI 2008/1438, SI 2008/1584, SI 2008/2360, SSI 2008/29
s.5A, enabling: SI 2008/1584, SI 2008/2360
s.6, applied: SI 2008/691 Art.6, SI 2008/1438 Art.6, SSI 2008/101 Sch.1 Part 1
s.6, enabling: SI 2008/691, SI 2008/1438
s.7, applied: SSI 2008/101 Sch.1 Part 1
s.15, enabling: SI 2008/691, SI 2008/1438, SI 2008/1584, SI 2008/1811, SI 2008/2360, SSI 2008/29

87. Abortion Act 1967

s.2, enabling: SI 2008/735, SI 2008/1338

88. Leasehold Reform Act 1967

see *Holding and Management (Solitaire) Ltd, Re* [2008] L. & T.R. 16 (Lands Tr), George Bartlett Q.C. (President)
s.1, amended: 2008 c.17 s.300, Sch.16
s.1A, repealed (in part): 2008 c.17 s.300, Sch.16
s.1AA, repealed: 2008 c.17 s.300, Sch.16
s.2, see *Boss Holdings Ltd v Grosvenor West End Properties Ltd* [2008] UKHL 5, [2008] 1 W.L.R. 289 (HL), Lord Hoffmann
s.4A, repealed: 2008 c.17 s.300
s.9, see *Pitts v Earl Cadogan* [2007] EWCA Civ 1280, [2008] R.V.R. 244 (CA (Civ Div)), Carnwath, L.J.
s.28, amended: 2008 c.17 Sch.8 para.6
s.29, amended: 2008 c.17 Sch.8 para.7
s.30, amended: 2008 c.17 Sch.8 para.8
s.33, amended: 2008 c.17 Sch.8 para.9
s.37, amended: 2008 c.17 Sch.8 para.10
Sch.4A, amended: 2008 c.17 s.301
Sch.4 Part II para.4, amended: 2008 c.17 Sch.8 para.11
Sch.4 Part II para.5, amended: 2008 c.17 Sch.8 para.11
Sch.4 Part II para.6, amended: 2008 c.17 Sch.8 para.11
Sch.4A para.2, amended: 2008 c.17 Sch.8 para.12
Sch.4A para.3A, amended: 2008 c.17 s.301
Sch.4A para.4A, added: 2008 c.17 s.302
Sch.4A para.5, amended: 2008 c.17 s.302
Sch.4A para.7, added: 2008 c.17 s.302

1968

xxxii. Port of London Act 1968

s.67, see *Port of London Authority v Transport for London* [2008] R.V.R. 93 (Lands Tr), PR Francis FRICS

CAP.

1968–cont.

4. Erskine Bridge Tolls Act 1968

repealed: 2008 asp 1 Sch.2 Part 1

13. National Loans Act 1968

applied: 2008 c.9 s.157
s.1, applied: 2008 c.9 s.159
s.4, applied: SI 2008/3004 Art.2
s.4, enabling: SI 2008/3004
s.5, applied: 2008 c.30 Sch.1 para.18
Sch.1, amended: 2008 c.17 Sch.8 para.13, Sch.16

14. Public Expenditure and Receipts Act 1968

s.5, applied: SI 2008/678 Sch.1 para.8
s.5, enabling: SI 2008/1166, SSI 2008/168
Sch.3, amended: SI 2008/678 Sch.2 para.8
Sch.3 para.1, referred to: SI 2008/678 Sch.1 para.8
Sch.3 para.2, referred to: SI 2008/678 Sch.1 para.8
Sch.3 para.3, applied: SI 2008/1166, SSI 2008/168

16. New Towns (Scotland) Act 1968

s.39, amended: SI 2008/948 Sch.1 para.1

19. Criminal Appeal Act 1968

see *R. v Adams (Terrance)* [2008] EWCA Crim 914, [2008] 4 All E.R. 574 (CA (Crim Div)), Latham, L.J.; see *R. v Reynolds (Michael Edwin)* [2007] EWCA Crim 538, [2008] 1 W.L.R. 1075 (CA (Crim Div)), Latham, L.J.
referred to: 2008 c.4 s.47
Part I, applied: 2008 c.4 Sch.27 para.14, SI 2008/1586 Sch.2 para.4, Sch.2 para.5, Sch.2 para.6
Part II, applied: SI 2008/1586 Sch.2 para.7
s.1, amended: 2008 c.4 Sch.8 para.2
s.4, amended: 2008 c.4 Sch.8 para.6, Sch.28 Part 3
s.6, amended: 2008 c.4 Sch.8 para.7, Sch.28 Part 3
s.6, repealed (in part): 2008 c.4 Sch.8 para.7, Sch.28 Part 3
s.10, amended: 2008 c.4 Sch.4 para.4
s.11, see *R. (on the application of Faithfull) v Ipswich Crown Court* [2007] EWHC 2763 (Admin), [2008] 1 W.L.R. 1636 (DC), Richards, L.J.; see *R. v Reynolds (Michael Edwin)* [2007] EWCA Crim 538, [2008] 1 W.L.R. 1075 (CA (Crim Div)), Latham, L.J.
s.11, amended: 2008 c.4 Sch.8 para.3
s.11, repealed (in part): 2008 c.4 Sch.8 para.7, Sch.28 Part 3
s.12, amended: 2008 c.4 Sch.8 para.4
s.14, amended: 2008 c.4 Sch.8 para.7, Sch.28 Part 3
s.14, repealed (in part): 2008 c.4 Sch.8 para.7, Sch.28 Part 3
s.15, amended: 2008 c.4 Sch.8 para.5
s.16B, repealed (in part): 2008 c.4 Sch.8 para.7, Sch.28 Part 3
s.16C, added: 2008 c.4 s.42
s.23, amended: 2008 c.4 Sch.8 para.10

CAP.

1968–cont.

19. Criminal Appeal Act 1968–*cont.*
s.30A, added: 2008 c.4 Sch.8 para.8
s.31, amended: 2008 c.4 Sch.8 para.9, Sch.8 para.11, Sch.28 Part 3
s.31C, repealed (in part): 2008 c.4 Sch.28 Part 3
s.33, referred to: SI 2008/1863 Art.43
s.37, amended: 2008 c.4 Sch.8 para.13, SI 2008/1587 Art.5
s.37, varied: SI 2008/1587 Art.5
s.37A, varied: SI 2008/1900 Sch.1 para.2
Sch.2 para.2, amended: 2008 c.4 s.22

20. Courts-Martial (Appeals) Act 1968
s.16, repealed (in part): 2008 c.4 Sch.25 para.3, Sch.28 Part 3
s.20, varied: SI 2008/1900 Sch.1 para.3
s.25B, repealed (in part): 2008 c.4 Sch.25 para.4, Sch.28 Part 3
s.25C, added: 2008 c.4 Sch.25 para.2
s.28, amended: 2008 c.4 Sch.25 para.7
s.35A, added: 2008 c.4 Sch.25 para.5
s.36, amended: 2008 c.4 Sch.25 para.6
s.36C, repealed (in part): 2008 c.4 Sch.25 para.8, Sch.28 Part 3
s.43, amended: 2008 c.4 Sch.25 para.9, Sch.28 Part 3
s.43A, varied: SI 2008/1900 Sch.1 para.2, Sch.1 para.3

27. Firearms Act 1968
applied: 2008 c.13 Sch.3, SI 2008/736 Sch.8 Part 9, SI 2008/3231 Art.16
s.1, see *Glasgow Housing Association Ltd v Fisher* 2008 S.L.T. (Sh Ct) 142 (Sh Ct (Glasgow)), Sheriff Principal J A Taylor
s.5, see *Glasgow Housing Association Ltd v Fisher* 2008 S.L.T. (Sh Ct) 142 (Sh Ct (Glasgow)), Sheriff Principal J A Taylor; see *R. v Deyemi (Danny)* [2007] EWCA Crim 2060, [2008] 1 Cr. App. R. 25 (CA (Crim Div)), Latham, L.J.
s.16A, see *Attorney General's Reference (No.54 of 2007), Re* [2007] EWCA Crim 1655, [2008] 1 Cr. App. R. (S.) 62 (CA (Crim Div)), Hooper, L.J.
s.17, see *R. v Sarwar (Sufyan)* [2007] EWCA Crim 3140, [2008] 2 Cr. App. R. (S.) 38 (CA (Crim Div)), Hooper, L.J.
s.21, amended: 2008 c.4 Sch.4 para.6
s.32A, applied: SI 2008/3231 Art.15
s.51, see *Attorney General's Reference (No.35 of 2007), Re* [2007] EWCA Crim 1523, [2008] 1 Cr. App. R. (S.) 26 (CA (Crim Div)), Scott Baker, L.J.
s.51A, see *R. v Beard (Thomas Howard)* [2007] EWCA Crim 3168, [2008] 2 Cr. App. R. (S.) 41 (CA (Crim Div)), Richards, L.J.
s.52, amended: 2008 c.4 Sch.4 para.7
Sch.1, see *R. v Sarwar (Sufyan)* [2007] EWCA Crim 3140, [2008] 2 Cr. App. R. (S.) 38 (CA (Crim Div)), Hooper, L.J.

CAP.

1968–cont.

29. Trade Descriptions Act 1968
applied: 2008 c.13 Sch.3
referred to: 2008 c.13 Sch.6
s.1, amended: SI 2008/1277 Sch.2 para.9
s.1, repealed (in part): SI 2008/1277 Sch.2 para.8, Sch.4 Part 1
s.5, applied: SI 2008/1277 Sch.3 para.1
s.5, repealed: SI 2008/1277 Sch.2 para.8, Sch.4 Part 1
s.6, repealed: SI 2008/1277 Sch.2 para.8, Sch.4 Part 1
s.7, repealed: SI 2008/1277 Sch.2 para.8, Sch.4 Part 1
s.8, repealed: SI 2008/1277 Sch.2 para.8, Sch.4 Part 1
s.9, repealed: SI 2008/1277 Sch.2 para.8, Sch.4 Part 1
s.10, repealed: SI 2008/1277 Sch.2 para.8, Sch.4 Part 1
s.12, amended: SI 2008/1277 Sch.2 para.10
s.13, repealed: SI 2008/1277 Sch.2 para.8, Sch.4 Part 1
s.14, repealed: SI 2008/1277 Sch.2 para.8, Sch.4 Part 1
s.15, repealed: SI 2008/1277 Sch.2 para.8, Sch.4 Part 1
s.19, applied: SI 2008/1277 Sch.3 para.2
s.19, repealed (in part): SI 2008/1277 Sch.4 Part 1
s.21, repealed (in part): SI 2008/1277 Sch.2 para.8, Sch.4 Part 1
s.22, repealed: SI 2008/1277 Sch.2 para.8, Sch.4 Part 1
s.24, referred to: SI 2008/1277 Sch.3 para.3
s.24, repealed (in part): SI 2008/1277 Sch.4 Part 1
s.32, repealed: SI 2008/1277 Sch.2 para.8, Sch.4 Part 1
s.37, repealed: SI 2008/1277 Sch.2 para.8, Sch.4 Part 1
s.38, amended: SI 2008/1277 Sch.2 para.11
s.39, amended: SI 2008/1277 Sch.2 para.12
s.39, referred to: SI 2008/1277 Sch.3 para.4
s.39, repealed (in part): SI 2008/1277 Sch.4 Part 1

34. Agriculture (Miscellaneous Provisions) Act 1968
applied: 2008 c.13 Sch.3

41. Countryside Act 1968
applied: 2008 c.13 Sch.3
s.6, applied: SI 2008/1961 Sch.4 para.8
s.6, referred to: SI 2008/1961 Sch.4 para.8
s.9, applied: SI 2008/1961 Sch.4 para.8
Sch.2, applied: SI 2008/1961 Sch.4 para.8

44. Finance Act 1968
s.43, repealed: 2008 c.12 Sch.1 Part 8
s.61, repealed (in part): 2008 c.12 Sch.1 Part 8

46. Health Services and Public Health Act 1968
s.62, repealed (in part): 2008 asp 5 Sch.3 Part 1

CAP.

1968–cont.

46. Health Services and Public Health Act 1968–*cont.*
s.63, applied: SI 2008/529 Sch.4 para.11, Sch.4 para.12, SI 2008/794 Reg.132, SI 2008/1273 Sch.5 para.8, Sch.5 para.11, Sch.6 para.7
s.64, amended: 2008 c.4 Sch.4 para.9
s.65, amended: 2008 c.4 Sch.4 para.10
s.71, repealed: 2008 asp 5 Sch.3 Part 1
s.71A, repealed: 2008 asp 5 Sch.3 Part 1
s.72, repealed: 2008 asp 5 Sch.3 Part 1
s.73, repealed: 2008 asp 5 Sch.3 Part 1

47. Sewerage (Scotland) Act 1968
referred to: SSI 2008/263 Sch.2
Sch.1 para.2, repealed: 2008 asp 5 Sch.3 Part 1

48. International Organisations Act 1968
s.1, enabling: SI 2008/3124
s.10, applied: SI 2008/3124

49. Social Work (Scotland) Act 1968
referred to: SI 2008/794 Sch.8 para.56
s.12, applied: SI 2008/794 Sch.8 para.30, Sch.9 para.22
s.12B, applied: SI 2008/794 Sch.8 para.53, Sch.9 para.56
s.14, applied: SSI 2008/228 Reg.4
s.86, amended: 2008 c.4 Sch.4 para.12
s.87, amended: 2008 c.14 s.147
s.87, applied: SSI 2008/13, SSI 2008/14, SSI 2008/14 Reg.2
s.94, amended: 2008 c.4 Sch.4 para.13, Sch.28 Part 1

50. Hearing Aid Council Act 1968
repealed: 2008 c.14 s.123, Sch.15 Part 2

52. Caravan Sites Act 1968
see *Doherty v Birmingham City Council* [2008] UKHL 57, [2008] 3 W.L.R. 636 (HL), Lord Hope of Craighead
s.2, see *Smith v Buckland* [2007] EWCA Civ 1318, [2008] 1 W.L.R. 661 (CA (Civ Div)), Mummery, L.J.
s.4, see *Smith v Buckland* [2007] EWCA Civ 1318, [2008] 1 W.L.R. 661 (CA (Civ Div)), Mummery, L.J.

54. Theatres Act 1968
applied: 2008 c.13 Sch.3
s.2, see *R. (on the application of Green) v City of Westminster Magistrates' Court* [2007] EWHC 2785 (Admin), [2008] E.M.L.R. 15 (DC), Hughes, L.J.

55. Friendly and Industrial and Provident Societies Act 1968
applied: 2008 c.17 s.271
referred to: SI 2008/565 Reg.14, Sch.1 para.1
s.3, disapplied: SI 2008/565 Sch.1 para.2
s.3A, varied: SI 2008/565 Sch.1 para.3
s.4, disapplied: 2008 c.17 s.134
s.4A, referred to: 2008 c.17 s.134
s.4A, repealed (in part): SI 2008/565 Reg.15
s.4A, varied: SI 2008/565 Sch.1 para.4
s.5, varied: SI 2008/565 Sch.1 para.5

CAP.

1968–cont.

55. Friendly and Industrial and Provident Societies Act 1968–*cont.*
s.5A, varied: SI 2008/565 Sch.1 para.6
s.7, amended: SI 2008/948 Sch.1 para.1
s.7, varied: SI 2008/565 Sch.1 para.7
s.8, amended: SI 2008/948 Sch.1 para.5
s.8, varied: SI 2008/565 Sch.1 para.8
s.9, varied: SI 2008/565 Sch.1 para.9
s.9A, varied: 2008 c.17 s.134, SI 2008/565 Sch.1 para.10
s.9B, varied: SI 2008/565 Sch.1 para.10
s.9C, varied: SI 2008/565 Sch.1 para.10
s.10, varied: SI 2008/565 Sch.1 para.11
s.11, varied: SI 2008/565 Sch.1 para.12
s.13, varied: SI 2008/565 Sch.1 para.13
s.14, varied: SI 2008/565 Sch.1 para.14
s.15, varied: SI 2008/565 Sch.1 para.15
s.18, varied: SI 2008/565 Sch.1 para.16
s.19, varied: SI 2008/565 Sch.1 para.17
s.21, varied: SI 2008/565 Sch.1 para.18

59. Hovercraft Act 1968
applied: SSI 2008/182 Art.28
s.1, applied: 2008 c.13 Sch.7

60. Theft Act 1968
applied: 2008 c.13 Sch.3

65. Gaming Act 1968
s.8, see *R. v Kelly (Derek)* [2008] EWCA Crim 137, [2008] 2 All E.R. 840 (CA (Crim Div)), Thomas, L.J.
s.21, see *Rank Group Ltd v Revenue and Customs Commissioners* [2008] 3 C.M.L.R. 31 (V&DTr (London)), Theodore Wallace (Chairman)
s.26, see *Rank Group Ltd v Revenue and Customs Commissioners* [2008] 3 C.M.L.R. 31 (V&DTr (London)), Theodore Wallace (Chairman)
s.31, see *Rank Group Ltd v Revenue and Customs Commissioners* [2008] 3 C.M.L.R. 31 (V&DTr (London)), Theodore Wallace (Chairman)
s.34, see *Rank Group Ltd v Revenue and Customs Commissioners* [2008] 3 C.M.L.R. 31 (V&DTr (London)), Theodore Wallace (Chairman)
s.52, see *R. v Kelly (Derek)* [2008] EWCA Crim 137, [2008] 2 All E.R. 840 (CA (Crim Div)), Thomas, L.J.

67. Medicines Act 1968
applied: 2008 c.13 Sch.3
referred to: 2008 c.13 Sch.6
s.2A, applied: SI 2008/552 Sch.5 para.2, Sch.5 para.4
s.4, applied: SI 2008/552 Sch.5 para.2, Sch.5 para.4
s.7, applied: SI 2008/944 Art.5, SI 2008/1270 Art.5
s.8, amended: SI 2008/3097 Reg.4
s.30, applied: SI 2008/552 Reg.18
s.44, applied: SI 2008/552 Sch.5 para.4
s.50, applied: SI 2008/552 Reg.14

CAP.

1968–cont.

67. Medicines Act 1968–*cont.*
s.51, applied: SI 2008/552 Reg.5, Sch.1 para.9
s.57, enabling: SI 2008/1161
s.58, applied: SI 2008/464, SI 2008/1161, SI 2008/1692 Reg.2, Reg.3, Reg.5
s.58, disapplied: SI 2008/1692 Reg.6
s.58, enabling: SI 2008/464, SI 2008/1161
s.62, applied: SI 2008/548
s.62, enabling: SI 2008/548
s.64, see *R. v Guy's and St Thomas' NHS Trust* [2008] EWCA Crim 2187, [2008] 4 All E.R. 1174 (CA (Crim Div)), Toulson, L.J.
s.66, enabling: SI 2008/1162
s.72A, enabling: SI 2008/2789
s.75, enabling: SI 2008/2946
s.76, enabling: SI 2008/2946
s.87, enabling: SI 2008/1162
s.91, applied: 2008 c.13 Sch.7
s.91, enabling: SI 2008/1162
s.95, applied: 2008 c.13 Sch.7
s.118, amended: SSI 2008/339 Art.4
s.129, applied: SI 2008/464, SI 2008/548, SI 2008/1161, SI 2008/1162, SI 2008/2789, SI 2008/2946
s.129, enabling: SI 2008/464, SI 2008/1161, SI 2008/1162, SI 2008/2789, SI 2008/2946
s.132, amended: SI 2008/3097 Reg.4

73. Transport Act 1968
see *R. v Livingston (Lee Craig)* [2008] EWCA Crim 789, [2008] 2 Cr. App. R. (S.) 96 (CA (Crim Div)), Thomas, L.J.
applied: SI 2008/230 Sch.1 para.2
Part II, amended: 2008 c.26 Sch.4 para.11
Part VI, referred to: 2008 c.13 Sch.6
s.9, amended: 2008 c.26 s.98, Sch.4 para.2, Sch.4 para.11, Sch.7 Part 4
s.9, applied: 2008 c.26 s.77, s.99, SSI 2008/228 Sch.2
s.9, substituted: 2008 c.26 Sch.4 para.2
s.9A, amended: 2008 c.26 s.10, s.67, Sch.4 para.3, Sch.4 para.11, Sch.7 Part 1
s.9A, repealed (in part): 2008 c.26 Sch.7 Part 1
s.9A, substituted: 2008 c.26 Sch.4 para.3
s.9B, amended: 2008 c.26 Sch.4 para.11
s.10, amended: 2008 c.26 s.66, Sch.4 para.4, Sch.4 para.11, Sch.7 Part 3
s.10, applied: 2008 c.26 s.66
s.10, repealed (in part): 2008 c.26 s.66, Sch.7 Part 3
s.11, amended: 2008 c.26 Sch.4 para.11
s.12, amended: 2008 c.26 Sch.4 para.5, Sch.4 para.11
s.13, amended: 2008 c.26 Sch.4 para.11
s.13A, amended: 2008 c.26 Sch.4 para.11
s.14, amended: 2008 c.26 Sch.4 para.6, Sch.4 para.11, SI 2008/948 Sch.1 para.1
s.15, amended: 2008 c.26 Sch.4 para.7, Sch.4 para.11

CAP.

1968–cont.

73. Transport Act 1968–*cont.*
s.15A, amended: 2008 c.26 Sch.4 para.11
s.16, amended: 2008 c.26 Sch.4 para.8, Sch.4 para.11
s.17, amended: 2008 c.26 Sch.4 para.11
s.18, amended: 2008 c.26 Sch.4 para.11
s.19, amended: 2008 c.26 Sch.4 para.11
s.20, amended: 2008 c.26 Sch.4 para.9, Sch.4 para.11
s.21, amended: 2008 c.26 Sch.4 para.11
s.22, amended: 2008 c.26 Sch.4 para.11
s.23, amended: 2008 c.26 Sch.4 para.10, Sch.4 para.11
s.23A, amended: 2008 c.26 Sch.4 para.11
s.24, repealed (in part): 2008 c.26 s.66, Sch.7 Part 3
s.28, applied: 2008 c.26 s.77
s.56, amended: 2008 c.26 Sch.4 para.12
s.56, substituted: 2008 c.26 Sch.4 para.12
s.64, amended: 2008 c.26 Sch.4 para.21
s.95, enabling: SI 2008/198
s.96, amended: SI 2008/198 Reg.4
s.97, amended: SI 2008/198 Reg.4
s.97A, repealed: SI 2008/198 Reg.4
s.97C, added: SI 2008/198 Reg.2
s.97D, added: SI 2008/198 Reg.2
s.97E, added: SI 2008/198 Reg.2
s.97F, added: SI 2008/198 Reg.2
s.97G, added: SI 2008/198 Reg.2
s.97H, added: SI 2008/198 Reg.2
s.101, applied: SI 2008/198
s.101, enabling: SI 2008/198
s.102B, added: SI 2008/198 Reg.3
s.102C, added: SI 2008/198 Reg.3
s.103, amended: SI 2008/198 Reg.4
s.105, applied: SI 2008/230 Sch.1 para.5
s.108, repealed (in part): 2008 asp 5 Sch.3 Part 1
s.112, amended: 2008 asp 5 Sch.3 Part 1
s.134, amended: 2008 c.26 Sch.4 para.13
s.137, amended: 2008 c.26 Sch.4 para.14
s.141, amended: 2008 c.26 Sch.4 para.15
s.142, repealed: 2008 c.12 Sch.1 Part 11
s.160, amended: 2008 c.26 Sch.4 para.16
Sch.5 Part I para.1, amended: 2008 c.26 Sch.4 para.17
Sch.5 Part I para.3, amended: 2008 c.26 Sch.4 para.17
Sch.5 Part I para.4, amended: 2008 c.26 Sch.4 para.17
Sch.5 Part I para.5, amended: 2008 c.26 Sch.4 para.17
Sch.5 Part II para.1, amended: 2008 c.26 Sch.4 para.17
Sch.5 Part II para.2, amended: 2008 c.26 Sch.4 para.17
Sch.5 Part II para.3, amended: 2008 c.26 Sch.4 para.17
Sch.5 Part II para.4, amended: 2008 c.26 Sch.4 para.17

CAP.

1968–cont.

73. Transport Act 1968–*cont.*
Sch.5 Part II para.5, amended: 2008 c.26 Sch.4 para.17
Sch.5 Part III para.1, amended: 2008 c.26 Sch.4 para.17
Sch.5 Part III para.2, amended: 2008 c.26 Sch.4 para.17
Sch.5 Part III para.3, amended: 2008 c.26 Sch.4 para.17
Sch.5 Part III para.4, amended: 2008 c.26 Sch.4 para.17
Sch.5 Part III para.5, amended: 2008 c.26 Sch.4 para.17
Sch.5 Part III para.6, amended: 2008 c.26 Sch.4 para.17
Sch.5 Part III para.7, amended: 2008 c.26 Sch.4 para.17
Sch.5 Part III para.8, amended: 2008 c.26 Sch.4 para.17
Sch.5 Part III para.9, amended: 2008 c.26 Sch.4 para.17
Sch.5 Part III para.10, amended: 2008 c.26 Sch.4 para.17
Sch.5 Part III para.11, amended: 2008 c.26 Sch.4 para.17
Sch.5 Part III para.12, amended: 2008 c.26 Sch.4 para.17
Sch.5 Part III para.13, amended: 2008 c.26 Sch.4 para.17
Sch.5 Part III para.14, amended: 2008 c.26 Sch.4 para.17
Sch.5 Part III para.15, amended: 2008 c.26 Sch.4 para.17
Sch.5 Part III para.16, amended: 2008 c.26 Sch.4 para.17
Sch.5 Part III para.17, amended: 2008 c.26 Sch.4 para.17

77. Sea Fisheries Act 1968
referred to: 2008 c.13 Sch.6
s.5, applied: SSI 2008/101 Sch.1 Part 1

1969

6. Mines Act (Northern Ireland) 1969
s.85, disapplied: SI 2008/1597 Reg.27

10. Mines and Quarries (Tips) Act 1969
applied: 2008 c.13 Sch.3
Part II, referred to: 2008 c.13 Sch.6

22. Redundant Churches and Other Religious Buildings Act 1969
s.1, applied: SI 2008/842, SI 2008/842 Art.2, Art.3
s.1, enabling: SI 2008/842

32. Finance Act 1969
Sch.17 Part I, referred to: 2008 c.9 Sch.4 para.10

46. Family Law Reform Act 1969
see *F (Children) (DNA Evidence), Re* [2007] EWHC 3235 (Fam), [2008] 1 F.L.R. 348 (Fam Div), Anthony Hayden QC
s.20, applied: SI 2008/972 Reg.3

CAP.

1969–cont.

46. Family Law Reform Act 1969–*cont.*
s.22, enabling: SI 2008/972
s.25, amended: 2008 c.22 Sch.6 para.13

48. Post Office Act 1969
Sch.9 para.17, amended: 2008 asp 5 Sch.3 Part 1

51. Development of Tourism Act 1969
applied: 2008 c.13 Sch.3
s.1, applied: SSI 2008/228 Sch.2

54. Children and Young Persons Act 1969
s.23, amended: SI 2008/912 Sch.1 para.13
s.23AA, amended: 2008 c.4 Sch.26 para.5
s.23AA, referred to: 2008 c.4 Sch.26 para.5
s.23AA, repealed (in part): 2008 c.4 Sch.26 para.5, Sch.28 Part 4
s.25, repealed: 2008 c.4 Sch.4 para.15, Sch.28 Part 1
s.26, amended: 2008 c.4 Sch.4 para.16
s.26, applied: 2008 c.4 s.152
s.32, amended: 2008 c.4 Sch.4 para.17, Sch.4 para.101
s.34, amended: SI 2008/912 Sch.1 para.3
s.70, amended: 2008 c.4 Sch.4 para.18, Sch.28 Part 1
s.70, applied: 2008 c.4 s.152
s.73, amended: 2008 c.4 Sch.4 para.19
Sch.3 para.6, amended: SI 2008/912 Sch.1 para.3
Sch.3 para.9, amended: SI 2008/912 Sch.1 para.3
Sch.3 para.10, amended: SI 2008/912 Sch.1 para.3

57. Employers Liability (Compulsory Insurance) Act 1969
s.3, applied: SI 2008/1963 Reg.2
s.4, enabling: SI 2008/1765
s.6, enabling: SI 2008/1765

58. Administration of Justice Act 1969
s.22, see *Wilson v Dunbar Bank Plc* [2008] CSIH 27, 2008 S.C. 457 (IH (Ex Div)), Lord Kingarth

1970

9. Taxes Management Act 1970
see *Arnold v Williams* [2008] EWHC 218 (Ch), [2008] B.P.I.R. 247 (Ch D (Birmingham)), Judge Purle Q.C.; see *Monro v Revenue and Customs Commissioners* [2008] EWCA Civ 306, [2008] 3 W.L.R. 734 (CA (Civ Div)), Mummery, L.J.; see *Pipe v Revenue and Customs Commissioners* [2008] EWHC 646 (Ch), [2008] S.T.C. 1911 (Ch D), Henderson, J; see *Smith v Revenue and Customs Commissioners* [2008] S.T.C. (S.C.D.) 779 (Sp Comm), Michael Tildesley; see *Stockler Charity (A Firm) v Revenue and Customs Commissioners* [2007] EWHC 2967 (Ch), [2008] S.T.C. 2070 (Ch D (Companies Ct)), Warren, J.

CAP.

1970–cont.

9. Taxes Management Act 1970–*cont.*

Part V, applied: 2008 c.9 Sch.36 para.48, SI 2008/562 Reg.20

s.1, see *Oriel Support Ltd v Revenue and Customs Commissioners* [2008] S.T.C. (S.C.D.) 292 (Sp Comm), AN Brice

s.2, applied: SI 2008/2696 Art.4

s.2A, applied: SI 2008/2696 Art.4

s.3, applied: SI 2008/2696 Art.4

s.3A, applied: SI 2008/2696 Art.4

s.7, see *Director of the Assets Recovery Agency v McCormack* [2007] EWHC 908 (QB), [2008] S.T.C. 1097 (QBD), Pitchers, J.

s.7, amended: 2008 c.9 Sch.1 para.38

s.7, applied: 2008 c.9 Sch.41 para.1

s.7, repealed (in part): 2008 c.9 Sch.41 para.25

s.8, see *Director of the Assets Recovery Agency v McCormack* [2007] EWHC 908 (QB), [2008] S.T.C. 1097 (QBD), Pitchers, J.; see *Pipe v Revenue and Customs Commissioners* [2008] EWHC 646 (Ch), [2008] S.T.C. 1911 (Ch D), Henderson, J

s.8, amended: 2008 c.9 Sch.12 para.8

s.8, applied: 2008 c.9 Sch.36 para.21, 2008 c.18 Sch.13 para.44

s.8A, amended: 2008 c.9 Sch.12 para.9

s.8A, applied: 2008 c.9 Sch.36 para.21, 2008 c.18 Sch.13 para.44

s.9, amended: 2008 c.9 Sch.12 para.10

s.9A, see *Floyd v Revenue and Customs Commissioners* [2008] S.T.C. (S.C.D.) 353 (Sp Comm), Dr John F Avery Jones

s.9ZA, applied: 2008 c.18 Sch.13 para.44

s.9ZB, amended: 2008 c.9 s.119

s.12AA, amended: 2008 c.9 Sch.12 para.11

s.12AA, applied: 2008 c.9 Sch.36 para.21, Sch.36 para.37, 2008 c.18 Sch.13 para.44

s.12AB, amended: 2008 c.9 Sch.12 para.12

s.12ABA, applied: 2008 c.18 Sch.13 para.44

s.12ABB, amended: 2008 c.9 s.119

s.12AC, see *Flaxmode Ltd v Revenue and Customs Commissioners* [2008] S.T.C. (S.C.D.) 666 (Sp Comm), Charles Hellier

s.12AE, amended: 2008 c.9 Sch.17 para.25

s.12B, amended: 2008 c.9 Sch.37 para.2

s.12B, repealed (in part): 2008 c.9 Sch.37 para.2

s.17, referred to: 2008 c.9 s.39

s.17, enabling: SI 2008/2688

s.18, enabling: SI 2008/2688

s.19A, see *A v Revenue and Customs Commissioners* [2008] S.T.C. (S.C.D.) 380 (Sp Comm), Stephen Oliver Q.C. (Chairman); see *Afsar v Revenue and Customs Commissioners* [2008] S.T.C. (S.C.D.) 348 (Sp Comm), David Demack; see *Bryant v Revenue and Customs Commissioners* [2008] S.T.C. (S.C.D.) 85 (Sp Comm), John Clark; see *R. (on the application of Revenue and Customs Commissioners) v General Income Tax Commissioners (Berkshire)* [2007] EWHC 871 (Admin), [2008] S.T.C. 1494 (QBD (Admin)), Wyn Williams, J.; see *Sokoya v Revenue and Customs Commissioners* [2008] S.T.C. (S.C.D.) 51 (Sp Comm), John F Avery Jones; see *Uyar v Revenue and Customs Commissioners* [2008] S.T.C. (S.C.D.) 609 (Sp Comm), J Gordon Reid Q.C.

s.19A, repealed: 2008 c.9 Sch.36 para.66

s.20, see *Floyd v Revenue and Customs Commissioners* [2008] S.T.C. (S.C.D.) 353 (Sp Comm), Dr John F Avery Jones

s.20, repealed: 2008 c.9 Sch.36 para.67

s.20B, see *Revenue and Customs Commissioners Application (Section 20(3) Notice: Plc), Re (SpC 647)* [2008] S.T.C. (S.C.D.) 358 (Sp Comm), John F Avery Jones (Chairman)

s.20B, amended: 2008 c.9 Sch.36 para.68

s.20B, repealed (in part): 2008 c.9 Sch.36 para.68

s.20BB, amended: 2008 c.9 Sch.36 para.69

s.20D, amended: 2008 c.9 Sch.36 para.70

s.20D, repealed (in part): 2008 c.9 Sch.36 para.70

s.28A, see *Bryant v Revenue and Customs Commissioners* [2008] S.T.C. (S.C.D.) 85 (Sp Comm), John Clark; see *Kilbride v Revenue and Customs Commissioners* [2008] S.T.C. (S.C.D.) 517 (Sp Comm), Richard Barlow

s.28C, amended: 2008 c.9 Sch.39 para.2

s.29, see *Collins v Revenue and Customs Commissioners* [2008] S.T.C. (S.C.D.) 718 (Sp Comm), Theodore Wallace; see *Corbally-Stourton v Revenue and Customs Commissioners* [2008] S.T.C. (S.C.D.) 907 (Sp Comm), Charles Hellier; see *Director of the Assets Recovery Agency v McCormack* [2007] EWHC 908 (QB), [2008] S.T.C. 1097 (QBD), Pitchers, J.; see *Employee v Revenue and Customs Commissioners* [2008] S.T.C. (S.C.D.) 688 (Sp Comm), AN Brice (Chairman); see *Moran v Revenue and Customs Commissioners* [2008] S.T.C. (S.C.D.) 787 (Sp Comm), Michael Tildesley (Chairman); see *Smith v Revenue and Customs Commissioners* [2008] S.T.C. (S.C.D.) 779 (Sp Comm), Michael Tildesley; see *Walker v Revenue and Customs Commissioners* [2008] S.T.C. (S.C.D.) 130 (Sp Comm), Adrian Shipwright (Chairman)

s.29, amended: 2008 c.9 Sch.36 para.71, Sch.39 para.3

s.29, applied: 2008 c.18 Sch.13 para.44

s.30, applied: 2008 c.9 Sch.19 para.4

CAP.

1970–cont.

9. **Taxes Management Act 1970**–*cont.*

s.30A, see *Arnold v Williams* [2008] EWHC 218 (Ch), [2008] B.P.I.R. 247 (Ch D (Birmingham)), Judge Purle Q.C.

s.30B, see *Stockler Charity (A Firm) v Revenue and Customs Commissioners* [2007] EWHC 2967 (Ch), [2008] S.T.C. 2070 (Ch D (Companies Ct)), Warren, J.

s.30B, amended: 2008 c.9 Sch.39 para.4

s.30B, applied: 2008 c.18 Sch.13 para.44

s.31, see *Oriel Support Ltd v Revenue and Customs Commissioners* [2008] S.T.C. (S.C.D.) 292 (Sp Comm), AN Brice; see *Tower MCashback LLP v Revenue and Customs Commissioners* [2008] EWHC 2387 (Ch), [2008] S.T.C. 3366 (Ch D), Henderson, J.

s.33, see *Monro v Revenue and Customs Commissioners* [2008] EWCA Civ 306, [2008] 3 W.L.R. 734 (CA (Civ Div)), Mummery, L.J.

s.33, amended: 2008 c.9 Sch.7 para.65, Sch.39 para.5

s.33A, amended: 2008 c.9 Sch.39 para.6

s.34, amended: 2008 c.9 Sch.39 para.7

s.35, amended: 2008 c.9 Sch.39 para.8

s.36, amended: 2008 c.9 Sch.39 para.9

s.37A, amended: 2008 c.9 Sch.39 para.10

s.40, amended: 2008 c.9 Sch.39 para.11

s.43, amended: 2008 c.9 Sch.39 para.12

s.43A, amended: 2008 c.9 Sch.39 para.13

s.43C, amended: 2008 c.9 Sch.39 para.14

s.44, varied: 2008 c.9 Sch.36 para.32

s.45, varied: 2008 c.9 Sch.36 para.32

s.46, varied: 2008 c.9 Sch.36 para.32

s.46A, varied: 2008 c.9 Sch.36 para.32

s.46B, see *Walker v Revenue and Customs Commissioners* [2008] S.T.C. (S.C.D.) 130 (Sp Comm), Adrian Shipwright (Chairman)

s.46B, amended: 2008 c.9 s.119, Sch.7 para.161

s.46B, varied: 2008 c.9 Sch.36 para.32

s.46C, amended: 2008 c.9 s.119

s.46C, varied: 2008 c.9 Sch.36 para.32

s.46D, amended: 2008 c.9 s.119

s.46D, varied: 2008 c.9 Sch.36 para.32

s.47, varied: 2008 c.9 Sch.36 para.32

s.47A, varied: 2008 c.9 Sch.36 para.32

s.47B, varied: 2008 c.9 Sch.36 para.32

s.47C, varied: 2008 c.9 Sch.36 para.32

s.48, varied: 2008 c.9 Sch.36 para.32

s.49, varied: 2008 c.9 Sch.36 para.32

s.49A, varied: 2008 c.9 Sch.36 para.32

s.49B, varied: 2008 c.9 Sch.36 para.32

s.49C, varied: 2008 c.9 Sch.36 para.32

s.49D, varied: 2008 c.9 Sch.36 para.32

s.49E, varied: 2008 c.9 Sch.36 para.32

s.49F, varied: 2008 c.9 Sch.36 para.32

s.49G, varied: 2008 c.9 Sch.36 para.32

s.49H, varied: 2008 c.9 Sch.36 para.32

s.49I, varied: 2008 c.9 Sch.36 para.32

CAP.

1970–cont.

9. **Taxes Management Act 1970**–*cont.*

s.50, see *Walsh v Revenue and Customs Commissioners* [2008] S.T.C. (S.C.D.) 742 (Sp Comm), John F Avery Jones

s.50, varied: 2008 c.9 Sch.36 para.32

s.51, varied: 2008 c.9 Sch.36 para.32

s.52, varied: 2008 c.9 Sch.36 para.32

s.53, varied: 2008 c.9 Sch.36 para.32

s.54, varied: 2008 c.9 Sch.36 para.32

s.55, amended: 2008 c.9 s.119

s.55, varied: 2008 c.9 Sch.36 para.32

s.56, applied: SI 2008/2696 Art.4

s.56, varied: 2008 c.9 Sch.36 para.32

s.56A, varied: 2008 c.9 Sch.36 para.32

s.56B, varied: 2008 c.9 Sch.36 para.32

s.56C, varied: 2008 c.9 Sch.36 para.32

s.56D, varied: 2008 c.9 Sch.36 para.32

s.57, varied: 2008 c.9 Sch.36 para.32

s.57A, varied: 2008 c.9 Sch.36 para.32

s.57B, varied: 2008 c.9 Sch.36 para.32

s.58, varied: 2008 c.9 Sch.36 para.32

s.59, varied: 2008 c.9 Sch.36 para.32

s.59A, amended: 2008 c.9 Sch.12 para.13

s.59A, referred to: SI 2008/838 Reg.2

s.59A, enabling: SI 2008/838

s.59B, amended: 2008 c.9 Sch.12 para.14

s.59E, enabling: SI 2008/2649

s.61, amended: 2008 c.9 Sch.43 para.1

s.61, repealed (in part): 2008 c.9 Sch.43 para.1

s.63, repealed: 2008 c.9 Sch.43 para.12

s.63A, repealed: 2008 c.9 Sch.43 para.12

s.66, amended: 2008 c.9 s.137

s.66, repealed (in part): 2008 c.9 s.137

s.70, see *Advocate General for Scotland v Montgomery* 2008 S.C.L.R. 1 (OH), Lady Paton

s.70, repealed (in part): 2008 c.9 Sch.44 para.1

s.87A, amended: 2008 c.9 Sch.35 para.1

s.91, amended: 2008 c.9 Sch.1 para.39

s.93, see *Pipe v Revenue and Customs Commissioners* [2008] EWHC 646 (Ch), [2008] S.T.C. 1911 (Ch D), Henderson, J

s.95, see *Revenue and Customs Commissioners v Khawaja* [2008] EWHC 1687 (Ch), [2008] S.T.C. 2880 (Ch D), Mann, J.; see *Stockler Charity (A Firm) v Revenue and Customs Commissioners* [2007] EWHC 2967 (Ch), [2008] S.T.C. 2070 (Ch D (Companies Ct)), Warren, J.

s.95A, see *Stockler Charity (A Firm) v Revenue and Customs Commissioners* [2007] EWHC 2967 (Ch), [2008] S.T.C. 2070 (Ch D (Companies Ct)), Warren, J.

s.97A, referred to: 2008 c.9 Sch.36 para.50

s.97AA, repealed: 2008 c.9 Sch.36 para.72

s.98, amended: 2008 c.9 s.76, Sch.36 para.73, Sch.41 para.25, SI 2008/562 Reg.26

CAP.

1970–cont.

9. Taxes Management Act 1970–*cont.*

s.98A, see *Bysermaw Properties Ltd v Revenue and Customs Commissioners* [2008] S.T.C. (S.C.D.) 322 (Sp Comm), Malcolm Gammie Q.C.

s.98C, amended: 2008 c.9 Sch.38 para.7

s.100, amended: 2008 c.9 Sch.36 para.74

s.107A, amended: 2008 c.9 Sch.36 para.75

s.108, applied: 2008 c.9 Sch.36 para.56, SI 2008/562 Reg.11

s.109, see *Advocate General for Scotland v Montgomery* 2008 S.C.L.R. 1 (OH), Lady Paton

s.114, see *Pipe v Revenue and Customs Commissioners* [2008] EWHC 646 (Ch), [2008] S.T.C. 1911 (Ch D), Henderson, J

s.114, applied: 2008 c.9 Sch.36 para.56

s.115, applied: 2008 c.9 Sch.36 para.56

s.118, amended: 2008 c.9 Sch.36 para.76, Sch.39 para.15

Sch.1A para.2A, amended: 2008 c.9 Sch.37 para.3

Sch.1A para.6, repealed: 2008 c.9 Sch.36 para.77

Sch.1A para.6A, repealed: 2008 c.9 Sch.36 para.77

10. Income and Corporation Taxes Act 1970

s.153, applied: 2008 c.9 s.58

30. Conservation of Seals Act 1970

referred to: 2008 c.13 Sch.6

31. Administration of Justice Act 1970

s.40, amended: SI 2008/1277 Sch.2 para.13

s.40, applied: 2008 c.13 Sch.3

s.40, referred to: 2008 c.13 Sch.6

Sch.8 para.7, repealed: 2008 c.14 Sch.15 Part 5

32. Riding Establishments Act 1970

applied: 2008 c.13 Sch.3

34. Marriage (Registrar General's Licence) Act 1970

s.18, amended: SI 2008/678 Sch.2 para.9

s.18, applied: SI 2008/678 Sch.1 para.9

35. Conveyancing and Feudal Reform (Scotland) Act 1970

s.19B, applied: SSI 2008/324 Reg.2

s.24, applied: SSI 2008/324 Reg.2

s.25, see *Wilson v Dunbar Bank Plc* [2008] CSIH 27, 2008 S.C. 457 (IH (Ex Div)), Lord Kingarth

39. Local Authorities (Goods and Services) Act 1970

s.1, amended: SI 2008/912 Sch.1 para.4

40. Agriculture Act 1970

applied: 2008 c.13 Sch.3

referred to: 2008 c.13 Sch.6

s.66, enabling: SI 2008/1523, SI 2008/1806, SSI 2008/201, SSI 2008/215

s.68, enabling: SI 2008/1523, SI 2008/1806, SSI 2008/215

CAP.

1970–cont.

40. Agriculture Act 1970–*cont.*

s.74A, enabling: SI 2008/1523, SI 2008/1806, SSI 2008/201, SSI 2008/215

s.78, enabling: SSI 2008/201

s.79, enabling: SSI 2008/201

s.84, applied: SSI 2008/215

s.84, enabling: SI 2008/1523, SI 2008/1806, SSI 2008/201, SSI 2008/215

s.106, repealed (in part): SI 2008/576 Sch.5 para.7

s.108, repealed: SI 2008/576 Sch.5 para.7

41. Equal Pay Act 1970

see *British Airways Plc v Grundy* [2008] EWCA Civ 875, [2008] I.R.L.R. 815 (CA (Civ Div)), Waller, L.J. (V-P); see *Chief Constable of West Midlands v Blackburn* [2008] I.C.R. 505 (EAT), Elias, J (President); see *Pike v Somerset CC* [2008] Pens. L.R. 403 (EAT), Judge McMullen Q.C.; see *Potter v North Cumbria Acute Hospitals NHS Trust* [2008] I.C.R. 910 (EAT), Underhill, J.

s.1, see *Cumbria CC v Dow (No.1)* [2008] I.R.L.R. 91 (EAT), Elias, J (President); see *Grundy v British Airways Plc* [2007] EWCA Civ 1020, [2008] I.R.L.R. 74 (CA (Civ Div)), Waller, L.J.; see *Redcar & Cleveland BC v Bainbridge* [2008] EWCA Civ 885, [2008] I.R.L.R. 776 (CA (Civ Div)), Mummery, L.J.; see *Redcar and Cleveland BC v Bainbridge* [2008] I.C.R. 249 (EAT), Elias, J.

s.2, see *Cumbria CC v Dow (No.2)* [2008] I.R.L.R. 109 (EAT), Elias, J (President); see *Unison v Allen* [2008] I.C.R. 114 (EAT), Elias, J (President)

s.2, referred to: SI 2008/3232 Sch.1 Part 3

s.2ZA, see *Sodexo v Gutridge* [2008] I.R.L.R. 752 (EAT), Elias, J.

42. Local Authority Social Services Act 1970

s.7, see *R. (on the application of B) v Lewisham LBC* [2008] EWHC 738 (Admin), [2008] 2 F.L.R. 523 (QBD (Admin)), Black, J.; see *R. (on the application of Chavda) v Harrow LBC* [2007] EWHC 3064 (Admin), [2008] B.L.G.R. 657 (QBD (Admin)), Judge Mackie Q.C.

Sch.1, amended: 2008 c.14 s.147, 2008 c.23 s.5, SI 2008/2828 Art.3, SI 2008/2833 Sch.3 para.27

44. Chronically Sick and Disabled Persons Act 1970

s.2, see *R. (on the application of Chavda) v Harrow LBC* [2007] EWHC 3064 (Admin), [2008] B.L.G.R. 657 (QBD (Admin)), Judge Mackie Q.C.; see *Sandford v Waltham Forest LBC* [2008] EWHC 1106 (QB), [2008] B.L.G.R. 816 (QBD), Judge Richard Seymour Q.C.

s.2, amended: 2008 c.14 s.148

CAP.

1970–cont.

44. Chronically Sick and Disabled Persons Act 1970–*cont.*
s.21, applied: SI 2008/614 Reg.8, SI 2008/1214 Reg.8
s.21, referred to: 2008 c.13 Sch.6
s.21A, applied: SI 2008/614 Reg.8, SI 2008/1214 Reg.8

45. Matrimonial Proceedings and Property Act 1970
s.37, see *Bindra v Chopra* [2008] EWHC 1715 (Ch), [2008] 3 F.C.R. 341 (Ch D), Etherton, J.

1971

22. Animals Act 1971
s.2, see *Welsh v Stokes* [2007] EWCA Civ 796, [2008] 1 W.L.R. 1224 (CA (Civ Div)), Dyson, L.J.

29. National Savings Bank Act 1971
s.2, enabling: SI 2008/734, SI 2008/1142, SI 2008/1164, SI 2008/3098
s.3, applied: SI 2008/734, SI 2008/1142
s.3, referred to: SI 2008/1164
s.4, applied: SI 2008/734
s.4, referred to: SI 2008/1164
s.6, referred to: SI 2008/1164
s.7, referred to: SI 2008/1164
s.8, applied: SI 2008/1142
s.8, referred to: SI 2008/1164
s.12, amended: 2008 c.9 Sch.36 Part 10

30. Unsolicited Goods and Services Act 1971
applied: 2008 c.13 Sch.3
s.2, referred to: 2008 c.13 Sch.6
s.3, referred to: 2008 c.13 Sch.6

32. Attachment of Earnings Act 1971
s.23, applied: SI 2008/1054 Sch.1
Sch.1 para.8, repealed: 2008 c.14 Sch.15 Part 5

38. Misuse of Drugs Act 1971
see *B v DPP* [2008] EWHC 1655 (Admin), (2008) 172 J.P. 449 (DC), Moses, L.J.; see *R. v Deyemi (Danny)* [2007] EWCA Crim 2060, [2008] 1 Cr. App. R. 25 (CA (Crim Div)), Latham, L.J.
s.2, applied: SI 2008/3130
s.2, enabling: SI 2008/3130
s.4, see *HM Advocate v Grant (Emma Jean)* 2008 S.L.T. 339 (HCJ), Lord Hamilton L.J.G.; see *Zhi Pen Lin v HM Advocate* 2008 J.C. 142 (HCJ), Lord Hamilton L.J.G.
s.5, see *HM Advocate v Grant (Emma Jean)* 2008 S.L.T. 339 (HCJ), Lord Hamilton L.J.G.
s.23, see *Brown v Donaldson* 2008 J.C. 83 (HCJ), Lord Gill L.J.C.; see *R. v Bristol (Christopher)* [2007] EWCA Crim 3214, (2008) 172 J.P. 161 (CA (Crim Div)), Thomas, L.J.

CAP.

1971–cont.

38. Misuse of Drugs Act 1971–*cont.*
s.23, varied: SI 2008/295 Reg.8, SI 2008/296 Reg.10
s.28, see *R. v Deyemi (Danny)* [2007] EWCA Crim 2060, [2008] 1 Cr. App. R. 25 (CA (Crim Div)), Latham, L.J.
Sch.2 Part II para.1, amended: SI 2008/3130 Art.2
Sch.2 Part II para.2A, added: SI 2008/3130 Art.2
Sch.2 Part II para.3, amended: SI 2008/3130 Art.2
Sch.2 Part III para.1, amended: SI 2008/3130 Art.2

45. Redemption of Standard Securities (Scotland) Act 1971
s.2, amended: SI 2008/948 Sch.1 para.42

48. Criminal Damage Act 1971
s.1, see *R. v Ratcliffe (Daniel James)* [2008] EWCA Crim 471, [2008] 2 Cr. App. R. (S.) 79 (CA (Crim Div)), Moses, L.J.

56. Pensions (Increase) Act 1971
applied: SI 2008/653 Reg.1, Reg.2, Reg.3, Reg.4, Reg.5, Reg.11, Reg.15, Reg.17, Reg.20, Reg.20A, SSI 2008/224 Reg.1, Reg.2, Reg.3, Reg.4, Reg.5, Reg.15, Reg.17, Reg.20, SSI 2008/230 Reg.4, Reg.38
s.1, applied: SI 2008/711 Art.3, Art.4
s.5, applied: SI 2008/653 Reg.10, Reg.11, SSI 2008/224 Reg.10, Reg.11
s.8, referred to: SI 2008/711 Art.2
Sch.2 Part I para.36, repealed: 2008 c.12 Sch.1 Part 1
Sch.2 Part II para.53B, added: SI 2008/912 Sch.1 para.5

58. Sheriff Courts (Scotland) Act 1971
s.1, repealed: 2008 asp 6 s.48
s.2, amended: 2008 asp 6 s.50
s.3, amended: 2008 asp 6 s.51
s.8, repealed: 2008 asp 6 s.52
s.9, repealed: 2008 asp 6 s.48
s.10, amended: 2008 asp 6 s.53
s.11, see *Dickson (Kenneth Robert) v HM Advocate* 2008 J.C. 181 (HCJ), Lord Hamilton L.J.G.
s.11, amended: 2008 asp 6 s.24, s.64
s.11A, amended: 2008 asp 6 s.26, s.64
s.11A, repealed (in part): 2008 asp 6 Sch.5 para.2
s.11C, repealed: 2008 asp 6 Sch.5 para.2
s.11D, amended: 2008 asp 6 Sch.5 para.2
s.12, substituted: 2008 asp 6 s.40
s.13, amended: 2008 asp 6 s.54
s.14, amended: 2008 asp 6 s.55
s.14, repealed (in part): 2008 asp 6 s.55
s.14A, added: 2008 asp 6 s.25
s.15, applied: 2008 asp 6 s.62
s.15, substituted: 2008 asp 6 s.47
s.16, amended: 2008 asp 6 s.47, s.56
s.16, applied: 2008 asp 6 s.62

CAP.

1971–cont.

58. Sheriff Courts (Scotland) Act 1971– *cont.*

s.17, amended: 2008 asp 6 s.47
s.17, applied: 2008 asp 6 s.62
s.17A, added: 2008 asp 6 s.49
s.18, repealed: 2008 asp 6 s.49
s.20, amended: 2008 asp 6 s.47
s.23, repealed: 2008 asp 6 Sch.5 para.2
s.24, repealed: 2008 asp 6 Sch.5 para.2
s.25, repealed: 2008 asp 6 Sch.5 para.2
s.26, repealed: 2008 asp 6 Sch.5 para.2
s.27, repealed: 2008 asp 6 Sch.5 para.2
s.28, repealed: 2008 asp 6 Sch.5 para.2
s.29, repealed: 2008 asp 6 Sch.5 para.2
s.30, repealed: 2008 asp 6 Sch.5 para.2
s.32, applied: 2008 asp 5 s.71
s.32, enabling: SSI 2008/9, SSI 2008/41, SSI 2008/111, SSI 2008/119, SSI 2008/121, SSI 2008/223, SSI 2008/335, SSI 2008/365, SSI 2008/375, SSI 2008/435, SSI 2008/436
s.33, amended: 2008 asp 6 Sch.5 para.2
s.34, applied: SSI 2008/9, SSI 2008/41, SSI 2008/111, SSI 2008/119, SSI 2008/223, SSI 2008/335, SSI 2008/365, SSI 2008/375, SSI 2008/435, SSI 2008/436

60. Prevention of Oil Pollution Act 1971

applied: SSI 2008/188 Art.53
disapplied: SSI 2008/189 Art.53, SSI 2008/190 Art.53

69. Medicines Act 1971

s.1, amended: SI 2008/2297 Reg.45
s.1, enabling: SI 2008/552

75. Civil Aviation Act 1971

s.62, referred to: SI 2008/3119

77. Immigration Act 1971

see *Odelola v Secretary of State for the Home Department* [2008] EWCA Civ 308, [2008] Imm. A.R. 632 (CA (Civ Div)), Buxton, L.J.; see *R. v Abdi (Liban)* [2007] EWCA Crim 1913, [2008] 1 Cr. App. R. (S.) 87 (CA (Crim Div)), Toulson, L.J.
applied: SI 2008/239 Reg.11, SI 2008/794 Reg.11, SSI 2008/228 Reg.8
s.1, varied: SI 2008/680 Art.5, Art.6, Sch.3 para.1
s.2, applied: SI 2008/1183 Reg.12, SI 2008/3048 Reg.11
s.2, varied: SI 2008/680 Art.5, Art.6, Sch.3 para.2
s.2A, varied: SI 2008/680 Art.5, Art.6, Sch.3 para.3
s.3, see *EO (Turkey) v Secretary of State for the Home Department* [2008] EWCA Civ 671, [2008] I.N.L.R. 295 (CA (Civ Div)), Tuckey, L.J.; see *Obed v Secretary of State for the Home Department* [2008] EWCA Civ 747, [2008] Imm. A.R. 747 (CA (Civ Div)), Sedley, L.J.
s.3, applied: SI 2008/99 Art.3, SI 2008/794 Reg.70, SI 2008/1216 Art.19

CAP.

1971–cont.

77. Immigration Act 1971–*cont.*

s.3, varied: SI 2008/680 Art.5, Art.6, Sch.3 para.4
s.3A, varied: SI 2008/680 Art.5, Art.6, Sch.3 para.5
s.3B, varied: SI 2008/680 Art.5, Art.6, Sch.3 para.6
s.3C, see *Liu v Secretary of State for the Home Department* [2007] EWCA Civ 1275, [2008] 1 C.M.L.R. 27 (CA (Civ Div)), Buxton, L.J.
s.3C, varied: SI 2008/680 Art.5, Art.6, Sch.3 para.7
s.3D, varied: SI 2008/680 Art.5, Art.6, Sch.3 para.8
s.4, varied: SI 2008/680 Art.5, Art.6, Sch.3 para.9
s.5, see *EO (Turkey) v Secretary of State for the Home Department* [2008] EWCA Civ 671, [2008] I.N.L.R. 295 (CA (Civ Div)), Tuckey, L.J.
s.5, applied: 2008 c.4 s.136, SI 2008/1818 Art.3
s.5, varied: SI 2008/680 Art.5, Art.6, Sch.3 para.10
s.6, see *R. v Abdi (Liban)* [2007] EWCA Crim 1913, [2008] 1 Cr. App. R. (S.) 87 (CA (Crim Div)), Toulson, L.J.
s.6, varied: SI 2008/680 Art.5, Art.6, Sch.3 para.11
s.7, varied: SI 2008/680 Art.5, Art.6, Sch.3 para.12
s.8, varied: SI 2008/680 Art.5, Art.6, Sch.3 para.13
s.8A, varied: SI 2008/680 Art.5, Art.6, Sch.3 para.14
s.8B, varied: SI 2008/680 Art.5, Art.6, Sch.3 para.15
s.8B, enabling: SI 2008/3052
s.9, varied: SI 2008/680 Art.5, Art.6, Sch.3 para.16
s.10, varied: SI 2008/680 Art.5, Art.6, Sch.3 para.17
s.11, varied: SI 2008/680 Art.5, Art.6, Sch.3 para.18
s.24, applied: 2008 c.4 s.133
s.24, varied: SI 2008/680 Art.5, Art.6, Sch.3 para.19
s.24A, varied: SI 2008/680 Art.5, Art.6, Sch.3 para.20
s.25, varied: SI 2008/680 Art.5, Art.6, Sch.3 para.21
s.25A, varied: SI 2008/680 Art.5, Art.6, Sch.3 para.22
s.25B, varied: SI 2008/680 Art.5, Art.6, Sch.3 para.23
s.25C, applied: SI 2008/786 Reg.4
s.25C, varied: SI 2008/680 Art.5, Art.6, Sch.3 para.24
s.25D, varied: SI 2008/680 Art.5, Art.6, Sch.3 para.25

CAP.

1971–cont.

77. Immigration Act 1971–*cont.*

s.26, varied: SI 2008/680 Art.5, Art.6, Sch.3 para.26
s.26A, amended: SI 2008/1693 Art.2
s.26A, applied: SI 2008/1693
s.26A, varied: SI 2008/680 Art.5, Art.6, Sch.3 para.27
s.26A, enabling: SI 2008/1693
s.26B, varied: SI 2008/680 Art.5, Art.6, Sch.3 para.28
s.27, varied: SI 2008/680 Art.5, Art.6, Sch.3 para.29
s.28, varied: SI 2008/680 Art.5, Art.6, Sch.3 para.30
s.28A, varied: SI 2008/680 Art.5, Art.6, Sch.3 para.31
s.28AA, applied: SI 2008/309 Art.5
s.28AA, varied: SI 2008/680 Art.5, Art.6, Sch.3 para.32
s.28B, varied: SI 2008/680 Art.5, Art.6, Sch.3 para.33
s.28C, varied: SI 2008/680 Art.5, Art.6
s.28CA, varied: SI 2008/680 Art.5, Art.6, Sch.3 para.34
s.28D, varied: SI 2008/680 Art.5, Art.6, Sch.3 para.35
s.28E, varied: SI 2008/680 Art.5, Art.6
s.28F, varied: SI 2008/680 Art.5, Art.6
s.28FA, applied: SI 2008/309 Art.5
s.28FA, varied: SI 2008/680 Art.5, Art.6, Sch.3 para.36
s.28FB, varied: SI 2008/680 Art.5, Art.6, Sch.3 para.37
s.28G, varied: SI 2008/680 Art.5, Art.6
s.28H, varied: SI 2008/680 Art.5, Art.6, Sch.3 para.38
s.28I, varied: SI 2008/680 Art.5, Art.6
s.28J, varied: SI 2008/680 Art.5, Art.6, Sch.3 para.39
s.28K, varied: SI 2008/680 Art.5, Art.6, Sch.3 para.40
s.28L, varied: SI 2008/680 Art.5, Art.6, Sch.3 para.41
s.30, varied: SI 2008/680 Sch.3 para.42
s.31, varied: SI 2008/680 Art.5, Art.6, Sch.3 para.43
s.31A, varied: SI 2008/680 Art.5, Art.6, Sch.3 para.44
s.32, varied: SI 2008/680 Art.5, Art.6, Sch.3 para.45
s.33, applied: SI 2008/1216 Art.19
s.33, varied: SI 2008/680 Art.5, Art.6, Sch.3 para.46
s.36, enabling: SI 2008/680
s.37, varied: SI 2008/680 Art.5, Art.6, Sch.3 para.47
Sch.2, referred to: SI 2008/680 Sch.3 para.48
Sch.2 Part I para.1, varied: SI 2008/680 Sch.3 para.49

CAP.

1971–cont.

77. Immigration Act 1971–*cont.*

Sch.2 Part I para.2, applied: SI 2008/3048 Reg.21
Sch.2 Part I para.2, varied: SI 2008/680 Sch.3 para.50
Sch.2 Part I para.2A, applied: SI 2008/3048 Reg.21
Sch.2 Part I para.2A, varied: SI 2008/680 Sch.3 para.51
Sch.2 Part I para.3, applied: SI 2008/3048 Reg.21
Sch.2 Part I para.3, varied: SI 2008/680 Sch.3 para.52
Sch.2 Part I para.4, varied: SI 2008/680 Sch.3 para.53
Sch.2 Part I para.5, varied: SI 2008/680 Sch.3 para.54
Sch.2 Part I para.6, applied: 2008 c.4 s.132
Sch.2 Part I para.6, varied: SI 2008/680 Sch.3 para.55
Sch.2 Part I para.7, varied: SI 2008/680 Sch.3 para.56
Sch.2 Part I para.8, varied: SI 2008/680 Sch.3 para.57
Sch.2 Part I para.9, varied: SI 2008/680 Sch.3 para.58
Sch.2 Part I para.10, varied: SI 2008/680 Sch.3 para.59
Sch.2 Part I para.12, varied: SI 2008/680 Sch.3 para.60
Sch.2 Part I para.13, varied: SI 2008/680 Sch.3 para.61
Sch.2 Part I para.14, varied: SI 2008/680 Sch.3 para.62
Sch.2 Part I para.16, varied: SI 2008/680 Sch.3 para.63
Sch.2 Part I para.17, varied: SI 2008/680 Sch.3 para.64
Sch.2 Part I para.18, varied: SI 2008/680 Sch.3 para.65
Sch.2 Part I para.19, varied: SI 2008/680 Sch.3 para.66
Sch.2 Part I para.20, varied: SI 2008/680 Sch.3 para.67
Sch.2 Part I para.21, applied: 2008 c.4 s.132, s.133
Sch.2 Part I para.21, varied: SI 2008/680 Sch.3 para.68
Sch.2 Part I para.22, varied: SI 2008/680 Sch.3 para.69
Sch.2 Part I para.23, varied: SI 2008/680 Sch.3 para.70
Sch.2 Part I para.24, varied: SI 2008/680 Sch.3 para.71
Sch.2 Part I para.25A, varied: SI 2008/680 Sch.3 para.72
Sch.2 Part I para.25B, varied: SI 2008/680 Sch.3 para.73
Sch.2 Part I para.25C, varied: SI 2008/680 Sch.3 para.74

CAP.

1971–cont.

77. Immigration Act 1971–*cont.*

Sch.2 Part I para.26, varied: SI 2008/680 Sch.3 para.75

Sch.2 Part I para.27, applied: SI 2008/5 Art.3, SI 2008/539 Sch.1 para.1

Sch.2 Part I para.27, varied: SI 2008/680 Sch.3 para.76

Sch.2 Part I para.27, enabling: SI 2008/5

Sch.2 Part I para.27B, applied: SI 2008/5 Art.5, SI 2008/539 Sch.1 para.1

Sch.2 Part I para.27B, varied: SI 2008/680 Sch.3 para.77

Sch.2 Part I para.27B, enabling: SI 2008/5

Sch.2 Part I para.27C, applied: SI 2008/539 Sch.1 para.1

Sch.2 Part I para.27C, varied: SI 2008/680 Sch.3 para.78

Sch.2 Part II para.28, varied: SI 2008/680 Sch.3 para.79

Sch.2 Part II para.29, varied: SI 2008/680 Sch.3 para.80

Sch.2 Part II para.30, varied: SI 2008/680 Sch.3 para.81

Sch.2 Part II para.31, varied: SI 2008/680 Sch.3 para.82

Sch.2 Part II para.32, varied: SI 2008/680 Sch.3 para.83

Sch.2 Part II para.33, varied: SI 2008/680 Sch.3 para.84

Sch.2 Part II para.34, varied: SI 2008/680 Sch.3 para.85

Sch.2 para.21, see *R. (on the application of A) v West Middlesex University Hospital NHS Trust* [2008] EWHC 855 (Admin), [2008] H.R.L.R. 29 (QBD (Admin)), Mitting, J.

Sch.3 para.1, varied: SI 2008/680 Sch.3 para.86

Sch.3 para.2, see *R. (on the application of SK (Zimbabwe)) v Secretary of State for the Home Department* [2008] EWCA Civ 1204, Times, November 21, 2008 (CA (Civ Div)), Laws, L.J.; see *R. (on the application of SK (Zimbabwe)) v Secretary of State for the Home Department* [2008] EWHC 98 (Admin), Times, February 26, 2008 (QBD (Admin)), Munby, J.

Sch.3 para.2, varied: SI 2008/680 Sch.3 para.87

Sch.3 para.6, varied: SI 2008/680 Sch.3 para.88

Sch.3 para.7, varied: SI 2008/680 Sch.3 para.89

Sch.3 para.8, varied: SI 2008/680 Sch.3 para.90

Sch.3 para.9, varied: SI 2008/680 Sch.3 para.91

Sch.3 para.10, varied: SI 2008/680 Sch.3 para.92

Sch.4 para.1, varied: SI 2008/680 Sch.3 para.93, Sch.3 para.94

Sch.4 para.2, varied: SI 2008/680 Sch.3 para.93, Sch.3 para.95

Sch.4 para.3, varied: SI 2008/680 Sch.3 para.93, Sch.3 para.96

Sch.4 para.4, varied: SI 2008/680 Sch.3 para.93, Sch.3 para.97

80. Banking and Financial Dealings Act 1971

applied: SI 2008/635 Art.10, SI 2008/1848 Reg.14, SI 2008/2841 Reg.2, SI 2008/3231 Art.40

s.1, applied: SI 2008/1738 r.15

1972

11. Superannuation Act 1972

applied: 2008 c.14 Sch.6 para.16, 2008 c.27 Sch.1 para.14

s.1, applied: SI 2008/653 Reg.2, SSI 2008/224 Reg.2

s.1, enabling: SI 2008/1891

s.7, applied: SI 2008/238, SI 2008/239, SI 2008/239 Reg.12, SI 2008/2176 Reg.1, SI 2008/2425, SI 2008/2867 Reg.1, SI 2008/2989, SI 2008/3245, SSI 2008/228, SSI 2008/228 Reg.9, SSI 2008/229, SSI 2008/230

s.7, enabling: SI 2008/238, SI 2008/239, SI 2008/1083, SI 2008/2425, SI 2008/2989, SI 2008/3245, SSI 2008/228, SSI 2008/229, SSI 2008/230

s.9, applied: SI 2008/653 Reg.2, SSI 2008/224 Reg.2, SSI 2008/227

s.9, enabling: SI 2008/541, SSI 2008/227

s.10, applied: SI 2008/653, SI 2008/653 Reg.11, SI 2008/654, SI 2008/655, SI 2008/906, SSI 2008/92, SSI 2008/224 Reg.1, SSI 2008/225, SSI 2008/226

s.10, disapplied: SSI 2008/228 Reg.9

s.10, enabling: SI 2008/653, SI 2008/654, SI 2008/655, SI 2008/906, SI 2008/2263, SSI 2008/92, SSI 2008/224, SSI 2008/225, SSI 2008/226

s.12, enabling: SI 2008/214, SI 2008/238, SI 2008/541, SI 2008/653, SI 2008/654, SI 2008/655, SI 2008/906, SI 2008/1083, SI 2008/2263, SI 2008/2425, SI 2008/2989, SI 2008/3245, SSI 2008/92, SSI 2008/161, SSI 2008/224, SSI 2008/225, SSI 2008/226, SSI 2008/227, SSI 2008/229, SSI 2008/230

s.16, applied: SI 2008/214

s.16, enabling: SI 2008/214, SSI 2008/161

s.24, enabling: SI 2008/655, SSI 2008/92, SSI 2008/225, SSI 2008/227

Sch.1, added: SI 2008/1891 Art.2

Sch.1, amended: 2008 c.14 Sch.6 para.15, 2008 c.27 Sch.1 para.14, SI 2008/1891 Art.2, Art.3, Art.4

Sch.3, enabling: SI 2008/541, SI 2008/653, SI 2008/654, SI 2008/906, SI 2008/2263, SSI 2008/92, SSI 2008/224, SSI 2008/225, SSI 2008/226, SSI 2008/

CAP.

1972–cont.

11. Superannuation Act 1972–*cont.*
Sch.3, enabling:–*cont.*
227, SSI 2008/228, SSI 2008/229, SSI 2008/230
Sch.4, amended: SI 2008/576 Sch.5 para.7
Sch.7 para.5, referred to: SI 2008/239 Reg.79, Reg.81, SSI 2008/228 Reg.74, Reg.76

18. Maintenance Orders (Reciprocal Enforcement) Act 1972
applied: SI 2008/1054 Sch.1, SI 2008/1202 Art.4
Part I, applied: SI 2008/1202, SI 2008/1202 Art.3
s.1, enabling: SI 2008/1202
s.2, applied: SI 2008/1202 Art.4
s.3, applied: SI 2008/1202 Art.4
s.4, applied: SI 2008/1202 Art.4
s.5, applied: SI 2008/1202 Art.4
s.7, applied: SI 2008/1202 Art.4
s.8, applied: SI 2008/1202 Art.4
s.9, applied: SI 2008/1202 Art.4
s.10, applied: SI 2008/1202 Art.4
s.11, applied: SI 2008/1202 Art.4
s.12, applied: SI 2008/1202 Art.4
s.13, applied: SI 2008/1202 Art.4
s.14, applied: SI 2008/1202 Art.4
s.15, applied: SI 2008/1202 Art.4
s.16, applied: SI 2008/1202 Art.4
s.17, applied: SI 2008/1202 Art.4
s.18, applied: SI 2008/1202 Art.4
s.19, applied: SI 2008/1202 Art.4
s.20, applied: SI 2008/1202 Art.4
s.21, applied: SI 2008/1202 Art.4
s.24, applied: SI 2008/1202
s.24, enabling: SI 2008/1202

27. Road Traffic (Foreign Vehicles) Act 1972
applied: 2008 c.13 Sch.3
s.3, referred to: 2008 c.13 Sch.6

35. Defective Premises Act 1972
applied: 2008 c.13 Sch.3

45. Trading Representations (Disabled Persons) Amendment Act 1972
repealed: SI 2008/1277 Sch.4 Part 1

58. National Health Service (Scotland) Act 1972
s.53, repealed: 2008 asp 5 Sch.3 Part 1

62. Agriculture (Miscellaneous Provisions) Act 1972
s.16, repealed: SI 2008/576 Sch.5 para.7
s.20, applied: SSI 2008/299, SSI 2008/300, SSI 2008/350

65. National Debt Act 1972
s.10, amended: 2008 c.9 s.163

66. Poisons Act 1972
applied: 2008 c.13 Sch.3
referred to: 2008 c.13 Sch.6

CAP.

1972–cont.

68. European Communities Act 1972
applied: 2008 c.3 Sch.2 Part 2, 2008 c.8 Sch.2 Part 24
s.1, amended: 2008 c.1 s.1, 2008 c.7 s.2, s.3, Sch.1 Part 1
s.1, referred to: SI 2008/297 Art.2, SI 2008/3116 Art.2
s.1, enabling: SI 2008/297, SI 2008/3116
s.2, see *Vodafone 2 v Revenue and Customs Commissioners* [2008] S.T.C. (S.C.D.) 55 (Sp Comm), John Walters Q.C. (Chairman)
s.2, amended: 2008 c.7 Sch.1 Part 1
s.2, applied: 2008 c.13 s.4, 2008 c.27 s.70, SI 2008/9, SI 2008/91, SI 2008/97, SI 2008/753, SI 2008/1276, SI 2008/1284, SI 2008/1317, SI 2008/1647, SI 2008/1660, SI 2008/1682, SI 2008/1718, SI 2008/2347, SI 2008/2500, SI 2008/2794, SI 2008/3144, SI 2008/3154, SI 2008/3203, SI 2008/3231, SSI 2008/395
s.2, referred to: SI 2008/644, SI 2008/916, SI 2008/1040, SI 2008/1237, SI 2008/1284, SI 2008/2411, SI 2008/2549, SI 2008/2716, SI 2008/2781, SI 2008/3196, SI 2008/3200, SSI 2008/119, SSI 2008/127, SSI 2008/129, SSI 2008/156, SSI 2008/223, SSI 2008/266, SSI 2008/300, SSI 2008/349, SSI 2008/365
s.2, enabling: SI 2008/6, SI 2008/9, SI 2008/15, SI 2008/37, SI 2008/41, SI 2008/51, SI 2008/80, SI 2008/81, SI 2008/91, SI 2008/97, SI 2008/163, SI 2008/198, SI 2008/295, SI 2008/296, SI 2008/301, SI 2008/346, SI 2008/375, SI 2008/438, SI 2008/439, SI 2008/447, SI 2008/462, SI 2008/465, SI 2008/489, SI 2008/499, SI 2008/525, SI 2008/530, SI 2008/552, SI 2008/557, SI 2008/565, SI 2008/567, SI 2008/569, SI 2008/573, SI 2008/583, SI 2008/601, SI 2008/622, SI 2008/646, SI 2008/647, SI 2008/656, SI 2008/665, SI 2008/677, SI 2008/685, SI 2008/690, SI 2008/702, SI 2008/719, SI 2008/728, SI 2008/736, SI 2008/738, SI 2008/753, SI 2008/781, SI 2008/941, SI 2008/962, SI 2008/963, SI 2008/1040, SI 2008/1064, SI 2008/1067, SI 2008/1079, SI 2008/1080, SI 2008/1090, SI 2008/1097, SI 2008/1098, SI 2008/1139, SI 2008/1140, SI 2008/1163, SI 2008/1180, SI 2008/1182, SI 2008/1267, SI 2008/1275, SI 2008/1276, SI 2008/1277, SI 2008/1284, SI 2008/1322, SI 2008/1331, SI 2008/1342, SI 2008/1428, SI 2008/1434, SI 2008/1439, SI 2008/1469, SI 2008/1519, SI 2008/1556, SI 2008/1583, SI 2008/1597, SI 2008/1646, SI 2008/1647, SI 2008/1660, SI 2008/1692, SI 2008/1714, SI 2008/1718, SI 2008/1741, SI 2008/1746, SI 2008/1792, SI 2008/1811, SI 2008/1816, SI 2008/1824, SI 2008/1881, SI 2008/1888, SI 2008/1897, SI 2008/1950, SI

CAP.

1972–cont.

68. European Communities Act 1972–*cont.*

s.2, enabling:–*cont.*

2008/1965, SI 2008/1980, SI 2008/2011, SI 2008/2072, SI 2008/2093, SI 2008/2108, SI 2008/2141, SI 2008/2164, SI 2008/2165, SI 2008/2166, SI 2008/2172, SI 2008/2256, SI 2008/2297, SI 2008/2335, SI 2008/2337, SI 2008/2349, SI 2008/2363, SI 2008/2500, SI 2008/2564, SI 2008/2570, SI 2008/2598, SI 2008/2648, SI 2008/2794, SI 2008/2795, SI 2008/2844, SI 2008/2847, SI 2008/2848, SI 2008/2851, SI 2008/2852, SI 2008/2871, SI 2008/2936, SI 2008/2986, SI 2008/3008, SI 2008/3053, SI 2008/3063, SI 2008/3073, SI 2008/3087, SI 2008/3097, SI 2008/3117, SI 2008/3143, SI 2008/3144, SI 2008/3145, SI 2008/3154, SI 2008/3203, SI 2008/3206, SI 2008/3230, SI 2008/3231, SI 2008/3252, SI 2008/3266, SI 2008/3295, SSI 2008/11, SSI 2008/17, SSI 2008/58, SSI 2008/64, SSI 2008/65, SSI 2008/66, SSI 2008/87, SSI 2008/94, SSI 2008/98, SSI 2008/99, SSI 2008/100, SSI 2008/129, SSI 2008/135, SSI 2008/148, SSI 2008/153, SSI 2008/155, SSI 2008/159, SSI 2008/162, SSI 2008/166, SSI 2008/170, SSI 2008/176, SSI 2008/184, SSI 2008/201, SSI 2008/202, SSI 2008/218, SSI 2008/233, SSI 2008/246, SSI 2008/266, SSI 2008/291, SSI 2008/294, SSI 2008/298, SSI 2008/309, SSI 2008/342, SSI 2008/350, SSI 2008/368, SSI 2008/372, SSI 2008/376, SSI 2008/389, SSI 2008/394, SSI 2008/395, SSI 2008/404, SSI 2008/417, SSI 2008/418, SSI 2008/425, SSI 2008/432

s.3, amended: 2008 c.7 Sch.1 Part 1

s.4, amended: 2008 c.7 Sch.1 Part 1

s.4, enabling: SI 2008/530

s.5, amended: 2008 c.7 Sch.1 Part 1

s.6, amended: 2008 c.7 Sch.1 Part 1

s.11, amended: 2008 c.7 Sch.1 Part 1

s.12, amended: 2008 c.7 Sch.1 Part 1

Sch.1 Part I para.1, amended: 2008 c.7 Sch.1 Part 1

Sch.1 Part I para.2, amended: 2008 c.7 Sch.1 Part 1

Sch.1 Part I para.3, amended: 2008 c.7 Sch.1 Part 1

Sch.1 Part I para.4, amended: 2008 c.7 Sch.1 Part 1

Sch.1 Part I para.5, amended: 2008 c.7 Sch.1 Part 1

Sch.1 Part I para.6, amended: 2008 c.7 Sch.1 Part 1

Sch.1 Part I para.7, amended: 2008 c.7 Sch.1 Part 1

Sch.1 Part II, amended: 2008 c.7 Sch.1 Part 1

CAP.

1972–cont.

68. European Communities Act 1972–*cont.*

Sch.2 para.1A, amended: 2008 c.7 Sch.1 Part 1

Sch.2 para.1A, applied: SI 2008/81, SI 2008/916, SI 2008/1284, SI 2008/1331, SI 2008/1682, SI 2008/1824, SI 2008/2500, SI 2008/2716, SI 2008/2781, SI 2008/3144, SSI 2008/119, SSI 2008/300

Sch.2 para.1A, referred to: SI 2008/1237, SI 2008/2570

Sch.2 para.1A, enabling: SI 2008/6, SI 2008/9, SI 2008/15, SI 2008/438, SI 2008/439, SI 2008/447, SI 2008/601, SI 2008/644, SI 2008/685, SI 2008/962, SI 2008/1040, SI 2008/1090, SI 2008/1098, SI 2008/1317, SI 2008/1428, SI 2008/1718, SI 2008/1811, SI 2008/1881, SI 2008/2072, SI 2008/2108, SI 2008/2141, SI 2008/2347, SI 2008/2411, SI 2008/2500, SI 2008/2549, SI 2008/3087, SI 2008/3143, SI 2008/3144, SI 2008/3154, SI 2008/3196, SI 2008/3203, SI 2008/3206, SI 2008/3230, SI 2008/3231, SSI 2008/11, SSI 2008/64, SSI 2008/98, SSI 2008/100, SSI 2008/102, SSI 2008/119, SSI 2008/127, SSI 2008/129, SSI 2008/135, SSI 2008/156, SSI 2008/159, SSI 2008/162, SSI 2008/223, SSI 2008/266, SSI 2008/300, SSI 2008/342, SSI 2008/349, SSI 2008/350, SSI 2008/365, SSI 2008/395, SSI 2008/418

Sch.2 para.2, applied: SI 2008/198, SI 2008/963, SI 2008/1277, SI 2008/1746, SI 2008/1816

Sch.2 para.2A, applied: SI 2008/1746

Sch.2 para.4, amended: 2008 c.7 Sch.1 Part 1

70. Local Government Act 1972

applied: SI 2008/570 Sch.1 para.1, SI 2008/634 Art.3, Art.4, SI 2008/700 Sch.1 para.1, SI 2008/907 Art.4, SI 2008/1848 Reg.11

referred to: SI 2008/1184 Reg.21, SI 2008/2439 Reg.37

varied: SI 2008/1848 Reg.11

Part V, applied: SI 2008/634 Art.9, SI 2008/907 Art.20, SI 2008/1572 Art.6

Part VA, applied: SI 2008/580 Art.9, SI 2008/634 Art.9, SI 2008/907 Art.20, SI 2008/1085 Reg.8

Part VA, disapplied: SI 2008/1085 Reg.8

Part VI, referred to: 2008 c.29 s.207

Part IX, applied: 2008 c.13 Sch.3

Part XI, applied: 2008 c.13 Sch.3

s.2, disapplied: SI 2008/907 Art.3, Art.4

s.2, varied: SI 2008/634 Art.3, Art.4, SI 2008/907 Art.4

s.3, applied: SI 2008/634 Art.9, SI 2008/907 Art.20

s.5, applied: SI 2008/634 Art.9, SI 2008/907 Art.20

CAP.

1972–cont.

70. Local Government Act 1972–*cont.*

s.7, disapplied: SI 2008/491 Art.12, SI 2008/492 Art.12, SI 2008/494 Art.13, SI 2008/634 Art.12, SI 2008/907 Art.12, Art.13, Art.23, Art.25

s.16, disapplied: SI 2008/490 Art.12, SI 2008/491 Art.13, SI 2008/492 Art.13, SI 2008/493 Art.14, SI 2008/494 Art.14, SI 2008/625 Reg.10, SI 2008/634 Art.15, SI 2008/907 Art.26

s.22, applied: SI 2008/788 Sch.1

s.24, applied: SI 2008/788 Sch.1

s.54, applied: SI 2008/584, SI 2008/3152

s.54, enabling: SI 2008/584

s.58, applied: SI 2008/584

s.58, enabling: SI 2008/584, SI 2008/3152

s.67, enabling: SI 2008/584

s.83, varied: SI 2008/634 Art.9

s.89, applied: SI 2008/907 Art.5

s.89, disapplied: SI 2008/491 Art.12, SI 2008/492 Art.12, SI 2008/634 Art.5, Art.12, SI 2008/907 Art.12, Art.23, Art.24, SI 2008/2113 Reg.13

s.89, varied: SI 2008/2857 Art.5

s.92, applied: SI 2008/1572 Art.6

s.94, applied: SI 2008/788 Art.4

s.95, applied: SI 2008/788 Art.4

s.96, applied: SI 2008/788 Art.4

s.97, applied: SI 2008/788 Art.4

s.98, applied: SI 2008/788 Art.4

s.100A, applied: SI 2008/1085 Reg.8

s.100A, varied: SI 2008/580 Art.9

s.100B, applied: SI 2008/1085 Reg.8

s.100B, varied: SI 2008/580 Art.9

s.100C, applied: SI 2008/1085 Reg.8

s.100E, applied: SI 2008/1085 Reg.8

s.100E, disapplied: SI 2008/580 Art.9

s.100EA, disapplied: SI 2008/580 Art.9

s.100F, disapplied: SI 2008/580 Art.9

s.100G, applied: SI 2008/1085 Reg.8

s.100G, disapplied: SI 2008/580 Art.9

s.100G, varied: SI 2008/580 Art.9

s.100H, varied: SI 2008/580 Art.9

s.100J, amended: 2008 c.17 Sch.8 para.15

s.100J, applied: SI 2008/1085 Reg.8

s.100K, amended: 2008 c.17 Sch.8 para.16

s.100K, applied: SI 2008/1085 Reg.8

s.100K, varied: SI 2008/580 Art.9

s.101, amended: 2008 c.29 s.224

s.101, applied: SI 2008/490 Art.8, SI 2008/491 Art.8, SI 2008/492 Art.8, SI 2008/493 Art.8, SI 2008/494 Art.8, SI 2008/609 Reg.8, SI 2008/634 Art.17, SI 2008/907 Art.9, SI 2008/1184 Reg.21

s.101, disapplied: SI 2008/3095 Art.3

s.102, applied: SI 2008/609 Reg.8

s.102, disapplied: SI 2008/2867 Reg.16

s.103, applied: SI 2008/634 Art.9, SI 2008/907 Art.20

s.105, applied: SI 2008/788 Art.4

CAP.

1972–cont.

70. Local Government Act 1972–*cont.*

s.106, applied: SI 2008/634 Art.9, SI 2008/907 Art.20

s.111, see *Ramblers' Association v Coventry City Council* [2008] EWHC 796 (Admin), Times, May 27, 2008 (QBD (Admin)), Michael Supperstone Q.C.

s.117, see *Kynnersley v Wolverhampton City Council* [2008] W.T.L.R. 65 (Ch D (Birmingham)), Judge Norris Q.C.

s.146, applied: SI 2008/634 Art.9, SI 2008/907 Art.20

s.146A, referred to: 2008 c.12 Sch.2 para.8

s.151, applied: SI 2008/228 Sch.1 para.20, SI 2008/3248 Reg.9

s.173, applied: 2008 c.25 s.48, SI 2008/532 Sch.1 para.5, SI 2008/788 Sch.1

s.173A, applied: 2008 c.25 s.48, SI 2008/788 Sch.1

s.174, applied: 2008 c.25 s.48, SI 2008/532 Sch.1 para.5, SI 2008/788 Sch.1

s.175, applied: SI 2008/788 Sch.1

s.176, applied: SI 2008/788 Sch.1

s.177, amended: 2008 c.25 Sch.1 para.42, Sch.2

s.178, applied: SI 2008/634 Art.9, SI 2008/907 Art.20

s.233, applied: 2008 c.29 s.229

s.236, amended: 2008 c.26 Sch.4 para.48

s.236, applied: SI 2008/1261 Art.5

s.236, varied: SI 2008/230 Art.6, SI 2008/1261 Art.5

s.236B, amended: 2008 c.26 Sch.4 para.48

s.238, amended: 2008 c.26 Sch.4 para.48

s.238, applied: SI 2008/1261 Art.5

s.238, varied: SI 2008/1261 Art.5

s.249, varied: SI 2008/2867 Reg.32

s.250, applied: 2008 c.14 s.75, 2008 c.29 s.113

s.250, varied: 2008 c.29 s.113, SI 2008/1261 Art.68

s.262, enabling: SI 2008/1285

Sch.12 Part IA para.6A, varied: SI 2008/2857 Art.6

Sch.12 Part III para.14, varied: SI 2008/2857 Art.6

Sch.12A Part I, applied: SI 2008/1085 Reg.8

Sch.12A Part I para.1, varied: SI 2008/580 Art.9

Sch.12A Part I para.2, varied: SI 2008/580 Art.9

Sch.12A Part I para.2A, varied: SI 2008/580 Art.9

Sch.12A Part I para.3, varied: SI 2008/580 Art.9

Sch.12A Part I para.4, varied: SI 2008/580 Art.9

Sch.12A Part I para.5, varied: SI 2008/580 Art.9

Sch.12A Part I para.6, varied: SI 2008/580 Art.9

CAP.

1972–cont.

70. Local Government Act 1972–*cont.*

Sch.12A Part I para.6A, varied: SI 2008/580 Art.9

Sch.12A Part I para.6B, varied: SI 2008/580 Art.9

Sch.12A Part I para.7, varied: SI 2008/580 Art.9

Sch.12A Part I para.7A, varied: SI 2008/580 Art.9, SI 2008/1085 Reg.8

Sch.12A Part I para.7B, varied: SI 2008/580 Art.9, SI 2008/1085 Reg.8

Sch.12A Part I para.7C, varied: SI 2008/580 Art.9, SI 2008/1085 Reg.8

Sch.12A Part I para.8, varied: SI 2008/580 Art.9

Sch.12A Part I para.9, varied: SI 2008/580 Art.9

Sch.12A Part I para.10, varied: SI 2008/580 Art.9

Sch.12A Part I para.11, varied: SI 2008/580 Art.9

Sch.12A Part I para.12, varied: SI 2008/580 Art.9

Sch.12A Part I para.13, varied: SI 2008/580 Art.9

Sch.12A Part I para.14, varied: SI 2008/580 Art.9

Sch.12A Part I para.15, varied: SI 2008/580 Art.9

Sch.12A Part II, applied: SI 2008/1085 Reg.8

Sch.12A Part II para.1, varied: SI 2008/580 Art.9

Sch.12A Part II para.2, varied: SI 2008/580 Art.9

Sch.12A Part II para.3, varied: SI 2008/580 Art.9

Sch.12A Part II para.4, varied: SI 2008/580 Art.9

Sch.12A Part II para.5, varied: SI 2008/580 Art.9

Sch.12A Part II para.6, varied: SI 2008/580 Art.9

Sch.12A Part II para.6B, varied: SI 2008/580 Art.9

Sch.12A Part II para.7, varied: SI 2008/580 Art.9

Sch.12A Part II para.8, varied: SI 2008/580 Art.9

Sch.12A Part II para.9, varied: SI 2008/580 Art.9

Sch.12A Part II para.10, varied: SI 2008/580 Art.9

Sch.12A Part III, applied: SI 2008/1085 Reg.8

Sch.12A Part III para.1, varied: SI 2008/580 Art.9

Sch.12A Part III para.2, varied: SI 2008/580 Art.9

Sch.12A Part III para.11, varied: SI 2008/580 Art.9

Sch.12A Part IV para.12, varied: SI 2008/580 Art.9

CAP.

1972–cont.

70. Local Government Act 1972–*cont.*

Sch.12A Part IV para.13, varied: SI 2008/580 Art.9

Sch.12A Part IV para.14, varied: SI 2008/580 Art.9

Sch.12A Part IV para.15, varied: SI 2008/580 Art.9

Sch.12A Part IV para.16, varied: SI 2008/580 Art.9

Sch.12A Part IV para.17, varied: SI 2008/580 Art.9

Sch.12A Part IV para.18, varied: SI 2008/580 Art.9

Sch.12A Part IV para.18A, varied: SI 2008/580 Art.9

Sch.12A Part IV para.18B, varied: SI 2008/580 Art.9

Sch.12A Part IV para.18C, varied: SI 2008/580 Art.9

Sch.12A Part IV para.19, varied: SI 2008/580 Art.9

Sch.12A Part IV para.20, varied: SI 2008/580 Art.9

Sch.12A Part IV para.21, varied: SI 2008/580 Art.9

Sch.12A Part IV para.22, varied: SI 2008/580 Art.9

Sch.12A Part IV para.23, varied: SI 2008/580 Art.9

Sch.12A Part IV para.24, varied: SI 2008/580 Art.9

Sch.12A Part IV para.25, varied: SI 2008/580 Art.9

Sch.12A Part IV para.26, varied: SI 2008/580 Art.9

Sch.12A Part IV para.27, varied: SI 2008/580 Art.9

Sch.12A Part V para.19, varied: SI 2008/580 Art.9

Sch.12A Part V para.20, varied: SI 2008/580 Art.9

Sch.12A Part V para.21, varied: SI 2008/580 Art.9

Sch.12A Part V para.28, varied: SI 2008/580 Art.9

Sch.12A Part V para.29, varied: SI 2008/580 Art.9

Sch.12A Part V para.30, varied: SI 2008/580 Art.9

Sch.12A Part V para.31, varied: SI 2008/580 Art.9

Sch.12A Part V para.32, varied: SI 2008/580 Art.9

Sch.12A Part V para.33, varied: SI 2008/580 Art.9

Sch.12A Part V para.34, varied: SI 2008/580 Art.9

Sch.12A Part VI para.22, varied: SI 2008/580 Art.9

Sch.12A Part VI para.35, varied: SI 2008/580 Art.9

CAP.

1972–cont.

70. Local Government Act 1972–*cont.*
Sch.14 Part II para.25, amended: SI 2008/2840 Art.3
Sch.14 Part II para.25, applied: SI 2008/2840 Art.3
Sch.14 Part II para.25, repealed (in part): SI 2008/2840 Art.3
Sch.29 Part II para.44, repealed (in part): SI 2008/1277 Sch.4 Part 1

71. Criminal Justice Act 1972
s.31, repealed: 2008 c.12 Sch.1 Part 3
s.59, repealed: 2008 c.12 Sch.1 Part 3
s.66, amended: 2008 c.12 Sch.1 Part 3
s.66, repealed (in part): 2008 c.12 Sch.1 Part 3

1973

13. Supply of Goods (Implied Terms) Act 1973
applied: 2008 c.13 Sch.3

16. Education Act 1973
s.3, enabling: SI 2008/1477

18. Matrimonial Causes Act 1973
see *MT v OT (Financial Provision: Costs)* [2007] EWHC 838 (Fam), [2008] 2 F.L.R. 1311 (Fam Div), Charles, J.; see *Whig v Whig* [2007] EWHC 1856 (Fam), [2008] 1 F.L.R. 453 (Fam Div), Munby, J.
applied: 2008 c.30 s.109
Part II, applied: 2008 c.30 s.118
s.11, see *Burns v Burns* [2007] EWHC 2492 (Fam), [2008] 1 F.L.R. 813 (Fam Div), Coleridge, J.
s.12, see *Westminster City Council v C* [2008] EWCA Civ 198, [2008] 2 F.L.R. 267 (CA (Civ Div)), Thorpe, L.J.
s.14, see *Burns v Burns* [2007] EWHC 2492 (Fam), [2008] 1 F.L.R. 813 (Fam Div), Coleridge, J.
s.21B, added: 2008 c.30 Sch.6 para.2
s.21C, added: 2008 c.30 Sch.6 para.2
s.23, applied: SI 2008/1582 Sch.4 para.1, SI 2008/3170 Sch.5 para.1, Sch.6 para.1
s.24, see *K v K* [2007] EWHC 3485 (Fam), [2008] 3 F.C.R. 773 (Fam Div), Richard Anelay Q.C.
s.24E, added: 2008 c.30 Sch.6 para.3
s.24F, added: 2008 c.30 Sch.6 para.3
s.24G, added: 2008 c.30 Sch.6 para.3
s.25, see *B v B (Ancillary Relief)* [2008] EWCA Civ 543, [2008] 1 W.L.R. 2362 (CA (Civ Div)), Sir Mark Potter (President, Fam); see *B v P* [2008] EWHC 112 (Fam), [2008] 1 F.L.R. 742 (Fam Div), Sir Mark Potter (President, Fam); see *Behzadi v Behzadi* [2008] EWCA Civ 1070, [2008] 3 F.C.R. 705 (CA (Civ Div)), Rix, L.J.; see *CR v CR* [2007] EWHC 3334 (Fam), [2008] 1 F.L.R. 323 (Fam Div), Bodey, J.; see *Crossley v Crossley* [2007] EWCA Civ 1491, [2008] 1 F.L.R. 1467 (CA (Civ Div)), Thorpe, L.J.; see *L v L (Ancillary Relief)*

CAP.

1973–cont.

18. Matrimonial Causes Act 1973–*cont.*
s.25–*cont.*
[2008] EWHC 3328 (Fam), [2008] 1 F.L.R. 142 (Fam Div), Richard Anelay Q.C.; see *McCartney v Mills McCartney* [2008] EWHC 401 (Fam), [2008] 1 F.L.R. 1508 (Fam Div), Bennett, J.; see *Williams v Thompson Leatherdale (A Firm)* [2008] EWHC 2574 (QB), [2008] 3 F.C.R. 613 (QBD), Field, J.
s.25, amended: 2008 c.30 Sch.6 para.4
s.25A, see *S v S* [2008] EWHC 519 (Fam), [2008] 2 F.L.R. 113 (Fam Div), Sir Mark Potter (President)
s.25A, amended: 2008 c.30 Sch.6 para.5
s.25B, applied: SI 2008/1582 Sch.4 para.1, SI 2008/3170 Sch.5 para.1, Sch.6 para.1
s.25E, amended: 2008 c.30 Sch.6 para.6, Sch.11 Part 4
s.25E, applied: SI 2008/1582 Sch.4 para.1, SI 2008/3170 Sch.5 para.1, Sch.6 para.1
s.25F, added: 2008 c.30 Sch.6 para.7
s.25G, added: 2008 c.30 Sch.6 para.7
s.28, see *E v E (Premature Remarriage)* [2008] 1 F.L.R. 220 (Fam Div), Singer, J.
s.31, see *L v L* [2006] EWHC 956 (Fam), [2008] 1 F.L.R. 26 (Fam Div), Munby, J.; see *North v North* [2007] EWCA Civ 760, [2008] 1 F.L.R. 158 (CA (Civ Div)), Thorpe, L.J.
s.31, amended: 2008 c.30 Sch.6 para.8, Sch.11 Part 4
s.37, see *Burke v Chapman & Chubb (A Firm)* [2008] EWHC 341 (QB), [2008] 2 F.L.R. 1207 (QBD), Plender, J; see *C v C (Privilege)* [2006] EWHC 336 (Fam), [2008] 1 F.L.R. 115 (Fam Div), Munby, J.
s.40B, added: 2008 c.30 Sch.6 para.9

24. Employment of Children Act 1973
repealed: 2008 c.12 Sch.1 Part 11

26. Land Compensation Act 1973
s.1, varied: 2008 c.29 s.152
s.2, varied: 2008 c.29 s.152
s.3, varied: 2008 c.29 s.152
s.4, varied: 2008 c.29 s.152
s.5, varied: 2008 c.29 s.152
s.6, varied: 2008 c.29 s.152
s.7, varied: 2008 c.29 s.152
s.8, see *Lall v Transport for London* [2008] R.V.R. 183 (Lands Tr), George Bartlett Q.C. (President)
s.8, varied: 2008 c.29 s.152
s.9, varied: 2008 c.29 s.152
s.10, varied: 2008 c.29 s.152
s.11, varied: 2008 c.29 s.152
s.12, varied: 2008 c.29 s.152
s.12A, varied: 2008 c.29 s.152
s.13, varied: 2008 c.29 s.152
s.14, varied: 2008 c.29 s.152
s.15, varied: 2008 c.29 s.152
s.16, varied: 2008 c.29 s.152

1973–cont.

26. Land Compensation Act 1973–*cont.*
s.17, varied: 2008 c.29 s.152
s.18, varied: 2008 c.29 s.152
s.19, varied: 2008 c.29 s.152
s.30, amended: SI 2008/1598 Reg.2
s.30, applied: SI 2008/2845 Reg.2
s.30, enabling: SI 2008/1598, SI 2008/2845
s.32, varied: SI 2008/2839 Sch.1 para.1
s.39, amended: 2008 c.17 Sch.8 para.17
s.44, varied: 2008 c.18 Sch.6 para.7, SI 2008/1238 Sch.1 para.2, SI 2008/2512 Sch.6 para.2
s.52, see *Lall v Transport for London* [2008] R.V.R. 183 (Lands Tr), George Bartlett Q.C. (President)
s.52A, see *Lall v Transport for London* [2008] R.V.R. 183 (Lands Tr), George Bartlett Q.C. (President)
s.58, varied: 2008 c.18 Sch.6 para.7, SI 2008/1238 Sch.1 para.2, SI 2008/2512 Sch.6 para.2

33. Protection of Wrecks Act 1973
applied: SI 2008/2775 Art.2
referred to: 2008 c.13 Sch.6
s.1, enabling: SI 2008/2775

35. Employment Agencies Act 1973
applied: 2008 c.13 Sch.3, SI 2008/1909 Sch.1
s.3B, amended: 2008 c.24 s.15
s.5, amended: 2008 c.24 s.15
s.5, referred to: 2008 c.13 Sch.6
s.6, amended: 2008 c.24 s.15
s.6, referred to: 2008 c.13 Sch.6
s.9, amended: 2008 c.24 s.16, s.18, Sch.1 Part 5
s.9, repealed (in part): 2008 c.24 s.16, Sch.1 Part 5
s.10, referred to: 2008 c.13 Sch.6
s.11, substituted: 2008 c.24 s.17
s.11A, amended: 2008 c.24 Sch.1 Part 5

41. Fair Trading Act 1973
applied: 2008 c.13 Sch.3
Part II, applied: SI 2008/1277 Sch.3 para.15
Part XI, see *Secretary of State for Business, Enterprise and Regulatory Reform v Amway (UK) Ltd* [2008] EWHC 1054 (Ch), [2008] B.C.C. 713 (Ch D), Norris, J.
s.23, applied: SI 2008/1277 Sch.3 para.9
s.23, referred to: 2008 c.13 Sch.6
s.23, repealed: SI 2008/1277 Sch.4 Part 1
s.24, repealed: SI 2008/1277 Sch.4 Part 1
s.25, repealed: SI 2008/1277 Sch.4 Part 1
s.26, repealed: SI 2008/1277 Sch.4 Part 1
s.27, repealed: SI 2008/1277 Sch.4 Part 1
s.28, repealed: SI 2008/1277 Sch.4 Part 1
s.29, repealed: SI 2008/1277 Sch.4 Part 1
s.30, referred to: 2008 c.13 Sch.6
s.30, repealed: SI 2008/1277 Sch.4 Part 1
s.31, repealed: SI 2008/1277 Sch.4 Part 1
s.32, repealed: SI 2008/1277 Sch.4 Part 1

1973–cont.

41. Fair Trading Act 1973–*cont.*
s.33, repealed: SI 2008/1277 Sch.4 Part 1
s.120, referred to: 2008 c.13 Sch.6
s.132, amended: SI 2008/1277 Sch.4 Part 1

43. Hallmarking Act 1973
applied: 2008 c.13 Sch.3
s.1, amended: SI 2008/1277 Sch.2 para.16
s.1, applied: SI 2008/1277 Sch.3 para.1, Sch.3 para.4
s.1, referred to: 2008 c.13 Sch.6
s.1, repealed (in part): SI 2008/1277 Sch.4 Part 1
s.3, referred to: 2008 c.13 Sch.6
s.5, referred to: 2008 c.13 Sch.6
s.6, referred to: 2008 c.13 Sch.6
s.7, referred to: 2008 c.13 Sch.6
s.11, referred to: 2008 c.13 Sch.6
Sch.1 Part III para.1, amended: SI 2008/1277 Sch.2 para.16
Sch.4 para.19, amended: SI 2008/948 Sch.1 para.1

50. Employment and Training Act 1973
s.2, applied: SI 2008/529 Reg.120, Reg.137, SI 2008/794 Reg.32, Reg.45, Reg.91, Reg.105, Reg.106, Reg.107, Reg.115, Sch.4 para.4, Sch.5 Part 1, Sch.6 para.15, Sch.8 para.15, Sch.9 para.32, SI 2008/1273 Reg.67, Reg.82, SI 2008/1582 Reg.120, Reg.137, SI 2008/1909 Sch.1, SI 2008/3170 Reg.67, Reg.82
s.4, applied: SI 2008/792 Art.6
s.10, applied: SI 2008/3093 Reg.10

51. Finance Act 1973
applied: SI 2008/1578, SI 2008/1580, SI 2008/1581
s.56, applied: SI 2008/1881, SI 2008/3154
s.56, enabling: SI 2008/506, SI 2008/525, SI 2008/530, SI 2008/552, SI 2008/732, SI 2008/1576, SI 2008/1577, SI 2008/1578, SI 2008/1580, SI 2008/1581, SI 2008/1881, SI 2008/1965, SI 2008/2269, SI 2008/2270, SI 2008/2297, SI 2008/2716, SI 2008/3153, SI 2008/3154, SI 2008/3196, SI 2008/3233, SSI 2008/378, SSI 2008/423

52. Prescription and Limitation (Scotland) Act 1973
s.6, see *Royal Insurance (UK) Ltd v Amec Construction (Scotland) Ltd* [2008] CSOH 107, 2008 S.L.T. 825 (OH), Lord Emslie
s.9, see *Royal Insurance (UK) Ltd v Amec Construction (Scotland) Ltd* [2008] CSOH 107, 2008 S.L.T. 825 (OH), Lord Emslie
s.11, see *Royal Insurance (UK) Ltd v Amec Construction (Scotland) Ltd* [2008] CSOH 107, 2008 S.L.T. 825 (OH), Lord Emslie
s.17, see *B v Murray (No.2)* [2008] UKHL 32, 2008 S.C. (H.L.) 146 (HL), Lord Hoffmann

CAP.

1973–cont.

52. Prescription and Limitation (Scotland) Act 1973–*cont.*
s.23A, amended: SSI 2008/404 Reg.3

60. Breeding of Dogs Act 1973
applied: 2008 c.13 Sch.3
referred to: 2008 c.13 Sch.6

63. Government Trading Funds Act 1973
applied: SI 2008/563, SI 2008/590
s.1, enabling: SI 2008/563, SI 2008/590, SI 2008/628, SI 2008/1208
s.2, applied: SI 2008/563, SI 2008/590
s.2, enabling: SI 2008/563, SI 2008/590, SI 2008/628
s.2A, applied: SI 2008/563 Art.5, SI 2008/590 Art.5
s.2A, enabling: SI 2008/563, SI 2008/590, SI 2008/628
s.2AA, enabling: SI 2008/563, SI 2008/590, SI 2008/628
s.2B, applied: SI 2008/563 Art.5, SI 2008/590 Art.5
s.2C, enabling: SI 2008/563, SI 2008/590
s.6, applied: SI 2008/590
s.6, enabling: SI 2008/563, SI 2008/628, SI 2008/1208

65. Local Government (Scotland) Act 1973
applied: SSI 2008/199 Art.8
s.26, applied: SSI 2008/325
s.26, enabling: SSI 2008/325
s.35, applied: SI 2008/2252 Sch.1 para.18
s.50, enabling: SSI 2008/414
s.85, applied: SI 2008/2252 Sch.1 para.16
s.97, amended: SI 2008/948 Sch.1 para.1
s.202, applied: SSI 2008/189 Art.28, SSI 2008/190 Art.28
s.202, referred to: SSI 2008/188 Art.28
s.202, repealed (in part): 2008 asp 5 Sch.3 Part 1
s.210, applied: 2008 c.29 s.113, SSI 2008/199 Art.8, SSI 2008/200 Art.7
s.210, varied: 2008 c.29 s.113
s.233, enabling: SSI 2008/325
Sch.27 Part II para.26, repealed: 2008 asp 5 Sch.3 Part 1
Sch.27 Part II para.27, repealed: 2008 asp 5 Sch.3 Part 1
Sch.27 Part II para.28, repealed: 2008 asp 5 Sch.3 Part 1
Sch.27 Part II para.29, repealed: 2008 asp 5 Sch.3 Part 1
Sch.27 Part II para.33, repealed: 2008 asp 5 Sch.3 Part 1
Sch.27 Part II para.34, repealed: 2008 asp 5 Sch.3 Part 1
Sch.27 Part II para.35, repealed: 2008 asp 5 Sch.3 Part 1
Sch.27 Part II para.36, repealed: 2008 asp 5 Sch.3 Part 1
Sch.27 Part II para.39, repealed: 2008 asp 5 Sch.3 Part 1

CAP.

1973–cont.

65. Local Government (Scotland) Act 1973–*cont.*
Sch.27 Part II para.40, repealed: 2008 asp 5 Sch.3 Part 1
Sch.27 Part II para.41, repealed: 2008 asp 5 Sch.3 Part 1
Sch.27 Part II para.42, repealed: 2008 asp 5 Sch.3 Part 1
Sch.27 Part II para.43, repealed: 2008 asp 5 Sch.3 Part 1
Sch.27 Part II para.44, repealed: 2008 asp 5 Sch.3 Part 1
Sch.27 Part II para.45, repealed: 2008 asp 5 Sch.3 Part 1
Sch.27 Part II para.46, repealed: 2008 asp 5 Sch.3 Part 1
Sch.27 Part II para.47, repealed: 2008 asp 5 Sch.3 Part 1
Sch.27 Part II para.48, repealed: 2008 asp 5 Sch.3 Part 1

66. Channel Tunnel (Initial Finance) Act 1973
repealed: 2008 c.12 Sch.1 Part 11

1974

xxiv. Greater London Council (General Powers) Act 1974
s.15, see *Wolman v Islington LBC* [2007] EWCA Civ 823, [2008] 1 All E.R. 1259 (CA (Civ Div)), Waller, L.J.

xxxvi. Port of Tyne (North Shields Fish Harbour) Act 1974
referred to: SI 2008/1817 Art.1

3. Slaughterhouses Act 1974
applied: 2008 c.13 Sch.3

6. Biological Weapons Act 1974
s.1, applied: 2008 c.28 Sch.2

7. Local Government Act 1974
Part III, applied: SI 2008/239 Reg.9
s.25, amended: 2008 c.17 Sch.8 para.18
s.25, repealed (in part): 2008 c.17 Sch.8 para.18, Sch.16
s.26, amended: 2008 c.17 Sch.8 para.18
s.26, repealed (in part): 2008 c.17 Sch.8 para.18, Sch.16
s.26, varied: SI 2008/3068 Art.11
Sch.5 para.8, amended: 2008 c.17 Sch.8 para.18

8. Statutory Corporations (Financial Provisions) Act 1974
s.4, amended: 2008 c.17 Sch.16

9. Pensions (Increase) Act 1974
applied: SSI 2008/230 Reg.38

23. Juries Act 1974
s.11, see *R. v B* [2008] EWCA Crim 1997, Times, October 8, 2008 (CA (Crim Div)), Toulson, L.J.

24. Prices Act 1974
applied: 2008 c.13 Sch.3
referred to: 2008 c.13 Sch.6

CAP.

1974–cont.

32. Town and Country Amenities Act 1974

repealed: 2008 c.12 Sch.1 Part 9

s.12, referred to: 2008 c.12 Sch.2 para.7

37. Health and Safety at Work etc Act 1974

applied: 2008 c.13 Sch.3, SI 2008/228 Sch.1 para.20, Sch.5 para.21, SI 2008/736 Reg.15, Reg.16, Reg.17, Reg.18, SI 2008/1597 Sch.5 para.17

see *R. v FJ Chalcroft Construction Ltd* [2008] EWCA Crim 770, [2008] 2 Cr. App. R. (S.) 105 (CA (Crim Div)), Toulson, L.J.

Part I, applied: 2008 c.32 s.99

s.2, see *R. v John Pointon & Sons Ltd* [2008] EWCA Crim 513, [2008] 2 Cr. App. R. (S.) 82 (CA (Crim Div)), Gage, L.J.

s.3, applied: SI 2008/1660 Sch.2 para.8

s.3, see *R. v N Ltd* [2008] EWCA Crim 1223, [2008] 1 W.L.R. 2684 (CA (Crim Div)), Hughes, L.J.; see *R. v Porter (James Godfrey)* [2008] EWCA Crim 1271, [2008] I.C.R. 1259 (CA (Crim Div)), Moses, L.J.

s.10, applied: SI 2008/960 Art.2, Sch.2 para.3

s.10, substituted: SI 2008/960 Art.4

s.11, applied: SI 2008/1087(b), SI 2008/2337(b), SI 2008/736 Sch.14, SI 2008/736(b), SI 2008/960 Sch.2 para.10

s.11, substituted: SI 2008/960 Art.5

s.12, applied: SI 2008/960 Sch.2 para.10

s.12, substituted: SI 2008/960 Art.5

s.13, applied: SI 2008/960 Sch.2 para.7, SI 2008/1660 Sch.2 para.8

s.13, substituted: SI 2008/960 Art.5

s.14, amended: SI 2008/960 Art.6

s.14, applied: SI 2008/960 Sch.2 para.5, Sch.2 para.6

s.15, amended: SI 2008/960 Art.7

s.15, applied: 2008 c.32 s.99

s.15, repealed (in part): 2008 c.20 Sch.3 para.2, Sch.4

s.15, enabling: SI 2008/2323, SI 2008/2337

s.16, amended: SI 2008/960 Art.8

s.16, applied: SI 2008/960 Sch.2 para.8

s.17, amended: SI 2008/960 Art.9

s.18, amended: SI 2008/960 Art.10

s.18, applied: SI 2008/960 Sch.2 para.10, SI 2008/1597 Sch.5 para.3

s.19, applied: SI 2008/960 Sch.2 para.10, SI 2008/1597 Sch.5 para.7, SI 2008/2852 Sch.7 para.3

s.19, varied: SI 2008/1597 Sch.5 para.8, SI 2008/2108 Reg.4

s.20, applied: SI 2008/1597 Reg.21, Sch.5 para.7

s.20, varied: SI 2008/1597 Sch.5 para.8, SI 2008/2108 Reg.4

s.21, applied: SI 2008/101 Reg.11, Reg.12, SI 2008/540 Reg.11, Reg.12, SI 2008/1597 Sch.5 para.7

CAP.

1974–cont.

37. Health and Safety at Work etc Act 1974–*cont.*

s.21, varied: SI 2008/1597 Sch.5 para.8

s.22, applied: SI 2008/101 Reg.11, Reg.12, SI 2008/540 Reg.11, Reg.12, SI 2008/1597 Sch.5 para.7

s.22, varied: SI 2008/1597 Sch.5 para.8

s.23, applied: SI 2008/1597 Sch.5 para.7

s.23, varied: SI 2008/1597 Sch.5 para.8

s.24, applied: SI 2008/736 Reg.18, SI 2008/1597 Sch.5 para.7

s.24, varied: SI 2008/1597 Sch.5 para.8

s.25, applied: SI 2008/1597 Sch.5 para.7

s.25, varied: SI 2008/1597 Sch.5 para.8

s.25A, applied: SI 2008/1597 Sch.5 para.7, SI 2008/2852 Reg.9

s.25A, varied: SI 2008/1597 Sch.5 para.8, SI 2008/2108 Reg.4

s.26, applied: SI 2008/1597 Sch.5 para.7

s.26, varied: SI 2008/1597 Sch.5 para.8, SI 2008/2108 Reg.4

s.27, amended: SI 2008/960 Art.11

s.27, applied: SI 2008/960 Sch.2 para.9, SI 2008/1597 Sch.5 para.7

s.27, varied: SI 2008/1597 Sch.5 para.8, SI 2008/2108 Reg.4

s.27A, applied: SI 2008/1597 Sch.5 para.7

s.27A, varied: SI 2008/1597 Sch.5 para.8, SI 2008/2108 Reg.4

s.28, amended: SI 2008/960 Art.12, SSI 2008/339 Art.5

s.28, applied: SI 2008/960 Sch.2 para.9, SI 2008/1597 Sch.5 para.7

s.28, varied: SI 2008/1597 Sch.5 para.8, SI 2008/2108 Reg.4

s.33, amended: 2008 c.20 s.1

s.33, applied: SI 2008/1597 Sch.5 para.7, SI 2008/2108 Reg.4

s.33, referred to: 2008 c.13 Sch.6

s.33, varied: SI 2008/1597 Sch.5 para.8, SI 2008/2108 Reg.4

s.33, see *R. v Chargot Ltd (t/a Contract Services)* [2007] EWCA Crim 3032, [2008] 2 All E.R. 1077 (CA (Crim Div)), Latham, L.J.; see *R. v John Pointon & Sons Ltd* [2008] EWCA Crim 513, [2008] 2 Cr. App. R. (S.) 82 (CA (Crim Div)), Gage, L.J.; see *R. v N Ltd* [2008] EWCA Crim 1223, [2008] 1 W.L.R. 2684 (CA (Crim Div)), Hughes, L.J.

s.34, amended: SI 2008/960 Art.13

s.34, applied: SI 2008/1597 Sch.5 para.7

s.34, varied: SI 2008/1597 Sch.5 para.8, Sch.5 para.13, SI 2008/2108 Reg.4

s.35, applied: SI 2008/1597 Sch.5 para.7

s.35, varied: SI 2008/1597 Sch.5 para.8, SI 2008/2108 Reg.4

s.36, applied: SI 2008/1597 Sch.5 para.7

s.36, varied: SI 2008/1597 Sch.5 para.8, SI 2008/2108 Reg.4

s.37, applied: SI 2008/1597 Sch.5 para.7

CAP.

1974–cont.

37. Health and Safety at Work etc Act 1974–*cont.*

s.37, varied: SI 2008/1597 Sch.5 para.8, SI 2008/2108 Reg.4
s.38, applied: SI 2008/1597 Sch.5 para.7
s.38, varied: SI 2008/1597 Sch.5 para.8, SI 2008/2108 Reg.4
s.39, applied: SI 2008/1597 Sch.5 para.7
s.39, varied: SI 2008/1597 Sch.5 para.8, SI 2008/2108 Reg.4
s.40, varied: SI 2008/2108 Reg.4
s.40, see *R. v Chargot Ltd (t/a Contract Services)* [2007] EWCA Crim 3032, [2008] 2 All E.R. 1077 (CA (Crim Div)), Latham, L.J.
s.41, applied: SI 2008/1597 Sch.5 para.7
s.41, varied: SI 2008/1597 Sch.5 para.8, SI 2008/2108 Reg.4
s.42, amended: 2008 c.20 Sch.3 para.2
s.42, applied: SI 2008/1597 Sch.5 para.7
s.42, varied: SI 2008/1597 Sch.5 para.8, SI 2008/2108 Reg.4
s.43, amended: SI 2008/960 Art.14
s.43, enabling: SI 2008/736, SI 2008/1087
s.45, amended: SI 2008/960 Art.15
s.50, amended: SI 2008/960 Art.16
s.50, applied: SI 2008/2337(b), SI 2008/960 Sch.2 para.10
s.53, amended: SI 2008/960 Art.17
s.53, applied: SSI 2008/189 Art.53
s.53, disapplied: SSI 2008/190 Art.53
s.53, referred to: SI 2008/228 Sch.1 para.20, SSI 2008/188 Art.53
s.55, amended: SI 2008/960 Art.18
s.59, amended: SI 2008/960 Art.19
s.80, applied: SSI 2008/188 Art.53, SSI 2008/189 Art.53, SSI 2008/190 Art.53
s.82, enabling: SI 2008/736, SI 2008/1087, SI 2008/2323
Sch.2 para.1, substituted: SI 2008/960 Sch.1
Sch.2 para.2, applied: SI 2008/960 Sch.2 para.2
Sch.2 para.2, substituted: SI 2008/960 Sch.1
Sch.2 para.3, substituted: SI 2008/960 Sch.1
Sch.2 para.4, substituted: SI 2008/960 Sch.1
Sch.2 para.5, substituted: SI 2008/960 Sch.1
Sch.2 para.6, substituted: SI 2008/960 Sch.1
Sch.2 para.7, substituted: SI 2008/960 Sch.1
Sch.2 para.8, substituted: SI 2008/960 Sch.1
Sch.2 para.8, applied: SI 2008/960 Sch.2 para.3
Sch.2 para.8, substituted: SI 2008/960 Sch.1
Sch.2 para.9, substituted: SI 2008/960 Sch.1
Sch.2 para.10, substituted: SI 2008/960 Sch.1
Sch.2 para.10, applied: SI 2008/960 Sch.2 para.4
Sch.2 para.10, substituted: SI 2008/960 Sch.1

CAP.

1974–cont.

37. Health and Safety at Work etc Act 1974–*cont.*

Sch.2 para.11, applied: SI 2008/960 Sch.2 para.3
Sch.2 para.11, substituted: SI 2008/960 Sch.1
Sch.2 para.12, substituted: SI 2008/960 Sch.1
Sch.2 para.13, substituted: SI 2008/960 Sch.1
Sch.2 para.14, substituted: SI 2008/960 Sch.1
Sch.2 para.15, applied: SI 2008/960 Sch.2 para.4
Sch.2 para.15, substituted: SI 2008/960 Sch.1
Sch.2 para.16, substituted: SI 2008/960 Sch.1
Sch.2 para.17, substituted: SI 2008/960 Sch.1
Sch.2 para.18, substituted: SI 2008/960 Sch.1
Sch.2 para.19, substituted: SI 2008/960 Sch.1
Sch.2 para.20, substituted: SI 2008/960 Sch.1
Sch.3 para.1, enabling: SI 2008/2337
Sch.3 para.3, enabling: SI 2008/2337
Sch.3A para.1, added: 2008 c.20 Sch.1
Sch.3A para.2, added: 2008 c.20 Sch.1

38. Land Tenure Reform (Scotland) Act 1974

s.11, amended: SI 2008/948 Sch.1 para.44

39. Consumer Credit Act 1974

applied: 2008 c.13 Sch.3, SI 2008/570 Sch.1 para.11, SI 2008/668 r.15, SI 2008/700 Sch.1 para.12, SI 2008/794 Sch.8 para.33, SI 2008/1816 Reg.6, Reg.11, Sch.3 para.5, SI 2008/2551 Reg.4
disapplied: 2008 c.10 s.8
referred to: 2008 c.13 Sch.6, SI 2008/668 r.26
Part III, applied: SI 2008/1741 Reg.112
s.8, amended: SI 2008/2826 Art.3
s.15, see *TRM Copy Centres (UK) Ltd v Lanwall Services Ltd* [2008] EWCA Civ 382, [2008] Bus. L.R. 1231 (CA (Civ Div)), Sir Mark Potter (President, Fam)
s.16, amended: SI 2008/3002 Sch.1 para.1
s.16, applied: SI 2008/529 Reg.93, SI 2008/645, SI 2008/1273 Reg.51, SI 2008/1582 Reg.93, SI 2008/3170 Reg.51, SSI 2008/235 Reg.11
s.16, varied: SI 2008/2839 Sch.1 para.1
s.16, enabling: SI 2008/645
s.16C, added: SI 2008/2826 Art.3
s.40A, enabling: SI 2008/668
s.41A, enabling: SI 2008/668
s.46, repealed: SI 2008/1277 Sch.2 para.18, Sch.4 Part 1
s.47, amended: SI 2008/1277 Sch.4 Part 1

CAP.

1974–cont.

39. Consumer Credit Act 1974–*cont.*
s.74, amended: SI 2008/1816 Sch.1 para.1
s.75, see *Office of Fair Trading v Lloyds TSB Bank Plc* [2007] UKHL 48, [2008] 1 A.C. 316 (HL), Lord Hoffmann
s.77, repealed (in part): SI 2008/1277 Sch.4 Part 1
s.77A, amended: SI 2008/2826 Art.4
s.77A, applied: SI 2008/2826 Art.5
s.77A, repealed (in part): SI 2008/2826 Art.4
s.77A, varied: SI 2008/2826 Art.5
s.77A, enabling: SI 2008/1751
s.78, repealed (in part): SI 2008/1277 Sch.4 Part 1
s.78, enabling: SI 2008/1751
s.79, repealed (in part): SI 2008/1277 Sch.4 Part 1
s.82, amended: SI 2008/733 Art.2, SI 2008/2826 Art.3
s.82, applied: SI 2008/831 Art.4
s.85, repealed (in part): SI 2008/1277 Sch.4 Part 1
s.86B, amended: SI 2008/2826 Art.8
s.86B, enabling: SI 2008/1751
s.86C, amended: SI 2008/2826 Art.9
s.97, repealed (in part): SI 2008/1277 Sch.4 Part 1
s.103, amended: SI 2008/1277 Sch.2 para.24
s.103, repealed (in part): SI 2008/1277 Sch.2 para.24, Sch.4 Part 1
s.107, repealed (in part): SI 2008/1277 Sch.2 para.25, Sch.4 Part 1
s.108, repealed (in part): SI 2008/1277 Sch.2 para.26, Sch.4 Part 1
s.109, repealed (in part): SI 2008/1277 Sch.2 para.27, Sch.4 Part 1
s.110, repealed (in part): SI 2008/1277 Sch.2 para.28, Sch.4 Part 1
s.113, see *Bank of Scotland v Euclidian (No.1) Ltd* [2007] EWHC 1732 (Comm), [2008] Lloyd's Rep. I.R. 182 (QBD (Comm)), Field, J.
s.130A, enabling: SI 2008/1751
s.139, applied: SSI 2008/223 r.15
s.151, amended: SI 2008/1277 Sch.4 Part 1
s.182, enabling: SI 2008/645, SI 2008/1751
s.189, amended: SI 2008/2826 Art.3
s.189, enabling: SI 2008/1751
Sch.A1 Part 4 para.10, enabling: SI 2008/668
Sch.1, amended: SI 2008/1277 Sch.4 Part 1

40. Control of Pollution Act 1974
applied: 2008 c.13 Sch.3, SSI 2008/188 Art.53
disapplied: SSI 2008/189 Art.53, SSI 2008/190 Art.53
Part III, applied: 2008 c.18 s.20
Part III, referred to: 2008 c.13 Sch.6
s.17, applied: 2008 c.13 Sch.7
s.47, repealed (in part): 2008 asp 5 Sch.3 Part 1

CAP.

1974–cont.

40. Control of Pollution Act 1974–*cont.*
s.60, applied: SI 2008/1160 Art.16, SI 2008/1261 Art.27, SI 2008/2512 Art.40
s.60, disapplied: 2008 c.18 s.21
s.60, varied: 2008 c.18 s.20
s.61, applied: SI 2008/1160 Art.16, SI 2008/1261 Art.27, SI 2008/2512 Art.40
s.61, disapplied: 2008 c.18 s.21, SI 2008/1261 Art.27, SI 2008/2512 Art.40
s.61, varied: 2008 c.18 s.20
s.65, applied: SI 2008/1160 Art.16, SI 2008/1261 Art.27, SI 2008/2512 Art.40
s.65, disapplied: 2008 c.18 s.21, SI 2008/1261 Art.27, SI 2008/2512 Art.40
s.106, repealed (in part): 2008 asp 5 Sch.3 Part 1
Sch.4, amended: 2008 asp 5 Sch.3 Part 1

44. Housing Act 1974
s.20, applied: 2008 c.17 s.262
s.29, applied: 2008 c.17 s.77
s.29A, applied: 2008 c.17 s.77
s.31, applied: 2008 c.17 s.274

46. Friendly Societies Act 1974
s.36, amended: SI 2008/948 Sch.1 para.1

47. Solicitors Act 1974
Part III, applied: SI 2008/1053 Sch.1, SI 2008/1054 Sch.1
s.20, referred to: 2008 c.13 Sch.6
s.36, see *Law Society v Shah* [2007] EWHC 2841 (Ch), [2008] 3 W.L.R. 1401 (Ch D), Floyd, J
s.46, varied: SI 2008/1436 Art.4
s.46A, varied: SI 2008/1436 Art.4
s.70, see *Mastercigars Direct Ltd v Withers LLP* [2007] EWHC 2733 (Ch), [2008] 3 All E.R. 417 (Ch D), Morgan, J.
s.73, see *Mastercigars Direct Ltd v Withers LLP* [2007] EWHC 2733 (Ch), [2008] 3 All E.R. 417 (Ch D), Morgan, J.
s.79, varied: SI 2008/222 Art.7

53. Rehabilitation of Offenders Act 1974
referred to: 2008 c.4 s.49
s.1, applied: SI 2008/1976 Reg.6
s.4, enabling: SI 2008/3259
s.5, amended: 2008 c.4 Sch.4 para.21
s.6, amended: 2008 c.4 Sch.10 para.2
s.7, amended: 2008 c.4 Sch.4 para.22
s.7, enabling: SI 2008/3259
s.8A, added: 2008 c.4 Sch.10 para.3
s.8A, referred to: 2008 c.4 Sch.27 para.19
s.9A, added: 2008 c.4 Sch.10 para.4
s.10, enabling: SI 2008/3259
Sch.1 para.1, substituted: 2008 c.4 Sch.10 para.5
Sch.1 para.2, substituted: 2008 c.4 Sch.10 para.5
Sch.1 para.3, substituted: 2008 c.4 Sch.10 para.5
Sch.1 para.4, substituted: 2008 c.4 Sch.10 para.5

CAP.

1974–cont.

53. Rehabilitation of Offenders Act 1974– *cont.*

Sch.1 para.5, substituted: 2008 c.4 Sch.10 para.5

Sch.1 para.6, substituted: 2008 c.4 Sch.10 para.5

Sch.1 para.7, substituted: 2008 c.4 Sch.10 para.5

Sch.2, applied: 2008 c.4 Sch.27 para.19

Sch.2 para.1, added: 2008 c.4 Sch.10 para.6

Sch.2 para.2, added: 2008 c.4 Sch.10 para.6

Sch.2 para.3, added: 2008 c.4 Sch.10 para.6

Sch.2 para.4, added: 2008 c.4 Sch.10 para.6

Sch.2 para.4, enabling: SI 2008/3259

Sch.2 para.5, added: 2008 c.4 Sch.10 para.6

Sch.2 para.6, added: 2008 c.4 Sch.10 para.6

Sch.2 para.6, enabling: SI 2008/3259

1975

4. Biological Standards Act 1975

repealed: 2008 c.14 s.159, Sch.15 Part 7

7. Finance Act 1975

s.22, referred to: 2008 c.9 Sch.4 para.10, Sch.4 para.11

s.37, referred to: 2008 c.9 Sch.4 para.11

Sch.9 para.2, referred to: 2008 c.9 Sch.4 para.11

8. Offshore Petroleum Development (Scotland) Act 1975

applied: SSI 2008/188 Art.53

disapplied: SSI 2008/189 Art.53, SSI 2008/190 Art.53

14. Social Security Act 1975

applied: SI 2008/794 Sch.1 para.10

s.126A, varied: SI 2008/632 Art.4

20. District Courts (Scotland) Act 1975

referred to: SSI 2008/93 Art.6

s.1A, repealed: SSI 2008/328 Sch.1

s.1A, varied: SSI 2008/31 Sch.4 Part 2, SSI 2008/93 Sch.3, SSI 2008/363 Sch.3

s.5, repealed (in part): SSI 2008/31 Sch.4 Part 1, SSI 2008/328 Sch.1

s.5, varied: SSI 2008/31 Sch.4 Part 2, SSI 2008/93 Sch.3, SSI 2008/363 Sch.3

s.7, repealed: SSI 2008/328 Sch.1

s.7, varied: SSI 2008/31 Sch.4 Part 2, SSI 2008/93 Sch.3, SSI 2008/363 Sch.3

s.8, repealed: SSI 2008/328 Sch.1

s.8, varied: SSI 2008/31 Sch.4 Part 2, SSI 2008/93 Sch.3, SSI 2008/363 Sch.3

s.17, repealed: SSI 2008/328 Sch.1

s.17, varied: SSI 2008/31 Sch.4 Part 2, SSI 2008/93 Sch.3, SSI 2008/363 Sch.3

s.18, repealed: SSI 2008/328 Sch.1

s.18, varied: SSI 2008/31 Sch.4 Part 2, SSI 2008/93 Sch.3, SSI 2008/363 Sch.3

s.20, repealed: SSI 2008/328 Sch.1

s.20, varied: SSI 2008/31 Sch.4 Part 2, SSI 2008/93 Sch.3, SSI 2008/363 Sch.3

s.23, repealed: SSI 2008/328 Sch.1

CAP.

1975–cont.

20. District Courts (Scotland) Act 1975– *cont.*

s.23, varied: SSI 2008/31 Sch.4 Part 2, SSI 2008/93 Sch.3, SSI 2008/363 Sch.3

22. Oil Taxation Act 1975

applied: SI 2008/225 Sch.1 para.14

s.6, amended: 2008 c.9 Sch.33 para.2

s.10, see *Shell UK Ltd v Revenue and Customs Commissioners* [2008] S.T.C. (S.C.D.) 91 (Sp Comm), AN Brice

s.12, amended: 2008 c.9 s.102

Sch.1 para.1, applied: 2008 c.9 Sch.39 para.66

Sch.2 para.1, amended: 2008 c.9 Sch.44 para.2

Sch.2 para.8, repealed: 2008 c.9 Sch.40 para.21

Sch.2 para.9, repealed: 2008 c.9 Sch.40 para.21

Sch.5 para.2A, substituted: 2008 c.9 s.103

23. Reservoirs Act 1975

s.28, applied: 2008 c.29 s.151

Sch.2, applied: 2008 c.29 s.151

24. House of Commons Disqualification Act 1975

Sch.1 Part I, amended: SI 2008/2833 Sch.3 para.28

Sch.1 Part II, amended: 2008 c.6 Sch.1 para.27, 2008 c.13 Sch.1 para.17, 2008 c.14 Sch.5 para.57, Sch.10 para.4, Sch.14 para.3, Sch.15 Part 1, Sch.15 Part 6, 2008 c.17 Sch.8 para.19, Sch.9 para.3, Sch.16, 2008 c.27 Sch.1 para.30, 2008 c.29 Sch.1 para.25, 2008 c.30 Sch.1 para.21, SI 2008/576 Sch.5 para.2, Sch.5 para.7

Sch.1 Part III, amended: 2008 c.14 Sch.5 para.57, Sch.15 Part 1, SI 2008/576 Sch.5 para.7, SI 2008/960 Sch.3, SI 2008/1241 Art.2, SI 2008/1889 Art.6, SI 2008/2833 Sch.3 para.28

25. Northern Ireland Assembly Disqualification Act 1975

Sch.1 Part I, amended: SI 2008/2833 Sch.3 para.29

Sch.1 Part II, amended: 2008 c.6 Sch.1 para.28, 2008 c.14 Sch.5 para.58, Sch.10 para.5, Sch.15 Part 1, 2008 c.17 Sch.8 para.20, Sch.16, 2008 c.27 Sch.1 para.31, 2008 c.29 Sch.1 para.25, 2008 c.30 Sch.1 para.22, SI 2008/576 Sch.5 para.3, Sch.5 para.7

Sch.1 Part III, amended: SI 2008/1216 Sch.5 para.2, Sch.6 Part 1, SI 2008/2833 Sch.3 para.29

26. Ministers of the Crown Act 1975

s.1, applied: SI 2008/678

s.1, enabling: SI 2008/678, SI 2008/1034, SI 2008/3134

s.2, enabling: SI 2008/1034

s.5A, enabling: SI 2008/3134

CAP.

1975–cont.

27. Ministerial and other Salaries Act 1975
s.1, amended: SI 2008/1781 Art.2
s.1, applied: SI 2008/1781 Art.2
s.1A, applied: SI 2008/1781 Art.2
s.1B, enabling: SI 2008/1781

30. Local Government (Scotland) Act 1975
s.7B, applied: SSI 2008/32 Art.2
s.7B, enabling: SSI 2008/32
s.37, enabling: SSI 2008/32

34. Evidence (Proceedings in Other Jurisdictions) Act 1975
see *Michael Wilson & Partners Ltd v Emmott* [2008] EWCA Civ 184, [2008] Bus. L.R. 1361 (CA (Civ Div)), Carnwath, L.J.

35. Farriers (Registration) Act 1975
applied: 2008 c.13 Sch.3
referred to: 2008 c.13 Sch.6
s.3, amended: SI 2008/646 Reg.3
s.4, amended: SI 2008/646 Reg.4
s.7, substituted: SI 2008/646 Reg.5
s.7A, substituted: SI 2008/646 Reg.5
s.7B, substituted: SI 2008/646 Reg.5
s.8, substituted: SI 2008/646 Reg.5
s.9, substituted: SI 2008/646 Reg.5
s.10, amended: SI 2008/646 Reg.6
s.15, amended: SI 2008/646 Reg.7
s.15A, amended: SI 2008/646 Reg.8
s.16, amended: SI 2008/646 Reg.9
Sch.1 Part I para.1, repealed: SI 2008/646 Reg.10
Sch.1 Part I para.2, repealed: SI 2008/646 Reg.10
Sch.1 Part I para.3, repealed: SI 2008/646 Reg.10
Sch.1 Part II para.12, amended: SI 2008/948 Sch.1 para.1

39. Hearing Aid Council (Extension) Act 1975
repealed: 2008 c.14 s.123, Sch.15 Part 2

47. Litigants in Person (Costs and Expenses) Act 1975
applied: SSI 2008/119 Sch.1 para.16

50. Guard Dogs Act 1975
applied: 2008 c.13 Sch.3

51. Salmon and Freshwater Fisheries Act 1975
applied: SI 2008/1261 Sch.10 para.12
referred to: 2008 c.13 Sch.6

52. Safety of Sports Grounds Act 1975
applied: 2008 c.13 Sch.3, SI 2008/55 Art.2, SI 2008/1644 Art.2, Art.3
s.1, enabling: SI 2008/55, SI 2008/1644
s.6, applied: 2008 c.13 Sch.7
s.12, referred to: 2008 c.13 Sch.6
s.18, applied: SI 2008/55, SI 2008/1644
s.18, enabling: SI 2008/55

60. Social Security Pensions Act 1975
s.59, amended: 2008 c.30 s.137, Sch.11 Part 6

CAP.

1975–cont.

60. Social Security Pensions Act 1975– *cont.*
s.59, applied: SI 2008/653 Reg.1, Reg.3, Reg.5, Reg.6, SI 2008/711 Art.6, SSI 2008/224 Reg.1, Reg.3, Reg.5, Reg.6
s.59, enabling: SI 2008/711
s.59A, applied: SI 2008/711 Art.5

63. Inheritance (Provision for Family and Dependants) Act 1975
see *Baker v Baker* [2008] EWHC 937 (Ch), [2008] 2 F.L.R. 767 (Ch D), Paul Girolami Q.C.
s.1, see *Baker v Baker* [2008] EWHC 937 (Ch), [2008] 2 F.L.R. 767 (Ch D), Paul Girolami Q.C.; see *Baker v Baker* [2008] EWHC 977 (Ch), [2008] 2 F.L.R. 1956 (Ch D), Paul Chaisty Q.C.; see *Baynes v Hedger* [2008] EWHC 1587 (Ch), [2008] 2 F.L.R. 1805 (Ch D), Lewison, J.; see *Negus v Bahouse* [2007] EWHC 2628 (Ch), [2008] 1 F.L.R. 381 (Ch D), Judge Roger Kaye Q.C.
s.2, see *Negus v Bahouse* [2007] EWHC 2628 (Ch), [2008] 1 F.L.R. 381 (Ch D), Judge Roger Kaye Q.C.
s.3, see *Baker v Baker* [2008] EWHC 977 (Ch), [2008] 2 F.L.R. 1956 (Ch D), Paul Chaisty Q.C.; see *Negus v Bahouse* [2007] EWHC 2628 (Ch), [2008] 1 F.L.R. 381 (Ch D), Judge Roger Kaye Q.C.

65. Sex Discrimination Act 1975
s.1, amended: SI 2008/963 Sch.1 para.1
s.2A, amended: SI 2008/963 Sch.1 para.2
s.3A, amended: SI 2008/656 Reg.2
s.3B, added: SI 2008/963 Sch.1 para.3
s.4A, see *English v Thomas Sanderson Blinds Ltd* [2008] I.C.R. 607 (EAT), Judge Peter Clark
s.4A, amended: SI 2008/656 Reg.3
s.5, amended: SI 2008/963 Sch.1 para.3, Sch.1 para.9
s.6, amended: SI 2008/656 Reg.4
s.6A, substituted: SI 2008/656 Reg.5
s.29, amended: SI 2008/963 Sch.1 para.4
s.30, amended: SI 2008/963 Sch.1 para.5
s.31, amended: SI 2008/963 Sch.1 para.6
s.34, amended: SI 2008/963 Sch.1 para.7
s.35, amended: SI 2008/963 Sch.1 para.8
s.35C, amended: SI 2008/963 Sch.1 para.10
s.35ZA, added: SI 2008/963 Sch.1 para.9
s.43, amended: SI 2008/963 Sch.1 para.11
s.44, substituted: SI 2008/963 Sch.1 para.12
s.45, substituted: SI 2008/963 Sch.1 para.13
s.46, amended: SI 2008/963 Sch.1 para.14
s.51, amended: SI 2008/963 Sch.1 para.15
s.51A, amended: SI 2008/963 Sch.1 para.16
s.55, amended: SI 2008/960 Sch.3
s.62, see *UNISON v Brennan* [2008] I.C.R. 955 (EAT), Elias, J (President)
s.63, referred to: SI 2008/3232 Sch.1 Part 2
s.66A, amended: SI 2008/963 Sch.1 para.17

CAP.

1975–cont.

65. Sex Discrimination Act 1975–*cont.*
s.74, amended: SI 2008/963 Sch.1 para.18
s.77, see *UNISON v Brennan* [2008] I.C.R. 955 (EAT), Elias, J (President)
s.82, amended: SI 2008/963 Sch.1 para.9

70. Welsh Development Agency Act 1975
s.21A, applied: 2008 c.29 s.194
Sch.4, applied: 2008 c.29 s.194

76. Local Land Charges Act 1975
s.2, disapplied: 2008 c.18 s.44

1976

13. Damages (Scotland) Act 1976
s.1, applied: SI 2008/1596 Reg.10, Reg.12
Sch.1, see *McGibbon v McAllister* [2008] CSOH 4, 2008 S.L.T. 459 (OH), Lord Brodie

14. Fatal Accidents and Sudden Deaths Inquiry (Scotland) Act 1976
s.1, see *Kennedy v Lord Advocate* [2008] CSOH 21, 2008 S.L.T. 195 (OH), Lord Mackay of Drumadoon

26. Explosives (Age of Purchase &c.) Act 1976
applied: 2008 c.13 Sch.3

27. Theatres Trust Act 1976
referred to: SSI 2008/432 Sch.5 para.11
Sch.1 para.14, amended: SI 2008/948 Sch.1 para.1

28. Congenital Disabilities (Civil Liability) Act 1976
referred to: 2008 c.22 s.53
s.1, amended: 2008 c.22 Sch.6 para.14
s.4, amended: 2008 c.22 Sch.6 para.15, Sch.7 para.1

30. Fatal Accidents Act 1976
see *Jones v Royal Devon and Exeter NHS Foundation Trust* [2008] EWHC 558 (QB), (2008) 101 B.M.L.R. 154 (QBD), King, J.
applied: SI 2008/1596 Reg.10, Reg.12
s.1, see *Corr v IBC Vehicles Ltd* [2008] UKHL 13, [2008] 1 A.C. 884 (HL), Lord Bingham of Cornhill
s.3, see *Jones v Royal Devon and Exeter NHS Foundation Trust* [2008] EWHC 558 (QB), (2008) 101 B.M.L.R. 154 (QBD), King, J.
s.4, see *Arnup v MW White Ltd* [2008] EWCA Civ 447, [2008] I.C.R. 1064 (CA (Civ Div)), Ward, L.J.; see *Cameron v Vinters Defence Systems Ltd* [2007] EWHC 2267 (QB), [2008] P.I.Q.R. P5 (QBD), Holland, J.

31. Legitimacy Act 1976
referred to: 2008 c.22 s.53
s.2A, added: 2008 c.22 Sch.6 para.16
s.3, substituted: 2008 c.22 Sch.6 para.17
s.9, amended: 2008 c.22 Sch.6 para.18
s.10, amended: 2008 c.22 Sch.6 para.19

CAP.

1976–cont.

32. Lotteries and Amusements Act 1976
s.1, see *Secretary of State for Business, Enterprise and Regulatory Reform v Amway (UK) Ltd* [2008] EWHC 1054 (Ch), [2008] B.C.C. 713 (Ch D), Norris, J.
s.16, see *Rank Group Ltd v Revenue and Customs Commissioners* [2008] 3 C.M.L.R. 31 (V&DTr (London)), Theodore Wallace (Chairman)

35. Police Pensions Act 1976
s.1, applied: SI 2008/1887, SSI 2008/387
s.1, enabling: SI 2008/1887, SSI 2008/387
s.11, see *R. (on the application of Ashton) v Police Medical Appeal Board* [2008] EWHC 1833 (Admin), [2008] Pens. L.R. 391 (QBD (Admin)), Charles, J.

36. Adoption Act 1976
referred to: 2008 c.4 s.73
s.18, see *H (A Child) (Leave to Apply for Residence Order), Re* [2008] EWCA Civ 503, [2008] 2 F.L.R. 848 (CA (Civ Div)), Buxton, L.J.
s.47, amended: 2008 c.4 Sch.15 para.7

38. Dangerous Wild Animals Act 1976
applied: 2008 c.13 Sch.3
referred to: 2008 c.13 Sch.6
s.8, enabling: SSI 2008/302
Sch.1, referred to: SSI 2008/302
Sch.1, substituted: SSI 2008/302 Sch.1

40. Finance Act 1976
s.78, referred to: 2008 c.9 Sch.4 para.11

52. Armed Forces Act 1976
Sch.3 para.1, applied: SI 2008/635 Art.19
Sch.3 para.15, applied: SI 2008/635 Art.19
Sch.3 para.20, amended: SI 2008/1694 Art.26
Sch.3 para.20, applied: SI 2008/1694 Sch.1 para.8
Sch.3 para.20, repealed (in part): SI 2008/1694 Art.26
Sch.3 para.21, added: SI 2008/1694 Art.27

55. Agriculture (Miscellaneous Provisions) Act 1976
s.3, repealed: SI 2008/576 Sch.5 para.7
Sch.1 para.1, repealed: SI 2008/576 Sch.5 para.7
Sch.1 para.2, repealed: SI 2008/576 Sch.5 para.7
Sch.1 para.3, repealed: SI 2008/576 Sch.5 para.7
Sch.1 para.4, repealed: SI 2008/576 Sch.5 para.7

57. Local Government (Miscellaneous Provisions) Act 1976
applied: 2008 c.13 Sch.3
Part II, referred to: 2008 c.13 Sch.6

58. International Carriage of Perishable Foodstuffs Act 1976
s.6, referred to: 2008 c.13 Sch.6
s.7, referred to: 2008 c.13 Sch.6
s.8, referred to: 2008 c.13 Sch.6

CAP.

1976–cont.

58. International Carriage of Perishable Foodstuffs Act 1976–*cont.*
s.9, referred to: 2008 c.13 Sch.6
s.10, referred to: 2008 c.13 Sch.6
s.11, referred to: 2008 c.13 Sch.6

63. Bail Act 1976
applied: SI 2008/1263 Reg.5
s.2, see *R. v Scott (Casim)* [2007] EWCA Crim 2757, (2008) 172 J.P. 149 (CA (Crim Div)), Toulson, L.J.
s.3, amended: 2008 c.4 Sch.11 para.2, Sch.12 para.2
s.3AA, amended: 2008 c.4 Sch.11 para.3
s.3AA, repealed (in part): 2008 c.4 Sch.11 para.3, Sch.28 Part 4
s.3AB, added: 2008 c.4 Sch.11 para.4
s.3AC, added: 2008 c.4 Sch.11 para.4
s.3AC, enabling: SI 2008/2713
s.4, amended: 2008 c.4 Sch.4 para.23, Sch.4 para.102, Sch.28 Part 1
s.9A, added: 2008 c.4 Sch.12 para.3
Sch.1, referred to: 2008 c.4 s.52
Sch.1 Part I para.1, amended: 2008 c.4 Sch.12 para.5
Sch.1 Part IA para.1, added: 2008 c.4 Sch.12 para.6
Sch.1 Part IA para.2, added: 2008 c.4 Sch.12 para.6
Sch.1 Part IA para.3, added: 2008 c.4 Sch.12 para.6
Sch.1 Part IA para.4, added: 2008 c.4 Sch.12 para.6
Sch.1 Part IA para.5, added: 2008 c.4 Sch.12 para.6
Sch.1 Part IA para.6, added: 2008 c.4 Sch.12 para.6
Sch.1 Part IA para.7, added: 2008 c.4 Sch.12 para.6
Sch.1 Part IA para.8, added: 2008 c.4 Sch.12 para.6
Sch.1 Part IA para.9, added: 2008 c.4 Sch.12 para.6

64. Valuation and Rating (Exempted Classes) (Scotland) Act 1976
s.1, applied: SSI 2008/80
s.1, enabling: SSI 2008/80

66. Licensing (Scotland) Act 1976
s.23, referred to: SSI 2008/194 Art.2
s.26, applied: SSI 2008/194 Art.2

71. Supplementary Benefits Act 1976
Sch.7 para.4, repealed (in part): 2008 c.14 Sch.15 Part 5

74. Race Relations Act 1976
see *D'Silva v NATFHE (now known as University & College Union)* [2008] I.R.L.R. 412 (EAT), Underhill, J.; see *R. (on the application of Al-Rawi) v Secretary of State for Foreign and Commonwealth Affairs* [2006] EWCA Civ 1279, [2008] Q.B. 289 (CA (Civ Div)), Brooke, L.J.; see *R. (on the application of Watkins-Singh) v

CAP.

1976–cont.

74. Race Relations Act 1976–*cont.*
see–*cont.*
Aberdare Girls' High School Governors [2008] EWHC 1865 (Admin), [2008] 3 F.C.R. 203 (QBD (Admin)), Silber, J.; see *R.(on the application of E) v JFS Governing Body* [2008] EWHC1535 (Admin), [2008] E.L.R. 445 (QBD (Admin)), Munby, J.
applied: SI 2008/532 Sch.1 para.4
s.1, see *Oyarce v Cheshire CC* [2008] EWCA Civ 434, [2008] 4 All E.R. 907 (CA (Civ Div)), Buxton, L.J.; see *R. (on the application of Al-Rawi) v Secretary of State for Foreign and Commonwealth Affairs* [2006] EWCA Civ 1279, [2008] Q.B. 289 (CA (Civ Div)), Brooke, L.J.; see *R. (on the application of Watkins-Singh) v Aberdare Girls' High School Governors* [2008] EWHC 1865 (Admin), [2008] 3 F.C.R. 203 (QBD (Admin)), Silber, J.; see *R.(on the application of E) v JFS Governing Body* [2008] EWHC 1535 (Admin), [2008] E.L.R. 445 (QBD (Admin)), Munby, J.
s.1, amended: SI 2008/3008 Reg.2
s.3, see *Okonu v G4S Security Services (UK) Ltd* [2008] I.C.R. 598 (EAT), Judge Birtles
s.12, see *Carter v Ahsan (No.1)* [2007] UKHL 51, [2008] 1 A.C. 696 (HL), Lord Hoffmann
s.19B, see *R. (on the application of Al-Rawi) v Secretary of State for Foreign and Commonwealth Affairs* [2006] EWCA Civ 1279, [2008] Q.B. 289 (CA (Civ Div)), Brooke, L.J.
s.25, see *Carter v Ahsan (No.1)* [2007] UKHL 51, [2008] 1 A.C. 696 (HL), Lord Hoffmann
s.33, see *Bird v Sylvester* [2007] EWCA Civ 1052, [2008] I.C.R. 208 (CA (Civ Div)), Laws, L.J.
s.54, referred to: SI 2008/3232 Sch.1 Part 2
s.54A, see *Okonu v G4S Security Services (UK) Ltd* [2008] I.C.R. 598 (EAT), Judge Birtles; see *Oyarce v Cheshire CC* [2008] EWCA Civ 434, [2008] 4 All E.R. 907 (CA (Civ Div)), Buxton, L.J.
s.71, see *R. (on the application of Baker) v Secretary of State for Communities and Local Government* [2008] EWCA Civ 141, [2008] B.L.G.R. 239 (CA (Civ Div)), May, L.J.; see *R. (on the application of C) v Secretary of State for Justice* [2008] EWCA Civ 882, Times, October 14, 2008 (CA (Civ Div)), Buxton, L.J.; see *R. (on the application of Watkins-Singh) v Aberdare Girls' High School Governors* [2008] EWHC 1865 (Admin), [2008] 3 F.C.R. 203 (QBD (Admin)), Silber, J.; see *R.(on the application of E) v JFS Governing Body* [2008] EWHC 1535 (Admin), [2008] E.L.R. 445 (QBD (Admin)), Munby, J.

CAP.

1976–cont.

74. Race Relations Act 1976–*cont.*

s.76ZA, see *Oyarce v Cheshire CC* [2008] EWCA Civ 434, [2008] 4 All E.R. 907 (CA (Civ Div)), Buxton, L.J.

Sch.1A Part I para.38, amended: 2008 c.26 Sch.4 para.49

Sch.1A Part I para.52, amended: 2008 c.17 Sch.9 para.4

Sch.1A Part I para.52A, added: 2008 c.17 Sch.8 para.21

Sch.1A Part II, amended: 2008 c.14 Sch.5 para.59, Sch.10 para.6, Sch.15 Part 1, Sch.15 Part 7, 2008 c.17 Sch.8 para.21, Sch.16, 2008 c.27 Sch.1 para.32, 2008 c.30 Sch.1 para.25, SI 2008/576 Sch.5 para.4, Sch.5 para.7, SI 2008/960 Sch.3

Sch.1A Part III, amended: 2008 c.14 Sch.10 para.6

Sch.1A Part IV, amended: 2008 c.14 Sch.5 para.59, Sch.15 Part 1

76. Energy Act 1976

applied: 2008 c.13 Sch.3

s.14, amended: 2008 c.29 Sch.2 para.15

s.14, applied: 2008 c.29 s.33

s.18, referred to: 2008 c.13 Sch.6

77. Weights and Measures etc Act 1976

applied: 2008 c.13 Sch.3

s.12, applied: 2008 c.13 Sch.7

80. Rent (Agriculture) Act 1976

applied: SI 2008/188 Sch.1 para.1

s.5, amended: 2008 c.17 Sch.8 para.22

s.5, varied: SI 2008/2839 Sch.1 para.1

86. Fishery Limits Act 1976

referred to: 2008 c.13 Sch.6

s.2, applied: SSI 2008/101 Sch.1 Part 1

1977

3. Aircraft and Shipbuilding Industries Act 1977

s.17, amended: SI 2008/948 Sch.1 para.1, Sch.1 para.45

5. Social Security (Miscellaneous Provisions) Act 1977

s.12, enabling: SI 2008/679

s.24, enabling: SI 2008/679

30. Rentcharges Act 1977

s.1, applied: SI 2008/794 Sch.6 para.18

32. Torts (Interference with Goods) Act 1977

s.11, see *Uzinterimpex JSC v Standard Bank Plc* [2008] EWCA Civ 819, [2008] Bus. L.R. 1762 (CA (Civ Div)), Sir Anthony Clarke, M.R.

37. Patents Act 1977

see *Generics (UK) Ltd v H Lundbeck A/S* [2008] EWCA Civ 311, [2008] R.P.C. 19 (CA (Civ Div)), Lord Hoffmann; see *Parkes v MacGregor* 2008 S.C.L.R. 345 (OH), Lady Paton

CAP.

1977–cont.

37. Patents Act 1977–*cont.*

s.1, see *Blacklight Power Inc v Comptroller-General of Patents* [2008] EWHC 2763 (Pat), Times, December 10, 2008 (Ch D (Patents Ct)), Floyd, J; see *Conor Medsystems Inc v Angiotech Pharmaceuticals Inc* [2008] UKHL 49, [2008] 4 All E.R. 621 (HL), Lord Hoffmann; see *Eli Lilly & Co v Human Genome Sciences Inc* [2008] EWHC 1903 (Pat), [2008] R.P.C. 29 (Ch D (Patents Ct)), Kitchin, J.; see *Generics (UK) Ltd v H Lundbeck A/S* [2008] EWCA Civ 311, [2008] R.P.C. 19 (CA (Civ Div)), Lord Hoffmann; see *Symbian Ltd v Comptroller General of Patents, Designs and Trademarks* [2008] EWCA Civ 1066, Times, October 28, 2008 (CA (Civ Div)), Jacob, L.J.

s.7, see *Cinpres Gas Injection Ltd v Melea Ltd* [2008] EWCA Civ 9, [2008] Bus. L.R. 1157 (CA (Civ Div)), Sir Igor Judge (President, QB)

s.12, see *Cinpres Gas Injection Ltd v Melea Ltd* [2008] EWCA Civ 9, [2008] Bus. L.R. 1157 (CA (Civ Div)), Sir Igor Judge (President, QB)

s.14, see *Blacklight Power Inc v Comptroller-General of Patents* [2008] EWHC 2763 (Pat), Times, December 10, 2008 (Ch D (Patents Ct)), Floyd, J

s.28, see *Matsushita Electrical Industrial Co v Comptroller General of Patents* [2008] EWHC 2071 (Pat), [2008] R.P.C. 35 (Ch D (Patents Ct)), Mann, J.

s.37, see *Cinpres Gas Injection Ltd v Melea Ltd* [2008] EWCA Civ 9, [2008] Bus. L.R. 1157 (CA (Civ Div)), Sir Igor Judge (President, QB)

s.66, see *MMI Research Ltd v Cellxion Ltd* [2007] EWHC 2611 (Pat), [2008] F.S.R. 23 (Ch D (Patents Ct)), Warren, J.

s.72, see *Eli Lilly & Co v Human Genome Sciences Inc* [2008] EWHC 1903 (Pat), [2008] R.P.C. 29 (Ch D (Patents Ct)), Kitchin, J.

s.74, see *Arrow Generics Ltd v Merck & Co Inc* [2007] EWHC 1900 (Pat), [2008] Bus. L.R. 487 (Ch D (Patents Ct)), Kitchin, J.

s.74A, see *DLP Ltd v Comptroller-General of Patents, Designs and Trade Marks* [2007] EWHC 2669 (Pat), [2008] Bus. L.R. 778 (Ch D (Patents Ct)), Kitchin, J.

s.74B, see *DLP Ltd v Comptroller-General of Patents, Designs and Trade Marks* [2007] EWHC 2669 (Pat), [2008] Bus. L.R. 778 (Ch D (Patents Ct)), Kitchin, J.

42. Rent Act 1977

see *Truro Diocesan Board of Finance Ltd v Foley* [2008] EWCA Civ 1162, Times, December 1, 2008 (CA (Civ Div)), May, L.J.

applied: SI 2008/188 Sch.1 para.1

s.14, amended: 2008 c.17 Sch.8 para.23

CAP.

1977–cont.

42. Rent Act 1977–*cont.*
s.15, varied: SI 2008/2839 Sch.1 para.1
s.63, amended: SI 2008/3134 Sch.1 para.1
s.63, applied: SI 2008/239 Reg.10
s.77, referred to: 2008 c.13 Sch.6
s.81, referred to: 2008 c.13 Sch.6
s.86, varied: SI 2008/2839 Sch.1 para.1
s.93, varied: SI 2008/2839 Sch.1 para.1

43. Protection from Eviction Act 1977
s.1, referred to: 2008 c.13 Sch.6
s.3, see *Polarpark Enterprises Inc v Allason* [2007] EWHC 1088 (Ch), [2008] 1 P. & C.R. 4 (Ch D), Briggs, J.
s.3A, see *Polarpark Enterprises Inc v Allason* [2007] EWHC 1088 (Ch), [2008] 1 P. & C.R. 4 (Ch D), Briggs, J.
s.3A, amended: 2008 c.17 Sch.8 para.24
s.3A, varied: SI 2008/2839 Sch.1 para.1

45. Criminal Law Act 1977
s.1, see *R. v Kenning (David Matthew)* [2008] EWCA Crim 1534, [2008] 3 W.L.R. 1306 (CA (Crim Div)), Lord Phillips of Worth Matravers, L.C.J.; see *R. v May (Raymond George)* [2008] UKHL 28, [2008] 1 A.C. 1028 (HL), Lord Bingham of Cornhill
s.12A, varied: SI 2008/2839 Sch.1 para.1

49. National Health Service Act 1977
s.16A, applied: SI 2008/794 Sch.8 para.29
s.16BA, applied: SI 2008/794 Sch.8 para.29
s.16CD, enabling: SI 2008/1186, SI 2008/1700
s.16CE, enabling: SI 2008/1186
s.28WB, enabling: SI 2008/1185
s.28WC, enabling: SI 2008/1185
s.28WE, enabling: SI 2008/1185, SI 2008/1700
s.28WF, enabling: SI 2008/1185
s.28X, applied: SI 2008/2699 Sch.1
s.28X, enabling: SI 2008/1187, SI 2008/1700
s.121, see *R. (on the application of A) v West Middlesex University Hospital NHS Trust* [2008] EWHC 855 (Admin), [2008] H.R.L.R. 29 (QBD (Admin)), Mitting, J.
s.126, enabling: SI 2008/553, SI 2008/1185, SI 2008/1186, SI 2008/1187, SI 2008/1657
Sch.12 para.2A, enabling: SI 2008/553, SI 2008/1657
Sch.12 para.2B, enabling: SI 2008/1657

50. Unfair Contract Terms Act 1977
see *Ferryways NV v Associated British Ports (The Humber Way)* [2008] EWHC 225 (Comm), [2008] 2 All E.R. (Comm) 504 (QBD (Comm)), Teare, J.; see *Macquarie Internationale Investments Ltd v Glencore (UK) Ltd* [2008] EWHC 1716 (Comm), [2008] 2 B.C.L.C. 565 (QBD (Comm)), Walker, J.; see *Trident Turboprop (Dublin) Ltd v First Flight Couriers Ltd* [2008] EWHC 1686 (Comm), [2008] 2 Lloyd's Rep. 581 (QBD (Comm)), Aikens, J.

CAP.

1977–cont.

50. Unfair Contract Terms Act 1977–*cont.*
applied: 2008 c.13 Sch.3
s.26, see *Trident Turboprop (Dublin) Ltd v First Flight Couriers Ltd* [2008] EWHC 1686 (Comm), [2008] 2 Lloyd's Rep. 581 (QBD (Comm)), Aikens, J.

1978

3. Refuse Disposal (Amenity) Act 1978
applied: 2008 c.13 Sch.3
s.2, applied: SSI 2008/189 Art.26, SSI 2008/190 Art.26
s.2, referred to: 2008 c.13 Sch.6
s.2A, applied: SI 2008/663 Reg.3
s.2A, enabling: SI 2008/663
s.2B, referred to: 2008 c.13 Sch.6
s.4, applied: SI 2008/2095 Reg.4, Reg.5, Reg.6
s.4, enabling: SI 2008/2095
s.5, applied: SI 2008/2095 Reg.4, Reg.5, Reg.6
s.5, enabling: SI 2008/2095
s.10, enabling: SI 2008/2095
s.11, referred to: SI 2008/663(a)
s.11, enabling: SI 2008/2095

10. European Parliamentary Elections Act 1978
Sch.1 para.2, applied: SSI 2008/228 Reg.8

22. Domestic Proceedings and Magistrates Courts Act 1978
applied: SI 2008/1052 Sch.1

23. Judicature (Northern Ireland) Act 1978
s.49, amended: 2008 c.4 Sch.8 para.27, Sch.28 Part 3
s.49, repealed (in part): 2008 c.4 Sch.8 para.27, Sch.28 Part 3
s.56, disapplied: 2008 c.28 s.72
s.67, applied: 2008 c.14 s.106
Sch.5, repealed: SI 2008/1216 Sch.6 Part 1

28. Adoption (Scotland) Act 1978
s.16, see *Scottish Borders Council v T* [2008] CSOH 17, 2008 Fam. L.R. 38 (OH), Lord Menzies
s.18, see *Scottish Borders Council v T* [2008] CSOH 17, 2008 Fam. L.R. 38 (OH), Lord Menzies
s.51A, applied: SI 2008/794 Sch.8 para.26

29. National Health Service (Scotland) Act 1978
applied: SSI 2008/315 Art.2
Part II, applied: SSI 2008/27 Reg.6
Part III, applied: SSI 2008/228 Reg.4
s.1, referred to: 2008 asp 5 s.1
s.1A, referred to: 2008 asp 5 s.1
s.2, applied: 2008 asp 5 s.2, SI 2008/1582 Reg.38, SI 2008/3170 Reg.23
s.2, enabling: SSI 2008/60
s.2A, referred to: 2008 asp 5 s.2
s.2C, applied: SSI 2008/224 Reg.7

CAP.

1978–cont.

29. National Health Service (Scotland) Act 1978–*cont.*
s.10, enabling: SSI 2008/312
s.13, referred to: 2008 asp 5 s.6
s.14, repealed: 2008 asp 5 Sch.3 Part 1
s.17E, enabling: SSI 2008/27
s.17K, enabling: SSI 2008/27
s.17N, enabling: SSI 2008/27
s.17P, enabling: SSI 2008/27
s.25, enabling: SSI 2008/27
s.26, enabling: SSI 2008/106
s.27, enabling: SSI 2008/27, SSI 2008/105
s.28, enabling: SSI 2008/27
s.36, applied: SSI 2008/312 Art.2
s.36, referred to: SSI 2008/312 Art.2
s.40, applied: SSI 2008/312 Art.2
s.44, applied: SSI 2008/312 Art.2
s.48, applied: SSI 2008/312 Art.2
s.69, enabling: SSI 2008/27, SSI 2008/105
s.70, enabling: SSI 2008/106, SSI 2008/289
s.73, applied: SSI 2008/224 Reg.7
s.73, enabling: SSI 2008/106
s.74, enabling: SSI 2008/106
s.75, enabling: SSI 2008/27
s.75A, enabling: SSI 2008/27, SSI 2008/105, SSI 2008/147, SSI 2008/288, SSI 2008/390
s.79, applied: SSI 2008/312 Art.2
s.85B, enabling: SSI 2008/60
s.88, applied: SSI 2008/315 Art.2
s.88, referred to: SSI 2008/315 Art.2
s.88, enabling: SSI 2008/315
s.98, enabling: SSI 2008/290
s.102, applied: SI 2008/794 Reg.156
s.105, enabling: SSI 2008/27, SSI 2008/60, SSI 2008/105, SSI 2008/106, SSI 2008/147, SSI 2008/288, SSI 2008/289, SSI 2008/290, SSI 2008/312, SSI 2008/315, SSI 2008/390
s.108, amended: 2008 asp 5 Sch.3 Part 1
s.108, enabling: SSI 2008/27, SSI 2008/60, SSI 2008/105, SSI 2008/106, SSI 2008/147, SSI 2008/288, SSI 2008/289, SSI 2008/290, SSI 2008/390
Sch.11 para.1, applied: SSI 2008/27 Reg.7
Sch.11 para.2, enabling: SSI 2008/106, SSI 2008/289
Sch.11 para.2A, enabling: SSI 2008/106, SSI 2008/289
Sch.11 para.4, applied: SSI 2008/27 Reg.7
Sch.11 para.7, applied: SSI 2008/27 Reg.7

30. Interpretation Act 1978
see *Odelola v Secretary of State for the Home Department* [2008] EWCA Civ 308, [2008] Imm. A.R. 632 (CA (Civ Div)), Buxton, L.J.
applied: 2008 c.01 s.12, 2008 c.4 s.85, s.91, 2008 c.30 s.73
referred to: SI 2008/2556 Art.3

CAP.

1978–cont.

30. Interpretation Act 1978–*cont.*
s.5, see *R. (on the application of Ashton) v Police Medical Appeal Board* [2008] EWHC 1833 (Admin), [2008] Pens. L.R. 391 (QBD (Admin)), Charles, J.
s.7, applied: 2008 c.14 s.93, 2008 c.17 s.55, 2008 c.18 s.53, SI 2008/37 Reg.23, SI 2008/608 Sch.1 para.17, SI 2008/1238 Art.12, SI 2008/2164 Reg.22, SI 2008/2512 Art.50, SI 2008/3206 Reg.30
s.14, applied: 2008 c.17 s.13, SI 2008/490 Art.7, SI 2008/491 Art.7, SI 2008/492 Art.7, SI 2008/493 Art.7, SI 2008/494 Art.7, SI 2008/634 Art.9, SI 2008/907 Art.8, Art.20
s.14, disapplied: SI 2008/2846 Sch.1
s.16, see *Odelola v Secretary of State for the Home Department* [2008] EWCA Civ 308, [2008] Imm. A.R. 632 (CA (Civ Div)), Buxton, L.J.
s.16, applied: SI 2008/2846 Sch.1
s.16, disapplied: SSI 2008/27 Reg.12
s.16, varied: SI 2008/788 Art.4
s.17, disapplied: SI 2008/2682 Sch.2 para.7
s.20A, amended: 2008 c.7 Sch.1 Part 2
Sch.1, amended: 2008 c.7 Sch.1 Part 2, 2008 c.17 Sch.9 para.5

31. Theft Act 1978
applied: 2008 c.13 Sch.3

33. State Immunity Act 1978
see *KOO Golden East Mongolia v Bank of Nova Scotia* [2008] EWHC 1120 (QB), [2008] P.N.L.R. 32 (QBD), Silber, J.; see *Ministry of Trade of Iraq v Tsavliris Salvage (International) Ltd (The Altair)* [2008] EWHC 612 (Comm), [2008] 2 All E.R. (Comm) 805 (QBD (Comm)), Gross, J.
s.1, see *Koo Golden East Mongolia v Bank of Nova Scotia* [2007] EWCA Civ 1443, [2008] Q.B. 717 (CA (Civ Div)), Sir Anthony Clarke, M.R.
s.3, see *Orascom Telecom Holding SAE v Chad* [2008] EWHC 1841 (Comm), [2008] 2 Lloyd's Rep. 396 (QBD (Comm)), Burton, J.
s.13, see *ETI Euro Telecom International NV v Bolivia* [2008] EWCA Civ 880, [2008] 2 Lloyd's Rep. 421 (CA (Civ Div)), Tuckey, L.J.; see *Koo Golden East Mongolia v Bank of Nova Scotia* [2007] EWCA Civ 1443, [2008] Q.B. 717 (CA (Civ Div)), Sir Anthony Clarke, M.R.; see *Orascom Telecom Holding SAE v Chad* [2008] EWHC 1841 (Comm), [2008] 2 Lloyd's Rep. 396 (QBD (Comm)), Burton, J.
s.14, see *Koo Golden East Mongolia v Bank of Nova Scotia* [2007] EWCA Civ 1443, [2008] Q.B. 717 (CA (Civ Div)), Sir Anthony Clarke, M.R.

CAP.

1978–cont.

33. State Immunity Act 1978–*cont.*
s.17, see *Orascom Telecom Holding SAE v Chad* [2008] EWHC 1841 (Comm), [2008] 2 Lloyd's Rep. 396 (QBD (Comm)), Burton, J.
s.20, see *Aziz v Aziz* [2007] EWCA Civ 712, [2008] 2 All E.R. 501 (CA (Civ Div)), Sedley, L.J.

36. House of Commons (Administration) Act 1978
s.3, applied: 2008 c.8 Sch.2 Part 53

37. Protection of Children Act 1978
s.1, referred to: 2008 c.4 Sch.27 para.24
s.1B, amended: 2008 c.4 s.69
s.7, amended: 2008 c.4 s.69

40. Rating (Disabled Persons) Act 1978
applied: SSI 2008/85 Reg.3

42. Finance Act 1978
s.62, referred to: 2008 c.9 Sch.4 para.11

47. Civil Liability (Contribution) Act 1978
see *BRB (Residuary) Ltd v Connex South Eastern Ltd (fomerly South Eastern Train Co Ltd)* [2008] EWHC 1172 (QB), [2008] 1 W.L.R. 2867 (QBD), Cranston, J.; see *City Index Ltd v Gawler* [2007] EWCA Civ 1382, [2008] Ch. 313 (CA (Civ Div)), Mummery, L.J.; see *Pulvers (A Firm) v Chan* [2007] EWHC 2406 (Ch), [2008] P.N.L.R. 9 (Ch D), Morgan, J.; see *West London Pipeline & Storage Ltd v Total UK Ltd* [2008] EWHC 1296 (Comm), [2008] C.P. Rep. 35 (QBD (Comm)), David Steel, J.
s.1, see *BRB (Residuary) Ltd v Connex South Eastern Ltd (fomerly South Eastern Train Co Ltd)* [2008] EWHC 1172 (QB), [2008] 1 W.L.R. 2867 (QBD), Cranston, J.; see *City Index Ltd v Gawler* [2007] EWCA Civ 1382, [2008] Ch. 313 (CA (Civ Div)), Mummery, L.J.; see *Revenue and Customs Commissioners v Yousef* [2008] EWHC 423 (Ch), [2008] B.C.C. 805 (Ch D), Judge Purle Q.C.
s.2, see *City Index Ltd v Gawler* [2007] EWCA Civ 1382, [2008] Ch. 313 (CA (Civ Div)), Mummery, L.J.; see *Pritchard Joyce & Hinds (A Firm) v Batcup* [2008] EWHC 20 (QB), [2008] P.N.L.R. 18 (QBD), Underhill, J.
s.6, see *City Index Ltd v Gawler* [2007] EWCA Civ 1382, [2008] Ch. 313 (CA (Civ Div)), Mummery, L.J.; see *Revenue and Customs Commissioners v Yousef* [2008] EWHC 423 (Ch), [2008] B.C.C. 805 (Ch D), Judge Purle Q.C.

1979

2. Customs and Excise Management Act 1979
applied: SI 2008/41 Reg.13, SI 2008/2108 Reg.4, SI 2008/2852 Sch.6 para.7
referred to: 2008 c.4 s.75

CAP.

1979–cont.

2. Customs and Excise Management Act 1979–*cont.*
s.1, amended: 2008 c.4 Sch.17 para.8, 2008 c.9 s.117
s.1, applied: 2008 c.4 Sch.17 para.9
s.35, applied: SI 2008/539 Sch.1 para.1
s.50, amended: 2008 c.4 Sch.17 para.8
s.50, applied: 2008 c.4 Sch.17 para.9, SI 2008/296 Reg.7
s.50, referred to: SI 2008/296 Reg.7
s.50, varied: SI 2008/296 Reg.7
s.64, applied: SI 2008/539 Sch.1 para.1
s.68, amended: 2008 c.4 Sch.17 para.8
s.68, applied: 2008 c.4 Sch.17 para.9, SI 2008/296 Reg.6
s.68, referred to: SI 2008/296 Reg.6
s.68, varied: SI 2008/296 Reg.6, SI 2008/1098 Art.10, SI 2008/3231 Art.42
s.77, applied: SI 2008/539 Sch.1 para.1
s.77A, applied: SI 2008/1098 Art.11, SI 2008/3231 Art.41
s.92, applied: 2008 c.9 Sch.41 para.1
s.93, enabling: SI 2008/2832
s.100G, applied: 2008 c.9 Sch.41 para.1
s.100G, enabling: SI 2008/753
s.100H, applied: 2008 c.9 Sch.41 para.1
s.100H, enabling: SI 2008/753
s.137, repealed (in part): 2008 c.9 s.162
s.138, applied: SI 2008/1098 Art.11, SI 2008/3231 Art.41
s.139, see *Revenue & Customs Commissioners v James (t/a M&D Enterprise)* [2008] EWHC 230 (QB), [2008] R.T.R. 18 (QBD), Eady, J.
s.145, applied: SI 2008/1098 Art.11, SI 2008/3231 Art.41
s.146, applied: SI 2008/1098 Art.11, SI 2008/3231 Art.41
s.146A, applied: SI 2008/1098 Art.11, SI 2008/3231 Art.41
s.147, applied: SI 2008/1098 Art.11, SI 2008/3231 Art.41
s.148, applied: SI 2008/1098 Art.11, SI 2008/3231 Art.41
s.150, applied: SI 2008/1098 Art.11, SI 2008/3231 Art.41
s.151, applied: SI 2008/1098 Art.11, SI 2008/3231 Art.41
s.152, see *Revenue & Customs Commissioners v James (t/a M&D Enterprise)* [2008] EWHC 230 (QB), [2008] R.T.R. 18 (QBD), Eady, J.
s.152, applied: SI 2008/1098 Art.11, SI 2008/3231 Art.41
s.154, applied: SI 2008/1098 Art.11, SI 2008/3231 Art.41
s.155, applied: SI 2008/1098 Art.11, SI 2008/3231 Art.41
s.159, amended: 2008 c.9 s.117
s.170, amended: 2008 c.4 Sch.17 para.8

CAP.

1979–cont.

2. **Customs and Excise Management Act 1979**–*cont.*
   - s.170, applied: 2008 c.4 Sch.17 para.9, SI 2008/41 Reg.12, SI 2008/1216 Sch.2 para.9
   - s.170, varied: SI 2008/1098 Art.10, SI 2008/3231 Art.42
   - s.170A, repealed: 2008 c.9 Sch.41 para.25
   - s.171, see *Chaudhry v Revenue and Customs Commissioners* [2007] EWHC 1805 (Admin), [2008] S.T.C. 2357 (DC), Sedley, L.J.
   - Sch.3, see *Revenue & Customs Commissioners v James (t/a M&D Enterprise)* [2008] EWHC 230 (QB), [2008] R.T.R. 18 (QBD), Eady, J.
   - Sch.3 para.5, see *Revenue & Customs Commissioners v James (t/a M&D Enterprise)* [2008] EWHC 230 (QB), [2008] R.T.R. 18 (QBD), Eady, J.
   - Sch.4 para.12, amended: 2008 c.12 Sch.1 Part 8, SI 2008/1277 Sch.4 Part 1
3. **Customs and Excise Duties (General Reliefs) Act 1979**
   - s.13, enabling: SI 2008/3058
4. **Alcoholic Liquor Duties Act 1979**
   - s.5, amended: 2008 c.9 s.11
   - s.8, applied: 2008 c.9 Sch.41 para.3
   - s.10, applied: 2008 c.9 Sch.41 para.3
   - s.11, applied: 2008 c.9 Sch.41 para.3
   - s.12, applied: 2008 c.9 Sch.41 para.1
   - s.15, applied: 2008 c.9 Sch.41 para.1
   - s.36, amended: 2008 c.9 s.11
   - s.41A, enabling: SI 2008/1885
   - s.46, enabling: SI 2008/1885
   - s.47, amended: 2008 c.9 Sch.41 para.25
   - s.47, applied: 2008 c.9 Sch.41 para.1
   - s.49, enabling: SI 2008/1885
   - s.54, amended: 2008 c.9 Sch.41 para.25
   - s.54, applied: 2008 c.9 Sch.41 para.1
   - s.55, amended: 2008 c.9 Sch.41 para.25
   - s.55, applied: 2008 c.9 Sch.41 para.1
   - s.61, enabling: SI 2008/1885
   - s.62, amended: 2008 c.9 s.11, Sch.41 para.25
   - s.62, applied: 2008 c.9 Sch.41 para.1
   - s.62, enabling: SI 2008/1885
   - s.64, enabling: SI 2008/1885
   - Sch.1, amended: 2008 c.9 s.11
   - Sch.2A para.4, applied: 2008 c.9 Sch.41 para.1
5. **Hydrocarbon Oil Duties Act 1979**
   - applied: SI 2008/753 Reg.2, SI 2008/3124 Art.7, Art.9
   - referred to: SI 2008/2168 Art.2
   - s.1, amended: 2008 c.9 s.13, Sch.5 para.2, Sch.6 para.2
   - s.1, repealed (in part): 2008 c.9 s.13, s.161
   - s.2A, amended: 2008 c.9 Sch.5 para.3, Sch.6 para.3
   - s.2A, repealed (in part): 2008 c.9 Sch.5 para.3

CAP.

1979–cont.

5. **Hydrocarbon Oil Duties Act 1979**–*cont.*
   - s.6, amended: 2008 c.9 s.13, s.15, s.16, Sch.6 para.4
   - s.6, repealed (in part): 2008 c.9 Sch.6 para.4
   - s.6A, enabling: SI 2008/754
   - s.6AA, amended: 2008 c.9 s.15, Sch.5 para.4
   - s.6AA, applied: SI 2008/2168 Art.3
   - s.6AB, amended: 2008 c.9 s.13, Sch.5 para.5
   - s.6AC, enabling: SI 2008/753
   - s.6AD, amended: 2008 c.9 s.15
   - s.6AD, applied: SI 2008/2168 Art.3
   - s.6AF, enabling: SI 2008/753
   - s.8, amended: 2008 c.9 s.15, Sch.5 para.6
   - s.8, repealed (in part): 2008 c.9 Sch.5 para.6
   - s.10, applied: 2008 c.9 Sch.41 para.3
   - s.10, repealed (in part): 2008 c.9 Sch.5 para.7
   - s.11, amended: 2008 c.9 s.13, s.15, Sch.6 para.25
   - s.11, applied: SI 2008/2168 Art.4, SI 2008/2599 Reg.4
   - s.11, repealed (in part): 2008 c.9 s.13
   - s.12, amended: 2008 c.9 Sch.6 para.26
   - s.12, repealed (in part): 2008 c.9 Sch.5 para.8
   - s.13, amended: 2008 c.9 Sch.6 para.27
   - s.13, applied: 2008 c.9 Sch.41 para.3
   - s.13, repealed (in part): 2008 c.9 Sch.5 para.9
   - s.13A, repealed: 2008 c.9 s.13
   - s.13AA, amended: 2008 c.9 s.13
   - s.13AA, applied: SI 2008/2168 Art.4
   - s.13AA, repealed (in part): 2008 c.9 Sch.5 para.10
   - s.13AB, amended: 2008 c.9 Sch.6 para.10
   - s.13AB, applied: 2008 c.9 Sch.41 para.3
   - s.13AB, repealed (in part): 2008 c.9 Sch.5 para.11
   - s.13AB, substituted: 2008 c.9 Sch.6 para.10
   - s.13AC, added: 2008 c.9 Sch.6 para.11
   - s.13AC, applied: SI 2008/2599 Reg.3, Reg.4, Reg.5
   - s.13AC, enabling: SI 2008/2599
   - s.13AD, added: 2008 c.9 Sch.6 para.11
   - s.13AD, applied: 2008 c.9 Sch.41 para.3, SI 2008/2599 Reg.5
   - s.13AD, repealed (in part): 2008 c.9 Sch.41 para.25
   - s.13ZA, added: 2008 c.9 Sch.6 para.28
   - s.13ZA, applied: SI 2008/2168 Art.4
   - s.13ZB, added: 2008 c.9 Sch.6 para.28
   - s.13ZB, applied: 2008 c.9 Sch.41 para.3, SI 2008/2600 Reg.3
   - s.13ZB, enabling: SI 2008/2600
   - s.14, amended: 2008 c.9 s.15
   - s.14, applied: 2008 c.9 Sch.41 para.3, SI 2008/2168 Art.4
   - s.14, repealed (in part): 2008 c.9 Sch.5 para.12
   - s.14A, added: 2008 c.9 Sch.5 para.13
   - s.14A, amended: 2008 c.9 s.15, Sch.6 para.13
   - s.14A, applied: SI 2008/2168 Art.4
   - s.14B, added: 2008 c.9 Sch.5 para.13

CAP.

1979–*cont.*

5. **Hydrocarbon Oil Duties Act 1979**–*cont.*
s.14C, added: 2008 c.9 Sch.5 para.13
s.14C, amended: 2008 c.9 Sch.6 para.14
s.14D, added: 2008 c.9 Sch.5 para.13
s.14D, applied: 2008 c.9 Sch.41 para.3
s.14E, added: 2008 c.9 Sch.6 para.15
s.14E, applied: SI 2008/2599 Reg.7, Reg.8, Reg.9
s.14E, referred to: SI 2008/2599 Reg.8
s.14E, enabling: SI 2008/2599
s.14F, added: 2008 c.9 Sch.6 para.15
s.14F, applied: 2008 c.9 Sch.41 para.3, SI 2008/2599 Reg.9
s.14F, repealed (in part): 2008 c.9 Sch.41 para.25
s.15, applied: SI 2008/753 Reg.2
s.17, applied: SI 2008/753 Reg.2
s.17A, repealed: 2008 c.9 Sch.5 para.14
s.19, applied: SI 2008/753 Reg.2
s.20A, amended: 2008 c.9 Sch.5 para.15
s.20A, applied: SI 2008/753 Reg.2
s.20A, enabling: SI 2008/753
s.20AA, amended: 2008 c.9 Sch.5 para.17, Sch.6 para.30
s.20AA, applied: SI 2008/753 Reg.2
s.20AA, enabling: SI 2008/753, SI 2008/2167, SI 2008/3019
s.20AAA, amended: 2008 c.9 s.13, Sch.5 para.16, Sch.6 para.29
s.20AAA, repealed (in part): 2008 c.9 Sch.5 para.16
s.20AB, enabling: SI 2008/753
s.20AC, added: 2008 c.9 Sch.5 para.18
s.20AC, applied: SI 2008/753 Reg.2
s.20AC, enabling: SI 2008/753
s.21, applied: 2008 c.9 Sch.41 para.1
s.21, enabling: SI 2008/753
s.23, applied: 2008 c.9 Sch.41 para.3
s.23, repealed (in part): 2008 c.9 Sch.5 para.19
s.23B, enabling: SI 2008/753
s.24, amended: 2008 c.9 Sch.5 para.20, Sch.6 para.5, Sch.6 para.16, Sch.6 para.31
s.24, applied: 2008 c.9 Sch.41 para.3, SI 2008/753 Reg.2
s.24, enabling: SI 2008/753, SI 2008/2599, SI 2008/2600
s.24A, repealed (in part): 2008 c.9 Sch.5 para.21
s.27, amended: 2008 c.9 s.13, Sch.5 para.22, Sch.6 para.6, Sch.6 para.32
Sch.3, enabling: SI 2008/753
Sch.3 Part I para.10A, repealed: 2008 c.9 Sch.6 para.7
Sch.4, enabling: SI 2008/753
Sch.4 para.3, amended: 2008 c.9 Sch.5 para.23
Sch.4 para.22, amended: 2008 c.9 Sch.5 para.23
Sch.5 para.3, amended: 2008 c.9 Sch.5 para.24

CAP.

1979–*cont.*

7. **Tobacco Products Duty Act 1979**
s.6, enabling: SI 2008/3026
s.7, applied: 2008 c.9 Sch.41 para.1
s.7D, amended: SI 2008/954 Art.5
Sch.1, amended: 2008 c.9 s.12, SI 2008/3026 Sch.2

8. **Excise Duties (Surcharges or Rebates) Act 1979**
s.1, enabling: SI 2008/2168, SI 2008/3018, SI 2008/3026, SI 2008/3062
s.2, enabling: SI 2008/2168, SI 2008/3018, SI 2008/3062

11. **Electricity (Scotland) Act 1979**
s.5, applied: SSI 2008/263 Sch.2

17. **Vaccine Damage Payments Act 1979**
applied: SI 2008/1596 Reg.7, SI 2008/2103 Art.2, SI 2008/2685 Sch.1
s.1, enabling: SI 2008/2103
s.2, varied: SI 2008/2103 Art.3
s.2, enabling: SI 2008/2103
s.3A, amended: SI 2008/2833 Sch.3 para.31
s.4, amended: SI 2008/2833 Sch.3 para.32, Sch.3 para.33
s.4, repealed (in part): SI 2008/2833 Sch.3 para.32, Sch.3 para.33
s.7A, amended: SI 2008/2833 Sch.3 para.34
s.7A, repealed (in part): SI 2008/2833 Sch.3 para.34
s.9A, repealed: SI 2008/2833 Sch.3 para.35
s.12, amended: SI 2008/2833 Sch.3 para.36
s.12, repealed (in part): SI 2008/2833 Sch.3 para.36

34. **Credit Unions Act 1979**
applied: SI 2008/2770 Art.9

38. **Estate Agents Act 1979**
applied: 2008 c.13 Sch.3
referred to: 2008 c.13 Sch.6
s.14, amended: SI 2008/948 Sch.1 para.8
s.23A, enabling: SI 2008/1712
s.23B, applied: SI 2008/1713 Reg.2
Sch.3, applied: SI 2008/1712
Sch.4 para.2, enabling: SI 2008/1713

41. **Pneumoconiosis etc (Workers Compensation) Act 1979**
applied: 2008 c.6 s.47, SI 2008/650 Reg.1
see *Cameron v Vinters Defence Systems Ltd* [2007] EWHC 2267 (QB), [2008] P.I.Q.R. P5 (QBD), Holland, J.
s.1, enabling: SI 2008/650, SI 2008/1963
s.2, see *Cameron v Vinters Defence Systems Ltd* [2007] EWHC 2267 (QB), [2008] P.I.Q.R. P5 (QBD), Holland, J.
s.5, applied: 2008 c.6 s.47
s.7, applied: SI 2008/650, SI 2008/1963
s.7, enabling: SI 2008/650

42. **Arbitration Act 1979**
s.1, see *CTI Group Inc v Transclear SA (The Mary Nour)* [2007] EWHC 2340 (Comm), [2008] 1 All E.R. (Comm) 203 (QBD (Comm)), Field, J.

CAP.

1979–cont.

43. Crown Agents Act 1979
s.22, amended: SI 2008/948 Sch.1 para.1, Sch.1 para.46
s.25, applied: SI 2008/921
Sch.5 para.20, applied: SI 2008/948 Sch.1 para.1
Sch.5 para.23, applied: SI 2008/921, SI 2008/921 Art.3
Sch.5 para.23, enabling: SI 2008/921
Sch.5 para.24, applied: SI 2008/921 Art.3

46. Ancient Monuments and Archaeological Areas Act 1979
applied: 2008 c.18 Sch.10 para.1, SI 2008/2512 Art.21, SSI 2008/100 Sch.2 Part 1, Sch.4 Part 2, SSI 2008/159 Sch.2, Sch.3 Part 2
referred to: 2008 c.13 Sch.6, 2008 c.18 Sch.9 para.4
s.1, applied: SI 2008/386 Reg.4, SI 2008/2499 Reg.4
s.2, amended: 2008 c.29 Sch.2 para.17
s.2, applied: 2008 c.29 s.33
s.2, disapplied: 2008 c.18 Sch.9 para.4
s.3, applied: 2008 c.29 s.33
s.6, disapplied: 2008 c.18 Sch.9 para.4
s.6A, disapplied: 2008 c.18 Sch.9 para.4
s.17, applied: 2008 c.18 Sch.9 para.4
s.19, applied: 2008 c.18 Sch.9 para.4
s.19, disapplied: 2008 c.18 Sch.9 para.4
s.25, disapplied: 2008 c.18 Sch.9 para.4
s.26, disapplied: 2008 c.18 Sch.9 para.4
s.28, amended: 2008 c.29 Sch.2 para.18
s.28, disapplied: 2008 c.18 Sch.9 para.4
s.35, applied: 2008 c.29 s.33
s.35, disapplied: 2008 c.18 Sch.9 para.4
s.37, amended: 2008 c.29 Sch.2 para.19
s.39, varied: 2008 c.18 Sch.9 para.4
s.42, disapplied: 2008 c.18 Sch.9 para.4
s.61, amended: 2008 c.29 Sch.2 para.20

53. Charging Orders Act 1979
s.2, see *Nelson v Greening & Sykes (Builders) Ltd* [2007] EWCA Civ 1358, [2008] 8 E.G. 158 (CA (Civ Div)), Ward, L.J.

54. Sale of Goods Act 1979
applied: 2008 c.13 Sch.3
s.18, see *Fairfax Gerrard Holdings Ltd v Capital Bank Plc* [2007] EWCA Civ 1226, [2008] 1 All E.R. (Comm) 632 (CA (Civ Div)), Waller, L.J. (V-P)
s.32, see *Scottish & Newcastle International Ltd v Othon Ghalanos Ltd* [2008] UKHL 11, [2008] Bus. L.R. 583 (HL), Lord Bingham of Cornhill
s.35, see *Whitecap Leisure Ltd v John H Rundle Ltd* [2008] EWCA Civ 429, [2008] 2 Lloyd's Rep. 216 (CA (Civ Div)), Ward, L.J.
s.51, see *CTI Group Inc v Transclear SA (The Mary Nour)* [2007] EWHC 2340 (Comm), [2008] 1 All E.R. (Comm) 203 (QBD (Comm)), Field, J.

CAP.

1980

1. Petroleum Revenue Tax Act 1980
s.1, amended: 2008 c.9 Sch.40 para.21

12. Bees Act 1980
s.1, referred to: 2008 c.13 Sch.6

9. Reserve Forces Act 1980
s.14, applied: SSI 2008/228 Reg.16
s.34, applied: SSI 2008/228 Reg.16

23. Consular Fees Act 1980
s.1, enabling: SI 2008/676

26. British Aerospace Act 1980
s.4, amended: SI 2008/948 Sch.1 para.48

27. Import of Live Fish (England and Wales) Act 1980
s.3, referred to: 2008 c.13 Sch.6

33. Industry Act 1980
s.3, amended: SI 2008/948 Sch.1 para.49

43. Magistrates Courts Act 1980
applied: SI 2008/41 Reg.25, SI 2008/2297 Reg.39, Reg.41, SI 2008/3206 Reg.12, Reg.14, SI 2008/3252 Reg.5
disapplied: 2008 c.4 Sch.2 para.22
Part III, applied: 2008 c.4 s.85, SI 2008/2347 Art.12
Part III, referred to: 2008 c.4 s.152
s.10, disapplied: 2008 c.4 Sch.2 para.22
s.11, amended: 2008 c.4 s.54
s.11, applied: SI 2008/2795 Reg.4
s.13, repealed (in part): 2008 c.4 Sch.28 Part 4
s.24, repealed (in part): 2008 c.4 Sch.28 Part 4
s.43A, applied: 2008 c.4 Sch.2 para.21
s.43A, varied: 2008 c.4 Sch.2 para.21
s.65, amended: 2008 c.22 Sch.6 para.20
s.65, repealed (in part): 2008 c.14 Sch.15 Part 5
s.67, applied: SI 2008/2836 Art.15
s.75, see *Crown Prosecution Service v Greenacre* [2007] EWHC 1193 (Admin), [2008] 1 W.L.R. 438 (DC), Laws, L.J.
s.75, applied: 2008 c.25 s.56, s.57, s.58
s.76, see *Crown Prosecution Service v Greenacre* [2007] EWHC 1193 (Admin), [2008] 1 W.L.R. 438 (DC), Laws, L.J.
s.76, applied: 2008 c.25 s.56
s.77, see *Crown Prosecution Service v Greenacre* [2007] EWHC 1193 (Admin), [2008] 1 W.L.R. 438 (DC), Laws, L.J.
s.77, applied: SI 2008/2347 Art.12
s.78, applied: SI 2008/2347 Art.12
s.80, applied: 2008 c.25 s.57
s.81, amended: 2008 c.4 Sch.26 para.1
s.81, applied: 2008 c.4 s.39, 2008 c.25 s.56
s.83, applied: SI 2008/1052 Art.3
s.85A, applied: 2008 c.25 s.56, s.58
s.88, applied: SI 2008/1052 Art.3
s.89, applied: SI 2008/1052 Art.3
s.90, applied: SSI 2008/102 Art.9, SSI 2008/151 Art.25

CAP.

1980–cont.

43. Magistrates Courts Act 1980–*cont.*

s.111, see *Haw v Westminster Magistrates Court* [2007] EWHC 2960 (Admin), [2008] Q.B. 888 (DC), Thomas, L.J.

s.111, applied: SI 2008/1052 Sch.1, SI 2008/1597 Sch.5 para.14, SI 2008/2852 Sch.6 para.26

s.114, applied: SI 2008/1052 Sch.1

s.127, see *R. (on the application of Thornhill) v Uxbridge Magistrates Court* [2008] EWHC 508 (Admin), (2008) 172 J.P. 297 (QBD (Admin)), Silber, J.

s.127, applied: 2008 c.29 s.58

s.127, disapplied: SI 2008/1276 Reg.10, SI 2008/1277 Reg.14, SI 2008/2668 Art.10

s.128, applied: 2008 c.4 Sch.2 para.21

s.128, varied: 2008 c.4 Sch.2 para.21

s.133, see *R. v James (Liam Martin)* [2007] EWCA Crim 1906, [2008] 1 Cr. App. R. (S.) 44 (CA (Crim Div)), Longmore, L.J.

s.136, applied: SI 2008/1052 Art.3

s.142, see *R. (on the application of Green & Green Scaffolding Ltd) v Staines Magstrates Court* [2008] EWHC 1443 (Admin), (2008) 172 J.P. 353 (DC), Maurice Kay, L.J.; see *R. (on the application of M) v Tower Bridge Magistrates' Court* [2007] EWHC 2766 (Admin), (2008) 172 J.P. 155 (DC), Keene, L.J.; see *Royal Society for the Prevention of Cruelty to Animals (RSPCA) v Munur* [2008] EWHC 199 (Admin), (2008) 172 J.P. 174 (DC), Latham, L.J.

s.144, applied: SI 2008/2858, SI 2008/2859

s.144, enabling: SI 2008/2858, SI 2008/2859

s.150, applied: SI 2008/794 Reg.147

Sch.1 para.2, repealed: 2008 c.12 Sch.1 Part 3

Sch.2, referred to: 2008 c.4 s.52

Sch.3, applied: 2008 c.14 s.92, 2008 c.25 s.136, 2008 c.28 Sch.7 para.37, 2008 c.30 s.47

Sch.5, applied: 2008 c.4 s.85

Sch.6, applied: 2008 c.4 s.85

Sch.6A, amended: 2008 c.4 Sch.4 para.24, Sch.4 para.103

Sch.6A, repealed: 2008 c.4 Sch.28 Part 1

44. Education (Scotland) Act 1980

see *D v Glasgow City Council* 2008 S.C. 117 (IH (1 Div)), Lord Hamilton L.P.

s.28A, see *D v Glasgow City Council* 2008 S.C. 117 (IH (1 Div)), Lord Hamilton L.P.; see *East Lothian Council, Petitioner* [2008] CSOH 137, 2008 S.L.T. 921 (OH), Lord Woolman; see *G v Inverclyde Council* 2008 S.L.T. (Sh Ct) 87 (Sh Ct (North Strathclyde) (Greenock)), Sheriff J P Herald

s.49, applied: SI 2008/794 Sch.8 para.13, Sch.9 para.52

s.53, applied: SSI 2008/265 Reg.3

s.53, disapplied: SSI 2008/400 Art.3

CAP.

1980–cont.

44. Education (Scotland) Act 1980–*cont.*

s.53, referred to: SSI 2008/400

s.56A, enabling: SSI 2008/265

s.56B, enabling: SSI 2008/265

s.56D, enabling: SSI 2008/265

s.73, applied: SI 2008/529 Reg.119, Reg.136, SI 2008/794 Reg.139, Sch.8 para.13, Sch.9 para.52, SI 2008/1273 Reg.66, Reg.79, SI 2008/1582 Reg.119, Reg.136, SI 2008/3170 Reg.66, Reg.79

s.73, enabling: SI 2008/546, SI 2008/2715, SSI 2008/205, SSI 2008/206, SSI 2008/214, SSI 2008/235

s.73B, applied: SI 2008/529 Reg.119, Reg.136, SI 2008/1273 Reg.66, Reg.79, SI 2008/1582 Reg.119, Reg.136, SI 2008/3170 Reg.66, Reg.79

s.73B, enabling: SI 2008/546, SI 2008/2715, SSI 2008/235

s.73ZA, applied: SI 2008/794 Sch.8 para.13, Sch.9 para.52

s.74, applied: SI 2008/529 Reg.119, Reg.136, SI 2008/1273 Reg.66, Reg.79, SI 2008/1582 Reg.119, Reg.136, SI 2008/3170 Reg.66, Reg.79

s.74, enabling: SSI 2008/205, SSI 2008/206, SSI 2008/214

s.75A, applied: SSI 2008/213

s.75A, enabling: SSI 2008/213

s.75B, enabling: SSI 2008/213

s.111, amended: SI 2008/948 Sch.1 para.1

s.133, applied: SSI 2008/265

s.135, enabling: SSI 2008/163, SSI 2008/178

45. Water (Scotland) Act 1980

referred to: SSI 2008/263 Sch.2

s.17, applied: SSI 2008/429

s.17, enabling: SSI 2008/429

s.29, enabling: SSI 2008/429

s.45, applied: SI 2008/794 Sch.6 para.7

s.107, enabling: SSI 2008/429

Sch.4 Part II para.2, referred to: SSI 2008/429 Art.3

Sch.4 Part II para.2, varied: SSI 2008/429 Sch.2 para.1

Sch.4 Part III para.10, referred to: SSI 2008/429 Art.3

Sch.4 Part III para.10, varied: SSI 2008/429 Sch.2 para.2

46. Solicitors (Scotland) Act 1980

applied: SI 2008/2341 Art.4, SSI 2008/332 Art.4

referred to: SSI 2008/332 Art.4

s.25A, applied: 2008 c.28 s.68

s.41, applied: SI 2008/794 Reg.107, Reg.115

s.51, repealed (in part): SSI 2008/332 Art.4

47. Criminal Appeal (Northern Ireland) Act 1980

referred to: 2008 c.4 s.47

Part I, applied: 2008 c.4 s.43, SI 2008/1586 Sch.2 para.8

Part II, applied: SI 2008/1586 Sch.2 para.10

CAP.

1980–cont.

47. Criminal Appeal (Northern Ireland) Act 1980–*cont.*

.13A, amended: 2008 c.4 Sch.26 para.6

s.1 (b), amended: 2008 c.4 Sch.8 para.15

s.4, amended: 2008 c.4 Sch.8 para.18

s.10, repealed (in part): 2008 c.4 Sch.8 para.19, Sch.28 Part 3

s.12, amended: 2008 c.4 Sch.8 para.16

s.13A, amended: 2008 c.4 Sch.8 para.17

s.13B, added: 2008 c.4 s.43

s.24(2A), amended: SI 2008/1216 Art.83

s.24(2D), amended: SI 2008/1216 Art.83

s.25, amended: 2008 c.4 Sch.8 para.22, SI 2008/1216 Art.83

s.26, amended: 2008 c.4 Sch.8 para.23

s.29A, added: 2008 c.4 Sch.8 para.20

s.30, amended: 2008 c.4 Sch.8 para.20

s.31, referred to: SI 2008/1863 Art.62

s.36, amended: 2008 c.4 Sch.8 para.24, SI 2008/1587 Art.6

s.36, varied: SI 2008/1587 Art.6

s.45, amended: 2008 c.4 Sch.8 para.21, Sch.8 para.25, SI 2008/1216 Art.83

Sch.4, repealed: SI 2008/1216 Sch.6 Part 1

48. Finance Act 1980

s.3, repealed: 2008 c.12 Sch.1 Part 8

s.7, repealed: 2008 c.12 Sch.1 Part 8

s.61, repealed: 2008 c.12 Sch.1 Part 8

s.103, repealed: 2008 c.12 Sch.1 Part 8

Sch.15, referred to: 2008 c.9 Sch.4 para.11

Sch.17 Part III para.15, amended: 2008 c.9 Sch.33 para.3

58. Limitation Act 1980

see *Ashe v National Westminster Bank Plc* [2008] EWCA Civ 55, [2008] 1 W.L.R. 710 (CA (Civ Div)), Mummery, L.J.; see *Byrne v Motor Insurers' Bureau* [2008] EWCA Civ 574, [2008] 3 W.L.R. 1421 (CA (Civ Div)), Waller, L.J.; see *Eurocruit Europe Ltd (In Liquidation), Re* [2007] EWHC 1433 (Ch), [2008] Bus. L.R. 146 (Ch D), Blackburne, J.; see *Roberts v Swangrove Estates Ltd* [2008] EWCA Civ 98, [2008] Ch. 439 (CA (Civ Div)), Mummery, L.J.; see *Shore v Sedgwick Financial Services Ltd* [2007] EWHC 2509 (Admin), [2008] P.N.L.R. 10 (QBD), Beatson, J.; see *Yorkshire Bank Finance Ltd v Mulhall* [2008] EWCA Civ 1156, [2008] 50 E.G. 74 (CA (Civ Div)), Sir Anthony May (President, QB)

applied: 2008 c.01 s.6

s.2, see *Shore v Sedgwick Financial Services Ltd* [2007] EWHC 2509 (Admin), [2008] P.N.L.R. 10 (QBD), Beatson, J.; see *Spencer v Secretary of State for Work and Pensions* [2008] EWCA Civ 750, [2008] C.P. Rep. 40 (CA (Civ Div)), Waller, L.J.

CAP.

1980–cont.

58. Limitation Act 1980–*cont.*

s.7, see *ED&F Man Sugar Ltd v Lendoudis* [2007] EWHC 2268 (Comm), [2008] 1 All E.R. 952 (QBD (Comm)), Christopher Clarke, J.

s.9, see *Legal Services Commission v Rasool* [2008] EWCA Civ 154, [2008] 1 W.L.R. 2711 (CA (Civ Div)), Ward, L.J.; see *Welford v Transport for London* [2008] R.V.R. 178 (Lands Tr), George Bartlett Q.C. (President)

s.11, see *A v Hoare* [2008] UKHL 6, [2008] 1 A.C. 844 (HL), Lord Hoffmann; see *Giles v Rhind* [2008] EWCA Civ 118, [2008] 3 W.L.R. 1233 (CA (Civ Div)), Buxton, L.J.

s.12, see *Thompson v Arnold* [2007] EWHC 1875 (QB), [2008] P.I.Q.R. P1 (QBD), Langstaff, J.

s.14, see *A v Hoare* [2008] UKHL 6, [2008] 1 A.C. 844 (HL), Lord Hoffmann

s.14A, see *Harris Springs Ltd v Howes* [2007] EWHC 3271 (TCC), [2008] B.L.R. 229 (QBD (TCC)), Judge Raynor QC; see *Shore v Sedgwick Financial Services Ltd* [2007] EWHC 2509 (Admin), [2008] P.N.L.R. 10 (QBD), Beatson, J.; see *Shore v Sedgwick Financial Services Ltd* [2008] EWCA Civ 863, [2008] P.N.L.R. 37 (CA (Civ Div)), Buxton, L.J.

s.14B, see *Rind v Theodore Goddard (A Firm)* [2008] EWHC 459 (Ch), [2008] P.N.L.R. 24 (Ch D), Morgan, J.

s.15, see *Ashe v National Westminster Bank Plc* [2008] EWCA Civ 55, [2008] 1 W.L.R. 710 (CA (Civ Div)), Mummery, L.J.; see *JA Pye (Oxford) Ltd v United Kingdom (44302/02)* (2008) 46 E.H.R.R. 45 (ECHR (Grand Chamber)), Judge Costa (President)

s.17, see *Ashe v National Westminster Bank Plc* [2008] EWCA Civ 55, [2008] 1 W.L.R. 710 (CA (Civ Div)), Mummery, L.J.

s.20, see *Yorkshire Bank Finance Ltd v Mulhall* [2008] EWCA Civ 1156, [2008] 50 E.G. 74 (CA (Civ Div)), Sir Anthony May (President, QB)

s.21, see *Statek Corp v Alford* [2008] EWHC 32 (Ch), [2008] B.C.C. 266 (Ch D), Evans-Lombe, J.

s.24, see *Yorkshire Bank Finance Ltd v Mulhall* [2008] EWCA Civ 1156, [2008] 50 E.G. 74 (CA (Civ Div)), Sir Anthony May (President, QB)

s.27B, amended: SI 2008/302 Art.4

s.28, see *Byrne v Motor Insurers' Bureau* [2007] EWHC 1268 (QB), [2008] 2 W.L.R. 234 (QBD), Flaux, J.; see *Byrne v Motor Insurers' Bureau* [2008] EWCA Civ 574, [2008] 3 W.L.R. 1421 (CA (Civ Div)), Waller, L.J.

s.29, see *Ofulue v Bossert* [2008] EWCA Civ 7, [2008] 3 W.L.R. 1253 (CA (Civ Div)), May, L.J.

CAP.

1980–cont.

58. Limitation Act 1980–*cont.*

s.32, see *Barnstaple Boat Co Ltd v Jones* [2007] EWCA Civ 727, [2008] 1 All E.R. 1124 (CA (Civ Div)), Waller, L.J. (V-P); see *Bell v Brown* [2007] EWHC 2788 (QB), [2008] B.P.I.R. 829 (QBD), Tugendhat, J.; see *Bocardo SA v Star Energy UK Onshore Ltd* [2008] EWHC1756 (Ch), [2008] 2 P. & C.R. 23 (Ch D), Peter Smith, J.; see *Europcar UK Ltd v Revenue and Customs Commissioners* [2008] EWHC 1363 (Ch), [2008] S.T.C. 2751 (Ch D), Henderson, J.; see *Giles v Rhind* [2008] EWCA Civ 118, [2008] 3 W.L.R. 1233 (CA (Civ Div)), Buxton, L.J.

s.33, see *A v Hoare* [2008] UKHL 6, [2008] 1 A.C. 844 (HL), Lord Hoffmann; see *Dobson v Thames Water Utilities Ltd* [2007] EWHC 2021 (TCC), [2008] 2 All E.R. 362 (QBD (TCC)), Ramsey, J.; see *Leeson v Marsden* [2008] EWHC 1011 (QB), (2008) 103 B.M.L.R. 49 (QBD), Cox, J.

s.35, see *Adelson v Associated Newspapers Ltd* [2007] EWCA Civ 701, [2008] 1 W.L.R. 585 (CA (Civ Div)), Lord Phillips, L.C.J.; see *Giles v Rhind* [2008] EWCA Civ 118, [2008] 3 W.L.R. 1233 (CA (Civ Div)), Buxton, L.J.; see *O'Byrne v Aventis Pasteur MSD Ltd* [2008] UKHL 34, [2008] 4 All E.R. 881 (HL), Lord Hoffmann

s.37, see *Roberts v Swangrove Estates Ltd* [2008] EWCA Civ 98, [2008] Ch. 439 (CA (Civ Div)), Mummery, L.J.

Sch.1 para.8, see *Ashe v National Westminster Bank Plc* [2008] EWCA Civ 55, [2008] 1 W.L.R. 710 (CA (Civ Div)), Mummery, L.J.

Sch.1 para.10, see *Roberts v Swangrove Estates Ltd* [2008] EWCA Civ 98, [2008] Ch. 439 (CA (Civ Div)), Mummery, L.J.

60. Civil Aviation Act 1980

s.5, amended: SI 2008/948 Sch.1 para.50

65. Local Government, Planning and Land Act 1980

s.4, repealed (in part): 2008 c.17 Sch.8 para.26, Sch.16

s.4A, repealed: 2008 c.17 Sch.16

s.9, amended: 2008 c.17 Sch.16

s.9A, amended: 2008 c.17 Sch.16

s.25, repealed (in part): 2008 c.12 Sch.1 Part 9

s.32A, amended: 2008 c.17 Sch.16

s.86, repealed: 2008 c.12 Sch.1 Part 9

s.93, amended: 2008 c.17 Sch.8 para.27

s.99, amended: 2008 c.17 Sch.8 para.28, Sch.16

s.149, applied: 2008 c.18 Sch.7 para.36

s.159, repealed (in part): 2008 c.14 Sch.11 para.2, Sch.15 Part 3

s.165, applied: 2008 c.17 s.52

s.165A, amended: 2008 c.17 Sch.8 para.29

s.165B, amended: 2008 c.17 Sch.8 para.30

s.165B, applied: 2008 c.17 s.52

CAP.

1980–cont.

65. Local Government, Planning and Land Act 1980–*cont.*

s.173, repealed: 2008 c.12 Sch.1 Part 9

s.174, repealed: 2008 c.12 Sch.1 Part 9

s.175, repealed: 2008 c.12 Sch.1 Part 9

s.178, repealed: 2008 c.12 Sch.1 Part 9

s.183, repealed (in part): 2008 c.12 Sch.1 Part 9

Sch.3 para.6, repealed (in part): 2008 c.17 Sch.16

Sch.4 para.4, amended: 2008 c.17 Sch.16

Sch.16 para.6, repealed: 2008 c.17 Sch.8 para.31, Sch.16

Sch.16 para.9, substituted: 2008 c.17 Sch.9 para.6

Sch.23 Part III para.4, repealed: 2008 c.12 Sch.1 Part 9

Sch.23 Part III para.6, repealed: 2008 c.12 Sch.1 Part 9

Sch.23 Part III para.7, repealed: 2008 c.12 Sch.1 Part 9

Sch.23 Part V para.13, repealed: 2008 c.12 Sch.1 Part 9

Sch.23 Part V para.15, repealed: 2008 c.12 Sch.1 Part 9

Sch.23 Part V para.18, repealed: 2008 c.12 Sch.1 Part 9

Sch.28 Part III para.6, amended: 2008 c.29 Sch.9 para.1

Sch.31 Part II para.8, referred to: 2008 c.12 Sch.2 para.9

Sch.31 Part III para.11, amended: SI 2008/948 Sch.1 para.1

66. Highways Act 1980

applied: 2008 c.13 Sch.3, SI 2008/2512 Sch.9 para.3

Part IX, referred to: 2008 c.13 Sch.6

s.10, amended: 2008 c.29 Sch.2 para.22

s.10, applied: 2008 c.29 s.33

s.10, enabling: SI 2008/233, SI 2008/234, SI 2008/342, SI 2008/585, SI 2008/2107, SI 2008/2109, SI 2008/2254, SI 2008/2350, SI 2008/2502, SI 2008/2510, SI 2008/2511, SI 2008/2701, SI 2008/3138, SI 2008/3291, SI 2008/3292

s.12, enabling: SI 2008/234, SI 2008/342, SI 2008/585, SI 2008/2107, SI 2008/2109, SI 2008/2254, SI 2008/2350, SI 2008/2502, SI 2008/2510, SI 2008/2511, SI 2008/3138, SI 2008/3199, SI 2008/3291, SI 2008/3292

s.14, amended: 2008 c.29 Sch.2 para.23

s.14, applied: 2008 c.29 s.33

s.16, amended: 2008 c.29 Sch.2 para.24

s.16, applied: 2008 c.29 s.33

s.16, enabling: SI 2008/231, SI 2008/232, SI 2008/2110, SI 2008/2253, SI 2008/3325

s.17, enabling: SI 2008/231, SI 2008/232, SI 2008/2110, SI 2008/2253, SI 2008/3325 Sch.1

s.18, amended: 2008 c.29 Sch.2 para.25

CAP.

1980–cont.

66. Highways Act 1980–*cont.*
s.18, applied: 2008 c.29 s.33
s.19, enabling: SI 2008/231, SI 2008/232, SI 2008/2110, SI 2008/2253
s.20, enabling: SI 2008/3199
s.26, applied: SI 2008/442 Reg.3, Sch.1 para.1
s.31, see *R. (on the application of Godmanchester Town Council) v Secretary of State for the Environment, Food and Rural Affairs* [2007] UKHL 28, [2008] 1 A.C. 221 (HL), Lord Hoffmann
s.41, enabling: SI 2008/2107, SI 2008/2109
s.64, applied: 2008 c.18 Sch.3 para.8, SI 2008/1261 Art.6, SI 2008/2512 Art.4
s.106, amended: 2008 c.29 Sch.2 para.26
s.106, applied: 2008 c.29 s.33, SI 2008/1373 Sch.1, SI 2008/3298 Sch.1
s.106, enabling: SI 2008/1373, SI 2008/2988, SI 2008/3138, SI 2008/3298
s.108, amended: 2008 c.29 Sch.2 para.27
s.108, applied: 2008 c.29 s.33
s.110, amended: 2008 c.29 Sch.2 para.28
s.110, applied: 2008 c.29 s.33
s.118, applied: SI 2008/442 Reg.3, Sch.1 para.2
s.118A, applied: SI 2008/442 Reg.3, Sch.1 para.3
s.118B, applied: SI 2008/442 Reg.3, Sch.1 para.4, Sch.1 para.7
s.118B, referred to: SI 2008/442 Sch.1 para.4
s.119, applied: SI 2008/442 Reg.3, Sch.1 para.5
s.119A, applied: SI 2008/442 Reg.3, Sch.1 para.6
s.119B, applied: SI 2008/442 Reg.3, Sch.1 para.7
s.119B, referred to: SI 2008/442 Sch.1 para.7
s.119D, applied: SI 2008/442 Reg.3
s.129A, see *Ramblers' Association v Coventry City Council* [2008] EWHC 796 (Admin), Times, May 27, 2008 (QBD (Admin)), Michael Supperstone Q.C.
s.141, disapplied: 2008 c.18 Sch.14 para.7
s.167, disapplied: 2008 c.18 Sch.14 para.7
s.169, disapplied: 2008 c.18 Sch.14 para.7
s.184, applied: 2008 c.18 Sch.3 para.8, SI 2008/1261 Art.6
s.219, amended: 2008 c.17 Sch.8 para.32
s.250, see *Lall v Transport for London* [2008] R.V.R. 183 (Lands Tr), George Bartlett Q.C. (President)
s.261, see *Esso Petroleum Co Ltd v Secretary of State for Transport* [2008] R.V.R. 351 (Lands Tr), George Bartlett Q.C. (President)
s.278, applied: 2008 c.29 s.223, SI 2008/1261 Art.58
s.278, referred to: SI 2008/1261 Art.58
s.329, amended: 2008 c.29 Sch.2 para.29
s.337, substituted: 2008 c.29 Sch.2 para.30
Sch.2 para.1, applied: SI 2008/3325 Art.1

CAP.

1980–cont.

66. Highways Act 1980–*cont.*
Sch.4, referred to: SI 2008/2110 Art.3, SI 2008/2253 Art.3, SI 2008/3325 Sch.1

1981

14. Public Passenger Vehicles Act 1981
applied: 2008 c.13 Sch.3
Part II, referred to: 2008 c.13 Sch.6
s.3, amended: 2008 c.26 s.1
s.4, amended: 2008 c.26 s.2, s.3
s.4, disapplied: 2008 c.26 s.5
s.4A, added: 2008 c.26 s.3
s.4A, applied: 2008 c.26 s.3
s.4A, referred to: 2008 c.26 s.3
s.4B, added: 2008 c.26 s.3
s.4C, added: 2008 c.26 s.3
s.4D, added: 2008 c.26 s.3
s.10, enabling: SI 2008/1458
s.12A, added: 2008 c.26 s.47
s.14, applied: SI 2008/1473 Reg.3
s.46, amended: 2008 c.02 Sch.1 para.1, Sch.2
s.52, enabling: SI 2008/1458, SI 2008/1465, SI 2008/1470, SI 2008/1473, SSI 2008/253
s.60, applied: 2008 c.13 Sch.7
s.60, enabling: SI 2008/1458, SI 2008/1465, SI 2008/1470, SI 2008/1473, SSI 2008/2, SSI 2008/253
s.61, applied: SI 2008/1458, SI 2008/1465, SI 2008/1470, SI 2008/1473, SSI 2008/2, SSI 2008/253
s.67, referred to: 2008 c.13 Sch.6
s.82, amended: 2008 c.26 s.2
Sch.2, applied: 2008 c.26 s.3
Sch.2, amended: 2008 c.26 s.4
Sch.2 para.1, amended: 2008 c.26 s.4
Sch.2 para.1, applied: 2008 c.26 s.5
Sch.2 para.2A, added: 2008 c.26 s.4
Sch.2 para.2B, added: 2008 c.26 s.4
Sch.2 para.5A, amended: 2008 c.26 s.4
Sch.2 para.5A, applied: 2008 c.26 s.5
Sch.2 para.6, amended: 2008 c.26 s.4
Sch.2 para.8, substituted: 2008 c.26 s.3
Sch.2 para.9, amended: 2008 c.26 s.4
Sch.2A para.1, added: 2008 c.26 Sch.3
Sch.2A para.2, added: 2008 c.26 Sch.3
Sch.2A para.3, added: 2008 c.26 Sch.3
Sch.2A para.4, added: 2008 c.26 Sch.3
Sch.2A para.5, added: 2008 c.26 Sch.3
Sch.2A para.6, added: 2008 c.26 Sch.3
Sch.2A para.7, added: 2008 c.26 Sch.3
Sch.2A para.8, added: 2008 c.26 Sch.3
Sch.2A para.9, added: 2008 c.26 Sch.3
Sch.2A para.10, added: 2008 c.26 Sch.3
Sch.2A para.11, added: 2008 c.26 Sch.3
Sch.2A para.12, added: 2008 c.26 Sch.3
Sch.2A para.13, added: 2008 c.26 Sch.3
Sch.2A para.14, added: 2008 c.26 Sch.3
Sch.2A para.15, added: 2008 c.26 Sch.3

CAP.

1981–cont.

14. Public Passenger Vehicles Act 1981– *cont.*
Sch.2A para.16, added: 2008 c.26 Sch.3
Sch.2A para.17, added: 2008 c.26 Sch.3
Sch.2A para.18, added: 2008 c.26 Sch.3
Sch.2A para.19, added: 2008 c.26 Sch.3

19. Statute Law (Repeals) Act 1981
Sch.2, repealed: 2008 c.12 Sch.1 Part 1

20. Judicial Pensions Act 1981
s.13, repealed (in part): SI 2008/2833 Sch.3 para.37

22. Animal Health Act 1981
applied: 2008 c.13 Sch.3, Sch.7, SSI 2008/11 Art.8, SSI 2008/219 Art.3, Art.10
referred to: 2008 c.13 Sch.6, SI 2008/130 Art.35, SI 2008/944 Art.6, SI 2008/1270 Art.6
varied: SI 2008/465 Reg.21
s.1, enabling: SI 2008/130, SI 2008/524, SI 2008/618, SI 2008/944, SI 2008/1066, SI 2008/1270, SI 2008/1314, SI 2008/1742, SSI 2008/11, SSI 2008/158, SSI 2008/219, SSI 2008/234, SSI 2008/266, SSI 2008/327, SSI 2008/369
s.6, applied: SI 2008/1040 Reg.3
s.7, enabling: SI 2008/789, SI 2008/944, SI 2008/1066, SI 2008/1270, SI 2008/1314, SSI 2008/11, SSI 2008/158
s.8, applied: SI 2008/1040 Reg.3
s.8, enabling: SI 2008/130, SI 2008/524, SI 2008/618, SI 2008/1066, SI 2008/1314, SI 2008/1742, SSI 2008/11, SSI 2008/158, SSI 2008/234, SSI 2008/266, SSI 2008/327
s.11, enabling: SSI 2008/158
s.15, enabling: SSI 2008/11, SSI 2008/158
s.17, applied: SI 2008/1040 Reg.3
s.17, enabling: SSI 2008/11, SSI 2008/234, SSI 2008/327
s.23, applied: SI 2008/1040 Reg.3
s.23, enabling: SSI 2008/11, SSI 2008/158, SSI 2008/234, SSI 2008/327
s.25, applied: SI 2008/1040 Reg.3
s.25, enabling: SSI 2008/11
s.26, applied: SI 2008/1040 Reg.3
s.28, enabling: SSI 2008/11, SSI 2008/158, SSI 2008/234, SSI 2008/327
s.29, applied: SI 2008/1040 Reg.3
s.32, applied: SSI 2008/11 Art.20
s.32, enabling: SSI 2008/11
s.35, enabling: SI 2008/944, SI 2008/1270, SSI 2008/11, SSI 2008/158
s.37, enabling: SI 2008/789
s.62D, applied: SI 2008/2774, SI 2008/2774 Art.2
s.62D, enabling: SI 2008/2774
s.64, enabling: SSI 2008/158
s.66, applied: SI 2008/1275 Reg.21
s.66, varied: SI 2008/465 Reg.21
s.71A, applied: SI 2008/1275 Reg.21
s.71A, varied: SI 2008/465 Reg.21

CAP.

1981–cont.

22. Animal Health Act 1981–*cont.*
s.72, enabling: SSI 2008/11
s.73, applied: SI 2008/1275 Reg.21
s.73, varied: SI 2008/465 Reg.21
s.75, applied: SI 2008/1275 Reg.21
s.75, varied: SI 2008/465 Reg.21
s.77, applied: SI 2008/1275 Reg.21
s.77, varied: SI 2008/465 Reg.21
s.79, applied: SI 2008/1275 Reg.21
s.83, enabling: SI 2008/130, SSI 2008/11, SSI 2008/158
s.84, enabling: SI 2008/652
s.87, varied: SI 2008/1270 Art.2, SSI 2008/158 Art.3
s.87, enabling: SI 2008/944, SI 2008/1270, SSI 2008/158, SSI 2008/327
s.88, varied: SI 2008/1270 Art.2, SSI 2008/158 Art.3
s.88, enabling: SI 2008/944, SI 2008/1270, SSI 2008/11, SSI 2008/158
Sch.5 para.7, repealed: SI 2008/576 Sch.5 para.7

23. Local Government (Miscellaneous Provisions) (Scotland) Act 1981
Sch.2 para.2, repealed: 2008 asp 5 Sch.3 Part 1

25. Industrial Diseases (Notification) Act 1981
s.1, amended: SI 2008/678 Sch.2 para.10
s.1, applied: SI 2008/678 Sch.1 para.10

28. Licensing (Alcohol Education and Research) Act 1981
s.10, amended: SI 2008/948 Sch.1 para.1

29. Fisheries Act 1981
referred to: 2008 c.13 Sch.6
s.30, applied: 2008 c.13 Sch.7, SSI 2008/101 Art.2, Sch.1 Part 1, SSI 2008/102 Art.8, SSI 2008/151 Art.1, Art.32
s.30, enabling: SI 2008/984, SI 2008/2347, SSI 2008/102, SSI 2008/151, SSI 2008/156

37. Zoo Licensing Act 1981
applied: 2008 c.13 Sch.3
s.19, referred to: 2008 c.13 Sch.6

45. Forgery and Counterfeiting Act 1981
applied: 2008 c.13 Sch.3

47. Criminal Attempts Act 1981
see *R. v R* [2008] EWCA Crim 619, [2008] 2 Cr. App. R. 38 (CA (Crim Div)), Moses, L.J.
s.1, see *R. v Kenning (David Matthew)* [2008] EWCA Crim 1534, [2008] 3 W.L.R. 1306 (CA (Crim Div)), Lord Phillips of Worth Matravers, L.C.J.

49. Contempt of Court Act 1981
s.4, see *R. v Times Newspapers Ltd* [2007] EWCA Crim 1925, [2008] 1 W.L.R. 234 (CA (Crim Div)), Lord Phillips, L.C.J.
s.11, see *R. (on the application of Trinity Mirror Plc) v Croydon Crown Court* [2008] EWCA Crim 50, [2008] Q.B. 770 (CA (Crim Div)), Sir Igor Judge (President, QB); see *R. v*

CAP.

1981–cont.

49. Contempt of Court Act 1981–*cont.*

s.11–*cont.*

Times Newspapers Ltd [2007] EWCA Crim 1925, [2008] 1 W.L.R. 234 (CA (Crim Div)), Lord Phillips, L.C.J.; see *Times Newspapers Ltd v R* [2008] EWCA Crim 2559, Times, October 31, 2008 (CMAC), Latham, L.J.

s.12, see *Haw v Westminster Magistrates Court* [2007] EWHC 2960 (Admin), [2008] Q.B. 888 (DC), Thomas, L.J.

s.14, repealed (in part): 2008 c.4 Sch.4 para.25, Sch.28 Part 1

54. Supreme Court Act 1981

s.2, amended: SI 2008/1777 Art.2

s.2, applied: SI 2008/1777

s.2, enabling: SI 2008/1777

s.24, see *Brown v Executors of the Estate of HM Queen Elizabeth the Queen Mother* [2008] EWCA Civ 56, [2008] 1 W.L.R. 2327 (CA (Civ Div)), Lord Phillips of Worth Matravers, L.C.J.

s.29, see *R. (on the application of Faithfull) v Ipswich Crown Court* [2007] EWHC 2763 (Admin), [2008] 1 W.L.R. 1636 (DC), Richards, L.J.

s.32A, see *Grieves v FT Everard & Sons Ltd* [2007] UKHL 39, [2008] 1 A.C. 281 (HL), Lord Hoffmann

s.35A, see *Ringway Infrastructure Services Ltd v Vauxhall Motors Ltd* [2007] EWHC 2507 (TCC), [2008] T.C.L.R. 2 (QBD (TCC)), Akenhead, J.

s.36, applied: 2008 c.14 s.106

s.37, see *Masri v Consolidated Contractors International Co SAL* [2007] EWHC 3010 (Comm), [2008] 1 All E.R. (Comm) 305 (QBD (Comm)), Gloster, J.; see *Masri v Consolidated Contractors International Co SAL* [2008] EWCA Civ 303, [2008] 2 All E.R. (Comm) 1099 (CA (Civ Div)), Ward, L.J.; see *Mobil Cerro Negro Ltd v Petroleos de Venezuela SA* [2008] EWHC 532 (Comm), [2008] 2 All E.R. (Comm) 1034 (QBD (Comm)), Walker, J.; see *Starlight Shipping Co v Tai Ping Insurance Co Ltd (Hubei Branch)* [2007] EWHC 1893 (Comm), [2008] 1 All E.R. (Comm) 593 (QBD (Comm)), Cooke, J.

s.42, applied: SI 2008/221 r.27

s.45, see *R. (on the application of Trinity Mirror Plc) v Croydon Crown Court* [2008] EWCA Crim 50, [2008] Q.B. 770 (CA (Crim Div)), Sir Igor Judge (President, QB); see *R. v M* [2008] EWCA Crim 1901, Times, October 24, 2008 (CA (Crim Div)), Toulson, L.J.

s.51, see *Dolphin Quays Developments Ltd v Mills* [2008] EWCA Civ 385, [2008] 1 W.L.R. 1829 (CA (Civ Div)), Mummery, L.J.; see *Jackson v Thakrar* [2007] EWHC 626 (TCC), [2008] 1 All E.R. 601 (QBD (TCC)), Judge Peter Coulson Q.C.; see

CAP.

1981–cont.

54. Supreme Court Act 1981–*cont.*

s.51–*cont.*

Lobster Group Ltd v Heidelberg Graphic Equipment Ltd [2008] EWHC 413 (TCC), [2008] 2 All E.R. 1173 (QBD (TCC)), Coulson, J.; see *Nelson v Greening & Sykes (Builders) Ltd* [2007] EWCA Civ 1358, [2008] 8 E.G. 158 (CA (Civ Div)), Ward, L.J.; see *Newall v Lewis* [2008] EWHC 910 (Ch), [2008] W.T.L.R. 1649 (Ch D), Briggs, J.; see *Palmer v Palmer* [2008] EWCA Civ 46, [2008] C.P. Rep. 21 (CA (Civ Div)), Pill, L.J.; see *Sims v Hawkins* [2007] EWCA Civ 1175, [2008] C.P. Rep. 7 (CA (Civ Div)), Rix, L.J.

s.81, disapplied: 2008 c.4 Sch.2 para.21

s.116, see *Burrows v HM Coroner for Preston* [2008] EWHC 1387 (Admin), [2008] 2 F.L.R. 1225 (QBD), Cranston, J.

Sch.1, see *Practice Note (Family Proceedings: Court Dress)* [2008] 1 W.L.R. 1701 (Fam Div), Sir Mark Potter (President)

Sch.1 para.2, amended: 2008 c.28 s.71

Sch.1 para.3, amended: 2008 c.22 Sch.6 para.21

Sch.5 Part 2, amended: 2008 c.14 Sch.15 Part 2

56. Transport Act 1981

applied: 2008 c.13 Sch.3

s.10, amended: SI 2008/948 Sch.1 para.51

s.11, amended: SI 2008/948 Sch.1 para.52

57. Employment and Training Act 1981

s.10, amended: SI 2008/960 Sch.3

59. Matrimonial Homes (Family Protection) (Scotland) Act 1981

s.1, see *Blackburn v Cowie* [2008] CSIH 30, 2008 S.C. 504 (IH (Ex Div)), Lord Osborne

61. British Nationality Act 1981

applied: 2008 c.28 Sch.7 para.44, SI 2008/676 Sch.1 Part VIII, SI 2008/2668 Art.1

referred to: 2008 c.22 s.53

s.2, enabling: SI 2008/135

s.16, enabling: SI 2008/1240

s.39, varied: SI 2008/680 Art.5, Art.8

s.40A, enabling: SI 2008/1088, SI 2008/1089

s.50, amended: 2008 c.22 Sch.6 para.22

Sch.4 para.1, varied: SI 2008/680 Art.5, Art.8

Sch.4 para.2, varied: SI 2008/680 Art.5, Art.8

Sch.4 para.3, varied: SI 2008/680 Art.5, Art.8

Sch.4 para.5, varied: SI 2008/680 Art.5, Art.8

Sch.4 para.7, varied: SI 2008/680 Art.5, Art.8

62. Companies Act 1981

applied: SI 2008/1789 Sch.1 Part 2

63. Betting and Gaming Duties Act 1981

s.21, applied: 2008 c.9 Sch.41 para.1

s.23, amended: 2008 c.9 s.23

s.26J, applied: 2008 c.9 Sch.41 para.1

CAP.

1981–cont.

63. Betting and Gaming Duties Act 1981– *cont.*

Sch.1 para.4, applied: 2008 c.9 Sch.41 para.1
Sch.1 para.5, applied: 2008 c.9 Sch.41 para.1
Sch.3 Part II para.10, applied: 2008 c.9 Sch.41 para.1
Sch.4 Part II para.5, enabling: SI 2008/2693
Sch.4 Part II para.12, enabling: SI 2008/2693

64. New Towns Act 1981

applied: SI 2008/1961 Sch.4 para.8
referred to: 2008 c.17 Sch.5 para.1
s.19, amended: 2008 c.29 Sch.9 para.2
s.35, amended: 2008 c.17 Sch.5 para.2, Sch.5 para.3
s.35, repealed: 2008 c.17 Sch.5 para.4, Sch.16
s.36, amended: 2008 c.17 Sch.5 para.2, Sch.5 para.5, Sch.16
s.36, referred to: 2008 c.17 Sch.5 para.5
s.36, repealed (in part): 2008 c.17 Sch.5 para.5, Sch.16
s.37, amended: 2008 c.17 Sch.5 para.2
s.37, repealed: 2008 c.17 Sch.5 para.6, Sch.16
s.38, amended: 2008 c.17 Sch.5 para.2
s.38, repealed: 2008 c.17 Sch.5 para.6, Sch.16
s.39, amended: 2008 c.17 Sch.5 para.2, Sch.5 para.7
s.39, referred to: 2008 c.17 Sch.5 para.7
s.40, amended: 2008 c.17 Sch.5 para.2
s.41, amended: 2008 c.17 Sch.5 para.2, Sch.5 para.8, Sch.16
s.41, applied: 2008 c.17 s.52
s.41, referred to: 2008 c.17 Sch.5 para.8
s.41A, added: 2008 c.17 Sch.5 para.9
s.41A, amended: 2008 c.17 Sch.5 para.2
s.58, amended: 2008 c.17 Sch.5 para.10, Sch.16
s.58, referred to: 2008 c.17 Sch.5 para.10
s.58, repealed (in part): 2008 c.17 Sch.5 para.10, Sch.16
s.58A, amended: 2008 c.17 Sch.5 para.11, Sch.16
s.58A, referred to: 2008 c.17 Sch.5 para.11
s.58A, repealed (in part): 2008 c.17 Sch.5 para.11, Sch.16
s.59, amended: 2008 c.17 Sch.5 para.12, Sch.16
s.60, amended: 2008 c.17 Sch.5 para.13, Sch.16
s.60, referred to: 2008 c.17 Sch.5 para.13
s.60, repealed (in part): 2008 c.17 Sch.5 para.13, Sch.16
s.61, amended: 2008 c.17 Sch.5 para.14, Sch.16
s.61, referred to: 2008 c.17 Sch.5 para.14
s.62, amended: 2008 c.17 Sch.5 para.15
s.62, referred to: 2008 c.17 Sch.5 para.15
s.62B, repealed: 2008 c.17 Sch.5 para.16, Sch.16

CAP.

1981–cont.

64. New Towns Act 1981–*cont.*

s.63, amended: 2008 c.17 Sch.5 para.17, Sch.16
s.63, referred to: 2008 c.17 Sch.5 para.17
s.65, amended: 2008 c.17 Sch.5 para.18
s.65, referred to: 2008 c.17 Sch.5 para.18
s.66, amended: 2008 c.17 Sch.5 para.19
s.67, amended: 2008 c.17 Sch.5 para.20, Sch.16
s.67, referred to: 2008 c.17 Sch.5 para.20
s.67, repealed (in part): 2008 c.17 Sch.5 para.20, Sch.16
s.68, amended: 2008 c.17 Sch.5 para.21, Sch.16, SI 2008/948 Sch.1 para.1
s.68, referred to: 2008 c.17 Sch.5 para.21
s.68, repealed (in part): 2008 c.17 Sch.5 para.21, Sch.16
s.69, amended: 2008 c.17 Sch.5 para.22, Sch.16
s.69, referred to: 2008 c.17 Sch.5 para.22
s.69, repealed (in part): 2008 c.17 Sch.5 para.22, Sch.16
s.70, amended: 2008 c.17 Sch.5 para.23, Sch.16
s.70, referred to: 2008 c.17 Sch.5 para.23
s.70, repealed (in part): 2008 c.17 Sch.5 para.23, Sch.16
s.71, amended: 2008 c.17 Sch.5 para.24, Sch.16
s.71, referred to: 2008 c.17 Sch.5 para.24
s.72, amended: 2008 c.17 Sch.5 para.25, Sch.16
s.74, amended: 2008 c.17 Sch.5 para.26
s.77, amended: 2008 c.17 Sch.5 para.27, Sch.16
s.78, applied: SI 2008/1034 Art.5
s.80, amended: 2008 c.17 Sch.5 para.28, Sch.16
s.80, referred to: SI 2008/1961 Sch.4 para.8
s.82, amended: 2008 c.17 Sch.5 para.29, Sch.16
s.82, referred to: 2008 c.17 Sch.5 para.29
Sch.4 Part IV para.13, applied: SI 2008/1961 Sch.4 para.8
Sch.9 para.1, repealed: 2008 c.17 Sch.5 para.30, Sch.16
Sch.9 para.2, repealed: 2008 c.17 Sch.5 para.30, Sch.16
Sch.9 para.3, repealed: 2008 c.17 Sch.5 para.30, Sch.16
Sch.9 para.4, repealed: 2008 c.17 Sch.5 para.30, Sch.16
Sch.9 para.5, repealed: 2008 c.17 Sch.5 para.30, Sch.16
Sch.9 para.6, repealed: 2008 c.17 Sch.5 para.30, Sch.16
Sch.9 para.7, repealed: 2008 c.17 Sch.5 para.30, Sch.16
Sch.9 para.8, repealed: 2008 c.17 Sch.5 para.30, Sch.16
Sch.10, amended: 2008 c.17 Sch.16

CAP.

1981–cont.

64. New Towns Act 1981–*cont.*
Sch.10, applied: 2008 c.17 s.52
Sch.10, referred to: 2008 c.17 Sch.5 para.31
Sch.10 para.1, amended: 2008 c.17 Sch.5 para.31
Sch.10 para.1, referred to: 2008 c.17 Sch.5 para.31
Sch.10 para.2, amended: 2008 c.17 Sch.5 para.31
Sch.10 para.2, referred to: 2008 c.17 Sch.5 para.31
Sch.10 para.3, amended: 2008 c.17 Sch.5 para.31
Sch.10 para.3, referred to: 2008 c.17 Sch.5 para.31
Sch.10 para.4, amended: 2008 c.17 Sch.5 para.31
Sch.10 para.4, repealed: 2008 c.17 Sch.5 para.31, Sch.16
Sch.10 para.5, amended: 2008 c.17 Sch.5 para.31
Sch.10 para.5, referred to: 2008 c.17 Sch.5 para.31
Sch.10 para.5, repealed (in part): 2008 c.17 Sch.5 para.31, Sch.16
Sch.10 para.6, amended: 2008 c.17 Sch.5 para.31
Sch.11, referred to: 2008 c.17 Sch.5 para.32
Sch.11, amended: 2008 c.17 Sch.16
Sch.11 para.3, amended: 2008 c.17 Sch.5 para.32
Sch.11 para.3, repealed: 2008 c.17 Sch.5 para.32, Sch.16
Sch.11 para.5, repealed: 2008 c.17 Sch.5 para.32, Sch.16
Sch.11 para.12, repealed: 2008 c.17 Sch.5 para.32, Sch.16

66. Compulsory Purchase (Vesting Declarations) Act 1981
applied: SI 2008/2512 Art.24
varied: 2008 c.18 Sch.6 para.4, SI 2008/1261 Art.30, SI 2008/2512 Art.24, SI 2008/3163 Art.5
s.3, varied: 2008 c.18 Sch.6 para.5, SI 2008/1261 Art.30, SI 2008/2512 Art.24, SI 2008/3163 Art.5
s.4, applied: 2008 c.18 s.6, Sch.6 para.18, SI 2008/1261 Art.33, SI 2008/2512 Art.33, SI 2008/3163 Art.13
s.5, varied: 2008 c.18 Sch.6 para.5, SI 2008/1261 Art.30, SI 2008/2512 Art.24, SI 2008/3163 Art.5
s.7, varied: SI 2008/1261 Art.30, SI 2008/2512 Art.24, SI 2008/3163 Art.5
s.15, amended: 2008 c.17 Sch.16
Sch.1, disapplied: 2008 c.18 Sch.6 para.11
Sch.2 para.1, amended: 2008 c.17 Sch.8 para.33, Sch.16
Sch.2 para.3, amended: 2008 c.17 Sch.8 para.33

CAP.

1981–cont.

67. Acquisition of Land Act 1981
applied: 2008 c.17 Sch.2 para.1, 2008 c.18 s.7, SI 2008/1238 Art.4, SI 2008/1261 Art.29, SI 2008/2512 Art.23, SI 2008/3163 Art.4
varied: SI 2008/1261 Art.29
Part II, applied: 2008 c.29 s.125
s.4, varied: 2008 c.18 Sch.6 para.20
s.6, varied: 2008 c.18 Sch.2 para.5, Sch.2 para.6
s.7, referred to: SI 2008/1961 Sch.4 para.8
s.12, applied: 2008 c.29 s.134
s.17, varied: 2008 c.17 Sch.2 para.1
s.19, applied: SI 2008/1961 Sch.4 para.8
s.32, applied: SI 2008/442 Reg.3
Sch.2 Part I para.1, varied: 2008 c.18 Sch.6 para.17
Sch.2 Part II para.2, varied: 2008 c.18 Sch.6 para.17
Sch.2 Part III, varied: 2008 c.18 Sch.3 para.3
Sch.2 Part III para.3, varied: 2008 c.18 Sch.3 para.3
Sch.2 Part III para.4, varied: 2008 c.18 Sch.3 para.3
Sch.2 Part III para.5, varied: 2008 c.18 Sch.3 para.3
Sch.2 Part III para.6, varied: 2008 c.18 Sch.3 para.3
Sch.2 Part III para.7, varied: 2008 c.18 Sch.3 para.3
Sch.2 Part III para.8, varied: 2008 c.18 Sch.3 para.3
Sch.2 Part III para.9, varied: 2008 c.18 Sch.3 para.3
Sch.3, applied: 2008 c.17 Sch.2 para.2
Sch.3 Part II para.4, varied: 2008 c.17 Sch.2 para.2
Sch.3 Part II para.6, applied: SI 2008/1961 Sch.4 para.8

69. Wildlife and Countryside Act 1981
see *R. (on the application of Winchester College) v Hampshire CC* [2007] EWHC 2786 (Admin), [2008] R.T.R. 15 (QBD (Admin)), George Bartlett Q.C.
applied: 2008 c.13 Sch.3, SI 2008/2349 Reg.21, SI 2008/3143 Reg.21, SSI 2008/100 Sch.4 Part 2, SSI 2008/159 Sch.3 Part 2
referred to: SI 2008/2512 Art.9
Part I, referred to: 2008 c.13 Sch.6
Part II, referred to: 2008 c.13 Sch.6
s.7, enabling: SI 2008/2357
s.8, see *Royal Society for the Prevention of Cruelty to Animals (RSPCA) v Munur* [2008] EWHC 199 (Admin), (2008) 172 J.P. 174 (DC), Latham, L.J.
s.19XA, amended: 2008 c.4 Sch.26 para.7
s.21, see *Royal Society for the Prevention of Cruelty to Animals (RSPCA) v Munur* [2008] EWHC 199 (Admin), (2008) 172 J.P. 174 (DC), Latham, L.J.

CAP.

1981–cont.

69. Wildlife and Countryside Act 1981– *cont.*

s.22, enabling: SI 2008/431, SI 2008/1927, SI 2008/2356

s.26, applied: SI 2008/431(b), SI 2008/1927(b), SI 2008/2356

s.26A, enabling: SSI 2008/17, SSI 2008/425

s.53, see *R. (on the application of Winchester College) v Hampshire CC* [2007] EWHC 2786 (Admin), [2008] R.T.R. 15 (QBD (Admin)), George Bartlett Q.C.

s.53A, applied: SI 2008/442 Reg.3, Reg.4, Reg.5, Reg.6

s.53A, referred to: SI 2008/442 Reg.3

s.53A, enabling: SI 2008/442

s.56, enabling: SI 2008/442

s.57, enabling: SI 2008/442

Sch.4, amended: SI 2008/2356 Art.3

Sch.5, amended: SI 2008/431 Art.2, Sch.1, SI 2008/1927 Art.2, SI 2008/2172 Reg.4

Sch.14, see *R. (on the application of Winchester College) v Hampshire CC* [2007] EWHC 2786 (Admin), [2008] R.T.R. 15 (QBD (Admin)), George Bartlett Q.C.

Sch.14 para.1, see *R. (on the application of Winchester College) v Hampshire CC* [2007] EWHC 2786 (Admin), [2008] R.T.R. 15 (QBD (Admin)), George Bartlett Q.C.; see *R. (on the application of Winchester College) v Hampshire CC* [2008] EWCA Civ 431, [2008] 3 All E.R. 717 (CA (Civ Div)), Ward, L.J.

Sch.14 para.2, see *R. (on the application of Winchester College) v Hampshire CC* [2007] EWHC 2786 (Admin), [2008] R.T.R. 15 (QBD (Admin)), George Bartlett Q.C.

Sch.14 para.3, see *R. (on the application of Winchester College) v Hampshire CC* [2007] EWHC 2786 (Admin), [2008] R.T.R. 15 (QBD (Admin)), George Bartlett Q.C.

1982

10. Industrial Training Act 1982

s.8, amended: SI 2008/948 Sch.1 para.1

s.11, applied: SI 2008/534, SI 2008/535, SI 2008/1639 Reg.3, Reg.4

s.11, enabling: SI 2008/534, SI 2008/535, SI 2008/1639

s.12, applied: SI 2008/534, SI 2008/535

s.12, enabling: SI 2008/534, SI 2008/535

16. Civil Aviation Act 1982

applied: SI 2008/1909 Sch.1

s.15, amended: SI 2008/948 Sch.1 para.1

s.60, enabling: SI 2008/1487, SI 2008/1782, SI 2008/2562, SI 2008/3121, SI 2008/3133

CAP.

1982–cont.

16. Civil Aviation Act 1982–*cont.*

s.61, enabling: SI 2008/1487, SI 2008/2562, SI 2008/3121, SI 2008/3125, SI 2008/3133

s.77, enabling: SI 2008/2562, SI 2008/3121

s.101, enabling: SI 2008/2562, SI 2008/3121, SI 2008/3133

s.102, enabling: SI 2008/1782, SI 2008/2562, SI 2008/3121, SI 2008/3133

s.108, enabling: SI 2008/3120

Sch.13, enabling: SI 2008/1782, SI 2008/2562, SI 2008/3121, SI 2008/3133

27. Civil Jurisdiction and Judgments Act 1982

see *Parkes v MacGregor* 2008 S.C.L.R. 345 (OH), Lady Paton

s.17, disapplied: SI 2008/1889 Art.4

s.18, see *Parkes v MacGregor* 2008 S.C.L.R. 345 (OH), Lady Paton

s.21, disapplied: SI 2008/1889 Art.5

s.25, see *Banco Nacional de Comercio Exterior SNC v Empresa de Telecomunicationes de Cuba SA* [2007] EWCA Civ 662, [2008] 1 W.L.R. 1936 (CA (Civ Div)), Lord Philips, L.C.J.; see *ETI Euro Telecom International NV v Bolivia* [2008] EWCA Civ 880, [2008] 2 Lloyd's Rep. 421 (CA (Civ Div)), Tuckey, L.J.; see *Masri v Consolidated Contractors International Co SAL* [2007] EWHC 3010 (Comm), [2008] 1 All E.R. (Comm) 305 (QBD (Comm)), Gloster, J.

Sch.4, varied: SI 2008/1889 Art.4

Sch.4 para.1, varied: SI 2008/1889 Art.4

Sch.4 para.2, varied: SI 2008/1889 Art.4

Sch.4 para.3, varied: SI 2008/1889 Art.4

Sch.4 para.4, varied: SI 2008/1889 Art.4

Sch.4 para.5, varied: SI 2008/1889 Art.4

Sch.4 para.6, varied: SI 2008/1889 Art.4

Sch.4 para.7, varied: SI 2008/1889 Art.4

Sch.4 para.8, varied: SI 2008/1889 Art.4

Sch.4 para.9, varied: SI 2008/1889 Art.4

Sch.4 para.10, varied: SI 2008/1889 Art.4

Sch.4 para.11, varied: SI 2008/1889 Art.4

Sch.4 para.12, varied: SI 2008/1889 Art.4

Sch.4 para.13, varied: SI 2008/1889 Art.4

Sch.4 para.14, varied: SI 2008/1889 Art.4

Sch.4 para.15, varied: SI 2008/1889 Art.4

Sch.4 para.16, varied: SI 2008/1889 Art.4

Sch.5 para.5, amended: 2008 c.14 Sch.15 Part 5

Sch.6, see *Parkes v MacGregor* 2008 S.C.L.R. 345 (OH), Lady Paton

Sch.8 para.1, varied: SI 2008/1889 Art.5

Sch.8 para.2, varied: SI 2008/1889 Art.5

Sch.8 para.3, varied: SI 2008/1889 Art.5

Sch.8 para.4, varied: SI 2008/1889 Art.5

Sch.8 para.5, varied: SI 2008/1889 Art.5

Sch.8 para.6, varied: SI 2008/1889 Art.5

Sch.8 para.7, varied: SI 2008/1889 Art.5

Sch.8 para.8, varied: SI 2008/1889 Art.5

CAP.

1982–cont.

27. Civil Jurisdiction and Judgments Act 1982–*cont.*
Sch.8 para.9, varied: SI 2008/1889 Art.5

28. Taking of Hostages Act 1982
s.1, applied: 2008 c.28 Sch.2, SI 2008/1216 Sch.1 para.20, Sch.2 para.19

29. Supply of Goods and Services Act 1982
applied: 2008 c.13 Sch.3
s.11, see *Trident Turboprop (Dublin) Ltd v First Flight Couriers Ltd* [2008] EWHC 1686 (Comm), [2008] 2 Lloyd's Rep. 581 (QBD (Comm)), Aikens, J.
s.15, see *Mastercigars Direct Ltd v Withers LLP* [2007] EWHC 2733 (Ch), [2008] 3 All E.R. 417 (Ch D), Morgan, J.

30. Local Government (Miscellaneous Provisions) Act 1982
applied: 2008 c.13 Sch.3
Part VIII, referred to: 2008 c.13 Sch.6
Sch.3, referred to: 2008 c.13 Sch.6
Sch.4, referred to: 2008 c.13 Sch.6
Sch.4 para.2, amended: 2008 c.17 Sch.8 para.34

31. Firearms Act 1982
applied: 2008 c.13 Sch.3

34. Forfeiture Act 1982
applied: SI 2008/2698 r.44
s.4, amended: SI 2008/2833 Sch.3 para.38
s.4, applied: SI 2008/2698 r.10, r.26
s.4, repealed (in part): SI 2008/2833 Sch.3 para.38

36. Aviation Security Act 1982
Part II, referred to: 2008 c.13 Sch.6
s.1, applied: 2008 c.28 Sch.2, SI 2008/1216 Sch.1 para.21, Sch 2 para.20
s.2, applied: 2008 c.28 Sch.2, SI 2008/1216 Sch.1 para.21, Sch.2 para.20
s.3, applied: 2008 c.28 Sch.2, SI 2008/1216 Sch.1 para.21, Sch.2 para.20
s.4, applied: 2008 c.28 Sch.2, SI 2008/1216 Sch.2 para.20
s.6, applied: 2008 c.28 Sch.2
s.20A, applied: 2008 c.13 Sch.7
s.21F, applied: 2008 c.13 Sch.7
s.21G, applied: 2008 c.13 Sch.7

37. Merchant Shipping (Liner Conferences) Act 1982
s.2, repealed: SI 2008/163 Reg.3
s.2, varied: SI 2008/1794 Art.3
s.3, repealed: SI 2008/163 Reg.3
s.3, varied: SI 2008/1794 Art.3
s.4, repealed: SI 2008/163 Reg.3
s.4, varied: SI 2008/1794 Art.3
s.11, repealed: SI 2008/163 Reg.3
s.11, varied: SI 2008/1794 Art.3
s.12, repealed: SI 2008/163 Reg.3
s.13, repealed: SI 2008/163 Reg.3
s.15, enabling: SI 2008/1794
Sch.1, varied: SI 2008/163 Reg.3

CAP.

1982–cont.

39. Finance Act 1982
s.1, repealed (in part): 2008 c.12 Sch.1 Part 8
s.3, repealed: 2008 c.12 Sch.1 Part 8
s.4, repealed (in part): 2008 c.9 Sch.6 para.8
s.129, amended: 2008 c.9 Sch.32 para.12
s.137, repealed: 2008 c.12 Sch.1 Part 8
s.150, repealed: 2008 c.12 Sch.1 Part 8
Sch.1 para.24, repealed: 2008 c.12 Sch.1 Part 8

45. Civic Government (Scotland) Act 1982
see *Burns (George Francis) v HM Advocate* 2008 J.C. 204 (HCJ), Lord Hamilton L.J.G.
referred to: SSI 2008/263 Sch.2
s.10, see *Wilson v Aberdeen City Council* [2008] CSIH 8, 2008 S.C. 231 (IH (Ex Div)), Lord Philip
s.29, amended: SI 2008/948 Sch.1 para.9
s.52, see *Jordan (Jason Alexander) v HM Advocate* [2008] HCJAC 24, 2008 S.L.T. 489 (HCJ), Lord Nimmo Smith
s.87, amended: 2008 asp 5 Sch.3 Part 1
Sch.1 para.5, see *Wilson v Aberdeen City Council* [2008] CSIH 8, 2008 S.C. 231 (IH (Ex Div)), Lord Philip
Sch.1 para.18, see *Habib v Central Fife Area Regulation Sub-Committee* 2008 S.L.T. (Sh Ct) 57 (Sh Ct (Tayside)), Sheriff W Holligan

47. Duchy of Cornwall Management Act 1982
s.9, amended: SI 2008/948 Sch.1 para.1

48. Criminal Justice Act 1982
s.28, repealed: 2008 c.12 Sch.1 Part 3
s.30, repealed: 2008 c.12 Sch.1 Part 3
s.31, repealed: 2008 c.12 Sch.1 Part 3
s.64, varied: SI 2008/680 Art.5, Art.9
s.68, repealed (in part): 2008 c.12 Sch.1 Part 3
s.72, repealed (in part): 2008 c.12 Sch.1 Part 3
s.81, enabling: SI 2008/680
Sch.10 para.1, varied: SI 2008/680 Art.5, Art.9
Sch.10 para.2, varied: SI 2008/680 Art.5, Art.9
Sch.12 para.1, repealed: 2008 c.12 Sch.1 Part 3
Sch.12 para.2, repealed: 2008 c.12 Sch.1 Part 3
Sch.13 Part III para.7, amended: 2008 c.4 Sch.4 para.27, Sch.28 Part 1, SI 2008/912 Sch.1 para.6
Sch.13 Part III para.9, amended: 2008 c.4 Sch.4 para.28, Sch.28 Part 1
Sch.13 Part III para.10, added: 2008 c.4 Sch.4 para.29
Sch.14 para.60, repealed: 2008 c.4 Sch.28 Part 1

52. Industrial Development Act 1982
s.8, amended: SI 2008/1272 Art.2
s.8, applied: SI 2008/1272
s.8, enabling: SI 2008/1272

CAP.

1982–cont.

53. Administration of Justice Act 1982
s.20, see *Pengelly v Pengelly* [2007] EWHC 3227 (Ch), [2008] Ch. 375 (Ch D), Judge Hodge Q.C.

1983

2. Representation of the People Act 1983
applied: SI 2008/634 Art.13, SI 2008/1741 Reg.14, SI 2008/1848 Reg.11, Sch.3
varied: SI 2008/1741 Reg.3
s.1, varied: SI 2008/634 Art.13
s.2, applied: SI 2008/1741 Reg.14
s.2, varied: SI 2008/634 Art.13
s.3, varied: SI 2008/634 Art.13
s.3A, varied: SI 2008/634 Art.13
s.4, varied: SI 2008/634 Art.13
s.4, applied: SI 2008/1741 Reg.25
s.4, referred to: SI 2008/1741 Reg.34, Reg.35, Reg.36, Reg.38, Reg.39
s.4, varied: SI 2008/634 Art.13, SI 2008/1741 Sch.4
s.4, enabling: SI 2008/1741
s.5, varied: SI 2008/634 Art.13
s.6, varied: SI 2008/634 Art.13
s.6, applied: SI 2008/1741 Reg.27
s.6, varied: SI 2008/634 Art.13
s.7, varied: SI 2008/634 Art.13
s.7, applied: SI 2008/1741 Reg.34
s.7, varied: SI 2008/634 Art.13
s.7, enabling: SI 2008/1741
s.7A, applied: SI 2008/1741 Reg.34
s.7A, varied: SI 2008/634 Art.13
s.7A, enabling: SI 2008/1741
s.7B, applied: SI 2008/1741 Reg.49
s.7B, varied: SI 2008/634 Art.13
s.7C, applied: SI 2008/1741 Reg.34
s.7C, varied: SI 2008/634 Art.13
s.7C, enabling: SI 2008/1741
s.8, applied: SI 2008/2867 Reg.9
s.8, varied: SI 2008/634 Art.13
s.9, disapplied: SI 2008/1741 Reg.49
s.9, varied: SI 2008/634 Art.13, SI 2008/1741 Sch.4
s.9, enabling: SI 2008/1741
s.9A, varied: SI 2008/634 Art.13
s.9B, varied: SI 2008/634 Art.13
s.9C, varied: SI 2008/634 Art.13
s.10, referred to: SI 2008/1741 Reg.93
s.10, varied: SI 2008/634 Art.13
s.10A, applied: SI 2008/1741 Reg.27, Reg.30, Reg.34
s.10A, varied: SI 2008/634 Art.13
s.10A, enabling: SI 2008/1741
s.10ZA, varied: SI 2008/634 Art.13
s.10ZB, varied: SI 2008/634 Art.13
s.11, varied: SI 2008/634 Art.13
s.12, varied: SI 2008/634 Art.13

CAP.

1983–cont.

2. Representation of the People Act 1983–*cont.*
s.13, applied: SI 2008/1741 Reg.33, Reg.44, Reg.52, Reg.53, Reg.93, Reg.96, Reg.97, Reg.98, Reg.99, Reg.100, Reg.101
s.13, varied: SI 2008/634 Art.13, SI 2008/1741 Sch.4
s.13, enabling: SI 2008/1741
s.13A, applied: SI 2008/1741 Reg.27, Reg.28, Reg.30, Reg.33, Reg.44, Reg.97, Reg.98, Reg.99, Reg.100, Reg.101, Reg.109
s.13A, varied: SI 2008/634 Art.13, SI 2008/1741 Sch.4
s.13A, enabling: SI 2008/1741
s.13B, varied: SI 2008/634 Art.13, SI 2008/1848 Sch.3, Sch.4 para.1
s.13BA, applied: SI 2008/1741 Reg.25, Reg.40, Reg.44, Reg.45, Reg.97, Reg.98, Reg.99, Reg.100, Reg.101, Reg.109
s.13BA, varied: SI 2008/634 Art.13
s.13BA, enabling: SI 2008/1741
s.13C, applied: SI 2008/1741 Reg.13, Reg.25
s.13C, varied: SI 2008/634 Art.13
s.13C, enabling: SI 2008/1741
s.13CA, varied: SI 2008/634 Art.13
s.13D, varied: SI 2008/634 Art.13
s.14, applied: SI 2008/1741 Reg.16, Reg.19
s.14, referred to: SI 2008/1726 Art.2
s.14, varied: SI 2008/634 Art.13
s.14, enabling: SI 2008/1741
s.15, applied: SI 2008/1726, SI 2008/1741 Reg.19, Reg.34, Reg.69
s.15, varied: SI 2008/634 Art.13, SI 2008/1726 Art.2
s.15, enabling: SI 2008/1726, SI 2008/1741
s.16, applied: SI 2008/1741 Reg.19
s.16, referred to: SI 2008/1741 Reg.17
s.16, varied: SI 2008/634 Art.13
s.16, enabling: SI 2008/1741
s.17, varied: SI 2008/634 Art.13
s.18, varied: SI 2008/634 Art.13
s.18A, varied: SI 2008/634 Art.13
s.18B, varied: SI 2008/634 Art.13
s.18C, varied: SI 2008/634 Art.13
s.18D, varied: SI 2008/634 Art.13
s.18E, varied: SI 2008/634 Art.13
s.19, varied: SI 2008/634 Art.13
s.20, varied: SI 2008/634 Art.13
s.21, varied: SI 2008/634 Art.13
s.22, varied: SI 2008/634 Art.13
s.23, varied: SI 2008/634 Art.13
s.24, varied: SI 2008/634 Art.13
s.25, varied: SI 2008/634 Art.13
s.26, varied: SI 2008/634 Art.13
s.27, varied: SI 2008/634 Art.13
s.28, referred to: SI 2008/2867 Reg.9
s.28, varied: SI 2008/634 Art.13, SI 2008/2867 Reg.9
s.29, varied: SI 2008/634 Art.13
s.30, varied: SI 2008/634 Art.13

CAP.

1983–cont.

2. Representation of the People Act 1983–*cont.*

s.31, varied: SI 2008/634 Art.13, SI 2008/1848 Sch.4 para.1
s.32, varied: SI 2008/634 Art.13
s.33, varied: SI 2008/634 Art.13
s.34, varied: SI 2008/634 Art.13
s.35, applied: SI 2008/1848 Reg.9
s.35, varied: SI 2008/634 Art.13, SI 2008/1848 Sch.4 para.1
s.36, applied: SI 2008/634 Art.13
s.36, varied: SI 2008/634 Art.13, SI 2008/1848 Sch.4 para.1
s.37, varied: SI 2008/634 Art.13
s.37A, applied: SI 2008/2857
s.37A, varied: SI 2008/634 Art.13
s.37A, enabling: SI 2008/2857
s.37B, varied: SI 2008/634 Art.13
s.38, varied: SI 2008/634 Art.13
s.39, varied: SI 2008/634 Art.13
s.40, varied: SI 2008/634 Art.13
s.41, varied: SI 2008/634 Art.13
s.42, varied: SI 2008/634 Art.13
s.43, varied: SI 2008/634 Art.13
s.44, varied: SI 2008/634 Art.13
s.45, varied: SI 2008/634 Art.13
s.46, varied: SI 2008/634 Art.13
s.47, varied: SI 2008/634 Art.13, SI 2008/1848 Sch.4 para.1
s.48, varied: SI 2008/634 Art.13
s.49, varied: SI 2008/634 Art.13, SI 2008/1848 Sch.4 para.1
s.50, varied: SI 2008/634 Art.13, SI 2008/1741 Sch.4
s.51, varied: SI 2008/634 Art.13
s.52, applied: SI 2008/1741 Reg.92, Reg.115
s.52, varied: SI 2008/634 Art.13, SI 2008/1741 Sch.4
s.53, varied: SI 2008/634 Art.13
s.53, enabling: SI 2008/305, SI 2008/1741
s.54, varied: SI 2008/634 Art.13, SI 2008/1741 Sch.4
s.55, varied: SI 2008/634 Art.13
s.56, varied: SI 2008/634 Art.13
s.57, varied: SI 2008/634 Art.13
s.58, applied: SI 2008/1741 Reg.39, Reg.63
s.58, varied: SI 2008/634 Art.13, SI 2008/1741 Sch.4
s.58, enabling: SI 2008/1741
s.59, applied: SI 2008/1741 Reg.16, Reg.17
s.59, varied: SI 2008/634 Art.13
s.60, varied: SI 2008/634 Art.13, SI 2008/1848 Sch.4 para.1
s.61, varied: SI 2008/634 Art.13, SI 2008/1848 Sch.4 para.1
s.62, varied: SI 2008/634 Art.13
s.62A, varied: SI 2008/634 Art.13, SI 2008/1848 Sch.4 para.1
s.62B, varied: SI 2008/634 Art.13

CAP.

1983–cont.

2. Representation of the People Act 1983–*cont.*

s.63, varied: SI 2008/634 Art.13, SI 2008/1741 Sch.4, SI 2008/1848 Sch.4 para.1
s.64, varied: SI 2008/634 Art.13
s.65, varied: SI 2008/634 Art.13, SI 2008/1848 Sch.4 para.1
s.65A, varied: SI 2008/634 Art.13
s.65B, varied: SI 2008/634 Art.13
s.66, applied: SI 2008/1848 Sch.3
s.66, referred to: SI 2008/1741 Reg.74
s.66, varied: SI 2008/634 Art.13, SI 2008/1848 Sch.4 para.1
s.66A, varied: SI 2008/634 Art.13, SI 2008/1848 Sch.4 para.1
s.66B, varied: SI 2008/634 Art.13
s.67, disapplied: SI 2008/634 Art.13
s.67, varied: SI 2008/634 Art.13
s.68, varied: SI 2008/634 Art.13
s.69, varied: SI 2008/634 Art.13
s.70, varied: SI 2008/634 Art.13
s.70A, varied: SI 2008/634 Art.13
s.71, varied: SI 2008/634 Art.13
s.71A, varied: SI 2008/634 Art.13
s.72, varied: SI 2008/634 Art.13
s.73, varied: SI 2008/634 Art.13
s.74, varied: SI 2008/634 Art.13
s.74A, varied: SI 2008/634 Art.13
s.75, applied: SI 2008/1741 Reg.10
s.75, varied: SI 2008/634 Art.13
s.75, enabling: SI 2008/1741
s.75A, varied: SI 2008/634 Art.13
s.76, varied: SI 2008/634 Art.13
s.76A, varied: SI 2008/634 Art.13
s.77, varied: SI 2008/634 Art.13
s.78, varied: SI 2008/634 Art.13
s.79, varied: SI 2008/634 Art.13
s.80, varied: SI 2008/634 Art.13
s.81, varied: SI 2008/634 Art.13
s.82, varied: SI 2008/634 Art.13
s.83, varied: SI 2008/634 Art.13
s.84, varied: SI 2008/634 Art.13
s.85, varied: SI 2008/634 Art.13
s.85A, varied: SI 2008/634 Art.13
s.86, varied: SI 2008/634 Art.13
s.87, varied: SI 2008/634 Art.13
s.87A, varied: SI 2008/634 Art.13
s.88, varied: SI 2008/634 Art.13
s.89, referred to: SI 2008/305(b)
s.89, varied: SI 2008/634 Art.13
s.89, enabling: SI 2008/1741
s.90, varied: SI 2008/634 Art.13
s.90A, varied: SI 2008/634 Art.13
s.90B, varied: SI 2008/634 Art.13
s.90C, varied: SI 2008/634 Art.13
s.90D, varied: SI 2008/634 Art.13
s.90ZA, varied: SI 2008/634 Art.13
s.90ZB, varied: SI 2008/634 Art.13
s.91, varied: SI 2008/634 Art.13

CAP.

1983–cont.

2. **Representation of the People Act 1983**–*cont.*

s.92, varied: SI 2008/634 Art.13, SI 2008/1848 Sch.4 para.1
s.93, varied: SI 2008/634 Art.13
s.94, varied: SI 2008/634 Art.13, SI 2008/1848 Sch.4 para.1
s.95, varied: SI 2008/634 Art.13
s.96, varied: SI 2008/634 Art.13, SI 2008/1848 Sch.4 para.1
s.97, varied: SI 2008/634 Art.13, SI 2008/1848 Sch.4 para.1
s.98, varied: SI 2008/634 Art.13
s.99, varied: SI 2008/634 Art.13
s.100, varied: SI 2008/634 Art.13, SI 2008/1848 Sch.4 para.1
s.101, varied: SI 2008/634 Art.13
s.102, varied: SI 2008/634 Art.13
s.103, varied: SI 2008/634 Art.13
s.104, varied: SI 2008/634 Art.13
s.105, varied: SI 2008/634 Art.13
s.106, varied: SI 2008/634 Art.13
s.107, varied: SI 2008/634 Art.13
s.108, varied: SI 2008/634 Art.13
s.109, varied: SI 2008/634 Art.13, SI 2008/1848 Sch.4 para.1
s.110, varied: SI 2008/634 Art.13, SI 2008/1848 Sch.4 para.1
s.110A, varied: SI 2008/634 Art.13
s.111, varied: SI 2008/634 Art.13, SI 2008/1848 Sch.4 para.1
s.112, varied: SI 2008/634 Art.13, SI 2008/1848 Sch.4 para.1
s.113, varied: SI 2008/634 Art.13, SI 2008/1848 Sch.4 para.1
s.114, varied: SI 2008/634 Art.13, SI 2008/1848 Sch.4 para.1
s.115, varied: SI 2008/634 Art.13, SI 2008/1848 Sch.4 para.1
s.116, varied: SI 2008/634 Art.13, SI 2008/1848 Sch.4 para.1
s.117, varied: SI 2008/634 Art.13
s.118, varied: SI 2008/634 Art.13, SI 2008/1848 Sch.4 para.1
s.118A, varied: SI 2008/634 Art.13
s.119, varied: SI 2008/634 Art.13, SI 2008/1848 Sch.4 para.1
s.128, varied: SI 2008/1848 Sch.5
s.129, varied: SI 2008/1848 Sch.5
s.130, applied: SI 2008/1848 Reg.11
s.130, varied: SI 2008/1848 Sch.5
s.131, varied: SI 2008/1848 Sch.5
s.131BA, varied: SI 2008/634 Art.13
s.132, varied: SI 2008/1848 Sch.5
s.133, varied: SI 2008/1848 Sch.5
s.136, varied: SI 2008/1848 Sch.5
s.137, varied: SI 2008/1848 Sch.5
s.138, varied: SI 2008/1848 Sch.5
s.139, varied: SI 2008/1848 Sch.5
s.140, varied: SI 2008/1848 Sch.5
s.141, varied: SI 2008/1848 Sch.5

CAP.

1983–cont.

2. **Representation of the People Act 1983**–*cont.*

s.143, varied: SI 2008/1848 Sch.5
s.145, varied: SI 2008/1848 Sch.5
s.146, varied: SI 2008/1848 Sch.5
s.147, varied: SI 2008/1848 Sch.5
s.154, varied: SI 2008/1848 Sch.5
s.155, varied: SI 2008/1848 Sch.5
s.156, varied: SI 2008/1848 Sch.5
s.157, varied: SI 2008/1848 Sch.5
s.160, varied: SI 2008/1848 Sch.5
s.161, varied: SI 2008/1848 Sch.5
s.162, varied: SI 2008/1848 Sch.5
s.163, varied: SI 2008/1848 Sch.5
s.164, applied: SI 2008/1848 Reg.11
s.164, varied: SI 2008/1848 Sch.5
s.167, varied: SI 2008/1848 Sch.4 para.1, Sch.5
s.168, varied: SI 2008/1848 Sch.4 para.1
s.169, varied: SI 2008/1848 Sch.4 para.1
s.170, varied: SI 2008/1848 Sch.4 para.1
s.173, varied: SI 2008/1848 Sch.4 para.1
s.174, varied: SI 2008/1848 Sch.4 para.1
s.175, varied: SI 2008/1848 Sch.4 para.1
s.176, varied: SI 2008/1848 Sch.4 para.1
s.177, varied: SI 2008/1848 Sch.4 para.1
s.178, varied: SI 2008/1848 Sch.4 para.1
s.179, varied: SI 2008/1848 Sch.4 para.1
s.180, varied: SI 2008/1848 Sch.5
s.181, varied: SI 2008/1848 Sch.4 para.1
s.183, varied: SI 2008/1848 Sch.5
s.184, varied: SI 2008/1848 Sch.5
s.185, varied: SI 2008/1848 Sch.4 para.1, Sch.5
s.199B, varied: SI 2008/1848 Sch.4 para.1
s.200, varied: SI 2008/1848 Sch.4 para.1
s.201, applied: SI 2008/305, SI 2008/1741, SI 2008/1901
s.201, enabling: SI 2008/1741
s.202, applied: SI 2008/1741, SI 2008/1901
s.202, referred to: SI 2008/305
s.202, varied: SI 2008/1848 Sch.4 para.1
Sch.1, enabling: SI 2008/1741
Sch.1 Part III para.19A, applied: SI 2008/1741 Reg.69
Sch.1 Part III para.19A, enabling: SI 2008/1741
Sch.1 Part III para.24, referred to: SI 2008/305(b)
Sch.1 Part III para.24, enabling: SI 2008/1741
Sch.1 Part III para.28, referred to: SI 2008/305(b)
Sch.1 Part III para.28, enabling: SI 2008/1741
Sch.1 Part III para.29, applied: SI 2008/1741 Reg.69
Sch.1 Part III para.29, referred to: SI 2008/1741 Reg.12
Sch.1 Part III para.29, enabling: SI 2008/1741
Sch.1 Part III para.31A, referred to: SI 2008/305(b)

CAP.

1983–cont.

2. Representation of the People Act 1983–*cont.*
Sch.1 Part III para.32, applied: SI 2008/1741 Reg.68
Sch.1 Part III para.32, enabling: SI 2008/1741
Sch.1 Part III para.37, amended: SI 2008/1741 Reg.15
Sch.1 Part III para.37, applied: SI 2008/1741 Reg.69
Sch.1 Part III para.37, enabling: SI 2008/1741
Sch.1 Part III para.45, referred to: SI 2008/305(b)
Sch.1 Part V para.55, referred to: SI 2008/1741 Reg.91
Sch.1 Part V para.56, applied: SI 2008/1741 Reg.91
Sch.1 Part V para.57, applied: SI 2008/1741 Reg.91
Sch.1 Part V para.57, enabling: SI 2008/1741, SI 2008/1901
Sch.2, enabling: SI 2008/1741
Sch.2A, applied: SI 2008/1741 Reg.103
Sch.2 para.1, referred to: SI 2008/1741 Reg.41, Reg.43
Sch.2 para.5A, enabling: SI 2008/305
Sch.2 para.12, enabling: SI 2008/305

3. Agricultural Marketing Act 1983
s.5, amended: SI 2008/948 Sch.1 para.1

10. Transport Act 1983
s.1, amended: 2008 c.26 Sch.4 para.50

18. Nuclear Material (Offences) Act 1983
referred to: 2008 c.4 s.75
s.1, amended: 2008 c.4 Sch.17 para.2
s.1, repealed (in part): 2008 c.4 Sch.17 para.2, Sch.28 Part 5
s.1A, added: 2008 c.4 Sch.17 para.3
s.1B, added: 2008 c.4 Sch.17 para.3
s.1B, applied: 2008 c.28 Sch.2
s.1C, added: 2008 c.4 Sch.17 para.3
s.1C, applied: 2008 c.28 Sch.2
s.1D, added: 2008 c.4 Sch.17 para.3
s.2, applied: 2008 c.28 Sch.2
s.2, substituted: 2008 c.4 Sch.17 para.4
s.3A, added: 2008 c.4 Sch.17 para.5
s.4, repealed (in part): 2008 c.12 Sch.1 Part 3
s.5A, repealed: 2008 c.12 Sch.1 Part 3
s.6, amended: 2008 c.4 Sch.17 para.6, Sch.28 Part 5
s.7, amended: 2008 c.4 Sch.17 para.7
s.7, referred to: 2008 c.4 s.152

20. Mental Health Act 1983
see *Crown Prosecution Service v P* [2007] EWHC 946 (Admin), [2008] 1 W.L.R. 1005 (DC), Smith, L.J.; see *R. (on the application of Rayner) v Secretary of State for the Home Department* [2008] EWCA Civ 176, [2008] U.K.H.R.R. 847 (CA (Civ Div)), Ward, L.J.
applied: 2008 c.4 Sch.1 para.20, 2008 c.14 s.2, s.4, s.59, s.83, s.84, SI 2008/1184 Reg.10, Reg.15, Reg.23, SI 2008/1204

CAP.

1983–cont.

20. Mental Health Act 1983–*cont.*
applied: 2008 c.4 Sch.1 para.20–*cont.*
Reg.3, SI 2008/1210 Art.10, SI 2008/1858 Reg.16, SI 2008/2436 Sch.2 para.1.1, SI 2008/2437 Reg.3, SI 2008/2684 Art.5, SI 2008/2698 r.11, SI 2008/2699 r.11, SI 2008/2705 r.13, Sch.1 para.4, Sch.1 para.7
referred to: SI 2008/1184 Reg.22, SI 2008/1210 Art.1, SI 2008/2436 Sch.2 para.2.3, SI 2008/2699 r.32, SI 2008/2705 r.14, r.22
Part II, applied: SI 2008/1184 Reg.3, Reg.4, Reg.24, SI 2008/1900 Sch.1 para.13, SI 2008/2439 Reg.3, Reg.33, Reg.37
Part II, applied: SI 2008/2439 Reg.4
Part III, applied: SI 2008/2439 Reg.37
Part IVA, applied: SI 2008/1184 Reg.28, SI 2008/2439 Reg.39
s.1, varied: SI 2008/1210 Art.1, Art.6
s.2, see *Savage v South Essex Partnership NHS Foundation Trust* [2007] EWCA Civ 1375, [2008] 1 W.L.R. 1667 (CA (Civ Div)), Sir Anthony Clarke, M.R.
s.2, applied: SI 2008/1184 Reg.4, SI 2008/1210 Art.8, SI 2008/2439 Reg.4
s.2, referred to: SI 2008/1210 Art.8
s.3, see *R. v Samuel (Perry)* [2007] EWCA Crim 1954, [2008] 1 Cr. App. R. (S.) 76 (CA (Crim Div)), Latham, L.J. (VP, CA Crim); see *Savage v South Essex Partnership NHS Foundation Trust* [2007] EWCA Civ 1375, [2008] 1 W.L.R. 1667 (CA (Civ Div)), Sir Anthony Clarke, M.R.
s.3, applied: SI 2008/1184 Reg.4, SI 2008/1210 Art.8, SI 2008/2439 Reg.4
s.3, referred to: SI 2008/1210 Art.8
s.4, applied: SI 2008/1184 Reg.4, SI 2008/2439 Reg.4
s.5, applied: SI 2008/1184 Reg.3, Reg.4, SI 2008/1207 Art.2, SI 2008/2439 Reg.3, Reg.4, SI 2008/2441 Art.2
s.5, enabling: SI 2008/1207, SI 2008/2441
s.6, applied: SI 2008/1184 Reg.3, SI 2008/2439 Reg.3
s.7, applied: SI 2008/1184 Reg.4, Reg.5, SI 2008/1210 Art.8, SI 2008/2439 Reg.9
s.7, referred to: SI 2008/1210 Art.8
s.8, applied: SI 2008/1184 Reg.3, SI 2008/2439 Reg.3
s.9, enabling: SI 2008/1184, SI 2008/2439
s.10, applied: SI 2008/1184 Reg.26
s.11, applied: SI 2008/2439 Reg.24
s.11, varied: SI 2008/1184 Reg.8
s.12, applied: 2008 c.4 Sch.1 para.20, SI 2008/1184 Reg.8, Reg.23, SI 2008/1204 Reg.2, SI 2008/1210 Art.8, SI 2008/1858 Reg.4, Reg.7, SI 2008/2439 Reg.10, Reg.24, SI 2008/2440 Reg.4
s.12A, applied: SI 2008/1205 Reg.3
s.12A, enabling: SI 2008/1205, SI 2008/2440

CAP.

1983–cont.

20. Mental Health Act 1983–*cont.*

s.13, applied: SI 2008/1210 Art.8, SI 2008/2439 Reg.24
s.13, varied: SI 2008/1184 Reg.8
s.14, applied: SI 2008/1184 Reg.19, SI 2008/2439 Reg.35
s.15, applied: SI 2008/1184 Reg.4, SI 2008/2439 Reg.4
s.17, applied: SI 2008/1184 Reg.19, SI 2008/2439 Reg.35
s.17A, applied: SI 2008/1184 Reg.6, SI 2008/1210 Art.8, SI 2008/2439 Reg.16
s.17A, referred to: SI 2008/1210 Art.8
s.17A, varied: SI 2008/1210 Art.1, Art.6, Art.11
s.17B, applied: SI 2008/1184 Reg.6, SI 2008/2439 Reg.16, SI 2008/2705 Sch.1 para.9
s.17B, varied: SI 2008/1210 Art.1, Art.6
s.17C, varied: SI 2008/1210 Art.1, Art.11
s.17D, varied: SI 2008/1210 Art.1, Art.11
s.17E, applied: SI 2008/1184 Reg.6, Reg.12, Reg.17, SI 2008/2439 Reg.19, Reg.22, Reg.26, Reg.27
s.17F, applied: SI 2008/1184 Reg.6, SI 2008/2439 Reg.19, Reg.20
s.17F, enabling: SI 2008/1184, SI 2008/2439
s.17G, varied: SI 2008/1210 Art.1, Art.11
s.18, applied: SI 2008/1184 Reg.19, SI 2008/2439 Reg.35
s.19, applied: SI 2008/1184 Reg.7, Reg.26, SI 2008/2439 Reg.23, Reg.27
s.19, enabling: SI 2008/1184, SI 2008/2439
s.19A, enabling: SI 2008/1184, SI 2008/2439, SI 2008/2560
s.20, applied: SI 2008/1184 Reg.13, Reg.26, SI 2008/2439 Reg.5, Reg.12, Reg.15
s.20A, applied: SI 2008/1184 Reg.13, Reg.26, SI 2008/1210 Art.10, SI 2008/2439 Reg.17, Reg.22
s.20B, varied: SI 2008/1210 Art.1, Art.11
s.21, amended: SI 2008/2833 Sch.3 para.40
s.21B, applied: SI 2008/1184 Reg.14, Reg.26, SI 2008/2439 Reg.6, Reg.8, Reg.13, Reg.15, Reg.18, Reg.22
s.23, applied: SI 2008/1184 Reg.3, Reg.18, Reg.26, SI 2008/2439 Reg.3, Reg.7, Reg.14, Reg.15, Reg.21, Reg.37, SI 2008/2699 r.33, SI 2008/2705 r.11, r.16, Sch.1 para.16
s.25, applied: SI 2008/1184 Reg.3, Reg.25, SI 2008/2439 Reg.3, Reg.34
s.25A, varied: SI 2008/1210 Art.1
s.25C, varied: SI 2008/1210 Art.1
s.25D, varied: SI 2008/1210 Art.1
s.25E, varied: SI 2008/1210 Art.1
s.25F, varied: SI 2008/1210 Art.1
s.25G, applied: SI 2008/1210 Art.9
s.25G, varied: SI 2008/1210 Art.1
s.25H, applied: SI 2008/1210 Art.8, Art.9
s.25H, varied: SI 2008/1210 Art.1
s.25I, varied: SI 2008/1210 Art.1

CAP.

1983–cont.

20. Mental Health Act 1983–*cont.*

s.26, applied: SI 2008/2439 Reg.33
s.26, referred to: SI 2008/1184 Reg.24
s.29, applied: SI 2008/2439 Reg.33
s.29, referred to: SI 2008/1184 Reg.24
s.32, varied: SI 2008/1210 Art.1, Art.6
s.32, enabling: SI 2008/1184, SI 2008/2439, SI 2008/2560
s.33, varied: SI 2008/1210 Art.1, Art.6
s.34, varied: SI 2008/1210 Art.1
s.35, applied: SI 2008/1900 Sch.1 para.13
s.36, see *R. v Simpson (Jonathan Paul)* [2007] EWCA Crim 2666, [2008] 1 Cr. App. R. (S.) 111 (CA (Crim Div)), Toulson, L.J.
s.36, applied: SI 2008/1900 Sch.1 para.13
s.37, see *Gray v Thames Trains Ltd* [2008] EWCA Civ 713, [2008] P.I.Q.R. P20 (CA (Civ Div)), Sir Anthony Clarke, M.R.; see *R. (on the application of Rayner) v Secretary of State for the Home Department* [2008] EWCA Civ 176, [2008] U.K.H.R.R. 847 (CA (Civ Div)), Ward, L.J.; see *R. v Simpson (Jonathan Paul)* [2007] EWCA Crim 2666, [2008] 1 Cr. App. R. (S.) 111 (CA (Crim Div)), Toulson, L.J.
s.37, amended: 2008 c.4 Sch.4 para.30, Sch.26 para.8, Sch.28 Part 1
s.37, applied: 2008 c.4 Sch.1 para.20, SI 2008/1184 Reg.26, SI 2008/1900 Sch.1 para.13, SI 2008/2439 Reg.15
s.38, applied: SI 2008/1900 Sch.1 para.13
s.41, see *R. (on the application of Rayner) v Secretary of State for the Home Department* [2008] EWCA Civ 176, [2008] U.K.H.R.R. 847 (CA (Civ Div)), Ward, L.J.; see *R. v Simpson (Jonathan Paul)* [2007] EWCA Crim 2666, [2008] 1 Cr. App. R. (S.) 111 (CA (Crim Div)), Toulson, L.J.
s.41, amended: SI 2008/2833 Sch.3 para.41
s.41, applied: SI 2008/1786 Art.2, SI 2008/1900 Sch.1 para.13
s.42, see *R. (on the application of Rayner) v Secretary of State for the Home Department* [2008] EWCA Civ 176, [2008] U.K.H.R.R. 847 (CA (Civ Div)), Ward, L.J.
s.44, applied: SI 2008/1900 Sch.1 para.13
s.45A, applied: SI 2008/794 Reg.160, Sch.5 Part 2, SI 2008/1786 Art.2, SI 2008/1900 Sch.1 para.13, SI 2008/2705 Sch.1 para.6
s.45B, applied: SI 2008/1900 Sch.1 para.13
s.47, applied: SI 2008/794 Reg.160, Sch.5 Part 2, SI 2008/2705 Sch.1 para.6
s.48, applied: SI 2008/2705 Sch.1 para.6
s.49, applied: SI 2008/1786 Art.2, SI 2008/1900 Sch.1 para.13
s.50, amended: SI 2008/2833 Sch.3 para.42
s.50, applied: SI 2008/1900 Sch.1 para.13
s.51, amended: SI 2008/2833 Sch.3 para.43

CAP.

1983–cont.

20. Mental Health Act 1983–*cont.*

s.51, applied: SI 2008/1900 Sch.1 para.13
s.52, applied: SI 2008/1900 Sch.1 para.13
s.53, amended: SI 2008/2833 Sch.3 para.44
s.53, applied: SI 2008/1900 Sch.1 para.13
s.54, applied: 2008 c.4 Sch.1 para.20
s.56, applied: SI 2008/2439 Reg.22
s.56, referred to: SI 2008/1184 Reg.6
s.57, amended: 2008 c.14 Sch.3 para.2
s.57, applied: 2008 c.14 s.52, SI 2008/1184 Reg.27, SI 2008/1900 Sch.1 para.13, SI 2008/2439, SI 2008/2439 Reg.22, Reg.38, Reg.40
s.57, referred to: SI 2008/1184 Reg.6
s.57, enabling: SI 2008/1184, SI 2008/2439
s.57A, applied: SI 2008/1184, SI 2008/2439 Reg.22
s.57A, referred to: SI 2008/1184 Reg.6
s.58, amended: 2008 c.14 Sch.3 para.3
s.58, applied: 2008 c.14 s.52, SI 2008/1184 Reg.27, SI 2008/1900 Sch.1 para.13, SI 2008/2439 Reg.22, Reg.40
s.58, referred to: SI 2008/1184 Reg.6
s.58A, applied: SI 2008/1184, SI 2008/1184 Reg.27, SI 2008/2439, SI 2008/2439 Reg.22, Reg.38, Reg.40
s.58A, referred to: SI 2008/1184 Reg.6
s.58A, enabling: SI 2008/1184, SI 2008/2439
s.59, applied: SI 2008/2439 Reg.22
s.59, referred to: SI 2008/1184 Reg.6
s.60, applied: SI 2008/2439 Reg.22
s.60, referred to: SI 2008/1184 Reg.6
s.61, amended: 2008 c.14 Sch.3 para.4
s.61, applied: 2008 c.14 s.52, SI 2008/1900 Sch.1 para.13, SI 2008/2439 Reg.22
s.61, referred to: SI 2008/1184 Reg.6
s.62, applied: SI 2008/1184 Reg.27, SI 2008/2439 Reg.22, Reg.38
s.62, referred to: SI 2008/1184 Reg.6
s.62A, applied: SI 2008/2439 Reg.22
s.62A, referred to: SI 2008/1184 Reg.6
s.63, applied: SI 2008/1900 Sch.1 para.13, SI 2008/2439 Reg.22
s.63, referred to: SI 2008/1184 Reg.6
s.64, applied: SI 2008/2439 Reg.22
s.64, referred to: SI 2008/1184 Reg.6
s.64, enabling: SI 2008/1184, SI 2008/2439
s.64B, applied: SI 2008/1184 Reg.28, SI 2008/2439 Reg.39, Reg.40
s.64C, applied: SI 2008/1184 Reg.28, SI 2008/2439 Reg.39
s.64E, applied: SI 2008/1184 Reg.28, SI 2008/2439 Reg.39, Reg.40
s.64G, applied: SI 2008/1184 Reg.28, SI 2008/2439 Reg.39
s.64H, amended: 2008 c.14 Sch.3 para.5
s.64H, applied: 2008 c.14 s.52
s.64H, enabling: SI 2008/1184, SI 2008/2439
s.65, amended: SI 2008/2833 Sch.3 para.45

CAP.

1983–cont.

20. Mental Health Act 1983–*cont.*

s.65, applied: SI 2008/2684 Art.7, SI 2008/2833 Art.6, Sch.1
s.66, amended: SI 2008/2833 Sch.3 para.46
s.66, applied: SI 2008/1184 Reg.24, Reg.26, SI 2008/2439 Reg.15, Reg.33, SI 2008/2699 r.32, r.41, SI 2008/2705 r.15, r.21, r.24, r.28
s.66, varied: SI 2008/1210 Art.1, Art.6
s.67, amended: SI 2008/2833 Sch.3 para.47
s.67, applied: SI 2008/2699 r.17
s.67, varied: SI 2008/1210 Art.1, Art.6
s.68, amended: SI 2008/2833 Sch.3 para.48
s.68, applied: SI 2008/2699 r.17
s.68A, amended: SI 2008/2833 Sch.3 para.49
s.69, amended: SI 2008/2833 Sch.3 para.50
s.69, applied: SI 2008/1184 Reg.26, SI 2008/2439 Reg.15
s.70, amended: SI 2008/2833 Sch.3 para.51
s.71, amended: SI 2008/2833 Sch.3 para.52
s.71, applied: SI 2008/2699 r.17
s.72, amended: SI 2008/2833 Sch.3 para.53
s.72, applied: SI 2008/1210 Art.9, SI 2008/2699 r.42
s.72, varied: SI 2008/1210 Art.1, Art.5
s.73, see *R. (on the application of Rayner) v Secretary of State for the Home Department* [2008] EWCA Civ 176, [2008] U.K.H.R.R. 847 (CA (Civ Div)), Ward, L.J.
s.73, amended: SI 2008/2833 Sch.3 para.54
s.73, applied: SI 2008/2699 r.42
s.74, amended: SI 2008/2833 Sch.3 para.55
s.75, see *R. (on the application of Rayner) v Secretary of State for the Home Department* [2008] EWCA Civ 176, [2008] U.K.H.R.R. 847 (CA (Civ Div)), Ward, L.J.
s.75, amended: SI 2008/2833 Sch.3 para.56
s.75, applied: SI 2008/2699 r.17, r.32, SI 2008/2705 r.15, r.24
s.76, amended: SI 2008/2833 Sch.3 para.57
s.76, varied: SI 2008/1210 Art.1, Art.6
s.77, amended: SI 2008/2833 Sch.3 para.58
s.77, varied: SI 2008/1210 Art.1, Art.6
s.78, amended: SI 2008/2833 Sch.3 para.59
s.78, repealed (in part): SI 2008/2833 Sch.3 para.59
s.78, enabling: SI 2008/2705
s.78A, added: SI 2008/2833 Sch.3 para.60
s.78A, applied: SI 2008/2705 r.30
s.79, repealed (in part): SI 2008/2833 Sch.3 para.61
s.80C, applied: SI 2008/1184 Reg.16, SI 2008/2439 Reg.29
s.82, applied: SI 2008/1184 Reg.15, SI 2008/2439 Reg.29
s.84, applied: SI 2008/1184 Reg.15, SI 2008/2439 Reg.29

CAP.

1983–cont.

20. Mental Health Act 1983–*cont.*

s.85, applied: SI 2008/1184 Reg.15, SI 2008/2439 Reg.29

s.85ZA, applied: SI 2008/1184 Reg.16, SI 2008/2439 Reg.29

s.86, amended: SI 2008/2833 Sch.3 para.62

s.86, applied: SI 2008/1786 Art.2, SI 2008/2699 r.32, SI 2008/2705 r.15

s.101, applied: SI 2008/2439 Reg.37

s.114, applied: 2008 c.14 Sch.9 para.2

s.114, enabling: SI 2008/1206, SI 2008/2436

s.117, see *K v Central and North West London Mental Health NHS Trust* [2008] EWHC 1217 (QB), (2008) 11 C.C.L. Rep. 543 (QBD), King, J.

s.117, applied: SI 2008/794 Sch.8 para.56, SI 2008/2705 Sch.1 para.4, Sch.1 para.17

s.117, varied: SI 2008/1210 Art.1, Art.6

s.118, amended: 2008 c.14 Sch.3 para.6

s.118, applied: 2008 c.14 s.52

s.118, varied: SI 2008/1210 Art.1, Art.6

s.119, amended: 2008 c.14 Sch.3 para.7, Sch.15 Part 1

s.119, applied: 2008 c.14 s.52

s.120, applied: 2008 c.14 s.52

s.120, referred to: 2008 c.14 s.59

s.120, substituted: 2008 c.14 Sch.3 para.8

s.120A, added: 2008 c.14 Sch.3 para.9

s.120B, added: 2008 c.14 Sch.3 para.9

s.120C, added: 2008 c.14 Sch.3 para.9

s.120D, added: 2008 c.14 Sch.3 para.9

s.121, applied: 2008 c.14 s.52, SI 2008/1184 Reg.30

s.121, repealed: 2008 c.14 Sch.15 Part 1

s.123, applied: SI 2008/1184 Reg.7, Reg.26, SI 2008/2439 Reg.23, Reg.27

s.127, varied: SI 2008/1210 Art.1

s.129, amended: 2008 c.14 Sch.3 para.10

s.130A, applied: SI 2008/2437 Reg.4, SI 2008/3166 Reg.3, Reg.7

s.130A, enabling: SI 2008/2437, SI 2008/3166

s.130B, applied: SI 2008/2437 Reg.4

s.130C, applied: SI 2008/2437 Reg.3

s.132, amended: SI 2008/2833 Sch.3 para.63

s.132A, amended: SI 2008/2833 Sch.3 para.64

s.134, amended: 2008 c.14 Sch.3 para.11, SI 2008/912 Sch.1 para.7, SI 2008/2833 Sch.3 para.65

s.134, applied: SI 2008/1184 Reg.29, Reg.30, Reg.31, SI 2008/1900 Sch.1 para.13, SI 2008/2439 Reg.41, Reg.42

s.134, enabling: SI 2008/1184, SI 2008/2439

s.134A, added: 2008 c.14 Sch.3 para.12

s.135, varied: SI 2008/800 Art.3

s.136, varied: SI 2008/800 Art.3

s.142A, enabling: SI 2008/1204

s.143, enabling: SI 2008/2441

CAP.

1983–cont.

20. Mental Health Act 1983–*cont.*

s.145, amended: 2008 c.14 Sch.3 para.13, SI 2008/2833 Sch.3 para.66

s.145, varied: SI 2008/1210 Art.1

Sch.1, referred to: SI 2008/1184 Reg.24

Sch.1 Part I para.1, varied: SI 2008/1210 Art.1, Art.6

Sch.1 Part I para.2, varied: SI 2008/1210 Art.1, Art.6

Sch.2 para.1, amended: SI 2008/2833 Sch.3 para.67

Sch.2 para.1, applied: SI 2008/2833 Sch.2

Sch.2 para.1A, amended: SI 2008/2833 Sch.3 para.67

Sch.2 para.2, amended: SI 2008/2833 Sch.3 para.67

Sch.2 para.2A, amended: SI 2008/2833 Sch.3 para.67

Sch.2 para.3, amended: SI 2008/2833 Sch.3 para.67

Sch.2 para.3, applied: SI 2008/2833 Sch.2

Sch.2 para.3, repealed (in part): SI 2008/2833 Sch.3 para.67

Sch.2 para.4, amended: SI 2008/2833 Sch.3 para.67

Sch.2 para.5, amended: SI 2008/2833 Sch.3 para.67

Sch.2 para.5, repealed: SI 2008/2833 Sch.3 para.67

Sch.2 para.6, amended: SI 2008/2833 Sch.3 para.67

Sch.4 para.23, repealed (in part): 2008 c.4 Sch.28 Part 3

Sch.5 para.34, amended: SI 2008/2833 Sch.3 para.68

28. Finance Act 1983

s.1, repealed (in part): 2008 c.12 Sch.1 Part 8

s.3, repealed: 2008 c.12 Sch.1 Part 8

Sch.1, repealed: 2008 c.12 Sch.1 Part 8

Sch.1 para.8, repealed: 2008 c.12 Sch.1 Part 8

30. Diseases of Fish Act 1983

referred to: 2008 c.13 Sch.6

s.7, enabling: SSI 2008/222

s.9, amended: SSI 2008/339 Art.6

34. Mobile Homes Act 1983

see *Doherty v Birmingham City Council* [2008] UKHL 57, [2008] 3 W.L.R. 636 (HL), Lord Hope of Craighead

referred to: 2008 c.17 s.324

s.5, see *Doherty v Birmingham City Council* [2008] UKHL 57, [2008] 3 W.L.R. 636 (HL), Lord Hope of Craighead

s.5, amended: 2008 c.17 s.318, Sch.16

35. Litter Act 1983

applied: 2008 c.13 Sch.3

40. Education (Fees and Awards) Act 1983

s.1, enabling: SI 2008/1259

s.2, enabling: SI 2008/1259

CAP.

1983–cont.

41. **Health and Social Services and Social Security Adjudications Act 1983**
Sch.2 para.15, repealed (in part): 2008 c.4 Sch.28 Part 1
Sch.2 para.16, repealed: 2008 c.4 Sch.28 Part 1

44. **National Audit Act 1983**
s.13, applied: 2008 c.2 s.2
s.13, referred to: 2008 c.2 s.2

47. **National Heritage Act 1983**
s.36, applied: 2008 c.18 Sch.9 para.5
s.36, disapplied: 2008 c.18 Sch.9 para.5
Sch.3 para.12, amended: SI 2008/948 Sch.1 para.1

54. **Medical Act 1983**
applied: 2008 c.14 s.98, s.100, s.105, s.108, s.109, SI 2008/2927 Reg.2, SSI 2008/230 Reg.40
s.1, amended: 2008 c.14 Sch.7 para.2, SI 2008/1774 Sch.1 para.1, SI 2008/3131 Sch.1 para.1
s.1, applied: SI 2008/1774 Art.4
s.1, repealed (in part): 2008 c.14 Sch.7 para.2, Sch.15 Part 2, SI 2008/3131 Sch.1 para.1
s.1, enabling: SI 2008/2554
s.2, amended: SI 2008/1774 Sch.1 para.2
s.3, applied: SI 2008/1284 Reg.18
s.4, amended: SI 2008/1037 Art.2, SI 2008/1774 Sch.1 para.3, SI 2008/3131 Sch.1 para.7
s.5, amended: SI 2008/1774 Sch.1 para.4, SI 2008/3131 Sch.1 para.7
s.6, amended: SI 2008/1774 Sch.1 para.5, SI 2008/3131 Sch.1 para.7
s.7, amended: SI 2008/1774 Sch.1 para.6, SI 2008/3131 Sch.1 para.7
s.7, repealed (in part): SI 2008/1774 Sch.1 para.6
s.8, applied: SI 2008/1037
s.8, repealed: SI 2008/1774 Sch.1 para.7
s.8, enabling: SI 2008/1037
s.9, repealed: SI 2008/1774 Sch.1 para.8
s.10A, amended: SI 2008/3131 Sch.1 para.2
s.10A, repealed (in part): SI 2008/3131 Sch.1 para.2
s.16, amended: SI 2008/1774 Sch.1 para.9, SI 2008/3131 Sch.1 para.7
s.18A, added: SI 2008/1774 Sch.1 para.10
s.29A, amended: SI 2008/3131 Sch.1 para.8
s.29B, amended: SI 2008/3131 Sch.1 para.9
s.29C, amended: 2008 c.14 Sch.7 para.3
s.29C, substituted: SI 2008/3131 Sch.1 para.10
s.29D, amended: SI 2008/3131 Sch.1 para.11
s.29E, amended: SI 2008/3131 Sch.1 para.12
s.29EA, added: SI 2008/3131 Sch.1 para.13
s.29F, amended: SI 2008/3131 Sch.1 para.14
s.29G, amended: SI 2008/3131 Sch.1 para.15
s.29J, amended: SI 2008/3131 Sch.1 para.16
s.30, amended: SI 2008/1774 Sch.1 para.11
s.30A, added: SI 2008/1774 Sch.1 para.12

CAP.

1983–cont.

54. **Medical Act 1983**–*cont.*
s.32, amended: SI 2008/1774 Sch.1 para.13
s.35A, amended: SI 2008/1774 Sch.1 para.14
s.35B, amended: 2008 c.14 Sch.7 para.5
s.35C, see *R. (on the application of Calhaem) v General Medical Council* [2007] EWHC 2606 (Admin), [2008] LS Law Medical 96 (QBD (Admin)), Jackson, J.
s.35C, amended: 2008 c.14 Sch.7 para.6, SI 2008/1774 Sch.1 para.15, SI 2008/3131 Sch.1 para.17
s.35CC, amended: SI 2008/3131 Sch.1 para.18
s.35D, amended: 2008 c.14 Sch.7 para.7
s.35E, amended: 2008 c.14 Sch.7 para.8
s.35ZA, added: 2008 c.14 Sch.7 para.4
s.36, see *Swanney v General Medical Council* [2008] CSIH 35, 2008 S.L.T. 646 (IH (Ex Div)), Lord Osborne
s.38, amended: 2008 c.14 Sch.7 para.9
s.38, applied: SI 2008/2554 Art.5, Art.7
s.38, repealed (in part): 2008 c.14 Sch.7 para.9, Sch.15 Part 2
s.40, amended: 2008 c.14 Sch.7 para.10
s.40A, added: 2008 c.14 Sch.7 para.11
s.41, amended: 2008 c.14 Sch.7 para.12, Sch.15 Part 2
s.41, repealed (in part): 2008 c.14 Sch.7 para.12, Sch.15 Part 2
s.41A, amended: 2008 c.14 Sch.7 para.13, Sch.15 Part 2
s.41A, applied: SI 2008/2554 Art.7
s.41C, amended: 2008 c.14 Sch.7 para.14
s.43, amended: 2008 c.14 Sch.7 para.15
s.43, enabling: SI 2008/1256
s.44, amended: 2008 c.14 Sch.7 para.16
s.45A, added: 2008 c.14 s.119
s.45A, applied: 2008 c.14 s.120
s.45A, varied: 2008 c.14 s.120
s.45B, added: 2008 c.14 s.119
s.45B, varied: 2008 c.14 s.120
s.45C, added: 2008 c.14 s.119
s.45C, varied: 2008 c.14 s.120
s.45D, added: 2008 c.14 s.119
s.45E, added: 2008 c.14 s.119
s.45F, added: 2008 c.14 s.119
s.47, amended: 2008 c.14 Sch.7 para.17
s.49B, amended: SI 2008/1774 Sch.1 para.16
s.50, amended: SI 2008/3131 Sch.1 para.3
s.50, repealed (in part): SI 2008/3131 Sch.1 para.3
s.51, amended: SI 2008/1774 Sch.1 para.17, SI 2008/3131 Sch.1 para.4
s.51, repealed (in part): SI 2008/1774 Sch.1 para.17
s.52A, substituted: SI 2008/1774 Sch.1 para.18
s.53, repealed (in part): 2008 c.14 Sch.7 para.18, Sch.15 Part 2, SI 2008/1774 Sch.1 para.19

CAP.

1983–cont.

54. Medical Act 1983–*cont.*

s.55, amended: 2008 c.14 Sch.7 para.19, SI 2008/1774 Sch.1 para.20

Sch.1 Part I para.1, substituted: SI 2008/1774 Sch.1 para.21

Sch.1 Part I para.1A, referred to: SI 2008/2554 Art.6

Sch.1 Part I para.1A, substituted: SI 2008/1774 Sch.1 para.21

Sch.1 Part I para.1A, varied: SI 2008/2556 Art.3

Sch.1 Part I para.1B, substituted: SI 2008/1774 Sch.1 para.21

Sch.1 Part I para.1B, enabling: SI 2008/2554

Sch.1 Part I para.1C, substituted: SI 2008/1774 Sch.1 para.21

Sch.1 Part I para.2, substituted: SI 2008/1774 Sch.1 para.21

Sch.1 Part I para.3, substituted: SI 2008/1774 Sch.1 para.21

Sch.1 Part I para.4, substituted: SI 2008/1774 Sch.1 para.21

Sch.1 Part I para.4A, substituted: SI 2008/1774 Sch.1 para.21

Sch.1 Part I para.4B, substituted: SI 2008/1774 Sch.1 para.21

Sch.1 Part I para.4ZA, substituted: SI 2008/1774 Sch.1 para.21

Sch.1 Part I para.5, substituted: SI 2008/1774 Sch.1 para.21

Sch.1 Part I para.6, substituted: SI 2008/1774 Sch.1 para.21

Sch.1 Part I para.7, substituted: SI 2008/1774 Sch.1 para.21

Sch.1 Part I para.8, substituted: SI 2008/1774 Sch.1 para.21

Sch.1 Part II para.9A, substituted: SI 2008/1774 Sch.1 para.21

Sch.1 Part II para.12, repealed: SI 2008/1774 Sch.1 para.21

Sch.1 Part II para.13, repealed: SI 2008/1774 Sch.1 para.21

Sch.1 Part II para.14, amended: SI 2008/1774 Sch.1 para.21

Sch.1 Part II para.15, amended: SI 2008/1774 Sch.1 para.21, SI 2008/3131 Sch.1 para.5

Sch.1 Part II para.16, amended: SI 2008/1774 Sch.1 para.21

Sch.1 Part II para.18, amended: SI 2008/948 Sch.1 para.1

Sch.1 Part III para.19, repealed: SI 2008/3131 Sch.1 para.5

Sch.1 Part III para.19A, repealed: 2008 c.14 Sch.7 para.20, Sch.15 Part 2

Sch.1 Part III para.19E, repealed: 2008 c.14 Sch.7 para.20, Sch.15 Part 2

Sch.1 Part III para.23, amended: 2008 c.14 Sch.7 para.20

Sch.1 Part III para.23, repealed (in part): 2008 c.14 Sch.7 para.20, Sch.15 Part 2

CAP.

1983–cont.

54. Medical Act 1983–*cont.*

Sch.1 Part III para.23B, amended: 2008 c.14 Sch.7 para.20

Sch.1 Part III para.23C, added: SI 2008/1774 Sch.1 para.21

Sch.1 Part III para.24, amended: 2008 c.14 Sch.7 para.20

Sch.1 Part III para.25, amended: SI 2008/3131 Sch.1 para.5

Sch.3 para.3, amended: SI 2008/1774 Sch.1 para.22

Sch.3A para.4, amended: 2008 c.14 Sch.7 para.21

Sch.3B para.3, amended: 2008 c.14 Sch.7 para.22

Sch.3B para.5, amended: SI 2008/3131 Sch.1 para.19

Sch.3B para.6, amended: SI 2008/3131 Sch.1 para.19

Sch.3B para.7, amended: SI 2008/3131 Sch.1 para.19

Sch.4, amended: 2008 c.14 Sch.7 para.23, Sch.15 Part 2

Sch.4 para.1, amended: 2008 c.14 Sch.7 para.23, Sch.15 Part 2

Sch.4 para.1, applied: SI 2008/1256, SI 2008/2554 Art.5, Art.6

Sch.4 para.1, repealed (in part): 2008 c.14 Sch.7 para.23, Sch.15 Part 2

Sch.4 para.1, enabling: SI 2008/1256

Sch.4 para.2, amended: 2008 c.14 Sch.7 para.23, Sch.15 Part 2

Sch.4 para.2, repealed (in part): 2008 c.14 Sch.7 para.23, Sch.15 Part 2

Sch.4 para.3, amended: 2008 c.14 Sch.7 para.23, Sch.15 Part 2

Sch.4 para.3A, amended: 2008 c.14 Sch.7 para.23

Sch.4 para.3A, substituted: 2008 c.14 Sch.7 para.23

Sch.4 para.4, amended: 2008 c.14 Sch.7 para.23

Sch.4 para.5, amended: 2008 c.14 Sch.7 para.23

Sch.4 para.5A, amended: 2008 c.14 Sch.7 para.23

Sch.4 para.5A, repealed (in part): 2008 c.14 Sch.7 para.23, Sch.15 Part 2

Sch.4 para.5B, amended: 2008 c.14 Sch.7 para.23

Sch.4 para.6, amended: 2008 c.14 Sch.7 para.23

Sch.4 para.7, amended: 2008 c.14 Sch.7 para.23, Sch.15 Part 2

Sch.4 para.7, repealed (in part): 2008 c.14 Sch.7 para.23, Sch.15 Part 2

Sch.4 para.8, amended: 2008 c.14 Sch.7 para.23

Sch.4 para.9, amended: 2008 c.14 Sch.7 para.23

CAP.

1983–cont.

54. Medical Act 1983–*cont.*
Sch.4 para.10, amended: 2008 c.14 Sch.7 para.23
Sch.4 para.10A, added: 2008 c.14 Sch.7 para.23
Sch.4 para.10A, amended: 2008 c.14 Sch.7 para.23
Sch.4 para.11, amended: 2008 c.14 Sch.7 para.23
Sch.4 para.12, amended: 2008 c.14 Sch.7 para.23
Sch.4 para.13, amended: 2008 c.14 Sch.7 para.23, Sch.15 Part 2
Sch.4 para.14, amended: 2008 c.14 Sch.7 para.23
Sch.6 para.14, repealed: SI 2008/3131 Sch.1 para.6

56. Oil Taxation Act 1983
s.9, amended: 2008 c.9 Sch.33 para.4

1984

12. Telecommunications Act 1984
applied: SSI 2008/182 Art.20
s.101, amended: SI 2008/1277 Sch.2 para.29
s.101, repealed (in part): SI 2008/1277 Sch.4 Part 1
Sch.2, applied: SI 2008/2512 Sch.10 para.30
Sch.2 para.9, applied: 2008 c.18 Sch.17 para.3
Sch.2 para.21, disapplied: 2008 c.18 Sch.17 para.2
Sch.2 para.23, applied: 2008 c.18 Sch.17 para.2, Sch.17 para.4
Sch.2 para.23, disapplied: 2008 c.18 Sch.17 para.2

16. Foreign Limitation Periods Act 1984
s.8, added: SI 2008/2986 Reg.4

21. Somerset House Act 1984
s.1, amended: SI 2008/1034 Sch.1 para.3
s.1, applied: SI 2008/1034 Art.4

22. Public Health (Control of Disease) Act 1984
s.1, amended: 2008 c.14 Sch.11 para.3
s.1, repealed (in part): 2008 c.14 Sch.11 para.3, Sch.15 Part 3
s.2, applied: SI 2008/622 Reg.2, SI 2008/781 Reg.2, SI 2008/1079 Reg.2, SI 2008/1080 Reg.2
s.2, disapplied: SI 2008/1261 Art.56
s.5, amended: 2008 c.14 Sch.11 para.4, Sch.15 Part 3
s.7, applied: SI 2008/622 Reg.2, SI 2008/1079 Reg.2
s.7, repealed (in part): 2008 c.14 Sch.11 para.5, Sch.15 Part 3
s.9, repealed: 2008 c.14 Sch.11 para.6, Sch.15 Part 3
s.10, repealed: 2008 c.14 s.130, Sch.15 Part 3
s.11, repealed: 2008 c.14 s.130, Sch.15 Part 3
s.12, repealed: 2008 c.14 s.130, Sch.15 Part 3

CAP.

1984–cont.

22. Public Health (Control of Disease) Act 1984–*cont.*
s.13, applied: 2008 c.13 Sch.7
s.13, repealed: 2008 c.14 s.130, Sch.15 Part 3
s.14, repealed: 2008 c.14 s.130, Sch.15 Part 3
s.15, referred to: 2008 c.13 Sch.6
s.15, repealed: 2008 c.14 s.130, Sch.15 Part 3
s.16, referred to: 2008 c.13 Sch.6
s.16, repealed: 2008 c.14 s.130, Sch.15 Part 3
s.17, referred to: 2008 c.13 Sch.6
s.17, repealed: 2008 c.14 s.130, Sch.15 Part 3
s.18, referred to: 2008 c.13 Sch.6
s.18, repealed: 2008 c.14 s.130, Sch.15 Part 3
s.19, referred to: 2008 c.13 Sch.6
s.19, repealed: 2008 c.14 s.130, Sch.15 Part 3
s.20, referred to: 2008 c.13 Sch.6
s.20, repealed: 2008 c.14 s.130, Sch.15 Part 3
s.21, referred to: 2008 c.13 Sch.6
s.21, repealed: 2008 c.14 s.130, Sch.15 Part 3
s.22, referred to: 2008 c.13 Sch.6
s.22, repealed: 2008 c.14 s.130, Sch.15 Part 3
s.23, referred to: 2008 c.13 Sch.6
s.23, repealed: 2008 c.14 s.130, Sch.15 Part 3
s.24, referred to: 2008 c.13 Sch.6
s.24, repealed: 2008 c.14 s.130, Sch.15 Part 3
s.25, referred to: 2008 c.13 Sch.6
s.25, repealed: 2008 c.14 s.130, Sch.15 Part 3
s.26, referred to: 2008 c.13 Sch.6
s.26, repealed: 2008 c.14 s.130, Sch.15 Part 3
s.27, referred to: 2008 c.13 Sch.6
s.27, repealed: 2008 c.14 s.130, Sch.15 Part 3
s.28, referred to: 2008 c.13 Sch.6
s.28, repealed: 2008 c.14 s.130, Sch.15 Part 3
s.29, referred to: 2008 c.13 Sch.6
s.29, repealed: 2008 c.14 s.130, Sch.15 Part 3
s.30, referred to: 2008 c.13 Sch.6
s.30, repealed: 2008 c.14 s.130, Sch.15 Part 3
s.31, referred to: 2008 c.13 Sch.6
s.31, repealed: 2008 c.14 s.130, Sch.15 Part 3
s.32, referred to: 2008 c.13 Sch.6
s.32, repealed: 2008 c.14 s.130, Sch.15 Part 3
s.33, referred to: 2008 c.13 Sch.6
s.33, repealed: 2008 c.14 s.130, Sch.15 Part 3
s.34, referred to: 2008 c.13 Sch.6
s.34, repealed: 2008 c.14 s.130, Sch.15 Part 3
s.35, referred to: 2008 c.13 Sch.6
s.35, repealed: 2008 c.14 s.130, Sch.15 Part 3
s.36, referred to: 2008 c.13 Sch.6
s.36, repealed: 2008 c.14 s.130, Sch.15 Part 3
s.37, referred to: 2008 c.13 Sch.6
s.37, repealed: 2008 c.14 s.130, Sch.15 Part 3
s.38, referred to: 2008 c.13 Sch.6
s.38, repealed: 2008 c.14 s.130, Sch.15 Part 3
s.39, referred to: 2008 c.13 Sch.6
s.39, repealed: 2008 c.14 s.130, Sch.15 Part 3
s.40, referred to: 2008 c.13 Sch.6
s.40, repealed: 2008 c.14 s.130, Sch.15 Part 3
s.41, referred to: 2008 c.13 Sch.6
s.41, repealed: 2008 c.14 s.130, Sch.15 Part 3
s.42, referred to: 2008 c.13 Sch.6

CAP.

1984–cont.

22. Public Health (Control of Disease) Act 1984–*cont.*

s.42, repealed: 2008 c.14 s.130, Sch.15 Part 3
s.43, referred to: 2008 c.13 Sch.6
s.43, repealed: 2008 c.14 s.130, Sch.15 Part 3
s.44, referred to: 2008 c.13 Sch.6
s.44, repealed: 2008 c.14 s.130, Sch.15 Part 3
s.45, referred to: 2008 c.13 Sch.6
s.45, repealed: 2008 c.14 s.130, Sch.15 Part 3
s.45A, added: 2008 c.14 s.129
s.45A, referred to: 2008 c.13 Sch.6
s.45B, added: 2008 c.14 s.129
s.45B, referred to: 2008 c.13 Sch.6
s.45C, added: 2008 c.14 s.129
s.45C, referred to: 2008 c.13 Sch.6
s.45D, added: 2008 c.14 s.129
s.45D, referred to: 2008 c.13 Sch.6
s.45E, added: 2008 c.14 s.129
s.45E, referred to: 2008 c.13 Sch.6
s.45F, added: 2008 c.14 s.129
s.45F, referred to: 2008 c.13 Sch.6
s.45G, added: 2008 c.14 s.129
s.45G, referred to: 2008 c.13 Sch.6
s.45H, added: 2008 c.14 s.129
s.45H, referred to: 2008 c.13 Sch.6
s.45I, added: 2008 c.14 s.129
s.45I, referred to: 2008 c.13 Sch.6
s.45J, added: 2008 c.14 s.129
s.45J, referred to: 2008 c.13 Sch.6
s.45K, added: 2008 c.14 s.129
s.45K, referred to: 2008 c.13 Sch.6
s.45L, added: 2008 c.14 s.129
s.45L, referred to: 2008 c.13 Sch.6
s.45M, added: 2008 c.14 s.129
s.45M, referred to: 2008 c.13 Sch.6
s.45N, added: 2008 c.14 s.129
s.45N, referred to: 2008 c.13 Sch.6
s.45O, added: 2008 c.14 s.129
s.45O, referred to: 2008 c.13 Sch.6
s.45P, added: 2008 c.14 s.129
s.45P, referred to: 2008 c.13 Sch.6
s.45Q, added: 2008 c.14 s.129
s.45Q, referred to: 2008 c.13 Sch.6
s.45R, added: 2008 c.14 s.129
s.45R, referred to: 2008 c.13 Sch.6
s.45S, added: 2008 c.14 s.129
s.45S, referred to: 2008 c.13 Sch.6
s.45T, added: 2008 c.14 s.129
s.45T, referred to: 2008 c.13 Sch.6
s.46, amended: 2008 c.14 s.147, Sch.15 Part 5
s.46, applied: 2008 c.14 Sch.13 para.8
s.48, amended: 2008 c.14 Sch.11 para.7
s.49, amended: 2008 c.14 Sch.11 para.8
s.49, repealed (in part): 2008 c.14 Sch.11 para.8, Sch.15 Part 3
s.50, amended: 2008 c.14 Sch.11 para.9, Sch.15 Part 3
s.50, repealed (in part): 2008 c.14 Sch.11 para.9, Sch.15 Part 3

CAP.

1984–cont.

22. Public Health (Control of Disease) Act 1984–*cont.*

s.51, amended: 2008 c.14 Sch.11 para.10, Sch.15 Part 3
s.51, repealed (in part): 2008 c.14 Sch.11 para.10, Sch.15 Part 3
s.52, repealed: 2008 c.14 Sch.11 para.11, Sch.15 Part 3
s.54, repealed: 2008 c.14 Sch.11 para.12, Sch.15 Part 3
s.55, repealed: 2008 c.14 Sch.11 para.12, Sch.15 Part 3
s.56, repealed: 2008 c.14 Sch.11 para.12, Sch.15 Part 3
s.57, repealed: 2008 c.14 Sch.11 para.12, Sch.15 Part 3
s.58, amended: 2008 c.14 Sch.11 para.13
s.59, amended: 2008 c.14 Sch.11 para.14
s.60, amended: 2008 c.14 Sch.11 para.15
s.60A, added: 2008 c.14 Sch.11 para.16
s.61, amended: 2008 c.14 Sch.11 para.17, Sch.15 Part 3
s.62, amended: 2008 c.14 Sch.11 para.18
s.62, repealed (in part): 2008 c.14 Sch.11 para.18, Sch.15 Part 3
s.63, substituted: 2008 c.14 Sch.11 para.19
s.63A, added: 2008 c.14 Sch.11 para.20
s.63B, added: 2008 c.14 Sch.11 para.20
s.64, amended: 2008 c.14 Sch.11 para.21
s.64, repealed (in part): 2008 c.14 Sch.11 para.21, Sch.15 Part 3
s.64A, added: 2008 c.14 Sch.11 para.22
s.67, amended: 2008 c.14 Sch.11 para.23
s.67, repealed (in part): 2008 c.14 Sch.11 para.23, Sch.15 Part 3
s.69, substituted: 2008 c.14 Sch.11 para.24
s.70, repealed: 2008 c.14 Sch.11 para.25, Sch.15 Part 3
s.71, substituted: 2008 c.14 Sch.11 para.26
s.72, amended: 2008 c.14 Sch.11 para.27
s.73, amended: 2008 c.14 Sch.11 para.28
s.74, amended: 2008 c.14 Sch.11 para.29, Sch.15 Part 3
s.76, repealed: 2008 c.14 Sch.11 para.30

23. Registered Homes Act 1984

applied: 2008 c.14 s.17

24. Dentists Act 1984

applied: SI 2008/2852 Sch.3 para.2, SI 2008/2927 Reg.2
s.1, enabling: SI 2008/3238
s.2C, amended: SI 2008/948 Sch.1 para.3
s.3, varied: SI 2008/1774 Art.5
s.27, amended: 2008 c.14 Sch.10 para.7
s.34A, enabling: SI 2008/1822
s.34AA, referred to: SI 2008/1822 Sch.1
s.34B, enabling: SI 2008/1822
s.36A, amended: 2008 c.14 Sch.10 para.8
s.36N, amended: 2008 c.14 Sch.10 para.9
s.36Z1, enabling: SI 2008/1823
s.36Z2, enabling: SI 2008/1823

CAP.

1984–cont.

24. Dentists Act 1984–*cont.*

s.36Z4, referred to: SI 2008/1823 Sch.1
s.37, amended: SI 2008/1774 Sch.5 para.1
s.50A, enabling: SI 2008/1822, SI 2008/1823
s.50C, applied: SI 2008/1822, SI 2008/1823
s.50C, enabling: SI 2008/1822, SI 2008/1823
Sch.2A para.3, applied: SI 2008/1822 Sch.1
Sch.4A para.3, applied: SI 2008/1823 Sch.1

26. Inshore Fishing (Scotland) Act 1984

s.1, applied: SSI 2008/317
s.1, enabling: SSI 2008/317
s.2A, enabling: SSI 2008/317
s.4, applied: SSI 2008/101 Sch.1 Part 1

27. Road Traffic Regulation Act 1984

applied: 2008 asp 4 s.39, 2008 c.18 Sch.3 para.5, SI 2008/2512 Art.11
referred to: 2008 asp 4 Sch.1, SI 2008/2367 Reg.2
s.1, amended: 2008 c.26 s.45
s.1, applied: SSI 2008/88 Reg.12
s.1, referred to: SI 2008/2367 Reg.3, Reg.5
s.1, enabling: SI 2008/2821
s.2, enabling: SI 2008/2821
s.5, referred to: 2008 c.13 Sch.6
s.6, referred to: SI 2008/2367 Reg.3, Reg.5
s.9, applied: SSI 2008/88 Reg.12
s.9, referred to: SI 2008/2367 Reg.3, Reg.5
s.14, see *DPP v Wells* [2007] EWHC 3259 (Admin), [2008] R.T.R. 23 (DC), Maurice Kay, L.J.
s.14, applied: 2008 asp 4 s.38, s.39, SI 2008/101 Reg.4, SI 2008/540 Reg.4, SI 2008/2512 Art.11
s.14, referred to: 2008 asp 4 s.38, SI 2008/2367 Reg.3, Reg.5
s.16, see *DPP v Wells* [2007] EWHC 3259 (Admin), [2008] R.T.R. 23 (DC), Maurice Kay, L.J.
s.16, referred to: 2008 asp 4 s.38, 2008 c.13 Sch.6
s.16A, referred to: SI 2008/2367 Reg.3, Reg.5
s.17, referred to: SI 2008/2367 Reg.3, Reg.5
s.17, enabling: SI 2008/2262
s.25, referred to: SI 2008/2367 Reg.3, Reg.5
s.26, applied: SI 2008/228 Reg.6
s.28, enabling: SSI 2008/4
s.32, applied: SI 2008/1055 Art.2, SI 2008/2442 Art.2
s.46, varied: SI 2008/226 Sch.2 para.1
s.47, referred to: 2008 c.13 Sch.6
s.55, applied: SI 2008/614 Reg.11, SI 2008/1214 Reg.11
s.55, varied: SI 2008/226 Sch.2 para.2, SI 2008/614 Reg.10, SI 2008/1214 Reg.10
s.63A, varied: SI 2008/226 Sch.2 para.3
s.64, applied: SI 2008/1261 Art.25
s.64, enabling: SI 2008/2177 Reg.1, Reg.2, Reg.3, Reg.4

CAP.

1984–cont.

27. Road Traffic Regulation Act 1984–*cont.*

s.65, enabling: SI 2008/2177 Reg.1, Reg.2, Reg.3, Reg.4, Reg.5, Reg.6, Reg.7
s.66, referred to: SI 2008/2367 Reg.3
s.67, referred to: SI 2008/2367 Reg.3, Reg.5
s.81, applied: SI 2008/2820 Art.3
s.82, enabling: SI 2008/2820
s.83, enabling: SI 2008/2820
s.85, enabling: SI 2008/2177 Reg.1, Reg.2, Reg.3, Reg.4
s.89, see *DPP v Wells* [2007] EWHC 3259 (Admin), [2008] R.T.R. 23 (DC), Maurice Kay, L.J.
s.99, applied: SI 2008/615 Reg.3, SI 2008/616 Reg.2, SI 2008/2367 Reg.8, Reg.9, Reg.10
s.99, enabling: SI 2008/612, SI 2008/2367
s.100, amended: SI 2008/2367 Reg.13
s.100, applied: SI 2008/2367 Reg.4, Reg.6, Reg.8
s.101, amended: SI 2008/2367 Reg.13
s.101, applied: SI 2008/2367 Reg.14, Reg.16, Reg.17
s.101, varied: SI 2008/226 Sch.2 para.4
s.101, enabling: SI 2008/2367
s.101A, applied: SI 2008/615 Reg.3, Reg.4, SI 2008/2095 Reg.4, Reg.5, SI 2008/2367 Reg.18
s.101A, enabling: SI 2008/2095, SI 2008/2367
s.101B, enabling: SI 2008/615
s.102, amended: SI 2008/2367 Reg.13
s.102, applied: SI 2008/2095 Reg.4, Reg.5, Reg.6
s.102, varied: SI 2008/226 Sch.2 para.5
s.102, enabling: SI 2008/2095, SI 2008/3013
s.103, enabling: SI 2008/2095, SI 2008/2367, SI 2008/3013
s.115, referred to: 2008 c.13 Sch.6
s.117, applied: SI 2008/614 Reg.8, SI 2008/1214 Reg.8
s.117, referred to: 2008 c.13 Sch.6
s.124, enabling: SSI 2008/3
s.134, applied: SI 2008/612, SI 2008/2095, SI 2008/2262, SI 2008/2367, SI 2008/3013, SSI 2008/3, SSI 2008/4
s.142, varied: SI 2008/226 Sch.2 para.6
s.142, enabling: SI 2008/2095
Sch.9 Part III, enabling: SSI 2008/3
Sch.9 Part V para.31, amended: 2008 c.26 Sch.4 para.51
Sch.9 Part VI, applied: SI 2008/608 Reg.4

28. County Courts Act 1984

s.6, applied: SI 2008/2995 Sch.1 Part 2
s.8, applied: SI 2008/2995 Sch.1 Part 1
s.23, see *National Westminster Bank Plc v King* [2008] EWHC 280 (Ch), [2008] Ch. 385 (Ch D), David Richards, J.

CAP.

1984–cont.

28. County Courts Act 1984–*cont.*

s.40, see *National Westminster Bank Plc v King* [2008] EWHC 280 (Ch), [2008] Ch. 385 (Ch D), David Richards, J.

s.71, applied: 2008 c.25 s.58

s.72, see *Revenue and Customs Commissioners v Xicom Systems Ltd* [2008] EWHC 1945 (Ch), [2008] S.T.C. 3492 (Ch D), David Richards, J.

s.85, applied: 2008 c.30 s.42

s.97, applied: SI 2008/1054 Sch.1

30. Food Act 1984

applied: 2008 c.13 Sch.3

33. Rates Act 1984

repealed: 2008 c.12 Sch.1 Part 7

s.2, amended: 2008 c.26 Sch.4 para.52

36. Mental Health (Scotland) Act 1984

applied: SSI 2008/228 Reg.4

37. Child Abduction Act 1984

Sch.1 para.2, amended: 2008 c.4 Sch.4 para.31, Sch.4 para.104

39. Video Recordings Act 1984

applied: 2008 c.13 Sch.3

s.4A, see *R. (on the application of British Board of Film Classification) v Video Appeals Committee* [2008] EWHC 203 (Admin), [2008] 1 W.L.R. 1658 (QBD (Admin)), Mitting, J.

s.9, referred to: 2008 c.13 Sch.6

s.10, referred to: 2008 c.13 Sch.6

s.11, referred to: 2008 c.13 Sch.6

s.12, referred to: 2008 c.13 Sch.6

s.13, referred to: 2008 c.13 Sch.6

s.14, referred to: 2008 c.13 Sch.6

s.22, applied: 2008 c.4 s.64

40. Animal Health and Welfare Act 1984

applied: 2008 c.13 Sch.3

s.10, referred to: 2008 c.13 Sch.6

s.10, enabling: SI 2008/1040

42. Matrimonial and Family Proceedings Act 1984

Part III, applied: 2008 c.30 s.109, s.118

s.17, amended: 2008 c.30 Sch.6 para.11

s.18, amended: 2008 c.30 Sch.6 para.12

s.28, applied: 2008 c.30 s.110

s.32, see *Practice Note (Family Proceedings: Court Dress)* [2008] 1 W.L.R. 1701 (Fam Div), Sir Mark Potter (President)

s.38, applied: SI 2008/2836 Art.12

s.39, applied: SI 2008/2836 Art.12

s.40, enabling: SI 2008/2446, SI 2008/2861

43. Finance Act 1984

s.57, repealed (in part): 2008 c.9 s.137

47. Repatriation of Prisoners Act 1984

applied: 2008 c.4 Sch.26 para.9

referred to: 2008 c.4 Sch.26 para.11, Sch.26 para.14, SI 2008/2699 r.32, SI 2008/2705 r.14

s.1, amended: 2008 c.4 Sch.26 para.11, Sch.28 Part 6

s.1, applied: 2008 c.28 s.55

CAP.

1984–cont.

47. Repatriation of Prisoners Act 1984–*cont.*

s.1, amended: 2008 c.4 Sch.26 para.10, Sch.26 para.11, Sch.26 para.17

s.1, applied: 2008 c.4 s.96, Sch.27 para.9, Sch.27 para.11, Sch.27 para.30, SI 2008/1466 Art.4

s.2, amended: 2008 c.4 s.93, s.96, Sch.26 para.11, Sch.26 para.12

s.2, varied: 2008 c.4 Sch.26 para.12

s.2, amended: 2008 c.4 Sch.26 para.10, Sch.26 para.17, SI 2008/1216 Sch.5 para.4

s.2, varied: 2008 c.4 Sch.26 para.19

s.3, amended: 2008 c.4 Sch.26 para.11, Sch.26 para.13

s.3, repealed (in part): 2008 c.4 Sch.28 Part 6

s.3, amended: 2008 c.4 Sch.26 para.10, Sch.26 para.17

s.4, amended: 2008 c.4 Sch.26 para.11, Sch.26 para.14

s.4, amended: 2008 c.4 Sch.26 para.10, Sch.26 para.17

s.4A, added: 2008 c.4 s.94

s.4A, amended: 2008 c.4 Sch.26 para.11

s.4B, added: 2008 c.4 s.94

s.4B, amended: 2008 c.4 Sch.26 para.11

s.4C, added: 2008 c.4 s.94

s.4C, amended: 2008 c.4 Sch.26 para.11

s.4D, added: 2008 c.4 s.95

s.4D, amended: 2008 c.4 Sch.26 para.11

s.4E, added: 2008 c.4 s.95

s.4E, amended: 2008 c.4 Sch.26 para.11

s.4F, added: 2008 c.4 s.95

s.4F, amended: 2008 c.4 Sch.26 para.11

s.5, amended: 2008 c.4 Sch.26 para.11, Sch.26 para.16

s.5, amended: 2008 c.4 Sch.26 para.15, Sch.26 para.17

s.6, amended: 2008 c.4 Sch.26 para.11, Sch.26 para.17

s.6, amended: 2008 c.4 Sch.26 para.15, Sch.26 para.17

s.7, amended: 2008 c.4 Sch.26 para.11, Sch.26 para.17

s.7, amended: 2008 c.4 Sch.26 para.15

s.8, amended: 2008 c.4 s.96, Sch.26 para.11, Sch.26 para.17, Sch.26 para.18, Sch.28 Part 6

s.8, amended: 2008 c.4 Sch.26 para.15

s.8, amended: 2008 c.4 s.96, Sch.26 para.18, Sch.28 Part 6

s.8, referred to: 2008 c.4 Sch.26 para.18

s.9, amended: 2008 c.4 Sch.26 para.11, Sch.26 para.17

s.9, amended: 2008 c.4 Sch.26 para.15

s.9, referred to: 2008 c.4 s.152

Sch.1 para.1, amended: 2008 c.4 Sch.26 para.19

Sch.1 para.1, substituted: 2008 c.4 Sch.26 para.19

CAP.

1984–cont.

47. Repatriation of Prisoners Act 1984–*cont.*

Sch.1 Part 1 para.5, amended: SI 2008/2833 Sch.3 para.69

Sch.1 Part 1 para.5, applied: SI 2008/2684 Art.5

Sch.1 para.2, substituted: 2008 c.4 Sch.26 para.19

Sch.1 para.2, varied: 2008 c.4 Sch.26 para.19

Sch.1 para.2A, added: SI 2008/1216 Sch.5 para.4

Sch.1 para.2A, substituted: 2008 c.4 Sch.26 para.19

Sch.1 Part 2 para.9, added: 2008 c.4 Sch.26 para.19

Sch.1 Part 2 para.10, added: 2008 c.4 Sch.26 para.19

Sch.1 Part 2 para.11, added: 2008 c.4 Sch.26 para.19

Sch.1 Part 2 para.12, added: 2008 c.4 Sch.26 para.19

Sch.1 Part 2 para.13, added: 2008 c.4 Sch.26 para.19

Sch.1 Part 2 para.14, added: 2008 c.4 Sch.26 para.19

Sch.1 para.3, substituted: 2008 c.4 Sch.26 para.19

Sch.1 para.4, substituted: 2008 c.4 Sch.26 para.19

Sch.1 para.5, substituted: 2008 c.4 Sch.26 para.19

Sch.1 para.6, substituted: 2008 c.4 Sch.26 para.19

Sch.1 para.7, substituted: 2008 c.4 Sch.26 para.19

Sch.1 para.8, substituted: 2008 c.4 Sch.26 para.19

51. Inheritance Tax Act 1984

referred to: SI 2008/606 Reg.4

s.3, see *Nelson Dance Family Settlement Trustees v Revenue and Customs Commissioners* [2008] S.T.C. (S.C.D.) 792 (Sp Comm), John F Avery Jones

s.3A, see *McKelvey v Revenue and Customs Commissioners* [2008] S.T.C. (S.C.D.) 944 (Sp Comm), Colin Bishopp

s.4, see *Wells (Personal Representative of Glowacki (Deceased)) v Revenue and Customs Commissioners* [2008] S.T.C. (S.C.D.) 188 (Sp Comm), Malcolm Gammie Q.C.

s.4, referred to: 2008 c.9 Sch.4 para.10, Sch.4 para.11

s.5, see *Taylor v Revenue and Customs Commissioners* [2008] S.T.C. (S.C.D.) 1159 (Sp Comm), Nuala Brice

s.7, see *Ogden v Trustees of the RHS Griffiths 2003 Settlement* [2008] EWHC 118 (Ch), [2008] 2 All E.R. 655 (Ch D (Birmingham)), Lewison, J.

s.8A, added: 2008 c.9 Sch.4 para.2

s.8A, referred to: 2008 c.9 Sch.4 para.10

CAP.

1984–cont.

51. Inheritance Tax Act 1984–*cont.*

s.8A, varied: 2008 c.9 Sch.4 para.10

s.8B, added: 2008 c.9 Sch.4 para.2

s.8C, added: 2008 c.9 Sch.4 para.2

s.8C, referred to: 2008 c.9 Sch.4 para.11

s.8C, varied: 2008 c.9 Sch.4 para.11

s.11, see *McKelvey v Revenue and Customs Commissioners* [2008] S.T.C. (S.C.D.) 944 (Sp Comm), Colin Bishopp

s.12, amended: 2008 c.9 Sch.29 para.18

s.13, see *A Trust Co Ltd (2007/84), Re* [2008] W.T.L.R. 377 (Royal Ct (Jer)), Commissioner Clyde-Smith

s.17, see *Wells (Personal Representative of Glowacki (Deceased)) v Revenue and Customs Commissioners* [2008] S.T.C. (S.C.D.) 188 (Sp Comm), Malcolm Gammie Q.C.

s.23, see *Bailhache Labesse Trustees Ltd v Revenue and Customs Commissioners* [2008] S.T.C. (S.C.D.) 869 (Sp Comm), Howard M Nowlan (Chairman)

s.24A, amended: 2008 c.17 Sch.9 para.7

s.32, referred to: 2008 c.9 Sch.4 para.11

s.32A, referred to: 2008 c.9 Sch.4 para.11

s.44, see *Stow v Stow* [2008] EWHC 495 (Ch), [2008] Ch. 461 (Ch D), Warren, J.

s.49, see *Ridgwell v Ridgwell* [2007] EWHC 2666 (Ch), [2008] S.T.C. 1883 (Ch D), Judge Behrens

s.49C, amended: 2008 c.9 s.141

s.49D, see *Ridgwell v Ridgwell* [2007] EWHC 2666 (Ch), [2008] S.T.C. 1883 (Ch D), Judge Behrens

s.49D, amended: 2008 c.9 s.141

s.49E, amended: 2008 c.9 s.141

s.53, amended: 2008 c.9 s.140

s.57, applied: SI 2008/605 Reg.5

s.58, amended: 2008 c.9 Sch.29 para.18

s.64, applied: SI 2008/606 Reg.4

s.65, applied: SI 2008/606 Reg.4

s.66, referred to: SI 2008/606 Reg.4

s.68, referred to: SI 2008/606 Reg.4

s.69, applied: SI 2008/606 Reg.4

s.71E, applied: SI 2008/606 Reg.4

s.71F, referred to: SI 2008/606 Reg.4

s.104, see *Nelson Dance Family Settlement Trustees v Revenue and Customs Commissioners* [2008] S.T.C. (S.C.D.) 792 (Sp Comm), John F Avery Jones

s.104, applied: SI 2008/605 Reg.5

s.105, see *McCall v Revenue and Customs Commissioners* [2008] S.T.C. (S.C.D.) 752 (Sp Comm), Charles Hellier; see *Piercy's Executors v Revenue and Customs Commissioners* [2008] S.T.C. (S.C.D.) 858 (Sp Comm), Howard M Nowlan

s.106, see *Vinton v Revenue and Customs Commissioners* [2008] S.T.C. (S.C.D.) 592 (Sp Comm), Judith Powell

CAP.

1984–cont.

51. Inheritance Tax Act 1984–*cont.*

s.107, see *Vinton v Revenue and Customs Commissioners* [2008] S.T.C. (S.C.D.) 592 (Sp Comm), Judith Powell

s.116, see *Nelson Dance Family Settlement Trustees v Revenue and Customs Commissioners* [2008] S.T.C. (S.C.D.) 792 (Sp Comm), John F Avery Jones

s.116, applied: SI 2008/605 Reg.5

s.126, referred to: 2008 c.9 Sch.4 para.11

s.142, see *Wells (Personal Representative of Glowacki (Deceased)) v Revenue and Customs Commissioners* [2008] S.T.C. (S.C.D.) 188 (Sp Comm), Malcolm Gammie Q.C.; see *Wills v Gibbs* [2007] EWHC 3361 (Ch), [2008] S.T.C. 786 (Ch D), Rimer, J.

s.144, see *Bailhache Labesse Trustees Ltd v Revenue and Customs Commissioners* [2008] S.T.C. (S.C.D.) 869 (Sp Comm), Howard M Nowlan (Chairman)

s.147, amended: 2008 c.9 Sch.4 para.3

s.151, amended: 2008 c.9 Sch.29 para.18

s.151A, amended: 2008 c.9 Sch.28 para.7

s.151BA, amended: 2008 c.9 Sch.4 para.4, Sch.28 para.8

s.151BA, repealed (in part): 2008 c.9 Sch.28 para.8

s.151C, amended: 2008 c.9 Sch.28 para.9

s.151D, added: 2008 c.9 Sch.28 para.10

s.151E, added: 2008 c.9 Sch.28 para.10

s.152, amended: 2008 c.9 Sch.29 para.18

s.199, see *Stow v Stow* [2008] EWHC 495 (Ch), [2008] Ch. 461 (Ch D), Warren, J.

s.210, amended: 2008 c.9 Sch.28 para.11

s.216, amended: 2008 c.9 Sch.28 para.12

s.216, applied: SI 2008/605 Reg.3, SI 2008/606 Reg.3, Reg.4

s.221, see *Wells (Personal Representative of Glowacki (Deceased)) v Revenue and Customs Commissioners* [2008] S.T.C. (S.C.D.) 188 (Sp Comm), Malcolm Gammie Q.C.

s.226, amended: 2008 c.9 Sch.28 para.13

s.233, amended: 2008 c.9 Sch.28 para.14

s.239, amended: 2008 c.9 Sch.4 para.5

s.244, amended: 2008 c.9 s.137

s.247, amended: 2008 c.9 Sch.4 para.6

s.247, repealed (in part): 2008 c.9 Sch.40 para.21

s.248, amended: 2008 c.9 Sch.40 para.21

s.250, repealed (in part): 2008 c.9 Sch.40 para.21

s.254, repealed (in part): 2008 c.9 Sch.44 para.3

s.256, applied: SI 2008/605, SI 2008/606

s.256, enabling: SI 2008/605, SI 2008/606

s.263, see *Smith v Revenue and Customs Commissioners* [2007] EWHC 2304 (Ch), [2008] S.T.C. 1649 (Ch D), Lightman, J.

CAP.

1984–cont.

51. Inheritance Tax Act 1984–*cont.*

s.264, applied: SI 2008/605 Reg.8, SI 2008/606 Reg.7

s.271A, added: 2008 c.9 Sch.29 para.18

s.272, amended: 2008 c.9 Sch.4 para.7

Sch.1, referred to: 2008 c.9 Sch.4 para.11

54. Roads (Scotland) Act 1984

see *Lerwick Port Authority v Scottish Ministers* 2008 S.L.T. 74 (OH), Lord Reed

applied: SSI 2008/88 Reg.12, SSI 2008/432 Sch.5 para.5

referred to: SSI 2008/263 Sch.1, Sch.2

s.7, applied: SSI 2008/432 Sch.5 para.5

s.56, applied: SSI 2008/88 Sch.1

s.58, applied: SSI 2008/88 Sch.1

s.61, applied: SSI 2008/88 Sch.1

s.85, applied: SSI 2008/88 Sch.1

s.86, applied: SSI 2008/88 Sch.1

s.88, applied: SSI 2008/88 Sch.1

s.90, applied: SSI 2008/88 Sch.1

s.91, applied: SSI 2008/88 Sch.1

s.92, applied: SSI 2008/88 Sch.1

s.113, applied: SSI 2008/88 Sch.2 para.2, Sch.2 para.6

s.151, see *Hamilton v Dumfries and Galloway Council* 2008 S.C. 197 (IH (Ex Div)), Lord Johnston; see *Teale v MacLeod* 2008 S.C.C.R. 12 (HCJ), Lord Osborne

Sch.8B, applied: SSI 2008/243 Reg.4, Reg.9

Sch.8B para.2, enabling: SSI 2008/243

Sch.8B para.4, amended: SSI 2008/243 Reg.7

Sch.8B para.4, enabling: SSI 2008/243

Sch.8B para.5, amended: SSI 2008/243 Reg.7

Sch.8B para.5, referred to: SSI 2008/243 Reg.6

Sch.8B para.5, enabling: SSI 2008/243

Sch.8B para.8, applied: SSI 2008/243 Reg.8

Sch.8B para.12, enabling: SSI 2008/243

Sch.8B para.13, enabling: SSI 2008/243

Sch.9 para.17, repealed: 2008 asp 5 Sch.3 Part 1

Sch.11, amended: 2008 asp 5 Sch.3 Part 1

55. Building Act 1984

referred to: 2008 c.13 Sch.6

Part I, disapplied: 2008 c.18 Sch.14 para.8

s.1, enabling: SI 2008/671, SI 2008/2363

s.4, applied: 2008 c.18 Sch.14 para.8

s.35, enabling: SI 2008/2363

s.35A, amended: 2008 c.17 s.317, Sch.16

s.35A, repealed (in part): 2008 c.17 s.317, Sch.16

s.35A, enabling: SI 2008/671

s.47, enabling: SI 2008/2363

s.94A, added: SI 2008/2334 Art.2

Sch.1 para.1, enabling: SI 2008/2363

Sch.1 para.2, enabling: SI 2008/2363

Sch.1 para.4, enabling: SI 2008/671, SI 2008/2363

CAP.

1984–cont.

55. Building Act 1984–*cont.*
Sch.1 para.4A, enabling: SI 2008/2363
Sch.1 para.7, enabling: SI 2008/2363
Sch.1 para.8, enabling: SI 2008/2363
Sch.1 para.10, enabling: SI 2008/2363

58. Rent (Scotland) Act 1984
s.12A, applied: SSI 2008/324 Reg.2
s.43, applied: SSI 2008/228 Reg.7

60. Police and Criminal Evidence Act 1984
see *R. v Ibrahim (Muktar)* [2008] EWCA Crim 880, [2008] 4 All E.R. 208 (CA (Crim Div)), Sir Igor Judge (President, QB); see *R. v Lynch (William Stewart)* [2007] EWCA Crim 3035, [2008] 1 Cr. App. R. 24 (CA (Crim Div)), Keene, L.J.
Part I, applied: SI 2008/1261 Art.52
Part II, applied: SI 2008/1261 Art.52
Part III, applied: SI 2008/1261 Art.52
Part IV, applied: SI 2008/1261 Art.52
Part V, applied: SI 2008/1261 Art.52
Part XI, applied: SI 2008/1261 Art.52
s.2, see *B v DPP* [2008] EWHC 1655 (Admin), (2008) 172 J.P. 449 (DC), Moses, L.J.; see *R. v Bristol (Christopher)* [2007] EWCA Crim 3214, (2008) 172 J.P. 161 (CA (Crim Div)), Thomas, L.J.
s.8, see *Khan v Commissioner of Police of the Metropolis* [2008] EWCA Civ 723, Times, June 16, 2008 (CA (Civ Div)), Pill, L.J.; see *Redknapp v Commissioner of Police of the Metropolis* [2008] EWHC 1177 (Admin), [2008] 1 All E.R. 229 (DC), Latham, L.J.
s.9, see *Redknapp v Commissioner of Police of the Metropolis* [2008] EWHC 1177 (Admin), [2008] 1 All E.R. 229 (DC), Latham, L.J.
s.9, referred to: 2008 c.25 s.97, s.110
s.12, referred to: 2008 c.9 Sch.36 para.19
s.13, referred to: 2008 c.9 Sch.36 para.19
s.16, see *Redknapp v Commissioner of Police of the Metropolis* [2008] EWHC 1177 (Admin), [2008] 1 All E.R. 229 (DC), Latham, L.J.
s.18, see *Khan v Commissioner of Police of the Metropolis* [2008] EWCA Civ 723, Times, June 16, 2008 (CA (Civ Div)), Pill, L.J.
s.32, see *Khan v Commissioner of Police of the Metropolis* [2008] EWCA Civ 723, Times, June 16, 2008 (CA (Civ Div)), Pill, L.J.
s.37, see *R. (on the application of G) v Chief Constable of West Yorkshire* [2008] EWCA Civ 28, [2008] 1 W.L.R. 550 (CA (Civ Div)), Sir Igor Judge
s.37A, see *R. (on the application of G) v Chief Constable of West Yorkshire* [2008] EWCA Civ 28, [2008] 1 W.L.R. 550 (CA (Civ Div)), Sir Igor Judge
s.37B, see *R. (on the application of G) v Chief Constable of West Yorkshire* [2008] EWCA Civ 28, [2008] 1 W.L.R. 550 (CA (Civ Div)), Sir Igor Judge

CAP.

1984–cont.

60. Police and Criminal Evidence Act 1984–*cont.*
s.37B, amended: 2008 c.4 Sch.26 para.20
s.60, applied: SI 2008/167
s.60, referred to: SI 2008/167 Art.2
s.61, amended: 2008 c.28 s.10
s.63, amended: 2008 c.28 s.10
s.63A, amended: 2008 c.28 s.10, s.14
s.63A, applied: 2008 c.28 s.18
s.63A, referred to: 2008 c.28 s.11
s.63B, amended: 2008 c.4 Sch.26 para.20
s.64, amended: 2008 c.28 s.10, s.14
s.64, applied: 2008 c.28 s.18
s.65, amended: 2008 c.28 s.10
s.66, see *R. v Lynch (William Stewart)* [2007] EWCA Crim 3035, [2008] 1 Cr. App. R. 24 (CA (Crim Div)), Keene, L.J.
s.66, applied: 2008 c.28 s.22, SI 2008/167
s.66, referred to: SI 2008/167 Art.2
s.67, see *R. v Doncaster (Roger George)* [2008] EWCA Crim 5, (2008) 172 J.P. 202 (CA (Crim Div)), Rix, L.J.; see *R. v Lynch (William Stewart)* [2007] EWCA Crim 3035, [2008] 1 Cr. App. R. 24 (CA (Crim Div)), Keene, L.J.
s.67, applied: SI 2008/2638
s.67, enabling: SI 2008/167, SI 2008/2638, SI 2008/3146
s.74, see *R. v Miell (Richard Andrew)* [2007] EWCA Crim 3130, [2008] 1 W.L.R. 627 (CA (Crim Div)), Lord Philips, L.C.J.
s.76, see *R. v Doncaster (Roger George)* [2008] EWCA Crim 5, (2008) 172 J.P. 202 (CA (Crim Div)), Rix, L.J.
s.78, see *C Plc v P* [2007] EWCA Civ 493, [2008] Ch. 1 (CA (Civ Div)), Longmore, L.J.; see *R. v D* [2008] EWCA Crim 1156, (2008) 172 J.P. 358 (CA (Crim Div)), Rix, L.J.; see *R. v Doncaster (Roger George)* [2008] EWCA Crim 5, (2008) 172 J.P. 202 (CA (Crim Div)), Rix, L.J.; see *R. v Flynn (Kris Ronald)* [2008] EWCA Crim 970, [2008] 2 Cr. App. R. 20 (CA (Crim Div)), Gage, L.J.; see *R. v Ibrahim (Muktar)* [2008] EWCA Crim 880, [2008] 4 All E.R. 208 (CA (Crim Div)), Sir Igor Judge (President, QB); see *R. v McNeill (Tracy)* [2007] EWCA Crim 2927, (2008) 172 J.P. 50 (CA (Crim Div)), Rix, L.J.
s.80, see *R. v L* [2008] EWCA Crim 973, [2008] 2 Cr. App. R. 18 (CA (Crim Div)), Lord Phillips, L.C.J.
s.108, repealed: 2008 c.12 Sch.1 Part 6
s.110, repealed: 2008 c.12 Sch.1 Part 6
s.120, amended: 2008 c.12 Sch.1 Part 6
Sch.1, applied: SI 2008/1261 Art.52
Sch.1 para.12, see *Redknapp v Commissioner of Police of the Metropolis* [2008] EWHC 1177 (Admin), [2008] 1 All E.R. 229 (DC), Latham, L.J.
Sch.2, applied: SI 2008/1261 Art.52

CAP.

1984–cont.

60. Police and Criminal Evidence Act 1984–*cont.*

Sch.5, applied: SI 2008/1261 Art.52
Sch.6, applied: SI 2008/1261 Art.52
Sch.7, applied: SI 2008/1261 Art.52

1985

5. New Towns and Urban Development Corporations Act 1985

s.1, repealed (in part): 2008 c.17 Sch.16
s.2, repealed: 2008 c.17 Sch.16
Sch.3 para.3, repealed: 2008 c.17 Sch.16
Sch.3 para.5, repealed: 2008 c.17 Sch.16
Sch.3 para.6, repealed (in part): 2008 c.17 Sch.16
Sch.3 para.8, repealed (in part): 2008 c.17 Sch.16
Sch.3 para.12, repealed (in part): 2008 c.17 Sch.16
Sch.3 para.16, repealed: 2008 c.17 Sch.16

6. Companies Act 1985

applied: 2008 c.2 s.15, SI 2008/432 Art.3, Art.8, SI 2008/629 Reg.25, SI 2008/948 Art.11, SI 2008/1053 Sch.1, SI 2008/1860 Reg.2, SI 2008/1886 Art.7, SI 2008/2546 Art.4, Art.9, SI 2008/2860 Sch.2 para.3, Sch.2 para.22, Sch.2 para.26, Sch.2 para.29, Sch.2 para.68, Sch.2 para.70, Sch.2 para.72, Sch.2 para.81, Sch.2 para.82, Sch.2 para.84, Sch.2 para.88, Sch.2 para.95, Sch.2 para.97, Sch.2 para.99, Sch.2 para.100, Sch.2 para.101, Sch.2 para.105, Sch.2 para.106, Sch.2 para.107, Sch.2 para.109, Sch.2 para.115, Sch.2 para.116, SI 2008/3229 Sch.1, Sch.2, Sch.3, SSI 2008/182
referred to: SI 2008/674 Art.6, SI 2008/1886 Art.6, SI 2008/1911 Reg.2
Part I, applied: SI 2008/2860 Sch.2 para.2
Part V c.IV, applied: SI 2008/1886 Art.7
Part VII, applied: SI 2008/629 Reg.20, Reg.25, Reg.31
Part VII c.I, applied: SI 2008/629 Reg.25
Part XI c.I, applied: 2008 c.13 Sch.3
Part XIV, applied: SI 2008/1909 Sch.1, SI 2008/2860 Sch.2 para.114
Part XV, applied: SI 2008/2860 Sch.2 para.114
Part XVI, applied: SI 2008/2860 Sch.2 para.114
Part XX, applied: SI 2008/653 Reg.15, Reg.16, SSI 2008/224 Reg.15
Part XXII c.II, applied: SI 2008/2860 Sch.2 para.93
s.4, applied: SI 2008/2860 Sch.2 para.110
s.5, applied: SI 2008/2860 Sch.2 para.110
s.6, applied: SI 2008/2860 Sch.2 para.110
s.7, applied: SI 2008/2860 Sch.2 para.3
s.8, applied: SI 2008/2860 Sch.2 para.3
s.8, enabling: SI 2008/739
s.10, amended: SI 2008/948 Sch.1 para.54

CAP.

1985–cont.

6. Companies Act 1985–*cont.*

s.11, amended: SI 2008/948 Sch.1 para.55
s.13, amended: SI 2008/948 Sch.1 para.56
s.17, amended: SI 2008/948 Sch.1 para.57
s.18, applied: SI 2008/2860 Sch.2 para.6, Sch.2 para.12
s.19, applied: SI 2008/2860 Sch.2 para.11
s.24, applied: SI 2008/432 Art.6, SI 2008/2860 Sch.2 para.24
s.24, disapplied: SI 2008/2546 Art.8
s.28, applied: SI 2008/2860 Sch.2 para.19
s.29, applied: SI 2008/2860 Sch.2 para.18
s.30, applied: SI 2008/495 Reg.7
s.31, applied: SI 2008/2860 Sch.2 para.20
s.32, applied: SI 2008/2860 Sch.2 para.21
s.35, applied: SI 2008/2860 Sch.2 para.15
s.36A, referred to: SI 2008/948 Art.7
s.38, applied: SI 2008/2860 Sch.2 para.16
s.43, amended: SI 2008/948 Sch.1 para.58
s.44, amended: SI 2008/948 Sch.1 para.59
s.45, amended: SI 2008/948 Sch.1 para.60
s.46, amended: SI 2008/948 Sch.1 para.61
s.47, amended: SI 2008/948 Sch.1 para.62
s.80, applied: SI 2008/2860 Sch.2 para.44, Sch.2 para.45
s.80A, applied: SI 2008/2860 Sch.2 para.44, Sch.2 para.45
s.84, applied: SI 2008/2860 Sch.2 para.56
s.85, applied: SI 2008/2860 Sch.2 para.56
s.88, applied: SI 2008/2860 Sch.2 para.47
s.89, applied: SI 2008/2860 Sch.2 para.50, Sch.2 para.52, Sch.2 para.53, Sch.2 para.55
s.90, applied: SI 2008/2860 Sch.2 para.49, Sch.2 para.50
s.90, referred to: SI 2008/2860 Sch.2 para.51
s.91, applied: SI 2008/2860 Sch.2 para.50
s.95, applied: SI 2008/2860 Sch.2 para.52, Sch.2 para.53, Sch.2 para.54, Sch.2 para.55
s.103, amended: SI 2008/948 Sch.1 para.63
s.104, amended: SI 2008/948 Sch.1 para.64
s.114, applied: SI 2008/2860 Sch.2 para.57
s.120, applied: SI 2008/2860 Sch.2 para.67
s.121, applied: SI 2008/2860 Sch.2 para.42
s.122, applied: SI 2008/2860 Sch.2 para.41, Sch.2 para.59, Sch.2 para.60, Sch.2 para.71, Sch.2 para.74
s.122, referred to: SI 2008/2860 Sch.2 para.71
s.124, applied: SI 2008/2860 Sch.2 para.67
s.126, amended: SI 2008/948 Sch.1 para.65
s.128, applied: SI 2008/2860 Sch.2 para.48, Sch.2 para.62, Sch.2 para.63
s.129, applied: SI 2008/2860 Sch.2 para.64, Sch.2 para.65, Sch.2 para.66
s.131, amended: SI 2008/948 Sch.1 para.66
s.136, see *Martin Currie Ltd, Petitioners* 2008 S.L.T. 57 (OH), Lord Drummond Young
s.136, amended: SI 2008/719 Reg.2

CAP.

1985–cont.

6. Companies Act 1985–*cont.*

s.136, applied: SI 2008/2860 Sch.2 para.68
s.137, applied: SI 2008/729 Reg.3, Reg.4
s.138, applied: SI 2008/729 Reg.5
s.139, applied: SI 2008/729 Reg.3, Reg.5
s.140, applied: SI 2008/1886 Art.7, SI 2008/2860 Sch.2 para.69
s.143, amended: SI 2008/948 Sch.1 para.67
s.143, applied: SI 2008/409 Sch.5 para.6, SI 2008/410 Sch.7 para.8
s.143, referred to: SI 2008/1579 Reg.6
s.146, applied: SI 2008/409 Sch.5 para.6, SI 2008/410 Sch.7 para.8, SI 2008/729 Reg.3, Reg.5, Reg.6, SI 2008/2860 Sch.2 para.70
s.146, referred to: SI 2008/2860 Sch.2 para.70
s.147, applied: SI 2008/729 Reg.5, SI 2008/2860 Sch.2 para.72
s.148, referred to: SI 2008/2860 Sch.2 para.70
s.149, amended: SI 2008/948 Sch.1 para.68
s.149, applied: SI 2008/729 Reg.6
s.150, applied: SI 2008/409 Sch.5 para.6, SI 2008/410 Sch.7 para.8
s.151, see *AMG Global Nominees (Private) Ltd v SMM Holdings Ltd* [2008] EWHC 221 (Ch), [2008] B.C.C. 307 (Ch D), Evans-Lombe, J.
s.152, amended: SI 2008/948 Sch.1 para.69
s.152, applied: SI 2008/948 Art.9
s.153, amended: SI 2008/948 Sch.1 para.70
s.159, applied: SI 2008/2860 Sch.2 para.73
s.162C, amended: SI 2008/948 Sch.1 para.71
s.162D, applied: SI 2008/2860 Sch.2 para.79
s.162F, amended: SI 2008/948 Sch.1 para.72
s.164, see *Dashfield v Davidson* [2008] B.C.C. 222 (Ch D (Bristol)), Judge McCahill Q.C.
s.164, applied: SI 2008/2860 Sch.2 para.76
s.164, referred to: SI 2008/2860 Sch.2 para.75
s.165, applied: SI 2008/2860 Sch.2 para.76
s.165, referred to: SI 2008/2860 Sch.2 para.75
s.166, referred to: SI 2008/2860 Sch.2 para.75
s.167, referred to: SI 2008/2860 Sch.2 para.75
s.169, applied: SI 2008/2860 Sch.2 para.77
s.169A, applied: SI 2008/2860 Sch.2 para.80
s.171, amended: SI 2008/948 Sch.1 para.73
s.171, applied: SI 2008/2860 Sch.2 para.78
s.172, amended: SI 2008/948 Sch.1 para.74, Sch.4
s.172, applied: SI 2008/948 Art.9, SI 2008/2860 Sch.2 para.78
s.173, applied: SI 2008/2860 Sch.2 para.78
s.174, applied: SI 2008/2860 Sch.2 para.78
s.175, applied: SI 2008/2860 Sch.2 para.78

CAP.

1985–cont.

6. Companies Act 1985–*cont.*

s.176, applied: SI 2008/2860 Sch.2 para.78
s.177, applied: SI 2008/2860 Sch.2 para.78
s.178, applied: SI 2008/2860 Sch.2 para.78
s.181, amended: SI 2008/948 Sch.1 para.75
s.185, varied: SI 2008/432 Art.3
s.196, see *Oval 1742 Ltd (In Creditors Voluntary Liquidation), Re* [2007] EWCA Civ 1262, [2008] Bus. L.R. 1213 (CA (Civ Div)), Smith, L.J.
s.196, disapplied: SI 2008/346 Sch.1 para.1
s.221, applied: SI 2008/629 Reg.25, Reg.31
s.225, applied: SI 2008/1911 Reg.7
s.226A, applied: SI 2008/629 Reg.25, Reg.31
s.227, applied: SI 2008/629 Reg.30
s.232, amended: SI 2008/948 Sch.2
s.234, applied: SI 2008/629 Reg.25, Reg.30, Reg.31
s.241, applied: SI 2008/674 Sch.3 para.4
s.242, applied: SI 2008/497 Reg.3, Reg.5
s.242A, amended: SI 2008/497 Reg.3, Reg.5
s.245B, applied: SI 2008/623 Art.6
s.247, applied: SI 2008/552 Reg.39
s.247, referred to: SI 2008/552 Reg.39
s.256, applied: SI 2008/651 Reg.4
s.257, applied: SI 2008/497
s.257, enabling: SI 2008/497
s.258, applied: 2008 c.2 s.15
s.259, applied: 2008 c.2 s.15
s.263, see *AG (Manchester) Ltd (formerly The Accident Group Ltd) (In Liquidation), Re* [2008] EWHC 64 (Ch), [2008] B.C.C. 497 (Ch D (Manchester)), Patten, J.
s.285, applied: SI 2008/432 Sch.1 para.1
s.288, applied: SI 2008/2860 Sch.2 para.25, Sch.2 para.31, Sch.2 para.38
s.289, amended: SI 2008/948 Sch.1 para.77
s.289, applied: SI 2008/2860 Sch.2 para.27, Sch.2 para.31
s.290, amended: SI 2008/948 Sch.1 para.78
s.290, applied: SI 2008/2860 Sch.2 para.27, Sch.2 para.31
s.305, applied: SI 2008/432 Sch.1 para.1
s.317, applied: SI 2008/432 Sch.1 para.1, SI 2008/2644 Art.26, Sch.2 para.1
s.320, see *Lexi Holdings (In Administration) v Luqman* [2008] EWHC 1639 (Ch), [2008] 2 B.C.L.C. 725 (Ch D), Briggs, J.
s.320, applied: SI 2008/432 Sch.1 para.1
s.322, see *Lexi Holdings (In Administration) v Luqman* [2008] EWHC 1639 (Ch), [2008] 2 B.C.L.C. 725 (Ch D), Briggs, J.
s.323, applied: SI 2008/432 Sch.1 para.1
s.324, applied: SI 2008/432 Sch.1 para.1
s.325, applied: SI 2008/432 Sch.1 para.1
s.330, see *Lexi Holdings (In Administration) v Luqman* [2008] EWHC 1639 (Ch), [2008] 2 B.C.L.C. 725 (Ch D), Briggs, J.
s.330, applied: SI 2008/432 Sch.1 para.1

CAP.

1985–cont.

6. **Companies Act 1985**–*cont.*

s.351, amended: SI 2008/948 Sch.1 para.79
s.359, see *AMG Global Nominees (Private) Ltd v SMM Holdings Ltd* [2008] EWHC 221 (Ch), [2008] B.C.C. 307 (Ch D), Evans-Lombe, J.
s.363, applied: SI 2008/1861 Reg.2, SI 2008/2860 Sch.2 para.81
s.363, enabling: SI 2008/1860, SI 2008/1861
s.364, amended: SI 2008/948 Sch.1 para.80, SI 2008/1659 Reg.2
s.364, applied: SI 2008/2860 Sch.2 para.81
s.364, enabling: SI 2008/1659
s.364A, amended: SI 2008/1659 Reg.3
s.364A, applied: SI 2008/2860 Sch.2 para.81
s.364A, repealed (in part): SI 2008/1659 Reg.3
s.364B, added: SI 2008/1659 Reg.4
s.364B, applied: SI 2008/2860 Sch.2 para.81
s.364C, added: SI 2008/1659 Reg.4
s.364C, applied: SI 2008/2860 Sch.2 para.81
s.364D, added: SI 2008/1659 Reg.4
s.364D, applied: SI 2008/2860 Sch.2 para.81
s.365, applied: SI 2008/2860 Sch.2 para.81
s.365, enabling: SI 2008/1659
s.380, amended: SI 2008/948 Sch.1 para.81
s.380, applied: SI 2008/2860 Sch.2 para.14
s.391, applied: SI 2008/1911 Reg.43
s.400, applied: SI 2008/2860 Sch.2 para.83
s.403, applied: SI 2008/2860 Sch.2 para.87
s.405, applied: SI 2008/2860 Sch.2 para.86
s.416, applied: SI 2008/2860 Sch.2 para.83
s.419, applied: SI 2008/2860 Sch.2 para.87
s.425, see *Linton Park Plc, Re* [2005] EWHC 3545 (Ch), [2008] B.C.C. 17 (Ch D), Lewison, J.
s.453D, added: SI 2008/948 Sch.1 para.82
s.458, see *R. v Bright (Michael John)* [2008] EWCA Crim 462, [2008] 2 Cr. App. R. (S.) 102 (CA (Crim Div)), Sir Igor Judge (President, QB)
s.459, see *Cuddy v Hawkes* [2007] EWCA Civ 1072, [2008] B.C.C. 125 (CA (Civ Div)), Chadwick, L.J.; see *Minrealm Ltd, Re* [2007] EWHC 3078 (Ch), [2008] 2 B.C.L.C. 141 (Ch D (Companies Ct)), Morgan, J.
s.651, see *Laroche v Spirit of Adventure (UK) Ltd* [2008] EWHC 788 (QB), [2008] 4 All E.R. 494 (QBD), Eady, J.
s.651, referred to: SI 2008/2860 Sch.2 para.89
s.652, applied: SI 2008/2860 Sch.2 para.91
s.652A, applied: SI 2008/2860 Sch.2 para.91
s.653, applied: SI 2008/2860 Sch.2 para.91

CAP.

1985–cont.

6. **Companies Act 1985**–*cont.*

s.653, referred to: SI 2008/2860 Sch.2 para.89
s.685, amended: SI 2008/948 Sch.1 para.83
s.693, applied: 2008 c.13 Sch.3
s.699, amended: SI 2008/948 Sch.1 para.84
s.701, amended: SI 2008/948 Sch.1 para.85
s.702, amended: SI 2008/948 Sch.1 para.86
s.705, amended: SI 2008/948 Sch.3 para.2
s.707B, applied: SI 2008/2860 Sch.2 para.115
s.708, applied: SI 2008/2860 Sch.2 para.94
s.710A, applied: SI 2008/2860 Sch.2 para.111
s.719, applied: SI 2008/2860 Sch.2 para.40
s.723B, applied: SI 2008/2860 Sch.2 para.36, Sch.2 para.37, Sch.2 para.38, Sch.2 para.39
s.723D, referred to: SI 2008/2860 Sch.2 para.36
s.723E, applied: SI 2008/2860 Sch.2 para.36, Sch.2 para.37
s.726, see *Jirehouse Capital v Beller* [2008] EWCA Civ 908, [2008] C.P. Rep. 44 (CA (Civ Div)), Mummery, L.J.
s.727, see *First Independent Factors and Finance Ltd v Mountford* [2008] EWHC 835 (Ch), [2008] B.C.C. 598 (Ch D (Birmingham)), Lewison, J.; see *Green v Walkling* [2007] EWHC 3251 (Ch), [2008] B.C.C. 256 (Ch D), Bernard Livesey Q.C.; see *Paycheck Services 3 Ltd, Re* [2008] EWHC 2200 (Ch), [2008] S.T.C. 3142 (Ch D (Companies Ct)), Mark Cawson Q.C.
s.733, applied: SI 2008/432 Sch.1 para.1, SI 2008/2644 Art.26, Sch.2 para.1
s.736, applied: 2008 c.2 s.15
s.742, amended: SI 2008/948 Sch.1 para.87
s.742, repealed (in part): SI 2008/948 Sch.2
Sch.1 para.2, amended: SI 2008/948 Sch.1 para.88
Sch.2 Part II para.6, repealed: SI 2008/948 Sch.2
Sch.2 Part II para.7, repealed: SI 2008/948 Sch.2
Sch.2 Part II para.8, repealed: SI 2008/948 Sch.2
Sch.2 Part II para.9, repealed: SI 2008/948 Sch.2
Sch.4 Part VII para.88, referred to: SI 2008/948 Art.9
Sch.4 Part VII para.89, referred to: SI 2008/948 Art.9
Sch.6 Part II para.15, amended: SI 2008/948 Sch.2
Sch.6 Part II para.16, amended: SI 2008/948 Sch.2
Sch.6 Part II para.17, amended: SI 2008/948 Sch.2

CAP.

1985–cont.

6. Companies Act 1985–*cont.*

Sch.6 Part II para.19, amended: SI 2008/948 Sch.2

Sch.6 Part II para.22, amended: SI 2008/948 Sch.2

Sch.6 Part II para.24, amended: SI 2008/948 Sch.2

Sch.6 Part II para.27, repealed (in part): SI 2008/948 Sch.2

Sch.9 Part IV para.3, amended: SI 2008/948 Sch.2

Sch.9 Part IV para.3, repealed (in part): SI 2008/948 Sch.2

Sch.15D para.1, amended: SI 2008/948 Sch.1 para.92

Sch.15D para.17, amended: SI 2008/1277 Sch.2 para.30

Sch.15D para.17, repealed (in part): SI 2008/1277 Sch.2 para.30, Sch.4 Part 1

Sch.21C Part II para.11, amended: SI 2008/948 Sch.1 para.93

Sch.21C Part II para.13, amended: SI 2008/948 Sch.1 para.93

Sch.21D Part II para.9, amended: SI 2008/948 Sch.1 para.94

Sch.21D Part II para.12, amended: SI 2008/948 Sch.1 para.94

Sch.24, applied: SI 2008/2860 Sch.2 para.116

7. Business Names Act 1985

applied: 2008 c.13 Sch.3

9. Companies Consolidation (Consequential Provisions) Act 1985

applied: SI 2008/2546 Art.4, SI 2008/3229 Sch.1, Sch.2, Sch.3

s.3, amended: SI 2008/948 Sch.1 para.95, Sch.2

10. London Regional Transport (Amendment) Act 1985

repealed: 2008 c.12 Sch.1 Part 5

13. Cinemas Act 1985

applied: 2008 c.13 Sch.3

17. Reserve Forces (Safeguard of Employment) Act 1985

applied: SSI 2008/82 Reg.10

21. Films Act 1985

Sch.1 para.4, enabling: SI 2008/1783

22. Dangerous Vessels Act 1985

s.5, referred to: 2008 c.13 Sch.6

23. Prosecution of Offences Act 1985

s.7A, amended: 2008 c.4 s.55

s.7A, repealed (in part): 2008 c.4 s.55, Sch.28 Part 4

s.10, see *R. (on the application of Purdy) v DPP* [2008] EWHC 2565 (Admin), (2008) 104 B.M.L.R. 231 (DC), Scott Baker, L.J.

s.12, repealed: 2008 c.12 Sch.1 Part 3

s.13, repealed: 2008 c.12 Sch.1 Part 3

s.15, amended: 2008 c.4 s.55

s.15, repealed (in part): 2008 c.12 Sch.1 Part 3

s.19, amended: 2008 c.4 Sch.4 para.32

CAP.

1985–cont.

23. Prosecution of Offences Act 1985–*cont.*

s.19, enabling: SI 2008/2448

s.19B, enabling: SI 2008/2448

s.20, enabling: SI 2008/2448

s.21, see *R. v Hayes (Costs)* [2008] 1 Costs L.R. 186 (Sup Ct Costs Office), Costs Judge Gordon-Saker

s.28, repealed: 2008 c.12 Sch.1 Part 3

s.31, repealed (in part): 2008 c.12 Sch.1 Part 3

26. Intoxicating Substances (Supply) Act 1985

applied: 2008 c.13 Sch.3

s.1, referred to: 2008 c.13 Sch.6

30. Ports (Finance) Act 1985

s.4, amended: SI 2008/948 Sch.1 para.1

37. Family Law (Scotland) Act 1985

see *C v S* [2008] CSOH 125, 2008 S.L.T. 871 (OH), Lord Matthews; see *Hodge v Hodge* 2008 Fam. L.R. 51 (Sh Pr), Sheriff Principal BA Lockhart; see *McKinnon v McKinnon* 2008 Fam. L.R. 25 (Sh Pr), Sheriff Principal JA Taylor

s.8, amended: 2008 c.30 Sch.7 para.2

s.8, applied: 2008 c.30 s.109, s.118

s.8, repealed (in part): 2008 c.30 Sch.7 para.2, Sch.11 Part 4

s.8B, added: 2008 c.30 Sch.7 para.3

s.9, amended: 2008 c.22 Sch.6 para.46

s.10, see *Armstrong v Armstrong* 2008 Fam. L.R. 125 (Sh Ct (South Strathclyde) (Dumfries)), Sheriff KA Ross

s.10, amended: 2008 c.30 Sch.7 para.4

s.10, enabling: SSI 2008/293

s.12A, amended: 2008 c.30 Sch.7 para.5

s.12B, added: 2008 c.30 Sch.7 para.6

s.12B, applied: 2008 c.30 s.109

s.13, amended: 2008 c.30 Sch.7 para.7

s.16, amended: 2008 c.30 Sch.7 para.8

s.27, amended: 2008 c.22 Sch.6 para.47, 2008 c.30 Sch.7 para.9

48. Food and Environment Protection Act 1985

applied: 2008 c.29 Sch.5 para.30, Sch.6 para.2, Sch.6 para.5

referred to: SSI 2008/263 Sch.1

Part I, applied: 2008 c.13 Sch.3

Part I, referred to: 2008 c.13 Sch.6

Part II, applied: 2008 c.13 Sch.3, 2008 c.29 s.149, Sch.5 para.29, SI 2008/1261 Art.13, SSI 2008/188 Art.53

Part II, disapplied: SSI 2008/189 Art.53, SSI 2008/190 Art.53

Part II, referred to: 2008 c.13 Sch.6

Part III, referred to: 2008 c.13 Sch.6

s.1, applied: SSI 2008/101 Sch.1 Part 1

s.1, enabling: SSI 2008/63

s.5, applied: SI 2008/969 Art.7

s.5, disapplied: 2008 c.18 Sch.14 para.9

s.7A, substituted: 2008 c.32 Sch.1 para.2

s.16, amended: SI 2008/960 Sch.3

CAP.

1985–cont.

48. Food and Environment Protection Act 1985–*cont.*
s.24, amended: 2008 c.32 Sch.1 para.3
s.24, enabling: SSI 2008/63
s.25, amended: SI 2008/960 Sch.3
Sch.3 para.1, disapplied: 2008 c.29 s.149
Sch.3 para.2, disapplied: 2008 c.29 s.149

49. Surrogacy Arrangements Act 1985
s.1, amended: 2008 c.22 s.59
s.2, amended: 2008 c.22 s.59, Sch.8 Part 1
s.3, amended: 2008 c.22 s.59

50. Representation of the People Act 1985
applied: SI 2008/1741 Reg.14
s.1, applied: SI 2008/1741 Reg.21, Reg.23
s.1, referred to: SI 2008/1741 Reg.20
s.2, applied: SI 2008/1741 Reg.20, Reg.23, Reg.30, Reg.34, Reg.49, Reg.53
s.2, varied: SI 2008/1741 Sch.4
s.2, enabling: SI 2008/1741
s.3, applied: SI 2008/1741 Reg.14
s.3, enabling: SI 2008/1741
s.6, applied: SI 2008/1741 Reg.55, Reg.57, Reg.58, Reg.61, Reg.62, Reg.64, Reg.65, Reg.66
s.6, referred to: SI 2008/1741 Reg.57, Reg.65
s.6, enabling: SI 2008/1741
s.7, applied: SI 2008/1741 Reg.55, Reg.59, Reg.61, Reg.62, Reg.66
s.7, enabling: SI 2008/1741
s.8, applied: SI 2008/1741 Reg.55, Reg.56, Reg.61, Reg.62, Reg.64
s.8, enabling: SI 2008/1741
s.9, applied: SI 2008/1741 Reg.55, Reg.60, Reg.61, Reg.62, Reg.66, Reg.76
s.9, enabling: SI 2008/1741
s.12, varied: SI 2008/1741 Sch.4
s.15, applied: SI 2008/1741 Reg.69
s.15, enabling: SI 2008/1741
s.16, disapplied: SI 2008/2857 Art.3
s.27, applied: SI 2008/1741

51. Local Government Act 1985
Part II, applied: 2008 c.13 Sch.3
Part IV, applied: 2008 c.26 s.77
s.15, applied: SI 2008/622 Reg.2
s.28, amended: 2008 c.26 Sch.4 para.53
s.28, applied: 2008 c.26 s.77, SI 2008/3112 Reg.2
s.29, applied: SI 2008/566, SI 2008/3112 Reg.2
s.29, enabling: SI 2008/566
s.31, applied: SI 2008/3112 Reg.2
s.32, applied: SI 2008/3112 Reg.2
s.35, amended: 2008 c.26 Sch.4 para.53
s.40, amended: 2008 c.26 Sch.4 para.53
s.42, amended: 2008 c.26 s.98, Sch.7 Part 4
s.42, referred to: 2008 c.26 s.98
s.42, repealed (in part): 2008 c.26 s.98, Sch.7 Part 4
Sch.8 para.15, applied: SI 2008/1079 Reg.2

CAP.

1985–cont.

51. Local Government Act 1985–*cont.*
Sch.10, applied: SI 2008/3112 Reg.2
Sch.10 Part II, amended: 2008 c.26 Sch.4 para.53
Sch.10 Part III, amended: 2008 c.26 Sch.4 para.53
Sch.10 Part IV, amended: 2008 c.26 Sch.4 para.53
Sch.10 Part V, amended: 2008 c.26 Sch.4 para.53, SI 2008/566 Art.2
Sch.10 Part VI, amended: 2008 c.26 Sch.4 para.53
Sch.10 Part VII, amended: 2008 c.26 Sch.4 para.53
Sch.12 para.3, repealed (in part): 2008 c.26 Sch.7 Part 4
Sch.14 Part I para.31, repealed (in part): 2008 c.26 Sch.7 Part 4

54. Finance Act 1985
s.10, repealed: 2008 c.9 s.114
s.82, repealed (in part): 2008 c.9 s.100
s.83, repealed (in part): 2008 c.9 Sch.32 para.2
s.84, amended: 2008 c.9 Sch.32 para.3
s.84, repealed (in part): 2008 c.9 Sch.32 para.3

60. Child Abduction and Custody Act 1985
see *G (Children) (Abduction: Withdrawal of Proceedings, Acquiescence, and Habitual Residence), Re* [2007] EWHC 2807 (Fam), [2008] 2 F.L.R. 351 (Fam Div), Sir Mark Potter (President, Fam)

61. Administration of Justice Act 1985
s.21, amended: SI 2008/537 Art.2
s.22, amended: SI 2008/948 Sch.1 para.1
s.50, see *Thomas & Agnes Carvel Foundation v Carvel* [2007] EWHC 1314 (Ch), [2008] Ch. 395 (Ch D), Lewison, J.
Sch.3 para.11, amended: SI 2008/948 Sch.1 para.1
Sch.6 para.15, amended: SI 2008/948 Sch.1 para.10

62. Oil and Pipelines Act 1985
Sch.3 para.9, amended: SI 2008/948 Sch.1 para.1, Sch.1 para.96

66. Bankruptcy (Scotland) Act 1985
applied: SSI 2008/82 Reg.3, SSI 2008/119 r.2, Sch.1 para.2, Sch.1 para.5, Sch.1 para.7, Sch.1 para.8
s.1A, applied: SSI 2008/119 Sch.1 para.9
s.1A, referred to: SSI 2008/143 Reg.17
s.1A, enabling: SSI 2008/119
s.2, applied: SSI 2008/119 Sch.1 para.3
s.5, applied: SSI 2008/82 Reg.12, Reg.14, SSI 2008/119 r.3, Sch.1 para.3
s.5, disapplied: SSI 2008/82 Reg.12
s.5, referred to: SSI 2008/82 Reg.15
s.5, enabling: SSI 2008/82, SSI 2008/334
s.5A, applied: SSI 2008/81 Reg.2, Reg.3
s.5A, enabling: SSI 2008/81

CAP.

1985–cont.

66. Bankruptcy (Scotland) Act 1985–*cont.*
s.6, applied: SSI 2008/119 r.3, SSI 2008/143 Reg.4
s.6, referred to: SSI 2008/82 Reg.14
s.6, enabling: SSI 2008/82
s.7, see *Parkes v MacGregor* 2008 S.C.L.R. 345 (OH), Lady Paton
s.7, applied: SSI 2008/82 Reg.13
s.7, referred to: SSI 2008/82 Reg.15
s.7, enabling: SSI 2008/82
s.8, applied: SSI 2008/143 Reg.12
s.8, enabling: SSI 2008/82
s.9, referred to: SSI 2008/143 Reg.13, Reg.23
s.9, varied: SSI 2008/82 Reg.9
s.11, enabling: SSI 2008/82
s.12, applied: SSI 2008/119 Sch.1 para.15
s.14, applied: SSI 2008/82 Reg.14, SSI 2008/119 Sch.1 para.9
s.14, disapplied: SSI 2008/82 Reg.9
s.14, enabling: SSI 2008/119
s.15, applied: SSI 2008/82 Reg.11, SSI 2008/119 Sch.1 para.8
s.15, disapplied: SSI 2008/82 Reg.9
s.15, referred to: SSI 2008/82 Reg.15
s.15, enabling: SSI 2008/82
s.17, disapplied: SSI 2008/82 Reg.9
s.19, enabling: SSI 2008/82
s.21B, referred to: SSI 2008/82 Reg.16
s.22, applied: SSI 2008/82 Reg.4
s.22, enabling: SSI 2008/82
s.23, applied: SSI 2008/82 Reg.5
s.23, enabling: SSI 2008/82
s.24, applied: SSI 2008/119 Sch.1 para.10
s.24, disapplied: SSI 2008/143 Reg.5
s.25, enabling: SSI 2008/82
s.28, applied: SSI 2008/82 Reg.17
s.28A, enabling: SSI 2008/122
s.29, applied: SSI 2008/119 Sch.1 para.8
s.32, applied: SSI 2008/82 Reg.18, Reg.19, SSI 2008/119 Sch.1 para.6, SSI 2008/228 Reg.49, SSI 2008/235 Reg.12
s.33, applied: SSI 2008/81 Reg.3
s.33, referred to: SSI 2008/143 Reg.6
s.39A, amended: SSI 2008/81 Reg.4
s.39A, enabling: SSI 2008/81
s.40, see *Blackburn v Cowie* [2008] CSIH 30, 2008 S.C. 504 (IH (Ex Div)), Lord Osborne
s.43A, applied: SSI 2008/82 Reg.20
s.45, enabling: SSI 2008/82
s.48, applied: SSI 2008/82 Reg.4
s.48, enabling: SSI 2008/82
s.49, applied: SSI 2008/82 Reg.5
s.49, enabling: SSI 2008/82
s.51, applied: SSI 2008/82 Reg.6
s.51, enabling: SSI 2008/82
s.54, applied: SSI 2008/119 Sch.1 para.8, SSI 2008/235 Reg.12
s.54, enabling: SSI 2008/82
s.55, applied: SSI 2008/143 Reg.19
s.56J, applied: SSI 2008/119 Sch.1 para.8

CAP.

1985–cont.

66. Bankruptcy (Scotland) Act 1985–*cont.*
s.57, applied: SSI 2008/119 Sch.1 para.11
s.62, enabling: SSI 2008/119
s.67, enabling: SSI 2008/82
s.69, enabling: SSI 2008/82
s.69A, enabling: SSI 2008/5, SSI 2008/79
s.72, applied: SSI 2008/81, SSI 2008/143
s.72, enabling: SSI 2008/5, SSI 2008/79, SSI 2008/143, SSI 2008/334
s.73, referred to: SSI 2008/82 Reg.14
s.73, enabling: SSI 2008/79, SSI 2008/82, SSI 2008/334
s.74, amended: SSI 2008/82 Reg.8
s.74, enabling: SSI 2008/82
s.75, applied: SSI 2008/235 Reg.12
Sch.3 Part I para.5, applied: SSI 2008/82 Reg.10
Sch.3 Part I para.6, applied: SSI 2008/82 Reg.10
Sch.4 para.8, applied: SSI 2008/119 Sch.1 para.8
Sch.4 para.11, applied: SSI 2008/235 Reg.12
Sch.5, see *Junespear Ltd v Dear* 2008 S.L.T. (Sh Ct) 69 (Sh Pr), Sheriff Principal RA Dunlop Q.C.
Sch.5 para.1, applied: SSI 2008/143 Reg.18
Sch.5 para.1A, applied: SSI 2008/143 Reg.18
Sch.5 para.2, applied: SSI 2008/119 Sch.1 para.9, SSI 2008/143 Reg.19
Sch.5 para.2, enabling: SSI 2008/119
Sch.5 para.5, enabling: SSI 2008/143
Sch.5 para.6, see *Junespear Ltd v Dear* 2008 S.L.T. (Sh Ct) 69 (Sh Pr), Sheriff Principal RA Dunlop Q.C.

67. Transport Act 1985
Part IV, amended: 2008 c.26 Sch.4 para.19
s.2, referred to: SI 2008/1951 Sch.4 para.11
s.3, repealed (in part): 2008 c.12 Sch.1 Part 11
s.6, amended: 2008 c.02 Sch.1 para.2, Sch.2, 2008 c.26 s.48, s.49, s.65
s.6A, added: 2008 c.26 s.48
s.6B, added: 2008 c.26 s.49
s.7, amended: 2008 c.26 s.50
s.7, enabling: SSI 2008/2
s.9, amended: 2008 c.26 s.51
s.9, repealed (in part): 2008 c.26 s.51, Sch.7 Part 3
s.12, amended: 2008 c.26 s.53
s.13, amended: 2008 c.26 s.54
s.13A, added: 2008 c.26 s.54
s.19, amended: 2008 c.26 s.57
s.19, applied: 2008 c.26 s.60
s.20, amended: 2008 c.26 s.58
s.21, amended: 2008 c.26 s.58
s.22, amended: 2008 c.26 s.59, Sch.7 Part 3
s.22, applied: 2008 c.26 s.60
s.23, amended: 2008 c.26 s.59
s.23, referred to: 2008 c.13 Sch.6
s.23, repealed (in part): 2008 c.26 s.59, Sch.7 Part 3

CAP.

1985–cont.

67. Transport Act 1985–*cont.*
s.23A, added: 2008 c.26 s.60
s.23A, referred to: 2008 c.26 s.60
s.26, amended: 2008 c.26 s.44, s.62
s.27A, added: 2008 c.26 s.63
s.27B, added: 2008 c.26 s.63
s.30, referred to: 2008 c.13 Sch.6
s.57, amended: 2008 c.26 Sch.4 para.19
s.58, repealed (in part): 2008 c.26 Sch.7 Part 4
s.60, applied: 2008 c.26 s.66
s.60, repealed (in part): 2008 c.26 s.66, Sch.7 Part 3
s.63, amended: 2008 c.26 s.10, s.68, Sch.4 para.20, Sch.7 Part 1
s.63, repealed (in part): 2008 c.26 s.10, Sch.7 Part 1
s.66, amended: 2008 c.26 s.40
s.72, amended: 2008 c.26 Sch.4 para.22
s.73, amended: 2008 c.26 Sch.4 para.23
s.74, amended: 2008 c.26 Sch.4 para.24
s.74, repealed (in part): 2008 c.26 s.71, Sch.7 Part 3
s.75, amended: 2008 c.26 Sch.4 para.25
s.75, repealed (in part): 2008 c.26 s.71, Sch.7 Part 3
s.76, amended: SI 2008/948 Sch.1 para.11
s.77, amended: SI 2008/948 Sch.1 para.11
s.79, amended: 2008 c.26 Sch.4 para.26, Sch.7 Part 3
s.79, repealed (in part): 2008 c.26 s.71, Sch.7 Part 3
s.80, amended: 2008 c.26 Sch.4 para.27
s.81, amended: 2008 c.26 Sch.4 para.28
s.84, amended: 2008 c.26 Sch.4 para.29
s.85, amended: 2008 c.26 Sch.4 para.30
s.86, amended: 2008 c.26 Sch.4 para.31
s.89, repealed (in part): 2008 c.26 s.10, Sch.7 Part 1
s.90, amended: 2008 c.26 s.70
s.93, amended: 2008 c.26 Sch.4 para.32
s.95, amended: 2008 c.26 Sch.4 para.33
s.96, amended: 2008 c.26 Sch.4 para.34
s.97, amended: 2008 c.26 Sch.4 para.35
s.101, referred to: 2008 c.13 Sch.6
s.104, amended: 2008 c.26 Sch.4 para.36
s.106, amended: 2008 c.26 Sch.4 para.37
s.125A, added: 2008 c.26 s.73
s.125B, added: 2008 c.26 s.73
s.125C, added: 2008 c.26 s.73
s.126, amended: 2008 c.26 s.52, s.61
s.126, enabling: SI 2008/1465, SI 2008/1470
s.130, amended: 2008 c.26 Sch.4 para.38
s.133, amended: 2008 c.26 Sch.4 para.39
s.134, varied: 2008 c.26 s.60
s.134, enabling: SI 2008/1465, SI 2008/1470
s.135, amended: 2008 c.26 s.73
s.135, varied: 2008 c.26 s.60
s.137, amended: 2008 c.26 Sch.4 para.40

CAP.

1985–cont.

67. Transport Act 1985–*cont.*
Sch.1 para.16, see *Bugbugs Ltd v Transport for London* [2007] EWHC 2987 (QB), [2008] R.T.R. 21 (QBD), Swift, J.
Sch.3 para.18, repealed (in part): 2008 c.26 Sch.7 Part 4
Sch.4, referred to: 2008 c.26 s.75
Sch.4 para.9, amended: 2008 c.26 s.76
Sch.4 para.11, enabling: SI 2008/2142
Sch.5 para.2, amended: 2008 c.26 s.72

68. Housing Act 1985
see *Mansfield DC v Langridge* [2008] EWCA Civ 264, [2008] H.L.R. 34 (CA (Civ Div)), Sir Mark Potter (President, Fam); see *McCann v United Kingdom (19009/04)* [2008] 2 F.L.R. 899 (ECHR), Judge Garlicki (President); see *Westminster City Council v Boraliu* [2007] EWCA Civ 1339, [2008] 1 W.L.R. 2408 (CA (Civ Div)), Chadwick, L.J.
applied: SI 2008/2839 Art.2
Part IV, applied: SI 2008/188 Sch.1 para.1
Part V, applied: 2008 c.17 s.149, s.173, s.180
Part VIII, applied: 2008 c.13 Sch.3
Part IX, applied: 2008 c.13 Sch.3
Part X, applied: 2008 c.13 Sch.3
Part IV, see *Jones v Merton LBC* [2008] EWCA Civ 660, [2008] 4 All E.R. 287 (CA (Civ Div)), Arden, L.J.
Part V, see *Hanoman v Southwark LBC* [2008] EWCA Civ 624, Times, June 24, 2008 (CA (Civ Div)), Sir Anthony Clarke, M.R.; see *Islington LBC v Honeygan-Green* [2008] EWCA Civ 363, [2008] 1 W.L.R. 1350 (CA (Civ Div)), Pill, L.J.
s.4, amended: SI 2008/3002 Sch.1 para.3
s.5, varied: SI 2008/2839 Sch.1 para.2
s.6A, amended: SI 2008/3002 Sch.1 para.4
s.6A, varied: SI 2008/2839 Sch.1 para.2
s.27, applied: SI 2008/239 Sch.2 para.22, SI 2008/2361 Reg.16, Reg.19, Reg.21
s.27, enabling: SI 2008/2361
s.27AB, amended: 2008 c.17 s.295
s.27AB, applied: 2008 c.17 Sch.11 para.22, SI 2008/2361 Reg.21
s.27AB, enabling: SI 2008/2361
s.30, amended: SI 2008/3002 Sch.1 para.5
s.32, see *Swords v Secretary of State for Communities and Local Government* [2007] EWCA Civ 795, [2008] H.L.R. 17 (CA (Civ Div)), Smith, L.J.
s.34, amended: 2008 c.17 Sch.14 para.1
s.34, applied: 2008 c.17 s.274
s.34A, added: 2008 c.17 s.296
s.36, amended: 2008 c.17 s.307
s.41, applied: 2008 c.17 s.274
s.43, see *Swords v Secretary of State for Communities and Local Government* [2007] EWCA Civ 795, [2008] H.L.R. 17 (CA (Civ Div)), Smith, L.J.
s.43, amended: 2008 c.17 Sch.14 para.1

CAP.

1985–*cont.*

68. Housing Act 1985–*cont.*

s.45, amended: SI 2008/3002 Sch.1 para.6
s.45, varied: SI 2008/2839 Sch.1 para.2
s.50, amended: SI 2008/3002 Sch.1 para.7, Sch.3
s.51, amended: SI 2008/948 Sch.1 para.1, SI 2008/3002 Sch.1 para.8
s.57, amended: SI 2008/3002 Sch.1 para.9
s.79, see *Mansfield DC v Langridge* [2008] EWCA Civ 264, [2008] H.L.R. 34 (CA (Civ Div)), Sir Mark Potter (President, Fam)
s.80, amended: SI 2008/3002 Sch.1 para.10
s.82, amended: 2008 c.17 Sch.11 para.2
s.84, see *McCann v United Kingdom (19009/04)* [2008] 2 F.L.R. 899 (ECHR), Judge Garlicki (President); see *Wandsworth LBC v Randall* [2007] EWCA Civ 1126, [2008] 1 W.L.R. 359 (CA (Civ Div)), Sir Anthony Clarke, M.R.
s.85, see *Islington LBC v Honeygan-Green* [2008] EWCA Civ 363, [2008] 1 W.L.R. 1350 (CA (Civ Div)), Pill, L.J.; see *Jones v Merton LBC* [2008] EWCA Civ 660, [2008] 4 All E.R. 287 (CA (Civ Div)), Arden, L.J.; see *Porter v Shepherds Bush Housing Association* [2008] EWCA Civ 196, [2008] H.L.R. 35 (CA (Civ Div)), Pill, L.J.; see *Sandwell MBC v Hensley* [2007] EWCA Civ 1425, [2008] H.L.R. 22 (CA (Civ Div)), Sir Andrew Morritt (Chancellor)
s.85, amended: 2008 c.17 Sch.11 para.3, Sch.16
s.85, repealed (in part): 2008 c.17 Sch.11 para.3, Sch.16
s.92, varied: SI 2008/2839 Sch.1 para.2
s.93, see *Malcolm v Lewisham LBC* [2007] EWCA Civ 763, [2008] Ch. 129 (CA (Civ Div)), Arden, L.J.; see *Malcolm v Lewisham LBC* [2008] UKHL 43, [2008] 1 A.C. 1399 (HL), Lord Bingham of Cornhill
s.103, see *Peabody Trust Governors v Reeve* [2008] EWHC 1432 (Ch), [2008] 43 E.G. 196 (Ch D), Gabriel Moss Q.C.
s.105, applied: 2008 c.17 Sch.11 para.22
s.118, see *Laskar v Laskar* [2008] EWCA Civ 347, [2008] 1 W.L.R. 2695 (CA (Civ Div)), Lord Neuberger of Abbotsbury
s.121, see *Islington LBC v Honeygan-Green* [2008] EWCA Civ 363, [2008] 1 W.L.R. 1350 (CA (Civ Div)), Pill, L.J.; see *Manchester City Council v Benjamin* [2008] EWCA Civ 189, [2008] H.L.R. 38 (CA (Civ Div)), Dyson, L.J.
s.121, amended: 2008 c.17 s.304
s.122, see *Islington LBC v Honeygan-Green* [2008] EWCA Civ 363, [2008] 1 W.L.R. 1350 (CA (Civ Div)), Pill, L.J.
s.125D, amended: 2008 c.17 s.306, Sch.16
s.128, amended: 2008 c.17 s.306, Sch.16
s.128A, added: 2008 c.17 s.306
s.128B, added: 2008 c.17 s.306
s.129, see *Laskar v Laskar* [2008] EWCA Civ 347, [2008] 1 W.L.R. 2695 (CA (Civ Div)), Lord Neuberger of Abbotsbury
s.136, amended: 2008 c.17 s.306, Sch.16
s.138, see *Islington LBC v Honeygan-Green* [2008] EWCA Civ 363, [2008] 1 W.L.R. 1350 (CA (Civ Div)), Pill, L.J.
s.140, amended: 2008 c.17 s.306
s.151B, amended: 2008 c.17 s.307
s.151B, applied: SI 2008/2839 Art.2
s.151B, varied: SI 2008/2839 Sch.1 para.2
s.153A, see *Hanoman v Southwark LBC* [2008] EWCA Civ 624, Times, June 24, 2008 (CA (Civ Div)), Sir Anthony Clarke, M.R.; see *Southwark LBC v Dennett* [2007] EWCA Civ 1091, [2008] H.L.R. 23 (CA (Civ Div)), May, L.J.
s.153B, see *Hanoman v Southwark LBC* [2008] EWCA Civ 624, Times, June 24, 2008 (CA (Civ Div)), Sir Anthony Clarke, M.R.
s.155, see *Hanoman v Southwark LBC* [2008] EWCA Civ 624, Times, June 24, 2008 (CA (Civ Div)), Sir Anthony Clarke, M.R.
s.156, amended: 2008 c.17 s.307
s.156, applied: SI 2008/371 Art.2, SI 2008/2839 Art.2
s.156, repealed (in part): 2008 c.17 Sch.16
s.156, varied: SI 2008/2839 Sch.1 para.2
s.156, enabling: SI 2008/371
s.171, varied: SI 2008/2839 Sch.1 para.2
s.171D, amended: 2008 c.17 s.191
s.171D, applied: 2008 c.17 s.75, s.190
s.181, see *Hanoman v Southwark LBC* [2008] EWCA Civ 624, Times, June 24, 2008 (CA (Civ Div)), Sir Anthony Clarke, M.R.
s.181, amended: 2008 c.17 s.306
s.184, applied: 2008 c.17 s.180
s.294, applied: SI 2008/442 Reg.3, Sch.1 para.8
s.421, amended: SI 2008/3002 Sch.1 para.11
s.422, amended: SI 2008/3002 Sch.1 para.12
s.423, amended: SI 2008/3002 Sch.1 para.13
s.424, amended: SI 2008/3002 Sch.1 para.14
s.425, amended: SI 2008/3002 Sch.1 para.15
s.427, amended: SI 2008/3002 Sch.1 para.16
s.427A, amended: SI 2008/3002 Sch.1 para.17
s.429A, varied: SI 2008/2839 Sch.1 para.2
s.431, amended: SI 2008/3002 Sch.1 para.18
s.434, amended: SI 2008/3002 Sch.1 para.19, Sch.3
s.447, amended: SI 2008/3002 Sch.1 para.20
s.450A, amended: SI 2008/3002 Sch.1 para.21
s.450B, amended: SI 2008/3002 Sch.1 para.22
s.450B, applied: SI 2008/3002 Sch.2 para.6
s.450C, amended: 2008 c.17 s.308

CAP.

1985–cont.

68. Housing Act 1985–*cont.*

s.450C, varied: 2008 c.17 s.308

s.450D, added: 2008 c.17 s.309

s.453, amended: SI 2008/3002 Sch.1 para.23

s.458, amended: SI 2008/3002 Sch.1 para.24

s.459, amended: SI 2008/3002 Sch.1 para.25

s.554, amended: SI 2008/3002 Sch.1 para.26

s.577, amended: SI 2008/3002 Sch.1 para.27

s.609, see *Cantrell v Wycombe DC* [2008] EWCA Civ 866, [2008] 41 E.G. 158 (CA (Civ Div)), Moore-Bick, L.J.

s.610, see *Lawntown Ltd v Camenzuli* [2007] EWCA Civ 949, [2008] 1 W.L.R. 2656 (CA (Civ Div)), Gage, L.J.

s.622, amended: 2008 c.17 s.307, s.316

s.622, applied: 2008 c.29 s.215

Sch.1 para.2, see *Holmes v South Yorkshire Police Authority* [2008] EWCA Civ 51, [2008] H.L.R. 33 (CA (Civ Div)), Sedley, L.J.; see *Wragg v Surrey CC* [2008] EWCA Civ 19, [2008] H.L.R. 30 (CA (Civ Div)), Pill, L.J.

Sch.1 para.2, amended: SI 2008/3002 Sch.1 para.28

Sch.1 para.2, applied: 2008 c.17 s.173

Sch.1 para.2, referred to: 2008 c.17 s.149

Sch.1 para.3, applied: 2008 c.17 s.173

Sch.1 para.3, referred to: 2008 c.17 s.149

Sch.1 para.4, see *Westminster City Council v Boraliu* [2007] EWCA Civ 1339, [2008] 1 W.L.R. 2408 (CA (Civ Div)), Chadwick, L.J.

Sch.1 para.4, applied: 2008 c.17 s.173

Sch.1 para.4, referred to: 2008 c.17 s.149

Sch.1 para.4A, applied: 2008 c.17 s.173

Sch.1 para.4A, referred to: 2008 c.17 s.149

Sch.1 para.4B, applied: 2008 c.17 s.173

Sch.1 para.4B, referred to: 2008 c.17 s.149

Sch.1 para.4ZA, applied: 2008 c.17 s.173

Sch.1 para.4ZA, referred to: 2008 c.17 s.149

Sch.1 para.4ZA, added: 2008 c.17 s.297

Sch.1 para.4ZA, applied: 2008 c.17 s.173

Sch.1 para.4ZA, referred to: 2008 c.17 s.149

Sch.1 para.5, applied: 2008 c.17 s.173

Sch.1 para.5, referred to: 2008 c.17 s.149

Sch.1 para.6, see *Westminster City Council v Boraliu* [2007] EWCA Civ 1339, [2008] 1 W.L.R. 2408 (CA (Civ Div)), Chadwick, L.J.

Sch.1 para.6, applied: 2008 c.17 s.173

Sch.1 para.6, referred to: 2008 c.17 s.149

Sch.1 para.7, applied: 2008 c.17 s.173

Sch.1 para.7, referred to: 2008 c.17 s.149

Sch.1 para.8, applied: 2008 c.17 s.173

Sch.1 para.8, referred to: 2008 c.17 s.149

Sch.1 para.9, applied: 2008 c.17 s.173

Sch.1 para.9, referred to: 2008 c.17 s.149

CAP.

1985–cont.

68. Housing Act 1985–*cont.*

Sch.1 para.10, applied: 2008 c.17 s.173

Sch.1 para.10, referred to: 2008 c.17 s.149

Sch.1 para.11, applied: 2008 c.17 s.173

Sch.1 para.11, referred to: 2008 c.17 s.149

Sch.1 para.12, applied: 2008 c.17 s.173, SI 2008/188 Sch.1 para.1

Sch.1 para.12, referred to: 2008 c.17 s.149

Sch.1 para.12ZA, added: 2008 c.17 s.297

Sch.2, see *Manchester City Council v Benjamin* [2008] EWCA Civ 189, [2008] H.L.R. 38 (CA (Civ Div)), Dyson, L.J.; see *Sandwell MBC v Hensley* [2007] EWCA Civ 1425, [2008] H.L.R. 22 (CA (Civ Div)), Sir Andrew Morritt (Chancellor); see *Wandsworth LBC v Randall* [2007] EWCA Civ 1126, [2008] 1 W.L.R. 359 (CA (Civ Div)), Sir Anthony Clarke, M.R.

Sch.2 Part I, amended: SI 2008/3002 Sch.1 para.29

Sch.2 Part I, applied: 2008 c.17 Sch.11 para.21

Sch.2 Part II, varied: SI 2008/2839 Sch.1 para.2

Sch.2 Part III, amended: SI 2008/3002 Sch.1 para.29

Sch.2 Part V para.6, varied: SI 2008/2839 Sch.1 para.2

Sch.3A, see *Swords v Secretary of State for Communities and Local Government* [2007] EWCA Civ 795, [2008] H.L.R. 17 (CA (Civ Div)), Smith, L.J.

Sch.3 Part 1, amended: 2008 c.17 Sch.11 para.4

Sch.3 Part 5, amended: SI 2008/3002 Sch.1 para.30

Sch.3A para.3, amended: 2008 c.17 s.294

Sch.3A para.3, applied: 2008 c.17 s.294, Sch.11 para.22

Sch.3A para.4, applied: 2008 c.17 Sch.11 para.22

Sch.3A para.5, amended: 2008 c.17 s.294

Sch.3A para.5A, added: 2008 c.17 s.294

Sch.3A para.6, see *Swords v Secretary of State for Communities and Local Government* [2007] EWCA Civ 795, [2008] H.L.R. 17 (CA (Civ Div)), Smith, L.J.

Sch.4, applied: 2008 c.17 Sch.11 para.21

Sch.4 para.4, see *Manchester City Council v Benjamin* [2008] EWCA Civ 189, [2008] H.L.R. 38 (CA (Civ Div)), Dyson, L.J.

Sch.4 para.7, amended: SI 2008/3002 Sch.1 para.31

Sch.4 para.7, varied: SI 2008/2839 Sch.1 para.2

Sch.4 para.7B, added: SI 2008/3002 Sch.1 para.31

Sch.5 para.3, amended: 2008 c.17 Sch.8 para.35

Sch.5 para.5, amended: SI 2008/3002 Sch.1 para.32

Sch.5 para.11, amended: 2008 c.17 s.310

CAP.

1985–cont.

68. Housing Act 1985–*cont.*
Sch.5 para.13, amended: 2008 c.17 Sch.13 para.2, Sch.16
Sch.5 para.15, amended: 2008 c.17 Sch.13 para.3
Sch.5 para.15A, added: 2008 c.17 Sch.13 para.4
Sch.5 para.16, amended: 2008 c.17 Sch.13 para.5
Sch.5A para.1, amended: 2008 c.17 Sch.13 para.7
Sch.5A para.2, amended: 2008 c.17 Sch.13 para.8
Sch.5A para.3, amended: 2008 c.17 Sch.13 para.9
Sch.5A para.3A, added: 2008 c.17 Sch.13 para.10
Sch.5A para.4, amended: 2008 c.17 Sch.13 para.11
Sch.5A para.5, amended: 2008 c.17 s.310, Sch.13 para.12
Sch.5A para.6, amended: 2008 c.17 Sch.13 para.13
Sch.6 Part III para.16D, enabling: SI 2008/533

69. Housing Associations Act 1985
s.1, applied: 2008 c.17 s.97, s.115, s.122
s.1, referred to: SI 2008/794 Sch.9 para.13
s.2B, referred to: 2008 c.17 s.97
s.9, amended: 2008 c.17 Sch.9 para.9
s.9, applied: SI 2008/2839 Art.2
s.9, varied: SI 2008/2839 Sch.1 para.3
s.10, amended: 2008 c.17 Sch.9 para.10
s.10, applied: SI 2008/2839 Art.2
s.10, repealed (in part): 2008 c.17 Sch.9 para.10, Sch.16
s.10, varied: SI 2008/2839 Sch.1 para.3
s.30, applied: 2008 c.17 s.262
s.33A, applied: SI 2008/2839 Art.2
s.33A, repealed: 2008 c.17 s.64, Sch.16
s.33A, varied: SI 2008/2839 Sch.1 para.3
s.41, applied: 2008 c.17 s.77
s.54, applied: 2008 c.17 s.274
s.55, applied: 2008 c.17 s.274
s.69, applied: SI 2008/2839 Art.2
s.69, varied: SI 2008/2839 Sch.1 para.3
s.74, referred to: SI 2008/2839 Sch.1 para.3, Sch.1 para.5
s.74, varied: SI 2008/2839 Sch.1 para.3
s.75, applied: SI 2008/2839 Art.2
s.75, disapplied: SI 2008/2839 Art.2
s.75, referred to: SI 2008/2839 Sch.1 para.3, Sch.1 para.5
s.75, varied: SI 2008/2839 Sch.1 para.3
s.76, varied: SI 2008/2839 Sch.1 para.3
s.77, applied: SI 2008/2839 Art.2
s.77, varied: SI 2008/2839 Sch.1 para.3
s.79, applied: 2008 c.17 s.274, SI 2008/2839 Art.2
s.79, varied: SI 2008/2839 Sch.1 para.3
s.80, applied: SI 2008/2839 Art.2

CAP.

1985–cont.

69. Housing Associations Act 1985–*cont.*
s.80, varied: SI 2008/2839 Sch.1 para.3
s.81, applied: SI 2008/2839 Art.2
s.81, varied: SI 2008/2839 Sch.1 para.3
s.82, applied: SI 2008/2839 Art.2
s.83, applied: SI 2008/2839 Art.2
s.83, varied: SI 2008/2839 Sch.1 para.3
s.84, referred to: SI 2008/2839 Sch.1 para.3, Sch.1 para.5
s.85, amended: SI 2008/3002 Sch.1 para.34
s.87, applied: SI 2008/2839 Art.2
s.87, varied: SI 2008/2839 Sch.1 para.3
s.88, referred to: SI 2008/2839 Sch.1 para.3, Sch.1 para.5
s.89, referred to: SI 2008/2839 Sch.1 para.3, Sch.1 para.5
s.90, referred to: SI 2008/2839 Sch.1 para.3, Sch.1 para.5
s.97, amended: SI 2008/948 Sch.1 para.1
s.106, amended: SI 2008/3002 Sch.1 para.35, Sch.3
Sch.1 para.2, applied: 2008 c.17 s.274
Sch.1 para.3, applied: 2008 c.17 s.274
Sch.5 Part I para.6, varied: SI 2008/2839 Sch.1 para.3
Sch.5 Part VI para.2, varied: SI 2008/2839 Sch.1 para.3
Sch.7, applied: SI 2008/2839 Art.2
Sch.7 para.1, varied: SI 2008/2839 Sch.1 para.3
Sch.7 para.2, varied: SI 2008/2839 Sch.1 para.3
Sch.7 para.3, varied: SI 2008/2839 Sch.1 para.3
Sch.7 para.4, varied: SI 2008/2839 Sch.1 para.3
Sch.7 para.5, varied: SI 2008/2839 Sch.1 para.3

70. Landlord and Tenant Act 1985
see *Eltham Properties Ltd v Kenny* [2008] L. & T.R. 14 (Lands Tr), AJ Trott FRICS
s.18, see *King v Udlaw Ltd* [2008] L. & T.R. 28 (Lands Tr), George Bartlett Q.C. (President)
s.20, see *Islington LBC v Abdel-Malek* [2008] L. & T.R. 2 (Lands Tr), AJ Trott FRICS
s.20B, see *Islington LBC v Abdel-Malek* [2008] L. & T.R. 2 (Lands Tr), AJ Trott FRICS
s.20ZA, see *Eltham Properties Ltd v Kenny* [2008] L. & T.R. 14 (Lands Tr), AJ Trott FRICS
s.21, substituted: 2008 c.17 Sch.12 para.2
s.21A, amended: 2008 c.17 Sch.12 para.3
s.22, amended: 2008 c.17 Sch.12 para.4
s.23, amended: 2008 c.17 Sch.12 para.5
s.23A, amended: 2008 c.17 Sch.12 para.6
s.26, amended: 2008 c.17 Sch.12 para.7
s.27, amended: 2008 c.17 Sch.12 para.8
s.28, amended: SI 2008/948 Sch.1 para.1
s.28, repealed: 2008 c.17 Sch.12 para.9, Sch.16

CAP.

1985–cont.

70. Landlord and Tenant Act 1985–*cont.*
s.38, amended: 2008 c.17 Sch.8 para.36
s.39, amended: 2008 c.17 Sch.12 para.10, Sch.16

72. Weights and Measures Act 1985
applied: 2008 c.13 Sch.3
Part II, referred to: 2008 c.13 Sch.6
Part III, referred to: 2008 c.13 Sch.6
Part IV, referred to: 2008 c.13 Sch.6
Part V, referred to: 2008 c.13 Sch.6
Part VI, referred to: 2008 c.13 Sch.6
Part VII, referred to: 2008 c.13 Sch.6
s.11A, amended: SI 2008/3262 Art.2
s.15, enabling: SI 2008/738
s.22, applied: 2008 c.13 Sch.7
s.29, applied: SI 2008/1277 Sch.3 para.9, Sch.3 para.11
s.29, repealed: SI 2008/1277 Sch.4 Part 1
s.72, applied: 2008 asp 4 s.21, SI 2008/1430 Reg.15, SI 2008/2852 Sch.7 para.5
s.86, enabling: SI 2008/738
Sch.12 para.2, repealed: SI 2008/576 Sch.5 para.7
Sch.12 para.3, repealed: SI 2008/1277 Sch.4 Part 1
Sch.12 para.4, repealed: SI 2008/1277 Sch.4 Part 1

73. Law Reform (Miscellaneous Provisions) (Scotland) Act 1985
s.4, see *Tawne Overseas Holdings Ltd v Firm of Newmiln Farm* [2008] CSOH 12, 2008 Hous. L.R. 18 (OH), Lord Malcolm
s.22, amended: 2008 asp 6 s.23, s.64

1986

5. Agricultural Holdings Act 1986
s.49, see *Shirley Children's Settlement Trustees v Crabtree* [2007] EWHC 1532 (Admin), [2008] 1 W.L.R. 18 (QBD (Admin)), Beatson, J.
s.50, see *Shirley Children's Settlement Trustees v Crabtree* [2007] EWHC 1532 (Admin), [2008] 1 W.L.R. 18 (QBD (Admin)), Beatson, J.
s.53, see *Shirley Children's Settlement Trustees v Crabtree* [2007] EWHC 1532 (Admin), [2008] 1 W.L.R. 18 (QBD (Admin)), Beatson, J.
Sch.6 Part I para.3, applied: SI 2008/253 Art.2, SI 2008/2708 Art.2, SI 2008/3200 Art.2
Sch.6 Part I para.4, enabling: SI 2008/253, SI 2008/2708, SI 2008/3200

14. Animals (Scientific Procedures) Act 1986
see *Secretary of State for the Home Department v British Union for the Abolition of Vivisection* [2008] EWCA Civ 870, Times, August 5, 2008 (CA (Civ Div)), Lord Phillips of Worth Matravers, L.C.J.

CAP.

1986–cont.

14. Animals (Scientific Procedures) Act 1986–*cont.*
applied: 2008 c.3 Sch.2 Part 2, Sch.2 Part 3, 2008 c.8 Sch.2 Part 9, SI 2008/2297 Reg.3, Reg.25, Sch.7 para.48
disapplied: SI 2008/1040 Reg.3
referred to: 2008 c.13 Sch.6
s.24, see *Secretary of State for the Home Department v British Union for the Abolition of Vivisection* [2008] EWCA Civ 870, Times, August 5, 2008 (CA (Civ Div)), Lord Phillips of Worth Matravers, L.C.J.

20. Horticultural Produce Act 1986
referred to: 2008 c.13 Sch.6

31. Airports Act 1986
s.8, amended: SI 2008/948 Sch.1 para.97
s.13, amended: 2008 c.26 Sch.4 para.54
s.22, amended: SI 2008/948 Sch.1 para.12
s.23, amended: SI 2008/948 Sch.1 para.12
s.35, enabling: SI 2008/2562
s.40, amended: SI 2008/948 Sch.1 para.97
s.40, enabling: SI 2008/2702
s.57, amended: 2008 c.26 Sch.4 para.54
s.69, applied: SI 2008/1909 Sch.1
s.73, applied: SI 2008/1909 Sch.1
s.74, amended: SI 2008/1277 Sch.2 para.32
s.74, repealed (in part): SI 2008/1277 Sch.4 Part 1

32. Drug Trafficking Offences Act 1986
see *Togher v Revenue and Customs Prosecution Office* [2007] EWCA Civ 686, [2008] Q.B. 476 (CA (Civ Div)), Chadwick, L.J.

33. Disabled Persons (Services, Consultation and Representation) Act 1986
s.7, amended: SI 2008/2833 Sch.3 para.70

35. Protection of Military Remains Act 1986
s.1, applied: SSI 2008/432 Sch.5 para.14
s.1, enabling: SI 2008/950

41. Finance Act 1986
s.66, repealed (in part): 2008 c.9 Sch.32 para.5
s.67, amended: 2008 c.9 Sch.32 para.6, Sch.32 para.14
s.70, amended: 2008 c.9 Sch.32 para.7, Sch.32 para.15
s.72A, amended: 2008 c.9 Sch.32 para.8
s.78, amended: 2008 c.9 s.154
s.79, amended: 2008 c.9 s.101, s.154
s.89AA, amended: SI 2008/3236 Reg.2
s.89AA, enabling: SI 2008/3236
s.97A, see *HSBC Holdings Plc v Revenue and Customs Commissioners* [2008] S.T.C. (S.C.D.) 502 (Sp Comm), John Clark
s.99, amended: 2008 c.9 s.154
s.102, see *Taylor v Revenue and Customs Commissioners* [2008] S.T.C. (S.C.D.) 1159 (Sp Comm), Nuala Brice

CAP.

1986–cont.

44. Gas Act 1986

Part I, applied: 2008 c.32 s.90, s.94, SI 2008/188 Art.23, SI 2008/2375 Reg.3
Part I, referred to: 2008 c.28 s.89
s.4A, amended: SI 2008/960 Sch.3
s.4A, applied: 2008 c.32 s.102
s.4A, disapplied: 2008 c.28 s.89
s.4AA, amended: 2008 c.32 s.83, s.102
s.4AA, applied: 2008 c.32 s.102
s.4AA, disapplied: 2008 c.28 s.89
s.4AA, repealed (in part): 2008 c.32 s.83, Sch.6
s.4AB, applied: 2008 c.32 s.102
s.4AB, disapplied: 2008 c.28 s.89
s.4B, applied: 2008 c.32 s.102
s.6A, applied: SI 2008/2375 Sch.2 para.2
s.7, applied: 2008 c.28 s.87, s.88, 2008 c.32 s.88, s.94, SI 2008/2551 Reg.4
s.7A, applied: 2008 c.32 s.88, SI 2008/188 Art.4, SI 2008/1898 Reg.4, SI 2008/2375 Sch.2 para.3, SI 2008/2551 Reg.4
s.7A, referred to: SI 2008/2375 Sch.2 para.1
s.7B, applied: 2008 c.32 s.88, SI 2008/2375 Reg.8
s.7B, enabling: SI 2008/2375
s.8, applied: 2008 c.32 s.88, s.94
s.8, referred to: SI 2008/2375 Reg.6
s.10, referred to: SI 2008/2375 Sch.2 para.2
s.17, amended: 2008 c.32 s.93, Sch.6
s.17, applied: 2008 c.32 s.92, s.94
s.18, applied: 2008 c.13 Sch.7
s.19E, amended: SI 2008/948 Sch.1 para.98
s.33A, enabling: SI 2008/696
s.33AA, applied: SI 2008/696
s.33AA, enabling: SI 2008/696
s.33BAA, applied: SI 2008/696
s.33BC, amended: 2008 c.27 Sch.8 para.1
s.33BC, applied: SI 2008/188
s.33BC, enabling: SI 2008/188
s.33D, enabling: SI 2008/696
s.34, amended: SI 2008/960 Sch.3
s.41E, amended: SI 2008/960 Sch.3
s.41HA, added: 2008 c.32 Sch.4 para.1
s.41HB, added: 2008 c.32 Sch.4 para.1
s.41HC, added: 2008 c.32 Sch.4 para.1
s.47, applied: 2008 c.13 Sch.7
s.47, enabling: SI 2008/696, SI 2008/2375
s.64, amended: 2008 c.32 Sch.5 para.2

45. Insolvency Act 1986

see *Avis v Turner* [2007] EWCA Civ 748, [2008] Ch. 218 (CA (Civ Div)), Ward, L.J.; see *Halabi v Camden LBC* [2008] EWHC 322 (Ch), [2008] B.P.I.R. 370 (Ch D), John Jarvis Q.C.; see *Jones (A Bankrupt), Re* [2008] 2 F.L.R. 1969 (Ch D), Chief Registrar Baister; see *Official Receiver v Bathurst* [2008] EWHC 1724 (Ch), [2008] B.P.I.R. 1548 (Ch D), Sir Andrew Morritt (Chancellor); see *Pannell v Official Receiver* [2008] EWHC 736 (Ch), [2008] B.P.I.R. 629 (Ch D (Bristol)), Judge

CAP.

1986–cont.

45. Insolvency Act 1986–*cont.*

see–*cont.*

Havelock-Allan Q.C.; see *Phoenix Kapitaldienst GmbH, Re* [2008] B.P.I.R. 1082 (Ch D), Registrar Jacques; see *R. v Neuberg (Karen Jayne)* [2007] EWCA Crim 1994, [2008] 1 Cr. App. R. (S.) 84 (CA (Crim Div)), Leveson, L.J.; see *Rich (A Bankrupt), Re* [2008] B.P.I.R. 485 (CC (Bristol)), Judge Weeks Q.C.; see *Ruttle Plant Hire Ltd v Secretary of State for the Environment Food and Rural Affairs* [2007] EWHC 2870 (TCC), [2008] 2 All E.R. (Comm) 264 (QBD (TCC)), Ramsey, J.

applied: 2008 c.17 s.162, s.164, s.166, s.167, SI 2008/50 Sch.1 para.8, SI 2008/386 Reg.4, SI 2008/1053 Sch.1, SI 2008/1734 Sch.1 para.8, SI 2008/1748 Sch.2 para.4, SI 2008/1790 Sch.1 para.8, SI 2008/2499 Reg.4, SI 2008/2644 Art.19, SI 2008/3084 Sch.1 para.8
disapplied: 2008 c.17 s.167, 2008 c.32 s.56, SI 2008/2644 Art.21, SI 2008/2674 Art.22
Part I, applied: 2008 c.17 s.160, SI 2008/653 Reg.15, Reg.16, SSI 2008/224 Reg.15
Part III, applied: SI 2008/653 Reg.15, Reg.16, SSI 2008/224 Reg.15
Part IV, applied: SI 2008/653 Reg.15, Reg.16, SI 2008/1185 Sch.1 para.44, SSI 2008/224 Reg.15
Part V, applied: SI 2008/653 Reg.15, Reg.16, SSI 2008/224 Reg.15
s.2, applied: SI 2008/1053 Sch.1
s.5, see *Rusjon Ltd (In Liquidation), Re* [2007] EWHC 2943 (Ch), [2008] 2 B.C.L.C. 234 (Ch D (Companies Ct)), Henderson, J
s.6, see *Beloit Walmsley Ltd, Re* [2008] EWHC 1888 (Ch), [2008] B.P.I.R. 1445 (Ch D (Manchester)), Judge Pelling Q.C.
s.7, see *Federal-Mogul Aftermarket UK Ltd, Re* [2008] EWHC 1099 (Ch), [2008] Bus. L.R. 1443 (Ch D (Companies Ct)), David Richards, J.
s.8, varied: SI 2008/948 Sch.1 para.101
s.27, see *Metronet Rail BCV Ltd (In Administration), Re* [2007] EWHC 2697 (Ch), [2008] Bus. L.R. 823 (Ch D), Patten, J.
s.27, varied: SI 2008/948 Sch.1 para.101
s.36, see *Delberry Ltd, Re* [2008] EWHC 925 (Ch), [2008] B.C.C. 653 (Ch D), Terence Mowschenson Q.C.
s.39, amended: SI 2008/1897 Reg.2
s.40, varied: SI 2008/346 Sch.1 para.2
s.43, varied: SI 2008/346 Sch.1 para.2
s.64, amended: SI 2008/1897 Reg.2
s.84, applied: 2008 c.17 s.164
s.107, varied: SI 2008/346 Sch.1 para.2
s.112, see *Cooper v PRG Powerhouse Ltd* [2008] EWHC 498 (Ch), [2008] 2 All E.R. (Comm) 964 (Ch D), Evans-Lombe, J.

CAP.

1986–cont.

45. Insolvency Act 1986–*cont.*

s.112, applied: SI 2008/386 Reg.4, SI 2008/2499 Reg.4

s.115, applied: SI 2008/346 Reg.27

s.122, see *Minrealm Ltd, Re* [2007] EWHC 3078 (Ch), [2008] 2 B.C.L.C. 141 (Ch D (Companies Ct)), Morgan, J.

s.122, amended: SI 2008/948 Sch.1 para.102

s.123, see *Cheyne Finance Plc (In Receivership), Re* [2007] EWHC 2116 (Ch), [2008] 1 B.C.L.C. 732 (Ch D (Companies Ct)), Briggs, J.; see *Cheyne Finance Plc (In Receivership), Re* [2007] EWHC 2402 (Ch), [2008] Bus. L.R. 1562 (Ch D (Companies Ct)), Briggs, J.; see *Hammonds (A Firm) v Pro-Fit USA Ltd* [2007] EWHC 1998 (Ch), [2008] 2 B.C.L.C. 159 (Ch D (Companies Ct)), Warren, J.; see *Minrealm Ltd, Re* [2007] EWHC 3078 (Ch), [2008] 2 B.C.L.C. 141 (Ch D (Companies Ct)), Morgan, J.

s.123, applied: 2008 c.17 s.166, SI 2008/1185 Sch.1 para.17

s.124, see *Minrealm Ltd, Re* [2007] EWHC 3078 (Ch), [2008] 2 B.C.L.C. 141 (Ch D (Companies Ct)), Morgan, J.

s.145, applied: SI 2008/386 Reg.4, SI 2008/2499 Reg.4

s.146, see *Morris, Petitioner* 2008 S.C. 111 (OH), Lord Drummond Young

s.156, varied: SI 2008/346 Sch.1 para.2

s.167, see *Cooper v PRG Powerhouse Ltd* [2008] EWHC 498 (Ch), [2008] 2 All E.R. (Comm) 964 (Ch D), Evans-Lombe, J.

s.175, see *Oval 1742 Ltd (In Creditors Voluntary Liquidation), Re* [2007] EWCA Civ 1262, [2008] Bus. L.R. 1213 (CA (Civ Div)), Smith, L.J.

s.175, varied: SI 2008/346 Sch.1 para.2

s.176A, see *Courts Plc (In Liquidation), Re* [2008] EWHC 2339 (Ch), [2008] B.C.C. 917 (Ch D (Companies Ct)), Blackburne, J.; see *Hydroserve Ltd, Re* [2007] EWHC 3026 (Ch), [2008] B.C.C. 175 (Ch D), Rimer, J.; see *Permacell Finesse Ltd (In Liquidation), Re* [2007] EWHC 3233 (Ch), [2008] B.C.C. 208 (Ch D (Birmingham)), Judge Purle Q.C.; see *Thorniley v Revenue and Customs Commissioners* [2008] EWHC 124 (Ch), [2008] 1 W.L.R. 1516 (Ch D (Companies Ct)), Patten, J.

s.176A, amended: SI 2008/948 Sch.1 para.103

s.176A, varied: SI 2008/346 Sch.1 para.2

s.188, amended: SI 2008/1897 Reg.5

s.206, see *R. (on the application of Griffin) v Richmond Magistrates' Court* [2008] EWHC 84 (Admin), [2008] 1 W.L.R. 1525 (DC), Dyson, L.J.

CAP.

1986–cont.

45. Insolvency Act 1986–*cont.*

s.208, see *R. (on the application of Griffin) v Richmond Magistrates' Court* [2008] EWHC 84 (Admin), [2008] 1 W.L.R. 1525 (DC), Dyson, L.J.

s.212, see *Eurocruit Europe Ltd (In Liquidation), Re* [2007] EWHC 1433 (Ch), [2008] Bus. L.R. 146 (Ch D), Blackburne, J.; see *Gemma Ltd (In Liquidation) v Davies* [2008] EWHC 546 (Ch), [2008] B.C.C. 812 (Ch D (Companies Ct)), Jonathan Gaunt, Q.C.; see *Krug International (UK) Ltd, Re* [2008] EWHC 2256 (Ch), [2008] B.P.I.R. 1512 (Ch D (Birmingham)), Judge Purle Q.C.

s.213, see *Walker v Mark Holt & Co* [2007] EWHC 3324 (Ch), [2008] B.C.C. 458 (Ch D (Bristol)), Judge McCahill Q.C.

s.214, applied: SI 2008/432 Sch.1 para.3, SI 2008/2546 Art.13, SI 2008/2644 Art.26, Sch.2 para.3

s.216, see *Cuddy v Hawkes* [2007] EWCA Civ 1072, [2008] B.C.C. 125 (CA (Civ Div)), Chadwick, L.J.; see *First Independent Factors and Finance Ltd v Mountford* [2008] EWHC 835 (Ch), [2008] B.C.C. 598 (Ch D (Birmingham)), Lewison, J.; see *R. (on the application of Griffin) v Richmond Magistrates' Court* [2008] EWHC 84 (Admin), [2008] 1 W.L.R. 1525 (DC), Dyson, L.J.; see *Revenue and Customs Commissioners v Yousef* [2008] EWHC 423 (Ch), [2008] B.C.C. 805 (Ch D), Judge Purle Q.C.

s.217, see *First Independent Factors and Finance Ltd v Mountford* [2008] EWHC 835 (Ch), [2008] B.C.C. 598 (Ch D (Birmingham)), Lewison, J.; see *Revenue and Customs Commissioners v Yousef* [2008] EWHC 423 (Ch), [2008] B.C.C. 805 (Ch D), Judge Purle Q.C.

s.236, see *Delberry Ltd, Re* [2008] EWHC 925 (Ch), [2008] B.C.C. 653 (Ch D), Terence Mowschenson Q.C.; see *Sefton v Gallucci* [2008] EWHC 738 (Ch), [2008] B.P.I.R. 1588 (Ch D (Birmingham)), Judge Purle Q.C.

s.237, see *Sefton v Gallucci* [2008] EWHC 738 (Ch), [2008] B.P.I.R. 1588 (Ch D (Birmingham)), Judge Purle Q.C.

s.238, see *HHO Licensing Ltd (In Liquidation), Re* [2007] EWHC 2953 (Ch), [2008] 1 B.C.L.C. 223 (Ch D (Companies Ct)), Peter Leaver Q.C.

s.239, see *Gemma Ltd (In Liquidation) v Davies* [2008] EWHC 546 (Ch), [2008] B.C.C. 812 (Ch D (Companies Ct)), Jonathan Gaunt, Q.C.; see *HHO Licensing Ltd (In Liquidation), Re* [2007] EWHC 2953 (Ch), [2008] 1 B.C.L.C. 223 (Ch D (Companies Ct)), Peter Leaver Q.C.

CAP.

1986–cont.

45. Insolvency Act 1986–*cont.*

s.240, see *HHO Licensing Ltd (In Liquidation), Re* [2007] EWHC 2953 (Ch), [2008] 1 B.C.L.C. 223 (Ch D (Companies Ct)), Peter Leaver Q.C.

s.249, applied: SI 2008/432 Sch.1 para.3, SI 2008/2546 Art.13, SI 2008/2644 Art.26, Sch.2 para.3

s.262, see *Monecor (London) Ltd v Ahmed* [2008] B.P.I.R. 458 (Ch D), Paul Chaisty Q.C.

s.267, see *Evans v Clarke Wilmott & Clarke* [2007] EWHC 852 (Ch), [2008] B.P.I.R. 37 (Ch D), Philip Sales Q.C.

s.268, see *Evans v Clarke Wilmott & Clarke* [2007] EWHC 852 (Ch), [2008] B.P.I.R. 37 (Ch D), Philip Sales Q.C.

s.271, see *Revenue and Customs Commissioners v Potter* [2008] B.P.I.R. 1033 (Ch D), Deputy Registrar Nicholas Briggs

s.281, see *R. (on the application of Balding) v Secretary of State for Work and Pensions* [2007] EWCA Civ 1327, [2008] 1 W.L.R. 564 (CA (Civ Div)), Mummery, L.J.

s.282, see *Halabi v Camden LBC* [2008] EWHC 322 (Ch), [2008] B.P.I.R. 370 (Ch D), John Jarvis Q.C.; see *Johnson v Tandrige DC* [2007] EWHC 3325 (Ch), [2008] B.P.I.R. 405 (Ch D), Judge Roger Kaye Q.C.; see *Tetteh v Lambeth LBC* [2008] B.P.I.R. 241 (Ch D), Registrar Nicholls; see *Whig v Whig* [2007] EWHC 1856 (Fam), [2008] 1 F.L.R. 453 (Fam Div), Munby, J.

s.283, see *Avis v Turner* [2007] EWCA Civ 748, [2008] Ch. 218 (CA (Civ Div)), Ward, L.J.

s.283A, see *Lewis v Metropolitan Property Realizations Ltd* [2008] EWHC 2760 (Ch), Times, December 9, 2008 (Ch D), Proudman, J; see *Pannell v Official Receiver* [2008] EWHC 736 (Ch), [2008] B.P.I.R. 629 (Ch D (Bristol)), Judge Havelock-Allan Q.C.

s.288, applied: SI 2008/2546 Art.13

s.292, see *Donaldson v O'Sullivan* [2008] EWHC 387 (Ch), [2008] B.C.C. 328 (Ch D (Bristol)), Judge Havelock-Allan Q.C.

s.297, see *Donaldson v O'Sullivan* [2008] EWHC 387 (Ch), [2008] B.C.C. 328 (Ch D (Bristol)), Judge Havelock-Allan Q.C.

s.298, see *Donaldson v O'Sullivan* [2008] EWHC 387 (Ch), [2008] B.C.C. 328 (Ch D (Bristol)), Judge Havelock-Allan Q.C.

s.303, see *Dadourian Group International Inc v Simms* [2008] EWHC 723 (Ch), [2008] B.P.I.R. 508 (Ch D), Warren, J.; see *Donaldson v O'Sullivan* [2008] EWHC 387 (Ch), [2008] B.C.C. 328 (Ch D (Bristol)), Judge Havelock-Allan Q.C.

CAP.

1986–cont.

45. Insolvency Act 1986–*cont.*

s.305, see *Lewis v Metropolitan Property Realizations Ltd* [2008] EWHC 2760 (Ch), Times, December 9, 2008 (Ch D), Proudman, J

s.305, applied: SI 2008/2546 Art.13

s.306, see *Raymond Saul & Co v Holden* [2008] EWHC 2731 (Ch), [2008] W.T.L.R. 1833 (Ch D), Richard Snowden QC

s.307, see *Arnold v Williams* [2008] EWHC 218 (Ch), [2008] B.P.I.R. 247 (Ch D (Birmingham)), Judge Purle Q.C.

s.307, applied: SI 2008/529 Reg.94, SI 2008/1582 Reg.94

s.310, see *Thurmond v Rajapakse* [2008] B.P.I.R. 283 (Ch D), Registrar Nicholls

s.310, applied: SI 2008/239 Reg.53, SI 2008/529 Reg.94, SI 2008/653 Reg.13, SI 2008/1582 Reg.94, SSI 2008/224 Reg.12

s.310, referred to: SI 2008/653 Reg.13

s.310A, applied: SI 2008/239 Reg.53

s.317, applied: SI 2008/2546 Art.13

s.330, see *Lewis v Metropolitan Property Realizations Ltd* [2008] EWHC 2760 (Ch), Times, December 9, 2008 (Ch D), Proudman, J

s.335A, see *Avis v Turner* [2007] EWCA Civ 748, [2008] Ch. 218 (CA (Civ Div)), Ward, L.J.; see *Turner v Avis* [2008] B.P.I.R. 1143 (Ch D (Liverpool)), Judge Pelling Q.C.

s.339, see *Rich (A Bankrupt), Re* [2008] B.P.I.R. 485 (CC (Bristol)), Judge Weeks Q.C.; see *Singla v Brown* [2007] EWHC 405 (Ch), [2008] Ch. 357 (Ch D), Thomas Ivory Q.C.; see *Stow v Stow* [2008] EWHC 495 (Ch), [2008] Ch. 461 (Ch D), Warren, J.; see *Whig v Whig* [2007] EWHC 1856 (Fam), [2008] 1 F.L.R. 453 (Fam Div), Munby, J.

s.340, see *Jones (A Bankrupt), Re* [2008] 2 F.L.R. 1969 (Ch D), Chief Registrar Baister

s.363, see *Donaldson v O'Sullivan* [2008] EWHC 387 (Ch), [2008] B.C.C. 328 (Ch D (Bristol)), Judge Havelock-Allan Q.C.; see *Expandable Ltd v Rubin* [2008] EWCA Civ 59, [2008] 1 W.L.R. 1099 (CA (Civ Div)), Rix, L.J.

s.375, see *Skeete v Pick* [2007] EWHC 2211 (Ch), [2008] 2 F.L.R. 2043 (Ch D), David Donaldson Q.C.

s.375, applied: SI 2008/50 Sch.1 para.8, SI 2008/1734 Sch.1 para.8, SI 2008/1790 Sch.1 para.8, SI 2008/3084 Sch.1 para.8

s.381, applied: SI 2008/386 Reg.4, SI 2008/2499 Reg.4

s.382, see *Day v Haine* [2007] EWHC 2691 (Ch), [2008] B.C.C. 199 (Ch D (Companies Ct)), Sir Donald Rattee; see *R. (on the application of Balding) v Secretary of State*

CAP.

1986–cont.

45. Insolvency Act 1986–*cont.*

s.382–*cont.*

for Work and Pensions [2007] EWCA Civ 1327, [2008] 1 W.L.R. 564 (CA (Civ Div)), Mummery, L.J.

s.391, applied: SI 2008/3 Art.4

s.411, applied: SI 2008/737

s.411, enabling: SI 2008/662, SI 2008/670, SI 2008/737, SSI 2008/393

s.413, applied: SI 2008/737

s.414, enabling: SI 2008/714, SI 2008/1053

s.415, enabling: SI 2008/714, SI 2008/1053

s.415A, enabling: SI 2008/3, SI 2008/672

s.423, see *Barnett v Semenyuk* [2008] B.P.I.R. 1427 (Ch D), Peter Leaver Q.C.; see *Brittain v Courtway Estates Holdings SA* [2008] EWHC 1791 (Ch), [2008] B.P.I.R. 1229 (Ch D), Evans-Lombe, J.; see *Eurocruit Europe Ltd (In Liquidation), Re* [2007] EWHC 1433 (Ch), [2008] Bus. L.R. 146 (Ch D), Blackburne, J.; see *Giles v Rhind* [2008] EWCA Civ 118, [2008] 3 W.L.R. 1233 (CA (Civ Div)), Buxton, L.J.; see *Griffin v Awoderu* [2008] EWHC 349 (Ch), [2008] B.P.I.R. 877 (Ch D), David Phillips, Q.C.; see *Kali Ltd v Chawla* [2007] EWHC 2357 (Ch), [2008] B.P.I.R. 415 (Ch D), Judge Hodge Q.C.; see *Krug International (UK) Ltd, Re* [2008] EWHC 2256 (Ch), [2008] B.P.I.R. 1512 (Ch D (Birmingham)), Judge Purle Q.C.; see *Stow v Stow* [2008] EWHC 495 (Ch), [2008] Ch. 461 (Ch D), Warren, J.

s.426, see *HIH Casualty & General Insurance Ltd, Re* [2008] UKHL 21, [2008] 1 W.L.R. 852 (HL), Lord Hoffmann; see *Phoenix Kapitaldienst GmbH, Re* [2008] B.P.I.R. 1082 (Ch D), Registrar Jacques

s.429, applied: 2008 c.17 s.266, SI 2008/630 Reg.14, SI 2008/631 Reg.12, SI 2008/1185 Reg.4, Sch.1 para.44, SI 2008/2252 Sch.1 para.13, SI 2008/2553 Art.5, SI 2008/2554 Art.5, SI 2008/2558 Reg.3, SI 2008/2927 Reg.2, SI 2008/3047 Art.5, SI 2008/3148 Sch.1

s.434A, added: SI 2008/948 Sch.1 para.105

s.434B, added: SI 2008/948 Sch.1 para.105

s.434C, added: SI 2008/948 Sch.1 para.105

s.436, see *Raymond Saul & Co v Holden* [2008] EWHC 2731 (Ch), [2008] W.T.L.R. 1833 (Ch D), Richard Snowden QC

Sch.A1 Part I para.3, amended: SI 2008/948 Sch.1 para.99

Sch.A1 Part II para.7, applied: SI 2008/1053 Sch.1

Sch.A1 Part III para.16, amended: SI 2008/1897 Reg.3

Sch.B1, applied: SI 2008/653 Reg.15, Reg.16, SI 2008/1185 Sch.1 para.44, SSI 2008/224 Reg.15

CAP.

1986–cont.

45. Insolvency Act 1986–*cont.*

Sch.B1 Part 1 para.1, applied: SI 2008/386 Reg.4, SI 2008/2499 Reg.4

Sch.B1 Part 1 para.3, applied: SI 2008/2644 Art.20, SI 2008/2674 Art.21

Sch.B1 Part 2 para.12, applied: 2008 c.17 s.144

Sch.B1 Part 2 para.13, applied: 2008 c.17 s.145, SI 2008/2644 Art.13, Art.15, Art.18, Art.24

Sch.B1 para.3, see *Hammonds (A Firm) v Pro-Fit USA Ltd* [2007] EWHC 1998 (Ch), [2008] 2 B.C.L.C. 159 (Ch D (Companies Ct)), Warren, J.

Sch.B1 Part 3 para.14, applied: 2008 c.17 s.144, s.145, SI 2008/1053 Sch.1

Sch.B1 Part 3 para.18, applied: SI 2008/1053 Sch.1

Sch.B1 Part 4 para.22, applied: 2008 c.17 s.144, s.145

Sch.B1 Part 4 para.27, applied: SI 2008/1053 Sch.1

Sch.B1 Part 4 para.29, applied: SI 2008/1053 Sch.1

Sch.B1 Part 6 para.45, substituted: SI 2008/1897 Reg.4

Sch.B1 Part 7 para.46, substituted: SI 2008/1897 Reg.4

Sch.B1 Part 7 para.49, amended: SI 2008/948 Sch.1 para.100

Sch.B1 Part 7 para.49, applied: SI 2008/2644 Art.20, SI 2008/2674 Art.21

Sch.B1 Part 7 para.51, applied: SI 2008/2644 Art.20, SI 2008/2674 Art.21

Sch.B1 Part 7 para.54, applied: SI 2008/2644 Art.20, SI 2008/2674 Art.21

Sch.B1 Part 8 para.62, applied: SI 2008/2644 Art.20, SI 2008/2674 Art.21

Sch.B1 Part 8 para.65, varied: SI 2008/346 Sch.1 para.2

Sch.B1 Part 8 para.66, varied: SI 2008/346 Sch.1 para.2

Sch.B1 Part 8 para.73, amended: SI 2008/948 Sch.1 para.100

Sch.B1 Part 8 para.74, amended: SI 2008/948 Sch.1 para.100

Sch.B1 Part 10 para.99, applied: SI 2008/2644 Art.15, SI 2008/2674 Art.16

Sch.B1 para.11, see *Hammonds (A Firm) v Pro-Fit USA Ltd* [2007] EWHC 1998 (Ch), [2008] 2 B.C.L.C. 159 (Ch D (Companies Ct)), Warren, J.

Sch.B1 para.12, see *Hammonds (A Firm) v Pro-Fit USA Ltd* [2007] EWHC 1998 (Ch), [2008] 2 B.C.L.C. 159 (Ch D (Companies Ct)), Warren, J.

Sch.B1 para.15, see *OMP Leisure Ltd, Re* [2008] B.C.C. 67 (Ch D (Manchester)), Judge Hodge Q.C.

Sch.B1 para.43, see *Fashoff (UK) Ltd (t/a Moschino) v Linton* [2008] EWHC 537 (Ch), [2008] B.C.C. 542 (Ch D), Judge

CAP.

1986–cont.

45. Insolvency Act 1986–*cont.*

Sch.B1 para.43–*cont.*

Toulmin Q.C.; see *Magical Marking Ltd v Phillips* [2008] EWHC 1640 (Pat), [2008] F.S.R. 36 (Ch D (Patents Ct)), Norris, J.; see *Metro Nominees (Wandsworth) (No.1) Ltd v Rayment* [2008] B.C.C. 40 (CC (Birmingham)), Judge Norris Q.C.

Sch.B1 para.84, see *Secretary of State for Trade and Industry v Arnold* [2007] EWHC 1933 (Ch), [2008] B.C.C. 119 (Ch D (Manchester)), Judge Pelling Q.C.

Sch.B1 para.88, see *Coyne v DRC Distribution Ltd* [2008] EWCA Civ 488, [2008] B.C.C. 612 (CA (Civ Div)), Ward, L.J.

Sch.B1 para.99, see *Sports Betting Media Ltd (In Administration), Re* [2007] EWHC 2085 (Ch), [2008] B.C.C. 177 (Ch D), Briggs, J.

Sch.4A, see *Official Receiver v May* [2008] EWHC 1778 (Ch), [2008] B.P.I.R. 1562 (Ch D), Christopher Nugee Q.C.

Sch.4A, applied: SI 2008/1185 Reg.4, Sch.1 para.44, SI 2008/2553 Art.5, SI 2008/2554 Art.5, SI 2008/2927 Reg.2, SI 2008/3047 Art.5, SI 2008/3148 Sch.1

Sch.4A para.2, see *Official Receiver v Bathurst* [2008] EWHC 1724 (Ch), [2008] B.P.I.R. 1548 (Ch D), Sir Andrew Morritt (Chancellor)

Sch.5 para.3, see *Lewis v Metropolitan Property Realizations Ltd* [2008] EWHC 2760 (Ch), Times, December 9, 2008 (Ch D), Proudman, J

Sch.5 para.8, see *Lewis v Metropolitan Property Realizations Ltd* [2008] EWHC 2760 (Ch), Times, December 9, 2008 (Ch D), Proudman, J

Sch.6 para.14, amended: SI 2008/948 Sch.1 para.104

Sch.8 para.27, enabling: SI 2008/670

46. Company Directors Disqualification Act 1986

see *Secretary of State for Business Enterprise and Regulatory Reform v Aaron* [2008] EWCA Civ 1146, Times, November 10, 2008 (CA (Civ Div)), Buxton, L.J.

applied: 2008 c.17 s.266, SI 2008/630 Reg.14, SI 2008/631 Reg.12, SI 2008/1185 Reg.4, Sch.1 para.44, SI 2008/2252 Sch.1 para.13, SI 2008/2553 Art.5, SI 2008/2554 Art.5, SI 2008/2558 Reg.3, SI 2008/2927 Reg.2, SI 2008/3047 Art.5, SI 2008/3148 Sch.1

s.1A, see *Morija Plc, Re* [2007] EWHC 3055 (Ch), [2008] 2 B.C.L.C. 313 (Ch D), Sir Andrew Park

s.3, amended: SI 2008/948 Sch.1 para.106

s.6, see *AG (Manchester) Ltd (formerly The Accident Group Ltd) (In Liquidation), Re* [2008] EWHC 64 (Ch), [2008] B.C.C. 497 (Ch D (Manchester)), Patten, J.; see *City Truck Group Ltd, Re* [2007] EWHC 350 (Ch), [2008] B.C.C. 76 (Ch D (Companies Ct)), Mann, J.; see *Official Receiver v Stojevic* [2007] EWHC 1186 (Ch), [2008] Bus. L.R. 641 (Ch D), Judge Pelling Q.C.; see *Secretary of State for Business Enterprise and Regulatory Reform v Aaron* [2008] EWCA Civ 1146, Times, November 10, 2008 (CA (Civ Div)), Buxton, L.J.; see *Secretary of State for Trade and Industry v Arnold* [2007] EWHC 1933 (Ch), [2008] B.C.C. 119 (Ch D (Manchester)), Judge Pelling Q.C.; see *Secretary of State for Trade and Industry v Thornbury* [2007] EWHC 3202 (Ch), [2008] B.C.C. 768 (Ch D (Leeds)), Judge Roger Kaye Q.C.; see *Vintage Hallmark Plc, Re* [2006] EWHC 2761 (Ch), [2008] B.C.C. 150 (Ch D (Companies Ct)), Judge Richard Havery Q.C.

s.7, see *Secretary of State for Business Enterprise and Regulatory Reform v Aaron* [2008] EWCA Civ 1146, Times, November 10, 2008 (CA (Civ Div)), Buxton, L.J.

s.8, see *Secretary of State for Business Enterprise and Regulatory Reform v Aaron* [2008] EWCA Civ 1146, Times, November 10, 2008 (CA (Civ Div)), Buxton, L.J.

s.20A, added: SI 2008/948 Sch.1 para.106

s.22, amended: SI 2008/948 Sch.1 para.106

s.22A, amended: SI 2008/948 Sch.1 para.106

s.22B, amended: SI 2008/948 Sch.1 para.106

s.22C, amended: SI 2008/948 Sch.1 para.106

Sch.1 Part I para.4, substituted: SI 2008/948 Sch.1 para.106

Sch.1 Part I para.5, substituted: SI 2008/948 Sch.1 para.106

Sch.1 Part I para.5A, amended: SI 2008/948 Sch.1 para.106

47. Legal Aid (Scotland) Act 1986

applied: SSI 2008/240 Reg.5, Reg.6, Reg.7

s.8, amended: SSI 2008/137 Reg.3, Reg.4

s.9, enabling: SSI 2008/251

s.11, amended: SSI 2008/137 Reg.5

s.11, applied: SSI 2008/137 Reg.6, Reg.7

s.11, enabling: SSI 2008/137, SSI 2008/251

s.12, enabling: SSI 2008/47, SSI 2008/240

s.13, applied: SSI 2008/52 Reg.3

s.15, amended: SSI 2008/138 Reg.3, Reg.4

s.17, amended: SSI 2008/138 Reg.5, Reg.6

s.17, enabling: SSI 2008/48

s.33, enabling: SSI 2008/240

s.36, applied: SSI 2008/52 Reg.3

s.36, enabling: SSI 2008/48, SSI 2008/137, SSI 2008/138, SSI 2008/240, SSI 2008/251

s.37, applied: SSI 2008/137, SSI 2008/138, SSI 2008/251

CAP.

1986–cont.

47. Legal Aid (Scotland) Act 1986–*cont.*
s.41A, enabling: SSI 2008/240

49. Agriculture Act 1986
s.4, repealed: SI 2008/576 Sch.5 para.7
s.5, repealed: SI 2008/576 Sch.5 para.7
s.6, repealed: SI 2008/576 Sch.5 para.7
s.7, repealed: SI 2008/576 Sch.5 para.7
Sch.3 para.2, repealed: SI 2008/576 Sch.5 para.7

50. Social Security Act 1986
s.63, varied: SI 2008/632 Art.4
Sch.10 Part I para.41, repealed (in part): 2008 c.14 Sch.15 Part 5

53. Building Societies Act 1986
applied: SI 2008/570 Sch.1 para.9, SI 2008/700 Sch.1 para.10
referred to: 2008 c.2 s.11
varied: 2008 c.2 s.11
s.1, applied: SI 2008/1427 Art.3, Art.4
s.5, applied: SI 2008/1427 Art.3, Art.4
s.5, referred to: 2008 c.31 s.2, SI 2008/1427 Art.3
s.5, varied: 2008 c.2 s.11
s.6, varied: 2008 c.2 s.11
s.6, disapplied: SI 2008/1427 Art.4
s.6, varied: 2008 c.2 s.11
s.6A, varied: 2008 c.2 s.11
s.6B, varied: 2008 c.2 s.11
s.6C, varied: 2008 c.2 s.11
s.7, applied: SI 2008/1427 Art.5
s.7, varied: 2008 c.2 s.11
s.8, disapplied: SI 2008/1427 Art.6
s.8, varied: 2008 c.2 s.11
s.9A, varied: 2008 c.2 s.11
s.9B, disapplied: SI 2008/1427 Art.7
s.9B, varied: 2008 c.2 s.11
s.36, applied: SI 2008/1427 Art.3, Art.4
s.36, referred to: SI 2008/1427 Art.3
s.37, applied: SI 2008/1427 Art.3, Art.4
s.72C, enabling: SI 2008/1143
s.72G, enabling: SI 2008/1143
s.72I, amended: SI 2008/948 Sch.1 para.107
s.72L, added: SI 2008/1519 Art.3
s.72M, added: SI 2008/1519 Art.4
s.74, amended: SI 2008/1519 Sch.2 para.2
s.76, amended: SI 2008/1519 Sch.2 para.3
s.76, enabling: SI 2008/1143
s.77, amended: SI 2008/948 Sch.1 para.13, Sch.2
s.78, amended: SI 2008/1519 Sch.2 para.4
s.78, substituted: SI 2008/1519 Sch.2 para.4
s.78A, substituted: SI 2008/1519 Art.5
s.79, amended: SI 2008/1519 Sch.2 para.5
s.79, substituted: SI 2008/1519 Sch.2 para.5
s.80, amended: SI 2008/1519 Sch.2 para.6
s.81A, amended: SI 2008/1519 Sch.2 para.7
s.90, varied: 2008 c.2 s.11
s.90A, varied: 2008 c.2 s.11, SI 2008/1427 Art.10
s.97, amended: SI 2008/1519 Art.8

CAP.

1986–cont.

53. Building Societies Act 1986–*cont.*
s.104, applied: SI 2008/1519
s.104, enabling: SI 2008/1519
s.119, amended: SI 2008/948 Sch.1 para.108, Sch.2
s.119A, added: SI 2008/948 Sch.1 para.109
Sch.2 Part I para.1, varied: 2008 c.2 s.11
Sch.2 Part I para.2, varied: 2008 c.2 s.11, SI 2008/1427 Art.8
Sch.2 Part I para.3, varied: 2008 c.2 s.11, SI 2008/1427 Art.8
Sch.2 Part I para.4, varied: 2008 c.2 s.11
Sch.2 Part I para.5, varied: 2008 c.2 s.11
Sch.2 Part I para.6, varied: 2008 c.2 s.11
Sch.2 Part I para.7, varied: 2008 c.2 s.11
Sch.2 Part I para.8, varied: 2008 c.2 s.11
Sch.2 Part I para.9, varied: 2008 c.2 s.11
Sch.2 Part I para.10, varied: 2008 c.2 s.11
Sch.2 Part I para.10A, varied: 2008 c.2 s.11
Sch.2 Part I para.10B, varied: 2008 c.2 s.11
Sch.2 Part I para.10C, varied: 2008 c.2 s.11
Sch.2 Part I para.11, varied: 2008 c.2 s.11
Sch.2 Part I para.12, varied: 2008 c.2 s.11
Sch.2 Part I para.13, varied: 2008 c.2 s.11
Sch.2 Part I para.14, varied: 2008 c.2 s.11
Sch.2 Part I para.15, varied: 2008 c.2 s.11
Sch.2 Part II para.16, applied: SI 2008/1427 Art.8
Sch.2 Part II para.16, disapplied: SI 2008/1427 Art.8
Sch.2 Part II para.16, varied: 2008 c.2 s.11
Sch.2 Part II para.17, varied: 2008 c.2 s.11
Sch.2 Part II para.18, varied: 2008 c.2 s.11
Sch.2 Part II para.19, varied: 2008 c.2 s.11
Sch.2 Part III para.20, varied: 2008 c.2 s.11
Sch.2 Part III para.20A, varied: 2008 c.2 s.11
Sch.2 Part III para.20B, varied: 2008 c.2 s.11
Sch.2 Part III para.21, varied: 2008 c.2 s.11
Sch.2 Part III para.22, varied: 2008 c.2 s.11
Sch.2 Part III para.22A, varied: 2008 c.2 s.11
Sch.2 Part III para.22B, varied: 2008 c.2 s.11
Sch.2 Part III para.23, varied: 2008 c.2 s.11
Sch.2 Part III para.24, varied: 2008 c.2 s.11
Sch.2 Part III para.25, varied: 2008 c.2 s.11
Sch.2 Part III para.26, varied: 2008 c.2 s.11
Sch.2 Part III para.27, varied: 2008 c.2 s.11
Sch.2 Part III para.27A, varied: 2008 c.2 s.11
Sch.2 Part III para.28, varied: 2008 c.2 s.11
Sch.2 Part III para.29, varied: 2008 c.2 s.11
Sch.2 Part III para.30, varied: 2008 c.2 s.11
Sch.2 Part III para.31, varied: 2008 c.2 s.11
Sch.2 Part III para.32, varied: 2008 c.2 s.11
Sch.2 Part III para.33, varied: 2008 c.2 s.11
Sch.2 Part III para.33A, varied: 2008 c.2 s.11
Sch.2 Part III para.34, varied: 2008 c.2 s.11
Sch.2 Part III para.35, varied: 2008 c.2 s.11
Sch.2 Part III para.36, varied: 2008 c.2 s.11
Sch.10A Part I para.1, amended: SI 2008/948 Sch.1 para.110

CAP.

1986–cont.

53. Building Societies Act 1986–*cont.*
Sch.10A Part I para.11, repealed: SI 2008/1519 Art.4
Sch.10A Part I para.12, repealed: SI 2008/1519 Art.4
Sch.10B Part I para.3, amended: SI 2008/948 Sch.1 para.111
Sch.10B Part I para.7, amended: SI 2008/948 Sch.1 para.111
Sch.10B Part II para.9, amended: SI 2008/948 Sch.1 para.111
Sch.10B Part II para.11, amended: SI 2008/948 Sch.1 para.111
Sch.10B Part II para.15, amended: SI 2008/948 Sch.1 para.111
Sch.10B Part II para.18, amended: SI 2008/948 Sch.1 para.111
Sch.10C para.1, added: SI 2008/1519 Sch.1 para.1
Sch.10C para.2, added: SI 2008/1519 Sch.1 para.1
Sch.10C para.3, added: SI 2008/1519 Sch.1 para.1
Sch.10C para.4, added: SI 2008/1519 Sch.1 para.1
Sch.10C para.5, added: SI 2008/1519 Sch.1 para.1
Sch.10C para.6, added: SI 2008/1519 Sch.1 para.1
Sch.11 para.1, amended: SI 2008/948 Sch.2, SI 2008/1519 Sch.2 para.8
Sch.11 para.2, amended: SI 2008/948 Sch.2
Sch.11 para.3, amended: SI 2008/948 Sch.2, SI 2008/1519 Sch.2 para.8
Sch.11 para.4, amended: SI 2008/948 Sch.2
Sch.11 para.5, amended: SI 2008/948 Sch.2
Sch.11 para.5, repealed: SI 2008/948 Sch.2
Sch.11 para.6, amended: SI 2008/948 Sch.2
Sch.11 para.6A, added: SI 2008/1519 Art.6
Sch.11 para.6A, amended: SI 2008/948 Sch.2
Sch.11 para.7, amended: SI 2008/948 Sch.2
Sch.11 para.8, amended: SI 2008/948 Sch.2
Sch.11 para.8A, added: SI 2008/1519 Art.6
Sch.11 para.8A, amended: SI 2008/948 Sch.2
Sch.11 para.8B, added: SI 2008/1519 Art.6
Sch.11 para.8B, amended: SI 2008/948 Sch.2
Sch.11 para.8C, added: SI 2008/1519 Art.6
Sch.11 para.8C, amended: SI 2008/948 Sch.2
Sch.11 para.9, amended: SI 2008/948 Sch.2
Sch.15 Part I para.1, varied: 2008 c.2 s.11
Sch.15 Part I para.2, varied: 2008 c.2 s.11
Sch.15 Part I para.3, varied: 2008 c.2 s.11, SI 2008/1427 Art.9
Sch.15 Part I para.4, varied: 2008 c.2 s.11
Sch.15 Part I para.5, varied: 2008 c.2 s.11
Sch.15 Part II para.6, varied: 2008 c.2 s.11
Sch.15 Part II para.7, varied: 2008 c.2 s.11

CAP.

1986–cont.

53. Building Societies Act 1986–*cont.*
Sch.15 Part II para.8, varied: 2008 c.2 s.11
Sch.15 Part II para.9, varied: 2008 c.2 s.11
Sch.15 Part II para.10, varied: 2008 c.2 s.11
Sch.15 Part II para.11, varied: 2008 c.2 s.11
Sch.15 Part II para.12, varied: 2008 c.2 s.11
Sch.15 Part II para.13, varied: 2008 c.2 s.11
Sch.15 Part II para.14, varied: 2008 c.2 s.11
Sch.15 Part II para.15, varied: 2008 c.2 s.11
Sch.15 Part II para.16, varied: 2008 c.2 s.11
Sch.15 Part II para.17, varied: 2008 c.2 s.11
Sch.15 Part II para.18, varied: 2008 c.2 s.11
Sch.15 Part II para.19, varied: 2008 c.2 s.11
Sch.15 Part II para.20, varied: 2008 c.2 s.11
Sch.15 Part II para.21, varied: 2008 c.2 s.11
Sch.15 Part II para.22, varied: 2008 c.2 s.11
Sch.15 Part II para.23, varied: 2008 c.2 s.11
Sch.15 Part II para.24, varied: 2008 c.2 s.11
Sch.15 Part II para.25, varied: 2008 c.2 s.11
Sch.15 Part II para.26, varied: 2008 c.2 s.11
Sch.15 Part II para.27, varied: 2008 c.2 s.11
Sch.15 Part II para.28, varied: 2008 c.2 s.11
Sch.15 Part II para.29, varied: 2008 c.2 s.11
Sch.15 Part II para.30, varied: 2008 c.2 s.11
Sch.15 Part II para.31, varied: 2008 c.2 s.11
Sch.15 Part II para.32, varied: 2008 c.2 s.11
Sch.15 Part II para.33, varied: 2008 c.2 s.11, SI 2008/1427 Art.9
Sch.15 Part III para.34, varied: 2008 c.2 s.11
Sch.15 Part III para.35, varied: 2008 c.2 s.11
Sch.15 Part III para.36, varied: 2008 c.2 s.11
Sch.15 Part III para.37, varied: 2008 c.2 s.11
Sch.15 Part III para.38, varied: 2008 c.2 s.11
Sch.15 Part III para.39, varied: 2008 c.2 s.11
Sch.15 Part III para.40, varied: 2008 c.2 s.11
Sch.15 Part III para.41, varied: 2008 c.2 s.11
Sch.15 Part III para.42, varied: 2008 c.2 s.11
Sch.15 Part III para.43, varied: 2008 c.2 s.11
Sch.15 Part III para.44, varied: 2008 c.2 s.11
Sch.15 Part III para.45, varied: 2008 c.2 s.11
Sch.15 Part III para.46, varied: 2008 c.2 s.11
Sch.15 Part III para.47, varied: 2008 c.2 s.11
Sch.15 Part III para.48, varied: 2008 c.2 s.11
Sch.15 Part III para.49, varied: 2008 c.2 s.11
Sch.15 Part III para.50, varied: 2008 c.2 s.11
Sch.15 Part III para.51, varied: 2008 c.2 s.11
Sch.15 Part III para.52, varied: 2008 c.2 s.11
Sch.15 Part III para.53, varied: 2008 c.2 s.11
Sch.15 Part III para.54, varied: 2008 c.2 s.11
Sch.15 Part III para.55, varied: 2008 c.2 s.11
Sch.15 Part III para.55A, varied: 2008 c.2 s.11
Sch.15 Part III para.55B, varied: 2008 c.2 s.11
Sch.15 Part III para.55C, varied: 2008 c.2 s.11
Sch.15 Part III para.55D, varied: 2008 c.2 s.11
Sch.15 Part III para.55E, varied: 2008 c.2 s.11, SI 2008/1427 Art.9
Sch.15 Part IV para.56, varied: 2008 c.2 s.11
Sch.15 Part IV para.57, varied: 2008 c.2 s.11
Sch.15 Part IV para.58, varied: 2008 c.2 s.11
Sch.15 Part IV para.59, varied: 2008 c.2 s.11

CAP.

1986–cont.

53. Building Societies Act 1986–*cont.*

Sch.15A Part I para.1, amended: SI 2008/1427 Art.11
Sch.15A Part I para.1, varied: 2008 c.2 s.11
Sch.15A Part I para.2, varied: 2008 c.2 s.11, SI 2008/1427 Art.11
Sch.15A Part I para.3, varied: 2008 c.2 s.11
Sch.15A Part I para.4, varied: 2008 c.2 s.11
Sch.15A Part I para.5, varied: 2008 c.2 s.11
Sch.15A Part I para.5A, varied: 2008 c.2 s.11
Sch.15A Part II para.6, varied: 2008 c.2 s.11
Sch.15A Part II para.7, varied: 2008 c.2 s.11
Sch.15A Part II para.8, varied: 2008 c.2 s.11
Sch.15A Part II para.8A, varied: 2008 c.2 s.11
Sch.15A Part II para.9, varied: 2008 c.2 s.11
Sch.15A Part II para.9A, varied: 2008 c.2 s.11
Sch.15A Part II para.10, varied: 2008 c.2 s.11
Sch.15A Part II para.11, amended: SI 2008/1427 Art.11
Sch.15A Part II para.11, varied: 2008 c.2 s.11, SI 2008/1427 Art.11
Sch.15A Part II para.12, varied: 2008 c.2 s.11, SI 2008/1427 Art.11
Sch.15A Part II para.13, varied: 2008 c.2 s.11, SI 2008/1427 Art.11
Sch.15A Part II para.14, varied: 2008 c.2 s.11
Sch.15A Part II para.15, varied: 2008 c.2 s.11
Sch.15A Part II para.16, varied: 2008 c.2 s.11
Sch.15A Part II para.17, varied: 2008 c.2 s.11
Sch.15A Part II para.18, varied: 2008 c.2 s.11, SI 2008/1427 Art.11
Sch.15A Part II para.19, varied: 2008 c.2 s.11
Sch.15A Part II para.20, varied: 2008 c.2 s.11, SI 2008/1427 Art.11
Sch.15A Part II para.21, varied: 2008 c.2 s.11
Sch.15A Part II para.22, varied: 2008 c.2 s.11
Sch.15A Part II para.23, varied: 2008 c.2 s.11
Sch.15A Part II para.24, varied: 2008 c.2 s.11
Sch.15A Part II para.25, varied: 2008 c.2 s.11
Sch.15A Part II para.26, varied: 2008 c.2 s.11
Sch.15A Part II para.27, varied: 2008 c.2 s.11, SI 2008/1427 Art.11
Sch.15A Part II para.27A, varied: 2008 c.2 s.11, SI 2008/1427 Art.11
Sch.15A Part II para.27B, varied: 2008 c.2 s.11, SI 2008/1427 Art.11
Sch.15A Part II para.27C, varied: 2008 c.2 s.11, SI 2008/1427 Art.11
Sch.15A Part II para.27D, varied: 2008 c.2 s.11, SI 2008/1427 Art.11
Sch.15A Part III para.28, varied: 2008 c.2 s.11
Sch.15A Part III para.29, varied: 2008 c.2 s.11
Sch.15A Part III para.30, varied: 2008 c.2 s.11
Sch.15A Part III para.30A, varied: 2008 c.2 s.11
Sch.15A Part III para.31, varied: 2008 c.2 s.11
Sch.15A Part III para.31A, varied: 2008 c.2 s.11
Sch.15A Part III para.32, varied: 2008 c.2 s.11
Sch.15A Part III para.33, amended: SI 2008/1427 Art.11

CAP.

1986–cont.

53. Building Societies Act 1986–*cont.*

Sch.15A Part III para.33, varied: 2008 c.2 s.11, SI 2008/1427 Art.11
Sch.15A Part III para.34, varied: 2008 c.2 s.11, SI 2008/1427 Art.11
Sch.15A Part III para.35, varied: 2008 c.2 s.11, SI 2008/1427 Art.11
Sch.15A Part III para.36, varied: 2008 c.2 s.11
Sch.15A Part III para.37, varied: 2008 c.2 s.11
Sch.15A Part III para.38, varied: 2008 c.2 s.11
Sch.15A Part III para.39, varied: 2008 c.2 s.11
Sch.15A Part III para.40, varied: 2008 c.2 s.11, SI 2008/1427 Art.11
Sch.15A Part III para.41, varied: 2008 c.2 s.11
Sch.15A Part III para.42, varied: 2008 c.2 s.11, SI 2008/1427 Art.11
Sch.15A Part III para.43, varied: 2008 c.2 s.11
Sch.15A Part III para.44, varied: 2008 c.2 s.11
Sch.15A Part III para.45, varied: 2008 c.2 s.11
Sch.15A Part III para.46, varied: 2008 c.2 s.11
Sch.15A Part III para.47, varied: 2008 c.2 s.11
Sch.15A Part III para.48, varied: 2008 c.2 s.11
Sch.15A Part III para.49, varied: 2008 c.2 s.11, SI 2008/1427 Art.11
Sch.15A Part III para.49A, varied: 2008 c.2 s.11, SI 2008/1427 Art.11
Sch.15A Part III para.49B, varied: 2008 c.2 s.11, SI 2008/1427 Art.11
Sch.15A Part III para.49C, varied: 2008 c.2 s.11, SI 2008/1427 Art.11
Sch.15A Part III para.49D, varied: 2008 c.2 s.11, SI 2008/1427 Art.11

55. Family Law Act 1986

see *Westminster City Council v C* [2008] EWCA Civ 198, [2008] 2 F.L.R. 267 (CA (Civ Div)), Thorpe, L.J.
applied: SI 2008/1052 Sch.1
s.46, see *H v H (Talaq Divorce)* [2007] EWHC 2945 (Fam), [2008] 2 F.L.R. 857 (Fam Div), Sumner, J.
s.56, amended: 2008 c.22 Sch.6 para.23

56. Parliamentary Constituencies Act 1986

s.3, applied: SI 2008/1486, SI 2008/1791
s.4, applied: SI 2008/1791 Art.1
s.4, enabling: SI 2008/1486, SI 2008/1791

59. Sex Discrimination Act 1986

s.6, see *UNISON v Brennan* [2008] I.C.R. 955 (EAT), Elias, J (President)

60. Financial Services Act 1986

s.45, applied: 2008 c.28 Sch.7 para.6
s.62, see *Shore v Sedgwick Financial Services Ltd* [2007] EWHC 2509 (Admin), [2008] P.N.L.R. 10 (QBD), Beatson, J.

62. Salmon Act 1986

s.31, applied: 2008 c.13 Sch.7
s.32, referred to: 2008 c.13 Sch.6

63. Housing and Planning Act 1986

s.2, repealed (in part): 2008 c.12 Sch.1 Part 9
s.4, repealed (in part): 2008 c.12 Sch.1 Part 9
s.11, repealed: 2008 c.12 Sch.1 Part 9

CAP.

1986–cont.

63. Housing and Planning Act 1986–*cont.*

s.47, repealed: 2008 c.12 Sch.1 Part 9

s.52, repealed: 2008 c.12 Sch.1 Part 9

s.53, repealed (in part): 2008 c.12 Sch.1 Part 9

s.54, repealed: 2008 c.12 Sch.1 Part 9

s.58, amended: 2008 c.12 Sch.1 Part 9

Sch.11 Part II para.28, repealed: 2008 c.12 Sch.1 Part 9

Sch.11 Part II para.29, repealed: 2008 c.12 Sch.1 Part 9

Sch.11 Part II para.30, repealed: 2008 c.12 Sch.1 Part 9

Sch.11 Part II para.31, repealed: 2008 c.12 Sch.1 Part 9

Sch.11 Part II para.32, repealed: 2008 c.12 Sch.1 Part 9

Sch.11 Part II para.33, repealed: 2008 c.12 Sch.1 Part 9

Sch.11 Part II para.34, repealed: 2008 c.12 Sch.1 Part 9

Sch.11 Part II para.35, repealed: 2008 c.12 Sch.1 Part 9

Sch.11 Part II para.36, repealed: 2008 c.12 Sch.1 Part 9

Sch.11 Part II para.37, repealed: 2008 c.12 Sch.1 Part 9

Sch.11 Part II para.38, repealed: 2008 c.12 Sch.1 Part 9

Sch.11 Part II para.39, repealed: 2008 c.12 Sch.1 Part 9

Sch.11 Part II para.40, repealed: 2008 c.12 Sch.1 Part 9

Sch.11 Part II para.41, repealed: 2008 c.12 Sch.1 Part 9

Sch.11 Part II para.42, repealed: 2008 c.12 Sch.1 Part 9

Sch.11 Part II para.43, repealed: 2008 c.12 Sch.1 Part 9

Sch.11 Part II para.44, repealed: 2008 c.12 Sch.1 Part 9

Sch.11 Part II para.45, repealed: 2008 c.12 Sch.1 Part 9

Sch.11 Part II para.46, repealed: 2008 c.12 Sch.1 Part 9

Sch.11 Part II para.47, repealed: 2008 c.12 Sch.1 Part 9

Sch.11 Part II para.48, repealed: 2008 c.12 Sch.1 Part 9

Sch.11 Part II para.49, repealed: 2008 c.12 Sch.1 Part 9

Sch.11 Part II para.50, repealed: 2008 c.12 Sch.1 Part 9

Sch.11 Part II para.51, repealed: 2008 c.12 Sch.1 Part 9

Sch.11 Part II para.52, repealed: 2008 c.12 Sch.1 Part 9

Sch.11 Part II para.53, repealed: 2008 c.12 Sch.1 Part 9

Sch.11 Part II para.54, repealed: 2008 c.12 Sch.1 Part 9

CAP.

1986–cont.

63. Housing and Planning Act 1986–*cont.*

Sch.11 Part II para.55, repealed: 2008 c.12 Sch.1 Part 9

Sch.11 Part II para.56, repealed: 2008 c.12 Sch.1 Part 9

Sch.11 Part II para.57, repealed: 2008 c.12 Sch.1 Part 9

Sch.11 Part II para.58, repealed: 2008 c.12 Sch.1 Part 9

Sch.11 Part II para.59, repealed: 2008 c.12 Sch.1 Part 9

Sch.11 Part II para.60, repealed: 2008 c.12 Sch.1 Part 9

Sch.11 Part II para.61, repealed: 2008 c.12 Sch.1 Part 9

Sch.11 Part II para.62, repealed: 2008 c.12 Sch.1 Part 9

64. Public Order Act 1986

Part IIIA, amended: 2008 c.4 Sch.16 para.3

Part IIIA, referred to: 2008 c.4 s.74, s.153

Part IIIA, amended: 2008 c.4 Sch.16 para.5

s.5, see *DPP v Beaumont* [2008] EWHC 523 (Admin), [2008] 1 W.L.R. 2186 (DC), Richards, L.J.; see *Johnson v DPP* [2008] EWHC 509 (Admin), Times, April 9, 2008 (DC), Richards, L.J.; see *McMillan v Crown Prosecution Service* [2008] EWHC 1457 (Admin), (2008) 172 J.P. 485 (DC), Maurice Kay, L.J.

s.11, see *Kay v Commissioner of Police of the Metropolis* [2008] UKHL 69, [2008] 1 W.L.R. 2723 (HL), Lord Phillips of Worth Matravers

s.24, see *Wood v DPP* [2008] EWHC 1056 (Admin), Times, May 23, 2008 (DC), Latham, L.J.

s.29A, amended: 2008 c.4 Sch.16 para.2

s.29B, added: 2008 c.4 Sch.16 para.4

s.29B, amended: 2008 c.4 Sch.16 para.2

s.29B, amended: 2008 c.4 Sch.16 para.2, Sch.16 para.6

s.29B, repealed (in part): 2008 c.4 Sch.28 Part 5

s.29C, amended: 2008 c.4 Sch.16 para.2, Sch.16 para.7

s.29D, amended: 2008 c.4 Sch.16 para.2, Sch.16 para.8

s.29E, amended: 2008 c.4 Sch.16 para.2, Sch.16 para.9

s.29F, amended: 2008 c.4 Sch.16 para.2, Sch.16 para.10

s.29G, amended: 2008 c.4 Sch.16 para.2, Sch.16 para.11

s.29H, amended: 2008 c.4 Sch.16 para.2, Sch.28 Part 5

s.29H, repealed (in part): 2008 c.4 Sch.28 Part 5

s.29I, amended: 2008 c.4 Sch.16 para.2, Sch.28 Part 5

s.29I, repealed (in part): 2008 c.4 Sch.28 Part 5

CAP.

1986–cont.

64. Public Order Act 1986–*cont.*
s.29J, amended: 2008 c.4 Sch.16 para.2
s.29JA, added: 2008 c.4 Sch.16 para.14
s.29JA, amended: 2008 c.4 Sch.16 para.2
s.29K, amended: 2008 c.4 Sch.16 para.2, Sch.16 para.15
s.29L, amended: 2008 c.4 Sch.16 para.2, Sch.16 para.16, Sch.28 Part 5
s.29M, amended: 2008 c.4 Sch.16 para.2
s.29N, amended: 2008 c.4 Sch.16 para.2, Sch.16 para.17

1987

3. Coal Industry Act 1987
referred to: SI 2008/751 Art.4

4. Ministry of Defence Police Act 1987
applied: 2008 c.4 s.126
s.3, amended: 2008 c.4 Sch.22 para.13
s.3A, amended: 2008 c.4 Sch.22 para.14
s.4, substituted: 2008 c.4 Sch.22 para.15
s.4A, substituted: 2008 c.4 Sch.22 para.16
s.4A, enabling: SI 2008/2059

9. Animals (Scotland) Act 1987
s.1, see *Welsh v Brady* [2008] CSOH 45, 2008 S.L.T. 363 (OH), Lord Malcolm

12. Petroleum Act 1987
s.21, amended: 2008 c.32 Sch.1 para.4
s.21, applied: 2008 c.32 s.32, SI 2008/1522 Art.2, SI 2008/2157 Art.2, SI 2008/2454 Art.2, SI 2008/3011 Art.2
s.22, enabling: SI 2008/1522, SI 2008/2157, SI 2008/2454, SI 2008/3011
s.23, applied: 2008 c.32 s.32
s.24, amended: SI 2008/960 Sch.3
s.24, applied: 2008 c.32 s.32, SI 2008/2454(b), SI 2008/3011(b), SI 2008/1522, SI 2008/2157

14. Recognition of Trusts Act 1987
see *CIS/213/2004, Re* [2008] W.T.L.R. 189 (SS Comm), Charles Turnbull

15. Reverter of Sites Act 1987
referred to: SI 2008/751 Art.4

16. Finance Act 1987
s.1, repealed (in part): 2008 c.9 s.13, Sch.5 para.25
s.50, amended: 2008 c.9 Sch.32 para.17
s.55, amended: 2008 c.9 Sch.32 para.18
s.62, amended: 2008 c.9 s.106
s.62, repealed (in part): 2008 c.9 s.106

18. Debtors (Scotland) Act 1987
s.1, amended: 2008 c.9 Sch.43 para.13
s.1, repealed (in part): 2008 c.6 Sch.8, 2008 c.9 Sch.43 para.13
s.5, amended: 2008 c.9 Sch.43 para.13
s.5, repealed (in part): 2008 c.9 Sch.43 para.13
s.15D, enabling: SSI 2008/121, SSI 2008/122
s.15L, enabling: SSI 2008/121, SSI 2008/122
s.50, varied: SSI 2008/104 Reg.2
s.57, varied: SSI 2008/104 Reg.2

CAP.

1987–cont.

18. Debtors (Scotland) Act 1987–*cont.*
s.65, varied: SSI 2008/104 Reg.2
s.66, varied: SSI 2008/104 Reg.2
s.70A, varied: SSI 2008/115 Art.12
s.70C, varied: SSI 2008/104 Reg.2
s.75, enabling: SSI 2008/366
s.90, varied: SSI 2008/104 Reg.2
s.106, amended: 2008 c.9 Sch.43 para.13
s.106, repealed (in part): 2008 c.9 Sch.43 para.13
s.106, varied: SSI 2008/104 Reg.2

21. Pilotage Act 1987
referred to: 2008 c.13 Sch.6

26. Housing (Scotland) Act 1987
see *Rizza v Glasgow Housing Association* 2008 S.L.T. (Lands Tr) 13 (Lands Tr (Scot)), Lord McGhie
s.20, amended: 2008 c.17 Sch.15 para.10
s.30, amended: 2008 c.17 Sch.15 para.11
s.31, amended: 2008 c.17 Sch.15 para.12
s.32, amended: 2008 c.17 Sch.15 para.13
s.34, amended: 2008 c.17 Sch.15 para.14
s.34, repealed (in part): 2008 c.17 Sch.15 para.14, Sch.16
s.35A, amended: 2008 c.17 Sch.15 para.15
s.43, amended: 2008 c.17 Sch.15 para.16
s.191, varied: SSI 2008/28 Art.2
s.191, enabling: SSI 2008/133
s.192, varied: SSI 2008/28 Art.2
s.192, enabling: SSI 2008/133
s.193, varied: SSI 2008/28 Art.2
s.203, varied: SSI 2008/28 Art.2
s.204, enabling: SSI 2008/34
s.237, enabling: SSI 2008/283
s.240A, applied: SSI 2008/336
s.240A, enabling: SSI 2008/336
s.330, enabling: SSI 2008/283
s.338, referred to: SI 2008/794 Sch.9 para.13
Sch.15 Part II para.3, applied: SSI 2008/133 Sch.1 para.2

27. Fire Safety and Safety of Places of Sport Act 1987
applied: 2008 c.13 Sch.3
referred to: 2008 c.13 Sch.6

31. Landlord and Tenant Act 1987
Part I, see *Dartmouth Court Blackheath Ltd v Berisworth Ltd* [2008] EWHC 350 (Ch), [2008] 2 P. & C.R. 3 (Ch D), Warren, J.
Part II, see *Cawsand Fort Management Co Ltd v Stafford* [2007] EWCA Civ 1187, [2008] 1 W.L.R. 371 (CA (Civ Div)), Mummery, L.J.
s.3, see *Dartmouth Court Blackheath Ltd v Berisworth Ltd* [2008] EWHC 350 (Ch), [2008] 2 P. & C.R. 3 (Ch D), Warren, J.
s.4, see *Dartmouth Court Blackheath Ltd v Berisworth Ltd* [2008] EWHC 350 (Ch), [2008] 2 P. & C.R. 3 (Ch D), Warren, J.
s.5, see *Chinnock v Hocaoglu* [2007] EWHC 2933 (Ch), [2008] 29 E.G. 92 (Ch D), Blackburne, J.

CAP.

1987–cont.

31. **Landlord and Tenant Act 1987**–*cont.*
s.21, see *Cawsand Fort Management Co Ltd v Stafford* [2007] EWCA Civ 1187, [2008] 1 W.L.R. 371 (CA (Civ Div)), Mummery, L.J.
s.21, amended: 2008 c.17 Sch.8 para.38
s.24, see *Cawsand Fort Management Co Ltd v Stafford* [2007] EWCA Civ 1187, [2008] 1 W.L.R. 371 (CA (Civ Div)), Mummery, L.J.
s.29, amended: 2008 c.17 Sch.8 para.39
s.42A, amended: 2008 c.17 Sch.12 para.12
s.53, amended: 2008 c.17 Sch.12 para.13, Sch.16
s.58, amended: 2008 c.17 Sch.8 para.40, Sch.16
s.58, varied: SI 2008/2839 Sch.1 para.1
s.60, amended: 2008 c.17 Sch.8 para.41
Sch.2 para.9, repealed: 2008 c.17 Sch.16

32. **Crossbows Act 1987**
applied: 2008 c.13 Sch.3

33. **AIDS (Control) Act 1987**
repealed: 2008 asp 5 Sch.3 Part 1

34. **Motor Cycle Noise Act 1987**
applied: 2008 c.13 Sch.3
referred to: 2008 c.13 Sch.6

38. **Criminal Justice Act 1987**
s.1, see *R. (on the application of Corner House Research) v Director of Serious Fraud Office* [2008] EWHC 714 (Admin), Times, April 16, 2008 (DC), Moses, L.J.
s.1, amended: 2008 c.4 Sch.26 para.21
s.2A, added: 2008 c.4 s.59
s.12, see *R. v Bright (Michael John)* [2008] EWCA Crim 462, [2008] 2 Cr. App. R. (S.) 102 (CA (Crim Div)), Sir Igor Judge (President, QB)
s.17, amended: 2008 c.4 s.59

42. **Family Law Reform Act 1987**
referred to: 2008 c.22 s.53
s.1, amended: 2008 c.22 Sch.6 para.24
s.1, applied: 2008 c.22 s.53
s.2, repealed (in part): 2008 c.14 Sch.15 Part 5
s.18, amended: 2008 c.22 Sch.6 para.25
Sch.2 para.5, amended: 2008 c.14 Sch.15 Part 5
Sch.2 para.6, repealed: 2008 c.14 Sch.15 Part 5
Sch.2 para.8, repealed: 2008 c.14 Sch.15 Part 5

43. **Consumer Protection Act 1987**
applied: 2008 c.13 Sch.3, SI 2008/1284 Reg.22, SI 2008/1597 Sch.5 para.17
Part III, applied: SI 2008/1277 Sch.3 para.9, Sch.3 para.11
Part IV, referred to: SI 2008/1277 Sch.3 para.6
Part V, referred to: SI 2008/1277 Sch.3 para.6
s.11, amended: SI 2008/960 Sch.3
s.11, applied: SI 2008/1284, SI 2008/1284 Reg.22, SI 2008/1654, SI 2008/2173, SI 2008/2566, SI 2008/2936

CAP.

1987–cont.

43. **Consumer Protection Act 1987**–*cont.*
s.11, enabling: SI 2008/1284, SI 2008/1654, SI 2008/2173, SI 2008/2566, SI 2008/2936
s.12, applied: SI 2008/1654 Reg.4
s.12, referred to: 2008 c.13 Sch.6
s.14, applied: SI 2008/1597 Sch.5 para.11
s.14, varied: SI 2008/1597 Sch.5 para.12
s.15, applied: SI 2008/1597 Sch.5 para.11, Sch.5 para.14
s.15, varied: SI 2008/1597 Sch.5 para.12
s.20, repealed: SI 2008/1277 Sch.4 Part 1
s.21, repealed: SI 2008/1277 Sch.4 Part 1
s.22, repealed: SI 2008/1277 Sch.4 Part 1
s.23, repealed: SI 2008/1277 Sch.4 Part 1
s.24, repealed: SI 2008/1277 Sch.4 Part 1
s.25, repealed: SI 2008/1277 Sch.4 Part 1
s.26, referred to: SI 2008/1277 Sch.3 para.5
s.26, repealed: SI 2008/1277 Sch.4 Part 1
s.27, amended: SI 2008/1277 Sch.4 Part 1
s.27, applied: SI 2008/2852 Sch.7 para.5
s.28, amended: SI 2008/1277 Sch.4 Part 1
s.28, applied: SI 2008/1284 Reg.24, SI 2008/1597 Sch.5 para.11
s.28, varied: SI 2008/1597 Sch.5 para.12
s.29, amended: SI 2008/1277 Sch.4 Part 1
s.29, applied: SI 2008/1284 Reg.24, SI 2008/1597 Reg.21, Sch.5 para.11
s.29, varied: SI 2008/1597 Sch.5 para.12
s.30, amended: SI 2008/1277 Sch.4 Part 1
s.30, applied: SI 2008/1597 Sch.5 para.11
s.30, varied: SI 2008/1597 Sch.5 para.12
s.31, applied: SI 2008/1597 Sch.5 para.11
s.31, varied: SI 2008/1597 Sch.5 para.12
s.32, applied: SI 2008/1597 Sch.5 para.11
s.32, varied: SI 2008/1597 Sch.5 para.12
s.33, amended: SI 2008/1277 Sch.4 Part 1
s.33, applied: SI 2008/1597 Sch.5 para.11, Sch.5 para.14
s.33, varied: SI 2008/1597 Sch.5 para.12
s.34, amended: SI 2008/1277 Sch.4 Part 1
s.34, applied: SI 2008/1597 Sch.5 para.11
s.34, varied: SI 2008/1597 Sch.5 para.12
s.35, amended: SI 2008/1277 Sch.4 Part 1
s.35, applied: SI 2008/1597 Sch.5 para.11, Sch.5 para.14
s.35, varied: SI 2008/1597 Sch.5 para.12
s.37, applied: SI 2008/1597 Sch.5 para.11
s.37, varied: SI 2008/1597 Sch.5 para.12
s.39, amended: SI 2008/1277 Sch.2 para.35
s.39, applied: SI 2008/1597 Sch.5 para.11
s.39, varied: SI 2008/1597 Sch.5 para.12
s.40, applied: SI 2008/1597 Sch.5 para.11
s.40, varied: SI 2008/1597 Sch.5 para.12
s.41, amended: SI 2008/1277 Sch.4 Part 1
s.44, applied: SI 2008/1597 Sch.5 para.11
s.44, varied: SI 2008/1597 Sch.5 para.12
s.46, amended: SI 2008/1277 Sch.2 para.36, Sch.4 Part 1
s.46, applied: SI 2008/2852 Sch.6 para.40

CAP.

1987–cont.

43. Consumer Protection Act 1987–*cont.*
s.47, applied: SI 2008/1597 Sch.5 para.11
s.47, varied: SI 2008/1597 Sch.5 para.12
s.49, amended: SI 2008/1277 Sch.2 para.37

51. Finance (No.2) Act 1987
s.62, applied: 2008 c.9 s.58
s.102, applied: SI 2008/908
s.102, enabling: SI 2008/908

53. Channel Tunnel Act 1987
s.1, applied: SI 2008/2852 Sch.3 para.7
s.11, applied: 2008 c.13 Sch.7, SI 2008/539 Art.1
s.11, enabling: SI 2008/2366

57. Urban Development Corporations (Financial Limits) Act 1987
repealed: 2008 c.12 Sch.1 Part 9
s.1, referred to: 2008 c.12 Sch.2 para.9

1988

1. Income and Corporation Taxes Act 1988
see *A Trust Co Ltd (2007/84), Re* [2008] W.T.L.R. 377 (Royal Ct (Jer)), Commissioner Clyde-Smith; see *Paycheck Services 3 Ltd, Re* [2008] EWHC 2200 (Ch), [2008] S.T.C. 3142 (Ch D (Companies Ct)), Mark Cawson Q.C.; see *Test Claimants in the CFC and Dividend Group Litigation v Inland Revenue Commissioners (C-201/05)* [2008] S.T.C. 1513 (ECJ (4th Chamber)), Judge Lenaerts (President)
referred to: SI 2008/1942 Reg.3
Part IV c.I, applied: SI 2008/1273 Sch.5 para.5
Part VII c.I, applied: SI 2008/18 Sch.3 para.4, SI 2008/529 Sch.4 para.5, SI 2008/538 Reg.10, SI 2008/1582 Sch.4 para.5, SI 2008/3170 Sch.5 para.5, Sch.6 para.4
Part VII c.I, referred to: SI 2008/1273 Sch.6 para.5
Part XIII c.II, applied: 2008 c.9 Sch.13 para.6
Part XIV, applied: SSI 2008/228 Reg.91
Part XVII c.IV, applied: 2008 c.9 s.64
s.12, repealed (in part): SI 2008/381 Art.3
s.13, amended: 2008 c.9 s.35
s.13, referred to: 2008 c.9 s.7
s.18, see *Minto v Revenue and Customs Commissioners* [2008] S.T.C. (S.C.D.) 121 (Sp Comm), John Walters Q.C.
s.19, see *Barrett v Revenue and Customs Commissioners* [2008] S.T.C. (S.C.D.) 268 (Sp Comm), Adrian Shipwright; see *Minto v Revenue and Customs Commissioners* [2008] S.T.C. (S.C.D.) 121 (Sp Comm), John Walters Q.C.
s.31ZA, applied: SI 2008/1520 Reg.2
s.31ZA, enabling: SI 2008/1520
s.31ZC, enabling: SI 2008/1520
s.36, amended: 2008 c.9 Sch.39 para.17
s.42, applied: SI 2008/1520 Reg.7

CAP.

1988–cont.

1. Income and Corporation Taxes Act 1988–*cont.*
s.42, referred to: SI 2008/1520 Reg.7
s.53, amended: 2008 c.9 Sch.17 para.28
s.55, amended: 2008 c.9 Sch.17 para.28
s.56, repealed (in part): 2008 c.9 Sch.17 para.24
s.65, applied: 2008 c.9 Sch.7 para.83, Sch.7 para.85
s.74, see *Micro Fusion 2004-1 LLP v Revenue and Customs Commissioners* [2008] S.T.C. (S.C.D.) 952 (Sp Comm), Edward Sadler; see *Sempra Metals Ltd v Revenue and Customs Commissioners* [2008] S.T.C. (S.C.D.) 1062 (Sp Comm), AN Brice
s.74, amended: 2008 c.9 s.73
s.75, applied: 2008 c.9 s.112, Sch.17 para.5
s.76, amended: 2008 c.9 Sch.17 para.5
s.76, applied: 2008 c.9 Sch.17 para.5
s.95ZA, added: 2008 c.9 Sch.17 para.16
s.100, referred to: 2008 c.18 Sch.13 para.18, Sch.13 para.34
s.112, applied: 2008 c.9 s.58
s.115, amended: 2008 c.9 s.58
s.115, applied: 2008 c.9 s.58
s.122, see *Bute v Revenue and Customs Commissioners* [2008] S.T.C. (S.C.D.) 258 (Sp Comm), Colin Bishopp
s.125, see *Revenue and Customs Commissioners v Bank of Ireland Britain Holdings Ltd* [2007] EWHC 941 (Ch), [2008] S.T.C. 253 (Ch D), Henderson, J
s.135, see *Employee v Revenue and Customs Commissioners* [2008] S.T.C. (S.C.D.) 688 (Sp Comm), AN Brice (Chairman)
s.138, repealed: 2008 c.9 s.50
s.139, repealed: 2008 c.9 s.50
s.145, disapplied: 2008 c.9 s.45
s.198, see *Emms v Revenue and Customs Commissioners* [2008] S.T.C. (S.C.D.) 618 (Sp Comm), Michael Tildesley (Chairman); see *Lewis v Revenue and Customs Commissioners* [2008] S.T.C. (S.C.D.) 895 (Sp Comm), John F Avery Jones
s.221, amended: SI 2008/954 Art.7
s.231, see *Japan Post v Revenue and Customs Commissioners* [2008] EWHC 1511 (Admin), [2008] S.T.C. 3295 (QBD (Admin)), Collins, J.
s.232, see *Japan Post v Revenue and Customs Commissioners* [2008] EWHC 1511 (Admin), [2008] S.T.C. 3295 (QBD (Admin)), Collins, J.
s.256B, amended: SI 2008/673 Art.2, SI 2008/3024 Art.2
s.257, amended: 2008 c.9 s.2, s.3, SI 2008/673 Art.2, SI 2008/3024 Art.2
s.257, applied: SI 2008/794 Reg.109
s.257, referred to: 2008 c.9 s.2, s.3
s.257A, amended: SI 2008/673 Art.2, SI 2008/3024 Art.2

CAP.

1988–cont.

1. **Income and Corporation Taxes Act 1988**–*cont.*

s.257AB, amended: 2008 c.9 Sch.39 para.18, SI 2008/673 Art.2, SI 2008/3024 Art.2
s.257BB, amended: 2008 c.9 Sch.39 para.19
s.257C, disapplied: 2008 c.9 s.2, s.3
s.257C, referred to: SI 2008/673 Art.2
s.257C, enabling: SI 2008/673, SI 2008/3024
s.265, amended: 2008 c.9 Sch.39 para.20, SI 2008/673 Art.3, SI 2008/3024 Art.3
s.265, enabling: SI 2008/673, SI 2008/3024
s.270, see *Paycheck Services 3 Ltd, Re* [2008] EWHC 2200 (Ch), [2008] S.T.C. 3142 (Ch D (Companies Ct)), Mark Cawson Q.C.
s.270, amended: 2008 c.9 Sch.39 para.21
s.273, applied: SI 2008/18 Sch.3 para.3, Sch.3 para.4, SI 2008/529 Sch.4 para.4, Sch.4 para.5, SI 2008/538 Reg.9, Reg.10, SI 2008/1273 Sch.5 para.4, Sch.5 para.5, Sch.6 para.4, Sch.6 para.5, SI 2008/1582 Sch.4 para.4, Sch.4 para.5, SI 2008/3170 Sch.5 para.4, Sch.5 para.5, Sch.6 para.3, Sch.6 para.4
s.278, amended: 2008 c.9 s.70
s.278, repealed (in part): 2008 c.9 s.70
s.289, see *GC Trading Ltd v Revenue and Customs Commissioners* [2008] S.T.C. (S.C.D.) 178 (Sp Comm), Adrian Shipwright (Chairman)
s.306, see *Ashley v Revenue and Customs Commissioners* [2008] S.T.C. (S.C.D.) 219 (Sp Comm), Adrian Shipwright
s.313, see *Kent Foods Ltd v Revenue and Customs Commissioners* [2008] S.T.C. (S.C.D.) 307 (Sp Comm), J Gordon Reid Q.C.
s.329AA, see *Minto v Revenue and Customs Commissioners* [2008] S.T.C. (S.C.D.) 121 (Sp Comm), John Walters Q.C.
s.334, see *Barrett v Revenue and Customs Commissioners* [2008] S.T.C. (S.C.D.) 268 (Sp Comm), Adrian Shipwright; see *Grace v Revenue and Customs Commissioners* [2008] S.T.C. (S.C.D.) 531 (Sp Comm), AN Brice
s.336, see *Grace v Revenue and Customs Commissioners* [2008] EWHC 2708 (Ch), [2008] B.T.C. 843 (Ch D), Lewison, J.; see *Grace v Revenue and Customs Commissioners* [2008] S.T.C. (S.C.D.) 531 (Sp Comm), AN Brice
s.338, see *Revenue and Customs Commissioners v Bank of Ireland Britain Holdings Ltd* [2007] EWHC 941 (Ch), [2008] S.T.C. 253 (Ch D), Henderson, J
s.343, see *Barkers of Malton Ltd v Revenue and Customs Commissioners* [2008] S.T.C. (S.C.D.) 884 (Sp Comm), Michael Tildesley (Chairman)
s.343, amended: 2008 c.9 Sch.35 para.3
s.343, applied: 2008 c.17 Sch.7 para.5

CAP.

1988–cont.

1. **Income and Corporation Taxes Act 1988**–*cont.*

s.343, repealed (in part): 2008 c.9 s.66
s.343ZA, added: 2008 c.9 s.89
s.369, applied: SI 2008/794 Sch.8 para.18, Sch.9 para.24
s.376, amended: 2008 c.17 Sch.8 para.42, Sch.9 para.12
s.376, varied: SI 2008/2839 Sch.1 para.1
s.393, see *Sun Life Assurance Co of Canada (UK) Ltd v Revenue and Customs Commissioners* [2008] S.T.C. (S.C.D.) 486 (Sp Comm), Julian Ghosh Q.C.
s.393, amended: 2008 c.9 Sch.35 para.4
s.393A, amended: 2008 c.9 s.110, Sch.34 para.1, Sch.35 para.5
s.393B, added: 2008 c.9 s.111
s.395, amended: 2008 c.9 Sch.24 para.17
s.410, applied: 2008 c.18 Sch.13 para.42
s.416, see *Kellogg Brown & Root Holdings Ltd v Revenue and Customs Commissioners* [2008] S.T.C. (S.C.D.) 928 (Sp Comm), Dr John F Avery Jones
s.416, applied: SI 2008/225 Sch.1 para.40, Sch.1 para.41
s.416, referred to: SI 2008/225 Sch.1 para.40
s.416, varied: SI 2008/225 Sch.1 para.40
s.419, amended: 2008 c.9 Sch.39 para.22
s.419, applied: 2008 c.9 Sch.41 para.7
s.431, amended: 2008 c.9 Sch.17 para.8, Sch.17 para.9, Sch.17 para.10, Sch.17 para.11, Sch.17 para.18, Sch.17 para.19, Sch.17 para.34, SI 2008/381 Art.4
s.431, repealed (in part): 2008 c.9 Sch.17 para.19
s.431, varied: SI 2008/2646 Reg.3
s.431A, amended: 2008 c.9 Sch.17 para.20
s.431A, enabling: SI 2008/1905, SI 2008/1923, SI 2008/3096
s.431D, amended: 2008 c.9 Sch.17 para.26
s.431D, enabling: SI 2008/2625
s.431E, enabling: SI 2008/2627
s.431ZA, added: 2008 c.9 Sch.17 para.10
s.432A, amended: 2008 c.9 Sch.17 para.10, Sch.17 para.17, SI 2008/954 Art.9
s.432A, repealed (in part): 2008 c.9 Sch.17 para.17, Sch.17 para.19
s.432AB, amended: 2008 c.9 Sch.17 para.28
s.432AB, repealed (in part): 2008 c.9 Sch.17 para.17
s.432B, repealed (in part): 2008 c.9 Sch.17 para.19
s.432C, amended: 2008 c.9 Sch.17 para.10
s.432E, amended: 2008 c.9 Sch.17 para.10, SI 2008/381 Art.6
s.432YA, amended: SI 2008/954 Art.8, SI 2008/3096 Art.2
s.432YA, repealed (in part): SI 2008/381 Art.5
s.432ZA, varied: SI 2008/1942 Reg.4

CAP.

1988–cont.

1. **Income and Corporation Taxes Act 1988**–*cont.*
s.434A, amended: 2008 c.9 Sch.17 para.21, Sch.17 para.22
s.436A, amended: 2008 c.9 Sch.17 para.40
s.437, amended: 2008 c.9 Sch.14 para.2
s.437, repealed (in part): 2008 c.9 Sch.14 para.2
s.440, amended: 2008 c.9 Sch.17 para.10
s.440B, amended: SI 2008/381 Art.7
s.442A, enabling: SI 2008/1944, SI 2008/2670
s.444A, amended: SI 2008/381 Art.8
s.444A, repealed (in part): SI 2008/381 Art.8
s.444AA, substituted: SI 2008/381 Art.10
s.444AB, amended: 2008 c.9 Sch.17 para.31, SI 2008/381 Art.11, SI 2008/1923 Art.2
s.444ABA, amended: SI 2008/381 Art.12
s.444ABA, repealed (in part): SI 2008/381 Art.12
s.444ABB, amended: 2008 c.9 Sch.17 para.32, SI 2008/381 Art.13
s.444ABBA, added: SI 2008/381 Art.14
s.444ABC, repealed: SI 2008/381 Art.15
s.444ABD, amended: 2008 c.9 Sch.17 para.33, SI 2008/381 Art.16
s.444AC, amended: SI 2008/381 Art.17
s.444AC, repealed (in part): SI 2008/381 Art.17
s.444ACZA, repealed: SI 2008/381 Art.18
s.444AE, substituted: 2008 c.9 Sch.17 para.2
s.444AEA, amended: SI 2008/381 Art.19
s.444AEB, amended: SI 2008/381 Art.20
s.444AEC, amended: SI 2008/381 Art.21
s.444AECA, added: SI 2008/381 Art.22
s.444AECB, added: SI 2008/381 Art.22
s.444AECC, added: SI 2008/381 Art.22
s.444AED, amended: SI 2008/381 Art.23
s.444AZA, added: SI 2008/381 Art.9
s.444AZB, added: SI 2008/381 Art.9
s.444BA, amended: SI 2008/2673 Art.2
s.444BB, enabling: SI 2008/2679
s.444BC, enabling: SI 2008/2679
s.444BD, enabling: SI 2008/2679
s.461, varied: SI 2008/1942 Reg.5
s.461B, varied: SI 2008/1942 Reg.6
s.461D, added: 2008 c.9 Sch.18 para.3
s.461D, varied: SI 2008/1942 Reg.2
s.461D, enabling: SI 2008/1942
s.461E, varied: SI 2008/1942 Reg.7
s.461F, varied: SI 2008/1942 Reg.7
s.461G, varied: SI 2008/1942 Reg.7
s.462, amended: 2008 c.9 Sch.18 para.5
s.462, repealed (in part): 2008 c.9 Sch.18 para.5
s.462A, repealed: 2008 c.9 Sch.18 para.5
s.463, amended: 2008 c.9 Sch.18 para.4
s.463, enabling: SI 2008/1937
s.466, amended: 2008 c.9 Sch.18 para.2
s.468, amended: 2008 c.9 Sch.1 para.41

CAP.

1988–cont.

1. **Income and Corporation Taxes Act 1988**–*cont.*
s.468A, amended: 2008 c.9 Sch.1 para.42
s.488, amended: 2008 c.17 Sch.9 para.13
s.488, varied: SI 2008/2839 Sch.1 para.1
s.489, amended: 2008 c.17 Sch.9 para.14
s.489, varied: SI 2008/2839 Sch.1 para.1
s.492, amended: 2008 c.9 s.112
s.495, amended: 2008 c.9 Sch.27 para.21
s.500, amended: 2008 c.9 Sch.39 para.23
s.502B, applied: 2008 c.9 Sch.20 para.11
s.502B, disapplied: 2008 c.9 Sch.20 para.11
s.502C, disapplied: 2008 c.9 Sch.20 para.11
s.502D, applied: 2008 c.9 Sch.20 para.11
s.502GA, added: 2008 c.9 Sch.20 para.9
s.502GB, added: 2008 c.9 Sch.20 para.9
s.502GB, referred to: 2008 c.9 Sch.20 para.9
s.502GC, added: 2008 c.9 Sch.20 para.9
s.502H, repealed: 2008 c.9 Sch.17 para.17
s.505, applied: 2008 c.9 Sch.19 para.1
s.506, applied: SI 2008/534 Art.5, SI 2008/535 Art.5
s.506B, amended: 2008 c.17 Sch.9 para.15
s.539, repealed: 2008 c.9 Sch.14 para.3
s.539A, repealed: 2008 c.9 Sch.14 para.3
s.539ZA, repealed: 2008 c.9 Sch.14 para.3
s.540, repealed: 2008 c.9 Sch.14 para.3
s.541, see *Drummond v Revenue and Customs Commissioners* [2008] EWHC 1758 (Ch), [2008] S.T.C. 2707 (Ch D), Norris, J.
s.541, repealed: 2008 c.9 Sch.14 para.3
s.542, repealed: 2008 c.9 Sch.14 para.3
s.543, repealed: 2008 c.9 Sch.14 para.3
s.544, repealed: 2008 c.9 Sch.14 para.3
s.545, repealed: 2008 c.9 Sch.14 para.3
s.546, repealed: 2008 c.9 Sch.14 para.3
s.546A, repealed: 2008 c.9 Sch.14 para.3
s.546B, repealed: 2008 c.9 Sch.14 para.3
s.546C, repealed: 2008 c.9 Sch.14 para.3
s.546D, repealed: 2008 c.9 Sch.14 para.3
s.547, see *Drummond v Revenue and Customs Commissioners* [2008] EWHC 1758 (Ch), [2008] S.T.C. 2707 (Ch D), Norris, J.
s.547, repealed: 2008 c.9 Sch.14 para.3
s.547A, repealed: 2008 c.9 Sch.14 para.3
s.548, repealed: 2008 c.9 Sch.14 para.3
s.548A, repealed: 2008 c.9 Sch.14 para.3
s.548B, repealed: 2008 c.9 Sch.14 para.3
s.549, repealed: 2008 c.9 Sch.14 para.3
s.550, repealed: 2008 c.9 Sch.14 para.3
s.551, repealed: 2008 c.9 Sch.14 para.3
s.551A, repealed: 2008 c.9 Sch.14 para.3
s.552, amended: 2008 c.9 Sch.1 para.43, Sch.14 para.4
s.552, repealed (in part): 2008 c.9 Sch.14 para.4
s.552A, amended: 2008 c.9 Sch.14 para.6
s.552A, enabling: SI 2008/2626

CAP.

1988–cont.

1. **Income and Corporation Taxes Act 1988**–*cont.*

s.552ZA, amended: 2008 c.9 Sch.14 para.5
s.552ZA, enabling: SI 2008/2628
s.553, repealed: 2008 c.9 Sch.14 para.7
s.553A, repealed: 2008 c.9 Sch.14 para.7
s.553B, repealed: 2008 c.9 Sch.14 para.7
s.553C, repealed: 2008 c.9 Sch.14 para.7
s.565, see *Revenue and Customs Commissioners v Smith* [2007] EWHC 488 (Ch), [2008] S.T.C. 1941 (Ch D), Warren, J.
s.576H, amended: SI 2008/954 Art.10
s.578A, applied: 2008 c.9 s.77
s.590C, applied: SI 2008/653 Reg.12, SSI 2008/224 Reg.12
s.591, see *Thorpe v Revenue and Customs Commissioners* [2008] S.T.C. (S.C.D.) 802 (Sp Comm), Julian Ghosh Q.C.
s.591, applied: SI 2008/653 Reg.8
s.591C, see *Thorpe v Revenue and Customs Commissioners* [2008] S.T.C. (S.C.D.) 802 (Sp Comm), Julian Ghosh Q.C.
s.592, see *Irving v Revenue and Customs Commissioners* [2008] EWCA Civ 6, [2008] S.T.C. 597 (CA (Civ Div)), Sedley, L.J.; see *Thorpe v Revenue and Customs Commissioners* [2008] S.T.C. (S.C.D.) 802 (Sp Comm), Julian Ghosh Q.C.
s.592, varied: 2008 c.9 Sch.29 para.17
s.595, see *Irving v Revenue and Customs Commissioners* [2008] EWCA Civ 6, [2008] S.T.C. 597 (CA (Civ Div)), Sedley, L.J.
s.596, see *Irving v Revenue and Customs Commissioners* [2008] EWCA Civ 6, [2008] S.T.C. 597 (CA (Civ Div)), Sedley, L.J.
s.596A, see *Barclays Bank Plc v Revenue and Customs Commissioners* [2007] EWCA Civ 442, [2008] S.T.C. 476 (CA (Civ Div)), May, L.J.; see *Irving v Revenue and Customs Commissioners* [2008] EWCA Civ 6, [2008] S.T.C. 597 (CA (Civ Div)), Sedley, L.J.; see *Thorpe v Revenue and Customs Commissioners* [2008] S.T.C. (S.C.D.) 802 (Sp Comm), Julian Ghosh Q.C.
s.611, see *Telent Plc v Revenue and Customs Commissioners* [2008] S.T.C. (S.C.D.) 202 (Sp Comm), John Clark
s.612, see *Barclays Bank Plc v Revenue and Customs Commissioners* [2007] EWCA Civ 442, [2008] S.T.C. 476 (CA (Civ Div)), May, L.J.
s.619, applied: SI 2008/18 Sch.3 para.3, Sch.3 para.4
s.639, applied: SI 2008/18 Sch.3 para.3, Sch.3 para.4
s.656, repealed (in part): 2008 c.9 Sch.14 para.8

CAP.

1988–cont.

1. **Income and Corporation Taxes Act 1988**–*cont.*

s.657, repealed (in part): 2008 c.9 Sch.14 para.8
s.658, repealed (in part): 2008 c.9 Sch.14 para.8
s.658, enabling: SI 2008/562, SI 2008/1481
s.686, see *Peter Clay Discretionary Trust Trustees v Revenue and Customs Commissioners* [2007] EWHC 2661 (Ch), [2008] Ch. 291 (Ch D), Lindsay, J.
s.699A, amended: 2008 c.9 Sch.1 para.44
s.701, amended: 2008 c.9 Sch.1 para.45
s.701, repealed (in part): 2008 c.9 Sch.1 para.45
s.703, see *Lloyd v Revenue and Customs Commissioners* [2008] S.T.C. (S.C.D.) 681 (Sp Comm), John F Avery Jones; see *Snell v Revenue and Customs Commissioners* [2008] S.T.C. (S.C.D.) 1094 (Sp Comm), Richard Barlow
s.704, see *Lloyd v Revenue and Customs Commissioners* [2008] S.T.C. (S.C.D.) 681 (Sp Comm), John F Avery Jones
s.704, repealed (in part): 2008 c.9 s.66
s.709, repealed (in part): 2008 c.9 s.66
s.710, see *Revenue and Customs Commissioners v D'Arcy* [2007] EWHC 163 (Ch), [2008] S.T.C. 1329 (Ch D), Henderson, J
s.715, see *Revenue and Customs Commissioners v D'Arcy* [2007] EWHC 163 (Ch), [2008] S.T.C. 1329 (Ch D), Henderson, J
s.730A, see *DCC Holdings (UK) Ltd v Revenue and Customs Commissioners* [2008] EWHC 2429 (Ch), [2008] B.T.C. 755 (Ch D), Norris, J.; see *Revenue and Customs Commissioners v Bank of Ireland Britain Holdings Ltd* [2007] EWHC 941 (Ch), [2008] S.T.C. 253 (Ch D), Henderson, J; see *Revenue and Customs Commissioners v Bank of Ireland Britain Holdings Ltd* [2008] EWCA Civ 58, [2008] S.T.C. 398 (CA (Civ Div)), Maurice Kay, L.J.
s.731, applied: 2008 c.9 s.66
s.731, repealed: 2008 c.9 s.66
s.732, repealed: 2008 c.9 s.66
s.733, repealed: 2008 c.9 s.66
s.734, repealed: 2008 c.9 s.66
s.735, repealed: 2008 c.9 s.66
s.736, repealed: 2008 c.9 s.66
s.737A, see *Revenue and Customs Commissioners v Bank of Ireland Britain Holdings Ltd* [2007] EWHC 941 (Ch), [2008] S.T.C. 253 (Ch D), Henderson, J; see *Revenue and Customs Commissioners v Bank of Ireland Britain Holdings Ltd* [2008] EWCA Civ 58, [2008] S.T.C. 398 (CA (Civ Div)), Maurice Kay, L.J.
s.737D, repealed: 2008 c.9 Sch.17 para.35

CAP.

1988–cont.

1. **Income and Corporation Taxes Act 1988**–*cont.*

s.738, repealed: 2008 c.9 s.66
s.747, see *Vodafone 2 v Revenue and Customs Commissioners* [2008] EWHC 1569 (Ch), [2008] S.T.C. 2391 (Ch D), Evans-Lombe, J.; see *Vodafone 2 v Revenue and Customs Commissioners* [2008] S.T.C. (S.C.D.) 55 (Sp Comm), John Walters Q.C. (Chairman)
s.747, amended: 2008 c.9 s.64
s.748, see *Vodafone 2 v Revenue and Customs Commissioners* [2008] EWHC 1569 (Ch), [2008] S.T.C. 2391 (Ch D), Evans-Lombe, J.; see *Vodafone 2 v Revenue and Customs Commissioners* [2008] S.T.C. (S.C.D.) 55 (Sp Comm), John Walters Q.C. (Chairman)
s.754, amended: 2008 c.9 s.119
s.755A, amended: 2008 c.9 Sch.17 para.14
s.755A, repealed (in part): 2008 c.9 Sch.17 para.18
s.755C, enabling: SI 2008/2643
s.755D, amended: 2008 c.9 s.64
s.756, see *Vodafone 2 v Revenue and Customs Commissioners* [2008] EWHC 1569 (Ch), [2008] S.T.C. 2391 (Ch D), Evans-Lombe, J.; see *Vodafone 2 v Revenue and Customs Commissioners* [2008] S.T.C. (S.C.D.) 55 (Sp Comm), John Walters Q.C. (Chairman)
s.756A, repealed (in part): 2008 c.9 s.41
s.756B, amended: 2008 c.9 s.41
s.756B, applied: 2008 c.9 s.42
s.756B, repealed (in part): 2008 c.9 s.41
s.756C, applied: 2008 c.9 s.42
s.756C, repealed (in part): 2008 c.9 s.41
s.757, amended: 2008 c.9 Sch.17 para.30
s.757, repealed: 2008 c.9 s.41
s.758, repealed: 2008 c.9 s.41
s.759, repealed: 2008 c.9 s.41
s.760, repealed: 2008 c.9 s.41
s.761, amended: 2008 c.9 Sch.7 para.92
s.761, applied: 2008 c.9 Sch.7 para.100, Sch.7 para.101, Sch.7 para.102
s.761, repealed: 2008 c.9 s.41
s.762, amended: 2008 c.9 Sch.7 para.93
s.762, applied: 2008 c.9 Sch.7 para.100, Sch.7 para.101, Sch.7 para.102, Sch.7 para.122
s.762, repealed: 2008 c.9 s.41
s.762A, repealed: 2008 c.9 s.41
s.762ZA, added: 2008 c.9 Sch.7 para.94
s.762ZA, repealed: 2008 c.9 s.41
s.762ZB, added: 2008 c.9 Sch.7 para.94
s.762ZB, repealed: 2008 c.9 s.41
s.763, repealed: 2008 c.9 s.41
s.767, amended: SI 2008/954 Art.11
s.767A, applied: 2008 c.9 Sch.36 para.36
s.767AA, applied: 2008 c.9 Sch.36 para.36
s.767B, amended: 2008 c.9 Sch.36 para.80

CAP.

1988–cont.

1. **Income and Corporation Taxes Act 1988**–*cont.*

s.767C, repealed: 2008 c.9 Sch.36 para.81
s.768, applied: 2008 c.18 Sch.13 para.30
s.768A, amended: 2008 c.9 Sch.35 para.6
s.768A, applied: 2008 c.18 Sch.13 para.30
s.768B, applied: 2008 c.18 Sch.13 para.30
s.768C, applied: 2008 c.18 Sch.13 para.30
s.768D, applied: 2008 c.18 Sch.13 para.30
s.768E, applied: 2008 c.18 Sch.13 para.30
s.769, amended: 2008 c.9 Sch.36 para.82
s.769, applied: 2008 c.9 Sch.36 para.36
s.774E, amended: 2008 c.9 Sch.20 para.12
s.774E, repealed (in part): 2008 c.9 Sch.20 para.6
s.781, applied: 2008 c.18 Sch.13 para.16, Sch.13 para.25
s.781, referred to: 2008 c.18 Sch.13 para.16, Sch.13 para.25
s.782, referred to: 2008 c.18 Sch.13 para.16, Sch.13 para.25
s.783, disapplied: 2008 c.18 Sch.13 para.16, Sch.13 para.25
s.783, referred to: 2008 c.18 Sch.13 para.16, Sch.13 para.25
s.784, referred to: 2008 c.18 Sch.13 para.16, Sch.13 para.25
s.785, referred to: 2008 c.18 Sch.13 para.16, Sch.13 para.25
s.785A, amended: 2008 c.9 Sch.20 para.3, Sch.22 para.1
s.785A, repealed (in part): 2008 c.9 Sch.22 para.1
s.785B, added: 2008 c.9 Sch.20 para.1
s.785B, varied: 2008 c.9 Sch.20 para.1
s.785C, added: 2008 c.9 Sch.20 para.1
s.785C, varied: 2008 c.9 Sch.20 para.1
s.785D, added: 2008 c.9 Sch.20 para.1
s.785D, varied: 2008 c.9 Sch.20 para.1
s.785E, added: 2008 c.9 Sch.20 para.1
s.785E, varied: 2008 c.9 Sch.20 para.1
s.788, applied: SI 2008/1770, SI 2008/1793, SI 2008/1795, SI 2008/1796
s.788, enabling: SI 2008/1770, SI 2008/1793, SI 2008/1795, SI 2008/1796
s.789, repealed (in part): 2008 c.9 Sch.1 para.46
s.793, see *Snell v Revenue and Customs Commissioners* [2008] S.T.C. (S.C.D.) 1094 (Sp Comm), Richard Barlow
s.798, amended: 2008 c.9 s.57
s.804B, amended: 2008 c.9 Sch.17 para.10
s.804E, amended: SI 2008/954 Art.12
s.806, amended: 2008 c.9 Sch.39 para.24
s.806G, amended: 2008 c.9 Sch.39 para.25
s.806H, enabling: SI 2008/2681
s.806M, amended: 2008 c.9 Sch.39 para.26
s.807A, amended: 2008 c.9 Sch.22 para.2
s.807A, repealed (in part): 2008 c.9 Sch.22 para.2
s.815AZA, added: 2008 c.9 s.59

CAP.

1988–cont.

1. **Income and Corporation Taxes Act 1988**–*cont.*
s.824, see *Japan Post v Revenue and Customs Commissioners* [2008] EWHC 1511 (Admin), [2008] S.T.C. 3295 (QBD (Admin)), Collins, J.
s.824, amended: 2008 c.9 Sch.12 para.15
s.826, amended: 2008 c.9 Sch.25 para.7, Sch.35 para.7
s.828, amended: 2008 c.9 Sch.16 para.3
s.834, amended: SI 2008/954 Art.13
s.839, applied: 2008 c.18 Sch.13 para.18, Sch.13 para.34, SI 2008/562 Reg.19
Sch.15 Part I para.20, amended: 2008 c.9 Sch.14 para.9
Sch.15 Part I para.20, repealed (in part): 2008 c.9 Sch.14 para.9
Sch.18 para.1, amended: 2008 c.9 Sch.24 para.18
Sch.18 para.5B, applied: 2008 c.18 Sch.13 para.42
Sch.18A Part 2, applied: SI 2008/2646 Reg.2
Sch.18A Part 2 para.16, enabling: SI 2008/2646
Sch.19ABA Part 2 para.8, substituted: SI 2008/1923 Art.3
Sch.19ABA Part 2 para.8A, added: SI 2008/1923 Art.3
Sch.19ABA Part 2 para.8B, added: SI 2008/1923 Art.3
Sch.19ABA Part 2 para.8C, added: SI 2008/1923 Art.3
Sch.19ABA Part 2 para.8D, added: SI 2008/1923 Art.3
Sch.19ABA Part 2 para.8E, added: SI 2008/1923 Art.3
Sch.19ABA Part 2 para.8F, added: SI 2008/1923 Art.3
Sch.19ABA Part 3 para.20A, added: SI 2008/1923 Art.3
Sch.19B Part I para.1, amended: 2008 c.9 Sch.35 para.8
Sch.19B Part IV para.17, amended: 2008 c.9 Sch.35 para.8
Sch.19C Part 1 para.1, amended: 2008 c.9 Sch.35 para.9
Sch.19C Part 4 para.17, amended: 2008 c.9 Sch.35 para.9
Sch.24, see *Vodafone 2 v Revenue and Customs Commissioners* [2008] EWHC 1569 (Ch), [2008] S.T.C. 2391 (Ch D), Evans-Lombe, J.; see *Vodafone 2 v Revenue and Customs Commissioners* [2008] S.T.C. (S.C.D.) 55 (Sp Comm), John Walters Q.C. (Chairman)
Sch.25 Part I para.2A, amended: 2008 c.9 s.64
Sch.25 Part I para.4, amended: 2008 c.9 Sch.17 para.29
Sch.25 Part II para.6, amended: 2008 c.9 s.64

CAP.

1988–cont.

1. **Income and Corporation Taxes Act 1988**–*cont.*
Sch.25 Part II para.11A, amended: SI 2008/954 Art.14, Sch.1
Sch.25 Part II para.11B, amended: SI 2008/954 Art.14
Sch.26, see *Vodafone 2 v Revenue and Customs Commissioners* [2008] S.T.C. (S.C.D.) 55 (Sp Comm), John Walters Q.C. (Chairman)
Sch.26, see *Vodafone 2 v Revenue and Customs Commissioners* [2008] EWHC 1569 (Ch), [2008] S.T.C. 2391 (Ch D), Evans-Lombe, J.; see *Vodafone 2 v Revenue and Customs Commissioners* [2008] S.T.C. (S.C.D.) 55 (Sp Comm), John Walters Q.C. (Chairman)
Sch.27 Part I para.1, repealed: 2008 c.9 s.41
Sch.27 Part I para.1, repealed: 2008 c.9 s.41
Sch.27 Part I para.2, repealed: 2008 c.9 s.41
Sch.27 Part I para.3, repealed: 2008 c.9 s.41
Sch.27 Part I para.4, repealed: 2008 c.9 s.41
Sch.27 Part I para.5, repealed: 2008 c.9 s.41
Sch.27 Part II para.6, repealed: 2008 c.9 s.41
Sch.27 Part II para.7, repealed: 2008 c.9 s.41
Sch.27 Part II para.8, repealed: 2008 c.9 s.41
Sch.27 Part II para.9, repealed: 2008 c.9 s.41
Sch.27 Part II para.10, repealed: 2008 c.9 s.41
Sch.27 Part II para.11, repealed: 2008 c.9 s.41
Sch.27 Part II para.12, repealed: 2008 c.9 s.41
Sch.27 Part II para.13, repealed: 2008 c.9 s.41
Sch.27 Part II para.14, repealed: 2008 c.9 s.41
Sch.27 Part III para.15, repealed: 2008 c.9 s.41
Sch.27 Part III para.16, repealed: 2008 c.9 s.41
Sch.27 Part IV para.17, repealed: 2008 c.9 s.41
Sch.27 Part IV para.18, repealed: 2008 c.9 s.41
Sch.27 Part IV para.19, repealed: 2008 c.9 s.41
Sch.27 Part IV para.20, repealed: 2008 c.9 s.41
Sch.27 Part IV para.21, repealed: 2008 c.9 s.41
Sch.28AA, applied: 2008 c.9 Sch.15 para.10
Sch.28 Part I para.1, repealed: 2008 c.9 s.41
Sch.28 Part I para.2, repealed: 2008 c.9 s.41
Sch.28 Part I para.3, repealed: 2008 c.9 s.41
Sch.28 Part I para.4, repealed: 2008 c.9 s.41
Sch.28 Part I para.5, repealed: 2008 c.9 s.41
Sch.28 Part II para.6, repealed: 2008 c.9 s.41
Sch.28 Part II para.7, repealed: 2008 c.9 s.41
Sch.28 Part II para.8, repealed: 2008 c.9 s.41
Sch.28 Part III para.9, repealed: 2008 c.9 s.41
Sch.28AA para.5A, amended: SI 2008/954 Art.15
Sch.36, applied: SSI 2008/224 Reg.8

4. **Norfolk and Suffolk Broads Act 1988**
s.2, applied: 2008 c.29 s.206

CAP.

1988–cont.

4. Norfolk and Suffolk Broads Act 1988– *cont.*
s.9, amended: 2008 c.29 s.224

7. Social Security Act 1988
s.13, applied: SI 2008/408, SI 2008/794 Sch.8 para.46, Sch.9 para.38
s.13, enabling: SI 2008/408

9. Local Government Act 1988
Part IV, applied: 2008 c.13 Sch.3
s.24, applied: 2008 c.17 s.274
Sch.2 Part 1, amended: 2008 c.17 Sch.8 para.43, 2008 c.26 Sch.4 para.55, SI 2008/912 Sch.1 para.8

13. Coroners Act 1988
s.8, see *R. (on the application of Bicknell) v HM Coroner for Birmingham and Solihull* [2007] EWHC 2547 (Admin), (2008) 11 C.C.L. Rep. 431 (QBD (Admin)), McCombe, J.; see *R. (on the application of Paul) v Deputy Coroner of the Queen's Household* [2007] EWHC 408 (Admin), [2008] Q.B.172 (DC), Smith, L.J.
s.14, see *R. (on the application of Paul) v Deputy Coroner of the Queen's Household* [2007] EWHC 408 (Admin), [2008] Q.B. 172 (DC), Smith, L.J.
s.15, see *R. (on the application of Bicknell) v HM Coroner for Birmingham and Solihull* [2007] EWHC 2547 (Admin), (2008) 11 C.C.L. Rep. 431 (QBD (Admin)), McCombe, J.
s.19, applied: SI 2008/2841 Reg.18
s.29, see *R. (on the application of Paul) v Deputy Coroner of the Queen's Household* [2007] EWHC 408 (Admin), [2008] Q.B. 172 (DC), Smith, L.J.
s.32, enabling: SI 2008/1652

14. Immigration Act 1988
s.2, varied: SI 2008/680 Art.5, Art.10, Sch.4 para.1
s.3, varied: SI 2008/680 Art.5, Art.10
s.6, varied: SI 2008/680 Art.5, Art.10
s.7, varied: SI 2008/680 Art.5, Art.10, Sch.4 para.2
s.10, varied: SI 2008/680 Art.5, Art.10
s.11, varied: SI 2008/680 Art.5, Art.10, Sch.4 para.3
s.12, varied: SI 2008/680 Art.5, Art.10, Sch.4 para.4
Sch.1 para.1, varied: SI 2008/680 Art.5, Art.10
Sch.1 para.2, varied: SI 2008/680 Art.5, Art.10
Sch.1 para.5, varied: SI 2008/680 Art.5, Art.10
Sch.1 para.7, varied: SI 2008/680 Art.5, Art.10
Sch.1 para.8, varied: SI 2008/680 Art.5, Art.10
Sch.1 para.9, varied: SI 2008/680 Art.5, Art.10

CAP.

1988–cont.

14. Immigration Act 1988– *cont.*
Sch.1 para.10, varied: SI 2008/680 Art.5, Art.10

20. Dartford-Thurrock Crossing Act 1988
s.25, enabling: SI 2008/2171
s.33, amended: SI 2008/948 Sch.1 para.152

22. Scotch Whisky Act 1988
applied: 2008 c.13 Sch.3

27. Malicious Communications Act 1988
applied: 2008 c.13 Sch.3
s.1, see *Connolly v DPP* [2007] EWHC 237 (Admin), [2008] 1 W.L.R. 276 (DC), Dyson, L.J.

30. Environment and Safety Information Act 1988
applied: 2008 c.13 Sch.3

31. Protection against Cruel Tethering Act 1988
applied: 2008 c.13 Sch.3

33. Criminal Justice Act 1988
see *CPS v Moulden (Leanne)* [2008] EWCA Crim 2648, Times, November 26, 2008 (CA (Crim Div)), Pill, L.J.; see *R. v Summers (Michael John)* [2008] EWCA Crim 872, [2008] 2 Cr. App. R. (S.) 101 (CA (Crim Div)), Dyson, L.J.; see *R. v W Stevenson & Sons (A Partnership)* [2008] EWCA Crim 273, [2008] Bus. L.R. 1200 (CA (Crim Div)), Lord Phillips, L.C.J.
applied: 2008 c.4 Sch.26 para.22
s.36, amended: 2008 c.4 s.46, Sch.26 para.23, Sch.28 Part 3, SI 2008/1216 Sch.5 para.6
s.40, see *R. v James (Liam Martin)* [2007] EWCA Crim 1906, [2008] 1 Cr. App. R. (S.) 44 (CA (Crim Div)), Longmore, L.J.; see *R. v Plant (Ricardo)* [2008] EWCA Crim 960, [2008] 2 Cr. App. R. 27 (CA (Crim Div)), Lord Phillips of Worth Matravers, L.C.J.
s.49, repealed: 2008 c.12 Sch.1 Part 3
s.64, repealed: 2008 c.12 Sch.1 Part 3
s.71, see *Jennings v Crown Prosecution Service* [2008] UKHL 29, [2008] 1 A.C. 1046 (HL), Lord Bingham of Cornhill; see *R. v Farquhar (Ian)* [2008] EWCA Crim 806, [2008] 2 Cr. App. R. (S.) 104 (CA (Crim Div)), Sir Igor Judge (President); see *R. v Hashash (Amiram)* [2006] EWCA Crim 2518, [2008] S.T.C. 1158 (CA (Crim Div)), Hooper, L.J.
s.72AA, see *CPS v Moulden (Leanne)* [2008] EWCA Crim 2648, Times, November 26, 2008 (CA (Crim Div)), Pill, L.J.; see *R. v Neuberg (Karen Jayne)* [2007] EWCA Crim 1994, [2008] 1 Cr. App. R. (S.) 84 (CA (Crim Div)), Leveson, L.J.
s.74, see *B (Confiscation Order), Re* [2008] EWHC 690 (Admin), [2008] 2 F.L.R. 1 (QBD (Admin)), Cranston, J.

CAP.

1988–cont.

33. Criminal Justice Act 1988–*cont.*

s.75, see *Crown Prosecution Service v Greenacre* [2007] EWHC 1193 (Admin), [2008] 1 W.L.R. 438 (DC), Laws, L.J.

s.75A, see *Crown Prosecution Service v Greenacre* [2007] EWHC 1193 (Admin), [2008] 1 W.L.R. 438 (DC), Laws, L.J.; see *Hansford v Southampton Magistrates' Court* [2008] EWHC 67 (Admin), [2008] 4 All E.R. 432 (DC), Dyson, L.J.

s.81, see *Hansford v Southampton Magistrates' Court* [2008] EWHC 67 (Admin), [2008] 4 All E.R. 432 (DC), Dyson, L.J.

s.93C, see *Ali v Revenue and Customs Prosecutions Office* [2008] EWCA Crim 1466, (2008) 172 J.P. 516 (CA (Crim Div)), Moses, L.J.

s.100, repealed: 2008 c.12 Sch.1 Part 3

s.103, repealed: 2008 c.12 Sch.1 Part 3

s.123, repealed (in part): 2008 c.12 Sch.1 Part 3

s.125, repealed: 2008 c.12 Sch.1 Part 3

s.133, amended: 2008 c.4 s.61

s.133, applied: 2008 c.4 Sch.27 para.22

s.133A, added: 2008 c.4 s.61

s.133B, added: 2008 c.4 s.61

s.134, applied: SI 2008/1216 Sch.1 para.22, Sch.2 para.22

s.139, amended: SI 2008/1216 Art.90

s.139A, amended: SI 2008/1216 Art.90

s.141, amended: SI 2008/1216 Art.90

s.141, applied: SI 2008/973, SI 2008/2039

s.141, referred to: SI 2008/973 Art.2

s.141, enabling: SI 2008/973, SI 2008/2039

s.160, amended: 2008 c.4 Sch.26 para.24

s.160, referred to: 2008 c.4 Sch.27 para.24

s.172, amended: 2008 c.4 s.61

Sch.5 Part I para.1, repealed: 2008 c.12 Sch.1 Part 3

Sch.5 Part I para.2, repealed: 2008 c.12 Sch.1 Part 3

Sch.5 Part I para.3, repealed: 2008 c.12 Sch.1 Part 3

Sch.5 Part I para.4, repealed: 2008 c.12 Sch.1 Part 3

Sch.5 Part I para.5, repealed: 2008 c.12 Sch.1 Part 3

Sch.5 Part I para.6, repealed: 2008 c.12 Sch.1 Part 3

Sch.5 Part I para.7, repealed: 2008 c.12 Sch.1 Part 3

Sch.5 Part I para.8, repealed: 2008 c.12 Sch.1 Part 3

Sch.5 Part I para.9, repealed: 2008 c.12 Sch.1 Part 3

Sch.5 Part I para.10, repealed: 2008 c.12 Sch.1 Part 3

Sch.5 Part I para.11, repealed: 2008 c.12 Sch.1 Part 3

CAP.

1988–cont.

33. Criminal Justice Act 1988–*cont.*

Sch.5 Part I para.12, repealed: 2008 c.12 Sch.1 Part 3

Sch.5 Part I para.13, repealed: 2008 c.12 Sch.1 Part 3

Sch.5 Part I para.14, repealed: 2008 c.12 Sch.1 Part 3

Sch.5 Part I para.15, repealed: 2008 c.12 Sch.1 Part 3

Sch.5 Part I para.16, repealed: 2008 c.12 Sch.1 Part 3

Sch.5 Part I para.17, repealed: 2008 c.12 Sch.1 Part 3

Sch.5 Part II para.18, repealed: 2008 c.12 Sch.1 Part 3

Sch.5 Part II para.19, repealed: 2008 c.12 Sch.1 Part 3

Sch.5 Part II para.20, repealed: 2008 c.12 Sch.1 Part 3

Sch.5 Part II para.21, repealed: 2008 c.12 Sch.1 Part 3

Sch.5 Part II para.22, repealed: 2008 c.12 Sch.1 Part 3

Sch.5 Part II para.23, repealed: 2008 c.12 Sch.1 Part 3

Sch.8 Part II para.11, repealed: 2008 c.12 Sch.1 Part 3

Sch.8 Part II para.12, repealed: 2008 c.12 Sch.1 Part 3

Sch.8 Part II para.13, repealed: 2008 c.12 Sch.1 Part 3

Sch.8 Part II para.14, repealed: 2008 c.12 Sch.1 Part 3

Sch.8 Part II para.15, repealed: 2008 c.12 Sch.1 Part 3

Sch.8 Part II para.16, repealed: 2008 c.12 Sch.1 Part 3

35. British Steel Act 1988

s.7, amended: SI 2008/948 Sch.1 para.153

36. Court of Session Act 1988

see *Tonner v Reiach & Hall (A Firm)* 2008 S.C. 1 (IH (Ex Div)), Lord Abernethy

s.1, amended: 2008 asp 6 s.44

s.1, enabling: SSI 2008/123

s.2, amended: 2008 asp 6 s.45, s.46

s.5, see *Stuart v Bulger* [2008] CSOH 102, 2008 S.L.T. 817 (OH), Lord Mackay of Drumadoon

s.5, amended: 2008 asp 6 s.46

s.5, enabling: SSI 2008/39, SSI 2008/120, SSI 2008/122, SSI 2008/123, SSI 2008/349, SSI 2008/401, SSI 2008/431

s.8, referred to: 2008 asp 6 s.62

s.45, applied: SI 2008/346 Reg.30

39. Finance Act 1988

s.126, repealed: 2008 c.9 Sch.36 para.92

s.127, repealed: 2008 c.9 s.114

Sch.13 Part I para.12, repealed: 2008 c.9 s.41

40. Education Reform Act 1988

applied: 2008 c.25 s.91

s.124B, amended: SI 2008/948 Sch.1 para.1

CAP.

1988–cont.

40. Education Reform Act 1988–*cont.*
s.129, enabling: SI 2008/1643
s.214, referred to: 2008 c.13 Sch.6
s.215, applied: 2008 c.13 Sch.3
s.216, enabling: SI 2008/2888, SI 2008/2889
s.232, enabling: SI 2008/2888
Sch.7 para.18, amended: SI 2008/948 Sch.1 para.1
Sch.10 para.1, applied: SI 2008/136 Reg.10
Sch.10 para.2, applied: SI 2008/136 Reg.10
Sch.12 Part II para.45, repealed: 2008 c.26 Sch.7 Part 4
Sch.12 Part II para.46, repealed: 2008 c.26 Sch.7 Part 4

41. Local Government Finance Act 1988
applied: SI 2008/3022 Reg.3, Reg.4
Part III, applied: SI 2008/3022 Reg.8, Reg.9
s.43, applied: SI 2008/2770 Art.3, Art.4
s.43, enabling: SI 2008/2770
s.44, applied: SI 2008/2770 Art.11
s.44, enabling: SI 2008/2770
s.45, applied: SI 2008/386 Reg.3, SI 2008/2499 Reg.3
s.45, enabling: SI 2008/386, SI 2008/2499
s.53, enabling: SI 2008/429, SI 2008/2672
s.55, applied: SI 2008/2770 Art.9, Art.10
s.55, enabling: SI 2008/2333, SI 2008/2671
s.60, enabling: SI 2008/2838, SI 2008/2929
s.61, applied: 2008 c.29 s.215
s.62, enabling: SI 2008/7, SI 2008/3075
s.64, enabling: SI 2008/429, SI 2008/2672
s.65, varied: SI 2008/1848 Reg.16
s.65, enabling: SI 2008/429, SI 2008/2672
s.66, see *Allen (Valuation Officer) v Mansfield DC* [2008] R.A. 338 (Lands Tr), Judge Huskinson
s.66, applied: SI 2008/794 Sch.6 para.7
s.74, applied: SI 2008/239 Sch.2 para.2
s.75, applied: SI 2008/239 Sch.2 para.2
s.78, applied: 2008 c.8 Sch.2 Part 10
s.78, applied: 2008 c.3 Sch.2 Part 2
s.88B, amended: 2008 c.26 Sch.4 para.56
s.88B, applied: 2008 c.3 Sch.2 Part 2
s.111, amended: 2008 c.26 Sch.4 para.56
s.114, varied: SI 2008/634 Art.8, SI 2008/907 Art.17
s.114A, varied: SI 2008/634 Art.8, SI 2008/907 Art.17
s.115, varied: SI 2008/634 Art.8, SI 2008/907 Art.17
s.115A, varied: SI 2008/634 Art.8, SI 2008/907 Art.17
s.115B, varied: SI 2008/634 Art.8, SI 2008/907 Art.17
s.116, varied: SI 2008/634 Art.8, SI 2008/907 Art.17
s.136, see *Womersley (Valuation Officer) v Hart DC* [2008] R.A. 279 (Lands Tr), Judge Huskinson

CAP.

1988–cont.

41. Local Government Finance Act 1988–*cont.*
s.140, enabling: SI 2008/2838, SI 2008/2929
s.143, enabling: SI 2008/7, SI 2008/216, SI 2008/315, SI 2008/386, SI 2008/387, SI 2008/429, SI 2008/2332, SI 2008/2333, SI 2008/2499, SI 2008/2671, SI 2008/2672, SI 2008/2770, SI 2008/2838, SI 2008/2929, SI 2008/2997, SI 2008/3075, SI 2008/3078
s.146, enabling: SI 2008/7, SI 2008/386, SI 2008/387, SI 2008/429, SI 2008/2333, SI 2008/2499, SI 2008/2671, SI 2008/2672, SI 2008/2770, SI 2008/3075
Sch.4A, applied: SI 2008/386 Reg.6, SI 2008/2499 Reg.6
Sch.5 para.11, see *Gallagher (Valuation Officer) v Church of Jesus Christ of Latter-Day Saints* [2008] UKHL 56, [2008] 1 W.L.R. 1852 (HL), Lord Hoffmann; see *Webb v Thornton (Valuation Officer)* [2008] R.A. 89 (VT)
Sch.6 para.2, see *Chilton-Merryweather (Listing Officer) v Hunt* [2008] EWCA Civ 1025, [2008] R.A. 357 (CA (Civ Div)), Waller, L.J.; see *Schofield (Valuation Officer) v RBNB (An Unlimited Co)* [2008] R.A. 121 (Lands Tr), George Bartlett Q.C. (President, LTr)
Sch.6 para.2, applied: SI 2008/2333 Reg.3, Reg.4, SI 2008/2671 Reg.3, Reg.4
Sch.6 para.2, enabling: SI 2008/216, SI 2008/2332, SI 2008/2333, SI 2008/2671, SI 2008/2997
Sch.8 Part II para.4, enabling: SI 2008/2838, SI 2008/2929, SI 2008/3078
Sch.8 Part II para.6, enabling: SI 2008/2838, SI 2008/2929, SI 2008/3078
Sch.9 para.1, enabling: SI 2008/7, SI 2008/387, SI 2008/3075
Sch.9 para.2, enabling: SI 2008/7, SI 2008/387, SI 2008/3075
Sch.9 para.5, see *Bournemouth & West Hampshire Water Plc v Central Valuation Officer* [2008] R.V.R. 102 (VT)
Sch.9 para.5C, see *Bournemouth & West Hampshire Water Plc v Central Valuation Officer* [2008] R.V.R. 102 (VT)
Sch.11, see *Womersley (Valuation Officer) v Hart DC* [2008] R.A. 279 (Lands Tr), Judge Huskinson
Sch.11 para.1, enabling: SI 2008/315
Sch.11 para.5, enabling: SI 2008/315
Sch.11 para.8, enabling: SI 2008/315

43. Housing (Scotland) Act 1988
s.19A, applied: SSI 2008/324 Reg.2
s.66, applied: SI 2008/794 Sch.9 para.36

45. Firearms (Amendment) Act 1988
s.17, applied: SI 2008/3231 Art.16

CAP.

1988–cont.

48. Copyright, Designs and Patents Act 1988

see *Experience Hendrix LLC v Purple Haze Records Ltd* [2007] EWCA Civ 501, [2008] E.C.C. 9 (CA (Civ Div)), Keene, L.J.; see *HRH Prince of Wales v Associated Newspapers Ltd* [2006] EWCA Civ 1776, [2008] Ch. 57 (CA (Civ Div)), Lord Philips, L.C.J.; see *Lucasfilm Ltd v Ainsworth* [2008] EWHC 1878 (Ch), [2008] E.C.D.R. 17 (Ch D), Mann, J.

Part I, applied: SI 2008/677 Art.2, Art.3, Art.4, Art.5

Part I, disapplied: SI 2008/677 Art.4

Part I, referred to: SI 2008/677 Art.3, Art.4

Part II, see *Experience Hendrix LLC v Purple Haze Records Ltd* [2007] EWCA Civ 501, [2008] E.C.C. 9 (CA (Civ Div)), Keene, L.J.

Part II, applied: SI 2008/677 Art.6

Part II, referred to: SI 2008/677 Art.6

Part II, see *Experience Hendrix LLC v Purple Haze Records Ltd* [2007] EWCA Civ 501, [2008] E.C.C. 9 (CA (Civ Div)), Keene, L.J.

s.4, see *Lucasfilm Ltd v Ainsworth* [2008] EWHC 1878 (Ch), [2008] E.C.D.R. 17 (Ch D), Mann, J.

s.6, see *Murphy v Media Protection Services Ltd* [2007] EWHC 3091 (Admin), [2008] 1 W.L.R. 1869 (DC), Pumfrey, L.J

s.14, applied: SI 2008/677 Art.4

s.16, see *Performing Right Society Ltd v Kwik-Fit Group Ltd* [2008] E.C.D.R. 2 (OH), Lord Emslie

s.17, see *Football Association Premier League Ltd v QC Leisure* [2008] EWHC 1411 (Ch), [2008] U.K.C.L.R. 329 (Ch D), Kitchin, J.

s.18A, applied: SI 2008/677 Art.3, Art.4

s.19, see *Football Association Premier League Ltd v QC Leisure* [2008] EWHC 1411 (Ch), [2008] U.K.C.L.R. 329 (Ch D), Kitchin, J.

s.19, applied: SI 2008/677 Art.3, Art.4

s.20, see *Football Association Premier League Ltd v QC Leisure* [2008] EWHC 1411 (Ch), [2008] U.K.C.L.R. 329 (Ch D), Kitchin, J.

s.20, applied: SI 2008/677 Art.3, Art.4

s.26, see *Performing Right Society Ltd v Kwik-Fit Group Ltd* [2008] E.C.D.R. 2 (OH), Lord Emslie

s.26, applied: SI 2008/677 Art.3, Art.4

s.28A, see *Football Association Premier League Ltd v QC Leisure* [2008] EWHC 1411 (Ch), [2008] U.K.C.L.R. 329 (Ch D), Kitchin, J.

s.30, see *HRH Prince of Wales v Associated Newspapers Ltd* [2006] EWCA Civ 1776, [2008] Ch. 57 (CA (Civ Div)), Lord Philips, L.C.J.

s.35, applied: SI 2008/211

s.48, amended: 2008 c.14 Sch.5 para.60

s.48, varied: SI 2008/2250 Art.3

CAP.

1988–cont.

48. Copyright, Designs and Patents Act 1988–*cont.*

s.51, see *Lucasfilm Ltd v Ainsworth* [2008] EWHC 1878 (Ch), [2008] E.C.D.R. 17 (Ch D), Mann, J.

s.52, see *Jules Rimet Cup Ltd v Football Association Ltd* [2007] EWHC 2376 (Ch), [2008] E.C.D.R. 4 (Ch D), Roger Wyand Q.C.; see *Lucasfilm Ltd v Ainsworth* [2008] EWHC 1878 (Ch), [2008] E.C.D.R. 17 (Ch D), Mann, J.

s.72, see *Football Association Premier League Ltd v QC Leisure* [2008] EWHC 1411 (Ch), [2008] U.K.C.L.R. 329 (Ch D), Kitchin, J.

s.107, applied: SI 2008/677 Art.3, Art.4

s.107A, applied: 2008 c.13 Sch.3

s.114A, amended: SI 2008/1277 Sch.2 para.40

s.114B, amended: SI 2008/1277 Sch.2 para.41

s.143, enabling: SI 2008/211

s.145, applied: SI 2008/2995 Sch.2

s.154, applied: SI 2008/677 Art.2

s.159, enabling: SI 2008/677

s.171, see *HRH Prince of Wales v Associated Newspapers Ltd* [2006] EWCA Civ 1776, [2008] Ch. 57 (CA (Civ Div)), Lord Philips, L.C.J.

s.180, see *Experience Hendrix LLC v Purple Haze Records Ltd* [2007] EWCA Civ 501, [2008] E.C.C. 9 (CA (Civ Div)), Keene, L.J.

s.182C, disapplied: SI 2008/677 Art.6

s.182CA, disapplied: SI 2008/677 Art.6

s.182D, disapplied: SI 2008/677 Art.6

s.183, disapplied: SI 2008/677 Art.6

s.185, disapplied: SI 2008/677 Art.6

s.186, disapplied: SI 2008/677 Art.6

s.187, disapplied: SI 2008/677 Art.6

s.188, disapplied: SI 2008/677 Art.6

s.198, disapplied: SI 2008/677 Art.6

s.198A, applied: 2008 c.13 Sch.3

s.204A, amended: SI 2008/1277 Sch.2 para.42

s.204B, amended: SI 2008/1277 Sch.2 para.43

s.208, enabling: SI 2008/677

s.226, see *Rolawn Ltd v Turfmech Machinery Ltd* [2008] EWHC 989 (Pat), [2008] E.C.D.R. 13 (Ch D (Patents Ct)), Mann, J.; see *Societa Esplosivi Industriali SpA v Ordnance Technologies (UK) Ltd (formerly SEI (UK) Ltd)* [2007] EWHC 2875 (Ch), [2008] 2 All E.R. 622 (Ch D), Lindsay, J.

s.296ZF, see *R. v Higgs (Neil Stanley)* [2008] EWCA Crim 1324, [2008] F.S.R. 34 (CA (Crim Div)), Jacob, L.J.

s.297, see *Murphy v Media Protection Services Ltd* [2007] EWHC 3091 (Admin), [2008] 1 W.L.R. 1869 (DC), Pumfrey, L.J; see *Murphy v Media Protection Services Ltd* [2008] EWHC

CAP.

1988–cont.

48. Copyright, Designs and Patents Act 1988–*cont.*

s.297–*cont.*

1666 (Admin), [2008] U.K.C.L.R. 427 (DC), Stanley Burnton, L.J.

s.297C, amended: SI 2008/1277 Sch.2 para.44

s.297D, amended: SI 2008/1277 Sch.2 para.45

s.298, see *Football Association Premier League Ltd v QC Leisure* [2008] EWHC 44 (Ch), [2008] U.K.C.L.R. 65 (Ch D), Barling, J

s.299, see *Football Association Premier League Ltd v QC Leisure* [2008] EWHC 44 (Ch), [2008] U.K.C.L.R. 65 (Ch D), Barling, J

Sch.2 para.6, applied: SI 2008/211

Sch.2A para.16, enabling: SI 2008/211

49. Health and Medicines Act 1988

s.5, amended: SI 2008/948 Sch.1 para.154

50. Housing Act 1988

Part I, applied: SI 2008/188 Sch.1 para.1

Part II, amended: 2008 c.17 Sch.8 para.45, Sch.16

s.1, see *Richardson v Midland Heart Ltd (formerly Focus Homes Options)* [2008] L. & T.R. 31 (Ch D (Birmingham)), Jonathan Gaunt, Q.C.

s.5, amended: 2008 c.17 Sch.11 para.6

s.7, see *Richardson v Midland Heart Ltd (formerly Focus Homes Options)* [2008] L. & T.R. 31 (Ch D (Birmingham)), Jonathan Gaunt, Q.C.

s.7, amended: 2008 c.17 Sch.11 para.7

s.8, see *Richardson v Midland Heart Ltd (formerly Focus Homes Options)* [2008] L. & T.R. 31 (Ch D (Birmingham)), Jonathan Gaunt, Q.C.

s.9, see *Hastoe Housing Association v Ellis* [2007] EWCA Civ 1238, [2008] H.L.R. 25 (CA (Civ Div)), Mummery, L.J.

s.9, amended: 2008 c.17 Sch.11 para.8, Sch.16

s.9, repealed (in part): 2008 c.17 Sch.11 para.8, Sch.16

s.19A, see *Truro Diocesan Board of Finance Ltd v Foley* [2008] EWCA Civ 1162, Times, December 1, 2008 (CA (Civ Div)), May, L.J.; see *Vesely v Levy* [2007] EWCA Civ 367, [2008] L. & T.R. 9 (CA (Civ Div)), Mummery, L.J.

s.20B, applied: 2008 c.17 Sch.11 para.17

s.20B, referred to: 2008 c.17 Sch.11 para.19

s.21, see *Andrews v Cunningham* [2007] EWCA Civ 762, [2008] H.L.R. 13 (CA (Civ Div)), Waller, L.J.; see *Truro Diocesan Board of Finance Ltd v Foley* [2008] EWCA Civ 1162, Times, December 1, 2008 (CA (Civ Div)), May, L.J.

s.21, amended: 2008 c.17 Sch.11 para.9

CAP.

1988–cont.

50. Housing Act 1988–*cont.*

s.34, see *Truro Diocesan Board of Finance Ltd v Foley* [2008] EWCA Civ 1162, Times, December 1, 2008 (CA (Civ Div)), May, L.J.

s.34, amended: SI 2008/3002 Sch.1 para.37

s.35, amended: SI 2008/3002 Sch.1 para.38

s.35, varied: SI 2008/2839 Sch.1 para.1

s.38, amended: SI 2008/3002 Sch.1 para.39

s.45, see *Truro Diocesan Board of Finance Ltd v Foley* [2008] EWCA Civ 1162, Times, December 1, 2008 (CA (Civ Div)), May, L.J.

s.50, applied: 2008 c.17 s.77, s.274, SI 2008/2839 Art.2

s.50, referred to: 2008 c.17 s.324

s.50, repealed (in part): 2008 c.17 Sch.8 para.46, Sch.16

s.50, varied: SI 2008/2839 Sch.1 para.4

s.51, applied: 2008 c.17 s.274, SI 2008/2839 Art.2

s.51, referred to: 2008 c.17 s.324

s.51, repealed (in part): 2008 c.17 Sch.8 para.46, Sch.16

s.51, varied: SI 2008/2839 Sch.1 para.4

s.52, amended: 2008 c.17 Sch.8 para.47

s.52, applied: SI 2008/2839 Art.2

s.52, disapplied: 2008 c.17 s.177

s.52, referred to: 2008 c.17 s.324

s.52, varied: SI 2008/2839 Sch.1 para.4

s.53, amended: 2008 c.17 Sch.8 para.48

s.53, applied: SI 2008/2839 Art.2

s.53, referred to: 2008 c.17 s.324

s.53, varied: SI 2008/2839 Sch.1 para.4

s.54, amended: 2008 c.17 Sch.8 para.49

s.54, referred to: 2008 c.17 s.324

s.59, amended: 2008 c.17 Sch.8 para.50

s.59, referred to: 2008 c.17 s.324

s.81, amended: 2008 c.17 s.191

s.81, applied: 2008 c.17 s.75, s.149, s.173, s.190

s.81, repealed (in part): 2008 c.17 s.191, Sch.16

s.81, varied: SI 2008/2839 Sch.1 para.1

s.82, applied: SI 2008/2839 Art.2

s.129, applied: SI 2008/794 Sch.9 para.36

s.133, amended: 2008 c.17 s.191, Sch.14 para.2

s.133, applied: 2008 c.17 s.75, s.149, s.173, s.190

s.133, repealed (in part): 2008 c.17 s.191, Sch.16

s.133, varied: SI 2008/2839 Sch.1 para.1

Sch.1 Part I para.4, applied: 2008 c.17 s.173

Sch.1 Part I para.4, referred to: 2008 c.17 s.149

Sch.1 Part I para.5, applied: 2008 c.17 s.173

Sch.1 Part I para.5, referred to: 2008 c.17 s.149

Sch.1 Part I para.6, applied: 2008 c.17 s.173

Sch.1 Part I para.6, referred to: 2008 c.17 s.149

Sch.1 Part I para.7, applied: 2008 c.17 s.173

Sch.1 Part I para.7, referred to: 2008 c.17 s.149

Sch.1 Part I para.8, applied: 2008 c.17 s.173

CAP.

1988–cont.

50. Housing Act 1988–*cont.*

Sch.1 Part I para.8, referred to: 2008 c.17 s.149

Sch.1 Part I para.12, amended: SI 2008/3002 Sch.1 para.40

Sch.1 Part I para.12, applied: 2008 c.17 s.173

Sch.1 Part I para.12, referred to: 2008 c.17 s.149

Sch.1 Part I para.12B, applied: 2008 c.17 s.173

Sch.1 Part I para.12B, referred to: 2008 c.17 s.149

Sch.1 Part I para.12ZA, applied: 2008 c.17 s.173

Sch.1 Part I para.12ZA, referred to: 2008 c.17 s.149

Sch.2, see *R. (on the application of Weaver) v London & Quadrant Housing Trust* [2008] EWHC 1377 (Admin), Times, July 8, 2008 (DC), Richards, L.J.; see *Richardson v Midland Heart Ltd (formerly Focus Homes Options)* [2008] L. & T.R. 31 (Ch D (Birmingham)), Jonathan Gaunt, Q.C.; see *S v Floyd* [2008] EWCA Civ 201, [2008] 1 W.L.R. 1274 (CA (Civ Div)), Mummery, L.J.

Sch.2A para.1, see *Andrews v Cunningham* [2007] EWCA Civ 762, [2008] H.L.R. 13 (CA (Civ Div)), Waller, L.J.

Sch.2A para.2, see *Andrews v Cunningham* [2007] EWCA Civ 762, [2008] H.L.R. 13 (CA (Civ Div)), Waller, L.J.

Sch.6 Part I para.7, repealed (in part): 2008 c.17 Sch.16

Sch.6 Part I para.24, repealed: 2008 c.17 Sch.16

Sch.8 Part III para.11, amended: SI 2008/948 Sch.1 para.1

Sch.10 Part II para.5, amended: 2008 c.29 Sch.9 para.3

Sch.11 para.2, amended: 2008 c.17 s.307

52. Road Traffic Act 1988

see *AXA Insurance UK Plc v Norwich Union Insurance Ltd* [2007] EWHC 1046 (Comm), [2008] Lloyd's Rep. I.R. 122 (QBD (Comm)), Andrew Smith, J.; see *Longstaff v DPP* [2008] EWHC 303 (Admin), [2008] R.T.R. 17 (DC), Maurice Kay, L.J.; see *McNeil v DPP* [2008] EWHC 1254 (Admin), [2008] R.T.R. 27 (DC), Latham, L.J.; see *R. (on the application of Irving) v Secretary of State for Transport* [2008] EWHC 1200 (Admin), (2008) 172 J.P. 425 (QBD (Admin)), Saunders, J.; see *R. v Stranney (Andrew Paul)* [2007] EWCA Crim 2847, [2008] 1 Cr. App. R. (S.) 104 (CA (Crim Div)), Toulson, L.J.

referred to: 2008 c.13 Sch.6

Part III, applied: SI 2008/2077 Art.2

s.2A, see *R. v McKenzie (Mark Anthony)* [2008] EWCA Crim 758, (2008) 172 J.P. 377 (CA (Crim Div)), Toulson, L.J.

CAP.

1988–cont.

52. Road Traffic Act 1988–*cont.*

s.4, see *Crown Prosecution Service v Gloucester Justices* [2008] EWHC 1488 (Admin), (2008) 172 J.P. 506 (DC), Richards, L.J.

s.5, see *Crown Prosecution Service v Gloucester Justices* [2008] EWHC 1488 (Admin), (2008) 172 J.P. 506 (DC), Richards, L.J.; see *Crown Prosecution Service v Thompson* [2007] EWHC 1841 (Admin), [2008] R.T.R. 5 (DC), Hughes, L.J.

s.7, see *Hussain v DPP* [2008] EWHC 901 (Admin), (2008) 172 J.P. 434 (DC), Leveson, L.J.; see *McKeon v DPP* [2007] EWHC 3216 (Admin), [2008] R.T.R. 14 (DC), Dyson, L.J.; see *McNeil v DPP* [2008] EWHC 1254 (Admin), [2008] R.T.R. 27 (DC), Latham, L.J.; see *Piggott v DPP* [2008] EWHC 305 (Admin), [2008] R.T.R. 16 (DC), Moses, L.J.

s.11, see *Hussain v DPP* [2008] EWHC 901 (Admin), (2008) 172 J.P. 434 (DC), Leveson, L.J.

s.15A, applied: 2008 c.13 Sch.3

s.17, applied: 2008 c.13 Sch.3

s.18, applied: 2008 c.13 Sch.3

s.36, referred to: SI 2008/2367 Reg.3, Reg.5

s.41, applied: 2008 c.13 Sch.3

s.41, enabling: SI 2008/1702

s.45, enabling: SI 2008/1402, SI 2008/1461

s.46, enabling: SI 2008/1402, SI 2008/1461

s.49, applied: 2008 c.13 Sch.7

s.49, enabling: SI 2008/1460

s.51, enabling: SI 2008/1460

s.61, applied: 2008 c.13 Sch.7

s.61, enabling: SI 2008/1443, SI 2008/1462

s.71, applied: 2008 c.13 Sch.3

s.80, amended: SI 2008/1277 Sch.4 Part 1

s.81, applied: 2008 c.13 Sch.3

s.82, applied: 2008 c.13 Sch.3

s.89, applied: SI 2008/3010 Reg.3

s.89, enabling: SI 2008/508, SI 2008/1435, SI 2008/2508

s.92, see *R. (on the application of Irving) v Secretary of State for Transport* [2008] EWHC 1200 (Admin), (2008) 172 J.P. 425 (QBD (Admin)), Saunders, J.

s.97, applied: SI 2008/2551 Reg.4

s.97, enabling: SI 2008/508, SI 2008/1038, SI 2008/1312

s.98, applied: SI 2008/2551 Reg.4

s.98A, applied: SI 2008/2551 Reg.4

s.99, applied: SI 2008/2551 Reg.4

s.99, enabling: SI 2008/1312

s.99A, applied: SI 2008/2551 Reg.4

s.99ZA, applied: SI 2008/2551 Reg.4

s.99ZB, applied: SI 2008/2551 Reg.4

s.99ZC, applied: SI 2008/2551 Reg.4

CAP.

1988–cont.

52. Road Traffic Act 1988–*cont.*

s.103, see *Horribine v Thomson* [2008] HCJAC 21, 2008 J.C. 306 (HCJ), Lord Hamilton L.J.G.; see *Logan v Harrower* [2008] HCJAC 61, 2008 S.L.T. 1049 (HCJ), Lord Nimmo Smith; see *Teale v MacLeod* 2008 S.C.C.R. 12 (HCJ), Lord Osborne

s.105, applied: 2008 c.13 Sch.7

s.105, enabling: SI 2008/508, SI 2008/1038, SI 2008/1312, SI 2008/1435, SI 2008/2508

s.120, applied: 2008 c.13 Sch.7

s.123, enabling: SI 2008/419

s.125, enabling: SI 2008/419

s.125A, enabling: SI 2008/419

s.127, enabling: SI 2008/419

s.129, enabling: SI 2008/419

s.132, enabling: SI 2008/419

s.141, enabling: SI 2008/419

s.143, see *Teale v MacLeod* 2008 S.C.C.R. 12 (HCJ), Lord Osborne

s.144, amended: 2008 c.14 Sch.5 para.61

s.145, see *AXA Insurance UK Plc v Norwich Union Insurance Ltd* [2007] EWHC 1046 (Comm), [2008] Lloyd's Rep. I.R. 122 (QBD (Comm)), Andrew Smith, J.

s.165B, enabling: SI 2008/2097

s.172, see *O'Halloran v United Kingdom (15809/02)* (2008) 46 E.H.R.R. 21 (ECHR (Grand Chamber)), Judge Costa (President)

s.185, see *DPP v King* [2008] EWHC 447 (Admin), (2008) 172 J.P. 401 (DC), Maurice Kay, L.J.

s.192, see *Teale v MacLeod* 2008 S.C.C.R. 12 (HCJ), Lord Osborne

s.195, applied: SI 2008/508, SI 2008/1038, SI 2008/1312, SI 2008/1402, SI 2008/1435, SI 2008/1443, SI 2008/1460, SI 2008/1461, SI 2008/1702, SI 2008/2097, SI 2008/2508

s.196, applied: 2008 c.13 Sch.3

Sch.2A, applied: 2008 c.13 Sch.7

53. Road Traffic Offenders Act 1988

s.1, see *Service v Cotton* [2008] HCJAC 8, 2008 S.C.C.R. 272 (HCJ), Lord Johnston

s.7, see *Breckon v DPP* [2007] EWHC 2013 (Admin), [2008] R.T.R. 8 (DC), Sedley, L.J.

s.15, see *Breckon v DPP* [2007] EWHC 2013 (Admin), [2008] R.T.R. 8 (DC), Sedley, L.J.

s.20, applied: SI 2008/1332 Art.3

s.20, enabling: SI 2008/1332

s.25, referred to: 2008 c.13 Sch.6

s.36, see *R. v Kirkby (Adam)* [2007] EWCA Crim 3410, [2008] 2 Cr. App. R. (S.) 46 (CA (Crim Div)), Longmore, L.J.

s.52, referred to: SI 2008/614 Reg.6, SI 2008/1214 Reg.6

s.62, referred to: 2008 c.13 Sch.6

s.67, referred to: 2008 c.13 Sch.6

CAP.

1988–cont.

53. Road Traffic Offenders Act 1988–*cont.*

s.90D, referred to: 2008 c.13 Sch.6

s.90F, amended: 2008 c.26 s.128

s.91, referred to: 2008 c.13 Sch.6

Sch.2, see *Logan v Harrower* [2008] HCJAC 61, 2008 S.L.T. 1049 (HCJ), Lord Nimmo Smith

54. Road Traffic (Consequential Provisions) Act 1988

applied: 2008 c.13 Sch.3

1989

3. Elected Authorities (Northern Ireland) Act 1989

s.2, applied: SI 2008/1741

s.2, referred to: SI 2008/1741 Reg.3

Sch.1, applied: SI 2008/1741

Sch.1, referred to: SI 2008/1741 Reg.3

5. Security Service Act 1989

s.1, referred to: 2008 c.28 s.21

s.2, applied: 2008 c.28 s.18, s.20

6. Official Secrets Act 1989

applied: SI 2008/239 Reg.75, SSI 2008/224 Reg.7, SSI 2008/228 Reg.69

12. Hearing Aid Council (Amendment) Act 1989

repealed: 2008 c.14 Sch.15 Part 2

14. Control of Pollution (Amendment) Act 1989

applied: 2008 c.13 Sch.3

s.1, referred to: 2008 c.13 Sch.6

s.2, applied: 2008 c.13 Sch.7

s.5, referred to: 2008 c.13 Sch.6

s.5B, applied: SI 2008/663 Reg.3

s.5B, enabling: SI 2008/663

s.7, referred to: 2008 c.13 Sch.6

s.9, referred to: SI 2008/663(b)

15. Water Act 1989

s.91, amended: SI 2008/948 Sch.1 para.155

s.174, amended: SI 2008/960 Sch.3, SI 2008/1277 Sch.2 para.47

18. Common Land (Rectification of Registers) Act 1989

applied: SI 2008/1961 Reg.14

22. Road Traffic (Driver Licensing and Information Systems) Act 1989

s.9, referred to: 2008 c.13 Sch.6

s.11, referred to: 2008 c.13 Sch.6

26. Finance Act 1989

s.43, see *Revenue and Customs Commissioners v Household Estate Agents Ltd* [2007] EWHC 1684 (Ch), [2008] S.T.C. 2045 (Ch D), Henderson, J; see *Sempra Metals Ltd v Revenue and Customs Commissioners* [2008] S.T.C. (S.C.D.) 1062 (Sp Comm), AN Brice

s.76, see *Irving v Revenue and Customs Commissioners* [2008] EWCA Civ 6, [2008] S.T.C. 597 (CA (Civ Div)), Sedley, L.J.

CAP.

1989–cont.

26. Finance Act 1989–*cont.*

s.82A, enabling: SI 2008/1906
s.82D, repealed (in part): SI 2008/381 Art.25
s.82E, amended: SI 2008/3096 Art.3
s.82F, amended: SI 2008/1905 Art.2, SI 2008/3096 Art.4
s.83, see *Scottish Widows Plc v Revenue and Customs Commissioners* [2008] S.T.C. (S.C.D.) 544 (Sp Comm), J Gordon Reid Q.C.
s.83, amended: 2008 c.9 Sch.17 para.1
s.83XA, amended: 2008 c.9 Sch.17 para.7
s.83XA, repealed (in part): 2008 c.9 Sch.17 para.7
s.83YA, amended: SI 2008/381 Art.26
s.83YC, added: 2008 c.9 Sch.17 para.1
s.83YC, applied: SI 2008/1926 Reg.3, Reg.4, Reg.5, Reg.6, Reg.7, Reg.8, Reg.10, Reg.11, Reg.12, Reg.13, Reg.14
s.83YD, added: 2008 c.9 Sch.17 para.1
s.83YD, applied: SI 2008/1926 Reg.9, Reg.10, Reg.11, Reg.12, Reg.13, Reg.14
s.83YE, added: 2008 c.9 Sch.17 para.1
s.83YE, enabling: SI 2008/1926
s.83YF, added: 2008 c.9 Sch.17 para.1
s.85, amended: 2008 c.9 Sch.17 para.6
s.85A, amended: 2008 c.9 Sch.17 para.18
s.86, applied: 2008 c.9 Sch.17 para.5
s.88, see *Sun Life Assurance Co of Canada (UK) Ltd v Revenue and Customs Commissioners* [2008] S.T.C. (S.C.D.) 486 (Sp Comm), Julian Ghosh Q.C.
s.88, amended: 2008 c.9 Sch.17 para.18, Sch.17 para.41, Sch.1 para.47
s.88, applied: 2008 c.9 Sch.13 para.3
s.89, see *Sun Life Assurance Co of Canada (UK) Ltd v Revenue and Customs Commissioners* [2008] S.T.C. (S.C.D.) 486 (Sp Comm), Julian Ghosh Q.C.
s.89, amended: 2008 c.9 Sch.17 para.37
s.89, applied: 2008 c.9 Sch.17 para.37
s.89, repealed (in part): 2008 c.9 Sch.17 para.18
s.90, repealed: 2008 c.9 Sch.14 para.17
s.142, repealed (in part): 2008 c.9 Sch.36 para.92
s.144, repealed (in part): 2008 c.9 Sch.36 para.92
s.149, repealed (in part): 2008 c.9 Sch.39 para.65
s.178, enabling: SI 2008/778, SI 2008/3234
s.182, see *Franbar Holdings Ltd v Patel* [2008] EWHC 1534 (Ch), [2008] B.C.C. 885 (Ch D), William Trower QC
s.182, referred to: SI 2008/2682 Reg.18
Sch.9 para.1, repealed: 2008 c.9 Sch.14 para.17
Sch.9 para.2, repealed: 2008 c.9 Sch.14 para.17
Sch.9 para.3, repealed: 2008 c.9 Sch.14 para.17
Sch.9 para.4, repealed: 2008 c.9 Sch.14 para.17
Sch.9 para.5, repealed: 2008 c.9 Sch.14 para.17
Sch.9 para.6, repealed: 2008 c.9 Sch.14 para.17
Sch.9 para.7, repealed: 2008 c.9 Sch.14 para.17
Sch.9 para.8, repealed: 2008 c.9 Sch.14 para.17
Sch.9 para.18, repealed: 2008 c.9 Sch.14 para.17

29. Electricity Act 1989

applied: SI 2008/2551 Reg.4
referred to: SSI 2008/263 Sch.2
Part I, applied: 2008 c.32 s.43, s.86, s.90, s.97, SI 2008/188 Art.23, SI 2008/2376 Reg.3
s.3A, amended: 2008 c.32 s.83, s.102
s.3A, applied: 2008 c.32 s.102
s.3A, repealed (in part): 2008 c.32 s.83, Sch.6
s.3B, applied: 2008 c.32 s.102
s.3C, amended: SI 2008/960 Sch.3
s.3C, applied: 2008 c.32 s.102
s.3D, applied: 2008 c.32 s.102
s.4, disapplied: SI 2008/3045 Art.3, SI 2008/3046 Art.3
s.5, applied: SI 2008/2376 Sch.2 para.3, SI 2008/3045, SI 2008/3046
s.5, enabling: SI 2008/3045, SI 2008/3046
s.6, amended: 2008 c.27 Sch.8 para.2
s.6, applied: 2008 c.32 s.41, s.45, s.84, s.88, s.97, SI 2008/188 Art.4, SI 2008/1898 Reg.4, SI 2008/2376 Sch.2 para.3, SI 2008/3045 Art.4, SI 2008/3046 Art.4
s.6, referred to: SI 2008/2376 Sch.2 para.1
s.6A, applied: SI 2008/2376 Reg.8
s.6A, enabling: SI 2008/2376
s.6D, added: 2008 c.32 s.44
s.6E, added: 2008 c.32 s.44
s.7, applied: 2008 c.32 s.84, s.88
s.8A, applied: 2008 c.32 s.41, s.84, s.88, s.97
s.16, referred to: SI 2008/2376 Sch.2 para.5
s.16A, amended: 2008 c.32 s.98
s.25, amended: 2008 c.32 Sch.5 para.3
s.29, applied: 2008 c.13 Sch.7, 2008 c.32 s.99
s.32, applied: 2008 c.32 s.38
s.32, substituted: 2008 c.32 s.37
s.32, enabling: SSI 2008/132
s.32A, applied: 2008 c.32 s.38
s.32A, substituted: 2008 c.32 s.37
s.32A, enabling: SSI 2008/132
s.32B, applied: 2008 c.32 s.38
s.32B, substituted: 2008 c.32 s.37
s.32BA, applied: 2008 c.32 s.38
s.32BA, substituted: 2008 c.32 s.37
s.32C, applied: 2008 c.32 s.38

CAP.

1989–cont.

29. Electricity Act 1989–*cont.*
s.32C, substituted: 2008 c.32 s.37
s.32D, applied: 2008 c.32 s.38
s.32D, substituted: 2008 c.32 s.37
s.32E, applied: 2008 c.32 s.38
s.32E, substituted: 2008 c.32 s.37
s.32F, applied: 2008 c.32 s.38
s.32F, substituted: 2008 c.32 s.37
s.32G, applied: 2008 c.32 s.38
s.32G, substituted: 2008 c.32 s.37
s.32H, applied: 2008 c.32 s.38
s.32H, substituted: 2008 c.32 s.37
s.32I, applied: 2008 c.32 s.38
s.32I, substituted: 2008 c.32 s.37
s.32J, applied: 2008 c.32 s.38
s.32J, substituted: 2008 c.32 s.37
s.32K, applied: 2008 c.32 s.38
s.32K, substituted: 2008 c.32 s.37
s.32K, varied: 2008 c.32 s.38
s.32L, applied: 2008 c.32 s.38
s.32L, substituted: 2008 c.32 s.37
s.32M, applied: 2008 c.32 s.38, s.100
s.32M, substituted: 2008 c.32 s.37
s.36, amended: 2008 c.29 Sch.2 para.32
s.36, applied: 2008 c.29 s.33
s.37, amended: 2008 c.29 Sch.2 para.33
s.37, applied: 2008 c.29 s.33
s.37, disapplied: 2008 c.18 s.4
s.37, referred to: 2008 c.18 Sch.4 para.1
s.37, enabling: SSI 2008/202
s.41A, amended: 2008 c.27 Sch.8 para.3
s.41A, applied: SI 2008/188
s.41A, enabling: SI 2008/188
s.42AA, amended: 2008 c.27 Sch.8 para.4
s.47, amended: 2008 c.32 Sch.5 para.4
s.56C, amended: SI 2008/960 Sch.3
s.56FA, added: 2008 c.32 Sch.4 para.2
s.56FB, added: 2008 c.32 Sch.4 para.2
s.56FC, added: 2008 c.32 Sch.4 para.2
s.60, enabling: SI 2008/2376, SSI 2008/202
s.64, amended: 2008 c.27 Sch.8 para.5, 2008 c.32 s.44
s.64, referred to: SSI 2008/182 Art.21, Art.22, SSI 2008/188 Art.30, Art.31, SSI 2008/189 Art.30, Art.31, SSI 2008/190 Art.31
s.80, amended: SI 2008/948 Sch.1 para.156
s.106, amended: 2008 c.32 s.96, Sch.5 para.5, Sch.5 para.6
Sch.2A para.1, added: 2008 c.32 Sch.2
Sch.2A para.2, added: 2008 c.32 Sch.2
Sch.2A para.3, added: 2008 c.32 Sch.2
Sch.2A para.4, added: 2008 c.32 Sch.2
Sch.2A para.5, added: 2008 c.32 Sch.2
Sch.2A para.6, added: 2008 c.32 Sch.2
Sch.2A para.7, added: 2008 c.32 Sch.2
Sch.2A para.8, added: 2008 c.32 Sch.2
Sch.2A para.9, added: 2008 c.32 Sch.2
Sch.2A para.10, added: 2008 c.32 Sch.2
Sch.2A para.11, added: 2008 c.32 Sch.2

CAP.

1989–cont.

29. Electricity Act 1989–*cont.*
Sch.2A para.12, added: 2008 c.32 Sch.2
Sch.2A para.13, added: 2008 c.32 Sch.2
Sch.2A para.14, added: 2008 c.32 Sch.2
Sch.2A para.15, added: 2008 c.32 Sch.2
Sch.2A para.16, added: 2008 c.32 Sch.2
Sch.2A para.17, added: 2008 c.32 Sch.2
Sch.2A para.18, added: 2008 c.32 Sch.2
Sch.2A para.19, added: 2008 c.32 Sch.2
Sch.2A para.20, added: 2008 c.32 Sch.2
Sch.2A para.21, added: 2008 c.32 Sch.2
Sch.2A para.22, added: 2008 c.32 Sch.2
Sch.2A para.23, added: 2008 c.32 Sch.2
Sch.2A para.24, added: 2008 c.32 Sch.2
Sch.2A para.25, added: 2008 c.32 Sch.2
Sch.2A para.26, added: 2008 c.32 Sch.2
Sch.2A para.27, added: 2008 c.32 Sch.2
Sch.2A para.28, added: 2008 c.32 Sch.2
Sch.2A para.29, added: 2008 c.32 Sch.2
Sch.2A para.30, added: 2008 c.32 Sch.2
Sch.2A para.31, added: 2008 c.32 Sch.2
Sch.2A para.32, added: 2008 c.32 Sch.2
Sch.2A para.33, added: 2008 c.32 Sch.2
Sch.2A para.34, added: 2008 c.32 Sch.2
Sch.2A para.35, added: 2008 c.32 Sch.2
Sch.2A para.36, added: 2008 c.32 Sch.2
Sch.2A para.37, added: 2008 c.32 Sch.2
Sch.2A para.38, added: 2008 c.32 Sch.2
Sch.3, applied: SI 2008/2376 Sch.2 para.2
Sch.4, applied: SI 2008/2376 Sch.2 para.2
Sch.6 para.3, applied: SI 2008/2376 Sch.2 para.2
Sch.7, applied: 2008 c.32 s.95, s.97
Sch.7 para.1, amended: 2008 c.32 s.96
Sch.7 para.4, amended: 2008 c.32 s.96
Sch.7 para.4, applied: 2008 c.32 s.97
Sch.7 para.5, amended: 2008 c.32 s.96
Sch.7 para.6, amended: 2008 c.32 s.96
Sch.7 para.7, amended: 2008 c.32 s.96
Sch.7 para.10, amended: 2008 c.32 s.96
Sch.7 para.13, amended: 2008 c.32 s.96

30. Dangerous Dogs Act 1989
referred to: 2008 c.13 Sch.6

33. Extradition Act 1989
see *R. (on the application of Wellington) v Secretary of State for the Home Department* [2007] EWHC 1109 (Admin), [2008] 3 All E.R. 248 (DC), Laws, L.J.

34. Law of Property (Miscellaneous Provisions) Act 1989
s.2, see *Hanoman v Southwark LBC* [2008] EWCA Civ 624, Times, June 24, 2008 (CA (Civ Div)), Sir Anthony Clarke, M.R.; see *Walters (Deceased), Re* [2007] EWHC 3060 (Ch), [2008] W.T.L.R. 339 (Ch D), Norris, J.

37. Football Spectators Act 1989
see *DPP v Beaumont* [2008] EWHC 523 (Admin), [2008] 1 W.L.R. 2186 (DC), Richards, L.J.

CAP.

1989–cont.

37. Football Spectators Act 1989–*cont.*
Part II, applied: SI 2008/1165 Art.3
Part II, referred to: SI 2008/1165
s.1, see *DPP v Beaumont* [2008] EWHC 523 (Admin), [2008] 1 W.L.R. 2186 (DC), Richards, L.J.
s.11, applied: SI 2008/1749
s.11, enabling: SI 2008/1749
s.14, varied: SI 2008/1165 Art.2
s.14, enabling: SI 2008/1165
s.14A, see *DPP v Beaumont* [2008] EWHC 523 (Admin), [2008] 1 W.L.R. 2186 (DC), Richards, L.J.; see *R. (on the application of White) v Blackfriars Crown Court* [2008] EWHC 510 (Admin), [2008] 2 Cr. App. R. (S.) 97 (DC), Richards, L.J.; see *R. v Arbery (Mark)* [2008] EWCA Crim 702, (2008) 172 J.P. 291 (CA (Crim Div)), Moore-Bick, L.J.
s.14B, see *R. (on the application of White) v Blackfriars Crown Court* [2008] EWHC 510 (Admin), [2008] 2 Cr. App. R. (S.) 97 (DC), Richards, L.J.
s.14E, see *R. (on the application of White) v Blackfriars Crown Court* [2008] EWHC 510 (Admin), [2008] 2 Cr. App. R. (S.) 97 (DC), Richards, L.J.
s.22A, enabling: SI 2008/1165
Sch.1 para.1, see *DPP v Beaumont* [2008] EWHC 523 (Admin), [2008] 1 W.L.R. 2186 (DC), Richards, L.J.; see *R. v Arbery (Mark)* [2008] EWCA Crim 702, (2008) 172 J.P. 291 (CA (Crim Div)), Moore-Bick, L.J.
Sch.1 para.1, amended: 2008 c.4 Sch.26 para.26

39. Self-Governing Schools etc (Scotland) Act 1989
s.19, applied: SSI 2008/228 Sch.2

40. Companies Act 1989
s.46, enabling: SI 2008/496
s.50, applied: SI 2008/948 Art.10
s.50, referred to: SI 2008/948 Art.10
s.82, amended: SI 2008/948 Sch.1 para.157
s.87, amended: SI 2008/948 Sch.1 para.158
s.112, amended: SI 2008/948 Sch.3 para.6
s.135, amended: SI 2008/948 Sch.1 para.159, Sch.2
Sch.10 Part I para.18, repealed (in part): SI 2008/948 Sch.2

41. Children Act 1989
see *Bush v Bush* [2008] EWCA Civ 865, [2008] 2 F.L.R. 1437 (CA (Civ Div)), Thorpe, L.J.; see *C (A Child) (Children Proceedings: Powers of Transfer), Re* [2008] EWCA Civ 502, [2008] 2 F.L.R. 815 (CA (Civ Div)), Wilson, L.J.; see *EN (A Child), Re* [2007] EWCA Civ 264, [2008] 2 F.C.R. 229 (CA (Civ Div)), Thorpe, L.J.; see *O v Lewisham LBC* [2007] EWHC 2130 (Admin), [2008] B.L.G.R. 765 (QBD (Admin)), Andrew

CAP.

1989–cont.

41. Children Act 1989–*cont.*
see–*cont.*
Nicol Q.C.; see *R (A Child), Re* Times, August 29, 2008 (CA (Civ Div)), Thorpe, L.J.; see *R. (on the application of G) v Nottingham City Council* [2008] EWHC 400 (Admin), [2008] 1 F.L.R. 1668 (QBD (Admin)), Munby, J.; see *R. (on the application of M) v Hammersmith and Fulham LBC* [2008] UKHL 14, [2008] 1 W.L.R. 535 (HL), Lord Hoffmann; see *T (A Child) v Wakefield MDC* [2008] EWCA Civ 199, [2008] 3 W.L.R. 1316 (CA (Civ Div)), Thorpe, L.J.
applied: SI 2008/170 Reg.4, SI 2008/228 Sch.1 para.6, SI 2008/542 Reg.9, SI 2008/1052 Sch.1, SI 2008/1054 Sch.1, SI 2008/1185 Sch.1 para.1, Sch.1 para.23, SI 2008/2261 Sch.2 para.14
referred to: 2008 c.23 s.1, SI 2008/1206 Sch.2 para.2, SI 2008/2436 Sch.2 para.2.1
Part I, applied: SI 2008/2836 Art.9, Art.20
Part I, referred to: 2008 c.22 s.53
Part II, applied: SI 2008/2836 Art.9, Art.20
Part II, referred to: 2008 c.22 s.53, 2008 c.23
Part III, applied: SI 2008/2836 Art.9, Art.20
Part III, referred to: 2008 c.23
Part IV, applied: SI 2008/2836 Art.9, Art.20
Part V, applied: SI 2008/2836 Art.9, Art.20
Part XA, applied: SI 2008/976 Reg.5, SI 2008/2261 Sch.2 para.23, SI 2008/2770 Art.8
Part III, see *R. (on the application of M) v Hammersmith and Fulham LBC* [2008] UKHL 14, [2008] 1 W.L.R. 535 (HL), Lord Hoffmann; see *R. (on the application of M) v Lambeth LBC* [2008] EWHC 1364 (Admin), [2008] 2 F.L.R. 1026 (QBD (Admin)), Bennett, J.
Part IV, see *B, Re* [2007] EWHC 1622 (Fam), [2008] 1 F.L.R. 482 (Fam Div), Munby, J.
Part V, see *B, Re* [2007] EWHC 1622 (Fam), [2008] 1 F.L.R. 482 (Fam Div), Munby, J.
s.1, see *B (Children) (Sexual Abuse: Standard of Proof), Re* [2008] UKHL 35, [2008] 3 W.L.R. 1 (HL), Lord Hoffmann; see *Chief Constable of Greater Manchester v I* [2007] EWHC 1837 (Fam), [2008] 1 F.L.R. 504 (Fam Div), Ryder, J.; see *M v H* [2008] EWHC 324 (Fam), [2008] 1 F.L.R. 1400 (Fam Div), Charles, J.; see *P (A Child), Re* [2008] EWCA Civ 535, [2008] 2 F.L.R. 625 (CA (Civ Div)), Thorpe, L.J.; see *S (Brussels II (Revised): Enforcement of Contact Order), Re* [2008] 2 F.L.R. 1358 (Fam Div), Roderic Wood, J.
s.2, amended: 2008 c.22 Sch.6 para.26
s.3, applied: SI 2008/788 Sch.1
s.3, referred to: SI 2008/2699 r.15
s.4, applied: SI 2008/1052 Sch.1, SI 2008/1054 Sch.1, SI 2008/2836 Art.5
s.4A, applied: SI 2008/1052 Sch.1, SI 2008/1054 Sch.1, SI 2008/2836 Art.5

CAP.

1989–cont.

41. Children Act 1989–*cont.*

s.4ZA, added: 2008 c.22 Sch.6 para.27

s.4ZA, applied: SI 2008/2836 Art.5

s.5, applied: SI 2008/1052 Sch.1, SI 2008/1054 Sch.1

s.6, applied: SI 2008/1052 Sch.1, SI 2008/1054 Sch.1

s.7, see *Practice Direction (Fam Div: Residence and Contact Orders: Domestic Violence)* [2008] 1 W.L.R. 1062 (Fam Div), Sir Mark Potter (President); see *B v B* [2008] EWHC 938 (Fam), [2008] 2 F.L.R. 1588 (Fam Div), Sumner, J.

s.8, see *B (A Child) (Prohibited Steps Order), Re* [2007] EWCA Civ 1055, [2008] 1 F.L.R. 613 (CA (Civ Div)), Thorpe, L.J.; see *F (Children) (Paternity: Jurisdiction), Re* [2007] EWCA Civ 873, [2008] 1 F.L.R. 225 (CA (Civ Div)), Thorpe, L.J.; see *H (A Child) (Leave to Apply for Residence Order), Re* [2008] EWCA Civ 503, [2008] 2 F.L.R. 848 (CA (Civ Div)), Buxton, L.J.

s.8, applied: SI 2008/2836 Art.5, Art.8

s.9, see *M (A Child) (Education: s.91(14) Order), Re* [2007] EWCA Civ 1550, [2008] 2 F.L.R. 404 (CA (Civ Div)), Wall, L.J.

s.9, amended: 2008 c.23 s.37

s.10, see *H (A Child) (Leave to Apply for Residence Order), Re* [2008] EWCA Civ 503, [2008] 2 F.L.R. 848 (CA (Civ Div)), Buxton, L.J.

s.10, amended: 2008 c.23 s.36

s.10, applied: SI 2008/1052 Sch.1, SI 2008/1054 Sch.1, SI 2008/2836 Art.6

s.11, see *B (A Child) (Prohibited Steps Order), Re* [2007] EWCA Civ 1055, [2008] 1 F.L.R. 613 (CA (Civ Div)), Thorpe, L.J.

s.11A, referred to: SI 2008/2940 Reg.3

s.11F, enabling: SI 2008/2940, SI 2008/2943

s.11J, applied: SI 2008/1054 Sch.1, SI 2008/2836 Art.6, SI 2008/2859 r.3

s.11L, applied: SI 2008/2859 r.3

s.11M, applied: SI 2008/2859 r.3

s.11O, applied: SI 2008/1054 Sch.1, SI 2008/2836 Art.6, SI 2008/2859 r.3

s.12, see *A (A Child) (Joint Residence: Parental Responsibility), Re* [2008] EWCA Civ 867, [2008] 2 F.L.R. 1593 (CA (Civ Div)), Sir Mark Potter (President)

s.12, amended: 2008 c.22 Sch.6 para.28

s.12, repealed (in part): 2008 c.23 s.37, Sch.4

s.13, see *B (A Child) (Prohibited Steps Order), Re* [2007] EWCA Civ 1055, [2008] 1 F.L.R. 613 (CA (Civ Div)), Thorpe, L.J.

s.13, applied: SI 2008/1052 Sch.1, SI 2008/1054 Sch.1

s.14A, amended: 2008 c.23 s.38

s.14A, applied: SI 2008/1052 Sch.1, SI 2008/1054 Sch.1, SI 2008/2836 Art.8

s.14C, applied: SI 2008/1052 Sch.1, SI 2008/1054 Sch.1

CAP.

1989–cont.

41. Children Act 1989–*cont.*

s.14D, applied: SI 2008/1052 Sch.1, SI 2008/1054 Sch.1

s.14F, applied: SI 2008/794 Sch.8 para.26, Sch.9 para.58

s.15, applied: SI 2008/18 Reg.32, SI 2008/529 Reg.46, SI 2008/794 Sch.8 para.26, SI 2008/1273 Reg.83G, Reg.30, SI 2008/1582 Reg.42, SI 2008/3170 Reg.30

s.17, see *R. (on the application of M) v Hammersmith and Fulham LBC* [2008] UKHL 14, [2008] 1 W.L.R. 535 (HL), Lord Hoffmann; see *R. (on the application of M) v Lambeth LBC* [2008] EWHC 1364 (Admin), [2008] 2 F.L.R. 1026 (QBD (Admin)), Bennett, J.; see *Westminster City Council v Boraliu* [2007] EWCA Civ 1339, [2008] 1 W.L.R. 2408 (CA (Civ Div)), Chadwick, L.J.

s.17, amended: 2008 c.23 s.24, Sch.1 para.1, Sch.3 para.2, Sch.4

s.17, applied: SI 2008/794 Sch.8 para.30, Sch.9 para.22

s.17A, amended: 2008 c.14 Sch.14 para.1, 2008 c.23 Sch.3 para.3

s.17B, amended: 2008 c.23 Sch.3 para.4

s.20, see *B County Council v H* [2008] EWHC 1070 (Admin), [2008] E.L.R. 333 (QBD (Admin)), Judge Mackie Q.C.; see *R. (on the application of Liverpool City Council) v Hillingdon LBC* [2008] EWHC 1702 (Admin), (2008) 11 C.C.L. Rep. 693 (QBD (Admin)), James Goudie Q.C.; see *R. (on the application of M) v Hammersmith and Fulham LBC* [2008] UKHL 14, [2008] 1 W.L.R. 535 (HL), Lord Hoffmann; see *R. (on the application of M) v Lambeth LBC* [2008] EWHC 1364 (Admin), [2008] 2 F.L.R. 1026 (QBD (Admin)), Bennett, J.

s.21, amended: 2008 c.4 Sch.4 para.34, Sch.4 para.105, Sch.28 Part 1, 2008 c.23 Sch.3 para.5

s.22, see *L (Adoption: Contacting Natural Father), Re* [2007] EWHC 1771 (Fam), [2008] 1 F.L.R. 1079 (Fam Div), Munby, J.; see *R. (on the application of MG) v Tower Hamlets LBC* [2008] EWHC 1577 (Admin), [2008] E.L.R. 523 (QBD (Admin)), Langstaff, J.

s.22, amended: 2008 c.23 Sch.3 para.6

s.22, applied: 2008 c.23 s.1, SI 2008/529 Sch.4 para.2, SI 2008/538 Reg.13, SI 2008/1273 Sch.5 para.2, Sch.6 para.1, SI 2008/1582 Sch.4 para.2, SI 2008/3170 Sch.5 para.2

s.22G, added: 2008 c.23 s.9

s.23, amended: 2008 c.23 Sch.3 para.7

s.23, applied: 2008 c.4 Sch.1 para.18, SI 2008/18 Reg.32, SI 2008/529 Reg.46, SI 2008/794 Reg.156, Sch.8 para.28, SI 2008/1273 Reg.83G, Reg.30, SI 2008/1582 Reg.42, SI 2008/3170 Reg.30

CAP.

1989–cont.

41. Children Act 1989–*cont.*

s.23, substituted: 2008 c.23 s.8
s.23A, amended: 2008 c.23 Sch.3 para.8
s.23A, applied: 2008 c.23 s.20
s.23B, amended: 2008 c.23 Sch.3 para.9
s.23B, applied: 2008 c.23 s.1, SI 2008/794 Sch.8 para.30, Sch.9 para.22
s.23B, repealed (in part): 2008 c.23 s.22, Sch.4
s.23C, amended: 2008 c.23 s.21
s.23C, applied: 2008 c.23 s.1, s.7, s.20, SI 2008/794 Sch.8 para.30, Sch.9 para.22
s.23CA, added: 2008 c.23 s.22
s.23CA, applied: 2008 c.23 s.1, s.7
s.23D, amended: 2008 c.23 s.23, Sch.3 para.10
s.23E, amended: 2008 c.23 s.22, Sch.3 para.11
s.23ZA, added: 2008 c.23 s.15
s.23ZB, added: 2008 c.23 s.16
s.24, amended: 2008 c.23 Sch.3 para.12
s.24, applied: 2008 c.23 s.1, s.7, SI 2008/18 Reg.32, SI 2008/529 Reg.46, SI 2008/1273 Reg.83G, Reg.30, SI 2008/1582 Reg.42, SI 2008/3170 Reg.30
s.24A, applied: 2008 c.23 s.1, s.7, SI 2008/794 Sch.8 para.30, Sch.9 para.22
s.24B, amended: 2008 c.23 s.23, Sch.3 para.13
s.24B, applied: 2008 c.23 s.1, s.7
s.24C, applied: 2008 c.23 s.1, s.7
s.24D, amended: 2008 c.23 Sch.3 para.14
s.24D, applied: 2008 c.23 s.1, s.7
s.25, see *Birmingham City Council v M* [2008] EWHC 1085 (Fam), [2008] 2 F.L.R. 542 (Fam Div), McFarlane, J.
s.25, amended: 2008 c.23 Sch.3 para.15
s.25, applied: SI 2008/1052 Sch.1, SI 2008/1054 Sch.1, SI 2008/2836 Art.5, Art.15
s.25A, added: 2008 c.23 s.10
s.25A, applied: 2008 c.23 s.2
s.25B, added: 2008 c.23 s.10
s.25C, added: 2008 c.23 s.10
s.26, amended: 2008 c.23 Sch.3 para.16
s.26, applied: 2008 c.23 s.2
s.26, repealed (in part): 2008 c.23 s.10, Sch.4
s.26A, amended: 2008 c.23 Sch.3 para.18
s.26ZB, amended: 2008 c.23 Sch.3 para.17
s.27, amended: 2008 c.23 Sch.3 para.19
s.29, amended: 2008 c.23 Sch.3 para.20
s.30, amended: 2008 c.23 Sch.3 para.21
s.30A, added: 2008 c.23 Sch.3 para.22
s.31, see *B (Children) (Sexual Abuse: Standard of Proof), Re* [2008] EWCA Civ 282, [2008] 2 F.L.R. 168 (CA (Civ Div)), Thorpe, L.J.; see *B (Children) (Sexual Abuse: Standard of Proof), Re* [2008] UKHL 35, [2008] 3 W.L.R. 1 (HL), Lord Hoffmann; see *JFM v Neath Port Talbot BC* [2008] EWCA Civ 3, [2008] 1 F.C.R. 97 (CA (Civ Div)), Thorpe, L.J.; see

CAP.

1989–cont.

41. Children Act 1989–*cont.*

s.31–*cont.*
Lewisham LBC v D [2008] 2 F.L.R. 1449 (Fam Div), Bodey, J.; see *P (Children) (Care Proceedings: Split Hearing), Re* [2007] EWCA Civ 1265, [2008] 1 F.C.R. 74 (CA (Civ Div)), Wilson, L.J.; see *T (A Child) v Wakefield MDC* [2008] EWCA Civ 199, [2008] 3 W.L.R. 1316 (CA (Civ Div)), Thorpe, L.J.
s.31, amended: 2008 c.4 Sch.4 para.35
s.31, applied: 2008 c.25 s.120, SI 2008/1052 Sch.1, SI 2008/1054 Sch.1, SI 2008/2836 Art.5
s.33, see *R. (on the application of MG) v Tower Hamlets LBC* [2008] EWHC 1577 (Admin), [2008] E.L.R. 523 (QBD (Admin)), Langstaff, J.
s.33, applied: SI 2008/1052 Sch.1, SI 2008/1054 Sch.1, SI 2008/2836 Art.5
s.34, see *J (A Child) (Restrictions on Applications), Re* [2007] EWCA Civ 906, [2008] 1 F.L.R. 369 (CA (Civ Div)), Dyson, L.J.; see *K (Care Proceedings: Care Plan), Re* [2007] EWHC 393 (Fam), [2008] 1 F.L.R. 1 (Fam Div), Munby, J.; see *Nottingham City Council v G* [2008] EWHC 540 (Fam), [2008] 2 F.L.R. 581 (Fam Div), Munby, J.
s.34, applied: SI 2008/1052 Sch.1, SI 2008/1054 Sch.1, SI 2008/2836 Art.5
s.36, amended: 2008 c.25 Sch.1 para.43
s.36, applied: SI 2008/1052 Sch.1, SI 2008/1054 Sch.1, SI 2008/2836 Art.5
s.37, see *JFM v Neath Port Talbot BC* [2008] EWCA Civ 3, [2008] 1 F.C.R. 97 (CA (Civ Div)), Thorpe, L.J.; see *Lambeth LBC v TK* [2008] EWCA Civ 103, [2008] 1 F.L.R. 1229 (CA (Civ Div)), Dyson, L.J.; see *Lewisham LBC v D* [2008] 2 F.L.R. 1449 (Fam Div), Bodey, J.; see *R. (on the application of M) v Lambeth LBC* [2008] EWHC 1364 (Admin), [2008] 2 F.L.R. 1026 (QBD (Admin)), Bennett, J.
s.39, applied: SI 2008/1052 Sch.1, SI 2008/1054 Sch.1
s.43, applied: SI 2008/1052 Sch.1, SI 2008/1054 Sch.1, SI 2008/2836 Art.5
s.44, see *LLBC v TG* [2007] EWHC 2640 (Fam), (2008) 11 C.C.L. Rep. 161 (Fam Div), McFarlane, J.
s.44, applied: SI 2008/1052 Sch.1, SI 2008/1054 Sch.1, SI 2008/2836 Art.5
s.44A, applied: SI 2008/1052 Sch.1, SI 2008/1054 Sch.1
s.44B, applied: SI 2008/1052 Sch.1, SI 2008/1054 Sch.1
s.45, applied: SI 2008/1052 Sch.1, SI 2008/1054 Sch.1, SI 2008/2836 Art.5
s.45, repealed (in part): 2008 c.23 s.30, Sch.4

CAP.

1989–cont.

41. Children Act 1989–*cont.*

s.46, applied: SI 2008/1052 Sch.1, SI 2008/1054 Sch.1, SI 2008/2836 Art.5

s.48, applied: SI 2008/1052 Sch.1, SI 2008/1054 Sch.1, SI 2008/2836 Art.5

s.50, applied: SI 2008/1052 Sch.1, SI 2008/1054 Sch.1, SI 2008/2836 Art.5

s.59, amended: 2008 c.23 Sch.1 para.2, Sch.3 para.23, Sch.4

s.59, applied: SI 2008/794 Reg.156, Sch.8 para.28

s.62, amended: 2008 c.23 Sch.3 para.24

s.65, amended: SI 2008/2833 Sch.3 para.72

s.65A, amended: SI 2008/2833 Sch.3 para.73

s.65A, applied: SI 2008/2699 Sch.1

s.68, applied: SI 2008/542 Reg.9

s.68, enabling: SI 2008/2691

s.79B, applied: SI 2008/2261 Sch.2 para.9, Sch.2 para.10

s.79B, repealed (in part): SI 2008/2833 Sch.3 para.74

s.79C, disapplied: SI 2008/2261 Sch.2 para.23

s.79C, enabling: SI 2008/2691

s.79D, applied: SI 2008/2261 Sch.2 para.21

s.79E, applied: SI 2008/2261 Sch.2 para.15

s.79F, applied: SI 2008/975 Sch.3 para.11, SI 2008/1729 Reg.3

s.79F, applied: SI 2008/1804 Reg.9, Reg.10, Reg.11, Reg.12, Reg.14, Reg.15, SI 2008/2261 Sch.2 para.1, Sch.2 para.4, Sch.2 para.5, Sch.2 para.7, Sch.2 para.8, Sch.2 para.11, Sch.2 para.12, Sch.2 para.14

s.79H, amended: SI 2008/2833 Sch.3 para.75

s.79H, enabling: SI 2008/2689

s.79K, applied: SI 2008/1052 Sch.1, SI 2008/2261 Sch.2 para.19, Sch.2 para.26, SI 2008/2836 Art.5

s.79L, applied: SI 2008/2261 Sch.2 para.16, Sch.2 para.17, SI 2008/2699 Sch.1

s.79L, referred to: SI 2008/2261 Sch.2 para.17, Sch.2 para.18

s.79M, amended: SI 2008/2833 Sch.3 para.76

s.79M, applied: SI 2008/2261 Sch.2 para.18, Sch.2 para.19, Sch.2 para.20, SI 2008/2699 Sch.1

s.79M, enabling: SI 2008/2691

s.79Q, applied: SI 2008/2261 Sch.2 para.27

s.79Q, referred to: SI 2008/2261 Sch.2 para.27

s.79R, applied: SI 2008/2261 Sch.2 para.27

s.83, amended: 2008 c.23 s.33

s.85, amended: 2008 c.23 s.17

s.86, amended: 2008 c.23 s.17

s.86A, added: 2008 c.23 s.18

s.91, see *A (A Child) (Joint Residence: Parental Responsibility), Re* [2008] EWCA Civ 867, [2008] 2 F.L.R. 1593 (CA (Civ Div)), Sir Mark Potter (President); see *F (Children) (Contact: Change of Name), Re* [2007] EWHC 2543 (Fam), [2008] 1 F.L.R. 1163 (Fam Div), Sumner, J.; see *J (A Child) (Restrictions on Applications), Re* [2007] EWCA Civ 906, [2008] 1 F.L.R. 369 (CA (Civ Div)), Dyson, L.J.; see *M (A Child) (Education: s.91(14) Order), Re* [2007] EWCA Civ 1550, [2008] 2 F.L.R. 404 (CA (Civ Div)), Wall, L.J.; see *R. (on the application of MG) v Tower Hamlets LBC* [2008] EWHC 1577 (Admin), [2008] E.L.R. 523 (QBD (Admin)), Langstaff, J.

s.91, amended: 2008 c.22 Sch.6 para.29, 2008 c.23 s.37, Sch.4

s.92, applied: 2008 c.22 s.54

s.92, enabling: SI 2008/2836

s.94, applied: SI 2008/1054 Sch.1

s.94, enabling: SI 2008/2836

s.97, see *X Council v B* [2008] EWHC 270 (Fam), [2008] 1 F.L.R. 1460 (Fam Div (Liverpool)), Munby, J.; see *Z County Council v S* [2008] EWHC 1773 (Fam), [2008] 2 F.L.R. 1800 (Fam Div), Hedley, J.

s.98, see *A District Council v M* [2008] 2 F.L.R. 390 (Fam Div), Baron, J.; see *X (Children) (Disclosure for Purposes of Criminal Proceedings), Re* [2008] EWHC 242 (Fam), [2008] 3 All E.R. 958 (Fam Div), Munby, J.; see *X (Children), Re* [2007] EWHC 1719 (Fam), [2008] 1 F.L.R. 589 (Fam Div), Munby, J.

s.100, see *Lewisham LBC v D* [2008] 2 F.L.R. 1449 (Fam Div), Bodey, J.

s.102, applied: SI 2008/1052 Sch.1, SI 2008/1054 Sch.1, SI 2008/2836 Art.5

s.104, amended: 2008 c.22 Sch.6 para.30, 2008 c.23 Sch.3 para.25, Sch.4

s.104, repealed (in part): 2008 c.23 Sch.3 para.25, Sch.4

s.104, enabling: SI 2008/2689, SI 2008/2691, SI 2008/2940, SI 2008/2943

s.104A, added: 2008 c.23 Sch.3 para.26

s.105, amended: 2008 c.4 Sch.4 para.36, Sch.28 Part 1, 2008 c.22 Sch.6 para.31, 2008 c.23 Sch.1 para.3, Sch.4

Sch.A1 Part II para.4, applied: SI 2008/2836 Art.9, Art.20, SI 2008/2859 r.3

Sch.A1 Part II para.5, applied: SI 2008/2836 Art.9, Art.20, SI 2008/2859 r.3

Sch.A1 Part II para.6, applied: SI 2008/2836 Art.9, Art.20, SI 2008/2859 r.3

Sch.A1 Part II para.7, applied: SI 2008/2836 Art.9, Art.20, SI 2008/2859 r.3

Sch.A1 Part II para.9, applied: SI 2008/2836 Art.6, Art.9, Art.20, SI 2008/2859 r.3

Sch.1, see *MT v OT (Financial Provision: Costs)* [2007] EWHC 838 (Fam), [2008] 2 F.L.R. 1311 (Fam Div), Charles, J.; see *N v D*

CAP.

1989–cont.

41. Children Act 1989–*cont.*

Sch.1–*cont.*

[2008] 1 F.L.R. 1629 (Fam Div), District Judge Harper

Sch.1, applied: SI 2008/18 Reg.32, SI 2008/529 Reg.46, SI 2008/1273 Reg.83G, Reg.30, SI 2008/1582 Reg.42, SI 2008/2836 Art.9, Art.20, SI 2008/3170 Reg.30

Sch.1 para.1, see *MT v OT (Financial Provision: Costs)* [2007] EWHC 838 (Fam), [2008] 2 F.L.R. 1311 (Fam Div), Charles, J.; see *W v C* [2008] EWHC 73 (Fam), [2008] 1 F.L.R. 1703 (Fam Div), Singer, J.

Sch.1 para.1, applied: SI 2008/1052 Sch.1, SI 2008/1054 Sch.1

Sch.1 para.2, applied: SI 2008/1052 Sch.1, Sch.2 para.2, SI 2008/1054 Sch.1, Sch.2 para.2

Sch.1 para.4, amended: 2008 c.22 Sch.6 para.32

Sch.1 para.5, applied: SI 2008/1052 Sch.1, SI 2008/1054 Sch.1

Sch.1 para.6, see *W v C* [2008] EWHC 73 (Fam), [2008] 1 F.L.R. 1703 (Fam Div), Singer, J.

Sch.1 para.6, applied: SI 2008/1052 Sch.1, SI 2008/1054 Sch.1

Sch.3 para.6, see *T (A Child) v Wakefield MDC* [2008] EWCA Civ 199, Times, April 14, 2008 (CA (Civ Div)), Thorpe, L.J.

Sch.1 para.8, applied: SI 2008/1052 Sch.1, SI 2008/1054 Sch.1

Sch.1 para.10, amended: 2008 c.22 Sch.6 para.32

Sch.1 para.10, applied: SI 2008/1052 Sch.1, SI 2008/1054 Sch.1

Sch.1 para.11, applied: SI 2008/1052 Sch.1, SI 2008/1054 Sch.1

Sch.1 para.14, applied: SI 2008/1052 Sch.1, SI 2008/1054 Sch.1

Sch.1 para.15, applied: SI 2008/794 Sch.8 para.26

Sch.2 Part I para.6, added: 2008 c.23 s.25

Sch.2 Part I para.6, amended: 2008 c.23 Sch.4

Sch.2 Part I para.8A, added: 2008 c.23 s.19

Sch.2 Part II para.12, amended: 2008 c.23 Sch.2 para.1

Sch.2 Part II para.12, repealed (in part): 2008 c.23 Sch.2 para.1

Sch.2 Part II para.12, substituted: 2008 c.23 Sch.1 para.4

Sch.2 Part II para.12A, added: 2008 c.23 Sch.2 para.2

Sch.2 Part II para.12A, repealed: 2008 c.23 Sch.2 para.2

Sch.2 Part II para.12A, substituted: 2008 c.23 Sch.1 para.4

Sch.2 Part II para.12B, added: 2008 c.23 Sch.2 para.2

Sch.2 Part II para.12B, repealed: 2008 c.23 Sch.2 para.2

CAP.

1989–cont.

41. Children Act 1989–*cont.*

Sch.2 Part II para.12B, substituted: 2008 c.23 Sch.1 para.4

Sch.2 Part II para.12B, varied: 2008 c.23 Sch.2 para.2

Sch.2 Part II para.12C, substituted: 2008 c.23 Sch.1 para.4

Sch.2 Part II para.12D, substituted: 2008 c.23 Sch.1 para.4

Sch.2 Part II para.12E, substituted: 2008 c.23 Sch.1 para.4

Sch.2 Part II para.12F, substituted: 2008 c.23 Sch.1 para.4

Sch.2 Part II para.12G, substituted: 2008 c.23 Sch.1 para.4

Sch.2 Part II para.13, substituted: 2008 c.23 Sch.1 para.4

Sch.2 Part II para.14, substituted: 2008 c.23 Sch.1 para.4

Sch.2 Part II para.17, amended: 2008 c.23 Sch.3 para.27

Sch.2 Part II para.17, repealed: 2008 c.23 s.16, Sch.4

Sch.2 Part II para.19, applied: SI 2008/1052 Sch.1, SI 2008/1054 Sch.1, SI 2008/2836 Art.5

Sch.2 Part II para.19B, amended: 2008 c.23 Sch.3 para.27

Sch.2 Part II para.20, amended: 2008 c.23 Sch.3 para.27

Sch.2 Part III para.21, amended: 2008 c.23 Sch.1 para.5

Sch.2 Part III para.23, applied: SI 2008/1054 Sch.1, SI 2008/2836 Art.5

Sch.2 Part III para.25, amended: 2008 c.23 Sch.3 para.27

Sch.2 para.19, see *A LBC v A* [2008] EWHC 1722 (Fam), [2008] 2 F.L.R. 1857 (Fam Div), Charles, J.

Sch.3 Part II para.6, applied: SI 2008/1052 Sch.1, SI 2008/1054 Sch.1

Sch.3 Part III para.13, amended: 2008 c.4 Sch.4 para.37

Sch.3 Part III para.14, amended: 2008 c.4 Sch.4 para.37

Sch.3 Part III para.15, applied: SI 2008/1052 Sch.1, SI 2008/1054 Sch.1

Sch.3 Part III para.17, applied: SI 2008/1052 Sch.1, SI 2008/1054 Sch.1

Sch.3 para.6, see *T (A Child) v Wakefield MDC* [2008] EWCA Civ 199, [2008] 3 W.L.R. 1316 (CA (Civ Div)), Thorpe, L.J.

Sch.5 Part II para.7, amended: 2008 c.23 Sch.3 para.28

Sch.8 para.3, amended: 2008 c.4 Sch.4 para.38

Sch.8 para.8, applied: SI 2008/1052 Sch.1, SI 2008/2836 Art.5

Sch.8 para.9, amended: 2008 c.23 Sch.1 para.6

CAP.

1989–cont.

41. Children Act 1989–*cont.*
Sch.9A para.2, amended: 2008 c.23 Sch.1 para.7
Sch.9A para.4, enabling: SI 2008/2691
Sch.9A para.6, applied: SI 2008/2261 Sch.2 para.13
Sch.11 Part I, applied: 2008 c.22 s.54
Sch.11 Part I, enabling: SI 2008/2836
Sch.13 para.32, repealed: 2008 c.12 Sch.1 Part 11
Sch.13 para.35, repealed (in part): 2008 c.4 Sch.28 Part 1

42. Local Government and Housing Act 1989
s.2, applied: SI 2008/220 Reg.3
s.2, enabling: SI 2008/220
s.4, applied: SI 2008/907 Art.17, SI 2008/1430 Reg.15
s.4, varied: SI 2008/907 Art.17
s.5, applied: SI 2008/634 Art.8, SI 2008/907 Art.17
s.5, varied: SI 2008/634 Art.8, SI 2008/907 Art.17
s.5A, applied: SI 2008/634 Art.8, SI 2008/907 Art.17
s.5A, varied: SI 2008/634 Art.8, SI 2008/907 Art.17
s.6, applied: SI 2008/3248 Reg.9
s.13, disapplied: SI 2008/2867 Reg.16
s.15, disapplied: SI 2008/2867 Reg.17
s.15, referred to: 2008 c.26 s.93
s.16, referred to: 2008 c.26 s.93
s.17, applied: SI 2008/2867 Reg.17
s.17, referred to: 2008 c.26 s.93
s.18, applied: SI 2008/788 Sch.1
s.18, enabling: SSI 2008/414, SSI 2008/415
s.19, applied: SI 2008/788 Art.4
s.31, applied: SI 2008/788 Art.4
s.68, amended: SI 2008/948 Sch.1 para.160
s.69, amended: SI 2008/948 Sch.1 para.160
s.69, applied: SI 2008/239 Reg.5
s.69, varied: SI 2008/239 Reg.5
s.71, amended: SI 2008/948 Sch.1 para.160
s.73, applied: SI 2008/239 Sch.2 para.5
s.74, varied: SI 2008/2867 Reg.26
s.75, varied: SI 2008/2867 Reg.26
s.76, varied: SI 2008/2867 Reg.26
s.77, varied: SI 2008/2867 Reg.26
s.78, varied: SI 2008/2867 Reg.26
s.78A, varied: SI 2008/2867 Reg.26
s.78B, varied: SI 2008/2867 Reg.26
s.79, varied: SI 2008/2867 Reg.26
s.80, varied: SI 2008/2867 Reg.26
s.80A, varied: SI 2008/2867 Reg.26
s.80B, added: 2008 c.17 s.313
s.80B, varied: SI 2008/2867 Reg.26
s.80ZA, varied: SI 2008/2867 Reg.26
s.81, varied: SI 2008/2867 Reg.26
s.82, varied: SI 2008/2867 Reg.26
s.83, varied: SI 2008/2867 Reg.26

CAP.

1989–cont.

42. Local Government and Housing Act 1989–*cont.*
s.84, varied: SI 2008/2867 Reg.26
s.85, varied: SI 2008/2867 Reg.26
s.86, varied: SI 2008/2867 Reg.26
s.87, varied: SI 2008/2867 Reg.26
s.87A, varied: SI 2008/2867 Reg.26
s.88, amended: 2008 c.17 s.313
s.88, varied: SI 2008/2867 Reg.26
s.150, applied: SI 2008/3248
s.150, enabling: SI 2008/3248
s.152, applied: SI 2008/3248
s.152, repealed (in part): 2008 asp 5 Sch.3 Part 1
s.155, amended: 2008 c.26 Sch.4 para.57
s.172, amended: 2008 c.17 Sch.16
s.172, varied: SI 2008/2839 Sch.1 para.1
s.173, amended: 2008 c.17 s.191
s.173, applied: 2008 c.17 s.149, s.173, s.190
s.173, repealed (in part): 2008 c.17 s.191, Sch.16
s.173, varied: SI 2008/2839 Sch.1 para.1
s.190, enabling: SI 2008/220
Sch.1, referred to: 2008 c.26 s.93
Sch.4 Part III para.2, substituted: 2008 c.17 s.313
Sch.11 para.58, repealed: 2008 c.17 Sch.16

44. Opticians Act 1989
applied: 2008 c.13 Sch.3, 2008 c.14 s.98, s.100, s.105, s.108, s.109, SI 2008/1185 Sch.1 para.15, SI 2008/2927 Reg.2
s.1, amended: SI 2008/1774 Sch.2 para.1
s.1, applied: SI 2008/1774 Art.4
s.2, enabling: SI 2008/3113
s.3, amended: 2008 c.14 Sch.7 para.25
s.3, applied: SI 2008/3113
s.3, enabling: SI 2008/3113
s.4, amended: 2008 c.14 Sch.7 para.26
s.4, enabling: SI 2008/3113
s.5, enabling: SI 2008/3113
s.5A, amended: 2008 c.14 Sch.7 para.27
s.5A, enabling: SI 2008/3113
s.5B, enabling: SI 2008/3113
s.5C, repealed: 2008 c.14 Sch.7 para.28, Sch.15 Part 2
s.5C, enabling: SI 2008/3113
s.5D, amended: 2008 c.14 Sch.7 para.29, Sch.15 Part 2
s.5D, enabling: SI 2008/3113
s.10, enabling: SI 2008/1940
s.11A, enabling: SI 2008/1940
s.11B, enabling: SI 2008/1940
s.13AA, added: 2008 c.14 Sch.7 para.30
s.13D, amended: 2008 c.14 Sch.7 para.31, SI 2008/1774 Sch.2 para.2
s.13F, amended: 2008 c.14 Sch.7 para.32
s.13F, applied: SI 2008/1185 Sch.1 para.47
s.13G, amended: 2008 c.14 Sch.7 para.33
s.13H, amended: 2008 c.14 Sch.7 para.34
s.13H, applied: SI 2008/1185 Sch.1 para.47

CAP.

1989–cont.

44. Opticians Act 1989–*cont.*

s.13I, amended: 2008 c.14 Sch.7 para.35
s.13J, amended: 2008 c.14 Sch.7 para.36
s.13K, amended: 2008 c.14 Sch.7 para.37
s.13L, amended: 2008 c.14 Sch.7 para.38, Sch.15 Part 2
s.23AA, added: 2008 c.14 Sch.7 para.39
s.23B, amended: 2008 c.14 Sch.7 para.40, Sch.15 Part 2
s.23B, repealed (in part): 2008 c.14 Sch.7 para.40, Sch.15 Part 2
s.23C, applied: SI 2008/2690, SI 2008/2690 Sch.1
s.23C, repealed (in part): 2008 c.14 Sch.7 para.41, Sch.15 Part 2
s.23C, enabling: SI 2008/2690
s.23CA, added: 2008 c.14 Sch.7 para.42
s.23D, repealed (in part): 2008 c.14 Sch.7 para.43, Sch.15 Part 2
s.23E, amended: 2008 c.14 Sch.7 para.44
s.23E, repealed (in part): 2008 c.14 Sch.15 Part 2
s.23G, amended: 2008 c.14 Sch.7 para.45
s.23I, added: 2008 c.14 Sch.7 para.46
s.25, enabling: SI 2008/1940
s.26, applied: SI 2008/1185 Reg.13
s.29, amended: 2008 c.14 Sch.7 para.47
s.31A, applied: SI 2008/2690 Sch.1
s.31A, enabling: SI 2008/1940, SI 2008/2690, SI 2008/3113
s.32, amended: SI 2008/948 Sch.1 para.1
s.32A, added: SI 2008/1774 Sch.2 para.3
s.33, amended: 2008 c.14 Sch.7 para.48
s.34, amended: 2008 c.14 Sch.7 para.49, SI 2008/1774 Sch.2 para.4
s.34, applied: SI 2008/1940, SI 2008/1940 Sch.1, SI 2008/2690, SI 2008/3113
s.34, repealed (in part): SI 2008/1774 Sch.2 para.4
s.36, amended: 2008 c.14 Sch.7 para.50, SI 2008/1774 Sch.2 para.5
Sch.1 para.1, substituted: SI 2008/1774 Sch.2 para.6
Sch.1 para.1A, substituted: SI 2008/1774 Sch.2 para.6
Sch.1 para.1B, substituted: SI 2008/1774 Sch.2 para.6
Sch.1 para.1C, substituted: SI 2008/1774 Sch.2 para.6
Sch.1 para.2, substituted: SI 2008/1774 Sch.2 para.6
Sch.1 para.2A, substituted: SI 2008/1774 Sch.2 para.6
Sch.1 para.3, substituted: SI 2008/1774 Sch.2 para.6
Sch.1 para.4, substituted: SI 2008/1774 Sch.2 para.6
Sch.1 para.5, substituted: SI 2008/1774 Sch.2 para.6
Sch.1 para.6, substituted: SI 2008/1774 Sch.2 para.6

CAP.

1989–cont.

44. Opticians Act 1989–*cont.*

Sch.1 para.7, substituted: SI 2008/1774 Sch.2 para.6
Sch.1 para.8, substituted: SI 2008/1774 Sch.2 para.6
Sch.1 para.9, substituted: SI 2008/1774 Sch.2 para.6
Sch.1 para.11, amended: SI 2008/1774 Sch.2 para.6
Sch.1 para.11A, added: SI 2008/1774 Sch.2 para.6
Sch.1 para.12, amended: 2008 c.14 Sch.7 para.51, SI 2008/1774 Sch.2 para.6
Sch.1 para.12A, enabling: SI 2008/3113
Sch.1 para.12B, added: SI 2008/1774 Sch.2 para.6
Sch.1 para.13, repealed: SI 2008/1774 Sch.2 para.6

45. Prisons (Scotland) Act 1989

applied: SI 2008/794 Reg.156, SI 2008/2551 Reg.4
s.14, applied: SSI 2008/8
s.14, enabling: SSI 2008/8, SSI 2008/35
s.17, applied: SI 2008/794 Reg.112
s.39, enabling: SSI 2008/8, SSI 2008/35, SSI 2008/377

1990

1. Capital Allowances Act 1990

s.3, see *Maco Door & Window Hardware (UK) Ltd v Revenue and Customs Commissioners* [2008] UKHL 54, [2008] 1 W.L.R. 1790 (HL), Lord Hoffmann
s.18, see *Maco Door & Window Hardware (UK) Ltd v Revenue and Customs Commissioners* [2008] UKHL 54, [2008] 1 W.L.R. 1790 (HL), Lord Hoffmann
s.24, see *JD Wetherspoon Plc v Revenue and Customs Commissioners* [2008] S.T.C. (S.C.D.) 460 (Sp Comm), Theodore Wallace
s.66, see *JD Wetherspoon Plc v Revenue and Customs Commissioners* [2008] S.T.C. (S.C.D.) 460 (Sp Comm), Theodore Wallace
Sch.AA1, see *JD Wetherspoon Plc v Revenue and Customs Commissioners* [2008] S.T.C. (S.C.D.) 460 (Sp Comm), Theodore Wallace

5. Criminal Justice (International Co-operation) Act 1990

Part II, applied: SI 2008/295 Reg.6, SI 2008/296 Reg.5
s.6, amended: 2008 c.4 Sch.26 para.27
s.13, applied: SI 2008/295 Reg.6, SI 2008/296 Reg.5
s.13, referred to: SI 2008/295 Reg.6
s.13, varied: SI 2008/295 Reg.6, SI 2008/296 Reg.5

6. Education (Student Loans) Act 1990

applied: SI 2008/529 Reg.4, SI 2008/1273 Reg.4, SI 2008/1582 Reg.5, SI 2008/3170 Reg.4
s.1, enabling: SI 2008/1479

CAP.

1990–cont.

6. Education (Student Loans) Act 1990– *cont.*

Sch.1 para.1, enabling: SI 2008/1479

8. Town and Country Planning Act 1990

applied: 2008 c.29 s.206, s.209, SI 2008/1261 Sch.2 para.25, Sch.6 para.20, SI 2008/2512 Art.34

varied: 2008 c.18 s.9

Part III, applied: 2008 c.18 s.10, Sch.16 para.2, SI 2008/2512 Art.34

Part IV, referred to: 2008 c.17 s.17

Part VI c.II, applied: 2008 c.29 s.204

Part XI, applied: 2008 c.29 s.137

s.2A, applied: SI 2008/580 Art.7, Art.8, Sch.1 para.1

s.2A, disapplied: SI 2008/580 Art.3

s.2A, enabling: SI 2008/580

s.2D, enabling: SI 2008/580

s.2F, enabling: SI 2008/580

s.5, amended: 2008 c.29 s.190

s.8A, amended: 2008 c.17 Sch.8 para.52

s.8A, repealed (in part): 2008 c.17 Sch.8 para.52, Sch.16

s.8A, varied: SI 2008/3068 Art.11

s.35B, referred to: 2008 c.12 Sch.2 para.10

s.55, see *Sumption v Greenwich LBC* [2007] EWHC 2776 (Admin), [2008] 1 P. & C.R. 20 (QBD (Admin)), Collins, J.

s.57, amended: 2008 c.29 Sch.2 para.35

s.59, enabling: SI 2008/502, SI 2008/550, SI 2008/580, SI 2008/675, SI 2008/2336, SI 2008/2362

s.60, enabling: SI 2008/502, SI 2008/675, SI 2008/2362

s.61, enabling: SI 2008/550, SI 2008/675, SI 2008/2336, SI 2008/2362

s.61A, amended: 2008 c.29 s.188

s.61A, repealed (in part): 2008 c.29 s.188, Sch.13

s.62, enabling: SI 2008/550, SI 2008/2336

s.65, enabling: SI 2008/550

s.69, amended: 2008 c.29 s.190

s.70, applied: SI 2008/1261 Sch.2 para.25, Sch.6 para.20

s.70A, amended: 2008 c.29 Sch.7 para.2

s.70B, amended: 2008 c.29 Sch.7 para.3

s.73, applied: SI 2008/1261 Sch.2 para.25, Sch.6 para.20

s.73, disapplied: SI 2008/580 Art.1

s.73A, applied: SI 2008/1261 Sch.2 para.25, Sch.6 para.20

s.74, enabling: SI 2008/550, SI 2008/580

s.77, see *R. (on the application of Persimmon Homes Ltd) v Secretary of State for Communities and Local Government* [2007] EWHC 1985 (Admin), [2008] J.P.L. 323 (QBD (Admin)), Sullivan, J.

s.77, amended: 2008 c.29 Sch.10 para.2

s.78, amended: 2008 c.29 Sch.10 para.3, Sch.11 para.2

CAP.

1990–cont.

8. Town and Country Planning Act 1990– *cont.*

s.78, applied: 2008 c.18 Sch.7 para.31, Sch.16 para.2

s.78, enabling: SI 2008/550

s.79, see *Jefferson v National Assembly for Wales* [2007] EWHC 3351 (Admin), [2008] 1 W.L.R. 2193 (QBD (Admin)), Judge Hickinbottom

s.79, amended: 2008 c.29 Sch.10 para.4

s.90, applied: SI 2008/969 Art.18, SI 2008/2512 Art.34

s.90, varied: SI 2008/2512 Art.34

s.91, disapplied: 2008 c.18 s.11

s.96A, added: 2008 c.29 s.190

s.97, applied: SI 2008/1261 Sch.2 para.25, Sch.6 para.20

s.106, see *Atlantic Housing Ltd v Secretary of State for Communities and Local Government* [2008] EWHC 1373 (Admin), [2008] 29 E.G. 97 (QBD (Admin)), Collins, J.; see *R. (on the application of Hall) v First Secretary of State* [2007] EWCA Civ 612, [2008] J.P.L. 63 (CA (Civ Div)), Ward, L.J.; see *Residents Against Waste Site Ltd v Lancashire CC* [2007] EWHC 2558 (Admin), [2008] Env. L.R. 27 (QBD (Admin)), Irwin, J.; see *Watson v Croft Promo-Sport Ltd* [2008] EWHC 759 (QB), [2008] 3 All E.R. 1171 (QBD (Newcastle)), Simon, J.; see *Yewbelle Ltd v London Green Developments Ltd* [2007] EWCA Civ 475, [2008] 1 P. & C.R. 17 (CA (Civ Div)), Waller, L.J. (V-P)

s.106, amended: 2008 c.29 s.174

s.106, referred to: 2008 c.29 s.223

s.106A, amended: 2008 c.29 s.174

s.106B, amended: 2008 c.29 s.174

s.106C, added: 2008 c.29 s.174

s.108, amended: 2008 c.29 s.189

s.118, applied: 2008 c.17 s.17

s.137, see *White v Herefordshire Council* [2007] EWCA Civ 1204, [2008] 1 W.L.R. 954 (CA (Civ Div)), Latham, L.J.

s.139, see *White v Herefordshire Council* [2007] EWCA Civ 1204, [2008] 1 W.L.R. 954 (CA (Civ Div)), Latham, L.J.

s.143, see *White v Herefordshire Council* [2007] EWCA Civ 1204, [2008] 1 W.L.R. 954 (CA (Civ Div)), Latham, L.J.

s.149, see *Aardvark SRE Ltd v Sedgfield BC* [2008] R.V.R. 213 (Lands Tr), AJ Trott FRICS

s.150, see *Aardvark SRE Ltd v Sedgfield BC* [2008] R.V.R. 213 (Lands Tr), AJ Trott FRICS

s.150, amended: 2008 c.29 s.175

s.151, see *Aardvark SRE Ltd v Sedgfield BC* [2008] R.V.R. 213 (Lands Tr), AJ Trott FRICS

s.151, amended: 2008 c.29 s.175

s.165A, added: 2008 c.29 s.175

CAP.

1990–cont.

8. **Town and Country Planning Act 1990–** *cont.*

s.168, see *Aardvark SRE Ltd v Sedgfield BC* [2008] R.V.R. 213 (Lands Tr), A.J Trott FRICS

s.169, amended: 2008 c.29 s.175

s.170, amended: 2008 c.29 s.175

s.171, amended: 2008 c.29 s.175

s.171B, see *Revenue and Customs Commissioners v Tallington Lakes Ltd* [2007] EWHC 1955 (Ch), [2008] S.T.C. 2734 (Ch D), David Richards, J.

s.174, see *Goodall v Peak District National Park Authority* [2008] EWHC 734 (Admin), [2008] 1 W.L.R. 2705 (DC), Keene, L.J.; see *R. (on the application of JRP Holdings Ltd) v Spelthorne BC* [2007] EWCA Civ 1122, [2008] J.P.L. 696 (CA (Civ Div)), Dyson, L.J.; see *R. v Challinor (Basil John)* [2007] EWCA Crim 2102, [2008] 1 P. & C.R. 9 (CA (Crim Div)), Rix, L.J.

s.175, amended: 2008 c.29 Sch.10 para.5

s.176, amended: 2008 c.29 Sch.10 para.6

s.179, see *Sevenoaks DC v Harber* [2008] EWHC 708 (Admin), [2008] 23 E.G. 118 (DC), Keene, L.J.

s.183, see *R. (on the application of JRP Holdings Ltd) v Spelthorne BC* [2007] EWCA Civ 1122, [2008] J.P.L. 696 (CA (Civ Div)), Dyson, L.J.

s.187B, see *Aylesbury Vale DC v Florent* [2007] EWHC 724 (QB), [2008] J.P.L. 70 (QBD), Gray, J.

s.192, see *Sumption v Greenwich LBC* [2007] EWHC 2776 (Admin), [2008] 1 P. & C.R. 20 (QBD (Admin)), Collins, J.

s.193, enabling: SI 2008/550

s.195, amended: 2008 c.29 Sch.10 para.7, Sch.11 para.3

s.196, amended: 2008 c.29 Sch.10 para.8

s.198, see *Perrin v Northampton BC* [2007] EWCA Civ 1353, [2008] 1 W.L.R. 1307 (CA (Civ Div)), Wall, L.J.

s.198, amended: 2008 c.29 Sch.8 para.8

s.198, disapplied: 2008 c.18 s.19

s.198, repealed (in part): 2008 c.29 s.192, Sch.13

s.198, enabling: SI 2008/2260

s.199, repealed: 2008 c.29 s.192, Sch.13

s.199, enabling: SI 2008/2260, SI 2008/3202

s.200, amended: 2008 c.29 Sch.8 para.9

s.201, repealed: 2008 c.29 s.192, Sch.13

s.202, amended: 2008 c.29 Sch.8 para.10

s.202, repealed (in part): 2008 c.29 s.192, Sch.13

s.202A, added: 2008 c.29 s.192

s.202B, added: 2008 c.29 s.192

s.202C, added: 2008 c.29 s.192

s.202D, added: 2008 c.29 s.192

s.202E, added: 2008 c.29 s.192

CAP.

1990–cont.

8. **Town and Country Planning Act 1990–** *cont.*

s.202F, added: 2008 c.29 s.192

s.202G, added: 2008 c.29 s.192

s.203, repealed: 2008 c.29 s.192, Sch.13

s.204, repealed: 2008 c.29 s.192, Sch.13

s.205, repealed: 2008 c.29 s.192, Sch.13

s.206, amended: 2008 c.29 Sch.8 para.11

s.207, amended: 2008 c.29 Sch.8 para.12

s.208, amended: 2008 c.29 Sch.10 para.9, Sch.11 para.4

s.210, amended: 2008 c.29 Sch.8 para.13

s.211, amended: 2008 c.29 Sch.2 para.36, Sch.8 para.14

s.211, disapplied: 2008 c.18 s.19

s.212, repealed (in part): 2008 c.29 Sch.8 para.15, Sch.13

s.213, amended: 2008 c.29 Sch.8 para.16

s.226, see *R. (on the application of Hall) v First Secretary of State* [2007] EWCA Civ 612, [2008] J.P.L. 63 (CA (Civ Div)), Ward, L.J.

s.229, applied: SI 2008/1961 Sch.4 para.8

s.237, amended: 2008 c.29 Sch.9 para.4

s.247, applied: SI 2008/442 Reg.3

s.257, applied: SI 2008/442 Reg.3, Sch.1 para.9

s.258, applied: SI 2008/442 Reg.3, Sch.1 para.10

s.264, applied: 2008 c.18 s.10, SI 2008/969 Art.18, SI 2008/2512 Art.34

s.266, amended: 2008 c.29 s.195

s.271, applied: 2008 c.18 s.8, s.9, SI 2008/1238 Sch.2 para.1, Sch.2 para.3, SI 2008/1261 Art.32, Sch.11 para.1, SI 2008/2512 Art.32, Sch.9 para.1, Sch.10 para.4, SI 2008/3163 Art.12

s.271, disapplied: SI 2008/1238 Art.8, Sch.2 para.5, SI 2008/1261 Sch.11 para.1, SI 2008/2512 Sch.9 para.1

s.271, referred to: 2008 c.18 s.9

s.271, varied: 2008 c.18 s.9, SI 2008/1261 Sch.11 para.1, SI 2008/2512 Sch.9 para.1

s.272, applied: 2008 c.18 s.8, s.9, Sch.17 para.2, SI 2008/1238 Sch.2 para.1, Sch.2 para.3, SI 2008/1261 Art.32, Sch.11 para.1, SI 2008/2512 Art.32, Sch.9 para.1, Sch.10 para.4, SI 2008/3163 Art.12

s.272, disapplied: SI 2008/1238 Art.8, Sch.2 para.5, SI 2008/1261 Sch.11 para.1, SI 2008/2512 Sch.9 para.1

s.272, referred to: SI 2008/1238 Sch.2 para.2

s.272, varied: 2008 c.18 s.9, SI 2008/1261 Sch.11 para.1, SI 2008/2512 Sch.9 para.1

s.273, applied: 2008 c.18 s.9, SI 2008/1238 Sch.2 para.1, Sch.2 para.3, SI 2008/1261 Sch.11 para.1, SI 2008/2512 Sch.9 para.1

s.273, disapplied: SI 2008/1238 Sch.2 para.5, SI 2008/1261 Sch.11 para.1, SI 2008/2512 Sch.9 para.1

s.273, referred to: SI 2008/1238 Sch.2 para.2

CAP.

1990–cont.

8. Town and Country Planning Act 1990– *cont.*

s.273, varied: 2008 c.18 s.9, SI 2008/1261 Sch.11 para.1, SI 2008/2512 Sch.9 para.1
s.274, applied: SI 2008/1238 Sch.2 para.1, SI 2008/1261 Sch.11 para.1, SI 2008/2512 Sch.9 para.1
s.274, disapplied: SI 2008/1238 Sch.2 para.5, SI 2008/1261 Sch.11 para.1, SI 2008/2512 Sch.9 para.1
s.274, referred to: SI 2008/1238 Sch.2 para.2
s.274, varied: 2008 c.18 s.9, SI 2008/1261 Sch.11 para.1, SI 2008/2512 Sch.9 para.1
s.275, applied: SI 2008/1261 Sch.11 para.1
s.275, disapplied: SI 2008/1238 Sch.2 para.5, SI 2008/1261 Sch.11 para.1, SI 2008/2512 Sch.9 para.1
s.275, referred to: SI 2008/1238 Sch.2 para.1, Sch.2 para.2, SI 2008/2512 Sch.9 para.1
s.275, varied: SI 2008/1261 Sch.11 para.1, SI 2008/2512 Sch.9 para.1
s.276, applied: SI 2008/1261 Sch.11 para.1
s.276, disapplied: SI 2008/1238 Sch.2 para.5, SI 2008/1261 Sch.11 para.1, SI 2008/2512 Sch.9 para.1
s.276, referred to: SI 2008/1238 Sch.2 para.1, Sch.2 para.2, SI 2008/2512 Sch.9 para.1
s.276, varied: SI 2008/1261 Sch.11 para.1, SI 2008/2512 Sch.9 para.1
s.277, applied: SI 2008/1261 Sch.11 para.1
s.277, disapplied: SI 2008/1238 Sch.2 para.5, SI 2008/1261 Sch.11 para.1, SI 2008/2512 Sch.9 para.1
s.277, referred to: SI 2008/1238 Sch.2 para.1, Sch.2 para.2, SI 2008/2512 Sch.9 para.1
s.277, varied: SI 2008/1261 Sch.11 para.1, SI 2008/2512 Sch.9 para.1
s.278, applied: SI 2008/1261 Sch.11 para.1
s.278, disapplied: SI 2008/1238 Sch.2 para.5, SI 2008/1261 Sch.11 para.1, SI 2008/2512 Sch.9 para.1
s.278, referred to: SI 2008/1238 Sch.2 para.1, Sch.2 para.2, SI 2008/2512 Sch.9 para.1
s.278, varied: SI 2008/1261 Sch.11 para.1, SI 2008/2512 Sch.9 para.1
s.279, applied: 2008 c.17 Sch.4 para.7, Sch.4 para.14, SI 2008/1261 Sch.11 para.1, SI 2008/2512 Sch.9 para.1
s.279, disapplied: SI 2008/1238 Sch.2 para.5, SI 2008/1261 Sch.11 para.1, SI 2008/2512 Sch.9 para.1
s.279, referred to: SI 2008/1238 Sch.2 para.1, Sch.2 para.2
s.279, varied: 2008 c.18 s.9, SI 2008/1261 Sch.11 para.1, SI 2008/2512 Sch.9 para.1
s.280, applied: 2008 c.17 Sch.4 para.7, Sch.4 para.14, SI 2008/1261 Sch.11 para.1, SI 2008/2512 Sch.9 para.1
s.280, disapplied: SI 2008/1238 Sch.2 para.5, SI 2008/1261 Sch.11 para.1, SI 2008/2512 Sch.9 para.1

CAP.

1990–cont.

8. Town and Country Planning Act 1990– *cont.*

s.280, referred to: SI 2008/1238 Sch.2 para.1, Sch.2 para.2
s.280, varied: 2008 c.18 s.9, SI 2008/1261 Sch.11 para.1, SI 2008/2512 Sch.9 para.1
s.281, referred to: SI 2008/1238 Sch.2 para.2
s.282, applied: 2008 c.17 Sch.4 para.7, Sch.4 para.14, SI 2008/2512 Sch.9 para.1
s.282, disapplied: SI 2008/1238 Sch.2 para.5, SI 2008/1261 Sch.11 para.1, SI 2008/2512 Sch.9 para.1
s.282, referred to: SI 2008/1238 Sch.2 para.1, Sch.2 para.2
s.282, varied: SI 2008/1261 Sch.11 para.1, SI 2008/2512 Sch.9 para.1
s.284, amended: 2008 c.29 s.191, Sch.8 para.17, Sch.13
s.285, see *R. (on the application of JRP Holdings Ltd) v Spelthorne BC* [2007] EWCA Civ 1122, [2008] J.P.L. 696 (CA (Civ Div)), Dyson, L.J.; see *R. v Challinor (Basil John)* [2007] EWCA Crim 2102, [2008] 1 P. & C.R. 9 (CA (Crim Div)), Rix, L.J.; see *Staffordshire CC v Challinor* [2007] EWCA Civ 864, [2008] 1 P. & C.R. 10 (CA (Civ Div)), Rix, L.J.
s.286, amended: 2008 c.29 s.190
s.287, see *MA Holdings Ltd v George Wimpey UK Ltd* [2008] EWCA Civ 12, [2008] 1 W.L.R. 1649 (CA (Civ Div)), Dyson, L.J.
s.287, varied: 2008 c.29 s.186
s.288, see *McCarthy v First Secretary of State* [2007] EWCA Civ 510, [2008] J.P.L. 712 (CA (Civ Div)), Buxton, L.J.; see *R. (on the application of Davies) v Secretary of State for Communities and Local Government* [2008] EWHC 2223 (Admin), Times, October 15, 2008 (QBD), Sullivan, J.
s.289, see *R. (on the application of Davies) v Secretary of State for Communities and Local Government* [2008] EWHC 2223 (Admin), Times, October 15, 2008 (QBD), Sullivan, J.; see *Staffordshire CC v Challinor* [2007] EWCA Civ 864, [2008] 1 P. & C.R. 10 (CA (Civ Div)), Rix, L.J.
s.303, disapplied: 2008 c.18 s.12
s.303, substituted: 2008 c.29 s.199
s.303, enabling: SI 2008/958
s.303A, referred to: 2008 c.12 Sch.2 para.10
s.303ZA, added: 2008 c.29 s.200
s.304A, amended: 2008 c.29 s.177
s.319A, added: 2008 c.29 s.196
s.322, amended: 2008 c.29 Sch.10 para.10
s.322A, amended: 2008 c.29 Sch.10 para.11
s.323, amended: 2008 c.29 Sch.10 para.12
s.323, enabling: SI 2008/2260, SI 2008/3202
s.325, referred to: 2008 c.17 s.18
s.329, amended: 2008 c.29 Sch.8 para.18
s.333, amended: 2008 c.29 Sch.10 para.13

CAP.

1990–cont.

8. Town and Country Planning Act 1990–*cont.*

s.333, enabling: SI 2008/502, SI 2008/550, SI 2008/595, SI 2008/675, SI 2008/2093, SI 2008/2260, SI 2008/2335, SI 2008/2336, SI 2008/2362, SI 2008/3202

s.336, amended: 2008 c.29 s.201, Sch.2 para.37, Sch.8 para.19

s.337, enabling: SI 2008/675, SI 2008/2362

Sch.1 para.3, amended: 2008 c.29 s.190

Sch.1 para.17, repealed: 2008 c.29 Sch.13

Sch.1A para.9, repealed: 2008 c.29 Sch.13

Sch.2 Part IA, applied: 2008 c.29 s.204

Sch.3 para.1, see *Greenweb Ltd v Wandsworth LBC* [2008] EWCA Civ 910, [2008] R.V.R. 294 (CA (Civ Div)), Buxton, L.J.

Sch.4A para.2, repealed (in part): 2008 c.29 s.188, Sch.13

Sch.6 para.1, amended: 2008 c.29 s.198

Sch.6 para.1, enabling: SI 2008/595, SI 2008/2093, SI 2008/2335

Sch.6 para.2, amended: 2008 c.29 s.198, Sch.10 para.14

Sch.6 para.3, amended: 2008 c.29 Sch.10 para.14

Sch.6 para.6, amended: 2008 c.29 Sch.10 para.14

Sch.9 para.3, applied: SI 2008/1556 Reg.4

Sch.9 para.3, varied: SI 2008/1556 Reg.4

Sch.9 para.4, varied: SI 2008/1556 Reg.4

Sch.13 para.1, referred to: 2008 c.29 s.204

Sch.13 para.2, referred to: 2008 c.29 s.204

Sch.13 para.3, referred to: 2008 c.29 s.204

Sch.13 para.4, referred to: 2008 c.29 s.204

Sch.13 para.24, added: 2008 c.29 s.175

Sch.13 para.25, added: 2008 c.29 s.175

9. Planning (Listed Buildings and Conservation Areas) Act 1990

see *Chambers v Guildford BC* [2008] EWHC 826 (QB), [2008] J.P.L. 1459 (QBD), McCombe, J.

applied: SI 2008/386 Reg.4, SI 2008/2499 Reg.4

referred to: 2008 c.13 Sch.6

s.1, see *Chambers v Guildford BC* [2008] EWHC 826 (QB), [2008] J.P.L. 1459 (QBD), McCombe, J.

s.1, applied: 2008 c.18 Sch.9 para.1, Sch.9 para.2, SI 2008/386 Reg.4, SI 2008/2499 Reg.4

s.7, see *Chambers v Guildford BC* [2008] EWHC 826 (QB), [2008] J.P.L. 1459 (QBD), McCombe, J.

s.7, amended: 2008 c.29 Sch.2 para.39

s.7, disapplied: 2008 c.18 Sch.9 para.1, Sch.9 para.2

s.8, applied: 2008 c.29 s.33

s.10, enabling: SI 2008/551

s.11, enabling: SI 2008/551

s.12, amended: 2008 c.29 Sch.10 para.16

CAP.

1990–cont.

9. Planning (Listed Buildings and Conservation Areas) Act 1990–*cont.*

s.20, see *Chambers v Guildford BC* [2008] EWHC 826 (QB), [2008] J.P.L. 1459 (QBD), McCombe, J.

s.20, amended: 2008 c.29 Sch.10 para.17

s.21, amended: 2008 c.29 Sch.11 para.5

s.22, amended: 2008 c.29 Sch.10 para.18

s.38, applied: 2008 c.18 Sch.9 para.1, Sch.9 para.2

s.40, amended: 2008 c.29 Sch.10 para.19

s.41, amended: 2008 c.29 Sch.10 para.20

s.42, applied: 2008 c.18 Sch.9 para.1, Sch.9 para.2

s.54, applied: 2008 c.18 Sch.9 para.1, Sch.9 para.2

s.59, amended: 2008 c.29 Sch.2 para.40

s.59, disapplied: 2008 c.18 Sch.9 para.3

s.72, see *R. (on the application of Park Pharmacy Trust) v Plymouth City Council* [2008] EWHC 445 (Admin), [2008] 2 P. & C.R. 11 (QBD (Admin)), Sullivan, J.

s.74, amended: 2008 c.29 Sch.2 para.41, Sch.10 para.21

s.74, applied: 2008 c.29 s.33

s.74, disapplied: 2008 c.18 Sch.9 para.1

s.81A, amended: 2008 c.29 Sch.7 para.5

s.81B, amended: 2008 c.29 Sch.7 para.6

s.88D, added: 2008 c.29 s.196

s.89, amended: 2008 c.29 Sch.10 para.22

s.93, amended: 2008 c.29 Sch.10 para.23

s.93, enabling: SI 2008/595

Sch.3 para.1, enabling: SI 2008/595

Sch.3 para.2, amended: 2008 c.29 Sch.10 para.24

Sch.3 para.3, amended: 2008 c.29 Sch.10 para.24

Sch.3 para.6, amended: 2008 c.29 Sch.10 para.24

Sch.4 para.2, amended: 2008 c.17 Sch.8 para.53

10. Planning (Hazardous Substances) Act 1990

s.3, amended: 2008 c.17 Sch.8 para.54

s.3, varied: SI 2008/3068 Art.11

s.9, amended: 2008 c.29 Sch.2 para.43

s.10, amended: 2008 c.29 Sch.2 para.44

s.12, amended: 2008 c.29 Sch.2 para.45, SI 2008/960 Sch.3

s.14, amended: 2008 c.29 Sch.2 para.46

s.20, amended: 2008 c.29 Sch.10 para.26

s.21, amended: 2008 c.29 Sch.10 para.27, Sch.11 para.6

s.21A, added: 2008 c.29 s.196

s.25, amended: 2008 c.29 Sch.10 para.28

s.26, repealed: 2008 c.12 Sch.1 Part 9

s.37, amended: 2008 c.29 Sch.10 para.29

s.39, amended: 2008 c.29 Sch.2 para.47

s.40, enabling: SI 2008/595

s.41, amended: 2008 c.12 Sch.1 Part 9

s.41, repealed (in part): 2008 c.12 Sch.1 Part 9

CAP.

1990–cont.

10. Planning (Hazardous Substances) Act 1990–*cont.*

Sch.1 para.1, enabling: SI 2008/595

Sch.1 para.2, amended: 2008 c.29 Sch.10 para.30

Sch.1 para.3, amended: 2008 c.29 Sch.10 para.30

Sch.1 para.6, amended: 2008 c.29 Sch.10 para.30

11. Planning (Consequential Provisions) Act 1990

Sch.2 para.22, repealed (in part): 2008 c.12 Sch.1 Part 11

16. Food Safety Act 1990

applied: SI 2008/622 Reg.2, SI 2008/781 Reg.2, SI 2008/1079 Reg.2, SI 2008/1718, SSI 2008/129

referred to: SI 2008/622 Reg.5

Part II, applied: 2008 c.13 Sch.3, Sch.7

Part II, referred to: 2008 c.13 Sch.6

Part III, applied: 2008 c.13 Sch.3

Part III, referred to: 2008 c.13 Sch.6

s.2, varied: SI 2008/1287 Reg.7, SI 2008/1317 Reg.7, SI 2008/1341 Reg.7, SSI 2008/216 Reg.7

s.3, applied: SI 2008/1237 Reg.26, SI 2008/1682 Reg.26, SSI 2008/127 Reg.23, SSI 2008/395 Reg.20

s.3, varied: SI 2008/56 Reg.11, SI 2008/916 Reg.26, SI 2008/1287 Reg.7, SI 2008/1317 Reg.7, SI 2008/1341 Reg.7, SI 2008/1718 Reg.21, SSI 2008/129 Reg.20, SSI 2008/216 Reg.7

s.5, amended: 2008 asp 5 Sch.3 Part 1

s.5, applied: SI 2008/548 Art.3

s.6, enabling: SI 2008/1317, SI 2008/1718, SI 2008/2999, SSI 2008/129, SSI 2008/216, SSI 2008/395

s.14, applied: SI 2008/1341 Reg.7

s.14, varied: SI 2008/622 Reg.5

s.15, applied: SI 2008/1341 Reg.7

s.15, varied: SI 2008/622 Reg.5

s.16, enabling: SI 2008/42, SI 2008/56, SI 2008/85, SI 2008/137, SI 2008/138, SI 2008/517, SI 2008/543, SI 2008/713, SI 2008/916, SI 2008/1188, SI 2008/1237, SI 2008/1268, SI 2008/1287, SI 2008/1317, SI 2008/1341, SI 2008/1642, SI 2008/1682, SI 2008/1718, SI 2008/2445, SI 2008/2602, SSI 2008/12, SSI 2008/97, SSI 2008/127, SSI 2008/129, SSI 2008/180, SSI 2008/216, SSI 2008/261, SSI 2008/322, SSI 2008/395

s.17, enabling: SI 2008/42, SI 2008/56, SI 2008/85, SI 2008/137, SI 2008/138, SI 2008/543, SI 2008/916, SI 2008/1188, SI 2008/1237, SI 2008/1268, SI 2008/1287, SI 2008/1317, SI 2008/1341, SI 2008/1642, SI 2008/1682, SI 2008/1718, SI 2008/2445, SI 2008/2602, SSI 2008/12, SSI 2008/127, SSI 2008/129,

CAP.

1990–cont.

16. Food Safety Act 1990–*cont.*

s.17, enabling:–*cont.*

SSI 2008/180, SSI 2008/216, SSI 2008/261, SSI 2008/322, SSI 2008/395

s.20, applied: SSI 2008/127 Reg.23

s.20, varied: SI 2008/622 Reg.5, SI 2008/781 Reg.5, SI 2008/1079 Reg.6, SI 2008/1080 Reg.6, SI 2008/1287 Reg.7, SI 2008/1317 Reg.7, SI 2008/1341 Reg.7, SI 2008/1718 Reg.21, SSI 2008/87 Reg.6, SSI 2008/129 Reg.20, SSI 2008/148 Reg.7, SSI 2008/176 Reg.6, SSI 2008/216 Reg.7, SSI 2008/395 Reg.20

s.21, applied: SI 2008/622 Reg.5, SSI 2008/395 Reg.20

s.21, varied: SI 2008/622 Reg.5, SI 2008/781 Reg.5, SI 2008/1079 Reg.6, SI 2008/1080 Reg.6, SI 2008/1287 Reg.7, SI 2008/1317 Reg.7, SI 2008/1341 Reg.7, SI 2008/1718 Reg.21, SSI 2008/87 Reg.6, SSI 2008/129 Reg.20, SSI 2008/148 Reg.7, SSI 2008/176 Reg.6, SSI 2008/216 Reg.7

s.22, varied: SI 2008/1287 Reg.7, SI 2008/1341 Reg.7, SSI 2008/216 Reg.7

s.26, enabling: SI 2008/56, SI 2008/138, SI 2008/543, SI 2008/916, SI 2008/1188, SI 2008/1237, SI 2008/1268, SI 2008/1287, SI 2008/1317, SI 2008/1341, SI 2008/1642, SI 2008/1682, SI 2008/1718, SI 2008/2445, SI 2008/2602, SSI 2008/127, SSI 2008/129, SSI 2008/180, SSI 2008/216, SSI 2008/261, SSI 2008/322, SSI 2008/395

s.29, applied: SI 2008/56 Reg.9, SI 2008/916 Reg.23, SI 2008/1237 Reg.23, SI 2008/1682 Reg.23, SSI 2008/127 Reg.20

s.29, varied: SI 2008/1718 Reg.21, SSI 2008/129 Reg.20, SSI 2008/395 Reg.20

s.30, applied: SI 2008/56 Reg.9, SI 2008/548 Art.3, SI 2008/916 Reg.23, SI 2008/1237 Reg.23, Reg.26, SI 2008/1682 Reg.23, Reg.26, SSI 2008/127 Reg.20, Reg.23, SSI 2008/395 Reg.20

s.30, varied: SI 2008/56 Reg.11, SI 2008/916 Reg.26, SI 2008/1287 Reg.7, SI 2008/1317 Reg.7, SI 2008/1341 Reg.7, SI 2008/1718 Reg.21, SSI 2008/129 Reg.20, SSI 2008/216 Reg.7, SSI 2008/395 Reg.20

s.31, enabling: SI 2008/916, SI 2008/1237, SI 2008/1682, SSI 2008/127

s.32, applied: SSI 2008/87 Reg.4, SSI 2008/148 Reg.5, SSI 2008/176 Reg.4

s.32, varied: SI 2008/622 Reg.5, SI 2008/781 Reg.5, SI 2008/1079 Reg.6, SI 2008/1080 Reg.6, SI 2008/1718 Reg.21, SSI 2008/129 Reg.20, SSI 2008/395 Reg.20

s.33, applied: SI 2008/1341 Reg.7

s.33, varied: SI 2008/622 Reg.5, SI 2008/781 Reg.5, SI 2008/1079 Reg.6, SI 2008/1080 Reg.6, SI 2008/1287 Reg.7, SI 2008/1317 Reg.7, SI 2008/1341 Reg.7, SSI 2008/

CAP.

1990–cont.

16. Food Safety Act 1990–*cont.*

s.33, varied:–*cont.*

87 Reg.6, SSI 2008/148 Reg.7, SSI 2008/176 Reg.6, SSI 2008/216 Reg.7

s.35, varied: SI 2008/622 Reg.5, SI 2008/781 Reg.5, SI 2008/1079 Reg.6, SI 2008/1080 Reg.6, SI 2008/1287 Reg.7, SI 2008/1317 Reg.7, SI 2008/1341 Reg.7, SSI 2008/87 Reg.6, SSI 2008/148 Reg.7, SSI 2008/176 Reg.6, SSI 2008/216 Reg.7

s.36, applied: SSI 2008/127 Reg.23, SSI 2008/395 Reg.20

s.36, varied: SI 2008/622 Reg.5, SI 2008/781 Reg.5, SI 2008/1079 Reg.6, SI 2008/1080 Reg.6, SI 2008/1287 Reg.7, SI 2008/1317 Reg.7, SI 2008/1341 Reg.7, SI 2008/1718 Reg.21, SSI 2008/87 Reg.6, SSI 2008/129 Reg.20, SSI 2008/148 Reg.7, SSI 2008/176 Reg.6, SSI 2008/216 Reg.7

s.36A, applied: SSI 2008/127 Reg.23, SSI 2008/395 Reg.20

s.36A, varied: SI 2008/622 Reg.5, SI 2008/781 Reg.5, SI 2008/1079 Reg.6, SI 2008/1080 Reg.6, SI 2008/1287 Reg.7, SI 2008/1341 Reg.7, SI 2008/1718 Reg.21, SSI 2008/87 Reg.6, SSI 2008/129 Reg.20, SSI 2008/148 Reg.7, SSI 2008/176 Reg.6, SSI 2008/216 Reg.7

s.37, varied: SI 2008/1718 Reg.18, SSI 2008/129 Reg.17, SSI 2008/395 Reg.17

s.44, applied: SI 2008/1237 Reg.26, SI 2008/1682 Reg.26, SSI 2008/127 Reg.23, SSI 2008/216 Reg.7

s.44, varied: SI 2008/56 Reg.11, SI 2008/622 Reg.5, SI 2008/781 Reg.5, SI 2008/916 Reg.26, SI 2008/1079 Reg.6, SI 2008/1080 Reg.6, SI 2008/1287 Reg.7, SI 2008/1317 Reg.7, SI 2008/1341 Reg.7, SI 2008/1718 Reg.21, SSI 2008/87 Reg.6, SSI 2008/129 Reg.20, SSI 2008/148 Reg.7, SSI 2008/176 Reg.6, SSI 2008/395 Reg.20

s.45, enabling: SI 2008/2999

s.46, applied: SSI 2008/395 Reg.20

s.46, varied: SI 2008/1718 Reg.21, SSI 2008/129 Reg.20

s.48, applied: SI 2008/42, SI 2008/56, SI 2008/85, SI 2008/137, SI 2008/138, SI 2008/517, SI 2008/543, SI 2008/713, SI 2008/1188, SI 2008/1237, SI 2008/1268, SI 2008/1287, SI 2008/1317, SI 2008/1341, SI 2008/1642, SI 2008/1682, SI 2008/2445, SI 2008/2602, SI 2008/2999, SSI 2008/12, SSI 2008/97, SSI 2008/127, SSI 2008/129, SSI 2008/180, SSI 2008/216, SSI 2008/261, SSI 2008/322, SSI 2008/395

s.48, enabling: SI 2008/42, SI 2008/56, SI 2008/85, SI 2008/137, SI 2008/138, SI 2008/517, SI 2008/543, SI 2008/713, SI 2008/916, SI 2008/1188, SI 2008/1237, SI 2008/1268, SI 2008/1287, SI 2008/1317, SI 2008/1341, SI 2008/1642, SI 2008/1682, SI 2008/1718, SI 2008/2445, SI 2008/2602, SI 2008/2999, SSI 2008/12, SSI 2008/97, SSI 2008/127, SSI 2008/129, SSI 2008/180, SSI 2008/216, SSI 2008/261, SSI 2008/322, SSI 2008/395

s.48A, applied: SI 2008/916

s.50, applied: SSI 2008/395 Reg.20

s.50, varied: SI 2008/1718 Reg.21, SSI 2008/129 Reg.20

Sch.1 para.1, enabling: SI 2008/42, SI 2008/138

Sch.3 para.1, applied: SI 2008/548 Art.3

19. National Health Service and Community Care Act 1990

see *Sandford v Waltham Forest LBC* [2008] EWHC 1106 (QB), [2008] B.L.G.R. 816 (QBD), Judge Richard Seymour Q.C.

s.60, referred to: 2008 c.29 s.127, s.128

Sch.9 para.1, repealed: 2008 asp 5 Sch.3 Part 1

Sch.9 para.4, repealed: 2008 asp 5 Sch.3 Part 1

27. Social Security Act 1990

s.15, enabling: SSI 2008/38

29. Finance Act 1990

s.3, repealed (in part): 2008 c.9 Sch.6 para.8

s.25, amended: 2008 c.9 Sch.19 para.8

s.53, repealed: 2008 c.9 s.66

s.64, referred to: SSI 2008/190 Art.30

s.108, amended: 2008 c.9 Sch.32 para.19

s.108, applied: 2008 c.9 Sch.32 para.23

s.111, applied: 2008 c.9 Sch.32 para.23

s.125, amended: 2008 c.9 Sch.36 para.83

s.125, repealed (in part): 2008 c.9 Sch.36 para.83

s.128, enabling: SI 2008/1443

Sch.9 para.3, repealed: SI 2008/381 Sch.1 Part 1

Sch.14 Part I para.10, repealed: 2008 c.9 s.41

Sch.14 Part I para.11, repealed: 2008 c.9 s.41

31. Aviation and Maritime Security Act 1990

Part III, referred to: 2008 c.13 Sch.6

s.1, applied: 2008 c.28 Sch.2, SI 2008/1216 Sch.1 para.23, Sch.2 para.23

s.9, applied: 2008 c.28 Sch.2, SI 2008/1216 Sch.1 para.23, Sch.2 para.23

s.10, applied: 2008 c.28 Sch.2, SI 2008/1216 Sch.1 para.23, Sch.2 para.23

s.11, applied: 2008 c.28 Sch.2, SI 2008/1216 Sch.1 para.23, Sch.2 para.23

s.12, applied: SI 2008/1216 Sch.1 para.23, Sch.2 para.23

s.13, applied: SI 2008/1216 Sch.1 para.23, Sch.2 para.23

s.14, applied: 2008 c.28 Sch.2

s.15, referred to: 2008 c.13 Sch.6

CAP.

1990–cont.

31. Aviation and Maritime Security Act 1990–*cont.*
s.36A, applied: 2008 c.13 Sch.7
s.41, applied: 2008 c.13 Sch.7
s.42, applied: 2008 c.13 Sch.7
s.48, referred to: 2008 c.13 Sch.6

35. Enterprise and New Towns (Scotland) Act 1990
applied: SSI 2008/426 Reg.28
s.2, applied: SI 2008/794 Reg.32, Reg.45, Sch.4 para.4, Sch.5 Part 1, Sch.6 para.15, Sch.8 para.15, Sch.9 para.32
s.21, applied: SSI 2008/426 Reg.28
s.25, applied: 2008 asp 2 Sch.5
s.26, applied: 2008 asp 2 Sch.5

37. Human Fertilisation and Embryology Act 1990
see *L v Human Fertilisation and Embryology Authority* [2008] EWHC 2149 (Fam), [2008] 2 F.L.R. 1999 (Fam Div), Charles, J.; see *Yearworth v North Bristol NHS Trust* [2008] LS Law Medical 535 (CC (Exeter)), Judge Griggs
applied: SI 2008/1052 Sch.1
referred to: 2008 c.22 s.58
s.1, amended: 2008 c.22 s.1
s.2, amended: 2008 c.22 s.2, Sch.7 para.2
s.3, amended: 2008 c.22 s.3
s.3, repealed (in part): 2008 c.22 s.3, Sch.8 Part 1
s.3ZA, added: 2008 c.22 s.3
s.4, amended: 2008 c.22 s.4
s.4, repealed (in part): 2008 c.22 s.4, Sch.8 Part 1
s.4A, added: 2008 c.22 s.4
s.7, amended: 2008 c.22 Sch.7 para.3
s.8, amended: 2008 c.22 s.6, Sch.8 Part 1
s.8, substituted: 2008 c.22 s.6
s.8B, added: 2008 c.22 s.8
s.8C, added: 2008 c.22 s.8
s.8D, added: 2008 c.22 s.8
s.8E, added: 2008 c.22 s.9
s.8ZA, added: 2008 c.22 s.7
s.9, substituted: 2008 c.22 s.10
s.10, repealed: 2008 c.22 Sch.7 para.4, Sch.8 Part 1
s.11, amended: 2008 c.22 s.11
s.12, amended: 2008 c.22 s.12, Sch.8 Part 1
s.13, amended: 2008 c.22 s.14, Sch.8 Part 1
s.13A, repealed (in part): 2008 c.22 Sch.7 para.5, Sch.8 Part 1
s.14, amended: 2008 c.22 s.15, Sch.8 Part 1
s.14A, amended: 2008 c.22 Sch.7 para.6, Sch.8 Part 1
s.15, amended: 2008 c.22 Sch.7 para.7
s.16, amended: 2008 c.22 s.16
s.16, repealed (in part): 2008 c.22 s.16, Sch.8 Part 1
s.17, amended: 2008 c.22 s.17
s.17, repealed (in part): 2008 c.22 s.17, Sch.8 Part 1

CAP.

1990–cont.

37. Human Fertilisation and Embryology Act 1990–*cont.*
s.18, substituted: 2008 c.22 s.18
s.19, substituted: 2008 c.22 s.19
s.19C, added: 2008 c.22 s.20
s.20, substituted: 2008 c.22 s.21
s.20A, substituted: 2008 c.22 s.21
s.20B, substituted: 2008 c.22 s.21
s.21, substituted: 2008 c.22 s.21
s.22, repealed: 2008 c.22 Sch.7 para.8, Sch.8 Part 1
s.23, amended: 2008 c.22 Sch.7 para.9
s.23, repealed (in part): 2008 c.22 Sch.7 para.9, Sch.8 Part 1
s.24, see *L v Human Fertilisation and Embryology Authority* [2008] EWHC 2149 (Fam), [2008] 2 F.L.R. 1999 (Fam Div), Charles, J.
s.24, amended: 2008 c.22 s.22
s.25, amended: 2008 c.22 s.23
s.27, disapplied: 2008 c.22 s.57
s.28, see *G (Surrogacy: Foreign Domicile), Re* [2007] EWHC 2814 (Fam), [2008] 1 F.L.R. 1047 (Fam Div), McFarlane, J.; see *N (A Child), Re* [2007] EWCA Civ 1053, [2008] 1 F.L.R. 198 (CA (Civ Div)), Thorpe, L.J.
s.28, disapplied: 2008 c.22 s.57
s.29, disapplied: 2008 c.22 s.57
s.30, see *G (Surrogacy: Foreign Domicile), Re* [2007] EWHC 2814 (Fam), [2008] 1 F.L.R. 1047 (Fam Div), McFarlane, J.
s.30, applied: 2008 c.22 s.54, s.57, SI 2008/2836 Art.5
s.30, repealed: 2008 c.22 s.57, Sch.8 Part 1
s.31, substituted: 2008 c.22 s.24
s.31A, amended: 2008 c.22 Sch.7 para.10, Sch.8 Part 1
s.32, amended: 2008 c.22 Sch.6 para.33, Sch.7 para.11
s.33, substituted: 2008 c.22 s.25
s.34, amended: 2008 c.22 Sch.6 para.34, Sch.7 para.12
s.35, amended: 2008 c.22 Sch.6 para.35
s.35A, added: 2008 c.22 s.26
s.35B, added: 2008 c.22 s.27
s.38A, added: 2008 c.22 s.28
s.39, repealed: 2008 c.22 s.28, Sch.8 Part 1
s.40, repealed: 2008 c.22 s.28, Sch.8 Part 1
s.41, amended: 2008 c.22 s.29, Sch.8 Part 1
s.41, applied: 2008 c.22 s.29
s.41, repealed (in part): 2008 c.22 s.29, Sch.8 Part 1
s.45, amended: 2008 c.22 s.30
s.45A, added: 2008 c.22 s.31
s.45B, added: 2008 c.22 s.32
s.47, amended: 2008 c.22 Sch.7 para.13, Sch.8 Part 1
s.48, amended: 2008 c.22 Sch.7 para.14
Sch.1, added: 2008 c.22 Sch.7 para.15
Sch.1 para.4A, added: 2008 c.22 Sch.1 para.2

CAP.

1990–cont.

37. Human Fertilisation and Embryology Act 1990–*cont.*

Sch.1 para.5, amended: 2008 c.22 Sch.1 para.3

Sch.1 para.5, repealed (in part): 2008 c.22 Sch.1 para.3, Sch.8 Part 1

Sch.1 para.9, amended: 2008 c.22 Sch.7 para.15

Sch.1 para.10, amended: 2008 c.22 Sch.7 para.15, Sch.8 Part 1

Sch.2 para.1, amended: 2008 c.22 Sch.2 para.2, Sch.8 Part 1

Sch.2 para.1A, amended: 2008 c.22 Sch.2 para.4

Sch.2 para.1ZA, added: 2008 c.22 Sch.2 para.3

Sch.2 para.1ZB, added: 2008 c.22 Sch.2 para.3

Sch.2 para.1ZC, added: 2008 c.22 Sch.2 para.3

Sch.2 para.2, amended: 2008 c.22 Sch.2 para.5

Sch.2 para.3, substituted: 2008 c.22 Sch.2 para.6

Sch.3 para.1, amended: 2008 c.22 Sch.3 para.2

Sch.3 para.1, substituted: 2008 c.22 Sch.3 para.3

Sch.3 para.2, amended: 2008 c.22 Sch.3 para.2, Sch.3 para.4

Sch.3 para.3, amended: 2008 c.22 Sch.3 para.2, Sch.3 para.5

Sch.3 para.4, amended: 2008 c.22 Sch.3 para.2, Sch.3 para.6

Sch.3 para.4A, added: 2008 c.22 Sch.3 para.7

Sch.3 para.4A, amended: 2008 c.22 Sch.3 para.2

Sch.3 para.5, amended: 2008 c.22 Sch.3 para.2, Sch.3 para.8

Sch.3 para.5, applied: 2008 c.22 s.41

Sch.3 para.6, amended: 2008 c.22 Sch.3 para.2, Sch.3 para.9

Sch.3 para.7, amended: 2008 c.22 Sch.3 para.2, Sch.3 para.10

Sch.3 para.8, amended: 2008 c.22 Sch.3 para.2, Sch.3 para.11

Sch.3 para.9, added: 2008 c.22 Sch.3 para.12

Sch.3 para.9, amended: 2008 c.22 Sch.3 para.2

Sch.3 para.10, added: 2008 c.22 Sch.3 para.12

Sch.3 para.10, amended: 2008 c.22 Sch.3 para.2

Sch.3 para.11, added: 2008 c.22 Sch.3 para.12

Sch.3 para.11, amended: 2008 c.22 Sch.3 para.2

Sch.3 para.12, added: 2008 c.22 Sch.3 para.13

CAP.

1990–cont.

37. Human Fertilisation and Embryology Act 1990–*cont.*

Sch.3 para.12, amended: 2008 c.22 Sch.3 para.2

Sch.3 para.13, added: 2008 c.22 Sch.3 para.13

Sch.3 para.13, amended: 2008 c.22 Sch.3 para.2

Sch.3 para.14, added: 2008 c.22 Sch.3 para.13

Sch.3 para.14, amended: 2008 c.22 Sch.3 para.2

Sch.3 para.15, added: 2008 c.22 Sch.3 para.14

Sch.3 para.15, amended: 2008 c.22 Sch.3 para.2

Sch.3 para.16, added: 2008 c.22 Sch.3 para.14

Sch.3 para.16, amended: 2008 c.22 Sch.3 para.2

Sch.3 para.17, added: 2008 c.22 Sch.3 para.14

Sch.3 para.17, amended: 2008 c.22 Sch.3 para.2

Sch.3 para.18, added: 2008 c.22 Sch.3 para.14

Sch.3 para.18, amended: 2008 c.22 Sch.3 para.2

Sch.3 para.19, added: 2008 c.22 Sch.3 para.14

Sch.3 para.19, amended: 2008 c.22 Sch.3 para.2

Sch.3 para.20, added: 2008 c.22 Sch.3 para.14

Sch.3 para.20, amended: 2008 c.22 Sch.3 para.2

Sch.3 para.21, added: 2008 c.22 Sch.3 para.14

Sch.3 para.21, amended: 2008 c.22 Sch.3 para.2

Sch.3 para.22, added: 2008 c.22 Sch.3 para.15

Sch.3 para.22, amended: 2008 c.22 Sch.3 para.2

Sch.3B para.1, added: 2008 c.22 Sch.5

Sch.3B para.2, added: 2008 c.22 Sch.5

Sch.3B para.3, added: 2008 c.22 Sch.5

Sch.3B para.4, added: 2008 c.22 Sch.5

Sch.3B para.5, added: 2008 c.22 Sch.5

Sch.3B para.6, added: 2008 c.22 Sch.5

Sch.3B para.7, added: 2008 c.22 Sch.5

Sch.3B para.8, added: 2008 c.22 Sch.5

Sch.3B para.9, added: 2008 c.22 Sch.5

Sch.3B para.10, added: 2008 c.22 Sch.5

Sch.3B para.11, added: 2008 c.22 Sch.5

Sch.3ZA Part 1 para.1, added: 2008 c.22 Sch.4

Sch.3ZA Part 1 para.2, added: 2008 c.22 Sch.4

Sch.3ZA Part 1 para.3, added: 2008 c.22 Sch.4

CAP.

1990–cont.

37. Human Fertilisation and Embryology Act 1990–*cont.*

Sch.3ZA Part 2 para.4, added: 2008 c.22 Sch.4

Sch.3ZA Part 2 para.5, added: 2008 c.22 Sch.4

Sch.3ZA Part 2 para.6, added: 2008 c.22 Sch.4

Sch.3ZA Part 2 para.7, added: 2008 c.22 Sch.4

40. Law Reform (Miscellaneous Provisions) (Scotland) Act 1990

referred to: SSI 2008/332 Art.4

s.7, applied: SI 2008/1185 Reg.4, Sch.1 para.44, SI 2008/2252 Sch.1 para.14, SI 2008/2553 Art.5, SI 2008/2554 Art.5, SI 2008/2558 Reg.3, SI 2008/2927 Reg.2, SI 2008/3047 Art.5, SI 2008/3148 Sch.1

s.33, applied: SI 2008/2341 Art.2, SSI 2008/332 Art.2

s.33, referred to: SSI 2008/332 Art.2

s.34, repealed: SSI 2008/332 Art.3

s.34, varied: SI 2008/2341 Art.3, SSI 2008/332 Art.3

s.34A, applied: SI 2008/2341 Art.7, SSI 2008/332 Art.7

s.34A, repealed: SSI 2008/332 Art.3

s.34A, varied: SI 2008/2341 Art.3, SSI 2008/332 Art.3

s.34B, repealed: SSI 2008/332 Art.3

s.34B, varied: SI 2008/2341 Art.3, SSI 2008/332 Art.3

Sch.3 para.1, repealed: SSI 2008/332 Art.3

Sch.3 para.2, repealed: SSI 2008/332 Art.3

Sch.3 para.3, repealed: SSI 2008/332 Art.3

Sch.3 para.4, repealed: SSI 2008/332 Art.3

Sch.3 para.5, repealed: SSI 2008/332 Art.3

Sch.3 para.6, repealed: SSI 2008/332 Art.3

Sch.3 para.6, varied: SI 2008/2341 Art.3, SSI 2008/332 Art.3

Sch.3 para.7, repealed: SSI 2008/332 Art.3

Sch.3 para.8, repealed: SSI 2008/332 Art.3

Sch.3 para.9, repealed: SSI 2008/332 Art.3

Sch.3 para.9A, repealed: SSI 2008/332 Art.3

Sch.3 para.9B, repealed: SSI 2008/332 Art.3

Sch.3 para.10, repealed: SSI 2008/332 Art.3

Sch.3 para.11, repealed: SSI 2008/332 Art.3

Sch.4 para.1, amended: 2008 asp 6 s.21

Sch.4 para.5, amended: 2008 asp 6 s.22

Sch.4 para.10, amended: 2008 asp 6 s.64

41. Courts and Legal Services Act 1990

see *Practice Direction (Sup Ct: Court Dress) (No.4)* [2008] 1 W.L.R. 357 (Sup Ct), Lord Phillips of Worth Matravers, L.C.J.

Part IV, applied: 2008 c.13 Sch.3

Part VI, applied: 2008 c.13 Sch.3

s.1, enabling: SI 2008/2934

s.27, see *Anderson, Petitioner* 2008 S.C.L.R. 59 (OH), Lord Mackay of Drumadoon

s.50, amended: SI 2008/1277 Sch.2 para.48, Sch.4 Part 1

CAP.

1990–cont.

41. Courts and Legal Services Act 1990–*cont.*

s.50, repealed (in part): SI 2008/1277 Sch.2 para.48, Sch.4 Part 1

s.53, enabling: SI 2008/537

s.55, applied: SI 2008/1865 Art.2

s.55, enabling: SI 2008/1865

s.58, see *Fenton v Holmes* [2007] EWHC 2476 (Ch), [2008] 2 Costs L.R. 238 (Ch D), Mann, J.; see *Gloucestershire CC v Evans* [2008] EWCA Civ 21, [2008] 1 W.L.R. 1883 (CA (Civ Div)), Buxton, L.J.

s.71, applied: 2008 c.14 Sch.6 para.6, 2008 c.28 s.68, SI 2008/1216 Sch.4 para.1

s.120, applied: SI 2008/1865

s.120, enabling: SI 2008/2934

Sch.5 para.9, amended: SI 2008/948 Sch.1 para.1

Sch.9 para.4, enabling: SI 2008/1865

Sch.10 para.29, repealed: 2008 c.14 Sch.15 Part 2

42. Broadcasting Act 1990

referred to: 2008 c.4 Sch.26 para.29, SI 2008/1420 Art.2

s.138, amended: SI 2008/948 Sch.1 para.175

s.138, referred to: SI 2008/948 Sch.1 para.175

s.167, amended: 2008 c.4 Sch.26 para.28

s.167, referred to: 2008 c.4 Sch.26 para.28

Sch.2 Part I, applied: SI 2008/1420 Art.2

Sch.2 Part I, referred to: SI 2008/948 Sch.1 para.176

Sch.2 Part I para.2, amended: SI 2008/948 Sch.1 para.176

Sch.2 Part II, applied: SI 2008/1420 Art.6

Sch.3 para.12, amended: SI 2008/948 Sch.1 para.1

Sch.6 para.12, amended: SI 2008/948 Sch.1 para.1

Sch.15 para.6, see *R. (on the application of Green) v City of Westminster Magistrates' Court* [2007] EWHC 2785 (Admin), [2008] E.M.L.R. 15 (DC), Hughes, L.J.

Sch.19 para.11, amended: SI 2008/948 Sch.1 para.1

Sch.20 para.48, repealed: SI 2008/1277 Sch.4 Part 1

Sch.20 para.49, repealed: SI 2008/1277 Sch.4 Part 1

43. Environmental Protection Act 1990

applied: 2008 c.13 Sch.3

referred to: SSI 2008/100 Sch.2 Part 1, SSI 2008/263 Sch.2

Part II, referred to: 2008 c.13 Sch.6

Part IIA, referred to: 2008 c.13 Sch.6

Part III, referred to: 2008 c.13 Sch.6

Part IIA, see *R. (on the application of Thames Water Utilities Ltd) v Bromley Magistrates Court* [2008] EWHC 1763 (QB), Times, August 28, 2008 (DC), Carnwath, L.J.

CAP.

1990–cont.

43. Environmental Protection Act 1990– *cont.*

Part III, see *R. (on the application of Thames Water Utilities Ltd) v Bromley Magistrates Court* [2008] EWHC 1763 (QB), Times, August 28, 2008 (DC), Carnwath, L.J.

s.29, referred to: SI 2008/663(c)

s.33, see *Neal Soil Suppliers Ltd v Environment Agency* [2007] EWHC 2592 (Admin), [2008] Env. L.R. 15 (DC), Keene, L.J.; see *R. (on the application of Thames Water Utilities Ltd) v Bromley Magistrates Court* [2008] EWHC 1763 (QB), Times, August 28, 2008 (DC), Carnwath, L.J.

s.34, applied: SI 2008/314 Reg.6, Reg.8

s.34A, applied: SI 2008/663 Reg.3

s.34A, enabling: SI 2008/663

s.44A, applied: SI 2008/580 Art.6

s.46, amended: 2008 c.27 s.76, Sch.5 para.3

s.46, referred to: 2008 c.27 Sch.5 para.3

s.47ZB, applied: SI 2008/663 Reg.2, Reg.3

s.47ZB, enabling: SI 2008/663

s.59, see *Neal Soil Suppliers Ltd v Environment Agency* [2007] EWHC 2592 (Admin), [2008] Env. L.R. 15 (DC), Keene, L.J.

s.60A, amended: 2008 c.27 Sch.5 para.1

s.78A, enabling: SI 2008/520

s.78YC, enabling: SI 2008/520

s.79, see *Manley v New Forest DC* [2007] EWHC 3188 (Admin), [2008] Env. L.R. 26 (DC), Moses, L.J.

s.79, amended: 2008 asp 5 s.109, s.110, s.111, s.112, Sch.3 Part 1

s.79, applied: 2008 c.18 s.21, SI 2008/1160 Art.16, SI 2008/2512 Art.40

s.79, referred to: SI 2008/1261 Art.27

s.80, amended: 2008 asp 5 s.113

s.80ZA, added: 2008 asp 5 s.113

s.81, amended: 2008 asp 5 s.113

s.82, applied: 2008 c.18 s.21, SI 2008/1160 Art.16, SI 2008/1261 Art.27, SI 2008/2512 Art.40

s.88, applied: SI 2008/663 Reg.2, Reg.3, Reg.4

s.88, enabling: SI 2008/663

s.94, applied: SI 2008/663 Reg.2

s.94A, applied: SI 2008/663 Reg.3

s.97A, enabling: SI 2008/663

s.98, referred to: SI 2008/663(d)

s.106, amended: 2008 c.22 s.60

s.118, referred to: 2008 c.13 Sch.6

s.140, applied: 2008 c.13 Sch.7

s.150, referred to: 2008 c.13 Sch.6

s.153, amended: SI 2008/3243 Art.2

s.153, enabling: SI 2008/3243

s.156, applied: 2008 c.13 Sch.7

s.160, see *Butland v Powys CC* [2007] EWCA Civ 1298, [2008] Env. L.R. 16 (CA (Civ Div)), Latham, L.J. (VP, CA Crim)

CAP.

1990–cont.

43. Environmental Protection Act 1990– *cont.*

s.161, amended: 2008 asp 5 s.114, 2008 c.27 Sch.5 para.4

s.161, referred to: 2008 c.27 Sch.5 para.4

Sch.2AA para.1, added: 2008 c.27 Sch.5 para.2

Sch.2AA para.2, added: 2008 c.27 Sch.5 para.2

Sch.2AA para.3, added: 2008 c.27 Sch.5 para.2

Sch.2AA para.4, added: 2008 c.27 Sch.5 para.2

Sch.2AA para.5, added: 2008 c.27 Sch.5 para.2

Sch.2AA para.6, added: 2008 c.27 Sch.5 para.2

Sch.2AA para.7, added: 2008 c.27 Sch.5 para.2

Sch.2AA para.8, added: 2008 c.27 Sch.5 para.2

Sch.2AA para.9, added: 2008 c.27 Sch.5 para.2

Sch.2AA para.10, added: 2008 c.27 Sch.5 para.2

Sch.2AA para.11, added: 2008 c.27 Sch.5 para.2

Sch.2AA para.12, added: 2008 c.27 Sch.5 para.2

Sch.2AA para.13, added: 2008 c.27 Sch.5 para.2

Sch.2AA para.14, added: 2008 c.27 Sch.5 para.2

Sch.2AA para.15, added: 2008 c.27 Sch.5 para.2

Sch.2AA para.16, added: 2008 c.27 Sch.5 para.2

Sch.3A para.7, applied: SI 2008/663 Reg.2, Reg.3

Sch.13 Part I para.10, repealed: 2008 c.29 Sch.13

1991

15. Local Government Finance (Publicity for Auditors Reports) Act 1991

applied: SI 2008/1079 Reg.6

19. Football (Offences) Act 1991

s.4, see *R. (on the application of White) v Blackfriars Crown Court* [2008] EWHC 510 (Admin), [2008] 2 Cr. App. R. (S.) 97 (DC), Richards, L.J.

s.5, see *R. (on the application of White) v Blackfriars Crown Court* [2008] EWHC 510 (Admin), [2008] 2 Cr. App. R. (S.) 97 (DC), Richards, L.J.

22. New Roads and Street Works Act 1991

applied: 2008 c.18 Sch.17 para.2, SI 2008/101 Reg.6, SI 2008/540 Reg.5, Reg.6, SSI 2008/88 Reg.5

referred to: SSI 2008/88 Reg.4

CAP.

1991–cont.

22. New Roads and Street Works Act 1991–*cont.*

Part III, applied: 2008 c.18 Sch.3 para.8, Sch.3 para.9, Sch.3 para.11, Sch.17 para.4, Sch.17 para.5, SI 2008/101 Reg.5, Reg.6, Reg.7, SI 2008/540 Reg.6, Reg.7, SI 2008/1238 Sch.2 para.5, SI 2008/1261 Art.6, SI 2008/2512 Art.4, Sch.9 para.1, Sch.9 para.2, Sch.9 para.3
Part III, disapplied: 2008 c.18 Sch.17 para.1
Part III, referred to: SI 2008/1261 Sch.11 para.1
Part IV, applied: SSI 2008/88 Reg.4
s.6, amended: 2008 c.29 Sch.2 para.49
s.6, applied: 2008 c.29 s.33
s.7, applied: 2008 c.29 s.144
s.8, applied: 2008 c.29 s.144
s.9, applied: 2008 c.29 s.144
s.10, applied: 2008 c.29 s.144
s.11, applied: 2008 c.29 s.144
s.12, applied: 2008 c.29 s.144
s.13, applied: 2008 c.29 s.144
s.14, applied: 2008 c.29 s.144
s.15, applied: 2008 c.29 s.144
s.16, applied: 2008 c.29 s.144
s.17, applied: 2008 c.29 s.144
s.18, applied: 2008 c.29 s.144
s.48, amended: 2008 c.26 s.124
s.48, applied: SI 2008/540 Reg.5, Reg.6
s.48, varied: SI 2008/1261 Art.6
s.48, enabling: SI 2008/101, SI 2008/102, SI 2008/466, SI 2008/540
s.49, applied: SI 2008/540 Reg.5, Reg.6
s.49, varied: SI 2008/1261 Art.6
s.49, enabling: SI 2008/101, SI 2008/540
s.50, amended: 2008 c.26 s.124
s.50, applied: SI 2008/540 Reg.5, Reg.6
s.50, varied: SI 2008/1261 Art.6
s.51, applied: SI 2008/540 Reg.5, Reg.6
s.51, referred to: 2008 c.13 Sch.6
s.51, varied: SI 2008/1261 Art.6
s.52, applied: SI 2008/540 Reg.5, Reg.6
s.52, varied: SI 2008/1261 Art.6
s.53, applied: SI 2008/101 Reg.4, SI 2008/540 Reg.4, Reg.5, Reg.6, Reg.13
s.53, varied: SI 2008/101 Reg.13, SI 2008/1261 Art.6
s.53, enabling: SI 2008/101, SI 2008/540
s.53A, applied: SI 2008/540 Reg.5, Reg.6
s.53A, varied: SI 2008/1261 Art.6
s.54, applied: 2008 c.18 Sch.14 para.14, SI 2008/101 Reg.4, Reg.5, Reg.8, Reg.12, Reg.19, Sch.1 para.3, Sch.1 para.7, SI 2008/102 Sch.2, SI 2008/540 Reg.4, Reg.5, Reg.6, Reg.8, Reg.12, Reg.19, Sch.1 para.3, Sch.1 para.7, SI 2008/1261 Art.6, SI 2008/2512 Art.4
s.54, varied: SI 2008/1261 Art.6, SI 2008/2512 Art.4
s.54, enabling: SI 2008/101, SI 2008/540

CAP.

1991–cont.

22. New Roads and Street Works Act 1991–*cont.*

s.55, applied: 2008 c.18 Sch.14 para.14, SI 2008/101 Reg.4, Reg.5, Reg.8, Reg.9, Reg.12, Reg.19, Sch.1 para.3, Sch.1 para.7, SI 2008/102 Sch.2, SI 2008/540 Reg.4, Reg.5, Reg.6, Reg.8, Reg.9, Reg.12, Reg.19, Sch.1 para.3, Sch.1 para.7, SI 2008/1261 Art.6, SI 2008/2512 Art.4
s.55, varied: SI 2008/1261 Art.6, SI 2008/2512 Art.4
s.55, enabling: SI 2008/101, SI 2008/540
s.56, applied: SI 2008/101 Reg.4, Reg.10, SI 2008/540 Reg.4, Reg.5, Reg.6, Reg.10
s.56, disapplied: 2008 c.18 Sch.14 para.14, SI 2008/1261 Art.6
s.56, varied: SI 2008/1261 Art.6
s.56, enabling: SI 2008/101, SI 2008/540
s.56A, applied: SI 2008/101 Reg.4, Reg.10, SI 2008/540 Reg.4, Reg.5, Reg.6, Reg.10
s.56A, disapplied: 2008 c.18 Sch.14 para.14, SI 2008/1261 Art.6
s.56A, varied: SI 2008/1261 Art.6
s.56A, enabling: SI 2008/101, SI 2008/540
s.57, applied: SI 2008/101 Reg.4, Reg.5, Reg.19, SI 2008/102 Sch.2, SI 2008/540 Reg.4, Reg.5, Reg.6, Reg.19, SI 2008/1261 Art.6, SI 2008/2512 Art.4
s.57, varied: SI 2008/1261 Art.6, SI 2008/2512 Art.4
s.57, enabling: SI 2008/101, SI 2008/540
s.58, applied: 2008 c.18 Sch.14 para.14, SI 2008/101 Reg.4, Reg.5, Reg.9, Reg.11, SI 2008/540 Reg.4, Reg.5, Reg.6, Reg.9, Reg.11
s.58, disapplied: SI 2008/1261 Art.6
s.58, varied: SI 2008/1261 Art.6
s.58, enabling: SI 2008/101, SI 2008/540
s.58A, applied: SI 2008/101 Reg.4, Reg.5, SI 2008/540 Reg.4, Reg.5, Reg.6
s.58A, disapplied: SI 2008/1261 Art.6
s.58A, varied: SI 2008/1261 Art.6
s.58A, enabling: SI 2008/101, SI 2008/540
s.59, applied: SI 2008/540 Reg.5, Reg.6, SI 2008/1261 Art.6, SI 2008/2512 Art.4
s.59, varied: SI 2008/1261 Art.6
s.60, applied: SI 2008/540 Reg.5, Reg.6, SI 2008/1261 Art.6, SI 2008/2512 Art.4
s.60, varied: SI 2008/1261 Art.6
s.61, applied: SI 2008/101 Reg.4, Reg.14, Sch.1 para.1, SI 2008/540 Reg.4, Reg.5, Reg.6, Reg.14, Sch.1 para.1, Sch.1 para.3
s.61, disapplied: 2008 c.18 Sch.14 para.14, SI 2008/101 Reg.13, SI 2008/540 Reg.13
s.61, varied: SI 2008/1261 Art.6
s.62, applied: SI 2008/101 Reg.4, SI 2008/540 Reg.4, Reg.5, Reg.6
s.62, disapplied: 2008 c.18 Sch.14 para.14
s.62, varied: SI 2008/1261 Art.6
s.62, enabling: SI 2008/101, SI 2008/540

CAP.

1991–cont.

22. New Roads and Street Works Act 1991–*cont.*

s.63, applied: SI 2008/101 Reg.15, Sch.1 para.7, Sch.1 para.12, SI 2008/540 Reg.5, Reg.6, Reg.15, Sch.1 para.7, Sch.1 para.12
s.63, disapplied: 2008 c.18 Sch.14 para.14
s.63, varied: SI 2008/1261 Art.6
s.63, enabling: SI 2008/101, SI 2008/540
s.64, applied: SI 2008/101 Reg.16, SI 2008/540 Reg.5, Reg.6, Reg.16
s.64, varied: SI 2008/1261 Art.6
s.64, enabling: SI 2008/101, SI 2008/540
s.65, applied: SI 2008/540 Reg.5, Reg.6
s.65, varied: SI 2008/1261 Art.6
s.66, applied: SI 2008/101 Reg.4, Reg.5, SI 2008/540 Reg.4, Reg.5, Reg.6
s.66, varied: SI 2008/1261 Art.6
s.67, applied: SI 2008/540 Reg.5, Reg.6
s.67, varied: SI 2008/1261 Art.6
s.68, applied: SI 2008/540 Reg.5, Reg.6, SI 2008/1261 Art.6, SI 2008/2512 Art.4
s.68, varied: SI 2008/1261 Art.6
s.69, applied: SI 2008/540 Reg.5, Reg.6, SI 2008/1261 Art.6, SI 2008/2512 Art.4
s.69, varied: SI 2008/1261 Art.6
s.70, amended: SI 2008/540 Reg.17
s.70, applied: SI 2008/101 Reg.4, Reg.5, Reg.18, SI 2008/102 Sch.2, SI 2008/540 Reg.4, Reg.5, Reg.6, Reg.18
s.70, varied: SI 2008/101 Reg.17, SI 2008/1261 Art.6
s.70, enabling: SI 2008/101, SI 2008/540
s.71, see *Hertfordshire CC v National Grid Gas Plc* [2007] EWHC 2535 (Admin), [2008] 1 W.L.R. 2562 (DC), Richards, L.J.
s.71, applied: 2008 c.18 Sch.17 para.15, SI 2008/540 Reg.5, Reg.6
s.71, varied: SI 2008/1261 Art.6
s.72, applied: SI 2008/101 Reg.4, Reg.5, SI 2008/540 Reg.4, Reg.5, Reg.6
s.72, varied: SI 2008/1261 Art.6
s.73, applied: SI 2008/540 Reg.5, Reg.6
s.73, varied: SI 2008/1261 Art.6
s.73A, applied: 2008 c.18 Sch.14 para.14, SI 2008/540 Reg.5, Reg.6
s.73A, disapplied: 2008 c.18 Sch.14 para.14, SI 2008/1261 Art.6
s.73A, varied: SI 2008/1261 Art.6
s.73B, applied: SI 2008/540 Reg.5, Reg.6
s.73B, disapplied: SI 2008/1261 Art.6
s.73B, varied: SI 2008/1261 Art.6
s.73C, applied: SI 2008/540 Reg.5, Reg.6
s.73C, disapplied: SI 2008/1261 Art.6
s.73C, varied: SI 2008/1261 Art.6
s.73D, applied: SI 2008/540 Reg.5, Reg.6
s.73D, varied: SI 2008/1261 Art.6
s.73E, applied: SI 2008/540 Reg.5, Reg.6
s.73E, varied: SI 2008/1261 Art.6
s.73F, applied: SI 2008/540 Reg.5, Reg.6
s.73F, varied: SI 2008/1261 Art.6
s.74, applied: SI 2008/101 Reg.4, Reg.10, SI 2008/102 Sch.2, SI 2008/540 Reg.4, Reg.10
s.74, disapplied: SI 2008/101 Reg.5, Reg.6, SI 2008/540 Reg.6
s.74, varied: SI 2008/1261 Art.6
s.74A, applied: SI 2008/540 Reg.5, Reg.6
s.74A, varied: SI 2008/1261 Art.6
s.74B, applied: SI 2008/540 Reg.5, Reg.6
s.74B, varied: SI 2008/1261 Art.6
s.75, applied: SI 2008/540 Reg.5, Reg.6, SI 2008/1261 Art.6
s.75, varied: SI 2008/1261 Art.6
s.75, enabling: SI 2008/589, SI 2008/600, SI 2008/1213
s.76, applied: SI 2008/540 Reg.5, Reg.6, SI 2008/1261 Art.6, SI 2008/2512 Art.4
s.76, varied: SI 2008/1261 Art.6
s.77, applied: SI 2008/540 Reg.5, Reg.6, SI 2008/1261 Art.6, SI 2008/2512 Art.4
s.77, varied: SI 2008/1261 Art.6
s.78, applied: SI 2008/540 Reg.5, Reg.6
s.78, varied: SI 2008/1261 Art.6
s.78A, applied: 2008 c.18 Sch.14 para.14, SI 2008/540 Reg.5, Reg.6
s.78A, disapplied: SI 2008/1261 Art.6
s.78A, varied: SI 2008/1261 Art.6
s.79, applied: SI 2008/540 Reg.5, Reg.6
s.79, varied: SI 2008/1261 Art.6
s.80, applied: SI 2008/101 Reg.4, SI 2008/540 Reg.4, Reg.5, Reg.6, Reg.13
s.80, varied: SI 2008/101 Reg.13, SI 2008/1261 Art.6
s.81, applied: SI 2008/540 Reg.5, Reg.6
s.81, varied: SI 2008/1261 Art.6
s.82, applied: SI 2008/540 Reg.5, Reg.6
s.82, varied: SI 2008/1261 Art.6
s.83, applied: SI 2008/540 Reg.5, Reg.6
s.83, varied: SI 2008/1261 Art.6
s.84, applied: SI 2008/540 Reg.5, Reg.6
s.84, varied: SI 2008/1261 Art.6
s.85, applied: 2008 c.18 Sch.17 para.4, SI 2008/101 Reg.4, SI 2008/540 Reg.4, Reg.5, Reg.6, SI 2008/2512 Art.26, Sch.9 para.2, SI 2008/3163 Art.8
s.85, varied: SI 2008/1261 Art.6
s.86, applied: 2008 c.18 Sch.3 para.8, SI 2008/540 Reg.5, Reg.6
s.86, referred to: SI 2008/1261 Art.6, SI 2008/2512 Art.4
s.86, varied: SI 2008/1261 Art.6
s.87, applied: SI 2008/540 Reg.5, Reg.6
s.87, referred to: 2008 c.18 Sch.3 para.11, SI 2008/2512 Art.4
s.87, varied: SI 2008/1261 Art.6
s.88, applied: SI 2008/540 Reg.5, Reg.6
s.88, varied: SI 2008/1261 Art.6
s.89, applied: SI 2008/540 Reg.5, Reg.6
s.89, varied: SI 2008/1261 Art.6

CAP.

1991–cont.

22. New Roads and Street Works Act 1991–*cont.*

s.90, applied: SI 2008/540 Reg.5, Reg.6
s.90, varied: SI 2008/1261 Art.6
s.91, applied: SI 2008/540 Reg.5, Reg.6
s.91, varied: SI 2008/1261 Art.6
s.92, applied: SI 2008/540 Reg.5, Reg.6
s.92, varied: SI 2008/1261 Art.6
s.93, applied: SI 2008/540 Reg.5, Reg.6
s.93, varied: SI 2008/1261 Art.6
s.94, applied: SI 2008/540 Reg.5, Reg.6
s.94, varied: SI 2008/1261 Art.6
s.95, applied: SI 2008/540 Reg.5, Reg.6
s.95, varied: SI 2008/1261 Art.6
s.95A, applied: SI 2008/540 Reg.5, Reg.6
s.95A, disapplied: SI 2008/102 Reg.3
s.95A, varied: SI 2008/1261 Art.6
s.95A, enabling: SI 2008/102, SI 2008/466
s.96, applied: SI 2008/540 Reg.5, Reg.6
s.96, varied: SI 2008/1261 Art.6
s.97, applied: SI 2008/540 Reg.5, Reg.6
s.97, varied: SI 2008/1261 Art.6
s.97, enabling: SI 2008/101, SI 2008/102, SI 2008/466, SI 2008/540
s.98, applied: SI 2008/101 Reg.6, SI 2008/102 Reg.5, SI 2008/540 Reg.5, Reg.6
s.98, varied: SI 2008/1261 Art.6
s.99, applied: SI 2008/540 Reg.5, Reg.6
s.99, varied: SI 2008/1261 Art.6
s.100, applied: SI 2008/540 Reg.5, Reg.6
s.100, varied: SI 2008/1261 Art.6
s.101, applied: SI 2008/540 Reg.5, Reg.6
s.101, varied: SI 2008/1261 Art.6
s.102, applied: SI 2008/540 Reg.5, Reg.6
s.102, varied: SI 2008/1261 Art.6
s.103, applied: SI 2008/540 Reg.5, Reg.6
s.103, varied: SI 2008/1261 Art.6
s.104, applied: SI 2008/540 Reg.5, Reg.6
s.104, varied: SI 2008/1261 Art.6
s.104, enabling: SI 2008/101, SI 2008/102, SI 2008/466, SI 2008/540, SI 2008/589, SI 2008/600, SI 2008/1213
s.105, applied: SI 2008/540 Reg.5, Reg.6
s.105, varied: SI 2008/1261 Art.6
s.106, applied: SI 2008/540 Reg.5, Reg.6
s.106, varied: SI 2008/1261 Art.6
s.108, enabling: SSI 2008/88, SSI 2008/244
s.112A, applied: SSI 2008/16 Reg.3, Reg.4, SSI 2008/88 Reg.3
s.112A, referred to: SSI 2008/16 Reg.4
s.112A, enabling: SSI 2008/16, SSI 2008/88
s.112B, applied: SSI 2008/15 Art.3, SSI 2008/88 Reg.3, Reg.15
s.112B, disapplied: SSI 2008/15 Art.3
s.112B, enabling: SSI 2008/88
s.113, applied: SSI 2008/15 Art.3, SSI 2008/88 Reg.4, Reg.6, Reg.8
s.113, enabling: SSI 2008/88
s.114, applied: SSI 2008/15 Art.3, SSI 2008/88 Reg.4, Reg.7, Reg.8
s.114, enabling: SSI 2008/88
s.115, applied: SSI 2008/88 Reg.8, SSI 2008/89 Reg.4
s.115, enabling: SSI 2008/88, SSI 2008/89
s.115A, applied: SSI 2008/88 Reg.8, SSI 2008/89 Reg.4
s.115A, enabling: SSI 2008/88, SSI 2008/89
s.116, applied: SSI 2008/88 Reg.4, Reg.8
s.116, enabling: SSI 2008/88
s.117, applied: SSI 2008/88 Reg.7, Reg.9, Reg.15, SSI 2008/89 Reg.2
s.117, enabling: SSI 2008/88, SSI 2008/89
s.118, applied: SSI 2008/88 Reg.15
s.120, applied: SSI 2008/88 Reg.10, SSI 2008/89 Reg.2
s.120, enabling: SSI 2008/89
s.121, applied: SSI 2008/88 Reg.3, SSI 2008/89 Reg.2
s.121, enabling: SSI 2008/88, SSI 2008/89
s.122, applied: SSI 2008/88 Reg.3, Reg.4, Reg.11
s.122, enabling: SSI 2008/88
s.123, applied: SSI 2008/15 Art.3, SSI 2008/88 Reg.12
s.123, enabling: SSI 2008/88
s.129, applied: SSI 2008/88 Reg.13
s.129, enabling: SSI 2008/88
s.131, applied: SSI 2008/88 Reg.14
s.131, enabling: SSI 2008/88
s.133, applied: SSI 2008/89 Reg.2
s.133, enabling: SSI 2008/89
s.134, enabling: SSI 2008/43
s.139, applied: SSI 2008/88 Reg.3
s.143, applied: SSI 2008/89 Reg.2
s.143, enabling: SSI 2008/89
s.144, applied: SSI 2008/88 Reg.3
s.149, applied: SSI 2008/88 Reg.14
s.149, enabling: SSI 2008/88
s.154A, applied: SSI 2008/244 Reg.3
s.154A, disapplied: SSI 2008/88 Reg.4
s.155, applied: SSI 2008/89 Reg.2
s.155, enabling: SSI 2008/89
s.156, enabling: SSI 2008/88, SSI 2008/243, SSI 2008/244
s.157, applied: SSI 2008/244 Reg.5
s.157A, enabling: SSI 2008/89
s.163, enabling: SSI 2008/16, SSI 2008/88, SSI 2008/89
s.163A, applied: SSI 2008/16, SSI 2008/43, SSI 2008/88, SSI 2008/89, SSI 2008/243, SSI 2008/244
Sch.3A, applied: SI 2008/101 Reg.12, SI 2008/540 Reg.12
Sch.3A, disapplied: 2008 c.18 Sch.14 para.14, SI 2008/1261 Art.6
Sch.3A para.1, enabling: SI 2008/101, SI 2008/540

CAP.

1991–cont.

22. New Roads and Street Works Act 1991–*cont.*

Sch.3A para.2, applied: 2008 c.18 Sch.14 para.14, SI 2008/101 Reg.4, Reg.8, Reg.9, Reg.12, SI 2008/540 Reg.4, Reg.8, Reg.9, Reg.12

Sch.3A para.2, enabling: SI 2008/101, SI 2008/540

Sch.3A para.3, applied: 2008 c.18 Sch.14 para.14, SI 2008/540 Reg.12

Sch.3A para.3, disapplied: 2008 c.18 Sch.14 para.14, SI 2008/101 Reg.12

Sch.3A para.3, referred to: SI 2008/101 Reg.12

Sch.3A para.3, enabling: SI 2008/101, SI 2008/540

Sch.3A para.4, applied: SI 2008/101 Reg.12, SI 2008/540 Reg.12

Sch.3A para.4, enabling: SI 2008/101, SI 2008/540

Sch.3A para.5, applied: SI 2008/101 Reg.12, SI 2008/540 Reg.12

Sch.3A para.5, disapplied: 2008 c.18 Sch.14 para.14, SI 2008/101 Reg.12, SI 2008/540 Reg.12

Sch.3A para.5, referred to: SI 2008/101 Reg.12

Sch.3A para.5, enabling: SI 2008/101, SI 2008/540

Sch.4, applied: 2008 c.18 Sch.14 para.14, SI 2008/101 Reg.4, SI 2008/540 Reg.4

Sch.4A, disapplied: SI 2008/102 Reg.3

Sch.4B, applied: SI 2008/102 Reg.5, SI 2008/540 Reg.5

Sch.4B, disapplied: SI 2008/101 Reg.5, Reg.6, SI 2008/540 Reg.6

Sch.4B, applied: SI 2008/102 Reg.9

Sch.4B para.2, enabling: SI 2008/102, SI 2008/466

Sch.4B para.4, amended: SI 2008/102 Reg.8

Sch.4B para.4, enabling: SI 2008/102, SI 2008/466

Sch.4B para.5, amended: SI 2008/102 Reg.8

Sch.4B para.5, applied: SI 2008/102 Reg.7

Sch.4B para.5, enabling: SI 2008/102, SI 2008/466

Sch.4B para.7, applied: SI 2008/102 Reg.10

Sch.4B para.8, enabling: SI 2008/102, SI 2008/466

Sch.4B para.9, enabling: SI 2008/102, SI 2008/466

Sch.6, applied: SSI 2008/88 Reg.3

Sch.6B, applied: SSI 2008/244 Reg.3, Reg.5, Reg.10

Sch.6B, disapplied: SSI 2008/88 Reg.4

Sch.6 para.2, applied: SSI 2008/89 Reg.2

Sch.6 para.2, enabling: SSI 2008/89

Sch.6 para.12, applied: SSI 2008/89 Reg.2

Sch.6 para.12, enabling: SSI 2008/89

Sch.6B para.2, enabling: SSI 2008/244

CAP.

1991–cont.

22. New Roads and Street Works Act 1991–*cont.*

Sch.6B para.4, amended: SSI 2008/244 Reg.8

Sch.6B para.4, enabling: SSI 2008/244

Sch.6B para.5, amended: SSI 2008/244 Reg.8

Sch.6B para.5, applied: SSI 2008/244 Reg.7

Sch.6B para.5, referred to: SSI 2008/244 Reg.7

Sch.6B para.5, enabling: SSI 2008/244

Sch.6B para.8, applied: SSI 2008/244 Reg.9

Sch.6B para.12, enabling: SSI 2008/244

Sch.6B para.13, enabling: SSI 2008/244

23. Children and Young Persons (Protection from Tobacco) Act 1991

applied: 2008 c.13 Sch.3

referred to: 2008 c.13 Sch.6

27. Radioactive Material (Road Transport) Act 1991

s.2, referred to: 2008 c.13 Sch.6

s.3, referred to: 2008 c.13 Sch.6

s.4, referred to: 2008 c.13 Sch.6

s.5, referred to: 2008 c.13 Sch.6

s.6, referred to: 2008 c.13 Sch.6

28. Natural Heritage (Scotland) Act 1991

referred to: SSI 2008/263 Sch.1, Sch.2

29. Property Misdescriptions Act 1991

applied: 2008 c.13 Sch.3

referred to: 2008 c.13 Sch.6

30. Welfare of Animals at Slaughter Act 1991

applied: 2008 c.13 Sch.3

31. Finance Act 1991

s.55, repealed: 2008 c.9 s.66

s.56, repealed: 2008 c.9 s.66

s.64, amended: 2008 c.9 s.104

s.65, amended: 2008 c.9 s.104, Sch.39 para.27

s.76, repealed (in part): 2008 c.9 Sch.14 para.17

s.108, amended: 2008 c.9 s.105

s.116, applied: SI 2008/1814 Reg.3, SI 2008/2777 Reg.3, SI 2008/3235 Reg.3

s.116, enabling: SI 2008/52, SI 2008/164, SI 2008/914, SI 2008/1814, SI 2008/2777, SI 2008/3235

s.117, applied: SI 2008/52 Reg.3, SI 2008/1814 Reg.3, SI 2008/2777 Reg.3, SI 2008/3235 Reg.3

s.117, enabling: SI 2008/52, SI 2008/164, SI 2008/914, SI 2008/1814, SI 2008/2777, SI 2008/3235

Sch.9 para.2, repealed: 2008 c.9 Sch.18 para.5

34. Planning and Compensation Act 1991

s.6, repealed (in part): 2008 c.29 Sch.13

Sch.2 para.5, amended: 2008 c.29 s.198

Sch.18 Part I, amended: 2008 c.14 Sch.11 para.31, Sch.15 Part 3, 2008 c.29 Sch.8 para.20, Sch.13

CAP.

1991–cont.

40. Road Traffic Act 1991

see *Teale v MacLeod* 2008 S.C.C.R. 12 (HCJ), Lord Osborne
s.66, varied: SI 2008/226 Sch.1 para.1
s.69, varied: SI 2008/226 Sch.1 para.2
s.71, varied: SI 2008/226 Sch.1 para.3
s.73, applied: SI 2008/609 Reg.8, Reg.9
s.73, varied: SI 2008/226 Sch.1 para.4
s.74, varied: SI 2008/226 Sch.1 para.5
s.78, varied: SI 2008/226 Sch.1 para.6
s.82, varied: SI 2008/226 Sch.1 para.7
Sch.3, applied: SI 2008/614 Reg.11, SI 2008/1214 Reg.11
Sch.3 para.1, enabling: SI 2008/226
Sch.3 para.2, disapplied: 2008 asp 4 s.38
Sch.3 para.2, enabling: SI 2008/226
Sch.3 para.3, enabling: SI 2008/226
Sch.6, referred to: SI 2008/226 Sch.1 para.8
Sch.6 para.1, varied: SI 2008/226 Sch.1 para.8
Sch.6 para.2, varied: SI 2008/226 Sch.1 para.8
Sch.6 para.3, varied: SI 2008/226 Sch.1 para.8
Sch.6 para.4, varied: SI 2008/226 Sch.1 para.8
Sch.6 para.5, varied: SI 2008/226 Sch.1 para.8
Sch.6 para.6, varied: SI 2008/226 Sch.1 para.8
Sch.6 para.7, varied: SI 2008/226 Sch.1 para.8
Sch.6 para.8, varied: SI 2008/226 Sch.1 para.8

48. Child Support Act 1991

see *Kehoe v United Kingdom (2010/06)* [2008] 2 F.L.R. 1014 (ECHR), Judge Garlicki (President)
applied: 2008 c.6 s.2, s.6, s.12, s.13, s.60, Sch.5 para.6, SI 2008/2551 Reg.4, Reg.12, Reg.13, SI 2008/2685 r.19, r.23, SI 2008/2698 r.19, r.20
referred to: 2008 c.6 s.56, s.59, SI 2008/2551 Reg.2, Reg.12
varied: 2008 c.6 s.59
s.2, amended: 2008 c.6 Sch.3 para.2
s.4, amended: 2008 c.6 s.35, Sch.3 para.3
s.4, applied: SI 2008/2548 Art.4, SI 2008/2551 Reg.3, Reg.13
s.4, repealed (in part): 2008 c.6 Sch.8
s.4, enabling: SI 2008/2551
s.6, amended: 2008 c.6 Sch.3 para.4
s.6, applied: SI 2008/1476 Art.2, SI 2008/2548 Art.4
s.6, referred to: 2008 c.6 s.59, SI 2008/2548 Art.4
s.6, repealed: 2008 c.6 Sch.8
s.6, varied: SI 2008/1476 Art.2
s.7, amended: 2008 c.6 s.35, Sch.3 para.5
s.7, applied: SI 2008/2551 Reg.3, Reg.13
s.7, repealed (in part): 2008 c.6 Sch.8

CAP.

1991–cont.

48. Child Support Act 1991–*cont.*

s.7, enabling: SI 2008/2551
s.8, amended: 2008 c.6 Sch.3 para.6, Sch.7 para.1, Sch.8
s.9, amended: 2008 c.6 s.35
s.9, repealed (in part): 2008 c.6 Sch.8
s.10, amended: 2008 c.6 Sch.3 para.7
s.11, amended: 2008 c.6 Sch.3 para.8
s.11, repealed (in part): 2008 c.6 Sch.7 para.1, Sch.8
s.12, amended: 2008 c.6 Sch.3 para.9, Sch.8
s.14, amended: 2008 c.6 Sch.3 para.10, Sch.8
s.14, enabling: SI 2008/536, SI 2008/2551
s.14A, amended: 2008 c.6 s.36
s.14A, applied: SI 2008/2551 Reg.15
s.14A, referred to: SI 2008/2551 Reg.8
s.15, amended: 2008 c.6 Sch.3 para.11
s.15, applied: SI 2008/2551 Reg.11
s.16, amended: 2008 c.6 Sch.3 para.12, SI 2008/2833 Sch.3 para.78
s.16, applied: SI 2008/2551 Reg.13
s.16, repealed (in part): 2008 c.6 Sch.8
s.17, amended: 2008 c.6 s.17, Sch.3 para.13, SI 2008/2833 Sch.3 para.79
s.17, applied: SI 2008/2551 Reg.13
s.17, repealed (in part): 2008 c.6 Sch.8
s.20, amended: 2008 c.6 Sch.3 para.14, Sch.7 para.1, SI 2008/2833 Sch.3 para.80, Sch.3 para.81
s.20, applied: 2008 c.6 s.6, SI 2008/1052 Sch.1, SI 2008/2685 r.21, SI 2008/2836 Art.5
s.20, repealed (in part): 2008 c.6 Sch.8, SI 2008/2833 Sch.3 para.80, Sch.3 para.81
s.20, varied: 2008 c.6 s.59
s.22, applied: SI 2008/1149 Art.2, SI 2008/2833 Sch.1, Sch.2
s.22, repealed: SI 2008/2833 Sch.3 para.82
s.23, amended: SI 2008/2833 Sch.3 para.83
s.23A, amended: 2008 c.6 Sch.3 para.15, SI 2008/2833 Sch.3 para.84
s.23A, applied: 2008 c.6 s.13
s.23A, repealed (in part): SI 2008/2833 Sch.3 para.84
s.24, amended: 2008 c.6 Sch.3 para.16, SI 2008/2833 Sch.3 para.85
s.24, applied: 2008 c.6 s.13, SI 2008/1955
s.24, substituted: SI 2008/2833 Sch.3 para.85
s.24, enabling: SI 2008/1955
s.25, amended: 2008 c.6 Sch.3 para.17
s.25, applied: 2008 c.6 s.13, SI 2008/1955
s.25, repealed (in part): SI 2008/2833 Sch.3 para.86
s.25, enabling: SI 2008/1955
s.26, amended: 2008 c.6 Sch.3 para.18, Sch.8, 2008 c.22 Sch.6 para.36
s.26, referred to: SI 2008/2551 Reg.5
s.27, amended: 2008 c.6 Sch.3 para.19, Sch.8
s.27A, amended: 2008 c.6 Sch.3 para.20, Sch.8

CAP.

1991–cont.

48. Child Support Act 1991–*cont.*

s.28, amended: 2008 c.6 Sch.3 para.21, Sch.8
s.28A, amended: 2008 c.6 Sch.3 para.25, Sch.8
s.28B, amended: 2008 c.6 Sch.3 para.26
s.28C, amended: 2008 c.6 Sch.3 para.27
s.28D, amended: 2008 c.6 s.18, Sch.3 para.28, SI 2008/2833 Sch.3 para.91
s.28D, applied: SI 2008/2551 Reg.12, SI 2008/2685 r.26
s.28E, amended: 2008 c.6 Sch.3 para.29
s.28F, amended: 2008 c.6 Sch.3 para.30, Sch.8
s.28J, amended: 2008 c.6 Sch.3 para.31, Sch.8
s.28ZA, amended: 2008 c.6 Sch.3 para.22, Sch.8, SI 2008/2833 Sch.3 para.87
s.28ZB, amended: 2008 c.6 Sch.3 para.23, SI 2008/2833 Sch.3 para.88
s.28ZC, amended: 2008 c.6 Sch.3 para.24, Sch.8, SI 2008/2833 Sch.3 para.89
s.28ZD, amended: SI 2008/2833 Sch.3 para.90
s.28ZD, repealed (in part): SI 2008/2833 Sch.3 para.90
s.29, amended: 2008 c.6 s.20, Sch.3 para.32
s.29, applied: SI 2008/2551 Reg.13
s.29, repealed (in part): 2008 c.6 Sch.8
s.29, enabling: SI 2008/2544
s.30, amended: 2008 c.6 Sch.3 para.33, Sch.7 para.1
s.31, amended: 2008 c.6 s.21, Sch.3 para.34
s.32, amended: 2008 c.6 Sch.3 para.35, Sch.7 para.1
s.32, repealed (in part): 2008 c.6 Sch.8
s.32, enabling: SI 2008/536, SI 2008/2544
s.32A, added: 2008 c.6 s.22
s.32A, varied: 2008 c.6 s.59
s.32B, added: 2008 c.6 s.22
s.32C, added: 2008 c.6 s.22
s.32C, varied: 2008 c.6 s.59
s.32D, added: 2008 c.6 s.22
s.32E, added: 2008 c.6 s.23
s.32E, varied: 2008 c.6 s.59
s.32F, added: 2008 c.6 s.23
s.32F, varied: 2008 c.6 s.59
s.32G, added: 2008 c.6 s.23
s.32H, added: 2008 c.6 s.23
s.32I, added: 2008 c.6 s.23
s.32J, added: 2008 c.6 s.23
s.32J, varied: 2008 c.6 s.59
s.32K, added: 2008 c.6 s.23
s.32L, added: 2008 c.6 s.24
s.32L, varied: 2008 c.6 s.59
s.32M, added: 2008 c.6 s.25
s.32M, applied: 2008 c.6 s.59
s.32M, varied: 2008 c.6 s.59
s.32N, added: 2008 c.6 s.25
s.33, amended: 2008 c.6 Sch.3 para.36

CAP.

1991–cont.

48. Child Support Act 1991–*cont.*

s.33, applied: 2008 c.6 s.59
s.33, repealed: 2008 c.6 Sch.8
s.34, amended: 2008 c.6 Sch.3 para.37
s.34, repealed: 2008 c.6 Sch.8
s.35, amended: 2008 c.6 Sch.3 para.38
s.35, varied: 2008 c.6 s.59
s.36, amended: 2008 c.6 s.26, Sch.7 para.1, Sch.8
s.36, repealed (in part): 2008 c.6 Sch.8
s.36, varied: 2008 c.6 s.59
s.37, amended: 2008 c.6 Sch.3 para.39
s.37, repealed: 2008 c.6 Sch.8
s.38, amended: 2008 c.6 Sch.3 para.40
s.38, varied: 2008 c.6 s.59
s.39, substituted: 2008 c.6 Sch.7 para.1
s.39A, amended: 2008 c.6 Sch.3 para.41
s.39A, repealed: 2008 c.6 Sch.8
s.39B, added: 2008 c.6 s.27
s.39B, varied: 2008 c.6 s.59
s.39C, added: 2008 c.6 s.27
s.39D, added: 2008 c.6 s.27
s.39E, added: 2008 c.6 s.27
s.39F, added: 2008 c.6 s.27
s.39G, added: 2008 c.6 s.27
s.39H, added: 2008 c.6 s.28
s.39H, varied: 2008 c.6 s.59
s.39I, added: 2008 c.6 s.28
s.39J, added: 2008 c.6 s.28
s.39K, added: 2008 c.6 s.28
s.39K, varied: 2008 c.6 s.59
s.39L, added: 2008 c.6 s.28
s.39M, added: 2008 c.6 s.28
s.39N, added: 2008 c.6 s.28
s.39O, added: 2008 c.6 s.28
s.39P, added: 2008 c.6 s.28
s.39Q, added: 2008 c.6 s.28
s.40, amended: 2008 c.6 s.29, Sch.7 para.1
s.40, varied: 2008 c.6 s.59
s.40A, amended: 2008 c.6 s.29, Sch.7 para.1
s.40A, repealed (in part): 2008 c.6 Sch.8
s.40A, varied: 2008 c.6 s.59
s.40B, amended: 2008 c.6 s.30, Sch.3 para.42, Sch.7 para.1
s.40B, repealed (in part): 2008 c.6 Sch.8
s.40B, varied: 2008 c.6 s.59
s.41, amended: 2008 c.6 Sch.3 para.43, Sch.8
s.41, applied: SI 2008/2548 Art.4
s.41, repealed (in part): 2008 c.6 Sch.7 para.1
s.41A, amended: 2008 c.6 Sch.3 para.44
s.41A, repealed (in part): 2008 c.6 Sch.7 para.1
s.41B, amended: 2008 c.6 Sch.3 para.45
s.41C, added: 2008 c.6 s.31
s.41C, varied: 2008 c.6 s.59
s.41D, added: 2008 c.6 s.32
s.41D, varied: 2008 c.6 s.59
s.41E, added: 2008 c.6 s.33
s.41E, varied: 2008 c.6 s.59

CAP.

1991–cont.

48. Child Support Act 1991–*cont.*

s.42, amended: 2008 c.6 s.37
s.42, applied: SI 2008/2551 Reg.2
s.43A, varied: 2008 c.6 s.59
s.43A, added: 2008 c.6 s.38
s.44, amended: 2008 c.6 Sch.3 para.46
s.44, applied: SI 2008/2551 Reg.5, Reg.10
s.45, amended: SI 2008/2833 Sch.3 para.92
s.45, repealed (in part): SI 2008/2833 Sch.3 para.92
s.46, amended: 2008 c.6 Sch.3 para.47
s.46, applied: 2008 c.6 s.13, s.59
s.46, referred to: 2008 c.6 s.59, SI 2008/2685 r.19
s.46, repealed: 2008 c.6 Sch.8
s.46A, amended: 2008 c.6 Sch.3 para.48, SI 2008/2833 Sch.3 para.93
s.46B, amended: 2008 c.6 Sch.3 para.49, SI 2008/2833 Sch.3 para.94
s.47, repealed: 2008 c.6 Sch.8
s.48, amended: 2008 c.6 Sch.3 para.50
s.49A, added: 2008 c.6 s.34
s.49A, varied: 2008 c.6 s.59
s.49B, varied: 2008 c.6 s.59
s.49B, added: 2008 c.6 s.39
s.49B, varied: 2008 c.6 s.59
s.49C, added: 2008 c.6 s.39
s.49D, varied: 2008 c.6 s.59
s.49D, added: 2008 c.6 s.40
s.49D, varied: 2008 c.6 s.59
s.50, amended: 2008 c.6 Sch.7 para.1, SI 2008/2833 Sch.3 para.95
s.50, applied: 2008 c.6 s.13, SI 2008/2551 Reg.14
s.50, repealed (in part): 2008 c.6 Sch.8
s.50, enabling: SI 2008/2551
s.50A, added: 2008 c.6 Sch.3 para.51
s.51, enabling: SI 2008/2544, SI 2008/2551
s.51A, added: 2008 c.6 s.41
s.52, amended: 2008 c.6 Sch.7 para.1, Sch.8
s.52, enabling: SI 2008/2544, SI 2008/2551
s.54, amended: 2008 c.6 Sch.7 para.1, SI 2008/2833 Sch.3 para.96
s.54, enabling: SI 2008/536, SI 2008/2544, SI 2008/2551
s.55, applied: SI 2008/2551 Reg.10
s.55, substituted: 2008 c.6 s.42
s.57, amended: 2008 c.6 Sch.7 para.1
s.57, enabling: SI 2008/2551
s.58, applied: 2008 c.6 s.13
Sch.1 Part I, applied: 2008 c.6 Sch.5 para.1
Sch.1 Part I para.1, amended: 2008 c.6 Sch.4 para.5
Sch.1 Part I para.2, amended: 2008 c.6 Sch.4 para.2
Sch.1 Part I para.2, substituted: 2008 c.6 Sch.4 para.3
Sch.1 Part I para.3, amended: 2008 c.6 Sch.4 para.2, Sch.4 para.4

CAP.

1991–cont.

48. Child Support Act 1991–*cont.*

Sch.1 Part I para.4, amended: 2008 c.6 Sch.4 para.2, Sch.4 para.4
Sch.1 Part I para.5, amended: 2008 c.6 Sch.4 para.2
Sch.1 Part I para.5, amended: 2008 c.6 Sch.4 para.2, Sch.7 para.1
Sch.1 Part I para.5A, added: 2008 c.6 Sch.4 para.5
Sch.1 Part I para.7, amended: 2008 c.6 Sch.3 para.52, Sch.4 para.4, Sch.4 para.6, Sch.7 para.1
Sch.1 Part I para.8, amended: 2008 c.6 Sch.4 para.7
Sch.1 Part I para.9, amended: 2008 c.6 Sch.4 para.2
Sch.1 Part I para.9, amended: 2008 c.6 Sch.4 para.8, Sch.8
Sch.1 Part I para.9, substituted: 2008 c.6 Sch.4 para.8
Sch.1 Part I para.10, amended: 2008 c.6 Sch.3 para.52, Sch.4 para.2, Sch.4 para.9, Sch.4 para.10
Sch.1 Part I para.10, enabling: SI 2008/2544
Sch.1 Part I para.10A, amended: 2008 c.6 Sch.7 para.1
Sch.1 Part I para.10B, amended: 2008 c.6 Sch.3 para.52, Sch.4 para.2
Sch.1 Part I para.10C, amended: 2008 c.6 Sch.7 para.1
Sch.1 Part II para.11, enabling: SI 2008/2544
Sch.1 Part II para.12, amended: 2008 c.6 Sch.3 para.52
Sch.1 Part II para.13, amended: 2008 c.6 Sch.3 para.52
Sch.1 Part II para.14, substituted: 2008 c.6 Sch.7 para.1
Sch.1 Part II para.15, amended: 2008 c.6 Sch.3 para.52
Sch.1 Part II para.16, amended: 2008 c.6 Sch.3 para.52
Sch.1 Part II para.16, applied: SI 2008/2551 Reg.10
Sch.1 Part II para.16, repealed (in part): 2008 c.6 Sch.7 para.1
Sch.1 Part II para.16, enabling: SI 2008/2551
Sch.2 para.1, repealed: 2008 c.6 Sch.8
Sch.2 para.1A, repealed: 2008 c.6 Sch.8
Sch.2 para.2, repealed: 2008 c.6 Sch.8
Sch.2 para.3, repealed: 2008 c.6 Sch.8
Sch.4 para.1, amended: SI 2008/2833 Sch.3 para.97
Sch.4 para.1, repealed (in part): SI 2008/2833 Sch.3 para.97
Sch.4 para.2, amended: SI 2008/2833 Sch.3 para.97
Sch.4 para.2A, amended: SI 2008/2833 Sch.3 para.97
Sch.4 para.2A, applied: 2008 c.6 s.13
Sch.4 para.2A, repealed: SI 2008/2833 Sch.3 para.97

CAP.

1991–cont.

48. Child Support Act 1991–*cont.*

Sch.4 para.3, amended: SI 2008/2833 Sch.3 para.97

Sch.4 para.3, substituted: SI 2008/2833 Sch.3 para.97

Sch.4 para.4, amended: SI 2008/2833 Sch.3 para.97

Sch.4 para.4, applied: SI 2008/2833 Sch.2

Sch.4 para.4A, amended: SI 2008/2833 Sch.3 para.97

Sch.4 para.4A, repealed: SI 2008/2833 Sch.3 para.97

Sch.4 para.5, amended: SI 2008/2833 Sch.3 para.97

Sch.4 para.5, repealed: SI 2008/2833 Sch.3 para.97

Sch.4 para.6, amended: SI 2008/2833 Sch.3 para.97

Sch.4 para.6, repealed: SI 2008/2833 Sch.3 para.97

Sch.4 para.7, amended: SI 2008/2833 Sch.3 para.97

Sch.4 para.7, repealed: SI 2008/2833 Sch.3 para.97

Sch.4 para.8, amended: SI 2008/2833 Sch.3 para.97

Sch.4 para.8, repealed: SI 2008/2833 Sch.3 para.97

Sch.4A para.2, repealed (in part): SI 2008/2833 Sch.3 para.98, Sch.3 para.99

Sch.4A para.4, amended: 2008 c.6 Sch.3 para.53

Sch.4A para.5, repealed (in part): 2008 c.6 Sch.8, SI 2008/2833 Sch.3 para.99

Sch.4A para.8, repealed (in part): SI 2008/2833 Sch.3 para.98

Sch.4B Part I para.2, amended: 2008 c.6 Sch.8

Sch.4C para.1, amended: 2008 c.6 Sch.7 para.1, SI 2008/2833 Sch.3 para.100

Sch.4C para.2, amended: 2008 c.6 Sch.7 para.1, SI 2008/2833 Sch.3 para.100

Sch.4C para.3, amended: SI 2008/2833 Sch.3 para.100

Sch.4C para.3, repealed (in part): 2008 c.6 Sch.7 para.1

Sch.4C para.4, amended: 2008 c.6 Sch.7 para.1, SI 2008/2833 Sch.3 para.100

Sch.4C para.5, amended: SI 2008/2833 Sch.3 para.100

Sch.4C para.6, amended: 2008 c.6 Sch.7 para.1, SI 2008/2833 Sch.3 para.100

Sch.5 para.8, repealed (in part): 2008 c.6 Sch.8

50. Age of Legal Capacity (Scotland) Act 1991

s.2, amended: 2008 c.22 Sch.7 para.16

52. Ports Act 1991

Sch.1, referred to: SI 2008/948 Sch.1 para.179

Sch.1 Part II para.11, amended: SI 2008/948 Sch.1 para.179

CAP.

1991–cont.

52. Ports Act 1991–*cont.*

Sch.1 Part II para.13, amended: SI 2008/948 Sch.1 para.179

53. Criminal Justice Act 1991

see *Gibson v Secretary of State for Justice* [2008] EWCA Civ 177, [2008] 3 W.L.R. 1044 (CA (Civ Div)), Sir Anthony Clarke, M.R.; see *R. v Giga (Zulfikar)* [2008] EWCA Crim 703, [2008] 2 Cr. App. R. (S.) 112 (CA (Crim Div)), Moore-Bick, L.J.

Part II, applied: 2008 c.4 Sch.27 para.8, Sch.27 para.12, SI 2008/2793 r.3

s.32, see *R. v Strachan (Greig)* [2007] EWCA Crim 1571, [2008] 1 Cr. App. R. (S.) 43 (CA (Crim Div)), Pill, L.J.

s.33, see *Gibson v Secretary of State for Justice* [2008] EWCA Civ 177, [2008] 3 W.L.R. 1044 (CA (Civ Div)), Sir Anthony Clarke, M.R.

s.33, amended: 2008 c.4 s.26

s.34A, applied: SI 2008/1788 Sch.1

s.35, see *R. (on the application of Black) v Secretary of State for the Home Department* [2008] EWCA Civ 359, [2008] 3 W.L.R. 845 (CA (Civ Div)), May, L.J.

s.35, amended: 2008 c.4 s.26

s.36, applied: 2008 c.4 s.32, Sch.27 para.10

s.37, see *Gibson v Secretary of State for Justice* [2008] EWCA Civ 177, [2008] 3 W.L.R. 1044 (CA (Civ Div)), Sir Anthony Clarke, M.R.

s.37, amended: 2008 c.4 s.26, SI 2008/912 Sch.1 para.9

s.37A, applied: SI 2008/1788 Sch.1, SI 2008/2768 Art.2, SI 2008/2793 r.3

s.37A, enabling: SI 2008/2768

s.37ZA, added: 2008 c.4 s.26

s.39, see *Dunn v Parole Board* [2008] EWCA Civ 374, [2008] H.R.L.R. 32 (CA (Civ Div)), Smith, L.J.; see *Gibson v Secretary of State for Justice* [2008] EWCA Civ 177, [2008] 3 W.L.R. 1044 (CA (Civ Div)), Sir Anthony Clarke, M.R.

s.39, referred to: 2008 c.4 Sch.26 para.32

s.40A, see *West Midlands Probation Board v French* [2008] EWHC 2631 (Admin), (2008) 172 J.P. 617 (DC), Scott Baker, L.J.

s.43, amended: 2008 c.4 Sch.26 para.29, SI 2008/912 Sch.1 para.9

s.43, referred to: 2008 c.4 Sch.26 para.29

s.44, amended: 2008 c.4 Sch.26 para.29

s.45, amended: 2008 c.4 s.28, Sch.28 Part 2

s.45, repealed (in part): 2008 c.4 s.28, Sch.28 Part 2

s.46, amended: 2008 c.4 Sch.26 para.29

s.46, repealed (in part): 2008 c.4 s.27, Sch.28 Part 2

s.46A, amended: 2008 c.4 s.33, Sch.28 Part 2, SI 2008/977 Art.2

s.46A, applied: SI 2008/977

CAP.

1991–cont.

53. Criminal Justice Act 1991–*cont.*

s.46A, repealed (in part): 2008 c.4 s.33, Sch.28 Part 2
s.46A, enabling: SI 2008/977
s.46B, amended: 2008 c.4 Sch.26 para.29
s.46ZA, added: 2008 c.4 s.33
s.50, amended: 2008 c.4 s.27, Sch.28 Part 2
s.50A, added: 2008 c.4 s.32
s.50A, applied: 2008 c.4 s.32
s.61, amended: 2008 c.23 Sch.1 para.8, Sch.4
s.65, amended: SI 2008/912 Sch.1 para.9
s.65, applied: SI 2008/1263 Reg.5, Reg.9, Reg.10
s.69, repealed: 2008 c.12 Sch.1 Part 3
s.72, repealed: 2008 c.12 Sch.1 Part 3
Sch.3 Part III para.10, amended: 2008 c.4 Sch.4 para.40, Sch.26 para.29, SI 2008/912 Sch.1 para.9
Sch.3 Part III para.11, amended: 2008 c.4 Sch.4 para.41, Sch.28 Part 1, SI 2008/912 Sch.1 para.9
Sch.11 para.3, repealed: 2008 c.4 Sch.28 Part 1
Sch.12 para.8, applied: SI 2008/1466 Art.3

54. Deer Act 1991

referred to: 2008 c.13 Sch.6

55. Agricultural Holdings (Scotland) Act 1991

see *O'Donnell v McDonald* 2008 S.C.189 (IH (2 Div)), Lord Gill L.J.C.

56. Water Industry Act 1991

see *Dobson v Thames Water Utilities Ltd* [2007] EWHC 2021 (TCC), [2008] 2 All E.R. 362 (QBD (TCC)), Ramsey, J.; see *R. (on the application of Thames Water Utilities Ltd) v Bromley Magistrates Court* [2008] EWHC 1763 (QB), Times, August 28, 2008 (DC), Carnwath, L.J.
s.18, see *Dobson v Thames Water Utilities Ltd* [2007] EWHC 2021 (TCC), [2008] 2 All E.R. 362 (QBD (TCC)), Ramsey, J.
s.38, enabling: SI 2008/594
s.39, applied: SI 2008/594
s.41, amended: 2008 c.17 Sch.8 para.56
s.60, applied: SI 2008/594 Reg.8
s.69, applied: 2008 c.13 Sch.7
s.70, referred to: 2008 c.13 Sch.6
s.77, applied: 2008 c.13 Sch.3
s.78, applied: 2008 c.13 Sch.3
s.79, applied: 2008 c.13 Sch.3
s.80, applied: 2008 c.13 Sch.3
s.81, applied: 2008 c.13 Sch.3
s.82, applied: 2008 c.13 Sch.3
s.83, applied: 2008 c.13 Sch.3
s.84, applied: 2008 c.13 Sch.3
s.85, applied: 2008 c.13 Sch.3
s.86, referred to: 2008 c.13 Sch.6
s.94, see *Dobson v Thames Water Utilities Ltd* [2007] EWHC 2021 (TCC), [2008] 2 All E.R. 362 (QBD (TCC)), Ramsey, J.
s.95, enabling: SI 2008/594

CAP.

1991–cont.

56. Water Industry Act 1991–*cont.*

s.96, applied: SI 2008/594
s.97, amended: 2008 c.17 Sch.8 para.57
s.98, amended: 2008 c.17 Sch.8 para.58
s.106, applied: SI 2008/2512 Art.19
s.106, disapplied: 2008 c.18 Sch.14 para.16
s.109, referred to: 2008 c.13 Sch.6
s.111, referred to: 2008 c.13 Sch.6
s.118, referred to: 2008 c.13 Sch.6
s.167, amended: 2008 c.29 Sch.2 para.50
s.206, amended: SI 2008/960 Sch.3
s.209, applied: 2008 c.29 s.151
s.213, enabling: SI 2008/594
s.219, amended: 2008 c.17 Sch.8 para.59
Sch.15 Part II, amended: SI 2008/1277 Sch.2 para.49, Sch.4 Part 1

57. Water Resources Act 1991

applied: 2008 c.13 Sch.3, SI 2008/1261 Sch.10 para.8, Sch.10 para.12
referred to: 2008 c.13 Sch.6, 2008 c.18 Sch.2 para.8, SI 2008/2512 Art.19
Part II c.II, applied: 2008 c.18 Sch.17 para.11
s.24, disapplied: 2008 c.18 Sch.14 para.15
s.30, applied: 2008 c.18 Sch.17 para.11
s.37, enabling: SI 2008/165
s.48A, applied: 2008 c.18 s.46, 2008 c.29 s.151
s.48A, disapplied: 2008 c.18 s.46
s.51, enabling: SI 2008/165
s.72, amended: 2008 c.17 Sch.8 para.60
s.83, applied: SI 2008/1097 Reg.18
s.85, applied: SI 2008/1261 Art.54, SI 2008/2512 Art.19
s.85, disapplied: 2008 c.18 Sch.17 para.4
s.85, referred to: 2008 c.18 Sch.2 para.8
s.92, applied: 2008 c.13 Sch.7
s.104, varied: SI 2008/1097 Reg.3
s.109, applied: 2008 c.18 Sch.17 para.11, SI 2008/1261 Sch.10 para.12
s.189, enabling: SI 2008/165
s.202, varied: SI 2008/1097 Reg.16
s.204, amended: SI 2008/960 Sch.3
s.219, enabling: SI 2008/165
s.221, enabling: SI 2008/165
Sch.24 Part II, amended: SI 2008/1277 Sch.2 para.50, Sch.4 Part 1

58. Statutory Water Companies Act 1991

s.9, amended: SI 2008/948 Sch.1 para.180

59. Land Drainage Act 1991

applied: SI 2008/1261 Sch.10 para.12
s.3, applied: SI 2008/750, SI 2008/1422, SI 2008/1423
s.3, enabling: SI 2008/750, SI 2008/1422, SI 2008/1423
s.23, disapplied: SI 2008/1261 Sch.10 para.12, SI 2008/2512 Art.48
Sch.3 para.1, applied: SI 2008/750 Sch.2 app.001
Sch.3 para.2, applied: SI 2008/750, SI 2008/1422, SI 2008/1423

CAP.

1991–cont.

59. Land Drainage Act 1991–*cont.*
Sch.3 para.2, referred to: SI 2008/750
Sch.3 para.4, applied: SI 2008/750 Sch.2 app.001
Sch.3 para.5, applied: SI 2008/750 Sch.2 app.001, SI 2008/1422 Art.1, SI 2008/1423 Art.1

60. Water Consolidation (Consequential Provisions) Act 1991
Sch.1 para.40, amended: SI 2008/948 Sch.1 para.182

64. Breeding of Dogs Act 1991
applied: 2008 c.13 Sch.3
referred to: 2008 c.13 Sch.6

65. Dangerous Dogs Act 1991
see *R. v Bogdal (Michael Edward) (aka Tadeusz (Marjan))* [2008] EWCA Crim 1, (2008) 172 J.P. 178 (CA (Crim Div)), Smith, L.J.
applied: 2008 c.13 Sch.3
referred to: 2008 c.13 Sch.6
s.3, see *R. v Gedminintaite (Edita)* [2008] EWCA Crim 814, (2008) 172 J.P. 413 (CA (Crim Div)), Keene, L.J.
s.4, see *R. v Flack (Michael James)* [2008] EWCA Crim 204, [2008] 2 Cr. App. R. (S.) 70 (CA (Crim Div)), Hooper, L.J.
s.10, see *R. v Bogdal (Michael Edward) (aka Tadeusz (Marjan))* [2008] EWCA Crim 1, (2008) 172 J.P. 178 (CA (Crim Div)), Smith, L.J.; see *R. v Gedminintaite (Edita)* [2008] EWCA Crim 814, (2008) 172 J.P. 413 (CA (Crim Div)), Keene, L.J.

66. British Technology Group Act 1991
s.8, amended: SI 2008/948 Sch.1 para.181

1992

3. Severn Bridges Act 1992
s.8, referred to: SI 2008/3263 Art.2
s.9, applied: SI 2008/3263 Art.1
s.9, enabling: SI 2008/3263

4. Social Security Contributions and Benefits Act 1992
see *CIS/213/2004, Re* [2008] W.T.L.R. 189 (SS Comm), Charles Turnbull
applied: SI 2008/632 Art.6, SI 2008/794 Reg.98, Reg.104, Reg.107, Reg.115, Sch.8 para.4, SI 2008/1052 Sch.2 para.2, Sch.2 para.5, SI 2008/1053 Sch.2 para.2, Sch.2 para.5, SI 2008/1054 Sch.2 para.2, Sch.2 para.5, SI 2008/2685 Sch.2
Part I, applied: SI 2008/1052 Sch.2 para.5, SI 2008/1054 Sch.2 para.5
Part I, referred to: SI 2008/579
Part II, applied: SI 2008/794 Sch.8 para.50
Part III, applied: SI 2008/794 Sch.8 para.50
Part IV, applied: SI 2008/794 Sch.8 para.50
Part V, applied: SI 2008/794 Sch.8 para.50

CAP.

1992–cont.

4. Social Security Contributions and Benefits Act 1992–*cont.*
Part VII, applied: SI 2008/529 Reg.120, Reg.137, SI 2008/1273 Reg.67, Reg.82, SI 2008/1582 Reg.120, Reg.137, SI 2008/3170 Reg.67, Reg.82
Part VIII, applied: SI 2008/794 Sch.6 para.5, Sch.8 para.35, Sch.9 para.23
Part IX, applied: SI 2008/18 Reg.32, SI 2008/529 Reg.46, SI 2008/1273 Reg.83G, Reg.30, SI 2008/1582 Reg.42, SI 2008/3170 Reg.30
Part X, applied: SI 2008/794 Sch.8 para.37
Part XI, applied: SI 2008/788 Sch.1, SI 2008/794 Sch.8 para.4
Part XII, applied: SI 2008/794 Reg.80, Sch.8 para.4
Part XIIZA, applied: SI 2008/794 Reg.82, Sch.8 para.4
Part XIIZB, applied: SI 2008/794 Reg.81, Sch.8 para.4
s.1, amended: 2008 c.30 s.135
s.1, applied: SI 2008/2682 Reg.9
s.3, see *Telent Plc v Revenue and Customs Commissioners* [2008] S.T.C. (S.C.D.) 202 (Sp Comm), John Clark
s.3, enabling: SI 2008/607, SI 2008/1431, SI 2008/2624
s.5, amended: 2008 c.16 s.1, Sch.2
s.5, repealed (in part): 2008 c.16 s.1, Sch.2
s.5, enabling: SI 2008/133
s.6, see *Telent Plc v Revenue and Customs Commissioners* [2008] S.T.C. (S.C.D.) 202 (Sp Comm), John Clark; see *Walker v United Kingdom (37212/02)* [2008] S.T.C. 786 (ECHR), Judge Casadevall (President)
s.6, applied: SI 2008/794 Reg.96, Reg.109
s.8, applied: SI 2008/794 Reg.109
s.11, amended: SI 2008/579 Art.2
s.11, applied: SI 2008/794 Reg.99
s.11, referred to: SI 2008/794 Reg.99
s.12, enabling: SI 2008/607, SI 2008/3099
s.13, amended: SI 2008/579 Art.3
s.13, enabling: SI 2008/607, SI 2008/3099
s.13A, added: 2008 c.30 s.135
s.15, amended: SI 2008/579 Art.4
s.15, applied: SI 2008/794 Reg.99
s.18, amended: SI 2008/579 Art.4
s.20, referred to: 2008 c.30 s.140
s.21, amended: 2008 c.30 Sch.4 para.2
s.22, amended: 2008 c.16 s.3, Sch.1 para.2
s.23, amended: 2008 c.16 Sch.1 para.3
s.30B, applied: SI 2008/632 Art.6
s.30C, applied: SI 2008/795 Reg.2
s.30C, enabling: SI 2008/2365
s.30DD, enabling: SI 2008/2365
s.30E, enabling: SI 2008/2365
s.35, applied: SI 2008/794 Reg.20
s.37, applied: SI 2008/794 Sch.8 para.17
s.37, referred to: SI 2008/2101 Art.3
s.39, amended: 2008 c.30 Sch.4 para.3

CAP.

1992–*cont.*

4. **Social Security Contributions and Benefits Act 1992**–*cont.*
s.39, applied: 2008 c.30 Sch.4 para.5
s.39A, applied: SI 2008/794 Sch.8 para.17
s.39A, referred to: SI 2008/2101 Art.3
s.39C, amended: 2008 c.30 Sch.4 para.4
s.44, amended: 2008 c.16 s.3, SI 2008/632 Art.4
s.44, applied: 2008 c.30 Sch.4 para.5
s.44A, amended: 2008 c.16 Sch.1 para.4, SI 2008/1554 Reg.47
s.44B, amended: 2008 c.16 Sch.1 para.5
s.44B, repealed (in part): 2008 c.16 Sch.2
s.45, amended: 2008 c.30 s.102
s.45, applied: 2008 c.30 Sch.4 para.5
s.45AA, added: 2008 c.30 Sch.4 para.5
s.46, amended: 2008 c.30 Sch.4 para.6
s.47, amended: 2008 c.30 s.102
s.47, applied: SI 2008/632 Art.6
s.48A, amended: 2008 c.30 Sch.4 para.7
s.48A, applied: 2008 c.30 Sch.4 para.5
s.48B, amended: 2008 c.30 Sch.4 para.8
s.48B, applied: 2008 c.30 Sch.4 para.5
s.48BB, amended: 2008 c.30 Sch.4 para.9
s.48C, amended: 2008 c.30 Sch.4 para.10
s.48C, applied: SI 2008/632 Art.6
s.51, amended: 2008 c.30 Sch.4 para.11
s.55A, varied: SI 2008/632 Art.4
s.62, referred to: 2008 c.30 s.102
s.64, referred to: SI 2008/2685 Sch.2
s.65, referred to: SI 2008/2685 Sch.2
s.68, applied: SI 2008/2685 r.25, Sch.2
s.69, applied: SI 2008/3270 Reg.2
s.70, applied: SI 2008/794 Sch.4 para.6, Sch.4 para.8
s.72, applied: SI 2008/794 Sch.4 para.4, Sch.4 para.7
s.72, referred to: SI 2008/2685 Sch.2
s.73, referred to: SI 2008/2685 Sch.2
s.77, applied: SI 2008/18 Reg.32, SI 2008/529 Reg.46, SI 2008/1273 Reg.83G, Reg.30, SI 2008/1582 Reg.42, SI 2008/3170 Reg.30
s.79, applied: SI 2008/632 Art.3
s.80, amended: SI 2008/632 Art.8
s.90, enabling: SI 2008/667
s.103, applied: SI 2008/2685 r.25, Sch.2
s.106, applied: SI 2008/794 Sch.8 para.50
s.107, applied: SI 2008/632 Art.6
s.108, applied: SI 2008/2685 r.25
s.108, enabling: SI 2008/14, SI 2008/1552
s.111, applied: SI 2008/2685 Sch.2
s.113, applied: SI 2008/794 Sch.4 para.7
s.113, enabling: SI 2008/667, SI 2008/840
s.117, enabling: SI 2008/703
s.122, amended: 2008 c.16 s.3
s.122, repealed (in part): 2008 c.16 s.3, Sch.2
s.122, enabling: SI 2008/14, SI 2008/133, SI 2008/667, SI 2008/840, SI 2008/1552

CAP.

1992–*cont.*

4. **Social Security Contributions and Benefits Act 1992**–*cont.*
s.123, enabling: SI 2008/586, SI 2008/698, SI 2008/1042, SI 2008/1599, SI 2008/1826, SI 2008/2111, SI 2008/2767, SI 2008/2824, SI 2008/3051, SI 2008/3140, SI 2008/3157, SI 2008/3195
s.124, applied: SI 2008/529 Reg.58, SI 2008/794 Reg.43, SI 2008/1273 Reg.37, SI 2008/1582 Reg.59, SI 2008/3170 Reg.37
s.124, enabling: SI 2008/698, SI 2008/1826, SI 2008/2767, SI 2008/3051
s.126, amended: SI 2008/632 Art.18
s.126, applied: SI 2008/794 Reg.43
s.127, referred to: SI 2008/794 Reg.43
s.129, referred to: SI 2008/2685 Sch.2
s.130, applied: SI 2008/529 Reg.58, SI 2008/1273 Reg.37, SI 2008/1582 Reg.59, SI 2008/3170 Reg.37
s.130, enabling: SI 2008/1082, SI 2008/2767, SI 2008/3157
s.130A, enabling: SI 2008/586, SI 2008/2767, SI 2008/2824
s.131, enabling: SI 2008/2767
s.134, enabling: SI 2008/959
s.135, enabling: SI 2008/698, SI 2008/1042, SI 2008/2428, SI 2008/2767, SI 2008/3195
s.136, enabling: SI 2008/698, SI 2008/1042, SI 2008/1599, SI 2008/2111, SI 2008/2428, SI 2008/2767, SI 2008/3140, SI 2008/3157
s.136A, enabling: SI 2008/1042, SI 2008/2767, SI 2008/3157
s.137, enabling: SI 2008/586, SI 2008/698, SI 2008/1042, SI 2008/1082, SI 2008/1599, SI 2008/1826, SI 2008/2111, SI 2008/2428, SI 2008/2767, SI 2008/2824, SI 2008/3051, SI 2008/3140, SI 2008/3157, SI 2008/3195
s.138, applied: SI 2008/2265 Reg.2
s.138, enabling: SI 2008/1778, SI 2008/2569
s.140A, added: 2008 c.14 s.131
s.140A, applied: SI 2008/3108 Reg.4, Reg.5
s.140A, enabling: SI 2008/3108
s.140B, added: 2008 c.14 s.131
s.140B, enabling: SI 2008/3108
s.145, enabling: SI 2008/3246, SI 2008/3247
s.147, enabling: SI 2008/3246
s.148, applied: SI 2008/3255 Art.2
s.148, enabling: SI 2008/3255
s.150, applied: SI 2008/3064 Art.2
s.150, enabling: SI 2008/3064
s.151, see *Revenue and Customs Commissioners v Thorn Baker Ltd* [2007] EWCA Civ 626, [2008] I.C.R. 46 (CA (Civ Div)), Auld, L.J.
s.153, enabling: SI 2008/1735

CAP.

1992–cont.

4. Social Security Contributions and Benefits Act 1992–*cont.*

s.157, amended: SI 2008/632 Art.9
s.171D, enabling: SI 2008/2365
s.171G, enabling: SI 2008/2365
s.175, enabling: SI 2008/14, SI 2008/133, SI 2008/408, SI 2008/498, SI 2008/586, SI 2008/607, SI 2008/636, SI 2008/667, SI 2008/698, SI 2008/703, SI 2008/840, SI 2008/1042, SI 2008/1431, SI 2008/1552, SI 2008/1599, SI 2008/1778, SI 2008/1826, SI 2008/2111, SI 2008/2365, SI 2008/2424, SI 2008/2428, SI 2008/2569, SI 2008/2624, SI 2008/2767, SI 2008/2824, SI 2008/3051, SI 2008/3108, SI 2008/3140, SI 2008/3157, SI 2008/3195, SI 2008/3255
s.176, amended: 2008 c.16 s.1, Sch.2
s.176, applied: SI 2008/3246, SI 2008/3255
Sch.1 para.1, amended: 2008 c.16 Sch.1 para.6, Sch.2
Sch.1 para.1, repealed (in part): 2008 c.16 Sch.1 para.6, Sch.2
Sch.1 para.6, enabling: SI 2008/636
Sch.1 para.7, enabling: SI 2008/636
Sch.3 Part I para.5, enabling: SI 2008/498
Sch.4 Part I, referred to: SI 2008/632 Art.3
Sch.4 Part I, substituted: SI 2008/632 Sch.1
Sch.4 Part I para.2, substituted: SI 2008/632 Sch.1
Sch.4 Part I para.2A, substituted: SI 2008/632 Sch.1
Sch.4 Part II, substituted: SI 2008/632 Sch.1
Sch.4 Part III, amended: SI 2008/798 Art.2
Sch.4 Part III, referred to: SI 2008/632 Art.3
Sch.4 Part III, substituted: SI 2008/632 Sch.1
Sch.4 Part IV, referred to: SI 2008/632 Art.3
Sch.4 Part IV, substituted: SI 2008/632 Sch.1
Sch.4 Part IV para.1A, substituted: SI 2008/632 Sch.1
Sch.4 Part IV para.2, substituted: SI 2008/632 Sch.1
Sch.4 Part IV para.5, substituted: SI 2008/632 Sch.1
Sch.4 Part IV para.6, substituted: SI 2008/632 Sch.1
Sch.4 Part V, referred to: SI 2008/632 Art.3
Sch.4 Part V, substituted: SI 2008/632 Sch.1
Sch.4A Part II para.2, amended: 2008 c.16 Sch.2
Sch.4A Part III para.5, amended: 2008 c.16 Sch.2
Sch.4A Part III para.7, amended: 2008 c.16 Sch.2
Sch.4A Part III para.8, repealed (in part): 2008 c.16 Sch.2
Sch.4B Part II para.2, substituted: 2008 c.30 Sch.4 para.12
Sch.4B Part II para.3, amended: 2008 c.30 Sch.4 para.12

CAP.

1992–cont.

4. Social Security Contributions and Benefits Act 1992–*cont.*

Sch.4B Part II para.5, amended: 2008 c.16 Sch.2, 2008 c.30 Sch.4 para.12
Sch.4B Part III para.6, amended: 2008 c.30 Sch.4 para.12
Sch.4B Part III para.8, amended: 2008 c.30 Sch.4 para.12
Sch.4B Part III para.9, amended: 2008 c.16 Sch.2, 2008 c.30 Sch.4 para.12
Sch.4B Part III para.10, amended: 2008 c.16 Sch.2, 2008 c.30 Sch.4 para.12
Sch.4B Part V para.12, amended: 2008 c.16 Sch.2, 2008 c.30 Sch.4 para.12, Sch.11 Part 2
Sch.4C para.1, added: 2008 c.30 Sch.3
Sch.4C para.2, added: 2008 c.30 Sch.3
Sch.4C para.3, added: 2008 c.30 Sch.3
Sch.4C para.4, added: 2008 c.30 Sch.3
Sch.4C para.5, added: 2008 c.30 Sch.3
Sch.4C para.6, added: 2008 c.30 Sch.3
Sch.4C para.7, added: 2008 c.30 Sch.3
Sch.4C para.8, added: 2008 c.30 Sch.3
Sch.4C para.9, added: 2008 c.30 Sch.3
Sch.5 paraA.1, varied: SI 2008/632 Art.4
Sch.5 para.1, varied: SI 2008/632 Art.4
Sch.5 para.2, varied: SI 2008/632 Art.4
Sch.5 para.2A, varied: SI 2008/632 Art.4
Sch.5 para.3, varied: SI 2008/632 Art.4
Sch.5 para.3A, varied: SI 2008/632 Art.4
Sch.5 para.3B, varied: SI 2008/632 Art.4
Sch.5 para.3C, varied: SI 2008/632 Art.4
Sch.5 para.4, varied: SI 2008/632 Art.4
Sch.5 para.5, varied: SI 2008/632 Art.4
Sch.5 para.5A, varied: SI 2008/632 Art.4
Sch.5 para.6, varied: SI 2008/632 Art.4
Sch.5 para.6A, varied: SI 2008/632 Art.4
Sch.5 para.7, varied: SI 2008/632 Art.4
Sch.5 para.7A, varied: SI 2008/632 Art.4
Sch.5 para.7B, varied: SI 2008/632 Art.4
Sch.5 para.7C, varied: SI 2008/632 Art.4
Sch.5 para.8, varied: SI 2008/632 Art.4
Sch.5 para.9, varied: SI 2008/632 Art.4
Sch.5A para.2, varied: SI 2008/632 Art.4
Sch.6, applied: SI 2008/2685 r.25, Sch.2
Sch.7 Part I para.2, enabling: SI 2008/2365
Sch.7 Part I para.3, amended: 2008 c.30 Sch.4 para.13
Sch.7 Part I para.4, amended: SI 2008/699 Art.2
Sch.7 Part I para.4, enabling: SI 2008/699
Sch.7 Part II para.9, applied: SI 2008/632 Art.6
Sch.7 Part V para.13, applied: SI 2008/632 Art.4, Art.6
Sch.7 Part V para.13, varied: SI 2008/632 Art.4
Sch.8, applied: SI 2008/2685 Sch.2
Sch.8 Part I para.2, amended: SI 2008/632 Art.7

CAP.

1992–cont.

4. Social Security Contributions and Benefits Act 1992–*cont.*
Sch.8 Part I para.2, enabling: SI 2008/721
Sch.8 Part I para.6, amended: SI 2008/632 Art.7
Sch.11 para.2, see *Revenue and Customs Commissioners v Thorn Baker Ltd* [2007] EWCA Civ 626, [2008] I.C.R. 46 (CA (Civ Div)), Auld, L.J.
Sch.11 para.2, amended: SI 2008/1554 Reg.44

5. Social Security Administration Act 1992
applied: SI 2008/726 Art.2
s.1, applied: SI 2008/795 Reg.4
s.1, enabling: SI 2008/441, SI 2008/2667
s.2A, amended: 2008 c.25 Sch.1 para.45
s.2A, enabling: SI 2008/2928, SI 2008/3051
s.2AA, amended: 2008 c.25 Sch.1 para.46
s.2AA, enabling: SI 2008/759
s.2B, amended: SI 2008/2833 Sch.3 para.102
s.2B, applied: SI 2008/2928 Reg.8
s.2B, enabling: SI 2008/2928, SI 2008/3051
s.2C, amended: 2008 c.25 Sch.1 para.47
s.5, amended: 2008 c.14 s.132
s.5, applied: SI 2008/794 Reg.47, Reg.66
s.5, enabling: SI 2008/586, SI 2008/667, SI 2008/698, SI 2008/794, SI 2008/959, SI 2008/1042, SI 2008/1082, SI 2008/1599, SI 2008/2299, SI 2008/2424, SI 2008/2667, SI 2008/2767, SI 2008/2824, SI 2008/2987, SI 2008/3109
s.6, enabling: SI 2008/959, SI 2008/1042, SI 2008/1082, SI 2008/2299, SI 2008/2424, SI 2008/2767, SI 2008/2824, SI 2008/2987
s.12, enabling: SI 2008/2265
s.12A, added: 2008 c.14 s.132
s.12A, disapplied: SI 2008/3109 Reg.5
s.12A, enabling: SI 2008/3109
s.71, see *R. (on the application of Balding) v Secretary of State for Work and Pensions* [2007] EWCA Civ 1327, [2008] 1 W.L.R. 564 (CA (Civ Div)), Mummery, L.J.
s.71, amended: 2008 c.14 s.132, SI 2008/2833 Sch.3 para.103
s.71, varied: 2008 c.14 s.132
s.74, amended: SI 2008/2428 Reg.23
s.74A, applied: SI 2008/794 Reg.121, Reg.130
s.75, enabling: SI 2008/586, SI 2008/1042, SI 2008/1082, SI 2008/2824
s.76, enabling: SI 2008/2824
s.105, amended: 2008 c.6 s.45
s.106, repealed (in part): 2008 c.6 Sch.8
s.107, repealed: 2008 c.6 Sch.8
s.108, amended: 2008 c.6 Sch.7 para.2
s.109A, referred to: SI 2008/463 Reg.2
s.110A, applied: SI 2008/463 Reg.2

CAP.

1992–cont.

5. Social Security Administration Act 1992–*cont.*
s.110A, enabling: SI 2008/463
s.110ZA, amended: 2008 c.9 Sch.36 para.84
s.112, see *R. (on the application of Pearson) v Greenwich Magistrates' Court* [2008] EWHC 300 (Admin), [2008] R.V.R. 234 (DC), Maurice Kay, L.J.
s.113, enabling: SI 2008/2299
s.113C, added: 2008 c.14 s.133
s.115A, applied: SI 2008/1185 Sch.3 para.5
s.116A, applied: SI 2008/463 Reg.3
s.116A, enabling: SI 2008/463
s.118, repealed (in part): 2008 c.9 Sch.44 para.4
s.121A, repealed: 2008 c.9 Sch.43 para.2
s.121B, repealed: 2008 c.9 Sch.43 para.14
s.121E, amended: 2008 c.6 Sch.7 para.2, 2008 c.14 s.132
s.121F, amended: 2008 c.6 Sch.7 para.2, 2008 c.14 s.132
s.122, amended: 2008 c.6 Sch.7 para.2, Sch.8
s.122C, enabling: SI 2008/2299
s.122E, enabling: SI 2008/959, SI 2008/2299
s.128A, enabling: SI 2008/959
s.130, enabling: SI 2008/1735
s.132A, enabling: SI 2008/2678
s.134, see *Hanoman v Southwark LBC* [2008] EWCA Civ 624, Times, June 24, 2008 (CA (Civ Div)), Sir Anthony Clarke, M.R.
s.134, enabling: SI 2008/1042, SI 2008/2824, SI 2008/3157
s.139, enabling: SI 2008/3157
s.140B, enabling: SI 2008/196, SI 2008/695, SI 2008/1167, SI 2008/1649
s.140C, enabling: SI 2008/196, SI 2008/1167, SI 2008/1649
s.140F, enabling: SI 2008/196, SI 2008/695, SI 2008/1649
s.141, applied: SI 2008/579, SI 2008/703
s.141, enabling: SI 2008/579
s.142, enabling: SI 2008/579
s.148, applied: 2008 c.30 s.14, SI 2008/730, SI 2008/909
s.148, enabling: SI 2008/730
s.148A, enabling: SI 2008/726
s.148AB, added: 2008 c.30 Sch.4 para.14
s.150, applied: SI 2008/632, SI 2008/667, SI 2008/711, SI 2008/797, SI 2008/798
s.150, referred to: SI 2008/799
s.150, varied: SI 2008/632 Art.4, SI 2008/3270 Reg.2
s.150, enabling: SI 2008/632, SI 2008/797, SI 2008/798
s.150A, applied: SI 2008/632, SI 2008/667
s.150A, enabling: SI 2008/632
s.151, applied: SI 2008/711
s.151, enabling: SI 2008/632

CAP.

1992–cont.

5. **Social Security Administration Act 1992**–*cont.*
   s.155, disapplied: SI 2008/667 Reg.2, SI 2008/840 Reg.2
   s.155, enabling: SI 2008/667, SI 2008/840
   s.171, applied: SI 2008/14
   s.172, applied: SI 2008/14, SI 2008/1552, SI 2008/2424, SI 2008/2783
   s.173, applied: SI 2008/441, SI 2008/2667
   s.176, applied: SI 2008/196, SI 2008/463, SI 2008/586, SI 2008/637, SI 2008/695, SI 2008/959, SI 2008/1042, SI 2008/1082, SI 2008/1649, SI 2008/2299, SI 2008/2424, SI 2008/2428, SI 2008/2667, SI 2008/2824, SI 2008/2987
   s.182C, enabling: SI 2008/223
   s.189, applied: SI 2008/196, SI 2008/695, SI 2008/1649
   s.189, enabling: SI 2008/196, SI 2008/223, SI 2008/441, SI 2008/463, SI 2008/586, SI 2008/632, SI 2008/637, SI 2008/667, SI 2008/695, SI 2008/698, SI 2008/730, SI 2008/759, SI 2008/797, SI 2008/798, SI 2008/840, SI 2008/1042, SI 2008/1082, SI 2008/1167, SI 2008/1596, SI 2008/1599, SI 2008/1649, SI 2008/2265, SI 2008/2299, SI 2008/2365, SI 2008/2424, SI 2008/2667, SI 2008/2678, SI 2008/2767, SI 2008/2824, SI 2008/2928, SI 2008/2987, SI 2008/3051, SI 2008/3109
   s.190, applied: SI 2008/579, SI 2008/632, SI 2008/711, SI 2008/797, SI 2008/798
   s.191, amended: 2008 c.17 Sch.8 para.61
   s.191, referred to: SSI 2008/81 Reg.2
   s.191, enabling: SI 2008/441, SI 2008/463, SI 2008/586, SI 2008/667, SI 2008/759, SI 2008/840, SI 2008/1042, SI 2008/1082, SI 2008/1599, SI 2008/2265, SI 2008/2299, SI 2008/2424, SI 2008/2667, SI 2008/2824, SI 2008/2928, SI 2008/2987, SI 2008/3051, SI 2008/3109
   Sch.3A para.1, added: 2008 c.14 s.133
   Sch.3A para.2, added: 2008 c.14 s.133
   Sch.3A para.3, added: 2008 c.14 s.133
   Sch.3A para.4, added: 2008 c.14 s.133
   Sch.3A para.5, added: 2008 c.14 s.133
   Sch.4 Part I, amended: SI 2008/2833 Sch.3 para.104
   Sch.4 Part II para.3, amended: SI 2008/2833 Sch.3 para.104
   Sch.4 Part II para.3ZA, added: SI 2008/2833 Sch.3 para.104
   Sch.9 para.1, enabling: SI 2008/721
6. **Social Security (Consequential Provisions) Act 1992**
   Sch.2 para.63, repealed (in part): SI 2008/2833 Sch.3 para.228
7. **Social Security Contributions and Benefits (Northern Ireland) Act 1992**
   applied: SI 2008/794 Sch.8 para.5
   Part XI, applied: SI 2008/794 Sch.8 para.5

CAP.

1992–cont.

7. **Social Security Contributions and Benefits (Northern Ireland) Act 1992**–*cont.*
   Part XII, applied: SI 2008/794 Sch.8 para.5
   Part XIIZA, applied: SI 2008/794 Sch.8 para.5
   Part XIIZB, applied: SI 2008/794 Sch.8 para.5
   s.1, amended: 2008 c.30 s.136
   s.3, enabling: SI 2008/607
   s.5, amended: 2008 c.16 s.2, Sch.2
   s.5, repealed (in part): 2008 c.16 s.2, Sch.2
   s.5, enabling: SI 2008/133
   s.11, amended: SI 2008/579 Art.2
   s.12, enabling: SI 2008/607, SI 2008/3099
   s.13, amended: SI 2008/579 Art.3
   s.13, enabling: SI 2008/607, SI 2008/3099
   s.13A, added: 2008 c.30 s.136
   s.15, amended: SI 2008/579 Art.4
   s.18, amended: SI 2008/579 Art.4
   s.20, referred to: 2008 c.30 s.140
   s.73, applied: SI 2008/1741 Reg.57
   s.113, enabling: SI 2008/840
   s.117, enabling: SI 2008/703
   s.121, enabling: SI 2008/133, SI 2008/840
   s.136A, added: 2008 c.14 s.134
   s.136A, applied: SI 2008/3108 Reg.4
   s.136A, enabling: SI 2008/3108
   s.136B, added: 2008 c.14 s.134
   s.136B, enabling: SI 2008/3108
   s.141, enabling: SI 2008/3246, SI 2008/3247
   s.171, enabling: SI 2008/133, SI 2008/607, SI 2008/636, SI 2008/703, SI 2008/840, SI 2008/3108
   s.172, amended: 2008 c.16 s.2
   s.172, applied: SI 2008/3246
   s.173, enabling: SI 2008/3246
   Sch.1 para.6, enabling: SI 2008/636
   Sch.1 para.7, enabling: SI 2008/636
8. **Social Security Administration (Northern Ireland) Act 1992**
   s.5, amended: 2008 c.14 s.135
   s.5, enabling: SI 2008/3109
   s.10A, added: 2008 c.14 s.135
   s.10A, enabling: SI 2008/3109
   s.69, amended: 2008 c.14 s.135
   s.69, varied: 2008 c.14 s.135
   s.104ZA, amended: 2008 c.9 Sch.36 para.85
   s.107C, added: 2008 c.14 s.136
   s.115D, amended: 2008 c.14 s.135
   s.115E, amended: 2008 c.14 s.135
   s.129, applied: SI 2008/703
   s.129, enabling: SI 2008/579
   s.132, applied: SI 2008/797
   s.132, enabling: SI 2008/797, SI 2008/799
   s.135, disapplied: SI 2008/840 Reg.2
   s.135, enabling: SI 2008/840
   s.165, applied: SI 2008/797
   s.165, enabling: SI 2008/579, SI 2008/797, SI 2008/799, SI 2008/840, SI 2008/3109

CAP.

1992–cont.

8. Social Security Administration (Northern Ireland) Act 1992–*cont.*

s.166, applied: SI 2008/579, SI 2008/797, SI 2008/799

s.167, enabling: SI 2008/840, SI 2008/3109

Sch.3A para.1, added: 2008 c.14 s.136

Sch.3A para.2, added: 2008 c.14 s.136

Sch.3A para.3, added: 2008 c.14 s.136

Sch.3A para.4, added: 2008 c.14 s.136

Sch.3A para.5, added: 2008 c.14 s.136

Sch.4 Part III para.5, amended: SI 2008/799 Art.2

12. Taxation of Chargeable Gains Act 1992

see *Collins v Revenue and Customs Commissioners* [2008] S.T.C. (S.C.D.) 718 (Sp Comm), Theodore Wallace; see *Corbally-Stourton v Revenue and Customs Commissioners* [2008] S.T.C. (S.C.D.) 907 (Sp Comm), Charles Hellier

applied: 2008 c.9 Sch.7 para.171, 2008 c.17 Sch.7 para.7, 2008 c.18 Sch.13 para.11, Sch.13 para.22

referred to: 2008 c.9 Sch.3 para.7, Sch.3 para.8

Part V c.III, applied: 2008 c.9 Sch.3 para.7, Sch.3 para.8

s.2, amended: 2008 c.9 Sch.2 para.2, Sch.2 para.24

s.2, repealed (in part): 2008 c.9 Sch.2 para.24

s.2A, repealed: 2008 c.9 Sch.2 para.25

s.3, amended: 2008 c.9 Sch.2 para.26, Sch.7 para.56, SI 2008/708 Art.2

s.3, enabling: SI 2008/708

s.3A, amended: 2008 c.9 Sch.2 para.27, Sch.7 para.57

s.3A, repealed (in part): 2008 c.9 Sch.2 para.27

s.4, substituted: 2008 c.9 s.8

s.6, repealed: 2008 c.9 Sch.2 para.3

s.9, amended: 2008 c.9 s.24

s.9, repealed (in part): 2008 c.9 Sch.7 para.58

s.10A, amended: 2008 c.9 Sch.7 para.59

s.10A, disapplied: 2008 c.9 Sch.7 para.84

s.12, applied: 2008 c.9 Sch.7 para.84

s.12, substituted: 2008 c.9 Sch.7 para.60

s.12, varied: 2008 c.9 Sch.7 para.84

s.13, see *Coombes v Revenue and Customs Commissioners* [2007] EWHC 3160 (Ch), [2008] S.T.C. 2984 (Ch D), Sir Donald Rattee

s.13, amended: 2008 c.9 Sch.7 para.103

s.13, applied: 2008 c.9 Sch.7 para.126, Sch.7 para.127

s.13, repealed (in part): 2008 c.9 Sch.2 para.4, Sch.2 para.28

s.14, applied: 2008 c.9 Sch.7 para.126

s.14A, added: 2008 c.9 Sch.7 para.104

s.16, repealed (in part): 2008 c.9 Sch.7 para.61

s.16ZA, added: 2008 c.9 Sch.7 para.62

CAP.

1992–cont.

12. Taxation of Chargeable Gains Act 1992–*cont.*

s.16ZB, added: 2008 c.9 Sch.7 para.62

s.16ZC, added: 2008 c.9 Sch.7 para.62

s.16ZD, added: 2008 c.9 Sch.7 para.62

s.17, disapplied: 2008 c.17 Sch.7 para.7, 2008 c.18 Sch.13 para.39

s.18, see *Kellogg Brown & Root Holdings Ltd v Revenue and Customs Commissioners* [2008] S.T.C. (S.C.D.) 928 (Sp Comm), Dr John F Avery Jones

s.24, see *Fletcher v Revenue and Customs Commissioners* [2008] S.T.C. (S.C.D.) 1219 (Sp Comm), Howard M Nowlan

s.25A, amended: 2008 c.9 Sch.20 para.5

s.26A, added: 2008 c.9 s.39

s.28, see *Burt v Revenue and Customs Commissioners* [2008] S.T.C. (S.C.D.) 814 (Sp Comm), Julian Ghosh Q.C.; see *Kellogg Brown & Root Holdings Ltd v Revenue and Customs Commissioners* [2008] S.T.C. (S.C.D.) 928 (Sp Comm), Dr John F Avery Jones; see *Underwood v Revenue and Customs Commissioners* [2008] EWHC 108 (Ch), [2008] S.T.C. 1138 (Ch D), Briggs, J.

s.30, applied: 2008 c.17 Sch.7 para.8, 2008 c.18 Sch.13 para.41

s.35, amended: 2008 c.9 Sch.2 para.58, 2008 c.17 Sch.7 para.9, 2008 c.18 Sch.13 para.46

s.35, repealed (in part): 2008 c.9 Sch.2 para.58, SI 2008/3002 Sch.1 para.42, Sch.3

s.35A, added: 2008 c.9 Sch.2 para.59

s.36, amended: 2008 c.9 Sch.2 para.73

s.37, see *Drummond v Revenue and Customs Commissioners* [2008] EWHC 1758 (Ch), [2008] S.T.C. 2707 (Ch D), Norris, J.

s.38, see *Drummond v Revenue and Customs Commissioners* [2008] EWHC 1758 (Ch), [2008] S.T.C. 2707 (Ch D), Norris, J.

s.43, applied: 2008 c.9 Sch.7 para.126

s.52A, added: 2008 c.9 Sch.2 para.78

s.53, amended: 2008 c.9 Sch.2 para.79

s.53, repealed (in part): 2008 c.9 Sch.2 para.79

s.54, amended: 2008 c.9 Sch.2 para.80

s.54, repealed (in part): 2008 c.9 Sch.2 para.80

s.55, amended: 2008 c.9 Sch.2 para.60

s.59, amended: 2008 c.9 s.58

s.60, see *Coombes v Revenue and Customs Commissioners* [2007] EWHC 3160 (Ch), [2008] S.T.C. 2984 (Ch D), Sir Donald Rattee

s.62, see *Wills v Gibbs* [2007] EWHC 3361 (Ch), [2008] S.T.C. 786 (Ch D), Rimer, J.

s.62, amended: 2008 c.9 Sch.2 para.29

s.62, repealed (in part): 2008 c.9 Sch.2 para.29

CAP.

1992–cont.

12. **Taxation of Chargeable Gains Act 1992**–*cont.*

s.68, see *Coombes v Revenue and Customs Commissioners* [2007] EWHC 3160 (Ch), [2008] S.T.C. 2984 (Ch D), Sir Donald Rattee

s.69, see *Jasmine Trustees Ltd v Wells & Hind (A Firm)* [2007] EWHC 38 (Ch), [2008] Ch. 194 (Ch D), Mann, J.

s.73, amended: 2008 c.9 Sch.2 para.61

s.77, see *Smallwood v Revenue and Customs Commissioners* [2008] S.T.C. (S.C.D.) 629 (Sp Comm), AN Brice

s.77, repealed: 2008 c.9 Sch.2 para.5

s.78, repealed: 2008 c.9 Sch.2 para.5

s.79, repealed: 2008 c.9 Sch.2 para.5

s.85, amended: 2008 c.9 Sch.7 para.107

s.85A, amended: 2008 c.9 Sch.7 para.129

s.86, see *Coombes v Revenue and Customs Commissioners* [2007] EWHC 3160 (Ch), [2008] S.T.C. 2984 (Ch D), Sir Donald Rattee; see *Smallwood v Revenue and Customs Commissioners* [2008] S.T.C. (S.C.D.) 629 (Sp Comm), AN Brice

s.86, amended: 2008 c.9 Sch.2 para.30

s.86A, amended: 2008 c.9 Sch.2 para.31

s.86A, repealed (in part): 2008 c.9 Sch.2 para.31

s.87, applied: 2008 c.9 Sch.7 para.100, Sch.7 para.116, Sch.7 para.117, Sch.7 para.118, Sch.7 para.120, Sch.7 para.122, Sch.7 para.124, Sch.7 para.125, Sch.7 para.126, Sch.7 para.127, Sch.7 para.155

s.87, substituted: 2008 c.9 Sch.7 para.108

s.87, varied: 2008 c.9 Sch.7 para.120

s.87A, applied: 2008 c.9 Sch.7 para.101, Sch.7 para.102, Sch.7 para.116, Sch.7 para.125, Sch.7 para.148

s.87B, applied: 2008 c.9 Sch.7 para.125

s.87C, applied: 2008 c.9 Sch.7 para.125

s.87C, disapplied: 2008 c.9 Sch.7 para.119

s.88, amended: 2008 c.9 Sch.7 para.109

s.88, applied: 2008 c.9 Sch.7 para.117, Sch.7 para.125

s.88, repealed (in part): 2008 c.9 Sch.2 para.6, Sch.7 para.109

s.89, amended: 2008 c.9 Sch.7 para.110

s.89, applied: 2008 c.9 Sch.7 para.100, Sch.7 para.120, Sch.7 para.122, Sch.7 para.123, Sch.7 para.124, Sch.7 para.125, Sch.7 para.126, Sch.7 para.127, Sch.7 para.155

s.90, applied: 2008 c.9 Sch.7 para.102, Sch.7 para.120, Sch.7 para.121, Sch.7 para.126, Sch.7 para.127

s.90, substituted: 2008 c.9 Sch.7 para.111

s.91, amended: 2008 c.9 Sch.7 para.112

s.91, repealed (in part): 2008 c.9 Sch.7 para.112

s.92, repealed: 2008 c.9 Sch.7 para.113

s.93, repealed: 2008 c.9 Sch.7 para.113

s.94, repealed: 2008 c.9 Sch.7 para.113

CAP.

1992–cont.

12. **Taxation of Chargeable Gains Act 1992**–*cont.*

s.95, repealed: 2008 c.9 Sch.7 para.113

s.104, amended: 2008 c.9 Sch.2 para.85

s.105, amended: 2008 c.9 Sch.2 para.86

s.106A, amended: 2008 c.9 Sch.2 para.87

s.106A, repealed (in part): 2008 c.9 Sch.2 para.87

s.107, amended: 2008 c.9 Sch.2 para.88

s.108, amended: 2008 c.9 Sch.2 para.89

s.109, amended: 2008 c.9 Sch.2 para.90

s.110, amended: 2008 c.9 Sch.2 para.91

s.110A, repealed: 2008 c.9 Sch.2 para.92

s.112, amended: 2008 c.9 Sch.2 para.93

s.113, amended: 2008 c.9 Sch.2 para.94

s.114, amended: 2008 c.9 Sch.2 para.95

s.116, amended: SI 2008/1579 Sch.1 para.2

s.116, applied: 2008 c.9 Sch.3 para.5, Sch.3 para.7

s.116, referred to: 2008 c.9 Sch.3 para.7

s.117, see *Harding v Revenue and Customs Commissioners* [2008] EWCA Civ 1164, [2008] S.T.C. 3499 (CA (Civ Div)), Rix, L.J.; see *Harding v Revenue and Customs Commissioners* [2008] EWHC 99 (Ch), [2008] S.T.C. 1965 (Ch D), Briggs, J.

s.119A, amended: 2008 c.9 Sch.7 para.63

s.119B, added: 2008 c.9 Sch.7 para.64

s.126, see *Fletcher v Revenue and Customs Commissioners* [2008] S.T.C. (S.C.D.) 1219 (Sp Comm), Howard M Nowlan

s.140A, varied: SI 2008/1579 Sch.4 para.2

s.140C, varied: SI 2008/1579 Sch.4 para.2

s.140E, varied: SI 2008/1579 Sch.4 para.2

s.140F, amended: SI 2008/1579 Sch.1 para.3

s.140F, varied: SI 2008/1579 Sch.4 para.2

s.140GA, added: SI 2008/1579 Sch.1 para.4

s.140I, amended: SI 2008/1579 Sch.1 para.5

s.140J, amended: SI 2008/1579 Sch.1 para.6

s.140L, amended: SI 2008/1579 Sch.1 para.7

s.145, amended: 2008 c.9 Sch.2 para.81

s.145, repealed (in part): 2008 c.9 Sch.2 para.81

s.149AA, amended: 2008 c.9 s.49

s.150A, amended: 2008 c.9 Sch.1 para.48

s.150D, repealed: 2008 c.9 Sch.2 para.32

s.151, applied: SI 2008/1934

s.151, enabling: SI 2008/1934, SI 2008/3025

s.154, varied: 2008 c.18 Sch.13 para.12

s.164A, see *Pegasus Management Holdings SCA v Ernst & Young (A Firm)* [2008] EWHC 2720 (Ch), [2008] B.T.C. 856 (Ch D), Lewison, J.

s.164N, see *Pegasus Management Holdings SCA v Ernst & Young (A Firm)* [2008] EWHC 2720 (Ch), [2008] B.T.C. 856 (Ch D), Lewison, J.

s.165, amended: 2008 c.9 Sch.2 para.33

s.165A, added: 2008 c.9 Sch.2 para.34

s.169H, added: 2008 c.9 Sch.3 para.2

s.169I, added: 2008 c.9 Sch.3 para.2

CAP.

1992–cont.

12. Taxation of Chargeable Gains Act 1992–*cont.*

s.169J, added: 2008 c.9 Sch.3 para.2
s.169K, added: 2008 c.9 Sch.3 para.2
s.169L, added: 2008 c.9 Sch.3 para.2
s.169M, added: 2008 c.9 Sch.3 para.2
s.169N, added: 2008 c.9 Sch.3 para.2
s.169N, applied: 2008 c.9 Sch.3 para.7, Sch.3 para.8
s.169O, added: 2008 c.9 Sch.3 para.2
s.169P, added: 2008 c.9 Sch.3 para.2
s.169P, applied: 2008 c.9 Sch.3 para.6
s.169Q, added: 2008 c.9 Sch.3 para.2
s.169Q, applied: 2008 c.9 Sch.3 para.5
s.169R, added: 2008 c.9 Sch.3 para.2
s.169S, added: 2008 c.9 Sch.3 para.2
s.170, see *Limitgood Ltd v Revenue and Customs Commissioners* [2008] EWHC 19 (Ch), [2008] S.T.C. 361 (Ch D), Blackburne, J.
s.170, applied: 2008 c.9 Sch.26 para.16
s.171, applied: 2008 c.9 Sch.7 para.126
s.175, amended: 2008 c.9 Sch.2 para.62
s.179, see *Johnston Publishing (North) Ltd v Revenue and Customs Commissioners* [2008] EWCA Civ 858, [2008] S.T.C. 3116 (CA (Civ Div)), Tuckey, L.J.; see *Limitgood Ltd v Revenue and Customs Commissioners* [2008] EWHC 19 (Ch), [2008] S.T.C. 361 (Ch D), Blackburne, J.
s.179, applied: 2008 c.18 Sch.13 para.31
s.203, amended: 2008 c.9 Sch.39 para.29
s.210A, amended: 2008 c.9 Sch.17 para.13, Sch.17 para.18
s.211ZA, amended: SI 2008/381 Art.28
s.213, amended: SI 2008/381 Art.29
s.213, repealed (in part): SI 2008/381 Art.29
s.214C, repealed: 2008 c.9 Sch.2 para.35
s.218, amended: 2008 c.17 Sch.9 para.17
s.218, varied: SI 2008/2839 Sch.1 para.1
s.219, amended: 2008 c.17 Sch.8 para.62, Sch.9 para.18
s.219, varied: SI 2008/2839 Sch.1 para.1
s.228, amended: 2008 c.9 Sch.2 para.36
s.241, amended: 2008 c.9 Sch.2 para.37, Sch.3 para.3
s.251, see *Fletcher v Revenue and Customs Commissioners* [2008] S.T.C. (S.C.D.) 1219 (Sp Comm), Howard M Nowlan
s.253, amended: 2008 c.9 Sch.2 para.38, Sch.39 para.30
s.259, amended: 2008 c.17 Sch.9 para.19
s.261C, repealed (in part): 2008 c.9 Sch.2 para.39
s.263D, amended: 2008 c.9 Sch.23 para.11
s.274, amended: 2008 c.9 Sch.4 para.8
s.277, see *Smallwood v Revenue and Customs Commissioners* [2008] S.T.C. (S.C.D.) 629 (Sp Comm), AN Brice
s.279, amended: 2008 c.9 Sch.2 para.40, Sch.39 para.31

CAP.

1992–cont.

12. Taxation of Chargeable Gains Act 1992–*cont.*

s.279A, amended: 2008 c.9 Sch.2 para.41
s.279B, amended: 2008 c.9 Sch.2 para.42
s.279C, amended: 2008 c.9 Sch.2 para.43
s.279C, repealed (in part): 2008 c.9 Sch.2 para.43
s.284B, repealed (in part): 2008 c.9 Sch.2 para.44
s.286, see *Kellogg Brown & Root Holdings Ltd v Revenue and Customs Commissioners* [2008] S.T.C. (S.C.D.) 928 (Sp Comm), Dr John F Avery Jones
s.288, amended: 2008 c.9 Sch.2 para.63, Sch.2 para.101, SI 2008/3002 Sch.1 para.43
Sch.A1 para.1, repealed: 2008 c.9 Sch.2 para.45
Sch.A1 para.2, repealed: 2008 c.9 Sch.2 para.45
Sch.A1 para.3, repealed: 2008 c.9 Sch.2 para.45
Sch.A1 para.4, repealed: 2008 c.9 Sch.2 para.45
Sch.A1 para.5, repealed: 2008 c.9 Sch.2 para.45
Sch.A1 para.6, repealed: 2008 c.9 Sch.2 para.45
Sch.A1 para.6A, repealed: 2008 c.9 Sch.2 para.45
Sch.A1 para.7, repealed: 2008 c.9 Sch.2 para.45
Sch.A1 para.8, repealed: 2008 c.9 Sch.2 para.45
Sch.A1 para.9, repealed: 2008 c.9 Sch.2 para.45
Sch.A1 para.10, repealed: 2008 c.9 Sch.2 para.45
Sch.A1 para.11, repealed: 2008 c.9 Sch.2 para.45
Sch.A1 para.11A, repealed: 2008 c.9 Sch.2 para.45
Sch.A1 para.12, repealed: 2008 c.9 Sch.2 para.45
Sch.A1 para.13, repealed: 2008 c.9 Sch.2 para.45
Sch.A1 para.14, repealed: 2008 c.9 Sch.2 para.45
Sch.A1 para.15, repealed: 2008 c.9 Sch.2 para.45
Sch.A1 para.16, repealed: 2008 c.9 Sch.2 para.45
Sch.A1 para.17, repealed: 2008 c.9 Sch.2 para.45
Sch.A1 para.18, repealed: 2008 c.9 Sch.2 para.45
Sch.A1 para.19, repealed: 2008 c.9 Sch.2 para.45
Sch.A1 para.20, repealed: 2008 c.9 Sch.2 para.45

CAP.

1992–*cont.*

12. **Taxation of Chargeable Gains Act 1992**–*cont.*

Sch.A1 para.21, repealed: 2008 c.9 Sch.2 para.45

Sch.A1 para.22, repealed: 2008 c.9 Sch.2 para.45

Sch.A1 para.22A, repealed: 2008 c.9 Sch.2 para.45

Sch.A1 para.22B, repealed: 2008 c.9 Sch.2 para.45

Sch.A1 para.23, repealed: 2008 c.9 Sch.2 para.45

Sch.A1 para.24, repealed: 2008 c.9 Sch.2 para.45

Sch.2 Part I para.1, repealed (in part): 2008 c.9 Sch.2 para.64

Sch.2 Part I para.4, amended: 2008 c.9 Sch.2 para.64

Sch.2 Part I para.4, repealed (in part): 2008 c.9 Sch.2 para.64

Sch.2 Part III para.17, amended: 2008 c.9 Sch.2 para.64

Sch.2 Part III para.17, repealed (in part): 2008 c.9 Sch.2 para.64

Sch.2 Part IV para.22, repealed: 2008 c.9 Sch.2 para.64

Sch.3 para.1, amended: 2008 c.9 Sch.2 para.65

Sch.3 para.2, amended: 2008 c.9 Sch.2 para.65

Sch.4, applied: 2008 c.9 Sch.2 para.76

Sch.4B, applied: 2008 c.9 Sch.7 para.120, Sch.7 para.121

Sch.4B, amended: 2008 c.9 Sch.2 para.8

Sch.4C, applied: 2008 c.9 Sch.7 para.100, Sch.7 para.120, Sch.7 para.121, Sch.7 para.126, Sch.7 para.153, Sch.7 para.155

Sch.4 paraA.1, added: 2008 c.9 Sch.2 para.74

Sch.4 para.2, amended: 2008 c.9 Sch.2 para.74

Sch.4 para.4, amended: 2008 c.9 Sch.2 para.74

Sch.4 para.7, amended: 2008 c.9 Sch.2 para.66

Sch.4 para.9, amended: 2008 c.9 Sch.2 para.74

Sch.4 para.9, repealed (in part): 2008 c.9 Sch.2 para.74

Sch.4A para.7, amended: 2008 c.9 Sch.2 para.7

Sch.4A para.12, amended: 2008 c.9 Sch.2 para.7

Sch.4A para.13, see *Domain Dynamics (Holdings) Ltd v Revenue and Customs Commissioners* [2008] S.T.C. (S.C.D.) 1136 (Sp Comm), AN Brice

Sch.4B para.1, amended: 2008 c.9 Sch.2 para.8

Sch.4B para.3, amended: 2008 c.9 Sch.2 para.8, Sch.7 para.130

CAP.

1992–*cont.*

12. **Taxation of Chargeable Gains Act 1992**–*cont.*

Sch.4B para.3, repealed (in part): 2008 c.9 Sch.2 para.8

Sch.4C para.1, amended: 2008 c.9 Sch.7 para.132

Sch.4C para.1A, added: 2008 c.9 Sch.7 para.133

Sch.4C para.4, amended: 2008 c.9 Sch.7 para.134

Sch.4C para.5, amended: 2008 c.9 Sch.7 para.135

Sch.4C para.6, amended: 2008 c.9 Sch.2 para.47

Sch.4C para.6, repealed (in part): 2008 c.9 Sch.2 para.9, Sch.2 para.47

Sch.4C para.7A, repealed: 2008 c.9 Sch.7 para.136

Sch.4C para.7B, substituted: 2008 c.9 Sch.7 para.137

Sch.4C para.7B, varied: 2008 c.9 Sch.7 para.152

Sch.4C para.8, applied: 2008 c.9 Sch.7 para.122, Sch.7 para.126, Sch.7 para.127, Sch.7 para.148, Sch.7 para.150, Sch.7 para.151, Sch.7 para.154

Sch.4C para.8, substituted: 2008 c.9 Sch.7 para.138

Sch.4C para.8A, applied: 2008 c.9 Sch.7 para.126

Sch.4C para.8AA, added: 2008 c.9 Sch.7 para.139

Sch.4C para.8B, repealed: 2008 c.9 Sch.7 para.140

Sch.4C para.8C, repealed: 2008 c.9 Sch.7 para.140

Sch.4C para.9, applied: 2008 c.9 Sch.7 para.149

Sch.4C para.9, substituted: 2008 c.9 Sch.7 para.141

Sch.4C para.9, varied: 2008 c.9 Sch.7 para.152

Sch.4C para.10, amended: 2008 c.9 Sch.7 para.142

Sch.4C para.10, repealed (in part): 2008 c.9 Sch.7 para.142

Sch.4C para.11, repealed: 2008 c.9 Sch.2 para.48

Sch.4C para.12, amended: 2008 c.9 Sch.7 para.143

Sch.4C para.12A, amended: 2008 c.9 Sch.7 para.144

Sch.4C para.13, amended: 2008 c.9 Sch.7 para.145

Sch.4ZA para.7, amended: 2008 c.9 Sch.2 para.67

Sch.5B, see *GC Trading Ltd v Revenue and Customs Commissioners* [2008] S.T.C. (S.C.D.) 178 (Sp Comm), Adrian Shipwright (Chairman)

Sch.5B, referred to: 2008 c.9 Sch.3 para.8

CAP.

1992–cont.

12. Taxation of Chargeable Gains Act 1992–*cont.*

Sch.5C, referred to: 2008 c.9 Sch.3 para.8

Sch.5 para.1, amended: 2008 c.9 Sch.2 para.10

Sch.5 para.7, see *Coombes v Revenue and Customs Commissioners* [2007] EWHC 3160 (Ch), [2008] S.T.C. 2984 (Ch D), Sir Donald Rattee

Sch.5 para.8, see *Coombes v Revenue and Customs Commissioners* [2007] EWHC 3160 (Ch), [2008] S.T.C. 2984 (Ch D), Sir Donald Rattee

Sch.5AA para.5, amended: SI 2008/954 Art.17

Sch.5BA para.1, repealed: 2008 c.9 Sch.2 para.49

Sch.5BA para.2, repealed: 2008 c.9 Sch.2 para.49

Sch.5BA para.3, repealed: 2008 c.9 Sch.2 para.49

Sch.5BA para.4, repealed: 2008 c.9 Sch.2 para.49

Sch.5BA para.5, repealed: 2008 c.9 Sch.2 para.49

Sch.5BA para.6, repealed: 2008 c.9 Sch.2 para.49

Sch.5BA para.7, repealed: 2008 c.9 Sch.2 para.49

Sch.5BA para.8, repealed: 2008 c.9 Sch.2 para.49

Sch.5BA para.9, repealed: 2008 c.9 Sch.2 para.49

Sch.5B para.1, see *Domain Dynamics (Holdings) Ltd v Revenue and Customs Commissioners* [2008] S.T.C. (S.C.D.) 1136 (Sp Comm), AN Brice; see *GC Trading Ltd v Revenue and Customs Commissioners* [2008] S.T.C. (S.C.D.) 178 (Sp Comm), Adrian Shipwright (Chairman)

Sch.5B para.1, amended: 2008 c.9 Sch.3 para.4

Sch.5B para.13, see *Blackburn v Revenue and Customs Commissioners* [2008] EWHC 266 (Ch), [2008] S.T.C. 842 (Ch D), Peter Smith, J.; see *Domain Dynamics (Holdings) Ltd v Revenue and Customs Commissioners* [2008] S.T.C. (S.C.D.) 1136 (Sp Comm), AN Brice

Sch.5B para.14, amended: SI 2008/954 Art.18

Sch.5B para.14, repealed (in part): SI 2008/954 Sch.1

Sch.5B para.19, see *Domain Dynamics (Holdings) Ltd v Revenue and Customs Commissioners* [2008] S.T.C. (S.C.D.) 1136 (Sp Comm), AN Brice

Sch.7A para.1, see *Limitgood Ltd v Revenue and Customs Commissioners* [2008] EWHC 19 (Ch), [2008] S.T.C. 361 (Ch D), Blackburne, J.

CAP.

1992–cont.

12. Taxation of Chargeable Gains Act 1992–*cont.*

Sch.7A para.12, amended: 2008 c.9 Sch.2 para.68

Sch.7D Part 4 para.15, repealed: 2008 c.9 Sch.2 para.50

Sch.9, applied: SI 2008/1588 Art.2

Sch.9 Part I para.1, enabling: SI 2008/1588

Sch.10 para.14, repealed (in part): 2008 c.9 s.41, s.66, Sch.7 para.95

13. Further and Higher Education Act 1992

s.16, applied: SI 2008/3083

s.16, enabling: SI 2008/49, SI 2008/1733, SI 2008/1773, SI 2008/3083

s.17, enabling: SI 2008/49, SI 2008/1733, SI 2008/1773, SI 2008/3083

s.20, enabling: SI 2008/50, SI 2008/1734, SI 2008/1790, SI 2008/3084

s.21, enabling: SI 2008/50, SI 2008/1734, SI 2008/1790, SI 2008/3084

s.26, applied: SI 2008/1418 Art.3, SI 2008/2773 Art.3, SI 2008/2992 Art.3

s.26, varied: SI 2008/633 Art.3, SI 2008/812 Art.3, SI 2008/1771 Art.3, SI 2008/1772 Art.3

s.27, enabling: SI 2008/633, SI 2008/812, SI 2008/1418, SI 2008/1771, SI 2008/1772, SI 2008/2773, SI 2008/2992

s.51, applied: SI 2008/49, SI 2008/1733, SI 2008/1773, SI 2008/3083

s.57, amended: 2008 c.02 Sch.1 para.3

s.65, see *R. (on the application of Queen Mary, University of London) v Higher Education Funding Council for England* [2008] EWHC 1472 (Admin), [2008] E.L.R. 540 (QBD (Admin)), Burnett, J.

s.65, applied: SI 2008/529 Reg.5, Reg.34, Reg.134, Reg.151, SI 2008/1273 Reg.5, Reg.12, Reg.80, Reg.93, SI 2008/1582 Reg.6, Reg.14, Reg.134, Reg.151, SI 2008/3170 Reg.5, Reg.12, Reg.80, Reg.104

Sch.4, enabling: SI 2008/50, SI 2008/1734, SI 2008/1790, SI 2008/3084

14. Local Government Finance Act 1992

applied: SI 2008/3022 Reg.15

Part I, applied: SI 2008/3022 Reg.7, Reg.8, Reg.9

s.1, applied: 2008 c.17 Sch.11 para.26

s.13, applied: SI 2008/794 Sch.8 para.44, Sch.9 para.35

s.14, enabling: SI 2008/981

s.21, enabling: SI 2008/315

s.22, applied: SI 2008/315 Reg.1

s.22B, applied: SI 2008/315 Reg.1

s.24, see *Chilton-Merryweather (Listing Officer) v Hunt* [2007] EWHC 3190 (Admin), [2008] Env. L.R. 29 (QBD (Admin)), Collins, J.; see *Chilton-Merryweather (Listing Officer) v Hunt* [2008] EWCA Civ 1025, [2008] R.A. 357

CAP.

1992–cont.

14. Local Government Finance Act 1992–*cont.*

s.24–*cont.*

(CA (Civ Div)), Waller, L.J.; see *McKenzie (Listing Officer) v Marshall* [2008] EWHC 641 (Admin), [2008] R.A. 269 (QBD (Admin)), Dobbs, J.

s.24, enabling: SI 2008/315

s.30, varied: SI 2008/584 Art.20, SI 2008/626 Reg.4, SI 2008/3022 Sch.2 para.1

s.31, varied: SI 2008/584 Art.20, SI 2008/626 Reg.4

s.32, applied: SI 2008/626 Reg.3, Reg.4, SI 2008/3022 Reg.3, Reg.4, Reg.15

s.32, varied: SI 2008/227 Reg.3, SI 2008/476 Reg.2, SI 2008/584 Art.20, SI 2008/626 Reg.3, Reg.4

s.32, enabling: SI 2008/227, SI 2008/476, SI 2008/626

s.33, applied: SI 2008/3022 Reg.3, Reg.4, Reg.15

s.33, referred to: SI 2008/3022 Reg.16

s.33, varied: SI 2008/227 Reg.4, SI 2008/476 Reg.3, SI 2008/584 Art.20, SI 2008/626 Reg.4, SI 2008/3022 Sch.2 para.2

s.33, enabling: SI 2008/227, SI 2008/476

s.34, applied: SI 2008/626 Reg.4, SI 2008/3022 Reg.3, Reg.4, Reg.15

s.34, varied: SI 2008/584 Art.20, SI 2008/626 Reg.4, SI 2008/3022 Sch.2 para.3

s.35, applied: SI 2008/3022 Reg.3, Reg.4, Reg.15

s.35, referred to: SI 2008/626 Reg.4

s.35, varied: SI 2008/584 Art.20, SI 2008/626 Reg.4

s.36, applied: SI 2008/3022 Reg.3, Reg.4, Reg.15

s.36, varied: SI 2008/584 Art.20, SI 2008/626 Reg.4, SI 2008/3022 Sch.2 para.4

s.37, applied: SI 2008/3022 Reg.3, Reg.4

s.37, varied: SI 2008/584 Art.20, SI 2008/626 Reg.4, SI 2008/3022 Sch.2 para.5

s.38, varied: SI 2008/584 Art.20, SI 2008/626 Reg.4

s.41, applied: SI 2008/626 Reg.6

s.41, varied: SI 2008/584 Art.20, SI 2008/626 Reg.5

s.42, varied: SI 2008/626 Reg.5

s.43, varied: SI 2008/227 Reg.5, SI 2008/476 Reg.4

s.43, enabling: SI 2008/227, SI 2008/476

s.44, varied: SI 2008/227 Reg.6, SI 2008/476 Reg.5

s.44, enabling: SI 2008/476

s.50, applied: SI 2008/626 Reg.3

s.50, referred to: SI 2008/584 Art.20

s.52B, applied: SI 2008/1850

s.52D, applied: SI 2008/1850

s.52E, applied: SI 2008/1850

s.52F, enabling: SI 2008/1850

CAP.

1992–cont.

14. Local Government Finance Act 1992–*cont.*

s.52I, applied: SI 2008/3022 Reg.3, Reg.4, Sch.1 para.1

s.52I, varied: SI 2008/3022 Sch.2 para.6

s.52T, applied: SI 2008/3022 Reg.3, Reg.4, Sch.1 para.1

s.52T, varied: SI 2008/3022 Sch.2 para.7

s.52X, varied: SI 2008/626 Reg.6

s.52Y, varied: SI 2008/626 Reg.6

s.54, varied: SI 2008/584 Art.20

s.66, varied: SI 2008/3022 Sch.2 para.8

s.67, varied: SI 2008/3022 Sch.2 para.9

s.69, referred to: SI 2008/239 Sch.2 para.2

s.69, varied: SI 2008/3022 Sch.2 para.10

s.80, applied: SI 2008/794 Sch.8 para.44, Sch.9 para.35

s.113, enabling: SI 2008/227, SI 2008/315, SI 2008/387, SI 2008/476, SI 2008/981, SI 2008/3264

s.116, enabling: SI 2008/387, SI 2008/3264

Sch.2 para.1, enabling: SI 2008/387, SI 2008/3264

Sch.2 para.2, enabling: SI 2008/387, SI 2008/3264

Sch.2 para.4, enabling: SI 2008/387

Sch.3 para.1, amended: SI 2008/981 Art.2

Sch.3 para.5, enabling: SI 2008/981

Sch.3 para.6, enabling: SI 2008/387

Sch.12 Part I para.1, enabling: SSI 2008/33, SSI 2008/136

Sch.12 Part I para.2, applied: SSI 2008/33, SSI 2008/136

Sch.12 Part II para.9, applied: SSI 2008/33 Art.3

Sch.12 Part II para.9, enabling: SSI 2008/33

Sch.13 para.2, repealed: 2008 asp 5 Sch.3 Part 1

15. Offshore Safety Act 1992

applied: 2008 c.13 Sch.3

s.4, repealed: 2008 c.20 Sch.4

19. Local Government Act 1992

see *Shrewsbury and Atcham BC v Secretary of State for Communities and Local Government* [2008] EWCA Civ 148, [2008] 3 All E.R. 548 (CA (Civ Div)), Waller, L.J. (V-P)

s.15, applied: SI 2008/423, SI 2008/424, SI 2008/425, SI 2008/427, SI 2008/2435

s.15, enabling: SI 2008/425

s.17, enabling: SI 2008/423, SI 2008/424, SI 2008/425, SI 2008/427, SI 2008/2435

s.20, applied: SI 2008/337 Sch.1 para.3

s.26, enabling: SI 2008/423, SI 2008/424, SI 2008/425, SI 2008/427, SI 2008/2435

34. Sexual Offences (Amendment) Act 1992

s.2, amended: SI 2008/1769 Sch.1 para.22

35. Timeshare Act 1992

applied: 2008 c.13 Sch.3

referred to: 2008 c.13 Sch.6

CAP.

1992–cont.

37. Further and Higher Education (Scotland) Act 1992

Part I, applied: SSI 2008/228 Sch.2, SSI 2008/229 Reg.14
Part II, applied: SSI 2008/163 Art.2, SSI 2008/177 Art.2, SSI 2008/229 Reg.14
s.12, applied: SI 2008/794 Sch.8 para.13, Sch.9 para.52
s.38, applied: 2008 c.25 s.91
s.44, enabling: SSI 2008/163, SSI 2008/177
s.45, enabling: SSI 2008/388
s.47, amended: SSI 2008/262 Art.2
s.48, applied: SSI 2008/212 Art.3, SSI 2008/220 Art.3
s.48, enabling: SSI 2008/212, SSI 2008/220
s.60, enabling: SSI 2008/163, SSI 2008/177, SSI 2008/212, SSI 2008/220, SSI 2008/388
Sch.5 para.1, applied: SI 2008/136 Reg.10
Sch.5 para.2, applied: SI 2008/136 Reg.10
Sch.5 para.3, applied: SI 2008/136 Reg.10
Sch.5 para.4, applied: SI 2008/136 Reg.10

40. Friendly Societies Act 1992

applied: SI 2008/1140 Art.1
s.69C, enabling: SI 2008/1144
s.69G, enabling: SI 2008/1144
s.69I, amended: SI 2008/948 Sch.1 para.183
s.69L, added: SI 2008/1140 Art.3
s.69M, added: SI 2008/1140 Art.4
s.73, amended: SI 2008/1140 Sch.2 para.2
s.74, substituted: SI 2008/1140 Art.5
s.74A, substituted: SI 2008/1140 Art.5
s.74B, substituted: SI 2008/1140 Art.5
s.74C, substituted: SI 2008/1140 Art.5
s.75, amended: SI 2008/1140 Sch.2 para.3
s.78, amended: SI 2008/1140 Sch.2 para.4
s.78A, amended: SI 2008/948 Sch.1 para.15, Sch.1 para.184, SI 2008/1140 Art.7
s.102, enabling: SI 2008/1140
s.119, amended: SI 2008/1140 Art.10
s.121, amended: SI 2008/1140 Art.8
s.121, enabling: SI 2008/1144
Sch.11 Part II para.8, substituted: SI 2008/948 Sch.1 para.185
Sch.13D Part I para.12, repealed: SI 2008/1140 Art.4
Sch.13E Part I para.3, amended: SI 2008/948 Sch.1 para.186
Sch.13E Part I para.7, amended: SI 2008/948 Sch.1 para.186
Sch.13E Part II para.9, amended: SI 2008/948 Sch.1 para.186
Sch.13E Part II para.11, amended: SI 2008/948 Sch.1 para.186
Sch.13E Part II para.15, amended: SI 2008/948 Sch.1 para.186
Sch.13E Part II para.18, amended: SI 2008/948 Sch.1 para.186
Sch.13F para.1, added: SI 2008/1140 Sch.1 para.1

CAP.

1992–cont.

40. Friendly Societies Act 1992–*cont.*

Sch.13F para.2, added: SI 2008/1140 Sch.1 para.1
Sch.13F para.3, added: SI 2008/1140 Sch.1 para.1
Sch.13F para.4, added: SI 2008/1140 Sch.1 para.1
Sch.13F para.5, added: SI 2008/1140 Sch.1 para.1
Sch.13F para.6, added: SI 2008/1140 Sch.1 para.1
Sch.13F para.7, added: SI 2008/1140 Sch.1 para.1
Sch.14 para.1, amended: SI 2008/1140 Sch.2 para.5
Sch.14 para.3, amended: SI 2008/1140 Sch.2 para.5
Sch.14 para.3A, added: SI 2008/948 Sch.1 para.16
Sch.14 para.4, amended: SI 2008/948 Sch.1 para.16, SI 2008/1140 Art.7
Sch.14 para.5, amended: SI 2008/948 Sch.1 para.16, Sch.1 para.187
Sch.14 para.10A, added: SI 2008/1140 Art.6
Sch.14 para.15A, added: SI 2008/1140 Art.6
Sch.14 para.15B, added: SI 2008/1140 Art.6
Sch.14 para.15C, added: SI 2008/1140 Art.6
Sch.14 para.16, amended: SI 2008/1140 Art.4, Sch.2 para.5
Sch.14 para.16, repealed (in part): SI 2008/1140 Art.4
Sch.14 para.17, repealed: SI 2008/1140 Art.4
Sch.16 para.1, amended: SI 2008/1140 Sch.2 para.5
Sch.16 para.2, amended: SI 2008/1140 Sch.2 para.5

41. Charities Act 1992

s.58, applied: SI 2008/629 Sch.1 para.17
s.64, applied: 2008 c.13 Sch.7
s.64A, applied: 2008 c.13 Sch.7

42. Transport and Works Act 1992

s.1, amended: 2008 c.29 Sch.2 para.52
s.1, applied: 2008 c.18 s.48, 2008 c.29 s.33, SI 2008/3163
s.1, disapplied: 2008 c.29 s.120
s.1, enabling: SI 2008/2512, SI 2008/3163
s.3, amended: 2008 c.29 Sch.2 para.53
s.3, applied: 2008 c.29 s.33, s.34, SI 2008/1238
s.3, disapplied: 2008 c.29 s.120
s.3, enabling: SI 2008/969, SI 2008/1238
s.5, applied: SI 2008/1238, SI 2008/3163
s.5, enabling: SI 2008/969, SI 2008/1238, SI 2008/2512, SI 2008/3163
s.6, applied: SI 2008/969
s.11, applied: SI 2008/2512, SI 2008/3163
s.13, applied: SI 2008/969
Sch.1 para.1, enabling: SI 2008/969, SI 2008/2512
Sch.1 para.2, enabling: SI 2008/969, SI 2008/2512

CAP.

1992–cont.

42. Transport and Works Act 1992–*cont.*

Sch.1 para.3, enabling: SI 2008/969, SI 2008/1238, SI 2008/2512, SI 2008/3163
Sch.1 para.4, enabling: SI 2008/969, SI 2008/1238, SI 2008/2512, SI 2008/3163
Sch.1 para.5, enabling: SI 2008/969, SI 2008/1238, SI 2008/2512, SI 2008/3163
Sch.1 para.6, enabling: SI 2008/2512
Sch.1 para.7, enabling: SI 2008/969, SI 2008/1238, SI 2008/2512, SI 2008/3163
Sch.1 para.8, enabling: SI 2008/969, SI 2008/1238, SI 2008/2512
Sch.1 para.10, enabling: SI 2008/969, SI 2008/2512
Sch.1 para.11, enabling: SI 2008/969, SI 2008/1238, SI 2008/2512, SI 2008/3163
Sch.1 para.12, enabling: SI 2008/2512
Sch.1 para.15, enabling: SI 2008/969, SI 2008/2512
Sch.1 para.16, enabling: SI 2008/969, SI 2008/1238, SI 2008/2512, SI 2008/3163
Sch.1 para.17, enabling: SI 2008/969, SI 2008/2512

44. Museums and Galleries Act 1992

Sch.2 para.2, amended: SI 2008/919 Art.2
Sch.2 para.2, enabling: SI 2008/919

48. Finance (No.2) Act 1992

s.1, enabling: SI 2008/753, SI 2008/1885
s.2, applied: SI 2008/753 Reg.2
s.2, enabling: SI 2008/1885
s.28, repealed (in part): 2008 c.9 Sch.36 para.86
s.40B, see *Halcyon Films LLP v Revenue and Customs Commissioners* [2008] S.T.C. (S.C.D.) 1016 (Sp Comm), Edward Sadler
s.42, see *Halcyon Films LLP v Revenue and Customs Commissioners* [2008] S.T.C. (S.C.D.) 1016 (Sp Comm), Edward Sadler; see *Micro Fusion 2004-1 LLP v Revenue and Customs Commissioners* [2008] S.T.C. (S.C.D.) 952 (Sp Comm), Edward Sadler
s.46, repealed (in part): 2008 c.9 Sch.2 para.70
Sch.9 para.9, repealed: 2008 c.9 Sch.18 para.5
Sch.9 para.15, repealed: 2008 c.9 Sch.14 para.17
Sch.9 para.21, repealed (in part): 2008 c.9 Sch.2 para.70
Sch.17 para.5, repealed (in part): 2008 c.9 Sch.2 para.70

51. Protection of Badgers Act 1992

s.1, referred to: 2008 c.13 Sch.6
s.2, referred to: 2008 c.13 Sch.6
s.3, referred to: 2008 c.13 Sch.6
s.4, referred to: 2008 c.13 Sch.6
s.5, referred to: 2008 c.13 Sch.6
s.10, referred to: 2008 c.13 Sch.6

CAP.

1992–cont.

52. Trade Union and Labour Relations (Consolidation) Act 1992

Part IV c.II, applied: SI 2008/228 Sch.2 para.20
s.30, amended: SI 2008/948 Sch.1 para.1
s.34, amended: SI 2008/948 Sch.1 para.1
s.46, see *Corrigan v GMB Union (No.1)* [2008] I.C.R. 197 (EAT), Elias, J.
s.67, see *UNIFI v Massey* [2007] EWCA Civ 800, [2008] I.C.R. 62 (CA (Civ Div)), Pill, L.J.
s.105, see *Unison v Allen* [2008] I.C.R. 114 (EAT), Elias, J (President)
s.131, amended: SI 2008/948 Sch.2
s.145A, referred to: SI 2008/3232 Sch.1 Part 2
s.145B, referred to: SI 2008/3232 Sch.1 Part 2
s.145E, amended: SI 2008/3055 Sch.1
s.146, referred to: SI 2008/3232 Sch.1 Part 2
s.156, amended: SI 2008/3055 Sch.1
s.168, applied: SI 2008/228 Sch.2 para.20
s.168A, applied: SI 2008/228 Sch.2 para.20
s.170, applied: SI 2008/228 Sch.2 para.20
s.174, amended: 2008 c.24 s.19
s.176, amended: 2008 c.24 s.19, SI 2008/3055 Sch.1
s.188, see *Day v Haine* [2007] EWHC 2691 (Ch), [2008] B.C.C. 199 (Ch D (Companies Ct)), Sir Donald Rattee; see *Northgate HR Ltd v Mercy* [2007] EWCA Civ 1304, [2008] I.C.R. 410 (CA (Civ Div)), Sir Mark Potter (President, Fam); see *UK Coal Mining Ltd v National Union of Mineworkers (Northumberland Area)* [2008] I.C.R. 163 (EAT), Elias, J (President)
s.189, see *Day v Haine* [2007] EWHC 2691 (Ch), [2008] B.C.C. 199 (Ch D (Companies Ct)), Sir Donald Rattee; see *Day v Haine* [2008] EWCA Civ 626, [2008] B.C.C. 845 (CA (Civ Div)), Thomas, L.J.; see *Northgate HR Ltd v Mercy* [2007] EWCA Civ 1304, [2008] I.C.R. 410 (CA (Civ Div)), Sir Mark Potter (President, Fam)
s.196, referred to: SI 2008/228 Sch.2 para.20
s.207A, added: 2008 c.24 s.3
s.218, referred to: SSI 2008/228 Reg.17
s.237, amended: 2008 c.30 s.57
s.238, amended: 2008 c.30 s.57
s.238, applied: SI 2008/3232 Sch.1 para.3
s.238, disapplied: SI 2008/3232 Sch.1 para.3
Sch.A1, see *R. (on the application of Cable & Wireless Services UK Ltd) v Central Arbitration Committee* [2008] EWHC 115 (Admin), [2008] I.C.R. 693 (QBD (Admin)), Collins, J.
Sch.A1 para.1, see *R. (on the application of Cable & Wireless Services UK Ltd) v Central Arbitration Committee* [2008] EWHC 115 (Admin), [2008] I.C.R. 693 (QBD (Admin)), Collins, J.

CAP.

1992–cont.

52. Trade Union and Labour Relations (Consolidation) Act 1992–*cont.*
Sch.A1 Part VIII para.156, referred to: SI 2008/3232 Sch.1 Part 2
Sch.A1 para.11, see *R. (on the application of Cable & Wireless Services UK Ltd) v Central Arbitration Committee* [2008] EWHC 115 (Admin), [2008] I.C.R. 693 (QBD (Admin)), Collins, J.
Sch.A1 para.19B, see *R. (on the application of Cable & Wireless Services UK Ltd) v Central Arbitration Committee* [2008] EWHC 115 (Admin), [2008] I.C.R. 693 (QBD (Admin)), Collins, J.
Sch.A2, added: 2008 c.24 s.3

53. Tribunals and Inquiries Act 1992
applied: SI 2008/315
s.8, applied: SI 2008/532, SI 2008/668, SI 2008/1088, SI 2008/1089, SI 2008/1497, SI 2008/1731, SI 2008/1797, SI 2008/1802, SI 2008/2206, SI 2008/2705
s.11, amended: SI 2008/2833 Sch.3 para.106
Sch.1 Part I, amended: SI 2008/2833 Sch.3 para.107

54. Human Fertilisation and Embryology (Disclosure of Information) Act 1992
repealed: 2008 c.22 Sch.8 Part 1

1993

8. Judicial Pensions and Retirement Act 1993
s.1, applied: SI 2008/2697 Reg.2
s.1, enabling: SI 2008/171, SI 2008/2947, SI 2008/3139
s.26, enabling: SI 2008/3139
s.29, enabling: SI 2008/171
s.30, enabling: SI 2008/171, SI 2008/3139
Sch.1 Part II, amended: SI 2008/171 Art.2, SI 2008/2833 Sch.3 para.109, SI 2008/2947 Art.2, SI 2008/3139 Art.2
Sch.5, amended: SI 2008/2833 Sch.3 para.110, SI 2008/3139 Art.3
Sch.6 para.23, repealed (in part): SI 2008/2833 Sch.3 para.228

9. Prisoners and Criminal Proceedings (Scotland) Act 1993
Part I, applied: SSI 2008/232 Art.3
s.2, see *Locke (John) v HM Advocate* [2008] HCJAC 6, 2008 S.L.T. 159 (HCJ), Lord Hamilton L.J.G.
s.3AA, amended: SSI 2008/126 Art.2
s.3AA, applied: SI 2008/1788 Sch.2, SSI 2008/36, SSI 2008/125
s.3AA, referred to: SSI 2008/125 Art.2
s.3AA, enabling: SSI 2008/126
s.10, amended: 2008 c.4 Sch.26 para.30
s.12, amended: SI 2008/912 Sch.1 para.10
s.12AA, applied: SSI 2008/36, SSI 2008/36 Art.2, SSI 2008/125, SSI 2008/125 Art.2
s.12AA, referred to: SSI 2008/36 Art.2

CAP.

1993–cont.

9. Prisoners and Criminal Proceedings (Scotland) Act 1993–*cont.*
s.12AA, enabling: SSI 2008/36, SSI 2008/125
s.12AB, applied: SI 2008/1788 Sch.2, SSI 2008/125 Sch.1 para.3, Sch.1 para.4
s.12AB, referred to: SSI 2008/125 Sch.1 para.3
s.15, amended: SI 2008/912 Sch.1 para.10
s.45, applied: SSI 2008/126

10. Charities Act 1993
applied: 2008 c.17 s.138, SI 2008/221 r.29, SI 2008/629 Reg.3
referred to: SI 2008/751 Art.4, SI 2008/3267 Art.3
s.2A, applied: SI 2008/751 Art.3
s.2B, applied: SI 2008/221 r.33
s.2B, enabling: SI 2008/221
s.2D, applied: SI 2008/221 r.22
s.3, applied: 2008 c.29 s.210, SI 2008/3267 Art.3, Art.4, Art.5, Art.9
s.3, varied: SI 2008/3267 Art.7
s.3A, applied: SI 2008/3267 Art.4, Art.5, Art.9, Art.11, SI 2008/3268 Reg.2
s.3A, referred to: SI 2008/3267 Art.7, Art.8, SI 2008/3268 Reg.2
s.3A, enabling: SI 2008/3268
s.4, applied: SI 2008/945 Art.10
s.4, disapplied: SI 2008/945 Art.5
s.6, disapplied: SI 2008/3267 Art.17
s.8, applied: SI 2008/3267 Art.17
s.9, varied: SI 2008/3267 Art.17
s.10, amended: SI 2008/948 Sch.1 para.192
s.10B, amended: SI 2008/948 Sch.1 para.192
s.16, varied: SI 2008/3267 Art.17
s.17, disapplied: SI 2008/3267 Art.17
s.18, disapplied: SI 2008/3267 Art.17
s.24, applied: SI 2008/629 Sch.1 para.3
s.24, varied: SI 2008/3267 Art.17
s.25, varied: SI 2008/3267 Art.17
s.28, disapplied: SI 2008/3267 Art.17
s.33, varied: SI 2008/3267 Art.17
s.36, disapplied: SI 2008/3267 Art.17
s.37, applied: SI 2008/3267 Art.17
s.38, disapplied: SI 2008/3267 Art.17
s.41, applied: 2008 c.17 s.135, SI 2008/629 Reg.24, Reg.26, Reg.31, Reg.32
s.41, disapplied: SI 2008/3267 Art.13
s.42, applied: 2008 c.17 s.135, SI 2008/629 Reg.5, Reg.6, Reg.7, Reg.8, Reg.15, Reg.20, Reg.24, Reg.26, Reg.27, Reg.28, Reg.31, Reg.32, Reg.40, SI 2008/945 Art.7
s.42, disapplied: SI 2008/3267 Art.13
s.42, enabling: SI 2008/629
s.43, amended: SI 2008/527 Art.2, SI 2008/948 Sch.1 para.17, Sch.1 para.192
s.43, applied: 2008 c.17 s.135, SI 2008/629 Reg.20, Reg.22, Reg.24, Reg.25, Reg.26, Reg.30, Reg.31, Reg.33, Reg.34
s.43, disapplied: SI 2008/3267 Art.13

CAP.

1993–cont.

10. Charities Act 1993–*cont.*

s.43, referred to: 2008 c.17 s.136, SI 2008/629 Reg.31
s.43A, applied: 2008 c.17 s.135, SI 2008/629 Reg.20, Reg.23, Reg.27, Reg.32, Reg.33, Reg.35
s.43A, referred to: SI 2008/629 Reg.30
s.43B, applied: 2008 c.17 s.135, SI 2008/629 Reg.20, Reg.23, Reg.28, Reg.32, Reg.33
s.43B, referred to: SI 2008/629 Reg.30
s.44, amended: SI 2008/527 Art.3, SI 2008/948 Sch.1 para.192
s.44, applied: 2008 c.17 s.135, SI 2008/629 Reg.24, Reg.25, Reg.26, Reg.30
s.44, disapplied: SI 2008/3267 Art.13
s.44, enabling: SI 2008/629
s.44A, applied: 2008 c.17 s.135, SI 2008/945 Sch.1
s.44A, disapplied: SI 2008/3267 Art.13
s.45, amended: SI 2008/527 Art.4, SI 2008/948 Sch.1 para.192
s.45, applied: 2008 c.17 s.135, SI 2008/629 Reg.24, Reg.25, Reg.30, Reg.31, Reg.32, Reg.38, Reg.39, Reg.40, Reg.41
s.45, disapplied: SI 2008/3267 Art.13
s.45, referred to: SI 2008/3267 Art.13
s.45, enabling: SI 2008/629
s.46, applied: SI 2008/629 Reg.40, Reg.41, SI 2008/945 Art.8, SI 2008/3267 Art.12, Art.14
s.46, varied: SI 2008/3267 Art.10
s.47, amended: SI 2008/527 Art.5, SI 2008/948 Sch.1 para.192
s.47, applied: SI 2008/3267 Art.16
s.48, disapplied: SI 2008/3267 Art.13
s.49, disapplied: SI 2008/3267 Art.13
s.49A, disapplied: SI 2008/3267 Art.13
s.67, repealed: SI 2008/948 Sch.4
s.68, substituted: SI 2008/948 Sch.3 para.7
s.68A, amended: SI 2008/527 Art.6
s.68ZA, substituted: SI 2008/948 Sch.3 para.7
s.68ZB, substituted: SI 2008/948 Sch.3 para.7
s.69, amended: SI 2008/527 Art.7, SI 2008/948 Sch.1 para.1, Sch.1 para.192
s.69C, amended: SI 2008/948 Sch.3 para.8
s.69CA, added: SI 2008/948 Sch.3 para.9
s.69D, amended: SI 2008/948 Sch.3 para.10
s.69D, repealed (in part): SI 2008/948 Sch.3 para.10
s.69G, varied: SI 2008/3267 Art.17
s.72, applied: 2008 c.17 s.266
s.73, varied: SI 2008/3267 Art.17
s.73D, amended: SI 2008/948 Sch.3 para.11
s.73E, amended: SI 2008/948 Sch.3 para.12
s.76, applied: 2008 c.13 Sch.3
s.77, applied: 2008 c.13 Sch.3
s.78, applied: 2008 c.13 Sch.3
s.86, applied: SI 2008/629
s.86, enabling: SI 2008/629, SI 2008/3268

CAP.

1993–cont.

10. Charities Act 1993–*cont.*

s.97, amended: SI 2008/948 Sch.1 para.192
s.97, applied: SI 2008/629 Reg.10
s.97, enabling: SI 2008/3268
Sch.1C, applied: SI 2008/221 r.17, SI 2008/3267 Art.4
Sch.5A, applied: SI 2008/629 Reg.9, Reg.10
Sch.5A, disapplied: SI 2008/3267 Art.13
Sch.5 para.3, applied: SI 2008/629 Sch.1 para.17
Sch.5 para.4, applied: SI 2008/629 Sch.1 para.17
Sch.5A para.1, amended: SI 2008/527 Art.8, SI 2008/948 Sch.1 para.192
Sch.5A para.2, amended: SI 2008/527 Art.8, SI 2008/948 Sch.1 para.192
Sch.5A para.3, amended: SI 2008/527 Art.8, SI 2008/948 Sch.1 para.192
Sch.5A para.3, applied: SI 2008/629 Reg.12, Reg.13, Reg.14, Reg.15, Reg.16, Reg.19, Reg.30
Sch.5A para.3, enabling: SI 2008/629
Sch.5A para.4, applied: SI 2008/629 Reg.18
Sch.5A para.4, enabling: SI 2008/629
Sch.5A para.5, amended: SI 2008/527 Art.8
Sch.5A para.6, amended: SI 2008/527 Art.8, SI 2008/948 Sch.1 para.192
Sch.5A para.6, applied: SI 2008/629 Reg.21, Reg.29, Reg.30, Reg.33, Reg.34
Sch.5A para.6, enabling: SI 2008/629
Sch.5A para.8, amended: SI 2008/948 Sch.1 para.192
Sch.5A para.8, applied: SI 2008/629 Reg.30
Sch.5A para.10, enabling: SI 2008/629
Sch.5A para.15, enabling: SI 2008/629

11. Clean Air Act 1993

applied: 2008 c.13 Sch.3, SSI 2008/100 Sch.4 Part 2, SSI 2008/159 Sch.3 Part 2
referred to: 2008 c.13 Sch.6
Part III, applied: SI 2008/514 Reg.2, SI 2008/3100 Reg.2, SSI 2008/154 Reg.2, SSI 2008/295 Reg.2, Reg.3
s.20, applied: SI 2008/515 Art.2, SI 2008/2343 Art.2
s.20, disapplied: SI 2008/3101 Art.2, SSI 2008/296 Art.2
s.20, referred to: SSI 2008/157 Art.2
s.20, enabling: SI 2008/514, SI 2008/2342, SI 2008/3100, SSI 2008/154, SSI 2008/295
s.21, enabling: SI 2008/515, SI 2008/2343, SI 2008/3101, SSI 2008/157, SSI 2008/296
s.61, amended: 2008 asp 5 Sch.3 Part 1
s.61, repealed (in part): 2008 asp 5 Sch.3 Part 1
s.63, enabling: SI 2008/514, SI 2008/3100, SSI 2008/154, SSI 2008/295
s.64, amended: 2008 asp 5 Sch.3 Part 1

12. Radioactive Substances Act 1993

applied: 2008 c.32 s.59

CAP.

1993–cont.

21. Osteopaths Act 1993
applied: 2008 c.13 Sch.3, SI 2008/2927 Reg.2
s.1, amended: SI 2008/1774 Sch.3 para.1
s.1, applied: SI 2008/1774 Art.4
s.1, repealed (in part): SI 2008/1774 Sch.3 para.1
s.3, amended: SI 2008/1774 Sch.3 para.2
s.17, amended: SI 2008/1774 Sch.3 para.3
s.20, amended: SI 2008/1774 Sch.3 para.4
s.35, amended: SI 2008/1774 Sch.3 para.5
s.36, amended: SI 2008/1774 Sch.3 para.6
s.40, amended: SI 2008/948 Sch.1 para.3
s.40A, added: SI 2008/1774 Sch.3 para.7
s.41, amended: SI 2008/1774 Sch.3 para.8
Sch.1 Part I para.1, substituted: SI 2008/1774 Sch.3 para.9
Sch.1 Part I para.1B, substituted: SI 2008/1774 Sch.3 para.9
Sch.1 Part I para.1C, substituted: SI 2008/1774 Sch.3 para.9
Sch.1 Part I para.1D, substituted: SI 2008/1774 Sch.3 para.9
Sch.1 Part I para.2, substituted: SI 2008/1774 Sch.3 para.9
Sch.1 Part I para.3, substituted: SI 2008/1774 Sch.3 para.9
Sch.1 Part I para.4, substituted: SI 2008/1774 Sch.3 para.9
Sch.1 Part I para.5, substituted: SI 2008/1774 Sch.3 para.9
Sch.1 Part I para.6, substituted: SI 2008/1774 Sch.3 para.9
Sch.1 Part I para.7, substituted: SI 2008/1774 Sch.3 para.9
Sch.1 Part I para.8, substituted: SI 2008/1774 Sch.3 para.9
Sch.1 Part I para.9, substituted: SI 2008/1774 Sch.3 para.9
Sch.1 Part I para.10, substituted: SI 2008/1774 Sch.3 para.9
Sch.1 Part I para.11, substituted: SI 2008/1774 Sch.3 para.9
Sch.1 Part I para.11A, substituted: SI 2008/1774 Sch.3 para.9
Sch.1 Part I para.12, substituted: SI 2008/1774 Sch.3 para.9
Sch.1 Part I para.13, substituted: SI 2008/1774 Sch.3 para.9
Sch.1 Part I para.14, substituted: SI 2008/1774 Sch.3 para.9
Sch.1 Part I para.15, amended: SI 2008/1774 Sch.3 para.9
Sch.1 Part I para.15, repealed (in part): SI 2008/1774 Sch.3 para.9
Sch.1 Part II para.16, amended: SI 2008/1774 Sch.3 para.9
Sch.1 Part II para.19, repealed: SI 2008/1774 Sch.3 para.9
Sch.1 Part II para.21, amended: SI 2008/1774 Sch.3 para.9

CAP.

1993–cont.

21. Osteopaths Act 1993–*cont.*
Sch.1 Part II para.25, substituted: SI 2008/1774 Sch.3 para.9
Sch.1 Part II para.26, repealed: SI 2008/1774 Sch.3 para.9
Sch.1 Part II para.27, repealed: SI 2008/1774 Sch.3 para.9
Sch.1 Part II para.28, repealed: SI 2008/1774 Sch.3 para.9
Sch.1 Part II para.29, repealed: SI 2008/1774 Sch.3 para.9
Sch.1 Part II para.30, substituted: SI 2008/1774 Sch.3 para.9
Sch.1 Part II para.31, repealed: SI 2008/1774 Sch.3 para.9
Sch.1 Part II para.32, repealed: SI 2008/1774 Sch.3 para.9
Sch.1 Part II para.33, repealed: SI 2008/1774 Sch.3 para.9
Sch.1 Part II para.34, substituted: SI 2008/1774 Sch.3 para.9
Sch.1 Part II para.35, repealed: SI 2008/1774 Sch.3 para.9
Sch.1 Part II para.36, repealed: SI 2008/1774 Sch.3 para.9
Sch.1 Part II para.37, repealed: SI 2008/1774 Sch.3 para.9
Sch.1 Part II para.38, substituted: SI 2008/1774 Sch.3 para.9
Sch.1 Part II para.39, repealed: SI 2008/1774 Sch.3 para.9
Sch.1 Part II para.40, repealed: SI 2008/1774 Sch.3 para.9
Sch.1 Part II para.41, repealed: SI 2008/1774 Sch.3 para.9

24. Video Recordings Act 1993
referred to: 2008 c.13 Sch.6

25. Local Government (Overseas Assistance) Act 1993
s.1, amended: SI 2008/2840 Art.4
s.1, repealed (in part): SI 2008/2840 Art.4

28. Leasehold Reform, Housing and Urban Development Act 1993
see *Howard de Walden Estates Ltd v Aggio* [2007] EWCA Civ 499, [2008] Ch. 26 (CA (Civ Div)), Mummery, L.J.; see *Howard de Walden Estates Ltd v Aggio* [2008] UKHL 44, [2008] 3 W.L.R. 244 (HL), Lord Hoffmann
s.1, see *Ulterra Ltd v Glenbarr (RTE) Co Ltd* [2008] 4 E.G. 174 (Lands Tr), Judge Reid Q.C.
s.4, see *Marine Court (St Leonards on Sea) Freeholders Ltd v Rother District Investments Ltd* [2008] 2 E.G. 148 (CC (Hastings)), Judge Hollis
s.4A, see *Elizabeth Court (Bournemouth) Ltd v Revenue and Customs Commissioners* [2008] S.T.C. (S.C.D.) 366 (Sp Comm), AN Brice

CAP.

1993–cont.

28. Leasehold Reform, Housing and Urban Development Act 1993–*cont.*

s.4C, see *Elizabeth Court (Bournemouth) Ltd v Revenue and Customs Commissioners* [2008] S.T.C. (S.C.D.) 366 (Sp Comm), AN Brice

s.5, see *Howard de Walden Estates Ltd v Aggio* [2008] UKHL 44, [2008] 3 W.L.R. 244 (HL), Lord Hoffmann

s.9, applied: SI 2008/3068 Art.10

s.13, see *Cascades and Quayside Ltd v Cascades Freehold Ltd* [2007] EWCA Civ 1555, [2008] L. & T.R. 23 (CA (Civ Div)), Dyson, L.J.; see *Midhage v 60 Coolhurst Road Ltd* [2008] L. & T.R. 5 (Lands Tr), Andrew Trott; see *Renshaw v Magnet Properties South East LLP* [2008] 4 E.G. 170 (CC (Central London)), Judge Collins; see *Sinclair Gardens Investments (Kensington) Ltd v Poets Chase Freehold Co Ltd* [2007] EWHC 1776 (Ch), [2008] 1 W.L.R. 768 (Ch D), Morgan, J.; see *Ulterra Ltd v Glenbarr (RTE) Co Ltd* [2008] 4 E.G. 174 (Lands Tr), Judge Reid Q.C.

s.16, applied: 2008 c.17 s.184

s.19, see *Renshaw v Magnet Properties South East LLP* [2008] 4 E.G. 170 (CC (Central London)), Judge Collins

s.21, see *Sinclair Gardens Investments (Kensington) Ltd v Poets Chase Freehold Co Ltd* [2007] EWHC 1776 (Ch), [2008] 1 W.L.R. 768 (Ch D), Morgan, J.; see *Ulterra Ltd v Glenbarr (RTE) Co Ltd* [2008] 4 E.G. 174 (Lands Tr), Judge Reid Q.C.

s.22, see *Sinclair Gardens Investments (Kensington) Ltd v Poets Chase Freehold Co Ltd* [2007] EWHC 1776 (Ch), [2008] 1 W.L.R. 768 (Ch D), Morgan, J.

s.24, see *Goldeagle Properties Ltd v Thornbury Court Ltd* [2008] EWCA Civ 864, [2008] 45 E.G. 102 (CA (Civ Div)), Tuckey, L.J.

s.25, see *Renshaw v Magnet Properties South East LLP* [2008] 4 E.G. 170 (CC (Central London)), Judge Collins

s.28, see *Sinclair Gardens Investments (Kensington) Ltd v Poets Chase Freehold Co Ltd* [2007] EWHC 1776 (Ch), [2008] 1 W.L.R. 768 (Ch D), Morgan, J.

s.29, see *Sinclair Gardens Investments (Kensington) Ltd v Poets Chase Freehold Co Ltd* [2007] EWHC 1776 (Ch), [2008] 1 W.L.R. 768 (Ch D), Morgan, J.

s.39, see *Howard de Walden Estates Ltd v Aggio* [2007] EWCA Civ 499, [2008] Ch. 26 (CA (Civ Div)), Mummery, L.J.; see *Howard de Walden Estates Ltd v Aggio* [2008] UKHL 44, [2008] 3 W.L.R. 244 (HL), Lord Hoffmann

CAP.

1993–cont.

28. Leasehold Reform, Housing and Urban Development Act 1993–*cont.*

s.47, see *Majorstake Ltd v Curtis* [2008] UKHL 10, [2008] 1 A.C. 787 (HL), Lord Hope of Craighead

s.57, see *Howard de Walden Estates Ltd v Aggio* [2008] UKHL 44, [2008] 3 W.L.R. 244 (HL), Lord Hoffmann

s.62, see *Howard de Walden Estates Ltd v Aggio* [2007] EWCA Civ 499, [2008] Ch. 26 (CA (Civ Div)), Mummery, L.J.

s.65, repealed: 2008 c.17 Sch.16

s.78, amended: 2008 c.17 Sch.12 para.15

s.79, amended: 2008 c.17 Sch.12 para.16

s.91, see *Howard de Walden Estates Ltd v Aggio* [2008] UKHL 44, [2008] 3 W.L.R. 244 (HL), Lord Hoffmann

s.99, see *Cascades and Quayside Ltd v Cascades Freehold Ltd* [2007] EWCA Civ 1555, [2008] L. & T.R. 23 (CA (Civ Div)), Dyson, L.J.

s.101, see *Howard de Walden Estates Ltd v Aggio* [2007] EWCA Civ 499, [2008] Ch. 26 (CA (Civ Div)), Mummery, L.J.; see *Howard de Walden Estates Ltd v Aggio* [2008] UKHL 44, [2008] 3 W.L.R. 244 (HL), Lord Hoffmann

s.135, applied: 2008 c.17 s.274

s.135, repealed: 2008 c.17 Sch.14 para.3, Sch.16

s.136, amended: 2008 c.17 Sch.14 para.3

s.137, repealed (in part): 2008 c.17 Sch.14 para.3, Sch.16

s.158, repealed: 2008 c.17 Sch.8 para.63, Sch.16

s.159, repealed: 2008 c.17 Sch.8 para.63, Sch.16

s.160, repealed: 2008 c.17 Sch.8 para.63, Sch.16

s.161, repealed: 2008 c.17 Sch.8 para.63, Sch.16

s.162, applied: SI 2008/3068 Art.10

s.162, repealed: 2008 c.17 Sch.8 para.63, Sch.16

s.163, repealed: 2008 c.17 Sch.8 para.63, Sch.16

s.164, repealed: 2008 c.17 Sch.8 para.63, Sch.16

s.165, repealed: 2008 c.17 Sch.8 para.63, Sch.16

s.166, repealed: 2008 c.17 Sch.8 para.63, Sch.16

s.167, repealed: 2008 c.17 Sch.8 para.63, Sch.16

s.168, repealed: 2008 c.17 Sch.8 para.63, Sch.16

s.169, repealed: 2008 c.17 Sch.8 para.63, Sch.16

s.170, repealed: 2008 c.17 Sch.8 para.63, Sch.16

s.171, repealed: 2008 c.17 Sch.8 para.63, Sch.16

CAP.

1993–cont.

28. Leasehold Reform, Housing and Urban Development Act 1993–*cont.*

s.172, repealed: 2008 c.17 Sch.8 para.63, Sch.16
s.173, repealed: 2008 c.17 Sch.8 para.63, Sch.16
s.175, repealed: 2008 c.17 Sch.8 para.63, Sch.16
s.177, repealed: 2008 c.17 Sch.8 para.63, Sch.16
s.181, repealed (in part): 2008 c.17 Sch.16
s.183, repealed: 2008 c.17 Sch.8 para.63, Sch.16
s.184, repealed: 2008 c.17 Sch.8 para.63, Sch.16
s.185, repealed: 2008 c.17 Sch.8 para.63, Sch.16
s.188, repealed (in part): 2008 c.17 Sch.8 para.63, Sch.16
Sch.9, see *Midhage v 60 Coolhurst Road Ltd* [2008] L. & T.R. 5 (Lands Tr), Andrew Trott
Sch.9 Part II para.3, applied: 2008 c.17 s.182
Sch.17 para.1, amended: 2008 c.17 s.53
Sch.17 para.1, repealed: 2008 c.17 Sch.8 para.63, Sch.16
Sch.17 para.2, repealed: 2008 c.17 Sch.8 para.63, Sch.16
Sch.17 para.3, repealed: 2008 c.17 Sch.8 para.63, Sch.16
Sch.17 para.4, repealed: 2008 c.17 Sch.8 para.63, Sch.16
Sch.17 para.5, repealed: 2008 c.17 Sch.8 para.63, Sch.16
Sch.17 para.6, repealed: 2008 c.17 Sch.8 para.63, Sch.16
Sch.17 para.7, repealed: 2008 c.17 Sch.8 para.63, Sch.16
Sch.17 para.8, repealed: 2008 c.17 Sch.8 para.63, Sch.16
Sch.18 para.1, repealed: 2008 c.17 Sch.8 para.63, Sch.16
Sch.18 para.2, repealed: 2008 c.17 Sch.8 para.63, Sch.16
Sch.18 para.3, repealed: 2008 c.17 Sch.8 para.63, Sch.16
Sch.18 para.4, repealed: 2008 c.17 Sch.8 para.63, Sch.16
Sch.18 para.5, repealed: 2008 c.17 Sch.8 para.63, Sch.16
Sch.18 para.6, repealed: 2008 c.17 Sch.8 para.63, Sch.16
Sch.18 para.7, repealed: 2008 c.17 Sch.8 para.63, Sch.16
Sch.18 para.8, repealed: 2008 c.17 Sch.8 para.63, Sch.16
Sch.18 para.9, repealed: 2008 c.17 Sch.8 para.63, Sch.16
Sch.18 para.10, amended: SI 2008/948 Sch.1 para.18
Sch.18 para.10, repealed: 2008 c.17 Sch.8 para.63, Sch.16

CAP.

1993–cont.

28. Leasehold Reform, Housing and Urban Development Act 1993–*cont.*

Sch.18 para.11, repealed: 2008 c.17 Sch.8 para.63, Sch.16
Sch.18 para.12, repealed: 2008 c.17 Sch.8 para.63, Sch.16
Sch.18 para.13, repealed: 2008 c.17 Sch.8 para.63, Sch.16
Sch.19 para.1, repealed: 2008 c.17 Sch.8 para.63, Sch.16
Sch.19 para.2, repealed: 2008 c.17 Sch.8 para.63, Sch.16
Sch.19 para.3, repealed: 2008 c.17 Sch.8 para.63, Sch.16
Sch.19 para.4, repealed: 2008 c.17 Sch.8 para.63, Sch.16
Sch.19 para.5, repealed: 2008 c.17 Sch.8 para.63, Sch.16
Sch.19 para.6, repealed: 2008 c.17 Sch.8 para.63, Sch.16
Sch.19 para.7, repealed: 2008 c.17 Sch.8 para.63, Sch.16
Sch.20 Part I para.1, repealed: 2008 c.17 Sch.8 para.63, Sch.16
Sch.20 Part I para.2, repealed: 2008 c.17 Sch.8 para.63, Sch.16
Sch.20 Part I para.3, repealed: 2008 c.17 Sch.8 para.63, Sch.16
Sch.20 Part II para.4, repealed: 2008 c.17 Sch.8 para.63, Sch.16
Sch.20 Part II para.5, amended: 2008 c.29 Sch.9 para.5
Sch.20 Part II para.5, repealed: 2008 c.17 Sch.8 para.63, Sch.16
Sch.20 Part II para.6, repealed: 2008 c.17 Sch.8 para.63, Sch.16
Sch.20 Part II para.7, repealed: 2008 c.17 Sch.8 para.63, Sch.16
Sch.20 Part II para.8, repealed: 2008 c.17 Sch.8 para.63, Sch.16
Sch.20 Part II para.9, repealed: 2008 c.17 Sch.8 para.63, Sch.16
Sch.20 Part II para.10, repealed: 2008 c.17 Sch.8 para.63, Sch.16
Sch.20 Part II para.11, repealed: 2008 c.17 Sch.8 para.63, Sch.16
Sch.20 Part II para.12, repealed: 2008 c.17 Sch.8 para.63, Sch.16
Sch.20 Part II para.13, repealed: 2008 c.17 Sch.8 para.63, Sch.16
Sch.20 Part II para.14, repealed: 2008 c.17 Sch.8 para.63, Sch.16
Sch.20 Part II para.15, repealed: 2008 c.17 Sch.8 para.63, Sch.16
Sch.20 Part II para.16, repealed: 2008 c.17 Sch.8 para.63, Sch.16
Sch.20 Part II para.17, repealed: 2008 c.17 Sch.8 para.63, Sch.16
Sch.20 Part II para.18, repealed: 2008 c.17 Sch.8 para.63, Sch.16

CAP.

1993–cont.

28. Leasehold Reform, Housing and Urban Development Act 1993–*cont.*

Sch.20 Part II para.19, repealed: 2008 c.17 Sch.8 para.63, Sch.16

Sch.20 Part III para.20, repealed: 2008 c.17 Sch.8 para.63, Sch.16

Sch.20 Part III para.21, repealed: 2008 c.17 Sch.8 para.63, Sch.16

Sch.20 Part III para.22, repealed: 2008 c.17 Sch.8 para.63, Sch.16

Sch.20 Part III para.23, repealed: 2008 c.17 Sch.8 para.63, Sch.16

Sch.21 para.2, repealed (in part): SI 2008/3002 Sch.1 para.44, Sch.3

Sch.21 para.3, repealed: 2008 c.17 Sch.16

Sch.21 para.32, repealed: 2008 c.17 Sch.16

34. Finance Act 1993

s.12, enabling: SI 2008/753

s.29, applied: 2008 c.9 Sch.41 para.1

s.92E, amended: SI 2008/954 Art.19

s.171, amended: 2008 c.9 Sch.12 para.16

s.178, amended: 2008 c.9 Sch.39 para.63

s.185, amended: 2008 c.9 s.107

Sch.20A Part I para.1, added: 2008 c.9 Sch.33 para.1

Sch.20A Part I para.2, added: 2008 c.9 Sch.33 para.1

Sch.20A Part I para.3, added: 2008 c.9 Sch.33 para.1

Sch.20A Part I para.4, added: 2008 c.9 Sch.33 para.1

Sch.20A Part I para.5, added: 2008 c.9 Sch.33 para.1

Sch.20A Part II para.6, added: 2008 c.9 Sch.33 para.1

Sch.20A Part II para.7, added: 2008 c.9 Sch.33 para.1

Sch.20A Part II para.8, added: 2008 c.9 Sch.33 para.1

Sch.20A Part III para.9, added: 2008 c.9 Sch.33 para.1

Sch.20A Part III para.10, added: 2008 c.9 Sch.33 para.1

Sch.20A Part III para.11, added: 2008 c.9 Sch.33 para.1

Sch.20A Part III para.12, added: 2008 c.9 Sch.33 para.1

37. Agriculture Act 1993

s.57, amended: SI 2008/948 Sch.3 para.13

38. Welsh Language Act 1993

Part II, applied: SI 2008/1890 Art.2

s.6, enabling: SI 2008/1890

s.18, applied: SI 2008/716

s.25, enabling: SI 2008/712, SI 2008/716, SI 2008/717, SI 2008/1648

s.26, applied: SI 2008/1860

s.26, enabling: SI 2008/7, SI 2008/1159, SI 2008/1848, SI 2008/3075

39. National Lottery etc Act 1993

s.12, applied: 2008 c.13 Sch.3

s.13, applied: 2008 c.13 Sch.3

CAP.

1993–cont.

39. National Lottery etc Act 1993–*cont.*

s.22, applied: SI 2008/255 Art.2, Art.3, Art.4

s.23, applied: SI 2008/255 Art.3, Art.4

s.23, referred to: SI 2008/255, SI 2008/255 Art.2

s.25, applied: 2008 c.31 Sch.3 para.5, Sch.3 para.14

s.25E, referred to: 2008 c.31 Sch.3 para.14

s.29A, applied: SI 2008/255

s.29A, enabling: SI 2008/255

s.60, applied: SI 2008/255

Sch.3A para.2, enabling: SI 2008/3103

Sch.3A para.3, applied: SI 2008/3103 Art.2

Sch.3A para.3, enabling: SI 2008/3103

Sch.3A para.6, enabling: SI 2008/3103

Sch.4A Part I para.6, applied: 2008 c.31 s.22

Sch.4A Part I para.7, applied: 2008 c.31 Sch.3 para.8

Sch.4A Part III para.18, applied: 2008 c.31 s.22

Sch.4A Part III para.21, amended: 2008 c.31 Sch.3 para.11

40. Noise and Statutory Nuisance Act 1993

applied: 2008 c.13 Sch.3

43. Railways Act 1993

see *BRB (Residuary) Ltd v Connex South Eastern Ltd (fomerly South Eastern Train Co Ltd)* [2008] EWHC 1172 (QB), [2008] 1 W.L.R. 2867 (QBD), Cranston, J.

Part I, applied: 2008 c.18 s.29, SI 2008/1261 Art.45

Part I, referred to: 2008 c.18 s.24, SI 2008/2512 Art.36

s.4, applied: 2008 c.18 s.22

s.4, referred to: 2008 c.18 s.22

s.6, disapplied: 2008 c.18 s.24

s.7, applied: 2008 c.18 s.34, SI 2008/2512 Art.36, Art.38

s.8, applied: 2008 c.29 s.25, SI 2008/2512 Art.36, Art.38

s.23, applied: 2008 c.18 s.26

s.25, amended: 2008 c.26 Sch.4 para.58

s.25, disapplied: 2008 c.18 s.25

s.63, applied: 2008 c.3 Sch.2 Part 2

s.94, amended: SI 2008/948 Sch.1 para.193

s.106, amended: SI 2008/948 Sch.1 para.193

s.119, referred to: 2008 c.13 Sch.6

s.120, referred to: 2008 c.13 Sch.6

s.121, referred to: 2008 c.13 Sch.6

s.121A, applied: 2008 c.13 Sch.7

s.122, applied: 2008 c.18 s.34

s.122, referred to: SI 2008/1261 Art.27

s.136, amended: 2008 c.26 Sch.4 para.58

s.145, amended: SI 2008/960 Sch.3, SI 2008/1277 Sch.2 para.52

s.149, amended: 2008 c.26 Sch.4 para.58

44. Crofters (Scotland) Act 1993

applied: SSI 2008/426 Reg.28

CAP.

1993–cont.

44. Crofters (Scotland) Act 1993–*cont.*

s.10, see *Gardner v Curran* 2008 S.L.T. (Sh Ct) 105 (Sh Ct (Grampian)), Sheriff Sir Stephen Young

48. Pension Schemes Act 1993

applied: SI 2008/239 Reg.61, SI 2008/576 Sch.4 para.5, SI 2008/632 Art.6, SI 2008/649 Reg.2, SI 2008/653 Reg.6, Reg.26, SSI 2008/224 Reg.22, SSI 2008/228 Reg.57, SSI 2008/230 Reg.43

referred to: 2008 c.30 s.146

Part III, applied: SI 2008/730 Art.2

Part III c.III, applied: SI 2008/410 Sch.4 para.25

Part IV c.III, applied: SI 2008/239 Reg.48, SSI 2008/228 Reg.44

Part IV c.IV, applied: SI 2008/239 Reg.76, Reg.78, Reg.79, Reg.81, Reg.84, SI 2008/653 Reg.1, Reg.5, SSI 2008/224 Reg.1, Reg.5, SSI 2008/228 Reg.70, Reg.73, Reg.74, Reg.76, Reg.79, SSI 2008/229 Reg.15

Part IV c.IV, referred to: SI 2008/653 Reg.1, SI 2008/1050 Sch.2 para.1, SSI 2008/224 Reg.1

Part IV c.V, applied: SI 2008/239 Reg.76, Reg.79, Reg.81, Reg.84, SI 2008/653 Reg.1, Reg.16, Reg.18, SSI 2008/224 Reg.1, Reg.16, Reg.18, SSI 2008/228 Reg.70, Reg.73, Reg.74, Reg.76, Reg.79

Part IV c.V, referred to: SI 2008/653 Reg.1, SSI 2008/224 Reg.1

s.1, applied: 2008 c.30 s.18

s.7, applied: 2008 c.30 s.20, s.24, s.26

s.8, amended: 2008 c.16 Sch.1 para.8

s.9, applied: SI 2008/653 Reg.18, Reg.22, SSI 2008/224 Reg.18, Reg.22

s.9, referred to: SI 2008/239 Reg.80

s.9, enabling: SI 2008/1979

s.10, applied: SSI 2008/228 Reg.88

s.10, repealed: 2008 c.30 s.106, Sch.11 Part 3

s.12B, amended: 2008 c.16 Sch.1 para.9

s.12C, applied: SI 2008/239 Reg.78, SSI 2008/228 Reg.73

s.14, applied: SI 2008/653 Reg.3, Reg.10, Reg.14, Reg.18, Reg.22, SSI 2008/224 Reg.3, Reg.10, Reg.14, Reg.18, Reg.22

s.15, applied: SI 2008/632 Art.5, SI 2008/653 Reg.18, Reg.22, SSI 2008/224 Reg.18, Reg.22

s.15, varied: SI 2008/632 Art.5

s.15A, applied: SSI 2008/228 Reg.88

s.17, applied: SI 2008/632 Art.5, SI 2008/653 Reg.3, Reg.6, Reg.26, SSI 2008/224 Reg.3, Reg.6, Reg.26

s.19, applied: SI 2008/239 Reg.78, Reg.83, SSI 2008/228 Reg.73, Reg.78

s.20, applied: SI 2008/239 Reg.78, SSI 2008/228 Reg.73

s.25A, repealed: 2008 c.30 s.106, Sch.11 Part 3

CAP.

1993–cont.

48. Pension Schemes Act 1993–*cont.*

s.26, repealed: 2008 c.30 s.106, Sch.11 Part 3

s.26, enabling: SI 2008/1979

s.27, repealed: 2008 c.30 s.106, Sch.11 Part 3

s.27, enabling: SI 2008/1050

s.27A, repealed: 2008 c.30 s.106, Sch.11 Part 3

s.28, enabling: SI 2008/1979

s.30, repealed: 2008 c.30 s.106, Sch.11 Part 3

s.32, repealed: 2008 c.30 s.106, Sch.11 Part 3

s.32A, repealed: 2008 c.30 s.106, Sch.11 Part 3

s.33A, repealed: 2008 c.30 s.106, Sch.11 Part 3

s.41, amended: 2008 c.16 Sch.1 para.10

s.41, repealed (in part): 2008 c.16 Sch.1 para.10, Sch.2

s.42A, amended: 2008 c.16 Sch.1 para.11

s.45, amended: 2008 c.16 Sch.1 para.12

s.46, amended: 2008 c.30 s.103, Sch.4 para.16

s.46A, added: 2008 c.30 s.103

s.47, amended: 2008 c.30 Sch.4 para.17

s.48, amended: 2008 c.30 Sch.4 para.18

s.49, amended: 2008 c.30 Sch.4 para.19

s.50, amended: 2008 c.30 Sch.11 Part 2

s.50, repealed (in part): 2008 c.30 Sch.11 Part 2

s.52, amended: 2008 c.30 Sch.11 Part 2

s.52, repealed (in part): 2008 c.30 Sch.11 Part 2

s.55, applied: SI 2008/239 Reg.49, Reg.80, SI 2008/653 Reg.2, Reg.3, Reg.6, SSI 2008/224 Reg.2, Reg.3, Reg.6, SSI 2008/228 Reg.45, Reg.75

s.61, applied: SI 2008/239 Reg.49, SI 2008/409 Sch.2 para.14, SI 2008/410 Sch.4 para.25, SI 2008/653 Reg.16, Reg.18, SSI 2008/224 Reg.16, Reg.18, SSI 2008/228 Reg.45

s.68A, applied: SI 2008/653 Reg.13, Reg.17, SSI 2008/224 Reg.13, Reg.17

s.68A, repealed: 2008 c.30 s.100, Sch.11 Part 2

s.68B, repealed: 2008 c.30 s.100, Sch.11 Part 2

s.68C, repealed: 2008 c.30 s.100, Sch.11 Part 2

s.68D, repealed: 2008 c.30 s.100, Sch.11 Part 2

s.69, see *Trustee Solutions Ltd v Dubery* [2007] EWCA Civ 771, [2008] 1 All E.R. 826 (CA (Civ Div)), Ward, L.J.

s.93, amended: 2008 c.30 s.134

s.93, referred to: SI 2008/653 Reg.1, SSI 2008/224 Reg.1

s.93A, enabling: SI 2008/1050

s.95, applied: SI 2008/653 Reg.5, SSI 2008/224 Reg.5

s.95, enabling: SI 2008/1050

CAP.

1993–cont.

48. Pension Schemes Act 1993–*cont.*
s.96, applied: SI 2008/653 Reg.5, SSI 2008/224 Reg.5
s.97, applied: SI 2008/653 Reg.6, SSI 2008/224 Reg.6
s.97, enabling: SI 2008/1050, SI 2008/2450
s.101AA, applied: SSI 2008/228 Reg.73
s.101AA, referred to: SI 2008/239 Reg.78, SI 2008/653 Reg.1, SSI 2008/224 Reg.1
s.101AC, enabling: SI 2008/1050
s.101AF, enabling: SI 2008/1050, SI 2008/2450
s.101AH, enabling: SI 2008/1050
s.101F, amended: 2008 c.30 s.134
s.101H, enabling: SI 2008/1050
s.101I, enabling: SI 2008/1050
s.101L, enabling: SI 2008/1050
s.109, applied: SI 2008/581, SI 2008/581 Art.2
s.109, enabling: SI 2008/581
s.111A, amended: 2008 c.30 s.49
s.111A, applied: 2008 c.30 s.9, s.26
s.113, enabling: SI 2008/649, SI 2008/1050
s.127, amended: SI 2008/948 Sch.1 para.194
s.145, amended: SI 2008/817 Art.9
s.145, applied: SI 2008/649 Reg.2
s.146, amended: 2008 c.30 s.66
s.164, amended: 2008 c.30 Sch.4 para.20
s.165, amended: 2008 c.30 Sch.4 para.21
s.167, amended: 2008 c.30 Sch.4 para.22
s.170, amended: SI 2008/2833 Sch.3 para.112
s.171A, amended: SI 2008/2833 Sch.3 para.113
s.175, enabling: SI 2008/661
s.175A, added: 2008 c.30 Sch.10 para.1
s.180, see *Trustee Solutions Ltd v Dubery* [2007] EWCA Civ 771, [2008] 1 All E.R. 826 (CA (Civ Div)), Ward, L.J.
s.181, see *Bridge Trustees Ltd v Yates* [2008] EWHC 964 (Ch), [2008] Pens. L.R. 261 (Ch D), Sarah Asplin QC
s.181, amended: 2008 c.16 Sch.2, 2008 c.30 Sch.11 Part 2
s.181, enabling: SI 2008/649, SI 2008/661, SI 2008/1050, SI 2008/1903, SI 2008/1979, SI 2008/2450
s.182, enabling: SI 2008/649, SI 2008/661, SI 2008/1050, SI 2008/1979, SI 2008/2450
s.183, enabling: SI 2008/1050, SI 2008/2450
s.185, amended: 2008 c.30 s.103
s.185, applied: SI 2008/649, SI 2008/661, SI 2008/1050, SI 2008/1903, SI 2008/1979, SI 2008/2450
s.186, amended: 2008 c.30 s.103
Sch.2 Part I para.5, enabling: SI 2008/1903
Sch.3 para.1, amended: 2008 c.30 Sch.2 para.2

CAP.

1993–cont.

48. Pension Schemes Act 1993–*cont.*
Sch.3 para.2, amended: 2008 c.30 Sch.2 para.3
Sch.3 para.2, applied: SI 2008/3070 Art.2
Sch.3 para.2, enabling: SI 2008/3070
Sch.4 para.2, amended: 2008 c.16 Sch.1 para.13
Sch.4 para.2, repealed (in part): 2008 c.16 Sch.1 para.13, Sch.2
Sch.4 para.3, amended: SI 2008/948 Sch.1 para.194
Sch.4 para.4, amended: SI 2008/948 Sch.1 para.194
Sch.8 para.16, repealed (in part): SI 2008/948 Sch.2

49. Pension Schemes (Northern Ireland) Act 1993
Part III c.III, applied: SI 2008/409 Sch.2 para.14
s.57, applied: SI 2008/409 Sch.2 para.14, SI 2008/410 Sch.4 para.25
s.123, amended: SI 2008/948 Sch.1 para.195
Sch.1 Part I para.5, enabling: SI 2008/1903
Sch.3 para.3, amended: SI 2008/948 Sch.1 para.195

50. Statute Law (Repeals) Act 1993
Sch.2 Part I para.1, repealed: 2008 c.12 Sch.1 Part 3

1994

5. New Towns (Amendment) Act 1994
repealed: 2008 c.17 Sch.16

9. Finance Act 1994
s.8, repealed: 2008 c.9 Sch.40 para.21
s.10A, repealed: 2008 c.9 Sch.43 para.3
s.12A, amended: 2008 c.9 Sch.6 para.18, Sch.6 para.34
s.12B, amended: 2008 c.9 Sch.6 para.19, Sch.6 para.35
s.14, amended: 2008 c.9 Sch.6 para.20, Sch.6 para.36
s.30, amended: 2008 c.9 s.153
s.33, applied: 2008 c.9 Sch.41 para.1
s.33, repealed (in part): 2008 c.9 Sch.41 para.25
s.38, enabling: SI 2008/1482
s.42, enabling: SI 2008/1482
s.53, applied: 2008 c.9 Sch.41 para.1
s.53, enabling: SI 2008/1945
s.53AA, applied: 2008 c.9 Sch.41 para.1
s.54, enabling: SI 2008/1482, SI 2008/2693
s.57, repealed: 2008 c.9 s.142
s.58, repealed: 2008 c.9 s.142
s.65, amended: 2008 c.9 s.143
s.65, repealed (in part): 2008 c.9 s.142
s.65, enabling: SI 2008/1945
s.73, amended: 2008 c.9 s.142
s.74, enabling: SI 2008/1482, SI 2008/1945, SI 2008/2693

CAP.

1994–cont.

9. **Finance Act 1994**–*cont.*

s.150, see *Prudential Plc v Revenue and Customs Commissioners* [2008] EWHC 1839 (Ch), [2008] S.T.C. 2820 (Ch D), Sir Andrew Morritt (Chancellor)

s.151, see *Prudential Plc v Revenue and Customs Commissioners* [2008] EWHC 1839 (Ch), [2008] S.T.C. 2820 (Ch D), Sir Andrew Morritt (Chancellor); see *Prudential Plc v Revenue and Customs Commissioners* [2008] S.T.C. (S.C.D.) 239 (Sp Comm), Sir Stephen Oliver Q.C.

s.153, see *Prudential Plc v Revenue and Customs Commissioners* [2008] EWHC 1839 (Ch), [2008] S.T.C. 2820 (Ch D), Sir Andrew Morritt (Chancellor)

s.155, see *Prudential Plc v Revenue and Customs Commissioners* [2008] EWHC 1839 (Ch), [2008] S.T.C. 2820 (Ch D), Sir Andrew Morritt (Chancellor); see *Prudential Plc v Revenue and Customs Commissioners* [2008] S.T.C. (S.C.D.) 239 (Sp Comm), Sir Stephen Oliver Q.C.

s.156, see *Prudential Plc v Revenue and Customs Commissioners* [2008] S.T.C. (S.C.D.) 239 (Sp Comm), Sir Stephen Oliver Q.C.

s.168A, see *Prudential Plc v Revenue and Customs Commissioners* [2008] S.T.C. (S.C.D.) 239 (Sp Comm), Sir Stephen Oliver Q.C.

s.187, repealed: 2008 c.9 Sch.36 para.92

s.225, amended: 2008 c.9 Sch.39 para.64

s.255, repealed: 2008 c.9 Sch.36 para.92

Sch.4 Part I para.13, repealed: 2008 c.9 Sch.41 para.25

Sch.5 para.2, amended: 2008 c.9 s.126

Sch.5 para.3, amended: 2008 c.9 Sch.42 para.2, Sch.42 para.3, Sch.42 para.4, Sch.42 para.5, Sch.42 para.6

Sch.5 para.9ZA, added: 2008 c.9 Sch.42 para.7

Sch.7 Part IV para.12, repealed: 2008 c.9 Sch.40 para.21

Sch.7 Part IV para.13, repealed: 2008 c.9 Sch.40 para.21

Sch.7 Part IV para.14, repealed: 2008 c.9 Sch.41 para.25

Sch.7 Part IV para.18, repealed: 2008 c.9 s.142

Sch.7 Part IV para.18A, repealed: 2008 c.9 Sch.43 para.3

Sch.7 Part IV para.20, amended: 2008 c.9 s.142

Sch.7 Part VI para.29, amended: 2008 c.9 Sch.44 para.5

Sch.7 Part VI para.29, repealed (in part): 2008 c.9 Sch.44 para.5

Sch.16 Part IV para.17, repealed: 2008 c.9 s.66

Sch.19 Part I para.21, repealed: 2008 c.9 Sch.44 para.11

CAP.

1994–cont.

9. **Finance Act 1994**–*cont.*

Sch.19 Part I para.29, repealed: 2008 c.9 Sch.36 para.92

Sch.24 para.2, repealed (in part): 2008 c.9 Sch.2 para.70

Sch.25 para.4, repealed (in part): 2008 c.9 Sch.2 para.70

13. **Intelligence Services Act 1994**

s.1, applied: 2008 c.28 s.18, s.21

s.1, referred to: 2008 c.28 s.21

s.2, applied: 2008 c.28 s.20

s.3, applied: 2008 c.28 s.21

s.3, referred to: 2008 c.28 s.21

s.4, applied: 2008 c.28 s.20

15. **Antarctic Act 1994**

s.9, enabling: SI 2008/3066

s.10, enabling: SI 2008/3066

s.14, enabling: SI 2008/3066

s.25, enabling: SI 2008/3066

s.32, enabling: SI 2008/3066

17. **Chiropractors Act 1994**

applied: SI 2008/2927 Reg.2

s.1, amended: SI 2008/1774 Sch.4 para.1

s.1, applied: SI 2008/1774 Art.4

s.1, repealed (in part): SI 2008/1774 Sch.4 para.1

s.1, enabling: SI 2008/3047

s.3, amended: SI 2008/1774 Sch.4 para.2

s.17, amended: SI 2008/1774 Sch.4 para.3

s.20, amended: SI 2008/1774 Sch.4 para.4

s.21, see *Cobb v General Chiropractic Council* 2008 S.C. 73 (IH (1 Div)), Lord Macfadyen

s.22, see *Cobb v General Chiropractic Council* 2008 S.C. 73 (IH (1 Div)), Lord Macfadyen

s.24, see *Cobb v General Chiropractic Council* 2008 S.C. 73 (IH (1 Div)), Lord Macfadyen

s.24, applied: SI 2008/3047 Art.7

s.35, amended: SI 2008/1774 Sch.4 para.5

s.36, amended: SI 2008/1774 Sch.4 para.6

s.41, amended: SI 2008/948 Sch.1 para.3

s.41A, added: SI 2008/1774 Sch.4 para.7

s.43, amended: SI 2008/1774 Sch.4 para.8

Sch.1 Part I para.1, substituted: SI 2008/1774 Sch.4 para.9

Sch.1 Part I para.1A, applied: SI 2008/3047 Art.6

Sch.1 Part I para.1B, substituted: SI 2008/1774 Sch.4 para.9

Sch.1 Part I para.1B, enabling: SI 2008/3047

Sch.1 Part I para.1C, substituted: SI 2008/1774 Sch.4 para.9

Sch.1 Part I para.1D, substituted: SI 2008/1774 Sch.4 para.9

Sch.1 Part I para.2, substituted: SI 2008/1774 Sch.4 para.9

Sch.1 Part I para.3, substituted: SI 2008/1774 Sch.4 para.9

Sch.1 Part I para.4, substituted: SI 2008/1774 Sch.4 para.9

Sch.1 Part I para.5, substituted: SI 2008/1774 Sch.4 para.9

CAP.

1994–cont.

17. **Chiropractors Act 1994**–*cont.*
Sch.1 Part I para.6, substituted: SI 2008/1774 Sch.4 para.9
Sch.1 Part I para.7, substituted: SI 2008/1774 Sch.4 para.9
Sch.1 Part I para.8, substituted: SI 2008/1774 Sch.4 para.9
Sch.1 Part I para.9, substituted: SI 2008/1774 Sch.4 para.9
Sch.1 Part I para.10, substituted: SI 2008/1774 Sch.4 para.9
Sch.1 Part I para.11, substituted: SI 2008/1774 Sch.4 para.9
Sch.1 Part I para.11A, substituted: SI 2008/1774 Sch.4 para.9
Sch.1 Part I para.12, substituted: SI 2008/1774 Sch.4 para.9
Sch.1 Part I para.13, substituted: SI 2008/1774 Sch.4 para.9
Sch.1 Part I para.14, substituted: SI 2008/1774 Sch.4 para.9
Sch.1 Part I para.15, amended: SI 2008/1774 Sch.4 para.9
Sch.1 Part I para.15, repealed (in part): SI 2008/1774 Sch.4 para.9
Sch.1 Part II para.16, amended: SI 2008/1774 Sch.4 para.9
Sch.1 Part II para.19, repealed: SI 2008/1774 Sch.4 para.9
Sch.1 Part II para.21, amended: SI 2008/1774 Sch.4 para.9
Sch.1 Part II para.25, substituted: SI 2008/1774 Sch.4 para.9
Sch.1 Part II para.26, repealed: SI 2008/1774 Sch.4 para.9
Sch.1 Part II para.27, repealed: SI 2008/1774 Sch.4 para.9
Sch.1 Part II para.28, repealed: SI 2008/1774 Sch.4 para.9
Sch.1 Part II para.29, repealed: SI 2008/1774 Sch.4 para.9
Sch.1 Part II para.30, substituted: SI 2008/1774 Sch.4 para.9
Sch.1 Part II para.31, repealed: SI 2008/1774 Sch.4 para.9
Sch.1 Part II para.32, repealed: SI 2008/1774 Sch.4 para.9
Sch.1 Part II para.33, repealed: SI 2008/1774 Sch.4 para.9
Sch.1 Part II para.34, substituted: SI 2008/1774 Sch.4 para.9
Sch.1 Part II para.35, repealed: SI 2008/1774 Sch.4 para.9
Sch.1 Part II para.36, repealed: SI 2008/1774 Sch.4 para.9
Sch.1 Part II para.37, repealed: SI 2008/1774 Sch.4 para.9
Sch.1 Part II para.38, substituted: SI 2008/1774 Sch.4 para.9
Sch.1 Part II para.39, repealed: SI 2008/1774 Sch.4 para.9

CAP.

1994–cont.

17. **Chiropractors Act 1994**–*cont.*
Sch.1 Part II para.40, repealed: SI 2008/1774 Sch.4 para.9
Sch.1 Part II para.41, repealed: SI 2008/1774 Sch.4 para.9

19. **Local Government (Wales) Act 1994**
Sch.5 Part III, applied: 2008 c.29 s.204
Sch.16 para.13, repealed: SI 2008/1277 Sch.4 Part 1
Sch.16 para.63, repealed (in part): 2008 c.17 Sch.16
Sch.16 para.104, repealed: 2008 c.17 Sch.16

20. **Sunday Trading Act 1994**
applied: 2008 c.13 Sch.3
referred to: 2008 c.13 Sch.6

21. **Coal Industry Act 1994**
s.4, amended: SI 2008/960 Sch.3
s.19, applied: SI 2008/794 Reg.107
s.59, amended: SI 2008/960 Sch.3, SI 2008/1277 Sch.2 para.57
s.59, repealed (in part): SI 2008/1277 Sch.2 para.57, Sch.4 Part 1
Sch.3 para.6, amended: SI 2008/948 Sch.1 para.196
Sch.4 Part I para.2, repealed (in part): 2008 c.9 Sch.2 para.70

22. **Vehicle Excise and Registration Act 1994**
applied: SI 2008/614 Reg.2, SI 2008/1214 Reg.2, SI 2008/2367 Reg.14, SSI 2008/103 Reg.11
Part II, applied: SI 2008/2551 Reg.4
Part III, referred to: 2008 c.13 Sch.6
s.10, amended: 2008 c.9 s.144
s.10, repealed (in part): 2008 c.9 s.144
s.19, substituted: 2008 c.9 s.144
s.21, enabling: SI 2008/642
s.22, applied: SI 2008/1715 Sch.1 para.4
s.22, repealed (in part): 2008 c.9 s.144
s.22, enabling: SI 2008/1444, SI 2008/2849
s.22A, enabling: SI 2008/1444
s.24, applied: 2008 c.13 Sch.7
s.26, enabling: SI 2008/2850
s.27, enabling: SI 2008/2372
s.28, applied: 2008 c.13 Sch.7
s.28A, referred to: 2008 c.13 Sch.6
s.29, amended: 2008 c.9 Sch.45 para.2
s.30, amended: 2008 c.9 Sch.45 para.3
s.31, amended: 2008 c.9 s.144
s.31B, amended: 2008 c.9 s.144
s.31C, amended: 2008 c.9 s.144
s.32A, enabling: SI 2008/2266
s.33, amended: 2008 c.9 s.147
s.57, enabling: SI 2008/1444, SI 2008/2372, SI 2008/2850
s.59, referred to: 2008 c.13 Sch.6
s.61B, amended: 2008 c.9 s.148
s.61B, enabling: SI 2008/1444
Sch.1 Part I para.1, amended: 2008 c.9 s.17
Sch.1 Part IA para.1B, amended: 2008 c.9 s.17

CAP.

1994–*cont.*

22. Vehicle Excise and Registration Act 1994–*cont.*

Sch.1 Part IB para.1J, amended: 2008 c.9 s.17, s.146

Sch.1 Part IB para.1K, amended: 2008 c.9 s.146

Sch.1 Part IB para.1M, added: 2008 c.9 s.146

Sch.1 Part II para.2, amended: 2008 c.9 s.17

Sch.2, referred to: SI 2008/1951 Sch.4 para.11

Sch.2A, applied: 2008 c.13 Sch.7

Sch.2A, enabling: SI 2008/2266

Sch.2 para.7, amended: 2008 c.14 Sch.5 para.62

Sch.2 para.7, repealed (in part): 2008 c.14 Sch.5 para.62, Sch.15 Part 1

Sch.2A para.1, amended: 2008 c.9 Sch.45 para.5

Sch.2A para.2, amended: 2008 c.9 Sch.45 para.6

Sch.2A para.3, amended: 2008 c.9 Sch.45 para.7

Sch.2A para.4, amended: 2008 c.9 Sch.45 para.8

23. Value Added Tax Act 1994

see *Customs and Excise Commissioners v Total Network SL* [2008] UKHL19, [2008] 1 A.C. 1174 (HL), Lord Hope of Craighead; see *DCM (Optical Holdings) Ltd v Revenue and Customs Commissioners* [2008] S.T.C. 1294 (IH (1 Div)), Lord Nimmo Smith

applied: 2008 c.9 Sch.36 para.5, Sch.36 para.62

s.2, amended: SI 2008/3020 Art.3

s.2, enabling: SI 2008/3020

s.5, see *Revenue and Customs Commissioners v Loyalty Management UK Ltd* [2007] EWCA Civ 965, [2008] S.T.C. 59 (CA (Civ Div)), Chadwick, L.J.

s.5, applied: 2008 c.9 Sch.36 para.34

s.7, applied: 2008 c.9 Sch.41 para.7

s.8, see *Barclays Bank Plc v Revenue and Customs Commissioners* [2008] B.V.C. 2189 (V&DTr (London)), JF Avery Jones (Chairman)

s.11, applied: 2008 c.9 Sch.36 para.34

s.15, applied: 2008 c.9 Sch.36 para.34

s.19, see *Institute of Biomedical Science v Revenue and Customs Commissioners* [2008] B.V.C. 2259 (V&DTr (London)), Charles Hellier (Chairman)

s.21, amended: SI 2008/3020 Art.4

s.21, enabling: SI 2008/3020

s.24, see *Gracechurch Management Services Ltd v Revenue and Customs Commissioners* [2007] EWHC 755 (Ch), [2008] S.T.C. 795 (Ch D), Sir Andrew Morritt C.; see *RBS Deutschland Holdings GmbH v Revenue and Customs Commissioners* [2008] B.V.C. 2003 (V&DTr (Edinburgh)), Kenneth Mure Q.C. (Chairman)

CAP.

1994–*cont.*

23. Value Added Tax Act 1994–*cont.*

s.25, referred to: 2008 c.9 s.121

s.26, see *DCM (Optical Holdings) Ltd v Revenue and Customs Commissioners* [2008] S.T.C. 1294 (IH (1 Div)), Lord Nimmo Smith; see *Lincoln Assurance Ltd v Revenue and Customs Commissioners* [2008] B.V.C. 2307 (V&DTr (London)), AN Brice (Chairman); see *RBS Deutschland Holdings GmbH v Revenue and Customs Commissioners* [2008] B.V.C. 2003 (V&DTr (Edinburgh)), Kenneth Mure Q.C. (Chairman); see *University College London v Revenue and Customs Commissioners* [2008] B.V.C. 2376 (V&DTr (London)), John Clark (Chairman)

s.26B, enabling: SI 2008/3021

s.29A, enabling: SI 2008/1410, SI 2008/2676

s.30, see *Marks & Spencer Plc v Customs and Excise Commissioners (C-309/06)* [2008] S.T.C. 1408 (ECJ (3rd Chamber)), Judge Rosas (President)

s.31, enabling: SI 2008/1892, SI 2008/2547

s.33, amended: 2008 asp 5 Sch.3 Part 1, 2008 c.26 Sch.4 para.59

s.33A, amended: 2008 c.9 Sch.39 para.33

s.33A, enabling: SI 2008/1339

s.41, applied: 2008 asp 2 s.1, s.2

s.43, see *Gracechurch Management Services Ltd v Revenue and Customs Commissioners* [2007] EWHC 755 (Ch), [2008] S.T.C. 795 (Ch D), Sir Andrew Morritt C.

s.51A, repealed: SI 2008/1146 Art.5

s.53, see *Dunwood Travel Ltd v Revenue and Customs Commissioners* [2007] EWHC 319 (Ch), [2008] S.T.C. 412 (Ch D), Mann, J.

s.54, applied: 2008 c.9 Sch.41 para.2

s.57, amended: SI 2008/722 Art.2, Art.3

s.57, enabling: SI 2008/722

s.67, repealed: 2008 c.9 Sch.41 para.25

s.67A, repealed: 2008 c.9 Sch.43 para.4

s.72, see *Voudouri (Michael George) v HM Advocate* [2008] HCJAC 34, 2008 S.L.T. 746 (HCJ), Lord Eassie

s.73, see *BUPA Purchasing Ltd v Revenue and Customs Commissioners* [2007] EWCA Civ 542, [2008] S.T.C. 101 (CA (Civ Div)), Auld, L.J.; see *Revenue and Customs Commissioners v Potter* [2008] B.P.I.R. 1033 (Ch D), Deputy Registrar Nicholas Briggs; see *Westone Wholesale Ltd v Revenue and Customs Commissioners* [2007] EWHC 2676 (Ch), [2008] S.T.C. 828 (Ch D), Patten, J.

s.73, amended: 2008 c.9 s.120

s.77, see *Dunwood Travel Ltd v Revenue and Customs Commissioners* [2007] EWHC 319 (Ch), [2008] S.T.C. 412 (Ch D), Mann, J.; see *Dunwood Travel Ltd v*

CAP.

1994–cont.

23. Value Added Tax Act 1994–*cont.*

s.77–*cont.*

Revenue and Customs Commissioners [2008] EWCA Civ 174, [2008] S.T.C. 959 (CA (Civ Div)), Laws, L.J.

s.77, amended: 2008 c.9 Sch.39 para.34

s.77, repealed (in part): 2008 c.9 Sch.39 para.34

s.78, see *RSPCA v Revenue and Customs Commissioners* [2007] EWHC 422 (Ch), [2008] S.T.C. 885 (Ch D), Lawrence Collins, L.J.

s.78, amended: 2008 c.9 Sch.39 para.35

s.79, see *RSPCA v Revenue and Customs Commissioners* [2007] EWHC 422 (Ch), [2008] S.T.C. 885 (Ch D), Lawrence Collins, L.J.

s.80, see *Boots Co Plc v Revenue and Customs Commissioners* [2008] B.V.C. 2328 (V&DTr (London)), AN Brice; see *Fleming (t/a Bodycraft) v Customs and Excise Commissioners* [2008] UKHL 2, [2008] 1 W.L.R. 195 (HL), Lord Hope of Craighead; see *LA Leisure Ltd v Revenue and Customs Commissioners* [2008] B.V.C. 2352 (V&DTr (Manchester)), IE Vellins (Chairman); see *Marks & Spencer Plc v Customs and Excise Commissioners (C-309/06)* [2008] S.T.C. 1408 (ECJ (3rd Chamber)), Judge Rosas (President); see *Midlands Co-operative Society Ltd v Revenue and Customs Commissioners* [2008] EWCA Civ 305, [2008] Bus. L.R. 1187 (CA (Civ Div)), Arden, L.J.

s.80, amended: 2008 c.9 s.120, Sch.39 para.36

s.80, applied: 2008 c.9 s.121

s.80, referred to: 2008 c.9 s.121

s.81, amended: 2008 c.9 s.132

s.81, repealed (in part): 2008 c.9 s.132

s.83, see *DCM (Optical Holdings) Ltd v Revenue and Customs Commissioners* [2008] S.T.C. 1294 (IH (1 Div)), Lord Nimmo Smith; see *Revenue and Customs Commissioners v Mobilx Ltd* [2007] EWHC 1769 (Ch), [2008] S.T.C. 3071 (Ch D), Warren, J.; see *University College London v Revenue and Customs Commissioners* [2008] B.V.C. 2376 (V&DTr (London)), John Clark (Chairman)

s.83, amended: SI 2008/1146 Art.3

s.84, see *RSPCA v Revenue and Customs Commissioners* [2007] EWHC 422 (Ch), [2008] S.T.C. 885 (Ch D), Lawrence Collins, L.J.

s.84, amended: SI 2008/1146 Art.3

s.85, see *University College London v Revenue and Customs Commissioners* [2008] B.V.C. 2376 (V&DTr (London)), John Clark (Chairman)

s.88, enabling: SI 2008/3021

s.89, amended: SI 2008/1146 Sch.1 para.2

CAP.

1994–cont.

23. Value Added Tax Act 1994–*cont.*

s.96, amended: SI 2008/1146 Sch.1 para.3

s.96, enabling: SI 2008/1892, SI 2008/2547, SI 2008/2676

Sch.1 para.1, amended: SI 2008/707 Art.2

Sch.1 para.4, amended: SI 2008/707 Art.2

Sch.1 para.5, applied: 2008 c.9 Sch.41 para.1

Sch.1 para.6, applied: 2008 c.9 Sch.41 para.1

Sch.1 para.7, applied: 2008 c.9 Sch.41 para.1

Sch.1 para.14, applied: 2008 c.9 Sch.41 para.1

Sch.1 para.15, enabling: SI 2008/707

Sch.2 para.3, applied: 2008 c.9 Sch.41 para.1

Sch.3 para.1, amended: SI 2008/707 Art.2

Sch.3 para.2, amended: SI 2008/707 Art.2

Sch.3 para.3, applied: 2008 c.9 Sch.41 para.1

Sch.3 para.8, applied: 2008 c.9 Sch.41 para.1

Sch.3 para.9, enabling: SI 2008/707

Sch.3A para.3, applied: 2008 c.9 Sch.41 para.1

Sch.3A para.4, applied: 2008 c.9 Sch.41 para.1

Sch.3A para.7, applied: 2008 c.9 Sch.41 para.1

Sch.4, applied: 2008 c.9 Sch.36 para.34

Sch.6 para.1, see *Weald Leasing Ltd v Revenue and Customs Commissioners* [2008] EWHC 30 (Ch), [2008] S.T.C. 1601 (Ch D), Lindsay, J.

Sch.7A, see *University of Cambridge v Revenue and Customs Commissioners* [2008] B.V.C. 2274 (V&DTr (London)), Edward Sadler (Chairman)

Sch.7A Part II, amended: SI 2008/2676 Art.2

Sch.7A Part II, applied: SI 2008/1410 Art.3

Sch.8, see *Marks & Spencer Plc v Customs and Excise Commissioners (C-309/06)* [2008] S.T.C. 1408 (ECJ (3rd Chamber)), Judge Rosas (President); see *Revenue and Customs Commissioners v Premier Foods (Holdings) Ltd* [2007] EWHC 3134 (Ch), [2008] S.T.C. 176 (Ch D), Sir Andrew Morritt (Chancellor)

Sch.8 Group 1, see *Procter & Gamble UK v Revenue and Customs Commissioners* [2008] EWHC 1558 (Ch), [2008] S.T.C. 2650 (Ch D), Warren, J.

Sch.8 Group 5, see *Jeanfield Swifts Football Club v Revenue and Customs Commissioners* [2008] B.V.C. 2490 (V&DTr (Edinburgh)), T Gordon Coutts Q.C. (Chairman); see *Quarriers v Revenue and Customs Commissioners* [2008] B.V.C. 2366 (V&DTr (Edinburgh)), J Gordon Reid (Chairman)

Sch.8 Group 8, see *EB Central Services Ltd v Revenue and Customs Commissioners* [2008] EWCA Civ 486, [2008] S.T.C. 2209 (CA (Civ Div)), Mummery, L.J.; see *Stone v Revenue and Customs Commissioners* [2008] EWHC 1249 (Ch), [2008] S.T.C. 2501 (Ch D), Sir Andrew Park

CAP.

1994–cont.

23. Value Added Tax Act 1994–*cont.*

Sch.8 Group 9, see *Stone v Revenue and Customs Commissioners* [2008] EWHC 1249 (Ch), [2008] S.T.C. 2501 (Ch D), Sir Andrew Park

Sch.9, see *Denyer v Revenue and Customs Commissioners* [2007] EWHC 2750 (Ch), [2008] S.T.C. 633 (Ch D), Briggs, J.

Sch.9 Part II, amended: 2008 c.14 Sch.15 Part 2, SI 2008/1146 Sch.1 para.4, SI 2008/1892 Art.2, SI 2008/2547 Art.3

Sch.9 Part II, referred to: SI 2008/2547 Art.3

Sch.9 Part II, repealed (in part): SI 2008/1146 Art.4, Art.4, SI 2008/1892 Art.2, SI 2008/2547 Art.3

Sch.9 Part II, substituted: SI 2008/2547 Art.3

Sch.9 Group 1, see *Revenue and Customs Commissioners v Tallington Lakes Ltd* [2007] EWHC 1955 (Ch), [2008] S.T.C. 2734 (Ch D), David Richards, J.

Sch.9 Group 2, see *InsuranceWide.com Services Ltd v Revenue and Customs Commissioners* [2008] Lloyd's Rep. I.R. 422 (V&DTr (London)), JC Gort (Chairman)

Sch.9 Group 4, see *Rank Group Ltd v Revenue and Customs Commissioners* [2008] 3 C.M.L.R. 31 (V&DTr (London)), Theodore Wallace (Chairman)

Sch.9 Group 5, see *AXA UK Plc v Revenue and Customs Commissioners* [2008] B.V.C. 2023 (V&DTr (London)), John F Avery Jones (Chairman); see *AXA UK Plc v Revenue and Customs Commissioners* [2008] EWHC 1137 (Ch), [2008] S.T.C. 2091 (Ch D), Henderson, J; see *HBOS Plc v Revenue and Customs Commissioners* [2008] CSIH 69 (IH (Ex Div)), Lord Nimmo Smith; see *JP Morgan Fleming Claverhouse Investment Trust Plc v Revenue and Customs Commissioners (C-363/05)* [2008] S.T.C. 1180 (ECJ (3rd Chamber)), Judge Rosas (President); see *T-Mobile (UK) Ltd v Revenue and Customs Commissioners* [2008] B.V.C. 2169 (V&DTr (London)), JC Gort (Chairman)

Sch.9 Group 7, see *Healthcare at Home Ltd v Revenue and Customs Commissioners* [2008] B.V.C. 2066 (V&DTr (Manchester)), Colin Bishopp (Chairman)

Sch.9 Group 9, see *Camping and Caravanning Club v Revenue and Customs Commissioners* [2008] B.V.C. 2465 (V&DTr (Manchester)), Michael Tildesley (Chairman); see *Institute of Biomedical Science v Revenue and Customs Commissioners* [2008] B.V.C. 2259 (V&DTr (London)), Charles Hellier (Chairman)

CAP.

1994–cont.

23. Value Added Tax Act 1994–*cont.*

Sch.10, see *Newnham College, Cambridge v Customs and Excise Commissioners* [2008] UKHL 23, [2008] 1 W.L.R. 888 (HL), Lord Hoffmann

Sch.10A, see *Leisure Pass Group Ltd v Revenue and Customs Commissioners* [2008] B.V.C. 2044 (V&DTr (London)), JF Avery Jones (Chairman); see *Leisure Pass Group Ltd v Revenue and Customs Commissioners* [2008] EWHC 2158 (Ch), [2008] S.T.C. 3340 (Ch D), Sir Andrew Park

Sch.10 para.1, substituted: SI 2008/1146 Art.2

Sch.10 Part 1 para.1, substituted: SI 2008/1146 Art.2

Sch.10 Part 1 para.2, substituted: SI 2008/1146 Art.2

Sch.10 Part 1 para.3, substituted: SI 2008/1146 Art.2

Sch.10 Part 1 para.4, substituted: SI 2008/1146 Art.2

Sch.10 Part 1 para.5, substituted: SI 2008/1146 Art.2

Sch.10 Part 1 para.6, substituted: SI 2008/1146 Art.2

Sch.10 Part 1 para.7, substituted: SI 2008/1146 Art.2

Sch.10 Part 1 para.8, substituted: SI 2008/1146 Art.2

Sch.10 Part 1 para.9, substituted: SI 2008/1146 Art.2

Sch.10 Part 1 para.10, substituted: SI 2008/1146 Art.2

Sch.10 Part 1 para.11, substituted: SI 2008/1146 Art.2

Sch.10 Part 1 para.12, substituted: SI 2008/1146 Art.2

Sch.10 Part 1 para.13, substituted: SI 2008/1146 Art.2

Sch.10 Part 1 para.14, substituted: SI 2008/1146 Art.2

Sch.10 Part 1 para.15, substituted: SI 2008/1146 Art.2

Sch.10 Part 1 para.16, substituted: SI 2008/1146 Art.2

Sch.10 Part 1 para.17, substituted: SI 2008/1146 Art.2

Sch.10 Part 1 para.18, substituted: SI 2008/1146 Art.2

Sch.10 Part 1 para.19, substituted: SI 2008/1146 Art.2

Sch.10 Part 1 para.20, substituted: SI 2008/1146 Art.2

Sch.10 Part 1 para.21, substituted: SI 2008/1146 Art.2

Sch.10 Part 1 para.22, substituted: SI 2008/1146 Art.2

Sch.10 Part 1 para.23, substituted: SI 2008/1146 Art.2

CAP. CAP.

1994–cont.

23. Value Added Tax Act 1994–*cont.*

Sch.10 Part 1 para.24, substituted: SI 2008/1146 Art.2

Sch.10 Part 1 para.25, substituted: SI 2008/1146 Art.2

Sch.10 Part 1 para.26, substituted: SI 2008/1146 Art.2

Sch.10 Part 1 para.27, substituted: SI 2008/1146 Art.2

Sch.10 Part 1 para.28, substituted: SI 2008/1146 Art.2

Sch.10 Part 1 para.29, substituted: SI 2008/1146 Art.2

Sch.10 Part 1 para.30, substituted: SI 2008/1146 Art.2

Sch.10 Part 1 para.31, substituted: SI 2008/1146 Art.2

Sch.10 Part 1 para.32, substituted: SI 2008/1146 Art.2

Sch.10 Part 1 para.33, substituted: SI 2008/1146 Art.2

Sch.10 Part 1 para.34, substituted: SI 2008/1146 Art.2

Sch.10 para.2, see *Newnham College, Cambridge v Customs and Excise Commissioners* [2008] UKHL 23, [2008] 1 W.L.R. 888 (HL), Lord Hoffmann

Sch.10 para.2, substituted: SI 2008/1146 Art.2

Sch.10 Part 2 para.35, substituted: SI 2008/1146 Art.2

Sch.10 Part 2 para.36, substituted: SI 2008/1146 Art.2

Sch.10 Part 2 para.37, substituted: SI 2008/1146 Art.2

Sch.10 Part 2 para.38, substituted: SI 2008/1146 Art.2

Sch.10 Part 2 para.39, substituted: SI 2008/1146 Art.2

Sch.10 para.3, substituted: SI 2008/1146 Art.2

Sch.10 para.3A, see *Newnham College, Cambridge v Customs and Excise Commissioners* [2008] UKHL 23, [2008] 1 W.L.R. 888 (HL), Lord Hoffmann

Sch.10 para.3A, substituted: SI 2008/1146 Art.2

Sch.10 Part 3 para.40, substituted: SI 2008/1146 Art.2

Sch.10 para.4, substituted: SI 2008/1146 Art.2

Sch.10 para.5, substituted: SI 2008/1146 Art.2

Sch.10 para.6, substituted: SI 2008/1146 Art.2

Sch.10 para.7, substituted: SI 2008/1146 Art.2

Sch.10 para.8, repealed (in part): SI 2008/1146 Art.5

Sch.10 para.8, substituted: SI 2008/1146 Art.2

1994–cont.

23. Value Added Tax Act 1994–*cont.*

Sch.10 para.9, substituted: SI 2008/1146 Art.2

Sch.10A para.1, see *Leisure Pass Group Ltd v Revenue and Customs Commissioners* [2008] EWHC 2158 (Ch), [2008] S.T.C. 3340 (Ch D), Sir Andrew Park

Sch.11 para.2, see *Boots Co Plc v Revenue and Customs Commissioners* [2008] B.V.C. 2328 (V&DTr (London)), AN Brice

Sch.11 para.2, applied: 2008 c.9 Sch.41 para.1, Sch.41 para.7

Sch.11 para.2, enabling: SI 2008/556, SI 2008/1482, SI 2008/3021

Sch.11 para.2A, enabling: SI 2008/3021

Sch.11 para.6, amended: 2008 c.9 Sch.37 para.5

Sch.11 para.6A, amended: 2008 c.9 Sch.37 para.6

Sch.11 para.7, repealed (in part): 2008 c.9 Sch.36 para.87

Sch.11 para.10, repealed (in part): 2008 c.9 Sch.36 para.87

Sch.11 para.14, repealed (in part): 2008 c.9 Sch.44 para.6

Sch.11A para.7, amended: SI 2008/954 Art.20

Sch.13 para.8, amended: SI 2008/1146 Sch.1 para.5

Sch.13 para.10, repealed: SI 2008/1146 Sch.1 para.5

26. Trade Marks Act 1994

see *R. v Cheng (Costs)* [2008] 1 Costs L.R. 180 (Sup Ct Costs Office), Costs Judge Gordon-Saker; see *R. v Rose (Costs)* [2008] 1 Costs L.R. 198 (Sup Ct Costs Office), Costs Judge Rogers; see *R. v Singh (Jhalman)* [2008] EWCA Crim 243, [2008] 2 Cr. App. R. (S.) 69 (CA (Crim Div)), Richards, L.J.

applied: SI 2008/1797 r.3, r.4, r.11, r.58, r.60, r.61, r.62, r.63, r.64, r.67, r.68, r.82, SI 2008/2206 Art.3, Sch.4 para.1, Sch.4 para.2

referred to: SI 2008/1958 r.2

varied: SI 2008/2206 Art.3

s.3, see *Bignell (t/a Just Employment) v Just Employment Law Ltd* [2007] EWHC 2203 (Ch), [2008] F.S.R. 6 (Ch D (Patents Ct)), Robert Englehart Q.C.; see *Campbell v Sugar Media Ltd* [2008] E.T.M.R. 56 (TMR), David Landau; see *D Jacobson & Sons Ltd v Globe Ltd* [2008] EWHC 88 (Ch), [2008] F.S.R. 21 (Ch D), Etherton, J.; see *Jules Rimet Cup Ltd v Football Association Ltd* [2007] EWHC 2376 (Ch), [2008] E.C.D.R. 4 (Ch D), Roger Wyand Q.C.; see *Melly's Trade Mark Application (Costs)* [2008] E.T.M.R. 42 (App Person), Geoffrey Hobbs Q.C.; see *Melly's Trade Mark Application* [2008] E.T.M.R. 41 (App Person), Geoffrey Hobbs Q.C.

s.4, referred to: SI 2008/1797 r.10

CAP.

1994–cont.

26. Trade Marks Act 1994–*cont.*

s.4, enabling: SI 2008/1797

s.5, see *Bowerbank's Trade Mark Application (No.O-070-07)* [2008] E.T.M.R. 31 (TMR), David Landau; see *Campbell v Sugar Media Ltd* [2008] E.T.M.R. 56 (TMR), David Landau; see *Digipos Store Solutions Group Ltd v Digi International Inc* [2008] EWHC 3371 (Ch), [2008] Bus. L.R. 1621 (Ch D), Daniel Alexander Q.C.; see *esure Insurance Ltd v Direct Line Insurance Plc* [2008] EWCA Civ 842, [2008] E.T.M.R. 77 (CA (Civ Div)), Arden, L.J.; see *esure Insurance Ltd v Direct Line Insurance Plc* [2008] R.P.C. 5 (TMR), Allan James; see *Jules Rimet Cup Ltd v Football Association Ltd* [2007] EWHC 2376 (Ch), [2008] E.C.D.R. 4 (Ch D), Roger Wyand Q.C.; see *Melly's Trade Mark Application* [2008] E.T.M.R. 41 (App Person), Geoffrey Hobbs Q.C.; see *Ruhnke v Queen Productions Ltd* [2008] E.T.M.R. 30 (TMR), M Reynolds

s.5, applied: SI 2008/1797 r.47

s.5, referred to: SI 2008/1797 r.19, r.20, r.21, r.42

s.6, applied: SI 2008/1797 r.14, r.20, r.42

s.6A, amended: SI 2008/1067 Reg.4

s.6A, referred to: SI 2008/1797 r.17

s.10, see *Eli Lilly & Co v 8PM Chemist Ltd* [2007] EWHC 2829 (Ch), [2008] F.S.R. 11 (Ch D), Mann, J.; see *Eli Lilly & Co v 8PM Chemist Ltd* [2008] EWCA Civ 24, [2008] F.S.R. 12 (CA (Civ Div)), Rix, L.J.; see *Rxworks Ltd v Hunter (t/a Connect Computers)* [2007] EWHC 3061 (Ch), [2008] E.C.C. 15 (Ch D), Daniel Alexander Q.C.

s.13, applied: SI 2008/1797 r.47

s.13, enabling: SI 2008/1797

s.24, disapplied: SI 2008/2206 Sch.1 Part 1

s.25, applied: SI 2008/1797 r.49

s.25, referred to: SI 2008/1797 r.48

s.25, varied: SI 2008/2206 Sch.2 para.1

s.25, enabling: SI 2008/1797

s.27, applied: SI 2008/1797 r.49

s.32, applied: SI 2008/1797 r.5, r.13

s.32, disapplied: SI 2008/2206 Sch.1 Part 1

s.33, disapplied: SI 2008/2206 Sch.1 Part 1

s.33, varied: SI 2008/2206 Sch.2 para.2

s.34, disapplied: SI 2008/2206 Sch.1 Part 1

s.34, enabling: SI 2008/1797

s.35, applied: SI 2008/1797 r.6, r.47

s.35, varied: SI 2008/2206 Sch.2 para.3

s.35, enabling: SI 2008/1797

s.36, applied: SI 2008/1797 r.6, r.47

s.37, see *West v Hudson* [2007] EWHC 1938 (Ch), (2008) 31 (2) I.P.D. 31009 (Ch D), Sir Andrew Morritt (Chancellor)

s.37, varied: SI 2008/2206 Sch.2 para.4

s.38, applied: SI 2008/1797 r.17, r.22

CAP.

1994–cont.

26. Trade Marks Act 1994–*cont.*

s.38, varied: SI 2008/2206 Sch.2 para.5

s.38, enabling: SI 2008/1797

s.38A, varied: SI 2008/2206 Sch.2 para.6

s.38B, varied: SI 2008/2206 Sch.2 para.6

s.39, applied: SI 2008/1797 r.25

s.39, disapplied: SI 2008/2206 Sch.1 Part 1

s.39, varied: SI 2008/2206 Sch.2 para.7

s.39, enabling: SI 2008/1797

s.40, applied: SI 2008/1797 r.34, r.47

s.40, disapplied: SI 2008/2206 Sch.1 Part 1

s.40, enabling: SI 2008/1797

s.41, applied: SI 2008/1797 r.28

s.41, disapplied: SI 2008/2206 Sch.1 Part 1

s.41, enabling: SI 2008/1797

s.42, disapplied: SI 2008/2206 Sch.1 Part 1

s.43, disapplied: SI 2008/2206 Sch.1 Part 1

s.43, enabling: SI 2008/1797

s.44, applied: SI 2008/1797 r.32

s.44, disapplied: SI 2008/2206 Sch.1 Part 1

s.44, enabling: SI 2008/1797

s.45, disapplied: SI 2008/2206 Sch.1 Part 1

s.45, enabling: SI 2008/1797

s.46, see *BSA by B2 Trade Mark* [2008] R.P.C. 22 (App Person), Geoffrey Hobbs Q.C.; see *Pan World Brands Ltd v Tripp Ltd* [2008] R.P.C. 2 (App Person), Richard Arnold Q.C.

s.46, applied: SI 2008/1797 r.38, r.39

s.46, referred to: SI 2008/1797 r.38, r.39

s.47, see *Bignell (t/a Just Employment) v Just Employment Law Ltd* [2007] EWHC 2203 (Ch), [2008] F.S.R. 6 (Ch D (Patents Ct)), Robert Englehart Q.C.; see *Rousselon Freres et Cie v Horwood Homewares Ltd* [2008] EWHC 881 (Ch), [2008] R.P.C. 30 (Ch D), Warren, J.

s.47, amended: SI 2008/1067 Reg.5

s.47, applied: SI 2008/1797 r.41

s.47, disapplied: SI 2008/1797 r.41

s.47, referred to: SI 2008/1797 r.41

s.52, enabling: SI 2008/1959

s.54, enabling: SI 2008/2206, SI 2008/2207

s.56, see *Melly's Trade Mark Application* [2008] E.T.M.R. 41 (App Person), Geoffrey Hobbs Q.C.

s.63, applied: SI 2008/1797 r.46, r.47

s.63, varied: SI 2008/2206 Sch.2 para.8

s.63, enabling: SI 2008/1797

s.64, disapplied: SI 2008/2206 Sch.1 Part 1

s.64, enabling: SI 2008/1797

s.65, applied: SI 2008/1797 r.55

s.65, disapplied: SI 2008/2206 Sch.1 Part 1

s.65, enabling: SI 2008/1797

s.66, applied: SI 2008/1797 r.3

s.66, enabling: SI 2008/1797

s.67, disapplied: SI 2008/1797 r.57

s.67, varied: SI 2008/2206 Sch.2 para.9

s.67, enabling: SI 2008/1797

s.68, enabling: SI 2008/1797

s.69, enabling: SI 2008/1797

CAP.

1994–cont.

26. Trade Marks Act 1994–*cont.*
s.76, applied: SI 2008/1797 r.68, r.71
s.76, enabling: SI 2008/1797
s.78, enabling: SI 2008/11, SI 2008/1797, SI 2008/2300
s.79, applied: SI 2008/1797 r.4
s.79, disapplied: SI 2008/2206 Sch.1 Part 1
s.79, enabling: SI 2008/11, SI 2008/1958, SI 2008/2207
s.80, applied: SI 2008/1797 r.80, SI 2008/1958 r.3
s.80, enabling: SI 2008/1797
s.81, enabling: SI 2008/1797
s.82, applied: SI 2008/1797 r.60
s.82, enabling: SI 2008/1797
s.84, applied: SI 2008/1797 r.61
s.88, enabling: SI 2008/1797
s.91, amended: SI 2008/1277 Sch.2 para.54
s.93, applied: 2008 c.13 Sch.3
s.94, disapplied: SI 2008/2206 Sch.1 Part 1
s.97, amended: SI 2008/1277 Sch.2 para.55
s.98, amended: SI 2008/1277 Sch.2 para.56
Sch.1 para.6, applied: SI 2008/1797 r.30
Sch.1 para.6, referred to: SI 2008/1797 r.30
Sch.1 para.6, enabling: SI 2008/1797
Sch.2 para.7, applied: SI 2008/1797 r.30
Sch.2 para.7, referred to: SI 2008/1797 r.30
Sch.2 para.7, enabling: SI 2008/1797

29. Police and Magistrates Courts Act 1994
s.33, repealed: 2008 c.12 Sch.1 Part 6
s.41, repealed: 2008 c.12 Sch.1 Part 6

30. Education Act 1994
s.18B, amended: 2008 c.25 s.164

33. Criminal Justice and Public Order Act 1994
see *R. v Ibrahim (Muktar)* [2008] EWCA Crim 880, [2008] 4 All E.R. 208 (CA (Crim Div)), Sir Igor Judge (President, QB)
Part V, applied: 2008 c.13 Sch.3
Part VII, applied: 2008 c.13 Sch.3
Part XII, applied: 2008 c.13 Sch.3
s.25, amended: SI 2008/1779 Art.16
s.34, see *R. v Ibrahim (Muktar)* [2008] EWCA Crim 880, [2008] 4 All E.R. 208 (CA (Crim Div)), Sir Igor Judge (President, QB); see *R. v Maguire (Glen)* [2008] EWCA Crim 1028, (2008) 172 J.P. 417 (CA (Crim Div)), Hughes, L.J.
s.34, amended: 2008 c.28 s.22
s.35, see *R. v Anwoir* [2008] EWCA Crim 1354, [2008] 4 All E.R. 582 (CA (Crim Div)), Latham, L.J.
s.36, disapplied: 2008 c.28 s.22
s.37, disapplied: 2008 c.28 s.22
s.77, referred to: 2008 c.13 Sch.6
s.78, referred to: 2008 c.13 Sch.6
s.80, amended: 2008 c.17 Sch.16
s.127, amended: 2008 c.4 s.138
s.127A, added: 2008 c.4 s.139

CAP.

1994–cont.

33. Criminal Justice and Public Order Act 1994–*cont.*
s.128, amended: SI 2008/1216 Sch.6 Part 3
s.136, amended: 2008 c.4 Sch.4 para.42
s.166, referred to: 2008 c.13 Sch.6
s.166A, referred to: 2008 c.13 Sch.6
s.167, referred to: 2008 c.13 Sch.6

36. Law of Property (Miscellaneous Provisions) Act 1994
s.19, applied: SI 2008/611 Art.29

37. Drug Trafficking Act 1994
see *Gibson v Revenue and Customs Prosecution Office* [2008] EWCA Civ 645, [2008] 2 F.L.R. 1672 (CA (Civ Div)), May, L.J.; see *Togher v Revenue and Customs Prosecution Office* [2007] EWCA Civ 686, [2008] Q.B. 476 (CA (Civ Div)), Chadwick, L.J.
s.1, see *R. v Green (Mark)* [2008] UKHL 30, [2008] 1 A.C. 1053 (HL), Lord Bingham of Cornhill
s.2, see *R. v Green (Mark)* [2008] UKHL 30, [2008] 1 A.C. 1053 (HL), Lord Bingham of Cornhill
s.4, see *R. v Green (Mark)* [2008] UKHL 30, [2008] 1 A.C. 1053 (HL), Lord Bingham of Cornhill; see *Telli v Revenue and Customs Prosecutions Office* [2007] EWCA Civ 1385, [2008] 3 All E.R. 405 (CA (Civ Div)), Ward, L.J.
s.5, see *Telli v Revenue and Customs Prosecutions Office* [2007] EWCA Civ 1385, [2008] 3 All E.R. 405 (CA (Civ Div)), Ward, L.J.
s.9, see *Togher v Revenue and Customs Prosecution Office* [2007] EWCA Civ 686, [2008] Q.B. 476 (CA (Civ Div)), Chadwick, L.J.
s.11, see *Telli v Revenue and Customs Prosecutions Office* [2007] EWCA Civ 1385, [2008] 3 All E.R. 405 (CA (Civ Div)), Ward, L.J.
s.17, see *Telli v Revenue and Customs Prosecutions Office* [2007] EWCA Civ 1385, [2008] 3 All E.R. 405 (CA (Civ Div)), Ward, L.J.
s.31, see *Togher v Revenue and Customs Prosecution Office* [2007] EWCA Civ 686, [2008] Q.B. 476 (CA (Civ Div)), Chadwick, L.J.
s.49, see *Ali v Revenue and Customs Prosecutions Office* [2008] EWCA Crim 1466, (2008) 172 J.P. 516 (CA (Crim Div)), Moses, L.J.

39. Local Government etc (Scotland) Act 1994
applied: SI 2008/570 Sch.1 para.3, SI 2008/700 Sch.1 para.3
s.2, applied: 2008 asp 6 Sch.3 para.4, SI 2008/2852 Sch.3 para.5, SSI 2008/263 Sch.2
s.40, applied: SSI 2008/228 Sch.2

CAP.

1994–cont.

39. Local Government etc (Scotland) Act 1994–*cont.*

s.128, applied: SSI 2008/228 Sch.2

s.153, enabling: SSI 2008/85

Sch.13 para.9, repealed: 2008 asp 5 Sch.3 Part 1

Sch.13 para.26, repealed: 2008 asp 5 Sch.3 Part 1

Sch.13 para.51, repealed: SI 2008/1277 Sch.4 Part 1

Sch.14, amended: 2008 asp 5 Sch.3 Part 1

40. Deregulation and Contracting Out Act 1994

s.37, amended: SI 2008/960 Sch.3

s.69, applied: SI 2008/570 Sch.1 para.19, SI 2008/700 Sch.1 para.21

s.70, applied: SI 2008/700 Sch.1 para.22

s.71, amended: 2008 c.29 s.224

1995

4. Finance Act 1995

s.32, repealed: 2008 c.9 Sch.41 para.25

s.55, repealed (in part): 2008 c.9 Sch.14 para.17

s.81, repealed: 2008 c.9 s.66

s.83, repealed (in part): 2008 c.9 Sch.17 para.35

s.105, repealed (in part): 2008 c.9 Sch.37 para.11

s.127, amended: 2008 c.9 Sch.16 para.1, Sch.16 para.2

s.127, repealed (in part): 2008 c.9 Sch.16 para.1

s.134, repealed (in part): 2008 c.9 s.41

Sch.8 Part I para.21, repealed (in part): 2008 c.9 Sch.17 para.18

Sch.8 Part III para.58, enabling: SI 2008/1944

Sch.17 Part III para.27, repealed: 2008 c.9 Sch.2 para.21

Sch.17 Part III para.28, repealed: 2008 c.9 Sch.2 para.21

Sch.17 Part III para.29, repealed: 2008 c.9 Sch.2 para.21

7. Requirements of Writing (Scotland) Act 1995

applied: 2008 c.32 s.77

Sch.2 para.3, amended: SI 2008/948 Sch.1 para.199

13. Road Traffic (New Drivers) Act 1995

s.3, referred to: 2008 c.13 Sch.6

15. Activity Centres (Young Persons Safety) Act 1995

s.1, amended: SI 2008/960 Sch.3

s.1, enabling: SI 2008/1973

s.2, amended: 2008 c.20 Sch.3 para.4

s.2, applied: 2008 c.13 Sch.7

s.3, amended: SI 2008/960 Sch.3

s.3, applied: SI 2008/1973

CAP.

1995–cont.

16. Prisoners (Return to Custody) Act 1995

s.2, repealed (in part): 2008 c.4 Sch.28 Part 1

18. Jobseekers Act 1995

applied: SI 2008/794 Reg.104, Reg.107, Reg.115, SI 2008/795 Reg.5, SI 2008/1052 Sch.2 para.2, SI 2008/1053 Sch.2 para.2, SI 2008/1054 Sch.2 para.2

referred to: SI 2008/2551 Reg.12

Part I, applied: SI 2008/529 Reg.120, Reg.137, SI 2008/1273 Reg.67, Reg.82, SI 2008/1582 Reg.120, Reg.137, SI 2008/3170 Reg.67, Reg.82

s.1, referred to: SSI 2008/81 Reg.2

s.1, enabling: SI 2008/13

s.3, applied: SI 2008/794 Reg.68, Sch.4 para.1

s.4, enabling: SI 2008/698, SI 2008/2767, SI 2008/3195

s.6, enabling: SI 2008/1826, SI 2008/3051

s.7, enabling: SI 2008/3051

s.8, enabling: SI 2008/3051

s.12, enabling: SI 2008/698, SI 2008/1599, SI 2008/2111, SI 2008/2767, SI 2008/3140, SI 2008/3157

s.16, applied: SI 2008/794 Reg.68, Sch.4 para.1

s.19, enabling: SI 2008/3051

s.35, enabling: SI 2008/13, SI 2008/698, SI 2008/1599, SI 2008/1826, SI 2008/2111, SI 2008/2767, SI 2008/3051, SI 2008/3140, SI 2008/3157, SI 2008/3195

s.36, enabling: SI 2008/13, SI 2008/698, SI 2008/1599, SI 2008/1826, SI 2008/2111, SI 2008/2767, SI 2008/3051, SI 2008/3140, SI 2008/3157, SI 2008/3195

s.37, applied: SI 2008/1826, SI 2008/3051

Sch.1 para.1, enabling: SI 2008/698, SI 2008/2767

Sch.1 para.3, enabling: SI 2008/698, SI 2008/2767

Sch.1 para.8, enabling: SI 2008/3051

Sch.1 para.8A, enabling: SI 2008/13

Sch.1 para.10, enabling: SI 2008/3051

Sch.1 para.11, enabling: SI 2008/2767

21. Merchant Shipping Act 1995

applied: 2008 c.13 Sch.7, SI 2008/676 Sch.1 Part XIII, SI 2008/2077 Art.2, SSI 2008/188 Art.31, SSI 2008/189 Art.31, SSI 2008/190 Art.31

Part I, referred to: 2008 c.13 Sch.6

Part II, referred to: 2008 c.13 Sch.6

Part III, referred to: 2008 c.13 Sch.6

Part IV, referred to: 2008 c.13 Sch.6

Part V, referred to: 2008 c.13 Sch.6

Part IX, applied: SI 2008/1160 Art.7, SI 2008/1261 Art.13, SSI 2008/182 Art.10, Art.22, Art.41, SSI 2008/188 Art.6, Art.25, SSI 2008/189 Art.6, Art.25, SSI 2008/190 Art.4, Art.6, Art.25, SSI 2008/361 Art.7

Part IX, referred to: 2008 c.13 Sch.6

CAP.

1995–cont.

21. Merchant Shipping Act 1995–*cont.*
Part X, referred to: 2008 c.13 Sch.6
Part XI, referred to: 2008 c.13 Sch.6
Part XII, referred to: 2008 c.13 Sch.6
s.18, enabling: SI 2008/1243
s.47, enabling: SI 2008/2851
s.58, applied: SSI 2008/190 Art.15
s.85, enabling: SI 2008/2165, SI 2008/2166, SI 2008/2851, SI 2008/3145
s.86, applied: SI 2008/2165, SI 2008/2166, SI 2008/2851
s.86, referred to: SI 2008/3145
s.86, enabling: SI 2008/2165, SI 2008/2166, SI 2008/3145
s.94, see *Club Cruise Entertainment & Travelling Services Europe BV v Department for Transport (The Van Gogh)* [2008] EWHC 2794 (Comm), [2008] 2 C.L.C. 708 (QBD (Comm)), Flaux, J.
s.95, see *Club Cruise Entertainment & Travelling Services Europe BV v Department for Transport (The Van Gogh)* [2008] EWHC 2794 (Comm), [2008] 2 C.L.C. 708 (QBD (Comm)), Flaux, J.
s.97, see *Club Cruise Entertainment & Travelling Services Europe BV v Department for Transport (The Van Gogh)* [2008] EWHC 2794 (Comm), [2008] 2 C.L.C. 708 (QBD (Comm)), Flaux, J.
s.128, enabling: SI 2008/2924, SI 2008/3257
s.131, applied: SI 2008/2924 Reg.33
s.131, referred to: SI 2008/3257 Reg.42
s.143, varied: SI 2008/2924 Reg.33, SI 2008/3257 Reg.43
s.144, applied: SI 2008/2924 Reg.29, SI 2008/3257 Reg.39
s.145, varied: SI 2008/2924 Reg.28, Reg.29, SI 2008/3257 Reg.38, Reg.39
s.146, varied: SI 2008/2924 Reg.34, SI 2008/3257 Reg.44
s.187, see *Krysia Maritime Inc v Intership Ltd (The Krysia)* [2008] EWHC 1880 (Admlty), [2008] 2 Lloyd's Rep. 707 (QBD (Admlty)), Aikens, J.
s.193, disapplied: SI 2008/1261 Art.55
s.252, applied: SI 2008/1261 Sch.8 para.23
s.258, applied: SI 2008/3257 Reg.36
s.258, varied: SI 2008/2924 Reg.26
s.259, applied: SI 2008/2924 Reg.17, SI 2008/3257 Reg.17, Reg.36
s.259, varied: SI 2008/2924 Reg.26
s.271, applied: SI 2008/676 Sch.1 Part XIII
s.284, referred to: SI 2008/2924 Reg.28, SI 2008/3257 Reg.38
s.284, varied: SI 2008/2924 Reg.28, SI 2008/3257 Reg.38
s.306, applied: SI 2008/2851

23. Goods Vehicles (Licensing of Operators) Act 1995
referred to: 2008 c.13 Sch.6

CAP.

1995–cont.

23. Goods Vehicles (Licensing of Operators) Act 1995–*cont.*
s.1, amended: 2008 c.26 s.3
s.2, see *Romantiek Transport BVBA v Vehicle and Operator Services Agency* [2008] EWCA Civ 534, [2008] 2 Lloyd's Rep. 409 (CA (Civ Div)), Tuckey, L.J.
s.5, amended: 2008 c.26 s.125
s.13, applied: SI 2008/1474 Reg.3
s.17, applied: SI 2008/1474 Reg.3
s.24, applied: SI 2008/1474 Reg.3
s.25, applied: SI 2008/1474 Reg.3
s.45, enabling: SI 2008/1474
s.57, applied: SI 2008/1474
s.57, enabling: SI 2008/1474
Sch.1A, applied: 2008 c.13 Sch.7
Sch.1A para.8, substituted: 2008 c.26 s.126

24. Crown Agents Act 1995
s.5, amended: SI 2008/948 Sch.1 para.200

25. Environment Act 1995
applied: 2008 c.13 Sch.3
Part III, applied: SI 2008/239 Sch.2 para.17
s.20, applied: SSI 2008/228 Sch.2
s.31, applied: SI 2008/1776 Sch.1
s.40, applied: SI 2008/1776 Sch.1, SSI 2008/170 Reg.21
s.41, amended: SI 2008/3087 Reg.17
s.41, applied: SI 2008/1776 Sch.1, SI 2008/3087 Reg.17
s.42, applied: SI 2008/1776 Sch.1
s.46, amended: SI 2008/948 Sch.1 para.1, Sch.1 para.19
s.48, applied: 2008 asp 2 Sch.5
s.87, applied: 2008 c.13 Sch.7
s.93, applied: SI 2008/413
s.93, referred to: SI 2008/413
s.93, enabling: SI 2008/413, SI 2008/1941
s.94, enabling: SI 2008/413, SI 2008/1941
s.94A, enabling: SI 2008/413, SI 2008/1941
s.95, applied: 2008 c.13 Sch.7
s.95, enabling: SI 2008/413, SI 2008/1941
s.97, applied: 2008 c.13 Sch.7
s.108, applied: 2008 c.32 s.27, SI 2008/314 Reg.15, SI 2008/2852 Sch.7 para.1
s.108, referred to: 2008 c.32 s.13
s.108, varied: SI 2008/1097 Reg.16
s.110, referred to: 2008 c.13 Sch.6
Sch.7 para.9, applied: SI 2008/788 Art.4
Sch.7 para.10, applied: SI 2008/788 Art.4
Sch.10 para.25, repealed (in part): 2008 c.17 Sch.16
Sch.17 para.2, repealed (in part): 2008 asp 5 Sch.3 Part 1
Sch.22 para.30, amended: SI 2008/960 Sch.3
Sch.24, amended: 2008 asp 5 Sch.3 Part 1

CAP.

1995–cont.

26. Pensions Act 1995

see *R. (on the application of Bradley) v Secretary of State for Work and Pensions* [2008] EWCA Civ 36, [2008] 3 W.L.R. 1059 (CA (Civ Div)), Wall, L.J.

applied: SI 2008/576 Sch.4 para.5

referred to: 2008 c.30 s.146

Part I, see *R. (on the application of Bradley) v Secretary of State for Work and Pensions* [2008] EWCA Civ 36, [2008] 3 W.L.R. 1059 (CA (Civ Div)), Wall, L.J.

s.3, applied: 2008 c.30 Sch.1 para.3

s.4, applied: 2008 c.30 Sch.1 para.3

s.7, amended: 2008 c.30 s.131, Sch.11 Part 6

s.10, applied: 2008 c.30 s.60, SSI 2008/228 Reg.94

s.29, applied: 2008 c.30 Sch.1 para.4

s.37, amended: 2008 c.30 s.130

s.47, applied: 2008 c.30 s.22

s.49, applied: SI 2008/239 Reg.42, SSI 2008/228 Reg.38

s.50, applied: SI 2008/649 Reg.2, Reg.3, Reg.4, Reg.5, SI 2008/653 Reg.10

s.50, referred to: SI 2008/649 Reg.5, SI 2008/653 Reg.10, SSI 2008/224 Reg.10

s.50, enabling: SI 2008/649

s.51ZA, amended: 2008 c.30 Sch.2 para.8

s.58, see *Allied Domecq (Holdings) Ltd v Allied Domecq First Pension Trust Fund* [2008] EWCA Civ 1084, [2008] Pens. L.R. 425 (CA (Civ Div)), Ward, L.J.

s.67D, enabling: SI 2008/1050

s.68, enabling: SI 2008/731, SI 2008/1068

s.73, see *Alexander Forbes Trustee Services Ltd v Clarke* [2008] EWHC 153 (Ch), [2008] Pens. L.R. 145 (Ch D), Henderson, J; see *Bridge Trustees Ltd v Yates* [2008] EWHC 964 (Ch), [2008] Pens. L.R. 261 (Ch D), Sarah Asplin QC; see *Trustee Solutions Ltd v Dubery* [2007] EWCA Civ 771, [2008] 1 All E.R. 826 (CA (Civ Div)), Ward, L.J.

s.75, see *Federal-Mogul Aftermarket UK Ltd, Re* [2008] EWHC 1099 (Ch), [2008] Bus. L.R. 1443 (Ch D (Companies Ct)), David Richards, J.

s.75, applied: SI 2008/731 Reg.2

s.75, disapplied: SI 2008/2546 Sch.3 para.6, Sch.3 para.11

s.75, enabling: SI 2008/731, SI 2008/1068

s.75A, enabling: SI 2008/731, SI 2008/1068

s.116, applied: 2008 c.13 Sch.7

s.118, enabling: SI 2008/731

s.119, enabling: SI 2008/731

s.120, applied: SI 2008/649, SI 2008/731, SI 2008/1050

s.124, enabling: SI 2008/649, SI 2008/731, SI 2008/1050, SI 2008/1068

s.125, enabling: SI 2008/731

s.168, amended: 2008 c.30 s.138

CAP.

1995–cont.

26. Pensions Act 1995–*cont.*

s.174, enabling: SI 2008/649, SI 2008/731, SI 2008/1050, SI 2008/1068

30. Landlord and Tenant (Covenants) Act 1995

s.6, see *Wembley National Stadium Ltd v Wembley (London) Ltd* [2007] EWHC 756 (Ch), [2008] 1 P. & C.R. 3 (Ch D), Sir Andrew Morritt C.

s.16, see *Prudential Assurance Co Ltd v Ayres* [2008] EWCA Civ 52, [2008] 1 All E.R. 1266 (CA (Civ Div)), Ward, L.J.

s.17, see *Scottish & Newcastle Plc v Raguz (No.3)* [2008] UKHL 65, [2008] 1 W.L.R. 2494 (HL), Lord Hoffmann

s.25, see *Prudential Assurance Co Ltd v Ayres* [2008] EWCA Civ 52, [2008] 1 All E.R. 1266 (CA (Civ Div)), Ward, L.J.

32. Olympic Symbol etc (Protection) Act 1995

applied: 2008 c.13 Sch.3

s.8, referred to: 2008 c.13 Sch.6

34. Child Support Act 1995

applied: SI 2008/794 Sch.6 para.15

s.17, repealed: SI 2008/2833 Sch.3 para.228

Sch.1, applied: SI 2008/794 Sch.6 para.15

Sch.3 para.9, repealed: 2008 c.6 Sch.8

Sch.3 para.10, repealed: 2008 c.6 Sch.8

Sch.3 para.18, repealed: SI 2008/2833 Sch.3 para.228

35. Criminal Appeal Act 1995

Part II, applied: SI 2008/1586 Sch.2 para.4, Sch.2 para.8

36. Children (Scotland) Act 1995

applied: 2008 c.23 s.20

Part I, referred to: 2008 c.22 s.53

s.1, amended: 2008 c.22 Sch.6 para.48

s.2, amended: 2008 c.22 Sch.6 para.49

s.3, amended: 2008 c.22 Sch.6 para.50

s.4A, added: 2008 c.22 Sch.6 para.51

s.5, see *P v Children's Reporter* 2008 S.L.T. (Sh Ct) 85 (Sh Ct (Lothian)), Sheriff IG McColl

s.11, see *Children's Reporter v D* 2008 S.L.T. (Sh Ct) 21 (Sh Pr), Sheriff Principal JA Taylor

s.11, amended: 2008 c.22 Sch.6 para.52

s.12, amended: 2008 c.22 Sch.6 para.53

s.13, applied: SI 2008/794 Sch.9 para.44

s.15, amended: 2008 c.22 Sch.6 para.54, Sch.7 para.17

s.16, see *Authority Reporter, Edinburgh v RU* 2008 Fam. L.R. 70 (Sh Pr), Sheriff Principal EF Bowen Q.C.

s.17, enabling: SSI 2008/75

s.26, amended: 2008 c.23 Sch.1 para.9

s.26, applied: SI 2008/794 Sch.8 para.28

s.29, applied: SI 2008/794 Sch.8 para.30, Sch.9 para.22

s.30, applied: SI 2008/794 Sch.8 para.30, Sch.9 para.22

CAP.

1995–cont.

36. Children (Scotland) Act 1995–*cont.*
s.31, enabling: SSI 2008/75
s.51, see *Children's Reporter v D* 2008 S.L.T. (Sh Ct) 21 (Sh Pr), Sheriff Principal JA Taylor
s.52, see *M v McClafferty* 2008 Fam. L.R. 22 (IH (Ex Div)), Lord Nimmo Smith
s.70, see *Children's Reporter v D* 2008 S.L.T. (Sh Ct) 21 (Sh Pr), Sheriff Principal JA Taylor
s.70, applied: SSI 2008/75 Reg.3, Reg.7, Reg.8, Reg.9
s.70, enabling: SSI 2008/75
s.93, see *Children's Reporter v D* 2008 S.L.T. (Sh Ct) 21 (Sh Pr), Sheriff Principal JA Taylor
s.103, enabling: SSI 2008/75
Sch.4 para.19, repealed: 2008 c.12 Sch.1 Part 11

38. Civil Evidence Act 1995
s.1, see *Official Receiver v Stojevic* [2007] EWHC 1186 (Ch), [2008] Bus. L.R. 641 (Ch D), Judge Pelling Q.C.
Sch.1 para.6, repealed: 2008 c.9 Sch.36 para.92
Sch.1 para.11, repealed (in part): 2008 c.9 s.114
Sch.1 para.13, repealed (in part): 2008 c.9 s.114

39. Criminal Law (Consolidation) (Scotland) Act 1995
s.1, amended: 2008 c.22 Sch.6 para.55
s.1, referred to: 2008 c.22 s.53
s.5, referred to: SI 2008/1062 Sch.1 para.1
s.6, see *Paterson (Alexander) v HM Advocate* [2008] HCJAC 18, 2008 S.L.T. 465 (HCJ), Lord Hamilton L.J.G.
s.18, enabling: SSI 2008/379
s.23A, amended: 2008 c.24 s.12
s.44, applied: SI 2008/2852 Sch.6 para.14
s.47, see *Frame v Kennedy* [2008] HCJAC 25, 2008 J.C. 317 (HCJ), Lord Johnston

40. Criminal Procedure (Consequential Provisions) (Scotland) Act 1995
Sch.2 Part III, amended: 2008 asp 5 Sch.3 Part 1

42. Private International Law (Miscellaneous Provisions) Act 1995
s.11, see *R. (on the application of Al-Jedda) v Secretary of State for Defence* [2007] UKHL 58, [2008] 1 A.C. 332 (HL), Lord Bingham of Cornhill
s.12, see *R. (on the application of Al-Jedda) v Secretary of State for Defence* [2007] UKHL 58, [2008] 1 A.C. 332 (HL), Lord Bingham of Cornhill
s.15A, added: SI 2008/2986 Reg.2
s.15B, added: SSI 2008/404 Reg.2
s.18, amended: SI 2008/2986 Reg.3, SSI 2008/404 Reg.2

CAP.

1995–cont.

43. Proceeds of Crime (Scotland) Act 1995
Part II, applied: 2008 asp 4 s.23

44. Statute Law (Repeals) Act 1995
Sch.2 para.1, amended: 2008 c.12 Sch.1 Part 3
Sch.2 para.1, repealed (in part): 2008 c.12 Sch.1 Part 3

45. Gas Act 1995
s.12, amended: 2008 c.32 s.78, Sch.6

46. Criminal Procedure (Scotland) Act 1995
applied: SI 2008/1597 Sch.5 para.15, SI 2008/2852 Sch.6 para.38, SSI 2008/103 Reg.16, SSI 2008/356 Reg.5, Reg.8, Reg.13, Reg.16, Reg.19, Reg.22, Reg.25, Reg.33
referred to: SSI 2008/356 Reg.28
Part X, applied: SI 2008/2852 Sch.6 para.36
s.8, amended: 2008 asp 6 s.59
s.14, see *Gillies v Ralph* [2008] HCJAC 55, 2008 S.L.T. 978 (HCJ), Lord Wheatley; see *Jones (Grant) v HM Advocate* 2008 J.C. 78 (HCJ), Lord Macfadyen
s.18, applied: SSI 2008/117 Reg.12, Reg.13
s.18, referred to: 2008 c.28 s.11
s.19, applied: SSI 2008/117 Reg.12, Reg.13
s.19A, applied: SSI 2008/117 Reg.12, Reg.13
s.19AA, applied: SSI 2008/117 Reg.12, Reg.13
s.20, applied: 2008 c.28 s.11
s.55, applied: 2008 c.28 s.45
s.57A, referred to: SSI 2008/356 Reg.21
s.59A, applied: SI 2008/794 Reg.160, Sch.5 Part 2
s.66, see *Stevenson (Paul Daniel) v HM Advocate* [2008] HCJAC 12, 2008 J.C. 296 (HCJ), Lord Nimmo Smith
s.70, applied: 2008 c.28 Sch.7 para.37, 2008 c.30 s.47
s.72, see *Martin (David Joseph) v HM Advocate* 2008 J.C. 287 (HCJ), Lord Osborne
s.76, see *Coyle (James Thomas) v HM Advocate* 2008 J.C. 107 (HCJ), Lord Macfadyen; see *Jordan (Jason Alexander) v HM Advocate* [2008] HCJAC 24, 2008 S.L.T. 489 (HCJ), Lord Nimmo Smith
s.92, see *Hunt v Aitken* [2008] HCJAC 57, 2008 S.C.C.R. 919 (HCJ), Lord Reed
s.97, see *HM Advocate v L* 2008 S.C.C.R. 51 (HCJ), Lord Hodge
s.102A, amended: SSI 2008/109 Art.2
s.106, see *Anderson (Colin) v HM Advocate* 2008 J.C. 111 (HCJ), Lord Gill L.J.C.; see *Burzala (Steven) v HM Advocate* 2008 S.L.T. 61 (HCJ), Lord Macfadyen; see *Coubrough (Richard Joseph) v HM Advocate* [2008] HCJAC 13, 2008 S.C.C.R. 317 (HCJ), Lord Osborne; see *Fraser (Nat Gordon) v HM Advocate*

CAP.

1995–cont.

46. Criminal Procedure (Scotland) Act 1995–*cont.*

s.106–*cont.*

[2008] HCJAC 26, 2008 S.C.C.R. 407 (HCJ), Lord Gill L.J.C.; see *Martin (David Joseph) v HM Advocate* 2008 J.C. 287 (HCJ), Lord Osborne

s.118, see *Fletcher (Brian Paul) v HM Advocate* [2008] HCJAC 1, 2008 J.C. 246 (HCJ), Lord Hamilton L.J.G.; see *Pickett (Scott) v HM Advocate* 2008 S.L.T. 319 (HCJ), Lord Osborne; see *Zhi Pen Lin v HM Advocate* 2008 J.C. 142 (HCJ), Lord Hamilton L.J.G.

s.134, applied: SSI 2008/93 Art.5, SSI 2008/328 Art.6, SSI 2008/363 Art.6

s.134, referred to: SI 2008/1597 Sch.5 para.15

s.136, applied: 2008 c.28 Sch.7 para.35, SI 2008/1276 Reg.10, SI 2008/1277 Reg.14, SSI 2008/64 Reg.12, SSI 2008/66 Reg.23, SSI 2008/100 Reg.22, SSI 2008/135 Reg.15, SSI 2008/159 Reg.21, SSI 2008/162 Reg.13

s.136, disapplied: SI 2008/1276 Reg.10, SI 2008/1277 Reg.14

s.137, applied: SSI 2008/93 Art.5, SSI 2008/328 Art.6, SSI 2008/363 Art.6

s.137ZA, applied: SSI 2008/93 Art.5, SSI 2008/328 Art.6, SSI 2008/363 Art.6

s.147, see *Small v Griffiths* 2008 S.C.C.R. 600 (HCJ), Lord Osborne

s.156, enabling: SSI 2008/61

s.166A, referred to: SSI 2008/42 Art.5

s.174, applied: SSI 2008/240 Reg.7

s.178, see *Hunt v Aitken* [2008] HCJAC 57, 2008 S.C.C.R. 919 (HCJ), Lord Reed

s.179, see *Hunt v Aitken* [2008] HCJAC 57, 2008 S.C.C.R. 919 (HCJ), Lord Reed

s.182, applied: SI 2008/1597 Sch.5 para.15, SI 2008/2852 Sch.6 para.36

s.196, see *Jordan (Jason Alexander) v HM Advocate* [2008] HCJAC 24, 2008 S.L.T. 489 (HCJ), Lord Nimmo Smith; see *Leonard v Houston* 2008 J.C. 92 (HCJ), Lord Macfadyen; see *Spence (Paul) v HM Advocate* 2008 J.C. 174 (HCJ), Lord Hamilton L.J.G.

s.205, applied: 2008 c.28 s.45

s.208, applied: 2008 c.28 s.45

s.209, amended: SI 2008/912 Sch.1 para.11

s.210A, see *Clark (George Samuel) v HM Advocate* [2008] HCJAC 35, 2008 S.L.T. 787 (HCJ), Lord Eassie; see *Jordan (Jason Alexander) v HM Advocate* [2008] HCJAC 24, 2008 S.L.T. 489 (HCJ), Lord Nimmo Smith

s.210B, see *HM Advocate v Henderson (Stephen Michael)* [2008] HCJ 4, 2008 S.L.T. 1077 (HCJ), Lord Uist

s.210E, see *HM Advocate v Henderson (Stephen Michael)* [2008] HCJ 4, 2008 S.L.T. 1077 (HCJ), Lord Uist

s.210F, see *HM Advocate v Henderson (Stephen Michael)* [2008] HCJ 4, 2008 S.L.T. 1077 (HCJ), Lord Uist

s.210F, applied: 2008 c.28 s.45, s.53

s.221, applied: 2008 asp 4 s.36, SSI 2008/102 Art.9, SSI 2008/151 Art.25

s.222, applied: SI 2008/2347 Art.12, SSI 2008/102 Art.9, SSI 2008/151 Art.25

s.226D, applied: SSI 2008/103 Reg.10

s.226D, enabling: SSI 2008/103

s.226F, enabling: SSI 2008/61, SSI 2008/104

s.226H, applied: SSI 2008/103 Reg.10, Reg.16, Reg.17, Reg.26

s.228, amended: SI 2008/912 Sch.1 para.11

s.234, amended: 2008 c.4 Sch.4 para.44, SI 2008/912 Sch.1 para.11

s.242, amended: 2008 c.4 Sch.4 para.45, SI 2008/912 Sch.1 para.11

s.244, amended: 2008 c.4 Sch.4 para.46

s.245C, applied: SI 2008/1788 Sch.2

s.245C, enabling: SSI 2008/307

s.274, see *HM Advocate v A* 2008 S.C.C.R. 84 (HCJ), Lord Brodie

s.275, see *HM Advocate v A* 2008 S.C.C.R. 84 (HCJ), Lord Brodie

s.302, applied: SI 2008/1185 Sch.3 para.5, SSI 2008/42 Art.6, SSI 2008/108, SSI 2008/108 Art.1, Art.2, SSI 2008/109, SSI 2008/240 Reg.7

s.302, enabling: SSI 2008/108

s.302A, applied: SSI 2008/7 Art.2, SSI 2008/240 Reg.7

s.302A, enabling: SSI 2008/7

s.303ZA, applied: SSI 2008/240 Reg.7

s.305, enabling: SSI 2008/61, SSI 2008/62, SSI 2008/275

Sch.1, referred to: SI 2008/1185 Reg.4, Sch.1 para.44

Sch.3 para.2, see *Paterson (Alexander) v HM Advocate* [2008] HCJAC 18, 2008 S.L.T. 465 (HCJ), Lord Hamilton L.J.G.

49. Town and Country Planning (Costs of Inquiries etc.) Act 1995

repealed: 2008 c.12 Sch.1 Part 9

s.1, referred to: 2008 c.12 Sch.2 para.10

50. Disability Discrimination Act 1995

see *Environment Agency v Rowan* [2008] I.C.R. 218 (EAT), Judge Serota Q.C.; see *Gichura v Home Office* [2008] EWCA Civ 697, [2008] I.C.R. 1287 (CA (Civ Div)), Waller, L.J.; see *Malcolm v Lewisham LBC* [2007] EWCA Civ 763, [2008] Ch. 129 (CA (Civ Div)), Arden, L.J.; see *R. (on the application of Chavda) v Harrow LBC* [2007] EWHC 3064 (Admin), [2008] B.L.G.R. 657 (QBD (Admin)), Judge Mackie Q.C.; see *R. (on the application of N) v Independent Appeal Panel of Barking*

CAP.

1995–cont.

50. Disability Discrimination Act 1995–*cont.*

see–*cont.*

and Dagenham LBC [2008] EWHC 390 (Admin), [2008] E.L.R. 280 (QBD (Admin)), Michael Supperstone Q.C.; see *Richmond Adult Community College v McDougall* [2008] EWCA Civ 4, [2008] I.C.R. 431 (CA (Civ Div)), Pill, L.J.; see *S v Floyd* [2008] EWCA Civ 201, [2008] 1 W.L.R. 1274 (CA (Civ Div)), Mummery, L.J.; see *X School Governing Body v SP* [2008] EWHC 389 (Admin), [2008] E.L.R. 243 (QBD (Admin)), Michael Supperstone Q.C.

applied: 2008 c.13 Sch.3, SI 2008/228 Sch.1 para.20, SI 2008/532 Sch.1 para.4, SSI 2008/228 Reg.4, SSI 2008/230 Reg.26

Part II, applied: SI 2008/1335 Art.3, SI 2008/1336 Art.3

Part V, referred to: 2008 c.13 Sch.6

s.1, see *Malcolm v Lewisham LBC* [2007] EWCA Civ 763, [2008] Ch. 129 (CA (Civ Div)), Arden, L.J.; see *Ministry of Defence v Hay* [2008] I.C.R. 1247 (EAT), Langstaff, J.

s.1, applied: SI 2008/975 Sch.3 para.17, Sch.6 para.18

s.3A, see *Environment Agency v Rowan* [2008] I.C.R. 218 (EAT), Judge Serota Q.C.

s.4A, see *Environment Agency v Rowan* [2008] I.C.R. 218 (EAT), Judge Serota Q.C.

s.17A, referred to: SI 2008/3232 Sch.1 Part 2

s.19, see *Gichura v Home Office* [2008] EWCA Civ 697, [2008] I.C.R. 1287 (CA (Civ Div)), Waller, L.J.

s.21, see *Gichura v Home Office* [2008] EWCA Civ 697, [2008] I.C.R. 1287 (CA (Civ Div)), Waller, L.J.

s.21, applied: SI 2008/975 Sch.3 para.17, Sch.6 para.18

s.22, see *Malcolm v Lewisham LBC* [2007] EWCA Civ 763, [2008] Ch. 129 (CA (Civ Div)), Arden, L.J.; see *Malcolm v Lewisham LBC* [2008] UKHL 43, [2008] 1 A.C. 1399 (HL), Lord Bingham of Cornhill

s.24, see *Malcolm v Lewisham LBC* [2007] EWCA Civ 763, [2008] Ch. 129 (CA (Civ Div)), Arden, L.J.; see *Malcolm v Lewisham LBC* [2008] UKHL 43, [2008] 1 A.C. 1399 (HL), Lord Bingham of Cornhill

s.28B, see *WS v Whitefield School and Centre Governors* [2008] EWHC 1196 (Admin), [2008] E.L.R. 428 (QBD (Admin)), Dobbs, J.

s.28D, amended: 2008 c.25 Sch.1 para.2

s.28D, applied: SI 2008/2867 Reg.12

s.28D, varied: SI 2008/2867 Reg.12

s.28H, amended: SI 2008/2833 Sch.3 para.115

s.28H, applied: SI 2008/2833 Sch.1

CAP.

1995–cont.

50. Disability Discrimination Act 1995–*cont.*

s.28H, repealed (in part): SI 2008/2833 Sch.3 para.115

s.28I, amended: SI 2008/2833 Sch.3 para.116

s.28I, applied: SI 2008/2699 Sch.1

s.28J, amended: SI 2008/2833 Sch.3 para.117

s.28J, repealed (in part): SI 2008/2833 Sch.3 para.117

s.28JA, added: SI 2008/2833 Sch.3 para.118

s.28M, amended: 2008 c.25 Sch.1 para.3, SI 2008/2833 Sch.3 para.119

s.28N, amended: SI 2008/2833 Sch.3 para.120

s.28Q, amended: 2008 c.25 Sch.1 para.4

s.31AA, enabling: SI 2008/2159

s.31AD, enabling: SI 2008/2159

s.31AF, applied: SI 2008/2159

s.36, amended: 2008 c.26 s.55

s.36A, added: 2008 c.26 s.56

s.38, amended: 2008 c.26 s.56

s.38, substituted: 2008 c.26 s.56

s.45, applied: SI 2008/1459

s.45, enabling: SI 2008/1459

s.46, applied: SI 2008/1746

s.46, referred to: SI 2008/2975 Reg.3

s.46, enabling: SI 2008/1746

s.47, applied: SI 2008/2969, SI 2008/2975 Reg.2, Reg.5

s.47, enabling: SI 2008/925, SI 2008/2969

s.49A, see *R. (on the application of Chavda) v Harrow LBC* [2007] EWHC 3064 (Admin), [2008] B.L.G.R. 657 (QBD (Admin)), Judge Mackie Q.C.

s.49D, applied: SI 2008/641

s.49D, enabling: SI 2008/641

s.67, applied: SI 2008/925, SI 2008/2969, SI 2008/2975

s.67, enabling: SI 2008/641, SI 2008/925, SI 2008/1459, SI 2008/2969, SI 2008/2975

s.67A, applied: SI 2008/925, SI 2008/2969, SI 2008/2975, SI 2008/2975 Reg.2, Reg.5

s.67A, enabling: SI 2008/2975

s.68, amended: 2008 c.26 s.56, SI 2008/2828 Art.4

s.70, amended: 2008 c.26 s.56

Sch.1 para.2, see *Ministry of Defence v Hay* [2008] I.C.R. 1247 (EAT), Langstaff, J.; see *Richmond Adult Community College v McDougall* [2008] EWCA Civ 4, [2008] I.C.R. 431 (CA (Civ Div)), Pill, L.J.

Sch.3 Part III para.10, amended: SI 2008/2833 Sch.3 para.121

53. Criminal Injuries Compensation Act 1995

applied: SI 2008/1596 Reg.7

s.1, amended: SI 2008/2833 Sch.3 para.123

s.5, amended: SI 2008/2833 Sch.3 para.124

CAP.

1995–cont.

53. Criminal Injuries Compensation Act 1995–*cont.*

s.5, applied: SI 2008/1149 Art.2, SI 2008/2833 Sch.1, Sch.2

s.9, amended: SI 2008/2833 Sch.3 para.125

s.9, repealed (in part): SI 2008/2833 Sch.3 para.125

s.11, repealed (in part): SI 2008/2833 Sch.3 para.126

1996

6. Chemical Weapons Act 1996

s.2, applied: 2008 c.28 Sch.2

s.11, applied: 2008 c.28 Sch.2

8. Finance Act 1996

see *DCC Holdings (UK) Ltd v Revenue and Customs Commissioners* [2008] EWHC 2429 (Ch), [2008] B.T.C. 755 (Ch D), Norris, J.; see *Revenue and Customs Commissioners v Bank of Ireland Britain Holdings Ltd* [2008] EWCA Civ 58, [2008] S.T.C. 398 (CA (Civ Div)), Maurice Kay, L.J.

Part III, see *Waste Recycling Group Ltd v Revenue and Customs Commissioners* [2008] EWCA Civ 849, [2008] B.T.C. 8076 (CA (Civ Div)), Sir Andrew Morritt C.

Part IV c.II, applied: 2008 c.9 Sch.13 para.2, 2008 c.18 Sch.13 para.14, Sch.13 para.24

Part IV c.II, referred to: 2008 c.18 Sch.13 para.40

Part III, see *Waste Recycling Group Ltd v Revenue and Customs Commissioners* [2008] EWCA Civ 849, [2008] B.T.C. 8076 (CA (Civ Div)), Sir Andrew Morritt C.

s.5, repealed (in part): 2008 c.9 Sch.5 para.25

s.37, repealed: 2008 c.9 Sch.41 para.25

s.40, see *Waste Recycling Group Ltd v Revenue and Customs Commissioners* [2007] EWHC 3014 (Ch), [2008] S.T.C. 1037 (Ch D), Barling, J; see *Waste Recycling Group Ltd v Revenue and Customs Commissioners* [2008] EWCA Civ 849, [2008] B.T.C. 8076 (CA (Civ Div)), Sir Andrew Morritt C.

s.42, amended: 2008 c.9 s.18

s.43A, amended: 2008 c.17 Sch.8 para.64, Sch.16

s.43A, repealed (in part): 2008 c.17 Sch.8 para.64, Sch.16, SI 2008/2669 Art.4

s.43B, see *Augean Plc v Revenue and Customs Commissioners* [2008] EWHC 2026 (Ch), [2008] S.T.C. 2894 (Ch D), David Richards, J.

s.43B, amended: SI 2008/2669 Art.2

s.43B, repealed (in part): SI 2008/2669 Art.3, Art.4

s.43B, varied: SI 2008/3068 Art.12

s.46, enabling: SI 2008/2669

s.47, applied: 2008 c.9 Sch.41 para.1

CAP.

1996–cont.

8. Finance Act 1996–*cont.*

s.49, enabling: SI 2008/1482, SI 2008/2693

s.51, enabling: SI 2008/770

s.53, amended: 2008 c.9 s.151

s.53, enabling: SI 2008/770

s.54, amended: 2008 c.9 s.151, SI 2008/2669 Art.3

s.54, repealed (in part): SI 2008/2669 Art.3, Art.4

s.64, see *Waste Recycling Group Ltd v Revenue and Customs Commissioners* [2007] EWHC 3014 (Ch), [2008] S.T.C. 1037 (Ch D), Barling, J; see *Waste Recycling Group Ltd v Revenue and Customs Commissioners* [2008] EWCA Civ 849, [2008] B.T.C. 8076 (CA (Civ Div)), Sir Andrew Morritt C.

s.65, see *Waste Recycling Group Ltd v Revenue and Customs Commissioners* [2008] EWCA Civ 849, [2008] B.T.C. 8076 (CA (Civ Div)), Sir Andrew Morritt C.

s.71, enabling: SI 2008/1482, SI 2008/2669, SI 2008/2693

s.82, see *DCC Holdings (UK) Ltd v Revenue and Customs Commissioners* [2008] EWHC 2429 (Ch), [2008] B.T.C. 755 (Ch D), Norris, J.

s.84, see *DCC Holdings (UK) Ltd v Revenue and Customs Commissioners* [2008] EWHC 2429 (Ch), [2008] B.T.C. 755 (Ch D), Norris, J.

s.85, see *DCC Holdings (UK) Ltd v Revenue and Customs Commissioners* [2008] EWHC 2429 (Ch), [2008] B.T.C. 755 (Ch D), Norris, J.

s.85B, enabling: SI 2008/3237

s.91A, amended: 2008 c.9 Sch.22 para.6, Sch.22 para.7, Sch.22 para.10, Sch.22 para.19

s.91B, amended: 2008 c.9 Sch.22 para.6, Sch.22 para.8, Sch.22 para.13

s.91C, amended: 2008 c.9 Sch.22 para.11, Sch.22 para.14

s.91D, amended: 2008 c.9 Sch.22 para.15

s.91E, amended: 2008 c.9 Sch.22 para.16

s.91H, added: 2008 c.9 Sch.22 para.17

s.91I, added: 2008 c.9 Sch.22 para.17

s.94B, added: 2008 c.9 Sch.22 para.18

s.97, see *DCC Holdings (UK) Ltd v Revenue and Customs Commissioners* [2008] EWHC 2429 (Ch), [2008] B.T.C. 755 (Ch D), Norris, J.

s.100, amended: SI 2008/954 Art.21

s.103, repealed (in part): 2008 c.9 Sch.22 para.19

s.124, repealed (in part): 2008 c.9 Sch.37 para.11

s.145, repealed: 2008 c.9 s.70

s.151, enabling: SI 2008/1464, SI 2008/2603

s.164, repealed (in part): 2008 c.9 Sch.17 para.24

CAP.

1996–cont.

8. Finance Act 1996–*cont.*

s.168, repealed (in part): 2008 c.9 Sch.14 para.17

s.197, enabling: SI 2008/3234

Sch.3 para.17, repealed: 2008 c.9 Sch.36 para.92

Sch.5 Part V para.18, repealed: 2008 c.9 Sch.40 para.21

Sch.5 Part V para.19, repealed: 2008 c.9 Sch.40 para.21

Sch.5 Part V para.20, repealed: 2008 c.9 Sch.40 para.21

Sch.5 Part V para.21, repealed (in part): 2008 c.9 Sch.41 para.25

Sch.5 Part V para.23A, repealed: 2008 c.9 Sch.43 para.5

Sch.5 Part VII para.37, amended: 2008 c.9 Sch.44 para.7

Sch.5 Part VII para.37, repealed (in part): 2008 c.9 Sch.44 para.7

Sch.6 para.21, repealed: 2008 c.9 Sch.1 para.49

Sch.9, referred to: 2008 c.17 Sch.7 para.11

Sch.9 para.1, amended: 2008 c.9 Sch.22 para.3

Sch.9 para.1A, repealed: 2008 c.9 Sch.14 para.17

Sch.9 para.11, disapplied: 2008 c.18 Sch.13 para.40

Sch.9 para.11B, added: 2008 c.9 Sch.22 para.4

Sch.9 para.12, amended: 2008 c.9 Sch.22 para.5

Sch.9 para.12, applied: 2008 c.17 Sch.7 para.11, 2008 c.18 Sch.13 para.14

Sch.9 para.12A, amended: SI 2008/1579 Sch.2 para.2

Sch.9 para.12B, amended: SI 2008/1579 Sch.2 para.3

Sch.9 para.12B, repealed (in part): SI 2008/1579 Sch.2 para.3

Sch.9 para.12B, varied: SI 2008/1579 Sch.4 para.3

Sch.9 para.12C, amended: SI 2008/1579 Sch.2 para.4

Sch.9 para.12C, varied: SI 2008/1579 Sch.4 para.3

Sch.9 para.12D, amended: SI 2008/1579 Sch.2 para.5

Sch.9 para.12D, repealed (in part): SI 2008/1579 Sch.2 para.5

Sch.9 para.12D, varied: SI 2008/1579 Sch.4 para.3

Sch.9 para.12E, amended: SI 2008/1579 Sch.2 para.6

Sch.9 para.12E, varied: SI 2008/1579 Sch.4 para.3

Sch.9 para.12F, amended: SI 2008/1579 Sch.2 para.7

Sch.9 para.12G, substituted: SI 2008/1579 Sch.2 para.8

CAP.

1996–cont.

8. Finance Act 1996–*cont.*

Sch.9 para.12H, amended: SI 2008/1579 Sch.2 para.9

Sch.9 para.12I, amended: SI 2008/1579 Sch.2 para.10

Sch.9 para.12J, amended: SI 2008/1579 Sch.2 para.11

Sch.9 para.15, see *DCC Holdings (UK) Ltd v Revenue and Customs Commissioners* [2008] EWHC 2429 (Ch), [2008] B.T.C. 755 (Ch D), Norris, J.

Sch.9 para.19A, amended: SI 2008/1579 Sch.2 para.12

Sch.9 para.19B, enabling: SI 2008/3237

Sch.11 Part I para.2, repealed (in part): 2008 c.9 Sch.17 para.3, Sch.17 para.18

Sch.11 Part I para.3, repealed: 2008 c.9 Sch.17 para.17

Sch.11 Part I para.3A, amended: 2008 c.9 Sch.17 para.9

Sch.13 para.3, see *Astall v Revenue and Customs Commissioners* [2008] EWHC 1471 (Ch), [2008] S.T.C. 2920 (Ch D), Peter Smith, J.; see *Astall v Revenue and Customs Commissioners* [2008] S.T.C. (S.C.D.) 142 (Sp Comm), John F Avery Jones

Sch.14 para.56, repealed: 2008 c.9 Sch.17 para.18

Sch.19 para.3, repealed: 2008 c.9 Sch.36 para.92

Sch.20 para.36, repealed: 2008 c.9 s.66

Sch.21 para.4, repealed: 2008 c.9 Sch.39 para.65

Sch.21 para.6, repealed: 2008 c.9 Sch.39 para.65

Sch.21 para.43, repealed: 2008 c.9 Sch.2 para.75

Sch.22 para.2, repealed: 2008 c.9 Sch.36 para.92

Sch.28 para.6, amended: 2008 c.9 s.41

Sch.38 para.9, repealed: 2008 c.9 s.66

14. Reserve Forces Act 1996

Part I, applied: 2008 c.8 Sch.2 Part 21

Part III, applied: 2008 c.8 Sch.2 Part 21

Part IV, applied: 2008 c.8 Sch.2 Part 21

Part V, applied: 2008 c.8 Sch.2 Part 21

Part XI, applied: 2008 c.25 s.62

s.1, applied: SI 2008/228 Sch.2 para.20

16. Police Act 1996

applied: 2008 c.4 s.126, SI 2008/239 Sch.2 para.6, SI 2008/2712 Art.4, SI 2008/2993 Art.3

s.4, applied: SI 2008/630 Reg.6

s.4, enabling: SI 2008/630

s.5C, applied: SI 2008/631 Reg.5

s.6ZA, applied: SI 2008/82, SI 2008/312 Reg.4

s.6ZA, enabling: SI 2008/82

s.6ZB, applied: SI 2008/82 Art.3, Art.6, SI 2008/312

CAP.

1996–cont.

16. Police Act 1996–*cont.*

s.6ZB, referred to: SI 2008/312 Reg.4
s.6ZB, enabling: SI 2008/312
s.9, referred to: SI 2008/311 Art.3
s.9A, see *DPP v Haw* [2007] EWHC 1931 (Admin), [2008] 1 W.L.R. 379 (DC), Lord Phillips, L.C.J.
s.9F, see *DPP v Haw* [2007] EWHC 1931 (Admin), [2008] 1 W.L.R. 379 (DC), Lord Phillips, L.C.J.
s.29, applied: SI 2008/1261 Art.51
s.36, amended: 2008 c.4 Sch.22 para.2
s.37A, applied: SI 2008/312 Reg.4
s.38, applied: SI 2008/312 Reg.3, Reg.4
s.40, applied: SI 2008/312 Reg.3, Reg.4
s.50, see *Holmes v South Yorkshire Police Authority* [2008] EWCA Civ 51, [2008] H.L.R. 33 (CA (Civ Div)), Sedley, L.J.
s.50, amended: 2008 c.4 Sch.22 para.3, Sch.28 Part 8
s.50, enabling: SI 2008/273, SI 2008/2862, SI 2008/2864, SI 2008/2865
s.51, amended: 2008 c.4 Sch.22 para.4
s.51, enabling: SI 2008/2862, SI 2008/2864
s.54, amended: 2008 c.4 s.129, Sch.28 Part 8
s.57, amended: 2008 c.4 s.128
s.57, applied: 2008 c.4 s.128
s.59, amended: 2008 c.4 Sch.22 para.5
s.63, amended: 2008 c.4 Sch.22 para.6
s.63, applied: SI 2008/273, SI 2008/2862, SI 2008/2863, SI 2008/2864, SI 2008/2865, SI 2008/2866
s.84, applied: SI 2008/2862, SI 2008/2864
s.84, substituted: 2008 c.4 Sch.22 para.7
s.84, enabling: SI 2008/2862, SI 2008/2864
s.85, amended: 2008 c.4 Sch.22 para.8
s.85, applied: SI 2008/2863, SI 2008/2863 r.2
s.85, enabling: SI 2008/2863
s.87, amended: 2008 c.4 Sch.22 para.9
s.87, applied: SI 2008/2862 Reg.4, SI 2008/2864 Reg.3
s.89, see *R. (on the application of M) v Tower Bridge Magistrates' Court* [2007] EWHC 2766 (Admin), (2008) 172 J.P. 155 (DC), Keene, L.J.
s.97, amended: 2008 c.4 Sch.22 para.10, Sch.28 Part 8
s.97, applied: SI 2008/755 Art.14
s.101, see *R. (on the application of Ashton) v Police Medical Appeal Board* [2008] EWHC 1833 (Admin), [2008] Pens. L.R. 391 (QBD (Admin)), Charles, J.
s.101, applied: SI 2008/2841 Reg.35
Sch.2A, applied: SI 2008/631 Reg.4
Sch.2 para.1, enabling: SI 2008/630
Sch.2 para.2, applied: SI 2008/630 Reg.5
Sch.2 para.5, applied: SI 2008/630 Reg.5
Sch.2 para.7, enabling: SI 2008/630
Sch.2A para.1, enabling: SI 2008/631
Sch.2A para.2, applied: SI 2008/631 Reg.4

CAP.

1996–cont.

16. Police Act 1996–*cont.*

Sch.2A para.3, applied: SI 2008/631 Reg.4
Sch.2A para.6, applied: SI 2008/631
Sch.2A para.7, enabling: SI 2008/631
Sch.3 para.1, applied: SI 2008/630 Reg.5, SI 2008/631 Reg.4
Sch.4A para.2, amended: 2008 c.14 Sch.5 para.63, SI 2008/912 Sch.1 para.27
Sch.4A para.2, repealed (in part): 2008 c.14 Sch.5 para.63, Sch.15 Part 1
Sch.4A para.2, varied: SI 2008/2250 Art.3
Sch.4A para.3, amended: 2008 c.14 Sch.5 para.63, SI 2008/912 Sch.1 para.26
Sch.4A para.3, varied: SI 2008/2250 Art.3
Sch.4A para.4, amended: 2008 c.14 Sch.5 para.63, SI 2008/912 Sch.1 para.26
Sch.4A para.4, repealed (in part): 2008 c.14 Sch.5 para.63, Sch.15 Part 1
Sch.4A para.4, varied: SI 2008/2250 Art.3
Sch.4A para.5, amended: SI 2008/912 Sch.1 para.27
Sch.6 para.1, amended: 2008 c.4 Sch.22 para.11
Sch.6 para.2, amended: 2008 c.4 Sch.22 para.11
Sch.6 para.6, repealed: 2008 c.4 Sch.22 para.11, Sch.28 Part 8
Sch.6 para.7, amended: 2008 c.4 Sch.22 para.11
Sch.6 para.10, amended: 2008 c.4 Sch.22 para.11
Sch.8 para.1, see *Holmes v South Yorkshire Police Authority* [2008] EWCA Civ 51, [2008] H.L.R. 33 (CA (Civ Div)), Sedley, L.J.

17. Employment Tribunals Act 1996

s.1, enabling: SI 2008/2771, SI 2008/3240
s.4, amended: 2008 c.24 s.9
s.4, enabling: SI 2008/3240
s.7, amended: 2008 c.24 s.4
s.7, enabling: SI 2008/3240
s.9, enabling: SI 2008/3240
s.16, amended: SI 2008/2833 Sch.3 para.137
s.18, amended: 2008 c.24 s.5, 2008 c.30 s.56, SI 2008/1660 Sch.3 para.1
s.18, applied: 2008 c.30 s.58, SI 2008/1660 Reg.18
s.18, repealed (in part): 2008 c.24 s.6, Sch.1 Part 1
s.19, repealed (in part): 2008 c.24 s.6, Sch.1 Part 1
s.19, enabling: SI 2008/3240
s.21, amended: 2008 c.30 s.59, SI 2008/1660 Sch.3 para.1
s.33, applied: SI 2008/221 r.27
s.41, enabling: SI 2008/3240

18. Employment Rights Act 1996

applied: 2008 c.30 s.56, SI 2008/625 Reg.12
Part II, applied: 2008 c.14 Sch.2 para.3
Part III, applied: SI 2008/239 Reg.20, SSI 2008/228 Reg.17

CAP.

1996–cont.

18. Employment Rights Act 1996–*cont.*

Part X, applied: 2008 c.30 s.55

Part XI, applied: 2008 c.18 Sch.12 para.16, SI 2008/625 Reg.12

Part X, see *Kuzel v Roche Products Ltd* [2008] EWCA Civ 380, [2008] I.C.R. 799 (CA (Civ Div)), Mummery, L.J.

s.23, referred to: SI 2008/3232 Sch.1 Part 2

s.24, substituted: 2008 c.24 s.7

s.31, amended: SI 2008/3055 Sch.1

s.34, referred to: SI 2008/794 Sch.7 para.1

s.37, applied: 2008 c.25 s.67

s.38, applied: 2008 c.25 s.67

s.39, applied: 2008 c.25 s.67

s.43F, enabling: SI 2008/531

s.45A, amended: SI 2008/1660 Sch.3 para.2

s.47AA, added: 2008 c.25 s.37

s.47C, enabling: SI 2008/1966

s.48, applied: 2008 c.30 s.56

s.48, referred to: SI 2008/3232 Sch.1 Part 2

s.49, applied: 2008 c.30 s.56

s.50, applied: SI 2008/228 Sch.2 para.20

s.55, applied: SI 2008/228 Sch.2 para.20

s.61, applied: 2008 c.25 s.67

s.62, applied: 2008 c.25 s.67

s.63A, amended: 2008 c.25 s.39

s.65, applied: 2008 c.25 s.67

s.70, referred to: SI 2008/794 Sch.7 para.1

s.73, enabling: SI 2008/1966

s.75, enabling: SI 2008/1966

s.75B, enabling: SI 2008/1966

s.75D, enabling: SI 2008/1966

s.90, amended: SI 2008/1879 Reg.2

s.98, see *Airbus UK Ltd v Webb* [2008] EWCA Civ 49, [2008] I.C.R. 561 (CA (Civ Div)), Mummery, L.J.; see *First West Yorkshire Ltd (t/a First Leeds) v Haigh* [2008] I.R.L.R. 182 (EAT), Judge Richardson; see *Hounslow LBC v Klusova* [2007] EWCA Civ 1127, [2008] I.C.R. 396 (CA (Civ Div)), Mummery, L.J.; see *Kelly v University of Southampton* [2008] I.C.R. 357 (EAT), Judge Richardson; see *Kuzel v Roche Products Ltd* [2008] EWCA Civ 380, [2008] I.C.R. 799 (CA (Civ Div)), Mummery, L.J.

s.98A, see *Kelly v University of Southampton* [2008] I.C.R. 357 (EAT), Judge Richardson; see *Wilmot v Selvarajan* [2008] EWCA Civ 862, [2008] I.C.R. 1236 (CA (Civ Div)), Mummery, L.J.; see *Yorkshire Housing Ltd v Swanson* [2008] I.R.L.R. 607 (EAT), Cox, J.

s.98A, repealed: 2008 c.24 s.2, Sch.1 Part 1

s.98ZG, see *Johns v Solent SD Ltd* [2008] EWCA Civ 790, [2008] I.R.L.R. 820 (CA (Civ Div)), Pill, L.J.; see *Johns v Solent SD Ltd* [2008] I.R.L.R. 88 (EAT), Nelson, J.

s.99, see *Atkins v Coyle Personnel Plc* [2008] I.R.L.R. 420 (EAT), Nelson, J.

s.99, enabling: SI 2008/1966

CAP.

1996–cont.

18. Employment Rights Act 1996–*cont.*

s.101A, amended: SI 2008/1660 Sch.3 para.2

s.101B, added: 2008 c.25 s.38

s.103A, see *Kuzel v Roche Products Ltd* [2008] EWCA Civ 380, [2008] I.C.R. 799 (CA (Civ Div)), Mummery, L.J.

s.104, amended: SI 2008/1660 Sch.3 para.2

s.104D, added: 2008 c.30 s.57

s.105, amended: 2008 c.25 s.39, 2008 c.30 s.57

s.108, amended: 2008 c.25 s.39, 2008 c.30 s.57

s.111, see *Royal Bank of Scotland v Bevan* [2008] I.C.R. 682 (EAT), Judge Richardson

s.111, referred to: SI 2008/3232 Sch.1 Part 2

s.112, amended: 2008 c.24 Sch.1 Part 1

s.119, applied: 2008 c.30 s.56

s.120, amended: 2008 c.24 Sch.1 Part 1, SI 2008/3055 Sch.1

s.123, see *GAB Robins (UK) Ltd v Triggs* [2008] EWCA Civ 17, [2008] I.C.R. 529 (CA (Civ Div)), Tuckey, L.J.

s.124, amended: SI 2008/3055 Sch.1

s.124, applied: 2008 c.30 s.56

s.124A, amended: 2008 c.24 s.3

s.138, applied: SI 2008/625 Reg.12

s.163, amended: 2008 c.24 s.7

s.163, referred to: SI 2008/3232 Sch.1 Part 3

s.186, amended: SI 2008/3055 Sch.1

s.189, amended: SI 2008/948 Sch.1 para.201

s.194, amended: 2008 c.25 s.39

s.195, amended: 2008 c.25 s.39

s.201, referred to: 2008 c.30 s.97

s.203, see *M&P Steelcraft Ltd v Ellis* [2008] I.C.R. 578 (EAT), Elias, J (President)

s.204, see *Bleuse v MBT Transport Ltd* [2008] I.C.R. 488 (EAT), Elias, J.

s.221, see *British Airways Plc v Williams* [2008] I.C.R. 779 (EAT), Keith, J.

s.224, see *British Airways Plc v Williams* [2008] I.C.R. 779 (EAT), Keith, J.

s.227, amended: SI 2008/3055 Sch.1

s.230, applied: 2008 c.30 s.56

s.234, applied: 2008 c.25 s.5

s.236, applied: SI 2008/1966

Sch.1 para.34, repealed: SI 2008/1277 Sch.4 Part 1

21. London Regional Transport Act 1996

repealed: 2008 c.12 Sch.1 Part 5

23. Arbitration Act 1996

see *Albon (t/a NA Carriage Co) v Naza Motor Trading Sdn Bhd* [2007] EWCA Civ 1124, [2008] 1 All E.R. (Comm) 351 (CA (Civ Div)), Waller, L.J. (V-P); see *Braes of Doune Wind Farm (Scotland) Ltd v Alfred McAlpine Business Services Ltd* [2008] EWHC 426 (TCC), [2008] 2 All E.R. (Comm) 493 (QBD (TCC)), Akenhead, J.; see *C v D* [2007] EWCA Civ 1282, [2008]

CAP.

1996–cont.

23. Arbitration Act 1996–*cont.*

see–*cont.*

Bus. L.R. 843 (CA (Civ Div)), Sir Anthony Clarke, M.R.; see *Crest Nicholson (Eastern) Ltd v Western* [2008] EWHC 1325 (TCC), [2008] B.L.R. 426 (QBD (TCC)), Akenhead, J.; see *ETI Euro Telecom International NV v Bolivia* [2008] EWCA Civ 880, [2008] 2 Lloyd's Rep. 421 (CA (Civ Div)), Tuckey, L.J.; see *IPCO (Nigeria) Ltd v Nigerian National Petroleum Corp* [2008] EWCA Civ 1157, [2008] 2 C.L.C. 550 (CA (Civ Div)), Tuckey, L.J.

Part I, disapplied: SI 2008/2685 r.3, SI 2008/2686 r.3, SI 2008/2698 r.3, SI 2008/2699 r.3

Part III, see *IPCO (Nigeria) Ltd v Nigerian National Petroleum Corp* [2008] EWCA Civ 1157, [2008] 2 C.L.C. 550 (CA (Civ Div)), Tuckey, L.J.

s.1, see *Holloway v Chancery Mead Ltd* [2007] EWHC 2495 (TCC), [2008] 1 All E.R. (Comm) 653 (QBD (TCC)), Ramsey, J.; see *L Brown & Sons Ltd v Crosby Homes (North West) Ltd* [2008] EWHC 817 (TCC), [2008] B.L.R. 366 (QBD (TCC)), Akenhead, J.

s.2, see *Braes of Doune Wind Farm (Scotland) Ltd v Alfred McAlpine Business Services Ltd* [2008] EWHC 426 (TCC), [2008] 2 All E.R. (Comm) 493 (QBD (TCC)), Akenhead, J.; see *Mobil Cerro Negro Ltd v Petroleos de Venezuela SA* [2008] EWHC 532 (Comm), [2008] 2 All E.R. (Comm) 1034 (QBD (Comm)), Walker, J.

s.3, see *Braes of Doune Wind Farm (Scotland) Ltd v Alfred McAlpine Business Services Ltd* [2008] EWHC 426 (TCC), [2008] 2 All E.R. (Comm) 493 (QBD (TCC)), Akenhead, J.

s.5, see *Heifer International Inc v Christiansen* [2007] EWHC 3015 (TCC), [2008] 2 All E.R. (Comm) 831 (QBD (TCC)), Judge Toulmin Q.C.

s.7, see *El Nasharty v J Sainsbury Plc* [2007] EWHC 2618 (Comm), [2008] 1 Lloyd's Rep. 360 (QBD (Comm)), Tomlinson, J.

s.9, see *City of London v Sancheti* [2008] EWCA Civ 1283, [2008] 2 C.L.C. 730 (CA (Civ Div)), Laws, L.J.; see *Holloway v Chancery Mead Ltd* [2007] EWHC 2495 (TCC), [2008] 1 All E.R. (Comm) 653 (QBD (TCC)), Ramsey, J.

s.14, see *Taylor Woodrow Construction Ltd v RMD Kwikform Ltd* [2008] EWHC 825 (TCC), [2008] 2 Lloyd's Rep. 345 (QBD (TCC)), Ramsey, J.

s.33, see *Bandwidth Shipping Corp v Intaari (A Firm) (The Magdalena Oldendorff)* [2007] EWCA Civ 998, [2008] Bus. L.R. 702 (CA (Civ Div)), Waller, L.J. (V-P)

CAP.

1996–cont.

23. Arbitration Act 1996–*cont.*

s.44, see *ETI Euro Telecom International NV v Bolivia* [2008] EWCA Civ 880, [2008] 2 Lloyd's Rep. 421 (CA (Civ Div)), Tuckey, L.J.; see *Mobil Cerro Negro Ltd v Petroleos de Venezuela SA* [2008] EWHC 532 (Comm), [2008] 2 All E.R. (Comm) 1034 (QBD (Comm)), Walker, J.; see *Pacific Maritime (Asia) Ltd v Holystone Overseas Ltd* [2007] EWHC 2319 (Comm), [2008] 1 Lloyd's Rep. 371 (QBD (Comm)), Christopher Clarke, J.; see *Starlight Shipping Co v Tai Ping Insurance Co Ltd (Hubei Branch)* [2007] EWHC 1893 (Comm), [2008] 1 All E.R. (Comm) 593 (QBD (Comm)), Cooke, J.

s.46, see *Musawi v RE International (UK) Ltd* [2007] EWHC 2981 (Ch), [2008] 1 All E.R. (Comm) 607 (Ch D), David Richards, J.

s.49, see *Gater Assets Ltd v Nak Naftogaz Ukrainiy* [2008] EWHC 1108 (Comm), [2008] 2 Lloyd's Rep. 295 (QBD (Comm)), Beatson, J.

s.58, see *Kazakhstan v Istil Group Inc* [2007] EWHC 2729 (Comm), [2008] 1 Lloyd's Rep. 382 (QBD (Comm)), Tomlinson, J.

s.66, see *Colliers International Property Consultants v Colliers Jordan Lee Jafaar Sdn Bhd* [2008] EWHC 1524 (Comm), [2008] 2 Lloyd's Rep. 368 (QBD (Comm)), Beatson, J.; see *Gater Assets Ltd v Nak Naftogaz Ukrainiy* [2007] EWCA Civ 988, [2008] Bus. L.R. 388 (CA (Civ Div)), Buxton, L.J.

s.67, see *Gulf Import and Export Co v Bunge SA* [2007] EWHC 2667 (Comm), [2008] 2 All E.R. (Comm) 161 (QBD (Comm)), Flaux, J.; see *Syska v Vivendi Universal SA* [2008] EWHC 2155 (Comm), [2008] 2 Lloyd's Rep. 636 (QBD (Comm)), Christopher Clarke, J.

s.68, see *ASM Shipping Ltd v Harris* [2007] EWHC 1513 (Comm), [2008] 1 Lloyd's Rep. 61 (QBD (Comm)), Andrew Smith, J.; see *Bandwidth Shipping Corp v Intaari (A Firm) (The Magdalena Oldendorff)* [2007] EWCA Civ 998, [2008] Bus. L.R. 702 (CA (Civ Div)), Waller, L.J. (V-P); see *Colliers International Property Consultants v Colliers Jordan Lee Jafaar Sdn Bhd* [2008] EWHC 1524 (Comm), [2008] 2 Lloyd's Rep. 368 (QBD (Comm)), Beatson, J.; see *Gulf Import and Export Co v Bunge SA* [2007] EWHC 2667 (Comm), [2008] 2 All E.R. (Comm) 161 (QBD (Comm)), Flaux, J.; see *L Brown & Sons Ltd v Crosby Homes (North West) Ltd* [2008] EWHC 817 (TCC), [2008] B.L.R. 366 (QBD (TCC)), Akenhead, J.

s.69, see *Braes of Doune Wind Farm (Scotland) Ltd v Alfred McAlpine Business Services Ltd* [2008] EWHC 426 (TCC), [2008] 2 All E.R. (Comm) 493 (QBD

CAP.

1996–cont.

23. Arbitration Act 1996–*cont.*

s.69–*cont.*

(TCC)), Akenhead, J.; see *CTI Group Inc v Transclear SA (The Mary Nour)* [2007] EWHC 2340 (Comm), [2008] 1 All E.R. (Comm) 203 (QBD (Comm)), Field, J.; see *Gulf Import and Export Co v Bunge SA* [2007] EWHC 2667 (Comm), [2008] 2 All E.R. (Comm) 161 (QBD (Comm)), Flaux, J.; see *Royal & Sun Alliance Insurance Plc v BAE Systems (Operations) Ltd* [2008] EWHC 743 (Comm), [2008] 1 Lloyd's Rep. 712 (QBD (Comm)), Walker, J.

s.73, see *ASM Shipping Ltd v Harris* [2007] EWHC 1513 (Comm), [2008] 1 Lloyd's Rep. 61 (QBD (Comm)), Andrew Smith, J.; see *Colliers International Property Consultants v Colliers Jordan Lee Jafaar Sdn Bhd* [2008] EWHC 1524 (Comm), [2008] 2 Lloyd's Rep. 368 (QBD (Comm)), Beatson, J.; see *Kazakhstan v Istil Group Inc* [2007] EWHC 2729 (Comm), [2008] 1 Lloyd's Rep. 382 (QBD (Comm)), Tomlinson, J.

s.79, see *Kazakhstan v Istil Group Inc* [2007] EWHC 2729 (Comm), [2008] 1 Lloyd's Rep. 382 (QBD (Comm)), Tomlinson, J.

s.93, applied: SI 2008/1053 Sch.1

s.101, see *Colliers International Property Consultants v Colliers Jordan Lee Jafaar Sdn Bhd* [2008] EWHC 1524 (Comm), [2008] 2 Lloyd's Rep. 368 (QBD (Comm)), Beatson, J.; see *Gater Assets Ltd v Nak Naftogaz Ukrainiy* [2007] EWCA Civ 988, [2008] Bus. L.R. 388 (CA (Civ Div)), Buxton, L.J.; see *Gater Assets Ltd v Nak Naftogaz Ukrainiy* [2008] EWHC 1108 (Comm), [2008] 2 Lloyd's Rep. 295 (QBD (Comm)), Beatson, J.

s.103, see *Dallah Real Estate and Tourism Holding Co v Pakistan* [2008] EWHC 1901 (Comm), [2008] 2 Lloyd's Rep. 535 (QBD (Comm)), Aikens, J.; see *Gater Assets Ltd v Nak Naftogaz Ukrainiy* [2008] EWHC 237 (Comm), [2008] 1 Lloyd's Rep. 479 (QBD (Comm)), Tomlinson, J.; see *IPCO (Nigeria) Ltd v Nigerian National Petroleum Corp* [2008] EWCA Civ 1157, [2008] 2 C.L.C. 550 (CA (Civ Div)), Tuckey, L.J.; see *IPCO (Nigeria) Ltd v Nigerian National Petroleum Corp* [2008] EWHC 797 (Comm), [2008] 2 Lloyd's Rep. 59 (QBD (Comm)), Tomlinson, J.

25. Criminal Procedure and Investigations Act 1996

Part I, applied: SI 2008/2712 Art.3

s.1, applied: SI 2008/2712 Art.3

s.6A, amended: 2008 c.4 s.60

s.11, amended: 2008 c.4 s.60

s.24, referred to: SI 2008/635 Art.4

CAP.

1996–cont.

25. Criminal Procedure and Investigations Act 1996–*cont.*

s.46, repealed: 2008 c.12 Sch.1 Part 3

s.65, repealed: 2008 c.12 Sch.1 Part 3

s.78, applied: SI 2008/635 Art.3, Art.4, Art.12, Art.13

s.78, enabling: SI 2008/635, SI 2008/648

27. Family Law Act 1996

see *Gull v Gull* [2007] EWCA Civ 900, [2008] 1 F.L.R. 232 (CA (Civ Div)), Tuckey, L.J.

applied: SI 2008/2836 Art.22

Part IV, applied: SI 2008/1054 Sch.1, SI 2008/2836 Art.6

Part IVA, applied: SI 2008/1054 Sch.1, SI 2008/2836 Art.10

s.42A, see *K v P* [2008] EWCA Civ 600, [2008] 2 F.L.R. 2137 (CA (Civ Div)), Thorpe, L.J.

s.43, applied: SI 2008/2836 Art.6

s.47, applied: SI 2008/2836 Art.23

s.48, see *K v P* [2008] EWCA Civ 600, [2008] 2 F.L.R. 2137 (CA (Civ Div)), Thorpe, L.J.

s.57, enabling: SI 2008/2836

s.59, applied: SI 2008/2836 Art.17

s.63, amended: 2008 c.22 Sch.6 para.37

s.63H, applied: SI 2008/2836 Art.24

s.63I, applied: SI 2008/2836 Art.24

s.63J, applied: SI 2008/2836 Art.24

s.63L, amended: SI 2008/2828 Art.5

s.65, enabling: SI 2008/2836

Sch.8 Part III para.53, repealed: 2008 c.17 Sch.16

Sch.8 Part III para.59, repealed: 2008 c.17 Sch.16

29. Sexual Offences (Conspiracy and Incitement) Act 1996

Sch.1 para.2, amended: SI 2008/1769 Sch.1 para.24

Sch.1 para.2, repealed (in part): SI 2008/1769 Sch.1 para.24, Sch.3

30. Community Care (Direct Payments) Act 1996

applied: SI 2008/794 Sch.8 para.53, Sch.9 para.56

31. Defamation Act 1996

s.2, see *Club La Costa (UK) Ltd v Gebhard* [2008] EWHC 2552 (QB), Times, December 10, 2008 (QBD), Tugendhat, J.; see *Warren v Random House Group Ltd* [2007] EWHC 2856 (QB), [2008] 2 W.L.R. 1033 (QBD), Gray, J.

s.3, see *Club La Costa (UK) Ltd v Gebhard* [2008] EWHC 2552 (QB), Times, December 10, 2008 (QBD), Tugendhat, J.

s.4, see *Club La Costa (UK) Ltd v Gebhard* [2008] EWHC 2552 (QB), Times, December 10, 2008 (QBD), Tugendhat, J.; see *Warren v Random House Group Ltd* [2007] EWHC 2856 (QB), [2008] 2 W.L.R. 1033 (QBD), Gray, J.

CAP.

1996–cont.

37. Noise Act 1996
applied: 2008 c.13 Sch.3, SI 2008/1430 Reg.15
referred to: 2008 c.13 Sch.6
s.8A, applied: SI 2008/663 Reg.2, Reg.3
s.8A, enabling: SI 2008/663
s.11, referred to: SI 2008/663(e)

40. Party Wall etc Act 1996
see *Rodrigues v Sokal* [2008] EWHC 2005 (TCC), [2008] T.C.L.R. 11 (QBD (TCC)), Judge Toulmin Q.C.
s.1, applied: 2008 c.18 Sch.14 para.17
s.1, disapplied: 2008 c.18 Sch.14 para.17
s.2, disapplied: 2008 c.18 Sch.14 para.17
s.6, disapplied: 2008 c.18 Sch.14 para.17
s.10, see *Rodrigues v Sokal* [2008] EWHC 2005 (TCC), [2008] T.C.L.R. 11 (QBD (TCC)), Judge Toulmin Q.C.

47. Trusts of Land and Appointment of Trustees Act 1996
see *Avis v Turner* [2007] EWCA Civ 748, [2008] Ch. 218 (CA (Civ Div)), Ward, L.J.; see *Jasmine Trustees Ltd v Wells & Hind (A Firm)* [2007] EWHC 38 (Ch), [2008] Ch. 194 (Ch D), Mann, J.
s.4, see *Avis v Turner* [2007] EWCA Civ 748, [2008] Ch. 218 (CA (Civ Div)), Ward, L.J.
s.6, see *Avis v Turner* [2007] EWCA Civ 748, [2008] Ch. 218 (CA (Civ Div)), Ward, L.J.
s.12, see *Barcham, Re* [2008] EWHC 1505 (Ch), [2008] 2 F.C.R. 643 (Ch D), Blackburne, J.
s.13, see *Barcham, Re* [2008] EWHC 1505 (Ch), [2008] 2 F.C.R. 643 (Ch D), Blackburne, J.
s.14, see *Avis v Turner* [2007] EWCA Civ 748, [2008] Ch. 218 (CA (Civ Div)), Ward, L.J.; see *Close Invoice Finance Ltd v Pile* [2008] EWHC 1580 (Ch), [2008] B.P.I.R. 1465 (Ch D), Judge Purle Q.C.; see *Negus v Bahouse* [2007] EWHC 2628 (Ch), [2008] 1 F.L.R. 381 (Ch D), Judge Roger Kaye Q.C.; see *Turner v Avis* [2008] B.P.I.R. 1143 (Ch D (Liverpool)), Judge Pelling Q.C.
s.15, see *Avis v Turner* [2007] EWCA Civ 748, [2008] Ch. 218 (CA (Civ Div)), Ward, L.J.; see *Close Invoice Finance Ltd v Pile* [2008] EWHC 1580 (Ch), [2008] B.P.I.R. 1465 (Ch D), Judge Purle Q.C.

48. Damages Act 1996
s.2, see *Tameside and Glossop Acute Services NHS Trust v Thompstone* [2008] EWCA Civ 5, [2008] 1 W.L.R. 2207 (CA (Civ Div)), Waller, L.J. (V-P)

49. Asylum and Immigration Act 1996
s.6, varied: SI 2008/680 Art.5, Art.12
s.8, see *Hounslow LBC v Klusova* [2007] EWCA Civ 1127, [2008] I.C.R. 396 (CA (Civ Div)), Mummery, L.J.; see *Kelly v University of Southampton* [2008] I.C.R. 357 (EAT), Judge Richardson

CAP.

1996–cont.

49. Asylum and Immigration Act 1996– *cont.*
s.8, applied: SI 2008/309 Art.5, SI 2008/310 Art.5
s.8, varied: SI 2008/680 Art.5, Art.12, Sch.5 para.1
s.8A, applied: SI 2008/310 Art.5
s.8A, varied: SI 2008/680 Art.5, Art.12, Sch.5 para.2
s.12, varied: SI 2008/680 Art.5, Art.12
s.13, varied: SI 2008/680 Art.5, Art.12, Sch.5 para.3
s.13, enabling: SI 2008/680
Sch.2 para.1, varied: SI 2008/680 Art.5, Art.12
Sch.2 para.2, varied: SI 2008/680 Art.5, Art.12
Sch.2 para.4, varied: SI 2008/680 Art.5, Art.12
Sch.2 para.5, varied: SI 2008/680 Art.5, Art.12
Sch.2 para.6, varied: SI 2008/680 Art.5, Art.12
Sch.2 para.8, varied: SI 2008/680 Art.5, Art.12
Sch.2 para.9, varied: SI 2008/680 Art.5, Art.12
Sch.2 para.10, varied: SI 2008/680 Art.5, Art.12
Sch.2 para.11, varied: SI 2008/680 Art.5, Art.12
Sch.2 para.12, varied: SI 2008/680 Art.5, Art.12
Sch.2 para.13, varied: SI 2008/680 Art.5, Art.12

52. Housing Act 1996
see *R. (on the application of Weaver) v London & Quadrant Housing Trust* [2008] EWHC 1377 (Admin), Times, July 8, 2008 (DC), Richards, L.J.
applied: SI 2008/2839 Art.2
Part I, applied: 2008 c.17 s.60, s.77
Part I c.II, amended: 2008 c.17 s.61
Part V c.I, applied: SI 2008/188 Sch.1 para.1
Part VII, see *Williams v Birmingham City Council* [2007] EWCA Civ 691, [2008] H.L.R. 4 (CA (Civ Div)), Ward, L.J.
Part VIII, applied: 2008 c.13 Sch.3
Part VII, see *Lambeth LBC v Johnston* [2008] EWCA Civ 690, Times, June 30, 2008 (CA (Civ Div)), Smith, L.J.; see *Manchester City Council v Moran* [2008] EWCA Civ 378, [2008] 1 W.L.R. 2387 (CA (Civ Div)), Sir Anthony Clarke, M.R.; see *Westminster City Council v Boraliu* [2007] EWCA Civ 1339, [2008] 1 W.L.R. 2408 (CA (Civ Div)), Chadwick, L.J.
s.art I c.I sA.1, added: 2008 c.17 s.61
s.art I c.I sA.1, amended: 2008 c.17 s.61
s.1, amended: 2008 c.17 s.61
s.1, applied: 2008 c.17 s.278

CAP.

1996–cont.

52. Housing Act 1996–*cont.*

s.1, repealed (in part): 2008 c.17 s.61, Sch.16
s.1, varied: SI 2008/2839 Sch.1 para.5
s.1A, added: 2008 c.17 s.61
s.1A, amended: 2008 c.17 s.61
s.2, amended: 2008 c.17 s.61
s.3, amended: 2008 c.17 s.61
s.4, amended: 2008 c.17 s.61
s.5, amended: 2008 c.17 s.61
s.6, amended: 2008 c.17 s.61
s.7, amended: 2008 c.17 s.61
s.8, amended: 2008 c.17 s.61
s.9, amended: 2008 c.17 s.61, s.62
s.9, varied: 2008 c.17 s.179, SI 2008/2839 Sch.1 para.5
s.10, amended: 2008 c.17 s.61
s.11, amended: 2008 c.17 s.61
s.11, referred to: 2008 c.17 s.179
s.11, varied: 2008 c.17 s.179
s.11A, amended: 2008 c.17 s.61
s.11A, referred to: 2008 c.17 s.179
s.11A, varied: 2008 c.17 s.179
s.11B, amended: 2008 c.17 s.61
s.11B, referred to: 2008 c.17 s.179
s.11B, varied: 2008 c.17 s.179
s.12, amended: 2008 c.17 s.61, s.307
s.12, referred to: 2008 c.17 s.179
s.12, varied: 2008 c.17 s.179
s.12A, amended: 2008 c.17 s.61, s.62, s.63
s.12A, referred to: 2008 c.17 s.179
s.12A, varied: 2008 c.17 s.179
s.12B, amended: 2008 c.17 s.61
s.12B, referred to: 2008 c.17 s.179
s.12B, varied: 2008 c.17 s.179
s.13, amended: 2008 c.17 s.61
s.13, referred to: 2008 c.17 s.179
s.13, varied: 2008 c.17 s.179
s.14, amended: 2008 c.17 s.61
s.14, referred to: 2008 c.17 s.179
s.14, varied: 2008 c.17 s.179
s.15, amended: 2008 c.17 s.61
s.15, referred to: 2008 c.17 s.179
s.15, varied: 2008 c.17 s.179
s.15A, amended: 2008 c.17 s.61, s.62, s.63
s.16, amended: 2008 c.17 s.61, s.185
s.16, applied: 2008 c.17 s.149, s.173, s.177, s.181, SI 2008/2839 Art.2
s.16, varied: SI 2008/2839 Sch.1 para.5
s.16A, amended: 2008 c.17 s.61, s.185
s.16A, applied: SI 2008/2839 Art.2
s.16A, varied: SI 2008/2839 Sch.1 para.5
s.17, amended: 2008 c.17 s.61, s.62, s.63
s.17, varied: 2008 c.17 s.184
s.18, amended: 2008 c.17 s.61, s.62
s.18, applied: 2008 c.17 s.77, s.181, s.274, SI 2008/2839 Art.2
s.18, varied: SI 2008/2839 Sch.1 para.5
s.19, amended: 2008 c.17 s.61
s.20, amended: 2008 c.17 s.61, s.185

CAP.

1996–cont.

52. Housing Act 1996–*cont.*

s.20, applied: 2008 c.17 s.177, SI 2008/2839 Art.2
s.20, varied: SI 2008/2839 Sch.1 para.5
s.21, amended: 2008 c.17 s.61, s.185
s.21, applied: 2008 c.17 s.177, SI 2008/2839 Art.2
s.21, varied: SI 2008/2839 Sch.1 para.5
s.22, amended: 2008 c.17 s.61
s.22, applied: 2008 c.17 s.274
s.23, amended: 2008 c.17 s.61, s.62
s.24, amended: 2008 c.17 s.61
s.25, amended: 2008 c.17 s.61
s.25, applied: SI 2008/2839 Sch.1 para.5
s.25, varied: SI 2008/2839 Sch.1 para.5
s.26, amended: 2008 c.17 s.61
s.27, amended: 2008 c.17 s.61
s.27, applied: 2008 c.17 s.181, SI 2008/2839 Art.2, Art.5
s.27, disapplied: 2008 c.17 s.177
s.27, varied: SI 2008/2839 Sch.1 para.5
s.27A, amended: 2008 c.17 s.61, s.62, s.63
s.27A, applied: 2008 c.17 s.180, s.182, SI 2008/2839 Art.2
s.27A, varied: SI 2008/2839 Sch.1 para.5
s.27B, amended: 2008 c.17 s.61
s.27B, applied: 2008 c.17 s.182, SI 2008/2839 Art.2
s.27B, varied: SI 2008/2839 Sch.1 para.5
s.28, amended: 2008 c.17 s.61, Sch.8 para.65
s.28, repealed (in part): 2008 c.17 Sch.8 para.65, Sch.16
s.29, amended: 2008 c.17 s.61, s.62
s.29, varied: SI 2008/2839 Sch.1 para.5
s.30, amended: 2008 c.17 s.61, s.62
s.30, varied: SI 2008/2839 Sch.1 para.5
s.31, amended: 2008 c.17 s.61
s.32, amended: 2008 c.17 s.61
s.33, amended: 2008 c.17 s.61
s.34, amended: 2008 c.17 s.61
s.35, amended: 2008 c.17 s.61
s.36, amended: 2008 c.17 s.61
s.36, varied: SI 2008/2839 Sch.1 para.5
s.37, amended: 2008 c.17 s.61
s.38, amended: 2008 c.17 s.61
s.39, amended: 2008 c.17 s.61, s.62, s.63
s.40, amended: 2008 c.17 s.61
s.41, amended: 2008 c.17 s.61
s.41, applied: SI 2008/2839 Art.4
s.42, amended: 2008 c.17 s.61
s.42, applied: SI 2008/2839 Art.5
s.43, amended: 2008 c.17 s.61
s.44, amended: 2008 c.17 s.61
s.45, amended: 2008 c.17 s.61
s.46, amended: 2008 c.17 s.61, s.62
s.46, varied: SI 2008/2839 Sch.1 para.5
s.47, amended: 2008 c.17 s.61
s.48, amended: 2008 c.17 s.61
s.49, amended: 2008 c.17 s.61
s.49, varied: SI 2008/2839 Sch.1 para.5

CAP.

1996–cont.

52. Housing Act 1996–*cont.*

s.50, amended: 2008 c.17 s.61
s.51, amended: 2008 c.17 s.61, s.124, Sch.14 para.4
s.51, varied: SI 2008/2839 Sch.1 para.5
s.51A, amended: 2008 c.17 s.61
s.51B, amended: 2008 c.17 s.61
s.51C, amended: 2008 c.17 s.61
s.52, amended: 2008 c.17 s.61, s.62
s.53, amended: 2008 c.17 s.61, s.62
s.53, applied: SI 2008/2839 Art.2
s.53, varied: SI 2008/2839 Sch.1 para.5
s.54, amended: 2008 c.17 s.61
s.54, applied: SI 2008/2839 Art.2
s.54, varied: SI 2008/2839 Sch.1 para.5
s.55, amended: 2008 c.17 s.61, s.62, s.63
s.56, amended: 2008 c.17 s.61
s.56, applied: 2008 c.17 s.278
s.56, referred to: SI 2008/2839 Sch.1 para.4, Sch.1 para.5
s.56, repealed: 2008 c.17 s.61, Sch.16
s.56, varied: SI 2008/2839 Sch.1 para.5
s.57, amended: 2008 c.17 s.61
s.58, amended: 2008 c.17 s.61
s.58, applied: 2008 c.17 s.274
s.59, amended: 2008 c.17 s.61
s.60, amended: 2008 c.17 s.61
s.61, amended: 2008 c.17 s.61
s.62, amended: 2008 c.17 s.61
s.63, amended: 2008 c.17 s.61
s.64, amended: 2008 c.17 s.61
s.94, amended: 2008 c.17 s.312
s.96, see *Vesely v Levy* [2007] EWCA Civ 367, [2008] L. & T.R. 9 (CA (Civ Div)), Mummery, L.J.
s.105, repealed (in part): 2008 c.17 Sch.16
s.122, enabling: SI 2008/587, SI 2008/3156
s.124, applied: 2008 c.17 Sch.11 para.17
s.125, referred to: 2008 c.17 Sch.11 para.19
s.127, amended: 2008 c.17 Sch.11 para.11
s.127, repealed (in part): 2008 c.17 Sch.11 para.11, Sch.16
s.130, amended: 2008 c.17 Sch.11 para.12
s.137, applied: 2008 c.17 Sch.11 para.22
s.143A, applied: 2008 c.17 Sch.11 para.17
s.143B, referred to: 2008 c.17 Sch.11 para.19
s.143D, amended: 2008 c.17 Sch.11 para.13
s.143D, repealed (in part): 2008 c.17 Sch.11 para.13, Sch.16
s.143E, see *R. (on the application of Gilboy) v Liverpool City Council* [2008] EWCA Civ 751, [2008] 4 All E.R. 127 (CA (Civ Div)), Waller, L.J. (V-P)
s.143F, see *R. (on the application of Gilboy) v Liverpool City Council* [2008] EWCA Civ 751, [2008] 4 All E.R. 127 (CA (Civ Div)), Waller, L.J. (V-P)
s.160, enabling: SI 2008/3015
s.167, amended: 2008 c.17 Sch.15 para.2
s.167, applied: SI 2008/2867 Reg.12

CAP.

1996–cont.

52. Housing Act 1996–*cont.*

s.167, varied: SI 2008/2867 Reg.12
s.175, see *Manchester City Council v Moran* [2008] EWCA Civ 378, [2008] 1 W.L.R. 2387 (CA (Civ Div)), Sir Anthony Clarke, M.R.; see *R. (on the application of Aweys) v Birmingham City Council* [2008] EWCA Civ 48, [2008] 1 W.L.R. 2305 (CA (Civ Div)), Ward, L.J.; see *Waltham Forest LBC v Maloba* [2007] EWCA Civ 1281, [2008] 1 W.L.R. 2079 (CA (Civ Div)), Sir Igor Judge (President, QB)
s.184, see *Lambeth LBC v Johnston* [2008] EWCA Civ 690, Times, June 30, 2008 (CA (Civ Div)), Smith, L.J.
s.184, amended: 2008 c.17 Sch.15 para.3
s.185, amended: 2008 c.17 Sch.15 para.4
s.185, applied: 2008 c.4 s.134
s.188, see *R. (on the application of M) v Hammersmith and Fulham LBC* [2008] UKHL 14, [2008] 1 W.L.R. 535 (HL), Lord Hoffmann
s.189, see *Lambeth LBC v Johnston* [2008] EWCA Civ 690, Times, June 30, 2008 (CA (Civ Div)), Smith, L.J.; see *R. (on the application of M) v Hammersmith and Fulham LBC* [2008] UKHL 14, [2008] 1 W.L.R. 535 (HL), Lord Hoffmann
s.191, see *Denton v Southwark LBC* [2007] EWCA Civ 623, [2008] H.L.R. 11 (CA (Civ Div)), Mummery, L.J.; see *Gilby v Westminster City Council* [2007] EWCA Civ 604, [2008] H.L.R. 7 (CA (Civ Div)), Mummery, L.J.; see *Manchester City Council v Moran* [2008] EWCA Civ 378, [2008] 1 W.L.R. 2387 (CA (Civ Div)), Sir Anthony Clarke, M.R.
s.193, see *Ahmed v Leicester City Council* [2007] EWCA Civ 843, [2008] H.L.R. 6 (CA (Civ Div)), Pill, L.J.; see *Boreh v Ealing LBC* [2008] EWCA Civ 1176, Times, November 11, 2008 (CA (Civ Div)), Wall, L.J.; see *Osseily v Westminster City Council* [2007] EWCA Civ 1108, [2008] H.L.R. 18 (CA (Civ Div)), Laws, L.J.; see *R. (on the application of Aweys) v Birmingham City Council* [2008] EWCA Civ 48, [2008] 1 W.L.R. 2305 (CA (Civ Div)), Ward, L.J.
s.193, amended: 2008 c.17 Sch.15 para.5
s.195, amended: 2008 c.17 Sch.15 para.6
s.199, amended: 2008 c.17 s.315, Sch.16
s.199, repealed (in part): 2008 c.17 s.315, Sch.16
s.202, see *Osseily v Westminster City Council* [2007] EWCA Civ 1108, [2008] H.L.R. 18 (CA (Civ Div)), Laws, L.J.
s.202, amended: 2008 c.17 Sch.15 para.7, Sch.16
s.218, amended: 2008 c.17 Sch.15 para.8
s.218A, applied: 2008 c.17 s.193
s.219, amended: SI 2008/3002 Sch.1 para.46

CAP.

1996–cont.

52. Housing Act 1996–*cont.*

Sch.1 Part II para.5, amended: 2008 c.17 Sch.14 para.4

Sch.1 Part II para.6, applied: SI 2008/2839 Art.4

Sch.1 Part II para.7, applied: SI 2008/2839 Art.4

Sch.1 Part II para.8, applied: SI 2008/2839 Art.4

Sch.1 Part II para.9, amended: 2008 c.17 s.62

Sch.1 Part II para.9, varied: SI 2008/2839 Sch.1 para.5

Sch.1 Part II para.11, amended: 2008 c.17 s.62

Sch.1 Part II para.11, varied: SI 2008/2839 Sch.1 para.5

Sch.1 Part II para.12, varied: SI 2008/2839 Sch.1 para.5

Sch.1 Part II para.13, amended: SI 2008/948 Sch.1 para.202

Sch.1 Part II para.13, varied: SI 2008/2839 Sch.1 para.5

Sch.1 Part II para.15, amended: 2008 c.17 s.61

Sch.1 Part II para.15, varied: SI 2008/2839 Sch.1 para.5

Sch.1 Part II para.15A, amended: 2008 c.17 s.62, s.63

Sch.1 Part III, amended: 2008 c.17 s.61

Sch.1 Part III para.16, amended: 2008 c.17 s.61

Sch.1 Part III para.16A, amended: 2008 c.17 s.61

Sch.1 Part III para.16A, applied: SI 2008/674 Art.3

Sch.1 Part III para.16A, substituted: SI 2008/948 Sch.1 para.202

Sch.1 Part III para.17, amended: 2008 c.17 s.61

Sch.1 Part III para.18, amended: SI 2008/948 Sch.1 para.20

Sch.1 Part III para.18A, amended: 2008 c.17 s.61

Sch.1 Part III para.19, amended: 2008 c.17 s.61

Sch.1 Part III para.19A, amended: 2008 c.17 s.61

Sch.1 para.4, see *Westminster City Council v Boraliu* [2007] EWCA Civ 1339, [2008] 1 W.L.R. 2408 (CA (Civ Div)), Chadwick, L.J.

Sch.1 Part IV para.20, amended: 2008 c.17 s.61

Sch.1 Part IV para.20, applied: SI 2008/2839 Art.4

Sch.1 Part IV para.20, varied: SI 2008/2839 Sch.1 para.5

Sch.1 Part IV para.20A, amended: 2008 c.17 s.61

Sch.1 Part IV para.21, amended: 2008 c.17 s.61

Sch.1 Part IV para.24, applied: 2008 c.17 s.262

Sch.1 Part IV para.27, varied: SI 2008/2839 Sch.1 para.5

CAP.

1996–cont.

52. Housing Act 1996–*cont.*

Sch.1 Part IV para.28, amended: 2008 c.17 Sch.14 para.4

Sch.2 para.1, amended: 2008 c.17 s.124

Sch.2 para.2, amended: 2008 c.17 s.124

Sch.2 para.3, amended: 2008 c.17 s.124

Sch.2 para.4, amended: 2008 c.17 s.124

Sch.2 para.5, amended: 2008 c.17 s.124

Sch.2 para.6, amended: 2008 c.17 s.124

Sch.2 para.6, varied: SI 2008/2839 Sch.1 para.5

Sch.2 para.7, amended: 2008 c.17 s.124

Sch.2 para.8, amended: 2008 c.17 s.124

Sch.2 para.9, amended: 2008 c.17 s.124

Sch.2 para.10, amended: 2008 c.17 s.124

Sch.2 para.11, amended: 2008 c.17 s.124, Sch.16

Sch.2 para.11, varied: SI 2008/2839 Sch.1 para.5

Sch.2 para.12, added: 2008 c.17 s.124

Sch.2 para.12, amended: 2008 c.17 s.124

Sch.9 para.1, repealed: 2008 c.17 Sch.16

Sch.9 para.2, repealed (in part): 2008 c.17 Sch.16

Sch.13 para.4, repealed: 2008 c.17 Sch.16

Sch.18 Part IV para.22, repealed (in part): 2008 c.17 Sch.16

53. Housing Grants, Construction and Regeneration Act 1996

see *Makers UK Ltd v Camden LBC* [2008] EWHC 1836 (TCC), [2008] B.L.R. 470 (QBD (TCC)), Akenhead, J.

Part I c.I, applied: SI 2008/1189 Art.3, SI 2008/2370 Art.3

Part II, see *Reinwood Ltd v L Brown & Sons Ltd* [2008] UKHL 12, [2008] 1 W.L.R. 696 (HL), Lord Hope of Craighead

s.3, amended: SI 2008/3002 Sch.1 para.48

s.23, applied: SI 2008/1189 Art.2, SI 2008/2370 Art.2

s.23, enabling: SI 2008/1189, SI 2008/2370

s.30, enabling: SI 2008/1190, SI 2008/2377, SI 2008/3104

s.33, enabling: SI 2008/1189, SI 2008/2370

s.59, amended: SI 2008/3002 Sch.1 para.49, Sch.3

s.101, amended: SI 2008/3002 Sch.1 para.50

s.108, see *Cubitt Building & Interiors Ltd v Richardson Roofing (Industrial) Ltd* [2008] EWHC 1020 (TCC), [2008] B.L.R. 354 (QBD (TCC)), Akenhead, J.

s.110, see *Reinwood Ltd v L Brown & Sons Ltd* [2008] UKHL 12, [2008] 1 W.L.R. 696 (HL), Lord Hope of Craighead

s.111, see *Reinwood Ltd v L Brown & Sons Ltd* [2008] UKHL 12, [2008] 1 W.L.R. 696 (HL), Lord Hope of Craighead

s.129, repealed: 2008 c.17 Sch.16

s.145, repealed: 2008 c.17 Sch.16

CAP.

1996–cont.

53. Housing Grants, Construction and Regeneration Act 1996–*cont.*

s.146, enabling: SI 2008/1189, SI 2008/1190, SI 2008/2370, SI 2008/2377, SI 2008/3104

55. Broadcasting Act 1996

referred to: SI 2008/1420 Art.2

Part I, applied: SI 2008/1420 Art.6

s.3, applied: SI 2008/1420 Art.6

s.5, applied: SI 2008/1420 Art.6

s.5, referred to: SI 2008/1420 Art.6

s.12, varied: SI 2008/1420 Art.11

s.18, applied: SI 2008/1420 Art.6

s.18, varied: SI 2008/1420 Art.6

s.19, varied: SI 2008/1420 Art.7

s.25, applied: SI 2008/1420 Art.3

s.32, enabling: SI 2008/1421

Sch.6 para.2, amended: SI 2008/948 Sch.1 para.203

Sch.6 para.3, amended: SI 2008/948 Sch.1 para.203

Sch.6 para.4, amended: SI 2008/948 Sch.1 para.203

Sch.7 para.3, repealed: 2008 c.9 Sch.2 para.70

56. Education Act 1996

see *Dimmock v Secretary of State for Children, Schools and Families* [2007] EWHC 2288 (Admin), [2008] 1 All E.R. 367 (QBD (Admin)), Burton, J.

applied: SI 2008/239 Reg.8

Part IV, applied: SI 2008/2699 Sch.1

Part VI c.II, applied: SI 2008/228 Sch.1 para.11

s.6, amended: 2008 c.25 Sch.1 para.6

s.9, see *Ealing LBC v Special Educational Needs and Disability Tribunal* [2008] EWHC 193 (Admin), [2008] E.L.R. 183 (QBD (Admin)), Plender, J; see *O v Lewisham LBC* [2007] EWHC 2130 (Admin), [2008] B.L.G.R. 765 (QBD (Admin)), Andrew Nicol Q.C.

s.15A, applied: SI 2008/228 Sch.1 para.18, Sch.1 para.19

s.15B, applied: SI 2008/228 Sch.1 para.18

s.18, applied: SI 2008/228 Sch.2 para.18

s.19, applied: SI 2008/228 Sch.2 para.9, SI 2008/3093 Reg.8, Sch.3 para.17

s.29, enabling: SI 2008/4, SI 2008/3089, SI 2008/3093

s.312, applied: SI 2008/529 Reg.43, SI 2008/975 Sch.3 para.17, Sch.6 para.18, SI 2008/1273 Reg.83D, Reg.27, SI 2008/1582 Reg.45, SI 2008/3170 Reg.27, Reg.87

s.313, amended: 2008 c.25 Sch.1 para.7, SI 2008/2833 Sch.3 para.128

s.313, applied: SI 2008/228 Sch.2 para.7

s.317, applied: SI 2008/2945 Reg.3

s.317, referred to: SI 2008/3093 Reg.10

s.317, enabling: SI 2008/2945

s.320, applied: SI 2008/228 Sch.2 para.11

CAP.

1996–cont.

56. Education Act 1996–*cont.*

s.321, see *R. (on the application of Hill) v Bedfordshire CC* [2007] EWHC 2435 (Admin), [2008] E.L.R. 191 (QBD (Admin)), Wyn Williams, J.

s.321, applied: SI 2008/228 Sch.1 para.2

s.322, applied: SI 2008/228 Sch.1 para.2

s.323, applied: SI 2008/228 Sch.1 para.2

s.324, see *R. (on the application of Hill) v Bedfordshire CC* [2007] EWHC 2435 (Admin), [2008] E.L.R. 191 (QBD (Admin)), Wyn Williams, J.; see *R. (on the application of M) v Sutton LBC* [2007] EWCA Civ 1205, [2008] E.L.R. 123 (CA (Civ Div)), Pill, L.J.

s.324, applied: 2008 c.02 s.3, 2008 c.25 s.132, SI 2008/228 Sch.1 para.2

s.325, applied: SI 2008/228 Sch.1 para.2

s.326, see *B County Council v H* [2008] EWHC 1070 (Admin), [2008] E.L.R. 333 (QBD (Admin)), Judge Mackie Q.C.; see *R. (on the application of MG) v Tower Hamlets LBC* [2008] EWHC 1577 (Admin), [2008] E.L.R. 523 (QBD (Admin)), Langstaff, J.

s.326, applied: SI 2008/228 Sch.1 para.2

s.326A, amended: SI 2008/2833 Sch.3 para.129

s.326A, applied: SI 2008/228 Sch.1 para.2

s.327, applied: SI 2008/228 Sch.1 para.2

s.328, applied: SI 2008/228 Sch.1 para.2

s.329, applied: SI 2008/228 Sch.1 para.2

s.329A, applied: SI 2008/228 Sch.1 para.2

s.330, applied: SI 2008/228 Sch.1 para.2

s.331, applied: SI 2008/228 Sch.1 para.2

s.332A, applied: SI 2008/228 Sch.1 para.5

s.332C, added: 2008 c.11 s.1

s.332D, added: 2008 c.11 s.1

s.332E, added: 2008 c.11 s.1

s.333, amended: SI 2008/2833 Sch.3 para.130

s.333, applied: SI 2008/2833 Sch.1, Sch.2

s.333, repealed (in part): SI 2008/2833 Sch.3 para.130

s.334, amended: SI 2008/2833 Sch.3 para.131

s.335, amended: SI 2008/2833 Sch.3 para.132

s.336, amended: SI 2008/2833 Sch.3 para.133

s.336A, amended: SI 2008/2833 Sch.3 para.136

s.336ZA, applied: SI 2008/2833 Art.6

s.336ZA, repealed: SI 2008/2833 Sch.3 para.134

s.336ZB, added: SI 2008/2833 Sch.3 para.135

s.337, substituted: 2008 c.25 s.142

s.342, amended: 2008 c.25 s.142, s.143, Sch.2

s.342A, added: 2008 c.25 s.144

CAP.

1996–cont.

56. Education Act 1996–*cont.*

s.342B, added: 2008 c.25 s.145
s.342C, added: 2008 c.25 s.145
s.347, amended: 2008 c.25 s.146
s.347, applied: 2008 c.25 s.148, SI 2008/1801 Reg.2
s.347, enabling: SI 2008/1701
s.348, applied: SI 2008/228 Sch.2 para.11
s.349, amended: 2008 c.25 s.147, Sch.2
s.390, applied: SI 2008/228 Sch.1 para.24
s.406, see *Dimmock v Secretary of State for Children, Schools and Families* [2007] EWHC 2288 (Admin), [2008] 1 All E.R. 367 (QBD (Admin)), Burton, J.
s.407, see *Dimmock v Secretary of State for Children, Schools and Families* [2007] EWHC 2288 (Admin), [2008] 1 All E.R. 367 (QBD (Admin)), Burton, J.
s.408, enabling: SI 2008/1727, SI 2008/1747
s.439, amended: 2008 c.25 Sch.1 para.49
s.444, amended: 2008 c.02 s.20, Sch.2
s.444A, amended: 2008 c.25 Sch.1 para.50
s.444ZA, amended: 2008 c.25 s.155
s.455, amended: 2008 c.02 s.22, Sch.2
s.455, applied: 2008 c.02 s.6
s.456, amended: 2008 c.02 s.22
s.456, applied: 2008 c.02 s.6
s.482, applied: SI 2008/239 Sch.2 para.21, SI 2008/1801 Reg.2
s.483A, amended: 2008 c.25 s.147
s.493, applied: SI 2008/228 Sch.2 para.12
s.494, applied: SI 2008/228 Sch.2 para.12
s.496, varied: SI 2008/3090 Reg.10
s.497, varied: SI 2008/3090 Reg.10
s.497A, applied: SI 2008/239 Reg.6
s.507A, applied: SI 2008/228 Sch.1 para.19
s.507B, applied: SI 2008/228 Sch.1 para.19
s.508A, applied: SI 2008/228 Sch.1 para.10
s.508B, applied: SI 2008/3093 Sch.2 para.5, Sch.3 para.10
s.508C, applied: SI 2008/3093 Sch.2 para.5, Sch.3 para.10
s.508E, applied: SI 2008/228 Sch.1 para.10
s.509, applied: SI 2008/228 Sch.1 para.10
s.509, repealed (in part): 2008 c.02 Sch.2
s.509A, amended: 2008 c.02 Sch.1 para.4, Sch.2
s.509A, repealed (in part): 2008 c.02 Sch.1 para.4, Sch.2
s.509AA, amended: 2008 c.02 Sch.1 para.4, Sch.2
s.509AA, repealed (in part): 2008 c.02 Sch.1 para.4, Sch.2
s.509AB, amended: 2008 c.02 Sch.1 para.4, Sch.2, 2008 c.25 s.83, 2008 c.26 Sch.4 para.60
s.509AB, repealed (in part): 2008 c.02 Sch.1 para.4, Sch.2
s.509AC, amended: 2008 c.02 Sch.1 para.4, Sch.2

CAP.

1996–cont.

56. Education Act 1996–*cont.*

s.509AC, repealed (in part): 2008 c.02 Sch.1 para.4, Sch.2
s.509AD, amended: 2008 c.25 s.84
s.510, applied: SI 2008/228 Sch.1 para.10
s.512, applied: SI 2008/228 Sch.2 para.15
s.512ZA, applied: SI 2008/228 Sch.2 para.15
s.512ZA, referred to: SI 2008/3016 Art.2
s.512ZB, applied: SI 2008/228 Sch.2 para.15, SI 2008/3091 Reg.5
s.513, applied: SI 2008/228 Sch.2 para.15
s.514, applied: SI 2008/228 Sch.1 para.10
s.518, applied: SI 2008/228 Sch.1 para.10, SI 2008/794 Sch.8 para.13, Sch.9 para.52
s.519, applied: SI 2008/228 Sch.5 para.14
s.537, enabling: SI 2008/364, SI 2008/1727, SI 2008/3093
s.537A, enabling: SI 2008/364, SI 2008/1722, SI 2008/1727, SI 2008/3072
s.537AA, added: 2008 c.25 Sch.1 para.8
s.546, enabling: SI 2008/1701
s.548, amended: 2008 c.25 Sch.1 para.9
s.551, enabling: SI 2008/1739
s.559, repealed (in part): 2008 c.12 Sch.1 Part 11
s.562, amended: 2008 c.4 Sch.4 para.47
s.563, enabling: SI 2008/1701, SI 2008/1747
s.566, amended: 2008 c.25 Sch.1 para.51
s.569, enabling: SI 2008/4, SI 2008/364, SI 2008/1727, SI 2008/1739, SI 2008/1747, SI 2008/3072, SI 2008/3093
s.578, referred to: 2008 c.02 s.29
s.579, see *R. (on the application of L) v Waltham Forest LBC* [2007] EWHC 2060 (Admin), [2008] B.L.G.R. 495 (QBD (Admin)), Rabinder Singh Q.C.
s.580, amended: 2008 c.25 Sch.1 para.10, Sch.1 para.11
Sch.1 para.6, amended: SI 2008/2840 Art.5
Sch.1 para.15, applied: 2008 c.25 s.73
Sch.27, applied: SI 2008/2699 Sch.1
Sch.27 para.3, see *O v Lewisham LBC* [2007] EWHC 2130 (Admin), [2008] B.L.G.R. 765 (QBD (Admin)), Andrew Nicol Q.C.
Sch.27 para.8, see *Ealing LBC v Special Educational Needs and Disability Tribunal* [2008] EWHC 193 (Admin), [2008] E.L.R. 183 (QBD (Admin)), Plender, J
Sch.27 para.9, see *R. (on the application of Hill) v Bedfordshire CC* [2007] EWHC 2435 (Admin), [2008] E.L.R. 191 (QBD (Admin)), Wyn Williams, J.
Sch.27 para.10, see *R. (on the application of Hill) v Bedfordshire CC* [2007] EWHC 2435 (Admin), [2008] E.L.R. 191 (QBD (Admin)), Wyn Williams, J.
Sch.27 para.11, see *R. (on the application of Hill) v Bedfordshire CC* [2007] EWHC 2435 (Admin), [2008] E.L.R. 191 (QBD (Admin)), Wyn Williams, J.
Sch.31, applied: SI 2008/228 Sch.1 para.24

CAP.

1996–cont.

56. Education Act 1996–*cont.*
Sch.35B para.8, amended: 2008 c.25 Sch.1 para.52

61. Channel Tunnel Rail Link Act 1996
applied: SI 2008/3076 Art.5
s.1, applied: SI 2008/3076 Art.3
s.2, applied: SI 2008/3076 Art.3
s.3, applied: SI 2008/3076 Art.3
s.4, applied: SI 2008/3076 Art.3
s.5, applied: SI 2008/3076 Art.3
s.6, applied: SI 2008/3076 Art.3
s.7, applied: SI 2008/3076 Art.3
s.8, applied: SI 2008/3076 Art.3
s.9, applied: SI 2008/3076 Art.3
s.10, applied: SI 2008/3076 Art.3
s.11, applied: SI 2008/3076 Art.3
s.12, applied: SI 2008/3076 Art.3
s.13, applied: SI 2008/3076 Art.3
s.14, applied: SI 2008/3076 Art.3
s.15, applied: SI 2008/3076 Art.3
s.16, applied: SI 2008/3076 Art.3
s.17, amended: 2008 c.5 s.2
s.17, applied: SI 2008/3076 Art.3
s.17, repealed (in part): 2008 c.5 s.2
s.18, applied: SI 2008/3076 Art.3
s.19, applied: SI 2008/3076 Art.3
s.20, applied: SI 2008/3076 Art.3
s.21, amended: 2008 c.5 s.3
s.21, applied: SI 2008/3076 Art.3
s.21, repealed (in part): 2008 c.5 s.3
s.21A, added: 2008 c.5 s.4
s.21A, applied: SI 2008/3076 Art.3
s.22, applied: SI 2008/3076 Art.3
s.23, applied: SI 2008/3076 Art.3
s.24, applied: SI 2008/3076 Art.3
s.25, applied: SI 2008/3076 Art.3
s.26, applied: SI 2008/3076 Art.3
s.27, applied: SI 2008/3076 Art.3
s.28, applied: SI 2008/3076 Art.3
s.29, applied: SI 2008/3076 Art.3
s.30, applied: SI 2008/3076 Art.3
s.31, applied: SI 2008/3076 Art.3
s.31, disapplied: 2008 c.5 s.1
s.32, applied: SI 2008/3076 Art.3
s.32, disapplied: 2008 c.5 s.1
s.33, applied: SI 2008/3076 Art.3
s.33, disapplied: 2008 c.5 s.1
s.34, applied: SI 2008/3076 Art.3
s.34, enabling: SI 2008/3076
s.35, applied: SI 2008/3076 Art.3
s.36, applied: SI 2008/3076 Art.3
s.37, applied: SI 2008/3076 Art.3
s.38, applied: SI 2008/3076 Art.3
s.39, applied: SI 2008/3076 Art.3
s.40, applied: SI 2008/3076 Art.3
s.41, applied: SI 2008/3076 Art.3
s.42, applied: SI 2008/3076 Art.3
s.42A, applied: SI 2008/3076 Art.3
s.43, applied: SI 2008/3076 Art.3
s.56, amended: 2008 c.5 s.5

CAP.

1997

7. Northern Ireland Arms Decommissioning Act 1997
s.2, applied: SI 2008/378, SI 2008/378 Art.2
s.2, enabling: SI 2008/378

8. Town and Country Planning (Scotland) Act 1997
applied: SSI 2008/159 Sch.2, SSI 2008/188 Art.53, SSI 2008/189 Art.53, SSI 2008/190 Art.53, SSI 2008/331 Art.5, SSI 2008/432 Reg.44, Sch.2 para.2
referred to: SSI 2008/100 Sch.2 Part 1, SSI 2008/263 Sch.1, Sch.2
Part II, referred to: SSI 2008/165 Art.2
Part V, applied: SSI 2008/433 Sch.2 para.2
s.4, enabling: SSI 2008/195, SSI 2008/196, SSI 2008/197, SSI 2008/198
s.5, applied: SSI 2008/426 Reg.29, SSI 2008/427 Art.3
s.6, applied: SSI 2008/427 Art.2, Art.3
s.7, applied: SSI 2008/427 Art.2, Art.3
s.7, enabling: SSI 2008/426
s.8, applied: SSI 2008/426 Reg.29, SSI 2008/427 Art.2, Art.3
s.8, enabling: SSI 2008/426
s.9, applied: SSI 2008/426 Reg.4, Reg.5, Reg.28, Reg.29, SSI 2008/427 Art.2, Art.3
s.9, enabling: SSI 2008/426
s.10, applied: SSI 2008/426 Reg.3, Reg.6, Reg.7, Reg.10, Reg.20, Reg.28, SSI 2008/427 Art.2, Art.3
s.10, disapplied: SSI 2008/427 Art.3
s.10, enabling: SSI 2008/426
s.11, applied: SSI 2008/427 Art.3, Art.4, Art.5
s.11, applied: SSI 2008/427 Art.4
s.12, applied: SSI 2008/426 Reg.18, Reg.20, Reg.21, Reg.23, Reg.30, SSI 2008/427 Art.3, Art.4, Art.5
s.12, disapplied: SSI 2008/427 Art.3
s.12, enabling: SSI 2008/426
s.12, applied: SSI 2008/427 Art.4
s.12A, applied: SSI 2008/426 Reg.3, Reg.7, Reg.10, Reg.20, SSI 2008/427 Art.3, Art.4, Art.5
s.12A, enabling: SSI 2008/426
s.13, applied: SSI 2008/426 Reg.28, SSI 2008/427 Art.3, Art.4, Art.5
s.13, applied: SSI 2008/427 Art.4
s.14, applied: SSI 2008/427 Art.3, Art.4
s.14, applied: SSI 2008/427 Art.4
s.15, applied: SSI 2008/427 Art.4
s.15, referred to: SSI 2008/426 Reg.9
s.15, enabling: SSI 2008/426
s.16, applied: SSI 2008/427 Art.4, Art.7
s.16, enabling: SSI 2008/426
s.17, applied: SSI 2008/426 Reg.11, Reg.12, Reg.28, SSI 2008/427 Art.4
s.17, enabling: SSI 2008/426
s.18, applied: SSI 2008/426 Reg.10, Reg.13, Reg.15, Reg.16, Reg.20, Reg.28, SSI 2008/427 Art.4
s.18, enabling: SSI 2008/426

CAP.

1997–cont.

8. **Town and Country Planning (Scotland) Act 1997**–*cont.*

s.19, applied: SSI 2008/426 Reg.17, Reg.18, Reg.19, Reg.20, Reg.21, Reg.23, SSI 2008/427 Art.4, Art.5
s.19, disapplied: SSI 2008/427 Art.5
s.19, enabling: SSI 2008/426
s.19A, applied: SSI 2008/426 Reg.10, Reg.16, Reg.20, SSI 2008/427 Art.4, Art.5
s.19A, enabling: SSI 2008/426
s.20, applied: SSI 2008/427 Art.2, Art.4, Art.5
s.20, applied: SSI 2008/427 Art.4, Art.5
s.20A, applied: SSI 2008/427 Art.4, Art.5
s.20B, applied: SSI 2008/427 Art.4, Art.5
s.20B, enabling: SSI 2008/426
s.21, applied: SSI 2008/426 Reg.20, Reg.25, Reg.28, SSI 2008/427 Art.2, Art.3, Art.4, Art.5
s.21, enabling: SSI 2008/426
s.22, applied: SSI 2008/427 Art.5
s.22, applied: SSI 2008/426 Reg.27, SSI 2008/427 Art.5
s.22, enabling: SSI 2008/426
s.23, applied: SSI 2008/427 Art.5
s.23, applied: SSI 2008/427 Art.3
s.23A, applied: SSI 2008/427 Art.3, Art.5
s.23A, enabling: SSI 2008/426
s.23D, enabling: SSI 2008/426
s.24, applied: SSI 2008/427 Art.5
s.24, applied: SSI 2008/427 Art.3
s.25, see *Aberdeenshire Council v Scottish Ministers* [2008] CSIH 28, 2008 S.C. 485 (IH (Ex Div)), Lord Nimmo Smith
s.25, applied: SSI 2008/427 Art.5
s.25, see *Aberdeenshire Council v Scottish Ministers* [2008] CSIH 28, 2008 S.C. 485 (IH (Ex Div)), Lord Nimmo Smith
s.25, applied: SSI 2008/427 Art.3
s.26, applied: SSI 2008/432 Reg.39
s.27A, applied: SSI 2008/432 Reg.37
s.27A, enabling: SSI 2008/432
s.27C, applied: SSI 2008/432 Reg.38
s.27C, enabling: SSI 2008/432
s.28, amended: 2008 c.29 Sch.2 para.55
s.30, enabling: SSI 2008/74, SSI 2008/203, SSI 2008/432
s.31, enabling: SSI 2008/74, SSI 2008/203
s.31A, applied: SSI 2008/432 Reg.2
s.32, enabling: SSI 2008/432
s.32A, applied: SSI 2008/432 Reg.28, SSI 2008/433 Reg.21
s.34, applied: SSI 2008/432 Reg.26
s.34, referred to: SSI 2008/432 Reg.21
s.34, enabling: SSI 2008/432
s.35, applied: SSI 2008/432 Reg.15
s.35, enabling: SSI 2008/432
s.35A, applied: SSI 2008/432 Reg.4, Reg.5, Reg.18
s.35A, enabling: SSI 2008/432

CAP.

1997–cont.

8. **Town and Country Planning (Scotland) Act 1997**–*cont.*

s.35B, applied: SSI 2008/432 Reg.6, Reg.21
s.35B, referred to: SSI 2008/432 Reg.5
s.35B, enabling: SSI 2008/432
s.35C, enabling: SSI 2008/432
s.36, applied: SSI 2008/432 Reg.16, Sch.2 para.1
s.36, enabling: SSI 2008/432
s.36A, applied: SSI 2008/432 Reg.21
s.36A, enabling: SSI 2008/432
s.38, enabling: SSI 2008/432
s.38A, applied: SSI 2008/432 Reg.27
s.38A, enabling: SSI 2008/432
s.40, enabling: SSI 2008/202
s.41, applied: SSI 2008/76 Reg.8
s.42, applied: SSI 2008/432 Reg.11
s.43, applied: SSI 2008/432 Reg.28
s.43, enabling: SSI 2008/432
s.43A, applied: SSI 2008/432 Reg.17, Reg.28, Reg.29, Sch.2 para.3, SSI 2008/433 Reg.7, Reg.8, Reg.9, Reg.21
s.43A, enabling: SSI 2008/433
s.46, applied: SSI 2008/432 Reg.34, Sch.2 para.3, SSI 2008/434 Reg.1, Reg.17
s.47, applied: SSI 2008/432 Reg.17, Reg.26, SSI 2008/434 Reg.1, Reg.3, Reg.16, Reg.17, Reg.24
s.47, enabling: SSI 2008/434
s.58, applied: SSI 2008/432 Reg.11, Reg.28, SSI 2008/433 Reg.21
s.58, referred to: SSI 2008/432 Reg.28
s.59, applied: SSI 2008/432 Reg.11, Reg.28, SSI 2008/433 Reg.21
s.59, referred to: SSI 2008/432 Reg.28
s.59, enabling: SSI 2008/432
s.75, applied: SSI 2008/432 Reg.28, Sch.2 para.4, SSI 2008/433 Reg.21
s.100, amended: 2008 c.29 s.176
s.101, amended: 2008 c.29 s.176
s.102, amended: 2008 c.29 s.176
s.116A, added: 2008 c.29 s.176
s.120, amended: 2008 c.29 s.176
s.121, amended: 2008 c.29 s.176
s.122, amended: 2008 c.29 s.176
s.130, applied: SSI 2008/434 Reg.1, Reg.13
s.130, enabling: SSI 2008/434
s.131, enabling: SSI 2008/434
s.150, applied: SSI 2008/432 Reg.2, Reg.39, Reg.41, Reg.42, Sch.2 para.5
s.151, applied: SSI 2008/432 Reg.2, Reg.39, Reg.41, Reg.42, Sch.2 para.5
s.152, applied: SSI 2008/432, SSI 2008/432 Reg.42
s.152, enabling: SSI 2008/432
s.154, applied: SSI 2008/432 Reg.41, Reg.42, SSI 2008/434, SSI 2008/434 Reg.1, Reg.16, Reg.24
s.154, enabling: SSI 2008/434
s.160, amended: 2008 c.29 Sch.2 para.56

CAP.

1997–cont.

8. Town and Country Planning (Scotland) Act 1997–*cont.*
s.160, applied: SSI 2008/100 Sch.2 Part 1
s.164, applied: SSI 2008/100 Sch.2 Part 1
s.168, applied: SSI 2008/434 Reg.15
s.169, applied: SSI 2008/434, SSI 2008/434 Reg.1, Reg.13
s.169, enabling: SSI 2008/434
s.172, amended: 2008 c.29 Sch.2 para.57
s.179, applied: SSI 2008/434 Reg.15
s.180, applied: SSI 2008/434, SSI 2008/434 Reg.1, Reg.13
s.189, varied: 2008 asp 4 s.42
s.203, applied: SSI 2008/88 Reg.12
s.215, applied: SSI 2008/331 Art.3
s.237, applied: SSI 2008/427 Art.2, Art.3, Art.4, Art.5
s.238, applied: SSI 2008/427 Art.2, Art.3, Art.4, Art.5
s.242A, applied: SSI 2008/432 Reg.21
s.263, see *Lerwick Port Authority v Scottish Ministers* 2008 S.L.T. 74 (OH), Lord Reed
s.265A, applied: SI 2008/1590 r.3
s.265A, enabling: SI 2008/1590
s.267, applied: SSI 2008/434
s.267, enabling: SSI 2008/434
s.271, varied: SSI 2008/432 Reg.44
s.275, applied: SSI 2008/434
s.275, enabling: SSI 2008/74, SSI 2008/203, SSI 2008/426, SSI 2008/432, SSI 2008/433, SSI 2008/434
s.275A, applied: SSI 2008/434
s.275A, enabling: SSI 2008/433, SSI 2008/434
s.277, amended: 2008 c.29 Sch.2 para.58
Sch.1, applied: SSI 2008/427 Art.6
Sch.14 para.17, added: 2008 c.29 s.176
Sch.14 para.18, added: 2008 c.29 s.176

9. Planning (Listed Buildings and Conservation Areas) (Scotland) Act 1997
applied: SSI 2008/100 Sch.4 Part 2, SSI 2008/159 Sch.2, Sch.3 Part 2
referred to: SSI 2008/100 Sch.2 Part 1
s.60, applied: SSI 2008/432 Reg.20, Reg.26
s.61, applied: SSI 2008/100 Sch.2 Part 1
s.65, applied: SSI 2008/432 Reg.20, Reg.26
Sch.3 para.6, applied: SI 2008/1590 r.3
Sch.3 para.6, enabling: SI 2008/1590

10. Planning (Hazardous Substances) (Scotland) Act 1997
s.7, amended: 2008 c.29 Sch.2 para.60
s.8, amended: 2008 c.29 Sch.2 para.61
s.10, amended: 2008 c.29 Sch.2 para.62, SI 2008/960 Sch.3
s.12, amended: 2008 c.29 Sch.2 para.63
s.38, amended: 2008 c.29 Sch.2 para.64
Sch.1 para.6, applied: SI 2008/1590 r.3
Sch.1 para.6, enabling: SI 2008/1590

CAP.

1997–cont.

12. Civil Procedure Act 1997
s.1, applied: SI 2008/2178, SI 2008/3085, SI 2008/3327
s.2, applied: SI 2008/3327
s.2, enabling: SI 2008/2178, SI 2008/3327
s.3, disapplied: 2008 c.28 s.72

16. Finance Act 1997
s.7, repealed (in part): 2008 c.9 s.13, Sch.5 para.25
s.11, amended: 2008 c.9 s.22
s.12, enabling: SI 2008/1949
s.14, enabling: SI 2008/1949
s.27, repealed (in part): 2008 c.9 s.142, Sch.41 para.25
s.35, repealed (in part): SI 2008/1146 Sch.1 para.7
s.36, repealed: SI 2008/1146 Sch.1 para.8
s.37, repealed (in part): SI 2008/1146 Sch.1 para.9
s.47, repealed (in part): 2008 c.9 Sch.39 para.65
s.51, repealed (in part): 2008 c.9 Sch.43 para.6
s.52, repealed: 2008 c.9 Sch.43 para.15
s.73, repealed: 2008 c.9 s.66
s.77, repealed: 2008 c.9 s.66
s.79, repealed: 2008 c.9 Sch.14 para.17
s.89, amended: 2008 c.9 Sch.2 para.69
s.91, repealed (in part): 2008 c.9 Sch.22 para.2
Sch.1 Part I, applied: 2008 c.9 Sch.41 para.1
Sch.1 Part I para.3, applied: 2008 c.9 Sch.41 para.1
Sch.6 para.6, repealed (in part): 2008 c.9 Sch.5 para.25
Sch.12 Part I para.7, amended: 2008 c.9 Sch.2 para.69
Sch.12 Part III para.19, repealed (in part): 2008 c.9 Sch.17 para.17
Sch.12 Part IV para.28, amended: SI 2008/954 Art.22

21. Knives Act 1997
applied: 2008 c.13 Sch.3
referred to: 2008 c.13 Sch.6
s.1, amended: SI 2008/1216 Art.90
s.2, amended: SI 2008/1216 Art.90

22. Architects Act 1997
s.1A, added: SI 2008/1331 Reg.3
s.2, amended: SI 2008/1331 Reg.4
s.3, amended: SI 2008/1331 Reg.5
s.4, amended: SI 2008/1331 Reg.6
s.5, substituted: SI 2008/1331 Reg.7
s.5A, added: SI 2008/1331 Reg.8
s.5B, added: SI 2008/1331 Reg.8
s.5C, added: SI 2008/1331 Reg.8
s.5D, added: SI 2008/1331 Reg.8
s.5E, added: SI 2008/1331 Reg.8
s.6, amended: SI 2008/1331 Reg.9
s.6, repealed (in part): SI 2008/1331 Reg.9
s.6A, added: SI 2008/1331 Reg.10

CAP.

1997–cont.

22. Architects Act 1997–*cont.*

s.7, amended: SI 2008/1331 Reg.11
s.8, amended: SI 2008/1331 Reg.12
s.9, amended: SI 2008/1331 Reg.13
s.10, amended: SI 2008/1331 Reg.14
s.11, amended: SI 2008/1331 Reg.15
s.12, repealed: SI 2008/1331 Reg.16
s.15, repealed (in part): SI 2008/1331 Reg.17
s.19, repealed: SI 2008/1331 Reg.18
s.20, amended: SI 2008/1331 Reg.19
s.22, substituted: SI 2008/1331 Reg.20
s.22A, substituted: SI 2008/1331 Reg.20
s.22B, added: SI 2008/1331 Reg.21
s.22C, added: SI 2008/1331 Reg.21
s.25, amended: SI 2008/1331 Reg.22
s.25, repealed (in part): SI 2008/1331 Reg.22
Sch.1 Part I para.2, amended: SI 2008/1331 Reg.23
Sch.1 Part I para.3, amended: SI 2008/1331 Reg.23
Sch.1 Part I para.6, amended: SI 2008/1331 Reg.23
Sch.1 Part II para.13, amended: SI 2008/1331 Reg.23
Sch.1 Part II para.15, amended: SI 2008/1331 Reg.23
Sch.1A para.1, added: SI 2008/1331 Sch.1
Sch.1A para.2, added: SI 2008/1331 Sch.1
Sch.1A para.3, added: SI 2008/1331 Sch.1
Sch.1A para.4, added: SI 2008/1331 Sch.1
Sch.1A para.4, varied: SI 2008/1331 Reg.24
Sch.1A para.4, added: SI 2008/1331 Sch.1
Sch.1A para.5, added: SI 2008/1331 Sch.1
Sch.1A para.6, added: SI 2008/1331 Sch.1
Sch.1A para.7, added: SI 2008/1331 Sch.1
Sch.1A para.8, added: SI 2008/1331 Sch.1
Sch.1A para.9, added: SI 2008/1331 Sch.1

27. Social Security (Recovery of Benefits) Act 1997

applied: SI 2008/1596 Reg.8, Reg.18
s.1, applied: SI 2008/1596 Reg.2
s.1, varied: SI 2008/1596 Sch.1 para.2
s.1A, added: 2008 c.6 s.54
s.1A, applied: SI 2008/1596 Reg.4, Reg.9
s.1A, enabling: SI 2008/1596, SI 2008/2365
s.6, applied: SI 2008/1596 Reg.10, SI 2008/2685 Sch.1
s.8, applied: SI 2008/1596 Reg.12
s.10, applied: SI 2008/1596 Reg.2
s.10, varied: SI 2008/1596 Sch.1 para.3
s.11, applied: SI 2008/1596 Reg.2, Reg.5, SI 2008/2685 Sch.1
s.11, repealed (in part): SI 2008/2833 Sch.3 para.139
s.11, varied: SI 2008/1596 Sch.1 para.4
s.12, amended: SI 2008/2833 Sch.3 para.140
s.12, applied: SI 2008/1596 Reg.2
s.12, varied: SI 2008/1596 Sch.1 para.5
s.13, amended: SI 2008/2833 Sch.3 para.141
s.13, applied: SI 2008/1596 Reg.2, Reg.5

CAP.

1997–cont.

27. Social Security (Recovery of Benefits) Act 1997–*cont.*

s.13, repealed (in part): SI 2008/2833 Sch.3 para.141
s.13, varied: SI 2008/1596 Sch.1 para.6
s.14, applied: SI 2008/1596 Reg.2, Reg.19
s.14, varied: SI 2008/1596 Sch.1 para.7
s.14, enabling: SI 2008/1596
s.15, applied: SI 2008/1596 Reg.2, Reg.5
s.15, referred to: SI 2008/1596 Reg.5
s.15, varied: SI 2008/1596 Sch.1 para.8
s.17, applied: SI 2008/1596 Reg.2
s.17, varied: SI 2008/1596 Sch.1 para.9
s.18, applied: SI 2008/1596 Reg.2, Reg.5
s.18, varied: SI 2008/1596 Sch.1 para.10
s.18, enabling: SI 2008/1596
s.19, applied: SI 2008/1596 Reg.2, Reg.5
s.19, varied: SI 2008/1596 Sch.1 para.11
s.19, enabling: SI 2008/1596
s.20, applied: SI 2008/1596 Reg.2
s.20, varied: SI 2008/1596 Sch.1 para.12
s.21, applied: SI 2008/1596 Reg.2, Reg.5, Reg.15
s.21, varied: SI 2008/1596 Sch.1 para.13
s.21, enabling: SI 2008/1596
s.22, applied: SI 2008/1596 Reg.2
s.22, varied: SI 2008/1596 Sch.1 para.14
s.23, applied: SI 2008/1596 Reg.2, Reg.5, Reg.15, Reg.16
s.23, referred to: SI 2008/1596 Reg.5
s.23, varied: SI 2008/1596 Sch.1 para.15
s.23, enabling: SI 2008/1596
s.26, applied: SI 2008/1596 Reg.2, Reg.5
s.26, varied: SI 2008/1596 Sch.1 para.16
s.27, applied: SI 2008/1596 Reg.2, Reg.5
s.27, varied: SI 2008/1596 Sch.1 para.17
s.28, applied: SI 2008/1596 Reg.2
s.29, amended: SI 2008/1554 Reg.50, SI 2008/2833 Sch.3 para.142
s.29, applied: SI 2008/1596 Reg.2, Reg.5
s.29, varied: SI 2008/1596 Sch.1 para.18
s.29, enabling: SI 2008/1596
s.30, applied: SI 2008/1596 Reg.2
s.30, enabling: SI 2008/2365
s.31, applied: SI 2008/1596 Reg.2
s.33, applied: SI 2008/1596 Reg.2
s.34, applied: SI 2008/1596 Reg.2
s.57, enabling: SI 2008/2365
Sch.1, applied: SI 2008/1596 Reg.2
Sch.1 Part I, referred to: SI 2008/1596 Reg.4
Sch.1 Part I para.2, applied: SI 2008/1596 Reg.5
Sch.1 Part I para.2, varied: SI 2008/1596 Sch.1 para.19
Sch.1 Part I para.3, applied: SI 2008/1596 Reg.5
Sch.1 Part I para.3, referred to: SI 2008/1596 Reg.5
Sch.1 Part I para.3, varied: SI 2008/1596 Sch.1 para.19

CAP.

1997–cont.

27. Social Security (Recovery of Benefits) Act 1997–*cont.*

Sch.1 Part I para.4, applied: SI 2008/1596 Reg.7

Sch.1 Part I para.4, enabling: SI 2008/1596

Sch.1 Part I para.5, applied: SI 2008/1596 Reg.5

Sch.1 Part I para.5, referred to: SI 2008/1596 Reg.5

Sch.1 Part I para.5, varied: SI 2008/1596 Sch.1 para.19

Sch.1 Part I para.6, varied: SI 2008/1596 Sch.1 para.19

Sch.1 Part I para.8, applied: SI 2008/1596 Reg.7

Sch.1 Part I para.8, enabling: SI 2008/1596

Sch.1 Part II para.9, applied: SI 2008/1596 Reg.5

Sch.1 Part II para.9, varied: SI 2008/1596 Sch.1 para.20

Sch.2, amended: SI 2008/1554 Reg.50

29. Local Government and Rating Act 1997

Part II, applied: SI 2008/2113 Reg.7, SI 2008/2176 Reg.1, SI 2008/2867 Reg.1

s.9, applied: SI 2008/337 Sch.1 para.1, Sch.1 para.4, Sch.1 para.5, Sch.1 para.6, Sch.1 para.7, Sch.1 para.8

s.9, varied: SI 2008/337 Sch.1 para.4

s.10, applied: SI 2008/337 Sch.1 para.4, Sch.1 para.5, Sch.1 para.6, Sch.1 para.7

s.11, applied: SI 2008/337 Sch.1 para.1, Sch.1 para.9, Sch.1 para.10

s.12, applied: SI 2008/337 Sch.1 para.1, Sch.1 para.10

s.14, applied: SI 2008/337 Sch.1 para.1, Sch.1 para.2, Sch.1 para.3, Sch.1 para.8, Sch.1 para.10, SI 2008/2113 Reg.8

s.16, applied: SI 2008/337 Sch.1 para.1, Sch.1 para.2, Sch.1 para.3, SI 2008/2113 Reg.8

s.17, applied: SI 2008/337 Sch.1 para.1, Sch.1 para.2, Sch.1 para.3

s.18, applied: SI 2008/337 Sch.1 para.1, Sch.1 para.4, Sch.1 para.5, Sch.1 para.6

s.22, applied: SI 2008/337 Sch.1 para.1, Sch.1 para.4, Sch.1 para.5, Sch.1 para.6

s.23, applied: SI 2008/337 Sch.1 para.1, Sch.1 para.3

s.23, disapplied: SI 2008/337 Sch.1 para.3

s.24, applied: SI 2008/337 Sch.1 para.4, Sch.1 para.5, Sch.1 para.6

Sch.2 para.1, enabling: SSI 2008/370, SSI 2008/371

Sch.2 para.3, applied: SSI 2008/85 Reg.3

Sch.2 para.4, applied: SSI 2008/85 Reg.5

40. Protection from Harassment Act 1997

applied: 2008 c.13 Sch.3

43. Crime (Sentences) Act 1997

applied: 2008 c.4 Sch.26 para.31

CAP.

1997–cont.

43. Crime (Sentences) Act 1997–*cont.*

s.30, see *R. v Bieber (David Francis)* [2008] EWCA Crim 1601, [2008] H.R.L.R. 43 (CA (Crim Div)), Lord Phillips of Worth Matravers, L.C.J.

s.31, amended: 2008 c.4 Sch.28 Part 2, SI 2008/912 Sch.1 para.12

s.32, amended: 2008 c.4 s.31

Sch.1, referred to: 2008 c.4 Sch.26 para.32

Sch.1 Part II para.8, amended: SI 2008/912 Sch.1 para.12

Sch.1 Part II para.8, applied: SI 2008/1788 Sch.1

Sch.1 Part II para.8, referred to: 2008 c.4 Sch.26 para.32

Sch.1 Part II para.8, varied: 2008 c.4 Sch.26 para.32

Sch.1 Part II para.9, referred to: 2008 c.4 Sch.26 para.32

Sch.1 Part II para.9, varied: 2008 c.4 Sch.26 para.32

Sch.1 Part II para.10, applied: SI 2008/1788 Sch.2

Sch.1 Part II para.11, amended: SI 2008/912 Sch.1 para.12

Sch.1 Part II para.12, amended: SI 2008/1241 Art.3

Sch.1 Part II para.13, amended: SI 2008/1241 Art.3

Sch.2, referred to: 2008 c.4 Sch.26 para.33

Sch.2 para.2, amended: 2008 c.4 Sch.26 para.33

Sch.2 para.3, amended: 2008 c.4 Sch.26 para.33

Sch.2 para.5, amended: 2008 c.4 Sch.26 para.33

Sch.2 para.9, repealed: SI 2008/1216 Sch.6 Part 1

Sch.2 para.10, repealed: SI 2008/1216 Sch.6 Part 1

Sch.5 para.7, amended: 2008 c.4 Sch.28 Part 2

44. Education Act 1997

s.19, enabling: SI 2008/3086

s.23, applied: SI 2008/1744, SI 2008/1744 Art.2

s.23, disapplied: SI 2008/1744 Art.2

s.23, enabling: SI 2008/1744

s.24, amended: 2008 c.25 s.9, s.161, s.163

s.26, amended: 2008 c.25 s.161

s.26A, amended: 2008 c.25 s.161

s.30, amended: 2008 c.25 s.162

s.32, amended: 2008 c.25 s.162

s.32A, substituted: 2008 c.25 s.162

s.36, enabling: SI 2008/923

s.43, amended: 2008 c.25 s.81

s.45, amended: 2008 c.25 s.81

s.45A, added: 2008 c.25 s.81

s.54, enabling: SI 2008/923, SI 2008/3086

s.58, amended: 2008 c.25 s.163

CAP.

1997–cont.

45. Police (Insurance of Voluntary Assistants) Act 1997
repealed: 2008 c.12 Sch.1 Part 6
s.1, referred to: 2008 c.12 Sch.2 para.8

48. Crime and Punishment (Scotland) Act 1997
see *Locke (John) v HM Advocate* [2008] HCJAC 6, 2008 S.L.T. 159 (HCJ), Lord Hamilton L.J.G.

50. Police Act 1997
Commencement Orders: SI 2008/692 Art.2
s.112, amended: 2008 c.4 s.50
s.112, applied: SI 2008/542 Reg.5, Reg.7
s.112, enabling: SI 2008/542
s.113A, amended: 2008 c.4 s.50
s.113A, applied: SI 2008/528 Reg.3, Reg.9, SI 2008/542 Reg.6, Reg.7, SI 2008/976 Reg.5, SI 2008/1315 Reg.9, SI 2008/1858 Reg.3, SI 2008/2437 Reg.4, SI 2008/3166 Reg.6
s.113A, enabling: SI 2008/542
s.113B, applied: SI 2008/542 Reg.6, Reg.7, Reg.9, SI 2008/976 Reg.5, SI 2008/1187 Sch.1 para.11, SI 2008/1315 Reg.9, SI 2008/1858 Reg.3, SI 2008/2437 Reg.4, SI 2008/3166 Reg.6
s.113B, enabling: SI 2008/542, SI 2008/2143, SSI 2008/6
s.113BA, amended: 2008 c.25 Sch.1 para.12
s.113D, enabling: SI 2008/2143
s.114, applied: SI 2008/542 Reg.6, Reg.7
s.114, enabling: SI 2008/542
s.115, see *R. (on the application of L) v Commissioner of Police of the Metropolis* [2007] EWCA Civ 168, [2008] 1 W.L.R. 681 (CA (Civ Div)), Longmore, L.J.
s.115, applied: SI 2008/1976 Reg.5, Reg.13
s.116, applied: SI 2008/542 Reg.6, Reg.7
s.116, enabling: SI 2008/542
s.118, enabling: SSI 2008/6
s.119, enabling: SSI 2008/6
s.125, enabling: SI 2008/542, SI 2008/2143
s.135, enabling: SI 2008/692

51. Sex Offenders Act 1997
see *A v Scottish Ministers* 2008 S.L.T. 412 (OH), Lord Turnbull; see *Rumbold v General Medical Council* [2007] EWHC 2569 (Admin), [2008] LS Law Medical 169 (QBD (Admin)), Wyn Williams, J.

58. Finance (No.2) Act 1997
s.26, repealed: 2008 c.9 s.66
s.48, see *Halcyon Films LLP v Revenue and Customs Commissioners* [2008] S.T.C. (S.C.D.) 1016 (Sp Comm), Edward Sadler; see *Micro Fusion 2004-1 LLP v Revenue and Customs Commissioners* [2008] S.T.C. (S.C.D.) 952 (Sp Comm), Edward Sadler
Sch.4 Part I para.24, repealed: 2008 c.9 Sch.2 para.21

CAP.

1997–cont.

58. Finance (No.2) Act 1997–*cont.*
Sch.4 Part I para.25, repealed: 2008 c.9 Sch.2 para.21
Sch.6 para.14, repealed: 2008 c.9 s.66

59. Education (Schools) Act 1997
s.2, applied: SI 2008/509, SI 2008/510, SI 2008/1593
s.3, applied: SI 2008/509, SI 2008/510, SI 2008/1593
s.3, enabling: SI 2008/509, SI 2008/510, SI 2008/1593, SI 2008/1594

66. Plant Varieties Act 1997
s.19, referred to: 2008 c.13 Sch.6
s.31, referred to: 2008 c.13 Sch.6
s.32, referred to: 2008 c.13 Sch.6

68. Special Immigration Appeals Commission Act 1997
s.6, amended: 2008 c.28 s.91

1998

11. Bank of England Act 1998
Part II, applied: SI 2008/3229 Sch.3
s.7, amended: SI 2008/948 Sch.1 para.205
s.12, applied: SI 2008/2998 Sch.1 para.12
s.17, amended: SI 2008/948 Sch.1 para.205
s.19, applied: SI 2008/794 Sch.6 para.13
s.35, repealed: SI 2008/948 Sch.2
s.40, applied: SI 2008/1344
Sch.2 para.4, applied: SI 2008/1344 Art.3
Sch.2 para.5, enabling: SI 2008/1344
Sch.2 para.10, applied: SI 2008/1344
Sch.2 para.11, applied: SI 2008/1344

14. Social Security Act 1998
applied: SI 2008/667 Reg.2
Part I c.I, applied: 2008 c.6 s.50, SI 2008/794 Reg.6, Reg.30, Reg.40, SI 2008/1149 Art.2, SI 2008/2683 Art.4, Art.5, SI 2008/2833 Art.3, Art.4, Sch.1
s.3, amended: 2008 c.6 Sch.7 para.3, 2008 c.30 s.63
s.3, applied: 2008 c.25 s.91
s.4, repealed: SI 2008/2833 Sch.3 para.144
s.5, applied: SI 2008/2833 Sch.2
s.5, repealed (in part): SI 2008/2833 Sch.3 para.145
s.6, applied: SI 2008/2833 Sch.2
s.6, repealed (in part): SI 2008/2833 Sch.3 para.146
s.6, enabling: SI 2008/1957
s.7, applied: SI 2008/2995 Art.3
s.7, repealed (in part): SI 2008/2833 Sch.3 para.147
s.7, enabling: SI 2008/2995
s.8, applied: SI 2008/840 Reg.2
s.8, varied: 2008 c.14 s.132
s.9, applied: SI 2008/2928 Reg.10
s.9, varied: 2008 c.14 s.132
s.9, enabling: SI 2008/2667
s.10, amended: SI 2008/2833 Sch.3 para.148

CAP.

1998–cont.

14. **Social Security Act 1998**–*cont.*

s.10, applied: SI 2008/794 Reg.45, Reg.63, Sch.6 para.14, SI 2008/2928 Reg.9, Reg.10
s.10, varied: 2008 c.14 s.132
s.10, enabling: SI 2008/1042, SI 2008/2667
s.10A, varied: 2008 c.14 s.132
s.11, varied: 2008 c.14 s.132
s.12, amended: SI 2008/2833 Sch.3 para.149
s.12, applied: SI 2008/1595 Reg.6, SI 2008/2685 r.21, r.25, Sch.1, SI 2008/2698 r.20, SI 2008/2928 Reg.10
s.12, varied: 2008 c.14 s.132
s.13, amended: SI 2008/2833 Sch.3 para.150
s.13, repealed (in part): SI 2008/2833 Sch.3 para.150
s.13, varied: 2008 c.14 s.132
s.14, amended: SI 2008/2833 Sch.3 para.151
s.14, applied: 2008 c.6 s.51
s.14, repealed (in part): SI 2008/2833 Sch.3 para.151
s.14, varied: 2008 c.14 s.132
s.15, amended: SI 2008/2833 Sch.3 para.152
s.15, repealed (in part): SI 2008/2833 Sch.3 para.152
s.15, substituted: SI 2008/2833 Sch.3 para.152
s.15, varied: 2008 c.14 s.132
s.15A, added: SI 2008/2833 Sch.3 para.153
s.15A, varied: 2008 c.14 s.132
s.16, varied: 2008 c.14 s.132
s.17, amended: SI 2008/2833 Sch.3 para.155
s.17, varied: 2008 c.14 s.132
s.18, amended: SI 2008/2833 Sch.3 para.156
s.18, varied: 2008 c.14 s.132
s.19, varied: 2008 c.14 s.132
s.20, amended: SI 2008/2833 Sch.3 para.157
s.20, applied: SI 2008/2685 r.25
s.20, varied: 2008 c.14 s.132
s.20, enabling: SI 2008/2685
s.20A, added: SI 2008/2833 Sch.3 para.158
s.20A, varied: 2008 c.14 s.132
s.21, amended: SI 2008/2833 Sch.3 para.159
s.21, varied: 2008 c.14 s.132
s.21, enabling: SI 2008/794
s.22, varied: 2008 c.14 s.132
s.23, varied: 2008 c.14 s.132
s.24, varied: 2008 c.14 s.132
s.24A, amended: SI 2008/2833 Sch.3 para.160
s.24A, varied: 2008 c.14 s.132
s.25, amended: SI 2008/2833 Sch.3 para.161
s.25, varied: 2008 c.14 s.132
s.26, amended: SI 2008/2833 Sch.3 para.162
s.26, varied: 2008 c.14 s.132
s.27, amended: SI 2008/2833 Sch.3 para.163
s.27, varied: 2008 c.14 s.132

CAP.

1998–cont.

14. **Social Security Act 1998**–*cont.*

s.28, amended: SI 2008/2833 Sch.3 para.164
s.28, repealed (in part): SI 2008/2833 Sch.3 para.164
s.28, varied: 2008 c.14 s.132
s.29, amended: SI 2008/2833 Sch.3 para.165
s.29, varied: 2008 c.14 s.132
s.30, varied: 2008 c.14 s.132
s.31, varied: 2008 c.14 s.132
s.32, varied: 2008 c.14 s.132
s.33, varied: 2008 c.14 s.132
s.34, varied: 2008 c.14 s.132
s.34, enabling: SI 2008/1042, SI 2008/1082
s.35, varied: 2008 c.14 s.132
s.36, varied: 2008 c.14 s.132
s.37, varied: 2008 c.14 s.132
s.37A, varied: 2008 c.14 s.132
s.38, varied: 2008 c.14 s.132
s.39, varied: 2008 c.14 s.132
s.39ZA, added: SI 2008/2833 Sch.3 para.166
s.39ZA, varied: 2008 c.14 s.132
s.62, repealed (in part): 2008 c.9 Sch.44 para.11
s.79, amended: SI 2008/2833 Sch.3 para.168
s.79, repealed (in part): SI 2008/2833 Sch.3 para.168
s.79, enabling: SI 2008/1042, SI 2008/1082, SI 2008/1596, SI 2008/2667
s.80, amended: SI 2008/2833 Sch.3 para.169
s.80, applied: SI 2008/2995
s.80, repealed (in part): SI 2008/2833 Sch.3 para.169
s.80, substituted: SI 2008/2833 Sch.3 para.169
s.81, amended: 2008 c.6 Sch.7 para.3, SI 2008/2833 Sch.3 para.170
s.84, enabling: SI 2008/1042, SI 2008/1082, SI 2008/2667
Sch.1 para.1, repealed (in part): SI 2008/2833 Sch.3 para.171
Sch.1 para.2, repealed (in part): SI 2008/2833 Sch.3 para.171
Sch.1 para.3, repealed (in part): SI 2008/2833 Sch.3 para.171
Sch.1 para.4, repealed (in part): SI 2008/2833 Sch.3 para.171
Sch.1 para.5, repealed (in part): SI 2008/2833 Sch.3 para.171
Sch.1 para.6, repealed (in part): SI 2008/2833 Sch.3 para.171
Sch.1 para.7, repealed (in part): SI 2008/2833 Sch.3 para.171
Sch.1 para.8, repealed (in part): SI 2008/2833 Sch.3 para.171
Sch.1 para.9, repealed (in part): SI 2008/2833 Sch.3 para.171

CAP.

1998–cont.

14. Social Security Act 1998–*cont.*
Sch.1 para.10, amended: 2008 c.6 Sch.3 para.54
Sch.1 para.10, repealed (in part): SI 2008/2833 Sch.3 para.171
Sch.1 para.11, repealed (in part): SI 2008/2833 Sch.3 para.171
Sch.1 para.12, repealed (in part): SI 2008/2833 Sch.3 para.171
Sch.1 para.13, repealed (in part): SI 2008/2833 Sch.3 para.171
Sch.4, applied: SI 2008/2833 Sch.1
Sch.4 para.1, applied: SI 2008/2833 Sch.2
Sch.4 para.1, repealed (in part): SI 2008/2833 Sch.3 para.172
Sch.4 para.2, repealed (in part): SI 2008/2833 Sch.3 para.172
Sch.4 para.3, repealed (in part): SI 2008/2833 Sch.3 para.172
Sch.4 para.4, repealed (in part): SI 2008/2833 Sch.3 para.172
Sch.4 para.5, repealed (in part): SI 2008/2833 Sch.3 para.172
Sch.4 para.6, repealed (in part): SI 2008/2833 Sch.3 para.172
Sch.4 para.7, repealed (in part): SI 2008/2833 Sch.3 para.172
Sch.4 para.8, repealed (in part): SI 2008/2833 Sch.3 para.172
Sch.5 para.1, amended: SI 2008/2833 Sch.3 para.173
Sch.5 para.2, repealed (in part): SI 2008/2833 Sch.3 para.173
Sch.5 para.5, repealed (in part): SI 2008/2833 Sch.3 para.173
Sch.5 para.6, repealed (in part): SI 2008/2833 Sch.3 para.173
Sch.5 para.7, repealed (in part): SI 2008/2833 Sch.3 para.173
Sch.5 para.8, repealed (in part): SI 2008/2833 Sch.3 para.173
Sch.7 para.3, repealed (in part): SI 2008/2833 Sch.3 para.228
Sch.7 para.11, repealed: SI 2008/2833 Sch.3 para.228
Sch.7 para.29, repealed: SI 2008/2833 Sch.3 para.228
Sch.7 para.30, repealed: SI 2008/2833 Sch.3 para.228
Sch.7 para.36, repealed: SI 2008/2833 Sch.3 para.228
Sch.7 para.42, repealed: SI 2008/2833 Sch.3 para.228
Sch.7 para.47, repealed (in part): SI 2008/2833 Sch.3 para.228
Sch.7 para.51, repealed: SI 2008/2833 Sch.3 para.228
Sch.7 para.52, repealed: SI 2008/2833 Sch.3 para.228
Sch.7 para.113, repealed (in part): SI 2008/2833 Sch.3 para.228

CAP.

1998–cont.

14. Social Security Act 1998–*cont.*
Sch.7 para.152, repealed (in part): SI 2008/2833 Sch.3 para.228
Sch.7 para.153, repealed: SI 2008/2833 Sch.3 para.228

17. Petroleum Act 1998
applied: 2008 c.32 s.77, SI 2008/225 Sch.1 para.27, Sch.1 para.28
referred to: SI 2008/225 Sch.1 para.2
Part I, applied: 2008 c.32 s.15
Part I, referred to: 2008 c.32 s.33
Part IV, applied: 2008 c.32 s.30
s.1, applied: 2008 c.32 s.30
s.4, applied: SI 2008/225 Reg.2
s.4, enabling: SI 2008/225
s.5, amended: 2008 c.32 Sch.5 para.8
s.5A, added: 2008 c.32 s.76
s.5B, added: 2008 c.32 s.76
s.5C, added: 2008 c.32 s.76
s.11, amended: 2008 c.32 Sch.1 para.7
s.13, substituted: 2008 c.32 Sch.1 para.8
s.17E, amended: SI 2008/948 Sch.1 para.206
s.25, applied: 2008 c.13 Sch.7
s.26, amended: 2008 c.32 s.78
s.26, repealed (in part): 2008 c.32 s.78, Sch.6
s.28, amended: 2008 c.32 s.78, Sch.1 para.9, Sch.6
s.30, amended: 2008 c.32 s.72, Sch.1 para.10
s.31, amended: 2008 c.32 s.72, Sch.5 para.9, Sch.6
s.34, amended: 2008 c.32 s.72, Sch.5 para.10, Sch.6
s.38, amended: 2008 c.32 s.73
s.38A, added: 2008 c.32 s.74
s.38B, added: 2008 c.32 s.74
s.39, varied: 2008 c.32 s.30
s.44, amended: 2008 c.32 Sch.1 para.11
s.44, applied: 2008 c.32 s.30
s.45, amended: 2008 c.32 Sch.5 para.11
s.45A, added: 2008 c.32 s.75
s.47A, amended: 2008 c.32 Sch.1 para.12

18. Audit Commission Act 1998
Part II, applied: SI 2008/625 Reg.14, SI 2008/907 Art.20
s.2, varied: SI 2008/634 Art.9, SI 2008/907 Art.20
s.3, varied: SI 2008/634 Art.9, SI 2008/907 Art.20
s.4, amended: 2008 c.14 Sch.5 para.64, Sch.15 Part 1
s.4, varied: SI 2008/634 Art.9, SI 2008/907 Art.20
s.4A, varied: SI 2008/634 Art.9, SI 2008/907 Art.20
s.5, varied: SI 2008/634 Art.9, SI 2008/907 Art.20
s.6, varied: SI 2008/634 Art.9, SI 2008/907 Art.20
s.7, amended: 2008 c.14 Sch.5 para.65

CAP.

1998–cont.

18. Audit Commission Act 1998–*cont.*

s.7, varied: SI 2008/634 Art.9, SI 2008/907 Art.20
s.8, varied: SI 2008/634 Art.9, SI 2008/907 Art.20
s.9, varied: SI 2008/634 Art.9, SI 2008/907 Art.20
s.10, varied: SI 2008/634 Art.9, SI 2008/907 Art.20
s.11, varied: SI 2008/634 Art.9, SI 2008/907 Art.20
s.11A, varied: SI 2008/634 Art.9, SI 2008/907 Art.20
s.12, varied: SI 2008/634 Art.9, SI 2008/907 Art.20
s.13, varied: SI 2008/634 Art.9, SI 2008/907 Art.20
s.13A, varied: SI 2008/634 Art.9, SI 2008/907 Art.20
s.14, varied: SI 2008/634 Art.9, SI 2008/907 Art.20
s.15, varied: SI 2008/634 Art.9, SI 2008/907 Art.20
s.16, varied: SI 2008/634 Art.9, SI 2008/907 Art.20
s.17, varied: SI 2008/634 Art.9, SI 2008/907 Art.20
s.18, applied: SI 2008/625 Reg.14
s.18, varied: SI 2008/634 Art.9, SI 2008/907 Art.20
s.19, varied: SI 2008/634 Art.9, SI 2008/907 Art.20
s.19A, varied: SI 2008/634 Art.9, SI 2008/907 Art.20
s.19B, varied: SI 2008/634 Art.9, SI 2008/907 Art.20
s.19C, varied: SI 2008/634 Art.9, SI 2008/907 Art.20
s.20, varied: SI 2008/634 Art.9, SI 2008/907 Art.20
s.21, varied: SI 2008/634 Art.9, SI 2008/907 Art.20
s.22, varied: SI 2008/634 Art.9, SI 2008/907 Art.20
s.23, varied: SI 2008/634 Art.9, SI 2008/907 Art.20
s.24, varied: SI 2008/634 Art.9, SI 2008/907 Art.20
s.25, varied: SI 2008/634 Art.9, SI 2008/907 Art.20
s.26, varied: SI 2008/634 Art.9, SI 2008/907 Art.20
s.27, varied: SI 2008/634 Art.9, SI 2008/907 Art.20
s.28, varied: SI 2008/634 Art.9, SI 2008/907 Art.20
s.29, varied: SI 2008/634 Art.9, SI 2008/907 Art.20
s.30, amended: 2008 c.26 Sch.4 para.61
s.30, varied: SI 2008/634 Art.9, SI 2008/907 Art.20

CAP.

1998–cont.

18. Audit Commission Act 1998–*cont.*

s.31, amended: SI 2008/948 Sch.1 para.23
s.31, varied: SI 2008/634 Art.9, SI 2008/907 Art.20
s.32, varied: SI 2008/634 Art.9, SI 2008/907 Art.20
s.32D, varied: SI 2008/634 Art.9, SI 2008/907 Art.20
s.33, amended: 2008 c.14 Sch.5 para.66
s.33, applied: 2008 c.14 s.56
s.33, varied: SI 2008/2250 Art.3
s.34, amended: 2008 c.14 Sch.5 para.67
s.34, applied: 2008 c.14 s.56
s.34, varied: SI 2008/2250 Art.3
s.37, amended: SI 2008/912 Sch.1 para.26
s.40, substituted: 2008 c.17 Sch.9 para.21
s.40, varied: SI 2008/2839 Sch.1 para.1
s.41, repealed: 2008 c.17 Sch.9 para.22, Sch.16
s.41, varied: SI 2008/2839 Sch.1 para.1
s.41A, repealed: 2008 c.17 Sch.9 para.22, Sch.16
s.41A, varied: SI 2008/2839 Sch.1 para.1
s.41B, repealed: 2008 c.17 Sch.9 para.22, Sch.16
s.41B, varied: SI 2008/2839 Sch.1 para.1
s.41C, amended: 2008 c.17 Sch.9 para.23
s.43, repealed: 2008 c.17 Sch.9 para.24, Sch.16
s.49, amended: 2008 c.14 Sch.5 para.68, Sch.15 Part 1, 2008 c.17 Sch.9 para.25
s.49, repealed (in part): 2008 c.14 Sch.5 para.68, Sch.15 Part 1
s.53, amended: SI 2008/817 Art.4
Sch.1 para.8, repealed (in part): 2008 c.17 Sch.9 para.26, Sch.16
Sch.1 para.8A, repealed: 2008 c.17 Sch.9 para.26, Sch.16
Sch.2, applied: SI 2008/907 Art.20
Sch.2 para.1, amended: SI 2008/2038 Art.21
Sch.2 para.1, varied: SI 2008/634 Art.9
Sch.2 para.1A, varied: SI 2008/634 Art.9
Sch.2 para.1B, varied: SI 2008/634 Art.9
Sch.2 para.1C, varied: SI 2008/634 Art.9
Sch.2 para.2, varied: SI 2008/634 Art.9
Sch.2 para.3, varied: SI 2008/634 Art.9
Sch.2 para.4, varied: SI 2008/634 Art.9
Sch.2A Part 1 para.1, amended: 2008 c.14 Sch.5 para.69, SI 2008/912 Sch.1 para.26, Sch.1 para.27
Sch.2A Part 1 para.1, repealed (in part): 2008 c.14 Sch.5 para.69, Sch.15 Part 1
Sch.2A Part 1 para.1, varied: SI 2008/2250 Art.3
Sch.2A Part 1 para.3, repealed (in part): 2008 c.17 Sch.9 para.27, Sch.16

29. Data Protection Act 1998

Commencement Orders: SI 2008/1592 Art.2
see *Afsar v Revenue and Customs Commissioners* [2008] S.T.C. (S.C.D.) 348 (Sp Comm), David Demack; see

CAP.

1998–cont.

29. Data Protection Act 1998–*cont.*

see–*cont.*

Johnson v Medical Defence Union Ltd [2007] EWCA Civ 262, [2008] Bus. L.R. 503 (CA (Civ Div)), Buxton, L.J.

applied: 2008 c.4 s.114, 2008 c.13 s.70, 2008 c.28 s.20

referred to: 2008 asp 5 s.117, 2008 c.4 s.77

s.1, see *Common Services Agency v Scottish Information Commissioner* [2008] UKHL 47, [2008] 1 W.L.R. 1550 (HL), Lord Hoffmann; see *Johnson v Medical Defence Union Ltd* [2007] EWCA Civ 262, [2008] Bus. L.R. 503 (CA (Civ Div)), Buxton, L.J.

s.7, see *R. (on the application of Secretary of State for the Home Department) v Information Tribunal* [2006] EWHC 2958 (Admin), [2008] 1 W.L.R. 58 (DC), Latham, L.J.

s.13, see *Johnson v Medical Defence Union Ltd* [2007] EWCA Civ 262, [2008] Bus. L.R. 503 (CA (Civ Div)), Buxton, L.J.

s.28, see *R. (on the application of Secretary of State for the Home Department) v Information Tribunal* [2006] EWHC 2958 (Admin), [2008] 1 W.L.R. 58 (DC), Latham, L.J.

s.33, applied: SI 2008/1741 Reg.118

s.35, see *R. (on the application of Davies) v Commissioners Office* [2008] EWHC 334 (Admin), [2008] 1 F.L.R. 1651 (QBD (Admin)), Black J.

s.35, applied: SI 2008/3239 Reg.25, Reg.26, Reg.29

s.42, see *R. (on the application of Secretary of State for the Home Department) v Information Tribunal* [2006] EWHC 2958 (Admin), [2008] 1 W.L.R. 58 (DC), Latham, L.J.

s.43, see *R. (on the application of Secretary of State for the Home Department) v Information Tribunal* [2006] EWHC 2958 (Admin), [2008] 1 W.L.R. 58 (DC), Latham, L.J.

s.51, see *R. (on the application of Secretary of State for the Home Department) v Information Tribunal* [2006] EWHC 2958 (Admin), [2008] 1 W.L.R. 58 (DC), Latham, L.J.

s.55, amended: 2008 c.4 s.78

s.55, applied: 2008 c.4 s.77

s.55A, added: 2008 c.4 s.144

s.55B, added: 2008 c.4 s.144

s.55C, added: 2008 c.4 s.144

s.55D, added: 2008 c.4 s.144

s.55E, added: 2008 c.4 s.144

s.67, amended: 2008 c.4 s.144

s.75, enabling: SI 2008/1592

CAP.

1998–cont.

29. Data Protection Act 1998–*cont.*

Sch.1 para.1, see *Common Services Agency v Scottish Information Commissioner* [2008] UKHL 47, [2008] 1 W.L.R. 1550 (HL), Lord Hoffmann

Sch.3, see *Common Services Agency v Scottish Information Commissioner* [2008] UKHL 47, [2008] 1 W.L.R. 1550 (HL), Lord Hoffmann

Sch.3 para.7, see *Common Services Agency v Scottish Information Commissioner* [2008] UKHL 47, [2008] 1 W.L.R. 1550 (HL), Lord Hoffmann

30. Teaching and Higher Education Act 1998

applied: SI 2008/529 Reg.95, SI 2008/1273 Reg.53, SI 2008/1582 Reg.95

s.3, enabling: SI 2008/1884

s.4, applied: SI 2008/228 Sch.1 para.20

s.12, applied: SI 2008/228 Sch.1 para.20

s.15, enabling: SI 2008/3256

s.15A, enabling: SI 2008/3256

s.19, applied: SI 2008/228 Sch.1 para.26, Sch.1 para.27, SI 2008/657 Sch.2 para.6, SI 2008/2945 Reg.3

s.19, enabling: SI 2008/657

s.22, applied: 2008 c.10 s.2, s.5, s.8, SI 2008/18 Reg.11, SI 2008/228 Sch.1 para.12, SI 2008/529 Reg.4, Reg.5, Reg.19, Reg.22, Reg.23, Reg.26, Reg.93, Reg.115, Reg.117, Reg.119, Reg.131, Reg.132, Reg.134, Reg.136, Reg.139, Reg.148, Reg.149, Reg.151, Reg.158, SI 2008/794 Reg.139, SI 2008/1273 Reg.4, Reg.5, Reg.15, Reg.51, Reg.60, Reg.62, Reg.64, Reg.66, Reg.78, Reg.79, Reg.80, Reg.85, Reg.91, Reg.92, Reg.93, Reg.100, SI 2008/1582 Reg.5, Reg.6, Reg.22, Reg.25, Reg.26, Reg.29, Reg.93, Reg.114, Reg.115, Reg.117, Reg.119, Reg.131, Reg.132, Reg.134, Reg.136, Reg.139, Reg.148, Reg.149, Reg.151, Reg.158, SI 2008/3170 Reg.4, Reg.5, Reg.6, Reg.15, Reg.51, Reg.60, Reg.62, Reg.64, Reg.66, Reg.78, Reg.79, Reg.80, Reg.95, Reg.102, Reg.103, Reg.104, Reg.111

s.22, enabling: SI 2008/18, SI 2008/235, SI 2008/529, SI 2008/538, SI 2008/546, SI 2008/1273, SI 2008/1324, SI 2008/1478, SI 2008/1582, SI 2008/2094, SI 2008/2140, SI 2008/2715, SI 2008/2939, SI 2008/3054, SI 2008/3114, SI 2008/3170

s.24, varied: 2008 c.10 s.7

s.42, applied: SI 2008/1884, SI 2008/3256

s.42, enabling: SI 2008/18, SI 2008/235, SI 2008/529, SI 2008/538, SI 2008/546, SI 2008/657, SI 2008/1273, SI 2008/1324, SI 2008/1478, SI 2008/1582, SI 2008/2094, SI 2008/2140, SI 2008/2715, SI 2008/2939, SI 2008/3054, SI 2008/3114, SI 2008/3170

s.43, applied: SI 2008/657 Reg.7

CAP.

1998–cont.

30. Teaching and Higher Education Act 1998–*cont.*

s.43, enabling: SI 2008/18, SI 2008/1273, SI 2008/1324, SI 2008/1478, SI 2008/2140, SI 2008/3054, SI 2008/3114, SI 2008/3170

s.44, referred to: SI 2008/1273 Reg.3

Sch.2, applied: SI 2008/1884 Reg.2

Sch.2 para.8, see *Davies v General Teaching Council for Wales* [2008] EWHC 1175 (Admin), [2008] E.L.R. 401 (QBD (Admin)), Blair, J.

31. School Standards and Framework Act 1998

applied: SI 2008/239 Reg.5, Reg.8, SI 2008/657 Reg.6

referred to: SI 2008/3089 Reg.2

Part II c.IV, applied: SI 2008/228 Sch.1 para.20

Part III, applied: SI 2008/3089 Reg.21, Reg.32, Reg.33

Part III, referred to: SI 2008/3089 Reg.27, SI 2008/3091 Reg.5

Part III c.I, amended: 2008 c.25 s.151

Part III c.I, added: 2008 c.25 Sch.1 para.65

s.1, enabling: SI 2008/3089

s.10, applied: SI 2008/3268 Reg.2

s.11, applied: SI 2008/239 Sch.2 para.18

s.15, applied: SI 2008/657 Reg.8

s.23, applied: SI 2008/3268 Reg.2

s.45, enabling: SI 2008/228

s.45A, applied: SI 2008/228 Reg.3, Reg.5, SI 2008/377 Reg.4

s.45A, enabling: SI 2008/228

s.45AA, enabling: SI 2008/228

s.47, enabling: SI 2008/228, SI 2008/1866

s.47A, amended: 2008 c.25 s.165, Sch.2

s.47A, applied: SI 2008/228 Sch.2 para.31, SI 2008/2867 Reg.25

s.47A, enabling: SI 2008/47, SI 2008/228

s.48, applied: SI 2008/228 Reg.26, Sch.1 para.20

s.48, enabling: SI 2008/228

s.49, applied: SI 2008/228 Sch.5 para.9

s.49, enabling: SI 2008/228

s.50, applied: SI 2008/228 Sch.5 para.13

s.50, enabling: SI 2008/1866

s.51A, applied: SI 2008/228 Reg.6

s.52, applied: SI 2008/377 Reg.3, Reg.4, Reg.5, SI 2008/1575 Reg.4, Reg.5, Reg.6

s.52, enabling: SI 2008/377, SI 2008/1575

s.69, applied: SI 2008/3089 Reg.9, Reg.12, SI 2008/3091 Reg.8, SI 2008/3093 Sch.2 para.11

s.69, enabling: SI 2008/100, SI 2008/783, SI 2008/1867, SI 2008/1868, SI 2008/1869, SI 2008/1870, SI 2008/1871, SI 2008/1872, SI 2008/1873, SI 2008/1874, SI 2008/1875, SI 2008/1876, SI 2008/2078, SI 2008/2079, SI 2008/2080, SI 2008/2081, SI 2008/2082, SI 2008/

CAP.

1998–cont.

31. School Standards and Framework Act 1998–*cont.*

s.69, enabling:–*cont.*

2083, SI 2008/2084, SI 2008/2085, SI 2008/2087, SI 2008/2092, SI 2008/2340, SI 2008/3147

s.84, applied: 2008 c.25 s.153, SI 2008/53 Art.2

s.85, applied: 2008 c.25 s.153, SI 2008/53 Art.2

s.85, enabling: SI 2008/53

s.85A, applied: SI 2008/228 Sch.2 para.14, SI 2008/3090 Reg.5, SI 2008/3091 Reg.4, Reg.14, Reg.16, Reg.17, Reg.18, Reg.19, Reg.20

s.85A, enabling: SI 2008/3091

s.85B, enabling: SI 2008/3091

s.86, amended: 2008 c.25 Sch.1 para.54, Sch.2

s.86, applied: SI 2008/3089 Reg.23

s.86, repealed (in part): 2008 c.25 Sch.1 para.54, Sch.2

s.86A, added: 2008 c.25 s.150

s.86B, added: 2008 c.25 s.150

s.87, amended: 2008 c.25 Sch.1 para.55

s.88, applied: SI 2008/3089 Reg.24

s.88, referred to: SI 2008/228 Sch.2 para.13

s.88A, amended: 2008 c.25 s.151

s.88B, added: 2008 c.25 s.151

s.88B, enabling: SI 2008/3089

s.88C, added: 2008 c.25 s.151

s.88C, applied: SI 2008/3089 Reg.12, Reg.13, Reg.15, Reg.18, Reg.22, Reg.31, Reg.32

s.88C, disapplied: SI 2008/3089 Reg.13, Reg.23, Reg.33

s.88C, referred to: SI 2008/3089 Reg.17

s.88C, enabling: SI 2008/3089

s.88D, added: 2008 c.25 s.151

s.88D, applied: SI 2008/3089 Reg.4

s.88D, enabling: SI 2008/3089

s.88E, added: 2008 c.25 s.151

s.88E, applied: SI 2008/3089 Reg.21, Reg.22

s.88E, enabling: SI 2008/3089

s.88F, added: 2008 c.25 s.151

s.88F, applied: SI 2008/3089 Reg.18

s.88F, referred to: SI 2008/3089 Reg.22, Reg.24

s.88F, enabling: SI 2008/3089

s.88G, added: 2008 c.25 s.151

s.88G, applied: SI 2008/3089 Reg.23

s.88G, enabling: SI 2008/3089

s.88H, added: 2008 c.25 s.151

s.88H, applied: SI 2008/3089 Reg.24, Reg.25, Reg.26, Reg.27, Reg.28, Reg.29, Reg.30, Reg.31, Reg.32, SI 2008/3091 Reg.16, SI 2008/3093 Sch.2 para.15

s.88H, referred to: SI 2008/3089 Reg.19

s.88H, enabling: SI 2008/3089

s.88I, added: 2008 c.25 s.151

CAP.

1998–cont.

31. School Standards and Framework Act 1998–*cont.*

s.88I, applied: SI 2008/3089 Reg.29, Reg.30, Reg.32, Sch.3 para.10, Sch.3 para.11, SI 2008/3093 Sch.2 para.15
s.88I, enabling: SI 2008/3089
s.88J, applied: SI 2008/3089 Reg.29, Reg.33
s.88K, added: 2008 c.25 s.151
s.88K, applied: SI 2008/3089 Reg.31
s.88K, enabling: SI 2008/3089
s.88L, added: 2008 c.25 s.151
s.88L, applied: SI 2008/3089 Reg.33
s.88L, enabling: SI 2008/3089
s.88M, applied: SI 2008/3090 Reg.5, Reg.9, SI 2008/3091 Reg.16, SI 2008/3093 Sch.2 para.7
s.88M, enabling: SI 2008/3090
s.88N, enabling: SI 2008/3090
s.88O, enabling: SI 2008/3090
s.88P, added: 2008 c.25 s.151
s.88P, applied: SI 2008/3091 Reg.4
s.88P, enabling: SI 2008/3091
s.88Q, added: 2008 c.25 s.151
s.88Q, applied: SI 2008/3091 Reg.6
s.88Q, enabling: SI 2008/3091
s.88R, added: 2008 c.25 Sch.1 para.56
s.89, amended: 2008 c.25 s.151, Sch.1 para.57
s.89, applied: 2008 c.25 s.167, SI 2008/228 Sch.2 para.13
s.89, repealed (in part): 2008 c.25 Sch.2
s.89A, amended: 2008 c.25 s.151, Sch.1 para.58
s.89A, applied: 2008 c.25 s.167
s.89B, amended: 2008 c.25 s.151
s.89B, applied: 2008 c.25 s.167
s.89B, amended: 2008 c.25 Sch.1 para.59
s.89C, amended: 2008 c.25 s.151
s.89C, applied: 2008 c.25 s.167, SI 2008/3089 Reg.7
s.89C, amended: 2008 c.25 Sch.1 para.60
s.89D, amended: 2008 c.25 s.151
s.89D, applied: 2008 c.25 s.167
s.89D, repealed: 2008 c.25 Sch.2
s.90, amended: 2008 c.25 s.151, Sch.1 para.62
s.90, applied: 2008 c.25 s.167
s.90, repealed (in part): 2008 c.25 Sch.2
s.90, enabling: SI 2008/1258
s.90A, amended: 2008 c.25 s.151
s.90A, repealed: 2008 c.25 Sch.2
s.90ZA, added: 2008 c.25 Sch.1 para.63
s.90ZA, amended: 2008 c.25 s.151
s.92, amended: 2008 c.25 Sch.1 para.65
s.92, enabling: SI 2008/3089, SI 2008/3093
s.94, amended: 2008 c.25 s.152
s.94, applied: SI 2008/3091 Reg.4, Reg.6
s.94, repealed (in part): 2008 c.25 Sch.1 para.66, Sch.2
s.94, enabling: SI 2008/3092
s.95, amended: 2008 c.25 Sch.1 para.67
s.95, enabling: SI 2008/3092
s.98, amended: 2008 c.25 Sch.1 para.68
s.98A, added: 2008 c.25 s.153
s.100, applied: SI 2008/3089 Reg.5
s.100, enabling: SI 2008/3089
s.101, applied: SI 2008/3089 Reg.11
s.102, applied: SI 2008/3089 Reg.5, Reg.6
s.102, enabling: SI 2008/3089
s.103, amended: 2008 c.25 Sch.1 para.69
s.103, applied: SI 2008/3089 Reg.13
s.104, applied: SI 2008/3089 Reg.24
s.104, referred to: SI 2008/3089 Reg.8, Reg.13
s.105, applied: SI 2008/3089 Reg.24
s.106, applied: SI 2008/3089 Reg.24
s.107, applied: SI 2008/3089 Reg.24
s.108, amended: 2008 c.25 Sch.1 para.70
s.108, applied: SI 2008/3089 Reg.13, Reg.24
s.109, applied: SI 2008/3089 Reg.13, Reg.24
s.114A, enabling: SI 2008/1800
s.124B, applied: SI 2008/783, SI 2008/2340, SI 2008/3091 Reg.8
s.138, enabling: SI 2008/47, SI 2008/228, SI 2008/377, SI 2008/1575, SI 2008/1800, SI 2008/3089, SI 2008/3090, SI 2008/3091, SI 2008/3092, SI 2008/3147
s.138A, added: 2008 c.25 Sch.1 para.71
s.142, amended: 2008 c.25 Sch.1 para.72
s.143, amended: 2008 c.25 Sch.1 para.73
s.144, enabling: SI 2008/3090
Sch.14 para.2A, applied: SI 2008/228 Reg.27
Sch.14 para.2B, enabling: SI 2008/228
Sch.19, applied: SI 2008/100 Art.2, SI 2008/1867 Art.2, SI 2008/1868 Art.2, SI 2008/1869 Art.2, SI 2008/1870 Art.2, SI 2008/1871 Art.2, SI 2008/1872 Art.2, SI 2008/1873 Art.2, SI 2008/1874 Art.2, SI 2008/1875 Art.2, SI 2008/1876 Art.2, SI 2008/2078 Art.2, SI 2008/2079 Art.2, SI 2008/2080 Art.2, SI 2008/2081 Art.2, SI 2008/2082 Art.2, SI 2008/2083 Art.2, SI 2008/2084 Art.2, SI 2008/2085 Art.2, SI 2008/2087 Art.2, SI 2008/2092 Art.2
Sch.26 para.10, applied: SI 2008/2699 Sch.1
Sch.30 para.60, repealed: 2008 c.25 Sch.2
Sch.30 para.133, repealed (in part): 2008 c.02 Sch.2

32. Police (Northern Ireland) Act 1998

s.27, applied: SI 2008/755 Art.14
s.66, applied: SI 2008/1216 Sch.2 para.27
Sch.4 para.18, repealed (in part): SI 2008/1216 Sch.6 Part 2

34. Private Hire Vehicles (London) Act 1998

applied: 2008 c.13 Sch.3

CAP.

1998–cont.

35. Northern Ireland (Sentences) Act 1998
applied: SI 2008/1975 Art.2
s.3, enabling: SI 2008/1975
s.19, applied: SI 2008/1975

36. Finance Act 1998
Commencement Orders: SI 2008/2302 Art.2, Art.3
s.6, repealed (in part): 2008 c.9 Sch.6 para.8
s.42, amended: SI 2008/954 Art.24
s.88, repealed: 2008 c.9 Sch.14 para.17
s.89, repealed: 2008 c.9 Sch.14 para.17
s.115, repealed: 2008 c.9 Sch.36 para.92
s.120, repealed: 2008 c.9 Sch.2 para.21
s.121, repealed (in part): 2008 c.9 Sch.2 para.55
s.122, repealed (in part): 2008 c.9 Sch.2 para.82
s.123, repealed (in part): 2008 c.9 Sch.2 para.96
s.125, repealed (in part): 2008 c.9 Sch.2 para.96
s.130, repealed (in part): 2008 c.9 Sch.7 para.114
s.140, repealed (in part): 2008 c.9 Sch.2 para.55
s.163, enabling: SI 2008/2647
Sch.2 para.12, enabling: SI 2008/2302
Sch.14 para.1, repealed: 2008 c.9 Sch.14 para.17
Sch.14 para.2, repealed: 2008 c.9 Sch.14 para.17
Sch.14 para.3, repealed: 2008 c.9 Sch.14 para.17
Sch.14 para.4, repealed: 2008 c.9 Sch.14 para.17
Sch.18, referred to: 2008 c.18 Sch.13 para.43
Sch.18 Part I para.2, applied: 2008 c.9 Sch.41 para.1
Sch.18 Part I para.2, repealed (in part): 2008 c.9 Sch.41 para.25
Sch.18 Part II para.3, applied: 2008 c.9 Sch.36 para.21
Sch.18 Part II para.10, amended: 2008 c.9 Sch.25 para.8
Sch.18 Part II para.11, substituted: SI 2008/954 Art.25
Sch.18 Part II para.15, applied: 2008 c.18 Sch.13 para.43
Sch.18 Part II para.16, amended: 2008 c.9 s.119
Sch.18 Part II para.19, substituted: SI 2008/954 Art.25
Sch.18 Part III, amended: 2008 c.9 Sch.37 para.9
Sch.18 Part III para.21, amended: 2008 c.9 Sch.37 para.8
Sch.18 Part III para.22, amended: 2008 c.9 Sch.37 para.9
Sch.18 Part III para.22, repealed (in part): 2008 c.9 Sch.37 para.9

CAP.

1998–cont.

36. Finance Act 1998–*cont.*
Sch.18 Part IV para.24, amended: SI 2008/954 Art.25
Sch.18 Part IV para.27, repealed: 2008 c.9 Sch.36 para.88
Sch.18 Part IV para.28, repealed: 2008 c.9 Sch.36 para.88
Sch.18 Part IV para.29, repealed: 2008 c.9 Sch.36 para.88
Sch.18 Part IV para.31, amended: 2008 c.9 s.119
Sch.18 Part IV para.34, amended: 2008 c.9 s.119
Sch.18 Part V, amended: 2008 c.9 Sch.39 para.41
Sch.18 Part V para.36, amended: 2008 c.9 Sch.39 para.38
Sch.18 Part V para.37, amended: 2008 c.9 Sch.39 para.39
Sch.18 Part V para.40, amended: 2008 c.9 Sch.39 para.40
Sch.18 Part V para.43, amended: 2008 c.9 Sch.39 para.41
Sch.18 Part V para.46, amended: 2008 c.9 Sch.39 para.42
Sch.18 Part VI para.51, amended: 2008 c.9 Sch.39 para.43
Sch.18 Part VI para.52, amended: 2008 c.9 Sch.25 para.8
Sch.18 Part VI para.52, applied: 2008 c.9 Sch.19 para.4
Sch.18 Part VI para.53, amended: 2008 c.9 Sch.39 para.44
Sch.18 Part VII, amended: 2008 c.9 Sch.39 para.47
Sch.18 Part VII para.55, amended: 2008 c.9 Sch.39 para.45
Sch.18 Part VII para.61, amended: 2008 c.9 s.119, Sch.39 para.46
Sch.18 Part VII para.65, amended: 2008 c.9 Sch.39 para.47
Sch.18 Part IXA para.83F, repealed: 2008 c.9 Sch.40 para.21
Sch.18 Part IXB para.83L, repealed: 2008 c.9 Sch.40 para.21
Sch.18 Part IX para.83ZA, added: 2008 c.9 Sch.25 para.8
Sch.18 Part IX para.83ZA, repealed (in part): 2008 c.9 Sch.40 para.21
Sch.18 Part XI para.88, amended: 2008 c.9 s.119
Sch.18 Part XI para.93, amended: 2008 c.9 s.119
Sch.18 para.33, see *Kilbride v Revenue and Customs Commissioners* [2008] S.T.C. (S.C.D.) 517 (Sp Comm), Richard Barlow
Sch.18 para.41, see *Revenue and Customs Commissioners v Household Estate Agents Ltd* [2007] EWHC 1684 (Ch), [2008] S.T.C. 2045 (Ch D), Henderson, J

CAP.

1998–cont.

36. Finance Act 1998–*cont.*

Sch.18 para.44, see *Revenue and Customs Commissioners v Household Estate Agents Ltd* [2007] EWHC 1684 (Ch), [2008] S.T.C. 2045 (Ch D), Henderson, J

Sch.18 para.45, see *Revenue and Customs Commissioners v Household Estate Agents Ltd* [2007] EWHC 1684 (Ch), [2008] S.T.C. 2045 (Ch D), Henderson, J

Sch.18 Part IXC para.83R, repealed: 2008 c.9 Sch.40 para.21

Sch.18 Part IXD para.83X, repealed: 2008 c.9 Sch.40 para.21

Sch.19 para.18, repealed: 2008 c.9 Sch.39 para.65

Sch.19 para.32, repealed: 2008 c.9 Sch.44 para.11

Sch.19 para.36, repealed: 2008 c.9 Sch.36 para.92

Sch.19 para.42, repealed (in part): 2008 c.9 Sch.36 para.92

Sch.20, repealed: 2008 c.9 Sch.2 para.55

Sch.21 para.2, repealed: 2008 c.9 Sch.2 para.55

Sch.21 para.4, repealed: 2008 c.9 Sch.2 para.55

Sch.21 para.6, repealed (in part): 2008 c.9 Sch.2 para.21, Sch.2 para.55, Sch.7 para.114

Sch.21 para.7, repealed: 2008 c.9 Sch.2 para.55

Sch.21 para.9, repealed: 2008 c.9 Sch.2 para.55

37. Crime and Disorder Act 1998

referred to: 2008 c.4 s.48

Part I c.I, applied: SI 2008/2163 Art.2, Art.3

s.1, amended: 2008 c.4 s.123, s.124

s.1AA, amended: 2008 c.4 s.124

s.1AB, amended: 2008 c.4 s.124

s.1B, amended: 2008 c.4 s.124

s.1C, see *R. v Dolan (Thomas James)* [2007] EWCA Crim 2791, [2008] 2 Cr. App. R. (S.) 11 (CA (Crim Div)), Latham, L.J.

s.1C, amended: 2008 c.4 s.123, s.124

s.1J, added: 2008 c.4 s.123

s.1K, added: 2008 c.4 s.123

s.5, amended: SI 2008/912 Sch.1 para.13

s.5, enabling: SI 2008/2163

s.6, applied: SI 2008/312 Reg.3, Reg.4, SI 2008/2163 Art.2, Art.3

s.6A, applied: SI 2008/2163 Art.2, Art.3

s.7, applied: SI 2008/2163 Art.2, Art.3

s.8, amended: SI 2008/912 Sch.1 para.13

s.8, referred to: 2008 c.25 s.42

s.9, amended: SI 2008/912 Sch.1 para.13

s.9, applied: 2008 c.25 s.42

s.10, applied: 2008 c.25 s.43

s.17, amended: SI 2008/78 Art.2

s.17, enabling: SI 2008/78

s.17A, enabling: SI 2008/1406

s.18, amended: SI 2008/912 Sch.1 para.13

CAP.

1998–cont.

37. Crime and Disorder Act 1998–*cont.*

s.31, see *Johnson v DPP* [2008] EWHC 509 (Admin), Times, April 9, 2008 (DC), Richards, L.J.

s.34, see *Crown Prosecution Service v P* [2007] EWHC 946 (Admin), [2008] 1 W.L.R. 1005 (DC), Smith, L.J.; see *R. v T* [2008] EWCA Crim 815, [2008] 3 W.L.R. 923 (CA (Crim Div)), Latham, L.J. (VP, CA Crim)

s.35, repealed: 2008 c.12 Sch.1 Part 3

s.36, repealed (in part): 2008 c.12 Sch.1 Part 3

s.38, amended: 2008 c.4 Sch.4 para.49, Sch.26 para.34, Sch.28 Part 1

s.38, referred to: 2008 c.4 Sch.26 para.34

s.38, repealed (in part): 2008 c.4 Sch.4 para.49, Sch.28 Part 1

s.41, enabling: SI 2008/3155

s.42, amended: 2008 c.4 s.9

s.65, amended: 2008 c.4 Sch.9 para.2

s.66A, added: 2008 c.4 Sch.9 para.3

s.66B, added: 2008 c.4 Sch.9 para.3

s.66C, added: 2008 c.4 Sch.9 para.3

s.66D, added: 2008 c.4 Sch.9 para.3

s.66E, added: 2008 c.4 Sch.9 para.3

s.66F, added: 2008 c.4 Sch.9 para.3

s.66G, added: 2008 c.4 Sch.9 para.3

s.66H, added: 2008 c.4 Sch.9 para.3

s.97, repealed (in part): 2008 c.12 Sch.1 Part 3

s.98, varied: SI 2008/912 Sch.1 para.13

s.107, repealed: 2008 c.12 Sch.1 Part 3

s.108, repealed: 2008 c.12 Sch.1 Part 3

s.114, amended: 2008 c.4 Sch.9 para.4

s.114, applied: SI 2008/78, SI 2008/3155

s.114, enabling: SI 2008/1406

s.115, amended: SI 2008/912 Sch.1 para.13

s.116, repealed: 2008 c.12 Sch.1 Part 3

Sch.8 para.13, amended: 2008 c.4 Sch.4 para.50

Sch.8 para.13, repealed (in part): 2008 c.4 Sch.28 Part 1

38. Government of Wales Act 1998

s.144, amended: SI 2008/948 Sch.1 para.207

s.146A, enabling: SI 2008/420

Sch.15 para.8, repealed: SI 2008/3002 Sch.3

Sch.15 para.13, repealed: 2008 c.17 Sch.16

Sch.16 para.24, repealed: 2008 c.17 Sch.16

Sch.16 para.25, repealed: 2008 c.17 Sch.16

Sch.16 para.26, repealed: 2008 c.17 Sch.16

Sch.16 para.61, repealed (in part): 2008 c.17 Sch.16

Sch.16 para.64, repealed: 2008 c.17 Sch.16

Sch.16 para.65, repealed: 2008 c.17 Sch.16

Sch.16 para.68, repealed (in part): 2008 c.17 Sch.16

Sch.16 para.83, repealed (in part): 2008 c.17 Sch.16

Sch.16 para.94, repealed: 2008 c.17 Sch.16

Sch.16 para.97, repealed (in part): 2008 c.17 Sch.16

CAP.

1998–cont.

39. National Minimum Wage Act 1998

applied: 2008 c.24 s.8, s.9

s.1, see *Revenue and Customs Commissioners v Annabel's (Berkeley Square) Ltd* [2008] I.C.R. 1076 (EAT), Wilkie, J.

s.1, enabling: SI 2008/1894

s.2, enabling: SI 2008/1894

s.3, enabling: SI 2008/1894

s.14, amended: 2008 c.24 s.10, Sch.1 Part 3

s.14, applied: 2008 c.24 s.10

s.15, amended: 2008 c.24 s.18

s.17, amended: 2008 c.24 s.8

s.17, applied: 2008 c.24 s.8

s.19, substituted: 2008 c.24 s.9

s.19A, substituted: 2008 c.24 s.9

s.19B, substituted: 2008 c.24 s.9

s.19C, substituted: 2008 c.24 s.9

s.19D, substituted: 2008 c.24 s.9

s.19E, substituted: 2008 c.24 s.9

s.19E, varied: 2008 c.24 s.9

s.19F, substituted: 2008 c.24 s.9

s.19G, substituted: 2008 c.24 s.9

s.19H, substituted: 2008 c.24 s.9

s.20, substituted: 2008 c.24 s.9

s.21, substituted: 2008 c.24 s.9

s.22, substituted: 2008 c.24 s.9

s.22A, substituted: 2008 c.24 s.9

s.22B, substituted: 2008 c.24 s.9

s.22C, substituted: 2008 c.24 s.9

s.22D, substituted: 2008 c.24 s.9

s.22E, substituted: 2008 c.24 s.9

s.22F, substituted: 2008 c.24 s.9

s.24, referred to: SI 2008/3232 Sch.1 Part 2

s.31, amended: 2008 c.24 s.11

s.31, applied: 2008 c.24 s.11

s.33, applied: 2008 c.24 s.11

s.33, repealed (in part): 2008 c.24 s.11, Sch.1 Part 4

s.37A, added: 2008 c.24 s.13

s.44, amended: 2008 c.24 s.14

s.51, amended: 2008 c.24 s.9, Sch.1 Part 2

s.51, applied: SI 2008/1894

s.51, enabling: SI 2008/1894

40. Criminal Justice (Terrorism and Conspiracy) Act 1998

s.8, repealed (in part): 2008 c.4 Sch.28 Part 4, Sch.28 Part 4

41. Competition Act 1998

see *Independent Media Support Ltd v Office of Communications* [2008] CAT 13, [2008] Comp. A.R. 161 (CAT), Vivien Rose (Chairman)

Part I c.I, disapplied: SI 2008/1820 Art.4

Part I c.I, referred to: SI 2008/1820

s.2, see *Independent Media Support Ltd v Office of Communications* [2008] CAT 13, [2008] Comp. A.R. 161 (CAT), Vivien Rose (Chairman); see *Independent Media Support Ltd v Office of Communications* [2008] Comp. A.R. 48 (CAT), Vivien Rose (Chairman)

CAP.

1998–cont.

41. Competition Act 1998–*cont.*

s.2–*cont.*

s.18, see *Albion Water Ltd v Water Services Regulation Authority (formerly Director General of Water Services)* [2008] EWCA Civ 536, [2008] Bus. L.R. 1655 (CA (Civ Div)), Sir Anthony Clarke, M.R.; see *Independent Media Support Ltd v Office of Communications* [2008] Comp. A.R. 48 (CAT), Vivien Rose (Chairman)

s.46, see *Independent Media Support Ltd v Office of Communications* [2008] Comp. A.R. 48 (CAT), Vivien Rose (Chairman)

s.47A, see *BCL Old Co Ltd v BASF SE* [2008] CAT 24, [2008] Comp. A.R. 210 (CAT), Barling, J; see *Devenish Nutrition Ltd v Sanofi-Aventis SA* [2008] EWCA Civ 1086, [2008] U.K.C.L.R. 783 (CA (Civ Div)), Tuckey, L.J.; see *Emerson Electric Co v Morgan Crucible Co Plc* [2008] C.P. Rep. 5 (CAT), Marion Simmons Q.C. (Chairman); see *Emerson Electric Co v Morgan Crucible Co Plc* [2008] CAT 8, [2008] Comp. A.R. 118 (CAT), Marion Simmons Q.C. (Chairman)

Sch.3 para.7, enabling: SI 2008/1820

Sch.8 para.3, see *Albion Water Ltd v Water Services Regulation Authority (formerly Director General of Water Services)* [2008] EWCA Civ 536, [2008] Bus. L.R. 1655 (CA (Civ Div)), Sir Anthony Clarke, M.R.

42. Human Rights Act 1998

see *A v B (Investigatory Powers Tribunal: Jurisdiction)* [2008] EWHC 1512 (Admin), [2008] 4 All E.R. 511 (QBD (Admin)), Collins, J.; see *C Plc v P* [2007] EWCA Civ 493, [2008] Ch. 1 (CA (Civ Div)), Longmore, L.J.; see *Chief Constable of Greater Manchester v I* [2007] EWHC 1837 (Fam), [2008] 1 F.L.R. 504 (Fam Div), Ryder, J.; see *Dickson (Kenneth Robert) v HM Advocate* 2008 J.C. 181 (HCJ), Lord Hamilton L.J.G.; see *Dunn v Parole Board* [2008] EWCA Civ 374, [2008] H.R.L.R. 32 (CA (Civ Div)), Smith, L.J.; see *Gillies v Ralph* [2008] HCJAC 55, 2008 S.L.T. 978 (HCJ), Lord Wheatley; see *Hinds v Liverpool County Court* [2008] EWHC 665 (QB), [2008] 2 F.L.R. 63 (QBD (Liverpool)), Akenhead, J.; see *K v Central and North West London Mental Health NHS Trust* [2008] EWHC 1217 (QB), (2008) 11 C.C.L. Rep. 543 (QBD), King, J.; see *L v Birmingham City Council* [2007] EWCA Civ 26, [2008] Q.B. 1 (CA (Civ Div)), Sir Anthony Clarke, M.R.; see *Mote v Secretary of State for Work and Pensions* [2007] EWCA Civ 1324, [2008] C.P. Rep. 13 (CA (Civ Div)), Lloyd, L.J.; see *Nasseri v Secretary of State for the Home Department* [2008] EWCA

CAP.

1998–cont.

42. Human Rights Act 1998–*cont.*

see–*cont.*

Civ 464, [2008] 3 W.L.R. 1386 (CA (Civ Div)), Sir Anthony Clarke, M.R.; see *P (A Child) (Adoption: Unmarried Couples), Re* [2008] UKHL 38, [2008] 3 W.L.R. 76 (HL (NI)), Lord Hoffmann; see *R. (on the application of Animal Defenders International) v Secretary of State for Culture, Media and Sport* [2008] UKHL 15, [2008] 1 A.C. 1312 (HL), Lord Bingham of Cornhill; see *R. (on the application of Chavda) v Harrow LBC* [2007] EWHC 3064 (Admin), [2008] B.L.G.R. 657 (QBD (Admin)), Judge Mackie Q.C.; see *R. (on the application of Smith) v Oxfordshire Assistant Deputy Coroner* [2008] EWHC 694 (Admin), [2008] 3 W.L.R. 1284 (QBD (Admin)), Collins, J.; see *Savage v South Essex Partnership NHS Foundation Trust* [2007] EWCA Civ 1375, [2008] 1 W.L.R. 1667 (CA (Civ Div)), Sir Anthony Clarke, M.R.; see *Tabernacle v Secretary of State for Defence* [2008] EWHC 416 (Admin), Times, April 9, 2008 (DC), Maurice Kay, L.J.

applied: SI 2008/5, SI 2008/82 Art.3, SI 2008/539

referred to: SI 2008/1206 Sch.2 para.2, SI 2008/2436 Sch.2 para.2.1

s.1, see *Dickson (Kenneth Robert) v HM Advocate* 2008 J.C. 181 (HCJ), Lord Hamilton L.J.G.

s.1, applied: SI 2008/718 Sch.1, SI 2008/3249 Sch.1

s.3, see *AS (Somalia) v Entry Clearance Officer (Addis Ababa)* [2008] EWCA Civ 149, [2008] Imm. A.R. 510 (CA (Civ Div)), Waller, L.J.; see *Doherty v Birmingham City Council* [2008] UKHL 57, [2008] 3 W.L.R. 636 (HL), Lord Hope of Craighead; see *Entico Corp Ltd v United Nations Educational Scientific and Cultural Association* [2008] EWHC 531 (Comm), [2008] 2 All E.R. (Comm) 97 (QBD (Comm)), Tomlinson, J.; see *F (A Child), Re* [2008] EWCA Civ 439, [2008] 2 F.L.R. 550 (CA (Civ Div)), Thorpe, L.J.; see *Khan v Commissioner of Police of the Metropolis* [2008] EWCA Civ 723, Times, June 16, 2008 (CA (Civ Div)), Pill, L.J.; see *Tabernacle v Secretary of State for Defence* [2008] EWHC 416 (Admin), Times, April 9, 2008 (DC), Maurice Kay, L.J.; see *Truro Diocesan Board of Finance Ltd v Foley* [2008] EWCA Civ 1162, Times, December 1, 2008 (CA (Civ Div)), May, L.J.; see *Warren v Random House Group Ltd* [2007] EWHC 2856 (QB), [2008] 2 W.L.R. 1033 (QBD), Gray, J.

s.4, see *AP v Crown Prosecution Service* [2007] EWCA Crim 3128, [2008] 1 Cr. App. R. 39 (CA (Crim Div)), Latham, L.J.; see *ES's Application for Judicial Review, Re* [2008] N.I. 11 (QBD (NI)), Gillen, J.; see *R. (on the application of Black) v Secretary of State for the Home Department* [2008] EWCA Civ 359, [2008] 3 W.L.R. 845 (CA (Civ Div)), May, L.J.

s.6, see *Dickson (Kenneth Robert) v HM Advocate* 2008 J.C. 181 (HCJ), Lord Hamilton L.J.G.; see *Doherty v Birmingham City Council* [2008] UKHL 57, [2008] 3 W.L.R. 636 (HL), Lord Hope of Craighead; see *Kennedy v Lord Advocate* [2008] CSOH 21, 2008 S.L.T. 195 (OH), Lord Mackay of Drumadoon; see *L v Birmingham City Council* [2007] EWCA Civ 26, [2008] Q.B. 1 (CA (Civ Div)), Sir Anthony Clarke, M.R.; see *L v Birmingham City Council* [2007] UKHL 27, [2008] 1 A.C. 95 (HL), Lord Bingham of Cornhill; see *McDonald (John) v HM Advocate* 2008 S.L.T. 144 (HCJ), Lord Hamilton L.J.G.; see *R. (on the application of Al-Skeini) v Secretary of State for Defence* [2007] UKHL 26, [2008] 1 A.C. 153 (HL), Lord Bingham of Cornhill; see *R. (on the application of M) v Lambeth LBC* [2008] EWHC 1364 (Admin), [2008] 2 F.L.R. 1026 (QBD (Admin)), Bennett, J.; see *Togher v Revenue and Customs Prosecution Office* [2007] EWCA Civ 686, [2008] Q.B. 476 (CA (Civ Div)), Chadwick, L.J.

s.6, applied: 2008 c.4 s.130, 2008 c.14 s.145, 2008 c.23 s.3, SI 2008/2674 Art.33

s.6, referred to: SI 2008/532 Sch.1 para.4

s.7, see *A v B (Investigatory Powers Tribunal: Jurisdiction)* [2008] EWHC 1512 (Admin), [2008] 4 All E.R. 511 (QBD (Admin)), Collins, J.; see *B v Secretary of State for the Home Department* [2008] UKHL 39, [2008] 3 W.L.R. 166 (HL), Lord Bingham of Cornhill; see *Dobson v Thames Water Utilities Ltd* [2007] EWHC 2021 (TCC), [2008] 2 All E.R. 362 (QBD (TCC)), Ramsey, J.; see *Dunn v Parole Board* [2008] EWCA Civ 374, [2008] H.R.L.R. 32 (CA (Civ Div)), Smith, L.J.; see *R. (on the application of Al-Skeini) v Secretary of State for Defence* [2007] UKHL 26, [2008] 1 A.C. 153 (HL), Lord Bingham of Cornhill

s.8, see *Dobson v Thames Water Utilities Ltd* [2007] EWHC 2021 (TCC), [2008] 2 All E.R. 362 (QBD (TCC)), Ramsey, J.

s.10, applied: 2008 c.4 s.135

s.12, see *Browne v Associated Newspapers Ltd* [2007] EWCA Civ 295, [2008] Q.B. 103 (CA (Civ Div)), Sir Anthony Clarke, M.R.; see *Response Handling Ltd v BBC* 2008 S.L.T. 51 (OH), Lord Bracadale

s.21, see *ES's Application for Judicial Review, Re* [2008] N.I. 11 (QBD (NI)), Gillen, J.

CAP.

1998–cont.

42. Human Rights Act 1998–*cont.*

Sch.1, see *HRH Prince of Wales v Associated Newspapers Ltd* [2006] EWCA Civ 1776, [2008] Ch. 57 (CA (Civ Div)), Lord Philips, L.C.J.; see *L v Birmingham City Council* [2007] EWCA Civ 26, [2008] Q.B. 1 (CA (Civ Div)), Sir Anthony Clarke, M.R.; see *McKennitt v Ash* [2006] EWCA Civ 1714, [2008] Q.B. 73 (CA (Civ Div)), Buxton, L.J.; see *R. (on the application of Al-Skeini) v Secretary of State for Defence* [2007] UKHL 26, [2008] 1 A.C. 153 (HL), Lord Bingham of Cornhill

45. Regional Development Agencies Act 1998

applied: 2008 c.17 s.51
s.5, varied: SI 2008/1342 Reg.10
s.8, amended: 2008 c.29 s.179
s.11, amended: 2008 c.29 s.179
s.18, amended: 2008 c.29 s.179
s.27, varied: SI 2008/1342 Reg.6
s.36, repealed: 2008 c.17 Sch.8 para.67, Sch.16
s.37, repealed: 2008 c.17 Sch.8 para.68, Sch.16
s.38, amended: 2008 c.17 Sch.8 para.69
s.38, repealed (in part): 2008 c.17 Sch.8 para.69, Sch.16
s.39, amended: 2008 c.17 Sch.8 para.70
Sch.2 para.7, amended: 2008 c.29 s.179
Sch.6 para.2, amended: 2008 c.29 Sch.9 para.6
Sch.9 para.1, repealed: 2008 c.17 Sch.8 para.71, Sch.16
Sch.9 para.2, repealed: 2008 c.17 Sch.8 para.71, Sch.16
Sch.9 para.3, repealed: 2008 c.17 Sch.8 para.71, Sch.16
Sch.9 para.4, repealed: 2008 c.17 Sch.8 para.71, Sch.16
Sch.9 para.5, repealed: 2008 c.17 Sch.8 para.71, Sch.16
Sch.9 para.6, repealed: 2008 c.17 Sch.8 para.71, Sch.16
Sch.9 para.7, repealed: 2008 c.17 Sch.8 para.71, Sch.16
Sch.9 para.8, repealed: 2008 c.17 Sch.8 para.71, Sch.16
Sch.9 para.9, repealed: 2008 c.17 Sch.8 para.71, Sch.16
Sch.9 para.10, repealed: 2008 c.17 Sch.8 para.71, Sch.16
Sch.9 para.11, repealed: 2008 c.17 Sch.8 para.71, Sch.16

46. Scotland Act 1998

see *A v Scottish Ministers* 2008 S.L.T. 412 (OH), Lord Turnbull; see *Dickson (Kenneth Robert) v HM Advocate* 2008 J.C. 181 (HCJ), Lord Hamilton L.J.G.; see *Kennedy v Lord Advocate* [2008] CSOH 21, 2008 S.L.T. 195 (OH), Lord Mackay of Drumadoon

CAP.

1998–cont.

46. Scotland Act 1998–*cont.*

applied: 2008 c.26 s.6, s.119, 2008 c.27 Sch.1 para.27
s.12, enabling: SI 2008/307
s.23, applied: 2008 c.27 Sch.1 para.27
s.29, see *Friend v Lord Advocate* [2007] UKHL 53, 2008 S.C. (H.L.) 107 (HL), Lord Bingham; see *Logan v Harrower* [2008] HCJAC 61, 2008 S.L.T. 1049 (HCJ), Lord Nimmo Smith
s.35, see *Friend v Lord Advocate* [2007] UKHL 53, 2008 S.C. (H.L.) 107 (HL), Lord Bingham
s.48, see *Kennedy v Lord Advocate* [2008] CSOH 21, 2008 S.L.T. 195 (OH), Lord Mackay of Drumadoon
s.51, see *Goatley (Stephen Maurice) v HM Advocate* 2008 J.C. 1 (HCJ), Lord Nimmo Smith
s.57, see *Coia (Raymond) v HM Advocate* 2008 S.L.T. 1115 (HCJ), Lord Osborne; see *Dickson (Kenneth Robert) v HM Advocate* 2008 J.C. 181 (HCJ), Lord Hamilton L.J.G.; see *Goatley (Stephen Maurice) v HM Advocate* 2008 J.C. 1 (HCJ), Lord Nimmo Smith; see *Kennedy v Lord Advocate* [2008] CSOH 21, 2008 S.L.T. 195 (OH), Lord Mackay of Drumadoon; see *La Torre (Antonio) v HM Advocate* 2008 J.C. 23 (HCJ), Lord Gill L.J.C.; see *Sinclair (Angus Robertson) v HM Advocate* 2008 S.L.T. 189 (HCJ), Lord Hamilton L.J.G.
s.57, applied: 2008 c.27 s.70
s.58, see *Friend v Lord Advocate* [2007] UKHL 53, 2008 S.C. (H.L.) 107 (HL), Lord Bingham
s.58, applied: 2008 c.27 s.70
s.63, enabling: SI 2008/1776
s.64, applied: 2008 c.31 s.26
s.65, applied: 2008 asp 2 s.4, s.6
s.70, applied: 2008 c.27 Sch.1 para.27
s.88, applied: SI 2008/534, SI 2008/535, SI 2008/1639
s.93, applied: SI 2008/1035 Art.2, SI 2008/1788 Art.2
s.93, enabling: SI 2008/1035, SI 2008/1788
s.95, applied: 2008 asp 6 s.19
s.104, enabling: SI 2008/1889
s.112, enabling: SI 2008/1889
s.113, enabling: SI 2008/307, SI 2008/1776, SI 2008/1788, SI 2008/1889
s.115, applied: SI 2008/307, SI 2008/1776, SI 2008/1889
s.117, applied: SI 2008/1776 Art.3
s.117, varied: SI 2008/1776 Art.3
s.118, applied: SI 2008/1776 Art.3
s.118, varied: SI 2008/1776 Art.3
s.124, enabling: SI 2008/1776

CAP.

1998–cont.

46. Scotland Act 1998–*cont.*

s.126, see *Friend v Lord Advocate* [2007] UKHL 53, 2008 S.C. (H.L.) 107 (HL), Lord Bingham

s.126, applied: 2008 c.29 s.227, s.235, 2008 c.32 s.35

s.126, referred to: SI 2008/984 Art.2, SI 2008/2347 Art.2

Sch.5 para.E1, see *Logan v Harrower* [2008] HCJAC 61, 2008 S.L.T. 1049 (HCJ), Lord Nimmo Smith

Sch.5 Part II, applied: 2008 c.14 s.172

Sch.5 Part II para H.2, amended: SI 2008/960 Sch.3

Sch.5 Part II para D.5, applied: SI 2008/1776 Art.2

Sch.5 para.7, see *Friend v Lord Advocate* [2007] UKHL 53, 2008 S.C. (H.L.) 107 (HL), Lord Bingham

Sch.6 para.13, see *McDonald (John) v HM Advocate* [2008] UKPC 46, 2008 S.L.T. 993 (PC (Sc)), Lord Hope of Craighead

Sch.7, applied: SI 2008/307

Sch.7 para.1, applied: SI 2008/1776, SI 2008/1889

Sch.7 para.2, applied: SI 2008/1776, SI 2008/1889

Sch.7 para.3, applied: SI 2008/1889

47. Northern Ireland Act 1998

applied: 2008 c.3 Sch.2 Part 2, 2008 c.8 Sch.2 Part 38, 2008 c.27 s.47, s.48

s.19, applied: SI 2008/2998 Sch.1 para.15

s.27, applied: 2008 c.27 s.70

s.28, applied: 2008 c.27 s.70

s.84, enabling: SI 2008/1241, SI 2008/1779

s.85, applied: SI 2008/1769(a), SI 2008/1216

s.85, referred to: SI 2008/1769(c), SI 2008/1216

s.85, enabling: SI 2008/1216, SI 2008/1769

s.87, amended: SI 2008/1242 Art.2

s.87, applied: SI 2008/1242

s.87, enabling: SI 2008/1242

s.98, referred to: SI 2008/984 Art.2, SI 2008/2347 Art.2

Sch.2 para.10B, amended: 2008 c.14 s.137

1999

2. Social Security Contributions (Transfer of Functions, etc.) Act 1999

see *Westek Ltd v Revenue and Customs Commissioners* [2008] S.T.C. (S.C.D.) 169 (Sp Comm), Howard M Nowlan

s.8, see *Westek Ltd v Revenue and Customs Commissioners* [2008] S.T.C. (S.C.D.) 169 (Sp Comm), Howard M Nowlan

Sch.4 para.3, amended: 2008 c.9 s.137

Sch.4 para.3, repealed (in part): 2008 c.9 s.137

CAP.

1999–cont.

2. Social Security Contributions (Transfer of Functions, etc.) Act 1999–*cont.*

Sch.5 para.7, repealed (in part): 2008 c.9 Sch.44 para.11

Sch.5 para.8, repealed: 2008 c.9 Sch.43 para.11

3. Road Traffic (NHS Charges) Act 1999

s.1, applied: SI 2008/2685 Sch.1

s.7, applied: SI 2008/2685 Sch.1

8. Health Act 1999

s.31, applied: SI 2008/228 Sch.1 para.7

s.60, amended: 2008 c.14 Sch.8 para.1, Sch.10 para.10, Sch.15 Part 2

s.60, applied: 2008 c.14 s.123

s.60, referred to: 2008 c.14 s.123, s.172

s.60, enabling: SI 2008/1485, SI 2008/1774, SI 2008/3131

s.60A, added: 2008 c.14 s.112

s.62, amended: 2008 c.14 Sch.8 para.2, Sch.10 para.11

s.62, applied: SI 2008/1485, SI 2008/1774, SI 2008/3131

s.62, enabling: SI 2008/1485, SI 2008/1774, SI 2008/3131

Sch.3, enabling: SI 2008/1485, SI 2008/1774, SI 2008/3131

Sch.3 para.5, amended: 2008 c.14 Sch.8 para.4

Sch.3 para.7, amended: 2008 c.14 Sch.8 para.5, Sch.10 para.12

Sch.3 para.7, referred to: 2008 c.14 s.172

Sch.3 para.7, repealed (in part): 2008 c.14 Sch.8 para.5, Sch.15 Part 2

Sch.3 para.8, amended: 2008 c.14 Sch.8 para.6

Sch.3 para.8, referred to: 2008 c.14 s.172

Sch.3 para.8, repealed (in part): 2008 c.14 Sch.8 para.6

Sch.3 para.9, amended: 2008 c.14 Sch.8 para.7

Sch.3 para.9, applied: SI 2008/1485, SI 2008/1774, SI 2008/3131

Sch.3 para.9, referred to: 2008 c.14 s.172, SI 2008/1485, SI 2008/1774, SI 2008/3131

Sch.3 para.10, amended: 2008 c.14 Sch.8 para.8, Sch.15 Part 2

Sch.3 para.11, amended: 2008 c.14 Sch.8 para.9

Sch.3 para.12, repealed: 2008 c.14 Sch.8 para.10, Sch.15 Part 2

11. Breeding and Sale of Dogs (Welfare) Act 1999

applied: 2008 c.13 Sch.3

14. Protection of Children Act 1999

see *R. (on the application of L) v Commissioner of Police of the Metropolis* [2007] EWCA Civ 168, [2008] 1 W.L.R. 681 (CA (Civ Div)), Longmore, L.J.

applied: SI 2008/473 Art.2, Art.3

CAP.

1999–cont.

14. Protection of Children Act 1999–*cont.*
s.1, applied: SI 2008/473 Art.2, Art.3, SI 2008/474 Reg.4, SI 2008/2252 Sch.1 para.20
s.3, applied: SI 2008/473 Art.3
s.4, applied: SI 2008/2699 r.19, Sch.1
s.9, amended: SI 2008/2833 Sch.3 para.175
s.9, applied: SI 2008/2833 Sch.1
s.9, repealed (in part): SI 2008/2833 Sch.3 para.175
s.9, enabling: SI 2008/1802
s.12, amended: SI 2008/2833 Sch.3 para.176
Sch.1 para.1, applied: SI 2008/2833 Sch.2
Sch.1 para.1, repealed: SI 2008/2833 Sch.3 para.177
Sch.1 para.2, repealed: SI 2008/2833 Sch.3 para.177
Sch.1 para.3, repealed: SI 2008/2833 Sch.3 para.177
Sch.1 para.4, repealed: SI 2008/2833 Sch.3 para.177
Sch.1 para.5, repealed: SI 2008/2833 Sch.3 para.177
Sch.1 para.6, repealed: SI 2008/2833 Sch.3 para.177
Sch.1 para.7, repealed: SI 2008/2833 Sch.3 para.177
Sch.1 para.8, repealed: SI 2008/2833 Sch.3 para.177, Sch.3 para.228

16. Finance Act 1999
s.13, amended: 2008 c.9 Sch.37 para.10
s.13, repealed (in part): 2008 c.9 Sch.36 para.89
s.15, repealed (in part): 2008 c.9 Sch.36 para.92
s.26, repealed: 2008 c.9 Sch.2 para.21
s.72, repealed: 2008 c.9 Sch.2 para.55
s.80, repealed: 2008 c.9 Sch.14 para.17
s.108, repealed (in part): 2008 c.9 Sch.40 para.21
Sch.4 para.16, repealed: 2008 c.9 Sch.14 para.17
Sch.4 para.18, repealed (in part): 2008 c.9 Sch.14 para.17
Sch.7, repealed: 2008 c.9 Sch.2 para.55
Sch.10, applied: SSI 2008/228 Reg.97
Sch.10 para.18, applied: SSI 2008/228 Reg.97
Sch.13 Part I para.1, amended: 2008 c.9 s.98, Sch.32 para.10
Sch.13 Part I para.6, amended: 2008 c.9 s.98
Sch.13 Part III para.16, repealed: 2008 c.9 Sch.32 para.10
Sch.13 Part III para.17, repealed: 2008 c.9 Sch.32 para.10
Sch.13 Part III para.18, repealed (in part): 2008 c.9 Sch.32 para.10
Sch.13 Part III para.19, repealed (in part): 2008 c.9 Sch.32 para.10
Sch.13 Part III para.21, repealed (in part): 2008 c.9 Sch.32 para.10

CAP.

1999–cont.

16. Finance Act 1999–*cont.*
Sch.13 Part III para.22, repealed: 2008 c.9 Sch.32 para.10
Sch.13 Part III para.23, repealed: 2008 c.9 Sch.32 para.10
Sch.14 para.9, repealed: 2008 c.9 s.100
Sch.14 para.10, repealed (in part): 2008 c.9 Sch.32 para.20
Sch.14 para.11, repealed (in part): 2008 c.9 Sch.32 para.20
Sch.14 para.12, repealed (in part): 2008 c.9 Sch.32 para.20
Sch.14 para.13, repealed (in part): 2008 c.9 Sch.32 para.20
Sch.15 Part I para.6, repealed: 2008 c.9 Sch.32 para.11
Sch.15 Part II para.12A, added: 2008 c.9 Sch.32 para.11
Sch.15 Part II para.20, amended: 2008 c.9 Sch.32 para.11
Sch.15 Part III para.26, repealed (in part): 2008 c.9 Sch.32 para.11

20. Commonwealth Development Corporation Act 1999
s.15, amended: SI 2008/948 Sch.3 para.14
s.26, amended: SI 2008/948 Sch.1 para.208
Sch.2 Part II para.9, amended: SI 2008/948 Sch.1 para.209
Sch.2 Part II para.11, amended: SI 2008/948 Sch.1 para.209
Sch.2 Part II para.12, amended: SI 2008/948 Sch.1 para.209
Sch.2 Part II para.14, amended: SI 2008/948 Sch.1 para.209
Sch.2 Part II para.15, amended: SI 2008/948 Sch.3 para.14

22. Access to Justice Act 1999
s.6, enabling: SI 2008/666, SI 2008/1328, SI 2008/2704
s.7, enabling: SI 2008/658, SI 2008/2703
s.10, enabling: SI 2008/658
s.12, enabling: SI 2008/725
s.13, enabling: SI 2008/725
s.14, amended: 2008 c.4 s.56
s.14, enabling: SI 2008/957, SI 2008/2930
s.15, amended: 2008 c.4 s.56
s.15, enabling: SI 2008/40
s.17, enabling: SI 2008/2430
s.17A, repealed (in part): 2008 c.4 Sch.28 Part 4
s.18A, added: 2008 c.4 s.58
s.25, amended: 2008 c.4 s.56, s.57, s.58
s.25, applied: SI 2008/40, SI 2008/666, SI 2008/957, SI 2008/1328, SI 2008/2704, SI 2008/2930
s.25, referred to: SI 2008/666, SI 2008/1328, SI 2008/2704, SI 2008/2930
s.26, amended: 2008 c.4 s.56
Sch.2 para.2, amended: 2008 c.22 Sch.6 para.38, SI 2008/2833 Sch.3 para.178
Sch.3 para.1A, added: 2008 c.4 s.56

CAP.

1999–cont.

22. Access to Justice Act 1999–*cont.*
Sch.3 para.2A, amended: 2008 c.4 s.56
Sch.3 para.3A, amended: 2008 c.4 s.56
Sch.3 para.3B, amended: 2008 c.4 s.56
Sch.3 para.3B, enabling: SI 2008/723
Sch.3 para.4, amended: 2008 c.4 s.56
Sch.3 para.5, amended: 2008 c.4 s.56
Sch.3 para.6, added: 2008 c.4 s.57
Sch.3 para.7, added: 2008 c.4 s.57
Sch.3 para.8, added: 2008 c.4 s.57

23. Youth Justice and Criminal Evidence Act 1999
see *R. v R* [2008] EWCA Crim 678, [2008] 1 W.L.R. 2044 (CA (Crim Div)), Thomas, L.J.
applied: 2008 c.4 Sch.26 para.35
s.17, see *R. v R* [2008] EWCA Crim 678, [2008] 1 W.L.R. 2044 (CA (Crim Div)), Thomas, L.J.
s.18, see *R. v R* [2008] EWCA Crim 678, [2008] 1 W.L.R. 2044 (CA (Crim Div)), Thomas, L.J.
s.27, see *R. v R* [2008] EWCA Crim 678, [2008] 1 W.L.R. 2044 (CA (Crim Div)), Thomas, L.J.
s.35, amended: 2008 c.4 Sch.26 para.36
s.62, amended: 2008 c.4 Sch.26 para.37
s.62, referred to: 2008 c.4 Sch.26 para.37

24. Pollution Prevention and Control Act 1999
applied: 2008 c.13 Sch.3, 2008 c.27 s.88
s.2, applied: 2008 c.13 Sch.7, SI 2008/1776 Sch.1, SSI 2008/410
s.2, enabling: SSI 2008/410
s.3, applied: 2008 c.13 Sch.7
Sch.1 Part I para.20, applied: SI 2008/1776 Sch.1, SI 2008/2549 Art.2, SSI 2008/86 Art.2
Sch.1 Part I para.20, enabling: SI 2008/2549, SSI 2008/86

26. Employment Relations Act 1999
s.34, enabling: SI 2008/3055
Sch.7 para.4, repealed (in part): 2008 c.24 Sch.1 Part 5

27. Local Government Act 1999
Part I, applied: SI 2008/228 Sch.1 para.20
s.1, amended: 2008 c.26 Sch.4 para.62
s.4, applied: SI 2008/450
s.4, enabling: SI 2008/450, SI 2008/503, SI 2008/659
s.4, applied: SI 2008/312 Reg.6, SI 2008/503, SI 2008/659
s.4, enabling: SI 2008/503
s.6, enabling: SI 2008/199
s.7, applied: SI 2008/199 Art.3
s.7, enabling: SI 2008/199
s.15, applied: SI 2008/239 Reg.6
s.25, amended: 2008 c.14 Sch.5 para.70
s.25, varied: SI 2008/2250 Art.3
s.29, enabling: SI 2008/199, SI 2008/450, SI 2008/503

CAP.

1999–cont.

28. Food Standards Act 1999
applied: 2008 c.13 Sch.3
referred to: 2008 c.13 Sch.6
s.27, applied: 2008 c.13 Sch.7

29. Greater London Authority Act 1999
Part IV c.VIII, applied: SI 2008/417 Reg.3
s.17A, applied: SI 2008/507
s.17A, enabling: SI 2008/507
s.25, enabling: SI 2008/724
s.30, applied: SI 2008/1342 Reg.7
s.38, amended: 2008 c.29 s.224
s.38, disapplied: SI 2008/1342 Reg.7
s.39, disapplied: SI 2008/1342 Reg.7
s.41, applied: SI 2008/580 Art.6
s.60A, amended: SI 2008/2038 Art.21
s.60A, enabling: SI 2008/2038
s.85, applied: SI 2008/1342 Reg.10
s.85, varied: SI 2008/227 Reg.7
s.86, enabling: SI 2008/227
s.88, varied: SI 2008/227 Reg.8
s.88, enabling: SI 2008/227
s.89, varied: SI 2008/227 Reg.9
s.89, enabling: SI 2008/227
s.99, varied: SI 2008/227 Reg.10
s.102, varied: SI 2008/227 Reg.11
s.154, disapplied: 2008 c.18 s.38
s.155, disapplied: 2008 c.18 s.38
s.163, applied: 2008 c.18 s.38
s.211, amended: 2008 c.26 Sch.4 para.63
s.216, disapplied: 2008 c.18 s.28
s.220, see *Metronet Rail BCV Ltd (In Administration), Re* [2007] EWHC 2697 (Ch), [2008] Bus. L.R. 823 (Ch D), Patten, J.
s.233, amended: SI 2008/948 Sch.1 para.210
s.235, amended: SI 2008/960 Sch.3, SI 2008/1277 Sch.2 para.59
s.243, enabling: SI 2008/417, SI 2008/2091
s.333A, amended: 2008 c.17 Sch.8 para.73, Sch.16
s.333A, varied: SI 2008/2839 Sch.1 para.6
s.333D, amended: 2008 c.17 Sch.8 para.74
s.333D, varied: SI 2008/2839 Sch.1 para.6
s.356, see *R. (on the application of Enfield LBC) v Mayor of London* [2007] EWHC 1795 (Admin), [2008] Env. L.R. 9 (QBD (Admin)), Mitting, J.; see *R. (on the application of Enfield LBC) v Mayor of London* [2008] EWCA Civ 202, [2008] Env. L.R. 33 (CA (Civ Div)), May, L.J.
s.356B, enabling: SI 2008/2038
s.362, see *R. (on the application of Eco-Power Co UK Ltd) v Transport for London* [2008] EWHC 846 (Admin), [2008] Env. L.R. 44 (QBD (Admin)), Judge Hickinbottom
s.377A, applied: SI 2008/701 Art.2
s.377A, enabling: SI 2008/701
s.405, enabling: SI 2008/2038
s.408, repealed (in part): 2008 c.17 Sch.8 para.75, Sch.16

CAP.

1999–cont.

29. Greater London Authority Act 1999–*cont.*

s.409, repealed (in part): 2008 c.17 Sch.8 para.76, Sch.16
s.420, applied: SI 2008/507, SI 2008/2038
s.420, enabling: SI 2008/227, SI 2008/417, SI 2008/724
Sch.14, see *Metronet Rail BCV Ltd (In Administration), Re* [2007] EWHC 2697 (Ch), [2008] Bus. L.R. 823 (Ch D), Patten, J.
Sch.15, see *Metronet Rail BCV Ltd (In Administration), Re* [2007] EWHC 2697 (Ch), [2008] Bus. L.R. 823 (Ch D), Patten, J.
Sch.15 para.1, see *Metronet Rail BCV Ltd (In Administration), Re* [2007] EWHC 2697 (Ch), [2008] Bus. L.R. 823 (Ch D), Patten, J.
Sch.15 para.2, see *Metronet Rail BCV Ltd (In Administration), Re* [2007] EWHC 2697 (Ch), [2008] Bus. L.R. 823 (Ch D), Patten, J.
Sch.18 para.8, amended: SI 2008/948 Sch.1 para.24
Sch.23 para.9, amended: 2008 c.26 s.113
Sch.23 para.10, amended: 2008 c.26 s.112
Sch.23 para.10A, added: 2008 c.26 s.113
Sch.23 para.12, enabling: SI 2008/1956
Sch.23 para.16, amended: 2008 c.26 Sch.6 para.10, Sch.7 Part 5
Sch.23 para.16, repealed (in part): 2008 c.26 Sch.6 para.10, Sch.7 Part 5
Sch.23 para.17, repealed (in part): 2008 c.26 Sch.6 para.11, Sch.7 Part 5
Sch.23 para.18, amended: 2008 c.26 Sch.6 para.12, Sch.7 Part 5
Sch.23 para.19, repealed (in part): 2008 c.26 s.120, Sch.7 Part 5
Sch.23 para.20, amended: 2008 c.26 s.120
Sch.23 para.20, repealed (in part): 2008 c.26 s.120, Sch.7 Part 5
Sch.23 para.21, amended: 2008 c.26 s.120, Sch.7 Part 5
Sch.23 para.21, repealed (in part): 2008 c.26 s.120, Sch.7 Part 5
Sch.23 para.22, amended: 2008 c.26 s.120, Sch.7 Part 5
Sch.23 para.22, repealed (in part): 2008 c.26 s.120, Sch.7 Part 5
Sch.23 para.23, amended: 2008 c.26 s.120, Sch.7 Part 5
Sch.23 para.24, amended: 2008 c.26 s.120, Sch.7 Part 5
Sch.23 para.24, repealed (in part): 2008 c.26 s.120, Sch.7 Part 5
Sch.23 para.24, substituted: 2008 c.26 s.120
Sch.23 para.25, amended: 2008 c.26 s.115
Sch.23 para.26, amended: 2008 c.26 s.115
Sch.23 para.28, enabling: SI 2008/1956
Sch.23 para.29, amended: 2008 c.26 s.116

CAP.

1999–cont.

29. Greater London Authority Act 1999–*cont.*

Sch.23 para.34A, amended: 2008 c.26 s.118
Sch.23 para.34B, added: 2008 c.26 s.117
Sch.27 para.95, repealed: 2008 c.4 Sch.28 Part 8
Sch.27 para.107, repealed: 2008 c.4 Sch.28 Part 8

30. Welfare Reform and Pensions Act 1999

see *Twizell v United Kingdom (25379/02)* (2008) 47 E.H.R.R. 49 (ECHR), Judge Garlicki (President)
Part I, applied: SI 2008/576 Sch.4 para.5
Part I, referred to: 2008 c.30 s.146
Part II, referred to: 2008 c.30 s.146
Part III, referred to: 2008 c.30 s.146
Part IV, referred to: 2008 c.30 s.146
s.3, amended: 2008 c.30 s.87, Sch.11 Part 1
s.3, repealed (in part): 2008 c.30 s.87, Sch.11 Part 1
s.6, repealed (in part): 2008 c.30 s.87, Sch.11 Part 1
s.8, amended: 2008 c.30 s.87, Sch.11 Part 1
s.11, see *Thurmond v Rajapakse* [2008] B.P.I.R. 283 (Ch D), Registrar Nicholls
s.23, enabling: SI 2008/1050
s.26, enabling: SI 2008/1050
s.28, amended: 2008 c.30 s.128
s.28, applied: 2008 c.30 s.118, SSI 2008/228 Reg.93
s.29, applied: SSI 2008/230 Reg.42
s.30, applied: SSI 2008/228 Reg.89
s.30, enabling: SI 2008/1050
s.31, applied: SI 2008/653 Reg.12, Reg.16, SSI 2008/224 Reg.12, Reg.16
s.33, applied: SI 2008/576 Sch.4 para.5, SSI 2008/228 Reg.94
s.34, applied: SSI 2008/228 Reg.93
s.36, repealed: 2008 c.30 Sch.11 Part 2
s.40, amended: 2008 c.30 Sch.11 Part 2
s.40, repealed (in part): 2008 c.30 Sch.11 Part 2
s.41, applied: SSI 2008/228 Reg.93, Reg.101
s.41, enabling: SI 2008/1050
s.48, amended: 2008 c.30 s.128
s.72, amended: 2008 c.25 Sch.1 para.74, Sch.2
s.80, repealed: 2008 c.6 Sch.8
s.83, applied: SI 2008/1050
s.83, enabling: SI 2008/1050
Sch.5 para.1, applied: SSI 2008/228 Reg.89
Sch.5 para.5, applied: SI 2008/653 Reg.2, SSI 2008/224 Reg.2
Sch.5 para.5, enabling: SI 2008/1050
Sch.5 para.6, applied: SSI 2008/228 Reg.90
Sch.5 para.7, applied: SSI 2008/228 Reg.91
Sch.5 para.7, repealed (in part): 2008 c.30 Sch.11 Part 2
Sch.5 para.8, enabling: SI 2008/1050

CAP.

1999–cont.

30. Welfare Reform and Pensions Act 1999–*cont.*

Sch.11 para.6, repealed: 2008 c.9 Sch.43 para.11

Sch.12 Part I para.29, repealed: 2008 c.30 Sch.11 Part 2

Sch.12 Part I para.30, repealed: 2008 c.30 Sch.11 Part 2

Sch.12 Part I para.41, repealed (in part): 2008 c.30 Sch.11 Part 2

31. Contracts (Rights of Third Parties) Act 1999

see *HSBC Bank Plc v 5th Avenue Partners Ltd* [2007] EWHC 2819 (Comm), [2008] 2 C.L.C. 770 (QBD (Comm)), Walker, J.

33. Immigration and Asylum Act 1999

Part VI, applied: 2008 c.4 s.134, s.135

s.1, varied: SI 2008/680 Art.5, Art.14

s.2, varied: SI 2008/680 Art.5, Art.14

s.3, varied: SI 2008/680 Art.5, Art.14

s.4, applied: SI 2008/2077 Art.3

s.4, disapplied: 2008 c.4 s.134

s.6, varied: SI 2008/680 Art.5, Art.14

s.7, varied: SI 2008/680 Art.5, Art.14

s.8, varied: SI 2008/680 Art.5, Art.14

s.10, see *R. (on the application of Lim) v Secretary of State for the Home Department* [2007] EWCA Civ 773, [2008] I.N.L.R. 60 (CA (Civ Div)), Sir Mark Potter (President, Fam)

s.10, applied: SI 2008/1216 Art.19

s.10, varied: SI 2008/680 Art.5, Art.14, Sch.6 para.1

s.13, varied: SI 2008/680 Art.5, Art.14, Sch.6 para.2

s.14, varied: SI 2008/680 Art.5, Art.14, Sch.6 para.3

s.16, varied: SI 2008/680 Art.5, Art.14, Sch.6 para.4

s.17, varied: SI 2008/680 Art.5, Art.14, Sch.6 para.5

s.18, varied: SI 2008/680 Art.5, Art.14

s.19, varied: SI 2008/680 Art.5, Art.14

s.20, applied: SI 2008/2077 Art.2, Art.3

s.20, enabling: SI 2008/2077

s.22, varied: SI 2008/680 Art.5, Art.14

s.23, disapplied: SI 2008/310 Art.4

s.24, amended: SI 2008/678 Sch.2 para.11

s.24, applied: SI 2008/678 Sch.1 para.11

s.24, varied: SI 2008/680 Art.5, Art.14, Sch.6 para.6

s.24A, amended: SI 2008/678 Sch.2 para.11

s.24A, applied: SI 2008/678 Sch.1 para.11

s.25, varied: SI 2008/680 Art.5, Art.14, Sch.6 para.7

s.26, varied: SI 2008/680 Art.5, Art.14, Sch.6 para.8

s.28, varied: SI 2008/680 Art.5, Art.14

s.30, varied: SI 2008/680 Art.5, Art.14

CAP.

1999–cont.

33. Immigration and Asylum Act 1999–*cont.*

s.31, see *R. v Asfaw (Fregenet)* [2008] UKHL 31, [2008] 1 A.C. 1061 (HL), Lord Bingham of Cornhill

s.32, varied: SI 2008/680 Art.5, Art.14, Sch.6 para.9

s.32A, varied: SI 2008/680 Art.5, Art.14, Sch.6 para.10

s.33, varied: SI 2008/680 Art.5, Art.14, Sch.6 para.11

s.34, varied: SI 2008/680 Art.5, Art.14, Sch.6 para.12

s.35, varied: SI 2008/680 Art.5, Art.14, Sch.6 para.13

s.35A, varied: SI 2008/680 Art.5, Art.14, Sch.6 para.14

s.36, varied: SI 2008/680 Art.5, Art.14, Sch.6 para.15

s.36A, varied: SI 2008/680 Art.5, Art.14, Sch.6 para.16

s.37, varied: SI 2008/680 Art.5, Art.14, Sch.6 para.17

s.38, varied: SI 2008/680 Art.5, Art.14

s.40, varied: SI 2008/680 Art.5, Art.14, Sch.6 para.18

s.40A, varied: SI 2008/680 Art.5, Art.14, Sch.6 para.19

s.40B, varied: SI 2008/680 Art.5, Art.14, Sch.6 para.20

s.43, varied: SI 2008/680 Art.5, Art.14, Sch.6 para.21

s.54, varied: SI 2008/680 Art.5, Art.14

s.65, see *B v Secretary of State for the Home Department* [2008] UKHL 39, [2008] 3 W.L.R. 166 (HL), Lord Bingham of Cornhill; see *C v Secretary of State for the Home Department* [2008] UKHL 40, [2008] 1 W.L.R. 1420 (HL), Lord Bingham of Cornhill

s.77, see *B v Secretary of State for the Home Department* [2008] UKHL 39, [2008] 3 W.L.R. 166 (HL), Lord Bingham of Cornhill

s.84, see *R. v K* [2008] EWCA Crim 1900, Times, October 8, 2008 (CA (Crim Div)), Toulson, L.J.

s.86, enabling: SI 2008/505

s.91, see *R. v K* [2008] EWCA Crim 1900, Times, October 8, 2008 (CA (Crim Div)), Toulson, L.J.

s.94, amended: SI 2008/2833 Sch.3 para.180

s.95, applied: 2008 c.4 s.134, SI 2008/794 Reg.104, Sch.8 para.22

s.95, referred to: SI 2008/794 Sch.8 para.22

s.96, disapplied: 2008 c.4 s.134

s.97, disapplied: 2008 c.4 s.134

s.98, applied: SI 2008/794 Reg.104, Sch.8 para.22

s.98, referred to: SI 2008/794 Sch.8 para.22

s.100, applied: 2008 c.17 s.77

CAP.

1999–cont.

33. Immigration and Asylum Act 1999– *cont.*

s.100, disapplied: 2008 c.4 s.134
s.101, disapplied: 2008 c.4 s.134
s.102, applied: SI 2008/2707 Art.2, SI 2008/2833 Sch.1, Sch.2
s.102, repealed: SI 2008/2833 Sch.3 para.181
s.103, amended: SI 2008/2833 Sch.3 para.182, Sch.3 para.183
s.103, applied: SI 2008/2707 Art.2
s.103, repealed (in part): SI 2008/2833 Sch.3 para.182, Sch.3 para.183
s.103A, amended: SI 2008/2833 Sch.3 para.184
s.103A, applied: SI 2008/2707 Art.2
s.104, applied: 2008 c.4 s.135
s.104, repealed: SI 2008/2833 Sch.3 para.185
s.108, disapplied: 2008 c.4 s.134
s.111, disapplied: 2008 c.4 s.134
s.113, disapplied: 2008 c.4 s.134
s.115, amended: 2008 c.14 s.138
s.115, applied: SI 2008/794 Reg.11, Reg.70, Sch.5 Part 1
s.115, disapplied: SI 2008/794 Sch.5 Part 1
s.115, enabling: SI 2008/3108
s.118, enabling: SI 2008/1768
s.119, amended: 2008 c.17 Sch.15 para.22
s.119, applied: 2008 c.4 s.134
s.119, enabling: SI 2008/1768
s.128, varied: SI 2008/680 Art.5, Art.14
s.129, varied: SI 2008/680 Art.5, Art.14
s.130, varied: SI 2008/680 Art.5, Art.14
s.131, varied: SI 2008/680 Art.5, Art.14
s.132, varied: SI 2008/680 Art.5, Art.14
s.133, varied: SI 2008/680 Art.5, Art.14
s.134, varied: SI 2008/680 Art.5, Art.14
s.135, varied: SI 2008/680 Art.5, Art.14
s.136, varied: SI 2008/680 Art.5, Art.14
s.137, varied: SI 2008/680 Art.5, Art.14
s.138, varied: SI 2008/680 Art.5, Art.14
s.139, varied: SI 2008/680 Art.5, Art.14
s.140, varied: SI 2008/680 Art.5, Art.14
s.141, varied: SI 2008/680 Art.5, Art.14, Sch.6 para.22
s.142, varied: SI 2008/680 Art.5, Art.14, Sch.6 para.23
s.143, varied: SI 2008/680 Art.5, Art.14, Sch.6 para.24
s.144, varied: SI 2008/680 Art.5, Art.14, Sch.6 para.25
s.145, varied: SI 2008/680 Art.5, Art.14, Sch.6 para.26
s.146, varied: SI 2008/680 Art.5, Art.14
s.165, varied: SI 2008/680 Art.5, Art.14
s.166, applied: SI 2008/2077
s.166, varied: SI 2008/680 Art.5, Art.14, Sch.6 para.27
s.166, enabling: SI 2008/760, SI 2008/1768

CAP.

1999–cont.

33. Immigration and Asylum Act 1999– *cont.*

s.167, varied: SI 2008/680 Art.5, Art.14, Sch.6 para.28
s.168, varied: SI 2008/680 Art.5, Art.14, Sch.6 para.29
s.169, varied: SI 2008/680 Art.5, Art.14
s.170, varied: SI 2008/680 Art.5, Art.14, Sch.6 para.30
s.170, enabling: SI 2008/680
Sch.1 para.1, varied: SI 2008/680 Art.5, Art.14, Sch.6 para.31
Sch.1 para.2, varied: SI 2008/680 Art.5, Art.14, Sch.6 para.31
Sch.1 para.2A, varied: SI 2008/680 Art.5, Art.14, Sch.6 para.31
Sch.1 para.3, varied: SI 2008/680 Art.5, Art.14, Sch.6 para.31
Sch.1 para.4, varied: SI 2008/680 Art.5, Art.14, Sch.6 para.31
Sch.1 para.5, varied: SI 2008/680 Art.5, Art.14, Sch.6 para.31
Sch.8 para.1, enabling: SI 2008/760
Sch.8 para.3, applied: SI 2008/794 Reg.104, Sch.8 para.22
Sch.8 para.3, enabling: SI 2008/760
Sch.8 para.9, varied: 2008 c.4 s.135
Sch.9, applied: SI 2008/794 Reg.104, Sch.8 para.22
Sch.9, referred to: SI 2008/794 Sch.8 para.22
Sch.10 para.1, applied: SI 2008/2833 Sch.2
Sch.10 para.1, repealed: SI 2008/2833 Sch.3 para.186
Sch.10 para.2, repealed: SI 2008/2833 Sch.3 para.186
Sch.10 para.3, repealed: SI 2008/2833 Sch.3 para.186
Sch.10 para.4, repealed: SI 2008/2833 Sch.3 para.186
Sch.10 para.5, repealed: SI 2008/2833 Sch.3 para.186
Sch.10 para.6, repealed: SI 2008/2833 Sch.3 para.186
Sch.10 para.7, repealed: SI 2008/2833 Sch.3 para.186
Sch.14 para.43, varied: SI 2008/680 Art.5, Art.14
Sch.14 para.44, varied: SI 2008/680 Art.5, Art.14
Sch.14 para.45, varied: SI 2008/680 Art.5, Art.14
Sch.14 para.52, varied: SI 2008/680 Art.5, Art.14
Sch.14 para.54, varied: SI 2008/680 Art.5, Art.14
Sch.14 para.55, varied: SI 2008/680 Art.5, Art.14
Sch.14 para.56, varied: SI 2008/680 Art.5, Art.14

CAP.

1999–cont.

33. Immigration and Asylum Act 1999– *cont.*
Sch.14 para.57, varied: SI 2008/680 Art.5, Art.14
Sch.14 para.58, varied: SI 2008/680 Art.5, Art.14
Sch.14 para.59, varied: SI 2008/680 Art.5, Art.14
Sch.14 para.60, varied: SI 2008/680 Art.5, Art.14
Sch.14 para.61, varied: SI 2008/680 Art.5, Art.14
Sch.14 para.62, varied: SI 2008/680 Art.5, Art.14
Sch.14 para.63, varied: SI 2008/680 Art.5, Art.14
Sch.14 para.64, varied: SI 2008/680 Art.5, Art.14
Sch.14 para.65, varied: SI 2008/680 Art.5, Art.14
Sch.14 para.67, varied: SI 2008/680 Art.5, Art.14
Sch.14 para.68, varied: SI 2008/680 Art.5, Art.14
Sch.14 para.70, varied: SI 2008/680 Art.5, Art.14
Sch.14 para.71, repealed (in part): SI 2008/2833 Sch.3 para.228
Sch.14 para.72, repealed (in part): SI 2008/2833 Sch.3 para.228
Sch.14 para.95, repealed: SI 2008/2833 Sch.3 para.228
Sch.16, varied: SI 2008/680 Art.5, Art.14

2000

vii. London Local Authorities Act 2000
s.15, see *Wolman v Islington LBC* [2007] EWCA Civ 823, [2008] 1 All E.R. 1259 (CA (Civ Div)), Waller, L.J.

1. Northern Ireland Act 2000
applied: 2008 c.3 Sch.2 Part 2, 2008 c.8 Sch.2 Part 38

2. Representation of the People Act 2000
s.10, varied: SI 2008/1848 Sch.4 para.1
s.12, varied: SI 2008/1848 Sch.4 para.1
Sch.4 para.1, referred to: SI 2008/305(c)
Sch.4 para.1, varied: SI 2008/1848 Sch.4 para.1
Sch.4 para.2, varied: SI 2008/1848 Sch.4 para.1
Sch.4 para.3, referred to: SI 2008/305(c)
Sch.4 para.3, varied: SI 2008/1848 Sch.4 para.1
Sch.4 para.4, referred to: SI 2008/305(c)
Sch.4 para.4, varied: SI 2008/1848 Sch.4 para.1
Sch.4 para.5, varied: SI 2008/1848 Sch.4 para.1
Sch.4 para.6, referred to: SI 2008/305(c)

CAP.

2000–cont.

2. Representation of the People Act 2000–*cont.*
Sch.4 para.6, varied: SI 2008/1848 Sch.4 para.1
Sch.4 para.7, referred to: SI 2008/305(c)
Sch.4 para.7, varied: SI 2008/1848 Sch.4 para.1
Sch.4 para.7A, varied: SI 2008/1848 Sch.4 para.1
Sch.4 para.7B, varied: SI 2008/1848 Sch.4 para.1
Sch.4 para.7C, varied: SI 2008/1848 Sch.4 para.1
Sch.4 para.7D, varied: SI 2008/1848 Sch.4 para.1
Sch.4 para.8, varied: SI 2008/1848 Sch.4 para.1

6. Powers of Criminal Courts (Sentencing) Act 2000
see *R. (on the application of Faithfull) v Ipswich Crown Court* [2007] EWHC 2763 (Admin), [2008] 1 W.L.R. 1636 (DC), Richards, L.J.
applied: 2008 c.4 Sch.27 para.1
referred to: 2008 c.4 Sch.26 para.40
s.1, amended: 2008 c.4 Sch.26 para.49, SI 2008/912 Sch.1 para.14
s.1A, amended: 2008 c.4 Sch.26 para.49, SI 2008/912 Sch.1 para.14
s.1B, amended: 2008 c.4 Sch.26 para.49
s.1C, amended: 2008 c.4 Sch.26 para.49
s.1D, amended: 2008 c.4 Sch.26 para.49
s.2, amended: 2008 c.4 Sch.26 para.49
s.3, amended: 2008 c.4 Sch.26 para.49, Sch.28 Part 4
s.3, repealed (in part): 2008 c.4 Sch.28 Part 4
s.3A, amended: 2008 c.4 Sch.26 para.49
s.3B, amended: 2008 c.4 Sch.26 para.49
s.3C, amended: 2008 c.4 Sch.26 para.49
s.4, amended: 2008 c.4 Sch.26 para.49
s.4A, amended: 2008 c.4 Sch.26 para.49
s.5, amended: 2008 c.4 Sch.26 para.49
s.5A, amended: 2008 c.4 Sch.26 para.49
s.6, amended: 2008 c.4 Sch.26 para.49
s.7, amended: 2008 c.4 Sch.26 para.49
s.8, amended: 2008 c.4 Sch.26 para.49
s.9, amended: 2008 c.4 Sch.26 para.49
s.10, amended: 2008 c.4 Sch.26 para.49
s.11, amended: 2008 c.4 Sch.26 para.49
s.12, amended: 2008 c.4 Sch.26 para.41
s.17, amended: 2008 c.4 s.35
s.17, repealed (in part): 2008 c.4 s.35, Sch.28 Part 2
s.19, amended: 2008 c.4 Sch.4 para.52
s.24, amended: 2008 c.4 Sch.26 para.42
s.27A, added: 2008 c.4 s.36
s.27B, added: 2008 c.4 s.37
s.28, amended: 2008 c.4 Sch.26 para.43
s.33, repealed: 2008 c.4 s.6, Sch.28 Part 1
s.34, repealed: 2008 c.4 s.6, Sch.28 Part 1
s.35, repealed: 2008 c.4 s.6, Sch.28 Part 1

CAP.

2000–cont.

6. Powers of Criminal Courts (Sentencing) Act 2000–*cont.*

s.36, repealed: 2008 c.4 s.6, Sch.28 Part 1
s.36A, repealed: 2008 c.4 s.6, Sch.28 Part 1
s.36B, repealed: 2008 c.4 s.6, Sch.28 Part 1
s.37, applied: SI 2008/2793 r.3
s.37, repealed: 2008 c.4 s.6, Sch.28 Part 1
s.38, repealed: 2008 c.4 s.6, Sch.28 Part 1
s.39, repealed: 2008 c.4 s.6, Sch.28 Part 1
s.40, repealed: 2008 c.4 s.6, Sch.28 Part 1
s.40A, repealed: 2008 c.4 s.6, Sch.28 Part 1
s.40B, repealed: 2008 c.4 s.6, Sch.28 Part 1
s.40C, repealed: 2008 c.4 s.6, Sch.28 Part 1
s.41, amended: SI 2008/912 Sch.1 para.14
s.46, amended: SI 2008/912 Sch.1 para.14
s.47, amended: SI 2008/912 Sch.1 para.14
s.54, amended: SI 2008/912 Sch.1 para.14
s.57, amended: SI 2008/912 Sch.1 para.14
s.60, repealed: 2008 c.4 s.6, Sch.28 Part 1
s.61, repealed: 2008 c.4 s.6, Sch.28 Part 1
s.62, applied: 2008 c.4 Sch.27 para.7
s.62, repealed: 2008 c.4 s.6, Sch.28 Part 1
s.63, amended: SI 2008/912 Sch.1 para.14
s.63, repealed: 2008 c.4 s.6, Sch.28 Part 1
s.64, amended: SI 2008/912 Sch.1 para.14
s.64, repealed: 2008 c.4 s.6, Sch.28 Part 1
s.64A, repealed: 2008 c.4 s.6, Sch.28 Part 1
s.65, repealed: 2008 c.4 s.6, Sch.28 Part 1
s.66, amended: SI 2008/912 Sch.1 para.14
s.66, repealed: 2008 c.4 s.6, Sch.28 Part 1
s.67, repealed: 2008 c.4 s.6, Sch.28 Part 1
s.68, repealed: 2008 c.4 s.6, Sch.28 Part 1
s.69, amended: SI 2008/912 Sch.1 para.14
s.69, repealed: 2008 c.4 s.6, Sch.28 Part 1
s.70, amended: SI 2008/912 Sch.1 para.14
s.70, repealed: 2008 c.4 s.6, Sch.28 Part 1
s.71, repealed: 2008 c.4 s.6, Sch.28 Part 1
s.72, repealed: 2008 c.4 s.6, Sch.28 Part 1
s.73, amended: 2008 c.4 Sch.4 para.53, SI 2008/912 Sch.1 para.14
s.73, applied: 2008 c.4 Sch.1 para.30
s.74, amended: 2008 c.4 Sch.4 para.54, Sch.28 Part 1, SI 2008/912 Sch.1 para.14
s.75, amended: 2008 c.4 Sch.4 para.55, Sch.28 Part 1
s.76, see *K v P* [2008] EWCA Civ 600, [2008] 2 F.L.R. 2137 (CA (Civ Div)), Thorpe, L.J.
s.82A, see *R. v Hogg (Brian Maurice)* [2007] EWCA Crim 1357, [2008] 1 Cr. App. R. (S.) 22 (CA (Crim Div)), Sir Igor Judge (President, QB)
s.82A, amended: 2008 c.4 s.19, s.22
s.84, see *R. v Jesson (Anthony Wayne)* [2007] EWCA Crim 1399, [2008] 1 Cr. App. R. (S.) 36 (CA (Crim Div)), Latham, L.J. (VP, CA Crim)
s.84, varied: 2008 c.4 s.20
s.86, see *R. v Strachan (Greig)* [2007] EWCA Crim 1571, [2008] 1 Cr. App. R. (S.) 43 (CA (Crim Div)), Pill, L.J.
s.89, disapplied: 2008 c.4 s.39
s.91, amended: 2008 c.4 Sch.4 para.56
s.91, applied: 2008 c.28 s.45
s.92, repealed (in part): 2008 c.4 Sch.26 para.44, Sch.28 Part 2
s.100, applied: 2008 c.28 s.45
s.101, amended: 2008 c.4 s.22
s.102, applied: SI 2008/2793 r.3
s.103, amended: SI 2008/912 Sch.1 para.14
s.103, applied: 2008 c.4 Sch.1 para.30, SI 2008/2793 r.3
s.103, referred to: 2008 c.4 Sch.1 para.30
s.109, see *R. v Stanley (Dean Mark)* [2008] EWCA Crim 655, [2008] 2 Cr. App. R. (S.) 107 (CA (Crim Div)), Toulson, L.J.
s.110, see *R. v Reid (Gary)* [2008] EWCA Crim 202, [2008] 2 Cr. App. R. (S.) 68 (CA (Crim Div)), Hooper, L.J.
s.116, see *R. v Jesson (Anthony Wayne)* [2007] EWCA Crim 1399, [2008] 1 Cr. App. R. (S.) 36 (CA (Crim Div)), Latham, L.J. (VP, CA Crim)
s.116, amended: 2008 c.4 Sch.26 para.45
s.130, amended: 2008 c.4 Sch.26 para.46
s.134, see *Revenue and Customs Prosecution Office v Duffy* [2008] EWHC 848 (Admin), [2008] 2 Cr. App. R. (S.) 103 (DC), Richards, L.J.
s.137, amended: 2008 c.4 Sch.4 para.57, Sch.28 Part 1
s.137, applied: 2008 c.25 s.56
s.137, repealed (in part): 2008 c.4 Sch.28 Part 1
s.140, see *Crown Prosecution Service v Greenacre* [2007] EWHC 1193 (Admin), [2008] 1 W.L.R. 438 (DC), Laws, L.J.
s.146, amended: 2008 c.4 Sch.26 para.47
s.150, amended: 2008 c.4 Sch.4 para.58
s.154, see *R. v Hills (Christopher Carl)* [2008] EWCA Crim 1871, Times, August 7, 2008 (CA (Crim Div)), Latham, L.J.
s.155, see *R. v Fairbrother (Barry James)* [2007] EWCA Crim 3280, [2008] 2 Cr. App. R. (S.) 43 (CA (Crim Div)), Latham, L.J. (VP, CA Crim); see *R. v Reynolds (Michael Edwin)* [2007] EWCA Crim 538, [2008] 1 W.L.R. 1075 (CA (Crim Div)), Latham, L.J.
s.155, amended: 2008 c.4 Sch.8 para.28, Sch.28 Part 3
s.155, repealed (in part): 2008 c.4 Sch.28 Part 3
s.159, amended: 2008 c.4 Sch.4 para.59, Sch.28 Part 1
s.160, amended: 2008 c.4 Sch.4 para.60, Sch.28 Part 1
s.160, repealed (in part): 2008 c.4 Sch.4 para.60, Sch.28 Part 1

CAP.

2000–cont.

6. Powers of Criminal Courts (Sentencing) Act 2000–*cont.*

s.163, amended: 2008 c.4 Sch.4 para.61, Sch.28 Part 1

s.163, repealed (in part): 2008 c.4 Sch.4 para.61, Sch.28 Part 1

s.164, amended: 2008 c.4 Sch.26 para.48

Sch.1, referred to: 2008 c.4 Sch.26 para.49

Sch.1 Part I para.1, amended: 2008 c.4 s.36

Sch.1 Part I para.5, amended: 2008 c.4 Sch.26 para.49

Sch.1 Part I para.9, amended: 2008 c.4 Sch.26 para.49

Sch.1 Part I para.9ZA, added: 2008 c.4 Sch.4 para.107

Sch.1 Part 1ZA para.9ZB, added: 2008 c.4 s.37

Sch.1 Part 1ZA para.9ZC, added: 2008 c.4 s.37

Sch.1 Part 1ZA para.9ZD, added: 2008 c.4 s.37

Sch.1 Part 1ZA para.9ZE, added: 2008 c.4 s.37

Sch.1 Part II para.14, amended: 2008 c.4 Sch.26 para.49

Sch.3 Part I para.1, repealed: 2008 c.4 s.6, Sch.28 Part 1

Sch.3 Part I para.2, repealed: 2008 c.4 s.6, Sch.28 Part 1

Sch.3 Part II para.2A, repealed: 2008 c.4 s.6, Sch.28 Part 1

Sch.3 Part II para.3, repealed: 2008 c.4 s.6, Sch.28 Part 1

Sch.3 Part II para.4, repealed: 2008 c.4 s.6, Sch.28 Part 1

Sch.3 Part II para.5, repealed: 2008 c.4 s.6, Sch.28 Part 1

Sch.3 Part II para.6, repealed: 2008 c.4 s.6, Sch.28 Part 1

Sch.3 Part II para.6A, repealed: 2008 c.4 s.6, Sch.28 Part 1

Sch.3 Part II para.7, repealed: 2008 c.4 s.6, Sch.28 Part 1

Sch.3 Part II para.8, repealed: 2008 c.4 s.6, Sch.28 Part 1

Sch.3 Part II para.9, repealed: 2008 c.4 s.6, Sch.28 Part 1

Sch.3 Part III para.10, repealed: 2008 c.4 s.6, Sch.28 Part 1

Sch.3 Part III para.11, repealed: 2008 c.4 s.6, Sch.28 Part 1

Sch.3 Part III para.12, repealed: 2008 c.4 s.6, Sch.28 Part 1

Sch.3 Part III para.13, repealed: 2008 c.4 s.6, Sch.28 Part 1

Sch.3 Part III para.14, repealed: 2008 c.4 s.6, Sch.28 Part 1

Sch.3 Part III para.15, repealed: 2008 c.4 s.6, Sch.28 Part 1

Sch.3 Part III para.16, repealed: 2008 c.4 s.6, Sch.28 Part 1

CAP.

2000–cont.

6. Powers of Criminal Courts (Sentencing) Act 2000–*cont.*

Sch.3 Part III para.17, repealed: 2008 c.4 s.6, Sch.28 Part 1

Sch.3 Part IV para.18, repealed: 2008 c.4 s.6, Sch.28 Part 1

Sch.3 Part IV para.19, repealed: 2008 c.4 s.6, Sch.28 Part 1

Sch.3 Part IV para.20, repealed: 2008 c.4 s.6, Sch.28 Part 1

Sch.3 Part IV para.21, repealed: 2008 c.4 s.6, Sch.28 Part 1

Sch.3 Part IV para.22, repealed: 2008 c.4 s.6, Sch.28 Part 1

Sch.3 Part IV para.23, repealed: 2008 c.4 s.6, Sch.28 Part 1

Sch.3 Part IV para.24, repealed: 2008 c.4 s.6, Sch.28 Part 1

Sch.3 Part IV para.25, repealed: 2008 c.4 s.6, Sch.28 Part 1

Sch.3 Part IV para.26, repealed: 2008 c.4 s.6, Sch.28 Part 1

Sch.5 para.1, repealed: 2008 c.4 s.6, Sch.28 Part 1

Sch.5 para.2, repealed: 2008 c.4 s.6, Sch.28 Part 1

Sch.5 para.3, repealed: 2008 c.4 s.6, Sch.28 Part 1

Sch.5 para.4, repealed: 2008 c.4 s.6, Sch.28 Part 1

Sch.5 para.5, repealed: 2008 c.4 s.6, Sch.28 Part 1

Sch.5 para.6, repealed: 2008 c.4 s.6, Sch.28 Part 1

Sch.5 para.7, repealed: 2008 c.4 s.6, Sch.28 Part 1

Sch.6 para.1, repealed: 2008 c.4 s.6, Sch.28 Part 1

Sch.6 para.2, repealed: 2008 c.4 s.6, Sch.28 Part 1

Sch.6 para.3, repealed: 2008 c.4 s.6, Sch.28 Part 1

Sch.6 para.4, repealed: 2008 c.4 s.6, Sch.28 Part 1

Sch.6 para.5, repealed: 2008 c.4 s.6, Sch.28 Part 1

Sch.6 para.5A, amended: 2008 c.23 Sch.1 para.10

Sch.6 para.5A, repealed: 2008 c.4 s.6, Sch.28 Part 1

Sch.6 para.6, repealed: 2008 c.4 s.6, Sch.28 Part 1

Sch.6 para.6A, amended: SI 2008/912 Sch.1 para.14

Sch.6 para.6A, repealed: 2008 c.4 s.6, Sch.28 Part 1

Sch.6 para.7, repealed: 2008 c.4 s.6, Sch.28 Part 1

Sch.6 para.8, repealed: 2008 c.4 s.6, Sch.28 Part 1

CAP.

2000–cont.

6. Powers of Criminal Courts (Sentencing) Act 2000–*cont.*

Sch.7 para.1, repealed: 2008 c.4 s.6, Sch.28 Part 1

Sch.7 para.2, repealed: 2008 c.4 s.6, Sch.28 Part 1

Sch.7 para.3, repealed: 2008 c.4 s.6, Sch.28 Part 1

Sch.7 para.4, repealed: 2008 c.4 s.6, Sch.28 Part 1

Sch.7 para.5, repealed: 2008 c.4 s.6, Sch.28 Part 1

Sch.7 para.6, repealed: 2008 c.4 s.6, Sch.28 Part 1

Sch.7 para.7, repealed: 2008 c.4 s.6, Sch.28 Part 1

Sch.7 para.8, repealed: 2008 c.4 s.6, Sch.28 Part 1

Sch.7 para.9, repealed: 2008 c.4 s.6, Sch.28 Part 1

Sch.7 para.10, repealed: 2008 c.4 s.6, Sch.28 Part 1

Sch.7 para.11, repealed: 2008 c.4 s.6, Sch.28 Part 1

Sch.7 para.12, repealed: 2008 c.4 s.6, Sch.28 Part 1

Sch.8, applied: 2008 c.4 Sch.27 para.2

Sch.8 para.1, amended: 2008 c.4 Sch.4 para.62, Sch.28 Part 1

Sch.8 para.1, repealed: 2008 c.4 Sch.4 para.108, Sch.28 Part 1

Sch.8 para.1, varied: 2008 c.4 Sch.27 para.2

Sch.8 para.2, amended: 2008 c.4 Sch.4 para.62, Sch.4 para.108, Sch.28 Part 1

Sch.8 para.2, repealed (in part): 2008 c.4 Sch.4 para.62, Sch.28 Part 1

Sch.8 para.3, amended: 2008 c.4 Sch.4 para.62, Sch.28 Part 1

Sch.8 para.3, repealed: 2008 c.4 Sch.4 para.62, Sch.28 Part 1

Sch.8 para.3, varied: 2008 c.4 Sch.27 para.2

Sch.8 para.4, amended: 2008 c.4 Sch.4 para.62, Sch.28 Part 1

Sch.8 para.4, repealed: 2008 c.4 Sch.4 para.62, Sch.28 Part 1

Sch.8 para.5, amended: 2008 c.4 Sch.4 para.62, Sch.4 para.108, Sch.28 Part 1

Sch.8 para.6, amended: 2008 c.4 Sch.4 para.62, Sch.4 para.108, Sch.28 Part 1

Sch.8 para.6A, added: 2008 c.4 Sch.4 para.108

Sch.8 para.6A, amended: 2008 c.4 Sch.4 para.62, Sch.28 Part 1

Sch.8 para.7, amended: 2008 c.4 Sch.4 para.62, Sch.28 Part 1

Sch.9 para.1, repealed: 2008 c.4 Sch.28 Part 1

Sch.9 para.2, repealed (in part): 2008 c.4 Sch.28 Part 1

Sch.9 para.28, repealed (in part): 2008 c.4 Sch.28 Part 1

CAP.

2000–cont.

6. Powers of Criminal Courts (Sentencing) Act 2000–*cont.*

Sch.9 para.33, repealed: 2008 c.4 Sch.28 Part 1

Sch.9 para.34, repealed (in part): 2008 c.4 Sch.28 Part 1

Sch.9 para.39, repealed: 2008 c.4 Sch.28 Part 1

Sch.9 para.41, repealed: 2008 c.4 Sch.28 Part 1

Sch.9 para.42, repealed: 2008 c.4 Sch.28 Part 1

Sch.9 para.49, repealed: 2008 c.4 Sch.28 Part 1

Sch.9 para.80, repealed: 2008 c.4 Sch.28 Part 1

Sch.9 para.93, repealed (in part): 2008 c.4 Sch.28 Part 1

Sch.9 para.126, repealed (in part): 2008 c.4 Sch.28 Part 1

Sch.9 para.127, repealed: 2008 c.4 Sch.28 Part 1

Sch.9 para.129, repealed: 2008 c.4 Sch.28 Part 1

Sch.9 para.131, repealed: 2008 c.4 Sch.28 Part 1

Sch.9 para.132, repealed: 2008 c.4 Sch.28 Part 1

Sch.10 para.4, repealed: 2008 c.4 Sch.4 para.63, Sch.28 Part 1

Sch.10 para.5, repealed: 2008 c.4 Sch.4 para.63, Sch.28 Part 1

Sch.10 para.6, repealed: 2008 c.4 Sch.4 para.63, Sch.28 Part 1

Sch.10 para.12, repealed: 2008 c.4 Sch.4 para.63, Sch.28 Part 1

Sch.10 para.13, repealed: 2008 c.4 Sch.4 para.63, Sch.28 Part 1

Sch.10 para.14, repealed: 2008 c.4 Sch.4 para.63, Sch.28 Part 1

Sch.10 para.15, repealed: 2008 c.4 Sch.4 para.63, Sch.28 Part 1

Sch.11 Part II para.4, repealed (in part): 2008 c.4 Sch.4 para.64, Sch.28 Part 1

Sch.11 Part II para.5, repealed: 2008 c.4 Sch.4 para.64, Sch.28 Part 1

7. Electronic Communications Act 2000

applied: SSI 2008/129 Reg.5, Reg.8, SSI 2008/395 Reg.5, Reg.8

referred to: SSI 2008/64 Reg.2, SSI 2008/66 Reg.2, SSI 2008/135 Reg.2, SSI 2008/219 Art.2, SSI 2008/303 Reg.2

s.7, applied: SSI 2008/386 Reg.2

s.8, enabling: SI 2008/316, SI 2008/2334, SSI 2008/380

s.9, applied: SSI 2008/380

s.9, enabling: SSI 2008/380

s.15, applied: SSI 2008/386 Reg.2

s.15, referred to: SI 2008/653 Reg.2, SSI 2008/100 Reg.2, SSI 2008/162 Reg.2, SSI 2008/342 Reg.2

CAP.

2000–cont.

8. **Financial Services and Markets Act 2000**

applied: 2008 c.28 Sch.7 para.41, 2008 c.30 s.26, 2008 c.31 s.14, SI 2008/239 Reg.6, SI 2008/346 Reg.38, Reg.40, Reg.42, SI 2008/1816 Reg.6, SI 2008/1908 Art.2, SI 2008/1909 Art.3, SI 2008/1950 Reg.29, SI 2008/2644 Art.10, SI 2008/2674 Art.7, SSI 2008/228 Reg.5

Part IV, applied: SI 2008/239 Reg.6, SI 2008/346 Reg.9, SI 2008/629 Sch.1 para.11, SI 2008/729 Reg.4, SSI 2008/228 Reg.5

Part VI, applied: SI 2008/2860 Sch.2 para.56

Part IX, applied: SI 2008/346 Reg.40

Part X, applied: SI 2008/410 Sch.3 para.56

Part XI, applied: SI 2008/1909 Sch.1

Part XIV, applied: SI 2008/346 Reg.36

Part XV, applied: SI 2008/2546 Art.29, SI 2008/2644 Art.14, SI 2008/2674 Art.15

Part XXVI, applied: SI 2008/346 Reg.44

Part VII, see *Save & Prosper Pensions Ltd, Petitioner* 2008 S.L.T. 317 (OH), Lord Glennie; see *Standard Life Assurance Ltd v Oak Dedicated Ltd* [2008] EWHC 222 (Comm), [2008] 2 All E.R. (Comm) 916 (QBD (Comm)), Tomlinson, J.

s.19, applied: 2008 c.30 s.26

s.22, applied: SI 2008/410 Sch.3 para.7, Sch.3 para.10, SI 2008/567 Reg.3, SI 2008/700 Art.1, SI 2008/1816 Sch.3 para.8, SSI 2008/228 Reg.2, Reg.90

s.22, referred to: SI 2008/570 Art.1

s.38, enabling: SI 2008/682

s.59, applied: SI 2008/432 Art.14, SI 2008/2546 Art.15

s.89F, amended: SI 2008/3053 Art.2

s.96A, applied: SI 2008/432 Sch.1 para.4, SI 2008/2546 Art.13, SI 2008/2644 Art.26, Sch.2 para.4

s.96B, applied: SI 2008/432 Sch.1 para.4, SI 2008/2546 Art.13, SI 2008/2644 Art.26, Sch.2 para.4

s.102A, amended: SI 2008/3053 Art.3

s.105, see *Save & Prosper Pensions Ltd, Petitioner* 2008 S.L.T. 317 (OH), Lord Glennie

s.105, amended: SI 2008/948 Sch.1 para.211

s.106, amended: SI 2008/948 Sch.1 para.211

s.106A, added: 2008 c.31 Sch.2 para.2

s.107, see *Save & Prosper Pensions Ltd, Petitioner* 2008 S.L.T. 317 (OH), Lord Glennie

s.107, amended: 2008 c.31 Sch.2 para.3

s.108, enabling: SI 2008/1467

s.111, amended: 2008 c.31 Sch.2 para.4

s.112, amended: SI 2008/948 Sch.1 para.211, SI 2008/1468 Reg.2

s.112, repealed (in part): SI 2008/948 Sch.2

s.112A, added: SI 2008/1468 Reg.2

s.117, enabling: SI 2008/1468

CAP.

2000–cont.

8. **Financial Services and Markets Act 2000**–*cont.*

s.118, amended: SI 2008/1439 Reg.3

s.118A, amended: SI 2008/1439 Reg.3

s.133, varied: SI 2008/3249 Sch.1

s.134, varied: SI 2008/3249 Sch.1

s.135, varied: SI 2008/3249 Sch.1

s.136, varied: SI 2008/3249 Sch.1

s.138, varied: SI 2008/432 Art.15, SI 2008/2546 Art.37, SI 2008/2644 Art.27, SI 2008/2666 Art.18, SI 2008/2674 Art.29

s.146, applied: SI 2008/1741 Reg.112

s.148, applied: SI 2008/2546 Art.37, SI 2008/2644 Art.27, SI 2008/2666 Art.18, SI 2008/2674 Art.29

s.148, disapplied: SI 2008/2546 Art.37, SI 2008/2644 Art.27, SI 2008/2666 Art.18, SI 2008/2674 Art.29

s.148, varied: SI 2008/432 Art.15, SI 2008/2674 Art.29

s.155, applied: SI 2008/346 Reg.42

s.155, varied: SI 2008/432 Art.16, SI 2008/2546 Art.38, SI 2008/2644 Art.28, SI 2008/2666 Art.19, SI 2008/2674 Art.30

s.157, varied: SI 2008/432 Art.16, SI 2008/2546 Art.38, SI 2008/2644 Art.28, SI 2008/2666 Art.19, SI 2008/2674 Art.30

s.165, varied: SI 2008/346 Sch.1 para.3

s.166, varied: SI 2008/346 Sch.1 para.4

s.168, amended: 2008 c.28 Sch.7 para.33

s.168, applied: 2008 c.13 Sch.7

s.170, see *Secretary of State for Business Enterprise and Regulatory Reform v Aaron* [2008] EWCA Civ 1146, Times, November 10, 2008 (CA (Civ Div)), Buxton, L.J.

s.210, applied: SI 2008/346 Reg.36

s.211, applied: SI 2008/346 Reg.36

s.213, see *Beloit Walmsley Ltd, Re* [2008] EWHC 1888 (Ch), [2008] B.P.I.R. 1445 (Ch D (Manchester)), Judge Pelling Q.C.

s.219, applied: SI 2008/2546 Art.31, SI 2008/2644 Art.16, SI 2008/2666 Art.13, SI 2008/2674 Art.17

s.222, applied: SI 2008/2546 Art.32, SI 2008/2644 Art.17, SI 2008/2666 Art.14, SI 2008/2674 Art.18

s.227, applied: SI 2008/2644 Art.25

s.228, see *R. (on the application of Heather Moor & Edgecomb Ltd) v Financial Ombudsman Service* [2008] EWCA Civ 642, [2008] Bus. L.R. 1486 (CA (Civ Div)), Laws, L.J.

s.229, see *Bunney v Burns Anderson Plc* [2007] EWHC 1240 (Ch), [2008] Bus. L.R. 22 (Ch D), Lewison, J.

s.235, enabling: SI 2008/1641, SI 2008/1813

s.291, varied: SI 2008/432 Art.20, SI 2008/2546 Art.39

s.323, amended: SI 2008/1469 Reg.2

s.323, enabling: SI 2008/1725

s.348, applied: SI 2008/346 Reg.43

CAP.

2000–cont.

8. Financial Services and Markets Act 2000–*cont.*

s.349, applied: SI 2008/346 Reg.43
s.352, applied: SI 2008/346 Reg.43
s.359, amended: 2008 c.31 Sch.2 para.6
s.362, amended: SI 2008/948 Sch.1 para.211
s.365, amended: SI 2008/948 Sch.1 para.211
s.369A, added: 2008 c.31 Sch.2 para.7
s.371, amended: SI 2008/948 Sch.1 para.211
s.398, applied: SI 2008/346 Reg.38
s.400, applied: SI 2008/346 Reg.38
s.401, applied: SI 2008/346 Reg.38
s.402, amended: 2008 c.28 Sch.7 para.33
s.417, applied: SI 2008/2546 Art.13, SI 2008/2644 Art.26
s.417, referred to: SI 2008/432 Art.17
s.420, amended: SI 2008/948 Sch.1 para.212
s.421, amended: SI 2008/948 Sch.1 para.212
s.421A, added: SI 2008/948 Sch.1 para.212
s.426, enabling: SI 2008/733, SI 2008/2673
s.428, enabling: SI 2008/682, SI 2008/1467, SI 2008/1468, SI 2008/1641, SI 2008/1725, SI 2008/1813, SI 2008/2673
Sch.1 Part I, applied: 2008 c.28 Sch.7 para.41
Sch.1 Part I para.10, amended: SI 2008/948 Sch.1 para.213
Sch.1 Part II, applied: 2008 c.28 Sch.7 para.41
Sch.1 Part III para.17, varied: SI 2008/346 Sch.1 para.5
Sch.1 Part IV, applied: 2008 c.28 Sch.7 para.41
Sch.1 Part IV para.19, applied: SI 2008/346 Reg.45
Sch.2, applied: SI 2008/410 Sch.3 para.7, Sch.3 para.10, SI 2008/567 Reg.3, SI 2008/1816 Sch.3 para.8, SSI 2008/228 Reg.90
Sch.2, referred to: SI 2008/570 Art.1, SSI 2008/228 Reg.2
Sch.2 Part I para.1, amended: 2008 c.31 Sch.2 para.1
Sch.2 Part I para.2, amended: 2008 c.31 Sch.2 para.1
Sch.2 Part I para.3, amended: 2008 c.31 Sch.2 para.1
Sch.2 Part I para.4, amended: 2008 c.31 Sch.2 para.1
Sch.2 Part I para.5, amended: 2008 c.31 Sch.2 para.1
Sch.2 Part I para.6, amended: 2008 c.31 Sch.2 para.1
Sch.2 Part I para.7, amended: 2008 c.31 Sch.2 para.1
Sch.2 Part I para.8, amended: 2008 c.31 Sch.2 para.1
Sch.2 Part I para.9, amended: 2008 c.31 Sch.2 para.1
Sch.2 Part IA para.9A, added: 2008 c.31 Sch.2 para.1
Sch.3, applied: SI 2008/729 Reg.4

CAP.

2000–cont.

8. Financial Services and Markets Act 2000–*cont.*

Sch.3 Part I para.5, referred to: SI 2008/239 Reg.6, SSI 2008/228 Reg.5
Sch.3 Part II para.12, applied: SI 2008/239 Reg.6, SSI 2008/228 Reg.5
Sch.3 Part II para.15, applied: SI 2008/239 Reg.6, SSI 2008/228 Reg.5
Sch.12, see *Save & Prosper Pensions Ltd, Petitioner* 2008 S.L.T. 317 (OH), Lord Glennie
Sch.12 Part IIA para.9A, added: 2008 c.31 Sch.2 para.5
Sch.13 Part I para.1, varied: SI 2008/3249 Sch.1
Sch.13 Part II para.2, varied: SI 2008/3249 Sch.1
Sch.13 Part II para.3, varied: SI 2008/3249 Sch.1
Sch.13 Part II para.4, varied: SI 2008/3249 Sch.1
Sch.13 Part II para.5, varied: SI 2008/3249 Sch.1
Sch.13 Part II para.6, varied: SI 2008/3249 Sch.1
Sch.13 Part III para.7, varied: SI 2008/3249 Sch.1
Sch.13 Part IV para.8, varied: SI 2008/3249 Sch.1
Sch.13 Part IV para.9, varied: SI 2008/3249 Sch.1
Sch.13 Part IV para.10, varied: SI 2008/3249 Sch.1
Sch.13 Part IV para.11, varied: SI 2008/3249 Sch.1
Sch.13 Part IV para.12, varied: SI 2008/3249 Sch.1
Sch.13 Part IV para.13, varied: SI 2008/3249 Sch.1

10. Crown Prosecution Service Inspectorate Act 2000

Sch.1 para.2, amended: 2008 c.14 Sch.5 para.71, SI 2008/912 Sch.1 para.27
Sch.1 para.2, repealed (in part): 2008 c.14 Sch.5 para.71, Sch.15 Part 1
Sch.1 para.2, varied: SI 2008/2250 Art.3
Sch.1 para.4, amended: 2008 c.14 Sch.5 para.71, SI 2008/912 Sch.1 para.26
Sch.1 para.4, repealed (in part): 2008 c.14 Sch.5 para.71, Sch.15 Part 1
Sch.1 para.4, varied: SI 2008/2250 Art.3
Sch.1 para.5, amended: SI 2008/912 Sch.1 para.27

11. Terrorism Act 2000

s.1, amended: 2008 c.28 s.75
s.3, see *Secretary of State for the Home Department v Lord Alton of Liverpool* [2008] EWCA Civ 443, [2008] 1 W.L.R. 2341 (CA (Civ Div)), Lord Phillips, L.C.J.
s.3, enabling: SI 2008/1645, SI 2008/1931

CAP.

2000–cont.

11. Terrorism Act 2000–*cont.*

s.11, applied: 2008 c.28 s.28, s.41, SI 2008/1466 Art.3
s.12, applied: 2008 c.28 s.28, s.41, SI 2008/1466 Art.3
s.13, applied: 2008 c.28 s.28
s.15, applied: 2008 c.28 s.28, s.41, SI 2008/1466 Art.3
s.16, applied: 2008 c.28 s.28, s.41, SI 2008/1466 Art.3
s.17, applied: 2008 c.28 s.28, s.41, SI 2008/1466 Art.3
s.18, applied: 2008 c.28 s.28, s.41, SI 2008/1466 Art.3
s.19, see *R. (on the application of Malik) v Manchester Crown Court* [2008] EWHC 1362 (Admin), [2008] 4 All E.R. 403 (DC), Dyson, L.J.
s.19, amended: 2008 c.28 s.77
s.19, applied: 2008 c.28 s.28
s.19, varied: 2008 c.28 s.77
s.21, varied: 2008 c.28 s.77
s.21A, applied: 2008 c.28 s.28
s.21A, varied: 2008 c.28 s.77
s.21D, applied: 2008 c.28 s.28
s.22A, added: 2008 c.28 s.77
s.23, substituted: 2008 c.28 s.34
s.23A, added: 2008 c.28 s.35
s.23B, added: 2008 c.28 s.36
s.38B, see *R. (on the application of Malik) v Manchester Crown Court* [2008] EWHC 1362 (Admin), [2008] 4 All E.R. 403 (DC), Dyson, L.J.
s.38B, applied: 2008 c.28 s.28, s.41
s.39, applied: 2008 c.28 s.28
s.43, appliod: 2008 c.28 s.1
s.47, applied: 2008 c.28 s.28
s.51, applied: 2008 c.28 s.28
s.54, applied: 2008 c.28 s.28, s.41, SI 2008/1466 Art.3
s.54, repealed (in part): 2008 c.28 Sch.3 para.2, Sch.9 Part 3
s.56, applied: 2008 c.28 s.28, s.41, SI 2008/1466 Art.3
s.57, see *R. v Rahman (Abdul)* [2008] EWCA Crim 1465, [2008] 4 All E.R. 661 (CA (Crim Div)), Lord Phillips of Worth Matravers, L.C.J.; see *R. v Zafar (Aitzaz)* [2008] EWCA Crim 184, [2008] Q.B. 810 (CA (Crim Div)), Lord Phillips of Worth Matravers, L.C.J.
s.57, applied: 2008 c.28 s.28, s.41, SI 2008/1466 Art.3
s.58, see *R. v K* [2008] EWCA Crim 185, [2008] Q.B. 827 (CA (Crim Div)), Lord Phillips of Worth Matravers, L.C.J.
s.58, applied: 2008 c.28 s.28, s.41, SI 2008/1466 Art.3
s.58, repealed (in part): 2008 c.28 Sch.3 para.3, Sch.9 Part 3
s.58A, added: 2008 c.28 s.76

CAP.

2000–cont.

11. Terrorism Act 2000–*cont.*

s.58A, applied: 2008 c.28 s.28, s.41, SI 2008/1466 Art.3
s.58A, varied: 2008 c.28 s.76
s.59, applied: 2008 c.28 s.41, SI 2008/1466 Art.3
s.60, applied: 2008 c.28 s.41, SI 2008/1466 Art.3
s.61, applied: 2008 c.28 s.41, SI 2008/1466 Art.3
s.62, applied: 2008 c.28 s.41, SI 2008/1466 Art.3
s.63, applied: 2008 c.28 s.41, SI 2008/1466 Art.3
s.63A, applied: 2008 c.28 s.41
s.63B, applied: 2008 c.28 s.41
s.63C, applied: 2008 c.28 s.41
s.63D, applied: 2008 c.28 s.41
s.116, applied: 2008 c.28 s.28
s.117, amended: 2008 c.28 s.29
s.118, amended: 2008 c.28 s.76
s.119, amended: 2008 c.28 Sch.3 para.4
s.120A, substituted: 2008 c.28 s.38
s.123, amended: 2008 c.28 s.35
s.123, applied: SI 2008/1645, SI 2008/1931
Sch.2, amended: SI 2008/1645 Art.2, SI 2008/1931 Art.2
Sch.2, referred to: SI 2008/1931
Sch.3A, applied: SI 2008/2668 Sch.1, Sch.1 para.3
Sch.3 para.7, amended: 2008 c.28 s.91
Sch.3A Part I para.1, amended: SI 2008/948 Sch.1 para.25
Sch.4 Part I para.1, amended: 2008 c.28 Sch.3 para.5
Sch.4 Part I para.2, amended: 2008 c.28 Sch.3 para.5
Sch.4 Part I para.4, amended: 2008 c.28 Sch.3 para.5
Sch.4 Part I para.4A, added: 2008 c.28 s.37
Sch.4 Part I para.5, amended: 2008 c.28 Sch.3 para.5
Sch.4 Part I para.6, amended: 2008 c.28 Sch.3 para.5
Sch.4 Part I para.9, amended: 2008 c.28 Sch.3 para.5
Sch.4 Part I para.9, repealed: 2008 c.28 Sch.3 para.5
Sch.4 Part I para.10, amended: 2008 c.28 Sch.3 para.5
Sch.4 Part I para.10, repealed: 2008 c.28 Sch.3 para.5
Sch.4 Part I para.12, amended: 2008 c.28 Sch.3 para.5
Sch.4 Part II para.15, amended: 2008 c.28 Sch.3 para.5
Sch.4 Part II para.16, amended: 2008 c.28 Sch.3 para.5
Sch.4 Part II para.17A, added: 2008 c.28 s.37
Sch.4 Part II para.18, amended: 2008 c.28 Sch.3 para.5

CAP.

2000–*cont.*

11. Terrorism Act 2000–*cont.*

Sch.4 Part II para.19, amended: 2008 c.28 Sch.3 para.5
Sch.4 Part II para.23, amended: 2008 c.28 Sch.3 para.5
Sch.4 Part II para.23, repealed: 2008 c.28 Sch.3 para.5
Sch.4 Part II para.24, amended: 2008 c.28 Sch.3 para.5
Sch.4 Part II para.24, repealed: 2008 c.28 Sch.3 para.5
Sch.4 Part II para.26, amended: 2008 c.28 Sch.3 para.5
Sch.4 Part III para.29, amended: 2008 c.28 Sch.3 para.5
Sch.4 Part III para.30, amended: 2008 c.28 Sch.3 para.5
Sch.4 Part III para.32, amended: 2008 c.28 Sch.3 para.5
Sch.4 Part III para.32A, added: 2008 c.28 s.37
Sch.4 Part III para.33, amended: 2008 c.28 Sch.3 para.5
Sch.4 Part III para.34, amended: 2008 c.28 Sch.3 para.5
Sch.4 Part III para.38, amended: 2008 c.28 Sch.3 para.5
Sch.4 Part III para.39, amended: 2008 c.28 Sch.3 para.5
Sch.4 Part III para.39, repealed: 2008 c.28 Sch.3 para.5
Sch.4 Part III para.40, amended: 2008 c.28 Sch.3 para.5
Sch.4 Part III para.40, repealed: 2008 c.28 Sch.3 para.5
Sch.4 Part III para.42, amended: 2008 c.28 Sch.3 para.5
Sch.4 Part IV para.45, amended: 2008 c.28 Sch.3 para.5
Sch.5, see *R. (on the application of Malik) v Manchester Crown Court* [2008] EWHC 1362 (Admin), [2008] 4 All E.R. 403 (DC), Dyson, L.J.
Sch.5 Part I para.1, applied: 2008 c.28 s.1
Sch.5 Part I para.3, applied: 2008 c.28 s.1
Sch.5 Part I para.11, applied: 2008 c.28 s.1
Sch.5 Part I para.15, applied: 2008 c.28 s.1
Sch.5 Part II para.28, applied: 2008 c.28 s.1
Sch.5 Part II para.31, applied: 2008 c.28 s.1
Sch.5 para.5, see *R. (on the application of Malik) v Manchester Crown Court* [2008] EWHC1362 (Admin), [2008] 4 All E.R. 403 (DC), Dyson, L.J.
Sch.5 para.6, see *R. (on the application of Malik) v Manchester Crown Court* [2008] EWHC1362 (Admin), [2008] 4 All E.R. 403 (DC), Dyson, L.J.
Sch.6 para.1, applied: 2008 c.28 s.28
Sch.7 para.18, applied: 2008 c.28 s.28
Sch.8 Part I para.8, amended: 2008 c.28 Sch.3 para.6

CAP.

2000–*cont.*

11. Terrorism Act 2000–*cont.*

Sch.8 Part I para.9, amended: 2008 c.28 s.82
Sch.8 Part I para.14, amended: 2008 c.28 s.16
Sch.8 Part I para.14, applied: 2008 c.28 s.18
Sch.8 Part I para.14, repealed (in part): 2008 c.28 s.16, Sch.9 Part 1
Sch.8 Part I para.17, amended: 2008 c.28 Sch.3 para.6
Sch.8 Part I para.20, amended: 2008 c.28 s.17
Sch.8 Part I para.20, applied: 2008 c.28 s.18
Sch.8 Part I para.21, added: 2008 c.28 s.17
Sch.8 Part III para.29, amended: 2008 c.28 s.82, Sch.9 Part 6
Sch.8 Part III para.34, amended: 2008 c.28 Sch.3 para.6
Sch.8 para.7, see *R. v Ibrahim (Muktar)* [2008] EWCA Crim 880, [2008] 4 All E.R. 208 (CA (Crim Div)), Sir Igor Judge (President, QB)
Sch.8 para.9, see *R. v Ibrahim (Muktar)* [2008] EWCA Crim 880, [2008] 4 All E.R. 208 (CA (Crim Div)), Sir Igor Judge (President, QB)
Sch.8A para.1, added: 2008 c.28 Sch.8
Sch.8A para.2, added: 2008 c.28 Sch.8
Sch.8A para.3, added: 2008 c.28 Sch.8
Sch.8A para.4, added: 2008 c.28 Sch.8
Sch.8A para.5, added: 2008 c.28 Sch.8
Sch.8A para.6, added: 2008 c.28 Sch.8
Sch.8A para.7, added: 2008 c.28 Sch.8

12. Limited Liability Partnerships Act 2000

applied: SI 2008/1715 Reg.4, Reg.6, SI 2008/1750 Sch.1 para.1
s.15, enabling: SI 2008/497, SI 2008/1911, SI 2008/1912, SI 2008/1913
s.17, applied: SI 2008/497, SI 2008/1911, SI 2008/1912, SI 2008/1913
s.17, enabling: SI 2008/1911, SI 2008/1912, SI 2008/1913

14. Care Standards Act 2000

applied: 2008 c.4 Sch.1 para.20, 2008 c.14 s.8, Sch.9 para.8, 2008 c.17 s.77, 2008 c.25 s.123
referred to: 2008 c.14 Sch.9 para.3, SI 2008/170 Reg.4
Part II, applied: 2008 c.14 s.17, SI 2008/1976 Reg.3, SI 2008/2252 Sch.1 para.21, SI 2008/3239 Reg.23
Part II, see *Welsh Ministers v Care Standards Tribunal* [2008] EWHC 49 (Admin), [2008] 1 W.L.R. 2097 (QBD (Admin)), Davis, J.
s.1, amended: 2008 c.14 Sch.5 para.2
s.1, referred to: 2008 c.25 s.123
s.2, amended: 2008 c.14 Sch.5 para.3
s.2, enabling: SI 2008/2352
s.3, amended: 2008 c.14 Sch.5 para.4
s.4, amended: 2008 c.14 Sch.5 para.5, 2008 c.23 s.4

CAP.

2000–cont.

14. Care Standards Act 2000–*cont.*

s.5, amended: 2008 c.14 Sch.5 para.6, 2008 c.23 s.4, Sch.4
s.5A, repealed: 2008 c.14 Sch.5 para.7, Sch.15 Part 1
s.5B, repealed: 2008 c.14 Sch.5 para.7, Sch.15 Part 1
s.8, amended: 2008 c.14 Sch.5 para.8, Sch.15 Part 1
s.10, repealed (in part): 2008 c.14 Sch.5 para.9, Sch.15 Part 1
s.11, amended: 2008 c.14 Sch.5 para.10, Sch.15 Part 1
s.11, repealed (in part): 2008 c.14 Sch.5 para.10, Sch.15 Part 1
s.11, varied: SI 2008/1976 Sch.1
s.12, amended: 2008 c.14 Sch.5 para.11
s.12, varied: SI 2008/1976 Sch.1
s.12, enabling: SI 2008/1976
s.13, varied: SI 2008/1976 Sch.1
s.14, amended: 2008 c.14 Sch.5 para.12, 2008 c.23 s.26
s.14, applied: SI 2008/1976 Reg.11, SI 2008/2252 Sch.1 para.21
s.14, varied: SI 2008/1976 Sch.1
s.14, enabling: SI 2008/1976
s.14A, added: 2008 c.14 Sch.5 para.13
s.14A, varied: SI 2008/1976 Sch.1
s.15, amended: 2008 c.14 Sch.5 para.14
s.15, applied: SI 2008/2252 Sch.1 para.21
s.15, varied: SI 2008/1976 Sch.1
s.15, enabling: SI 2008/1976
s.16, amended: 2008 c.14 Sch.5 para.15
s.16, varied: SI 2008/1976 Sch.1
s.16, enabling: SI 2008/1976
s.17, amended: 2008 c.14 Sch.5 para.16
s.17, varied: SI 2008/1976 Sch.1
s.18, varied: SI 2008/1976 Sch.1
s.19, amended: 2008 c.14 Sch.5 para.17, Sch.15 Part 1
s.19, varied: SI 2008/1976 Sch.1
s.20, amended: 2008 c.14 Sch.5 para.18
s.20, varied: SI 2008/1976 Sch.1
s.20A, added: 2008 c.14 Sch.5 para.19
s.20A, varied: SI 2008/1976 Sch.1
s.20B, added: 2008 c.14 Sch.5 para.19
s.20B, varied: SI 2008/1976 Sch.1
s.21, amended: 2008 c.14 Sch.5 para.20, Sch.15 Part 1, 2008 c.23 s.28, Sch.4
s.21, applied: SI 2008/2252 Sch.1 para.21, SI 2008/2699 Sch.1
s.21, varied: SI 2008/1976 Sch.1
s.22, amended: 2008 c.14 Sch.5 para.21, 2008 c.23 Sch.1 para.11
s.22, applied: SI 2008/2352
s.22, varied: SI 2008/1976 Sch.1
s.22, enabling: SI 2008/640, SI 2008/1976, SI 2008/2352
s.22A, added: 2008 c.23 s.26
s.22A, varied: SI 2008/1976 Sch.1

CAP.

2000–cont.

14. Care Standards Act 2000–*cont.*

s.22B, added: 2008 c.23 s.27
s.22B, varied: SI 2008/1976 Sch.1
s.23, amended: 2008 c.23 s.28
s.23, varied: SI 2008/1976 Sch.1
s.24, varied: SI 2008/1976 Sch.1
s.24A, added: 2008 c.14 Sch.5 para.22
s.24A, varied: SI 2008/1976 Sch.1
s.25, varied: SI 2008/1976 Sch.1
s.25, enabling: SI 2008/1976
s.26, amended: 2008 c.14 Sch.5 para.23
s.26, varied: SI 2008/1976 Sch.1
s.27, varied: SI 2008/1976 Sch.1
s.28, varied: SI 2008/1976 Reg.4, Sch.1
s.29, amended: 2008 c.14 Sch.5 para.24
s.29, varied: SI 2008/1976 Sch.1
s.30, varied: SI 2008/1976 Sch.1
s.30A, added: 2008 c.23 s.29
s.30A, amended: 2008 c.14 Sch.5 para.26, Sch.15 Part 1
s.30A, varied: SI 2008/1976 Sch.1
s.30ZA, added: 2008 c.14 Sch.5 para.25
s.30ZA, varied: SI 2008/1976 Sch.1
s.30ZB, added: 2008 c.14 Sch.5 para.25
s.30ZB, varied: SI 2008/1976 Sch.1
s.31, amended: 2008 c.14 Sch.5 para.27, 2008 c.23 Sch.1 para.12
s.31, varied: SI 2008/1976 Sch.1
s.32, varied: SI 2008/1976 Sch.1
s.33, varied: SI 2008/1976 Sch.1
s.34, varied: SI 2008/1976 Sch.1
s.35, varied: SI 2008/1976 Sch.1
s.36, varied: SI 2008/1976 Sch.1
s.36A, varied: SI 2008/1976 Sch.1
s.37, varied: SI 2008/1976 Sch.1
s.38, varied: SI 2008/1976 Sch.1
s.39, varied: SI 2008/1976 Sch.1
s.40, varied: SI 2008/1976 Sch.1
s.41, varied: SI 2008/1976 Sch.1
s.42, amended: 2008 c.14 Sch.5 para.28
s.42, applied: SI 2008/1976 Reg.3
s.42, repealed (in part): 2008 c.14 Sch.5 para.28, Sch.15 Part 1
s.42, varied: SI 2008/1976 Sch.1
s.42, enabling: SI 2008/1976
s.43, amended: 2008 c.23 Sch.1 para.13
s.55, amended: 2008 c.14 Sch.5 para.29, Sch.15 Part 1
s.56, applied: SI 2008/2252 Sch.1 para.26
s.58, applied: SI 2008/2699 Sch.1
s.59, applied: SI 2008/2252 Sch.1 para.26
s.67, applied: SI 2008/529 Reg.149, SI 2008/1273 Reg.92, SI 2008/1582 Reg.149, SI 2008/3170 Reg.103
s.68, applied: SI 2008/2699 Sch.1
s.71, applied: SI 2008/2252 Sch.1 para.26
s.81, applied: SI 2008/473 Art.4, SI 2008/474 Reg.8, SI 2008/2252 Sch.1 para.20

CAP.

2000–*cont.*

14. Care Standards Act 2000–*cont.*

s.82, see *Joyce v Secretary of State for Health* [2008] EWHC 1891 (Admin), (2008) 11 C.C.L. Rep. 761 (QBD (Admin)), Goldring, J.

s.86, see *Joyce v Secretary of State for Health* [2008] EWHC 1891 (Admin), (2008) 11 C.C.L. Rep. 761 (QBD (Admin)), Goldring, J.

s.86, applied: SI 2008/2699 r.19, Sch.1

s.113, repealed (in part): 2008 c.14 Sch.5 para.30, Sch.15 Part 1

s.113A, repealed: 2008 c.14 Sch.5 para.31, Sch.15 Part 1

s.118, enabling: SI 2008/640, SI 2008/1976, SI 2008/2352

s.118A, added: 2008 c.14 Sch.5 para.32

s.120, repealed (in part): 2008 c.14 Sch.5 para.33, Sch.15 Part 1

s.121, amended: 2008 c.14 Sch.5 para.34, Sch.15 Part 1, 2008 c.23 s.4, SI 2008/2833 Sch.3 para.187

Sch.4 para.21, repealed: SI 2008/2833 Sch.3 para.228

Sch.4 para.28, repealed (in part): 2008 c.4 Sch.28 Part 1

17. Finance Act 2000

s.5, repealed (in part): 2008 c.9 s.13

s.37, repealed: 2008 c.9 Sch.2 para.21

s.46, amended: 2008 c.9 Sch.14 para.17

s.66, repealed: 2008 c.9 Sch.2 para.55

s.67, repealed: 2008 c.9 Sch.2 para.55

s.136, repealed (in part): 2008 c.9 Sch.41 para.25

Sch.6, applied: 2008 c.27 Sch.4 para.3

Sch.6 Part II para.19, repealed (in part): 2008 c.9 s.149

Sch.6 Part IV para.41, enabling: SI 2008/1482, SI 2008/2693

Sch.6 Part IV para.42, amended: 2008 c.9 s.19

Sch.6 Part V para.53, applied: 2008 c.9 Sch.41 para.1

Sch.6 Part V para.55, applied: 2008 c.9 Sch.41 para.1

Sch.6 Part V para.55, repealed (in part): 2008 c.9 Sch.41 para.25

Sch.6 Part VII para.89A, repealed: 2008 c.9 Sch.43 para.7

Sch.6 Part VIII para.98, repealed: 2008 c.9 Sch.40 para.21

Sch.6 Part VIII para.99, repealed: 2008 c.9 Sch.40 para.21

Sch.6 Part VIII para.100, repealed: 2008 c.9 Sch.40 para.21

Sch.6 Part XII para.135, amended: 2008 c.9 Sch.44 para.8

Sch.6 Part XII para.135, repealed (in part): 2008 c.9 Sch.44 para.8

Sch.6 Part XIII para.143, repealed (in part): 2008 c.9 s.150

CAP.

2000–*cont.*

17. Finance Act 2000–*cont.*

Sch.6 Part XIII para.146, enabling: SI 2008/1482, SI 2008/2693

Sch.10 para.1, see *MKM Computing Ltd v Revenue and Customs Commissioners* [2008] S.T.C. (S.C.D.) 403 (Sp Comm), Charles Hellier

Sch.12, see *Dragonfly Consulting Ltd v Revenue and Customs Commissioners* [2008] EWHC 2113 (Ch), [2008] S.T.C. 3030 (Ch D), Henderson, J.; see *Dragonfly Consulting Ltd v Revenue and Customs Commissioners* [2008] S.T.C. (S.C.D.) 430 (Sp Comm), Charles Hellier; see *First Word Software Ltd v Revenue and Customs Commissioners* [2008] S.T.C. (S.C.D.) 389 (Sp Comm), AN Brice (Chairman); see *MKM Computing Ltd v Revenue and Customs Commissioners* [2008] S.T.C. (S.C.D.) 403 (Sp Comm), Charles Hellier

Sch.15 Part III para.26, amended: 2008 c.9 Sch.11 para.2

Sch.15 Part III para.30A, added: 2008 c.9 Sch.11 para.3

Sch.15 Part III para.30B, added: 2008 c.9 Sch.11 para.3

Sch.15 Part III para.30C, added: 2008 c.9 Sch.11 para.3

Sch.15 Part VI para.58, amended: SI 2008/954 Art.26

Sch.15 Part VI para.58, repealed (in part): SI 2008/954 Sch.1

Sch.20 Part I para.1, amended: 2008 c.9 Sch.10 para.8

Sch.20 Part I para.5, amended: 2008 c.9 s.27

Sch.20 Part II para.13, amended: 2008 c.9 Sch.8 para.1, Sch.9 para.1

Sch.20 Part II para.14, amended: 2008 c.9 Sch.8 para.1, Sch.9 para.1

Sch.20 Part II para.15, amended: 2008 c.9 Sch.8 para.1, Sch.9 para.1, Sch.35 para.10

Sch.20 Part II para.16, amended: 2008 c.9 Sch.8 para.1

Sch.20 Part II para.18, amended: 2008 c.9 Sch.9 para.1

Sch.20 Part II para.18A, added: 2008 c.9 Sch.9 para.1

Sch.20 Part III para.23, amended: 2008 c.9 Sch.35 para.10

Sch.22 Part IV para.29, enabling: SI 2008/2264

Sch.22 Part IV para.31, enabling: SI 2008/2264

Sch.22 Part IV para.36, enabling: SI 2008/2264

Sch.22 Part IX para.84, repealed: 2008 c.9 Sch.27 para.22

Sch.22 Part IX para.86, repealed: 2008 c.9 Sch.27 para.22

Sch.22 Part IX para.87, amended: 2008 c.9 Sch.24 para.19

CAP.

2000–cont.

17. Finance Act 2000–*cont.*

Sch.22 Part X para.94, amended: 2008 c.9 s.80, Sch.24 para.19
Sch.22 Part X para.94, referred to: 2008 c.9 s.80
Sch.22 Part X para.95, amended: 2008 c.9 s.80
Sch.22 Part X para.95, referred to: 2008 c.9 s.80
Sch.22 Part X para.97, amended: 2008 c.9 s.80
Sch.22 Part X para.97, referred to: 2008 c.9 s.80
Sch.22 Part X para.98, amended: 2008 c.9 s.80
Sch.22 Part X para.98, referred to: 2008 c.9 s.80
Sch.22 Part X para.99, amended: 2008 c.9 s.80
Sch.22 Part X para.99, referred to: 2008 c.9 s.80

19. Child Support, Pensions and Social Security Act 2000

Commencement Orders: SI 2008/2545 Art.2, Art.3, Art.4
referred to: 2008 c.6 s.56
Part II c.II, referred to: 2008 c.30 s.146
s.3, repealed: 2008 c.6 Sch.8
s.16, repealed (in part): 2008 c.6 Sch.8
s.19, repealed: 2008 c.6 Sch.8
s.28, repealed: 2008 c.6 Sch.8
s.29, enabling: SI 2008/2544
s.58, see *Secretary of State for Defence v Pensions Appeal Tribunal* [2007] EWHC 1177 (Admin), [2008] 1 All E.R. 287 (QBD (Admin)), Stanley Burnton, J.
s.62, amended: 2008 c.4 Sch.4 para.66
s.64, amended: 2008 c.4 Sch.4 para.67, SI 2008/912 Sch.1 para.15
s.69, enabling: SI 2008/637
s.70, enabling: SI 2008/1167
s.86, enabling: SI 2008/2545
Sch.3 para.11, repealed (in part): 2008 c.6 Sch.8
Sch.7 para.4, amended: SI 2008/2833 Sch.3 para.190
Sch.7 para.4, enabling: SI 2008/586, SI 2008/1082, SI 2008/2428, SI 2008/2667
Sch.7 para.6, amended: SI 2008/2833 Sch.3 para.190
Sch.7 para.6, applied: SI 2008/2685 r.21, SI 2008/2698 r.20
Sch.7 para.7, amended: SI 2008/2833 Sch.3 para.190
Sch.7 para.7, repealed (in part): SI 2008/2833 Sch.3 para.190
Sch.7 para.8, amended: SI 2008/2833 Sch.3 para.190
Sch.7 para.8, repealed (in part): SI 2008/2833 Sch.3 para.190

CAP.

2000–cont.

19. Child Support, Pensions and Social Security Act 2000–*cont.*

Sch.7 para.9, amended: SI 2008/2833 Sch.3 para.190
Sch.7 para.9, repealed (in part): SI 2008/2833 Sch.3 para.190
Sch.7 para.10, repealed (in part): SI 2008/2833 Sch.3 para.190
Sch.7 para.11, amended: SI 2008/2833 Sch.3 para.190
Sch.7 para.12, amended: SI 2008/2833 Sch.3 para.190
Sch.7 para.12, enabling: SI 2008/2667
Sch.7 para.13, amended: SI 2008/2833 Sch.3 para.190
Sch.7 para.13, enabling: SI 2008/2667
Sch.7 para.16, amended: SI 2008/2833 Sch.3 para.190
Sch.7 para.17, amended: SI 2008/2833 Sch.3 para.190
Sch.7 para.18, amended: SI 2008/2833 Sch.3 para.190
Sch.7 para.19, amended: SI 2008/2833 Sch.3 para.190
Sch.7 para.19, repealed (in part): SI 2008/2833 Sch.3 para.190
Sch.7 para.20, amended: SI 2008/2833 Sch.3 para.190
Sch.7 para.20, repealed (in part): SI 2008/2833 Sch.3 para.190
Sch.7 para.20, enabling: SI 2008/1082, SI 2008/2428, SI 2008/2667
Sch.7 para.22, repealed (in part): SI 2008/2833 Sch.3 para.228
Sch.7 para.23, amended: SI 2008/2833 Sch.3 para.190
Sch.7 para.23, enabling: SI 2008/1082, SI 2008/2428

20. Government Resources and Accounts Act 2000

s.2, applied: 2008 c.3 s.4, Sch.2 Part 1, Sch.2 Part 2, Sch.2 Part 3, 2008 c.8 s.3, Sch.2 Part 1, Sch.2 Part 2, Sch.2 Part 3, Sch.2 Part 4, Sch.2 Part 5, Sch.2 Part 6, Sch.2 Part 7, Sch.2 Part 8, Sch.2 Part 9, Sch.2 Part 10, Sch.2 Part 11, Sch.2 Part 12, Sch.2 Part 13, Sch.2 Part 14, Sch.2 Part 15, Sch.2 Part 16, Sch.2 Part 17, Sch.2 Part 18, Sch.2 Part 19, Sch.2 Part 20, Sch.2 Part 21, Sch.2 Part 22, Sch.2 Part 23, Sch.2 Part 24, Sch.2 Part 25, Sch.2 Part 26, Sch.2 Part 27, Sch.2 Part 28, Sch.2 Part 29, Sch.2 Part 30, Sch.2 Part 31, Sch.2 Part 32, Sch.2 Part 33, Sch.2 Part 34, Sch.2 Part 35, Sch.2 Part 36, Sch.2 Part 37, Sch.2 Part 38, Sch.2 Part 39, Sch.2 Part 40, Sch.2 Part 41, Sch.2 Part 42, Sch.2 Part 43, Sch.2 Part 44, Sch.2 Part 45, Sch.2 Part 46, Sch.2 Part 47, Sch.2 Part 48, Sch.2 Part 49, Sch.2 Part 50, Sch.2 Part 51, Sch.2 Part 52, Sch.2 Part 54, Sch.2 Part 55
s.5, amended: SI 2008/948 Sch.1 para.214
s.9, amended: SI 2008/948 Sch.1 para.214

CAP.

2000–cont.

20. Government Resources and Accounts Act 2000–*cont.*

s.10, applied: SI 2008/1440 Art.2, SI 2008/1907 Art.2

s.10, enabling: SI 2008/1440, SI 2008/1907

s.25, applied: SI 2008/817

s.25, enabling: SI 2008/817

21. Learning and Skills Act 2000

s.2, amended: 2008 c.25 s.82

s.3, amended: 2008 c.25 s.82, s.86

s.3, referred to: SI 2008/119 Art.2

s.4, substituted: 2008 c.25 s.82

s.4A, added: 2008 c.25 s.86

s.4B, added: 2008 c.25 s.86

s.4C, added: 2008 c.25 s.86

s.6, amended: 2008 c.25 Sch.1 para.76

s.7, applied: SI 2008/228 Reg.23, Sch.4 para.1

s.13, amended: 2008 c.25 s.86, Sch.1 para.76

s.13, applied: 2008 c.25 s.4, s.47

s.18A, enabling: SI 2008/741

s.24B, applied: SI 2008/118 Reg.2, SI 2008/119 Art.2

s.24B, enabling: SI 2008/118, SI 2008/119

s.35, amended: 2008 c.25 Sch.1 para.76

s.41, amended: 2008 c.25 Sch.1 para.76

s.98, amended: 2008 c.25 s.159

s.98, repealed (in part): 2008 c.25 s.159, Sch.2

s.99, amended: 2008 c.25 s.160

s.99, repealed (in part): 2008 c.25 s.160, Sch.2

s.114, repealed (in part): 2008 c.25 s.79, Sch.2, Sch.2

s.115, amended: SI 2008/912 Sch.1 para.16

s.115, repealed: 2008 c.25 s.79, Sch.2

s.116, applied: SI 2008/228 Sch.1 para.19

s.116, repealed: 2008 c.25 s.79, Sch.2

s.117, repealed: 2008 c.25 s.79, Sch.2

s.118, repealed: 2008 c.25 s.79, Sch.2

s.119, repealed: 2008 c.25 s.79, Sch.2

s.120, amended: SI 2008/912 Sch.1 para.16

s.120, repealed: 2008 c.25 s.79, Sch.2

s.121, repealed: 2008 c.25 s.79, Sch.2

s.125, amended: SI 2008/912 Sch.1 para.16

s.138, amended: SI 2008/912 Sch.1 para.16

s.139A, added: 2008 c.25 s.80

s.139B, added: 2008 c.25 s.80

s.139C, added: 2008 c.25 s.80

s.140, amended: 2008 c.25 Sch.1 para.77

s.140, repealed (in part): 2008 c.25 Sch.2

s.152, amended: 2008 c.25 s.86

s.152, applied: SI 2008/741

Sch.1A Part I para.1, added: 2008 c.25 s.86

Sch.1A Part I para.2, added: 2008 c.25 s.86

Sch.1A Part II para.3, added: 2008 c.25 s.86

Sch.1A Part II para.4, added: 2008 c.25 s.86

Sch.1A Part II para.5, added: 2008 c.25 s.86

Sch.1A Part II para.6, added: 2008 c.25 s.86

Sch.1A Part II para.7, added: 2008 c.25 s.86

CAP.

2000–cont.

21. Learning and Skills Act 2000–*cont.*

Sch.1A Part II para.8, added: 2008 c.25 s.86

Sch.1A Part II para.9, added: 2008 c.25 s.86

Sch.9 para.59, repealed (in part): 2008 c.02 Sch.2

22. Local Government Act 2000

applied: SI 2008/490 Art.8, SI 2008/493 Art.8, Art.11, SI 2008/494 Art.8, Art.11

Part I, applied: 2008 c.13 Sch.3

Part II, applied: SI 2008/634 Art.7, SI 2008/907 Art.16, SI 2008/1085 Reg.4, SI 2008/1848 Reg.10, Reg.13

Part III, applied: SI 2008/788 Art.6, SI 2008/1085 Reg.19

s.1, enabling: SI 2008/3095

s.2, see *R. (on the application of Hill) v Bedfordshire CC* [2007] EWHC 2435 (Admin), [2008] E.L.R. 191 (QBD (Admin)), Wyn Williams, J.

s.2, applied: SI 2008/239 Sch.2 para.22, SI 2008/3095 Art.4, Sch.1 para.4

s.4, applied: 2008 c.17 s.126, SI 2008/2867 Reg.13

s.7, disapplied: SI 2008/493 Art.13

s.10, applied: SI 2008/907 Art.18

s.10, varied: SI 2008/634 Art.7, SI 2008/907 Art.16, SI 2008/2113 Reg.10

s.11, applied: SI 2008/634 Art.19

s.11, referred to: SI 2008/907 Art.18

s.11, varied: SI 2008/634 Art.7, SI 2008/907 Art.16, SI 2008/2113 Reg.10

s.12, varied: SI 2008/634 Art.7, SI 2008/907 Art.16, SI 2008/2113 Reg.10

s.13, applied: SI 2008/907 Art.21

s.13, varied: SI 2008/490 Art.8, SI 2008/491 Art.8, SI 2008/492 Art.8, SI 2008/493 Art.8, SI 2008/494 Art.8, SI 2008/634 Art.7, SI 2008/907 Art.9, Art.16, SI 2008/2113 Reg.10

s.13, enabling: SI 2008/516, SI 2008/744, SI 2008/1430, SI 2008/2787

s.14, varied: SI 2008/634 Art.7, SI 2008/907 Art.7, Art.9, Art.16, SI 2008/2113 Reg.10

s.15, varied: SI 2008/490 Art.6, Art.8, SI 2008/491 Art.6, Art.8, SI 2008/492 Art.6, Art.8, SI 2008/493 Art.6, Art.8, Art.11, SI 2008/494 Art.6, Art.8, Art.11, SI 2008/634 Art.7, SI 2008/907 Art.16, SI 2008/2113 Reg.10

s.16, varied: SI 2008/634 Art.7, SI 2008/907 Art.16, SI 2008/2113 Reg.10

s.17, varied: SI 2008/634 Art.7, SI 2008/907 Art.16, SI 2008/2113 Reg.10

s.18, varied: SI 2008/634 Art.7, SI 2008/907 Art.16, SI 2008/2113 Reg.10

s.19, varied: SI 2008/634 Art.7, SI 2008/907 Art.16, SI 2008/2113 Reg.10

s.20, varied: SI 2008/634 Art.7, SI 2008/907 Art.16, SI 2008/2113 Reg.10

CAP.

2000–cont.

22. Local Government Act 2000–*cont.*

s.21, disapplied: SI 2008/490 Art.8, SI 2008/491 Art.8, SI 2008/492 Art.8, SI 2008/494 Art.8

s.21, varied: SI 2008/493 Art.8, SI 2008/634 Art.7, SI 2008/907 Art.9, Art.16, SI 2008/2113 Reg.10

s.21A, applied: SI 2008/3261 Art.1, Art.2

s.21A, varied: SI 2008/634 Art.7, SI 2008/907 Art.16, SI 2008/2113 Reg.10

s.21A, enabling: SI 2008/3261

s.21B, varied: SI 2008/634 Art.7, SI 2008/907 Art.16, SI 2008/2113 Reg.10

s.21C, varied: SI 2008/634 Art.7, SI 2008/907 Art.16, SI 2008/2113 Reg.10

s.21D, varied: SI 2008/634 Art.7, SI 2008/907 Art.16, SI 2008/2113 Reg.10

s.21E, varied: SI 2008/634 Art.7, SI 2008/907 Art.16, SI 2008/2113 Reg.10

s.22, varied: SI 2008/634 Art.7, SI 2008/907 Art.16, SI 2008/2113 Reg.10

s.22A, varied: SI 2008/634 Art.7, SI 2008/907 Art.16, SI 2008/2113 Reg.10

s.23, varied: SI 2008/634 Art.7, SI 2008/907 Art.16, SI 2008/2113 Reg.10

s.24, varied: SI 2008/634 Art.7, SI 2008/907 Art.16, SI 2008/2113 Reg.10

s.25, applied: SI 2008/907 Art.16, SI 2008/1848 Reg.4, Reg.10, Reg.13

s.25, varied: SI 2008/907 Art.16, SI 2008/2113 Reg.10

s.26, applied: SI 2008/907 Art.16

s.26, varied: SI 2008/907 Art.16, SI 2008/2113 Reg.10

s.27, applied: SI 2008/907 Art.16, SI 2008/1848 Reg.10, Reg.13

s.27, varied: SI 2008/907 Art.16, SI 2008/1848 Reg.10, Reg.13, SI 2008/2113 Reg.10

s.28, applied: SI 2008/907 Art.16

s.28, varied: SI 2008/907 Art.16, SI 2008/2113 Reg.10

s.29, applied: SI 2008/907 Art.16, SI 2008/1848 Reg.12, Reg.13

s.29, varied: SI 2008/907 Art.16, SI 2008/1848 Reg.13, SI 2008/2113 Reg.10

s.30, applied: SI 2008/1848 Reg.4

s.30, varied: SI 2008/634 Art.7, SI 2008/907 Art.16, SI 2008/2113 Reg.10

s.31, varied: SI 2008/634 Art.7, SI 2008/907 Art.16, SI 2008/2113 Reg.10

s.32, varied: SI 2008/634 Art.7, SI 2008/907 Art.16, SI 2008/2113 Reg.10

s.33, applied: SI 2008/1848 Reg.4, Reg.12, Reg.13

s.33, varied: SI 2008/634 Art.7, SI 2008/907 Art.16, SI 2008/2113 Reg.10

s.33A, varied: SI 2008/634 Art.7, SI 2008/907 Art.16, SI 2008/2113 Reg.10

s.33B, varied: SI 2008/634 Art.7, SI 2008/907 Art.16, SI 2008/2113 Reg.10

CAP.

2000–cont.

22. Local Government Act 2000–*cont.*

s.33C, varied: SI 2008/634 Art.7, SI 2008/907 Art.16, SI 2008/2113 Reg.10

s.33D, varied: SI 2008/634 Art.7, SI 2008/907 Art.16, SI 2008/2113 Reg.10

s.33E, varied: SI 2008/634 Art.7, SI 2008/907 Art.16, SI 2008/2113 Reg.10

s.33F, varied: SI 2008/634 Art.7, SI 2008/907 Art.16, SI 2008/2113 Reg.10

s.33G, disapplied: SI 2008/2867 Reg.29

s.33G, varied: SI 2008/634 Art.7, SI 2008/907 Art.16, SI 2008/2113 Reg.10, SI 2008/2867 Reg.29

s.33H, varied: SI 2008/634 Art.7, SI 2008/907 Art.16, SI 2008/2113 Reg.10

s.33I, varied: SI 2008/634 Art.7, SI 2008/907 Art.16, SI 2008/2113 Reg.10

s.33J, varied: SI 2008/634 Art.7, SI 2008/907 Art.16, SI 2008/2113 Reg.10

s.33K, varied: SI 2008/634 Art.7, SI 2008/907 Art.16, SI 2008/2113 Reg.10

s.33L, varied: SI 2008/634 Art.7, SI 2008/907 Art.16, SI 2008/2113 Reg.10

s.33M, varied: SI 2008/634 Art.7, SI 2008/907 Art.16, SI 2008/2113 Reg.10

s.33N, varied: SI 2008/634 Art.7, SI 2008/907 Art.16, SI 2008/2113 Reg.10

s.33O, varied: SI 2008/634 Art.7, SI 2008/907 Art.16, SI 2008/2113 Reg.10

s.33P, varied: SI 2008/634 Art.7, SI 2008/907 Art.16, SI 2008/2113 Reg.10

s.34, varied: SI 2008/634 Art.7, SI 2008/907 Art.16, SI 2008/2113 Reg.10

s.35, varied: SI 2008/634 Art.7, SI 2008/907 Art.16, SI 2008/2113 Reg.10

s.36, applied: SI 2008/1848 Reg.4

s.36, varied: SI 2008/634 Art.7, SI 2008/907 Art.16, SI 2008/2113 Reg.10

s.37, varied: SI 2008/634 Art.7, SI 2008/907 Art.16, SI 2008/2113 Reg.10

s.38, applied: SI 2008/1848 Reg.4

s.38, varied: SI 2008/634 Art.7, SI 2008/907 Art.16, SI 2008/2113 Reg.10

s.39, varied: SI 2008/634 Art.7, SI 2008/907 Art.16, SI 2008/2113 Reg.10

s.39, enabling: SI 2008/3112

s.40, referred to: SI 2008/907 Art.12

s.40, varied: SI 2008/634 Art.7, SI 2008/907 Art.16, SI 2008/2113 Reg.10

s.41, varied: SI 2008/634 Art.7, SI 2008/907 Art.16, SI 2008/2113 Reg.10

s.42, varied: SI 2008/634 Art.7, SI 2008/907 Art.16, SI 2008/2113 Reg.10

s.43, varied: SI 2008/634 Art.7, SI 2008/907 Art.16, SI 2008/2113 Reg.10

s.44, varied: SI 2008/634 Art.7, SI 2008/907 Art.16, SI 2008/2113 Reg.10

s.44A, applied: SI 2008/2867 Reg.30

s.44A, varied: SI 2008/634 Art.7, SI 2008/907 Art.16, SI 2008/2113 Reg.10

CAP.

2000–cont.

22. Local Government Act 2000–*cont.*

s.44B, varied: SI 2008/634 Art.7, SI 2008/907 Art.16, SI 2008/2113 Reg.10
s.44C, varied: SI 2008/634 Art.7, SI 2008/907 Art.16, SI 2008/2113 Reg.10
s.44D, varied: SI 2008/634 Art.7, SI 2008/907 Art.16, SI 2008/2113 Reg.10
s.44E, varied: SI 2008/634 Art.7, SI 2008/907 Art.16, SI 2008/2113 Reg.10
s.44F, varied: SI 2008/634 Art.7, SI 2008/907 Art.16, SI 2008/2113 Reg.10
s.44G, varied: SI 2008/634 Art.7, SI 2008/907 Art.16, SI 2008/2113 Reg.10
s.44H, varied: SI 2008/634 Art.7, SI 2008/907 Art.16, SI 2008/2113 Reg.10
s.45, varied: SI 2008/634 Art.7, SI 2008/907 Art.16, SI 2008/2113 Reg.10
s.45, enabling: SI 2008/1848
s.46, varied: SI 2008/634 Art.7, SI 2008/907 Art.16, SI 2008/2113 Reg.10
s.47, varied: SI 2008/634 Art.7, SI 2008/907 Art.16, SI 2008/2113 Reg.10
s.48, varied: SI 2008/634 Art.7, SI 2008/907 Art.16, SI 2008/2113 Reg.10
s.49, applied: SI 2008/788, SI 2008/788 Sch.1
s.49, varied: SI 2008/634 Art.7, SI 2008/907 Art.16
s.50, applied: SI 2008/788, SI 2008/788 Art.3
s.50, varied: SI 2008/634 Art.7, SI 2008/907 Art.16
s.50, enabling: SI 2008/788
s.51, applied: SI 2008/634 Art.7, Art.20, SI 2008/788 Art.6, SI 2008/907 Art.18
s.51, referred to: SI 2008/634 Art.7
s.51, varied: SI 2008/634 Art.7, SI 2008/907 Art.16
s.52, applied: SI 2008/929 Art.1
s.52, varied: SI 2008/634 Art.7, SI 2008/907 Art.16
s.53, varied: SI 2008/634 Art.7, SI 2008/907 Art.16
s.53, enabling: SI 2008/1085
s.54, varied: SI 2008/634 Art.7, SI 2008/907 Art.16
s.54, enabling: SI 2008/1085
s.54A, applied: SI 2008/1085 Reg.6
s.54A, varied: SI 2008/634 Art.7, SI 2008/907 Art.16
s.54A, enabling: SI 2008/1085
s.55, varied: SI 2008/634 Art.7, SI 2008/907 Art.16
s.55, enabling: SI 2008/1085
s.56, applied: SI 2008/788 Sch.1
s.56, varied: SI 2008/634 Art.7, SI 2008/907 Art.16
s.56A, varied: SI 2008/634 Art.7, SI 2008/907 Art.16
s.57, varied: SI 2008/634 Art.7, SI 2008/907 Art.16

CAP.

2000–cont.

22. Local Government Act 2000–*cont.*

s.57A, applied: SI 2008/1085 Reg.6, Reg.7, Reg.8, Reg.10, Reg.13, Reg.14, Reg.16, SI 2008/2938 Reg.5
s.57A, referred to: SI 2008/1085 Reg.7
s.57A, varied: SI 2008/634 Art.7, SI 2008/907 Art.16
s.57B, applied: SI 2008/1085 Reg.6, Reg.7, Reg.8
s.57B, referred to: SI 2008/1085 Reg.7
s.57B, varied: SI 2008/634 Art.7, SI 2008/907 Art.16
s.57C, applied: SI 2008/1085 Reg.8
s.57C, referred to: SI 2008/1085 Reg.11
s.57C, varied: SI 2008/634 Art.7, SI 2008/907 Art.16
s.57C, enabling: SI 2008/1085
s.57D, varied: SI 2008/634 Art.7, SI 2008/907 Art.16
s.58, varied: SI 2008/634 Art.7, SI 2008/907 Art.16
s.58, applied: SI 2008/1085 Reg.8
s.58, varied: SI 2008/634 Art.7, SI 2008/907 Art.16
s.59, varied: SI 2008/634 Art.7, SI 2008/907 Art.16
s.60, applied: SI 2008/1085 Reg.13, Reg.14
s.60, varied: SI 2008/634 Art.7, SI 2008/907 Art.16
s.61, varied: SI 2008/634 Art.7, SI 2008/907 Art.16
s.62, varied: SI 2008/634 Art.7, SI 2008/907 Art.16
s.63, applied: SI 2008/1085 Reg.12
s.63, varied: SI 2008/634 Art.7, SI 2008/907 Art.16, SI 2008/1085 Reg.12
s.64, applied: SI 2008/1085 Reg.15, Reg.17, Reg.18, SI 2008/2938 Reg.5
s.64, varied: SI 2008/634 Art.7, SI 2008/907 Art.16
s.64, enabling: SI 2008/2938
s.65, applied: SI 2008/2938 Reg.5
s.65, varied: SI 2008/634 Art.7, SI 2008/907 Art.16
s.65, enabling: SI 2008/2938
s.65A, varied: SI 2008/634 Art.7, SI 2008/907 Art.16
s.66, varied: SI 2008/634 Art.7, SI 2008/907 Art.16
s.66, enabling: SI 2008/1085
s.66A, varied: SI 2008/634 Art.7, SI 2008/907 Art.16
s.66B, varied: SI 2008/634 Art.7, SI 2008/907 Art.16
s.66C, varied: SI 2008/634 Art.7, SI 2008/907 Art.16
s.67, varied: SI 2008/634 Art.7, SI 2008/907 Art.16
s.68, varied: SI 2008/634 Art.7, SI 2008/907 Art.16

CAP.

2000–cont.

22. Local Government Act 2000–*cont.*

s.69, varied: SI 2008/634 Art.7, SI 2008/907 Art.16
s.70, varied: SI 2008/634 Art.7, SI 2008/907 Art.16
s.71, varied: SI 2008/634 Art.7, SI 2008/907 Art.16
s.72, varied: SI 2008/634 Art.7, SI 2008/907 Art.16
s.73, varied: SI 2008/634 Art.7, SI 2008/907 Art.16
s.73, enabling: SI 2008/1085
s.74, varied: SI 2008/634 Art.7, SI 2008/907 Art.16
s.75, varied: SI 2008/634 Art.7, SI 2008/907 Art.16
s.76, varied: SI 2008/634 Art.7, SI 2008/907 Art.16
s.77, varied: SI 2008/634 Art.7, SI 2008/907 Art.16
s.77, enabling: SI 2008/2938
s.78, varied: SI 2008/634 Art.7, SI 2008/907 Art.16
s.78A, applied: SI 2008/2252 Sch.1 para.17, SI 2008/2938 Reg.3, Reg.4
s.78A, varied: SI 2008/634 Art.7, SI 2008/907 Art.16
s.78A, enabling: SI 2008/2938
s.78B, applied: SI 2008/2938 Reg.4
s.78B, varied: SI 2008/634 Art.7, SI 2008/907 Art.16
s.79, applied: SI 2008/2252 Sch.1 para.17
s.79, varied: SI 2008/634 Art.7, SI 2008/907 Art.16
s.80, varied: SI 2008/634 Art.7, SI 2008/907 Art.16
s.81, applied: SI 2008/788 Sch.1
s.81, varied: SI 2008/634 Art.7, SI 2008/907 Art.16
s.81, enabling: SI 2008/788
s.82, varied: SI 2008/634 Art.7, SI 2008/907 Art.16
s.82A, varied: SI 2008/634 Art.7, SI 2008/907 Art.16
s.83, varied: SI 2008/634 Art.7, SI 2008/907 Art.16
s.93, referred to: SI 2008/2114 Art.2
s.94, referred to: SI 2008/2101 Art.3
s.95, referred to: SI 2008/2101 Art.3
s.100, applied: SI 2008/788 Sch.1
s.101, applied: SI 2008/907 Art.20
s.105, enabling: SI 2008/516, SI 2008/744, SI 2008/788, SI 2008/1085, SI 2008/1430, SI 2008/1848, SI 2008/2787, SI 2008/2938, SI 2008/3095
s.106, enabling: SI 2008/1848
Sch.4, applied: SI 2008/48 Reg.3, Reg.5
Sch.4 para.1, referred to: SI 2008/48 Reg.5
Sch.4 para.5, disapplied: SI 2008/2867 Reg.29

CAP.

2000–cont.

23. Regulation of Investigatory Powers Act 2000

see *A v B (Investigatory Powers Tribunal: Jurisdiction)* [2008] EWHC 1512 (Admin), [2008] 4 All E.R. 511 (QBD (Admin)), Collins, J.
Part I, applied: 2008 c.13 s.70, 2008 c.28 s.20
Part II, applied: SI 2008/212 Reg.3
s.5, applied: SI 2008/648 Sch.1
s.15, referred to: SI 2008/648 Sch.1
s.17, see *A v HM Treasury* [2008] EWCA Civ 1187, Times, November 12, 2008 (CA (Civ Div)), Sir Anthony Clarke, M.R.
s.17, applied: SI 2008/635 Art.3, Art.12, Art.13
s.18, amended: 2008 c.28 s.69, s.74
s.49, see *R. v S* [2008] EWCA Crim 2177, Times, October 15, 2008 (CA (Crim Div)), Sir Igor Judge (President, QB)
s.53, see *R. v S* [2008] EWCA Crim 2177, Times, October 15, 2008 (CA (Crim Div)), Sir Igor Judge (President, QB)
s.65, see *A v B (Investigatory Powers Tribunal: Jurisdiction)* [2008] EWHC 1512 (Admin), [2008] 4 All E.R. 511 (QBD (Admin)), Collins, J.
s.66, see *A v B (Investigatory Powers Tribunal: Jurisdiction)* [2008] EWHC 1512 (Admin), [2008] 4 All E.R. 511 (QBD (Admin)), Collins, J.
s.81, applied: 2008 c.28 s.21
Sch.1 Part I para.20F, substituted: 2008 c.14 Sch.5 para.72

26. Postal Services Act 2000

s.72, amended: SI 2008/948 Sch.1 para.215
s.73, amended: SI 2008/948 Sch.1 para.216
s 77, amended: SI 2008/948 Sch.1 para.217
s.80, amended: SI 2008/948 Sch.3 para.15
s.125, referred to: 2008 c.14 s.93
Sch.7 para.3, amended: SI 2008/960 Sch.3, SI 2008/1277 Sch.2 para.60

27. Utilities Act 2000

Part I, applied: SI 2008/2375 Reg.3, SI 2008/2376 Reg.3
s.3, applied: 2008 c.32 s.92, s.95
s.33, amended: 2008 c.32 Sch.5 para.13, Sch.6
s.33, applied: SI 2008/1163 Reg.2, Reg.3, SI 2008/2376 Reg.3
s.67, amended: 2008 c.32 s.39
s.81, amended: 2008 c.32 Sch.5 para.14
s.81, applied: SI 2008/2375 Reg.3
s.103, amended: 2008 c.27 Sch.8 para.6
s.103, applied: SI 2008/188
s.103, enabling: SI 2008/188
s.105, amended: 2008 c.32 Sch.5 para.15, SI 2008/960 Sch.3, SI 2008/1277 Sch.2 para.61
s.105, repealed (in part): SI 2008/1277 Sch.4 Part 1

CAP.

2000–cont.

29. Trustee Act 2000
applied: 2008 c.30 s.68
Sch.2 Part II para.35, repealed: SI 2008/576 Sch.5 para.7
Sch.2 Part II para.36, repealed: SI 2008/576 Sch.5 para.7

32. Police (Northern Ireland) Act 2000
s.2, applied: SI 2008/2852 Sch.3 para.6

36. Freedom of Information Act 2000
see *BBC v Sugar* [2008] EWCA Civ 191, [2008] 1 W.L.R. 2289 (CA (Civ Div)), Buxton, L.J.; see *Secretary of State for the Home Department v British Union for the Abolition of Vivisection* [2008] EWCA Civ 870, Times, August 5, 2008 (CA (Civ Div)), Lord Phillips of Worth Matravers, L.C.J.
applied: 2008 c.27 s.63, s.68, Sch.1 para.26
s.1, see *Corporate Officer of the House of Commons v Information Commissioner* [2008] EWHC 1084 (Admin), Times, May 22, 2008 (DC), Sir Igor Judge (President, QB)
s.3, applied: SI 2008/432 Art.18, SI 2008/2546 Art.41, SI 2008/2644 Art.29, SI 2008/2674 Art.31
s.4, enabling: SI 2008/1271
s.7, applied: SI 2008/1967
s.7, enabling: SI 2008/1967
s.19, see *Corporate Officer of the House of Commons v Information Commissioner* [2008] EWHC 1084 (Admin), Times, May 22, 2008 (DC), Sir Igor Judge (President, QB)
s.41, see *Secretary of State for the Home Department v British Union for the Abolition of Vivisection* [2008] EWCA Civ 870, Times, August 5, 2008 (CA (Civ Div)), Lord Phillips of Worth Matravers, L.C.J.
s.44, see *Secretary of State for the Home Department v British Union for the Abolition of Vivisection* [2008] EWCA Civ 870, Times, August 5, 2008 (CA (Civ Div)), Lord Phillips of Worth Matravers, L.C.J.
s.50, see *BBC v Sugar* [2008] EWCA Civ 191, [2008] 1 W.L.R. 2289 (CA (Civ Div)), Buxton, L.J.; see *Corporate Officer of the House of Commons v Information Commissioner* [2008] EWHC 1084 (Admin), Times, May 22, 2008 (DC), Sir Igor Judge (President, QB)
s.57, see *BBC v Sugar* [2008] EWCA Civ 191, [2008] 1 W.L.R. 2289 (CA (Civ Div)), Buxton, L.J.; see *Corporate Officer of the House of Commons v Information Commissioner* [2008] EWHC 1084 (Admin), Times, May 22, 2008 (DC), Sir Igor Judge (President, QB)
s.82, applied: SI 2008/1967
Sch.1 Part I, referred to: SI 2008/1967 Art.2
Sch.1 Part I para.2, amended: SI 2008/1967 Art.2

CAP.

2000–cont.

36. Freedom of Information Act 2000– *cont.*
Sch.1 Part I para.3, amended: SI 2008/1967 Art.2
Sch.1 Part I para.5, amended: SI 2008/1967 Art.2
Sch.1 Part I para.6, amended: 2008 c.29 Sch.1 para.27
Sch.1 Part II para.28, substituted: 2008 c.26 Sch.4 para.64
Sch.1 Part VI, amended: 2008 c.6 Sch.1 para.29, 2008 c.13 Sch.1 para.19, 2008 c.14 Sch.5 para.73, Sch.10 para.13, Sch.14 para.4, Sch.15 Part 1, Sch.15 Part 2, Sch.15 Part 6, Sch.15 Part 7, 2008 c.17 Sch.8 para.77, Sch.9 para.28, Sch.16, 2008 c.27 Sch.1 para.33, 2008 c.29 Sch.1 para.27, 2008 c.30 Sch.1 para.24, SI 2008/576 Sch.5 para.5, Sch.5 para.7, SI 2008/912 Sch.1 para.17, SI 2008/960 Sch.3, SI 2008/1271 Sch.1, SI 2008/2833 Sch.3 para.188
Sch.1 Part VII, amended: SI 2008/1241 Art.4

37. Countryside and Rights of Way Act 2000
Commencement Orders: SI 2008/308 Art.2
s.86, applied: SI 2008/239 Sch.2 para.24
s.98, see *Betterment Properties (Weymouth) Ltd v Dorset CC* [2008] EWCA Civ 22, [2008] 3 All E.R. 736 (CA (Civ Div)), Laws, L.J.
s.103, enabling: SI 2008/308

38. Transport Act 2000
Part I, applied: SI 2008/1909 Sch.1
Part III, applied: 2008 c.26 s.87
Part III, referred to: 2008 c.13 Sch.6
s.48, amended: SI 2008/948 Sch.1 para.218
s.56, amended: SI 2008/948 Sch.3 para.16
s.59, amended: SI 2008/948 Sch.1 para.218
s.77, enabling: SI 2008/518
s.108, amended: 2008 c.26 s.7, s.8, s.9, Sch.4 para.42, Sch.7 Part 1
s.108, applied: 2008 c.26 s.90, s.91
s.109, amended: 2008 c.26 s.9
s.109, repealed (in part): 2008 c.26 s.9, Sch.7 Part 1
s.109C, enabling: SI 2008/1286
s.110, repealed (in part): 2008 c.26 s.10, Sch.7 Part 1
s.111, repealed (in part): 2008 c.26 s.10, Sch.7 Part 1
s.112, amended: 2008 c.26 s.10, s.11, Sch.7 Part 1
s.113, amended: 2008 c.26 s.12
s.113, repealed (in part): 2008 c.26 s.12, Sch.7 Part 1
s.113A, amended: 2008 c.26 s.10
s.113B, amended: 2008 c.26 s.10
s.114, amended: 2008 c.26 s.13
s.115, amended: 2008 c.26 s.14
s.116, amended: 2008 c.26 s.15, Sch.7 Part 2

CAP.

2000–cont.

38. Transport Act 2000–*cont.*

s.117, amended: 2008 c.26 s.16
s.117, substituted: 2008 c.26 s.16
s.118, amended: 2008 c.26 s.17
s.122, amended: 2008 c.26 s.18
s.124, amended: 2008 c.26 s.19, Sch.1 para.2, Sch.4 para.43
s.124, repealed (in part): 2008 c.26 Sch.1 para.2, Sch.7 Part 1
s.125, amended: 2008 c.26 s.20
s.125, repealed (in part): 2008 c.26 s.20, Sch.7 Part 2
s.126, amended: 2008 c.26 s.21, Sch.7 Part 2
s.126, substituted: 2008 c.26 s.21
s.126A, added: 2008 c.26 s.22
s.126B, added: 2008 c.26 s.23
s.126C, added: 2008 c.26 s.24
s.126D, added: 2008 c.26 s.24
s.126E, added: 2008 c.26 s.25
s.127, amended: 2008 c.26 s.26
s.127A, added: 2008 c.26 s.27
s.127B, added: 2008 c.26 s.27
s.128, amended: 2008 c.26 s.28
s.129, amended: 2008 c.26 s.29
s.129, repealed (in part): 2008 c.26 s.29, Sch.7 Part 2
s.130, amended: 2008 c.26 s.30
s.131A, added: 2008 c.26 s.31
s.131B, added: 2008 c.26 s.32
s.131C, added: 2008 c.26 s.33
s.131D, added: 2008 c.26 s.34
s.131E, added: 2008 c.26 s.35
s.131F, added: 2008 c.26 s.36
s.132, amended: 2008 c.26 s.37
s.132A, added: 2008 c.26 s.38
s.132B, added: 2008 c.26 s.39
s.132C, added: 2008 c.26 s.40
s.132D, added: 2008 c.26 s.40
s.133, amended: 2008 c.26 s.41
s.134, amended: 2008 c.26 s.42
s.134A, added: 2008 c.26 s.43
s.134B, added: 2008 c.26 s.44
s.135, amended: 2008 c.26 Sch.1 para.3
s.139, amended: 2008 c.26 Sch.1 para.4
s.145, applied: SI 2008/417 Reg.4
s.145A, enabling: SI 2008/417, SI 2008/2091
s.146, amended: 2008 c.26 Sch.4 para.44
s.148, referred to: 2008 c.13 Sch.6
s.153, substituted: 2008 c.26 s.46
s.155, amended: 2008 c.26 s.44, s.63, s.64, s.65
s.155, repealed (in part): 2008 c.26 s.64, Sch.7 Part 3
s.156, repealed: 2008 c.26 Sch.7 Part 4
s.157, amended: 2008 c.26 Sch.4 para.45
s.160, amended: 2008 c.26 s.64
s.160, enabling: SI 2008/417

CAP.

2000–cont.

38. Transport Act 2000–*cont.*

s.162, amended: 2008 c.26 s.7, s.10, s.15, s.22, s.26, s.27, s.32, s.40, s.46, Sch.4 para.46, Sch.7 Part 2
s.162, repealed (in part): 2008 c.26 s.12, Sch.7 Part 1
s.163, amended: 2008 c.26 s.103, Sch.5 para.2
s.164, amended: 2008 c.26 s.104
s.165, amended: 2008 c.26 s.105
s.165A, added: 2008 c.26 s.106
s.166, amended: 2008 c.26 s.107, Sch.7 Part 5
s.166A, added: 2008 c.26 s.108
s.167, amended: 2008 c.26 Sch.5 para.3
s.167, enabling: SI 2008/1951
s.168, amended: 2008 c.26 Sch.5 para.4
s.168, enabling: SI 2008/1951
s.169, amended: 2008 c.26 s.110, Sch.5 para.5
s.169, applied: SI 2008/101 Reg.16, SI 2008/540 Reg.16
s.169, repealed (in part): 2008 c.26 s.110, Sch.7 Part 5
s.170, amended: 2008 c.26 s.111, Sch.5 para.6
s.170, applied: SI 2008/1951
s.170, repealed (in part): 2008 c.26 s.111, Sch.7 Part 5
s.171, amended: 2008 c.26 s.112, Sch.7 Part 5
s.171, enabling: SI 2008/1951
s.172, amended: 2008 c.26 s.113
s.172, enabling: SI 2008/1951
s.172A, added: 2008 c.26 s.114
s.173, amended: 2008 c.26 s.115
s.174, amended: 2008 c.26 s.115
s.176, amended: 2008 c.26 s.116
s.177, amended: 2008 c.26 Sch.5 para.7
s.177A, added: 2008 c.26 s.117
s.179, amended: 2008 c.26 Sch.1 para.5
s.180, amended: 2008 c.26 Sch.1 para.6
s.181, amended: 2008 c.26 Sch.1 para.7, Sch.7 Part 1
s.193, amended: 2008 c.26 Sch.5 para.8
s.194, amended: 2008 c.26 s.118
s.197, amended: 2008 c.26 Sch.6 para.8, Sch.7 Part 5
s.198, amended: 2008 c.26 s.7, s.12, Sch.4 para.47, Sch.5 para.9, Sch.7 Part 1
s.247, enabling: SI 2008/1746
s.263, substituted: 2008 c.26 s.125
Sch.5 para.17, repealed: 2008 c.17 Sch.16
Sch.7 para.2, repealed (in part): 2008 c.9 Sch.2 para.70
Sch.9 para.3, amended: SI 2008/960 Sch.3, SI 2008/1277 Sch.2 para.62
Sch.10 para.1, amended: 2008 c.26 Sch.2 para.16
Sch.10 Part 1 para.1, added: 2008 c.26 Sch.2 para.2
Sch.10 Part 1 para.1, amended: 2008 c.26 Sch.2 para.3, Sch.2 para.16

CAP.

2000–cont.

38. Transport Act 2000–*cont.*

Sch.10 Part 1 para.1, substituted: 2008 c.26 Sch.2 para.2
Sch.10 Part 1 para.2, amended: 2008 c.26 Sch.2 para.4, Sch.2 para.16
Sch.10 Part 1 para.2, substituted: 2008 c.26 Sch.2 para.2
Sch.10 Part 1 para.3, amended: 2008 c.26 Sch.2 para.16
Sch.10 Part 1 para.3, repealed (in part): 2008 c.26 Sch.2 para.5
Sch.10 Part 1 para.3, substituted: 2008 c.26 Sch.2 para.2
Sch.10 Part 1 para.4, amended: 2008 c.26 Sch.2 para.16
Sch.10 Part 1 para.4, repealed (in part): 2008 c.26 Sch.2 para.5
Sch.10 Part 1 para.4, substituted: 2008 c.26 Sch.2 para.2
Sch.10 Part 1 para.5, amended: 2008 c.26 Sch.2 para.6, Sch.2 para.16
Sch.10 Part 1 para.5, substituted: 2008 c.26 Sch.2 para.2
Sch.10 Part 1 para.6, amended: 2008 c.26 Sch.2 para.16
Sch.10 Part 1 para.6, substituted: 2008 c.26 Sch.2 para.2
Sch.10 Part 1 para.7, amended: 2008 c.26 Sch.2 para.16
Sch.10 Part 1 para.7, substituted: 2008 c.26 Sch.2 para.2
Sch.10 Part 1 para.8, amended: 2008 c.26 Sch.2 para.16
Sch.10 Part 1 para.8, substituted: 2008 c.26 Sch.2 para.2
Sch.10 Part 1 para.9, amended: 2008 c.26 Sch.2 para.16
Sch.10 Part 1 para.9, substituted: 2008 c.26 Sch.2 para.2
Sch.10 Part 1 para.10, amended: 2008 c.26 Sch.2 para.16
Sch.10 Part 1 para.10, repealed (in part): 2008 c.26 Sch.2 para.7
Sch.10 Part 1 para.10, substituted: 2008 c.26 Sch.2 para.2
Sch.10 Part 1 para.11, amended: 2008 c.26 Sch.2 para.16
Sch.10 Part 1 para.11, repealed (in part): 2008 c.26 Sch.2 para.8
Sch.10 Part 1 para.11, substituted: 2008 c.26 Sch.2 para.2
Sch.10 Part 1 para.12, amended: 2008 c.26 Sch.2 para.9, Sch.2 para.16
Sch.10 Part 1 para.12, substituted: 2008 c.26 Sch.2 para.2
Sch.10 Part 1 para.13, amended: 2008 c.26 Sch.2 para.10, Sch.2 para.16
Sch.10 Part 1 para.13, substituted: 2008 c.26 Sch.2 para.2
Sch.10 Part 1 para.14, amended: 2008 c.26 Sch.2 para.11, Sch.2 para.16

CAP.

2000–cont.

38. Transport Act 2000–*cont.*

Sch.10 Part 1 para.14, substituted: 2008 c.26 Sch.2 para.2
Sch.10 Part 1 para.14A, added: 2008 c.26 Sch.2 para.12
Sch.10 Part 1 para.14A, amended: 2008 c.26 Sch.2 para.16
Sch.10 Part 1 para.14A, substituted: 2008 c.26 Sch.2 para.2
Sch.10 Part 1 para.15, amended: 2008 c.26 Sch.2 para.13, Sch.2 para.16
Sch.10 Part 1 para.15, substituted: 2008 c.26 Sch.2 para.2
Sch.10 Part 1 para.16, amended: 2008 c.26 Sch.2 para.14, Sch.2 para.16
Sch.10 Part 1 para.16, repealed (in part): 2008 c.26 Sch.2 para.14
Sch.10 Part 1 para.16, substituted: 2008 c.26 Sch.2 para.2
Sch.10 para.2, amended: 2008 c.26 Sch.2 para.16, Sch.7 Part 2
Sch.10 Part 2 para.17, added: 2008 c.26 Sch.2 para.15
Sch.10 Part 2 para.17, amended: 2008 c.26 Sch.2 para.16
Sch.10 Part 2 para.18, added: 2008 c.26 Sch.2 para.15
Sch.10 Part 2 para.18, amended: 2008 c.26 Sch.2 para.16
Sch.10 Part 2 para.19, added: 2008 c.26 Sch.2 para.15
Sch.10 Part 2 para.19, amended: 2008 c.26 Sch.2 para.16
Sch.10 Part 2 para.20, added: 2008 c.26 Sch.2 para.15
Sch.10 Part 2 para.20, amended: 2008 c.26 Sch.2 para.16
Sch.10 Part 2 para.21, added: 2008 c.26 Sch.2 para.15
Sch.10 Part 2 para.21, amended: 2008 c.26 Sch.2 para.16
Sch.10 Part 2 para.22, added: 2008 c.26 Sch.2 para.15
Sch.10 Part 2 para.22, amended: 2008 c.26 Sch.2 para.16
Sch.10 Part 2 para.23, added: 2008 c.26 Sch.2 para.15
Sch.10 Part 2 para.23, amended: 2008 c.26 Sch.2 para.16
Sch.10 para.3, amended: 2008 c.26 Sch.2 para.16
Sch.10 para.3, repealed (in part): 2008 c.26 Sch.7 Part 2
Sch.10 para.4, amended: 2008 c.26 Sch.2 para.16
Sch.10 para.4, repealed (in part): 2008 c.26 Sch.7 Part 2
Sch.10 para.5, amended: 2008 c.26 Sch.2 para.16
Sch.10 para.6, amended: 2008 c.26 Sch.2 para.16

CAP.

2000–cont.

38. Transport Act 2000–*cont.*

Sch.10 para.7, amended: 2008 c.26 Sch.2 para.16

Sch.10 para.8, amended: 2008 c.26 Sch.2 para.16

Sch.10 para.9, amended: 2008 c.26 Sch.2 para.16

Sch.10 para.10, amended: 2008 c.26 Sch.2 para.16

Sch.10 para.10, repealed (in part): 2008 c.26 Sch.7 Part 2

Sch.10 para.11, amended: 2008 c.26 Sch.2 para.16

Sch.10 para.11, repealed (in part): 2008 c.26 Sch.7 Part 2

Sch.10 para.12, amended: 2008 c.26 Sch.2 para.16

Sch.10 para.13, amended: 2008 c.26 Sch.2 para.16

Sch.10 para.14, amended: 2008 c.26 Sch.2 para.16

Sch.10 para.15, amended: 2008 c.26 Sch.2 para.16

Sch.10 para.16, amended: 2008 c.26 Sch.2 para.16

Sch.10 para.16, repealed (in part): 2008 c.26 Sch.7 Part 2

Sch.10 para.22, amended: 2008 c.26 Sch.2 para.16

Sch.11 para.3, repealed (in part): 2008 c.26 Sch.7 Part 1

Sch.11 para.11, repealed (in part): 2008 c.26 Sch.7 Part 1

Sch.11 para.13, repealed (in part): 2008 c.26 Sch.7 Part 3

Sch.12 para.2, amended: 2008 c.26 Sch.5 para.11

Sch.12 para.3, amended: 2008 c.26 Sch.5 para.12

Sch.12 para.7, amended: 2008 c.26 Sch.5 para.13

Sch.12 para.8, amended: 2008 c.26 Sch.1 para.8, Sch.5 para.14, Sch.6 para.2

Sch.12 para.8, repealed (in part): 2008 c.26 Sch.6 para.2, Sch.7 Part 5

Sch.12 para.9, repealed (in part): 2008 c.26 Sch.6 para.3, Sch.7 Part 5

Sch.12 para.10, amended: 2008 c.26 Sch.6 para.4

Sch.12 para.11, amended: 2008 c.26 Sch.6 para.5

Sch.12 para.11A, added: 2008 c.26 Sch.5 para.15

Sch.12 para.11B, added: 2008 c.26 Sch.5 para.15

Sch.12 para.11C, added: 2008 c.26 Sch.5 para.15

Sch.12 para.12, amended: 2008 c.26 Sch.6 para.6

Sch.12 para.12, repealed (in part): 2008 c.26 Sch.6 para.6, Sch.7 Part 5

CAP.

2000–cont.

38. Transport Act 2000–*cont.*

Sch.12 para.13, amended: 2008 c.26 Sch.6 para.7, Sch.7 Part 5

Sch.12 para.13, repealed (in part): 2008 c.26 Sch.6 para.7, Sch.7 Part 5

Sch.26 Part VII para.37, repealed: 2008 c.9 Sch.2 para.70

41. Political Parties, Elections and Referendums Act 2000

applied: 2008 c.8 Sch.2 Part 55, SI 2008/491 Art.6, SI 2008/1319 Art.5, SI 2008/1741 Reg.99

referred to: SI 2008/907 Art.7, SI 2008/1319 Art.6, SI 2008/1656 Sch.1 para.1

Part IV, applied: SI 2008/1741 Reg.105

Part IV, referred to: SI 2008/1741 Reg.99

Part IVA, applied: SI 2008/1741 Reg.105

Part IVA, referred to: SI 2008/1741 Reg.99

s.6A, applied: SI 2008/1848 Sch.3

s.6A, referred to: SI 2008/1741 Reg.72

s.6A, varied: SI 2008/1848 Sch.4 para.1

s.6B, applied: SI 2008/1848 Sch.3

s.6B, referred to: SI 2008/1741 Reg.72

s.6B, varied: SI 2008/1848 Sch.4 para.1

s.6C, applied: SI 2008/1848 Sch.3

s.6C, referred to: SI 2008/1741 Reg.72

s.6C, varied: SI 2008/1848 Sch.4 para.1

s.6D, applied: SI 2008/1848 Sch.3

s.6D, referred to: SI 2008/1741 Reg.72

s.6D, varied: SI 2008/1848 Sch.4 para.1

s.6E, referred to: SI 2008/1741 Reg.72

s.6E, varied: SI 2008/1848 Sch.4 para.1

s.7, applied: SI 2008/305, SI 2008/307, SI 2008/507, SI 2008/1741, SI 2008/1901, SI 2008/1914

s.22, applied: SI 2008/1316 Art.4

s.24, applied: SI 2008/1741 Reg.104

s.42, varied: SI 2008/1848 Sch.4 para.1

s.43, varied: SI 2008/1848 Sch.4 para.1

s.44, varied: SI 2008/1848 Sch.4 para.1

s.46, varied: SI 2008/1848 Sch.4 para.1

s.54, referred to: SI 2008/1737 Art.10

s.65, applied: SI 2008/2869 Reg.3

s.65, enabling: SI 2008/2869

s.69, varied: SI 2008/1848 Sch.4 para.1

s.71A, substituted: SI 2008/1319 Art.3

s.71B, substituted: SI 2008/1319 Art.3

s.71C, substituted: SI 2008/1319 Art.3

s.71D, substituted: SI 2008/1319 Art.3

s.71E, substituted: SI 2008/1319 Art.3

s.71F, substituted: SI 2008/1319 Art.3

s.71G, substituted: SI 2008/1319 Art.3

s.71GA, substituted: SI 2008/1319 Art.3

s.71H, substituted: SI 2008/1319 Art.3

s.71HA, substituted: SI 2008/1319 Art.3

s.71I, substituted: SI 2008/1319 Art.3

s.71I, applied: SI 2008/1737 Art.10

s.71I, substituted: SI 2008/1319 Art.3

s.71J, substituted: SI 2008/1319 Art.3

s.71J, applied: SI 2008/1737 Art.10

CAP.

2000–cont.

41. Political Parties, Elections and Referendums Act 2000–*cont.*

s.71J, substituted: SI 2008/1319 Art.3
s.71K, substituted: SI 2008/1319 Art.3
s.71L, substituted: SI 2008/1319 Art.3
s.71M, substituted: SI 2008/1319 Art.3
s.71M, applied: SI 2008/1656 Sch.1 para.3
s.71M, substituted: SI 2008/1319 Art.3
s.71M, varied: SI 2008/1656 Sch.1 para.2, Sch.1 para.3
s.71N, substituted: SI 2008/1319 Art.3
s.71N, varied: SI 2008/1656 Sch.1 para.3
s.71O, substituted: SI 2008/1319 Art.3
s.71O, applied: SI 2008/1656 Sch.1 para.3
s.71O, substituted: SI 2008/1319 Art.3
s.71P, substituted: SI 2008/1319 Art.3
s.71Q, substituted: SI 2008/1319 Art.3
s.71R, substituted: SI 2008/1319 Art.3
s.71S, substituted: SI 2008/1319 Art.3
s.71T, substituted: SI 2008/1319 Art.3
s.71T, varied: SI 2008/1656 Sch.1 para.3
s.71U, substituted: SI 2008/1319 Art.3
s.71V, substituted: SI 2008/1319 Art.3
s.71W, substituted: SI 2008/1319 Art.3
s.71X, substituted: SI 2008/1319 Art.3
s.71Y, substituted: SI 2008/1319 Art.3
s.71Z, applied: SI 2008/1737
s.71Z, substituted: SI 2008/1319 Art.3
s.71Z1, applied: SI 2008/1737 Art.3, Art.4
s.71Z1, substituted: SI 2008/1319 Art.3
s.71Z1, enabling: SI 2008/1737
s.71Z2, referred to: SI 2008/1319 Art.6
s.71Z2, substituted: SI 2008/1319 Art.3
s.71Z3, applied: SI 2008/1737 Art.7
s.71Z3, substituted: SI 2008/1319 Art.3
s.71Z3, varied: SI 2008/1319 Sch.1 para.1
s.71Z3, enabling: SI 2008/1737
s.71Z4, applied: SI 2008/1737 Art.11
s.71Z4, substituted: SI 2008/1319 Art.3
s.71Z4, varied: SI 2008/1319 Sch.1 para.1
s.71Z4, enabling: SI 2008/1737
s.85, applied: SI 2008/1741 Reg.105
s.105, applied: SI 2008/1741 Reg.105
s.106, applied: SI 2008/1741 Reg.105
s.149, varied: SI 2008/1319 Sch.1 para.3
s.150, amended: SI 2008/1319 Sch.2 para.1
s.156, amended: SI 2008/1319 Art.4
s.156, applied: SI 2008/1737
s.156, enabling: SI 2008/1737
s.159A, amended: SI 2008/1319 Art.4
s.160, amended: SI 2008/948 Sch.1 para.26
s.160, applied: SI 2008/1741 Reg.105
Sch.6 para.2, applied: SI 2008/2869 Reg.3
Sch.6 para.2, enabling: SI 2008/2869
Sch.6 para.3, applied: SI 2008/2869 Reg.3
Sch.6 para.3, enabling: SI 2008/2869
Sch.6A para.2, amended: SI 2008/1737 Sch.1 para.2
Sch.6A para.2, applied: SI 2008/2869 Reg.3
Sch.6A para.2, enabling: SI 2008/2869
Sch.6A para.2A, added: SI 2008/1737 Sch.1 para.3
Sch.6A para.2A, applied: SI 2008/1737 Art.11
Sch.6A para.3, amended: SI 2008/1737 Sch.1 para.4
Sch.6A para.3A, added: SI 2008/1737 Sch.1 para.4
Sch.6A para.4, amended: SI 2008/1737 Sch.1 para.4
Sch.6A para.4, varied: SI 2008/1656 Sch.1 para.3
Sch.6A para.4A, added: SI 2008/1737 Sch.1 para.4
Sch.6A para.4A, varied: SI 2008/1656 Sch.1 para.3
Sch.7, referred to: SI 2008/1741 Reg.103
Sch.7A, referred to: SI 2008/1741 Reg.103
Sch.7 Part I para.1, applied: SI 2008/1741 Reg.103
Sch.7 Part III para.10, applied: SI 2008/2869 Reg.3
Sch.7 Part III para.10, enabling: SI 2008/2869
Sch.7A para.5, applied: SI 2008/1737 Art.10
Sch.7A para.6, applied: SI 2008/1737 Art.10
Sch.7A para.9, amended: SI 2008/1737 Sch.2 para.2
Sch.7A para.9, varied: SI 2008/1656 Sch.1 para.4
Sch.7A para.10, amended: SI 2008/1737 Sch.2 para.3, Sch.2 para.4, Sch.2 para.5
Sch.7A para.10, varied: SI 2008/1656 Sch.1 para.5
Sch.7A para.11, varied: SI 2008/1656 Sch.1 para.5
Sch.7A para.12, varied: SI 2008/1656 Sch.1 para.5
Sch.7A para.13, varied: SI 2008/1656 Sch.1 para.5
Sch.7A para.14, applied: SI 2008/1656 Sch.1 para.4, Sch.1 para.5
Sch.7A para.15, amended: SI 2008/1737 Sch.2 para.6
Sch.11, applied: SI 2008/1741 Reg.105
Sch.11 Part III para.10, applied: SI 2008/2869 Reg.3
Sch.11 Part III para.10, enabling: SI 2008/2869
Sch.15, applied: SI 2008/1741 Reg.105
Sch.15 Part III para.10, applied: SI 2008/2869 Reg.3
Sch.15 Part III para.10, enabling: SI 2008/2869
Sch.20, varied: SI 2008/1319 Sch.1 para.2

43. Criminal Justice and Court Services Act 2000

applied: SI 2008/473 Art.2
s.1, amended: 2008 c.4 Sch.4 para.69, Sch.26 para.50

CAP.

2000–cont.

43. Criminal Justice and Court Services Act 2000–*cont.*

s.32, applied: SI 2008/2699 r.19
s.40, repealed (in part): SI 2008/1769 Sch.1 para.28, Sch.3
s.42, amended: SI 2008/2833 Sch.3 para.189
s.46, repealed: 2008 c.4 Sch.28 Part 1
s.52, repealed: 2008 c.4 Sch.28 Part 1
s.61, applied: 2008 c.28 Sch.6 para.5
s.61, referred to: 2008 c.28 s.45
s.64, amended: SI 2008/912 Sch.1 para.18
s.70, repealed (in part): 2008 c.4 Sch.4 para.70, Sch.28 Part 1
s.71, applied: SI 2008/1965
s.71, enabling: SI 2008/1965
Sch.1A para.2, amended: 2008 c.14 Sch.5 para.74
Sch.1A para.2, repealed (in part): 2008 c.14 Sch.5 para.74, Sch.15 Part 1
Sch.1A para.2, varied: SI 2008/2250 Art.3
Sch.1A para.3, amended: 2008 c.14 Sch.5 para.74
Sch.1A para.3, repealed (in part): 2008 c.14 Sch.5 para.74, Sch.15 Part 1
Sch.1A para.3, varied: SI 2008/2250 Art.3
Sch.1A para.4, amended: 2008 c.14 Sch.5 para.74
Sch.1A para.4, repealed (in part): 2008 c.14 Sch.5 para.74, Sch.15 Part 1
Sch.1A para.4, varied: SI 2008/2250 Art.3
Sch.7 Part I para.4, amended: 2008 c.4 Sch.28 Part 1
Sch.7 Part II para.37, repealed (in part): 2008 c.4 Sch.28 Part 1
Sch.7 Part II para.69, repealed: 2008 c.4 Sch.28 Part 1
Sch.7 Part II para.163, repealed: 2008 c.4 Sch.28 Part 1
Sch.7 Part II para.164, repealed: 2008 c.4 Sch.28 Part 1
Sch.7 Part II para.174, repealed: 2008 c.4 Sch.28 Part 1
Sch.7 Part II para.175, repealed: 2008 c.4 Sch.28 Part 1
Sch.7 Part II para.192, repealed: 2008 c.4 Sch.28 Part 1
Sch.7 Part II para.196, repealed (in part): 2008 c.4 Sch.28 Part 1
Sch.7 Part II para.197, amended: 2008 c.4 Sch.28 Part 1
Sch.7 Part II para.197, repealed (in part): 2008 c.4 Sch.28 Part 1
Sch.7 Part II para.201, repealed: 2008 c.4 Sch.28 Part 1
Sch.7 Part II para.202, repealed (in part): 2008 c.4 Sch.28 Part 1
Sch.7 Part II para.204, repealed: 2008 c.4 Sch.28 Part 1
Sch.7 Part II para.208, repealed: 2008 c.25 Sch.2

CAP.

2000–cont.

43. Criminal Justice and Court Services Act 2000–*cont.*

Sch.7 Part II para.209, repealed: 2008 c.25 Sch.2
Sch.7 Part II para.210, repealed: 2008 c.25 Sch.2

2001

2. Capital Allowances Act 2001

applied: 2008 c.9 s.83, s.85, Sch.27 para.30, Sch.27 para.35, 2008 c.18 Sch.13 para.7, Sch.13 para.8, Sch.13 para.9, Sch.13 para.27
Part 2, applied: 2008 c.9 Sch.26 para.17, 2008 c.18 Sch.13 para.19, Sch.13 para.20, Sch.13 para.35, Sch.13 para.36, Sch.13 para.37
Part 2, referred to: 2008 c.18 Sch.13 para.9, Sch.13 para.27
Part 2 c.10, applied: 2008 c.9 Sch.26 para.14
Part 2 c.17, amended: 2008 c.9 Sch.20 para.6
Part 2 c.18, applied: 2008 c.9 s.75, s.76
Part 2 c.6A, applied: 2008 c.9 Sch.20 para.11
Part 3, applied: 2008 c.9 s.85, s.86, s.87, Sch.27 para.31, Sch.27 para.32, 2008 c.18 Sch.13 para.10, Sch.13 para.21, Sch.13 para.38
Part 3, referred to: 2008 c.9 Sch.27 para.31, Sch.27 para.33, Sch.27 para.34, 2008 c.18 Sch.13 para.28
Part 3 c.2, applied: 2008 c.9 Sch.27 para.33
Part 4, applied: 2008 c.9 s.85
s.1, amended: 2008 c.9 Sch.27 para.2
s.1, repealed (in part): 2008 c.9 Sch.27 para.2
s.2, amended: 2008 c.9 Sch.25 para.2, Sch.27 para.3
s.3, amended: 2008 c.9 Sch.25 para.3
s.3, repealed (in part): 2008 c.9 Sch.27 para.4
s.5, see *Tower MCashback LLP v Revenue and Customs Commissioners* [2008] S.T.C. (S.C.D.) 1 (Sp Comm), Howard M Nowlan
s.11, see *Tower MCashback LLP v Revenue and Customs Commissioners* [2008] EWHC 2387 (Ch), [2008] S.T.C. 3366 (Ch D), Henderson, J.
s.13, amended: 2008 c.9 Sch.20 para.6
s.22, applied: 2008 c.9 Sch.27 para.33
s.23, amended: 2008 c.9 s.71, s.72, s.73
s.26, amended: 2008 c.9 Sch.34 para.3
s.28, amended: 2008 c.9 s.71
s.28, repealed (in part): 2008 c.9 s.71
s.29, repealed: 2008 c.9 s.72
s.33A, added: 2008 c.9 s.73
s.33B, added: 2008 c.9 s.73
s.38A, added: 2008 c.9 Sch.24 para.2
s.38B, added: 2008 c.9 Sch.24 para.2
s.39, amended: 2008 c.9 s.75, s.76
s.40, repealed: 2008 c.9 s.76
s.41, repealed: 2008 c.9 s.76
s.42, repealed: 2008 c.9 s.76

CAP.

2001–cont.

2. **Capital Allowances Act 2001**–*cont.*
s.43, repealed: 2008 c.9 s.76
s.44, applied: 2008 c.9 s.75
s.44, repealed: 2008 c.9 s.75
s.45, repealed: 2008 c.9 s.76
s.45A, enabling: SI 2008/1916
s.45D, amended: 2008 c.9 s.77
s.45E, amended: 2008 c.9 s.78
s.45H, enabling: SI 2008/1917
s.45I, enabling: SI 2008/1917
s.46, amended: 2008 c.9 s.75, s.76
s.47, amended: SI 2008/954 Art.28
s.47, repealed (in part): 2008 c.9 s.75, SI 2008/954 Sch.1
s.48, amended: SI 2008/954 Art.29
s.48, repealed (in part): 2008 c.9 s.75, SI 2008/954 Sch.1
s.49, amended: SI 2008/954 Art.30
s.49, repealed (in part): 2008 c.9 s.75
s.51, repealed: 2008 c.9 s.76
s.51A, added: 2008 c.9 Sch.24 para.3
s.51B, added: 2008 c.9 Sch.24 para.3
s.51C, added: 2008 c.9 Sch.24 para.3
s.51D, added: 2008 c.9 Sch.24 para.3
s.51E, added: 2008 c.9 Sch.24 para.3
s.51F, added: 2008 c.9 Sch.24 para.3
s.51G, added: 2008 c.9 Sch.24 para.3
s.51H, added: 2008 c.9 Sch.24 para.3
s.51I, added: 2008 c.9 Sch.24 para.3
s.51J, added: 2008 c.9 Sch.24 para.3
s.51K, added: 2008 c.9 Sch.24 para.3
s.51L, added: 2008 c.9 Sch.24 para.3
s.51M, added: 2008 c.9 Sch.24 para.3
s.51N, added: 2008 c.9 Sch.24 para.3
s.52, amended: 2008 c.9 s.75, s.76, s.108, Sch.20 para.6
s.52A, added: 2008 c.9 Sch.24 para.4
s.54, amended: 2008 c.9 Sch.26 para.3
s.56, amended: 2008 c.9 s.80, s.81, Sch.26 para.4
s.56, referred to: 2008 c.9 s.80
s.56A, added: 2008 c.9 s.81
s.57, amended: 2008 c.9 Sch.20 para.6, Sch.34 para.4
s.58, amended: 2008 c.9 Sch.24 para.5
s.59, amended: 2008 c.9 s.81
s.61, amended: 2008 c.9 Sch.20 para.4
s.61, applied: 2008 c.18 Sch.13 para.19, Sch.13 para.35
s.63, applied: 2008 c.18 Sch.13 para.19, Sch.13 para.20, Sch.13 para.35, Sch.13 para.36
s.65, amended: 2008 c.9 Sch.26 para.5
s.66, amended: 2008 c.9 Sch.20 para.6, Sch.26 para.6
s.68, applied: 2008 c.18 Sch.13 para.19, Sch.13 para.35
s.70H, amended: 2008 c.9 Sch.20 para.8
s.70H, applied: 2008 c.9 Sch.20 para.11

CAP.

2001–cont.

2. **Capital Allowances Act 2001**–*cont.*
s.70I, amended: 2008 c.9 Sch.20 para.6, Sch.20 para.7
s.70I, varied: 2008 c.9 Sch.20 para.6
s.84, amended: 2008 c.9 Sch.26 para.7
s.88, disapplied: 2008 c.18 Sch.13 para.19, Sch.13 para.35
s.89, amended: 2008 c.9 Sch.20 para.6
s.92, repealed: 2008 c.9 Sch.26 para.8
s.101, substituted: 2008 c.9 Sch.26 para.9
s.102, applied: 2008 c.9 s.83
s.102, referred to: 2008 c.9 s.83
s.102, substituted: 2008 c.9 Sch.26 para.10
s.102, varied: 2008 c.9 s.83
s.104, repealed: 2008 c.9 Sch.26 para.11
s.104A, added: 2008 c.9 Sch.26 para.2
s.104B, added: 2008 c.9 Sch.26 para.2
s.104C, added: 2008 c.9 Sch.26 para.2
s.104D, added: 2008 c.9 Sch.26 para.2
s.104D, referred to: 2008 c.9 s.83
s.104E, added: 2008 c.9 Sch.26 para.2
s.104E, applied: 2008 c.9 s.83
s.163, amended: 2008 c.9 s.109
s.164, amended: 2008 c.9 Sch.34 para.5
s.165, amended: 2008 c.9 s.110, Sch.34 para.6
s.181, applied: 2008 c.18 Sch.13 para.9, Sch.13 para.27
s.182, applied: 2008 c.18 Sch.13 para.9, Sch.13 para.27
s.186, amended: 2008 c.9 Sch.27 para.5
s.186, applied: 2008 c.9 Sch.27 para.30
s.188, applied: 2008 c.18 Sch.13 para.20, Sch.13 para.36
s.196, applied: 2008 c.18 Sch.13 para.20, Sch.13 para.36
s.205, amended: 2008 c.9 Sch.24 para.6
s.210, amended: 2008 c.9 Sch.24 para.7
s.217, amended: 2008 c.9 Sch.20 para.6, Sch.24 para.8
s.218, amended: 2008 c.9 Sch.20 para.6
s.218A, added: 2008 c.9 Sch.24 para.9
s.219, amended: 2008 c.9 Sch.20 para.6
s.221, amended: 2008 c.9 Sch.20 para.6
s.221, applied: 2008 c.9 Sch.20 para.6
s.221, referred to: 2008 c.9 Sch.20 para.6
s.222, repealed: 2008 c.9 Sch.20 para.6
s.223, repealed: 2008 c.9 Sch.20 para.6
s.224, repealed: 2008 c.9 Sch.20 para.6
s.226, repealed: 2008 c.9 Sch.20 para.6
s.227, amended: 2008 c.9 Sch.20 para.6
s.227, repealed (in part): 2008 c.9 Sch.20 para.6
s.228, amended: 2008 c.9 Sch.20 para.6
s.228, repealed (in part): 2008 c.9 Sch.20 para.6
s.228A, referred to: 2008 c.9 Sch.20 para.7, Sch.20 para.12, Sch.20 para.13
s.228A, substituted: 2008 c.9 Sch.20 para.12

CAP.

2001–cont.

2. **Capital Allowances Act 2001**–*cont.*
s.228B, amended: 2008 c.9 Sch.20 para.12, Sch.20 para.13
s.228C, amended: 2008 c.9 Sch.20 para.12
s.228D, repealed: 2008 c.9 Sch.20 para.12
s.228E, repealed: 2008 c.9 Sch.20 para.12
s.228F, repealed: 2008 c.9 Sch.20 para.12
s.228G, amended: 2008 c.9 Sch.20 para.12
s.228H, amended: 2008 c.9 Sch.20 para.12
s.228J, amended: 2008 c.9 Sch.20 para.12
s.230, amended: 2008 c.9 Sch.20 para.6
s.235, applied: 2008 c.9 s.75, s.76
s.236, amended: 2008 c.9 Sch.24 para.10
s.237, amended: 2008 c.9 Sch.24 para.11
s.237, repealed (in part): 2008 c.9 s.76
s.241, amended: 2008 c.9 Sch.20 para.6, Sch.24 para.12
s.243, repealed: 2008 c.9 Sch.20 para.6
s.257A, varied: SI 2008/1942 Reg.8
s.262A, added: 2008 c.9 Sch.25 para.4
s.263, amended: 2008 c.9 Sch.24 para.13
s.265, amended: 2008 c.9 Sch.24 para.14
s.265, disapplied: 2008 c.18 Sch.13 para.37
s.266, amended: 2008 c.9 Sch.26 para.12
s.271, repealed: 2008 c.9 s.84
s.272, repealed: 2008 c.9 s.84
s.273, repealed: 2008 c.9 s.84
s.274, applied: 2008 c.9 Sch.27 para.34
s.274, repealed: 2008 c.9 s.84
s.275, repealed: 2008 c.9 s.84
s.276, applied: 2008 c.9 Sch.27 para.34
s.276, repealed: 2008 c.9 s.84
s.277, repealed: 2008 c.9 s.84
s.278, repealed: 2008 c.9 s.84
s.279, repealed: 2008 c.9 s.84
s.280, repealed: 2008 c.9 s.84
s.281, repealed: 2008 c.9 s.84
s.282, repealed: 2008 c.9 s.84
s.283, repealed: 2008 c.9 s.84
s.284, repealed: 2008 c.9 s.84
s.285, repealed: 2008 c.9 s.84
s.286, repealed: 2008 c.9 s.84
s.287, repealed: 2008 c.9 s.84
s.288, repealed: 2008 c.9 s.84
s.289, repealed: 2008 c.9 s.84
s.290, repealed: 2008 c.9 s.84
s.291, repealed: 2008 c.9 s.84
s.292, repealed: 2008 c.9 s.84
s.293, repealed: 2008 c.9 s.84
s.294, repealed: 2008 c.9 s.84
s.295, repealed: 2008 c.9 s.84
s.296, repealed: 2008 c.9 s.84
s.297, repealed: 2008 c.9 s.84
s.298, repealed: 2008 c.9 s.84
s.299, repealed: 2008 c.9 s.84
s.300, repealed: 2008 c.9 s.84
s.301, repealed: 2008 c.9 s.84
s.302, repealed: 2008 c.9 s.84
s.303, repealed: 2008 c.9 s.84
s.304, repealed: 2008 c.9 s.84

CAP.

2001–cont.

2. **Capital Allowances Act 2001**–*cont.*
s.305, repealed: 2008 c.9 s.84
s.306, repealed: 2008 c.9 s.84
s.307, referred to: 2008 c.9 Sch.27 para.32
s.307, repealed: 2008 c.9 s.84
s.308, repealed: 2008 c.9 s.84
s.309, repealed: 2008 c.9 s.84
s.310, repealed: 2008 c.9 s.84
s.311, applied: 2008 c.18 Sch.13 para.28
s.311, repealed: 2008 c.9 s.84
s.312, repealed: 2008 c.9 s.84
s.313, repealed: 2008 c.9 s.84
s.313A, added: 2008 c.9 s.87
s.313A, repealed: 2008 c.9 s.84
s.314, repealed: 2008 c.9 s.84
s.315, repealed: 2008 c.9 s.84
s.316, repealed: 2008 c.9 s.84
s.317, repealed: 2008 c.9 s.84
s.318, repealed: 2008 c.9 s.84
s.319, repealed: 2008 c.9 s.84
s.320, repealed: 2008 c.9 s.84
s.321, repealed: 2008 c.9 s.84
s.322, repealed: 2008 c.9 s.84
s.323, repealed: 2008 c.9 s.84
s.324, repealed: 2008 c.9 s.84
s.325, repealed: 2008 c.9 s.84
s.326, repealed: 2008 c.9 s.84
s.327, repealed: 2008 c.9 s.84
s.328, repealed: 2008 c.9 s.84
s.329, repealed: 2008 c.9 s.84
s.330, repealed: 2008 c.9 s.84
s.331, repealed: 2008 c.9 s.84
s.332, repealed: 2008 c.9 s.84
s.333, repealed: 2008 c.9 s.84
s.334, repealed: 2008 c.9 s.84
s.335, repealed: 2008 c.9 s.84
s.336, repealed: 2008 c.9 s.84
s.337, repealed: 2008 c.9 s.84
s.338, repealed: 2008 c.9 s.84
s.339, repealed: 2008 c.9 s.84
s.340, repealed: 2008 c.9 s.84
s.341, applied: 2008 c.9 Sch.27 para.34
s.341, repealed: 2008 c.9 s.84
s.342, repealed: 2008 c.9 s.84
s.343, repealed: 2008 c.9 s.84
s.344, repealed: 2008 c.9 s.84
s.345, repealed: 2008 c.9 s.84
s.346, repealed: 2008 c.9 s.84
s.347, repealed: 2008 c.9 s.84
s.348, repealed: 2008 c.9 s.84
s.349, repealed: 2008 c.9 s.84
s.350, repealed: 2008 c.9 s.84
s.351, repealed: 2008 c.9 s.84
s.352, repealed: 2008 c.9 s.84
s.353, repealed: 2008 c.9 s.84
s.354, repealed: 2008 c.9 s.84
s.355, repealed: 2008 c.9 s.84
s.356, repealed: 2008 c.9 s.84
s.357, repealed: 2008 c.9 s.84
s.358, repealed: 2008 c.9 s.84

CAP.

2001–cont.

2. **Capital Allowances Act 2001**–*cont.*
s.359, repealed: 2008 c.9 s.84
s.360, repealed: 2008 c.9 s.84
s.361, repealed: 2008 c.9 s.84
s.362, repealed: 2008 c.9 s.84
s.363, repealed: 2008 c.9 s.84
s.364, repealed: 2008 c.9 s.84
s.365, repealed: 2008 c.9 s.84
s.366, repealed: 2008 c.9 s.84
s.367, repealed: 2008 c.9 s.84
s.368, repealed: 2008 c.9 s.84
s.369, repealed: 2008 c.9 s.84
s.370, repealed: 2008 c.9 s.84
s.371, repealed: 2008 c.9 s.84
s.372, repealed: 2008 c.9 s.84
s.373, repealed: 2008 c.9 s.84
s.374, repealed: 2008 c.9 s.84
s.375, repealed: 2008 c.9 s.84
s.376, repealed: 2008 c.9 s.84
s.377, repealed: 2008 c.9 s.84
s.378, repealed: 2008 c.9 s.84
s.379, repealed: 2008 c.9 s.84
s.380, repealed: 2008 c.9 s.84
s.381, repealed: 2008 c.9 s.84
s.382, repealed: 2008 c.9 s.84
s.383, repealed: 2008 c.9 s.84
s.384, repealed: 2008 c.9 s.84
s.385, repealed: 2008 c.9 s.84
s.386, repealed: 2008 c.9 s.84
s.387, repealed: 2008 c.9 s.84
s.388, repealed: 2008 c.9 s.84
s.389, repealed: 2008 c.9 s.84
s.390, repealed: 2008 c.9 s.84
s.391, repealed: 2008 c.9 s.84
s.392, repealed: 2008 c.9 s.84
s.393, repealed: 2008 c.9 s.84
s.443, amended: 2008 c.9 Sch.27 para.6
s.448, amended: 2008 c.9 Sch.27 para.7
s.484, applied: 2008 c.9 Sch.27 para.34
s.537, amended: 2008 c.9 Sch.27 para.8
s.539, repealed: 2008 c.9 Sch.27 para.9
s.540, repealed: 2008 c.9 Sch.27 para.10
s.542, amended: 2008 c.9 Sch.27 para.11
s.546, repealed (in part): 2008 c.9 Sch.27 para.12
s.559, disapplied: 2008 c.18 Sch.13 para.10
s.564, amended: 2008 c.9 Sch.27 para.13
s.564, repealed (in part): 2008 c.9 Sch.27 para.13
s.567, amended: 2008 c.9 Sch.27 para.14
s.567, disapplied: 2008 c.18 Sch.13 para.21, Sch.13 para.38
s.568, disapplied: 2008 c.18 Sch.13 para.21, Sch.13 para.38
s.569, amended: 2008 c.9 Sch.27 para.15
s.569, disapplied: 2008 c.18 Sch.13 para.21, Sch.13 para.38
s.570, amended: 2008 c.9 Sch.27 para.16
s.570, disapplied: 2008 c.18 Sch.13 para.21, Sch.13 para.38

CAP.

2001–cont.

2. **Capital Allowances Act 2001**–*cont.*
s.570A, amended: 2008 c.9 Sch.27 para.17
s.573, amended: 2008 c.9 Sch.27 para.18
s.573, disapplied: 2008 c.18 Sch.13 para.10
s.575, applied: 2008 c.9 Sch.26 para.15
Sch.A1 Part 1 para.1, added: 2008 c.9 Sch.25 para.5
Sch.A1 Part 1 para.2, added: 2008 c.9 Sch.25 para.5
Sch.A1 Part 1 para.3, added: 2008 c.9 Sch.25 para.5
Sch.A1 Part 1 para.4, added: 2008 c.9 Sch.25 para.5
Sch.A1 Part 1 para.5, added: 2008 c.9 Sch.25 para.5
Sch.A1 Part 1 para.6, added: 2008 c.9 Sch.25 para.5
Sch.A1 Part 1 para.7, added: 2008 c.9 Sch.25 para.5
Sch.A1 Part 1 para.8, added: 2008 c.9 Sch.25 para.5
Sch.A1 Part 1 para.9, added: 2008 c.9 Sch.25 para.5
Sch.A1 Part 1 para.10, added: 2008 c.9 Sch.25 para.5
Sch.A1 Part 1 para.11, added: 2008 c.9 Sch.25 para.5
Sch.A1 Part 1 para.12, added: 2008 c.9 Sch.25 para.5
Sch.A1 Part 1 para.13, added: 2008 c.9 Sch.25 para.5
Sch.A1 Part 1 para.14, added: 2008 c.9 Sch.25 para.5
Sch.A1 Part 1 para.15, added: 2008 c.9 Sch.25 para.5
Sch.A1 Part 1 para.16, added: 2008 c.9 Sch.25 para.5
Sch.A1 Part 1 para.17, added: 2008 c.9 Sch.25 para.5
Sch.A1 Part 2 para.18, added: 2008 c.9 Sch.25 para.5
Sch.A1 Part 2 para.19, added: 2008 c.9 Sch.25 para.5
Sch.A1 Part 2 para.20, added: 2008 c.9 Sch.25 para.5
Sch.A1 Part 2 para.21, added: 2008 c.9 Sch.25 para.5
Sch.A1 Part 2 para.22, added: 2008 c.9 Sch.25 para.5
Sch.A1 Part 2 para.23, added: 2008 c.9 Sch.25 para.5
Sch.A1 Part 3 para.24, added: 2008 c.9 Sch.25 para.5
Sch.A1 Part 3 para.25, added: 2008 c.9 Sch.25 para.5
Sch.A1 Part 3 para.26, added: 2008 c.9 Sch.25 para.5
Sch.A1 Part 3 para.27, added: 2008 c.9 Sch.25 para.5
Sch.A1 Part 4 para.28, added: 2008 c.9 Sch.25 para.5

CAP.

2001–cont.

2. **Capital Allowances Act 2001**–*cont.*
Sch.A1 Part 4 para.29, added: 2008 c.9 Sch.25 para.5
Sch.1 Part 1, amended: 2008 c.9 Sch.25 para.6
Sch.1 Part 2, amended: 2008 c.9 Sch.24 para.15, Sch.26 para.13, Sch.27 para.19
Sch.3 Part 4 para.14, repealed: 2008 c.9 s.76
Sch.3 Part 4 para.46, repealed: 2008 c.9 s.76
Sch.3 Part 4 para.47, repealed: 2008 c.9 s.76
Sch.3 Part 4 para.48, repealed: 2008 c.9 s.76
Sch.3 Part 4 para.49, repealed: 2008 c.9 s.76
Sch.3 Part 4 para.50, repealed: 2008 c.9 s.76
Sch.3 Part 4 para.51, repealed: 2008 c.9 s.76
Sch.3 Part 5 para.56, repealed: 2008 c.9 Sch.27 para.20
Sch.3 Part 5 para.57, repealed: 2008 c.9 Sch.27 para.20
Sch.3 Part 5 para.58, repealed: 2008 c.9 Sch.27 para.20
Sch.3 Part 5 para.59, repealed: 2008 c.9 Sch.27 para.20
Sch.3 Part 5 para.60, repealed: 2008 c.9 Sch.27 para.20
Sch.3 Part 5 para.61, repealed: 2008 c.9 Sch.27 para.20
Sch.3 Part 5 para.62, repealed: 2008 c.9 Sch.27 para.20
Sch.3 Part 5 para.63, repealed: 2008 c.9 Sch.27 para.20
Sch.3 Part 5 para.64, repealed: 2008 c.9 Sch.27 para.20
Sch.3 Part 5 para.65, repealed: 2008 c.9 Sch.27 para.20
Sch.3 Part 5 para.66, repealed: 2008 c.9 Sch.27 para.20
Sch.3 Part 5 para.67, repealed: 2008 c.9 Sch.27 para.20
Sch.3 Part 5 para.68, repealed: 2008 c.9 Sch.27 para.20
Sch.3 Part 5 para.69, repealed: 2008 c.9 Sch.27 para.20
Sch.3 Part 5 para.70, repealed: 2008 c.9 Sch.27 para.20
Sch.3 Part 5 para.71, repealed: 2008 c.9 Sch.27 para.20
Sch.3 Part 5 para.72, repealed: 2008 c.9 Sch.27 para.20
Sch.3 Part 5 para.73, repealed: 2008 c.9 Sch.27 para.20
Sch.3 Part 5 para.74, repealed: 2008 c.9 Sch.27 para.20
Sch.3 Part 5 para.75, repealed: 2008 c.9 Sch.27 para.20
Sch.3 Part 5 para.76, repealed: 2008 c.9 Sch.27 para.20
Sch.3 Part 5 para.77, repealed: 2008 c.9 Sch.27 para.20
Sch.3 Part 5 para.78, repealed: 2008 c.9 Sch.27 para.20

CAP.

2001–cont.

2. **Capital Allowances Act 2001**–*cont.*
Sch.3 Part 5 para.79, repealed: 2008 c.9 Sch.27 para.20
Sch.3 Part 11 para.110, repealed: 2008 c.9 Sch.27 para.20

3. **Vehicles (Crime) Act 2001**
applied: 2008 c.13 Sch.3, SI 2008/1715 Reg.4
referred to: 2008 c.13 Sch.6
Part 2, applied: SI 2008/1715 Reg.3, Reg.4
s.17, enabling: SI 2008/1715
s.18, enabling: SI 2008/1715
s.19, applied: SI 2008/1715 Reg.5
s.19, enabling: SI 2008/1715
s.24, applied: SI 2008/1715 Reg.7
s.24, enabling: SI 2008/1715
s.25, applied: SI 2008/1715 Reg.6
s.25, enabling: SI 2008/1715
s.41, enabling: SI 2008/1715

6. **Regulatory Reform Act 2001**
s.1, applied: 2008 c.13 Sch.7

9. **Finance Act 2001**
s.2, repealed (in part): 2008 c.9 s.13
s.14, repealed: 2008 c.9 s.144
s.16, amended: 2008 c.9 s.20
s.24, applied: 2008 c.9 Sch.41 para.1
s.25, enabling: SI 2008/1482, SI 2008/2693
s.45, enabling: SI 2008/1482, SI 2008/2693
s.78, repealed: 2008 c.9 Sch.2 para.55
s.83, repealed (in part): 2008 c.9 Sch.14 para.17
s.89, repealed (in part): 2008 c.9 Sch.44 para.11
s.107, repealed: 2008 c.9 s.135
Sch.4 para.1, applied: 2008 c.9 Sch.41 para.1
Sch.4 para.1, repealed (in part): 2008 c.9 Sch.41 para.25
Sch.5 para.14A, repealed: 2008 c.9 Sch.43 para.8
Sch.6 Part 2 para.7, repealed: 2008 c.9 Sch.40 para.21
Sch.6 Part 2 para.8, repealed: 2008 c.9 Sch.40 para.21
Sch.6 Part 2 para.9, repealed: 2008 c.9 Sch.40 para.21
Sch.6 Part 2 para.9A, repealed (in part): 2008 c.9 Sch.40 para.21
Sch.7 para.12, amended: 2008 c.9 Sch.44 para.9
Sch.7 para.12, repealed (in part): 2008 c.9 Sch.44 para.9
Sch.19 Part 2 para.4, repealed: 2008 c.9 Sch.27 para.23
Sch.21 para.5, repealed: 2008 c.9 Sch.27 para.23
Sch.21 para.6, repealed: 2008 c.9 Sch.27 para.23
Sch.22 Part 3 para.14, amended: 2008 c.9 Sch.17 para.23
Sch.22 Part 3 para.17, amended: 2008 c.9 Sch.17 para.23

CAP.

2001–cont.

9. **Finance Act 2001**–*cont.*
Sch.22 Part 4 para.21, amended: 2008 c.9 Sch.17 para.23
Sch.22 Part 4 para.22, amended: 2008 c.9 Sch.17 para.23
Sch.22 Part 4 para.24, amended: 2008 c.9 Sch.17 para.23
Sch.22 Part 4 para.27, amended: 2008 c.9 Sch.17 para.23
Sch.26 para.1, repealed: 2008 c.9 Sch.2 para.55
Sch.26 para.2, repealed: 2008 c.9 Sch.2 para.55
Sch.26 para.3, repealed: 2008 c.9 Sch.2 para.55
Sch.26 para.4, repealed: 2008 c.9 Sch.2 para.55
Sch.26 para.5, repealed: 2008 c.9 Sch.2 para.55
Sch.26 para.6, repealed: 2008 c.9 Sch.2 para.55
Sch.26 para.7, repealed: 2008 c.9 Sch.2 para.55
Sch.28 Part 1 para.1, repealed: 2008 c.9 Sch.14 para.17
Sch.28 Part 1 para.2, repealed: 2008 c.9 Sch.14 para.17
Sch.28 Part 1 para.3, repealed: 2008 c.9 Sch.14 para.17
Sch.28 Part 1 para.4, repealed: 2008 c.9 Sch.14 para.17
Sch.28 Part 1 para.5, repealed: 2008 c.9 Sch.14 para.17
Sch.28 Part 1 para.6, repealed: 2008 c.9 Sch.14 para.17
Sch.28 Part 1 para.7, repealed: 2008 c.9 Sch.14 para.17
Sch.28 Part 1 para.8, repealed: 2008 c.9 Sch.14 para.17
Sch.28 Part 1 para.9, repealed: 2008 c.9 Sch.14 para.17
Sch.28 Part 1 para.10, repealed: 2008 c.9 Sch.14 para.17
Sch.28 Part 1 para.11, repealed: 2008 c.9 Sch.14 para.17
Sch.28 Part 1 para.12, repealed: 2008 c.9 Sch.14 para.17
Sch.28 Part 1 para.13, repealed: 2008 c.9 Sch.14 para.17
Sch.28 Part 1 para.14, repealed: 2008 c.9 Sch.14 para.17
Sch.28 Part 1 para.15, repealed: 2008 c.9 Sch.14 para.17
Sch.28 Part 1 para.16, repealed: 2008 c.9 Sch.14 para.17
Sch.28 Part 1 para.17, repealed: 2008 c.9 Sch.14 para.17
Sch.29 Part 5 para.21, repealed: 2008 c.9 Sch.36 para.92
Sch.29 Part 5 para.38, repealed (in part): 2008 c.9 Sch.36 para.92

CAP.

2001–cont.

10. **Special Educational Needs and Disability Act 2001**
Sch.8 Part 2 para.20, repealed (in part): SI 2008/2833 Sch.3 para.228

11. **Social Security Fraud Act 2001**
s.7, applied: SI 2008/794 Reg.157, Sch.4 para.6

12. **Private Security Industry Act 2001**
see *Security Industry Authority v Stewart* [2007] EWHC 2338 (Admin), [2008] 2 All E.R. 1003 (DC), Laws, L.J.
applied: 2008 c.13 Sch.3
s.8, see *Security Industry Authority v Stewart* [2007] EWHC 2338 (Admin), [2008] 2 All E.R. 1003 (DC), Laws, L.J.
s.11, see *Security Industry Authority v Stewart* [2007] EWHC 2338 (Admin), [2008] 2 All E.R. 1003 (DC), Laws, L.J.

15. **Health and Social Care Act 2001**
s.54, amended: 2008 c.14 Sch.15 Part 5
s.57, see *Casewell v Secretary of State for Work and Pensions* [2008] EWCA Civ 524, (2008) 11 C.C.L. Rep. 684 (CA (Civ Div)), Tuckey, L.J.
s.57, amended: 2008 c.14 s.146
s.57, applied: SI 2008/794 Sch.8 para.53, Sch.9 para.56
s.64, amended: 2008 c.14 s.146
Sch.5 Part 3 para.17, repealed: 2008 c.14 Sch.15 Part 6
Sch.5 Part 3 para.18, repealed: 2008 c.14 Sch.15 Part 6

16. **Criminal Justice and Police Act 2001**
Part 1, applied: 2008 c.13 Sch.3
s.3, enabling: SI 2008/3297
s.57, amended: 2008 c.22 Sch.7 para.19
s.66, amended: 2008 c.22 Sch.7 para.20, SI 2008/1277 Sch.2 para.63
s.66, repealed (in part): 2008 c.22 Sch.7 para.20, Sch.8 Part 1, SI 2008/1277 Sch.4 Part 1
s.125, repealed (in part): 2008 c.4 Sch.28 Part 8
Sch.1 Part 1 para.46, repealed: SI 2008/1277 Sch.4 Part 1
Sch.1 Part 1 para.52, substituted: 2008 c.22 Sch.7 para.21
Sch.1 Part 1 para.73Ji, added: SI 2008/1277 Sch.2 para.64
Sch.1 Part 1 para.73Ki, added: SI 2008/1277 Sch.2 para.64
Sch.2 Part 1 para.4, repealed: SI 2008/1277 Sch.4 Part 1
Sch.2 Part 1 para.4B, added: SI 2008/1277 Sch.2 para.65
Sch.2 Part 1 para.4C, added: SI 2008/1277 Sch.2 para.65
Sch.2 Part 1 para.9, repealed: SI 2008/1277 Sch.4 Part 1
Sch.2 Part 1 para.9B, added: SI 2008/1277 Sch.2 para.65

CAP.

2001–cont.

16. Criminal Justice and Police Act 2001– *cont.*

Sch.2 Part 1 para.9C, added: SI 2008/1277 Sch.2 para.65

Sch.2 Part 2 para.16, repealed (in part): 2008 c.22 Sch.8 Part 1

17. International Criminal Court Act 2001

s.2, referred to: SI 2008/3135 Art.2

s.4, enabling: SI 2008/3135

s.51, applied: SI 2008/1216 Sch.1 para.26, Sch.2 para.28

s.52, applied: SI 2008/1216 Sch.1 para.26, Sch.2 para.28

Sch.1 para.3, enabling: SI 2008/3135

Sch.7 para.2, amended: 2008 c.4 s.22

Sch.7 para.3, amended: SI 2008/1241 Art.5

19. Armed Forces Act 2001

Part 2, applied: SI 2008/648 Sch.1

s.9, amended: SI 2008/1694 Art.14

s.10, amended: SI 2008/1694 Art.15

s.10, enabling: SI 2008/1698

s.11, amended: SI 2008/1694 Art.15

s.11, enabling: SI 2008/1698

s.31, enabling: SI 2008/1698

Sch.6 Part 5 para.30, repealed: 2008 c.17 Sch.16

22. European Communities (Finance) Act 2001

repealed: 2008 c.1 s.2

23. Human Reproductive Cloning Act 2001

repealed: 2008 c.22 s.3, Sch.8 Part 1

24. Anti-terrorism, Crime and Security Act 2001

Part 2, applied: 2008 c.28 s.63

s.4, enabling: SI 2008/2668, SI 2008/2766

s.14, enabling: SI 2008/2668, SI 2008/2766

s.19, repealed (in part): 2008 c.28 Sch.1 para.1, Sch.9 Part 2

s.37, repealed: 2008 c.12 Sch.1 Part 3

s.38, repealed: 2008 c.12 Sch.1 Part 3

s.47, applied: 2008 c.28 Sch.2, SI 2008/1466 Art.3

s.50, applied: SI 2008/1466 Art.3

s.52, applied: 2008 c.28 s.1, s.9

s.77, amended: SI 2008/960 Sch.3

s.80A, added: 2008 c.32 s.101

s.113, applied: 2008 c.28 s.28, s.41, SI 2008/1466 Art.3

s.113A, amended: 2008 c.28 s.75

s.114, applied: 2008 c.28 Sch.2

s.122, repealed: 2008 c.12 Sch.1 Part 3

s.123, repealed: 2008 c.12 Sch.1 Part 3

Sch.1 Part 2 para.3, amended: 2008 c.28 s.83

Sch.1 Part 2 para.4, amended: 2008 c.28 s.83

Sch.1 Part 3 para.7, substituted: 2008 c.28 s.84

Sch.1 Part 4 para.10, amended: 2008 c.28 s.83

CAP.

2001–cont.

24. Anti-terrorism, Crime and Security Act 2001–*cont.*

Sch.3, enabling: SI 2008/2668, SI 2008/2766

Sch.3 para.11, substituted: 2008 c.28 s.70

Sch.6 para.6, amended: 2008 c.28 s.91

2002

1. International Development Act 2002

applied: 2008 c.3 Sch.2 Part 2, 2008 c.8 Sch.2 Part 24

s.11, applied: SI 2008/2088 Art.3, SI 2008/2090 Art.3

s.11, enabling: SI 2008/2086, SI 2008/2088, SI 2008/2089, SI 2008/2090

7. Homelessness Act 2002

applied: SI 2008/2867 Reg.12

varied: SI 2008/2867 Reg.27

s.1, disapplied: SI 2008/2867 Reg.12

s.1, varied: SI 2008/2867 Reg.12

s.2, varied: SI 2008/2867 Reg.12

s.3, varied: SI 2008/2867 Reg.12

s.4, varied: SI 2008/2867 Reg.12

9. Land Registration Act 2002

applied: SI 2008/1730 r.3

s.1, enabling: SI 2008/1750, SI 2008/1919

s.4, amended: SI 2008/2872 Art.2

s.5, applied: SI 2008/2872

s.5, enabling: SI 2008/2872

s.7, amended: SI 2008/2872 Art.3

s.13, enabling: SI 2008/1919

s.14, enabling: SI 2008/1919

s.21, enabling: SI 2008/1919

s.22, enabling: SI 2008/1919

s.25, enabling: SI 2008/1750, SI 2008/1919

s.27, enabling: SI 2008/1919

s.29, see *Fitzkriston LLP v Panayi* [2008] EWCA Civ 283, [2008] L. & T.R. 26 (CA (Civ Div)), Laws, L.J.

s.36, enabling: SI 2008/1919

s.43, enabling: SI 2008/1919

s.47, enabling: SI 2008/1919

s.60, enabling: SI 2008/1919

s.66, enabling: SI 2008/1750, SI 2008/1919

s.67, enabling: SI 2008/1750, SI 2008/1919

s.70, enabling: SI 2008/1919

s.71, enabling: SI 2008/1750

s.73, enabling: SI 2008/1750, SI 2008/1919

s.88, enabling: SI 2008/1919

s.91, amended: SI 2008/948 Sch.1 para.224

s.91, applied: SI 2008/1750 r.3

s.91, enabling: SI 2008/1750

s.92, enabling: SI 2008/1748, SI 2008/1750

s.95, enabling: SI 2008/1750

s.100, enabling: SI 2008/1921, SI 2008/3201

s.102, applied: SI 2008/1748 Sch.1 para.5

s.109, applied: SI 2008/1730 r.27

s.109, enabling: SI 2008/1730, SI 2008/1731

s.110, enabling: SI 2008/1731

CAP.

2002–*cont.*

9. Land Registration Act 2002–*cont.*
s.111, applied: SI 2008/1730 r.31
s.114, enabling: SI 2008/1730, SI 2008/1731
s.126, enabling: SI 2008/1750, SI 2008/1919
s.127, applied: SI 2008/1750, SI 2008/1919, SI 2008/1920
s.127, enabling: SI 2008/1919
s.128, applied: SI 2008/1748
s.128, enabling: SI 2008/1731, SI 2008/1748, SI 2008/1750, SI 2008/1919
s.134, enabling: SI 2008/1919
Sch.2 Part 1 para.2, enabling: SI 2008/1919
Sch.2 Part 1 para.7, enabling: SI 2008/1919
Sch.4 para.7, enabling: SI 2008/1919
Sch.5 para.1, applied: SI 2008/1750 Sch.2 para.1
Sch.5 para.1, referred to: SI 2008/1748 r.4
Sch.5 para.1, enabling: SI 2008/1748
Sch.5 para.2, enabling: SI 2008/1748
Sch.5 para.3, applied: SI 2008/1748, SI 2008/1748 r.8, r.10
Sch.5 para.3, enabling: SI 2008/1748
Sch.5 para.4, applied: SI 2008/1748 r.10, Sch.1 para.8
Sch.5 para.4, referred to: SI 2008/1748 r.7, r.8
Sch.5 para.4, enabling: SI 2008/1730
Sch.5 para.5, enabling: SI 2008/1750
Sch.5 para.11, applied: SI 2008/1748
Sch.5 para.11, referred to: SI 2008/1748
Sch.5 para.11, enabling: SI 2008/1748
Sch.6 para.2, enabling: SI 2008/1919
Sch.6 para.10, enabling: SI 2008/1919
Sch.6 para.15, enabling: SI 2008/1919
Sch.7 para.4, applied: SI 2008/1748 Sch.2 para.13
Sch.8, applied: SI 2008/1748 Sch.2 para.13
Sch.8 para.9, enabling: SI 2008/1919
Sch.10 Part 1 para.3, enabling: SI 2008/1919
Sch.10 Part 2 para.5, enabling: SI 2008/1919
Sch.10 Part 2 para.6, enabling: SI 2008/1750, SI 2008/1919
Sch.10 Part 2 para.8, enabling: SI 2008/1750, SI 2008/1919
Sch.12 para.2, enabling: SI 2008/1919

15. Commonhold and Leasehold Reform Act 2002
see *Elizabeth Court (Bournemouth) Ltd v Revenue and Customs Commissioners* [2008] S.T.C. (S.C.D.) 366 (Sp Comm), AN Brice
s.62, amended: 2008 c.17 s.319
s.65, enabling: SI 2008/1920
s.72, see *Holding and Management (Solitaire) Ltd, Re* [2008] L. & T.R. 16 (Lands Tr), George Bartlett Q.C. (President)
s.121, see *Elizabeth Court (Bournemouth) Ltd v Revenue and Customs Commissioners* [2008] S.T.C. (S.C.D.) 366 (Sp Comm), AN Brice

CAP.

2002–*cont.*

15. Commonhold and Leasehold Reform Act 2002–*cont.*
s.122, see *Elizabeth Court (Bournemouth) Ltd v Revenue and Customs Commissioners* [2008] S.T.C. (S.C.D.) 366 (Sp Comm), AN Brice
s.125, see *Elizabeth Court (Bournemouth) Ltd v Revenue and Customs Commissioners* [2008] S.T.C. (S.C.D.) 366 (Sp Comm), AN Brice
s.141, repealed: 2008 c.17 Sch.16
s.156, repealed (in part): 2008 c.17 Sch.16
s.168, see *Swanston Grange (Luton) Management Ltd v Langley-Essen* [2008] L. & T.R. 20 (Lands Tr), Judge Huskinson
Sch.10 para.6, repealed: 2008 c.17 Sch.16
Sch.10 para.7, repealed: 2008 c.17 Sch.16

16. State Pension Credit Act 2002
applied: SI 2008/1052 Sch.2 para.2, SI 2008/1053 Sch.2 para.2, SI 2008/1054 Sch.2 para.2
s.1, enabling: SI 2008/2424, SI 2008/2767
s.2, enabling: SI 2008/698, SI 2008/2767, SI 2008/3195
s.6, applied: 2008 c.30 s.105
s.9, amended: 2008 c.30 s.105
s.9, repealed (in part): 2008 c.30 s.105
s.15, enabling: SI 2008/2767, SI 2008/3157
s.17, enabling: SI 2008/698, SI 2008/2424, SI 2008/2767, SI 2008/3157, SI 2008/3195
s.19, enabling: SI 2008/698, SI 2008/2424, SI 2008/2767, SI 2008/3157, SI 2008/3195

17. National Health Service Reform and Health Care Professions Act 2002
s.25, amended: 2008 c.14 s.113, Sch.10 para.16, Sch.10 para.17, Sch.15 Part 2
s.25, referred to: SI 2008/2927 Reg.2
s.25, varied: 2008 c.14 Sch.10 para.1
s.26, amended: 2008 c.14 s.115, Sch.10 para.18
s.26, repealed (in part): 2008 c.14 s.116, Sch.15 Part 2
s.26, varied: 2008 c.14 Sch.10 para.1
s.26A, added: 2008 c.14 s.116
s.26B, added: 2008 c.14 s.117
s.29, amended: 2008 c.14 s.118, Sch.15 Part 2
s.29, repealed (in part): 2008 c.14 s.118, Sch.15 Part 2
s.29, varied: 2008 c.14 s.118
s.38, enabling: SI 2008/2927
Sch.7 para.1, amended: 2008 c.14 Sch.10 para.19
Sch.7 para.2, amended: 2008 c.14 Sch.10 para.19
Sch.7 para.3, amended: 2008 c.14 Sch.10 para.19
Sch.7 para.4, amended: 2008 c.14 Sch.10 para.19
Sch.7 para.4, substituted: 2008 c.14 s.114

CAP.

2002–cont.

17. **National Health Service Reform and Health Care Professions Act 2002–** *cont.*

Sch.7 para.5, amended: 2008 c.14 Sch.10 para.19

Sch.7 para.6, amended: 2008 c.14 s.114, Sch.10 para.19

Sch.7 para.6, enabling: SI 2008/2927

Sch.7 para.7, amended: 2008 c.14 Sch.10 para.19

Sch.7 para.8, amended: 2008 c.14 Sch.10 para.19

Sch.7 para.9, amended: 2008 c.14 Sch.10 para.19

Sch.7 para.10, amended: 2008 c.14 s.114, Sch.10 para.19

Sch.7 para.11, amended: 2008 c.14 Sch.10 para.19

Sch.7 para.11, substituted: 2008 c.14 s.114

Sch.7 para.12, amended: 2008 c.14 Sch.10 para.19

Sch.7 para.13, amended: 2008 c.14 Sch.10 para.19

Sch.7 para.14, amended: 2008 c.14 Sch.10 para.19

Sch.7 para.15, amended: 2008 c.14 Sch.10 para.19

Sch.7 para.16, amended: 2008 c.14 s.114, Sch.10 para.19

Sch.7 para.17, amended: 2008 c.14 Sch.10 para.19

Sch.7 para.18, amended: 2008 c.14 Sch.10 para.19

Sch.7 para.19, amended: 2008 c.14 Sch.10 para.19

Sch.7 para.20, amended: 2008 c.14 Sch.10 para.19

Sch.7 para.20, repealed: 2008 c.14 Sch.15 Part 2

Sch.7 para.20, varied: 2008 c.14 Sch.10 para.1

Sch.7 para.21, amended: 2008 c.14 Sch.10 para.19

Sch.7 para.21, repealed: 2008 c.14 Sch.15 Part 2

Sch.7 para.21, varied: 2008 c.14 Sch.10 para.1

Sch.7 para.22, amended: 2008 c.14 Sch.10 para.19

Sch.7 para.22, repealed: 2008 c.14 Sch.15 Part 2

Sch.7 para.22, varied: 2008 c.14 Sch.10 para.1

Sch.7 para.23, amended: 2008 c.14 Sch.10 para.19

Sch.7 para.23, repealed: 2008 c.14 Sch.15 Part 2

Sch.7 para.23, varied: 2008 c.14 Sch.10 para.1

Sch.7 para.24, amended: 2008 c.14 Sch.10 para.19

CAP.

2002–cont.

17. **National Health Service Reform and Health Care Professions Act 2002–** *cont.*

Sch.7 para.24, repealed: 2008 c.14 Sch.15 Part 2

Sch.7 para.24, varied: 2008 c.14 Sch.10 para.1

21. **Tax Credits Act 2002**

Commencement Orders: SI 2008/3151 Art.3

applied: SI 2008/2685 Sch.1

Part 1, applied: SI 2008/18 Reg.32, SI 2008/529 Reg.43, Reg.46, SI 2008/794 Reg.145, SI 2008/1273 Reg.83D, Reg.83G, Reg.27, Reg.30, SI 2008/1582 Reg.42, Reg.45, SI 2008/3170 Reg.27, Reg.30, Reg.87

s.3, applied: SI 2008/3151 Art.2

s.4, enabling: SI 2008/604, SI 2008/2169

s.7, enabling: SI 2008/604, SI 2008/796, SI 2008/2169

s.8, enabling: SI 2008/2169

s.9, applied: SI 2008/794 Sch.6 para.1, Sch.6 para.5

s.9, enabling: SI 2008/796

s.11, enabling: SI 2008/796

s.12, applied: SI 2008/2687, SI 2008/3170 Reg.27

s.12, enabling: SI 2008/604, SI 2008/2169, SI 2008/2687

s.13, enabling: SI 2008/796

s.14, applied: SI 2008/1186 Reg.3

s.24, enabling: SI 2008/604

s.25, repealed (in part): 2008 c.9 Sch.36 para.90

s.35, see *Revenue and Customs Prosecution Office v Duffy* [2008] EWHC 848 (Admin), [2008] 2 Cr. App. R. (S.) 103 (DC), Richards, L.J.

s.41, applied: SI 2008/796

s.41, referred to: SI 2008/796

s.41, enabling: SI 2008/796

s.62, enabling: SI 2008/3151

s.63, applied: SI 2008/2707 Art.2

s.65, enabling: SI 2008/604, SI 2008/796, SI 2008/2169, SI 2008/2687

s.66, applied: SI 2008/796

s.67, enabling: SI 2008/604, SI 2008/2169

Sch.2 para.3, applied: SI 2008/2685 r.23, r.26

Sch.5 para.4, amended: 2008 c.6 Sch.7 para.4

Sch.5 para.6, amended: 2008 c.6 Sch.7 para.4

Sch.5 para.10, repealed: 2008 c.25 Sch.1 para.78, Sch.2

22. **Employment Act 2002**

s.13, amended: SI 2008/2656 Reg.2

s.24, repealed (in part): 2008 c.24 Sch.1 Part 1

s.29, repealed: 2008 c.24 s.1, Sch.1 Part 1

CAP.

2002–*cont.*

22. Employment Act 2002–*cont.*

s.30, see *Redcar & Cleveland BC v Bainbridge* [2008] EWCA Civ 885, [2008] I.R.L.R. 776 (CA (Civ Div)), Mummery, L.J.

s.30, repealed: 2008 c.24 s.1, Sch.1 Part 1

s.31, see *Clyde Valley Housing Association v MacAulay* [2008] I.R.L.R. 616 (EAT (SC)), Lady Smith; see *McKindless Group v McLaughlin* [2008] I.R.L.R. 678 (EAT (SC)), Lady Smith; see *Royal Bank of Scotland v Bevan* [2008] I.C.R. 682 (EAT), Judge Richardson; see *Yorkshire Housing Ltd v Swanson* [2008] I.R.L.R. 607 (EAT), Cox, J.

s.31, repealed: 2008 c.24 s.1, Sch.1 Part 1

s.32, see *Alitalia Airport SpA v Akrif* [2008] I.C.R. 813 (EAT), Elias, J.; see *Cannop v Highland Council* [2008] CSIH 38, 2008 S.L.T. 625 (IH (1 Div)), Lord Hamilton L.P.; see *Clyde Valley Housing Association v MacAulay* [2008] I.R.L.R. 616 (EAT (SC)), Lady Smith; see *Highland Council v TGWU* [2008] I.C.R. 1150 (EAT (SC)), Lady Smith; see *Highland Council v TGWU/Unison* [2008] I.R.L.R. 272 (EAT (SC)), Lady Smith; see *Sarti (Sauchiehall St) Ltd v Polito* [2008] I.C.R. 1279 (EAT (SC)), Lady Smith

s.32, repealed: 2008 c.24 s.1, Sch.1 Part 1

s.33, repealed: 2008 c.24 s.1, Sch.1 Part 1

s.34, repealed (in part): 2008 c.24 Sch.1 Part 1

s.40, amended: 2008 c.24 Sch.1 Part 1

s.45, enabling: SI 2008/2776

s.51, amended: 2008 c.24 Sch.1 Part 1

s.51, applied: SI 2008/2776

s.51, enabling: SI 2008/2776

Sch.2, see *Alitalia Airport SpA v Akrif* [2008] I.C.R. 813 (EAT), Elias, J.; see *Davies v Farnborough College of Technology* [2008] I.R.L.R. 14 (EAT), Burton, J.; see *Wilmot v Selvarajan* [2008] EWCA Civ 862, [2008] I.C.R. 1236 (CA (Civ Div)), Mummery, L.J.; see *Yorkshire Housing Ltd v Swanson* [2008] I.R.L.R. 607 (EAT), Cox, J.

Sch.2 Part 1 para.1, applied: SI 2008/3232 Sch.1 para.2

Sch.2 Part 1 para.1, repealed: 2008 c.24 s.1, Sch.1 Part 1

Sch.2 Part 1 para.2, applied: SI 2008/3232 Sch.1 para.2

Sch.2 Part 1 para.2, repealed: 2008 c.24 s.1, Sch.1 Part 1

Sch.2 Part 1 para.3, repealed: 2008 c.24 s.1, Sch.1 Part 1

Sch.2 Part 1 para.4, applied: SI 2008/3232 Sch.1 para.2

Sch.2 Part 1 para.4, repealed: 2008 c.24 s.1, Sch.1 Part 1

Sch.2 Part 1 para.5, repealed: 2008 c.24 s.1, Sch.1 Part 1

CAP.

2002–*cont.*

22. Employment Act 2002–*cont.*

Sch.2 Part 2 para.6, applied: SI 2008/3232 Sch.1 para.3

Sch.2 Part 2 para.6, repealed: 2008 c.24 s.1, Sch.1 Part 1

Sch.2 Part 2 para.7, repealed: 2008 c.24 s.1, Sch.1 Part 1

Sch.2 Part 2 para.8, repealed: 2008 c.24 s.1, Sch.1 Part 1

Sch.2 Part 2 para.9, applied: SI 2008/3232 Sch.1 para.3

Sch.2 Part 2 para.9, repealed: 2008 c.24 s.1, Sch.1 Part 1

Sch.2 Part 2 para.10, repealed: 2008 c.24 s.1, Sch.1 Part 1

Sch.2 Part 3 para.11, repealed: 2008 c.24 s.1, Sch.1 Part 1

Sch.2 Part 3 para.12, repealed: 2008 c.24 s.1, Sch.1 Part 1

Sch.2 Part 3 para.13, repealed: 2008 c.24 s.1, Sch.1 Part 1

Sch.2 Part 4 para.14, repealed: 2008 c.24 s.1, Sch.1 Part 1

Sch.2 Part 4 para.15, repealed: 2008 c.24 s.1, Sch.1 Part 1

Sch.2 para.6, see *Alitalia Airport SpA v Akrif* [2008] I.C.R. 813 (EAT), Elias, J.; see *Cannop v Highland Council* [2008] CSIH 38, 2008 S.L.T. 625 (IH (1 Div)), Lord Hamilton L.P.; see *Highland Council v TGWU* [2008] I.C.R. 1150 (EAT (SC)), Lady Smith; see *Highland Council v TGWU/Unison* [2008] I.R.L.R. 272 (EAT (SC)), Lady Smith

Sch.3, amended: SI 2008/1660 Sch.3 para.3

Sch.3, repealed: 2008 c.24 s.1, Sch.1 Part 1

Sch.4, amended: SI 2008/1660 Sch.3 para.3

Sch.4, repealed: 2008 c.24 s.1, Sch.1 Part 1

Sch.5, amended: SI 2008/1660 Sch.3 para.3

Sch.6 para.11, repealed (in part): 2008 c.6 Sch.8

Sch.6 para.13, repealed (in part): 2008 c.6 Sch.8

23. Finance Act 2002

s.5, repealed (in part): 2008 c.9 Sch.5 para.25

s.29, applied: 2008 c.13 Sch.2 para.3

s.46, repealed: 2008 c.9 Sch.2 para.55

s.47, repealed: 2008 c.9 Sch.2 para.55

s.60, amended: 2008 c.9 s.77

s.87, repealed: 2008 c.9 Sch.14 para.17

s.101, see *Halcyon Films LLP v Revenue and Customs Commissioners* [2008] S.T.C. (S.C.D.) 1016 (Sp Comm), Edward Sadler

s.126, repealed: 2008 c.9 s.149

s.133, repealed (in part): 2008 c.9 Sch.40 para.21

s.134, amended: SI 2008/2871 Reg.3

s.134, repealed (in part): SI 2008/2871 Reg.3

Sch.2 para.4, repealed: 2008 c.9 Sch.5 para.25

CAP.

2002–cont.

23. Finance Act 2002–*cont.*

Sch.9 Part 2 para.4, repealed (in part): 2008 c.9 s.41

Sch.9 Part 2 para.5, repealed (in part): 2008 c.9 Sch.2 para.55

Sch.10 para.1, repealed: 2008 c.9 Sch.2 para.55

Sch.10 para.2, repealed: 2008 c.9 Sch.2 para.55

Sch.10 para.3, repealed: 2008 c.9 Sch.2 para.55

Sch.10 para.4, repealed: 2008 c.9 Sch.2 para.55

Sch.10 para.5, repealed: 2008 c.9 Sch.2 para.55

Sch.10 para.6, repealed: 2008 c.9 Sch.2 para.55

Sch.10 para.7, repealed: 2008 c.9 Sch.2 para.55

Sch.10 para.8, repealed: 2008 c.9 Sch.2 para.55

Sch.10 para.9, repealed: 2008 c.9 Sch.2 para.55

Sch.10 para.10, repealed: 2008 c.9 Sch.2 para.55

Sch.10 para.11, repealed: 2008 c.9 Sch.2 para.55

Sch.10 para.12, repealed: 2008 c.9 Sch.2 para.55

Sch.11 para.2, repealed (in part): 2008 c.9 Sch.2 para.55

Sch.11 para.3, repealed: 2008 c.9 Sch.2 para.21

Sch.11 para.4, repealed: 2008 c.9 Sch.2 para.55

Sch.11 para.5, repealed: 2008 c.9 Sch.2 para.55

Sch.11 para.6, repealed: 2008 c.9 Sch.2 para.55, Sch.7 para.114

Sch.12 Part 2A para.10C, added: 2008 c.9 Sch.10 para.9

Sch.12 Part 3 para.11, amended: 2008 c.9 Sch.8 para.2, Sch.10 para.9

Sch.12 Part 4 para.12, amended: 2008 c.9 Sch.17 para.36

Sch.12 Part 5 para.15, amended: 2008 c.9 Sch.8 para.2, Sch.10 para.9

Sch.13 Part 1 para.1, amended: 2008 c.9 Sch.10 para.10

Sch.13 Part 1 para.2, amended: 2008 c.9 s.27

Sch.13 Part 1 para.2, repealed (in part): 2008 c.9 s.27

Sch.13 Part 1 para.6, amended: 2008 c.9 s.27

Sch.13 Part 1 para.6, referred to: 2008 c.9 s.27

Sch.13 Part 1 para.6, repealed (in part): 2008 c.9 s.27

Sch.13 Part 1 para.10, disapplied: 2008 c.9 s.27

Sch.13 Part 1 para.12, repealed: 2008 c.9 s.27

Sch.13 Part 2 para.14, amended: 2008 c.9 Sch.8 para.3, Sch.9 para.2

CAP.

2002–cont.

23. Finance Act 2002–*cont.*

Sch.13 Part 2 para.15, amended: 2008 c.9 Sch.8 para.3, Sch.9 para.2

Sch.13 Part 2 para.15A, amended: 2008 c.9 Sch.8 para.3

Sch.13 Part 2 para.16, amended: 2008 c.9 Sch.9 para.2

Sch.13 Part 2 para.16A, amended: 2008 c.9 Sch.8 para.3

Sch.13 Part 2 para.18, amended: 2008 c.9 Sch.9 para.2

Sch.13 Part 2 para.18A, added: 2008 c.9 Sch.9 para.2

Sch.13 Part 3 para.21, amended: 2008 c.9 s.30, Sch.8 para.3

Sch.13 Part 5 para.25, amended: 2008 c.9 Sch.8 para.3

Sch.13 Part 5 para.25, repealed: 2008 c.9 s.27

Sch.16 Part 2 para.4, enabling: SI 2008/383

Sch.16 Part 6 para.27, amended: 2008 c.9 Sch.39 para.48

Sch.16 Part 6 para.35, amended: 2008 c.9 s.54

Sch.18 Part 2 para.5, applied: 2008 c.9 Sch.19 para.1

Sch.25 Part 1 para.21, repealed: 2008 c.9 Sch.14 para.17

Sch.26, applied: 2008 c.9 Sch.22 para.20, 2008 c.18 Sch.13 para.15, Sch.13 para.24

Sch.26 Part 2 para.3, amended: 2008 c.9 Sch.22 para.20

Sch.26 Part 2 para.4, amended: 2008 c.9 Sch.22 para.20

Sch.26 Part 4 para.17C, enabling: SI 2008/3237

Sch.26 Part 6 para.27A, added: 2008 c.9 Sch.22 para.4

Sch.26 Part 6 para.28, amended: 2008 c.9 Sch.22 para.5

Sch.26 Part 6 para.28, applied: 2008 c.18 Sch.13 para.15

Sch.26 Part 6 para.30A, amended: SI 2008/1579 Sch.3 para.2

Sch.26 Part 6 para.30B, amended: SI 2008/1579 Sch.3 para.3

Sch.26 Part 6 para.30B, repealed (in part): SI 2008/1579 Sch.3 para.3

Sch.26 Part 6 para.30B, varied: SI 2008/1579 Sch.4 para.4

Sch.26 Part 6 para.30C, amended: SI 2008/1579 Sch.3 para.4

Sch.26 Part 6 para.30C, varied: SI 2008/1579 Sch.4 para.4

Sch.26 Part 6 para.30D, amended: SI 2008/1579 Sch.3 para.5

Sch.26 Part 6 para.30D, repealed (in part): SI 2008/1579 Sch.3 para.5

Sch.26 Part 6 para.30D, varied: SI 2008/1579 Sch.4 para.4

CAP.

2002–cont.

23. Finance Act 2002–*cont.*

Sch.26 Part 6 para.30E, varied: SI 2008/1579 Sch.4 para.4

Sch.26 Part 6 para.30G, amended: SI 2008/1579 Sch.3 para.6

Sch.26 Part 6 para.30H, amended: SI 2008/1579 Sch.3 para.7

Sch.26 Part 6 para.30I, amended: SI 2008/1579 Sch.3 para.8

Sch.26 Part 8 para.41, amended: 2008 c.9 Sch.17 para.12

Sch.26 Part 8 para.41A, added: 2008 c.9 Sch.17 para.12

Sch.26 Part 8 para.42, repealed: 2008 c.9 Sch.17 para.12

Sch.26 Part 8 para.43, added: 2008 c.9 Sch.17 para.12

Sch.26 Part 9 para.43A, applied: 2008 c.9 Sch.22 para.20

Sch.26 Part 9 para.45D, amended: 2008 c.9 Sch.2 para.51

Sch.26 Part 9 para.50A, amended: SI 2008/1579 Sch.3 para.9

Sch.29, applied: 2008 c.17 Sch.7 para.10, 2008 c.18 Sch.13 para.13, Sch.13 para.23

Sch.29, referred to: 2008 c.17 Sch.7 para.10, 2008 c.18 Sch.13 para.13

Sch.29 Part 6 para.36, repealed (in part): 2008 c.9 Sch.17 para.17

Sch.29 Part 11 para.85, repealed (in part): SI 2008/1579 Sch.3 para.11

Sch.29 Part 11 para.85, varied: SI 2008/1579 Sch.4 para.4

Sch.29 Part 11 para.85A, amended: SI 2008/1579 Sch.3 para.12

Sch.29 Part 11 para.85A, repealed (in part): SI 2008/1579 Sch.3 para.12

Sch.29 Part 11 para.85A, varied: SI 2008/1579 Sch.4 para.4

Sch.29 Part 11 para.85B, amended: SI 2008/1579 Sch.3 para.13

Sch.29 Part 11 para.85C, amended: SI 2008/1579 Sch.3 para.14

Sch.29 Part 11 para.85D, amended: SI 2008/1579 Sch.3 para.15

Sch.29 Part 11 para.87, amended: SI 2008/1579 Sch.3 para.16

Sch.29 Part 11 para.87, varied: SI 2008/1579 Sch.4 para.4

Sch.29 Part 11 para.87A, amended: SI 2008/1579 Sch.3 para.17

Sch.29 Part 11 para.87A, repealed (in part): SI 2008/1579 Sch.3 para.17

Sch.29 Part 11 para.87A, varied: SI 2008/1579 Sch.4 para.4

Sch.29 Part 11 para.88, amended: SI 2008/1579 Sch.3 para.18

Sch.29 Part 12 para.92, applied: 2008 c.9 s.65

Sch.29 Part 12 para.95A, added: 2008 c.9 s.65

CAP.

2002–cont.

23. Finance Act 2002–*cont.*

Sch.29 Part 15 para.138, repealed (in part): 2008 c.9 Sch.17 para.17

Sch.39 para.6, see *Revenue and Customs Commissioners v Morris* [2007] EWHC 3345 (Ch), [2008] B.P.I.R. 391 (Ch D), Judge Pelling Q.C.

24. European Parliamentary Elections Act 2002

s.1, amended: SI 2008/1954 Art.2

s.4, enabling: SI 2008/3102

s.6, disapplied: SI 2008/2857 Art.7

s.6, enabling: SI 2008/1914

s.7, enabling: SI 2008/1741

s.12, applied: 2008 c.7 s.4

26. Justice (Northern Ireland) Act 2002

Commencement Orders: SI 2008/2833 Sch.3 para.228

s.27, applied: SI 2008/1216 Sch.4 para.4

s.46, amended: SI 2008/1216 Sch.5 para.9

Sch.3 para.22, repealed: SI 2008/2833 Sch.3 para.228

Sch.4 para.1, repealed (in part): SI 2008/1216 Sch.6 Part 3

Sch.7 para.18, repealed: SI 2008/1216 Sch.6 Part 1

Sch.11 para.12, repealed: SI 2008/1216 Sch.6 Part 1

Sch.12 para.47, repealed: SI 2008/2833 Sch.3 para.228

Sch.13, amended: SI 2008/1216 Art.95, Sch.6 Part 2

28. Export Control Act 2002

applied: SI 2008/3231 Art.43

s.1, enabling: SI 2008/639, SI 2008/1098, SI 2008/1281, SI 2008/3063, SI 2008/3161, SI 2008/3231

s.2, enabling: SI 2008/639, SI 2008/1098, SI 2008/1281, SI 2008/3063, SI 2008/3161, SI 2008/3231

s.3, enabling: SI 2008/131, SI 2008/1098, SI 2008/1964, SI 2008/3063, SI 2008/3231

s.4, enabling: SI 2008/131, SI 2008/639, SI 2008/1098, SI 2008/1281, SI 2008/1805, SI 2008/1964, SI 2008/3063, SI 2008/3161, SI 2008/3231

s.5, enabling: SI 2008/131, SI 2008/639, SI 2008/1098, SI 2008/1281, SI 2008/1805, SI 2008/1964, SI 2008/3063, SI 2008/3161, SI 2008/3231

s.7, enabling: SI 2008/131, SI 2008/639, SI 2008/1098, SI 2008/1281, SI 2008/1805, SI 2008/1964, SI 2008/3063, SI 2008/3161, SI 2008/3231

s.8, referred to: SI 2008/3231

29. Proceeds of Crime Act 2002

see *Assets Recovery Agency v Virtosu* [2008] EWHC 149 (QB), [2008] 3 All E.R. 637 (QBD), Tugendhat, J.; see *CPS v Moulden (Leanne)* [2008] EWCA Crim 2648, Times, November 26, 2008 (CA (Crim Div)), Pill,

CAP.

2002–cont.

29. Proceeds of Crime Act 2002–*cont.*

see–*cont.*

L.J.; see *Green v Walkling* [2007] EWHC 3251 (Ch), [2008] B.C.C. 256 (Ch D), Bernard Livesey Q.C.; see *R. v Singh (Jhalman)* [2008] EWCA Crim 243, [2008] 2 Cr. App. R. (S.) 69 (CA (Crim Div)), Richards, L.J.; see *Telli v Revenue and Customs Prosecutions Office* [2007] EWCA Civ 1385, [2008] 3 All E.R. 405 (CA (Civ Div)), Ward, L.J.

applied: 2008 asp 2 Sch.1, SI 2008/1978

Part 6, see *Director of the Assets Recovery Agency v McCormack* [2007] EWHC 908 (QB), [2008] S.T.C. 1097 (QBD), Pitchers, J.

Part 6, applied: SI 2008/755 Art.7

Part 8 c.2, applied: SI 2008/946, SI 2008/946 Art.3

Part 5, see *Director of the Assets Recovery Agency v Olupitan* [2008] EWCA Civ 104, [2008] C.P. Rep. 24 (CA (Civ Div)), Sir Igor Judge (President, QB); see *R. v W* [2008] EWCA Crim 2, [2008] 3 All E.R. 533 (CA (Crim Div)), Laws, L.J.

Part 7, see *R. v W* [2008] EWCA Crim 2, [2008] 3 All E.R. 533 (CA (Crim Div)), Laws, L.J.

s.6, see *CPS v Moulden (Leanne)* [2008] EWCA Crim 2648, Times, November 26, 2008 (CA (Crim Div)), Pill, L.J.; see *Crown Prosecution Service (Nottinghamshire) v Rose* [2008] EWCA Crim 239, [2008] 1 W.L.R. 2113 (CA (Crim Div)), Richards, L.J.; see *R. v Hockey (Terence John)* [2007] EWCA Crim 1577, [2008] 1 Cr. App. R. (S.) 50 (CA (Crim Div)), Pill, L.J.

s.6, applied: 2008 c.4 s.39, SI 2008/755 Art.4

s.6, varied: SI 2008/755 Art.4

s.7, varied: SI 2008/755 Art.4

s.8, varied: SI 2008/755 Art.4

s.9, varied: SI 2008/755 Art.4

s.10, varied: SI 2008/755 Art.4

s.11, varied: SI 2008/755 Art.4

s.12, varied: SI 2008/755 Art.4

s.13, see *R. (on the application of Faithfull) v Ipswich Crown Court* [2007] EWHC 2763 (Admin), [2008] 1 W.L.R. 1636 (DC), Richards, L.J.

s.13, amended: 2008 c.28 Sch.3 para.7

s.13, varied: SI 2008/755 Art.4

s.14, varied: SI 2008/755 Art.4

s.15, varied: SI 2008/755 Art.4

s.16, varied: SI 2008/755 Art.4

s.17, varied: SI 2008/755 Art.4

s.18, varied: SI 2008/755 Art.4

s.19, applied: SI 2008/755 Art.4

s.19, varied: SI 2008/755 Art.4

s.20, applied: SI 2008/755 Art.4

CAP.

2002–cont.

29. Proceeds of Crime Act 2002–*cont.*

s.20, varied: SI 2008/755 Art.4

s.21, varied: SI 2008/755 Art.4

s.22, varied: SI 2008/755 Art.4

s.23, varied: SI 2008/755 Art.4

s.24, varied: SI 2008/755 Art.4

s.24A, varied: SI 2008/755 Art.4

s.25, varied: SI 2008/755 Art.4

s.26, varied: SI 2008/755 Art.4

s.27, applied: SI 2008/755 Art.4

s.27, varied: SI 2008/755 Art.4

s.28, applied: SI 2008/755 Art.4

s.28, varied: SI 2008/755 Art.4

s.29, varied: SI 2008/755 Art.4

s.30, varied: SI 2008/755 Art.4

s.31, see *CPS v Moulden (Leanne)* [2008] EWCA Crim 2648, Times, November 26, 2008 (CA (Crim Div)), Pill, L.J.; see *R. v Hockey (Terence John)* [2007] EWCA Crim 1577, [2008] 1 Cr. App. R. (S.) 50 (CA (Crim Div)), Pill, L.J.

s.31, varied: SI 2008/755 Art.4

s.32, see *R. v Hockey (Terence John)* [2007] EWCA Crim 1577, [2008] 1 Cr. App. R. (S.) 50 (CA (Crim Div)), Pill, L.J.

s.32, varied: SI 2008/755 Art.4

s.33, varied: SI 2008/755 Art.4

s.34, varied: SI 2008/755 Art.4

s.35, varied: SI 2008/755 Art.4

s.36, varied: SI 2008/755 Art.4

s.37, varied: SI 2008/755 Art.4

s.38, varied: SI 2008/755 Art.4

s.39, varied: SI 2008/755 Art.4

s.40, see *King v Serious Fraud Office* [2008] EWCA Crim 530, [2008] 1 W.L.R. 2634 (CA (Crim Div)), Gage, L.J.

s.40, varied: SI 2008/755 Art.4

s.41, see *AP v Crown Prosecution Service* [2007] EWCA Crim 3128, [2008] 1 Cr. App. R. 39 (CA (Crim Div)), Latham, L.J.; see *Irwin Mitchell (A Firm) v Revenue & Customs Prosecutions Office* [2008] EWCA Crim 1741, Times, August 27, 2008 (CA (Crim Div)), Toulson, L.J.; see *King v Serious Fraud Office* [2008] EWCA Crim 530, [2008] 1 W.L.R. 2634 (CA (Crim Div)), Gage, L.J.; see *R. v M* [2008] EWCA Crim 1901, Times, October 24, 2008 (CA (Crim Div)), Toulson, L.J.

s.41, varied: SI 2008/755 Art.4

s.42, varied: SI 2008/755 Art.4

s.43, varied: SI 2008/755 Art.4

s.44, varied: SI 2008/755 Art.4

s.45, varied: SI 2008/755 Art.4

s.46, varied: SI 2008/755 Art.4

s.47, varied: SI 2008/755 Art.4

s.48, varied: SI 2008/755 Art.4

s.49, applied: SI 2008/755 Art.17

s.49, varied: SI 2008/755 Art.4

s.50, varied: SI 2008/755 Art.4

s.51, applied: SI 2008/755 Art.17

CAP.

2002–cont.

29. Proceeds of Crime Act 2002–*cont.*

s.51, varied: SI 2008/755 Art.4
s.52, varied: SI 2008/755 Art.4
s.53, varied: SI 2008/755 Art.4
s.54, varied: SI 2008/755 Art.4
s.55, varied: SI 2008/755 Art.4
s.56, applied: SI 2008/755 Art.5
s.56, varied: SI 2008/755 Art.4
s.57, applied: SI 2008/755 Art.5
s.57, varied: SI 2008/755 Art.4
s.58, varied: SI 2008/755 Art.4
s.59, varied: SI 2008/755 Art.4
s.60, varied: SI 2008/755 Art.4
s.61, varied: SI 2008/755 Art.4
s.62, varied: SI 2008/755 Art.4
s.63, varied: SI 2008/755 Art.4
s.64, varied: SI 2008/755 Art.4
s.65, varied: SI 2008/755 Art.4
s.66, varied: SI 2008/755 Art.4
s.67, varied: SI 2008/755 Art.4
s.68, varied: SI 2008/755 Art.4
s.69, see *Serious Fraud Office v Lexi Holdings Plc (In Administration)* [2008] EWCA Crim 1443, [2008] B.P.I.R. 1598 (CA (Crim Div)), Keene, L.J.
s.69, varied: SI 2008/755 Art.4
s.70, varied: SI 2008/755 Art.4
s.71, varied: SI 2008/755 Art.4
s.72, varied: SI 2008/755 Art.4
s.73, varied: SI 2008/755 Art.4
s.74, varied: SI 2008/755 Art.4
s.75, varied: SI 2008/755 Art.4
s.76, see *Crown Prosecution Service (Nottinghamshire) v Rose* [2008] EWCA Crim 239, [2008] 1 W.L.R. 2113 (CA (Crim Div)), Richards, L.J.
s.76, varied: SI 2008/755 Art.4
s.77, varied: SI 2008/755 Art.4
s.78, varied: SI 2008/755 Art.4
s.79, see *Crown Prosecution Service (Nottinghamshire) v Rose* [2008] EWCA Crim 239, [2008] 1 W.L.R. 2113 (CA (Crim Div)), Richards, L.J.
s.79, varied: SI 2008/755 Art.4
s.80, see *Crown Prosecution Service (Nottinghamshire) v Rose* [2008] EWCA Crim 239, [2008] 1 W.L.R. 2113 (CA (Crim Div)), Richards, L.J.; see *R. v Pattison (Leslie)* [2007] EWCA Crim 1536, [2008] 1 Cr. App. R. (S.) 51 (CA (Crim Div)), Toulson, L.J.
s.80, varied: SI 2008/755 Art.4
s.81, varied: SI 2008/755 Art.4
s.82, amended: 2008 c.28 Sch.3 para.7
s.82, varied: SI 2008/755 Art.4
s.83, varied: SI 2008/755 Art.4
s.84, varied: SI 2008/755 Art.4
s.85, varied: SI 2008/755 Art.4
s.86, varied: SI 2008/755 Art.4
s.87, varied: SI 2008/755 Art.4

CAP.

2002–cont.

29. Proceeds of Crime Act 2002–*cont.*

s.88, varied: SI 2008/755 Art.4
s.89, varied: SI 2008/755 Art.4
s.90, varied: SI 2008/755 Art.4
s.91, varied: SI 2008/755 Art.4
s.97, amended: 2008 c.28 Sch.3 para.7
s.148, amended: 2008 c.28 Sch.3 para.7
s.156, applied: SI 2008/755 Art.4
s.156, varied: SI 2008/755 Art.4
s.157, varied: SI 2008/755 Art.4
s.158, varied: SI 2008/755 Art.4
s.159, varied: SI 2008/755 Art.4
s.160, varied: SI 2008/755 Art.4
s.161, varied: SI 2008/755 Art.4
s.162, varied: SI 2008/755 Art.4
s.163, amended: 2008 c.28 Sch.3 para.7
s.163, varied: SI 2008/755 Art.4
s.164, varied: SI 2008/755 Art.4
s.165, varied: SI 2008/755 Art.4
s.166, varied: SI 2008/755 Art.4
s.167, varied: SI 2008/755 Art.4
s.168, varied: SI 2008/755 Art.4
s.169, applied: SI 2008/755 Art.4
s.169, varied: SI 2008/755 Art.4
s.170, applied: SI 2008/755 Art.4
s.170, varied: SI 2008/755 Art.4
s.171, varied: SI 2008/755 Art.4
s.172, varied: SI 2008/755 Art.4
s.173, varied: SI 2008/755 Art.4
s.174, varied: SI 2008/755 Art.4
s.175, varied: SI 2008/755 Art.4
s.176, varied: SI 2008/755 Art.4
s.177, applied: SI 2008/755 Art.4
s.177, varied: SI 2008/755 Art.4
s.178, applied: SI 2008/755 Art.4
s.178, varied: SI 2008/755 Art.4
s.179, varied: SI 2008/755 Art.4
s.180, varied: SI 2008/755 Art.4
s.181, varied: SI 2008/755 Art.4
s.182, varied: SI 2008/755 Art.4
s.183, varied: SI 2008/755 Art.4
s.184, varied: SI 2008/755 Art.4
s.185, varied: SI 2008/755 Art.4
s.186, varied: SI 2008/755 Art.4
s.187, varied: SI 2008/755 Art.4
s.188, varied: SI 2008/755 Art.4
s.189, varied: SI 2008/755 Art.4
s.190, varied: SI 2008/755 Art.4
s.191, varied: SI 2008/755 Art.4
s.192, varied: SI 2008/755 Art.4
s.193, varied: SI 2008/755 Art.4
s.194, varied: SI 2008/755 Art.4
s.195, varied: SI 2008/755 Art.4
s.196, varied: SI 2008/755 Art.4
s.197, applied: SI 2008/755 Art.17
s.197, varied: SI 2008/755 Art.4
s.198, varied: SI 2008/755 Art.4
s.199, applied: SI 2008/755 Art.17
s.199, varied: SI 2008/755 Art.4
s.200, varied: SI 2008/755 Art.4

CAP.

2002–cont.

29. Proceeds of Crime Act 2002–*cont.*

s.201, varied: SI 2008/755 Art.4
s.202, varied: SI 2008/755 Art.4
s.203, varied: SI 2008/755 Art.4
s.204, applied: SI 2008/755 Art.5
s.204, varied: SI 2008/755 Art.4
s.205, applied: SI 2008/755 Art.5
s.205, varied: SI 2008/755 Art.4
s.206, varied: SI 2008/755 Art.4
s.207, varied: SI 2008/755 Art.4
s.208, varied: SI 2008/755 Art.4
s.209, varied: SI 2008/755 Art.4
s.210, varied: SI 2008/755 Art.4
s.211, varied: SI 2008/755 Art.4
s.212, varied: SI 2008/755 Art.4
s.213, varied: SI 2008/755 Art.4
s.214, varied: SI 2008/755 Art.4
s.215, varied: SI 2008/755 Art.4
s.216, varied: SI 2008/755 Art.4
s.217, varied: SI 2008/755 Art.4
s.218, varied: SI 2008/755 Art.4
s.219, varied: SI 2008/755 Art.4
s.220, varied: SI 2008/755 Art.4
s.221, varied: SI 2008/755 Art.4
s.222, varied: SI 2008/755 Art.4
s.223, varied: SI 2008/755 Art.4
s.224, varied: SI 2008/755 Art.4
s.225, varied: SI 2008/755 Art.4
s.226, varied: SI 2008/755 Art.4
s.227, varied: SI 2008/755 Art.4
s.228, varied: SI 2008/755 Art.4
s.229, varied: SI 2008/755 Art.4
s.230, amended: 2008 c.28 Sch.3 para.7
s.230, varied: SI 2008/755 Art.4
s.231, varied: SI 2008/755 Art.4
s.232, varied: SI 2008/755 Art.4
s.233, varied: SI 2008/755 Art.4
s.234, varied: SI 2008/755 Art.4
s.235, varied: SI 2008/755 Art.4
s.236, varied: SI 2008/755 Art.4
s.237, varied: SI 2008/755 Art.4
s.238, varied: SI 2008/755 Art.4
s.239, varied: SI 2008/755 Art.4
s.240, see *Assets Recovery Agency v Virtosu* [2008] EWHC 149 (QB), [2008] 3 All E.R. 637 (QBD), Tugendhat, J.
s.241, see *Assets Recovery Agency v Virtosu* [2008] EWHC 149 (QB), [2008] 3 All E.R. 637 (QBD), Tugendhat, J.; see *Director of the Assets Recovery Agency v Olupitan* [2008] EWCA Civ 104, [2008] C.P. Rep. 24 (CA (Civ Div)), Sir Igor Judge (President, QB)
s.242, see *R. (on the application of the Chief Constable of Greater Manchester) v City of Salford Magistrates' Court* [2008] EWHC 1651 (Admin), (2008) 172 J.P. 497 (DC), Richards, L.J.

CAP.

2002–cont.

29. Proceeds of Crime Act 2002–*cont.*

s.256, see *Scottish Ministers v Stirton* [2008] CSOH 20, 2008 S.L.T. 505 (OH), Lord Glennie
s.280, amended: SI 2008/949 Art.2
s.280, applied: SI 2008/755 Art.6
s.280, referred to: SI 2008/755 Art.6
s.286A, applied: SI 2008/523
s.286A, enabling: SI 2008/523
s.286B, applied: SI 2008/523
s.286B, enabling: SI 2008/523
s.289, applied: SI 2008/947 Art.3
s.292, applied: SI 2008/947, SI 2008/947 Art.2
s.292, enabling: SI 2008/947
s.294, see *R. (on the application of the Chief Constable of Greater Manchester) v City of Salford Magistrates' Court* [2008] EWHC 1651 (Admin), (2008) 172 J.P. 497 (DC), Richards, L.J.
s.295, see *R. (on the application of the Chief Constable of Greater Manchester) v City of Salford Magistrates' Court* [2008] EWHC 1651 (Admin), (2008) 172 J.P. 497 (DC), Richards, L.J.
s.297, see *R. (on the application of the Chief Constable of Greater Manchester) v City of Salford Magistrates' Court* [2008] EWHC 1651 (Admin), (2008) 172 J.P. 497 (DC), Richards, L.J.
s.298, see *R. (on the application of the Chief Constable of Greater Manchester) v City of Salford Magistrates' Court* [2008] EWHC 1651 (Admin), (2008) 172 J.P. 497 (DC), Richards, L.J.
s.304, see *Assets Recovery Agency v Virtosu* [2008] EWHC 149 (QB), [2008] 3 All E.R. 637 (QBD), Tugendhat, J.
s.305, see *Assets Recovery Agency v Virtosu* [2008] EWHC 149 (QB), [2008] 3 All E.R. 637 (QBD), Tugendhat, J.
s.325, applied: SI 2008/755 Art.3, Art.7
s.325, referred to: SI 2008/755 Art.7
s.327, see *R. v W* [2008] EWCA Crim 2, [2008] 3 All E.R. 533 (CA (Crim Div)), Laws, L.J.
s.328, see *R. v Anwoir* [2008] EWCA Crim 1354, [2008] 4 All E.R. 582 (CA (Crim Div)), Latham, L.J.; see *R. v W* [2008] EWCA Crim 2, [2008] 3 All E.R. 533 (CA (Crim Div)), Laws, L.J.
s.333, see *Green v Walkling* [2007] EWHC 3251 (Ch), [2008] B.C.C. 256 (Ch D), Bernard Livesey Q.C.
s.340, see *R. v W* [2008] EWCA Crim 2, [2008] 3 All E.R. 533 (CA (Crim Div)), Laws, L.J.
s.345, see *Redknapp v Commissioner of Police of the Metropolis* [2008] EWHC 1177 (Admin), [2008] 1 All E.R. 229 (DC), Latham, L.J.
s.352, applied: SI 2008/755 Art.8

CAP.

2002–*cont.*

29. Proceeds of Crime Act 2002–*cont.*
s.356, applied: SI 2008/755 Art.8
s.357, applied: SI 2008/755 Art.3, Art.9
s.376, varied: SI 2008/755 Art.10
s.377, applied: SI 2008/946, SI 2008/946 Art.2, Art.3
s.377, enabling: SI 2008/946
s.377A, applied: SI 2008/1978, SI 2008/1978 Art.2
s.377A, enabling: SI 2008/1978
s.429, enabling: SI 2008/946
s.436, applied: SI 2008/1909 Art.2
s.436, enabling: SI 2008/1909
s.438, applied: SI 2008/1909 Art.3
s.438, enabling: SI 2008/1909
s.443, enabling: SI 2008/298
s.444, applied: SI 2008/755 Art.11
s.444, enabling: SI 2008/302
s.459, applied: SI 2008/1909
s.459, enabling: SI 2008/523, SI 2008/946, SI 2008/947
Sch.1 para.7, applied: SI 2008/755 Art.12
Sch.1 para.7, disapplied: SI 2008/755 Art.12
Sch.5 para.8, amended: SI 2008/1769 Sch.1 para.29
Sch.5 para.8, repealed (in part): SI 2008/1769 Sch.1 para.29, Sch.3
Sch.10 Part 2 para.18, repealed: 2008 c.9 Sch.27 para.24
Sch.10 Part 2 para.19, repealed: 2008 c.9 Sch.27 para.24
Sch.10 Part 2 para.20, repealed: 2008 c.9 Sch.27 para.24
Sch.10 Part 2 para.21, repealed: 2008 c.9 Sch.27 para.24
Sch.11 para.22, repealed (in part): 2008 c.30 Sch.11 Part 2

30. Police Reform Act 2002
see *R. (on the application of Reynolds) v Chief Constable of Sussex* [2008] EWCA Civ 1160, Times, November 6, 2008 (CA (Civ Div)), Ward, L.J.
applied: 2008 c.4 s.127, SI 2008/2712 Art.4, SI 2008/2993 Art.3
Part 2, applied: SI 2008/212 Reg.5, Reg.7
s.10, see *R. (on the application of Reynolds) v Chief Constable of Sussex* [2008] EWCA Civ 1160, Times, November 6, 2008 (CA (Civ Div)), Ward, L.J.
s.10, varied: SI 2008/212 Sch.1 para.1
s.11, varied: SI 2008/212 Sch.1 para.2
s.12, varied: SI 2008/212 Sch.1 para.3
s.13, enabling: SI 2008/2866
s.14, varied: SI 2008/212 Sch.1 para.4
s.15, varied: SI 2008/212 Sch.1 para.5
s.16, varied: SI 2008/212 Sch.1 para.6
s.16A, varied: SI 2008/212 Sch.1 para.7
s.17, varied: SI 2008/212 Sch.1 para.8
s.18, varied: SI 2008/212 Sch.1 para.9
s.20, varied: SI 2008/212 Sch.1 para.10

CAP.

2002–*cont.*

30. Police Reform Act 2002–*cont.*
s.21, see *R. (on the application of Saunders) v Independent Police Complaints Commission* [2008] EWHC 2372 (Admin), Times, October 22, 2008 (QBD (Admin)), Underhill, J.
s.21, varied: SI 2008/212 Sch.1 para.11
s.22, varied: SI 2008/212 Sch.1 para.12
s.23, amended: 2008 c.4 Sch.23 para.2
s.23, varied: SI 2008/212 Sch.1 para.13
s.23, enabling: SI 2008/2866
s.24, applied: SI 2008/2866
s.24, varied: SI 2008/212 Sch.1 para.14
s.26, varied: SI 2008/212 Sch.1 para.15
s.26A, varied: SI 2008/212 Sch.1 para.15
s.26B, varied: SI 2008/212 Sch.1 para.15
s.29, applied: SI 2008/2864 Reg.3
s.29, varied: SI 2008/212 Sch.1 para.16
s.38, applied: SI 2008/1430 Reg.15
s.60, enabling: SI 2008/2096
s.82, enabling: SSI 2008/117
s.105, enabling: SI 2008/2096, SI 2008/2866
Sch.3, applied: SI 2008/212 Reg.5
Sch.3, referred to: SI 2008/2863 r.4
Sch.3 Part 1 para.1, varied: SI 2008/212 Sch.2 para.2
Sch.3 Part 1 para.2, varied: SI 2008/212 Sch.2 para.3
Sch.3 Part 1 para.3, varied: SI 2008/212 Sch.2 para.4
Sch.3 Part 1 para.4, varied: SI 2008/212 Sch.2 para.5
Sch.3 Part 1 para.5, varied: SI 2008/212 Sch.2 para.6
Sch.3 Part 1 para.6, amended: 2008 c.4 Sch.23 para.4
Sch.3 Part 1 para.6, varied: SI 2008/212 Sch.2 para.7
Sch.3 Part 1 para.7, varied: SI 2008/212 Sch.2 para.8
Sch.3 Part 1 para.8, varied: SI 2008/212 Sch.2 para.8
Sch.3 Part 1 para.9, varied: SI 2008/212 Sch.2 para.8
Sch.3 Part 2A para.14A, varied: SI 2008/212 Sch.2 para.14
Sch.3 Part 2A para.14B, varied: SI 2008/212 Sch.2 para.15
Sch.3 Part 2A para.14D, varied: SI 2008/212 Sch.2 para.16
Sch.3 Part 2 para.10, varied: SI 2008/212 Sch.2 para.9
Sch.3 Part 2 para.11, varied: SI 2008/212 Sch.2 para.10
Sch.3 Part 2 para.12, varied: SI 2008/212 Sch.2 para.11
Sch.3 Part 2 para.13, varied: SI 2008/212 Sch.2 para.12
Sch.3 Part 2 para.14, varied: SI 2008/212 Sch.2 para.13

CAP.

2002–cont.

30. Police Reform Act 2002–*cont.*

Sch.3 Part 3 para.15, varied: SI 2008/212 Sch.2 para.17

Sch.3 Part 3 para.16, applied: SI 2008/2864 Reg.11, Reg.20, Reg.30, Reg.31, Reg.32, Reg.39, Reg.40, Reg.51, Reg.52, Reg.53

Sch.3 Part 3 para.16, varied: SI 2008/212 Sch.2 para.18

Sch.3 Part 3 para.17, applied: SI 2008/2864 Reg.10, Reg.11, Reg.20, Reg.30, Reg.31, Reg.32, Reg.39, Reg.40, Reg.51, Reg.52, Reg.53

Sch.3 Part 3 para.17, varied: SI 2008/212 Sch.2 para.19

Sch.3 Part 3 para.17A, varied: SI 2008/212 Sch.2 para.20

Sch.3 Part 3 para.18, applied: SI 2008/2864 Reg.10, Reg.11, Reg.20, Reg.30, Reg.31, Reg.32, Reg.39, Reg.40, Reg.51, Reg.52, Reg.53

Sch.3 Part 3 para.18, varied: SI 2008/212 Sch.2 para.21

Sch.3 Part 3 para.18A, varied: SI 2008/212 Sch.2 para.22

Sch.3 Part 3 para.19, applied: SI 2008/2864 Reg.10, Reg.11, Reg.20, Reg.30, Reg.31, Reg.32, Reg.39, Reg.40, Reg.51, Reg.52, Reg.53

Sch.3 Part 3 para.19, varied: SI 2008/212 Sch.2 para.23

Sch.3 Part 3 para.19A, added: 2008 c.4 Sch.23 para.5

Sch.3 Part 3 para.19A, applied: SI 2008/2863 r.19, r.22

Sch.3 Part 3 para.19B, added: 2008 c.4 Sch.23 para.5

Sch.3 Part 3 para.19B, applied: SI 2008/2864 Reg.31, Reg.39, Reg.52

Sch.3 Part 3 para.19B, enabling: SI 2008/2866

Sch.3 Part 3 para.19C, added: 2008 c.4 Sch.23 para.5

Sch.3 Part 3 para.19C, applied: SI 2008/2864 Reg.34, Reg.54

Sch.3 Part 3 para.19C, enabling: SI 2008/2866

Sch.3 Part 3 para.19D, added: 2008 c.4 Sch.23 para.5

Sch.3 Part 3 para.19D, enabling: SI 2008/2866

Sch.3 Part 3 para.19E, added: 2008 c.4 Sch.23 para.5

Sch.3 Part 3 para.20, varied: SI 2008/212 Sch.2 para.24

Sch.3 Part 3 para.20A, amended: 2008 c.4 Sch.23 para.6

Sch.3 Part 3 para.20A, repealed (in part): 2008 c.4 Sch.23 para.6, Sch.28 Part 8

Sch.3 Part 3 para.20A, varied: SI 2008/212 Sch.2 para.25

Sch.3 Part 3 para.20B, amended: 2008 c.4 Sch.23 para.7

CAP.

2002–cont.

30. Police Reform Act 2002–*cont.*

Sch.3 Part 3 para.20B, repealed (in part): 2008 c.4 Sch.23 para.7, Sch.28 Part 8

Sch.3 Part 3 para.20B, varied: SI 2008/212 Sch.2 para.25

Sch.3 Part 3 para.20C, varied: SI 2008/212 Sch.2 para.25

Sch.3 Part 3 para.20D, amended: 2008 c.4 Sch.23 para.8

Sch.3 Part 3 para.20D, varied: SI 2008/212 Sch.2 para.25

Sch.3 Part 3 para.20E, amended: 2008 c.4 Sch.23 para.9

Sch.3 Part 3 para.20E, repealed (in part): 2008 c.4 Sch.23 para.9, Sch.28 Part 8

Sch.3 Part 3 para.20E, varied: SI 2008/212 Sch.2 para.25

Sch.3 Part 3 para.20F, varied: SI 2008/212 Sch.2 para.25

Sch.3 Part 3 para.20G, repealed: 2008 c.4 Sch.23 para.10, Sch.28 Part 8

Sch.3 Part 3 para.20G, varied: SI 2008/212 Sch.2 para.25

Sch.3 Part 3 para.20H, applied: SI 2008/2864 Reg.42, Reg.51, Reg.53

Sch.3 Part 3 para.20H, varied: SI 2008/212 Sch.2 para.25

Sch.3 Part 3 para.20I, varied: SI 2008/212 Sch.2 para.25

Sch.3 Part 3 para.21, varied: SI 2008/212 Sch.2 para.26

Sch.3 Part 3 para.21A, amended: 2008 c.4 Sch.23 para.11, Sch.28 Part 8

Sch.3 Part 3 para.21A, varied: SI 2008/212 Sch.2 para.27

Sch.3 Part 3 para.22, amended: 2008 c.4 Sch.23 para.12, Sch.28 Part 8

Sch.3 Part 3 para.22, applied: SI 2008/2864 Reg.19

Sch.3 Part 3 para.22, repealed (in part): 2008 c.4 Sch.23 para.12

Sch.3 Part 3 para.22, varied: SI 2008/212 Sch.2 para.28

Sch.3 Part 3 para.22, enabling: SI 2008/2866

Sch.3 Part 3 para.23, amended: 2008 c.4 Sch.23 para.13

Sch.3 Part 3 para.23, applied: SI 2008/2864 Reg.19

Sch.3 Part 3 para.24, amended: 2008 c.4 Sch.23 para.14

Sch.3 Part 3 para.24, applied: SI 2008/2864 Reg.19

Sch.3 Part 3 para.24A, amended: 2008 c.4 Sch.23 para.15

Sch.3 Part 3 para.24A, varied: SI 2008/212 Sch.2 para.29

Sch.3 Part 3 para.24B, amended: 2008 c.4 Sch.23 para.16, Sch.28 Part 8

Sch.3 Part 3 para.24B, varied: SI 2008/212 Sch.2 para.30

CAP.

2002–cont.

30. Police Reform Act 2002–*cont.*

Sch.3 Part 3 para.24C, varied: SI 2008/212 Sch.2 para.31

Sch.3 Part 3 para.25, amended: 2008 c.4 Sch.23 para.17, Sch.28 Part 8

Sch.3 Part 3 para.25, varied: SI 2008/212 Sch.2 para.32

Sch.3 Part 3 para.27, amended: 2008 c.4 Sch.23 para.18

Sch.3 Part 3 para.27, applied: SI 2008/2864 Reg.19, Reg.30, Reg.32, Reg.40

Sch.3 Part 3 para.27, varied: SI 2008/212 Sch.2 para.33

Sch.3 Part 3 para.28, varied: SI 2008/212 Sch.2 para.34

Sch.3 Part 3 para.29, added: 2008 c.4 Sch.23 para.19

Sch.3 Part 3 para.29, enabling: SI 2008/2866

Sch.3 para.14D, see *R. (on the application of Reynolds) v Chief Constable of Sussex* [2008] EWCA Civ 1160, Times, November 6, 2008 (CA (Civ Div)), Ward, L.J.

Sch.4 Part 1 para.2, amended: 2008 c.26 Sch.4 para.65

32. Education Act 2002

Commencement Orders: SI 2008/1728 Art.3, Sch.1 Part 1, 2

applied: SI 2008/136 Reg.3, SI 2008/473 Art.2, Art.3

disapplied: SI 2008/136 Reg.5

Part 10 c.1, applied: 2008 c.25 s.130, s.139

Part 10 c.1, referred to: 2008 c.25 s.93

s.1, amended: 2008 c.25 Sch.1 para.14

s.1, referred to: SI 2008/3016

s.2, enabling: SI 2008/3016

s.4, applied: SI 2008/3016

s.12, applied: SI 2008/228 Sch.1 para.20

s.14, applied: SI 2008/228 Sch.2 para.1, SI 2008/794 Sch.8 para.13, Sch.9 para.52

s.19, enabling: SI 2008/168

s.23, enabling: SI 2008/168

s.26, enabling: SI 2008/168

s.27, applied: SI 2008/228 Sch.1 para.20, Sch.5 para.26, SI 2008/1866 Reg.2

s.29A, added: 2008 c.25 s.154

s.29B, added: 2008 c.25 s.157

s.31, enabling: SI 2008/136, SI 2008/555

s.32, amended: 2008 c.02 s.21

s.44, applied: SI 2008/228 Sch.1 para.20

s.44, enabling: SI 2008/46

s.52, see *W v Independent Appeal Panel of Bexley LBC* [2008] EWHC 758 (Admin), [2008] E.L.R. 301 (QBD (Admin)), Burton, J.

s.52, applied: SI 2008/228 Reg.23, SI 2008/532 Reg.3, Reg.4, Reg.7, Reg.8, Reg.9

s.52, enabling: SI 2008/532

s.67, applied: SI 2008/239 Sch.2 para.21

s.82, referred to: SI 2008/4 Sch.1 para.4

s.84, applied: SI 2008/657 Reg.8, SI 2008/1766 Art.2

CAP.

2002–cont.

32. Education Act 2002–*cont.*

s.84, enabling: SI 2008/1766

s.85, applied: SI 2008/657 Reg.8

s.87, applied: SI 2008/228 Sch.1 para.23

s.87, enabling: SI 2008/1752, SI 2008/1753, SI 2008/1754, SI 2008/1755, SI 2008/1756, SI 2008/1757, SI 2008/1758, SI 2008/1759, SI 2008/1760, SI 2008/1761, SI 2008/1762, SI 2008/1763, SI 2008/3081

s.88, amended: 2008 c.25 s.156

s.96, applied: SI 2008/1752, SI 2008/1753, SI 2008/1754, SI 2008/1755, SI 2008/1756, SI 2008/1757, SI 2008/1758, SI 2008/1759, SI 2008/1760, SI 2008/1761, SI 2008/1762, SI 2008/1763

s.101, amended: SI 2008/1899 Art.2

s.101, enabling: SI 2008/1899

s.102, applied: SI 2008/1736 Reg.2

s.102, enabling: SI 2008/1732, SI 2008/2629

s.103, applied: SI 2008/1409 Art.2

s.105, amended: SI 2008/1899 Art.3

s.105, applied: SI 2008/1408 Art.4

s.105, referred to: SI 2008/1736 Reg.3

s.105, enabling: SI 2008/1408, SI 2008/1899

s.108, applied: SI 2008/1736 Reg.3

s.108, enabling: SI 2008/1409, SI 2008/1732, SI 2008/1787, SI 2008/1899, SI 2008/2629

s.112, enabling: SI 2008/1736

s.117, applied: SI 2008/1409, SI 2008/1732, SI 2008/1736, SI 2008/1787, SI 2008/1899, SI 2008/2629

s.120, applied: SI 2008/2155

s.121, referred to: SI 2008/2155

s.122, applied: SI 2008/228 Sch.3 para.19, Sch.3 para.20, SI 2008/2099 Art.3

s.122, enabling: SI 2008/2155

s.123, enabling: SI 2008/2099, SI 2008/2155

s.124, enabling: SI 2008/2155

s.125, applied: SI 2008/2155

s.126, applied: SI 2008/2155

s.132, applied: SI 2008/215

s.132, enabling: SI 2008/215

s.134, enabling: SI 2008/1883

s.135, applied: SI 2008/2945 Reg.3

s.142, see *R. (on the application of L) v Commissioner of Police of the Metropolis* [2007] EWCA Civ 168, [2008] 1 W.L.R. 681 (CA (Civ Div)), Longmore, L.J.

s.142, applied: 2008 c.25 s.141, SI 2008/473 Art.2, Art.3, SI 2008/474 Reg.6, SI 2008/1884 Reg.2

s.144, amended: SI 2008/2833 Sch.3 para.193

s.144, applied: 2008 c.25 s.141

s.145, enabling: SI 2008/215, SI 2008/1883

s.156A, added: 2008 c.25 Sch.1 para.15

CAP.

2002–cont.

32. Education Act 2002–*cont.*

s.157, repealed (in part): 2008 c.25 Sch.1 para.16, Sch.2
s.157, enabling: SI 2008/3253
s.158, amended: 2008 c.25 Sch.1 para.17
s.158, repealed (in part): 2008 c.25 Sch.1 para.17, Sch.2
s.159, applied: SI 2008/2699 r.22
s.161, applied: SI 2008/1801 Reg.2
s.162A, applied: SI 2008/1801 Reg.2, Reg.8
s.162A, repealed: 2008 c.25 Sch.1 para.18, Sch.2
s.162A, enabling: SI 2008/1801
s.162B, applied: 2008 c.25 s.140
s.162B, repealed: 2008 c.25 Sch.1 para.18, Sch.2
s.162B, enabling: SI 2008/1801
s.163, amended: 2008 c.25 Sch.1 para.19, Sch.2
s.164, amended: 2008 c.25 Sch.1 para.20, Sch.2
s.165, amended: 2008 c.25 Sch.1 para.21, Sch.2
s.165, applied: SI 2008/2699 r.22
s.166, amended: SI 2008/2833 Sch.3 para.194
s.166, applied: SI 2008/2699 r.22, r.25, Sch.1
s.167, amended: SI 2008/2833 Sch.3 para.195
s.167A, amended: 2008 c.25 Sch.1 para.22, Sch.2
s.167A, applied: 2008 c.25 s.131
s.167A, repealed (in part): 2008 c.25 Sch.1 para.22, Sch.2
s.167B, amended: SI 2008/2833 Sch.3 para.196
s.167B, applied: 2008 c.25 s.131
s.167C, applied: 2008 c.25 s.131
s.167C, substituted: 2008 c.25 Sch.1 para.23
s.167D, applied: 2008 c.25 s.131
s.167D, substituted: 2008 c.25 Sch.1 para.23
s.171, amended: 2008 c.25 Sch.1 para.24, Sch.2
s.171, repealed (in part): 2008 c.25 Sch.1 para.24, Sch.2
s.175, applied: SI 2008/228 Sch.1 para.6
s.176, amended: 2008 c.25 s.158
s.176, repealed (in part): 2008 c.25 s.158, Sch.2
s.181, applied: SI 2008/794 Sch.8 para.13, Sch.9 para.52
s.186, applied: 2008 c.10 s.2, s.5
s.207, applied: SI 2008/228 Sch.2 para.12
s.210, amended: 2008 c.02 s.21
s.210, applied: SI 2008/1899
s.210, enabling: SI 2008/136, SI 2008/168, SI 2008/215, SI 2008/532, SI 2008/555, SI 2008/1408, SI 2008/1409, SI 2008/1732, SI 2008/1736, SI 2008/1752, SI 2008/1753, SI 2008/1754, SI 2008/1755, SI 2008/1756, SI 2008/1757, SI

CAP.

2002–cont.

32. Education Act 2002–*cont.*

s.210, enabling:–*cont.*
2008/1758, SI 2008/1759, SI 2008/1760, SI 2008/1761, SI 2008/1762, SI 2008/1763, SI 2008/1766, SI 2008/1787, SI 2008/1801, SI 2008/1883, SI 2008/1899, SI 2008/2629, SI 2008/3016, SI 2008/3081, SI 2008/3253
s.210A, added: 2008 c.25 Sch.1 para.79
s.214, enabling: SI 2008/532
s.216, enabling: SI 2008/1728
Sch.4 para.3, repealed (in part): 2008 c.25 Sch.2
Sch.4 para.8, repealed (in part): 2008 c.25 Sch.2
Sch.7 Part 2 para.10, repealed: 2008 c.25 Sch.2
Sch.17 para.8, repealed: 2008 c.25 Sch.2
Sch.18 para.4, repealed: SI 2008/2833 Sch.3 para.228
Sch.18 para.5, repealed: SI 2008/2833 Sch.3 para.228
Sch.18 para.10, repealed (in part): SI 2008/2833 Sch.3 para.228
Sch.19 para.2, repealed (in part): 2008 c.02 Sch.2
Sch.21 para.51, repealed (in part): 2008 c.02 Sch.2

36. Tobacco Advertising and Promotion Act 2002

applied: 2008 c.13 Sch.3

38. Adoption and Children Act 2002

see *B (Children) (Placement Order: Expert Reports), Re* [2008] EWCA Civ 835, [2008] 2 F.L.R. 1404 (CA (Civ Div)), Thorpe, L.J.; see *D v D* [2008] EWHC 403 (Fam), [2008] 1 F.L.R. 1475 (Fam Div), Ryder, J.; see *EN (A Child), Re* [2007] EWCA Civ 264, [2008] 2 F.C.R. 229 (CA (Civ Div)), Thorpe, L.J.
applied: SI 2008/794 Reg.156, SI 2008/1052 Sch.1, SI 2008/1054 Sch.1, SI 2008/2836 Art.6, Art.11, Art.21, Art.25
Part 1, applied: SI 2008/1052 Sch.1, SI 2008/1054 Sch.1
s.1, see *P (A Child), Re* [2008] EWCA Civ 535, [2008] 2 F.L.R. 625 (CA (Civ Div)), Thorpe, L.J.
s.2, applied: SI 2008/18 Reg.32, SI 2008/529 Reg.46, SI 2008/794 Sch.8 para.26, Sch.9 para.57, SI 2008/1273 Reg.83G, Reg.30, SI 2008/1582 Reg.42, SI 2008/3170 Reg.30
s.3, applied: SI 2008/18 Reg.32, SI 2008/529 Reg.46, SI 2008/794 Sch.8 para.26, Sch.9 para.57, SI 2008/1273 Reg.83G, Reg.30, SI 2008/1582 Reg.42, SI 2008/3170 Reg.30
s.4, applied: SI 2008/18 Reg.32, SI 2008/529 Reg.46, SI 2008/794 Sch.8 para.26, Sch.9 para.57, SI 2008/1273 Reg.83G,

CAP.

2002–cont.

38. Adoption and Children Act 2002–*cont.*

s.4, applied:–*cont.*
Reg.30, SI 2008/1582 Reg.42, SI 2008/3170 Reg.30
s.12, amended: 2008 c.23 s.34, Sch.4
s.18, see *A LBC v A* [2008] EWHC 1722 (Fam), [2008] 2 F.L.R. 1857 (Fam Div), Charles, J.
s.22, see *P (A Child), Re* [2008] EWCA Civ 535, [2008] 2 F.L.R. 625 (CA (Civ Div)), Thorpe, L.J.
s.22, applied: SI 2008/1052 Sch.1, SI 2008/2836 Art.8
s.22, disapplied: SI 2008/1052 Sch.1, SI 2008/1054 Sch.1
s.23, applied: SI 2008/2836 Art.5
s.24, see *F (A Child), Re* [2008] EWCA Civ 439, [2008] 2 F.L.R. 550 (CA (Civ Div)), Thorpe, L.J.; see *NS-H v Kingston Upon Hull City Council* [2008] EWCA Civ 493, [2008] 2 F.L.R. 918 (CA (Civ Div)), Pill, L.J.
s.26, see *EN (A Child), Re* [2007] EWCA Civ 264, [2008] 2 F.C.R. 229 (CA (Civ Div)), Thorpe, L.J.; see *P (A Child), Re* [2008] EWCA Civ 535, [2008] 2 F.L.R. 625 (CA (Civ Div)), Thorpe, L.J.
s.27, see *P (A Child), Re* [2008] EWCA Civ 535, [2008] 2 F.L.R. 625 (CA (Civ Div)), Thorpe, L.J.
s.28, applied: SI 2008/2836 Art.8
s.29, applied: SI 2008/2836 Art.8
s.30, applied: SI 2008/2836 Art.8
s.37, applied: SI 2008/2836 Art.8
s.38, applied: SI 2008/2836 Art.8
s.40, applied: SI 2008/2836 Art.8
s.42, see *A (A Child) (Adoption), Re* [2007] EWCA Civ 1383, [2008] 1 F.L.R. 959 (CA (Civ Div)), Ward, L.J.; see *A LBC v A* [2008] EWHC 1722 (Fam), [2008] 2 F.L.R. 1857 (Fam Div), Charles, J.
s.42, applied: SI 2008/2836 Art.8
s.47, applied: SI 2008/2836 Art.8
s.50, applied: SI 2008/2836 Art.5, Art.8
s.51, amended: 2008 c.22 Sch.6 para.39
s.51, applied: SI 2008/2836 Art.5, Art.8
s.52, see *P (A Child), Re* [2008] EWCA Civ 535, [2008] 2 F.L.R. 625 (CA (Civ Div)), Thorpe, L.J.
s.66, see *D v D* [2008] EWHC 403 (Fam), [2008] 1 F.L.R. 1475 (Fam Div), Ryder, J.
s.78, amended: SI 2008/678 Sch.2 para.12
s.78, applied: SI 2008/678 Sch.1 para.12
s.79, amended: SI 2008/678 Sch.2 para.12
s.79, applied: SI 2008/678 Sch.1 para.12
s.81, amended: SI 2008/678 Sch.2 para.12
s.81, applied: SI 2008/678 Sch.1 para.12
s.83, see *MN (India) v Secretary of State for the Home Department* [2008] EWCA Civ 38, [2008] 2 F.L.R. 87 (CA (Civ Div)), Ward, L.J.
s.83, applied: SI 2008/2836 Art.6, Art.11, Art.21

CAP.

2002–cont.

38. Adoption and Children Act 2002–*cont.*

s.84, see *A LBC v A* [2008] EWHC 1722 (Fam), [2008] 2 F.L.R. 1857 (Fam Div), Charles, J.; see *G (A Child) (Adoption: Placement outside Jurisdiction), Re* [2008] EWCA Civ 105, [2008] Fam. 97 (CA (Civ Div)), Sir Mark Potter (President, Fam); see *G (Surrogacy: Foreign Domicile), Re* [2007] EWHC 2814 (Fam), [2008] 1 F.L.R. 1047 (Fam Div), McFarlane, J.
s.98, amended: SI 2008/678 Sch.2 para.12
s.98, applied: SI 2008/678 Sch.1 para.12
s.118, repealed (in part): 2008 c.23 Sch.4
s.142, amended: SI 2008/678 Sch.2 para.12
s.142, applied: SI 2008/678 Sch.1 para.12
Sch.1 para.1, amended: SI 2008/678 Sch.2 para.12
Sch.1 para.1, applied: SI 2008/678 Sch.1 para.12
Sch.1 para.3, amended: SI 2008/678 Sch.2 para.12
Sch.1 para.3, applied: SI 2008/678 Sch.1 para.12
Sch.2 para.1, amended: SI 2008/678 Sch.2 para.12
Sch.2 para.1, applied: SI 2008/678 Sch.1 para.12
Sch.6, amended: 2008 c.23 Sch.1 para.14

40. Enterprise Act 2002

see *British Sky Broadcasting Group Plc v Competition Commission* [2008] CAT 1, [2008] Comp. A.R. 1 (CAT), Barling, J; see *Norris v United States* [2008] UKHL 16, [2008] 1 A.C. 920 (HL), Lord Bingham of Cornhill; see *Permacell Finesse Ltd (In Liquidation), Re* [2007] EWHC 3233 (Ch), [2008] B.C.C. 208 (Ch D (Birmingham)), Judge Purle Q.C.
disapplied: SI 2008/948 Sch.1 para.101
Part 3, disapplied: SI 2008/2546 Art.40
Part 8, applied: 2008 c.13 Sch.3
Part 9, see *Dumfries and Galloway Council v Scottish Information Commissioner* [2008] CSIH 12, 2008 S.C. 327 (IH (Ex Div)), Lord Nimmo Smith
s.10, repealed (in part): SI 2008/1277 Sch.4 Part 1
s.11, enabling: SI 2008/2161
s.26, see *British Sky Broadcasting Group Plc v Competition Commission* [2008] CAT 25, [2008] Comp. A.R. 223 (CAT), Barling, J
s.38, see *British Sky Broadcasting Group Plc v Competition Commission* [2008] CAT 7, [2008] Comp. A.R. 143 (CAT), Barling, J
s.54, see *British Sky Broadcasting Group Plc v Competition Commission* [2008] CAT 1, [2008] Comp. A.R. 1 (CAT), Barling, J
s.58, see *British Sky Broadcasting Group Plc v Competition Commission* [2008] CAT 25, [2008] Comp. A.R. 223 (CAT), Barling, J
s.58, amended: SI 2008/2645 Art.2
s.58, enabling: SI 2008/2645

CAP.

2002–cont.

40. Enterprise Act 2002–*cont.*

s.58A, see *British Sky Broadcasting Group Plc v Competition Commission* [2008] CAT 25, [2008] Comp. A.R. 223 (CAT), Barling, J

s.120, see *British Sky Broadcasting Group Plc v Competition Commission* [2008] CAT 7, [2008] Comp. A.R. 143 (CAT), Barling, J; see *British Sky Broadcasting Group Plc v Competition Commission* [2008] CAT 9, [2008] Comp. A.R. 156 (CAT), Barling, J

s.124, enabling: SI 2008/2645

s.129, amended: SI 2008/2645 Art.3

s.130, amended: SI 2008/2645 Art.3

s.188, see *Norris v United States* [2008] UKHL 16, [2008] 1 A.C. 920 (HL), Lord Bingham of Cornhill; see *R. v Whittle (Peter)* [2008] EWCA Crim 2560, Times, November 27, 2008 (CA (Crim Div)), Hallett, L.J.

s.211, applied: SI 2008/1277 Sch.3 para.11

s.212, applied: SI 2008/1277 Sch.3 para.13, Sch.3 para.14

s.218A, added: SI 2008/1277 Reg.27

s.227E, referred to: 2008 c.13 Sch.6

s.230, applied: SI 2008/1277 Sch.3 para.9

s.237, see *Dumfries and Galloway Council v Scottish Information Commissioner* [2008] CSIH 12, 2008 S.C. 327 (IH (Ex Div)), Lord Nimmo Smith

s.238, see *Dumfries and Galloway Council v Scottish Information Commissioner* [2008] CSIH 12, 2008 S.C. 327 (IH (Ex Div)), Lord Nimmo Smith

s.241, see *Dumfries and Galloway Council v Scottish Information Commissioner* [2008] CSIH 12, 2008 S.C. 327 (IH (Ex Div)), Lord Nimmo Smith

s.249, applied: SI 2008/948 Sch.1 para.101

s.255, amended: SI 2008/948 Sch.1 para.225

s.261, see *Lewis v Metropolitan Property Realizations Ltd* [2008] EWHC 2760 (Ch), Times, December 9, 2008 (Ch D), Proudman, J; see *Pannell v Official Receiver* [2008] EWHC 736 (Ch), [2008] B.P.I.R. 629 (Ch D (Bristol)), Judge Havelock-Allan Q.C.

Sch.4 para.11, see *Emerson Electric Co v Morgan Crucible Co Plc* [2008] C.P. Rep. 5 (CAT), Marion Simmons Q.C. (Chairman)

Sch.8 para.20B, added: SI 2008/2645 Art.4

Sch.13 Part 1 para.1, repealed: SI 2008/1277 Sch.2 para.70, Sch.4 Part 1

Sch.13 Part 1 para.7A, repealed: SI 2008/1277 Sch.2 para.70, Sch.4 Part 1

Sch.13 Part 1 para.9C, added: SI 2008/1277 Reg.26

Sch.13 Part 2 para.11, amended: SI 2008/1277 Sch.2 para.70

Sch.14, amended: SI 2008/1277 Sch.4 Part 1

Sch.25 para.16, repealed: SI 2008/1277 Sch.4 Part 1

CAP.

2002–cont.

40. Enterprise Act 2002–*cont.*

Sch.25 para.17, repealed: SI 2008/1277 Sch.4 Part 1

Sch.25 para.44, repealed (in part): 2008 c.26 Sch.7 Part 2

41. Nationality, Immigration and Asylum Act 2002

see *DK (Serbia) v Secretary of State for the Home Department* [2006] EWCA Civ 1747, [2008] 1 W.L.R. 1246 (CA (Civ Div)), Latham, L.J.

s.10, varied: SI 2008/680 Art.5, Art.16, Sch.7 para.1

s.36, amended: SI 2008/2833 Sch.3 para.197

s.62, varied: SI 2008/680 Art.5, Art.16, Sch.7 para.2

s.63, varied: SI 2008/680 Art.5, Art.16

s.69, applied: 2008 c.4 s.133

s.72, see *R. (on the application of TB) v Secretary of State for the Home Department* [2008] EWCA Civ 977, Times, September 9, 2008 (CA (Civ Div)), Thorpe, L.J.

s.72, applied: 2008 c.4 s.131

s.72, disapplied: 2008 c.4 s.131

s.72, varied: SI 2008/680 Art.5, Art.16, Sch.7 para.3

s.73, varied: SI 2008/680 Art.5, Art.16

s.74, varied: SI 2008/680 Art.5, Art.16

s.75, varied: SI 2008/680 Art.5, Art.16, Sch.7 para.4

s.76, varied: SI 2008/680 Art.5, Art.16, Sch.7 para.5

s.78, varied: SI 2008/680 Art.5, Art.16, Sch.7 para.6

s.79, varied: SI 2008/680 Art.5, Art.16

s.81, varied: SI 2008/680 Art.5, Art.16, Sch.7 para.7, Sch.7 para.8

s.82, see *R. (on the application of Lim) v Secretary of State for the Home Department* [2007] EWCA Civ 773, [2008] I.N.L.R. 60 (CA (Civ Div)), Sir Mark Potter (President, Fam); see *SA (Pakistan) v Secretary of State for the Home Department* [2008] Imm. A.R. 124 (AIT), CMG Ockelton (Deputy President)

s.82, varied: SI 2008/680 Art.5, Art.16, Sch.7 para.7, Sch.7 para.9

s.83, varied: SI 2008/680 Sch.7 para.7

s.83A, varied: SI 2008/680 Sch.7 para.7

s.84, see *B v Secretary of State for the Home Department* [2008] UKHL 39, [2008] 3 W.L.R. 166 (HL), Lord Bingham of Cornhill; see *R. (on the application of Lim) v Secretary of State for the Home Department* [2007] EWCA Civ 773, [2008] I.N.L.R. 60 (CA (Civ Div)), Sir Mark Potter (President, Fam)

s.84, varied: SI 2008/680 Art.5, Art.16, Sch.7 para.7, Sch.7 para.10

CAP.

2002–cont.

41. Nationality, Immigration and Asylum Act 2002–*cont.*

s.85, see *AS (Somalia) v Entry Clearance Officer (Addis Ababa)* [2008] EWCA Civ 149, [2008] Imm. A.R. 510 (CA (Civ Div)), Waller, L.J.

s.85, varied: SI 2008/680 Art.5, Art.16, Sch.7 para.7, Sch.7 para.11

s.85A, varied: SI 2008/680 Art.5, Art.16, Sch.7 para.7

s.86, see *AD (Afghanistan) v Secretary of State for the Home Department* [2008] Imm. A.R. 57 (AIT), Senior Immigration Judge Allen; see *AG (Kosovo) v Secretary of State for the Home Department* [2008] Imm. A.R.19 (AIT), CMG Ockelton (Deputy President)

s.86, varied: SI 2008/680 Art.5, Art.16, Sch.7 para.7, Sch.7 para.12

s.87, varied: SI 2008/680 Art.5, Art.16, Sch.7 para.7, Sch.7 para.13

s.88, varied: SI 2008/680 Art.5, Art.16, Sch.7 para.7, Sch.7 para.14

s.88A, disapplied: SI 2008/310 Art.4

s.88A, varied: SI 2008/680 Art.5, Art.16, Sch.7 para.7, Sch.7 para.15

s.89, varied: SI 2008/680 Art.5, Art.16, Sch.7 para.7, Sch.7 para.16

s.90, varied: SI 2008/680 Art.5, Art.16, Sch.7 para.7, Sch.7 para.17

s.91, varied: SI 2008/680 Art.5, Art.16, Sch.7 para.7

s.92, see *Etame v Secretary of State for the Home Department* [2008] EWHC 1140 (Admin), [2008] 4 All E.R. 798 (QBD), Blake, J

s.92, varied: SI 2008/680 Art.5, Art.16, Sch.7 para.7, Sch.7 para.18

s.93, varied: SI 2008/680 Sch.7 para.7

s.94, varied: SI 2008/680 Art.5, Art.16, Sch.7 para.7, Sch.7 para.19

s.94A, varied: SI 2008/680 Art.5, Art.16, Sch.7 para.7

s.95, varied: SI 2008/680 Art.5, Art.16, Sch.7 para.7, Sch.7 para.20

s.96, varied: SI 2008/680 Art.5, Art.16, Sch.7 para.7, Sch.7 para.21

s.97, varied: SI 2008/680 Art.5, Art.16, Sch.7 para.7, Sch.7 para.22

s.97A, varied: SI 2008/680 Art.5, Art.16, Sch.7 para.7, Sch.7 para.23

s.98, varied: SI 2008/680 Art.5, Art.16, Sch.7 para.7, Sch.7 para.24

s.99, varied: SI 2008/680 Art.5, Art.16, Sch.7 para.7

s.100, varied: SI 2008/680 Sch.7 para.7

s.101, varied: SI 2008/680 Sch.7 para.7

s.102, varied: SI 2008/680 Sch.7 para.7

s.103, varied: SI 2008/680 Sch.7 para.7

s.103A, see *DK (Serbia) v Secretary of State for the Home Department* [2006] EWCA Civ 1747, [2008] 1 W.L.R. 1246 (CA (Civ

CAP.

2002–cont.

41. Nationality, Immigration and Asylum Act 2002–*cont.*

s.103A–*cont.*

Div)), Latham, L.J.; see *FS (Eritrea) v Secretary of State for the Home Department* [2008] Imm. A.R. 47 (AIT), CMG Ockelton (Deputy President); see *R. (on the appplication of AM (Cameroon)) v Asylum and Immigration Tribunal* [2008] EWCA Civ 100, [2008] 1 W.L.R. 2062 (CA (Civ Div)), Waller, L.J. (V-P)

s.103A, varied: SI 2008/680 Sch.7 para.7, Sch.7 para.25

s.103B, varied: SI 2008/680 Sch.7 para.7, Sch.7 para.25

s.103C, varied: SI 2008/680 Sch.7 para.7, Sch.7 para.25

s.103D, varied: SI 2008/680 Sch.7 para.7, Sch.7 para.25

s.103E, varied: SI 2008/680 Art.5, Art.16, Sch.7 para.7, Sch.7 para.26

s.104, applied: SI 2008/18 Reg.10, SI 2008/529 Reg.4, Reg.115, Reg.132, Reg.149, SI 2008/1273 Reg.4, Reg.62, Reg.79, Reg.92, SI 2008/1582 Reg.5, Reg.115, Reg.132, Reg.149, SI 2008/3170 Reg.4, Reg.62, Reg.79, Reg.103

s.104, referred to: 2008 c.4 s.137

s.104, varied: SI 2008/680 Art.5, Art.16, Sch.7 para.7, Sch.7 para.27

s.105, varied: SI 2008/680 Art.5, Art.16, Sch.7 para.7, Sch.7 para.28

s.105, enabling: SI 2008/684, SI 2008/1819

s.106, varied: SI 2008/680 Art.5, Art.16, Sch.7 para.7, Sch.7 para.29

s.106, enabling: SI 2008/1088, SI 2008/1089

s.107, varied: SI 2008/680 Sch.7 para.7

s.108, see *OA (Nigeria) v Secretary of State for the Home Department* [2008] Imm. A.R. 201 (AIT), CMG Ockelton (Deputy President)

s.108, varied: SI 2008/680 Art.5, Art.16, Sch.7 para.7, Sch.7 para.30

s.109, varied: SI 2008/680 Art.5, Art.16, Sch.7 para.7, Sch.7 para.31

s.110, varied: SI 2008/680 Sch.7 para.7

s.111, varied: SI 2008/680 Sch.7 para.7

s.112, varied: SI 2008/680 Art.5, Art.16, Sch.7 para.7, Sch.7 para.32

s.112, enabling: SI 2008/684, SI 2008/1088, SI 2008/1089

s.113, varied: SI 2008/680 Art.5, Art.16, Sch.7 para.7, Sch.7 para.33

s.114, varied: SI 2008/680 Art.5, Art.16, Sch.7 para.7

s.115, varied: SI 2008/680 Sch.7 para.7

s.116, varied: SI 2008/680 Sch.7 para.7

s.117, varied: SI 2008/680 Sch.7 para.7

s.118, varied: SI 2008/680 Art.5, Art.16

s.119, varied: SI 2008/680 Art.5, Art.16

CAP.

2002–cont.

41. Nationality, Immigration and Asylum Act 2002–*cont.*

s.120, varied: SI 2008/680 Art.5, Art.16, Sch.7 para.34
s.121, varied: SI 2008/680 Art.5, Art.16
s.125, varied: SI 2008/680 Art.5, Art.16
s.126, varied: SI 2008/680 Art.5, Art.16, Sch.7 para.35
s.127, varied: SI 2008/680 Art.5, Art.16, Sch.7 para.36
s.128, varied: SI 2008/680 Art.5, Art.16
s.133, varied: SI 2008/680 Art.5, Art.16, Sch.7 para.37
s.134, varied: SI 2008/680 Art.5, Art.16, Sch.7 para.38
s.136, varied: SI 2008/680 Art.5, Art.16, Sch.7 para.39
s.137, varied: SI 2008/680 Art.5, Art.16, Sch.7 para.40
s.138, varied: SI 2008/680 Art.5, Art.16, Sch.7 para.41
s.139, varied: SI 2008/680 Art.5, Art.16, Sch.7 para.42
s.143, varied: SI 2008/680 Art.5, Art.16
s.144, varied: SI 2008/680 Art.5, Art.16, Sch.7 para.44
s.145, varied: SI 2008/680 Art.5, Art.16, Sch.7 para.45
s.146, varied: SI 2008/680 Art.5, Art.16, Sch.7 para.46
s.147, varied: SI 2008/680 Art.5, Art.16
s.148, varied: SI 2008/680 Art.5, Art.16
s.149, varied: SI 2008/680 Art.5, Art.16
s.150, varied: SI 2008/680 Art.5, Art.16
s.151, varied: SI 2008/680 Art.5, Art.16
s.152, varied: SI 2008/680 Art.5, Art.16
s.153, varied: SI 2008/680 Art.5, Art.16
s.154, varied: SI 2008/680 Art.5, Art.16
s.155, varied: SI 2008/680 Art.5, Art.16
s.159, varied: SI 2008/680 Art.5, Art.16
s.160, varied: SI 2008/680 Art.5, Art.16, Sch.7 para.47
s.161, varied: SI 2008/680 Art.5, Art.16
s.163, enabling: SI 2008/680
s.164, varied: SI 2008/680 Art.5, Art.16
Sch.3 para.1, amended: 2008 c.23 s.22
Sch.4 para.2, applied: SI 2008/2995 Sch.1 Part 1
Sch.7 para.1, varied: SI 2008/680 Art.5, Art.16
Sch.7 para.2, varied: SI 2008/680 Art.5, Art.16
Sch.7 para.4, varied: SI 2008/680 Art.5, Art.16
Sch.7 para.5, varied: SI 2008/680 Art.5, Art.16
Sch.7 para.6, varied: SI 2008/680 Art.5, Art.16
Sch.7 para.7, varied: SI 2008/680 Art.5, Art.16

CAP.

2002–cont.

41. Nationality, Immigration and Asylum Act 2002–*cont.*

Sch.7 para.8, varied: SI 2008/680 Art.5, Art.16
Sch.8 para.1, varied: SI 2008/680 Art.5, Art.16
Sch.8 para.2, varied: SI 2008/680 Art.5, Art.16, Sch.7 para.43
Sch.8 para.3, varied: SI 2008/680 Art.5, Art.16
Sch.8 para.4, varied: SI 2008/680 Art.5, Art.16
Sch.8 para.5, varied: SI 2008/680 Art.5, Art.16, Sch.7 para.43
Sch.8 para.6, varied: SI 2008/680 Art.5, Art.16, Sch.7 para.43
Sch.8 para.7, varied: SI 2008/680 Art.5, Art.16
Sch.8 para.8, varied: SI 2008/680 Art.5, Art.16
Sch.8 para.9, varied: SI 2008/680 Art.5, Art.16, Sch.7 para.43
Sch.8 para.10, varied: SI 2008/680 Art.5, Art.16
Sch.8 para.11, varied: SI 2008/680 Art.5, Art.16
Sch.8 para.13, varied: SI 2008/680 Art.5, Art.16
Sch.8 para.15, varied: SI 2008/680 Art.5, Art.16, Sch.7 para.43
Sch.8 para.16, varied: SI 2008/680 Art.5, Art.16
Sch.9, varied: SI 2008/680 Art.5, Art.16

2003

1. Income Tax (Earnings and Pensions) Act 2003

Part 2, applied: SI 2008/794 Reg.112, SI 2008/1464 Art.2
Part 2 c.4, amended: 2008 c.9 Sch.7 para.8
Part 2 c.5, amended: 2008 c.9 Sch.7 para.12
Part 2 c.5, amended: 2008 c.9 Sch.7 para.17
Part 3 c.5, disapplied: 2008 c.9 s.45
Part 7 c.2, applied: 2008 c.9 Sch.7 para.91
s.6, amended: 2008 c.9 Sch.7 para.3
s.10, amended: 2008 c.9 Sch.7 para.4
s.13, amended: 2008 c.9 Sch.7 para.5
s.14, amended: 2008 c.9 Sch.7 para.6, Sch.7 para.7
s.15, amended: 2008 c.9 Sch.7 para.6, Sch.7 para.9
s.16, amended: 2008 c.9 Sch.7 para.6
s.17, amended: 2008 c.9 Sch.7 para.6
s.18, amended: 2008 c.9 Sch.7 para.6
s.19, amended: 2008 c.9 Sch.7 para.6
s.20, amended: 2008 c.9 Sch.7 para.10, Sch.7 para.11
s.20, repealed (in part): 2008 c.9 Sch.7 para.11
s.21, amended: 2008 c.9 Sch.7 para.10

CAP.

2003–cont.

1. **Income Tax (Earnings and Pensions) Act 2003**–*cont.*
   s.21, repealed: 2008 c.9 Sch.7 para.13
   s.22, amended: 2008 c.9 Sch.7 para.10, Sch.7 para.14
   s.22, varied: 2008 c.9 Sch.7 para.82
   s.23, amended: 2008 c.9 Sch.7 para.10, Sch.7 para.15
   s.24, amended: 2008 c.9 Sch.7 para.10, Sch.7 para.16
   s.25, amended: 2008 c.9 Sch.7 para.10
   s.25, repealed: 2008 c.9 Sch.7 para.18
   s.26, amended: 2008 c.9 Sch.7 para.10, Sch.7 para.19
   s.26, varied: 2008 c.9 Sch.7 para.82
   s.27, amended: 2008 c.9 Sch.7 para.10, Sch.7 para.20
   s.28, amended: 2008 c.9 Sch.7 para.10
   s.29, amended: 2008 c.9 Sch.7 para.10
   s.30, amended: 2008 c.9 Sch.7 para.10
   s.31, amended: 2008 c.9 Sch.7 para.10
   s.31, repealed: 2008 c.9 Sch.7 para.21
   s.32, amended: 2008 c.9 Sch.7 para.10
   s.32, repealed: 2008 c.9 Sch.7 para.21
   s.33, amended: 2008 c.9 Sch.7 para.10
   s.33, repealed: 2008 c.9 Sch.7 para.21
   s.34, amended: 2008 c.9 Sch.7 para.10
   s.34, repealed: 2008 c.9 Sch.7 para.21
   s.35, amended: 2008 c.9 Sch.7 para.10
   s.35, repealed: 2008 c.9 Sch.7 para.21
   s.36, amended: 2008 c.9 Sch.7 para.10
   s.36, repealed: 2008 c.9 Sch.7 para.21
   s.37, amended: 2008 c.9 Sch.7 para.10
   s.37, repealed: 2008 c.9 Sch.7 para.21
   s.38, amended: 2008 c.9 Sch.7 para.10
   s.39, amended: 2008 c.9 Sch.7 para.10
   s.40, amended: 2008 c.9 Sch.7 para.10
   s.41, amended: 2008 c.9 Sch.7 para.10
   s.41A, added: 2008 c.9 Sch.7 para.22
   s.41B, added: 2008 c.9 Sch.7 para.22
   s.41C, added: 2008 c.9 Sch.7 para.22
   s.41D, added: 2008 c.9 Sch.7 para.22
   s.41E, added: 2008 c.9 Sch.7 para.22
   s.42, repealed: 2008 c.9 Sch.7 para.23
   s.43, repealed: 2008 c.9 Sch.7 para.23
   s.62, see *Resolute Management Services Ltd v Revenue and Customs Commissioners* [2008] S.T.C. (S.C.D.) 1202 (Sp Comm), Malcolm Gammie Q.C.
   s.100A, added: 2008 c.9 s.45
   s.100A, referred to: 2008 c.9 s.45
   s.100B, added: 2008 c.9 s.45
   s.139, amended: 2008 c.9 s.47
   s.150, amended: SI 2008/511 Art.2
   s.170, enabling: SI 2008/511
   s.225, amended: 2008 c.9 Sch.7 para.24
   s.239, amended: 2008 c.9 s.48
   s.269, amended: 2008 c.9 s.48
   s.271, amended: 2008 c.9 Sch.7 para.25
   s.291, amended: 2008 c.9 s.52

CAP.

2003–cont.

1. **Income Tax (Earnings and Pensions) Act 2003**–*cont.*
   s.297B, added: 2008 c.9 s.51
   s.318, amended: SI 2008/2170 Reg.2
   s.318C, amended: SI 2008/2170 Reg.3
   s.318C, repealed (in part): SI 2008/2170 Reg.3
   s.318D, enabling: SI 2008/2170
   s.335, amended: 2008 c.9 Sch.7 para.26
   s.336, see *Guarantor v Revenue and Customs Commissioners* [2008] S.T.C. (S.C.D.) 1154 (Sp Comm), Colin Bishopp (Chairman); see *Perrin v Revenue and Customs Commissioners* [2008] S.T.C. (S.C.D.) 672 (Sp Comm), Charles Hellier
   s.343, amended: 2008 c.14 Sch.15 Part 2, SI 2008/836 Art.2
   s.343, enabling: SI 2008/836
   s.370, amended: 2008 c.9 Sch.7 para.27
   s.371, amended: 2008 c.9 Sch.7 para.28
   s.378, amended: 2008 c.9 Sch.7 para.29
   s.401, see *Resolute Management Services Ltd v Revenue and Customs Commissioners* [2008] S.T.C. (S.C.D.) 1202 (Sp Comm), Malcolm Gammie Q.C.
   s.413, amended: 2008 c.9 Sch.7 para.30
   s.418, repealed (in part): 2008 c.9 s.50
   s.421E, amended: 2008 c.9 Sch.7 para.31
   s.428, amended: 2008 c.9 s.49
   s.431, varied: 2008 c.9 Sch.7 para.91
   s.446N, amended: 2008 c.9 Sch.7 para.32
   s.446T, amended: 2008 c.9 s.49
   s.474, amended: 2008 c.9 Sch.7 para.33
   s.480, amended: 2008 c.9 s.49
   s.536, amended: SI 2008/706 Art.2
   s.540, amended: 2008 c.9 Sch.7 para.34
   s.575, repealed (in part): 2008 c.9 Sch.7 para.45
   s.639, referred to: SI 2008/794 Reg.75
   s.641, repealed (in part): 2008 c.12 Sch.1 Part 1
   s.648, enabling: SI 2008/782
   s.677, amended: 2008 c.9 s.46, 2008 c.14 s.138
   s.684, see *Oriel Support Ltd v Revenue and Customs Commissioners* [2008] S.T.C. (S.C.D.) 292 (Sp Comm), AN Brice
   s.684, enabling: SI 2008/782, SI 2008/2601
   s.687, see *Oriel Support Ltd v Revenue and Customs Commissioners* [2008] S.T.C. (S.C.D.) 292 (Sp Comm), AN Brice
   s.690, amended: 2008 c.9 Sch.7 para.35
   s.698, amended: 2008 c.9 Sch.7 para.36
   s.700, amended: 2008 c.9 Sch.7 para.37
   s.700A, added: 2008 c.9 Sch.7 para.38
   s.711, amended: 2008 c.9 Sch.39 para.49
   s.721, amended: 2008 c.9 Sch.7 para.39
   s.721, varied: 2008 c.9 Sch.7 para.82
   Sch.1 Part 1, amended: 2008 c.9 s.46
   Sch.1 Part 2, amended: 2008 c.9 Sch.7 para.40

CAP.

2003–cont.

1. **Income Tax (Earnings and Pensions) Act 2003**–*cont.*
   Sch.2 Part 2 para.8, amended: 2008 c.9 Sch.7 para.41
   Sch.3 Part 2 para.6, amended: 2008 c.9 Sch.7 para.42
   Sch.3 Part 6 para.37, amended: SI 2008/954 Art.32
   Sch.3 Part 7 para.38, amended: SI 2008/954 Art.32
   Sch.4 Part 6 para.26, amended: SI 2008/954 Art.33
   Sch.5 Part 2 para.5, amended: SI 2008/706 Art.2
   Sch.5 Part 2 para.6, amended: SI 2008/706 Art.2
   Sch.5 Part 3 para.8, amended: 2008 c.9 s.33
   Sch.5 Part 3 para.12A, added: 2008 c.9 s.33
   Sch.5 Part 3 para.16, amended: 2008 c.9 s.33
   Sch.5 Part 3 para.20A, added: 2008 c.9 s.33
   Sch.5 Part 3 para.20B, added: 2008 c.9 s.33
   Sch.5 Part 3 para.20C, added: 2008 c.9 s.33
   Sch.5 Part 4 para.27, amended: 2008 c.9 Sch.7 para.43
   Sch.5 Part 6 para.39, amended: SI 2008/954 Art.34
   Sch.5 Part 8 para.54, enabling: SI 2008/706
   Sch.6 Part 2 para.135, repealed (in part): 2008 c.9 Sch.44 para.11
   Sch.6 Part 2 para.208, repealed: 2008 c.9 Sch.7 para.79
   Sch.7 Part 2 para.9, repealed: 2008 c.9 Sch.7 para.44
   Sch.7 Part 2 para.10, repealed: 2008 c.9 Sch.7 para.44
   Sch.7 Part 2 para.11, repealed: 2008 c.9 Sch.7 para.44
   Sch.7 Part 2 para.12, repealed: 2008 c.9 Sch.7 para.44
   Sch.7 Part 7 para.57, repealed: 2008 c.9 s.50
   Sch.7 Part 8 para.86, amended: 2008 c.9 Sch.2 para.52
7. **European Parliament (Representation) Act 2003**
   s.3, applied: SI 2008/1954
   s.5, applied: SI 2008/1954
   s.5, enabling: SI 2008/1954
   s.6, enabling: SI 2008/1954
8. **National Minimum Wage (Enforcement Notices) Act 2003**
   repealed: 2008 c.24 Sch.1 Part 2
14. **Finance Act 2003**
   see *Sun Life Assurance Co of Canada (UK) Ltd v Revenue and Customs Commissioners* [2008] S.T.C. (S.C.D.) 486 (Sp Comm), Julian Ghosh Q.C.
   s.58B, amended: 2008 c.9 s.93
   s.58B, enabling: SI 2008/1932
   s.58C, amended: 2008 c.9 s.93
   s.58C, enabling: SI 2008/1932

CAP.

2003–cont.

14. **Finance Act 2003**–*cont.*
   s.71, amended: 2008 c.17 Sch.8 para.79, Sch.9 para.30
   s.73A, amended: 2008 c.9 s.155
   s.73AB, added: 2008 c.9 s.155
   s.74, see *Elizabeth Court (Bournemouth) Ltd v Revenue and Customs Commissioners* [2008] S.T.C. (S.C.D.) 366 (Sp Comm), AN Brice
   s.77, substituted: 2008 c.9 s.94
   s.77A, amended: SI 2008/2338 Reg.2
   s.79, amended: 2008 c.9 s.94, Sch.30 para.2
   s.79, repealed (in part): 2008 c.9 Sch.30 para.2
   s.81B, amended: 2008 c.9 Sch.30 para.3
   s.102, enabling: SI 2008/710
   s.103, amended: 2008 c.9 Sch.30 para.4
   s.109, enabling: SI 2008/2338
   s.122, amended: 2008 c.9 Sch.30 para.5
   s.123, enabling: SI 2008/710
   s.138, repealed (in part): 2008 c.9 s.47
   s.143, see *Sempra Metals Ltd v Revenue and Customs Commissioners* [2008] S.T.C. (S.C.D.) 1062 (Sp Comm), AN Brice
   s.152, substituted: 2008 c.9 Sch.16 para.8
   s.156, enabling: SI 2008/1924
   s.160, repealed: 2008 c.9 Sch.2 para.55
   s.163, repealed (in part): 2008 c.9 Sch.7 para.114
   s.165, repealed: 2008 c.9 s.76
   s.166, repealed: 2008 c.9 s.76
   s.171, repealed: 2008 c.9 Sch.14 para.17
   s.192, repealed (in part): 2008 c.9 Sch.40 para.21
   Sch.3 para.2, amended: 2008 c.17 Sch.9 para.31
   Sch.3 para.5, enabling: SI 2008/2339
   Sch.4 para.2, amended: SI 2008/1146 Sch.1 para.11
   Sch.5 para.9, amended: 2008 c.9 s.95
   Sch.5 para.9, repealed (in part): 2008 c.9 s.95
   Sch.5 para.9A, added: 2008 c.9 s.95
   Sch.6 Part 2 para.5, repealed (in part): 2008 c.9 s.95
   Sch.6 Part 2 para.6, repealed (in part): 2008 c.9 s.95
   Sch.6 Part 3 para.9, repealed (in part): 2008 c.9 s.95
   Sch.6 Part 3 para.10, repealed (in part): 2008 c.9 s.95
   Sch.6 Part 4 para.12, amended: 2008 c.9 s.95
   Sch.6 Part 4 para.13, amended: 2008 c.9 Sch.30 para.6
   Sch.7 Part 1 para.3, amended: 2008 c.9 s.96
   Sch.7 Part 1 para.4, amended: 2008 c.9 s.96
   Sch.7 Part 1 para.4, repealed (in part): 2008 c.9 s.96
   Sch.7 Part 1 para.4A, amended: 2008 c.9 s.96
   Sch.7 Part 1 para.4ZA, added: 2008 c.9 s.96
   Sch.8 para.3, amended: 2008 c.9 s.95

CAP.

2003–cont.

14. Finance Act 2003–*cont.*

Sch.9, referred to: 2008 c.17 s.70
Sch.9 para.1, amended: 2008 c.17 Sch.8 para.80, Sch.9 para.32
Sch.9 para.1, varied: SI 2008/2839 Sch.1 para.1
Sch.9 para.4B, added: 2008 c.9 s.95
Sch.9 para.5, amended: 2008 c.17 Sch.8 para.80
Sch.9 para.7, referred to: 2008 c.17 s.73
Sch.9 para.10, amended: 2008 c.9 s.95
Sch.9 para.11, amended: 2008 c.9 s.95
Sch.9 para.12, added: 2008 c.9 s.95
Sch.10 Part 1 para.8, repealed: 2008 c.9 Sch.40 para.21
Sch.10 Part 7 para.36, amended: 2008 c.9 Sch.30 para.7
Sch.11 Part 1 para.1, amended: 2008 c.9 Sch.30 para.11
Sch.11 Part 1 para.1, repealed: 2008 c.9 Sch.30 para.8
Sch.11 Part 1 para.2, amended: 2008 c.9 Sch.30 para.11
Sch.11 Part 1 para.2, repealed: 2008 c.9 Sch.30 para.8
Sch.11 Part 1 para.2A, amended: 2008 c.9 Sch.30 para.11
Sch.11 Part 1 para.2A, repealed: 2008 c.9 Sch.30 para.8
Sch.11 Part 1 para.2B, amended: 2008 c.9 Sch.30 para.11
Sch.11 Part 1 para.2B, repealed: 2008 c.9 Sch.30 para.8
Sch.11 Part 1 para.3, amended: 2008 c.9 Sch.30 para.11
Sch.11 Part 1 para.3, repealed: 2008 c.9 Sch.30 para.8
Sch.11 Part 2 para.4, amended: 2008 c.9 Sch.30 para.9, Sch.30 para.11
Sch.11 Part 2 para.5, amended: 2008 c.9 Sch.30 para.11
Sch.11 Part 2 para.6, amended: 2008 c.9 Sch.30 para.11
Sch.11 Part 3 para.7, amended: 2008 c.9 Sch.30 para.11
Sch.11 Part 3 para.7, repealed: 2008 c.9 Sch.30 para.10
Sch.11 Part 3 para.8, amended: 2008 c.9 Sch.30 para.11
Sch.11 Part 3 para.8, repealed: 2008 c.9 Sch.30 para.10
Sch.11 Part 3 para.9, amended: 2008 c.9 Sch.30 para.11
Sch.11 Part 3 para.9, repealed: 2008 c.9 Sch.30 para.10
Sch.11 Part 3 para.10, amended: 2008 c.9 Sch.30 para.11
Sch.11 Part 3 para.10, repealed: 2008 c.9 Sch.30 para.10
Sch.11 Part 3 para.11, amended: 2008 c.9 Sch.30 para.11

CAP.

2003–cont.

14. Finance Act 2003–*cont.*

Sch.11 Part 3 para.11, repealed: 2008 c.9 Sch.30 para.10
Sch.11 Part 3 para.12, amended: 2008 c.9 Sch.30 para.11
Sch.11 Part 3 para.12, repealed: 2008 c.9 Sch.30 para.10
Sch.11 Part 3 para.13, amended: 2008 c.9 Sch.30 para.11
Sch.11 Part 3 para.13, repealed: 2008 c.9 Sch.30 para.10
Sch.11 Part 3 para.14, amended: 2008 c.9 Sch.30 para.11
Sch.11 Part 3 para.14, repealed: 2008 c.9 Sch.30 para.10
Sch.11 Part 3 para.15, amended: 2008 c.9 Sch.30 para.11
Sch.11 Part 3 para.15, repealed: 2008 c.9 Sch.30 para.10
Sch.11 Part 3 para.16, amended: 2008 c.9 Sch.30 para.11
Sch.11 Part 3 para.16, repealed: 2008 c.9 Sch.30 para.10
Sch.11 Part 3 para.17, amended: 2008 c.9 Sch.30 para.11
Sch.11 Part 3 para.17, repealed: 2008 c.9 Sch.30 para.10
Sch.12 Part 1 para.1A, repealed: 2008 c.9 Sch.43 para.9
Sch.12 Part 1 para.3, repealed: 2008 c.9 Sch.43 para.16
Sch.12 Part 2 para.5, amended: 2008 c.9 s.137
Sch.12 Part 2 para.5, repealed (in part): 2008 c.9 s.137
Sch.12 Part 2 para.7, repealed: 2008 c.9 Sch.44 para.10
Sch.15 Part 2 para.8, amended: 2008 c.9 Sch.30 para.12
Sch.15 Part 3 para.10, amended: 2008 c.9 Sch.31 para.5
Sch.15 Part 3 para.10, applied: 2008 c.9 Sch.31 para.11
Sch.15 Part 3 para.11, amended: 2008 c.9 s.95
Sch.15 Part 3 para.12A, added: 2008 c.9 Sch.31 para.6
Sch.15 Part 3 para.12A, applied: 2008 c.9 Sch.31 para.11
Sch.15 Part 3 para.12A, disapplied: 2008 c.9 Sch.31 para.11
Sch.15 Part 3 para.14, amended: 2008 c.9 Sch.31 para.1
Sch.15 Part 3 para.15, amended: 2008 c.9 Sch.31 para.2
Sch.15 Part 3 para.16, amended: 2008 c.9 Sch.31 para.3
Sch.15 Part 3 para.17A, amended: 2008 c.9 Sch.31 para.8
Sch.15 Part 3 para.18, amended: 2008 c.9 Sch.31 para.7

CAP.

2003–cont.

14. Finance Act 2003–*cont.*

Sch.15 Part 3 para.19, amended: 2008 c.9 s.95

Sch.15 Part 3 para.23, amended: 2008 c.9 s.95

Sch.15 Part 3 para.26, amended: 2008 c.9 Sch.31 para.4, Sch.31 para.9

Sch.16 para.6, amended: 2008 c.9 Sch.30 para.13

Sch.17A para.3, amended: 2008 c.9 Sch.30 para.14

Sch.17A para.4, amended: 2008 c.9 Sch.30 para.14

Sch.17A para.18A, amended: 2008 c.9 s.95

Sch.23 Part 4A para.22C, amended: 2008 c.9 s.49

Sch.23 Part 4 para.21, amended: 2008 c.9 s.49

Sch.24, see *Sempra Metals Ltd v Revenue and Customs Commissioners* [2008] S.T.C. (S.C.D.) 1062 (Sp Comm), AN Brice

Sch.24 para.9, see *Sempra Metals Ltd v Revenue and Customs Commissioners* [2008] S.T.C. (S.C.D.) 1062 (Sp Comm), AN Brice

Sch.26 para.3, amended: 2008 c.9 Sch.16 para.3, Sch.16 para.9

Sch.26 para.3, repealed (in part): 2008 c.9 Sch.16 para.9

Sch.26 para.4, repealed (in part): 2008 c.9 Sch.16 para.9

Sch.26 para.5A, added: 2008 c.9 Sch.16 para.9

Sch.29 para.3, repealed: 2008 c.9 Sch.7 para.146

Sch.29 para.5, repealed: 2008 c.9 Sch.2 para.55

Sch.29 para.6, repealed (in part): 2008 c.9 Sch.7 para.146

Sch.33 para.3, repealed: 2008 c.9 Sch.17 para.3

Sch.33 para.6, repealed (in part): 2008 c.9 Sch.17 para.18

Sch.33 para.24, repealed (in part): SI 2008/381 Sch.1 Part 1

Sch.34 Part 1 para.1, repealed: 2008 c.9 Sch.14 para.17

Sch.34 Part 1 para.2, repealed: 2008 c.9 Sch.14 para.17

Sch.34 Part 1 para.3, repealed: 2008 c.9 Sch.14 para.17

Sch.34 Part 1 para.4, repealed: 2008 c.9 Sch.14 para.17

Sch.34 Part 1 para.5, repealed: 2008 c.9 Sch.14 para.17

Sch.34 Part 2 para.6, repealed: 2008 c.9 Sch.14 para.17

Sch.34 Part 2 para.7, repealed: 2008 c.9 Sch.14 para.17

Sch.34 Part 2 para.8, repealed: 2008 c.9 Sch.14 para.17

CAP.

2003–cont.

14. Finance Act 2003–*cont.*

Sch.34 Part 2 para.9, repealed: 2008 c.9 Sch.14 para.17

Sch.34 Part 2 para.10, repealed: 2008 c.9 Sch.14 para.17

Sch.34 Part 2 para.11, repealed: 2008 c.9 Sch.14 para.17

Sch.34 Part 2 para.12, repealed: 2008 c.9 Sch.14 para.17

Sch.34 Part 3 para.13, repealed: 2008 c.9 Sch.14 para.17

Sch.34 Part 4 para.14, repealed: 2008 c.9 Sch.14 para.17

Sch.34 Part 4 para.15, repealed: 2008 c.9 Sch.14 para.17

Sch.38 para.6, repealed: 2008 c.9 s.66

Sch.40 para.2, repealed (in part): 2008 c.9 Sch.32 para.21

Sch.41 para.1, repealed (in part): SI 2008/381 Sch.1 Part 1

17. Licensing Act 2003

see *R. (on the application of Daniel Thwaites Plc) v Wirral Borough Magistrates Court* [2008] EWHC 838 (Admin), [2008] 1 All E.R. 239 (QBD (Admin)), Black J.; see *R. (on the application of Westminster City Council) v Metropolitan Stipendiary Magistrate* [2008] EWHC 1202 (Admin), (2008) 172 J.P. 462 (QBD (Admin)), Mitting, J.

applied: 2008 c.13 Sch.3

referred to: 2008 c.13 Sch.6

s.4, see *R. (on the application of Daniel Thwaites Plc) v Wirral Borough Magistrates Court* [2008] EWHC 838 (Admin), [2008] 1 All E.R. 239 (QBD (Admin)), Black J.

s.5, applied: SI 2008/2867 Reg.12

s.5, varied: SI 2008/2867 Reg.12

s.13, referred to: SI 2008/1430 Reg.5

s.57, applied: SI 2008/1430 Reg.15

s.59, applied: SI 2008/1430 Reg.15

s.94, applied: SI 2008/1430 Reg.15

s.96, applied: SI 2008/1430 Reg.15

s.154, applied: SI 2008/1430 Reg.15

Sch.4 para.22i, added: SI 2008/1277 Sch.2 para.71

Sch.4 para.23, added: SI 2008/1277 Sch.2 para.71

Sch.5 Part 1 para.1, applied: SI 2008/1052 Sch.1

Sch.5 Part 1 para.2, applied: SI 2008/1052 Sch.1

Sch.5 Part 1 para.3, applied: SI 2008/1052 Sch.1

Sch.5 Part 1 para.4, applied: SI 2008/1052 Sch.1

Sch.5 Part 1 para.7, applied: SI 2008/1052 Sch.1

Sch.5 Part 1 para.8, applied: SI 2008/1052 Sch.1

CAP.

2003–*cont.*

17. **Licensing Act 2003**–*cont.*
Sch.5 Part 1 para.8A, applied: SI 2008/1052 Sch.1
Sch.5 Part 2 para.10, applied: SI 2008/1052 Sch.1
Sch.5 Part 2 para.11, applied: SI 2008/1052 Sch.1
Sch.5 Part 2 para.12, applied: SI 2008/1052 Sch.1
Sch.5 Part 2 para.13, applied: SI 2008/1052 Sch.1
Sch.5 Part 2 para.14, applied: SI 2008/1052 Sch.1
Sch.5 Part 3 para.16, applied: SI 2008/1052 Sch.1
Sch.5 Part 3 para.17, applied: SI 2008/1052 Sch.1
Sch.5 Part 3 para.18, applied: SI 2008/1052 Sch.1
Sch.6 para.2, repealed: 2008 c.12 Sch.1 Part 3

20. **Railways and Transport Safety Act 2003**
applied: 2008 c.3 Sch.2 Part 2, 2008 c.4 s.126, 2008 c.8 Sch.2 Part 7
s.9, applied: 2008 c.13 Sch.7
s.11, applied: 2008 c.13 Sch.7
s.28, applied: SI 2008/1430 Reg.15
s.31, applied: SI 2008/1430 Reg.4, Reg.5, Reg.6, Reg.9, Reg.22
s.36, amended: 2008 c.4 Sch.22 para.18
s.37, amended: 2008 c.4 Sch.22 para.19
s.42, amended: 2008 c.4 Sch.22 para.20
s.43, repealed: 2008 c.4 Sch.22 para.21, Sch.28 Part 8
s.78, referred to: 2008 c.13 Sch.6
s.79, referred to: 2008 c.13 Sch.6
s.80, referred to: 2008 c.13 Sch.6

21. **Communications Act 2003**
see *R. (on the application of Animal Defenders International) v Secretary of State for Culture, Media and Sport* [2008] UKHL 15, [2008] 1 A.C. 1312 (HL), Lord Bingham of Cornhill
applied: SSI 2008/188 Art.29, SSI 2008/189 Art.29, SSI 2008/190 Art.29
referred to: SI 2008/1420 Art.2
s.67, amended: SI 2008/948 Sch.1 para.30
s.77, amended: SI 2008/948 Sch.1 para.30
s.91, amended: SI 2008/948 Sch.1 para.30
s.206, applied: SI 2008/693 Art.3
s.206, enabling: SI 2008/693
s.243, enabling: SI 2008/1420
s.264, applied: SI 2008/1420 Art.3
s.319, see *R. (on the application of Animal Defenders International) v Secretary of State for Culture, Media and Sport* [2008] UKHL 15, [2008] 1 A.C. 1312 (HL), Lord Bingham of Cornhill
s.320, see *R. (on the application of Animal Defenders International) v Secretary of State for Culture, Media and Sport* [2008]

CAP.

2003–*cont.*

21. **Communications Act 2003**–*cont.*
s.320–*cont.*
UKHL 15, [2008] 1 A.C. 1312 (HL), Lord Bingham of Cornhill
s.321, see *R. (on the application of Animal Defenders International) v Secretary of State for Culture, Media and Sport* [2008] UKHL 15, [2008] 1 A.C. 1312 (HL), Lord Bingham of Cornhill
s.365, enabling: SI 2008/643
s.393, amended: SI 2008/1277 Sch.2 para.72
s.402, enabling: SI 2008/643, SI 2008/1420
Sch.3, applied: SI 2008/2512 Sch.10 para.30
Sch.8, see *T Mobile (UK) Ltd v Office of Communications* [2008] EWCA Civ 1373, Times, December 18, 2008 (CA (Civ Div)), Tuckey, L.J.
Sch.17 para.1, applied: 2008 c.29 s.137
Sch.17 para.123, repealed: 2008 c.17 Sch.16

22. **Fireworks Act 2003**
applied: 2008 c.13 Sch.3
s.2, amended: SI 2008/960 Sch.3
s.11, referred to: 2008 c.13 Sch.6

24. **Human Fertilisation and Embryology (Deceased Fathers) Act 2003**
Sch.1 para.3, repealed: 2008 c.22 Sch.8 Part 1
Sch.1 para.5, repealed: 2008 c.22 Sch.8 Part 1
Sch.1 para.7, repealed: 2008 c.22 Sch.8 Part 1
Sch.1 para.9, repealed: 2008 c.22 Sch.8 Part 1
Sch.1 para.10, repealed: 2008 c.22 Sch.8 Part 1
Sch.1 para.12, repealed: 2008 c.22 Sch.8 Part 1
Sch.1 para.18, repealed: 2008 c.22 Sch.8 Part 1

26. **Local Government Act 2003**
Part 1, applied: SI 2008/634 Art.9, SI 2008/907 Art.20
s.9, enabling: SI 2008/414
s.20, applied: SSI 2008/400 Art.3
s.21, applied: 2008 c.17 s.113
s.21, enabling: SI 2008/414, SI 2008/588
s.24, enabling: SI 2008/588
s.31, applied: 2008 c.3 Sch.2 Part 2, 2008 c.8 Sch.2 Part 10
s.36, applied: 2008 c.8 Sch.2 Part 10
s.93, disapplied: SI 2008/2909 Art.3
s.94, enabling: SI 2008/2909
s.105, applied: SI 2008/239 Sch.2 para.23
s.105, varied: SI 2008/917 Art.7
s.109, repealed: 2008 c.17 Sch.16
s.123, enabling: SI 2008/588
s.127, enabling: SI 2008/428
Sch.4 para.1, varied: SI 2008/917 Art.7
Sch.4 para.4, varied: SI 2008/917 Art.7
Sch.4 para.27, varied: SI 2008/917 Art.7

CAP.

2003–cont.

30. Sustainable Energy Act 2003
s.1, amended: 2008 c.32 s.87
s.1, repealed (in part): 2008 c.32 s.87, Sch.6

31. Female Genital Mutilation Act 2003
s.1, applied: SI 2008/1216 Sch.1 para.27, Sch.2 para.29
s.2, applied: SI 2008/1216 Sch.1 para.27, Sch.2 para.29
s.3, applied: SI 2008/1216 Sch.1 para.27, Sch.2 para.29

32. Crime (International Co-operation) Act 2003
Commencement Orders: SI 2008/3009 Art.2, Art.3
s.13, see *R. (on the application of Hafner) v Westminster Magistrates Court* [2008] EWHC 524 (Admin), Times, March 19, 2008 (DC), Lord Phillips of Worth Matravers, L.C.J.
s.15, see *R. (on the application of Hafner) v Westminster Magistrates Court* [2008] EWHC 524 (Admin), Times, March 19, 2008 (DC), Lord Phillips of Worth Matravers, L.C.J.
s.27, amended: 2008 c.4 s.97
s.32, applied: SI 2008/2156 Art.3
s.35, applied: SI 2008/2156 Art.3
s.37, applied: SSI 2008/264 Art.2
s.40, applied: SSI 2008/264 Art.2
s.43, applied: SI 2008/2156 Art.3, SSI 2008/264 Art.2
s.44, applied: SI 2008/2156 Art.3, SSI 2008/264 Art.2
s.45, applied: SI 2008/2156 Art.3, SSI 2008/264 Art.2
s.48, amended: 2008 c.4 Sch.26 para.52
s.50, applied: SI 2008/2156, SSI 2008/264
s.51, applied: SI 2008/2156 Art.3
s.51, enabling: SI 2008/2156, SSI 2008/264
s.57, applied: SI 2008/3010 Reg.2, Reg.3
s.57, referred to: SI 2008/3010 Reg.2
s.57, enabling: SI 2008/3010
s.72, enabling: SI 2008/3010
s.94, enabling: SI 2008/3009
Sch.5 para.82, varied: SI 2008/755 Art.10
Sch.5 para.83, varied: SI 2008/755 Art.10

37. Water Act 2003
Commencement Orders: SI 2008/1922 Art.2
applied: 2008 c.3 Sch.2 Part 2, 2008 c.8 Sch.2 Part 33
s.105, enabling: SI 2008/1922

38. Anti-social Behaviour Act 2003
see *R. (on the application of Smith) v Snaresbrook Crown Court* [2008] EWHC 1282 (Admin), (2008) 172 J.P. 473 (DC), Latham, L.J.
applied: 2008 c.13 Sch.3
Part 1, see *R. (on the application of Smith) v Snaresbrook Crown Court* [2008] EWHC 1282 (Admin), (2008) 172 J.P. 473 (DC), Latham, L.J.

CAP.

2003–cont.

38. Anti-social Behaviour Act 2003–*cont.*
s.2, see *R. (on the application of Smith) v Snaresbrook Crown Court* [2008] EWHC 1282 (Admin), (2008) 172 J.P. 473 (DC), Latham, L.J.
s.5, see *R. (on the application of Smith) v Snaresbrook Crown Court* [2008] EWHC 1282 (Admin), (2008) 172 J.P. 473 (DC), Latham, L.J.
s.11A, added: 2008 c.4 Sch.20
s.11B, added: 2008 c.4 Sch.20
s.11C, added: 2008 c.4 Sch.20
s.11D, added: 2008 c.4 Sch.20
s.11E, added: 2008 c.4 Sch.20
s.11F, added: 2008 c.4 Sch.20
s.11G, added: 2008 c.4 Sch.20
s.11H, added: 2008 c.4 Sch.20
s.11I, added: 2008 c.4 Sch.20
s.11J, added: 2008 c.4 Sch.20
s.11K, added: 2008 c.4 Sch.20
s.11L, added: 2008 c.4 Sch.20
s.14, repealed (in part): 2008 c.17 Sch.16
s.19, amended: 2008 c.25 Sch.1 para.80
s.26B, amended: 2008 c.4 s.125
s.27, amended: 2008 c.4 s.125
s.29, amended: 2008 c.4 s.125
s.40, applied: SI 2008/1430 Reg.15
s.41, applied: SI 2008/1430 Reg.15
s.43, applied: SI 2008/663 Reg.4
s.43A, applied: SI 2008/663 Reg.2, Reg.3
s.43A, enabling: SI 2008/663
s.47, referred to: SI 2008/663(f)
s.47, enabling: SI 2008/663
s.54, referred to: 2008 c.13 Sch.6
s.75, referred to: 2008 c.13 Sch.6
s.88, repealed: 2008 c.4 Sch.28 Part 1
Sch.2 para.1, repealed: 2008 c.4 Sch.28 Part 1
Sch.2 para.2, repealed: 2008 c.4 Sch.28 Part 1
Sch.2 para.3, repealed: 2008 c.4 Sch.28 Part 1
Sch.2 para.4, repealed: 2008 c.4 Sch.28 Part 1
Sch.2 para.5, repealed: 2008 c.4 Sch.28 Part 1
Sch.2 para.6, repealed: 2008 c.4 Sch.28 Part 1

39. Courts Act 2003
applied: 2008 c.8 Sch.2 Part 13
s.2, applied: SI 2008/2791
s.2, enabling: SI 2008/2791
s.22, applied: SI 2008/2995 Sch.1 Part 2
s.24, applied: SI 2008/2995 Sch.1 Part 1
s.31, applied: 2008 c.8 Sch.2 Part 13
s.66, see *Crown Prosecution Service v Greenacre* [2007] EWHC 1193 (Admin), [2008] 1 W.L.R. 438 (DC), Laws, L.J.
s.69, enabling: SI 2008/2076, SI 2008/3269
s.72, applied: SI 2008/2076, SI 2008/3269

CAP.

2003–cont.

39. Courts Act 2003–*cont.*
s.75, enabling: SI 2008/2447
s.79, applied: SI 2008/2447
s.85, applied: 2008 c.28 s.72
s.92, applied: SI 2008/7, SI 2008/115, SI 2008/116, SI 2008/117, SI 2008/1052, SI 2008/1054, SI 2008/2853, SI 2008/2854, SI 2008/2855, SI 2008/2856, SI 2008/3106
s.92, enabling: SI 2008/115, SI 2008/116, SI 2008/117, SI 2008/1052, SI 2008/1053, SI 2008/1054, SI 2008/2853, SI 2008/2854, SI 2008/2855, SI 2008/2856, SI 2008/3106
s.97, enabling: SI 2008/621
s.98, applied: SI 2008/1053 Sch.1
Sch.3A para.2, amended: 2008 c.14 Sch.5 para.75, SI 2008/912 Sch.1 para.27
Sch.3A para.2, repealed (in part): 2008 c.14 Sch.5 para.75, Sch.15 Part 1
Sch.3A para.2, varied: SI 2008/2250 Art.3
Sch.3A para.4, amended: 2008 c.14 Sch.5 para.75, SI 2008/912 Sch.1 para.26
Sch.3A para.4, repealed (in part): 2008 c.14 Sch.5 para.75, Sch.15 Part 1
Sch.3A para.4, varied: SI 2008/2250 Art.3
Sch.3A para.5, amended: SI 2008/912 Sch.1 para.27
Sch.5, disapplied: 2008 c.4 s.80
Sch.5 Part 3 para.9A, added: 2008 c.4 s.41
Sch.5 Part 3 para.9A, applied: SI 2008/3242 Reg.2
Sch.5 Part 3 para.9B, added: 2008 c.4 s.41
Sch.5 Part 3 para.9B, applied: SI 2008/3242 Reg.2
Sch.5 Part 3 para.9C, added: 2008 c.4 s.41
Sch.5 Part 3 para.9C, applied: SI 2008/3242 Reg.2
Sch.5 Part 3 para.9C, enabling: SI 2008/3242
Sch.5 Part 9 para.38, amended: 2008 c.4 s.80
Sch.5 Part 9 para.39, applied: 2008 c.4 s.81
Sch.8 para.80, repealed (in part): 2008 c.14 Sch.15 Part 5

41. Extradition Act 2003
see *Chen v Romania* [2007] EWHC 520 (Admin), [2008] 1 All E.R. 851 (DC), Scott Baker, L.J.; see *Goatley (Stephen Maurice) v HM Advocate* 2008 J.C. 1 (HCJ), Lord Nimmo Smith; see *Hilali v Governor of Whitemoor Prison* [2008] UKHL 3, [2008] 1 A.C. 805 (HL), Lord Bingham of Cornhill; see *La Torre (Antonio) v HM Advocate* 2008 J.C. 23 (HCJ), Lord Gill L.J.C.; see *Norris v United States* [2008] UKHL 16, [2008] 1 A.C. 920 (HL), Lord Bingham of Cornhill
Part 1, see *Hilali v Governor of Whitemoor Prison* [2008] UKHL 3, [2008] 1 A.C. 805 (HL), Lord Bingham of Cornhill

CAP.

2003–cont.

41. Extradition Act 2003–*cont.*
s.2, see *Caldarelli v Italy* [2007] EWHC 1624 (Admin), [2008] 1 W.L.R. 31 (DC), Laws, L.J.; see *Caldarelli v Italy* [2008] UKHL 51, [2008] 1 W.L.R. 1724 (HL), Lord Bingham of Cornhill; see *Governor of Wandsworth Prison v Kinderis* [2007] EWHC 998 (Admin), [2008] Q.B. 347 (DC), Laws, L.J.; see *Kucera v Czech Republic* [2008] EWHC 414 (Admin), [2008] 4 All E.R. 80 (DC), Richards, L.J.; see *La Torre (Antonio) v HM Advocate* 2008 J.C. 23 (HCJ), Lord Gill L.J.C.; see *Pilecki v Poland* [2008] UKHL 7, [2008] 1 W.L.R. 325 (HL), Lord Bingham of Cornhill
s.7, see *Governor of Wandsworth Prison v Kinderis* [2007] EWHC 998 (Admin), [2008] Q.B. 347 (DC), Laws, L.J.
s.10, see *Campbell (Alistair Iain) v HM Advocate* [2008] HCJAC 11, 2008 J.C. 265 (HCJ), Lord Nimmo Smith; see *Pilecki v Poland* [2008] UKHL 7, [2008] 1 W.L.R. 325 (HL), Lord Bingham of Cornhill
s.11, see *Caldarelli v Italy* [2007] EWHC 1624 (Admin), [2008] 1 W.L.R. 31 (DC), Laws, L.J.; see *Caldarelli v Italy* [2008] UKHL 51, [2008] 1 W.L.R. 1724 (HL), Lord Bingham of Cornhill
s.14, see *Campbell (Alistair Iain) v HM Advocate* [2008] HCJAC 11, 2008 J.C. 265 (HCJ), Lord Nimmo Smith; see *Davis v Spain* [2008] EWHC 853 (Admin), [2008] 1 W.L.R. 2593 (DC), Moses, L.J.
s.20, see *Caldarelli v Italy* [2007] EWHC 1624 (Admin), [2008] 1 W.L.R. 31 (DC), Laws, L.J.; see *Campbell (Alistair Iain) v HM Advocate* [2008] HCJAC 11, 2008 J.C. 265 (HCJ), Lord Nimmo Smith
s.21, see *Campbell (Alistair Iain) v HM Advocate* [2008] HCJAC 11, 2008 J.C. 265 (HCJ), Lord Nimmo Smith; see *Goatley (Stephen Maurice) v HM Advocate* 2008 J.C. 1 (HCJ), Lord Nimmo Smith; see *Szklanny v City of Westminster Magistrates Court* [2007] EWHC 2646 (Admin), [2008] 1 W.L.R. 789 (DC), Richards, L.J.
s.22, see *Governor of Wandsworth Prison v Kinderis* [2007] EWHC 998 (Admin), [2008] Q.B. 347 (DC), Laws, L.J.
s.26, see *Hilali v Governor of Whitemoor Prison* [2008] UKHL 3, [2008] 1 A.C. 805 (HL), Lord Bingham of Cornhill; see *Moulai v France* [2008] EWHC 1024 (Admin), [2008] 1 W.L.R. 2460 (DC), Hooper, L.J.
s.32, see *Pilecki v Poland* [2008] UKHL 7, [2008] 1 W.L.R. 325 (HL), Lord Bingham of Cornhill
s.34, see *Hilali v Governor of Whitemoor Prison* [2008] UKHL 3, [2008] 1 A.C. 805 (HL), Lord Bingham of Cornhill

CAP.

2003–cont.

41. Extradition Act 2003–*cont.*

s.35, see *Governor of Wandsworth Prison v Kinderis* [2007] EWHC 998 (Admin), [2008] Q.B. 347 (DC), Laws, L.J.; see *Moulai v France* [2008] EWHC 1024 (Admin), [2008] 1 W.L.R. 2460 (DC), Hooper, L.J.; see *Szklanny v City of Westminster Magistrates Court* [2007] EWHC 2646 (Admin), [2008] 1 W.L.R. 789 (DC), Richards, L.J.

s.36, see *Governor of Wandsworth Prison v Kinderis* [2007] EWHC 998 (Admin), [2008] Q.B. 347 (DC), Laws, L.J.; see *Pilecki v Poland* [2008] UKHL 7, [2008] 1 W.L.R. 325 (HL), Lord Bingham of Cornhill

s.45, see *Governor of Wandsworth Prison v Kinderis* [2007] EWHC 998 (Admin), [2008] Q.B. 347 (DC), Laws, L.J.

s.46, see *Governor of Wandsworth Prison v Kinderis* [2007] EWHC 998 (Admin), [2008] Q.B. 347 (DC), Laws, L.J.

s.47, see *Governor of Wandsworth Prison v Kinderis* [2007] EWHC 998 (Admin), [2008] Q.B. 347 (DC), Laws, L.J.

s.64, see *La Torre (Antonio) v HM Advocate* 2008 J.C. 23 (HCJ), Lord Gill L.J.C.

s.65, see *Kucera v Czech Republic* [2008] EWHC 414 (Admin), [2008] 4 All E.R. 80 (DC), Richards, L.J.; see *Pilecki v Poland* [2008] UKHL 7, [2008] 1 W.L.R. 325 (HL), Lord Bingham of Cornhill

s.68A, see *Caldarelli v Italy* [2007] EWHC 1624 (Admin), [2008] 1 W.L.R. 31 (DC), Laws, L.J.; see *Caldarelli v Italy* [2008] UKHL 51, [2008] 1 W.L.R. 1724 (HL), Lord Bingham of Cornhill

s.69, enabling: SI 2008/1589

s.70, see *Akaroglu v Romania* [2007] EWHC 367 (Admin), [2008] 1 All E.R. 27 (DC), Scott Baker, L.J.; see *La Torre (Antonio) v HM Advocate* 2008 J.C. 23 (HCJ), Lord Gill L.J.C.

s.74, enabling: SI 2008/1589

s.78, see *Akaroglu v Romania* [2007] EWHC 367 (Admin), [2008] 1 All E.R. 27 (DC), Scott Baker, L.J.; see *La Torre (Antonio) v HM Advocate* 2008 J.C. 23 (HCJ), Lord Gill L.J.C.

s.79, see *Chen v Romania* [2007] EWHC 520 (Admin), [2008] 1 All E.R. 851 (DC), Scott Baker, L.J.; see *Mucelli v Albania* [2007] EWHC 2632 (Admin), [2008] 1 W.L.R. 2437 (DC), Richards, L.J.

s.80, see *La Torre (Antonio) v HM Advocate* 2008 J.C. 23 (HCJ), Lord Gill L.J.C.

s.82, see *Chen v Romania* [2007] EWHC 520 (Admin), [2008] 1 All E.R. 851 (DC), Scott Baker, L.J.

s.84, see *La Torre (Antonio) v HM Advocate* 2008 J.C. 23 (HCJ), Lord Gill L.J.C.

CAP.

2003–cont.

41. Extradition Act 2003–*cont.*

s.85, see *Chen v Romania* [2007] EWHC 520 (Admin), [2008] 1 All E.R. 851 (DC), Scott Baker, L.J.; see *Mucelli v Albania* [2007] EWHC 2632 (Admin), [2008] 1 W.L.R. 2437 (DC), Richards, L.J.

s.87, see *Chen v Romania* [2007] EWHC 520 (Admin), [2008] 1 All E.R. 851 (DC), Scott Baker, L.J.; see *Norris v United States* [2008] UKHL 16, [2008] 1 A.C. 920 (HL), Lord Bingham of Cornhill

s.103, see *Chen v Romania* [2007] EWHC 520 (Admin), [2008] 1 All E.R. 851 (DC), Scott Baker, L.J.; see *La Torre (Antonio) v Lord Advocate* 2008 J.C. 72 (HCJ), Lord Gill L.J.C.; see *Mucelli v Albania* [2007] EWHC 2632 (Admin), [2008] 1 W.L.R. 2437 (DC), Richards, L.J.; see *Mustafa v United States* [2008] EWHC 1357 (Admin), [2008] 1 W.L.R. 2760 (DC), Sir Igor Judge (President, QB)

s.104, see *Chen v Romania* [2007] EWHC 520 (Admin), [2008] 1 All E.R. 851 (DC), Scott Baker, L.J.; see *La Torre (Antonio) v Lord Advocate* 2008 J.C. 72 (HCJ), Lord Gill L.J.C.

s.137, see *Norris v United States* [2008] UKHL 16, [2008] 1 A.C. 920 (HL), Lord Bingham of Cornhill

s.213, see *Moulai v France* [2008] EWHC 1024 (Admin), [2008] 1 W.L.R. 2460 (DC), Hooper, L.J.

s.223, applied: SI 2008/1589

42. Sexual Offences Act 2003

see *A v Scottish Ministers* 2008 S.L.T. 412 (OH), Lord Turnbull; see *Attorney General's Reference (Nos.74 and 83 of 2007), Re* [2007] EWCA Crim 2550, [2008] 1 Cr. App. R. (S.) 110 (CA (Crim Div)), Latham, L.J. (VP, QBD); see *Clark (George Samuel) v HM Advocate* [2008] HCJAC 35, 2008 S.L.T. 787 (HCJ), Lord Eassie; see *R. v Fowkes (Danny)* [2007] EWCA Crim 3206, [2008] 2 Cr. App. R. (S.) 22 (CA (Crim Div)), Hallett, LJ

applied: 2008 c.4 Sch.26 para.53, Sch.27 para.38

Part 2, applied: SI 2008/1216 Art.19

s.1, referred to: SI 2008/1062 Sch.1 para.1

s.2, referred to: SI 2008/1062 Sch.1 para.1

s.3, see *R. v Heard (Lee)* [2007] EWCA Crim 125, [2008] Q.B. 43 (CA (Crim Div)), Hughes, L.J.

s.5, see *R. v G* [2008] UKHL 37, [2008] 1 W.L.R. 1379 (HL), Lord Hoffmann

s.5, referred to: SI 2008/1062 Sch.1 para.1

s.6, referred to: SI 2008/1062 Sch.1 para.1

s.7, see *R. v B* [2008] EWCA Crim 830, Times, April 18, 2008 (CA (Crim Div)), Rix, L.J.

s.7, referred to: SI 2008/1062 Sch.1 para.1

s.8, referred to: SI 2008/1062 Sch.1 para.1

CAP.

2003–*cont.*

42. Sexual Offences Act 2003–*cont.*

s.9, see *Attorney General's Reference (Nos.74 and 83 of 2007), Re* [2007] EWCA Crim 2550, [2008] 1 Cr. App. R. (S.) 110 (CA (Crim Div)), Latham, L.J. (VP, QBD)

s.11, see *R. v B* [2008] EWCA Crim 830, Times, April 18, 2008 (CA (Crim Div)), Rix, L.J.

s.12, see *R. v B* [2008] EWCA Crim 830, Times, April 18, 2008 (CA (Crim Div)), Rix, L.J.

s.13, see *R. v G* [2008] UKHL 37, [2008] 1 W.L.R. 1379 (HL), Lord Hoffmann

s.14, see *R. v R* [2008] EWCA Crim 619, [2008] 2 Cr. App. R. 38 (CA (Crim Div)), Moses, L.J.

s.15, amended: 2008 c.4 Sch.15 para.1, SI 2008/1779 Art.4

s.15, applied: SI 2008/1216 Sch.1 para.28, Sch.2 para.13

s.15, referred to: 2008 c.4 s.73

s.15, repealed (in part): SI 2008/1769 Art.78, Sch.3, SI 2008/1779 Art.4

s.16, applied: SI 2008/1216 Sch.2 para.13

s.16, repealed (in part): SI 2008/1769 Art.78, Sch.3

s.17, applied: SI 2008/1216 Sch.2 para.13

s.17, repealed (in part): SI 2008/1769 Art.78, Sch.3

s.18, applied: SI 2008/1216 Sch.2 para.13

s.18, repealed (in part): SI 2008/1769 Art.78, Sch.3

s.19, applied: SI 2008/1216 Sch.2 para.13

s.19, repealed (in part): SI 2008/1769 Art.78, Sch.3

s.20, amended: SI 2008/1779 Art.5

s.20, repealed (in part): SI 2008/1769 Art.78, Sch.3

s.21, amended: 2008 c.23 Sch.1 para.15, 2008 c.25 Sch.1 para.81, SI 2008/1779 Art.6

s.21, repealed (in part): SI 2008/1769 Art.78, Sch.3, SI 2008/1779 Art.6

s.22, amended: SI 2008/1779 Art.7

s.22, repealed (in part): SI 2008/1769 Art.78, Sch.3, SI 2008/1779 Art.7

s.23, repealed (in part): SI 2008/1769 Art.78, Sch.3

s.24, repealed (in part): SI 2008/1769 Art.78, Sch.3

s.27, amended: 2008 c.4 Sch.15 para.3, 2008 c.23 Sch.1 para.16

s.29, amended: 2008 c.4 Sch.15 para.4

s.30, see *R. v C* [2008] EWCA Crim 1155, Times, June 9, 2008 (CA (Crim Div)), Lord Philips, L.C.J.

s.30, referred to: SI 2008/1062 Sch.1 para.1, Sch.1 para.2

s.31, referred to: SI 2008/1062 Sch.1 para.1, Sch.1 para.2

CAP.

2003–*cont.*

42. Sexual Offences Act 2003–*cont.*

s.32, referred to: SI 2008/1062 Sch.1 para.1, Sch.1 para.2

s.33, referred to: SI 2008/1062 Sch.1 para.1, Sch.1 para.2

s.34, referred to: SI 2008/1062 Sch.1 para.1, Sch.1 para.2

s.35, referred to: SI 2008/1062 Sch.1 para.1, Sch.1 para.2

s.36, referred to: SI 2008/1062 Sch.1 para.1, Sch.1 para.2

s.37, referred to: SI 2008/1062 Sch.1 para.1, Sch.1 para.2

s.38, referred to: SI 2008/1062 Sch.1 para.1, Sch.1 para.2

s.39, referred to: SI 2008/1062 Sch.1 para.1, Sch.1 para.2

s.40, referred to: SI 2008/1062 Sch.1 para.1, Sch.1 para.2

s.41, referred to: SI 2008/1062 Sch.1 para.1, Sch.1 para.2

s.47, applied: SI 2008/1216 Sch.1 para.28, Sch.2 para.13

s.47, repealed (in part): SI 2008/1769 Art.78, Sch.3, SI 2008/1779 Art.8

s.48, applied: SI 2008/1216 Sch.1 para.28, Sch.2 para.13

s.48, repealed (in part): SI 2008/1769 Art.78, Sch.3

s.49, amended: 2008 c.23 Sch.1 para.17

s.49, applied: SI 2008/1216 Sch.1 para.28, Sch.2 para.13

s.49, repealed (in part): SI 2008/1769 Art.78, Sch.3

s.50, applied: SI 2008/1216 Sch.1 para.28, Sch.2 para.13

s.50, repealed (in part): SI 2008/1769 Art.78, Sch.3

s.51, repealed (in part): SI 2008/1769 Art.78, Sch.3

s.52, applied: SI 2008/1216 Sch.2 para.13

s.52, repealed (in part): SI 2008/1769 Art.78, Sch.3

s.53, applied: SI 2008/1216 Sch.2 para.13

s.53, repealed (in part): SI 2008/1769 Art.78, Sch.3

s.54, repealed (in part): SI 2008/1769 Art.78, Sch.3

s.57, see *R. v Makai (Atilla)* [2007] EWCA Crim 1652, [2008] 1 Cr. App. R. (S.) 73 (CA (Crim Div)), Pill, L.J.

s.57, applied: SI 2008/1216 Sch.1 para.28, Sch.2 para.13

s.58, applied: SI 2008/1216 Sch.1 para.28, Sch.2 para.13

s.59, applied: SI 2008/1216 Sch.1 para.28, Sch.2 para.13

s.60, amended: SI 2008/1779 Art.9

s.64, amended: 2008 c.4 Sch.15 para.5

s.64, applied: 2008 c.4 s.73

s.65, amended: 2008 c.4 Sch.15 para.6

CAP.

2003–cont.

42. Sexual Offences Act 2003–*cont.*

s.65, applied: 2008 c.4 s.73
s.66, applied: SI 2008/1216 Sch.2 para.13
s.66, repealed (in part): SI 2008/1769 Art.78, Sch.3
s.67, applied: SI 2008/1216 Sch.2 para.13
s.67, repealed (in part): SI 2008/1769 Art.78, Sch.3
s.68, see *R. v Bassett (Kevin)* [2008] EWCA Crim 1174, (2008) 172 J.P. 491 (CA (Crim Div)), Hughes, L.J.
s.68, repealed (in part): SI 2008/1769 Art.78, Sch.3
s.69, applied: SI 2008/1216 Sch.2 para.13
s.69, repealed (in part): SI 2008/1769 Art.78, Sch.3
s.70, applied: SI 2008/1216 Sch.2 para.13
s.70, repealed (in part): SI 2008/1769 Art.78, Sch.3
s.71, repealed (in part): SI 2008/1769 Art.78, Sch.3
s.72, amended: SI 2008/1779 Art.10
s.72, repealed (in part): SI 2008/1769 Art.78, Sch.3
s.72, substituted: 2008 c.4 s.72
s.74, see *R. v Bree (Benjamin)* [2007] EWCA Crim 804, [2008] Q.B. 131 (CA (Crim Div)), Sir Igor Judge (President, QB)
s.78, repealed (in part): SI 2008/1769 Art.78, Sch.3
s.79, repealed (in part): SI 2008/1769 Art.78, Sch.3
s.81, see *A v Scottish Ministers* 2008 S.L.T. 412 (OH), Lord Turnbull
s.82, see *A v Scottish Ministers* 2008 S.L.T. 412 (OH), Lord Turnbull
s.82, amended: SI 2008/1216 Sch.5 para.10
s.83, amended: 2008 c.4 s.142, Sch.26 para.54
s.84, amended: 2008 c.4 s.142
s.85, see *McDonagh v Pattison* 2008 J.C. 125 (HCJ), Lord Osborne
s.85, amended: 2008 c.4 s.142, Sch.26 para.55
s.86, repealed (in part): 2008 c.4 Sch.28 Part 4
s.87, applied: SSI 2008/117 Reg.12, Reg.13, SSI 2008/128 Reg.2
s.87, repealed (in part): 2008 c.4 Sch.28 Part 4
s.87, enabling: SSI 2008/128
s.91, see *McDonagh v Pattison* 2008 J.C. 125 (HCJ), Lord Osborne
s.91, applied: SI 2008/1216 Sch.2 para.13
s.94, amended: SI 2008/2656 Reg.3
s.95, amended: SI 2008/2656 Reg.3
s.104, see *R. v Terrell (Alexander James)* [2007] EWCA Crim 3079, [2008] 2 All E.R. 1065 (CA (Crim Div)), Lord Philips, L.C.J.

CAP.

2003–cont.

42. Sexual Offences Act 2003–*cont.*

s.106, see *R. v Terrell (Alexander James)* [2007] EWCA Crim 3079, [2008] 2 All E.R. 1065 (CA (Crim Div)), Lord Philips, L.C.J.
s.106, amended: 2008 c.4 s.141
s.113, applied: SI 2008/1216 Sch.2 para.13
s.122, applied: SI 2008/1216 Sch.2 para.13
s.128, applied: SI 2008/1216 Sch.2 para.13
s.131, amended: SI 2008/1216 Sch.5 para.10
s.133, amended: 2008 c.4 Sch.26 para.56
s.133, substituted: 2008 c.4 Sch.26 para.56
s.138, amended: 2008 c.4 s.142, Sch.26 para.57
s.142, amended: SI 2008/1779 Art.11
s.142, repealed (in part): SI 2008/1779 Art.11
Sch.2 para.1, amended: 2008 c.4 s.72, Sch.28 Part 5
Sch.2 para.2, amended: 2008 c.4 s.72
Sch.2 para.2, repealed: SI 2008/1779 Art.12
Sch.2 para.3, amended: SI 2008/1779 Art.12
Sch.3, referred to: 2008 c.4 Sch.26 para.58
Sch.3 para.35A, added: 2008 c.4 Sch.26 para.58
Sch.3 para.42, see *Clark (George Samuel) v HM Advocate* [2008] HCJAC 35, 2008 S.L.T. 787 (HCJ), Lord Eassie
Sch.3 para.60, see *Clark (George Samuel) v HM Advocate* [2008] HCJAC 35, 2008 S.L.T. 787 (HCJ), Lord Eassie
Sch.3 para.92A, added: 2008 c.4 Sch.26 para.58, SI 2008/1779 Art.13
Sch.3 para.92B, added: SI 2008/1779 Art.13
Sch.3 para.92C, added: SI 2008/1779 Art.13
Sch.3 para.92D, added: SI 2008/1779 Art.13
Sch.3 para.92E, added: SI 2008/1779 Art.13
Sch.3 para.92F, added: SI 2008/1779 Art.13
Sch.3 para.92G, added: SI 2008/1779 Art.13
Sch.3 para.92H, added: SI 2008/1779 Art.13
Sch.3 para.92I, added: SI 2008/1779 Art.13
Sch.3 para.92J, added: SI 2008/1779 Art.13
Sch.3 para.92K, added: SI 2008/1779 Art.13
Sch.3 para.92L, added: SI 2008/1779 Art.13
Sch.3 para.92M, added: SI 2008/1779 Art.13
Sch.3 para.92N, added: SI 2008/1779 Art.13
Sch.3 para.92O, added: SI 2008/1779 Art.13
Sch.3 para.92P, added: SI 2008/1779 Art.13
Sch.3 para.92Q, added: SI 2008/1779 Art.13
Sch.3 para.92R, added: SI 2008/1779 Art.13
Sch.3 para.92S, added: SI 2008/1779 Art.13
Sch.3 para.92T, added: SI 2008/1779 Art.13
Sch.3 para.92U, added: SI 2008/1779 Art.13
Sch.3 para.92V, added: SI 2008/1779 Art.13
Sch.3 para.93, amended: 2008 c.4 Sch.26 para.58
Sch.3 para.93A, amended: 2008 c.4 Sch.26 para.58
Sch.5 para.171, amended: SI 2008/1779 Art.14
Sch.5 para.171B, added: SI 2008/1779 Art.14

CAP.

2003–*cont.*

42. Sexual Offences Act 2003–*cont.*

Sch.6 para.18, repealed (in part): SI 2008/1779 Art.15

Sch.6 para.39, repealed: SI 2008/1779 Art.15

Sch.6 para.46, repealed (in part): SI 2008/1779 Art.15

43. Health and Social Care (Community Health and Standards) Act 2003

Commencement Orders: SI 2008/1334 Art.2

referred to: SI 2008/408

Part 2 c.3, repealed: 2008 c.14 Sch.15 Part 1

s.41, repealed: 2008 c.14 Sch.5 para.36, Sch.15 Part 1

s.42, repealed: 2008 c.14 Sch.5 para.36, Sch.15 Part 1

s.43, repealed: 2008 c.14 Sch.5 para.36, Sch.15 Part 1

s.43D, repealed: 2008 c.14 Sch.5 para.36, Sch.15 Part 1

s.44, repealed: 2008 c.14 Sch.5 para.36, Sch.15 Part 1

s.45, amended: 2008 c.14 Sch.5 para.37

s.46, repealed: 2008 c.14 Sch.5 para.38, Sch.15 Part 1

s.47A, repealed: 2008 c.14 Sch.5 para.39, Sch.15 Part 1

s.47B, repealed: 2008 c.14 Sch.5 para.39, Sch.15 Part 1

s.47C, repealed: 2008 c.14 Sch.5 para.39, Sch.15 Part 1

s.48, repealed: 2008 c.14 Sch.5 para.40

s.49, repealed: 2008 c.14 Sch.5 para.40

s.49N, repealed: 2008 c.14 Sch.5 para.40

s.49S, repealed: 2008 c.14 Sch.5 para.40

s.50, repealed: 2008 c.14 Sch.5 para.40

s.51, repealed: 2008 c.14 Sch.5 para.40

s.52, repealed: 2008 c.14 Sch.5 para.40

s.53, repealed: 2008 c.14 Sch.5 para.40

s.53A, repealed: 2008 c.14 Sch.5 para.40

s.53B, repealed: 2008 c.14 Sch.5 para.40

s.54, repealed: 2008 c.14 Sch.5 para.40

s.55, repealed: 2008 c.14 Sch.5 para.40

s.56, repealed: 2008 c.14 Sch.5 para.40

s.57, repealed: 2008 c.14 Sch.5 para.40

s.58, repealed: 2008 c.14 Sch.5 para.40

s.59, repealed: 2008 c.14 Sch.5 para.40

s.60, repealed: 2008 c.14 Sch.5 para.40

s.61, repealed: 2008 c.14 Sch.5 para.40

s.62, repealed: 2008 c.14 Sch.5 para.40

s.63, repealed: 2008 c.14 Sch.5 para.40

s.64, repealed: 2008 c.14 Sch.5 para.40

s.65, repealed: 2008 c.14 Sch.5 para.40

s.66, repealed: 2008 c.14 Sch.5 para.40

s.67, repealed: 2008 c.14 Sch.5 para.40

s.68, repealed: 2008 c.14 Sch.5 para.40

s.69, repealed: 2008 c.14 Sch.5 para.40

s.69A, repealed: 2008 c.14 Sch.5 para.40

s.76, repealed: 2008 c.14 Sch.5 para.41, Sch.15 Part 1

CAP.

2003–*cont.*

43. Health and Social Care (Community Health and Standards) Act 2003–*cont.*

s.77, repealed: 2008 c.14 Sch.5 para.41, Sch.15 Part 1

s.78, repealed: 2008 c.14 Sch.5 para.41, Sch.15 Part 1

s.79, repealed: 2008 c.14 Sch.5 para.41, Sch.15 Part 1

s.80, repealed: 2008 c.14 Sch.5 para.41, Sch.15 Part 1

s.81, repealed: 2008 c.14 Sch.5 para.41, Sch.15 Part 1

s.82, repealed: 2008 c.14 Sch.5 para.41, Sch.15 Part 1

s.83, repealed: 2008 c.14 Sch.5 para.41, Sch.15 Part 1

s.84, repealed: 2008 c.14 Sch.5 para.41, Sch.15 Part 1

s.85, repealed: 2008 c.14 Sch.5 para.41, Sch.15 Part 1

s.86, repealed: 2008 c.14 Sch.5 para.41, Sch.15 Part 1

s.87, repealed: 2008 c.14 Sch.5 para.41, Sch.15 Part 1

s.88, repealed: 2008 c.14 Sch.5 para.41, Sch.15 Part 1

s.89, repealed: 2008 c.14 Sch.5 para.41, Sch.15 Part 1

s.90, repealed: 2008 c.14 Sch.5 para.41, Sch.15 Part 1

s.90, varied: 2008 c.4 s.86

s.91, repealed: 2008 c.14 Sch.5 para.41, Sch.15 Part 1

s.96, amended: 2008 c.14 Sch.5 para.42

s.100, amended: 2008 c.14 Sch.5 para.43

s.102, repealed: 2008 c.14 Sch.5 para.44, Sch.15 Part 1

s.103, repealed: 2008 c.14 Sch.5 para.44, Sch.15 Part 1

s.104, repealed: 2008 c.14 Sch.5 para.44, Sch.15 Part 1

s.113, amended: 2008 c.01 s.10

s.113, applied: 2008 c.14 s.77, s.79

s.113, repealed (in part): 2008 c.14 Sch.5 para.45, Sch.15 Part 1

s.113, enabling: SI 2008/528

s.114, applied: 2008 c.14 s.77, s.79

s.114, repealed (in part): 2008 c.14 Sch.5 para.46, Sch.15 Part 1

s.120, repealed: 2008 c.14 Sch.5 para.47, Sch.15 Part 1

s.121, repealed: 2008 c.14 Sch.5 para.47, Sch.15 Part 1

s.122, repealed: 2008 c.14 Sch.5 para.47, Sch.15 Part 1

s.123, repealed: 2008 c.14 Sch.5 para.47, Sch.15 Part 1

s.124, applied: SI 2008/1181 Reg.3

s.124, repealed: 2008 c.14 Sch.5 para.47, Sch.15 Part 1

s.124, enabling: SI 2008/1181

CAP.

2003–cont.

43. Health and Social Care (Community Health and Standards) Act 2003–*cont.*

s.125, repealed: 2008 c.14 Sch.5 para.47, Sch.15 Part 1
s.126, repealed: 2008 c.14 Sch.5 para.47, Sch.15 Part 1
s.127, repealed: 2008 c.14 Sch.5 para.47, Sch.15 Part 1
s.128, repealed: 2008 c.14 Sch.5 para.47, Sch.15 Part 1
s.129, repealed: 2008 c.14 Sch.5 para.47, Sch.15 Part 1
s.130, repealed: 2008 c.14 Sch.5 para.47, Sch.15 Part 1
s.131, repealed: 2008 c.14 Sch.5 para.47, Sch.15 Part 1
s.132, repealed: 2008 c.14 Sch.5 para.47, Sch.15 Part 1
s.133, repealed: 2008 c.14 Sch.5 para.47, Sch.15 Part 1
s.134, repealed: 2008 c.14 Sch.5 para.47, Sch.15 Part 1
s.135, repealed: 2008 c.14 Sch.5 para.47, Sch.15 Part 1
s.136, repealed: 2008 c.14 Sch.5 para.47, Sch.15 Part 1
s.137, repealed: 2008 c.14 Sch.5 para.47, Sch.15 Part 1
s.138, repealed: 2008 c.14 Sch.5 para.47, Sch.15 Part 1
s.139, repealed: 2008 c.14 Sch.5 para.47, Sch.15 Part 1
s.140, repealed: 2008 c.14 Sch.5 para.47, Sch.15 Part 1
s.141, repealed: 2008 c.14 Sch.5 para.47, Sch.15 Part 1
s.143, substituted: 2008 c.14 Sch.5 para.48
s.144, repealed: 2008 c.14 Sch.5 para.49, Sch.15 Part 1
s.145, repealed: 2008 c.14 Sch.5 para.50, Sch.15 Part 1
s.145A, repealed: 2008 c.14 Sch.5 para.50, Sch.15 Part 1
s.148, amended: 2008 c.14 Sch.5 para.51, Sch.15 Part 1
s.153, enabling: SI 2008/252, SSI 2008/96
s.157, amended: SI 2008/2833 Sch.3 para.199
s.157, applied: SI 2008/2685 Sch.1
s.157, repealed (in part): SI 2008/2833 Sch.3 para.199
s.158, amended: SI 2008/2833 Sch.3 para.200
s.158, applied: SI 2008/2683 Art.4, SI 2008/2833 Art.3
s.158, repealed (in part): SI 2008/2833 Sch.3 para.200
s.159, applied: SI 2008/2683 Art.4, SI 2008/2833 Art.3
s.159, repealed (in part): SI 2008/2833 Sch.3 para.201

CAP.

2003–cont.

43. Health and Social Care (Community Health and Standards) Act 2003–*cont.*

s.168, enabling: SSI 2008/96
s.175, enabling: SI 2008/528
s.195, applied: SI 2008/252
s.195, enabling: SI 2008/252, SI 2008/1181, SSI 2008/96
s.199, enabling: SI 2008/1334
Sch.6 para.1, repealed: 2008 c.14 Sch.5 para.52, Sch.15 Part 1
Sch.6 para.2, repealed: 2008 c.14 Sch.5 para.52, Sch.15 Part 1
Sch.6 para.3, repealed: 2008 c.14 Sch.5 para.52, Sch.15 Part 1
Sch.6 para.4, repealed: 2008 c.14 Sch.5 para.52, Sch.15 Part 1
Sch.6 para.5, repealed: 2008 c.14 Sch.5 para.52, Sch.15 Part 1
Sch.6 para.6, repealed: 2008 c.14 Sch.5 para.52, Sch.15 Part 1
Sch.6 para.7, repealed: 2008 c.14 Sch.5 para.52, Sch.15 Part 1
Sch.6 para.8, repealed: 2008 c.14 Sch.5 para.52, Sch.15 Part 1
Sch.6 para.9, repealed: 2008 c.14 Sch.5 para.52, Sch.15 Part 1
Sch.6 para.10, repealed: 2008 c.14 Sch.5 para.52, Sch.15 Part 1
Sch.6 para.11, repealed: 2008 c.14 Sch.5 para.52, Sch.15 Part 1
Sch.6 para.12, repealed: 2008 c.14 Sch.5 para.52, Sch.15 Part 1
Sch.7 para.1, repealed: 2008 c.14 Sch.15 Part 1
Sch.7 para.2, repealed: 2008 c.14 Sch.15 Part 1
Sch.7 para.3, repealed: 2008 c.14 Sch.15 Part 1
Sch.7 para.4, repealed: 2008 c.14 Sch.15 Part 1
Sch.7 para.5, repealed: 2008 c.14 Sch.15 Part 1
Sch.7 para.6, repealed: 2008 c.14 Sch.15 Part 1
Sch.7 para.7, repealed: 2008 c.14 Sch.15 Part 1
Sch.7 para.8, repealed: 2008 c.14 Sch.15 Part 1
Sch.7 para.9, repealed: 2008 c.14 Sch.15 Part 1
Sch.7 para.10, repealed: 2008 c.14 Sch.15 Part 1
Sch.7 para.11, repealed: 2008 c.14 Sch.15 Part 1
Sch.7 para.12, repealed: 2008 c.14 Sch.15 Part 1
Sch.8 para.1, repealed: 2008 c.14 Sch.15 Part 1
Sch.8 para.2, repealed: 2008 c.14 Sch.15 Part 1

CAP.

2003–cont.

43. Health and Social Care (Community Health and Standards) Act 2003–*cont.*

Sch.8 para.3, repealed: 2008 c.14 Sch.15 Part 1

Sch.8 para.4, repealed: 2008 c.14 Sch.15 Part 1

Sch.8 para.5, repealed: 2008 c.14 Sch.15 Part 1

Sch.8 para.6, repealed: 2008 c.14 Sch.15 Part 1

44. Criminal Justice Act 2003

Commencement Orders: 2008 c.4 Sch.28 Part 4; SI 2008/576 Sch.5 para.7; SI 2008/694 Art.2; SI 2008/1424 Art.2, Art.3

see *R. v Ashes (Stephen Kenny)* [2007] EWCA Crim 1848, [2008] 1 All E.R. 113 (CA (Crim Div)), Hallett, L.J.; see *R. v D (Craig)* [2007] EWCA Crim 3200, [2008] 2 Cr. App. R. (S.) 23 (CA (Crim Div)), Rix, L.J.; see *R. v Herbert (Ricky Paul)* [2007] EWCA Crim 3034, [2008] 2 Cr. App. R. (S.) 28 (CA (Crim Div)), Keene, L.J.; see *R. v Hills (Christopher Carl)* [2008] EWCA Crim 1871, Times, August 7, 2008 (CA (Crim Div)), Latham, L.J.; see *R. v K* [2007] EWCA Crim 3150, (2008) 172 J.P. 538 (CA (Crim Div)), Richards, L.J.; see *R. v Khan (Bakish Alla)* [2008] EWCA Crim 531, [2008] 3 All E.R. 502 (CA (Crim Div)), Lord Philips, L.C.J.; see *R. v Lavery (Dominic Robert)* [2008] EWCA Crim 2499, Times, October 20, 2008 (CA (Crim Div)), Lord Judge, L.C.J.; see *R. v McNee (Michael)* [2007] EWCA Crim 1529, [2008] 1 Cr. App. R. (S.) 24 (CA (Crim Div)), Sir Igor Judge (President, QB); see *R. v Reynolds (Michael Edwin)* [2007] EWCA Crim 538, [2008] 1 W.L.R. 1075 (CA (Crim Div)), Latham, L.J.; see *R. v Seddon (Andrew)* [2007] EWCA Crim 3022, [2008] 2 Cr. App. R. (S.) 30 (CA (Crim Div)), Hughes, L.J.; see *R. v Wallace (James Andrew)* [2007] EWCA Crim 1760, [2008] 1 W.L.R. 572 (CA (Crim Div)), Scott Baker, L.J.; see *Wells v Parole Board* [2008] EWCA Civ 30, [2008] 1 W.L.R. 1977 (CA (Civ Div)), Lord Philips, L.C.J.

applied: 2008 c.4 Sch.26 para.59

referred to: 2008 c.4 Sch.26 para.2

Part 9, applied: 2008 c.4 Sch.27 para.16

Part 11, see *R. v Wallace (James Andrew)* [2007] EWCA Crim 1760, [2008] 1 W.L.R. 572 (CA (Crim Div)), Scott Baker, L.J.

Part 12 c.1, referred to: 2008 c.4 s.4, Sch.1 para.35

Part 12 c.6, applied: 2008 c.4 s.32, SI 2008/2793 r.3

Part 12 c.6, amended: 2008 c.4 s.21

Part 12 c.6, amended: 2008 c.4 s.34

CAP.

2003–cont.

44. Criminal Justice Act 2003–*cont.*

s.21, see *R. v Samuel (Perry)* [2007] EWCA Crim 1954, [2008] 1 Cr. App. R. (S.) 76 (CA (Crim Div)), Latham, L.J. (VP, CA Crim)

s.23A, amended: 2008 c.4 Sch.26 para.60

s.23A, repealed (in part): 2008 c.4 Sch.26 para.60, Sch.28 Part 4

s.23B, added: 2008 c.4 Sch.26 para.61

s.25, amended: 2008 c.4 Sch.26 para.62

s.29, applied: SI 2008/1424 Art.3

s.57, see *R. v B* [2008] EWCA Crim 1144, Times, May 22, 2008 (CA (Crim Div)), Sir Igor Judge (President)

s.58, see *R. v Arnold (Louise)* [2008] EWCA Crim 1034, [2008] 1 W.L.R. 2881 (CMAC), Hughes, L.J.

s.61, amended: 2008 c.4 s.44

s.62, see *R. v Y* [2008] EWCA Crim 10, [2008] 1 W.L.R. 1683 (CA (Crim Div)), Hughes, L.J.

s.78, see *R. v Miell (Richard Andrew)* [2007] EWCA Crim 3130, [2008] 1 W.L.R. 627 (CA (Crim Div)), Lord Philips, L.C.J.

s.88, amended: 2008 c.4 Sch.26 para.63

s.89, amended: 2008 c.4 Sch.26 para.63

s.91, amended: 2008 c.4 Sch.26 para.63

s.98, see *R. v McNeill (Tracy)* [2007] EWCA Crim 2927, (2008) 172 J.P. 50 (CA (Crim Div)), Rix, L.J.; see *R. v Wallace (James Andrew)* [2007] EWCA Crim 1760, [2008] 1 W.L.R. 572 (CA (Crim Div)), Scott Baker, L.J.

s.101, see *R. v Bullen (Lee David)* [2008] EWCA Crim 4, [2008] 2 Cr. App. R. 25 (CA (Crim Div)), Rix, L.J.; see *R. v D* [2008] EWCA Crim 1156, (2008) 172 J.P. 358 (CA (Crim Div)), Rix, L.J.; see *R. v Doncaster (Roger George)* [2008] EWCA Crim 5, (2008) 172 J.P. 202 (CA (Crim Div)), Rix, L.J.; see *R. v Freeman (Daniel Robert)* [2008] EWCA Crim 1863, (2008) 172 J.P. 529 (CA (Crim Div)), Latham, L.J.; see *R. v Lamaletie (Mervyn)* [2008] EWCA Crim 314, (2008) 172 J.P. 249 (CA (Crim Div)), Hooper, L.J.; see *R. v McKenzie (Mark Anthony)* [2008] EWCA Crim 758, (2008) 172 J.P. 377 (CA (Crim Div)), Toulson, L.J.; see *R. v McNeill (Tracy)* [2007] EWCA Crim 2927, (2008) 172 J.P. 50 (CA (Crim Div)), Rix, L.J.; see *R. v Ngyuen* [2008] EWCA Crim 585, [2008] 2 Cr. App. R. 9 (CA (Crim Div)), Dyson, L.J.; see *R. v Walker (Daniel)* [2007] EWCA Crim 2631, [2008] 2 Cr. App. R. (S.) 6 (CA (Crim Div)), Lord Philips, L.C.J.; see *R. v Wallace (James Andrew)* [2007] EWCA Crim 1760, [2008] 1 W.L.R. 572 (CA (Crim Div)), Scott Baker, L.J.; see *R. v Wilson (Jason Roger)* [2008] EWCA Crim 134, [2008] 2 Cr. App. R. 3 (CA (Crim Div)), Moses, L.J.

CAP.

2003–cont.

44. Criminal Justice Act 2003–*cont.*

s.102, see *R. v D* [2008] EWCA Crim 1156, (2008) 172 J.P. 358 (CA (Crim Div)), Rix, L.J.

s.103, see *R. v McKenzie (Mark Anthony)* [2008] EWCA Crim 758, (2008) 172 J.P. 377 (CA (Crim Div)), Toulson, L.J.

s.114, see *R. v Adams (Ishmael)* [2007] EWCA Crim 3025, [2008] 1 Cr. App. R. 35 (CA (Crim Div)), Hughes, L.J.; see *R. v K* [2007] EWCA Crim 3150, (2008) 172 J.P. 538 (CA (Crim Div)), Richards, L.J.; see *R. v L* [2008] EWCA Crim 973, [2008] 2 Cr. App. R. 18 (CA (Crim Div)), Lord Phillips, L.C.J.; see *R. v Lynch (William Stewart)* [2007] EWCA Crim 3035, [2008] 1 Cr. App. R. 24 (CA (Crim Div)), Keene, L.J.; see *R. v S* [2007] EWCA Crim 335, [2008] 2 Cr. App. R. 26 (CA (Crim Div)), Latham, L.J.; see *R. v Y* [2008] EWCA Crim 10, [2008] 1 W.L.R. 1683 (CA (Crim Div)), Hughes, L.J.; see *Sak v Crown Prosecution Service* [2007] EWHC 2886 (Admin), (2008) 172 J.P. 89 (DC), Thomas, L.J.; see *West Midlands Probation Board v French* [2008] EWHC 2631 (Admin), (2008) 172 J.P. 617 (DC), Scott Baker, L.J.; see *Williams (t/a Williams of Porthmadog) v Vehicle and Operator Services Agency* [2008] EWHC 849 (Admin), (2008) 172 J.P. 328 (DC), Keene, L.J.

s.115, see *R. v K* [2007] EWCA Crim 3150, (2008) 172 J.P. 538 (CA (Crim Div)), Richards, L.J.

s.116, see *R. v Adams (Ishmael)* [2007] EWCA Crim 3025, [2008] 1 Cr. App. R. 35 (CA (Crim Div)), Hughes, L.J.; see *R. v Chal (Amolak Singh)* [2007] EWCA Crim 2647, [2008] 1 Cr. App. R. 18 (CA (Crim Div)), Toulson, L.J.; see *Sak v Crown Prosecution Service* [2007] EWHC 2886 (Admin), (2008) 172 J.P. 89 (DC), Thomas, L.J.; see *West Midlands Probation Board v French* [2008] EWHC 2631 (Admin), (2008) 172 J.P. 617 (DC), Scott Baker, L.J.

s.117, see *West Midlands Probation Board v French* [2008] EWHC 2631 (Admin), (2008) 172 J.P. 617 (DC), Scott Baker, L.J.

s.118, see *R. v Y* [2008] EWCA Crim 10, [2008] 1 W.L.R. 1683 (CA (Crim Div)), Hughes, L.J.; see *West Midlands Probation Board v French* [2008] EWHC 2631 (Admin), (2008) 172 J.P. 617 (DC), Scott Baker, L.J.

s.134, see *R. v Chal (Amolak Singh)* [2007] EWCA Crim 2647, [2008] 1 Cr. App. R. 18 (CA (Crim Div)), Toulson, L.J.

s.139, see *Police Service of Northern Ireland v McClure* [2008] NICA 31, [2008] N.I. 49 (CA (NI)), Kerr, L.C.J.; see *R. v Lynch (William Stewart)* [2007] EWCA Crim

CAP.

2003–cont.

44. Criminal Justice Act 2003–*cont.*

s.139–*cont.*

3035, [2008] 1 Cr. App. R. 24 (CA (Crim Div)), Keene, L.J.

s.142, see *R. v Bowker (Anthony)* [2007] EWCA Crim 1608, [2008] 1 Cr. App. R. (S.) 72 (CA (Crim Div)), Latham, L.J.

s.142, amended: 2008 c.4 s.9, Sch.26 para.64, Sch.28 Part 2

s.142A, added: 2008 c.4 s.9

s.143, see *R. v Rahman (Abdul)* [2008] EWCA Crim 1465, [2008] 4 All E.R. 661 (CA (Crim Div)), Lord Phillips of Worth Matravers, L.C.J.

s.147, amended: 2008 c.4 Sch.4 para.72

s.147, applied: 2008 c.4 Sch.27 para.6

s.147, repealed (in part): 2008 c.4 Sch.4 para.72, Sch.28 Part 1

s.148, amended: 2008 c.4 s.10, Sch.4 para.73, Sch.28 Part 1

s.148, applied: 2008 c.4 s.1

s.148, disapplied: 2008 c.4 Sch.1 para.5

s.148, repealed (in part): 2008 c.4 Sch.4 para.73, Sch.28 Part 1

s.149, amended: 2008 c.4 Sch.4 para.74

s.150, amended: 2008 c.4 Sch.4 para.75, Sch.26 para.65

s.150, applied: 2008 c.4 s.1

s.150A, added: 2008 c.4 s.11

s.151, amended: 2008 c.4 s.11, Sch.4 para.76

s.152, amended: 2008 c.4 Sch.26 para.66

s.152, disapplied: 2008 c.4 Sch.2 para.6, Sch.2 para.8

s.153, amended: 2008 c.4 Sch.28 Part 2

s.154, applied: 2008 c.4 Sch.27 para.31, 2008 c.28 s.54, Sch.5 para.15

s.154, referred to: 2008 c.13 s.49, 2008 c.14 s.10, s.76, 2008 c.27 s.88, Sch.2 para.30, SI 2008/1848 Reg.6, SI 2008/3231 Art.34, Art.35, Art.36

s.156, amended: 2008 c.4 Sch.4 para.77, Sch.28 Part 1

s.158, amended: 2008 c.4 s.12, SI 2008/912 Sch.1 para.19

s.160, amended: SI 2008/912 Sch.1 para.19

s.161, amended: 2008 c.4 Sch.4 para.78, Sch.28 Part 1

s.161, applied: 2008 c.4 Sch.1 para.5

s.161, repealed (in part): 2008 c.4 Sch.4 para.78, Sch.28 Part 1

s.163, amended: 2008 c.4 Sch.26 para.68

s.166, amended: 2008 c.4 s.11, Sch.4 para.76, Sch.4 para.79

s.172, see *R. v Taylor (Barrington Robert)* [2008] EWCA Crim 465, [2008] 2 Cr. App. R. (S.) 83 (CA (Crim Div)), Hooper, L.J.

s.174, amended: 2008 c.4 Sch.4 para.80

s.176, amended: 2008 c.4 Sch.4 para.81, Sch.28 Part 1

s.177, amended: 2008 c.4 Sch.4 para.82

CAP.

2003–cont.

44. Criminal Justice Act 2003–*cont.*

s.177, applied: 2008 c.4 Sch.27 para.1, SI 2008/1586 Sch.2 para.1
s.177, referred to: SI 2008/2793 r.3
s.181, amended: 2008 c.4 s.20
s.184, amended: SI 2008/912 Sch.1 para.19
s.189, referred to: SI 2008/2793 r.3
s.191, referred to: 2008 c.4 Sch.1 para.35
s.192, referred to: 2008 c.4 Sch.1 para.35
s.197, amended: 2008 c.4 Sch.4 para.83, Sch.28 Part 1, SI 2008/912 Sch.1 para.19
s.199, amended: 2008 c.4 Sch.4 para.84, SI 2008/912 Sch.1 para.19
s.199, repealed (in part): 2008 c.4 Sch.4 para.84, Sch.28 Part 1
s.201, amended: 2008 c.4 Sch.4 para.85, SI 2008/912 Sch.1 para.19
s.202, amended: 2008 c.4 Sch.4 para.86, SI 2008/912 Sch.1 para.19
s.203, amended: 2008 c.4 Sch.4 para.87, SI 2008/912 Sch.1 para.19
s.204, referred to: SI 2008/2793 r.3
s.206, amended: SI 2008/912 Sch.1 para.19
s.209, amended: 2008 c.4 Sch.4 para.88, SI 2008/912 Sch.1 para.19
s.211, repealed (in part): 2008 c.4 Sch.4 para.89, Sch.28 Part 1
s.214, amended: 2008 c.4 Sch.4 para.90
s.217, amended: 2008 c.4 Sch.4 para.91
s.219, amended: SI 2008/912 Sch.1 para.19
s.220, see *Richards v National Probation Service* [2007] EWHC 3108 (Admin), (2008) 172 J.P. 100 (DC), Thomas, L.J.
s.221, amended: 2008 c.4 Sch.4 para.92, Sch.26 para.2
s.221, repealed (in part): 2008 c.4 Sch.4 para.92, Sch.28 Part 1
s.222, amended: 2008 c.4 Sch.4 para.93, SI 2008/912 Sch.1 para.19
s.222, applied: 2008 c.4 Sch.2 para.1
s.224, see *R. v McNee (Michael)* [2007] EWCA Crim 1529, [2008] 1 Cr. App. R. (S.) 24 (CA (Crim Div)), Sir Igor Judge (President, QB); see *R. v Reynolds (Michael Edwin)* [2007] EWCA Crim 538, [2008] 1 W.L.R. 1075 (CA (Crim Div)), Latham, L.J.; see *R. v Terrell (Alexander James)* [2007] EWCA Crim 3079, [2008] 2 All E.R. 1065 (CA (Crim Div)), Lord Philips, L.C.J.
s.224, amended: 2008 c.4 Sch.28 Part 2
s.225, see *Attorney General's Reference (No.54 of 2007), Re* [2007] EWCA Crim 1655, [2008] 1 Cr. App. R. (S.) 62 (CA (Crim Div)), Hooper, L.J.; see *R. v Bennett (Andrew)* [2007] EWCA Crim 1093, [2008] 1 Cr. App. R. (S.) 11 (CA (Crim Div)), Tuckey, L.J.; see *R. v Lavery (Dominic Robert)* [2008] EWCA Crim 2499, Times, October 20, 2008 (CA (Crim Div)), Lord Judge, L.C.J.; see *R. v Lewis (Terence)* [2007] EWCA Crim 2015,

CAP.

2003–cont.

44. Criminal Justice Act 2003–*cont.*

s.225–*cont.*
[2008] 1 Cr. App. R. (S.) 63 (CA (Crim Div)), Maurice Kay, L.J.; see *R. v Pressdee (Robert Christopher)* [2007] EWCA Crim 1289, [2008] 1 Cr. App. R. (S.) 25 (CA (Crim Div)), Laws, L.J.; see *R. v Reynolds (Michael Edwin)* [2007] EWCA Crim 538, [2008] 1 W.L.R. 1075 (CA (Crim Div)), Latham, L.J.; see *R. v Stanley (Dean Mark)* [2008] EWCA Crim 655, [2008] 2 Cr. App. R. (S.) 107 (CA (Crim Div)), Toulson, L.J.; see *R. v Terrell (Alexander James)* [2007] EWCA Crim 3079, [2008] 2 All E.R. 1065 (CA (Crim Div)), Lord Philips, L.C.J.; see *Wells v Parole Board* [2007] EWHC 1835 (Admin), [2008] 1 All E.R. 138 (DC), Laws, L.J.
s.225, amended: 2008 c.4 s.13, SI 2008/1587 Art.2
s.225, applied: 2008 c.28 s.45, s.53, Sch.6 para.5, Sch.6 para.7, SI 2008/1586 Sch.2 para.2
s.226, see *R. v Herbert (Ricky Paul)* [2007] EWCA Crim 3034, [2008] 2 Cr. App. R. (S.) 28 (CA (Crim Div)), Keene, L.J.; see *R. v Norris (Craig Dean)* [2007] EWCA Crim 1103, [2008] 1 Cr. App. R. (S.) 16 (CA (Crim Div)), Tuckey, L.J.; see *R. v Reynolds (Michael Edwin)* [2007] EWCA Crim 538, [2008] 1 W.L.R. 1075 (CA (Crim Div)), Latham, L.J.
s.226, amended: 2008 c.4 s.14
s.226, applied: 2008 c.28 s.45, Sch.6 para.5, SI 2008/1586 Sch.2 para.2
s.227, see *R. (on the application of O'Connell) v Parole Board* [2007] EWHC 2591 (Admin), [2008] 1 W.L.R. 979 (QBD (Admin)), Latham, L.J.; see *R. v Reynolds (Michael Edwin)* [2007] EWCA Crim 538, [2008] 1 W.L.R. 1075 (CA (Crim Div)), Latham, L.J.
s.227, amended: 2008 c.4 s.15, Sch.28 Part 2, SI 2008/1587 Art.2
s.227, applied: SI 2008/1586 Sch.2 para.2
s.227, varied: SI 2008/1587 Art.2
s.228, see *R. v Herbert (Ricky Paul)* [2007] EWCA Crim 3034, [2008] 2 Cr. App. R. (S.) 28 (CA (Crim Div)), Keene, L.J.; see *R. v Lavery (Dominic Robert)* [2008] EWCA Crim 2499, Times, October 20, 2008 (CA (Crim Div)), Lord Judge, L.C.J.
s.228, amended: 2008 c.4 s.16, Sch.28 Part 2
s.228, applied: SI 2008/1586 Sch.2 para.2
s.228, repealed (in part): 2008 c.4 Sch.28 Part 2
s.229, see *Attorney General's Reference (No.54 of 2007), Re* [2007] EWCA Crim 1655, [2008] 1 Cr. App. R. (S.) 62 (CA (Crim Div)), Hooper, L.J.; see *R. v Abdi (Liban)* [2007] EWCA Crim 1913, [2008] 1 Cr. App. R. (S.) 87 (CA (Crim Div)),

CAP.

2003–cont.

44. Criminal Justice Act 2003–*cont.*

s.229–*cont.*

Toulson, L.J.; see *R. v Henson (Daniel Thomas)* [2007] EWCA Crim 1308, [2008] 1 Cr. App. R. (S.) 19 (CA (Crim Div)), Rix, L.J.; see *R. v Lavery (Dominic Robert)* [2008] EWCA Crim 2499, Times, October 20, 2008 (CA (Crim Div)), Lord Judge, L.C.J.; see *R. v Nobes (David Allan)* [2007] EWCA Crim 1139, [2008] 1 Cr. App. R. (S.) 17 (CA (Crim Div)), Rix, L.J.; see *R. v Terrell (Alexander James)* [2007] EWCA Crim 3079, [2008] 2 All E.R. 1065 (CA (Crim Div)), Lord Philips, L.C.J.; see *R. v White (Paul)* [2007] EWCA Crim 1141, [2008] 1 Cr. App. R. (S.) 21 (CA (Crim Div)), Rix, L.J.

s.229, amended: 2008 c.4 s.17, Sch.28 Part 2

s.229, repealed (in part): 2008 c.4 Sch.28 Part 2

s.231, amended: 2008 c.4 s.18

s.232, amended: 2008 c.4 s.18

s.233, repealed: 2008 c.4 Sch.26 para.70, Sch.28 Part 2

s.234, repealed: 2008 c.4 s.18, Sch.28 Part 2

s.237, amended: 2008 c.4 s.21

s.240, see *K v P* [2008] EWCA Civ 600, [2008] 2 F.L.R. 2137 (CA (Civ Div)), Thorpe, L.J.; see *R. v Ashes (Stephen Kenny)* [2007] EWCA Crim 1848, [2008] 1 All E.R. 113 (CA (Crim Div)), Hallett, L.J.; see *R. v Stickley (Joanna)* [2007] EWCA Crim 3184, [2008] 2 Cr. App. R. (S.) 33 (CA (Crim Div)), Mackay, J.

s.240A, added: 2008 c.4 s.21

s.240A, applied: SI 2008/2793 r.2, r.3, r.4

s.240A, disapplied: SI 2008/2793 r.2, r.3, r.4

s.240A, referred to: SI 2008/2793 r.2

s.240A, enabling: SI 2008/2793

s.241, amended: 2008 c.4 s.21

s.242, amended: 2008 c.4 s.21

s.246, amended: 2008 c.4 s.22, s.24

s.246, applied: SI 2008/1788 Sch.1

s.247, see *R. (on the application of O'Connell) v Parole Board* [2007] EWHC 2591 (Admin), [2008] 1 W.L.R. 979 (QBD (Admin)), Latham, L.J.

s.247, repealed (in part): 2008 c.4 Sch.28 Part 2

s.249, applied: 2008 c.4 s.32

s.250, applied: 2008 c.4 s.32, SI 2008/1788 Sch.1, SI 2008/2793 r.3

s.253, amended: SI 2008/912 Sch.1 para.19

s.253, applied: SI 2008/2768 Art.2

s.253, enabling: SI 2008/2768

s.254, see *R. (on the application of Gulliver) v Parole Board* [2007] EWCA Civ 1386, [2008] 1 W.L.R. 1116 (CA (Civ Div)), Clarke, L.J, M.R.

s.254, amended: 2008 c.4 s.29

CAP.

2003–cont.

44. Criminal Justice Act 2003–*cont.*

s.254, applied: 2008 c.4 Sch.27 para.12, SI 2008/1586 Sch.2 para.3

s.254, referred to: 2008 c.4 Sch.26 para.32

s.254, repealed (in part): 2008 c.4 s.29, Sch.28 Part 2

s.255A, added: 2008 c.4 s.29

s.255A, amended: 2008 c.4 s.29, SI 2008/1587 Art.3

s.255A, varied: SI 2008/1587 Art.3

s.255B, added: 2008 c.4 s.29

s.255C, added: 2008 c.4 s.29

s.255D, added: 2008 c.4 s.29

s.256, amended: 2008 c.4 s.30, Sch.28 Part 2

s.256, repealed (in part): 2008 c.4 Sch.28 Part 2

s.256, substituted: 2008 c.4 s.30

s.256A, added: 2008 c.4 s.30

s.259A, added: 2008 c.4 s.34

s.260, amended: 2008 c.4 s.34, Sch.28 Part 2, SI 2008/978 Art.2

s.260, repealed (in part): 2008 c.4 s.34, Sch.28 Part 2

s.260, enabling: SI 2008/978

s.264, amended: 2008 c.4 Sch.26 para.71

s.264A, amended: 2008 c.4 s.20, Sch.28 Part 2

s.265, see *R. v MacDonald (James Terence)* [2008] EWCA Crim 707, [2008] 2 Cr. App. R. (S.) 100 (CA (Crim Div)), Dyson, L.J.

s.265, amended: 2008 c.4 s.20

s.266, amended: SI 2008/912 Sch.1 para.19

s.269, see *R. v Height (John)* [2008] EWCA Crim 2500, Times, November 24, 2008 (CA (Crim Div)), Lord Judge, L.C.J.; see *R. v Henson (Daniel Thomas)* [2007] EWCA Crim 1308, [2008] 1 Cr. App. R. (S.) 19 (CA (Crim Div)), Rix, L.J.; see *R. v McNee (Michael)* [2007] EWCA Crim 1529, [2008] 1 Cr. App. R. (S.) 24 (CA (Crim Div)), Sir Igor Judge (President, QB)

s.269, amended: 2008 c.4 s.22

s.272, repealed (in part): 2008 c.4 Sch.28 Part 3

s.273, amended: 2008 c.4 Sch.26 para.73

s.279, repealed: 2008 c.4 Sch.4 para.94, Sch.28 Part 1

s.281, applied: 2008 c.4 Sch.27 para.20

s.281, referred to: 2008 c.18 Sch.11 para.7, 2008 c.25 s.96, s.118, s.121, s.127, 2008 c.27 Sch.2 para.30, 2008 c.28 s.2

s.282, applied: 2008 c.22 s.29, 2008 c.25 s.76, s.90

s.282, referred to: 2008 c.4 s.77, 2008 c.17 s.264, 2008 c.25 s.15

s.283, referred to: 2008 c.29 s.218

s.300, amended: 2008 c.4 s.40, Sch.26 para.2, Sch.28 Part 2

CAP.

2003–cont.

44. Criminal Justice Act 2003–*cont.*

s.300, repealed (in part): 2008 c.4 Sch.26 para.2, Sch.28 Part 2
s.304, see *K v P* [2008] EWCA Civ 600, [2008] 2 F.L.R. 2137 (CA (Civ Div)), Thorpe, L.J.
s.305, amended: 2008 c.4 Sch.26 para.72, SI 2008/1587 Art.2
s.305, repealed (in part): 2008 c.4 Sch.28 Part 2
s.305, varied: SI 2008/1587 Art.2
s.325, amended: 2008 c.4 Sch.26 para.74, SI 2008/912 Sch.1 para.19
s.325, referred to: 2008 c.4 Sch.26 para.74
s.326, amended: 2008 c.4 Sch.26 para.75
s.327A, added: 2008 c.4 s.140
s.327B, added: 2008 c.4 s.140
s.330, amended: 2008 c.4 s.21, Sch.4 para.95, Sch.26 para.76, Sch.28 Part 1
s.330, applied: SI 2008/978, SI 2008/2793
s.330, enabling: SI 2008/2768
s.336, enabling: SI 2008/694, SI 2008/1424
Sch.3, referred to: 2008 c.4 s.53
Sch.3 Part 1 para.2, amended: 2008 c.4 Sch.13 para.2
Sch.3 Part 1 para.6, substituted: 2008 c.4 Sch.13 para.3
Sch.3 Part 1 para.8, amended: 2008 c.4 Sch.13 para.4
Sch.3 Part 1 para.9, amended: 2008 c.4 Sch.13 para.5
Sch.3 Part 1 para.13, referred to: 2008 c.4 s.153
Sch.3 Part 1 para.13, repealed: 2008 c.4 Sch.28 Part 4
Sch.3 Part 1 para.22, referred to: 2008 c.4 s.153
Sch.3 Part 1 para.22, repealed: 2008 c.4 Sch.28 Part 4
Sch.3 Part 1 para.22A, added: 2008 c.4 Sch.13 para.8
Sch.3 Part 1 para.23, amended: 2008 c.4 Sch.13 para.9
Sch.3 Part 1 para.24, amended: 2008 c.4 Sch.13 para.10
Sch.3 Part 2 para.57, repealed (in part): 2008 c.4 Sch.28 Part 4
Sch.5 Part 2 para.35A, added: SI 2008/1769 Sch.1 para.31
Sch.5 Part 2 para.36A, added: SI 2008/1769 Sch.1 para.31
Sch.5 Part 2 para.38A, added: SI 2008/1769 Sch.1 para.31
Sch.5 Part 2 para.38B, added: SI 2008/1769 Sch.1 para.31
Sch.5 Part 2 para.38C, added: SI 2008/1769 Sch.1 para.31
Sch.5 Part 2 para.38D, added: SI 2008/1769 Sch.1 para.31
Sch.5 Part 2 para.38E, added: SI 2008/1769 Sch.1 para.31

CAP.

2003–cont.

44. Criminal Justice Act 2003–*cont.*

Sch.5 Part 2 para.38F, added: SI 2008/1769 Sch.1 para.31
Sch.5 Part 2 para.38G, added: SI 2008/1769 Sch.1 para.31
Sch.5 Part 2 para.38H, added: SI 2008/1769 Sch.1 para.31
Sch.8, see *West Midlands Probation Board v Sutton Coldfield Magistrates Court* [2008] EWHC 15 (Admin), [2008] 1 W.L.R. 918 (DC), Dyson, L.J.
Sch.8 Part 2 para.9, amended: 2008 c.4 s.38
Sch.8 Part 2 para.10, amended: 2008 c.4 s.38
Sch.8 Part 2 para.12, repealed: 2008 c.4 Sch.4 para.96, Sch.28 Part 1
Sch.8 Part 3 para.15, repealed: 2008 c.4 Sch.4 para.96, Sch.28 Part 1
Sch.8 Part 4 para.17, repealed (in part): 2008 c.4 Sch.4 para.96, Sch.28 Part 1
Sch.8 Part 6 para.25A, added: 2008 c.4 Sch.4 para.109
Sch.8 Part 6 para.27, amended: SI 2008/912 Sch.1 para.19
Sch.10 para.9, amended: SI 2008/912 Sch.1 para.19
Sch.11 Part 4 para.17, amended: SI 2008/912 Sch.1 para.19
Sch.11 Part 4 para.22, amended: SI 2008/912 Sch.1 para.19
Sch.12 Part 3 para.22, amended: SI 2008/912 Sch.1 para.19
Sch.12 para.8, see *R. v Phipps (Stephen Donald)* [2007] EWCA Crim 2923, [2008] 2 Cr. App. R. (S.) 20 (CA (Crim Div)), Hallett, L.J.; see *R. v Sheppard (Craig Paul)* [2008] EWCA Crim 799, [2008] 2 Cr. App. R. (S.) 93 (CA (Crim Div)), Thomas, L.J.
Sch.13 Part 3 para.15, amended: SI 2008/912 Sch.1 para.19
Sch.13 Part 3 para.20, amended: SI 2008/912 Sch.1 para.19
Sch.15, applied: 2008 c.4 Sch.27 para.11
Sch.15, referred to: 2008 c.4 Sch.27 para.9
Sch.15A Part 1 para.1, added: 2008 c.4 Sch.5
Sch.15A Part 1 para.2, added: 2008 c.4 Sch.5
Sch.15A Part 1 para.3, added: 2008 c.4 Sch.5
Sch.15A Part 1 para.4, added: 2008 c.4 Sch.5
Sch.15A Part 1 para.5, added: 2008 c.4 Sch.5
Sch.15A Part 1 para.6, added: 2008 c.4 Sch.5
Sch.15A Part 1 para.7, added: 2008 c.4 Sch.5
Sch.15A Part 1 para.8, added: 2008 c.4 Sch.5
Sch.15A Part 1 para.9, added: 2008 c.4 Sch.5
Sch.15A Part 1 para.10, added: 2008 c.4 Sch.5
Sch.15A Part 1 para.11, added: 2008 c.4 Sch.5
Sch.15A Part 1 para.12, added: 2008 c.4 Sch.5
Sch.15A Part 1 para.13, added: 2008 c.4 Sch.5
Sch.15A Part 1 para.14, added: 2008 c.4 Sch.5
Sch.15A Part 1 para.15, added: 2008 c.4 Sch.5
Sch.15A Part 1 para.16, added: 2008 c.4 Sch.5
Sch.15A Part 1 para.17, added: 2008 c.4 Sch.5

CAP.

2003–cont.

44. Criminal Justice Act 2003–*cont.*

Sch.15A Part 1 para.18, added: 2008 c.4 Sch.5
Sch.15A Part 1 para.19, added: 2008 c.4 Sch.5
Sch.15A Part 1 para.20, added: 2008 c.4 Sch.5
Sch.15A Part 1 para.21, added: 2008 c.4 Sch.5
Sch.15A Part 1 para.22, added: 2008 c.4 Sch.5
Sch.15A Part 1 para.23, added: 2008 c.4 Sch.5
Sch.15A Part 2 para.24, added: 2008 c.4 Sch.5
Sch.15A Part 2 para.25, added: 2008 c.4 Sch.5
Sch.15A Part 2 para.26, added: 2008 c.4 Sch.5
Sch.15A Part 2 para.27, added: 2008 c.4 Sch.5
Sch.15A Part 2 para.28, added: 2008 c.4 Sch.5
Sch.15A Part 2 para.29, added: 2008 c.4 Sch.5
Sch.15A Part 2 para.30, added: 2008 c.4 Sch.5
Sch.15A Part 2 para.31, added: 2008 c.4 Sch.5
Sch.15A Part 2 para.32, added: 2008 c.4 Sch.5
Sch.15A Part 2 para.33, added: 2008 c.4 Sch.5
Sch.15A Part 2 para.34, added: 2008 c.4 Sch.5
Sch.15A Part 2 para.35, added: 2008 c.4 Sch.5
Sch.15A Part 3 para.36, added: 2008 c.4 Sch.5
Sch.15A Part 3 para.37, added: 2008 c.4 Sch.5
Sch.15A Part 3 para.38, added: 2008 c.4 Sch.5
Sch.15A Part 3 para.39, added: 2008 c.4 Sch.5
Sch.15A Part 3 para.40, added: 2008 c.4 Sch.5
Sch.15A Part 3 para.41, added: 2008 c.4 Sch.5
Sch.15A Part 3 para.42, added: 2008 c.4 Sch.5
Sch.15A Part 3 para.43, added: 2008 c.4 Sch.5
Sch.15A Part 3 para.44, added: 2008 c.4 Sch.5
Sch.15A Part 3 para.45, added: 2008 c.4 Sch.5
Sch.15A Part 3 para.46, added: 2008 c.4 Sch.5
Sch.15A Part 3 para.47, added: 2008 c.4 Sch.5
Sch.15A Part 3 para.48, added: 2008 c.4 Sch.5

CAP.

2003–cont.

44. Criminal Justice Act 2003–*cont.*

Sch.15A Part 3 para.49, added: 2008 c.4 Sch.5
Sch.15A Part 3 para.49A, added: 2008 c.4 Sch.5, SI 2008/1779 Art.17
Sch.15A Part 3 para.49B, added: 2008 c.4 Sch.5, SI 2008/1779 Art.17
Sch.15A Part 3 para.49C, added: 2008 c.4 Sch.5, SI 2008/1779 Art.17
Sch.15A Part 3 para.49D, added: 2008 c.4 Sch.5, SI 2008/1779 Art.17
Sch.15A Part 3 para.49E, added: 2008 c.4 Sch.5, SI 2008/1779 Art.17
Sch.15A Part 3 para.49F, added: 2008 c.4 Sch.5, SI 2008/1779 Art.17
Sch.15A Part 3 para.49G, added: 2008 c.4 Sch.5, SI 2008/1779 Art.17
Sch.15A Part 3 para.49H, added: 2008 c.4 Sch.5, SI 2008/1779 Art.17
Sch.15A Part 3 para.49I, added: 2008 c.4 Sch.5, SI 2008/1779 Art.17
Sch.15A Part 3 para.49J, added: 2008 c.4 Sch.5, SI 2008/1779 Art.17
Sch.15A Part 3 para.49K, added: 2008 c.4 Sch.5, SI 2008/1779 Art.17
Sch.15A Part 3 para.49L, added: 2008 c.4 Sch.5, SI 2008/1779 Art.17
Sch.15A Part 3 para.50, added: 2008 c.4 Sch.5
Sch.15A Part 4 para.51, added: 2008 c.4 Sch.5
Sch.15A Part 4 para.52, added: 2008 c.4 Sch.5
Sch.15A Part 5 para.53, added: 2008 c.4 Sch.5
Sch.16 para.1, repealed: 2008 c.4 Sch.28 Part 2
Sch.16 para.2, repealed: 2008 c.4 Sch.28 Part 2
Sch.16 para.3, repealed: 2008 c.4 Sch.28 Part 2
Sch.16 para.4, repealed: 2008 c.4 Sch.28 Part 2
Sch.16 para.5, repealed: 2008 c.4 Sch.28 Part 2
Sch.16 para.6, repealed: 2008 c.4 Sch.28 Part 2
Sch.16 para.7, repealed: 2008 c.4 Sch.28 Part 2
Sch.16 para.8, repealed: 2008 c.4 Sch.28 Part 2
Sch.16 para.9, repealed: 2008 c.4 Sch.28 Part 2
Sch.16 para.10, repealed: 2008 c.4 Sch.28 Part 2
Sch.16 para.11, repealed: 2008 c.4 Sch.28 Part 2
Sch.16 para.12, repealed: 2008 c.4 Sch.28 Part 2
Sch.16 para.13, repealed: 2008 c.4 Sch.28 Part 2

CAP.

2003–cont.

44. Criminal Justice Act 2003–*cont.*

Sch.16 para.14, repealed: 2008 c.4 Sch.28 Part 2
Sch.16 para.15, repealed: 2008 c.4 Sch.28 Part 2
Sch.16 para.16, repealed: 2008 c.4 Sch.28 Part 2
Sch.16 para.17, repealed: 2008 c.4 Sch.28 Part 2
Sch.16 para.18, repealed: 2008 c.4 Sch.28 Part 2
Sch.16 para.19, repealed: 2008 c.4 Sch.28 Part 2
Sch.16 para.20, repealed: 2008 c.4 Sch.28 Part 2
Sch.16 para.21, repealed: 2008 c.4 Sch.28 Part 2
Sch.16 para.22, repealed: 2008 c.4 Sch.28 Part 2
Sch.17 Part 1 para.1, repealed: 2008 c.4 Sch.28 Part 2
Sch.17 Part 1 para.2, repealed: 2008 c.4 Sch.28 Part 2
Sch.17 Part 1 para.3, repealed: 2008 c.4 Sch.28 Part 2
Sch.17 Part 1 para.4, repealed: 2008 c.4 Sch.28 Part 2
Sch.17 Part 1 para.5, repealed: 2008 c.4 Sch.28 Part 2
Sch.17 Part 1 para.6, repealed: 2008 c.4 Sch.28 Part 2
Sch.17 Part 1 para.7, repealed: 2008 c.4 Sch.28 Part 2
Sch.17 Part 1 para.8, repealed: 2008 c.4 Sch.28 Part 2
Sch.17 Part 1 para.9, repealed: 2008 c.4 Sch.28 Part 2
Sch.17 Part 1 para.10, repealed: 2008 c.4 Sch.28 Part 2
Sch.17 Part 1 para.11, repealed: 2008 c.4 Sch.28 Part 2
Sch.17 Part 1 para.12, repealed: 2008 c.4 Sch.28 Part 2
Sch.17 Part 1 para.13, repealed: 2008 c.4 Sch.28 Part 2
Sch.17 Part 1 para.14, repealed: 2008 c.4 Sch.28 Part 2
Sch.17 Part 1 para.15, repealed: 2008 c.4 Sch.28 Part 2
Sch.17 Part 1 para.16, repealed: 2008 c.4 Sch.28 Part 2
Sch.17 Part 1 para.17, repealed: 2008 c.4 Sch.28 Part 2
Sch.17 Part 1 para.18, repealed: 2008 c.4 Sch.28 Part 2
Sch.17 Part 1 para.19, repealed: 2008 c.4 Sch.28 Part 2
Sch.17 Part 1 para.20, repealed: 2008 c.4 Sch.28 Part 2
Sch.17 Part 1 para.21, repealed: 2008 c.4 Sch.28 Part 2

CAP.

2003–cont.

44. Criminal Justice Act 2003–*cont.*

Sch.17 Part 1 para.22, repealed: 2008 c.4 Sch.28 Part 2
Sch.17 Part 1 para.23, repealed: 2008 c.4 Sch.28 Part 2
Sch.17 Part 1 para.24, repealed: 2008 c.4 Sch.28 Part 2
Sch.17 Part 1 para.25, repealed: 2008 c.4 Sch.28 Part 2
Sch.17 Part 1 para.26, repealed: 2008 c.4 Sch.28 Part 2
Sch.17 Part 1 para.27, repealed: 2008 c.4 Sch.28 Part 2
Sch.17 Part 1 para.28, repealed: 2008 c.4 Sch.28 Part 2
Sch.17 Part 1 para.29, repealed: 2008 c.4 Sch.28 Part 2
Sch.17 Part 1 para.30, repealed: 2008 c.4 Sch.28 Part 2
Sch.17 Part 1 para.31, repealed: 2008 c.4 Sch.28 Part 2
Sch.17 Part 1 para.32, repealed: 2008 c.4 Sch.28 Part 2
Sch.17 Part 1 para.33, repealed: 2008 c.4 Sch.28 Part 2
Sch.17 Part 1 para.34, repealed: 2008 c.4 Sch.28 Part 2
Sch.17 Part 1 para.35, repealed: 2008 c.4 Sch.28 Part 2
Sch.17 Part 1 para.36, repealed: 2008 c.4 Sch.28 Part 2
Sch.17 Part 1 para.37, repealed: 2008 c.4 Sch.28 Part 2
Sch.17 Part 1 para.38, repealed: 2008 c.4 Sch.28 Part 2
Sch.17 Part 1 para.39, repealed: 2008 c.4 Sch.28 Part 2
Sch.17 Part 1 para.40, repealed: 2008 c.4 Sch.28 Part 2
Sch.17 Part 1 para.41, repealed: 2008 c.4 Sch.28 Part 2
Sch.17 Part 1 para.42, repealed: 2008 c.4 Sch.28 Part 2
Sch.17 Part 1 para.43, repealed: 2008 c.4 Sch.28 Part 2
Sch.17 Part 1 para.44, repealed: 2008 c.4 Sch.28 Part 2
Sch.17 Part 1 para.45, repealed: 2008 c.4 Sch.28 Part 2
Sch.17 Part 1 para.46, repealed: 2008 c.4 Sch.28 Part 2
Sch.17 Part 1 para.47, repealed: 2008 c.4 Sch.28 Part 2
Sch.17 Part 1 para.48, repealed: 2008 c.4 Sch.28 Part 2
Sch.17 Part 1 para.49, repealed: 2008 c.4 Sch.28 Part 2
Sch.17 Part 1 para.50, repealed: 2008 c.4 Sch.28 Part 2
Sch.17 Part 1 para.51, repealed: 2008 c.4 Sch.28 Part 2

CAP.

2003–cont.

44. Criminal Justice Act 2003–*cont.*
Sch.17 Part 1 para.52, repealed: 2008 c.4 Sch.28 Part 2
Sch.17 Part 1 para.53, repealed: 2008 c.4 Sch.28 Part 2
Sch.17 Part 1 para.54, repealed: 2008 c.4 Sch.28 Part 2
Sch.17 Part 1 para.55, repealed: 2008 c.4 Sch.28 Part 2
Sch.17 Part 1 para.56, repealed: 2008 c.4 Sch.28 Part 2
Sch.17 Part 1 para.57, repealed: 2008 c.4 Sch.28 Part 2
Sch.17 Part 1 para.58, repealed: 2008 c.4 Sch.28 Part 2
Sch.17 Part 1 para.59, repealed: 2008 c.4 Sch.28 Part 2
Sch.17 Part 1 para.60, repealed: 2008 c.4 Sch.28 Part 2
Sch.17 Part 1 para.60A, repealed: 2008 c.4 Sch.28 Part 2
Sch.17 Part 1 para.61, repealed: 2008 c.4 Sch.28 Part 2
Sch.17 Part 1 para.62, repealed: 2008 c.4 Sch.28 Part 2
Sch.17 Part 2 para.63, repealed: 2008 c.4 Sch.28 Part 2
Sch.17 Part 2 para.64, repealed: 2008 c.4 Sch.28 Part 2
Sch.17 Part 2 para.65, repealed: 2008 c.4 Sch.28 Part 2
Sch.17 Part 2 para.66, repealed: 2008 c.4 Sch.28 Part 2
Sch.17 Part 2 para.67, repealed: 2008 c.4 Sch.28 Part 2
Sch.17 Part 2 para.68, repealed: 2008 c.4 Sch.28 Part 2
Sch.17 Part 2 para.69, repealed: 2008 c.4 Sch.28 Part 2
Sch.17 Part 2 para.70, repealed: 2008 c.4 Sch.28 Part 2
Sch.17 Part 2 para.71, repealed: 2008 c.4 Sch.28 Part 2
Sch.17 Part 2 para.72, repealed: 2008 c.4 Sch.28 Part 2
Sch.17 Part 2 para.73, repealed: 2008 c.4 Sch.28 Part 2
Sch.17 Part 2 para.74, repealed: 2008 c.4 Sch.28 Part 2
Sch.17 Part 2 para.75, repealed: 2008 c.4 Sch.28 Part 2
Sch.17 Part 2 para.76, repealed: 2008 c.4 Sch.28 Part 2
Sch.17 Part 2 para.77, repealed: 2008 c.4 Sch.28 Part 2
Sch.17 Part 2 para.78, repealed: 2008 c.4 Sch.28 Part 2
Sch.17 Part 2 para.79, repealed: 2008 c.4 Sch.28 Part 2
Sch.17 Part 2 para.80, repealed: 2008 c.4 Sch.28 Part 2

CAP.

2003–cont.

44. Criminal Justice Act 2003–*cont.*
Sch.17 Part 2 para.81, repealed: 2008 c.4 Sch.28 Part 2
Sch.17 Part 2 para.82, repealed: 2008 c.4 Sch.28 Part 2
Sch.17 Part 2 para.83, repealed: 2008 c.4 Sch.28 Part 2
Sch.17 Part 2 para.84, repealed: 2008 c.4 Sch.28 Part 2
Sch.17 Part 2 para.85, repealed: 2008 c.4 Sch.28 Part 2
Sch.17 Part 2 para.86, repealed: 2008 c.4 Sch.28 Part 2
Sch.17 Part 2 para.87, repealed: 2008 c.4 Sch.28 Part 2
Sch.17 Part 2 para.88, repealed: 2008 c.4 Sch.28 Part 2
Sch.17 Part 2 para.89, repealed: 2008 c.4 Sch.28 Part 2
Sch.17 Part 2 para.90, repealed: 2008 c.4 Sch.28 Part 2
Sch.17 Part 2 para.91, repealed: 2008 c.4 Sch.28 Part 2
Sch.17 Part 2 para.92, repealed: 2008 c.4 Sch.28 Part 2
Sch.17 Part 2 para.93, repealed: 2008 c.4 Sch.28 Part 2
Sch.17 Part 2 para.94, repealed: 2008 c.4 Sch.28 Part 2
Sch.17 Part 2 para.95, repealed: 2008 c.4 Sch.28 Part 2
Sch.17 Part 2 para.96, repealed: 2008 c.4 Sch.28 Part 2
Sch.17 Part 2 para.97, repealed: 2008 c.4 Sch.28 Part 2
Sch.17 Part 2 para.98, repealed: 2008 c.4 Sch.28 Part 2
Sch.17 Part 2 para.99, repealed: 2008 c.4 Sch.28 Part 2
Sch.17 Part 2 para.100, repealed: 2008 c.4 Sch.28 Part 2
Sch.17 Part 2 para.101, repealed: 2008 c.4 Sch.28 Part 2
Sch.17 Part 2 para.102, repealed: 2008 c.4 Sch.28 Part 2
Sch.17 Part 2 para.103, repealed: 2008 c.4 Sch.28 Part 2
Sch.17 Part 2 para.104, repealed: 2008 c.4 Sch.28 Part 2
Sch.17 Part 2 para.105, repealed: 2008 c.4 Sch.28 Part 2
Sch.17 Part 2 para.106, repealed: 2008 c.4 Sch.28 Part 2
Sch.17 Part 2 para.107, repealed: 2008 c.4 Sch.28 Part 2
Sch.17 Part 2 para.108, repealed: 2008 c.4 Sch.28 Part 2
Sch.17 Part 2 para.109, repealed: 2008 c.4 Sch.28 Part 2
Sch.17 Part 2 para.110, repealed: 2008 c.4 Sch.28 Part 2

CAP.

2003–cont.

44. Criminal Justice Act 2003–*cont.*

Sch.17 Part 2 para.111, added: SI 2008/1779 Art.18
Sch.17 Part 2 para.111, repealed: 2008 c.4 Sch.28 Part 2
Sch.17 Part 2 para.112, added: SI 2008/1779 Art.18
Sch.17 Part 2 para.112, repealed: 2008 c.4 Sch.28 Part 2
Sch.17 Part 2 para.113, added: SI 2008/1779 Art.18
Sch.17 Part 2 para.113, repealed: 2008 c.4 Sch.28 Part 2
Sch.17 Part 2 para.114, added: SI 2008/1779 Art.18
Sch.17 Part 2 para.114, repealed: 2008 c.4 Sch.28 Part 2
Sch.17 Part 2 para.115, added: SI 2008/1779 Art.18
Sch.17 Part 2 para.115, repealed: 2008 c.4 Sch.28 Part 2
Sch.17 Part 2 para.116, added: SI 2008/1779 Art.18
Sch.17 Part 2 para.116, repealed: 2008 c.4 Sch.28 Part 2
Sch.17 Part 2 para.117, added: SI 2008/1779 Art.18
Sch.17 Part 2 para.117, repealed: 2008 c.4 Sch.28 Part 2
Sch.17 Part 2 para.118, added: SI 2008/1779 Art.18
Sch.17 Part 2 para.118, repealed: 2008 c.4 Sch.28 Part 2
Sch.17 Part 2 para.119, added: SI 2008/1779 Art.18
Sch.17 Part 2 para.119, repealed: 2008 c.4 Sch.28 Part 2
Sch.17 Part 2 para.120, added: SI 2008/1779 Art.18
Sch.17 Part 2 para.120, repealed: 2008 c.4 Sch.28 Part 2
Sch.17 Part 2 para.121, added: SI 2008/1779 Art.18
Sch.17 Part 2 para.121, repealed: 2008 c.4 Sch.28 Part 2
Sch.17 Part 2 para.122, added: SI 2008/1779 Art.18
Sch.17 Part 2 para.122, repealed: 2008 c.4 Sch.28 Part 2
Sch.17 Part 2 para.123, added: SI 2008/1779 Art.18
Sch.17 Part 2 para.123, repealed: 2008 c.4 Sch.28 Part 2
Sch.17 Part 2 para.124, added: SI 2008/1779 Art.18
Sch.17 Part 2 para.124, repealed: 2008 c.4 Sch.28 Part 2
Sch.17 Part 2 para.125, added: SI 2008/1779 Art.18
Sch.17 Part 2 para.125, repealed: 2008 c.4 Sch.28 Part 2

CAP.

2003–cont.

44. Criminal Justice Act 2003–*cont.*

Sch.17 Part 2 para.126, added: SI 2008/1779 Art.18
Sch.17 Part 2 para.126, repealed: 2008 c.4 Sch.28 Part 2
Sch.17 Part 2 para.127, added: SI 2008/1779 Art.18
Sch.17 Part 2 para.127, repealed: 2008 c.4 Sch.28 Part 2
Sch.17 Part 2 para.128, added: SI 2008/1779 Art.18
Sch.17 Part 2 para.128, repealed: 2008 c.4 Sch.28 Part 2
Sch.17 Part 2 para.129, added: SI 2008/1779 Art.18
Sch.17 Part 2 para.129, repealed: 2008 c.4 Sch.28 Part 2
Sch.17 Part 2 para.130, added: SI 2008/1779 Art.18
Sch.17 Part 2 para.130, repealed: 2008 c.4 Sch.28 Part 2
Sch.17 Part 2 para.131, added: SI 2008/1779 Art.18
Sch.17 Part 2 para.131, repealed: 2008 c.4 Sch.28 Part 2
Sch.17 Part 2 para.132, added: SI 2008/1779 Art.18
Sch.17 Part 2 para.132, repealed: 2008 c.4 Sch.28 Part 2
Sch.17 Part 2 para.133, added: SI 2008/1779 Art.18
Sch.17 Part 2 para.133, repealed: 2008 c.4 Sch.28 Part 2
Sch.17 Part 2 para.134, added: SI 2008/1779 Art.18
Sch.17 Part 2 para.134, repealed: 2008 c.4 Sch.28 Part 2
Sch.17 Part 2 para.135, added: SI 2008/1779 Art.18
Sch.17 Part 2 para.135, repealed: 2008 c.4 Sch.28 Part 2
Sch.17 Part 2 para.136, added: SI 2008/1779 Art.18
Sch.17 Part 2 para.136, repealed: 2008 c.4 Sch.28 Part 2
Sch.17 Part 2 para.137, added: SI 2008/1779 Art.18
Sch.17 Part 2 para.137, repealed: 2008 c.4 Sch.28 Part 2
Sch.17 Part 2 para.138, added: SI 2008/1779 Art.18
Sch.17 Part 2 para.138, repealed: 2008 c.4 Sch.28 Part 2
Sch.17 Part 2 para.139, added: SI 2008/1779 Art.18
Sch.17 Part 2 para.139, repealed: 2008 c.4 Sch.28 Part 2
Sch.17 Part 2 para.140, added: SI 2008/1779 Art.18
Sch.17 Part 2 para.140, repealed: 2008 c.4 Sch.28 Part 2

CAP.

2003–cont.

44. Criminal Justice Act 2003–*cont.*

Sch.17 Part 2 para.141, added: SI 2008/1779 Art.18

Sch.17 Part 2 para.141, repealed: 2008 c.4 Sch.28 Part 2

Sch.17 Part 2 para.142, added: SI 2008/1779 Art.18

Sch.17 Part 2 para.142, repealed: 2008 c.4 Sch.28 Part 2

Sch.17 Part 2 para.143, added: SI 2008/1779 Art.18

Sch.17 Part 2 para.143, repealed: 2008 c.4 Sch.28 Part 2

Sch.17 Part 2 para.144, added: SI 2008/1779 Art.18

Sch.17 Part 2 para.144, repealed: 2008 c.4 Sch.28 Part 2

Sch.17 Part 2 para.145, added: SI 2008/1779 Art.18

Sch.17 Part 2 para.145, repealed: 2008 c.4 Sch.28 Part 2

Sch.17 Part 2 para.146, added: SI 2008/1779 Art.18

Sch.17 Part 2 para.146, repealed: 2008 c.4 Sch.28 Part 2

Sch.17 Part 2 para.147, added: SI 2008/1779 Art.18

Sch.17 Part 2 para.147, repealed: 2008 c.4 Sch.28 Part 2

Sch.17 Part 2 para.148, added: SI 2008/1779 Art.18

Sch.17 Part 2 para.148, repealed: 2008 c.4 Sch.28 Part 2

Sch.17 Part 2 para.149, added: SI 2008/1779 Art.18

Sch.17 Part 2 para.149, repealed: 2008 c.4 Sch.28 Part 2

Sch.17 Part 2 para.150, added: SI 2008/1779 Art.18

Sch.17 Part 2 para.150, repealed: 2008 c.4 Sch.28 Part 2

Sch.17 Part 2 para.151, added: SI 2008/1779 Art.18

Sch.17 Part 2 para.151, repealed: 2008 c.4 Sch.28 Part 2

Sch.17 Part 2 para.152, added: SI 2008/1779 Art.18

Sch.17 Part 2 para.152, repealed: 2008 c.4 Sch.28 Part 2

Sch.17 Part 2 para.153, added: SI 2008/1779 Art.18

Sch.17 Part 2 para.153, repealed: 2008 c.4 Sch.28 Part 2

Sch.17 Part 2 para.154, added: SI 2008/1779 Art.18

Sch.17 Part 2 para.154, repealed: 2008 c.4 Sch.28 Part 2

Sch.17 Part 2 para.155, added: SI 2008/1779 Art.18

Sch.17 Part 2 para.155, repealed: 2008 c.4 Sch.28 Part 2

CAP.

2003–cont.

44. Criminal Justice Act 2003–*cont.*

Sch.17 Part 2 para.156, added: SI 2008/1779 Art.18

Sch.17 Part 2 para.156, repealed: 2008 c.4 Sch.28 Part 2

Sch.21, see *Attorney General's Reference (No.66 of 2007), Re* [2007] EWCA Crim 2630, [2008] 1 Cr. App. R. (S.) 107 (CA (Crim Div)), Toulson, L.J.; see *Attorney General's Reference (Nos.143 and 144 of 2006), Re* [2007] EWCA Crim 1245, [2008] 1 Cr. App. R. (S.) 28 (CA (Crim Div)), Lord Philips, L.C.J.; see *Attorney General's References (Nos.85, 86 & 87 of 2007), Re* [2007] EWCA Crim 3300, [2008] 2 Cr. App. R. (S.) 45 (CA (Crim Div)), Latham, L.J. (VP, CA Crim); see *R. v Height (John)* [2008] EWCA Crim 2500, Times, November 24, 2008 (CA (Crim Div)), Lord Judge, L.C.J.; see *R. v McNee (Michael)* [2007] EWCA Crim 1529, [2008] 1 Cr. App. R. (S.) 24 (CA (Crim Div)), Sir Igor Judge (President, QB)

Sch.21 para.4, see *R. v Height (John)* [2008] EWCA Crim 2500, Times, November 24, 2008 (CA (Crim Div)), Lord Judge, L.C.J.; see *R. v Mullen (Michael Patrick)* [2008] EWCA Crim 592, [2008] 2 Cr. App. R. (S.) 88 (CA (Crim Div)), Sir Igor Judge (President, QB)

Sch.21 para.4, amended: 2008 c.28 s.75

Sch.21 para.5, see *R. v Height (John)* [2008] EWCA Crim 2500, Times, November 24, 2008 (CA (Crim Div)), Lord Judge, L.C.J.; see *R. v Herbert* [2008] EWCA Crim 2501, Times, November 24, 2008 (CA (Crim Div)), Lord Chief Justice; see *R. v Tailor (Narendra)* [2007] EWCA Crim 1564, [2008] 1 Cr. App. R. (S.) 37 (CA (Crim Div)), Moses, L.J.; see *R. v Walker (Daniel)* [2007] EWCA Crim 2631, [2008] 2 Cr. App. R. (S.) 6 (CA (Crim Div)), Lord Philips, L.C.J.

Sch.21 para.6, see *R. v Rush (Ainsley)* [2007] EWCA Crim 1907, [2008] 1 Cr. App. R. (S.) 45 (CA (Crim Div)), Longmore, L.J.

Sch.22, see *R. v Henson (Daniel Thomas)* [2007] EWCA Crim 1308, [2008] 1 Cr. App. R. (S.) 19 (CA (Crim Div)), Rix, L.J.

Sch.24 para.1, repealed: 2008 c.4 Sch.4 para.97, Sch.28 Part 1

Sch.24 para.2, repealed: 2008 c.4 Sch.4 para.97, Sch.28 Part 1

Sch.24 para.3, repealed: 2008 c.4 Sch.4 para.97, Sch.28 Part 1

Sch.25 para.14, repealed: 2008 c.12 Sch.1 Part 1

Sch.26 para.12, amended: 2008 c.14 Sch.15 Part 5

Sch.26 para.19, repealed: SI 2008/576 Sch.5 para.7

CAP.

2003–*cont.*

44. **Criminal Justice Act 2003**–*cont.*

Sch.27 para.2, repealed: SI 2008/576 Sch.5 para.7

Sch.31 para.3A, added: 2008 c.4 Sch.26 para.2

Sch.31 para.4, amended: 2008 c.4 Sch.26 para.2, Sch.28 Part 2

Sch.31 para.5, amended: 2008 c.4 Sch.26 para.2

Sch.32 Part 1 para.1, repealed: SI 2008/1216 Sch.6 Part 1

Sch.32 Part 1 para.2, repealed (in part): 2008 c.4 Sch.28 Part 1, SI 2008/1216 Sch.6 Part 1

Sch.32 Part 1 para.3, repealed: SI 2008/1216 Sch.6 Part 1

Sch.32 Part 1 para.4, repealed: SI 2008/1216 Sch.6 Part 1

Sch.32 Part 1 para.5, repealed: SI 2008/1216 Sch.6 Part 1

Sch.32 Part 1 para.6, repealed: SI 2008/1216 Sch.6 Part 1

Sch.32 Part 1 para.7, repealed: SI 2008/1216 Sch.6 Part 1

Sch.32 Part 1 para.8, repealed (in part): 2008 c.4 Sch.28 Part 1, SI 2008/1216 Sch.6 Part 1

Sch.32 Part 1 para.9, repealed: SI 2008/1216 Sch.6 Part 1

Sch.32 Part 1 para.10, repealed: SI 2008/1216 Sch.6 Part 1

Sch.32 Part 1 para.11, repealed: SI 2008/1216 Sch.6 Part 1

Sch.32 Part 1 para.12, repealed: SI 2008/1216 Sch.6 Part 1

Sch.32 Part 1 para.13, repealed: SI 2008/1216 Sch.6 Part 1

Sch.32 Part 1 para.14, repealed: 2008 c.4 Sch.28 Part 1, SI 2008/1216 Sch.6 Part 1

Sch.32 Part 1 para.15, repealed: SI 2008/1216 Sch.6 Part 1

Sch.32 Part 1 para.16, repealed: SI 2008/1216 Sch.6 Part 1

Sch.32 Part 1 para.17, repealed: SI 2008/1216 Sch.6 Part 1

Sch.32 Part 1 para.18, repealed: SI 2008/1216 Sch.6 Part 1

Sch.32 Part 1 para.19, repealed: SI 2008/1216 Sch.6 Part 1

Sch.32 Part 1 para.20, repealed: SI 2008/1216 Sch.6 Part 1

Sch.32 Part 1 para.21, repealed: SI 2008/1216 Sch.6 Part 1

Sch.32 Part 1 para.22, repealed: SI 2008/1216 Sch.6 Part 1

Sch.32 Part 1 para.23, repealed: SI 2008/1216 Sch.6 Part 1

Sch.32 Part 1 para.24, repealed: SI 2008/1216 Sch.6 Part 1

Sch.32 Part 1 para.25, repealed: SI 2008/1216 Sch.6 Part 1

CAP.

2003–*cont.*

44. **Criminal Justice Act 2003**–*cont.*

Sch.32 Part 1 para.26, repealed: SI 2008/1216 Sch.6 Part 1

Sch.32 Part 1 para.27, repealed: SI 2008/1216 Sch.6 Part 1

Sch.32 Part 1 para.28, repealed: SI 2008/1216 Sch.6 Part 1

Sch.32 Part 1 para.29, repealed: SI 2008/1216 Sch.6 Part 1

Sch.32 Part 1 para.30, repealed: SI 2008/1216 Sch.6 Part 1

Sch.32 Part 1 para.31, repealed: SI 2008/1216 Sch.6 Part 1

Sch.32 Part 1 para.32, repealed: SI 2008/1216 Sch.6 Part 1

Sch.32 Part 1 para.33, repealed: SI 2008/1216 Sch.6 Part 1

Sch.32 Part 1 para.34, repealed: SI 2008/1216 Sch.6 Part 1

Sch.32 Part 1 para.35, repealed: SI 2008/1216 Sch.6 Part 1

Sch.32 Part 1 para.36, repealed: SI 2008/1216 Sch.6 Part 1

Sch.32 Part 1 para.37, repealed: SI 2008/1216 Sch.6 Part 1

Sch.32 Part 1 para.38, repealed: SI 2008/1216 Sch.6 Part 1

Sch.32 Part 1 para.39, repealed: SI 2008/1216 Sch.6 Part 1

Sch.32 Part 1 para.40, repealed: SI 2008/1216 Sch.6 Part 1

Sch.32 Part 1 para.41, repealed: SI 2008/1216 Sch.6 Part 1

Sch.32 Part 1 para.42, repealed: SI 2008/1216 Sch.6 Part 1

Sch.32 Part 1 para.43, repealed: SI 2008/1216 Sch.6 Part 1

Sch.32 Part 1 para.44, repealed: SI 2008/1216 Sch.6 Part 1

Sch.32 Part 1 para.45, repealed: SI 2008/1216 Sch.6 Part 1

Sch.32 Part 1 para.46, repealed: SI 2008/1216 Sch.6 Part 1

Sch.32 Part 1 para.47, repealed: SI 2008/1216 Sch.6 Part 1

Sch.32 Part 1 para.48, repealed: SI 2008/1216 Sch.6 Part 1

Sch.32 Part 1 para.49, repealed: SI 2008/1216 Sch.6 Part 1

Sch.32 Part 1 para.50, repealed: SI 2008/1216 Sch.6 Part 1

Sch.32 Part 1 para.51, repealed: SI 2008/1216 Sch.6 Part 1

Sch.32 Part 1 para.52, repealed: SI 2008/1216 Sch.6 Part 1

Sch.32 Part 1 para.53, repealed: SI 2008/1216 Sch.6 Part 1

Sch.32 Part 1 para.54, repealed: SI 2008/1216 Sch.6 Part 1

Sch.32 Part 1 para.55, repealed: SI 2008/1216 Sch.6 Part 1

CAP.

2003–cont.

44. Criminal Justice Act 2003–*cont.*

Sch.32 Part 1 para.56, repealed: SI 2008/1216 Sch.6 Part 1

Sch.32 Part 1 para.57, repealed: SI 2008/1216 Sch.6 Part 1

Sch.32 Part 1 para.58, repealed: SI 2008/1216 Sch.6 Part 1

Sch.32 Part 1 para.59, repealed: SI 2008/1216 Sch.6 Part 1

Sch.32 Part 1 para.60, repealed: SI 2008/1216 Sch.6 Part 1

Sch.32 Part 1 para.61, repealed: SI 2008/1216 Sch.6 Part 1

Sch.32 Part 1 para.62, repealed: SI 2008/1216 Sch.6 Part 1

Sch.32 Part 1 para.63, repealed: SI 2008/1216 Sch.6 Part 1

Sch.32 Part 1 para.64, repealed (in part): 2008 c.4 Sch.28 Part 1, SI 2008/1216 Sch.6 Part 1

Sch.32 Part 1 para.65, repealed: SI 2008/1216 Sch.6 Part 1

Sch.32 Part 1 para.66, repealed: SI 2008/1216 Sch.6 Part 1

Sch.32 Part 1 para.67, repealed: SI 2008/1216 Sch.6 Part 1

Sch.32 Part 1 para.68, repealed: SI 2008/1216 Sch.6 Part 1

Sch.32 Part 1 para.69, repealed: SI 2008/1216 Sch.6 Part 1

Sch.32 Part 1 para.70, repealed (in part): 2008 c.4 Sch.28 Part 1, SI 2008/1216 Sch.6 Part 1

Sch.32 Part 1 para.71, repealed: SI 2008/1216 Sch.6 Part 1

Sch.32 Part 1 para.72, repealed: SI 2008/1216 Sch.6 Part 1

Sch.32 Part 1 para.73, repealed: 2008 c.4 Sch.28 Part 1, SI 2008/1216 Sch.6 Part 1

Sch.32 Part 1 para.74, repealed: SI 2008/1216 Sch.6 Part 1

Sch.32 Part 1 para.75, repealed: SI 2008/1216 Sch.6 Part 1

Sch.32 Part 1 para.76, repealed: SI 2008/1216 Sch.6 Part 1

Sch.32 Part 1 para.77, repealed: SI 2008/1216 Sch.6 Part 1

Sch.32 Part 1 para.78, repealed: SI 2008/1216 Sch.6 Part 1

Sch.32 Part 1 para.79, repealed: SI 2008/1216 Sch.6 Part 1

Sch.32 Part 1 para.80, repealed: SI 2008/1216 Sch.6 Part 1

Sch.32 Part 1 para.81, repealed: SI 2008/1216 Sch.6 Part 1

Sch.32 Part 1 para.82, repealed: SI 2008/1216 Sch.6 Part 1

Sch.32 Part 1 para.83, repealed: SI 2008/1216 Sch.6 Part 1

Sch.32 Part 1 para.84, repealed: SI 2008/1216 Sch.6 Part 1

CAP.

2003–cont.

44. Criminal Justice Act 2003–*cont.*

Sch.32 Part 1 para.85, repealed: SI 2008/1216 Sch.6 Part 1

Sch.32 Part 1 para.86, repealed: SI 2008/1216 Sch.6 Part 1

Sch.32 Part 1 para.87, repealed: SI 2008/1216 Sch.6 Part 1

Sch.32 Part 1 para.88, repealed: SI 2008/1216 Sch.6 Part 1

Sch.32 Part 1 para.89, repealed (in part): 2008 c.4 Sch.28 Part 1, SI 2008/1216 Sch.6 Part 1

Sch.32 Part 1 para.90, repealed: SI 2008/1216 Sch.6 Part 1

Sch.32 Part 1 para.91, repealed: SI 2008/1216 Sch.6 Part 1

Sch.32 Part 1 para.92, repealed: SI 2008/1216 Sch.6 Part 1

Sch.32 Part 1 para.93, repealed: SI 2008/1216 Sch.6 Part 1

Sch.32 Part 1 para.94, repealed: SI 2008/1216 Sch.6 Part 1

Sch.32 Part 1 para.95, repealed: 2008 c.4 Sch.28 Part 1, SI 2008/1216 Sch.6 Part 1

Sch.32 Part 1 para.96, repealed: 2008 c.4 Sch.28 Part 1, SI 2008/1216 Sch.6 Part 1

Sch.32 Part 1 para.97, repealed: 2008 c.4 Sch.28 Part 1, SI 2008/1216 Sch.6 Part 1

Sch.32 Part 1 para.98, repealed: 2008 c.4 Sch.28 Part 1, SI 2008/1216 Sch.6 Part 1

Sch.32 Part 1 para.99, repealed: 2008 c.4 Sch.28 Part 1, SI 2008/1216 Sch.6 Part 1

Sch.32 Part 1 para.100, repealed: 2008 c.4 Sch.28 Part 1, SI 2008/1216 Sch.6 Part 1

Sch.32 Part 1 para.101, repealed: 2008 c.4 Sch.28 Part 1, SI 2008/1216 Sch.6 Part 1

Sch.32 Part 1 para.102, repealed: 2008 c.4 Sch.28 Part 1, SI 2008/1216 Sch.6 Part 1

Sch.32 Part 1 para.103, repealed: 2008 c.4 Sch.28 Part 1, SI 2008/1216 Sch.6 Part 1

Sch.32 Part 1 para.104, repealed: 2008 c.4 Sch.28 Part 1, SI 2008/1216 Sch.6 Part 1

Sch.32 Part 1 para.105, repealed: 2008 c.4 Sch.28 Part 1, SI 2008/1216 Sch.6 Part 1

Sch.32 Part 1 para.106, repealed (in part): 2008 c.4 Sch.28 Part 1, SI 2008/1216 Sch.6 Part 1

Sch.32 Part 1 para.107, repealed: 2008 c.4 Sch.28 Part 1, SI 2008/1216 Sch.6 Part 1

Sch.32 Part 1 para.108, repealed: SI 2008/1216 Sch.6 Part 1

Sch.32 Part 1 para.109, repealed: SI 2008/1216 Sch.6 Part 1

Sch.32 Part 1 para.110, repealed: SI 2008/1216 Sch.6 Part 1

Sch.32 Part 1 para.111, repealed: SI 2008/1216 Sch.6 Part 1

Sch.32 Part 1 para.112, repealed: SI 2008/1216 Sch.6 Part 1

Sch.32 Part 1 para.113, repealed: SI 2008/1216 Sch.6 Part 1

CAP.

2003–cont.

44. Criminal Justice Act 2003–*cont.*

Sch.32 Part 1 para.114, repealed: SI 2008/1216 Sch.6 Part 1

Sch.32 Part 1 para.115, repealed: SI 2008/1216 Sch.6 Part 1

Sch.32 Part 1 para.116, repealed: SI 2008/1216 Sch.6 Part 1

Sch.32 Part 1 para.117, repealed: SI 2008/1216 Sch.6 Part 1

Sch.32 Part 1 para.118, repealed: SI 2008/1216 Sch.6 Part 1

Sch.32 Part 1 para.119, repealed: SI 2008/1216 Sch.6 Part 1

Sch.32 Part 1 para.120, repealed: SI 2008/1216 Sch.6 Part 1

Sch.32 Part 1 para.121, repealed: SI 2008/1216 Sch.6 Part 1

Sch.32 Part 1 para.122, repealed: 2008 c.4 Sch.28 Part 1, SI 2008/1216 Sch.6 Part 1

Sch.32 Part 1 para.123, repealed (in part): 2008 c.4 Sch.28 Part 1, SI 2008/1216 Sch.6 Part 1

Sch.32 Part 1 para.124, repealed: SI 2008/1216 Sch.6 Part 1

Sch.32 Part 1 para.125, repealed: 2008 c.4 Sch.28 Part 1, SI 2008/1216 Sch.6 Part 1

Sch.32 Part 1 para.126, repealed: SI 2008/1216 Sch.6 Part 1

Sch.32 Part 1 para.127, repealed: 2008 c.4 Sch.28 Part 1, SI 2008/1216 Sch.6 Part 1

Sch.32 Part 1 para.128, repealed: 2008 c.4 Sch.28 Part 1, SI 2008/1216 Sch.6 Part 1

Sch.32 Part 1 para.129, repealed: 2008 c.4 Sch.28 Part 1, SI 2008/1216 Sch.6 Part 1

Sch.32 Part 1 para.130, repealed: SI 2008/1216 Sch.6 Part 1

Sch.32 Part 1 para.131, repealed (in part): 2008 c.4 Sch.28 Part 1, SI 2008/1216 Sch.6 Part 1

Sch.32 Part 1 para.132, repealed: SI 2008/1216 Sch.6 Part 1

Sch.32 Part 1 para.133, repealed: SI 2008/1216 Sch.6 Part 1

Sch.32 Part 1 para.134, repealed: SI 2008/1216 Sch.6 Part 1

Sch.32 Part 1 para.135, repealed: SI 2008/1216 Sch.6 Part 1

Sch.32 Part 1 para.136, repealed: SI 2008/1216 Sch.6 Part 1

Sch.32 Part 1 para.137, repealed: SI 2008/1216 Sch.6 Part 1

Sch.32 Part 1 para.138, repealed: 2008 c.4 Sch.28 Part 1, SI 2008/1216 Sch.6 Part 1

Sch.32 Part 1 para.139, repealed: SI 2008/1216 Sch.6 Part 1

Sch.32 Part 1 para.140, repealed: SI 2008/1216 Sch.6 Part 1

Sch.32 Part 1 para.141, repealed: SI 2008/1216 Sch.6 Part 1

Sch.32 Part 1 para.142, repealed: SI 2008/1216 Sch.6 Part 1

CAP.

2003–cont.

44. Criminal Justice Act 2003–*cont.*

Sch.32 Part 1 para.143, repealed: SI 2008/1216 Sch.6 Part 1

Sch.32 Part 1 para.144, repealed: SI 2008/1216 Sch.6 Part 1

Sch.32 Part 2 para.152, repealed: 2008 c.12 Sch.1 Part 1

Sch.34A para.1, added: 2008 c.4 Sch.24

Sch.34A para.2, added: 2008 c.4 Sch.24

Sch.34A para.3, added: 2008 c.4 Sch.24

Sch.34A para.4, added: 2008 c.4 Sch.24

Sch.34A para.5, added: 2008 c.4 Sch.24

Sch.34A para.6, added: 2008 c.4 Sch.24

Sch.34A para.7, added: 2008 c.4 Sch.24

Sch.34A para.8, added: 2008 c.4 Sch.24

Sch.34A para.9, added: 2008 c.4 Sch.24

Sch.34A para.10, added: 2008 c.4 Sch.24

Sch.34A para.11, added: 2008 c.4 Sch.24

Sch.34A para.12, added: 2008 c.4 Sch.24

Sch.34A para.13, added: 2008 c.4 Sch.24

Sch.34A para.14, added: 2008 c.4 Sch.24

Sch.34A para.15, added: 2008 c.4 Sch.24

Sch.36 Part 4 para.50, repealed: 2008 c.4 Sch.28 Part 4

Sch.37 Part 4, amended: 2008 c.4 Sch.28 Part 4

Sch.37 Part 4, referred to: 2008 c.4 s.153

2004

3. National Insurance Contributions and Statutory Payments Act 2004

s.5, repealed (in part): 2008 c.9 Sch.43 para.11

5. Planning and Compulsory Purchase Act 2004

Commencement Orders: 2008 c.29 Sch.13, s.225

see *R. (on the application of Howsmoor Developments Ltd) v South Gloucestershire CC* [2008] EWHC 262 (Admin), [2008] Env. L.R. 38 (QBD (Admin)), Sir George Newman

referred to: 2008 c.29 s.204

Part 2, applied: SI 2008/1572 Art.3, SI 2008/2867 Reg.24

s.1, amended: 2008 c.29 s.181

s.1, varied: SI 2008/2867 Reg.20

s.2, varied: SI 2008/2867 Reg.20

s.3, varied: SI 2008/2867 Reg.20

s.4, amended: 2008 c.17 s.16

s.4, varied: SI 2008/2867 Reg.20

s.4A, added: 2008 c.29 s.179

s.4A, varied: SI 2008/2867 Reg.20

s.5, varied: SI 2008/2867 Reg.20

s.6, varied: SI 2008/2867 Reg.20

s.7, varied: SI 2008/2867 Reg.20

s.8, varied: SI 2008/2867 Reg.20

s.9, varied: SI 2008/2867 Reg.20

s.10, varied: SI 2008/2867 Reg.20

s.11, varied: SI 2008/2867 Reg.20

CAP.

2004–cont.

5. **Planning and Compulsory Purchase Act 2004**–*cont.*

s.12, varied: SI 2008/2867 Reg.20
s.13, varied: SI 2008/2867 Reg.21, Reg.23
s.14, varied: SI 2008/2867 Reg.21, Reg.23
s.14, enabling: SI 2008/1371
s.15, amended: 2008 c.29 s.180
s.15, applied: SI 2008/2867 Reg.22, Reg.23
s.15, repealed (in part): 2008 c.29 s.180, Sch.13
s.15, varied: SI 2008/1572 Art.4, SI 2008/2867 Reg.21, Reg.22, Reg.23
s.15, enabling: SI 2008/1371
s.16, applied: SI 2008/2867 Reg.22
s.16, varied: SI 2008/2867 Reg.21, Reg.23
s.17, amended: 2008 c.29 s.180
s.17, repealed (in part): 2008 c.29 s.180, Sch.13
s.17, varied: SI 2008/2867 Reg.21, Reg.23
s.17, enabling: SI 2008/1371
s.18, amended: 2008 c.29 s.180
s.18, repealed (in part): 2008 c.29 s.180, Sch.13
s.18, varied: SI 2008/2867 Reg.21, Reg.23
s.19, amended: 2008 c.29 s.180, s.182
s.19, applied: 2008 c.21 s.1
s.19, varied: SI 2008/2867 Reg.21, Reg.23
s.20, applied: SI 2008/1371 Reg.3
s.20, disapplied: SI 2008/2867 Reg.23
s.20, varied: SI 2008/2867 Reg.21, Reg.23
s.20, enabling: SI 2008/1371
s.21, varied: SI 2008/2867 Reg.21, Reg.23
s.22, varied: SI 2008/2867 Reg.21, Reg.23
s.23, applied. SI 2008/2867 Reg.19
s.23, varied: SI 2008/2867 Reg.21, Reg.23
s.24, varied: SI 2008/2867 Reg.21, Reg.23
s.24, enabling: SI 2008/1371
s.25, varied: SI 2008/2867 Reg.21, Reg.23
s.26, varied: SI 2008/2867 Reg.21, Reg.23
s.27, varied: SI 2008/2867 Reg.21, Reg.23
s.28, varied: SI 2008/2867 Reg.21, Reg.23
s.29, applied: 2008 c.29 s.207, SI 2008/2867 Reg.24
s.29, varied: SI 2008/2867 Reg.21, Reg.23, Reg.24
s.29, enabling: SI 2008/1572
s.30, varied: SI 2008/2867 Reg.21, Reg.23
s.31, varied: SI 2008/2867 Reg.21, Reg.23
s.32, varied: SI 2008/2867 Reg.21, Reg.23
s.33, varied: SI 2008/2867 Reg.21, Reg.23
s.34, varied: SI 2008/2867 Reg.21, Reg.23
s.35, varied: SI 2008/2867 Reg.21, Reg.23
s.36, varied: SI 2008/2867 Reg.21, Reg.23
s.36, enabling: SI 2008/1371
s.37, amended: 2008 c.17 Sch.8 para.81, 2008 c.29 s.180
s.37, varied: SI 2008/2867 Reg.21, Reg.23
s.38, see *Jefferson v National Assembly for Wales* [2007] EWHC 3351 (Admin), [2008] 1 W.L.R. 2193 (QBD (Admin)), Judge Hickinbottom; see *South Cambridgeshire DC v Secretary of State for Communities and Local Government* [2007] EWHC 2117 (Admin), [2008] J.P.L. 519 (QBD (Admin)), Keith, J.

CAP.

2004–cont.

5. **Planning and Compulsory Purchase Act 2004**–*cont.*

s.38–*cont.*

s.38, amended: 2008 c.29 s.180
s.39, amended: 2008 c.29 s.183
s.42, repealed (in part): 2008 c.29 Sch.13
s.46, repealed: 2008 c.29 s.225, Sch.13
s.47, repealed: 2008 c.29 s.225, Sch.13
s.48, repealed: 2008 c.29 s.225, Sch.13
s.53, repealed: 2008 c.29 Sch.13
s.56, amended: 2008 c.29 s.184
s.62, applied: 2008 c.21 s.1
s.113, amended: 2008 c.29 s.185
s.121, amended: 2008 c.29 Sch.7 para.7
s.121, enabling: SI 2008/10, SI 2008/2162
s.122, amended: 2008 c.29 Sch.13
s.122, repealed (in part): 2008 c.29 Sch.13
s.122, enabling: SI 2008/10, SI 2008/1371, SI 2008/2162
Sch.6 para.5, repealed: 2008 c.29 s.225, Sch.13
Sch.7 para.18, repealed: SI 2008/3002 Sch.3

6. **Child Trust Funds Act 2004**

applied: SI 2008/2685 r.19, Sch.1, SI 2008/2698 r.19
s.3, applied: 2008 c.31 s.10
s.24, amended: SI 2008/2833 Sch.3 para.202
s.24, applied: SI 2008/2707 Art.2

7. **Gender Recognition Act 2004**

s.7, enabling: SI 2008/715
s.24, enabling: SI 2008/715
Sch.3 Part 1 para.3, amended: SI 2008/678 Sch.2 para.13
Sch.3 Part 1 para.3, applied: SI 2008/678 Sch.1 para.13

8. **Higher Education Act 2004**

see *R. (on the application of Carnell) v Regents Park College* [2008] EWHC 739 (Admin), [2008] E.L.R. 268 (QBD (Admin)), Black, J.; see *R. (on the application of Peng Hu Shi) v King's College London* [2008] EWHC 857 (Admin), [2008] E.L.R. 414 (QBD (Admin)), Mitting, J.; see *R. (on the application of Siborurema) v Office of the Independent Adjudicator* [2007] EWCA Civ 1365, [2008] E.L.R. 209 (CA (Civ Div)), Pill, L.J.
s.11, see *R. (on the application of Siborurema) v Office of the Independent Adjudicator* [2007] EWCA Civ 1365, [2008] E.L.R. 209 (CA (Civ Div)), Pill, L.J.
s.12, see *R. (on the application of Siborurema) v Office of the Independent Adjudicator* [2007] EWCA Civ 1365, [2008] E.L.R. 209 (CA (Civ Div)), Pill, L.J.

CAP.

2004–*cont.*

8. Higher Education Act 2004–*cont.*

s.24, enabling: SI 2008/1640, SI 2008/2507

s.26, applied: SI 2008/2507

s.44, referred to: SI 2008/1273 Reg.3, SI 2008/3170 Reg.3

s.47, enabling: SI 2008/1640, SI 2008/2507

11. Gangmasters (Licensing) Act 2004

s.8, applied: SI 2008/638

s.8, enabling: SI 2008/638

s.25, enabling: SI 2008/638

12. Finance Act 2004

applied: SI 2008/238 Reg.14, SI 2008/239 Reg.25, SI 2008/653 Reg.11, Reg.15, Reg.22, SSI 2008/224 Reg.11, Reg.15, Reg.22, SSI 2008/228 Reg.22, SSI 2008/230 Reg.22

Part 4, applied: SI 2008/653 Reg.1, Reg.5, Reg.10, Reg.12, Reg.14, Reg.18, SSI 2008/224 Reg.1, Reg.5, Reg.10, Reg.11, Reg.14, Reg.18

Part 4 c.2, applied: 2008 c.30 s.9, s.16, s.67, SI 2008/653 Reg.5, Reg.16, SSI 2008/224 Reg.5, Reg.16

Part 4 c.5, applied: SSI 2008/230 Reg.21

s.7, repealed (in part): 2008 c.9 s.13, Sch.5 para.25

s.10, repealed (in part): 2008 c.9 Sch.5 para.25

s.15, applied: SSI 2008/224 Reg.16

s.59, amended: 2008 c.17 Sch.8 para.82, Sch.9 para.33

s.59, varied: SI 2008/2839 Sch.1 para.1

s.61, applied: 2008 c.9 s.128

s.71, enabling: SI 2008/740

s.97, referred to: SSI 2008/224 Reg.6

s.131, amended: 2008 c.9 Sch.22 para.17

s.142, repealed: 2008 c.9 s.75

s.150, referred to: SSI 2008/228 Reg.9

s.160, referred to: SI 2008/653 Reg.12, SSI 2008/224 Reg.11

s.164, substituted: 2008 c.9 Sch.29 para.1

s.166, applied: SI 2008/238 Reg.14, SSI 2008/230 Reg.39

s.168, applied: SI 2008/238 Reg.14, SSI 2008/230 Reg.39

s.169, applied: SI 2008/239 Reg.79, SSI 2008/228 Reg.74

s.169, referred to: SI 2008/653 Reg.5, SSI 2008/224 Reg.5

s.172, amended: 2008 c.9 Sch.28 para.2

s.172A, amended: 2008 c.9 Sch.28 para.3

s.172A, applied: SI 2008/1946 Reg.1

s.172B, amended: 2008 c.9 Sch.28 para.4

s.172B, repealed (in part): 2008 c.9 Sch.28 para.4

s.185G, repealed (in part): 2008 c.9 Sch.2 para.53

s.188, applied: SI 2008/18 Sch.3 para.3, Sch.3 para.4, SI 2008/529 Sch.4 para.4, Sch.4 para.5, SI 2008/538 Reg.9, Reg.10, SI 2008/1273 Sch.5 para.4, Sch.5 para.5,

CAP.

2004–*cont.*

12. Finance Act 2004–*cont.*

s.188, applied:–*cont.*

Sch.6 para.4, Sch.6 para.5, SI 2008/1582 Sch.4 para.4, Sch.4 para.5, SI 2008/3170 Sch.5 para.4, Sch.5 para.5, Sch.6 para.3, Sch.6 para.4

s.197, amended: 2008 c.9 Sch.29 para.14

s.199, amended: 2008 c.9 Sch.29 para.14

s.199A, added: 2008 c.9 s.90

s.199A, applied: 2008 c.9 s.90

s.205, applied: SI 2008/653 Reg.16, Reg.18, SSI 2008/224 Reg.16, Reg.18

s.206, applied: SI 2008/653 Reg.8, Reg.22, SSI 2008/224 Reg.8, Reg.22

s.214, applied: SI 2008/653 Reg.8, SSI 2008/224 Reg.8

s.215, amended: 2008 c.9 Sch.29 para.15

s.216, amended: 2008 c.9 Sch.29 para.1, Sch.29 para.5

s.216, applied: SI 2008/653 Reg.8, SSI 2008/224 Reg.8

s.218, applied: SSI 2008/230 Reg.22

s.238, applied: SI 2008/239 Reg.33, SSI 2008/228 Reg.30

s.241, applied: SI 2008/653 Reg.14

s.241, referred to: SI 2008/653 Reg.10, SSI 2008/224 Reg.10, Reg.14

s.251, enabling: SI 2008/720

s.256, applied: SSI 2008/224 Reg.3

s.256, referred to: SI 2008/653 Reg.3

s.275, applied: SI 2008/239 Reg.26, SSI 2008/228 Reg.23

s.283, enabling: SI 2008/2990

s.295, repealed (in part): 2008 c.9 Sch.40 para.21

s.308, amended: 2008 c.9 Sch.38 para.2

s.311, amended: 2008 c.9 Sch.38 para.3

s.312, substituted: 2008 c.9 Sch.38 para.4

s.312, enabling: SI 2008/1947

s.312A, enabling: SI 2008/1947

s.313, amended: 2008 c.9 Sch.38 para.5

s.316, substituted: 2008 c.9 Sch.38 para.6

s.320, see *Europcar UK Ltd v Revenue and Customs Commissioners* [2008] EWHC 1363 (Ch), [2008] S.T.C. 2751 (Ch D), Henderson, J.

Sch.7 para.1, repealed: SI 2008/381 Sch.1 Part 1

Sch.7 para.9, amended: 2008 c.9 Sch.17 para.18

Sch.7 para.9, repealed (in part): 2008 c.9 Sch.17 para.18

Sch.11 Part 1 para.4, enabling: SI 2008/1282

Sch.11 Part 2 para.8, enabling: SI 2008/1282

Sch.11 Part 3 para.12, enabling: SI 2008/1282

Sch.21 para.2, repealed: 2008 c.9 Sch.2 para.21

Sch.21 para.3, repealed (in part): 2008 c.9 Sch.2 para.55

Sch.21 para.8, repealed: 2008 c.9 Sch.2 para.55

CAP.

2004–cont.

12. Finance Act 2004–*cont.*

Sch.21 para.10, amended: 2008 c.9 Sch.2 para.55
Sch.21 para.10, repealed (in part): 2008 c.9 Sch.2 para.55
Sch.26 para.1, repealed (in part): 2008 c.9 s.41
Sch.26 para.2, repealed (in part): 2008 c.9 s.41
Sch.26 para.4, repealed: 2008 c.9 s.41
Sch.26 para.5, repealed: 2008 c.9 s.41
Sch.26 para.6, repealed (in part): 2008 c.9 s.41
Sch.26 para.7, repealed: 2008 c.9 s.41
Sch.26 para.8, repealed: 2008 c.9 s.41
Sch.26 para.9, repealed: 2008 c.9 s.41
Sch.26 para.14, repealed (in part): 2008 c.9 s.41
Sch.26 para.15, repealed: 2008 c.9 s.41
Sch.26 para.16, repealed (in part): 2008 c.9 s.41
Sch.28, applied: SSI 2008/224 Reg.16
Sch.28 Part 1 para.3, amended: 2008 c.9 Sch.29 para.2
Sch.28 Part 1 para.3, enabling: SI 2008/1946
Sch.28 Part 2 para.15, applied: SI 2008/653 Reg.14, Reg.16, Reg.18, Reg.20, SSI 2008/224 Reg.14, Reg.18, Reg.20
Sch.28 Part 2 para.16, amended: 2008 c.9 Sch.28 para.5
Sch.28 Part 2 para.17, amended: 2008 c.9 Sch.29 para.2
Sch.28 Part 2 para.17, enabling: SI 2008/1946
Sch.29 Part 1 para.1, applied: SI 2008/653 Reg.14
Sch.29 Part 1 para.1, referred to: SI 2008/653 Reg.10, SSI 2008/224 Reg.10, Reg.14
Sch.29 Part 1 para.4, applied: SI 2008/653 Reg.15
Sch.29 Part 1 para.4, referred to: SI 2008/653 Reg.11, SSI 2008/224 Reg.11, Reg.15
Sch.29 Part 1 para.7, applied: SI 2008/239 Reg.51, SSI 2008/224 Reg.5, SSI 2008/228 Reg.47
Sch.29 Part 1 para.7, referred to: SI 2008/653 Reg.5
Sch.29 Part 2 para.14, applied: SI 2008/653 Reg.8, SSI 2008/224 Reg.8
Sch.29 Part 2 para.20, applied: SSI 2008/224 Reg.5
Sch.29 Part 2 para.20, referred to: SI 2008/653 Reg.5
Sch.29A Part 1 para.2, repealed (in part): 2008 c.9 Sch.29 para.3
Sch.32 para.10, substituted: 2008 c.9 Sch.29 para.7
Sch.32 para.10A, added: 2008 c.9 Sch.29 para.8
Sch.32 para.11, amended: 2008 c.9 Sch.29 para.9

CAP.

2004–cont.

12. Finance Act 2004–*cont.*

Sch.32 para.13, amended: 2008 c.9 Sch.29 para.10
Sch.34 para.7ZA, amended: 2008 c.9 Sch.29 para.16
Sch.34 para.10, amended: 2008 c.9 Sch.29 para.19
Sch.34 para.11, amended: 2008 c.9 Sch.29 para.19
Sch.34 para.11, applied: 2008 c.9 Sch.29 para.19
Sch.35 para.25, repealed: 2008 c.9 Sch.14 para.17
Sch.35 para.27, repealed: 2008 c.9 Sch.14 para.17
Sch.36, applied: SSI 2008/230 Reg.22
Sch.36 Part 3 para.34, amended: 2008 c.9 Sch.29 para.13
Sch.36 Part 3 para.34, repealed (in part): 2008 c.9 Sch.29 para.13
Sch.36 Part 4 para.56, amended: 2008 c.9 Sch.29 para.18

17. Health Protection Agency Act 2004

s.2A, added: 2008 c.14 s.159
s.3, amended: SI 2008/960 Sch.3
s.6, amended: 2008 c.14 s.159
s.8, amended: 2008 c.14 s.159
s.9, amended: 2008 c.14 s.159

18. Traffic Management Act 2004

Commencement Orders: SI 2008/757 Art.4
applied: 2008 c.13 Sch.3
Part 6, applied: SI 2008/609 Reg.9, SI 2008/613 Art.2, SI 2008/614 Reg.10
s.9, enabling: SI 2008/2367
s.60, applied: 2008 c.18 Sch.3 para.5
s.61, applied: 2008 c.18 Sch.3 para.5
s.72, enabling: SI 2008/614, SI 2008/1214, SI 2008/1513
s.73, enabling: SI 2008/614, SI 2008/1214, SI 2008/1513
s.76, amended: 2008 c.26 s.127
s.76, applied: SI 2008/616 Reg.2
s.76, enabling: SI 2008/616
s.78, applied: SI 2008/616 Reg.2
s.78, enabling: SI 2008/609, SI 2008/913, SI 2008/1513
s.79, applied: SI 2008/616 Reg.2
s.79, enabling: SI 2008/614, SI 2008/1214, SI 2008/1513
s.80, enabling: SI 2008/608
s.81, applied: SI 2008/609 Reg.8, Reg.10
s.81, enabling: SI 2008/609, SI 2008/913
s.82, enabling: SI 2008/609, SI 2008/913
s.85, amended: 2008 c.26 s.127
s.85, applied: SI 2008/613 Sch.1 app.001 para.3
s.86, amended: 2008 c.26 s.127
s.86, applied: SI 2008/613 Sch.1 app.001 para.4
s.87, amended: 2008 c.26 s.127
s.88, enabling: SI 2008/614, SI 2008/1214

CAP.

2004–cont.

18. Traffic Management Act 2004–*cont.*

s.89, applied: SI 2008/608

s.89, enabling: SI 2008/608, SI 2008/609, SI 2008/614, SI 2008/913, SI 2008/1055, SI 2008/1214, SI 2008/1513, SI 2008/2344

s.92, enabling: SI 2008/620, SI 2008/1215

s.99, enabling: SI 2008/757

Sch.7 Part 1 para.4, applied: SI 2008/613 Sch.1 app.001 para.1, Sch.1 app.001 para.5, Sch.1 app.001 para.6, Sch.1 app.001 para.7, Sch.1 app.001 para.8, Sch.1 app.001 para.9, Sch.1 app.001 para.10, SI 2008/614 Reg.3, SI 2008/1214 Reg.3

Sch.8 Part 2 para.8, applied: SI 2008/1051, SI 2008/1055, SI 2008/1084, SI 2008/1086, SI 2008/1211, SI 2008/1212, SI 2008/1340, SI 2008/1518, SI 2008/1764, SI 2008/1896, SI 2008/2344, SI 2008/2442, SI 2008/2567, SI 2008/3160, SI 2008/3198

Sch.8 Part 2 para.8, enabling: SI 2008/1051, SI 2008/1055, SI 2008/1084, SI 2008/1086, SI 2008/1211, SI 2008/1212, SI 2008/1340, SI 2008/1518, SI 2008/1764, SI 2008/1896, SI 2008/2344, SI 2008/2442, SI 2008/2567, SI 2008/3160, SI 2008/3198

Sch.9, applied: SI 2008/608 Reg.4

Sch.9 Part 3 para.8, applied: SI 2008/613 Sch.1 para.4

Sch.9 Part 3 para.8, enabling: SI 2008/613

Sch.10 para.3, applied: SI 2008/1051, SI 2008/1055, SI 2008/1084, SI 2008/1086, SI 2008/1211, SI 2008/1212, SI 2008/1340, SI 2008/1518, SI 2008/1764, SI 2008/1896, SI 2008/2344, SI 2008/2442, SI 2008/2567, SI 2008/3160, SI 2008/3198

Sch.10 para.3, enabling: SI 2008/1051, SI 2008/1055, SI 2008/1084, SI 2008/1086, SI 2008/1211, SI 2008/1212, SI 2008/1340, SI 2008/1518, SI 2008/1764, SI 2008/1896, SI 2008/2344, SI 2008/2442, SI 2008/2567, SI 2008/3160, SI 2008/3198

19. Asylum and Immigration (Treatment of Claimants, etc.) Act 2004

s.1, varied: SI 2008/680 Art.5, Art.18

s.2, varied: SI 2008/680 Art.5, Art.18, Sch.8 para.1

s.4, amended: SSI 2008/259 Art.2

s.4, varied: SI 2008/680 Art.5, Art.18, Sch.8 para.2

s.5, varied: SI 2008/680 Art.5, Art.18, Sch.8 para.3

s.6, varied: SI 2008/680 Art.5, Art.18, Sch.8 para.4

s.9, amended: SI 2008/2833 Sch.3 para.203

s.14, varied: SI 2008/680 Art.5, Art.18, Sch.8 para.5

s.15, varied: SI 2008/680 Art.5, Art.18

CAP.

2004–cont.

19. Asylum and Immigration (Treatment of Claimants, etc.) Act 2004–*cont.*

s.16, varied: SI 2008/680 Art.5, Art.18

s.17, varied: SI 2008/680 Art.5, Art.18, Sch.8 para.6

s.18, varied: SI 2008/680 Art.5, Art.18

s.19, varied: SI 2008/680 Art.5, Art.18, Sch.8 para.7

s.19, see *AB (Democratic Republic of Congo) v Secretary of State for the Home Department* [2007] EWCA Civ 1422, [2008] Imm. A.R. 283 (CA (Civ Div)), Judge, L.J.; see *R. (on the application of Baiai) v Secretary of State for the Home Department* [2008] UKHL 53, [2008] 3 W.L.R. 549 (HL), Lord Bingham of Cornhill

s.20, varied: SI 2008/680 Art.5, Art.18, Sch.8 para.8

s.25, varied: SI 2008/680 Art.5, Art.18, Sch.8 para.9

s.26, varied: SI 2008/680 Art.5, Art.18, Sch.8 para.10

s.27, varied: SI 2008/680 Art.5, Art.18

s.28, varied: SI 2008/680 Art.5, Art.18

s.29, varied: SI 2008/680 Art.5, Art.18

s.30, varied: SI 2008/680 Art.5, Art.18

s.31, varied: SI 2008/680 Art.5, Art.18

s.34, varied: SI 2008/680 Art.5, Art.18

s.35, varied: SI 2008/680 Art.5, Art.18, Sch.8 para.11

s.36, varied: 2008 c.4 s.133, SI 2008/680 Art.5, Art.18, Sch.8 para.12

s.42, applied: SI 2008/544, SI 2008/1695, SI 2008/3017

s.42, varied: SI 2008/680 Art.5, Art.18, Sch.8 para.13

s.45, varied: SI 2008/680 Art.5, Art.18, Sch.8 para.14

s.47, varied: SI 2008/680 Art.5, Art.18

s.49, enabling: SI 2008/680

s.50, varied: SI 2008/680 Art.5, Art.18

Sch.2 Part 1 para.16, varied: SI 2008/680 Art.5, Art.18

Sch.2 Part 1 para.21, varied: SI 2008/680 Art.5, Art.18

Sch.3 para.2, see *Nasseri v Secretary of State for the Home Department* [2007] EWHC 1548 (Admin), [2008] 2 W.L.R. 523 (QBD (Admin)), McCombe, J.; see *Nasseri v Secretary of State for the Home Department* [2008] EWCA Civ 464, [2008] 3 W.L.R. 1386 (CA (Civ Div)), Sir Anthony Clarke, M.R.

Sch.3 para.3, see *Nasseri v Secretary of State for the Home Department* [2007] EWHC 1548 (Admin), [2008] 2 W.L.R. 523 (QBD (Admin)), McCombe, J.

Sch.4, varied: SI 2008/680 Art.5, Art.18

20. Energy Act 2004

Part 1, applied: SI 2008/2375 Reg.3, SI 2008/2376 Reg.3

CAP.

2004–cont.

20. Energy Act 2004–*cont.*
s.29, amended: SI 2008/948 Sch.1 para.227
s.30, amended: SI 2008/948 Sch.1 para.227
s.37, referred to: 2008 c.32 s.45
s.81, repealed (in part): 2008 c.32 Sch.6
s.105, amended: 2008 c.32 s.69
s.105, repealed (in part): 2008 c.32 Sch.5 para.17, Sch.6
s.105A, added: 2008 c.32 s.69
s.107, repealed (in part): 2008 c.32 Sch.5 para.18, Sch.6
s.108, amended: 2008 c.32 s.69
s.110A, added: 2008 c.32 s.70
s.110B, added: 2008 c.32 s.70
s.112A, added: 2008 c.32 s.71
s.114, amended: 2008 c.32 s.70
s.116, repealed: 2008 c.32 Sch.6
s.121, amended: 2008 c.32 s.40
s.121A, added: SI 2008/1888 Reg.2
s.125, substituted: 2008 c.27 Sch.7 para.2
s.125A, substituted: 2008 c.27 Sch.7 para.2
s.125B, substituted: 2008 c.27 Sch.7 para.2
s.125C, substituted: 2008 c.27 Sch.7 para.2
s.126, amended: 2008 c.27 Sch.7 para.3
s.128, amended: 2008 c.27 Sch.7 para.4
s.129, amended: 2008 c.27 Sch.7 para.5
s.131A, added: 2008 c.27 Sch.7 para.6
s.131B, added: 2008 c.27 Sch.7 para.6
s.131C, added: 2008 c.27 Sch.7 para.6
s.132, amended: 2008 c.27 Sch.7 para.7, 2008 c.32 Sch.5 para.19
s.137, applied: SI 2008/2376 Reg.3
s.146, applied: SI 2008/2376 Reg.3
s.150, applied: SI 2008/2375 Reg.3
s.180, repealed (in part): 2008 c.32 Sch.6
s.185, amended: 2008 c.32 Sch.5 para.20
s.188, amended: 2008 c.32 Sch.1 para.13
s.188, applied: 2008 c.32 s.34
s.196, amended: 2008 c.27 Sch.7 para.7
Sch.4 para.5, repealed: 2008 c.9 Sch.27 para.25
Sch.4 para.6, repealed: 2008 c.9 Sch.27 para.25
Sch.6 para.6, amended: SI 2008/948 Sch.1 para.228
Sch.6 para.7, amended: SI 2008/948 Sch.1 para.228
Sch.7 para.8, amended: SI 2008/948 Sch.1 para.229
Sch.7 para.9, amended: SI 2008/948 Sch.1 para.229
Sch.9 Part 6 para.36, repealed: 2008 c.9 Sch.2 para.70
Sch.13 para.2, amended: 2008 c.32 Sch.5 para.21
Sch.20 Part 2 para.16, amended: SI 2008/948 Sch.1 para.230

CAP.

2004–cont.

21. Fire and Rescue Services Act 2004
applied: 2008 c.13 Sch.3, SI 2008/239 Sch.2 para.5, SI 2008/794 Reg.43, SI 2008/2852 Sch.3 para.5
s.1, applied: SI 2008/239 Reg.12
s.4, applied: SI 2008/199 Art.1, SI 2008/450 Art.1
s.21, enabling: SI 2008/1370, SI 2008/2298
s.29, applied: SI 2008/239 Sch.2 para.25
s.34, applied: SI 2008/213, SSI 2008/160
s.34, enabling: SI 2008/213, SSI 2008/160
s.60, enabling: SI 2008/213, SI 2008/2298, SSI 2008/160
s.62, enabling: SI 2008/2298
Sch.1 para.96, repealed: 2008 c.9 s.72

23. Public Audit (Wales) Act 2004
s.14, amended: SI 2008/948 Sch.1 para.1
s.62, amended: 2008 c.14 Sch.5 para.76
s.62, varied: SI 2008/2250 Art.3
s.64, amended: 2008 c.14 Sch.5 para.77
s.67A, amended: SI 2008/912 Sch.1 para.26
Sch.2 para.27, repealed: 2008 c.17 Sch.16
Sch.2 para.28, repealed: 2008 c.17 Sch.16
Sch.2 para.29, repealed: 2008 c.17 Sch.16
Sch.2 para.30, repealed: 2008 c.17 Sch.16
Sch.2 para.37, repealed: 2008 c.17 Sch.16

24. Employment Relations Act 2004
s.41, repealed (in part): 2008 c.30 Sch.11 Part 1
s.45, repealed: 2008 c.24 Sch.1 Part 2
s.46, repealed: 2008 c.24 Sch.1 Part 2

25. Horserace Betting and Olympic Lottery Act 2004
s.6, amended: SI 2008/948 Sch.1 para.231
s.12, amended: SI 2008/948 Sch.1 para.231
s.25, applied: SI 2008/255
s.25, enabling: SI 2008/255
s.36, applied: SI 2008/255
s.36, enabling: SI 2008/255

26. Christmas Day (Trading) Act 2004
applied: 2008 c.13 Sch.3
s.2, referred to: 2008 c.13 Sch.6
s.3, referred to: 2008 c.13 Sch.6

27. Companies (Audit, Investigations and Community Enterprise) Act 2004
Part 2, applied: SI 2008/2546 Art.4, SI 2008/3229 Sch.1, Sch.2, Sch.3
s.14, amended: SI 2008/948 Sch.1 para.232
s.14, applied: SI 2008/623 Art.7
s.14, enabling: SI 2008/623
s.15, repealed: SI 2008/948 Sch.2
s.15, substituted: SI 2008/948 Sch.1 para.232
s.16, amended: SI 2008/948 Sch.1 para.233
s.34, amended: SI 2008/948 Sch.1 para.234, Sch.2
s.43, amended: SI 2008/948 Sch.1 para.31, Sch.1 para.234
s.45, amended: SI 2008/948 Sch.2
s.53, amended: SI 2008/948 Sch.2

CAP.

2004–cont.

28. Domestic Violence, Crime and Victims Act 2004

Commencement Orders: SI 2008/3065 Art.2
Part 2, applied: SI 2008/1184 Reg.21
Part 3, applied: SI 2008/1184 Reg.21
s.5, see *R. v Ikram (Abid)* [2008] EWCA Crim 586, [2008] 4 All E.R. 253 (CA (Crim Div)), Sir Igor Judge (President, QB)
s.5, applied: SI 2008/1216 Sch.1 para.30, Sch.2 para.30
s.6, see *R. v Ikram (Abid)* [2008] EWCA Crim 586, [2008] 4 All E.R. 253 (CA (Crim Div)), Sir Igor Judge (President, QB)
s.9, amended: SI 2008/912 Sch.1 para.20
s.17, see *Practice Direction (Sup Ct: Criminal Proceedings: Arraignment)* [2008] 1 W.L.R. 154 (Sup Ct), Sir Igor Judge (President)
s.23, applied: SI 2008/1184 Reg.21
s.35, amended: SI 2008/912 Sch.1 para.20
s.35, applied: SI 2008/1184 Reg.20, SI 2008/2439 Reg.36
s.36, amended: SI 2008/912 Sch.1 para.20
s.36, applied: SI 2008/1184 Reg.20, SI 2008/2439 Reg.36
s.36A, applied: SI 2008/1184 Reg.20, SI 2008/2439 Reg.36
s.37, amended: SI 2008/912 Sch.1 para.20, SI 2008/2833 Sch.3 para.205
s.37, applied: SI 2008/1184 Reg.20, SI 2008/2439 Reg.36
s.37A, amended: SI 2008/2833 Sch.3 para.206
s.37A, applied: SI 2008/1184 Reg.20, SI 2008/2439 Reg.36
s.38, amended: SI 2008/912 Sch.1 para.20, SI 2008/2833 Sch.3 para.207
s.38, applied: SI 2008/1184 Reg.20, SI 2008/2439 Reg.36
s.38A, amended: SI 2008/2833 Sch.3 para.208
s.38A, applied: SI 2008/1184 Reg.20, SI 2008/2439 Reg.36
s.38B, applied: SI 2008/1184 Reg.20, SI 2008/2439 Reg.36
s.39, amended: SI 2008/912 Sch.1 para.20
s.39, applied: SI 2008/1184 Reg.20, SI 2008/2439 Reg.36
s.40, amended: SI 2008/912 Sch.1 para.20, SI 2008/2833 Sch.3 para.209
s.40, applied: SI 2008/1184 Reg.20, SI 2008/2439 Reg.36
s.41, amended: SI 2008/912 Sch.1 para.20, SI 2008/2833 Sch.3 para.210
s.41, applied: SI 2008/1184 Reg.20, SI 2008/2439 Reg.36
s.41A, applied: SI 2008/1184 Reg.20, SI 2008/2439 Reg.36
s.42, amended: SI 2008/912 Sch.1 para.20
s.42, applied: SI 2008/1184 Reg.20, SI 2008/2439 Reg.36

CAP.

2004–cont.

28. Domestic Violence, Crime and Victims Act 2004–*cont.*

s.42A, applied: SI 2008/1184 Reg.20, SI 2008/2439 Reg.36
s.43, amended: SI 2008/912 Sch.1 para.20, SI 2008/2833 Sch.3 para.211
s.43, applied: SI 2008/1184 Reg.20, SI 2008/2439 Reg.36
s.43A, amended: SI 2008/2833 Sch.3 para.212
s.43A, applied: SI 2008/1184 Reg.20, SI 2008/2439 Reg.36
s.44, amended: SI 2008/912 Sch.1 para.20, SI 2008/2833 Sch.3 para.213
s.44, applied: SI 2008/1184 Reg.20, SI 2008/2439 Reg.36
s.44A, amended: SI 2008/2833 Sch.3 para.214
s.44A, applied: SI 2008/1184 Reg.20, SI 2008/2439 Reg.36
s.44B, applied: SI 2008/1184 Reg.20, SI 2008/2439 Reg.36
s.54, amended: SI 2008/912 Sch.1 para.20
s.60, enabling: SI 2008/3065
Sch.9 para.17, amended: SI 2008/2833 Sch.3 para.215
Sch.9 para.19, repealed: SI 2008/960 Sch.3
Sch.9 para.25A, added: SI 2008/912 Sch.1 para.20

30. Human Tissue Act 2004

applied: SI 2008/2841 Reg.16, Reg.24
s.1, amended: 2008 c.22 Sch.7 para.22
s.14, amended: 2008 c.22 Sch.7 para.23
s.16, applied: SI 2008/2841 Reg.24
s.16, enabling: SI 2008/3067
s.52, applied: SI 2008/3067
s.52, enabling: SI 2008/3067
s.54, amended: 2008 c.22 Sch.7 para.24

31. Children Act 2004

Commencement Orders: SI 2008/752 Art.2; SI 2008/1904 Art.2
referred to: SI 2008/1206 Sch.2 para.2, SI 2008/2436 Sch.2 para.2.1
s.10, amended: 2008 c.25 Sch.1 para.83
s.10, applied: 2008 c.25 s.85
s.10, referred to: 2008 c.23 s.7
s.11, amended: 2008 c.25 Sch.1 para.84
s.12, applied: SI 2008/1722 Reg.8
s.13, amended: 2008 c.25 Sch.1 para.85
s.20, amended: 2008 c.14 Sch.5 para.78, SI 2008/912 Sch.1 para.27
s.26, referred to: SI 2008/170 Reg.7
s.47, amended: 2008 c.23 s.35
s.49, amended: 2008 c.23 Sch.1 para.17
s.67, enabling: SI 2008/752, SI 2008/1904
Sch.5 Part 1, enabling: SI 2008/1904
Sch.5 Part 3, enabling: SI 2008/1904

32. Armed Forces (Pensions and Compensation) Act 2004

s.1, enabling: SI 2008/39, SI 2008/229, SI 2008/2160, SI 2008/2942

CAP.

2004–cont.

32. Armed Forces (Pensions and Compensation) Act 2004–*cont.*
s.7, repealed (in part): SI 2008/2833 Sch.3 para.228
s.10, enabling: SI 2008/39, SI 2008/2160, SI 2008/2942

33. Civil Partnership Act 2004
applied: SI 2008/168 Sch.1 para.1, SI 2008/3082 Sch.1 para.1
s.6A, amended: SI 2008/678 Sch.2 para.14
s.6A, applied: SI 2008/678 Sch.1 para.14
s.34, amended: SI 2008/678 Sch.2 para.14
s.34, applied: SI 2008/678 Sch.1 para.14
s.35, amended: SI 2008/678 Sch.2 para.14
s.35, applied: SI 2008/678 Sch.1 para.14
s.36, amended: SI 2008/678 Sch.2 para.14
s.36, applied: SI 2008/678 Sch.1 para.14
s.246, applied: SI 2008/1205 Reg.7, SI 2008/1315 Reg.3, SI 2008/1858 Reg.10, SI 2008/2440 Reg.6
Sch.5, applied: 2008 c.30 s.109, s.118
Sch.5 Part 1, applied: SI 2008/1582 Sch.4 para.1, SI 2008/3170 Sch.5 para.1, Sch.6 para.1
Sch.5 Part 2 para.6, applied: SI 2008/3170 Sch.5 para.1
Sch.5 Part 2 para.7, applied: SI 2008/3170 Sch.5 para.1
Sch.5 Part 4A para.19A, added: 2008 c.30 Sch.6 para.15
Sch.5 Part 4A para.19B, added: 2008 c.30 Sch.6 para.15
Sch.5 Part 4A para.19C, added: 2008 c.30 Sch.6 para.15
Sch.5 Part 4A para.19D, added: 2008 c.30 Sch.6 para.15
Sch.5 Part 4A para.19E, added: 2008 c.30 Sch.6 para.15
Sch.5 Part 4A para.19F, added: 2008 c.30 Sch.6 para.15
Sch.5 Part 5 para.20, amended: 2008 c.30 Sch.6 para.16, Sch.11 Part 4
Sch.5 Part 5 para.21, amended: 2008 c.30 Sch.6 para.16, Sch.11 Part 4
Sch.5 Part 5 para.22, amended: 2008 c.30 Sch.6 para.16
Sch.5 Part 5 para.23, amended: 2008 c.30 Sch.6 para.16, Sch.11 Part 4
Sch.5 Part 6, applied: SI 2008/1582 Sch.4 para.1, SI 2008/3170 Sch.6 para.1
Sch.5 Part 7, applied: SI 2008/1582 Sch.4 para.1, SI 2008/3170 Sch.6 para.1
Sch.5 Part 7 para.30, amended: 2008 c.30 Sch.11 Part 4
Sch.5 Part 7 para.30, repealed (in part): 2008 c.30 Sch.6 para.17
Sch.5 Part 7 para.34A, added: 2008 c.30 Sch.6 para.17
Sch.5 Part 7 para.34B, added: 2008 c.30 Sch.6 para.17

CAP.

2004–cont.

33. Civil Partnership Act 2004–*cont.*
Sch.5 Part 7 para.37, amended: 2008 c.30 Sch.6 para.17
Sch.5 Part 11, amended: 2008 c.30 Sch.6 para.18
Sch.5 Part 11 para.50, amended: 2008 c.30 Sch.6 para.18, Sch.11 Part 4
Sch.5 Part 11 para.53, amended: 2008 c.30 Sch.6 para.18
Sch.5 Part 11 para.54, amended: 2008 c.30 Sch.6 para.18
Sch.5 Part 11 para.57, amended: 2008 c.30 Sch.6 para.18
Sch.5 Part 11 para.58, amended: 2008 c.30 Sch.6 para.18
Sch.5 Part 14 para.79A, added: 2008 c.30 Sch.6 para.19
Sch.6, applied: SI 2008/1052 Sch.1
Sch.7, applied: 2008 c.30 s.109, s.118
Sch.7 Part 1 para.9, amended: 2008 c.30 Sch.6 para.20
Sch.7 Part 1 para.10, amended: 2008 c.30 Sch.6 para.20, Sch.11 Part 4
Sch.7 Part 1 para.14, amended: 2008 c.30 Sch.6 para.20
Sch.9 Part 2 para.18, repealed: 2008 c.17 Sch.16
Sch.9 Part 2 para.23, repealed: 2008 c.17 Sch.16
Sch.11 Part 2 para.2, applied: 2008 c.30 s.110
Sch.24 Part 1 para.3, repealed: 2008 c.6 Sch.8

34. Housing Act 2004
Commencement Orders: SI 2008/898 Art.2
Part 2, applied: 2008 c.13 Sch.3, SI 2008/254 Reg.3
Part 3, applied: 2008 c.13 Sch.3, SI 2008/254 Reg.3
Part 4, applied: 2008 c.13 Sch.3
Part 4 c.1, applied: SI 2008/254 Reg.3
Part 5, applied: 2008 c.13 Sch.3, 2008 c.17 s.290
s.72, applied: SI 2008/254 Reg.3
s.73, applied: SI 2008/254 Reg.2, Reg.3
s.74, applied: SI 2008/254 Reg.3
s.74, enabling: SI 2008/254
s.95, applied: SI 2008/254 Reg.3
s.96, applied: SI 2008/254 Reg.2, Reg.3
s.97, applied: SI 2008/254 Reg.3
s.97, enabling: SI 2008/254
s.119, applied: SI 2008/254 Reg.3
s.155, applied: SI 2008/898 Art.2
s.156, applied: SI 2008/898 Art.2
s.157, applied: SI 2008/898 Art.2
s.158, applied: SI 2008/898 Art.2
s.159, applied: SI 2008/898 Art.2
s.163, enabling: SI 2008/572, SI 2008/1266, SI 2008/2363, SI 2008/3107
s.233, applied: SI 2008/2345 Art.2
s.233, referred to: SI 2008/2345
s.233, enabling: SI 2008/2345

CAP.

2004–*cont.*

34. Housing Act 2004–*cont.*

s.250, applied: SI 2008/572, SI 2008/1266, SI 2008/2363, SI 2008/3107

s.250, enabling: SI 2008/572, SI 2008/1266, SI 2008/3107

s.270, enabling: SI 2008/898

Sch.14 para.4, applied: SI 2008/2346 Reg.2

Sch.14 para.4, referred to: SI 2008/2345 Art.2

Sch.14 para.4, enabling: SI 2008/2346

35. Pensions Act 2004

Commencement Orders: SI 2008/627 Art.2; SI 2008/1882 Art.2

applied: SI 2008/239 Reg.25, SI 2008/576 Sch.4 para.5, SSI 2008/228 Reg.22

referred to: 2008 c.30 s.146

Part 1, applied: SI 2008/731 Reg.16

Part 2 c.3, applied: 2008 c.30 Sch.5 para.3

Part 3, see *British Vita Unlimited v British Vita Pension Fund Trustees Ltd* [2007] EWHC 953 (Ch), [2008] 1 All E.R. 37 (Ch D), Warren, J.

Part 3, applied: SI 2008/2546 Sch.3 para.5

Part 3, disapplied: SI 2008/2546 Sch.3 para.11

s.5, amended: 2008 c.30 s.65

s.9, applied: SI 2008/731 Reg.16

s.38, amended: 2008 c.30 Sch.9 para.2, Sch.9 para.7, Sch.9 para.8, Sch.11 Part 6

s.38, applied: SI 2008/2546 Sch.3 para.7

s.38, disapplied: SI 2008/2546 Sch.3 para.11

s.38A, added: 2008 c.30 Sch.9 para.2

s.38A, referred to: 2008 c.30 s.127

s.38B, added: 2008 c.30 Sch.9 para.2

s.38B, referred to: 2008 c.30 s.127

s.39, amended: 2008 c.30 Sch.9 para.8

s.39A, added: 2008 c.30 Sch.9 para.9

s.39B, added: 2008 c.30 Sch.9 para.9

s.43, applied: SI 2008/2546 Sch.3 para.7

s.43, disapplied: SI 2008/2546 Sch.3 para.11

s.43, referred to: 2008 c.30 Sch.9 para.15

s.43A, added: 2008 c.30 Sch.9 para.10

s.43B, added: 2008 c.30 Sch.9 para.10

s.44, amended: 2008 c.30 Sch.9 para.14

s.52, disapplied: SI 2008/2546 Sch.3 para.11

s.69, enabling: SI 2008/731

s.72, amended: 2008 c.30 s.61

s.72, applied: 2008 c.30 s.40, s.41

s.74, amended: 2008 c.30 s.61

s.75, amended: 2008 c.30 s.61

s.76, amended: 2008 c.30 s.61

s.80, amended: 2008 c.30 s.48, Sch.11 Part 1

s.82, amended: 2008 c.30 s.62, s.64

s.84, amended: 2008 c.30 s.83

s.88, substituted: 2008 c.30 s.62

s.90, amended: 2008 c.30 Sch.9 para.3

s.91, enabling: SI 2008/1882

s.93, enabling: SI 2008/731

s.96, amended: 2008 c.30 Sch.9 para.4

s.102, amended: 2008 c.30 s.44

CAP.

2004–*cont.*

35. Pensions Act 2004–*cont.*

s.103, amended: 2008 c.30 s.44

s.117, applied: SI 2008/910

s.117, enabling: SI 2008/910

s.117A, added: 2008 c.30 Sch.10 para.3

s.126, applied: SI 2008/3069 Reg.3

s.126, enabling: SI 2008/731, SI 2008/1810

s.127, applied: SI 2008/3069 Reg.3

s.162, applied: SI 2008/664 Reg.2

s.168A, added: 2008 c.30 s.121

s.173, amended: 2008 c.30 s.123, Sch.10 para.4, Sch.11 Part 4

s.173, enabling: SI 2008/664

s.177, applied: SI 2008/911 Art.2

s.178, applied: SI 2008/217, SI 2008/217 Art.2, SI 2008/911

s.178, enabling: SI 2008/217, SI 2008/911

s.181A, added: 2008 c.30 Sch.10 para.5

s.188, amended: 2008 c.30 Sch.10 para.6

s.189A, added: 2008 c.30 Sch.10 para.7

s.209, amended: 2008 c.30 Sch.10 para.8

s.212A, added: SI 2008/817 Art.8

s.222, see *British Vita Unlimited v British Vita Pension Fund Trustees Ltd* [2007] EWHC 953 (Ch), [2008] 1 All E.R. 37 (Ch D), Warren, J.

s.224, see *British Vita Unlimited v British Vita Pension Fund Trustees Ltd* [2007] EWHC 953 (Ch), [2008] 1 All E.R. 37 (Ch D), Warren, J.

s.225, see *British Vita Unlimited v British Vita Pension Fund Trustees Ltd* [2007] EWHC 953 (Ch), [2008] 1 All E.R. 37 (Ch D), Warren, J.

s.231, amended: 2008 c.30 s.132

s.232, enabling: SI 2008/731

s.242, applied: 2008 c.30 Sch.1 para.1

s.253, applied: SI 2008/624 Reg.2

s.253, enabling: SI 2008/624

s.257, applied: SI 2008/2546 Art.27

s.258, applied: SI 2008/2546 Art.27

s.286, amended: 2008 c.30 s.124, Sch.11 Part 5

s.286, enabling: SI 2008/1432, SI 2008/1903, SI 2008/3069

s.286A, added: 2008 c.30 s.125

s.293, referred to: SI 2008/239 Reg.83

s.306, amended: 2008 c.30 Sch.9 para.11

s.307, enabling: SI 2008/731

s.314, applied: 2008 c.13 Sch.7

s.315, enabling: SI 2008/624, SI 2008/627, SI 2008/664, SI 2008/731, SI 2008/909, SI 2008/910, SI 2008/911, SI 2008/1432, SI 2008/1810, SI 2008/1903, SI 2008/3069

s.316, amended: 2008 c.30 s.124, s.125, Sch.9 para.5, Sch.9 para.12

s.316, applied: SI 2008/909, SI 2008/910, SI 2008/911, SI 2008/1432, SI 2008/1903

CAP.

2004–cont.

35. Pensions Act 2004–*cont.*

s.317, applied: SI 2008/624, SI 2008/664, SI 2008/731, SI 2008/910, SI 2008/1432, SI 2008/1810, SI 2008/1903

s.318, enabling: SI 2008/624, SI 2008/664, SI 2008/731, SI 2008/910, SI 2008/1432, SI 2008/1810, SI 2008/1903, SI 2008/3069

s.321, repealed: 2008 c.30 Sch.11 Part 6

s.322, enabling: SI 2008/627

s.323, amended: 2008 c.30 s.63, Sch.10 para.9

Sch.1 Part 4 para.21, amended: 2008 c.30 s.133

Sch.1 Part 4 para.21, substituted: 2008 c.30 s.133

Sch.1 Part 4 para.21, enabling: SI 2008/731

Sch.1 Part 5 para.28, repealed: 2008 c.30 s.133, Sch.11 Part 6

Sch.2 Part 2 para.9, amended: 2008 c.30 s.131

Sch.2 Part 4 para.30A, added: 2008 c.30 Sch.9 para.13

Sch.2 Part 4 para.33A, added: 2008 c.30 Sch.9 para.13

Sch.4 Part 2 para.7, amended: 2008 c.30 s.44

Sch.4 Part 3 para.13, amended: 2008 c.30 s.44

Sch.5 Part 3 para.18, amended: 2008 c.30 s.123

Sch.7, applied: 2008 c.30 Sch.5 para.3

Sch.7 para.3, amended: 2008 c.30 Sch.8 para.2

Sch.7 para.5, amended: 2008 c.30 Sch.8 para.3

Sch.7 para.11, amended: 2008 c.30 Sch.8 para.4

Sch.7 para.12, amended: 2008 c.30 Sch.2 para.5

Sch.7 para.13, amended: 2008 c.30 Sch.8 para.5

Sch.7 para.14, amended: 2008 c.30 Sch.8 para.6

Sch.7 para.15, amended: 2008 c.30 Sch.8 para.7

Sch.7 para.17, amended: 2008 c.30 Sch.2 para.6

Sch.7 para.18, amended: 2008 c.30 Sch.8 para.8

Sch.7 para.19, amended: 2008 c.30 Sch.8 para.9

Sch.7 para.21, amended: 2008 c.30 Sch.8 para.10, Sch.8 para.11

Sch.7 para.23C, added: 2008 c.30 Sch.8 para.14

Sch.7 para.25, amended: 2008 c.30 Sch.8 para.12

Sch.7 para.25A, added: 2008 c.30 Sch.8 para.13

Sch.7 para.25B, added: 2008 c.30 Sch.8 para.14

CAP.

2004–cont.

35. Pensions Act 2004–*cont.*

Sch.7 para.25C, added: 2008 c.30 Sch.8 para.14

Sch.7 para.25D, added: 2008 c.30 Sch.8 para.14

Sch.7 para.25E, added: 2008 c.30 Sch.8 para.14

Sch.7 para.25F, added: 2008 c.30 Sch.8 para.14

Sch.7 para.26, applied: 2008 c.30 Sch.5 para.18, SI 2008/909 Art.2

Sch.7 para.26, enabling: SI 2008/909

Sch.7 para.27, enabling: SI 2008/909

Sch.7 para.28, applied: 2008 c.30 Sch.5 para.17

Sch.7 para.29, amended: 2008 c.30 Sch.2 para.7

Sch.7 para.33, substituted: 2008 c.30 Sch.8 para.15

Sch.7 para.34, amended: 2008 c.30 Sch.8 para.16

Sch.7 para.35, amended: 2008 c.30 Sch.8 para.17, Sch.8 para.18

Sch.10 para.4, added: 2008 c.30 s.63

36. Civil Contingencies Act 2004

applied: SI 2008/2867 Reg.11

s.2, referred to: SI 2008/2867 Reg.11

s.13, enabling: SI 2008/3012

s.17, applied: SI 2008/3012

Sch.1 Part 1 para.6, substituted: SI 2008/3012 Art.2

2005

2. Prevention of Terrorism Act 2005

see *Secretary of State for the Home Department v F* [2008] EWCA Civ 1148, Times, October 29, 2008 (CA (Civ Div)), Sir Anthony Clarke, M.R.

s.1, amended: 2008 c.28 s.79

s.1, referred to: SI 2008/559 Art.2

s.2, see *Secretary of State for the Home Department v E* [2007] UKHL 47, [2008] 1 A.C. 499 (HL), Lord Bingham of Cornhill

s.2, referred to: SI 2008/559 Art.2

s.3, see *Secretary of State for the Home Department v AF* [2008] EWCA Civ 117, [2008] 1 W.L.R. 2528 (CA (Civ Div)), Sir Anthony Clarke, M.R.; see *Secretary of State for the Home Department v JJ* [2007] UKHL 45, [2008] 1 A.C. 385 (HL), Lord Bingham of Cornhill; see *Secretary of State for the Home Department v MB* [2007] UKHL 46, [2008] 1 A.C. 440 (HL), Lord Bingham of Cornhill

s.3, amended: 2008 c.28 s.80, Sch.9 Part 5

s.3, referred to: SI 2008/559 Art.2

s.3, repealed (in part): 2008 c.28 Sch.9 Part 5

s.4, referred to: SI 2008/559 Art.2

s.5, referred to: SI 2008/559 Art.2

s.6, referred to: SI 2008/559 Art.2

CAP.

2005–*cont.*

2. Prevention of Terrorism Act 2005–*cont.*
s.7, referred to: SI 2008/559 Art.2
s.7A, added: 2008 c.28 s.78
s.7A, applied: 2008 c.28 s.1
s.7A, referred to: SI 2008/559 Art.2
s.7B, added: 2008 c.28 s.78
s.7B, applied: 2008 c.28 s.1
s.7B, referred to: SI 2008/559 Art.2
s.7C, added: 2008 c.28 s.78
s.7C, applied: 2008 c.28 s.1
s.7C, referred to: SI 2008/559 Art.2
s.8, see *Secretary of State for the Home Department v E* [2007] UKHL 47, [2008] 1 A.C. 499 (HL), Lord Bingham of Cornhill
s.8, referred to: SI 2008/559 Art.2
s.8, repealed (in part): 2008 c.28 Sch.9 Part 5
s.9, see *R. v Rahman (Abdul)* [2008] EWCA Crim 1465, [2008] 4 All E.R. 661 (CA (Crim Div)), Lord Phillips of Worth Matravers, L.C.J.
s.9, amended: 2008 c.28 s.78
s.9, referred to: SI 2008/559 Art.2
s.13, applied: SI 2008/559
s.13, enabling: SI 2008/559
s.14, applied: SI 2008/559
Sch.1 para.4, see *Secretary of State for the Home Department v MB* [2007] UKHL 46, [2008] 1 A.C. 440 (HL), Lord Bingham of Cornhill
Sch.1 para.5, amended: 2008 c.28 s.81, Sch.9 Part 5

4. Constitutional Reform Act 2005
Commencement Orders: SI 2008/2597 Art.2
s.3, repealed (in part): SI 2008/2833 Sch.3 para.217
s.8, referred to: SI 2008/2597 Art.2
s.59, referred to: SI 2008/1863 Art.13
s.94B, amended: SI 2008/2833 Sch.3 para.218
s.109, referred to: SI 2008/609 Reg.9, SI 2008/2705 r.11
s.115, enabling: SI 2008/2098
s.118, applied: SI 2008/2700, SI 2008/2700 Art.2
s.118, enabling: SI 2008/2700
s.120, applied: SI 2008/2700
s.120, enabling: SI 2008/2098
s.121, applied: SI 2008/2700
s.121, enabling: SI 2008/2098
s.148, enabling: SI 2008/2597
Sch.4 Part 1 para.25, repealed: SI 2008/2833 Sch.3 para.228
Sch.4 Part 1 para.28, repealed (in part): SI 2008/2833 Sch.3 para.228
Sch.4 Part 1 para.221, repealed: SI 2008/2833 Sch.3 para.228
Sch.4 Part 1 para.273, repealed (in part): SI 2008/2833 Sch.3 para.228
Sch.4 Part 1 para.274, repealed (in part): SI 2008/2833 Sch.3 para.228

CAP.

2005–*cont.*

4. Constitutional Reform Act 2005–*cont.*
Sch.7 para.4, amended: 2008 c.14 Sch.15 Part 2, SI 2008/2833 Sch.3 para.219
Sch.9 Part 1 para.13, referred to: SI 2008/1586 Sch.2 para.14
Sch.9 Part 1 para.16, applied: SI 2008/755 Art.15
Sch.9 Part 1 para.16, referred to: SI 2008/1586 Sch.2 para.14, SI 2008/1863 Art.43
Sch.9 Part 1 para.33, applied: SI 2008/755 Art.15
Sch.9 Part 1 para.33, referred to: SI 2008/1586 Sch.2 para.14, SI 2008/1863 Art.62
Sch.9 Part 1 para.42, repealed (in part): 2008 c.26 Sch.7 Part 3
Sch.11 Part 3 para.6, amended: 2008 c.14 Sch.15 Part 2
Sch.14 Part 1, amended: SI 2008/2833 Sch.3 para.220
Sch.14 Part 3, amended: SI 2008/2833 Sch.3 para.220

5. Income Tax (Trading and Other Income) Act 2005
Part 2, applied: SI 2008/794 Reg.112
Part 4 c.2, applied: 2008 c.9 s.39
Part 6 c.7, applied: SI 2008/562 Reg.21
s.25, amended: SI 2008/954 Art.36
s.50, amended: 2008 c.9 s.77
s.50, applied: 2008 c.9 s.77
s.55A, added: 2008 c.9 s.73
s.148A, applied: 2008 c.9 Sch.20 para.11
s.148A, disapplied: 2008 c.9 Sch.20 para.11
s.148B, disapplied: 2008 c.9 Sch.20 para.11
s.148C, applied: 2008 c.9 Sch.20 para.11
s.148FA, added: 2008 c.9 Sch.20 para.10
s.148FB, added: 2008 c.9 Sch.20 para.10
s.148FB, referred to: 2008 c.9 Sch.20 para.10
s.148FC, added: 2008 c.9 Sch.20 para.10
s.172A, added: 2008 c.9 Sch.15 para.2
s.172B, added: 2008 c.9 Sch.15 para.2
s.172C, added: 2008 c.9 Sch.15 para.2
s.172D, added: 2008 c.9 Sch.15 para.2
s.172E, added: 2008 c.9 Sch.15 para.2
s.172F, added: 2008 c.9 Sch.15 para.2
s.173, amended: 2008 c.9 Sch.15 para.3
s.174, amended: 2008 c.9 Sch.15 para.3
s.174, referred to: 2008 c.18 Sch.13 para.34
s.175, amended: 2008 c.9 Sch.15 para.3
s.176, amended: 2008 c.9 Sch.15 para.3
s.177, amended: 2008 c.9 Sch.15 para.3
s.178, amended: 2008 c.9 Sch.15 para.3
s.179, amended: 2008 c.9 Sch.15 para.3
s.180, amended: 2008 c.9 Sch.15 para.3
s.181, amended: 2008 c.9 Sch.15 para.3
s.182, amended: 2008 c.9 Sch.15 para.3
s.183, amended: 2008 c.9 Sch.15 para.3
s.184, amended: 2008 c.9 Sch.15 para.3
s.185, amended: 2008 c.9 Sch.15 para.3
s.186, amended: 2008 c.9 Sch.15 para.3
s.259, amended: SI 2008/954 Art.37

CAP.

2005–cont.

5. **Income Tax (Trading and Other Income) Act 2005**–*cont.*
s.260, amended: 2008 c.9 Sch.7 para.47
s.260, repealed (in part): 2008 c.9 Sch.7 para.47
s.269, repealed (in part): 2008 c.9 Sch.7 para.48
s.272, amended: 2008 c.9 s.73
s.301, amended: 2008 c.9 Sch.39 para.51
s.302, amended: 2008 c.9 Sch.39 para.52
s.357, repealed: 2008 c.9 Sch.7 para.49
s.358, repealed: 2008 c.9 Sch.7 para.49
s.359, repealed: 2008 c.9 Sch.7 para.49
s.360, repealed: 2008 c.9 Sch.7 para.49
s.360A, repealed: 2008 c.9 Sch.7 para.49
s.382, amended: 2008 c.9 Sch.12 para.2
s.383, amended: 2008 c.9 Sch.12 para.2
s.384, amended: 2008 c.9 Sch.12 para.2
s.385, amended: 2008 c.9 Sch.12 para.2
s.386, amended: 2008 c.9 Sch.12 para.2
s.387, amended: 2008 c.9 Sch.12 para.2
s.388, amended: 2008 c.9 Sch.12 para.2
s.389, amended: 2008 c.9 Sch.12 para.2
s.390, amended: 2008 c.9 Sch.12 para.2
s.391, amended: 2008 c.9 Sch.12 para.2
s.392, amended: 2008 c.9 Sch.12 para.2
s.393, amended: 2008 c.9 Sch.12 para.2
s.394, amended: 2008 c.9 Sch.12 para.2
s.395, amended: 2008 c.9 Sch.12 para.2
s.396, amended: 2008 c.9 Sch.12 para.2
s.397, amended: 2008 c.9 Sch.12 para.2, Sch.12 para.3
s.397A, added: 2008 c.9 Sch.12 para.4
s.397A, amended: 2008 c.9 Sch.12 para.2
s.397B, added: 2008 c.9 Sch.12 para.4
s.397B, amended: 2008 c.9 Sch.12 para.2
s.397C, added: 2008 c.9 Sch.12 para.4
s.397C, amended: 2008 c.9 Sch.12 para.2
s.398, amended: 2008 c.9 Sch.12 para.2, Sch.12 para.5
s.399, amended: 2008 c.9 Sch.12 para.2, Sch.12 para.6
s.400, amended: 2008 c.9 Sch.12 para.2
s.401, amended: 2008 c.9 Sch.12 para.2
s.403, amended: 2008 c.9 Sch.12 para.18
s.406, amended: 2008 c.9 Sch.12 para.19
s.407, amended: 2008 c.9 Sch.12 para.20
s.408, amended: 2008 c.9 Sch.12 para.21
s.465A, amended: 2008 c.9 Sch.1 para.51
s.466, amended: 2008 c.9 Sch.1 para.52
s.467, amended: 2008 c.9 Sch.1 para.53, Sch.14 para.11
s.469, amended: 2008 c.9 Sch.14 para.12
s.473, repealed (in part): 2008 c.9 Sch.14 para.17
s.476, amended: 2008 c.9 Sch.17 para.27
s.486, repealed: 2008 c.9 Sch.14 para.13
s.501, amended: 2008 c.9 Sch.14 para.14
s.501, repealed (in part): 2008 c.9 Sch.14 para.14

CAP.

2005–cont.

5. **Income Tax (Trading and Other Income) Act 2005**–*cont.*
s.530, amended: 2008 c.9 Sch.1 para.54
s.530, repealed (in part): 2008 c.9 Sch.1 para.54
s.535, amended: 2008 c.9 Sch.1 para.55
s.536, amended: 2008 c.9 Sch.1 para.56
s.537, amended: 2008 c.9 Sch.1 para.57
s.539, amended: 2008 c.9 Sch.1 para.58
s.541B, repealed (in part): 2008 c.9 Sch.14 para.15
s.629, applied: SI 2008/2682 Reg.4
s.669, amended: 2008 c.9 Sch.1 para.59
s.679, repealed (in part): 2008 c.9 Sch.1 para.60
s.680, amended: 2008 c.9 Sch.1 para.61
s.680A, amended: 2008 c.9 Sch.1 para.62
s.680A, repealed (in part): 2008 c.9 Sch.1 para.62
s.685A, amended: 2008 c.9 s.67
s.688, amended: 2008 c.9 Sch.12 para.22
s.694, enabling: SI 2008/704, SI 2008/1934, SI 2008/3025
s.695, enabling: SI 2008/704, SI 2008/1934, SI 2008/3025
s.696, enabling: SI 2008/704, SI 2008/1934, SI 2008/3025
s.697, enabling: SI 2008/704, SI 2008/1934, SI 2008/3025
s.698, enabling: SI 2008/704, SI 2008/1934, SI 2008/3025
s.699, enabling: SI 2008/704, SI 2008/1934, SI 2008/3025
s.700, enabling: SI 2008/704, SI 2008/1934, SI 2008/3025
s.701, amended: 2008 c.9 s.40
s.701, enabling: SI 2008/704, SI 2008/1934, SI 2008/3025
s.720, applied: SI 2008/562 Reg.7
s.721, applied: SI 2008/562 Reg.7
s.724, enabling: SI 2008/562, SI 2008/1481
s.776, amended: 2008 c.23 s.21
s.806, amended: 2008 c.23 Sch.1 para.18, Sch.4
s.829, amended: 2008 c.9 Sch.7 para.50
s.830, amended: 2008 c.9 Sch.7 para.51, Sch.7 para.96, Sch.7 para.156, Sch.7 para.162
s.830, repealed (in part): 2008 c.9 Sch.7 para.51
s.831, applied: 2008 c.9 Sch.7 para.83, Sch.7 para.85
s.831, repealed: 2008 c.9 Sch.7 para.52
s.832, disapplied: 2008 c.9 Sch.7 para.83
s.832, substituted: 2008 c.9 Sch.7 para.53
s.832, varied: 2008 c.9 Sch.7 para.83
s.832A, disapplied: 2008 c.9 Sch.7 para.83
s.833, repealed: 2008 c.9 Sch.7 para.54
s.834, repealed: 2008 c.9 Sch.7 para.54
s.835, repealed: 2008 c.9 Sch.7 para.54
s.836, repealed: 2008 c.9 Sch.7 para.54

CAP.

2005–cont.

5. **Income Tax (Trading and Other Income) Act 2005**–*cont.*

s.837, repealed: 2008 c.9 Sch.7 para.54
s.839, repealed (in part): 2008 c.9 Sch.7 para.67
s.840, repealed (in part): 2008 c.9 Sch.7 para.68
s.840A, added: 2008 c.9 Sch.7 para.69
s.840A, amended: 2008 c.9 Sch.39 para.53
s.857, amended: 2008 c.9 Sch.7 para.70
s.858, amended: 2008 c.9 s.58
s.878, repealed (in part): 2008 c.9 Sch.7 para.71
Sch.1 Part 1 para.210, repealed: 2008 c.9 Sch.14 para.16
Sch.1 Part 1 para.211, repealed: 2008 c.9 Sch.14 para.16
Sch.1 Part 1 para.212, repealed: 2008 c.9 Sch.14 para.16
Sch.1 Part 1 para.213, repealed: 2008 c.9 Sch.14 para.16
Sch.1 Part 1 para.214, repealed: 2008 c.9 Sch.14 para.16
Sch.1 Part 1 para.215, repealed: 2008 c.9 Sch.14 para.16
Sch.1 Part 1 para.216, repealed: 2008 c.9 Sch.14 para.16
Sch.1 Part 1 para.217, repealed: 2008 c.9 Sch.14 para.16
Sch.1 Part 1 para.218, repealed: 2008 c.9 Sch.14 para.16
Sch.1 Part 1 para.219, repealed: 2008 c.9 Sch.14 para.16
Sch.1 Part 1 para.220, repealed: 2008 c.9 Sch.14 para.16
Sch.1 Part 1 para.221, repealed: 2008 c.9 Sch.14 para.16
Sch.1 Part 1 para.226, repealed: 2008 c.9 Sch.14 para.16
Sch.1 Part 1 para.227, repealed: 2008 c.9 Sch.14 para.16
Sch.1 Part 1 para.228, repealed: 2008 c.9 Sch.14 para.16
Sch.1 Part 1 para.253, applied: 2008 c.9 Sch.29 para.17
Sch.1 Part 1 para.268, repealed (in part): 2008 c.9 Sch.14 para.17
Sch.1 Part 1 para.269, repealed: 2008 c.9 Sch.14 para.17
Sch.1 Part 1 para.302, repealed: 2008 c.9 s.66
Sch.1 Part 1 para.303, repealed: 2008 c.9 s.66
Sch.1 Part 1 para.308, repealed: 2008 c.9 s.41
Sch.1 Part 1 para.309, repealed: 2008 c.9 s.41
Sch.1 Part 1 para.350, repealed (in part): 2008 c.9 s.41
Sch.1 Part 2 para.389, repealed: 2008 c.14 Sch.15 Part 7
Sch.1 Part 2 para.390, repealed: 2008 c.14 Sch.15 Part 7
Sch.1 Part 2 para.427, repealed: 2008 c.9 Sch.2 para.21

CAP.

2005–cont.

5. **Income Tax (Trading and Other Income) Act 2005**–*cont.*

Sch.1 Part 2 para.428, repealed: 2008 c.9 Sch.2 para.21
Sch.1 Part 2 para.429, repealed: 2008 c.9 Sch.7 para.79
Sch.1 Part 2 para.493, repealed: 2008 c.9 Sch.14 para.17
Sch.1 Part 2 para.552, repealed: 2008 c.9 Sch.27 para.26
Sch.1 Part 2 para.553, repealed: 2008 c.9 Sch.27 para.26
Sch.1 Part 2 para.554, repealed: 2008 c.9 Sch.27 para.26
Sch.1 Part 2 para.555, repealed: 2008 c.9 Sch.27 para.26
Sch.1 Part 2 para.556, repealed: 2008 c.9 Sch.27 para.26
Sch.1 Part 2 para.557, repealed: 2008 c.9 Sch.27 para.26
Sch.1 Part 2 para.558, repealed: 2008 c.9 Sch.27 para.26
Sch.1 Part 2 para.648, repealed: 2008 c.9 Sch.29 para.14
Sch.2 Part 5 para.86, repealed (in part): 2008 c.9 Sch.14 para.17
Sch.2 Part 11 para.150, repealed: 2008 c.9 Sch.7 para.72
Sch.2 Part 11 para.151, repealed: 2008 c.9 Sch.7 para.72
Sch.4 Part 2, amended: 2008 c.9 Sch.1 para.63, Sch.7 para.73, Sch.15 para.4

7. **Finance Act 2005**

see *LA Leisure Ltd v Revenue and Customs Commissioners* [2008] B.V.C. 2352 (V&DTr (Manchester)), IE Vellins (Chairman)
s.23, amended: 2008 c.9 Sch.2 para.12
s.26, amended: 2008 c.9 Sch.2 para.13
s.28, amended: 2008 c.9 Sch.2 para.14
s.28, repealed (in part): 2008 c.9 Sch.2 para.14
s.30, repealed (in part): 2008 c.9 Sch.2 para.15
s.31, amended: 2008 c.9 Sch.2 para.16
s.32, amended: 2008 c.9 Sch.2 para.17
s.33, repealed: 2008 c.9 Sch.2 para.18
s.41, amended: 2008 c.9 Sch.2 para.19, Sch.2 para.102
s.44, repealed (in part): 2008 c.9 Sch.2 para.21
s.54A, added: SI 2008/1821 Art.2
s.60, see *Micro Fusion 2004-1 LLP v Revenue and Customs Commissioners* [2008] S.T.C. (S.C.D.) 952 (Sp Comm), Edward Sadler
Sch.1 para.1, repealed: 2008 c.9 Sch.2 para.20
Sch.1 para.2, repealed: 2008 c.9 Sch.2 para.20
Sch.1 para.4, repealed: 2008 c.9 Sch.2 para.20

CAP.

2005–cont.

7. **Finance Act 2005**–*cont.*
Sch.1 para.7, amended: 2008 c.9 Sch.2 para.20
Sch.4 Part 2 para.52, enabling: SI 2008/3237
Sch.10 para.44, repealed: 2008 c.9 Sch.29 para.11

9. **Mental Capacity Act 2005**
see *A Local Authority v E* [2007] EWHC 2396 (Fam), [2008] 1 F.L.R. 978 (Fam Div), Sir Mark Potter (President, Fam); see *Saulle v Nouvet* [2007] EWHC 2902 (QB), [2008] LS Law Medical 201 (QBD), Andrew Edis Q.C.
applied: 2008 c.6 s.52, 2008 c.14 s.4, SI 2008/1748 Sch.3 para.2, SI 2008/2836 Art.15
referred to: SI 2008/1206 Sch.2 para.2, SI 2008/1858 Reg.3, SI 2008/2436 Sch.2 para.2.1
s.1, see *Saulle v Nouvet* [2007] EWHC 2902 (QB), [2008] LS Law Medical 201 (QBD), Andrew Edis Q.C.
s.2, see *Saulle v Nouvet* [2007] EWHC 2902 (QB), [2008] LS Law Medical 201 (QBD), Andrew Edis Q.C.
s.3, see *Local Authority X v MM* [2007] EWHC 2003 (Fam), [2008] 3 F.C.R. 788 (Fam Div), Munby, J.
s.27, amended: 2008 c.22 Sch.6 para.40
s.30, amended: 2008 c.22 Sch.7 para.25
s.35, applied: SI 2008/1184 Reg.31, SI 2008/2439 Reg.42
s.36, applied: SI 2008/1184 Reg.31, SI 2008/2439 Reg.42
s.37, applied: SI 2008/1184 Reg.31, SI 2008/1315 Reg.12, Reg.14, SI 2008/1858 Reg.16, SI 2008/2439 Reg.42
s.38, applied: SI 2008/1184 Reg.31, SI 2008/1315 Reg.12, Reg.14, SI 2008/1858 Reg.16, SI 2008/2439 Reg.42
s.39, applied: SI 2008/1184 Reg.31, SI 2008/1315 Reg.12, Reg.14, SI 2008/1858 Reg.16, SI 2008/2439 Reg.42
s.39A, applied: SI 2008/1184 Reg.31, SI 2008/1315 Reg.12, Reg.14, SI 2008/1858 Reg.16, SI 2008/2439 Reg.42
s.39B, applied: SI 2008/1184 Reg.31, SI 2008/1315 Reg.12, Reg.14, SI 2008/1858 Reg.16, SI 2008/2439 Reg.42
s.39C, applied: SI 2008/1184 Reg.31, SI 2008/1315 Reg.12, Reg.14, SI 2008/1858 Reg.16, SI 2008/2439 Reg.42
s.39D, applied: SI 2008/1184 Reg.31, SI 2008/1315 Reg.12, Reg.14, SI 2008/1858 Reg.16, SI 2008/2439 Reg.42
s.39E, applied: SI 2008/1184 Reg.31, SI 2008/2439 Reg.42
s.40, applied: SI 2008/1184 Reg.31, SI 2008/2439 Reg.42
s.41, applied: SI 2008/1184 Reg.31, SI 2008/2439 Reg.42

CAP.

2005–cont.

9. **Mental Capacity Act 2005**–*cont.*
s.45, applied: SI 2008/2705 r.16, Sch.1 para.14
s.65, applied: SI 2008/1858
s.65, enabling: SI 2008/1315, SI 2008/1858, SI 2008/2368
Sch.A1 Part 4 para.24, applied: SI 2008/1858 Reg.17
Sch.A1 Part 4 para.25, applied: SI 2008/1858 Reg.17
Sch.A1 Part 4 para.29, applied: SI 2008/1858 Reg.16
Sch.A1 Part 4 para.30, applied: SI 2008/1858 Reg.16, Reg.17
Sch.A1 Part 4 para.31, enabling: SI 2008/1858
Sch.A1 Part 4 para.33, enabling: SI 2008/1858
Sch.A1 Part 4 para.47, enabling: SI 2008/1858
Sch.A1 Part 4 para.68, applied: SI 2008/1858 Reg.17
Sch.A1 Part 4 para.69, applied: SI 2008/1858 Reg.14, Reg.19
Sch.A1 Part 4 para.70, enabling: SI 2008/1858
Sch.A1 Part 5 para.76, applied: SI 2008/1858 Reg.13, Reg.16
Sch.A1 Part 9 para.129, enabling: SI 2008/1858
Sch.A1 Part 9 para.130, enabling: SI 2008/1858
Sch.A1 Part 10 para.138, enabling: SI 2008/1315, SI 2008/2368
Sch.A1 Part 10 para.142, enabling: SI 2008/1315
Sch.A1 Part 10 para.143, enabling: SI 2008/1315, SI 2008/2368
Sch.A1 Part 10 para.144, enabling: SI 2008/1315, SI 2008/2368
Sch.A1 Part 10 para.145, enabling: SI 2008/1315
Sch.A1 Part 10 para.148, enabling: SI 2008/1315
Sch.A1 Part 10 para.149, enabling: SI 2008/1315
Sch.A1 Part 10 para.151, enabling: SI 2008/1315
Sch.A1 Part 13 para.183, applied: SI 2008/1858 Reg.17, Reg.19
Sch.A1 Part 13 para.183, enabling: SI 2008/1858

10. **Public Services Ombudsman (Wales) Act 2005**
Sch.3, amended: 2008 c.27 Sch.1 para.35

11. **Commissioners for Revenue and Customs Act 2005**
s.2, applied: SI 2008/295 Reg.3, SI 2008/296 Reg.3
s.7, applied: SI 2008/539 Art.2, Art.4
s.9, applied: SI 2008/539 Sch.1 para.1

CAP.

2005–cont.

11. Commissioners for Revenue and Customs Act 2005–*cont.*
s.25, amended: 2008 c.9 s.137
s.25A, added: 2008 c.9 s.138
s.44, amended: 2008 c.10 s.6
s.44, repealed (in part): 2008 c.24 s.9, Sch.1 Part 2
Sch.2 Part 1 para.14, repealed: 2008 c.4 Sch.28 Part 6
Sch.4 para.84, repealed: 2008 c.9 s.76
Sch.4 para.102, repealed (in part): 2008 c.9 Sch.7 para.79
Sch.4 para.104, repealed: 2008 c.9 Sch.7 para.79

12. Inquiries Act 2005
applied: 2008 c.28 s.74
s.14, applied: 2008 c.28 s.74
s.28, see *Kennedy v Lord Advocate* [2008] CSOH 21, 2008 S.L.T. 195 (OH), Lord Mackay of Drumadoon
s.32, see *Kennedy v Lord Advocate* [2008] CSOH 21, 2008 S.L.T. 195 (OH), Lord Mackay of Drumadoon
s.33, see *Kennedy v Lord Advocate* [2008] CSOH 21, 2008 S.L.T. 195 (OH), Lord Mackay of Drumadoon

13. Disability Discrimination Act 2005
referred to: SI 2008/2975 Reg.3
s.6, amended: SI 2008/1746 Reg.3
Sch.1 Part 1 para.34, repealed (in part): SI 2008/2828 Art.6

14. Railways Act 2005
applied: 2008 c.18 s.27
s.3, enabling: SSI 2008/30
s.6, applied: 2008 c.3 Sch.2 Part 2, 2008 c.5 s.1, 2008 c.8 Sch.2 Part 7
s.13, amended: 2008 c.26 Sch.4 para.66
s.19A, added: 2008 c.26 s.74
s.22, referred to: 2008 c.18 s.27
s.22, enabling: SSI 2008/30
s.23, referred to: 2008 c.18 s.27
s.24, referred to: 2008 c.18 s.27
s.25, referred to: 2008 c.18 s.27
s.26, referred to: 2008 c.18 s.27
s.27, referred to: 2008 c.18 s.27
s.28, referred to: 2008 c.18 s.27
s.29, referred to: 2008 c.18 s.27
s.30, referred to: 2008 c.18 s.27
s.31, referred to: 2008 c.18 s.27
s.33, amended: 2008 c.26 Sch.4 para.66
s.37, referred to: 2008 c.18 s.27
s.58, amended: 2008 c.26 Sch.4 para.66
Sch.3 para.1, amended: SI 2008/960 Sch.3
Sch.3 para.2, applied: SI 2008/2323
Sch.3 para.10, amended: SI 2008/960 Sch.3
Sch.10 Part 4 para.33, repealed: 2008 c.9 Sch.2 para.70

15. Serious Organised Crime and Police Act 2005
Commencement Orders: SI 2008/306 Art.2; SI 2008/697 Art.2; SI 2008/1325 Art.2

CAP.

2005–cont.

15. Serious Organised Crime and Police Act 2005–*cont.*
see *DPP v Haw* [2007] EWHC 1931 (Admin), [2008] 1 W.L.R. 379 (DC), Lord Phillips, L.C.J.; see *Khan v Commissioner of Police of the Metropolis* [2008] EWCA Civ 723, Times, June 16, 2008 (CA (Civ Div)), Pill, L.J.
Part 4, applied: 2008 c.13 Sch.3
s.33, applied: SI 2008/1908 Art.2
s.33, enabling: SI 2008/1908
s.71, see *R. v P* [2007] EWCA Crim 2290, [2008] 2 All E.R. 6684 (CA (Crim Div)), Sir Igor Judge (President, QB)
s.73, see *R. v Z* [2007] EWCA Crim 1473, [2008] 1 Cr. App. R. (S.) 60 (CA (Crim Div)), Thomas, L.J.
s.74, see *R. v P* [2007] EWCA Crim 2290, [2008] 2 All E.R. 6684 (CA (Crim Div)), Sir Igor Judge (President, QB); see *R. v Z* [2007] EWCA Crim 1473, [2008] 1 Cr. App. R. (S.) 60 (CA (Crim Div)), Thomas, L.J.
s.75, see *R. v P* [2007] EWCA Crim 2290, [2008] 2 All E.R. 6684 (CA (Crim Div)), Sir Igor Judge (President, QB)
s.76, see *R. v Adams (Terrance)* [2008] EWCA Crim 914, [2008] 4 All E.R. 574 (CA (Crim Div)), Latham, L.J.
s.134, see *DPP v Haw* [2007] EWHC 1931 (Admin), [2008] 1 W.L.R. 379 (DC), Lord Phillips, L.C.J.
s.172, applied: SI 2008/1908
s.173, enabling: SI 2008/574
s.178, enabling: SI 2008/306, SI 2008/697, SI 2008/1325

16. Clean Neighbourhoods and Environment Act 2005
Commencement Orders: SI 2008/956 Art.2
Part 2, applied: 2008 c.13 Sch.3
Part 6, applied: 2008 c.13 Sch.3
Part 7, applied: 2008 c.13 Sch.3
Part 7, referred to: 2008 c.13 Sch.6
s.3, referred to: 2008 c.13 Sch.6
s.4, referred to: 2008 c.13 Sch.6
s.5, referred to: 2008 c.13 Sch.6
s.6, applied: SI 2008/663 Reg.3
s.6, referred to: 2008 c.13 Sch.6
s.6, enabling: SI 2008/663
s.7, referred to: 2008 c.13 Sch.6
s.9, referred to: SI 2008/663(g)
s.54, enabling: SI 2008/314
s.59, applied: SI 2008/663 Reg.4
s.59, enabling: SI 2008/663
s.60, applied: SI 2008/663 Reg.2, Reg.3
s.60, enabling: SI 2008/663
s.61, enabling: SI 2008/663
s.66, referred to: SI 2008/663(h)
s.67, enabling: SI 2008/663
s.74, applied: SI 2008/663 Reg.2, Reg.3
s.74, enabling: SI 2008/663
s.81, referred to: SI 2008/663(i)

CAP.

2005–cont.

16. Clean Neighbourhoods and Environment Act 2005–*cont.*
s.105, amended: 2008 c.27 s.88
s.105, applied: 2008 c.27 s.88
s.108, enabling: SI 2008/956

18. Education Act 2005
Part 1 c.3, applied: SI 2008/170 Reg.4
s.5, amended: 2008 c.25 Sch.1 para.26
s.10, applied: 2008 c.25 s.75
s.11, applied: 2008 c.25 s.75
s.11A, enabling: SI 2008/1723
s.14, enabling: SI 2008/1723
s.16, enabling: SI 2008/1723
s.19, applied: SI 2008/3118
s.19, enabling: SI 2008/3118
s.28, amended: 2008 c.25 Sch.1 para.27
s.58, applied: 2008 c.25 s.75, s.97, s.110
s.59, amended: 2008 c.25 Sch.1 para.28, Sch.2
s.62, amended: 2008 c.25 Sch.1 para.29
s.102, enabling: SI 2008/3086
s.106, repealed: 2008 c.25 Sch.2
s.120, enabling: SI 2008/3086
Sch.8 para.2, repealed: 2008 c.25 Sch.2
Sch.8 para.4, repealed: 2008 c.25 Sch.2
Sch.9 para.26, repealed: 2008 c.25 Sch.2

19. Gambling Act 2005
Commencement Orders: SI 2008/1326 Art.2, Sch.1
applied: 2008 c.13 Sch.3, SI 2008/469 Reg.7, SI 2008/1330 Reg.2
referred to: 2008 c.13 Sch.6, SI 2008/469 Reg.2
Part 2, applied: SI 2008/1909 Sch.1
s.7, enabling: SI 2008/1330
s.59, applied: 2008 c.13 Sch.7
s.69, enabling: SI 2008/1803, SI 2008/3105
s.100, enabling: SI 2008/1803, SI 2008/3105
s.103, enabling: SI 2008/1803
s.104, enabling: SI 2008/1803
s.146, applied: 2008 c.13 Sch.7
s.163, applied: SI 2008/469 Reg.6
s.175, enabling: SI 2008/1327
s.331, enabling: SI 2008/19, SI 2008/2829
s.349, applied: SI 2008/2867 Reg.12
s.349, varied: SI 2008/2867 Reg.12
s.355, applied: SI 2008/1327, SI 2008/1330
s.355, enabling: SI 2008/19, SI 2008/469, SI 2008/1327, SI 2008/1330, SI 2008/1803, SI 2008/2829, SI 2008/3105
s.358, enabling: SI 2008/1326
Sch.9 para.2, enabling: SI 2008/469
Sch.9 para.4, applied: SI 2008/469 Reg.6
Sch.9 para.5, applied: SI 2008/469 Reg.6

22. Finance (No.2) Act 2005
s.7, amended: 2008 c.9 Sch.1 para.64
s.7, repealed (in part): 2008 c.9 Sch.1 para.64
s.17, enabling: SI 2008/705, SI 2008/1463, SI 2008/3159

CAP.

2005–cont.

22. Finance (No.2) Act 2005–*cont.*
s.18, enabling: SI 2008/705, SI 2008/1463, SI 2008/3159
s.23, repealed: 2008 c.9 s.41
s.59, repealed (in part): 2008 c.9 Sch.2 para.70
Sch.6 para.7, amended: 2008 c.9 Sch.22 para.18
Sch.7 para.13, repealed: 2008 c.9 Sch.22 para.19
Sch.9 para.19, repealed (in part): 2008 c.9 Sch.17 para.17
Sch.9 para.20, repealed (in part): SI 2008/381 Sch.1 Part 1

2006

2. European Union (Accessions) Act 2006
applied: SI 2008/1954

3. Equality Act 2006
see *R. (on the application of Watkins-Singh) v Aberdare Girls' High School Governors* [2008] EWHC 1865 (Admin), [2008] 3 F.C.R. 203 (QBD (Admin)), Silber, J.
Part 4, applied: SI 2008/532 Sch.1 para.4
s.14, enabling: SI 2008/1335
s.15, applied: SI 2008/1336 Art.3
s.15, disapplied: SI 2008/1335 Art.3
s.39, enabling: SI 2008/1335, SI 2008/1336
s.42, enabling: SI 2008/1336
s.45, see *R. (on the application of Watkins-Singh) v Aberdare Girls' High School Governors* [2008] EWHC 1865 (Admin), [2008] 3 F.C.R. 203 (QBD (Admin)), Silber, J.
s.49, see *R. (on the application of Watkins-Singh) v Aberdare Girls' High School Governors* [2008] EWHC 1865 (Admin), [2008] 3 F.C.R. 203 (QBD (Admin)), Silber, J.

5. Transport (Wales) Act 2006
s.7, amended: 2008 c.26 s.69
Sch.1 para.2, repealed (in part): 2008 c.26 Sch.7 Part 1
Sch.1 para.3, repealed (in part): 2008 c.26 Sch.7 Part 1
Sch.1 para.5, repealed: 2008 c.26 Sch.7 Part 1

6. Appropriation Act 2006
repealed: 2008 c.8 Sch.3

11. Terrorism Act 2006
s.1, applied: 2008 c.28 s.28, s.41
s.2, see *R. v K* [2008] EWCA Crim 185, [2008] Q.B. 827 (CA (Crim Div)), Lord Phillips of Worth Matravers, L.C.J.; see *R. v Rahman (Abdul)* [2008] EWCA Crim 1465, [2008] 4 All E.R. 661 (CA (Crim Div)), Lord Phillips of Worth Matravers, L.C.J.
s.2, applied: 2008 c.28 s.28, s.41
s.5, applied: 2008 c.28 s.28, s.41
s.6, applied: 2008 c.28 s.28, s.41

CAP.

2006–cont.

11. Terrorism Act 2006–*cont.*
s.7, amended: 2008 c.28 s.38
s.8, applied: 2008 c.28 s.28, s.41
s.9, applied: 2008 c.28 s.28, s.41
s.10, applied: 2008 c.28 s.28, s.41
s.11, applied: 2008 c.28 s.28, s.41
s.11A, added: 2008 c.28 s.38
s.14, repealed: 2008 c.4 Sch.28 Part 5
s.17, applied: 2008 c.28 s.41
s.25, applied: SI 2008/1745
s.25, disapplied: SI 2008/1745 Art.2
s.25, enabling: SI 2008/1745
s.28, applied: 2008 c.28 s.1
Sch.1, referred to: 2008 c.4 Sch.26 para.79
Sch.1 para.6, amended: 2008 c.4 Sch.26 para.79
Sch.1 para.6A, added: 2008 c.4 Sch.26 para.79

12. London Olympic Games and Paralympic Games Act 2006
applied: 2008 c.13 Sch.3
s.5, applied: 2008 c.18 Sch.7 para.36

13. Immigration, Asylum and Nationality Act 2006
Commencement Orders: SI 2008/310 Art.2, Art.3, Art.4, Art.5
s.2, varied: SI 2008/680 Art.5, Art.20
s.4, applied: SI 2008/310 Art.4
s.4, disapplied: SI 2008/310 Art.4
s.5, varied: SI 2008/680 Art.5, Art.20
s.6, varied: SI 2008/680 Art.5, Art.20
s.7, varied: SI 2008/680 Art.5, Art.20, Sch.9 para.1
s.9, varied: SI 2008/680 Art.5, Art.20
s.11, varied: SI 2008/680 Art.5, Art.20, Sch.9 para.2
s.15, applied: SI 2008/132 Art.2, SI 2008/2077 Art.3
s.15, disapplied: SI 2008/310 Art.5
s.15, enabling: SI 2008/132
s.16, disapplied: SI 2008/310 Art.5
s.17, disapplied: SI 2008/310 Art.5
s.18, disapplied: SI 2008/310 Art.5
s.20, applied: SI 2008/132
s.21, disapplied: SI 2008/310 Art.5
s.22, disapplied: SI 2008/310 Art.5
s.24, disapplied: SI 2008/310 Art.5
s.25, disapplied: SI 2008/310 Art.5
s.26, disapplied: SI 2008/310 Art.5
s.27, varied: SI 2008/680 Art.5, Art.20, Sch.9 para.3
s.28, varied: SI 2008/680 Art.5, Art.20, Sch.9 para.4
s.29, varied: SI 2008/680 Art.5, Art.20
s.30, varied: SI 2008/680 Art.5, Art.20
s.32, applied: SI 2008/5 Art.6, Art.7, SI 2008/539 Sch.1 para.1
s.32, enabling: SI 2008/5
s.36, applied: SI 2008/539, SI 2008/539 Art.1, Art.2, Art.3

CAP.

2006–cont.

13. Immigration, Asylum and Nationality Act 2006–*cont.*
s.36, enabling: SI 2008/539
s.37, enabling: SI 2008/8
s.38, applied: SI 2008/539, SI 2008/539 Art.1, Art.4, Art.5
s.38, repealed: 2008 c.28 Sch.1 para.4, Sch.9 Part 2
s.38, enabling: SI 2008/539
s.42, varied: SI 2008/680 Art.5, Art.20
s.48, varied: SI 2008/680 Art.5, Art.20
s.50, varied: SI 2008/680 Art.5, Art.20, Sch.9 para.5
s.51, varied: SI 2008/680 Art.5, Art.20, Sch.9 para.6
s.51, enabling: SI 2008/166, SI 2008/218, SI 2008/544, SI 2008/1337, SI 2008/1695, SI 2008/2790, SI 2008/3017
s.52, applied: SI 2008/166
s.52, varied: SI 2008/680 Art.5, Art.20, Sch.9 para.7
s.52, enabling: SI 2008/218, SI 2008/544, SI 2008/1337, SI 2008/1695, SI 2008/2790, SI 2008/3017
s.53, varied: SI 2008/680 Art.5, Art.20
s.54, varied: SI 2008/680 Art.5, Art.20, Sch.9 para.8
s.57, varied: SI 2008/680 Art.5, Art.20
s.62, enabling: SI 2008/310
s.63, enabling: SI 2008/680
s.64, varied: SI 2008/680 Art.5, Art.20, Sch.9 para.9
Sch.2 para.4, varied: SI 2008/680 Art.5, Art.20
Sch.2 para.6, varied: SI 2008/680 Art.5, Art.20

14. Consumer Credit Act 2006
Commencement Orders: SI 2008/831 Art.3, Art.4, Sch.2, Sch.3; SI 2008/2444 Art.2
s.2, disapplied: SI 2008/831 Art.4
s.69, enabling: SI 2008/831
s.71, enabling: SI 2008/831, SI 2008/2444
Sch.3 para.2, repealed: SI 2008/2826 Art.6
Sch.3 para.15, applied: SSI 2008/223 r.15

15. Identity Cards Act 2006
s.25, see *R. v Zenasni (Safi)* [2007] EWCA Crim 2165, [2008] 1 Cr. App. R. (S.) 94 (CA (Crim Div)), Toulson, L.J.

16. Natural Environment and Rural Communities Act 2006
see *R. (on the application of Winchester College) v Hampshire CC* [2007] EWHC 2786 (Admin), [2008] R.T.R. 15 (QBD (Admin)), George Bartlett Q.C.
Part 2, applied: SI 2008/431 (a), SI 2008/1927 (a)
s.67, see *R. (on the application of Winchester College) v Hampshire CC* [2007] EWHC 2786 (Admin), [2008] R.T.R. 15 (QBD (Admin)), George Bartlett Q.C.; see *R. (on the application of Winchester College)*

2006–cont.

16. Natural Environment and Rural Communities Act 2006–*cont.*

s.67–*cont.*

v Hampshire CC [2008] EWCA Civ 431, [2008] 3 All E.R. 717 (CA (Civ Div)), Ward, L.J.

s.87, enabling: SI 2008/420, SI 2008/576, SSI 2008/77

s.88, enabling: SI 2008/420, SI 2008/576, SSI 2008/77

s.89, enabling: SI 2008/420, SI 2008/576, SSI 2008/77

s.90, enabling: SI 2008/420, SI 2008/576, SSI 2008/77

s.91, enabling: SI 2008/576

s.93, enabling: SI 2008/576

s.96, applied: SI 2008/576

s.96, enabling: SI 2008/576, SSI 2008/77

s.97, applied: SI 2008/420, SI 2008/576, SSI 2008/77

s.97, enabling: SI 2008/420, SI 2008/576, SSI 2008/77

Sch.5 Part 2 para.7, amended: 2008 c.4 Sch.26 para.80

Sch.8 para.5, enabling: SI 2008/420, SI 2008/576, SSI 2008/77

Sch.8 para.6, enabling: SI 2008/420, SI 2008/576, SSI 2008/77

Sch.8 para.7, enabling: SI 2008/420, SI 2008/576, SSI 2008/77

Sch.8 para.8, enabling: SI 2008/420, SI 2008/576, SSI 2008/77

Sch.8 para.9, enabling: SI 2008/420, SI 2008/576, SSI 2008/77

Sch.8 para.10, enabling: SI 2008/420, SI 2008/576, SSI 2008/77

Sch.8 para.11, enabling: SI 2008/420, SI 2008/576, SSI 2008/77

Sch.9, enabling: SI 2008/420, SI 2008/576, SSI 2008/77

Sch.10, enabling: SI 2008/420, SI 2008/576, SSI 2008/77

19. Climate Change and Sustainable Energy Act 2006

s.2, repealed: 2008 c.27 s.82

s.3, amended: 2008 c.27 s.81

s.3, repealed (in part): 2008 c.27 s.81

s.3A, added: 2008 c.27 s.81

s.5, amended: 2008 c.32 s.87, Sch.6

s.18, repealed: 2008 c.32 Sch.6

s.22, repealed (in part): 2008 c.32 Sch.6

s.23, repealed: 2008 c.32 Sch.6

s.24, repealed: 2008 c.32 Sch.6

s.26, amended: SI 2008/1767 Art.2

s.26, applied: SI 2008/1767

s.26, enabling: SI 2008/1767

20. Children and Adoption Act 2006

Commencement Orders: SI 2008/1798 Art.2; SI 2008/2870 Art.2

s.8, applied: SI 2008/2859 r.3

s.9, applied: SI 2008/1808, SI 2008/1809

2006–cont.

20. Children and Adoption Act 2006–*cont.*

s.9, referred to: SI 2008/1808 Art.2, SI 2008/1809 Art.2

s.9, enabling: SI 2008/1808, SI 2008/1809

s.11, referred to: SI 2008/1807 Reg.2

s.11, enabling: SI 2008/1807

s.12, applied: SI 2008/1807 Reg.7

s.12, enabling: SI 2008/1807

s.16, enabling: SI 2008/1807

s.17, applied: SI 2008/1798

s.17, enabling: SI 2008/1798, SI 2008/2870

21. Childcare Act 2006

Commencement Orders: SI 2008/17 Art.2, Art.3; SI 2008/785 Art.2; SI 2008/2261 Art.2, Art.3, Art.4, Sch.1 para.1, Sch.2 para.1, para.2, para.3, para.4, para.5, para.6, para.7, para.8, para.9, para.10, para.11, para.12, para.13, para.14, para.15, para.16, para.17, para.18, para.19, para.20, para.21, para.22, para.23, para.24, para.25, para.26, para.27

applied: SI 2008/2261 Sch.2 para.13, Sch.2 para.14, Sch.2 para.18

Part 3, applied: 2008 c.25 s.94, SI 2008/975 Reg.7, Reg.8, Reg.13, Reg.14, SI 2008/2261 Sch.2 para.23

Part 3 c.3, applied: SI 2008/975 Sch.3 para.24

Part 3 c.4, applied: SI 2008/975 Sch.6 para.26

s.1, enabling: SI 2008/1437

s.7, applied: SI 2008/1724 Reg.2, Reg.3, Reg.4

s.7, enabling: SI 2008/1724

s.8, applied: SI 2008/1722 Reg.5, Reg.7

s.13, amended: 2008 c.25 Sch.1 para.31

s.18, amended: 2008 c.23 Sch.1 para.19, Sch.4

s.26, enabling: SI 2008/169

s.27, applied: SI 2008/170 Reg.3, Reg.4, Reg.7

s.27, enabling: SI 2008/170, SI 2008/1716

s.33, applied: SI 2008/2261 Sch.2 para.21

s.33, disapplied: SI 2008/979 Art.2, SI 2008/2261 Sch.2 para.2, Sch.2 para.7

s.33, enabling: SI 2008/979

s.34, amended: 2008 c.25 Sch.1 para.32

s.34, applied: SI 2008/2261 Sch.2 para.5

s.34, disapplied: SI 2008/979 Art.2, SI 2008/2261 Sch.2 para.5

s.34, enabling: SI 2008/979

s.35, applied: SI 2008/974 Reg.3, Reg.4, SI 2008/1804 Reg.3, SI 2008/2261 Sch.2 para.15

s.35, enabling: SI 2008/974, SI 2008/1804

s.36, applied: SI 2008/974 Reg.3, Reg.4, SI 2008/1804 Reg.4, SI 2008/2261 Sch.2 para.15

s.36, enabling: SI 2008/974, SI 2008/1804

CAP.

2006–cont.

21. Childcare Act 2006–*cont.*

s.37, applied: SI 2008/1804 Reg.9, Reg.10, Reg.13, Reg.16, Reg.17, SI 2008/2261 Sch.2 para.1, Sch.2 para.2, Sch.2 para.4, Sch.2 para.5, Sch.2 para.7, Sch.2 para.9, Sch.2 para.11, Sch.2 para.12, Sch.2 para.13, Sch.2 para.14, Sch.2 para.15, Sch.2 para.22
s.37, enabling: SI 2008/976, SI 2008/1804
s.38, applied: SI 2008/976 Reg.6, SI 2008/2261 Sch.2 para.14
s.39, enabling: SI 2008/1952, SI 2008/1953
s.40, applied: SI 2008/1724 Reg.2
s.43, applied: SI 2008/1953
s.43, enabling: SI 2008/1953
s.44, enabling: SI 2008/1952, SI 2008/1953
s.46, applied: SI 2008/1724 Reg.2
s.46, enabling: SI 2008/1743
s.47, repealed (in part): 2008 c.25 Sch.2
s.49, amended: 2008 c.25 Sch.1 para.33
s.49, applied: SI 2008/1729 Reg.5
s.49, enabling: SI 2008/1729
s.50, applied: SI 2008/1729 Reg.5, Reg.8
s.50, enabling: SI 2008/1729
s.52, applied: SI 2008/2261 Sch.2 para.21
s.52, disapplied: SI 2008/979 Art.2, SI 2008/2261 Sch.2 para.2
s.52, enabling: SI 2008/979
s.53, amended: 2008 c.25 Sch.1 para.34
s.53, applied: SI 2008/2261 Sch.2 para.5, Sch.2 para.8
s.53, disapplied: SI 2008/979 Art.2, SI 2008/2261 Sch.2 para.5
s.53, enabling: SI 2008/979
s.54, applied: SI 2008/975 Reg.4, Reg.5, SI 2008/1804 Reg.5, SI 2008/2261 Sch.2 para.15
s.54, enabling: SI 2008/975, SI 2008/1804
s.55, applied: SI 2008/975 Reg.4, Reg.5, SI 2008/1804 Reg.6, SI 2008/2261 Sch.2 para.15
s.55, enabling: SI 2008/975, SI 2008/1804
s.56, applied: SI 2008/975 Sch.3 para.11, Sch.3 para.28, SI 2008/1804 Reg.11, Reg.12, Reg.16, Reg.17, SI 2008/2261 Sch.2 para.1, Sch.2 para.2, Sch.2 para.4, Sch.2 para.5, Sch.2 para.8, Sch.2 para.10, Sch.2 para.11, Sch.2 para.12, Sch.2 para.13, Sch.2 para.14, Sch.2 para.15
s.56, enabling: SI 2008/976, SI 2008/1804
s.58, applied: SI 2008/976 Reg.6, SI 2008/2261 Sch.2 para.14
s.59, applied: SI 2008/975, SI 2008/975 Reg.6, Reg.8
s.59, enabling: SI 2008/975
s.60, enabling: SI 2008/1729
s.61, applied: SI 2008/1729 Reg.14
s.61, enabling: SI 2008/1729
s.62, applied: SI 2008/975 Reg.10, Reg.11, SI 2008/1804 Reg.7
s.62, enabling: SI 2008/975, SI 2008/1804

CAP.

2006–cont.

21. Childcare Act 2006–*cont.*

s.63, amended: 2008 c.25 Sch.1 para.35
s.63, applied: SI 2008/975 Reg.10, Reg.11, SI 2008/1804 Reg.8, SI 2008/2261 Sch.2 para.5
s.63, enabling: SI 2008/975, SI 2008/1804
s.64, applied: SI 2008/975 Sch.6 para.31, SI 2008/1804 Reg.14, Reg.15, Reg.17, SI 2008/2261 Sch.2 para.1, Sch.2 para.2, Sch.2 para.3, Sch.2 para.4, Sch.2 para.5, Sch.2 para.6, Sch.2 para.7, Sch.2 para.8, Sch.2 para.13
s.64, enabling: SI 2008/976, SI 2008/1804
s.66, applied: SI 2008/976 Reg.6, SI 2008/2261 Sch.2 para.14
s.67, applied: SI 2008/975, SI 2008/1740
s.67, enabling: SI 2008/975, SI 2008/1740
s.69, amended: SI 2008/2833 Sch.3 para.221
s.69, applied: SI 2008/975 Sch.3 para.29, Sch.6 para.32, SI 2008/976 Reg.9
s.69, enabling: SI 2008/976
s.72, applied: SI 2008/2261 Sch.2 para.26
s.73, applied: SI 2008/2261 Sch.2 para.16, Sch.2 para.17
s.74, applied: SI 2008/2261 Sch.2 para.18, Sch.2 para.19, SI 2008/2699 Sch.1
s.75, enabling: SI 2008/1740
s.83, enabling: SI 2008/961
s.84, enabling: SI 2008/961
s.89, enabling: SI 2008/793, SI 2008/1804
s.90, applied: SI 2008/976 Reg.4, Reg.5
s.90, enabling: SI 2008/976
s.92, applied: SI 2008/975 Sch.3 para.28, Sch.6 para.31, SI 2008/976 Reg.7, SI 2008/1804 Reg.17, SI 2008/2261 Sch.2 para.13
s.92, enabling: SI 2008/976, SI 2008/1804
s.96, applied: SI 2008/974 Sch.2 para.14, Sch.2 para.24, SI 2008/975 Sch.2 para.11, Sch.2 para.17, Sch.5 para.9, Sch.5 para.17, SI 2008/976 Reg.3, SI 2008/2261 Sch.2 para.7, Sch.2 para.8
s.96, enabling: SI 2008/976
s.99, applied: SI 2008/1722 Reg.3, Reg.4, Reg.5, Reg.6, Reg.7, Reg.8
s.99, enabling: SI 2008/1722, SI 2008/3071
s.104, enabling: SI 2008/974, SI 2008/975, SI 2008/976, SI 2008/979, SI 2008/1722, SI 2008/1724, SI 2008/1740, SI 2008/1743, SI 2008/1804, SI 2008/1953, SI 2008/2261, SI 2008/3071
s.106, amended: 2008 c.25 Sch.1 para.36
s.109, enabling: SI 2008/17, SI 2008/785, SI 2008/2261
s.110, amended: 2008 c.02 Sch.1 para.5
Sch.1, referred to: SI 2008/2261 Sch.1 para.1
Sch.2, referred to: SI 2008/2261 Sch.1 para.1
Sch.3, referred to: SI 2008/2261 Sch.1 para.1

CAP.

2006–cont.

22. Electoral Administration Act 2006

Commencement Orders: SI 2008/610 Art.2; SI 2008/1316 Art.2, Art.3, Art.4, Art.5; SI 2008/1656 Art.2

applied: 2008 c.8 Sch.2 Part 55

s.14, enabling: SI 2008/48

s.42, applied: SI 2008/1741

s.42, enabling: SI 2008/1741, SI 2008/1901

s.61, referred to: SI 2008/1656 Sch.1 para.1

s.63, applied: SI 2008/1319

s.63, enabling: SI 2008/1319

s.77, enabling: SI 2008/610, SI 2008/1316, SI 2008/1656

Sch.1 Part 6, referred to: SI 2008/1656 Sch.1 para.1

24. Appropriation (No.2) Act 2006

repealed: 2008 c.8 Sch.3

25. Finance Act 2006

s.17, enabling: SI 2008/1146

s.20, repealed: 2008 c.9 Sch.36 para.92

s.26, repealed: SI 2008/1146 Art.5

s.28, enabling: SI 2008/1878

s.30, repealed: 2008 c.9 s.75

s.59, repealed (in part): 2008 c.9 s.47

s.98, amended: 2008 c.9 s.156

s.98, applied: SI 2008/1821

s.98, enabling: SI 2008/1821

s.139, repealed (in part): 2008 c.9 Sch.17 para.35

s.173, applied: SI 2008/1770, SI 2008/1789, SI 2008/1793, SI 2008/1795, SI 2008/1796

s.173, enabling: SI 2008/1770, SI 2008/1789, SI 2008/1793, SI 2008/1795, SI 2008/1796

s.174, repealed: 2008 c.9 Sch.36 para.91

Sch.10 Part 3 para.23, amended: 2008 c.9 s.56

Sch.10 Part 3 para.32, amended: 2008 c.9 s.56

Sch.10 Part 4 para.39, amended: 2008 c.9 s.56

Sch.11 para.8, repealed: 2008 c.9 Sch.17 para.3

Sch.12 Part 1 para.3, repealed: 2008 c.9 Sch.2 para.21

Sch.12 Part 3 para.13, repealed: 2008 c.9 Sch.2 para.21, Sch.2 para.55

Sch.12 Part 3 para.27, repealed: 2008 c.9 Sch.2 para.55

Sch.12 Part 3 para.29, repealed: 2008 c.9 Sch.2 para.21

Sch.12 Part 3 para.31, repealed: 2008 c.9 Sch.2 para.21

Sch.12 Part 3 para.34, repealed (in part): 2008 c.9 Sch.7 para.114

Sch.12 Part 3 para.36, repealed (in part): 2008 c.9 Sch.7 para.114

Sch.12 Part 3 para.47, repealed (in part): 2008 c.9 s.41

CAP.

2006–cont.

25. Finance Act 2006–*cont.*

Sch.12 Part 3 para.48, repealed (in part): 2008 c.9 Sch.2 para.21

Sch.20 Part 3 para.14, disapplied: 2008 c.9 s.140

26. Commons Act 2006

Commencement Orders: SI 2008/1960 Art.2, Sch.1

applied: 2008 c.29 s.139, SI 2008/1961 Reg.3, Reg.50

referred to: SI 2008/1961 Reg.24

Part 1, applied: SI 2008/1961 Reg.5

Part 1, disapplied: SI 2008/1961 Reg.5, Reg.10

Part 2, applied: SI 2008/1961 Reg.47

s.3, enabling: SI 2008/1961

s.4, applied: SI 2008/1961 Reg.5

s.5, applied: SI 2008/1961 Reg.5, Reg.10

s.6, applied: SI 2008/1961 Reg.36, Sch.4 para.1, Sch.5 para.5, Sch.6 para.2

s.7, applied: SI 2008/1961 Reg.36, Sch.4 para.2, Sch.4 para.3, Sch.5 para.5, Sch.6 para.2

s.8, applied: SI 2008/1961 Sch.4 para.2, Sch.4 para.3, Sch.4 para.5, Sch.4 para.7, Sch.4 para.8, Sch.4 para.12, Sch.5 para.2, Sch.5 para.5, Sch.6 para.2

s.8, enabling: SI 2008/1961

s.10, applied: SI 2008/1961 Sch.4 para.4, Sch.5 para.5, Sch.6 para.2

s.11, applied: SI 2008/1961 Sch.4 para.3, Sch.4 para.5, Sch.5 para.5, Sch.6 para.2

s.11, enabling: SI 2008/1961

s.12, applied: SI 2008/1961 Sch.4 para.6, Sch.5 para.5, Sch.6 para.2

s.13, applied: SI 2008/1961 Sch.4 para.3, Sch.4 para.7, Sch.5 para.5, Sch.6 para.2

s.14, applied: SI 2008/1961 Sch.5 para.5, Sch.6 para.2

s.14, enabling: SI 2008/1961

s.15, applied: SI 2008/1961 Reg.19, Reg.21, Sch.4 para.9, Sch.4 para.10, Sch.5 para.5, Sch.6 para.2

s.16, applied: SI 2008/1961 Reg.49

s.17, applied: SI 2008/1961 Reg.7, Reg.49

s.17, enabling: SI 2008/1961

s.19, applied: SI 2008/1961 Reg.21, Reg.27, Sch.4 para.11, Sch.5 para.5, Sch.6 para.2

s.20, applied: SI 2008/1961 Reg.53, Reg.54

s.20, enabling: SI 2008/1961

s.21, applied: SI 2008/1961 Reg.54

s.21, enabling: SI 2008/1961

s.24, enabling: SI 2008/1961

s.34, referred to: 2008 c.13 Sch.6

s.38, applied: 2008 c.29 s.139

s.56, enabling: SI 2008/1960

s.59, enabling: SI 2008/1960, SI 2008/1961

Sch.1, applied: SI 2008/1961 Sch.6 para.2

Sch.1 para.1, applied: SI 2008/1961 Reg.46, Sch.4 para.3, Sch.4 para.12, Sch.5 para.5, SI 2008/1962 Art.2

CAP.

2006–*cont.*

26. Commons Act 2006–*cont.*

Sch.1 para.1, enabling: SI 2008/1961, SI 2008/1962
Sch.1 para.3, applied: SI 2008/1961 Sch.4 para.3, Sch.4 para.13, Sch.5 para.5
Sch.2, applied: SI 2008/1961 Reg.18, Reg.21, Reg.38, Sch.4 para.14, Sch.6 para.2
Sch.2 para.2, applied: SI 2008/1961 Sch.4 para.14, Sch.5 para.5
Sch.2 para.2, enabling: SI 2008/1961
Sch.2 para.3, applied: SI 2008/1961 Sch.4 para.14, Sch.5 para.5
Sch.2 para.3, enabling: SI 2008/1961
Sch.2 para.4, applied: SI 2008/1961 Reg.27, Sch.4 para.14, Sch.5 para.5
Sch.2 para.4, enabling: SI 2008/1961
Sch.2 para.5, applied: SI 2008/1961 Reg.27, Sch.4 para.14, Sch.5 para.5
Sch.2 para.5, enabling: SI 2008/1961
Sch.2 para.6, applied: SI 2008/1961 Reg.27, Sch.4 para.14, Sch.5 para.5
Sch.2 para.6, enabling: SI 2008/1961
Sch.2 para.7, applied: SI 2008/1961 Reg.27, Sch.4 para.14, Sch.5 para.5
Sch.2 para.7, enabling: SI 2008/1961
Sch.2 para.8, applied: SI 2008/1961 Reg.27, Sch.4 para.14, Sch.5 para.5
Sch.2 para.8, enabling: SI 2008/1961
Sch.2 para.9, applied: SI 2008/1961 Reg.27, Sch.4 para.14, Sch.5 para.5
Sch.2 para.9, enabling: SI 2008/1961
Sch.2 para.10, enabling: SI 2008/1961
Sch.3, applied: SI 2008/1961 Reg.42, Sch.6 para.2
Sch.3, referred to: SI 2008/1961 Reg.40
Sch.3 para.2, applied: SI 2008/1961 Reg.18, Reg.39, Reg.42, Sch.4 para.15, Sch.4 para.16, Sch.4 para.17, Sch.4 para.18, Sch.4 para.19, Sch.4 para.20, Sch.4 para.21, Sch.5 para.2, Sch.5 para.5
Sch.3 para.2, enabling: SI 2008/1961
Sch.3 para.3, applied: SI 2008/1961 Reg.39, Reg.43
Sch.3 para.4, applied: SI 2008/1961 Reg.39, Reg.42, Sch.5 para.2, Sch.5 para.5
Sch.3 para.4, enabling: SI 2008/1961
Sch.3 para.5, applied: SI 2008/1961 Reg.39
Sch.3 para.5, enabling: SI 2008/1961
Sch.3 para.8, applied: SI 2008/1961 Reg.48
Sch.3 para.8, enabling: SI 2008/1961

28. Health Act 2006

Commencement Orders: SI 2008/1147 Art.2, Art.3, Art.4; SI 2008/1972 Art.2; SI 2008/2714 Art.2; SI 2008/3171 Art.2
see *R. (on the application of G) v Nottinghamshire Healthcare NHS Trust* [2008] EWHC 1096 (Admin), [2008] H.R.L.R. 42 (DC), Pill, L.J.
Part 1, applied: 2008 c.13 Sch.3

CAP.

2006–*cont.*

28. Health Act 2006–*cont.*

s.3, see *R. (on the application of G) v Nottinghamshire Healthcare NHS Trust* [2008] EWHC 1096 (Admin), [2008] H.R.L.R. 42 (DC), Pill, L.J.
s.17, applied: SI 2008/3239 Reg.3
s.17, enabling: SI 2008/3239
s.18, applied: SI 2008/3239 Reg.16, Reg.22
s.18, enabling: SI 2008/3239
s.19, applied: SI 2008/3239 Reg.23
s.19, referred to: SI 2008/3239 Reg.23
s.20, applied: SI 2008/3239 Reg.19, Reg.20
s.20, disapplied: SI 2008/3239 Reg.21
s.20, enabling: SI 2008/3239
s.43, applied: SI 2008/1185 Reg.3
s.43, enabling: SI 2008/1209, SI 2008/1700
s.50, varied: 2008 c.14 Sch.10 para.1
s.58, amended: 2008 c.14 Sch.10 para.20
s.60, amended: 2008 c.14 Sch.10 para.21
s.60, applied: SI 2008/1774 Art.4
s.61, amended: 2008 c.14 Sch.5 para.79, Sch.15 Part 1
s.63, amended: 2008 c.14 Sch.10 para.22
s.73, enabling: SI 2008/1209
s.79, enabling: SI 2008/1209, SI 2008/1700, SI 2008/3239
s.83, enabling: SI 2008/1147, SI 2008/1972, SI 2008/2714, SI 2008/3171
Sch.4 para.2, enabling: SI 2008/2792
Sch.5, amended: 2008 c.14 Sch.5 para.80, Sch.10 para.23, Sch.15 Part 1, Sch.15 Part 2, Sch.15 Part 7
Sch.8 para.52, varied: 2008 c.14 Sch.10 para.1

29. Compensation Act 2006

s.8, enabling: SI 2008/1441
s.9, enabling: SI 2008/1441
s.15, applied: SI 2008/1441
s.15, enabling: SI 2008/1441
Sch.1, enabling: SI 2008/1441

30. Commissioner for Older People (Wales) Act 2006

s.5, enabling: SI 2008/1512
s.6, enabling: SI 2008/1512
s.8, enabling: SI 2008/1512
s.10, enabling: SI 2008/1512
s.15, enabling: SI 2008/1512
Sch.1 para.8, enabling: SI 2008/1512

32. Government of Wales Act 2006

applied: 2008 c.8 Sch.2 Part 55
s.58, applied: 2008 c.25 s.167, SI 2008/1786
s.58, enabling: SI 2008/1786
s.59, applied: SI 2008/2716
s.82, applied: 2008 c.27 s.70
s.95, applied: SI 2008/1036, SI 2008/1785, SI 2008/3132
s.95, enabling: SI 2008/1036, SI 2008/1785, SI 2008/3132
s.105, applied: 2008 c.23 s.40
s.120, applied: 2008 c.31 s.26

CAP.

2006–cont.

32. Government of Wales Act 2006–*cont.*
s.134, amended: SI 2008/948 Sch.1 para.243
s.139, amended: SI 2008/948 Sch.1 para.243
s.141, amended: SI 2008/948 Sch.1 para.243
s.152, applied: 2008 c.27 s.70
s.158, applied: 2008 c.29 s.235
s.158, referred to: SI 2008/1438
Sch.1 para.8, applied: SI 2008/1791
Sch.1 para.10, applied: SI 2008/1791 Art.1
Sch.3 Part 2 para.5, applied: 2008 c.27 s.70
Sch.4 para.1, disapplied: SI 2008/1786 Art.3
Sch.4 para.2, enabling: SI 2008/1786
Sch.5 Part 1, amended: 2008 c.25 s.149, 2008 c.26 s.122, 2008 c.29 s.202, SI 2008/1036 Art.2, SI 2008/1785 Art.2, SI 2008/3132 Art.2, Art.3, Art.4, Art.5, Art.6
Sch.7 Part 1 para.9, amended: SI 2008/960 Sch.3
Sch.8 para.14, amended: SI 2008/948 Sch.1 para.1
Sch.8 para.21, amended: SI 2008/948 Sch.1 para.34
Sch.11 para.34, applied: SI 2008/1848, SI 2008/1899
Sch.11 para.35, applied: SI 2008/1512

33. Northern Ireland (Miscellaneous Provisions) Act 2006
Commencement Orders: SI 2008/1318 Art.2
applied: 2008 c.8 Sch.2 Part 55
s.13, repealed (in part): SI 2008/1319 Art.4
s.14, applied: SI 2008/1319 Art.5
s.31, enabling: SI 2008/1318

35. Fraud Act 2006
applied: 2008 c.13 Sch.3

36. Wireless Telegraphy Act 2006
see *T Mobile (UK) Ltd v Office of Communications* [2008] EWCA Civ 1373, Times, December 18, 2008 (CA (Civ Div)), Tuckey, L.J.
applied: SI 2008/2794 Reg.3
s.3, referred to: SI 2008/3197 Art.2
s.8, disapplied: SI 2008/2427 Reg.3
s.8, enabling: SI 2008/236, SI 2008/237, SI 2008/2426, SI 2008/2427
s.12, enabling: SI 2008/139, SI 2008/2106
s.13, enabling: SI 2008/139, SI 2008/2106
s.14, see *T Mobile (UK) Ltd v Office of Communications* [2008] EWCA Civ 1373, Times, December 18, 2008 (CA (Civ Div)), Tuckey, L.J.
s.14, enabling: SI 2008/686, SI 2008/3190, SI 2008/3191
s.29, enabling: SI 2008/687, SI 2008/3197
s.30, enabling: SI 2008/688, SI 2008/2105, SI 2008/3192
s.31, enabling: SI 2008/689, SI 2008/2104, SI 2008/3193
s.111, amended: SI 2008/1277 Sch.2 para.74
s.122, applied: SI 2008/139, SI 2008/236, SI 2008/237, SI 2008/686, SI 2008/687, SI 2008/688, SI 2008/689, SI 2008/2104,

CAP.

2006–cont.

36. Wireless Telegraphy Act 2006–*cont.*
s.122, applied:–*cont.*
SI 2008/2105, SI 2008/2106, SI 2008/2426, SI 2008/2427, SI 2008/3190, SI 2008/3191, SI 2008/3192, SI 2008/3193, SI 2008/3197
s.122, enabling: SI 2008/139, SI 2008/686, SI 2008/688, SI 2008/689, SI 2008/2104, SI 2008/2105, SI 2008/2106, SI 2008/3190, SI 2008/3191, SI 2008/3192, SI 2008/3193

38. Violent Crime Reduction Act 2006
Commencement Orders: SI 2008/791 Art.2, Art.3; SI 2008/1407 Art.2
applied: 2008 c.13 Sch.3, SI 2008/791
s.15, enabling: SI 2008/1430
s.16, applied: SI 2008/1430 Reg.4, Reg.5, Reg.6, Reg.7, Reg.8, Reg.9, Reg.14, Reg.17, Reg.22, Reg.24
s.16, enabling: SI 2008/1430
s.17, applied: SI 2008/1430 Reg.15, Reg.22, Reg.23
s.17, enabling: SI 2008/1430
s.20, applied: SI 2008/1430
s.20, enabling: SI 2008/1430
s.47, amended: 2008 c.4 Sch.4 para.98
s.66, applied: SI 2008/1407
s.66, enabling: SI 2008/791, SI 2008/1407
Sch.2 para.2, applied: SI 2008/1216 Art.4, Art.5, Art.91
Sch.2 para.2, referred to: SI 2008/1216 Art.7
Sch.4 para.3, repealed (in part): SI 2008/1769 Sch.3

40. Education and Inspections Act 2006
Commencement Orders: SI 2008/1429 Art.3, Sch.1 Part 1, 2, 3; SI 2008/1971 Art.2
applied: 2008 c.23 s.11
Part 2, applied: SI 2008/228 Sch.1 para.10
s.11, amended: 2008 c.25 Sch.1 para.38
s.15, enabling: SI 2008/2035
s.18, applied: SI 2008/228 Reg.22, Sch.3 para.15
s.46, repealed: 2008 c.25 Sch.2
s.47, repealed (in part): 2008 c.25 Sch.2
s.50, repealed (in part): 2008 c.25 Sch.2
s.52, repealed (in part): 2008 c.25 Sch.2
s.62, applied: SI 2008/657 Reg.8
s.63, applied: SI 2008/228 Sch.1 para.9
s.64, applied: SI 2008/228 Sch.1 para.9
s.65, applied: SI 2008/228 Sch.1 para.9
s.66, applied: SI 2008/228 Sch.1 para.9
s.74, amended: 2008 c.25 Sch.1 para.87
s.83, amended: 2008 c.02 Sch.2
s.83, repealed (in part): 2008 c.02 Sch.2
s.88, amended: 2008 c.25 Sch.1 para.39
s.89, amended: 2008 c.02 s.13
s.114, enabling: SI 2008/681, SI 2008/1484, SI 2008/1784, SI 2008/2563, SI 2008/3126
s.124, applied: SI 2008/657 Reg.8
s.162, amended: 2008 c.02 s.23

CAP.

2006–cont.

40. Education and Inspections Act 2006–*cont.*

s.166, applied: SI 2008/50 Sch.2 para.4, SI 2008/1734 Sch.2 para.4, SI 2008/1790 Sch.2 para.4, SI 2008/3084 Sch.2 para.4
s.166, enabling: SI 2008/3082
s.171, amended: 2008 c.25 Sch.1 para.40
s.180, amended: 2008 c.25 Sch.1 para.88
s.181, amended: 2008 c.02 s.23
s.181, enabling: SI 2008/54, SI 2008/1429, SI 2008/1971
s.182A, added: 2008 c.02 s.23
s.188, enabling: SI 2008/54, SI 2008/1429, SI 2008/1971
Sch.2, applied: SI 2008/228 Sch.1 para.10
Sch.6, applied: SI 2008/228 Sch.1 para.9
Sch.10 para.4, repealed: 2008 c.2 Sch.2
Sch.10 para.5, repealed (in part): 2008 c.02 Sch.2
Sch.13 para.1, amended: 2008 c.14 Sch.5 para.81, SI 2008/912 Sch.1 para.26, Sch.1 para.27
Sch.13 para.1, repealed (in part): 2008 c.14 Sch.5 para.81, Sch.15 Part 1
Sch.13 para.1, varied: SI 2008/2250 Art.3
Sch.14 para.62, repealed: 2008 c.25 Sch.2
Sch.14 para.73, repealed (in part): 2008 c.25 Sch.2
Sch.14 para.75, repealed: 2008 c.25 Sch.2

41. National Health Service Act 2006

Commencement Orders: SI 2008/1147 Art.3
applied: SI 2008/570 Sch.1 para.16, SI 2008/700 Sch.1 para.17, SI 2008/915 Reg.6, SI 2008/1185 Sch.1 para.33, SI 2008/1186 Reg.3
Part 10, referred to: SI 2008/1148 Reg.6, Reg.13
s.1, see *R. (on the application of St Helens BC) v Manchester Primary Care Trust* [2008] EWCA Civ 931, (2008) 11 C.C.L. Rep. 774 (CA (Civ Div)), May, L.J.
s.3, see *R. (on the application of St Helens BC) v Manchester Primary Care Trust* [2008] EWCA Civ 931, (2008) 11 C.C.L. Rep. 774 (CA (Civ Div)), May, L.J.
s.4, applied: SI 2008/794 Reg.156
s.6, applied: SI 2008/794 Reg.154
s.7, enabling: SI 2008/224, SI 2008/1148, SI 2008/2496, SI 2008/2677, SI 2008/3080, SI 2008/3166
s.8, applied: SI 2008/1185 Reg.15
s.8, enabling: SI 2008/224, SI 2008/2496, SI 2008/2677, SI 2008/3080, SI 2008/3166
s.9, amended: 2008 c.14 Sch.5 para.82
s.9, applied: SI 2008/1185 Reg.7, Reg.8, Sch.1 para.30, Sch.1 para.31
s.9, varied: SI 2008/2250 Art.3
s.9, enabling: SI 2008/1185
s.12, applied: SI 2008/794 Reg.154
s.13, applied: SI 2008/1582 Reg.38, SI 2008/3170 Reg.23

CAP.

2006–cont.

41. National Health Service Act 2006–*cont.*

s.13, enabling: SI 2008/528
s.14, enabling: SI 2008/3166
s.18, applied: SI 2008/794 Sch.8 para.29, SI 2008/1812
s.18, enabling: SI 2008/1812
s.19, enabling: SI 2008/3080, SI 2008/3166
s.23A, added: 2008 c.14 s.139
s.25, applied: SI 2008/1471, SI 2008/1775, SI 2008/1859, SI 2008/2769
s.25, referred to: SI 2008/2431, SI 2008/2431 Art.3
s.25, enabling: SI 2008/1471, SI 2008/1775, SI 2008/1859, SI 2008/2431, SI 2008/2769
s.28, applied: SI 2008/519, SI 2008/1582 Reg.38, SI 2008/3170 Reg.23
s.28, enabling: SI 2008/519, SI 2008/558
s.35, amended: 2008 c.14 Sch.5 para.83
s.51, enabling: SI 2008/1902
s.56, amended: 2008 c.14 Sch.5 para.84
s.64, enabling: SI 2008/1902
s.71, amended: 2008 c.14 s.142, Sch.5 para.85, Sch.15 Part 4
s.71, varied: SI 2008/2250 Art.3
s.75, applied: SI 2008/228 Sch.1 para.7, SI 2008/239 Reg.12
s.75, enabling: SI 2008/3166
s.83, applied: SI 2008/653 Reg.7
s.89, enabling: SI 2008/528, SI 2008/1514
s.91, applied: SI 2008/2252 Sch.1 para.6
s.94, applied: SI 2008/653 Reg.7
s.94, enabling: SI 2008/528, SI 2008/1514
s.103, applied: SI 2008/653 Reg.7
s.104, enabling: SI 2008/528, SI 2008/1514
s.106, applied: SI 2008/2252 Sch.1 para.6
s.109, applied: SI 2008/653 Reg.7
s.109, enabling: SI 2008/528, SI 2008/1514
s.115, applied: SI 2008/1185 Sch.1 para.16, SI 2008/1186 Reg.5
s.115, referred to: SI 2008/1186 Reg.5
s.115, enabling: SI 2008/2449
s.116, enabling: SI 2008/2449
s.118, applied: SI 2008/1185 Reg.4
s.120, applied: SI 2008/1185 Reg.13, Reg.15
s.121, enabling: SI 2008/528, SI 2008/1514
s.123, applied: SI 2008/2252 Sch.1 para.6
s.125, applied: SI 2008/1700 Reg.16
s.126, enabling: SI 2008/528, SI 2008/683, SI 2008/1514
s.129, applied: SI 2008/2252 Sch.1 para.7
s.129, enabling: SI 2008/683
s.146, applied: SI 2008/2252 Sch.1 para.6
s.148, amended: 2008 c.23 s.4, Sch.4
s.148, applied: SI 2008/2252 Sch.1 para.8
s.151, applied: SI 2008/1185 Reg.4, Sch.1 para.44, SI 2008/2252 Sch.1 para.9
s.152, applied: SI 2008/2252 Sch.1 para.10
s.154, applied: SI 2008/2252 Sch.1 para.11

CAP.

2006–cont.

41. National Health Service Act 2006– *cont.*

s.155, applied: SI 2008/2252 Sch.1 para.11
s.159, applied: SI 2008/2252 Sch.1 para.6
s.164, amended: 2008 c.14 s.141
s.164, repealed (in part): 2008 c.14 s.141, Sch.15 Part 4
s.164, enabling: SI 2008/683
s.172, enabling: SI 2008/571, SI 2008/1697, SI 2008/2593
s.174, enabling: SI 2008/571
s.175, see *R. (on the application of A) v West Middlesex University Hospital NHS Trust* [2008] EWHC 855 (Admin), [2008] H.R.L.R. 29 (QBD (Admin)), Mitting, J.
s.175, enabling: SI 2008/2251
s.176, enabling: SI 2008/547
s.180, applied: SI 2008/1185 Reg.16
s.180, enabling: SI 2008/2449
s.182, enabling: SI 2008/571, SI 2008/843, SI 2008/1697, SI 2008/2593, SI 2008/2868
s.183, enabling: SI 2008/571, SI 2008/843, SI 2008/1697, SI 2008/2868
s.184, enabling: SI 2008/571, SI 2008/843, SI 2008/1697, SI 2008/2593, SI 2008/2868
s.185, applied: SI 2008/653 Reg.7
s.197, applied: SI 2008/1148 Reg.2, Reg.7, Reg.12, Reg.13
s.198, applied: SI 2008/1148 Reg.2, Reg.7, Reg.12
s.199, enabling: SI 2008/1148
s.201, amended: 2008 c.14 Sch.10 para.24
s.209, enabling: SI 2008/1148
s.213, enabling: SI 2008/83, SI 2008/412, SI 2008/415, SI 2008/416, SI 2008/430, SI 2008/440, SI 2008/894, SI 2008/895, SI 2008/1323, SI 2008/2784, SI 2008/2786
s.217, enabling: SI 2008/83, SI 2008/412, SI 2008/416, SI 2008/430, SI 2008/440, SI 2008/894, SI 2008/895, SI 2008/1323, SI 2008/2784, SI 2008/2786
s.228, amended: 2008 c.14 Sch.12 para.2
s.228, repealed (in part): 2008 c.14 Sch.12 para.2, Sch.15 Part 4
s.229, amended: 2008 c.14 Sch.12 para.3, Sch.15 Part 4
s.230, repealed (in part): 2008 c.14 Sch.12 para.4, Sch.15 Part 4
s.235, applied: SSI 2008/224 Reg.1
s.242, applied: SI 2008/2496 Reg.2, Reg.3, SI 2008/2677 Reg.2, Reg.3
s.242B, applied: SI 2008/2434 Art.2
s.242B, enabling: SI 2008/2496, SI 2008/2677
s.243, enabling: SI 2008/528
s.244, enabling: SI 2008/528
s.248, applied: SI 2008/1185 Sch.1 para.22
s.250A, added: 2008 c.14 s.157

CAP.

2006–cont.

41. National Health Service Act 2006– *cont.*

s.250B, added: 2008 c.14 s.157
s.250C, added: 2008 c.14 s.157
s.250C, enabling: SI 2008/2558
s.250D, added: 2008 c.14 s.157
s.251, see *Lewis v Secretary of State for Health* [2008] EWHC 2196 (QB), [2008] LS Law Medical 559 (QBD), Foskett, J.
s.252, referred to: 2008 c.14 s.157
s.252, substituted: 2008 c.14 s.158
s.256, amended: SI 2008/3002 Sch.1 para.52
s.256, varied: SI 2008/2839 Sch.1 para.1
s.259, applied: SI 2008/1786 Art.2
s.261, applied: SI 2008/3258
s.261, enabling: SI 2008/1938, SI 2008/3258
s.262, applied: SI 2008/3258
s.262, enabling: SI 2008/1938, SI 2008/3258
s.263, applied: SI 2008/1938, SI 2008/3258
s.263, enabling: SI 2008/1938, SI 2008/3258
s.264, applied: SI 2008/1938, SI 2008/3258
s.264, enabling: SI 2008/1938, SI 2008/3258
s.265, applied: SI 2008/1938, SI 2008/1938 Reg.8, SI 2008/3258, SI 2008/3258 Reg.9
s.265, enabling: SI 2008/1938, SI 2008/3258
s.266, enabling: SI 2008/1938, SI 2008/3258
s.268, amended: SI 2008/3002 Sch.1 para.53
s.271, amended: 2008 c.14 Sch.14 para.5
s.272, enabling: SI 2008/83, SI 2008/224, SI 2008/412, SI 2008/415, SI 2008/416, SI 2008/430, SI 2008/440, SI 2008/519, SI 2008/528, SI 2008/547, SI 2008/558, SI 2008/571, SI 2008/683, SI 2008/843, SI 2008/894, SI 2008/895, SI 2008/1269, SI 2008/1323, SI 2008/1471, SI 2008/1514, SI 2008/1697, SI 2008/1775, SI 2008/1812, SI 2008/1859, SI 2008/1938, SI 2008/2251, SI 2008/2431, SI 2008/2496, SI 2008/2558, SI 2008/2593, SI 2008/2677, SI 2008/2769, SI 2008/2784, SI 2008/2786, SI 2008/2868, SI 2008/3080, SI 2008/3166, SI 2008/3258
s.273, enabling: SI 2008/224, SI 2008/558, SI 2008/1148, SI 2008/1471, SI 2008/1775, SI 2008/1812, SI 2008/1859, SI 2008/1902, SI 2008/2496, SI 2008/2677, SI 2008/2769, SI 2008/3080, SI 2008/3166
s.275, amended: SI 2008/3002 Sch.1 para.54
Sch.1 para.3, amended: 2008 c.14 Sch.14 para.6

CAP.

2006–*cont.*

41. National Health Service Act 2006– *cont.*

Sch.1 para.7A, added: 2008 c.14 s.143
Sch.1 para.7A, applied: SI 2008/3080 Reg.2, Reg.3
Sch.1 para.7A, varied: 2008 c.14 s.143
Sch.1 para.7B, added: 2008 c.14 s.143
Sch.1 para.7B, enabling: SI 2008/3080
Sch.3 Part 1 para.4, enabling: SI 2008/1269
Sch.3 Part 2 para.13, enabling: SI 2008/1812
Sch.4 Part 1 para.4, enabling: SI 2008/1269
Sch.4 Part 1 para.5, enabling: SI 2008/1471, SI 2008/1775, SI 2008/1859, SI 2008/2431, SI 2008/2769
Sch.4 Part 1 para.8, applied: SI 2008/2431 Art.6
Sch.4 Part 1 para.10, referred to: SI 2008/79 Art.2
Sch.4 Part 1 para.10, enabling: SI 2008/79
Sch.4 Part 1 para.12, amended: SI 2008/817 Art.5
Sch.4 Part 2 para.18, applied: SI 2008/794 Reg.154
Sch.5 para.1, applied: SI 2008/727
Sch.5 para.1, enabling: SI 2008/727
Sch.10 para.8, amended: 2008 c.14 Sch.5 para.86
Sch.12 para.2, enabling: SI 2008/528
Sch.12 para.3, enabling: SI 2008/528, SI 2008/1514
Sch.14 para.1, repealed: 2008 c.14 Sch.12 para.5, Sch.15 Part 4
Sch.14 para.2, repealed: 2008 c.14 Sch.12 para.5, Sch.15 Part 4
Sch.14 para.3A, added: 2008 c.14 Sch.12 para.5
Sch.14 para.4, amended: 2008 c.14 Sch.12 para.5, Sch.15 Part 4
Sch.15 para.1, amended: SI 2008/817 Art.6
Sch.15 para.4, amended: SI 2008/817 Art.6
Sch.15 para.5, amended: SI 2008/817 Art.6
Sch.15 para.6, amended: SI 2008/817 Art.6
Sch.21, applied: SI 2008/1786 Art.2

42. National Health Service (Wales) Act 2006

applied: SI 2008/570 Sch.1 para.17, SI 2008/700 Sch.1 para.18
disapplied: SI 2008/1976 Reg.3
s.4, applied: SI 2008/794 Reg.156
s.6, applied: SI 2008/794 Reg.154
s.7, amended: 2008 c.14 Sch.5 para.87
s.10, applied: SI 2008/794 Reg.154
s.11, applied: SI 2008/794 Sch.8 para.29, SI 2008/1582 Reg.38, SI 2008/3170 Reg.23
s.12, enabling: SI 2008/2437
s.18, applied: SI 2008/712, SI 2008/717, SI 2008/717 Art.3, SI 2008/1648
s.18, referred to: SI 2008/712 Art.3, SI 2008/716 Art.3, SI 2008/717 Art.3, SI 2008/1648 Art.3

CAP.

2006–*cont.*

42. National Health Service (Wales) Act 2006–*cont.*

s.18, enabling: SI 2008/712, SI 2008/716, SI 2008/717, SI 2008/1648
s.22, applied: SI 2008/1582 Reg.38, SI 2008/3170 Reg.23
s.30, amended: 2008 c.14 Sch.5 para.88
s.30, repealed (in part): 2008 c.14 Sch.5 para.88, Sch.15 Part 1
s.41, applied: SI 2008/653 Reg.7
s.47, enabling: SI 2008/1329, SI 2008/1425
s.49, enabling: SI 2008/1425
s.52, applied: SI 2008/653 Reg.7
s.60, applied: SI 2008/653 Reg.7
s.63, enabling: SI 2008/1425
s.66, applied: SI 2008/653 Reg.7
s.71, enabling: SI 2008/577, SI 2008/2552
s.76, enabling: SI 2008/577
s.77, enabling: SI 2008/577
s.88, amended: 2008 c.14 s.141
s.88, repealed (in part): 2008 c.14 s.141, Sch.15 Part 4
s.124, enabling: SI 2008/2364
s.128, enabling: SI 2008/577, SI 2008/2552
s.129, enabling: SI 2008/577, SI 2008/660, SI 2008/2552
s.130, enabling: SI 2008/1480, SI 2008/2568
s.131, enabling: SI 2008/1480, SI 2008/2568
s.132, enabling: SI 2008/1480, SI 2008/2568
s.133, applied: SI 2008/653 Reg.7
s.149, amended: 2008 c.14 Sch.10 para.25
s.174, amended: 2008 c.14 Sch.12 para.7, Sch.15 Part 4
s.175, amended: 2008 c.14 Sch.12 para.8, Sch.15 Part 4
s.176, amended: 2008 c.14 Sch.12 para.9, Sch.15 Part 4
s.194, amended: SI 2008/3002 Sch.1 para.56
s.194, varied: SI 2008/2839 Sch.1 para.1
s.196, amended: SI 2008/3002 Sch.1 para.57
s.199, amended: SI 2008/3002 Sch.1 para.58
s.203, enabling: SI 2008/577, SI 2008/660, SI 2008/922, SI 2008/924, SI 2008/926, SI 2008/927, SI 2008/931, SI 2008/935, SI 2008/936, SI 2008/1329, SI 2008/1425, SI 2008/1480, SI 2008/1720, SI 2008/1721, SI 2008/2364, SI 2008/2438, SI 2008/2443, SI 2008/2552, SI 2008/2568
s.204, enabling: SI 2008/932, SI 2008/933, SI 2008/934, SI 2008/937, SI 2008/938, SI 2008/939, SI 2008/940, SI 2008/1717, SI 2008/1719, SI 2008/2437
Sch.1 para.3, amended: 2008 c.14 Sch.14 para.7
Sch.1 para.7A, added: 2008 c.14 s.144
Sch.1 para.7B, added: 2008 c.14 s.144
Sch.2 Part 3 para.28, applied: SI 2008/1717, SI 2008/1719

CAP.

2006–cont.

42. National Health Service (Wales) Act 2006–*cont.*

Sch.3 Part 1 para.5, applied: SI 2008/712 Art.4, SI 2008/716 Art.4, SI 2008/717 Art.4, SI 2008/1648 Art.4

Sch.3 Part 1 para.5, enabling: SI 2008/712, SI 2008/716, SI 2008/717, SI 2008/1648

Sch.3 Part 1 para.7, enabling: SI 2008/712, SI 2008/716, SI 2008/717, SI 2008/1648

Sch.3 Part 1 para.9, enabling: SI 2008/2438, SI 2008/2443

Sch.3 Part 2 para.18, applied: SI 2008/794 Reg.154

Sch.3 Part 2 para.18, enabling: SI 2008/937

Sch.3 Part 3 para.28, applied: SI 2008/932, SI 2008/933, SI 2008/934, SI 2008/937, SI 2008/938, SI 2008/939, SI 2008/940

Sch.3 Part 3 para.28, enabling: SI 2008/932, SI 2008/933, SI 2008/934, SI 2008/937, SI 2008/938, SI 2008/939, SI 2008/940, SI 2008/1717, SI 2008/1719

Sch.3 Part 3 para.29, applied: SI 2008/922, SI 2008/924, SI 2008/926, SI 2008/927, SI 2008/931, SI 2008/935, SI 2008/936, SI 2008/1720, SI 2008/1721

Sch.3 Part 3 para.29, enabling: SI 2008/922, SI 2008/924, SI 2008/926, SI 2008/927, SI 2008/931, SI 2008/935, SI 2008/936, SI 2008/1720, SI 2008/1721

Sch.8, amended: 2008 c.14 Sch.12 para.10

Sch.8 para.1, amended: 2008 c.14 Sch.12 para.10, Sch.15 Part 4

Sch.8 para.1, repealed (in part): 2008 c.14 Sch.12 para.10, Sch.15 Part 4

Sch.8 para.2, substituted: 2008 c.14 Sch.12 para.10

Sch.8 para.3A, added: 2008 c.14 Sch.12 para.10

Sch.8 para.4, amended: 2008 c.14 Sch.12 para.10, Sch.15 Part 4

43. National Health Service (Consequential Provisions) Act 2006

Commencement Orders: SI 2008/1147 Art.3; SI 2008/1972 Art.2

Sch.1 para.202, repealed: 2008 c.25 Sch.2

44. NHS Redress Act 2006

s.5, amended: 2008 c.14 Sch.5 para.89

s.13, amended: 2008 c.14 Sch.5 para.90

45. Animal Welfare Act 2006

see *Hanchett-Stamford v Attorney General* [2008] EWHC 330 (Ch), [2008] 4 All E.R. 323 (Ch D), Lewison, J.

applied: 2008 c.13 Sch.3

referred to: 2008 c.13 Sch.6

s.5, applied: SI 2008/1426, SI 2008/3094

s.5, enabling: SI 2008/1426, SI 2008/3094

s.12, applied: 2008 c.13 Sch.7

s.61, applied: SI 2008/1426, SI 2008/3094

CAP.

2006–cont.

46. Companies Act 2006

Commencement Orders: SI 2008/674 Art.3, Art.5, Art.6, Sch.3 para.6; SI 2008/1886 Art.2, Art.7, Art.8; SI 2008/2860 Art.3, Art.4, Sch.1 Part 1, Sch.2 para.2, para.4, para.11, para.12, para.13, para.14, para.15, para.16, para.17, para.18, para.19, para.22, para.23, para.28, para.31, para.34, para.35, para.40, para.41, para.43, para.44, para.46, para.47, para.48, para.49, para.51, para.54, para.56, para.57, para.58, para.61, para.62, para.63, para.64, para.65, para.66, para.68, para.69, para.70, para.71, para.72, para.73, para.74, para.76, para.77, para.78, para.79, para.80, para.81, para.82, para.83, para.84, para.85, para.86, para.87, para.88, para.90, para.91, para.92, para.93, para.95, para.96, para.97, para.98, para.99, para.100, para.101, para.102, para.103, para.104, para.105, para.106, para.107, para.108, para.109, para.112, para.113

applied: 2008 c.2 s.15, 2008 c.17 s.271, 2008 c.31 s.13, SI 2008/373 Reg.7, SI 2008/374 Reg.8, SI 2008/409 Sch.6 para.30, Sch.6 para.33, SI 2008/432 Art.3, Art.8, SI 2008/565 Reg.3, SI 2008/623 Art.7, SI 2008/948 Art.6, SI 2008/1053 Sch.1, SI 2008/1715 Reg.4, Reg.6, SI 2008/1738 r.5, r.11, r.14, r.15, SI 2008/1886 Art.7, SI 2008/2361 Reg.17, SI 2008/2546 Art.9, SI 2008/2860 Art.7, Sch.2 para.22, Sch.2 para.26, Sch.2 para.29, Sch.2 para.93, Sch.2 para.97, SI 2008/3229 Reg.1, Sch.1, Sch.2, Sch.3

disapplied: 2008 c.17 s.167, SI 2008/2860 Sch.2 para.1, Sch.2 para.10

referred to: SI 2008/373 Reg.4, Reg.5, Reg.6, Reg.15, Reg.16, SI 2008/409 Sch.2 para.3, Sch.2 para.7, Sch.6 para.24, SI 2008/565 Reg.3, SI 2008/623, SI 2008/948 Art.6, SI 2008/1886 Art.6, SI 2008/1912 Reg.1, SI 2008/2860 Sch.2 para.75, Sch.2 para.81

varied: SI 2008/373 Reg.3, Reg.10, Reg.11, Reg.12

Part 1, applied: SI 2008/2546 Art.4

Part 2, applied: SI 2008/2546 Art.4

Part 3, applied: SI 2008/2546 Art.4

Part 3, referred to: SI 2008/2860 Sch.2 para.7

Part 3 c.2, applied: SI 2008/3229 Sch.1, Sch.2, Sch.3

Part 3 c.3, applied: SI 2008/2860 Sch.2 para.42, Sch.2 para.43

Part 3 c.4, applied: SI 2008/3229 Sch.1, Sch.2, Sch.3

Part 4, applied: SI 2008/2546 Art.4

Part 5, applied: SI 2008/2546 Art.4

Part 6, applied: SI 2008/2546 Art.4

Part 7, applied: SI 2008/2546 Art.4, SI 2008/2860 Sch.2 para.10, Sch.2 para.22

Part 8, applied: SI 2008/2546 Art.4

CAP.

2006–cont.

46. Companies Act 2006–*cont.*

Part 9, applied: SI 2008/2546 Art.4
Part 10, applied: SI 2008/2546 Art.4
Part 10 c.4, applied: SI 2008/2546 Art.13
Part 10 c.8, applied: SI 2008/2860 Sch.2 para.33
Part 10 c.8, referred to: SI 2008/2860 Sch.2 para.34
Part 11, applied: SI 2008/2546 Art.4
Part 11, disapplied: SI 2008/432 Art.11
Part 12, applied: SI 2008/2546 Art.4
Part 13, applied: SI 2008/2546 Art.4
Part 14, applied: SI 2008/2546 Art.4
Part 14, referred to: SI 2008/409 Sch.5 para.2, SI 2008/410 Sch.7 para.3
Part 15, applied: 2008 c.17 s.130, SI 2008/374 Reg.9, Reg.11, SI 2008/409 Reg.2, SI 2008/410 Reg.2, SI 2008/567 Reg.3, Reg.4, Sch.1 para.1, SI 2008/569 Reg.4, Sch.1 para.1, SI 2008/1912 Reg.2, SI 2008/1913 Reg.2, SI 2008/2546 Art.4
Part 15 c.4, applied: SI 2008/565 Reg.3
Part 15 c.5, applied: SI 2008/565 Reg.3
Part 16, applied: SI 2008/1911 Reg.48, SI 2008/2546 Art.4
Part 16 c.1, applied: SI 2008/373 Reg.8, SI 2008/567 Reg.4, Sch.1 para.1, SI 2008/569 Reg.4, Sch.1 para.1
Part 17, applied: SI 2008/2546 Art.4
Part 18, applied: SI 2008/2546 Art.4
Part 19, applied: SI 2008/2546 Art.4
Part 20, applied: SI 2008/2546 Art.4
Part 21, applied: SI 2008/2546 Art.4
Part 22, applied: SI 2008/2546 Art.4
Part 23, applied: SI 2008/948 Art.6, SI 2008/1915 Art.3, SI 2008/2546 Art.4
Part 24, applied: SI 2008/2546 Art.4, SI 2008/2860 Sch.2 para.81
Part 25, applied: SI 2008/2546 Art.4
Part 26, applied: SI 2008/2546 Art.4
Part 27, applied: SI 2008/2546 Art.4
Part 28, applied: SI 2008/2546 Art.4
Part 28 c.1, applied: 2008 c.30 Sch.1 para.13
Part 29, applied: SI 2008/2546 Art.4
Part 30, applied: SI 2008/729 Reg.6, SI 2008/2546 Art.4
Part 31, applied: SI 2008/2546 Art.4
Part 32, applied: SI 2008/2546 Art.4
Part 33, applied: SI 2008/2546 Art.4
Part 33 c.1, applied: SI 2008/2860 Sch.2 para.93
Part 34, applied: SI 2008/2546 Art.4
Part 35, applied: SI 2008/410 Sch.6 para.30, SI 2008/2546 Art.4
Part 36, applied: SI 2008/2546 Art.4
Part 37, applied: SI 2008/2546 Art.4
Part 38, applied: SI 2008/2546 Art.4
Part 39, applied: SI 2008/2546 Art.4
Part 42, applied: 2008 c.17 s.131, SI 2008/489 Reg.4, SI 2008/496 Art.4, SI 2008/948 Art.5

CAP.

2006–cont.

46. Companies Act 2006–*cont.*

Part 42 c.2, applied: SI 2008/1950 Reg.3
Part 45, applied: SI 2008/2546 Art.4
Part 46, applied: SI 2008/2546 Art.4
Part 47, applied: SI 2008/2546 Art.4
s.1, applied: SI 2008/3229 Sch.1, Sch.2, Sch.3
s.1, referred to: 2008 c.2 s.15
s.1, varied: SI 2008/2860 Sch.2 para.2
s.2, applied: SI 2008/3229 Sch.1, Sch.2, Sch.3
s.3, applied: SI 2008/3229 Sch.1, Sch.2, Sch.3
s.4, applied: SI 2008/3229 Sch.1, Sch.2, Sch.3
s.5, applied: SI 2008/3229 Sch.1, Sch.2, Sch.3
s.6, applied: SI 2008/3229 Sch.1, Sch.2, Sch.3
s.7, applied: SI 2008/2860 Sch.2 para.2, SI 2008/3229 Sch.1, Sch.2, Sch.3
s.8, applied: SI 2008/2860 Sch.2 para.2, SI 2008/3014 Reg.2, SI 2008/3229 Sch.1, Sch.2, Sch.3
s.8, enabling: SI 2008/3014
s.9, applied: SI 2008/2860 Sch.2 para.2, SI 2008/3229 Sch.1, Sch.2, Sch.3
s.10, applied: SI 2008/2860 Sch.2 para.2, SI 2008/3014 Reg.3, SI 2008/3229 Sch.1, Sch.2, Sch.3
s.10, enabling: SI 2008/3014
s.11, applied: SI 2008/2860 Sch.2 para.2, SI 2008/3014 Reg.4, SI 2008/3229 Sch.1, Sch.2, Sch.3
s.11, enabling: SI 2008/3014
s.12, applied: SI 2008/2860 Sch.2 para.2, SI 2008/3229 Sch.1, Sch.2, Sch.3
s.13, applied: SI 2008/2860 Sch.2 para.2, SI 2008/3229 Sch.1, Sch.2, Sch.3
s.14, applied: SI 2008/2860 Sch.2 para.2, SI 2008/3229 Sch.1, Sch.2, Sch.3
s.15, applied: SI 2008/2860 Sch.2 para.2, SI 2008/3229 Sch.1, Sch.2, Sch.3
s.16, applied: SI 2008/2860 Sch.2 para.2, SI 2008/3229 Sch.1, Sch.2, Sch.3
s.17, applied: SI 2008/3229 Sch.1, Sch.2, Sch.3
s.18, disapplied: SI 2008/2860 Sch.2 para.3
s.19, disapplied: SI 2008/2860 Sch.2 para.3
s.19, enabling: SI 2008/3229
s.20, disapplied: SI 2008/2860 Sch.2 para.3
s.21, disapplied: SI 2008/2860 Sch.2 para.4
s.22, disapplied: SI 2008/2860 Sch.2 para.4
s.23, disapplied: SI 2008/2860 Sch.2 para.5
s.26, applied: SI 2008/2860 Sch.2 para.6
s.28, applied: SI 2008/2860 Sch.2 para.4, Sch.2 para.7, Sch.2 para.9, Sch.2 para.110
s.28, referred to: SI 2008/2860 Sch.2 para.3, Sch.2 para.8
s.29, applied: SI 2008/3229 Sch.1, Sch.2, Sch.3

CAP.

2006–cont.

46. Companies Act 2006–*cont.*

s.30, applied: 2008 c.17 s.162, s.164, s.214, SI 2008/2860 Sch.2 para.19, SI 2008/3229 Sch.1, Sch.2, Sch.3
s.32, applied: SI 2008/2860 Sch.2 para.11
s.34, applied: SI 2008/2860 Sch.2 para.12
s.35, applied: SI 2008/2860 Sch.2 para.13
s.36, applied: SI 2008/2860 Sch.2 para.14
s.39, applied: SI 2008/2860 Sch.2 para.15, SI 2008/3229 Sch.1, Sch.2, Sch.3
s.44, applied: SI 2008/948 Art.7, Art.8
s.45, applied: SI 2008/3229 Sch.1, Sch.2, Sch.3
s.46, applied: SI 2008/3229 Sch.1, Sch.2, Sch.3
s.47, applied: SI 2008/2860 Sch.2 para.16, SI 2008/3229 Sch.1, Sch.2, Sch.3
s.54, applied: SI 2008/2860 Sch.2 para.18
s.54, disapplied: SI 2008/2860 Sch.2 para.17
s.55, applied: SI 2008/2860 Sch.2 para.18
s.55, disapplied: SI 2008/2860 Sch.2 para.17
s.56, applied: SI 2008/2860 Sch.2 para.18
s.57, disapplied: SI 2008/2860 Sch.2 para.17
s.65, disapplied: SI 2008/2860 Sch.2 para.17
s.66, disapplied: SI 2008/2860 Sch.2 para.17
s.69, applied: SI 2008/1738 r.3, r.5, r.8
s.71, enabling: SI 2008/1738
s.73, applied: SI 2008/1738 r.3
s.77, applied: SI 2008/2860 Sch.2 para.19
s.78, applied: SI 2008/2860 Sch.2 para.19
s.80, applied: SI 2008/2860 Sch.2 para.19
s.81, applied: SI 2008/2860 Sch.2 para.19
s.82, enabling: SI 2008/495
s.84, applied: SI 2008/432 Sch.1 para.2, SI 2008/2546 Art.13, SI 2008/2644 Art.26, Sch.2 para.2
s.84, enabling: SI 2008/495
s.89, applied: SI 2008/2860 Sch.2 para.22
s.90, applied: SI 2008/2860 Sch.2 para.22
s.91, applied: SI 2008/2860 Sch.2 para.22
s.92, applied: SI 2008/2860 Sch.2 para.22
s.93, applied: SI 2008/2860 Sch.2 para.22
s.94, applied: SI 2008/2860 Sch.2 para.22
s.95, applied: SI 2008/2860 Sch.2 para.22
s.96, applied: SI 2008/2860 Sch.2 para.22
s.97, applied: SI 2008/2860 Sch.2 para.22
s.98, applied: SI 2008/2860 Sch.2 para.22
s.99, applied: SI 2008/2860 Sch.2 para.22
s.100, applied: SI 2008/2860 Sch.2 para.22
s.101, applied: SI 2008/2860 Sch.2 para.22
s.102, applied: SI 2008/2860 Sch.2 para.22
s.103, applied: SI 2008/2860 Sch.2 para.22, SI 2008/3014 Reg.5
s.103, enabling: SI 2008/3014
s.104, applied: SI 2008/2860 Sch.2 para.22
s.105, applied: SI 2008/2860 Sch.2 para.22
s.106, applied: SI 2008/2860 Sch.2 para.22
s.107, applied: SI 2008/2860 Sch.2 para.22
s.108, applied: SI 2008/2860 Sch.2 para.22
s.110, applied: SI 2008/3014 Reg.6

CAP.

2006–cont.

46. Companies Act 2006–*cont.*

s.110, enabling: SI 2008/3014
s.120, applied: SI 2008/2860 Sch.2 para.23
s.146, applied: SI 2008/373 Reg.2, Reg.12, SI 2008/374 Reg.3
s.162, applied: SI 2008/432 Sch.1 para.2, SI 2008/2546 Art.13, SI 2008/2644 Art.26, Sch.2 para.2, SI 2008/2860 Sch.2 para.25, Sch.2 para.38, SI 2008/3007 Reg.2
s.162, enabling: SI 2008/3007
s.163, applied: SI 2008/2860 Sch.2 para.27
s.165, applied: SI 2008/432 Sch.1 para.2, SI 2008/2546 Art.13, SI 2008/2644 Art.26, Sch.2 para.2
s.167, applied: SI 2008/432 Sch.1 para.2, SI 2008/2546 Art.13, SI 2008/2644 Art.26, Sch.2 para.2, SI 2008/2860 Sch.2 para.27, Sch.2 para.28, Sch.2 para.29, Sch.2 para.30, Sch.2 para.31
s.170, applied: SI 2008/432 Sch.1 para.2, SI 2008/2546 Art.13, SI 2008/2644 Art.26, Sch.2 para.2
s.171, applied: SI 2008/432 Sch.1 para.2, SI 2008/2546 Art.13, SI 2008/2644 Art.26, Sch.2 para.2
s.172, see *Franbar Holdings Ltd v Patel* [2008] EWHC 1534 (Ch), [2008] B.C.C. 885 (Ch D), William Trower QC
s.172, applied: SI 2008/432 Sch.1 para.2, SI 2008/2546 Art.13, SI 2008/2644 Art.26, Sch.2 para.2
s.173, applied: SI 2008/432 Sch.1 para.2, SI 2008/2546 Art.13, SI 2008/2644 Art.26, Sch.2 para.2
s.174, applied: SI 2008/432 Sch.1 para.2, SI 2008/2546 Art.13, SI 2008/2644 Art.26, Sch.2 para.2
s.175, applied: SI 2008/432 Sch.1 para.2, SI 2008/2546 Art.13, SI 2008/2644 Art.26, Sch.2 para.2
s.176, applied: SI 2008/432 Sch.1 para.2, SI 2008/2546 Art.13, SI 2008/2644 Art.26, Sch.2 para.2
s.177, applied: SI 2008/432 Sch.1 para.2, SI 2008/2546 Art.13, SI 2008/2644 Art.26, Sch.2 para.2
s.182, applied: SI 2008/432 Sch.1 para.2, SI 2008/2546 Art.13, SI 2008/2644 Art.26, Sch.2 para.2
s.183, applied: SI 2008/432 Sch.1 para.2, SI 2008/2546 Art.13, SI 2008/2644 Art.26, Sch.2 para.2
s.184, applied: SI 2008/432 Sch.1 para.2, SI 2008/2546 Art.13, SI 2008/2644 Art.26, Sch.2 para.2
s.185, applied: SI 2008/432 Sch.1 para.2, SI 2008/2546 Art.13, SI 2008/2644 Art.26, Sch.2 para.2
s.185, varied: SI 2008/432 Art.3

CAP.

2006–cont.

46. Companies Act 2006–*cont.*

s.186, applied: SI 2008/432 Sch.1 para.2, SI 2008/2546 Art.13, SI 2008/2644 Art.26, Sch.2 para.2

s.187, applied: SI 2008/2546 Art.13

s.187, referred to: SI 2008/2644 Art.26, Sch.2 para.2

s.188, applied: SI 2008/432 Sch.1 para.2, SI 2008/2644 Art.26, Sch.2 para.2

s.189, applied: SI 2008/432 Sch.1 para.2, SI 2008/2644 Art.26, Sch.2 para.2

s.190, applied: SI 2008/432 Sch.1 para.2, SI 2008/2644 Art.26, Sch.2 para.2

s.191, applied: SI 2008/432 Sch.1 para.2, SI 2008/2644 Art.26, Sch.2 para.2

s.192, applied: SI 2008/432 Sch.1 para.2, SI 2008/2644 Art.26, Sch.2 para.2

s.193, applied: SI 2008/432 Sch.1 para.2, SI 2008/2644 Art.26, Sch.2 para.2

s.194, applied: SI 2008/432 Sch.1 para.2, SI 2008/2644 Art.26, Sch.2 para.2

s.195, applied: SI 2008/432 Sch.1 para.2, SI 2008/2644 Art.26, Sch.2 para.2

s.196, applied: SI 2008/432 Sch.1 para.2, SI 2008/2644 Art.26, Sch.2 para.2

s.197, applied: SI 2008/432 Sch.1 para.2, SI 2008/2644 Art.26, Sch.2 para.2

s.198, applied: SI 2008/432 Sch.1 para.2, SI 2008/2644 Art.26, Sch.2 para.2

s.199, applied: SI 2008/432 Sch.1 para.2, SI 2008/2644 Art.26, Sch.2 para.2

s.200, applied: SI 2008/432 Sch.1 para.2, SI 2008/2644 Art.26, Sch.2 para.2

s.201, applied: SI 2008/432 Sch.1 para.2, SI 2008/2644 Art.26, Sch.2 para.2

s.202, applied: SI 2008/432 Sch.1 para.2, SI 2008/2644 Art.26, Sch.2 para.2

s.203, applied: SI 2008/432 Sch.1 para.2, SI 2008/2644 Art.26, Sch.2 para.2

s.204, applied: SI 2008/432 Sch.1 para.2, SI 2008/2644 Art.26, Sch.2 para.2

s.205, applied: SI 2008/432 Sch.1 para.2, SI 2008/2644 Art.26, Sch.2 para.2

s.205, varied: SI 2008/674 Sch.3 para.1

s.206, applied: SI 2008/432 Sch.1 para.2, SI 2008/2644 Art.26, Sch.2 para.2

s.207, applied: SI 2008/432 Sch.1 para.2, SI 2008/2644 Art.26, Sch.2 para.2

s.208, applied: SI 2008/432 Sch.1 para.2, SI 2008/2644 Art.26, Sch.2 para.2

s.209, applied: SI 2008/432 Sch.1 para.2, SI 2008/2644 Art.26, Sch.2 para.2

s.210, applied: SI 2008/432 Sch.1 para.2, SI 2008/2644 Art.26, Sch.2 para.2

s.211, applied: SI 2008/432 Sch.1 para.2, SI 2008/2644 Art.26, Sch.2 para.2

s.212, applied: SI 2008/432 Sch.1 para.2, SI 2008/2644 Art.26, Sch.2 para.2

s.213, applied: SI 2008/432 Sch.1 para.2, SI 2008/2644 Art.26, Sch.2 para.2

CAP.

2006–cont.

46. Companies Act 2006–*cont.*

s.214, applied: SI 2008/432 Sch.1 para.2, SI 2008/2644 Art.26, Sch.2 para.2

s.215, applied: SI 2008/432 Sch.1 para.2, SI 2008/2644 Art.26, Sch.2 para.2

s.216, applied: SI 2008/432 Sch.1 para.2, SI 2008/2644 Art.26, Sch.2 para.2

s.217, applied: SI 2008/432 Sch.1 para.2, SI 2008/2644 Art.26, Sch.2 para.2

s.218, applied: SI 2008/432 Sch.1 para.2, SI 2008/2644 Art.26, Sch.2 para.2

s.219, applied: SI 2008/409 Sch.3 para.6, SI 2008/410 Sch.5 para.8, Sch.8 para.19, SI 2008/432 Sch.1 para.2, SI 2008/2644 Art.26, Sch.2 para.2

s.220, applied: SI 2008/432 Sch.1 para.2, SI 2008/2644 Art.26, Sch.2 para.2

s.221, applied: SI 2008/432 Sch.1 para.2, SI 2008/2644 Art.26, Sch.2 para.2

s.222, applied: SI 2008/409 Sch.3 para.6, SI 2008/410 Sch.5 para.8, SI 2008/432 Sch.1 para.2, SI 2008/2644 Art.26, Sch.2 para.2

s.223, applied: SI 2008/432 Sch.1 para.2, SI 2008/2546 Art.13

s.223, referred to: SI 2008/2644 Art.26, Sch.2 para.2

s.227, applied: SI 2008/432 Sch.1 para.2, SI 2008/2546 Art.13, SI 2008/2644 Art.26, Sch.2 para.2

s.228, applied: SI 2008/432 Sch.1 para.2, SI 2008/2546 Art.13, SI 2008/2644 Art.26, Sch.2 para.2

s.229, applied: SI 2008/432 Sch.1 para.2, SI 2008/2546 Art.13, SI 2008/2644 Art.26, Sch.2 para.2

s.230, applied: SI 2008/432 Sch.1 para.2, SI 2008/2546 Art.13, SI 2008/2644 Art.26, Sch.2 para.2

s.231, applied: SI 2008/432 Sch.1 para.2, SI 2008/2546 Art.13, SI 2008/2644 Art.26, Sch.2 para.2

s.232, disapplied: SI 2008/2546 Art.12, SI 2008/2644 Art.30, SI 2008/2674 Art.32

s.234, varied: SI 2008/674 Sch.3 para.1

s.235, applied: SI 2008/3229 Sch.1, Sch.2, Sch.3

s.242, disapplied: SI 2008/2860 Sch.2 para.34

s.242, referred to: SI 2008/2860 Sch.2 para.34

s.243, applied: SI 2008/2860 Sch.2 para.37

s.245, applied: SI 2008/2860 Sch.2 para.35

s.247, applied: SI 2008/2860 Sch.2 para.40

s.260, see *Franbar Holdings Ltd v Patel* [2008] EWHC 1534 (Ch), [2008] B.C.C. 885 (Ch D), William Trower QC

s.260, applied: SI 2008/432 Sch.1 para.2, SI 2008/2546 Art.13, SI 2008/2644 Art.26, Sch.2 para.2

CAP.

2006–cont.

46. Companies Act 2006–*cont.*

s.261, see *Franbar Holdings Ltd v Patel* [2008] EWHC 1534 (Ch), [2008] B.C.C. 885 (Ch D), William Trower QC

s.261, applied: SI 2008/432 Sch.1 para.2, SI 2008/2546 Art.13, SI 2008/2644 Art.26, Sch.2 para.2

s.262, applied: SI 2008/432 Sch.1 para.2, SI 2008/2546 Art.13, SI 2008/2644 Art.26, Sch.2 para.2

s.263, see *Franbar Holdings Ltd v Patel* [2008] EWHC 1534 (Ch), [2008] B.C.C. 885 (Ch D), William Trower QC

s.263, applied: SI 2008/432 Sch.1 para.2, SI 2008/2546 Art.13, SI 2008/2644 Art.26, Sch.2 para.2

s.264, applied: SI 2008/432 Sch.1 para.2, SI 2008/2546 Art.13, SI 2008/2644 Art.26, Sch.2 para.2

s.265, applied: SI 2008/432 Sch.1 para.2, SI 2008/2546 Art.13, SI 2008/2644 Art.26, Sch.2 para.2

s.266, applied: SI 2008/432 Sch.1 para.2, SI 2008/2546 Art.13, SI 2008/2644 Art.26, Sch.2 para.2

s.267, applied: SI 2008/432 Sch.1 para.2, SI 2008/2546 Art.13, SI 2008/2644 Art.26, Sch.2 para.2

s.268, applied: SI 2008/432 Sch.1 para.2, SI 2008/2546 Art.13, SI 2008/2644 Art.26, Sch.2 para.2

s.269, applied: SI 2008/432 Sch.1 para.2, SI 2008/2546 Art.13, SI 2008/2644 Art.26, Sch.2 para.2

s.275, applied: SI 2008/2860 Sch.2 para.25, Sch.2 para.38, SI 2008/3007 Reg.2

s.275, enabling: SI 2008/3007

s.276, applied: SI 2008/2860 Sch.2 para.27, Sch.2 para.29, Sch.2 para.31

s.277, applied: SI 2008/2860 Sch.2 para.27

s.297, applied: SI 2008/3006 Reg.4

s.380, varied: SI 2008/1911 Reg.4

s.381, amended: SI 2008/393 Reg.6

s.381, referred to: SI 2008/1912 Reg.2

s.381, varied: SI 2008/1911 Reg.5

s.382, amended: SI 2008/393 Reg.3

s.382, applied: SI 2008/393 Reg.2, SI 2008/410 Sch.7 para.12, SI 2008/1911 Reg.2

s.382, varied: SI 2008/1911 Reg.5

s.382A, applied: SI 2008/1911 Reg.2

s.382A, varied: SI 2008/1911 Reg.5

s.382B, applied: SI 2008/1911 Reg.2

s.382B, varied: SI 2008/1911 Reg.5

s.383, amended: SI 2008/393 Reg.3

s.383, applied: SI 2008/393 Reg.2, SI 2008/489 Reg.6, SI 2008/1911 Reg.2

s.383, varied: SI 2008/1911 Reg.5

s.384, applied: SI 2008/489 Reg.6, SI 2008/1911 Reg.2

s.384, varied: SI 2008/1911 Reg.5

CAP.

2006–cont.

46. Companies Act 2006–*cont.*

s.386, applied: 2008 c.17 s.130, SI 2008/410 Sch.1 para.50, Sch.2 para.61, Sch.3 para.68

s.386, varied: SI 2008/1911 Reg.6

s.387, varied: SI 2008/1911 Reg.6

s.388, varied: SI 2008/1911 Reg.6

s.389, varied: SI 2008/1911 Reg.6

s.390, disapplied: SI 2008/567 Sch.1 para.3

s.390, varied: SI 2008/1911 Reg.7

s.391, disapplied: SI 2008/567 Sch.1 para.3

s.391, varied: SI 2008/1911 Reg.7

s.392, disapplied: SI 2008/567 Sch.1 para.3

s.392, referred to: SI 2008/1911 Reg.7

s.392, varied: SI 2008/1911 Reg.7

s.393, applied: SI 2008/373 Reg.3, SI 2008/569 Sch.1 para.2

s.393, referred to: SI 2008/567 Sch.1 para.12

s.393, varied: SI 2008/373 Reg.3, SI 2008/1911 Reg.8

s.394, varied: SI 2008/1911 Reg.9

s.395, amended: SI 2008/393 Reg.9

s.395, varied: SI 2008/1911 Reg.9

s.396, applied: SI 2008/374 Reg.11, SI 2008/409 Reg.3, SI 2008/410 Reg.3, Reg.4, Reg.5, Reg.6, SI 2008/567 Sch.1 para.4, SI 2008/569 Sch.1 para.2

s.396, referred to: SI 2008/567 Sch.1 para.12

s.396, varied: SI 2008/373 Reg.3, SI 2008/1911 Reg.9

s.396, enabling: SI 2008/409, SI 2008/410

s.397, varied: SI 2008/1911 Reg.9

s.398, applied: SI 2008/409 Reg.8

s.398, varied: SI 2008/1911 Reg.10

s.399, varied: SI 2008/1911 Reg.10

s.400, applied: SI 2008/409 Sch.2 para.3, Sch.2 para.7, SI 2008/410 Sch.4 para.2, Sch.4 para.13

s.400, varied: SI 2008/1911 Reg.10

s.401, applied: SI 2008/409 Sch.2 para.3, Sch.2 para.7, SI 2008/410 Sch.4 para.2, Sch.4 para.13

s.401, varied: SI 2008/1911 Reg.10

s.402, varied: SI 2008/1911 Reg.10

s.403, applied: SI 2008/374 Reg.11, SI 2008/410 Reg.9

s.403, varied: SI 2008/1911 Reg.10

s.404, applied: SI 2008/567 Sch.1 para.7, SI 2008/569 Sch.1 para.2

s.404, referred to: SI 2008/567 Sch.1 para.12

s.404, varied: SI 2008/373 Reg.3, SI 2008/1911 Reg.10

s.404, enabling: SI 2008/409, SI 2008/410

s.405, applied: SI 2008/410 Sch.4 para.10, Sch.6 para.30

s.405, varied: SI 2008/1911 Reg.10

s.406, varied: SI 2008/1911 Reg.10

s.407, varied: SI 2008/1911 Reg.10

s.408, amended: SI 2008/393 Reg.10

CAP.

2006–cont.

46. Companies Act 2006–*cont.*

s.408, applied: SI 2008/409 Reg.3, Sch.1 para.59, SI 2008/410 Reg.3, Reg.5, Reg.6, Sch.1 para.65, Sch.1 para.71, Sch.2 para.85
s.408, varied: SI 2008/1911 Reg.10
s.409, referred to: SI 2008/409 Reg.4, Reg.10, SI 2008/410 Reg.7
s.409, varied: SI 2008/1911 Reg.11
s.409, enabling: SI 2008/409, SI 2008/410
s.410, varied: SI 2008/1911 Reg.11
s.410A, added: SI 2008/393 Reg.8
s.410A, varied: SI 2008/1911 Reg.11
s.411, amended: SI 2008/393 Reg.11
s.411, applied: SI 2008/1950 Sch.1 para.4
s.411, varied: SI 2008/1911 Reg.11
s.412, enabling: SI 2008/409, SI 2008/410
s.414, applied: SI 2008/373 Reg.4, SI 2008/409 Sch.1 para.13, SI 2008/410 Sch.1 para.13, Sch.2 para.19, Sch.3 para.18
s.414, varied: SI 2008/373 Reg.4, SI 2008/1911 Reg.12
s.415, applied: 2008 c.31 s.13, SI 2008/409 Reg.7, SI 2008/410 Reg.10
s.415A, added: SI 2008/393 Reg.6
s.416, amended: SI 2008/393 Reg.6
s.416, applied: 2008 c.27 s.85, SI 2008/409 Sch.5 para.1, SI 2008/410 Sch.7 Part 1
s.416, enabling: SI 2008/409, SI 2008/410
s.417, amended: SI 2008/393 Reg.6
s.419, amended: SI 2008/393 Reg.6
s.419, applied: SI 2008/373 Reg.5
s.419, varied: SI 2008/373 Reg.5
s.420, applied: SI 2008/410 Reg.11
s.421, enabling: SI 2008/410
s.422, applied: SI 2008/373 Reg.6
s.422, varied: SI 2008/373 Reg.6
s.423, applied: 2008 c.17 s.132, SI 2008/373 Reg.4, Reg.5, Reg.6, Reg.10, Reg.11, Reg.12, SI 2008/374 Reg.5, Reg.6, Reg.8
s.423, referred to: SI 2008/374 Reg.3
s.423, varied: SI 2008/1911 Reg.13
s.424, applied: 2008 c.17 s.132
s.425, applied: 2008 c.17 s.132
s.425, varied: SI 2008/373 Reg.12, SI 2008/1911 Reg.14
s.426, applied: SI 2008/373 Reg.12, Reg.17, SI 2008/374 Reg.4, Reg.7, Reg.12
s.426, enabling: SI 2008/374
s.427, applied: SI 2008/374 Reg.6, Reg.7
s.427, enabling: SI 2008/374
s.428, applied: SI 2008/374 Reg.6, Reg.7
s.428, enabling: SI 2008/374
s.429, varied: SI 2008/373 Reg.17
s.431, applied: 2008 c.17 s.132, SI 2008/373 Reg.10, Reg.11
s.431, varied: SI 2008/1911 Reg.15
s.432, applied: 2008 c.17 s.132, SI 2008/373 Reg.10, Reg.11
s.433, applied: SI 2008/565 Reg.3

CAP.

2006–cont.

46. Companies Act 2006–*cont.*

s.433, varied: SI 2008/1911 Reg.16
s.434, applied: 2008 c.17 s.132, SI 2008/373 Reg.10, Reg.17
s.434, varied: SI 2008/1911 Reg.16
s.435, applied: 2008 c.17 s.132, SI 2008/373 Reg.17
s.435, varied: SI 2008/1911 Reg.16
s.436, applied: 2008 c.17 s.132, SI 2008/565 Reg.3
s.436, varied: SI 2008/1911 Reg.16
s.437, applied: SI 2008/373 Reg.4, Reg.5, Reg.6, Reg.10, Reg.11, Reg.13
s.438, varied: SI 2008/373 Reg.13
s.441, amended: SI 2008/393 Reg.6
s.441, applied: 2008 c.17 s.132, SI 2008/373 Reg.4, Reg.5, Reg.6, Reg.10, Reg.11, Reg.14, SI 2008/410 Sch.6 para.30, SI 2008/497 Reg.2, Reg.4, SI 2008/569 Reg.5
s.441, varied: SI 2008/1911 Reg.17
s.442, applied: 2008 c.17 s.132, SI 2008/374 Reg.4
s.442, varied: SI 2008/1911 Reg.17
s.443, applied: 2008 c.17 s.132
s.443, varied: SI 2008/497 Sch.1 Part 1, SI 2008/1911 Reg.17
s.444, amended: SI 2008/393 Reg.12
s.444, applied: 2008 c.17 s.132, SI 2008/373 Reg.15, Reg.16, SI 2008/409 Reg.6, Reg.11, Sch.2 para.8, Sch.6 para.34, SI 2008/410 Sch.4 para.7
s.444, varied: SI 2008/1911 Reg.17
s.444, enabling: SI 2008/409
s.444A, added: SI 2008/393 Reg.6
s.444A, applied: 2008 c.17 s.132
s.445, amended: SI 2008/393 Reg.6
s.445, applied: SI 2008/373 Reg.15, Reg.16
s.445, varied: SI 2008/1911 Reg.18
s.445, enabling: SI 2008/410
s.446, amended: SI 2008/393 Reg.6
s.446, varied: SI 2008/1911 Reg.19
s.448, amended: SI 2008/393 Reg.13
s.449, varied: SI 2008/1911 Reg.20
s.450, varied: SI 2008/1911 Reg.21
s.451, varied: SI 2008/373 Reg.8, Reg.14, Reg.15, Reg.16, SI 2008/1911 Reg.22
s.452, varied: SI 2008/373 Reg.8, Reg.14, Reg.15, Reg.16, SI 2008/1911 Reg.22
s.453, applied: SI 2008/497, SI 2008/497 Reg.2, Reg.4
s.453, varied: SI 2008/1911 Reg.22
s.453, enabling: SI 2008/497
s.454, applied: 2008 c.17 s.132, SI 2008/373 Reg.7, Reg.9, Reg.12, Reg.13, Reg.14, Reg.15
s.454, varied: SI 2008/1911 Reg.23
s.454, enabling: SI 2008/373
s.455, varied: SI 2008/1911 Reg.23
s.456, applied: SI 2008/623 Art.2
s.456, varied: SI 2008/1911 Reg.23

CAP.

2006–cont.

46. Companies Act 2006–*cont.*

s.457, enabling: SI 2008/623
s.458, amended: SI 2008/948 Sch.1 para.244
s.458, varied: SI 2008/1911 Reg.24
s.459, varied: SI 2008/1911 Reg.24
s.460, amended: SI 2008/948 Sch.1 para.245
s.460, varied: SI 2008/1911 Reg.24
s.461, amended: SI 2008/948 Sch.1 para.246
s.461, varied: SI 2008/1911 Reg.24
s.464, applied: SI 2008/651 Reg.2, Reg.4
s.464, varied: SI 2008/1911 Reg.25
s.464, enabling: SI 2008/651
s.465, amended: SI 2008/393 Reg.4
s.465, applied: SI 2008/393 Reg.2, SI 2008/410 Reg.4, Sch.7 para.12, SI 2008/1911 Reg.2
s.465, varied: SI 2008/1911 Reg.26
s.466, amended: SI 2008/393 Reg.4
s.466, applied: SI 2008/393 Reg.2, SI 2008/489 Reg.6, SI 2008/1911 Reg.2
s.466, varied: SI 2008/1911 Reg.26
s.467, amended: SI 2008/393 Reg.7
s.467, applied: SI 2008/489 Reg.6, SI 2008/1911 Reg.2
s.467, varied: SI 2008/1911 Reg.26
s.468, varied: SI 2008/1911 Reg.27
s.468, enabling: SI 2008/393
s.469, applied: SI 2008/565 Reg.3
s.469, varied: SI 2008/1911 Reg.28
s.471, applied: 2008 c.31 Sch.1 para.3
s.471, varied: SI 2008/1911 Reg.29
s.472, varied: SI 2008/1911 Reg.30
s.473, applied: SI 2008/393, SI 2008/409, SI 2008/410
s.473, varied: SI 2008/1911 Reg.31
s.473, enabling: SI 2008/393
s.474, varied: SI 2008/1911 Reg.32
s.475, applied: SI 2008/565 Reg.3
s.475, varied: SI 2008/1911 Reg.33
s.477, amended: SI 2008/393 Reg.5
s.477, applied: 2008 c.17 s.129, s.130, SI 2008/373 Reg.18
s.477, varied: SI 2008/1911 Reg.34
s.478, varied: SI 2008/1911 Reg.34
s.479, amended: SI 2008/393 Reg.5
s.479, varied: SI 2008/1911 Reg.34
s.480, applied: SI 2008/373 Reg.18, SI 2008/409 Sch.1 para.63, Sch.4 para.10
s.480, varied: SI 2008/1911 Reg.35
s.481, varied: SI 2008/1911 Reg.35
s.483, applied: SSI 2008/144
s.483, enabling: SSI 2008/144
s.484, enabling: SI 2008/393
s.485, applied: SI 2008/565 Reg.6, SI 2008/567 Reg.7, Sch.1 para.1, Sch.1 para.9, SI 2008/1911 Reg.2
s.485, varied: SI 2008/565 Reg.6, SI 2008/567 Sch.1 para.9, SI 2008/1911 Reg.36

CAP.

2006–cont.

46. Companies Act 2006–*cont.*

s.486, applied: SI 2008/565 Reg.6, SI 2008/567 Reg.7, Sch.1 para.1, Sch.1 para.9, SI 2008/1911 Reg.2
s.486, varied: SI 2008/1911 Reg.36
s.487, applied: SI 2008/565 Reg.6, SI 2008/567 Reg.7, Sch.1 para.1, Sch.1 para.9, SI 2008/1911 Reg.2
s.487, varied: SI 2008/565 Reg.6, SI 2008/567 Sch.1 para.9, SI 2008/1911 Reg.36
s.488, applied: SI 2008/565 Reg.6, SI 2008/567 Reg.7, Sch.1 para.1, Sch.1 para.9, SI 2008/1911 Reg.2
s.488, varied: SI 2008/565 Reg.6, SI 2008/567 Sch.1 para.9, SI 2008/1911 Reg.36
s.492, applied: SI 2008/1911 Reg.2
s.492, varied: SI 2008/1911 Reg.37
s.494, applied: SI 2008/1911 Reg.2
s.494, varied: SI 2008/1911 Reg.38
s.494, enabling: SI 2008/489
s.495, applied: SI 2008/373 Reg.7, SI 2008/374 Reg.4, SI 2008/565 Reg.3, Reg.7, SI 2008/567 Reg.8, Sch.1 para.1, SI 2008/569 Reg.9, SI 2008/1911 Reg.2
s.495, disapplied: SI 2008/373 Reg.7
s.495, referred to: SI 2008/373 Reg.7
s.495, varied: SI 2008/1911 Reg.39
s.496, applied: SI 2008/373 Reg.9, SI 2008/374 Reg.4, SI 2008/565 Reg.3
s.497, applied: SI 2008/373 Reg.9, SI 2008/374 Reg.4, SI 2008/410 Reg.11
s.498, amended: SI 2008/393 Reg.6
s.498, applied: SI 2008/373 Reg.7, SI 2008/565 Reg.3, Reg.7, SI 2008/567 Reg.8, Sch.1 para.1, SI 2008/569 Reg.9, SI 2008/1911 Reg.2
s.498, varied: SI 2008/1911 Reg.40
s.499, applied: 2008 c.17 s.132, SI 2008/565 Reg.7, SI 2008/567 Reg.8, Sch.1 para.1, SI 2008/569 Reg.9, SI 2008/1911 Reg.2
s.499, varied: SI 2008/1911 Reg.40
s.500, applied: 2008 c.17 s.132, SI 2008/1911 Reg.2
s.500, varied: SI 2008/1911 Reg.40
s.501, applied: 2008 c.17 s.132, SI 2008/1911 Reg.2
s.501, varied: SI 2008/1911 Reg.40
s.502, applied: 2008 c.17 s.132, SI 2008/1911 Reg.2
s.502, varied: SI 2008/1911 Reg.40
s.503, applied: SI 2008/565 Reg.3, Reg.8, SI 2008/567 Reg.9, Sch.1 para.1, SI 2008/569 Reg.10, SI 2008/1911 Reg.2
s.503, referred to: SI 2008/373 Reg.7
s.503, varied: SI 2008/373 Reg.7, Reg.9, SI 2008/1911 Reg.41
s.504, applied: SI 2008/496 Art.11, SI 2008/565 Reg.8, SI 2008/567 Reg.9, Sch.1 para.1, SI 2008/569 Reg.10, SI 2008/1911 Reg.2

CAP.

2006–*cont.*

46. Companies Act 2006–*cont.*

s.504, varied: SI 2008/373 Reg.7, Reg.9, SI 2008/1911 Reg.41
s.504, enabling: SI 2008/496
s.505, applied: 2008 c.17 s.132, SI 2008/565 Reg.3, Reg.8, SI 2008/567 Reg.9, Sch.1 para.1, Sch.1 para.10, SI 2008/569 Reg.10, SI 2008/1911 Reg.2
s.505, varied: SI 2008/373 Reg.7, Reg.9, SI 2008/567 Sch.1 para.10, SI 2008/1911 Reg.41
s.506, applied: 2008 c.17 s.132, SI 2008/565 Reg.8, SI 2008/567 Reg.9, Sch.1 para.1, Sch.1 para.10, SI 2008/569 Reg.10, SI 2008/1911 Reg.2
s.506, varied: SI 2008/373 Reg.7, Reg.9, SI 2008/567 Sch.1 para.10, SI 2008/569 Sch.1 para.3, SI 2008/1911 Reg.41
s.507, applied: SI 2008/1911 Reg.2
s.507, varied: SI 2008/1911 Reg.42
s.508, applied: SI 2008/1911 Reg.2
s.508, varied: SI 2008/1911 Reg.42
s.509, applied: SI 2008/1911 Reg.2
s.509, varied: SI 2008/1911 Reg.42
s.510, applied: SI 2008/1911 Reg.2
s.510, varied: SI 2008/1911 Reg.43
s.511, applied: SI 2008/1911 Reg.2
s.511, varied: SI 2008/1911 Reg.43
s.512, applied: SI 2008/1911 Reg.2
s.512, referred to: SI 2008/1911 Reg.43
s.512, varied: SI 2008/1911 Reg.43
s.513, applied: SI 2008/1911 Reg.2
s.513, varied: SI 2008/1911 Reg.44
s.515, applied: SI 2008/1911 Reg.2
s.515, varied: SI 2008/1911 Reg.45
s.516, applied: SI 2008/1911 Reg.2
s.516, varied: SI 2008/1911 Reg.45
s.517, applied: SI 2008/1911 Reg.2
s.517, varied: SI 2008/1911 Reg.45
s.518, applied: SI 2008/1911 Reg.2
s.518, varied: SI 2008/1911 Reg.45
s.519, amended: SI 2008/948 Sch.1 para.247
s.519, applied: SI 2008/565 Reg.5, Reg.12, SI 2008/567 Reg.13, SI 2008/1911 Reg.2
s.519, varied: SI 2008/1911 Reg.46
s.520, applied: SI 2008/1911 Reg.2
s.520, varied: SI 2008/1911 Reg.46
s.521, amended: SI 2008/948 Sch.1 para.248
s.521, applied: SI 2008/1911 Reg.2
s.521, varied: SI 2008/1911 Reg.46
s.522, applied: SI 2008/496 Art.5, SI 2008/1911 Reg.2
s.522, varied: SI 2008/1911 Reg.46
s.523, applied: SI 2008/496 Art.5, SI 2008/1911 Reg.2
s.523, varied: SI 2008/1911 Reg.46
s.524, applied: SI 2008/1911 Reg.2
s.524, varied: SI 2008/1911 Reg.46
s.525, applied: SI 2008/496 Art.5, SI 2008/1911 Reg.2

CAP.

2006–*cont.*

46. Companies Act 2006–*cont.*

s.525, varied: SI 2008/1911 Reg.46
s.526, applied: SI 2008/1911 Reg.2
s.526, varied: SI 2008/1911 Reg.46
s.538, enabling: SI 2008/489
s.539, varied: SI 2008/1911 Reg.47
s.540, applied: SI 2008/2860 Sch.2 para.41
s.540, referred to: SI 2008/2860 Sch.2 para.41
s.550, applied: SI 2008/2860 Sch.2 para.43, Sch.2 para.44
s.551, applied: SI 2008/2860 Sch.2 para.45
s.554, applied: SI 2008/2860 Sch.2 para.46
s.555, applied: SI 2008/2860 Sch.2 para.47
s.556, applied: SI 2008/2860 Sch.2 para.48
s.561, applied: SI 2008/2860 Sch.2 para.49, Sch.2 para.50, Sch.2 para.52, Sch.2 para.53, Sch.2 para.55
s.562, applied: SI 2008/2860 Sch.2 para.49, Sch.2 para.50
s.562, referred to: SI 2008/2860 Sch.2 para.49, Sch.2 para.51
s.563, applied: SI 2008/2860 Sch.2 para.49, Sch.2 para.51
s.567, applied: SI 2008/2860 Sch.2 para.50
s.568, applied: SI 2008/2860 Sch.2 para.51
s.568, referred to: SI 2008/2860 Sch.2 para.51
s.570, applied: SI 2008/2860 Sch.2 para.52, Sch.2 para.55
s.571, applied: SI 2008/2860 Sch.2 para.53, Sch.2 para.54, Sch.2 para.55
s.572, applied: SI 2008/2860 Sch.2 para.54
s.573, applied: SI 2008/2860 Sch.2 para.55
s.578, applied: SI 2008/2860 Sch.2 para.56
s.579, applied: SI 2008/2860 Sch.2 para.56
s.583, applied: SI 2008/2860 Sch.2 para.57
s.589, varied: SI 2008/2860 Sch.2 para.58
s.606, varied: SI 2008/2860 Sch.2 para.58
s.607, applied: SI 2008/2860 Sch.2 para.57
s.631, referred to: SI 2008/2860 Sch.2 para.61
s.634, referred to: SI 2008/2860 Sch.2 para.61
s.636, applied: SI 2008/2860 Sch.2 para.62
s.637, applied: SI 2008/2860 Sch.2 para.63
s.638, applied: SI 2008/2860 Sch.2 para.64
s.639, applied: SI 2008/2860 Sch.2 para.65
s.640, applied: SI 2008/2860 Sch.2 para.66
s.641, varied: SI 2008/1886 Art.3
s.642, applied: SI 2008/1915 Art.2
s.643, applied: SI 2008/1915 Art.2
s.643, enabling: SI 2008/1915
s.644, varied: SI 2008/1886 Art.4
s.645, applied: SI 2008/2860 Sch.2 para.68
s.646, applied: SI 2008/2860 Sch.2 para.68
s.647, applied: SI 2008/2860 Sch.2 para.68
s.648, applied: SI 2008/1915 Art.3, SI 2008/2860 Sch.2 para.68
s.649, applied: SI 2008/2860 Sch.2 para.68

CAP.

2006–cont.

46. Companies Act 2006–*cont.*

s.650, applied: SI 2008/2860 Sch.2 para.68
s.651, applied: SI 2008/2860 Sch.2 para.68
s.652, referred to: SI 2008/2860 Sch.2 para.69
s.652, varied: SI 2008/1886 Art.5
s.653, referred to: SI 2008/2860 Sch.2 para.69
s.654, applied: SI 2008/1915
s.654, disapplied: SI 2008/1915 Art.3
s.654, enabling: SI 2008/1915
s.658, referred to: SI 2008/1579 Reg.6
s.659, applied: SI 2008/409 Sch.5 para.6, SI 2008/410 Sch.7 para.8
s.662, applied: SI 2008/409 Sch.5 para.6, SI 2008/410 Sch.7 para.8, SI 2008/2860 Sch.2 para.70, Sch.2 para.72
s.662, referred to: SI 2008/2860 Sch.2 para.70
s.663, applied: SI 2008/2860 Sch.2 para.71
s.663, referred to: SI 2008/2860 Sch.2 para.71
s.664, applied: SI 2008/2860 Sch.2 para.72
s.665, applied: SI 2008/2860 Sch.2 para.72
s.666, applied: SI 2008/2860 Sch.2 para.72
s.667, applied: SI 2008/2860 Sch.2 para.72
s.668, referred to: SI 2008/2860 Sch.2 para.70
s.670, applied: SI 2008/409 Sch.5 para.6, SI 2008/410 Sch.7 para.8
s.677, applied: SI 2008/409 Reg.12, Sch.7 para.3, SI 2008/410 Reg.12, Sch.9 para.3
s.677, enabling: SI 2008/409, SI 2008/410
s.682, applied: SI 2008/410 Sch.1 para.64, Sch.3 para.82
s.686, applied: SI 2008/2860 Sch.2 para.73
s.689, applied: SI 2008/2860 Sch.2 para.74
s.693, applied: SI 2008/2860 Sch.2 para.76
s.694, applied: SI 2008/2860 Sch.2 para.76
s.707, applied: SI 2008/2860 Sch.2 para.77
s.708, applied: SI 2008/2860 Sch.2 para.77
s.709, applied: SI 2008/2860 Sch.2 para.78
s.710, applied: SI 2008/2860 Sch.2 para.78
s.711, applied: SI 2008/2860 Sch.2 para.78
s.712, applied: SI 2008/409 Reg.12, Sch.7 para.4, SI 2008/410 Reg.12, Sch.9 para.4, SI 2008/2860 Sch.2 para.78
s.712, enabling: SI 2008/409, SI 2008/410
s.713, applied: SI 2008/2860 Sch.2 para.78
s.714, applied: SI 2008/2860 Sch.2 para.78
s.714, referred to: SI 2008/2860 Sch.2 para.78
s.715, applied: SI 2008/2860 Sch.2 para.78
s.716, applied: SI 2008/2860 Sch.2 para.78
s.717, applied: SI 2008/2860 Sch.2 para.78
s.718, applied: SI 2008/2860 Sch.2 para.78
s.719, applied: SI 2008/2860 Sch.2 para.78
s.720, applied: SI 2008/2860 Sch.2 para.78
s.721, applied: SI 2008/2860 Sch.2 para.78
s.722, applied: SI 2008/2860 Sch.2 para.78

CAP.

2006–cont.

46. Companies Act 2006–*cont.*

s.723, applied: SI 2008/2860 Sch.2 para.78
s.727, applied: SI 2008/2860 Sch.2 para.79
s.730, applied: SI 2008/2860 Sch.2 para.80
s.754, varied: SI 2008/346 Sch.1 para.6
s.757, applied: SI 2008/729 Reg.6
s.758, applied: SI 2008/729 Reg.6
s.763, varied: SI 2008/729 Reg.2
s.763, enabling: SI 2008/729
s.766, enabling: SI 2008/729
s.776, varied: SI 2008/2546 Art.4
s.777, varied: SI 2008/2546 Art.4
s.778, varied: SI 2008/2546 Art.4
s.831, applied: SI 2008/410 Reg.12, Sch.9 para.5
s.831, enabling: SI 2008/410
s.832, applied: SI 2008/410 Reg.12, Sch.1 para.75, Sch.9 para.6
s.832, enabling: SI 2008/410
s.833, applied: SI 2008/495 Reg.7
s.833, referred to: SI 2008/410 Sch.1 para.75
s.836, applied: SI 2008/409 Reg.12, Sch.7 para.5, SI 2008/410 Reg.12, Sch.9 para.7
s.836, enabling: SI 2008/409, SI 2008/410
s.843, applied: SI 2008/410 Sch.3 para.11
s.854, applied: SI 2008/432 Sch.1 para.2, SI 2008/2546 Art.13, SI 2008/2644 Art.26, Sch.2 para.2, SI 2008/2860 Sch.2 para.81
s.855, amended: SI 2008/3000 Reg.2, Reg.3, Reg.4
s.855, applied: SI 2008/432 Sch.1 para.2, SI 2008/2546 Art.13, SI 2008/2644 Art.26, Sch.2 para.2, SI 2008/2860 Sch.2 para.81, SI 2008/3000 Reg.5, Reg.6
s.855A, added: SI 2008/3000 Reg.2
s.855A, applied: SI 2008/432 Sch.1 para.2, SI 2008/2546 Art.13, SI 2008/2644 Art.26, Sch.2 para.2, SI 2008/2860 Sch.2 para.81
s.856, amended: SI 2008/3000 Reg.7
s.856, applied: SI 2008/432 Sch.1 para.2, SI 2008/2546 Art.13, SI 2008/2644 Art.26, Sch.2 para.2, SI 2008/2860 Sch.2 para.81
s.856, repealed (in part): SI 2008/3000 Reg.7
s.856A, added: SI 2008/3000 Reg.7
s.856A, applied: SI 2008/432 Sch.1 para.2, SI 2008/2546 Art.13, SI 2008/2644 Art.26, Sch.2 para.2, SI 2008/2860 Sch.2 para.81
s.856B, added: SI 2008/3000 Reg.7
s.856B, applied: SI 2008/432 Sch.1 para.2, SI 2008/2546 Art.13, SI 2008/2644 Art.26, Sch.2 para.2, SI 2008/2860 Sch.2 para.81
s.857, applied: SI 2008/432 Sch.1 para.2, SI 2008/2546 Art.13, SI 2008/2644 Art.26, Sch.2 para.2, SI 2008/2860 Sch.2 para.81
s.857, enabling: SI 2008/3000
s.858, amended: SI 2008/3000 Reg.8

CAP.

2006–*cont.*

46. Companies Act 2006–*cont.*

s.858, applied: SI 2008/432 Sch.1 para.2, SI 2008/2546 Art.13, SI 2008/2644 Art.26, Sch.2 para.2, SI 2008/2860 Sch.2 para.81
s.859, applied: SI 2008/432 Sch.1 para.2, SI 2008/2546 Art.13, SI 2008/2644 Art.26, Sch.2 para.2, SI 2008/2860 Sch.2 para.81
s.859, repealed: SI 2008/3000 Reg.8
s.860, applied: SI 2008/2860 Sch.2 para.82, SI 2008/2996 Reg.2
s.860, enabling: SI 2008/2996
s.862, applied: SI 2008/2860 Sch.2 para.83, SI 2008/2996 Reg.4
s.862, enabling: SI 2008/2996
s.863, applied: SI 2008/2860 Sch.2 para.84
s.868, applied: SI 2008/2860 Sch.2 para.85
s.871, applied: SI 2008/2860 Sch.2 para.86
s.872, applied: SI 2008/2860 Sch.2 para.87
s.877, applied: SI 2008/3007 Reg.2
s.877, enabling: SI 2008/3007
s.878, applied: SI 2008/2860 Sch.2 para.82, SI 2008/2996 Reg.3
s.878, enabling: SI 2008/2996
s.880, applied: SI 2008/2860 Sch.2 para.83, SI 2008/2996 Reg.4
s.880, enabling: SI 2008/2996
s.882, applied: SI 2008/2860 Sch.2 para.84
s.887, applied: SI 2008/2860 Sch.2 para.87
s.892, applied: SI 2008/3007 Reg.2
s.892, enabling: SI 2008/3007
s.896, amended: SI 2008/948 Sch.1 para.249
s.899, amended: SI 2008/948 Sch.1 para.250
s.899, applied: 2008 c.17 s.160
s.900, applied: 2008 c.17 s.160
s.909, amended: SI 2008/690 Reg.2
s.914, substituted: SI 2008/690 Reg.3
s.918A, added: SI 2008/690 Reg.2
s.930, substituted: SI 2008/690 Reg.4
s.938, amended: SI 2008/948 Sch.1 para.251
s.948, varied: SI 2008/3122 Sch.1 para.1
s.949, varied: SI 2008/3122 Sch.1 para.2
s.950, varied: SI 2008/3122 Sch.1 para.3
s.953, varied: SI 2008/3122 Sch.1 para.4
s.955, varied: SI 2008/3122 Sch.1 para.5
s.961, varied: SI 2008/3122 Sch.1 para.6
s.962, varied: SI 2008/3122 Sch.1 para.7
s.964, varied: SI 2008/3122 Sch.1 para.8
s.965, enabling: SI 2008/3122
s.994, see *Franbar Holdings Ltd v Patel* [2008] EWHC 1534 (Ch), [2008] B.C.C. 885 (Ch D), William Trower QC; see *Hawkes v Cuddy* [2007] EWHC 2999 (Ch), [2008] B.C.C. 390 (Ch D), Lewison, J.
s.1000, applied: SI 2008/2860 Sch.2 para.91
s.1003, applied: SI 2008/2860 Sch.2 para.91
s.1012, applied: SI 2008/2860 Sch.2 para.88
s.1013, applied: SI 2008/2860 Sch.2 para.88

CAP.

2006–*cont.*

46. Companies Act 2006–*cont.*

s.1014, applied: SI 2008/2860 Sch.2 para.88
s.1015, applied: SI 2008/2860 Sch.2 para.88
s.1016, applied: SI 2008/2860 Sch.2 para.88
s.1017, applied: SI 2008/2860 Sch.2 para.88
s.1018, applied: SI 2008/2860 Sch.2 para.88
s.1019, applied: SI 2008/2860 Sch.2 para.88
s.1020, applied: SI 2008/2860 Sch.2 para.88
s.1021, applied: SI 2008/2860 Sch.2 para.88
s.1022, applied: SI 2008/2860 Sch.2 para.88
s.1023, applied: SI 2008/2860 Sch.2 para.88
s.1029, applied: SI 2008/2860 Sch.2 para.90, Sch.2 para.91
s.1029, referred to: SI 2008/2860 Sch.2 para.91
s.1030, applied: SI 2008/2860 Sch.2 para.90, Sch.2 para.91
s.1030, disapplied: SI 2008/2860 Sch.2 para.91
s.1031, applied: SI 2008/2860 Sch.2 para.90
s.1032, applied: SI 2008/2860 Sch.2 para.90
s.1034, applied: SI 2008/2860 Sch.2 para.92
s.1034, varied: SI 2008/2860 Sch.2 para.92
s.1046, referred to: SI 2008/410 Sch.7 para.7
s.1063, applied: SI 2008/2860 Sch.2 para.94
s.1064, applied: SI 2008/2860 Sch.2 para.95
s.1065, applied: SI 2008/2860 Sch.2 para.96
s.1068, applied: SI 2008/2860 Sch.2 para.97
s.1069, applied: SI 2008/2860 Sch.2 para.97
s.1070, applied: SI 2008/2860 Sch.2 para.98
s.1071, applied: SI 2008/2860 Sch.2 para.99
s.1072, applied: SI 2008/2860 Sch.2 para.100, Sch.2 para.102
s.1073, applied: SI 2008/2860 Sch.2 para.100, Sch.2 para.102
s.1074, applied: SI 2008/2860 Sch.2 para.100, Sch.2 para.102
s.1075, applied: SI 2008/2860 Sch.2 para.101
s.1076, applied: SI 2008/2860 Sch.2 para.102
s.1078, applied: SI 2008/2860 Sch.2 para.103
s.1079, applied: SI 2008/2860 Sch.2 para.104
s.1081, applied: SI 2008/2860 Sch.2 para.105
s.1088, applied: SI 2008/2860 Sch.2 para.36
s.1094, applied: SI 2008/2860 Sch.2 para.107
s.1095, applied: SI 2008/2860 Sch.2 para.107
s.1096, applied: SI 2008/2860 Sch.2 para.107
s.1097, applied: SI 2008/2860 Sch.2 para.107
s.1098, applied: SI 2008/2860 Sch.2 para.107
s.1108, applied: SI 2008/2860 Sch.2 para.108

CAP.

2006–cont.

46. Companies Act 2006–*cont.*

s.1109, applied: SI 2008/2860 Sch.2 para.108
s.1110, applied: SI 2008/2860 Sch.2 para.108
s.1112, applied: SI 2008/2860 Sch.2 para.36, Sch.2 para.37, Sch.2 para.109
s.1115, disapplied: SI 2008/2860 Sch.2 para.111
s.1121, applied: SI 2008/565 Reg.6, Reg.12, SI 2008/567 Reg.7, Sch.1 para.1, SI 2008/569 Reg.16
s.1121, varied: SI 2008/1911 Reg.49
s.1122, applied: SI 2008/565 Reg.6, Reg.12, SI 2008/569 Reg.16
s.1122, varied: SI 2008/1911 Reg.49
s.1123, applied: SI 2008/565 Reg.6, Reg.12, SI 2008/567 Reg.7, Sch.1 para.1, SI 2008/569 Reg.16
s.1125, varied: SI 2008/1911 Reg.50
s.1126, varied: SI 2008/1911 Reg.50
s.1127, applied: SI 2008/565 Reg.13, SI 2008/567 Reg.6, Reg.13, SI 2008/569 Reg.15, Reg.16
s.1127, varied: SI 2008/1911 Reg.50, SI 2008/1950 Reg.4
s.1128, applied: SI 2008/565 Reg.13, SI 2008/567 Reg.6, Reg.13, SI 2008/569 Reg.15, Reg.16
s.1128, varied: SI 2008/1911 Reg.50, SI 2008/1950 Reg.4
s.1129, varied: SI 2008/1911 Reg.50
s.1130, applied: SI 2008/565 Reg.5, Reg.6, SI 2008/567 Reg.6, Reg.7, Sch.1 para.1, SI 2008/569 Reg.15, Reg.16
s.1130, varied: SI 2008/1911 Reg.50
s.1131, varied: SI 2008/1911 Reg.50
s.1132, varied: SI 2008/1911 Reg.50
s.1136, referred to: SI 2008/3006 Reg.3
s.1136, enabling: SI 2008/3006
s.1137, enabling: SI 2008/3006, SI 2008/3007
s.1141, enabling: SI 2008/3000
s.1145, applied: SI 2008/3006 Reg.8
s.1154, applied: SI 2008/2860 Sch.2 para.112
s.1155, applied: SI 2008/2860 Sch.2 para.112
s.1157, varied: SI 2008/1911 Reg.51
s.1159, referred to: 2008 c.2 s.15
s.1161, applied: SI 2008/567 Sch.1 para.1, SI 2008/569 Sch.1 para.1
s.1161, referred to: 2008 c.2 s.15
s.1161, varied: SI 2008/1911 Reg.52
s.1162, referred to: 2008 c.2 s.15, SI 2008/409 Sch.6 para.22, SI 2008/410 Sch.4 para.16
s.1162, varied: SI 2008/1911 Reg.52
s.1167, enabling: SI 2008/1659, SI 2008/1860, SI 2008/1861, SI 2008/1915, SI 2008/2996, SI 2008/3000, SI 2008/3007, SI 2008/3014
s.1169, varied: SI 2008/1911 Reg.53
s.1172, varied: SI 2008/1911 Reg.54

CAP.

2006–cont.

46. Companies Act 2006–*cont.*

s.1173, varied: SI 2008/1911 Reg.55
s.1209, varied: SI 2008/1950 Reg.6
s.1210, amended: SI 2008/565 Reg.15, SI 2008/567 Reg.14, SI 2008/1950 Reg.31
s.1210, applied: SI 2008/496 Art.4, SI 2008/569 Reg.14, SI 2008/1911 Reg.48
s.1210, repealed (in part): SI 2008/565 Reg.15
s.1210, varied: SI 2008/1950 Reg.6
s.1210, enabling: SI 2008/569, SI 2008/1911
s.1211, varied: SI 2008/1950 Reg.6
s.1212, varied: SI 2008/1950 Reg.6
s.1213, varied: SI 2008/1950 Reg.6
s.1214, applied: 2008 c.17 s.131, SI 2008/496 Art.4, SI 2008/948 Art.5
s.1214, varied: SI 2008/1950 Reg.6
s.1215, varied: SI 2008/1950 Reg.6
s.1216, applied: 2008 c.17 s.131, SI 2008/948 Art.5
s.1216, varied: SI 2008/948 Art.5, SI 2008/1950 Reg.6
s.1217, varied: SI 2008/1950 Reg.6
s.1218, varied: SI 2008/1950 Reg.6
s.1219, varied: SI 2008/1950 Reg.6
s.1220, varied: SI 2008/1950 Reg.6
s.1221, applied: SI 2008/496 Art.4
s.1221, referred to: SI 2008/496 Art.4
s.1221, varied: SI 2008/1950 Reg.6
s.1222, varied: SI 2008/1950 Reg.6
s.1223, applied: SI 2008/496 Art.9
s.1223, varied: SI 2008/1950 Reg.6
s.1223A, varied: SI 2008/1950 Reg.6
s.1224, applied: SI 2008/489 Reg.4, SI 2008/496 Art.4
s.1224, varied: SI 2008/1950 Reg.6
s.1224A, varied: SI 2008/1950 Reg.6
s.1224B, varied: SI 2008/1950 Reg.6
s.1225, varied: SI 2008/1950 Reg.6
s.1226, varied: SI 2008/1950 Reg.6
s.1227, varied: SI 2008/1950 Reg.6
s.1228, varied: SI 2008/1950 Reg.6
s.1229, varied: SI 2008/1950 Reg.6
s.1230, varied: SI 2008/1950 Reg.6
s.1231, applied: SI 2008/496 Art.4
s.1231, varied: SI 2008/1950 Reg.6
s.1232, varied: SI 2008/1950 Reg.6
s.1233, varied: SI 2008/1950 Reg.6
s.1234, varied: SI 2008/1950 Reg.6
s.1235, varied: SI 2008/1950 Reg.6
s.1236, varied: SI 2008/1950 Reg.6
s.1237, applied: SI 2008/496 Art.4
s.1237, varied: SI 2008/1950 Reg.6
s.1238, varied: SI 2008/1950 Reg.6
s.1239, applied: SI 2008/496 Art.3, Art.4, SI 2008/499
s.1239, varied: SI 2008/1950 Reg.6
s.1239, enabling: SI 2008/499, SI 2008/2639
s.1240, applied: SI 2008/496 Art.3

CAP.

2006–cont.

46. Companies Act 2006–*cont.*

s.1240, varied: SI 2008/1950 Reg.6
s.1241, applied: SI 2008/496 Art.4
s.1241, varied: SI 2008/1950 Reg.6
s.1242, varied: SI 2008/1950 Reg.6
s.1243, applied: SI 2008/496 Art.9
s.1243, varied: SI 2008/1950 Reg.6
s.1244, applied: SI 2008/496 Art.4
s.1244, varied: SI 2008/1950 Reg.6
s.1245, varied: SI 2008/1950 Reg.6
s.1246, applied: SI 2008/496 Art.4
s.1246, varied: SI 2008/1950 Reg.6
s.1246, enabling: SI 2008/2639
s.1247, varied: SI 2008/1950 Reg.6
s.1248, varied: SI 2008/1950 Reg.6
s.1249, varied: SI 2008/1950 Reg.6
s.1250, varied: SI 2008/1950 Reg.6
s.1251, varied: SI 2008/1950 Reg.6
s.1251A, varied: SI 2008/1950 Reg.6
s.1252, referred to: SI 2008/496 Art.4
s.1252, varied: SI 2008/1950 Reg.6
s.1252, enabling: SI 2008/496
s.1253, varied: SI 2008/1950 Reg.6
s.1253, enabling: SI 2008/496
s.1253A, applied: SI 2008/496 Art.4
s.1253A, varied: SI 2008/1950 Reg.6
s.1253B, applied: SI 2008/496 Art.4
s.1253B, referred to: SI 2008/496 Art.4
s.1253B, varied: SI 2008/1950 Reg.6
s.1253C, varied: SI 2008/1950 Reg.6
s.1253D, varied: SI 2008/1950 Reg.6
s.1253E, varied: SI 2008/1950 Reg.6
s.1253F, varied: SI 2008/1950 Reg.6
s.1254, applied: SI 2008/496 Art.4
s.1254, varied: SI 2008/1950 Reg.6
s.1255, varied: SI 2008/1950 Reg.6
s.1256, varied: SI 2008/496 Art.10, SI 2008/1950 Reg.6
s.1257, varied: SI 2008/1950 Reg.6
s.1258, varied: SI 2008/1950 Reg.6
s.1259, varied: SI 2008/1950 Reg.6
s.1260, varied: SI 2008/1950 Reg.6
s.1261, applied: SI 2008/496 Art.4
s.1261, varied: SI 2008/1950 Reg.6
s.1262, varied: SI 2008/1950 Reg.6
s.1263, applied: SI 2008/496 Art.4
s.1263, varied: SI 2008/1950 Reg.6
s.1264, varied: SI 2008/1950 Reg.6
s.1283, applied: SI 2008/2860 Sch.2 para.113
s.1284, referred to: SI 2008/2860 Sch.2 para.114
s.1288, varied: SI 2008/1911 Reg.56
s.1289, varied: SI 2008/1911 Reg.56
s.1290, applied: SI 2008/393, SI 2008/409, SI 2008/410, SI 2008/495, SI 2008/497, SI 2008/948, SI 2008/954, SI 2008/1911, SI 2008/1915
s.1290, varied: SI 2008/1911 Reg.56
s.1291, enabling: SI 2008/489

CAP.

2006–cont.

46. Companies Act 2006–*cont.*

s.1292, applied: SI 2008/393, SI 2008/1911, SI 2008/1915
s.1292, varied: SI 2008/1911 Reg.57
s.1292, enabling: SI 2008/374, SI 2008/393, SI 2008/409, SI 2008/410, SI 2008/489, SI 2008/495, SI 2008/497, SI 2008/569, SI 2008/674, SI 2008/729, SI 2008/948, SI 2008/954, SI 2008/1911, SI 2008/2639, SI 2008/2860, SI 2008/3000, SI 2008/3006, SI 2008/3007, SI 2008/3014
s.1294, applied: SI 2008/948, SI 2008/954
s.1294, enabling: SI 2008/495, SI 2008/948, SI 2008/954
s.1296, enabling: SI 2008/674, SI 2008/948, SI 2008/954, SI 2008/1886, SI 2008/2860
s.1297, applied: SI 2008/2860 Sch.2 para.2, Sch.2 para.22, Sch.2 para.93
s.1297, disapplied: SI 2008/2860 Sch.2 para.1
s.1297, referred to: SI 2008/674 Art.6, SI 2008/948 Art.12, SI 2008/954 Art.4, SI 2008/2860 Art.7, Art.8
s.1297, varied: SI 2008/2860 Sch.2 para.1
s.1300, enabling: SI 2008/674, SI 2008/1886, SI 2008/2860
Sch.2 Part 1 para.3A, varied: SI 2008/3122 Sch.1 para.9
Sch.2 Part 1 para.5A, varied: SI 2008/3122 Sch.1 para.9
Sch.2 Part 1 para.7A, varied: SI 2008/3122 Sch.1 para.9
Sch.2 Part 1 para.12A, varied: SI 2008/3122 Sch.1 para.9
Sch.2 Part 2 para.14A, varied: SI 2008/3122 Sch.1 para.10
Sch.2 Part 2 para.22A, varied: SI 2008/3122 Sch.1 para.10
Sch.2 Part 2 para.25A, varied: SI 2008/3122 Sch.1 para.10
Sch.2 Part 2 para.25B, varied: SI 2008/3122 Sch.1 para.10
Sch.2 Part 2 para.27A, varied: SI 2008/3122 Sch.1 para.10
Sch.2 Part 2 para.27B, varied: SI 2008/3122 Sch.1 para.10
Sch.2 Part 2 para.29A, varied: SI 2008/3122 Sch.1 para.10
Sch.2 Part 2 para.32A, varied: SI 2008/3122 Sch.1 para.10
Sch.2 Part 2 para.34, amended: SI 2008/1277 Sch.2 para.75
Sch.2 Part 2 para.34, repealed (in part): SI 2008/1277 Sch.4 Part 1
Sch.2 Part 2 para.39, varied: SI 2008/3122 Sch.1 para.10
Sch.2 Part 2 para.48A, varied: SI 2008/3122 Sch.1 para.10
Sch.2 Part 2 para.52A, varied: SI 2008/3122 Sch.1 para.10

CAP.

2006–cont.

46. Companies Act 2006–*cont.*

Sch.2 Part 2 para.55A, varied: SI 2008/3122 Sch.1 para.10

Sch.2 Part 2 para.70, varied: SI 2008/3122 Sch.1 para.10

Sch.7 para.1, varied: SI 2008/1911 Reg.52

Sch.7 para.2, varied: SI 2008/1911 Reg.52

Sch.7 para.3, varied: SI 2008/1911 Reg.52

Sch.7 para.4, varied: SI 2008/1911 Reg.52

Sch.7 para.5, applied: SI 2008/409 Sch.6 para.19, SI 2008/410 Sch.6 para.19

Sch.7 para.5, varied: SI 2008/1911 Reg.52

Sch.7 para.6, applied: SI 2008/409 Sch.6 para.19, SI 2008/410 Sch.6 para.19

Sch.7 para.6, varied: SI 2008/1911 Reg.52

Sch.7 para.7, applied: SI 2008/409 Sch.6 para.19, SI 2008/410 Sch.6 para.19

Sch.7 para.7, varied: SI 2008/1911 Reg.52

Sch.7 para.8, applied: SI 2008/409 Sch.6 para.19, SI 2008/410 Sch.6 para.19

Sch.7 para.8, varied: SI 2008/1911 Reg.52

Sch.7 para.9, applied: SI 2008/409 Sch.6 para.19, SI 2008/410 Sch.6 para.19

Sch.7 para.9, varied: SI 2008/1911 Reg.52

Sch.7 para.10, applied: SI 2008/409 Sch.6 para.19, SI 2008/410 Sch.6 para.19

Sch.7 para.10, varied: SI 2008/1911 Reg.52

Sch.7 para.11, applied: SI 2008/409 Sch.6 para.19, SI 2008/410 Sch.6 para.19

Sch.7 para.11, varied: SI 2008/1911 Reg.52

Sch.8, amended: SI 2008/393 Reg.6, SI 2008/3000 Reg.9

Sch.10 Part 2 para.16A, applied: SI 2008/496 Art.4

Sch.11 Part 2 para.8, applied: SI 2008/496 Art.3

Sch.13 para.7, enabling: SI 2008/496

Sch.13 para.11, enabling: SI 2008/496

47. Safeguarding Vulnerable Groups Act 2006

Commencement Orders: SI 2008/930 Art.2; SI 2008/1320 Art.2, Art.3, Art.4, Art.5; SI 2008/3204 Art.2

applied: 2008 c.25 s.141, SI 2008/1592 Art.2, SI 2008/2553 Art.5, SI 2008/2554 Art.5, SI 2008/2927 Reg.2, SI 2008/3047 Art.5, SI 2008/3148 Sch.1, SI 2008/3265 Sch.1 para.10

s.2, applied: SI 2008/2252 Sch.1 para.20

s.2, enabling: SI 2008/16

s.4, amended: SI 2008/2833 Sch.3 para.222

s.4, applied: SI 2008/473 Art.2, Art.4, SI 2008/1497 Reg.3, SI 2008/2684 Art.7, SI 2008/2698 r.20, r.21, r.22, SI 2008/2833 Sch.1

s.4, repealed (in part): SI 2008/2833 Sch.3 para.222

s.4, enabling: SI 2008/1497

s.6, amended: 2008 c.14 Sch.14 para.8

s.21, amended: 2008 c.25 Sch.1 para.89

s.24, applied: SI 2008/3265 Sch.1 para.1

CAP.

2006–cont.

47. Safeguarding Vulnerable Groups Act 2006–*cont.*

s.35, applied: SI 2008/3265 Reg.3, Sch.1 para.6

s.35, enabling: SI 2008/3265

s.36, applied: SI 2008/3265 Reg.4, Sch.1 para.6

s.36, enabling: SI 2008/3265

s.37, applied: SI 2008/3265 Reg.5

s.37, enabling: SI 2008/3265

s.39, applied: SI 2008/3265 Reg.6, Sch.1 para.6

s.39, enabling: SI 2008/3265

s.40, applied: SI 2008/3265 Reg.7

s.40, enabling: SI 2008/3265

s.41, applied: SI 2008/16 Reg.4, SI 2008/3265 Reg.8, Sch.1 para.3, Sch.1 para.6

s.41, enabling: SI 2008/3265

s.42, applied: SI 2008/3265 Reg.9

s.42, enabling: SI 2008/3265

s.44, referred to: SI 2008/2553 Art.1

s.45, amended: 2008 c.14 Sch.5 para.91

s.45, applied: SI 2008/16 Reg.4, SI 2008/3265 Reg.10, Sch.1 para.6

s.45, repealed (in part): 2008 c.14 Sch.5 para.91, Sch.15 Part 1

s.45, enabling: SI 2008/3265

s.46, applied: SI 2008/3265 Reg.11

s.46, enabling: SI 2008/3265

s.53, amended: 2008 c.23 Sch.1 para.20, Sch.4

s.56, applied: SI 2008/1062, SI 2008/1320, SI 2008/3050, SI 2008/3265

s.59, amended: 2008 c.25 s.147, SI 2008/912 Sch.1 para.21

s.60, enabling: SI 2008/16

s.61, applied: SI 2008/1062, SI 2008/3050

s.61, enabling: SI 2008/473, SI 2008/474, SI 2008/930, SI 2008/1062, SI 2008/1320, SI 2008/1497, SI 2008/3204, SI 2008/3265

s.64, enabling: SI 2008/473, SI 2008/474, SI 2008/1062, SI 2008/1497, SI 2008/3050

s.65, enabling: SI 2008/930, SI 2008/1320, SI 2008/3204

Sch.3, applied: SI 2008/473 Art.2, Art.4, SI 2008/474 Reg.2

Sch.3 Part 1 para.1, applied: SI 2008/473 Art.2, SI 2008/474 Reg.10, SI 2008/1062 Reg.2, SI 2008/3265 Reg.12

Sch.3 Part 1 para.1, referred to: SI 2008/3265 Reg.13

Sch.3 Part 1 para.1, enabling: SI 2008/1062

Sch.3 Part 1 para.2, applied: SI 2008/473 Art.2, SI 2008/474 Reg.10, SI 2008/3265 Reg.12

Sch.3 Part 1 para.2, referred to: SI 2008/3265 Reg.13

Sch.3 Part 1 para.3, applied: SI 2008/473 Art.3, SI 2008/3265 Reg.12

CAP.

2006–*cont.*

47. Safeguarding Vulnerable Groups Act 2006–*cont.*

Sch.3 Part 1 para.3, referred to: SI 2008/3265 Reg.13

Sch.3 Part 1 para.4, applied: SI 2008/473 Art.3, SI 2008/3265 Reg.12

Sch.3 Part 1 para.4, referred to: SI 2008/3265 Reg.13

Sch.3 Part 1 para.5, applied: SI 2008/473 Art.3, SI 2008/3265 Reg.12

Sch.3 Part 1 para.5, referred to: SI 2008/3265 Reg.13

Sch.3 Part 2 para.7, applied: SI 2008/473 Art.4, SI 2008/474 Reg.10, SI 2008/1062 Reg.3, SI 2008/3265 Reg.12

Sch.3 Part 2 para.7, referred to: SI 2008/3265 Reg.13

Sch.3 Part 2 para.7, enabling: SI 2008/1062

Sch.3 Part 2 para.8, applied: SI 2008/474 Reg.10, SI 2008/3265 Reg.12

Sch.3 Part 2 para.8, referred to: SI 2008/3265 Reg.13

Sch.3 Part 2 para.9, applied: SI 2008/3265 Reg.12

Sch.3 Part 2 para.9, referred to: SI 2008/3265 Reg.13

Sch.3 Part 2 para.10, applied: SI 2008/3265 Reg.12

Sch.3 Part 2 para.10, referred to: SI 2008/3265 Reg.13

Sch.3 Part 2 para.11, applied: SI 2008/3265 Reg.12

Sch.3 Part 2 para.11, referred to: SI 2008/3265 Reg.13

Sch.3 Part 3 para.15, enabling: SI 2008/474

Sch.3 Part 3 para.16, varied: SI 2008/473 Art.2, Art.4

Sch.3 Part 3 para.18, applied: SI 2008/474 Reg.11

Sch.3 Part 3 para.18, varied: SI 2008/473 Art.2, Art.4

Sch.3 Part 3 para.18, enabling: SI 2008/474

Sch.3 Part 3 para.19, applied: SI 2008/16 Reg.4, SI 2008/3265 Reg.12

Sch.3 Part 3 para.19, varied: SI 2008/473 Art.2, Art.4

Sch.3 Part 3 para.19, enabling: SI 2008/3265

Sch.3 Part 3 para.21, applied: SI 2008/3265 Reg.13

Sch.3 Part 3 para.21, enabling: SI 2008/3265

Sch.3 Part 3 para.24, amended: SI 2008/3050 Art.2

Sch.3 Part 3 para.24, enabling: SI 2008/1062

Sch.3 Part 3 para.25, substituted: SI 2008/3050 Art.3

Sch.4 Part 1 para.1, amended: 2008 c.14 Sch.5 para.92, 2008 c.25 Sch.1 para.41

Sch.4 Part 1 para.1, repealed (in part): 2008 c.14 Sch.5 para.92, Sch.15 Part 1

Sch.4 Part 2 para.7, amended: 2008 c.14 Sch.5 para.93

Sch.4 Part 2 para.7, repealed (in part): 2008 c.14 Sch.5 para.93, Sch.15 Part 1

Sch.8 para.2, enabling: SI 2008/473

Sch.8 para.3, enabling: SI 2008/473

48. Police and Justice Act 2006

Commencement Orders: SI 2008/311 Art.2, Art.3; SI 2008/617 Art.2; SI 2008/790 Art.2, Art.3; SI 2008/2503 Art.2, Art.3; SI 2008/2785 Art.2, Art.3

see *Caldarelli v Italy* [2007] EWHC 1624 (Admin), [2008] 1 W.L.R. 31 (DC), Laws, L.J.

referred to: 2008 c.4 Sch.26 para.81

s.13, amended: SI 2008/678 Sch.2 para.15

s.13, applied: SI 2008/678 Sch.1 para.15

s.13, enabling: SI 2008/570, SI 2008/700

s.41, enabling: SI 2008/212

s.42, see *Caldarelli v Italy* [2007] EWHC 1624 (Admin), [2008] 1 W.L.R. 31 (DC), Laws, L.J.

s.44, applied: 2008 c.4 s.96

s.44, repealed (in part): 2008 c.4 Sch.28 Part 6

s.49, amended: 2008 c.4 Sch.26 para.81

s.49, repealed (in part): 2008 c.4 Sch.28 Part 8

s.49, enabling: SI 2008/311, SI 2008/617, SI 2008/2785

s.51, enabling: SI 2008/82, SI 2008/312, SI 2008/619

s.53, enabling: SI 2008/311, SI 2008/617, SI 2008/790, SI 2008/2503, SI 2008/2785

Sch.1 Part 3 para.30, repealed (in part): 2008 c.4 Sch.28 Part 8

Sch.1 Part 6 para.48, amended: SI 2008/912 Sch.1 para.22

Sch.2, applied: SI 2008/700 Art.1

Sch.2 para.9, referred to: SI 2008/82 Art.6

Sch.2 para.10, referred to: SI 2008/311 Art.3

Sch.2 para.19, repealed: 2008 c.4 Sch.28 Part 8

Sch.13 para.1, see *Caldarelli v Italy* [2007] EWHC 1624 (Admin), [2008] 1 W.L.R. 31 (DC), Laws, L.J.

Sch.14 para.55, repealed (in part): 2008 c.4 Sch.28 Part 7

49. Road Safety Act 2006

Commencement Orders: SI 2008/1862 Art.2, Art.3, Art.4; SI 2008/1864 Art.2, Art.3; SI 2008/1918 Art.2; SI 2008/3164 Art.2, Art.3, Art.4

s.49A, added: 2008 c.26 s.129

s.49B, added: 2008 c.26 s.130

s.61, enabling: SI 2008/1862, SI 2008/1864, SI 2008/1918, SI 2008/3164

CAP.

2006–cont.

50. Charities Act 2006
Commencement Orders: SI 2008/751 Art.2, Sch.1; SI 2008/945 Art.2, Art.3, Art.4, Art.5, Art.6, Art.7, Art.8, Art.10, Art.11, Sch.1, Sch.2; SI 2008/3267 Art.2, Sch.1
see *Hanchett-Stamford v Attorney General* [2008] EWHC 330 (Ch), [2008] 4 All E.R. 323 (Ch D), Lewison, J.
applied: SI 2008/221 r.29
s.1, applied: 2008 c.29 s.210
s.2, applied: 2008 c.29 s.210
s.4, referred to: SI 2008/629 Reg.40, Reg.41
s.50, applied: 2008 c.13 Sch.3
s.51, enabling: SI 2008/218
s.52, enabling: SI 2008/218
s.63, applied: 2008 c.13 Sch.7
s.74, applied: SI 2008/527
s.74, enabling: SI 2008/527
s.77, enabling: SI 2008/527
s.78, enabling: SI 2008/3267
s.79, enabling: SI 2008/751, SI 2008/945, SI 2008/3267
Sch.8 para.190, repealed: 2008 c.17 Sch.16

51. Legislative and Regulatory Reform Act 2006
Part 1, applied: SI 2008/960, SI 2008/2840, SI 2008/3262
s.1, enabling: SI 2008/2826, SI 2008/2840, SI 2008/3001, SI 2008/3262
s.2, enabling: SI 2008/960
s.3, applied: SI 2008/960, SI 2008/2826, SI 2008/2840, SI 2008/3001, SI 2008/3262
s.11, applied: SI 2008/2840
s.13, applied: SI 2008/960, SI 2008/2826, SI 2008/2840, SI 2008/3001, SI 2008/3262
s.13, referred to: SI 2008/2840
s.14, applied: SI 2008/960, SI 2008/2826, SI 2008/2840, SI 2008/3001, SI 2008/3262
s.15, applied: SI 2008/960, SI 2008/2826, SI 2008/2840, SI 2008/3001, SI 2008/3262
s.17, applied: SI 2008/960, SI 2008/2826, SI 2008/3001, SI 2008/3262
s.18, applied: SI 2008/2840
s.22, applied: 2008 c.17 s.86

52. Armed Forces Act 2006
Commencement Orders: 2008 c.17 Sch.16, s.321; SI 2008/1650 Art.2, Art.4
applied: 2008 c.4 Sch.26 para.82, SI 2008/1062 Sch.1 para.1
referred to: 2008 c.4 s.148, SI 2008/1780 Art.2
Part 8 c.6, amended: 2008 c.4 Sch.25 para.13
s.42, applied: SI 2008/1651 Reg.12
s.42, referred to: SI 2008/1062 Sch.1 para.1, Sch.1 para.2
s.48, varied: 2008 c.4 s.98
s.110, applied: 2008 c.28 Sch.6 para.7, Sch.6 para.8
s.183, amended: SI 2008/912 Sch.1 para.23
s.188, amended: 2008 c.4 Sch.25 para.11
s.209, amended: 2008 c.4 Sch.25 para.12

CAP.

2006–cont.

52. Armed Forces Act 2006–*cont.*
s.209, applied: 2008 c.28 Sch.6 para.5
s.211, applied: 2008 c.4 Sch.1 para.30, 2008 c.28 Sch.6 para.5
s.213, referred to: 2008 c.4 Sch.1 para.30
s.219, amended: 2008 c.4 Sch.25 para.13
s.220, amended: 2008 c.4 Sch.25 para.14
s.221, amended: 2008 c.4 Sch.25 para.15, Sch.28 Part 2
s.221, repealed (in part): 2008 c.4 Sch.25 para.15, Sch.28 Part 2
s.222, amended: 2008 c.4 Sch.25 para.16
s.223, amended: 2008 c.4 Sch.25 para.17, Sch.28 Part 2
s.228, amended: 2008 c.4 Sch.25 para.18
s.237, amended: 2008 c.4 Sch.25 para.19
s.253, amended: 2008 c.4 Sch.25 para.24
s.254, amended: 2008 c.4 Sch.25 para.25
s.256, amended: 2008 c.4 Sch.25 para.20
s.260, amended: 2008 c.4 Sch.25 para.21
s.261, amended: 2008 c.4 Sch.25 para.22
s.270, amended: 2008 c.4 Sch.25 para.26, Sch.28 Part 2
s.270, repealed (in part): 2008 c.4 Sch.25 para.26, Sch.28 Part 2
s.270A, added: 2008 c.4 Sch.25 para.27
s.270B, added: 2008 c.4 Sch.25 para.27
s.273, amended: 2008 c.4 Sch.25 para.23, Sch.25 para.28
s.276, amended: 2008 c.4 Sch.25 para.29
s.276, applied: 2008 c.4 Sch.25 para.34
s.276A, added: 2008 c.4 Sch.25 para.30
s.276B, added: 2008 c.4 Sch.25 para.30
s.343, enabling: SI 2008/1651
s.362, varied: SI 2008/1651 Sch.3 para.3
s.370, varied: SI 2008/1651 Sch.3 para.1
s.373, amended: 2008 c.4 Sch.25 para.31
s.373, applied: SI 2008/1694, SI 2008/1696, SI 2008/3294
s.374, referred to: 2008 c.28 Sch.6 para.11
s.374, varied: SI 2008/1651 Sch.3 para.2
s.379, enabling: SI 2008/1696
s.380, applied: 2008 c.28 Sch.6 para.13
s.381, enabling: SI 2008/1694, SI 2008/3294
s.382, enabling: SI 2008/1780
s.383, enabling: SI 2008/1650
s.384, referred to: 2008 c.4 s.152
s.384, varied: 2008 c.15 s.15
Sch.2 para.12, amended: 2008 c.4 Sch.26 para.82
Sch.5 Part 1 para.1, amended: 2008 c.4 Sch.26 para.82
Sch.5 Part 2 para.10, amended: 2008 c.4 Sch.26 para.82
Sch.5 Part 2 para.14, amended: 2008 c.4 Sch.25 para.32
Sch.7 Part 2 para.9, amended: 2008 c.4 Sch.25 para.33
Sch.16 para.139, repealed: 2008 c.17 Sch.16

CAP.

2006–*cont.*

52. Armed Forces Act 2006–*cont.*
Sch.16 para.218, repealed: 2008 c.4 Sch.28 Part 2
Sch.16 para.225, repealed: 2008 c.4 Sch.28 Part 2

54. Consolidated Fund Act 2006
repealed: 2008 c.8 Sch.3

2007

2. Planning-gain Supplement (Preparations) Act 2007
referred to: 2008 c.29 s.225

3. Income Tax Act 2007
referred to: SI 2008/2682 Sch.2 para.5, SI 2008/3023 Art.1
Part 2 c.2, amended: 2008 c.9 Sch.1 para.9
Part 4 c.2, applied: 2008 c.9 Sch.21 para.6
Part 5 c.2, referred to: 2008 c.9 s.39
Part 5 c.3, referred to: 2008 c.9 s.39
s.2, amended: 2008 c.9 Sch.7 para.75
s.6, amended: 2008 c.9 s.5
s.6, repealed (in part): 2008 c.9 s.5
s.7, substituted: 2008 c.9 Sch.1 para.2
s.10, amended: 2008 c.9 s.4, Sch.1 para.3, SI 2008/3023 Art.2
s.10, repealed (in part): 2008 c.9 Sch.1 para.3
s.10, varied: 2008 c.9 s.4
s.11, amended: 2008 c.9 Sch.1 para.4
s.12, amended: SI 2008/3023 Art.3
s.12, substituted: 2008 c.9 Sch.1 para.5
s.13, amended: 2008 c.9 s.68, Sch.1 para.6
s.16, amended: 2008 c.9 Sch.1 para.7
s.17, amended: 2008 c.9 Sch.1 para.8
s.20, amended: SI 2008/709 Art.2
s.20, repealed: 2008 c.9 Sch.1 para.10
s.21, amended: 2008 c.9 Sch.1 para.11
s.21, repealed (in part): 2008 c.9 Sch.1 para.11
s.21, enabling: SI 2008/709, SI 2008/3023
s.24, amended: 2008 c.9 Sch.27 para.27
s.25, amended: 2008 c.9 Sch.27 para.27
s.31, amended: 2008 c.9 Sch.1 para.12
s.32, amended: 2008 c.9 Sch.21 para.3
s.34, amended: 2008 c.9 Sch.7 para.76
s.35, amended: 2008 c.9 s.2, SI 2008/3023 Art.4
s.35, applied: SI 2008/794 Reg.99, Reg.103
s.35, referred to: 2008 c.9 s.2
s.36, amended: 2008 c.9 s.3, SI 2008/3023 Art.4
s.36, referred to: 2008 c.9 s.3
s.37, amended: 2008 c.9 s.3, SI 2008/3023 Art.4
s.37, referred to: 2008 c.9 s.3
s.38, amended: SI 2008/3023 Art.4
s.38, applied: SI 2008/794 Reg.99
s.39, applied: SI 2008/794 Reg.99
s.40, amended: 2008 c.9 Sch.39 para.55
s.40, applied: SI 2008/794 Reg.99
s.42, amended: 2008 c.9 Sch.7 para.77

CAP.

2007–*cont.*

3. Income Tax Act 2007–*cont.*
s.43, amended: SI 2008/3023 Art.4
s.45, amended: SI 2008/3023 Art.4
s.45, applied: SI 2008/794 Reg.103
s.46, amended: 2008 c.9 Sch.39 para.56, SI 2008/3023 Art.4
s.46, applied: SI 2008/794 Reg.103
s.47, applied: SI 2008/794 Reg.103
s.48, applied: SI 2008/794 Reg.103
s.49, applied: SI 2008/794 Reg.103
s.50, applied: SI 2008/794 Reg.103
s.51, applied: SI 2008/794 Reg.103
s.52, applied: SI 2008/794 Reg.103
s.53, amended: 2008 c.9 Sch.39 para.57
s.53, applied: SI 2008/794 Reg.103
s.54, applied: SI 2008/794 Reg.103
s.55, applied: SI 2008/794 Reg.103
s.56, amended: 2008 c.9 s.70
s.57, disapplied: 2008 c.9 s.2, s.3
s.57, enabling: SI 2008/3023
s.64, amended: 2008 c.9 Sch.21 para.4
s.64, repealed (in part): 2008 c.9 s.66
s.72, amended: 2008 c.9 Sch.21 para.5
s.72, repealed (in part): 2008 c.9 s.66
s.74A, added: 2008 c.9 Sch.21 para.2
s.74A, applied: 2008 c.9 Sch.21 para.6
s.74B, added: 2008 c.9 Sch.21 para.2
s.74B, applied: 2008 c.9 Sch.21 para.7
s.74C, added: 2008 c.9 Sch.21 para.2
s.74D, added: 2008 c.9 Sch.21 para.2
s.74D, applied: 2008 c.9 Sch.21 para.6
s.76, amended: 2008 c.9 Sch.24 para.21
s.78, amended: 2008 c.9 Sch.24 para.22
s.103B, amended: 2008 c.9 s.61
s.147, amended: 2008 c.9 Sch.2 para.98
s.148, amended: 2008 c.9 Sch.2 para.99
s.155, amended: 2008 c.9 Sch.39 para.58
s.158, amended: 2008 c.9 s.31, Sch.1 para.13
s.161, repealed (in part): 2008 c.9 Sch.2 para.54
s.192, amended: 2008 c.9 Sch.11 para.5
s.196A, added: 2008 c.9 Sch.11 para.6
s.196B, added: 2008 c.9 Sch.11 para.6
s.196C, added: 2008 c.9 Sch.11 para.6
s.209, amended: 2008 c.9 Sch.1 para.14
s.210, amended: 2008 c.9 Sch.1 para.15
s.213, amended: 2008 c.9 Sch.1 para.16
s.220, amended: 2008 c.9 Sch.1 para.17
s.224, amended: 2008 c.9 Sch.1 para.18
s.229, amended: 2008 c.9 Sch.1 para.19
s.230, amended: SI 2008/954 Art.39
s.230, repealed (in part): SI 2008/954 Sch.1
s.237, amended: 2008 c.9 Sch.39 para.59
s.272, enabling: SI 2008/1893
s.284, enabling: SI 2008/1893
s.303, amended: 2008 c.9 Sch.11 para.8
s.307A, added: 2008 c.9 Sch.11 para.9
s.307B, added: 2008 c.9 Sch.11 para.9
s.307C, added: 2008 c.9 Sch.11 para.9
s.340, enabling: SI 2008/383

CAP.

2007–cont.

3. **Income Tax Act 2007**–*cont.*
s.341, enabling: SI 2008/383
s.372, amended: 2008 c.9 Sch.39 para.60
s.384, amended: 2008 c.9 Sch.22 para.21
s.384, varied: 2008 c.9 Sch.22 para.21
s.414, amended: 2008 c.9 Sch.1 para.20
s.425, amended: 2008 c.9 Sch.12 para.24
s.429, amended: 2008 c.9 s.130
s.429, applied: 2008 c.9 s.133
s.448, amended: 2008 c.9 s.66
s.449, amended: 2008 c.9 s.66
s.451, repealed: 2008 c.9 s.66
s.460, amended: 2008 c.9 Sch.7 para.78
s.486, amended: 2008 c.9 Sch.1 para.21
s.498, amended: 2008 c.9 Sch.1 para.22
s.504, amended: 2008 c.9 Sch.1 para.23, Sch.12 para.25
s.505, amended: 2008 c.9 s.66
s.506, repealed: 2008 c.9 s.66
s.521, amended: 2008 c.9 Sch.19 para.9
s.521, applied: 2008 c.9 Sch.19 para.1
s.555, amended: 2008 c.17 Sch.9 para.34
s.567, amended: 2008 c.9 Sch.12 para.26
s.572A, added: 2008 c.9 Sch.23 para.2
s.573, amended: 2008 c.9 Sch.23 para.3
s.574, amended: 2008 c.9 Sch.23 para.4
s.575, repealed: 2008 c.9 Sch.23 para.5
s.578, amended: 2008 c.9 Sch.23 para.6
s.579, amended: 2008 c.9 Sch.23 para.7
s.579, repealed (in part): 2008 c.9 Sch.23 para.7
s.580, repealed: 2008 c.9 Sch.23 para.8
s.581A, added: 2008 c.9 Sch.23 para.9
s.583, amended: 2008 c.9 Sch.23 para.10
s.592, amended: 2008 c.9 Sch.12 para.27
s.593, amended: 2008 c.9 Sch.12 para.28
s.594, amended: 2008 c.9 Sch.12 para.29
s.595, amended: 2008 c.9 Sch.12 para.30
s.617, amended: 2008 c.9 Sch.7 para.157
s.644, repealed: 2008 c.9 Sch.7 para.158
s.668, amended: 2008 c.9 Sch.39 para.61
s.669, amended: 2008 c.9 Sch.39 para.62
s.670A, added: 2008 c.9 Sch.7 para.159
s.684, amended: 2008 c.9 s.66
s.687, repealed: 2008 c.9 s.66
s.688, repealed (in part): 2008 c.9 s.66
s.720, amended: 2008 c.9 Sch.7 para.164
s.726, substituted: 2008 c.9 Sch.7 para.165
s.727, amended: 2008 c.9 Sch.7 para.166
s.730, substituted: 2008 c.9 Sch.7 para.167
s.731, amended: 2008 c.9 Sch.7 para.168
s.734, amended: 2008 c.9 Sch.7 para.97
s.735, substituted: 2008 c.9 Sch.7 para.169
s.745, amended: 2008 c.9 Sch.1 para.24
s.809A, added: 2008 c.9 Sch.7 para.1
s.809B, added: 2008 c.9 Sch.7 para.1
s.809B, applied: 2008 c.9 Sch.7 para.85
s.809C, added: 2008 c.9 Sch.7 para.1
s.809D, added: 2008 c.9 Sch.7 para.1
s.809D, applied: 2008 c.9 Sch.7 para.85

CAP.

2007–cont.

3. **Income Tax Act 2007**–*cont.*
s.809E, added: 2008 c.9 Sch.7 para.1
s.809E, applied: 2008 c.9 Sch.7 para.85
s.809E, referred to: 2008 c.9 Sch.7 para.85
s.809F, added: 2008 c.9 Sch.7 para.1
s.809G, added: 2008 c.9 Sch.7 para.1
s.809H, added: 2008 c.9 Sch.7 para.1
s.809I, added: 2008 c.9 Sch.7 para.1
s.809J, added: 2008 c.9 Sch.7 para.1
s.809K, added: 2008 c.9 Sch.7 para.1
s.809L, added: 2008 c.9 Sch.7 para.1
s.809L, varied: 2008 c.9 Sch.7 para.86
s.809M, added: 2008 c.9 Sch.7 para.1
s.809N, added: 2008 c.9 Sch.7 para.1
s.809N, varied: 2008 c.9 Sch.7 para.87
s.809O, added: 2008 c.9 Sch.7 para.1
s.809O, varied: 2008 c.9 Sch.7 para.88
s.809P, added: 2008 c.9 Sch.7 para.1
s.809Q, added: 2008 c.9 Sch.7 para.1
s.809Q, varied: 2008 c.9 Sch.7 para.89
s.809R, added: 2008 c.9 Sch.7 para.1
s.809R, varied: 2008 c.9 Sch.7 para.89
s.809S, added: 2008 c.9 Sch.7 para.1
s.809S, varied: 2008 c.9 Sch.7 para.89
s.809T, added: 2008 c.9 Sch.7 para.1
s.809U, added: 2008 c.9 Sch.7 para.1
s.809V, added: 2008 c.9 Sch.7 para.1
s.809W, added: 2008 c.9 Sch.7 para.1
s.809X, added: 2008 c.9 Sch.7 para.1
s.809Y, added: 2008 c.9 Sch.7 para.1
s.809Z, added: 2008 c.9 Sch.7 para.1
s.809ZA, added: 2008 c.9 Sch.20 para.2
s.809ZA, varied: 2008 c.9 Sch.20 para.2
s.809ZB, added: 2008 c.9 Sch.20 para.2
s.809ZB, varied: 2008 c.9 Sch.20 para.2
s.809ZC, added: 2008 c.9 Sch.20 para.2
s.809ZC, varied: 2008 c.9 Sch.20 para.2
s.809ZD, added: 2008 c.9 Sch.20 para.2
s.809ZD, varied: 2008 c.9 Sch.20 para.2
s.809Z1, added: 2008 c.9 Sch.7 para.1
s.809Z2, added: 2008 c.9 Sch.7 para.1
s.809Z3, added: 2008 c.9 Sch.7 para.1
s.809Z4, added: 2008 c.9 Sch.7 para.1
s.809Z5, added: 2008 c.9 Sch.7 para.1
s.809Z6, added: 2008 c.9 Sch.7 para.1
s.809Z7, added: 2008 c.9 Sch.7 para.1
s.818, amended: 2008 c.9 Sch.16 para.10
s.818, repealed (in part): 2008 c.9 Sch.16 para.10
s.827, amended: 2008 c.9 Sch.16 para.5
s.831, amended: 2008 c.9 s.24
s.832, amended: 2008 c.9 s.24
s.851, amended: 2008 c.9 Sch.1 para.25
s.851, applied: SI 2008/2682 Reg.12, Reg.13, Reg.15
s.851, disapplied: SI 2008/2682 Reg.4
s.852, enabling: SI 2008/2682
s.858, applied: SI 2008/2682 Reg.14, Reg.19, Sch.2 para.9

CAP.

2007–cont.

3. **Income Tax Act 2007**–*cont.*
   s.859, applied: SI 2008/2682 Reg.14, Reg.19, Sch.2 para.9
   s.860, applied: SI 2008/2682 Reg.14, Reg.19, Sch.2 para.9
   s.861, applied: SI 2008/2682 Reg.14, Reg.19, Sch.2 para.9
   s.871, enabling: SI 2008/2682
   s.874, amended: 2008 c.9 Sch.1 para.26
   s.889, amended: 2008 c.9 Sch.1 para.27
   s.892, amended: 2008 c.9 Sch.1 para.28
   s.895, amended: SI 2008/954 Art.40
   s.901, amended: 2008 c.9 Sch.1 para.29
   s.902, repealed: 2008 c.9 Sch.1 para.30
   s.919, amended: 2008 c.9 Sch.1 para.31
   s.939, amended: 2008 c.9 s.134, Sch.1 para.32
   s.939, repealed (in part): 2008 c.9 s.134
   s.940A, added: 2008 c.9 s.134
   s.964, repealed (in part): 2008 c.9 s.69
   s.975, applied: SI 2008/2682 Reg.4
   s.989, amended: 2008 c.9 Sch.12 para.31, Sch.1 para.33
   s.993, applied: 2008 c.18 Sch.13 para.34
   s.998, varied: 2008 c.9 Sch.19 para.3
   s.1012, amended: 2008 c.9 s.67
   s.1014, amended: 2008 c.9 Sch.16 para.2, Sch.16 para.6, Sch.1 para.34
   s.1014, disapplied: 2008 c.9 s.31
   s.1022, amended: SI 2008/954 Art.41
   Sch.1 Part 1 para.85, repealed (in part): 2008 c.9 Sch.1 para.35
   Sch.1 Part 1 para.86, repealed: 2008 c.9 Sch.1 para.35
   Sch.1 Part 1 para.111, repealed: 2008 c.9 Sch.14 para.17
   Sch.1 Part 1 para.112, repealed: 2008 c.9 Sch.1 para.35
   Sch.1 Part 1 para.141, repealed: 2008 c.9 Sch.14 para.17
   Sch.1 Part 1 para.151, repealed: 2008 c.9 Sch.1 para.35
   Sch.1 Part 1 para.152, repealed: 2008 c.9 Sch.1 para.35
   Sch.1 Part 1 para.155, repealed (in part): 2008 c.9 s.66
   Sch.1 Part 1 para.167, repealed: 2008 c.9 s.66
   Sch.1 Part 1 para.168, repealed: 2008 c.9 s.66
   Sch.1 Part 1 para.169, repealed: 2008 c.9 s.66
   Sch.1 Part 1 para.170, repealed: 2008 c.9 s.66
   Sch.1 Part 1 para.175, repealed: 2008 c.9 Sch.17 para.35
   Sch.1 Part 1 para.179, repealed (in part): 2008 c.9 s.41
   Sch.1 Part 1 para.180, repealed: 2008 c.9 s.41
   Sch.1 Part 1 para.181, repealed: 2008 c.9 s.41
   Sch.1 Part 1 para.191, repealed: 2008 c.9 Sch.1 para.35
   Sch.1 Part 2 para.244, repealed: 2008 c.9 Sch.1 para.35

CAP.

2007–cont.

3. **Income Tax Act 2007**–*cont.*
   Sch.1 Part 2 para.259, repealed: 2008 c.9 Sch.1 para.35
   Sch.1 Part 2 para.279, repealed: 2008 c.9 Sch.1 para.35
   Sch.1 Part 2 para.295, repealed: 2008 c.9 Sch.2 para.21
   Sch.1 Part 2 para.296, repealed: 2008 c.9 Sch.2 para.21
   Sch.1 Part 2 para.301, repealed: 2008 c.9 Sch.2 para.21
   Sch.1 Part 2 para.313, repealed: 2008 c.9 Sch.2 para.55
   Sch.1 Part 2 para.335, repealed (in part): 2008 c.9 Sch.23 para.12
   Sch.1 Part 2 para.342, repealed (in part): 2008 c.9 Sch.2 para.102
   Sch.1 Part 2 para.343, repealed: 2008 c.9 Sch.2 para.55
   Sch.1 Part 2 para.350, repealed: 2008 c.9 Sch.36 para.92
   Sch.1 Part 2 para.406, repealed: 2008 c.9 Sch.27 para.27
   Sch.1 Part 2 para.530, repealed: 2008 c.9 Sch.1 para.35
   Sch.1 Part 2 para.535, repealed (in part): 2008 c.9 Sch.1 para.35
   Sch.1 Part 2 para.536, repealed (in part): 2008 c.9 Sch.1 para.35
   Sch.1 Part 2 para.537, repealed: 2008 c.9 Sch.1 para.35
   Sch.1 Part 2 para.538, repealed: 2008 c.9 Sch.1 para.35
   Sch.1 Part 2 para.564, repealed: 2008 c.9 Sch.1 para.35
   Sch.1 Part 2 para.565, repealed: 2008 c.9 Sch.1 para.35
   Sch.1 Part 2 para.592, repealed (in part): 2008 c.9 Sch.1 para.35
   Sch.4, amended: 2008 c.9 Sch.1 para.36

5. **Welfare Reform Act 2007**
   Commencement Orders: SI 2008/411 Art.2; SI 2008/787 Art.2, Sch.1; SI 2008/2101 Art.2; SI 2008/2772 Art.2; SI 2008/3167 Art.2
   applied: SI 2008/794, SI 2008/1052 Sch.2 para.2, SI 2008/1053 Sch.2 para.2, SI 2008/1054 Sch.2 para.2, SI 2008/2428, SI 2008/2685 Sch.2
   Part 1, applied: SI 2008/794 Reg.19, Reg.34, Reg.104, Reg.107, Reg.115, SI 2008/1273 Reg.67, Reg.82, SI 2008/1554, SI 2008/1582 Reg.120, Reg.137, SI 2008/1879, SI 2008/3170 Reg.67, Reg.82
   Part 1, referred to: SI 2008/2551 Reg.12
   s.1, applied: SI 2008/794 Reg.80, Reg.81, Reg.82, Reg.111
   s.1, referred to: SI 2008/794 Reg.146
   s.2, applied: SI 2008/794 Reg.72A, Reg.43, Reg.67, Reg.72, Sch.4 para.1
   s.2, disapplied: SI 2008/794 Reg.7

CAP.

2007–cont.

5. **Welfare Reform Act 2007**–*cont.*
 s.2, enabling: SI 2008/794, SI 2008/2428, SI 2008/3051
 s.3, applied: SI 2008/794 Reg.72A, Reg.72, Reg.73, Reg.75, Reg.90
 s.3, enabling: SI 2008/794, SI 2008/2428
 s.4, applied: SI 2008/794 Reg.67, Reg.68, Reg.111, Sch.4 para.1, Sch.6 para.19
 s.4, disapplied: SI 2008/794 Reg.7, Reg.146
 s.4, enabling: SI 2008/794, SI 2008/2428, SI 2008/3051, SI 2008/3195
 s.5, applied: SI 2008/794 Reg.146
 s.5, enabling: SI 2008/794, SI 2008/2428
 s.8, enabling: SI 2008/794, SI 2008/2428
 s.9, enabling: SI 2008/794, SI 2008/2428
 s.11, applied: SI 2008/794 Reg.48
 s.11, varied: SI 2008/794 Reg.66
 s.11, enabling: SI 2008/794
 s.12, varied: SI 2008/794 Reg.66
 s.12, enabling: SI 2008/794
 s.14, enabling: SI 2008/794
 s.16, enabling: SI 2008/794
 s.17, enabling: SI 2008/794, SI 2008/1599, SI 2008/2428, SI 2008/3157
 s.18, applied: SI 2008/794 Reg.151, Sch.6 para.1
 s.18, disapplied: SI 2008/794 Reg.160
 s.18, referred to: SI 2008/794 Reg.161
 s.18, enabling: SI 2008/794, SI 2008/2428
 s.20, disapplied: SI 2008/794 Reg.80, Reg.81, Reg.82
 s.20, enabling: SI 2008/794
 s.22, enabling: SI 2008/794
 s.23, enabling: SI 2008/794
 s.24, applied: SI 2008/794 Reg.4
 s.24, enabling: SI 2008/794, SI 2008/1599, SI 2008/2428, SI 2008/3051, SI 2008/3157, SI 2008/3195, SI 2008/3270
 s.25, enabling: SI 2008/794, SI 2008/795, SI 2008/1599, SI 2008/2428, SI 2008/2783, SI 2008/3157, SI 2008/3195, SI 2008/3270
 s.26, enabling: SI 2008/794
 s.28, enabling: SI 2008/1554, SI 2008/1879, SI 2008/2428
 s.29, enabling: SI 2008/795, SI 2008/2783
 s.30, applied: SI 2008/586
 s.32, enabling: SI 2008/959, SI 2008/1082
 s.33, enabling: SI 2008/959
 s.34, applied: SI 2008/959
 s.34, enabling: SI 2008/959, SI 2008/1082
 s.35, applied: SI 2008/586
 s.42, applied: SI 2008/2112 Reg.4, SI 2008/2114 Art.2
 s.42, enabling: SI 2008/2112, SI 2008/2114
 s.46, applied: SI 2008/463
 s.47, applied: SI 2008/463
 s.50, referred to: SI 2008/2101 Art.3
 s.51, referred to: SI 2008/2101 Art.3
 s.68, enabling: SI 2008/787, SI 2008/2101

CAP.

2007–cont.

5. **Welfare Reform Act 2007**–*cont.*
 s.70, enabling: SI 2008/411, SI 2008/787, SI 2008/2101, SI 2008/2772, SI 2008/3167
 Sch.1 Part 1 para.1, enabling: SI 2008/794, SI 2008/2428
 Sch.1 Part 1 para.3, varied: SI 2008/794 Reg.13
 Sch.1 Part 1 para.3, enabling: SI 2008/794
 Sch.1 Part 1 para.4, applied: SI 2008/794 Reg.9, Reg.11, Reg.12, Reg.33
 Sch.1 Part 1 para.4, disapplied: SI 2008/794 Reg.10
 Sch.1 Part 1 para.4, enabling: SI 2008/794
 Sch.1 Part 2, applied: SI 2008/794 Reg.111
 Sch.1 Part 2, referred to: SI 2008/794 Reg.146
 Sch.1 Part 2 para.6, applied: SI 2008/794 Reg.15, Reg.41, Reg.42, Reg.83, Reg.90, Reg.110, Sch.6 para.2
 Sch.1 Part 2 para.6, disapplied: SI 2008/794 Reg.18, Reg.33
 Sch.1 Part 2 para.6, referred to: SI 2008/794 Reg.146, Sch.7 para.12
 Sch.1 Part 2 para.6, enabling: SI 2008/794, SI 2008/2428
 Sch.2 para.1, enabling: SI 2008/794, SI 2008/2428
 Sch.2 para.2, enabling: SI 2008/794, SI 2008/2428
 Sch.2 para.3, enabling: SI 2008/794
 Sch.2 para.4, enabling: SI 2008/794
 Sch.2 para.5, enabling: SI 2008/794
 Sch.2 para.6, enabling: SI 2008/794
 Sch.2 para.7, applied: SI 2008/794 Reg.11
 Sch.2 para.7, enabling: SI 2008/794
 Sch.2 para.8, enabling: SI 2008/794
 Sch.2 para.9, enabling: SI 2008/794
 Sch.2 para.10, applied: SI 2008/794 Reg.90
 Sch.2 para.10, enabling: SI 2008/794, SI 2008/2428
 Sch.2 para.12, enabling: SI 2008/794
 Sch.2 para.14, enabling: SI 2008/794
 Sch.3 para.7, repealed (in part): 2008 c.6 Sch.8
 Sch.3 para.12, disapplied: SI 2008/795 Reg.5
 Sch.4 para.1, enabling: SI 2008/795
 Sch.4 para.2, enabling: SI 2008/795, SI 2008/2783
 Sch.4 para.3, enabling: SI 2008/795, SI 2008/2783
 Sch.4 para.10, enabling: SI 2008/3270
 Sch.7 para.1, repealed (in part): SI 2008/2833 Sch.3 para.228

6. **Justice and Security (Northern Ireland) Act 2007**
 s.1, amended: 2008 c.28 s.28

8. **Digital Switchover (Disclosure of Information) Act 2007**
 s.2, enabling: SI 2008/2557

CAP.

2007–*cont.*

9. Rating (Empty Properties) Act 2007
Sch.1 para.8, enabling: SI 2008/428

10. Appropriation (No.2) Act 2007
Sch.2 Part 1, referred to: 2008 c.3 Sch.2 Part 3
Sch.2 Part 14, referred to: 2008 c.3 Sch.2 Part 3
Sch.2 Part 15, referred to: 2008 c.3 Sch.2 Part 3
Sch.2 Part 27, referred to: 2008 c.3 Sch.2 Part 3
Sch.2 Part 29, referred to: 2008 c.3 Sch.2 Part 3

11. Finance Act 2007
Commencement Orders: SI 2008/568 Art.2, Art.3, Art.4
s.3, applied: 2008 c.9 s.7
s.12, see *R. (on the application of Federation of Tour Operators) v HM Treasury* [2008] EWCA Civ 752, [2008] S.T.C. 2524 (CA (Civ Div)), Waller, L.J. (V-P)
s.16, amended: 2008 c.9 s.164
s.16, applied: SI 2008/1825
s.16, enabling: SI 2008/1825, SI 2008/1939
s.17, applied: SI 2008/1521 Art.2
s.17, enabling: SI 2008/1521
s.29, repealed (in part): 2008 c.9 Sch.14 para.17
s.36, applied: 2008 c.18 Sch.13 para.21, Sch.13 para.38
s.36, repealed: 2008 c.9 Sch.27 para.28
s.37, repealed: 2008 c.9 s.75
s.38, applied: 2008 c.9 Sch.17 para.27
s.45, repealed (in part): 2008 c.9 Sch.18 para.5
s.46, enabling: SI 2008/561
s.50, enabling: SI 2008/1880
s.72, repealed (in part): 2008 c.9 Sch.31 para.10
s.72, varied: 2008 c.9 s.97
s.81, repealed: 2008 c.9 Sch.30 para.15
s.84, amended: 2008 c.24 s.12
s.91, repealed (in part): 2008 c.9 Sch.39 para.65
s.97, enabling: SI 2008/568
s.110, applied: SI 2008/1579
s.110, enabling: SI 2008/1579
Sch.7, applied: 2008 c.9 Sch.17 para.27
Sch.7 Part 1 para.13, repealed (in part): 2008 c.9 Sch.17 para.17
Sch.7 Part 1 para.19, repealed (in part): 2008 c.9 Sch.17 para.10
Sch.7 Part 1 para.44, repealed: 2008 c.9 Sch.17 para.17
Sch.7 Part 1 para.45, repealed: 2008 c.9 Sch.14 para.17
Sch.7 Part 1 para.46, repealed: 2008 c.9 Sch.14 para.17
Sch.7 Part 1 para.58, repealed: 2008 c.9 Sch.17 para.18
Sch.7 Part 1 para.67, repealed (in part): 2008 c.9 Sch.17 para.18

CAP.

2007–*cont.*

11. Finance Act 2007–*cont.*
Sch.7 Part 1 para.78, repealed: 2008 c.9 Sch.17 para.27
Sch.7 Part 2 para.85, added: SI 2008/381 Art.30
Sch.7 Part 2 para.86, added: SI 2008/381 Art.30
Sch.8 Part 1 para.5, repealed: 2008 c.9 Sch.17 para.17
Sch.8 Part 1 para.15, repealed (in part): 2008 c.9 Sch.17 para.18
Sch.8 Part 1 para.16, repealed (in part): 2008 c.9 Sch.17 para.18
Sch.9 para.3, repealed (in part): SI 2008/381 Sch.1 Part 1
Sch.9 para.14, repealed (in part): 2008 c.9 Sch.2 para.70
Sch.9 para.16, enabling: SI 2008/381
Sch.9 para.17, amended: 2008 c.9 Sch.17 para.38
Sch.9 para.17, enabling: SI 2008/379
Sch.10 para.1, repealed: 2008 c.9 Sch.17 para.3
Sch.10 para.6, repealed (in part): 2008 c.9 Sch.14 para.17
Sch.11 para.3, amended: SI 2008/954 Art.42
Sch.14 para.6, repealed: 2008 c.9 s.66
Sch.24, applied: 2008 c.9 s.122
Sch.24 Part 1 para.1, amended: 2008 c.9 Sch.40 para.2
Sch.24 Part 1 para.1A, added: 2008 c.9 Sch.40 para.3
Sch.24 Part 1 para.2, amended: 2008 c.9 Sch.40 para.4
Sch.24 Part 1 para.3, amended: 2008 c.9 Sch.40 para.5
Sch.24 Part 2, amended: 2008 c.9 Sch.40 para.11
Sch.24 Part 2 para.4, amended: 2008 c.9 Sch.40 para.6
Sch.24 Part 2 para.5, amended: 2008 c.9 Sch.40 para.7
Sch.24 Part 2 para.6, amended: 2008 c.9 Sch.40 para.8
Sch.24 Part 2 para.9, amended: 2008 c.9 Sch.40 para.9
Sch.24 Part 2 para.11, amended: 2008 c.9 Sch.40 para.10
Sch.24 Part 2 para.12, amended: 2008 c.9 Sch.40 para.11
Sch.24 Part 2 para.12, referred to: 2008 c.9 Sch.36 para.50
Sch.24 Part 3 para.13, amended: 2008 c.9 Sch.40 para.12
Sch.24 Part 3 para.15, amended: 2008 c.9 Sch.40 para.13
Sch.24 Part 3 para.16, substituted: 2008 c.9 Sch.40 para.14
Sch.24 Part 4 para.18, amended: 2008 c.9 Sch.40 para.15

CAP.

2007–*cont.*

11. Finance Act 2007–*cont.*

Sch.24 Part 4 para.19, amended: 2008 c.9 Sch.40 para.16

Sch.24 Part 4 para.21, amended: 2008 c.9 Sch.40 para.17

Sch.24 Part 5 para.22, amended: 2008 c.9 Sch.40 para.18

Sch.24 Part 5 para.23A, added: 2008 c.9 Sch.40 para.19

Sch.24 Part 5 para.28, amended: 2008 c.9 Sch.40 para.20

Sch.24 Part 5 para.29, disapplied: SI 2008/568 Art.4

12. Mental Health Act 2007

Commencement Orders: SI 2008/745 Art.2, Art.3, Art.4; SI 2008/800 Art.2, Art.3; SI 2008/1210 Art.2, Art.4; SI 2008/1900 Art.1, Art.2; SI 2008/2561 Art.2; SI 2008/2788 Art.2

see *R. v Rush (Ainsley)* [2007] EWCA Crim 1907, [2008] 1 Cr. App. R. (S.) 45 (CA (Crim Div)), Longmore, L.J.

s.18, applied: SI 2008/800 Art.3

s.21, applied: SI 2008/800 Art.3

s.38, repealed (in part): SI 2008/2833 Sch.3 para.228

s.44, referred to: SI 2008/800 Art.3

s.54, applied: SI 2008/2828

s.54, enabling: SI 2008/1210, SI 2008/2828

s.56, enabling: SI 2008/745, SI 2008/800, SI 2008/1210, SI 2008/1900, SI 2008/2561, SI 2008/2788

s.57, enabling: SI 2008/1210

Sch.2, applied: SI 2008/800 Art.3

Sch.4 para.1, referred to: SI 2008/1900 Sch.1 para.2

Sch.4 para.2, referred to: SI 2008/1900 Sch.1 para.2

Sch.4 para.3, referred to: SI 2008/1900 Sch.1 para.2

Sch.6 para.3, amended: SI 2008/912 Sch.1 para.24

Sch.6 para.7, amended: SI 2008/912 Sch.1 para.24

Sch.6 para.9, amended: SI 2008/912 Sch.1 para.24

Sch.6 para.11, amended: SI 2008/912 Sch.1 para.24

Sch.6 para.15, amended: SI 2008/912 Sch.1 para.24

Sch.10 para.2, amended: SI 2008/2833 Sch.3 para.223

13. Concessionary Bus Travel Act 2007

s.9, amended: 2008 c.26 Sch.4 para.67

15. Tribunals, Courts and Enforcement Act 2007

Commencement Orders: SI 2008/749 Art.2; SI 2008/1158 Art.2; SI 2008/1653 Art.2, Art.3; SI 2008/2696 Art.6; SSI 2008/150 Art.2; SI 2008/2696 Art.5

CAP.

2007–*cont.*

15. Tribunals, Courts and Enforcement Act 2007–*cont.*

applied: 2008 c.9 s.124, SI 2008/2686 r.5, SI 2008/2698 r.5

s.3, applied: SSI 2008/357 Art.3

s.3, referred to: SI 2008/1210 Art.5

s.7, applied: SI 2008/2700 Art.2

s.7, enabling: SI 2008/2684

s.9, enabling: SI 2008/2685, SI 2008/2686, SI 2008/2699

s.10, enabling: SI 2008/2698

s.11, applied: SI 2008/2707 Art.2

s.11, varied: SI 2008/2683 Art.5, SI 2008/2833 Sch.4 para.4

s.11, enabling: SI 2008/2707, SI 2008/2780

s.13, varied: SI 2008/2833 Sch.4 para.5

s.13, enabling: SI 2008/2834

s.15, referred to: SI 2008/2684 Art.7

s.16, applied: SI 2008/2698 r.28

s.16, enabling: SI 2008/2698

s.20, applied: SI 2008/2698 r.27, r.30, SSI 2008/357 Art.2

s.20, enabling: SSI 2008/357

s.21, applied: SI 2008/2684 Art.7

s.22, enabling: SI 2008/2685, SI 2008/2686, SI 2008/2698, SI 2008/2699

s.25, applied: SI 2008/2685 r.7, SI 2008/2686 r.7, SI 2008/2698 r.7, SI 2008/2699 r.7

s.28, applied: SI 2008/2699

s.29, applied: SI 2008/2698 r.10, SI 2008/2699 r.10

s.29, enabling: SI 2008/2685, SI 2008/2686, SI 2008/2698, SI 2008/2699

s.30, applied: SI 2008/1210 Art.5, SI 2008/2696 Art.3, SI 2008/2835 Art.2

s.30, referred to: SI 2008/2833

s.30, enabling: SI 2008/2833

s.31, referred to: SI 2008/2700 Art.2

s.31, enabling: SI 2008/2683, SI 2008/2696, SI 2008/2833

s.32, enabling: SI 2008/2833

s.33, enabling: SI 2008/2833

s.34, enabling: SI 2008/2833

s.37, enabling: SI 2008/2833

s.38, enabling: SI 2008/2833

s.40, applied: SI 2008/2685 r.4, SI 2008/2686 r.4, SI 2008/2696 Art.3, SI 2008/2698 r.4, SI 2008/2699 r.4

s.44, applied: SI 2008/2938, SSI 2008/396

s.49, applied: SI 2008/2833, SI 2008/2834, SI 2008/2835

s.50, applied: SI 2008/2995 Art.5, Art.6, Art.7, Art.8

s.51, applied: SI 2008/2995

s.51, enabling: SI 2008/2995

s.134, applied: SI 2008/1159 Reg.4

s.134, enabling: SI 2008/1159

s.145, enabling: SI 2008/1653, SI 2008/2683, SI 2008/2833, SI 2008/2834, SI 2008/2835

CAP.

2007–*cont.*

15. Tribunals, Courts and Enforcement Act 2007–*cont.*

s.148, enabling: SI 2008/749, SI 2008/1158, SI 2008/1653, SI 2008/2696, SSI 2008/150
Sch.2 para.1, applied: SI 2008/2995 Sch.1 Part 1
Sch.2 para.2, enabling: SI 2008/2692
Sch.3 para.2, enabling: SI 2008/2692
Sch.4 Part 1 para.2, applied: SI 2008/2700 Art.2
Sch.4 Part 1 para.5, applied: SI 2008/2700 Art.2
Sch.4 Part 2 para.15, enabling: SI 2008/2834, SI 2008/2835
Sch.5, enabling: SI 2008/2685, SI 2008/2686, SI 2008/2698, SI 2008/2699
Sch.5 Part 2 para.22, referred to: SI 2008/1149 Art.2
Sch.5 Part 3 para.28, applied: SI 2008/2685, SI 2008/2686, SI 2008/2698, SI 2008/2699
Sch.5 Part 4 para.30, enabling: SI 2008/2683, SI 2008/2833
Sch.6, applied: SI 2008/2696 Art.3
Sch.6, referred to: SI 2008/2835 Art.2
Sch.6 Part 4, amended: SI 2008/2833 Art.2
Sch.7, applied: 2008 c.29 s.113
Sch.7 Part 3 para.24, applied: SI 2008/2142, SI 2008/2863, SI 2008/2938, SI 2008/3092, SI 2008/3240, SSI 2008/396
Sch.9 Part 1 para.2, enabling: SI 2008/1149
Sch.9 Part 3 para.11, applied: SI 2008/2697 Reg.2
Sch.9 Part 3 para.12, enabling: SI 2008/2697
Sch.10 Part 1 para.22, repealed (in part): SI 2008/2833 Sch.3 para.228
Sch.10 Part 1 para.29, repealed (in part): SI 2008/2833 Sch.3 para.228
Sch.10 Part 1 para.31, repealed: SI 2008/2833 Sch.3 para.228
Sch.12, applied: 2008 c.9 s.127, 2008 c.25 s.56
Sch.12 Part 2 para.6, referred to: 2008 c.25 s.56
Sch.12 Part 2 para.14, repealed (in part): 2008 c.9 Sch.43 para.10
Sch.12 Part 2 para.19, amended: 2008 c.9 Sch.43 para.10
Sch.13 para.33, repealed: 2008 c.9 Sch.43 para.11
Sch.13 para.96, repealed: 2008 c.6 Sch.8
Sch.13 para.97, repealed: 2008 c.6 Sch.8
Sch.13 para.104, repealed (in part): 2008 c.9 Sch.43 para.11
Sch.13 para.114, repealed: 2008 c.9 Sch.43 para.11
Sch.13 para.116, repealed (in part): 2008 c.9 Sch.43 para.11
Sch.13 para.119, repealed: 2008 c.9 Sch.43 para.11

CAP.

2007–*cont.*

15. Tribunals, Courts and Enforcement Act 2007–*cont.*

Sch.13 para.123, repealed: 2008 c.9 Sch.43 para.11
Sch.13 para.126, repealed (in part): 2008 c.9 Sch.43 para.11
Sch.13 para.128, repealed: 2008 c.24 Sch.1 Part 2
Sch.13 para.136, repealed: 2008 c.9 Sch.43 para.11
Sch.13 para.140, repealed: 2008 c.9 Sch.43 para.11
Sch.13 para.147, repealed (in part): 2008 c.9 Sch.43 para.11
Sch.22 para.8, repealed: 2008 c.17 Sch.16

17. Consumers, Estate Agents and Redress Act 2007

Commencement Orders: SI 2008/905 Art.3, Sch.1, Sch.2; SI 2008/1262 Art.3; SI 2008/2550 Art.2, Sch.1
s.5, applied: SI 2008/1262 Art.4
s.41, varied: SI 2008/1262 Art.4
s.43, applied: SI 2008/1898, SI 2008/2355
s.43, enabling: SI 2008/1898, SI 2008/2355
s.44, applied: SI 2008/1898, SI 2008/2355
s.44, enabling: SI 2008/1898, SI 2008/2355
s.46, enabling: SI 2008/1898, SI 2008/2355
s.47, applied: SI 2008/2267, SI 2008/2268
s.47, enabling: SI 2008/2267, SI 2008/2268
s.59, applied: 2008 c.13 Sch.7
s.59, enabling: SI 2008/1816
s.60, enabling: SI 2008/2550
s.62, applied: SI 2008/1262, SI 2008/1816
s.63, enabling: SI 2008/1262
s.66, enabling: SI 2008/905, SI 2008/1262, SI 2008/2550
Sch.7 para.11, repealed: 2008 c.9 Sch.2 para.70

18. Statistics and Registration Service Act 2007

Commencement Orders: SI 2008/839 Art.2, Art.3
referred to: 2008 c.3 Sch.2 Part 2
s.6, applied: SI 2008/928, SI 2008/928 Art.2, SSI 2008/131, SSI 2008/131 Art.2
s.6, enabling: SI 2008/928, SSI 2008/131
s.11, applied: SI 2008/2998, SSI 2008/399
s.11, enabling: SI 2008/2998, SSI 2008/399
s.12, applied: SSI 2008/399 Sch.1 para.1
s.13, applied: SSI 2008/399 Sch.1 para.1
s.14, applied: SSI 2008/399 Sch.1 para.1
s.24, enabling: SI 2008/792
s.39, repealed (in part): 2008 c.28 Sch.1 para.5, Sch.9 Part 2
s.65, applied: SI 2008/928, SI 2008/2998, SSI 2008/131, SSI 2008/399
s.67, amended: 2008 c.28 Sch.1 para.5
s.67, repealed (in part): 2008 c.28 Sch.9 Part 2
s.74, enabling: SI 2008/839

CAP.

2007–cont.

19. Corporate Manslaughter and Corporate Homicide Act 2007
Commencement Orders: SI 2008/401 Art.2
s.2, referred to: SI 2008/401 Art.2
s.2, varied: SI 2008/401 Art.2
s.3, varied: SI 2008/401 Art.2
s.5, varied: SI 2008/401 Art.2
s.7, amended: SI 2008/912 Sch.1 para.25
s.7, varied: SI 2008/401 Art.2
s.20, varied: SI 2008/401 Art.2
s.22, enabling: SI 2008/396
s.24, enabling: SI 2008/401
s.27, enabling: SI 2008/401
Sch.1, amended: SI 2008/396 Art.2

20. Forced Marriage (Civil Protection) Act 2007
Commencement Orders: SI 2008/2779 Art.2
s.4, enabling: SI 2008/2779

21. Offender Management Act 2007
Commencement Orders: SI 2008/504 Art.2, Art.3, Art.4
s.1, amended: 2008 c.4 Sch.4 para.99, Sch.26 para.83
s.2, referred to: SI 2008/598 Art.3
s.2, varied: SI 2008/504 Art.5
s.3, applied: SI 2008/598 Art.3
s.5, applied: SI 2008/239 Sch.2 para.7
s.5, enabling: SI 2008/598
s.13, applied: SI 2008/794 Sch.6 para.5
s.13, enabling: SI 2008/1263
s.36, applied: SI 2008/912
s.38, enabling: SI 2008/912
s.41, enabling: SI 2008/504

22. Pensions Act 2007
referred to: 2008 c.30 s.146
s.7, repealed (in part): 2008 c.16 Sch.2
s.8, repealed (in part): 2008 c.16 Sch.2
s.10, repealed (in part): 2008 c.16 Sch.2
s.18, amended: SI 2008/1432 Reg.3
s.18, applied: SI 2008/1432
s.18, enabling: SI 2008/1432
s.21, repealed: 2008 c.30 s.79, Sch.11 Part 1
s.23, amended: 2008 c.30 s.86
s.23, repealed (in part): 2008 c.30 s.86, Sch.11 Part 1
s.25, applied: SI 2008/1432
s.25, enabling: SI 2008/1432
s.27, enabling: SI 2008/2301
Sch.1 Part 7 para.35, repealed (in part): 2008 c.16 Sch.2
Sch.1 Part 7 para.37, repealed: 2008 c.16 Sch.2
Sch.1 Part 7 para.39, repealed: 2008 c.16 Sch.2
Sch.4 Part 1 para.5, repealed: 2008 c.30 Sch.11 Part 3
Sch.4 Part 1 para.8, repealed: 2008 c.30 Sch.11 Part 3
Sch.4 Part 1 para.9, referred to: 2008 c.30 s.106

CAP.

2007–cont.

22. Pensions Act 2007–*cont.*
Sch.4 Part 1 para.9, repealed: 2008 c.30 Sch.11 Part 3
Sch.4 Part 1 para.10, referred to: 2008 c.30 s.106
Sch.4 Part 1 para.10, repealed: 2008 c.30 Sch.11 Part 3
Sch.4 Part 1 para.12, referred to: 2008 c.30 s.106
Sch.4 Part 1 para.12, repealed: 2008 c.30 Sch.11 Part 3
Sch.4 Part 1 para.13, repealed: 2008 c.30 Sch.11 Part 3
Sch.4 Part 1 para.14, repealed: 2008 c.30 Sch.11 Part 3
Sch.4 Part 1 para.27, repealed: 2008 c.30 Sch.11 Part 2
Sch.4 Part 1 para.40, repealed: 2008 c.30 Sch.11 Part 2
Sch.6 Part 1 para.6, amended: 2008 c.30 s.84, s.85
Sch.6 Part 1 para.7, amended: 2008 c.30 s.84, s.85, Sch.11 Part 1
Sch.6 Part 2, amended: 2008 c.30 s.84
Sch.6 Part 2 para.8A, added: 2008 c.30 s.84
Sch.6 Part 2 para.11, amended: 2008 c.30 s.84
Sch.6 Part 2 para.17, amended: 2008 c.30 s.84
Sch.6 Part 3 para.18, substituted: 2008 c.30 s.82

23. Sustainable Communities Act 2007
s.2, applied: SI 2008/2694 Reg.4
s.5, applied: SI 2008/2694 Reg.4
s.5, enabling: SI 2008/2694

24. Greater London Authority Act 2007
Commencement Orders: SI 2008/113 Art.2; SI 2008/582 Art.2; SI 2008/1372 Art.2, Art.3; SI 2008/2037 Art.2
s.36, repealed: 2008 c.29 Sch.13
s.53, enabling: SI 2008/1372
s.59, enabling: SI 2008/113, SI 2008/582, SI 2008/1372, SI 2008/2037

25. Further Education and Training Act 2007
Commencement Orders: SI 2008/313 Art.2, Art.3; SI 2008/983 Art.2; SI 2008/1065 Art.2
s.32, enabling: SI 2008/313, SI 2008/983, SI 2008/1065

27. Serious Crime Act 2007
Commencement Orders: SI 2008/219 Art.2, Art.3; SI 2008/755 Art.18; SSI 2008/152 Art.2; SI 2008/755 Art.2, Art.3, Art.4, Art.5, Art.6, Art.7, Art.8, Art.9, Art.10, Art.11, Art.12, Art.13, Art.14, Art.15, Art.16, Art.17; SI 2008/2504 Art.2
Part 2, applied: SI 2008/1216 Sch.1 para.34, Sch.2 para.16, Sch.2 para.33, SI 2008/1769 Art.76

CAP.

2007–cont.

27. Serious Crime Act 2007–*cont.*

s.19, applied: SI 2008/1863 Art.7, Art.47, Art.49

s.20, applied: SI 2008/1863 Art.7, Art.47, Art.49

s.21, applied: SI 2008/1863 Art.7, Art.47, Art.49

s.24, applied: SI 2008/1863 Art.9, Art.13, Art.14, Art.15, Art.42, Art.47, Art.51, Art.54, Art.55, Art.59, Art.60, Art.61

s.24, varied: SI 2008/755 Art.15

s.24, enabling: SI 2008/1863

s.68, applied: SI 2008/2353 Art.2

s.68, enabling: SI 2008/2353

s.74, enabling: SI 2008/575

s.78, applied: SI 2008/755 Art.17

s.82, disapplied: SI 2008/755 Art.17

s.85, applied: SI 2008/403 Art.3

s.85, enabling: SI 2008/403

s.89, applied: SI 2008/949

s.89, enabling: SI 2008/403, SI 2008/1863

s.90, enabling: SI 2008/574, SI 2008/949

s.91, enabling: SI 2008/755

s.94, applied: SI 2008/755

s.94, enabling: SI 2008/219, SI 2008/755, SI 2008/2504, SSI 2008/152

Sch.8, applied: SI 2008/755 Art.3, Art.11

Sch.8 Part 1, applied: SI 2008/755 Art.4

Sch.8 Part 2, applied: SI 2008/755 Art.3

Sch.8 Part 2 para.88, referred to: SI 2008/755 Art.6

Sch.8 Part 3, applied: SI 2008/755 Art.3

Sch.8 Part 3 para.100, referred to: SI 2008/755 Art.7

Sch.8 Part 4, applied: SI 2008/755 Art.3

Sch.8 Part 4 para.108, applied: SI 2008/755 Art.3, Art.9

Sch.8 Part 4 para.108, disapplied: SI 2008/755 Art.9

Sch.8 Part 4 para.110, applied: SI 2008/755 Art.3, Art.9

Sch.8 Part 4 para.110, disapplied: SI 2008/755 Art.9

Sch.8 Part 4 para.113, disapplied: SI 2008/755 Art.10

Sch.8 Part 5, applied: SI 2008/755 Art.3

Sch.8 Part 6 para.140, applied: SI 2008/755 Art.3

Sch.8 Part 6 para.142, disapplied: SI 2008/755 Art.12

28. Local Government and Public Involvement in Health Act 2007

Commencement Orders: SI 2008/172 Art.2, Art.3, Art.4, Art.5, Art.6, Art.7, Art.8, Art.9; SI 2008/337 Art.2, Sch.1 para.1, para.2, para.3, para.4, para.5, para.6, para.7, para.8, para.9, para.10; SI 2008/461 Art.2, Sch.1; SI 2008/591 Art.1, Art.2; SI 2008/917 Art.2, Art.3, Art.4, Art.5, Art.6; SI 2008/1265 Art.2, Art.3; SI

CAP.

2007–cont.

28. Local Government and Public Involvement in Health Act 2007–*cont.*

–*cont.*

2008/2434 Art.2; SI 2008/3110 Art.2, Art.3, Art.4, Art.5, Art.6

see *Shrewsbury and Atcham BC v Secretary of State for Communities and Local Government* [2008] EWCA Civ 148, [2008] 3 All E.R. 548 (CA (Civ Div)), Waller, L.J. (V-P)

referred to: SI 2008/907 Art.7

Part 1 c.1, applied: SI 2008/2176 Reg.1, SI 2008/2867 Reg.1, SI 2008/3022 Reg.7

Part 4, applied: SI 2008/337 Sch.1 para.4, Sch.1 para.7, Sch.1 para.8, Sch.1 para.10, SI 2008/2113 Reg.7

s.2, applied: SI 2008/490, SI 2008/491, SI 2008/492, SI 2008/493, SI 2008/494, SI 2008/634, SI 2008/907

s.4, applied: SI 2008/490, SI 2008/491, SI 2008/492, SI 2008/493, SI 2008/494, SI 2008/634, SI 2008/907

s.7, applied: SI 2008/490 Art.7, SI 2008/491 Art.7, SI 2008/492 Art.7, SI 2008/493 Art.7, SI 2008/494 Art.7, SI 2008/634 Art.9, SI 2008/907 Art.8, Art.20

s.7, enabling: SI 2008/490, SI 2008/491, SI 2008/492, SI 2008/493, SI 2008/494, SI 2008/634, SI 2008/907

s.11, enabling: SI 2008/490, SI 2008/491, SI 2008/492, SI 2008/493, SI 2008/494, SI 2008/634, SI 2008/907

s.12, enabling: SI 2008/490, SI 2008/491, SI 2008/492, SI 2008/493, SI 2008/494, SI 2008/634, SI 2008/907

s.13, enabling: SI 2008/490, SI 2008/491, SI 2008/492, SI 2008/493, SI 2008/494, SI 2008/634, SI 2008/907

s.14, applied: SI 2008/490 Art.7, SI 2008/491 Art.7, SI 2008/492 Art.7, SI 2008/493 Art.7, SI 2008/494 Art.7, SI 2008/634 Art.9, SI 2008/907 Art.8, Art.20, SI 2008/2867 Reg.5, Reg.14

s.14, enabling: SI 2008/2113, SI 2008/2176, SI 2008/2867, SI 2008/3022

s.16, applied: SI 2008/2176 Reg.1, Reg.8, Reg.13, SI 2008/2867 Reg.1

s.20, applied: SI 2008/490 Art.7, SI 2008/491 Art.7, SI 2008/492 Art.7, SI 2008/493 Art.7, SI 2008/494 Art.7, SI 2008/634 Art.9, SI 2008/907 Art.8, Art.20, SI 2008/2176 Reg.1, SI 2008/2867 Reg.1

s.75, varied: SI 2008/337 Sch.1 para.9

s.76, varied: SI 2008/337 Sch.1 para.9

s.77, varied: SI 2008/337 Sch.1 para.9

s.78, varied: SI 2008/337 Sch.1 para.9

s.79, varied: SI 2008/337 Sch.1 para.9, SI 2008/2113 Reg.7

s.80, applied: SI 2008/337 Sch.1 para.9

s.80, referred to: SI 2008/337 Sch.1 para.9

s.80, varied: SI 2008/337 Sch.1 para.9

s.81, varied: SI 2008/337 Sch.1 para.9

CAP.

2007–cont.

28. Local Government and Public Involvement in Health Act 2007–*cont.*

s.82, varied: SI 2008/337 Sch.1 para.9
s.83, varied: SI 2008/337 Sch.1 para.9
s.84, varied: SI 2008/337 Sch.1 para.9
s.85, varied: SI 2008/337 Sch.1 para.9
s.86, applied: SI 2008/337 Sch.1 para.4, Sch.1 para.7, Sch.1 para.8, Sch.1 para.10, SI 2008/2113 Reg.7, SI 2008/2176 Reg.1, SI 2008/2867 Reg.1
s.86, varied: SI 2008/337 Sch.1 para.9, SI 2008/2113 Reg.7, Reg.8
s.87, applied: SI 2008/337 Sch.1 para.10
s.87, varied: SI 2008/337 Sch.1 para.9
s.88, varied: SI 2008/337 Sch.1 para.9
s.89, applied: SI 2008/337 Sch.1 para.7
s.89, varied: SI 2008/337 Sch.1 para.9
s.90, applied: SI 2008/337 Sch.1 para.7
s.90, varied: SI 2008/337 Sch.1 para.9
s.91, varied: SI 2008/337 Sch.1 para.9
s.92, applied: SI 2008/337 Sch.1 para.4, Sch.1 para.7
s.92, varied: SI 2008/337 Sch.1 para.9, SI 2008/2113 Reg.7
s.93, varied: SI 2008/337 Sch.1 para.9
s.94, varied: SI 2008/337 Sch.1 para.9
s.95, varied: SI 2008/337 Sch.1 para.9
s.96, applied: SI 2008/337 Sch.1 para.4, Sch.1 para.7, Sch.1 para.8, Sch.1 para.10
s.96, varied: SI 2008/337 Sch.1 para.9, SI 2008/2113 Reg.7
s.97, applied: SI 2008/337 Sch.1 para.4, Sch.1 para.7, Sch.1 para.8, Sch.1 para.10, SI 2008/2176 Reg.1, SI 2008/2867 Reg.1
s.97, varied: SI 2008/337 Sch.1 para.9, SI 2008/2113 Reg.7
s.97, enabling: SI 2008/625, SI 2008/626
s.98, applied: SI 2008/337 Sch.1 para.4, Sch.1 para.7, Sch.1 para.8, Sch.1 para.10
s.98, varied: SI 2008/337 Sch.1 para.9, SI 2008/2113 Reg.7, Reg.8
s.98, enabling: SI 2008/625, SI 2008/626
s.99, applied: SI 2008/337 Sch.1 para.4, Sch.1 para.7, Sch.1 para.8, Sch.1 para.10
s.99, varied: SI 2008/337 Sch.1 para.9, SI 2008/2113 Reg.7
s.100, applied: SI 2008/337 Sch.1 para.4, Sch.1 para.7, Sch.1 para.8, Sch.1 para.10
s.100, varied: SI 2008/337 Sch.1 para.9, SI 2008/2113 Reg.7
s.101, varied: SI 2008/337 Sch.1 para.9
s.102, varied: SI 2008/337 Sch.1 para.9
s.103, varied: SI 2008/2113 Reg.11, Reg.12
s.104, amended: 2008 c.17 Sch.8 para.83, 2008 c.26 Sch.4 para.68
s.104, varied: SI 2008/2113 Reg.11, Reg.12
s.105, varied: SI 2008/2113 Reg.11, Reg.12
s.106, varied: SI 2008/2113 Reg.11, Reg.12
s.107, varied: SI 2008/2113 Reg.11, Reg.12
s.108, applied: SI 2008/312 Reg.3, Reg.4
s.108, varied: SI 2008/2113 Reg.11, Reg.12

CAP.

2007–cont.

28. Local Government and Public Involvement in Health Act 2007–*cont.*

s.109, varied: SI 2008/2113 Reg.11, Reg.12
s.110, varied: SI 2008/2113 Reg.11, Reg.12
s.111, varied: SI 2008/2113 Reg.11, Reg.12
s.112, varied: SI 2008/2113 Reg.11, Reg.12
s.113, varied: SI 2008/2113 Reg.11, Reg.12
s.114, varied: SI 2008/2113 Reg.11, Reg.12
s.115, varied: SI 2008/2113 Reg.11, Reg.12
s.116, applied: SI 2008/2113 Reg.11
s.116, varied: SI 2008/2113 Reg.11, Reg.12
s.117, varied: SI 2008/2113 Reg.11, Reg.12
s.118, varied: SI 2008/2113 Reg.11, Reg.12
s.119, varied: SI 2008/2113 Reg.11, Reg.12
s.120, varied: SI 2008/2113 Reg.11, Reg.12
s.121, varied: SI 2008/2113 Reg.11, Reg.12
s.122, varied: SI 2008/2113 Reg.11, Reg.12
s.123, varied: SI 2008/2113 Reg.11, Reg.12
s.124, varied: SI 2008/2113 Reg.11, Reg.12
s.125, varied: SI 2008/2113 Reg.11, Reg.12
s.126, varied: SI 2008/2113 Reg.11, Reg.12
s.127, varied: SI 2008/2113 Reg.11, Reg.12
s.128, varied: SI 2008/2113 Reg.11, Reg.12
s.155, repealed (in part): 2008 c.17 Sch.16
s.183, applied: SI 2008/929 Art.2
s.183, enabling: SI 2008/929
s.188, referred to: SI 2008/172 Art.2
s.190, referred to: SI 2008/172 Art.2
s.221, applied: SI 2008/528 Reg.2, Reg.5, Reg.8, SI 2008/915 Reg.4
s.223, enabling: SI 2008/528
s.224, applied: SI 2008/528
s.224, enabling: SI 2008/528
s.225, applied: SI 2008/915 Reg.4, Reg.5, Reg.6
s.225, enabling: SI 2008/915
s.226, applied: SI 2008/528 Reg.17
s.226, enabling: SI 2008/528
s.227, amended: 2008 c.14 Sch.5 para.94
s.228, applied: SI 2008/528 Reg.7, Reg.8
s.228, enabling: SI 2008/528, SI 2008/1877
s.229, enabling: SI 2008/528, SI 2008/915
s.240, applied: SI 2008/490, SI 2008/491, SI 2008/492, SI 2008/493, SI 2008/494, SI 2008/634, SI 2008/907, SI 2008/915
s.240, enabling: SI 2008/528, SI 2008/929, SI 2008/2176, SI 2008/2867, SI 2008/3022
s.243, enabling: SI 2008/526
s.245, enabling: SI 2008/172, SI 2008/337, SI 2008/461, SI 2008/591, SI 2008/917, SI 2008/1265, SI 2008/2434, SI 2008/3110
Sch.4 Part 1, applied: SI 2008/634 Art.7, SI 2008/907 Art.16
Sch.4 Part 1 para.1, varied: SI 2008/2113 Reg.9
Sch.4 Part 1 para.2, varied: SI 2008/2113 Reg.9
Sch.4 Part 1 para.3, applied: SI 2008/2867 Reg.29

CAP.

2007–cont.

28. Local Government and Public Involvement in Health Act 2007–*cont.*

Sch.4 Part 1 para.3, disapplied: SI 2008/2867 Reg.29
Sch.4 Part 1 para.3, varied: SI 2008/2113 Reg.9
Sch.4 Part 1 para.4, varied: SI 2008/2113 Reg.9
Sch.4 Part 1 para.5, varied: SI 2008/2113 Reg.9
Sch.4 Part 2 para.6, varied: SI 2008/2113 Reg.9
Sch.4 Part 2 para.7, varied: SI 2008/2113 Reg.9
Sch.4 Part 2 para.8, varied: SI 2008/2113 Reg.9
Sch.4 Part 2 para.9, varied: SI 2008/2113 Reg.9
Sch.4 Part 2 para.10, varied: SI 2008/2113 Reg.9
Sch.4 Part 2 para.11, varied: SI 2008/2113 Reg.9
Sch.4 Part 2 para.12, varied: SI 2008/2113 Reg.9
Sch.4 Part 3 para.13, varied: SI 2008/2113 Reg.9

29. Legal Services Act 2007

Commencement Orders: SI 2008/222 Art.2, Art.3, Art.4, Art.5, Art.6, Art.7, Art.8; SI 2008/1436 Art.2, Art.3, Art.4; SI 2008/3149 Art.2, Art.3
applied: 2008 c.4 Sch.27 para.35
s.8, varied: SI 2008/3149 Art.3
s.13, applied: SI 2008/3149 Art.3
s.69, varied: SI 2008/222 Art.4
s.70, varied: SI 2008/222 Art.5
s.144, varied: SI 2008/3149 Art.3
s.173, varied: SI 2008/3149 Art.3
s.174, varied: SI 2008/3149 Art.3
s.180, varied: SI 2008/222 Art.6
s.194, applied: SI 2008/2680 Art.2
s.194, varied: SI 2008/1799 Art.2
s.194, enabling: SI 2008/2680
s.195, applied: SSI 2008/332 Art.2
s.195, referred to: SI 2008/2341 Art.2
s.196, disapplied: SI 2008/2341 Art.3
s.198, applied: 2008 c.13 Sch.3
s.204, enabling: SI 2008/3149
s.206, applied: SI 2008/3074
s.208, enabling: SI 2008/222, SI 2008/1436, SI 2008/1799, SI 2008/2341, SI 2008/3149
s.210, applied: SSI 2008/332 Art.2
s.210, referred to: SI 2008/2341 Art.2
s.211, enabling: SI 2008/222, SI 2008/1436, SI 2008/1591, SI 2008/3149
Sch.1 para.13, applied: SI 2008/1436 Art.4
Sch.4 Part 1 para.1, applied: SI 2008/3149 Art.3
Sch.16 Part 2 para.82, added: SI 2008/3074 Art.2

CAP.

2007–cont.

29. Legal Services Act 2007–*cont.*

Sch.16 Part 2 para.82, amended: SI 2008/3074 Art.2
Sch.20 para.2, applied: SSI 2008/332 Art.2
Sch.20 para.2, referred to: SI 2008/2341 Art.2
Sch.21 para.73, repealed: 2008 c.4 Sch.28 Part 8
Sch.21 para.119, repealed: 2008 c.4 Sch.28 Part 8
Sch.22 para.2, applied: SI 2008/3074
Sch.22 para.2, enabling: SI 2008/3074
Sch.22 para.3, applied: SI 2008/3074
Sch.23, applied: SSI 2008/332 Art.2
Sch.23, referred to: SI 2008/2341 Art.2

30. UK Borders Act 2007

Commencement Orders: SI 2008/99 Art.2, Art.4; SI 2008/309 Art.2, Art.3, Art.4, Art.5, Art.6, Art.7; SI 2008/1818 Art.2, Art.3, Sch.1; SI 2008/2822 Art.2; SI 2008/3136 Art.2
s.5, enabling: SI 2008/1183, SI 2008/3048
s.6, applied: SI 2008/1183, SI 2008/3048
s.6, enabling: SI 2008/1183, SI 2008/3048
s.7, enabling: SI 2008/1183, SI 2008/3048
s.8, enabling: SI 2008/1183, SI 2008/3048
s.9, applied: SI 2008/2830 Art.3, SI 2008/3048 Reg.23, SI 2008/3049 Art.2
s.10, applied: SI 2008/2830 Art.3, Art.7, Art.8
s.10, enabling: SI 2008/2830
s.11, applied: SI 2008/2830 Art.6
s.11, enabling: SSI 2008/365
s.13, applied: SI 2008/3049
s.13, enabling: SI 2008/3049
s.14, applied: SI 2008/3049
s.14, enabling: SI 2008/2830, SI 2008/3049
s.15, enabling: SI 2008/1183, SI 2008/3048
s.21, enabling: SI 2008/3158
s.25, applied: SI 2008/309 Art.6, SI 2008/786 Reg.4
s.26, applied: SI 2008/99 Art.4, SI 2008/309 Art.7, SI 2008/786 Reg.3
s.26, referred to: SI 2008/786 Reg.3
s.26, enabling: SI 2008/786
s.32, applied: SI 2008/1818 Art.2, Art.3
s.33, amended: 2008 c.4 s.146
s.59, enabling: SI 2008/99, SI 2008/309, SI 2008/1818, SI 2008/2822, SI 2008/3136

31. Consolidated Fund Act 2007

applied: 2008 c.8 s.3, Sch.1

2008

1. European Communities (Finance) Act 2008

Royal Assent, February 19, 2008

01. NHS Redress (Wales) Measure 2008

Royal Assent, July 09, 2008

2. Banking (Special Provisions) Act 2008

Royal Assent, February 21, 2008

CAP. CAP.

2008–cont.

2. **Banking (Special Provisions) Act 2008**–*cont.*
   applied: SI 2008/2644 Art.26, SI 2008/3073 Reg.2
   s.3, enabling: SI 2008/432, SI 2008/2546
   s.4, enabling: SI 2008/432, SI 2008/2546
   s.5, applied: SI 2008/718 Sch.1
   s.5, enabling: SI 2008/718, SI 2008/3249
   s.6, enabling: SI 2008/2644, SI 2008/2666, SI 2008/2674
   s.7, enabling: SI 2008/3250, SI 2008/3251
   s.8, enabling: SI 2008/2546, SI 2008/2666, SI 2008/2674
   s.9, enabling: SI 2008/718, SI 2008/3249
   s.11, enabling: SI 2008/1427
   s.12, enabling: SI 2008/432, SI 2008/718, SI 2008/1427, SI 2008/2546, SI 2008/2644, SI 2008/2666, SI 2008/2674, SI 2008/3249
   s.13, applied: SI 2008/718, SI 2008/1427, SI 2008/3249, SI 2008/3250, SI 2008/3251
   s.13, enabling: SI 2008/432, SI 2008/718, SI 2008/1427, SI 2008/2546, SI 2008/2644, SI 2008/2666, SI 2008/2674, SI 2008/3249
   Sch.1, enabling: SI 2008/2546
   Sch.2, enabling: SI 2008/2644, SI 2008/2666, SI 2008/2674

02. **Learner Travel (Wales) Measure 2008**
   Royal Assent, December 10, 2008

3. **Appropriation Act 2008**
   Royal Assent, March 20, 2008

4. **Criminal Justice and Immigration Act 2008**
   Commencement Orders: SI 2008/1466 Art.2; SI 2008/1586 Art.2, Sch.1 para.1, para.2, para.3, para.4, para.5, para.6, para.7, para.8, para.9, para.10, para.11, para.12, para.13, para.14, para.15, para.16, para.17, para.18, para.19, para.20, para.21, para.22, para.23, para.24, para.25, para.26, para.27, para.28, para.29, para.33, para.34, para.35, para.36, para.37, para.38, para.39, para.40, para.41, para.42, para.43, para.44, para.45, para.46, para.47, para.48, para.49, para.50; SI 2008/2712 Art.2, Sch.1 para.1, para.2, para.3, para.4, para.5, para.6, para.7, para.8, para.9, para.10, para.11, para.12, para.14, para.15, para.16, para.17, para.18, para.19; SI 2008/2993 Art.2; SI 2008/3260 Art.2
   Royal Assent, May 08, 2008
   s.11, referred to: SI 2008/1586 Sch.2 para.1
   s.13, referred to: SI 2008/1586 Sch.2 para.2
   s.14, referred to: SI 2008/1586 Sch.2 para.2
   s.15, referred to: SI 2008/1586 Sch.2 para.2
   s.16, referred to: SI 2008/1586 Sch.2 para.2
   s.17, referred to: SI 2008/1586 Sch.2 para.2
   s.18, referred to: SI 2008/1586 Sch.2 para.2
   s.26, disapplied: SI 2008/1466 Art.3

2008–cont.

4. **Criminal Justice and Immigration Act 2008**–*cont.*
   s.26, referred to: SI 2008/1466 Art.4
   s.29, referred to: SI 2008/1586 Sch.2 para.3
   s.30, referred to: SI 2008/1586 Sch.2 para.3
   s.39, applied: 2008 c.25 s.56
   s.60, referred to: SI 2008/2712 Art.3
   s.134, repealed (in part): 2008 c.17 Sch.15 para.24, Sch.16
   s.135, repealed (in part): 2008 c.17 Sch.15 para.25, Sch.16
   s.147, applied: SI 2008/2793
   s.148, enabling: SI 2008/1587
   s.153, enabling: SI 2008/1466, SI 2008/1586, SI 2008/2712, SI 2008/2993, SI 2008/3260
   Sch.1 Part 2 para.18, amended: 2008 c.23 Sch.1 para.21
   Sch.5, referred to: SI 2008/1586 Sch.2 para.2
   Sch.6 para.2, applied: SI 2008/2793 r.2, r.3, r.4
   Sch.6 para.2, disapplied: SI 2008/2793 r.2, r.3, r.4
   Sch.6 para.2, referred to: SI 2008/2793 r.2
   Sch.6 para.2, enabling: SI 2008/2793
   Sch.7 para.5, amended: 2008 c.25 Sch.1 para.90
   Sch.7 para.5A, added: 2008 c.25 Sch.1 para.90
   Sch.8 Part 1 para.6, referred to: SI 2008/1586 Sch.2 para.4
   Sch.8 Part 1 para.7, referred to: SI 2008/1586 Sch.2 para.5
   Sch.8 Part 1 para.8, referred to: SI 2008/1586 Sch.2 para.5
   Sch.8 Part 1 para.9, referred to: SI 2008/1586 Sch.2 para.5
   Sch.8 Part 1 para.12, referred to: SI 2008/1586 Sch.2 para.6
   Sch.8 Part 1 para.13, referred to: SI 2008/1586 Sch.2 para.7
   Sch.8 Part 2 para.18, referred to: SI 2008/1586 Sch.2 para.8
   Sch.8 Part 2 para.19, referred to: SI 2008/1586 Sch.2 para.9
   Sch.8 Part 2 para.20, referred to: SI 2008/1586 Sch.2 para.9
   Sch.8 Part 2 para.21, referred to: SI 2008/1586 Sch.2 para.9
   Sch.8 Part 2 para.24, referred to: SI 2008/1586 Sch.2 para.10
   Sch.8 Part 3 para.26, referred to: SI 2008/1586 Sch.2 para.11
   Sch.8 Part 3 para.27, referred to: SI 2008/1586 Sch.2 para.12
   Sch.8 Part 3 para.28, referred to: SI 2008/1586 Sch.2 para.13
   Sch.26 Part 2 para.19, disapplied: SI 2008/1466 Art.4

CAP.

2008–cont.

4. Criminal Justice and Immigration Act 2008–*cont.*
Sch.26 Part 2 para.71, referred to: SI 2008/1586 Sch.2 para.2
Sch.28, referred to: SI 2008/1586 Sch.2 para.4, Sch.2 para.5, Sch.2 para.6, Sch.2 para.12, Sch.2 para.13

5. Channel Tunnel Rail Link (Supplementary Provisions) Act 2008
Royal Assent, May 22, 2008

6. Child Maintenance and Other Payments Act 2008
Commencement Orders: SI 2008/1476 Art.2, Art.3, Sch.1; SI 2008/2033 Art.2; SI 2008/2548 Art.2, Art.3; SI 2008/2675 Art.2, Art.3
Royal Assent, June 05, 2008
s.6, amended: SI 2008/2833 Sch.3 para.225
s.13, applied: SI 2008/2675 Art.4
s.15, referred to: SI 2008/2685 r.19
s.46, applied: SI 2008/1963 Reg.5
s.46, enabling: SI 2008/1963
s.47, applied: SI 2008/1963 Reg.2, Reg.3
s.47, referred to: SI 2008/1963 Reg.2
s.47, enabling: SI 2008/1963, SI 2008/2365
s.48, enabling: SI 2008/1595
s.49, applied: SI 2008/1595 Reg.5, Reg.6
s.49, enabling: SI 2008/1595
s.50, amended: SI 2008/2833 Sch.3 para.226
s.50, repealed (in part): SI 2008/2833 Sch.3 para.226
s.50, enabling: SI 2008/1595, SI 2008/2706
s.51, repealed: SI 2008/2833 Sch.3 para.227
s.53, applied: SI 2008/1963
s.53, enabling: SI 2008/1595, SI 2008/1596, SI 2008/2365
s.54, applied: SI 2008/1596
s.54, referred to: SI 2008/1596 Reg.6
s.57, applied: SI 2008/1596
s.57, enabling: SI 2008/2543, SI 2008/2656
s.62, enabling: SI 2008/1476, SI 2008/2033, SI 2008/2548, SI 2008/2675
Sch.3 Part 1 para.16, repealed (in part): SI 2008/2833 Sch.3 para.228
Sch.3 Part 1 para.17, repealed: SI 2008/2833 Sch.3 para.228
Sch.3 Part 1 para.54, repealed: SI 2008/2833 Sch.3 para.228

7. European Union (Amendment) Act 2008
Royal Assent, June 19, 2008

8. Appropriation (No.2) Act 2008
Royal Assent, July 21, 2008

9. Finance Act 2008
Commencement Orders: SI 2008/1928 Art.2
Royal Assent, July 21, 2008
s.26, applied: SI 2008/1933 Art.2
s.26, enabling: SI 2008/1933
s.27, applied: SI 2008/1930 Art.2
s.27, enabling: SI 2008/1930

CAP.

2008–cont.

9. Finance Act 2008–*cont.*
s.28, applied: SI 2008/1929 Art.2
s.28, enabling: SI 2008/1929
s.29, enabling: SI 2008/1928
s.30, enabling: SI 2008/1925
s.31, enabling: SI 2008/3165
s.93, enabling: SI 2008/1932
s.116, enabling: SI 2008/1935
s.135, applied: SI 2008/1936 Art.2, Art.3
s.135, enabling: SI 2008/1936
s.136, enabling: SI 2008/1948, SI 2008/2991
Sch.8 para.1, enabling: SI 2008/1933
Sch.8 para.3, enabling: SI 2008/1933
Sch.9 para.3, enabling: SI 2008/1929

10. Sale of Student Loans Act 2008
Royal Assent, July 21, 2008
s.5, enabling: SI 2008/2715
s.6, enabling: SI 2008/2715

11. Special Educational Needs (Information) Act 2008
Royal Assent, July 21, 2008
s.2, enabling: SI 2008/2664

12. Statute Law (Repeals) Act 2008
Royal Assent, July 21, 2008

13. Regulatory Enforcement and Sanctions Act 2008
Commencement Orders: SI 2008/2371 Art.2
Royal Assent, July 21, 2008
s.76, enabling: SI 2008/2371

14. Health and Social Care Act 2008
Commencement Orders: SI 2008/2214 Art.2; SI 2008/2497 Art.2, Art.3, Art.4, Art.6, Art.7; SI 2008/2717 Art.2; SI 2008/2994 Art.2, Art.3; SI 2008/3137 Art.2; SI 2008/3168 Art.2, Art.3, Art.4, Art.5, Art.6, Art.7, Art.8; SI 2008/3244 Art.2, Art.3
Royal Assent, July 21, 2008
Part 1, applied: SI 2008/2252 Sch.1 para.22, Sch.1 para.23
Part 1 c.2, applied: SI 2008/3168 Art.7
s.11, applied: SI 2008/3168 Art.6, Art.7
s.11, varied: SI 2008/3168 Art.3
s.12, applied: SI 2008/2252 Sch.1 para.22, SI 2008/3168 Art.7, Art.8
s.12, varied: SI 2008/3168 Art.6
s.15, applied: SI 2008/2252 Sch.1 para.22
s.17, applied: SI 2008/2252 Sch.1 para.23
s.19, applied: SI 2008/2252 Sch.1 para.23
s.22, varied: SI 2008/3168 Art.4
s.26, applied: SI 2008/3168 Art.8
s.28, applied: SI 2008/3168 Art.8
s.32, amended: SI 2008/3168 Art.5
s.32, applied: SI 2008/2252 Sch.1 para.23, SI 2008/2699 Sch.1
s.32, varied: SI 2008/3168 Art.7
s.132, enabling: SI 2008/3109
s.135, enabling: SI 2008/3109
s.161, enabling: SI 2008/2252, SI 2008/3168

CAP.

2008–cont.

14. Health and Social Care Act 2008–*cont.*
s.167, enabling: SI 2008/2250, SI 2008/3168
s.170, enabling: SI 2008/2214, SI 2008/2497, SI 2008/2717, SI 2008/2994, SI 2008/3137, SI 2008/3168, SI 2008/3244
s.171, enabling: SI 2008/3137
s.172, applied: SI 2008/2497, SI 2008/2717, SI 2008/3244
Sch.1 para.3, referred to: SI 2008/2252 Reg.6, Reg.7
Sch.1 para.3, enabling: SI 2008/2252
Sch.5 Part 3 para.63, varied: SI 2008/2250 Art.3

15. Criminal Evidence (Witness Anonymity) Act 2008
Royal Assent, July 21, 2008

16. National Insurance Contributions Act 2008
Royal Assent, July 21, 2008

17. Housing and Regeneration Act 2008
Commencement Orders: SI 2008/2358 Art.2, Art.3, Art.4; SI 2008/3068 Art.2, Art.3, Art.4, Art.5, Sch.1
Royal Assent, July 22, 2008
see *Doherty v Birmingham City Council* [2008] UKHL 57, [2008] 3 W.L.R. 636 (HL), Lord Hope of Craighead
applied: SI 2008/3002 Sch.2 para.7
Part 2 c.3, applied: SI 2008/2358 Art.3
s.4, varied: SI 2008/3068 Art.11
s.9, applied: SI 2008/3068 Art.10
s.13, amended: 2008 c.29 Sch.2 para.65
s.67, enabling: SI 2008/2839
s.112, referred to: SI 2008/2358 Art.3
s.127, referred to: SI 2008/2358 Art.3
s.170, applied: SI 2008/3068 Art.11
s.171, applied: SI 2008/3068 Art.11
s.171, varied: SI 2008/3068 Art.11
s.174, referred to: SI 2008/2358 Art.3
s.179, referred to: SI 2008/2358 Art.3
s.196, referred to: SI 2008/2358 Art.3
s.197, referred to: SI 2008/2358 Art.3
s.216, referred to: SI 2008/2358 Art.3
s.298, applied: SI 2008/3111 Reg.4, Sch.1 para.1, Sch.1 para.2, Sch.2 para.14, Sch.2 para.15, Sch.2 para.16, Sch.2 para.17
s.298, enabling: SI 2008/3111
s.320, enabling: SI 2008/2358, SI 2008/2831, SI 2008/2839, SI 2008/3002
s.321, enabling: SI 2008/2831, SI 2008/3002
s.322, applied: SI 2008/3002 Sch.2 para.7
s.322, enabling: SI 2008/2358, SI 2008/3068
s.325, enabling: SI 2008/2358, SI 2008/3068
Sch.2, applied: SI 2008/3068 Art.10
Sch.7 para.9, repealed: SI 2008/3002 Sch.3

18. Crossrail Act 2008
Royal Assent, July 22, 2008

CAP.

2008–cont.

18. Crossrail Act 2008–*cont.*
applied: SI 2008/2036 Art.3, Art.4
referred to: SI 2008/2034 Art.2
s.1, applied: SI 2008/2036 Art.3, Art.4
s.12, enabling: SI 2008/2175
s.39, applied: SI 2008/2036
s.39, enabling: SI 2008/2036
s.48, amended: 2008 c.29 Sch.2 para.66
Sch.7 Part 1 para.1, enabling: SI 2008/2034
Sch.7 Part 2 para.9, referred to: SI 2008/2175 Reg.2, Sch.2
Sch.7 Part 3 para.17, referred to: SI 2008/2175 Reg.2, Sch.2
Sch.7 Part 4 para.30, applied: SI 2008/2175 Reg.5, Reg.6, Reg.7, SI 2008/2908 Reg.2, Reg.3, Reg.5
Sch.7 Part 4 para.30, referred to: SI 2008/2175 Sch.1 para.6
Sch.7 Part 4 para.30, enabling: SI 2008/2175, SI 2008/2908
Sch.7 Part 4 para.34, applied: SI 2008/2908 Reg.3
Sch.7 Part 4 para.34, enabling: SI 2008/2908
Sch.7 Part 4 para.35, enabling: SI 2008/2908

19. Appropriation (No.3) Act 2008
Royal Assent, October 16, 2008

20. Health and Safety (Offences) Act 2008
Royal Assent, October 16, 2008

21. Planning and Energy Act 2008
Royal Assent, November 13, 2008

22. Human Fertilisation and Embryology Act 2008
Royal Assent, November 13, 2008

23. Children and Young Persons Act 2008
Royal Assent, November 13, 2008

24. Employment Act 2008
Royal Assent, November 13, 2008
s.22, enabling: SI 2008/3232

25. Education and Skills Act 2008
Commencement Orders: SI 2008/3077 Art.2, Art.3, Art.4, Art.5
Royal Assent, November 26, 2008
s.173, enabling: SI 2008/3077

26. Local Transport Act 2008
Royal Assent, November 26, 2008
referred to: SI 2008/3132 Art.1
s.79, applied: SI 2008/3112 Reg.2
s.85, applied: SI 2008/3112 Reg.2

27. Climate Change Act 2008
Royal Assent, November 26, 2008

28. Counter-Terrorism Act 2008
Commencement Orders: SI 2008/3296 Art.2
Royal Assent, November 26, 2008
s.66, applied: SI 2008/3085
s.66, enabling: SSI 2008/401
s.67, applied: SI 2008/3085
s.67, enabling: SSI 2008/401
s.72, applied: SI 2008/3085
s.72, enabling: SI 2008/3085

CAP.

2008–cont.

28. Counter-Terrorism Act 2008–*cont.*
s.100, enabling: SI 2008/3296

29. Planning Act 2008
Royal Assent, November 26, 2008

30. Pensions Act 2008
Royal Assent, November 26, 2008
s.144, enabling: SI 2008/3241
s.149, enabling: SI 2008/3241

31. Dormant Bank and Building Society Accounts Act 2008
Royal Assent, November 26, 2008

CAP.

2008–cont.

31. Dormant Bank and Building Society Accounts Act 2008–*cont.*
s.1, applied: 2008 c.9 s.39
s.2, applied: 2008 c.9 s.39

32. Energy Act 2008
Royal Assent, November 26, 2008

33. Consolidated Fund Act 2008
Royal Assent, December 18, 2008

STATUTORY INSTRUMENT CITATOR 2008

The Statutory Instrument Citator covers the period 2008 and is up to date to **March 1, 2009** (orders and Acts received). It comprises in a single table:

(i) Statutory Instruments amended, repealed, modified, etc. by statute passed or Statutory Instrument issued during this period;

(ii) Statutory Instruments judicially considered during this period;

(iii) Statutory Instruments consolidated during this period;

(iv) Statutory Instruments made under the powers of any Statutory Instrument issued during this period.

The material is arranged in numerical order under the relevant year.

Definitions of legislative effects:

"added"	: new provisions are inserted by subsequent legislation
"amended"	: text of legislation is modified by subsequent legislation
"applied"	: brought to bear, or exercised by subsequent legislation
"consolidated"	: used where previous Acts in the same subject area are brought together in subsequent legislation, with or without amendments
"disapplied"	: an exception made to the application of an earlier enactment
"enabling"	: giving power for the relevant SI to be made
"referred to"	: direction from other legislation without specific effect or application
"repealed"	: rescinded by subsequent legislation
"restored"	: reinstated by subsequent legislation (where previously repealed/revoked)
"substituted"	: text of provision is completely replaced by subsequent legislation
"varied"	: provisions modified in relation to their application to specified areas or circumstances, however the text itself remains unchanged

STATUTORY INSTRUMENTS ISSUED BY THE SCOTTISH PARLIAMENT

NO.

1999

1. Environmental Impact Assessment (Scotland) Regulations 1999
see *Lerwick Port Authority v Scottish Ministers* 2008 S.L.T. 74 (OH), Lord Reed
Reg.2, amended: SSI 2008/202 Reg.4
Reg.55, amended: SSI 2008/202 Reg.4
Sch.2 para.2, referred to: SSI 2008/432 Reg.30

34. Spreadable Fats (Marketing Standards) (Scotland) Regulations 1999
revoked: SSI 2008/216 Reg.8

43. Environmental Impact Assessment (Forestry) (Scotland) Regulations 1999
Sch.2 para.1, amended: SSI 2008/202 Reg.5

88. Lobsters and Crawfish (Prohibition of Fishing and Landing) (Scotland) Order 1999
Art.3, applied: SSI 2008/101 Sch.1 Part 1

NO.

1999–cont.

88. Lobsters and Crawfish (Prohibition of Fishing and Landing) (Scotland) Order 1999–*cont.*
Art.4, applied: SSI 2008/101 Sch.1 Part 1

186. Beef Bones (Scotland) Regulations 1999
revoked: SSI 2008/166 Reg.3

2000

7. Sea Fishing (Enforcement of Community Control Measures) (Scotland) Order 2000
Art.2, amended: SSI 2008/151 Art.23
Art.3, applied: SSI 2008/101 Sch.1 Part 1

53. Sea Fishing (Enforcement of Community Conservation Measures) (Scotland) Order 2000
Art.3, applied: SSI 2008/101 Sch.1 Part 1

NO.

2000–cont.

54. National Health Service (Clinical Negligence and Other Risks Indemnity Scheme) (Scotland) Regulations 2000
Reg.1, amended: SSI 2008/60 Reg.2
Reg.7, amended: SSI 2008/60 Reg.2
Reg.7, revoked (in part): SSI 2008/60 Reg.2
Reg.9, revoked (in part): SSI 2008/60 Reg.2

58. Valuation for Rating (Plant and Machinery) (Scotland) Regulations 2000
Reg.2A, added: SSI 2008/360 Reg.2
Sch.1 Part 1, amended: SSI 2008/360 Reg.2
Sch.1 Part 2, amended: SSI 2008/360 Reg.2
Sch.1 Part 3, amended: SSI 2008/360 Reg.2
Sch.1 Part 4, added: SSI 2008/360 Reg.2

110. Repayment of Student Loans (Scotland) Regulations 2000
Reg.2, amended: SI 2008/1879 Reg.36

112. Divorce etc (Pensions) (Scotland) Regulations 2000
Reg.2, amended: SSI 2008/293 Reg.2
Reg.3, amended: SSI 2008/293 Reg.2

130. Foods for Special Medical Purposes (Scotland) Regulations 2000
Reg.8, added: SSI 2008/322 Reg.3

178. Contaminated Land (Scotland) Regulations 2000
applied: SSI 2008/100 Sch.4 Part 2

197. Undersized Lobsters (Scotland) Order 2000
Art.3, applied: SSI 2008/101 Sch.1 Part 1
Art.4, applied: SSI 2008/101 Sch.1 Part 1
Art.5, applied: SSI 2008/101 Sch.1 Part 1

199. Local Government Pension Scheme (Scotland) Amendment Regulations 2000
revoked: SSI 2008/229 Sch.1

224. National Health Service (Functions of the Common Services Agency) (Scotland) Amendment Order 2000
revoked: SSI 2008/312 Sch.1

227. Sea Fish (Specified Sea Areas) (Regulation of Nets and Other Fishing Gear) (Scotland) Order 2000
Art.4, applied: SSI 2008/101 Sch.1 Part 1
Art.5, applied: SSI 2008/101 Sch.1 Part 1
Art.5A, applied: SSI 2008/101 Sch.1 Part 1

228. Undersized Edible Crabs (Scotland) Order 2000
Art.3, applied: SSI 2008/101 Sch.1 Part 1

320. Electricity Works (Environmental Impact Assessment) (Scotland) Regulations 2000
Reg.2, amended: SSI 2008/246 Reg.2
Reg.4, amended: SSI 2008/246 Reg.3
Reg.6, amended: SSI 2008/246 Reg.4
Reg.7, amended: SSI 2008/246 Reg.5
Reg.8, amended: SSI 2008/246 Reg.6
Reg.9, amended: SSI 2008/246 Reg.7
Reg.10, amended: SSI 2008/246 Reg.8

NO.

2000–cont.

320. Electricity Works (Environmental Impact Assessment) (Scotland) Regulations 2000–*cont.*
Reg.10, substituted: SSI 2008/246 Reg.8
Reg.11, amended: SSI 2008/246 Reg.9
Reg.12, amended: SSI 2008/246 Reg.10
Reg.14, amended: SSI 2008/246 Reg.11
Reg.14A, added: SSI 2008/246 Reg.12
Sch.1, amended: SSI 2008/246 Reg.13
Sch.2, amended: SSI 2008/202 Reg.6, SSI 2008/246 Reg.13
Sch.2, revoked (in part): SSI 2008/246 Reg.13

323. Pollution Prevention and Control (Scotland) Regulations 2000
applied: SSI 2008/100 Sch.4 Part 2, SSI 2008/298 Reg.8
Reg.6, amended: SSI 2008/410 Reg.2
Sch.1 Part I, added: SSI 2008/410 Reg.2
Sch.1 Part I, amended: SSI 2008/410 Reg.2
Sch.3 Part 6 para.26, added: SSI 2008/410 Sch.1

405. Prohibition of Fishing with Multiple Trawls (No.2) (Scotland) Order 2000
Art.3, applied: SSI 2008/101 Sch.1 Part 1

418. Sheep and Goats Identification (Scotland) Regulations 2000
applied: SI 2008/130 Art.22, Art.30

2001

23. Local Government Pension Scheme (Pension Sharing on Divorce) (Scotland) Regulations 2001
revoked (in part): SSI 2008/229 Sch.1

45. Diseases of Animals (Approved Disinfectants) Amendment (Scotland) Order 2001
revoked: SSI 2008/219 Sch.1

75. Adults with Incapacity (Public Guardian's Fees) (Scotland) Regulations 2001
revoked: SSI 2008/52 Reg.4

76. Adults with Incapacity (Certificates from Medical Practitioners) (Accounts and Funds) (Scotland) Regulations 2001
revoked: SSI 2008/51 Reg.5

78. Adults with Incapacity (Countersignatories of Applications for Authority to Intromit) (Scotland) Regulations 2001
revoked: SSI 2008/50 Art.3

80. Adults with Incapacity (Certificates in Relation to Powers of Attorney) (Scotland) Regulations 2001
revoked: SSI 2008/56 Reg.5

172. European Communities (Service of Judicial and Extrajudicial Documents) (Scotland) Regulations 2001
referred to: SSI 2008/372 Reg.2

NO.

2001–cont.

172. European Communities (Service of Judicial and Extrajudicial Documents) (Scotland) Regulations 2001–*cont.*
Reg.2, amended: SSI 2008/372 Reg.2
Reg.3, amended: SSI 2008/372 Reg.2
Reg.3, revoked (in part): SSI 2008/372 Reg.2
Reg.4, amended: SSI 2008/372 Reg.2

219. Public Service Vehicles (Registration of Local Services) (Scotland) Regulations 2001
Reg.13, amended: SSI 2008/253 Reg.2

222. Education (Assisted Places) (Scotland) Regulations 2001
Reg.9, amended: SSI 2008/213 Reg.2
Reg.13, amended: SSI 2008/213 Reg.2
Reg.15, amended: SSI 2008/213 Reg.2
Reg.16, amended: SSI 2008/213 Reg.2
Reg.17, amended: SSI 2008/213 Reg.2
Sch.2, substituted: SSI 2008/213 Reg.2

223. St Mary's Music School (Aided Places) (Scotland) Regulations 2001
Sch.1 Part III para.10, amended: SSI 2008/214 Reg.2
Sch.1 Part III para.13, amended: SSI 2008/214 Reg.2
Sch.1 Part III para.14, amended: SSI 2008/214 Reg.2
Sch.1 Part IV para.18, amended: SSI 2008/214 Reg.2
Sch.1 Part IV para.24, amended: SSI 2008/214 Reg.2

252. Beef Labelling (Enforcement) (Scotland) Regulations 2001
revoked: SSI 2008/418 Reg.10

333. Potatoes Originating in Germany (Notification) (Scotland) Order 2001
revoked: SSI 2008/299 Art.5

430. National Health Service (Charges for Drugs and Appliances) (Scotland) Regulations 2001
applied: SSI 2008/27 Reg.12
Reg.7, applied: SSI 2008/27 Reg.12

433. Smoke Control Areas (Authorised Fuels) (Scotland) Regulations 2001
revoked: SSI 2008/154 Sch.2

460. Local Government Pension Scheme (Scotland) Amendment Regulations 2001
revoked: SSI 2008/229 Sch.1

725. Adults with Incapacity (Public Guardians Fees) (Scotland) Regulations 2001
revoked: SSI 2008/52 Reg.4

2002

32. Scottish Legal Services Ombudsman (Compensation) (Prescribed Amount) Order 2002
applied: SI 2008/2341 Art.7

NO.

2002–cont.

32. Scottish Legal Services Ombudsman (Compensation) (Prescribed Amount) Order 2002–*cont.*
revoked: SSI 2008/332 Art.7

38. Sheep and Goats Movement (Interim Measures) (Scotland) Order 2002
applied: SI 2008/130 Art.22, Art.30

69. Mobility and Access Committee for Scotland Regulations 2002
revoked: SSI 2008/187 Reg.2

96. Adults with Incapacity (Reports in Relation to Guardianship and Intervention Orders) (Scotland) Regulations 2002
Reg.3, amended: SSI 2008/55 Reg.2
Reg.4, amended: SSI 2008/55 Reg.2
Reg.5, amended: SSI 2008/55 Reg.2
Reg.6, amended: SSI 2008/55 Reg.2
Sch.1, amended: SSI 2008/55 Reg.2, Sch.1
Sch.2, amended: SSI 2008/55 Sch.2
Sch.3, substituted: SSI 2008/55 Sch.3
Sch.4, amended: SSI 2008/55 Sch.2
Sch.5, amended: SSI 2008/55 Sch.2
Sch.6, substituted: SSI 2008/55 Sch.4
Sch.7, amended: SSI 2008/55 Sch.2
Sch.8, amended: SSI 2008/55 Sch.2
Sch.9, substituted: SSI 2008/55 Sch.5
Sch.10, amended: SSI 2008/55 Sch.2

97. Adults with Incapacity (Recall of Guardians Powers) (Scotland) Regulations 2002
Sch.1, added: SSI 2008/53 Reg.2
Sch.1, amended: SSI 2008/53 Sch.1
Sch.2, amended: SSI 2008/53 Reg.2, Sch.1
Sch.4, amended: SSI 2008/53 Reg.2
Sch.5, amended: SSI 2008/53 Reg.2

132. Act of Sederunt (Summary Cause Rules) 2002
referred to: SSI 2008/121 r.5, r.6
Sch.1 Appendix, added: SSI 2008/121 Sch.2
Sch.1 Appendix, amended: SSI 2008/121 r.6, SSI 2008/223 Sch.3, SSI 2008/365 Sch.1
Sch.1 Appendix, revoked: SSI 2008/121 r.2
Sch.1 Part 5 para.5.6, amended: SSI 2008/121 r.6
Sch.1 Part 5 para.5.7, amended: SSI 2008/365 r.9
Sch.1 Part 6 para.6.A1, added: SSI 2008/121 r.6
Sch.1 Part 6 para.6.A1, amended: SSI 2008/121 r.6
Sch.1 Part 6 para.6.A2, added: SSI 2008/121 r.6
Sch.1 Part 6 para.6.A2, amended: SSI 2008/121 r.6
Sch.1 Part 6 para.6.A3, added: SSI 2008/121 r.6
Sch.1 Part 6 para.6.A3, amended: SSI 2008/121 r.6
Sch.1 Part 6 para.6.A4, added: SSI 2008/121 r.6

NO.

2002–cont.

132. Act of Sederunt (Summary Cause Rules) 2002–*cont.*
Sch.1 Part 6 para.6.A4, amended: SSI 2008/121 r.6
Sch.1 Part 6 para.6.A5, added: SSI 2008/121 r.6
Sch.1 Part 6 para.6.A5, amended: SSI 2008/121 r.6
Sch.1 Part 6 para.6.A6, added: SSI 2008/121 r.6
Sch.1 Part 6 para.6.A6, amended: SSI 2008/121 r.6
Sch.1 Part 6 para.6.A7, added: SSI 2008/121 r.6
Sch.1 Part 6 para.6.A7, amended: SSI 2008/121 r.6
Sch.1 Part 6 para.6.1, amended: SSI 2008/121 r.6
Sch.1 Part 6 para.6.2, amended: SSI 2008/121 r.6
Sch.1 Part 6 para.6.3, amended: SSI 2008/121 r.6
Sch.1 Part 14A para.14A.1, added: SSI 2008/223 r.6
Sch.1 Part 14A para.14A.2, added: SSI 2008/223 r.6
Sch.1 Part 14A para.14A.3, added: SSI 2008/223 r.6
Sch.1 Part 14A para.14A.4, added: SSI 2008/223 r.6
Sch.1 Part 14B para.14B.1, added: SSI 2008/223 r.6
Sch.1 Part 14B para.14B.2, added: SSI 2008/223 r.6
Sch.1 Part 14B para.14B.3, added: SSI 2008/223 r.6
Sch.1 Part 14B para.14B.4, added: SSI 2008/223 r.6
Sch.1 Part 30 para.30.9, added: SSI 2008/223 r.8
Sch.1 Part 31 para.31.1, revoked: SSI 2008/121 r.2
Sch.1 Part 31 para.31.2, revoked: SSI 2008/121 r.2
Sch.1 Part 31 para.31.3, revoked: SSI 2008/121 r.2
Sch.1 Part 31 para.31.4, revoked: SSI 2008/121 r.2
Sch.1 Part 31 para.31.5, revoked: SSI 2008/121 r.2
Sch.1 Part 31 para.31.6, revoked: SSI 2008/121 r.2
Sch.1 Part 31 para.31.7, revoked: SSI 2008/121 r.2
Sch.1 Part 36 para.36.1, amended: SSI 2008/223 r.6
Sch.1 Part 36 para.36.2, substituted: SSI 2008/223 r.6
Sch.1 Part 36 para.36.4, revoked: SSI 2008/223 r.6

NO.

2002–cont.

133. Act of Sederunt (Small Claim Rules) 2002
referred to: SSI 2008/121 r.7
Sch.1 Appendix1, added: SSI 2008/121 Sch.3
Sch.1 Appendix1, amended: SSI 2008/121 r.7, SSI 2008/223 Sch.4
Sch.1 Appendix1, revoked: SSI 2008/121 r.7
Sch.1 Part 6 para.6.5, amended: SSI 2008/365 r.10
Sch.1 Part 6 para.6.6, amended: SSI 2008/121 r.7
Sch.1 Part 7 para.7.A1, added: SSI 2008/121 r.7
Sch.1 Part 7 para.7.A1, amended: SSI 2008/121 r.7
Sch.1 Part 7 para.7.A2, added: SSI 2008/121 r.7
Sch.1 Part 7 para.7.A2, amended: SSI 2008/121 r.7
Sch.1 Part 7 para.7.A3, added: SSI 2008/121 r.7
Sch.1 Part 7 para.7.A3, amended: SSI 2008/121 r.7
Sch.1 Part 7 para.7.A4, added: SSI 2008/121 r.7
Sch.1 Part 7 para.7.A4, amended: SSI 2008/121 r.7
Sch.1 Part 7 para.7.A5, added: SSI 2008/121 r.7
Sch.1 Part 7 para.7.A5, amended: SSI 2008/121 r.7
Sch.1 Part 7 para.7.A6, added: SSI 2008/121 r.7
Sch.1 Part 7 para.7.A6, amended: SSI 2008/121 r.7
Sch.1 Part 7 para.7.A7, added: SSI 2008/121 r.7
Sch.1 Part 7 para.7.A7, amended: SSI 2008/121 r.7
Sch.1 Part 7 para.7.1, amended: SSI 2008/121 r.7
Sch.1 Part 7 para.7.2, amended: SSI 2008/121 r.7
Sch.1 Part 7 para.7.3, amended: SSI 2008/121 r.7
Sch.1 Part 13A para.13A.1, added: SSI 2008/223 r.7
Sch.1 Part 13A para.13A.2, added: SSI 2008/223 r.7
Sch.1 Part 13A para.13A.3, added: SSI 2008/223 r.7
Sch.1 Part 13A para.13A.4, added: SSI 2008/223 r.7
Sch.1 Part 13B para.13B.1, added: SSI 2008/223 r.7
Sch.1 Part 13B para.13B.2, added: SSI 2008/223 r.7
Sch.1 Part 13B para.13B.3, added: SSI 2008/223 r.7
Sch.1 Part 13B para.13B.4, added: SSI 2008/223 r.7

NO.

2002–cont.

133. Act of Sederunt (Small Claim Rules) 2002–*cont.*
Sch.1 Part 26 para.26.1, amended: SSI 2008/223 r.7
Sch.1 Part 26 para.26.2, substituted: SSI 2008/223 r.7
Sch.1 Part 26 para.26.4, revoked: SSI 2008/223 r.7

178. Forth Estuary Transport Authority Order 2002
Art.11, revoked: 2008 asp 1 Sch.2 Part 2
Art.13, amended: 2008 asp 1 Sch.1 para.3
Sch.3 para.2, revoked: 2008 asp 1 Sch.2 Part 2

289. Bus Service Operators Grant (Scotland) Regulations 2002
Reg.3, amended: SI 2008/1879 Reg.37

303. Community Care (Personal Care and Nursing Care) (Scotland) Regulations 2002
Reg.2, see *Argyll and Bute Council v Scottish Public Services Ombudsman* 2008 S.C. 155 (OH), Lord Macphail
Reg.2, amended: SSI 2008/78 Reg.2

311. Local Government Pension Scheme (Scotland) Amendment Regulations 2002
revoked: SSI 2008/229 Sch.1

318. Housing (Scotland) Act 2001 (Scottish Secure Tenancy etc.) Order 2002
Art.4, see *Rizza v Glasgow Housing Association* 2008 S.L.T. (Lands Tr) 13 (Lands Tr (Scot)), Lord McGhie

494. Civil Legal Aid (Scotland) Regulations 2002
Reg.2, amended: SI 2008/1879 Reg.38
Reg.14, amended: SSI 2008/50 Art.2
Reg.33, amended: SI 2008/1879 Reg.38, SSI 2008/48 Reg.3
Sch.2 para.5, amended: SI 2008/1879 Reg.38
Sch.3 para.7, amended: SI 2008/1879 Reg.38

527. Smoke Control Areas (Authorised Fuels) (Scotland) Amendment Regulations 2002
revoked: SSI 2008/154 Sch.2

549. School Crossing Patrol Sign (Scotland) Regulations 2002
revoked: SSI 2008/4 Reg.2

560. Act of Sederunt (Debt Arrangement and Attachment (Scotland) Act 2002) 2002
referred to: SSI 2008/121 r.8
Sch.1 Appendix, added: SSI 2008/121 Sch.4
Sch.1 Part Ch.1A para.6B, added: SSI 2008/121 r.8
Sch.1 Part Ch.1A para.6C, added: SSI 2008/121 r.8
Sch.1 Part Ch.1A para.6D, added: SSI 2008/121 r.8

NO.

2002–cont.

560. Act of Sederunt (Debt Arrangement and Attachment (Scotland) Act 2002) 2002–*cont.*
Sch.1 Part Ch.1A para.6E, added: SSI 2008/121 r.8

566. Act of Sederunt (Fees of Messengers-at-Arms) (No.2) 2002
Sch.1 para.15, amended: SSI 2008/431 Sch.1

567. Act of Sederunt (Fees of Sheriff Officers) (No.2) 2002
Sch.1 para.17, amended: SSI 2008/430 Sch.1

2003

1. Cairngorms National Park Designation, Transitional and Consequential Provisions (Scotland) Order 2003
Art.7, applied: SSI 2008/432 Reg.36

21. Police and Police (Special Constables) (Scotland) Amendment Regulations 2003
revoked: SSI 2008/117 Sch.3

51. Action Programme for Nitrate Vulnerable Zones (Scotland) Regulations 2003
applied: SSI 2008/100 Sch.4 Part 2
Reg.1, revoked: SSI 2008/298 Reg.2
Reg.2, revoked: SSI 2008/298 Reg.2
Reg.3, revoked: SSI 2008/298 Reg.2
Reg.4, revoked: SSI 2008/298 Reg.2
Reg.5, revoked: SSI 2008/298 Reg.2
Reg.6, revoked: SSI 2008/298 Reg.2
Reg.7, revoked: SSI 2008/298 Reg.2
Reg.8, revoked: SSI 2008/298 Reg.2
Reg.9, revoked: SSI 2008/298 Reg.2
Sch.1 para.1, revoked: SSI 2008/298 Reg.2
Sch.1 para.2, revoked: SSI 2008/298 Reg.2
Sch.1 para.3, revoked: SSI 2008/298 Reg.2
Sch.1 para.4, revoked: SSI 2008/298 Reg.2
Sch.1 para.5, revoked: SSI 2008/298 Reg.2
Sch.1 para.6, revoked: SSI 2008/298 Reg.2
Sch.1 para.7, revoked: SSI 2008/298 Reg.2
Sch.1 para.8, revoked: SSI 2008/298 Reg.2
Sch.1 para.9, revoked: SSI 2008/298 Reg.2
Sch.1 para.10, revoked: SSI 2008/298 Reg.2
Sch.1 para.11, revoked: SSI 2008/298 Reg.2
Sch.1 para.12, revoked: SSI 2008/298 Reg.2
Sch.1 para.13, revoked: SSI 2008/298 Reg.2
Sch.1 para.14, revoked: SSI 2008/298 Reg.2
Sch.1 para.15, revoked: SSI 2008/298 Reg.2
Sch.1 para.16, revoked: SSI 2008/298 Reg.2
Sch.1 para.17, revoked: SSI 2008/298 Reg.2
Sch.1 para.18, revoked: SSI 2008/298 Reg.2

91. Bluetongue (Scotland) Order 2003
revoked: SSI 2008/11 Art.30

159. National Health Service (Functions of the Common Services Agency) (Scotland) Amendment Order 2003
revoked: SSI 2008/312 Sch.1

NO.

2003–cont.

169. Action Programme for Nitrate Vulnerable Zones (Scotland) Amendment Regulations 2003
revoked: SSI 2008/298 Reg.2

176. Council Tax (Discounts) (Scotland) Consolidation and Amendment Order 2003
Art.4, amended: SI 2008/1879 Reg.39

179. Advice and Assistance (Assistance by Way of Representation) (Scotland) Regulations 2003
Reg.6, amended: SSI 2008/251 Reg.4
Reg.6, revoked (in part): SSI 2008/251 Reg.4
Reg.6A, amended: SSI 2008/251 Reg.4
Reg.6B, revoked: SSI 2008/251 Reg.4
Reg.7, amended: SSI 2008/251 Reg.4
Reg.9, revoked (in part): SSI 2008/251 Reg.4

229. Pet Travel Scheme (Scotland) Order 2003
Art.5, applied: SI 2008/1035 Sch.1 para.1
Art.7, applied: SI 2008/1035 Sch.1 para.2
Art.10, applied: SI 2008/1035 Sch.1 para.3
Sch.5 para.7, applied: SI 2008/1035 Sch.1 para.4

243. Community Care (Direct Payments) (Scotland) Regulations 2003
Reg.2, amended: SI 2008/2828 Art.17
Reg.2, revoked (in part): SI 2008/2828 Art.17

306. National Health Service (Functions of the Common Services Agency) (Scotland) Amendment (No.2) Order 2003
revoked: SSI 2008/312 Sch.1

311. Condensed Milk and Dried Milk (Scotland) Regulations 2003
Reg.2, amended: SSI 2008/12 Reg.3
Sch.1, amended: SSI 2008/12 Reg.4
Sch.1, substituted: SSI 2008/12 Reg.4

334. Diseases of Animals (Approved Disinfectants) Amendment (Scotland) Order 2003
revoked: SSI 2008/219 Sch.1

344. National Health Service (Compensation for Premature Retirement) (Scotland) Regulations 2003
Reg.4, amended: SSI 2008/225 Reg.4
Reg.15, substituted: SSI 2008/92 Reg.5

371. Prohibition of Fishing for Scallops (Scotland) Order 2003
Art.3, applied: SSI 2008/101 Sch.1 Part 1
Art.4, applied: SSI 2008/101 Sch.1 Part 1
Art.5, applied: SSI 2008/101 Sch.1 Part 1

411. Animal By-Products (Scotland) Regulations 2003
applied: SSI 2008/100 Sch.4 Part 2, SSI 2008/159 Sch.3 Part 2
Reg.19, applied: SI 2008/1035 Sch.1 para.1
Reg.21, applied: SI 2008/1035 Sch.1 para.2
Reg.26, applied: SI 2008/1035 Sch.1 para.3
Reg.27, applied: SI 2008/1035 Sch.1 para.4
Reg.30, applied: SI 2008/1035 Sch.1 para.5

NO.

2003–cont.

411. Animal By-Products (Scotland) Regulations 2003–*cont.*
Reg.40, applied: SI 2008/1035 Sch.1 para.6
Reg.41, applied: SI 2008/1035 Sch.1 para.7
Reg.42, applied: SI 2008/1035 Sch.1 para.8
Reg.49, applied: SI 2008/1035 Sch.1 para.9
Sch.1 Part 2 para.2, applied: SI 2008/1035 Sch.1 para.10
Sch.2 Part 2 para.6, applied: SI 2008/1035 Sch.1 para.11

415. Road Works (Inspection Fees) (Scotland) Regulations 2003
Reg.3, amended: SSI 2008/43 Reg.2

420. Housing Grants (Application Forms) (Scotland) Regulations 2003
Sch.1, amended: SSI 2008/283 Reg.3
Sch.2, amended: SSI 2008/283 Reg.4
Sch.3, amended: SSI 2008/283 Reg.5
Sch.4, amended: SSI 2008/283 Reg.6

435. Stornoway Harbour Revision (Constitution) Order 2003
Art.4, revoked: SSI 2008/422 Sch.3
Art.5, revoked: SSI 2008/422 Sch.3
Art.6, revoked: SSI 2008/422 Sch.3
Art.7, revoked: SSI 2008/422 Sch.3
Art.8, revoked: SSI 2008/422 Sch.3
Art.9, revoked: SSI 2008/422 Sch.3
Art.10, revoked: SSI 2008/422 Sch.3
Art.11, revoked: SSI 2008/422 Sch.3
Art.13, revoked: SSI 2008/422 Sch.3
Sch.1, revoked: SSI 2008/422 Sch.3
Sch.2 para.1, revoked: SSI 2008/422 Sch.3
Sch.2 para.2, revoked: SSI 2008/422 Sch.3
Sch.2 para.3, revoked: SSI 2008/422 Sch.3
Sch.2 para.4, revoked: SSI 2008/422 Sch.3
Sch.2 para.5, revoked: SSI 2008/422 Sch.3
Sch.2 para.6, revoked: SSI 2008/422 Sch.3
Sch.2 para.7, revoked: SSI 2008/422 Sch.3
Sch.2 para.8, revoked: SSI 2008/422 Sch.3
Sch.2 para.9, revoked: SSI 2008/422 Sch.3
Sch.2 para.10, revoked: SSI 2008/422 Sch.3
Sch.2 para.11, revoked: SSI 2008/422 Sch.3
Sch.2 para.12, revoked: SSI 2008/422 Sch.3
Sch.2 para.13, revoked: SSI 2008/422 Sch.3
Sch.2 para.14, revoked: SSI 2008/422 Sch.3
Sch.2 para.15, revoked: SSI 2008/422 Sch.3
Sch.2 para.16, revoked: SSI 2008/422 Sch.3
Sch.2 para.17, revoked: SSI 2008/422 Sch.3
Sch.2 para.18, revoked: SSI 2008/422 Sch.3
Sch.2 para.19, revoked: SSI 2008/422 Sch.3
Sch.2 para.20, revoked: SSI 2008/422 Sch.3
Sch.2 para.21, revoked: SSI 2008/422 Sch.3
Sch.2 para.22, revoked: SSI 2008/422 Sch.3
Sch.2 para.23, revoked: SSI 2008/422 Sch.3
Sch.2 para.24, revoked: SSI 2008/422 Sch.3
Sch.2 para.25, revoked: SSI 2008/422 Sch.3

453. Title Conditions (Scotland) Act 2003 (Conservation Bodies) Order 2003
Sch.1 Part II, amended: SSI 2008/217 Art.2

NO.

2003–cont.

460. National Health Service (Travelling Expenses and Remission of Charges) (Scotland) (No.2) Regulations 2003

Reg.2, amended: SSI 2008/27 Sch.3 para.2, SSI 2008/288 Reg.2
Reg.3, applied: SI 2008/794 Sch.8 para.45, Sch.9 para.37, SSI 2008/27 Reg.8
Reg.4, amended: SSI 2008/27 Sch.3 para.2, SSI 2008/288 Reg.2
Reg.5, applied: SI 2008/794 Sch.8 para.45, Sch.9 para.37
Reg.8, amended: SSI 2008/390 Reg.3
Reg.9, amended: SSI 2008/288 Reg.2
Reg.11, amended: SSI 2008/27 Sch.3 para.2
Reg.11, applied: SI 2008/794 Sch.8 para.45, Sch.9 para.37
Sch.1 Part I para.2, amended: SSI 2008/147 Reg.2, SSI 2008/390 Reg.4
Sch.1 Part II para.4, amended: SSI 2008/390 Reg.5

461. Housing Grants (Assessment of Contributions) (Scotland) Regulations 2003

Reg.2, amended: SSI 2008/336 Reg.3
Reg.9, amended: SSI 2008/336 Reg.4
Reg.26, amended: SSI 2008/336 Reg.5

531. Control of Pollution (Silage, Slurry and Agricultural Fuel Oil) (Scotland) Regulations 2003

applied: SSI 2008/100 Sch.2 Part 1, Sch.4 Part 2, SSI 2008/159 Sch.3 Part 2
Reg.1, amended: SSI 2008/54 Reg.3
Reg.3, amended: SSI 2008/54 Reg.3
Sch.1 para.2, amended: SSI 2008/54 Reg.3
Sch.1 para.2A, added: SSI 2008/54 Reg.3
Sch.1 para.10, added: SSI 2008/54 Reg.3

2004

6. Meat Products (Scotland) Regulations 2004

Reg.5, amended: SSI 2008/97 Reg.3
Sch.3 para.6, revoked: SSI 2008/97 Reg.4
Sch.3 para.7, revoked: SSI 2008/97 Reg.4
Sch.3 para.10, amended: SSI 2008/97 Reg.4

83. Individual Learning Account (Scotland) Regulations 2004

Reg.1, amended: SSI 2008/204 Reg.3
Reg.2, amended: SSI 2008/204 Reg.4
Reg.3, amended: SSI 2008/204 Reg.5
Reg.3, revoked (in part): SSI 2008/204 Reg.5
Reg.4, amended: SSI 2008/204 Reg.6
Reg.10, amended: SSI 2008/204 Reg.7
Reg.10, revoked (in part): SSI 2008/204 Reg.7
Reg.11, amended: SSI 2008/1 Reg.3, SSI 2008/204 Reg.8
Reg.11, revoked (in part): SSI 2008/204 Reg.8
Reg.12, amended: SSI 2008/204 Reg.9

NO.

2004–cont.

114. National Health Service (Primary Medical Services Performers Lists) (Scotland) Regulations 2004

Reg.2, amended: SSI 2008/27 Sch.3 para.3
Sch.1 para.3, amended: SSI 2008/27 Sch.3 para.3

115. National Health Service (General Medical Services Contracts) (Scotland) Regulations 2004

Reg.2, amended: SSI 2008/27 Sch.3 para.4
Sch.5 Part 3 para.44, amended: SSI 2008/27 Sch.3 para.4
Sch.5 Part 3 para.44, applied: SSI 2008/27 Reg.4

116. National Health Service (Primary Medical Services Section 17C Agreements) (Scotland) Regulations 2004

Reg.2, amended: SSI 2008/27 Sch.3 para.5
Sch.1 Part 3 para.15, amended: SSI 2008/27 Sch.3 para.5
Sch.1 Part 3 para.15, applied: SSI 2008/27 Reg.4

137. Sexual Offences Act 2003 (Prescribed Police Stations) (Scotland) Regulations 2004

revoked: SSI 2008/128 Sch.2

142. General Medical Services (Transitional and Other Ancillary Provisions) (Scotland) Order 2004

Art.13, applied: SSI 2008/27 Reg.2

143. Organic Aid (Scotland) Regulations 2004

applied: SSI 2008/100 Sch.2 Part 1, SSI 2008/159 Sch.2

163. General Medical Services and Section 17C Agreements (Transitional and other Ancillary Provisions) (Scotland) Order 2004

Art.1, referred to: SSI 2008/27 Reg.2

219. Town and Country Planning (Fees for Applications and Deemed Applications) (Scotland) Regulations 2004

applied: SSI 2008/432 Reg.9, Reg.10, Reg.12

249. Plant Health Fees (Scotland) Amendment Regulations 2004

revoked: SSI 2008/153 Reg.6

255. Potatoes Originating in Poland (Notification) (Scotland) Order 2004

Art.2, amended: SSI 2008/299 Art.3
Art.3, amended: SSI 2008/299 Art.4
Art.3, revoked (in part): SSI 2008/299 Art.4

261. Shrimp Fishing Nets (Scotland) Order 2004

Art.3, amended: SSI 2008/10 Art.2
Art.3, applied: SSI 2008/101 Sch.1 Part 1

276. Inshore Fishing (Prohibition of Fishing and Fishing Methods) (Scotland) Order 2004

Art.3, applied: SSI 2008/101 Sch.1 Part 1
Art.5, applied: SSI 2008/101 Sch.1 Part 1
Art.6, applied: SSI 2008/101 Sch.1 Part 1

NO.

2004–cont.

276. Inshore Fishing (Prohibition of Fishing and Fishing Methods) (Scotland) Order 2004–*cont.*
Art.7, applied: SSI 2008/101 Sch.1 Part 1
Art.9, applied: SSI 2008/101 Sch.1 Part 1
Art.10, applied: SSI 2008/101 Sch.1 Part 1

356. Sports Grounds and Sporting Events (Designation) (Scotland) Order 2004
Sch.1 Part I, amended: SSI 2008/379 Art.2

370. Sexual Offences Act 2003 (Prescribed Police Stations) (Scotland) Amendment Regulations 2004
revoked: SSI 2008/128 Sch.2

381. Agricultural Subsidies (Appeals) (Scotland) Regulations 2004
Reg.2, amended: SSI 2008/184 Sch.4 para.2
Reg.4, amended: SSI 2008/58 Art.3, SSI 2008/66 Reg.27, SSI 2008/100 Reg.23, SSI 2008/159 Reg.22, SSI 2008/294 Reg.6

392. Sea Fishing (Enforcement of Community Satellite Monitoring Measures) (Scotland) Order 2004
Art.9, applied: SSI 2008/101 Sch.1 Part 1

406. Building (Scotland) Regulations 2004
Reg.2, amended: SSI 2008/310 Reg.2
Sch.3 para.15A, added: SSI 2008/310 Reg.2
Sch.5 Part 6 para.6.9, amended: SSI 2008/310 Reg.2

428. Building (Procedure) (Scotland) Regulations 2004
Reg.41, applied: SSI 2008/309 Reg.6

472. Food Labelling Amendment (No.2) (Scotland) Regulations 2004
Sch.1, revoked: SSI 2008/180 Reg.3

477. Title Conditions (Scotland) Act 2003 (Rural Housing Bodies) Order 2004
Sch.1, amended: SSI 2008/391 Art.2

498. Sea Fish (Marketing Standards) (Scotland) Regulations 2004
Reg.3, applied: SSI 2008/101 Sch.1 Part 1

508. Building (Fees) (Scotland) Regulations 2004
substituted: SSI 2008/397 Reg.4
substituted: SSI 2008/397 Reg.5
Reg.3, amended: SSI 2008/397 Reg.3
Reg.5, amended: SSI 2008/397 Reg.4
Reg.6, amended: SSI 2008/397 Reg.5

518. Common Agricultural Policy Schemes (Cross-Compliance) (Scotland) Regulations 2004
Reg.2, amended: SSI 2008/184 Sch.3 para.1
Reg.4, applied: SSI 2008/159 Reg.10
Reg.4, referred to: SSI 2008/135 Reg.12
Reg.6, applied: SSI 2008/100 Reg.14
Reg.6, referred to: SSI 2008/159 Reg.13
Sch.1, applied: SSI 2008/159 Reg.10
Sch.1, referred to: SSI 2008/135 Reg.12

NO.

2005

9. Sexual Offences Act 2003 (Prescribed Police Stations) (Scotland) Amendment Regulations 2005
revoked: SSI 2008/128 Sch.2

73. Potatoes Originating in the Netherlands (Notification) (Scotland) Order 2005
revoked: SSI 2008/299 Art.5

103. Non Domestic Rating (Rural Areas and Rateable Value Limits) (Scotland) Order 2005
Sch.1, referred to: SSI 2008/370 Art.2
Sch.1, substituted: SSI 2008/370 Sch.1

143. Common Agricultural Policy Single Farm Payment and Support Schemes (Scotland) Regulations 2005
Reg.2, amended: SSI 2008/184 Sch.1 para.1
Reg.6, substituted: SSI 2008/184 Sch.1 para.2

156. Sexual Offences Act 2003 (Prescribed Police Stations) (Scotland) Amendment (No.2) Regulations 2005
revoked: SSI 2008/128 Sch.2

188. Act of Adjournal (Criminal Procedure Rules Amendment No.3) (Vulnerable Witnesses (Scotland) Act 2004) 2005
r.2, revoked (in part): SSI 2008/62 r.3

286. Registration of Fish Sellers and Buyers and Designation of Auction Sites (Scotland) Regulations 2005
Reg.3, applied: SSI 2008/101 Sch.1 Part 1
Reg.4, applied: SSI 2008/101 Sch.1 Part 1
Reg.5, applied: SSI 2008/101 Sch.1 Part 1
Reg.6, applied: SSI 2008/101 Sch.1 Part 1
Reg.7, applied: SSI 2008/101 Sch.1 Part 1
Reg.8, applied: SSI 2008/101 Sch.1 Part 1
Reg.9, applied: SSI 2008/101 Sch.1 Part 1
Reg.10, applied: SSI 2008/101 Sch.1 Part 1
Reg.11, applied: SSI 2008/101 Sch.1 Part 1

293. Local Government Pension Scheme (Scotland) Amendment Regulations 2005
revoked: SSI 2008/229 Sch.1

315. Local Government Pension Scheme (Scotland) Amendment (No.2) Regulations 2005
revoked: SSI 2008/229 Sch.1

330. Prevention and Monitoring of Cetacean Bycatch (Scotland) Order 2005
Art.3, applied: SSI 2008/101 Sch.1 Part 1
Art.4, applied: SSI 2008/101 Sch.1 Part 1

331. Plant Protection Products (Scotland) Regulations 2005
applied: SSI 2008/100 Sch.4 Part 2, SSI 2008/159 Sch.3 Part 2

332. Eggs (Marketing Standards) (Enforcement) (Scotland) Regulations 2005
revoked: SSI 2008/129 Reg.21

NO.

2005–cont.

348. Water Environment (Controlled Activities) (Scotland) Regulations 2005
applied: SSI 2008/100 Sch.2 Part 1, Sch.4 Part 2, SSI 2008/159 Sch.3 Part 2
referred to: SSI 2008/263 Sch.1
Sch.3 Part 1, amended: SSI 2008/54 Sch.1 para.1
Sch.3 Part 2, amended: SSI 2008/54 Sch.1 para.2
Sch.4 Part 2, amended: SSI 2008/170 Reg.20

380. Mental Health (Conflict of Interest) (Scotland) (No.2) Regulations 2005
referred to: SSI 2008/356 Reg.25

393. Teachers Superannuation (Scotland) Regulations 2005
Part C Reg.C1, amended: SSI 2008/227 Reg.3
Part C Reg.C1, revoked (in part): SSI 2008/227 Reg.3
Part C Reg.C1A, added: SSI 2008/227 Reg.4
Part C Reg.C2, amended: SSI 2008/227 Reg.5
Part C Reg.C4B, amended: SSI 2008/227 Reg.6
Part D Reg.D1, amended: SSI 2008/227 Reg.7
Part D Reg.D5, added: SSI 2008/227 Reg.8
Part E Reg.E6, amended: SSI 2008/227 Reg.10
Part E Reg.E7, amended: SSI 2008/227 Reg.11
Part E Reg.E8, amended: SSI 2008/227 Reg.12
Part E Reg.E8B, amended: SSI 2008/227 Reg.13
Part E Reg.E10A, amended: SSI 2008/227 Reg.14
Part E Reg.E13, amended: SSI 2008/227 Reg.15
Part E Reg.E26, amended: SSI 2008/227 Reg.16
Part E Reg.E29, amended: SSI 2008/227 Reg.17
Part E Reg.E31, amended: SSI 2008/227 Reg.18
Part E Reg.E34, amended: SSI 2008/227 Reg.19
Part E Reg.E36, amended: SSI 2008/227 Reg.20
Part E Reg.EA1, amended: SSI 2008/227 Reg.9
Part G Reg.G1, amended: SSI 2008/227 Reg.21
Part H Reg.H2, amended: SSI 2008/227 Reg.22
Part J Reg.J4, amended: SSI 2008/227 Reg.23
Part J Reg.J6A, amended: SSI 2008/227 Reg.24

NO.

2005–cont.

393. Teachers Superannuation (Scotland) Regulations 2005–*cont.*
Part J Reg.J8, substituted: SSI 2008/227 Reg.25
Part J Reg.J9, amended: SSI 2008/227 Reg.26
Sch.1, amended: SSI 2008/227 Reg.27
Sch.2A para.4, amended: SSI 2008/227 Reg.28
Sch.2A para.27, amended: SSI 2008/227 Reg.28
Sch.2A para.30, amended: SSI 2008/227 Reg.28
Sch.2A para.37, amended: SSI 2008/227 Reg.28
Sch.6 Part II para.11, amended: SSI 2008/227 Reg.29
Sch.6 Part IIA para.12B, amended: SSI 2008/227 Reg.29
Sch.6 Part IIA para.12C, amended: SSI 2008/227 Reg.29
Sch.6 Part IIB para.12E, amended: SSI 2008/227 Reg.29
Sch.6 Part IIB para.12F, amended: SSI 2008/227 Reg.29

443. Mental Health (Certificates for Medical Treatment) (Scotland) Regulations 2005
Sch.2, amended: SSI 2008/316 Sch.1

463. Mental Health (Absconding by mentally disordered offenders) (Scotland) Regulations 2005
Reg.2, amended: SSI 2008/356 Reg.34

519. Mental Health Tribunal for Scotland (Practice and Procedure) (No.2) Rules 2005
Part VII r.42, amended: SSI 2008/396 r.2
Part VII r.46, substituted: SSI 2008/396 r.2
Part VII r.59, amended: SSI 2008/396 r.2
Part VII r.66, amended: SSI 2008/396 r.2
Part VII r.72, amended: SSI 2008/396 r.2

542. Food Labelling Amendment (No.3) (Scotland) Regulations 2005
revoked: SSI 2008/180 Reg.3

554. Local Government Pensions Etc (Civil Partnership) (Scotland) Amendment Regulations 2005
revoked: SSI 2008/229 Sch.1

555. Plant Health Fees (Scotland) Amendment Regulations 2005
revoked: SSI 2008/153 Reg.6

557. Private Landlord Registration (Advice and Assistance) (Scotland) Regulations 2005
Reg.4, amended: SSI 2008/402 Reg.2

558. Private Landlord Registration (Information and Fees) (Scotland) Regulations 2005
Reg.4, amended: SSI 2008/403 Reg.2
Sch.2 para.1, substituted: SSI 2008/403 Reg.2

NO.

2005–cont.

558. Private Landlord Registration (Information and Fees) (Scotland) Regulations 2005–*cont.*
Sch.2 para.2, substituted: SSI 2008/403 Reg.2
Sch.2 para.3, substituted: SSI 2008/403 Reg.2
Sch.2 para.4, substituted: SSI 2008/403 Reg.2
Sch.2 para.5, substituted: SSI 2008/403 Reg.2

574. Act of Adjournal (Criminal Procedure Rules Amendment No.6) (Vulnerable Witnesses (Scotland) Act 2004) (Evidence on Commission) 2005
r.2, revoked (in part): SSI 2008/62 r.3

589. Mobility and Access Committee for Scotland Amendment Regulations 2005
revoked: SSI 2008/187 Reg.2

599. Pesticides (Maximum Residue Levels in Crops, Food and Feeding Stuffs) (Scotland) Regulations 2005
revoked: SSI 2008/342 Sch.2
Sch.2, amended: SSI 2008/65 Sch.1
Sch.2, varied: SSI 2008/65 Sch.1

605. Feeding Stuffs (Scotland) Regulations 2005
Sch.7 Part Ch, amended: SSI 2008/215 Sch.1

608. Feed (Hygiene and Enforcement) (Scotland) Regulations 2005
Reg.2, amended: SSI 2008/201 Reg.2
Reg.31A, added: SSI 2008/201 Reg.2
Reg.37, applied: SSI 2008/201 Reg.4
Sch.1, amended: SSI 2008/201 Reg.2

613. Plant Health (Scotland) Order 2005
Art.2, amended: SSI 2008/300 Art.3, SSI 2008/350 Art.3
Art.19, amended: SSI 2008/300 Art.4
Art.19A, added: SSI 2008/300 Art.4
Art.41, amended: SSI 2008/300 Art.5, SSI 2008/350 Art.4
Art.45, amended: SSI 2008/300 Art.6
Sch.1 Part A, amended: SSI 2008/350 Art.5
Sch.1 Part B, amended: SSI 2008/300 Art.7
Sch.2 Part B, amended: SSI 2008/300 Art.8, Art.9
Sch.3, amended: SSI 2008/300 Art.10
Sch.4 Part A, amended: SSI 2008/300 Art.11, Art.12, SSI 2008/350 Art.6
Sch.4 Part B, amended: SSI 2008/300 Art.13, SSI 2008/350 Art.6
Sch.6 Part A para.8, added: SSI 2008/350 Art.7
Sch.7 Part A para.8, added: SSI 2008/350 Art.7
Sch.8 Part A para.2, revoked: SSI 2008/300 Art.14
Sch.8 Part A para.5, amended: SSI 2008/300 Art.15

NO.

2005–cont.

614. Smoke Control Areas (Authorised Fuels) (Scotland) Amendment Regulations 2005
revoked: SSI 2008/154 Sch.2

2006

1. Public Contracts (Scotland) Regulations 2006
applied: SSI 2008/376 Reg.4
referred to: SSI 2008/376 Reg.4
see *Lightways (Contractors) Ltd v North Ayrshire Council* [2008] CSOH 91, 2008 S.L.T. 690 (OH), Lord Bracadale
Reg.2, amended: SSI 2008/291 Reg.2
Reg.3, amended: SSI 2008/94 Reg.2
Reg.5, amended: SSI 2008/94 Reg.2
Reg.8, amended: SSI 2008/94 Reg.2
Reg.13, amended: SSI 2008/94 Reg.2
Reg.14, amended: SSI 2008/94 Reg.2
Reg.23, amended: SSI 2008/94 Reg.2
Reg.31, amended: SSI 2008/94 Reg.2
Reg.32, amended: SSI 2008/94 Reg.2
Reg.32, see *Lightways (Contractors) Ltd v North Ayrshire Council* [2008] CSOH 91, 2008 S.L.T. 690 (OH), Lord Bracadale
Reg.33, amended: SSI 2008/94 Reg.2
Reg.37, amended: SSI 2008/94 Reg.2
Reg.40, referred to: SSI 2008/291 Reg.4
Sch.1, amended: SSI 2008/94 Reg.2, SSI 2008/376 Reg.2
Sch.2, amended: SSI 2008/376 Reg.2
Sch.2, substituted: SSI 2008/291 Sch.1
Sch.3 Part A, substituted: SSI 2008/291 Sch.2
Sch.3 Part B, amended: SSI 2008/94 Reg.2
Sch.3 Part B, substituted: SSI 2008/291 Sch.2
Sch.4, amended: SSI 2008/94 Reg.2
Sch.6 Part 001 para.1, substituted: SSI 2008/94 Sch.1
Sch.6 Part 002 para.2, substituted: SSI 2008/94 Sch.1
Sch.6 Part 003 para.3, substituted: SSI 2008/94 Sch.1

2. Utilities Contracts (Scotland) Regulations 2006
Reg.2, amended: SSI 2008/94 Reg.3, SSI 2008/291 Reg.3
Reg.5, amended: SSI 2008/94 Reg.3
Reg.6, amended: SSI 2008/376 Reg.3
Reg.7, amended: SSI 2008/94 Reg.3
Reg.11, amended: SSI 2008/94 Reg.3
Reg.34, amended: SSI 2008/94 Reg.3
Reg.34, revoked (in part): SSI 2008/94 Reg.3
Reg.38, amended: SSI 2008/94 Reg.3
Reg.38, referred to: SSI 2008/291 Reg.4
Sch.1, amended: SSI 2008/376 Sch.1
Sch.2, amended: SSI 2008/376 Reg.3
Sch.2, substituted: SSI 2008/291 Sch.1

NO.

2006–cont.

2. Utilities Contracts (Scotland) Regulations 2006–*cont.*

Sch.3 Part A, substituted: SSI 2008/291 Sch.2

Sch.3 Part B, substituted: SSI 2008/291 Sch.2

Sch.4, amended: SSI 2008/94 Reg.3

3. Food Hygiene (Scotland) Regulations 2006

Sch.4 para.2, amended: SSI 2008/129 Sch.3 para.3, SSI 2008/395 Sch.3 para.3

Sch.7 para.45, revoked: SSI 2008/129 Reg.21

8. Restriction of Liberty Order (Scotland) Regulations 2006

Reg.2, amended: SSI 2008/307 Reg.2

Sch.2, substituted: SSI 2008/307 Reg.2

Sch.2 para.1, substituted: SSI 2008/307 Reg.2

Sch.2 para.2, substituted: SSI 2008/307 Reg.2

Sch.2 para.3, substituted: SSI 2008/307 Reg.2

15. Intensive Support and Monitoring (Scotland) Regulations 2006

revoked: SSI 2008/75 Reg.1

24. Crofting Counties Agricultural Grants (Scotland) Scheme 2006

Art.2, amended: SSI 2008/58 Art.2

Art.2, substituted: SSI 2008/58 Art.2

Art.6, amended: SSI 2008/58 Art.2

Art.11A, added: SSI 2008/58 Art.2

Art.13, amended: SSI 2008/58 Art.2

Art.13A, added: SSI 2008/58 Art.2

44. Foot-and-Mouth Disease (Scotland) Order 2006

Art.59, revoked: SSI 2008/219 Sch.1

58. Inshore Fishing (Prohibition of Fishing for Cockles) (Scotland) Order 2006

Art.2, applied: SSI 2008/101 Sch.1 Part 1

73. Sheep and Goats (Identification and Traceability) (Scotland) Regulations 2006

applied: SI 2008/130 Art.22, Art.30

referred to: SSI 2008/368 Reg.2

Reg.2, amended: SSI 2008/368 Reg.2

Reg.3, amended: SSI 2008/368 Reg.2

Reg.18, amended: SSI 2008/368 Reg.2

Reg.30, substituted: SSI 2008/368 Reg.2

76. Act of Adjournal (Criminal Procedure Rules Amendment) (Vulnerable Witnesses (Scotland) Act 2004) 2006

r.2, revoked (in part): SSI 2008/62 r.3

94. Prisons and Young Offenders Institutions (Scotland) Rules 2006

Part 1 r.5, amended: SSI 2008/377 r.2

Sch.2, amended: SSI 2008/377 r.2

96. Police Act 1997 (Criminal Records) (Scotland) Regulations 2006

Reg.7A, added: SSI 2008/6 Reg.3

NO.

2006–cont.

96. Police Act 1997 (Criminal Records) (Scotland) Regulations 2006–*cont.*

Reg.8, amended: SSI 2008/6 Reg.4

Reg.11, amended: SSI 2008/6 Reg.5

Reg.12, amended: SSI 2008/6 Reg.6

Reg.16A, added: SSI 2008/6 Reg.7

Reg.17, amended: SSI 2008/6 Reg.8

123. Local Government Pension Scheme (Scotland) Amendment Regulations 2006

revoked: SSI 2008/229 Sch.1

126. Water Environment and Water Services (Scotland) Act 2003 (Designation of Responsible Authorities and Functions) Order 2006

revoked: SSI 2008/263 Art.4

151. Pesticides (Maximum Residue Levels in Crops, Food and Feeding Stuffs) (Scotland) Amendment Regulations 2006

revoked: SSI 2008/342 Sch.2

157. Erskine Bridge (Temporary Suspension of Tolls) Order 2006

revoked: 2008 asp 1 Sch.2 Part 2

182. Community Justice Authorities (Establishment, Constitution and Proceedings) (Scotland) Order 2006

Art.10, amended: SSI 2008/30 Art.3

218. Charities Accounts (Scotland) Regulations 2006

Reg.10, amended: SI 2008/948 Sch.1 para.35

220. Protection of Charities Assets (Exemption) (Scotland) Order 2006

Sch.1 Part 2, amended: SSI 2008/413 Art.2

Sch.1 Part 3, amended: SSI 2008/413 Art.3

233. Advice and Assistance (Scotland) Amendment (No.2) Regulations 2006

revoked: SSI 2008/240 Reg.8

250. Public Transport Users Committee for Scotland Order 2006

Art.6, amended: SSI 2008/186 Art.2

284. Sea Fishing (Marking and Identification of Passive Fishing Gear and Beam Trawls) (Scotland) Order 2006

Art.14, applied: SSI 2008/101 Sch.1 Part 1

312. Pesticides (Maximum Residue Levels in Crops, Food and Feeding Stuffs) (Scotland) Amendment (No.2) Regulations 2006

revoked: SSI 2008/342 Sch.2

314. Plastic Materials and Articles in Contact with Food (Scotland) Regulations 2006

Reg.24, referred to: SSI 2008/127 Reg.19

Sch.2 Part 1, referred to: SSI 2008/127 Reg.18

315. Home Detention Curfew Licence (Prescribed Standard Conditions) (Scotland) Order 2006

revoked: SSI 2008/36 Art.3, SSI 2008/125 Art.3

NO.

2006–cont.

336. Avian Influenza and Influenza of Avian Origin in Mammals (Scotland) Order 2006
Art.2, amended: SSI 2008/129 Sch.3 para.4, SSI 2008/395 Sch.3 para.4
Art.87, revoked (in part): SSI 2008/219 Sch.1

337. Avian Influenza (Slaughter and Vaccination) (Scotland) Regulations 2006
Reg.2, amended: SSI 2008/129 Sch.3 para.5, SSI 2008/395 Sch.3 para.5

338. Firefighters Compensation Scheme (Scotland) Order 2006
Sch.1, applied: SI 2008/649 Reg.4

352. Diseases of Animals (Approved Disinfectants) Amendment (Scotland) Order 2006
revoked: SSI 2008/219 Sch.1

434. Dumfries and Galloway (Electoral Arrangements) Order 2006
Sch.1, amended: SSI 2008/325 Art.2

468. Local Government Pension Scheme (Scotland) Amendment (No.2) Regulations 2006
revoked: SSI 2008/229 Sch.1

484. National Health Service Central Register (Scotland) Regulations 2006
Sch.1, amended: SSI 2008/358 Reg.2
Sch.2, amended: SSI 2008/358 Reg.2

505. Sea Fishing (Northern Hake Stock) (Scotland) Order 2006
Art.3, applied: SSI 2008/101 Sch.1 Part 1
Art.4, applied: SSI 2008/101 Sch.1 Part 1
Art.5, applied: SSI 2008/101 Sch.1 Part 1
Art.6, applied: SSI 2008/101 Sch.1 Part 1
Art.7, applied: SSI 2008/101 Sch.1 Part 1
Art.8, applied: SSI 2008/101 Sch.1 Part 1

514. Local Government Pension Scheme (Scotland) Amendment (No.3) Regulations 2006
revoked: SSI 2008/229 Sch.1

517. Plastic Materials and Articles in Contact with Food (Scotland) (No.2) Regulations 2006
revoked: SSI 2008/127 Reg.26

530. Transmissible Spongiform Encephalopathies (Scotland) Regulations 2006
Reg.2, amended: SSI 2008/166 Reg.2, SSI 2008/417 Reg.2
Reg.2, applied: SI 2008/1035 Sch.1 para.1
Reg.5, amended: SSI 2008/166 Reg.2, SSI 2008/417 Reg.2
Reg.6, applied: SI 2008/1035 Sch.1 para.2
Reg.8, applied: SI 2008/1035 Sch.1 para.3
Reg.9, applied: SI 2008/1035 Sch.1 para.4
Reg.10, applied: SI 2008/1035 Sch.1 para.5
Reg.11, applied: SI 2008/1035 Sch.1 para.6
Reg.12, amended: SSI 2008/417 Reg.2
Reg.12, applied: SI 2008/1035 Sch.1 para.7
Reg.20, amended: SSI 2008/417 Reg.2
Reg.20, applied: SI 2008/1035 Sch.1 para.8

NO.

2006–cont.

530. Transmissible Spongiform Encephalopathies (Scotland) Regulations 2006–*cont.*
Sch.2 Part 1 para.1, applied: SI 2008/1035 Sch.1 para.9
Sch.2 Part 1 para.1, substituted: SSI 2008/417 Reg.2
Sch.2 Part 1 para.2, substituted: SSI 2008/417 Reg.2
Sch.2 Part 1 para.3, applied: SI 2008/1035 Sch.1 para.9
Sch.2 Part 1 para.3, substituted: SSI 2008/417 Reg.2
Sch.2 Part 1 para.4, applied: SI 2008/1035 Sch.1 para.9
Sch.2 Part 1 para.4, substituted: SSI 2008/417 Reg.2
Sch.2 Part 1 para.5, applied: SI 2008/1035 Sch.1 para.9
Sch.2 Part 1 para.5, substituted: SSI 2008/417 Reg.2
Sch.2 Part 1 para.6, applied: SI 2008/1035 Sch.1 para.9
Sch.2 Part 1 para.6, substituted: SSI 2008/417 Reg.2
Sch.2 Part 1 para.7, substituted: SSI 2008/417 Reg.2
Sch.2 Part 1 para.8, substituted: SSI 2008/417 Reg.2
Sch.2 Part 1 para.9, substituted: SSI 2008/417 Reg.2
Sch.2 Part 1 para.10, substituted: SSI 2008/417 Reg.2
Sch.2 Part 1 para.11, substituted: SSI 2008/417 Reg.2
Sch.2 Part 1 para.12, substituted: SSI 2008/417 Reg.2
Sch.2 Part 1 para.13, substituted: SSI 2008/417 Reg.2
Sch.2 Part 1 para.14, substituted: SSI 2008/417 Reg.2
Sch.2 Part 2 para.7, substituted: SSI 2008/417 Reg.2
Sch.2 Part 2 para.8, substituted: SSI 2008/417 Reg.2
Sch.2 Part 2 para.9, substituted: SSI 2008/417 Reg.2
Sch.2 Part 2 para.10, substituted: SSI 2008/417 Reg.2
Sch.2 Part 2 para.11, substituted: SSI 2008/417 Reg.2
Sch.2 Part 2 para.12, substituted: SSI 2008/417 Reg.2
Sch.2 Part 2 para.13, substituted: SSI 2008/417 Reg.2
Sch.2 Part 2 para.14, substituted: SSI 2008/417 Reg.2
Sch.2 Part 2 para.15, substituted: SSI 2008/417 Reg.2
Sch.2 Part 2 para.16, substituted: SSI 2008/417 Reg.2

NO.

2006–cont.

530. Transmissible Spongiform Encephalopathies (Scotland) Regulations 2006–*cont.*

Sch.2 Part 2 para.17, substituted: SSI 2008/417 Reg.2

Sch.2 Part 2 para.18, substituted: SSI 2008/417 Reg.2

Sch.2 Part 2 para.19, substituted: SSI 2008/417 Reg.2

Sch.2 Part 2 para.20, substituted: SSI 2008/417 Reg.2

Sch.2 Part 2 para.21, substituted: SSI 2008/417 Reg.2

Sch.2 Part 2 para.22, substituted: SSI 2008/417 Reg.2

Sch.3 para.1, applied: SI 2008/1035 Sch.1 para.10

Sch.3 para.4, applied: SI 2008/1035 Sch.1 para.10

Sch.3 para.6, applied: SI 2008/1035 Sch.1 para.10

Sch.3 para.8, applied: SI 2008/1035 Sch.1 para.10

Sch.3 para.9, applied: SI 2008/1035 Sch.1 para.10

Sch.3 para.10, applied: SI 2008/1035 Sch.1 para.10

Sch.4 para.1, applied: SI 2008/1035 Sch.1 para.11

Sch.4 para.6, applied: SI 2008/1035 Sch.1 para.11

Sch.4 para.7, applied: SI 2008/1035 Sch.1 para.11

Sch.4 para.8, applied: SI 2008/1035 Sch.1 para.11

Sch.4 para.9, applied: SI 2008/1035 Sch.1 para.11

Sch.4 para.11, applied: SI 2008/1035 Sch.1 para.11

Sch.4 para.12, applied: SI 2008/1035 Sch.1 para.11

Sch.4 para.13, applied: SI 2008/1035 Sch.1 para.11

Sch.4 para.18, applied: SI 2008/1035 Sch.1 para.11

Sch.4 para.19, applied: SI 2008/1035 Sch.1 para.11

Sch.4 para.21, applied: SI 2008/1035 Sch.1 para.11

Sch.4 para.22, applied: SI 2008/1035 Sch.1 para.11

Sch.4 para.23, applied: SI 2008/1035 Sch.1 para.11

Sch.4 para.24, applied: SI 2008/1035 Sch.1 para.11

Sch.4 para.25, applied: SI 2008/1035 Sch.1 para.11

Sch.5 Part 1 para.2, applied: SI 2008/1035 Sch.1 para.12

Sch.5 Part 1 para.6, applied: SI 2008/1035 Sch.1 para.12

NO.

2006–cont.

530. Transmissible Spongiform Encephalopathies (Scotland) Regulations 2006–*cont.*

Sch.5 Part 2 para.21, applied: SI 2008/1035 Sch.1 para.13

Sch.5 Part 2 para.23, applied: SI 2008/1035 Sch.1 para.13

Sch.5 Part 2 para.24, applied: SI 2008/1035 Sch.1 para.13

Sch.6 para.1, substituted: SSI 2008/166 Sch.1

Sch.6 para.2, substituted: SSI 2008/166 Sch.1

Sch.6 para.3, substituted: SSI 2008/166 Sch.1

Sch.6 para.4, substituted: SSI 2008/166 Sch.1

Sch.6 para.5, substituted: SSI 2008/166 Sch.1

Sch.6 para.6, substituted: SSI 2008/166 Sch.1

Sch.6 para.7, substituted: SSI 2008/166 Sch.1

Sch.6 para.8, substituted: SSI 2008/166 Sch.1

Sch.6 para.9, substituted: SSI 2008/166 Sch.1

Sch.6 para.10, substituted: SSI 2008/166 Sch.1

Sch.6 para.11, substituted: SSI 2008/166 Sch.1

Sch.6 para.12, substituted: SSI 2008/166 Sch.1

Sch.6 para.13, substituted: SSI 2008/166 Sch.1

Sch.6 para.14, substituted: SSI 2008/166 Sch.1

Sch.6 para.15, substituted: SSI 2008/166 Sch.1

Sch.6 para.16, substituted: SSI 2008/166 Sch.1

Sch.6 para.17, substituted: SSI 2008/166 Sch.1

Sch.6 para.18, substituted: SSI 2008/166 Sch.1

Sch.6 para.19, applied: SI 2008/1035 Sch.1 para.14

Sch.6 para.19, substituted: SSI 2008/166 Sch.1

Sch.6 para.20, substituted: SSI 2008/166 Sch.1

Sch.6 para.21, substituted: SSI 2008/166 Sch.1

Sch.6 para.22, substituted: SSI 2008/166 Sch.1

Sch.6 para.23, substituted: SSI 2008/166 Sch.1

Sch.7 para.1, substituted: SSI 2008/417 Reg.2

Sch.7 para.2, substituted: SSI 2008/166 Reg.2, SSI 2008/417 Reg.2

NO.

2006–cont.

530. Transmissible Spongiform Encephalopathies (Scotland) Regulations 2006– *cont.*

Sch.7 para.3, substituted: SSI 2008/417 Reg.2

Sch.7 para.4, substituted: SSI 2008/417 Reg.2

542. Rice Products (Restriction on First Placing on the Market) (Scotland) Regulations 2006

revoked: SSI 2008/87 Reg.7

543. EC Fertilisers (Scotland) Regulations 2006

applied: SSI 2008/100 Sch.4 Part 2, SSI 2008/159 Sch.3 Part 2

548. Pesticides (Maximum Residue Levels in Crops, Food and Feeding Stuffs) (Scotland) Amendment (No.3) Regulations 2006

revoked: SSI 2008/342 Sch.2

554. Water Environment (Relevant Enactments) Order 2006

revoked: SSI 2008/263 Art.4

559. Health Protection Agency (Scottish Health Functions) Order 2006

applied: SSI 2008/312 Art.2

570. Home Energy Efficiency Scheme (Scotland) Regulations 2006

Reg.7, amended: SSI 2008/38 Reg.2

582. Environmental Impact Assessment (Agriculture) (Scotland) Regulations 2006

applied: SSI 2008/100 Sch.4 Part 2, SSI 2008/159 Sch.3 Part 2

referred to: SSI 2008/263 Sch.1

Reg.5, amended: SSI 2008/202 Reg.7

588. Personal Injuries (NHS Charges) (Amounts) (Scotland) Regulations 2006

Reg.2, amended: SSI 2008/96 Reg.2

Reg.2A, added: SSI 2008/96 Reg.2

Reg.3, amended: SSI 2008/96 Reg.2

Reg.6, amended: SSI 2008/96 Reg.2

603. National Health Service (Functions of the Common Services Agency) (Scotland) Amendment (No.2) Order 2006

revoked: SSI 2008/312 Sch.1

2007

1. Products of Animal Origin (Third Country Imports) (Scotland) Regulations 2007

Reg.4, applied: SI 2008/1035 Sch.1 para.1

Reg.5, applied: SI 2008/1035 Sch.1 para.2

Reg.30, applied: SI 2008/1035 Sch.1 para.3

Reg.32, applied: SI 2008/1035 Sch.1 para.4

4. Road Works (Inspection Fees) (Scotland) Amendment Regulations 2007

revoked: SSI 2008/43 Reg.3

NO.

2007–cont.

36. Non Domestic Rating (Rural Areas and Rateable Value Limits) (Scotland) Amendment Order 2007

revoked: SSI 2008/370 Art.3

39. Sea Fishing (Prohibition on the Removal of Shark Fins) (Scotland) Order 2007

Art.3, applied: SSI 2008/101 Sch.1 Part 1

40. Sea Fishing (Restriction on Days at Sea) (Scotland) Order 2007

revoked: SSI 2008/151 Art.33

55. Smoke Control Areas (Exempt Fireplaces) (Scotland) Order 2007

revoked: SSI 2008/157 Art.3

56. Smoke Control Areas (Authorised Fuels) (Scotland) Amendment Regulations 2007

revoked: SSI 2008/154 Sch.2

63. Sea Fish (Prohibited Methods of Fishing) (Firth of Clyde) Order 2007

revoked: SSI 2008/29 Art.5

65. Local Government Finance (Scotland) Order 2007

Art.2, revoked: SSI 2008/33 Art.5

Sch.1, amended: SSI 2008/33 Art.5

68. Police (Injury Benefit) (Scotland) Regulations 2007

Reg.3, amended: SSI 2008/387 Reg.32

Reg.6, amended: SSI 2008/387 Reg.33

Reg.31, applied: SI 2008/649 Reg.4

Sch.1 para.1, amended: SSI 2008/387 Reg.34

71. Local Government Pensions Etc (Councillors and VisitScotland) (Scotland) Amendment Regulations 2007

revoked: SSI 2008/229 Sch.1

72. Sexual Offences Act 2003 (Prescribed Police Stations) (Scotland) Amendment Regulations 2007

revoked: SSI 2008/128 Sch.2

85. Home Energy Efficiency Scheme (Scotland) Amendment Regulations 2007

revoked: SSI 2008/38 Reg.3

102. National Assistance (Assessment of Resources) Amendment (Scotland) Regulations 2007

Reg.2, revoked: SSI 2008/13 Reg.5

Reg.3, revoked: SSI 2008/13 Reg.5

Reg.4, revoked (in part): SSI 2008/13 Reg.5

103. National Assistance (Sums for Personal Requirements) (Scotland) Regulations 2007

revoked: SSI 2008/14 Reg.3

108. Local Government (Allowances and Expenses) (Scotland) Regulations 2007

Reg.2, amended: SSI 2008/414 Reg.2

Reg.4, amended: SSI 2008/414 Reg.2

Reg.5, amended: SSI 2008/414 Reg.2

Sch.2, amended: SSI 2008/414 Reg.2

NO.

2007–cont.

108. Local Government (Allowances and Expenses) (Scotland) Regulations 2007–*cont.*
Sch.3, amended: SSI 2008/414 Reg.2
Sch.4, amended: SSI 2008/414 Reg.2

109. Police Grant (Scotland) Order 2007
Art.2, amended: SSI 2008/20 Art.2
Art.3, amended: SSI 2008/20 Art.2

127. Sea Fishing (Enforcement of Community Quota and Third Country Fishing Measures) (Scotland) Order 2007
revoked: SSI 2008/151 Art.33
Art.2, amended: SSI 2008/102 Art.17
Art.2, revoked (in part): SSI 2008/102 Art.17
Art.4, revoked: SSI 2008/102 Art.17
Art.5, revoked: SSI 2008/102 Art.17
Art.6, revoked: SSI 2008/102 Art.17
Art.7, revoked: SSI 2008/102 Art.17
Art.11, revoked (in part): SSI 2008/102 Art.17
Art.12, amended: SSI 2008/102 Art.17
Art.14, amended: SSI 2008/102 Art.17
Art.20, amended: SSI 2008/102 Art.17
Sch.2, revoked: SSI 2008/102 Art.17

139. National Health Service (Charges for Drugs and Appliances) (Scotland) Regulations 2007
applied: SSI 2008/27 Reg.12
Reg.7, applied: SSI 2008/27 Reg.12
Reg.8, applied: SSI 2008/27 Reg.11

142. Pesticides (Maximum Residue Levels in Crops, Food and Feeding Stuffs) (Scotland) Amendment Regulations 2007
revoked: SSI 2008/342 Sch.2

151. Nursing and Midwifery Student Allowances (Scotland) Regulations 2007
applied: SI 2008/529 Reg.4, Reg.115, Reg.132, Reg.149, SI 2008/1273 Reg.4, Reg.62, Reg.79, Reg.92, SI 2008/1582 Reg.5, Reg.115, Reg.132, Reg.149, SI 2008/3170 Reg.4, Reg.62, Reg.79, Reg.103
Reg.2, amended: SSI 2008/206 Reg.6
Reg.4, amended: SSI 2008/206 Reg.7

153. Students Allowances (Scotland) Regulations 2007
Reg.2, amended: SSI 2008/206 Reg.3
Reg.4, amended: SSI 2008/206 Reg.4

154. Education (Student Loans) (Scotland) Regulations 2007
Reg.2, amended: SSI 2008/206 Reg.9
Reg.3, amended: SSI 2008/205 Reg.3
Reg.3, revoked (in part): SSI 2008/205 Reg.3
Reg.4, amended: SSI 2008/205 Reg.4
Reg.4, applied: SI 2008/794 Reg.14
Reg.6, amended: SSI 2008/205 Reg.5
Reg.6, revoked (in part): SSI 2008/205 Reg.5
Reg.7, amended: SSI 2008/205 Reg.6

NO.

2007–cont.

154. Education (Student Loans) (Scotland) Regulations 2007–*cont.*
Reg.11, amended: SSI 2008/206 Reg.10

155. Graduate Endowment (Scotland) Regulations 2007
revoked: 2008 asp 3 s.1

156. Education Maintenance Allowances (Scotland) Regulations 2007
Sch.2 para.3, amended: SI 2008/1879 Reg.40

183. Local Governance (Scotland) Act 2004 (Remuneration) Regulations 2007
Reg.6, amended: SSI 2008/415 Reg.2
Reg.7, amended: SSI 2008/415 Reg.2
Reg.10, substituted: SSI 2008/415 Reg.2
Reg.11, amended: SSI 2008/415 Reg.2
Reg.12, amended: SSI 2008/415 Reg.2

185. Inshore Fishing (Prohibited Methods of Fishing) (Loch Creran) Order 2007
Art.3, applied: SSI 2008/101 Sch.1 Part 1
Art.4, applied: SSI 2008/101 Sch.1 Part 1
Art.5, applied: SSI 2008/101 Sch.1 Part 1

194. Animals and Animal Products (Import and Export) (Scotland) Regulations 2007
applied: SSI 2008/11 Art.6
Reg.1, amended: SSI 2008/155 Reg.2
Reg.2, amended: SSI 2008/155 Reg.2
Reg.3, applied: SI 2008/1035 Sch.1 para.1
Reg.5, applied: SI 2008/1035 Sch.1 para.2
Reg.8, applied: SI 2008/1035 Sch.1 para.3
Reg.9, applied: SI 2008/1035 Sch.1 para.4
Reg.10, applied: SI 2008/1035 Sch.1 para.5
Reg.13, applied: SI 2008/1035 Sch.1 para.6
Reg.15, amended: SSI 2008/155 Reg.2
Reg.16, amended: SSI 2008/155 Reg.2
Reg.17, amended: SSI 2008/155 Reg.2
Reg.17, applied: SI 2008/1035 Sch.1 para.7
Reg.18, amended: SSI 2008/155 Reg.2
Reg.19, amended: SSI 2008/155 Reg.2
Reg.20, amended: SSI 2008/155 Reg.2
Reg.20, applied: SI 2008/1035 Sch.1 para.8
Reg.21, amended: SSI 2008/155 Reg.2
Reg.22, amended: SSI 2008/155 Reg.2
Reg.23, amended: SSI 2008/155 Reg.2
Reg.24, amended: SSI 2008/155 Reg.2
Reg.25, amended: SSI 2008/155 Reg.2
Reg.28A, added: SSI 2008/155 Reg.2
Reg.28B, added: SSI 2008/155 Reg.2
Sch.3 Part I para.10, applied: SI 2008/1035 Sch.1 para.9
Sch.3 Part I para.17, added: SSI 2008/155 Reg.2
Sch.3 Part II para.4, applied: SI 2008/1035 Sch.1 para.10
Sch.3 Part II para.5, applied: SI 2008/1035 Sch.1 para.10
Sch.3 Part III para.2, applied: SI 2008/1035 Sch.1 para.11

NO.

2007–cont.

194. Animals and Animal Products (Import and Export) (Scotland) Regulations 2007–*cont.*

Sch.3 Part III para.6, applied: SI 2008/1035 Sch.1 para.11

Sch.4 Part I para.3, applied: SI 2008/1035 Sch.1 para.12

Sch.4 Part I para.5, applied: SI 2008/1035 Sch.1 para.12

Sch.4 Part I para.7, applied: SI 2008/1035 Sch.1 para.12

Sch.4 Part I para.8, applied: SI 2008/1035 Sch.1 para.12

Sch.4 Part I para.9, applied: SI 2008/1035 Sch.1 para.12

Sch.4 Part I para.10, applied: SI 2008/1035 Sch.1 para.12

Sch.4 Part II para.11, applied: SI 2008/1035 Sch.1 para.13

Sch.4 Part III para.16, applied: SI 2008/1035 Sch.1 para.14

Sch.4 Part IV para.21, applied: SI 2008/1035 Sch.1 para.15

Sch.5 Part I para.1, applied: SI 2008/1035 Sch.1 para.16

Sch.5 Part I para.2, applied: SI 2008/1035 Sch.1 para.16

Sch.5 Part I para.3, applied: SI 2008/1035 Sch.1 para.16

Sch.5 Part I para.4, applied: SI 2008/1035 Sch.1 para.16

Sch.5 Part I para.5, applied: SI 2008/1035 Sch.1 para.16

Sch.5 Part II para.1, applied: SI 2008/1035 Sch.1 para.17

Sch.5 Part II para.2, applied: SI 2008/1035 Sch.1 para.17

Sch.7 Part I para.1, amended: SSI 2008/155 Reg.2

Sch.7 Part I para.2, amended: SSI 2008/155 Reg.2

Sch.7 Part I para.3, amended: SSI 2008/155 Reg.2

Sch.7 Part I para.4, amended: SSI 2008/155 Reg.2

Sch.7 Part I para.5, amended: SSI 2008/155 Reg.2

Sch.7 Part I para.6, amended: SSI 2008/155 Reg.2

Sch.7 Part I para.7, amended: SSI 2008/155 Reg.2

Sch.7 Part I para.8, amended: SSI 2008/155 Reg.2

Sch.7 Part II para.1, amended: SSI 2008/155 Reg.2

Sch.7 Part II para.2, amended: SSI 2008/155 Reg.2

Sch.7 Part II para.3, amended: SSI 2008/155 Reg.2

Sch.7 Part II para.4, amended: SSI 2008/155 Reg.2

NO.

2007–cont.

194. Animals and Animal Products (Import and Export) (Scotland) Regulations 2007–*cont.*

Sch.7 Part II para.5, amended: SSI 2008/155 Reg.2

Sch.7 Part II para.6, amended: SSI 2008/155 Reg.2

Sch.7 Part II para.7, amended: SSI 2008/155 Reg.2

Sch.7 Part II para.8, amended: SSI 2008/155 Reg.2

Sch.7 Part II para.9, amended: SSI 2008/155 Reg.2

Sch.7 Part II para.10, amended: SSI 2008/155 Reg.2

Sch.7 Part II para.11, amended: SSI 2008/155 Reg.2

Sch.8 Part I para.1, applied: SI 2008/1035 Sch.1 para.18

Sch.8 Part I para.2, applied: SI 2008/1035 Sch.1 para.18

Sch.8 Part I para.3, applied: SI 2008/1035 Sch.1 para.18

Sch.8 Part II para.1, applied: SI 2008/1035 Sch.1 para.19

Sch.8 Part II para.3, applied: SI 2008/1035 Sch.1 para.19

Sch.8 Part II para.4, applied: SI 2008/1035 Sch.1 para.19

Sch.8 Part II para.5, applied: SI 2008/1035 Sch.1 para.19

Sch.8A para.1, added: SSI 2008/155 Reg.2

199. Firefighters Pension Scheme (Scotland) Order 2007

Sch.1, added: SSI 2008/160 Sch.1 para.3, Sch.1 para.4, Sch.1 para.6, Sch.1 para.10

Sch.1, amended: SSI 2008/160 Sch.1 para.1, Sch.1 para.2, Sch.1 para.4, Sch.1 para.5, Sch.1 para.7, Sch.1 para.8, Sch.1 para.9, Sch.1 para.10, Sch.1 para.11, Sch.1 para.12, Sch.1 para.13

Sch.1, applied: SI 2008/649 Reg.4

Sch.1, referred to: SSI 2008/160 Art.2

Sch.1, revoked: SSI 2008/160 Sch.1 para.2, Sch.1 para.11

Sch.1, substituted: SSI 2008/160 Sch.1 para.2, Sch.1 para.3, Sch.1 para.5, Sch.1 para.6, Sch.1 para.7, Sch.1 para.10

201. Police Pensions (Scotland) Regulations 2007

Reg.3, amended: SSI 2008/387 Reg.36

Reg.5, amended: SSI 2008/387 Reg.37

Reg.17, amended: SSI 2008/387 Reg.38

Reg.18, amended: SSI 2008/387 Reg.39

Reg.19, amended: SSI 2008/387 Reg.40

Reg.20, amended: SSI 2008/387 Reg.41

Reg.23, amended: SSI 2008/387 Reg.42

Reg.51, amended: SSI 2008/387 Reg.43

Reg.72, applied: SI 2008/649 Reg.4

Sch.1, amended: SSI 2008/387 Reg.44

NO.

2007–cont.

202. Business Improvement Districts (Scotland) Regulations 2007
Reg.5, amended: SSI 2008/359 Reg.2
Sch.2 Part 001 para.1, amended: SSI 2008/359 Reg.3
Sch.2 Part 002 para.10, amended: SSI 2008/359 Reg.3
Sch.2 Part 002 para.11, amended: SSI 2008/359 Reg.3

203. Charities References in Documents (Scotland) Regulations 2007
Reg.4, amended: SSI 2008/59 Reg.2

216. Non-Domestic Rates (Levying) (Scotland) Regulations 2007
referred to: SSI 2008/85 Reg.6
revoked: SSI 2008/85 Reg.6

220. Bankruptcy Fees (Scotland) Amendment Regulations 2007
Reg.3, revoked: SSI 2008/5 Reg.3

240. Inshore Fishing (Prohibited Methods of Fishing) (Firth of Lorn) (No.2) Order 2007
Art.3, applied: SSI 2008/101 Sch.1 Part 1

247. Advice and Assistance (Financial Conditions) (Scotland) Regulations 2007
revoked: SSI 2008/137 Reg.8

249. Civil Legal Aid (Financial Conditions) (Scotland) Regulations 2007
revoked: SSI 2008/138 Reg.7

254. Poultry Breeding Flocks and Hatcheries (Scotland) Order 2007
revoked: SSI 2008/266 Art.14

267. Renewables Obligation (Scotland) Order 2007
Art.4, amended: SSI 2008/132 Art.2
Art.24, amended: SSI 2008/132 Art.2
Sch.1, substituted: SSI 2008/132 Sch.1

303. Spreadable Fats (Marketing Standards) (Scotland) Amendment Regulations 2007
revoked: SSI 2008/216 Reg.8

306. Pesticides (Maximum Residue Levels in Crops, Food and Feeding Stuffs) (Scotland) Amendment (No.2) Regulations 2007
revoked: SSI 2008/342 Sch.2

314. Plant Health Fees (Scotland) Amendment Regulations 2007
revoked: SSI 2008/153 Reg.6

330. Bovine Semen (Scotland) Regulations 2007
Reg.3, applied: SI 2008/1035 Sch.1 para.1
Reg.4, applied: SI 2008/1035 Sch.1 para.2
Reg.5, applied: SI 2008/1035 Sch.1 para.3
Reg.7, applied: SI 2008/1035 Sch.1 para.4
Reg.8, applied: SI 2008/1035 Sch.1 para.5
Reg.10, applied: SI 2008/1035 Sch.1 para.6
Reg.15, applied: SI 2008/1035 Sch.1 para.7
Reg.17, applied: SI 2008/1035 Sch.1 para.8
Reg.18, applied: SI 2008/1035 Sch.1 para.9

NO.

2007–cont.

330. Bovine Semen (Scotland) Regulations 2007–*cont.*
Reg.19, applied: SI 2008/1035 Sch.1 para.10
Reg.21, applied: SI 2008/1035 Sch.1 para.11
Reg.29, applied: SI 2008/1035 Sch.1 para.12
Reg.32, applied: SI 2008/1035 Sch.1 para.13
Reg.33, applied: SI 2008/1035 Sch.1 para.14
Reg.34, applied: SI 2008/1035 Sch.1 para.15
Reg.35, applied: SI 2008/1035 Sch.1 para.16
Reg.36, applied: SI 2008/1035 Sch.1 para.17
Reg.40, applied: SI 2008/1035 Sch.1 para.18
Reg.41, applied: SI 2008/1035 Sch.1 para.19
Reg.42, applied: SI 2008/1035 Sch.1 para.20
Sch.3 Part 3 para.1, applied: SI 2008/1035 Sch.1 para.21
Sch.4 para.2, applied: SI 2008/1035 Sch.1 para.22
Sch.6 para.2, applied: SI 2008/1035 Sch.1 para.23
Sch.7 para.1, applied: SI 2008/1035 Sch.1 para.24

389. National Health Service (Charges for Drugs and Appliances) (Scotland) (No.2) Regulations 2007
applied: SSI 2008/27 Reg.12
revoked: SSI 2008/27 Reg.12
Reg.7, applied: SSI 2008/27 Reg.12
Reg.8, applied: SSI 2008/27 Reg.11, Reg.12

433. Plastic Materials and Articles in Contact with Food (Lid Gaskets) (Scotland) Regulations 2007
revoked: SSI 2008/127 Reg.26
Reg.2, amended: SSI 2008/261 Reg.3

439. Less Favoured Area Support Scheme (Scotland) Regulations 2007
Reg.2, amended: SSI 2008/294 Reg.3
Reg.6, amended: SSI 2008/294 Reg.4
Reg.16A, added: SSI 2008/294 Reg.5

451. Provision of School Lunches (Disapplication of the Requirement to Charge) (Scotland) Order 2007
revoked: SSI 2008/400 Art.4

471. Materials and Articles in Contact with Food (Scotland) Regulations 2007
Reg.2, amended: SSI 2008/127 Reg.25
Reg.10, amended: SSI 2008/127 Reg.25
Reg.11, amended: SSI 2008/127 Reg.25, SSI 2008/261 Reg.4
Reg.21, revoked: SSI 2008/127 Reg.26

481. Pesticides (Maximum Residue Levels in Crops, Food and Feeding Stuffs) (Scotland) Amendment (No.3) Regulations 2007
revoked: SSI 2008/342 Sch.2

513. Licensing (Relevant Offences) (Scotland) Regulations 2007
Sch.1 Part 2 para.45, added: SI 2008/1277 Sch.2 para.114
Sch.1 Part 2 para.46, added: SI 2008/1277 Sch.2 para.114

NO.

2007–cont.

514. Local Government Pension Scheme (Scotland) Amendment Regulations 2007
revoked: SSI 2008/229 Sch.1

522. Official Feed and Food Controls (Scotland) Regulations 2007
Sch.2, amended: SSI 2008/218 Reg.2

523. Pesticides (Maximum Residue Levels in Crops, Food and Feeding Stuffs) (Scotland) Amendment (No.4) Regulations 2007
revoked: SSI 2008/342 Sch.2

534. Food Labelling (Declaration of Allergens) (Scotland) Regulations 2007
revoked (in part): SSI 2008/180 Reg.3

537. Fishery Products (Official Controls Charges) (Scotland) Regulations 2007
Reg.2, amended: SSI 2008/98 Reg.6

538. Meat (Official Controls Charges) (Scotland) (No.2) Regulations 2007
revoked: SSI 2008/98 Reg.7

549. Infant Formula and Follow-on Formula (Scotland) Regulations 2007
see *Infant and Dietetic Foods Association Ltd, Petitioners* [2008] CSOH 18, 2008 S.L.T. 137 (OH), Lord Macphail; see *Infant and Dietetic Foods Association Ltd, Petitioners* [2008] CSOH 87, 2008 S.L.T. 723 (OH), Lord Clarke
Reg.3, amended: SSI 2008/322 Reg.2
Reg.20, amended: SSI 2008/322 Reg.2
Reg.26, amended: SSI 2008/322 Reg.2
Reg.27, amended: SSI 2008/322 Reg.2
Reg.31, amended: SSI 2008/322 Reg.2
Sch.1, amended: SSI 2008/322 Reg.2

577. Zoonoses and Animal By-Products (Fees) (Scotland) Regulations 2007
Reg.2, amended: SSI 2008/378 Reg.3
Reg.3, amended: SSI 2008/378 Reg.4, SSI 2008/423 Reg.2
Reg.3, applied: SI 2008/1035 Sch.1 para.1
Reg.3, revoked (in part): SSI 2008/378 Reg.4

2008

8. Discontinuance of Legalised Police Cells (Scotland) Rules 2008
revoked: SSI 2008/35 r.2

11. Bluetongue (Scotland) Order 2008
Art.2, amended: SSI 2008/234 Art.2, SSI 2008/327 Art.2
Art.3, amended: SSI 2008/234 Art.2, SSI 2008/327 Art.2
Art.11, amended: SSI 2008/327 Art.2
Art.13, amended: SSI 2008/327 Art.2
Art.14, substituted: SSI 2008/327 Art.2
Art.15, revoked: SSI 2008/327 Art.2
Art.16, substituted: SSI 2008/327 Art.2
Art.16A, added: SSI 2008/234 Art.2
Art.16A, substituted: SSI 2008/327 Art.2

NO.

2008–cont.

11. Bluetongue (Scotland) Order 2008– *cont.*
Art.17, revoked: SSI 2008/234 Art.2
Art.18, amended: SSI 2008/234 Art.2
Art.19, substituted: SSI 2008/234 Art.2, SSI 2008/327 Art.2
Art.21, revoked: SSI 2008/234 Art.2
Art.22, revoked: SSI 2008/234 Art.2
Art.22A, added: SSI 2008/234 Art.2
Art.22A, revoked: SSI 2008/327 Art.2
Art.22B, added: SSI 2008/234 Art.2
Art.22C, added: SSI 2008/234 Art.2
Art.22D, added: SSI 2008/234 Art.2
Art.22E, added: SSI 2008/234 Art.2
Art.23, revoked: SSI 2008/234 Art.2
Art.24, revoked: SSI 2008/234 Art.2
Art.25, revoked: SSI 2008/234 Art.2

15. Transport (Scotland) Act 2005 (Commencement No.4) Order 2008
Art.3, added: SSI 2008/90 Art.2
Sch.1, amended: SSI 2008/90 Art.2

27. National Health Service (Charges for Drugs and Appliances) (Scotland) Regulations 2008
Reg.2, amended: SSI 2008/105 Reg.2
Reg.8, amended: SSI 2008/105 Reg.2
Reg.9, amended: SSI 2008/105 Reg.2
Sch.3 para.2, amended: SSI 2008/105 Reg.2

33. Local Government Finance (Scotland) Order 2008
Sch.1, substituted: SSI 2008/136 Sch.1

36. Home Detention Curfew Licence (Prescribed Standard Conditions) (Scotland) Order 2008
revoked: SSI 2008/124 Art.2

40. Act of Sederunt (Fees of Solicitors in the Sheriff Court) (Amendment) 2008
Art.2, amended: SSI 2008/72 Art.2

49. Adult Support and Protection (Scotland) Act 2007 (Commencement No.2 and Transitional Provisions) Order 2008
Art.2, amended: SSI 2008/116 Art.2, SSI 2008/314 Art.3

52. Adults with Incapacity (Public Guardian's Fees) (Scotland) Regulations 2008
Reg.2, substituted: SSI 2008/238 Reg.2
Sch.1, amended: SSI 2008/238 Sch.1, Sch.2, Sch.3

65. Pesticides (Maximum Residue Levels in Crops, Food and Feeding Stuffs) (Scotland) Amendment Regulations 2008
revoked: SSI 2008/342 Sch.2

82. Bankruptcy (Scotland) Regulations 2008
referred to: SSI 2008/334 Reg.3
Sch.1, amended: SSI 2008/334 Sch.1, Sch.2

NO.

2008–cont.

93. Justice of the Peace Courts (Sheriffdom of Grampian, Highland and Islands) Order 2008
referred to: SSI 2008/179 Art.2
Art.7, added: SSI 2008/179 Art.2
Art.8, added: SSI 2008/179 Art.2
Sch.4, added: SSI 2008/179 Art.2

100. Rural Development Contracts (Rural Priorities) (Scotland) Regulations 2008
applied: SSI 2008/159 Sch.2
Reg.2, amended: SSI 2008/233 Reg.3
Reg.9, amended: SSI 2008/233 Reg.4
Reg.12, amended: SSI 2008/233 Reg.5
Sch.1, amended: SSI 2008/233 Reg.6
Sch.2 Part 1, amended: SSI 2008/233 Reg.7, Sch.1

101. Aquaculture and Fisheries (Scotland) Act 2007 (Fixed Penalty Notices) Order 2008
Sch.1 Part 1, amended: SSI 2008/151 Art.34
Sch.1 Part 1, referred to: SSI 2008/151 Art.34

102. Sea Fishing (Control Procedures for Herring, Mackerel and Horse Mackerel) (Scotland) Order 2008
Art.3, applied: SSI 2008/101 Sch.1 Part 1
Art.4, applied: SSI 2008/101 Sch.1 Part 1
Art.6, applied: SSI 2008/101 Sch.1 Part 1
Art.7, applied: SSI 2008/101 Sch.1 Part 1
Art.7, substituted: SSI 2008/156 Art.2
Sch.1, amended: SSI 2008/156 Art.2

127. Plastic Materials and Articles in Contact with Food (Scotland) Regulations 2008
Reg.2, amended: SSI 2008/261 Reg.2
Reg.9, amended: SSI 2008/261 Reg.2
Reg.19, amended: SSI 2008/261 Reg.2
Reg.26, revoked (in part): SSI 2008/261 Reg.2
Sch.2 para.6, amended: SSI 2008/261 Reg.2
Sch.2 para.9, amended: SSI 2008/261 Reg.2
Sch.3 Part 3 para.3, amended: SSI 2008/261 Reg.2
Sch.3 Part 3 para.4, amended: SSI 2008/261 Reg.2
Sch.3 Part 4 para.4, amended: SSI 2008/261 Reg.2
Sch.3 Part 6 para.1, amended: SSI 2008/261 Reg.2
Sch.3 Part 7 para.1, amended: SSI 2008/261 Reg.2
Sch.3 Part 7 para.3, amended: SSI 2008/261 Reg.2

129. Eggs and Chicks (Scotland) Regulations 2008
referred to: SSI 2008/395 Reg.22
revoked: SSI 2008/395 Reg.21

137. Advice and Assistance (Financial Conditions) (Scotland) Regulations 2008
Reg.7, amended: SSI 2008/251 Reg.3

NO.

2008–cont.

151. Sea Fishing (Enforcement of Community Quota and Third Country Fishing Measures and Restriction on Days at Sea) (Scotland) Order 2008
applied: SSI 2008/101 Sch.1 Part 1

154. Smoke Control Areas (Authorised Fuels) (Scotland) Regulations 2008
revoked: SSI 2008/295 Reg.3

157. Smoke Control Areas (Exempt Fireplaces) (Scotland) Order 2008
revoked: SSI 2008/296 Art.3

163. Designation of Institutions of Higher Education (The Scottish Agricultural College) (Scotland) Order 2008
revoked: SSI 2008/177 Art.3

164. Planning etc (Scotland) Act 2006 (Commencement No.3) Order 2008
referred to: SSI 2008/165 Art.2
Art.1, amended: SSI 2008/191 Art.3
Sch.1, amended: SSI 2008/191 Art.3

170. Bathing Waters (Scotland) Regulations 2008
referred to: SSI 2008/263 Sch.1, Sch.2

186. Public Transport Users Committee for Scotland Amendment Order 2008
revoked: SSI 2008/248 Art.2

187. Mobility and Access Committee for Scotland Revocation Regulations 2008
revoked: SSI 2008/247 Reg.2

228. Local Government Pension Scheme (Administration) (Scotland) Regulations 2008
applied: SSI 2008/229 Reg.13
Part 2, applied: SSI 2008/230 Reg.3
Reg.3, applied: SSI 2008/230 Reg.3
Reg.7, applied: SSI 2008/230 Reg.29
Reg.10, applied: SSI 2008/229 Reg.4
Reg.13, applied: SSI 2008/230 Reg.7
Reg.14, applied: SSI 2008/229 Reg.6, Sch.2 para.4, SSI 2008/230 Reg.7
Reg.23, applied: SSI 2008/230 Reg.15
Reg.64, referred to: SSI 2008/229 Reg.13
Reg.65, referred to: SSI 2008/229 Reg.13
Reg.73, referred to: SSI 2008/229 Reg.15
Reg.74, applied: SSI 2008/230 Reg.6, Reg.29
Reg.75, applied: SSI 2008/230 Reg.6, Reg.29
Reg.76, applied: SSI 2008/230 Reg.6, Reg.29
Reg.77, applied: SSI 2008/230 Reg.6
Reg.78, applied: SSI 2008/230 Reg.7
Reg.79, applied: SSI 2008/230 Reg.7
Reg.80, applied: SSI 2008/230 Reg.7
Reg.81, applied: SSI 2008/230 Reg.7
Reg.82, applied: SSI 2008/230 Reg.7
Sch.1, applied: SSI 2008/230 Reg.3

NO.

2008–cont.

229. Local Government Pension Scheme (Transitional Provisions) (Scotland) Regulations 2008

applied: SSI 2008/228 Sch.3 para.3, Sch.3 para.7

referred to: SSI 2008/228 Reg.74

Reg.11, applied: SSI 2008/228 Reg.28

Reg.12, applied: SSI 2008/228 Reg.65

230. Local Government Pension Scheme (Benefits, Membership and Contributions) (Scotland) Regulations 2008

applied: SSI 2008/228 Reg.6, Reg.8, Reg.11, Reg.15, Reg.16, Reg.28, Reg.40, Reg.47, Reg.66, Reg.68, Reg.70, Sch.3 para.1, Sch.3 para.3, Sch.3 para.7, SSI 2008/229 Reg.7, Reg.8, Reg.13

referred to: SSI 2008/228 Reg.74, Reg.76, SSI 2008/229 Reg.11, Sch.2 para.6

Reg.3, applied: SSI 2008/228 Reg.3, SSI 2008/229 Reg.3, Reg.9, Reg.13

Reg.4, applied: SSI 2008/228 Reg.10, Reg.16, Reg.17, Reg.35, SSI 2008/229 Reg.9

Reg.4, referred to: SSI 2008/228 Reg.38

Reg.5, varied: SSI 2008/229 Reg.13

Reg.6, applied: SSI 2008/228 Reg.13

Reg.7, applied: SSI 2008/228 Reg.12

Reg.8, applied: SSI 2008/228 Reg.13, Reg.14, Reg.41

Reg.9, applied: SSI 2008/229 Reg.3

Reg.11, applied: SSI 2008/229 Reg.3

Reg.12, applied: SSI 2008/228 Reg.36, Reg.61, SSI 2008/229 Sch.2 para.6

Reg.12, disapplied: SSI 2008/229 Sch.2 para.3

Reg.13, applied: SSI 2008/228 Reg.36, Reg.61

Reg.14, applied: SSI 2008/228 Reg.20

Reg.15, referred to: SSI 2008/228 Reg.25

Reg.16, applied: SSI 2008/228 Reg.12, Reg.23, Reg.46, SSI 2008/229 Reg.3

Reg.17, applied: SSI 2008/228 Reg.12, Reg.23, Reg.46, SSI 2008/229 Reg.3

Reg.18, applied: SSI 2008/228 Reg.12, Reg.23, Reg.37, Reg.46, Reg.61, Reg.65, SSI 2008/229 Reg.3, Reg.10, Sch.2 para.1, Sch.2 para.3

Reg.18, referred to: SSI 2008/228 Reg.37

Reg.19, applied: SSI 2008/228 Reg.12, Reg.23, Reg.37, Reg.46, SSI 2008/229 Reg.3

Reg.20, applied: SSI 2008/228 Reg.12, Reg.13, Reg.21, Reg.23, Reg.37, Reg.46, Reg.52, SSI 2008/229 Reg.3

Reg.21, applied: SSI 2008/228 Reg.47

Reg.21, referred to: SSI 2008/228 Reg.23

Reg.23, applied: SSI 2008/228 Reg.47, Reg.95

Reg.24, applied: SSI 2008/228 Reg.46, Reg.47, SSI 2008/229 Reg.3

Reg.25, referred to: SSI 2008/228 Reg.54

NO.

2008–cont.

230. Local Government Pension Scheme (Benefits, Membership and Contributions) (Scotland) Regulations 2008– *cont.*

Reg.27, applied: SSI 2008/228 Reg.46, Reg.47

Reg.29, applied: SSI 2008/228 Reg.12

Reg.30, applied: SSI 2008/228 Reg.12, Reg.23, Reg.37, Reg.46, Reg.61, SSI 2008/229 Reg.3, Reg.10, Sch.2 para.1, Sch.2 para.3

Reg.30, varied: SSI 2008/229 Reg.13, Reg.14

Reg.31, applied: SSI 2008/228 Reg.12, Reg.23, Reg.37, Reg.46, Reg.52

Reg.32, applied: SSI 2008/228 Reg.47, Reg.95

Reg.33, applied: SSI 2008/228 Reg.46, Reg.47, SSI 2008/229 Reg.3

Reg.34, applied: SSI 2008/228 Reg.46

Reg.35, applied: SSI 2008/228 Reg.47, Reg.95

Reg.36, applied: SSI 2008/228 Reg.46, Reg.47, SSI 2008/229 Reg.3

Reg.37, applied: SSI 2008/228 Reg.46

Reg.39, applied: SSI 2008/228 Reg.47, Reg.98

268. Charity Test (Specified Bodies) (Scotland) Order 2008

Sch.1, substituted: SSI 2008/413 Art.4

298. Action Programme for Nitrate Vulnerable Zones (Scotland) Regulations 2008

Reg.9, amended: SSI 2008/394 Reg.2

Sch.3, amended: SSI 2008/394 Reg.3

Sch.3 Part C, amended: SSI 2008/394 Reg.3

300. Plant Health (Scotland) Amendment Order 2008

Art.11, revoked: SSI 2008/350 Art.8

Art.13, revoked: SSI 2008/350 Art.8

309. Energy Performance of Buildings (Scotland) Regulations 2008

Reg.17, amended: SSI 2008/389 Reg.2

328. Justice of the Peace Court (Sheriffdom of Glasgow and Strathkelvin) Order 2008

Art.8, amended: SSI 2008/374 Art.2

Art.9, added: SSI 2008/374 Art.2

Sch.1, substituted: SSI 2008/374 Art.2

Sch.2, added: SSI 2008/374 Art.2

370. Non-Domestic Rating (Rural Areas and Rateable Value Limits) (Scotland) Amendment Order 2008

Art.1, amended: SSI 2008/371 Art.2

432. Town and Country Planning (Development Management Procedure) (Scotland) Regulations 2008

Reg.18, applied: SSI 2008/433 Reg.19, SSI 2008/434 Reg.20

Reg.19, applied: SSI 2008/433 Reg.19, SSI 2008/434 Reg.20

Reg.20, applied: SSI 2008/434 Reg.20

NO.

2008–cont.

432. Town and Country Planning (Development Management Procedure) (Scotland) Regulations 2008–*cont.*
Reg.25, applied: SSI 2008/433 Reg.19, SSI 2008/434 Reg.20

NO.

STATUTORY INSTRUMENTS ISSUED BY THE UK PARLIAMENT

NO.

1912

348. Public Trustee Rules 1912
r.37, applied: SI 2008/611 Art.27

1915

769. Standing Orders and Regulations for the Constitution and Government of the Naval Medical Compassionate Fund Order in Council 1915
revoked: SI 2008/3129 Sch.1
Art.1, substituted: SI 2008/1488 Art.2
Art.2, substituted: SI 2008/1488 Art.2
Art.3, substituted: SI 2008/1488 Art.2
Art.4, revoked: SI 2008/1488 Art.2
Art.5, substituted: SI 2008/1488 Art.2
Art.6, substituted: SI 2008/1488 Art.2
Art.7, substituted: SI 2008/1488 Art.2
Art.8, substituted: SI 2008/1488 Art.2
Art.9, substituted: SI 2008/1488 Art.2
Art.10, substituted: SI 2008/1488 Art.2
Art.11, substituted: SI 2008/1488 Art.2
Art.12, substituted: SI 2008/1488 Art.2
Art.13, added: SI 2008/1488 Art.2

1919

884. Navel Medical Compassionate Fund Amending Order in Council 1919
revoked: SI 2008/3129 Sch.1

1926

129. Pensions Appeal Tribunals (England and Wales) Regulations 1926
revoked: SI 2008/2683 Sch.2

1928

206. Cattle Plaque Order 1928
applied: SI 2008/1275 Reg.15

1930

1016. Cremation Act 1902 Section 7, etc - Regulations 1930
revoked (in part): SI 2008/2841 Sch.2
Reg.10, applied: SI 2008/2841 Reg.37
Reg.17, applied: SI 2008/2841 Reg.37
Sch.1, applied: SI 2008/2841 Reg.37

NO.

1938

245. Local Government Superannuation (Administration) (Scotland) Regulations 1938
applied: SSI 2008/228 Reg.47, Reg.63, Reg.66
referred to: SSI 2008/228 Reg.74, Reg.76

1384. Local Government Superannuation (Administration) (No.2) (Scotland) Regulations 1938
applied: SSI 2008/228 Reg.47, Reg.63, Reg.66
referred to: SSI 2008/228 Reg.74, Reg.76

1948

1470. National Insurance (Married Women) Regulations 1948
see *Revenue and Customs Commissioners v Mayor* [2007] EWHC 3147 (Ch), [2008] S.T.C. 1958 (Ch D), Patten, J.

1950

942. Town and Country Planning (General Development) (Scotland) Order, 1950
applied: SSI 2008/432 Reg.47

1326. British Wool Marketing Scheme (Approval) Order 1950
Sch.1 Part V para.66, amended: SI 2008/948 Sch.1 para.1

1952

1568. Cremation Regulations 1952
revoked (in part): SI 2008/2841 Sch.2

1954

16. Legalised Police Cells (Kirkwall) Rules 1954
revoked: SSI 2008/8 r.2

1243. Local Government Superannuation (Administration) (Scotland) Regulations, 1954
applied: SSI 2008/228 Reg.47, Reg.63, Reg.66
referred to: SSI 2008/228 Reg.74, Reg.76

NO.

1956

1230. Income Tax (Purchased Life Annuities) Regulations 1956
applied: SI 2008/562 Reg.5
revoked: SI 2008/562 Reg.28

1771. Coal and Other Mines (Locomotives) Order 1956
Sch.1 Part II para.3, disapplied: SI 2008/1597 Reg.27

1778. Miscellaneous Mines Order 1956
Sch.1 Part IX para.52, disapplied: SI 2008/1597 Reg.27

1958

738. Orkney County Council (Loch of Boardhouse) Water Order 1958
revoked: SSI 2008/429 Art.7

1653. Town and Country Planning (General Development) (Scotland) (Amendment) Order, 1958
applied: SSI 2008/432 Reg.47

1959

377. Maintenance Orders (Facilities for Enforcement) Order 1959
Sch.1, amended: SI 2008/1203 Art.2

1361. Town and Country Planning (General Development) (Scotland) Order, 1959
applied: SSI 2008/432 Reg.47

1960

543. Election Petition Rules 1960
varied: SI 2008/1848 Reg.11
r.2, varied: SI 2008/1848 Sch.6
r.4, varied: SI 2008/1848 Sch.6
r.10, varied: SI 2008/1848 Sch.6
r.12, varied: SI 2008/1848 Sch.6
r.14, varied: SI 2008/1848 Sch.6
r.16, varied: SI 2008/1848 Sch.6
r.18, varied: SI 2008/1848 Sch.6
Sch.1, varied: SI 2008/1848 Sch.6

1015. Coal Mines (Fire damp Drainage) Regulations 1960
Reg.11, disapplied: SI 2008/1597 Reg.27

1722. Town and Country Planning (General Development) (Scotland) Amendment Order, 1960
applied: SSI 2008/432 Reg.47

2308. Income Tax (Purchased Life Annuities) (Amendment) Regulations 1960
revoked: SI 2008/562 Reg.28

1963

1767. Town and Country Planning (General Development) (Scotland) Amendment Order 1963
applied: SSI 2008/432 Reg.47

NO.

1964

1171. Artificial Insemination of Pigs (Scotland) Regulations 1964
Reg.2, applied: SI 2008/1035 Sch.1 para.1
Reg.4, applied: SI 2008/1035 Sch.1 para.2
Reg.5, applied: SI 2008/1035 Sch.1 para.3
Reg.6, applied: SI 2008/1035 Sch.1 para.4
Reg.7, applied: SI 2008/1035 Sch.1 para.5
Reg.8, applied: SI 2008/1035 Sch.1 para.6
Reg.9, applied: SI 2008/1035 Sch.1 para.7
Reg.10, applied: SI 2008/1035 Sch.1 para.8

1755. Ecclesiastical Jurisdiction (Discipline) Rules 1964
r.49, applied: SI 2008/1969 Sch.2 para.4

1791. Town and Country Planning (General Development) (Scotland) Amendment Order 1964
applied: SSI 2008/432 Reg.47

2058. War Pensions (Mercantile Marine) Scheme 1964
Sch.7 para.4, amended: SI 2008/2683 Sch.1 para.1
Sch.7 para.8, amended: SI 2008/2683 Sch.1 para.1

1965

1146. Cremation Regulations 1965
revoked (in part): SI 2008/2841 Sch.2

1776. Rules of the Supreme Court (Revision) 1965
Ord.20 r.5, see *Adelson v Associated Newspapers Ltd* [2007] EWCA Civ 701, [2008] 1 W.L.R. 585 (CA (Civ Div)), Lord Phillips, L.C.J.
Ord.38 r.2, see *West London Pipeline & Storage Ltd v Total UK Ltd* [2008] EWHC 1729 (Comm), [2008] 2 C.L.C. 258 (QBD (Comm)), Beatson, J.
Ord.52 r.5, see *R. v M* [2008] EWCA Crim 1901, Times, October 24, 2008 (CA (Crim Div)), Toulson, L.J.

1966

97. Police (Special Constables) (Scotland) Regulations 1966
revoked: SSI 2008/117 Sch.3
Reg.2, applied: SSI 2008/117 Reg.30
Reg.7, applied: SSI 2008/117 Reg.30
Reg.10, applied: SSI 2008/117 Reg.30

1967

480. Carriage by Air Acts (Application of Provisions) Order 1967
see *Laroche v Spirit of Adventure (UK) Ltd* [2008] EWHC 788 (QB), [2008] 4 All E.R. 494 (QBD), Eady, J.
Sch.1, see *Laroche v Spirit of Adventure (UK) Ltd* [2008] EWHC 788 (QB), [2008] 4 All E.R. 494 (QBD), Eady, J.

NO.

1967–cont.

1484. Naval Medical Compassionate Fund (Amendment) Order 1967
revoked: SI 2008/3129 Sch.1

1968

942. Port of Tyne Reorganisation Scheme 1967 Confirmation Order 1968
referred to: SI 2008/1817 Art.1
Sch, revoked: SI 2008/1817 Art.3

1969

17. Town and Country Planning (Tree Preservation Order) Regulations 1969
Sch.1, referred to: SI 2008/2512 Art.34

47. Firearms (Dangerous Air Weapons) Rules 1969
see *R. v Beard (Thomas Howard)* [2007] EWCA Crim 3168, [2008] 2 Cr. App. R. (S.) 41 (CA (Crim Div)), Richards, L.J.

592. Civil Aviation Act 1949 (Overseas Territories) Order 1969
applied: SI 2008/3125
referred to: SI 2008/3119
varied: SI 2008/3120 Art.2

1784. Export of Horses (Protection) Order 1969
Art.11, applied: SI 2008/1035 Sch.1 para.1
Art.12, applied: SI 2008/1035 Sch.1 para.2

1970

318. Foreign Fishing Boats (Stowage of Gear) Order 1970
Art.3, applied: SSI 2008/101 Sch.1 Part 1

348. Wool Textile Industry (Export Promotion Levy) Order 1970
revoked: SI 2008/2932 Art.2
Art.6, disapplied: SI 2008/2932 Art.1

600. Town and Country Planning (General Development) (Scotland) Amendment Order 1970
applied: SSI 2008/432 Reg.47

1539. Foreign Marriage Order 1970
applied: SI 2008/676 Sch.1 Part VI

1971

131. Public Health (Aircraft) (Scotland) Regulations 1971
revoked: 2008 asp 5 Sch.3 Part 2

132. Public Health (Ships) (Scotland) Regulations 1971
revoked: 2008 asp 5 Sch.3 Part 2

450. Road Vehicles (Registration and Licensing) Regulations 1971
applied: SSI 2008/182 Art.42, SSI 2008/189 Art.26, SSI 2008/190 Art.26

NO.

1971–cont.

880. Wool Textile Industry (Export Promotion Levy) (Amendment) Order 1971
revoked: SI 2008/2932 Art.2

1065. Rent Assessment Committees (England and Wales) Regulations 1971
Reg.3, amended: SI 2008/2683 Sch.1 para.2

1253. Indictment Rules 1971
r.4, see *R. v Marchese (Maria Del Carmen)* [2008] EWCA Crim 389, [2008] 2 Cr. App. R. 12 (CA (Crim Div)), Lord Phillips of Worth Matravers, L.C.J.
r.9, see *R. v Plant (Ricardo)* [2008] EWCA Crim 960, [2008] 2 Cr. App. R. 27 (CA (Crim Div)), Lord Phillips of Worth Matravers, L.C.J.

1267. Medicines (Surgical Materials) Order 1971
applied: SI 2008/552 Sch.3 para.6

1450. Medicines (Exemption from Licences) (Special and Transitional Cases) Order 1971
Art.2, applied: SI 2008/552 Reg.24, Sch.1 para.8, Sch.4 para.8

1861. Blood Tests (Evidence of Paternity) Regulations 1971
Reg.2, amended: SI 2008/972 Reg.4
Reg.2, revoked (in part): SI 2008/972 Reg.4
Reg.4, amended: SI 2008/972 Reg.5, Reg.6
Reg.6, amended: SI 2008/972 Reg.7, Reg.8, Reg.9
Reg.7, amended: SI 2008/972 Reg.10
Reg.8A, amended: SI 2008/972 Reg.11
Reg.12, amended: SI 2008/972 Reg.12
Sch.1, amended: SI 2008/972 Reg.13, Reg.14, Reg.15

1972

472. Boulby Mine (Storage Battery Locomotives) Special Regulations 1972
Reg.4, disapplied: SI 2008/1597 Reg.27
Reg.8, disapplied: SI 2008/1597 Reg.27

730. Explosives (Northern Ireland) Order 1972
applied: SI 2008/2852 Sch.2 para.3

733. Port of Tyne Revision Order 1972
referred to: SI 2008/1817 Art.1
revoked: SI 2008/1817 Art.3

764. National Savings Bank Regulations 1972
applied: SI 2008/1142 Reg.4
Reg.2, amended: SI 2008/734 Reg.3, SI 2008/3098 Reg.7
Reg.2A, amended: SI 2008/734 Reg.3, SI 2008/3098 Reg.5
Reg.2BA, added: SI 2008/1142 Reg.4
Reg.2BA, applied: SI 2008/1142 Reg.5
Reg.2BB, added: SI 2008/1142 Reg.4
Reg.2BB, applied: SI 2008/1142 Reg.5
Reg.21, amended: SI 2008/1164 Reg.2

NO.

1972–cont.

764. National Savings Bank Regulations 1972–*cont.*
Reg.21, revoked (in part): SI 2008/3098 Reg.8
Reg.28, amended: SI 2008/1164 Reg.4
Reg.29L, amended: SI 2008/734 Reg.3
Reg.29N, amended: SI 2008/3098 Reg.6
Reg.29P, amended: SI 2008/3098 Reg.9
Reg.42, amended: SI 2008/1164 Reg.3, Reg.4
Reg.42, revoked (in part): SI 2008/1164 Reg.3

963. Employers Liability (Defective Equipment and Compulsory Insurance) (Northern Ireland) Order 1972
Art.7, applied: SI 2008/1963 Reg.2

1073. Superannuation (Northern Ireland) Order 1972
Art.12, applied: SI 2008/653 Reg.11, SSI 2008/224 Reg.1

1101. Cayman Islands (Constitution) Order 1972
applied: SI 2008/3127 Art.1
Sch.2, amended: SI 2008/3127 Art.2

1264. Electoral Law (Northern Ireland) Order 1972
Art.9, applied: SI 2008/1741 Reg.97

1265. Health and Personal Social Services (Northern Ireland) Order 1972
Art.2, referred to: SI 2008/542 Reg.9
Art.15, applied: SI 2008/1741 Reg.57
Art.16, applied: SI 2008/1582 Reg.38, SI 2008/1769 Art.55
Art.90, applied: SI 2008/700 Sch.1 para.19

1667. Immigration (Particulars of Passengers and Crew) Order 1972
revoked: SI 2008/5 Art.8

1966. Salmon and Migratory Trout (Restrictions on Landing) Order 1972
Art.3, applied: SSI 2008/101 Sch.1 Part 1

1980. Swine Vesicular Disease Order 1972
applied: SI 2008/1275 Reg.15

1973

19. Adoption (Designation of Overseas Adoptions) Order 1973
see *D v D* [2008] EWHC 403 (Fam), [2008] 1 F.L.R. 1475 (Fam Div), Ryder, J.

207. Salmon and Migratory Trout (Prohibition of Fishing) (No.2) Order 1973
Art.3, applied: SSI 2008/101 Sch.1 Part 1

256. Transfer of Functions (Local Government, etc) (Northern Ireland) Order 1973
Sch.2, amended: 2008 c.4 Sch.28 Part 1

313. Local Government Superannuation (Miscellaneous Provisions) Regulations 1973
referred to: SI 2008/239 Reg.79, Reg.81, SSI 2008/228 Reg.74, Reg.76

NO.

1973–cont.

1311. Hydrocarbon Oil Regulations 1973
Reg.3, amended: SI 2008/753 Reg.3
Reg.6, amended: SI 2008/753 Reg.3
Reg.7, amended: SI 2008/753 Reg.3
Reg.8, amended: SI 2008/753 Reg.3
Reg.11, amended: SI 2008/753 Reg.3
Reg.12, amended: SI 2008/753 Reg.3
Reg.14, amended: SI 2008/753 Reg.3
Reg.46, amended: SI 2008/753 Reg.3
Reg.47, amended: SI 2008/753 Reg.3
Reg.48, amended: SI 2008/753 Reg.3
Reg.50, amended: SI 2008/753 Reg.3
Reg.51, amended: SI 2008/753 Reg.3

1822. Medicines (Pharmacies) (Applications for Registration and Fees) Regulations 1973
Reg.3, amended: SI 2008/2946 Reg.2

1952. Crystal Glass (Descriptions) Regulations 1973
Reg.8, applied: SI 2008/1277 Sch.3 para.1, Sch.3 para.2, Sch.3 para.3

1996. Local Government Superannuation (Miscellaneous Provisions) (No.2) Regulations 1973
referred to: SI 2008/239 Reg.79, Reg.81, SSI 2008/228 Reg.74, Reg.76

2163. Northern Ireland (Modification of Enactments-;No.1) Order 1973
Sch.1, amended: 2008 c.4 Sch.28 Part 1

1974

467. National Health Service (Functions of the Common Services Agency) (Scotland) Order 1974
revoked: SSI 2008/312 Sch.1
Art.3, applied: SI 2008/1909 Sch.1

470. National Health Service (Designated Medical Officers) (Scotland) Regulations 1974
revoked: 2008 asp 5 Sch.3 Part 2

520. Local Government Superannuation Regulations 1974
applied: SI 2008/239 Reg.51, Reg.69, Reg.72
referred to: SI 2008/239 Reg.79, Reg.81

812. Local Government Superannuation (Scotland) Regulations 1974
applied: SSI 2008/228 Reg.47, Reg.63, Reg.66
referred to: SSI 2008/228 Reg.74, Reg.76

923. Port of Tyne Authority (Constitution) Revision Order 1974
referred to: SI 2008/1817 Art.1

1008. Public Health (Ships) (Scotland) Amendment Regulations 1974
revoked: 2008 asp 5 Sch.3 Part 2

1017. Public Health (Aircraft) (Scotland) Amendment Regulations 1974
revoked: 2008 asp 5 Sch.3 Part 2

NO.

1974–cont.

1136. Plant Varieties and Seeds Tribunal Rules 1974

Part 2 r.10, revoked (in part): SI 2008/2683 Sch.1 para.3

1260. Specialized Agencies of the United Nations (Immunities and Privileges) Order 1974

see *Entico Corp Ltd v United Nations Educational Scientific and Cultural Association* [2008] EWHC 531 (Comm), [2008] 2 All E.R. (Comm) 97 (QBD (Comm)), Tomlinson, J.

1335. Industrial Training (Levy Exemption References) Regulations 1974

Sch.1 para.6, amended: SI 2008/2683 Sch.1 para.4

1555. Molluscan Shellfish (Control of Deposit) Order 1974

Art.5, applied: SSI 2008/101 Sch.1 Part 1

2010. Social Security (Benefit) (Married Women and Widows Special Provisions) Regulations 1974

Reg.1, amended: SI 2008/1554 Reg.64
Reg.3, amended: SI 2008/1554 Reg.64

2034. Agriculture (Tractor Cabs) Regulations 1974

applied: SI 2008/736 Reg.3

2211. Rabies (Importation of Dogs, Cats and Other Mammals) Order 1974

Art.4, applied: SI 2008/1035 Sch.1 para.1
Art.5, applied: SI 2008/1035 Sch.1 para.2
Art.5C, applied: SI 2008/1035 Sch.1 para.3
Art.6, applied: SI 2008/1035 Sch.1 para.4
Art.7, applied: SI 2008/1035 Sch.1 para.5
Art.9, applied: SI 2008/1035 Sch.1 para.6
Art.10, applied: SI 2008/1035 Sch.1 para.7
Art.11, applied: SI 2008/1035 Sch.1 para.8
Art.12, applied: SI 2008/1035 Sch.1 para.9
Art.13, applied: SI 2008/1035 Sch.1 para.10
Art.14, applied: SI 2008/1035 Sch.1 para.11

1975

148. Town and Country Planning (Tree Preservation Order) (Amendment) and (Trees in Conservation Areas) (Exempted Cases) Regulations 1975

Reg.3, applied: SI 2008/2512 Art.34

335. Health and Safety Inquiries (Procedure) Regulations 1975

Reg.2, amended: SI 2008/960 Sch.3
Reg.8, amended: SI 2008/2683 Sch.1 para.5

492. Social Security (Contributions) Regulations 1975

see *Revenue and Customs Commissioners v Mayor* [2007] EWHC 3147 (Ch), [2008] S.T.C. 1958 (Ch D), Patten, J.
Reg.91, see *Revenue and Customs Commissioners v Mayor* [2007] EWHC 3147 (Ch), [2008] S.T.C. 1958 (Ch D), Patten, J.

NO.

1975–cont.

493. Social Security (Benefit) (Members of the Forces) Regulations 1975

Reg.2, amended: SI 2008/1554 Reg.66

494. Social Security (Airmen's Benefits) Regulations 1975

Reg.1, amended: SI 2008/1554 Reg.65
Reg.2, amended: SI 2008/1554 Reg.65
Reg.3, amended: SI 2008/1554 Reg.65

529. Social Security (Mariners Benefits) Regulations 1975

applied: SI 2008/794 Reg.98
Reg.1, amended: SI 2008/1554 Reg.67
Reg.4, amended: SI 2008/1554 Reg.67
Reg.5, amended: SI 2008/1554 Reg.67
Reg.6, amended: SI 2008/1554 Reg.67

556. Social Security (Credits) Regulations 1975

Reg.2, amended: SI 2008/1554 Reg.48
Reg.3, amended: SI 2008/1554 Reg.48
Reg.8, amended: SI 2008/1554 Reg.48
Reg.8A, amended: SI 2008/1554 Reg.48
Reg.8A, applied: SI 2008/794 Sch.6 para.15
Reg.8B, amended: SI 2008/1554 Reg.48
Reg.8B, applied: SI 2008/794 Sch.6 para.15
Reg.8C, amended: SI 2008/1554 Reg.48
Reg.9D, applied: SI 2008/794 Reg.8

563. Social Security Benefit (Persons Abroad) Regulations 1975

Reg.5, applied: SI 2008/667 Reg.3, SI 2008/840 Reg.3

679. Town and Country Planning (General Development) (Scotland) Order 1975

applied: SSI 2008/432 Reg.47

980. Immigration (Particulars of Passengers and Crew) (Amendment) Order 1975

revoked: SI 2008/5 Art.8

1023. Rehabilitation of Offenders Act 1974 (Exceptions) Order 1975

applied: SI 2008/1976 Reg.6
Art.2, amended: SI 2008/3259 Art.3
Art.3, amended: SI 2008/3259 Art.4
Art.4, amended: SI 2008/3259 Art.5
Art.5, amended: SI 2008/3259 Art.6
Sch.1 Part III para.10, added: SI 2008/3259 Art.7
Sch.1 Part IV, amended: SI 2008/3259 Art.7
Sch.3 para.5, substituted: SI 2008/2683 Sch.1 para.6

1976

226. Treatment of Offenders (Northern Ireland) Order 1976

revoked: SI 2008/1216 Sch.6 Part 1

246. Local Government Area Changes Regulations 1976

Reg.41, applied: SI 2008/584 Art.21

NO.

1976–cont.

615. Social Security (Medical Evidence) Regulations 1976
applied: SI 2008/794 Reg.20, Reg.21, Reg.30, Reg.149
Reg.1, amended: SI 2008/1554 Reg.68
Reg.2, amended: SI 2008/1554 Reg.68
Reg.5, amended: SI 2008/1554 Reg.68

766. Employment Protection (Offshore Employment) Order 1976
applied: SI 2008/535 Art.2

1019. Offshore Installations (Operational Safety, Health and Welfare) Regulations 1976
Reg.5, see *Spencer-Franks v Kellogg Brown & Root Ltd* [2008] UKHL 46, 2008 S.L.T. 675 (HL), Lord Hoffmann

1041. Births and Deaths Registration (Northern Ireland) Order 1976
referred to: 2008 c.22 s.53
Art.10, amended: 2008 c.22 Sch.6 para.60
Art.14A, substituted: 2008 c.22 Sch.6 para.62
Art.14ZA, added: 2008 c.22 Sch.6 para.61
Art.18, amended: 2008 c.22 Sch.6 para.63
Art.19, amended: 2008 c.22 Sch.6 para.64
Art.20, amended: 2008 c.22 Sch.6 para.65
Art.37, amended: 2008 c.22 Sch.6 para.66

1042. Sex Discrimination (Northern Ireland) Order 1976
Art.2, amended: SI 2008/963 Sch.2 para.3, Sch.2 para.9
Art.3, amended: SI 2008/963 Sch.2 para.1
Art.4A, amended: SI 2008/963 Sch.2 para.2
Art.5B, added: SI 2008/963 Sch.2 para.3
Art.30, amended: SI 2008/963 Sch.2 para.4
Art.31, amended: SI 2008/963 Sch.2 para.5
Art.32, amended: SI 2008/963 Sch.2 para.6
Art.35, amended: SI 2008/963 Sch.2 para.7
Art.36, amended: SI 2008/963 Sch.2 para.8
Art.36A, amended: SI 2008/963 Sch.2 para.10
Art.36ZA, added: SI 2008/963 Sch.2 para.9
Art.44, amended: SI 2008/963 Sch.2 para.11
Art.45, substituted: SI 2008/963 Sch.2 para.12
Art.46, substituted: SI 2008/963 Sch.2 para.13
Art.47, amended: SI 2008/963 Sch.2 para.14
Art.52A, amended: SI 2008/963 Sch.2 para.15
Art.54, amended: SI 2008/963 Sch.2 para.16
Art.66A, amended: SI 2008/963 Sch.2 para.17
Art.74, amended: SI 2008/963 Sch.2 para.18

1213. Pharmacy (Northern Ireland) Order 1976
applied: SI 2008/2927 Reg.2
Art.6, applied: SI 2008/2789 Reg.5
Art.9, applied: SI 2008/2789 Reg.5

NO.

1976–cont.

1813. Consumer Transactions (Restrictions on Statements) Order 1976
applied: SI 2008/1277 Sch.3 para.11
Art.4, referred to: SI 2008/1277 Sch.3 para.13
Art.5, referred to: SI 2008/1277 Sch.3 para.13

1912. Civil Aviation Act 1971 (Overseas Territories) Order 1976
referred to: SI 2008/3119
varied: SI 2008/3120 Art.3

1977

181. Cereals Marketing Act 1965 (Amendment) Regulations 1977
revoked: SI 2008/576 Sch.5 para.8

343. Social Security Benefit (Dependency) Regulations 1977
Reg.1, amended: SI 2008/2683 Sch.1 para.7
Sch.2 Part I para.2B, amended: SI 2008/667 Reg.4

426. Criminal Damage (Northern Ireland) Order 1977
Art.3, applied: SI 2008/1216 Sch.1 para.16, Sch.1 para.17, Sch.2 para.16, Sch.2 para.17

500. Safety Representatives and Safety Committees Regulations 1977
applied: SI 2008/228 Sch.2 para.20
Reg.4, amended: SI 2008/960 Sch.3
Reg.5, amended: SI 2008/960 Sch.3
Reg.10, amended: SI 2008/960 Sch.3

670. Medicines (Bal Jivan Chamcho Prohibition) (No.2) Order 1977
Art.2, amended: SI 2008/548 Art.4

819. Naval Medical Compassionate Fund (Amendment) Order 1977
revoked: SI 2008/3129 Sch.1

944. Importation of Animals Order 1977
Art.3, applied: SI 2008/1035 Sch.1 para.1
Art.10, applied: SI 2008/1035 Sch.1 para.2
Art.11, applied: SI 2008/1035 Sch.1 para.3
Art.12, applied: SI 2008/1035 Sch.1 para.4
Art.13, applied: SI 2008/1035 Sch.1 para.5
Art.14, applied: SI 2008/1035 Sch.1 para.6
Art.16, applied: SI 2008/1035 Sch.1 para.7
Art.19, applied: SI 2008/1035 Sch.1 para.8

1210. National Savings Bank (Investment Deposits) (Limits) Order 1977
Art.2C, amended: SI 2008/734 Reg.4
Art.3, amended: SI 2008/1164 Reg.5
Art.3B, amended: SI 2008/734 Reg.4
Art.3C, revoked: SI 2008/734 Reg.4

1250. Family Law Reform (Northern Ireland) Order 1977
Art.13, amended: 2008 c.22 Sch.6 para.67

1251. Fatal Accidents (Northern Ireland) Order 1977
applied: SI 2008/1596 Reg.10, Reg.12

1491. Intestate Succession (Interest and Capitalisation) Order 1977
Art.3, amended: SI 2008/3162 Art.2
Sch.1, substituted: SI 2008/3162 Sch.1

NO.

1977–cont.

1877. Tourism (Sleeping Accommodation Price Display) Order 1977
revoked: SI 2008/1277 Sch.2 para.76, Sch.4 Part 2

1918. Business Advertisements (Disclosure) Order 1977
applied: SI 2008/1277 Sch.3 para.11

2151. Agricultural Wages (Regulation) (Northern Ireland) Order 1977
applied: 2008 c.24 s.8, s.9, s.10, s.11

1978

32. Diseases of Animals (Approved Disinfectants) Order 1978
applied: SSI 2008/219 Art.10
revoked (in part): SSI 2008/219 Sch.1
Art.5, applied: SI 2008/1035 Sch.1 para.1
Art.7, applied: SI 2008/1035 Sch.1 para.2
Art.9, applied: SI 2008/1035 Sch.1 para.3

369. Public Health (Ships) (Scotland) Amendment Regulations 1978
revoked: 2008 asp 5 Sch.3 Part 2

370. Public Health (Aircraft) (Scotland) Amendment Regulations 1978
revoked: 2008 asp 5 Sch.3 Part 2

374. Social Security (Modification of Coroners (Amendment) Act 1926) Order 1978
Art.3, applied: SI 2008/239 Reg.9

393. Social Security (Graduated Retirement Benefit) (No.2) Regulations 1978
Sch.2 para.1, varied: SI 2008/632 Art.12
Sch.2 para 2, varied: SI 2008/632 Art.12
Sch.2 para.3, varied: SI 2008/632 Art.12
Sch.2 para.4, varied: SI 2008/632 Art.12

639. Sheffield Assay Office Order 1978
Art.10, amended: SI 2008/948 Sch.1 para.1

1039. Health and Safety at Work (Northern Ireland) Order 1978
applied: SI 2008/1597 Sch.5 para.17
Art.2, applied: 2008 c.20 s.2
Art.17, revoked (in part): 2008 c.20 Sch.3 para.3, Sch.4
Art.21, applied: SI 2008/1597 Sch.5 para.9, SI 2008/2852 Sch.7 para.4
Art.21, varied: SI 2008/1597 Sch.5 para.10, SI 2008/2108 Reg.4
Art.22, applied: SI 2008/1597 Reg.21, Sch.5 para.9
Art.22, varied: SI 2008/1597 Sch.5 para.10, SI 2008/2108 Reg.4
Art.23, applied: SI 2008/1597 Sch.5 para.9
Art.23, varied: SI 2008/1597 Sch.5 para.10
Art.24, applied: SI 2008/1597 Sch.5 para.9
Art.24, varied: SI 2008/1597 Sch.5 para.10
Art.25, applied: SI 2008/1597 Sch.5 para.9
Art.25, varied: SI 2008/1597 Sch.5 para.10
Art.26, applied: SI 2008/1597 Sch.5 para.9
Art.26, varied: SI 2008/1597 Sch.5 para.10

NO.

1978–cont.

1039. Health and Safety at Work (Northern Ireland) Order 1978–*cont.*
Art.27, applied: SI 2008/1597 Sch.5 para.9
Art.27, varied: SI 2008/1597 Sch.5 para.10
Art.27A, applied: SI 2008/1597 Sch.5 para.9
Art.27A, varied: SI 2008/1597 Sch.5 para.10, SI 2008/2108 Reg.4
Art.28, applied: SI 2008/1597 Sch.5 para.9
Art.28, varied: SI 2008/1597 Sch.5 para.10, SI 2008/2108 Reg.4
Art.29, applied: SI 2008/1597 Sch.5 para.9
Art.29, varied: SI 2008/1597 Sch.5 para.10, SI 2008/2108 Reg.4
Art.29A, applied: SI 2008/1597 Sch.5 para.9
Art.29A, varied: SI 2008/1597 Sch.5 para.10, SI 2008/2108 Reg.4
Art.30, applied: SI 2008/1597 Sch.5 para.9
Art.30, varied: SI 2008/1597 Sch.5 para.10, SI 2008/2108 Reg.4
Art.31, amended: 2008 c.20 s.1
Art.31, applied: SI 2008/1597 Sch.5 para.9, SI 2008/2108 Reg.4
Art.31, varied: SI 2008/1597 Sch.5 para.10, SI 2008/2108 Reg.4
Art.32, applied: SI 2008/1597 Sch.5 para.9
Art.32, varied: SI 2008/1597 Sch.5 para.10, Sch.5 para.13, SI 2008/2108 Reg.4
Art.33, applied: SI 2008/1597 Sch.5 para.9
Art.33, varied: SI 2008/1597 Sch.5 para.10, SI 2008/2108 Reg.4
Art.34, applied: SI 2008/1597 Sch.5 para.9
Art.34, varied: SI 2008/1597 Sch.5 para.10, SI 2008/2108 Reg.4
Art.34A, applied: SI 2008/1597 Sch.5 para.9
Art.34A, varied: SI 2008/1597 Sch.5 para.10, SI 2008/2108 Reg.4
Art.35, applied: SI 2008/1597 Sch.5 para.9
Art.35, varied: SI 2008/1597 Sch.5 para.10, SI 2008/2108 Reg.4
Art.36, applied: SI 2008/1597 Sch.5 para.9
Art.36, varied: SI 2008/1597 Sch.5 para.10, SI 2008/2108 Reg.4
Art.37, varied: SI 2008/2108 Reg.4
Art.38, applied: SI 2008/1597 Sch.5 para.9
Art.38, varied: SI 2008/1597 Sch.5 para.10, SI 2008/2108 Reg.4
Art.39, amended: 2008 c.20 Sch.3 para.3
Art.39, applied: SI 2008/1597 Sch.5 para.9
Art.39, varied: SI 2008/1597 Sch.5 para.10, SI 2008/2108 Reg.4
Sch.3A, added: 2008 c.20 Sch.2

1047. Protection of Children (Northern Ireland) Order 1978
Art.2, amended: 2008 c.4 s.70, SI 2008/1769 Art.42
Art.3, amended: SI 2008/1769 Art.42
Art.3, applied: SI 2008/1216 Sch.1 para.18, Sch.2 para.8, SI 2008/1769 Art.76
Art.3, referred to: 2008 c.4 Sch.27 para.24
Art.3A, amended: 2008 c.4 s.70
Art.3B, added: SI 2008/1769 Art.42

NO.

1978–cont.

1047. Protection of Children (Northern Ireland) Order 1978–*cont.*
Art.7, amended: SI 2008/1769 Art.42

1723. Compressed Acetylene (Importation) Regulations 1978
applied: SI 2008/736 Sch.8 Part 3

1907. Health and Personal Social Services (Northern Ireland) Order 1978
Art.16, applied: SI 2008/3170 Reg.23

1908. Rehabilitation of Offenders (Northern Ireland) Order 1978
applied: SI 2008/542 Reg.6
Art.6, amended: SI 2008/1216 Art.95, Sch.5 para.3

1910. European Communities (Services of Lawyers) Order 1978
Art.2, amended: SI 2008/81 Reg.2

1979

26. Cereals Marketing Act 1965 (Amendment) Regulations 1979
revoked: SI 2008/576 Sch.5 para.8

294. Aircraft and Shipbuilding Industries (Northern Ireland) Order 1979
Art.12, amended: SI 2008/948 Sch.1 para.47

597. Social Security (Overlapping Benefits) Regulations 1979
applied: SI 2008/794 Sch.4 para.4
Reg.2, amended: SI 2008/1554 Reg.51
Reg.4, amended: SI 2008/1554 Reg.51
Reg.10, amended: SI 2008/1554 Reg.51
Reg.16, amended: SI 2008/1554 Reg.51
Reg.17, amended: SI 2008/1554 Reg.51
Sch.1, amended: SI 2008/1554 Reg.51

642. Social Security (Widow's Benefit and Retirement Pensions) Regulations 1979
Reg.1, amended: SI 2008/2683 Sch.1 para.8

643. Social Security (Widow's Benefit, Retirement Pensions and Other Benefits) (Transitional) Regulations 1979
applied: 2008 c.30 s.141

1138. Cremation Regulations 1979
revoked (in part): SI 2008/2841 Sch.2

1573. Statutory Rules (Northern Ireland) Order 1979
applied: 2008 c.4 s.147, 2008 c.14 s.161, 2008 c.20 s.2, 2008 c.27 s.90, 2008 c.31 s.21, SI 2008/1216 Art.100, SI 2008/1769 Art.80

1587. Edinburgh Assay Office Order 1979
Art.12, amended: SI 2008/948 Sch.1 para.1

1702. Importation of Birds, Poultry and Hatching Eggs Order 1979
Art.4, applied: SI 2008/1035 Sch.1 para.1
Art.9, applied: SI 2008/1035 Sch.1 para.2

1714. Perjury (Northern Ireland) Order 1979
Art.10, applied: SI 2008/2852 Sch.6 para.14

NO.

1980

12. Importation of Embryos, Ova and Semen Order 1980
Art.4, applied: SI 2008/1035 Sch.1 para.1
Art.6, applied: SI 2008/1035 Sch.1 para.2

51. Consumer Credit (Total Charge for Credit) Regulations 1980
applied: SI 2008/529 Reg.93, SI 2008/1273 Reg.51, SI 2008/1582 Reg.93, SI 2008/3170 Reg.51, SSI 2008/235 Reg.11

704. Criminal Justice (Northern Ireland) Order 1980
Art.9, applied: SI 2008/1216 Sch.2 para.10
Art.9, revoked: SI 2008/1769 Sch.1 para.14, Sch.3

1082. Pensions Appeal Tribunals (Posthumous Appeals) Order 1980
Art.1, amended: SI 2008/2683 Sch.1 para.10
Art.3, amended: SI 2008/2683 Sch.1 para.11
Art.4, amended: SI 2008/2683 Sch.1 para.12
Art.5, amended: SI 2008/2683 Sch.1 para.13
Art.5A, amended: SI 2008/2683 Sch.1 para.14
Art.6, amended: SI 2008/2683 Sch.1 para.15
Art.9, amended: SI 2008/2683 Sch.1 para.16

1120. Pensions Appeal Tribunals (England and Wales) Rules 1980
revoked: SI 2008/2683 Sch.2

1697. Rent Act 1977 (Forms etc.) Regulations 1980
Sch.1, amended: SI 2008/2831 Sch.1 para.1
Sch.1, varied: SI 2008/2839 Sch.1 para.1

1700. Rent Assessment Committees (England and Wales) (Rent Tribunal) Regulations 1980
Reg.7, amended: SI 2008/2683 Sch.1 para.17

1923. Medicines (Sale or Supply) (Miscellaneous Provisions) Regulations 1980
Reg.1, amended: SI 2008/1162 Reg.2
Sch.2 para.1, amended: SI 2008/1162 Reg.2

1924. Medicines (Pharmacy and General Sale Exemption) Order 1980
Art.1, amended: SI 2008/1161 Art.6
Art.4AA, amended: SI 2008/1161 Art.7
Sch.3 Part III, amended: SI 2008/1161 Art.8

1965. Air Navigation Order 1980
Art.70, applied: SI 2008/3121 Art.2

1981

15. Public Bodies Land (Appropriate Ministers) Order 1981
Art.2, amended: SI 2008/2831 Sch.2 para.1

154. Road Traffic (Northern Ireland) Order 1981
applied: SI 2008/2551 Reg.4
Part II, applied: SI 2008/1216 Art.91
Art.79A, applied: SI 2008/542 Reg.9
Art.172B, applied: SI 2008/1216 Sch.1 para.19, Sch.2 para.18
Art.180, varied: SI 2008/1216 Art.91
Art.180(4AA), varied: SI 2008/1216 Art.91

NO.

1981–cont.

155. Firearms (Northern Ireland) Order 1981
applied: SI 2008/3231 Art.16

226. Judgments Enforcement (Northern Ireland) Order 1981
Art.2, amended: SI 2008/948 Sch.1 para.53
Art.14, amended: SI 2008/948 Sch.1 para.53

228. Legal Aid, Advice and Assistance (Northern Ireland) Order 1981
Art.20, amended: SI 2008/948 Sch.1 para.2
Sch.1, amended: SI 2008/1216 Art.85

231. Weights and Measures (Northern Ireland) Order 1981
Art.22, applied: SI 2008/1277 Sch.3 para.11
Art.22, revoked (in part): SI 2008/1277 Sch.2 para.77, Sch.4 Part 2
Sch.10, revoked: SI 2008/1277 Sch.4 Part 2

257. Public Service Vehicles (Conditions of Fitness, Equipment, Use and Certification) Regulations 1981
Reg.46, amended: SI 2008/1458 Reg.3, Reg.4
Reg.50, amended: SI 2008/1458 Reg.4
Reg.53, amended: SI 2008/1458 Reg.4
Reg.57, amended: SI 2008/1458 Reg.4

552. Magistrates Courts Rules 1981
see *R. (on the application of Chief Constable of North Wales) v Anglesey Justices* [2008] EWHC 309 (Admin), (2008) 172 J.P. 225 (DC), Maurice Kay, L.J.
r.4, see *R. (on the application of Chief Constable of North Wales) v Anglesey Justices* [2008] EWHC 309 (Admin), (2008) 172 J.P. 225 (DC), Maurice Kay, L.J.

829. Town and Country Planning (Development by Planning Authorities) (Scotland) Regulations 1981
Reg.6, see *Lerwick Port Authority v Scottish Ministers* 2008 S.L.T. 74 (OH), Lord Reed

830. Town and Country Planning (General Development) (Scotland) Order 1981
applied: SSI 2008/432 Reg.47

917. Health and Safety (First-Aid) Regulations 1981
Reg.3, applied: SI 2008/736 Reg.19, Reg.21

994. Lobsters (Control of Deposit) Order 1981
Art.6, applied: SSI 2008/101 Sch.1 Part 1

995. Lobsters (Control of Importation) Order 1981
Art.5, applied: SSI 2008/101 Sch.1 Part 1

1121. Double Taxation Relief (Taxes on Income) (Mauritius) Order 1981
see *Smallwood v Revenue and Customs Commissioners* [2008] S.T.C. (S.C.D.) 629 (Sp Comm), AN Brice

1171. Air Navigation (Restriction of Flying) (Scottish Highlands) Regulations 1981
revoked: SI 2008/1239 Reg.2

NO.

1981–cont.

1675. Magistrates Courts (Northern Ireland) Order 1981
applied: SI 2008/3206 Reg.12, Reg.14
Part VIII, applied: 2008 c.28 Sch.5 para.5, Sch.5 para.10
Part IX, applied: 2008 c.4 s.88
Art.19, disapplied: SI 2008/1276 Reg.10, SI 2008/1277 Reg.14
Art.19, varied: SI 2008/2668 Art.10
Art.20, amended: SI 2008/1216 Art.92
Art.20, applied: SI 2008/1216 Art.92
Art.25, applied: SI 2008/1216 Art.92
Art.29, amended: SI 2008/1216 Art.90
Art.40, applied: SI 2008/2297 Reg.44
Art.92, varied: 2008 c.4 s.89
Art.95, applied: SI 2008/2347 Art.12, SSI 2008/102 Art.9, SSI 2008/151 Art.25
Art.95, varied: 2008 c.4 s.89
Art.132A, amended: SI 2008/1216 Art.87
Art.146, applied: SI 2008/1597 Sch.5 para.14, SI 2008/2852 Sch.6 para.26
Sch.2, revoked (in part): SI 2008/1769 Sch.1 para.15, Sch.1 para.15, Sch.3, Sch.3
Sch.4, applied: 2008 c.28 Sch.7 para.37

1687. County Court Rules 1981
Part 1 r.3, applied: SI 2008/2551 Reg.6
Ord.20 r.5, see *West London Pipeline & Storage Ltd v Total UK Ltd* [2008] EWHC 1729 (Comm), [2008] 2 C.L.C. 258 (QBD (Comm)), Beatson, J.

1694. Motor Vehicles (Tests) Regulations 1981
Reg.20, amended: SI 2008/1402 Reg.3, SI 2008/1461 Reg.2
Reg.25, amended: SI 2008/1402 Reg.4

1794. Transfer of Undertakings (Protection of Employment) Regulations 1981
applied: SSI 2008/229 Reg.13, Reg.14
see *Computershare Investor Services Plc v Jackson* [2007] EWCA Civ 1065, [2008] I.C.R. 341 (CA (Civ Div)), Mummery, L.J.; see *Power v Regent Security Services Ltd* [2007] EWCA Civ 1188, [2008] 2 All E.R. 977 (CA (Civ Div)), Mummery, L.J.; see *Sodexo v Gutridge* [2008] I.R.L.R. 752 (EAT), Elias, J.; see *Unison v Allen* [2008] I.C.R. 114 (EAT), Elias, J (President)
Reg.5, see *Capita Health Solutions v BBC* [2008] I.R.L.R. 595 (EAT (SC)), Smith, L.J.; see *Computershare Investor Services Plc v Jackson* [2007] EWCA Civ 1065, [2008] I.C.R. 341 (CA (Civ Div)), Mummery, L.J.; see *Power v Regent Security Services Ltd* [2007] EWCA Civ 1188, [2008] 2 All E.R. 977 (CA (Civ Div)), Mummery, L.J.
Reg.12, see *Power v Regent Security Services Ltd* [2007] EWCA Civ 1188, [2008] 2 All E.R. 977 (CA (Civ Div)), Mummery, L.J.

NO.

1981–cont.

1805. Air Navigation (Guernsey) Order 1981
revoked: SI 2008/3121 Art.2

1982

80. Receiving of Trans-shipped Sea Fish (Licensing) Order 1982
Art.3, applied: SSI 2008/101 Sch.1 Part 1

485. Wool Textile Industry (Export Promotion Levy) (Amendment) Order 1982
revoked: SI 2008/2932 Art.2

719. Public Lending Right Scheme 1982 (Commencement) Order 1982
applied: SI 2008/794 Reg.92

723. Port of Tyne Revision Order 1982
referred to: SI 2008/1817 Art.1
revoked: SI 2008/1817 Art.3

847. European Communities (Designation) (No.2) Order 1982
Sch.1, amended: SI 2008/301 Sch.1

894. Statutory Sick Pay (General) Regulations 1982
Reg.3, amended: SI 2008/1554 Reg.45
Reg.3A, revoked: SI 2008/1735 Reg.3
Reg.9A, amended: SI 2008/2683 Sch.1 para.18
Reg.15, amended: SI 2008/1735 Reg.2
Reg.15A, revoked: SI 2008/1735 Reg.3

1046. War Pensions (Commencing Dates of Past Awards) Order 1982
Art.1, amended: SI 2008/2683 Sch.1 para.20
Art.4, amended: SI 2008/2683 Sch.1 para.21
Sch.2, amended: SI 2008/2683 Sch.1 para.22

1221. Wildlife and Countryside (Registration and Ringing of Certain Captive Birds) Regulations 1982
Reg.1, amended: SI 2008/2357 Reg.4
Reg.3, amended: SI 2008/2357 Reg.5
Reg.4, amended: SI 2008/2357 Reg.6
Reg.5, amended: SI 2008/2357 Reg.7
Sch.1, added: SI 2008/2357 Reg.8
Sch.1 Part I, added: SI 2008/2357 Reg.8
Sch.1 Part II, added: SI 2008/2357 Reg.8

1408. Social Security (General Benefit) Regulations 1982
Reg.1, amended: SI 2008/2683 Sch.1 para.24
Reg.11, amended: SI 2008/2683 Sch.1 para.25
Reg.16, amended: SI 2008/2365 Reg.2

1489. Workmen's Compensation (Supplementation) Scheme 1982
Art.1, amended: SI 2008/2683 Sch.1 para.27
Art.5, amended: SI 2008/721 Art.2
Art.12, amended: SI 2008/2683 Sch.1 para.28
Sch.1 Part I, substituted: SI 2008/721 Art.3
Sch.1 Part II, substituted: SI 2008/721 Art.3
Sch.2, amended: SI 2008/2683 Sch.1 para.29

NO.

1982–cont.

1496. Notification of New Substances Regulations 1982
Reg.4, applied: SI 2008/736 Sch.11

1676. Judicial Committee (General Appellate Jurisdiction) Rules Order 1982
Sch.A para.1, amended: SI 2008/300 Art.6
Sch.A para.1, revoked (in part): SI 2008/300 Art.6
Sch.A para.2, added: SI 2008/300 Art.6
Sch.A para.3, revoked (in part): SI 2008/300 Art.6
Sch.A para.4, revoked (in part): SI 2008/300 Art.6
Sch.A para.6, revoked: SI 2008/300 Art.6
Sch.A para.7, revoked: SI 2008/300 Art.6
Sch.B Part II, revoked: SI 2008/300 Art.7
Sch.II Part 1 para.13, amended: SI 2008/300 Art.3
Sch.II Part 1 para.24, applied: SI 2008/300 Art.8
Sch.II Part 1 para.24, substituted: SI 2008/300 Art.4
Sch.II Part 1 para.26, revoked: SI 2008/300 Art.5
Sch.II Part 1 para.27, revoked: SI 2008/300 Art.5

1710. British Dependent Territories Citizenship (Designated Service) Order 1982
Sch.1 para.2, revoked: SI 2008/1240 Art.2
Sch.1 para.3, revoked: SI 2008/1240 Art.2

1983

6. Veterinary Surgery (Blood Sampling) Order 1983
Art.3, referred to: SI 2008/1040 Reg.17

136. Pneumoconiosis, Byssinosis and Miscellaneous Diseases Benefit Scheme 1983
Art.1, amended: SI 2008/2683 Sch.1 para.31
Art.12, amended: SI 2008/2683 Sch.1 para.32
Sch.3, amended: SI 2008/2683 Sch.1 para.33

686. Personal Injuries (Civilians) Scheme 1983
Art.27, applied: SI 2008/794 Sch.8 para.51
Art.56, amended: SI 2008/2683 Sch.1 para.35
Sch.3, substituted: SI 2008/592 Sch.2
Sch.4, referred to: SI 2008/794 Sch.8 para.51
Sch.4, substituted: SI 2008/592 Sch.3
Sch.5 para.4, amended: SI 2008/2683 Sch.1 para.36
Sch.5 para.8, amended: SI 2008/2683 Sch.1 para.36

NO.

1983–cont.

747. Act of Sederunt (Ordinary Cause Rules, Sheriff Court) 1983
see *Sinclair v Private Rented Housing Panel* 2008 S.L.T. (Sh Ct) 84 (Sh Ct (Grampian)), Sheriff Graeme Napier

892. Mental Health Act Commission (Establishment and Constitution) Order 1983
revoked: 2008 c.14 Sch.15 Part 1
Art.3, amended: SI 2008/2828 Art.7

893. Mental Health (Hospital, Guardianship and Consent to Treatment) Regulations 1983
revoked (in part): SI 2008/1184 Sch.2, SI 2008/2439 Sch.2

894. Mental Health Act Commission Regulations 1983
revoked: 2008 c.14 Sch.15 Part 1

942. Mental Health Review Tribunal Rules 1983
revoked: SI 2008/2705 r.31
r.29, see *R. (on the application of Rayner) v Secretary of State for the Home Department* [2008] EWCA Civ 176, [2008] U.K.H.R.R. 847 (CA (Civ Div)), Ward, L.J.

1120. Criminal Attempts and Conspiracy (Northern Ireland) Order 1983
Art.5, revoked (in part): SI 2008/1769 Sch.1 para.16, Sch.3

1140. Classification and Labelling of Explosives Regulations 1983
applied: SI 2008/736 Sch.8 Part 7, Sch.8 Part 8

1168. Electrically Assisted Pedal Cycles Regulations 1983
see *DPP v King* [2008] EWHC 447 (Admin), (2008) 172 J.P. 401 (DC), Maurice Kay, L.J.

1590. Town and Country Planning (Structure and Local Plans) (Scotland) Regulations 1983
applied: SSI 2008/427 Art.2, Art.4
referred to: SSI 2008/427 Art.4
revoked: SSI 2008/427 Art.10
Reg.1, applied: SSI 2008/427 Art.3, Art.5
Reg.2, applied: SSI 2008/427 Art.3, Art.5
Reg.2A, applied: SSI 2008/427 Art.3, Art.5
Reg.3, applied: SSI 2008/427 Art.3, Art.5
Reg.4, applied: SSI 2008/427 Art.3, Art.5
Reg.5, applied: SSI 2008/427 Art.3, Art.5
Reg.6, applied: SSI 2008/427 Art.3, Art.5
Reg.7, applied: SSI 2008/427 Art.3, Art.5
Reg.8, applied: SSI 2008/427 Art.3, Art.5
Reg.9, applied: SSI 2008/427 Art.3, Art.5
Reg.10, applied: SSI 2008/427 Art.3, Art.5
Reg.11, applied: SSI 2008/427 Art.5
Reg.12, applied: SSI 2008/427 Art.5
Reg.13, applied: SSI 2008/427 Art.5
Reg.14, applied: SSI 2008/427 Art.5
Reg.15, applied: SSI 2008/427 Art.5
Reg.16, applied: SSI 2008/427 Art.5

NO.

1983–cont.

1590. Town and Country Planning (Structure and Local Plans) (Scotland) Regulations 1983–*cont.*
Reg.17, applied: SSI 2008/427 Art.5
Reg.18, applied: SSI 2008/427 Art.5
Reg.19, applied: SSI 2008/427 Art.5
Reg.19A, applied: SSI 2008/427 Art.3, Art.5
Reg.20, applied: SSI 2008/427 Art.3, Art.5
Reg.21, applied: SSI 2008/427 Art.3, Art.5
Reg.22, applied: SSI 2008/427 Art.3, Art.5
Reg.23, applied: SSI 2008/427 Art.3, Art.5
Reg.24, applied: SSI 2008/427 Art.3, Art.5
Reg.25, applied: SSI 2008/427 Art.3, Art.5
Reg.26, applied: SSI 2008/427 Art.3, Art.5
Reg.27, applied: SSI 2008/427 Art.3, Art.5
Reg.28, applied: SSI 2008/427 Art.3, Art.5
Reg.29, applied: SSI 2008/427 Art.3, Art.5
Reg.30, applied: SSI 2008/427 Art.3, Art.5
Reg.31, applied: SSI 2008/427 Art.3, Art.5
Reg.32, applied: SSI 2008/427 Art.3
Reg.33, applied: SSI 2008/427 Art.3
Reg.34, applied: SSI 2008/426 Reg.30, SSI 2008/427 Art.3, Art.4, Art.5
Reg.35, applied: SSI 2008/427 Art.3
Reg.36, applied: SSI 2008/427 Art.3
Reg.37, applied: SSI 2008/427 Art.3
Reg.38, applied: SSI 2008/427 Art.3
Reg.39, applied: SSI 2008/427 Art.3
Reg.40, applied: SSI 2008/427 Art.3
Reg.41, applied: SSI 2008/427 Art.3, Art.5
Reg.41A, applied: SSI 2008/427 Art.3, Art.5
Reg.42, applied: SSI 2008/427 Art.3, Art.5
Reg.43, applied: SSI 2008/427 Art.3, Art.5
Reg.44, applied: SSI 2008/427 Art.3, Art.5
Reg.45, applied: SSI 2008/427 Art.3, Art.5
Reg.45A, applied: SSI 2008/427 Art.3, Art.5
Reg.46, applied: SSI 2008/427 Art.3, Art.5
Reg.47, applied: SSI 2008/427 Art.3, Art.5
Sch.1 Part I, applied: SSI 2008/427 Art.3, Art.5

1598. Social Security (Unemployment, Sickness and Invalidity Benefit) Regulations 1983
Reg.1, amended: SI 2008/2683 Sch.1 para.37
Reg.20, amended: SI 2008/2428 Reg.21

1964. Adoption Agencies Regulations 1983
applied: SI 2008/794 Reg.156

1984

252. High Court of Justiciary Fees Order 1984
Sch.1 Part 001, substituted: SSI 2008/237 Sch.1, Sch.2

291. Sea Fishing (Enforcement of Community Licensing Measures) (North of Scotland Box) Order 1984
Art.3, applied: SSI 2008/101 Sch.1 Part 1, Sch.1 Part 2

NO.

1984–cont.

353. European Communities (Designation) Order 1984
revoked: SI 2008/301 Art.6

360. District Electoral Areas Commissioner (Northern Ireland) Order 1984
Art.2, applied: SI 2008/1741 Reg.100
Art.3, applied: SI 2008/1741 Reg.100

365. Double Taxation Relief (Taxes on Income) (New Zealand) Order 1984
Sch.1, added: SI 2008/1793 Sch.1
Sch.1, substituted: SI 2008/1793 Sch.1

467. Town and Country Planning (Control of Advertisements) (Scotland) Regulations 1984
Reg.24, see *Site Projects Ltd v Scottish Ministers* [2008] CSOH 57, 2008 S.L.T. 445 (OH), Lord Brodie
Reg.25, see *Site Projects Ltd v Scottish Ministers* [2008] CSOH 57, 2008 S.L.T. 445 (OH), Lord Brodie

552. Coroners Rules 1984
see *R. (on the application of Smith) v Oxfordshire Assistant Deputy Coroner* [2008] EWHC 694 (Admin), [2008] 3 W.L.R. 1284 (QBD (Admin)), Collins, J.
Part VI r.43, applied: SI 2008/1652 r.4
Part VI r.43, substituted: SI 2008/1652 r.2
Part VIII r.57A, added: SI 2008/1652 r.3
r.42, see *R. (on the application of Smith) v Oxfordshire Assistant Deputy Coroner* [2008] EWHC 694 (Admin), [2008] 3 W.L.R. 1284 (QBD (Admin)), Collins, J.

748. Road Transport (International Passenger Services) Regulations 1984
Reg.14, amended: SI 2008/1577 Reg.2

1111. Dangerous Wild Animals Act 1976 (Modification) Order 1984
revoked (in part): SSI 2008/302 Art.3

1325. Importation of Bovine Semen Regulations 1984
revoked (in part): SI 2008/1040 Sch.10 Part 1

1345. Residential Care Homes Regulations 1984
applied: 2008 c.14 s.17

1522. Undersized Scallops (West Coast) Order 1984
Art.2, applied: SSI 2008/101 Sch.1 Part 1

1523. Scallops (Irish Sea) (Prohibition of Fishing) Order 1984
Art.2, applied: SSI 2008/101 Sch.1 Part 1

1578. Nursing Homes and Mental Nursing Homes Regulations 1984
applied: 2008 c.14 s.17

1890. Freight Containers (Safety Convention) Regulations 1984
applied: SI 2008/736 Reg.4

NO.

1985

153. Cremation (Amendment) Regulations 1985
revoked (in part): SI 2008/2841 Sch.2

406. Merchant Shipping (Liner Conferences) (Mandatory Provisions) Regulations 1985
referred to: SI 2008/163 Reg.3

444. Falkland Islands Constitution Order 1985
revoked: SI 2008/2846 Art.3

705. Act of Sederunt (Consumer Credit Act 1974) 1985
Art.2, amended: SSI 2008/223 r.15
Art.5A, amended: SSI 2008/223 r.15
Art.6, amended: SSI 2008/223 r.15

754. Foreign Limitation Periods (Northern Ireland) Order 1985
Art.9, added: SI 2008/2986 Reg.5

805. Companies (Tables A to F) Regulations 1985
applied: SI 2008/2860 Sch.2 para.1
Sch.1 Part Table C para.8, amended: SI 2008/739 Reg.2
Sch.1 Part Table E para.2, revoked: SI 2008/739 Reg.3

956. European Communities (Designation) (No.2) Order 1985
revoked: SI 2008/301 Art.6

960. Films Co-Production Agreements Order 1985
Sch.1, substituted: SI 2008/1783 Art.2

967. Social Security (Industrial Injuries) (Prescribed Diseases) Regulations 1985
Sch.1 Part I, amended: SI 2008/14 Reg.2, SI 2008/1552 Reg.2

1064. Safety of Sports Grounds (Rugby Football Grounds) (Designation) Order 1985
Sch.1, amended: SI 2008/55 Art.3

1163. Napier College of Commerce and Technology (No.2) Regulations 1985
Reg.3, amended: SSI 2008/388 Art.3

1204. Betting, Gaming, Lotteries and Amusements (Northern Ireland) Order 1985
Art.2, amended: SI 2008/948 Sch.1 para.2

1205. Credit Unions (Northern Ireland) Order 1985
Art.2, applied: SI 2008/1741 Reg.25
Art.46, amended: SI 2008/948 Sch.1 para.2

1391. Registration of Fish Farming and Shellfish Farming Businesses Order 1985
Sch.4, substituted: SSI 2008/222 Sch.1
Sch.5, substituted: SSI 2008/222 Sch.2

1450. Hydrocarbon Oil (Mixing of Oils) Regulations 1985
Reg.2, amended: SI 2008/753 Reg.4
Reg.3, substituted: SI 2008/753 Reg.4
Reg.4, amended: SI 2008/753 Reg.4

NO.

1985–cont.

1450. Hydrocarbon Oil (Mixing of Oils) Regulations 1985–*cont.*
Reg.6, amended: SI 2008/753 Reg.4
Reg.7, amended: SI 2008/753 Reg.4
Reg.9, amended: SI 2008/753 Reg.4

1803. Harwich Harbour Revision Order 1985
Art.2, revoked: SI 2008/2359 Sch.1

1861. Artificial Insemination of Cattle (Animal Health) (England and Wales) Regulations 1985
applied: SI 2008/1040 Reg.43
revoked (in part): SI 2008/1040 Sch.10 Part 1

1925. Bankruptcy (Scotland) Regulations 1985
referred to: SSI 2008/82 Reg.22
revoked: SSI 2008/82 Reg.21

1986

24. Local Government Superannuation Regulations 1986
applied: SI 2008/239 Reg.51, Reg.69, Reg.72
referred to: SI 2008/239 Reg.79, Reg.81

26. Textile Products (Indications of Fibre Content) Regulations 1986
applied: SI 2008/15 Reg.4
referred to: SI 2008/6 Reg.2
Reg.4, amended: SI 2008/6 Reg.2
Reg.11, applied: SI 2008/1277 Sch.3 para.2, Sch.3 para.3
Sch.1 para.2, amended: SI 2008/6 Reg.2
Sch.1 para.7, amended: SI 2008/6 Reg.2
Sch.1 para.8, amended: SI 2008/6 Reg.2
Sch.2 Part I, revoked: SI 2008/6 Reg.2
Sch.2 Part II, revoked: SI 2008/6 Reg.2
Sch.3, revoked: SI 2008/6 Reg.2

59. Inshore Fishing (Salmon and Migratory Trout) (Prohibition of Gill Nets) (Scotland) Order 1986
Art.3, applied: SSI 2008/101 Sch.1 Part 1

183. Removal and Disposal of Vehicles Regulations 1986
Reg.5C, added: SI 2008/612 Reg.2
Reg.5C, applied: SI 2008/615 Reg.3

366. Pensions Appeal Tribunals (England and Wales) (Amendment) Rules 1986
revoked: SI 2008/2683 Sch.2

428. Heather and Grass etc (Burning) Regulations 1986
revoked (in part): SI 2008/1081 Reg.11

457. Residential Care Homes (Amendment) Regulations 1986
applied: 2008 c.14 s.17

590. Value Added Tax Tribunals Rules 1986
r.19, see *University College London v Revenue and Customs Commissioners* [2008] B.V.C. 2376 (V&DTr (London)), John Clark (Chairman)

NO.

1986–cont.

594. Education and Libraries (Northern Ireland) Order 1986
Art.2, applied: SI 2008/542 Reg.9, SI 2008/1741 Reg.42
Art.3, applied: 2008 c.4 Sch.3 para.5

595. Mental Health (Northern Ireland) Order 1986
applied: SI 2008/1216 Art.19
Art.44, amended: SI 2008/1216 Sch.5 para.5
Art.56, amended: SI 2008/1216 Sch.5 para.5
Art.79, amended: SI 2008/1216 Sch.5 para.5
Art.121, applied: SI 2008/1216 Sch.2 para.21
Art.122, applied: SI 2008/1216 Sch.2 para.11
Art.122, referred to: SI 2008/1062 Sch.1 para.1, Sch.1 para.2
Art.122, revoked: SI 2008/1769 Sch.1 para.17, Sch.3
Art.123, applied: SI 2008/1216 Sch.2 para.11
Art.123, referred to: SI 2008/1062 Sch.1 para.1, Sch.1 para.2
Art.123, revoked: SI 2008/1769 Sch.1 para.17, Sch.3

975. National Health Service (General Ophthalmic Services) Regulations 1986
applied: SI 2008/1187 Sch.1 para.8, SI 2008/1209 Reg.4, SI 2008/1700 Reg.6, Reg.7, Reg.9
referred to: SI 2008/1209 Reg.4, SI 2008/1700 Reg.6, Reg.8
revoked (in part): SI 2008/1700 Sch.2
Reg.2, amended: SI 2008/2552 Reg.2
Reg.6, applied: SI 2008/1209 Reg.4
Reg.10, amended: SI 2008/577 Reg.3
Reg.10, applied: SI 2008/1700 Reg.7
Reg.12, applied: SI 2008/1700 Reg.6
Reg.12, referred to: SI 2008/1700 Reg.6
Reg.13, amended: SI 2008/2552 Reg.2
Reg.16, applied: SI 2008/1700 Reg.8
Sch.1 para.2, amended: SI 2008/1514 Reg.2
Sch.1 para.2, revoked (in part): SI 2008/528 Sch.1 para.1
Sch.1 para.4, disapplied: SI 2008/1209 Reg.4
Sch.1 para.6, applied: SI 2008/1700 Reg.9
Sch.1 para.6ZA, disapplied: SI 2008/1209 Reg.4
Sch.1 para.8A, applied: SI 2008/1700 Reg.5
Sch.1 para.8A, varied: SI 2008/1700 Reg.4
Sch.1 para.8B, applied: SI 2008/1700 Reg.5
Sch.1 para.8B, varied: SI 2008/1700 Reg.4
Sch.1 para.8C, applied: SI 2008/1700 Reg.5
Sch.1 para.8C, varied: SI 2008/1700 Reg.4

1030. Public Service Vehicles (Traffic Regulation Conditions) Regulations 1986
Reg.3, amended: SSI 2008/2 Reg.2

1032. Companies (Northern Ireland) Order 1986
applied: 2008 c.2 s.15, SI 2008/948 Art.11, SI 2008/1185 Reg.4, Sch.1 para.44, SI 2008/1750 Sch.1 para.1, SI 2008/1886 Art.7, SI

NO.

1986–cont.

1032. Companies (Northern Ireland) Order 1986–*cont.*

applied: 2008 c.2 s.15–*cont.*
2008/2860 Sch.2 para.3, Sch.2 para.22, Sch.2 para.26, Sch.2 para.29, Sch.2 para.68, Sch.2 para.70, Sch.2 para.72, Sch.2 para.81, Sch.2 para.82, Sch.2 para.84, Sch.2 para.88, Sch.2 para.95, Sch.2 para.97, Sch.2 para.99, Sch.2 para.100, Sch.2 para.101, Sch.2 para.105, Sch.2 para.106, Sch.2 para.107, Sch.2 para.109, Sch.2 para.115, Sch.2 para.116
referred to: SI 2008/674 Art.6, SI 2008/1886 Art.6, SI 2008/1911 Reg.2
Part II, applied: SI 2008/2553 Art.5, SI 2008/2554 Art.5, SI 2008/2860 Sch.2 para.2
Part IV, applied: SI 2008/1886 Art.7
Part XXII, applied: SI 2008/2860 Sch.2 para.93
Art.4, applied: 2008 c.2 s.15
Art.10, amended: SI 2008/948 Sch.1 para.112
Art.10, revoked (in part): SI 2008/948 Sch.1 para.112, Sch.2
Art.15, applied: SI 2008/2860 Sch.2 para.110
Art.16, applied: SI 2008/2860 Sch.2 para.110
Art.17, applied: SI 2008/2860 Sch.2 para.110
Art.18, applied: SI 2008/2860 Sch.2 para.3
Art.19, applied: SI 2008/2860 Sch.2 para.3
Art.21, amended: SI 2008/948 Sch.1 para.113
Art.22, amended: SI 2008/948 Sch.1 para.114
Art.24, amended: SI 2008/948 Sch.1 para.115
Art.28, amended: SI 2008/948 Sch.1 para.116
Art.29, applied: SI 2008/2860 Sch.2 para.6, Sch.2 para.12
Art.30, applied: SI 2008/2860 Sch.2 para.11
Art.34, applied: SI 2008/2860 Sch.2 para.24
Art.38, applied: SI 2008/2860 Sch.2 para.19
Art.39, applied: SI 2008/2860 Sch.2 para.18
Art.40, applied: SI 2008/495 Reg.7
Art.41, applied: SI 2008/2860 Sch.2 para.20
Art.42, applied: SI 2008/2860 Sch.2 para.21
Art.45, applied: SI 2008/2860 Sch.2 para.15
Art.46A, referred to: SI 2008/948 Art.8
Art.48, applied: SI 2008/2860 Sch.2 para.16
Art.53, amended: SI 2008/948 Sch.1 para.117
Art.54, amended: SI 2008/948 Sch.1 para.118
Art.55, amended: SI 2008/948 Sch.1 para.119
Art.56, amended: SI 2008/948 Sch.1 para.120
Art.57, amended: SI 2008/948 Sch.1 para.121
Art.90, applied: SI 2008/2860 Sch.2 para.44, Sch.2 para.45
Art.90A, applied: SI 2008/2860 Sch.2 para.44, Sch.2 para.45

NO.

1986–cont.

1032. Companies (Northern Ireland) Order 1986–*cont.*

Art.94, applied: SI 2008/2860 Sch.2 para.56
Art.95, applied: SI 2008/2860 Sch.2 para.56
Art.98, applied: SI 2008/2860 Sch.2 para.47
Art.99, applied: SI 2008/2860 Sch.2 para.50, Sch.2 para.52, Sch.2 para.53, Sch.2 para.55
Art.100, applied: SI 2008/2860 Sch.2 para.49
Art.100, referred to: SI 2008/2860 Sch.2 para.51
Art.101, applied: SI 2008/2860 Sch.2 para.50
Art.105, applied: SI 2008/2860 Sch.2 para.52, Sch.2 para.53, Sch.2 para.54, Sch.2 para.55
Art.113, amended: SI 2008/948 Sch.1 para.122
Art.114, amended: SI 2008/948 Sch.1 para.123
Art.124, applied: SI 2008/2860 Sch.2 para.57
Art.130, applied: SI 2008/2860 Sch.2 para.67
Art.131, applied: SI 2008/2860 Sch.2 para.42
Art.132, applied: SI 2008/2860 Sch.2 para.41, Sch.2 para.59, Sch.2 para.60, Sch.2 para.71, Sch.2 para.74
Art.132, referred to: SI 2008/2860 Sch.2 para.71
Art.134, applied: SI 2008/2860 Sch.2 para.67
Art.136, amended: SI 2008/948 Sch.1 para.124
Art.138, applied: SI 2008/2860 Sch.2 para.48, Sch.2 para.62, Sch.2 para.63
Art.139, applied: SI 2008/2860 Sch.2 para.64, Sch.2 para.65, Sch.2 para.66
Art.141, amended: SI 2008/948 Sch.1 para.125
Art.146, amended: SI 2008/719 Reg.3
Art.146, applied: SI 2008/729 Reg.5, SI 2008/2860 Sch.2 para.68
Art.147, applied: SI 2008/729 Reg.3, Reg.4
Art.148, applied: SI 2008/729 Reg.5
Art.149, applied: SI 2008/729 Reg.3, Reg.5
Art.150, applied: SI 2008/1886 Art.7, SI 2008/2860 Sch.2 para.69
Art.153, amended: SI 2008/948 Sch.1 para.126
Art.153, applied: SI 2008/409 Sch.5 para.6, SI 2008/410 Sch.7 para.8
Art.156, applied: SI 2008/409 Sch.5 para.6, SI 2008/410 Sch.7 para.8, SI 2008/729 Reg.3, Reg.5, Reg.6, SI 2008/2860 Sch.2 para.70
Art.156, referred to: SI 2008/2860 Sch.2 para.70

NO.

1986–cont.

1032. Companies (Northern Ireland) Order 1986–*cont.*

Art.157, applied: SI 2008/729 Reg.5, SI 2008/2860 Sch.2 para.72

Art.158, referred to: SI 2008/2860 Sch.2 para.70

Art.159, amended: SI 2008/948 Sch.1 para.127

Art.159, applied: SI 2008/729 Reg.6

Art.160, applied: SI 2008/409 Sch.5 para.6, SI 2008/410 Sch.7 para.8

Art.162, amended: SI 2008/948 Sch.1 para.128

Art.162, applied: SI 2008/948 Art.9

Art.163, amended: SI 2008/948 Sch.1 para.129

Art.169, applied: SI 2008/2860 Sch.2 para.73

Art.172C, amended: SI 2008/948 Sch.1 para.130

Art.172D, applied: SI 2008/2860 Sch.2 para.79

Art.172F, amended: SI 2008/948 Sch.1 para.131

Art.174, applied: SI 2008/2860 Sch.2 para.76

Art.174, referred to: SI 2008/2860 Sch.2 para.75

Art.175, applied: SI 2008/2860 Sch.2 para.76

Art.175, referred to: SI 2008/2860 Sch.2 para.75

Art.176, referred to: SI 2008/2860 Sch.2 para.75

Art.177, referred to: SI 2008/2860 Sch.2 para.75

Art.179, applied: SI 2008/2860 Sch.2 para.77

Art.179A, applied: SI 2008/2860 Sch.2 para.80

Art.181, amended: SI 2008/948 Sch.1 para.132

Art.181, applied: SI 2008/2860 Sch.2 para.78

Art.182, amended: SI 2008/948 Sch.1 para.133, Sch.3 para.3, Sch.4

Art.182, applied: SI 2008/948 Art.9

Art.183, applied: SI 2008/2860 Sch.2 para.78

Art.188, applied: SI 2008/2860 Sch.2 para.78

Art.191, amended: SI 2008/948 Sch.1 para.134

Art.233, applied: SI 2008/1911 Reg.7

Art.240, amended: SI 2008/948 Sch.1 para.135, Sch.2

Art.249, applied: SI 2008/674 Sch.3 para.4

Art.253B, applied: SI 2008/623 Art.6

Art.257A, applied: SI 2008/674 Art.4

Art.257A, varied: SI 2008/674 Sch.2 para.2

Art.257B, applied: SI 2008/674 Art.4

NO.

1986–cont.

1032. Companies (Northern Ireland) Order 1986–*cont.*

Art.257B, varied: SI 2008/674 Sch.2 para.3

Art.257C, applied: SI 2008/674 Art.4

Art.257C, varied: SI 2008/674 Sch.2 para.4

Art.257D, applied: SI 2008/674 Art.4

Art.257D, varied: SI 2008/674 Sch.2 para.5

Art.257E, applied: SI 2008/674 Art.4

Art.257E, varied: SI 2008/674 Sch.2 para.6

Art.264, applied: SI 2008/651 Reg.4

Art.266, applied: 2008 c.2 s.15

Art.267, applied: 2008 c.2 s.15

Art.296, applied: SI 2008/2860 Sch.2 para.25, Sch.2 para.31

Art.297, amended: SI 2008/948 Sch.1 para.136

Art.298, amended: SI 2008/948 Sch.1 para.137

Art.298, applied: SI 2008/2860 Sch.2 para.31

Art.359, amended: SI 2008/948 Sch.1 para.138

Art.371, applied: SI 2008/2860 Sch.2 para.81

Art.372, amended: SI 2008/948 Sch.1 para.139

Art.372, applied: SI 2008/2860 Sch.2 para.81

Art.372A, applied: SI 2008/2860 Sch.2 para.81

Art.373, applied: SI 2008/2860 Sch.2 para.81

Art.388, amended: SI 2008/948 Sch.1 para.140

Art.388, applied: SI 2008/2860 Sch.2 para.14

Art.399, applied: SI 2008/1911 Reg.43

Art.407, applied: SI 2008/2860 Sch.2 para.83

Art.408, applied: SI 2008/2860 Sch.2 para.85

Art.411, applied: SI 2008/2860 Sch.2 para.87

Art.413, applied: SI 2008/2860 Sch.2 para.86

Art.438, applied: SI 2008/2860 Sch.2 para.114

Art.446D, added: SI 2008/948 Sch.1 para.141

Art.449, applied: SI 2008/2860 Sch.2 para.114

Art.602, referred to: SI 2008/2860 Sch.2 para.89

Art.603, applied: SI 2008/2860 Sch.2 para.91

Art.603A, applied: SI 2008/2860 Sch.2 para.91

Art.604, applied: SI 2008/2860 Sch.2 para.91

Art.604, referred to: SI 2008/2860 Sch.2 para.89

NO.

1986–cont.

1032. Companies (Northern Ireland) Order 1986–*cont.*
Art.634, amended: SI 2008/948 Sch.1 para.142
Art.650, amended: SI 2008/948 Sch.1 para.143
Art.651, amended: SI 2008/948 Sch.1 para.144
Art.654, amended: SI 2008/948 Sch.3 para.4
Art.656B, applied: SI 2008/2860 Sch.2 para.115
Art.657, applied: SI 2008/2860 Sch.2 para.94
Art.659A, applied: SI 2008/2860 Sch.2 para.111
Art.668, applied: SI 2008/2860 Sch.2 para.40
Sch.1, amended: SI 2008/948 Sch.1 para.145
Sch.2, revoked: SI 2008/948 Sch.1 para.146, Sch.2
Sch.4, referred to: SI 2008/948 Art.9
Sch.6, amended: SI 2008/948 Sch.1 para.147, Sch.2
Sch.6, revoked (in part): SI 2008/948 Sch.1 para.147, Sch.2
Sch.9, amended: SI 2008/948 Sch.1 para.148, Sch.2
Sch.9, revoked (in part): SI 2008/948 Sch.1 para.148, Sch.2
Sch.15D, amended: SI 2008/948 Sch.1 para.149, SI 2008/1277 Sch.2 para.79
Sch.15D, revoked (in part): SI 2008/1277 Sch.2 para.79, Sch.4 Part 2
Sch.20C, amended: SI 2008/948 Sch.1 para.150
Sch.20D, amended: SI 2008/948 Sch.1 para.151
Sch.23, applied: SI 2008/2860 Sch.2 para.116

1078. Road Vehicles (Construction and Use) Regulations 1986
Reg.5, revoked: SI 2008/1277 Sch.4 Part 2
Sch.7B Part I para.7, amended: SI 2008/1702 Reg.2

1110. Horticultural Development Council Order 1986
revoked: SI 2008/576 Sch.5 para.8

1245. Community Bus Regulations 1986
Reg.4, amended: SI 2008/1465 Reg.2

1335. Costs in Criminal Cases (General) Regulations 1986
Reg.3, amended: SI 2008/2448 Reg.3
Reg.3E, amended: SI 2008/2448 Reg.4
Reg.3F, amended: SI 2008/2448 Reg.5
Reg.4, amended: SI 2008/2448 Reg.6
Reg.5, amended: SI 2008/2448 Reg.7
Reg.6, amended: SI 2008/2448 Reg.8, Reg.9
Reg.8, amended: SI 2008/2448 Reg.10
Reg.14, amended: SI 2008/2448 Reg.11

NO.

1986–cont.

1335. Costs in Criminal Cases (General) Regulations 1986–*cont.*
Reg.16, amended: SI 2008/2448 Reg.12
Reg.17, amended: SI 2008/2448 Reg.13
Reg.20, amended: SI 2008/2448 Reg.14
Reg.21, amended: SI 2008/2448 Reg.15
Reg.24, amended: SI 2008/2448 Reg.16

1502. Economic Regulation of Airports (Designation) Order 1986
Art.2, amended: SI 2008/2702 Art.3

1510. Control of Pesticides Regulations 1986
applied: SSI 2008/100 Sch.4 Part 2, SSI 2008/159 Sch.3 Part 2

1544. Civil Aviation Authority (Economic Regulation of Airports) Regulations 1986
Reg.13, amended: SI 2008/2683 Sch.1 para.38

1629. Public Service Vehicles (Traffic Commissioners Publication and Inquiries) Regulations 1986
Reg.7, amended: SI 2008/2683 Sch.1 para.39

1648. Tyne and Wear Passenger Transport Executive (Exclusion of Bus Operating Powers) Order 1986
Art.2, revoked (in part): 2008 c.26 s.66

1649. Greater Manchester Passenger Transport Executive (Exclusion of Bus Operating Powers) Order 1986
Art.2, revoked (in part): 2008 c.26 s.66

1650. Merseyside Passenger Transport Executive (Exclusion of Bus Operating Powers) Order 1986
Art.2, revoked (in part): 2008 c.26 s.66

1651. South Yorkshire Passenger Transport Executive (Exclusion of Bus Operating Powers) Order 1986
Art.2, revoked (in part): 2008 c.26 s.66

1652. West Midlands Passenger Transport Executive (Exclusion of Bus Operating Powers) Order 1986
Art.2, revoked (in part): 2008 c.26 s.66

1653. West Yorkshire Passenger Transport Executive (Exclusion of Bus Operating Powers) Order 1986
Art.2, revoked (in part): 2008 c.26 s.66

1671. Public Service Vehicles (Registration of Local Services) Regulations 1986
Reg.12, amended: SI 2008/1470 Reg.2

1761. Medicines Act 1968 (Hearings by Persons Appointed) Rules 1986
r.6, revoked (in part): SI 2008/2683 Sch.1 para.40

1883. Criminal Justice (Northern Ireland) Order 1986
Sch.1, revoked: SI 2008/1769 Sch.1 para.18, Sch.3

NO.

1986–cont.

1911. Animals (Scientific Procedures) (Procedure for Representations) Rules 1986
r.8, revoked (in part): SI 2008/2683 Sch.1 para.41

1915. Insolvency (Scotland) Rules 1986
applied: SI 2008/2644 Art.19
disapplied: SI 2008/2644 Art.21
Part 2 r.2.1, amended: SI 2008/662 r.4
Part 2 r.2.39B, added: SI 2008/662 r.5
Part 2 r.2.39B, applied: SI 2008/346 Sch.1 para.8, SI 2008/2644 Art.15
Part 2 r.2.41, amended: SI 2008/662 r.6
Part 3 r.3.4, applied: SI 2008/2644 Art.20
Part 4 r.4.16, amended: SSI 2008/393 r.3
Part 4 r.4.17, amended: SSI 2008/393 r.4
Part 4 r.4.67, varied: SI 2008/346 Sch.1 para.8
Part 7 r.7.36, added: SSI 2008/393 r.5
Sch.1 para.18, amended: SSI 2008/393 r.6

1925. Insolvency Rules 1986
applied: SI 2008/2644 Art.19
disapplied: SI 2008/2644 Art.21, SI 2008/2674 Art.22
see *Courts Plc (In Liquidation), Re* [2008] EWHC 2339 (Ch), [2008] B.C.C. 917 (Ch D (Companies Ct)), Blackburne, J.; see *Day v Haine* [2008] EWCA Civ 626, [2008] B.C.C. 845 (CA (Civ Div)), Thomas, L.J.; see *Halabi v Camden LBC* [2008] EWHC 322 (Ch), [2008] B.P.I.R. 370 (Ch D), John Jarvis Q.C.; see *Smedley v Brittain* [2008] B.P.I.R. 219 (Ch D), Registrar Nicholls; see *Stone v Vallance* [2008] B.P.I.R. 236 (Ch D), Registrar Simmonds
Part 2 r.2.50, applied: SI 2008/2644 Art.20, SI 2008/2674 Art.21
Part 2 r.2.67, applied: SI 2008/2644 Art.15, SI 2008/2674 Art.16
Part 2 r.2.67, varied: SI 2008/346 Sch.1 para.7
Part 4, see *First Independent Factors and Finance Ltd v Mountford* [2008] EWHC 835 (Ch), [2008] B.C.C. 598 (Ch D (Birmingham)), Lewison, J.
Part 4 r.4.18, varied: SI 2008/346 Sch.1 para.7
Part 4 r.4.21A, amended: SI 2008/737 r.7
Part 4 r.4.27, amended: SI 2008/737 r.7
Part 4 r.4.28, amended: SI 2008/737 r.7
Part 4 r.4.30, amended: SI 2008/737 r.7
Part 4 r.4.36, amended: SI 2008/737 r.7
Part 4 r.4.37, amended: SI 2008/737 r.7
Part 4 r.4.41, amended: SI 2008/737 r.7
Part 4 r.4.52, amended: SI 2008/737 r.7
Part 4 r.4.61, amended: SI 2008/737 r.7
Part 4 r.4.62, amended: SI 2008/737 r.7
Part 4 r.4.78, amended: SI 2008/737 r.7
Part 4 r.4.97, amended: SI 2008/737 r.7
Part 4 r.4.106, amended: SI 2008/737 r.7
Part 4 r.4.119, amended: SI 2008/737 r.7
Part 4 r.4.120, amended: SI 2008/737 r.7
Part 4 r.4.130, amended: SI 2008/737 r.7
Part 4 r.4.131, amended: SI 2008/737 r.7

NO.

1986–cont.

1925. Insolvency Rules 1986–*cont.*
Part 4 r.4.143, amended: SI 2008/737 r.7
Part 4 r.4.148A, amended: SI 2008/737 r.7
Part 4 r.4.150, amended: SI 2008/737 r.7
Part 4 r.4.169, amended: SI 2008/737 r.7
Part 4 r.4.170, amended: SI 2008/737 r.7
Part 4 r.4.180, see *Lomax Leisure Ltd (In Liquidation) v Miller* [2007] EWHC 2508 (Ch), [2008] 1 B.C.L.C. 262 (Ch D), Mark Cawson Q.C.
Part 4 r.4.182, see *Lomax Leisure Ltd (In Liquidation) v Miller* [2007] EWHC 2508 (Ch), [2008] 1 B.C.L.C. 262 (Ch D), Mark Cawson Q.C.
Part 4 r.4.186, amended: SI 2008/737 r.7
Part 4 r.4.207, amended: SI 2008/737 r.7
Part 4 r.4.214, amended: SI 2008/737 r.7
Part 4 r.4.217, amended: SI 2008/737 r.7
Part 4 r.4.218, amended: SI 2008/737 r.4
Part 4 r.4.218, varied: SI 2008/346 Sch.1 para.7
Part 4 r.4.218A, added: SI 2008/737 r.5
Part 4 r.4.218A, varied: SI 2008/346 Sch.1 para.7
Part 4 r.4.218B, added: SI 2008/737 r.5
Part 4 r.4.218B, varied: SI 2008/346 Sch.1 para.7
Part 4 r.4.218C, added: SI 2008/737 r.5
Part 4 r.4.218C, varied: SI 2008/346 Sch.1 para.7
Part 4 r.4.218D, added: SI 2008/737 r.5
Part 4 r.4.218D, varied: SI 2008/346 Sch.1 para.7
Part 4 r.4.218E, added: SI 2008/737 r.5
Part 4 r.4.218E, varied: SI 2008/346 Sch.1 para.7
Part 4 r.4.219, amended: SI 2008/737 r.7
Part 4 r.4.219, varied: SI 2008/346 Sch.1 para.7
Part 4 r.4.230, see *First Independent Factors and Finance Ltd v Mountford* [2008] EWHC 835 (Ch), [2008] B.C.C. 598 (Ch D (Birmingham)), Lewison, J.
Part 5 r.5.22, see *Monecor (London) Ltd v Ahmed* [2008] B.P.I.R. 458 (Ch D), Paul Chaisty Q.C.
Part 6 r.6.3, see *Johnson v Tandrige DC* [2007] EWHC 3325 (Ch), [2008] B.P.I.R. 405 (Ch D), Judge Roger Kaye Q.C.
Part 6 r.6.11, see *Johnson v Tandrige DC* [2007] EWHC 3325 (Ch), [2008] B.P.I.R. 405 (Ch D), Judge Roger Kaye Q.C.
Part 6 r.6.132, see *Donaldson v O'Sullivan* [2008] EWHC 387 (Ch), [2008] B.C.C. 328 (Ch D (Bristol)), Judge Havelock-Allan Q.C.
Part 6 r.6.211, see *Halabi v Camden LBC* [2008] EWHC 322 (Ch), [2008] B.P.I.R. 370 (Ch D), John Jarvis Q.C.

NO.

1986–cont.

1925. Insolvency Rules 1986–*cont.*

Part 6 r.6.235A, see *Smedley v Brittain* [2008] B.P.I.R. 219 (Ch D), Registrar Nicholls

Part 7 r.7.34, amended: SI 2008/737 r.7

Part 9 r.9.6, amended: SI 2008/737 r.7

Part 11 r.11.2, see *Lomax Leisure Ltd (In Liquidation) v Miller* [2007] EWHC 2508 (Ch), [2008] 1 B.C.L.C. 262 (Ch D), Mark Cawson Q.C.

Part 11 r.11.4, see *Lomax Leisure Ltd (In Liquidation) v Miller* [2007] EWHC 2508 (Ch), [2008] 1 B.C.L.C. 262 (Ch D), Mark Cawson Q.C.

Part 11 r.11.5, see *Lomax Leisure Ltd (In Liquidation) v Miller* [2007] EWHC 2508 (Ch), [2008] 1 B.C.L.C. 262 (Ch D), Mark Cawson Q.C.

Part 12 r.12.1, enabled: SI 2008/670

Part 4, see *First Independent Factors and Finance Ltd v Mountford* [2008] EWHC 835 (Ch), [2008] B.C.C. 598 (Ch D (Birmingham)), Lewison, J.

r.4.180, see *Lomax Leisure Ltd (In Liquidation) v Miller* [2007] EWHC 2508 (Ch), [2008] 1 B.C.L.C. 262 (Ch D), Mark Cawson Q.C.

r.4.182, see *Lomax Leisure Ltd (In Liquidation) v Miller* [2007] EWHC 2508 (Ch), [2008] 1 B.C.L.C. 262 (Ch D), Mark Cawson Q.C.

r.4.230, see *First Independent Factors and Finance Ltd v Mountford* [2008] EWHC 835 (Ch), [2008] B.C.C. 598 (Ch D (Birmingham)), Lewison, J.

r.5.22, see *Monecor (London) Ltd v Ahmed* [2008] B.P.I.R. 458 (Ch D), Paul Chaisty Q.C.

r.6.3, see *Johnson v Tandrige DC* [2007] EWHC 3325 (Ch), [2008] B.P.I.R. 405 (Ch D), Judge Roger Kaye Q.C.

r.6.11, see *Johnson v Tandrige DC* [2007] EWHC 3325 (Ch), [2008] B.P.I.R. 405 (Ch D), Judge Roger Kaye Q.C.

r.6.132, see *Donaldson v O'Sullivan* [2008] EWHC 387 (Ch), [2008] B.C.C. 328 (Ch D (Bristol)), Judge Havelock-Allan Q.C.

r.6.211, see *Halabi v Camden LBC* [2008] EWHC 322 (Ch), [2008] B.P.I.R. 370 (Ch D), John Jarvis Q.C.

r.6.235A, see *Smedley v Brittain* [2008] B.P.I.R. 219 (Ch D), Registrar Nicholls

r.7.31, see *Franbar Holdings Ltd v Patel* [2008] EWHC 1534 (Ch), [2008] B.C.C. 885 (Ch D), William Trower QC

r.11.2, see *Lomax Leisure Ltd (In Liquidation) v Miller* [2007] EWHC 2508 (Ch), [2008] 1 B.C.L.C. 262 (Ch D), Mark Cawson Q.C.

r.11.4, see *Lomax Leisure Ltd (In Liquidation) v Miller* [2007] EWHC 2508 (Ch), [2008] 1 B.C.L.C. 262 (Ch D), Mark Cawson Q.C.

r.11.5, see *Lomax Leisure Ltd (In Liquidation) v Miller* [2007] EWHC 2508 (Ch), [2008] 1 B.C.L.C. 262 (Ch D), Mark Cawson Q.C.

NO.

1986–cont.

1925. Insolvency Rules 1986–*cont.*

r.12.3, see *Day v Haine* [2007] EWHC 2691 (Ch), [2008] B.C.C. 199 (Ch D (Companies Ct)), Sir Donald Rattee; see *Day v Haine* [2008] EWCA Civ 626, [2008] B.C.C. 845 (CA (Civ Div)), Thomas, L.J.

r.12.12, see *Krug International (UK) Ltd, Re* [2008] EWHC 2256 (Ch), [2008] B.P.I.R. 1512 (Ch D (Birmingham)), Judge Purle Q.C.

r.13.7, see *Krug International (UK) Ltd, Re* [2008] EWHC 2256 (Ch), [2008] B.P.I.R. 1512 (Ch D (Birmingham)), Judge Purle Q.C.

r.13.12, see *Day v Haine* [2007] EWHC 2691 (Ch), [2008] B.C.C.199 (Ch D (Companies Ct)), Sir Donald Rattee; see *Day v Haine* [2008] EWCA Civ 626, [2008] B.C.C. 845 (CA (Civ Div)),Thomas, L.J.

Sch.4, amended: SI 2008/737 r.6, Sch.1

1960. Statutory Maternity Pay (General) Regulations 1986

Reg.6, amended: SI 2008/632 Art.10

Reg.7, amended: SI 2008/2683 Sch.1 para.42

Reg.25A, amended: SI 2008/1554 Reg.46

2092. Local Government Reorganisation (Preservation of Right to Buy) Order 1986

Art.11, amended: SI 2008/2831 Sch.1 para.2

2128. Passenger and Goods Vehicles (Recording Equipment) (Approval of fitters and workshops) (Fees) Regulations 1986

Reg.3, amended: SI 2008/1581 Reg.2

2194. Housing (Right to Buy) (Prescribed Forms) Regulations 1986

Sch.1, amended: SI 2008/2831 Sch.1 para.3

Sch.1, varied: SI 2008/2839 Sch.1 para.1

2195. Housing (Right to Buy) (Service Charges) Order 1986

Art.2, amended: SI 2008/533 Art.2

2215. Local Elections (Parishes and Communities) Rules 1986

r.8, varied: SI 2008/423 Art.10, SI 2008/425 Art.8

2297. Act of Sederunt (Sheriff Court Company Insolvency Rules) 1986

Part II r.10, amended: SSI 2008/223 r.10

Part IV r.18, amended: SSI 2008/223 r.10

r.3, amended: SSI 2008/223 r.10

r.3A, added: SSI 2008/223 r.12

r.3B, added: SSI 2008/223 r.12

1987

37. Dangerous Substances in Harbour Areas Regulations 1987

Part IX, applied: SI 2008/736 Reg.11

Sch.6 para.6, amended: SI 2008/960 Sch.3

NO.

1987–cont.

257. Police Pensions Regulations 1987

Reg.1, amended: SI 2008/1887 Reg.11, SSI 2008/387 Reg.11

Reg.1, revoked (in part): SI 2008/1887 Reg.11

Reg.1, amended: SI 2008/1887 Reg.17, SSI 2008/387 Reg.19

Reg.1, amended: SI 2008/1887 Reg.18, SSI 2008/387 Reg.21

Reg.2, amended: SI 2008/1887 Reg.12, SSI 2008/387 Reg.12

Reg.2, applied: SI 2008/649 Reg.4

Reg.2A, added: SI 2008/1887 Reg.13, SSI 2008/387 Reg.13

Reg.3, revoked (in part): SSI 2008/387 Reg.17

Reg.3, amended: SI 2008/1887 Reg.19, SSI 2008/387 Reg.22

Reg.3A, revoked (in part): SSI 2008/387 Reg.20

Reg.4, amended: SI 2008/1887 Reg.4, SSI 2008/387 Reg.4

Reg.6, amended: SI 2008/1887 Reg.5, SSI 2008/387 Reg.5

Reg.7, amended: SI 2008/1887 Reg.14, SSI 2008/387 Reg.14

Reg.8, amended: SI 2008/1887 Reg.15, SSI 2008/387 Reg.15

Reg.8A, amended: SSI 2008/387 Reg.18

Reg.8A, revoked (in part): SSI 2008/387 Reg.18

Reg.10, amended: SI 2008/1887 Reg.16, SSI 2008/387 Reg.16

Reg.11, see *Lothian and Borders Police Board v Smillie* [2008] CSOH 131, 2008 S.L.T. 1081 (OH), Lord Matthews

Reg.12, see *R. (on the application of Ashton) v Police Medical Appeal Board* [2008] EWHC 1833 (Admin), [2008] Pens. L.R. 391 (QBD (Admin)), Charles, J.

Reg.16, amended: SI 2008/1887 Reg.6, SSI 2008/387 Reg.6

Reg.16, substituted: SSI 2008/387 Reg.6

Reg.17, amended: SI 2008/1887 Reg.7, SSI 2008/387 Reg.7

Reg.17, revoked (in part): SSI 2008/387 Reg.7

Reg.18, amended: SI 2008/1887 Reg.8, SSI 2008/387 Reg.8

Reg.18, substituted: SI 2008/1887 Reg.9, SSI 2008/387 Reg.9

Reg.19, amended: SI 2008/1887 Reg.10, SSI 2008/387 Reg.10

Sch.A, see *R. (on the application of Ashton) v Police Medical Appeal Board* [2008] EWHC 1833 (Admin), [2008] Pens. L.R. 391 (QBD (Admin)), Charles, J.

Sch.A, added: SI 2008/1887 Reg.20

Sch.A, amended: SI 2008/1887 Reg.20, SSI 2008/387 Reg.23

Sch.B Part III para.5, amended: SI 2008/1887 Reg.21, SSI 2008/387 Reg.24

NO.

1987–cont.

257. Police Pensions Regulations 1987–*cont.*

Sch.B Part VI para.1, amended: SI 2008/1887 Reg.22, SSI 2008/387 Reg.25

Sch.F Part I para.1, amended: SI 2008/1887 Reg.23, SSI 2008/387 Reg.26

390. Artificial Insemination (Cattle and Pigs) (Fees) Regulations 1987

Reg.2, amended: SI 2008/1040 Reg.44

Reg.3, amended: SI 2008/1040 Reg.44

Reg.3, revoked (in part): SI 2008/1040 Reg.44

Reg.4, amended: SI 2008/1040 Reg.44

Sch.1, revoked (in part): SI 2008/1040 Reg.44

463. Public Order (Northern Ireland) Order 1987

Art.22, see *Police Service of Northern Ireland v McClure* [2008] NICA 31, [2008] N.I. 49 (CA (NI)), Kerr, L.C.J.

Art.22, amended: SI 2008/1216 Art.90

755. Secure Tenancies (Notices) Regulations 1987

Sch.1 Part I, varied: SI 2008/2839 Sch.1 para.1

Sch.1 Part II, varied: SI 2008/2839 Sch.1 para.1

Sch.1 Part III, varied: SI 2008/2839 Sch.1 para.1

764. Town and Country Planning (Use Classes) Order 1987

applied: SI 2008/1261 Sch.6 para.2, SI 2008/1430 Reg.12

see *McDonalds Real Estate Ltd Liability Partnership v Arundel Corp* [2008] EWHC 377 (Ch), [2008] 30 E.G. 84 (Ch D), Lewison, J.; see *Winchester City Council v Secretary of State for Communities and Local Government* [2007] EWHC 2303 (Admin), [2008] 1 P. & C.R. 15 (QBD (Admin)), Judge Mole Q.C.

Art.2, see *Winchester City Council v Secretary of State for Communities and Local Government* [2007] EWHC 2303 (Admin), [2008] 1 P. & C.R. 15 (QBD (Admin)), Judge Mole Q.C.

Art.3, see *Winchester City Council v Secretary of State for Communities and Local Government* [2007] EWHC 2303 (Admin), [2008] 1 P. & C.R. 15 (QBD (Admin)), Judge Mole Q.C.

851. Police Regulations 1987

Reg.72, see *Holmes v South Yorkshire Police Authority* [2008] EWCA Civ 51, [2008] H.L.R. 33 (CA (Civ Div)), Sedley, L.J.

904. Artificial Insemination of Cattle (Advertising Controls etc.) (Great Britain) Regulations 1987

revoked (in part): SI 2008/1040 Sch.10 Part 1

NO.

1987–cont.

1110. Personal Pension Schemes (Disclosure of Information) Regulations 1987
Reg.1, revoked (in part): SI 2008/2301 Sch.1 para.1

1112. Personal Pension Schemes (Transfer Values) Regulations 1987
Reg.1, amended: SI 2008/1050 Sch.2 para.1
Reg.3, amended: SI 2008/2450 Reg.2
Reg.3, substituted: SI 2008/1050 Sch.2 para.1
Reg.4, substituted: SI 2008/1050 Sch.2 para.1

1208. Heather and Grass etc (Burning) (Amendment) Regulations 1987
revoked (in part): SI 2008/1081 Reg.11

1806. Value Added Tax (Tour Operators) Order 1987
see *Dunwood Travel Ltd v Revenue and Customs Commissioners* [2007] EWHC 319 (Ch), [2008] S.T.C. 412 (Ch D), Mann, J.

1850. Local Government Superannuation (Scotland) Regulations 1987
applied: SSI 2008/228 Reg.47, Reg.63, Reg.66, SSI 2008/229 Reg.12
referred to: SSI 2008/228 Reg.74, Reg.76, SSI 2008/229 Reg.5, Reg.14
revoked: SSI 2008/229 Sch.1
Part E reg E.2, applied: SSI 2008/228 Reg.13
Part J, applied: SSI 2008/229 Reg.15
Part J reg J.6, applied: SSI 2008/229 Reg.15

1967. Income Support (General) Regulations 1987
applied: SI 2008/794 Sch.6 para.9
referred to: SI 2008/632 Art.16
Part V, amended: SI 2008/2111 Reg.2
Part V, revoked: SI 2008/2111 Reg.2
Reg.2, amended: SI 2008/698 Reg.2, SI 2008/1554 Reg.2, SI 2008/2767 Reg.2, SI 2008/3157 Reg.2
Reg.4, amended: SI 2008/2767 Reg.2
Reg.4ZA, amended: SI 2008/1826 Reg.2
Reg.5, amended: SI 2008/698 Reg.2
Reg.6, amended: SI 2008/1554 Reg.2
Reg.6, applied: SI 2008/794 Sch.7 para.13, Sch.9 para.51
Reg.6, referred to: SI 2008/794 Sch.6 para.15
Reg.13, amended: SI 2008/698 Reg.2, SI 2008/3157 Reg.2
Reg.14, amended: SI 2008/1554 Reg.2
Reg.17, referred to: SI 2008/632 Art.16
Reg.18, referred to: SI 2008/632 Art.16
Reg.21, referred to: SI 2008/632 Art.16
Reg.25, amended: SI 2008/2111 Reg.2
Reg.25A, revoked: SI 2008/2111 Reg.2
Reg.29, amended: SI 2008/698 Reg.2
Reg.29, revoked (in part): SI 2008/698 Reg.2
Reg.30, amended: SI 2008/698 Reg.2
Reg.31, amended: SI 2008/1554 Reg.2, SI 2008/2767 Reg.2

NO.

1987–cont.

1967. Income Support (General) Regulations 1987–*cont.*
Reg.31, revoked (in part): SI 2008/2767 Reg.2
Reg.32, amended: SI 2008/1554 Reg.2, SI 2008/2767 Reg.2
Reg.35, revoked (in part): SI 2008/698 Reg.2
Reg.40, amended: SI 2008/1554 Reg.2, SI 2008/1599 Reg.2
Reg.42, amended: SI 2008/698 Reg.2, SI 2008/2767 Reg.2, SI 2008/3157 Reg.2
Reg.48, amended: SI 2008/2767 Reg.2
Reg.48, revoked (in part): SI 2008/698 Reg.2
Reg.51, amended: SI 2008/698 Reg.2, SI 2008/2767 Reg.2, SI 2008/3157 Reg.2
Reg.51A, revoked (in part): SI 2008/2767 Reg.2
Reg.54, amended: SI 2008/2111 Reg.2
Reg.55, amended: SI 2008/2111 Reg.2
Reg.57, substituted: SI 2008/2111 Reg.2
Reg.58, amended: SI 2008/2111 Reg.2
Reg.59, amended: SI 2008/2111 Reg.2
Reg.60, revoked: SI 2008/2111 Reg.2
Reg.61, amended: SI 2008/2767 Reg.2, SI 2008/3157 Reg.2
Reg.62, amended: SI 2008/1599 Reg.2
Reg.66A, amended: SI 2008/1599 Reg.2, SI 2008/2767 Reg.2
Reg.66A, revoked (in part): SI 2008/2767 Reg.2
Reg.71, referred to: SI 2008/632 Art.16
Reg.72, amended: SI 2008/698 Reg.2, SI 2008/1554 Reg.2, SI 2008/2767 Reg.2
Reg.73, amended: SI 2008/1554 Reg.2
Reg.75, amended: SI 2008/1554 Reg.2
Sch.1B, referred to: SI 2008/3051 Reg.2
Sch.1B para.1, applied: SI 2008/3051 Reg.13
Sch.1B para.1, referred to: SI 2008/3051 Sch.1 para.1, Sch.1 para.2, Sch.1 para.6, Sch.1 para.8
Sch.1B para.1, substituted: SI 2008/3051 Reg.2, Reg.3, Reg.4
Sch.1B para.4, referred to: SI 2008/794 Reg.43, Sch.6 para.15
Sch.1B para.5, referred to: SI 2008/794 Sch.6 para.15
Sch.1B para.26, revoked: SI 2008/698 Reg.2
Sch.1B para.27, revoked: SI 2008/698 Reg.2
Sch.1B para.28, amended: SI 2008/3157 Reg.2
Sch.2 Part I, referred to: SI 2008/632 Art.16
Sch.2 Part I para.1, substituted: SI 2008/632 Sch.2
Sch.2 Part I para.1A, substituted: SI 2008/632 Sch.2
Sch.2 Part I para.1ZA, substituted: SI 2008/632 Sch.2
Sch.2 Part I para.2, substituted: SI 2008/632 Sch.2

NO.

1987–cont.

1967. Income Support (General) Regulations 1987–*cont.*

Sch.2 Part I para.2A, substituted: SI 2008/632 Sch.2
Sch.2 Part II para.3, amended: SI 2008/632 Art.16
Sch.2 Part III para.7, amended: SI 2008/698 Reg.2
Sch.2 Part III para.11, applied: SI 2008/794 Reg.7
Sch.2 Part III para.11A, applied: SI 2008/794 Reg.7
Sch.2 Part III para.12, applied: SI 2008/794 Reg.7, Sch.6 para.1
Sch.2 Part III para.13A, referred to: SI 2008/632 Art.16
Sch.2 Part III para.14, referred to: SI 2008/632 Art.16
Sch.2 Part IV, referred to: SI 2008/632 Art.16
Sch.2 Part IV para.15, substituted: SI 2008/632 Sch.3
Sch.3, applied: SI 2008/794 Sch.6 para.20
Sch.3 para.1, amended: SI 2008/1554 Reg.2
Sch.3 para.1, varied: SI 2008/3195 Reg.10
Sch.3 para.1A, amended: SI 2008/1554 Reg.2
Sch.3 para.1A, referred to: SI 2008/3195 Reg.8
Sch.3 para.3, amended: SI 2008/2767 Reg.2
Sch.3 para.4, amended: SI 2008/698 Reg.2, SI 2008/1554 Reg.2, SI 2008/2767 Reg.2
Sch.3 para.4, applied: SI 2008/794 Sch.6 para.6
Sch.3 para.5A, applied: SI 2008/794 Sch.6 para.6
Sch.3 para.6, amended: SI 2008/1554 Reg.2
Sch.3 para.6, applied: SI 2008/3195 Reg.3
Sch.3 para.6, referred to: SI 2008/3195 Reg.3
Sch.3 para.6, varied: SI 2008/3195 Reg.5, Reg.10
Sch.3 para.7, applied: SI 2008/794 Sch.6 para.20
Sch.3 para.8, amended: SI 2008/1554 Reg.2
Sch.3 para.8, applied: SI 2008/3195 Reg.3
Sch.3 para.8, referred to: SI 2008/3195 Reg.3
Sch.3 para.8, varied: SI 2008/3195 Reg.5, Reg.10
Sch.3 para.9, varied: SI 2008/3195 Reg.10
Sch.3 para.10, varied: SI 2008/3195 Reg.10
Sch.3 para.11, varied: SI 2008/3195 Reg.5, Reg.10
Sch.3 para.12, amended: SI 2008/3195 Reg.2
Sch.3 para.12, revoked (in part): SI 2008/3195 Reg.2
Sch.3 para.13, varied: SI 2008/3195 Reg.10
Sch.3 para.14, amended: SI 2008/698 Reg.2, SI 2008/1554 Reg.2, SI 2008/2767 Reg.2

NO.

1987–cont.

1967. Income Support (General) Regulations 1987–*cont.*

Sch.3 para.14, varied: SI 2008/3195 Reg.5, Reg.10
Sch.3 para.15, applied: SI 2008/794 Sch.6 para.3, SI 2008/3195 Reg.12
Sch.3 para.16, amended: SI 2008/2767 Reg.2
Sch.3 para.16, applied: SI 2008/794 Sch.6 para.3, SI 2008/3195 Reg.12
Sch.3 para.17, applied: SI 2008/794 Sch.6 para.3
Sch.3 para.18, amended: SI 2008/632 Art.16, SI 2008/1554 Reg.2, SI 2008/2767 Reg.2
Sch.7, see *R. (on the application of M) v Secretary of State for Work and Pensions* [2008] UKHL 63, [2008] 3 W.L.R. 1023 (HL), Lord Hope of Craighead
Sch.7, amended: SI 2008/1554 Reg.2
Sch.7, referred to: SI 2008/632 Art.16
Sch.8 para.4, amended: SI 2008/1554 Reg.2
Sch.9 para.4, amended: SI 2008/698 Reg.2
Sch.9 para.5, substituted: SI 2008/3157 Reg.2
Sch.9 para.5C, added: SI 2008/3140 Reg.2
Sch.9 para.6, amended: SI 2008/3157 Reg.2
Sch.9 para.7, amended: SI 2008/1554 Reg.2, SI 2008/3157 Reg.2
Sch.9 para.11, amended: SI 2008/3157 Reg.2
Sch.9 para.13, amended: SI 2008/1554 Reg.2
Sch.9 para.16, amended: SI 2008/3157 Reg.2
Sch.9 para.21, amended: SI 2008/2767 Reg.2
Sch.9 para.25, amended: SI 2008/3157 Reg.2
Sch.9 para.25, revoked (in part): SI 2008/3157 Reg.2
Sch.9 para.27, amended: SI 2008/3157 Reg.2
Sch.9 para.28, substituted: SI 2008/698 Reg.2
Sch.9 para.31, amended: SI 2008/3157 Reg.2
Sch.9 para.33, amended: SI 2008/3157 Reg.2
Sch.9 para.39, amended: SI 2008/2767 Reg.2
Sch.9 para.41, revoked: SI 2008/698 Reg.2
Sch.9 para.42, revoked: SI 2008/698 Reg.2
Sch.9 para.45, revoked: SI 2008/2767 Reg.2
Sch.9 para.46, substituted: SI 2008/698 Reg.2
Sch.9 para.47, revoked: SI 2008/3157 Reg.2
Sch.9 para.48, substituted: SI 2008/3157 Reg.2
Sch.9 para.49, substituted: SI 2008/3157 Reg.2
Sch.9 para.50, amended: SI 2008/3157 Reg.2

NO.

1987–cont.

1967. Income Support (General) Regulations 1987–*cont.*

Sch.9 para.52, substituted: SI 2008/3157 Reg.2
Sch.9 para.53, substituted: SI 2008/3157 Reg.2
Sch.9 para.54, substituted: SI 2008/3157 Reg.2
Sch.9 para.56, amended: SI 2008/3157 Reg.2
Sch.9 para.57, revoked: SI 2008/3157 Reg.2
Sch.9 para.73, amended: SI 2008/2111 Reg.2
Sch.9 para.76, amended: SI 2008/3157 Reg.2
Sch.10 para.7, amended: SI 2008/698 Reg.2, SI 2008/1554 Reg.2
Sch.10 para.10, amended: SI 2008/698 Reg.2
Sch.10 para.17, substituted: SI 2008/698 Reg.2
Sch.10 para.18, amended: SI 2008/3157 Reg.2
Sch.10 para.19, amended: SI 2008/3157 Reg.2
Sch.10 para.22, amended: SI 2008/2767 Reg.2
Sch.10 para.29, amended: SI 2008/2767 Reg.2
Sch.10 para.32, revoked: SI 2008/698 Reg.2
Sch.10 para.33, revoked: SI 2008/698 Reg.2
Sch.10 para.36, amended: SI 2008/698 Reg.2
Sch.10 para.38, substituted: SI 2008/3157 Reg.2
Sch.10 para.39, substituted: SI 2008/3157 Reg.2
Sch.10 para.40, amended: SI 2008/3157 Reg.2
Sch.10 para.41, substituted: SI 2008/3157 Reg.2
Sch.10 para.47, revoked: SI 2008/3157 Reg.2
Sch.10 para.48, revoked: SI 2008/3157 Reg.2
Sch.10 para.49, revoked: SI 2008/3157 Reg.2
Sch.10 para.63, amended: SI 2008/3157 Reg.2
Sch.10 para.65, amended: SI 2008/3157 Reg.2
Sch.10 para.66, amended: SI 2008/3157 Reg.2

1968. Social Security (Claims and Payments) Regulations 1987

Reg.2, amended: SI 2008/1554 Reg.10
Reg.3, amended: SI 2008/441 Reg.2, SI 2008/1554 Reg.11, SI 2008/2667 Reg.2
Reg.4, amended: SI 2008/1554 Reg.12, SI 2008/2667 Reg.2
Reg.4, applied: SI 2008/794 Sch.6 para.15
Reg.4G, added: SI 2008/1554 Reg.13
Reg.4H, added: SI 2008/1554 Reg.13

NO.

1987–cont.

1968. Social Security (Claims and Payments) Regulations 1987–*cont.*

Reg.4I, added: SI 2008/1554 Reg.13
Reg.4I, applied: SI 2008/794 Reg.144
Reg.6, amended: SI 2008/1554 Reg.14, SI 2008/2667 Reg.2, SI 2008/2683 Sch.1 para.43
Reg.7, amended: SI 2008/1554 Reg.15
Reg.7, applied: SI 2008/794 Reg.106
Reg.9, applied: SI 2008/795 Reg.2
Reg.10, amended: SI 2008/1554 Reg.16
Reg.11, amended: SI 2008/1554 Reg.17
Reg.13, amended: SI 2008/1554 Reg.18
Reg.16, amended: SI 2008/1554 Reg.19
Reg.16A, amended: SI 2008/1554 Reg.20
Reg.19, amended: SI 2008/2424 Reg.2
Reg.22, amended: SI 2008/2667 Reg.2
Reg.26C, added: SI 2008/1554 Reg.21
Reg.32, amended: SI 2008/1554 Reg.22, SI 2008/1599 Reg.3
Reg.33, applied: SI 2008/2265 Reg.5, SI 2008/2682 Reg.6
Reg.36, amended: SI 2008/1554 Reg.23
Reg.38, applied: SI 2008/794 Reg.161
Sch.1 Part I, amended: SI 2008/1554 Reg.24
Sch.1 Part I, applied: SI 2008/795 Reg.2
Sch.4, amended: SI 2008/1554 Reg.25, SI 2008/2424 Reg.2
Sch.9 para.1, amended: SI 2008/1554 Reg.26, SI 2008/2767 Reg.3
Sch.9 para.1, varied: SI 2008/2839 Sch.1 para.1
Sch.9 para.3, amended: SI 2008/1554 Reg.26
Sch.9 para.4, amended: SI 2008/667 Reg.5, SI 2008/1554 Reg.26
Sch.9 para.4A, amended: SI 2008/1554 Reg.26
Sch.9 para.5, amended: SI 2008/698 Reg.3
Sch.9 para.7B, amended: SI 2008/1554 Reg.26
Sch.9 para.7C, amended: SI 2008/698 Reg.3, SI 2008/1554 Reg.26
Sch.9 para.8, amended: SI 2008/1554 Reg.26
Sch.9 para.9, amended: SI 2008/2767 Reg.3
Sch.9A para.1, amended: SI 2008/1554 Reg.27
Sch.9A para.2, amended: SI 2008/1554 Reg.27
Sch.9A para.3, amended: SI 2008/1554 Reg.27
Sch.9A para.4, amended: SI 2008/1554 Reg.27
Sch.9A para.8, amended: SI 2008/2831 Sch.1 para.4
Sch.9A para.8, varied: SI 2008/2839 Sch.1 para.1
Sch.9A para.10, amended: SI 2008/1554 Reg.27

NO.

1987–cont.

1968. Social Security (Claims and Payments) Regulations 1987–*cont.*

Sch.9A para.11, amended: SI 2008/1554 Reg.27

Sch.9B para.2, amended: SI 2008/1554 Reg.28

Sch.9B para.3, amended: SI 2008/1554 Reg.28

Sch.9B para.5, amended: SI 2008/1554 Reg.28

Sch.9B para.6, amended: SI 2008/1554 Reg.28

Sch.9B para.8, amended: SI 2008/1554 Reg.28

1969. Income Support (Transitional) Regulations 1987

Reg.15, varied: SI 2008/632 Art.17

2023. Insolvent Companies (Disqualification of Unfit Directors) Proceedings Rules 1987

r.3, see *Official Receiver v Stojevic* [2007] EWHC 1186 (Ch), [2008] Bus. L.R. 641 (Ch D), Judge Pelling Q.C.

2024. Non-Contentious Probate Rules 1987

see *Caudle v LD Law Ltd* [2008] EWHC 374 (QB), [2008] 1 W.L.R. 1540 (QBD), Wyn Williams, J.

r.22, see *Burrows v HM Coroner for Preston* [2008] EWHC 1387 (Admin), [2008] 2 F.L.R. 1225 (QBD), Cranston, J.

2048. Charities (Northern Ireland) Order 1987

Art.9B, substituted: SI 2008/948 Sch.3 para.5

2049. Consumer Protection (Northern Ireland) Order 1987

referred to: SI 2008/1277 Sch.3 para.7

Part III, applied: SI 2008/1277 Sch.3 para.11

Part IV, referred to: SI 2008/1277 Sch.3 para.8

Part V, referred to: SI 2008/1277 Sch.3 para.8

Art.13, revoked: SI 2008/1277 Sch.2 para.80, Sch.4 Part 2

Art.19, referred to: SI 2008/1277 Sch.3 para.7

Art.27, revoked: SI 2008/1277 Sch.2 para.80, Sch.4 Part 2

Art.30, revoked: SI 2008/1277 Sch.2 para.80, Sch.4 Part 2

Art.33, revoked: SI 2008/1277 Sch.2 para.80, Sch.4 Part 2

2117. Consumer Protection (Cancellation of Contracts Concluded away from Business Premises) Regulations 1987

revoked: SI 2008/1816 Sch.2

2197. Civil Jurisdiction (Offshore Activities) Order 1987

applied: SI 2008/2852 Sch.8 para.6

Art.1, applied: SI 2008/736 Reg.18

Art.1, referred to: SI 2008/225 Sch.1 para.36, Sch.1 para.37, Sch.1 para.43

NO.

1987–cont.

2203. Adoption (Northern Ireland) Order 1987

Art.2, applied: SI 2008/542 Reg.9

Art.9, see *P (A Child) (Adoption: Unmarried Couples), Re* [2008] UKHL 38, [2008] 3 W.L.R. 76 (HL (NI)), Lord Hoffmann

Art.14, see *P (A Child) (Adoption: Unmarried Couples), Re* [2008] UKHL 38, [2008] 3 W.L.R. 76 (HL (NI)), Lord Hoffmann

Art.15, amended: 2008 c.22 Sch.6 para.68

Art.40, disapplied: SI 2008/1769 Art.34, Art.36

Art.47, amended: SI 2008/1769 Sch.1 para.19

2215. Police Pensions (Purchase of Increased Benefits) Regulations 1987

Reg.2, amended: SI 2008/1887 Reg.25, SSI 2008/387 Reg.28

Reg.3, amended: SI 2008/1887 Reg.26, SSI 2008/387 Reg.29

Sch.1 Part I para.3, amended: SI 2008/1887 Reg.27, SSI 2008/387 Reg.30

Sch.1 Part I para.3, revoked (in part): SI 2008/1887 Reg.27, SSI 2008/387 Reg.30

Sch.1 Part I para.4, amended: SI 2008/1887 Reg.27, SSI 2008/387 Reg.30

1988

35. Social Fund (Recovery by Deductions from Benefits) Regulations 1988

Reg.3, amended: SI 2008/1554 Reg.5

93. Department of Trade and Industry (Fees) Order 1988

enabled: SI 2008/11, SI 2008/1958, SI 2008/2206

186. Measuring Instruments (EEC Requirements) Regulations 1988

Sch.1 para.1, amended: SI 2008/1267 Reg.2

Sch.1 para.5, amended: SI 2008/1267 Reg.2

Sch.1 para.6, amended: SI 2008/1267 Sch.1

370. International Carriage of Dangerous Goods by Road (Fees) Regulations 1988

Reg.3, amended: SI 2008/1578 Reg.2

Reg.3A, amended: SI 2008/1578 Reg.2

Reg.4, amended: SI 2008/1578 Reg.2

Reg.5, amended: SI 2008/1578 Reg.2

371. International Transport of Goods under Cover of TIR Carnets (Fees) Regulations 1988

Reg.3, amended: SI 2008/1580 Reg.2

Reg.5, amended: SI 2008/1580 Reg.2

486. National Health Service (General Ophthalmic Services) Amendment Regulations 1988

revoked (in part): SI 2008/1700 Sch.2

524. Social Fund (Applications) Regulations 1988

revoked: SI 2008/2265 Reg.9

NO.

1988–cont.

625. Local Government Superannuation (Scotland) Amendment Regulations 1988
revoked: SSI 2008/229 Sch.1

643. Department of Transport (Fees) Order 1988
applied: SI 2008/508, SI 2008/1402, SI 2008/1460, SI 2008/1461, SI 2008/1465, SI 2008/1474, SI 2008/1576, SI 2008/1578
enabled: SI 2008/1443, SI 2008/1458, SI 2008/1470, SI 2008/1473, SI 2008/1577, SI 2008/1580, SI 2008/1581

664. Social Security (Payments on account, Overpayments and Recovery) Regulations 1988
Reg.1, amended: SI 2008/1554 Reg.52, SI 2008/2683 Sch.1 para.44
Reg.2, amended: SI 2008/1554 Reg.52
Reg.4, amended: SI 2008/1554 Reg.52
Reg.5, amended: SI 2008/1554 Reg.52
Reg.7, amended: SI 2008/1554 Reg.52, SI 2008/2428 Reg.22
Reg.8, amended: SI 2008/1554 Reg.52
Reg.8, applied: SI 2008/794 Reg.107
Reg.9, applied: SI 2008/794 Reg.107
Reg.13, amended: SI 2008/1554 Reg.52
Reg.14, amended: SI 2008/1554 Reg.52
Reg.15, amended: SI 2008/1554 Reg.52
Reg.16, amended: SI 2008/1554 Reg.52
Reg.17, amended: SI 2008/1554 Reg.52

668. Pneumoconiosis etc (Workers Compensation) (Payment of Claims) Regulations 1988
Reg.3, amended: SI 2008/1963 Reg.6
Reg.5, amended: SI 2008/650 Reg.2
Reg.6, amended: SI 2008/650 Reg.2
Reg.8, amended: SI 2008/650 Reg.2
Sch.1 Part 1, substituted: SI 2008/650 Sch.1
Sch.1 Part 2, substituted: SI 2008/650 Sch.1

785. European Communities (Designation) Order 1988
Sch.1, amended: SI 2008/301 Sch.1

794. Crossbows (Northern Ireland) Order 1988
Art.8, amended: SI 2008/1216 Art.90

809. Excise Warehousing (Etc.) Regulations 1988
Reg.10A, amended: SI 2008/2832 Reg.3
Reg.10A, revoked (in part): SI 2008/2832 Reg.3
Sch.5 para.1, added: SI 2008/2832 Reg.3
Sch.5 para.2, added: SI 2008/2832 Reg.3
Sch.5 para.3, added: SI 2008/2832 Reg.3
Sch.5 para.4, added: SI 2008/2832 Reg.3

915. Control of Misleading Advertisements Regulations 1988
applied: SI 2008/1277 Sch.3 para.11, Sch.3 para.15
revoked: SI 2008/1277 Sch.2 para.81, Sch.4 Part 2

NO.

1988–cont.

915. Control of Misleading Advertisements Regulations 1988–*cont.*
Reg.1, referred to: SI 2008/1277 Sch.3 para.13
Reg.2, referred to: SI 2008/1277 Sch.3 para.13
Reg.3, referred to: SI 2008/1277 Sch.3 para.13
Reg.4, referred to: SI 2008/1277 Sch.3 para.13
Reg.4A, referred to: SI 2008/1277 Sch.3 para.14
Reg.5, referred to: SI 2008/1277 Sch.3 para.13
Reg.6, referred to: SI 2008/1277 Sch.3 para.13
Reg.7, referred to: SI 2008/1277 Sch.3 para.13
Reg.8, referred to: SI 2008/1277 Sch.3 para.13
Reg.9, referred to: SI 2008/1277 Sch.3 para.13
Reg.10, referred to: SI 2008/1277 Sch.3 para.13
Reg.11, referred to: SI 2008/1277 Sch.3 para.13

958. Consumer Protection (Cancellation of Contracts Concluded away from Business Premises) (Amendment) Regulations 1988
revoked: SI 2008/1816 Sch.2

1191. Nursing Homes and Mental Nursing Homes (Amendment) Regulations 1988
applied: 2008 c.14 s.17

1192. Residential Care Homes (Amendment) Regulations 1988
applied: 2008 c.14 s.17

1199. Town and Country Planning (Assessment of Environmental Effects) Regulations 1988
Reg.4, see *Cooper v Attorney General* [2008] EWHC 2178 (QB), [2008] 3 C.M.L.R. 45 (QBD), Plender, J

1294. Naval Medical Compassionate Fund (Amendment) Order 1988
revoked: SI 2008/3129 Sch.1

1305. General Optical Council (Contact Lens (Qualifications etc.) Rules) Order of Council 1988
Sch.1 para.3, amended: SI 2008/1940 Sch.1

1478. Goods Vehicles (Plating and Testing) Regulations 1988
Reg.3, amended: SI 2008/1460 Reg.3
Reg.12, amended: SI 2008/1460 Reg.4, Reg.6
Reg.16, amended: SI 2008/1460 Reg.5, Reg.6
Reg.25, amended: SI 2008/1460 Reg.6
Reg.34, amended: SI 2008/1460 Reg.6
Reg.37B, amended: SI 2008/1460 Reg.6

NO.

1988–cont.

1550. Public Health (Notification of Infectious Diseases) (Scotland) Regulations 1988
revoked: 2008 asp 5 Sch.3 Part 2

1586. Electro-medical Equipment (EEC Requirements) Regulations 1988
revoked: SI 2008/2297 Reg.45
Reg.4, applied: SI 2008/1277 Sch.3 para.2, Sch.3 para.3

1652. Teachers Superannuation (Consolidation) Regulations 1988
see *Pike v Somerset CC* [2008] Pens. L.R. 403 (EAT), Judge McMullen Q.C.

1655. Docks Regulations 1988
Reg.13, disapplied: SI 2008/1597 Reg.27

1724. Social Fund Cold Weather Payments (General) Regulations 1988
Reg.1, amended: SI 2008/1554 Reg.6, SI 2008/2569 Reg.2
Reg.1A, amended: SI 2008/1554 Reg.6, SI 2008/2569 Reg.2
Reg.3, varied: SI 2008/2569 Reg.3
Sch.1, substituted: SI 2008/2569 Sch.1
Sch.2, substituted: SI 2008/2569 Sch.2

1847. Criminal Justice (Evidence etc.) (Northern Ireland) Order 1988
Art.15, amended: 2008 c.4 Sch.26 para.25, SI 2008/1769 Art.42
Art.15, applied: SI 2008/1216 Sch.2 para.12, SI 2008/1769 Art.76
Art.15, referred to: 2008 c.4 Sch.27 para.24
Art.15A, added: SI 2008/1769 Art.42

1909. Merchant Shipping (Fishing Vessels-Tonnage) Regulations 1988
Reg.7, applied: SI 2008/2924 Sch.1 para.6, SI 2008/3257 Sch.1 para.6

1987. Criminal Evidence (Northern Ireland) Order 1988
Art.3, amended: 2008 c.28 s.24
Art.5, disapplied: 2008 c.28 s.24
Art.6, disapplied: 2008 c.28 s.24

1990. Housing (Northern Ireland) Order 1988
Art.7A, amended: 2008 c.17 Sch.15 para.18
Art.9, amended: 2008 c.17 Sch.15 para.19
Art.10, amended: 2008 c.17 Sch.15 para.20
Art.11, amended: 2008 c.17 Sch.15 para.21

2013. Act of Sederunt (Proceedings in the Sheriff Court under the Debtors (Scotland) Act 1987) 1988
referred to: SSI 2008/121 r.3, r.10
Part IV r.38, amended: SSI 2008/121 r.10
Part IV r.65A, added: SSI 2008/121 r.10
Sch.1, added: SSI 2008/121 r.10, Sch.5
Sch.1, amended: SSI 2008/121 r.3, r.10
Sch.1, revoked: SSI 2008/121 r.3

2019. Criminal Justice Act 1988 (Offensive Weapons) Order 1988
Sch.1 para.1, amended: SI 2008/973 Art.2
Sch.1 para.3, added: SI 2008/973 Art.2

NO.

1988–cont.

2019. Criminal Justice Act 1988 (Offensive Weapons) Order 1988–*cont.*
Sch.1 para.3, substituted: SI 2008/2039 Art.2
Sch.1 para.4, added: SI 2008/973 Art.2
Sch.1 para.5, added: SI 2008/973 Art.2
Sch.1 para.5A, added: SI 2008/973 Art.2, SI 2008/2039 Art.2
Sch.1 para.6, added: SI 2008/973 Art.2
Sch.1 para.6, amended: SI 2008/2039 Art.2

2240. European Communities (Designation) (No.2) Order 1988
revoked: SI 2008/301 Art.6

1989

193. Town and Country Planning (Fees for Applications and Deemed Applications) Regulations 1989
Reg.1, amended: SI 2008/958 Reg.2
Reg.10A, amended: SI 2008/958 Reg.2
Reg.11A, amended: SI 2008/958 Reg.2
Reg.11D, added: SI 2008/958 Reg.2
Sch.1 Part I para.4, amended: SI 2008/958 Reg.2
Sch.1 Part I para.6, amended: SI 2008/958 Reg.2
Sch.1 Part I para.7, amended: SI 2008/958 Reg.2
Sch.1 Part I para.7A, amended: SI 2008/958 Reg.2
Sch.1 Part I para.7B, revoked (in part): SI 2008/958 Reg.2
Sch.1 Part I para.15, amended: SI 2008/958 Reg.2
Sch.1 Part II, substituted: SI 2008/958 Sch.1
Sch.2, substituted: SI 2008/958 Sch.2

282. Education (Designated Institutions) Order 1989
Sch.1, amended: SI 2008/1643 Art.3

306. National Health Service (Charges to Overseas Visitors) Regulations 1989
see *R. (on the application of A) v West Middlesex University Hospital NHS Trust* [2008] EWHC 855 (Admin), [2008] H.R.L.R. 29 (QBD (Admin)), Mitting, J.
Reg.4, amended: SI 2008/2251 Reg.2, SI 2008/2364 Reg.2

339. Civil Legal Aid (General) Regulations 1989
Reg.79, see *Legal Services Commission v Rasool* [2008] EWCA Civ 154, [2008] 1 W.L.R. 2711 (CA (Civ Div)), Ward, L.J.
Reg.86, see *Legal Services Commission v Rasool* [2008] EWCA Civ 154, [2008] 1 W.L.R. 2711 (CA (Civ Div)), Ward, L.J.

351. Education (Schools and Further and Higher Education) Regulations 1989
revoked (in part): SI 2008/1701 Reg.2

NO.

1989–cont.

364. National Health Service (Charges to Overseas Visitors) (Scotland) Regulations 1989
Reg.1, amended: SSI 2008/290 Reg.2
Reg.2, amended: SSI 2008/290 Reg.2
Reg.3, amended: SSI 2008/290 Reg.2
Reg.4, amended: SSI 2008/290 Reg.2
Reg.8, amended: SSI 2008/290 Reg.2

395. National Health Service (General Ophthalmic Services) Amendment Regulations 1989
revoked (in part): SI 2008/1700 Sch.2

422. Housing (Scotland) (Superannuation Fund) Regulations 1989
revoked: SSI 2008/229 Sch.1

507. Community Charges (Deductions from Income Support) (Scotland) Regulations 1989
Reg.1, amended: SI 2008/1879 Reg.34
Reg.2, amended: SI 2008/1879 Reg.34
Reg.3, amended: SI 2008/1879 Reg.34
Reg.4, amended: SI 2008/1879 Reg.34

530. Erskine Bridge Regulations 1989
revoked: 2008 asp 1 Sch.2 Part 2

635. Electricity at Work Regulations 1989
Reg.26, disapplied: SI 2008/1597 Reg.27

638. European Economic Interest Grouping Regulations 1989
Reg.2, amended: SI 2008/948 Sch.1 para.161
Reg.2, referred to: SI 2008/948 Sch.1 para.161
Reg.8, amended: SI 2008/948 Sch.1 para.162
Reg.18, substituted: SI 2008/948 Sch.1 para.163
Sch.4, referred to: SI 2008/948 Sch.1 para.164
Sch.4 para.1, amended: SI 2008/948 Sch.1 para.164
Sch.4 Part 1 para.1, added: SI 2008/948 Sch.1 para.164
Sch.4 Part 1 para.1, amended: SI 2008/948 Sch.1 para.164
Sch.4 Part 1 para.2, added: SI 2008/948 Sch.1 para.164
Sch.4 Part 1 para.2, amended: SI 2008/948 Sch.1 para.164
Sch.4 Part 1 para.3, added: SI 2008/948 Sch.1 para.164
Sch.4 Part 1 para.3, amended: SI 2008/948 Sch.1 para.164
Sch.4 Part 1 para.4, added: SI 2008/948 Sch.1 para.164
Sch.4 Part 1 para.4, amended: SI 2008/948 Sch.1 para.164
Sch.4 Part 1 para.5, added: SI 2008/948 Sch.1 para.164
Sch.4 Part 1 para.5, amended: SI 2008/948 Sch.1 para.164

NO.

1989–cont.

638. European Economic Interest Grouping Regulations 1989–*cont.*
Sch.4 Part 1 para.6, added: SI 2008/948 Sch.1 para.164
Sch.4 Part 1 para.6, amended: SI 2008/948 Sch.1 para.164
Sch.4 Part 1 para.7, added: SI 2008/948 Sch.1 para.164
Sch.4 Part 1 para.7, amended: SI 2008/948 Sch.1 para.164
Sch.4 Part 1 para.8, added: SI 2008/948 Sch.1 para.164
Sch.4 Part 1 para.8, amended: SI 2008/948 Sch.1 para.164
Sch.4 Part 1 para.9, added: SI 2008/948 Sch.1 para.164
Sch.4 Part 1 para.9, amended: SI 2008/948 Sch.1 para.164
Sch.4 Part 1 para.10, added: SI 2008/948 Sch.1 para.164
Sch.4 Part 1 para.10, amended: SI 2008/948 Sch.1 para.164
Sch.4 Part 1 para.11, added: SI 2008/948 Sch.1 para.164
Sch.4 Part 1 para.11, amended: SI 2008/948 Sch.1 para.164
Sch.4 Part 1 para.12, added: SI 2008/948 Sch.1 para.164
Sch.4 Part 1 para.12, amended: SI 2008/948 Sch.1 para.164
Sch.4 Part 1 para.12, revoked: SI 2008/948 Sch.1 para.164
Sch.4 Part 1 para.13, added: SI 2008/948 Sch.1 para.164
Sch.4 Part 1 para.13, amended: SI 2008/948 Sch.1 para.164
Sch.4 Part 1 para.14, added: SI 2008/948 Sch.1 para.164
Sch.4 Part 1 para.14, amended: SI 2008/948 Sch.1 para.164
Sch.4 Part 1 para.15, added: SI 2008/948 Sch.1 para.164
Sch.4 Part 1 para.15, amended: SI 2008/948 Sch.1 para.164
Sch.4 Part 1 para.16, added: SI 2008/948 Sch.1 para.164
Sch.4 Part 1 para.16, amended: SI 2008/948 Sch.1 para.164
Sch.4 Part 1 para.17, added: SI 2008/948 Sch.1 para.164
Sch.4 Part 1 para.17, amended: SI 2008/948 Sch.1 para.164
Sch.4 Part 1 para.18, added: SI 2008/948 Sch.1 para.164
Sch.4 Part 1 para.18, amended: SI 2008/948 Sch.1 para.164
Sch.4 Part 1 para.19, added: SI 2008/948 Sch.1 para.164
Sch.4 Part 1 para.19, amended: SI 2008/948 Sch.1 para.164

NO.

1989–cont.

638. European Economic Interest Grouping Regulations 1989–*cont.*

Sch.4 Part 1 para.20, added: SI 2008/948 Sch.1 para.164

Sch.4 Part 1 para.20, amended: SI 2008/948 Sch.1 para.164

Sch.4 Part 1 para.21, added: SI 2008/948 Sch.1 para.164

Sch.4 Part 1 para.21, amended: SI 2008/948 Sch.1 para.164

Sch.4 Part 1 para.22, added: SI 2008/948 Sch.1 para.164

Sch.4 Part 1 para.22, amended: SI 2008/948 Sch.1 para.164

Sch.4 Part 1 para.23, added: SI 2008/948 Sch.1 para.164

Sch.4 Part 1 para.23, amended: SI 2008/948 Sch.1 para.164

Sch.4 Part 1 para.24, added: SI 2008/948 Sch.1 para.164

Sch.4 Part 1 para.24, amended: SI 2008/948 Sch.1 para.164

Sch.4 Part 1 para.24, revoked: SI 2008/948 Sch.1 para.164

Sch.4 para.2, amended: SI 2008/948 Sch.1 para.164

Sch.4 Part 2 para.1, added: SI 2008/948 Sch.1 para.164

Sch.4 Part 2 para.1, amended: SI 2008/948 Sch.1 para.164

Sch.4 Part 2 para.2, added: SI 2008/948 Sch.1 para.164

Sch.4 Part 2 para.2, amended: SI 2008/948 Sch.1 para.164

Sch.4 para.3, amended: SI 2008/948 Sch.1 para.164

Sch.4 para.4, amended: SI 2008/948 Sch.1 para.164

Sch.4 para.5, amended: SI 2008/948 Sch.1 para.164

Sch.4 para.6, amended: SI 2008/948 Sch.1 para.164

Sch.4 para.7, amended: SI 2008/948 Sch.1 para.164

Sch.4 para.8, amended: SI 2008/948 Sch.1 para.164

Sch.4 para.9, amended: SI 2008/948 Sch.1 para.164

Sch.4 para.10, amended: SI 2008/948 Sch.1 para.164

Sch.4 para.11, amended: SI 2008/948 Sch.1 para.164

Sch.4 para.12, amended: SI 2008/948 Sch.1 para.164

Sch.4 para.13, amended: SI 2008/948 Sch.1 para.164

Sch.4 para.14, amended: SI 2008/948 Sch.1 para.164

Sch.4 para.15, amended: SI 2008/948 Sch.1 para.164

NO.

1989–cont.

638. European Economic Interest Grouping Regulations 1989–*cont.*

Sch.4 para.16, amended: SI 2008/948 Sch.1 para.164

Sch.4 para.17, amended: SI 2008/948 Sch.1 para.164

Sch.4 para.18, amended: SI 2008/948 Sch.1 para.164

Sch.4 para.19, amended: SI 2008/948 Sch.1 para.164

Sch.4 para.20, amended: SI 2008/948 Sch.1 para.164

Sch.4 para.21, amended: SI 2008/948 Sch.1 para.164

Sch.4 para.22, amended: SI 2008/948 Sch.1 para.164

Sch.4 para.23, amended: SI 2008/948 Sch.1 para.164

Sch.4 para.24, amended: SI 2008/948 Sch.1 para.164

744. Removal, Storage and Disposal of Vehicles (Prescribed Sums and Charges etc.) Regulations 1989

revoked (in part): SI 2008/2095 Reg.2

802. Local Government Superannuation (Scotland) Amendment Regulations 1989

revoked: SSI 2008/229 Sch.1

869. Consumer Credit (Exempt Agreements) Order 1989

Sch.1 Part II, amended: SI 2008/645 Art.2, SI 2008/2831 Sch.1 para.5

900. Birmingham Assay Office Order 1989

Art.10, amended: SI 2008/948 Sch.1 para.1

919. Undersized Velvet Crabs Order 1989

Art.2, applied: SSI 2008/101 Sch.1 Part 1

Art.3, applied: SSI 2008/101 Sch.1 Part 1

Art.4, applied: SSI 2008/101 Sch.1 Part 1

967. Local Government Superannuation (Scotland) Amendment (No.2) Regulations 1989

revoked: SSI 2008/229 Sch.1

1058. Non-Domestic Rating (Collection and Enforcement) (Local Lists) Regulations 1989

Reg.3, amended: SI 2008/428 Sch.1 para.1

1066. Sandeels Licensing Order 1989

Art.2, applied: SSI 2008/101 Sch.1 Part 1

1100. Design Right (Semiconductor Topographies) Regulations 1989

Sch.1, amended: SI 2008/1434 Reg.3

1159. Water Supply and Sewerage Services (Customer Service Standards) Regulations 1989

revoked: SI 2008/594 Sch.1

1175. National Health Service (General Ophthalmic Services) Amendment (No.2) Regulations 1989

revoked (in part): SI 2008/1700 Sch.2

NO.

1989–cont.

1200. Cereals Marketing Act (Application to Oilseeds) Order 1989
revoked: SI 2008/576 Sch.5 para.8

1230. Sight Testing (Examination and Prescription) (No.2) Regulations 1989
Reg.3, amended: SI 2008/1700 Sch.1 para.1

1263. Sludge (Use in Agriculture) Regulations 1989
applied: SSI 2008/100 Sch.4 Part 2, SSI 2008/159 Sch.3 Part 2

1285. Undersized Bass Order 1989
Art.3, applied: SSI 2008/101 Sch.1 Part 1

1297. Taxes (Interest Rate) Regulations 1989
Reg.2, amended: SI 2008/3234 Reg.2
Reg.2A, added: SI 2008/3234 Reg.2
Reg.3AB, amended: SI 2008/778 Reg.2

1339. Limitation (Northern Ireland) Order 1989
Art.72B, amended: SI 2008/302 Art.5

1341. Police and Criminal Evidence (Northern Ireland) Order 1989
Art.19, amended: SI 2008/1216 Art.86
Art.48, amended: SI 2008/1216 Art.87
Art.53, amended: 2008 c.28 s.12
Art.56A, amended: SI 2008/1216 Art.88
Art.61, amended: 2008 c.28 s.12
Art.63, amended: 2008 c.28 s.12
Art.63A, amended: 2008 c.28 s.12, s.15
Art.63A, applied: 2008 c.28 s.18
Art.64, amended: 2008 c.28 s.12, s.15
Art.64, applied: 2008 c.28 s.18
Art.65, applied: 2008 c.28 s.24
Art.84, substituted: SI 2008/1216 Art.89
Sch.2, amended: SI 2008/1769 Sch.1 para.20, Sch.3

1344. Treatment of Offenders (Northern Ireland) Order 1989
Art.12, revoked (in part): SI 2008/1769 Sch.1 para.21, Sch.3
Sch.1, revoked: SI 2008/1216 Sch.6 Part 1

1355. Cider and Perry Regulations 1989
referred to: SI 2008/2302 Art.3
Reg.4, amended: SI 2008/1885 Reg.3
Reg.12, amended: SI 2008/1885 Reg.3
Reg.23, amended: SI 2008/1885 Reg.3
Reg.25, substituted: SI 2008/1885 Reg.3
Reg.26, substituted: SI 2008/1885 Reg.3

1356. Wine and Made-wine Regulations 1989
referred to: SI 2008/2302 Art.3
Reg.4, amended: SI 2008/1885 Reg.4
Reg.12, amended: SI 2008/1885 Reg.4
Reg.23, amended: SI 2008/1885 Reg.4
Reg.25, substituted: SI 2008/1885 Reg.4
Reg.26, substituted: SI 2008/1885 Reg.4

NO.

1989–cont.

1383. Water Supply and Sewerage Services (Customer Service Standards) (Amendment) Regulations 1989
revoked: SI 2008/594 Sch.1

1407. Port of Tyne (Pilotage) Harbour Revision Order 1989
referred to: SI 2008/1817 Art.1

1491. Criminal Legal Aid (Scotland) (Fees) Regulations 1989
Reg.6, amended: SSI 2008/240 Reg.4

1671. Offshore Installations and Pipeline Works (First-Aid) Regulations 1989
Reg.5, applied: SI 2008/736 Reg.20

1676. Orkney Islands Council (Loch of Boardhouse) (Amendment) Water Order 1989
revoked: SSI 2008/429 Art.7

1796. Road Vehicles Lighting Regulations 1989
Reg.10, revoked: SI 2008/1277 Sch.2 para.82, Sch.4 Part 2

2261. Non-Domestic Rating (Unoccupied Property) Regulations 1989
revoked (in part): SI 2008/386 Reg.7, SI 2008/2499 Reg.7

2288. All-Terrain Motor Vehicles (Safety) Regulations 1989
Reg.4, revoked: SI 2008/1597 Sch.1
Reg.5, revoked: SI 2008/1597 Sch.1
Reg.6, revoked: SI 2008/1597 Sch.1

2303. Non-Domestic Rating (Miscellaneous Provisions) (No.2) Regulations 1989
Reg.2, amended: SI 2008/2997 Reg.2

2395. Air Navigation (Overseas Territories) Order 1989
varied: SI 2008/3119 Sch.1

2404. Companies (Northern Ireland) Order 1989
applied: SI 2008/631 Reg.12, SI 2008/2558 Reg.3
Part II, applied: SI 2008/630 Reg.14, SI 2008/2252 Sch.1 para.13, SI 2008/2927 Reg.2, SI 2008/3047 Art.5, SI 2008/3148 Sch.1

2405. Insolvency (Northern Ireland) Order 1989
disapplied: 2008 c.32 s.56
Part III, applied: SI 2008/948 Sch.1 para.167
Part XIV, added: SI 2008/948 Sch.1 para.171
Art.21, amended: SI 2008/948 Sch.1 para.167
Art.39, amended: SI 2008/948 Sch.1 para.167
Art.49, amended: SI 2008/1897 Reg.2
Art.50, disapplied: SI 2008/346 Sch.1 para.9
Art.93, varied: SI 2008/346 Sch.1 para.9
Art.100, applied: SI 2008/346 Reg.27
Art.102, amended: SI 2008/948 Sch.1 para.168
Art.134, varied: SI 2008/346 Sch.1 para.9

NO.

1989–cont.

2405. Insolvency (Northern Ireland) Order 1989–*cont.*

Art.149, varied: SI 2008/346 Sch.1 para.9

Art.150A, amended: SI 2008/948 Sch.1 para.169

Art.150A, varied: SI 2008/346 Sch.1 para.9

Art.159, amended: SI 2008/1897 Reg.5

Art.280, applied: SI 2008/529 Reg.94, SI 2008/1582 Reg.94

Art.283, applied: SI 2008/529 Reg.94, SI 2008/1582 Reg.94

Sch.A1, amended: SI 2008/948 Sch.1 para.165, SI 2008/1897 Reg.3

Sch.A1, referred to: SI 2008/948 Sch.1 para.165

Sch.B1, amended: SI 2008/948 Sch.1 para.166

Sch.B1, varied: SI 2008/346 Sch.1 para.9

Sch.2A, applied: SI 2008/2927 Reg.2, SI 2008/3047 Art.5, SI 2008/3148 Sch.1

Sch.4, amended: SI 2008/948 Sch.1 para.170

1990

145. Non-Domestic Rating (Collection and Enforcement) (Miscellaneous Provisions) Regulations 1990

Reg.3, amended: SI 2008/428 Sch.1 para.2

422. Local Government Superannuation (Scotland) Amendment Regulations 1990

revoked: SSI 2008/229 Sch.1

447. Housing (Prescribed Forms) Regulations 1990

Sch.1, varied: SI 2008/442 Sch.1 para.8

454. Horticultural Development Council (Amendment) Order 1990

revoked: SI 2008/576 Sch.5 para.8

545. Community Charges (Deductions from Income Support) (No.2) Regulations 1990

Reg.2, amended: SI 2008/1554 Reg.53

Reg.3, amended: SI 2008/1554 Reg.53

Reg.4, amended: SI 2008/1554 Reg.53

593. Companies (Northern Ireland) Order 1990

Art.52, applied: SI 2008/948 Art.10

Art.52, referred to: SI 2008/948 Art.10

607. Milk and Milk Products (Protection of Designations) Regulations 1990

revoked (in part): SI 2008/1287 Reg.8, SI 2008/1341 Reg.8

626. Income Tax (Purchased Life Annuities) (Amendment) Regulations 1990

revoked: SI 2008/562 Reg.28

816. Milk and Milk Products (Protection of Designations) (Scotland) Regulations 1990

revoked: SSI 2008/216 Reg.8

NO.

1990–cont.

1051. National Health Service (General Ophthalmic Services) Amendment Regulations 1990

revoked (in part): SI 2008/1700 Sch.2

1179. Spirit Drinks Regulations 1990

revoked: SI 2008/3206 Sch.1

1196. Spirit Drinks (Scotland) Regulations 1990

revoked: SI 2008/3206 Sch.1

1284. Local Government Superannuation (Scotland) Amendment (No.2) Regulations 1990

revoked: SSI 2008/229 Sch.1

1447. Local Government (Politically Restricted Posts) (No.2) Regulations 1990

revoked (in part): SI 2008/220 Reg.4

1457. Register of Patent Agents Rules 1990

applied: SI 2008/2995 Art.6

1458. Register of Trade Mark Agents Rules 1990

applied: SI 2008/2995 Art.6

1504. Companies (No.2) (Northern Ireland) Order 1990

Art.70, amended: SI 2008/948 Sch.1 para.177, Sch.2

Art.70, referred to: SI 2008/948 Sch.1 para.177

Art.224, revoked (in part): SI 2008/948 Sch.2

1506. Education (Student Loans) (Northern Ireland) Order 1990

applied: SI 2008/529 Reg.4, SI 2008/1273 Reg.4, SI 2008/1582 Reg.5, SI 2008/3170 Reg.4

Sch.2, amended: SI 2008/948 Sch.1 para.178

1508. Horse Racing (Northern Ireland) Order 1990

Art.10, amended: SI 2008/948 Sch.1 para.2

1519. Planning (Listed Buildings and Conservation Areas) Regulations 1990

Reg.3, substituted: SI 2008/551 Reg.2

Reg.4, amended: SI 2008/551 Reg.2

Reg.6, amended: SI 2008/551 Reg.2

Reg.6, applied: SI 2008/551 Reg.3

Sch.2 Part I, referred to: SI 2008/551 Reg.3

Sch.2 Part I, revoked (in part): SI 2008/551 Reg.2

1700. New Towns (Transfer of Housing Stock) Regulations 1990

Reg.5, varied: SI 2008/2839 Sch.1 para.1

1766. Companies (Forms Amendment No.2 and Company's Type and Principal Business Activities) Regulations 1990

Sch.3 Part II, amended: SI 2008/1659 Reg.5

1788. Social Fund (Miscellaneous Provisions) Regulations 1990

revoked: SI 2008/2265 Reg.9

NO.

1990–cont.

2024. National Health Service Trusts (Membership and Procedure) Regulations 1990
Reg.1, amended: SI 2008/1269 Reg.3
Reg.2, amended: SI 2008/1269 Reg.3
Reg.9A, added: SI 2008/1269 Reg.3
Reg.9B, added: SI 2008/1269 Reg.3
Reg.9C, added: SI 2008/1269 Reg.3
Reg.9D, added: SI 2008/1269 Reg.3
Reg.11, amended: SI 2008/1700 Sch.1 para.2
Reg.13, amended: SI 2008/1269 Reg.3
Reg.14, amended: SI 2008/1269 Reg.3

2035. Overhead Lines (Exemption) Regulations 1990
Reg.3, amended: SSI 2008/202 Reg.8

2051. Sea Fish (Specified Manx Waters) Licensing Order 1990
Art.3, applied: SSI 2008/101 Sch.1 Part 1

2052. Sea Fishing (Specified Western Waters) (Restrictions on Landing) Order 1990
Art.3, applied: SSI 2008/101 Sch.1 Part 1

2145. Civil Aviation Act 1982 (Jersey) Order 1990
applied: SI 2008/2562

2231. Income Tax (Building Societies) (Dividends and Interest) Regulations 1990
revoked: SI 2008/2682 Sch.3
Reg.11, applied: SI 2008/2682 Sch.2 para.9

2232. Income Tax (Deposit-takers) (Interest Payments) Regulations 1990
revoked: SI 2008/2682 Sch.3

2386. Central Institutions (Recognition) (Scotland) (No.2) Regulations 1990
revoked: SSI 2008/163 Art.3, SSI 2008/178 Reg.2

2404. Cardiothoracic Centre-Liverpool National Health Service Trust (Establishment) Order 1990
Art.1, amended: SI 2008/1471 Art.2
Art.2, amended: SI 2008/1471 Art.2
Art.3, amended: SI 2008/1471 Art.3

2463. Food Safety (Sampling and Qualifications) Regulations 1990
Sch.1, amended: SI 2008/56 Reg.12, SI 2008/916 Reg.27, SI 2008/1237 Reg.27, SI 2008/1682 Reg.27, SSI 2008/127 Reg.24

2570. Companies (Revision of Defective Accounts and Report) Regulations 1990
revoked: SI 2008/373 Reg.20

1991

20. Food Protection (Emergency Prohibitions) (Radioactivity in Sheep) Order 1991
Sch.1 Part II para.2, amended: SSI 2008/63 Sch.2

NO.

1991–cont.

20. Food Protection (Emergency Prohibitions) (Radioactivity in Sheep) Order 1991–*cont.*
Sch.1 Part II para.2, revoked (in part): SSI 2008/63 Sch.1

78. Local Government Superannuation (Scotland) Amendment Regulations 1991
revoked: SSI 2008/229 Sch.1

189. Air Navigation (Overseas Territories) (Amendment) Order 1991
varied: SI 2008/3119 Sch.1

194. Health and Personal Social Services (Northern Ireland) Order 1991
Art.10, applied: SI 2008/1769 Art.55

269. Companies (Defective Accounts) (Authorised Person) Order (Northern Ireland) 1991
revoked: SI 2008/623 Art.6

499. Abortion Regulations 1991
Reg.2, amended: SI 2008/1338 Reg.2
Reg.4, amended: SI 2008/1338 Reg.3
Reg.5, amended: SI 2008/735 Reg.2, SI 2008/1338 Reg.4

724. High Court and County Courts Jurisdiction Order 1991
see *National Westminster Bank Plc v King* [2008] EWHC 280 (Ch), [2008] Ch. 385 (Ch D), David Richards, J.
Art.1A, added: SI 2008/2934 Art.3
Art.2, amended: SI 2008/2934 Art.5
Art.2, revoked (in part): SI 2008/2934 Art.4
Art.4, amended: SI 2008/2934 Art.6
Art.6B, added: SI 2008/2934 Art.7

859. Estate Agents (Provision of Information) Regulations 1991
see *Foxtons Ltd v Bicknell* [2008] EWCA Civ 419, [2008] 24 E.G. 142 (CA (Civ Div)), Waller, L.J. (V-P)

890. Arrangements for Placement of Children (General) Regulations 1991
Reg.13, see *R. (on the application of L) v Merton LBC* [2008] EWHC 1628 (Admin), [2008] 2 F.L.R. 1481 (QBD (Admin)), Irwin, J.

900. Common Services Agency (Withdrawal and Amendment of Functions) (Scotland) Order 1991
revoked: SSI 2008/312 Sch.1

994. Naval Medical Compassionate Fund (Amendment) Order 1991
revoked: SI 2008/3129 Sch.1

1063. Manchester Ship Canal Harbour Revision Order 1991
varied: SI 2008/230 Art.5

1091. Estate Agents (Specified Offences) (No.2) Order 1991
Sch.1, amended: SI 2008/1277 Sch.2 para.83, Sch.4 Part 2

NO.

1991–cont.

1247. Family Proceedings Rules 1991

see *Crossley v Crossley* [2007] EWCA Civ 1491, [2008] 1 F.C.R. 323 (CA (Civ Div)), Thorpe, L.J.

applied: SI 2008/1054 Art.1

see *Crossley v Crossley* [2007] EWCA Civ 1491, [2008] 1 F.L.R. 1467 (CA (Civ Div)), Thorpe, L.J.; see *Oxfordshire CC v P* [2005] EWHC 2156 (Fam), [2008] 2 F.L.R. 1708 (Fam Div), McFarlane, J.

Part I r.1.2, amended: SI 2008/2861 r.4

Part II r.2.6, applied: SI 2008/1054 Sch.1

Part II r.2.39, amended: SI 2008/2836 Art.28

Part II r.2.40, revoked: SI 2008/2836 Art.28

Part III r.3.8, amended: SI 2008/2446 r.4, SI 2008/2836 Art.28

Part III r.3.22, amended: SI 2008/2446 r.5

Part III r.3.23, amended: SI 2008/2446 r.6

Part III r.3.25, added: SI 2008/2446 r.7

Part III r.3.26, added: SI 2008/2446 r.7

Part III r.3.27, added: SI 2008/2446 r.7

Part III r.3.28, added: SI 2008/2446 r.7

Part III r.3.29, added: SI 2008/2446 r.7

Part III r.3.30, added: SI 2008/2446 r.7

Part III r.3.31, added: SI 2008/2446 r.7

Part III r.3.32, added: SI 2008/2446 r.7

Part III r.3.33, added: SI 2008/2446 r.7

Part III r.3.34, added: SI 2008/2446 r.7

Part III r.3.35, added: SI 2008/2446 r.7

Part III r.3.36, added: SI 2008/2446 r.7

Part IV r.4.1, amended: SI 2008/2861 r.5

Part IV r.4.4, amended: SI 2008/2861 r.6

Part IV r.4.4A, added: SI 2008/2861 r.7

Part IV r.4.5, amended: SI 2008/2861 r.8

Part IV r.4.8, amended: SI 2008/2861 r.9

Part IV r.4.9, amended: SI 2008/2861 r.10

Part IV r.4.11, amended: SI 2008/2861 r.11

Part IV r.4.11AA, amended: SI 2008/2861 r.12

Part IV r.4.13B, added: SI 2008/2861 r.13

Part IV r.4.14, amended: SI 2008/2861 r.14

Part IV r.4.15, amended: SI 2008/2861 r.15

Part IV r.4.16, amended: SI 2008/2861 r.16

Part IV r.4.17, amended: SI 2008/2861 r.17

Part IV r.4.21, amended: SI 2008/2861 r.18

Part IV r.4.21AA, added: SI 2008/2861 r.19

Part IV r.4.21A, amended: SI 2008/2861 r.20

Part IV r.4.21B, added: SI 2008/2861 r.21

Part IV r.4.22, amended: SI 2008/2836 Art.28

Part IV r.4.26, amended: SI 2008/2836 Art.28

Part VIII r.8.1B, added: SI 2008/2446 r.8

Part IX r.9.1, amended: SI 2008/2446 r.9

Part IX r.9.5, applied: SI 2008/2836 Art.15

Part X r.10.20A, amended: SI 2008/2446 r.10

Part X r.10.21, amended: SI 2008/2446 r.11

Part X r.10.21A, amended: SI 2008/2446 r.12

Appendix 1, added: SI 2008/2861 Sch.1, Sch.3, Sch.4

NO.

1991–cont.

1247. Family Proceedings Rules 1991–*cont.*

Appendix 1, amended: SI 2008/2446 Sch.1, Sch.2, Sch.3, SI 2008/2861 r.22

Appendix 1, substituted: SI 2008/2861 Sch.2

Appendix 3, amended: SI 2008/2861 r.23

Pt VII, see *D (Brussels II Revised: Contact), Re* [2007] EWHC 822 (Fam), [2008] 1 F.L.R. 516 (Fam Div), Black, J.

r.2.61B, see *Crossley v Crossley* [2007] EWCA Civ 1491, [2008] 1 F.L.R. 1467 (CA (Civ Div)), Thorpe, L.J.

r.2.69B, see *A v A (Ancillary Relief: Costs)* [2007] EWHC 1810 (Fam), [2008] 1 F.L.R. 1428 (Fam Div), Munby, J.

r.4.6, see *C (A Child) (Children Proceedings: Powers of Transfer), Re* [2008] EWCA Civ 502, [2008] 2 F.L.R. 815 (CA (Civ Div)), Wilson, L.J.

r.4.14, see *C (A Child) (Children Proceedings: Powers of Transfer), Re* [2008] EWCA Civ 502, [2008] 2 F.L.R. 815 (CA (Civ Div)), Wilson, L.J.

r.4.22, see *W v C* [2008] EWHC 73 (Fam), [2008] 1 F.L.R. 1703 (Fam Div), Singer, J.

r.7.44, see *D (Brussels II Revised: Contact), Re* [2007] EWHC 822 (Fam), [2008] 1 F.L.R. 516 (Fam Div), Black, J.

r.10.20A, see *A District Council v M* [2008] 2 F.L.R. 390 (Fam Div), Baron, J.

1285. Controlled Drugs (Substances Useful for Manufacture) Regulations 1991

revoked: SI 2008/296 Reg.11

1395. Family Proceedings Courts (Children Act 1989) Rules 1991

Part I r.1, amended: SI 2008/2858 r.4

Part I r.1, varied: SI 2008/2859 r.6

Part I r.2, varied: SI 2008/2859 r.7

Part II r.4, amended: SI 2008/2858 r.5

Part II r.4, varied: SI 2008/2859 r.8

Part II r.4A, varied: SI 2008/2859 r.9

Part II r.4B, varied: SI 2008/2859 r.9

Part II r.5, amended: SI 2008/2858 r.6

Part II r.5, varied: SI 2008/2859 r.10

Part II r.8, varied: SI 2008/2859 r.11

Part II r.9, varied: SI 2008/2859 r.12

Part II r.11, amended: SI 2008/2858 r.7

Part II r.11AA, amended: SI 2008/2858 r.8

Part II r.11AA, varied: SI 2008/2859 r.13

Part II r.13B, varied: SI 2008/2859 r.14

Part II r.14, amended: SI 2008/2858 r.9

Part II r.14, varied: SI 2008/2859 r.15

Part II r.15, amended: SI 2008/2858 r.10

Part II r.15, varied: SI 2008/2859 r.16

Part II r.16, amended: SI 2008/2858 r.11

Part II r.16, varied: SI 2008/2859 r.17

Part II r.17, amended: SI 2008/2858 r.12

Part II r.17, varied: SI 2008/2859 r.18

Part II r.21, varied: SI 2008/2859 r.19

Part II r.21AA, varied: SI 2008/2859 r.20

Part III r.33, varied: SI 2008/2859 r.21

NO.

1991–cont.

1395. Family Proceedings Courts (Children Act 1989) Rules 1991–*cont.*

Sch.1, amended: SI 2008/2858 r.13, Sch.1, Sch.2

Sch.1, varied: SI 2008/2859 r.22

Sch.2, varied: SI 2008/2859 r.23

1531. Control of Explosives Regulations 1991

applied: SI 2008/736 Reg.9

Reg.4, applied: SI 2008/736 Reg.9, Sch.8 Part 9

1597. Bathing Waters (Classification) Regulations 1991

revoked: SI 2008/1097 Reg.19

Reg.2, amended: SI 2008/1097 Reg.18

Sch.1 para.1, revoked: SI 2008/1097 Reg.18

Sch.1 para.2, revoked: SI 2008/1097 Reg.18

Sch.1 para.3, revoked: SI 2008/1097 Reg.18

Sch.2 para.1, revoked: SI 2008/1097 Reg.18

Sch.2 para.2, revoked: SI 2008/1097 Reg.18

Sch.2 para.3, revoked: SI 2008/1097 Reg.18

Sch.2 para.4, revoked: SI 2008/1097 Reg.18

Sch.3, revoked: SI 2008/1097 Reg.18

1609. Bathing Waters (Classification) (Scotland) Regulations 1991

applied: SSI 2008/170 Reg.6

revoked: SSI 2008/170 Reg.22

Reg.2, varied: SSI 2008/170 Reg.21

Reg.3, varied: SSI 2008/170 Reg.21

Sch.1 para.1, varied: SSI 2008/170 Reg.21

Sch.1 para.2, varied: SSI 2008/170 Reg.21

Sch.1 para.3, varied: SSI 2008/170 Reg.21

Sch.2 para.1, varied: SSI 2008/170 Reg.21

Sch.2 para.2, varied: SSI 2008/170 Reg.21

Sch.2 para.3, varied: SSI 2008/170 Reg.21

Sch.2 para.4, varied: SSI 2008/170 Reg.21

Sch.3, varied: SSI 2008/170 Reg.21

1672. Civil Aviation Authority Regulations 1991

Reg.6, amended: SI 2008/2683 Sch.1 para.46

Reg.14, amended: SI 2008/2683 Sch.1 para.47

Reg.26, amended: SI 2008/2683 Sch.1 para.48

Reg.31D, amended: SI 2008/2683 Sch.1 para.49

Reg.31D, revoked (in part): SI 2008/2683 Sch.1 para.49

1677. Children (Allocation of Proceedings) Order 1991

revoked: SI 2008/2836 Sch.2

Art.11, see *C (A Child) (Children Proceedings: Powers of Transfer), Re* [2008] EWCA Civ 502, [2008] 2 F.L.R. 815 (CA (Civ Div)), Wilson, L.J.

1697. Air Navigation (Overseas Territories) (Amendment) (No.2) Order 1991

varied: SI 2008/3119 Sch.1

NO.

1991–cont.

1801. Children (Allocation of Proceedings) (Appeals) Order 1991

revoked: SI 2008/2836 Sch.2

1991. Family Proceedings Courts (Matrimonial Proceedings etc.) Rules 1991

Part II r.3A, amended: SI 2008/2836 Art.28

Sch.1, amended: SI 2008/2828 Art.8

1997. Companies Act 1989 (Eligibility for Appointment as Company Auditor) (Consequential Amendments) Regulations 1991

Sch.1 para.13, revoked: SI 2008/576 Sch.5 para.8

Sch.1 para.16, revoked: SI 2008/576 Sch.5 para.8

Sch.1 para.60, revoked: 2008 c.17 Sch.16

1998. Companies (Inspection and Copying of Registers, Indices and Documents) Regulations 1991

revoked: SI 2008/3006 Reg.2

2032. Children (Prescribed Orders-Northern Ireland, Guernsey and Isle of Man) Regulations 1991

Reg.8, revoked (in part): 2008 c.4 Sch.28 Part 1

2242. Beef Carcase (Classification) Regulations 1991

Reg.10, revoked (in part): SI 2008/576 Sch.5 para.8

2502. Residential Care Homes (Amendment) Regulations 1991

applied: 2008 c.14 s.17

2532. Nursing Homes and Mental Nursing Homes (Amendment) Regulations 1991

applied: 2008 c.14 s.17

2628. Child Support (Northern Ireland) Order 1991 (N.I.23) 1991

Art.27, amended: 2008 c.22 Sch.6 para.69

2630. Immigration (Isle of Man) Order 1991

revoked: SI 2008/680 Art.3

2704. Bank Accounts Directive (Miscellaneous Banks) Regulations 1991

revoked: SI 2008/567 Reg.15

2808. Income Tax (Purchased Life Annuities) (Amendment) Regulations 1991

revoked: SI 2008/562 Reg.28

2839. Environmental Protection (Duty of Care) Regulations 1991

applied: SI 2008/314 Reg.6

2890. Social Security (Disability Living Allowance) Regulations 1991

Reg.1, amended: SI 2008/2683 Sch.1 para.50

Reg.4, amended: SI 2008/632 Art.13

NO.

1992

10. Income Tax (Building Societies) (Audit Powers) Regulations 1992
revoked: SI 2008/2682 Sch.3

11. Income Tax (Building Societies) (Dividends and Interest) (Amendment) Regulations 1992
revoked: SI 2008/2682 Sch.3

12. Income Tax (Deposit-takers) (Audit Powers) Regulations 1992
revoked: SI 2008/2682 Sch.3

13. Income Tax (Deposit-takers) (Interest Payments) (Amendment) Regulations 1992
revoked: SI 2008/2682 Sch.3

14. Income Tax (Deposit-takers) (Non-residents) Regulations 1992
revoked: SI 2008/2682 Sch.3

15. Income Tax (Interest Payments) (Information Powers) Regulations 1992
Reg.2, amended: SI 2008/2688 Reg.3
Reg.3, amended: SI 2008/2688 Reg.4
Reg.3, revoked (in part): SI 2008/2688 Reg.4
Reg.5, amended: SI 2008/2688 Reg.5
Reg.6, amended: SI 2008/2688 Reg.6
Reg.8, amended: SI 2008/2688 Reg.7
Reg.9, amended: SI 2008/2688 Reg.8
Reg.10, amended: SI 2008/2688 Reg.9
Reg.11, amended: SI 2008/2688 Reg.10
Reg.12, amended: SI 2008/2688 Reg.11

129. Firemen's Pension Scheme Order 1992
Sch.2, added: SI 2008/214 Sch.1 para.1, Sch.1 para.2, SSI 2008/161 Sch.1 para.1, Sch.1 para.2
Sch.2, amended: SI 2008/214 Sch.1 para.2, SSI 2008/161 Sch.1 para.2
Sch.2, applied: SI 2008/649 Reg.4
Sch.2, substituted: SI 2008/214 Sch.1 para.2, SSI 2008/161 Sch.1 para.2

223. Town and Country Planning (General Permitted Development) (Scotland) Order 1992
applied: SSI 2008/100 Sch.2 Part 1, SSI 2008/188 Art.54, SSI 2008/189 Art.54, SSI 2008/190 Art.54, SSI 2008/432 Reg.14
referred to: SSI 2008/432 Reg.26
Art.2, amended: SSI 2008/203 Art.2
Art.3, applied: SSI 2008/361 Art.32
Sch.1 Part 12 para.33, amended: SSI 2008/427 Art.9
Sch.1 Part 25A para.72A, amended: SSI 2008/74 Art.2
Sch.2, applied: SSI 2008/361 Art.32

224. Town and Country Planning (General Development Procedure) (Scotland) Order 1992
applied: SSI 2008/432 Reg.47
revoked: SSI 2008/432 Reg.47

NO.

1992–cont.

230. Civil Aviation Act 1982 (Guernsey) Order 1992
referred to: SI 2008/3121

231. Electricity (Northern Ireland) Order 1992
Art.10, applied: 2008 c.32 s.45
Art.73, amended: SI 2008/948 Sch.1 para.189
Art.77, amended: SI 2008/948 Sch.1 para.189
Art.78, amended: SI 2008/948 Sch.1 para.189
Art.82, amended: SI 2008/948 Sch.1 para.189

272. Act of Sederunt (Judicial Factors Rules) 1992
Part I r.2, amended: SSI 2008/223 r.9
Part I r.2A, added: SSI 2008/223 r.13
Part I r.2B, added: SSI 2008/223 r.13
Part I r.4A, added: SSI 2008/223 r.9

433. Erskine Bridge Tolls Order 1992
revoked: 2008 asp 1 Sch.2 Part 2

434. National Health Service (Service Committees and Tribunal) (Scotland) Regulations 1992
applied: SSI 2008/224 Reg.13

548. Council Tax (Discount Disregards) Order 1992
Sch.1 para.4, see *Wirral BC v Farthing* [2008] EWHC 1919 (Ch), [2008] R.A. 303 (Ch D), Judge Hodge Q.C.

550. Council Tax (Situation and Valuation of Dwellings) Regulations 1992
see *Chilton-Merryweather (Listing Officer) v Hunt* [2008] EWCA Civ 1025, [2008] R.A. 357 (CA (Civ Div)), Waller, L.J.
Reg.6, amended: SI 2008/315 Reg.2
Reg.6, referred to: SI 2008/315 Reg.2
Reg.6, see *McKenzie (Listing Officer) v Marshall* [2008] EWHC 641 (Admin), [2008] R.A. 269 (QBD (Admin)), Dobbs, J.

556. Non-Domestic Rating (Material Day for List Alterations) Regulations 1992
see *O'Brien (t/a Poster Sites Southern) v Harding (Valuation Officer)* [2008] R.A. 73 (Lands Tr), Judge Mole Q.C.
Reg.3, varied: SI 2008/2333 Reg.6, SI 2008/2671 Reg.6

588. Controlled Waste Regulations 1992
referred to: SSI 2008/100 Sch.2 Part 1
Reg.7A, see *R. (on the application of Thames Water Utilities Ltd) v Bromley Magistrates Court* [2008] EWHC 1763 (QB), Times, August 28, 2008 (DC), Carnwath, L.J.

612. Local Authorities (Calculation of Council Tax Base) Regulations 1992
applied: SI 2008/3022 Reg.12, Reg.15
Reg.1, varied: SI 2008/3022 Sch.2 para.11
Reg.6, varied: SI 2008/3022 Sch.2 para.12
Reg.7, varied: SI 2008/3022 Sch.2 para.13

NO.

1992–cont.

664. National Health Service (Service Committees and Tribunal) Regulations 1992
applied: SI 2008/653 Reg.14, SI 2008/1700 Sch.1 para.3
Reg.2, amended: SI 2008/1700 Sch.1 para.3
Reg.2, revoked (in part): SI 2008/1700 Sch.1 para.3
Reg.2, varied: SI 2008/1700 Reg.11, Reg.12
Reg.3, revoked (in part): SI 2008/1700 Sch.1 para.3
Reg.3, varied: SI 2008/1700 Reg.11, Reg.12
Reg.4, amended: SI 2008/1700 Sch.1 para.3
Reg.4, applied: SI 2008/1700 Reg.11, Reg.12
Reg.4, referred to: SI 2008/1700 Reg.11
Reg.4, varied: SI 2008/1700 Reg.11, Reg.12
Reg.5, applied: SI 2008/1700 Reg.11, Reg.12
Reg.5, revoked (in part): SI 2008/1700 Sch.1 para.3
Reg.5, varied: SI 2008/1700 Reg.11, Reg.12
Reg.6, amended: SI 2008/1700 Sch.1 para.3
Reg.6, referred to: SI 2008/1700 Reg.11
Reg.6, varied: SI 2008/1700 Reg.11, Reg.12
Reg.7, applied: SI 2008/1700 Reg.11
Reg.7, varied: SI 2008/1700 Reg.11
Reg.8, applied: SI 2008/1700 Reg.13, Reg.14, Reg.15
Reg.8, varied: SI 2008/1700 Reg.11
Reg.9, applied: SI 2008/1700 Reg.13, Reg.15
Reg.9, referred to: SI 2008/1700 Reg.15
Reg.9, varied: SI 2008/1700 Reg.11
Reg.10, amended: SI 2008/2683 Sch.1 para.52
Reg.10, applied: SI 2008/1700 Reg.13, Reg.15
Reg.10, revoked (in part): SI 2008/1700 Sch.1 para.3
Reg.10, varied: SI 2008/1700 Reg.11, Reg.12
Reg.11, applied: SI 2008/1700 Reg.13, Reg.15, Sch.1 para.3
Reg.12, applied: SI 2008/1700 Reg.13, Sch.1 para.3
Reg.13, applied: SI 2008/1700 Sch.1 para.3
Reg.14, applied: SI 2008/1700 Reg.11, Reg.12, Sch.1 para.3
Reg.15, applied: SI 2008/1700 Sch.1 para.3
Reg.16, applied: SI 2008/1700 Sch.1 para.3
Reg.20, revoked (in part): SI 2008/1700 Sch.1 para.3
Reg.33, amended: SI 2008/2683 Sch.1 para.53
Reg.33, revoked (in part): SI 2008/2683 Sch.1 para.53
Sch.2 para.1, varied: SI 2008/1700 Reg.11, Reg.12
Sch.2 Part I para.1, varied: SI 2008/1700 Reg.11, Reg.12
Sch.2 Part I para.2, amended: SI 2008/1700 Sch.1 para.3
Sch.2 Part I para.2, varied: SI 2008/1700 Reg.11, Reg.12

NO.

1992–cont.

664. National Health Service (Service Committees and Tribunal) Regulations 1992–*cont.*
Sch.2 Part I para.3, varied: SI 2008/1700 Reg.11, Reg.12
Sch.2 Part I para.4, varied: SI 2008/1700 Reg.11, Reg.12
Sch.2 Part I para.5, varied: SI 2008/1700 Reg.11, Reg.12
Sch.2 Part I para.6, varied: SI 2008/1700 Reg.11, Reg.12
Sch.2 Part I para.7, varied: SI 2008/1700 Reg.11, Reg.12
Sch.2 Part I para.8, revoked (in part): SI 2008/1700 Sch.1 para.3
Sch.2 Part I para.8, varied: SI 2008/1700 Reg.11, Reg.12
Sch.2 para.2, amended: SI 2008/1700 Sch.1 para.3
Sch.2 para.2, varied: SI 2008/1700 Reg.11, Reg.12
Sch.2 para.3, varied: SI 2008/1700 Reg.11, Reg.12
Sch.2 para.4, varied: SI 2008/1700 Reg.11, Reg.12
Sch.2 para.5, varied: SI 2008/1700 Reg.11, Reg.12
Sch.2 para.6, varied: SI 2008/1700 Reg.11, Reg.12
Sch.2 para.7, varied: SI 2008/1700 Reg.11, Reg.12
Sch.2 para.8, varied: SI 2008/1700 Reg.11, Reg.12
Sch.2 para.9, varied: SI 2008/1700 Reg.11, Reg.12
Sch.2 para.10, varied: SI 2008/1700 Reg.11, Reg.12
Sch.2 para.11, varied: SI 2008/1700 Reg.11, Reg.12
Sch.4 para.1, varied: SI 2008/1700 Reg.11, Reg.12
Sch.4 para.2, varied: SI 2008/1700 Reg.11, Reg.12
Sch.4 para.3, varied: SI 2008/1700 Reg.11, Reg.12
Sch.4 para.4, varied: SI 2008/1700 Reg.11, Reg.12
Sch.4 para.5, amended: SI 2008/2683 Sch.1 para.54
Sch.4 para.5, varied: SI 2008/1700 Reg.11, Reg.12
Sch.4 para.6, varied: SI 2008/1700 Reg.11, Reg.12
Sch.4 para.7, varied: SI 2008/1700 Reg.11, Reg.12
Sch.4 para.8, varied: SI 2008/1700 Reg.11, Reg.12
Sch.4 para.9, revoked (in part): SI 2008/1700 Sch.1 para.3
Sch.4 para.9, varied: SI 2008/1700 Reg.11, Reg.12

NO.

1992–cont.

664. National Health Service (Service Committees and Tribunal) Regulations 1992–*cont.*
Sch.4 para.10, varied: SI 2008/1700 Reg.11, Reg.12
Sch.9 para.5, amended: SI 2008/2683 Sch.1 para.55

666. Town and Country Planning (Control of Advertisements) Regulations 1992
applied: SI 2008/1848 Reg.15

671. Artificial Insemination of Cattle (Animal Health) (England and Wales) (Amendment) Regulations 1992
revoked (in part): SI 2008/1040 Sch.10 Part 1

737. Price Indications (Bureaux de Change) (No.2) Regulations 1992
applied: SI 2008/1277 Sch.3 para.5, Sch.3 para.6, Sch.3 para.10, Sch.3 para.12

807. Industrial Relations (Northern Ireland) Order 1992
amended: SI 2008/948 Sch.1 para.2, Sch.1 para.190
Art.2, amended: SI 2008/948 Sch.1 para.2, Sch.1 para.190
Art.4, amended: SI 2008/948 Sch.1 para.2, Sch.1 para.190
Art.7, amended: SI 2008/948 Sch.1 para.2, Sch.1 para.190
Art.11, amended: SI 2008/948 Sch.1 para.2, Sch.1 para.190
Sch.1, amended: SI 2008/948 Sch.1 para.2, Sch.1 para.190
Sch.4, amended: SI 2008/948 Sch.1 para.2, Sch.1 para.190

1220. Local Government Superannuation (Reserve Forces) (Scotland) Regulations 1992
revoked: SSI 2008/229 Sch.1

1268. Manchester Ship Canal Harbour Revision Order 1992
varied: SI 2008/230 Art.5

1366. Army Terms of Service (Part-time Service in Northern Ireland) Regulations 1992
revoked: SI 2008/1849 Reg.3

1708. Housing (Service Charge Loans) Regulations 1992
applied: SI 2008/2831 Sch.3 para.4
Reg.1, amended: SI 2008/2831 Sch.1 para.6
Reg.2, amended: SI 2008/2831 Sch.1 para.6
Reg.5, amended: SI 2008/2831 Sch.1 para.6
Reg.5, applied: SI 2008/2831 Sch.3 para.4

1711. European Communities (Designation) (No.2) Order 1992
Sch.1, amended: SI 2008/301 Sch.1

1725. Housing (Northern Ireland) Order 1992
Art.29, amended: SI 2008/948 Sch.1 para.191

NO.

1992–cont.

1728. Offshore, and Pipelines, Safety (Northern Ireland) Order 1992
Art.6, revoked: 2008 c.20 Sch.4

1812. Child Support (Information, Evidence and Disclosure) Regulations 1992
applied: 2008 c.6 Sch.2
revoked: SI 2008/2551 Reg.15
Reg.1, amended: SI 2008/536 Reg.2
Reg.2, amended: SI 2008/536 Reg.2
Reg.3, amended: SI 2008/536 Reg.2

1813. Child Support (Maintenance Assessment Procedure) Regulations 1992
Reg.1, amended: SI 2008/2543 Reg.2, SI 2008/2683 Sch.1 para.57
Reg.1, applied: 2008 c.6 Sch.2
Reg.1, revoked (in part): SI 2008/2543 Reg.2
Reg.2, amended: SI 2008/2543 Reg.2
Reg.2, applied: 2008 c.6 Sch.2
Reg.3, applied: 2008 c.6 Sch.2
Reg.4, applied: 2008 c.6 Sch.2
Reg.5, applied: 2008 c.6 Sch.2, SI 2008/1476 Art.2, SI 2008/2548 Art.4
Reg.6, applied: 2008 c.6 Sch.2
Reg.7, applied: 2008 c.6 Sch.2
Reg.8, applied: 2008 c.6 Sch.2
Reg.8A, applied: 2008 c.6 Sch.2
Reg.8B, applied: 2008 c.6 Sch.2
Reg.8C, applied: 2008 c.6 Sch.2
Reg.8D, applied: 2008 c.6 Sch.2
Reg.9, applied: 2008 c.6 Sch.2
Reg.9A, applied: 2008 c.6 Sch.2
Reg.10, amended: SI 2008/2683 Sch.1 para.58
Reg.10, applied: 2008 c.6 Sch.2
Reg.10A, applied: 2008 c.6 Sch.2
Reg.11, applied: 2008 c.6 Sch.2
Reg.12, applied: 2008 c.6 Sch.2
Reg.13, applied: 2008 c.6 Sch.2
Reg.14, applied: 2008 c.6 Sch.2
Reg.15, applied: 2008 c.6 Sch.2
Reg.15A, applied: 2008 c.6 Sch.2
Reg.16, applied: 2008 c.6 Sch.2
Reg.16A, applied: 2008 c.6 Sch.2
Reg.17, amended: SI 2008/2543 Reg.2
Reg.17, applied: 2008 c.6 Sch.2, SI 2008/2685 Sch.1
Reg.18, amended: SI 2008/2683 Sch.1 para.59
Reg.18, applied: 2008 c.6 Sch.2
Reg.18A, applied: 2008 c.6 Sch.2
Reg.18B, applied: 2008 c.6 Sch.2
Reg.18C, applied: 2008 c.6 Sch.2
Reg.18D, applied: 2008 c.6 Sch.2
Reg.19, applied: 2008 c.6 Sch.2
Reg.20, amended: SI 2008/2543 Reg.2, SI 2008/2683 Sch.1 para.60
Reg.20, applied: 2008 c.6 Sch.2
Reg.21, applied: 2008 c.6 Sch.2
Reg.22, applied: 2008 c.6 Sch.2

NO.

1992–cont.

1813. Child Support (Maintenance Assessment Procedure) Regulations 1992– *cont.*

Reg.23, amended: SI 2008/2683 Sch.1 para.61
Reg.23, applied: 2008 c.6 Sch.2
Reg.23, revoked (in part): SI 2008/2543 Reg.2
Reg.23, applied: 2008 c.6 Sch.2
Reg.24, applied: 2008 c.6 Sch.2
Reg.25, applied: 2008 c.6 Sch.2
Reg.26, applied: 2008 c.6 Sch.2
Reg.26A, applied: 2008 c.6 Sch.2
Reg.27, applied: 2008 c.6 Sch.2
Reg.28, applied: 2008 c.6 Sch.2
Reg.29, applied: 2008 c.6 Sch.2
Reg.30, amended: SI 2008/2543 Reg.2
Reg.30, applied: 2008 c.6 Sch.2
Reg.30A, amended: SI 2008/2544 Reg.4
Reg.30A, applied: 2008 c.6 Sch.2
Reg.31, applied: 2008 c.6 Sch.2
Reg.31A, applied: 2008 c.6 Sch.2
Reg.31B, applied: 2008 c.6 Sch.2
Reg.31C, applied: 2008 c.6 Sch.2
Reg.32, amended: SI 2008/2543 Reg.2
Reg.32, applied: 2008 c.6 Sch.2
Reg.32A, applied: 2008 c.6 Sch.2
Reg.32B, applied: 2008 c.6 Sch.2
Reg.33, applied: 2008 c.6 Sch.2
Reg.34, applied: 2008 c.6 Sch.2
Reg.34, revoked: SI 2008/2543 Reg.2
Reg.35, applied: 2008 c.6 Sch.2
Reg.35, revoked: SI 2008/2543 Reg.2
Reg.35A, revoked: SI 2008/2543 Reg.2
Reg.36, revoked: SI 2008/2543 Reg.2
Reg.37, applied: 2008 c.6 Sch.2
Reg.37, revoked: SI 2008/2543 Reg.2
Reg.38, revoked: SI 2008/2543 Reg.2
Reg.39, applied: 2008 c.6 Sch.2
Reg.39, revoked: SI 2008/2543 Reg.2
Reg.40, applied: 2008 c.6 Sch.2
Reg.40, revoked: SI 2008/2543 Reg.2
Reg.40A, applied: 2008 c.6 Sch.2
Reg.40A, revoked: SI 2008/2543 Reg.2
Reg.40ZA, applied: 2008 c.6 Sch.2
Reg.40ZA, revoked: SI 2008/2543 Reg.2
Reg.41, applied: 2008 c.6 Sch.2
Reg.41, revoked: SI 2008/2543 Reg.2
Reg.42, applied: 2008 c.6 Sch.2
Reg.42, revoked: SI 2008/2543 Reg.2
Reg.43, applied: 2008 c.6 Sch.2
Reg.43, revoked: SI 2008/2543 Reg.2
Reg.44, applied: 2008 c.6 Sch.2
Reg.44, revoked: SI 2008/2543 Reg.2
Reg.45, applied: 2008 c.6 Sch.2
Reg.45, revoked: SI 2008/2543 Reg.2
Reg.46, applied: 2008 c.6 Sch.2
Reg.46, revoked: SI 2008/2543 Reg.2
Reg.47, revoked: SI 2008/2543 Reg.2
Reg.48, applied: 2008 c.6 Sch.2

NO.

1992–cont.

1813. Child Support (Maintenance Assessment Procedure) Regulations 1992– *cont.*

Reg.48, revoked: SI 2008/2543 Reg.2
Reg.49, revoked: SI 2008/2543 Reg.2
Reg.49A, applied: 2008 c.6 Sch.2
Reg.49A, revoked: SI 2008/2543 Reg.2
Reg.50, applied: 2008 c.6 Sch.2
Reg.50, revoked: SI 2008/2543 Reg.2
Sch.1, applied: 2008 c.6 Sch.2
Sch.2, applied: 2008 c.6 Sch.2
Sch.2 para.1, amended: SI 2008/2543 Reg.2
Sch.2 para.1, revoked (in part): SI 2008/2543 Reg.2
Sch.2 para.3, amended: SI 2008/2543 Reg.2
Sch.2 para.3, revoked (in part): SI 2008/2543 Reg.2
Sch.2 para.5, revoked: SI 2008/2543 Reg.2

1815. Child Support (Maintenance Assessments and Special Cases) Regulations 1992

applied: 2008 c.6 Sch.2
Sch.1 para.15, see *Chandler v Secretary of State for Work and Pensions* [2007] EWCA Civ 1211, [2008] 1 W.L.R. 734 (CA (Civ Div)), Latham, L.J.

1816. Child Support (Arrears, Interest and Adjustment of Maintenance Assessments) Regulations 1992

applied: 2008 c.6 Sch.2
referred to: 2008 c.6 s.43
Reg.14, amended: SI 2008/2683 Sch.1 para.62

1836. Horticultural Development Council (Amendment) Order 1992

revoked: SI 2008/576 Sch.5 para.8

1878. Act of Sederunt (Fees of Witnesses and Shorthand Writers in the Sheriff Court) 1992

Sch.2 para.1, amended: SSI 2008/118 Art.2
Sch.2 para.4, amended: SSI 2008/118 Art.2
Sch.2 para.5, amended: SSI 2008/118 Art.2

1989. Child Support (Collection and Enforcement) Regulations 1992

applied: 2008 c.6 Sch.2
Reg.3, amended: SI 2008/2544 Reg.2
Reg.3, revoked (in part): SI 2008/2544 Reg.2
Reg.4, applied: SI 2008/794 Reg.128
Reg.11, amended: SI 2008/2544 Reg.2
Reg.15, substituted: SI 2008/536 Reg.3
Reg.22, amended: SI 2008/2544 Reg.2

2007. Residential Care Homes (Amendment) Regulations 1992

applied: 2008 c.14 s.17

2051. Management of Health and Safety at Work Regulations 1992

see *Spencer v Secretary of State for Work and Pensions* [2007] EWHC1775 (QB), [2008] 1 C.M.L.R. 32 (QBD), Holland, J.; see *Spencer v Secretary of State for Work and*

NO.

1992–cont.

2051. Management of Health and Safety at Work Regulations 1992–*cont.*
see–*cont.*
Pensions [2008] EWCA Civ 750, [2008] C.P. Rep. 40 (CA (Civ Div)), Waller, L.J.

2182. Fines (Deductions from Income Support) Regulations 1992
Reg.1, amended: SI 2008/1554 Reg.54
Reg.2, amended: SI 2008/1554 Reg.54
Reg.2A, amended: SI 2008/1554 Reg.54
Reg.4, amended: SI 2008/1554 Reg.54
Reg.7, amended: SI 2008/1554 Reg.54

2241. Residential Care Homes (Amendment) (No.2) Regulations 1992
applied: 2008 c.14 s.17

2370. Zootechnical Standards Regulations 1992
referred to: SI 2008/1064 Reg.2
Reg.6, added: SI 2008/1064 Reg.2
Sch.3 Part V, substituted: SI 2008/1064 Reg.2

2633. Sea Fish Licensing Order 1992
Art.3, applied: SSI 2008/101 Sch.1 Part 1

2643. Child Support (Collection and Enforcement of Other Forms of Maintenance) Regulations 1992
applied: 2008 c.6 Sch.2

2645. Child Support (Maintenance Arrangements and Jurisdiction) Regulations 1992
applied: 2008 c.6 Sch.2

2735. Ceredigion and Mid Wales National Health Service Trust (Establishment) Order 1992
revoked: SI 2008/934 Art.2

2790. Statistics of Trade (Customs and Excise) Regulations 1992
Reg.3, amended: SI 2008/2847 Reg.2
Reg.4, amended: SI 2008/2847 Reg.2
Sch.1, substituted: SI 2008/557 Sch.1

2870. European Communities (Designation) (No.4) Order 1992
Sch.1, amended: SI 2008/301 Sch.1

2885. Offshore Installations (Safety Case) Regulations 1992
Reg.17, applied: SI 2008/736 Sch.12

2904. Local Authorities (Calculation of Council Tax Base) (Supply of Information) Regulations 1992
applied: SI 2008/3022 Reg.15
Reg.4, varied: SI 2008/3022 Sch.2 para.14

2914. Controlled Drugs (Substances Useful for Manufacture) (Amendment) Regulations 1992
revoked: SI 2008/296 Reg.11

2915. Income Tax (Building Societies) (Dividends and Interest) (Amendment No.2) Regulations 1992
revoked: SI 2008/2682 Sch.3

NO.

1992–cont.

2977. National Assistance (Assessment of Resources) Regulations 1992
Reg.20, amended: SI 2008/593 Reg.3, SSI 2008/13 Reg.2
Reg.28, amended: SI 2008/593 Reg.4, SSI 2008/13 Reg.3
Reg.28A, amended: SI 2008/743 Reg.4
Sch.3 Part I para.10, amended: SI 2008/593 Reg.5
Sch.3 Part I para.28G, amended: SSI 2008/13 Reg.4
Sch.3 Part I para.28H, amended: SI 2008/593 Reg.5, SI 2008/743 Reg.5
Sch.3 Part II para.30, revoked (in part): SI 2008/593 Reg.5
Sch.3 Part II para.31, amended: SI 2008/593 Reg.5
Sch.4 para.10A, added: SI 2008/593 Reg.6
Sch.4 para.19, substituted: SI 2008/593 Reg.6

2985. Street Works (Registers, Notices, Directions and Designations) Regulations 1992
applied: SI 2008/101 Reg.19, SI 2008/540 Reg.19
Reg.1A, added: SI 2008/101 Reg.2, SI 2008/540 Reg.2

2991. Road Works (Registers, Notices, Directions and Designations) (Scotland) Regulations 1992
revoked: SSI 2008/88 Reg.16

3004. Workplace (Health, Safety and Welfare) Regulations 1992
see *Wright v Edinburgh Royal Infirmary Joint Venture* 2008 S.L.T. (Sh Ct) 90 (Sh Ct (Lothian)), Sheriff F L Reith Q.C.
Reg.13, see *Mason v Satelcom Ltd* [2007] EWHC 2540 (QB), [2008] P.I.Q.R. P4 (QBD), Judge Reddihough; see *Mason v Satelcom Ltd* [2008] EWCA Civ 494, [2008] I.C.R. 971 (CA (Civ Div)), Ward, L.J.
Reg.18, see *Wright v Edinburgh Royal Infirmary Joint Venture* 2008 S.L.T. (Sh Ct) 90 (Sh Ct (Lothian)), Sheriff F L Reith Q.C.

3025. Local Government Superannuation (Scotland) Amendment Regulations 1992
revoked: SSI 2008/229 Sch.1

3045. Horses (Zootechnical Standards) Regulations 1992
revoked (in part): SSI 2008/99 Reg.11

3073. Supply of Machinery (Safety) Regulations 1992
applied: SI 2008/1597 Reg.16
referred to: SI 2008/1597 Reg.16
revoked: SI 2008/1597 Sch.1

3082. Non-Domestic Rating Contributions (England) Regulations 1992
referred to: SI 2008/3078 Reg.2
Sch.1 Part 1 para.1, amended: SI 2008/3078 Reg.3

NO.

1992–cont.

3082. Non-Domestic Rating Contributions (England) Regulations 1992–*cont.*
Sch.1 Part 1 para.4, amended: SI 2008/3078 Reg.3
Sch.1 Part II, substituted: SI 2008/3078 Reg.3
Sch.2 Part 1 para.2, amended: SI 2008/3078 Reg.4
Sch.2 Part 1 para.8, amended: SI 2008/3078 Reg.4

3094. Child Support Fees Regulations 1992
referred to: 2008 c.6 s.43

3161. Artificial Insemination of Pigs (EEC) Regulations 1992
Reg.2, applied: SI 2008/1035 Sch.1 para.1

3198. Air Navigation (Overseas Territories) (Amendment) Order 1992
varied: SI 2008/3119 Sch.1

3204. Registered Homes (Northern Ireland) Order 1992
applied: SI 2008/1741 Reg.57
Art.3, applied: SI 2008/1741 Reg.57
Art.16, applied: SI 2008/1741 Reg.57

3238. Non-Domestic Rating Contributions (Wales) Regulations 1992
Sch.4, substituted: SI 2008/2838 Sch.1, SI 2008/2929 Sch.1

3288. Package Travel, Package Holidays and Package Tours Regulations 1992
Reg.11, see *R. (on the application of Federation of Tour Operators) v HM Treasury* [2008] EWCA Civ 752, [2008] S.T.C. 2524 (CA (Civ Div)), Waller, L.J. (V-P)
Reg.15, see *Evans v Kosmar Villa Holiday Plc* [2007] EWCA Civ 1003, [2008] 1 W.L.R. 297 (CA (Civ Div)), Arden, L.J.

1993

9. Rail Crossing Extinguishment and Diversion Orders Regulations 1993
Sch.2, varied: SI 2008/442 Sch.1 para.3, Sch.1 para.6

10. Town and Country Planning (Public Path Orders) Regulations 1993
Sch.1, varied: SI 2008/442 Sch.1 para.9, Sch.1 para.10

11. Public Path Orders Regulations 1993
Sch.1, varied: SI 2008/442 Sch.1 para.1, Sch.1 para.2, Sch.1 para.5

202. Local Authorities (Standing Orders) Regulations 1993
applied: SI 2008/1419 Reg.4
Sch.1 Part I para.1, varied: SI 2008/1419 Reg.4
Sch.1 Part I para.1A, varied: SI 2008/1419 Reg.4

252. Non-Domestic Rating (Demand Notices) (Wales) Regulations 1993
referred to: SI 2008/7 Reg.2

NO.

1993–cont.

252. Non-Domestic Rating (Demand Notices) (Wales) Regulations 1993–*cont.*
Sch.2 Part I para.1, amended: SI 2008/7 Reg.2, SI 2008/3075 Reg.2
Sch.2 Part II para.1, amended: SI 2008/7 Reg.2, SI 2008/3075 Reg.2

290. Council Tax (Alteration of Lists and Appeals) Regulations 1993
referred to: SI 2008/315 Reg.3
see *Chilton-Merryweather (Listing Officer) v Hunt* [2008] EWCA Civ 1025, [2008] R.A. 357 (CA (Civ Div)), Waller, L.J.
Reg.2, amended: SI 2008/315 Reg.4
Reg.4, see *McKenzie (Listing Officer) v Marshall* [2008] EWHC 641 (Admin), [2008] R.A. 269 (QBD (Admin)), Dobbs, J.
Reg.8, amended: SI 2008/315 Reg.5
Reg.10, substituted: SI 2008/315 Reg.6
Reg.11, revoked (in part): SI 2008/315 Reg.7
Reg.12, revoked (in part): SI 2008/315 Reg.7
Reg.13, substituted: SI 2008/315 Reg.8
Reg.13, see *McKenzie (Listing Officer) v Marshall* [2008] EWHC 641 (Admin), [2008] R.A. 269 (QBD (Admin)), Dobbs, J.
Reg.14, see *McKenzie (Listing Officer) v Marshall* [2008] EWHC 641 (Admin), [2008] R.A. 269 (QBD (Admin)), Dobbs, J.
Reg.15, amended: SI 2008/315 Reg.9
Reg.16, amended: SI 2008/315 Reg.10
Reg.17, amended: SI 2008/315 Reg.11
Reg.18, amended: SI 2008/315 Reg.12
Reg.18A, added: SI 2008/315 Reg.13
Reg.18B, added: SI 2008/315 Reg.13
Reg.18C, added: SI 2008/315 Reg.13
Reg.18D, added: SI 2008/315 Reg.13
Reg.18E, added: SI 2008/315 Reg.13
Reg.19, substituted: SI 2008/315 Reg.14
Reg.19A, substituted: SI 2008/315 Reg.14
Reg.19B, substituted: SI 2008/315 Reg.14
Reg.23, amended: SI 2008/315 Reg.15
Reg.24, amended: SI 2008/315 Reg.16
Reg.32, see *McKenzie (Listing Officer) v Marshall* [2008] EWHC 641 (Admin), [2008] R.A. 269 (QBD (Admin)), Dobbs, J.
Reg.35, amended: SI 2008/315 Reg.17, SI 2008/316 Art.2

291. Non-Domestic Rating (Alteration of Lists and Appeals) Regulations 1993
Reg.4, see *Womersley (Valuation Officer) v Hart DC* [2008] R.A. 279 (Lands Tr), Judge Huskinson
Reg.7, see *Womersley (Valuation Officer) v Hart DC* [2008] R.A. 279 (Lands Tr), Judge Huskinson

NO.

1993–cont.

486. Bankruptcy Fees (Scotland) Regulations 1993
Reg.2, amended: SSI 2008/5 Reg.2, SSI 2008/79 Reg.3
Reg.3, amended: SSI 2008/79 Reg.4
Reg.4, amended: SSI 2008/79 Reg.5
Reg.5, amended: SSI 2008/79 Reg.6
Reg.6, amended: SSI 2008/79 Reg.7
Reg.7, amended: SSI 2008/79 Reg.8
Reg.8, amended: SSI 2008/79 Reg.9
Reg.9, amended: SSI 2008/79 Reg.10
Reg.10, added: SSI 2008/79 Reg.11
Reg.11, added: SSI 2008/79 Reg.11
Reg.12, added: SSI 2008/79 Reg.11
Sch.1, referred to: SSI 2008/143 Reg.18
Sch.1 Part I, amended: SSI 2008/79 Reg.12
Sch.1 Part I, substituted: SSI 2008/5 Sch.1
Sch.1 Part II, amended: SSI 2008/79 Reg.12
Sch.1 Part II, substituted: SSI 2008/5 Sch.1

494. Council Tax (Deductions from Income Support) Regulations 1993
Reg.1, amended: SI 2008/1554 Reg.55
Reg.2, amended: SI 2008/1554 Reg.55
Reg.3, amended: SI 2008/1554 Reg.55
Reg.4, amended: SI 2008/1554 Reg.55
Reg.5, amended: SI 2008/1554 Reg.55
Reg.8, amended: SI 2008/1554 Reg.55

500. Water Supply and Sewerage Services (Customer Service Standards) (Amendment) Regulations 1993
revoked: SI 2008/594 Sch.1

557. Napier University (Scotland) Order of Council 1993
Art.2, amended: SSI 2008/388 Art.2
Art.13, amended: SSI 2008/388 Art.2

595. European Communities (Designation) Order 1993
Sch.1, amended: SI 2008/301 Sch.1

624. Children (Allocation of Proceedings) (Amendment) Order 1993
revoked: SI 2008/2836 Sch.2

627. Family Proceedings Courts (Child Support Act 1991) Rules 1993
applied: 2008 c.6 Sch.2
r.5, amended: SI 2008/2683 Sch.1 para.63

920. Act of Sederunt (Child Support Rules) 1993
Sch.1, amended: SSI 2008/223 r.16

987. Retention of Registration Marks Regulations 1993
Reg.2, amended: SI 2008/2850 Reg.3
Reg.3, substituted: SI 2008/2850 Reg.4
Reg.4, amended: SI 2008/2850 Reg.5
Reg.4A, amended: SI 2008/2850 Reg.6
Reg.5, substituted: SI 2008/2850 Reg.7
Reg.7, amended: SI 2008/2850 Reg.8
Reg.8, amended: SI 2008/2850 Reg.9
Reg.9, amended: SI 2008/2850 Reg.10
Reg.10, amended: SI 2008/2850 Reg.11
Reg.11, amended: SI 2008/2850 Reg.12

NO.

1993–cont.

1202. Road Traffic (Parking Adjudicators) (London) Regulations 1993
Reg.9, amended: SI 2008/2683 Sch.1 para.64

1228. Beer Regulations 1993
referred to: SI 2008/2302 Art.3
Reg.26, substituted: SI 2008/1885 Reg.2
Reg.27, revoked: SI 2008/1885 Reg.2
Reg.28, amended: SI 2008/1885 Reg.2
Reg.29, amended: SI 2008/1885 Reg.2
Reg.30, substituted: SI 2008/1885 Reg.2
Reg.31, revoked: SI 2008/1885 Reg.2
Reg.32, amended: SI 2008/1885 Reg.2
Reg.33, amended: SI 2008/1885 Reg.2
Reg.33A, added: SI 2008/1885 Reg.2
Reg.33B, added: SI 2008/1885 Reg.2

1593. Local Government Superannuation (Scotland) Amendment Regulations 1993
revoked: SSI 2008/229 Sch.1

1679. Income Support (General) Amendment No.3 Regulations 1993
Reg.4, applied: SI 2008/794 Sch.6 para.12

1787. United Nations Arms Embargoes (Liberia, Somalia and the Former Yugoslavia) Order 1993
Art.2, amended: SI 2008/3128 Art.2
Art.2, revoked (in part): SI 2008/3128 Art.2
Art.3, revoked (in part): SI 2008/3128 Art.2
Art.7, revoked (in part): SI 2008/3128 Art.2
Art.8, amended: SI 2008/3128 Art.2
Art.10, amended: SI 2008/3128 Art.2
Sch.1 para.4, amended: SI 2008/3128 Art.2

1820. Partnerships and Unlimited Companies (Accounts) Regulations 1993
revoked: SI 2008/569 Reg.18
Reg.7, applied: SI 2008/409 Sch.2 para.8, Sch.6 para.34, SI 2008/410 Sch.4 para.7

1897. Management and Administration of Safety and Health at Mines Regulations 1993
Reg.20, amended: SI 2008/960 Sch.3

1956. Act of Sederunt (Sheriff Court Ordinary Cause Rules) 1993
see *Cultural and Educational Development Association of Scotland v Glasgow City Council* [2008] CSIH 23, 2008 S.C. 439 (IH (Ex Div)), Lord Macfadyen
Sch.1, applied: SI 2008/794 Sch.9 para.44
Sch.1, see *Barr Roads & Contracting v Lusk Construction Ltd* 2008 S.C.L.R. 749 (Sh Ct (North Strathclyde) (Kilmarnock)), Sheriff Ireland; see *Cultural and Educational Development Association of Scotland v Glasgow City Council* [2008] CSIH 23, 2008 S.C. 439 (IH (Ex Div)), Lord Macfadyen

1966. Importation of Bovine Semen (Amendment) Regulations 1993
revoked (in part): SI 2008/1040 Sch.10 Part 1

NO.

1993–cont.

2013. Local Government Superannuation (Scotland) Amendment (No.2) Regulations 1993
revoked: SSI 2008/229 Sch.1

2015. Fishing Boats (Marking and Documentation) (Enforcement) Order 1993
Art.3, applied: SSI 2008/101 Sch.1 Part 1, Sch.1 Part 2

2073. Enforcement of Road Traffic Debts Order 1993
applied: SI 2008/1053 Sch.1

2156. Mental Health (Hospital, Guardianship and Consent to Treatment) Amendment Regulations 1993
revoked (in part): SI 2008/1184 Sch.2, SI 2008/2439 Sch.2

2166. Controlled Drugs (Substances Useful for Manufacture) (Intra-Community Trade) Regulations 1993
revoked: SI 2008/295 Reg.9

2240. Housing (Extension of Right to Buy) Order 1993
Art.3, varied: SI 2008/2839 Sch.1 para.1

2241. Housing (Preservation of Right to Buy) Regulations 1993
varied: SI 2008/3002 Art.7

2661. European Communities (Designation) (No.3) Order 1993
Sch.1, amended: SI 2008/301 Sch.1

2854. Employment Appeal Tribunal Rules 1993
r.2A, see *Jurkowska v Hlmad Ltd* [2008] EWCA Civ 231, [2008] C.P. Rep. 27 (CA (Civ Div)), Sedley, L.J.

3031. Transfrontier Shipment of Radioactive Waste Regulations 1993
revoked: SI 2008/3087 Reg.19

3044. Local Government Superannuation (Scotland) Amendment (No.3) Regulations 1993
revoked: SSI 2008/229 Sch.1

3050. Notification of New Substances Regulations 1993
applied: SI 2008/736 Reg.14, Sch.11
referred to: SI 2008/2108
revoked: SI 2008/2852 Sch.10 Part 2
Reg.3, amended: SI 2008/2108 Reg.5
Reg.4, applied: SI 2008/736 Sch.11
Reg.5, applied: SI 2008/736 Sch.11
Reg.6, applied: SI 2008/736 Sch.11
Reg.11, applied: SI 2008/736 Sch.11
Reg.13, applied: SI 2008/736 Sch.11
Reg.23, applied: SI 2008/736 Sch.11

3053. Commercial Agents (Council Directive) Regulations 1993
see *Nigel Fryer Joinery Services Ltd v Ian Firth Hardware Ltd* [2008] EWHC 767 (Ch), [2008] 2 Lloyd's Rep. 108 (CC (Manchester)), Patten, J.; see *Sagal (t/a Bunz UK) v Atelier Bunz GmbH* [2008]

NO.

1993–cont.

3053. Commercial Agents (Council Directive) Regulations 1993–*cont.*
see–*cont.*
EWHC 789 (Comm), [2008] 2 Lloyd's Rep. 158 (QBD (Comm)), Judge Mackie Q.C.
Reg.2, see *Sagal (t/a Bunz UK) v Atelier Bunz GmbH* [2008] EWHC 789 (Comm), [2008] 2 Lloyd's Rep. 158 (QBD (Comm)), Judge Mackie Q.C.
Reg.15, see *Nigel Fryer Joinery Services Ltd v Ian Firth Hardware Ltd* [2008] EWHC 767 (Ch), [2008] 2 Lloyd's Rep. 108 (CC (Manchester)), Patten, J.
Reg.16, see *Nigel Fryer Joinery Services Ltd v Ian Firth Hardware Ltd* [2008] EWHC 767 (Ch), [2008] 2 Lloyd's Rep. 108 (CC (Manchester)), Patten, J.
Reg.17, see *Nigel Fryer Joinery Services Ltd v Ian Firth Hardware Ltd* [2008] EWHC 767 (Ch), [2008] 2 Lloyd's Rep. 108 (CC (Manchester)), Patten, J.
Reg.18, see *Nigel Fryer Joinery Services Ltd v Ian Firth Hardware Ltd* [2008] EWHC 767 (Ch), [2008] 2 Lloyd's Rep. 108 (CC (Manchester)), Patten, J.

3080. Act of Sederunt (Fees of Solicitors in the Sheriff Court) (Amendment and Further Provisions) 1993
see *Mitchell v Hass Tek Services Ltd* 2008 S.L.T. (Sh Ct) 112 (Sh Ct (South Strathclyde)), Sheriff KA Ross
Sch.1 Part 1, amended: SSI 2008/40 Sch.1
Sch.1 Part 1 para.1, amended: SSI 2008/40 Sch.1
Sch.1 Part 1 para.2, amended: SSI 2008/40 Sch.1
Sch.1 Part 1 para.3, amended: SSI 2008/40 Sch.1
Sch.1 para.14, amended: SSI 2008/40 Art.2

3187. Advice and Assistance (Financial Limit) (Scotland) Regulations 1993
Reg.3, amended: SSI 2008/251 Reg.2
Reg.3, referred to: SSI 2008/137 Reg.7
Reg.3, revoked (in part): SSI 2008/251 Reg.2
Reg.3, varied: SSI 2008/416 Art.2
Reg.4, revoked (in part): SSI 2008/251 Reg.2

3228. Public Services Contracts Regulations 1993
Reg.23, see *Partenaire Ltd v Department of Finance and Personnel* [2008] Eu. L.R. 501 (QBD (NI)), Coghlin, J.
Reg.32, see *Lion Apparel Systems Ltd v Firebuy Ltd* [2007] EWHC 2179 (Ch), [2008] Eu. L.R. 191 (Ch D), Morgan, J.; see *Lion Apparel Systems Ltd v Firebuy Ltd* [2008] EWHC 122 (Ch), [2008] Eu. L.R. 564 (Ch D), Morgan, J.; see *Partenaire Ltd v Department of Finance and Personnel* [2008] Eu. L.R. 501 (QBD (NI)), Coghlin, J.

NO.

1993–cont.

3245. Insurance Accounts Directive (Miscellaneous Insurance Undertakings) Regulations 1993
revoked: SI 2008/565 Reg.16

1994

105. Medicines (Homoeopathic Medicinal Products for Human Use) Regulations 1994
Reg.14, amended: SI 2008/552 Reg.47
Reg.15, amended: SI 2008/552 Reg.47
Sch.2 para.3, amended: SI 2008/552 Reg.47
Sch.2A para.2, amended: SI 2008/552 Reg.47

227. Child Support (Miscellaneous Amendments and Transitional Provisions) Regulations 1994
applied: 2008 c.6 Sch.2

232. Batteries and Accumulators (Containing Dangerous Substances) Regulations 1994
revoked: SI 2008/2164 Sch.2

295. Income Tax (Deposit-takers) (Interest Payments) (Amendment) Regulations 1994
revoked: SI 2008/2682 Sch.3

296. Income Tax (Building Societies) (Dividends and Interest) (Amendment) Regulations 1994
revoked: SI 2008/2682 Sch.3

426. Airports (Northern Ireland) Order 1994
Art.31, amended: SI 2008/948 Sch.1 para.197
Art.49, amended: SI 2008/1277 Sch.2 para.84
Art.49, revoked (in part): SI 2008/1277 Sch.2 para.84, Sch.4 Part 2
Art.50, amended: SI 2008/948 Sch.1 para.197
Art.57, amended: SI 2008/948 Sch.1 para.197
Art.60, amended: SI 2008/948 Sch.1 para.197
Art.61, amended: SI 2008/948 Sch.1 para.197

429. Health and Personal Social Services (Northern Ireland) Order 1994
Sch.1, amended: SI 2008/1769 Sch.1 para.23, Sch.3

531. Local Government Superannuation (Scotland) Amendment Regulations 1994
revoked: SSI 2008/229 Sch.1

570. Channel Tunnel (Security) Order 1994
Part II, applied: 2008 c.28 Sch.2, SI 2008/1216 Sch.1 para.24, Sch.2 para.24

574. Railways (Heathrow Express) (Exemptions) Order 1994
Art.3, applied: 2008 c.18 s.26
Art.3, referred to: 2008 c.18 s.26

NO.

1994–cont.

574. Railways (Heathrow Express) (Exemptions) Order 1994–*cont.*
Art.4, applied: 2008 c.18 s.26
Art.4, referred to: 2008 c.18 s.26

627. Housing (Right to Manage) Regulations 1994
applied: SI 2008/2361 Reg.22, Reg.25
revoked (in part): SI 2008/2361 Reg.2
Reg.2, applied: SI 2008/2361 Reg.23
Reg.2, referred to: SI 2008/2361 Reg.23
Reg.3, applied: SI 2008/2361 Reg.24
Reg.3, referred to: SI 2008/2361 Reg.24
Reg.4, applied: SI 2008/2361 Reg.25

651. Education (Special Educational Needs) (Approval of Independent Schools) Regulations 1994
Sch.1 para.7, revoked (in part): SI 2008/1701 Reg.3

704. Social Security Pensions (Home Responsibilities) Regulations 1994
Reg.2, amended: SI 2008/498 Reg.2

757. European Communities (Designation) Order 1994
Sch.1, amended: SI 2008/301 Sch.1

867. Local Government Changes for England Regulations 1994
applied: SI 2008/3252 Reg.3
Reg.5, amended: SI 2008/2867 Reg.34

950. Foreign Companies (Execution of Documents) Regulations 1994
applied: SI 2008/948 Art.7

955. Travellers Allowances Order 1994
Art.2, amended: SI 2008/3058 Sch.1 para.1, Sch.1 para.2, Sch.1 para.3
Art.2, referred to: SI 2008/3058 Art.1
Art.3, amended: SI 2008/3058 Sch.1 para.4
Art.4, amended: SI 2008/3058 Sch.1 para.5
Sch.1, amended: SI 2008/3058 Sch.1 para.6

1056. Waste Management Licensing Regulations 1994
applied: SSI 2008/100 Sch.2 Part 1, Sch.4 Part 2, SSI 2008/159 Sch.3 Part 2, SSI 2008/298 Reg.8

1062. Occupational and Personal Pension Schemes (Consequential Amendments) Regulations 1994
applied: SSI 2008/228 Reg.73

1151. Wildlife and Countryside Act 1981 (Variation of Schedule 4) Order 1994
Art.3, revoked (in part): SI 2008/2356 Art.4

1443. Act of Sederunt (Rules of the Court of Session 1994) 1994
referred to: SSI 2008/349 r.2
see *Stephen v Simon Mokster Shipping AS* [2008] CSOH 99, 2008 S.L.T. 743 (OH), Lord Clarke
Appendix 1, amended: SSI 2008/122 r.3, Sch.1, SSI 2008/123 r.4, SSI 2008/349 r.3, r.6
Sch.2 Part 2 para.4.11, revoked (in part): SSI 2008/122 r.3

NO.

1994–cont.

1443. Act of Sederunt (Rules of the Court of Session 1994) 1994–*cont.*

Sch.2 para.4.16, see *Billig v Council of the Law Society of Scotland* 2008 S.L.T. 227 (IH (1 Div)), Lord Hamilton L.P.

Sch.2 Part 3, applied: SSI 2008/122 r.3

Sch.2 Part 3, added: SSI 2008/122 r.3

Sch.2 Part 3, added: SSI 2008/349 r.4

Sch.2 Part 3 para.13.2, amended: SSI 2008/122 r.3, SSI 2008/349 r.3

Sch.2 Part 3 para.13.6A, revoked (in part): SSI 2008/122 r.3

Sch.2 Part 3 para.13.8A, revoked (in part): SSI 2008/122 r.3

Sch.2 Part 3 para.13.9, revoked: SSI 2008/122 r.3

Sch.2 Part 3 para.13.10, revoked: SSI 2008/122 r.3

Sch.2 Part 3 para.14.4, amended: SSI 2008/349 r.3

Sch.2 Part 3 para.15.1, amended: SSI 2008/349 r.4

Sch.2 Part 3 para.16.2A, amended: SSI 2008/349 r.5

Sch.2 Part 3 para.16.4, amended: SSI 2008/349 r.6

Sch.2 Part 3 para.16.15, amended: SSI 2008/122 r.3

Sch.2 Part 3 para.21A, added: SSI 2008/349 r.4

Sch.2 Part 3 para.21.2, amended: SSI 2008/349 r.6

Sch.2 Part 3 para.41.20, amended: SSI 2008/349 r.7

Sch.2 Part 3 para.41.21, amended: SSI 2008/349 r.7

Sch.2 Part 3 para.41.41, revoked (in part): SSI 2008/349 r.7

Sch.2 Part 3 para.41.44, amended: SSI 2008/349 r.7

Sch.2 Part 3 para.41.59, added: SSI 2008/349 r.7

Sch.2 Part 3 para.42.1, amended: SSI 2008/123 r.2

Sch.2 Part 3 para.42.9, amended: SSI 2008/39 r.2

Sch.2 Part 3 para.42.16, amended: SSI 2008/39 Sch.1, SSI 2008/120 r.2

Sch.2 para.4.16, see *Billig v Council of the Law Society of Scotland* 2008 S.C. 150 (IH (1 Div)), Lord Hamilton L.P.

Sch.2 Part 4 para.43.5, amended: SSI 2008/349 r.8

Sch.2 Part 4 para.47.3, amended: SSI 2008/349 r.3

Sch.2 Part 4 para.50.2, amended: SSI 2008/349 r.6

Sch.2 Part 4 para.50.5, amended: SSI 2008/349 r.6

Sch.2 Part 4 para.58.6, amended: SSI 2008/349 r.3

NO.

1994–cont.

1443. Act of Sederunt (Rules of the Court of Session 1994) 1994–*cont.*

Sch.2 Part 4 para.58.7A, added: SSI 2008/349 r.9

Sch.2 Part 4 para.58.8A, amended: SSI 2008/123 r.3

Sch.2 Part 4 para.58.11, added: SSI 2008/349 r.9

Sch.2 Part 5, applied: SSI 2008/122 r.4

Sch.2 Part 5, substituted: SSI 2008/122 r.4

Sch.2 Part 5, added: SSI 2008/123 r.3

Sch.2 Part 5 para.96.1, added: SSI 2008/401 r.2

Sch.2 Part 5 para.96.2, added: SSI 2008/401 r.2

Sch.2 Part 5 para.96.3, added: SSI 2008/401 r.2

Sch.2 Part 5 para.96.4, added: SSI 2008/401 r.2

Sch.2 Part 5 para.96.5, added: SSI 2008/401 r.2

Sch.2 Part 5 para.96.6, added: SSI 2008/401 r.2

Sch.2 Part 5 para.96.7, added: SSI 2008/401 r.2

Sch.2 Part 5 para.96.8, added: SSI 2008/401 r.2

Sch.2 Part 5 para.96.9, added: SSI 2008/401 r.2

Sch.2 Part 5 para.96.10, added: SSI 2008/401 r.2

Sch.2 Part 5 para.96.11, added: SSI 2008/401 r.2

Sch.2 Part 5 para.96.12, added: SSI 2008/401 r.2

Sch.2 Part 5 para.96.13, added: SSI 2008/401 r.2

Sch.2 para.42.7, see *Stuart v Bulger* [2008] CSOH 102, 2008 S.L.T. 817 (OH), Lord Mackay of Drumadoon

Sch.2 para.42.14, see *Trunature Ltd v Scotnet (1974) Ltd* [2008] CSIH 33, 2008 S.L.T. 653 (IH (2 Div)), Lord Gill L.J.C.

Sch.2 para.43.11, see *Fletcher v Lunan* 2008 Rep. L.R. 72 (OH), Lord Carloway

Sch.2 para.65.3, see *Royal Bank of Scotland Group Plc v Revenue and Customs Commissioners* [2008] S.T.C. 1485 (IH (2 Div)), Lord Gill L.J.C.

Sch.2 Part 5 para.95.1, added: SSI 2008/123 r.3

Sch.2 Part 5 para.95.2, added: SSI 2008/123 r.3

Sch.2 Part 5 para.95.3, added: SSI 2008/123 r.3

Sch.2 Part 5 para.95.4, added: SSI 2008/123 r.3

Sch.2 Part 5 para.95.5, added: SSI 2008/123 r.3

NO.

1994–cont.

1701. Organic Aid (Scotland) Regulations 1994

applied: SSI 2008/100 Sch.2 Part 1, SSI 2008/159 Sch.2

1729. Nitrate Sensitive Areas Regulations 1994

revoked: SI 2008/2349 Reg.50

1738. Air Passenger Duty Regulations 1994

Sch.3, amended: SI 2008/1482 Sch.2

1774. Insurance Premium Tax Regulations 1994

Reg.13, amended: SI 2008/1482 Reg.3, SI 2008/2693 Reg.4

Reg.29, revoked: SI 2008/1945 Reg.3

Reg.30, revoked: SI 2008/1945 Reg.3

Reg.31, revoked: SI 2008/1945 Reg.3

Reg.33, substituted: SI 2008/1945 Reg.4

Sch.1, amended: SI 2008/1482 Sch.1, SI 2008/1945 Sch.1

1806. Notification of Existing Substances (Enforcement) Regulations 1994

revoked: SI 2008/2852 Sch.10 Part 2

1811. Special Commissioners (Jurisdiction and Procedure) Regulations 1994

applied: SI 2008/562 Reg.20

Reg.2, amended: SI 2008/574 Sch.1 para.4

Reg.9, see *University College London v Revenue and Customs Commissioners* [2008] B.V.C. 2376 (V&DTr (London)), John Clark (Chairman)

Reg.19, see *Dunne v Revenue and Customs Commissioners* [2008] S.T.C. (S.C.D.) 527 (Sp Comm), Sir Stephen Oliver Q.C.

Reg.21, see *Businessman v Revenue and Customs Commissioners* [2008] S.T.C. (S.C.D.) 1151 (Sp Comm), Dr John F Avery Jones; see *GC Trading Ltd v Revenue and Customs Commissioners (Costs)* [2008] S.T.C. (S.C.D.) 855 (Sp Comm), Adrian Shipwright; see *Nightswood BV v Revenue and Customs Commissioners* [2008] S.T.C. (S.C.D.) 384 (Sp Comm), Adrian Shipwright

1812. General Commissioners (Jurisdiction and Procedure) Regulations 1994

applied: SI 2008/562 Reg.20

Reg.20, see *Rouf (t/a New Balaka Restaurant) v General Commissioners of Income Tax* [2008] S.T.C. 1557 (OH), Lord Macphail

1813. General and Special Commissioners (Amendment of Enactments) Regulations 1994

applied: SI 2008/562 Reg.20

1885. Local Authorities (Charges for Land Searches) Regulations 1994

applied: SI 2008/3248 Reg.3

revoked (in part): SI 2008/3248 Reg.3

1983. Friendly Societies (Accounts and Related Provisions) Regulations 1994

Reg.8, amended: SI 2008/1144 Sch.1 para.1

NO.

1994–cont.

1983. Friendly Societies (Accounts and Related Provisions) Regulations 1994–*cont.*

Reg.8, revoked (in part): SI 2008/1144 Sch.1 para.1

Reg.9, revoked: SI 2008/1144 Reg.3

Sch.2 Part III para.4, amended: SI 2008/1144 Sch.1 para.2

Sch.4 para.3, revoked: SI 2008/1144 Reg.4

Sch.4 para.4, revoked: SI 2008/1144 Reg.4

Sch.4 para.5, revoked: SI 2008/1144 Reg.4

Sch.4 para.6, revoked: SI 2008/1144 Reg.4

Sch.4 para.7, revoked: SI 2008/1144 Reg.4

Sch.4 para.8, revoked: SI 2008/1144 Reg.4

Sch.4 para.9, revoked: SI 2008/1144 Reg.4

Sch.4 para.10, revoked: SI 2008/1144 Reg.4

Sch.4 para.11, revoked: SI 2008/1144 Reg.4

Sch.4 para.12, revoked: SI 2008/1144 Reg.4

Sch.4 para.13, revoked: SI 2008/1144 Reg.4

Sch.4 para.14, revoked: SI 2008/1144 Reg.4

Sch.4 para.30, revoked (in part): SI 2008/1144 Reg.4

Sch.4 para.31, revoked: SI 2008/1144 Reg.4

Sch.4 para.35, added: SI 2008/1144 Reg.5

Sch.5 Part I para.1, revoked: SI 2008/1144 Reg.6

Sch.5 Part I para.2, revoked: SI 2008/1144 Reg.6

Sch.5 Part I para.3, revoked: SI 2008/1144 Reg.6

Sch.5 Part I para.4, revoked: SI 2008/1144 Reg.6

Sch.5 Part I para.5, revoked: SI 2008/1144 Reg.6

Sch.5 Part I para.6, revoked: SI 2008/1144 Reg.6

Sch.5 Part I para.7, revoked: SI 2008/1144 Reg.6

Sch.5 Part I para.8, revoked: SI 2008/1144 Reg.6

Sch.5 Part II para.9, revoked: SI 2008/1144 Reg.6

Sch.5 Part II para.10, revoked: SI 2008/1144 Reg.6

Sch.5 Part II para.11, revoked: SI 2008/1144 Reg.6

Sch.5 Part II para.12, revoked: SI 2008/1144 Reg.6

Sch.5 Part II para.13, revoked: SI 2008/1144 Reg.6

Sch.5 Part II para.14, revoked: SI 2008/1144 Reg.6

Sch.5 Part II para.15, revoked: SI 2008/1144 Reg.6

Sch.5 Part II para.16, revoked: SI 2008/1144 Reg.6

Sch.5 Part II para.17, revoked: SI 2008/1144 Reg.6

Sch.5 Part II para.18, revoked: SI 2008/1144 Reg.6

NO.

1994–cont.

1983. Friendly Societies (Accounts and Related Provisions) Regulations 1994–*cont.*

Sch.5 Part II para.19, revoked: SI 2008/1144 Reg.6

Sch.5 Part II para.20, revoked: SI 2008/1144 Reg.6

Sch.5 Part III para.21, revoked: SI 2008/1144 Reg.6

Sch.5 Part III para.22, revoked: SI 2008/1144 Reg.6

Sch.5 Part III para.32, revoked: SI 2008/1144 Reg.6

Sch.5 Part III para.33, revoked: SI 2008/1144 Reg.6

Sch.5 Part III para.34, revoked: SI 2008/1144 Reg.6

Sch.6 Part IVA para.24A, amended: SI 2008/1144 Reg.7

Sch.7 Part III, revoked (in part): SI 2008/1144 Sch.1 para.3

Sch.9 para.6, amended: SI 2008/1144 Sch.1 para.4

Sch.9 para.9, revoked: SI 2008/1144 Sch.1 para.4

2023. Police Authorities (Selection Panel) Regulations 1994

revoked: SI 2008/630 Reg.4

Reg.7, applied: SI 2008/630 Reg.5, SI 2008/631 Reg.4

2063. Supply of Machinery (Safety) (Amendment) Regulations 1994

revoked: SI 2008/1597 Sch.1

2155. Pig Carcase (Grading) Regulations 1994

Reg.7, revoked (in part): SI 2008/576 Sch.5 para.8

2164. Children (Allocation of Proceedings) (Amendment) Order 1994

revoked: SI 2008/2836 Sch.2

2195. Police (Amendment) (No.2) Regulations 1994

see *Holmes v South Yorkshire Police Authority* [2008] EWCA Civ 51, [2008] H.L.R. 33 (CA (Civ Div)), Sedley, L.J.

2507. Insolvency Regulations 1994

Reg.3B, added: SI 2008/670 Reg.3

Reg.3C, added: SI 2008/670 Reg.3

Reg.18, substituted: SI 2008/670 Reg.3

2616. Solicitors (Non-Contentious Business) Remuneration Order 1994

applied: SI 2008/1969 Sch.1 Part Table a, Sch.2 para.1, Sch.2 para.4

2716. Conservation (Natural Habitats, c.) Regulations 1994

applied: SSI 2008/100 Sch.4 Part 2, SSI 2008/159 Sch.3 Part 2, SSI 2008/427 Art.2, Art.3, Art.4, Art.5, SSI 2008/432 Sch.2 para.4

referred to: SSI 2008/263 Sch.2

Reg.37A, amended: SSI 2008/425 Reg.3

NO.

1994–cont.

2716. Conservation (Natural Habitats, c.) Regulations 1994–*cont.*

Reg.39, amended: SI 2008/2172 Reg.3, SSI 2008/17 Reg.2, SSI 2008/425 Reg.4

Reg.39, revoked (in part): SSI 2008/17 Reg.2

Reg.40, amended: SSI 2008/425 Reg.5

Reg.41A, substituted: SSI 2008/425 Reg.6

Reg.48, applied: SI 2008/1160 Art.18, SSI 2008/361 Art.32

Reg.60, applied: SSI 2008/361 Art.32

Reg.60, disapplied: SI 2008/1160 Art.18, SSI 2008/361 Art.32

Reg.85A, amended: SSI 2008/427 Art.8

Reg.85D, amended: SSI 2008/427 Art.8

Sch.2, amended: SI 2008/2172 Reg.2

Sch.2A, amended: SSI 2008/17 Reg.2

2809. Ports (Northern Ireland) Order 1994

Sch.1, amended: SI 2008/948 Sch.1 para.198

2841. Urban Waste Water Treatment (England and Wales) Regulations 1994

see *Dobson v Thames Water Utilities Ltd* [2007] EWHC 2021 (TCC), [2008] 2 All E.R. 362 (QBD (TCC)), Ramsey, J.; see *R. (on the application of Thames Water Utilities Ltd) v Bromley Magistrates Court* [2008] EWHC 1763 (QB), Times, August 28, 2008 (DC), Carnwath, L.J.

Reg.2, referred to: 2008 c.29 s.29

2842. Urban Waste Water Treatment (Scotland) Regulations 1994

referred to: SSI 2008/263 Sch.2

2924. Teachers Superannuation (Additional Voluntary Contributions) Regulations 1994

Reg.2, amended: SI 2008/541 Reg.3

Reg.7, amended: SI 2008/541 Reg.4

Reg.12, amended: SI 2008/541 Reg.5

Reg.16, amended: SI 2008/541 Reg.6

2946. Social Security (Incapacity Benefit) Regulations 1994

Reg.4A, amended: SI 2008/2683 Sch.1 para.65

Reg.8, amended: SI 2008/2365 Reg.3

Reg.10, amended: SI 2008/632 Art.14

Reg.10, applied: SI 2008/3270 Reg.2

Reg.21, amended: SI 2008/2365 Reg.3

3013. Value Added Tax (Buildings and Land) Order 1994

revoked: SI 2008/1146 Sch.1 para.12

3039. Police (Special Constables) (Scotland) Amendment Regulations 1994

revoked: SSI 2008/117 Sch.3

3138. Children (Allocation of Proceedings) (Amendment) (No.2) Order 1994

revoked: SI 2008/2836 Sch.2

3144. Medicines for Human Use (Marketing Authorisations Etc.) Regulations 1994

applied: SI 2008/944 Art.5, SI 2008/1270 Art.5

NO.

1994–cont.

3144. Medicines for Human Use (Marketing Authorisations Etc.) Regulations 1994–*cont.*
Reg.1, amended: SI 2008/3097 Reg.2
Reg.1, applied: SI 2008/548 Art.3
Reg.2, applied: SI 2008/548 Art.3
Reg.4, applied: SI 2008/552 Reg.18, Reg.35
Sch.2 Part 1 para.5, applied: SI 2008/552 Sch.5 para.2
Sch.2 Part 2 para.11, applied: SI 2008/552 Reg.35
Sch.2 Part 3 para.16, applied: SI 2008/552 Reg.35
Sch.2 Part 4 para.17, applied: SI 2008/552 Reg.35
Sch.3 para.6, amended: SI 2008/3097 Reg.3
Sch.3 para.6AA, added: SI 2008/3097 Reg.3
Sch.3 para.6BA, added: SI 2008/3097 Reg.3
Sch.3 para.6BB, added: SI 2008/3097 Reg.3
Sch.3 para.6G, added: SI 2008/3097 Reg.3
Sch.3 para.10, amended: SI 2008/3097 Reg.3
Sch.3 para.11, amended: SI 2008/3097 Reg.3
Sch.3 para.12, amended: SI 2008/3097 Reg.3
Sch.3 para.13B, added: SI 2008/3097 Reg.3
Sch.3 para.17, amended: SI 2008/3097 Reg.3

3200. Non-Domestic Rating (Unoccupied Property) (Scotland) Regulations 1994
Sch.1 Part 1, amended: SSI 2008/83 Reg.2

1995

11. Pigs (Records, Identification and Movement) Order 1995
referred to: SSI 2008/369 Art.2
Art.2, amended: SSI 2008/369 Art.2

35. Occupational and Personal Pension Schemes (Miscellaneous Amendments) Regulations 1995
applied: SSI 2008/228 Reg.73

214. Local Government Superannuation (Scotland) Amendment Regulations 1995
revoked: SSI 2008/229 Sch.1

235. Billing Authorities (Anticipation of Precepts) (Amendment) Regulations 1995
Reg.3, varied: SI 2008/626 Reg.5

239. Non-Domestic Rating (Telecommunications and Canals) (Scotland) Order 1995
Art.2B, substituted: SSI 2008/84 Art.2

262. European Communities (Designation) Order 1995
Sch.1, amended: SI 2008/301 Sch.1

NO.

1995–cont.

279. Value Added Tax (Buildings and Land) Order 1995
revoked: SI 2008/1146 Sch.1 para.13

300. National Health Service Pension Scheme Regulations 1995
applied: SI 2008/653 Reg.1
referred to: SI 2008/653 Reg.1, Reg.2
Reg.A2, amended: SI 2008/654 Reg.2, SI 2008/2263 Reg.3
Reg.B2, amended: SI 2008/2263 Reg.4
Reg.B2, substituted: SI 2008/654 Reg.3
Reg.B3, amended: SI 2008/654 Reg.4
Reg.C1, amended: SI 2008/654 Reg.5
Reg.C2, amended: SI 2008/654 Reg.6
Reg.D1, amended: SI 2008/654 Reg.7, SI 2008/2263 Reg.5
Reg.D2, amended: SI 2008/654 Reg.8, SI 2008/2263 Reg.6
Reg.D2, revoked (in part): SI 2008/654 Reg.8
Reg.E1, amended: SI 2008/654 Reg.9
Reg.E2, amended: SI 2008/654 Reg.10
Reg.E2A, added: SI 2008/654 Reg.11
Reg.E2B, added: SI 2008/654 Reg.11
Reg.E2B, amended: SI 2008/2263 Reg.7
Reg.E2C, added: SI 2008/654 Reg.11
Reg.E3, amended: SI 2008/654 Reg.12
Reg.E4, revoked: SI 2008/654 Reg.13
Reg.E7, added: SI 2008/654 Reg.14
Reg.F1, amended: SI 2008/654 Reg.15
Reg.F2, amended: SI 2008/654 Reg.16, SI 2008/2263 Reg.8
Reg.F5, amended: SI 2008/2263 Reg.17
Reg.F5, substituted: SI 2008/654 Reg.17
Reg.G1, amended: SI 2008/654 Reg.18, Reg.19
Reg.G2, amended: SI 2008/654 Reg.18, Reg.20
Reg.G3, amended: SI 2008/654 Reg.18, Reg.21
Reg.G4, amended: SI 2008/654 Reg.18, Reg.22
Reg.G7, amended: SI 2008/654 Reg.18, Reg.23
Reg.G9, amended: SI 2008/654 Reg.18, Reg.25
Reg.G10, amended: SI 2008/654 Reg.18, Reg.26
Reg.G11, amended: SI 2008/654 Reg.18, Reg.27
Reg.G13, amended: SI 2008/654 Reg.18, Reg.28
Reg.G14, added: SI 2008/654 Reg.29
Reg.G15, added: SI 2008/654 Reg.29
Reg.G16, added: SI 2008/654 Reg.29
Reg.G17, added: SI 2008/654 Reg.29
Reg.H1, amended: SI 2008/654 Reg.30
Reg.H3, amended: SI 2008/654 Reg.31
Reg.H4, amended: SI 2008/654 Reg.32
Reg.H5, amended: SI 2008/654 Reg.33, SI 2008/2263 Reg.9

NO.

1995–cont.

300. National Health Service Pension Scheme Regulations 1995–*cont.*

Reg.H7, amended: SI 2008/654 Reg.34
Reg.J1, amended: SI 2008/654 Reg.35
Reg.K1, substituted: SI 2008/654 Reg.36
Reg.K2, amended: SI 2008/654 Reg.37
Reg.L1, amended: SI 2008/654 Reg.38, SI 2008/2263 Reg.10
Reg.L2, amended: SI 2008/654 Reg.39, SI 2008/2263 Reg.11
Reg.L4, amended: SI 2008/654 Reg.40
Part M, applied: SI 2008/653 Reg.1
Reg.M1, substituted: SI 2008/654 Reg.41
Reg.M2, substituted: SI 2008/654 Reg.41
Reg.M3, amended: SI 2008/2263 Reg.12
Reg.M3, substituted: SI 2008/654 Reg.41
Reg.M4, substituted: SI 2008/654 Reg.41
Reg.M5, substituted: SI 2008/654 Reg.41
Reg.M6, substituted: SI 2008/654 Reg.41
Reg.M7, added: SI 2008/2263 Reg.13
Reg.M7, substituted: SI 2008/654 Reg.41
Reg.N1, amended: SI 2008/654 Reg.42
Reg.N5, revoked: SI 2008/654 Reg.43
Reg.P2, amended: SI 2008/654 Reg.44, SI 2008/2263 Reg.14
Reg.Q1, amended: SI 2008/654 Reg.45
Reg.Q2, amended: SI 2008/654 Reg.46
Reg.Q4, amended: SI 2008/654 Reg.47
Reg.Q4, revoked (in part): SI 2008/654 Reg.47
Reg.Q5, amended: SI 2008/654 Reg.48
Reg.Q6, amended: SI 2008/654 Reg.49
Reg.Q7, amended: SI 2008/654 Reg.50
Reg.G8, amended: SI 2008/654 Reg.18, Reg.24
Reg.Q8, added: SI 2008/654 Reg.51
Reg.Q9, added: SI 2008/654 Reg.51
Reg.Q10, added: SI 2008/654 Reg.51
Reg.Q11, added: SI 2008/654 Reg.51
Reg.Q12, added: SI 2008/654 Reg.51
Reg.Q13, added: SI 2008/654 Reg.51
Reg.Q14, added: SI 2008/654 Reg.51
Reg.Q15, added: SI 2008/654 Reg.51
Reg.Q16, added: SI 2008/654 Reg.51
Reg.Q17, added: SI 2008/654 Reg.51
Reg.R3, amended: SI 2008/654 Reg.52
Reg.R4, amended: SI 2008/654 Reg.53
Reg.R5, amended: SI 2008/654 Reg.54
Reg.R9, amended: SI 2008/654 Reg.55
Reg.S1, amended: SI 2008/654 Reg.56
Reg.S2, amended: SI 2008/654 Reg.57, SI 2008/2263 Reg.15
Reg.S3A, added: SI 2008/654 Reg.58
Reg.S4, amended: SI 2008/654 Reg.59, Reg.60, SI 2008/2263 Reg.16
Reg.S4A, added: SI 2008/654 Reg.61
Reg.T1, substituted: SI 2008/2263 Reg.18
Reg.T2A, amended: SI 2008/654 Reg.62
Reg.T6, amended: SI 2008/2263 Reg.19
Reg.T8, amended: SI 2008/2263 Reg.20

NO.

1995–cont.

300. National Health Service Pension Scheme Regulations 1995–*cont.*

Reg.U1A, amended: SI 2008/654 Reg.63, SI 2008/2263 Reg.21
Reg.U1A, substituted: SI 2008/2263 Reg.21
Reg.U4, added: SI 2008/654 Reg.64
Sch.2 para.1, amended: SI 2008/654 Reg.65, SI 2008/2263 Reg.22
Sch.2 para.2, amended: SI 2008/654 Reg.65, SI 2008/2263 Reg.22
Sch.2 para.2A, amended: SI 2008/654 Reg.65
Sch.2 para.2A, revoked (in part): SI 2008/654 Reg.65
Sch.2 para.3, amended: SI 2008/654 Reg.65, SI 2008/2263 Reg.22
Sch.2 para.5, amended: SI 2008/654 Reg.65, SI 2008/2263 Reg.22
Sch.2 para.8, amended: SI 2008/654 Reg.65, SI 2008/2263 Reg.22
Sch.2 para.9, amended: SI 2008/654 Reg.65, SI 2008/2263 Reg.22
Sch.2 para.9, revoked (in part): SI 2008/2263 Reg.22
Sch.2 para.10, amended: SI 2008/654 Reg.65, SI 2008/2263 Reg.22
Sch.2 para.11, amended: SI 2008/654 Reg.65
Sch.2 para.12, amended: SI 2008/654 Reg.65
Sch.2 para.16B, added: SI 2008/654 Reg.65
Sch.2 para.16C, added: SI 2008/654 Reg.65
Sch.2 para.17, substituted: SI 2008/654 Reg.65
Sch.2 para.17A, added: SI 2008/654 Reg.65
Sch.2 para.19, revoked (in part): SI 2008/654 Reg.65
Sch.2 para.22A, added: SI 2008/654 Reg.65
Sch.2 para.23, amended: SI 2008/2263 Reg.22
Sch.2A para.1, amended: SI 2008/654 Reg.66
Sch.2A para.7, amended: SI 2008/2263 Reg.23
Sch.2A para.9, amended: SI 2008/654 Reg.66
Sch.2A para.14, amended: SI 2008/2263 Reg.23

310. Social Security (Incapacity Benefit) (Transitional) Regulations 1995

Reg.18, amended: SI 2008/632 Art.15
Reg.18, applied: SI 2008/3270 Reg.2

311. Social Security (Incapacity for Work) (General) Regulations 1995

Reg.10, applied: SI 2008/2928 Reg.3
Reg.13A, applied: SI 2008/795 Reg.2
Reg.17, amended: SI 2008/2365 Reg.4, SI 2008/2683 Sch.1 para.66

NO.

1995–cont.

356. Milk Development Council Order 1995
revoked: SI 2008/576 Sch.5 para.8

365. National Health Service Superannuation Scheme (Scotland) Regulations 1995
applied: SSI 2008/224 Reg.1
referred to: SSI 2008/224 Reg.1, Reg.2, SSI 2008/229 Reg.14
Reg.A2, amended: SSI 2008/92 Reg.2, SSI 2008/226 Reg.3
Reg.B2, substituted: SSI 2008/226 Reg.4
Reg.B3, amended: SSI 2008/226 Reg.5
Reg.B5, referred to: SSI 2008/224 Reg.1
Reg.C1, amended: SSI 2008/226 Reg.6
Reg.C2, amended: SSI 2008/226 Reg.7
Reg.C4, amended: SSI 2008/92 Reg.2, SSI 2008/226 Reg.8
Reg.D1, amended: SSI 2008/226 Reg.9
Reg.D2, amended: SSI 2008/92 Reg.2, SSI 2008/226 Reg.10
Reg.E1, amended: SSI 2008/226 Reg.11
Reg.E2, amended: SSI 2008/226 Reg.12
Reg.E2A, added: SSI 2008/226 Reg.13
Reg.E2B, added: SSI 2008/226 Reg.13
Reg.E2C, added: SSI 2008/226 Reg.13
Reg.E3, amended: SSI 2008/226 Reg.14
Reg.E4, revoked: SSI 2008/226 Reg.15
Reg.E5, amended: SSI 2008/92 Reg.2
Reg.E6, amended: SSI 2008/226 Reg.16
Reg.E9, amended: SSI 2008/226 Reg.17
Reg.E11, added: SSI 2008/226 Reg.18
Reg.F1, amended: SSI 2008/92 Reg.2, SSI 2008/226 Reg.19
Reg.F2, amended: SSI 2008/226 Reg.20
Reg.F5, substituted: SSI 2008/226 Reg.21
Part G, amended: SSI 2008/226 Reg.22
Reg.G1, amended: SSI 2008/226 Reg.23
Reg.G2, amended: SSI 2008/92 Reg.2, SSI 2008/226 Reg.24
Reg.G3, amended: SSI 2008/226 Reg.25
Reg.G4, amended: SSI 2008/226 Reg.26
Reg.G7, amended: SSI 2008/226 Reg.27
Reg.G9, amended: SSI 2008/226 Reg.28
Reg.G14, added: SSI 2008/226 Reg.32
Reg.Q10, added: SSI 2008/226 Reg.52
Reg.G10, amended: SSI 2008/226 Reg.29
Reg.G11, amended: SSI 2008/226 Reg.30
Reg.G13, amended: SSI 2008/226 Reg.31
Reg.G15, added: SSI 2008/226 Reg.32
Reg.G16, added: SSI 2008/226 Reg.32
Reg.G17, added: SSI 2008/226 Reg.32
Reg.H1, amended: SSI 2008/226 Reg.33
Reg.H3, amended: SSI 2008/92 Reg.2, SSI 2008/226 Reg.34
Reg.H4, amended: SSI 2008/226 Reg.35
Reg.H5, amended: SSI 2008/226 Reg.36
Reg.H7, amended: SSI 2008/226 Reg.37
Reg.J1, amended: SSI 2008/92 Reg.2, SSI 2008/226 Reg.38

NO.

1995–cont.

365. National Health Service Superannuation Scheme (Scotland) Regulations 1995–*cont.*
Reg.K1, substituted: SSI 2008/226 Reg.39
Reg.K2, amended: SSI 2008/226 Reg.40
Reg.L1, amended: SSI 2008/226 Reg.41
Part M, applied: SSI 2008/224 Reg.1
Reg.M1, substituted: SSI 2008/226 Reg.42
Reg.M2, applied: SSI 2008/224 Pt 2 Reg.1
Reg.M2, substituted: SSI 2008/226 Reg.42
Reg.M3, substituted: SSI 2008/226 Reg.42
Reg.M4, substituted: SSI 2008/226 Reg.42
Reg.M5, substituted: SSI 2008/226 Reg.42
Reg.N1, amended: SSI 2008/226 Reg.43
Reg.N1A, added: SSI 2008/92 Reg.2
Reg.N3A, amended: SSI 2008/92 Reg.2
Reg.N5, revoked: SSI 2008/226 Reg.44
Reg.P1, amended: SSI 2008/92 Reg.2
Reg.P3, amended: SSI 2008/226 Reg.45
Reg.Q1, amended: SSI 2008/92 Reg.2, SSI 2008/226 Reg.46
Reg.Q2, amended: SSI 2008/226 Reg.47
Reg.Q3, amended: SSI 2008/226 Reg.48
Reg.Q3, revoked (in part): SSI 2008/226 Reg.48
Reg.Q4, amended: SSI 2008/226 Reg.49
Reg.Q5, amended: SSI 2008/226 Reg.50
Reg.Q7, amended: SSI 2008/92 Reg.2, SSI 2008/226 Reg.51
Reg.Q8, added: SSI 2008/226 Reg.52
Reg.Q9, added: SSI 2008/226 Reg.52
Reg.Q11, added: SSI 2008/226 Reg.52
Reg.Q12, added: SSI 2008/226 Reg.52
Reg.Q13, added: SSI 2008/226 Reg.52
Reg.Q14, added: SSI 2008/226 Reg.52
Reg.Q15, added: SSI 2008/226 Reg.52
Reg.Q16, added: SSI 2008/226 Reg.52
Reg.Q17, added: SSI 2008/226 Reg.52
Reg.R1, amended: SSI 2008/92 Reg.2
Reg.R3, amended: SSI 2008/226 Reg.53
Reg.R4, amended: SSI 2008/226 Reg.54
Reg.R8, amended: SSI 2008/226 Reg.55
Reg.S1, amended: SSI 2008/226 Reg.56
Reg.S2, amended: SSI 2008/226 Reg.57
Reg.S3A, added: SSI 2008/226 Reg.58
Reg.S4, amended: SSI 2008/92 Reg.2, SSI 2008/226 Reg.59
Reg.S4A, added: SSI 2008/226 Reg.60
Reg.T1, substituted: SSI 2008/92 Reg.2
Reg.T2A, amended: SSI 2008/226 Reg.61
Reg.T7, amended: SSI 2008/92 Reg.2
Reg.T9, amended: SSI 2008/92 Reg.2
Reg.U2, substituted: SSI 2008/92 Reg.2
Reg.U3, amended: SSI 2008/92 Reg.2
Reg.U4, added: SSI 2008/226 Reg.62
Sch.1 Part I para.1, amended: SSI 2008/92 Reg.2
Sch.1 Part I para.2A, amended: SSI 2008/226 Reg.63

NO.

1995–cont.

365. National Health Service Superannuation Scheme (Scotland) Regulations 1995–*cont.*

Sch.1 Part I para.2A, revoked (in part): SSI 2008/226 Reg.63

Sch.1 Part II para.8, amended: SSI 2008/226 Reg.63

Sch.1 Part III para.9, amended: SSI 2008/226 Reg.63

Sch.1 Part IV para.10, amended: SSI 2008/226 Reg.63

Sch.1 Part IV para.10, substituted: SSI 2008/92 Reg.2

Sch.1 Part V para.11, amended: SSI 2008/226 Reg.63

Sch.1 Part V para.12, amended: SSI 2008/226 Reg.63

Sch.1 Part VI para.16B, added: SSI 2008/226 Reg.63

Sch.1 Part VI para.16C, added: SSI 2008/226 Reg.63

Sch.1 Part VI para.17, substituted: SSI 2008/226 Reg.63

Sch.1 Part VII para.18, revoked (in part): SSI 2008/226 Reg.63

Sch.1 Part XI para.22A, added: SSI 2008/226 Reg.63

Sch.1A para.2, amended: SSI 2008/226 Reg.64

414. National Health Service (Pharmaceutical Services) (Scotland) Regulations 1995

Sch.1 para.3, amended: SSI 2008/27 Sch.3 para.1

418. Town and Country Planning (General Permitted Development) Order 1995

applied: SI 2008/1261 Sch.6 para.19

referred to: 2008 c.18 s.10, 2008 c.29 s.25

varied: 2008 c.18 s.13

Art.1, amended: SI 2008/675 Art.2, SI 2008/2362 Art.2

Art.3, applied: SI 2008/1160 Art.18

Art.3, disapplied: 2008 c.18 s.15

Sch.1 Part 1, amended: SI 2008/2362 Sch.1

Sch.1 Part 2, added: SI 2008/2362 Art.2

Sch.1 Part 2, substituted: SI 2008/2362 Art.2

Sch.2 Part 1 paraA, substituted: SI 2008/2362 Sch.1

Sch.2 Part 1 paraB, substituted: SI 2008/2362 Sch.1

Sch.2 Part 1 paraC, substituted: SI 2008/2362 Sch.1

Sch.2 Part 1 paraD, substituted: SI 2008/2362 Sch.1

Sch.2 Part 1 paraE, substituted: SI 2008/2362 Sch.1

Sch.2 Part 1 paraF, substituted: SI 2008/2362 Sch.1

Sch.2 Part 1, substituted: SI 2008/2362 Sch.1

NO.

1995–cont.

418. Town and Country Planning (General Permitted Development) Order 1995–*cont.*

Sch.2 Part 1 paraH, substituted: SI 2008/2362 Sch.1

Sch.2 Part 1 paraI, substituted: SI 2008/2362 Sch.1

Sch.2 para.A1, see *Sumption v Greenwich LBC* [2007] EWHC 2776 (Admin), [2008] 1 P. & C.R. 20 (QBD (Admin)), Collins, J.

Sch.2 Part 1 paraA.1, substituted: SI 2008/2362 Sch.1

Sch.2 Part 1 paraB.1, substituted: SI 2008/2362 Sch.1

Sch.2 Part 1 paraC.1, substituted: SI 2008/2362 Sch.1

Sch.2 Part 1 paraD.1, substituted: SI 2008/2362 Sch.1

Sch.2 Part 1 paraE.1, substituted: SI 2008/2362 Sch.1

Sch.2 Part 1 paraF.1, substituted: SI 2008/2362 Sch.1

Sch.2 Part 1 paraH.1, substituted: SI 2008/2362 Sch.1

Sch.2 Part 1 paraA.2, substituted: SI 2008/2362 Sch.1

Sch.2 Part 1 paraB.2, substituted: SI 2008/2362 Sch.1

Sch.2 Part 1 paraC.2, substituted: SI 2008/2362 Sch.1

Sch.2 Part 1 paraE.2, substituted: SI 2008/2362 Sch.1

Sch.2 Part 1 paraH.2, substituted: SI 2008/2362 Sch.1

Sch.2 Part 1 paraA.3, substituted: SI 2008/2362 Sch.1

Sch.2 Part 1 paraB.3, substituted: SI 2008/2362 Sch.1

Sch.2 Part 1 paraE.3, substituted: SI 2008/2362 Sch.1

Sch.2 Part 1 paraH.3, substituted: SI 2008/2362 Sch.1

Sch.2 Part 1 paraE.4, substituted: SI 2008/2362 Sch.1

Sch.2 Part 1 paraH.4, substituted: SI 2008/2362 Sch.1

Sch.2 Part 1 paraH.5, substituted: SI 2008/2362 Sch.1

Sch.2 Part 11, referred to: SI 2008/1160 Art.18

Sch.2 Part 39 paraA.2, amended: SI 2008/502 Art.2

Sch.2 Part 39 paraA.3, amended: SI 2008/502 Art.2

Sch.2 Part 40 paraA, added: SI 2008/675 Art.2

Sch.2 Part 40 paraB, added: SI 2008/675 Art.2

Sch.2 Part 40 paraC, added: SI 2008/675 Art.2

NO.

1995–cont.

418. Town and Country Planning (General Permitted Development) Order 1995–*cont.*

Sch.2 Part 40 paraD, added: SI 2008/675 Art.2
Sch.2 Part 40 paraE, added: SI 2008/675 Art.2
Sch.2 Part 40 paraF, added: SI 2008/675 Art.2
Sch.2 Part 40, added: SI 2008/675 Art.2
Sch.2 Part 40, amended: SI 2008/2362 Art.2
Sch.2 Part 40, substituted: SI 2008/2362 Art.2
Sch.2 Part 40 paraA.1, added: SI 2008/675 Art.2
Sch.2 Part 40 paraA.1, amended: SI 2008/2362 Art.4
Sch.2 Part 40 paraB.1, added: SI 2008/675 Art.2
Sch.2 Part 40 paraE.1, added: SI 2008/675 Art.2
Sch.2 Part 40 paraF.1, added: SI 2008/675 Art.2
Sch.2 Part 40 paraA.2, added: SI 2008/675 Art.2
Sch.2 Part 40 paraB.2, added: SI 2008/675 Art.2

419. Town and Country Planning (General Development Procedure) Order 1995

applied: SI 2008/1261 Sch.2 para.25
Art.1, amended: SI 2008/550 Art.2, SI 2008/2336 Art.3
Art.3, amended: SI 2008/2336 Art.3
Art.4E, added: SI 2008/550 Art.2
Art.5, substituted: SI 2008/550 Art.2
Art.7, amended: SI 2008/550 Art.2
Art.7, applied: SI 2008/550 Art.3
Art.20, amended: SI 2008/550 Art.2
Art.24, amended: SI 2008/550 Art.2
Art.24, revoked (in part): SI 2008/550 Art.2
Sch.2 Part 2, applied: SI 2008/550 Art.3
Sch.2 Part 2, revoked (in part): SI 2008/550 Art.2

449. Medical Devices (Consultation Requirements) (Fees) Regulations 1995

Reg.3, amended: SI 2008/530 Reg.2
Reg.3A, amended: SI 2008/530 Reg.2

484. Spirit Drinks (Scotland) Amendment Regulations 1995

revoked: SI 2008/3206 Sch.1

490. Antarctic Regulations 1995

Reg.4, amended: SI 2008/3066 Reg.2
Reg.6, amended: SI 2008/3066 Reg.3
Sch.1, amended: SI 2008/3066 Reg.4, Sch.1
Sch.2, amended: SI 2008/3066 Reg.4, Sch.2

516. Income-related Benefits Schemes (Miscellaneous Amendments) Regulations 1995

applied: SI 2008/794 Sch.6 para.12

NO.

1995–cont.

558. National Health Service (General Ophthalmic Services) Amendment Regulations 1995

revoked (in part): SI 2008/1700 Sch.2

572. Valuation Appeal Committee (Procedure in Appeals under the Valuation Acts) (Scotland) Regulations 1995

Reg.5, see *Marks & Spencer Plc v Glasgow Assessor* [2008] R.V.R. 81 (Lands Tr (Scot)), JN Wright Q.C.; see *North British Trust Hotels v Lothian Assessor* [2008] R.V.R. 83 (Lands Tr (Scot)), JN Wright Q.C.; see *Woolworths Plc v Renfrewshire Valuation Joint Board Assessor* [2008] R.V.R. 232 (Lands Tr (Scot)), JN Wright Q.C.
Reg.6, see *North British Trust Hotels v Lothian Assessor* [2008] R.V.R. 83 (Lands Tr (Scot)), JN Wright Q.C.
Reg.13, see *Belhaven Brewery Co Ltd v Highland and Western Isles Assessor* [2008] CSIH 3, 2008 S.C. 288 (LVAC), Lord Gill L.J.C.

614. Animal By-Products (Identification) Regulations 1995

Reg.3, amended: SSI 2008/417 Reg.3

632. Judicial Pensions (Miscellaneous) Regulations 1995

Part II, referred to: SI 2008/2697 Reg.2

731. Welfare of Animals (Slaughter or Killing) Regulations 1995

Sch.9, see *R. (on the application of Royal Society for the Prevention of Cruelty to Animals) v Secretary of State for the Environment, Food and Rural Affairs* [2008] EWHC 2321 (Admin), Times, October 16, 2008 (QBD (Admin)), Sir Robin Auld

732. Spirit Drinks (Amendment) Regulations 1995

revoked: SI 2008/3206 Sch.1

738. Offshore Installations and Pipeline Works (Management and Administration) Regulations 1995

Reg.3, see *Langley v Revenue and Customs Commissioners* [2008] S.T.C. (S.C.D.) 298 (Sp Comm), Howard M Nowlan; see *Torr v Revenue and Customs Commissioners* [2008] S.T.C. (S.C.D.) 772 (Sp Comm), Theodore Wallace
Reg.21, applied: SI 2008/1765

750. Local Government (Superannuation and Compensation for Premature Retirement) (Scotland) Amendment Regulations 1995

revoked: SSI 2008/229 Sch.1

755. Children (Northern Ireland) Order 1995

applied: SI 2008/542 Reg.9
see *ES's Application for Judicial Review, Re* [2008] N.I. 11 (QBD (NI)), Gillen, J.
Part II, referred to: 2008 c.22 s.53

NO | NO.

1995–cont.

755. Children (Northern Ireland) Order 1995–*cont.*
Part XI, applied: SI 2008/542 Reg.9, SI 2008/976 Reg.5
Part XIV, referred to: 2008 c.22 s.53
Art.2, amended: 2008 c.22 Sch.6 para.70
Art.2, referred to: SI 2008/794 Sch.8 para.26
Art.4, applied: SI 2008/1769 Art.28
Art.5, amended: 2008 c.22 Sch.6 para.71
Art.7, amended: 2008 c.22 Sch.6 para.72, Sch.8 Part 2
Art.8, amended: 2008 c.22 Sch.6 para.73
Art.12, amended: 2008 c.22 Sch.6 para.74
Art.15, applied: SI 2008/794 Sch.8 para.26
Art.21, applied: SI 2008/1769 Art.28
Art.23, applied: SI 2008/1769 Art.28
Art.27, applied: SI 2008/1769 Art.28, Art.34
Art.34A, applied: SI 2008/1769 Art.28
Art.34B, applied: 2008 c.23 s.20
Art.34C, applied: SI 2008/1769 Art.28
Art.34D, applied: 2008 c.23 s.20
Art.60, applied: SI 2008/1769 Art.28
Art.64, see *ES's Application for Judicial Review, Re* [2008] N.I. 11 (QBD (NI)), Gillen, J.
Art.75, applied: SI 2008/1769 Art.28, Art.34
Art.106, applied: SI 2008/1769 Art.34
Art.108, applied: SI 2008/542 Reg.9
Art.155, amended: 2008 c.22 Sch.6 para.75
Art.155(2), applied: 2008 c.22 s.53
Art.159, applied: SI 2008/1769 Art.28
Art.160, applied: SI 2008/1769 Art.28
Art.179, amended: 2008 c.22 Sch.6 para.76
Sch.1, amended: 2008 c.22 Sch.6 para.77
Sch.1, applied: SI 2008/794 Sch.8 para.26
Sch.6, amended: 2008 c.22 Sch.6 para.78
Sch.9, revoked: SI 2008/1769 Sch.3

866. National Health Service (Injury Benefits) Regulations 1995
applied: SI 2008/1596 Reg.7
referred to: SI 2008/2263 Reg.87
Reg.2, amended: SI 2008/655 Reg.3, SI 2008/2263 Reg.88
Reg.2A, added: SI 2008/655 Reg.3
Reg.4, amended: SI 2008/655 Reg.3, SI 2008/2263 Reg.89
Reg.4A, amended: SI 2008/2263 Reg.90
Reg.7, amended: SI 2008/655 Reg.3
Reg.8, amended: SI 2008/655 Reg.3
Reg.9, amended: SI 2008/655 Reg.3
Reg.11, amended: SI 2008/655 Reg.3
Reg.12, amended: SI 2008/655 Reg.3
Reg.18A, substituted: SI 2008/2263 Reg.91
Reg.21B, added: SI 2008/2263 Reg.92

1019. Local Government Pension Scheme Regulations 1995
applied: SI 2008/238 Reg.12, SI 2008/239 Reg.51, Reg.69, Reg.72
referred to: SI 2008/239 Reg.79, Reg.81

1032. United Nations Arms Embargoes (Dependent Territories) Order 1995
amended: SI 2008/3123 Art.2
Art.2, amended: SI 2008/3123 Art.2
Art.3, revoked (in part): SI 2008/3123 Art.2
Art.4, revoked (in part): SI 2008/3123 Art.2
Art.8, revoked (in part): SI 2008/3123 Art.2
Art.9, amended: SI 2008/3123 Art.2
Art.11, amended: SI 2008/3123 Art.2
Sch.3 para.4, amended: SI 2008/3123 Art.2

1045. Child Support and Income Support (Amendment) Regulations 1995
applied: 2008 c.6 Sch.2

1046. Excise Goods (Drawback) Regulations 1995
Reg.6, amended: SI 2008/1885 Reg.5

1053. Personal and Occupational Pension Schemes (Pensions Ombudsman) (Procedure) Rules 1995
r.12, revoked (in part): SI 2008/2683 Sch.1 para.67

1116. Medicines (Products for Human Use-Fees) Regulations 1995
varied: SI 2008/552 Sch.7

1184. Income Tax (Building Societies) (Dividends and Interest) (Amendment) Regulations 1995
revoked: SI 2008/2682 Sch.3

1239. Pipe-lines (Inquiries Procedure) Rules 1995
r.2, amended: SI 2008/2831 Sch.4 para.2
r.10, amended: SI 2008/2831 Sch.4 para.3

1268. Value Added Tax (Special Provisions) Order 1995
Art.5, amended: SI 2008/1146 Sch.1 para.15

1436. Petroleum (Production) (Landward Areas) Regulations 1995
Sch.3 para.8A, added: 2008 c.32 Sch.3 para.1
Sch.3 para.17, amended: 2008 c.32 Sch.3 para.1
Sch.3 para.38, amended: 2008 c.32 Sch.3 para.1
Sch.3 para.38A, added: 2008 c.32 Sch.3 para.1

1544. Eggs (Marketing Standards) Regulations 1995
applied: SI 2008/1718 Reg.22

1649. Children (Allocation of Proceedings) (Amendment) Order 1995
revoked: SI 2008/2836 Sch.2

1708. Nitrate Sensitive Areas (Amendment) Regulations 1995
revoked: SI 2008/2349 Reg.50

1730. Insurance Companies (Taxation of Reinsurance Business) Regulations 1995
Reg.2, amended: SI 2008/1944 Reg.3, SI 2008/2670 Reg.3
Reg.3, amended: SI 2008/1944 Reg.4

NO.

1995–cont.

1730. Insurance Companies (Taxation of Reinsurance Business) Regulations 1995–*cont.*
Reg.6, amended: SI 2008/1944 Reg.5, SI 2008/2670 Reg.4
Reg.7, amended: SI 2008/1944 Reg.6, SI 2008/2670 Reg.5
Reg.7, revoked (in part): SI 2008/2670 Reg.5
Reg.9, amended: SI 2008/1944 Reg.7
Reg.13, amended: SI 2008/1944 Reg.8

1965. Naval Medical Compassionate Fund (Amendment) Order 1995
revoked: SI 2008/3129 Sch.1

1979. Venture Capital Trust Regulations 1995
Reg.2, amended: SI 2008/1893 Reg.3
Reg.3, amended: SI 2008/1893 Reg.4, Reg.5
Reg.4, amended: SI 2008/1893 Reg.4, Reg.6
Reg.5, amended: SI 2008/1893 Reg.4, Reg.7
Reg.6, amended: SI 2008/1893 Reg.4, Reg.8
Reg.7, amended: SI 2008/1893 Reg.4
Reg.8, amended: SI 2008/1893 Reg.4
Reg.8, substituted: SI 2008/1893 Reg.9
Reg.8A, amended: SI 2008/1893 Reg.4
Reg.8B, amended: SI 2008/1893 Reg.4
Reg.8C, amended: SI 2008/1893 Reg.4
Reg.8D, amended: SI 2008/1893 Reg.4
Reg.8E, amended: SI 2008/1893 Reg.4
Reg.8F, amended: SI 2008/1893 Reg.4
Reg.8G, amended: SI 2008/1893 Reg.4
Reg.8H, amended: SI 2008/1893 Reg.4
Reg.8I, amended: SI 2008/1893 Reg.4
Reg.8J, amended: SI 2008/1893 Reg.4
Reg.9, amended: SI 2008/1893 Reg.10
Reg.22, amended: SI 2008/1893 Reg.11
Reg.23, amended: SI 2008/1893 Reg.12
Reg.24, amended: SI 2008/1893 Reg.13
Reg.25, amended: SI 2008/1893 Reg.14

2051. Stamp Duty Reserve Tax (Tradepoint) Regulations 1995
Reg.1, amended: SI 2008/914 Reg.2
Reg.2, amended: SI 2008/914 Reg.2
Reg.3, amended: SI 2008/914 Reg.2

2092. Companies (Summary Financial Statement) Regulations 1995
referred to: SI 2008/374 Reg.12
revoked: SI 2008/374 Reg.12

2093. Patents Rules 1995
r.41, see *Matsushita Electrical Industrial Co v Comptroller General of Patents* [2008] EWHC 2071 (Pat), [2008] R.P.C. 35 (Ch D (Patents Ct)), Mann, J.

2095. Nitrate Sensitive Areas (Amendment) (No.2) Regulations 1995
revoked: SI 2008/2349 Reg.50

2287. Income Support (General) Amendment and Transitional Regulations 1995
Reg.3, applied: SI 2008/794 Sch.6 para.20

NO.

1995–cont.

2294. Civil Aviation Authority (Economic Regulation of Airports) (Northern Ireland) Regulations 1995
Reg.13, amended: SI 2008/2683 Sch.1 para.68

2370. Motor Cycle Silencer and Exhaust Systems Regulations 1995
Reg.7, revoked: SI 2008/1277 Sch.2 para.85, Sch.4 Part 2

2478. Bovine Embryo (Collection, Production and Transfer) Regulations 1995
Reg.4, applied: SI 2008/1035 Sch.1 para.1
Reg.5, applied: SI 2008/1035 Sch.1 para.2
Reg.6, applied: SI 2008/1035 Sch.1 para.3
Reg.7, applied: SI 2008/1035 Sch.1 para.4
Reg.8, applied: SI 2008/1035 Sch.1 para.5
Reg.9, applied: SI 2008/1035 Sch.1 para.6
Reg.11, applied: SI 2008/1035 Sch.1 para.7
Reg.13, applied: SI 2008/1035 Sch.1 para.8
Reg.13, referred to: SI 2008/1040 Sch.4 para.2
Reg.14, referred to: SI 2008/1040 Sch.4 para.2
Reg.15, referred to: SI 2008/1040 Sch.4 para.2
Reg.16, applied: SI 2008/1035 Sch.1 para.9
Reg.16, referred to: SI 2008/1040 Sch.6 para.2
Reg.17, referred to: SI 2008/1040 Sch.6 para.2
Reg.18, referred to: SI 2008/1040 Sch.6 para.2
Sch.4 para.13, applied: SI 2008/1035 Sch.1 para.10
Sch.7 para.4, applied: SI 2008/1035 Sch.1 para.11
Sch.7 para.5, applied: SI 2008/1035 Sch.1 para.11

2489. Footwear (Indication of Composition) Labelling Regulations 1995
Reg.10, applied: SI 2008/1277 Sch.3 para.2, Sch.3 para.3

2498. Merchant Shipping (Reporting Requirements for Ships Carrying Dangerous or Polluting Goods) Regulations 1995
Reg.3, amended: SI 2008/3145 Reg.2

2518. Value Added Tax Regulations 1995
Reg.14, see *Revenue and Customs Commissioners v Dempster (t/a Boulevard)* [2008] EWHC 63 (Ch), [2008] S.T.C. 2079 (Ch D), Briggs, J.
Reg.15, amended: SI 2008/3021 Reg.3
Reg.23E, added: SI 2008/556 Reg.2
Reg.23F, added: SI 2008/556 Reg.2
Reg.25, see *Dunwood Travel Ltd v Revenue and Customs Commissioners* [2007] EWHC 319 (Ch), [2008] S.T.C. 412 (Ch D), Mann, J.; see *R. (on the application of BMW AG) v Revenue and Customs Commissioners* [2008] EWHC 712

NO.

1995–cont.

2518. Value Added Tax Regulations 1995–*cont.*

Reg.25–*cont.*

(Admin), [2008] S.T.C. 3090 (QBD (Admin)), Tugendhat, J.

Reg.29, see *Fleming (t/a Bodycraft) v Customs and Excise Commissioners* [2008] UKHL 2, [2008] 1 W.L.R. 195 (HL), Lord Hope of Craighead; see *LA Leisure Ltd v Revenue and Customs Commissioners* [2008] B.V.C. 2352 (V&DTr (Manchester)), IE Vellins (Chairman)

Reg.34, amended: SI 2008/1482 Reg.2

Reg.55K, amended: SI 2008/3021 Reg.4

Reg.66, see *Boots Co Plc v Revenue and Customs Commissioners* [2008] B.V.C. 2328 (V&DTr (London)), AN Brice

Reg.67, see *Boots Co Plc v Revenue and Customs Commissioners* [2008] B.V.C. 2328 (V&DTr (London)), AN Brice

Reg.84, amended: SI 2008/1146 Sch.1 para.17

Reg.94B, amended: SI 2008/954 Art.44, SI 2008/1146 Sch.1 para.18

Reg.101, see *Camden Motors (Holdings) Ltd v Revenue and Customs Commissioners* [2008] B.V.C. 2442 (V&DTr (London)), JC Gort (Chairman); see *Gracechurch Management Services Ltd v Revenue and Customs Commissioners* [2007] EWHC 755 (Ch), [2008] S.T.C. 795 (Ch D), Sir Andrew Morritt C.; see *Lincoln Assurance Ltd v Revenue and Customs Commissioners* [2008] B.V.C. 2307 (V&DTr (London)), AN Brice (Chairman)

Reg.103, see *Lincoln Assurance Ltd v Revenue and Customs Commissioners* [2008] B.V.C. 2307 (V&DTr (London)), AN Brice (Chairman)

Reg.106, see *Camden Motors (Holdings) Ltd v Revenue and Customs Commissioners* [2008] B.V.C. 2442 (V&DTr (London)), JC Gort (Chairman)

Reg.107, see *Camden Motors (Holdings) Ltd v Revenue and Customs Commissioners* [2008] B.V.C. 2442 (V&DTr (London)), JC Gort (Chairman)

Reg.107B, see *Camden Motors (Holdings) Ltd v Revenue and Customs Commissioners* [2008] B.V.C. 2442 (V&DTr (London)), JC Gort (Chairman)

Reg.107E, amended: SI 2008/954 Art.45

Reg.113, amended: SI 2008/1146 Sch.1 para.19

Reg.114, amended: SI 2008/1146 Sch.1 para.20

Reg.115, amended: SI 2008/1146 Sch.1 para.21

NO.

1995–cont.

2549. Artificial Insemination of Cattle (Animal Health) (England and Wales) (Amendment) Regulations 1995

revoked (in part): SI 2008/1040 Sch.10 Part 1

2562. Local Authorities (Precepts) (Wales) Regulations 1995

Reg.5, varied: SI 2008/584 Art.20

Sch.1 Part II para.8, varied: SI 2008/584 Art.20

2631. Amusement Machine Licence Duty Regulations 1995

Reg.3, amended: SI 2008/2693 Reg.2

Reg.5, added: SI 2008/2693 Reg.3

2644. Statutory Nuisance (Appeals) Regulations 1995

see *Manley v New Forest DC* [2007] EWHC 3188 (Admin), [2008] Env. L.R. 26 (DC), Moses, L.J.

2701. Air Navigation (Overseas Territories) (Amendment) Order 1995

varied: SI 2008/3119 Sch.1

2716. Other Fuel Substitutes (Rates of Excise Duty etc) Order 1995

applied: SI 2008/2168 Art.5

Art.2, amended: SI 2008/754 Art.3

Art.3, amended: SI 2008/754 Art.4

Art.4, amended: SI 2008/754 Art.5, Art.6

Art.5, amended: SI 2008/754 Art.7

2814. Teachers Superannuation (Additional Voluntary Contributions) (Scotland) Regulations 1995

Reg.2, amended: SSI 2008/227 Reg.32

Reg.12, amended: SSI 2008/227 Reg.33

Reg.16, amended: SSI 2008/227 Reg.34

Reg.19, substituted: SSI 2008/227 Reg.35

2869. Goods Vehicles (Licensing of Operators) Regulations 1995

Reg.33, see *Romantiek Transport BVBA v Vehicle and Operator Services Agency* [2008] EWCA Civ 534, [2008] 2 Lloyd's Rep. 409 (CA (Civ Div)), Tuckey, L.J.

Sch.3 para.23, see *Romantiek Transport BVBA v Vehicle and Operator Services Agency* [2008] EWCA Civ 534, [2008] 2 Lloyd's Rep. 409 (CA (Civ Div)), Tuckey, L.J.

2870. Escape and Rescue from Mines Regulations 1995

Reg.2, amended: SI 2008/960 Sch.3

Reg.13, amended: SI 2008/960 Sch.3

2880. Sale of Registration Marks Regulations 1995

Sch.1 para.1, amended: SI 2008/2372 Reg.3

Sch.1 para.2, amended: SI 2008/2372 Reg.4

Sch.1 para.3, amended: SI 2008/2372 Reg.5

Sch.1 para.3, revoked (in part): SI 2008/2372 Reg.5

Sch.1 para.4, amended: SI 2008/2372 Reg.6

Sch.1 para.5, substituted: SI 2008/2372 Reg.7

Sch.1 para.7, amended: SI 2008/2372 Reg.8

Sch.1 para.8, amended: SI 2008/2372 Reg.9

NO.

1995–cont.

2880. Sale of Registration Marks Regulations 1995–*cont.*
Sch.1 para.9, amended: SI 2008/2372 Reg.10
Sch.1 para.10, amended: SI 2008/2372 Reg.11

2909. Public Service Vehicles (Operators Licences) (Fees) Regulations 1995
Sch.1, amended: SI 2008/1473 Reg.2

2994. Road Traffic (Northern Ireland) Order 1995
Art.9, applied: SI 2008/1216 Sch.1 para.25, Sch.2 para.25
Art.11A, added: SI 2008/1216 Art.52
Art.12A, added: SI 2008/1216 Art.62
Art.12B, added: SI 2008/1216 Art.53
Art.14, amended: SI 2008/1216 Art.63
Art.14, applied: SI 2008/1216 Art.61, Sch.1 para.25, Sch.2 para.25
Art.17D, amended: SI 2008/1216 Art.59
Art.18, amended: SI 2008/1216 Art.59
Art.19, amended: SI 2008/1216 Art.59
Art.20, amended: SI 2008/1216 Art.59
Art.21, amended: SI 2008/1216 Art.59
Art.38B, varied: SI 2008/1216 Art.61
Art.55, amended: SI 2008/1216 Art.54
Art.57A, added: SI 2008/1216 Art.54
Art.58, amended: SI 2008/1216 Art.54

3000. Goods Vehicles (Licensing of Operators) (Fees) Regulations 1995
Sch.1, applied: SI 2008/1474 Reg.4
Sch.1 Part I, amended: SI 2008/1474 Reg.2
Sch.1 Part II, amended: SI 2008/1474 Reg.2

3002. Designation of Structure Plan Areas (Scotland) Order 1995
applied: SSI 2008/427 Art.2, Art.3
revoked: SSI 2008/427 Art.10

3044. Travellers Allowances Amendment Order 1995
revoked: SI 2008/3058 Art.3

3123. Sweeteners in Food Regulations 1995
Reg.2, amended: SI 2008/138 Reg.14
Sch.1, amended: SI 2008/138 Reg.14

3124. Colours in Food Regulations 1995
Reg.5, amended: SSI 2008/129 Sch.3 para.1, SSI 2008/395 Sch.3 para.1
Sch.2 para.6, amended: SI 2008/85 Reg.5, SI 2008/137 Reg.5, SSI 2008/12 Reg.5

3128. Merchant Shipping (Port State Control) Regulations 1995
Part I, applied: SI 2008/2924 Reg.31
Reg.11, varied: SI 2008/2924 Reg.31, SI 2008/3257 Reg.41
Reg.12, varied: SI 2008/2924 Reg.31, SI 2008/3257 Reg.41

3187. Miscellaneous Food Additives Regulations 1995
disapplied: SSI 2008/176 Reg.3
Reg.2, amended: SI 2008/138 Reg.3
Reg.11, amended: SI 2008/138 Reg.4
Sch.1, amended: SI 2008/138 Reg.5

NO.

1995–cont.

3187. Miscellaneous Food Additives Regulations 1995–*cont.*
Sch.2 Part A, amended: SI 2008/138 Reg.6
Sch.2 Part B, amended: SI 2008/138 Reg.7
Sch.2 Part C, amended: SI 2008/138 Sch.1
Sch.2 Part D, amended: SI 2008/138 Sch.2
Sch.3, amended: SI 2008/138 Reg.10
Sch.4, amended: SI 2008/138 Reg.11
Sch.7, amended: SI 2008/85 Reg.6, SI 2008/137 Reg.6, SI 2008/138 Reg.12, SSI 2008/12 Reg.6
Sch.8, amended: SI 2008/138 Reg.13
Sch.8 Part 3, amended: SI 2008/42 Reg.2, SI 2008/138 Reg.13
Sch.8 Part 4, amended: SI 2008/42 Reg.2, SI 2008/138 Reg.13

3213. Pensions (Northern Ireland) Order 1995
Art.3, applied: 2008 c.30 Sch.1 para.3
Art.4, applied: 2008 c.30 Sch.1 para.3
Art.29, applied: 2008 c.30 Sch.1 para.4

3237. Insurance Companies (Overseas Life Assurance Business) (Compliance) Regulations 1995
Reg.2, amended: SI 2008/2627 Reg.2
Reg.13, amended: SI 2008/2627 Reg.2
Reg.14, amended: SI 2008/2627 Reg.2
Reg.14A, amended: SI 2008/2627 Reg.2

3294. Local Government (Superannuation and Compensation for Redundancy or Premature Retirement) (Scotland) Amendment Regulations 1995
revoked (in part): SSI 2008/229 Sch.1

1996

207. Jobseeker's Allowance Regulations 1996
referred to: SI 2008/632 Art.24
Part VIII, amended: SI 2008/2111 Reg.3
Part VIII, revoked: SI 2008/2111 Reg.3
Reg.1, amended: SI 2008/698 Reg.4, SI 2008/1554 Reg.3, SI 2008/2767 Reg.4, SI 2008/3157 Reg.3
Reg.3A, amended: SI 2008/13 Reg.2
Reg.3E, amended: SI 2008/13 Reg.2
Reg.3F, revoked: SI 2008/13 Reg.2
Reg.4, amended: SI 2008/698 Reg.4
Reg.5, amended: SI 2008/3051 Reg.11
Reg.6, amended: SI 2008/3051 Reg.11
Reg.8, amended: SI 2008/3051 Reg.11
Reg.11, amended: SI 2008/1554 Reg.3, SI 2008/3051 Reg.11, SI 2008/3157 Reg.3
Reg.12, amended: SI 2008/3051 Reg.11
Reg.13, amended: SI 2008/3051 Reg.11
Reg.14, amended: SI 2008/698 Reg.4, SI 2008/1554 Reg.3, SI 2008/1826 Reg.3, SI 2008/3051 Reg.11
Reg.15, amended: SI 2008/698 Reg.4, SI 2008/1826 Reg.3
Reg.15, substituted: SI 2008/1826 Reg.3

NO.

1996–cont.

207. Jobseeker's Allowance Regulations 1996–*cont.*

Reg.17, amended: SI 2008/3051 Reg.11
Reg.17A, amended: SI 2008/1826 Reg.3
Reg.17A, referred to: SI 2008/794 Reg.107, Reg.115
Reg.19, amended: SI 2008/698 Reg.4, SI 2008/1554 Reg.3, SI 2008/2831 Sch.1 para.7, SI 2008/3051 Reg.11
Reg.19, applied: SI 2008/794 Reg.108
Reg.19, referred to: SI 2008/794 Reg.108, Sch.6 para.15
Reg.30, amended: SI 2008/3051 Reg.11
Reg.46, amended: SI 2008/1554 Reg.3
Reg.48, amended: SI 2008/698 Reg.4, SI 2008/1554 Reg.3
Reg.49, amended: SI 2008/1554 Reg.3
Reg.50, amended: SI 2008/2767 Reg.4
Reg.52, amended: SI 2008/698 Reg.4
Reg.55, amended: SI 2008/1554 Reg.3
Reg.55A, amended: SI 2008/1554 Reg.3
Reg.57, amended: SI 2008/3157 Reg.3
Reg.61, amended: SI 2008/1554 Reg.3
Reg.72, amended: SI 2008/3051 Reg.11
Reg.73A, added: SI 2008/3051 Reg.11
Reg.75, amended: SI 2008/698 Reg.4, SI 2008/3157 Reg.3
Reg.75, applied: SI 2008/794 Sch.6 para.6
Reg.75, referred to: SI 2008/794 Reg.107, Reg.108, Reg.115, Sch.6 para.15
Reg.76, amended: SI 2008/1554 Reg.3
Reg.78, amended: SI 2008/1554 Reg.3
Reg.79, amended: SI 2008/632 Art.23
Reg.83, referred to: SI 2008/632 Art.24
Reg.84, referred to: SI 2008/632 Art.24
Reg.85, referred to: SI 2008/632 Art.24
Reg.89, amended: SI 2008/2111 Reg.3
Reg.90, revoked: SI 2008/2111 Reg.3
Reg.94, amended: SI 2008/698 Reg.4
Reg.95, amended: SI 2008/698 Reg.4
Reg.96, amended: SI 2008/1554 Reg.3, SI 2008/2767 Reg.4
Reg.96, revoked (in part): SI 2008/2767 Reg.4
Reg.97, amended: SI 2008/1554 Reg.3, SI 2008/2767 Reg.4
Reg.103, amended: SI 2008/1554 Reg.3, SI 2008/1599 Reg.4
Reg.105, amended: SI 2008/698 Reg.4, SI 2008/2767 Reg.4, SI 2008/3157 Reg.3
Reg.110, amended: SI 2008/2767 Reg.4
Reg.113, amended: SI 2008/698 Reg.4, SI 2008/2767 Reg.4, SI 2008/3157 Reg.3
Reg.117, amended: SI 2008/2111 Reg.3
Reg.118, amended: SI 2008/2111 Reg.3
Reg.121, substituted: SI 2008/2111 Reg.3
Reg.122, amended: SI 2008/2111 Reg.3
Reg.123, amended: SI 2008/2111 Reg.3
Reg.124, revoked: SI 2008/2111 Reg.3

NO.

1996–cont.

207. Jobseeker's Allowance Regulations 1996–*cont.*

Reg.130, amended: SI 2008/2767 Reg.4, SI 2008/3157 Reg.3
Reg.131, amended: SI 2008/1599 Reg.4
Reg.136, amended: SI 2008/1599 Reg.4, SI 2008/2767 Reg.4
Reg.136, revoked (in part): SI 2008/2767 Reg.4
Reg.140, amended: SI 2008/1554 Reg.3, SI 2008/3051 Reg.11
Reg.146A, amended: SI 2008/1554 Reg.3
Reg.148, referred to: SI 2008/632 Art.24
Reg.149, amended: SI 2008/698 Reg.4, SI 2008/1554 Reg.3, SI 2008/2767 Reg.4
Reg.150, amended: SI 2008/1554 Reg.3
Reg.153, amended: SI 2008/1554 Reg.3
Reg.170, amended: SI 2008/3157 Reg.3
Reg.171, amended: SI 2008/1554 Reg.3
Reg.172, amended: SI 2008/632 Art.25
Sch.A1 para.6A, added: SI 2008/1554 Reg.3
Sch.A1 para.12, amended: SI 2008/1554 Reg.3
Sch.A1 para.16, amended: SI 2008/3157 Reg.3
Sch.1 Part I, referred to: SI 2008/632 Art.24
Sch.1 Part I para.1, amended: SI 2008/698 Reg.4, SI 2008/1554 Reg.3
Sch.1 Part I para.1, substituted: SI 2008/632 Sch.14
Sch.1 Part I para.2, substituted: SI 2008/632 Sch.14
Sch.1 Part I para.3, substituted: SI 2008/632 Sch.14
Sch.1 Part II para.4, amended: SI 2008/632 Art.24
Sch.1 Part III para.8, amended: SI 2008/698 Reg.4
Sch.1 Part III para.15A, referred to: SI 2008/632 Art.24
Sch.1 Part III para.16, referred to: SI 2008/632 Art.24
Sch.1 Part IV, referred to: SI 2008/632 Art.24
Sch.1 Part IV, substituted: SI 2008/632 Sch.15
Sch.1 Part IVA para.20H, amended: SI 2008/1554 Reg.3
Sch.1 Part IVB, referred to: SI 2008/632 Art.24
Sch.1 Part IVB para.20M, substituted: SI 2008/632 Sch.16
Sch.2 para.1, amended: SI 2008/1554 Reg.3
Sch.2 para.1, varied: SI 2008/3195 Reg.11
Sch.2 para.1A, amended: SI 2008/1554 Reg.3
Sch.2 para.1A, referred to: SI 2008/3195 Reg.8
Sch.2 para.3, amended: SI 2008/2767 Reg.4
Sch.2 para.4, amended: SI 2008/698 Reg.4, SI 2008/2767 Reg.4

NO.

1996–cont.

207. Jobseeker's Allowance Regulations 1996–*cont.*

Sch.2 para.4, applied: SI 2008/794 Sch.6 para.6
Sch.2 para.4A, varied: SI 2008/3195 Reg.6, Reg.11
Sch.2 para.6, amended: SI 2008/1554 Reg.3
Sch.2 para.6, applied: SI 2008/3195 Reg.3
Sch.2 para.6, referred to: SI 2008/3195 Reg.3
Sch.2 para.6, varied: SI 2008/3195 Reg.6, Reg.11
Sch.2 para.7, amended: SI 2008/1554 Reg.3
Sch.2 para.7, applied: SI 2008/3195 Reg.3
Sch.2 para.7, referred to: SI 2008/3195 Reg.3
Sch.2 para.7, varied: SI 2008/3195 Reg.6, Reg.11
Sch.2 para.8, varied: SI 2008/3195 Reg.11
Sch.2 para.9, varied: SI 2008/3195 Reg.11
Sch.2 para.10, varied: SI 2008/3195 Reg.6, Reg.11
Sch.2 para.11, amended: SI 2008/3195 Reg.2
Sch.2 para.11, revoked (in part): SI 2008/3195 Reg.2
Sch.2 para.12, varied: SI 2008/3195 Reg.11
Sch.2 para.13, amended: SI 2008/698 Reg.4, SI 2008/1554 Reg.3, SI 2008/1826 Reg.3, SI 2008/2767 Reg.4
Sch.2 para.13, varied: SI 2008/3195 Reg.6, Reg.11
Sch.2 para.14, applied: SI 2008/794 Sch.6 para.3, SI 2008/3195 Reg.12
Sch.2 para.15, amended: SI 2008/2767 Reg.4
Sch.2 para.15, applied: SI 2008/794 Sch.6 para.3, SI 2008/3195 Reg.12
Sch.2 para.16, applied: SI 2008/794 Sch.6 para.3
Sch.2 para.17, amended: SI 2008/632 Art.24, SI 2008/1554 Reg.3, SI 2008/2767 Reg.4
Sch.2 para.18, amended: SI 2008/1554 Reg.3
Sch.2 para.18, applied: SI 2008/794 Sch.6 para.20
Sch.2 para.18, varied: SI 2008/3195 Reg.11
Sch.5, referred to: SI 2008/632 Art.24
Sch.5A, referred to: SI 2008/632 Art.24
Sch.6 para.5, amended: SI 2008/1554 Reg.3
Sch.6A para.1, amended: SI 2008/1554 Reg.3
Sch.7 para.6C, added: SI 2008/3140 Reg.3
Sch.7 para.6C, revoked: SI 2008/3140 Reg.3
Sch.7 para.7, substituted: SI 2008/3157 Reg.3
Sch.7 para.8, amended: SI 2008/1554 Reg.3, SI 2008/3157 Reg.3
Sch.7 para.12, amended: SI 2008/3157 Reg.3
Sch.7 para.14, amended: SI 2008/1554 Reg.3
Sch.7 para.17, substituted: SI 2008/3157 Reg.3

NO.

1996–cont.

207. Jobseeker's Allowance Regulations 1996–*cont.*

Sch.7 para.22, amended: SI 2008/2767 Reg.4
Sch.7 para.26, amended: SI 2008/3157 Reg.3
Sch.7 para.26, revoked (in part): SI 2008/3157 Reg.3
Sch.7 para.28, amended: SI 2008/3157 Reg.3
Sch.7 para.29, substituted: SI 2008/698 Reg.4
Sch.7 para.40, revoked: SI 2008/3157 Reg.3
Sch.7 para.41, amended: SI 2008/2767 Reg.4
Sch.7 para.43, amended: SI 2008/3157 Reg.3
Sch.7 para.44, revoked: SI 2008/2767 Reg.4
Sch.7 para.45, substituted: SI 2008/698 Reg.4
Sch.7 para.46, revoked: SI 2008/3157 Reg.3
Sch.7 para.47, substituted: SI 2008/3157 Reg.3
Sch.7 para.48, substituted: SI 2008/3157 Reg.3
Sch.7 para.49, amended: SI 2008/3157 Reg.3
Sch.7 para.52, substituted: SI 2008/3157 Reg.3
Sch.7 para.53, substituted: SI 2008/3157 Reg.3
Sch.7 para.55, amended: SI 2008/3157 Reg.3
Sch.7 para.70, amended: SI 2008/2111 Reg.3
Sch.7 para.72, amended: SI 2008/3157 Reg.3
Sch.8 para.12, amended: SI 2008/698 Reg.4, SI 2008/1554 Reg.3, SI 2008/3157 Reg.3
Sch.8 para.22, substituted: SI 2008/698 Reg.4
Sch.8 para.27, amended: SI 2008/2767 Reg.4
Sch.8 para.31, amended: SI 2008/2767 Reg.4
Sch.8 para.34, amended: SI 2008/3157 Reg.3
Sch.8 para.35, amended: SI 2008/698 Reg.4
Sch.8 para.36, substituted: SI 2008/3157 Reg.3
Sch.8 para.37, substituted: SI 2008/3157 Reg.3
Sch.8 para.38, amended: SI 2008/3157 Reg.3
Sch.8 para.39, substituted: SI 2008/3157 Reg.3
Sch.8 para.52, amended: SI 2008/3157 Reg.3
Sch.8 para.58, amended: SI 2008/3157 Reg.3
Sch.8 para.59, amended: SI 2008/3157 Reg.3

NO.

1996–cont.

223. Income Tax (Building Societies) (Dividends and Interest) (Amendment) Regulations 1996
revoked: SI 2008/2682 Sch.3

259. North Glamorgan National Health Service Trust (Establishment) Order 1996
revoked: SI 2008/940 Art.2

275. Gas (Northern Ireland) Order 1996
Art.3, amended: 2008 c.32 Sch.1 para.5

282. Merchant Shipping (Prevention of Pollution) (Law of the Sea Convention) Order 1996
Art.2, enabled: SI 2008/2924, SI 2008/3257

294. Mental Health (After-care under Supervision) Regulations 1996
revoked: SI 2008/1210 Art.12

295. Mental Health (Patients in the Community) (Transfers from Scotland) Regulations 1996
revoked: SI 2008/2828 Art.9

314. Mental Health Review Tribunal (Amendment) Rules 1996
revoked: SI 2008/2705 r.31

414. Local Government Superannuation (Scotland) Amendment Regulations 1996
revoked: SSI 2008/229 Sch.1

428. Noise Insulation (Railways and Other Guided Transport Systems) Regulations 1996
Reg.7, applied: SI 2008/1261 Sch.6 para.17

513. Act of Adjournal (Criminal Procedure Rules) 1996
r.2, substituted: SSI 2008/61 r.2
Sch.2 Appendix, amended: SSI 2008/61 r.2, r.3, r.4, r.5, r.6, SSI 2008/62 r.3, Sch.1, SSI 2008/275 Sch.1
Sch.2 Part IV para.17.A1, added: SSI 2008/61 r.3
Sch.2 Part IV para.18.1, amended: SSI 2008/61 r.2
Sch.2 Part IV para.18.3, substituted: SSI 2008/61 r.4
Sch.2 Part IV para.18.3A, substituted: SSI 2008/61 r.4
Sch.2 Part IV para.18.3B, substituted: SSI 2008/61 r.4
Sch.2 Part IV para.18.3C, substituted: SSI 2008/61 r.4
Sch.2 Part V para.20.9A, added: SSI 2008/61 r.5
Sch.2 Part V para.20.9AA, added: SSI 2008/61 r.5, SSI 2008/275 r.2
Sch.2 Part V para.20.9B, added: SSI 2008/61 r.5
Sch.2 Part V para.20.9C, added: SSI 2008/61 r.5
Sch.2 Part V para.20.9D, added: SSI 2008/61 r.5

NO.

1996–cont.

513. Act of Adjournal (Criminal Procedure Rules) 1996–*cont.*
Sch.2 Part VII para.32.2, amended: SSI 2008/61 r.2
Sch.2 Part VII para.36.2, amended: SSI 2008/61 r.2
Sch.2 Part VII para.53.1, added: SSI 2008/61 r.6
Sch.2 para.40.2, see *McDonald (John) v HM Advocate* [2008] UKPC 46, 2008 S.L.T. 993 (PC (Sc)), Lord Hope of Craighead
Sch.2 para.40.5, see *McDonald (John) v HM Advocate* 2008 S.L.T. 144 (HCJ), Lord Hamilton L.J.G.
Sch.2 Part VII para.53.1, added: SSI 2008/61 r.6

540. Mental Health (Hospital, Guardianship and Consent to Treatment) (Amendment) Regulations 1996
revoked (in part): SI 2008/1184 Sch.2, SI 2008/2439 Sch.2

551. Gas Safety (Management) Regulations 1996
applied: SI 2008/736 Reg.16, Sch.13
Reg.11, applied: SI 2008/736 Sch.13

600. Energy Information (Washing Machines) Regulations 1996
Sch.5 Part III para.15, amended: SI 2008/1277 Sch.2 para.86
Sch.5 Part III para.15, revoked (in part): SI 2008/1277 Sch.2 para.86, Sch.4 Part 2

601. Energy Information (Tumble Driers) Regulations 1996
Sch.5 Part III para.15, amended: SI 2008/1277 Sch.2 para.87
Sch.5 Part III para.15, revoked (in part): SI 2008/1277 Sch.4 Part 2

615. Education (Areas to which Pupils and Students Belong) Regulations 1996
Reg.7, see *R. (on the application of L) v Waltham Forest LBC* [2007] EWHC 2060 (Admin), [2008] B.L.G.R. 495 (QBD (Admin)), Rabinder Singh Q.C.

617. Criminal Justice (Scotland) Act 1987 Fixed Penalty Order 1996
revoked: SSI 2008/108 Art.3

683. Medicines (Products for Human Use-Fees) Amendment Regulations 1996
revoked: SI 2008/552 Sch.7

707. Health Authorities (Membership and Procedure) Regulations 1996
Reg.1, amended: SI 2008/1700 Sch.1 para.4
Reg.10, amended: SI 2008/1700 Sch.1 para.4
Reg.14, amended: SI 2008/1700 Sch.1 para.4
Reg.16, amended: SI 2008/1700 Sch.1 para.4

710. Local Government Changes for England (Education) (Miscellaneous Provisions) Regulations 1996
Reg.13, amended: SI 2008/2683 Sch.1 para.70
Reg.16, revoked: SI 2008/2683 Sch.1 para.71

NO.

1996–cont.

714. Trade Marks (International Registration) Order 1996
applied: SI 2008/1958 r.4
revoked: SI 2008/2206 Sch.7

825. Pipelines Safety Regulations 1996
Reg.3, applied: SI 2008/2852 Sch.3 para.1
Reg.13A, applied: SI 2008/101 Reg.11, Reg.12, SI 2008/540 Reg.11, Reg.12
Reg.25, applied: SI 2008/2867 Reg.31
Reg.25, varied: SI 2008/2867 Reg.31

848. Deregulation (Corn Returns Act 1882) Order 1996
revoked: SI 2008/576 Sch.5 para.8

888. Protection of Water Against Agricultural Nitrate Pollution (England and Wales) Regulations 1996
applied: SI 2008/2349 Reg.4, SI 2008/3143 Reg.4
revoked (in part): SI 2008/2349 Reg.50, SI 2008/3143 Reg.50

913. Offshore Installations and Wells (Design and Construction, etc.) Regulations 1996
see *Spencer-Franks v Kellogg Brown & Root Ltd* [2008] UKHL 46, 2008 S.L.T. 675 (HL), Lord Hoffmann

1022. Lands Tribunal Rules 1996
r.50, see *Port of London Authority v Transport for London* [2008] R.V.R. 93 (Lands Tr), PR Francis FRICS

1076. Statutory Nuisance (Appeals) (Scotland) Regulations 1996
Reg.2, amended: 2008 asp 5 Sch.2 para.6

1172. Occupational Pension Schemes (Contracting-out) Regulations 1996
applied: SSI 2008/228 Reg.73
Reg.1, applied: SSI 2008/228 Reg.75
Reg.1, referred to: SI 2008/239 Reg.80
Reg.23, amended: SI 2008/2301 Sch.1 para.2
Reg.49, amended: SI 2008/1903 Reg.21
Reg.54, applied: SI 2008/239 Reg.49, SSI 2008/228 Reg.45
Reg.60, applied: SI 2008/653 Reg.18, Reg.22, SSI 2008/224 Reg.18, Reg.22

1241. Local Government (Superannuation and Compensation for Premature Retirement) (Scotland) Amendment Regulations 1996
revoked: SSI 2008/229 Sch.1

1270. Occupational Pension Schemes (Internal Dispute Resolution Procedures) Regulations 1996
revoked: SI 2008/649 Reg.7

1299. Proceeds of Crime (Northern Ireland) Order 1996
Art.3, see *Maye, Re* [2008] UKHL 9, [2008] 1 W.L.R. 315 (HL (NI)), Lord Bingham of Cornhill

NO.

1996–cont.

1299. Proceeds of Crime (Northern Ireland) Order 1996–*cont.*
Art.5, see *Maye, Re* [2008] UKHL 9, [2008] 1 W.L.R. 315 (HL (NI)), Lord Bingham of Cornhill
Art.5, amended: 2008 c.28 Sch.3 para.1
Art.6, see *Maye, Re* [2008] UKHL 9, [2008] 1 W.L.R. 315 (HL (NI)), Lord Bingham of Cornhill
Art.8, see *Maye, Re* [2008] UKHL 9, [2008] 1 W.L.R. 315 (HL (NI)), Lord Bingham of Cornhill
Art.21, see *Maye, Re* [2008] UKHL 9, [2008] 1 W.L.R. 315 (HL (NI)), Lord Bingham of Cornhill
Art.49, amended: SI 2008/574 Sch.1 para.5
Art.50, applied: SI 2008/1909 Sch.1
Sch.2, amended: SI 2008/574 Sch.1 para.5
Sch.2, applied: SI 2008/1909 Sch.1

1320. Road Traffic Offenders (Northern Ireland) Order 1996
Art.26, amended: SI 2008/1216 Art.52, Art.63, Art.64
Art.29, applied: SI 2008/1216 Art.91
Art.38A, added: SI 2008/1216 Art.60
Art.38A, applied: SI 2008/1216 Art.61
Art.38E, added: SI 2008/1216 Art.60
Art.46A, added: SI 2008/1216 Art.60
Art.47, applied: SI 2008/1216 Art.91
Sch.1, amended: SI 2008/1216 Art.52, Art.53, Art.54, Art.55, Art.56, Art.57, Art.58, Art.60

1373. Notification of Existing Substances (Enforcement) (Amendment) Regulations 1996
revoked: SI 2008/2852 Sch.10 Part 2

1462. Contracting-out (Transfer and Transfer Payment) Regulations 1996
applied: SSI 2008/228 Reg.73, Reg.90

1499. Food Labelling Regulations 1996
Reg.2, amended: SI 2008/1188 Reg.2, SI 2008/1268 Reg.2, SI 2008/1317 Reg.9, SSI 2008/180 Reg.2
Reg.4, amended: SSI 2008/129 Sch.3 para.2, SSI 2008/395 Sch.3 para.2
Reg.13, amended: SI 2008/1188 Reg.2, SI 2008/1268 Reg.2, SSI 2008/180 Reg.2
Reg.34B, amended: SI 2008/1188 Reg.2, SI 2008/1268 Reg.2, SSI 2008/180 Reg.2
Reg.34B, revoked (in part): SI 2008/1188 Reg.3, SI 2008/1268 Reg.3, SSI 2008/180 Reg.2
Reg.45, amended: SSI 2008/129 Sch.3 para.2, SSI 2008/395 Sch.3 para.2
Reg.50, amended: SI 2008/1188 Reg.2, SI 2008/1268 Reg.2, SSI 2008/180 Reg.2
Sch.AA1, substituted: SI 2008/1188 Sch.1, SI 2008/1268 Sch.1, SSI 2008/180 Sch.1
Sch.2A, revoked (in part): SI 2008/1188 Reg.3, SI 2008/1268 Reg.3, SSI 2008/180 Reg.2

NO.

1996–cont.

1507. Ancient Monuments (Class Consents) (Scotland) Order 1996
applied: SSI 2008/100 Sch.4 Part 2, SSI 2008/159 Sch.3 Part 2

1513. Health and Safety (Consultation with Employees) Regulations 1996
applied: SI 2008/228 Sch.2 para.20

1527. Landfill Tax Regulations 1996
Reg.13, amended: SI 2008/1482 Reg.5, Reg.8, SI 2008/2693 Reg.4
Reg.13, revoked (in part): SI 2008/1482 Reg.5
Reg.31, amended: SI 2008/770 Reg.2
Reg.33A, amended: SI 2008/770 Reg.3
Reg.34, amended: SI 2008/770 Reg.4
Reg.34, revoked (in part): SI 2008/770 Reg.4
Reg.35, amended: SI 2008/770 Reg.5
Sch.1, amended: SI 2008/1482 Sch.3

1536. Occupational Pension Schemes (Minimum Funding Requirement and Actuarial Valuations) Regulations 1996
Reg.16, see *Allied Domecq (Holdings) Ltd v Allied Domecq First Pension Trust Fund* [2008] EWCA Civ 1084, [2008] Pens. L.R. 425 (CA (Civ Div)), Ward, L.J.

1537. Personal and Occupational Pension Schemes (Protected Rights) Regulations 1996
Reg.1, amended: SI 2008/1050 Sch.2 para.2
Reg.2, substituted: SI 2008/1050 Sch.2 para.2
Reg.12, amended: SI 2008/1979 Reg.2
Reg.12, revoked (in part): SI 2008/1979 Reg.2

1564. Protection of Water Against Agricultural Nitrate Pollution (Scotland) Regulations 1996
referred to: SSI 2008/263 Sch.1

1592. Construction (Health, Safety and Welfare) Regulations 1996
see *Mason v Satelcom Ltd* [2007] EWHC 2540 (QB), [2008] P.I.Q.R. P4 (QBD), Judge Reddihough; see *Mason v Satelcom Ltd* [2008] EWCA Civ 494, [2008] I.C.R. 971 (CA (Civ Div)), Ward, L.J.; see *Wright v Edinburgh Royal Infirmary Joint Venture* 2008 S.L.T. (Sh Ct) 90 (Sh Ct (Lothian)), Sheriff F L Reith Q.C.
Reg.2, see *Wright v Edinburgh Royal Infirmary Joint Venture* 2008 S.L.T. (Sh Ct) 90 (Sh Ct (Lothian)), Sheriff F L Reith Q.C.
Reg.4, see *Mason v Satelcom Ltd* [2007] EWHC 2540 (QB), [2008] P.I.Q.R. P4 (QBD), Judge Reddihough
Reg.5, see *Mason v Satelcom Ltd* [2007] EWHC 2540 (QB), [2008] P.I.Q.R. P4 (QBD), Judge Reddihough; see *Wright v Edinburgh Royal Infirmary Joint Venture* 2008 S.L.T. (Sh Ct) 90 (Sh Ct (Lothian)), Sheriff F L Reith Q.C.

NO.

1996–cont.

1592. Construction (Health, Safety and Welfare) Regulations 1996–*cont.*
Reg.6, see *Mason v Satelcom Ltd* [2007] EWHC 2540 (QB), [2008] P.I.Q.R. P4 (QBD), Judge Reddihough; see *Wright v Edinburgh Royal Infirmary Joint Venture* 2008 S.L.T. (Sh Ct) 90 (Sh Ct (Lothian)), Sheriff F L Reith Q.C.
Reg.16, see *Wright v Edinburgh Royal Infirmary Joint Venture* 2008 S.L.T. (Sh Ct) 90 (Sh Ct (Lothian)), Sheriff F L Reith Q.C.

1648. A556(M) Motorway (M6 to M56 Link) and Connecting Roads Scheme 1996
revoked: SI 2008/231 Art.2

1649. A556(M) Motorway (M6 to M56 Link) Supplementary Connecting Roads Scheme 1996
revoked: SI 2008/232 Art.2

1650. A556 Trunk Road (Church Farm-Turnpike Wood, Over Tabley) Order 1996
revoked: SI 2008/233 Art.2

1651. A556 Trunk Road (Turnpike Wood, Over Tabley-A56 Bowdon Roundabout) (Detrunking) Order 1996
revoked: SI 2008/234 Art.2

1654. Income Tax (Payments on Account) Regulations 1996
Reg.3, amended: SI 2008/838 Reg.2

1655. Occupational Pension Schemes (Disclosure of Information) Regulations 1996
Reg.1, revoked (in part): SI 2008/2301 Sch.1 para.1
Sch.1 para.25, amended: SI 2008/649 Reg.6
Sch.1 para.26, amended: SI 2008/649 Reg.6

1656. Work in Compressed Air Regulations 1996
applied: SI 2008/736 Sch.5

1678. Deregulation (Model Appeal Provisions) Order 1996
Sch.1 Part I para.6, amended: SI 2008/2683 Sch.1 para.72
Sch.1 Part I para.25, revoked (in part): SI 2008/2683 Sch.1 para.72
Sch.1 Part I para.37, amended: SI 2008/2683 Sch.1 para.72

1685. Police (Promotion) Regulations 1996
Sch.1 para.5, amended: SI 2008/273 Reg.2

1715. Occupational Pension Schemes (Scheme Administration) Regulations 1996
Reg.4, amended: SI 2008/948 Sch.1 para.21

1784. Plant Health Fees (Scotland) Regulations 1996
revoked: SSI 2008/153 Reg.6

1830. A1 Motorway (North of Leeming to Scotch Corner Section and Connecting Roads) Scheme 1996
revoked: SI 2008/2253 Art.6

NO.

1996–cont.

1831. A1 Trunk Road (Lengths of A1 Carriageway between Catterick and Barton) (Detrunking) Order 1996
revoked: SI 2008/2254 Art.4

1847. Occupational Pension Schemes (Transfer Values) Regulations 1996
applied: SI 2008/653 Reg.6, SSI 2008/228 Reg.73
Reg.1, amended: SI 2008/1050 Reg.2
Reg.2, disapplied: SI 2008/239 Reg.78, SSI 2008/228 Reg.73
Reg.5, applied: SI 2008/239 Reg.78, SSI 2008/228 Reg.73
Reg.6, amended: SI 2008/1050 Reg.3
Reg.7, substituted: SI 2008/1050 Reg.4
Reg.7A, substituted: SI 2008/1050 Reg.4
Reg.7B, amended: SI 2008/2450 Reg.3
Reg.7B, substituted: SI 2008/1050 Reg.4
Reg.7C, amended: SI 2008/2450 Reg.3
Reg.7C, substituted: SI 2008/1050 Reg.4
Reg.7D, substituted: SI 2008/1050 Reg.4
Reg.7E, substituted: SI 2008/1050 Reg.4
Reg.8, substituted: SI 2008/1050 Reg.4
Reg.10, disapplied: SI 2008/239 Reg.78, SSI 2008/228 Reg.73
Reg.11, amended: SI 2008/1050 Reg.5
Reg.11, revoked (in part): SI 2008/1050 Reg.5
Reg.12, amended: SI 2008/1050 Reg.6
Reg.18, applied: SI 2008/239 Reg.78, SSI 2008/228 Reg.73
Sch.1 para.1, amended: SI 2008/1050 Reg.7
Sch.1 para.1, revoked (in part): SI 2008/1050 Reg.7
Sch.1 para.3, added: SI 2008/1050 Reg.7
Sch.1A para.1, added: SI 2008/1050 Sch.1
Sch.1A para.2, added: SI 2008/1050 Sch.1
Sch.1A para.3, added: SI 2008/1050 Sch.1
Sch.1A para.4, added: SI 2008/1050 Sch.1
Sch.1A para.5, added: SI 2008/1050 Sch.1
Sch.1A para.6, added: SI 2008/1050 Sch.1
Sch.1A para.7, added: SI 2008/1050 Sch.1
Sch.1A para.8, added: SI 2008/1050 Sch.1
Sch.1A para.9, added: SI 2008/1050 Sch.1
Sch.1A para.10, added: SI 2008/1050 Sch.1
Sch.1A para.11, added: SI 2008/1050 Sch.1
Sch.1A para.12, added: SI 2008/1050 Sch.1
Sch.1A para.13, added: SI 2008/1050 Sch.1
Sch.1A para.14, added: SI 2008/1050 Sch.1
Sch.1A para.15, added: SI 2008/1050 Sch.1
Sch.1B para.1, added: SI 2008/1050 Sch.1
Sch.1B para.2, added: SI 2008/1050 Sch.1
Sch.1B para.3, added: SI 2008/1050 Sch.1
Sch.1B para.4, added: SI 2008/1050 Sch.1
Sch.1B para.5, added: SI 2008/1050 Sch.1
Sch.1B para.6, added: SI 2008/1050 Sch.1
Sch.1B para.7, added: SI 2008/1050 Sch.1
Sch.1B para.8, added: SI 2008/1050 Sch.1
Sch.1B para.9, added: SI 2008/1050 Sch.1

NO.

1996–cont.

1907. Inshore Fishing (Monofilament Gill Nets) (Scotland) Order 1996
Art.2, applied: SSI 2008/101 Sch.1 Part 1
Art.3, applied: SSI 2008/101 Sch.1 Part 1

1919. Employment Rights (Northern Ireland) Order 1996
Art.132, see *Bombardier Aerospace/Short Bros Plc v McConnell* [2008] I.R.L.R. 51 (CA (NI)), Campbell, L.J.
Art.136, see *Bombardier Aerospace/Short Bros Plc v McConnell* [2008] I.R.L.R. 51 (CA (NI)), Campbell, L.J.
Art.137, see *Bombardier Aerospace/Short Bros Plc v McConnell* [2008] I.R.L.R. 51 (CA (NI)), Campbell, L.J.
Art.164, see *Bombardier Aerospace/Short Bros Plc v McConnell* [2008] I.R.L.R. 51 (CA (NI)), Campbell, L.J.
Art.234, amended: SI 2008/948 Sch.1 para.204

1921. Industrial Tribunals (Northern Ireland) Order 1996
Art.13, amended: SI 2008/1769 Sch.1 para.25

2089. Carriage of Dangerous Goods by Rail Regulations 1996
Reg.3, amended: SI 2008/960 Sch.3

2095. Carriage of Dangerous Goods by Road Regulations 1996
Reg.5, amended: SI 2008/960 Sch.3

2256. Social Landlords (Permissible Additional Purposes or Objects) Order 1996
Art.2, amended: SI 2008/2831 Sch.1 para.8

2317. Teachers (Compensation for Premature Retirement and Redundancy) (Scotland) Regulations 1996
Reg.16B, amended: SSI 2008/227 Reg.36

2325. Housing Act 1996 (Consequential Provisions) Order 1996
Sch.2 para.15, revoked (in part): 2008 c.17 Sch.16
Sch.2 para.18, revoked (in part): 2008 c.17 Sch.16
Sch.2 para.19, revoked (in part): 2008 c.17 Sch.16
Sch.2 para.21, revoked (in part): 2008 c.17 Sch.16

2349. Employment Protection (Recoupment of Jobseeker's Allowance and Income Support) Regulations 1996
Reg.10, amended: SI 2008/2683 Sch.1 para.73

2447. Advice and Assistance (Scotland) Regulations 1996
Reg.2, amended: SI 2008/1879 Reg.35
Reg.4, amended: SI 2008/1879 Reg.35
Reg.8B, applied: SSI 2008/137 Reg.7
Reg.8C, added: SSI 2008/240 Reg.3
Reg.13, amended: SSI 2008/240 Reg.3
Reg.14A, added: SSI 2008/240 Reg.3
Reg.15A, amended: SSI 2008/240 Reg.3

NO.

1996–cont.

2447. Advice and Assistance (Scotland) Regulations 1996–*cont.*
Reg.16, amended: SI 2008/1879 Reg.35, SSI 2008/47 Reg.3
Reg.17, amended: SSI 2008/240 Reg.3
Sch.2 para.2, amended: SSI 2008/240 Reg.3
Sch.2 para.2A, added: SSI 2008/240 Reg.3
Sch.2 para.5, amended: SI 2008/1879 Reg.35
Sch.3 Part I para.1, amended: SSI 2008/240 Reg.3
Sch.3 Part II para.1, amended: SSI 2008/240 Reg.3
Sch.3 Part II para.2, revoked: SSI 2008/240 Reg.3

2475. Personal and Occupational Pension Schemes (Pensions Ombudsman) Regulations 1996
Reg.3, amended: SI 2008/649 Reg.6

2507. Act of Sederunt (Sheriff Court Bankruptcy Rules) 1996
applied: SSI 2008/119 r.3
revoked: SSI 2008/119 r.3

2537. Hydrocarbon Oil Duties (Marine Voyages Reliefs) Regulations 1996
Reg.2, amended: SI 2008/753 Reg.5
Reg.3, amended: SI 2008/753 Reg.5
Reg.6, amended: SI 2008/753 Reg.5
Reg.10, amended: SI 2008/753 Reg.5
Reg.11, amended: SI 2008/753 Reg.5

2745. Social Security Benefit (Computation of Earnings) Regulations 1996
Reg.7, applied: SI 2008/632 Art.6

2758. Multiplex Licence (Broadcasting of Programmes in Gaelic) Order 1996
Art.2, substituted: SI 2008/1421 Art.2

2888. Disabled Facilities Grants and Home Repair Assistance (Maximum Amounts) Order 1996
Art.2, revoked (in part): SI 2008/1189 Art.4, SI 2008/2370 Art.4
Art.3, revoked (in part): SI 2008/1189 Art.4, SI 2008/2370 Art.4

2890. Housing Renewal Grants Regulations 1996
referred to: SI 2008/1190 Reg.3
Reg.5, substituted: SI 2008/1190 Reg.4, SI 2008/2377 Reg.3
Reg.10, substituted: SI 2008/1190 Reg.4, SI 2008/2377 Reg.3
Reg.12, amended: SI 2008/1190 Reg.4, SI 2008/2377 Reg.3
Reg.31, amended: SI 2008/1190 Reg.4, SI 2008/2377 Reg.3
Sch.1, referred to: SI 2008/1190 Reg.4
Sch.1A, referred to: SI 2008/1190 Reg.5
Sch.1 Part I para.1, amended: SI 2008/1190 Reg.4, SI 2008/2377 Reg.3
Sch.1 Part I para.2, amended: SI 2008/1190 Reg.4, SI 2008/2377 Reg.3

NO.

1996–cont.

2890. Housing Renewal Grants Regulations 1996–*cont.*
Sch.1 Part II para.3, amended: SI 2008/1190 Reg.4, SI 2008/2377 Reg.3
Sch.1 Part III para.13A, amended: SI 2008/1190 Reg.4, SI 2008/2377 Reg.3
Sch.1 Part III para.13A, revoked (in part): SI 2008/1190 Reg.4, SI 2008/2377 Reg.3
Sch.1 Part III para.14, amended: SI 2008/1190 Reg.4, SI 2008/2377 Reg.3
Sch.1 Part IV para.18, amended: SI 2008/1190 Reg.4, SI 2008/2377 Reg.3
Sch.1A Part I para.1, amended: SI 2008/1190 Reg.5, SI 2008/2377 Reg.4
Sch.1A Part I para.2, amended: SI 2008/1190 Reg.5, SI 2008/2377 Reg.4
Sch.1A Part II para.3, amended: SI 2008/1190 Reg.5, SI 2008/2377 Reg.4
Sch.1A Part III para.5, revoked (in part): SI 2008/1190 Reg.5, SI 2008/2377 Reg.4
Sch.1A Part III para.6, substituted: SI 2008/1190 Reg.5, SI 2008/2377 Reg.4
Sch.1A Part IV para.13, amended: SI 2008/1190 Reg.5, SI 2008/2377 Reg.4
Sch.2, referred to: SI 2008/1190 Reg.4
Sch.2 para.12, amended: SI 2008/1190 Reg.4, SI 2008/2377 Reg.3
Sch.2 para.12A, added: SI 2008/1190 Reg.4, SI 2008/2377 Reg.3
Sch.2 para.18, amended: SI 2008/1190 Reg.4, SI 2008/2377 Reg.3
Sch.3, referred to: SI 2008/1190 Reg.4
Sch.3 para.4, amended: SI 2008/1190 Reg.4, SI 2008/2377 Reg.3
Sch.3 para.4A, added: SI 2008/1190 Reg.4, SI 2008/2377 Reg.3
Sch.3 para.4B, added: SI 2008/3104 Reg.3
Sch.3 para.13, amended: SI 2008/1190 Reg.4, SI 2008/2377 Reg.3
Sch.3 para.50A, added: SI 2008/3104 Reg.3
Sch.3 para.50B, added: SI 2008/3104 Reg.3
Sch.4, referred to: SI 2008/1190 Reg.4
Sch.4 para.6, amended: SI 2008/1190 Reg.4, SI 2008/2377 Reg.3
Sch.4 para.6, substituted: SI 2008/3104 Reg.3
Sch.4 para.6A, added: SI 2008/1190 Reg.4, SI 2008/2377 Reg.3
Sch.4 para.9, amended: SI 2008/3104 Reg.3
Sch.4 para.67, added: SI 2008/3104 Reg.3

2907. Child Support Departure Direction and Consequential Amendments Regulations 1996
Reg.1, amended: SI 2008/2683 Sch.1 para.75
Reg.1, applied: 2008 c.6 Sch.2
Reg.2, applied: 2008 c.6 Sch.2
Reg.3, applied: 2008 c.6 Sch.2
Reg.4, applied: 2008 c.6 Sch.2
Reg.5, applied: 2008 c.6 Sch.2
Reg.6, applied: 2008 c.6 Sch.2
Reg.7, applied: 2008 c.6 Sch.2

NO.

1996–cont.

2907. Child Support Departure Direction and Consequential Amendments Regulations 1996–*cont.*

Reg.8, applied: 2008 c.6 Sch.2
Reg.8A, applied: 2008 c.6 Sch.2
Reg.9, applied: 2008 c.6 Sch.2
Reg.10, applied: 2008 c.6 Sch.2
Reg.11, applied: 2008 c.6 Sch.2
Reg.11A, applied: 2008 c.6 Sch.2
Reg.12, applied: 2008 c.6 Sch.2
Reg.13, applied: 2008 c.6 Sch.2
Reg.14, applied: 2008 c.6 Sch.2
Reg.15, applied: 2008 c.6 Sch.2
Reg.16, applied: 2008 c.6 Sch.2
Reg.17, applied: 2008 c.6 Sch.2
Reg.18, applied: 2008 c.6 Sch.2
Reg.19, applied: 2008 c.6 Sch.2
Reg.20, applied: 2008 c.6 Sch.2
Reg.21, applied: 2008 c.6 Sch.2
Reg.22, applied: 2008 c.6 Sch.2
Reg.23, applied: 2008 c.6 Sch.2
Reg.24, applied: 2008 c.6 Sch.2
Reg.25, applied: 2008 c.6 Sch.2
Reg.26, applied: 2008 c.6 Sch.2
Reg.27, applied: 2008 c.6 Sch.2
Reg.28, applied: 2008 c.6 Sch.2
Reg.29, applied: 2008 c.6 Sch.2
Reg.30, applied: 2008 c.6 Sch.2
Reg.31, applied: 2008 c.6 Sch.2
Reg.32, applied: 2008 c.6 Sch.2
Reg.32A, amended: SI 2008/2683 Sch.1 para.76
Reg.32A, applied: 2008 c.6 Sch.2
Reg.32B, amended: SI 2008/2683 Sch.1 para.77
Reg.32B, applied: 2008 c.6 Sch.2
Reg.32C, applied: 2008 c.6 Sch.2
Reg.32D, applied: 2008 c.6 Sch.2
Reg.32E, amended: SI 2008/2683 Sch.1 para.78
Reg.32E, applied: 2008 c.6 Sch.2
Reg.32F, applied: 2008 c.6 Sch.2
Reg.32G, applied: 2008 c.6 Sch.2
Reg.33, applied: 2008 c.6 Sch.2
Reg.34, applied: 2008 c.6 Sch.2
Reg.34A, amended: SI 2008/2683 Sch.1 para.79
Reg.34A, applied: 2008 c.6 Sch.2
Reg.35, applied: 2008 c.6 Sch.2
Reg.36, applied: 2008 c.6 Sch.2
Reg.37, applied: 2008 c.6 Sch.2
Reg.38, applied: 2008 c.6 Sch.2
Reg.39, applied: 2008 c.6 Sch.2
Reg.40, applied: 2008 c.6 Sch.2
Reg.41, applied: 2008 c.6 Sch.2
Reg.42, applied: 2008 c.6 Sch.2
Reg.42A, applied: 2008 c.6 Sch.2
Reg.43, applied: 2008 c.6 Sch.2
Reg.44, applied: 2008 c.6 Sch.2
Reg.45, applied: 2008 c.6 Sch.2

NO.

1996–cont.

2907. Child Support Departure Direction and Consequential Amendments Regulations 1996–*cont.*

Reg.46, amended: SI 2008/2543 Reg.3
Reg.46, applied: 2008 c.6 Sch.2
Reg.46A, applied: 2008 c.6 Sch.2
Reg.48, applied: 2008 c.6 Sch.2
Reg.49, applied: 2008 c.6 Sch.2
Reg.50, applied: 2008 c.6 Sch.2
Reg.51, applied: 2008 c.6 Sch.2
Reg.52, applied: 2008 c.6 Sch.2
Reg.53, applied: 2008 c.6 Sch.2
Reg.54, applied: 2008 c.6 Sch.2
Reg.55, applied: 2008 c.6 Sch.2
Reg.56, applied: 2008 c.6 Sch.2
Reg.57, applied: 2008 c.6 Sch.2
Reg.58, applied: 2008 c.6 Sch.2
Reg.59, applied: 2008 c.6 Sch.2
Reg.60, applied: 2008 c.6 Sch.2
Reg.61, applied: 2008 c.6 Sch.2
Reg.62, applied: 2008 c.6 Sch.2
Reg.63, applied: 2008 c.6 Sch.2
Reg.64, applied: 2008 c.6 Sch.2
Reg.65, applied: 2008 c.6 Sch.2
Reg.66, applied: 2008 c.6 Sch.2
Reg.67, applied: 2008 c.6 Sch.2
Reg.68, applied: 2008 c.6 Sch.2
Sch.1, applied: 2008 c.6 Sch.2

2991. Insurance Companies (Reserves) (Tax) Regulations 1996

Reg.2, amended: SI 2008/954 Art.46, SI 2008/2679 Reg.3
Reg.5, revoked: SI 2008/2679 Reg.4
Reg.7, amended: SI 2008/2679 Reg.5
Reg.8, varied: SI 2008/2646 Reg.4
Reg.8A, amended: SI 2008/2679 Reg.6
Reg.8A, revoked (in part): SI 2008/2679 Reg.6
Reg.8B, amended: SI 2008/2679 Reg.7
Reg.9, amended: SI 2008/2679 Reg.8
Reg.10, amended: SI 2008/2679 Reg.9
Reg.14, amended: SI 2008/2679 Reg.10

3065. Water Supply and Sewerage Services (Customer Service Standards) (Amendment) Regulations 1996

revoked: SI 2008/594 Sch.1

3105. Nitrate Sensitive Areas (Amendment) Regulations 1996

revoked: SI 2008/2349 Reg.50

3126. Occupational Pension Schemes (Winding Up) Regulations 1996

applied: SSI 2008/228 Reg.73
Reg.1, amended: SI 2008/2301 Sch.1 para.3
Reg.13, see *Bridge Trustees Ltd v Yates* [2008] EWHC 964 (Ch), [2008] Pens. L.R. 261 (Ch D), Sarah Asplin QC

NO.

1996–cont.

3128. Occupational Pension Schemes (Deficiency on Winding Up etc.) Regulations 1996

see *Federal-Mogul Aftermarket UK Ltd, Re* [2008] EWHC 1099 (Ch), [2008] Bus. L.R. 1443 (Ch D (Companies Ct)), David Richards, J.

Reg.2, amended: SI 2008/2301 Sch.1 para.4

3158. Licensing (Northern Ireland) Order 1996

Art.60A, added: SI 2008/1216 Art.67

3160. Criminal Justice (Northern Ireland) Order 1996

Part II, applied: SI 2008/1216 Art.35

Art.2, amended: SI 2008/1216 Sch.5 para.7, Sch.6 Part 1

Art.2, revoked (in part): SI 2008/1216 Sch.6 Part 1

Art.4, amended: SI 2008/1216 Sch.5 para.7

Art.10, amended: SI 2008/1216 Sch.5 para.7

Art.13, amended: SI 2008/1216 Sch.5 para.7

Art.15, amended: SI 2008/1216 Sch.5 para.7

Art.15, applied: SI 2008/1216 Art.35

Art.18, revoked: SI 2008/1216 Sch.6 Part 1

Art.22, revoked: SI 2008/1216 Sch.6 Part 1

Art.24, revoked: SI 2008/1216 Sch.6 Part 1

Art.25, amended: SI 2008/1216 Sch.5 para.7

Art.25, applied: SI 2008/1216 Art.35

Art.26, applied: SI 2008/1216 Art.35

Art.27, substituted: SI 2008/1216 Art.34

Art.28, revoked: SI 2008/1216 Sch.6 Part 1

Art.36, amended: SI 2008/1216 Sch.5 para.7

Art.39, amended: SI 2008/1216 Sch.5 para.7

Art.44A, amended: SI 2008/1216 Sch.5 para.7

Art.53, amended: SI 2008/1216 Art.90

Art.54, amended: SI 2008/1216 Art.90

Art.57, amended: SI 2008/1216 Sch.6 Part 1

Sch.2, amended: SI 2008/1216 Art.47, Sch.6 Part 1

Sch.2, revoked (in part): SI 2008/1216 Art.47, Sch.6 Part 1

3213. Naval Medical Compassionate Fund (Amendment) Order 1996

revoked: SI 2008/3129 Sch.1

3261. Children's Hearings (Scotland) Rules 1996

see *P v Children's Reporter* 2008 S.L.T. (Sh Ct) 85 (Sh Ct (Lothian)), Sheriff IG McColl

r.5, see *P v Children's Reporter* 2008 S.L.T. (Sh Ct) 85 (Sh Ct (Lothian)), Sheriff IG McColl

3263. Fostering of Children (Scotland) Regulations 1996

Reg.9, applied: SI 2008/794 Sch.8 para.28

3266. Adoption Agencies (Scotland) Regulations 1996

applied: SI 2008/794 Reg.156

NO.

1997

51. Value Added Tax (Registered Social Landlords) (No.2) Order 1997

revoked: SI 2008/1146 Sch.1 para.22

56. Road Traffic (Permitted Parking Area and Special Parking Area) (County of Buckinghamshire) (High Wycombe Town Centre) Order 1997

revoked: SI 2008/2344 Art.3

74. Housing Act 1996 (Consequential Amendments) Order 1997

Sch.1 para.9, revoked (in part): 2008 c.17 Sch.16

172. Standing Civilian Courts Order 1997

Art.6, applied: SI 2008/635 Art.2

264. London Underground (East London Line Extension) Order 1997

see *Spirerose Ltd v Transport for London* [2008] R.V.R. 12 (Lands Tr), George Bartlett Q.C.

265. Life Assurance and Other Policies (Keeping of Information and Duties of Insurers) Regulations 1997

Reg.2, amended: SI 2008/2628 Reg.2

266. Potato Industry Development Council Order 1997

revoked: SI 2008/576 Sch.5 para.8

275. Immigration (Isle of Man) Order 1997

revoked: SI 2008/680 Art.3

291. Act of Sederunt (Child Care and Maintenance Rules) 1997

r.3.47, see *G v McClafferty* 2008 Fam. L.R. 11 (Sh Pr), Sheriff Principal JA Taylor

302. Civil Jurisdiction and Judgments Act 1982 (Interim Relief) Order 1997

see *ETI Euro Telecom International NV v Bolivia* [2008] EWCA Civ 880, [2008] 2 Lloyd's Rep. 421 (CA (Civ Div)), Tuckey, L.J.; see *Masri v Consolidated Contractors International Co SAL* [2007] EWHC 3010 (Comm), [2008] 1 All E.R. (Comm) 305 (QBD (Comm)), Gloster, J.

312. Teachers Superannuation (Amendment) Regulations 1997

see *Pike v Somerset CC* [2008] Pens. L.R. 403 (EAT), Judge McMullen Q.C.

348. Merchant Shipping (Training and Certification) Regulations 1997

Reg.5, amended: SI 2008/2851 Reg.2

Reg.5A, amended: SI 2008/2851 Reg.2

Reg.17, amended: SI 2008/2851 Reg.2

Reg.18, amended: SI 2008/2851 Reg.2

Reg.21, revoked: SI 2008/2851 Reg.2

358. Occupational and Personal Pension Schemes (Contracting-out etc Review of Determinations) Regulations 1997

Reg.4, revoked (in part): SI 2008/2683 Sch.1 para.80

NO.

1997–cont.

420. Town and Country Planning (Determination of Appeals by Appointed Persons) (Prescribed Classes) Regulations 1997
Reg.3, amended: SI 2008/595 Reg.2
Reg.4, amended: SI 2008/2335 Reg.13
Reg.4, revoked (in part): SI 2008/595 Reg.2, SI 2008/2093 Reg.12, SI 2008/2335 Reg.13

470. Personal Pension Schemes (Appropriate Schemes) Regulations 1997
Reg.1, amended: SI 2008/1979 Reg.3
Reg.2, substituted: SI 2008/1979 Reg.3
Reg.3, revoked: SI 2008/1979 Reg.3
Reg.4, revoked (in part): SI 2008/1979 Reg.3
Reg.6, amended: SI 2008/1979 Reg.3
Reg.6, revoked (in part): SI 2008/1979 Reg.3
Reg.18, revoked: SI 2008/1979 Reg.3
Sch.1 Part I para.1, revoked: SI 2008/1979 Reg.3
Sch.1 Part I para.2, revoked: SI 2008/1979 Reg.3
Sch.1 Part I para.3, revoked: SI 2008/1979 Reg.3
Sch.1 Part I para.4, revoked: SI 2008/1979 Reg.3
Sch.1 Part II, revoked: SI 2008/1979 Reg.3
Sch.2 para.1, revoked: SI 2008/1979 Reg.3
Sch.2 para.2, revoked: SI 2008/1979 Reg.3
Sch.2 para.3, revoked: SI 2008/1979 Reg.3
Sch.2 para.4, revoked: SI 2008/1979 Reg.3
Sch.2 para.5, revoked: SI 2008/1979 Reg.3
Sch.2 para.6, revoked: SI 2008/1979 Reg.3
Sch.2 para.7, revoked: SI 2008/1979 Reg.3
Sch.2 para.8, revoked: SI 2008/1979 Reg.3
Sch.2 para.9, revoked: SI 2008/1979 Reg.3

674. Local Government Superannuation (Scotland) Amendment Regulations 1997
revoked: SSI 2008/229 Sch.1

687. Sheriff Court Fees Order 1997
Art.7, substituted: SSI 2008/239 Art.2
Sch.1, substituted: SSI 2008/239 Sch.1, Sch.2, Sch.3

688. Court of Session etc Fees Order 1997
Sch.1, amended: SSI 2008/236 Sch.1, Sch.2, Sch.3

784. Occupational Pension Schemes (Discharge of Liability) Regulations 1997
applied: SSI 2008/228 Reg.73

785. Occupational Pension Schemes (Assignment, Forfeiture, Bankruptcy etc.) Regulations 1997
Reg.2, applied: SI 2008/653 Reg.5, SSI 2008/224 Reg.5

786. Personal and Occupational Pension Schemes (Miscellaneous Amendments) Regulations 1997
applied: SSI 2008/228 Reg.73

NO.

1997–cont.

794. Occupational Pensions Regulatory Authority (Determinations and Review Procedure) Regulations 1997
Reg.13, revoked (in part): SI 2008/2683 Sch.1 para.81

801. Mental Health (Hospital, Guardianship and Consent to Treatment) Amendment Regulations 1997
revoked (in part): SI 2008/1184 Sch.2, SI 2008/2439 Sch.2

818. National Health Service (Optical Charges and Payments) Regulations 1997
applied: SI 2008/1185 Reg.16, Sch.1 para.13, SI 2008/1186 Reg.5
Reg.1, amended: SI 2008/577 Reg.2, SI 2008/1657 Reg.2, SI 2008/2449 Reg.3, SI 2008/2552 Reg.3
Reg.4, amended: SI 2008/1657 Sch.1 para.2, Sch.1 para.3, Sch.1 para.4
Reg.5, amended: SI 2008/1657 Sch.1 para.2
Reg.6, amended: SI 2008/1657 Sch.1 para.2, Sch.1 para.3
Reg.8, amended: SI 2008/2449 Reg.3, SI 2008/2552 Reg.3
Reg.8, applied: SI 2008/1186 Reg.5
Reg.9, amended: SI 2008/1657 Sch.1 para.2, Sch.1 para.5, Sch.1 para.6
Reg.11, amended: SI 2008/1657 Sch.1 para.2
Reg.19, amended: SI 2008/553 Reg.2, SI 2008/660 Reg.2
Reg.19A, added: SI 2008/1657 Reg.3
Reg.19B, added: SI 2008/1657 Reg.3
Reg.19C, added: SI 2008/1657 Reg.3
Sch.1, amended: SI 2008/553 Reg.3, SI 2008/660 Reg.3
Sch.1, revoked: SI 2008/553 Reg.3
Sch.2 para.1, amended: SI 2008/553 Reg.3, SI 2008/660 Reg.3
Sch.2 para.2, amended: SI 2008/553 Reg.3, SI 2008/660 Reg.3
Sch.3, substituted: SI 2008/553 Sch.1, SI 2008/660 Sch.1

831. Lifts Regulations 1997
Reg.2, amended: SI 2008/1597 Sch.6 para.2, Sch.6 para.3, Sch.6 para.4, Sch.6 para.5
Sch.1, amended: SI 2008/1597 Sch.6 para.6
Sch.14, amended: SI 2008/1597 Sch.6 para.7

864. Falkland Islands Constitution (Amendment) Order 1997
revoked: SI 2008/2846 Art.3

876. Pembrokeshire and Derwen National Health Service Trust (Establishment) Order 1997
revoked: SI 2008/937 Art.2

990. Nitrate Sensitive Areas (Amendment) Regulations 1997
revoked: SI 2008/2349 Reg.50

NO.

1997–cont.

1143. Local Government Superannuation (Scottish Environment Protection Agency) (Scotland) Regulations 1997
revoked: SSI 2008/229 Sch.1

1180. Protection from Harassment (Northern Ireland) Order 1997
Art.6, applied: SI 2008/1216 Sch.2 para.26

1373. Local Government Superannuation (Scotland) Amendment (No.2) Regulations 1997
revoked: SSI 2008/229 Sch.1

1435. Local Government Superannuation (Scotland) Amendment (No.3) Regulations 1997
revoked: SSI 2008/229 Sch.1

1505. Road Works (Registers, Notices, Directions and Designations) (Scotland) Amendment Regulations 1997
revoked: SSI 2008/88 Reg.16

1510. Merchant Shipping (Tonnage) Regulations 1997
Reg.6, applied: SI 2008/2924 Sch.1 para.3, Sch.1 para.4, Sch.1 para.5, SI 2008/3257 Sch.1 para.3, Sch.1 para.4, Sch.1 para.5
Reg.12, applied: SI 2008/2924 Sch.1 para.3, SI 2008/3257 Sch.1 para.3
Reg.12C, applied: SI 2008/2924 Sch.1 para.5, SI 2008/3257 Sch.1 para.5
Reg.14, applied: SI 2008/2924 Sch.1 para.7, SI 2008/3257 Sch.1 para.7

1612. Local Government Pension Scheme Regulations 1997
applied: SI 2008/239 Reg.51, Reg.69, Reg.72, Reg.76
referred to: SI 2008/238 Reg.13, SI 2008/239 Reg.79, Reg.81
Part II, revoked: SI 2008/238 Sch.1
Part IV, revoked: SI 2008/238 Sch.1
Reg.1, revoked: SI 2008/238 Sch.1
Reg.2, revoked: SI 2008/238 Sch.1
Reg.3, revoked: SI 2008/238 Sch.1
Reg.12, applied: SI 2008/238 Reg.9
Reg.13, revoked (in part): SI 2008/238 Sch.1
Reg.14, revoked: SI 2008/238 Sch.1
Reg.15, revoked: SI 2008/238 Sch.1
Reg.16, revoked: SI 2008/238 Sch.1
Reg.17, revoked: SI 2008/238 Sch.1
Reg.18, amended: SI 2008/2425 Reg.3
Reg.18, revoked: SI 2008/238 Sch.1
Reg.20, revoked (in part): SI 2008/238 Sch.1
Reg.20B, revoked: SI 2008/238 Sch.1
Reg.21, revoked: SI 2008/238 Sch.1
Reg.22, revoked: SI 2008/238 Sch.1
Reg.23, revoked: SI 2008/238 Sch.1
Reg.24, revoked: SI 2008/238 Sch.1
Reg.25, revoked: SI 2008/238 Sch.1
Reg.25A, revoked: SI 2008/238 Sch.1
Reg.26, revoked: SI 2008/238 Sch.1
Reg.27, revoked: SI 2008/238 Sch.1
Reg.28, revoked: SI 2008/238 Sch.1
Reg.29, revoked: SI 2008/238 Sch.1

NO.

1997–cont.

1612. Local Government Pension Scheme Regulations 1997–*cont.*
Reg.30, revoked: SI 2008/238 Sch.1
Reg.31, revoked: SI 2008/238 Sch.1
Reg.32, revoked: SI 2008/238 Sch.1
Reg.32A, applied: SI 2008/238 Reg.5
Reg.32A, revoked: SI 2008/238 Sch.1
Reg.33, revoked: SI 2008/238 Sch.1
Reg.34, revoked: SI 2008/238 Sch.1
Reg.35, revoked: SI 2008/238 Sch.1
Reg.36, revoked: SI 2008/238 Sch.1
Reg.37, revoked: SI 2008/238 Sch.1
Reg.38, amended: SI 2008/2425 Reg.4
Reg.38, revoked: SI 2008/238 Sch.1
Reg.39, revoked: SI 2008/238 Sch.1
Reg.40, revoked: SI 2008/238 Sch.1
Reg.41, revoked: SI 2008/238 Sch.1
Reg.42, applied: SI 2008/238 Reg.6
Reg.42, revoked: SI 2008/238 Sch.1
Reg.42A, revoked: SI 2008/238 Sch.1
Reg.43, revoked: SI 2008/238 Sch.1
Reg.44, revoked: SI 2008/238 Sch.1
Reg.44, substituted: SI 2008/2425 Reg.5
Reg.45, revoked: SI 2008/238 Sch.1
Reg.46, revoked: SI 2008/238 Sch.1
Reg.47, revoked: SI 2008/238 Sch.1
Reg.48, revoked: SI 2008/238 Sch.1
Reg.49, amended: SI 2008/2425 Reg.6
Reg.49, revoked: SI 2008/238 Sch.1
Reg.50, revoked: SI 2008/238 Sch.1
Reg.52, amended: SI 2008/2425 Reg.7
Reg.55, applied: SI 2008/238 Sch.2 para.5, SI 2008/239 Reg.18, Reg.19, Reg.20, Reg.21
Reg.55, revoked: SI 2008/238 Sch.1
Reg.56, revoked: SI 2008/238 Sch.1
Reg.57, revoked: SI 2008/238 Sch.1
Reg.58, revoked: SI 2008/238 Sch.1
Reg.59, revoked: SI 2008/238 Sch.1
Reg.60, revoked: SI 2008/238 Sch.1
Reg.61, revoked: SI 2008/238 Sch.1
Reg.62, revoked: SI 2008/238 Sch.1
Reg.63, revoked: SI 2008/238 Sch.1
Reg.64, revoked: SI 2008/238 Sch.1
Reg.65, revoked: SI 2008/238 Sch.1
Reg.66, revoked: SI 2008/238 Sch.1
Reg.67, revoked: SI 2008/238 Sch.1
Reg.68, revoked: SI 2008/238 Sch.1
Reg.69, revoked: SI 2008/238 Sch.1
Reg.70, revoked: SI 2008/238 Sch.1
Reg.71, revoked: SI 2008/238 Sch.1
Reg.72, revoked: SI 2008/238 Sch.1
Reg.73, revoked: SI 2008/238 Sch.1
Reg.73A, applied: SI 2008/239 Reg.31
Reg.73A, revoked: SI 2008/238 Sch.1
Reg.74, revoked: SI 2008/238 Sch.1
Reg.75, revoked: SI 2008/238 Sch.1
Reg.76, revoked: SI 2008/238 Sch.1
Reg.76A, applied: SI 2008/239 Reg.35
Reg.76A, revoked: SI 2008/238 Sch.1

1997–cont.

1612. Local Government Pension Scheme Regulations 1997–*cont.*

Reg.76B, revoked: SI 2008/238 Sch.1
Reg.76C, revoked: SI 2008/238 Sch.1
Reg.77, revoked: SI 2008/238 Sch.1
Reg.78, revoked: SI 2008/238 Sch.1
Reg.79, revoked: SI 2008/238 Sch.1
Reg.80, revoked: SI 2008/238 Sch.1
Reg.81, revoked: SI 2008/238 Sch.1
Reg.81A, revoked: SI 2008/238 Sch.1
Reg.81B, revoked: SI 2008/238 Sch.1
Reg.82, revoked: SI 2008/238 Sch.1
Reg.83, revoked (in part): SI 2008/238 Sch.1
Reg.84, revoked: SI 2008/238 Sch.1
Reg.85, revoked: SI 2008/238 Sch.1
Reg.86, revoked: SI 2008/238 Sch.1
Reg.87, amended: SI 2008/2425 Reg.8
Reg.87, revoked: SI 2008/238 Sch.1
Reg.88, applied: SI 2008/239 Reg.76
Reg.88, revoked: SI 2008/238 Sch.1
Reg.89, revoked: SI 2008/238 Sch.1
Reg.90, revoked: SI 2008/238 Sch.1
Reg.91, revoked: SI 2008/238 Sch.1
Reg.92, revoked: SI 2008/238 Sch.1
Reg.93, revoked: SI 2008/238 Sch.1
Reg.94, revoked: SI 2008/238 Sch.1
Reg.95, revoked: SI 2008/238 Sch.1
Reg.96, revoked: SI 2008/238 Sch.1
Reg.96A, revoked: SI 2008/238 Sch.1
Reg.106B, applied: SI 2008/239 Reg.67
Reg.109, revoked: SI 2008/238 Sch.1
Reg.110, referred to: SI 2008/238 Reg.12
Reg.110, revoked: SI 2008/238 Sch.1
Reg.111, revoked: SI 2008/238 Sch.1
Reg.112, revoked: SI 2008/238 Sch.1
Reg.113, revoked: SI 2008/238 Sch.1
Reg.114, revoked: SI 2008/238 Sch.1
Reg.115, revoked: SI 2008/238 Sch.1
Reg.116, revoked: SI 2008/238 Sch.1
Reg.117, revoked: SI 2008/238 Sch.1
Reg.118, revoked: SI 2008/238 Sch.1
Reg.119, revoked: SI 2008/238 Sch.1
Reg.120, revoked: SI 2008/238 Sch.1
Reg.121, revoked: SI 2008/238 Sch.1
Reg.122, revoked (in part): SI 2008/238 Sch.1
Reg.122A, amended: SI 2008/2425 Reg.9
Reg.123, applied: SI 2008/238 Sch.2 para.3
Reg.123, revoked: SI 2008/238 Sch.1
Reg.124, revoked: SI 2008/238 Sch.1
Reg.125, revoked: SI 2008/238 Sch.1
Reg.126, revoked: SI 2008/238 Sch.1
Reg.133, revoked: SI 2008/238 Sch.1
Reg.134, revoked: SI 2008/238 Sch.1
Reg.135, revoked: SI 2008/238 Sch.1
Reg.137A, applied: SI 2008/238 Reg.13
Reg.143, revoked: SI 2008/238 Sch.1
Reg.147, varied: SI 2008/238 Reg.14
Reg.151, amended: SI 2008/2425 Reg.9
Reg.152, referred to: SI 2008/238 Reg.14

1997–cont.

1612. Local Government Pension Scheme Regulations 1997–*cont.*

Reg.153, amended: SI 2008/2425 Reg.9
Reg.153, varied: SI 2008/239 Reg.68
Reg.155, varied: SI 2008/238 Reg.14
Reg.156, referred to: SI 2008/238 Reg.14
Sch.1, amended: SI 2008/2425 Reg.10
Sch.1, revoked: SI 2008/238 Sch.1
Sch.2, revoked: SI 2008/238 Sch.1
Sch.2A, revoked: SI 2008/238 Sch.1
Sch.2A para.1, revoked: SI 2008/238 Sch.1
Sch.2A para.2, revoked: SI 2008/238 Sch.1
Sch.2A para.3, revoked: SI 2008/238 Sch.1
Sch.2A para.4, revoked: SI 2008/238 Sch.1
Sch.2A para.5, revoked: SI 2008/238 Sch.1
Sch.2A para.6, revoked: SI 2008/238 Sch.1
Sch.2A para.7, revoked: SI 2008/238 Sch.1
Sch.2A para.8, revoked: SI 2008/238 Sch.1
Sch.2A para.9, revoked: SI 2008/238 Sch.1
Sch.2A para.10, revoked: SI 2008/238 Sch.1
Sch.2A para.11, revoked: SI 2008/238 Sch.1
Sch.2A para.12, revoked: SI 2008/238 Sch.1
Sch.3, revoked: SI 2008/238 Sch.1
Sch.3 para.1, revoked: SI 2008/238 Sch.1
Sch.4 para.1, revoked: SI 2008/238 Sch.1
Sch.4 para.2, revoked: SI 2008/238 Sch.1
Sch.4 para.3, revoked: SI 2008/238 Sch.1
Sch.4 para.4, revoked: SI 2008/238 Sch.1
Sch.4 para.5, revoked: SI 2008/238 Sch.1
Sch.4 para.6, revoked: SI 2008/238 Sch.1
Sch.4 para.7, revoked: SI 2008/238 Sch.1
Sch.4 para.8, revoked: SI 2008/238 Sch.1
Sch.4 para.9, revoked: SI 2008/238 Sch.1
Sch.4 para.10, revoked: SI 2008/238 Sch.1
Sch.5 Part I paral, revokod: SI 2008/238 Sch.1
Sch.5 Part II, applied: SI 2008/239 Sch.4 para.2, Sch.4 para.7
Sch.5 Part II, revoked: SI 2008/238 Sch.1
Sch.5 Part III, applied: SI 2008/239 Sch.4 para.7
Sch.5 Part III, revoked: SI 2008/238 Sch.1
Sch.8, referred to: SI 2008/238 Reg.13

1613. Local Government Pension Scheme (Transitional Provisions) Regulations 1997

applied: SI 2008/239 Reg.51, Reg.69, Reg.72
referred to: SI 2008/239 Reg.79, Reg.81
revoked: SI 2008/238 Sch.1
Reg.19, referred to: SI 2008/238 Reg.11

1624. Energy Information (Combined Washer-driers) Regulations 1997

Sch.5 Part III para.15, amended: SI 2008/1277 Sch.2 para.88
Sch.5 Part III para.15, revoked (in part): SI 2008/1277 Sch.2 para.88, Sch.4 Part 2

NO.

1997–cont.

1713. Confined Spaces Regulations 1997

Reg.4, see *R. v John Pointon & Sons Ltd* [2008] EWCA Crim 513, [2008] 2 Cr. App. R. (S.) 82 (CA (Crim Div)), Gage, L.J.

Reg.5, see *R. v John Pointon & Sons Ltd* [2008] EWCA Crim 513, [2008] 2 Cr. App. R. (S.) 82 (CA (Crim Div)), Gage, L.J.

1746. Air Navigation (Overseas Territories) (Amendment) Order 1997

varied: SI 2008/3119 Sch.1

1830. Prescription Only Medicines (Human Use) Order 1997

Art.1, amended: SI 2008/1161 Art.2

Art.2, amended: SI 2008/464 Art.2, SI 2008/1161 Art.3

Art.2, revoked (in part): SI 2008/464 Art.2

Art.3, amended: SI 2008/464 Art.3

Art.3A, revoked: SI 2008/464 Art.4

Art.3B, amended: SI 2008/464 Art.5

Art.3C, amended: SI 2008/464 Art.6

Art.5B, added: SI 2008/464 Art.7

Art.8, amended: SI 2008/1161 Art.4

Art.8, applied: SI 2008/1692 Reg.7

Art.8, disapplied: SI 2008/1692 Reg.7

Art.12, amended: SI 2008/464 Art.8

Art.13A, amended: SI 2008/464 Art.9

Art.15, amended: SI 2008/1161 Art.5

Sch.3A, revoked: SI 2008/464 Art.10

1896. Family Law Act 1996 (Part IV) (Allocation of Proceedings) Order 1997

revoked: SI 2008/2836 Sch.2

1897. Children (Allocation of Proceedings) (Amendment) Order 1997

revoked: SI 2008/2836 Sch.2

1968. Education (Assisted Places) Regulations 1997

Reg.10, amended: SI 2008/509 Reg.3, SI 2008/1593 Reg.2

Sch.2 para.1, amended: SI 2008/509 Reg.3, SI 2008/1593 Reg.2

Sch.2 para.2, amended: SI 2008/509 Reg.3, SI 2008/1593 Reg.2

1969. Education (Assisted Places) (Incidental Expenses) Regulations 1997

Reg.2, amended: SI 2008/510 Reg.3, SI 2008/1594 Reg.2

Reg.4, amended: SI 2008/510 Reg.3, SI 2008/1594 Reg.2

Reg.9, amended: SI 2008/1879 Reg.4

1984. Rent Officers (Housing Benefit Functions) Order 1997

see *R. (on the application of Heffernan) v Rent Service* [2007] EWCA Civ 544, [2008] H.L.R. 2 (CA (Civ Div)), Pill, L.J.

Art.4B, amended: SI 2008/3156 Art.2

Sch.1 Part I para.4, amended: SI 2008/3156 Art.2

Sch.1 Part I para.5, amended: SI 2008/3156 Art.2

NO.

1997–cont.

1984. Rent Officers (Housing Benefit Functions) Order 1997–*cont.*

Sch.1 para.4, see *R. (on the application of Heffernan) v Rent Service* [2007] EWCA Civ 544, [2008] H.L.R. 2 (CA (Civ Div)), Pill, L.J.; see *R. (on the application of Heffernan) v Rent Service* [2008] UKHL 58, [2008] 1 W.L.R. 1702 (HL), Lord Hope of Craighead

Sch.3B para.2, revoked (in part): SI 2008/3156 Art.2

Sch.3B para.4, substituted: SI 2008/3156 Art.2

1995. Rent Officers (Housing Benefit Functions) (Scotland) Order 1997

Art.4B, amended: SI 2008/3156 Art.3

Sch.1 Part I para.4, amended: SI 2008/3156 Art.3

Sch.1 Part I para.5, amended: SI 2008/3156 Art.3

Sch.3B para.2, revoked (in part): SI 2008/3156 Art.3

Sch.3B para.4, substituted: SI 2008/3156 Art.3

2196. Gaming Duty Regulations 1997

Reg.5, amended: SI 2008/1949 Reg.4

2389. Airports (Groundhandling) Regulations 1997

Sch.1 para.13, amended: SI 2008/2683 Sch.1 para.83

Sch.2 Part I para.5, amended: SI 2008/2683 Sch.1 para.84

2439. Vehicle Excise Duty (Immobilisation, Removal and Disposal of Vehicles) Regulations 1997

Reg.2, amended: SI 2008/2266 Reg.3

Reg.4, amended: SI 2008/2266 Reg.4

Reg.4, revoked (in part): SI 2008/2266 Reg.4

Reg.5, amended: SI 2008/2266 Reg.5

Reg.6, amended: SI 2008/2266 Reg.6

Reg.6, revoked (in part): SI 2008/2266 Reg.6

Reg.8, amended: SI 2008/2266 Reg.7

Reg.9, amended: SI 2008/2266 Reg.8

Reg.12, amended: SI 2008/2266 Reg.9

Reg.17, amended: SI 2008/2266 Reg.10

Sch.1 para.1, amended: SI 2008/2266 Reg.11

Sch.1 para.2, amended: SI 2008/2266 Reg.11

2567. Merchant Shipping (Oil Pollution Preparedness, Response and Cooperation Convention) Order 1997

Art.2, applied: 2008 c.13 Sch.7

2622. Food Protection (Emergency Prohibitions) (Dounreay Nuclear Establishment) Order 1997

Art.4, applied: SSI 2008/101 Sch.1 Part 1

Art.5, applied: SSI 2008/101 Sch.1 Part 1

Art.6, applied: SSI 2008/101 Sch.1 Part 1

NO.

1997–cont.

2778. Waste and Contaminated Land (Northern Ireland) Order 1997
see *Department of the Environment and Heritage Service v Felix O'Hare & Co Ltd* [2008] Env. L.R. 28 (CA (NI)), Girvan, L.J.
Art.2, see *Department of the Environment and Heritage Service v Felix O'Hare & Co Ltd* [2008] Env. L.R. 28 (CA (NI)), Girvan, L.J.
Art.72, applied: SI 2008/2852 Sch.7 para.2

2959. Beef Bones Regulations 1997
revoked (in part): SI 2008/1180 Reg.3, SI 2008/1182 Reg.3

2962. Merchant Shipping and Fishing Vessels (Health and Safety at Work) Regulations 1997
Reg.28, see *Club Cruise Entertainment & Travelling Services Europe BV v Department for Transport (The Van Gogh)* [2008] EWHC 2794 (Comm), [2008] 2 C.L.C. 708 (QBD (Comm)), Flaux, J.

2971. Secretary of State for the Environment, Transport and the Regions Order 1997
referred to: SI 2008/1034 Art.6

2974. Falkland Islands Constitution (Amendment) (No.2) Order 1997
revoked: SI 2008/2846 Art.3

3001. Teachers Pensions Regulations 1997
applied: SI 2008/541 Reg.18
see *Pike v Somerset CC* [2008] Pens. L.R. 403 (EAT), Judge McMullen Q.C.
Part E regA.1, amended: SI 2008/541 Reg.12
Reg.1, amended: SI 2008/541 Reg.8
Reg.1, amended: SI 2008/541 Reg.9
Reg.1, revoked (in part): SI 2008/541 Reg.9
Reg.1, amended: SI 2008/541 Reg.9, Reg.10
Reg.1, amended: SI 2008/541 Reg.16
Reg.1A, added: SI 2008/541 Reg.9
Reg.2, amended: SI 2008/541 Reg.10
Reg.3, amended: SI 2008/541 Reg.10
Reg.3C, amended: SI 2008/541 Reg.11
Reg.4, amended: SI 2008/541 Reg.10
Reg.5, added: SI 2008/541 Reg.9
Reg.5, amended: SI 2008/541 Reg.14
Reg.6, amended: SI 2008/541 Reg.14
Reg.6A, added: SI 2008/541 Reg.8
Reg.8A, amended: SI 2008/541 Reg.10
Reg.22, amended: SI 2008/541 Reg.15
Reg.22, referred to: SI 2008/541 Reg.15
Reg.24, applied: SI 2008/541 Reg.15
Reg.25, amended: SI 2008/541 Reg.10, Reg.16
Reg.25, applied: SI 2008/541 Reg.15
Reg.26, applied: SI 2008/541 Reg.15
Reg.27, applied: SI 2008/541 Reg.15
Reg.28, amended: SI 2008/541 Reg.9
Reg.28, applied: SI 2008/541 Reg.15
Reg.29, applied: SI 2008/541 Reg.15
Reg.29A, applied: SI 2008/541 Reg.15
Reg.30, applied: SI 2008/541 Reg.15
Reg.31, amended: SI 2008/541 Reg.10

NO.

1997–cont.

3001. Teachers Pensions Regulations 1997– *cont.*
Reg.33, amended: SI 2008/541 Reg.13
Sch.1, amended: SI 2008/541 Reg.9
Sch.2 Part I para.12, amended: SI 2008/2828 Art.10
Sch.2 Part II para.24, amended: SI 2008/541 Reg.17
Sch.2A para.4, amended: SI 2008/541 Reg.11
Sch.2A para.14, amended: SI 2008/541 Reg.16
Sch.2A para.27, amended: SI 2008/541 Reg.11

3048. Local Government Superannuation (Scotland) Amendment (No.4) Regulations 1997
revoked: SSI 2008/229 Sch.1

1998

79. Nitrate Sensitive Areas (Amendment) Regulations 1998
revoked: SI 2008/2349 Reg.50

85. Urban Development Corporations in England (Transfer of Property, Rights and Liabilities) (Commission for the New Towns) Order 1998
Art.3, revoked (in part): 2008 c.17 Sch.16

119. Local Government Finance (New Parishes) Regulations 1998
applied: SI 2008/337 Sch.1 para.2

211. Education (Student Loans) Regulations 1998
Reg.3, amended: SI 2008/1479 Reg.6
Reg.6, amended: SI 2008/1479 Reg.7

364. Local Government Pension Scheme (Transitional Provisions) (Scotland) Regulations 1998
referred to: SSI 2008/228 Reg.74, Reg.76
revoked: SSI 2008/229 Sch.1

366. Local Government Pension Scheme (Scotland) Regulations 1998
applied: SSI 2008/228 Reg.47, Reg.63, Reg.66, Reg.70, SSI 2008/229 Reg.8, SSI 2008/230 Reg.21
referred to: SSI 2008/228 Reg.74, Reg.76, SSI 2008/229 Reg.2, Reg.3, Reg.4, Reg.5, Reg.11, Sch.2 para.6
Part II, revoked: SSI 2008/229 Sch.1
Part IV, revoked: SSI 2008/229 Sch.1
Reg.1, revoked: SSI 2008/229 Sch.1
Reg.2, revoked: SSI 2008/229 Sch.1
Reg.12, revoked (in part): SSI 2008/229 Sch.1
Reg.13, revoked: SSI 2008/229 Sch.1
Reg.14, revoked: SSI 2008/229 Sch.1
Reg.15, revoked: SSI 2008/229 Sch.1
Reg.16, revoked: SSI 2008/229 Sch.1
Reg.17, revoked: SSI 2008/229 Sch.1
Reg.17A, revoked: SSI 2008/229 Sch.1

NO.

1998–cont.

366. Local Government Pension Scheme (Scotland) Regulations 1998–*cont.*
Reg.20, applied: SSI 2008/228 Reg.15
Reg.27, disapplied: SSI 2008/230 Reg.20
Reg.31A, applied: SSI 2008/229 Reg.6
Reg.41, applied: SSI 2008/229 Reg.7
Reg.41, revoked: SSI 2008/229 Sch.1
Reg.42, revoked: SSI 2008/229 Sch.1
Reg.43, revoked: SSI 2008/229 Sch.1
Reg.44, revoked: SSI 2008/229 Sch.1
Reg.45, revoked: SSI 2008/229 Sch.1
Reg.46, revoked: SSI 2008/229 Sch.1
Reg.47, revoked: SSI 2008/229 Sch.1
Reg.48, revoked: SSI 2008/229 Sch.1
Reg.49, revoked: SSI 2008/229 Sch.1
Reg.54, applied: SSI 2008/228 Reg.15, Reg.16, Reg.17, Reg.18, SSI 2008/229 Sch.2 para.5
Reg.54, revoked: SSI 2008/229 Sch.1
Reg.55, revoked: SSI 2008/229 Sch.1
Reg.55A, revoked: SSI 2008/229 Sch.1
Reg.56, revoked: SSI 2008/229 Sch.1
Reg.57, revoked: SSI 2008/229 Sch.1
Reg.58, revoked: SSI 2008/229 Sch.1
Reg.59, revoked: SSI 2008/229 Sch.1
Reg.60, revoked: SSI 2008/229 Sch.1
Reg.61, revoked: SSI 2008/229 Sch.1
Reg.62, revoked: SSI 2008/229 Sch.1
Reg.63, revoked: SSI 2008/229 Sch.1
Reg.64, revoked: SSI 2008/229 Sch.1
Reg.65, revoked (in part): SSI 2008/229 Sch.1
Reg.66, revoked: SSI 2008/229 Sch.1
Reg.67, revoked: SSI 2008/229 Sch.1
Reg.68, revoked: SSI 2008/229 Sch.1
Reg.69, revoked: SSI 2008/229 Sch.1
Reg.70, revoked: SSI 2008/229 Sch.1
Reg.71, revoked: SSI 2008/229 Sch.1
Reg.72, revoked: SSI 2008/229 Sch.1
Reg.73, revoked: SSI 2008/229 Sch.1
Reg.74, revoked: SSI 2008/229 Sch.1
Reg.75, revoked: SSI 2008/229 Sch.1
Reg.75A, applied: SSI 2008/228 Reg.31
Reg.75A, revoked: SSI 2008/229 Sch.1
Reg.76, revoked: SSI 2008/229 Sch.1
Reg.77, revoked: SSI 2008/229 Sch.1
Reg.78, revoked: SSI 2008/229 Sch.1
Reg.79, revoked: SSI 2008/229 Sch.1
Reg.80, revoked: SSI 2008/229 Sch.1
Reg.81, revoked: SSI 2008/229 Sch.1
Reg.83, revoked: SSI 2008/229 Sch.1
Reg.84, revoked: SSI 2008/229 Sch.1
Reg.85, revoked: SSI 2008/229 Sch.1
Reg.86, revoked: SSI 2008/229 Sch.1
Reg.87, applied: SSI 2008/228 Reg.70
Reg.87, revoked (in part): SSI 2008/229 Sch.1
Reg.88, revoked: SSI 2008/229 Sch.1
Reg.89, revoked: SSI 2008/229 Sch.1
Reg.90, revoked: SSI 2008/229 Sch.1

NO.

1998–cont.

366. Local Government Pension Scheme (Scotland) Regulations 1998–*cont.*
Reg.91, revoked: SSI 2008/229 Sch.1
Reg.92, revoked: SSI 2008/229 Sch.1
Reg.93, revoked: SSI 2008/229 Sch.1
Reg.94, revoked: SSI 2008/229 Sch.1
Reg.95, revoked: SSI 2008/229 Sch.1
Reg.110, applied: SSI 2008/229 Reg.12
Reg.110, disapplied: SSI 2008/229 Reg.12
Reg.110, revoked: SSI 2008/229 Sch.1
Reg.111, revoked: SSI 2008/229 Sch.1
Reg.112, revoked: SSI 2008/229 Sch.1
Reg.113, revoked: SSI 2008/229 Sch.1
Reg.114, revoked: SSI 2008/229 Sch.1
Reg.115, revoked: SSI 2008/229 Sch.1
Reg.116, revoked: SSI 2008/229 Sch.1
Reg.117, revoked: SSI 2008/229 Sch.1
Reg.118, revoked: SSI 2008/229 Sch.1
Reg.119, revoked: SSI 2008/229 Sch.1
Reg.120, revoked: SSI 2008/229 Sch.1
Reg.121, revoked: SSI 2008/229 Sch.1
Reg.122, revoked: SSI 2008/229 Sch.1
Reg.123, applied: SSI 2008/229 Sch.2 para.3
Reg.123, revoked: SSI 2008/229 Sch.1
Reg.124, revoked: SSI 2008/229 Sch.1
Reg.125, revoked: SSI 2008/229 Sch.1
Reg.126, revoked: SSI 2008/229 Sch.1
Reg.127, revoked: SSI 2008/229 Sch.1
Reg.132, revoked: SSI 2008/229 Sch.1
Reg.133, revoked: SSI 2008/229 Sch.1
Reg.136, revoked: SSI 2008/229 Sch.1
Reg.138, revoked: SSI 2008/229 Sch.1
Reg.139, revoked: SSI 2008/229 Sch.1
Reg.140, revoked: SSI 2008/229 Sch.1
Reg.141, revoked: SSI 2008/229 Sch.1
Reg.142, revoked: SSI 2008/229 Sch.1
Reg.143, revoked: SSI 2008/229 Sch.1
Reg.144, revoked: SSI 2008/229 Sch.1
Reg.145, revoked: SSI 2008/229 Sch.1
Reg.146, revoked: SSI 2008/229 Sch.1
Reg.147, revoked: SSI 2008/229 Sch.1
Reg.148, revoked: SSI 2008/229 Sch.1
Reg.149, revoked: SSI 2008/229 Sch.1
Reg.150, revoked: SSI 2008/229 Sch.1
Reg.151, revoked: SSI 2008/229 Sch.1
Reg.152, revoked: SSI 2008/229 Sch.1
Reg.153, revoked: SSI 2008/229 Sch.1
Reg.154, revoked: SSI 2008/229 Sch.1
Reg.155, revoked: SSI 2008/229 Sch.1
Reg.156, revoked: SSI 2008/229 Sch.1
Reg.157, revoked: SSI 2008/229 Sch.1
Reg.158, revoked: SSI 2008/229 Sch.1
Reg.159, revoked: SSI 2008/229 Sch.1
Reg.160, revoked: SSI 2008/229 Sch.1
Sch.1, revoked: SSI 2008/229 Sch.1
Sch.1A, revoked: SSI 2008/229 Sch.1
Sch.2A, revoked: SSI 2008/229 Sch.1
Sch.2 para.1, revoked: SSI 2008/229 Sch.1
Sch.2 para.2, revoked: SSI 2008/229 Sch.1
Sch.2 para.3, revoked: SSI 2008/229 Sch.1

NO.

1998–cont.

366. Local Government Pension Scheme (Scotland) Regulations 1998–*cont.*

Sch.2 para.4, revoked: SSI 2008/229 Sch.1
Sch.2 para.5, revoked: SSI 2008/229 Sch.1
Sch.2 para.6, revoked: SSI 2008/229 Sch.1
Sch.2 para.7, revoked: SSI 2008/229 Sch.1
Sch.2 para.8, revoked: SSI 2008/229 Sch.1
Sch.2 para.9, revoked: SSI 2008/229 Sch.1
Sch.2 para.10, revoked: SSI 2008/229 Sch.1
Sch.2 para.11, revoked: SSI 2008/229 Sch.1
Sch.2 para.12, revoked: SSI 2008/229 Sch.1
Sch.2A para.1, revoked: SSI 2008/229 Sch.1
Sch.2A para.2, revoked: SSI 2008/229 Sch.1
Sch.2A para.3, revoked: SSI 2008/229 Sch.1
Sch.2A para.4, revoked: SSI 2008/229 Sch.1
Sch.2A para.5, revoked: SSI 2008/229 Sch.1
Sch.2A para.6, revoked: SSI 2008/229 Sch.1
Sch.2A para.7, revoked: SSI 2008/229 Sch.1
Sch.2A para.8, revoked: SSI 2008/229 Sch.1
Sch.2A para.9, revoked: SSI 2008/229 Sch.1
Sch.2A para.10, revoked: SSI 2008/229 Sch.1
Sch.2A para.11, revoked: SSI 2008/229 Sch.1
Sch.2A para.12, revoked: SSI 2008/229 Sch.1
Sch.3, revoked: SSI 2008/229 Sch.1
Sch.3 para.1, revoked: SSI 2008/229 Sch.1
Sch.3 para.2, revoked: SSI 2008/229 Sch.1
Sch.3 para.3, revoked: SSI 2008/229 Sch.1
Sch.3 para.4, revoked: SSI 2008/229 Sch.1
Sch.3 para.5, revoked: SSI 2008/229 Sch.1
Sch.3 para.6, revoked: SSI 2008/229 Sch.1
Sch.3 para.7, revoked: SSI 2008/229 Sch.1
Sch.4 para.1, revoked: SSI 2008/229 Sch.1
Sch.4 para.2, revoked: SSI 2008/229 Sch.1
Sch.4 para.3, revoked: SSI 2008/229 Sch.1
Sch.4 para.4, revoked: SSI 2008/229 Sch.1
Sch.4 para.5, revoked: SSI 2008/229 Sch.1
Sch.4 para.6, revoked: SSI 2008/229 Sch.1
Sch.4 para.7, revoked: SSI 2008/229 Sch.1
Sch.4 para.8, revoked: SSI 2008/229 Sch.1
Sch.4 para.9, revoked: SSI 2008/229 Sch.1
Sch.4 para.10, revoked: SSI 2008/229 Sch.1
Sch.5 Part I para.1, revoked: SSI 2008/229 Sch.1
Sch.5 Part I para.2, revoked: SSI 2008/229 Sch.1
Sch.5 Part I para.3, revoked: SSI 2008/229 Sch.1
Sch.5 Part I para.4, revoked: SSI 2008/229 Sch.1
Sch.5 Part I para.5, revoked: SSI 2008/229 Sch.1
Sch.5 Part I para.6, revoked: SSI 2008/229 Sch.1
Sch.5 Part II, revoked: SSI 2008/229 Sch.1
Sch.7 Part I para.1, revoked: SSI 2008/229 Sch.1

NO.

1998–cont.

366. Local Government Pension Scheme (Scotland) Regulations 1998–*cont.*

Sch.7 Part I para.2, revoked: SSI 2008/229 Sch.1
Sch.7 Part I para.3, revoked: SSI 2008/229 Sch.1
Sch.7 Part I para.4, revoked: SSI 2008/229 Sch.1
Sch.7 Part I para.5, revoked: SSI 2008/229 Sch.1
Sch.7 Part I para.6, revoked: SSI 2008/229 Sch.1
Sch.7 Part I para.7, revoked: SSI 2008/229 Sch.1
Sch.7 Part I para.8, revoked: SSI 2008/229 Sch.1
Sch.7 Part I para.9, revoked: SSI 2008/229 Sch.1
Sch.7 Part I para.10, revoked: SSI 2008/229 Sch.1
Sch.7 Part I para.11, revoked: SSI 2008/229 Sch.1
Sch.7 Part I para.12, revoked: SSI 2008/229 Sch.1
Sch.7 Part I para.13, revoked: SSI 2008/229 Sch.1
Sch.7 Part I para.14, revoked: SSI 2008/229 Sch.1
Sch.7 Part I para.15, revoked: SSI 2008/229 Sch.1
Sch.7 Part I para.16, revoked: SSI 2008/229 Sch.1
Sch.7 Part I para.17, revoked: SSI 2008/229 Sch.1
Sch.7 Part I para.18, revoked: SSI 2008/229 Sch.1
Sch.7 Part I para.19, revoked: SSI 2008/229 Sch.1
Sch.7 Part I para.20, revoked: SSI 2008/229 Sch.1
Sch.7 Part I para.21, revoked: SSI 2008/229 Sch.1
Sch.7 Part I para.22, revoked: SSI 2008/229 Sch.1
Sch.7 Part I para.23, revoked: SSI 2008/229 Sch.1
Sch.7 Part I para.24, revoked: SSI 2008/229 Sch.1
Sch.7 Part I para.25, revoked: SSI 2008/229 Sch.1
Sch.7 Part I para.26, revoked: SSI 2008/229 Sch.1
Sch.7 Part I para.27, revoked: SSI 2008/229 Sch.1
Sch.8 para.1, revoked: SSI 2008/229 Sch.1
Sch.8 para.2, revoked: SSI 2008/229 Sch.1
Sch.8 para.3, revoked: SSI 2008/229 Sch.1
Sch.8 para.4, revoked: SSI 2008/229 Sch.1
Sch.8 para.5, revoked: SSI 2008/229 Sch.1
Sch.8 para.6, revoked: SSI 2008/229 Sch.1

NO.

1998–cont.

463. Specified Animal Pathogens Order 1998
applied: SI 2008/1090 Reg.3, SSI 2008/11 Art.6
disapplied: SI 2008/962 Reg.3
revoked (in part): SI 2008/944 Art.12, SI 2008/1270 Art.12

472. Secure Training Centre Rules 1998
r.5, applied: SI 2008/2793 r.4

494. Health and Safety (Enforcing Authority) Regulations 1998
Reg.2, amended: SI 2008/960 Sch.3
Reg.5, amended: SI 2008/960 Sch.3
Reg.5, applied: SI 2008/2323 Reg.6
Reg.6, amended: SI 2008/960 Sch.3
Reg.6, applied: SI 2008/2323 Reg.6

504. Building Societies (Accounts and Related Provisions) Regulations 1998
Reg.10, amended: SI 2008/1143 Reg.3
Sch.5 para.38, added: SI 2008/1143 Reg.4
Sch.7 Part VIA para.31A, amended: SI 2008/1143 Reg.5

530. Local Government Pension Scheme (Amendment) Regulations 1998
revoked: SI 2008/238 Sch.1

562. Income-related Benefits (Subsidy to Authorities) Order 1998
Art.13, amended: SI 2008/196 Art.2
Art.18, amended: SI 2008/196 Art.2
Art.18, revoked (in part): SI 2008/196 Art.2
Art.21, revoked: SI 2008/196 Art.2
Sch.1, substituted: SI 2008/196 Sch.1, SI 2008/1649 Sch.1
Sch.4A Part II para.2, amended: SI 2008/695 Sch.1 para.1
Sch.4A Part III, substituted: SI 2008/695 Sch.1 para.2
Sch.4A Part IV para.4, amended: SI 2008/695 Sch.1 para.3
Sch.4A Part V, substituted: SI 2008/695 Sch.1 para.4

568. Local Government Pension Scheme (Amendment) (Environment Agency) Regulations 1998
revoked: SI 2008/238 Sch.1

574. Medicines for Human Use and Medical Devices (Fees and Miscellaneous Amendments) Regulations 1998
revoked: SI 2008/552 Sch.7

642. National Health Service (Optical Charges and Payments) (Scotland) Regulations 1998
Reg.1, amended: SSI 2008/289 Reg.2
Reg.8, amended: SSI 2008/106 Reg.2, SSI 2008/289 Reg.2
Reg.12, applied: SSI 2008/106 Reg.3
Reg.17, applied: SSI 2008/106 Reg.3
Reg.19, amended: SSI 2008/106 Reg.2
Sch.1, amended: SSI 2008/106 Reg.2
Sch.2, substituted: SSI 2008/106 Sch.1
Sch.3 para.1, amended: SSI 2008/106 Reg.2

NO.

1998–cont.

642. National Health Service (Optical Charges and Payments) (Scotland) Regulations 1998–*cont.*
Sch.3 para.2, amended: SSI 2008/106 Reg.2

745. European Communities (Designation) Order 1998
Sch.1, amended: SI 2008/301 Sch.1

902. Residential Care Homes and the Nursing Homes and Mental Nursing Homes (Amendment) Regulations 1998
applied: 2008 c.14 s.17

1019. General Osteopathic Council (Constitution and Procedure) Rules Order of Council 1998
revoked: SI 2008/1774 Sch.5 para.4

1027. Plant Breeders Rights Regulations 1998
Reg.8, revoked (in part): SI 2008/2683 Sch.1 para.85

1069. Activity Centres (Young Person's Safety) (Northern Ireland) Order 1998
Art.4, amended: 2008 c.20 Sch.3 para.5

1071. Family Homes and Domestic Violence (Northern Ireland) Order 1998
Art.2, amended: 2008 c.22 Sch.6 para.79

1189. Mental Health Review Tribunal (Amendment) Rules 1998
revoked: SI 2008/2705 r.31

1201. Pensions Appeal Tribunals (England and Wales) (Amendment) Rules 1998
revoked: SI 2008/2683 Sch.2

1202. Action Programme for Nitrate Vulnerable Zones (England and Wales) Regulations 1998
revoked (in part): SI 2008/2349 Reg.50, SI 2008/3143 Reg.50

1238. Local Government Pension Scheme Regulations 1997 (Amendment) Regulations 1998
revoked: SI 2008/238 Sch.1

1376. Plastic Materials and Articles in Contact with Food Regulations 1998
applied: SI 2008/916 Reg.22, SSI 2008/127 Reg.19
disapplied: SI 2008/1237 Reg.22, SI 2008/1682 Reg.22
Reg.3, applied: SI 2008/916 Reg.22, SI 2008/1237 Reg.22, SI 2008/1682 Reg.22, SSI 2008/127 Reg.19
Reg.10, applied: SI 2008/916 Reg.22, SI 2008/1237 Reg.22, SI 2008/1682 Reg.22, SSI 2008/127 Reg.19

1377. Merchant Shipping (Prevention of Pollution by Garbage) Regulations 1998
revoked: SI 2008/3257 Reg.5

NO.

1998–cont.

1451. National Health Service Superannuation Scheme (Scotland) (Additional Voluntary Contributions) Regulations 1998

applied: SSI 2008/224 Reg.4, Reg.7
Reg.2, amended: SSI 2008/225 Reg.2
Reg.3, amended: SSI 2008/225 Reg.2
Reg.4, amended: SSI 2008/225 Reg.2
Reg.5, amended: SSI 2008/225 Reg.2
Reg.6, amended: SSI 2008/225 Reg.2
Reg.10, amended: SSI 2008/225 Reg.2
Reg.11, amended: SSI 2008/225 Reg.2
Reg.14, amended: SSI 2008/225 Reg.2
Reg.15, amended: SSI 2008/225 Reg.2
Reg.19, amended: SSI 2008/225 Reg.2
Reg.20, amended: SSI 2008/225 Reg.2
Reg.21, substituted: SSI 2008/92 Reg.4
Reg.22, substituted: SSI 2008/225 Reg.2
Sch.2 para.1, amended: SSI 2008/225 Reg.2
Sch.2 para.4, amended: SSI 2008/225 Reg.2
Sch.2 para.7, amended: SSI 2008/225 Reg.2
Sch.2 para.11, amended: SSI 2008/225 Reg.2
Sch.2 para.13, amended: SSI 2008/225 Reg.2
Sch.2 para.14, amended: SSI 2008/225 Reg.2

1461. Air Passenger Duty and Other Indirect Taxes (Interest Rate) Regulations 1998

Reg.2, amended: SI 2008/3234 Reg.3
Reg.2A, added: SI 2008/3234 Reg.3

1504. Criminal Justice (Children) (Northern Ireland) Order 1998

Art.5, revoked: SI 2008/1216 Sch.6 Part 4
Art.12, applied: SI 2008/1216 Art.43
Art.13, amended: SI 2008/1216 Art.96
Art.30A, substituted: SI 2008/1216 Art.97
Art.33, amended: SI 2008/1216 Art.99
Art.36J, amended: SI 2008/1216 Art.98
Art.39, amended: SI 2008/1216 Art.36, Art.96
Art.39, applied: 2008 c.28 s.45
Art.40, amended: SI 2008/1216 Art.36
Art.41, amended: SI 2008/1216 Art.36
Art.43, revoked: SI 2008/1216 Art.99, Sch.6 Part 2
Art.45, applied: 2008 c.28 s.45, s.53, SI 2008/1216 Art.7, Art.35
Art.46, applied: SI 2008/1216 Art.35
Art.50, referred to: 2008 c.4 Sch.3 para.5
Sch.1, amended: SI 2008/1769 Sch.1 para.26, Sch.3
Sch.1, revoked (in part): SI 2008/1769 Sch.1 para.26, Sch.3
Sch.1A, amended: SI 2008/1216 Art.48
Sch.1A, revoked (in part): SI 2008/1216 Art.48, Sch.6 Part 1
Sch.5, revoked: SI 2008/1216 Sch.6 Part 1

NO.

1998–cont.

1506. Social Security (Northern Ireland) Order 1998

Part II, varied: 2008 c.14 s.135
Art.9, applied: SI 2008/840 Reg.2

1594. National Health Service (Scotland) (Injury Benefits) Regulations 1998

applied: SI 2008/1596 Reg.7
Reg.2, amended: SSI 2008/92 Reg.3, SSI 2008/225 Reg.3
Reg.4, amended: SSI 2008/92 Reg.3, SSI 2008/225 Reg.3
Reg.4A, amended: SSI 2008/92 Reg.3
Reg.7, amended: SSI 2008/225 Reg.3
Reg.8, amended: SSI 2008/225 Reg.3
Reg.9, amended: SSI 2008/225 Reg.3
Reg.11, amended: SSI 2008/225 Reg.3
Reg.12, amended: SSI 2008/225 Reg.3
Reg.18A, added: SSI 2008/92 Reg.3
Reg.22, substituted: SSI 2008/92 Reg.3

1715. National Institutions of The Church of England (Transfer of Functions) Order 1998

referred to: SI 2008/2470

1759. Education (Northern Ireland) Order 1998

Art.36, applied: SI 2008/1884 Reg.2

1760. Education (Student Support) (Northern Ireland) Order 1998

Art.3, applied: SI 2008/529 Reg.119, Reg.136, Reg.139, SI 2008/794 Reg.139, SI 2008/1273 Reg.66, Reg.79, Reg.85, SI 2008/1582 Reg.119, Reg.136, Reg.139, SI 2008/3170 Reg.66, Reg.79, Reg.95
Art.8, applied: SI 2008/529 Reg.119, Reg.136, Reg.139, SI 2008/1273 Reg.66, Reg.79, Reg.85, SI 2008/1582 Reg.119, Reg.136, Reg.139, SI 2008/3170 Reg.66, Reg.79, Reg.95

1807. Motor Cycles (Protective Helmets) Regulations 1998

Reg.6, amended: SI 2008/1277 Sch.2 para.89, Sch.4 Part 2

1831. Local Government Pension Scheme (Management and Investment of Funds) Regulations 1998

Reg.2, amended: SI 2008/2425 Reg.12
Reg.5, amended: SI 2008/2425 Reg.13
Reg.5, applied: SI 2008/239 Reg.42
Reg.5, revoked (in part): SI 2008/2425 Reg.13
Reg.9A, applied: SI 2008/239 Reg.34, Reg.35
Sch.2 para.3, revoked: SI 2008/2425 Reg.14

1833. Working Time Regulations 1998

see *Bleuse v MBT Transport Ltd* [2008] I.C.R. 488 (EAT), Elias, J.
Reg.10, see *Miles v Linkage Community Trust Ltd* [2008] I.R.L.R. 602 (EAT), Judge McMullen Q.C.

NO.

1998–cont.

1833. Working Time Regulations 1998–*cont.*
Reg.16, see *British Airways Plc v Williams* [2008] I.C.R. 779 (EAT), Keith, J.; see *Lyddon v Englefield Brickwork Ltd* [2008] I.R.L.R. 198 (EAT), Elias, J (President)
Reg.18, amended: SI 2008/1660 Sch.3 para.4
Reg.18, see *British Airways Plc v Williams* [2008] I.C.R. 779 (EAT), Keith, J.
Reg.24, see *Miles v Linkage Community Trust Ltd* [2008] I.R.L.R. 602 (EAT), Judge McMullen Q.C.
Reg.28, amended: SI 2008/960 Sch.3
Reg.28, revoked (in part): SI 2008/960 Sch.3
Reg.30, referred to: SI 2008/3232 Sch.1 Part 2
Reg.30, see *Miles v Linkage Community Trust Ltd* [2008] I.R.L.R. 602 (EAT), Judge McMullen Q.C.
Reg.38, amended: SI 2008/1696 Art.2

1870. Individual Savings Account Regulations 1998
referred to: SI 2008/1934 Reg.2
Reg.2, amended: SI 2008/704 Reg.3, SI 2008/3025 Reg.3
Reg.4, amended: SI 2008/704 Reg.4
Reg.5A, added: SI 2008/1934 Reg.3
Reg.6, amended: SI 2008/704 Reg.5
Reg.7, amended: SI 2008/704 Reg.6, SI 2008/3025 Reg.4
Reg.7, revoked (in part): SI 2008/704 Reg.6
Reg.8, amended: SI 2008/704 Reg.7, SI 2008/1934 Reg.4
Reg.8, revoked (in part): SI 2008/704 Reg.7
Reg.9, amended: SI 2008/704 Reg.8
Reg.10, amended: SI 2008/704 Reg.9
Reg.12, amended: SI 2008/704 Reg.10
Reg.16, amended: SI 2008/704 Reg.11
Reg.22, amended: SI 2008/704 Reg.12
Reg.23, amended: SI 2008/1934 Reg.5
Reg.24, amended: SI 2008/704 Reg.13
Reg.31, amended: SI 2008/704 Reg.14
Reg.31, revoked (in part): SI 2008/704 Reg.14
Reg.34, amended: SI 2008/704 Reg.15
Reg.35, amended: SI 2008/704 Reg.16
Reg.36, amended: SI 2008/704 Reg.17, SI 2008/1934 Reg.6
Reg.36, revoked (in part): SI 2008/1934 Reg.6

1908. Dartford-Thurrock Crossing Regulations 1998
Reg.5, amended: SI 2008/2171 Reg.2

1967. Assured and Protected Tenancies (Lettings to Students) Regulations 1998
Reg.5, varied: SI 2008/2839 Sch.1 para.1

1973. Education (Infant Class Sizes) (England) Regulations 1998
Reg.2, amended: SI 2008/3089 Reg.34
Reg.3, amended: SI 2008/3089 Reg.34

NO.

1998–cont.

2003. Education (Student Support) Regulations 1998
applied: SI 2008/529 Reg.3, SI 2008/1273 Reg.3, SI 2008/1582 Reg.4, SI 2008/3170 Reg.3

2051. Motor Vehicles (EC Type Approval) Regulations 1998
Reg.3, amended: SI 2008/2844 Reg.2, Reg.3
Reg.4, amended: SI 2008/2844 Reg.3
Reg.5, amended: SI 2008/2844 Reg.3
Reg.7, amended: SI 2008/2844 Reg.3
Reg.12, amended: SI 2008/2844 Reg.3
Sch.1, amended: SI 2008/2844 Reg.3, Reg.4
Sch.1, substituted: SI 2008/2844 Reg.3
Sch.2 Part I para.1, amended: SI 2008/2844 Reg.3
Sch.2 Part II para.3, amended: SI 2008/2844 Reg.3

2118. Local Government Pension Scheme (Transitional Provisions etc.) (Amendment) Regulations 1998
revoked: SI 2008/238 Sch.1

2138. Nitrate Sensitive Areas (Amendment) (No.2) Regulations 1998
revoked (in part): SI 2008/2349 Reg.50

2166. Children (Allocation of Proceedings) (Amendment) Order 1998
revoked: SI 2008/2836 Sch.2

2229. Education (Proportion of Selective Admissions) Regulations 1998
Reg.1A, added: SI 2008/3089 Reg.36

2254. Road Works (Registers, Notices, Directions and Designations) (Scotland) Amendment Regulations 1998
revoked: SSI 2008/88 Reg.16

2306. Provision and Use of Work Equipment Regulations 1998
see *Mason v Satelcom Ltd* [2007] EWHC 2540 (QB), [2008] P.I.Q.R. P4 (QBD), Judge Reddihough; see *Mason v Satelcom Ltd* [2008] EWCA Civ 494, [2008] I.C.R. 971 (CA (Civ Div)), Ward, L.J.; see *Smith v Northamptonshire CC* [2008] EWCA Civ 181, [2008] 3 All E.R. 1054 (CA (Civ Div)), Waller, L.J. (V-P); see *Spencer-Franks v Kellogg Brown & Root Ltd* [2008] UKHL 46, 2008 S.L.T. 675 (HL), Lord Hoffmann
Reg.2, see *Spencer-Franks v Kellogg Brown & Root Ltd* [2008] UKHL 46, 2008 S.L.T. 675 (HL), Lord Hoffmann
Reg.3, see *Jennings v Forestry Commission* [2008] EWCA Civ 581, [2008] I.C.R. 988 (CA (Civ Div)), May, L.J.; see *Mason v Satelcom Ltd* [2007] EWHC 2540 (QB), [2008] P.I.Q.R. P4 (QBD), Judge Reddihough
Reg.4, see *Mason v Satelcom Ltd* [2007] EWHC 2540 (QB), [2008] P.I.Q.R. P4 (QBD), Judge Reddihough; see *Mason v Satelcom Ltd* [2008] EWCA Civ 494,

NO.

1998–cont.

2306. Provision and Use of Work Equipment Regulations 1998–*cont.*

Reg.4–*cont.*

[2008] I.C.R. 971 (CA (Civ Div)), Ward, L.J.; see *Reid v Sundolitt Ltd* 2008 S.C. 49 (IH (Ex Div)), Lord Johnston; see *Smith v Northamptonshire CC* [2008] EWCA Civ 181, [2008] 3 All E.R. 1054 (CA (Civ Div)), Waller, L.J. (V-P)

Reg.5, see *Smith v Northamptonshire CC* [2008] EWCA Civ 181, [2008] 3 All E.R. 1054 (CA (Civ Div)), Waller, L.J. (V-P)

Reg.9, see *Allison v London Underground Ltd* [2008] EWCA Civ 71, [2008] I.C.R. 719 (CA (Civ Div)), Sir Anthony Clarke, M.R.

Sch.1, amended: SI 2008/1597 Sch.7 para.1

2307. Lifting Operations and Lifting Equipment Regulations 1998

Reg.2, amended: SI 2008/1597 Sch.7 para.2

2424. Drinking Milk Regulations 1998

revoked (in part): SI 2008/1317 Reg.8

2451. Gas Safety (Installation and Use) Regulations 1998

Reg.16, applied: SI 2008/101 Reg.11, Reg.12, SI 2008/540 Reg.11, Reg.12

2456. Rail Vehicle Accessibility Regulations 1998

Reg.2, amended: SI 2008/1746 Reg.2
Reg.3, amended: SI 2008/1746 Reg.2
Reg.4, applied: SI 2008/925 Art.6
Reg.4, disapplied: SI 2008/925 Art.3
Reg.4, referred to: SI 2008/925 Art.4, Art.5
Reg.5, applied: SI 2008/925 Art.6
Reg.5, disapplied: SI 2008/925 Art.3
Reg.5, referred to: SI 2008/925 Art.4, Art.5
Reg.11, applied: SI 2008/925 Art.6
Reg.11, disapplied: SI 2008/925 Art.3
Reg.13, applied: SI 2008/925 Art.6
Reg.13, disapplied: SI 2008/925 Art.3
Reg.13, referred to: SI 2008/925 Art.4, Art.5
Reg.16, applied: SI 2008/925 Art.6
Reg.16, disapplied: SI 2008/925 Art.3
Reg.23, applied: SI 2008/925 Art.6
Reg.23, disapplied: SI 2008/925 Art.3
Reg.23, referred to: SI 2008/925 Art.4, Art.5

2535. Religious Character of Schools (Designation Procedure) Regulations 1998

referred to: SI 2008/100, SI 2008/1867, SI 2008/1868, SI 2008/1869, SI 2008/1870, SI 2008/1871, SI 2008/1872, SI 2008/1873, SI 2008/1874, SI 2008/1875, SI 2008/1876, SI 2008/2078, SI 2008/2079, SI 2008/2080, SI 2008/2081, SI 2008/2082, SI 2008/2083, SI 2008/2084, SI 2008/2085, SI 2008/2087, SI 2008/2092, SI 2008/3147

2548. District of South Lakeland (Electoral Changes) Order 1998

Art.2, revoked: SI 2008/423 Art.13
Art.3, revoked (in part): SI 2008/423 Art.13

NO.

1998–cont.

2548. District of South Lakeland (Electoral Changes) Order 1998–*cont.*

Art.4, revoked: SI 2008/423 Art.13
Art.5, revoked: SI 2008/423 Art.13
Art.6, revoked: SI 2008/423 Art.13
Art.8, amended: SI 2008/423 Art.13
Sch.1, revoked: SI 2008/423 Art.13
Sch.2, revoked: SI 2008/423 Art.13

2560. District of Welwyn Hatfield (Electoral Changes) Order 1998

Art.2, revoked: SI 2008/424 Art.10
Art.3, revoked (in part): SI 2008/424 Art.10
Art.4, revoked: SI 2008/424 Art.10
Sch.1, revoked: SI 2008/424 Art.10
Sch.2, revoked: SI 2008/424 Art.10

2571. Borough of Barrow-in-Furness (Electoral Changes) Order 1998

Art.1, revoked: SI 2008/427 Art.8
Art.2, revoked: SI 2008/427 Art.8
Art.3, revoked (in part): SI 2008/427 Art.8
Art.4, revoked: SI 2008/427 Art.8
Art.5, revoked: SI 2008/427 Art.8
Sch.1, revoked: SI 2008/427 Art.8

2573. Employers Liability (Compulsory Insurance) Regulations 1998

Reg.4, revoked (in part): SI 2008/1765 Reg.2
Reg.5, amended: SI 2008/1765 Reg.2
Reg.6, amended: SI 2008/1765 Reg.2

2624. Mental Health (Hospital, Guardianship and Consent to Treatment) Amendment Regulations 1998

revoked (in part): SI 2008/1184 Sch.2, SI 2008/2439 Sch.2

2625. Mental Health (Nurses) Order 1998

revoked (in part): SI 2008/1207 Art.3, SI 2008/2441 Art.3

2746. Groundwater Regulations 1998

Reg.4, see *R. (on the application of Anti-Waste Ltd) v Environment Agency* [2007] EWCA Civ 1377, [2008] 1 W.L.R. 923 (CA (Civ Div)), Pill, L.J.

2793. European Communities (Designation) (No.3) Order 1998

Sch.1, amended: SI 2008/301 Sch.1

2839. Criminal Justice (Northern Ireland) Order 1998

Art.4, revoked: SI 2008/1216 Sch.6 Part 2
Art.8, applied: SI 2008/1216 Art.5
Sch.1 Part I para.3, revoked: SI 2008/1216 Sch.6 Part 1
Sch.1 Part I para.7, revoked (in part): SI 2008/1216 Sch.6 Part 1

2843. Borough of Congleton (Electoral Changes) Order 1998

Art.9, revoked: SI 2008/634 Art.23

2845. Borough of Crewe and Nantwich (Electoral Changes) Order 1998

Art.10, revoked: SI 2008/634 Art.24

2847. Borough of Macclesfield (Electoral Changes) Order 1998

Art.7, revoked: SI 2008/634 Art.25

NO.

1998–cont.

2866. City of Chester (Electoral Changes) Order 1998
Art.5, revoked: SI 2008/634 Art.26

2888. Local Government Pension Scheme (Management and Investment of Funds) (Scotland) Regulations 1998
Reg.5, applied: SSI 2008/228 Reg.38
Reg.9A, applied: SSI 2008/228 Reg.31

2963. Non-Domestic Rating (Rural Settlements) (Wales) Order 1998
referred to: SI 2008/2770 Art.12

3050. Consumer Protection (Cancellation of Contracts Concluded away from Business Premises) (Amendment) Regulations 1998
revoked: SI 2008/1816 Sch.2

3117. General Optical Council (Membership) Order of Council 1998
revoked: SI 2008/1774 Sch.5 para.3

3132. Civil Procedure Rules 1998
applied: SI 2008/1053 Sch.1, SI 2008/2698 r.10, SI 2008/2699 r.10
see *Jackson v Marina Homes Ltd* [2007] EWCA Civ 1404, [2008] C.P. Rep. 17 (CA (Civ Div)), Sedley, L.J.; see *Jones v Wrexham BC* [2007] EWCA Civ 1356, [2008] 1 W.L.R. 1590 (CA (Civ Div)), Waller, L.J. (V-P); see *Kostic v Chaplin* [2007] EWHC 2909 (Ch), [2008] 2 Costs L.R. 271 (Ch D), Henderson, J; see *Monsanto Technology LLC v Cargill International SA* [2007] EWHC 3113 (Pat), [2008] F.S.R. 16 (Ch D (Patents Ct)), Pumfrey, L.J; see *Roberts v Gill & Co* [2008] EWCA Civ 803, [2008] W.T.L.R. 1429 (CA (Civ Div)), Pill, L.J.; see *Ul-Haq v Shah* [2008] EWHC 1896 (QB), [2008] R.T.R. 31 (QBD (Birmingham)), Walker, J.; see *Whitecap Leisure Ltd v John H Rundle Ltd* [2008] EWCA Civ 429, [2008] 2 Lloyd's Rep. 216 (CA (Civ Div)), Ward, L.J.
see *Haji-Ioannou v Frangos* [2006] EWCA Civ 1663, [2008] 1 W.L.R. 144 (CA (Civ Div)), Sir Andrew Morritt C.
Part 1 r.1.2, amended: SI 2008/3085 r.3
Part 2 r.2.3, amended: SI 2008/2178 r.3
Part 3 r.3.1, amended: SI 2008/3327 r.3
Part 3 r.3.7, amended: SI 2008/2178 r.4
Part 5, referred to: SI 2008/609 Reg.15
Part 6 r.6.1, substituted: SI 2008/2178 Sch.1
Part 6 r.6.2, substituted: SI 2008/2178 Sch.1
Part 6 r.6.3, substituted: SI 2008/2178 Sch.1
Part 6 r.6.4, substituted: SI 2008/2178 Sch.1
Part 6 r.6.5, substituted: SI 2008/2178 Sch.1
Part 6 r.6.6, substituted: SI 2008/2178 Sch.1
Part 6 r.6.7, substituted: SI 2008/2178 Sch.1
Part 6 r.6.8, substituted: SI 2008/2178 Sch.1
Part 6 r.6.9, substituted: SI 2008/2178 Sch.1
Part 6 r.6.10, substituted: SI 2008/2178 Sch.1
Part 6 r.6.11, substituted: SI 2008/2178 Sch.1

NO.

1998–cont.

3132. Civil Procedure Rules 1998–*cont.*
Part 6 r.6.11A, substituted: SI 2008/2178 Sch.1
Part 6 r.6.12, substituted: SI 2008/2178 Sch.1
Part 6 r.6.13, substituted: SI 2008/2178 Sch.1
Part 6 r.6.14, substituted: SI 2008/2178 Sch.1
Part 6 r.6.15, substituted: SI 2008/2178 Sch.1
Part 6 r.6.16, substituted: SI 2008/2178 Sch.1
Part 6 r.6.17, substituted: SI 2008/2178 Sch.1
Part 6 r.6.18, substituted: SI 2008/2178 Sch.1
Part 6 r.6.19, substituted: SI 2008/2178 Sch.1
Part 6 r.6.20, substituted: SI 2008/2178 Sch.1
Part 6 r.6.21, substituted: SI 2008/2178 Sch.1
Part 6 r.6.22, substituted: SI 2008/2178 Sch.1
Part 6 r.6.23, substituted: SI 2008/2178 Sch.1
Part 6 r.6.24, substituted: SI 2008/2178 Sch.1
Part 6 r.6.25, substituted: SI 2008/2178 Sch.1
Part 6 r.6.26, substituted: SI 2008/2178 Sch.1
Part 6 r.6.26A, substituted: SI 2008/2178 Sch.1
Part 6 r.6.27, substituted: SI 2008/2178 Sch.1
Part 6 r.6.28, substituted: SI 2008/2178 Sch.1
Part 6 r.6.29, substituted: SI 2008/2178 Sch.1
Part 6 r.6.30, substituted: SI 2008/2178 Sch.1
Part 6 r.6.31, substituted: SI 2008/2178 Sch.1
Part 6 r.6.32, substituted: SI 2008/2178 Sch.1
Part 6 r.6.33, substituted: SI 2008/2178 Sch.1
Part 6 r.6.34, substituted: SI 2008/2178 Sch.1
Part 6 r.6.35, substituted: SI 2008/2178 Sch.1
Part 6 r.6.36, substituted: SI 2008/2178 Sch.1
Part 6 r.6.37, substituted: SI 2008/2178 Sch.1
Part 6 r.6.38, substituted: SI 2008/2178 Sch.1
Part 6 r.6.39, substituted: SI 2008/2178 Sch.1
Part 6 r.6.40, substituted: SI 2008/2178 Sch.1
Part 6 r.6.41, substituted: SI 2008/2178 Sch.1
Part 6 r.6.42, substituted: SI 2008/2178 Sch.1
Part 6 r.6.43, substituted: SI 2008/2178 Sch.1
Part 6 r.6.44, substituted: SI 2008/2178 Sch.1
Part 6 r.6.45, substituted: SI 2008/2178 Sch.1
Part 6 r.6.46, substituted: SI 2008/2178 Sch.1

NO.

1998–cont.

3132. Civil Procedure Rules 1998–*cont.*

Part 6 r.6.47, substituted: SI 2008/2178 Sch.1
Part 6 r.6.48, substituted: SI 2008/2178 Sch.1
Part 6 r.6.49, substituted: SI 2008/2178 Sch.1
Part 6 r.6.50, substituted: SI 2008/2178 Sch.1
Part 6 r.6.51, substituted: SI 2008/2178 Sch.1
Part 6 r.6.52, substituted: SI 2008/2178 Sch.1
Part 7 r.7.2, amended: SI 2008/2178 r.6
Part 7 r.7.4, amended: SI 2008/2178 r.6, SI 2008/3327 r.4
Part 7 r.7.5, substituted: SI 2008/2178 r.6
Part 7 r.7.6, substituted: SI 2008/2178 r.6
Part 8, referred to: SI 2008/1053 Sch.1
Part 8 r.8.1, amended: SI 2008/2178 r.7
Part 10 r.10.3, amended: SI 2008/2178 r.8
Part 10 r.10.5, amended: SI 2008/2178 r.8
Part 11, see *Dunn v Parole Board* [2008] EWCA Civ 374, [2008] H.R.L.R. 32 (CA (Civ Div)), Smith, L.J.
Part 12 r.12.3, amended: SI 2008/2178 r.9
Part 12 r.12.4, amended: SI 2008/2178 r.9
Part 12 r.12.10, amended: SI 2008/2178 r.9
Part 12 r.12.11, amended: SI 2008/2178 r.9
Part 12 r.12.11, revoked (in part): SI 2008/2178 r.9
Part 13 r.13.3, amended: SI 2008/2178 r.10
Part 14 r.14.1A, amended: SI 2008/3327 r.5
Part 14 r.14.2, amended: SI 2008/2178 r.11
Part 15 r.15.4, amended: SI 2008/2178 r.12
Part 16 r.16.3, amended: SI 2008/3327 r.6
Part 16 r.16.5, amended: SI 2008/2178 r.13
Part 18, see *Harcourt v FEF Griffin* [2007] EWHC 1500 (QB), [2008] Lloyd's Rep. I.R. 386 (QBD), Irwin, J.
Part 18, see *Martin v Triggs Turner Barton (A Firm)* [2008] EWHC 89 (Ch), [2008] W.T.L.R. 509 (Ch D), Susan Prevezer Q.C.; see *West London Pipeline and Storage Ltd v Total UK Ltd* [2008] EWHC 1296 (Comm), [2008] 1 C.L.C. 935 (QBD (Comm)), David Steel, J.
Part 20 r.20.13, amended: SI 2008/2178 r.14
Part 21, see *S v Floyd* [2008] EWCA Civ 201, [2008] 1 W.L.R. 1274 (CA (Civ Div)), Mummery, L.J.
Part 21 r.21.1, amended: SI 2008/2178 r.15
Part 21 r.21.5, amended: SI 2008/2178 r.15
Part 21 r.21.8, amended: SI 2008/2178 r.15
Part 21 r.21.11, applied: SI 2008/794 Sch.9 para.43
Part 24, see *Walsh v Staines* [2007] EWHC 1814 (Ch), [2008] P.N.L.R. 8 (Ch D), Sarah Asplin QC
Part 26 r.26.3, amended: SI 2008/2178 r.16
Part 26 r.26.6, amended: SI 2008/3327 r.7
Part 30 r.30.6, amended: SI 2008/3327 r.8
Part 31, see *British Sky Broadcasting Plc v Virgin Media Communications Ltd (formerly NTL Communications Ltd)* [2008] EWCA Civ 612, Times, June 11, 2008 (CA (Civ Div)), Lord Philips, L.C.J.; see *West London Pipeline and Storage Ltd v Total UK Ltd* [2008] EWHC 1296 (Comm), [2008] 1 C.L.C. 935 (QBD (Comm)), David Steel, J.
Part 36, see *Carver v BAA Plc* [2008] EWCA Civ 412, [2008] 3 All E.R. 911 (CA (Civ Div)), Ward, L.J.
Part 36 r.36.9, amended: SI 2008/2178 r.17
Part 36 r.36.10, amended: SI 2008/2178 r.17
Part 36 r.36.15, amended: SI 2008/2178 r.17
Part 38, see *Sheltam Rail Co (Proprietary) Ltd v Mirambo Holdings Ltd* [2008] EWHC 829 (Comm), [2008] 2 Lloyd's Rep. 195 (QBD (Comm)), Aikens, J.
Part 38 r.38.6, amended: SI 2008/2178 r.18
Part 38 r.38.8, amended: SI 2008/2178 r.19
Part 40 r.40.4, amended: SI 2008/2178 r.20
Part 42 r.42.2, amended: SI 2008/2178 r.21
Part 43 r.43.2, amended: SI 2008/2178 r.22
Part 44 r.44.1, amended: SI 2008/2178 r.23
Part 44 r.44.3, amended: SI 2008/3327 r.9
Part 44 r.44.3C, added: SI 2008/2178 r.23
Part 44 r.44.12, amended: SI 2008/2178 r.23
Part 44 r.44.13, amended: SI 2008/2178 r.23
Part 44 r.44.18, added: SI 2008/3327 r.9
Part 44 r.44.19, added: SI 2008/3327 r.9
Part 44 r.44.20, added: SI 2008/3327 r.9
Part 45, see *Amber Construction Services Ltd v London Interspace HG Ltd* [2007] EWHC 3042 (TCC), [2008] B.L.R. 74 (QBD (TCC)), Akenhead, J.
Part 47, see *Harris v Moat Housing Group-South Ltd* [2007] EWHC 3092 (QB), [2008] 1 W.L.R. 1578 (QBD), Christopher Clarke, J.
Part 45 r.45.5, amended: SI 2008/2178 r.24
Part 46 r.46.2, amended: SI 2008/3327 r.10
Part 47 r.47.5, substituted: SI 2008/2178 r.25
Part 47 r.47.11, amended: SI 2008/2178 r.25
Part 47 r.47.12, amended: SI 2008/2178 r.25
Part 47 r.47.15, amended: SI 2008/2178 r.25
Part 47 r.47.16, amended: SI 2008/2178 r.25
Part 47 r.47.18, amended: SI 2008/2178 r.25
Part 52, applied: SI 2008/1863 Art.27
Part 52 r.52.3, amended: SI 2008/2178 r.26
Part 54, see *Bunney v Burns Anderson Plc* [2007] EWHC 1240 (Ch), [2008] Bus. L.R. 22 (Ch D), Lewison, J.
Part 54 r.54.28, amended: SI 2008/2178 r.27
Part 54 r.54.28B, amended: SI 2008/2178 r.27
Part 55 r.55.8, amended: SI 2008/2178 r.28
Part 55 r.55.10, amended: SI 2008/3327 r.11
Part 55 r.55.23, amended: SI 2008/2178 r.28
Part 56 r.56.1, amended: SI 2008/2178 r.29

NO.

1998–cont.

3132. Civil Procedure Rules 1998–*cont.*

Part 56 r.56.2, amended: SI 2008/2178 r.29
Part 56 r.56.3, amended: SI 2008/2178 r.29
Part 56 r.56.3, revoked (in part): SI 2008/2178 r.29
Part 57 r.57.4, amended: SI 2008/2178 r.30
Part 57 r.57.8, applied: SI 2008/1053 Sch.1
Part 57 r.57.16, amended: SI 2008/2178 r.30
Part 58 r.58.6, amended: SI 2008/2178 r.31
Part 58 r.58.10, amended: SI 2008/2178 r.31
Part 59 r.59.5, amended: SI 2008/2178 r.32
Part 59 r.59.9, amended: SI 2008/2178 r.32
Part 61 r.61.4, amended: SI 2008/2178 r.33
Part 61 r.61.11, amended: SI 2008/2178 r.33
Part 62, see *Gater Assets Ltd v Nak Naftogaz Ukrainiy* [2007] EWCA Civ 988, [2008] Bus. L.R. 388 (CA (Civ Div)), Buxton, L.J.
Part 62, see *Sheltam Rail Co (Proprietary) Ltd v Mirambo Holdings Ltd* [2008] EWHC 829 (Comm), [2008] 2 Lloyd's Rep. 195 (QBD (Comm)), Aikens, J.
Part 62 r.62.5, amended: SI 2008/2178 r.34
Part 62 r.62.16, amended: SI 2008/2178 r.34
Part 62 r.62.18, amended: SI 2008/2178 r.34
Part 62 r.62.20, amended: SI 2008/2178 r.34
Part 63 r.63.16, amended: SI 2008/2178 r.35
Part 65, revoked: SI 2008/2178 r.36
Part 65 r.65.1, amended: SI 2008/2178 r.36
Part 65 r.65.1, revoked (in part): SI 2008/2178 r.36
Part 65 r.65.18, amended: SI 2008/2178 r.36
Part 67, see *Mastercigars Direct Ltd v Withers LLP* [2007] EWHC 2733 (Ch), [2008] 3 All E.R. 417 (Ch D), Morgan, J.
Part 70 r.70.5, substituted: SI 2008/3327 r.12
Part 71, see *Islamic Investment Co of the Gulf (Bahamas) Ltd v Symphony Gems NV* [2008] EWCA Civ 389, Times, April 4, 2008 (CA (Civ Div)), Tuckey, L.J.
Part 74 r.74.6, amended: SI 2008/2178 r.37
Part 74 r.74.31, amended: SI 2008/2178 r.37
Part 74 r.74.32, amended: SI 2008/2178 r.37
Part 74 r.74.33, amended: SI 2008/2178 r.37
Part 74 r.74.33, substituted: SI 2008/2178 r.37
Part 75 r.75.5, substituted: SI 2008/3327 r.13
Part 75 r.75.5A, added: SI 2008/3327 r.13
Part 75 r.75.7, amended: SI 2008/3327 r.13
Part 76, see *Secretary of State for the Home Department v MB* [2007] UKHL 46, [2008] 1 A.C. 440 (HL), Lord Bingham of Cornhill
Part 78 r.78.1, added: SI 2008/2178 Sch.2
Part 78 r.78.2, added: SI 2008/2178 Sch.2
Part 78 r.78.3, added: SI 2008/2178 Sch.2
Part 78 r.78.4, added: SI 2008/2178 Sch.2
Part 78 r.78.5, added: SI 2008/2178 Sch.2
Part 78 r.78.6, added: SI 2008/2178 Sch.2
Part 78 r.78.7, added: SI 2008/2178 Sch.2
Part 78 r.78.8, added: SI 2008/2178 Sch.2
Part 78 r.78.9, added: SI 2008/2178 Sch.2

NO.

1998–cont.

3132. Civil Procedure Rules 1998–*cont.*

Part 78 r.78.10, added: SI 2008/2178 Sch.2
Part 78 r.78.11, added: SI 2008/2178 Sch.2
Part 78 r.78.12, added: SI 2008/2178 Sch.2
Part 78 r.78.13, added: SI 2008/2178 Sch.2
Part 78 r.78.14, added: SI 2008/2178 Sch.2
Part 78 r.78.15, added: SI 2008/2178 Sch.2
Part 78 r.78.16, added: SI 2008/2178 Sch.2
Part 78 r.78.17, added: SI 2008/2178 Sch.2
Part 78 r.78.18, added: SI 2008/2178 Sch.2
Part 78 r.78.19, added: SI 2008/2178 Sch.2
Part 78 r.78.20, added: SI 2008/2178 Sch.2
Part 78 r.78.21, added: SI 2008/2178 Sch.2
Part 78 r.78.22, added: SI 2008/2178 Sch.2
Part 79 r.79.1, added: SI 2008/3085 Sch.1
Part 79 r.79.2, added: SI 2008/3085 Sch.1
Part 79 r.79.3, added: SI 2008/3085 Sch.1
Part 79 r.79.4, added: SI 2008/3085 Sch.1
Part 79 r.79.5, added: SI 2008/3085 Sch.1
Part 79 r.79.6, added: SI 2008/3085 Sch.1
Part 79 r.79.7, added: SI 2008/3085 Sch.1
Part 79 r.79.8, added: SI 2008/3085 Sch.1
Part 79 r.79.9, added: SI 2008/3085 Sch.1
Part 79 r.79.10, added: SI 2008/3085 Sch.1
Part 79 r.79.11, added: SI 2008/3085 Sch.1
Part 79 r.79.12, added: SI 2008/3085 Sch.1
Part 79 r.79.13, added: SI 2008/3085 Sch.1
Part 79 r.79.14, added: SI 2008/3085 Sch.1
Part 79 r.79.15, added: SI 2008/3085 Sch.1
Part 79 r.79.16, added: SI 2008/3085 Sch.1
Part 79 r.79.17, added: SI 2008/3085 Sch.1
Part 79 r.79.18, added: SI 2008/3085 Sch.1
Part 79 r.79.19, added: SI 2008/3085 Sch.1
Part 79 r.79.20, added: SI 2008/3085 Sch.1
Part 79 r.79.21, added: SI 2008/3085 Sch.1
Part 79 r.79.22, added: SI 2008/3085 Sch.1
Part 79 r.79.23, added: SI 2008/3085 Sch.1
Part 79 r.79.24, added: SI 2008/3085 Sch.1
Part 79 r.79.25, added: SI 2008/3085 Sch.1
Part 79 r.79.26, added: SI 2008/3085 Sch.1
Part 79 r.79.27, added: SI 2008/3085 Sch.1
Part 79 r.79.28, added: SI 2008/3085 Sch.1
Part 79 r.79.29, added: SI 2008/3085 Sch.1
Part 79 r.79.30, added: SI 2008/3085 Sch.1
Pt 11, see *Dunn v Parole Board* [2008] EWCA Civ 374, [2008] H.R.L.R. 32 (CA (Civ Div)), Smith, L.J.
Pt 18, see *Martin v Triggs Turner Barton (A Firm)* [2008] EWHC 89 (Ch), [2008] W.T.L.R. 509 (Ch D), Susan Prevezer Q.C.; see *West London Pipeline & Storage Ltd v Total UK Ltd* [2008] EWHC 1296 (Comm), [2008] C.P. Rep. 35 (QBD (Comm)), David Steel, J.
Pt 19, see *Smithson v Hamilton* [2008] EWCA Civ 996, [2008] Pens. L.R. 363 (CA (Civ Div)), Mummery, L.J.
Pt 21, see *S v Floyd* [2008] EWCA Civ 201, [2008] 1 W.L.R. 1274 (CA (Civ Div)), Mummery, L.J.

NO.

1998–cont.

3132. Civil Procedure Rules 1998–*cont.*

Pt 30, see *Neath Port Talbot CBC v Currie & Brown Project Management Ltd* [2008] EWHC 1508 (TCC), [2008] C.P. Rep. 39 (QBD (Bristol)), Ramsey, J.

Pt 31, see *British Sky Broadcasting Plc v Virgin Media Communications Ltd (formerly NTL Communications Ltd)* [2008] EWCA Civ 612, [2008] 1 W.L.R. 2854 (CA (Civ Div)), Lord Philips, L.C.J.; see *West London Pipeline & Storage Ltd v Total UK Ltd* [2008] EWHC 1296 (Comm), [2008] C.P. Rep. 35 (QBD (Comm)), David Steel, J.

Pt 36, see *Carver v BAA Plc* [2008] EWCA Civ 412, [2008] 3 All E.R. 911 (CA (Civ Div)), Ward, L.J.

Pt 38, see *Sheltam Rail Co (Proprietary) Ltd v Mirambo Holdings Ltd* [2008] EWHC 829 (Comm), [2008] 2 Lloyd's Rep. 195 (QBD (Comm)), Aikens, J.

Pt 45, see *Amber Construction Services Ltd v London Interspace HG Ltd* [2007] EWHC 3042 (TCC), [2008] B.L.R. 74 (QBD (TCC)), Akenhead, J.

Pt 47, see *Harris v Moat Housing Group-South Ltd* [2007] EWHC 3092 (QB), [2008] 1 W.L.R. 1578 (QBD), Christopher Clarke, J.

Pt 62, see *Sheltam Rail Co (Proprietary) Ltd v Mirambo Holdings Ltd* [2008] EWHC 829 (Comm), [2008] 2 Lloyd's Rep. 195 (QBD (Comm)), Aikens, J.

Pt 67, see *Mastercigars Direct Ltd v Withers LLP* [2007] EWHC 2733 (Ch), [2008] 3 All E.R. 417 (Ch D), Morgan, J.

Pt 71, see *Islamic Investment Co of the Gulf (Bahamas) Ltd v Symphony Gems NV* [2008] EWCA Civ 389, Times, April 4, 2008 (CA (Civ Div)), Tuckey, L.J.

Pt 76, see *Secretary of State for the Home Department v F* [2008] EWCA Civ 1148, Times, October 29, 2008 (CA (Civ Div)), Sir Anthony Clarke, M.R.; see *Secretary of State for the Home Department v MB* [2007] UKHL 46, [2008] 1 A.C. 440 (HL), Lord Bingham of Cornhill

r.1.1, see *Albon (t/a NA Carriage Co) v Naza Motor Trading Sdn Bhd* [2007] EWHC 2613 (Ch), [2008] 1 W.L.R. 2380 (Ch D), Lightman, J.; see *Phillips v Symes* [2006] EWHC 2595 (Ch), [2008] B.P.I.R. 212 (Ch D), Peter Smith, J.

r.2.3, see *R. (on the application of Corner House Research) v Director of the Serious Fraud Office* [2008] EWHC 246 (Admin), [2008] C.P. Rep. 20 (QBD (Admin)), Collins, J.

r.3.1, see *Moulai v France* [2008] EWHC 1024 (Admin), [2008] 1 W.L.R. 2460 (DC), Hooper, L.J.; see *Phillips v Symes* [2006] EWHC 2595 (Ch), [2008] B.P.I.R. 212 (Ch D), Peter Smith, J.; see *Porter v Shepherds Bush Housing Association* [2008] EWCA

NO.

1998–cont.

3132. Civil Procedure Rules 1998–*cont.*

r.3.1–*cont.*

Civ 196, [2008] H.L.R. 35 (CA (Civ Div)), Pill, L.J.

r.3.2, see *Beloit Walmsley Ltd, Re* [2008] EWHC 1888 (Ch), [2008] B.P.I.R. 1445 (Ch D (Manchester)), Judge Pelling Q.C.

r.3.4, see *Barrett v Barrett* [2008] EWHC 1061 (Ch), [2008] B.P.I.R. 817 (Ch D), David Richards, J.; see *Emerson Electric Co v Morgan Crucible Co Plc* [2008] Comp. A.R. 37 (CAT), Marion Simmons Q.C. (Chairman); see *Ul-Haq v Shah* [2008] EWHC 1896 (QB), [2008] R.T.R. 31 (QBD (Birmingham)), Walker, J.; see *Walsh v Staines* [2007] EWHC 1814 (Ch), [2008] P.N.L.R. 8 (Ch D), Sarah Asplin QC

r.3.5, see *Serious Fraud Office v Lexi Holdings Plc (In Administration)* [2008] EWCA Crim 1443, [2008] B.P.I.R. 1598 (CA (Crim Div)), Keene, L.J.

r.3.9, see *R. (on the application of Howes) v Child Support Commissioners* [2007] EWHC 559 (admin), [2008] 1 F.L.R. 1691 (QBD (Admin)), Black J.

r.3.10, see *Moulai v France* [2008] EWHC 1024 (Admin), [2008] 1 W.L.R. 2460 (DC), Hooper, L.J.; see *Phillips v Symes (A Bankrupt)* [2008] UKHL 1, [2008] 1 W.L.R. 180 (HL), Lord Bingham of Cornhill, L.C.J.

r.5.4C, see *R. (on the application of Corner House Research) v Director of the Serious Fraud Office* [2008] EWHC 246 (Admin), [2008] C.P. Rep. 20 (QBD (Admin)), Collins, J.

r.6.9, see *Moulai v France* [2008] EWHC 1024 (Admin), [2008] 1 W.L.R. 2460 (DC), Hooper, L.J.; see *Mucelli v Albania* [2007] EWHC 2632 (Admin), [2008] 1 W.L.R. 2437 (DC), Richards, L.J.; see *Phillips v Symes (A Bankrupt)* [2008] UKHL 1, [2008] 1 W.L.R. 180 (HL), Lord Bingham of Cornhill, L.C.J.

r.6.19, see *Olafsson v Gissurarson* [2008] EWCA Civ 152, [2008] 1 W.L.R. 2016 (CA (Civ Div)), Sir Anthony Clarke, M.R.

r.6.20, see *Cooley v Ramsey* [2008] EWHC 129 (QB), [2008] I.L.Pr. 27 (QBD), Tugendhat, J.; see *Elektrim SA v Vivendi Holdings 1 Corp* [2008] EWCA Civ 1178, [2008] 2 C.L.C. 564 (CA (Civ Div)), Sir Anthony May (President, QB); see *Krug International (UK) Ltd, Re* [2008] EWHC 2256 (Ch), [2008] B.P.I.R. 1512 (Ch D (Birmingham)), Judge Purle Q.C.; see *Vitol SA v Capri Marine Ltd* [2008] EWHC 378 (Comm), [2008] B.P.I.R. 1629 (QBD (Comm)), Tomlinson, J.

r.6.21, see *Cooley v Ramsey* [2008] EWHC 129 (QB), [2008] I.L.Pr. 27 (QBD), Tugendhat, J.; see *Krug International (UK) Ltd, Re* [2008] EWHC 2256 (Ch), [2008]

NO.

1998–cont.

3132. Civil Procedure Rules 1998–*cont.*

r.6.21–*cont.*

B.P.I.R. 1512 (Ch D (Birmingham)), Judge Purle Q.C.

r.6.30, see *Vitol SA v Capri Marine Ltd* [2008] EWHC 378 (Comm), [2008] B.P.I.R. 1629 (QBD (Comm)), Tomlinson, J.

r.7.5, see *Phillips v Symes (A Bankrupt)* [2008] UKHL 1, [2008] 1 W.L.R. 180 (HL), Lord Bingham of Cornhill, L.C.J.

r.7.6, see *Hoddinott v Persimmon Homes (Wessex) Ltd* [2007] EWCA Civ 1203, [2008] 1 W.L.R. 806 (CA (Civ Div)), Sir Anthony Clarke, M.R.

r.11, see *Hoddinott v Persimmon Homes (Wessex) Ltd* [2007] EWCA Civ 1203, [2008] 1 W.L.R. 806 (CA (Civ Div)), Sir Anthony Clarke, M.R.

r.12.8, see *MMI Research Ltd v Cellxion Ltd* [2007] EWHC 2611 (Pat), [2008] F.S.R. 23 (Ch D (Patents Ct)), Warren, J.

r.13.3, see *Bell v Brown* [2007] EWHC 2788 (QB), [2008] B.P.I.R. 829 (QBD), Tugendhat, J.

r.16.2, see *Nomura International Plc v Granada Group Ltd* [2007] EWHC 642 (Comm), [2008] Bus. L.R. 1 (QBD (Comm)), Cooke, J.

r.17.4, see *Adelson v Associated Newspapers Ltd* [2007] EWCA Civ 701, [2008] 1 W.L.R. 585 (CA (Civ Div)), Lord Phillips, L.C.J.; see *Evans v Cig Mon Cymru Ltd* [2008] EWCA Civ 390, [2008] 1 W.L.R. 2675 (CA (Civ Div)), Laws, L.J.; see *Society of Lloyd's v Henderson* [2007] EWCA Civ 930, [2008] 1 W.L.R. 2255 (CA (Civ Div)), Buxton, L.J.

r.18.1, see *Harcourt v FEF Griffin* [2007] EWHC 1500 (QB), [2008] Lloyd's Rep. I.R. 386 (QBD), Irwin, J.

r.19.2, see *Dunlop Haywards (DHL) Ltd (formerly Dunlop Heywood Lorenz Ltd) v Erinaceous Insurance Services Ltd (formerly Hanover Park Commercial Ltd)* [2008] EWHC 520 (Comm), [2008] Lloyd's Rep. I.R. 676 (QBD (Comm)), Field, J.

r.19.5, see *Adelson v Associated Newspapers Ltd* [2007] EWCA Civ 701, [2008] 1 W.L.R. 585 (CA (Civ Div)), Lord Phillips, L.C.J.; see *Roberts v Gill & Co* [2008] EWCA Civ 803, [2008] W.T.L.R. 1429 (CA (Civ Div)), Pill, L.J.

r.19.7, see *Smithson v Hamilton* [2008] EWCA Civ 996, [2008] Pens. L.R. 363 (CA (Civ Div)), Mummery, L.J.

r.21.1, see *Saulle v Nouvet* [2007] EWHC 2902 (QB), [2008] LS Law Medical 201 (QBD), Andrew Edis Q.C.

r.25.1, see *Bank of Scotland v Neath Port Talbot CBC (Costs)* [2006] EWHC 2930 (Ch), [2008] B.C.C. 376 (Ch D), David

NO.

1998–cont.

3132. Civil Procedure Rules 1998–*cont.*

r.25.1–*cont.*

Richards, J.; see *Bell v Brown* [2007] EWHC 2788 (QB), [2008] B.P.I.R. 829 (QBD), Tugendhat, J.; see *Lichter v Rubin* [2008] EWHC 450 (Ch), Times, April 18, 2008 (Ch D), Henderson, J; see *Masri v Consolidated Contractors International Co SAL* [2007] EWHC 3010 (Comm), [2008] 1 All E.R. (Comm) 305 (QBD (Comm)), Gloster, J.

r.25.12, see *Gater Assets Ltd v Nak Naftogaz Ukrainiy* [2007] EWCA Civ 988, [2008] Bus. L.R. 388 (CA (Civ Div)), Buxton, L.J.

r.25.13, see *Jirehouse Capital v Beller* [2008] EWCA Civ 908, [2008] C.P. Rep. 44 (CA (Civ Div)), Mummery, L.J.

r.30.2, see *Collins v Drumgold* [2008] EWHC 584 (TCC), [2008] T.C.L.R. 5 (QBD (TCC)), Coulson, J.; see *Neath Port Talbot CBC v Currie & Brown Project Management Ltd* [2008] EWHC1508 (TCC), [2008] C.P. Rep. 39 (QBD (Bristol)), Ramsey, J.

r.30.3, see *Collins v Drumgold* [2008] EWHC 584 (TCC), [2008] T.C.L.R. 5 (QBD (TCC)), Coulson, J.

r.30.5, see *Collins v Drumgold* [2008] EWHC 584 (TCC), [2008] T.C.L.R. 5 (QBD (TCC)), Coulson, J.

r.31.3, see *Expandable Ltd v Rubin* [2008] EWCA Civ 59, [2008] 1 W.L.R. 1099 (CA (Civ Div)), Rix, L.J.

r.31.6, see *OCS Group Ltd v Wells* [2008] EWHC 919 (QB), [2008] 4 All E.R. 818 (QBD), Nelson, J.

r.31.12, see *Martin v Triggs Turner Barton (A Firm)* [2008] EWHC 89 (Ch), [2008] W.T.L.R. 509 (Ch D), Susan Prevezer Q.C.

r.31.14, see *Expandable Ltd v Rubin* [2008] EWCA Civ 59, [2008] 1 W.L.R. 1099 (CA (Civ Div)), Rix, L.J.

r.31.16, see *Hutchison 3G UK Ltd v O2 (UK) Ltd* [2008] EWHC 55 (Comm), [2008] U.K.C.L.R. 83 (QBD (Comm)), David Steel, J.; see *OCS Group Ltd v Wells* [2008] EWHC 919 (QB), [2008] 4 All E.R. 818 (QBD), Nelson, J.; see *SES Contracting Ltd v UK Coal Plc* [2007] EWHC 161 (QB), (2008) 24 Const. L.J. 518 (QBD), Judge Seymour Q.C.

r.31.19, see *Expandable Ltd v Rubin* [2008] EWCA Civ 59, [2008] 1 W.L.R. 1099 (CA (Civ Div)), Rix, L.J.; see *West London Pipeline & Storage Ltd v Total UK Ltd* [2008] EWHC 1729 (Comm), [2008] 2 C.L.C. 258 (QBD (Comm)), Beatson, J.

r.31.22, see *Hellard v Money* [2008] EWHC 2275 (Ch), [2008] B.P.I.R. 1487 (Ch D), Lewison, J.

NO.

1998–cont.

3132. Civil Procedure Rules 1998–*cont.*

r.32.7, see *West London Pipeline & Storage Ltd v Total UK Ltd* [2008] EWHC 1729 (Comm), [2008] 2 C.L.C. 258 (QBD (Comm)), Beatson, J.

r.35.15, see *Balcombe Group Plc v London Development Agency* [2008] EWHC 1392 (TCC), [2008] T.C.L.R. 8 (QBD (TCC)), Coulson, J.

r.36.14, see *Carver v BAA Plc* [2008] EWCA Civ 412, [2008] 3 All E.R. 911 (CA (Civ Div)), Ward, L.J.; see *Jones v Associated Newspapers Ltd* [2007] EWHC 1489 (QB), [2008] 1 All E.R. 240 (QBD), Eady, J.

r.38.2, see *Sheltam Rail Co (Proprietary) Ltd v Mirambo Holdings Ltd* [2008] EWHC 829 (Comm), [2008] 2 Lloyd's Rep. 195 (QBD (Comm)), Aikens, J.

r.38.4, see *Sheltam Rail Co (Proprietary) Ltd v Mirambo Holdings Ltd* [2008] EWHC 829 (Comm), [2008] 2 Lloyd's Rep. 195 (QBD (Comm)), Aikens, J.

r.40.8, see *Gater Assets Ltd v Nak Naftogaz Ukrainiy* [2008] EWHC 1108 (Comm), [2008] 2 Lloyd's Rep. 295 (QBD (Comm)), Beatson, J.

r.40.9, see *Thomas & Agnes Carvel Foundation v Carvel* [2007] EWHC 1314 (Ch), [2008] Ch. 395 (Ch D), Lewison, J.; see *West v Hudson* [2007] EWHC 1938 (Ch), (2008) 31 (2) I.P.D. 31009 (Ch D), Sir Andrew Morritt (Chancellor)

r.44.3, see *Aspin v Metric Group Ltd* [2007] EWCA Civ 922, [2008] 2 Costs L.R. 259 (CA (Civ Div)), Chadwick, L.J.; see *Hall v Stone* [2007] EWCA Civ 1354, [2008] C.P. Rep. 14 (CA (Civ Div)), Waller, L.J. (V-P); see *Kostic v Chaplin* [2007] EWHC 2909 (Ch), [2008] 2 Costs L.R. 271 (Ch D), Henderson, J; see *Krysia Maritime Inc v Intership Ltd (The Krysia)* [2008] EWHC 1880 (Admlty), [2008] 2 Lloyd's Rep. 707 (QBD (Admlty)), Aikens, J.; see *McGlinn v Waltham Contractors Ltd* [2007] EWHC 698 (TCC), [2008] Bus. L.R. 278 (QBD (TCC)), Judge Peter Coulson Q.C.

r.44.4, see *National Westminster Bank Plc v Rabobank Nederland* [2007] EWHC 3163 (Comm), [2008] 1 All E.R. (Comm) 266 (QBD (Comm)), Sir Anthony Colman; see *Newall v Lewis* [2008] EWHC 910 (Ch), [2008] W.T.L.R. 1649 (Ch D), Briggs, J.

r.44.5, see *Brown v Russell Young & Co* [2007] EWCA Civ 43, [2008] 1 W.L.R. 525 (CA (Civ Div)), Buxton, L.J.

r.44.14, see *Haji-Ioannou v Frangos* [2006] EWCA Civ 1663, [2008] 1 W.L.R. 144 (CA (Civ Div)), Sir Andrew Morritt C.

r.45.2, see *Amber Construction Services Ltd v London Interspace HG Ltd* [2007] EWHC 3042 (TCC), [2008] B.L.R. 74 (QBD (TCC)), Akenhead, J.

NO.

1998–cont.

3132. Civil Procedure Rules 1998–*cont.*

r.45.3, see *Amber Construction Services Ltd v London Interspace HG Ltd* [2007] EWHC 3042 (TCC), [2008] B.L.R. 74 (QBD (TCC)), Akenhead, J.

r.45.11, see *Kilby v Gawith* [2008] EWCA Civ 812, [2008] C.P. Rep. 33 (CA (Civ Div)), Sir Anthony Clarke, M.R.

r.47.6, see *Harris v Moat Housing Group-South Ltd* [2007] EWHC 3092 (QB), [2008] 1 W.L.R. 1578 (QBD), Christopher Clarke, J.

r.47.8, see *Haji-Ioannou v Frangos* [2006] EWCA Civ 1663, [2008] 1 W.L.R. 144 (CA (Civ Div)), Sir Andrew Morritt C.

r.47.18, see *Richardson Roofing Co Ltd v Ballast Plc (Dissolved)* [2008] EWHC 1806 (TCC), [2008] T.C.L.R. 12 (QBD (TCC)), Judge Toulmin Q.C.

r.48.2, see *PR Records Ltd v Vinyl 2000 Ltd* [2007] EWHC 1721 (Ch), [2008] 1 Costs L.R. 19 (Ch D), Morgan, J.

r.52.1, see *MA Holdings Ltd v George Wimpey UK Ltd* [2008] EWCA Civ 12, [2008] 1 W.L.R. 1649 (CA (Civ Div)), Dyson, L.J.

r.52.3, see *Poole BC v Hambridge* [2007] EWCA Civ 990, [2008] C.P. Rep. 1 (CA (Civ Div)), Pill, L.J.

r.52.10, see *Hicks v Russell Jones & Walker* [2007] EWCA Civ 844, [2008] 2 All E.R. 1089 (CA (Civ Div)), Lloyds, L.J.

r.52.17, see *Jaffray v Society of Lloyds* [2007] EWCA Civ 586, [2008] 1 W.L.R. 75 (CA (Civ Div)), Buxton, L.J.

r.62.18, see *Colliers International Property Consultants v Colliers Jordan Lee Jafaar Sdn Bhd* [2008] EWHC 1524 (Comm), [2008] 2 Lloyd's Rep. 368 (QBD (Comm)), Beatson, J.

r.71.2, see *Vitol SA v Capri Marine Ltd* [2008] EWHC 378 (Comm), [2008] B.P.I.R. 1629 (QBD (Comm)), Tomlinson, J.

r.73.10, see *Close Invoice Finance Ltd v Pile* [2008] EWHC 1580 (Ch), [2008] B.P.I.R. 1465 (Ch D), Judge Purle Q.C.

Sch.1 Part 115 para.16, amended: SI 2008/3327 r.14

Sch.1 Part 115 para.17, amended: SI 2008/2178 r.39

Sch.1 Part 115 para.32, amended: SI 2008/3327 r.14

Sch.1 Part 115 para.33, amended: SI 2008/2178 r.39

Sch.2 Part 26 para.17, amended: SI 2008/3327 r.15

Sch.2 Part 27 para.5, amended: SI 2008/2178 r.40

Sch.2 Part 27 para.17, amended: SI 2008/2178 r.40

Sch.2 Part 28 para.2, amended: SI 2008/2178 r.41

NO.

1998–cont.

3132. Civil Procedure Rules 1998–*cont.*
Sch.2 Part 28 para.3, amended: SI 2008/2178 r.41
Sch.2 Part 29 para.1, amended: SI 2008/2178 r.42
Sch.2 Part 33 para.4, amended: SI 2008/2178 r.43

3175. Corporation Tax (Instalment Payments) Regulations 1998
Reg.3, amended: SI 2008/2649 Reg.2

3177. European Single Currency (Taxes) Regulations 1998
Reg.6, amended: SI 2008/2647 Reg.2

3218. Parole Board (Transfer of Functions) Order 1998
varied: 2008 c.4 s.27

3277. Port of Tyne Harbour Revision Order 1998
referred to: SI 2008/1817 Art.1

3315. Swansea (1999) National Health Service Trust (Establishment) Order 1998
revoked: SI 2008/938 Art.2

3316. Carmarthenshire National Health Service Trust (Establishment) Order 1998
revoked: SI 2008/933 Art.2

3317. Conwy and Denbighshire National Health Service Trust (Establishment) Order 1998
revoked: SI 2008/1719 Art.2

3318. Pontypridd and Rhondda National Health Service Trust (Establishment) Order 1998
revoked: SI 2008/932 Art.2

3319. Bro Morgannwg National Health Service Trust (Establishment) Order 1998
revoked: SI 2008/939 Art.2

3320. North East Wales National Health Service Trust (Establishment) Order 1998
revoked: SI 2008/1717 Art.2

1999

2. Education (School Premises) Regulations 1999
see *Charterhouse School Governing Body v Hannaford Upright* [2007] EWHC 2718 (TCC), [2008] B.L.R. 239 (QBD (TCC)), Akenhead, J.

9. Curfew Condition (Responsible Officer) Order 1999
revoked: SI 2008/2768 Art.3

71. Allocation of Housing and Homelessness (Review Procedures) Regulations 1999
see *Gilby v Westminster City Council* [2007] EWCA Civ 604, [2008] H.L.R. 7 (CA (Civ Div)), Mummery, L.J.

NO.

1999–cont.

71. Allocation of Housing and Homelessness (Review Procedures) Regulations 1999–*cont.*
Reg.8, see *Gilby v Westminster City Council* [2007] EWCA Civ 604, [2008] H.L.R. 7 (CA (Civ Div)), Mummery, L.J.; see *Lambeth LBC v Johnston* [2008] EWCA Civ 690, Times, June 30, 2008 (CA (Civ Div)), Smith, L.J.

126. Education (Determination of Admission Arrangements) Regulations 1999
revoked (in part): SI 2008/3089 Sch.1

137. National Lottery (Imposition of Penalties and Revocation of Licences) Procedure Regulations 1999
Reg.7, revoked (in part): SI 2008/2683 Sch.1 para.87
Reg.14, revoked (in part): SI 2008/2683 Sch.1 para.88

160. Petroleum (Current Model Clauses) Order 1999
Sch.2 Part II para.7A, added: 2008 c.32 Sch.3 para.3
Sch.2 Part II para.17, amended: 2008 c.32 Sch.3 para.3
Sch.2 Part II para.39, amended: 2008 c.32 Sch.3 para.3
Sch.2 Part II para.39A, added: 2008 c.32 Sch.3 para.3
Sch.3 Part II para.7A, added: 2008 c.32 Sch.3 para.4
Sch.3 Part II para.17, amended: 2008 c.32 Sch.3 para.4
Sch.3 Part II para.37, amended: 2008 c.32 Sch.3 para.4
Sch.3 Part II para.37A, added: 2008 c.32 Sch.3 para.4
Sch.4 Part II para.7A, added: 2008 c.32 Sch.3 para.5
Sch.4 Part II para.17, amended: 2008 c.32 Sch.3 para.5
Sch.4 Part II para.38, amended: 2008 c.32 Sch.3 para.5
Sch.4 Part II para.38A, added: 2008 c.32 Sch.3 para.5
Sch.5 Part II para.7A, added: 2008 c.32 Sch.3 para.6
Sch.5 Part II para.17, amended: 2008 c.32 Sch.3 para.6
Sch.5 Part II para.40, amended: 2008 c.32 Sch.3 para.6
Sch.5 Part II para.40A, added: 2008 c.32 Sch.3 para.6
Sch.6 Part II para.6A, added: 2008 c.32 Sch.3 para.7
Sch.6 Part II para.16, amended: 2008 c.32 Sch.3 para.7
Sch.6 Part II para.39, amended: 2008 c.32 Sch.3 para.7
Sch.6 Part II para.39A, added: 2008 c.32 Sch.3 para.7

NO.

1999–cont.

160. Petroleum (Current Model Clauses) Order 1999–*cont.*

Sch.8 Part II para.6A, added: 2008 c.32 Sch.3 para.8

Sch.8 Part II para.15, amended: 2008 c.32 Sch.3 para.8

Sch.8 Part II para.36, amended: 2008 c.32 Sch.3 para.8

Sch.8 Part II para.36A, added: 2008 c.32 Sch.3 para.8

Sch.9 Part II para.8A, added: 2008 c.32 Sch.3 para.9

Sch.9 Part II para.19, amended: 2008 c.32 Sch.3 para.9

Sch.9 Part II para.42, amended: 2008 c.32 Sch.3 para.9

Sch.9 Part II para.42A, added: 2008 c.32 Sch.3 para.9

Sch.10 Part II para.8A, added: 2008 c.32 Sch.3 para.10

Sch.10 Part II para.19, amended: 2008 c.32 Sch.3 para.10

Sch.10 Part II para.42, amended: 2008 c.32 Sch.3 para.10

Sch.10 Part II para.42A, added: 2008 c.32 Sch.3 para.10

Sch.11 Part II para.5A, added: 2008 c.32 Sch.3 para.11

Sch.11 Part II para.7, amended: 2008 c.32 Sch.3 para.11

Sch.11 Part II para.21A, added: 2008 c.32 Sch.3 para.11

Sch.12 Part II para.6A, added: 2008 c.32 Sch.3 para.12

Sch.12 Part II para.10, amended: 2008 c.32 Sch.3 para.12

Sch.12 Part II para.28, amended: 2008 c.32 Sch.3 para.12

Sch.12 Part II para.28A, added: 2008 c.32 Sch.3 para.12

Sch.13 Part II para.6A, added: 2008 c.32 Sch.3 para.13

Sch.13 Part II para.14, amended: 2008 c.32 Sch.3 para.13

Sch.13 Part II para.33, amended: 2008 c.32 Sch.3 para.13

Sch.13 Part II para.33A, added: 2008 c.32 Sch.3 para.13

Sch.14 Part II para.6A, added: 2008 c.32 Sch.3 para.14

Sch.14 Part II para.15, amended: 2008 c.32 Sch.3 para.14

Sch.14 Part II para.35, amended: 2008 c.32 Sch.3 para.14

Sch.14 Part II para.35A, added: 2008 c.32 Sch.3 para.14

258. Education (Aptitude for Particular Subjects) Regulations 1999

Reg.1A, added: SI 2008/3089 Reg.37

NO.

1999–cont.

260. National Institute for Clinical Excellence Regulations 1999

Reg.1, amended: SI 2008/2250 Art.2

265. Education (Registered Inspectors of Schools Appeal Tribunal and Registered Nursery Education Inspectors Appeal Tribunal) (Procedure) Regulations 1999

Reg.24, amended: SI 2008/2683 Sch.1 para.89

293. Town and Country Planning (Environmental Impact Assessment) (England and Wales) Regulations 1999

applied: 2008 c.18 s.10, SI 2008/1556 Reg.2

referred to: SI 2008/2335 Reg.2

Reg.1, amended: SI 2008/2335 Reg.3

Reg.2, amended: SI 2008/2093 Reg.3, SI 2008/2335 Reg.3

Reg.2, varied: 2008 c.18 s.10, s.14

Reg.3, substituted: SI 2008/2093 Reg.3, SI 2008/2335 Reg.3

Reg.5, amended: SI 2008/2093 Reg.4, SI 2008/2335 Reg.4

Reg.5, varied: SI 2008/1556 Reg.2

Reg.6, varied: SI 2008/1556 Reg.2

Reg.7, substituted: SI 2008/2093 Reg.5, SI 2008/2335 Reg.5

Reg.7, varied: SI 2008/1556 Reg.2

Reg.8, amended: SI 2008/2093 Reg.5, SI 2008/2335 Reg.5

Reg.8, varied: SI 2008/1556 Reg.2

Reg.9, amended: SI 2008/2093 Reg.5, SI 2008/2335 Reg.5

Reg.9, varied: SI 2008/1556 Reg.2

Reg.10, amended: SI 2008/2093 Reg.6, SI 2008/2335 Reg.6

Reg.10, applied: SI 2008/1556 Reg.2

Reg.10, varied: SI 2008/1556 Reg.2

Reg.11, amended: SI 2008/2093 Reg.6, SI 2008/2335 Reg.6

Reg.11, applied: SI 2008/1556 Reg.2

Reg.11, varied: SI 2008/1556 Reg.2

Reg.12, amended: SI 2008/2093 Reg.6, SI 2008/2335 Reg.6

Reg.13, amended: SI 2008/2093 Reg.7, SI 2008/2335 Reg.7

Reg.14, amended: SI 2008/2093 Reg.7, SI 2008/2335 Reg.7

Reg.15, amended: SI 2008/2093 Reg.7, SI 2008/2335 Reg.7

Reg.17, amended: SI 2008/2093 Reg.7, SI 2008/2335 Reg.7

Reg.19, amended: SI 2008/2093 Reg.7, SI 2008/2335 Reg.7

Reg.20, amended: SI 2008/2093 Reg.8, SI 2008/2335 Reg.8

Reg.20, varied: SI 2008/1556 Reg.2

Reg.22, amended: SI 2008/2093 Reg.9, SI 2008/2335 Reg.9

Reg.25, amended: SI 2008/2093 Reg.9, SI 2008/2335 Reg.9

NO.

1999–cont.

293. Town and Country Planning (Environmental Impact Assessment) (England and Wales) Regulations 1999–*cont.*

Reg.26A, amended: SI 2008/1556 Reg.3, SI 2008/2093 Reg.9, SI 2008/2335 Reg.9

Reg.26A, applied: SI 2008/1556 Reg.4

Reg.26A, referred to: SI 2008/1556 Reg.4

Reg.26A, varied: SI 2008/1556 Reg.2

Reg.26B, added: SI 2008/2093 Reg.9

Reg.27, amended: SI 2008/2093 Reg.10, SI 2008/2335 Reg.10

Reg.30, amended: SI 2008/2093 Reg.11, SI 2008/2335 Reg.11

Reg.37, amended: SI 2008/2335 Reg.12

Sch.1, referred to: 2008 c.18 s.10

Sch.2 para.2, referred to: 2008 c.18 s.10

391. Channel Tunnel Rail Link (Nomination) Order 1999

revoked: SI 2008/3076 Art.4

437. Control of Substances Hazardous to Health Regulations 1999

see *Miller v Greater Glasgow Health Board* [2008] CSOH 71, 2008 S.L.T. 567 (OH), Lady Clark of Calton

Reg.5, see *Miller v Greater Glasgow Health Board* [2008] CSOH 71, 2008 S.L.T. 567 (OH), Lady Clark of Calton

491. Criminal Legal Aid (Fixed Payments) (Scotland) Regulations 1999

referred to: SSI 2008/240 Reg.8

Reg.2, amended: SSI 2008/240 Reg.2

Reg.3, amended: SSI 2008/240 Reg.2

Reg.4, amended: SSI 2008/240 Reg.2

Reg.5, amended: SSI 2008/240 Reg.2

Sch.1A, added: SSI 2008/240 Sch.1

Sch.1 Part 1, amended: SSI 2008/240 Reg.2

Sch.1B Part 1, added: SSI 2008/240 Sch.1

Sch.1B Part 2, added: SSI 2008/240 Sch.1

524. Children (Allocation of Proceedings) (Amendment) Order 1999

revoked: SI 2008/2836 Sch.2

545. Local Government (Parishes and Parish Councils) Regulations 1999

applied: SI 2008/337 Sch.1 para.2

Reg.17, applied: SI 2008/337 Sch.1 para.2

584. National Minimum Wage Regulations 1999

Reg.2, amended: SI 2008/1894 Reg.2

Reg.3, see *Burrow Down Support Services Ltd v Rossiter* [2008] I.C.R. 1172 (EAT), Elias, J (President)

Reg.11, amended: SI 2008/1894 Reg.3

Reg.11, referred to: SSI 2008/81 Reg.2

Reg.12, amended: SI 2008/1879 Reg.3, SI 2008/1894 Reg.4

Reg.13, amended: SI 2008/1894 Reg.5

Reg.15, see *Burrow Down Support Services Ltd v Rossiter* [2008] I.C.R. 1172 (EAT), Elias, J (President)

Reg.36, amended: SI 2008/1894 Reg.6

NO.

1999–cont.

584. National Minimum Wage Regulations 1999–*cont.*

Reg.38, see *Revenue and Customs Commissioners v Annabel's (Berkeley Square) Ltd* [2008] I.C.R. 1076 (EAT), Wilkie, J.

593. Value Added Tax (Buildings and Land) Order 1999

revoked: SI 2008/1146 Sch.1 para.23

614. Local Authorities Traffic Orders (Procedure) (Scotland) Regulations 1999

Reg.8, amended: SSI 2008/3 Reg.2

662. Water (Northern Ireland) Order 1999

Art.25, applied: SI 2008/2852 Sch.7 para.2

678. Transfer of Functions (Lord Advocate and Secretary of State) Order 1999

Sch.1, amended: SI 2008/2833 Sch.3 para.228

728. Prison Rules 1999

Part I r.2, amended: SI 2008/597 r.3

Part II r.9, applied: SI 2008/2793 r.4

Part II r.11, amended: SI 2008/597 r.4

Part II r.22, amended: SI 2008/597 r.4

Part II r.35, amended: SI 2008/597 r.4

Part II r.43, amended: SI 2008/597 r.4

Part II r.49, amended: SI 2008/597 r.4

Part II r.61, amended: SI 2008/597 r.5

Part IV r.70, amended: SI 2008/597 r.6

Part IV r.70A, added: SI 2008/597 r.7

Part IV r.73, amended: SI 2008/597 r.4

Part V r.74, amended: SI 2008/597 r.4

Part V r.75, amended: SI 2008/597 r.4

Part V r.76, amended: SI 2008/597 r.4

Part V r.77, amended: SI 2008/597 r.4

Part V r.78, amended: SI 2008/597 r.4

Part V r.79, amended: SI 2008/597 r.4

Part V r.80, amended: SI 2008/597 r.4

r.2, see *R. (on the application of Edwards-Sayer) v Secretary of State for the Home Department* [2008] EWHC 467 (Admin), [2008] 1 W.L.R. 2280 (DC), Richards, L.J.

r.9, see *Lexi Holdings Plc (In Administration) v Luqman* [2008] EWHC 151 (Ch), Times, February 19, 2008 (Ch D), Henderson, J

732. Police (Efficiency) Regulations 1999

applied: SI 2008/2863 r.2

revoked: SI 2008/2862 Reg.3

743. Control of Major Accident Hazards Regulations 1999

applied: SI 2008/2867 Reg.11

Reg.10, applied: SI 2008/2867 Reg.11

Reg.20, amended: SI 2008/960 Sch.3, SI 2008/2337 Reg.7

Reg.22, amended: SI 2008/736 Reg.22, SI 2008/1087 Reg.2

752. Bankruptcy Fees (Scotland) Amendment Regulations 1999

Reg.4, revoked: SSI 2008/5 Reg.3

NO.

1999–cont.

786. Road Traffic (NHS Charges) (Reviews and Appeals) Regulations 1999
Reg.1, amended: SI 2008/2683 Sch.1 para.91
Reg.1, revoked (in part): SI 2008/2683 Sch.1 para.91
Reg.3, amended: SI 2008/2683 Sch.1 para.92
Reg.3, revoked (in part): SI 2008/2683 Sch.1 para.92
Reg.4, revoked: SI 2008/2683 Sch.1 para.93
Reg.5, revoked: SI 2008/2683 Sch.1 para.93
Reg.6, revoked: SI 2008/2683 Sch.1 para.93
Reg.7, revoked: SI 2008/2683 Sch.1 para.93
Reg.8, revoked: SI 2008/2683 Sch.1 para.93
Reg.9, revoked: SI 2008/2683 Sch.1 para.93
Reg.10, revoked: SI 2008/2683 Sch.1 para.93
Reg.11, revoked: SI 2008/2683 Sch.1 para.93
Reg.12, applied: SI 2008/2683 Art.5
Reg.12, revoked: SI 2008/2683 Sch.1 para.93

818. Police Appeals Tribunals Rules 1999
revoked (in part): SI 2008/2863 r.2
r.9, revoked (in part): SI 2008/2683 Sch.1 para.94

855. Public Trustee (Fees) Order 1999
revoked: SI 2008/611 Art.32

881. Overseas Insurers (Tax Representatives) Regulations 1999
Reg.2, amended: SI 2008/2626 Reg.3
Reg.4, amended: SI 2008/2626 Reg.4
Reg.10, amended: SI 2008/2626 Reg.5
Reg.12, amended: SI 2008/2626 Reg.6
Sch.1 Part I para.1, amended: SI 2008/2626 Reg.7
Sch.1 Part I para.2, revoked: SI 2008/2626 Reg.7
Sch.1 Part II para.3, amended: SI 2008/2626 Reg.7
Sch.1 Part II para.4, amended: SI 2008/2626 Reg.7
Sch.1 Part II para.5, amended: SI 2008/2626 Reg.7
Sch.1 Part III para.7, amended: SI 2008/2626 Reg.7
Sch.1 Part III para.8, substituted: SI 2008/2626 Reg.7
Sch.1 Part III para.9, amended: SI 2008/2626 Reg.7
Sch.1 Part III para.10, amended: SI 2008/2626 Reg.7

896. East Kent Hospitals National Health Service Trust (Establishment) Order 1999
Art.1, amended: SI 2008/1859 Art.2, Art.3
Art.2, amended: SI 2008/1859 Art.3
Art.3, amended: SI 2008/1859 Art.4
Art.4, substituted: SI 2008/1859 Art.5

903. Education (Individual Pupil Information) (Prescribed Persons) Regulations 1999
Reg.3, amended: SI 2008/1722 Reg.9

NO.

1999–cont.

919. Diseases of Animals (Approved Disinfectants) (Amendment) Order 1999
revoked (in part): SSI 2008/219 Sch.1

929. Act of Sederunt (Summary Applications, Statutory Applications and Appeals etc Rules) 1999
Part 2 r.2.12, amended: SSI 2008/365 r.8
Part 2 r.2.33, substituted: SSI 2008/223 r.14
Part 2 r.2.33i, substituted: SSI 2008/223 r.14
Part 2 r.2.34, substituted: SSI 2008/223 r.14
Part 2 r.2.37, added: SSI 2008/223 r.5
Part 2 r.2.38, added: SSI 2008/223 r.5
Part 2 r.2.39, added: SSI 2008/223 r.5
Part 2 r.2.40, added: SSI 2008/223 r.5
Part 2 r.2.41, added: SSI 2008/223 r.5
Part 3, revoked: SSI 2008/223 r.14
Part 3, amended: SSI 2008/223 r.14
Part 3, added: SSI 2008/9 r.2
Part 3, added: SSI 2008/335 r.2
Part 3 r.3.11.1, amended: SSI 2008/41 r.2
Part 3 r.3.11.22, added: SSI 2008/41 r.2
Part 3 r.3.11.23, added: SSI 2008/41 r.2
Part 3 r.3.11.24, added: SSI 2008/41 r.2
Part 3 r.3.16.1, amended: SSI 2008/111 r.2, r.3
Part 3 r.3.16.4, amended: SSI 2008/111 r.2
Part 3 r.3.16.8, amended: SSI 2008/111 r.3
Part 3 r.3.16.10, amended: SSI 2008/111 r.4
Part 3 r.3.33.1, amended: SSI 2008/223 r.5
Part 3 r.3.33.2, substituted: SSI 2008/223 r.5
Part 3 r.3.33.4, revoked: SSI 2008/223 r.5
Part 3 r.3.35.4, revoked (in part): SSI 2008/375 r.2
Part 3 r.3.35.5, substituted: SSI 2008/375 r.2
Part 3 r.3.35.6, amended: SSI 2008/375 r.2
Part 3 r.3.36.1, added: SSI 2008/365 r.6
Part 3 r.3.36.2, added: SSI 2008/365 r.6
Sch.1, amended: SSI 2008/9 Sch.1, SSI 2008/111 r.2, SSI 2008/223 Sch.2, SSI 2008/335 Sch.1, SSI 2008/375 Sch.1

985. Social Landlords (Additional Purposes or Objects) Order 1999
Art.3, amended: SI 2008/2831 Sch.1 para.9

991. Social Security and Child Support (Decisions and Appeals) Regulations 1999
see *Mote v Secretary of State for Work and Pensions* [2007] EWCA Civ 1324, [2008] C.P. Rep. 13 (CA (Civ Div)), Lloyd, L.J.
applied: SI 2008/794 Reg.7, Reg.144
see *Mote v Secretary of State for Work and Pensions* [2007] EWCA Civ 1324, [2008] C.P. Rep. 13 (CA (Civ Div)), Lloyd, L.J.
Part V, revoked: SI 2008/2683 Sch.1 para.126
Reg.1, amended: SI 2008/1554 Reg.30, SI 2008/1596 Sch.2 para.1, SI 2008/2543 Reg.4, SI 2008/2656 Reg.4, SI 2008/2683 Sch.1 para.96
Reg.1, applied: SI 2008/794 Sch.9 para.11
Reg.1, referred to: SI 2008/794 Reg.40
Reg.2, amended: SI 2008/2683 Sch.1 para.97

NO.

1999–cont.

991. Social Security and Child Support (Decisions and Appeals) Regulations 1999–*cont.*

Reg.3, amended: SI 2008/1554 Reg.31, SI 2008/2667 Reg.3, SI 2008/2683 Sch.1 para.98
Reg.3, applied: SI 2008/2685 Sch.1
Reg.3A, amended: SI 2008/2543 Reg.4, SI 2008/2544 Reg.3, SI 2008/2683 Sch.1 para.99
Reg.3A, applied: 2008 c.6 Sch.2, SI 2008/2685 Sch.1
Reg.4, amended: SI 2008/2683 Sch.1 para.100
Reg.4, applied: 2008 c.6 Sch.2
Reg.6, amended: SI 2008/1554 Reg.32, SI 2008/2667 Reg.3, SI 2008/2683 Sch.1 para.101
Reg.6A, amended: SI 2008/2683 Sch.1 para.102
Reg.6A, applied: 2008 c.6 Sch.2
Reg.6B, amended: SI 2008/2683 Sch.1 para.103
Reg.6B, applied: 2008 c.6 Sch.2
Reg.7, amended: SI 2008/1042 Reg.2, SI 2008/1554 Reg.33, SI 2008/2667 Reg.3, SI 2008/2683 Sch.1 para.104
Reg.7, revoked (in part): SI 2008/1042 Reg.2, SI 2008/2667 Reg.3
Reg.7A, amended: SI 2008/1554 Reg.34
Reg.7B, amended: SI 2008/1554 Reg.35, SI 2008/2543 Reg.4, SI 2008/2683 Sch.1 para.105
Reg.7B, applied: 2008 c.6 Sch.2
Reg.7B, revoked (in part): SI 2008/2543 Reg.4
Reg.7C, applied: 2008 c.6 Sch.2
Reg.8, amended: SI 2008/2683 Sch.1 para.106
Reg.9A, amended: SI 2008/2683 Sch.1 para.108
Reg.9ZA, added: SI 2008/1596 Sch.2 para.1
Reg.9ZA, amended: SI 2008/1596 Sch.2 para.1, SI 2008/2683 Sch.1 para.107
Reg.10, substituted: SI 2008/1554 Reg.36
Reg.11, amended: SI 2008/1554 Reg.37
Reg.13, amended: SI 2008/1554 Reg.38
Reg.14A, amended: SI 2008/1554 Reg.39
Reg.15A, applied: 2008 c.6 Sch.2
Reg.15B, applied: 2008 c.6 Sch.2
Reg.15C, applied: 2008 c.6 Sch.2
Reg.15D, applied: 2008 c.6 Sch.2
Reg.16, amended: SI 2008/2683 Sch.1 para.109
Reg.17, amended: SI 2008/1554 Reg.40
Reg.19, amended: SI 2008/1554 Reg.41
Reg.20, amended: SI 2008/2683 Sch.1 para.110
Reg.21, amended: SI 2008/2683 Sch.1 para.111

NO.

1999–cont.

991. Social Security and Child Support (Decisions and Appeals) Regulations 1999–*cont.*

Reg.22, amended: SI 2008/2683 Sch.1 para.112
Reg.23, amended: SI 2008/2683 Sch.1 para.113
Reg.23, applied: 2008 c.6 Sch.2
Reg.24, amended: SI 2008/2683 Sch.1 para.114
Reg.24, applied: 2008 c.6 Sch.2
Reg.25, amended: SI 2008/2683 Sch.1 para.115
Reg.26, amended: SI 2008/2683 Sch.1 para.116
Reg.27, amended: SI 2008/2683 Sch.1 para.117
Reg.27, revoked (in part): SI 2008/2683 Sch.1 para.117
Reg.29, amended: SI 2008/1596 Sch.2 para.1, SI 2008/2683 Sch.1 para.118
Reg.29, revoked (in part): SI 2008/2683 Sch.1 para.118
Reg.30, amended: SI 2008/2683 Sch.1 para.119
Reg.30A, amended: SI 2008/2683 Sch.1 para.120
Reg.31, amended: SI 2008/1596 Sch.2 para.1
Reg.31, revoked: SI 2008/2683 Sch.1 para.121
Reg.32, amended: SI 2008/2683 Sch.1 para.122
Reg.32, applied: 2008 c.6 Sch.2
Reg.32, revoked (in part): SI 2008/2683 Sch.1 para.122
Reg.33, amended: SI 2008/1596 Sch.2 para.1, SI 2008/2683 Sch.1 para.123
Reg.33, applied: 2008 c.6 Sch.2, SI 2008/1595 Reg.6
Reg.33, revoked (in part): SI 2008/2683 Sch.1 para.123
Reg.33, substituted: SI 2008/2683 Sch.1 para.123
Reg.33, varied: SI 2008/1596 Sch.2 para.1
Reg.34, applied: 2008 c.6 Sch.2, SI 2008/2551 Reg.13
Reg.35, revoked (in part): SI 2008/2683 Sch.1 para.124
Reg.36, revoked (in part): SI 2008/2683 Sch.1 para.124
Reg.37, revoked (in part): SI 2008/2683 Sch.1 para.124
Reg.38, revoked (in part): SI 2008/2683 Sch.1 para.124
Reg.38A, amended: SI 2008/2683 Sch.1 para.125
Reg.39, applied: 2008 c.6 Sch.2
Reg.39, revoked (in part): SI 2008/2683 Sch.1 para.126
Reg.40, applied: 2008 c.6 Sch.2

NO.

1999–cont.

991. Social Security and Child Support (Decisions and Appeals) Regulations 1999–*cont.*

Reg.40, revoked (in part): SI 2008/2683 Sch.1 para.126

Reg.41, revoked: SI 2008/2683 Sch.1 para.126

Reg.42, revoked (in part): SI 2008/2683 Sch.1 para.126

Reg.43, revoked (in part): SI 2008/2683 Sch.1 para.126

Reg.44, revoked: SI 2008/2683 Sch.1 para.126

Reg.45, revoked: SI 2008/2683 Sch.1 para.126

Reg.46, revoked (in part): SI 2008/2683 Sch.1 para.126

Reg.47, revoked (in part): SI 2008/2683 Sch.1 para.126

Reg.49, revoked (in part): SI 2008/2683 Sch.1 para.126

Reg.50, revoked: SI 2008/2683 Sch.1 para.126

Reg.51, revoked (in part): SI 2008/2683 Sch.1 para.126

Reg.52, revoked: SI 2008/2683 Sch.1 para.126

Reg.53, revoked (in part): SI 2008/2683 Sch.1 para.126

Reg.54, revoked (in part): SI 2008/2683 Sch.1 para.126

Reg.55, revoked (in part): SI 2008/2683 Sch.1 para.126

Reg.56, revoked (in part): SI 2008/2683 Sch.1 para.126

Reg.57, revoked (in part): SI 2008/2683 Sch.1 para.126

Reg.57A, revoked (in part): SI 2008/2683 Sch.1 para.126

Reg.57AA, revoked (in part): SI 2008/2683 Sch.1 para.126

Reg.57B, revoked (in part): SI 2008/2683 Sch.1 para.126

Reg.58, revoked (in part): SI 2008/2683 Sch.1 para.126

Reg.58A, amended: SI 2008/2683 Sch.1 para.127

Sch.1, applied: 2008 c.6 Sch.2

Sch.2, applied: 2008 c.6 Sch.2

Sch.2 para.5, amended: SI 2008/1554 Reg.42

Sch.2 para.27, amended: SI 2008/787 Art.3

Sch.3, applied: 2008 c.6 Sch.2

Sch.3A, applied: 2008 c.6 Sch.2

Sch.3B, applied: 2008 c.6 Sch.2

Sch.3C, applied: 2008 c.6 Sch.2

Sch.3 para.1, amended: SI 2008/1957 Reg.2

Sch.3 para.1, revoked (in part): SI 2008/2683 Sch.1 para.128

Sch.3 para.1, varied: SI 2008/1957 Reg.3

NO.

1999–cont.

991. Social Security and Child Support (Decisions and Appeals) Regulations 1999–*cont.*

Sch.3 para.2, revoked (in part): SI 2008/2683 Sch.1 para.128

Sch.3 para.3, revoked (in part): SI 2008/2683 Sch.1 para.128

Sch.3 para.4, revoked (in part): SI 2008/2683 Sch.1 para.128

Sch.3 para.5, revoked (in part): SI 2008/2683 Sch.1 para.128

Sch.3C para.1, added: SI 2008/1554 Reg.43

Sch.3C para.2, added: SI 2008/1554 Reg.43

Sch.3C para.3, added: SI 2008/1554 Reg.43

Sch.3C para.4, added: SI 2008/1554 Reg.43

Sch.3C para.5, added: SI 2008/1554 Reg.43

Sch.3C para.6, added: SI 2008/1554 Reg.43

Sch.3C para.7, added: SI 2008/1554 Reg.43

Sch.3C para.8, added: SI 2008/1554 Reg.43

Sch.3C para.9, added: SI 2008/1554 Reg.43

Sch.3C para.10, added: SI 2008/1554 Reg.43

Sch.4, applied: 2008 c.6 Sch.2

1017. Scotland Act 1998 (Transitory and Transitional Provisions) (Removal of Judges) Order 1999

revoked: 2008 asp 6 Sch.5 para.3

1027. Social Security Contributions (Decisions and Appeals) Regulations 1999

Reg.3, see *Westek Ltd v Revenue and Customs Commissioners* [2008] S.T.C. (S.C.D.) 169 (Sp Comm), Howard M Nowlan

Reg.10, see *Revenue and Customs Commissioners v Mayor* [2007] EWHC 3147 (Ch), [2008] S.T.C. 1958 (Ch D), Patten, J.

1047. Child Support (Miscellaneous Amendments) (No.2) Regulations 1999

Reg.46, revoked: SI 2008/2683 Sch.2

1053. Non-Road Mobile Machinery (Emission of Gaseous and Particulate Pollutants) Regulations 1999

Reg.2, amended: SI 2008/2011 Reg.2

1066. Education (Information as to Provision of Education) (England) Regulations 1999

revoked: SI 2008/4 Sch.3

1080. Education (Lower Primary Class Sizes) (Scotland) Regulations 1999

see *East Lothian Council, Petitioner* [2008] CSOH 137, 2008 S.L.T. 921 (OH), Lord Woolman

1096. Scotland Act 1998 (Transitory and Transitional Provisions) (Statutory Instruments) Order 1999

Art.11, enabled: SSI 2008/124

1212. Local Government Pension Scheme (Miscellaneous Provisions) Regulations 1999

revoked: SI 2008/238 Sch.1

NO.

1999–cont.

1305. Child Support Commissioners (Procedure) Regulations 1999
revoked: SI 2008/2683 Sch.2
see *R. (on the application of Howes) v Child Support Commissioners* [2007] EWHC 559 (admin), [2008] 1 F.L.R. 1691 (QBD (Admin)), Black J.
Reg.4, amended: SI 2008/1955 Reg.2
Reg.11, see *R. (on the application of Howes) v Child Support Commissioners* [2007] EWHC 559 (admin), [2008] 1 F.L.R. 1691 (QBD (Admin)), Black J.
Reg.20, applied: 2008 c.6 Sch.2

1319. Scotland Act 1998 (Cross-Border Public Authorities) (Specification) Order 1999
Sch.1, amended: SI 2008/2683 Sch.1 para.129

1321. Swansea (1999) National Health Service Trust (Change of Name) Order 1999
revoked: SI 2008/938 Art.2

1408. Non-resident Companies (General Insurance Business) Regulations 1999
Reg.4, amended: SI 2008/954 Art.47
Reg.6, revoked: SI 2008/2643 Reg.2

1413. Potato Industry Development Council (Amendment) Order 1999
revoked: SI 2008/576 Sch.5 para.8

1466. Social Security and Child Support (Decisions and Appeals) (Amendment) Regulations 1999
referred to: SI 2008/2683 Art.3
Reg.2, revoked (in part): SI 2008/2683 Sch.2

1495. Social Security Commissioners (Procedure) Regulations 1999
amended: SI 2008/2683 Sch.1 para.131
Reg.1, amended: SI 2008/2683 Sch.1 para.131
Reg.2, revoked: SI 2008/2683 Sch.1 para.132
Reg.3, revoked: SI 2008/2683 Sch.1 para.132
Reg.4, amended: SI 2008/2683 Sch.1 para.133
Reg.4, revoked (in part): SI 2008/2683 Sch.1 para.133
Reg.5, revoked (in part): SI 2008/2683 Sch.1 para.134
Reg.6, revoked (in part): SI 2008/2683 Sch.1 para.134
Reg.7, revoked (in part): SI 2008/2683 Sch.1 para.134
Reg.8, revoked (in part): SI 2008/2683 Sch.1 para.134
Reg.8A, revoked (in part): SI 2008/2683 Sch.1 para.134
Reg.9, revoked (in part): SI 2008/2683 Sch.1 para.134
Reg.10, revoked (in part): SI 2008/2683 Sch.1 para.134

NO.

1999–cont.

1495. Social Security Commissioners (Procedure) Regulations 1999–*cont.*
Reg.11, revoked (in part): SI 2008/2683 Sch.1 para.134
Reg.12, revoked (in part): SI 2008/2683 Sch.1 para.134
Reg.13, revoked (in part): SI 2008/2683 Sch.1 para.134
Reg.14, revoked (in part): SI 2008/2683 Sch.1 para.135
Reg.15, revoked: SI 2008/2683 Sch.1 para.136
Reg.16, revoked (in part): SI 2008/2683 Sch.1 para.136
Reg.17, revoked (in part): SI 2008/2683 Sch.1 para.136
Reg.18, revoked (in part): SI 2008/2683 Sch.1 para.136
Reg.19, revoked (in part): SI 2008/2683 Sch.1 para.136
Reg.20, revoked (in part): SI 2008/2683 Sch.1 para.136
Reg.21, revoked (in part): SI 2008/2683 Sch.1 para.136
Reg.22, revoked (in part): SI 2008/2683 Sch.1 para.136
Reg.23, revoked (in part): SI 2008/2683 Sch.1 para.136
Reg.24, revoked (in part): SI 2008/2683 Sch.1 para.136
Reg.25, revoked (in part): SI 2008/2683 Sch.1 para.136
Reg.26, revoked (in part): SI 2008/2683 Sch.1 para.136
Reg.27, revoked (in part): SI 2008/2683 Sch.1 para.136
Reg.28, revoked (in part): SI 2008/2683 Sch.1 para.136
Reg.29, revoked: SI 2008/2683 Sch.1 para.136
Reg.30, revoked (in part): SI 2008/2683 Sch.1 para.136
Reg.31, revoked (in part): SI 2008/2683 Sch.1 para.136
Reg.32, revoked (in part): SI 2008/2683 Sch.1 para.136
Reg.33, revoked (in part): SI 2008/2683 Sch.1 para.136

1510. Social Security Act 1998 (Commencement No.7 and Consequential and Transitional Provisions) Order 1999
applied: 2008 c.6 Sch.2

1517. Energy Information (Lamps) Regulations 1999
Sch.4 Part III para.12, amended: SI 2008/1277 Sch.2 para.92
Sch.4 Part III para.12, revoked (in part): SI 2008/1277 Sch.4 Part 2

NO.

1999–cont.

1537. General Chiropractic Council (Constitution and Procedure) Rules Order 1999
revoked: SI 2008/1774 Sch.5 para.5

1549. Public Interest Disclosure (Prescribed Persons) Order 1999
Sch.1, amended: SI 2008/531 Sch.1, SI 2008/2831 Sch.2 para.2

1667. Road Traffic (Permitted Parking Area and Special Parking Area) (County of Buckinghamshire) (High Wycombe Town Centre) (Amendment) Order 1999
revoked: SI 2008/2344 Art.3

1670. Social Security and Child Support (Decisions and Appeals) Amendment (No.3) Regulations 1999
Reg.2, revoked (in part): SI 2008/2683 Sch.2

1672. Public Gas Transporter Pipe-line Works (Environmental Impact Assessment) Regulations 1999
Reg.2, amended: SSI 2008/202 Reg.3

1676. Energy Information (Dishwashers) Regulations 1999
Sch.5 Part III para.12, amended: SI 2008/1277 Sch.2 para.93
Sch.5 Part III para.12, revoked (in part): SI 2008/1277 Sch.4 Part 2

1747. Scotland Act 1998 (Cross-Border Public Authorities) (Adaptation of Functions etc.) Order 1999
Sch.1, amended: SI 2008/2683 Sch.1 para.137
Sch.10 Part II para.2, revoked: SI 2008/2833 Sch.3 para.228

1750. Scotland Act 1998 (Transfer of Functions to the Scottish Ministers etc.) Order 1999
Sch.1, amended: SI 2008/2833 Sch.3 para.228

1892. Town and Country Planning (Trees) Regulations 1999
Reg.9A, added: SI 2008/2260 Reg.3
Reg.10, applied: SI 2008/2512 Art.34
Reg.11, amended: SI 2008/3202 Reg.2
Reg.11, substituted: SI 2008/2260 Reg.5
Reg.12, substituted: SI 2008/2260 Reg.5
Reg.13, substituted: SI 2008/2260 Reg.5
Reg.14, substituted: SI 2008/2260 Reg.5
Reg.15, substituted: SI 2008/2260 Reg.5
Reg.16, substituted: SI 2008/2260 Reg.5
Reg.17, substituted: SI 2008/2260 Reg.5
Sch.1, amended: SI 2008/2260 Reg.4
Sch.1, referred to: SI 2008/2512 Art.34
Sch.1, revoked: SI 2008/2260 Reg.4

1918. Road Traffic (Parking Adjudicators) (England and Wales) Regulations 1999
Reg.9, amended: SI 2008/2683 Sch.1 para.138

NO.

1999–cont.

1957. Merchant Shipping (Marine Equipment) Regulations 1999
applied: SI 2008/3257 Reg.21

2001. Pressure Equipment Regulations 1999
Reg.2, amended: SI 2008/1597 Sch.7 para.3
Sch.6, amended: SI 2008/1597 Sch.7 para.3
Sch.8 para.1, revoked (in part): SI 2008/960 Sch.3

2024. Quarries Regulations 1999
Reg.45, applied: SI 2008/2852 Sch.3 para.1

2083. Unfair Terms in Consumer Contracts Regulations 1999
see *Heifer International Inc v Christiansen* [2007] EWHC 3015 (TCC), [2008] 2 All E.R. (Comm) 831 (QBD (TCC)), Judge Toulmin Q.C.; see *Office of Fair Trading v Abbey National Plc* [2008] EWHC 875 (Comm), [2008] 2 All E.R. (Comm) 625 (QBD (Comm)), Andrew Smith, J.
Reg.3, see *Heifer International Inc v Christiansen* [2007] EWHC 3015 (TCC), [2008] 2 All E.R. (Comm) 831 (QBD (TCC)), Judge Toulmin Q.C.
Reg.5, see *Heifer International Inc v Christiansen* [2007] EWHC 3015 (TCC), [2008] 2 All E.R. (Comm) 831 (QBD (TCC)), Judge Toulmin Q.C.; see *Office of Fair Trading v Abbey National Plc* [2008] EWHC 875 (Comm), [2008] 2 All E.R. (Comm) 625 (QBD (Comm)), Andrew Smith, J.
Reg.6, see *Office of Fair Trading v Abbey National Plc* [2008] EWHC 875 (Comm), [2008] 2 All E.R. (Comm) 625 (QBD (Comm)), Andrew Smith, J.
Reg.7, see *County Homesearch Co (Thames & Chilterns) Ltd v Cowham* [2008] EWCA Civ 26, [2008] 1 W.L.R. 909 (CA (Civ Div)), Sir Anthony Clarke, M.R.; see *Peabody Trust Governors v Reeve* [2008] EWHC 1432 (Ch), [2008] 43 E.G. 196 (Ch D), Gabriel Moss Q.C.
Reg.8, see *Heifer International Inc v Christiansen* [2007] EWHC 3015 (TCC), [2008] 2 All E.R. (Comm) 831 (QBD (TCC)), Judge Toulmin Q.C.; see *Peabody Trust Governors v Reeve* [2008] EWHC 1432 (Ch), [2008] 43 E.G. 196 (Ch D), Gabriel Moss Q.C.

2131. Northern Ireland Act Tribunal (Procedure) Rules 1999
Part II r.9, amended: 2008 c.28 s.91

2228. Environmental Impact Assessment (Forestry) (England and Wales) Regulations 1999
see *R. (on the application of Tree and Wildlife Action Committee Ltd) v Forestry Commissioners* [2007] EWHC 1623 (Admin), [2008] Env. L.R. 5 (QBD (Admin)), Collins, J.

NO.

1999–cont.

2228. Environmental Impact Assessment (Forestry) (England and Wales) Regulations 1999–*cont.*
Sch.3 para.1, see *R. (on the application of Tree and Wildlife Action Committee Ltd) v Forestry Commissioners* [2007] EWHC 1623 (Admin), [2008] Env. L.R. 5 (QBD (Admin)), Collins, J.

2257. Education (Non-Maintained Special Schools) (England) Regulations 1999
Sch.1 Part II para.12, amended: SI 2008/1879 Reg.5

2263. Education (Student Support) (Dance and Drama) Regulations 1999
Reg.4, applied: SI 2008/529 Reg.34, SI 2008/1273 Reg.12, SI 2008/1582 Reg.14, SI 2008/3170 Reg.12

2277. Redundancy Payments (Continuity of Employment in Local Government, etc.) (Modification) Order 1999
Sch.1 para.4B, added: SI 2008/912 Sch.2 para.1
Sch.1 para.6AA, added: SI 2008/2250 Art.2
Sch.1 para.13, amended: SI 2008/2831 Sch.1 para.10
Sch.1 para.17, amended: SI 2008/2831 Sch.2 para.3

2337. Primary Care Trusts (Consultation on Establishment, Dissolution and Transfer of Staff) Regulations 1999
Reg.1, amended: SI 2008/1700 Sch.1 para.5
Reg.2, amended: SI 2008/1700 Sch.1 para.5
Reg.3, amended: SI 2008/1700 Sch.1 para.5

2356. Companies (Forms) (Amendment) Regulations 1999
Sch.1, revoked: SI 2008/1861 Reg.3

2357. Companies (Welsh Language Forms) (Amendment) Regulations 1999
Sch.1, amended: SI 2008/1860 Reg.3

2383. Stamp Duty Reserve Tax (UK Depositary Interests in Foreign Securities) Regulations 1999
Reg.2, amended: SI 2008/954 Art.48

2403. Administration of the Rent Officer Service (England) Order 1999
applied: SI 2008/239 Reg.10, SI 2008/3134
Art.1A, added: SI 2008/3134 Sch.1 para.2
Art.3, amended: SI 2008/3134 Sch.1 para.2
Art.4, amended: SI 2008/3134 Sch.1 para.2
Art.5, amended: SI 2008/3134 Sch.1 para.2
Art.6, disapplied: SI 2008/3134

2457. Spreadable Fats (Marketing Standards) (England) Regulations 1999
revoked: SI 2008/1287 Reg.8

2506. Education (Special Educational Needs) (Information) (England) Regulations 1999
applied: SI 2008/2945 Reg.5

2570. Tax Credits (Decisions and Appeals) (Amendment) Regulations 1999
Reg.22, revoked: SI 2008/2683 Sch.2

NO.

1999–cont.

2570. Tax Credits (Decisions and Appeals) (Amendment) Regulations 1999–*cont.*
Reg.23, revoked (in part): SI 2008/2683 Sch.2
Reg.25, revoked: SI 2008/2683 Sch.2
Reg.26, revoked: SI 2008/2683 Sch.2
Reg.27, revoked: SI 2008/2683 Sch.2

2571. Tax Credits (Payments on Account, Overpayments and Recovery) (Amendment) Regulations 1999
Reg.3, amended: SI 2008/2683 Sch.1 para.139

2677. Social Security and Child Support (Decisions and Appeals), Vaccine Damage Payments and Jobseeker's Allowance (Amendment) Regulations 1999
referred to: SI 2008/2683 Art.3
Reg.9, revoked: SI 2008/2683 Sch.2
Reg.10, revoked (in part): SI 2008/2683 Sch.2

2714. National Health Service (General Ophthalmic Services) (Amendment) Regulations 1999
revoked: SI 2008/1700 Sch.2

2789. Criminal Evidence (Northern Ireland) Order 1999
Art.2, amended: SI 2008/1216 Art.82
Art.3, amended: SI 2008/1769 Sch.1 para.27
Art.3, revoked (in part): SI 2008/1769 Sch.1 para.27, Sch.3
Art.8, see *JA's Application for Judicial Review, Re* [2008] N.I. 74 (QBD (NI)), Kerr, L.C.J.
Art.21A, added: SI 2008/1216 Art.82
Art.21B, added: SI 2008/1216 Art.82
Art.21C, added: SI 2008/1216 Art.82
Art.23, amended: SI 2008/1769 Sch.1 para.27

2864. Motor Vehicles (Driving Licences) Regulations 1999
referred to: SI 2008/1435 Reg.2
Reg.3, amended: SI 2008/1435 Reg.3
Reg.3A, added: SI 2008/1435 Reg.3
Reg.22, amended: SI 2008/1435 Reg.4
Reg.23, amended: SI 2008/508 Reg.3, SI 2008/1435 Reg.5
Reg.23, revoked (in part): SI 2008/508 Reg.3
Reg.23A, added: SI 2008/1435 Reg.6
Reg.24, amended: SI 2008/508 Reg.4, SI 2008/1435 Reg.7
Reg.27, amended: SI 2008/1435 Reg.8
Reg.27, revoked (in part): SI 2008/1435 Reg.8
Reg.28, amended: SI 2008/1435 Reg.9
Reg.28, revoked (in part): SI 2008/1435 Reg.9
Reg.30, amended: SI 2008/508 Reg.5, SI 2008/1435 Reg.10
Reg.35, amended: SI 2008/508 Reg.6, SI 2008/1435 Reg.11

NO.

1999–cont.

2864. Motor Vehicles (Driving Licences) Regulations 1999–*cont.*

Reg.38, amended: SI 2008/1435 Reg.12
Reg.40, amended: SI 2008/508 Reg.7
Reg.40, substituted: SI 2008/1435 Reg.13
Reg.40A, added: SI 2008/1435 Reg.14
Reg.40B, added: SI 2008/1435 Reg.14
Reg.40B, amended: SI 2008/2508 Reg.3
Reg.40C, added: SI 2008/1435 Reg.14
Reg.40C, amended: SI 2008/2508 Reg.4
Reg.41, amended: SI 2008/1435 Reg.15
Reg.47, amended: SI 2008/508 Reg.8, SI 2008/1435 Reg.16
Reg.47A, added: SI 2008/1435 Reg.17
Reg.47B, added: SI 2008/1435 Reg.17
Reg.48, amended: SI 2008/508 Reg.9, SI 2008/1435 Reg.18
Sch.3 Part 1, amended: SI 2008/508 Sch.1, SI 2008/1038 Reg.3, SI 2008/1312 Reg.4
Sch.5 Part 1, substituted: SI 2008/508 Sch.2
Sch.5 Part 2, substituted: SI 2008/508 Sch.2
Sch.7 Part 1, amended: SI 2008/1435 Reg.19
Sch.7 Part 1 paraA, amended: SI 2008/1435 Reg.19
Sch.7 Part 1 paraB, amended: SI 2008/1435 Reg.19
Sch.7 Part 1 paraC, amended: SI 2008/1435 Reg.19
Sch.7 Part 1 paraD, amended: SI 2008/1435 Reg.19
Sch.7 Part 1 paraE, amended: SI 2008/1435 Reg.19
Sch.7 Part 1 paraF, amended: SI 2008/1435 Reg.19
Sch.7 Part 1, amended: SI 2008/1435 Reg.19
Sch.7 Part 2, amended: SI 2008/1435 Reg.19
Sch.7 Part 2 paraA, amended: SI 2008/1435 Reg.19
Sch.7 Part 2 paraB, amended: SI 2008/1435 Reg.19
Sch.7 Part 2 paraC, amended: SI 2008/1435 Reg.19
Sch.7 Part 2 paraD, amended: SI 2008/1435 Reg.19
Sch.7 Part 2 paraE, amended: SI 2008/1435 Reg.19
Sch.7 Part 2 paraF, amended: SI 2008/1435 Reg.19
Sch.7 Part 2, amended: SI 2008/1435 Reg.19
Sch.7 Part 3, amended: SI 2008/1435 Reg.19
Sch.7 Part 3 paraA, amended: SI 2008/1435 Reg.19
Sch.7 Part 3 paraB, amended: SI 2008/1435 Reg.19
Sch.7 Part 3 paraC, amended: SI 2008/1435 Reg.19
Sch.7 Part 3 paraD, amended: SI 2008/1435 Reg.19
Sch.7 Part 3 paraE, amended: SI 2008/1435 Reg.19

NO.

1999–cont.

2864. Motor Vehicles (Driving Licences) Regulations 1999–*cont.*

Sch.7 Part 3 paraF, amended: SI 2008/1435 Reg.19
Sch.7 Part 3, amended: SI 2008/1435 Reg.19
Sch.7 Part 3 paraH, amended: SI 2008/1435 Reg.19
Sch.7 Part 4, amended: SI 2008/1435 Reg.19
Sch.7 Part 4 paraA, amended: SI 2008/1435 Reg.19
Sch.7 Part 4 paraB, amended: SI 2008/1435 Reg.19
Sch.7 Part 4 paraC, amended: SI 2008/1435 Reg.19
Sch.7 Part 4 paraD, amended: SI 2008/1435 Reg.19
Sch.7 Part 4 paraE, amended: SI 2008/1435 Reg.19
Sch.7 Part 4 paraF, amended: SI 2008/1435 Reg.19
Sch.7 Part 4, amended: SI 2008/1435 Reg.19
Sch.7 Part 4 paraH, amended: SI 2008/1435 Reg.19
Sch.8 Part 1 paraD, amended: SI 2008/508 Reg.12
Sch.8 Part 1 paraD, revoked (in part): SI 2008/508 Reg.12
Sch.10C, added: SI 2008/1435 Reg.21
Sch.10 Part 1, amended: SI 2008/1435 Reg.20
Sch.10A Part 1, added: SI 2008/1435 Reg.21
Sch.10A Part 2, added: SI 2008/1435 Reg.21
Sch.10B Part 1, added: SI 2008/1435 Reg.21
Sch.10B Part 2, added: SI 2008/1435 Reg.21

2892. Nuclear Reactors (Environmental Impact Assessment for Decommissioning) Regulations 1999

Reg.16, amended: SI 2008/960 Sch.3

2979. Financial Markets and Insolvency (Settlement Finality) Regulations 1999

Reg.14, varied: SI 2008/1427 Art.12

3121. Value Added Tax (Input Tax) (Specified Supplies) Order 1999

see *Standard Life Assurance Co v Revenue and Customs Commissioners* [2008] B.V.C. 2054 (V&DTr (Edinburgh)), T Gordon Coutts Q.C. (Chairman)

3198. Personal and Occupational Pension Schemes (Miscellaneous Amendments) Regulations 1999

applied: SSI 2008/228 Reg.73

3232. Ionising Radiations Regulations 1999

applied: SI 2008/736 Reg.8, Sch.5
Reg.6, applied: SI 2008/736 Sch.7
Reg.24, amended: SI 2008/960 Sch.3
Reg.35, applied: SI 2008/736 Sch.7
Sch.1, referred to: SI 2008/2852 Sch.3 para.1
Sch.1 para.1, applied: SI 2008/736 Reg.8, Sch.7

NO.

1999–cont.

3242. Management of Health and Safety at Work Regulations 1999
Reg.3, see *R. v John Pointon & Sons Ltd* [2008] EWCA Crim 513, [2008] 2 Cr. App. R. (S.) 82 (CA (Crim Div)), Gage, L.J.

3292. Special Commissioners (Jurisdiction and Procedure) (Amendment) Regulations 1999
applied: SI 2008/562 Reg.20

3293. General Commissioners (Jurisdiction and Procedure) (Amendment) Regulations 1999
applied: SI 2008/562 Reg.20

3294. Special Commissioners (Amendment of the Taxes Management Act 1970) Regulations 1999
applied: SI 2008/562 Reg.20

3312. Maternity and Parental Leave etc Regulations 1999
Reg.2, referred to: SI 2008/656 Reg.1
Reg.7, applied: SI 2008/657 Reg.11
Reg.9, amended: SI 2008/1966 Reg.4
Reg.12A, applied: SI 2008/239 Reg.18, SSI 2008/228 Reg.15
Reg.17, amended: SI 2008/1966 Reg.4
Reg.18A, amended: SI 2008/1966 Reg.5
Reg.19, amended: SI 2008/1966 Reg.6
Reg.19, revoked (in part): SI 2008/1966 Reg.6
Reg.20, amended: SI 2008/1966 Reg.7
Reg.20, revoked (in part): SI 2008/1966 Reg.7

3323. Transnational Information and Consultation of Employees Regulations 1999
Reg.32, referred to: SI 2008/3232 Sch.1 Part 2

3438. Local Government Pension Scheme (Amendment etc.) Regulations 1999
revoked: SI 2008/238 Sch.1

3441. Water Industry (Charges) (Vulnerable Groups) Regulations 1999
Reg.2, amended: SI 2008/1879 Reg.8

2000

51. Sea Fishing (Enforcement of Community Control Measures) Order 2000
Art.3, applied: SSI 2008/101 Sch.1 Part 2

58. Cremation (Amendment) Regulations 2000
revoked: SI 2008/2841 Sch.2

89. Primary Care Trusts (Membership, Procedure and Administration Arrangements) Regulations 2000
Reg.1, amended: SI 2008/1269 Reg.2, SI 2008/1700 Sch.1 para.6, SI 2008/2250 Art.2
Reg.2, amended: SI 2008/1269 Reg.2
Reg.4A, added: SI 2008/1269 Reg.2
Reg.4B, added: SI 2008/1269 Reg.2

NO.

2000–cont.

89. Primary Care Trusts (Membership, Procedure and Administration Arrangements) Regulations 2000–*cont.*
Reg.4C, added: SI 2008/1269 Reg.2
Reg.5, amended: SI 2008/1700 Sch.1 para.6, SI 2008/2250 Art.2
Reg.7, amended: SI 2008/1269 Reg.2
Reg.8, substituted: SI 2008/1269 Reg.2

136. Trade Marks Rules 2000
revoked: SI 2008/1797 Sch.2
r.5, amended: SI 2008/11 r.3
r.11B, added: SI 2008/11 r.4
r.13, see *West v Hudson* [2007] EWHC 1938 (Ch), (2008) 31 (2) I.P.D. 31009 (Ch D), Sir Andrew Morritt (Chancellor)
r.31, see *BSA by B2 Trade Mark* [2008] R.P.C. 22 (App Person), Geoffrey Hobbs Q.C.

137. Trade Marks (Fees) Rules 2000
revoked (in part): SI 2008/1958 r.4, SI 2008/2207 r.2
r.3A, added: SI 2008/11 r.6
Sch.1, amended: SI 2008/11 r.7

138. Trade Marks (International Registration) (Amendment) Order 2000
revoked: SI 2008/2206 Sch.7

212. National Health Service Trusts (Trust Funds Appointment of Trustees) Order 2000
applied: SI 2008/1902 Art.4
Sch.1, amended: SI 2008/1902 Art.3

227. Contaminated Land (England) Regulations 2000
applied: SSI 2008/159 Sch.3 Part 2

288. Special Commissioners (Jurisdiction and Procedure) (Amendment) Regulations 2000
applied: SI 2008/562 Reg.20

432. Greater London Authority (Disqualification) Order 2000
Sch.1 Part II para.10, amended: SI 2008/960 Sch.3

516. Community Legal Service (Financial) Regulations 2000
applied: SI 2008/2940 Reg.3, SI 2008/2943 Reg.3
Reg.3, amended: SI 2008/658 Reg.4, SI 2008/2703 Reg.4
Reg.4, amended: SI 2008/1879 Reg.13
Reg.5, amended: SI 2008/658 Reg.5
Reg.5A, amended: SI 2008/658 Reg.6
Reg.6, amended: SI 2008/658 Reg.7
Reg.15, amended: SI 2008/658 Reg.8, Reg.9
Reg.24, see *R. (on the application of Southwark Law Centre) v Legal Services Commission* [2007] EWHC 1715 (Admin), [2008] 1 W.L.R. 1368 (QBD (Admin)), Collins, J.
Reg.35, amended: SI 2008/658 Reg.10
Reg.38, amended: SI 2008/658 Reg.11
Reg.43, amended: SI 2008/658 Reg.12

NO.

2000–cont.

540. Valuation for Rating (Plant and Machinery) (England) Regulations 2000

Reg.2A, added: SI 2008/2332 Reg.2

541. Asylum Support Appeals (Procedure) Rules 2000

revoked: SI 2008/2683 Sch.2

592. Medicines for Human Use and Medical Devices (Fees and Miscellaneous Amendments) Regulations 2000

Reg.4, revoked: SI 2008/552 Sch.7

Sch.1, revoked: SI 2008/552 Sch.7

617. NHS Bodies and Local Authorities Partnership Arrangements Regulations 2000

Reg.5, amended: SI 2008/2828 Art.11, SI 2008/3166 Reg.4

618. National Health Service (Payments by Local Authorities to NHS Bodies) (Prescribed Functions) Regulations 2000

Reg.2, amended: SI 2008/2828 Art.12

619. National Health Service Pension Scheme (Additional Voluntary Contributions) Regulations 2000

applied: SI 2008/653 Reg.4, Reg.7

Reg.2, amended: SI 2008/655 Reg.2

Reg.3, amended: SI 2008/655 Reg.2

Reg.4, amended: SI 2008/655 Reg.2

Reg.5, amended: SI 2008/655 Reg.2

Reg.6, amended: SI 2008/655 Reg.2

Reg.9, amended: SI 2008/655 Reg.2

Reg.10, amended: SI 2008/655 Reg.2

Reg.11, amended: SI 2008/655 Reg.2

Reg.14, amended: SI 2008/655 Reg.2

Reg.15, amended: SI 2008/655 Reg.2

Reg.19, amended: SI 2008/655 Reg.2

Reg.20, amended: SI 2008/655 Reg.2

Reg.22, added: SI 2008/655 Reg.2

Sch.2 para.1, amended: SI 2008/655 Reg.2

Sch.2 para.4, amended: SI 2008/655 Reg.2

Sch.2 para.7, amended: SI 2008/655 Reg.2

Sch.2 para.11, amended: SI 2008/655 Reg.2

Sch.2 para.13, amended: SI 2008/655 Reg.2

Sch.2 para.14, amended: SI 2008/655 Reg.2

620. National Health Service (Charges for Drugs and Appliances) Regulations 2000

Reg.2, amended: SI 2008/571 Reg.3, SI 2008/1697 Reg.2, SI 2008/1700 Sch.1 para.7, SI 2008/2593 Reg.2

Reg.3, amended: SI 2008/571 Reg.2, Reg.4

Reg.3, referred to: SI 2008/1186 Reg.3, SSI 2008/27 Reg.3

Reg.4, amended: SI 2008/571 Reg.2, Reg.5

Reg.4A, amended: SI 2008/571 Reg.2

Reg.5, amended: SI 2008/571 Reg.2, SI 2008/2593 Reg.2

Reg.6, amended: SI 2008/571 Reg.2

Reg.6A, amended: SI 2008/571 Reg.2, SI 2008/2593 Reg.2

NO.

2000–cont.

620. National Health Service (Charges for Drugs and Appliances) Regulations 2000–*cont.*

Reg.7A, amended: SI 2008/571 Reg.6

Reg.7A, substituted: SI 2008/571 Reg.6

Reg.7B, added: SI 2008/571 Reg.7

Reg.9, amended: SI 2008/571 Reg.2

Sch.1, amended: SI 2008/571 Reg.2

627. Community Legal Service (Funding) Order 2000

applied: SI 2008/2704 Art.3

see *R. (on the application of Niazi) v Secretary of State for the Home Department* [2008] EWCA Civ 755, Times, July 21, 2008 (CA (Civ Div)), Sir Anthony Clarke, M.R.

636. Social Security (Immigration and Asylum) Consequential Amendments Regulations 2000

Reg.1, amended: SI 2008/1554 Reg.69

Reg.2, amended: SI 2008/1554 Reg.69, SI 2008/3108 Reg.8

Reg.2, applied: SI 2008/794 Sch.5 Part 1

Reg.12, amended: SI 2008/1554 Reg.69

Sch.1 Part I para.1, amended: SI 2008/1554 Reg.69

Sch.1 Part I para.2, amended: SI 2008/1554 Reg.69

Sch.1 Part I para.3, amended: SI 2008/1554 Reg.69

Sch.1 Part I para.4, amended: SI 2008/1554 Reg.69

Sch.1 Part II para.1, amended: SI 2008/3108 Reg.8

Sch.1 Part II para.2, amended: SI 2008/3108 Reg.8

Sch.1 Part II para.3, amended: SI 2008/3108 Reg.8

Sch.1 Part II para.4, amended: SI 2008/3108 Reg.8

656. Food Standards Act 1999 (Transitional and Consequential Provisions and Savings) (England and Wales) Regulations 2000

Reg.14, applied: SI 2008/1523

692. Conditional Fee Agreements Regulations 2000

see *Fenton v Holmes* [2007] EWHC 2476 (Ch), [2008] 2 Costs L.R. 238 (Ch D), Mann, J.

Reg.3, see *Fenton v Holmes* [2007] EWHC 2476 (Ch), [2008] 2 Costs L.R. 238 (Ch D), Mann, J.

Reg.3A, see *Jones v Wrexham BC* [2007] EWCA Civ 1356, [2008] 1 W.L.R. 1590 (CA (Civ Div)), Waller, L.J. (V-P)

Reg.4, see *Jones v Wrexham BC* [2007] EWCA Civ 1356, [2008] 1 W.L.R. 1590 (CA (Civ Div)), Waller, L.J. (V-P)

Reg.5, see *Fenton v Holmes* [2007] EWHC 2476 (Ch), [2008] 2 Costs L.R. 238 (Ch D), Mann, J.

NO.

2000–cont.

704. Asylum Support Regulations 2000
Reg.4, amended: SI 2008/1879 Reg.11
Reg.10, amended: SI 2008/760 Reg.2

706. Persons subject to Immigration Control (Housing Authority Accommodation and Homelessness) Order 2000
Art.2, amended: SI 2008/1768 Art.2
Art.3, revoked (in part): SI 2008/1768 Art.2
Art.7, amended: SI 2008/1768 Art.2
Art.8, substituted: SI 2008/1768 Art.2
Art.9, substituted: SI 2008/1768 Art.2

727. Social Security Contributions (Intermediaries) Regulations 2000
Reg.6, see *Dragonfly Consulting Ltd v Revenue and Customs Commissioners* [2008] EWHC 2113 (Ch), [2008] S.T.C. 3030 (Ch D), Henderson, J.; see *Dragonfly Consulting Ltd v Revenue and Customs Commissioners* [2008] S.T.C. (S.C.D.) 430 (Sp Comm), Charles Hellier; see *First Word Software Ltd v Revenue and Customs Commissioners* [2008] S.T.C. (S.C.D.) 389 (Sp Comm), AN Brice (Chairman); see *MKM Computing Ltd v Revenue and Customs Commissioners* [2008] S.T.C. (S.C.D.) 403 (Sp Comm), Charles Hellier

729. Social Fund Winter Fuel Payment Regulations 2000
Reg.1, amended: SI 2008/1554 Reg.7
Reg.2, amended: SI 2008/1554 Reg.7
Reg.2, varied: SI 2008/1778 Reg.2
Reg.3, amended: SI 2008/1554 Reg.7
Reg.4, amended: SI 2008/1554 Reg.7

845. Medical Food (England) Regulations 2000
Reg.8, added: SI 2008/2445 Reg.3

878. Milk Development Council (Amendment) Order 2000
revoked: SI 2008/576 Sch.5 para.8

897. Social Security (Work-focused Interviews) Regulations 2000
applied: SI 2008/2928 Reg.3

912. Immigration (Passenger Information) Order 2000
revoked: SI 2008/5 Art.8

914. Control of Misleading Advertisements (Amendment) Regulations 2000
revoked: SI 2008/1277 Sch.2 para.95, Sch.4 Part 2

944. Education (Student Loans) (Repayment) Regulations 2000
Reg.2, amended: SI 2008/2715 Reg.4, Reg.15
Reg.3, amended: SI 2008/2715 Reg.5
Reg.4, amended: SI 2008/2715 Reg.6
Reg.4A, added: SI 2008/2715 Reg.7
Reg.7, amended: SI 2008/546 Reg.3
Reg.9, amended: SI 2008/2715 Reg.8
Reg.10, amended: SI 2008/2715 Reg.9

NO.

2000–cont.

944. Education (Student Loans) (Repayment) Regulations 2000–*cont.*
Reg.13D, substituted: SI 2008/2715 Reg.10
Reg.14, amended: SI 2008/2715 Reg.11
Reg.15, amended: SI 2008/1879 Reg.6
Reg.26, amended: SI 2008/546 Reg.4
Reg.27, amended: SI 2008/2715 Reg.16
Reg.28, amended: SI 2008/2715 Reg.12
Reg.35, amended: SI 2008/2715 Reg.13
Reg.39B, amended: SI 2008/2715 Reg.17
Reg.40, amended: SI 2008/2715 Reg.18
Reg.40, revoked (in part): SI 2008/2715 Reg.18
Reg.41, amended: SI 2008/2715 Reg.19
Reg.67, added: SI 2008/2715 Reg.14

976. Sea Fishing (Enforcement of Measures for the Recovery of the Stock of Cod) (Irish Sea) (Wales) Order 2000
Art.3, applied: SSI 2008/101 Sch.1 Part 2

1005. Local Government Pension Scheme (Amendment) Regulations 2000
revoked: SI 2008/238 Sch.1

1032. Greater London Authority (Limitation of Salaries) Order 2000
Art.3, substituted: SI 2008/724 Art.2

1048. Pensions on Divorce etc (Provision of Information) Regulations 2000
Reg.1, amended: SI 2008/1050 Sch.2 para.3
Reg.3, amended: SI 2008/1050 Sch.2 para.3
Reg.4, amended: SI 2008/1050 Sch.2 para.3

1049. Pensions on Divorce etc (Charging) Regulations 2000
Reg.9, amended: SI 2008/1050 Sch.2 para.4

1052. Pension Sharing (Valuation) Regulations 2000
Reg.1, amended: SI 2008/1050 Sch.2 para.5
Reg.4, substituted: SI 2008/1050 Sch.2 para.5
Reg.5, substituted: SI 2008/1050 Sch.2 para.5
Reg.6, substituted: SI 2008/1050 Sch.2 para.5
Reg.7, amended: SI 2008/1050 Sch.2 para.5
Reg.7, substituted: SI 2008/1050 Sch.2 para.5

1053. Pension Sharing (Implementation and Discharge of Liability) Regulations 2000
Reg.1, amended: SI 2008/1050 Sch.2 para.6
Reg.10, substituted: SI 2008/1050 Sch.2 para.6
Reg.16, amended: SI 2008/1050 Sch.2 para.6

1054. Pension Sharing (Pension Credit Benefit) Regulations 2000
Reg.1, amended: SI 2008/1050 Sch.2 para.7
Reg.3, applied: SI 2008/653 Reg.5, SSI 2008/224 Reg.5
Reg.7, applied: SI 2008/653 Reg.13, Reg.17, SSI 2008/224 Reg.13, Reg.17

NO.

2000–cont.

1054. Pension Sharing (Pension Credit Benefit) Regulations 2000–*cont.*

Reg.23, amended: SI 2008/1050 Sch.2 para.7

Reg.24, substituted: SI 2008/1050 Sch.2 para.7

Reg.27, revoked: SI 2008/1050 Sch.2 para.7

1076. Bro Morgannwg National Health Service Trust (Establishment) Amendment Order 2000

revoked: SI 2008/939 Art.2

1098. Education (National Curriculum) (Attainment Targets and Programmes of Study in Physical Education) (Wales) Order 2000

revoked: SI 2008/1409 Sch.1 para.1

1099. Education (National Curriculum) (Attainment Targets and Programmes of Study in Science) (Wales) Order 2000

revoked: SI 2008/1409 Sch.1 para.1

1100. Education (National Curriculum) (Attainment Targets and Programmes of Study in Mathematics) (Wales) Order 2000

revoked: SI 2008/1409 Sch.1 para.1

1101. Education (National Curriculum) (Attainment Targets and Programmes of Study in Welsh) Order 2000

revoked: SI 2008/1409 Sch.1 para.1

1111. Airports Act 1986 (Jersey) Order 2000

applied: SI 2008/2562

1119. European Communities (Lawyer's Practice) Regulations 2000

Reg.1, varied: SI 2008/81 Reg.4

Reg.2, amended: SI 2008/81 Reg.3

Reg.2, referred to: SI 2008/81 Reg.4

Reg.21, applied: SI 2008/81 Reg.4

1153. Education (National Curriculum) (Attainment Targets and Programmes of Study in Art) (Wales) Order 2000

revoked: SI 2008/1409 Sch.1 para.1

1154. Education (National Curriculum) (Attainment Targets and Programmes of Study in English) (Wales) Order 2000

revoked: SI 2008/1409 Sch.1 para.1

1155. Education (National Curriculum) (Attainment Targets and Programmes of Study in Geography) (Wales) Order 2000

revoked: SI 2008/1409 Sch.1 para.1

1156. Education (National Curriculum) (Attainment Targets and Programmes of Study in History) (Wales) Order 2000

revoked: SI 2008/1409 Sch.1 para.1

NO.

2000–cont.

1157. Education (National Curriculum) (Attainment Targets and Programmes of Study in Modern Foreign Languages) (Wales) Order 2000

revoked: SI 2008/1409 Sch.1 para.1

1158. Education (National Curriculum) (Attainment Targets and Programmes of Study in Music) (Wales) Order 2000

revoked: SI 2008/1409 Sch.1 para.1

1159. Education (National Curriculum) (Attainment Targets and Programmes of Study in Technology) (Wales) Order 2000

revoked: SI 2008/1409 Sch.1 para.1

1160. Youth Justice Board for England and Wales Order 2000

Art.2, amended: SI 2008/3155 Art.2

Art.4, amended: SI 2008/3155 Art.2

1161. Immigration (Leave to Enter and Remain) Order 2000

Art.7, applied: SI 2008/3048 Reg.21

1164. Local Government Pension Scheme (Greater London Authority etc.) Regulations 2000

revoked: SI 2008/238 Sch.1

1346. Air Navigation (Jersey) Order 2000

revoked: SI 2008/2562 Art.2

1403. Stakeholder Pension Schemes Regulations 2000

Reg.1, revoked (in part): SI 2008/2301 Sch.1 para.1

Sch.2, amended: SI 2008/649 Reg.6

1493. Town and Country Planning (Mayor of London) Order 2000

revoked: SI 2008/580 Art.10

1551. Part-time Workers (Prevention of Less Favourable Treatment) Regulations 2000

see *Revenue and Customs Commissioners v Smith* [2007] EWHC 488 (Ch), [2008] S.T.C. 1941 (Ch D), Warren, J.; see *Sharma v Manchester City Council* [2008] I.C.R. 623 (EAT), Elias, J (President)

Reg.13, amended: SI 2008/1696 Art.3

1596. Social Security and Child Support (Miscellaneous Amendments) Regulations 2000

referred to: SI 2008/2683 Art.3

Reg.24, revoked (in part): SI 2008/2683 Sch.2

Reg.25, revoked (in part): SI 2008/2683 Sch.2

Reg.29, revoked (in part): SI 2008/2683 Sch.2

Reg.30, revoked: SI 2008/2683 Sch.2

Reg.31, revoked (in part): SI 2008/2683 Sch.2

Reg.32, revoked: SI 2008/2683 Sch.2

NO.

2000–cont.

1597. Education (National Curriculum) (Attainment Targets and Programmes of Study in Music) (England) Order 2000

revoked (in part): SI 2008/1761 Art.5

1598. Education (National Curriculum) (Attainment Targets and Programmes of Study in Mathematics) (England) Order 2000

revoked (in part): SI 2008/1759 Art.6

1601. Education (National Curriculum) (Attainment Targets and Programmes of Study in Information and Communication Technology) (England) Order 2000

revoked (in part): SI 2008/1758 Art.6

1602. Education (National Curriculum) (Attainment Targets and Programmes of Study in Art and Design) (England) Order 2000

revoked (in part): SI 2008/1752 Art.5

1603. Education (National Curriculum) (Attainment Target and Programmes of Study in Citizenship) (England) Order 2000

revoked: SI 2008/1753 Art.6

1604. Education (National Curriculum) (Attainment Targets and Programmes of Study in English) (England) Order 2000

revoked (in part): SI 2008/1755 Art.6

1605. Education (National Curriculum) (Attainment Targets and Programmes of Study in Geography) (England) Order 2000

revoked (in part): SI 2008/1756 Art.5

1606. Education (National Curriculum) (Attainment Targets and Programmes of Study in History) (England) Order 2000

revoked (in part): SI 2008/1757 Art.5

1607. Education (National Curriculum) (Attainment Targets and Programmes of Study in Physical Education) (England) Order 2000

revoked (in part): SI 2008/1762 Art.6

1624. Town and Country Planning (Inquiries Procedure) (England) Rules 2000

r.11, amended: SI 2008/2831 Sch.4 para.1

1625. Town and Country Planning Appeals (Determination by Inspectors) (Inquiries Procedure) (England) Rules 2000

r.11, amended: SI 2008/2831 Sch.4 para.1

1725. Borough of Shrewsbury and Atcham (Electoral Changes) Order 2000

Art.4, revoked (in part): SI 2008/492 Art.14

1843. Sea Fishing (North-East Atlantic Control Measures) Order 2000

Art.4, applied: SSI 2008/101 Sch.1 Part 1, Sch.1 Part 2

NO.

2000–cont.

1866. Medical Food (Wales) Regulations 2000

Reg.8, added: SI 2008/2602 Reg.3

1926. Social Security (Work-focused Interviews for Lone Parents) and Miscellaneous Amendments Regulations 2000

applied: SI 2008/3051 Reg.13, Sch.1 para.5
Reg.2, amended: SI 2008/3051 Reg.5
Reg.2ZA, added: SI 2008/3051 Reg.5
Reg.2ZA, amended: SI 2008/3051 Reg.6, Reg.7
Reg.4, amended: SI 2008/2928 Reg.12, SI 2008/3051 Reg.5
Reg.5, amended: SI 2008/3051 Reg.5
Reg.6, amended: SI 2008/3051 Reg.5
Reg.7, amended: SI 2008/3051 Reg.5
Reg.9, amended: SI 2008/2683 Sch.1 para.140

1970. Public Service Vehicles Accessibility Regulations 2000

Reg.7, amended: SI 2008/1459 Reg.2
Reg.12, amended: SI 2008/1459 Reg.2
Reg.17, amended: SI 2008/1459 Reg.2
Reg.18, amended: SI 2008/1459 Reg.2

1973. Pollution Prevention and Control (England and Wales) Regulations 2000

applied: SSI 2008/159 Sch.3 Part 2
see *R. (on the application of Anti-Waste Ltd) v Environment Agency* [2007] EWCA Civ 1377, [2008] 1 W.L.R. 923 (CA (Civ Div)), Pill, L.J.; see *R. (on the application of Edwards) v Environment Agency (No.2)* [2008] UKHL 22, [2008] 1 W.L.R. 1587 (HL), Lord Hoffmann
Reg.2, see *R. (on the application of Anti-Waste Ltd) v Environment Agency* [2007] EWCA Civ 1377, [2008] 1 W.L.R. 923 (CA (Civ Div)), Pill, L.J.
Reg.10, see *R. (on the application of Anti-Waste Ltd) v Environment Agency* [2007] EWCA Civ 1377, [2008] 1 W.L.R. 923 (CA (Civ Div)), Pill, L.J.
Reg.11, see *R. (on the application of Edwards) v Environment Agency (No.2)* [2008] UKHL 22, [2008] 1 W.L.R. 1587 (HL), Lord Hoffmann

1975. Horticultural Development Council (Amendment) Order 2000

revoked: SI 2008/576 Sch.5 para.8

1980. Education (National Curriculum) (Modern Foreign Languages) (Wales) Order 2000

revoked: SI 2008/1408 Art.2

2027. Sheep and Goats Identification (England) Order 2000

applied: SI 2008/130 Art.22, Art.30

2055. Brucellosis (England) Order 2000

Art.4, substituted: SI 2008/618 Art.2
Art.5, amended: SI 2008/618 Art.2

NO.

2000–cont.

2055. Brucellosis (England) Order 2000–*cont.*
Art.13, substituted: SI 2008/618 Art.2

2089. Insurance Companies (Overseas Life Assurance Business) (Excluded Business) Regulations 2000
Reg.2, amended: SI 2008/2625 Reg.3
Reg.8, amended: SI 2008/2625 Reg.4

2129. Tonnage Tax (Training Requirement) Regulations 2000
applied: SI 2008/2264 Reg.2
Reg.15, amended: SI 2008/2264 Reg.3
Reg.21, amended: SI 2008/2264 Reg.3

2190. Transport and Works (Applications and Objections Procedure) (England and Wales) Rules 2000
applied: SI 2008/1238, SI 2008/2512

2230. Sea Fishing (Enforcement of Community Conservation Measures) (Wales) Order 2000
Art.3, applied: SSI 2008/101 Sch.1 Part 2

2301. Water Supply and Sewerage Services (Customer Service Standards) (Amendment) Regulations 2000
revoked: SI 2008/594 Sch.1

2326. Immigration (European Economic Area) Regulations 2000
Reg.5, see *Zalewska v Department for Social Development* [2008] N.I. 1 (CA (NI)), Girvan, L.J.; see *Zalewska v Department for Social Development* [2008] UKHL 67, [2008] 1 W.L.R. 2602 (HL (NI)), Lord Hope of Craighead

2334. Consumer Protection (Distance Selling) Regulations 2000
Reg.19, applied: SI 2008/1277 Sch.1 para.29
Reg.24, revoked (in part): SI 2008/1277 Sch.4 Part 2

2413. Companies (Welsh Language Forms) (Amendment) Regulations 2000
Sch.1, amended: SI 2008/1860 Reg.3

2531. Building Regulations 2000
Reg.12, amended: SI 2008/671 Reg.2
Reg.17E, amended: SI 2008/2363 Reg.3
Reg.20D, amended: SI 2008/2363 Reg.3
Reg.22A, added: SI 2008/671 Reg.2
Reg.22B, added: SI 2008/2334 Art.3
Sch.2A, amended: SI 2008/671 Reg.2

2532. Building (Approved Inspectors etc.) Regulations 2000
Reg.12, amended: SI 2008/2363 Reg.4
Reg.12D, amended: SI 2008/2363 Reg.4
Reg.31A, added: SI 2008/2334 Art.4

2670. Children (Allocation of Proceedings) (Amendment) Order 2000
revoked: SI 2008/2836 Sch.2

2724. Immigration (Designation of Travel Bans) Order 2000
Sch.1 Part 1, substituted: SI 2008/3052 Sch.1

NO.

2000–cont.

2724. Immigration (Designation of Travel Bans) Order 2000–*cont.*
Sch.1 Part 2, substituted: SI 2008/3052 Sch.1

2826. Local Government Pension Scheme (Merseyside Transport Limited) Regulations 2000
revoked: SI 2008/238 Sch.1

2831. Genetically Modified Organisms (Contained Use) Regulations 2000
applied: SI 2008/736 Reg.13
Reg.9, applied: SI 2008/736 Sch.10
Reg.10, applied: SI 2008/736 Sch.10
Reg.11, applied: SI 2008/736 Sch.10
Reg.12, applied: SI 2008/736 Sch.10
Reg.14, applied: SI 2008/736 Reg.13
Reg.15, applied: SI 2008/736 Reg.13, Sch.10
Reg.18, applied: SI 2008/736 Sch.10
Reg.26, amended: SI 2008/960 Sch.3

2853. Local Authorities (Functions and Responsibilities) (England) Regulations 2000
disapplied: SI 2008/3022 Reg.4, Sch.1 para.1
varied: SI 2008/2113 Reg.6
Reg.1, amended: SI 2008/516 Reg.3
Reg.2, amended: SI 2008/516 Reg.4, SI 2008/2787 Reg.3
Reg.2, revoked (in part): SI 2008/2787 Reg.3
Reg.2, varied: SI 2008/1419 Reg.4, SI 2008/2113 Sch.1
Reg.4, amended: SI 2008/516 Reg.6
Sch.1, amended: SI 2008/516 Reg.5, SI 2008/1430 Reg.25, SI 2008/2787 Reg.4, Reg.5, Reg.6
Sch.1, varied: SI 2008/2113 Sch.1
Sch.2 para.9, revoked: SI 2008/516 Reg.7
Sch.2 para.22, revoked: SI 2008/516 Reg.7
Sch.2 para.22, varied: SI 2008/2113 Sch.1
Sch.3, amended: SI 2008/516 Reg.6, SI 2008/744 Reg.2

2854. Social Security Commissioners (Procedure) (Amendment) Regulations 2000
revoked: SI 2008/2683 Sch.2

2993. National Health Service Bodies and Local Authorities Partnership Arrangements (Wales) Regulations 2000
Reg.5, amended: SI 2008/2828 Art.13

3025. Local Government Pension Scheme (Pension Sharing on Divorce) Regulations 2000
revoked: SI 2008/238 Sch.1

3031. Medicines (Products for Human Use-Fees) Amendment Regulations 2000
revoked: SI 2008/552 Sch.7

3047. Beef Labelling (Enforcement) (England) Regulations 2000
revoked: SI 2008/3252 Reg.11

NO.

2000–cont.

3097. Batteries and Accumulators (Containing Dangerous Substances) (Amendment) Regulations 2000
revoked: SI 2008/2164 Sch.2

3173. Child Support (Variations) (Modification of Statutory Provisions) Regulations 2000
applied: 2008 c.6 Sch.2

3174. Child Support (Temporary Compensation Payment Scheme) Regulations 2000
Reg.2, amended: SI 2008/2683 Sch.1 para.141

3177. Child Support (Voluntary Payments) Regulations 2000
applied: 2008 c.6 Sch.2
Reg.1, amended: SI 2008/2543 Reg.5

3185. Child Support (Decisions and Appeals) (Amendment) Regulations 2000
Reg.13, revoked: SI 2008/2683 Sch.2

3186. Child Support (Transitional Provisions) Regulations 2000
applied: 2008 c.6 Sch.2
Reg.3, amended: SI 2008/2543 Reg.6
Reg.11, amended: SI 2008/2543 Reg.6
Reg.15, amended: SI 2008/2543 Reg.6, SI 2008/2544 Reg.7
Reg.25, amended: SI 2008/2543 Reg.6
Reg.28, amended: SI 2008/2543 Reg.6
Reg.30, amended: SI 2008/2543 Reg.6

3226. Transport Tribunal Rules 2000
Part I r.3, amended: SI 2008/2142 r.4
Part IVA r.18E, revoked: SI 2008/2142 r.5
Part IVB r.18F, added: SI 2008/2142 r.6
Part IVB r.18G, added: SI 2008/2142 r.6
Part IVB r.18H, added: SI 2008/2142 r.6
Part IVB r.18J, added: SI 2008/2142 r.6
Part V r.24, substituted: SI 2008/2142 r.7
Part V r.28, amended: SI 2008/2142 r.8
Part V r.35, amended: SI 2008/2142 r.9

3236. Non-automatic Weighing Instruments Regulations 2000
Reg.2, amended: SI 2008/738 Reg.2, Reg.4, Reg.5
Reg.2A, added: SI 2008/738 Reg.2
Reg.11, revoked (in part): SI 2008/738 Reg.4
Reg.12, revoked (in part): SI 2008/738 Reg.4
Reg.13, revoked (in part): SI 2008/738 Reg.4
Reg.18, revoked (in part): SI 2008/738 Reg.4
Reg.24A, added: SI 2008/738 Reg.3
Reg.27, amended: SI 2008/738 Reg.5
Reg.40, amended: SI 2008/738 Reg.5
Sch.2, amended: SI 2008/738 Reg.5
Sch.5 para.1, substituted: SI 2008/738 Reg.5
Sch.5 Part II para.5, revoked: SI 2008/738 Reg.5

3246. Air Navigation (Jersey) (Amendment) Order 2000
revoked: SI 2008/2562 Art.2

NO.

2000–cont.

3255. Social Security (Australia) Order 2000
see *Secretary of State for Work and Pensions v Burley* [2008] EWCA Civ 376, [2008] 3 All E.R. 343 (CA (Civ Div)), Mummery, L.J.

3371. Young Offender Institution Rules 2000
Part I r.2, amended: SI 2008/599 r.3
Part II r.5, applied: SI 2008/2793 r.4
Part II r.8, amended: SI 2008/599 r.4
Part II r.10, amended: SI 2008/599 r.4
Part II r.13, substituted: SI 2008/3155 Art.3
Part II r.29, amended: SI 2008/599 r.4
Part II r.52, amended: SI 2008/599 r.4
Part II r.64, amended: SI 2008/599 r.5
Part IV r.74A, added: SI 2008/599 r.6
Part IV r.77, amended: SI 2008/599 r.4
Part V r.78, amended: SI 2008/599 r.4
Part V r.79, amended: SI 2008/599 r.4
Part V r.80, amended: SI 2008/599 r.4
Part V r.81, amended: SI 2008/599 r.4
Part V r.82, amended: SI 2008/599 r.4
Part V r.83, amended: SI 2008/599 r.4, r.7
Part V r.84, amended: SI 2008/599 r.4

2001

155. Child Support (Maintenance Calculations and Special Cases) Regulations 2001
applied: 2008 c.6 Sch.2
Reg.1, amended: SI 2008/1554 Reg.61, SI 2008/2543 Reg.7
Reg.4, amended: SI 2008/1554 Reg.61
Reg.5, amended: SI 2008/1554 Reg.61
Reg.8, amended: SI 2008/2543 Reg.7
Reg.11, amended: SI 2008/2543 Reg.7
Sch.Part II para.6, amended: SI 2008/2544 Reg.6

156. Child Support (Variations) Regulations (2000) 2001
applied: 2008 c.6 Sch.2
Reg.19, amended: SI 2008/2543 Reg.8
Reg.20, amended: SI 2008/2543 Reg.8
Reg.32, amended: SI 2008/1554 Reg.62
Sch.1 para.1, amended: SI 2008/1554 Reg.63

157. Child Support (Maintenance Calculation Procedure) Regulations 2001
Reg.1, amended: SI 2008/2543 Reg.9
Reg.1, applied: 2008 c.6 Sch.2
Reg.2, applied: 2008 c.6 Sch.2
Reg.3, applied: 2008 c.6 Sch.2, SI 2008/2551 Reg.7
Reg.4, applied: 2008 c.6 Sch.2
Reg.5, amended: SI 2008/2543 Reg.9
Reg.5, applied: 2008 c.6 Sch.2, SI 2008/1476 Art.2, SI 2008/2548 Art.4
Reg.6, amended: SI 2008/2543 Reg.9
Reg.6, applied: 2008 c.6 Sch.2
Reg.7, applied: 2008 c.6 Sch.2
Reg.8, applied: 2008 c.6 Sch.2

NO.

2001–cont.

157. Child Support (Maintenance Calculation Procedure) Regulations 2001– *cont.*

Reg.8, revoked: SI 2008/2543 Reg.9
Reg.9, applied: 2008 c.6 Sch.2
Reg.9, revoked: SI 2008/2543 Reg.9
Reg.9A, applied: 2008 c.6 Sch.2
Reg.9A, revoked: SI 2008/2543 Reg.9
Reg.10, revoked: SI 2008/2543 Reg.9
Reg.11, revoked: SI 2008/2543 Reg.9
Reg.12, revoked: SI 2008/2543 Reg.9
Reg.13, revoked: SI 2008/2543 Reg.9
Reg.14, revoked: SI 2008/2543 Reg.9
Reg.15, revoked: SI 2008/2543 Reg.9
Reg.16, revoked: SI 2008/2543 Reg.9
Reg.17, revoked: SI 2008/2543 Reg.9
Reg.18, revoked: SI 2008/2543 Reg.9
Reg.19, revoked: SI 2008/2543 Reg.9
Reg.20, applied: 2008 c.6 Sch.2
Reg.20, revoked: SI 2008/2543 Reg.9
Reg.21, applied: 2008 c.6 Sch.2
Reg.22, applied: 2008 c.6 Sch.2
Reg.23, applied: 2008 c.6 Sch.2, SI 2008/2551 Reg.13
Reg.24, applied: 2008 c.6 Sch.2
Reg.25, amended: SI 2008/2543 Reg.9, SI 2008/2544 Reg.5
Reg.25, applied: 2008 c.6 Sch.2
Reg.25, revoked (in part): SI 2008/2543 Reg.9
Reg.26, amended: SI 2008/2544 Reg.5
Reg.26, applied: 2008 c.6 Sch.2
Reg.27, applied: 2008 c.6 Sch.2
Reg.27, revoked: SI 2008/2543 Reg.9
Reg.28, amended: SI 2008/2543 Reg.9, SI 2008/2544 Reg.5
Reg.28, applied: 2008 c.6 Sch.2
Reg.29, amended: SI 2008/2543 Reg.9, SI 2008/2544 Reg.5
Reg.29, applied: 2008 c.6 Sch.2
Reg.29, revoked (in part): SI 2008/2543 Reg.9
Reg.29A, applied: 2008 c.6 Sch.2
Reg.29B, added: SI 2008/2544 Reg.5
Reg.29B, applied: 2008 c.6 Sch.2
Reg.30, applied: 2008 c.6 Sch.2
Reg.31, amended: SI 2008/2543 Reg.9, SI 2008/2544 Reg.5
Reg.31, applied: 2008 c.6 Sch.2
Reg.31, revoked (in part): SI 2008/2543 Reg.9
Sch.1, applied: 2008 c.6 Sch.2
Sch.2, applied: 2008 c.6 Sch.2
Sch.2 para.1, amended: SI 2008/2543 Reg.9
Sch.2 para.1, revoked (in part): SI 2008/2543 Reg.9
Sch.2 para.3, amended: SI 2008/2543 Reg.9
Sch.2 para.3, revoked (in part): SI 2008/2543 Reg.9
Sch.2 para.4, amended: SI 2008/2543 Reg.9

NO.

2001–cont.

157. Child Support (Maintenance Calculation Procedure) Regulations 2001– *cont.*

Sch.3, applied: 2008 c.6 Sch.2
Sch.3 para.1, amended: SI 2008/2543 Reg.9
Sch.3 para.1, revoked (in part): SI 2008/2543 Reg.9
Sch.3 para.3, amended: SI 2008/2543 Reg.9
Sch.3 para.3, revoked (in part): SI 2008/2543 Reg.9
Sch.3 para.4, amended: SI 2008/2543 Reg.9

158. Child Support (Consequential Amendments and Transitional Provisions) Regulations 2001

Reg.4, revoked (in part): SI 2008/2683 Sch.2

188. Human Fertilisation and Embryology (Research Purposes) Regulations 2001

revoked: 2008 c.22 s.11, Sch.8 Part 2

238. Detention Centre Rules 2001

r.9, see *R. (on the application of SK (Zimbabwe)) v Secretary of State for the Home Department* [2008] EWCA Civ 1204, Times, November 21, 2008 (CA (Civ Div)), Laws, L.J.; see *R. (on the application of SK (Zimbabwe)) v Secretary of State for the Home Department* [2008] EWHC 98 (Admin), Times, February 26, 2008 (QBD (Admin)), Munby, J.

257. Pensions Appeal Tribunals (England and Wales) (Amendment) Rules 2001

revoked: SI 2008/2683 Sch.2

275. School Milk (Wales) Regulations 2001

revoked: SI 2008/2141 Reg.9

341. Representation of the People (England and Wales) Regulations 2001

applied: SI 2008/1741 Reg.92
Reg.3, varied: SI 2008/1848 Sch.4 para.1
Reg.4, varied: SI 2008/1848 Sch.4 para.1
Reg.5, varied: SI 2008/1848 Sch.4 para.1
Reg.6, varied: SI 2008/1848 Sch.4 para.1
Reg.7, varied: SI 2008/1848 Sch.4 para.1
Reg.8, varied: SI 2008/1848 Sch.4 para.1
Reg.11, varied: SI 2008/1848 Sch.4 para.1
Reg.45E, revoked (in part): 2008 c.28 Sch.1 para.2, Sch.9 Part 2
Reg.45G, applied: SI 2008/2869 Reg.3
Reg.50, varied: SI 2008/1848 Sch.4 para.1
Reg.51, varied: SI 2008/1848 Sch.4 para.1
Reg.51A, varied: SI 2008/1848 Sch.4 para.1
Reg.51AA, varied: SI 2008/1848 Sch.4 para.1
Reg.51B, varied: SI 2008/1848 Sch.4 para.1
Reg.52, varied: SI 2008/1848 Sch.4 para.1
Reg.55, varied: SI 2008/1848 Sch.4 para.1
Reg.56, varied: SI 2008/1848 Sch.4 para.1
Reg.57, varied: SI 2008/1848 Sch.4 para.1
Reg.58, varied: SI 2008/1848 Sch.4 para.1
Reg.59, varied: SI 2008/1848 Sch.4 para.1

NO.

2001–cont.

341. Representation of the People (England and Wales) Regulations 2001–*cont.*

Reg.61B, varied: SI 2008/1848 Sch.4 para.1
Reg.62, varied: SI 2008/1848 Sch.4 para.1
Reg.64, varied: SI 2008/1848 Sch.4 para.1
Reg.66, varied: SI 2008/1848 Sch.4 para.1
Reg.67, varied: SI 2008/1848 Sch.4 para.1
Reg.68, varied: SI 2008/1848 Sch.4 para.1
Reg.69, varied: SI 2008/1848 Sch.4 para.1
Reg.70, varied: SI 2008/1848 Sch.4 para.1
Reg.71, varied: SI 2008/1848 Sch.4 para.1
Reg.72, varied: SI 2008/1848 Sch.4 para.1
Reg.73, varied: SI 2008/1848 Sch.4 para.1
Reg.74, varied: SI 2008/1848 Sch.4 para.1
Reg.75, varied: SI 2008/1848 Sch.4 para.1
Reg.76, varied: SI 2008/1848 Sch.4 para.1
Reg.77, varied: SI 2008/1848 Sch.4 para.1
Reg.78, varied: SI 2008/1848 Sch.4 para.1
Reg.79, varied: SI 2008/1848 Sch.4 para.1
Reg.80, varied: SI 2008/1848 Sch.4 para.1
Reg.81, varied: SI 2008/1848 Sch.4 para.1
Reg.82, varied: SI 2008/1848 Sch.4 para.1
Reg.83, varied: SI 2008/1848 Sch.4 para.1
Reg.84, varied: SI 2008/1848 Sch.4 para.1
Reg.84A, varied: SI 2008/1848 Sch.4 para.1
Reg.85, varied: SI 2008/1848 Sch.4 para.1
Reg.85A, varied: SI 2008/1848 Sch.4 para.1
Reg.85B, varied: SI 2008/1848 Sch.4 para.1
Reg.86, varied: SI 2008/1848 Sch.4 para.1
Reg.86A, varied: SI 2008/1848 Sch.4 para.1
Reg.87, varied: SI 2008/1848 Sch.4 para.1
Reg.88, varied: SI 2008/1848 Sch.4 para.1
Reg.89, varied: SI 2008/1848 Sch.4 para.1
Reg.91, varied: SI 2008/1848 Sch.4 para.1
Reg.102, amended: 2008 c.28 Sch.1 para.2
Reg.108A, added: 2008 c.28 Sch.1 para.2
Reg.109, amended: 2008 c.28 Sch.1 para.2, Sch.9 Part 2
Reg.109, revoked (in part): 2008 c.28 Sch.1 para.2, Sch.9 Part 2
Reg.113, amended: 2008 c.28 Sch.1 para.2
Reg.115, amended: 2008 c.28 Sch.1 para.2, Sch.9 Part 2
Reg.116, amended: SI 2008/1901 Reg.4
Reg.116, varied: SI 2008/1848 Sch.4 para.1
Reg.117, applied: SI 2008/1901 Reg.2
Reg.118, amended: 2008 c.28 Sch.1 para.2
Reg.118, varied: SI 2008/1848 Sch.4 para.1
Reg.119, amended: 2008 c.28 Sch.1 para.2
Reg.119, varied: SI 2008/1848 Sch.4 para.1
Reg.120, substituted: SI 2008/1901 Reg.5
Reg.121, amended: SI 2008/1901 Reg.4
Sch.3, varied: SI 2008/1848 Sch.4 para.1

354. Aerodromes (Designation) (Chargeable Air Services) Order 2001

Sch.1, amended: SI 2008/518 Art.2

400. Representation of the People (Northern Ireland) Regulations 2001

revoked: SI 2008/1741 Sch.2

NO.

2001–cont.

404. Income Tax (Building Societies) (Dividends and Interest) (Amendment) Regulations 2001

revoked: SI 2008/2682 Sch.3

406. Income Tax (Deposit-takers) (Interest Payments) (Amendment) Regulations 2001

revoked: SI 2008/2682 Sch.3

416. Port of Tyne Harbour Revision Order 2001

referred to: SI 2008/1817 Art.1

497. Representation of the People (Scotland) Regulations 2001

applied: SI 2008/307 Art.21, SI 2008/1741 Reg.92
Reg.10, amended: SI 2008/305 Reg.13
Reg.10, revoked (in part): SI 2008/305 Reg.13
Reg.45D, revoked (in part): 2008 c.28 Sch.1 para.3
Reg.45F, applied: SI 2008/2869 Reg.3
Reg.50, amended: SI 2008/305 Reg.2
Reg.51, amended: SI 2008/305 Reg.3
Reg.51A, substituted: SI 2008/305 Reg.4
Reg.57, varied: SI 2008/48 Reg.5
Reg.58, varied: SI 2008/48 Reg.5
Reg.60A, added: SI 2008/305 Reg.5
Reg.61B, added: SI 2008/305 Reg.6
Reg.63A, amended: SI 2008/305 Reg.14
Reg.64, amended: SI 2008/305 Reg.2
Reg.81, amended: SI 2008/305 Reg.7
Reg.84, amended: SI 2008/305 Reg.8
Reg.85, amended: SI 2008/305 Reg.9
Reg.85A, added: SI 2008/305 Reg.10
Reg.85B, added: SI 2008/305 Reg.10
Reg.89, amended: SI 2008/305 Reg.11
Reg.101, amended: 2008 c.28 Sch.1 para.3
Reg.107A, added: 2008 c.28 Sch.1 para.3
Reg.108, amended: 2008 c.28 Sch.1 para.3
Reg.108, revoked (in part): 2008 c.28 Sch.1 para.3
Reg.112, amended: 2008 c.28 Sch.1 para.3
Reg.115, amended: 2008 c.28 Sch.1 para.3
Reg.116, amended: SI 2008/305 Reg.14, SI 2008/1901 Reg.7
Reg.117, amended: SI 2008/305 Reg.14
Reg.117, applied: SI 2008/1901 Reg.2
Reg.118, amended: 2008 c.28 Sch.1 para.3
Reg.119, amended: 2008 c.28 Sch.1 para.3
Reg.120, substituted: SI 2008/1901 Reg.8
Sch.3, amended: SI 2008/305 Sch.1

500. North Tees Primary Care Trust (Establishment) Order 2001

Art.1, amended: SI 2008/1812 Art.2
Art.2, amended: SI 2008/1812 Art.2

544. Financial Services and Markets Act 2000 (Regulated Activities) Order 2001

applied: SI 2008/410 Sch.3 para.7, Sch.3 para.10, SI 2008/567 Reg.3

NO.

2001–cont.

544. Financial Services and Markets Act 2000 (Regulated Activities) Order 2001–*cont.*
Art.5, applied: SI 2008/346 Reg.9
Art.5, referred to: SI 2008/2644 Art.10, SI 2008/2674 Art.7
Art.60, amended: SI 2008/948 Sch.1 para.1

600. Special Educational Needs Tribunal Regulations 2001
Reg.2, amended: SI 2008/2683 Sch.1 para.143
Reg.24, see *R. (on the application of MG) v Tower Hamlets LBC* [2008] EWHC 1577 (Admin), [2008] E.L.R. 523 (QBD (Admin)), Langstaff, J.
Reg.30, revoked (in part): SI 2008/2683 Sch.1 para.144
Reg.33, see *R. (on the application of R) v Special Educational Needs and Disability Tribunal* [2008] EWHC 473 (Admin), [2008] E.L.R. 291 (QBD (Admin)), Mitting, J.
Reg.39A, added: SI 2008/2683 Sch.1 para.145
Reg.48, amended: SI 2008/2683 Sch.1 para.146

656. North Cumbria Acute Hospitals National Health Service Trust (Establishment) Order 2001
Art.1, amended: SI 2008/1775 Art.2, Art.3
Art.2, amended: SI 2008/1775 Art.3
Art.3, amended: SI 2008/1775 Art.4
Art.4, substituted: SI 2008/1775 Art.5

769. Social Security (Crediting and Treatment of Contributions, and National Insurance Numbers) Regulations 2001
referred to: SI 2008/223 Reg.2
Reg.1, amended: SI 2008/1554 Reg.49, SI 2008/2683 Sch.1 para.147
Reg.4, amended: SI 2008/1554 Reg.49
Reg.5, amended: SI 2008/1554 Reg.49
Reg.5A, amended: SI 2008/1554 Reg.49
Reg.9, amended: SI 2008/223 Reg.2
Reg.12, amended: SI 2008/223 Reg.2
Sch.1, added: SI 2008/223 Reg.2
Sch.1, substituted: SI 2008/223 Reg.2
Sch.1 para.1, added: SI 2008/223 Reg.2
Sch.1 para.2, added: SI 2008/223 Reg.2
Sch.1 para.3, added: SI 2008/223 Reg.2

770. Local Government Pension Scheme (Miscellaneous) Regulations 2001
revoked: SI 2008/238 Sch.1

775. Children (Allocation of Proceedings) (Amendment) Order 2001
revoked: SI 2008/2836 Sch.2

795. Medicines for Human Use and Medical Devices (Fees and Miscellaneous Amendments) Regulations 2001
Reg.5, revoked: SI 2008/552 Sch.7
Sch, revoked: SI 2008/552 Sch.7

NO.

2001–cont.

838. Climate Change Levy (General) Regulations 2001
Reg.14, amended: SI 2008/1482 Reg.6
Reg.17, amended: SI 2008/1482 Reg.6
Reg.28, amended: SI 2008/1482 Reg.6, Reg.8, SI 2008/2693 Reg.4
Reg.47, revoked (in part): 2008 c.9 s.149
Sch.para.8, amended: SI 2008/1482 Reg.6

850. Criminal Justice and Court Services Act 2000 (Approved Premises) Regulations 2001
revoked: SI 2008/1263 Reg.4

855. Criminal Defence Service (Funding) Order 2001
see *R. v Rose (Costs)* [2008] 1 Costs L.R. 198 (Sup Ct Costs Office), Costs Judge Rogers
Sch.1 para.23, see *R. v Mahmood (Costs)* [2008] 2 Costs L.R. 326 (Sup Ct Costs Office), Costs Judge Gordon-Saker
Sch.2 para.4, see *R. v Cheng (Costs)* [2008] 1 Costs L.R. 180 (Sup Ct Costs Office), Costs Judge Gordon-Saker
Sch.3 para.4, see *R. v Hayes (Costs)* [2008] 1 Costs L.R. 186 (Sup Ct Costs Office), Costs Judge Gordon-Saker
Sch.4 para.5, see *R. v Rose (Costs)* [2008] 1 Costs L.R. 198 (Sup Ct Costs Office), Costs Judge Rogers
Sch.4 para.6, see *R. v Tanimowo (Costs)* [2008] 2 Costs L.R. 331 (Sup Ct Costs Office), Costs Judge Campbell
Sch.4 para.23, see *R. v Leigh (John) (Costs)* [2008] 1 Costs L.R. 191 (Sup Ct Costs Office), Costs Judge Rogers

856. Criminal Defence Service (Recovery of Defence Costs Orders) Regulations 2001
Reg.3, amended: SI 2008/2430 Reg.4
Reg.4, substituted: SI 2008/2430 Reg.5
Reg.6, substituted: SI 2008/2430 Reg.6
Reg.7A, added: SI 2008/2430 Reg.7
Reg.8, amended: SI 2008/2430 Reg.8
Reg.9, amended: SI 2008/2430 Reg.9
Reg.10, amended: SI 2008/2430 Reg.10
Reg.11, substituted: SI 2008/2430 Reg.11
Reg.12, revoked: SI 2008/2430 Reg.12
Reg.13, amended: SI 2008/2430 Reg.13
Reg.14, amended: SI 2008/2430 Reg.14

880. Biocidal Products Regulations 2001
applied: SSI 2008/219 Art.3, Art.6
Sch.11 para.2, amended: SI 2008/960 Sch.3

943. Occupational and Personal Pension Schemes (Perpetuities and Contracting-out) Amendment Regulations 2001
Reg.4, revoked: SI 2008/1979 Reg.4

964. Stamp Duty and Stamp Duty Reserve Tax (Definition of Unit Trust Scheme and Open-ended Investment Company) Regulations 2001
Reg.2, amended: SI 2008/954 Art.49

NO.

2001–cont.

971. Education (Student Loans) (Repayment) (Amendment) Regulations 2001

Sch.para.1, revoked: SI 2008/2715 Reg.15

994. Milk and Milk Products (Pupils in Educational Establishments) (England) Regulations 2001

revoked: SI 2008/2072 Reg.5

996. Financial Services and Markets Act 2000 (Prescribed Markets and Qualifying Investments) Order 2001

Art.5, amended: SI 2008/3053 Art.4

1002. Housing Benefit and Council Tax Benefit (Decisions and Appeals) Regulations 2001

Reg.1, amended: SI 2008/1082 Reg.3, SI 2008/2683 Sch.1 para.149
Reg.2, amended: SI 2008/2683 Sch.1 para.150
Reg.4, amended: SI 2008/2683 Sch.1 para.151
Reg.5, amended: SI 2008/2683 Sch.1 para.152
Reg.7, amended: SI 2008/1082 Reg.3, SI 2008/2683 Sch.1 para.153
Reg.8, amended: SI 2008/1082 Reg.3, SI 2008/2683 Sch.1 para.154
Reg.9, amended: SI 2008/2683 Sch.1 para.155
Reg.10A, amended: SI 2008/2683 Sch.1 para.156
Reg.11, amended: SI 2008/2667 Reg.4, SI 2008/2683 Sch.1 para.157
Reg.16, revoked (in part): SI 2008/2683 Sch.1 para.158
Reg.17, amended: SI 2008/2683 Sch.1 para.159
Reg.18, revoked: SI 2008/2683 Sch.1 para.160
Reg.19, amended: SI 2008/2683 Sch.1 para.161
Reg.19, revoked (in part): SI 2008/2683 Sch.1 para.161
Reg.20, amended: SI 2008/2683 Sch.1 para.162
Reg.20, substituted: SI 2008/2683 Sch.1 para.162
Reg.21, amended: SI 2008/2667 Reg.4
Reg.22, revoked: SI 2008/2683 Sch.1 para.163
Reg.23, revoked: SI 2008/2683 Sch.1 para.163

1004. Social Security (Contributions) Regulations 2001

Reg.1, amended: SI 2008/954 Art.50, SI 2008/2683 Sch.1 para.164
Reg.10, amended: SI 2008/133 Reg.3
Reg.11, amended: SI 2008/133 Reg.4
Reg.48, see *Clements v Revenue and Customs Commissioners* [2008] S.T.C. (S.C.D.) 744 (Sp Comm), David Williams

NO.

2001–cont.

1004. Social Security (Contributions) Regulations 2001–*cont.*

Reg.50, see *Clements v Revenue and Customs Commissioners* [2008] S.T.C. (S.C.D.) 744 (Sp Comm), David Williams; see *Revenue and Customs Commissioners v Kearney* [2008] EWHC 842 (Ch), [2008] S.T.C. 1506 (Ch D), Lewison, J.
Reg.65C, added: SI 2008/607 Reg.3
Reg.65D, added: SI 2008/3099 Reg.2
Reg.67, amended: SI 2008/636 Reg.3
Reg.125, amended: SI 2008/703 Reg.2
Sch.2 para.13, see *Telent Plc v Revenue and Customs Commissioners* [2008] S.T.C. (S.C.D.) 202 (Sp Comm), John Clark
Sch.3 para.1, see *Telent Plc v Revenue and Customs Commissioners* [2008] S.T.C. (S.C.D.) 202 (Sp Comm), John Clark
Sch.3 Part V para.1, amended: SI 2008/607 Reg.4
Sch.3 Part VIII para.7E, added: SI 2008/607 Reg.4
Sch.3 Part VIII para.12B, added: SI 2008/607 Reg.4
Sch.3 Part X para.1, amended: SI 2008/607 Reg.4, SI 2008/1431 Reg.2, SI 2008/2624 Reg.2
Sch.3 Part X para.18, added: SI 2008/607 Reg.4
Sch.3 Part X para.19, added: SI 2008/607 Reg.4
Sch.3 Part X para.20, added: SI 2008/1431 Reg.2
Sch.3 Part X para.21, added: SI 2008/2624 Reg.2
Sch.4 Part III para.15, amended: SI 2008/636 Reg.4
Sch.4 Part III para.16, amended: SI 2008/636 Reg.5
Sch.4 Part III para.17, amended: SI 2008/636 Reg.6
Sch.4 Part III para.22, amended: SI 2008/636 Reg.7
Sch.4 Part IV para.31, amended: SI 2008/636 Reg.7
Sch.6 Part 1, referred to: SI 2008/794 Reg.43, Sch.7 para.12

1019. Borough of Basingstoke and Deane (Electoral Changes) Order 2001

Art.2, revoked: SI 2008/425 Art.11
Art.3, revoked (in part): SI 2008/425 Art.11
Art.6, revoked: SI 2008/425 Art.11
Art.8, amended: SI 2008/425 Art.11
Sch.1, revoked: SI 2008/425 Art.11
Sch.2, revoked: SI 2008/425 Art.11

1032. Pensions Appeal Tribunals (Late Appeals) Regulations 2001

see *Secretary of State for Defence v Pensions Appeal Tribunal* [2007] EWHC 1177 (Admin), [2008] 1 All E.R. 287 (QBD (Admin)), Stanley Burnton, J.

NO.

2001–cont.

1032. Pensions Appeal Tribunals (Late Appeals) Regulations 2001–*cont.*
Reg.4, see *Secretary of State for Defence v Pensions Appeal Tribunal* [2007] EWHC 1177 (Admin), [2008] 1 All E.R. 287 (QBD (Admin)), Stanley Burnton, J.

1055. Notification of New Substances (Amendment) Regulations 2001
revoked: SI 2008/2852 Sch.10 Part 2

1062. Financial Services and Markets Act 2000 (Collective Investment Schemes) Order 2001
Sch.para.9, substituted: SI 2008/1641 Art.2

1077. Community Legal Service (Funding) (Counsel in Family Proceedings) Order 2001
Art.2, amended: SI 2008/666 Art.3
Art.2, referred to: SI 2008/666 Art.2
Art.2D, amended: SI 2008/666 Art.4
Art.2E, amended: SI 2008/666 Art.5
Art.6, amended: SI 2008/666 Art.6
Art.8, amended: SI 2008/666 Art.7, Art.8
Art.9, amended: SI 2008/666 Art.9

1090. Limited Liability Partnerships Regulations 2001
applied: SI 2008/674 Art.6, SI 2008/948 Art.11, SI 2008/1886 Art.7, SI 2008/1911 Reg.2
Reg.3, revoked: SI 2008/1911 Reg.58
Sch.1, amended: SI 2008/497 Sch.1 para.1, Sch.1 para.2, Sch.1 para.3
Sch.1, revoked: SI 2008/1911 Reg.58
Sch.2 Part I, amended: SI 2008/1911 Reg.58
Sch.6 Part I para.1, amended: SI 2008/1911 Reg.58
Sch.6 Part I para.2, amended: SI 2008/1911 Reg.58
Sch.6 Part I para.3, amended: SI 2008/1911 Reg.58
Sch.6 Part I para.4, amended: SI 2008/1911 Reg.58
Sch.6 Part I para.5, amended: SI 2008/1911 Reg.58
Sch.6 Part I para.6, revoked: SI 2008/1911 Reg.58
Sch.6 Part I para.7, amended: SI 2008/1911 Reg.58

1095. Social Security Commissioners (Procedure) (Amendment) Regulations 2001
Reg.2, revoked: SI 2008/2683 Sch.2
Reg.3, revoked (in part): SI 2008/2683 Sch.2
Reg.4, revoked: SI 2008/2683 Sch.2
Reg.5, revoked (in part): SI 2008/2683 Sch.2
Reg.6, revoked: SI 2008/2683 Sch.2
Reg.7, revoked: SI 2008/2683 Sch.2
Reg.8, revoked: SI 2008/2683 Sch.2
Reg.9, revoked: SI 2008/2683 Sch.2
Reg.10, revoked: SI 2008/2683 Sch.2
Reg.11, revoked: SI 2008/2683 Sch.2
Reg.12, revoked: SI 2008/2683 Sch.2

NO.

2001–cont.

1095. Social Security Commissioners (Procedure) (Amendment) Regulations 2001–*cont.*
Reg.13, revoked: SI 2008/2683 Sch.2
Reg.14, revoked: SI 2008/2683 Sch.2

1117. Fisheries and Aquaculture Structures (Grants) (England) Regulations 2001
Reg.17, amended: SI 2008/1322 Reg.2

1149. Postal Services Act 2000 (Consequential Modifications No.1) Order 2001
Sch.1 Part 1 para.98, revoked: 2008 c.17 Sch.16

1163. Double Taxation Relief (Surrender of Relievable Tax Within a Group) Regulations 2001
Reg.4, amended: SI 2008/2681 Reg.2

1165. Defence Aviation Repair Agency Trading Fund Order 2001
revoked: SI 2008/1208 Art.2
Art.4, substituted: SI 2008/628 Art.2
Sch.2, substituted: SI 2008/628 Art.2

1167. Discretionary Financial Assistance Regulations 2001
Reg.2, applied: SI 2008/794 Sch.8 para.62, Sch.9 para.11
Reg.3, amended: SI 2008/637 Reg.2
Reg.5, substituted: SI 2008/637 Reg.3

1169. Criminal Defence Service (Choice in Very High Cost Cases) Regulations 2001
revoked: SI 2008/40 Reg.5

1183. Pensions Appeal Tribunals (England and Wales) (Amendment No.2) Rules 2001
revoked: SI 2008/2683 Sch.2

1201. Financial Services and Markets Act 2000 (Exemption) Order 2001
Sch.Part I para.1, applied: 2008 c.28 Sch.7 para.6
Sch.Part I para.2, applied: 2008 c.28 Sch.7 para.6
Sch.Part I para.3, applied: 2008 c.28 Sch.7 para.6
Sch.Part I para.4, applied: 2008 c.28 Sch.7 para.6
Sch.Part I para.5, applied: 2008 c.28 Sch.7 para.6
Sch.Part I para.6, applied: 2008 c.28 Sch.7 para.6
Sch.Part I para.7, applied: 2008 c.28 Sch.7 para.6
Sch.Part I para.8, applied: 2008 c.28 Sch.7 para.6
Sch.Part I para.9, applied: 2008 c.28 Sch.7 para.6
Sch.Part I para.10, applied: 2008 c.28 Sch.7 para.6
Sch.Part I para.11, applied: 2008 c.28 Sch.7 para.6

NO.

2001–cont.

1201. Financial Services and Markets Act 2000 (Exemption) Order 2001–*cont.*
Sch.Part I para.12, applied: 2008 c.28 Sch.7 para.6
Sch.Part I para.13, applied: 2008 c.28 Sch.7 para.6
Sch.Part I para.14, applied: 2008 c.28 Sch.7 para.6
Sch.Part I para.15, applied: 2008 c.28 Sch.7 para.6
Sch.Part I para.15A, applied: 2008 c.28 Sch.7 para.6
Sch.Part I para.15B, applied: 2008 c.28 Sch.7 para.6
Sch.Part II para.16, applied: 2008 c.28 Sch.7 para.6
Sch.Part II para.17, applied: 2008 c.28 Sch.7 para.6
Sch.Part II para.18, applied: 2008 c.28 Sch.7 para.6
Sch.Part II para.19, applied: 2008 c.28 Sch.7 para.6
Sch.Part II para.20, applied: 2008 c.28 Sch.7 para.6
Sch.Part II para.21, applied: 2008 c.28 Sch.7 para.6
Sch.Part II para.22, applied: 2008 c.28 Sch.7 para.6
Sch.Part II para.23, applied: 2008 c.28 Sch.7 para.6
Sch.Part II para.25, applied: 2008 c.28 Sch.7 para.6
Sch.Part III para.26, applied: 2008 c.28 Sch.7 para.6
Sch.Part III para.27, applied: 2008 c.28 Sch.7 para.6
Sch.Part III para.28, applied: 2008 c.28 Sch.7 para.6
Sch.Part III para.29, applied: 2008 c.28 Sch.7 para.6
Sch.Part III para.30, applied: 2008 c.28 Sch.7 para.6
Sch.Part III para.31, applied: 2008 c.28 Sch.7 para.6
Sch.Part III para.32, applied: 2008 c.28 Sch.7 para.6
Sch.Part III para.33, applied: 2008 c.28 Sch.7 para.6
Sch.Part III para.33A, applied: 2008 c.28 Sch.7 para.6
Sch.Part III para.34, applied: 2008 c.28 Sch.7 para.6
Sch.Part III para.34A, applied: 2008 c.28 Sch.7 para.6
Sch.Part III para.34B, added: SI 2008/682 Art.2
Sch.Part III para.34B, applied: 2008 c.28 Sch.7 para.6
Sch.Part III para.35, applied: 2008 c.28 Sch.7 para.6

NO.

2001–cont.

1201. Financial Services and Markets Act 2000 (Exemption) Order 2001–*cont.*
Sch.Part III para.36, applied: 2008 c.28 Sch.7 para.6
Sch.Part III para.37, applied: 2008 c.28 Sch.7 para.6
Sch.Part III para.38, applied: 2008 c.28 Sch.7 para.6
Sch.Part III para.39, applied: 2008 c.28 Sch.7 para.6
Sch.Part IV para.40, applied: 2008 c.28 Sch.7 para.6
Sch.Part IV para.41, applied: 2008 c.28 Sch.7 para.6
Sch.Part IV para.42, applied: 2008 c.28 Sch.7 para.6
Sch.Part IV para.43, applied: 2008 c.28 Sch.7 para.6
Sch.Part IV para.44, applied: 2008 c.28 Sch.7 para.6
Sch.Part IV para.45, applied: 2008 c.28 Sch.7 para.6
Sch.Part IV para.46, applied: 2008 c.28 Sch.7 para.6
Sch.Part IV para.47, applied: 2008 c.28 Sch.7 para.6
Sch.Part IV para.48, amended: SI 2008/2831 Sch.1 para.11, Sch.2 para.4
Sch.Part IV para.48, applied: 2008 c.28 Sch.7 para.6
Sch.Part IV para.49, applied: 2008 c.28 Sch.7 para.6
Sch.Part IV para.50, applied: 2008 c.28 Sch.7 para.6
Sch.Part IV para.51, applied: 2008 c.28 Sch.7 para.6

1208. Weighing Equipment (Beltweighers) Regulations 2001
Reg.15, applied: SSI 2008/102 Art.4

1228. Open-Ended Investment Companies Regulations 2001
Reg.2, amended: SI 2008/948 Sch.1 para.220
Reg.13, amended: SI 2008/948 Sch.1 para.221
Sch.5 para.1, amended: SI 2008/948 Sch.1 para.28
Sch.5 para.2, amended: SI 2008/948 Sch.1 para.28
Sch.5 para.11, amended: SI 2008/948 Sch.1 para.222
Sch.6 para.2, amended: SI 2008/948 Sch.1 para.223
Sch.6 para.3, amended: SI 2008/948 Sch.1 para.223
Sch.6 para.5, substituted: SI 2008/948 Sch.1 para.223
Sch.6 para.6, amended: SI 2008/948 Sch.1 para.223
Sch.6 para.6, revoked (in part): SI 2008/948 Sch.1 para.223

NO.

2001–cont.

1261. Terrorism Act 2000 (Proscribed Organisations) (Amendment) Order 2001
see *Secretary of State for the Home Department v Lord Alton of Liverpool* [2008] EWCA Civ 443, [2008] 1 W.L.R. 2341 (CA (Civ Div)), Lord Phillips, L.C.J.

1268. General Teaching Council for England (Disciplinary Functions) Regulations 2001
Reg.29, amended: SI 2008/3256 Reg.2

1361. Spreadable Fats (Marketing Standards) (Wales) Regulations 2001
revoked: SI 2008/1341 Reg.8

1436. Immigration (Restrictions on Employment) (Code of Practice) Order 2001
applied: SI 2008/310 Art.5

1437. Criminal Defence Service (General) (No.2) Regulations 2001
applied: SI 2008/40 Reg.4
Reg.2, amended: SI 2008/1879 Reg.14
Reg.3, amended: SI 2008/725 Reg.2
Reg.5, amended: SI 2008/725 Reg.3, SI 2008/1879 Reg.14
Reg.22, see *R. v Hayes (Costs)* [2008] 1 Costs L.R. 186 (Sup Ct Costs Office), Costs Judge Gordon-Saker

1452. Civil Aviation Act 1982 (Overseas Territories) Order 2001
applied: SI 2008/3125

1481. Local Government Pension Scheme (Amendment) Regulations 2001
revoked: SI 2008/238 Sch.1

1539. Artificial Insemination of Cattle (Emergency Licences) (Wales) Regulations 2001
revoked: SI 2008/1040 Sch.10 Part 2

1543. National Health Service (Payments by Local Authorities to Health Authorities) (Prescribed Functions) (Wales) Regulations 2001
Reg.2, amended: SI 2008/2828 Art.14

1656. Children (Allocation of Proceedings) (Amendment No.2) Order 2001
revoked: SI 2008/2836 Sch.2

1701. Noise Emission in the Environment by Equipment for use Outdoors Regulations 2001
Reg.2, amended: SI 2008/1597 Sch.7 para.4
Reg.3, amended: SI 2008/1597 Sch.7 para.4

1712. Tobacco Products Regulations 2001
Sch.1 para.11, substituted: SI 2008/954 Art.51

1829. Child Minding and Day Care (Applications for Registration) (England) Regulations 2001
Sch.1 para.1C, applied: SI 2008/2261 Sch.2 para.12

1841. Medicines (Aristolochia and Mu Tong etc.) (Prohibition) Order 2001
Art.1, amended: SI 2008/548 Art.5

NO.

2001–cont.

1841. Medicines (Aristolochia and Mu Tong etc.) (Prohibition) Order 2001–*cont.*
Art.4, amended: SI 2008/548 Art.5

1877. Representation of the People (Northern Ireland) (Amendment) Regulations 2001
revoked: SI 2008/1741 Sch.2

2234. Curfew Order and Curfew Requirement (Responsible Officer) Order 2001
Art.2, amended: SI 2008/912 Sch.2 para.2
Art.4, amended: SI 2008/912 Sch.2 para.2

2276. Conduct of Members (Principles) (Wales) Order 2001
applied: SI 2008/788

2289. Conduct of Members (Model Code of Conduct) (Wales) Order 2001
revoked: SI 2008/788 Art.5

2292. Local Authorities (Referendums) (Petitions and Directions) (Wales) Regulations 2001
Reg.17, applied: SI 2008/1848 Reg.4, Reg.13
Reg.19, applied: SI 2008/1848 Reg.4, Reg.13
Reg.20, applied: SI 2008/1848 Reg.13
Reg.23, applied: SI 2008/1848 Reg.10
Reg.24, applied: SI 2008/1848 Reg.10

2313. Road User Charging (Enforcement and Adjudication) (London) Regulations 2001
Reg.3, amended: SI 2008/1956 Reg.2
Reg.3, applied: SI 2008/2995 Sch.1 Part 1
Sch.1 Part II para.8, revoked (in part): SI 2008/2683 Sch.1 para.165

2340. Discretionary Housing Payments (Grants) Order 2001
Art.3, revoked (in part): SI 2008/1167 Art.2
Art.4, revoked (in part): SI 2008/1167 Art.2
Art.5, revoked: SI 2008/1167 Art.2
Art.6, substituted: SI 2008/1167 Art.2

2476. Financial Services and Markets Tribunal Rules 2001
varied: SI 2008/3249 Sch.1
Part I r.2, varied: SI 2008/3249 Sch.1
Part II r.4, varied: SI 2008/3249 Sch.1
Part II r.5, varied: SI 2008/3249 Sch.1
Part II r.6, varied: SI 2008/3249 Sch.1
Part II r.7, varied: SI 2008/3249 Sch.1
Part II r.8, varied: SI 2008/3249 Sch.1
Part II r.10, varied: SI 2008/3249 Sch.1
Part II r.10A, varied: SI 2008/3249 Sch.1
Part II r.10B, varied: SI 2008/3249 Sch.1
Part II r.11, varied: SI 2008/3249 Sch.1
Part II r.12, varied: SI 2008/3249 Sch.1
Part II r.14, varied: SI 2008/3249 Sch.1
Part II r.15, varied: SI 2008/3249 Sch.1
Part III r.19, varied: SI 2008/3249 Sch.1
Part IV r.23, varied: SI 2008/3249 Sch.1

2486. Motor Vehicles (Approval) (Fees) Regulations 2001
Reg.4, amended: SI 2008/1443 Reg.3, Reg.4

NO.

2001–cont.

2486. Motor Vehicles (Approval) (Fees) Regulations 2001–*cont.*
Reg.5, amended: SI 2008/1443 Reg.3
Reg.9, amended: SI 2008/1443 Reg.3

2541. Capital Allowances (Energy-saving Plant and Machinery) Order 2001
Art.2, amended: SI 2008/1916 Art.2

2550. Welsh Language Schemes (Public Bodies) Order 2001
Sch.1, amended: SI 2008/912 Sch.2 para.3

2551. Batteries and Accumulators (Containing Dangerous Substances) (Amendment) Regulations 2001
revoked: SI 2008/2164 Sch.2

2564. Life Sentences (Northern Ireland) Order 2001
applied: SI 2008/1216 Art.35, Art.46
Art.2, amended: SI 2008/1216 Sch.5 para.8
Art.3, revoked: SI 2008/1216 Sch.6 Part 1
Art.4, revoked: SI 2008/1216 Sch.6 Part 1
Art.10, amended: 2008 c.4 Sch.26 para.51
Sch.1 para.1, revoked: SI 2008/1216 Sch.6 Part 1
Sch.1 para.2, revoked: SI 2008/1216 Sch.6 Part 1
Sch.1 para.3, revoked: SI 2008/1216 Sch.6 Part 1
Sch.1 para.4, revoked: SI 2008/1216 Sch.6 Part 1
Sch.1 para.5, revoked: SI 2008/1216 Sch.6 Part 1
Sch.1 para.6, revoked: SI 2008/1216 Sch.6 Part 1
Sch.1 para.7, revoked: SI 2008/1216 Sch.6 Part 1
Sch.1 para.8, revoked: SI 2008/1216 Sch.6 Part 1
Sch.2 para.1, revoked: SI 2008/1216 Sch.6 Part 1
Sch.2 para.2, revoked: SI 2008/1216 Sch.6 Part 1
Sch.2 para.3, revoked: SI 2008/1216 Sch.6 Part 1
Sch.2 para.4, revoked: SI 2008/1216 Sch.6 Part 1
Sch.2 para.5, revoked: SI 2008/1216 Sch.6 Part 1
Sch.2 para.6, revoked: SI 2008/1216 Sch.6 Part 1

2590. Immigration (Leave to Enter) Order 2001
Art.3, applied: SI 2008/3048 Reg.21

2793. Road User Charging And Workplace Parking Levy (Classes Of Motor Vehicles) (England) Regulations 2001
applied: SI 2008/1951 Sch.2 para.1

2812. Relevant Authorities (Standards Committee) Regulations 2001
applied: SI 2008/1265 Art.3
Reg.1, amended: SI 2008/1085 Sch.1
Reg.2, amended: SI 2008/1085 Sch.1

NO.

2001–cont.

2812. Relevant Authorities (Standards Committee) Regulations 2001–*cont.*
Reg.3, substituted: SI 2008/1085 Sch.1
Reg.7, amended: SI 2008/1085 Sch.1
Reg.7, revoked (in part): SI 2008/1085 Sch.1

2866. Local Government Pension Scheme (Her Majesty's Chief Inspector of Schools in England) (Transfers) Regulations 2001
revoked: SI 2008/238 Sch.1

2874. Children (Leaving Care) (England) Regulations 2001
see *R. (on the application of G) v Nottingham City Council* [2008] EWHC 400 (Admin), [2008] 1 F.L.R. 1668 (QBD (Admin)), Munby, J.

2879. Value Added Tax (Refund of Tax to Museums and Galleries) Order 2001
Sch.1, amended: SI 2008/1339 Art.3, Art.4, Art.5, Art.6, Art.7, Art.8, Art.9, Art.10

2897. Education (Induction Arrangements for School Teachers) (Consolidation) (England) Regulations 2001
applied: SI 2008/657 Reg.2
revoked: SI 2008/657 Sch.1

2975. Radiation (Emergency Preparedness and Public Information) Regulations 2001
applied: SI 2008/2867 Reg.11
Reg.4, applied: SI 2008/2867 Reg.11
Reg.5, applied: SI 2008/2867 Reg.11
Reg.9, applied: SI 2008/2867 Reg.11
Reg.14, applied: SI 2008/736 Reg.8, Sch.7

3022. Excise Duty Points (Duty Suspended Movements of Excise Goods) Regulations 2001
Reg.7, see *Garrett Trading Ltd v Revenue and Customs Commissioners* [2008] 3 C.M.L.R. 42 (V&DTr (London)), JF Avery Jones (Chairman)

3057. General Optical Council (Membership) Order of Council 2001
revoked: SI 2008/1774 Sch.5 para.3

3074. Children (Leaving Care) Social Security Benefits Regulations 2001
Reg.2, amended: SI 2008/1554 Reg.70

3194. Potatoes Originating in Germany (Notification) (England) Order 2001
revoked: SI 2008/2411 Art.3

3210. Social Security (Jobcentre Plus Interviews) Regulations 2001
applied: SI 2008/2928 Reg.3

3343. Motor Vehicles (Access to Driver Licensing Records) Regulations 2001
Reg.2, amended: SI 2008/1965 Reg.2

3363. Terrorism (United Nations Measures) (Channel Islands) Order 2001
Art.3, amended: 2008 c.28 s.75

3364. Terrorism (United Nations Measures) (Isle of Man) Order 2001
Art.3, amended: 2008 c.28 s.75

NO.

2001–cont.

3365. Terrorism (United Nations Measures) Order 2001
referred to: 2008 c.28 s.64
Art.4, revoked (in part): 2008 c.28 Sch.9 Part 4

3366. Terrorism (United Nations Measures) (Overseas Territories) Order 2001
Art.2, amended: 2008 c.28 s.75

3367. Civil Aviation Act 1982 (Overseas Territories) (No.2) Order 2001
varied: SI 2008/3120 Art.4

3384. Local Authorities (Standing Orders) (England) Regulations 2001
applied: SI 2008/634 Art.9, SI 2008/907 Art.20, SI 2008/1419 Reg.4

3401. Local Government Pension Scheme (Amendment No.2) Regulations 2001
revoked: SI 2008/238 Sch.1

3455. Education (Special Educational Needs) (England) (Consolidation) Regulations 2001
Reg.2, amended: SI 2008/2683 Sch.1 para.167
Reg.12, amended: SI 2008/2683 Sch.1 para.168
Reg.16, amended: SI 2008/2683 Sch.1 para.169
Reg.17, amended: SI 2008/2683 Sch.1 para.170
Reg.23, see *R. (on the application of L) v Waltham Forest LBC* [2007] EWHC 2060 (Admin), [2008] B.L.G.R. 495 (QBD (Admin)), Rabinder Singh Q.C.
Reg.25, amended: SI 2008/2683 Sch.1 para.171
Reg.26, amended: SI 2008/2683 Sch.1 para.172
Sch.1 Part A, amended: SI 2008/2683 Sch.1 para.173
Sch.1 Part B, amended: SI 2008/2683 Sch.1 para.173

3457. Race Relations Act 1976 (General Statutory Duty) Order 2001
Sch.1, amended: SI 2008/576 Sch.5 para.8, SI 2008/2683 Sch.1 para.174

3458. Race Relations Act 1976 (Statutory Duties) Order 2001
Art.2, varied: SI 2008/912 Sch.2 para.4
Art.4, applied: SI 2008/228 Sch.1 para.20
Art.5, varied: SI 2008/912 Sch.2 para.4
Sch.1, amended: SI 2008/912 Sch.2 para.4, SI 2008/960 Sch.3, SI 2008/2831 Sch.1 para.12, Sch.2 para.5
Sch.3, amended: SI 2008/2683 Sch.1 para.175

3510. Seeds (National Lists of Varieties) Regulations 2001
Reg.16, amended: SI 2008/2683 Sch.1 para.176

NO.

2001–cont.

3541. Potatoes Originating in Germany, Notification (Wales) Order 2001
revoked: SI 2008/2781 Art.3

3561. Rent Officers (Housing Benefit Functions) (Amendment) Order 2001
see *R. (on the application of Heffernan) v Rent Service* [2008] UKHL 58, [2008] 1 W.L.R. 1702 (HL), Lord Hope of Craighead

3606. Goods Vehicles (Authorisation of International Journeys) (Fees) Regulations 2001
Reg.3, amended: SI 2008/1576 Reg.2

3625. Financial Services and Markets Act 2000 (Control of Business Transfers) (Requirements on Applicants) Regulations 2001
Reg.3, amended: SI 2008/1467 Reg.2
Reg.4, amended: SI 2008/1467 Reg.2

3626. Financial Services and Markets Act 2000 (Control of Transfers of Business Done at Lloyd's) Order 2001
Art.2, amended: SI 2008/1725 Art.2
Art.3, amended: SI 2008/1725 Art.2
Art.4, amended: SI 2008/1725 Art.2
Art.5, amended: SI 2008/1725 Art.2

3629. Financial Services and Markets Act 2000 (Consequential Amendments) (Taxes) Order 2001
Art.14, revoked: SI 2008/381 Sch.1 Part 2

3649. Financial Services and Markets Act 2000 (Consequential Amendments and Repeals) Order 2001
Art.386, revoked: SI 2008/1816 Sch.2

3686. Intervention Board for Agricultural Produce (Abolition) Regulations 2001
Reg.6, revoked (in part): SI 2008/576 Sch.5 para.8

3698. Contracting Out (Administrative and Other Court Staff) Order 2001
Art.2, substituted: SI 2008/2791 Art.2

3712. Mental Health Act 1983 (Remedial) Order 2001
revoked: SI 2008/2828 Art.15

3744. Abolition of the NHS Tribunal (Consequential Provisions) Regulations 2001
Reg.6, applied: SI 2008/2252 Sch.1 para.6

3745. Smoke Control Areas (Authorised Fuels) (England) Regulations 2001
revoked: SI 2008/514 Sch.2

3750. Family Health Services Appeal Authority (Procedure) Rules 2001
referred to: SI 2008/1700 Reg.17
Part I r.2, amended: SI 2008/1700 Sch.1 para.8
Part II r.5, referred to: SI 2008/1187 Sch.1 para.12
Part II r.6, applied: SI 2008/1187 Sch.1 para.13
Part III, applied: SI 2008/1187 Sch.1 para.14

NO.

2001–cont.

3750. Family Health Services Appeal Authority (Procedure) Rules 2001–*cont.*

Part IV r.32, applied: SI 2008/1187 Sch.1 para.15

Part IV r.33, applied: SI 2008/1187 Sch.1 para.15

Part IV r.37, applied: SI 2008/1187 Sch.1 para.15

Part IV r.42, applied: SI 2008/1187 Sch.1 para.16

Part IV r.43, applied: SI 2008/1187 Sch.1 para.16

Part IV r.44, applied: SI 2008/1187 Sch.1 para.15

Part IV r.45, applied: SI 2008/1187 Sch.1 para.15

Part V r.46, applied: SI 2008/1187 Sch.1 para.17

3832. Trade Marks (Amendment) Rules 2001

revoked: SI 2008/1797 Sch.2

3929. Civil Jurisdiction and Judgments Order 2001

Sch.1 para.12, see *Gomez v Gomez-Monche Vives* [2008] EWCA Civ 1065, [2008] 2 C.L.C. 494 (CA (Civ Div)), Jacob, L.J.; see *Gomez v Gomez-Monche Vives* [2008] EWHC 259 (Ch), [2008] 3 W.L.R. 309 (Ch D), Morgan, J.

3938. Education (Induction Arrangements for School Teachers) (Consolidation) (England) (Amendment) Regulations 2001

revoked: SI 2008/657 Sch.1

3965. Care Homes Regulations 2001

applied: 2008 c.14 s.17

3967. Children's Homes Regulations 2001

applied: 2008 c.14 s.17

3968. Private and Voluntary Health Care (England) Regulations 2001

applied: 2008 c.14 s.17

Reg.2, amended: SI 2008/2352 Reg.2

Reg.3, amended: SI 2008/2352 Reg.3

Reg.3, revoked (in part): SI 2008/2352 Reg.3

Reg.4, amended: SI 2008/2352 Reg.4

Reg.5, substituted: SI 2008/2352 Reg.5

Reg.26, amended: SI 2008/2352 Reg.6

Reg.47, amended: SI 2008/2828 Art.16

3969. National Care Standards Commission (Registration) Regulations 2001

applied: 2008 c.14 s.17

3981. Goods Vehicles (Enforcement Powers) Regulations 2001

Reg.11, revoked (in part): SI 2008/2683 Sch.1 para.177

3998. Misuse of Drugs Regulations 2001

referred to: SI 2008/2297 Sch.3 para.6

Sch.2, referred to: SI 2008/3239 Reg.9

NO.

2001–cont.

4011. Electricity and Gas (Energy Efficiency Obligations) Order 2001

applied: SI 2008/188 Art.2, Art.12

4022. Social Security (Loss of Benefit) Regulations 2001

Reg.2, amended: SI 2008/787 Art.3, SI 2008/1554 Reg.56

Reg.3, amended: SI 2008/1554 Reg.56

4066. Borough of Bedford (Electoral Changes) Order 2001

Art.3, revoked: SI 2008/907 Art.29

Art.9, revoked: SI 2008/907 Art.29

4067. District of Mid Bedfordshire (Electoral Changes) Order 2001

Art.3, revoked: SI 2008/907 Art.30

4068. District of South Bedfordshire (Electoral Changes) Order 2001

Art.2, revoked: SI 2008/907 Art.31

Art.3, revoked: SI 2008/907 Art.31

Art.8, revoked: SI 2008/907 Art.31

2002

57. Fostering Services Regulations 2002

applied: 2008 c.14 s.17

Reg.24, amended: SI 2008/640 Reg.2

111. Al-Qa'ida and Taliban (United Nations Measures) Order 2002

referred to: 2008 c.28 s.64

Art.8, revoked (in part): 2008 c.28 Sch.9 Part 4

206. Local Government Pension Scheme (Amendment) Regulations 2002

revoked: SI 2008/238 Sch.1

233. Police Act 1997 (Criminal Records) Regulations 2002

Reg.5A, amended: SI 2008/2143 Reg.2

Reg.8A, substituted: SI 2008/2143 Reg.3

236. Medicines (Codification Amendments Etc.) Regulations 2002

Reg.16, revoked: SI 2008/552 Sch.7

240. Sheep and Goats Identification and Movement (Interim Measures) (England) Order 2002

applied: SI 2008/130 Art.22, Art.30

253. Nursing and Midwifery Order (2001) 2002

applied: SI 2008/2927 Reg.2

Art.3, amended: SI 2008/1485 Sch.1 para.1

Art.3, enabled: SI 2008/2553

Art.3, revoked (in part): SI 2008/1485 Sch.1 para.1

Art.3, varied: 2008 c.14 Sch.10 para.1

Art.5, applied: SI 2008/1206 Sch.1, SI 2008/1207 Art.2, SI 2008/1741 Reg.57, SI 2008/1858 Reg.5, SI 2008/2436 Sch.1 para.1, SI 2008/2441 Art.2

Art.6A, added: SI 2008/1485 Sch.1 para.2

Art.7, amended: SI 2008/1485 Sch.1 para.3

Art.22, amended: 2008 c.14 Sch.10 para.14, SI 2008/1485 Sch.1 para.4

NO.

2002–cont.

253. Nursing and Midwifery Order (2001) 2002–*cont.*

Art.22, applied: SI 2008/3148 Sch.1
Art.22, enabled: SI 2008/3148
Art.26, applied: SI 2008/3148 Sch.1
Art.26, enabled: SI 2008/3148
Art.30, applied: SI 2008/3148 Sch.1
Art.30, enabled: SI 2008/3148
Art.31, applied: SI 2008/2553 Art.7
Art.32, amended: SI 2008/1485 Sch.1 para.5
Art.32, applied: SI 2008/3148 Sch.1
Art.32, enabled: SI 2008/3148
Art.33, applied: SI 2008/3148 Sch.1
Art.33, enabled: SI 2008/3148
Art.37, amended: SI 2008/1485 Sch.1 para.6
Art.47, applied: SI 2008/3148, SI 2008/3148 Sch.1
Art.47, enabled: SI 2008/3148
Art.48, amended: SI 2008/1485 Sch.1 para.7
Art.48, applied: SI 2008/3148
Art.50, substituted: SI 2008/1485 Sch.1 para.8
Art.52, amended: SI 2008/1485 Sch.1 para.9
Sch.1 Part I para.1, amended: SI 2008/1485 Sch.1 para.12
Sch.1 Part I para.1, revoked: SI 2008/1485 Sch.1 para.10
Sch.1 Part I para.1, substituted: SI 2008/1485 Sch.1 para.10
Sch.1 Part I para.1A, applied: SI 2008/2553 Art.6
Sch.1 Part I para.1B, enabled: SI 2008/2553
Sch.1 Part I para.2, amended: SI 2008/1485 Sch.1 para.12
Sch.1 Part I para.2, revoked: SI 2008/1485 Sch.1 para.10
Sch.1 Part I para.2, substituted: SI 2008/1485 Sch.1 para.10
Sch.1 Part I para.3, revoked: SI 2008/1485 Sch.1 para.10
Sch.1 Part I para.3, substituted: SI 2008/1485 Sch.1 para.10
Sch.1 Part I para.4, revoked: SI 2008/1485 Sch.1 para.10
Sch.1 Part I para.4, substituted: SI 2008/1485 Sch.1 para.10
Sch.1 Part I para.5, revoked: SI 2008/1485 Sch.1 para.10
Sch.1 Part I para.5, substituted: SI 2008/1485 Sch.1 para.10
Sch.1 Part I para.6, revoked: SI 2008/1485 Sch.1 para.10
Sch.1 Part I para.6, substituted: SI 2008/1485 Sch.1 para.10
Sch.1 Part I para.7, revoked: SI 2008/1485 Sch.1 para.10
Sch.1 Part I para.7, substituted: SI 2008/1485 Sch.1 para.10
Sch.1 Part I para.8, amended: SI 2008/1485 Sch.1 para.12

NO.

2002–cont.

253. Nursing and Midwifery Order (2001) 2002–*cont.*

Sch.1 Part I para.8, revoked: SI 2008/1485 Sch.1 para.10
Sch.1 Part I para.8, substituted: SI 2008/1485 Sch.1 para.10
Sch.1 Part I para.9, revoked: SI 2008/1485 Sch.1 para.10
Sch.1 Part I para.9, substituted: SI 2008/1485 Sch.1 para.10
Sch.1 Part I para.10, revoked: SI 2008/1485 Sch.1 para.10
Sch.1 Part I para.10, substituted: SI 2008/1485 Sch.1 para.10
Sch.1 Part I para.11, revoked: SI 2008/1485 Sch.1 para.10
Sch.1 Part I para.11, substituted: SI 2008/1485 Sch.1 para.10
Sch.1 Part I para.12, substituted: SI 2008/1485 Sch.1 para.10
Sch.1 Part I para.14, amended: SI 2008/1485 Sch.1 para.10
Sch.1 Part I para.14, revoked (in part): SI 2008/1485 Sch.1 para.10
Sch.1 Part I para.15, revoked (in part): SI 2008/1485 Sch.1 para.10
Sch.1 Part II para.16, amended: SI 2008/1485 Sch.1 para.10
Sch.1 Part II para.16, applied: SI 2008/3148 Sch.1
Sch.1 Part II para.16, enabled: SI 2008/3148
Sch.1 Part II para.17, applied: SI 2008/3148 Sch.1
Sch.1 Part II para.17, enabled: SI 2008/3148
Sch.1 Part II para.17, substituted: SI 2008/1485 Sch.1 para.10
Sch.1 Part II para.18, amended: SI 2008/1485 Sch.1 para.10
Sch.1 Part II para.18, revoked (in part): SI 2008/1485 Sch.1 para.10
Sch.2 para.6, revoked: SI 2008/1485 Sch.1 para.12
Sch.4, amended: SI 2008/1485 Sch.1 para.11
Sch.4, revoked (in part): SI 2008/1485 Sch.1 para.11

254. Health Professions Order 2001. 2002

applied: SI 2008/2927 Reg.2
Art.5, applied: SI 2008/1206 Sch.1, SI 2008/1858 Reg.5, SI 2008/2436 Sch.1 para.1, SSI 2008/306 Art.3
Art.11, applied: SSI 2008/306 Art.4
Art.14, applied: SSI 2008/306 Art.4
Art.16, applied: SSI 2008/306 Art.4
Art.18, applied: SSI 2008/306 Art.4
Art.22, amended: 2008 c.14 Sch.10 para.15

274. Sheep and Goats Identification and Movement (Interim Measures) (Wales) Regulations 2002

applied: SI 2008/130 Art.22, Art.30

NO.

2002–cont.

303. Community Care (Personal Care and Nursing Care) (Scotland) Regulations 2002
Reg.2, see *Argyll and Bute Council v Scottish Public Services Ombudsman* 2008 S.L.T. 168 (OH), Lord Macphail

324. Care Homes (Wales) Regulations 2002
applied: 2008 c.14 s.17
see *Welsh Ministers v Care Standards Tribunal* [2008] EWHC 49 (Admin), [2008] 1 W.L.R. 2097 (QBD (Admin)), Davis, J.

325. Private and Voluntary Health Care (Wales) Regulations 2002
applied: 2008 c.14 s.17

327. Children's Homes (Wales) Regulations 2002
applied: 2008 c.14 s.17

331. Non-Domestic Rating (Rural Rate Relief) (Wales) Order 2002
referred to: SI 2008/2770 Art.12

367. Deregulation (Disposals of Dwelling-houses by Local Authorities) Order 2002
revoked: 2008 c.17 Sch.16

378. School Budget Shares (Prescribed Purposes) (England) Regulations 2002
referred to: SI 2008/228 Sch.3 para.28

435. Education (QCA Levy) Regulations 2002
revoked: SI 2008/923 Reg.2
Reg.8, amended: SI 2008/948 Sch.1 para.29

458. Dairy Produce Quotas (General Provisions) Regulations 2002
Reg.2, substituted: SI 2008/438 Reg.2
Reg.4, amended: SI 2008/438 Reg.2

528. Environmental Protection (Controls on Ozone-Depleting Substances) Regulations 2002
Reg.1A, added: SI 2008/91 Sch.1 para.1
Reg.2, amended: SI 2008/91 Sch.1 para.2
Reg.3, substituted: SI 2008/91 Sch.1 para.3
Reg.7, amended: SI 2008/91 Sch.1 para.4
Reg.9, substituted: SI 2008/91 Sch.1 para.5
Reg.10, substituted: SI 2008/91 Sch.1 para.5
Reg.11, substituted: SI 2008/91 Sch.1 para.5
Reg.12, substituted: SI 2008/91 Sch.1 para.5
Reg.13, substituted: SI 2008/91 Sch.1 para.5
Reg.14, substituted: SI 2008/91 Sch.1 para.5
Sch.1 Part 1 para.1, amended: SI 2008/91 Sch.1 para.6
Sch.1 Part II para.12, amended: SI 2008/91 Sch.1 para.7

542. Medicines for Human Use and Medical Devices (Fees and Miscellaneous Amendments) Regulations 2002
Reg.5, revoked: SI 2008/552 Sch.7
Sch.1, revoked: SI 2008/552 Sch.7

NO.

2002–cont.

546. Children Act (Miscellaneous Amendments) (England) Regulations 2002
applied: 2008 c.14 s.17

618. Medical Devices Regulations 2002
see *Hyaltech Ltd, Petitioners* [2008] CSIH 64 (IH (Ex Div)), Lady Paton
Reg.2, amended: SI 2008/2936 Reg.2
Reg.2, see *Hyaltech Ltd, Petitioners* [2008] CSIH 64 (IH (Ex Div)), Lady Paton
Reg.3, amended: SI 2008/2936 Reg.3
Reg.3, revoked (in part): SI 2008/2936 Reg.3
Reg.5, amended: SI 2008/2936 Reg.4
Reg.8, amended: SI 2008/2936 Reg.5
Reg.9, amended: SI 2008/2936 Reg.6
Reg.14, amended: SI 2008/2936 Reg.7
Reg.15, amended: SI 2008/2936 Reg.8
Reg.16, amended: SI 2008/2936 Reg.9
Reg.18, amended: SI 2008/2936 Reg.10
Reg.19, amended: SI 2008/2936 Reg.11
Reg.21, substituted: SI 2008/2936 Reg.12
Reg.29, amended: SI 2008/2936 Reg.13
Reg.30, amended: SI 2008/2936 Reg.14
Reg.31, amended: SI 2008/2936 Reg.15
Reg.47, amended: SI 2008/2936 Reg.16
Reg.54, amended: SI 2008/530 Reg.3
Reg.55, amended: SI 2008/530 Reg.3
Reg.56, amended: SI 2008/530 Reg.3
Reg.60, amended: SI 2008/2936 Reg.17
Reg.63, amended: SI 2008/2936 Reg.18
Reg.63, revoked (in part): SI 2008/2936 Reg.18

691. Companies (Forms) (Amendment) Regulations 2002
Sch.1, revoked: SI 2008/1861 Reg.3

692. Trade Marks (International Registration) (Amendment) Order 2002
revoked: SI 2008/2206 Sch.7

719. ABRO Trading Fund Order 2002
revoked: SI 2008/563 Art.6

744. Nitrate Sensitive Areas (Amendment) Regulations 2002
revoked: SI 2008/2349 Reg.50

761. Aggregates Levy (General) Regulations 2002
Reg.15, amended: SI 2008/1482 Reg.7
Reg.18, amended: SI 2008/1482 Reg.7
Reg.29, amended: SI 2008/1482 Reg.7, Reg.8, SI 2008/2693 Reg.4

794. Ministry of Agriculture, Fisheries and Food (Dissolution) Order 2002
Art.2, applied: SI 2008/1523
Art.6, applied: SI 2008/1523

796. Criminal Injuries Compensation (Northern Ireland) Order 2002
applied: SI 2008/1596 Reg.7

798. Air Navigation (Environmental Standards) Order 2002
revoked: SI 2008/3133 Art.2

NO.

2002–cont.

816. Protection of Children and Vulnerable Adults and Care Standards Tribunal Regulations 2002
revoked: SI 2008/2683 Sch.2
Reg.1, amended: SI 2008/1802 Reg.2
Reg.4, amended: SI 2008/1802 Reg.3
Sch.2 para.3, amended: SI 2008/1802 Reg.4
Sch.7 para.1, amended: SI 2008/1802 Reg.5

819. Local Government Pension Scheme (Miscellaneous) Regulations 2002
revoked: SI 2008/238 Sch.1

827. General Osteopathic Council (Election of Members and Chairman of Council) Rules Order of Council 2002
revoked: SI 2008/1774 Sch.5 para.4

844. Bail (Electronic Monitoring of Requirements) (Responsible Officer) Order 2002
revoked: SI 2008/2713 Art.4

865. Care Standards Act 2000 (Establishments and Agencies) (Miscellaneous Amendments) Regulations 2002
applied: 2008 c.14 s.17

881. Nursing and Midwifery Order 2001 (Consequential Amendments) Order 2002
Sch.1 para.22, revoked (in part): SI 2008/1741 Sch.2

919. Registration of Social Care and Independent Health Care (Wales) Regulations 2002
applied: 2008 c.14 s.17
Reg.1, amended: SI 2008/1976 Reg.21
Reg.2, amended: SI 2008/1976 Reg.21

1015. Bus Service Operators Grant (England) Regulations 2002
Reg.3, amended: SI 2008/1879 Reg.12

1040. A282 Trunk Road (Dartford-Thurrock Crossing Charging Scheme) Order 2002
revoked: SI 2008/1951 Art.7

1078. Air Navigation (Jersey) (Amendment No.2) Order 2002
revoked: SI 2008/2562 Art.2

1102. Value Added Tax (Buildings and Land) Order 2002
revoked: SI 2008/1146 Sch.1 para.24

1131. Artificial Insemination of Cattle (Animal Health) (Amendment) (Wales) Regulations 2002
revoked: SI 2008/1040 Sch.10 Part 2

1263. General Chiropractic Council (Election of Members and Chairman of Council) Rules Order 2002
revoked: SI 2008/1774 Sch.5 para.5

1311. National Health Service (Compensation for Premature Retirement) Regulations 2002
Reg.4, amended: SI 2008/655 Reg.4

NO.

2002–cont.

1331. Education (QCA Levy) (Amendment) Regulations 2002
revoked: SI 2008/923 Reg.2

1355. Offshore Chemicals Regulations 2002
applied: SI 2008/2852 Sch.6 para.1
Reg.16, applied: SI 2008/2852 Sch.7 para.6
Reg.18, applied: SI 2008/2852 Sch.6 para.14

1357. Sheep and Goats Identification and Movement (Interim Measures) (Wales) Order 2002
applied: SI 2008/130 Art.22, Art.30

1379. Social Security and Child Support (Decisions and Appeals) (Miscellaneous Amendments) Regulations 2002
referred to: SI 2008/2683 Art.3
Reg.9, revoked: SI 2008/2683 Sch.2
Reg.10, revoked (in part): SI 2008/2683 Sch.2
Reg.13, revoked (in part): SI 2008/2683 Sch.2
Reg.14, revoked (in part): SI 2008/2683 Sch.2
Reg.15, revoked (in part): SI 2008/2683 Sch.2
Reg.16, revoked (in part): SI 2008/2683 Sch.2
Reg.17, revoked (in part): SI 2008/2683 Sch.2
Reg.18, revoked (in part): SI 2008/2683 Sch.2
Reg.19, revoked: SI 2008/2683 Sch.2
Reg.20, revoked (in part): SI 2008/2683 Sch.2
Reg.22, revoked: SI 2008/2683 Sch.2
Reg.27, revoked (in part): SI 2008/2683 Sch.2
Reg.28, revoked: SI 2008/2683 Sch.2

1438. Health Service (Control of Patient Information) Regulations 2002
see *Lewis v Secretary of State for Health* [2008] EWHC 2196 (QB), [2008] LS Law Medical 559 (QBD), Foskett, J.

1505. National Care Standards Commission (Fees and Frequency of Inspections) (Amendment) Regulations 2002
applied: 2008 c.14 s.17

1676. Horticultural Development Council (Amendment) Order 2002
revoked: SI 2008/576 Sch.5 para.8

1689. Chemicals (Hazard Information and Packaging for Supply) Regulations 2002
referred to: SI 2008/2108
Reg.2, amended: SI 2008/2337 Reg.2, SI 2008/2852 Sch.10 para.2
Reg.3, amended: SI 2008/2108 Reg.5
Reg.4, amended: SI 2008/2852 Sch.10 para.3

NO.

2002–*cont.*

1689. Chemicals (Hazard Information and Packaging for Supply) Regulations 2002–*cont.*

Reg.5, substituted: SI 2008/2852 Sch.10 para.4
Reg.8, revoked (in part): SI 2008/2852 Sch.10 Part 2
Reg.8A, amended: SI 2008/2337 Reg.3
Reg.9, amended: SI 2008/2337 Reg.3
Reg.12, revoked (in part): SI 2008/2852 Sch.10 Part 2
Reg.14, amended: SI 2008/960 Sch.3
Sch.3 Part I para.19, revoked (in part): SI 2008/2337 Reg.4
Sch.3 Part II para.2, amended: SI 2008/2337 Reg.4
Sch.3 Part II para.2a, amended: SI 2008/2337 Reg.4
Sch.3 Part II para.6, amended: SI 2008/2337 Sch.1
Sch.3 Part II para.6a, amended: SI 2008/2337 Sch.1
Sch.3 Part III para.1, amended: SI 2008/2337 Sch.2
Sch.3 Part III para.2, amended: SI 2008/2337 Sch.3
Sch.4, revoked: SI 2008/2852 Sch.10 Part 2
Sch.4 para.1, revoked: SI 2008/2852 Sch.10 Part 2
Sch.4 para.2, revoked: SI 2008/2852 Sch.10 Part 2
Sch.4 para.3, revoked: SI 2008/2852 Sch.10 Part 2
Sch.4 para.4, revoked: SI 2008/2852 Sch.10 Part 2
Sch.4 para.5, revoked: SI 2008/2852 Sch.10 Part 2
Sch.4 para.6, revoked: SI 2008/2852 Sch.10 Part 2
Sch.4 para.7, revoked: SI 2008/2852 Sch.10 Part 2
Sch.4 para.8, revoked: SI 2008/2852 Sch.10 Part 2
Sch.4 para.9, revoked: SI 2008/2852 Sch.10 Part 2
Sch.4 para.10, revoked: SI 2008/2852 Sch.10 Part 2
Sch.4 para.11, revoked: SI 2008/2852 Sch.10 Part 2
Sch.4 para.12, revoked: SI 2008/2852 Sch.10 Part 2
Sch.4 para.13, revoked: SI 2008/2852 Sch.10 Part 2
Sch.4 para.14, revoked: SI 2008/2852 Sch.10 Part 2
Sch.4 para.15, revoked: SI 2008/2852 Sch.10 Part 2
Sch.4 para.16, revoked: SI 2008/2852 Sch.10 Part 2
Sch.5 Part II para.1, substituted: SI 2008/2337 Sch.4

NO.

2002–*cont.*

1689. Chemicals (Hazard Information and Packaging for Supply) Regulations 2002–*cont.*

Sch.5 Part II para.2, substituted: SI 2008/2337 Sch.4
Sch.5 Part II para.3, substituted: SI 2008/2337 Sch.4
Sch.5 Part II para.4, substituted: SI 2008/2337 Sch.4
Sch.5 Part II para.5, substituted: SI 2008/2337 Sch.4
Sch.5 Part II para.6, substituted: SI 2008/2337 Sch.4
Sch.5 Part II para.7, substituted: SI 2008/2337 Sch.4
Sch.5 Part II para.8, substituted: SI 2008/2337 Sch.4
Sch.5 Part II para.9, substituted: SI 2008/2337 Sch.4
Sch.5 Part II para.10, substituted: SI 2008/2337 Sch.4
Sch.5 Part II para.11, substituted: SI 2008/2337 Sch.4
Sch.5 Part II para.12, substituted: SI 2008/2337 Sch.4

1703. Social Security (Jobcentre Plus Interviews) Regulations 2002

applied: SI 2008/3051 Reg.13, Sch.1 para.5
Reg.4, amended: SI 2008/3051 Reg.8
Reg.4A, added: SI 2008/3051 Reg.8
Reg.4A, amended: SI 2008/3051 Reg.9, Reg.10
Reg.5, amended: SI 2008/3051 Reg.8
Reg.6, amended: SI 2008/3051 Reg.8
Reg.8, amended: SI 2008/2928 Reg.12, SI 2008/3051 Reg.8
Reg.12, amended: SI 2008/3051 Reg.8
Reg.15, amended: SI 2008/2683 Sch.1 para.178
Reg.16, referred to: SI 2008/2928 Reg.3

1731. Inheritance Tax (Delivery of Accounts) (Excepted Transfers and Excepted Terminations) Regulations 2002

revoked: SI 2008/605 Reg.9

1732. Inheritance Tax (Delivery of Accounts) (Excepted Settlements) Regulations 2002

revoked: SI 2008/606 Reg.8

1739. Youth Justice and Criminal Evidence Act 1999 (Commencement No.7) Order 2002

see *R. v R* [2008] EWCA Crim 678, [2008] 1 W.L.R. 2044 (CA (Crim Div)), Thomas, L.J.

1773. Hydrocarbon Oil (Marking) Regulations 2002

Reg.2, amended: SI 2008/753 Reg.6
Reg.3, amended: SI 2008/753 Reg.6
Reg.4A, added: SI 2008/753 Reg.6
Reg.6, amended: SI 2008/753 Reg.6
Reg.7, amended: SI 2008/753 Reg.6

NO.

2002–cont.

1773. Hydrocarbon Oil (Marking) Regulations 2002–*cont.*
Reg.8, amended: SI 2008/753 Reg.6
Reg.9, amended: SI 2008/753 Reg.6
Reg.11, amended: SI 2008/753 Reg.6
Reg.12, amended: SI 2008/753 Reg.6
Reg.13, amended: SI 2008/753 Reg.6
Reg.14, amended: SI 2008/753 Reg.6
Reg.15, amended: SI 2008/753 Reg.6
Reg.16, amended: SI 2008/753 Reg.6

1792. State Pension Credit Regulations 2002
referred to: SI 2008/632 Art.26
Reg.1, amended: SI 2008/1554 Reg.4, SI 2008/2767 Reg.5, SI 2008/3157 Reg.4
Reg.3, substituted: SI 2008/2424 Reg.3
Reg.3A, added: SI 2008/2424 Reg.3
Reg.4, amended: SI 2008/2767 Reg.5
Reg.5, amended: SI 2008/2424 Reg.3
Reg.5, revoked (in part): SI 2008/2424 Reg.3
Reg.6, amended: SI 2008/632 Art.26
Reg.7, amended: SI 2008/632 Art.26
Reg.9, amended: SI 2008/1554 Reg.4
Reg.13A, amended: SI 2008/1554 Reg.4
Reg.13B, amended: SI 2008/1554 Reg.4
Reg.15, amended: SI 2008/1554 Reg.4, SI 2008/3157 Reg.4
Reg.17B, amended: SI 2008/3157 Reg.4
Sch.1 Part III para.6, amended: SI 2008/1554 Reg.4
Sch.2 para.1, amended: SI 2008/1554 Reg.4
Sch.2 para.4, amended: SI 2008/2767 Reg.5
Sch.2 para.5, amended: SI 2008/698 Reg.5, SI 2008/1554 Reg.4
Sch.2 para.5, applied: SI 2008/794 Sch.6 para.6
Sch.2 para.7, amended: SI 2008/1554 Reg.4
Sch.2 para.8, varied: SI 2008/3195 Reg.12
Sch.2 para.9, amended: SI 2008/3195 Reg.2
Sch.2 para.9, revoked (in part): SI 2008/3195 Reg.2
Sch.2 para.10, amended: SI 2008/1554 Reg.4, SI 2008/2767 Reg.5
Sch.2 para.11, applied: SI 2008/794 Sch.6 para.3
Sch.2 para.12, applied: SI 2008/794 Sch.6 para.3
Sch.2 para.13, applied: SI 2008/794 Sch.6 para.3
Sch.2 para.14, amended: SI 2008/632 Art.26, SI 2008/1554 Reg.4, SI 2008/2767 Reg.5
Sch.3 para.1, amended: SI 2008/632 Art.26, SI 2008/2424 Reg.3
Sch.4 para.1, amended: SI 2008/3157 Reg.4
Sch.4 para.3, amended: SI 2008/3157 Reg.4
Sch.4 para.4, substituted: SI 2008/3157 Reg.4
Sch.4 para.6, amended: SI 2008/3157 Reg.4
Sch.4 para.12, amended: SI 2008/3157 Reg.4

NO.

2002–cont.

1792. State Pension Credit Regulations 2002–*cont.*
Sch.4 para.17, revoked: SI 2008/3157 Reg.4
Sch.5 Part I para.14, substituted: SI 2008/3157 Reg.4
Sch.5 Part I para.15, amended: SI 2008/2767 Reg.5
Sch.5 Part I para.17, amended: SI 2008/3157 Reg.4
Sch.5 Part I para.20, amended: SI 2008/1554 Reg.4, SI 2008/3157 Reg.4
Sch.5 Part I para.20A, amended: SI 2008/1554 Reg.4, SI 2008/3157 Reg.4
Sch.5 Part I para.20A, revoked (in part): SI 2008/3157 Reg.4
Sch.5 Part I para.20B, added: SI 2008/3157 Reg.4
Sch.6 para.4, amended: SI 2008/1554 Reg.4, SI 2008/3157 Reg.4

1822. Anti-terrorism (Financial and Other Measures) (Overseas Territories) Order 2002
Art.4, amended: 2008 c.28 s.75

1837. Penalties for Disorderly Behaviour (Amount of Penalty) Order 2002
Sch.1 Part I, substituted: SI 2008/3297 Sch.1
Sch.1 Part II, substituted: SI 2008/3297 Sch.1

1860. Regulatory Reform (Housing Assistance) (England and Wales) Order 2002
Art.3, applied: SI 2008/2867 Reg.12
Art.3, varied: SI 2008/2867 Reg.12

1873. Representation of the People (Northern Ireland) (Amendment) Regulations 2002
revoked: SI 2008/1741 Sch.2

1915. Child Support Appeals (Jurisdiction of Courts) Order 2002
applied: SI 2008/2836 Art.5
Art.3, amended: SI 2008/2683 Sch.1 para.180
Art.5, substituted: SI 2008/2683 Sch.1 para.181

1920. Abolition of the NHS Tribunal (Consequential Provisions) Regulations 2002
Reg.6, applied: SI 2008/2252 Sch.1 para.6

1985. Special Educational Needs and Disability Tribunal (General Provisions and Disability Claims Procedure) Regulations 2002
Reg.1, amended: SI 2008/2683 Sch.1 para.183
Reg.2, amended: SI 2008/2683 Sch.1 para.184
Reg.3, amended: SI 2008/2683 Sch.1 para.185
Reg.4, amended: SI 2008/2683 Sch.1 para.186
Reg.30, revoked (in part): SI 2008/2683 Sch.1 para.187

NO.

2002–cont.

1985. Special Educational Needs and Disability Tribunal (General Provisions and Disability Claims Procedure) Regulations 2002–*cont.*

Reg.39A, added: SI 2008/2683 Sch.1 para.188

Reg.48, amended: SI 2008/2683 Sch.1 para.189

2005. Working Tax Credit (Entitlement and Maximum Rate) Regulations 2002

Reg.2, amended: SI 2008/1879 Reg.20

Reg.6, amended: SI 2008/1879 Reg.20

Reg.9, amended: SI 2008/1879 Reg.20

Reg.13, amended: SI 2008/1879 Reg.20

Reg.14, amended: SI 2008/604 Reg.3, SI 2008/2169 Reg.2

Reg.14, revoked (in part): SI 2008/604 Reg.3, SI 2008/2169 Reg.2

Reg.18, amended: SI 2008/1879 Reg.20

Reg.20, referred to: SI 2008/794 Reg.8

Sch.2, amended: SI 2008/796 Sch.1

2006. Tax Credits (Definition and Calculation of Income) Regulations 2002

Reg.4, amended: SI 2008/604 Reg.2, SI 2008/2169 Reg.4

Reg.5, revoked (in part): SI 2008/604 Reg.2

Reg.7, amended: SI 2008/1879 Reg.21

Reg.8, amended: SI 2008/2169 Reg.5

2007. Child Tax Credit Regulations 2002

Reg.2, amended: SI 2008/2169 Reg.7

Reg.3, amended: SI 2008/1879 Reg.22, SI 2008/2169 Reg.8

Reg.4, substituted: SI 2008/2169 Reg.9

Reg.5, amended: SI 2008/1879 Reg.22, SI 2008/2169 Reg.10

Reg.7, amended: SI 2008/796 Reg.2

2008. Tax Credits (Income Thresholds and Determination of Rates) Regulations 2002

Reg.3, amended: SI 2008/796 Reg.4

Reg.4, amended: SI 2008/1879 Reg.23

Reg.7, amended: SI 2008/796 Reg.4

Reg.8, amended: SI 2008/796 Reg.4

2014. Tax Credits (Claims and Notifications) Regulations 2002

Reg.5, amended: SI 2008/2169 Reg.12

Reg.5, applied: SI 2008/3151 Art.2

Reg.11, amended: SI 2008/604 Reg.4

Reg.13, amended: SI 2008/2169 Reg.13

2022. Bus Service Operators Grant (Wales) Regulations 2002

Reg.3, amended: SI 2008/1879 Reg.25

2034. Fixed-term Employees (Prevention of Less Favourable Treatment) Regulations 2002

Reg.11, see *Revenue and Customs Commissioners v Thorn Baker Ltd* [2007] EWCA Civ 626, [2008] I.C.R. 46 (CA (Civ Div)), Auld, L.J.

NO.

2002–cont.

2034. Fixed-term Employees (Prevention of Less Favourable Treatment) Regulations 2002–*cont.*

Reg.19, see *Revenue and Customs Commissioners v Thorn Baker Ltd* [2007] EWCA Civ 626, [2008] I.C.R. 46 (CA (Civ Div)), Auld, L.J.

Reg.19, amended: SI 2008/2776 Reg.2

2063. Education (Induction Arrangements for School Teachers) (Consolidation) (Amendment) (England) Regulations 2002

revoked: SI 2008/657 Sch.1

2070. National Care Standards Commission (Fees and Frequency of Inspections) Amendment (No.2) Regulations 2002

applied: 2008 c.14 s.17

2086. Education (Teacher Student Loans) (Repayment etc.) Regulations 2002

Reg.11, applied: SI 2008/794 Sch.8 para.14

2092. Street Works (Inspection Fees) (England) Regulations 2002

Reg.3, amended: SI 2008/589 Reg.3

2114. Schools Forums (England) Regulations 2002

applied: SI 2008/2867 Reg.25

varied: SI 2008/2867 Reg.25

Reg.1, amended: SI 2008/47 Reg.2

Reg.2, varied: SI 2008/2867 Reg.25

Reg.3, amended: SI 2008/47 Reg.2

Reg.4, amended: SI 2008/47 Reg.2

Reg.4A, amended: SI 2008/47 Reg.2

Reg.5, substituted: SI 2008/47 Reg.2

Reg.6, amended: SI 2008/47 Reg.2

Reg.7, revoked: SI 2008/47 Reg.2

Reg.9, varied: SI 2008/2867 Reg.25

2153. Sheep and Goats Identification and Movement (Interim Measures) (England) (No.2) Order 2002

applied: SI 2008/130 Art.22, Art.30

2173. Tax Credits (Payments by the Commissioners) Regulations 2002

Reg.11, amended: SI 2008/2683 Sch.1 para.190

Reg.12, amended: SI 2008/604 Reg.5

2176. Notification of New Substances (Amendment) Regulations 2002

revoked: SI 2008/2852 Sch.10 Part 2

2202. National Health Service Reform and Health Care Professions Act 2002 (Commencement No.1) Order 2002

Art.2, varied: 2008 c.14 Sch.10 para.1

2232. Public Trustee (Fees) (Amendment) Order 2002

revoked: SI 2008/611 Art.32

2297. Protection of Water Against Agricultural Nitrate Pollution (Amendment) (Wales) Regulations 2002

applied: SI 2008/3143 Reg.4

revoked: SI 2008/3143 Reg.50

NO.

2002–cont.

2302. Sheep and Goats Identification and Movement (Interim Measures) (Wales) (No.2) Order 2002
applied: SI 2008/130 Art.22, Art.30

2315. Beef Labelling (Enforcement) (England) (Amendment) Regulations 2002
revoked: SI 2008/3252 Reg.11

2323. Social Fund (Miscellaneous Amendments) Regulations 2002
revoked: SI 2008/2265 Reg.9

2375. National Health Service (Functions of Strategic Health Authorities and Primary Care Trusts and Administration Arrangements) (England) Regulations 2002
Reg.2, amended: SI 2008/3166 Reg.5
Reg.3, amended: SI 2008/3166 Reg.5
Reg.6, amended: SI 2008/2496 Reg.6, SI 2008/2677 Reg.6
Reg.10, amended: SI 2008/3166 Reg.5
Sch.1 Part 1, amended: SI 2008/1700 Sch.1 para.9
Sch.1 Part 2, amended: SI 2008/3166 Reg.5
Sch.5, amended: SI 2008/224 Reg.2
Sch.5, referred to: SI 2008/224 Reg.2

2376. Council for the Regulation of Health Care Professionals (Appointment etc.) Regulations 2002
revoked: SI 2008/2927 Reg.9

2593. District of Penwith (Electoral Changes) Order 2002
Art.9, revoked: SI 2008/491 Art.14

2614. Nitrate Vulnerable Zones (Additional Designations) (England) (No.2) Regulations 2002
applied: SI 2008/2349 Reg.4
revoked: SI 2008/2349 Reg.50

2622. Children Act 1989 and the Care Standards Act 2000 (Miscellaneous Regulations) (Amendment) (Wales) Regulations 2002
applied: 2008 c.14 s.17

2676. Control of Lead at Work Regulations 2002
applied: SI 2008/736 Reg.7
Reg.2, amended: SI 2008/960 Sch.3
Reg.10, amended: SI 2008/960 Sch.3

2677. Control of Substances Hazardous to Health Regulations 2002
applied: SI 2008/736 Sch.5, SSI 2008/100 Sch.2 Part 1
Reg.2, amended: SI 2008/960 Sch.3
Reg.4, revoked (in part): SI 2008/2852 Sch.10 para.6, Sch.10 Part 2
Reg.11, amended: SI 2008/960 Sch.3
Sch.2, amended: SI 2008/2852 Sch.10 Part 2
Sch.3 Part I para.3, amended: SI 2008/960 Sch.3
Sch.5, amended: SI 2008/960 Sch.3

NO.

2002–cont.

2685. Town and Country Planning (Enforcement) (Determination by Inspectors) (Inquiries Procedure) (England) Rules 2002
r.11, amended: SI 2008/2831 Sch.4 para.1

2686. Town and Country Planning (Enforcement) (Inquiries Procedure) (England) Rules 2002
r.13, amended: SI 2008/2831 Sch.4 para.1

2742. Road Vehicles (Registration and Licensing) Regulations 2002
Reg.10, amended: SI 2008/642 Reg.2
Reg.27, amended: SI 2008/2849 Reg.2
Reg.27, revoked (in part): SI 2008/2849 Reg.2
Sch.2 para.12, amended: SI 2008/1444 Reg.3
Sch.2 para.13, amended: SI 2008/1444 Reg.3
Sch.3 para.7, amended: SI 2008/1444 Reg.4

2786. Air Navigation (Dangerous Goods) Regulations 2002
Reg.3, amended: SI 2008/1943 Reg.2, SI 2008/2429 Reg.2

2788. Paternity and Adoption Leave Regulations 2002
Reg.19, amended: SI 2008/1966 Reg.9
Reg.21, revoked: SI 2008/1966 Reg.9
Reg.21A, applied: SI 2008/239 Reg.18, SSI 2008/228 Reg.15
Reg.27, amended: SI 2008/1966 Reg.10
Reg.29, see *Atkins v Coyle Personnel Plc* [2008] I.R.L.R. 420 (EAT), Nelson, J.

2818. Statutory Paternity Pay and Statutory Adoption Pay (Weekly Rates) Regulations 2002
Reg.2, amended: SI 2008/632 Art.11
Reg.3, amended: SI 2008/632 Art.11

2842. Architects Qualifications (EC Recognition) Order 2002
Art.3, revoked: SI 2008/1331 Reg.25
Art.5, revoked: SI 2008/1331 Reg.25
Art.6, amended: SI 2008/1331 Reg.25
Art.6, revoked (in part): SI 2008/1331 Reg.25

2896. Education (Determination of Admission Arrangements) (Amendment) (England) Regulations 2002
revoked: SI 2008/3089 Sch.1

2897. Education (School Information) (England) Regulations 2002
revoked: SI 2008/3093 Sch.1

2899. Education (Admissions Appeals Arrangements) (England) Regulations 2002
Reg.2, amended: SI 2008/3092 Reg.3
Reg.4, revoked (in part): SI 2008/3092 Reg.4
Reg.6, substituted: SI 2008/3092 Reg.5
Sch.2 para.1, substituted: SI 2008/3092 Reg.6
Sch.2 para.2, substituted: SI 2008/3092 Reg.6

NO.

2002–cont.

2900. Education (Admission Forums) (England) Regulations 2002

revoked: SI 2008/3091 Reg.3

2926. Tax Credits (Appeals) Regulations 2002

amended: SI 2008/2683 Sch.1 para.201

Reg.2, amended: SI 2008/2683 Sch.1 para.192

Reg.3, amended: SI 2008/2683 Sch.1 para.193

Reg.4, amended: SI 2008/2683 Sch.1 para.194

Reg.5, amended: SI 2008/2683 Sch.1 para.195

Reg.6, amended: SI 2008/2683 Sch.1 para.196

Reg.6, revoked (in part): SI 2008/2683 Sch.1 para.196

Reg.7, amended: SI 2008/2683 Sch.1 para.197

Reg.8, amended: SI 2008/2683 Sch.1 para.198

Reg.9, amended: SI 2008/2683 Sch.1 para.199

Reg.10, amended: SI 2008/2683 Sch.1 para.200

Reg.11, amended: SI 2008/2683 Sch.1 para.201

Reg.11, revoked (in part): SI 2008/2683 Sch.1 para.201

Reg.12, amended: SI 2008/2683 Sch.1 para.202

2935. Children Act 1989 and the Care Standards Act 2000 (Miscellaneous Regulations) (Amendment) (Wales) (No.2) Regulations 2002

applied: 2008 c.14 s.17

2977. Vehicles Crime (Registration of Registration Plate Suppliers) (England and Wales) Regulations 2002

revoked: SI 2008/1715 Reg.8

3007. Commission for Patient and Public Involvement in Health (Functions) Regulations 2002

Reg.2, revoked: SI 2008/528 Sch.1 para.2

Reg.7, amended: SI 2008/528 Sch.1 para.2

Reg.7, revoked (in part): SI 2008/528 Sch.1 para.2

Reg.8, revoked (in part): SI 2008/528 Sch.1 para.2

3026. Forest Reproductive Material (Great Britain) Regulations 2002

Reg.4, applied: SSI 2008/100 Sch.2 Part 2

3038. Commission for Patient and Public Involvement in Health (Membership and Procedure) Regulations 2002

Reg.5, revoked (in part): SI 2008/528 Sch.1 para.3

NO.

2002–cont.

3045. Sale and Supply of Goods to Consumers Regulations 2002

Reg.15, amended: SI 2008/1277 Sch.2 para.97

3046. Smoke Control Areas (Authorised Fuels) (England) (Amendment) Regulations 2002

revoked: SI 2008/514 Sch.2

3048. Local Authority (Overview and Scrutiny Committees Health Scrutiny Functions) Regulations 2002

Reg.2, amended: SI 2008/528 Reg.18

3049. Police (Retention and Disposal of Motor Vehicles) Regulations 2002

Reg.2, amended: SI 2008/2096 Reg.3

Reg.6, substituted: SI 2008/2096 Reg.4

3057. Hydrocarbon Oil (Registered Dealers in Controlled Oil) Regulations 2002

Reg.3, amended: SI 2008/753 Reg.7

3062. Potato Industry Development Council (Amendment) Order 2002

revoked: SI 2008/576 Sch.5 para.8

3113. Traffic Signs Regulations and General Directions 2002

Reg.8, amended: SI 2008/2177 Reg.3

Reg.10, amended: SI 2008/2177 Reg.4

Reg.11, amended: SI 2008/2177 Reg.5

Reg.18, amended: SI 2008/2177 Reg.6

Reg.32, substituted: SI 2008/2177 Reg.7

Reg.002, amended: SI 2008/2177 Reg.4

Reg.004, added: SI 2008/2177 Sch.1

Reg.004, amended: SI 2008/2177 Reg.4

Reg.006, amended: SI 2008/2177 Reg.4

Reg.041, amended: SI 2008/2177 Reg.3

3135. Medical Act 1983 (Amendment) Order 2002

Sch.1 Part I para.10, applied: SI 2008/2556 Art.3

3136. General Medical Council (Constitution) Order 2002

revoked: SI 2008/1774 Sch.5 para.2

3150. Company Directors Disqualification (Northern Ireland) Order 2002

applied: SI 2008/630 Reg.14, SI 2008/631 Reg.12, SI 2008/2252 Sch.1 para.13, SI 2008/2553 Art.5, SI 2008/2554 Art.5, SI 2008/2558 Reg.3, SI 2008/2927 Reg.2, SI 2008/3047 Art.5, SI 2008/3148 Sch.1

Art.2, amended: SI 2008/948 Sch.1 para.226

Art.2, revoked (in part): SI 2008/948 Sch.2

Art.6, amended: SI 2008/948 Sch.1 para.226

Art.23A, added: SI 2008/948 Sch.1 para.226

Art.25, amended: SI 2008/948 Sch.1 para.226

Sch.1 Part I para.4, amended: SI 2008/948 Sch.1 para.226

Sch.1 Part I para.5, substituted: SI 2008/948 Sch.1 para.226

Sch.1 Part I para.6, amended: SI 2008/948 Sch.1 para.226

NO.

2002–cont.

3150. Company Directors Disqualification (Northern Ireland) Order 2002–*cont.*
Sch.1 Part I para.7, amended: SI 2008/948 Sch.1 para.226

3170. Medicines for Human Use (Kava-kava) (Prohibition) Order 2002
Art.1, amended: SI 2008/548 Art.6
Art.3, amended: SI 2008/548 Art.6

3178. Education (Pupil Exclusions and Appeals) (Maintained Schools) (England) Regulations 2002
applied: SI 2008/532 Sch.1 para.6
see *R. (on the application of B) v Headteacher of St Michael's Church of England School* [2007] EWHC 2052 (Admin), [2008] E.L.R. 116 (QBD (Admin)), Beatson, J.
Sch.1 para.11, substituted: SI 2008/2683 Sch.1 para.203

3179. Education (Pupil Exclusions and Appeals) (Pupil Referral Units) (England) Regulations 2002
applied: SI 2008/532 Sch.1 para.4
referred to: SI 2008/532 Reg.11, Sch.1 para.4
revoked: SI 2008/532 Reg.11

3196. Tax Credits (Appeals) (No.2) Regulations 2002
Reg.1, amended: SI 2008/2683 Sch.1 para.205
Reg.2, amended: SI 2008/2683 Sch.1 para.206
Reg.3, amended: SI 2008/2683 Sch.1 para.207
Reg.4, amended: SI 2008/2683 Sch.1 para.208
Reg.5, amended: SI 2008/2683 Sch.1 para.209
Reg.5, revoked (in part): SI 2008/2683 Sch.1 para.209
Reg.6, revoked: SI 2008/2683 Sch.1 para.210
Reg.7, revoked: SI 2008/2683 Sch.1 para.210
Reg.9, revoked: SI 2008/2683 Sch.1 para.210
Reg.10, revoked: SI 2008/2683 Sch.1 para.210
Reg.11, revoked: SI 2008/2683 Sch.1 para.210
Reg.12, revoked: SI 2008/2683 Sch.1 para.210
Reg.13, revoked: SI 2008/2683 Sch.1 para.210
Reg.14, revoked: SI 2008/2683 Sch.1 para.210
Reg.15, revoked: SI 2008/2683 Sch.1 para.210
Reg.16, revoked: SI 2008/2683 Sch.1 para.210
Reg.17, revoked: SI 2008/2683 Sch.1 para.210
Reg.18, revoked: SI 2008/2683 Sch.1 para.210

NO.

2002–cont.

3196. Tax Credits (Appeals) (No.2) Regulations 2002–*cont.*
Reg.19, revoked: SI 2008/2683 Sch.1 para.210
Reg.20, revoked: SI 2008/2683 Sch.1 para.210
Reg.21, revoked: SI 2008/2683 Sch.1 para.210
Reg.22, revoked: SI 2008/2683 Sch.1 para.210
Reg.23, revoked: SI 2008/2683 Sch.1 para.210
Reg.24, revoked: SI 2008/2683 Sch.1 para.210
Reg.25, revoked: SI 2008/2683 Sch.1 para.210
Reg.26, revoked: SI 2008/2683 Sch.1 para.210
Reg.26A, revoked: SI 2008/2683 Sch.1 para.210
Reg.27, revoked: SI 2008/2683 Sch.1 para.210

3200. Education (Student Support) (No.2) Regulations 2002
applied: SI 2008/3170 Reg.3

3211. National Care Standards Commission (Fees and Frequency of Inspections) Amendment (No.3) Regulations 2002
applied: 2008 c.14 s.17

3212. Nurses Agencies Regulations 2002
applied: 2008 c.14 s.17

3213. Residential Family Centres Regulations 2002
applied: 2008 c.14 s.17

3214. Domiciliary Care Agencies Regulations 2002
applied: 2008 c.14 s.17

3237. Social Security Commissioners (Procedure) (Tax Credits Appeals) Regulations 2002
revoked: SI 2008/2683 Sch.2

3264. Allocation of Housing (England) Regulations 2002
Reg.2, amended: SI 2008/3015 Reg.2
Reg.3, amended: SI 2008/3015 Reg.2

2003

62. Companies (Welsh Language Forms) Regulations 2003
Sch.1, amended: SI 2008/1860 Reg.3

74. Wireless Telegraphy (Exemption) Regulations 2003
Reg.3, amended: SI 2008/2426 Reg.3
Sch.5 Part III, amended: SI 2008/2426 Reg.4
Sch.6 Part III, amended: SI 2008/2426 Reg.5
Sch.7 Part III, amended: SI 2008/236 Reg.2
Sch.11 Part I, added: SI 2008/2426 Reg.6
Sch.11 Part II, added: SI 2008/2426 Reg.6
Sch.11 Part III, added: SI 2008/2426 Reg.6

NO.

2003–cont.

92. Crown Office Fees Order 2003
revoked: SI 2008/1977 Art.3

96. Community Investment Tax Relief (Accreditation of Community Development Finance Institutions) Regulations 2003
Reg.2, amended: SI 2008/383 Reg.3
Reg.3, amended: SI 2008/383 Reg.4
Reg.7, amended: SI 2008/383 Reg.5
Reg.8, substituted: SI 2008/383 Reg.6
Reg.10, amended: SI 2008/383 Reg.9
Reg.12, amended: SI 2008/383 Reg.5
Reg.13, amended: SI 2008/383 Reg.5
Reg.15, amended: SI 2008/383 Reg.5, Reg.7
Reg.15A, added: SI 2008/383 Reg.8
Reg.15B, added: SI 2008/383 Reg.8
Reg.15C, added: SI 2008/383 Reg.8
Reg.15D, added: SI 2008/383 Reg.8
Reg.15E, added: SI 2008/383 Reg.8
Reg.16, amended: SI 2008/383 Reg.5
Sch.1 para.2, amended: SI 2008/383 Reg.5
Sch.1 para.3A, added: SI 2008/383 Reg.10
Sch.1 para.4, amended: SI 2008/383 Reg.5

106. Education (Induction Arrangements for School Teachers) (Consolidation) (England) (Amendment) Regulations 2003
revoked: SI 2008/657 Sch.1

120. Proceeds of Crime Act 2002 (Commencement No.4, Transitional Provisions and Savings) Order 2003
see *R. v Anwoir* [2008] EWCA Crim 1354, [2008] 4 All E.R. 582 (CA (Crim Div)), Latham, L.J.

150. Local Health Boards (Functions) (Wales) Regulations 2003
Reg.2, applied: SI 2008/2437 Reg.3

190. Education (Information as to Provision of Education) (England) (Amendment) Regulations 2003
revoked: SI 2008/4 Sch.3

228. Vehicles Crime (Registration of Registration Plate Suppliers) (England and Wales) (Amendment) Regulations 2003
revoked: SI 2008/1715 Reg.8

237. Fostering Services (Wales) Regulations 2003
applied: 2008 c.14 s.17

329. Rating Lists (Valuation Date) (England) Order 2003
revoked: SI 2008/216 Art.3

331. Children (Allocation of Proceedings) (Amendment) Order 2003
revoked: SI 2008/2836 Sch.2

332. Child Minding and Day Care (Suspension of Registration) (England) Regulations 2003
Reg.3, applied: SI 2008/2261 Sch.2 para.1, Sch.2 para.4, Sch.2 para.24
Reg.8, applied: SI 2008/2261 Sch.2 para.24

NO.

2003–cont.

333. Proceeds of Crime Act 2002 (Commencement No.5, Transitional Provisions, Savings and Amendment) Order 2003
Art.3, see *CPS v Moulden (Leanne)* [2008] EWCA Crim 2648, Times, November 26, 2008 (CA (Crim Div)), Pill, L.J.

335. Proceeds of Crime Act 2002 (Disclosure of Information) Order 2003
revoked: SI 2008/1909 Art.4

367. Voluntary Adoption Agencies and the Adoption Agencies (Miscellaneous Amendments) Regulations 2003
applied: 2008 c.14 s.17

369. National Care Standards Commission (Registration) (Amendment) Regulations 2003
applied: 2008 c.14 s.17

373. Consistent Financial Reporting (England) Regulations 2003
Sch.1, amended: SI 2008/46 Reg.2

399. Movement of Animals (Restrictions) (Wales) Order 2003
applied: SI 2008/1275 Reg.15

417. Protection of Children and Vulnerable Adults (Northern Ireland) Order 2003
applied: SI 2008/1769 Sch.2 para.2
Art.48, referred to: SI 2008/542 Reg.9
Sch.1 para.1, varied: SI 2008/1769 Sch.2 para.2
Sch.1 para.2, varied: SI 2008/1769 Sch.2 para.2
Sch.1 para.3, varied: SI 2008/1769 Sch.2 para.2

419. Energy (Northern Ireland) Order 2003
Art.52, applied: 2008 c.32 s.40
Art.56, varied: 2008 c.32 s.40
Art.63, amended: SI 2008/1277 Sch.2 para.98
Art.63, revoked (in part): SI 2008/1277 Sch.2 para.98, Sch.4 Part 2

425. Proceeds of Crime Act 2002 (Investigations in different parts of the United Kingdom) Order 2003
Art.2, amended: SI 2008/298 Art.2
Art.5, amended: SI 2008/298 Art.2
Art.7, amended: SI 2008/298 Art.2
Art.8, amended: SI 2008/298 Art.2
Art.15, amended: SI 2008/298 Art.2
Art.17, amended: SI 2008/298 Art.2
Art.18, amended: SI 2008/298 Art.2
Art.27, amended: SI 2008/298 Art.2
Art.28, amended: SI 2008/298 Art.2

431. Health and Personal Social Services (Quality, Improvement and Regulation) (Northern Ireland) Order 2003
applied: SI 2008/542 Reg.9
referred to: SI 2008/542 Reg.9
Part III, applied: SI 2008/542 Reg.9
Part VI, applied: SI 2008/542 Reg.9

NO.

2003–cont.

435. Access to Justice (Northern Ireland) Order 2003
Art.25, amended: SI 2008/1216 Sch.5 para.11
Art.26, applied: SI 2008/1216 Art.92
Art.26, referred to: SI 2008/1216 Art.92
Sch.2 para.2, amended: SI 2008/1216 Art.84
Sch.2 para.2, revoked (in part): SI 2008/1216 Sch.6 Part 2
Sch.2 para.3, amended: SI 2008/1216 Art.85

455. Social Security (Working Tax Credit and Child Tax Credit) (Consequential Amendments) Regulations 2003
Sch.1 para.15, revoked: SI 2008/2111 Reg.4
Sch.2 para.15, revoked: SI 2008/2111 Reg.4

492. Child Benefit and Guardian's Allowance (Administration) Regulations 2003
Reg.2, amended: SI 2008/2683 Sch.1 para.211
Reg.28, applied: SI 2008/2682 Reg.6

527. Police Regulations 2003
Reg.15, amended: SI 2008/2865 Reg.2
Reg.33, applied: SI 2008/2864 Reg.3

528. Police (Efficiency) (Amendment) Regulations 2003
revoked: SI 2008/2862 Reg.3

533. Accounts and Audit Regulations 2003
varied: SI 2008/1342 Reg.10
Reg.2, amended: SI 2008/912 Sch.2 para.5

534. Care Homes (Amendment) Regulations 2003
applied: 2008 c.14 s.17

562. Farm Waste Grant (Nitrate Vulnerable Zones) (England) Scheme 2003
revoked: SI 2008/2349 Reg.50

625. Medicines for Human Use and Medical Devices (Fees Amendments) Regulations 2003
Reg.4, revoked: SI 2008/552 Sch.7
Sch.1, revoked: SI 2008/552 Sch.7

626. Protection of Children and Vulnerable Adults and Care Standards Tribunal (Amendment) Regulations 2003
revoked: SI 2008/2683 Sch.2

628. National Assistance (Sums for Personal Requirements) (England) Regulations 2003
Reg.2, amended: SI 2008/593 Reg.2

658. Immigration (Notices) Regulations 2003
Reg.2, amended: SI 2008/1819 Reg.2
Reg.5, amended: SI 2008/684 Reg.2, SI 2008/1819 Reg.2
Reg.7, amended: SI 2008/684 Reg.2

690. Public Trustee (Fees) (Amendment) Order 2003
revoked: SI 2008/611 Art.32

NO.

2003–cont.

751. Energy Information (Household Electric Ovens) Regulations 2003
Sch.6 Part III para.12, amended: SI 2008/1277 Sch.2 para.99
Sch.6 Part III para.12, revoked (in part): SI 2008/1277 Sch.4 Part 2

762. Community Care, Services for Carers and Children's Services (Direct Payments) (England) Regulations 2003
Reg.2, amended: SI 2008/2828 Art.18
Reg.2, revoked (in part): SI 2008/2828 Art.18
Reg.4, see *Casewell v Secretary of State for Work and Pensions* [2008] EWCA Civ 524, (2008) 11 C.C.L. Rep. 684 (CA (Civ Div)), Tuckey, L.J.
Reg.6, see *Casewell v Secretary of State for Work and Pensions* [2008] EWCA Civ 524, (2008) 11 C.C.L. Rep. 684 (CA (Civ Div)), Tuckey, L.J.

781. Residential Family Centres (Wales) Regulations 2003
applied: 2008 c.14 s.17

896. Fostering Services (Wales) (Amendment) Regulations 2003
applied: 2008 c.14 s.17

908. Horticultural Development Council (Amendment) Order 2003
revoked: SI 2008/576 Sch.5 para.8

916. Child Benefit and Guardian's Allowance (Decisions and Appeals) Regulations 2003
Reg.2, amended: SI 2008/2683 Sch.1 para.213
Reg.2, revoked (in part): SI 2008/2683 Sch.1 para.213
Reg.6, amended: SI 2008/2683 Sch.1 para.214
Reg.8, amended: SI 2008/2683 Sch.1 para.215
Reg.10, amended: SI 2008/2683 Sch.1 para.216
Reg.13, amended: SI 2008/2683 Sch.1 para.217
Reg.16, amended: SI 2008/2683 Sch.1 para.218
Reg.17, amended: SI 2008/2683 Sch.1 para.219
Reg.18, amended: SI 2008/2683 Sch.1 para.220
Reg.21, amended: SI 2008/2683 Sch.1 para.221
Reg.23, amended: SI 2008/2683 Sch.1 para.222
Reg.25, amended: SI 2008/2683 Sch.1 para.223
Reg.28, amended: SI 2008/2683 Sch.1 para.224
Reg.28, referred to: SI 2008/2685 Sch.1

NO.

2003–cont.

916. Child Benefit and Guardian's Allowance (Decisions and Appeals) Regulations 2003–*cont.*
Reg.29, amended: SI 2008/2683 Sch.1 para.225
Reg.29A, added: SI 2008/2683 Sch.1 para.226
Reg.30, amended: SI 2008/2683 Sch.1 para.227
Reg.31, amended: SI 2008/2683 Sch.1 para.228
Reg.32, amended: SI 2008/2683 Sch.1 para.229

918. Individual Learning Accounts Wales Regulations 2003
Sch.1 para.8, added: SI 2008/1879 Reg.26

921. Paternity and Adoption Leave (Adoption from Overseas) Regulations 2003
applied: SI 2008/1966 Reg.2

938. Tax Credits Act 2002 (Commencement No.3 and Transitional Provisions and Savings) Order 2003
Art.3, applied: SI 2008/2101 Art.3
Art.4, applied: SI 2008/2101 Art.3

947. Care Homes (Amendment) (Wales) Regulations 2003
applied: 2008 c.14 s.17

962. Tax Credits Act 2002 (Commencement No.4, Transitional Provisions and Savings) Order 2003
Art.2, amended: SI 2008/3151 Art.3
Art.5, amended: SI 2008/3151 Art.3

968. Special Commissioners (Jurisdiction and Procedure) (Amendment) Regulations 2003
applied: SI 2008/562 Reg.20

1004. Care Homes (Wales) (Amendment No.2) Regulations 2003
applied: 2008 c.14 s.17

1021. Local Authorities (Members Allowances) (England) Regulations 2003
Part 1, applied: SI 2008/634 Art.11
Part 2, applied: SI 2008/634 Art.11
Part 3, applied: SI 2008/634 Art.11
Part 4, applied: SI 2008/634 Art.11
Part 5, disapplied: SI 2008/907 Art.16
Part 6, applied: SI 2008/634 Art.11
Reg.4, varied: SI 2008/634 Art.11
Reg.6, disapplied: SI 2008/634 Art.11, SI 2008/907 Art.16
Reg.10, referred to: SI 2008/634 Art.11
Reg.10, varied: SI 2008/634 Art.11
Reg.16, varied: SI 2008/634 Art.11
Reg.17, disapplied: SI 2008/634 Art.11, SI 2008/907 Art.16

1022. Local Government Pension Scheme and Discretionary Compensation (Local Authority Members in England) Regulations 2003
revoked: SI 2008/238 Sch.1

NO.

2003–cont.

1039. Education (National Curriculum) (Key Stage 3 Assessment Arrangements) (England) Order 2003
referred to: SI 2008/3081 Art.2
Art.3, amended: SI 2008/3081 Art.2
Art.8, revoked: SI 2008/3081 Art.2
Art.9, revoked: SI 2008/3081 Art.2
Art.10, applied: SI 2008/3081 Art.3
Art.10, revoked: SI 2008/3081 Art.2
Art.11, amended: SI 2008/3081 Art.2
Art.12, amended: SI 2008/3081 Art.2

1050. Social Security and Child Support (Miscellaneous Amendments) Regulations 2003
referred to: SI 2008/2683 Art.3
Reg.3, revoked (in part): SI 2008/2683 Sch.2

1060. Protection of Children and Vulnerable Adults and Care Standards Tribunal (Amendment No.2) Regulations 2003
revoked: SI 2008/2683 Sch.2

1079. Diseases of Poultry (Wales) Order 2003
applied: SI 2008/1275 Reg.15

1184. Education (Prohibition from Teaching or Working with Children) Regulations 2003
applied: SI 2008/2699 Sch.1
Reg.2, amended: SI 2008/2683 Sch.1 para.231
Reg.10, amended: SI 2008/2683 Sch.1 para.232
Reg.10A, amended: SI 2008/2683 Sch.1 para.233
Reg.11, amended: SI 2008/2683 Sch.1 para.234
Reg.12, amended: SI 2008/2683 Sch.1 para.235
Reg.13, amended: SI 2008/2683 Sch.1 para.236
Sch.2 Part 1, applied: SI 2008/474 Reg.6

1238. Bathing Waters (Classification) (England) Regulations 2003
revoked: SI 2008/1097 Reg.19

1240. Conditional Fee Agreements (Miscellaneous Amendments) Regulations 2003
see *Jones v Wrexham BC* [2007] EWCA Civ 1356, [2008] 1 W.L.R. 1590 (CA (Civ Div)), Waller, L.J. (V-P)

1246. European Communities (Designation) (No.2) Order 2003
Sch.1, amended: SI 2008/1792 Sch.1

1247. Criminal Justice (Northern Ireland) Order 2003
Art.6, applied: SI 2008/1216 Art.92
Art.18, revoked: SI 2008/1769 Sch.1 para.32, Sch.3
Art.19, revoked: SI 2008/1769 Sch.1 para.32, Sch.3

NO.

2003–cont.

1247. Criminal Justice (Northern Ireland) Order 2003–*cont.*

Art.20, applied: SI 2008/1216 Sch.1 para.29, Sch.2 para.14

Art.20, revoked: SI 2008/1769 Sch.1 para.32, Sch.3

Art.21, applied: SI 2008/1216 Sch.1 para.29, Sch.2 para.14

Art.21, revoked: SI 2008/1769 Sch.1 para.32, Sch.3

Art.22, revoked: SI 2008/1769 Sch.1 para.32, Sch.3

Art.32, revoked: SI 2008/1216 Sch.6 Part 1

Art.33, revoked: SI 2008/1216 Sch.6 Part 4

Sch.1 para.4, revoked: SI 2008/1769 Sch.1 para.32

Sch.1 para.6, revoked (in part): SI 2008/1769 Sch.1 para.32

Sch.1 para.7, revoked: SI 2008/1769 Sch.1 para.32

Sch.1 para.9, revoked: SI 2008/1769 Sch.1 para.32

Sch.1 para.22, revoked: SI 2008/1769 Sch.1 para.32

1248. Merchant Shipping (Categorisation of Registries of Relevant British Possessions) Order 2003

Sch.1, substituted: SI 2008/1243 Art.2

1250. General and Specialist Medical Practice (Education, Training and Qualifications) Order 2003

Art.8, applied: SI 2008/554 Sch.1

Art.11, applied: SI 2008/554 Sch.1

Art.11A, applied: SI 2008/554 Sch.1

Art.12, applied: SI 2008/554 Sch.1

Art.13, applied: SI 2008/554 Sch.1

Art.14, amended: SI 2008/3131 Sch.2 para.20

Art.14, applied: SI 2008/554 Sch.1

Art.14A, applied: SI 2008/554 Sch.1

Art.15B, added: SI 2008/3131 Sch.2 para.21

Art.19, applied: SI 2008/554 Sch.1

Art.21, applied: SI 2008/554 Sch.1

Art.21, referred to: SI 2008/554 Sch.1

Art.24, applied: SI 2008/554 Sch.1

Art.24, enabled: SI 2008/554

Art.25, applied: SI 2008/554, SI 2008/554 Sch.1

Art.25, enabled: SI 2008/554

Sch.3, referred to: SI 2008/554 Sch.1

Sch.7A Part 2, applied: SI 2008/554 Sch.1

1326. Government Resources and Accounts Act 2000 (Audit of Public Bodies) Order 2003

Art.5, revoked: SI 2008/576 Sch.5 para.8

Art.6, revoked: SI 2008/576 Sch.5 para.8

Art.11, revoked (in part): 2008 c.17 Sch.16

Art.18, revoked: 2008 c.17 Sch.16

NO.

2003–cont.

1372. Competition Appeal Tribunal Rules 2003

r.8, see *British Sky Broadcasting Group Plc v Competition Commission* [2008] CAT 1, [2008] Comp. A.R.1 (CAT), Barling, J

r.19, see *Albion Water Ltd v Water Services Regulation Authority* [2008] CAT 3, [2008] Comp. A.R. 103 (CAT), Marion Simmons Q.C. (Chairman); see *British Sky Broadcasting Group Plc v Competition Commission* [2008] CAT 7, [2008] Comp. A.R. 143 (CAT), Barling, J; see *Emerson Electric Co v Morgan Crucible Co Plc* [2008] C.P. Rep. 5 (CAT), Marion Simmons Q.C. (Chairman)

r.26, see *British Sky Broadcasting Group Plc v Competition Commission* [2008] CAT 1, [2008] Comp. A.R.1 (CAT), Barling, J

r.31, see *BCL Old Co Ltd v BASF SE* [2008] CAT 24, [2008] Comp. A.R. 210 (CAT), Barling, J; see *Emerson Electric Co v Morgan Crucible Co Plc* [2008] C.P. Rep. 5 (CAT), Marion Simmons Q.C. (Chairman)

r.40, see *Emerson Electric Co v Morgan Crucible Co Plc* [2008] Comp. A.R. 37 (CAT), Marion Simmons Q.C. (Chairman)

1374. Enterprise Act 2002 (Part 8 Community Infringements Specified UK Laws) Order 2003

referred to: SI 2008/1277 Sch.3 para.13

Sch.1, amended: SI 2008/1277 Sch.2 para.100, Sch.4 Part 2, SI 2008/1816 Sch.1 para.2

1376. Enterprise Act 2002 (Part 8 Notice to OFT of Intended Prosecution Specified Enactments, Revocation and Transitional Provision) Order 2003

referred to: SI 2008/1277 Sch.3 para.9, Sch.3 para.10

Sch.1, amended: SI 2008/1277 Sch.2 para.101, Sch.4 Part 2, SI 2008/1816 Sch.1 para.3

1400. Enterprise Act 2002 (Part 9 Restrictions on Disclosure of Information) (Amendment and Specification) Order 2003

Sch.3, amended: SI 2008/1277 Sch.2 para.103, Sch.4 Part 2, SI 2008/1816 Sch.1 para.4

Sch.4, amended: SI 2008/1277 Sch.2 para.103, Sch.4 Part 2, SI 2008/1816 Sch.1 para.4

Sch.5, amended: SI 2008/1816 Sch.2

1417. Land Registration Rules 2003

Part 1 r.5, amended: SI 2008/1919 Sch.1 para.1

Part 1 r.6, amended: SI 2008/1919 Sch.1 para.2

Part 1 r.7, amended: SI 2008/1919 Sch.1 para.3

Part 1 r.8, amended: SI 2008/1919 Sch.1 para.4

NO.

2003–cont.

1417. Land Registration Rules 2003–*cont.*
Part 1 r.8, applied: SI 2008/1919 r.6
Part 1 r.8, revoked (in part): SI 2008/1919 Sch.1 para.4
Part 1 r.9, amended: SI 2008/1919 Sch.1 para.5
Part 2 r.11, amended: SI 2008/1919 Sch.1 para.6
Part 2 r.12, amended: SI 2008/1750 Sch.2 para.1
Part 3, disapplied: SI 2008/1750 Sch.2 para.1
Part 3 r.15, amended: SI 2008/1750 Sch.2 para.2
Part 3 r.19, amended: SI 2008/1919 Sch.1 para.7
Part 4 r.27, amended: SI 2008/1919 Sch.1 para.8
Part 4 r.27, substituted: SI 2008/1919 Sch.1 para.8
Part 4 r.33, amended: SI 2008/1919 Sch.1 para.9
Part 4 r.37, amended: SI 2008/1919 Sch.1 para.10
Part 4 r.38, applied: SI 2008/1750 r.3
Part 5 r.49, substituted: SI 2008/1919 Sch.1 para.11
Part 5 r.51, amended: SI 2008/1919 Sch.1 para.12
Part 5 r.52, substituted: SI 2008/1919 Sch.1 para.13
Part 6 r.54, amended: SI 2008/1919 Sch.1 para.14
Part 6 r.57, disapplied: SI 2008/1750 Sch.2 para.2
Part 6 r.58, amended: SI 2008/1919 Sch.1 para.15
Part 6 r.62, amended: SI 2008/1919 Sch.1 para.16
Part 6 r.63, amended: SI 2008/1919 Sch.1 para.17
Part 6 r.67, amended: SI 2008/1919 Sch.1 para.18
Part 6 r.68, substituted: SI 2008/1919 Sch.1 para.19
Part 6 r.70, substituted: SI 2008/1919 Sch.1 para.20
Part 6 r.71, substituted: SI 2008/1919 Sch.1 para.21
Part 6 r.72, substituted: SI 2008/1919 Sch.1 para.22
Part 6 r.72B, added: SI 2008/1919 Sch.1 para.23
Part 6 r.72C, added: SI 2008/1919 Sch.1 para.23
Part 6 r.73, substituted: SI 2008/1919 Sch.1 para.24
Part 6 r.73A, substituted: SI 2008/1919 Sch.1 para.24
Part 6 r.74, substituted: SI 2008/1919 Sch.1 para.24

NO.

2003–cont.

1417. Land Registration Rules 2003–*cont.*
Part 6 r.75, substituted: SI 2008/1919 Sch.1 para.24
Part 6 r.77, substituted: SI 2008/1919 Sch.1 para.25
Part 6 r.78, revoked: SI 2008/1919 Sch.1 para.26
Part 6 r.79A, added: SI 2008/1919 Sch.1 para.27
Part 7 r.81, disapplied: SI 2008/1750 Sch.2 para.3
Part 7 r.86, amended: SI 2008/1919 Sch.1 para.28
Part 7 r.87, amended: SI 2008/1919 Sch.1 para.29
Part 7 r.87A, added: SI 2008/1919 Sch.1 para.30
Part 8 r.91A, amended: SI 2008/1919 Sch.1 para.31
Part 8 r.91B, added: SI 2008/1919 Sch.1 para.32
Part 8 r.92, amended: SI 2008/1750 Sch.2 para.3, SI 2008/1919 Sch.1 para.33
Part 8 r.93, amended: SI 2008/1919 Sch.1 para.34
Part 8 r.94, amended: SI 2008/1919 Sch.1 para.35
Part 8 r.96, amended: SI 2008/1919 Sch.1 para.36
Part 8 r.98, substituted: SI 2008/1919 Sch.1 para.37
Part 9 r.107, amended: SI 2008/1919 Sch.1 para.38
Part 9 r.108, amended: SI 2008/1750 Sch.2 para.4, SI 2008/1919 Sch.1 para.39
Part 9 r.111, substituted: SI 2008/1919 Sch.1 para.40
Part 9 r.113, substituted: SI 2008/1919 Sch.1 para.41
Part 9 r.116, amended: SI 2008/1919 Sch.1 para.42
Part 9 r.116A, added: SI 2008/1919 Sch.1 para.43
Part 10 r.119, amended: SI 2008/1919 Sch.1 para.44
Part 13 r.131, amended: SI 2008/1919 Sch.1 para.45
Part 13 r.133, amended: SI 2008/1750 Sch.2 para.5
Part 13 r.133, substituted: SI 2008/1919 Sch.1 para.46
Part 13 r.135, amended: SI 2008/1750 Sch.2 para.6
Part 13 r.135, substituted: SI 2008/1919 Sch.1 para.47
Part 13 r.136, amended: SI 2008/1919 Sch.1 para.48
Part 13 r.139, revoked: SI 2008/1919 Sch.1 para.49
Part 13 r.140, amended: SI 2008/1919 Sch.1 para.50

NO.

2003–cont.

1417. Land Registration Rules 2003–*cont.*
Part 14 r.162, amended: SI 2008/1919 Sch.1 para.51
Part 14 r.163, amended: SI 2008/1919 Sch.1 para.52
Part 14 r.175, amended: SI 2008/1919 Sch.1 para.53
Part 14 r.181, revoked: SI 2008/1919 Sch.1 para.54
Part 14 r.182, amended: SI 2008/1919 Sch.1 para.55
Part 14 r.182, revoked (in part): SI 2008/1919 Sch.1 para.55
Part 14 r.183, substituted: SI 2008/1919 Sch.1 para.56
Part 14 r.183A, added: SI 2008/1919 Sch.1 para.57
Part 14 r.187, substituted: SI 2008/1919 Sch.1 para.58
Part 14 r.188, amended: SI 2008/1919 Sch.1 para.59
Part 14 r.188A, added: SI 2008/1919 Sch.1 para.60
Part 14 r.194A, added: SI 2008/1919 Sch.1 para.61
Part 14 r.194B, added: SI 2008/1919 Sch.1 para.61
Part 14 r.194C, added: SI 2008/1919 Sch.1 para.61
Part 14 r.194D, added: SI 2008/1919 Sch.1 para.61
Part 14 r.194E, added: SI 2008/1919 Sch.1 para.61
Part 14 r.194F, added: SI 2008/1919 Sch.1 para.61
Part 14 r.194G, added: SI 2008/1919 Sch.1 para.61
Part 14 r.195, substituted: SI 2008/1919 Sch.1 para.62
Part 14 r.196A, added: SI 2008/1919 Sch.1 para.63
Part 14 r.196B, added: SI 2008/1919 Sch.1 para.63
Part 15 r.198, amended: SI 2008/1919 Sch.1 para.64
Part 15 r.199, revoked (in part): SI 2008/1919 Sch.1 para.65
Part 15 r.203, amended: SI 2008/1919 Sch.1 para.66
Part 15 r.203, disapplied: SI 2008/1750 Sch.2 para.4
Part 15 r.206, amended: SI 2008/1919 Sch.1 para.67
Part 15 r.207, revoked: SI 2008/1919 Sch.1 para.68
Part 15 r.207A, added: SI 2008/1919 Sch.1 para.69
Part 15 r.210, amended: SI 2008/1919 Sch.1 para.70
Part 15 r.211, amended: SI 2008/1919 Sch.1 para.71

NO.

2003–cont.

1417. Land Registration Rules 2003–*cont.*
Part 15 r.215A, added: SI 2008/1919 Sch.1 para.72
Part 15 r.216, amended: SI 2008/1919 Sch.1 para.73
Part 15 r.217, amended: SI 2008/1750 Sch.2 para.7, SI 2008/1919 Sch.1 para.74
Part 16 r.223, amended: SI 2008/1919 Sch.1 para.75
Sch.1, amended: SI 2008/574 Sch.1 para.6
Sch.1, substituted: SI 2008/1919 Sch.2
Sch.1A, amended: SI 2008/1919 r.4
Sch.2, applied: SI 2008/3201 Art.2
Sch.2 para.5, amended: SI 2008/1919 r.4
Sch.3, amended: SI 2008/1919 Sch.3 para.1, Sch.3 para.2, Sch.3 para.3
Sch.4, substituted: SI 2008/1919 Sch.4
Sch.5, amended: SI 2008/574 Sch.1 para.6, SI 2008/1919 r.4
Sch.6 Part 3, amended: SI 2008/1919 Sch.5 para.1
Sch.6 Part 3 paraH, amended: SI 2008/1919 Sch.5 para.1
Sch.6 Part 4 paraI, amended: SI 2008/1919 Sch.5 para.2
Sch.6 Part 5 paraE, amended: SI 2008/1919 Sch.5 para.3
Sch.6 Part 5 paraF, amended: SI 2008/1919 Sch.5 para.3
Sch.9, amended: SI 2008/1919 Sch.6 para.1, Sch.6 para.2

1479. Highways, Crime Prevention etc.(Special Extinguishment and Special Diversion Orders) Regulations 2003
Sch.1, varied: SI 2008/442 Sch.1 para.4, Sch.1 para.7

1483. Local Authorities (Code of Conduct) (Local Determination) Regulations 2003
applied: SI 2008/1265 Art.3
Reg.1, amended: SI 2008/1085 Sch.1
Reg.2, amended: SI 2008/1085 Sch.1
Reg.2, revoked (in part): SI 2008/1085 Sch.1
Reg.4, revoked (in part): SI 2008/1085 Sch.1
Reg.5, amended: SI 2008/1085 Sch.1
Reg.6, amended: SI 2008/1085 Sch.1
Reg.8, amended: SI 2008/1085 Sch.1
Reg.9, amended: SI 2008/1085 Sch.1
Reg.12, amended: SI 2008/1085 Sch.1
Reg.13, amended: SI 2008/1085 Sch.1

1511. Creosote (Prohibition on Use and Marketing) (No.2) Regulations 2003
revoked: SI 2008/2852 Sch.10 Part 1

1557. Local and European Parliamentary Elections (Registration of Citizens of Accession States) Regulations 2003
Sch.2 para.4, revoked (in part): SI 2008/1741 Sch.2

NO.

2003–cont.

1593. Enterprise Act 2002 (Part 8 Domestic Infringements) Order 2003
referred to: SI 2008/1277 Sch.3 para.11, Sch.3 para.12
Sch.1 Part I, amended: SI 2008/1277 Sch.2 para.102, Sch.4 Part 2
Sch.1 Part II, amended: SI 2008/1277 Sch.2 para.102, Sch.4 Part 2

1596. Condensed Milk and Dried Milk (England) Regulations 2003
Reg.2, amended: SI 2008/85 Reg.3
Sch.1, added: SI 2008/85 Reg.4
Sch.1, amended: SI 2008/85 Reg.4
Sch.1, substituted: SI 2008/85 Reg.4

1605. Referral Orders (Amendment of Referral Conditions) Regulations 2003
Reg.2, revoked (in part): 2008 c.4 Sch.28 Part 2

1617. Strategic Health Authorities (Consultation on Changes) Regulations 2003
Reg.2, amended: SI 2008/528 Sch.1 para.4
Reg.2, revoked (in part): SI 2008/528 Sch.1 para.4

1633. Uncertificated Securities (Amendment) (Eligible Debt Securities) Regulations 2003
Sch.2 para.8, amended: SI 2008/1816 Sch.1 para.5

1660. Employment Equality (Religion or Belief) Regulations 2003
Reg.3, see *McClintock v Department of Constitutional Affairs* [2008] I.R.L.R. 29 (EAT), Elias, J (President)
Reg.28, referred to: SI 2008/3232 Sch.1 Part 2
Reg.36, amended: SI 2008/1696 Art.4

1661. Employment Equality (Sexual Orientation) Regulations 2003
Reg.5, see *English v Thomas Sanderson Blinds Ltd* [2008] I.C.R. 607 (EAT), Judge Peter Clark
Reg.28, referred to: SI 2008/3232 Sch.1 Part 2
Reg.36, amended: SI 2008/1696 Art.5

1662. Education (School Teachers Qualifications) (England) Regulations 2003
Sch.2 Part 1 para.5, applied: SI 2008/657 Sch.2 para.17, Sch.2 para.19
Sch.2 Part 1 para.9, applied: SI 2008/657 Sch.2 para.18
Sch.2 Part 1 para.10, applied: SI 2008/657 Sch.2 para.18
Sch.2 Part 1 para.12, applied: SI 2008/657 Sch.2 para.17
Sch.2 Part 1 para.13, applied: SI 2008/657 Sch.2 para.19

1663. Education (Specified Work and Registration) (England) Regulations 2003
Reg.3, amended: SI 2008/1883 Reg.3

NO.

2003–cont.

1663. Education (Specified Work and Registration) (England) Regulations 2003–*cont.*
Reg.7, amended: SI 2008/1883 Reg.4
Reg.8, added: SI 2008/1883 Reg.4
Reg.9, added: SI 2008/1883 Reg.4
Sch.2 para.1, amended: SI 2008/1883 Reg.5
Sch.3 para.1, substituted: SI 2008/1883 Reg.6
Sch.3 Part 1 para.1, substituted: SI 2008/1883 Reg.6
Sch.3 Part 1 para.2, substituted: SI 2008/1883 Reg.6
Sch.3 Part 1 para.3, substituted: SI 2008/1883 Reg.6
Sch.3 para.2, substituted: SI 2008/1883 Reg.6
Sch.3 Part 2 para.4, substituted: SI 2008/1883 Reg.6
Sch.3 para.3, substituted: SI 2008/1883 Reg.6
Sch.3 Part 3 para.5, substituted: SI 2008/1883 Reg.6

1703. Care Homes (Amendment No.2) Regulations 2003
applied: 2008 c.14 s.17

1727. Occupational Pension Schemes (Transfer Values and Miscellaneous Amendments) Regulations 2003
applied: SSI 2008/228 Reg.73

1729. Disease Control (England) Order 2003
Art.2, amended: SI 2008/1066 Art.2
Art.14, amended: SI 2008/1066 Art.2
Art.20, amended: SI 2008/1066 Art.2

1735. Asylum Support Appeals (Procedure) (Amendment) Rules 2003
revoked: SI 2008/2683 Sch.2

1845. Care Homes (Adult Placements) (Amendment) Regulations 2003
applied: 2008 c.14 s.17

1852. Action Programme for Nitrate Vulnerable Zones (Amendment) (Wales) Regulations 2003
applied: SSI 2008/159 Sch.3 Part 2

1886. Social Security (Jobcentre Plus Interviews for Partners) Regulations 2003
Reg.2, amended: SI 2008/759 Reg.2
Reg.2, revoked (in part): SI 2008/759 Reg.2
Reg.3, substituted: SI 2008/759 Reg.2
Reg.4, amended: SI 2008/759 Reg.2
Reg.5, amended: SI 2008/759 Reg.2
Reg.6, amended: SI 2008/759 Reg.2
Reg.7, amended: SI 2008/759 Reg.2
Reg.11, amended: SI 2008/759 Reg.2, SI 2008/1554 Reg.71
Reg.12, amended: SI 2008/759 Reg.2
Reg.14, amended: SI 2008/2683 Sch.1 para.237

NO.

2003–cont.

1888. European Communities (Designation) (No.3) Order 2003
Sch.1, amended: SI 2008/301 Sch.1

1907. Greater London Authority Elections (Election Addresses) Order 2003
Art.2, amended: SI 2008/507 Art.3, Art.4
Art.2, substituted: SI 2008/507 Art.3
Art.5, amended: SI 2008/507 Art.5, Art.6
Art.7, amended: SI 2008/507 Art.7
Art.8, amended: SI 2008/507 Art.8
Art.9, amended: SI 2008/507 Art.9

1910. Education (Independent School Standards) (England) Regulations 2003
Reg.3, substituted: SI 2008/3253 Reg.3
Reg.4, amended: SI 2008/3253 Reg.4
Sch.1 para.1, amended: SI 2008/3253 Reg.5
Sch.1 para.3, amended: SI 2008/3253 Reg.6
Sch.1 para.6, substituted: SI 2008/3253 Reg.7
Sch.1 para.7, amended: SI 2008/3253 Reg.8

1926. Education (Independent School Inspection Fees and Publication) (England) Regulations 2003
revoked: SI 2008/1801 Reg.9

1942. Representation of the People (Form of Canvass) (Northern Ireland) Regulations 2003
revoked: SI 2008/1741 Sch.2

1960. Motor Cycles Etc (Single Vehicle Approval) (Fees) Regulations 2003
Reg.3, amended: SI 2008/1462 Reg.2
Reg.6, amended: SI 2008/1462 Reg.2

1966. Disease Control (Wales) Order 2003
applied: SI 2008/1742 Art.14
Art.2, amended: SI 2008/1314 Art.2
Art.14, amended: SI 2008/1314 Art.2

1968. Transport of Animals (Cleansing and Disinfection) (Wales) (No.3) Order 2003
applied: SI 2008/1040 Reg.23
Art.3, amended: SI 2008/789 Art.2
Art.3, revoked (in part): SI 2008/789 Art.2
Sch.1A para.1, added: SI 2008/789 Art.2
Sch.1A para.2, added: SI 2008/789 Art.2
Sch.1A para.3, added: SI 2008/789 Art.2
Sch.1A para.4, added: SI 2008/789 Art.2

1987. Service Charges (Consultation Requirements) (England) Regulations 2003
see *Eltham Properties Ltd v Kenny* [2008] L. & T.R. 14 (Lands Tr), AJ Trott FRICS

1994. Education (Mandatory Awards) Regulations 2003
applied: SI 2008/529 Sch.4 para.11, Sch.4 para.12, SI 2008/1273 Sch.5 para.8, Sch.5 para.11, Sch.6 para.7
Reg.2, amended: SI 2008/1477 Reg.5
Reg.7, amended: SI 2008/1477 Reg.6
Reg.21, amended: SI 2008/1477 Sch.1
Sch.1, amended: SI 2008/1477 Reg.7, Sch.1

NO.

2003–cont.

1994. Education (Mandatory Awards) Regulations 2003–*cont.*
Sch.2 Part 1 para.2, amended: SI 2008/1477 Sch.1
Sch.2 Part 1 para.3, amended: SI 2008/1477 Sch.1
Sch.2 Part 2 para.5, amended: SI 2008/1477 Sch.1
Sch.2 Part 2 para.7, amended: SI 2008/1477 Sch.1
Sch.2 Part 2 para.7, referred to: SI 2008/794 Reg.133
Sch.2 Part 2 para.9, amended: SI 2008/1477 Sch.1
Sch.2 Part 3, applied: SI 2008/794 Reg.132
Sch.2 Part 3 para.12, amended: SI 2008/1477 Sch.1
Sch.2 Part 3 para.13, amended: SI 2008/1477 Sch.1
Sch.2 Part 3 para.14, amended: SI 2008/1477 Sch.1
Sch.3 Part 1 para.1, amended: SI 2008/1477 Sch.1
Sch.3 Part 2 para.4, amended: SI 2008/1477 Reg.8, Sch.1
Sch.3 Part 2 para.6, amended: SI 2008/1477 Sch.1
Sch.3 Part 3 para.8, amended: SI 2008/1477 Sch.1
Sch.3 Part 3A para.10, amended: SI 2008/1477 Sch.1
Sch.4 para.2, amended: SI 2008/1477 Sch.1
Sch.5 para.4, amended: SI 2008/1477 Sch.1

1996. Day Care and Child Minding (National Standards) (England) Regulations 2003
Reg.4, applied: SI 2008/2261 Sch.2 para.23
Reg.8, applied: SI 2008/2261 Sch.2 para.22
Sch.2 para.2, applied: SI 2008/2261 Sch.2 para.12

2042. Mental Health (Correspondence of Patients, Patient Advocacy and Liaison Services) Regulations 2003
revoked: SI 2008/1184 Sch.2

2043. Protection of Children and Vulnerable Adults and Care Standards Tribunal (Amendment No.3) Regulations 2003
revoked: SI 2008/2683 Sch.2

2075. Meat Products (England) Regulations 2003
Reg.5, amended: SI 2008/517 Reg.3
Sch.3 para.6, revoked: SI 2008/517 Reg.4
Sch.3 para.7, revoked: SI 2008/517 Reg.4
Sch.3 para.10, revoked: SI 2008/517 Reg.4

2076. Capital Allowances (Environmentally Beneficial Plant and Machinery) Order 2003
Art.2, amended: SI 2008/1917 Art.2
Art.3, amended: SI 2008/1917 Art.2
Art.5, amended: SI 2008/1917 Art.2

NO.

2003–cont.

2082. Insurance Companies (Calculation of Profits Policy Holders Tax) Regulations 2003

Reg.4, amended: SI 2008/1906 Reg.2

2093. Enterprise Act 2002 (Commencement No.4 and Transitional Provisions and Savings) Order 2003

Art.3, applied: SI 2008/386 Reg.4, SI 2008/948 Sch.1 para.101, SI 2008/2499 Reg.4

2098. Leasehold Valuation Tribunals (Fees) (England) Regulations 2003

Reg.8, amended: SI 2008/1879 Reg.15

2099. Leasehold Valuation Tribunals (Procedure) (England) Regulations 2003

Reg.20, see *Grosvenor Estate Belgravia v Adams* [2008] R.V.R. 173 (Lands Tr), George Bartlett Q.C. (President, LTr)

Reg.21, substituted: SI 2008/2683 Sch.1 para.238

Reg.24, see *Grosvenor Estate Belgravia v Adams* [2008] R.V.R. 173 (Lands Tr), George Bartlett Q.C. (President, LTr)

2148. Education (Induction Arrangements for School Teachers) (Consolidation) (England) (Amendment No.2) Regulations 2003

revoked: SI 2008/657 Sch.1

2171. Adjudicator to Her Majesty's Land Registry (Practice and Procedure) Rules 2003

Part 1 r.2, amended: SI 2008/1731 r.5
Part 2 r.5, applied: SI 2008/1731 r.3
Part 2 r.8, amended: SI 2008/1731 r.6
Part 2 r.9, amended: SI 2008/1731 r.7
Part 2 r.12, amended: SI 2008/1731 r.8
Part 2 r.13, amended: SI 2008/1731 r.9
Part 2 r.14, amended: SI 2008/1731 r.10
Part 2 r.14, revoked (in part): SI 2008/1731 r.10
Part 3 r.16, amended: SI 2008/1731 r.11
Part 3 r.16, revoked (in part): SI 2008/1731 r.11
Part 3 r.17, amended: SI 2008/1731 r.12
Part 3 r.17, applied: SI 2008/1731 r.3
Part 3 r.18, amended: SI 2008/1731 r.13
Part 3 r.18, revoked (in part): SI 2008/1731 r.13
Part 4 r.20, substituted: SI 2008/1731 r.14
Part 4 r.21, amended: SI 2008/1731 r.15
Part 4 r.24, amended: SI 2008/1731 r.16
Part 4 r.27, amended: SI 2008/1731 r.17
Part 4 r.28, amended: SI 2008/1731 r.18
Part 4 r.30, amended: SI 2008/1731 r.19
Part 5 r.32A, added: SI 2008/1731 r.20
Part 5 r.37, revoked: SI 2008/1731 r.21
Part 5 r.40, amended: SI 2008/1731 r.22
Part 5 r.41A, added: SI 2008/1731 r.23
Part 5 r.42, amended: SI 2008/1731 r.24
Part 5 r.42, applied: SI 2008/1730 r.32
Part 5 r.43, amended: SI 2008/1731 r.25
Part 6 r.45, amended: SI 2008/1731 r.26
Part 7 r.47, amended: SI 2008/1731 r.27
Part 7 r.47, revoked (in part): SI 2008/1731 r.27

NO.

2003–cont.

2171. Adjudicator to Her Majesty's Land Registry (Practice and Procedure) Rules 2003–*cont.*

Part 7 r.48, amended: SI 2008/1731 r.28
Part 7 r.50, amended: SI 2008/1731 r.29
Part 7 r.50, revoked (in part): SI 2008/1731 r.29
Part 7 r.51, amended: SI 2008/1731 r.30

2249. Local Government Pension Scheme (Amendment) Regulations 2003

revoked: SI 2008/238 Sch.1

2251. Mental Health Review Tribunals (Regions) Order 2003

revoked: SI 2008/2683 Sch.2

2253. Price Marking (Food and Drink Services) Order 2003

revoked: SI 2008/1277 Sch.2 para.104, Sch.4 Part 2

2273. Armed Forces (Entry, Search and Seizure) Order 2003

Art.12, amended: SI 2008/1698 Art.2
Art.13, amended: SI 2008/1698 Art.3
Art.17, applied: SI 2008/648 Sch.1

2314. Religious Character of Schools (Designation Procedure) (Independent Schools) (England) Regulations 2003

applied: SI 2008/2340
referred to: SI 2008/783

2317. Medicines (Child Safety) Regulations 2003

Reg.1, amended: SI 2008/1162 Reg.3
Reg.3, amended: SI 2008/1162 Reg.3

2323. Care Standards Act 2000 (Domiciliary Care Agencies and Nurses Agencies) (Amendment) (England) Regulations 2003

applied: 2008 c.14 s.17

2382. National Health Service (Travel Expenses and Remission of Charges) Regulations 2003

Part II, applied: SI 2008/1186 Reg.3
Reg.2, amended: SI 2008/571 Reg.9, SI 2008/1697 Reg.3
Reg.3, amended: SI 2008/571 Reg.10, SI 2008/1700 Sch.1 para.10
Reg.5, amended: SI 2008/1697 Reg.4
Reg.5, applied: SI 2008/794 Sch.8 para.45, Sch.9 para.37
Reg.6, applied: SI 2008/794 Sch.8 para.45, Sch.9 para.37
Reg.12, applied: SI 2008/794 Sch.8 para.45, Sch.9 para.37
Reg.15, amended: SI 2008/2868 Reg.2
Sch.1, amended: SI 2008/843 Reg.2, SI 2008/1697 Reg.5, SI 2008/2868 Reg.3, Reg.4
Sch.1, applied: SI 2008/1186 Reg.3

NO.

2003–cont.

2439. Social Security (Incapacity Benefit Work-focused Interviews) Regulations 2003

applied: SI 2008/2928 Reg.3, Reg.12

revoked: SI 2008/2928 Reg.12

Reg.10, applied: SI 2008/2928 Reg.12

Reg.10, disapplied: SI 2008/2928 Reg.12

Reg.12, amended: SI 2008/2683 Sch.1 para.239

2456. Classical Swine Fever (Wales) Order 2003

applied: SI 2008/1275 Reg.15

2495. Income Tax (Incentive Payments for Voluntary Electronic Communication of PAYE Returns) Regulations 2003

see *ZXCV Ltd v Revenue and Customs Commissioners* [2008] S.T.C. (S.C.D.) 1171 (Sp Comm), Sir Stephen Oliver Q.C.

Reg.1, see *ZXCV Ltd v Revenue and Customs Commissioners* [2008] S.T.C. (S.C.D.) 1171 (Sp Comm), Sir Stephen Oliver Q.C.

2527. Nurses Agencies (Wales) Regulations 2003

applied: 2008 c.14 s.17

2589. Judicial Pensions and Retirement Act 1993 (Addition of Qualifying Judicial Offices) (No.2) Order 2003

revoked: SI 2008/2833 Sch.3 para.228

2600. Police (Efficiency) (Amendment No.2) Regulations 2003

revoked: SI 2008/2862 Reg.3

2603. Freedom of Information Act 2000 (Commencement No.3) Order 2003

Sch.1 Part 1, varied: 2008 c.14 Sch.10 para.1

2613. Council Tax and Non-Domestic Rating (Demand Notices) (England) Regulations 2003

Reg.1, amended: SI 2008/387 Reg.3, SI 2008/3264 Reg.3

Reg.1A, added: SI 2008/3264 Reg.4

Reg.3, amended: SI 2008/387 Reg.4, SI 2008/3264 Reg.5

Sch.1 para.1, substituted: SI 2008/387 Sch.1 Part 1

Sch.1 para.1, amended: SI 2008/3264 Reg.6

Sch.1 para.1, substituted: SI 2008/387 Sch.1 Part 1

Sch.1 para.2, substituted: SI 2008/387 Sch.1 Part 1

Sch.1 para.3, substituted: SI 2008/387 Sch.1 Part 1

Sch.1 para.4, substituted: SI 2008/387 Sch.1 Part 1

Sch.1 para.5, substituted: SI 2008/387 Sch.1 Part 1

Sch.1 para.6, substituted: SI 2008/387 Sch.1 Part 1

Sch.1 para.7, substituted: SI 2008/387 Sch.1 Part 1

Sch.1 para.8, substituted: SI 2008/387 Sch.1 Part 1

NO.

2003–cont.

2613. Council Tax and Non-Domestic Rating (Demand Notices) (England) Regulations 2003–*cont.*

Sch.1 para.8A, substituted: SI 2008/387 Sch.1 Part 1

Sch.1 para.9, substituted: SI 2008/387 Sch.1 Part 1

Sch.1 para.10, substituted: SI 2008/387 Sch.1 Part 1

Sch.1 para.11, substituted: SI 2008/387 Sch.1 Part 1

Sch.1 para.12, substituted: SI 2008/387 Sch.1 Part 1

Sch.1 para.13, substituted: SI 2008/387 Sch.1 Part 1

Sch.1 para.14, substituted: SI 2008/387 Sch.1 Part 1

Sch.1 para.15, substituted: SI 2008/387 Sch.1 Part 1

Sch.1 para.16, substituted: SI 2008/387 Sch.1 Part 1

Sch.1 para.17, substituted: SI 2008/387 Sch.1 Part 1

Sch.1 para.18, substituted: SI 2008/387 Sch.1 Part 1

Sch.1 para.19, substituted: SI 2008/387 Sch.1 Part 1

Sch.1 para.20, substituted: SI 2008/387 Sch.1 Part 1

Sch.1 para.21, substituted: SI 2008/387 Sch.1 Part 1

Sch.1 para.22, substituted: SI 2008/387 Sch.1 Part 1

Sch.1 para.23, substituted: SI 2008/387 Sch.1 Part 1

Sch.1 para.23A, added: SI 2008/3264 Reg.6

Sch.1 para.23A, substituted: SI 2008/387 Sch.1 Part 1

Sch.1 para.23B, added: SI 2008/3264 Reg.6

Sch.1 para.23B, substituted: SI 2008/387 Sch.1 Part 1

Sch.1 para.23C, added: SI 2008/3264 Reg.6

Sch.1 para.23C, substituted: SI 2008/387 Sch.1 Part 1

Sch.1 para.24, substituted: SI 2008/387 Sch.1 Part 1

Sch.2 Part 1 para.1, substituted: SI 2008/387 Sch.1 Part 2

Sch.2 Part 1 para.2, substituted: SI 2008/387 Sch.1 Part 2

Sch.2 Part 1 para.3, substituted: SI 2008/387 Sch.1 Part 2

Sch.2 Part 1 para.4, substituted: SI 2008/387 Sch.1 Part 2

Sch.2 Part 1 para.5, substituted: SI 2008/387 Sch.1 Part 2

Sch.2 Part 1 para.6, substituted: SI 2008/387 Sch.1 Part 2

Sch.2 Part 1 para.7, substituted: SI 2008/387 Sch.1 Part 2

NO.

2003–cont.

2613. Council Tax and Non-Domestic Rating (Demand Notices) (England) Regulations 2003–*cont.*

Sch.2 Part 2, substituted: SI 2008/387 Sch.1 Part 2

Sch.2 Part 3 para.1, substituted: SI 2008/387 Sch.1 Part 2

Sch.2 Part 3 para.2, substituted: SI 2008/387 Sch.1 Part 2

Sch.2 Part 3 para.3, substituted: SI 2008/387 Sch.1 Part 2

Sch.2 Part 3 para.4, substituted: SI 2008/387 Sch.1 Part 2

Sch.3 Part 1 para.7A, added: SI 2008/3264 Reg.7

Sch.3 Part 1 para.7B, added: SI 2008/3264 Reg.7

Sch.3 Part 1 para.7C, added: SI 2008/3264 Reg.7

Sch.3 Part 3 para.3A, added: SI 2008/3264 Reg.7

Sch.3 Part 3 para.3B, added: SI 2008/3264 Reg.7

Sch.3 Part 3 para.3C, added: SI 2008/3264 Reg.7

Sch.3 Part 3 para.3D, added: SI 2008/3264 Reg.7

2635. End-of-Life Vehicles Regulations 2003

Reg.6, applied: SI 2008/2164 Reg.4

2650. Creosote (Prohibition on Use and Marketing) (No.2) Amendment Regulations 2003

revoked: SI 2008/2852 Sch.10 Part 1

2682. Income Tax (Pay As You Earn) Regulations 2003

see *Westek Ltd v Revenue and Customs Commissioners* [2008] S.T.C. (S.C.D.) 169 (Sp Comm), Howard M Nowlan

Part 8, added: SI 2008/2601 Reg.3

Reg.2, amended: SI 2008/782 Reg.3

Reg.7, amended: SI 2008/782 Reg.4

Reg.12, see *Oriel Support Ltd v Revenue and Customs Commissioners* [2008] S.T.C. (S.C.D.) 292 (Sp Comm), AN Brice

Reg.70, amended: SI 2008/782 Reg.5

Reg.72D, amended: SI 2008/782 Reg.6

Reg.72E, added: SI 2008/782 Reg.7

Reg.72F, added: SI 2008/782 Reg.7

Reg.72G, added: SI 2008/782 Reg.7

Reg.78, amended: SI 2008/782 Reg.8

Reg.80, amended: SI 2008/782 Reg.9

Reg.80, see *Oriel Support Ltd v Revenue and Customs Commissioners* [2008] S.T.C. (S.C.D.) 292 (Sp Comm), AN Brice; see *Westek Ltd v Revenue and Customs Commissioners* [2008] S.T.C. (S.C.D.) 169 (Sp Comm), Howard M Nowlan

Reg.82, amended: SI 2008/782 Reg.10

Reg.84, amended: SI 2008/782 Reg.11

Reg.108, amended: SI 2008/782 Reg.12

NO.

2003–cont.

2682. Income Tax (Pay As You Earn) Regulations 2003–*cont.*

Reg.133D, revoked (in part): SI 2008/782 Reg.13

Reg.185, amended: SI 2008/782 Reg.14

Reg.188, amended: SI 2008/782 Reg.15

Reg.211, amended: SI 2008/2601 Reg.4

Reg.214, amended: SI 2008/2601 Reg.5

Reg.215, amended: SI 2008/2601 Reg.6

Reg.218, amended: SI 2008/782 Reg.16

Sch.1 Part 2 para.21, amended: SI 2008/782 Reg.17

2714. Non-resident Insurance Companies Regulations 2003

Reg.3, amended: SI 2008/954 Art.52

2764. Export of Goods, Transfer of Technology and Provision of Technical Assistance (Control) Order 2003

revoked: SI 2008/3231 Sch.6

Art.11, amended: SI 2008/1281 Art.2

Sch.1, substituted: SI 2008/1281 Sch.1

Sch.1 Part I, amended: SI 2008/3161 Art.2

Sch.1 Part I, substituted: SI 2008/1281 Sch.1, SI 2008/3161 Art.2

Sch.1 Part I para ML.1, substituted: SI 2008/1281 Sch.1

Sch.1 Part I para ML.2, substituted: SI 2008/1281 Sch.1

Sch.1 Part I para ML.3, substituted: SI 2008/1281 Sch.1

Sch.1 Part I para ML.4, substituted: SI 2008/1281 Sch.1

Sch.1 Part I para ML.5, substituted: SI 2008/1281 Sch.1

Sch.1 Part I para ML.6, substituted: SI 2008/1281 Sch.1

Sch.1 Part I para ML.7, substituted: SI 2008/1281 Sch.1

Sch.1 Part I para ML.8, substituted: SI 2008/1281 Sch.1

Sch.1 Part I para ML.9, substituted: SI 2008/1281 Sch.1

Sch.1 Part I para ML.10, substituted: SI 2008/1281 Sch.1

Sch.1 Part I para ML.11, substituted: SI 2008/1281 Sch.1

Sch.1 Part I para ML.12, substituted: SI 2008/1281 Sch.1

Sch.1 Part I para ML.13, substituted: SI 2008/1281 Sch.1

Sch.1 Part I para ML.14, substituted: SI 2008/1281 Sch.1

Sch.1 Part I para ML.15, substituted: SI 2008/1281 Sch.1

Sch.1 Part I para ML.16, substituted: SI 2008/1281 Sch.1

Sch.1 Part I para ML.17, substituted: SI 2008/1281 Sch.1

Sch.1 Part I para ML.18, substituted: SI 2008/1281 Sch.1

NO.

2003–cont.

2764. Export of Goods, Transfer of Technology and Provision of Technical Assistance (Control) Order 2003–*cont.*

Sch.1 Part I paraML.19, substituted: SI 2008/1281 Sch.1

Sch.1 Part I paraML.20, substituted: SI 2008/1281 Sch.1

Sch.1 Part I paraML.21, amended: SI 2008/639 Art.2

Sch.1 Part I paraML.21, substituted: SI 2008/1281 Sch.1

Sch.1 Part I paraML.22, substituted: SI 2008/1281 Sch.1

Sch.1 Part II, amended: SI 2008/3161 Art.2

Sch.1 Part II, substituted: SI 2008/1281 Sch.1

Sch.1 Part II paraPL.8001, substituted: SI 2008/1281 Sch.1

Sch.2 Part 002 paraPL.9005, amended: SI 2008/1281 Sch.2 para.1

Sch.2 Part 003 paraPL.9008, amended: SI 2008/1281 Sch.2 para.2, Sch.2 para.3, Sch.2 para.4, Sch.2 para.5

Sch.2 Part 004 paraPL.9009, amended: SI 2008/1281 Sch.2 para.6, Sch.2 para.7

Sch.5, amended: SI 2008/1281 Art.2, SI 2008/3161 Art.2

2765. Trade in Goods (Control) Order 2003

referred to: SI 2008/1281 Art.2, SI 2008/1805 Art.2, SI 2008/3161 Art.2

revoked: SI 2008/3231 Sch.6

Art.1, amended: SI 2008/1805 Sch.1 para.1

Art.2, amended: SI 2008/1805 Sch.1 para.2

Art.3, amended: SI 2008/1805 Sch.1 para.3

Art.3A, added: SI 2008/1805 Sch.1 para.4

Art.4, amended: SI 2008/1805 Sch.1 para.5

Art.7, amended: SI 2008/1805 Sch.1 para.6

Art.9, see *R. v Knight (John)* [2008] EWCA Crim 478, [2008] 2 Cr. App. R. (S.) 76 (CA (Crim Div)), Sir Igor Judge (President, QB)

Art.9, amended: SI 2008/1805 Sch.1 para.7

Art.9, revoked (in part): SI 2008/1805 Sch.1 para.7

Art.12, amended: SI 2008/1805 Sch.1 para.8

Art.13, amended: SI 2008/1805 Sch.1 para.9

Sch.1, substituted: SI 2008/1805 Sch.1 para.10

Sch.1 para.1, substituted: SI 2008/1805 Sch.1 para.10

Sch.1 para.2, substituted: SI 2008/1805 Sch.1 para.10

Sch.1 para.3, substituted: SI 2008/1805 Sch.1 para.10

Sch.1 para.4, substituted: SI 2008/1805 Sch.1 para.10

Sch.1 para.5, substituted: SI 2008/1805 Sch.1 para.10

Sch.1 para.6, substituted: SI 2008/1805 Sch.1 para.10

Sch.1 para.7, substituted: SI 2008/1805 Sch.1 para.10

NO.

2003–cont.

2765. Trade in Goods (Control) Order 2003–*cont.*

Sch.1 para.8, substituted: SI 2008/1805 Sch.1 para.10

Sch.1 para.9, substituted: SI 2008/1805 Sch.1 para.10

Sch.1 para.10, substituted: SI 2008/1805 Sch.1 para.10

Sch.1 para.11, substituted: SI 2008/1805 Sch.1 para.10

Sch.2, substituted: SI 2008/1805 Sch.1 para.11

Sch.2 para.1, substituted: SI 2008/1805 Sch.1 para.11

Sch.2 para.2, substituted: SI 2008/1805 Sch.1 para.11

Sch.2 para.3, substituted: SI 2008/1805 Sch.1 para.11

Sch.2 para.4, substituted: SI 2008/1805 Sch.1 para.11

Sch.2 para.4A, added: SI 2008/639 Art.2

Sch.2 para.4A, substituted: SI 2008/1805 Sch.1 para.11

Sch.2 para.5, substituted: SI 2008/1805 Sch.1 para.11

Sch.2 para.6, substituted: SI 2008/1805 Sch.1 para.11

Sch.2 para.7, substituted: SI 2008/1805 Sch.1 para.11

Sch.2 para.8, substituted: SI 2008/1805 Sch.1 para.11

Sch.2 para.9, substituted: SI 2008/1805 Sch.1 para.11

Sch.3, added: SI 2008/1805 Sch.1 para.12

Sch.3 para.1, added: SI 2008/1805 Sch.1 para.12

Sch.3 para.2, added: SI 2008/1805 Sch.1 para.12

2901. European Communities (Designation) (No.4)Order 2003

Sch.1, amended: SI 2008/301 Sch.1

Sch.3, amended: SI 2008/301 Sch.1

2909. Schools Forums (Wales) Regulations 2003

applied: SI 2008/2867 Reg.25

2919. Veterinary Surgeons&apos Qualifications (European Recognition) Order 2003

Art.2, revoked: SI 2008/1824 Reg.3

Art.3, revoked: SI 2008/1824 Reg.3

Art.4, revoked: SI 2008/1824 Reg.3

Art.5, revoked: SI 2008/1824 Reg.3

Art.6, revoked: SI 2008/1824 Reg.3

Art.7, revoked: SI 2008/1824 Reg.3

Art.8, revoked: SI 2008/1824 Reg.3

Art.9, revoked: SI 2008/1824 Reg.3

Art.10, revoked: SI 2008/1824 Reg.3

Art.11, revoked: SI 2008/1824 Reg.3

Sch.1 para.2, revoked: SI 2008/1824 Reg.3

Sch.1 para.3, revoked: SI 2008/1824 Reg.3

Sch.1 para.4, revoked: SI 2008/1824 Reg.3

NO.

2003–*cont.*

2919. Veterinary Surgeons&apos Qualifications (European Recognition) Order 2003–*cont.*

Sch.1 para.7, amended: SI 2008/1824 Reg.3

Sch.1 para.7, revoked (in part): SI 2008/1824 Reg.3

Sch.1 para.8, revoked: SI 2008/1824 Reg.3

2994. Department for Transport (Driver Licensing and Vehicle Registration Fees) Order 2003

applied: SI 2008/508, SI 2008/1038, SI 2008/1312

Art.2, amended: SI 2008/908 Art.3

3004. Local Government Pension Scheme (Amendment) (No.2) Regulations 2003

revoked: SI 2008/238 Sch.1

3006. Race Relations Act 1976 (Statutory Duties) Order 2003

Sch.1, amended: SI 2008/526 Art.2

Sch.2, varied: 2008 c.14 Sch.10 para.1

3007. Race Relations Act 1976 (General Statutory Duty) Order 2003

Sch.1, varied: 2008 c.14 Sch.10 para.1

3035. Shrimp Fishing Nets (Wales) Order 2003

revoked: SI 2008/1811 Art.5

3044. Honey (Wales) Regulations 2003

Sch.2, amended: SI 2008/543 Reg.3

3053. Condensed Milk and Dried Milk (Wales) Regulations 2003

Reg.2, amended: SI 2008/137 Reg.3

Sch.1, amended: SI 2008/137 Reg.4

3054. Nurses Agencies (Wales) (Amendment) Regulations 2003

applied: 2008 c.14 s.17

3059. NHS Professionals Special Health Authority (Establishment and Constitution) Order 2003

Art.4, substituted: SI 2008/558 Art.2

3060. NHS Professionals Special Health Authority Regulations 2003

Reg.1, amended: SI 2008/2250 Art.2

3075. Money Laundering Regulations 2003

referred to: SI 2008/1741 Reg.112

Sch.2 Part II para.6, revoked (in part): SI 2008/1741 Sch.2

3096. Regulatory Reform (Business Tenancies) (England and Wales) Order 2003

Sch.1, see *Chiltern Railway Co Ltd v Patel* [2008] EWCA Civ 178, [2008] Bus. L.R. 1295 (CA (Civ Div)), Mummery, L.J.

Sch.2 para.3, see *Chiltern Railway Co Ltd v Patel* [2008] EWCA Civ 178, [2008] Bus. L.R. 1295 (CA (Civ Div)), Mummery, L.J.

Sch.2 para.4, see *Chiltern Railway Co Ltd v Patel* [2008] EWCA Civ 178, [2008] Bus. L.R. 1295 (CA (Civ Div)), Mummery, L.J.

NO.

2003–*cont.*

3096. Regulatory Reform (Business Tenancies) (England and Wales) Order 2003–*cont.*

Sch.2 para.7, see *Chiltern Railway Co Ltd v Patel* [2008] EWCA Civ 178, [2008] Bus. L.R. 1295 (CA (Civ Div)), Mummery, L.J.

Sch.2 para.8, see *Chiltern Railway Co Ltd v Patel* [2008] EWCA Civ 178, [2008] Bus. L.R. 1295 (CA (Civ Div)), Mummery, L.J.

3146. Local Authorities (Capital Finance and Accounting) (England) Regulations 2003

Reg.7A, added: SI 2008/414 Reg.3

Reg.28, substituted: SI 2008/414 Reg.4

Reg.29, substituted: SI 2008/414 Reg.4

Reg.30C, amended: SI 2008/414 Reg.5

Reg.30E, added: SI 2008/414 Reg.6

Reg.30F, added: SI 2008/414 Reg.6

3150. Extradition Act 2003 (Multiple Offences) Order 2003

Sch.1 para.2, see *Pilecki v Poland* [2008] UKHL 7, [2008] 1 W.L.R. 325 (HL), Lord Bingham of Cornhill

3172. Regulation of Investigatory Powers (Communications Data) Order 2003

applied: SI 2008/212 Reg.6

3183. Control of Misleading Advertisements (Amendment) Regulations 2003

revoked: SI 2008/1277 Sch.2 para.105, Sch.4 Part 2

3195. Communications (Bailiwick of Guernsey) Order 2003

applied: SI 2008/643

3197. Communications (Jersey) Order 2003

applied: SI 2008/643

3198. Communications (Isle of Man) Order 2003

applied: SI 2008/643

3200. Double Taxation Relief (Taxes on Income)(Chile) Order 2003

applied: SI 2008/3170 Reg.3

3201. Misuse of Drugs Act 1971 (Modification) (No.2) Order 2003

revoked: SI 2008/3130 Art.1

see *R. v Xiong Xu* [2007] EWCA Crim 3129, [2008] 2 Cr. App. R. (S.) 50 (CA (Crim Div)), Latham, L.J.

3227. Education (Pupil Exclusions and Appeals) (Maintained Schools) (Wales) Regulations 2003

Reg.4, see *R. (on the application of Watkins-Singh) v Aberdare Girls' High School Governors* [2008] EWHC 1865 (Admin), [2008] 3 F.C.R. 203 (QBD (Admin)), Silber, J.

3231. Education (School Day and School Year) (Wales) Regulations 2003

Reg.3, amended: SI 2008/1739 Reg.2

Reg.5, amended: SI 2008/1739 Reg.2

NO.

2003–cont.

3239. Local Authorities (Capital Finance and Accounting) (Wales) Regulations 2003
Reg.22, substituted: SI 2008/588 Reg.3
Reg.24C, amended: SI 2008/588 Reg.4
Reg.24E, added: SI 2008/588 Reg.5
Reg.24F, added: SI 2008/588 Reg.5

3242. Water Environment (Water Framework Directive) (England and Wales) Regulations 2003
applied: SI 2008/1097 Reg.7
Sch.2 Part 2 para.11, revoked: SI 2008/1097 Reg.19
Sch.2 Part 2 para.26, revoked: SI 2008/1097 Reg.19
Sch.2 Part 2 para.29, added: SI 2008/1097 Reg.5

3245. Water Environment (Water Framework Directive) (Northumbria River Basin District) Regulations 2003
applied: SI 2008/1097 Reg.7, SSI 2008/170 Reg.6

3273. African Swine Fever (Wales) Order 2003
applied: SI 2008/1275 Reg.15

3297. Reporting of Savings Income Information Regulations 2003
Reg.16, amended: SI 2008/2682 Sch.1 para.2, Sch.1 para.3
Reg.16, revoked (in part): SI 2008/2682 Sch.1 para.2, Sch.1 para.3

3310. Controls on Certain Azo Dyes and Blue Colourant Regulations 2003
revoked: SI 2008/2852 Sch.10 Part 1

3319. Conduct of Employment Agencies and Employment Businesses Regulations 2003
Sch.4, applied: SI 2008/3265 Reg.4

3334. Extradition Act 2003 (Designation of Part 2 Territories) Order 2003
Art.2, amended: SI 2008/1589 Art.2
Art.4, amended: SI 2008/1589 Art.3

3363. Insolvency Practitioners and Insolvency Services Account (Fees) Order 2003
Art.2, amended: SI 2008/3 Art.3
Art.2, applied: SI 2008/3 Art.4
Art.3, amended: SI 2008/672 Art.3
Sch.1 para.2, amended: SI 2008/672 Art.4

2004

99. Water Environment (Water Framework Directive) (Solway Tweed River Basin District) Regulations 2004
applied: SI 2008/1097 Reg.7, SSI 2008/170 Reg.6
Sch.2 Part 2 para.11, revoked: SI 2008/1097 Reg.19
Sch.2 Part 2 para.26, revoked: SI 2008/1097 Reg.19

NO.

2004–cont.

99. Water Environment (Water Framework Directive) (Solway Tweed River Basin District) Regulations 2004–*cont.*
Sch.2 Part 2 para.28, added: SI 2008/1097 Reg.5

129. Cableway Installations Regulations 2004
Reg.23, amended: SI 2008/960 Sch.3

160. Charities (Alexandra Park and Palace) Order 2004
see *R. (on the application of O'Callaghan) v Charity Commission for England and Wales* [2007] EWHC 2491 (Admin), [2008] W.T.L.R. 117 (QBD (Admin)), Sullivan, J.

163. Conduct of Members (Model Code of Conduct) (Amendment) (Wales) Order 2004
revoked: SI 2008/788 Art.5

219. Domiciliary Care Agencies (Wales) Regulations 2004
applied: 2008 c.14 s.17

260. Education (National Curriculum) (Modern Foreign Languages) (England) Order 2004
revoked: SI 2008/1766 Art.3

291. National Health Service (General Medical Services Contracts) Regulations 2004
Reg.2, amended: SI 2008/528 Sch.1 para.5, SI 2008/1700 Sch.1 para.12
Sch.6 Part 3 para.48, amended: SI 2008/528 Sch.1 para.5
Sch.6 Part 5 para.78, revoked: SI 2008/528 Sch.1 para.5
Sch.6 Part 5 para.90, revoked: SI 2008/528 Sch.1 para.5
Sch.6 Part 5 para.91A, added: SI 2008/1514 Reg.3

293. European Parliamentary Elections Regulations 2004
Reg.2, applied: SI 2008/2867 Reg.9
Reg.2, varied: SI 2008/2857 Art.7
Reg.6, applied: SI 2008/2857 Art.7
Reg.83, applied: SI 2008/1647 Reg.3
Sch.1 Part 4 para.56, applied: SI 2008/1647 Reg.3

307. Communications (Bailiwick of Guernsey) Order 2004
applied: SI 2008/643

308. Broadcasting and Communications (Jersey) Order 2004
applied: SI 2008/643

318. Trade in Controlled Goods (Embargoed Destinations) Order 2004
referred to: SI 2008/1281 Art.2, SI 2008/3161 Art.2
revoked: SI 2008/3231 Sch.6
Art.2, amended: SI 2008/1805 Art.3
Art.2, referred to: SI 2008/639 Art.2

NO.

2004–cont.

352. Petroleum Licensing (Exploration and Production) (Seaward and Landward Areas) Regulations 2004

Reg.3, disapplied: SI 2008/225 Reg.2
Sch.1 para.5A, added: 2008 c.32 Sch.3 para.16
Sch.1 para.7, amended: 2008 c.32 Sch.3 para.16
Sch.1 para.20A, added: 2008 c.32 Sch.3 para.16
Sch.2, disapplied: SI 2008/225 Reg.2
Sch.2 para.9A, added: 2008 c.32 Sch.3 para.17
Sch.2 para.16, amended: 2008 c.32 Sch.3 para.17
Sch.2 para.38, amended: 2008 c.32 Sch.3 para.17
Sch.2 para.38A, added: 2008 c.32 Sch.3 para.17
Sch.3, disapplied: SI 2008/225 Reg.2
Sch.3 para.10A, added: 2008 c.32 Sch.3 para.18
Sch.3 para.17, amended: 2008 c.32 Sch.3 para.18
Sch.3 para.39, amended: 2008 c.32 Sch.3 para.18
Sch.3 para.39A, added: 2008 c.32 Sch.3 para.18
Sch.4, disapplied: SI 2008/225 Reg.2
Sch.4 para.8A, added: 2008 c.32 Sch.3 para.19
Sch.4 para.15, amended: 2008 c.32 Sch.3 para.19
Sch.4 para.37, amended: 2008 c.32 Sch.3 para.19
Sch.4 para.37A, added: 2008 c.32 Sch.3 para.19
Sch.5, disapplied: SI 2008/225 Reg.2
Sch.6 para.8A, added: 2008 c.32 Sch.3 para.20
Sch.6 para.15, amended: 2008 c.32 Sch.3 para.20
Sch.6 para.36, amended: 2008 c.32 Sch.3 para.20
Sch.6 para.36A, added: 2008 c.32 Sch.3 para.20

402. Education (Pupil Exclusions) (Miscellaneous Amendments) (England) Regulations 2004

Reg.5, revoked: SI 2008/532 Reg.11
Reg.10, revoked: SI 2008/532 Reg.11

447. Schools Forums (England) (Amendment) Regulations 2004

applied: SI 2008/2867 Reg.25

478. National Health Service (General Medical Services Contracts) (Wales) Regulations 2004

Reg.2, amended: SI 2008/1329 Reg.2, SI 2008/1425 Reg.2
Reg.5, amended: SI 2008/1425 Reg.3

NO.

2004–cont.

478. National Health Service (General Medical Services Contracts) (Wales) Regulations 2004–*cont.*

Sch.6 Part 2 para.15, amended: SI 2008/1425 Reg.4
Sch.6 Part 2 para.17, amended: SI 2008/1425 Reg.4
Sch.6 Part 2 para.18, amended: SI 2008/1425 Reg.4
Sch.6 Part 2 para.19, amended: SI 2008/1425 Reg.4
Sch.6 Part 3 para.38, substituted: SI 2008/1329 Reg.3
Sch.6 Part 3 para.39, amended: SI 2008/1329 Reg.3
Sch.6 Part 4 para.52, amended: SI 2008/1425 Reg.4
Sch.6 Part 4 para.56, amended: SI 2008/1425 Reg.4
Sch.6 Part 4 para.58, amended: SI 2008/1425 Reg.4
Sch.6 Part 4 para.65, substituted: SI 2008/1329 Reg.3
Sch.6 Part 6 para.91, amended: SI 2008/1425 Reg.4
Sch.6 Part 8 para.111, amended: SI 2008/1425 Reg.4
Sch.6 Part 8 para.113, amended: SI 2008/1425 Reg.4
Sch.6 Part 8 para.118, amended: SI 2008/1425 Reg.4
Sch.6 Part 9 para.119, amended: SI 2008/1425 Reg.4

573. Local Government Pension Scheme (Amendment) Regulations 2004

revoked: SI 2008/238 Sch.1

585. National Health Service (Performers Lists) Regulations 2004

applied: SI 2008/1700 Reg.13, Reg.14, Reg.15
Part 4, referred to: SI 2008/1187 Sch.1 para.1
Reg.2, amended: SI 2008/1187 Reg.2
Reg.3, amended: SI 2008/1187 Reg.3
Reg.6, applied: SI 2008/2252 Sch.1 para.7
Reg.8, applied: SI 2008/2252 Sch.1 para.8
Reg.9, amended: SI 2008/1187 Reg.4
Reg.10, applied: SI 2008/2252 Sch.1 para.9
Reg.12, applied: SI 2008/2252 Sch.1 para.10
Reg.13, applied: SI 2008/2252 Sch.1 para.11
Reg.34, added: SI 2008/1187 Reg.5
Reg.34, amended: SI 2008/1700 Sch.1 para.14
Reg.35, added: SI 2008/1187 Reg.5
Reg.36, added: SI 2008/1187 Reg.5
Reg.37, added: SI 2008/1187 Reg.5
Reg.38, added: SI 2008/1187 Reg.5
Reg.39, added: SI 2008/1187 Reg.5
Reg.40, added: SI 2008/1187 Reg.5
Reg.41, added: SI 2008/1187 Reg.5
Reg.42, added: SI 2008/1187 Reg.5

NO.

2004–cont.

593. Insolvency Proceedings (Fees) Order 2004

Art.5, amended: SI 2008/714 Art.2
Art.6, amended: SI 2008/714 Art.2
Sch.2 para.2, amended: SI 2008/714 Art.2

627. National Health Service (Personal Medical Services Agreements) Regulations 2004

Reg.2, amended: SI 2008/528 Sch.1 para.7, SI 2008/1700 Sch.1 para.13
Sch.5 Part 3 para.47, amended: SI 2008/528 Sch.1 para.7
Sch.5 Part 5 para.74, revoked: SI 2008/528 Sch.1 para.7
Sch.5 Part 5 para.84, revoked: SI 2008/528 Sch.1 para.7
Sch.5 Part 5 para.85A, added: SI 2008/1514 Reg.4

643. Police (Complaints and Misconduct) Regulations 2004

applied: SI 2008/212 Reg.6, Reg.7
referred to: SI 2008/2863 r.4
Reg.1, amended: SI 2008/2866 Reg.3
Reg.1, varied: SI 2008/212 Sch.3 para.2
Reg.2, varied: SI 2008/212 Sch.3 para.3
Reg.3, varied: SI 2008/212 Sch.3 para.4
Reg.4, varied: SI 2008/212 Sch.3 para.4
Reg.5, varied: SI 2008/212 Sch.3 para.5
Reg.6, varied: SI 2008/212 Sch.3 para.6
Reg.8, varied: SI 2008/212 Sch.3 para.7
Reg.9, varied: SI 2008/212 Sch.3 para.8
Reg.11, varied: SI 2008/212 Sch.3 para.9
Reg.14A, added: SI 2008/2866 Reg.3
Reg.14A, applied: SI 2008/2864 Reg.19, Reg.34, Reg.35, Reg.54, Reg.55
Reg.14B, added: SI 2008/2866 Reg.3
Reg.14C, added: SI 2008/2866 Reg.3
Reg.14D, added: SI 2008/2866 Reg.3
Reg.14E, added: SI 2008/2866 Reg.3
Reg.18, amended: SI 2008/2866 Reg.3
Reg.18, revoked (in part): SI 2008/2866 Reg.3
Reg.18, varied: SI 2008/212 Sch.3 para.10
Reg.21, varied: SI 2008/212 Sch.3 para.11
Reg.24, varied: SI 2008/212 Sch.3 para.11
Reg.25, varied: SI 2008/212 Sch.3 para.12
Reg.26, varied: SI 2008/212 Sch.3 para.13
Reg.28, varied: SI 2008/212 Sch.3 para.13
Reg.30, varied: SI 2008/212 Sch.3 para.13

645. Police (Conduct) Regulations 2004

applied: SI 2008/2863 r.2, SI 2008/2864 Reg.19
revoked: SI 2008/2864 Reg.2

652. Ministry of Defence Police Appeal Tribunals Regulations 2004

Reg.4, amended: SI 2008/2059 Reg.2

660. Independent Police Complaints Commission (Staff Conduct) Regulations 2004

applied: SI 2008/212 Reg.6

NO.

2004–cont.

660. Independent Police Complaints Commission (Staff Conduct) Regulations 2004–*cont.*

Reg.1, varied: SI 2008/212 Sch.4 para.1
Reg.2, varied: SI 2008/212 Sch.4 para.2

664. Health and Social Care (Community Health and Standards) Act 2003 (Commission for Healthcare Audit and Inspection and Commission for Social Care Inspection) (Transitional and Consequential Provisions) Order 2004

Sch.1 para.7, revoked: SI 2008/2683 Sch.2

674. Recovery of Duties and Taxes Etc Due in Other Member States (Corresponding UK Claims, Procedure and Supplementary) Regulations 2004

see *Revenue and Customs Commissioners v Morris* [2007] EWHC 3345 (Ch), [2008] B.P.I.R. 391 (Ch D), Judge Pelling Q.C.
Reg.6, see *Revenue and Customs Commissioners v Morris* [2007] EWHC 3345 (Ch), [2008] B.P.I.R. 391 (Ch D), Judge Pelling Q.C.

683. Leasehold Valuation Tribunals (Fees) (Wales) Regulations 2004

Reg.8, amended: SI 2008/1879 Reg.27

692. Communications (Television Licensing) Regulations 2004

Sch.1, amended: SI 2008/643 Reg.3
Sch.1, referred to: SI 2008/643 Reg.7
Sch.2, referred to: SI 2008/643 Reg.7
Sch.2 Part 1 para.2, amended: SI 2008/643 Reg.4
Sch.2 Part 2 para.5, amended: SI 2008/643 Reg.4, Sch.1
Sch.2 Part 2 para.6, amended: SI 2008/643 Reg.4, Sch.1
Sch.2 Part 2 para.7, amended: SI 2008/643 Reg.4, Sch.1
Sch.2 Part 3 para.9, amended: SI 2008/643 Reg.4
Sch.2 Part 3 para.11, amended: SI 2008/643 Reg.4
Sch.2 Part 3 para.12, amended: SI 2008/643 Reg.4
Sch.2 Part 3 para.13, amended: SI 2008/643 Reg.4
Sch.2 Part 3 para.14, amended: SI 2008/643 Reg.4
Sch.2 Part 3 para.15, amended: SI 2008/643 Reg.4
Sch.2 Part 3 para.16, amended: SI 2008/643 Reg.4
Sch.2 Part 3 para.17, amended: SI 2008/643 Reg.4
Sch.3, referred to: SI 2008/643 Reg.7
Sch.3 Part 1, amended: SI 2008/643 Reg.5
Sch.3 Part 2 para.1, amended: SI 2008/643 Reg.5
Sch.4, referred to: SI 2008/643 Reg.7

NO.

2004–cont.

692. Communications (Television Licensing) Regulations 2004–*cont.*
Sch.5, referred to: SI 2008/643 Reg.7
Sch.5 para.1, amended: SI 2008/643 Reg.6
Sch.5 para.3, amended: SI 2008/643 Reg.6

693. Enterprise Act 2002 (Part 9 Restrictions on Disclosure of Information) (Specification) Order 2004
Sch.1, amended: SI 2008/37 Reg.26, SI 2008/1597 Sch.7 para.5, SI 2008/2164 Reg.24

702. Firearms (Northern Ireland) Order 2004
Art.58, applied: SI 2008/1216 Sch.1 para.31, Sch.2 para.31
Art.59, applied: SI 2008/1216 Sch.1 para.31, Sch.2 para.31
Art.60, applied: SI 2008/1216 Sch.1 para.31, Sch.2 para.31
Art.64, applied: SI 2008/1216 Sch.1 para.31, Sch.2 para.31
Art.70, applied: SI 2008/1216 Art.4, Art.5, Art.91
Art.70, referred to: SI 2008/1216 Art.7
Sch.4 para.1, substituted: SI 2008/1769 Sch.1 para.34
Sch.4 para.2, amended: SI 2008/1769 Sch.1 para.34, Sch.3
Sch.7 para.18, revoked: SI 2008/1216 Sch.6 Part 1
Sch.7 para.19, revoked: SI 2008/1216 Sch.6 Part 1
Sch.7 para.20, revoked: SI 2008/1216 Sch.6 Part 1

706. European Communities (Designation) Order 2004
Sch.1, amended: SI 2008/301 Sch.1
Sch.2, revoked: SI 2008/301 Sch.1

752. Employment Act 2002 (Dispute Resolution) Regulations 2004
see *Highland Council v TGWU* [2008] I.C.R. 1150 (EAT (SC)), Lady Smith; see *Yorkshire Housing Ltd v Swanson* [2008] I.R.L.R. 607 (EAT), Cox, J.
Reg.2, see *Yorkshire Housing Ltd v Swanson* [2008] I.R.L.R. 607 (EAT), Cox, J.
Reg.3, applied: SI 2008/3232 Sch.1 para.2
Reg.3, see *Harris v Towergate London Market Ltd* [2008] EWCA Civ 433, [2008] I.C.R. 1200 (CA (Civ Div)), Ward, L.J.
Reg.6, applied: SI 2008/3232 Sch.1 para.3
Reg.9, see *Alitalia Airport SpA v Akrif* [2008] I.C.R. 813 (EAT), Elias, J.; see *Highland Council v TGWU* [2008] I.C.R. 1150 (EAT (SC)), Lady Smith
Reg.12, see *Yorkshire Housing Ltd v Swanson* [2008] I.R.L.R. 607 (EAT), Cox, J.
Reg.15, applied: SI 2008/1660 Reg.17
Reg.15, see *Ashcroft v Haberdashers Aske's Boys School* [2008] I.C.R. 613 (EAT), Burton, J.; see *Harris v Towergate London*

NO.

2004–cont.

752. Employment Act 2002 (Dispute Resolution) Regulations 2004–*cont.*
Reg.15–*cont.*
Market Ltd [2008] EWCA Civ 433, [2008] I.C.R. 1200 (CA (Civ Div)), Ward, L.J.; see *Royal Bank of Scotland v Bevan* [2008] I.C.R. 682 (EAT), Judge Richardson
Reg.18, see *Highland Council v TGWU* [2008] I.C.R. 1150 (EAT (SC)), Lady Smith

755. Immigration (Restrictions on Employment) Order 2004
applied: SI 2008/310 Art.5
see *Kelly v University of Southampton* [2008] I.C.R. 357 (EAT), Judge Richardson
Art.3, see *Kelly v University of Southampton* [2008] I.C.R. 357 (EAT), Judge Richardson

756. Civil Aviation (Working Time) Regulations 2004
Reg.3, amended: SI 2008/960 Sch.3
Reg.4, see *British Airways Plc v Williams* [2008] I.C.R. 779 (EAT), Keith, J.
Sch.2 para.8, amended: SI 2008/960 Sch.3

778. Value Added Tax (Buildings and Land) Order 2004
revoked: SI 2008/1146 Sch.1 para.25

799. Public Trustee (Fees) (Amendment) Order 2004
revoked: SI 2008/611 Art.32

815. Independent Police Complaints Commission (Investigatory Powers) Order 2004
applied: SI 2008/212 Reg.6

850. Controlled Drugs (Substances Useful for Manufacture) (Intra-Community Trade) (Amendment) Regulations 2004
revoked: SI 2008/295 Reg.9

870. Local Authorities (Conduct of Referendums) (Wales) Regulations 2004
revoked: SI 2008/1848 Reg.1

928. Local Government Pension Scheme and Discretionary Compensation (Members of County and County Borough Councils in Wales) Regulations 2004
revoked: SI 2008/238 Sch.1

947. Trade Marks (Amendment) Rules 2004
revoked: SI 2008/1797 Sch.2

948. Trade Marks (International Registration) (Amendment) Order 2004
revoked: SI 2008/2206 Sch.7

964. Milk Development Council (Amendment) Order 2004
revoked: SI 2008/576 Sch.5 para.8

996. Pigs (Records, Identification and Movement) (Wales) Order 2004
revoked: SI 2008/1742 Art.19

NO.

2004–cont.

1020. National Health Service (Performers Lists) (Wales) Regulations 2004
Reg.4A, amended: SI 2008/1425 Reg.5
Reg.13, amended: SI 2008/1425 Reg.6
Reg.22, amended: SI 2008/1425 Reg.7
Reg.23A, amended: SI 2008/1425 Reg.8
Reg.29, amended: SI 2008/1425 Reg.9

1031. Medicines for Human Use (Clinical Trials) Regulations 2004
applied: SI 2008/552 Sch.1 para.10
Reg.2, amended: SI 2008/941 Reg.2
Reg.15, amended: SI 2008/941 Reg.3
Reg.19, applied: SI 2008/552 Reg.32
Reg.20, applied: SI 2008/552 Reg.32
Reg.24, applied: SI 2008/552 Reg.19
Reg.27, applied: SI 2008/552 Reg.2
Reg.28, applied: SI 2008/552 Reg.30
Reg.31, applied: SI 2008/552 Reg.2
Reg.44, applied: SI 2008/552 Reg.18
Reg.51, applied: SI 2008/552 Sch.2 para.7
Sch.1 Part 1 para.1, amended: SI 2008/941 Reg.4
Sch.1 Part 1 para.1, referred to: SI 2008/941 Reg.4
Sch.1 Part 2 para.15, referred to: SI 2008/941 Reg.3
Sch.2, referred to: SI 2008/941 Reg.5
Sch.2 para.1, amended: SI 2008/941 Reg.5
Sch.2 para.3, amended: SI 2008/941 Reg.5
Sch.2 para.6, amended: SI 2008/941 Reg.5
Sch.2 para.7, amended: SI 2008/941 Reg.5
Sch.2 para.8, amended: SI 2008/941 Reg.5
Sch.3 Part 1 para.2, amended: SI 2008/941 Reg.6
Sch.3 Part 2 para.11, applied: SI 2008/552 Reg.19, Sch.5 para.9

1049. Trade in Controlled Goods (Embargoed Destinations) (Amendment) Order 2004
revoked: SI 2008/3231 Sch.6

1050. Export of Goods, Transfer of Technology and Provision of Technical Assistance (Control) (Amendment) Order 2004
revoked: SI 2008/3231 Sch.6

1056. European Parliamentary Elections (Returning Officers) Order 2004
revoked: SI 2008/1914 Art.2

1110. European Communities (Designation) (No.2) Order 2004
revoked: SI 2008/3117 Art.5

1140. Occupational Pension Schemes (Winding Up) (Amendment) Regulations 2004
applied: SSI 2008/228 Reg.73

1157. Medicines for Human Use (Clinical Trials Fees Amendments) Regulations 2004
revoked: SI 2008/552 Sch.7

NO.

2004–cont.

1219. Accession (Immigration and Worker Registration) Regulations 2004
Reg.4, see *Zalewska v Department for Social Development* [2008] UKHL 67, [2008] 1 W.L.R. 2602 (HL (NI)), Lord Hope of Craighead
Reg.5, applied: SI 2008/794 Reg.70
Reg.7, see *Zalewska v Department for Social Development* [2008] UKHL 67, [2008] 1 W.L.R. 2602 (HL (NI)), Lord Hope of Craighead
Reg.8, see *Zalewska v Department for Social Development* [2008] UKHL 67, [2008] 1 W.L.R. 2602 (HL (NI)), Lord Hope of Craighead

1245. European Parliament (Number of MEPs) (United Kingdom and Gibraltar) Order 2004
revoked: SI 2008/1954 Art.3

1270. Cash Ratio Deposits (Value Bands and Ratios) Order 2004
revoked: SI 2008/1344 Art.2

1300. Measuring Instruments (EEC Requirements) (Fees) Regulations 2004
Sch.1, amended: SI 2008/732 Reg.2

1309. Adventure Activities Licensing Regulations 2004
Reg.5, amended: SI 2008/1973 Reg.2
Reg.18, amended: SI 2008/960 Sch.3

1314. Care Homes (Wales) (Amendment) Regulations 2004
applied: 2008 c.14 s.17

1363. Stamp Duty Land Tax (Appeals) Regulations 2004
applied: SI 2008/562 Reg.20

1396. Meat Products (Wales) Regulations 2004
Reg.5, amended: SI 2008/713 Reg.3
Sch.3 para.6, revoked: SI 2008/713 Reg.4
Sch.3 para.7, revoked: SI 2008/713 Reg.4
Sch.3 para.10, revoked: SI 2008/713 Reg.4

1452. Polish Potatoes (Notification) (England) Order 2004
revoked: SI 2008/2411 Art.3

1468. Energy Information (Household Refrigerators and Freezers) Regulations 2004
Sch.6 Part 3 para.12, amended: SI 2008/1277 Sch.2 para.107
Sch.6 Part 3 para.12, revoked (in part): SI 2008/1277 Sch.2 para.107, Sch.4 Part 2

1484. Consumer Credit (Advertisements) Regulations 2004
Reg.1, amended: SI 2008/1277 Sch.2 para.108, Sch.4 Part 2
Reg.2, amended: SI 2008/1277 Sch.2 para.108, Sch.4 Part 2
Reg.3, amended: SI 2008/1277 Sch.2 para.108, Sch.4 Part 2

NO.

2004–cont.

1484. Consumer Credit (Advertisements) Regulations 2004–*cont.*

Reg.4, amended: SI 2008/1277 Sch.2 para.108, Sch.4 Part 2

Reg.7, amended: SI 2008/1277 Sch.2 para.108, Sch.4 Part 2

Reg.7, revoked (in part): SI 2008/1277 Sch.2 para.108, Sch.4 Part 2

Reg.9, amended: SI 2008/1277 Sch.2 para.108, Sch.4 Part 2

Sch.3 para.1, revoked: SI 2008/1277 Sch.2 para.108, Sch.4 Part 2

Sch.3 para.2, revoked: SI 2008/1277 Sch.2 para.108, Sch.4 Part 2

Sch.3 para.3, revoked: SI 2008/1277 Sch.2 para.108, Sch.4 Part 2

Sch.3 para.4, revoked: SI 2008/1277 Sch.2 para.108, Sch.4 Part 2

Sch.3 para.5, revoked: SI 2008/1277 Sch.2 para.108, Sch.4 Part 2

Sch.3 para.6, revoked: SI 2008/1277 Sch.2 para.108, Sch.4 Part 2

1500. Criminal Justice (Northern Ireland) Order 2004

Part IV, applied: 2008 c.4 Sch.27 para.17

Art.20, amended: 2008 c.4 s.45

Sch.4 para.7A, added: SI 2008/1769 Sch.1 para.33

Sch.4 para.10A, added: SI 2008/1769 Sch.1 para.33

1501. Criminal Justice (Evidence) (Northern Ireland) Order 2004

Art.18, see *JA's Application for Judicial Review, Re* [2008] N.I. 74 (QBD (NI)), Kerr, L.C.J.

Art.22, see *JA's Application for Judicial Review, Re* [2008] N.I. 74 (QBD (NI)), Kerr, L.C.J.

1510. Conduct of Members (Model Code of Conduct) (Wales) (Amendment) (No.2) Order 2004

revoked: SI 2008/788 Art.5

1517. Enterprise Act 2002 (Bodies Designated to make Super-complaints) Order 2004

Sch.1, substituted: SI 2008/2161 Art.2

1633. Environmental Assessment of Plans and Programmes Regulations 2004

see *R. (on the application of Howsmoor Developments Ltd) v South Gloucestershire CC* [2008] EWHC 262 (Admin), [2008] Env. L.R. 38 (QBD (Admin)), Sir George Newman

1679. Demoted Tenancies (Review of Decisions) (England) Regulations 2004

see *R. (on the application of Gilboy) v Liverpool City Council* [2008] EWCA Civ 751, [2008] 4 All E.R. 127 (CA (Civ Div)), Waller, L.J. (V-P)

1729. Education (School Teachers Qualifications) (Wales) Regulations 2004

Reg.6, amended: SI 2008/215 Reg.10

NO.

2004–cont.

1729. Education (School Teachers Qualifications) (Wales) Regulations 2004–*cont.*

Sch.2 Part 1 para.5, amended: SI 2008/215 Reg.4, Reg.5, Reg.6

Sch.2 Part 1 para.11, amended: SI 2008/215 Reg.7, Reg.9, Reg.10

Sch.2 Part 1 para.11, revoked (in part): SI 2008/215 Reg.8

1748. Community Care, Services for Carers and Children's Services (Direct Payments) (Wales) Regulations 2004

Sch.1, amended: SI 2008/2828 Art.19

Sch.1, revoked (in part): SI 2008/2828 Art.19

1756. Adult Placement Schemes (Wales)-Regulations 2004

applied: 2008 c.14 s.17

1761. Nursing and Midwifery Council (Fitness to Practise) Rules Order of Council 2004

Sch.1, amended: SI 2008/3148 Sch.1

1767. Nursing and Midwifery Council (Education, Registration and Registration Appeals) Rules Order of Council 2004

Sch.1, added: SI 2008/1485 Sch.2 para.1

1768. National Health Service (Complaints) Regulations 2004

Reg.2, amended: SI 2008/528 Sch.1 para.6, SI 2008/1700 Sch.1 para.11

Reg.20, amended: SI 2008/528 Sch.1 para.6

1770. Care Standards Act 2000 (Establishments and Agencies) (Miscellaneous Amendments) Regulations 2004

applied: 2008 c.14 s.17

1771. Health Act 1999 (Consequential Amendments) (Nursing and Midwifery) Order 2004

Sch.1 Part 2 para.27, revoked (in part): SI 2008/1741 Sch.2

1793. Education (National Curriculum) (Attainment Targets and Programmes of Study in Modern Foreign Languages in respect of the Third Key Stage) (England) (No.2) Order 2004

revoked: SI 2008/1760 Art.5

1794. Education (National Curriculum) (Attainment Targets and Programmes of Study in Design and Technology in respect of the First, Second and Third Key Stages) (England) (No.2) Order 2004

revoked (in part): SI 2008/1754 Art.5

1800. Education (National Curriculum) (Attainment Targets and Programmes of Study in Science in respect of the First, Second Third and Fourth Key Stages) (England) (No.2) Order 2004

revoked (in part): SI 2008/1763 Art.5

NO.

2004–cont.

1830. Commonhold (Land Registration) Rules 2004

r.5, amended: SI 2008/1920 r.3
r.6, amended: SI 2008/1920 r.4
r.14, amended: SI 2008/1920 r.5
r.20, amended: SI 2008/1920 r.6
r.25, amended: SI 2008/1920 r.7
Sch.1, amended: SI 2008/1920 Sch.1

1861. Employment Tribunals (Constitution and Rules of Procedure) Regulations 2004

applied: SI 2008/534 Art.9, SI 2008/535 Art.9
Reg.2, amended: SI 2008/2683 Sch.1 para.241
Reg.3, amended: SI 2008/2683 Sch.1 para.242
Reg.4, amended: SI 2008/2683 Sch.1 para.243, SI 2008/2771 Reg.3, Reg.4, SI 2008/3240 Reg.3
Reg.5, amended: SI 2008/2683 Sch.1 para.244
Reg.6, amended: SI 2008/2683 Sch.1 para.245
Reg.7, amended: SI 2008/2683 Sch.1 para.246
Reg.8, amended: SI 2008/2683 Sch.1 para.247, SI 2008/2771 Reg.5, Reg.6, SI 2008/3240 Reg.3
Reg.8, applied: SI 2008/2995 Sch.1 Part 1
Reg.9, amended: SI 2008/2683 Sch.1 para.248, SI 2008/3240 Reg.3
Reg.10, amended: SI 2008/2683 Sch.1 para.249
Reg.11, amended: SI 2008/2683 Sch.1 para.250
Reg.13, amended: SI 2008/2683 Sch.1 para.251
Reg.15, amended: SI 2008/2683 Sch.1 para.252
Reg.16, amended: SI 2008/2683 Sch.1 para.253
Reg.16, applied: SI 2008/736 Reg.18
Reg.17, amended: SI 2008/2683 Sch.1 para.254
Sch.1, applied: SI 2008/736 Reg.18
Sch.1 para.1, amended: SI 2008/2683 Sch.1 para.255, SI 2008/3240 Reg.4
Sch.1 para.1, revoked (in part): SI 2008/3240 Reg.4
Sch.1 para.2, amended: SI 2008/3240 Reg.4
Sch.1 para.2, revoked (in part): SI 2008/3240 Reg.4
Sch.1 para.3, amended: SI 2008/2683 Sch.1 para.255, SI 2008/3240 Reg.4
Sch.1 para.3, revoked (in part): SI 2008/3240 Reg.4
Sch.1 para.4, amended: SI 2008/2683 Sch.1 para.255, SI 2008/3240 Reg.4
Sch.1 para.6, amended: SI 2008/2683 Sch.1 para.255, SI 2008/3240 Reg.4

NO.

2004–cont.

1861. Employment Tribunals (Constitution and Rules of Procedure) Regulations 2004–*cont.*

Sch.1 para.7, amended: SI 2008/2683 Sch.1 para.255
Sch.1 para.8, amended: SI 2008/2683 Sch.1 para.255, SI 2008/3240 Reg.4
Sch.1 para.9, amended: SI 2008/3240 Reg.4
Sch.1 para.10, amended: SI 2008/2683 Sch.1 para.255, SI 2008/3240 Reg.4
Sch.1 para.10, revoked (in part): SI 2008/3240 Reg.4
Sch.1 para.11, amended: SI 2008/2683 Sch.1 para.255, SI 2008/3240 Reg.4
Sch.1 para.12, amended: SI 2008/2683 Sch.1 para.255, SI 2008/3240 Reg.4
Sch.1 para.13, amended: SI 2008/2683 Sch.1 para.255
Sch.1 para.14, amended: SI 2008/2683 Sch.1 para.255, SI 2008/3240 Reg.4
Sch.1 para.15, amended: SI 2008/2683 Sch.1 para.255
Sch.1 para.15, substituted: SI 2008/3240 Reg.4
Sch.1 para.16, amended: SI 2008/2683 Sch.1 para.255
Sch.1 para.17, amended: SI 2008/2683 Sch.1 para.255
Sch.1 para.18, amended: SI 2008/2683 Sch.1 para.255, SI 2008/3240 Reg.4
Sch.1 para.18, revoked (in part): SI 2008/3240 Reg.4
Sch.1 para.18A, added: SI 2008/3240 Reg.4
Sch.1 para.19, amended: SI 2008/2683 Sch.1 para.255
Sch.1 para.20, amended: SI 2008/2683 Sch.1 para.255
Sch.1 para.22, amended: SI 2008/2683 Sch.1 para.255
Sch.1 para.22, revoked: SI 2008/3240 Reg.4
Sch.1 para.23, amended: SI 2008/2683 Sch.1 para.255
Sch.1 para.23, revoked: SI 2008/3240 Reg.4
Sch.1 para.24, revoked: SI 2008/3240 Reg.4
Sch.1 para.25, see *British Association for Shooting and Conservation v Cokayne* [2008] I.C.R. 185 (EAT), Judge David Richardson
Sch.1 para.25, amended: SI 2008/2683 Sch.1 para.255, SI 2008/3240 Reg.4
Sch.1 para.25A, added: SI 2008/3240 Reg.4
Sch.1 para.26, amended: SI 2008/3240 Reg.4
Sch.1 para.27, amended: SI 2008/2683 Sch.1 para.255
Sch.1 para.27, revoked (in part): SI 2008/3240 Reg.4
Sch.1 para.28, amended: SI 2008/2683 Sch.1 para.255
Sch.1 para.29, amended: SI 2008/2683 Sch.1 para.255

NO.

2004–cont.

1861. Employment Tribunals (Constitution and Rules of Procedure) Regulations 2004–*cont.*

Sch.1 para.30, amended: SI 2008/2683 Sch.1 para.255

Sch.1 para.31, amended: SI 2008/2683 Sch.1 para.255

Sch.1 para.32, amended: SI 2008/2683 Sch.1 para.255

Sch.1 para.33, amended: SI 2008/2683 Sch.1 para.255, SI 2008/3240 Reg.4

Sch.1 para.34, amended: SI 2008/2683 Sch.1 para.255, SI 2008/3240 Reg.4

Sch.1 para.35, amended: SI 2008/2683 Sch.1 para.255

Sch.1 para.36, amended: SI 2008/2683 Sch.1 para.255

Sch.1 para.37, see *Newham LBC v Bone* [2008] EWCA Civ 435, [2008] I.C.R. 923 (CA (Civ Div)), Buxton, L.J.

Sch.1 para.37, amended: SI 2008/2683 Sch.1 para.255

Sch.1 para.38, amended: SI 2008/2683 Sch.1 para.255

Sch.1 para.39, amended: SI 2008/2683 Sch.1 para.255

Sch.1 para.40, amended: SI 2008/2683 Sch.1 para.255

Sch.1 para.41, amended: SI 2008/2683 Sch.1 para.255

Sch.1 para.42, amended: SI 2008/2683 Sch.1 para.255

Sch.1 para.43, amended: SI 2008/2683 Sch.1 para.255

Sch.1 para.44, amended: SI 2008/2683 Sch.1 para.255

Sch.1 para.45, amended: SI 2008/2683 Sch.1 para.255

Sch.1 para.46, amended: SI 2008/2683 Sch.1 para.255

Sch.1 para.47, amended: SI 2008/2683 Sch.1 para.255

Sch.1 para.48, amended: SI 2008/2683 Sch.1 para.255

Sch.1 para.49, amended: SI 2008/2683 Sch.1 para.255

Sch.1 para.50, amended: SI 2008/2683 Sch.1 para.255, SI 2008/3240 Reg.4

Sch.1 para.52, amended: SI 2008/2683 Sch.1 para.255

Sch.1 para.54, amended: SI 2008/2683 Sch.1 para.255, SI 2008/3240 Reg.4

Sch.1 para.55, amended: SI 2008/2683 Sch.1 para.255

Sch.1 para.57, amended: SI 2008/2683 Sch.1 para.255

Sch.1 para.58, amended: SI 2008/2683 Sch.1 para.255

Sch.1 para.60, amended: SI 2008/2683 Sch.1 para.255, SI 2008/3240 Reg.4

NO.

2004–cont.

1861. Employment Tribunals (Constitution and Rules of Procedure) Regulations 2004–*cont.*

Sch.1 para.61, amended: SI 2008/2683 Sch.1 para.255, SI 2008/3240 Reg.4

Sch.2 para.3, amended: SI 2008/2683 Sch.1 para.256, SI 2008/3240 Reg.5

Sch.2 para.4, amended: SI 2008/2683 Sch.1 para.256

Sch.2 para.6, amended: SI 2008/2683 Sch.1 para.256

Sch.2 para.8, amended: SI 2008/2683 Sch.1 para.256

Sch.2 para.9, amended: SI 2008/2683 Sch.1 para.256

Sch.2 para.10, amended: SI 2008/2683 Sch.1 para.256, SI 2008/3240 Reg.5

Sch.3 para.8, amended: SI 2008/2683 Sch.1 para.257

Sch.4, applied: SI 2008/736 Reg.18, SI 2008/2852 Sch.8 para.2

Sch.4 para.6, amended: SI 2008/2683 Sch.1 para.258, SI 2008/3240 Reg.6

Sch.4 para.7, amended: SI 2008/2683 Sch.1 para.258

Sch.4 para.8, amended: SI 2008/2683 Sch.1 para.258

Sch.4 para.9, amended: SI 2008/2683 Sch.1 para.258

Sch.4 para.10, amended: SI 2008/2683 Sch.1 para.258, SI 2008/3240 Reg.6

Sch.6 para.3, amended: SI 2008/2683 Sch.1 para.259

Sch.6 para.4, amended: SI 2008/3240 Reg.7

Sch.6 para.4, revoked (in part): SI 2008/3240 Reg.7

Sch.6 para.5, amended: SI 2008/2683 Sch.1 para.259

Sch.6 para.6, amended: SI 2008/2683 Sch.1 para.259

Sch.6 para.10, amended: SI 2008/2683 Sch.1 para.259

Sch.6 para.11, amended: SI 2008/2683 Sch.1 para.259

Sch.6 para.12, amended: SI 2008/2683 Sch.1 para.259

Sch.6 para.13, amended: SI 2008/2683 Sch.1 para.259

1864. Tax Avoidance Schemes (Information) Regulations 2004

referred to: SI 2008/1947 Reg.2

Reg.7, substituted: SI 2008/1947 Reg.3

Reg.7A, added: SI 2008/1947 Reg.4

Reg.7B, added: SI 2008/1947 Reg.4

1932. Student Fees (Amounts) (England) Regulations 2004

Reg.4, amended: SI 2008/2507 Reg.2

Reg.5, amended: SI 2008/2507 Reg.2

NO.

2004–cont.

1933. Value Added Tax (Disclosure of Avoidance Schemes) (Designations) Order 2004
Art.2, amended: SI 2008/954 Art.53

1972. Care Standards Act 2000 (Extension of the Application of Part 2 to Adult Placement Schemes) (England) Regulations 2004
applied: 2008 c.14 s.17

1975. Contracting Out (Functions relating to Broadcast Advertising) and Specification of Relevant Functions Order 2004
Art.2, amended: SI 2008/1277 Sch.2 para.109, Sch.4 Part 2
Art.6, revoked: SI 2008/1277 Sch.2 para.109, Sch.4 Part 2
Art.8, revoked (in part): SI 2008/1277 Sch.2 para.109, Sch.4 Part 2
Art.12, amended: SI 2008/1277 Sch.4 Part 2

1984. European Communities (Designation) (No.4) Order 2004
Sch.1, amended: SI 2008/301 Sch.1
Sch.2, revoked: SI 2008/301 Sch.1

1988. Anti-social Behaviour (Northern Ireland) Order 2004
Art.4, amended: SI 2008/1216 Art.93
Art.6C, amended: SI 2008/1216 Art.94

2065. Biofuels and Other Fuel Substitutes (Payment of Excise Duties etc.) Regulations 2004
Reg.3, amended: SI 2008/753 Reg.8
Reg.3, enabled: SI 2008/753
Reg.19A, amended: SI 2008/753 Reg.8
Reg.28, revoked: SI 2008/753 Reg.8
Sch.1 para.1, amended: SI 2008/753 Reg.8
Sch.1 para.2, amended: SI 2008/753 Reg.8

2071. Adult Placement Schemes (England) Regulations 2004
applied: 2008 c.14 s.17

2073. Protection of Children and Vulnerable Adults and Care Standards Tribunal (Amendment) Regulations 2004
revoked: SI 2008/2683 Sch.2

2085. A26 and A27 Trunk Roads (Beddingham) (40 Miles Per Hour Speed Limit) Order 2004
revoked: SI 2008/2820 Art.2

2095. Financial Services (Distance Marketing) Regulations 2004
Reg.15, revoked (in part): SI 2008/1277 Sch.4 Part 2
Reg.22, amended: SI 2008/1277 Sch.4 Part 2

2110. Merchant Shipping (Vessel Traffic Monitoring and Reporting Requirements) Regulations 2004
Reg.4, amended: SI 2008/3145 Reg.3
Reg.5, amended: SI 2008/3145 Reg.3
Reg.16, amended: SI 2008/3145 Reg.3

NO.

2004–cont.

2152. Cosmetic Products (Safety) Regulations 2004
revoked: SI 2008/1284 Sch.1

2198. Discharge of Fines by Unpaid Work (Pilot Schemes) Order 2004
Art.2, amended: SI 2008/621 Art.2
Sch.1, amended: SI 2008/621 Art.2

2199. Venture Capital Trust (Winding up and Mergers) (Tax) Regulations 2004
Reg.9, amended: SI 2008/954 Art.54

2203. Town and Country Planning (Regional Planning) (England) Regulations 2004
varied: SI 2008/2867 Reg.20

2204. Town and Country Planning (Local Development) (England) Regulations 2004
applied: SI 2008/2867 Reg.21
Part 6, applied: SI 2008/2867 Reg.23
Reg.2, amended: SI 2008/1371 Reg.2
Reg.2, revoked (in part): SI 2008/1371 Reg.2
Reg.5, amended: SI 2008/1371 Reg.2
Reg.6, amended: SI 2008/1371 Reg.2
Reg.7, see *R. (on the application of Howsmoor Developments Ltd) v South Gloucestershire CC* [2008] EWHC 262 (Admin), [2008] Env. L.R. 38 (QBD (Admin)), Sir George Newman
Reg.8, amended: SI 2008/1371 Reg.2
Reg.8, revoked (in part): SI 2008/1371 Reg.2
Reg.9, amended: SI 2008/1371 Reg.2
Reg.10, substituted: SI 2008/1371 Reg.2
Reg.11, substituted: SI 2008/1371 Reg.2
Reg.11A, substituted: SI 2008/1371 Reg.2
Reg.14, amended: SI 2008/1371 Reg.2
Reg.16, amended: SI 2008/1371 Reg.2
Reg.24, substituted: SI 2008/1371 Reg.2
Reg.25, applied: SI 2008/1371 Reg.3
Reg.25, substituted: SI 2008/1371 Reg.2
Reg.26, applied: SI 2008/1371 Reg.3
Reg.26, substituted: SI 2008/1371 Reg.2
Reg.27, applied: SI 2008/1371 Reg.3
Reg.27, substituted: SI 2008/1371 Reg.2
Reg.27, varied: SI 2008/1371 Reg.3
Reg.28, substituted: SI 2008/1371 Reg.2
Reg.29, substituted: SI 2008/1371 Reg.2
Reg.30, substituted: SI 2008/1371 Reg.2
Reg.30, varied: SI 2008/1371 Reg.3
Reg.31, substituted: SI 2008/1371 Reg.2
Reg.32, substituted: SI 2008/1371 Reg.2
Reg.33, substituted: SI 2008/1371 Reg.2
Reg.34, amended: SI 2008/1371 Reg.2
Reg.35, amended: SI 2008/1371 Reg.2
Reg.36, amended: SI 2008/1371 Reg.2
Reg.37, substituted: SI 2008/1371 Reg.2
Reg.37, varied: SI 2008/1371 Reg.3
Reg.38, amended: SI 2008/1371 Reg.2
Reg.39, amended: SI 2008/1371 Reg.2
Reg.40, substituted: SI 2008/1371 Reg.2
Reg.41, amended: SI 2008/1371 Reg.2

NO.

2004–*cont.*

2204. Town and Country Planning (Local Development) (England) Regulations 2004–*cont.*
Reg.43, amended: SI 2008/1371 Reg.2
Reg.44, amended: SI 2008/1371 Reg.2
Reg.44A, added: SI 2008/1371 Reg.2
Reg.45, substituted: SI 2008/1371 Reg.2
Reg.45A, substituted: SI 2008/1371 Reg.2

2302. Disability Discrimination Codes of Practice (Employment and Occupation, and Trade Organisations and Qualifications Bodies) Appointed Day Order 2004
revoked: SI 2008/1336 Art.2

2326. European Public Limited-Liability Company Regulations 2004
Reg.3, amended: SI 2008/948 Sch.1 para.235
Reg.13, amended: SI 2008/948 Sch.1 para.235
Reg.45, referred to: SI 2008/3232 Sch.1 Part 2
Reg.79, amended: SI 2008/948 Sch.1 para.235
Reg.80, amended: SI 2008/948 Sch.1 para.235
Reg.83, amended: SI 2008/948 Sch.1 para.235
Reg.88, amended: SI 2008/948 Sch.1 para.235
Reg.89, amended: SI 2008/948 Sch.1 para.235
Sch.4 para.1, amended: SI 2008/948 Sch.1 para.235
Sch.4 para.2, amended: SI 2008/948 Sch.1 para.235
Sch.4 para.3, amended: SI 2008/948 Sch.1 para.235
Sch.4 para.4, amended: SI 2008/948 Sch.1 para.235
Sch.4 para.5, amended: SI 2008/948 Sch.1 para.235
Sch.4 para.6, amended: SI 2008/948 Sch.1 para.235
Sch.4 para.7, amended: SI 2008/948 Sch.1 para.235
Sch.4 para.8, amended: SI 2008/948 Sch.1 para.235
Sch.4 para.9, amended: SI 2008/948 Sch.1 para.235
Sch.4 para.10, amended: SI 2008/948 Sch.1 para.235
Sch.4 para.11, amended: SI 2008/948 Sch.1 para.235

2361. Cosmetic Products (Safety) (Amendment) Regulations 2004
revoked: SI 2008/1284 Sch.1

2412. Genetically Modified Organisms (Traceability and Labelling) (England) Regulations 2004
Reg.8, amended: SI 2008/2598 Reg.2

NO.

2004–*cont.*

2412. Genetically Modified Organisms (Traceability and Labelling) (England) Regulations 2004–*cont.*
Reg.8, revoked (in part): SI 2008/2598 Reg.2

2414. Care Standards Act 2000 and the Children Act 1989 (Amendment of Miscellaneous Regulations) (Wales) Regulations 2004
applied: 2008 c.14 s.17

2468. Penalties for Disorderly Behaviour (Amount of Penalty) (Amendment No.2) Order 2004
revoked: SI 2008/3297 Art.3

2506. Schools Budget Shares (Wales) Regulations 2004
Sch.1 para.37, added: SI 2008/1866 Reg.4

2561. Export of Goods, Transfer of Technology and Provision of Technical Assistance (Control) (Amendment No.2) Order 2004
revoked: SI 2008/3231 Sch.6

2608. General Medical Council (Fitness to Practise) Rules Order of Council 2004
see *R. (on the application of Gwynn) v General Medical Council* [2007] EWHC 3145 (Admin), [2008] LS Law Medical 112 (QBD (Admin)), Sullivan, J.
Sch.1, added: SI 2008/1256 Sch.1

2692. Genetically Modified Organisms (Transboundary Movements) (England) Regulations 2004
Reg.8, amended: SI 2008/2598 Reg.3

2695. Disqualification from Caring for Children (Wales) Regulations 2004
Reg.3, amended: SI 2008/2691 Reg.2
Sch.1 Part I para.1, amended: SI 2008/2691 Reg.2
Sch.1 Part I para.2, amended: SI 2008/2691 Reg.2

2697. Polish Potatoes (Notification) (Wales) Order 2004
revoked: SI 2008/2781 Art.3

2741. Export Control (Libya Embargo) Order 2004
revoked: SI 2008/3231 Sch.6

2824. Food Labelling (Amendment) (England) (No.2) Regulations 2004
Sch.1, revoked: SI 2008/1188 Reg.3

2858. Education (School Performance Targets) (England) Regulations 2004
applied: SI 2008/3086 Reg.2
Reg.2, amended: SI 2008/3086 Reg.2
Reg.4, revoked: SI 2008/3086 Reg.2
Reg.5, amended: SI 2008/3086 Reg.2
Reg.6, amended: SI 2008/3086 Reg.2
Reg.8, amended: SI 2008/3086 Reg.2

NO.

2004–cont.

2913. Controls on Certain Azo Dyes and Blue Colourant (Amendment) Regulations 2004
revoked: SI 2008/2852 Sch.10 Part 1

2988. Cosmetic Products (Safety) (Amendment) (No.2) Regulations 2004
revoked: SI 2008/1284 Sch.1

3022. Food Labelling (Amendment) (No.2) (Wales) Regulations 2004
Sch.1, revoked: SI 2008/1268 Reg.3

3114. Family Proceedings Fees Order 2004
revoked: SI 2008/1054 Sch.3
Sch.1A para.2, amended: SI 2008/115 Art.2

3120. Non-Contentious Probate Fees Order 2004
Sch.1, amended: SI 2008/2854 Art.3
Sch.1, referred to: SI 2008/2854 Art.2
Sch.1A para.1, amended: SI 2008/2854 Art.4
Sch.1A para.3, amended: SI 2008/2854 Art.5
Sch.1A para.3, referred to: SI 2008/2854 Art.5

3121. Civil Proceedings Fees Order 2004
referred to: SI 2008/116 Art.2
revoked: SI 2008/1053 Sch.3
Sch.1, amended: SI 2008/116 Art.3
Sch.1A para.2, amended: SI 2008/116 Art.4

3130. Financing of Maintained Schools (England) Regulations 2004
revoked: SI 2008/228 Reg.2

3131. LEA Budget, Schools Budget and Individual Schools Budget (England) Regulations 2004
revoked: SI 2008/228 Reg.2

3154. Wireless Telegraphy (Spectrum Trading) Regulations 2004
Reg.4, amended: SI 2008/2105 Reg.3
Reg.6, amended: SI 2008/2105 Reg.4
Sch.1 Part 4, amended: SI 2008/688 Reg.2, SI 2008/2105 Reg.5, SI 2008/3192 Reg.2
Sch.1 Part 8, added: SI 2008/2105 Reg.5
Sch.1 Part 9, added: SI 2008/2105 Reg.5

3155. Wireless Telegraphy (Register) Regulations 2004
Reg.4, amended: SI 2008/2104 Reg.2
Sch.1 Part 4, amended: SI 2008/689 Reg.2, SI 2008/3193 Reg.2
Sch.1 Part 10, added: SI 2008/2104 Reg.2

3219. Insurance Accounts Directive (Lloyd's Syndicate and Aggregate Accounts) Regulations 2004
revoked: SI 2008/1950 Reg.30

3226. Sea Fishing (Enforcement of Community Satellite Monitoring Measures) Order 2004
Art.5, applied: SSI 2008/101 Sch.1 Part 2
Art.6, applied: SSI 2008/101 Sch.1 Part 2
Art.7, applied: SSI 2008/101 Sch.1 Part 2
Art.8, applied: SSI 2008/101 Sch.1 Part 2
Art.9, applied: SSI 2008/101 Sch.1 Part 2
Art.11, applied: SSI 2008/101 Sch.1 Part 2

NO.

2004–cont.

3226. Sea Fishing (Enforcement of Community Satellite Monitoring Measures) Order 2004–*cont.*
Art.12, applied: SSI 2008/101 Sch.1 Part 2
Art.13, applied: SSI 2008/101 Sch.1 Part 2
Art.14, applied: SSI 2008/101 Sch.1 Part 2

3271. Loan Relationships and Derivative Contracts (Change Of Accounting Practice) Regulations 2004
Reg.2, amended: SI 2008/3237 Reg.3
Reg.3A, amended: SI 2008/3237 Reg.4
Reg.3C, amended: SI 2008/3237 Reg.5

3280. Common Agricultural Policy Single Payment and Support Schemes (Cross Compliance) (Wales) Regulations 2004
Sch.1 para.16, substituted: SI 2008/1081 Reg.10

3282. Suspension of Day Care Providers and Child Minders (Wales) Regulations 2004
Reg.2, amended: SI 2008/2689 Reg.2
Reg.8, amended: SI 2008/2689 Reg.2

3328. European Communities (Designation) (No.7) Order 2004
Sch.1, amended: SI 2008/301 Sch.1
Sch.2, amended: SI 2008/301 Sch.1

3354. Protection of Children and Vulnerable Adults and Care Standards Tribunal (Amendment No.2) Regulations 2004
revoked: SI 2008/2683 Sch.2

3368. Social Security, Child Support and Tax Credits (Decisions and Appeals) Amendment Regulations 2004
referred to: SI 2008/2683 Art.3
Reg 2, revoked (in part): SI 2008/2683 Sch.2
Reg.3, revoked (in part): SI 2008/2683 Sch.2
Reg.6, revoked: SI 2008/2683 Sch.2

3372. Local Government Pension Scheme (Amendment) (No.2) Regulations 2004
revoked: SI 2008/238 Sch.1

3386. Control of Substances Hazardous to Health (Amendment) Regulations 2004
Reg.2, revoked (in part): SI 2008/2852 Sch.10 Part 2

3387. Non-Domestic Rating (Chargeable Amounts) (England) Regulations 2004
Reg.4, amended: SI 2008/428 Sch.1 para.3
Reg.10, amended: SI 2008/428 Sch.1 para.3
Reg.11, amended: SI 2008/428 Sch.1 para.3
Sch.2 para.4, amended: SI 2008/428 Sch.1 para.3
Sch.2 para.5, amended: SI 2008/428 Sch.1 para.3

3391. Environmental Information Regulations 2004
applied: 2008 c.27 s.63, s.68, Sch.1 para.26

NO.

2004–cont.

3391. Environmental Information Regulations 2004–*cont.*
see *R. (on the application of Hardy) v Milford Haven Port Authority* [2007] EWHC 1883 (Admin), [2008] J.P.L. 702 (QBD), Beatson, J.
Reg.5, see *Export Credits Guarantee Department v Friends of the Earth* [2008] EWHC 638 (Admin), [2008] Env. L.R. 40 (QBD (Admin)), Mitting, J.
Reg.11, see *R. (on the application of Hardy) v Milford Haven Port Authority* [2007] EWHC 1883 (Admin), [2008] J.P.L. 702 (QBD), Beatson, J.
Reg.12, see *Export Credits Guarantee Department v Friends of the Earth* [2008] EWHC 638 (Admin), [2008] Env. L.R. 40 (QBD (Admin)), Mitting, J.; see *R. (on the application of Hardy) v Milford Haven Port Authority* [2007] EWHC 1883 (Admin), [2008] J.P.L. 702 (QBD), Beatson, J.

3392. Electricity and Gas (Energy Efficiency Obligations) Order 2004
applied: SI 2008/188 Art.17

3426. Information and Consultation of Employees Regulations 2004
see *UK Coal Mining Ltd v National Union of Mineworkers (Northumberland Area)* [2008] I.C.R. 163 (EAT), Elias, J (President)
Reg.33, referred to: SI 2008/3232 Sch.1 Part 2

2005

3. Social Security (Incapacity Benefit Work-focused Interviews) Amendment Regulations 2005
revoked: SI 2008/2928 Reg.12

15. Immigration (Procedure for Marriage) Regulations 2005
see *R. (on the application of Baiai) v Secretary of State for the Home Department* [2008] UKHL 53, [2008] 3 W.L.R. 549 (HL), Lord Bingham of Cornhill

17. Incidental Catches of Cetaceans in Fisheries (England) Order 2005
Art.4, applied: SSI 2008/101 Sch.1 Part 2

50. Blood Safety and Quality Regulations 2005
Reg.8, amended: SI 2008/941 Reg.7
Reg.9, amended: SI 2008/941 Reg.8
Reg.12B, amended: SI 2008/941 Reg.9
Reg.22, amended: SI 2008/525 Reg.2
Reg.22, revoked (in part): SI 2008/525 Reg.2

52. Education (Student Support) Regulations 2005
applied: SI 2008/3170 Reg.3

176. County of Durham (Electoral Changes) Order 2005
applied: SI 2008/493 Art.13

NO.

2005–cont.

191. Child Trust Funds (Non-tax Appeals) Regulations 2005
Reg.2, amended: SI 2008/2683 Sch.1 para.261
Reg.3, amended: SI 2008/2683 Sch.1 para.262
Reg.4, amended: SI 2008/2683 Sch.1 para.263
Reg.5, amended: SI 2008/2683 Sch.1 para.264
Reg.5, revoked (in part): SI 2008/2683 Sch.1 para.264
Reg.6, amended: SI 2008/2683 Sch.1 para.265
Reg.7, amended: SI 2008/2683 Sch.1 para.266
Reg.8, amended: SI 2008/2683 Sch.1 para.267
Reg.8, revoked (in part): SI 2008/2683 Sch.1 para.267
Reg.9, amended: SI 2008/2683 Sch.1 para.268
Reg.10, amended: SI 2008/2683 Sch.1 para.269
Reg.11, amended: SI 2008/2683 Sch.1 para.270
Reg.12, amended: SI 2008/2683 Sch.1 para.271
Reg.13, amended: SI 2008/2683 Sch.1 para.272
Reg.13, revoked (in part): SI 2008/2683 Sch.1 para.272
Reg.14, amended: SI 2008/2683 Sch.1 para.273
Reg.15, revoked (in part): SI 2008/2683 Sch.1 para.274

207. Social Security and Child Support Commissioners (Procedure) (Amendment) Regulations 2005
revoked: SI 2008/2683 Sch.2

218. Common Agricultural Policy Single Payment and Support Schemes (Integrated Administration and Control System) Regulations 2005
applied: SSI 2008/159 Reg.3
Reg.2, amended: SSI 2008/184 Sch.2 para.1

219. Common Agricultural Policy Single Payment and Support Schemes Regulations 2005
Reg.6, substituted: SI 2008/1139 Reg.3
Reg.9, substituted: SI 2008/1139 Reg.4

222. Copyright (Certification of Licensing Scheme for Educational Recording of Broadcasts) (Educational Recording Agency Limited) Order 2005
referred to: SI 2008/211
revoked: SI 2008/211 Art.2

230. Asylum and Immigration Tribunal (Procedure) Rules 2005
referred to: SI 2008/1088 r.1

NO.

2005–cont.

230. Asylum and Immigration Tribunal (Procedure) Rules 2005–*cont.*

see *DK (Serbia) v Secretary of State for the Home Department* [2006] EWCA Civ 1747, [2008] 1 W.L.R. 1246 (CA (Civ Div)), Latham, L.J.; see *FS (Eritrea) v Secretary of State for the Home Department* [2008] Imm. A.R. 47 (AIT), CMG Ockelton (Deputy President)

Part 2 r.8, amended: SI 2008/1088 r.2

Part 2 r.9, amended: SI 2008/1088 r.3

Part 2 r.15, amended: SI 2008/1088 r.4

Part 3 r.30, amended: SI 2008/1088 r.5

Part 3 r.31, amended: SI 2008/1088 r.6

Part 3 r.33, amended: SI 2008/1088 r.7

Part 3 r.36, amended: SI 2008/1088 r.8

Part 5 r.45, amended: SI 2008/1088 r.9

Part 5 r.54, revoked (in part): SI 2008/2683 Sch.1 para.275

Part 5 r.56, amended: SI 2008/1088 r.10

r.17, see *AP (Pakistan) v Secretary of State for the Home Department* [2008] I.N.L.R. 118 (AIT), Senior Immigration Judge Mackey

r.22, see *SK (Sri Lanka) v Secretary of State for the Home Department* [2008] EWCA Civ 495, Times, May 27, 2008 (CA (Civ Div)), Longmore, L.J.

r.32, see *DK (Serbia) v Secretary of State for the Home Department* [2006] EWCA Civ 1747, [2008] 1 W.L.R. 1246 (CA (Civ Div)), Latham, L.J.; see *Saber v Secretary of State for the Home Department* [2007] UKHL 57, [2008] 3 All E.R. 97 (HL), Lord Bingham of Cornhill

r.45, see *SK (Sri Lanka) v Secretary of State for the Home Department* [2008] EWCA Civ 495, Times, May 27, 2008 (CA (Civ Div)), Longmore, L.J.

r.59, see *AP (Pakistan) v Secretary of State for the Home Department* [2008] I.N.L.R. 118 (AIT), Senior Immigration Judge Mackey

232. Export Control (Iraq and Ivory Coast) Order 2005

Art.1, amended: SI 2008/3231 Sch.6

Art.6, revoked: SI 2008/3231 Sch.6

Art.7, revoked: SI 2008/3231 Sch.6

255. Pensions (Northern Ireland) Order 2005

Art.110, applied: SI 2008/3069 Reg.3

Art.111, applied: SI 2008/3069 Reg.3

Art.146, applied: SI 2008/664 Reg.2

279. Dutch Potatoes (Notification) (England) Order 2005

revoked: SI 2008/2411 Art.3

337. Social Security, Child Support and Tax Credits (Miscellaneous Amendments) Regulations 2005

referred to: SI 2008/2683 Art.3

Reg.2, revoked (in part): SI 2008/2683 Sch.2

Reg.4, revoked (in part): SI 2008/2683 Sch.2

NO.

2005–cont.

340. General Commissioners (Jurisdiction and Procedure) (Amendment) Regulations 2005

applied: SI 2008/562 Reg.20

341. Special Commissioners (Jurisdiction and Procedure) (Amendment) Regulations 2005

applied: SI 2008/562 Reg.20

346. Education (Information as to Provision of Education) (England) (Amendment) Regulations 2005

revoked: SI 2008/4 Sch.3

351. Public Trustee (Fees) (Amendment) Order 2005

revoked: SI 2008/611 Art.32

360. Common Agricultural Policy Single Payment and Support Schemes (Wales) Regulations 2005

Reg.2, substituted: SI 2008/2500 Reg.3

Reg.6, substituted: SI 2008/2500 Reg.4

Reg.7A, substituted: SI 2008/2500 Reg.5

Reg.8, revoked: SI 2008/2500 Reg.6

Reg.10, amended: SI 2008/2500 Reg.7

368. Accounts and Audit (Wales) Regulations 2005

Reg.2, amended: SI 2008/912 Sch.2 para.6

384. Criminal Procedure Rules 2005

applied: 2008 c.4 Sch.27 para.16, SI 2008/1586 Sch.2 para.4

referred to: SI 2008/2076 r.2

see *King v Serious Fraud Office* [2008] EWCA Crim 530, [2008] 1 W.L.R. 2634 (CA (Crim Div)), Gage, L.J.; see *R. v Scott (Casim)* [2007] EWCA Crim 2757, (2008) 172 J.P. 149 (CA (Crim Div)), Toulson, L.J.

Part 2 r.2.1, amended: SI 2008/2076 r.4, SI 2008/3269 r.3

Part 2 r.2.2, amended: SI 2008/3269 r.4

Part 2 r.2.5, added: SI 2008/2076 r.5

Part 4 r.4.4, amended: SI 2008/2076 r.6, r.7

Part 7 r.7.1, amended: SI 2008/3269 r.12

Part 7 r.7.1, substituted: SI 2008/2076 Sch.1

Part 7 r.7.2, amended: SI 2008/3269 r.5, r.12

Part 7 r.7.2, substituted: SI 2008/2076 Sch.1

Part 7 r.7.3, amended: SI 2008/3269 r.12

Part 7 r.7.3, substituted: SI 2008/2076 Sch.1

Part 7 r.7.4, amended: SI 2008/3269 r.6, r.12

Part 7 r.7.4, substituted: SI 2008/2076 Sch.1

Part 7 r.7.5, amended: SI 2008/3269 r.12

Part 7 r.7.5, substituted: SI 2008/2076 Sch.1

Part 7 r.7.6, amended: SI 2008/3269 r.12

Part 7 r.7.6, substituted: SI 2008/2076 Sch.1

Part 7 r.7.7, amended: SI 2008/3269 r.12

Part 7 r.7.7, substituted: SI 2008/2076 Sch.1

Part 7 r.7.8, amended: SI 2008/3269 r.12

Part 7 r.7.8, substituted: SI 2008/2076 Sch.1

Part 7 r.7.9, amended: SI 2008/3269 r.12

Part 7 r.7.9, substituted: SI 2008/2076 Sch.1

Part 19 r.19.1, amended: SI 2008/3269 r.7

Part 19 r.19.2, amended: SI 2008/3269 r.7

Part 19 r.19.3, amended: SI 2008/3269 r.7

NO.

2005–cont.

384. Criminal Procedure Rules 2005–*cont.*
Part 19 r.19.4, amended: SI 2008/3269 r.7
Part 19 r.19.5, amended: SI 2008/3269 r.7
Part 19 r.19.6, amended: SI 2008/3269 r.7
Part 19 r.19.7, amended: SI 2008/3269 r.7
Part 19 r.19.8, amended: SI 2008/3269 r.7
Part 19 r.19.9, amended: SI 2008/3269 r.7
Part 19 r.19.10, amended: SI 2008/3269 r.7
Part 19 r.19.11, amended: SI 2008/3269 r.7
Part 19 r.19.12, amended: SI 2008/3269 r.7
Part 19 r.19.13, amended: SI 2008/3269 r.7
Part 19 r.19.14, amended: SI 2008/3269 r.7
Part 19 r.19.15, amended: SI 2008/3269 r.7
Part 19 r.19.16, amended: SI 2008/3269 r.7
Part 19 r.19.17, amended: SI 2008/3269 r.7
Part 19 r.19.18, amended: SI 2008/3269 r.7
Part 19 r.19.19, amended: SI 2008/3269 r.7
Part 19 r.19.20, amended: SI 2008/3269 r.7
Part 19 r.19.21, amended: SI 2008/3269 r.7
Part 19 r.19.22, amended: SI 2008/3269 r.7
Part 19 r.19.23, amended: SI 2008/3269 r.7
Part 19 r.19.24, amended: SI 2008/3269 r.7
Part 19 r.19.25, added: SI 2008/3269 r.7
Part 19 r.19.25, amended: SI 2008/3269 r.7
Part 21 r.21.1, amended: SI 2008/3269 r.12
Part 21 r.21.1, substituted: SI 2008/3269 Sch.1
Part 21 r.21.2, amended: SI 2008/3269 r.12
Part 21 r.21.2, substituted: SI 2008/3269 Sch.1
Part 21 r.21.3, amended: SI 2008/3269 r.12
Part 21 r.21.3, substituted: SI 2008/3269 Sch.1
Part 21 r.21.4, amended: SI 2008/3269 r.12
Part 21 r.21.4, substituted: SI 2008/3269 Sch.1
Part 21 r.21.5, amended: SI 2008/3269 r.12
Part 21 r.21.5, substituted: SI 2008/3269 Sch.1
Part 21 r.21.6, amended: SI 2008/3269 r.12
Part 21 r.21.6, substituted: SI 2008/3269 Sch.1
Part 37 r.37.1, amended: SI 2008/3269 r.12
Part 37 r.37.1, substituted: SI 2008/3269 Sch.2
Part 37 r.37.2, amended: SI 2008/3269 r.12
Part 37 r.37.2, substituted: SI 2008/3269 Sch.2
Part 37 r.37.3, amended: SI 2008/3269 r.12
Part 37 r.37.3, substituted: SI 2008/3269 Sch.2
Part 37 r.37.4, amended: SI 2008/3269 r.12
Part 37 r.37.4, substituted: SI 2008/3269 Sch.2
Part 37 r.37.5, amended: SI 2008/3269 r.12
Part 37 r.37.5, substituted: SI 2008/3269 Sch.2
Part 37 r.37.6, amended: SI 2008/3269 r.12
Part 37 r.37.6, substituted: SI 2008/3269 Sch.2

NO.

2005–cont.

384. Criminal Procedure Rules 2005–*cont.*
Part 37 r.37.7, amended: SI 2008/3269 r.12
Part 37 r.37.7, substituted: SI 2008/3269 Sch.2
Part 37 r.37.8, amended: SI 2008/3269 r.12
Part 37 r.37.8, substituted: SI 2008/3269 Sch.2
Part 37 r.37.9, added: SI 2008/2076 r.10
Part 37 r.37.9, amended: SI 2008/3269 r.12
Part 37 r.37.9, substituted: SI 2008/3269 Sch.2
Part 37 r.37.10, added: SI 2008/2076 r.10
Part 37 r.37.10, amended: SI 2008/3269 r.12
Part 37 r.37.10, substituted: SI 2008/3269 Sch.2
Part 37 r.37.11, added: SI 2008/2076 r.10
Part 37 r.37.11, amended: SI 2008/3269 r.12
Part 37 r.37.11, substituted: SI 2008/3269 Sch.2
Part 37 r.37.12, amended: SI 2008/3269 r.12
Part 37 r.37.12, substituted: SI 2008/3269 Sch.2
Part 37 r.37.13, amended: SI 2008/3269 r.12
Part 37 r.37.13, substituted: SI 2008/3269 Sch.2
Part 37 r.37.14, amended: SI 2008/3269 r.12
Part 37 r.37.14, substituted: SI 2008/3269 Sch.2
Part 37 r.37.15, amended: SI 2008/3269 r.12
Part 37 r.37.15, substituted: SI 2008/3269 Sch.2
Part 38 r.38.1, amended: SI 2008/3269 r.12
Part 38 r.38.1, revoked: SI 2008/3269 r.10
Part 38 r.38.2, amended: SI 2008/3269 r.12
Part 38 r.38.2, revoked: SI 2008/3269 r.10
Part 38 r.38.3, amended: SI 2008/3269 r.12
Part 38 r.38.3, revoked: SI 2008/3269 r.10
Part 38 r.38.4, amended: SI 2008/3269 r.12
Part 38 r.38.4, revoked: SI 2008/3269 r.10
Part 38 r.38.5, amended: SI 2008/3269 r.12
Part 38 r.38.5, revoked: SI 2008/3269 r.10
Part 38 r.38.6, amended: SI 2008/3269 r.12
Part 38 r.38.6, revoked: SI 2008/3269 r.10
Part 44 r.44.1, amended: SI 2008/2076 r.11, SI 2008/3269 r.12
Part 44 r.44.1, substituted: SI 2008/3269 Sch.3
Part 44 r.44.2, amended: SI 2008/3269 r.12
Part 44 r.44.2, substituted: SI 2008/3269 Sch.3
Part 44 r.44.3, amended: SI 2008/3269 r.12
Part 44 r.44.3, substituted: SI 2008/3269 Sch.3
Part 44 r.44.4, amended: SI 2008/3269 r.12
Part 44 r.44.4, substituted: SI 2008/3269 Sch.3
Part 48 r.48.1, amended: SI 2008/912 Sch.2 para.7
Part 50 r.50, amended: SI 2008/3269 r.12
Part 50 r.50.1, amended: SI 2008/3269 r.12

NO.

2005–cont.

384. Criminal Procedure Rules 2005–*cont.*
Part 50 r.50.2, amended: SI 2008/3269 r.12
Part 50 r.50.3, amended: SI 2008/3269 r.12
Part 50 r.50.4, amended: SI 2008/3269 r.12
Part 50 r.50.5, amended: SI 2008/3269 r.12
Part 50 r.50.6, amended: SI 2008/3269 r.12
Part 50 r.50.7, amended: SI 2008/3269 r.12
Part 50 r.50.8, amended: SI 2008/3269 r.12
Part 50 r.50.9, amended: SI 2008/3269 r.12
Part 55 r.55.4, added: SI 2008/2076 r.13
Part 58 r.58.1, amended: SI 2008/3269 r.12
Part 58 r.58.2, amended: SI 2008/3269 r.12
Part 58 r.58.3, amended: SI 2008/3269 r.12
Part 58 r.58.4, amended: SI 2008/3269 r.12
Part 58 r.58.5, amended: SI 2008/3269 r.12
Part 58 r.58.6, amended: SI 2008/3269 r.12
Part 58 r.58.7, amended: SI 2008/3269 r.12
Part 58 r.58.8, amended: SI 2008/3269 r.12
Part 58 r.58.9, amended: SI 2008/3269 r.12
Part 58 r.58.10, amended: SI 2008/3269 r.12
Part 58 r.58.11, amended: SI 2008/3269 r.12
Part 58 r.58.12, amended: SI 2008/3269 r.12
Part 59 r.59.4, see *King v Serious Fraud Office* [2008] EWCA Crim 530, [2008] 3 All E.R. 830 (CA (Crim Div)), Gage, L.J.
Part 60 r.60.1, amended: SI 2008/3269 r.12
Part 60 r.60.2, amended: SI 2008/3269 r.12
Part 60 r.60.3, amended: SI 2008/3269 r.12
Part 60 r.60.4, amended: SI 2008/3269 r.12
Part 60 r.60.5, amended: SI 2008/3269 r.12
Part 60 r.60.6, amended: SI 2008/3269 r.12
Part 60 r.60.7, amended: SI 2008/3269 r.12
Part 60 r.60.8, amended: SI 2008/3269 r.12
Part 61 r.61.1, amended: SI 2008/3269 r.12
Part 61 r.61.2, amended: SI 2008/3269 r.12
Part 61 r.61.3, amended: SI 2008/3269 r.12
Part 61 r.61.4, amended: SI 2008/3269 r.12
Part 61 r.61.5, amended: SI 2008/3269 r.12
Part 61 r.61.6, amended: SI 2008/3269 r.12
Part 61 r.61.7, amended: SI 2008/3269 r.12
Part 61 r.61.8, amended: SI 2008/3269 r.12
Part 61 r.61.9, amended: SI 2008/3269 r.12
Part 61 r.61.10, amended: SI 2008/3269 r.12
Part 61 r.61.11, amended: SI 2008/3269 r.12
Part 61 r.61.12, amended: SI 2008/3269 r.12
Part 61 r.61.13, amended: SI 2008/3269 r.12
Part 61 r.61.14, amended: SI 2008/3269 r.12
Part 61 r.61.15, amended: SI 2008/3269 r.12
Part 61 r.61.16, amended: SI 2008/3269 r.12
Part 61 r.61.17, amended: SI 2008/3269 r.12
Part 61 r.61.18, amended: SI 2008/3269 r.12
Part 61 r.61.19, amended: SI 2008/3269 r.12
Part 61 r.61.20, amended: SI 2008/3269 r.12
Part 61 r.61.21, amended: SI 2008/3269 r.12
Part 61 r.61.22, amended: SI 2008/3269 r.12
Part 62 r.62.1, amended: SI 2008/3269 r.12
Part 62 r.62.2, amended: SI 2008/3269 r.12
Part 62 r.62.3, amended: SI 2008/3269 r.12
Part 63 r.63.1, amended: SI 2008/3269 r.12

NO.

2005–cont.

384. Criminal Procedure Rules 2005–*cont.*
Part 63 r.63.1, substituted: SI 2008/2076 Sch.2
Part 63 r.63.2, amended: SI 2008/3269 r.12
Part 63 r.63.2, substituted: SI 2008/2076 Sch.2
Part 63 r.63.3, amended: SI 2008/3269 r.12
Part 63 r.63.3, substituted: SI 2008/2076 Sch.2
Part 63 r.63.4, amended: SI 2008/3269 r.12
Part 63 r.63.4, substituted: SI 2008/2076 Sch.2
Part 63 r.63.5, amended: SI 2008/3269 r.12
Part 63 r.63.5, substituted: SI 2008/2076 Sch.2
Part 63 r.63.6, amended: SI 2008/3269 r.12
Part 63 r.63.6, substituted: SI 2008/2076 Sch.2
Part 63 r.63.7, amended: SI 2008/3269 r.12
Part 63 r.63.7, substituted: SI 2008/2076 Sch.2
Part 63 r.63.8, amended: SI 2008/3269 r.12
Part 63 r.63.8, substituted: SI 2008/2076 Sch.2
Part 63 r.63.9, amended: SI 2008/3269 r.12
Part 63 r.63.9, substituted: SI 2008/2076 Sch.2
Part 63 r.63.10, amended: SI 2008/3269 r.12
Part 63 r.63.10, substituted: SI 2008/2076 Sch.2
Part 64 r.64.1, amended: SI 2008/3269 r.12
Part 64 r.64.2, amended: SI 2008/3269 r.12
Part 64 r.64.3, amended: SI 2008/3269 r.12
Part 64 r.64.4, amended: SI 2008/3269 r.12
Part 64 r.64.5, amended: SI 2008/3269 r.12
Part 64 r.64.6, amended: SI 2008/3269 r.12
Part 64 r.64.7, amended: SI 2008/3269 r.12
Part 65 r.65.1, amended: SI 2008/2076 r.15, SI 2008/3269 r.12
Part 65 r.65.2, amended: SI 2008/3269 r.12
Part 65 r.65.3, amended: SI 2008/3269 r.12
Part 65 r.65.4, amended: SI 2008/3269 r.12
Part 65 r.65.5, amended: SI 2008/2076 r.16, r.17, SI 2008/3269 r.12
Part 65 r.65.6, amended: SI 2008/3269 r.12
Part 65 r.65.7, amended: SI 2008/3269 r.12
Part 65 r.65.8, amended: SI 2008/3269 r.12
Part 65 r.65.9, amended: SI 2008/3269 r.12
Part 65 r.65.10, amended: SI 2008/3269 r.12
Part 65 r.65.11, amended: SI 2008/3269 r.12
Part 65 r.65.11, substituted: SI 2008/2076 r.18
Part 65 r.65.12, amended: SI 2008/3269 r.12
Part 65 r.65.13, amended: SI 2008/3269 r.12
Part 65 r.65.14, amended: SI 2008/3269 r.12
Part 66 r.66.1, amended: SI 2008/3269 r.12
Part 66 r.66.2, amended: SI 2008/3269 r.12
Part 66 r.66.3, amended: SI 2008/3269 r.12
Part 66 r.66.4, amended: SI 2008/3269 r.12
Part 66 r.66.5, amended: SI 2008/3269 r.12

NO.

2005–cont.

384. Criminal Procedure Rules 2005–*cont.*

Part 66 r.66.6, amended: SI 2008/2076 r.19, SI 2008/3269 r.12
Part 66 r.66.7, amended: SI 2008/3269 r.12
Part 66 r.66.8, amended: SI 2008/3269 r.12
Part 66 r.66.9, amended: SI 2008/3269 r.12
Part 66 r.66.10, amended: SI 2008/3269 r.12
Part 66 r.66.11, amended: SI 2008/3269 r.12
Part 66 r.66.12, amended: SI 2008/3269 r.12
Part 66 r.66.13, amended: SI 2008/3269 r.12
Part 66 r.66.14, amended: SI 2008/3269 r.12
Part 66 r.66.15, amended: SI 2008/3269 r.12
Part 66 r.66.16, amended: SI 2008/3269 r.12
Part 66 r.66.17, amended: SI 2008/3269 r.12
Part 67 r.67.1, amended: SI 2008/3269 r.12
Part 67 r.67.2, amended: SI 2008/3269 r.12
Part 67 r.67.3, amended: SI 2008/3269 r.12
Part 67 r.67.4, amended: SI 2008/3269 r.12
Part 67 r.67.5, amended: SI 2008/3269 r.12
Part 67 r.67.6, amended: SI 2008/3269 r.12
Part 67 r.67.7, amended: SI 2008/3269 r.12
Part 67 r.67.8, amended: SI 2008/3269 r.12
Part 67 r.67.9, amended: SI 2008/3269 r.12
Part 67 r.67.10, amended: SI 2008/3269 r.12
Part 67 r.67.11, amended: SI 2008/3269 r.12
Part 68 r.68.1, amended: SI 2008/2076 r.20, r.21, SI 2008/3269 r.12
Part 68 r.68.2, amended: SI 2008/2076 r.22, SI 2008/3269 r.12
Part 68 r.68.3, amended: SI 2008/2076 r.23, SI 2008/3269 r.12
Part 68 r.68.4, amended: SI 2008/2076 r.24, SI 2008/3269 r.12
Part 68 r.68.5, amended: SI 2008/3269 r.12
Part 68 r.68.6, amended: SI 2008/3269 r.12
Part 68 r.68.7, amended: SI 2008/3269 r.12
Part 68 r.68.8, amended: SI 2008/3269 r.12
Part 68 r.68.9, amended: SI 2008/3269 r.12
Part 68 r.68.10, amended: SI 2008/3269 r.12
Part 68 r.68.11, amended: SI 2008/3269 r.12
Part 68 r.68.12, amended: SI 2008/3269 r.12
Part 68 r.68.13, amended: SI 2008/3269 r.12
Part 68 r.68.14, amended: SI 2008/3269 r.12
Part 68 r.68.15, amended: SI 2008/3269 r.12
Part 68 r.68.16, amended: SI 2008/3269 r.12
Part 68 r.68.17, amended: SI 2008/3269 r.12
Part 68 r.68.18, amended: SI 2008/3269 r.12
Part 68 r.68.19, amended: SI 2008/3269 r.12
Part 68 r.68.20, amended: SI 2008/3269 r.12
Part 68 r.68.21, amended: SI 2008/3269 r.12
Part 68 r.68.22, amended: SI 2008/3269 r.12
Part 68 r.68.23, amended: SI 2008/3269 r.12
Part 68 r.68.24, amended: SI 2008/3269 r.12
Part 68 r.68.25, amended: SI 2008/3269 r.12
Part 68 r.68.26, amended: SI 2008/3269 r.12
Part 68 r.68.27, amended: SI 2008/3269 r.12
Part 68 r.68.28, amended: SI 2008/3269 r.12
Part 68 r.68.29, amended: SI 2008/3269 r.12
Part 68 r.68.30, amended: SI 2008/3269 r.12
Part 68 r.68.31, amended: SI 2008/3269 r.12

NO.

2005–cont.

384. Criminal Procedure Rules 2005–*cont.*

Part 69 r.69.1, substituted: SI 2008/3269 r.12
Part 69 r.69.2, substituted: SI 2008/3269 r.12
Part 69 r.69.3, substituted: SI 2008/3269 r.12
Part 69 r.69.4, substituted: SI 2008/3269 r.12
Part 69 r.69.5, substituted: SI 2008/3269 r.12
Part 69 r.69.6, substituted: SI 2008/3269 r.12
Part 69 r.69.7, substituted: SI 2008/3269 r.12
Part 69 r.69.8, substituted: SI 2008/3269 r.12
Part 69 r.69.9, substituted: SI 2008/3269 r.12
Part 70 r.70.1, amended: SI 2008/3269 r.12
Part 70 r.70.2, amended: SI 2008/3269 r.12
Part 70 r.70.3, amended: SI 2008/3269 r.12
Part 70 r.70.4, amended: SI 2008/3269 r.12
Part 70 r.70.5, amended: SI 2008/3269 r.12
Part 70 r.70.6, amended: SI 2008/3269 r.12
Part 70 r.70.7, amended: SI 2008/3269 r.12
Part 70 r.70.8, amended: SI 2008/3269 r.12
Part 74 r.74.1, amended: SI 2008/3269 r.12
Part 74 r.74.2, amended: SI 2008/3269 r.12
Part 74 r.74.3, amended: SI 2008/3269 r.12
Part 74 r.74.4, amended: SI 2008/3269 r.12
Part 78 r.78.1, amended: SI 2008/2076 r.25
Part 78 r.78.1, revoked (in part): SI 2008/2076 r.25
r.4.7, see *R. v Popat (Harish)* [2008] EWCA Crim 1921, Times, September 10, 2008 (CA (Crim Div)), Hughes, L.J.
r.59.4, see *King v Serious Fraud Office* [2008] EWCA Crim 530, [2008] 1 W.L.R. 2634 (CA (Crim Div)), Gage, L.J.

390. Tractor etc (EC Type-Approval) Regulations 2005

Reg.2, amended: SI 2008/1980 Reg.2

392. Adoptions with a Foreign Element Regulations 2005

Pt 2, see *MN (India) v Secretary of State for the Home Department* [2008] EWCA Civ 38, [2008] 2 F.L.R. 87 (CA (Civ Div)), Ward, L.J.
Reg.10, see *G (A Child) (Adoption: Placement outside Jurisdiction), Re* [2008] EWCA Civ 105, [2008] Fam. 97 (CA (Civ Div)), Sir Mark Potter (President, Fam)

393. Sea Fishing (Restriction on Days at Sea) Order 2005

revoked: SI 2008/2347 Art.21

408. Health Protection Agency Regulations 2005

Reg.1, amended: SI 2008/2250 Art.2

422. Central Rating List (Wales) Regulations 2005

Reg.8, substituted: SI 2008/2672 Reg.2

437. Armed Forces Early Departure Payments Scheme Order 2005

referred to: SI 2008/229 Art.3
Art.4, amended: SI 2008/229 Art.3

438. Armed Forces Pension Scheme Order 2005

Sch.1, added: SI 2008/229 Art.2
Sch.1, amended: SI 2008/229 Art.2

NO.

2005–cont.

438. Armed Forces Pension Scheme Order 2005–*cont.*

Sch.1, referred to: SI 2008/229 Art.2

439. Armed Forces and Reserve Forces (Compensation Scheme) Order 2005

applied: SI 2008/1963 Reg.2

referred to: SI 2008/39 Art.2

Art.2, amended: SI 2008/39 Art.3, SI 2008/2683 Sch.1 para.277, SI 2008/2942 Art.3

Art.7, amended: SI 2008/39 Art.4, SI 2008/2942 Art.4

Art.8, amended: SI 2008/2942 Art.5

Art.13, amended: SI 2008/39 Art.5, SI 2008/2683 Sch.1 para.278, SI 2008/2942 Art.6

Art.14, amended: SI 2008/39 Art.6

Art.15, amended: SI 2008/39 Art.7, SI 2008/2942 Art.7

Art.15A, added: SI 2008/39 Art.8

Art.15A, amended: SI 2008/2942 Art.8

Art.15B, added: SI 2008/39 Art.8

Art.15B, amended: SI 2008/2683 Sch.1 para.279, SI 2008/2942 Art.9

Art.15B, revoked (in part): SI 2008/2942 Art.9

Art.15C, added: SI 2008/2942 Art.10

Art.15D, added: SI 2008/2942 Art.10

Art.19, amended: SI 2008/2942 Art.11

Art.20, amended: SI 2008/39 Art.9, SI 2008/2160 Art.2

Art.37, amended: SI 2008/39 Art.10, SI 2008/2942 Art.12

Art.43, amended: SI 2008/2683 Sch.1 para.280

Art.44, amended: SI 2008/39 Art.11, SI 2008/2942 Art.13

Art.45, amended: SI 2008/2683 Sch.1 para.281, SI 2008/2942 Art.14

Art.47, amended: SI 2008/39 Art.12, SI 2008/2683 Sch.1 para.282, SI 2008/2942 Art.15

Art.48, amended: SI 2008/39 Art.13, SI 2008/2683 Sch.1 para.283, SI 2008/2942 Art.16

Art.49, amended: SI 2008/2683 Sch.1 para.284, SI 2008/2942 Art.17

Art.54, amended: SI 2008/39 Art.14, SI 2008/2683 Sch.1 para.285, SI 2008/2942 Art.18

Art.56, amended: SI 2008/2683 Sch.1 para.286

Art.57, amended: SI 2008/2683 Sch.1 para.287

Sch.4, amended: SI 2008/39 Art.15, SI 2008/2160 Art.3, SI 2008/2942 Art.19

441. Pension Protection Fund (Multi-employer Schemes) (Modification) Regulations 2005

Reg.15, revoked (in part): SI 2008/731 Reg.17

Reg.62, revoked (in part): SI 2008/731 Reg.17

NO.

2005–cont.

443. Trade in Goods (Control) (Amendment) Order 2005

revoked: SI 2008/3231 Sch.6

445. Trade in Controlled Goods (Embargoed Destinations) (Amendment) Order 2005

revoked: SI 2008/3231 Sch.6

454. Social Security (Graduated Retirement Benefit) Regulations 2005

Sch.1 Part 1 para.1, varied: SI 2008/632 Art.12

Sch.1 Part 1 para.2, varied: SI 2008/632 Art.12

Sch.1 Part 1 para.3, varied: SI 2008/632 Art.12

Sch.1 Part 1 para.4, varied: SI 2008/632 Art.12

Sch.1 Part 1 para.5, varied: SI 2008/632 Art.12

Sch.1 Part 1 para.6, varied: SI 2008/632 Art.12

Sch.1 Part 1 para.7, varied: SI 2008/632 Art.12

Sch.1 Part 1 para.8, varied: SI 2008/632 Art.12

Sch.1 Part 1 para.9, varied: SI 2008/632 Art.12

Sch.1 Part 1 para.10, varied: SI 2008/632 Art.12

Sch.1 Part 2A para.20A, varied: SI 2008/632 Art.12

Sch.1 Part 2A para.20B, varied: SI 2008/632 Art.12

Sch.1 Part 2A para.20C, varied: SI 2008/632 Art.12

Sch.1 Part 2A para.20D, varied: SI 2008/632 Art.12

Sch.1 Part 2 para.11, varied: SI 2008/632 Art.12

Sch.1 Part 2 para.12, varied: SI 2008/632 Art.12

Sch.1 Part 2 para.13, varied: SI 2008/632 Art.12

Sch.1 Part 2 para.14, varied: SI 2008/632 Art.12

Sch.1 Part 2 para.15, varied: SI 2008/632 Art.12

Sch.1 Part 2 para.16, varied: SI 2008/632 Art.12

Sch.1 Part 2 para.17, varied: SI 2008/632 Art.12

Sch.1 Part 2 para.18, varied: SI 2008/632 Art.12

Sch.1 Part 2 para.19, varied: SI 2008/632 Art.12

Sch.1 Part 2 para.20, varied: SI 2008/632 Art.12

Sch.1 Part 2 para.20ZA, varied: SI 2008/632 Art.12

Sch.1 Part 2 para.20ZB, varied: SI 2008/632 Art.12

Sch.1 Part 3 para.21, varied: SI 2008/632 Art.12

465. Dairy Produce Quotas Regulations 2005

Reg.2, amended: SI 2008/439 Sch.1 para.1

Reg.4, amended: SI 2008/439 Sch.1 para.2

Reg.9, amended: SI 2008/439 Sch.1 para.3

Reg.13, amended: SI 2008/439 Sch.1 para.4

Reg.15, amended: SI 2008/439 Sch.1 para.5

NO.

2005–cont.

465. Dairy Produce Quotas Regulations 2005–*cont.*
Reg.19, amended: SI 2008/439 Sch.1 para.6
Reg.21, amended: SI 2008/439 Sch.1 para.7
Reg.22, amended: SI 2008/439 Sch.1 para.8
Reg.23, amended: SI 2008/439 Sch.1 para.9
Reg.25, amended: SI 2008/439 Sch.1 para.10
Reg.27, amended: SI 2008/439 Sch.1 para.11
Reg.28, amended: SI 2008/439 Sch.1 para.12
Reg.30, amended: SI 2008/439 Sch.1 para.13
Reg.31, amended: SI 2008/439 Sch.1 para.14
Reg.33, amended: SI 2008/439 Sch.1 para.15
Reg.38, amended: SI 2008/439 Sch.1 para.16
Reg.39, amended: SI 2008/439 Sch.1 para.17

466. Dairy Produce Quotas (General Provisions) (Amendment) Regulations 2005
revoked: SI 2008/438 Reg.3

468. Export of Goods, Transfer of Technology and Provision of Technical Assistance (Control) (Amendment) Order 2005
revoked: SI 2008/3231 Sch.6

470. Police Authorities (Best Value) Performance Indicators Order 2005
applied: SI 2008/659 Art.3
revoked: SI 2008/659 Art.3

472. Family Proceedings Fees (Amendment) Order 2005
revoked: SI 2008/1054 Sch.3

473. Civil Proceedings Fees (Amendment) Order 2005
revoked: SI 2008/1053 Sch.3

480. National Health Service (General Ophthalmic Services Supplementary List) and (General Ophthalmic Services Amendment and Consequential Amendment) Regulations 2005
applied: SI 2008/1187 Sch.1 para.8
revoked: SI 2008/1700 Sch.2

520. Children (Allocation of Proceedings) (Amendment) Order 2005
revoked: SI 2008/2836 Sch.2

526. LEA Budget, Schools Budget and Individual Schools Budget (Amendment) (England) Regulations 2005
revoked: SI 2008/228 Reg.2

537. Dairy Produce Quotas (Wales) Regulations 2005
Reg.2, amended: SI 2008/685 Sch.1 para.1
Reg.4, amended: SI 2008/685 Sch.1 para.2
Reg.9, amended: SI 2008/685 Sch.1 para.3
Reg.13, amended: SI 2008/685 Sch.1 para.4
Reg.15, amended: SI 2008/685 Sch.1 para.5
Reg.19, amended: SI 2008/685 Sch.1 para.6
Reg.21, amended: SI 2008/685 Sch.1 para.7
Reg.22, amended: SI 2008/685 Sch.1 para.8
Reg.23, amended: SI 2008/685 Sch.1 para.9
Reg.25, amended: SI 2008/685 Sch.1 para.10

NO.

2005–cont.

537. Dairy Produce Quotas (Wales) Regulations 2005–*cont.*
Reg.27, amended: SI 2008/685 Sch.1 para.11
Reg.28, amended: SI 2008/685 Sch.1 para.12
Reg.30, amended: SI 2008/685 Sch.1 para.13
Reg.31, amended: SI 2008/685 Sch.1 para.14
Reg.33, amended: SI 2008/685 Sch.1 para.15
Reg.38, amended: SI 2008/685 Sch.1 para.16
Reg.39, amended: SI 2008/685 Sch.1 para.17

551. Central Rating List (England) Regulations 2005
Reg.8, revoked (in part): SI 2008/429 Reg.2
Sch.1 Part 12, amended: SI 2008/429 Reg.2

555. Contracting-out, Protected Rights and Safeguarded Rights (Transfer Payment) Amendment Regulations 2005
applied: SSI 2008/228 Reg.73

560. Asylum and Immigration Tribunal (Fast Track Procedure) Rules 2005
applied: SI 2008/1089 r.1
Part 2 r.6, amended: SI 2008/1089 r.2
Part 2 r.6, revoked (in part): SI 2008/1089 r.2
Part 2 r.13, substituted: SI 2008/1089 r.3
Sch.2, amended: SI 2008/1089 r.4

572. Charities (Accounts and Reports) Regulations 2005
applied: SI 2008/629 Reg.4
referred to: SI 2008/629 Reg.4
revoked: SI 2008/629 Reg.4
Reg.7, referred to: SI 2008/629 Reg.4

581. Penalties for Disorderly Behaviour (Amount of Penalty) (Amendment) Order 2005
revoked: SI 2008/3297 Art.3

590. Pension Protection Fund (Entry Rules) Regulations 2005
applied: SI 2008/1810 Reg.2
Reg.2, amended: SI 2008/731 Reg.18
Reg.3, amended: SI 2008/1810 Reg.2

626. Occupational and Personal Pension Schemes (General Levy) Regulations 2005
Reg.6, amended: SI 2008/661 Reg.2
Reg.7, amended: SI 2008/661 Reg.2

640. National Care Standards Commission (Commission for Social Care Inspection) (Fees and Frequency of Inspections) (Adoption Agencies) (Amendment) Regulations 2005
applied: 2008 c.14 s.17

641. National Health Service (Pharmaceutical Services) Regulations 2005
Reg.2, amended: SI 2008/528 Sch.1 para.8
Reg.23, amended: SI 2008/528 Sch.1 para.8
Reg.27, revoked (in part): SI 2008/528 Sch.1 para.8

NO.

2005–cont.

641. National Health Service (Pharmaceutical Services) Regulations 2005– *cont.*
Reg.33, amended: SI 2008/528 Sch.1 para.8
Reg.56A, added: SI 2008/683 Reg.2
Sch.1 Part 1 para.1, amended: SI 2008/1514 Reg.5
Sch.1 Part 1 para.1, revoked (in part): SI 2008/528 Sch.1 para.8
Sch.1 Part 4 para.26, amended: SI 2008/683 Reg.3
Sch.1 Part 4 para.26, revoked (in part): SI 2008/528 Sch.1 para.8
Sch.1 Part 4 para.28, amended: SI 2008/683 Reg.3
Sch.2 para.1, amended: SI 2008/1514 Reg.5
Sch.2 para.1, revoked (in part): SI 2008/528 Sch.1 para.8
Sch.3 para.1, amended: SI 2008/1514 Reg.5
Sch.3 para.1, revoked (in part): SI 2008/528 Sch.1 para.8
Sch.4 Part 1 para.2, amended: SI 2008/683 Reg.4

659. Non-Domestic Rating (Alteration of Lists and Appeals) (England) Regulations 2005
see *O'Brien (t/a Poster Sites Southern) v Harding (Valuation Officer)* [2008] R.A. 73 (Lands Tr), Judge Mole Q.C.
Part 3, applied: SI 2008/2333 Reg.4
Reg.4, applied: SI 2008/2333 Reg.4
Reg.4, varied: SI 2008/2333 Reg.4
Reg.6, varied: SI 2008/2333 Reg.5

665. Local Government (Best Value Performance Indicators) (Wales) Order 2005
revoked: SI 2008/503 Art.3

669. Pension Protection Fund (Review and Reconsideration of Reviewable Matters) Regulations 2005
Reg.27, amended: SI 2008/2683 Sch.1 para.288

678. Occupational Pension Schemes (Employer Debt) Regulations 2005
applied: SI 2008/731 Reg.2
Reg.1, amended: SI 2008/731 Reg.4
Reg.2, amended: SI 2008/731 Reg.4, SI 2008/1068 Reg.2
Reg.2, revoked (in part): SI 2008/731 Reg.4
Reg.5, applied: SI 2008/731 Reg.2
Reg.5, substituted: SI 2008/731 Reg.5
Reg.6, amended: SI 2008/731 Reg.6
Reg.6, applied: SI 2008/731 Reg.2
Reg.6, referred to: SI 2008/731 Reg.2
Reg.6A, added: SI 2008/731 Reg.7
Reg.6B, added: SI 2008/731 Reg.7
Reg.6C, added: SI 2008/731 Reg.7
Reg.6D, added: SI 2008/731 Reg.7
Reg.7, applied: SI 2008/731 Reg.16
Reg.7, substituted: SI 2008/731 Reg.8
Reg.7A, amended: SI 2008/1068 Reg.2

NO.

2005–cont.

678. Occupational Pension Schemes (Employer Debt) Regulations 2005– *cont.*
Reg.7A, applied: SI 2008/731 Reg.16
Reg.7A, substituted: SI 2008/731 Reg.8
Reg.7B, substituted: SI 2008/731 Reg.8
Reg.8, substituted: SI 2008/731 Reg.9
Reg.9, substituted: SI 2008/731 Reg.10
Reg.11, amended: SI 2008/731 Reg.11
Reg.12, amended: SI 2008/731 Reg.11
Reg.16, amended: SI 2008/1068 Reg.2
Reg.16, substituted: SI 2008/731 Reg.12
Sch.1, substituted: SI 2008/731 Sch.1
Sch.1B, substituted: SI 2008/731 Sch.3
Sch.1C, substituted: SI 2008/731 Sch.3
Sch.1D, substituted: SI 2008/731 Sch.3
Sch.1A para.1, substituted: SI 2008/731 Sch.2
Sch.1A para.2, substituted: SI 2008/731 Sch.2
Sch.1A para.3, substituted: SI 2008/731 Sch.2
Sch.1A para.4, substituted: SI 2008/731 Sch.2
Sch.1A para.5, substituted: SI 2008/731 Sch.2
Sch.1A para.6, substituted: SI 2008/731 Sch.2
Sch.1A para.7, substituted: SI 2008/731 Sch.2
Sch.1B para.1, substituted: SI 2008/731 Sch.3
Sch.1B para.2, substituted: SI 2008/731 Sch.3
Sch.1B para.3, substituted: SI 2008/731 Sch.3

686. Pensions Regulator (Freezing Orders and Consequential Amendments) Regulations 2005
applied: SSI 2008/228 Reg.73

697. Accounting Standards (Prescribed Body) Regulations 2005
revoked: SI 2008/651 Reg.3

699. Companies (Defective Accounts) (Authorised Person) Order 2005
revoked: SI 2008/623 Art.6

704. Personal and Occupational Pension Schemes (Indexation and Disclosure of Information) (Miscellaneous Amendments) Regulations 2005
applied: SSI 2008/228 Reg.73

706. Occupational Pension Schemes (Winding up etc.) Regulations 2005
applied: SSI 2008/228 Reg.73

709. Pensions Appeal Tribunals (England and Wales) (Amendment) Rules 2005
revoked: SI 2008/2683 Sch.2

715. Supervision of Accounts and Reports (Prescribed Body) Order 2005
applied: SI 2008/623 Art.7

NO.

2005–cont.

758. Non-Domestic Rating (Alteration of Lists and Appeals) (Wales) Regulations 2005
Part 3, applied: SI 2008/2671 Reg.4
Reg.4, applied: SI 2008/2671 Reg.4
Reg.4, varied: SI 2008/2671 Reg.4
Reg.6, varied: SI 2008/2671 Reg.5

774. Children Act 2004 (Amendment of Miscellaneous Regulations) (Wales) Regulations 2005
applied: 2008 c.14 s.17

824. Pension Protection Fund (PPF Ombudsman) Order 2005
Art.7, amended: SI 2008/2683 Sch.1 para.289

831. Supply of Machinery (Safety) (Amendment) Regulations 2005
revoked: SI 2008/1597 Sch.1

842. Occupational Pension Schemes (Levies) Regulations 2005
Reg.6, amended: SI 2008/910 Reg.2

843. Town and Country Planning (Fees for Applications and Deemed Applications) (Amendment) (England) Regulations 2005
revoked: SI 2008/958 Reg.3

870. Social Security Commissioners (Procedure) (Amendment) Regulations 2005
referred to: SI 2008/2683 Art.3
Reg.1, revoked: SI 2008/2683 Sch.2
Reg.2, substituted: SI 2008/2683 Sch.2
Reg.3, revoked: SI 2008/2683 Sch.2
Reg.4, revoked: SI 2008/2683 Sch.2
Reg.5, revoked: SI 2008/2683 Sch.2
Reg.6, revoked: SI 2008/2683 Sch.2
Reg.7, revoked: SI 2008/2683 Sch.2
Reg.8, revoked: SI 2008/2683 Sch.2

894. Hazardous Waste (England and Wales) Regulations 2005
Reg.5, referred to: 2008 c.29 s.30

895. List of Wastes (England) Regulations 2005
Sch.1, applied: SI 2008/2841 Reg.29

928. Export and Import of Dangerous Chemicals Regulations 2005
revoked: SI 2008/2108 Reg.5
Reg.1, amended: SI 2008/960 Sch.3
Reg.2, amended: SI 2008/960 Sch.3
Reg.4, amended: SI 2008/960 Sch.3

950. Criminal Justice Act 2003 (Commencement No.8 and Transitional and Saving Provisions) Order 2005
see *Gibson v Secretary of State for Justice* [2008] EWCA Civ 177, [2008] 3 W.L.R. 1044 (CA (Civ Div)), Sir Anthony Clarke, M.R.
Sch.2 Part 003 para.14, amended: 2008 c.4 Sch.26 para.78

NO.

2005–cont.

950. Criminal Justice Act 2003 (Commencement No.8 and Transitional and Saving Provisions) Order 2005–*cont.*
Sch.2 Part 003 para.19, disapplied: 2008 c.4 s.32
Sch.2 Part 003 para.19, referred to: 2008 c.4 Sch.26 para.32
Sch.2 Part 003 para.30, revoked: 2008 c.4 Sch.28 Part 2
Sch.2 para.23, see *Gibson v Secretary of State for Justice* [2008] EWCA Civ 177, [2008] 3 W.L.R. 1044 (CA (Civ Div)), Sir Anthony Clarke, M.R.

986. Criminal Justice (Sentencing) (Curfew Condition) Order 2005
revoked: SI 2008/2768 Art.3

990. Child Trust Funds (Appeals) Regulations 2005
Reg.1, amended: SI 2008/2683 Sch.1 para.291
Reg.1, revoked (in part): SI 2008/2683 Sch.1 para.291
Reg.2, amended: SI 2008/2683 Sch.1 para.292
Reg.3, amended: SI 2008/2683 Sch.1 para.293
Reg.4, amended: SI 2008/2683 Sch.1 para.294
Reg.4, revoked (in part): SI 2008/2683 Sch.1 para.294
Reg.6, revoked: SI 2008/2683 Sch.1 para.295
Reg.7, revoked: SI 2008/2683 Sch.1 para.295
Reg.8, revoked: SI 2008/2683 Sch.1 para.295
Reg.9, revoked: SI 2008/2683 Sch.1 para.295
Reg.10, revoked: SI 2008/2683 Sch.1 para.295
Reg.11, revoked: SI 2008/2683 Sch.1 para.295
Reg.12, revoked: SI 2008/2683 Sch.1 para.295
Reg.13, revoked: SI 2008/2683 Sch.1 para.295
Reg.14, revoked: SI 2008/2683 Sch.1 para.295
Reg.15, revoked: SI 2008/2683 Sch.1 para.295
Reg.16, revoked: SI 2008/2683 Sch.1 para.295
Reg.17, revoked: SI 2008/2683 Sch.1 para.295
Reg.18, revoked: SI 2008/2683 Sch.1 para.295
Reg.19, revoked: SI 2008/2683 Sch.1 para.295
Reg.20, revoked: SI 2008/2683 Sch.1 para.295

NO.

2005–cont.

990. Child Trust Funds (Appeals) Regulations 2005–*cont.*

Reg.21, revoked: SI 2008/2683 Sch.1 para.295

Reg.22, revoked: SI 2008/2683 Sch.1 para.295

Reg.23, revoked: SI 2008/2683 Sch.1 para.295

Reg.24, revoked: SI 2008/2683 Sch.1 para.295

Reg.25, revoked: SI 2008/2683 Sch.1 para.295

1031. Social Security Commissioners (Procedure) (Child Trust Funds) Regulations 2005

revoked: SI 2008/2683 Sch.2

1082. Manufacture and Storage of Explosives Regulations 2005

applied: SI 2008/2852 Sch.3 para.1

Reg.2, applied: SI 2008/736 Sch.8 Part 1

Reg.9, applied: SI 2008/736 Sch.8 Part 1

Reg.10, applied: SI 2008/736 Sch.8 Part 1, Sch.8 Part 2

Reg.11, applied: SI 2008/736 Sch.8 Part 2

Reg.16, applied: SI 2008/736 Sch.8 Part 1, Sch.8 Part 2

Reg.20, applied: SI 2008/736 Sch.8 Part 1, Sch.8 Part 2

Reg.27, applied: 2008 c.20 Sch.3 para.1

Sch.1 para.1, applied: SI 2008/736 Reg.9

Sch.1 para.2, applied: SI 2008/736 Reg.9

1109. Special Guardianship Regulations 2005

Reg.6, see *R. (on the application of B) v Lewisham LBC* [2008] EWHC 738 (Admin), [2008] 2 F.L.R. 523 (QBD (Admin)), Black, J.

Reg.9, amended: SI 2008/1879 Reg.7

1124. Medicines for Human Use (Fees Amendments) Regulations 2005

revoked: SI 2008/552 Sch.7

1135. Gas (Standards of Performance) Regulations 2005

Reg.3, amended: SI 2008/696 Reg.2

Reg.7, amended: SI 2008/696 Reg.3

Reg.8, amended: SI 2008/696 Reg.4

Reg.9, amended: SI 2008/696 Reg.5

Reg.10, amended: SI 2008/696 Reg.6

Reg.10A, added: SI 2008/696 Reg.7

Reg.10B, added: SI 2008/696 Reg.8

Reg.12, amended: SI 2008/696 Reg.9

Reg.13, amended: SI 2008/696 Reg.10

Reg.16, amended: SI 2008/696 Reg.11

Sch.1 Part I, amended: SI 2008/696 Reg.12

1162. Potatoes Originating in the Netherlands (Notification) (Wales) Order 2005

revoked: SI 2008/2781 Art.3

NO.

2005–cont.

1313. Adoption Agencies (Wales) Regulations 2005

see *B (Children) (Placement Order: Expert Reports), Re* [2008] EWCA Civ 835, [2008] 2 F.L.R. 1404 (CA (Civ Div)), Thorpe, L.J.

1378. Wireless Telegraphy (Licence Charges) Regulations 2005

Reg.3, amended: SI 2008/2106 Reg.3

Sch.2, amended: SI 2008/139 Reg.3, SI 2008/2106 Reg.4

Sch.2, referred to: SI 2008/139 Reg.3

Sch.8 Part 1 para.4, substituted: SI 2008/139 Reg.4

Sch.8 Part 1 para.5, substituted: SI 2008/139 Reg.4

Sch.8 Part 1 para.6, substituted: SI 2008/139 Reg.4

Sch.8 Part 2, substituted: SI 2008/139 Reg.4

Sch.8 Part 2 para.7, substituted: SI 2008/139 Reg.4

Sch.8 Part 2 para.8, substituted: SI 2008/139 Reg.4

Sch.8 Part 2 para.9, substituted: SI 2008/139 Reg.4

Sch.8 Part 3, substituted: SI 2008/139 Reg.4

Sch.8 Part 3 para.7, substituted: SI 2008/139 Reg.4

Sch.8 Part 3 para.8, substituted: SI 2008/139 Reg.4

Sch.8 Part 4 para.10, substituted: SI 2008/139 Reg.4

Sch.8 Part 4 para.11, substituted: SI 2008/139 Reg.4

Sch.9, added: SI 2008/2106 Reg.5

Sch.10, added: SI 2008/2106 Reg.5

Sch.11 Part 1, added: SI 2008/2106 Reg.5

Sch.11 Part 2, added: SI 2008/2106 Reg.5

Sch.11 Part 3, added: SI 2008/2106 Reg.5

1388. Unfitness to Stand Trial and Insanity (Royal Air Force) Regulations 2005

Reg.4, amended: SI 2008/912 Sch.2 para.8

1389. Unfitness to Stand Trial and Insanity (Royal Navy) Regulations 2005

Reg.4, amended: SI 2008/912 Sch.2 para.9

1390. Unfitness to Stand Trial and Insanity (Army) Regulations 2005

Reg.4, amended: SI 2008/912 Sch.2 para.10

1394. National Curriculum (Key Stage 3 Assessment Arrangements) (Wales) Order 2005

Art.3, amended: SI 2008/1899 Art.4

Art.7, amended: SI 2008/1899 Art.4

Art.7, revoked (in part): SI 2008/1899 Art.4

1437. Education (Pupil Information) (England) Regulations 2005

Reg.2, amended: SI 2008/1747 Reg.3

Reg.6, amended: SI 2008/1747 Reg.4

Reg.9, amended: SI 2008/1747 Reg.5

Sch.1 para.2, amended: SI 2008/1747 Reg.6

Sch.2 para.1, amended: SI 2008/1747 Reg.7

NO.

2005–*cont.*

1437. Education (Pupil Information) (England) Regulations 2005–*cont.*
Sch.2 para.4, amended: SI 2008/1747 Reg.7
Sch.2 para.5, amended: SI 2008/1747 Reg.7
Sch.2 para.6, amended: SI 2008/1747 Reg.7
Sch.2 para.6, revoked (in part): SI 2008/1747 Reg.7

1441. Reporting of Prices of Milk Products (England) Regulations 2005
revoked: SI 2008/1428 Reg.5

1447. NHS Institute for Innovation and Improvement Regulations 2005
Reg.1, amended: SI 2008/2250 Art.2

1455. Insolvency (Northern Ireland) Order 2005
Art.4, applied: SI 2008/948 Sch.1 para.167
Sch.5, applied: SI 2008/2558 Reg.3

1472. Opticians Act 1989 (Transitional Provisions) Order 2005
Art.13, varied: 2008 c.14 Sch.10 para.1

1473. General Optical Council (Continuing Education and Training Rules) Order of Council 2005
Sch.1, added: SI 2008/1940 Sch.1
Sch.1, amended: SI 2008/1940 Sch.1
Sch.1, revoked: SI 2008/1940 Sch.1

1474. General Optical Council (Committee Constitution Rules) Order of Council 2005
revoked: SI 2008/1774 Sch.5 para.3
Sch.1, added: SI 2008/3113 Sch.1
Sch.1, amended: SI 2008/3113 Sch.1
Sch.1, revoked: SI 2008/3113 Sch.1
Sch.1, substituted: SI 2008/3113 Sch.1

1475. General Optical Council (Fitness to Practise Rules) Order of Council 2005
Sch.1, added: SI 2008/2690 Sch.1

1478. General Optical Council (Registration Rules) Order of Council 2005
Sch.1, added: SI 2008/1940 Sch.1
Sch.1, amended: SI 2008/1940 Sch.1
Sch.1, substituted: SI 2008/1940 Sch.1

1479. Recovery of Taxes etc Due in Other Member States (Amendment of Section 134 of the Finance Act 2002) Regulations 2005
revoked: SI 2008/2871 Reg.5

1509. Residential Property Tribunal (Right to Buy Determinations) Procedure (England) Regulations 2005
Reg.12, amended: SI 2008/2683 Sch.1 para.297
Reg.26, revoked (in part): SI 2008/2683 Sch.1 para.298

1512. Adoption Support Services (Local Authorities) (Wales) Regulations 2005
Reg.17, amended: SI 2008/1879 Reg.28

NO.

2005–*cont.*

1513. Special Guardianship (Wales) Regulations 2005
Reg.12, amended: SI 2008/1879 Reg.29

1514. Adoption Support Agencies (Wales) Regulations 2005
applied: 2008 c.14 s.17

1530. Home Energy Efficiency Scheme (England) Regulations 2005
Reg.4, amended: SI 2008/1879 Reg.9

1541. Regulatory Reform (Fire Safety) Order 2005
applied: 2008 c.13 Sch.3
Art.26, amended: SI 2008/960 Sch.3

1585. Wireless Telegraphy (Automotive Short Range Radar) (Exemption) (No.2) Regulations 2005
Reg.3, amended: SI 2008/237 Reg.2
Reg.4, amended: SI 2008/237 Reg.2

1606. Road Traffic Act 1988 (Retention and Disposal of Seized Motor Vehicles) Regulations 2005
Reg.2, amended: SI 2008/2097 Reg.3
Reg.6, substituted: SI 2008/2097 Reg.4

1677. Export Control (Democratic Republic of Congo) Order 2005
referred to: SI 2008/131 Art.2
Art.1, amended: SI 2008/131 Sch.1 para.1, SI 2008/1964 Art.3
Art.3, amended: SI 2008/131 Sch.1 para.2, SI 2008/1964 Art.4
Art.3A, added: SI 2008/131 Sch.1 para.3

1740. Education (Induction Arrangements for School Teachers) (Consolidation) (England) (Amendment) Regulations 2005
revoked: SI 2008/657 Sch.1

1788. Community Interest Company Regulations 2005
Reg.2, amended: SI 2008/948 Sch.1 para.242
Reg.26, revoked (in part): SI 2008/948 Sch.2
Reg.29, substituted: SI 2008/948 Sch.1 para.242
Sch.1 para.3, amended: SI 2008/948 Sch.1 para.242
Sch.2 para.3, amended: SI 2008/948 Sch.1 para.242
Sch.3 para.3, amended: SI 2008/948 Sch.1 para.242

1815. Cosmetic Products (Safety) (Amendment) Regulations 2005
revoked: SI 2008/1284 Sch.1

1818. Education (Induction Arrangements for School Teachers) (Wales) Regulations 2005
Reg.10, applied: SI 2008/657 Reg.11, Reg.17
Reg.14, applied: SI 2008/657 Reg.18, Sch.2 para.2
Sch.2 para.2, applied: SI 2008/657 Reg.18

NO.

2005–cont.

1820. List of Wastes (Wales) Regulations 2005
Sch.1, applied: SI 2008/2841 Reg.29

1902. Motor Cars (Driving Instruction) Regulations 2005
Reg.17, amended: SI 2008/419 Reg.2
Reg.20, amended: SI 2008/419 Reg.2
Sch.4 Part 1, amended: SI 2008/419 Reg.2
Sch.4 Part 2, amended: SI 2008/419 Reg.2
Sch.5 Part 1, amended: SI 2008/419 Reg.2
Sch.5 Part 2, amended: SI 2008/419 Reg.2

1903. Local Government Pension Scheme (Amendment) Regulations 2005
revoked: SI 2008/238 Sch.1

1965. Criminal Justice (Northern Ireland) Order 2005
Art.8, revoked: SI 2008/1216 Art.84, Sch.6 Part 2
Art.16, revoked (in part): SI 2008/1216 Sch.6 Part 1

1970. Air Navigation Order 2005
referred to: SI 2008/2562 Art.4
Art.1, applied: SI 2008/2562 Sch.1 Part 1
Art.1, varied: SI 2008/2562 Sch.1 para.1
Art.3, applied: SI 2008/2562 Sch.1 Part 1
Art.3, varied: SI 2008/2562 Sch.1 para.2
Art.5, applied: SI 2008/2562 Sch.1 Part 1
Art.5, varied: SI 2008/2562 Sch.1 para.3
Art.8, applied: SI 2008/2562 Sch.1 Part 1
Art.8, varied: SI 2008/2562 Sch.1 para.4
Art.19, applied: SI 2008/2562 Sch.1 Part 1
Art.19, varied: SI 2008/2562 Sch.1 para.5
Art.20, applied: SI 2008/2562 Sch.1 Part 1
Art.20, varied: SI 2008/2562 Sch.1 para.6
Art.25, applied: SI 2008/2562 Sch.1 Part 1
Art.25, varied: SI 2008/2562 Sch.1 para.7
Art.26, applied: SI 2008/2562 Sch.1 Part 1
Art.26, varied: SI 2008/2562 Sch.1 para.8
Art.36, applied: SI 2008/2562 Sch.1 Part 1
Art.36, varied: SI 2008/2562 Sch.1 para.9
Art.46, applied: SI 2008/2562 Sch.1 Part 1
Art.46, varied: SI 2008/2562 Sch.1 para.10, Sch.1 para.11
Art.48, applied: SI 2008/2562 Sch.1 Part 1
Art.48, varied: SI 2008/2562 Sch.1 para.12, Sch.1 para.13
Art.49, applied: SI 2008/2562 Sch.1 Part 1
Art.49, varied: SI 2008/2562 Sch.1 para.14
Art.50, applied: SI 2008/2562 Sch.1 Part 1
Art.50, varied: SI 2008/2562 Sch.1 para.15
Art.55, applied: SI 2008/2562 Sch.1 Part 1
Art.55, varied: SI 2008/2562 Sch.1 para.16
Art.60, applied: SI 2008/2562 Sch.1 Part 1
Art.60, varied: SI 2008/2562 Sch.1 para.17, Sch.1 para.18
Art.61, applied: SI 2008/2562 Sch.1 Part 1
Art.61, varied: SI 2008/2562 Sch.1 para.19
Art.62, applied: SI 2008/2562 Sch.1 Part 1
Art.62, varied: SI 2008/2562 Sch.1 para.20
Art.63, applied: SI 2008/2562 Sch.1 Part 1

NO.

2005–cont.

1970. Air Navigation Order 2005–*cont.*
Art.63, varied: SI 2008/2562 Sch.1 para.21
Art.64, applied: SI 2008/2562 Sch.1 Part 1
Art.65, applied: SI 2008/2562 Sch.1 Part 1
Art.65, varied: SI 2008/2562 Sch.1 para.22
Art.66, applied: SI 2008/2562 Sch.1 Part 1
Art.66, varied: SI 2008/2562 Sch.1 para.23
Art.67, applied: SI 2008/2562 Sch.1 Part 1
Art.67, varied: SI 2008/2562 Sch.1 para.24
Art.69, applied: SI 2008/2562 Sch.1 Part 1
Art.69, varied: SI 2008/2562 Sch.1 para.25
Art.70, applied: SI 2008/2562 Sch.1 Part 1
Art.70, enabled: SI 2008/1943, SI 2008/2429
Art.70, varied: SI 2008/2562 Sch.1 para.26
Art.71, applied: SI 2008/2562 Sch.1 Part 1
Art.71, varied: SI 2008/2562 Sch.1 para.27
Art.73, applied: SI 2008/2562 Sch.1 Part 1
Art.74, applied: SI 2008/2562 Sch.1 Part 1
Art.75, applied: SI 2008/2562 Sch.1 Part 1
Art.77, applied: SI 2008/2562 Sch.1 Part 1
Art.78, applied: SI 2008/2562 Sch.1 Part 1
Art.79, applied: SI 2008/2562 Sch.1 Part 1
Art.80, applied: SI 2008/2562 Sch.1 Part 1
Art.80, varied: SI 2008/2562 Sch.1 para.28
Art.80A, varied: SI 2008/2562 Sch.1 para.29
Art.86, applied: SI 2008/2562 Sch.1 Part 1
Art.86, varied: SI 2008/2562 Sch.1 para.30
Art.88, applied: SI 2008/2562 Sch.1 Part 1
Art.88, varied: SI 2008/2562 Sch.1 para.31
Art.89, applied: SI 2008/2562 Sch.1 Part 1
Art.90, applied: SI 2008/2562 Sch.1 Part 1
Art.90, varied: SI 2008/2562 Sch.1 para.32
Art.91, applied: SI 2008/2562 Sch.1 Part 1
Art.91, varied: SI 2008/2562 Sch.1 para.33
Art.92, applied: SI 2008/2562 Sch.1 Part 1
Art.92, varied: SI 2008/2562 Sch.1 para.34
Art.93, applied: SI 2008/2562 Sch.1 Part 1
Art.93, varied: SI 2008/2562 Sch.1 para.35, Sch.1 para.36
Art.94, applied: SI 2008/2562 Sch.1 Part 1
Art.94, varied: SI 2008/2562 Sch.1 para.37
Art.95, applied: SI 2008/2562 Sch.1 Part 1
Art.95, enabled: SI 2008/669
Art.95, varied: SI 2008/2562 Sch.1 para.38
Art.96, applied: SI 2008/2562 Sch.1 Part 1
Art.96, enabled: SI 2008/1239, SI 2008/3169
Art.96, varied: SI 2008/2562 Sch.1 para.39
Art.97, applied: SI 2008/2562 Sch.1 Part 1
Art.97, varied: SI 2008/2562 Sch.1 para.40, Sch.1 para.41
Art.98, applied: SI 2008/2562 Sch.1 Part 1
Art.98, varied: SI 2008/2562 Sch.1 para.42
Art.99, applied: SI 2008/2562 Sch.1 Part 1
Art.99, varied: SI 2008/2562 Sch.1 para.43
Art.100, applied: SI 2008/2562 Sch.1 Part 1
Art.100, varied: SI 2008/2562 Sch.1 para.44
Art.101, applied: SI 2008/2562 Sch.1 Part 1
Art.102, applied: SI 2008/2562 Sch.1 Part 1

NO.

2005–cont.

1970. Air Navigation Order 2005–*cont.*
Art.102, varied: SI 2008/2562 Sch.1 para.45
Art.103, applied: SI 2008/2562 Sch.1 Part 1
Art.103, varied: SI 2008/2562 Sch.1 para.46
Art.105, applied: SI 2008/2562 Sch.1 Part 1
Art.105, varied: SI 2008/2562 Sch.1 para.47
Art.106, applied: SI 2008/2562 Sch.1 Part 1
Art.107, applied: SI 2008/2562 Sch.1 Part 1
Art.107, varied: SI 2008/2562 Sch.1 para.48
Art.108, applied: SI 2008/2562 Sch.1 Part 1
Art.108, varied: SI 2008/2562 Sch.1 para.49
Art.109, applied: SI 2008/2562 Sch.1 Part 1
Art.109, varied: SI 2008/2562 Sch.1 para.50
Art.110, applied: SI 2008/2562 Sch.1 Part 1
Art.110, varied: SI 2008/2562 Sch.1 para.51
Art.112, applied: SI 2008/2562 Sch.1 Part 1
Art.112, varied: SI 2008/2562 Sch.1 para.52
Art.113, applied: SI 2008/2562 Sch.1 Part 1
Art.113, varied: SI 2008/2562 Sch.1 para.53
Art.114, applied: SI 2008/2562 Sch.1 Part 1
Art.114, varied: SI 2008/2562 Sch.1 para.54
Art.115, applied: SI 2008/2562 Sch.1 Part 1
Art.116, applied: SI 2008/2562 Sch.1 Part 1
Art.117, applied: SI 2008/2562 Sch.1 Part 1
Art.117A, varied: SI 2008/2562 Sch.1 para.55
Art.117B, varied: SI 2008/2562 Sch.1 para.55
Art.120, applied: SI 2008/2562 Sch.1 Part 1
Art.120A, varied: SI 2008/2562 Sch.1 para.56
Art.124, applied: SI 2008/2562 Sch.1 Part 1
Art.124, varied: SI 2008/2562 Sch.1 para.57
Art.125, applied: SI 2008/2562 Sch.1 Part 1
Art.125, varied: SI 2008/2562 Sch.1 para.58
Art.126, applied: SI 2008/2562 Sch.1 Part 1
Art.126, varied: SI 2008/2562 Sch.1 para.59
Art.128, applied: SI 2008/2562 Sch.1 Part 1
Art.128, varied: SI 2008/2562 Sch.1 para.60
Art.129, applied: SI 2008/2562 Sch.1 Part 1
Art.129, varied: SI 2008/2562 Sch.1 para.61
Art.130, applied: SI 2008/2562 Sch.1 Part 1
Art.130, varied: SI 2008/2562 Sch.1 para.62
Art.131, applied: SI 2008/2562 Sch.1 Part 1
Art.131, varied: SI 2008/2562 Sch.1 para.63
Art.132, applied: SI 2008/2562 Sch.1 Part 1
Art.132, varied: SI 2008/2562 Sch.1 para.64
Art.135, applied: SI 2008/2562 Sch.1 Part 1
Art.135, varied: SI 2008/2562 Sch.1 para.65
Art.136, applied: SI 2008/2562 Sch.1 Part 1
Art.136, varied: SI 2008/2562 Sch.1 para.66
Art.137, applied: SI 2008/2562 Sch.1 Part 1
Art.137, varied: SI 2008/2562 Sch.1 para.67
Art.137A, applied: SI 2008/2562 Sch.1 Part 1
Art.137A, varied: SI 2008/2562 Sch.1 para.68
Art.137C, applied: SI 2008/2562 Sch.1 Part 1
Art.137C, varied: SI 2008/2562 Sch.1 para.68
Art.138, applied: SI 2008/2562 Sch.1 Part 1
Art.138, varied: SI 2008/2562 Sch.1 para.69
Art.140, applied: SI 2008/2562 Sch.1 Part 1

NO.

2005–cont.

1970. Air Navigation Order 2005–*cont.*
Art.140, varied: SI 2008/2562 Sch.1 para.70, Sch.1 para.71
Art.142, applied: SI 2008/2562 Sch.1 Part 1
Art.142, varied: SI 2008/2562 Sch.1 para.72
Art.143, applied: SI 2008/2562 Sch.1 Part 1
Art.143, varied: SI 2008/2562 Sch.1 para.73
Art.144, applied: SI 2008/2562 Sch.1 Part 1
Art.144, varied: SI 2008/2562 Sch.1 para.74
Art.145, applied: SI 2008/2562 Sch.1 Part 1
Art.145, varied: SI 2008/2562 Sch.1 para.75
Art.146, applied: SI 2008/2562 Sch.1 Part 1
Art.147, applied: SI 2008/2562 Sch.1 Part 1
Art.147, varied: SI 2008/2562 Sch.1 para.76
Art.148, applied: SI 2008/2562 Sch.1 Part 1
Art.148, varied: SI 2008/2562 Sch.1 para.77
Art.148A, applied: SI 2008/2562 Sch.1 Part 1
Art.148A, varied: SI 2008/2562 Sch.1 para.78
Art.149, applied: SI 2008/2562 Sch.1 Part 1
Art.149, varied: SI 2008/2562 Sch.1 para.79
Art.152, applied: SI 2008/2562 Sch.1 Part 1
Art.152, varied: SI 2008/2562 Sch.1 para.80
Art.153, applied: SI 2008/2562 Sch.1 Part 1
Art.153, varied: SI 2008/2562 Sch.1 para.81
Art.154, applied: SI 2008/2562 Sch.1 Part 1
Art.154, varied: SI 2008/2562 Sch.1 para.82
Art.155, applied: SI 2008/2562 Sch.1 Part 1
Art.155, varied: SI 2008/2562 Sch.1 para.83, Sch.1 para.84
Art.156, applied: SI 2008/2562 Sch.1 Part 1
Art.156, varied: SI 2008/2562 Sch.1 para.85
Art.157, applied: SI 2008/2562 Sch.1 Part 1
Art.157, varied: SI 2008/2562 Sch.1 para.86
Art.158, applied: SI 2008/2562 Sch.1 Part 1
Art.158, varied: SI 2008/2562 Sch.1 para.87
Art.159, applied: SI 2008/2562 Sch.1 Part 1
Art.159, varied: SI 2008/2562 Sch.1 para.88
Art.160, applied: SI 2008/2562 Sch.1 Part 1
Art.160, varied: SI 2008/2562 Sch.1 para.89
Art.161, applied: SI 2008/2562 Sch.1 Part 1
Art.161, varied: SI 2008/2562 Sch.1 para.90
Art.162, applied: SI 2008/2562 Sch.1 Part 1
Art.162, varied: SI 2008/2562 Sch.1 para.91
Art.163, applied: SI 2008/2562 Sch.1 Part 1
Art.163, varied: SI 2008/2562 Sch.1 para.92
Art.164, applied: SI 2008/2562 Sch.1 Part 1
Art.164, varied: SI 2008/2562 Sch.1 para.93
Art.165, applied: SI 2008/2562 Sch.1 Part 1
Art.165, varied: SI 2008/2562 Sch.1 para.94
Art.166, applied: SI 2008/2562 Sch.1 Part 1
Art.166, varied: SI 2008/2562 Sch.1 para.95
Art.167, amended: SI 2008/1782 Art.2
Art.168, applied: SI 2008/2562 Sch.1 Part 1
Art.168, varied: SI 2008/2562 Sch.1 para.96
Sch.2, applied: SI 2008/2562 Sch.1 Part 1
Sch.2 Part B para.1, varied: SI 2008/2562 Sch.1 para.97
Sch.2 Part B para.2, varied: SI 2008/2562 Sch.1 para.97

NO.

2005–cont.

1970. Air Navigation Order 2005–*cont.*
Sch.2 Part B para.3, varied: SI 2008/2562 Sch.1 para.97
Sch.2 Part C, varied: SI 2008/2562 Sch.1 para.97
Sch.3 Part A, applied: SI 2008/3133 Art.5, Art.18
Sch.5, applied: SI 2008/2562 Sch.1 Part 1
Sch.5 para.2, varied: SI 2008/2562 Sch.1 para.98
Sch.5 para.3, varied: SI 2008/2562 Sch.1 para.98
Sch.11, applied: SI 2008/2562 Sch.1 Part 1
Sch.11 Part A para.1, varied: SI 2008/2562 Sch.1 para.99
Sch.11 Part A para.2, varied: SI 2008/2562 Sch.1 para.99
Sch.11 Part B para.1, varied: SI 2008/2562 Sch.1 para.99
Sch.11 Part B para.2, varied: SI 2008/2562 Sch.1 para.99
Sch.11 Part B para.3, varied: SI 2008/2562 Sch.1 para.99
Sch.11 Part B para.4, varied: SI 2008/2562 Sch.1 para.99
Sch.12, applied: SI 2008/2562 Sch.1 Part 1
Sch.12 Part A, varied: SI 2008/2562 Sch.1 para.100
Sch.12 Part B, varied: SI 2008/2562 Sch.1 para.100
Sch.12 Part C, varied: SI 2008/2562 Sch.1 para.100
Sch.13, applied: SI 2008/2562 Sch.1 Part 1
Sch.14, applied: SI 2008/2562 Sch.1 Part 1
Sch.14 Part A, varied: SI 2008/2562 Sch.1 para.101
Sch.14 Part B, varied: SI 2008/2562 Sch.1 para.101

1972. Children Act 2004 (Children's Services) Regulations 2005
Reg.2, amended: SI 2008/912 Sch.2 para.11

1983. Age-Related Payments Regulations 2005
Reg.2, amended: SI 2008/1554 Reg.72

1986. Financial Assistance Scheme Regulations 2005
applied: SI 2008/794 Reg.72A
Reg.2, amended: SI 2008/1432 Reg.5, SI 2008/1903 Reg.5
Reg.4, amended: SI 2008/1903 Reg.5
Reg.5A, added: SI 2008/1903 Reg.6
Reg.9, amended: SI 2008/1903 Reg.7, SI 2008/3069 Reg.2
Reg.11, amended: SI 2008/1903 Reg.7
Reg.12, amended: SI 2008/1903 Reg.7
Reg.12A, added: SI 2008/1903 Reg.7
Reg.12B, added: SI 2008/1903 Reg.7
Reg.15, amended: SI 2008/1903 Reg.8
Reg.15A, added: SI 2008/3241 Art.3
Reg.17, amended: SI 2008/1432 Reg.6, SI 2008/1903 Reg.9

NO.

2005–cont.

1986. Financial Assistance Scheme Regulations 2005–*cont.*
Reg.17A, added: SI 2008/1903 Reg.10
Reg.17B, added: SI 2008/1903 Reg.10
Reg.18, amended: SI 2008/1432 Reg.6, SI 2008/1903 Reg.11
Reg.18, revoked (in part): SI 2008/1903 Reg.11
Reg.19, amended: SI 2008/1903 Reg.12
Sch.1 para.3A, added: SI 2008/1903 Reg.13
Sch.1 para.6, substituted: SI 2008/1903 Reg.13
Sch.2 para.1, amended: SI 2008/1903 Reg.14
Sch.2 para.1, revoked (in part): SI 2008/1432 Reg.7
Sch.2 para.3, amended: SI 2008/1432 Reg.7
Sch.2 para.4, amended: SI 2008/1432 Reg.7
Sch.2 para.5, amended: SI 2008/1432 Reg.7
Sch.2 para.7, amended: SI 2008/1432 Reg.7
Sch.2 para.9, amended: SI 2008/1432 Reg.7
Sch.2 para.10, amended: SI 2008/1432 Reg.7, SI 2008/1903 Reg.14
Sch.2A para.1, added: SI 2008/1903 Reg.15
Sch.2A para.2, added: SI 2008/1903 Reg.15
Sch.2A para.3, added: SI 2008/1903 Reg.15
Sch.2A para.4, added: SI 2008/1903 Reg.15
Sch.2A para.5, added: SI 2008/1903 Reg.15
Sch.2A para.6, added: SI 2008/1903 Reg.15
Sch.2A para.7, added: SI 2008/1903 Reg.15
Sch.2A para.8, added: SI 2008/1903 Reg.15

1994. Financial Assistance Scheme (Internal Review) Regulations 2005
Reg.2, amended: SI 2008/1903 Reg.19
Reg.3, amended: SI 2008/1903 Reg.19
Reg.5, amended: SI 2008/1903 Reg.19
Reg.6, amended: SI 2008/1903 Reg.19
Reg.11, amended: SI 2008/1903 Reg.19
Reg.16, amended: SI 2008/1903 Reg.19

2001. Dangerous Substances and Preparations (Nickel) (Safety) Regulations 2005
revoked: SI 2008/2852 Sch.10 Part 1

2004. Local Government Pension Scheme and Management and Investment of Funds (Amendment) Regulations 2005
Reg.2, revoked: SI 2008/238 Sch.1
Reg.3, revoked: SI 2008/238 Sch.1
Reg.4, revoked: SI 2008/238 Sch.1
Reg.5, revoked: SI 2008/238 Sch.1
Reg.6, revoked: SI 2008/238 Sch.1
Reg.7, revoked: SI 2008/238 Sch.1

2011. Dentists Act 1984 (Amendment) Order 2005
Art.29, varied: 2008 c.14 Sch.10 para.1

2014. Friendly Societies (Modification of the Corporation Tax Acts) Regulations 2005
Reg.5, amended: SI 2008/1937 Reg.3
Reg.6, amended: SI 2008/1937 Reg.4

NO.

2005–*cont.*

2014. Friendly Societies (Modification of the Corporation Tax Acts) Regulations 2005–*cont.*
Reg.7A, amended: SI 2008/1937 Reg.5
Reg.9, amended: SI 2008/1937 Reg.6
Reg.9A, revoked: SI 2008/1937 Reg.7
Reg.10, amended: SI 2008/1937 Reg.8
Reg.20A, revoked: SI 2008/1937 Reg.9
Reg.23, amended: SI 2008/1937 Reg.10
Reg.32, amended: SI 2008/1937 Reg.11
Reg.40, amended: SI 2008/1937 Reg.12
Reg.43A, amended: SI 2008/1937 Reg.13

2024. Pension Protection Fund (Reference of Reviewable Matters to the PPF Ombudsman) Regulations 2005
Reg.14, amended: SI 2008/2683 Sch.1 para.299

2038. Education (School Inspection) (England) Regulations 2005
Reg.8, substituted: SI 2008/1723 Reg.2

2045. Income Tax (Construction Industry Scheme) Regulations 2005
Reg.2, amended: SI 2008/740 Reg.3
Reg.7, amended: SI 2008/740 Reg.4
Reg.8, amended: SI 2008/740 Reg.5
Reg.11, amended: SI 2008/740 Reg.6
Reg.16, amended: SI 2008/740 Reg.7
Reg.32, amended: SI 2008/1282 Reg.2
Reg.57, amended: SI 2008/740 Reg.8

2054. Remand in Custody (Effect of Concurrent and Consecutive Sentences of Imprisonment) Rules 2005
r.2, see *R. v Ashes (Stephen Kenny)* [2007] EWCA Crim 1848, [2008] 1 All E.R. 113 (CA (Crim Div)), Hallett, L.J.

2057. Food Labelling (Amendment) (England) (No.2) Regulations 2005
revoked: SI 2008/1188 Reg.3

2078. Mental Health (Care and Treatment) (Scotland) Act 2003 (Consequential Provisions) Order 2005
Art.8, amended: SI 2008/2828 Art.20

2114. Civil Partnership Act 2004 (Amendments to Subordinate Legislation) Order 2005
Sch.9 para.1, revoked (in part): SI 2008/1741 Sch.2

2115. Town and Country Planning (Major Infrastructure Project Inquiries Procedure) (England) Rules 2005
r.15, amended: SI 2008/2831 Sch.4 para.1

2149. Children and Young People's Plan (England) Regulations 2005
applied: SI 2008/228 Sch.1 para.20
varied: SI 2008/2867 Reg.12
Reg.3, applied: SI 2008/2867 Reg.12

2152. Education (School Information) (England) (Amendment) Regulations 2005
revoked: SI 2008/3093 Sch.1

NO.

2005–*cont.*

2188. Pensions Regulator (Financial Support Directions etc.) Regulations 2005
Reg.15, amended: SI 2008/731 Reg.19

2189. Financial Assistance Scheme (Provision of Information and Administration of Payments) Regulations 2005
Reg.2, amended: SI 2008/1903 Reg.17
Sch.1 para.1, amended: SI 2008/1903 Reg.18

2224. Occupational Pension Schemes (Employer Debt etc.) (Amendment) Regulations 2005
Reg.3, revoked: SI 2008/731 Reg.16

2250. Nursing and Midwifery Council (Election Scheme) Rules Order of Council 2005
revoked: SI 2008/1485 Sch.2 para.2

2296. Day Care and Child Minding (Disqualification) (England) Regulations 2005
Reg.9, applied: SI 2008/2261 Sch.2 para.20, Sch.2 para.25

2300. Day Care and Child Minding (Inspection) (England) Regulations 2005
Reg.5, applied: SI 2008/2261 Sch.2 para.27
Reg.6, applied: SI 2008/2261 Sch.2 para.27

2337. Companies Act 1989 (Delegation) Order 2005
revoked: SI 2008/496 Art.12
Art.2, amended: SI 2008/496 Art.12

2347. Animal By-Products Regulations 2005
Reg.21, applied: SI 2008/2270 Sch.1, SI 2008/3196 Sch.1

2415. NHS Business Services Authority (Awdurdod Gwasanaethau Busnes y GIG) Regulations 2005
Reg.1, amended: SI 2008/2250 Art.2

2417. Companies (Disclosure of Auditor Remuneration) Regulations 2005
revoked: SI 2008/489 Reg.2

2450. Education (Local Education Authority Performance Targets) (England) Regulations 2005
referred to: SI 2008/3086 Reg.3
Reg.2, amended: SI 2008/3086 Reg.4
Sch.1 para.2, revoked: SI 2008/3086 Reg.5
Sch.1 para.3, amended: SI 2008/3086 Reg.6
Sch.1 para.4, substituted: SI 2008/3086 Reg.7
Sch.1 para.8, added: SI 2008/3086 Reg.8
Sch.1 para.9, added: SI 2008/3086 Reg.8
Sch.1 para.10, added: SI 2008/3086 Reg.8

2517. Plant Health (Forestry) Order 2005
Art.2, amended: SI 2008/644 Art.2
Sch.1 para.4A, added: SI 2008/644 Art.2
Sch.1 para.8A, added: SI 2008/644 Art.2
Sch.4 Part A, amended: SI 2008/644 Art.2
Sch.4 Part B, amended: SI 2008/644 Art.2
Sch.5 Part A para.1a, added: SI 2008/644 Art.2

NO.

2005–cont.

2517. Plant Health (Forestry) Order 2005–*cont.*

Sch.6 Part A para.2, amended: SI 2008/644 Art.2

Sch.6 Part A para.4, added: SI 2008/644 Art.2

Sch.6 Part A para.5, added: SI 2008/644 Art.2

Sch.7 Part A para.2, amended: SI 2008/644 Art.2

Sch.7 Part A para.4, added: SI 2008/644 Art.2

Sch.7 Part A para.5, added: SI 2008/644 Art.2

2530. Plant Health (England) Order 2005

Art.2, amended: SI 2008/2411 Art.2

Art.19, amended: SI 2008/2411 Art.2

Art.22, amended: SI 2008/2411 Art.2

Art.39A, added: SI 2008/2411 Art.2

Art.41, amended: SI 2008/2411 Art.2

Art.45, amended: SI 2008/2411 Art.2

Sch.1 Part A para.4, amended: SI 2008/2765 Art.2

Sch.1 Part A para.6, revoked: SI 2008/2765 Art.2

Sch.1 Part B para.4, revoked: SI 2008/2411 Art.2

Sch.2 Part B, amended: SI 2008/2411 Art.2

Sch.3, amended: SI 2008/2411 Art.2

Sch.4 Part A, amended: SI 2008/2411 Art.2, SI 2008/2765 Art.2

Sch.4 Part B, amended: SI 2008/2411 Art.2, SI 2008/2765 Art.2

Sch.6 Part A para.8, added: SI 2008/2765 Art.2

Sch.7 Part A para.8, added: SI 2008/2765 Art.2

Sch.8 Part A para.2, amended: SI 2008/2411 Art.2

Sch.8 Part A para.5, amended: SI 2008/2411 Art.2

2531. NHS Blood and Transplant (Gwaed a Thrawsblaniadau'r GIG) Regulations 2005

Reg.1, amended: SI 2008/2250 Art.2

2558. Northern Ireland (Sentences) Act 1998 (Specified Organisations) Order 2005

revoked: SI 2008/1975 Art.1

2571. Chemicals (Hazard Information and Packaging for Supply) (Amendment) Regulations 2005

Reg.2, revoked (in part): SI 2008/2337 Reg.6, SI 2008/2852 Sch.10 Part 2

2604. Social Security (Incapacity Benefit Work-focused Interviews) Amendment (No.2) Regulations 2005

revoked: SI 2008/2928 Reg.12

NO.

2005–cont.

2720. Adoption Support Agencies (England) and Adoption Agencies (Miscellaneous Amendments) Regulations 2005

applied: 2008 c.14 s.17

2721. London Thames Gateway Development Corporation (Planning Functions) Order 2005

Art.3, referred to: SI 2008/580 Art.3

2722. Planning and Compulsory Purchase Act 2004 (Commencement No.4 and Consequential, Transitional and Savings Provisions) (Wales) Order 2005

Sch.1, amended: SI 2008/10 Art.2, SI 2008/2162 Art.2

2750. Medicines (Traditional Herbal Medicinal Products for Human Use) Regulations 2005

Reg.2, applied: SI 2008/548 Art.3

Reg.6, applied: SI 2008/552 Reg.18

2757. Bus Lane Contraventions (Penalty Charges, Adjudication and Enforcement) (England) Regulations 2005

Reg.20, amended: SI 2008/2683 Sch.1 para.300

2761. Civil Partnership (Registration Abroad and Certificates) Order 2005

applied: SI 2008/676 Sch.1 Part VI

2795. Family Procedure (Adoption) Rules 2005

Part 7 r.55, amended: SI 2008/2447 r.2

Part 9 r.95, amended: SI 2008/2447 r.2

2797. Children (Allocation of Proceedings) (Amendment No.2) Order 2005

revoked: SI 2008/2836 Sch.2

2835. Food Labelling (Amendment) (Wales) (No.2) Regulations 2005

revoked: SI 2008/1268 Reg.3

2847. Planning and Compulsory Purchase Act 2004 (Commencement No.6, Transitional Provisions and Savings) Order 2005

Art.2, referred to: 2008 c.29 s.204

Art.3, applied: 2008 c.29 s.204

2877. Civil Partnership (Pensions, Social Security and Child Support) (Consequential, etc Provisions) Order 2005

Sch.3 para.36, revoked (in part): SI 2008/2683 Sch.2

2878. Social Security (Civil Partnership) (Consequential Amendments) Regulations 2005

Reg.9, revoked (in part): SI 2008/2683 Sch.2

2895. Smoke Control Areas (Authorised Fuels) (England) (Amendment) Regulations 2005

revoked: SI 2008/514 Sch.2

NO.

2005–cont.

2914. Government of Maintained Schools (Wales) Regulations 2005
Reg.24, applied: SI 2008/168 Reg.6, SI 2008/3082 Reg.6
Reg.49, applied: SI 2008/168 Reg.7, SI 2008/3082 Reg.7
Reg.50, applied: SI 2008/168 Reg.3, SI 2008/3082 Reg.3
Reg.50, referred to: SI 2008/168 Reg.3
Reg.51, applied: SI 2008/168 Reg.3, SI 2008/3082 Reg.3
Reg.51, referred to: SI 2008/168 Reg.3
Reg.52, applied: SI 2008/168 Reg.3, SI 2008/3082 Reg.3
Reg.52, referred to: SI 2008/168 Reg.3
Reg.55, referred to: SI 2008/168 Reg.7, SI 2008/3082 Reg.7
Reg.56, referred to: SI 2008/168 Reg.7, SI 2008/3082 Reg.7
Sch.4 para.2, applied: SI 2008/168 Sch.1 para.2, SI 2008/3082 Sch.1 para.2
Sch.5 para.2, applied: SI 2008/168 Reg.6, SI 2008/3082 Reg.6
Sch.5 para.3, applied: SI 2008/168 Reg.6, SI 2008/3082 Reg.6
Sch.5 para.4, applied: SI 2008/168 Reg.6, SI 2008/3082 Reg.6
Sch.5 para.5, applied: SI 2008/168 Reg.6, SI 2008/3082 Reg.6
Sch.5 para.6, applied: SI 2008/168 Reg.6, SI 2008/3082 Reg.6
Sch.5 para.7, applied: SI 2008/168 Reg.6, SI 2008/3082 Reg.6
Sch.5 para.8, applied: SI 2008/168 Reg.6, SI 2008/3082 Reg.6
Sch.5 para.9, applied: SI 2008/168 Reg.6, SI 2008/3082 Reg.6
Sch.5 para.10, applied: SI 2008/168 Reg.6, SI 2008/3082 Reg.6
Sch.5 para.11, applied: SI 2008/168 Reg.6, SI 2008/3082 Reg.6
Sch.5 para.12, applied: SI 2008/168 Reg.6, SI 2008/3082 Reg.6

2915. Governor Allowances (Wales) Regulations 2005
applied: SI 2008/168 Sch.1 para.1

2924. Family Law Act 1996 (Part IV) (Allocation of Proceedings) (Amendment) Order 2005
revoked: SI 2008/2836 Sch.2

2966. Disability Discrimination (Public Authorities) (Statutory Duties) Regulations 2005
Reg.2, amended: SI 2008/641 Reg.2
Reg.2, varied: SI 2008/912 Sch.2 para.12
Sch.1 Part I, amended: SI 2008/526 Art.3, SI 2008/641 Reg.3, SI 2008/912 Sch.2 para.12, SI 2008/960 Sch.3, SI 2008/2831 Sch.1 para.13, Sch.2 para.6
Sch.1 Part V, amended: SI 2008/641 Reg.3
Sch.1 Part V, varied: 2008 c.14 Sch.10 para.1

NO.

2005–cont.

2966. Disability Discrimination (Public Authorities) (Statutory Duties) Regulations 2005–*cont.*
Sch.1 Part VI, added: SI 2008/641 Reg.4

2969. Food Labelling (Amendment) (England) (No.2) (Amendment) Regulations 2005
revoked: SI 2008/1188 Reg.3

2979. Medicines for Human Use (Fees Amendments) (No.2) Regulations 2005
revoked: SI 2008/552 Sch.7

2981. Vehicles Crime (Registration of Registration Plate Suppliers) (England and Wales) (Amendment) Regulations 2005
revoked: SI 2008/1715 Reg.8

3061. Social Fund Maternity and Funeral Expenses (General) Regulations 2005
Reg.3, amended: SI 2008/1554 Reg.8
Reg.5, amended: SI 2008/1554 Reg.8
Reg.7, amended: SI 2008/1554 Reg.8

3068. Bovine Products (Restriction on Placing on the Market) (England) (No.2) Regulations 2005
revoked: SI 2008/1881 Reg.21

3069. Local Government Pension Scheme (Civil Partnership) (Amendment) (England and Wales) Regulations 2005
revoked: SI 2008/238 Sch.1

3100. Sheep and Goats (Records, Identification and Movement) (England) Order 2005
applied: SI 2008/130 Art.22, Art.30
Art.14, referred to: SI 2008/51 Sch.5 para.4
Art.17, referred to: SI 2008/51 Sch.5 para.4
Art.20, referred to: SI 2008/51 Sch.5 para.4

3115. Local Authority Adoption Service (Wales) Regulations 2005
applied: 2008 c.14 s.17

3117. Offshore Installations (Safety Case) Regulations 2005
applied: SI 2008/736 Reg.15, Sch.12
Reg.2, applied: SI 2008/736 Reg.18
Reg.6, applied: SI 2008/736 Sch.12
Reg.9, applied: SI 2008/736 Sch.12
Reg.23, applied: SI 2008/736 Sch.12
Reg.26, applied: SI 2008/736 Sch.12

3164. Occupational and Personal Pension Schemes (Civil Partnership) (Miscellaneous Amendments) Regulations 2005
applied: SSI 2008/228 Reg.73

3181. Proceeds of Crime Act 2002 (External Requests and Orders) Order 2005
Art.2, amended: SI 2008/302 Art.2
Art.3, amended: SI 2008/302 Art.2
Art.5, enabled: SI 2008/523

NO.

2005–cont.

3181. Proceeds of Crime Act 2002 (External Requests and Orders) Order 2005–*cont.*

Art.6, see *King v Serious Fraud Office* [2008] EWCA Crim 530, [2008] 1 W.L.R. 2634 (CA (Crim Div)), Gage, L.J.
Art.6, revoked (in part): SI 2008/302 Art.2
Art.7, see *King v Serious Fraud Office* [2008] EWCA Crim 530, [2008] 1 W.L.R. 2634 (CA (Crim Div)), Gage, L.J.
Art.8, see *King v Serious Fraud Office* [2008] EWCA Crim 530, [2008] 1 W.L.R. 2634 (CA (Crim Div)), Gage, L.J.
Art.16, amended: SI 2008/302 Art.2
Art.17, amended: SI 2008/302 Art.2
Art.18, see *King v Serious Fraud Office* [2008] EWCA Crim 530, [2008] 1 W.L.R. 2634 (CA (Crim Div)), Gage, L.J.
Art.18, revoked (in part): SI 2008/302 Art.2
Art.27, amended: SI 2008/302 Art.2
Art.28, amended: SI 2008/302 Art.2
Art.29, amended: SI 2008/302 Art.2
Art.30, revoked: SI 2008/302 Art.2
Art.31, revoked: SI 2008/302 Art.2
Art.32, revoked: SI 2008/302 Art.2
Art.35, revoked: SI 2008/302 Art.2
Art.36, revoked: SI 2008/302 Art.2
Art.38, amended: SI 2008/302 Art.2
Art.39, revoked: SI 2008/302 Art.2
Art.40, amended: SI 2008/302 Art.2
Art.41, amended: SI 2008/302 Art.2
Art.42, amended: SI 2008/302 Art.2
Art.43, amended: SI 2008/302 Art.2
Art.43, revoked (in part): SI 2008/302 Art.2
Art.44, amended: SI 2008/302 Art.2
Art.46, amended: SI 2008/302 Art.2
Art.93, revoked (in part): SI 2008/302 Art.2
Art.102, amended: SI 2008/302 Art.2
Art.103, amended: SI 2008/302 Art.2
Art.104, revoked (in part): SI 2008/302 Art.2
Art.113, amended: SI 2008/302 Art.2
Art.114, amended: SI 2008/302 Art.2
Art.114, revoked (in part): SI 2008/302 Art.2
Art.115, amended: SI 2008/302 Art.2
Art.116, revoked: SI 2008/302 Art.2
Art.117, revoked: SI 2008/302 Art.2
Art.118, revoked: SI 2008/302 Art.2
Art.121, revoked: SI 2008/302 Art.2
Art.122, revoked: SI 2008/302 Art.2
Art.124, amended: SI 2008/302 Art.2
Art.125, revoked: SI 2008/302 Art.2
Art.126, amended: SI 2008/302 Art.2
Art.127, amended: SI 2008/302 Art.2
Art.128, amended: SI 2008/302 Art.2
Art.129, amended: SI 2008/302 Art.2
Art.129, revoked (in part): SI 2008/302 Art.2
Art.130, amended: SI 2008/302 Art.2
Art.132, amended: SI 2008/302 Art.2
Art.150A, added: SI 2008/302 Art.3
Art.150B, added: SI 2008/302 Art.3

NO.

2005–cont.

3181. Proceeds of Crime Act 2002 (External Requests and Orders) Order 2005–*cont.*

Art.150C, added: SI 2008/302 Art.3
Art.151, amended: SI 2008/302 Art.2
Art.183, amended: SI 2008/302 Art.2
Art.184, amended: SI 2008/302 Art.3
Art.188, amended: SI 2008/302 Art.3
Art.191, amended: SI 2008/302 Art.2
Art.194, amended: SI 2008/302 Art.2
Art.198, applied: SI 2008/523
Art.198, enabled: SI 2008/523
Art.199, applied: SI 2008/523
Art.199, enabled: SI 2008/523
Art.210, revoked: SI 2008/302 Art.2
Art.213, amended: SI 2008/302 Art.2

3185. Naval Medical Compassionate Fund (Amendment) Order 2005

revoked: SI 2008/3129 Sch.1

3199. Local Government Pension Scheme (Amendment) (No.2) Regulations 2005

revoked: SI 2008/238 Sch.1

3202. Payments to the Churches Conservation Trust Order 2005

revoked: SI 2008/1968 Art.5

3207. Channel Tunnel (International Arrangements) Order 2005

Art.2, amended: SI 2008/2366 Art.2
Art.4A, added: SI 2008/2366 Art.2

3239. Qualifications, Curriculum and Assessment Authority for Wales (Transfer of Functions to the National Assembly for Wales and Abolition) Order 2005

Sch.1 para.19, revoked: 2008 c.25 Sch.2
Sch.1 para.20, revoked: 2008 c.25 Sch.2

3240. Veterinary Surgeons (Examination of Commonwealth and Foreign Candidates) Regulations Order of Council 2005

referred to: SI 2008/2501 Sch.1
Sch.1, substituted: SI 2008/2501 Sch.1

3257. Export Control (Uzbekistan) Order 2005

Art.1, amended: SI 2008/3231 Sch.6
Art.7, revoked: SI 2008/3231 Sch.6
Art.8, revoked: SI 2008/3231 Sch.6

3262. Healthy Start Scheme and Welfare Food (Amendment) Regulations 2005

Reg.2, amended: SI 2008/1879 Reg.10
Reg.3, amended: SI 2008/408 Reg.2, SI 2008/1879 Reg.10
Reg.8, amended: SI 2008/408 Reg.3
Sch.2 para.4, amended: SI 2008/408 Reg.4, SI 2008/1879 Reg.10

3273. Financial Assistance Scheme (Appeals) Regulations 2005

Reg.2, amended: SI 2008/1903 Reg.20
Reg.6, amended: SI 2008/1903 Reg.20

NO.

2005–cont.

3273. Financial Assistance Scheme (Appeals) Regulations 2005–*cont.*

Reg.17, amended: SI 2008/1903 Reg.20

Reg.21, amended: SI 2008/2683 Sch.1 para.302

Reg.28, amended: SI 2008/2683 Sch.1 para.303

3274. Parks for People (England) Joint Scheme (Authorisation) Order 2005

revoked: SI 2008/3103 Art.3

3281. Feeding Stuffs (England) Regulations 2005

Sch.7 Part Ch.A, amended: SI 2008/1523 Sch.1

3286. Pesticides (Maximum Residue Levels in Crops, Food and Feeding Stuffs) (England and Wales) Regulations 2005

revoked: SI 2008/2570 Sch.2

Sch.2, amended: SI 2008/665 Sch.1

3296. Bovine Products (Restriction on Placing on the Market) (Wales) (No.2) Regulations 2005

revoked: SI 2008/3154 Reg.21

3320. Hydrocarbon Oil Duties (Reliefs for Electricity Generation) Regulations 2005

Reg.2, amended: SI 2008/753 Reg.9

Reg.3, amended: SI 2008/753 Reg.9

Reg.9, amended: SI 2008/753 Reg.9

Reg.10, amended: SI 2008/753 Reg.9

Reg.13, amended: SI 2008/753 Reg.9

Sch.1, amended: SI 2008/753 Reg.9

3346. Cosmetic Products (Safety) (Amendment) (No.2) Regulations 2005

revoked: SI 2008/1284 Sch.1

3361. National Health Service (General Dental Services Contracts) Regulations 2005

Reg.2, amended: SI 2008/1700 Sch.1 para.15

Sch.3 Part 5 para.36, revoked: SI 2008/528 Sch.1 para.9

Sch.3 Part 5 para.44, amended: SI 2008/528 Sch.1 para.9

Sch.3 Part 5 para.45, revoked: SI 2008/528 Sch.1 para.9

Sch.3 Part 5 para.46A, added: SI 2008/1514 Reg.6

3362. Feeding Stuffs (Application to Zootechnical Additives etc.) (Scotland) Regulations 2005

Reg.5, revoked: SSI 2008/201 Reg.3

Reg.6, revoked: SSI 2008/201 Reg.3

3364. Valuation Tribunals (Wales) Regulations 2005

Reg.5, applied: SI 2008/239 Sch.2 para.23

NO.

2005–cont.

3373. National Health Service (Personal Dental Services Agreements) Regulations 2005

Sch.3 Part 5 para.37, revoked: SI 2008/528 Sch.1 para.10

Sch.3 Part 5 para.44, amended: SI 2008/528 Sch.1 para.10

Sch.3 Part 5 para.45, revoked: SI 2008/528 Sch.1 para.10

Sch.3 Part 5 para.46A, added: SI 2008/1514 Reg.7

3377. Occupational Pension Schemes (Scheme Funding) Regulations 2005

see *British Vita Unlimited v British Vita Pension Fund Trustees Ltd* [2007] EWHC 953 (Ch), [2008] 1 All E.R. 37 (Ch D), Warren, J.

Reg.5, see *Allied Domecq (Holdings) Ltd v Allied Domecq First Pension Trust Fund* [2007] EWHC 2911 (Ch), [2008] Pens. L.R. 1 (Ch D), Blackburne, J.; see *Allied Domecq (Holdings) Ltd v Allied Domecq First Pension Trust Fund* [2008] EWCA Civ 1084, [2008] Pens. L.R. 425 (CA (Civ Div)), Ward, L.J.

Reg.8, see *Allied Domecq (Holdings) Ltd v Allied Domecq First Pension Trust Fund* [2007] EWHC 2911 (Ch), [2008] Pens. L.R. 1 (Ch D), Blackburne, J.; see *Allied Domecq (Holdings) Ltd v Allied Domecq First Pension Trust Fund* [2008] EWCA Civ 1084, [2008] Pens. L.R. 425 (CA (Civ Div)), Ward, L.J.

Reg.15, amended: SI 2008/2301 Sch.1 para.5

Sch.2 para.3, substituted: SI 2008/731 Reg.20

Sch.2 para.9, see *Allied Domecq (Holdings) Ltd v Allied Domecq First Pension Trust Fund* [2007] EWHC 2911 (Ch), [2008] Pens. L.R. 1 (Ch D), Blackburne, J.; see *Allied Domecq (Holdings) Ltd v Allied Domecq First Pension Trust Fund* [2008] EWCA Civ 1084, [2008] Pens. L.R. 425 (CA (Civ Div)), Ward, L.J.

3382. Proceeds of Crime Act 2002 (Legal Expenses in Civil Recovery Proceedings) Regulations 2005

referred to: SI 2008/523 Reg.1

Reg.2, amended: SI 2008/523 Reg.2

Reg.5, amended: SI 2008/523 Reg.2

Reg.8, amended: SI 2008/523 Reg.2

Reg.9, amended: SI 2008/523 Reg.2

Reg.10, amended: SI 2008/523 Reg.2

Reg.12, amended: SI 2008/523 Reg.2

Reg.13, amended: SI 2008/523 Reg.2

3396. Victims of Violent Intentional Crime (Arrangements for Compensation) (European Communities) Regulations 2005

Reg.4, amended: SI 2008/2683 Sch.1 para.305

Reg.11, amended: SI 2008/2683 Sch.1 para.306

NO.

2005–cont.

3430. Parliamentary Commissioner (No.2) Order 2005
Sch.1, revoked: SI 2008/576 Sch.5 para.8

3443. Family Proceedings Fees (Amendment No.2) Order 2005
revoked: SI 2008/1054 Sch.3

3444. Magistrates Courts Fees Order 2005
revoked: SI 2008/1052 Sch.3
Sch.2 para.2, amended: SI 2008/117 Art.2

3445. Civil Proceedings Fees (Amendment) Order 2005
revoked: SI 2008/1053 Sch.3

3456. Registered Pension Schemes (Audited Accounts) (Specified Persons) Regulations 2005
Reg.2, amended: SI 2008/948 Sch.1 para.33, SI 2008/954 Art.56
Reg.3, amended: SI 2008/954 Art.57

3459. Common Agricultural Policy Single Payment and Support Schemes (Cross-compliance) (England) Regulations 2005
Sch.1 para.7, amended: SI 2008/80 Reg.2

3472. Hydrocarbon Oil (Registered Remote Markers) Regulations 2005
Reg.2, amended: SI 2008/753 Reg.10
Reg.3, amended: SI 2008/753 Reg.10
Reg.4, amended: SI 2008/753 Reg.10
Reg.6, amended: SI 2008/753 Reg.10
Reg.8, amended: SI 2008/753 Reg.10
Reg.9, amended: SI 2008/753 Reg.10
Reg.11, amended: SI 2008/753 Reg.10
Reg.12, amended: SI 2008/753 Reg.10
Reg.13, amended: SI 2008/753 Reg.10

3474. Income Tax (Building Societies) (Dividends and Interest) (Amendment) Regulations 2005
revoked: SI 2008/2682 Sch.3

3477. National Health Service (Dental Charges) Regulations 2005
Reg.4, amended: SI 2008/547 Reg.3
Sch.3, amended: SI 2008/547 Reg.3

3504. Adoption and Children Act 2002 (Consequential Amendments) Order 2005
Art.6, revoked: SI 2008/2683 Sch.2

3517. Veterinary Surgeons and Veterinary Practitioners (Registration) Regulations Order of Council 2005
Sch.1, amended: SI 2008/2933 Sch.1

3626. Food Labelling (Amendment) (Wales) (No.2) (Amendment) Regulations 2005
revoked: SI 2008/1268 Reg.3

2006

5. Public Contracts Regulations 2006
applied: SI 2008/2848 Reg.4

NO.

2006–cont.

5. Public Contracts Regulations 2006–*cont.*
see *Letting International Ltd v Newham LBC* [2007] EWCA Civ 1522, [2008] Eu. L.R. 517 (CA (Civ Div)), Ward, L.J.; see *Risk Management Partners Ltd v Brent LBC* [2008] EWHC 1094 (Admin), [2008] Eu. L.R. 660 (QBD), Stanley Burnton, L.J.
Reg.2, amended: SI 2008/2256 Reg.2
Reg.6, amended: SI 2008/2848 Reg.3
Reg.32, see *McConnell Archive Storage Ltd v Belfast City Council* [2008] NICh 3, [2008] Eu. L.R. 549 (Ch D (NI)), Deeny, J.
Reg.40, referred to: SI 2008/2256 Reg.4
Reg.47, see *Letting International Ltd v Newham LBC* [2007] EWCA Civ 1522, [2008] Eu. L.R. 517 (CA (Civ Div)), Ward, L.J.
Sch.1, amended: SI 2008/2683 Sch.1 para.307, SI 2008/2848 Reg.2
Sch.2, substituted: SI 2008/2256 Sch.1
Sch.3, substituted: SI 2008/2256 Sch.2

6. Utilities Contracts Regulations 2006
Reg.2, amended: SI 2008/2256 Reg.3
Reg.38, amended: SI 2008/2256 Reg.3
Reg.38, referred to: SI 2008/2256 Reg.4
Sch.1, added: SI 2008/2848 Sch.1
Sch.2, substituted: SI 2008/2256 Sch.1
Sch.3, substituted: SI 2008/2256 Sch.2

33. Occupational Pension Schemes (Early Leavers Cash Transfer Sums and Contribution Refunds) Regulations 2006
applied: SSI 2008/228 Reg.73
Reg.1, amended: SI 2008/1050 Sch.2 para.8
Reg.2, substituted: SI 2008/1050 Sch.2 para.8
Reg.2B, amended: SI 2008/2450 Reg.4
Reg.2C, amended: SI 2008/2450 Reg.4
Reg.2D, amended: SI 2008/2450 Reg.4
Reg.4, substituted: SI 2008/1050 Sch.2 para.8
Reg.5, amended: SI 2008/1050 Sch.2 para.8
Reg.7, amended: SI 2008/1050 Sch.2 para.8

34. Occupational Pension Schemes (Transfer Values etc.) (Coal Staff and Mineworkers Schemes) (Amendment) Regulations 2006
applied: SSI 2008/228 Reg.73

91. Transport for London (Best Value) (Contracting Out of Investment and Highway Functions) Order 2006
varied: SI 2008/917 Art.6

92. Cremation (Amendment) Regulations 2006
revoked: SI 2008/2841 Sch.2

116. Feeding Stuffs (Wales) Regulations 2006
Sch.7 Part CHAPTER, amended: SI 2008/1806 Sch.1

NO.

2006–cont.

126. Assembly Learning Grants and Loans (Higher Education) (Wales) Regulations 2006
applied: SI 2008/3170 Reg.3

128. Education (Admission of Looked After Children) (England) Regulations 2006
revoked: SI 2008/3089 Sch.1

131. Registered Pension Schemes (Enhanced Lifetime Allowance) Regulations 2006
applied: SI 2008/653 Reg.3, SSI 2008/224 Reg.3

147. Personal Pension Schemes (Appropriate Schemes) (Amendment) Regulations 2006
revoked: SI 2008/1979 Reg.5

202. Duty Stamps Regulations 2006
Reg.10, amended: SI 2008/1277 Sch.2 para.111

213. Housing Benefit Regulations 2006
applied: SI 2008/254 Reg.2
referred to: SI 2008/632 Art.19, SI 2008/959 Reg.2, Reg.3, Reg.4
Reg.2, amended: SI 2008/698 Reg.6, SI 2008/959 Reg.4, SI 2008/1042 Reg.3, SI 2008/1082 Reg.5, SI 2008/2299 Reg.2, SI 2008/2767 Reg.6, SI 2008/3157 Reg.5
Reg.2, applied: SI 2008/794 Reg.116
Reg.2, varied: SI 2008/2839 Sch.1 para.1
Reg.5, amended: SI 2008/959 Reg.4, SI 2008/1082 Reg.6
Reg.5, revoked (in part): SI 2008/959 Reg.4
Reg.6, amended: SI 2008/1082 Reg.7
Reg.7, amended: SI 2008/1042 Reg.3, SI 2008/1082 Reg.7A, SI 2008/2767 Reg.6
Reg.10, amended: SI 2008/1082 Reg.8
Reg.11, amended: SI 2008/1082 Reg.9
Reg.13C, applied: SI 2008/2112 Reg.5
Reg.19, amended: SI 2008/1082 Reg.10
Reg.22, amended: SI 2008/1082 Reg.11
Reg.23, amended: SI 2008/1082 Reg.12
Reg.26, amended: SI 2008/1082 Reg.13
Reg.28, amended: SI 2008/1042 Reg.3, SI 2008/1082 Reg.14, SI 2008/3157 Reg.5
Reg.37, amended: SI 2008/698 Reg.6
Reg.40, amended: SI 2008/1082 Reg.15, SI 2008/1599 Reg.5
Reg.42, amended: SI 2008/698 Reg.6, SI 2008/2767 Reg.6
Reg.42, revoked (in part): SI 2008/1042 Reg.3
Reg.46, amended: SI 2008/2767 Reg.6
Reg.49, amended: SI 2008/698 Reg.6, SI 2008/2767 Reg.6
Reg.50, amended: SI 2008/1082 Reg.16
Reg.53, amended: SI 2008/1042 Reg.3, SI 2008/2767 Reg.6, SI 2008/3157 Reg.5
Reg.56, amended: SI 2008/1042 Reg.3, SI 2008/1082 Reg.17
Reg.59, amended: SI 2008/1599 Reg.5
Reg.63, amended: SI 2008/1042 Reg.3

NO.

2006–cont.

213. Housing Benefit Regulations 2006– *cont.*
Reg.64, amended: SI 2008/1599 Reg.5
Reg.72, substituted: SI 2008/959 Reg.2
Reg.73, substituted: SI 2008/959 Reg.3
Reg.73A, substituted: SI 2008/959 Reg.3
Reg.73B, substituted: SI 2008/959 Reg.3
Reg.73C, substituted: SI 2008/959 Reg.3
Reg.73D, substituted: SI 2008/959 Reg.3
Reg.74, amended: SI 2008/632 Art.19, SI 2008/1082 Reg.18, SI 2008/2767 Reg.6
Reg.74, applied: SI 2008/794 Sch.6 para.19
Reg.74, referred to: SI 2008/632 Art.19
Reg.77, revoked: SI 2008/959 Reg.4
Reg.78, revoked: SI 2008/959 Reg.4
Reg.79, amended: SI 2008/2667 Reg.5
Reg.80, revoked (in part): SI 2008/959 Reg.4
Reg.82, revoked (in part): SI 2008/2299 Reg.2
Reg.83, amended: SI 2008/1082 Reg.19, SI 2008/2299 Reg.2, SI 2008/2424 Reg.4, SI 2008/2987 Reg.2
Reg.83, revoked (in part): SI 2008/2299 Reg.2
Reg.84, revoked: SI 2008/2299 Reg.2
Reg.85, revoked: SI 2008/2299 Reg.2
Reg.86, amended: SI 2008/2767 Reg.6, SI 2008/2987 Reg.2
Reg.87, substituted: SI 2008/2299 Reg.2
Reg.88, amended: SI 2008/1042 Reg.3, SI 2008/1082 Reg.20, SI 2008/2299 Reg.2, SI 2008/2987 Reg.2
Reg.88, revoked (in part): SI 2008/2299 Reg.2
Reg.89, revoked (in part): SI 2008/959 Reg.4
Reg.91A, amended: SI 2008/2824 Reg.2
Reg.95, amended: SI 2008/1082 Reg.21
Reg.96, applied: SI 2008/2112 Reg.5
Reg.101, amended: SI 2008/586 Reg.2, SI 2008/2824 Reg.4
Reg.101, revoked (in part): SI 2008/2824 Reg.4
Reg.102, amended: SI 2008/2824 Reg.4
Reg.105, amended: SI 2008/1082 Reg.22, SI 2008/2824 Reg.4
Reg.115, substituted: SI 2008/959 Reg.2
Reg.116, substituted: SI 2008/959 Reg.3
Reg.121, substituted: SI 2008/2299 Reg.2
Reg.121A, added: SI 2008/2299 Reg.2
Sch.1 Part 1 para.1, amended: SI 2008/3157 Reg.5
Sch.1 Part 1 para.1, applied: SI 2008/794 Sch.6 para.18
Sch.1 Part 1 para.2, amended: SI 2008/632 Art.19
Sch.1 Part 2 para.6, referred to: SI 2008/794 Sch.6 para.18
Sch.2, applied: SI 2008/2824 Reg.2, Reg.3
Sch.2 para.3, substituted: SI 2008/2824 Reg.2

NO.

2006–cont.

213. Housing Benefit Regulations 2006– *cont.*

Sch.2 para.9, amended: SI 2008/2767 Reg.6
Sch.3 Part 1, referred to: SI 2008/632 Art.19
Sch.3 Part 1 para.1, amended: SI 2008/1082 Reg.23
Sch.3 Part 1 para.1, substituted: SI 2008/632 Sch.6
Sch.3 Part 1 para.2, substituted: SI 2008/632 Sch.6
Sch.3 Part 2 para.3, amended: SI 2008/632 Art.19, SI 2008/1042 Reg.3
Sch.3 Part 3 para.6, substituted: SI 2008/1042 Reg.3
Sch.3 Part 3 para.9, revoked: SI 2008/1042 Reg.3
Sch.3 Part 3 para.10, revoked: SI 2008/1042 Reg.3
Sch.3 Part 3 para.11, revoked: SI 2008/1042 Reg.3
Sch.3 Part 3 para.13, amended: SI 2008/1042 Reg.3, SI 2008/1082 Reg.23
Sch.3 Part 3 para.13, revoked (in part): SI 2008/1042 Reg.3
Sch.3 Part 3 para.15, amended: SI 2008/1082 Reg.23, SI 2008/2767 Reg.6
Sch.3 Part 4, amended: SI 2008/1042 Reg.3
Sch.3 Part 4, referred to: SI 2008/632 Art.19
Sch.3 Part 4, substituted: SI 2008/632 Sch.7
Sch.3 Part 5 para.21, added: SI 2008/1082 Reg.23
Sch.3 Part 5 para.21, substituted: SI 2008/1082 Reg.23
Sch.3 Part 5 para.22, added: SI 2008/1082 Reg.23
Sch.3 Part 5 para.22, substituted: SI 2008/1082 Reg.23
Sch.3 Part 5 para.23, added: SI 2008/1082 Reg.23
Sch.3 Part 5 para.23, substituted: SI 2008/1082 Reg.23
Sch.3 Part 5 para.24, added: SI 2008/1082 Reg.23
Sch.3 Part 5 para.24, substituted: SI 2008/1082 Reg.23
Sch.3 Part 6 para.25, added: SI 2008/1082 Reg.23
Sch.3 Part 6 para.25, substituted: SI 2008/1082 Reg.23
Sch.3 Part 6 para.26, added: SI 2008/1082 Reg.23
Sch.3 Part 6 para.26, substituted: SI 2008/1082 Reg.23
Sch.4 para.3, amended: SI 2008/1042 Reg.3, SI 2008/1082 Reg.24
Sch.4 para.3, revoked (in part): SI 2008/1042 Reg.3
Sch.4 para.9, amended: SI 2008/1042 Reg.3
Sch.4 para.12, amended: SI 2008/1082 Reg.24

NO.

2006–cont.

213. Housing Benefit Regulations 2006– *cont.*

Sch.4 para.17, amended: SI 2008/632 Art.19, SI 2008/1042 Reg.3, SI 2008/1082 Reg.24
Sch.5 para.4, amended: SI 2008/1082 Reg.25
Sch.5 para.7, amended: SI 2008/1082 Reg.25
Sch.5 para.8, amended: SI 2008/3157 Reg.5
Sch.5 para.11, amended: SI 2008/3157 Reg.5
Sch.5 para.15, amended: SI 2008/1042 Reg.3, SI 2008/3157 Reg.5
Sch.5 para.18, revoked: SI 2008/1042 Reg.3
Sch.5 para.25, amended: SI 2008/1042 Reg.3, SI 2008/3157 Reg.5
Sch.5 para.25, revoked (in part): SI 2008/3157 Reg.5
Sch.5 para.27, amended: SI 2008/3157 Reg.5
Sch.5 para.28, amended: SI 2008/2767 Reg.6
Sch.5 para.28A, added: SI 2008/698 Reg.6
Sch.5 para.35, amended: SI 2008/2767 Reg.6, SI 2008/3157 Reg.5
Sch.5 para.37, revoked: SI 2008/698 Reg.6
Sch.5 para.38, revoked: SI 2008/3157 Reg.5
Sch.5 para.40, revoked: SI 2008/2767 Reg.6
Sch.5 para.41, amended: SI 2008/698 Reg.6
Sch.5 para.43, revoked: SI 2008/3157 Reg.5
Sch.5 para.44, amended: SI 2008/1042 Reg.3
Sch.5 para.44, substituted: SI 2008/3157 Reg.5
Sch.5 para.45, amended: SI 2008/1042 Reg.3
Sch.5 para.45, substituted: SI 2008/3157 Reg.5
Sch.5 para.47, substituted: SI 2008/1042 Reg.3
Sch.5 para.48, revoked: SI 2008/698 Reg.6
Sch.5 para.51, substituted: SI 2008/3157 Reg.5
Sch.5 para.52, substituted: SI 2008/3157 Reg.5
Sch.5 para.53, substituted: SI 2008/3157 Reg.5
Sch.5 para.55, amended: SI 2008/3157 Reg.5
Sch.5 para.55A, revoked: SI 2008/3157 Reg.5
Sch.5 para.55B, revoked: SI 2008/3157 Reg.5
Sch.5 para.56, amended: SI 2008/632 Art.19
Sch.5 para.63, amended: SI 2008/3157 Reg.5
Sch.5 para.64, added: SI 2008/3140 Reg.4
Sch.5 para.64, revoked (in part): SI 2008/3140 Reg.4
Sch.6 para.5, amended: SI 2008/1082 Reg.26

NO.

2006–cont.

213. Housing Benefit Regulations 2006– *cont.*

Sch.6 para.9, amended: SI 2008/698 Reg.6, SI 2008/1082 Reg.26
Sch.6 para.16, amended: SI 2008/1042 Reg.3
Sch.6 para.19, amended: SI 2008/2767 Reg.6
Sch.6 para.19A, added: SI 2008/698 Reg.6
Sch.6 para.24, amended: SI 2008/2767 Reg.6
Sch.6 para.29, revoked: SI 2008/698 Reg.6
Sch.6 para.34, amended: SI 2008/2767 Reg.6
Sch.6 para.36, revoked: SI 2008/2767 Reg.6
Sch.6 para.39, substituted: SI 2008/3157 Reg.5
Sch.6 para.40, amended: SI 2008/1042 Reg.3
Sch.6 para.40, substituted: SI 2008/3157 Reg.5
Sch.6 para.41, amended: SI 2008/1042 Reg.3
Sch.6 para.41, substituted: SI 2008/3157 Reg.5
Sch.6 para.43, amended: SI 2008/1042 Reg.3
Sch.6 para.48A, revoked: SI 2008/3157 Reg.5
Sch.6 para.48B, revoked: SI 2008/3157 Reg.5
Sch.6 para.51, amended: SI 2008/3157 Reg.5
Sch.6 para.55, amended: SI 2008/1042 Reg.3
Sch.6 para.56, amended: SI 2008/3157 Reg.5
Sch.6 para.57, amended: SI 2008/3157 Reg.5
Sch.7 Part 1 para.1, revoked: SI 2008/959 Reg.4
Sch.7 Part 1 para.2, revoked: SI 2008/959 Reg.4
Sch.7 Part 2 para.3, revoked: SI 2008/959 Reg.4
Sch.7 Part 2 para.4, revoked: SI 2008/959 Reg.4
Sch.7 Part 2 para.5, revoked: SI 2008/959 Reg.4
Sch.7 Part 2 para.6, revoked: SI 2008/959 Reg.4
Sch.7 Part 2 para.7, revoked: SI 2008/959 Reg.4
Sch.7 Part 2 para.8, revoked: SI 2008/959 Reg.4
Sch.7 Part 2 para.9, revoked: SI 2008/959 Reg.4
Sch.7 Part 3 para.10, revoked: SI 2008/959 Reg.4
Sch.7 Part 4 para.11, revoked: SI 2008/959 Reg.4

NO.

2006–cont.

213. Housing Benefit Regulations 2006– *cont.*

Sch.8 para.1, revoked: SI 2008/959 Reg.4
Sch.8 para.2, revoked: SI 2008/959 Reg.4
Sch.8 para.3, revoked: SI 2008/959 Reg.4
Sch.8 para.4, revoked: SI 2008/959 Reg.4
Sch.8 para.5, revoked: SI 2008/959 Reg.4
Sch.8 para.6, revoked: SI 2008/959 Reg.4
Sch.8 para.7, revoked: SI 2008/959 Reg.4
Sch.8 para.8, revoked: SI 2008/959 Reg.4
Sch.8 para.9, revoked: SI 2008/959 Reg.4
Sch.8 para.10, revoked: SI 2008/959 Reg.4
Sch.9 Part 2 para.9, amended: SI 2008/959 Reg.4, SI 2008/1082 Reg.27
Sch.9 Part 3 para.10, amended: SI 2008/1082 Reg.27
Sch.9 Part 6 para.14, amended: SI 2008/1082 Reg.27

214. Housing Benefit (Persons who have attained the qualifying age for state pension credit) Regulations 2006

applied: SI 2008/254 Reg.2
referred to: SI 2008/632 Art.20, SI 2008/959 Reg.5, Reg.6
Reg.2, amended: SI 2008/959 Reg.6, SI 2008/1042 Reg.4, SI 2008/1082 Reg.29, SI 2008/2299 Reg.3, SI 2008/2767 Reg.7, SI 2008/3157 Reg.6
Reg.2, varied: SI 2008/2839 Sch.1 para.1
Reg.5, amended: SI 2008/1082 Reg.30
Reg.6, amended: SI 2008/1082 Reg.31
Reg.7, amended: SI 2008/1042 Reg.4, SI 2008/2767 Reg.7
Reg.13C, applied: SI 2008/2112 Reg.5
Reg.19, amended: SI 2008/1082 Reg.32
Reg.22, amended: SI 2008/1042 Reg.4
Reg.24, amended: SI 2008/3157 Reg.6
Reg.29, amended: SI 2008/1082 Reg.33, SI 2008/3157 Reg.6
Reg.31, amended: SI 2008/1042 Reg.4, SI 2008/1082 Reg.34, SI 2008/3157 Reg.6
Reg.38, amended: SI 2008/3157 Reg.6
Reg.48, amended: SI 2008/1082 Reg.35
Reg.52, substituted: SI 2008/959 Reg.6
Reg.53, substituted: SI 2008/959 Reg.5
Reg.54, amended: SI 2008/1082 Reg.36
Reg.55, amended: SI 2008/632 Art.20, SI 2008/1082 Reg.37, SI 2008/2767 Reg.7
Reg.55, referred to: SI 2008/632 Art.20
Reg.58, revoked: SI 2008/959 Reg.6
Reg.59, amended: SI 2008/2667 Reg.6
Reg.61, revoked (in part): SI 2008/959 Reg.6
Reg.63, revoked (in part): SI 2008/2299 Reg.3
Reg.64, amended: SI 2008/1082 Reg.38, SI 2008/2299 Reg.3, SI 2008/2424 Reg.5, SI 2008/2987 Reg.3
Reg.64, revoked (in part): SI 2008/2299 Reg.3, SI 2008/2824 Reg.8
Reg.65, revoked: SI 2008/2299 Reg.3
Reg.66, revoked: SI 2008/2299 Reg.3

NO.

2006–cont.

214. Housing Benefit (Persons who have attained the qualifying age for state pension credit) Regulations 2006– *cont.*

Reg.67, amended: SI 2008/1042 Reg.4, SI 2008/2767 Reg.7, SI 2008/2987 Reg.3
Reg.68, substituted: SI 2008/2299 Reg.3
Reg.69, amended: SI 2008/2299 Reg.3, SI 2008/2987 Reg.3
Reg.69, revoked (in part): SI 2008/2299 Reg.3
Reg.70, revoked (in part): SI 2008/959 Reg.6
Reg.72A, amended: SI 2008/2824 Reg.3
Reg.77, applied: SI 2008/2112 Reg.5
Reg.82, amended: SI 2008/586 Reg.3, SI 2008/2824 Reg.5
Reg.82, revoked (in part): SI 2008/2824 Reg.5
Reg.83, amended: SI 2008/1042 Reg.4, SI 2008/2824 Reg.5
Reg.86, amended: SI 2008/1082 Reg.39, SI 2008/2824 Reg.5
Reg.96, substituted: SI 2008/959 Reg.5
Reg.97, substituted: SI 2008/959 Reg.5
Reg.102, substituted: SI 2008/2299 Reg.3
Reg.102A, added: SI 2008/2299 Reg.3
Sch.1 Part 1 para.1, amended: SI 2008/3157 Reg.6
Sch.1 Part 1 para.2, amended: SI 2008/632 Art.20
Sch.2 para.3, substituted: SI 2008/2824 Reg.3
Sch.2 para.9, amended: SI 2008/2767 Reg.7
Sch.3 Part 1, referred to: SI 2008/632 Art.20
Sch.3 Part 1 para.1, substituted: SI 2008/632 Sch.8
Sch.3 Part 1 para.2, substituted: SI 2008/632 Sch.8
Sch.3 Part 2 para.3, amended: SI 2008/632 Art.20
Sch.3 Part 4, referred to: SI 2008/632 Art.20
Sch.3 Part 4, substituted: SI 2008/632 Sch.9
Sch.4 para.5, amended: SI 2008/1082 Reg.40, SI 2008/3157 Reg.6
Sch.4 para.9, amended: SI 2008/632 Art.20
Sch.5 para.1, amended: SI 2008/1042 Reg.4, SI 2008/3157 Reg.6
Sch.5 para.3, amended: SI 2008/3157 Reg.6
Sch.5 para.4, substituted: SI 2008/3157 Reg.6
Sch.5 para.6, amended: SI 2008/3157 Reg.6
Sch.5 para.12, amended: SI 2008/1042 Reg.4
Sch.5 para.13, amended: SI 2008/3157 Reg.6
Sch.5 para.21, amended: SI 2008/632 Art.20, SI 2008/3157 Reg.6
Sch.5 para.23, revoked: SI 2008/3157 Reg.6
Sch.6 Part 1 para.15, amended: SI 2008/3157 Reg.6

NO.

2006–cont.

214. Housing Benefit (Persons who have attained the qualifying age for state pension credit) Regulations 2006– *cont.*

Sch.6 Part 1 para.16, amended: SI 2008/2767 Reg.7
Sch.6 Part 1 para.18, amended: SI 2008/3157 Reg.6
Sch.6 Part 1 para.21, amended: SI 2008/1082 Reg.41, SI 2008/3157 Reg.6
Sch.6 Part 1 para.22, amended: SI 2008/1042 Reg.4, SI 2008/1082 Reg.41
Sch.6 Part 1 para.26B, added: SI 2008/3157 Reg.6
Sch.7 para.1, revoked: SI 2008/959 Reg.6
Sch.7 para.2, revoked: SI 2008/959 Reg.6
Sch.7 para.3, revoked: SI 2008/959 Reg.6
Sch.7 para.4, revoked: SI 2008/959 Reg.6
Sch.7 para.5, revoked: SI 2008/959 Reg.6
Sch.7 para.6, revoked: SI 2008/959 Reg.6
Sch.7 para.7, revoked: SI 2008/959 Reg.6
Sch.7 para.8, revoked: SI 2008/959 Reg.6
Sch.7 para.9, revoked: SI 2008/959 Reg.6
Sch.7 para.10, revoked: SI 2008/959 Reg.6
Sch.8 Part 2 para.9, amended: SI 2008/959 Reg.6, SI 2008/1042 Reg.4
Sch.8 Part 6 para.14, amended: SI 2008/2767 Reg.7

215. Council Tax Benefit Regulations 2006

referred to: SI 2008/632 Art.21, SI 2008/959 Reg.7, Reg.8, Reg.9
Reg.2, amended: SI 2008/698 Reg.7, SI 2008/959 Reg.9, SI 2008/1042 Reg.5, SI 2008/1082 Reg.43, SI 2008/2299 Reg.4, SI 2008/2767 Reg.8, SI 2008/3157 Reg.7
Reg.5, amended: SI 2008/959 Reg.9, SI 2008/1082 Reg.44
Reg.5, revoked (in part): SI 2008/959 Reg.9
Reg.6, amended: SI 2008/1082 Reg.45
Reg.7, amended: SI 2008/1082 Reg.46
Reg.8, amended: SI 2008/2767 Reg.8
Reg.9, amended: SI 2008/1082 Reg.47
Reg.12, amended: SI 2008/1082 Reg.48
Reg.13, amended: SI 2008/1082 Reg.49
Reg.16, amended: SI 2008/1082 Reg.50
Reg.18, amended: SI 2008/1042 Reg.5, SI 2008/1082 Reg.51, SI 2008/3157 Reg.7
Reg.27, amended: SI 2008/698 Reg.7
Reg.30, amended: SI 2008/1082 Reg.52, SI 2008/1599 Reg.6
Reg.32, amended: SI 2008/698 Reg.7, SI 2008/2767 Reg.8
Reg.32, revoked (in part): SI 2008/1042 Reg.5
Reg.36, amended: SI 2008/2767 Reg.8
Reg.39, amended: SI 2008/698 Reg.7, SI 2008/2767 Reg.8
Reg.40, amended: SI 2008/1082 Reg.53
Reg.43, amended: SI 2008/1042 Reg.5, SI 2008/2767 Reg.8, SI 2008/3157 Reg.7
Reg.45, amended: SI 2008/1082 Reg.54

NO.

2006–cont.

215. Council Tax Benefit Regulations 2006–*cont.*

Reg.46, amended: SI 2008/1599 Reg.6
Reg.50, amended: SI 2008/1042 Reg.5
Reg.51, amended: SI 2008/1599 Reg.6
Reg.57, amended: SI 2008/959 Reg.9
Reg.57, revoked (in part): SI 2008/959 Reg.9
Reg.58, amended: SI 2008/632 Art.21, SI 2008/1082 Reg.55, SI 2008/2767 Reg.8
Reg.60, substituted: SI 2008/959 Reg.7
Reg.61, substituted: SI 2008/959 Reg.8
Reg.65, revoked: SI 2008/959 Reg.9
Reg.66, revoked: SI 2008/959 Reg.9
Reg.68, revoked (in part): SI 2008/2299 Reg.4
Reg.69, amended: SI 2008/1082 Reg.56, SI 2008/2299 Reg.4, SI 2008/2424 Reg.6, SI 2008/2987 Reg.4
Reg.69, revoked (in part): SI 2008/2299 Reg.4
Reg.70, amended: SI 2008/1042 Reg.5
Reg.70, revoked: SI 2008/2299 Reg.4
Reg.71, amended: SI 2008/1042 Reg.5
Reg.71, revoked: SI 2008/2299 Reg.4
Reg.72, amended: SI 2008/1042 Reg.5, SI 2008/2767 Reg.8, SI 2008/2987 Reg.4
Reg.73, substituted: SI 2008/2299 Reg.4
Reg.74, amended: SI 2008/1082 Reg.57, SI 2008/2299 Reg.4, SI 2008/2767 Reg.8, SI 2008/2987 Reg.4
Reg.74, revoked (in part): SI 2008/2299 Reg.4
Reg.75, revoked (in part): SI 2008/959 Reg.9
Reg.85, substituted: SI 2008/2824 Reg.6
Reg.86, amended: SI 2008/2824 Reg.6
Reg.90, amended: SI 2008/1082 Reg.58, SI 2008/2824 Reg.6
Reg.96, substituted: SI 2008/959 Reg.7
Reg.97, substituted: SI 2008/959 Reg.8
Reg.98, added: SI 2008/2299 Reg.4
Sch.1 Part 1, referred to: SI 2008/632 Art.21
Sch.1 Part 1 para.1, amended: SI 2008/1082 Reg.59
Sch.1 Part 1 para.1, substituted: SI 2008/632 Sch.10
Sch.1 Part 1 para.2, substituted: SI 2008/632 Sch.10
Sch.1 Part 2 para.3, amended: SI 2008/632 Art.21, SI 2008/1042 Reg.5
Sch.1 Part 3 para.6, substituted: SI 2008/1042 Reg.5
Sch.1 Part 3 para.9, revoked: SI 2008/1042 Reg.5
Sch.1 Part 3 para.10, revoked: SI 2008/1042 Reg.5
Sch.1 Part 3 para.11, revoked: SI 2008/1042 Reg.5
Sch.1 Part 3 para.13, amended: SI 2008/1042 Reg.5, SI 2008/1082 Reg.59, SI 2008/2767 Reg.8

NO.

2006–cont.

215. Council Tax Benefit Regulations 2006–*cont.*

Sch.1 Part 3 para.13, revoked (in part): SI 2008/1042 Reg.5
Sch.1 Part 3 para.15, amended: SI 2008/1082 Reg.59
Sch.1 Part 4, amended: SI 2008/1042 Reg.5
Sch.1 Part 4, referred to: SI 2008/632 Art.21
Sch.1 Part 4, substituted: SI 2008/632 Sch.11
Sch.1 Part 5 para.21, added: SI 2008/1082 Reg.59
Sch.1 Part 5 para.21, substituted: SI 2008/1082 Reg.59
Sch.1 Part 5 para.22, added: SI 2008/1082 Reg.59
Sch.1 Part 5 para.22, substituted: SI 2008/1082 Reg.59
Sch.1 Part 5 para.23, added: SI 2008/1082 Reg.59
Sch.1 Part 5 para.23, substituted: SI 2008/1082 Reg.59
Sch.1 Part 5 para.24, added: SI 2008/1082 Reg.59
Sch.1 Part 5 para.24, substituted: SI 2008/1082 Reg.59
Sch.1 Part 6 para.25, added: SI 2008/1082 Reg.59
Sch.1 Part 6 para.25, substituted: SI 2008/1082 Reg.59
Sch.1 Part 6 para.26, added: SI 2008/1082 Reg.59
Sch.1 Part 6 para.26, substituted: SI 2008/1082 Reg.59
Sch.2 para.1, amended: SI 2008/632 Art.21, SI 2008/1082 Reg.60
Sch.2 para.2, amended: SI 2008/2767 Reg.8
Sch.3 para.3, amended: SI 2008/1042 Reg.5, SI 2008/1082 Reg.61
Sch.3 para.3, revoked (in part): SI 2008/1042 Reg.5
Sch.3 para.9, amended: SI 2008/1042 Reg.5
Sch.3 para.12, amended: SI 2008/1082 Reg.61
Sch.3 para.16, amended: SI 2008/632 Art.21, SI 2008/1042 Reg.5, SI 2008/1082 Reg.61
Sch.4 para.4, amended: SI 2008/1082 Reg.62
Sch.4 para.8, amended: SI 2008/1082 Reg.62
Sch.4 para.9, amended: SI 2008/3157 Reg.7
Sch.4 para.12, amended: SI 2008/3157 Reg.7
Sch.4 para.16, amended: SI 2008/1042 Reg.5, SI 2008/3157 Reg.7
Sch.4 para.26, amended: SI 2008/3157 Reg.7
Sch.4 para.26, revoked (in part): SI 2008/3157 Reg.7
Sch.4 para.28, amended: SI 2008/3157 Reg.7

NO.

2006–cont.

215. Council Tax Benefit Regulations 2006–*cont.*

Sch.4 para.29, amended: SI 2008/2767 Reg.8
Sch.4 para.29A, added: SI 2008/698 Reg.7
Sch.4 para.33, amended: SI 2008/3157 Reg.7
Sch.4 para.36, amended: SI 2008/2767 Reg.8
Sch.4 para.37, substituted: SI 2008/3157 Reg.7
Sch.4 para.39, revoked: SI 2008/698 Reg.7
Sch.4 para.40, revoked: SI 2008/3157 Reg.7
Sch.4 para.42, revoked: SI 2008/2767 Reg.8
Sch.4 para.43, amended: SI 2008/698 Reg.7
Sch.4 para.44, revoked: SI 2008/3157 Reg.7
Sch.4 para.45, amended: SI 2008/1042 Reg.5
Sch.4 para.45, substituted: SI 2008/3157 Reg.7
Sch.4 para.46, amended: SI 2008/1042 Reg.5
Sch.4 para.46, substituted: SI 2008/3157 Reg.7
Sch.4 para.47, amended: SI 2008/3157 Reg.7
Sch.4 para.48, substituted: SI 2008/1042 Reg.5
Sch.4 para.49, revoked: SI 2008/698 Reg.7
Sch.4 para.52, substituted: SI 2008/3157 Reg.7
Sch.4 para.53, substituted: SI 2008/3157 Reg.7
Sch.4 para.55, amended: SI 2008/3157 Reg.7
Sch.4 para.55A, added: SI 2008/3157 Reg.7
Sch.4 para.56, amended: SI 2008/632 Art.21
Sch.4 para.56A, revoked: SI 2008/3157 Reg.7
Sch.4 para.56B, revoked: SI 2008/3157 Reg.7
Sch.4 para.63, amended: SI 2008/3157 Reg.7
Sch.4 para.64, revoked: SI 2008/1042 Reg.5
Sch.4 para.65, added: SI 2008/3140 Reg.5
Sch.4 para.65, revoked: SI 2008/3140 Reg.2, Reg.5
Sch.5 para.1, amended: SI 2008/3157 Reg.7
Sch.5 para.5, amended: SI 2008/1082 Reg.63
Sch.5 para.9, amended: SI 2008/698 Reg.7, SI 2008/1082 Reg.63
Sch.5 para.19, amended: SI 2008/2767 Reg.8
Sch.5 para.19A, added: SI 2008/698 Reg.7
Sch.5 para.24, amended: SI 2008/2767 Reg.8, SI 2008/3157 Reg.7
Sch.5 para.30, revoked: SI 2008/698 Reg.7
Sch.5 para.34, amended: SI 2008/2767 Reg.8

NO.

2006–cont.

215. Council Tax Benefit Regulations 2006–*cont.*

Sch.5 para.36, revoked: SI 2008/2767 Reg.8
Sch.5 para.39, substituted: SI 2008/3157 Reg.7
Sch.5 para.40, amended: SI 2008/1042 Reg.5
Sch.5 para.40, substituted: SI 2008/3157 Reg.7
Sch.5 para.41, amended: SI 2008/1042 Reg.5
Sch.5 para.41, substituted: SI 2008/3157 Reg.7
Sch.5 para.43, amended: SI 2008/1042 Reg.5
Sch.5 para.44, revoked: SI 2008/698 Reg.7
Sch.5 para.53, amended: SI 2008/3157 Reg.7
Sch.5 para.53A, revoked: SI 2008/3157 Reg.7
Sch.5 para.53B, revoked: SI 2008/3157 Reg.7
Sch.5 para.57, amended: SI 2008/1042 Reg.5, SI 2008/3157 Reg.7
Sch.5 para.58, amended: SI 2008/3157 Reg.7
Sch.5 para.59, amended: SI 2008/3157 Reg.7
Sch.6 Part 1 para.1, revoked: SI 2008/959 Reg.9
Sch.6 Part 1 para.2, revoked: SI 2008/959 Reg.9
Sch.6 Part 2 para.3, revoked: SI 2008/959 Reg.9
Sch.6 Part 2 para.4, revoked: SI 2008/959 Reg.9
Sch.6 Part 2 para.5, revoked: SI 2008/959 Reg.9
Sch.6 Part 3 para.6, revoked: SI 2008/959 Reg.9
Sch.6 Part 4 para.7, revoked: SI 2008/959 Reg.9
Sch.7 para.1, revoked: SI 2008/959 Reg.9
Sch.7 para.2, revoked: SI 2008/959 Reg.9
Sch.7 para.3, revoked: SI 2008/959 Reg.9
Sch.7 para.4, revoked: SI 2008/959 Reg.9
Sch.7 para.5, revoked: SI 2008/959 Reg.9
Sch.7 para.6, revoked: SI 2008/959 Reg.9
Sch.7 para.7, revoked: SI 2008/959 Reg.9
Sch.8 Part 2 para.9, amended: SI 2008/959 Reg.9, SI 2008/1082 Reg.64
Sch.8 Part 3 para.10, amended: SI 2008/1082 Reg.64
Sch.8 Part 5 para.12, amended: SI 2008/1082 Reg.64
Sch.8 Part 6 para.13, amended: SI 2008/1082 Reg.64

NO.

2006–cont.

216. Council Tax Benefit (Persons who have attained the qualifying age for state pension credit) Regulations 2006

referred to: SI 2008/632 Art.22, SI 2008/959 Reg.10, Reg.11

Reg.2, amended: SI 2008/959 Reg.11, SI 2008/1042 Reg.6, SI 2008/1082 Reg.66, SI 2008/2299 Reg.5, SI 2008/2767 Reg.9, SI 2008/3157 Reg.8

Reg.5, amended: SI 2008/1082 Reg.67

Reg.6, amended: SI 2008/1082 Reg.68

Reg.8, amended: SI 2008/2767 Reg.9

Reg.9, amended: SI 2008/1082 Reg.69

Reg.14, amended: SI 2008/3157 Reg.8

Reg.19, amended: SI 2008/1082 Reg.70, SI 2008/3157 Reg.8

Reg.21, amended: SI 2008/1042 Reg.6, SI 2008/1082 Reg.71, SI 2008/3157 Reg.8

Reg.28, amended: SI 2008/3157 Reg.8

Reg.38, amended: SI 2008/1082 Reg.72

Reg.40, amended: SI 2008/959 Reg.11

Reg.40, revoked (in part): SI 2008/959 Reg.11

Reg.41, substituted: SI 2008/959 Reg.11

Reg.42, amended: SI 2008/632 Art.22, SI 2008/1082 Reg.73, SI 2008/2767 Reg.9

Reg.44, substituted: SI 2008/959 Reg.10

Reg.45, amended: SI 2008/1082 Reg.74

Reg.49, revoked: SI 2008/959 Reg.11

Reg.52, revoked (in part): SI 2008/2299 Reg.5

Reg.53, amended: SI 2008/1042 Reg.6, SI 2008/1082 Reg.75, SI 2008/2299 Reg.5, SI 2008/2424 Reg.7, SI 2008/2824 Reg.9, SI 2008/2987 Reg.5

Reg.53, revoked (in part): SI 2008/2299 Reg.5, SI 2008/2824 Reg.9

Reg.54, revoked: SI 2008/2299 Reg.5

Reg.55, revoked: SI 2008/2299 Reg.5

Reg.56, amended: SI 2008/2424 Reg.7

Reg.57, amended: SI 2008/2767 Reg.9, SI 2008/2987 Reg.5

Reg.58, substituted: SI 2008/2299 Reg.5

Reg.59, amended: SI 2008/1082 Reg.76, SI 2008/2767 Reg.9, SI 2008/2987 Reg.5

Reg.59, revoked (in part): SI 2008/2299 Reg.5

Reg.60, revoked (in part): SI 2008/959 Reg.11

Reg.70, substituted: SI 2008/2824 Reg.7

Reg.71, amended: SI 2008/2824 Reg.7

Reg.75, amended: SI 2008/1082 Reg.77, SI 2008/2824 Reg.7

Reg.81, substituted: SI 2008/959 Reg.10

Reg.82, substituted: SI 2008/959 Reg.10

Reg.83, added: SI 2008/2299 Reg.5

Sch.1 Part 1, referred to: SI 2008/632 Art.22

Sch.1 Part 1 para.1, substituted: SI 2008/632 Sch.12

NO.

2006–cont.

216. Council Tax Benefit (Persons who have attained the qualifying age for state pension credit) Regulations 2006–*cont.*

Sch.1 Part 1 para.2, substituted: SI 2008/632 Sch.12

Sch.1 Part 2 para.3, amended: SI 2008/632 Art.22

Sch.1 Part 4, referred to: SI 2008/632 Art.22

Sch.1 Part 4, substituted: SI 2008/632 Sch.13

Sch.2 para.5, amended: SI 2008/1082 Reg.78, SI 2008/3157 Reg.8

Sch.2 para.9, amended: SI 2008/632 Art.22

Sch.3 para.1, amended: SI 2008/1042 Reg.6, SI 2008/3157 Reg.8

Sch.3 para.3, amended: SI 2008/3157 Reg.8

Sch.3 para.4, substituted: SI 2008/3157 Reg.8

Sch.3 para.6, amended: SI 2008/3157 Reg.8

Sch.3 para.12, amended: SI 2008/1042 Reg.6

Sch.3 para.13, amended: SI 2008/3157 Reg.8

Sch.3 para.21, amended: SI 2008/632 Art.22, SI 2008/3157 Reg.8

Sch.3 para.22, revoked: SI 2008/3157 Reg.8

Sch.3 para.25, added: SI 2008/1042 Reg.6

Sch.4 Part 1 para.15, amended: SI 2008/3157 Reg.8

Sch.4 Part 1 para.16, amended: SI 2008/2767 Reg.9

Sch.4 Part 1 para.18, amended: SI 2008/3157 Reg.8

Sch.4 Part 1 para.21, amended: SI 2008/1082 Reg.79

Sch.4 Part 1 para.22, amended: SI 2008/1082 Reg.79

Sch.4 Part 1 para.25A, added: SI 2008/3157 Reg.8

Sch.4 Part 1 para.26A, added: SI 2008/1042 Reg.6

Sch.5 para.1, revoked: SI 2008/959 Reg.11

Sch.5 para.2, revoked: SI 2008/959 Reg.11

Sch.5 para.3, revoked: SI 2008/959 Reg.11

Sch.5 para.4, revoked: SI 2008/959 Reg.11

Sch.5 para.5, revoked: SI 2008/959 Reg.11

Sch.5 para.6, revoked: SI 2008/959 Reg.11

Sch.5 para.7, revoked: SI 2008/959 Reg.11

Sch.6 para.1, amended: SI 2008/632 Art.22, SI 2008/1082 Reg.80

Sch.6 para.2, amended: SI 2008/2767 Reg.9

Sch.7 Part 2 para.9, amended: SI 2008/959 Reg.11

Sch.7 Part 6 para.13, amended: SI 2008/1082 Reg.81

217. Housing Benefit and Council Tax Benefit (Consequential Provisions) Regulations 2006

Sch.2 para.15, revoked: SI 2008/2683 Sch.2

Sch.3 para.3, amended: SI 2008/1042 Reg.7

NO.

2006–cont.

217. Housing Benefit and Council Tax Benefit (Consequential Provisions) Regulations 2006–*cont.*

Sch.3 para.5, amended: SI 2008/1042 Reg.7, SI 2008/1082 Reg.2

Sch.3 para.9, amended: SI 2008/1042 Reg.7

Sch.4 para.3, amended: SI 2008/1042 Reg.7

Sch.4 para.4, revoked (in part): SI 2008/3157 Reg.9

223. Child Benefit (General) Regulations 2006

Reg.8, amended: SI 2008/1879 Reg.24

Reg.38, amended: SI 2008/2683 Sch.1 para.308

246. Transfer of Undertakings (Protection of Employment) Regulations 2006

applied: 2008 c.6 s.11, 2008 c.13 s.18, 2008 c.23 s.13, SI 2008/239 Reg.16, SI 2008/2546 Art.27, SSI 2008/230 Reg.18

referred to: SI 2008/2546 Sch.3 para.12

see *Holis Metal Industries Ltd v GMB* [2008] I.C.R. 464 (EAT), Judge Ansell; see *Kimberley Group Housing Ltd v Hambley* [2008] I.C.R. 1030 (EAT), Langstaff, J.; see *Lightways (Contractors) Ltd v North Ayrshire Council* [2008] CSOH 91, 2008 S.L.T. 690 (OH), Lord Bracadale; see *Print Factory (London) 1991 Ltd v Millam* [2007] EWCA Civ 322, [2008] B.C.C. 169 (CA (Civ Div)), Buxton, L.J.

Reg.2, applied: SI 2008/239 Reg.16

Reg.2, see *Kimberley Group Housing Ltd v Hambley* [2008] I.C.R. 1030 (EAT), Langstaff, J.

Reg.3, applied: SI 2008/239 Reg.16

Reg.3, disapplied: SI 2008/239 Reg.16, SI 2008/1419 Reg.3

Reg.3, see *Holis Metal Industries Ltd v GMB* [2008] I.C.R. 464 (EAT), Judge Ansell; see *Kimberley Group Housing Ltd v Hambley* [2008] I.C.R. 1030 (EAT), Langstaff, J.

Reg.4, see *Kimberley Group Housing Ltd v Hambley* [2008] I.C.R. 1030 (EAT), Langstaff, J.

Reg.13, referred to: SI 2008/228 Sch.2 para.20

264. Community Benefit Societies (Restriction on Use of Assets) Regulations 2006

Reg.2, varied: SI 2008/2839 Sch.1 para.1

300. Export Control (Bosnia and Herzegovina) Order 2006

revoked: SI 2008/3231 Sch.6

349. Occupational and Personal Pension Schemes (Consultation by Employers and Miscellaneous Amendment) Regulations 2006

Sch.1 para.8, referred to: SI 2008/3232 Sch.1 Part 2

397. Railways (Interoperability) Regulations 2006

Reg.2, amended: SI 2008/1746 Reg.4

NO.

2006–cont.

397. Railways (Interoperability) Regulations 2006–*cont.*

Reg.3, amended: SI 2008/1746 Reg.4

Reg.4, amended: SI 2008/1746 Reg.4

Reg.4A, added: SI 2008/1746 Reg.4

Reg.4B, added: SI 2008/1746 Reg.4

Reg.5, amended: SI 2008/1746 Reg.4

Reg.11, amended: SI 2008/1746 Reg.4

Reg.12, amended: SI 2008/1746 Reg.4

Reg.33, amended: SI 2008/1746 Reg.4

468. School Finance (England) Regulations 2006

Sch.2 para.35, applied: SI 2008/228 Sch.2 para.36 proviso.001

494. Medicines for Human Use and Medical Devices (Fees Amendments) Regulations 2006

Reg.2, revoked: SI 2008/552 Sch.7

Sch.1, revoked: SI 2008/552 Sch.7

499. Registered Pension Schemes (Transfer of Sums and Assets) Regulations 2006

Reg.6, amended: SI 2008/1946 Reg.2

Reg.10, substituted: SI 2008/1946 Reg.2

536. Social Security (Incapacity Benefit Work-focused Interviews) Amendment Regulations 2006

revoked: SI 2008/2928 Reg.12

539. Private and Voluntary Health Care (England) (Amendment) Regulations 2006

applied: 2008 c.14 s.17

552. National Health Service (Local Pharmaceutical Services etc.) Regulations 2006

Reg.2, amended: SI 2008/528 Sch.1 para.11, SI 2008/1700 Sch.1 para.16

Reg.4, revoked (in part): SI 2008/528 Sch.1 para.11

Reg.15, revoked (in part): SI 2008/528 Sch.1 para.11

Sch.2 para.1, amended: SI 2008/1514 Reg.8

Sch.2 para.1, revoked (in part): SI 2008/528 Sch.1 para.11

557. Health and Safety (Enforcing Authority for Railways and Other Guided Transport Systems) Regulations 2006

applied: SI 2008/1597 Sch.5 para.3

Reg.2, amended: SI 2008/2323 Reg.3

Reg.4, amended: SI 2008/2323 Reg.4

Reg.5, substituted: SI 2008/2323 Reg.5

567. Registered Pension Schemes (Provision of Information) Regulations 2006

Reg.3, amended: SI 2008/720 Reg.3

Reg.4, amended: SI 2008/720 Reg.4

Reg.4, revoked (in part): SI 2008/720 Reg.4

Reg.8, amended: SI 2008/720 Reg.5

Reg.14, amended: SI 2008/720 Reg.6

Reg.17A, added: SI 2008/720 Reg.7

NO.

2006–cont.

572. Taxation of Pension Schemes (Transitional Provisions) Order 2006
Art.5A, added: SI 2008/2990 Art.3
Art.23, amended: SI 2008/2990 Art.4
Art.23, revoked (in part): SI 2008/2990 Art.4

583. Social Housing (Grants to Bodies other than Registered Social Landlords) (Additional Purposes) (England) Order 2006
Art.2, amended: SI 2008/2831 Sch.1 para.14

594. Serious Organised Crime and Police Act 2005 (Consequential and Supplementary Amendments to Secondary Legislation) Order 2006
Sch.1 para.19, revoked (in part): SI 2008/2863 r.2

604. Measuring Instruments (EEC Requirements) (Fees) (Amendment) Regulations 2006
Reg.2, revoked (in part): SI 2008/732 Reg.3

606. Naval, Military and Air Forces Etc (Disablement and Death) Service Pensions Order 2006
applied: SI 2008/794 Sch.8 para.49, Sch.8 para.50, SI 2008/1963 Reg.2
Part II, applied: SI 2008/794 Sch.8 para.50
Part III, applied: SI 2008/794 Sch.8 para.50
Art.7, amended: SI 2008/679 Sch.1 para.1
Art.10, amended: SI 2008/679 Sch.1 para.10, Sch.1 para.11
Art.23, amended: SI 2008/679 Sch.1 para.2
Art.23, applied: SI 2008/794 Sch.8 para.49
Art.23, referred to: SI 2008/794 Sch.8 para.52
Art.27, revoked (in part): SI 2008/679 Sch.1 para.3
Art.33, amended: SI 2008/679 Sch.1 para.4
Art.40, amended: SI 2008/679 Sch.1 para.5
Art.43, amended: SI 2008/2683 Sch.1 para.310
Art.44, amended: SI 2008/679 Sch.1 para.6, SI 2008/2683 Sch.1 para.311
Art.50, amended: SI 2008/679 Sch.1 para.12
Art.56, amended: SI 2008/679 Sch.1 para.13
Art.61, amended: SI 2008/2683 Sch.1 para.312
Art.62, amended: SI 2008/2683 Sch.1 para.313
Sch.1 Part II, amended: SI 2008/679 Sch.2
Sch.1 Part III, amended: SI 2008/679 Sch.3
Sch.1 Part IV, amended: SI 2008/679 Sch.4
Sch.2 Part II, amended: SI 2008/679 Sch.5
Sch.2 Part III, amended: SI 2008/679 Sch.6
Sch.3 para.1, amended: SI 2008/679 Sch.1 para.9
Sch.3 para.3, amended: SI 2008/679 Sch.1 para.9, SI 2008/2683 Sch.1 para.314
Sch.3 para.12, added: SI 2008/2683 Sch.1 para.314

NO.

2006–cont.

620. Police Authorities (Best Value) Performance Indicators (Amendment) Order 2006
revoked: SI 2008/659 Art.3

636. Gambling Act 2005 (Licensing Authority Policy Statement) (England and Wales) Regulations 2006
applied: SI 2008/2867 Reg.12

641. Water Resources (Abstraction and Impounding) Regulations 2006
Reg.6, amended: SI 2008/165 Reg.2
Reg.12, amended: SI 2008/165 Reg.2
Reg.34, amended: SI 2008/165 Reg.2

646. Housing (Approval of Codes of Management Practice) (Student Accommodation) (England) Order 2006
Art.2, revoked (in part): SI 2008/2345 Art.3

676. Judicial Discipline (Prescribed Procedures) Regulations 2006
Reg.2, amended: SI 2008/2098 Reg.3
Reg.3, amended: SI 2008/2098 Reg.4
Reg.9, amended: SI 2008/2098 Reg.5
Reg.10, amended: SI 2008/2098 Reg.6
Reg.13, amended: SI 2008/2098 Reg.7
Reg.14, amended: SI 2008/2098 Reg.8
Reg.15, amended: SI 2008/2098 Reg.9
Reg.17, amended: SI 2008/2098 Reg.10
Reg.18, amended: SI 2008/2098 Reg.11
Reg.22, substituted: SI 2008/2098 Reg.12
Reg.23, substituted: SI 2008/2098 Reg.13
Reg.24, substituted: SI 2008/2098 Reg.13
Reg.25, amended: SI 2008/2098 Reg.14
Reg.27, amended: SI 2008/2098 Reg.15
Reg.29, amended: SI 2008/2098 Reg.16
Reg.30, amended: SI 2008/2098 Reg.17
Reg.31, substituted: SI 2008/2098 Reg.18
Reg.32, substituted: SI 2008/2098 Reg.18
Reg.34, amended: SI 2008/2098 Reg.19
Reg.36, amended: SI 2008/2098 Reg.20

715. Magistrates Courts Fees (Amendment) Order 2006
revoked: SI 2008/1052 Sch.3

719. Civil Proceedings Fees (Amendment) Order 2006
revoked: SI 2008/1053 Sch.3

739. Family Proceedings Fees (Amendment) Order 2006
revoked: SI 2008/1054 Sch.3

758. Gender Recognition (Application Fees) Order 2006
Art.2, amended: SI 2008/715 Art.3
Art.3, amended: SI 2008/715 Art.4
Art.5, amended: SI 2008/715 Art.5, SI 2008/1879 Reg.16

759. Occupational Pension Schemes (Modification of Schemes) Regulations 2006
Reg.5, amended: SI 2008/1050 Sch.2 para.9

NO.

2006–cont.

760. Patents, Trade Marks and Designs (Address For Service and Time Limits, etc) Rules 2006
r.15, revoked: SI 2008/1797 Sch.2
r.16, revoked: SI 2008/1797 Sch.2
r.17, revoked: SI 2008/1797 Sch.2
r.18, revoked: SI 2008/1797 Sch.2
r.19, revoked: SI 2008/1797 Sch.2
r.20, revoked: SI 2008/1797 Sch.2

763. Trade Marks (International Registration) (Amendment) Order 2006
revoked: SI 2008/2206 Sch.7

830. Residential Property Tribunal (Fees) (England) Regulations 2006
Reg.5, amended: SI 2008/1879 Reg.17

831. Residential Property Tribunal Procedure (England) Regulations 2006
Reg.21, amended: SI 2008/2683 Sch.1 para.316
Reg.29, revoked (in part): SI 2008/2683 Sch.1 para.317

873. Staffing of Maintained Schools (Wales) Regulations 2006
applied: SI 2008/168 Reg.3, SI 2008/3082 Reg.3
Reg.9, applied: SI 2008/168 Reg.7
Reg.9, referred to: SI 2008/3082 Reg.7
Reg.9A, applied: SI 2008/168 Reg.7
Reg.9A, referred to: SI 2008/3082 Reg.7
Reg.9B, applied: SI 2008/168 Reg.7
Reg.9B, referred to: SI 2008/3082 Reg.7
Reg.10, applied: SI 2008/168 Reg.7
Reg.10, referred to: SI 2008/3082 Reg.7
Reg.11, applied: SI 2008/168 Reg.7
Reg.11, roferred to: SI 2008/3082 Reg.7
Reg.12, applied: SI 2008/168 Reg.7
Reg.12, referred to: SI 2008/3082 Reg.7
Reg.13, applied: SI 2008/168 Reg.7
Reg.13, referred to: SI 2008/3082 Reg.7
Reg.14, applied: SI 2008/168 Reg.7
Reg.14, referred to: SI 2008/3082 Reg.7
Reg.15, applied: SI 2008/168 Reg.7
Reg.15, referred to: SI 2008/3082 Reg.7
Reg.15A, applied: SI 2008/168 Reg.7
Reg.15A, referred to: SI 2008/3082 Reg.7
Reg.16, applied: SI 2008/168 Reg.7
Reg.16, referred to: SI 2008/3082 Reg.7
Reg.17, applied: SI 2008/168 Reg.7
Reg.17, referred to: SI 2008/3082 Reg.7
Reg.18, applied: SI 2008/168 Reg.7
Reg.18, referred to: SI 2008/3082 Reg.7
Reg.18A, applied: SI 2008/168 Reg.7
Reg.18A, referred to: SI 2008/3082 Reg.7
Reg.19, applied: SI 2008/168 Reg.7
Reg.19, referred to: SI 2008/3082 Reg.7
Reg.20, applied: SI 2008/168 Reg.7
Reg.20, referred to: SI 2008/3082 Reg.7
Reg.20A, applied: SI 2008/168 Reg.7
Reg.20A, referred to: SI 2008/3082 Reg.7
Reg.21, applied: SI 2008/168 Reg.7

NO.

2006–cont.

873. Staffing of Maintained Schools (Wales) Regulations 2006–*cont.*
Reg.21, referred to: SI 2008/3082 Reg.7
Reg.22, applied: SI 2008/168 Reg.7
Reg.22, referred to: SI 2008/3082 Reg.7
Reg.23, applied: SI 2008/168 Reg.7
Reg.23, referred to: SI 2008/3082 Reg.7
Reg.24, applied: SI 2008/168 Reg.7
Reg.24, referred to: SI 2008/3082 Reg.7
Reg.24A, applied: SI 2008/168 Reg.7
Reg.24A, referred to: SI 2008/3082 Reg.7
Reg.25, applied: SI 2008/168 Reg.7
Reg.25, referred to: SI 2008/3082 Reg.7
Reg.26, applied: SI 2008/168 Reg.7
Reg.26, referred to: SI 2008/3082 Reg.7
Reg.26A, applied: SI 2008/168 Reg.7
Reg.26A, referred to: SI 2008/3082 Reg.7
Reg.27, applied: SI 2008/168 Reg.7
Reg.27, referred to: SI 2008/3082 Reg.7
Reg.28, applied: SI 2008/168 Reg.7
Reg.28, referred to: SI 2008/3082 Reg.7
Reg.29, applied: SI 2008/168 Reg.7
Reg.29, referred to: SI 2008/3082 Reg.7
Reg.30, applied: SI 2008/168 Reg.7
Reg.30, referred to: SI 2008/3082 Reg.7
Reg.31, applied: SI 2008/168 Reg.7
Reg.31, referred to: SI 2008/3082 Reg.7
Reg.32, applied: SI 2008/168 Reg.7
Reg.32, referred to: SI 2008/3082 Reg.7
Reg.33, applied: SI 2008/168 Reg.7
Reg.33, referred to: SI 2008/3082 Reg.7
Reg.34, applied: SI 2008/168 Reg.7
Reg.34, referred to: SI 2008/3082 Reg.7

878. Care Standards Act 2000 and the Children Act 1989 (Abolition of Fees) (Wales) Regulations 2006
applied: 2008 c.14 s.17
Reg.1, amended: SI 2008/1976 Reg.22

932. Police (Injury Benefit) Regulations 2006
Reg.3, amended: SI 2008/1887 Reg.29
Reg.6, amended: SI 2008/1887 Reg.30
Reg.31, applied: SI 2008/649 Reg.4
Sch.1, added: SI 2008/1887 Reg.31
Sch.1, amended: SI 2008/1887 Reg.31

964. Authorised Investment Funds (Tax) Regulations 2006
referred to: SI 2008/705 Reg.2
Part 4, revoked: SI 2008/3159 Reg.17
Reg.2, amended: SI 2008/705 Reg.3, SI 2008/3159 Reg.4
Reg.10, amended: SI 2008/3159 Reg.5
Reg.11, amended: SI 2008/3159 Reg.6
Reg.12, amended: SI 2008/705 Reg.4, SI 2008/3159 Reg.7
Reg.13, amended: SI 2008/3159 Reg.8
Reg.14, amended: SI 2008/3159 Reg.9
Reg.14A, added: SI 2008/3159 Reg.10
Reg.14B, added: SI 2008/3159 Reg.11
Reg.14C, added: SI 2008/3159 Reg.11

NO.

2006–cont.

964. Authorised Investment Funds (Tax) Regulations 2006–*cont.*
Reg.14C, applied: SI 2008/3159 Reg.30
Reg.14D, added: SI 2008/3159 Reg.11
Reg.24, amended: SI 2008/3159 Reg.12
Reg.48, amended: SI 2008/3159 Reg.13
Reg.49, amended: SI 2008/3159 Reg.14
Reg.51, substituted: SI 2008/3159 Reg.15
Reg.52A, substituted: SI 2008/3159 Reg.16
Reg.55, applied: SI 2008/3159 Reg.31
Reg.55, varied: SI 2008/3159 Reg.31
Reg.56, applied: SI 2008/3159 Reg.31
Reg.56, varied: SI 2008/3159 Reg.31
Reg.69A, added: SI 2008/705 Reg.5
Reg.69B, added: SI 2008/705 Reg.5
Reg.69C, added: SI 2008/705 Reg.5
Reg.69D, added: SI 2008/705 Reg.5
Reg.69DA, added: SI 2008/705 Reg.5, SI 2008/3159 Reg.18
Reg.69E, added: SI 2008/705 Reg.5
Reg.69F, added: SI 2008/705 Reg.5
Reg.69G, added: SI 2008/705 Reg.5
Reg.69G, amended: SI 2008/3159 Reg.19
Reg.69H, added: SI 2008/705 Reg.5
Reg.69I, added: SI 2008/705 Reg.5
Reg.69J, added: SI 2008/705 Reg.5
Reg.69J, amended: SI 2008/3159 Reg.20
Reg.69K, added: SI 2008/705 Reg.5
Reg.69K, amended: SI 2008/3159 Reg.21
Reg.69L, added: SI 2008/705 Reg.5
Reg.69L, amended: SI 2008/3159 Reg.22
Reg.69M, added: SI 2008/705 Reg.5
Reg.69N, added: SI 2008/705 Reg.5
Reg.69O, added: SI 2008/705 Reg.5
Reg.69P, added: SI 2008/705 Reg.5
Reg.69Q, added: SI 2008/705 Reg.5
Reg.69R, added: SI 2008/705 Reg.5
Reg.69T, added: SI 2008/705 Reg.5
Reg.69U, added: SI 2008/705 Reg.5
Reg.69V, added: SI 2008/705 Reg.5
Reg.69W, added: SI 2008/705 Reg.5
Reg.69X, added: SI 2008/705 Reg.5
Reg.69Y, added: SI 2008/705 Reg.5
Reg.69Z, added: SI 2008/705 Reg.5
Reg.69Z, amended: SI 2008/3159 Reg.23
Reg.69Z1, added: SI 2008/705 Reg.5
Reg.69Z2, added: SI 2008/705 Reg.5
Reg.69Z3, added: SI 2008/705 Reg.5
Reg.69Z4, added: SI 2008/705 Reg.5
Reg.69Z5, added: SI 2008/705 Reg.5
Reg.69Z6, added: SI 2008/705 Reg.5
Reg.69Z7, added: SI 2008/705 Reg.5
Reg.69Z8, added: SI 2008/705 Reg.5
Reg.69Z9, added: SI 2008/705 Reg.5
Reg.69Z10, added: SI 2008/705 Reg.5
Reg.69Z11, added: SI 2008/705 Reg.5
Reg.69Z12, added: SI 2008/705 Reg.5
Reg.69Z13, added: SI 2008/705 Reg.5
Reg.69Z14, added: SI 2008/705 Reg.5
Reg.69Z15, added: SI 2008/705 Reg.5

NO.

2006–cont.

964. Authorised Investment Funds (Tax) Regulations 2006–*cont.*
Reg.69Z16, added: SI 2008/705 Reg.5
Reg.69Z17, added: SI 2008/705 Reg.5
Reg.69Z18, added: SI 2008/705 Reg.5
Reg.69Z19, added: SI 2008/705 Reg.5
Reg.69Z19, amended: SI 2008/3159 Reg.24
Reg.69Z20, added: SI 2008/705 Reg.5
Reg.69Z21, added: SI 2008/705 Reg.5
Reg.69Z22, added: SI 2008/705 Reg.5
Reg.69Z23, added: SI 2008/705 Reg.5
Reg.69Z23, amended: SI 2008/3159 Reg.25
Reg.69Z23, revoked (in part): SI 2008/3159 Reg.25
Reg.69Z24, added: SI 2008/705 Reg.5
Reg.69Z24, amended: SI 2008/3159 Reg.26
Reg.69Z24A, added: SI 2008/705 Reg.5, SI 2008/3159 Reg.27
Reg.69Z24B, added: SI 2008/705 Reg.5, SI 2008/3159 Reg.27
Reg.69Z24C, added: SI 2008/705 Reg.5, SI 2008/3159 Reg.27
Reg.69Z24D, added: SI 2008/705 Reg.5, SI 2008/3159 Reg.27
Reg.69Z25, added: SI 2008/705 Reg.5
Reg.69Z26, added: SI 2008/705 Reg.5
Reg.69Z27, added: SI 2008/705 Reg.5
Reg.69Z28, added: SI 2008/705 Reg.5
Reg.69Z29, added: SI 2008/705 Reg.5
Reg.69Z30, added: SI 2008/705 Reg.5
Reg.69Z31, added: SI 2008/705 Reg.5
Reg.69Z32, added: SI 2008/705 Reg.5
Reg.69Z33, added: SI 2008/705 Reg.5
Reg.69Z34, added: SI 2008/705 Reg.5
Reg.69Z35, added: SI 2008/705 Reg.5
Reg.69Z36, added: SI 2008/705 Reg.5
Reg.69Z37, added: SI 2008/705 Reg.5
Reg.69Z38, added: SI 2008/705 Reg.5
Reg.69Z39, added: SI 2008/705 Reg.5
Reg.69Z40, added: SI 2008/705 Reg.5
Reg.69Z41, added: SI 2008/705 Reg.5
Reg.94, amended: SI 2008/3159 Reg.28
Reg.95, substituted: SI 2008/1463 Reg.2
s.Art.4A Reg.69S, added: SI 2008/705 Reg.5
Sch.1 Part 1, amended: SI 2008/705 Reg.6
Sch.1 Part 2, amended: SI 2008/705 Reg.7, SI 2008/3159 Reg.29

965. Child Benefit (Rates) Regulations 2006
Reg.2, amended: SI 2008/797 Art.2, SI 2008/3246 Reg.3

966. Local Government Pension Scheme (Amendment) Regulations 2006
revoked: SI 2008/238 Sch.1

985. Pesticides (Maximum Residue Levels in Crops, Food and Feeding Stuffs) (England and Wales) (Amendment) Regulations 2006
revoked: SI 2008/2570 Sch.2

NO.

2006–cont.

1003. Immigration (European Economic Area) Regulations 2006

see *B v Secretary of State for the Home Department* [2008] EWCA Civ 806, [2008] 3 C.M.L.R. 24 (CA (Civ Div)), Waller, L.J.; see *Harrow LBC v Ibrahim* [2008] EWCA Civ 386, [2008] 2 C.M.L.R. 30 (CA (Civ Div)), Rix, L.J.; see *KG (Sri Lanka) v Secretary of State for the Home Department* [2008] EWCA Civ 13, [2008] Imm. A.R. 343 (CA (Civ Div)), Buxton, L.J.; see *McCarthy v Secretary of State for the Home Department* [2008] EWCA Civ 641, [2008] 3 C.M.L.R. 7 (CA (Civ Div)), Pill, L.J.

Reg.2, see *McCarthy v Secretary of State for the Home Department* [2008] EWCA Civ 641, [2008] 3 C.M.L.R. 7 (CA (Civ Div)), Pill, L.J.

Reg.4, see *Abdirahman v Secretary of State for Work and Pensions* [2007] EWCA Civ 657, [2008] 1 W.L.R. 254 (CA (Civ Div)), Sir Andrew Morritt C.; see *AG (Germany) v Secretary of State for the Home Department* [2008] Imm. A.R. 78 (AIT), Senior Immigration Judge Storey

Reg.6, applied: SI 2008/794 Reg.70

Reg.6, see *AG (Germany) v Secretary of State for the Home Department* [2008] Imm. A.R. 78 (AIT), Senior Immigration Judge Storey

Reg.7, applied: SI 2008/794 Reg.70

Reg.8, see *KG (Sri Lanka) v Secretary of State for the Home Department* [2008] EWCA Civ 13, [2008] Imm. A.R. 343 (CA (Civ Div)), Buxton, L.J.; see *TR (Sri Lanka) v Secretary of State for the Home Department* [2008] UKAIT 4, [2008] Imm. A.R. 223 (AIT), Hodge, J. (President)

Reg.11, see *CO (Nigeria) v Entry Clearance Officer, Lagos* [2008] Imm. A.R. 70 (AIT), CMG Ockelton (Deputy President)

Reg.12, see *CO (Nigeria) v Entry Clearance Officer, Lagos* [2008] Imm. A.R. 70 (AIT), CMG Ockelton (Deputy President)

Reg.13, applied: SI 2008/794 Reg.70

Reg.14, applied: SI 2008/794 Reg.70

Reg.14, see *Abdirahman v Secretary of State for Work and Pensions* [2007] EWCA Civ 657, [2008] 1 W.L.R. 254 (CA (Civ Div)), Sir Andrew Morritt C.

Reg.15, see *McCarthy v Secretary of State for the Home Department* [2008] EWCA Civ 641, [2008] 3 C.M.L.R. 7 (CA (Civ Div)), Pill, L.J.

Reg.21, see *B v Secretary of State for the Home Department* [2008] EWCA Civ 806, [2008] 3 C.M.L.R. 24 (CA (Civ Div)), Waller, L.J.

1008. Grants to the Churches Conservation Trust Order 2006

revoked: SI 2008/842 Art.4

NO.

2006–cont.

1027. Community Trade Mark Regulations 2006

Reg.4, amended: SI 2008/1959 Reg.2

1029. Trade Marks and Designs (Address For Service) (Amendment) Rules 2006

revoked: SI 2008/1797 Sch.2

1030. Cross-Border Insolvency Regulations 2006

varied: SI 2008/346 Sch.1 para.11

Sch.1, applied: SSI 2008/119 Sch.1 para.3, Sch.1 para.13

Sch.3 Part 3 para.11, applied: SSI 2008/119 Sch.1 para.13

1031. Employment Equality (Age) Regulations 2006

see *Johns v Solent SD Ltd* [2008] EWCA Civ 790, [2008] I.R.L.R. 820 (CA (Civ Div)), Pill, L.J.

Pt 2, see *Standard Life Bank Ltd v Wilson* [2008] I.C.R. 947 (EAT (SC)), Lady Smith

Reg.3, see *Hampton v Lord Chancellor* [2008] I.R.L.R. 258 (ET), M Zuke (Chairman); see *Loxley v BAE Systems Land Systems (Munitions & Ordnance) Ltd* [2008] I.C.R. 1348 (EAT), Elias, J (President)

Reg.24, see *Standard Life Bank Ltd v Wilson* [2008] I.C.R. 947 (EAT (SC)), Lady Smith

Reg.30, see *Johns v Solent SD Ltd* [2008] EWCA Civ 790, [2008] I.R.L.R. 820 (CA (Civ Div)), Pill, L.J.; see *Johns v Solent SD Ltd* [2008] I.R.L.R. 88 (EAT), Nelson, J.

Reg.32, amended: SI 2008/573 Reg.3

Reg.36, referred to: SI 2008/3232 Sch.1 Part 2

Rog.41, amended: SI 2008/573 Reg.4

Reg.42, amended: SI 2008/573 Reg.5

1033. Education (Information as to Provision of Education) (England) (Amendment) Regulations 2006

revoked: SI 2008/4 Sch.3

1036. Sheep and Goats (Records, Identification and Movement) (Wales) Order 2006

applied: SI 2008/130 Art.22, Art.30

revoked: SI 2008/130 Art.37

1041. Parliamentary Constituencies and Assembly Electoral Regions (Wales) Order 2006

Art.1, amended: SI 2008/1791 Art.2

1080. Trade Marks (International Registration) (Amendment No.2) Order 2006

revoked: SI 2008/2206 Sch.7

1161. Seed Potatoes (England) Regulations 2006

Sch.3 Part II, amended: SI 2008/560 Reg.2

1198. Cosmetic Products (Safety) (Amendment) Regulations 2006

revoked: SI 2008/1284 Sch.1

NO.

2006–cont.

1199. Nursing and Midwifery Council (Practice Committees) (Constitution) Rules Order of Council 2006

revoked: SI 2008/1485 Sch.2 para.3

1226. Transmissible Spongiform Encephalopathies (Wales) Regulations 2006

revoked: SI 2008/3154 Reg.21

Reg.2, amended: SI 2008/1182 Reg.2

Sch.6 para.1, substituted: SI 2008/1182 Sch.1

Sch.6 para.2, substituted: SI 2008/1182 Sch.1

Sch.6 para.3, substituted: SI 2008/1182 Sch.1

Sch.6 para.4, substituted: SI 2008/1182 Sch.1

Sch.6 para.5, substituted: SI 2008/1182 Sch.1

Sch.6 para.6, substituted: SI 2008/1182 Sch.1

Sch.6 para.7, substituted: SI 2008/1182 Sch.1

Sch.6 para.8, substituted: SI 2008/1182 Sch.1

Sch.6 para.9, substituted: SI 2008/1182 Sch.1

Sch.6 para.10, substituted: SI 2008/1182 Sch.1

Sch.6 para.11, substituted: SI 2008/1182 Sch.1

Sch.6 para.12, substituted: SI 2008/1182 Sch.1

Sch.6 para.13, substituted: SI 2008/1182 Sch.1

Sch.6 para.14, substituted: SI 2008/1182 Sch.1

Sch.6 para.15, substituted: SI 2008/1182 Sch.1

Sch.6 para.16, substituted: SI 2008/1182 Sch.1

Sch.6 para.17, substituted: SI 2008/1182 Sch.1

Sch.6 para.18, substituted: SI 2008/1182 Sch.1

Sch.6 para.19, substituted: SI 2008/1182 Sch.1

Sch.6 para.20, substituted: SI 2008/1182 Sch.1

Sch.6 para.21, substituted: SI 2008/1182 Sch.1

Sch.6 para.22, substituted: SI 2008/1182 Sch.1

Sch.6 para.23, substituted: SI 2008/1182 Sch.1

Sch.7 para.2, substituted: SI 2008/1182 Reg.2

1228. Transmissible Spongiform Encephalopathies (No.2) Regulations 2006

revoked: SI 2008/1881 Reg.21

Reg.2, amended: SI 2008/1180 Reg.2

Sch.6 para.1, substituted: SI 2008/1180 Sch.1

NO.

2006–cont.

1228. Transmissible Spongiform Encephalopathies (No.2) Regulations 2006–*cont.*

Sch.6 para.2, substituted: SI 2008/1180 Sch.1

Sch.6 para.3, substituted: SI 2008/1180 Sch.1

Sch.6 para.4, substituted: SI 2008/1180 Sch.1

Sch.6 para.5, substituted: SI 2008/1180 Sch.1

Sch.6 para.6, substituted: SI 2008/1180 Sch.1

Sch.6 para.7, substituted: SI 2008/1180 Sch.1

Sch.6 para.8, substituted: SI 2008/1180 Sch.1

Sch.6 para.9, substituted: SI 2008/1180 Sch.1

Sch.6 para.10, substituted: SI 2008/1180 Sch.1

Sch.6 para.11, substituted: SI 2008/1180 Sch.1

Sch.6 para.12, substituted: SI 2008/1180 Sch.1

Sch.6 para.13, substituted: SI 2008/1180 Sch.1

Sch.6 para.14, substituted: SI 2008/1180 Sch.1

Sch.6 para.15, substituted: SI 2008/1180 Sch.1

Sch.6 para.16, substituted: SI 2008/1180 Sch.1

Sch.6 para.17, substituted: SI 2008/1180 Sch.1

Sch.6 para.18, substituted: SI 2008/1180 Sch.1

Sch.6 para.19, substituted: SI 2008/1180 Sch.1

Sch.6 para.20, substituted: SI 2008/1180 Sch.1

Sch.6 para.21, substituted: SI 2008/1180 Sch.1

Sch.6 para.22, substituted: SI 2008/1180 Sch.1

Sch.6 para.23, substituted: SI 2008/1180 Sch.1

Sch.7 para.2, substituted: SI 2008/1180 Reg.2

1248. Merchant Shipping (Prevention of Air Pollution from Ships) Order 2006

Art.2, enabled: SI 2008/2924

Art.3, enabled: SI 2008/2924

1254. Fire and Rescue Services (Northern Ireland) Order 2006

Art.3, applied: SI 2008/2852 Sch.3 para.6

Sch.3 para.24, revoked: 2008 c.9 s.72

Sch.4, amended: 2008 c.9 s.72

NO.

2006–cont.

1260. Human Tissue Act 2004 (Ethical Approval, Exceptions from Licensing and Supply of Information about Transplants) Regulations 2006
Reg.3, amended: SI 2008/3067 Reg.2

1289. Protection of Water Against Agricultural Nitrate Pollution (England and Wales) (Amendment) Regulations 2006
revoked (in part): SI 2008/2349 Reg.50, SI 2008/3143 Reg.50

1293. Animal By-Products (Wales) Regulations 2006
applied: SI 2008/3154 Sch.6 para.3
Reg.21, applied: SI 2008/2716 Reg.3

1327. Sea Fishing (Restriction on Days at Sea) (Monitoring, Inspection and Surveillance) Order 2006
revoked: SI 2008/2347 Art.21

1331. Export Control Order 2006
revoked: SI 2008/3231 Sch.6

1379. Radioactive Contaminated Land (Modification of Enactments) (England) Regulations 2006
Reg.5, amended: SI 2008/520 Reg.2
Reg.17, substituted: SI 2008/520 Reg.2

1390. British Citizenship (Designated Service) Order 2006
Sch.2 para.15, added: SI 2008/135 Art.2

1401. Plastic Materials and Articles in Contact with Food (England) Regulations 2006
Reg.24, referred to: SI 2008/916 Reg.22

1463. Restriction of the Use of Certain Hazardous Substances in Electrical and Electronic Equipment Regulations 2006
revoked: SI 2008/37 Reg.2
Reg.7, referred to: SI 2008/37 Reg.24
Reg.8, referred to: SI 2008/37 Reg.24
Reg.9, referred to: SI 2008/37 Reg.24

1466. Transport and Works (Applications and Objections Procedure) (England and Wales) Rules 2006
applied: SI 2008/969, SI 2008/3163
r.10, applied: SI 2008/969 Art.19

1471. Animals and Animal Products (Import and Export) (England) Regulations 2006
disapplied: SI 2008/962 Reg.3
Reg.1, amended: SI 2008/3203 Reg.2
Reg.35, amended: SI 2008/3203 Reg.2
Sch.1 para.1, revoked: SI 2008/3203 Reg.2
Sch.1 para.2, revoked: SI 2008/3203 Reg.2
Sch.2, substituted: SI 2008/3203 Sch.1
Sch.3 Part I para.1, substituted: SI 2008/3203 Sch.1
Sch.3 Part I para.2, substituted: SI 2008/3203 Sch.1
Sch.3 Part I para.3, substituted: SI 2008/3203 Sch.1

NO.

2006–cont.

1471. Animals and Animal Products (Import and Export) (England) Regulations 2006–*cont.*
Sch.3 Part I para.4, substituted: SI 2008/3203 Sch.1
Sch.3 Part I para.5, substituted: SI 2008/3203 Sch.1
Sch.3 Part I para.6, substituted: SI 2008/3203 Sch.1
Sch.3 Part I para.7, substituted: SI 2008/3203 Sch.1
Sch.3 Part I para.8, substituted: SI 2008/3203 Sch.1
Sch.3 Part I para.9, substituted: SI 2008/3203 Sch.1
Sch.3 Part I para.10, substituted: SI 2008/3203 Sch.1
Sch.3 Part I para.10A, substituted: SI 2008/3203 Sch.1
Sch.3 Part I para.11, substituted: SI 2008/3203 Sch.1
Sch.3 Part I para.12, substituted: SI 2008/3203 Sch.1
Sch.3 Part I para.13, substituted: SI 2008/3203 Sch.1
Sch.3 Part I para.14, substituted: SI 2008/3203 Sch.1
Sch.3 Part I para.15, substituted: SI 2008/3203 Sch.1
Sch.3 Part I para.16, substituted: SI 2008/3203 Sch.1
Sch.3 Part I para.17, substituted: SI 2008/3203 Sch.1
Sch.3 Part I para.18, substituted: SI 2008/3203 Sch.1
Sch.3 Part II para.1, substituted: SI 2008/3203 Sch.1
Sch.3 Part II para.2, substituted: SI 2008/3203 Sch.1
Sch.3 Part II para.3, substituted: SI 2008/3203 Sch.1
Sch.3 Part III para.1, substituted: SI 2008/3203 Sch.1
Sch.3 Part III para.2, substituted: SI 2008/3203 Sch.1
Sch.3 Part III para.3, substituted: SI 2008/3203 Sch.1
Sch.3 Part III para.4, substituted: SI 2008/3203 Sch.1
Sch.3 Part III para.5, substituted: SI 2008/3203 Sch.1
Sch.3 Part III para.6, substituted: SI 2008/3203 Sch.1
Sch.7 Part I para.1, substituted: SI 2008/3203 Sch.1
Sch.7 Part I para.2, substituted: SI 2008/3203 Sch.1
Sch.7 Part I para.3, substituted: SI 2008/3203 Sch.1
Sch.7 Part I para.4, substituted: SI 2008/3203 Sch.1

NO.

2006–cont.

1471. Animals and Animal Products (Import and Export) (England) Regulations 2006–*cont.*
Sch.7 Part I para.5, substituted: SI 2008/3203 Sch.1
Sch.7 Part I para.6, substituted: SI 2008/3203 Sch.1
Sch.7 Part I para.7, substituted: SI 2008/3203 Sch.1
Sch.7 Part I para.8, substituted: SI 2008/3203 Sch.1
Sch.7 Part II para.1, substituted: SI 2008/3203 Sch.1
Sch.7 Part II para.2, substituted: SI 2008/3203 Sch.1
Sch.7 Part II para.3, substituted: SI 2008/3203 Sch.1
Sch.7 Part II para.4, substituted: SI 2008/3203 Sch.1
Sch.7 Part II para.5, substituted: SI 2008/3203 Sch.1
Sch.7 Part II para.6, substituted: SI 2008/3203 Sch.1
Sch.7 Part II para.7, substituted: SI 2008/3203 Sch.1
Sch.7 Part II para.8, substituted: SI 2008/3203 Sch.1
Sch.7 Part II para.9, substituted: SI 2008/3203 Sch.1
Sch.7 Part II para.10, substituted: SI 2008/3203 Sch.1
Sch.7 Part II para.11, substituted: SI 2008/3203 Sch.1
Sch.7 Part II para.12, substituted: SI 2008/3203 Sch.1
Sch.7 Part II para.13, substituted: SI 2008/3203 Sch.1
Sch.7 Part II para.14, substituted: SI 2008/3203 Sch.1
Sch.7 Part II para.15, substituted: SI 2008/3203 Sch.1
Sch.7 Part II para.16, substituted: SI 2008/3203 Sch.1
Sch.7 Part II para.17, substituted: SI 2008/3203 Sch.1
Sch.7 Part II para.18, substituted: SI 2008/3203 Sch.1
Sch.7 Part II para.19, substituted: SI 2008/3203 Sch.1
Sch.7 Part II para.20, substituted: SI 2008/3203 Sch.1
Sch.7 Part II para.21, substituted: SI 2008/3203 Sch.1
Sch.7 Part II para.22, substituted: SI 2008/3203 Sch.1
Sch.7 Part II para.23, substituted: SI 2008/3203 Sch.1
Sch.7 Part II para.24, substituted: SI 2008/3203 Sch.1
Sch.7 Part II para.25, substituted: SI 2008/3203 Sch.1

NO.

2006–cont.

1493. Care Standards Act 2000 (Establishments and Agencies) (Miscellaneous Amendments) Regulations 2006
applied: 2008 c.14 s.17

1506. Specified Animal Pathogens (Amendment) (England) Order 2006
revoked: SI 2008/944 Art.12

1510. Ozone Depleting Substances (Qualifications) Regulations 2006
Reg.3, amended: SI 2008/97 Reg.2
Sch.1, amended: SI 2008/97 Reg.2

1512. Bovine Spongiform Encephalopathy (BSE) Compensation (Wales) Regulations 2006
revoked: SI 2008/3154 Reg.21

1513. Sheep and Goats Transmissible Spongiform Encephalopathy (TSE) Compensation (Wales) Regulations 2006
revoked: SI 2008/3154 Reg.21

1532. Street Works (Inspection Fees) (Wales) Regulations 2006
Reg.3, amended: SI 2008/600 Reg.3, SI 2008/1213 Reg.3

1536. Animals and Animal Products (Import and Export) (Wales) Regulations 2006
applied: SI 2008/1090 Reg.3

1541. Children (Allocation of Proceedings) (Amendment) Order 2006
revoked: SI 2008/2836 Sch.2

1549. Sea Fishing (Marking and Identification of Passive Fishing Gear and Beam Trawls) (England) Order 2006
Art.4, applied: SSI 2008/101 Sch.1 Part 2

1642. Residential Property Tribunal (Fees) (Wales) Regulations 2006
Reg.5, amended: SI 2008/1879 Reg.30

1643. Plant Health (Wales) Order 2006
Art.2, amended: SI 2008/2781 Art.2
Art.19, amended: SI 2008/2781 Art.2
Art.22, amended: SI 2008/2781 Art.2
Art.39A, added: SI 2008/2781 Art.2
Art.41, amended: SI 2008/2781 Art.2
Art.45, amended: SI 2008/2781 Art.2
Sch.1 Part A para.4, substituted: SI 2008/2913 Art.2
Sch.1 Part A para.6, revoked: SI 2008/2913 Art.2
Sch.1 Part B para.4, revoked: SI 2008/2781 Art.2
Sch.2 Part B, amended: SI 2008/2781 Art.2
Sch.3, amended: SI 2008/2781 Art.2
Sch.4 Part A, amended: SI 2008/2781 Art.2, SI 2008/2913 Art.2
Sch.4 Part B, amended: SI 2008/2781 Art.2, SI 2008/2913 Art.2
Sch.6 Part A para.8, added: SI 2008/2913 Art.2
Sch.8 Part A para.2, amended: SI 2008/2781 Art.2

NO.

2006–cont.

1643. Plant Health (Wales) Order 2006– *cont.*

Sch.8 Part A para.5, amended: SI 2008/2781 Art.2

1666. General Dental Council (Constitution) Order of Council 2006

Art.4, amended: SI 2008/3238 Art.2

1671. Dentists Act 1984 (Amendment) Order 2005 Transitional Provisions Order of Council 2006

Art.11, varied: 2008 c.14 Sch.10 para.1

1696. Export Control (Security and Paramilitary Goods) Order 2006

revoked: SI 2008/3231 Sch.6

1703. Private and Voluntary Health Care and Miscellaneous (Wales) (Amendment) Regulations 2006

applied: 2008 c.14 s.17

1705. Local Safeguarding Children Boards (Wales) Regulations 2006

Reg.5, amended: SI 2008/912 Sch.2 para.13

1719. Technical Assistance Control Regulations 2006

revoked: SI 2008/3231 Sch.6

1722. Enterprise Act 2002 (Disqualification from Office General) Order 2006

Sch.2 Part 2 para.20, varied: 2008 c.14 Sch.10 para.1

1734. Private and Voluntary Health Care (England) (Amendment No.2) Regulations 2006

applied: 2008 c.14 s.17

1742. Pesticides (Maximum Residue Levels in Crops, Food and Feeding Stuffs) (England and Wales) (Amendment) (No.2) Regulations 2006

revoked: SI 2008/2570 Sch.2

1786. Courts-Martial (Prosecution Appeals) Order 2006

Art.4, see *R. v Arnold (Louise)* [2008] EWCA Crim 1034, [2008] 1 W.L.R. 2881 (CMAC), Hughes, L.J.

1796. Sea Fishing (Northern Hake Stock) (Wales) Order 2006

revoked: SI 2008/2347 Art.21

Art.3, applied: SSI 2008/101 Sch.1 Part 2

Art.4, applied: SSI 2008/101 Sch.1 Part 2

Art.5, applied: SSI 2008/101 Sch.1 Part 2

Art.6, applied: SSI 2008/101 Sch.1 Part 2

Art.7, applied: SSI 2008/101 Sch.1 Part 2

Art.8, applied: SSI 2008/101 Sch.1 Part 2

1811. Firefighters Compensation Scheme (England) Order 2006

Sch.1, applied: SI 2008/649 Reg.4

1869. Smoke Control Areas (Authorised Fuels) (England) (Amendment) Regulations 2006

revoked: SI 2008/514 Sch.2

1879. Plant Health (Import Inspection Fees) (England) Regulations 2006

Reg.4, amended: SI 2008/3233 Reg.2

NO.

2006–cont.

1879. Plant Health (Import Inspection Fees) (England) Regulations 2006– *cont.*

Sch.2, substituted: SI 2008/3233 Reg.2

1930. Protection of Children and Vulnerable Adults and Care Standards Tribunal (Amendment) Regulations 2006

revoked: SI 2008/2683 Sch.2

1954. Transport and Works (Model Clauses for Railways and Tramways) Order 2006

Sch.1, amended: SI 2008/2831 Sch.1 para.16

Sch.2, amended: SI 2008/2831 Sch.1 para.16

1975. Registered Designs Rules 2006

Part 4 r.20, revoked (in part): SI 2008/2683 Sch.1 para.318

1999. Gaming Duty (Amendment) Regulations 2006

revoked: SI 2008/1949 Reg.3

2008. Local Government Pension Scheme (Amendment) (No.2) Regulations 2006

revoked: SI 2008/238 Sch.1

2055. Merchant Shipping (Fees) Regulations 2006

applied: SI 2008/2924 Reg.11, Reg.13, SI 2008/3257 Reg.11, Reg.13

2059. European Cooperative Society (Involvement of Employees) Regulations 2006

Reg.34, referred to: SI 2008/3232 Sch.1 Part 2

2125. Medicines for Human Use (Fees Amendments) Regulations 2006

Reg.2, revoked: SI 2008/552 Sch.7

Reg.3, revoked: SI 2008/552 Sch.7

Reg.4, revoked: SI 2008/552 Sch.7

2183. Merchant Shipping and Fishing Vessels (Provision and Use of Work Equipment) Regulations 2006

Reg.6, amended: SI 2008/2165 Reg.2

Sch.1, amended: SI 2008/1597 Sch.7 para.6, SI 2008/2165 Reg.2

2184. Merchant Shipping and Fishing Vessels (Lifting Operations and Lifting Equipment) Regulations 2006

Reg.11, amended: SI 2008/2166 Reg.2

2185. Olympic Delivery Authority (Planning Functions) Order 2006

referred to: SI 2008/580 Art.3

2189. Education (Pupil Exclusions and Appeals) (Miscellaneous Amendments) (England) Regulations 2006

Reg.2, revoked (in part): SI 2008/532 Reg.11

Reg.4, revoked: SI 2008/532 Reg.11

Reg.5, revoked (in part): SI 2008/532 Reg.11

2231. Cosmetic Products (Safety) (Amendment) (No.2) Regulations 2006

revoked: SI 2008/1284 Sch.1

NO.

2006–cont.

2238. Environmental Noise (England) Regulations 2006
Reg.19, amended: SI 2008/375 Reg.3
Sch.2 para.2, amended: SI 2008/375 Reg.3
Sch.2 para.3, amended: SI 2008/375 Reg.3

2271. Export Control (Amendment) Order 2006
revoked: SI 2008/3231 Sch.6

2285. Charges for Residues Surveillance Regulations 2006
Reg.2, amended: SI 2008/2999 Reg.2
Sch.1, amended: SI 2008/2999 Sch.1

2321. African Development Fund (Multilateral Debt Relief Initiative) Order 2006
Art.3, amended: SI 2008/2089 Art.2

2323. International Development Association (Multilateral Debt Relief Initiative) Order 2006
Art.3, amended: SI 2008/2086 Art.2

2373. Gangmasters (Licensing Conditions) (No.2) Rules 2006
r.7, amended: SI 2008/638 r.2
r.7, revoked (in part): SI 2008/638 r.2
r.8, amended: SI 2008/638 r.2
r.8, revoked (in part): SI 2008/638 r.2

2380. Appointments Commission Regulations 2006
Reg.1, amended: SI 2008/2250 Art.2
Reg.2, amended: SI 2008/2792 Reg.2

2492. Criminal Defence Service (Financial Eligibility) Regulations 2006
Reg.5, amended: SI 2008/1879 Reg.18
Reg.9, amended: SI 2008/723 Reg.2
Reg.10, amended: SI 2008/723 Reg.3
Sch.1, amended: SI 2008/723 Reg.4

2525. Refugee or Person in Need of International Protection (Qualification) Regulations 2006
see *AA (Uganda) v Secretary of State for the Home Department* [2008] EWCA Civ 579, [2008] I.N.L.R. 307 (CA (Civ Div)), Buxton, L.J.

2601. Education (Information About Individual Pupils) (England) Regulations 2006
Reg.2, amended: SI 2008/3072 Reg.2
Sch.1 Part 1 para.2, amended: SI 2008/3072 Reg.2

2616. Protection of Military Remains Act 1986 (Designation of Vessels and Controlled Sites) Order 2006
revoked: SI 2008/950 Art.4

2646. Homelessness (Wales) Regulations 2006
Reg.2, amended: SI 2008/1879 Reg.31
Reg.3, amended: SI 2008/1879 Reg.31

2657. Terrorism (United Nations Measures) Order 2006
referred to: 2008 c.28 s.64

NO.

2006–cont.

2657. Terrorism (United Nations Measures) Order 2006–*cont.*
see *A v HM Treasury* [2008] EWCA Civ 1187, Times, November 12, 2008 (CA (Civ Div)), Sir Anthony Clarke, M.R.; see *A v HM Treasury* [2008] EWHC 869 (Admin), [2008] 3 All E.R. 361 (QBD (Admin)), Collins, J.
Art.2, amended: 2008 c.28 s.75
Art.5, revoked (in part): 2008 c.28 Sch.9 Part 4
Art.7, see *A v HM Treasury* [2008] EWCA Civ 1187, Times, November 12, 2008 (CA (Civ Div)), Sir Anthony Clarke, M.R.
Art.8, see *A v HM Treasury* [2008] EWCA Civ 1187, Times, November 12, 2008 (CA (Civ Div)), Sir Anthony Clarke, M.R.

2679. Measuring Instruments (EEC Requirements) (Fees) (Amendment No.2) Regulations 2006
Reg.2, revoked (in part): SI 2008/732 Reg.3

2682. Burma (Sale, Supply, Export, Technical Assistance, Financing and Financial Assistance) (Penalties and Licences) Regulations 2006
revoked: SI 2008/1098 Art.12

2683. Export Control (Lebanon, etc.) Order 2006
revoked: SI 2008/3231 Sch.6

2687. Plastic Materials and Articles in Contact with Food (England) (No.2) Regulations 2006
revoked: SI 2008/916 Reg.29

2697. Plant Health (Fees) (Forestry) Regulations 2006
Reg.3, amended: SI 2008/702 Reg.2
Sch.3A, added: SI 2008/702 Reg.2

2739. Control of Asbestos Regulations 2006
applied: SI 2008/736 Reg.5, Reg.6, Sch.5
Reg.2, amended: SI 2008/960 Sch.3
Reg.3, amended: SI 2008/960 Sch.3
Reg.25, amended: SI 2008/2852 Sch.10 para.8
Reg.25, revoked (in part): SI 2008/2852 Sch.10 Part 2
Reg.27, revoked: SI 2008/2852 Sch.10 Part 2
Reg.28, revoked: SI 2008/2852 Sch.10 Part 2
Reg.29, revoked: SI 2008/2852 Sch.10 Part 2
Reg.32, amended: SI 2008/2852 Sch.10 para.9
Reg.32, revoked (in part): SI 2008/2852 Sch.10 Part 2
Reg.33, amended: SI 2008/2852 Sch.10 para.10
Reg.35, amended: SI 2008/2852 Sch.10 para.11

NO.

2006–cont.

2798. Sea Fishing (Enforcement of Community Satellite Monitoring Measures) (Wales) Order 2006

Art.5, applied: SSI 2008/101 Sch.1 Part 2
Art.6, applied: SSI 2008/101 Sch.1 Part 2
Art.7, applied: SSI 2008/101 Sch.1 Part 2
Art.8, applied: SSI 2008/101 Sch.1 Part 2
Art.9, applied: SSI 2008/101 Sch.1 Part 2
Art.11, applied: SSI 2008/101 Sch.1 Part 2
Art.12, applied: SSI 2008/101 Sch.1 Part 2
Art.13, applied: SSI 2008/101 Sch.1 Part 2
Art.14, applied: SSI 2008/101 Sch.1 Part 2

2841. Products of Animal Origin (Third Country Imports) (England) Regulations 2006

Sch.1 Part I para.1, substituted: SI 2008/3230 Sch.1
Sch.1 Part I para.2, substituted: SI 2008/3230 Sch.1
Sch.1 Part I para.3, substituted: SI 2008/3230 Sch.1
Sch.1 Part I para.4, substituted: SI 2008/3230 Sch.1
Sch.1 Part I para.5, substituted: SI 2008/3230 Sch.1
Sch.1 Part I para.6, substituted: SI 2008/3230 Sch.1
Sch.1 Part I para.7, substituted: SI 2008/3230 Sch.1
Sch.1 Part I para.8, substituted: SI 2008/3230 Sch.1
Sch.1 Part I para.9, substituted: SI 2008/3230 Sch.1
Sch.1 Part I para.10, substituted: SI 2008/3230 Sch.1
Sch.1 Part I para.11, substituted: SI 2008/3230 Sch.1
Sch.1 Part I para.12, substituted: SI 2008/3230 Sch.1
Sch.1 Part I para.13, substituted: SI 2008/3230 Sch.1
Sch.1 Part I para.14, substituted: SI 2008/3230 Sch.1
Sch.1 Part I para.15, substituted: SI 2008/3230 Sch.1
Sch.1 Part I para.16, substituted: SI 2008/3230 Sch.1
Sch.1 Part I para.17, substituted: SI 2008/3230 Sch.1
Sch.1 Part I para.18, substituted: SI 2008/3230 Sch.1
Sch.1 Part I para.19, substituted: SI 2008/3230 Sch.1
Sch.1 Part I para.20, substituted: SI 2008/3230 Sch.1
Sch.1 Part I para.21, substituted: SI 2008/3230 Sch.1
Sch.1 Part I para.22, substituted: SI 2008/3230 Sch.1
Sch.1 Part II para.1, substituted: SI 2008/3230 Sch.1

NO.

2006–cont.

2841. Products of Animal Origin (Third Country Imports) (England) Regulations 2006–*cont.*

Sch.1 Part II para.2, substituted: SI 2008/3230 Sch.1
Sch.1 Part II para.3, substituted: SI 2008/3230 Sch.1
Sch.1 Part II para.4, substituted: SI 2008/3230 Sch.1
Sch.1 Part II para.5, substituted: SI 2008/3230 Sch.1
Sch.1 Part II para.6, substituted: SI 2008/3230 Sch.1
Sch.1 Part II para.7, substituted: SI 2008/3230 Sch.1
Sch.1 Part II para.8, substituted: SI 2008/3230 Sch.1
Sch.1 Part II para.9, substituted: SI 2008/3230 Sch.1
Sch.1 Part II para.10, substituted: SI 2008/3230 Sch.1
Sch.1 Part II para.11, substituted: SI 2008/3230 Sch.1
Sch.1 Part II para.12, substituted: SI 2008/3230 Sch.1
Sch.1 Part II para.13, substituted: SI 2008/3230 Sch.1
Sch.1 Part II para.14, substituted: SI 2008/3230 Sch.1
Sch.1 Part II para.15, substituted: SI 2008/3230 Sch.1
Sch.1 Part II para.16, substituted: SI 2008/3230 Sch.1
Sch.1 Part II para.17, substituted: SI 2008/3230 Sch.1
Sch.1 Part II para.18, substituted: SI 2008/3230 Sch.1
Sch.1 Part II para.19, substituted: SI 2008/3230 Sch.1
Sch.1 Part II para.20, substituted: SI 2008/3230 Sch.1
Sch.1 Part II para.21, substituted: SI 2008/3230 Sch.1
Sch.1 Part II para.22, substituted: SI 2008/3230 Sch.1
Sch.1 Part II para.23, substituted: SI 2008/3230 Sch.1
Sch.1 Part II para.24, substituted: SI 2008/3230 Sch.1
Sch.1 Part II para.25, substituted: SI 2008/3230 Sch.1
Sch.1 Part II para.26, substituted: SI 2008/3230 Sch.1
Sch.1 Part II para.27, substituted: SI 2008/3230 Sch.1
Sch.1 Part II para.28, substituted: SI 2008/3230 Sch.1
Sch.1 Part II para.29, substituted: SI 2008/3230 Sch.1
Sch.1 Part II para.30, substituted: SI 2008/3230 Sch.1

NO.

2006–cont.

2841. Products of Animal Origin (Third Country Imports) (England) Regulations 2006–*cont.*

Sch.1 Part II para.31, substituted: SI 2008/3230 Sch.1
Sch.1 Part III para.1, substituted: SI 2008/3230 Sch.1
Sch.1 Part III para.2, substituted: SI 2008/3230 Sch.1
Sch.1 Part III para.3, substituted: SI 2008/3230 Sch.1
Sch.1 Part III para.4, substituted: SI 2008/3230 Sch.1
Sch.1 Part III para.5, substituted: SI 2008/3230 Sch.1
Sch.1 Part III para.6, substituted: SI 2008/3230 Sch.1
Sch.1 Part III para.7, substituted: SI 2008/3230 Sch.1
Sch.1 Part III para.8, substituted: SI 2008/3230 Sch.1
Sch.1 Part III para.9, substituted: SI 2008/3230 Sch.1
Sch.1 Part III para.10, substituted: SI 2008/3230 Sch.1
Sch.1 Part IV para.1, substituted: SI 2008/3230 Sch.1
Sch.1 Part IV para.2, substituted: SI 2008/3230 Sch.1
Sch.1 Part IV para.3, substituted: SI 2008/3230 Sch.1
Sch.1 Part V para.1, substituted: SI 2008/3230 Sch.1
Sch.1 Part V para.2, substituted: SI 2008/3230 Sch.1
Sch.1 Part V para.3, substituted: SI 2008/3230 Sch.1
Sch.1 Part V para.4, substituted: SI 2008/3230 Sch.1
Sch.1 Part VI para.1, substituted: SI 2008/3230 Sch.1
Sch.1 Part VI para.2, substituted: SI 2008/3230 Sch.1
Sch.1 Part VII para.1, substituted: SI 2008/3230 Sch.1
Sch.1 Part VII para.2, substituted: SI 2008/3230 Sch.1
Sch.1 Part VII para.3, substituted: SI 2008/3230 Sch.1
Sch.1 Part VIII para.1, substituted: SI 2008/3230 Sch.1
Sch.1 Part VIII para.2, substituted: SI 2008/3230 Sch.1
Sch.1 Part VIII para.3, substituted: SI 2008/3230 Sch.1
Sch.1 Part VIII para.4, substituted: SI 2008/3230 Sch.1
Sch.1 Part VIII para.5, substituted: SI 2008/3230 Sch.1
Sch.1 Part VIII para.6, substituted: SI 2008/3230 Sch.1

NO.

2006–cont.

2841. Products of Animal Origin (Third Country Imports) (England) Regulations 2006–*cont.*

Sch.1 Part VIII para.7, substituted: SI 2008/3230 Sch.1
Sch.1 Part VIII para.8, substituted: SI 2008/3230 Sch.1
Sch.1 Part VIII para.9, substituted: SI 2008/3230 Sch.1
Sch.1 Part VIII para.10, substituted: SI 2008/3230 Sch.1
Sch.1 Part VIII para.11, substituted: SI 2008/3230 Sch.1
Sch.1 Part VIII para.12, substituted: SI 2008/3230 Sch.1
Sch.1 Part VIII para.13, substituted: SI 2008/3230 Sch.1
Sch.1 Part VIII para.14, substituted: SI 2008/3230 Sch.1
Sch.1 Part VIII para.15, substituted: SI 2008/3230 Sch.1
Sch.1 Part VIII para.16, substituted: SI 2008/3230 Sch.1
Sch.1 Part VIII para.17, substituted: SI 2008/3230 Sch.1
Sch.1 Part VIII para.18, substituted: SI 2008/3230 Sch.1
Sch.1 Part VIII para.19, substituted: SI 2008/3230 Sch.1
Sch.1 Part VIII para.20, substituted: SI 2008/3230 Sch.1
Sch.1 Part IX para.1, substituted: SI 2008/3230 Sch.1
Sch.1 Part IX para.2, substituted: SI 2008/3230 Sch.1
Sch.1 Part IX para.3, substituted: SI 2008/3230 Sch.1
Sch.1 Part IX para.4, substituted: SI 2008/3230 Sch.1
Sch.1 Part IX para.5, substituted: SI 2008/3230 Sch.1
Sch.1 Part IX para.6, substituted: SI 2008/3230 Sch.1
Sch.1 Part IX para.7, substituted: SI 2008/3230 Sch.1
Sch.1 Part IX para.8, substituted: SI 2008/3230 Sch.1
Sch.1 Part IX para.9, substituted: SI 2008/3230 Sch.1
Sch.1 Part IX para.10, substituted: SI 2008/3230 Sch.1
Sch.1 Part IX para.11, substituted: SI 2008/3230 Sch.1
Sch.1 Part IX para.12, substituted: SI 2008/3230 Sch.1
Sch.1 Part IX para.13, substituted: SI 2008/3230 Sch.1
Sch.1 Part IX para.14, substituted: SI 2008/3230 Sch.1
Sch.1 Part IX para.15, substituted: SI 2008/3230 Sch.1

NO.

2006–cont.

2841. Products of Animal Origin (Third Country Imports) (England) Regulations 2006–*cont.*

Sch.1 Part IX para.16, substituted: SI 2008/3230 Sch.1

Sch.1 Part IX para.17, substituted: SI 2008/3230 Sch.1

Sch.1 Part X para.1, substituted: SI 2008/3230 Sch.1

Sch.1 Part X para.2, substituted: SI 2008/3230 Sch.1

Sch.1 Part X para.3, substituted: SI 2008/3230 Sch.1

Sch.1 Part X para.4, substituted: SI 2008/3230 Sch.1

Sch.1 Part X para.5, substituted: SI 2008/3230 Sch.1

Sch.1 Part X para.6, substituted: SI 2008/3230 Sch.1

Sch.1 Part X para.7, substituted: SI 2008/3230 Sch.1

Sch.1 Part X para.8, substituted: SI 2008/3230 Sch.1

Sch.1 Part X para.9, substituted: SI 2008/3230 Sch.1

Sch.1 Part X para.10, substituted: SI 2008/3230 Sch.1

Sch.1 Part X para.11, substituted: SI 2008/3230 Sch.1

Sch.1 Part X para.12, substituted: SI 2008/3230 Sch.1

Sch.1 Part X para.13, substituted: SI 2008/3230 Sch.1

Sch.1 Part X para.14, substituted: SI 2008/3230 Sch.1

Sch.1 Part X para.15, substituted: SI 2008/3230 Sch.1

Sch.1 Part X para.16, substituted: SI 2008/3230 Sch.1

Sch.1 Part X para.17, substituted: SI 2008/3230 Sch.1

Sch.1 Part X para.18, substituted: SI 2008/3230 Sch.1

Sch.1 Part X para.19, substituted: SI 2008/3230 Sch.1

Sch.1 Part X para.20, substituted: SI 2008/3230 Sch.1

Sch.1 Part X para.21, substituted: SI 2008/3230 Sch.1

Sch.1 Part X para.22, substituted: SI 2008/3230 Sch.1

Sch.1 Part X para.23, substituted: SI 2008/3230 Sch.1

Sch.1 Part X para.24, substituted: SI 2008/3230 Sch.1

Sch.1 Part X para.25, substituted: SI 2008/3230 Sch.1

Sch.1 Part X para.26, substituted: SI 2008/3230 Sch.1

Sch.1 Part X para.27, substituted: SI 2008/3230 Sch.1

NO.

2006–cont.

2841. Products of Animal Origin (Third Country Imports) (England) Regulations 2006–*cont.*

Sch.1 Part X para.28, substituted: SI 2008/3230 Sch.1

Sch.1 Part X para.29, substituted: SI 2008/3230 Sch.1

Sch.1 Part X para.30, substituted: SI 2008/3230 Sch.1

Sch.1 Part X para.31, substituted: SI 2008/3230 Sch.1

Sch.1 Part X para.32, substituted: SI 2008/3230 Sch.1

Sch.1 Part X para.33, substituted: SI 2008/3230 Sch.1

Sch.1 Part X para.34, substituted: SI 2008/3230 Sch.1

Sch.1 Part X para.35, substituted: SI 2008/3230 Sch.1

Sch.1 Part X para.36, substituted: SI 2008/3230 Sch.1

Sch.1 Part X para.37, substituted: SI 2008/3230 Sch.1

Sch.1 Part X para.38, substituted: SI 2008/3230 Sch.1

Sch.1 Part X para.39, substituted: SI 2008/3230 Sch.1

Sch.1 Part X para.40, substituted: SI 2008/3230 Sch.1

Sch.1 Part X para.41, substituted: SI 2008/3230 Sch.1

Sch.1 Part X para.42, substituted: SI 2008/3230 Sch.1

Sch.1 Part X para.43, substituted: SI 2008/3230 Sch.1

Sch.1 Part X para.44, substituted: SI 2008/3230 Sch.1

Sch.1 Part X para.45, substituted: SI 2008/3230 Sch.1

Sch.1 Part X para.46, substituted: SI 2008/3230 Sch.1

Sch.1 Part X para.47, substituted: SI 2008/3230 Sch.1

Sch.1 Part X para.48, substituted: SI 2008/3230 Sch.1

Sch.1 Part X para.49, substituted: SI 2008/3230 Sch.1

Sch.1 Part X para.50, substituted: SI 2008/3230 Sch.1

Sch.1 Part X para.51, substituted: SI 2008/3230 Sch.1

Sch.1 Part X para.52, substituted: SI 2008/3230 Sch.1

Sch.1 Part X para.53, substituted: SI 2008/3230 Sch.1

Sch.1 Part X para.54, substituted: SI 2008/3230 Sch.1

Sch.1 Part X para.55, substituted: SI 2008/3230 Sch.1

Sch.1 Part X para.56, substituted: SI 2008/3230 Sch.1

NO.

2006–cont.

2841. Products of Animal Origin (Third Country Imports) (England) Regulations 2006–*cont.*
Sch.1 Part X para.57, substituted: SI 2008/3230 Sch.1
Sch.1 Part X para.58, substituted: SI 2008/3230 Sch.1
Sch.1 Part X para.59, substituted: SI 2008/3230 Sch.1
Sch.1 Part X para.60, substituted: SI 2008/3230 Sch.1
Sch.1 Part X para.61, substituted: SI 2008/3230 Sch.1
Sch.1 Part X para.62, substituted: SI 2008/3230 Sch.1
Sch.1 Part X para.63, substituted: SI 2008/3230 Sch.1
Sch.1 Part X para.64, substituted: SI 2008/3230 Sch.1
Sch.1 Part X para.65, substituted: SI 2008/3230 Sch.1
Sch.1 Part X para.66, substituted: SI 2008/3230 Sch.1
Sch.1 Part X para.67, substituted: SI 2008/3230 Sch.1
Sch.1 Part X para.68, substituted: SI 2008/3230 Sch.1
Sch.1 Part X para.69, substituted: SI 2008/3230 Sch.1
Sch.1 Part X para.70, substituted: SI 2008/3230 Sch.1
Sch.1 Part X para.71, substituted: SI 2008/3230 Sch.1
Sch.1 Part X para.72, substituted: SI 2008/3230 Sch.1
Sch.1 Part X para.73, substituted: SI 2008/3230 Sch.1
Sch.1 Part X para.74, substituted: SI 2008/3230 Sch.1
Sch.1 Part X para.75, substituted: SI 2008/3230 Sch.1
Sch.1 Part X para.76, substituted: SI 2008/3230 Sch.1
Sch.1 Part X para.77, substituted: SI 2008/3230 Sch.1
Sch.1 Part X para.78, substituted: SI 2008/3230 Sch.1
Sch.1 Part X para.79, substituted: SI 2008/3230 Sch.1
Sch.1 Part X para.80, substituted: SI 2008/3230 Sch.1
Sch.1 Part X para.81, substituted: SI 2008/3230 Sch.1
Sch.1 Part X para.82, substituted: SI 2008/3230 Sch.1
Sch.1 Part X para.83, substituted: SI 2008/3230 Sch.1
Sch.1 Part X para.84, substituted: SI 2008/3230 Sch.1
Sch.1 Part X para.85, substituted: SI 2008/3230 Sch.1

NO.

2006–cont.

2841. Products of Animal Origin (Third Country Imports) (England) Regulations 2006–*cont.*
Sch.1 Part X para.86, substituted: SI 2008/3230 Sch.1
Sch.1 Part X para.87, substituted: SI 2008/3230 Sch.1
Sch.1 Part X para.88, substituted: SI 2008/3230 Sch.1
Sch.1 Part X para.89, substituted: SI 2008/3230 Sch.1
Sch.1 Part X para.90, substituted: SI 2008/3230 Sch.1
Sch.1 Part X para.91, substituted: SI 2008/3230 Sch.1
Sch.1 Part X para.92, substituted: SI 2008/3230 Sch.1
Sch.1 Part X para.93, substituted: SI 2008/3230 Sch.1
Sch.1 Part X para.94, substituted: SI 2008/3230 Sch.1
Sch.1 Part X para.95, substituted: SI 2008/3230 Sch.1
Sch.1 Part X para.96, substituted: SI 2008/3230 Sch.1
Sch.1 Part X para.97, substituted: SI 2008/3230 Sch.1
Sch.1 Part X para.98, substituted: SI 2008/3230 Sch.1
Sch.1 Part X para.99, substituted: SI 2008/3230 Sch.1
Sch.1 Part X para.100, substituted: SI 2008/3230 Sch.1
Sch.1 Part X para.101, substituted: SI 2008/3230 Sch.1
Sch.1 Part X para.102, substituted: SI 2008/3230 Sch.1
Sch.1 Part X para.103, substituted: SI 2008/3230 Sch.1
Sch.1 Part X para.104, substituted: SI 2008/3230 Sch.1
Sch.1 Part X para.105, substituted: SI 2008/3230 Sch.1
Sch.1 Part X para.106, substituted: SI 2008/3230 Sch.1
Sch.1 Part X para.107, substituted: SI 2008/3230 Sch.1
Sch.1 Part X para.108, substituted: SI 2008/3230 Sch.1
Sch.1 Part X para.109, substituted: SI 2008/3230 Sch.1
Sch.1 Part X para.110, substituted: SI 2008/3230 Sch.1
Sch.1 Part X para.111, substituted: SI 2008/3230 Sch.1
Sch.1 Part X para.112, substituted: SI 2008/3230 Sch.1
Sch.1 Part X para.113, substituted: SI 2008/3230 Sch.1
Sch.1 Part X para.114, substituted: SI 2008/3230 Sch.1

NO.

2006–cont.

2841. Products of Animal Origin (Third Country Imports) (England) Regulations 2006–*cont.*
Sch.1 Part X para.115, substituted: SI 2008/3230 Sch.1
Sch.1 Part X para.116, substituted: SI 2008/3230 Sch.1
Sch.1 Part X para.117, substituted: SI 2008/3230 Sch.1
Sch.1 Part X para.118, substituted: SI 2008/3230 Sch.1
Sch.1 Part XI para.1, substituted: SI 2008/3230 Sch.1

2907. Cosmetic Products (Safety) (Amendment) (No.3) Regulations 2006
revoked: SI 2008/1284 Sch.1

2914. Local Government (Early Termination of Employment) (Discretionary Compensation) (England and Wales) Regulations 2006
applied: SI 2008/1419 Reg.5

2916. Dangerous Substances and Preparations (Safety) Regulations 2006
revoked: SI 2008/2852 Sch.10 Part 1

2921. Rice Products (Restriction on First Placing on the Market) (England) Regulations 2006
revoked: SI 2008/622 Reg.6

2922. Pesticides (Maximum Residue Levels in Crops, Food and Feeding Stuffs) (England and Wales) (Amendment) (No.3) Regulations 2006
revoked: SI 2008/2570 Sch.2

2923. Rice Products (Restriction on First Placing on the Market) (Wales) Regulations 2006
revoked: SI 2008/781 Reg.6

2926. Sheep and Goats (Records, Identification and Movement) (Wales) (Amendment) Order 2006
revoked: SI 2008/130 Art.37

2929. Seed Potatoes (Wales) Regulations 2006
referred to: SI 2008/1063 Reg.2
Sch.3 Part II, amended: SI 2008/1063 Reg.2
Sch.3 Part III, amended: SI 2008/1063 Reg.2

2930. Sex Discrimination Act 1975 (Public Authorities) (Statutory Duties) Order 2006
Art.2, varied: SI 2008/912 Sch.2 para.14
Sch.1, amended: SI 2008/912 Sch.2 para.14, SI 2008/960 Sch.3, SI 2008/2831 Sch.1 para.15, Sch.2 para.7
Sch.1, varied: 2008 c.14 Sch.10 para.1

2950. Merchant Shipping (Prevention of Pollution by Sewage and Garbage) Order 2006
Art.3, enabled: SI 2008/3257
Art.4, enabled: SI 2008/3257
Art.5, enabled: SI 2008/3257

NO.

2006–cont.

2950. Merchant Shipping (Prevention of Pollution by Sewage and Garbage) Order 2006–*cont.*
Art.6, applied: SI 2008/3257 Reg.42

2952. Al-Qaida and Taliban (United Nations Measures) Order 2006
referred to: 2008 c.28 s.64
see *A v HM Treasury* [2008] EWCA Civ 1187, Times, November 12, 2008 (CA (Civ Div)), Sir Anthony Clarke, M.R.; see *A v HM Treasury* [2008] EWHC 869 (Admin), [2008] 3 All E.R. 361 (QBD (Admin)), Collins, J.
Art.5, revoked (in part): 2008 c.28 Sch.9 Part 4
Art.5, see *A v HM Treasury* [2008] EWCA Civ 1187, Times, November 12, 2008 (CA (Civ Div)), Sir Anthony Clarke, M.R.

2974. Political Donations and Regulated Transactions (Anonymous Electors) (England and Wales) Regulations 2006
revoked: SI 2008/2869 Reg.2

2979. Smoke Control Areas (Authorised Fuels) (Wales) Regulations 2006
referred to: SI 2008/3100 Reg.3
revoked: SI 2008/3100 Reg.3

2980. Smoke Control Areas (Exempted Fireplaces) (Wales) Order 2006
revoked: SI 2008/3101 Art.3

2981. Specified Animal Pathogens (Amendment) (Wales) Order 2006
revoked: SI 2008/1270 Art.12

2982. Plastic Materials and Articles in Contact with Food (Wales) Regulations 2006
revoked: SI 2008/1237 Reg.29
Reg.25, applied: SI 2008/1682 Reg.22
Reg.25, referred to: SI 2008/1237 Reg.22
Sch.2, applied: SI 2008/1682 Reg.21
Sch.2, referred to: SI 2008/1237 Reg.21

2988. Radioactive Contaminated Land (Modification of Enactments) (Wales) Regulations 2006
Reg.5, amended: SI 2008/521 Reg.2
Reg.17, substituted: SI 2008/521 Reg.2

2990. Education and Inspections Act 2006 (Commencement No.1 and Saving Provisions) Order 2006
Art.4, amended: SI 2008/54 Art.2

2993. Regional Transport Planning (Wales) Order 2006
Art.5, amended: SI 2008/1286 Art.2

3039. Trade Marks (Amendment) Rules 2006
revoked: SI 2008/1797 Sch.2

3088. Social Security (Incapacity Benefit Work-focused Interviews) Amendment (No.2) Regulations 2006
revoked: SI 2008/2928 Reg.12

NO.

2006–cont.

3097. Education (Assisted Places) (Amendment) (Wales) Regulations 2006
Reg.1, amended: SI 2008/509 Reg.2

3098. Education (Assisted Places) (Incidental Expenses) (Amendment) (Wales) Regulations 2006
Reg.1, amended: SI 2008/510 Reg.2

3117. Network Rail (Thameslink 2000) Order 2006
Art.2, varied: SI 2008/3163 Art.15
Art.46, varied: SI 2008/3163 Art.15
Art.47, varied: SI 2008/3163 Art.15
Art.49, varied: SI 2008/3163 Art.15
Art.50, varied: SI 2008/3163 Art.15
Art.51, varied: SI 2008/3163 Art.15
Sch.7, applied: SI 2008/3163 Art.6
Sch.7 para.1, varied: SI 2008/3163 Art.15
Sch.7 para.2, varied: SI 2008/3163 Art.15
Sch.7 para.3, varied: SI 2008/3163 Art.15
Sch.7 para.4, varied: SI 2008/3163 Art.15
Sch.7 para.5, varied: SI 2008/3163 Art.15
Sch.7 para.6, varied: SI 2008/3163 Art.15
Sch.7 para.7, varied: SI 2008/3163 Art.15
Sch.7 para.8, varied: SI 2008/3163 Art.15
Sch.7 para.9, varied: SI 2008/3163 Art.15
Sch.9 para.1, varied: SI 2008/3163 Art.15
Sch.9 para.2, applied: SI 2008/3163 Art.12
Sch.9 para.2, varied: SI 2008/3163 Art.15
Sch.9 para.3, varied: SI 2008/3163 Art.15
Sch.10 Part 1 para.1, varied: SI 2008/3163 Art.15
Sch.10 Part 1 para.2, varied: SI 2008/3163 Art.15
Sch.10 Part 1 para.3, varied: SI 2008/3163 Art.15
Sch.10 Part 1 para.4, varied: SI 2008/3163 Art.15
Sch.10 Part 1 para.5, varied: SI 2008/3163 Art.15
Sch.10 Part 1 para.6, varied: SI 2008/3163 Art.15
Sch.10 Part 1 para.7, varied: SI 2008/3163 Art.15
Sch.10 Part 1 para.8, varied: SI 2008/3163 Art.15
Sch.10 Part 1 para.9, varied: SI 2008/3163 Art.15
Sch.10 Part 1 para.10, varied: SI 2008/3163 Art.15
Sch.10 Part 1 para.11, varied: SI 2008/3163 Art.15
Sch.10 Part 1 para.12, varied: SI 2008/3163 Art.15
Sch.10 Part 1 para.13, varied: SI 2008/3163 Art.15
Sch.10 Part 2 para.14, varied: SI 2008/3163 Art.15
Sch.10 Part 2 para.15, varied: SI 2008/3163 Art.15
Sch.10 Part 2 para.16, varied: SI 2008/3163 Art.15

NO.

2006–cont.

3117. Network Rail (Thameslink 2000) Order 2006–*cont.*
Sch.10 Part 2 para.17, varied: SI 2008/3163 Art.15
Sch.10 Part 3 para.18, varied: SI 2008/3163 Art.15
Sch.10 Part 3 para.19, varied: SI 2008/3163 Art.15
Sch.10 Part 3 para.20, varied: SI 2008/3163 Art.15
Sch.10 Part 3 para.21, varied: SI 2008/3163 Art.15
Sch.10 Part 3 para.22, varied: SI 2008/3163 Art.15
Sch.10 Part 3 para.23, varied: SI 2008/3163 Art.15
Sch.10 Part 3 para.24, varied: SI 2008/3163 Art.15
Sch.10 Part 3 para.25, varied: SI 2008/3163 Art.15
Sch.10 Part 3 para.26, varied: SI 2008/3163 Art.15
Sch.10 Part 3 para.27, varied: SI 2008/3163 Art.15
Sch.10 Part 4 para.28, varied: SI 2008/3163 Art.15
Sch.10 Part 4 para.29, varied: SI 2008/3163 Art.15
Sch.10 Part 4 para.30, varied: SI 2008/3163 Art.15
Sch.10 Part 4 para.31, varied: SI 2008/3163 Art.15
Sch.10 Part 4 para.32, varied: SI 2008/3163 Art.15
Sch.10 Part 4 para.33, varied: SI 2008/3163 Art.15
Sch.10 Part 4 para.34, varied: SI 2008/3163 Art.15
Sch.10 Part 4 para.35, varied: SI 2008/3163 Art.15
Sch.10 Part 4 para.36, varied: SI 2008/3163 Art.15
Sch.10 Part 4 para.37, varied: SI 2008/3163 Art.15
Sch.10 Part 4 para.38, varied: SI 2008/3163 Art.15
Sch.10 Part 4 para.39, varied: SI 2008/3163 Art.15
Sch.10 Part 4 para.40, varied: SI 2008/3163 Art.15
Sch.10 Part 4 para.41, varied: SI 2008/3163 Art.15
Sch.10 Part 4 para.42, varied: SI 2008/3163 Art.15
Sch.10 Part 4 para.43, varied: SI 2008/3163 Art.15
Sch.10 Part 4 para.44, varied: SI 2008/3163 Art.15
Sch.10 Part 4 para.45, varied: SI 2008/3163 Art.15

NO.

2006–cont.

3117. Network Rail (Thameslink 2000) Order 2006–*cont.*

Sch.10 Part 4 para.46, varied: SI 2008/3163 Art.15

Sch.10 Part 4 para.47, varied: SI 2008/3163 Art.15

Sch.10 Part 4 para.48, varied: SI 2008/3163 Art.15

Sch.10 Part 4 para.49, varied: SI 2008/3163 Art.15

Sch.10 Part 4 para.50, varied: SI 2008/3163 Art.15

Sch.10 Part 4 para.51, varied: SI 2008/3163 Art.15

Sch.10 Part 5 para.52, varied: SI 2008/3163 Art.15

Sch.10 Part 5 para.53, varied: SI 2008/3163 Art.15

Sch.10 Part 5 para.54, varied: SI 2008/3163 Art.15

Sch.10 Part 5 para.55, varied: SI 2008/3163 Art.15

Sch.10 Part 6 para.56, varied: SI 2008/3163 Art.15

Sch.10 Part 6 para.57, varied: SI 2008/3163 Art.15

Sch.10 Part 6 para.58, varied: SI 2008/3163 Art.15

Sch.10 Part 6 para.59, varied: SI 2008/3163 Art.15

Sch.10 Part 6 para.60, varied: SI 2008/3163 Art.15

Sch.10 Part 6 para.61, varied: SI 2008/3163 Art.15

Sch.10 Part 6 para.62, varied: SI 2008/3163 Art.15

Sch.10 Part 6 para.63, varied: SI 2008/3163 Art.15

Sch.10 Part 6 para.64, varied: SI 2008/3163 Art.15

Sch.10 Part 6 para.65, varied: SI 2008/3163 Art.15

Sch.10 Part 6 para.66, varied: SI 2008/3163 Art.15

Sch.10 Part 6 para.67, varied: SI 2008/3163 Art.15

Sch.10 Part 6 para.68, varied: SI 2008/3163 Art.15

Sch.10 Part 6 para.69, varied: SI 2008/3163 Art.15

3148. Controlled Drugs (Supervision of Management and Use) Regulations 2006

Reg.2, varied: 2008 c.14 Sch.10 para.1

3156. Education (Student Support) (European Institutions) (No.2) Regulations 2006

Reg.3, amended: SI 2008/3054 Reg.5

Reg.8, amended: SI 2008/3054 Reg.6

Reg.9, amended: SI 2008/3054 Reg.7

Reg.17, amended: SI 2008/1478 Reg.3

NO.

2006–cont.

3156. Education (Student Support) (European Institutions) (No.2) Regulations 2006–*cont.*

Reg.18, amended: SI 2008/3054 Sch.1

Reg.19, amended: SI 2008/3054 Sch.1

Reg.21, amended: SI 2008/3054 Sch.1

Reg.24, amended: SI 2008/3054 Sch.1

Reg.26, amended: SI 2008/3054 Sch.1

Reg.27, amended: SI 2008/3054 Sch.1

Reg.28, amended: SI 2008/3054 Sch.1

Reg.29, amended: SI 2008/3054 Sch.1

Sch.1 Part 2 para.8, amended: SI 2008/1478 Reg.4

Sch.2 Part 2 para.2, amended: SI 2008/3054 Sch.1

Sch.2 Part 2 para.7, amended: SI 2008/3054 Sch.1

3243. Armed Forces (Entry, Search and Seizure) Order 2006

Art.2, amended: SI 2008/1698 Art.4

Art.3, amended: SI 2008/1698 Art.5

Art.4, amended: SI 2008/1698 Art.6

3251. Care Standards Act 2000 and the Children Act 1989 (Regulatory Reform and Complaints) (Wales) Regulations 2006

applied: 2008 c.14 s.17

3271. Overseas Life Insurance Companies Regulations 2006

Reg.5, amended: SI 2008/1924 Reg.3

Reg.6, amended: SI 2008/1924 Reg.4

Reg.6, revoked (in part): SI 2008/1924 Reg.4

Reg.6, substituted: SI 2008/1924 Reg.4

Reg.8, revoked (in part): SI 2008/1924 Reg.5

Reg.9, revoked (in part): SI 2008/1924 Reg.6

Reg.14A, substituted: SI 2008/1924 Reg.8

Reg.14ZA, added: SI 2008/1924 Reg.7

Reg.14ZB, added: SI 2008/1924 Reg.7

Reg.14ZC, added: SI 2008/1924 Reg.7

Reg.15, substituted: SI 2008/1924 Reg.9

Reg.15A, revoked: SI 2008/1924 Reg.10

Reg.15B, added: SI 2008/1924 Reg.11

Reg.15C, added: SI 2008/1924 Reg.12

Reg.22, amended: SI 2008/1924 Reg.13

Reg.22B, added: SI 2008/1924 Reg.14

Reg.23, revoked: SI 2008/1924 Reg.15

Reg.25, revoked: SI 2008/1924 Reg.16

Reg.26, revoked (in part): SI 2008/1924 Reg.17

3284. Gambling (Operating Licence and Single-Machine Permit Fees) Regulations 2006

Reg.2, amended: SI 2008/1803 Reg.3

Reg.4, amended: SI 2008/1803 Reg.4

Reg.4A, added: SI 2008/1803 Reg.5

Reg.6, amended: SI 2008/1803 Reg.6

Reg.9, amended: SI 2008/1803 Reg.7

Reg.10, amended: SI 2008/1803 Reg.8

Reg.14A, added: SI 2008/1803 Reg.9

Reg.15, amended: SI 2008/1803 Reg.10

NO.

2006–cont.

3284. Gambling (Operating Licence and Single-Machine Permit Fees) Regulations 2006–*cont.*
Reg.20, amended: SI 2008/1803 Reg.11
Reg.21, amended: SI 2008/1803 Reg.12
Reg.23, substituted: SI 2008/1803 Reg.13
Reg.24, amended: SI 2008/1803 Reg.14
Sch.1, amended: SI 2008/1803 Sch.1
Sch.1, substituted: SI 2008/3105 Sch.1
Sch.2, amended: SI 2008/1803 Sch.2
Sch.3, amended: SI 2008/1803 Sch.3
Sch.4, amended: SI 2008/1803 Sch.4
Sch.4, substituted: SI 2008/3105 Sch.2
Sch.5, amended: SI 2008/1803 Sch.5
Sch.6, amended: SI 2008/1803 Sch.6

3287. Gambling Appeals Tribunal Fees Regulations 2006
Reg.3, amended: SI 2008/1879 Reg.19

3297. Textile Products (Indications of Fibre Content) (Amendment and Consolidation of Schedules of Textile Names and Allowances) Regulations 2006
revoked: SI 2008/6 Reg.1

3298. Textile Products (Determination of Composition) Regulations 2006
revoked: SI 2008/15 Reg.1

3305. Local Elections (Parishes and Communities) (England and Wales) Rules 2006
r.5, varied: SI 2008/2857 Art.5

3311. Controls on Dangerous Substances and Preparations Regulations 2006
revoked: SI 2008/2852 Sch.10 Part 1

3317. Accession (Immigration and Worker Authorisation) Regulations 2006
Reg.6, applied: SI 2008/794 Reg.70

3322. Compensation (Claims Management Services) Regulations 2006
Reg.21, substituted: SI 2008/1441 Reg.3
Reg.21A, substituted: SI 2008/1441 Reg.3
Reg.21B, substituted: SI 2008/1441 Reg.3
Reg.40, amended: SI 2008/1441 Reg.4
Reg.42, amended: SI 2008/1441 Reg.5
Reg.43, amended: SI 2008/1441 Reg.6
Reg.44A, added: SI 2008/1441 Reg.7

3335. National Assembly for Wales (Disqualification) Order 2006
Sch.1 Part 1, amended: 2008 c.14 Sch.10 para.26, SI 2008/2250 Art.2

3336. Water and Sewerage Services (Northern Ireland) Order 2006
Art.265, amended: SI 2008/1277 Sch.2 para.112
Art.265, revoked (in part): SI 2008/1277 Sch.2 para.112, Sch.4 Part 2
Art.268, amended: SI 2008/948 Sch.1 para.252
Art.275, amended: SI 2008/948 Sch.1 para.252
Art.276, amended: SI 2008/948 Sch.1 para.252

NO.

2006–cont.

3343. Rural Development Programmes (Wales) Regulations 2006
Reg.3, applied: SI 2008/253 Sch.1, SI 2008/3200 Sch.1

3345. Non-Domestic Rating (Small Business Relief) (Wales) Order 2006
revoked: SI 2008/2770 Art.12

3364. Police and Justice Act 2006 (Commencement No.1, Transitional and Saving Provisions) Order 2006
Art.3, amended: SI 2008/617 Art.2

3365. Police and Justice Act 2006 (Supplementary and Transitional Provisions) Order 2006
Art.2, amended: SI 2008/619 Art.2
Art.3, amended: SI 2008/619 Art.2

3372. Enterprise Act 2002 (Part 8 Community Infringements Specified UK Laws) Order 2006
referred to: SI 2008/1277 Sch.3 para.14
Sch.1, amended: SI 2008/1277 Sch.2 para.113

3384. Financial Services and Markets Act 2000 (Regulated Activities) (Amendment No.3) Order 2006
Art.34, revoked: SI 2008/1816 Sch.2

3389. Group Relief for Overseas Losses (Modification of the Corporation Tax Acts for Non-resident Insurance Companies) (No.2) Regulations 2006
revoked: SI 2008/2646 Reg.5

3397. Health and Social Care (Community Health and Standards) Act 2003 (Commencement) (No.11) Order 2006
Art.4, amended: SI 2008/2683 Sch.1 para.319

3398. Personal Injuries (NHS Charges) (Reviews and Appeals) and Road Traffic (NHS Charges) (Reviews and Appeals) (Amendment) Regulations 2006
Reg.1, amended: SI 2008/2683 Sch.1 para.321
Reg.4, amended: SI 2008/2683 Sch.1 para.322
Reg.4, revoked (in part): SI 2008/2683 Sch.1 para.322
Reg.5, amended: SI 2008/2683 Sch.1 para.323
Reg.5, revoked (in part): SI 2008/2683 Sch.1 para.323
Reg.6, amended: SI 2008/2683 Sch.1 para.324
Reg.6, revoked (in part): SI 2008/2683 Sch.1 para.324
Reg.7, amended: SI 2008/2683 Sch.1 para.325
Reg.7, revoked (in part): SI 2008/2683 Sch.1 para.325
Reg.8, substituted: SI 2008/2683 Sch.1 para.326

NO.

2006–cont.

3398. Personal Injuries (NHS Charges) (Reviews and Appeals) and Road Traffic (NHS Charges) (Reviews and Appeals) (Amendment) Regulations 2006–*cont.*

Reg.9, revoked: SI 2008/2683 Sch.1 para.327

3408. Education (Aptitude for Particular Subjects) (Amendment) (England) Regulations 2006

revoked: SI 2008/3089 Sch.1

3415. Police Pensions Regulations 2006

Reg.3, amended: SI 2008/1887 Reg.33
Reg.5, amended: SI 2008/1887 Reg.34
Reg.17, amended: SI 2008/1887 Reg.35
Reg.18, amended: SI 2008/1887 Reg.36
Reg.19, amended: SI 2008/1887 Reg.37
Reg.20, amended: SI 2008/1887 Reg.38
Reg.23, amended: SI 2008/1887 Reg.39
Reg.51, amended: SI 2008/1887 Reg.40
Reg.72, applied: SI 2008/649 Reg.4
Sch.1, amended: SI 2008/1887 Reg.41
Sch.5 para.13, revoked: SI 2008/1887 Reg.42

3426. Hydrocarbon Oil Duties (Hydrogenation of Biomass) (Reliefs) Regulations 2006

substituted: SI 2008/753 Reg.11
Reg.1, amended: SI 2008/753 Reg.11
Reg.3, amended: SI 2008/753 Reg.11
Reg.5, amended: SI 2008/753 Reg.11

3428. Companies Act 2006 (Commencement No.1, Transitional Provisions and Savings) Order 2006

Sch.1 para.1, revoked: SI 2008/2860 Art.6
Sch.1 para.2, revoked: SI 2008/2860 Art.6
Sch.1 para.3, revoked: SI 2008/2860 Art.6
Sch.1 para.4, revoked: SI 2008/2860 Art.6
Sch.1 para.5, referred to: SI 2008/2860 Sch.2 para.103
Sch.1 para.5, revoked: SI 2008/2860 Art.6
Sch.1 para.6, referred to: SI 2008/2860 Sch.2 para.104
Sch.1 para.6, revoked: SI 2008/2860 Art.6
Sch.1 para.7, revoked: SI 2008/2860 Art.6
Sch.1 para.8, revoked: SI 2008/2860 Art.6
Sch.1 para.9, revoked: SI 2008/2860 Art.6
Sch.1 para.10, revoked: SI 2008/2860 Art.6
Sch.1 para.11, revoked: SI 2008/2860 Art.6
Sch.1 para.12, revoked: SI 2008/2860 Art.6
Sch.1 para.13, revoked: SI 2008/2860 Art.6
Sch.1 para.14, revoked: SI 2008/2860 Art.6
Sch.1 para.15, revoked: SI 2008/2860 Art.6
Sch.1 para.16, revoked: SI 2008/2860 Art.6

3429. Companies (Registrar, Languages and Trading Disclosures) Regulations 2006

Reg.6, revoked: SI 2008/495 Reg.11
Sch.1 para.1, revoked: SI 2008/495 Reg.11
Sch.1 para.2, revoked: SI 2008/495 Reg.11
Sch.1 para.3, revoked: SI 2008/495 Reg.11

NO.

2006–cont.

3429. Companies (Registrar, Languages and Trading Disclosures) Regulations 2006–*cont.*

Sch.1 para.4, revoked: SI 2008/495 Reg.11
Sch.2 para.1, revoked: SI 2008/495 Reg.11
Sch.2 para.2, revoked: SI 2008/495 Reg.11
Sch.2 para.3, revoked: SI 2008/495 Reg.11
Sch.2 para.4, revoked: SI 2008/495 Reg.11

3432. Firefighters Pension Scheme (England) Order 2006

Sch.1, added: SI 2008/213 Sch.1 para.3, Sch.1 para.4, Sch.1 para.7, Sch.1 para.11
Sch.1, amended: SI 2008/213 Sch.1 para.1, Sch.1 para.2, Sch.1 para.4, Sch.1 para.5, Sch.1 para.6, Sch.1 para.8, Sch.1 para.9, Sch.1 para.10, Sch.1 para.11, Sch.1 para.12, Sch.1 para.14, Sch.1 para.15
Sch.1, applied: SI 2008/649 Reg.4
Sch.1, revoked: SI 2008/213 Sch.1 para.12
Sch.1, substituted: SI 2008/213 Sch.1 para.2, Sch.1 para.3, Sch.1 para.6, Sch.1 para.7, Sch.1 para.8, Sch.1 para.11, Sch.1 para.13

3435. Civil Procedure (Amendment No.3) Rules 2006

see *Carver v BAA Plc* [2008] EWCA Civ 412, [2008] 3 All E.R. 911 (CA (Civ Div)), Ward, L.J.
r.7, see *Carver v BAA Plc* [2008] EWCA Civ 412, [2008] 3 All E.R. 911 (CA (Civ Div)), Ward, L.J.

2007

60. Occupational and Personal Pension Schemes (Prescribed Bodies) Regulations 2007

applied: SSI 2008/228 Reg.73

106. Dairy Produce Quotas (Amendment) Regulations 2007

Reg.2, revoked (in part): SI 2008/439 Reg.3

115. Personal Injuries (NHS Charges) (Amounts) Regulations 2007

Reg.2, amended: SI 2008/252 Reg.2

172. Education (Induction Arrangements for School Teachers) (Consolidation) (England) (Amendment) Regulations 2007

revoked: SI 2008/657 Sch.1
Reg.3, revoked: SI 2008/657 Sch.1

176. Education (Student Support) Regulations 2007

applied: SI 2008/529 Reg.3
revoked: SI 2008/529 Reg.3
Reg.2, applied: SI 2008/794 Reg.14
Reg.4, applied: SI 2008/529 Reg.3
Reg.38, amended: SI 2008/235 Reg.5
Reg.62, amended: SI 2008/235 Reg.6
Reg.63, amended: SI 2008/235 Reg.7
Reg.108A, added: SI 2008/235 Reg.8

NO.

2007–cont.

192. Education (Admission Forums) (England) (Amendment) Regulations 2007
revoked: SI 2008/3091 Reg.3

193. European Communities (Designation) Order 2007
Art.2, revoked (in part): SI 2008/301 Sch.1

194. School Admissions (Co-ordination of Admission Arrangements) (England) Regulations 2007
revoked: SI 2008/3090 Reg.2
Reg.1, amended: SI 2008/3090 Sch.2 para.1
Reg.3, amended: SI 2008/3090 Sch.2 para.2
Reg.10, amended: SI 2008/3090 Sch.2 para.3
Reg.11, added: SI 2008/3090 Sch.2 para.4
Sch.4 para.1, added: SI 2008/3090 Sch.2 para.5
Sch.4 para.2, added: SI 2008/3090 Sch.2 para.5
Sch.4 para.3, added: SI 2008/3090 Sch.2 para.5
Sch.4 para.4, added: SI 2008/3090 Sch.2 para.5

226. Tax Credits (Approval of Child Care Providers) (Wales) Scheme 2007
referred to: SI 2008/2687
Art.2, amended: SI 2008/2687 Art.3
Art.11, amended: SI 2008/2687 Art.3
Art.11, revoked (in part): SI 2008/2687 Art.3

228. Local Government Pension Scheme (Amendment) Regulations 2007
revoked: SI 2008/238 Sch.1

266. Copyright (Certification of Licensing Scheme for Educational Recording of Broadcasts) (Educational Recording Agency Limited) Order 2007
referred to: SI 2008/211
Sch.1, substituted: SI 2008/211 Sch.1

273. Copyright and Performances (Application to Other Countries) Order 2007
revoked: SI 2008/677 Art.1

275. Transfer of Functions (Asylum Support Adjudicators) Order 2007
Art.6, revoked (in part): SI 2008/2683 Sch.2

285. Scottish Parliament (Disqualification) Order 2007
Sch.1 Part I, amended: SI 2008/960 Sch.3, SI 2008/2683 Sch.1 para.328
Sch.1 Part I, varied: 2008 c.14 Sch.10 para.1

288. Police and Criminal Evidence (Amendment) (Northern Ireland) Order 2007
Art.39, revoked: SI 2008/1216 Sch.6 Part 2

289. Pharmacists and Pharmacy Technicians Order 2007
applied: SI 2008/2927 Reg.2
Art.10, applied: SI 2008/2789 Reg.5
Art.11, applied: SI 2008/1284 Reg.18
Art.17, enabled: SI 2008/1553

NO.

2007–cont.

289. Pharmacists and Pharmacy Technicians Order 2007–*cont.*
Art.40, applied: SI 2008/1553
Art.40, enabled: SI 2008/1553
Art.48, amended: 2008 c.14 Sch.10 para.27
Art.66, applied: SI 2008/1553
Art.66, enabled: SI 2008/1553
Sch.1 Part 1 para.8, varied: 2008 c.14 Sch.10 para.1

311. Children's Homes (Wales) (Miscellaneous Amendments) Regulations 2007
applied: 2008 c.14 s.17

314. Fuel-testing Pilot Projects (Biomix Project) Regulations 2007
Reg.2, amended: SI 2008/753 Reg.12
Reg.5, amended: SI 2008/753 Reg.12
Sch.1, amended: SI 2008/753 Reg.12

320. Construction (Design and Management) Regulations 2007
Reg.2, applied: SI 2008/2852 Sch.3 para.1

375. Home Energy Efficiency Schemes (Wales) Regulations 2007
Reg.5, amended: SI 2008/1879 Reg.32

386. Dangerous Substances and Preparations (Safety) (Amendment) Regulations 2007
revoked: SI 2008/2852 Sch.10 Part 1

398. Commissioner for Older People in Wales Regulations 2007
Reg.4, amended: SI 2008/1512 Reg.3
Reg.5, amended: SI 2008/1512 Reg.3
Reg.8, amended: SI 2008/1512 Reg.3
Reg.11, amended: SI 2008/1512 Reg.3
Reg.14, amended: SI 2008/1512 Reg.3
Reg.15, amended: SI 2008/1512 Reg.3
Reg.16, amended: SI 2008/1512 Reg.3

399. Local Authorities (Executive Arrangements) (Functions and Responsibilities) (Wales) Regulations 2007
Sch.1, amended: SI 2008/1430 Reg.26

401. Gangmasters (Licensing Conditions) (No.2) (Amendment) Rules 2007
revoked: SI 2008/638 r.3

441. Royal Pharmaceutical Society of Great Britain (Registration Rules) Order of Council 2007
Sch.1, amended: SI 2008/1553 Sch.1
Sch.1, substituted: SI 2008/1553 Sch.1

447. Adventure Activities (Licensing) (Designation) Order 2007
Art.2, amended: SI 2008/960 Sch.3

448. Diseases of Animals (Approved Disinfectants) (England) Order 2007
Art.3, applied: SI 2008/652 Art.2

457. Commons (Registration of Town or Village Greens) (Interim Arrangements) (England) Regulations 2007
applied: SI 2008/1961 Reg.14
revoked (in part): SI 2008/1961 Reg.55

NO.

2007–cont.

477. Dairy Produce (Miscellaneous Provisions) Regulations 2007
Reg.3, revoked (in part): SI 2008/438 Reg.3

478. NHS Direct National Health Service Trust (Establishment) Order 2007
Art.1, amended: SI 2008/2769 Art.2
Art.1, varied: 2008 c.14 Sch.10 para.1
Art.3, amended: SI 2008/2769 Art.3

496. School Admissions (Alteration and Variation of, and Objections to, Arrangements) (England) Regulations 2007
revoked: SI 2008/3089 Sch.1
Reg.7, substituted: SI 2008/1258 Reg.3

497. Education (Determination of Admission Arrangements) (Amendment) (England) Regulations 2007
revoked: SI 2008/3089 Sch.1

529. Cattle Identification Regulations 2007
Sch.2, applied: SI 2008/51 Sch.5 para.1

556. Commission for Social Care Inspection (Fees and Frequency of Inspections) Regulations 2007
applied: 2008 c.14 s.17

561. Royal Pharmaceutical Society of Great Britain (Fitness to Practise and Registration Appeals Committees and their Advisers Rules) Order of Council 2007
Sch.1, varied: 2008 c.14 Sch.10 para.1

565. Postgraduate Medical Education and Training Board (Fees) Rules Order 2007
revoked: SI 2008/554 Sch.1

603. Education and Inspections Act 2006 (Consequential Amendments) Regulations 2007
Reg.11, revoked: SI 2008/2683 Sch.2

605. Vehicle Drivers (Certificates of Professional Competence) Regulations 2007
Reg.2, amended: SI 2008/1965 Reg.4
Reg.4, amended: SI 2008/1965 Reg.5
Reg.5, amended: SI 2008/1965 Reg.6
Reg.5A, added: SI 2008/1965 Reg.7
Reg.6, amended: SI 2008/506 Reg.2, SI 2008/1965 Reg.8
Reg.6A, added: SI 2008/1965 Reg.9
Reg.7, amended: SI 2008/1965 Reg.10
Reg.8, amended: SI 2008/1965 Reg.11
Reg.8, revoked (in part): SI 2008/1965 Reg.11
Reg.8A, added: SI 2008/1965 Reg.12
Reg.8B, added: SI 2008/1965 Reg.12
Reg.9, revoked (in part): SI 2008/1965 Reg.13
Reg.11, amended: SI 2008/1965 Reg.14
Reg.12, amended: SI 2008/1965 Reg.15
Reg.13, amended: SI 2008/1965 Reg.16

NO.

2007–cont.

614. Civil Aviation (Isle of Man) Order 2007
applied: SI 2008/1487

616. General Medical Council (Constitution) (Amendment) Order 2007
revoked: SI 2008/1774 Sch.5 para.2

618. Disability Discrimination (Public Authorities) (Statutory Duties) (Amendment) Regulations 2007
Reg.4, varied: 2008 c.14 Sch.10 para.1

649. Consular Fees Order 2007
revoked: SI 2008/676 Sch.2

651. Air Force Act 1955 (Part 1) Regulations 2007
Reg.3, substituted: SI 2008/1585 Reg.3
Sch.1 Part 1, substituted: SI 2008/1585 Reg.4
Sch.1 Part 2, substituted: SI 2008/1585 Reg.4
Sch.4, substituted: SI 2008/1585 Reg.5

680. Civil Proceedings Fees (Amendment) Order 2007
revoked: SI 2008/1053 Sch.3

681. Public Trustee (Fees) (Amendment) Order 2007
revoked: SI 2008/611 Art.32

682. Family Proceedings Fees (Amendment) Order 2007
revoked: SI 2008/1054 Sch.3

688. Social Security Benefits Up-rating Order 2007
revoked: SI 2008/632 Art.27

706. Prevention of Terrorism Act 2005 (Continuance in force of sections 1 to 9) Order 2007
Art.2, applied: SI 2008/559 Art.2

712. Education (Provision of Information About Young Children) (England) Regulations 2007
revoked: SI 2008/1722 Reg.10

715. Northern Ireland Arms Decommissioning Act 1997 (Amnesty Period) Order 2007
revoked: SI 2008/378 Art.3

722. Childcare (Supply and Disclosure of Information) (England) Regulations 2007
Reg.2, amended: SI 2008/961 Reg.3
Reg.4, amended: SI 2008/961 Reg.4
Reg.5, amended: SI 2008/961 Reg.5
Reg.7, amended: SI 2008/961 Reg.6
Reg.9, amended: SI 2008/961 Reg.7
Reg.10, amended: SI 2008/961 Reg.8
Sch.1 Part 1 para.5, amended: SI 2008/961 Reg.9
Sch.1 Part 1 para.5A, added: SI 2008/961 Reg.9
Sch.1 Part 2 para.6, amended: SI 2008/961 Reg.9
Sch.1 Part 3 para.16, amended: SI 2008/961 Reg.9

NO.

2007–cont.

722. Childcare (Supply and Disclosure of Information) (England) Regulations 2007–*cont.*
Sch.1 Part 3 para.18, added: SI 2008/961 Reg.9

723. Childcare (Disqualification) Regulations 2007
Reg.6A, added: SI 2008/1740 Reg.3
Reg.8, amended: SI 2008/1740 Reg.4
Reg.8, applied: SI 2008/2261 Sch.2 para.25
Reg.9, applied: SI 2008/2261 Sch.2 para.20
Reg.10, amended: SI 2008/1740 Reg.5
Sch.1 para.4, amended: SI 2008/1740 Reg.6
Sch.1 para.15, amended: SI 2008/1740 Reg.6
Sch.3 para.4, substituted: SI 2008/1740 Reg.7

730. Childcare (Voluntary Registration) Regulations 2007
revoked: SI 2008/975 Reg.3
Reg.7A, added: SI 2008/793 Reg.2

734. Rules of the Air Regulations 2007
Sch.1, added: SI 2008/669 Reg.2
Sch.1, amended: SI 2008/669 Reg.2

739. Environmental Offences (Use of Fixed Penalty Receipts) (Wales) Regulations 2007
amended: SI 2008/663 Reg.6
Reg.1, revoked: SI 2008/663 Reg.5
Reg.2, revoked: SI 2008/663 Reg.5
Reg.3, revoked: SI 2008/663 Reg.5
Reg.4, revoked: SI 2008/663 Reg.5

765. Smoke-free (Exemptions and Vehicles) Regulations 2007
Reg.10, see *R. (on the application of G) v Nottinghamshire Healthcare NHS Trust* [2008] EWHC 1096 (Admin), [2008] H.R.L.R. 42 (DC), Pill, L.J.

775. Social Security Benefits Up-rating Regulations 2007
revoked: SI 2008/667 Reg.6

778. Student Fees (Qualifying Courses and Persons) (England) Regulations 2007
Reg.2, amended: SI 2008/1640 Reg.3
Reg.5, amended: SI 2008/1640 Reg.4

785. National Insurance Contributions (Application of Part 7 of the Finance Act 2004) Regulations 2007
referred to: SI 2008/2678 Reg.2
Part 2, applied: SI 2008/2678 Reg.1
Reg.1, amended: SI 2008/2678 Reg.3
Reg.2, amended: SI 2008/2678 Reg.4
Reg.2, referred to: SI 2008/2678 Reg.4
Reg.3, amended: SI 2008/2678 Reg.5
Reg.3, referred to: SI 2008/2678 Reg.5
Reg.4, amended: SI 2008/2678 Reg.6, Reg.7, Reg.8
Reg.4, referred to: SI 2008/2678 Reg.8
Reg.5, amended: SI 2008/2678 Reg.6
Reg.5A, added: SI 2008/2678 Reg.9
Reg.5A, amended: SI 2008/2678 Reg.6

NO.

2007–cont.

785. National Insurance Contributions (Application of Part 7 of the Finance Act 2004) Regulations 2007–*cont.*
Reg.6, amended: SI 2008/2678 Reg.6, Reg.10
Reg.7, amended: SI 2008/2678 Reg.6, Reg.11
Reg.7, referred to: SI 2008/2678 Reg.11
Reg.7A, added: SI 2008/2678 Reg.12
Reg.7A, amended: SI 2008/2678 Reg.6
Reg.8, amended: SI 2008/2678 Reg.6
Reg.9, amended: SI 2008/2678 Reg.6
Reg.10, amended: SI 2008/2678 Reg.6, Reg.13
Reg.11, amended: SI 2008/2678 Reg.6
Reg.11, substituted: SI 2008/2678 Reg.14
Reg.11A, amended: SI 2008/2678 Reg.6
Reg.12, amended: SI 2008/2678 Reg.6, Reg.15
Reg.12, referred to: SI 2008/2678 Reg.15
Reg.12A, added: SI 2008/2678 Reg.16
Reg.12A, amended: SI 2008/2678 Reg.6
Reg.12B, added: SI 2008/2678 Reg.16
Reg.12B, amended: SI 2008/2678 Reg.6
Reg.12C, added: SI 2008/2678 Reg.16
Reg.12C, amended: SI 2008/2678 Reg.6
Reg.13, amended: SI 2008/2678 Reg.6
Reg.13, substituted: SI 2008/2678 Reg.17
Reg.13A, amended: SI 2008/2678 Reg.6
Reg.14, amended: SI 2008/2678 Reg.18, Reg.19
Reg.14, referred to: SI 2008/2678 Reg.19
Reg.14A, added: SI 2008/2678 Reg.20
Reg.14A, amended: SI 2008/2678 Reg.18
Reg.15, amended: SI 2008/2678 Reg.18
Reg.16, amended: SI 2008/2678 Reg.21
Reg.17, amended: SI 2008/2678 Reg.22
Reg.17, referred to: SI 2008/2678 Reg.22
Reg.18, amended: SI 2008/2678 Reg.23
Reg.19, added: SI 2008/2678 Reg.24

803. Medicines for Human Use and Medical Devices (Fees Amendments) (No.2) Regulations 2007
Reg.3, revoked: SI 2008/552 Sch.7
Reg.4, revoked: SI 2008/552 Sch.7
Reg.5, revoked: SI 2008/552 Sch.7
Reg.6, revoked: SI 2008/552 Sch.7
Reg.7, revoked: SI 2008/552 Sch.7
Reg.8, revoked: SI 2008/552 Sch.7
Reg.9, revoked: SI 2008/552 Sch.7
Reg.10, revoked: SI 2008/552 Sch.7
Reg.11, revoked: SI 2008/552 Sch.7
Sch.1, revoked: SI 2008/552 Sch.7

807. Immigration and Nationality (Fees) Order 2007
referred to: SI 2008/166 Art.2
Art.2, amended: SI 2008/166 Art.3
Art.3, amended: SI 2008/166 Art.4, Art.5, Art.6, Art.7
Art.5, added: SI 2008/166 Art.8

NO.

2007–cont.

813. Health and Safety (Fees) Regulations 2007
revoked: SI 2008/736 Reg.23

814. Occupational and Personal Pension Schemes (Miscellaneous Amendments) Regulations 2007
applied: SSI 2008/228 Reg.73

817. Designation of Rural Primary Schools (England) Order 2007
revoked: SI 2008/2035 Art.3

841. Electricity Generating Stations and Overhead Lines (Inquiries Procedure) (England and Wales) Rules 2007
r.2, amended: SI 2008/2831 Sch.4 para.2
r.15, amended: SI 2008/2831 Sch.4 para.4

844. Dairy Produce Quotas (Wales) (Amendment) Regulations 2007
Reg.2, revoked (in part): SI 2008/685 Reg.3

863. Asylum Support (Amendment) Regulations 2007
revoked: SI 2008/760 Reg.3

871. Producer Responsibility Obligations (Packaging Waste) Regulations 2007
Reg.23, amended: SI 2008/1941 Reg.3
Reg.24, amended: SI 2008/1941 Reg.4
Reg.26, amended: SI 2008/1941 Reg.5
Sch.2 para.5, amended: SI 2008/413 Reg.2
Sch.2 para.6, amended: SI 2008/413 Reg.2
Sch.5 para.1, amended: SI 2008/1941 Reg.6

917. Health and Social Care (Community Health and Standards) Act 2003 Consequential Provisions (Recovery of NHS Charges) Order 2007
revoked: SI 2008/2683 Sch.2

936. Immigration and Nationality (Cost Recovery Fees) Regulations 2007
Reg.2, amended: SI 2008/218 Reg.2, SI 2008/1337 Reg.2
Reg.3, amended: SI 2008/2790 Reg.3
Reg.3, revoked (in part): SI 2008/218 Reg.2, SI 2008/1337 Reg.2
Reg.4, amended: SI 2008/2790 Reg.3
Reg.4A, added: SI 2008/1337 Reg.2
Reg.6, amended: SI 2008/1337 Reg.2
Reg.7, amended: SI 2008/1337 Reg.2
Reg.8, amended: SI 2008/1337 Reg.2
Reg.8A, added: SI 2008/1337 Reg.2
Reg.10, amended: SI 2008/1337 Reg.2
Reg.10A, added: SI 2008/218 Reg.2
Reg.10A, amended: SI 2008/1337 Reg.2
Reg.10A, substituted: SI 2008/2790 Reg.3
Reg.10B, added: SI 2008/218 Reg.2
Reg.10B, amended: SI 2008/1337 Reg.2, SI 2008/2790 Reg.3
Reg.10B, revoked (in part): SI 2008/2790 Reg.3
Reg.10C, added: SI 2008/218 Reg.2
Reg.13, amended: SI 2008/218 Reg.2
Reg.14, revoked: SI 2008/1337 Reg.2
Reg.14A, added: SI 2008/218 Reg.2
Reg.14B, added: SI 2008/218 Reg.2

NO.

2007–cont.

936. Immigration and Nationality (Cost Recovery Fees) Regulations 2007–*cont.*
Reg.15A, added: SI 2008/218 Reg.2
Reg.15A, substituted: SI 2008/1337 Reg.2
Reg.16, substituted: SI 2008/2790 Reg.3

937. Scottish Parliament (Elections etc.) Order 2007
Appendix 1, amended: SI 2008/307 Sch.1
Art.3, amended: SI 2008/307 Art.2
Art.8, amended: SI 2008/307 Art.25
Art.9, amended: SI 2008/307 Art.3
Art.9, applied: SI 2008/307 Art.20, Art.22, Art.24
Art.10, amended: SI 2008/307 Art.4
Art.10, applied: SI 2008/307 Art.20, Art.22, Art.24
Art.11, amended: SI 2008/307 Art.5
Art.11, applied: SI 2008/307 Art.24
Art.12, amended: SI 2008/307 Art.6
Art.12, applied: SI 2008/307 Art.20, Art.22, Art.24
Art.28, amended: SI 2008/307 Art.7
Sch.2, added: SI 2008/307 Art.8
Sch.2, amended: SI 2008/307 Art.8, Art.26
Sch.2, applied: SI 2008/307 Art.24
Sch.3 para.1, amended: SI 2008/307 Art.9
Sch.3 para.1A, added: SI 2008/307 Art.10
Sch.3 para.1B, added: SI 2008/307 Art.10
Sch.3 para.8, varied: SI 2008/307 Art.24
Sch.3 para.9, varied: SI 2008/307 Art.24
Sch.3 para.11A, added: SI 2008/307 Art.11
Sch.3 para.12A, added: SI 2008/307 Art.12
Sch.3 para.12B, added: SI 2008/307 Art.12
Sch.4 para.1, amended: SI 2008/307 Art.2
Sch.4 para.16, amended: SI 2008/307 Art.13
Sch.4 para.19, amended: SI 2008/307 Art.14
Sch.4 para.20, amended: SI 2008/307 Art.15
Sch.4 para.20A, added: SI 2008/307 Art.16
Sch.4 para.20B, added: SI 2008/307 Art.16
Sch.4 para.26, amended: SI 2008/307 Art.17
Sch.5 Part II para.7, amended: SI 2008/307 Art.27
Sch.5 Part II para.11, amended: SI 2008/307 Art.27

971. Pesticides (Maximum Residue Levels in Crops, Food and Feeding Stuffs) (England and Wales) (Amendment) Regulations 2007
revoked: SI 2008/2570 Sch.2

989. Pension Protection Fund (Pension Compensation Cap) Order 2007
revoked: SI 2008/909 Art.3

991. Energy Performance of Buildings (Certificates and Inspections) (England and Wales) Regulations 2007
referred to: SI 2008/647 Reg.2
Reg.11, amended: SI 2008/2363 Reg.2
Reg.14, amended: SI 2008/647 Reg.2, SI 2008/2363 Reg.2

NO.

2007–cont.

991. Energy Performance of Buildings (Certificates and Inspections) (England and Wales) Regulations 2007–*cont.*
Reg.17, amended: SI 2008/2363 Reg.2
Reg.31, amended: SI 2008/2363 Reg.2
Reg.32, substituted: SI 2008/647 Reg.2
Reg.34A, added: SI 2008/2363 Reg.2
Reg.35A, added: SI 2008/2363 Reg.2
Reg.35B, added: SI 2008/2363 Reg.2
Reg.36, amended: SI 2008/647 Reg.2
Reg.36A, added: SI 2008/2363 Reg.2
Reg.51, added: SI 2008/647 Reg.2
Reg.51, amended: SI 2008/2363 Reg.2
Sch.1, amended: SI 2008/647 Reg.2

1012. Occupational Pension Schemes (Levy Ceiling) Order 2007
revoked: SI 2008/911 Art.3

1029. Mutilations (Permitted Procedures) (Wales) Regulations 2007
Reg.3, amended: SI 2008/3094 Reg.3
Reg.4, amended: SI 2008/3094 Reg.4
Reg.5, substituted: SI 2008/3094 Reg.5
Sch.1, amended: SI 2008/3094 Reg.6
Sch.4 paraA.1, added: SI 2008/3094 Reg.7
Sch.4 paraA.2, added: SI 2008/3094 Reg.7
Sch.4 paraA.3, added: SI 2008/3094 Reg.7
Sch.4 paraA.4, added: SI 2008/3094 Reg.7
Sch.4 paraA.5, added: SI 2008/3094 Reg.7
Sch.4 para.5, amended: SI 2008/3094 Reg.7
Sch.5 para.1A, added: SI 2008/3094 Reg.8
Sch.5 para.2A, added: SI 2008/3094 Reg.8
Sch.5 para.2B, added: SI 2008/3094 Reg.8
Sch.6 para.1A, added: SI 2008/3094 Reg.9
Sch.6 para.2A, added: SI 2008/3094 Reg.9
Sch.6 para.2B, added: SI 2008/3094 Reg.9

1041. National Assistance (Assessment of Resources and Sums for Personal Requirements) (Amendments) (Wales) Regulations 2007
Reg.2, revoked: SI 2008/743 Reg.3
Reg.3, revoked: SI 2008/743 Reg.3
Reg.4, revoked: SI 2008/743 Reg.3
Reg.5, revoked: SI 2008/743 Reg.3
Reg.6, revoked (in part): SI 2008/743 Reg.3

1045. Assembly Learning Grants and Loans (Higher Education) (Wales) Regulations 2007
applied: SI 2008/3170 Reg.3
Part 4, revoked: SI 2008/1273 Reg.3
Part 6, revoked: SI 2008/1273 Reg.3
Reg.1, revoked: SI 2008/1273 Reg.3
Reg.2, revoked: SI 2008/1273 Reg.3
Reg.3, revoked (in part): SI 2008/1273 Reg.3
Reg.4, revoked: SI 2008/1273 Reg.3
Reg.5, revoked: SI 2008/1273 Reg.3
Reg.6, revoked: SI 2008/1273 Reg.3
Reg.7, revoked: SI 2008/1273 Reg.3
Reg.8, revoked: SI 2008/1273 Reg.3
Reg.9, revoked: SI 2008/1273 Reg.3

NO.

2007–cont.

1045. Assembly Learning Grants and Loans (Higher Education) (Wales) Regulations 2007–*cont.*
Reg.10, revoked: SI 2008/1273 Reg.3
Reg.11, revoked: SI 2008/1273 Reg.3
Reg.23, revoked: SI 2008/1273 Reg.3
Reg.23A, revoked: SI 2008/1273 Reg.3
Reg.24, revoked: SI 2008/1273 Reg.3
Reg.25, revoked: SI 2008/1273 Reg.3
Reg.26, revoked: SI 2008/1273 Reg.3
Reg.27, revoked: SI 2008/1273 Reg.3
Reg.28, revoked: SI 2008/1273 Reg.3
Reg.29, revoked: SI 2008/1273 Reg.3
Reg.30, revoked: SI 2008/1273 Reg.3
Reg.31, revoked: SI 2008/1273 Reg.3
Reg.32, revoked: SI 2008/1273 Reg.3
Reg.33, revoked: SI 2008/1273 Reg.3
Reg.34, revoked: SI 2008/1273 Reg.3
Reg.35, revoked: SI 2008/1273 Reg.3
Reg.36, revoked: SI 2008/1273 Reg.3
Reg.37, revoked: SI 2008/1273 Reg.3
Reg.50, revoked: SI 2008/1273 Reg.3
Reg.51, revoked: SI 2008/1273 Reg.3
Reg.52, revoked: SI 2008/1273 Reg.3
Reg.53, revoked: SI 2008/1273 Reg.3
Reg.54, revoked: SI 2008/1273 Reg.3
Reg.55, revoked: SI 2008/1273 Reg.3
Reg.56, revoked: SI 2008/1273 Reg.3
Reg.57, revoked: SI 2008/1273 Reg.3
Reg.58, revoked: SI 2008/1273 Reg.3
Reg.59, revoked: SI 2008/1273 Reg.3
Reg.60, revoked: SI 2008/1273 Reg.3
Reg.61, revoked: SI 2008/1273 Reg.3
Reg.61A, revoked: SI 2008/1273 Reg.3
Reg.61B, revoked: SI 2008/1273 Reg.3
Reg.61C, revoked: SI 2008/1273 Reg.3
Reg.61D, revoked: SI 2008/1273 Reg.3
Reg.61E, revoked: SI 2008/1273 Reg.3
Reg.61F, revoked: SI 2008/1273 Reg.3
Reg.61G, revoked: SI 2008/1273 Reg.3
Reg.61H, revoked: SI 2008/1273 Reg.3
Reg.61I, revoked: SI 2008/1273 Reg.3
Reg.61J, revoked: SI 2008/1273 Reg.3
Reg.61K, revoked: SI 2008/1273 Reg.3
Reg.61L, revoked: SI 2008/1273 Reg.3
Reg.61M, revoked: SI 2008/1273 Reg.3
Reg.61N, revoked: SI 2008/1273 Reg.3
Reg.61O, revoked: SI 2008/1273 Reg.3
Reg.61P, revoked: SI 2008/1273 Reg.3
Reg.61Q, revoked: SI 2008/1273 Reg.3
Reg.61R, revoked: SI 2008/1273 Reg.3
Reg.62, revoked: SI 2008/1273 Reg.3
Reg.63, revoked: SI 2008/1273 Reg.3
Reg.64, revoked: SI 2008/1273 Reg.3
Reg.65, revoked: SI 2008/1273 Reg.3
Reg.66, revoked: SI 2008/1273 Reg.3
Reg.67, revoked: SI 2008/1273 Reg.3
Reg.68, revoked: SI 2008/1273 Reg.3
Reg.69, revoked: SI 2008/1273 Reg.3
Reg.70, revoked: SI 2008/1273 Reg.3

NO.

2007–cont.

1045. Assembly Learning Grants and Loans (Higher Education) (Wales) Regulations 2007–*cont.*

Reg.71, revoked: SI 2008/1273 Reg.3
Reg.72, revoked: SI 2008/1273 Reg.3
Reg.73, revoked: SI 2008/1273 Reg.3
Reg.74, revoked: SI 2008/1273 Reg.3
Reg.75, revoked: SI 2008/1273 Reg.3
Reg.76, revoked: SI 2008/1273 Reg.3
Reg.77, revoked: SI 2008/1273 Reg.3
Reg.78, revoked: SI 2008/1273 Reg.3
Reg.79, revoked: SI 2008/1273 Reg.3
Reg.80, revoked: SI 2008/1273 Reg.3
Reg.81, revoked: SI 2008/1273 Reg.3
Reg.82, revoked: SI 2008/1273 Reg.3
Sch.1 Part 1 para.1, revoked: SI 2008/1273 Reg.3
Sch.1 Part 2, applied: SI 2008/538 Reg.3
Sch.1 Part 2, referred to: SI 2008/538 Reg.9
Sch.1 Part 2, revoked: SI 2008/1273 Reg.3
Sch.4 para.1, revoked: SI 2008/1273 Reg.3
Sch.4 para.2, revoked: SI 2008/1273 Reg.3
Sch.4 para.3, revoked: SI 2008/1273 Reg.3
Sch.4 para.4, revoked: SI 2008/1273 Reg.3
Sch.4 para.5, revoked: SI 2008/1273 Reg.3
Sch.4 para.6, revoked: SI 2008/1273 Reg.3
Sch.4 para.7, revoked: SI 2008/1273 Reg.3
Sch.4 para.8, revoked: SI 2008/1273 Reg.3
Sch.4 para.9, revoked: SI 2008/1273 Reg.3
Sch.4 para.10, revoked: SI 2008/1273 Reg.3
Sch.4 para.11, revoked: SI 2008/1273 Reg.3
Sch.4 para.12, revoked: SI 2008/1273 Reg.3

1072. Firefighters Pension Scheme (Wales) Order 2007

Sch.1, applied: SI 2008/649 Reg.4

1073. Firefighters Compensation Scheme (Wales) Order 2007

Sch.1, applied: SI 2008/649 Reg.4

1089. Education (Investigation of Parents Complaints) (England) Regulations 2007

Reg.3, amended: SI 2008/1723 Reg.3

1093. Companies Act 2006 (Commencement No.2, Consequential Amendments, Transitional Provisions and Savings) Order 2007

Sch.1 para.1, revoked: SI 2008/2860 Art.6
Sch.1 para.2, revoked: SI 2008/2860 Art.6
Sch.1 para.3, revoked: SI 2008/2860 Art.6
Sch.1 para.4, revoked: SI 2008/2860 Art.6
Sch.1 para.5, revoked: SI 2008/2860 Art.6
Sch.4 Part 1 para.4, revoked: SI 2008/948 Sch.2

1097. Stamp Duty and Stamp Duty Reserve Tax (Investment Exchanges and Clearing Houses) (Eurex Clearing AG) Regulations 2007

Reg.2, amended: SI 2008/164 Reg.4
Reg.3, substituted: SI 2008/164 Reg.5
Reg.4, amended: SI 2008/164 Reg.6

NO.

2007–cont.

1097. Stamp Duty and Stamp Duty Reserve Tax (Investment Exchanges and Clearing Houses) (Eurex Clearing AG) Regulations 2007–*cont.*

Reg.5, amended: SI 2008/164 Reg.7

1099. Children (Allocation of Proceedings) (Amendment No.2) Order 2007

revoked: SI 2008/2836 Sch.2

1100. Mutilations (Permitted Procedures) (England) Regulations 2007

Reg.3, amended: SI 2008/1426 Reg.3
Reg.4, amended: SI 2008/1426 Reg.4
Reg.5, substituted: SI 2008/1426 Reg.5
Sch.1, amended: SI 2008/1426 Reg.6
Sch.4 paraA.1, added: SI 2008/1426 Reg.7
Sch.4 paraA.2, added: SI 2008/1426 Reg.7
Sch.4 paraA.3, added: SI 2008/1426 Reg.7
Sch.4 paraA.4, added: SI 2008/1426 Reg.7
Sch.4 paraA.5, added: SI 2008/1426 Reg.7
Sch.4 para.5, amended: SI 2008/1426 Reg.7
Sch.5 para.1A, added: SI 2008/1426 Reg.8
Sch.5 para.2A, added: SI 2008/1426 Reg.8
Sch.5 para.2B, added: SI 2008/1426 Reg.8
Sch.6 para.1A, added: SI 2008/1426 Reg.9
Sch.6 para.2A, added: SI 2008/1426 Reg.9
Sch.6 para.2B, added: SI 2008/1426 Reg.9

1104. National Health Service (Travelling Expenses and Remission of Charges) (Wales) Regulations 2007

Reg.2, amended: SI 2008/1879 Reg.33, SI 2008/2568 Reg.2
Reg.5, amended: SI 2008/1879 Reg.33, SI 2008/2568 Reg.3
Reg.5, applied: SI 2008/794 Sch.8 para.45, Sch.9 para.37
Reg.6, applied: SI 2008/794 Sch.8 para.45, Sch.9 para.37
Reg.11, applied: SI 2008/794 Sch.8 para.45, Sch.9 para.37
Sch.1, amended: SI 2008/1480 Reg.2

1115. Air Navigation (Isle of Man) Order 2007

Art.3, revoked (in part): SI 2008/1487 Art.5
Art.12, amended: SI 2008/1487 Art.5
Art.13, amended: SI 2008/1487 Art.5
Art.17, amended: SI 2008/1487 Art.5
Art.21, amended: SI 2008/1487 Art.5
Art.22, substituted: SI 2008/1487 Art.5
Art.25, amended: SI 2008/1487 Art.3
Art.26, amended: SI 2008/1487 Art.3
Art.27, amended: SI 2008/1487 Art.3
Art.27A, added: SI 2008/1487 Art.3
Art.28A, added: SI 2008/1487 Art.3
Art.37A, added: SI 2008/1487 Art.3
Art.68, amended: SI 2008/1487 Art.3, Art.5
Sch.3 para.5, amended: SI 2008/1487 Art.5
Sch.3 para.6, substituted: SI 2008/1487 Art.5
Sch.4 para.2, amended: SI 2008/1487 Art.4
Sch.4 para.4, amended: SI 2008/1487 Art.4

NO.

2007–cont.

1158. Immigration and Nationality (Fees) Regulations 2007
Reg.2, amended: SI 2008/544 Reg.2, SI 2008/1695 Reg.2, SI 2008/3017 Reg.2
Reg.4, revoked: SI 2008/544 Reg.2
Reg.5, revoked (in part): SI 2008/1695 Reg.2
Reg.5A, added: SI 2008/544 Reg.2
Reg.5A, amended: SI 2008/3017 Reg.2
Reg.5A, substituted: SI 2008/1695 Reg.2
Reg.5B, added: SI 2008/544 Reg.2
Reg.5B, amended: SI 2008/1695 Reg.2
Reg.5B, revoked (in part): SI 2008/1695 Reg.2
Reg.5C, added: SI 2008/1695 Reg.2
Reg.7, amended: SI 2008/544 Reg.2
Reg.9, amended: SI 2008/544 Reg.2, SI 2008/1695 Reg.2
Reg.9, substituted: SI 2008/3017 Reg.2
Reg.10, amended: SI 2008/544 Reg.2
Reg.11, amended: SI 2008/544 Reg.2
Reg.12, amended: SI 2008/544 Reg.2, SI 2008/1695 Reg.2, SI 2008/3017 Reg.2
Reg.15, revoked (in part): SI 2008/1695 Reg.2, SI 2008/3017 Reg.2
Reg.16, revoked: SI 2008/3017 Reg.2
Reg.17, amended: SI 2008/544 Reg.2
Reg.17, revoked: SI 2008/1695 Reg.2
Reg.18, revoked: SI 2008/3017 Reg.2
Reg.20, amended: SI 2008/1695 Reg.2
Reg.20A, added: SI 2008/544 Reg.2
Reg.20A, amended: SI 2008/3017 Reg.2
Reg.20A, substituted: SI 2008/1695 Reg.2
Reg.20AA, added: SI 2008/3017 Reg.2
Reg.20B, added: SI 2008/544 Reg.2
Reg.20B, amended: SI 2008/1695 Reg.2
Reg.20B, substituted: SI 2008/3017 Reg.2
Reg.20C, added: SI 2008/544 Reg.2
Reg.20C, amended: SI 2008/1695 Reg.2, SI 2008/3017 Reg.2
Reg.20C, revoked (in part): SI 2008/3017 Reg.2
Reg.20D, added: SI 2008/544 Reg.2
Reg.20E, added: SI 2008/544 Reg.2
Reg.20F, added: SI 2008/1695 Reg.2

1166. Local Government Pension Scheme (Benefits, Membership and Contributions) Regulations 2007
applied: SI 2008/238 Reg.6, SI 2008/239 Reg.5, Reg.7, Reg.11, Reg.14, Reg.18, Reg.19, Reg.30, Reg.43, Reg.45, Reg.51, Reg.72, Reg.76, Sch.3 para.1, Sch.3 para.3, Sch.3 para.7, SI 2008/1419 Reg.5
referred to: SI 2008/239 Reg.79, Reg.81
Reg.1, amended: SI 2008/1083 Reg.3, SI 2008/2425 Reg.16
Reg.2, applied: SI 2008/238 Reg.3, Reg.8, SI 2008/239 Reg.4
Reg.2, substituted: SI 2008/1083 Reg.4
Reg.3, amended: SI 2008/1083 Reg.5
Reg.3, applied: SI 2008/238 Reg.8, Reg.9, SI 2008/239 Reg.13, Reg.19, Reg.20, Reg.39

NO.

2007–cont.

1166. Local Government Pension Scheme (Benefits, Membership and Contributions) Regulations 2007–*cont.*
Reg.3, referred to: SI 2008/239 Reg.42
Reg.5, amended: SI 2008/1083 Reg.6
Reg.6, applied: SI 2008/239 Reg.15
Reg.6, substituted: SI 2008/1083 Reg.7
Reg.7, amended: SI 2008/1083 Reg.8
Reg.7, applied: SI 2008/239 Reg.17, Reg.46
Reg.8, amended: SI 2008/1083 Reg.9
Reg.8, applied: SI 2008/238 Reg.3
Reg.8, revoked (in part): SI 2008/1083 Reg.9
Reg.9, applied: SI 2008/238 Reg.3
Reg.9, revoked (in part): SI 2008/1083 Reg.10
Reg.10, applied: SI 2008/238 Reg.3
Reg.10, substituted: SI 2008/1083 Reg.11
Reg.11, applied: SI 2008/238 Reg.3
Reg.12, amended: SI 2008/2425 Reg.17
Reg.12, applied: SI 2008/238 Sch.2 para.3, Sch.2 para.6, SI 2008/239 Reg.40, Reg.66
Reg.13, applied: SI 2008/239 Reg.40, Reg.66
Reg.15, referred to: SI 2008/239 Reg.28
Reg.16, applied: SI 2008/238 Reg.3, SI 2008/239 Reg.15, Reg.26, Reg.50
Reg.17, applied: SI 2008/238 Reg.3, SI 2008/239 Reg.15, Reg.26, Reg.50
Reg.18, amended: SI 2008/1083 Reg.12
Reg.18, applied: SI 2008/238 Reg.3, Sch.2 para.1, Sch.2 para.3, SI 2008/239 Reg.15, Reg.26, Reg.41, Reg.50, Reg.66, Reg.71
Reg.18, referred to: SI 2008/239 Reg.41
Reg.19, applied: SI 2008/238 Reg.3, SI 2008/239 Reg.15, Reg.26, Reg.41, Reg.50
Reg.20, applied: SI 2008/238 Reg.3, SI 2008/239 Reg.15, Reg.26, Reg.41, Reg.50, Reg.56
Reg.20, substituted: SI 2008/1083 Reg.13
Reg.21, applied: SI 2008/239 Reg.51
Reg.23, amended: SI 2008/2425 Reg.18
Reg.23, applied: SI 2008/239 Reg.51
Reg.24, applied: SI 2008/238 Reg.3, SI 2008/239 Reg.50
Reg.25, amended: SI 2008/1083 Reg.14
Reg.25, applied: SI 2008/239 Reg.58
Reg.26, substituted: SI 2008/1083 Reg.15
Reg.27, applied: SI 2008/239 Reg.50
Reg.29, amended: SI 2008/2425 Reg.19
Reg.29, applied: SI 2008/239 Reg.15
Reg.29, substituted: SI 2008/1083 Reg.16
Reg.30, amended: SI 2008/1083 Reg.17
Reg.30, applied: SI 2008/238 Reg.3, Reg.10, SI 2008/239 Reg.15, Reg.26, Reg.50, Reg.66
Reg.31, applied: SI 2008/239 Reg.15, Reg.26, Reg.41, Reg.50, Reg.56
Reg.31, substituted: SI 2008/1083 Reg.18
Reg.32, amended: SI 2008/2425 Reg.20
Reg.32, applied: SI 2008/239 Reg.51
Reg.33, amended: SI 2008/1083 Reg.19

NO.

2007–cont.

1166. Local Government Pension Scheme (Benefits, Membership and Contributions) Regulations 2007–*cont.*
Reg.33, applied: SI 2008/238 Reg.3, SI 2008/239 Reg.50
Reg.35, amended: SI 2008/1083 Reg.20
Reg.35, applied: SI 2008/239 Reg.51
Reg.36, amended: SI 2008/1083 Reg.21
Reg.36, applied: SI 2008/238 Reg.3, SI 2008/239 Reg.50, Reg.51
Reg.37, applied: SI 2008/239 Reg.50
Reg.39, applied: SI 2008/239 Reg.51
Reg.39, substituted: SI 2008/1083 Reg.22
Reg.41, added: SI 2008/1083 Reg.23
Reg.42, added: SI 2008/1083 Reg.23

1167. Consumer Credit (Information Requirements and Duration of Licences and Charges) Regulations 2007
Reg.6, amended: SI 2008/1751 Reg.2
Reg.7, amended: SI 2008/1751 Reg.2
Reg.9, amended: SI 2008/1751 Reg.2
Reg.9, revoked (in part): SI 2008/1751 Reg.2
Reg.10, amended: SI 2008/1751 Reg.2
Reg.11, revoked: SI 2008/2826 Art.7
Reg.12, amended: SI 2008/1751 Reg.2
Reg.14, substituted: SI 2008/1751 Reg.2
Reg.15, revoked: SI 2008/1751 Reg.2
Reg.16, substituted: SI 2008/1751 Reg.2
Reg.17, amended: SI 2008/1751 Reg.2
Reg.19, amended: SI 2008/1751 Reg.2
Reg.20, amended: SI 2008/1751 Reg.2
Reg.21, amended: SI 2008/1751 Reg.2
Reg.22, amended: SI 2008/1751 Reg.2
Reg.23, amended: SI 2008/1751 Reg.2
Reg.38, revoked (in part): SI 2008/1751 Reg.2
Reg.40, amended: SI 2008/1751 Reg.2
Reg.50, amended: SI 2008/1751 Reg.2
Sch.3 Part 3 para.8, amended: SI 2008/1751 Reg.2
Sch.3 Part 3 para.10, amended: SI 2008/1751 Reg.2
Sch.5 Part 1 para.6, substituted: SI 2008/1751 Reg.2

1174. Criminal Defence Service (Funding) Order 2007
referred to: SI 2008/2930 Art.2
Art.3, amended: SI 2008/957 Art.2
Sch.2 Part 4 para.25, added: SI 2008/957 Art.3
Sch.2 Part 4 para.25, amended: SI 2008/2930 Art.3, Art.4
Sch.2 Part 4 para.25, applied: SI 2008/2930 Art.1

1320. Health Service Medicines (Information Relating to Sales of Branded Medicines etc.) Regulations 2007
Reg.2, amended: SI 2008/3258 Reg.8
Reg.3, substituted: SI 2008/1938 Reg.7, SI 2008/3258 Reg.8

NO.

2007–cont.

1320. Health Service Medicines (Information Relating to Sales of Branded Medicines etc.) Regulations 2007–*cont.*
Reg.4, amended: SI 2008/3258 Reg.8
Reg.5, amended: SI 2008/3258 Reg.8
Sch.1 para.1, amended: SI 2008/3258 Reg.8
Sch.1 para.2, amended: SI 2008/3258 Reg.8

1334. Export Control (North Korea) Order 2007
Art.1, amended: SI 2008/3231 Sch.6
Art.2, revoked: SI 2008/3231 Sch.6
Art.3, revoked: SI 2008/3231 Sch.6

1336. Education (Student Fees, Awards and Support) (Amendment) Regulations 2007
Reg.11, revoked: SI 2008/529 Reg.3
Reg.12, revoked: SI 2008/529 Reg.3
Reg.13, revoked: SI 2008/529 Reg.3
Reg.14, revoked: SI 2008/529 Reg.3
Reg.15, revoked: SI 2008/529 Reg.3
Reg.16, revoked: SI 2008/529 Reg.3
Reg.17, revoked: SI 2008/529 Reg.3
Reg.18, revoked: SI 2008/529 Reg.3
Reg.19, revoked: SI 2008/529 Reg.3
Reg.20, revoked: SI 2008/529 Reg.3
Reg.21, revoked: SI 2008/529 Reg.3
Reg.27, revoked: SI 2008/529 Reg.3
Reg.28, revoked: SI 2008/529 Reg.3
Reg.29, revoked: SI 2008/529 Reg.3
Reg.30, revoked: SI 2008/529 Reg.3
Reg.31, revoked: SI 2008/529 Reg.3
Reg.32, revoked: SI 2008/529 Reg.3
Reg.33, revoked: SI 2008/529 Reg.3
Reg.34, revoked: SI 2008/529 Reg.3
Reg.35, revoked: SI 2008/529 Reg.3
Reg.36, revoked: SI 2008/529 Reg.3
Reg.37, revoked: SI 2008/529 Reg.3

1348. Veterinary Surgeons Qualifications (European Recognition) Order 2007
revoked: SI 2008/1824 Reg.3

1349. European Communities (Designation) (No.2) Order 2007
Sch.1, amended: SI 2008/1792 Sch.1

1351. Safeguarding Vulnerable Groups (Northern Ireland) Order 2007
applied: SI 2008/1592 Art.2, SI 2008/2553 Art.5, SI 2008/2554 Art.5, SI 2008/2927 Reg.2, SI 2008/3047 Art.5, SI 2008/3148 Sch.1
Art.60, referred to: SI 2008/1769 Sch.2 para.2
Sch.8, referred to: SI 2008/1769 Sch.2 para.2

1365. Education (School Information) (England) (Amendment) Regulations 2007
revoked: SI 2008/3093 Sch.1

NO.

2007–cont.

1388. Government of Wales Act 2006 (Consequential Modifications and Transitional Provisions) Order 2007
Sch.1 para.53, revoked: SI 2008/2833 Sch.3 para.228

1415. Local Authority Targets (Well-Being of Young Children) Regulations 2007
Reg.1, amended: SI 2008/1437 Reg.3
Reg.3, amended: SI 2008/1437 Reg.4

1488. Local Government Pension Scheme (Amendment) (No.2) Regulations 2007
revoked: SI 2008/238 Sch.1

1492. Whole of Government Accounts (Designation of Bodies) Order 2007
Sch.1, varied: 2008 c.14 Sch.10 para.1

1518. Marine Works (Environmental Impact Assessment) Regulations 2007
applied: SSI 2008/331 Art.5

1526. Export Control (Iran) Order 2007
Art.1, amended: SI 2008/3063 Art.2

1561. Local Government Pension Scheme (Amendment) (No.3) Regulations 2007
revoked: SI 2008/238 Sch.1

1596. Controls on Dangerous Substances and Preparations (Amendment) Regulations 2007
revoked: SI 2008/2852 Sch.10 Part 1

1601. Value Added Tax (Reduced Rate) Order 2007
Art.5, applied: SI 2008/1410 Art.3

1612. Representation of the People (Northern Ireland) (Amendment) Regulations 2007
revoked: SI 2008/1741 Sch.2

1615. Spreadable Fats (Marketing Standards) (England) (Amendment) Regulations 2007
revoked: SI 2008/1287 Reg.8

1619. Housing Benefit and Council Tax Benefit (War Pension Disregards) Regulations 2007
Sch.1 Part 1 para.1, substituted: SI 2008/3157 Reg.10
Sch.1 Part 2 para.2, substituted: SI 2008/3157 Reg.10
Sch.1 Part 2 para.3, substituted: SI 2008/3157 Reg.10

1623. Cosmetic Products (Safety) (Amendment) Regulations 2007
revoked: SI 2008/1284 Sch.1

1629. Education (Mandatory Awards) (Amendment) Regulations 2007
Reg.13, revoked: SI 2008/1477 Reg.3
Sch.1, revoked: SI 2008/1477 Reg.3

1630. Education (Student Loans) (Amendment) (England and Wales) Regulations 2007
Reg.9, revoked: SI 2008/1479 Reg.4

NO.

2007–cont.

1655. Civil Jurisdiction and Judgments Regulations 2007
see *Crucial Music Corp (formerly Onemusic Corp) v Klondyke Management AG (formerly Point Classics AG)* [2007] EWHC 1782 (Ch), [2008] Bus. L.R. 327 (Ch D), Bernard Livesey Q.C.

1667. Home Information Pack (No.2) Regulations 2007
applied: SI 2008/898 Art.2
referred to: SI 2008/1266 Reg.2
Reg.1, amended: SI 2008/572 Reg.3
Reg.2, amended: SI 2008/572 Reg.3, SI 2008/3107 Reg.8
Reg.8, amended: SI 2008/572 Reg.2, SI 2008/3107 Reg.3, Reg.9
Reg.8, revoked (in part): SI 2008/3107 Reg.3
Reg.9, amended: SI 2008/3107 Reg.4
Reg.10A, amended: SI 2008/1266 Reg.2
Reg.13, amended: SI 2008/572 Reg.3, SI 2008/3107 Reg.11
Reg.14, amended: SI 2008/572 Reg.3, SI 2008/3107 Reg.12
Reg.15, amended: SI 2008/2363 Reg.5
Reg.16, amended: SI 2008/1266 Reg.2, SI 2008/3107 Reg.5
Reg.22A, added: SI 2008/572 Reg.3
Reg.30, revoked (in part): SI 2008/3107 Reg.6
Reg.34, amended: SI 2008/1266 Reg.2, SI 2008/3107 Reg.5
Reg.34A, added: SI 2008/572 Reg.3
Sch.2A para.1, added: SI 2008/572 Reg.2
Sch.2A para.2, added: SI 2008/572 Reg.2
Sch.2A para.3, added: SI 2008/572 Reg.2
Sch.2A para.4, added: SI 2008/572 Reg.2
Sch.5 para.1, amended: SI 2008/3107 Reg.7
Sch.5 para.1, revoked (in part): SI 2008/3107 Reg.7
Sch.5 para.1, amended: SI 2008/3107 Reg.7
Sch.5 para.1A, amended: SI 2008/3107 Reg.7
Sch.5 para.2, amended: SI 2008/3107 Reg.7
Sch.5 para.2, revoked (in part): SI 2008/3107 Reg.7
Sch.5 para.2, amended: SI 2008/3107 Reg.7
Sch.5 para.3, amended: SI 2008/3107 Reg.7
Sch.5 para.3A, amended: SI 2008/3107 Reg.7
Sch.5 para.4, amended: SI 2008/3107 Reg.7
Sch.6 Part 2 para.4, amended: SI 2008/572 Reg.4, SI 2008/3107 Reg.5
Sch.11 Part 1 para.1, added: SI 2008/3107 Reg.10
Sch.11 Part 2 para.2, added: SI 2008/3107 Reg.10
Sch.11 Part 2 para.3, added: SI 2008/3107 Reg.10
Sch.11 Part 2 para.4, added: SI 2008/3107 Reg.10

NO.

2007–cont.

1667. Home Information Pack (No.2) Regulations 2007–*cont.*
Sch.11 Part 3 para.5, added: SI 2008/3107 Reg.10
Sch.12 Part 1 para.1, added: SI 2008/3107 Reg.10
Sch.12 Part 2 para.2, added: SI 2008/3107 Reg.10
Sch.12 Part 2 para.3, added: SI 2008/3107 Reg.10
Sch.12 Part 2 para.4, added: SI 2008/3107 Reg.10
Sch.12 Part 3 para.5, added: SI 2008/3107 Reg.10

1672. Health and Safety (Fees) (Amendment) Regulations 2007
revoked: SI 2008/736 Reg.23

1680. Consular Fees (Amendment) Order 2007
revoked: SI 2008/676 Sch.2

1684. Protection of Children and Vulnerable Adults and Care Standards Tribunal (Amendment) Regulations 2007
revoked: SI 2008/2683 Sch.2

1708. Poultry Breeding Flocks and Hatcheries (Wales) Order 2007
revoked: SI 2008/524 Art.14

1709. Secure Training Centre (Amendment) Rules 2007
see *R. (on the application of C) v Secretary of State for Justice* [2008] EWCA Civ 882, Times, October 14, 2008 (CA (Civ Div)), Buxton, L.J.

1711. Transfrontier Shipment of Waste Regulations 2007
Reg.4, amended: SI 2008/9 Reg.3
Reg.19, amended: SI 2008/9 Reg.4
Reg.23A, added: SI 2008/9 Reg.5
Reg.23B, added: SI 2008/9 Reg.5

1720. Education (Outturn Statements) (England) Regulations 2007
revoked: SI 2008/1575 Reg.3

1750. Home Loss Payments (Prescribed Amounts) (England) Regulations 2007
revoked: SI 2008/1598 Reg.3

1764. Disability Discrimination (General Qualifications Bodies) (Relevant Qualifications, Reasonable Steps and Physical Features) Regulations 2007
Reg.3, amended: SI 2008/2159 Reg.2
Sch.1, amended: SI 2008/2159 Reg.2

1766. NHS Foundation Trusts (Trust Funds Appointment of Trustees) Order 2007
applied: SI 2008/1902 Art.4
Sch.1, amended: SI 2008/1902 Art.2

1768. Digital Switchover (Disclosure of Information) Act 2007 (Prescription of Information) Order 2007
Art.3, amended: SI 2008/2557 Art.2

NO.

2007–cont.

1771. Early Years Foundation Stage (Welfare Requirements) Regulations 2007
Reg.2, amended: SI 2008/1953 Reg.3
Reg.3, amended: SI 2008/1953 Reg.4
Reg.3A, added: SI 2008/1953 Reg.5
Reg.3A, applied: SI 2008/2261 Sch.2 para.7
Reg.3B, added: SI 2008/1953 Reg.5
Reg.3C, added: SI 2008/1953 Reg.5
Reg.7, amended: SI 2008/1953 Reg.6
Reg.8, amended: SI 2008/1953 Reg.6, Reg.7
Reg.9, amended: SI 2008/1953 Reg.6
Reg.9, applied: SI 2008/2261 Sch.2 para.22
Reg.10, amended: SI 2008/1953 Reg.6
Reg.11, amended: SI 2008/1953 Reg.6
Sch.1 para.5, amended: SI 2008/1953 Reg.8
Sch.1 para.8, amended: SI 2008/1953 Reg.8
Sch.1 para.9, amended: SI 2008/1953 Reg.8
Sch.1 para.12, added: SI 2008/1953 Reg.8

1772. Early Years Foundation Stage (Learning and Development Requirements) Order 2007
Art.2, amended: SI 2008/1952 Art.2

1831. Crime and Disorder (Prescribed Information) Regulations 2007
Sch.1 para.1, amended: SI 2008/1406 Reg.3
Sch.1 para.2, amended: SI 2008/1406 Reg.3

1863. Export and Trade Control Order 2007
revoked: SI 2008/3231 Sch.6

1865. Student Fees (Amounts) (England) (Amendment) Regulations 2007
revoked: SI 2008/2507 Reg.3

1870. Education (Provision of Full-Time Education for Excluded Pupils) (England) Regulations 2007
Reg.10, revoked (in part): SI 2008/532 Reg.11

1894. Coal Mines (Control of Inhalable Dust) Regulations 2007
Reg.2, amended: SI 2008/960 Sch.3

1898. Mental Capacity Act 2005 (Transitional and Consequential Provisions) Order 2007
Sch.1 para.23, revoked: SI 2008/2836 Sch.2

1905. Spreadable Fats (Marketing Standards) (Wales) (Amendment) Regulations 2007
revoked: SI 2008/1341 Reg.8

1929. Air Navigation (Restriction of Flying) (Nuclear Installations) Regulations 2007
Sch.2, amended: SI 2008/3169 Reg.3

1932. Police Pension Fund Regulations 2007
Reg.2, amended: SI 2008/1887 Reg.44
Reg.4, amended: SI 2008/1887 Reg.45
Reg.5, amended: SI 2008/1887 Reg.46
Reg.12, amended: SI 2008/1887 Reg.47
Reg.12A, added: SI 2008/1887 Reg.48

NO.

2007–cont.

1949. European Grouping of Territorial Cooperation Regulations 2007
Reg.2, amended: SI 2008/728 Reg.2
Reg.4, revoked (in part): SI 2008/728 Reg.2
Reg.6, amended: SI 2008/728 Reg.2, SI 2008/948 Sch.1 para.36
Reg.6, revoked (in part): SI 2008/728 Reg.2
Sch.1 Part 1 para.1, revoked: SI 2008/728 Reg.2
Sch.1 Part 1 para.2, revoked: SI 2008/728 Reg.2
Sch.1 Part 1 para.3, revoked: SI 2008/728 Reg.2
Sch.1 Part 1 para.4, revoked: SI 2008/728 Reg.2
Sch.1 Part 1 para.5, revoked: SI 2008/728 Reg.2

1971. Gas (Applications for Licences and Extensions and Restrictions of Licences) Regulations 2007
applied: SI 2008/2375 Reg.2
revoked: SI 2008/2375 Reg.1

1972. Electricity (Applications for Licences, Modifications of an Area and Extensions and Restrictions of Licences) Regulations 2007
applied: SI 2008/2376 Reg.2
revoked: SI 2008/2376 Reg.1

1976. Trade Marks (Relative Grounds) Order 2007
applied: SI 2008/2206 Art.3
varied: SI 2008/2206 Art.3
see *West v Hudson* [2007] EWHC 1938 (Ch), (2008) 31 (2) I.P.D. 31009 (Ch D), Sir Andrew Morritt (Chancellor)
Art.4, applied: SI 2008/1797 r.14

2053. Traffic Management Act 2004 (Commencement No.5 and Transitional Provisions) (England) Order 2007
Art.1, amended: SI 2008/757 Art.3
Art.3, amended: SI 2008/757 Art.4
Art.5, added: SI 2008/757 Art.5
Art.6, added: SI 2008/757 Art.5
Art.7, added: SI 2008/757 Art.5
Art.8, added: SI 2008/757 Art.5

2074. Zoonoses and Animal By-Products (Fees) (England) Regulations 2007
revoked: SI 2008/2270 Reg.4

2076. Trade Marks (Amendment) Rules 2007
revoked: SI 2008/1797 Sch.2

2077. Trade Marks (Fees) (Amendment) Rules 2007
revoked: SI 2008/1958 r.4

2083. Pesticides (Maximum Residue Levels in Crops, Food and Feeding Stuffs) (England and Wales) (Amendment) (No.2) Regulations 2007
revoked: SI 2008/2570 Sch.2

NO.

2007–cont.

2124. Consular Fees (Amendment) (No.2) Order 2007
revoked: SI 2008/676 Sch.2

2125. Films Co-Production Agreements (Amendment) Order 2007
revoked: SI 2008/1783 Art.3

2147. Group Relief for Overseas Losses (Modification of the Corporation Tax Acts for Non-resident Insurance Companies) (No.2) (Amendment) Regulations 2007
revoked: SI 2008/2646 Reg.5

2157. Money Laundering Regulations 2007
applied: SI 2008/668 r.15
referred to: SI 2008/668 r.26

2175. Family Proceedings Fees (Amendment) (No.2) Order 2007
revoked: SI 2008/1054 Sch.3

2176. Civil Proceedings Fees (Amendment) (No.2) Order 2007
revoked: SI 2008/1053 Sch.3

2182. Children Act 2004 Information Database (England) Regulations 2007
Sch.3 para.5, substituted: SI 2008/912 Sch.2 para.15
Sch.4 para.4, added: SI 2008/912 Sch.2 para.15

2185. Judicial Pensions and Retirement Act 1993 (Addition of Qualifying Judicial Offices) (No.2) Order 2007
revoked: SI 2008/2833 Sch.3 para.228

2194. Companies Act 2006 (Commencement No.3, Consequential Amendments, Transitional Provisions and Savings) Order 2007
Sch.1 para.1, revoked: SI 2008/2860 Art.6
Sch.1 para.2, revoked: SI 2008/2860 Art.6
Sch.1 para.3, revoked: SI 2008/2860 Art.6
Sch.1 para.4, revoked: SI 2008/2860 Art.6
Sch.1 para.5, revoked: SI 2008/2860 Art.6
Sch.1 para.6, revoked: SI 2008/2860 Art.6
Sch.1 para.7, revoked: SI 2008/2860 Art.6
Sch.1 para.8, revoked: SI 2008/2860 Art.6
Sch.1 para.9, revoked: SI 2008/2860 Art.6
Sch.1 para.10, revoked: SI 2008/2860 Art.6
Sch.1 para.11, revoked: SI 2008/2860 Art.6
Sch.1 para.12, revoked: SI 2008/2860 Art.6
Sch.1 para.13, revoked: SI 2008/2860 Art.6
Sch.1 para.14, revoked: SI 2008/2860 Art.6
Sch.1 para.15, referred to: SI 2008/674 Sch.3 para.4
Sch.1 para.15, revoked: SI 2008/2860 Art.6
Sch.1 para.16, revoked: SI 2008/2860 Art.6
Sch.1 para.17, revoked: SI 2008/2860 Art.6
Sch.1 para.18, revoked: SI 2008/2860 Art.6
Sch.1 para.19, revoked: SI 2008/2860 Art.6
Sch.1 para.20, revoked: SI 2008/2860 Art.6
Sch.1 para.21, revoked: SI 2008/2860 Art.6
Sch.3 para.26A, added: SI 2008/674 Sch.3 para.2

NO.

2007–cont.

2194. Companies Act 2006 (Commencement No.3, Consequential Amendments, Transitional Provisions and Savings) Order 2007–*cont.*
Sch.3 para.48, amended: SI 2008/674 Sch.3 para.2
Sch.4 Part 1 para.1, revoked (in part): SI 2008/948 Sch.2
Sch.4 Part 2 para.17, revoked (in part): SI 2008/948 Sch.2
Sch.4 Part 3 para.83, revoked: 2008 c.17 Sch.16

2203. Diseases of Animals (Approved Disinfectants) (Fees) (England) Order 2007
revoked: SI 2008/652 Art.3

2204. Civil Procedure (Amendment) Rules 2007
see *Saulle v Nouvet* [2007] EWHC 2902 (QB), [2008] LS Law Medical 201 (QBD), Andrew Edis Q.C.

2245. Eggs and Chicks (England) Regulations 2007
applied: SI 2008/1718 Reg.22
revoked: SI 2008/1718 Reg.2
varied: SI 2008/1718 Reg.22

2263. Education (Student Fees, Awards and Support) (Amendment) (No.2) Regulations 2007
Reg.9, revoked: SI 2008/529 Reg.3
Reg.10, revoked: SI 2008/529 Reg.3
Reg.11, revoked: SI 2008/529 Reg.3
Reg.12, revoked: SI 2008/529 Reg.3
Reg.13, revoked: SI 2008/529 Reg.3
Reg.14, revoked: SI 2008/529 Reg.3
Reg.15, revoked: SI 2008/529 Reg.3
Reg.16, revoked: SI 2008/529 Reg.3
Reg.17, revoked: SI 2008/529 Reg.3
Reg.18, revoked: SI 2008/529 Reg.3
Reg.19, revoked: SI 2008/529 Reg.3
Reg.20, revoked: SI 2008/529 Reg.3
Reg.21, revoked: SI 2008/529 Reg.3
Reg.22, revoked: SI 2008/529 Reg.3
Reg.23, revoked: SI 2008/529 Reg.3
Reg.24, revoked: SI 2008/529 Reg.3

2282. Education (School Teachers Pay and Conditions) Order 2007
revoked: SI 2008/2155 Art.3

2310. Education (Fees and Awards) (Wales) Regulations 2007
Reg.2, amended: SI 2008/1259 Reg.4
Sch.1 para.3, amended: SI 2008/1259 Reg.5
Sch.1 para.6, substituted: SI 2008/1259 Reg.5
Sch.1 para.7, amended: SI 2008/1259 Reg.5
Sch.1 para.8, amended: SI 2008/1259 Reg.5
Sch.1 para.9, amended: SI 2008/1259 Reg.5
Sch.1 para.9, revoked (in part): SI 2008/1259 Reg.5
Sch.1 para.10, amended: SI 2008/1259 Reg.5
Sch.1 para.11, amended: SI 2008/1259 Reg.5

NO.

2007–cont.

2310. Education (Fees and Awards) (Wales) Regulations 2007–*cont.*
Sch.1 para.12, amended: SI 2008/1259 Reg.5

2313. Assembly Learning Grants (European Institutions) (Wales) Regulations 2007
revoked (in part): SI 2008/18 Reg.5
Reg.9, amended: SI 2008/18 Sch.1 para.1
Reg.10, amended: SI 2008/18 Sch.1 para.2, Sch.1 para.3
Reg.17, amended: SI 2008/18 Sch.1 para.4
Sch.2 Part 2 para.6, amended: SI 2008/18 Sch.1 para.5
Sch.3 Part 2 para.2, amended: SI 2008/18 Sch.1 para.6
Sch.3 Part 2 para.2, revoked (in part): SI 2008/18 Sch.1 para.7

2318. National Minimum Wage Regulations 1999 (Amendment) Regulations 2007
Reg.2, revoked: SI 2008/1894 Reg.8
Reg.4, revoked: SI 2008/1894 Reg.8
Reg.8, revoked: SI 2008/1894 Reg.8

2324. Education (School Performance Information) (England) Regulations 2007
referred to: SI 2008/364 Reg.2
Reg.10, revoked: SI 2008/1727 Reg.3
Sch.3 para.2, amended: SI 2008/364 Reg.2
Sch.4 Part 2 para.1, amended: SI 2008/1727 Reg.4
Sch.5 para.1, revoked: SI 2008/1727 Reg.3
Sch.5 para.2, revoked: SI 2008/1727 Reg.3
Sch.5 para.3, revoked: SI 2008/1727 Reg.3
Sch.5 para.4, revoked: SI 2008/1727 Reg.3
Sch.5 para.5, revoked: SI 2008/1727 Reg.3
Sch.6 para.6, amended: SI 2008/1727 Reg.5

2329. Gambling Act 2005 (Advertising of Foreign Gambling) Regulations 2007
Reg.2, amended: SI 2008/2829 Reg.2
Reg.2, substituted: SI 2008/19 Reg.2, SI 2008/2829 Reg.2

2336. Legal Officers (Annual Fees) Order 2007
revoked: SI 2008/1969 Art.4

2340. Ecclesiastical Judges, Legal Officers and Others (Fees) Order 2007
revoked: SI 2008/1970 Art.3
Sch.1 Part Table, substituted: SI 2008/1970 Sch.1 Part Table
Sch.1 Part Table a, substituted: SI 2008/1970 Sch.1 Part Table a
Sch.1 Part Table b, substituted: SI 2008/1970 Sch.1 Part Table b
Sch.1 Part Table c, substituted: SI 2008/1970 Sch.1 Part Table c
Sch.1 Part Table d, substituted: SI 2008/1970 Sch.1 Part Table d
Sch.1 Part Table e, substituted: SI 2008/1970 Sch.1 Part Table e

NO.

2007–cont.

2359. Education (Nutritional Standards and Requirements for School Food) (England) Regulations 2007
Reg.2, amended: SI 2008/1800 Reg.3
Reg.10, substituted: SI 2008/1800 Reg.4
Sch.1, amended: SI 2008/1800 Reg.5
Sch.3 Part 2 para.11, amended: SI 2008/1800 Reg.6
Sch.3 Part 2 para.13, amended: SI 2008/1800 Reg.7
Sch.3 Part 2 para.14, amended: SI 2008/1800 Reg.8, Reg.10
Sch.3 Part 2 para.15, added: SI 2008/1800 Reg.9
Sch.3 Part 2 para.16, added: SI 2008/1800 Reg.9

2372. Home Loss Payments (Prescribed Amounts) (Wales) Regulations 2007
referred to: SI 2008/2845 Reg.3
revoked: SI 2008/2845 Reg.3

2398. Agricultural Holdings (Units of Production) (Wales) Order 2007
revoked: SI 2008/253 Art.3

2400. Cosmetic Products (Safety) (Amendment) (No.2) Regulations 2007
revoked: SI 2008/1284 Sch.1

2439. Charges for Residues Surveillance (Amendment) Regulations 2007
revoked: SI 2008/2999 Reg.3

2441. Community Legal Service (Funding) Order 2007
Art.2, applied: SI 2008/2704 Art.3
Art.3, amended: SI 2008/1328 Art.3, SI 2008/2704 Art.6
Art.5, amended: SI 2008/1328 Art.4, SI 2008/2704 Art.7
Sch.1, substituted: SI 2008/1328 Sch.1
Sch.1 Part 001, amended: SI 2008/2704 Art.8
Sch.1 Part 001, substituted: SI 2008/1328 Sch.1
Sch.1 Part 002, amended: SI 2008/2704 Art.9
Sch.1 Part 002, substituted: SI 2008/1328 Sch.1
Sch.1 Part 003, substituted: SI 2008/1328 Sch.1

2460. Smoke Control Areas (Authorised Fuels) (England) (Amendment) Regulations 2007
revoked: SI 2008/514 Sch.2

2462. Smoke Control Areas (Exempted Fireplaces) (England) Order 2007
revoked: SI 2008/515 Art.3

2481. Tax Credits (Child Care Providers) (Miscellaneous Revocation and Transitional Provisions) (England) Scheme 2007
Art.4, amended: SI 2008/2683 Sch.1 para.329

NO.

2007–cont.

2496. Zoonoses and Animal By-Products (Fees) (Wales) Regulations 2007
revoked: SI 2008/2716 Reg.4

2539. Veterinary Medicines Regulations 2007
applied: SI 2008/962 Reg.17, SI 2008/1090 Reg.3, Reg.17
disapplied: SI 2008/962 Reg.3
revoked: SI 2008/2297 Reg.45

2583. Supervision of Accounts and Reports (Prescribed Body) Order 2007
revoked: SI 2008/623 Art.7
Art.2, applied: SI 2008/623 Art.7

2585. Commons (Deregistration and Exchange Orders) (Interim Arrangements) (England) Regulations 2007
applied: SI 2008/1961 Reg.14
revoked (in part): SI 2008/1961 Reg.55

2601. Houses in Multiple Occupation (Specified Educational Establishments) (England) (No.2) Regulations 2007
revoked: SI 2008/2346 Reg.3

2619. Magistrates Courts Fees (Amendment) Order 2007
revoked: SI 2008/1052 Sch.3

2620. Protection of Children and Vulnerable Adults and Care Standards Tribunal (Review of Inclusion in the PoCA List and Review of Section 142 Directions) Regulations 2007
revoked: SI 2008/2683 Sch.2

2687. Education (Listed Bodies) (England) Order 2007
Sch.1 Part 1, amended: SI 2008/2888 Art.3, Art.4, Art.5, Art.6

2688. Education (Recognised Bodies) (England) Order 2007
Sch.1, amended: SI 2008/2889 Art.3, Art.4

2781. European Communities (Recognition of Professional Qualifications) Regulations 2007
Part 2, applied: SI 2008/657 Sch.2 para.10
Part 3, applied: SI 2008/554 Sch.1, SI 2008/657 Sch.2 para.10
Part 3, applied: SI 2008/657 Sch.2 para.10
Reg.3, referred to: SI 2008/554 Sch.1
Reg.7, applied: SI 2008/1284 Reg.18
Reg.20, applied: SI 2008/554 Sch.1
Reg.21, applied: SI 2008/554 Sch.1
Reg.22, applied: SI 2008/554 Sch.1
Reg.23, applied: SI 2008/554 Sch.1
Reg.24, applied: SI 2008/554 Sch.1
Reg.25, applied: SI 2008/554 Sch.1
Reg.26, applied: SI 2008/554 Sch.1
Sch.5, amended: SI 2008/2683 Sch.1 para.330

NO.

2007–cont.

2782. Education (Recognition of School Teachers Professional Qualifications) (Consequential Provisions) (England) Regulations 2007
Reg.3, revoked: SI 2008/657 Sch.1

2786. Plastic Materials and Articles in Contact with Food (Lid Gaskets) (England) Regulations 2007
revoked: SI 2008/916 Reg.29
Reg.2, amended: SI 2008/1642 Reg.6

2790. Materials and Articles in Contact with Food (England) Regulations 2007
Reg.2, amended: SI 2008/916 Reg.28
Reg.9, referred to: SI 2008/916 Reg.13
Reg.10, amended: SI 2008/916 Reg.28
Reg.11, amended: SI 2008/916 Reg.28, SI 2008/1642 Reg.5
Reg.24, revoked: SI 2008/916 Reg.29

2800. Family Proceedings Fees (Amendment) (No.2) (Amendment) Order 2007
revoked: SI 2008/1054 Sch.3

2801. Civil Proceedings Fees (Amendment) (No.2) (Amendment) Order 2007
revoked: SI 2008/1053 Sch.3

2850. Parochial Fees Order 2007
revoked: SI 2008/2470 Art.6

2868. Housing Benefit (Local Housing Allowance and Information Sharing) Amendment Regulations 2007
Reg.3, amended: SI 2008/586 Reg.4
Reg.4, amended: SI 2008/586 Reg.4
Reg.7, amended: SI 2008/586 Reg.4
Reg.8, amended: SI 2008/586 Reg.4
Reg.14, referred to: SI 2008/632 Art.19
Reg.18, applied: SI 2008/2824 Reg.2, Reg.3
Reg.19, amended: SI 2008/586 Reg.4

2869. Housing Benefit (State Pension Credit) (Local Housing Allowance and Information Sharing) Amendment Regulations 2007
Reg.3, amended: SI 2008/586 Reg.5
Reg.4, amended: SI 2008/586 Reg.5
Reg.7, amended: SI 2008/586 Reg.5
Reg.8, amended: SI 2008/586 Reg.5
Reg.14, referred to: SI 2008/632 Art.20
Reg.15, amended: SI 2008/586 Reg.5

2870. Housing Benefit (Local Housing Allowance, Miscellaneous and Consequential) Amendment Regulations 2007
Reg.4, amended: SI 2008/586 Reg.6

2871. Rent Officers (Housing Benefit Functions) Amendment Order 2007
Art.4, amended: SI 2008/587 Art.2
Art.6, amended: SI 2008/587 Art.2
Art.6, revoked (in part): SI 2008/587 Art.2
Art.13, amended: SI 2008/587 Art.2
Art.15, amended: SI 2008/587 Art.2
Art.15, revoked (in part): SI 2008/587 Art.2

NO.

2007–cont.

2951. Administrative Justice and Tribunals Council (Listed Tribunals) Order 2007
Art.2, amended: SI 2008/2683 Sch.1 para.331

2968. Agricultural Holdings (Units of Production) (England) Order 2007
revoked: SI 2008/2708 Art.3

2974. Companies (Cross-Border Mergers) Regulations 2007
Reg.19, amended: SI 2008/583 Reg.2
Reg.51, referred to: SI 2008/3232 Sch.1 Part 2

2979. Education (Pupil Referral Units) (Application of Enactments) (England) Regulations 2007
Sch.3 para.1, revoked: SI 2008/3093 Sch.1

2998. Pesticides (Maximum Residue Levels in Crops, Food and Feeding Stuffs) (England and Wales) (Amendment) (No.3) Regulations 2007
revoked: SI 2008/2570 Sch.2

3009. Education (Determination of Admission Arrangements) (Amendment No.2) (England) Regulations 2007
revoked: SI 2008/3089 Sch.1

3072. Renewable Transport Fuel Obligations Order 2007
Art.21, amended: 2008 c.9 s.13

3101. European Qualifications (Health and Social Care Professions) Regulations 2007
Reg.1, amended: SI 2008/462 Reg.2

3134. Nursing and Midwifery Council (Election Scheme) (Amendment) Rules Order of Council 2007
revoked: SI 2008/1485 Sch.2 para.2

3186. Corporation Tax (Implementation of the Mergers Directive) Regulations 2007
Reg.3, applied: SI 2008/1579 Reg.6
Reg.3, varied: SI 2008/1579 Reg.4
Sch.1 Part 1 para.1, varied: SI 2008/1579 Reg.4
Sch.1 Part 1 para.2, varied: SI 2008/1579 Reg.4
Sch.1 Part 1 para.3, varied: SI 2008/1579 Reg.4
Sch.1 Part 1 para.4, varied: SI 2008/1579 Reg.4
Sch.1 Part 1 para.5, varied: SI 2008/1579 Reg.4
Sch.1 Part 1 para.6, varied: SI 2008/1579 Reg.4
Sch.1 Part 1 para.7, varied: SI 2008/1579 Reg.4
Sch.1 Part 1 para.8, varied: SI 2008/1579 Reg.4
Sch.1 Part 1 para.9, varied: SI 2008/1579 Reg.4
Sch.1 Part 1 para.10, revoked: SI 2008/1579 Reg.5

NO.

2007–cont.

3186. Corporation Tax (Implementation of the Mergers Directive) Regulations 2007–*cont.*

Sch.1 Part 1 para.10, varied: SI 2008/1579 Reg.4

Sch.1 Part 2 para.11, varied: SI 2008/1579 Reg.4

Sch.1 Part 2 para.12, varied: SI 2008/1579 Reg.4

Sch.1 Part 2 para.13, varied: SI 2008/1579 Reg.4

Sch.1 Part 2 para.14, varied: SI 2008/1579 Reg.4

Sch.1 Part 3 para.15, varied: SI 2008/1579 Reg.4

Sch.1 Part 3 para.16, varied: SI 2008/1579 Reg.4

Sch.1 Part 3 para.17, varied: SI 2008/1579 Reg.4

Sch.1 Part 4 para.18, varied: SI 2008/1579 Reg.4

Sch.1 Part 4 para.19, varied: SI 2008/1579 Reg.4

Sch.1 Part 4 para.20, varied: SI 2008/1579 Reg.4

Sch.1 Part 4 para.21, varied: SI 2008/1579 Reg.4

Sch.1 Part 4 para.22, varied: SI 2008/1579 Reg.4

Sch.1 Part 4 para.23, varied: SI 2008/1579 Reg.4

Sch.1 Part 4 para.24, varied: SI 2008/1579 Reg.4

Sch.1 Part 5 para.25, varied: SI 2008/1579 Reg.4

Sch.3 Part 1 para.1, varied: SI 2008/1579 Reg.4

Sch.3 Part 2 para.2, varied: SI 2008/1579 Reg.4

Sch.3 Part 3 para.3, varied: SI 2008/1579 Reg.4

Sch.3 Part 3 para.4, varied: SI 2008/1579 Reg.4

Sch.3 Part 3 para.5, varied: SI 2008/1579 Reg.4

3224. Secretaries of State for Children, Schools and Families, for Innovation, Universities and Skills and for Business, Enterprise and Regulatory Reform Order 2007

Sch.1 Part 2 para.32, revoked: SI 2008/2683 Sch.2

Sch.1 Part 2 para.63, revoked (in part): SI 2008/1722 Reg.10

3245. Radioactive Contaminated Land (Modification of Enactments) (England) (Amendment) Regulations 2007

Reg.3, amended: SI 2008/520 Reg.3

Reg.3, revoked (in part): SI 2008/520 Reg.3

NO.

2007–cont.

3250. Radioactive Contaminated Land (Modification of Enactments) (Wales) (Amendment) Regulations 2007

Reg.3, amended: SI 2008/521 Reg.3

Reg.3, revoked (in part): SI 2008/521 Reg.3

3252. Materials and Articles in Contact with Food (Wales) Regulations 2007

referred to: SI 2008/1237 Reg.28

Reg.2, amended: SI 2008/1237 Reg.28, SI 2008/1682 Reg.28

Reg.9, referred to: SI 2008/1237 Reg.13, SI 2008/1682 Reg.13

Reg.10, amended: SI 2008/1237 Reg.28

Reg.11, amended: SI 2008/1237 Reg.28, SI 2008/1682 Reg.28

Reg.24, revoked: SI 2008/1237 Reg.29, SI 2008/1682 Reg.30

3256. Food Labelling (Declaration of Allergens) (England) Regulations 2007

revoked: SI 2008/1188 Reg.3

3277. Animals and Animal Products (Import and Export) (England) (Amendment) Regulations 2007

Reg.2, revoked (in part): SI 2008/3203 Reg.3

3297. Pesticides (Maximum Residue Levels in Crops, Food and Feeding Stuffs) (England and Wales) (Amendment) (No.4) Regulations 2007

revoked: SI 2008/2570 Sch.2

3304. Bluetongue (No.2) Order 2007

revoked: SI 2008/962 Reg.29

3309. Bluetongue (No.2) (Wales) Order 2007

revoked: SI 2008/1090 Reg.29

3379. Food Labelling (Declaration of Allergens) (Wales) Regulations 2007

revoked: SI 2008/1268 Reg.3

3382. Army Terms of Service Regulations 2007

Reg.11, amended: SI 2008/1849 Reg.2

3385. Meat (Official Controls Charges) (England) (No.2) Regulations 2007

revoked: SI 2008/447 Reg.6

3390. Supply of Information (Register of Deaths) (Northern Ireland) Regulations 2007

revoked: SI 2008/700 Art.2

3428. Drinking Milk (Amendment) (England) Regulations 2007

revoked: SI 2008/1317 Reg.8

3429. Milk and Milk Products (Pupils in Educational Establishments) (England) (Amendment) Regulations 2007

revoked: SI 2008/2072 Reg.5

3436. Education (Provision of Information About Young Children) (England) (Amendment) Regulations 2007

revoked: SI 2008/1722 Reg.10

NO.

2007–cont.

3437. Stamp Duty Land Tax (Zero-Carbon Homes Relief) Regulations 2007
Reg.6, amended: SI 2008/1932 Reg.2

3438. Controls on Dangerous Substances and Preparations (Amendment) (No.2) Regulations 2007
revoked: SI 2008/2852 Sch.10 Part 1

3440. Immigration (Designation of Travel Bans) (Amendment) Order 2007
revoked: SI 2008/3052 Art.3

3442. Courts-Martial (Army) Rules 2007
Part 2 r.8, revoked: SI 2008/1699 r.2
Part 2 r.16, revoked: SI 2008/1699 r.2

3443. Courts-Martial (Royal Navy) Rules 2007
Part 2 r.6, revoked: SI 2008/1699 r.4
Part 2 r.13, revoked: SI 2008/1699 r.4

3444. Courts-Martial (Royal Air Force) Rules 2007
Part 2 r.8, revoked: SI 2008/1699 r.3
Part 2 r.16, revoked: SI 2008/1699 r.3

3452. Cosmetic Products (Safety) (Amendment) (No.3) Regulations 2007
revoked: SI 2008/1284 Sch.1

3460. Supply of Information (Register of Deaths) Regulations 2007
revoked: SI 2008/570 Art.2

3461. Meat (Official Controls Charges) (Wales) (No.2) Regulations 2007
revoked: SI 2008/601 Reg.6

3468. Air Navigation (Overseas Territories) Order 2007
Art.19, amended: SI 2008/3125 Art.3
Art.64, amended: SI 2008/3125 Art.4
Art.73, revoked (in part): SI 2008/3125 Art.5
Art.74, substituted: SI 2008/3125 Art.6
Art.104, amended: SI 2008/3125 Art.7
Art.105, amended: SI 2008/3125 Art.8
Art.107, amended: SI 2008/3125 Art.9
Art.135, amended: SI 2008/3125 Art.10
Art.141, amended: SI 2008/3125 Art.11
Art.142, amended: SI 2008/3125 Art.12
Art.155, amended: SI 2008/3125 Art.13
Art.156, amended: SI 2008/3125 Art.14, Art.15, Art.16
Sch.9 para.2, amended: SI 2008/3125 Art.17
Sch.11, amended: SI 2008/3125 Art.18

3483. Civil Enforcement of Parking Contraventions (England) General Regulations 2007
Reg.2, amended: SI 2008/1513 Reg.3
Reg.6, substituted: SI 2008/1513 Reg.4
Reg.17, applied: SI 2008/2995 Sch.1 Part 1

3494. Statutory Auditors and Third Country Auditors Regulations 2007
Reg.1, amended: SI 2008/499 Reg.2
Reg.7, revoked (in part): SI 2008/499 Reg.2
Reg.15, amended: SI 2008/499 Reg.2
Reg.29, substituted: SI 2008/2639 Reg.2

NO.

2007–cont.

3494. Statutory Auditors and Third Country Auditors Regulations 2007–*cont.*
Reg.34, amended: SI 2008/499 Reg.2
Reg.35, amended: SI 2008/2639 Reg.2
Reg.35, applied: SI 2008/2639 Reg.3
Reg.36, amended: SI 2008/499 Reg.2
Reg.37, varied: SI 2008/2639 Reg.3
Reg.39, amended: SI 2008/2639 Reg.2
Reg.40, amended: SI 2008/2639 Reg.2

3495. Companies Act 2006 (Commencement No.5, Transitional Provisions and Savings) Order 2007
Art.9, amended: SI 2008/674 Sch.3 para.3
Art.10, referred to: SI 2008/674 Sch.3 para.4
Sch.1 Part 1 para.1, revoked: SI 2008/674 Sch.3 para.5, SI 2008/2860 Art.6
Sch.1 Part 1 para.2, revoked: SI 2008/674 Sch.3 para.5, SI 2008/2860 Art.6
Sch.1 Part 1 para.3, revoked: SI 2008/2860 Art.6
Sch.1 Part 1 para.4, revoked: SI 2008/2860 Art.6
Sch.1 Part 1 para.5, revoked: SI 2008/2860 Art.6
Sch.1 Part 1 para.6, revoked: SI 2008/2860 Art.6
Sch.1 Part 1 para.7, revoked: SI 2008/2860 Art.6
Sch.1 Part 1 para.8, revoked: SI 2008/2860 Art.6
Sch.1 Part 1 para.9, revoked: SI 2008/2860 Art.6
Sch.1 Part 1 para.10, revoked: SI 2008/2860 Art.6
Sch.1 Part 1 para.11, revoked: SI 2008/2860 Art.6
Sch.1 Part 1 para.12, revoked: SI 2008/2860 Art.6
Sch.1 Part 1 para.13, revoked: SI 2008/2860 Art.6
Sch.1 Part 1 para.14, revoked: SI 2008/2860 Art.6
Sch.1 Part 1 para.15, revoked: SI 2008/2860 Art.6
Sch.1 Part 1 para.16, revoked: SI 2008/2860 Art.6
Sch.1 Part 1 para.17, revoked: SI 2008/2860 Art.6
Sch.1 Part 1 para.18, revoked: SI 2008/2860 Art.6
Sch.1 Part 1 para.19, revoked: SI 2008/2860 Art.6
Sch.1 Part 1 para.20, revoked: SI 2008/2860 Art.6
Sch.1 Part 1 para.21, revoked: SI 2008/2860 Art.6
Sch.1 Part 2 para.22, revoked: SI 2008/2860 Art.6
Sch.1 Part 2 para.23, revoked: SI 2008/2860 Art.6

NO.

2007–cont.

3495. Companies Act 2006 (Commencement No.5, Transitional Provisions and Savings) Order 2007–*cont.*
Sch.1 Part 2 para.24, revoked: SI 2008/2860 Art.6
Sch.4 Part 1 para.2, amended: SI 2008/674 Sch.3 para.6
Sch.4 Part 1 para.15, amended: SI 2008/1886 Art.8
Sch.4 Part 1 para.35, amended: SI 2008/674 Sch.3 para.6
Sch.4 Part 1 para.35, applied: SI 2008/948 Art.6
Sch.4 Part 1 para.38, amended: SI 2008/674 Sch.3 para.6
Sch.4 Part 1 para.43, substituted: SI 2008/674 Sch.3 para.6
Sch.5 para.2, amended: SI 2008/674 Sch.3 para.7

3496. Severn Bridges Tolls Order 2007
revoked: SI 2008/3263 Art.3

3517. Land Registration (Proper Office) Order 2007
revoked: SI 2008/3201 Art.4
Art.2, amended: SI 2008/1921 Art.2

3521. Infant Formula and Follow-on Formula (England) Regulations 2007
Reg.3, amended: SI 2008/2445 Reg.2
Reg.20, amended: SI 2008/2445 Reg.2
Reg.26, amended: SI 2008/2445 Reg.2
Reg.27, amended: SI 2008/2445 Reg.2
Reg.31, amended: SI 2008/2445 Reg.2

3538. Environmental Permitting (England and Wales) Regulations 2007
applied: SI 2008/314 Reg.8
referred to: SI 2008/314 Reg.3
Reg.39, revoked (in part): 2008 c.27 s.88

3544. Legislative and Regulatory Reform (Regulatory Functions) Order 2007
Sch.1 Part 1, added: SI 2008/574 Sch.1 para.9
Sch.1 Part 1, amended: SI 2008/574 Sch.1 para.9, SI 2008/960 Sch.3
Sch.1 Part 3, amended: SI 2008/1277 Sch.2 para.115, Sch.4 Part 2, SI 2008/1284 Reg.26, SI 2008/1597 Sch.7 para.7, SI 2008/1816 Sch.1 para.6, Sch.2

3570. Employment Rights (Increase of Limits) Order 2007
revoked: SI 2008/3055 Art.2

3573. Infant Formula and Follow-on Formula (Wales) Regulations 2007
Reg.3, substituted: SI 2008/2602 Reg.2
Reg.20, amended: SI 2008/2602 Reg.2
Reg.26, amended: SI 2008/2602 Reg.2
Reg.27, amended: SI 2008/2602 Reg.2
Reg.31, amended: SI 2008/2602 Reg.2

3612. General Commissioners and Special Commissioners (Jurisdiction and Procedure) (Amendment) Regulations 2007
applied: SI 2008/562 Reg.20

NO.

2008

4. Information as to Provision of Education (England) Regulations 2008
Reg.3, amended: SI 2008/3089 Reg.35

11. Trade Marks and Trade Marks (Fees) (Amendment) Rules 2008
revoked: SI 2008/1958 r.4
r.2, revoked: SI 2008/1797 Sch.2
r.3, revoked: SI 2008/1797 Sch.2
r.4, revoked: SI 2008/1797 Sch.2

18. Assembly Learning Grants (European Institutions) (Wales) Regulations 2008
Reg.3, amended: SI 2008/3114 Reg.4
Reg.9, amended: SI 2008/3114 Reg.5
Reg.10, amended: SI 2008/3114 Reg.6
Reg.18, amended: SI 2008/1324 Reg.5
Reg.22, amended: SI 2008/3114 Reg.7
Reg.25, amended: SI 2008/3114 Sch.1
Reg.27, amended: SI 2008/3114 Sch.1
Reg.28, amended: SI 2008/3114 Sch.1
Reg.29, amended: SI 2008/3114 Sch.1
Reg.30, amended: SI 2008/3114 Sch.1
Sch.2 Part 2 para.8, amended: SI 2008/1324 Reg.6
Sch.3 Part 2 para.2, amended: SI 2008/3114 Sch.1
Sch.3 Part 2 para.4, amended: SI 2008/1324 Reg.7, SI 2008/3114 Sch.1
Sch.3 Part 2 para.7, amended: SI 2008/3114 Sch.1

19. Gambling Act 2005 (Advertising of Foreign Gambling) (Amendment) Regulations 2008
revoked: SI 2008/2829 Reg.3

47. Schools Forums (England) (Amendment) Regulations 2008
applied: SI 2008/2867 Reg.25

48. Absent Voting (Transitional Provisions) (Scotland) Regulations 2008
applied: SI 2008/307 Art.21

51. Hill Farm Allowance Regulations 2008
applied: SI 2008/2708 Sch.1
Reg.2, referred to: SI 2008/2708 Sch.1

56. Plastic Materials and Articles in Contact with Food (Lid Gaskets) (Wales) Regulations 2008
revoked: SI 2008/1237 Reg.29
Reg.2, amended: SI 2008/1682 Reg.29

101. Street Works (Registers, Notices, Directions and Designations) (Wales) Regulations 2008
revoked: SI 2008/540 Reg.20

102. Street Works (Fixed Penalty) (Wales) Regulations 2008
Reg.5, amended: SI 2008/466 Reg.2

115. Family Proceedings Fees (Amendment) Order 2008
revoked: SI 2008/1054 Sch.3

116. Civil Proceedings Fees (Amendment) Order 2008
revoked: SI 2008/1053 Sch.3

NO.

2008-cont.

117. Magistrates Courts Fees (Amendment) Order 2008
revoked: SI 2008/1052 Sch.3

136. Control of School Premises (Wales) Regulations 2008
Reg.10, amended: SI 2008/555 Reg.2

170. Childcare Act 2006 (Provision of Information) (Wales) Regulations 2008
Reg.4, amended: SI 2008/1716 Reg.2

172. Local Government and Public Involvement in Health Act 2007 (Commencement No.2 and Savings) Order 2008
Art.7, amended: SI 2008/337 Art.3

228. School Finance (England) Regulations 2008
applied: SI 2008/2867 Reg.25
Reg.7, disapplied: SI 2008/3016 Art.4
Reg.9, disapplied: SI 2008/3016 Art.4
Reg.12, applied: SI 2008/377 Reg.5
Reg.15, applied: SI 2008/377 Reg.2
Reg.17, applied: SI 2008/377 Reg.2
Sch.2 para.15, referred to: SI 2008/3016 Art.4
Sch.2 para.15, varied: SI 2008/3016 Art.3

235. Education (Student Support) (Amendment) Regulations 2008
revoked: SI 2008/1582 Reg.4

238. Local Government Pension Scheme (Transitional Provisions) Regulations 2008
applied: SI 2008/239 Reg.51, Sch.3 para.3, Sch.3 para.7
referred to: SI 2008/239 Reg.79
Reg.9, amended: SI 2008/1083 Reg.25
Reg.11, applied: SI 2008/239 Reg.30
Reg.12, applied: SI 2008/239 Reg.71
Sch.1, amended: SI 2008/1083 Reg.25, SI 2008/2425 Reg.21
Sch.2 para.2, amended: SI 2008/1083 Reg.25
Sch.2 para.6, amended: SI 2008/1083 Reg.25
Sch.2 para.7, amended: SI 2008/1083 Reg.25

239. Local Government Pension Scheme (Administration) Regulations 2008
Reg.5, revoked (in part): SI 2008/2989 Reg.3
Reg.13, applied: SI 2008/238 Reg.4
Reg.16, amended: SI 2008/3245 Reg.3
Reg.16, applied: SI 2008/238 Sch.2 para.4
Reg.17, applied: SI 2008/238 Reg.5
Reg.31, amended: SI 2008/2425 Reg.22
Reg.38, amended: SI 2008/2989 Reg.4
Reg.56, amended: SI 2008/1083 Reg.24
Reg.83, amended: SI 2008/2425 Reg.22
Sch.1, amended: SI 2008/2425 Reg.22, SI 2008/3245 Reg.4
Sch.2 Part 1 para.2, applied: SI 2008/1419 Reg.6

NO.

2008–cont.

239. Local Government Pension Scheme (Administration) Regulations 2008–*cont.*
Sch.4 para.1, substituted: SI 2008/3245 Reg.5
Sch.4 Part 1 para.1, substituted: SI 2008/3245 Reg.5
Sch.4 Part 1 para.2, substituted: SI 2008/3245 Reg.5
Sch.4 Part 1 para.3, substituted: SI 2008/3245 Reg.5
Sch.4 Part 1 para.4, substituted: SI 2008/3245 Reg.5
Sch.4 Part 1 para.5, substituted: SI 2008/3245 Reg.5
Sch.4 Part 1 para.6, substituted: SI 2008/3245 Reg.5
Sch.4 Part 1 para.7, substituted: SI 2008/3245 Reg.5
Sch.4 para.2, substituted: SI 2008/3245 Reg.5
Sch.4 Part 2, added: SI 2008/3245 Reg.7
Sch.4 Part 2, substituted: SI 2008/3245 Reg.5
Sch.4 para.3, substituted: SI 2008/3245 Reg.5
Sch.4 para.4, substituted: SI 2008/3245 Reg.5
Sch.4 para.5, substituted: SI 2008/3245 Reg.5
Sch.4 para.6, substituted: SI 2008/3245 Reg.5
Sch.4 para.7, substituted: SI 2008/3245 Reg.5, Reg.6

253. Agricultural Holdings (Units of Production) (Wales) Order 2008
revoked: SI 2008/3200 Art.3

337. Local Government and Public Involvement in Health Act 2007 (Commencement No.3, Transitional and Saving Provisions and Commencement No.2 (Amendment)) Order 2008
Sch.1, applied: SI 2008/2113 Reg.7

346. Regulated Covered Bonds Regulations 2008
Reg.1, amended: SI 2008/1714 Reg.2
Reg.21, amended: SI 2008/1714 Reg.2
Reg.22, substituted: SI 2008/1714 Reg.2
Reg.28, amended: SI 2008/1714 Reg.2
Reg.29, substituted: SI 2008/1714 Reg.2
Sch.1 Part 2 para.8, substituted: SI 2008/1714 Reg.2
Sch.1 Part 2 para.9, amended: SI 2008/1714 Reg.2

374. Companies (Summary Financial Statement) Regulations 2008
applied: SI 2008/373 Reg.17
Reg.3, referred to: SI 2008/373 Reg.17

NO.

2008–cont.

381. Insurance Business Transfer Schemes (Amendment of the Corporation Tax Acts) Order 2008
Art.1, amended: 2008 c.9 Sch.17 para.39
Art.29, amended: 2008 c.9 Sch.17 para.39

409. Small Companies and Groups (Accounts and Directors Report) Regulations 2008
applied: SI 2008/373 Reg.2, SI 2008/569 Reg.4, Sch.1 para.1
Reg.3, varied: SI 2008/1912 Reg.3
Reg.4, varied: SI 2008/1912 Reg.4
Reg.6, varied: SI 2008/1912 Reg.5
Reg.8, varied: SI 2008/1912 Reg.6
Reg.10, varied: SI 2008/1912 Reg.7
Reg.13, varied: SI 2008/1912 Reg.8
Sch.1 Part 1, referred to: SI 2008/374 Sch.1 para.3
Sch.1 Part 1, varied: SI 2008/1912 Sch.1
Sch.1 Part 1 para.1, varied: SI 2008/1912 Sch.1
Sch.1 Part 1 para.2, varied: SI 2008/1912 Sch.1
Sch.1 Part 1 para.3, disapplied: SI 2008/569 Sch.1 para.1
Sch.1 Part 1 para.3, varied: SI 2008/1912 Sch.1
Sch.1 Part 1 para.4, varied: SI 2008/1912 Sch.1
Sch.1 Part 1 para.5, varied: SI 2008/1912 Sch.1
Sch.1 Part 1 para.6, disapplied: SI 2008/569 Sch.1 para.1
Sch.1 Part 1 para.6, varied: SI 2008/1912 Sch.1
Sch.1 Part 1 para.7, varied: SI 2008/1912 Sch.1
Sch.1 Part 1 para.8, varied: SI 2008/1912 Sch.1
Sch.1 Part 1 para.9, varied: SI 2008/1912 Sch.1
Sch.1 Part 2 para.10, varied: SI 2008/1912 Sch.1
Sch.1 Part 2 para.11, varied: SI 2008/1912 Sch.1
Sch.1 Part 2 para.12, varied: SI 2008/1912 Sch.1
Sch.1 Part 2 para.13, varied: SI 2008/373 Reg.3, SI 2008/1912 Sch.1
Sch.1 Part 2 para.14, varied: SI 2008/1912 Sch.1
Sch.1 Part 2 para.15, varied: SI 2008/1912 Sch.1
Sch.1 Part 2 para.16, varied: SI 2008/1912 Sch.1
Sch.1 Part 2 para.17, varied: SI 2008/1912 Sch.1
Sch.1 Part 2 para.18, varied: SI 2008/1912 Sch.1
Sch.1 Part 2 para.19, varied: SI 2008/1912 Sch.1
Sch.1 Part 2 para.20, varied: SI 2008/1912 Sch.1
Sch.1 Part 2 para.21, disapplied: SI 2008/569 Sch.1 para.1

NO.

2008–cont.

409. Small Companies and Groups (Accounts and Directors Report) Regulations 2008–*cont.*
Sch.1 Part 2 para.21, varied: SI 2008/1912 Sch.1
Sch.1 Part 2 para.22, varied: SI 2008/1912 Sch.1
Sch.1 Part 2 para.23, varied: SI 2008/1912 Sch.1
Sch.1 Part 2 para.24, varied: SI 2008/1912 Sch.1
Sch.1 Part 2 para.25, varied: SI 2008/1912 Sch.1
Sch.1 Part 2 para.26, varied: SI 2008/1912 Sch.1
Sch.1 Part 2 para.27, varied: SI 2008/1912 Sch.1
Sch.1 Part 2 para.28, varied: SI 2008/1912 Sch.1
Sch.1 Part 2 para.29, varied: SI 2008/1912 Sch.1
Sch.1 Part 2 para.30, varied: SI 2008/1912 Sch.1
Sch.1 Part 2 para.31, varied: SI 2008/1912 Sch.1
Sch.1 Part 2 para.32, varied: SI 2008/1912 Sch.1
Sch.1 Part 2 para.33, varied: SI 2008/1912 Sch.1
Sch.1 Part 2 para.34, varied: SI 2008/1912 Sch.1
Sch.1 Part 2 para.35, varied: SI 2008/1912 Sch.1
Sch.1 Part 2 para.36, varied: SI 2008/1912 Sch.1
Sch.1 Part 2 para.37, varied: SI 2008/1912 Sch.1
Sch.1 Part 2 para.38, varied: SI 2008/1912 Sch.1
Sch.1 Part 2 para.39, varied: SI 2008/1912 Sch.1
Sch.1 Part 2 para.40, varied: SI 2008/1912 Sch.1
Sch.1 Part 2 para.41, varied: SI 2008/1912 Sch.1
Sch.1 Part 3 para.42, varied: SI 2008/1912 Sch.1
Sch.1 Part 3 para.43, varied: SI 2008/1912 Sch.1
Sch.1 Part 3 para.44, varied: SI 2008/1912 Sch.1
Sch.1 Part 3 para.45, varied: SI 2008/1912 Sch.1
Sch.1 Part 3 para.46, varied: SI 2008/1912 Sch.1
Sch.1 Part 3 para.47, varied: SI 2008/1912 Sch.1
Sch.1 Part 3 para.48, varied: SI 2008/1912 Sch.1
Sch.1 Part 3 para.49, disapplied: SI 2008/569 Sch.1 para.1

NO.

2008–cont.

409. Small Companies and Groups (Accounts and Directors Report) Regulations 2008–*cont.*

Sch.1 Part 3 para.49, varied: SI 2008/1912 Sch.1

Sch.1 Part 3 para.50, disapplied: SI 2008/569 Sch.1 para.1

Sch.1 Part 3 para.50, varied: SI 2008/1912 Sch.1

Sch.1 Part 3 para.51, varied: SI 2008/1912 Sch.1

Sch.1 Part 3 para.52, varied: SI 2008/1912 Sch.1

Sch.1 Part 3 para.53, varied: SI 2008/1912 Sch.1

Sch.1 Part 3 para.54, varied: SI 2008/1912 Sch.1

Sch.1 Part 3 para.55, varied: SI 2008/1912 Sch.1

Sch.1 Part 3 para.56, varied: SI 2008/1912 Sch.1

Sch.1 Part 3 para.57, varied: SI 2008/1912 Sch.1

Sch.1 Part 3 para.58, varied: SI 2008/1912 Sch.1

Sch.1 Part 3 para.59, varied: SI 2008/1912 Sch.1

Sch.1 Part 3 para.60, varied: SI 2008/1912 Sch.1

Sch.1 Part 3 para.61, varied: SI 2008/1912 Sch.1

Sch.1 Part 3 para.62, varied: SI 2008/1912 Sch.1

Sch.1 Part 3 para.63, varied: SI 2008/1912 Sch.1

Sch.2 Part 1 para.1, varied: SI 2008/1912 Reg.4, Sch.2

Sch.2 Part 1 para.2, varied: SI 2008/1912 Reg.4, Sch.2

Sch.2 Part 1 para.3, varied: SI 2008/1912 Reg.4, Sch.2

Sch.2 Part 1 para.4, varied: SI 2008/1912 Reg.4, Sch.2

Sch.2 Part 1 para.5, varied: SI 2008/1912 Reg.4, Sch.2

Sch.2 Part 1 para.6, varied: SI 2008/1912 Reg.4, Sch.2

Sch.2 Part 1 para.7, varied: SI 2008/1912 Reg.4, Sch.2

Sch.2 Part 1 para.8, amended: SI 2008/569 Reg.17

Sch.2 Part 1 para.8, varied: SI 2008/1912 Reg.4, Sch.2

Sch.2 Part 1 para.9, varied: SI 2008/1912 Reg.4, Sch.2

Sch.2 Part 1 para.10, disapplied: SI 2008/569 Sch.1 para.1

Sch.2 Part 1 para.10, varied: SI 2008/1912 Reg.4, Sch.2

Sch.2 Part 1 para.11, varied: SI 2008/1912 Reg.4, Sch.2

NO.

2008–cont.

409. Small Companies and Groups (Accounts and Directors Report) Regulations 2008–*cont.*

Sch.2 Part 2 para.12, varied: SI 2008/1912 Reg.4, Sch.2

Sch.2 Part 2 para.13, varied: SI 2008/1912 Reg.4, Sch.2

Sch.2 Part 2 para.14, varied: SI 2008/1912 Reg.4, Sch.2

Sch.2 Part 2 para.15, varied: SI 2008/1912 Reg.4, Sch.2

Sch.2 Part 2 para.16, varied: SI 2008/1912 Reg.4, Sch.2

Sch.2 Part 2 para.17, varied: SI 2008/1912 Reg.4, Sch.2

Sch.3 Part 1 para.1, applied: SI 2008/374 Reg.9

Sch.3 Part 1 para.3, disapplied: SI 2008/569 Sch.1 para.1

Sch.4 Part 1 para.1, varied: SI 2008/1912 Sch.3

Sch.4 Part 2 para.2, varied: SI 2008/1912 Sch.3

Sch.4 Part 2 para.3, varied: SI 2008/1912 Sch.3

Sch.4 Part 2 para.4, varied: SI 2008/1912 Sch.3

Sch.4 Part 2 para.5, varied: SI 2008/1912 Sch.3

Sch.4 Part 2 para.6, varied: SI 2008/1912 Sch.3

Sch.4 Part 2 para.7, varied: SI 2008/1912 Sch.3

Sch.4 Part 2 para.8, varied: SI 2008/1912 Sch.3

Sch.4 Part 2 para.9, varied: SI 2008/1912 Sch.3

Sch.4 Part 2 para.10, varied: SI 2008/1912 Sch.3

Sch.5, disapplied: SI 2008/569 Sch.1 para.1

Sch.6 Part 1 para.1, varied: SI 2008/1912 Sch.4 Part 1

Sch.6 Part 1 para.2, varied: SI 2008/1912 Sch.4 Part 1

Sch.6 Part 1 para.3, varied: SI 2008/1912 Sch.4 Part 1

Sch.6 Part 1 para.4, varied: SI 2008/1912 Sch.4 Part 1

Sch.6 Part 1 para.5, varied: SI 2008/1912 Sch.4 Part 1

Sch.6 Part 1 para.6, varied: SI 2008/1912 Sch.4 Part 1

Sch.6 Part 1 para.7, varied: SI 2008/1912 Sch.4 Part 1

Sch.6 Part 1 para.8, varied: SI 2008/1912 Sch.4 Part 1

Sch.6 Part 1 para.9, varied: SI 2008/1912 Sch.4 Part 1

Sch.6 Part 1 para.10, varied: SI 2008/1912 Sch.4 Part 1

NO.

2008–cont.

409. Small Companies and Groups (Accounts and Directors Report) Regulations 2008–*cont.*

Sch.6 Part 1 para.11, varied: SI 2008/1912 Sch.4 Part 1
Sch.6 Part 1 para.12, varied: SI 2008/1912 Sch.4 Part 1
Sch.6 Part 1 para.13, disapplied: SI 2008/569 Sch.1 para.1
Sch.6 Part 1 para.13, varied: SI 2008/1912 Sch.4 Part 1
Sch.6 Part 1 para.14, disapplied: SI 2008/569 Sch.1 para.1
Sch.6 Part 1 para.14, varied: SI 2008/1912 Sch.4 Part 1
Sch.6 Part 1 para.15, disapplied: SI 2008/569 Sch.1 para.1
Sch.6 Part 1 para.15, varied: SI 2008/1912 Sch.4 Part 1
Sch.6 Part 1 para.16, varied: SI 2008/1912 Sch.4 Part 1
Sch.6 Part 1 para.17, varied: SI 2008/1912 Sch.4 Part 1
Sch.6 Part 1 para.18, varied: SI 2008/1912 Sch.4 Part 1
Sch.6 Part 1 para.19, varied: SI 2008/1912 Sch.4 Part 1
Sch.6 Part 1 para.20, varied: SI 2008/1912 Sch.4 Part 1
Sch.6 Part 2 para.21, varied: SI 2008/1912 Sch.4 Part 2
Sch.6 Part 2 para.22, varied: SI 2008/1912 Sch.4 Part 2
Sch.6 Part 2 para.23, varied: SI 2008/1912 Sch.4 Part 2
Sch.6 Part 2 para.24, varied: SI 2008/1912 Sch.4 Part 2
Sch.6 Part 2 para.25, varied: SI 2008/1912 Sch.4 Part 2
Sch.6 Part 2 para.26, varied: SI 2008/1912 Sch.4 Part 2
Sch.6 Part 2 para.27, varied: SI 2008/1912 Sch.4 Part 2
Sch.6 Part 2 para.28, varied: SI 2008/1912 Sch.4 Part 2
Sch.6 Part 2 para.29, varied: SI 2008/1912 Sch.4 Part 2
Sch.6 Part 2 para.30, varied: SI 2008/1912 Sch.4 Part 2
Sch.6 Part 2 para.31, varied: SI 2008/1912 Sch.4 Part 2
Sch.6 Part 2 para.32, varied: SI 2008/1912 Sch.4 Part 2
Sch.6 Part 2 para.33, varied: SI 2008/1912 Sch.4 Part 2
Sch.6 Part 2 para.34, amended: SI 2008/569 Reg.17
Sch.6 Part 2 para.34, varied: SI 2008/1912 Sch.4 Part 2
Sch.6 Part 2 para.35, varied: SI 2008/1912 Sch.4 Part 2

NO.

2008–cont.

409. Small Companies and Groups (Accounts and Directors Report) Regulations 2008–*cont.*

Sch.6 Part 2 para.36, disapplied: SI 2008/569 Sch.1 para.1
Sch.6 Part 2 para.36, varied: SI 2008/1912 Sch.4 Part 2
Sch.6 Part 2 para.37, varied: SI 2008/1912 Sch.4 Part 2
Sch.8 para.1, varied: SI 2008/1912 Sch.5
Sch.8 para.2, varied: SI 2008/1912 Sch.5
Sch.8 para.3, varied: SI 2008/1912 Sch.5
Sch.8 para.4, varied: SI 2008/1912 Sch.5
Sch.8 para.5, varied: SI 2008/1912 Sch.5
Sch.8 para.6, varied: SI 2008/1912 Sch.5
Sch.8 para.7, varied: SI 2008/1912 Sch.5
Sch.8 para.8, varied: SI 2008/1912 Sch.5
Sch.8 para.9, varied: SI 2008/1912 Sch.5
Sch.8 para.10, varied: SI 2008/1912 Sch.5
Sch.8 para.11, varied: SI 2008/1912 Sch.5

410. Large and Medium-sized Companies and Groups (Accounts and Reports) Regulations 2008

applied: SI 2008/373 Reg.2, SI 2008/565 Reg.3, SI 2008/567 Reg.4, Sch.1 para.1, SI 2008/569 Reg.4, Sch.1 para.1
referred to: SI 2008/565 Reg.3
Reg.3, varied: SI 2008/1913 Reg.3
Reg.4, varied: SI 2008/1913 Reg.4
Reg.7, applied: SI 2008/1950 Sch.1 para.3
Reg.7, varied: SI 2008/1913 Reg.5
Reg.9, varied: SI 2008/1913 Reg.6
Reg.13, varied: SI 2008/1913 Reg.7
Sch.1, referred to: SI 2008/409 Reg.3
Sch.1 Part 1, referred to: SI 2008/374 Sch.1 para.3
Sch.1 Part 1, varied: SI 2008/1913 Sch.1
Sch.1 Part 1 para.1, varied: SI 2008/1913 Sch.1
Sch.1 Part 1 para.2, varied: SI 2008/1913 Sch.1
Sch.1 Part 1 para.3, disapplied: SI 2008/569 Sch.1 para.1
Sch.1 Part 1 para.3, varied: SI 2008/1913 Sch.1
Sch.1 Part 1 para.4, varied: SI 2008/1913 Sch.1
Sch.1 Part 1 para.5, varied: SI 2008/1913 Sch.1
Sch.1 Part 1 para.6, disapplied: SI 2008/569 Sch.1 para.1
Sch.1 Part 1 para.6, varied: SI 2008/1913 Sch.1
Sch.1 Part 1 para.7, varied: SI 2008/1913 Sch.1
Sch.1 Part 1 para.8, varied: SI 2008/1913 Sch.1
Sch.1 Part 1 para.9, varied: SI 2008/1913 Sch.1
Sch.1 Part 2 para.10, varied: SI 2008/1913 Sch.1
Sch.1 Part 2 para.11, varied: SI 2008/1913 Sch.1
Sch.1 Part 2 para.12, varied: SI 2008/1913 Sch.1

NO.

2008–cont.

410. Large and Medium-sized Companies and Groups (Accounts and Reports) Regulations 2008–*cont.*

Sch.1 Part 2 para.13, varied: SI 2008/373 Reg.3, SI 2008/1913 Sch.1

Sch.1 Part 2 para.14, varied: SI 2008/1913 Sch.1

Sch.1 Part 2 para.15, varied: SI 2008/1913 Sch.1

Sch.1 Part 2 para.16, varied: SI 2008/1913 Sch.1

Sch.1 Part 2 para.17, varied: SI 2008/1913 Sch.1

Sch.1 Part 2 para.18, varied: SI 2008/1913 Sch.1

Sch.1 Part 2 para.19, varied: SI 2008/1913 Sch.1

Sch.1 Part 2 para.20, varied: SI 2008/1913 Sch.1

Sch.1 Part 2 para.21, disapplied: SI 2008/569 Sch.1 para.1

Sch.1 Part 2 para.21, varied: SI 2008/1913 Sch.1

Sch.1 Part 2 para.22, varied: SI 2008/1913 Sch.1

Sch.1 Part 2 para.23, varied: SI 2008/1913 Sch.1

Sch.1 Part 2 para.24, varied: SI 2008/1913 Sch.1

Sch.1 Part 2 para.25, varied: SI 2008/1913 Sch.1

Sch.1 Part 2 para.26, varied: SI 2008/1913 Sch.1

Sch.1 Part 2 para.27, varied: SI 2008/1913 Sch.1

Sch.1 Part 2 para.28, varied: SI 2008/1913 Sch.1

Sch.1 Part 2 para.29, varied: SI 2008/1913 Sch.1

Sch.1 Part 2 para.30, varied: SI 2008/1913 Sch.1

Sch.1 Part 2 para.31, varied: SI 2008/1913 Sch.1

Sch.1 Part 2 para.32, varied: SI 2008/1913 Sch.1

Sch.1 Part 2 para.33, varied: SI 2008/1913 Sch.1

Sch.1 Part 2 para.34, varied: SI 2008/1913 Sch.1

Sch.1 Part 2 para.35, varied: SI 2008/1913 Sch.1

Sch.1 Part 2 para.36, varied: SI 2008/1913 Sch.1

Sch.1 Part 2 para.37, varied: SI 2008/1913 Sch.1

Sch.1 Part 2 para.38, varied: SI 2008/1913 Sch.1

Sch.1 Part 2 para.39, varied: SI 2008/1913 Sch.1

Sch.1 Part 2 para.40, varied: SI 2008/1913 Sch.1

NO.

2008–cont.

410. Large and Medium-sized Companies and Groups (Accounts and Reports) Regulations 2008–*cont.*

Sch.1 Part 2 para.41, varied: SI 2008/1913 Sch.1

Sch.1 Part 3 para.42, varied: SI 2008/1913 Sch.1

Sch.1 Part 3 para.43, varied: SI 2008/1913 Sch.1

Sch.1 Part 3 para.44, varied: SI 2008/1913 Sch.1

Sch.1 Part 3 para.45, disapplied: SI 2008/569 Sch.1 para.1

Sch.1 Part 3 para.45, varied: SI 2008/1913 Sch.1

Sch.1 Part 3 para.46, varied: SI 2008/1913 Sch.1

Sch.1 Part 3 para.47, varied: SI 2008/1913 Sch.1

Sch.1 Part 3 para.48, varied: SI 2008/1913 Sch.1

Sch.1 Part 3 para.49, varied: SI 2008/1913 Sch.1

Sch.1 Part 3 para.50, disapplied: SI 2008/569 Sch.1 para.1

Sch.1 Part 3 para.50, varied: SI 2008/1913 Sch.1

Sch.1 Part 3 para.51, varied: SI 2008/1913 Sch.1

Sch.1 Part 3 para.52, disapplied: SI 2008/569 Sch.1 para.1

Sch.1 Part 3 para.52, varied: SI 2008/1913 Sch.1

Sch.1 Part 3 para.53, disapplied: SI 2008/569 Sch.1 para.1

Sch.1 Part 3 para.53, varied: SI 2008/1913 Sch.1

Sch.1 Part 3 para.54, disapplied: SI 2008/569 Sch.1 para.1

Sch.1 Part 3 para.54, varied: SI 2008/1913 Sch.1

Sch.1 Part 3 para.55, varied: SI 2008/1913 Sch.1

Sch.1 Part 3 para.56, varied: SI 2008/1913 Sch.1

Sch.1 Part 3 para.57, varied: SI 2008/1913 Sch.1

Sch.1 Part 3 para.58, varied: SI 2008/1913 Sch.1

Sch.1 Part 3 para.59, varied: SI 2008/1913 Sch.1

Sch.1 Part 3 para.60, varied: SI 2008/1913 Sch.1

Sch.1 Part 3 para.61, varied: SI 2008/1913 Sch.1

Sch.1 Part 3 para.62, varied: SI 2008/1913 Sch.1

Sch.1 Part 3 para.63, varied: SI 2008/1913 Sch.1

Sch.1 Part 3 para.64, disapplied: SI 2008/569 Sch.1 para.1

NO.

2008–cont.

410. Large and Medium-sized Companies and Groups (Accounts and Reports) Regulations 2008–*cont.*

Sch.1 Part 3 para.64, varied: SI 2008/1913 Sch.1
Sch.1 Part 3 para.65, varied: SI 2008/1913 Sch.1
Sch.1 Part 3 para.66, disapplied: SI 2008/569 Sch.1 para.1
Sch.1 Part 3 para.66, varied: SI 2008/1913 Sch.1
Sch.1 Part 3 para.67, disapplied: SI 2008/569 Sch.1 para.1
Sch.1 Part 3 para.67, varied: SI 2008/1913 Sch.1
Sch.1 Part 3 para.68, varied: SI 2008/1913 Sch.1
Sch.1 Part 3 para.69, varied: SI 2008/1913 Sch.1
Sch.1 Part 3 para.70, varied: SI 2008/1913 Sch.1
Sch.1 Part 3 para.71, varied: SI 2008/1913 Sch.1
Sch.1 Part 3 para.72, varied: SI 2008/1913 Sch.1
Sch.1 Part 4 para.73, varied: SI 2008/1913 Sch.1
Sch.1 Part 5 para.74, varied: SI 2008/1913 Sch.1
Sch.1 Part 5 para.75, varied: SI 2008/1913 Sch.1
Sch.2 Part 1, applied: SI 2008/567 Sch.1 para.4
Sch.2 Part 1, varied: SI 2008/567 Sch.1 para.4
Sch.2 Part 3 para.54, disapplied: SI 2008/567 Sch.1 para.4
Sch.2 Part 3 para.61, disapplied: SI 2008/567 Sch.1 para.4
Sch.2 Part 3 para.63, disapplied: SI 2008/567 Sch.1 para.4
Sch.2 Part 3 para.64, disapplied: SI 2008/567 Sch.1 para.4
Sch.2 Part 3 para.79, disapplied: SI 2008/567 Sch.1 para.4
Sch.2 Part 3 para.84, disapplied: SI 2008/567 Sch.1 para.4
Sch.2 Part 3 para.86, disapplied: SI 2008/567 Sch.1 para.4
Sch.3, applied: SI 2008/565 Reg.3, SI 2008/1950 Reg.18, Sch.1 para.1, Sch.1 para.2
Sch.3 Part 1 para.2, disapplied: SI 2008/565 Reg.3, SI 2008/1950 Reg.18
Sch.3 Part 1 para.2, referred to: SI 2008/1950 Sch.1 para.1
Sch.3 Part 1 para.11, disapplied: SI 2008/565 Reg.3, SI 2008/1950 Reg.18, Sch.1 para.1
Sch.3 Part 3 para.62, disapplied: SI 2008/565 Reg.3
Sch.3 Part 3 para.68, disapplied: SI 2008/565 Reg.3, SI 2008/1950 Reg.18, Sch.1 para.1

NO.

2008–cont.

410. Large and Medium-sized Companies and Groups (Accounts and Reports) Regulations 2008–*cont.*

Sch.3 Part 3 para.70, disapplied: SI 2008/565 Reg.3
Sch.3 Part 3 para.71, disapplied: SI 2008/565 Reg.3, SI 2008/1950 Reg.18, Sch.1 para.1
Sch.3 Part 3 para.72, disapplied: SI 2008/565 Reg.3, SI 2008/1950 Reg.18, Sch.1 para.1
Sch.3 Part 3 para.79, disapplied: SI 2008/1950 Reg.18
Sch.3 Part 3 para.81, disapplied: SI 2008/1950 Reg.18
Sch.3 Part 3 para.82, disapplied: SI 2008/565 Reg.3, SI 2008/1950 Reg.18, Sch.1 para.1
Sch.3 Part 3 para.83, disapplied: SI 2008/565 Reg.3, SI 2008/1950 Reg.18, Sch.1 para.1
Sch.3 Part 3 para.84, disapplied: SI 2008/565 Reg.3
Sch.3 Part 3 para.90, applied: SI 2008/1950 Sch.1 para.1
Sch.4, applied: SI 2008/565 Reg.3
Sch.4 Part 1 para.1, varied: SI 2008/1913 Sch.2
Sch.4 Part 1 para.2, varied: SI 2008/1913 Sch.2
Sch.4 Part 1 para.3, varied: SI 2008/1913 Sch.2
Sch.4 Part 1 para.4, varied: SI 2008/1913 Sch.2
Sch.4 Part 1 para.5, varied: SI 2008/1913 Sch.2
Sch.4 Part 1 para.6, varied: SI 2008/1913 Sch.2
Sch.4 Part 1 para.7, amended: SI 2008/569 Reg.17
Sch.4 Part 1 para.7, varied: SI 2008/1913 Sch.2
Sch.4 Part 1 para.8, varied: SI 2008/1913 Sch.2
Sch.4 Part 1 para.9, disapplied: SI 2008/565 Reg.3, SI 2008/569 Sch.1 para.1
Sch.4 Part 1 para.9, varied: SI 2008/1913 Sch.2
Sch.4 Part 2 para.10, varied: SI 2008/1913 Sch.2
Sch.4 Part 2 para.11, varied: SI 2008/1913 Sch.2
Sch.4 Part 2 para.12, disapplied: SI 2008/565 Reg.3, SI 2008/569 Sch.1 para.1
Sch.4 Part 2 para.12, varied: SI 2008/567 Sch.1 para.5, SI 2008/1913 Sch.2
Sch.4 Part 2 para.13, varied: SI 2008/1913 Sch.2
Sch.4 Part 2 para.14, varied: SI 2008/1913 Sch.2
Sch.4 Part 3 para.15, varied: SI 2008/1913 Sch.2

NO.

2008–cont.

410. Large and Medium-sized Companies and Groups (Accounts and Reports) Regulations 2008–*cont.*

Sch.4 Part 3 para.16, varied: SI 2008/1913 Sch.2
Sch.4 Part 3 para.17, varied: SI 2008/1913 Sch.2
Sch.4 Part 3 para.18, varied: SI 2008/1913 Sch.2
Sch.4 Part 3 para.19, varied: SI 2008/1913 Sch.2
Sch.4 Part 3 para.20, varied: SI 2008/1913 Sch.2
Sch.4 Part 3 para.21, varied: SI 2008/1913 Sch.2
Sch.4 Part 3 para.22, varied: SI 2008/1913 Sch.2
Sch.4 Part 4 para.23, varied: SI 2008/1913 Sch.2
Sch.4 Part 5 para.24, varied: SI 2008/1913 Sch.2
Sch.4 Part 5 para.25, varied: SI 2008/1913 Sch.2
Sch.4 Part 5 para.26, varied: SI 2008/1913 Sch.2
Sch.4 Part 5 para.27, varied: SI 2008/1913 Sch.2
Sch.5, applied: SI 2008/565 Reg.3
Sch.5 Part 1 para.1, applied: SI 2008/374 Reg.9
Sch.5 Part 2 para.2, disapplied: SI 2008/565 Reg.3, SI 2008/569 Sch.1 para.1
Sch.5 Part 2 para.2, varied: SI 2008/567 Sch.1 para.6
Sch.5 Part 2 para.4, disapplied: SI 2008/565 Reg.3, SI 2008/569 Sch.1 para.1
Sch.5 Part 2 para.4, varied: SI 2008/567 Sch.1 para.6
Sch.5 Part 2 para.5, applied: SI 2008/565 Reg.3
Sch.5 Part 2 para.5, disapplied: SI 2008/565 Reg.3, SI 2008/569 Sch.1 para.1
Sch.5 Part 2 para.5, varied: SI 2008/567 Sch.1 para.6
Sch.6, referred to: SI 2008/409 Reg.8
Sch.6 Part 1 para.1, varied: SI 2008/1913 Sch.3
Sch.6 Part 1 para.2, varied: SI 2008/1913 Sch.3
Sch.6 Part 1 para.3, varied: SI 2008/1913 Sch.3
Sch.6 Part 1 para.4, varied: SI 2008/1913 Sch.3
Sch.6 Part 1 para.5, varied: SI 2008/1913 Sch.3
Sch.6 Part 1 para.6, varied: SI 2008/1913 Sch.3
Sch.6 Part 1 para.7, varied: SI 2008/1913 Sch.3
Sch.6 Part 1 para.8, varied: SI 2008/1913 Sch.3

NO.

2008–cont.

410. Large and Medium-sized Companies and Groups (Accounts and Reports) Regulations 2008–*cont.*

Sch.6 Part 1 para.9, varied: SI 2008/1913 Sch.3
Sch.6 Part 1 para.10, varied: SI 2008/1913 Sch.3
Sch.6 Part 1 para.11, varied: SI 2008/1913 Sch.3
Sch.6 Part 1 para.12, varied: SI 2008/1913 Sch.3
Sch.6 Part 1 para.13, disapplied: SI 2008/569 Sch.1 para.1
Sch.6 Part 1 para.13, varied: SI 2008/567 Sch.1 para.7, SI 2008/1913 Sch.3
Sch.6 Part 1 para.14, disapplied: SI 2008/569 Sch.1 para.1
Sch.6 Part 1 para.14, varied: SI 2008/567 Sch.1 para.7, SI 2008/1913 Sch.3
Sch.6 Part 1 para.15, disapplied: SI 2008/569 Sch.1 para.1
Sch.6 Part 1 para.15, varied: SI 2008/567 Sch.1 para.7, SI 2008/1913 Sch.3
Sch.6 Part 1 para.16, varied: SI 2008/1913 Sch.3
Sch.6 Part 1 para.17, varied: SI 2008/1913 Sch.3
Sch.6 Part 1 para.18, varied: SI 2008/1913 Sch.3
Sch.6 Part 1 para.19, varied: SI 2008/1913 Sch.3
Sch.6 Part 1 para.20, varied: SI 2008/1913 Sch.3
Sch.6 Part 1 para.21, varied: SI 2008/1913 Sch.3
Sch.6 Part 1 para.22, varied: SI 2008/1913 Sch.3
Sch.7, disapplied: SI 2008/567 Sch.1 para.8
Sch.7 Part 1 para.1, disapplied: SI 2008/569 Sch.1 para.1
Sch.7 Part 1 para.2, disapplied: SI 2008/569 Sch.1 para.1
Sch.7 Part 1 para.3, disapplied: SI 2008/569 Sch.1 para.1
Sch.7 Part 1 para.4, disapplied: SI 2008/569 Sch.1 para.1
Sch.7 Part 1 para.5, disapplied: SI 2008/569 Sch.1 para.1
Sch.7 Part 1 para.6, applied: SI 2008/565 Reg.3, SI 2008/567 Sch.1 para.8
Sch.7 Part 1 para.6, disapplied: SI 2008/569 Sch.1 para.1
Sch.7 Part 1 para.7, applied: SI 2008/565 Reg.3, SI 2008/567 Sch.1 para.8
Sch.7 Part 2 para.8, disapplied: SI 2008/569 Sch.1 para.1
Sch.7 Part 2 para.9, disapplied: SI 2008/569 Sch.1 para.1
Sch.7 Part 3 para.10, disapplied: SI 2008/569 Sch.1 para.1

NO.

2008–cont.

410. Large and Medium-sized Companies and Groups (Accounts and Reports) Regulations 2008–*cont.*

Sch.7 Part 4 para.11, disapplied: SI 2008/569 Sch.1 para.1
Sch.7 Part 5 para.12, disapplied: SI 2008/569 Sch.1 para.1
Sch.7 Part 6 para.13, disapplied: SI 2008/569 Sch.1 para.1
Sch.7 Part 6 para.13, referred to: SI 2008/374 Reg.10
Sch.7 Part 6 para.14, applied: SI 2008/374 Reg.10
Sch.7 Part 6 para.14, disapplied: SI 2008/569 Sch.1 para.1
Sch.8 Part 2 para.3, applied: SI 2008/374 Reg.10
Sch.8 Part 2 para.5, applied: SI 2008/374 Reg.10
Sch.8 Part 3, applied: SI 2008/373 Reg.9
Sch.10 para.1, varied: SI 2008/1913 Sch.4
Sch.10 para.2, varied: SI 2008/1913 Sch.4
Sch.10 para.3, varied: SI 2008/1913 Sch.4
Sch.10 para.4, varied: SI 2008/1913 Sch.4
Sch.10 para.5, varied: SI 2008/1913 Sch.4
Sch.10 para.6, varied: SI 2008/1913 Sch.4
Sch.10 para.7, varied: SI 2008/1913 Sch.4
Sch.10 para.8, varied: SI 2008/1913 Sch.4
Sch.10 para.9, varied: SI 2008/1913 Sch.4
Sch.10 para.10, varied: SI 2008/1913 Sch.4
Sch.10 para.11, varied: SI 2008/1913 Sch.4
Sch.10 para.12, varied: SI 2008/1913 Sch.4
Sch.10 para.13, varied: SI 2008/1913 Sch.4
Sch.10 para.14, varied: SI 2008/1913 Sch.4
Sch.10 para.15, varied: SI 2008/1913 Sch.4

417. Concessionary Bus Travel (Permits) (England) Regulations 2008

Reg.2, amended: SI 2008/2091 Reg.2

432. Northern Rock plc Transfer Order 2008

Art.3, applied: SI 2008/718 Sch.1
Art.4, applied: SI 2008/718 Sch.1
Art.12, applied: SI 2008/718 Sch.1

473. Safeguarding Vulnerable Groups Act 2006 (Transitional Provisions) Order 2008

Art.1, amended: SI 2008/2683 Sch.1 para.333
Art.2, amended: SI 2008/2683 Sch.1 para.334
Art.2, applied: SI 2008/474 Reg.3, SI 2008/1062 Reg.2, SI 2008/1497 Reg.3
Art.3, applied: SI 2008/1497 Reg.3
Art.4, amended: SI 2008/2683 Sch.1 para.335
Art.4, applied: SI 2008/474 Reg.8, SI 2008/1062 Reg.3, SI 2008/1497 Reg.3

NO.

2008–cont.

474. Safeguarding Vulnerable Groups Act 2006 (Barring Procedure) Regulations 2008

Reg.1, amended: SI 2008/2683 Sch.1 para.337
Reg.2, applied: SI 2008/473 Art.2, Art.4
Reg.4, amended: SI 2008/2683 Sch.1 para.338
Reg.5, amended: SI 2008/2683 Sch.1 para.339
Reg.6, amended: SI 2008/2683 Sch.1 para.340
Reg.8, amended: SI 2008/2683 Sch.1 para.341

489. Companies (Disclosure of Auditor Remuneration and Liability Limitation Agreements) Regulations 2008

applied: SI 2008/565 Reg.3
Reg.4, applied: SI 2008/569 Reg.4
Reg.5, applied: SI 2008/567 Reg.4, SI 2008/569 Reg.4
Reg.6, applied: SI 2008/567 Reg.4, SI 2008/569 Reg.4

497. Companies (Late Filing Penalties) and Limited Liability Partnerships (Filing Periods and Late Filing Penalties) Regulations 2008

Reg.6, amended: SI 2008/1911 Reg.22

514. Smoke Control Areas (Authorised Fuels) (England) Regulations 2008

Sch.1 para.42A, added: SI 2008/2342 Reg.2

515. Smoke Control Areas (Exempted Fireplaces) (England) Order 2008

revoked: SI 2008/2343 Art.3

516. Local Authorities (Functions and Responsibilities) (England) (Amendment) Regulations 2008

Reg.4, amended: SI 2008/2787 Reg.7
Reg.4, revoked (in part): SI 2008/2787 Reg.7

528. Local Involvement Networks Regulations 2008

Reg.7, amended: SI 2008/1877 Reg.2

529. Education (Student Support) Regulations 2008

Part 4, revoked: SI 2008/1582 Reg.4
Part 5, revoked: SI 2008/1582 Reg.4
Part 6, revoked: SI 2008/1582 Reg.4
Part 7, revoked: SI 2008/1582 Reg.4
Part 10, revoked: SI 2008/1582 Reg.4
Reg.1, revoked: SI 2008/1582 Reg.4
Reg.2, amended: SI 2008/1582 Sch.5 para.1, SI 2008/2939 Sch.1 para.1
Reg.2, revoked: SI 2008/1582 Reg.4
Reg.3, revoked (in part): SI 2008/1582 Reg.4
Reg.4, amended: SI 2008/1582 Sch.5 para.2, Sch.5 para.3
Reg.4, revoked: SI 2008/1582 Reg.4
Reg.5, revoked: SI 2008/1582 Reg.4
Reg.6, revoked: SI 2008/1582 Reg.4
Reg.7, revoked: SI 2008/1582 Reg.4
Reg.8, revoked: SI 2008/1582 Reg.4

NO.

2008–cont.

529. Education (Student Support) Regulations 2008–*cont.*
Reg.9, revoked: SI 2008/1582 Reg.4
Reg.10, revoked: SI 2008/1582 Reg.4
Reg.65, amended: SI 2008/2094 Sch.1 para.1
Reg.66, substituted: SI 2008/2094 Sch.1 para.2
Reg.66A, added: SI 2008/2094 Sch.1 para.3
Reg.93, revoked: SI 2008/1582 Reg.4
Reg.94, revoked: SI 2008/1582 Reg.4
Reg.95, revoked: SI 2008/1582 Reg.4
Reg.96, revoked: SI 2008/1582 Reg.4
Reg.97, revoked: SI 2008/1582 Reg.4
Reg.98, revoked: SI 2008/1582 Reg.4
Reg.99, revoked: SI 2008/1582 Reg.4
Reg.100, revoked: SI 2008/1582 Reg.4
Reg.101, amended: SI 2008/2094 Sch.1 para.4
Reg.101, revoked: SI 2008/1582 Reg.4
Reg.102, revoked: SI 2008/1582 Reg.4
Reg.104, amended: SI 2008/1582 Sch.5 para.4
Reg.110, amended: SI 2008/1582 Sch.5 para.5
Reg.115, revoked: SI 2008/1582 Reg.4
Reg.116, revoked: SI 2008/1582 Reg.4
Reg.117, revoked: SI 2008/1582 Reg.4
Reg.118, revoked: SI 2008/1582 Reg.4
Reg.119, revoked: SI 2008/1582 Reg.4
Reg.120, amended: SI 2008/1582 Sch.5 para.6, SI 2008/2094 Sch.1 para.5, Sch.1 para.6
Reg.120, revoked: SI 2008/1582 Reg.4
Reg.121, revoked: SI 2008/1582 Reg.4
Reg.122, revoked: SI 2008/1582 Reg.4
Reg.123, revoked: SI 2008/1582 Reg.4
Reg.124, revoked: SI 2008/1582 Reg.4
Reg.125, revoked: SI 2008/1582 Reg.4
Reg.126, revoked: SI 2008/1582 Reg.4
Reg.127, revoked: SI 2008/1582 Reg.4
Reg.128, revoked: SI 2008/1582 Reg.4
Reg.129, revoked: SI 2008/1582 Reg.4
Reg.130, revoked: SI 2008/1582 Reg.4
Reg.131, revoked: SI 2008/1582 Reg.4
Reg.132, amended: SI 2008/1582 Sch.5 para.7, Sch.5 para.8
Reg.132, revoked: SI 2008/1582 Reg.4
Reg.133, revoked: SI 2008/1582 Reg.4
Reg.134, revoked: SI 2008/1582 Reg.4
Reg.135, revoked: SI 2008/1582 Reg.4
Reg.136, revoked: SI 2008/1582 Reg.4
Reg.137, amended: SI 2008/2094 Sch.1 para.7, Sch.1 para.8
Reg.137, revoked: SI 2008/1582 Reg.4
Reg.138, revoked: SI 2008/1582 Reg.4
Reg.139, revoked: SI 2008/1582 Reg.4
Reg.140, revoked: SI 2008/1582 Reg.4
Reg.141, revoked: SI 2008/1582 Reg.4
Reg.142, revoked: SI 2008/1582 Reg.4

NO.

2008–cont.

529. Education (Student Support) Regulations 2008–*cont.*
Reg.143, revoked: SI 2008/1582 Reg.4
Reg.144, revoked: SI 2008/1582 Reg.4
Reg.145, revoked: SI 2008/1582 Reg.4
Reg.146, revoked: SI 2008/1582 Reg.4
Reg.147, revoked: SI 2008/1582 Reg.4
Reg.148, revoked: SI 2008/1582 Reg.4
Reg.149, revoked: SI 2008/1582 Reg.4
Reg.150, revoked: SI 2008/1582 Reg.4
Reg.151, revoked: SI 2008/1582 Reg.4
Reg.152, revoked: SI 2008/1582 Reg.4
Reg.153, revoked: SI 2008/1582 Reg.4
Reg.154, revoked: SI 2008/1582 Reg.4
Reg.155, revoked: SI 2008/1582 Reg.4
Reg.156, revoked: SI 2008/1582 Reg.4
Reg.157, revoked: SI 2008/1582 Reg.4
Reg.158, revoked: SI 2008/1582 Reg.4
Sch.1 Part 1 para.1, revoked: SI 2008/1582 Reg.4
Sch.1 Part 2, revoked: SI 2008/1582 Reg.4
Sch.1 Part 2 para.8, amended: SI 2008/1582 Sch.5 para.9
Sch.2 Part 1 para.1, revoked: SI 2008/1582 Reg.4
Sch.2 Part 1 para.2, revoked: SI 2008/1582 Reg.4
Sch.2 Part 1 para.3, revoked: SI 2008/1582 Reg.4
Sch.2 Part 1 para.4, revoked: SI 2008/1582 Reg.4
Sch.2 Part 1 para.5, revoked: SI 2008/1582 Reg.4
Sch.2 Part 1 para.6, revoked: SI 2008/1582 Reg.4
Sch.2 Part 1 para.7, revoked: SI 2008/1582 Reg.4
Sch.2 Part 1 para.8, revoked: SI 2008/1582 Reg.4

562. Income Tax (Purchased Life Annuities) Regulations 2008
Reg.19, amended: SI 2008/1481 Reg.2

569. Partnerships (Accounts) Regulations 2008
Reg.7, applied: SI 2008/409 Sch.2 para.8, Sch.6 para.34, SI 2008/410 Sch.4 para.7

600. Street Works (Inspection Fees) (Wales) (Amendment) Regulations 2008
revoked: SI 2008/1213 Reg.4

608. Civil Enforcement of Parking Contraventions (Representations and Appeals) (Wales) Regulations 2008
applied: SI 2008/609 Reg.13, SI 2008/615 Reg.6
Reg.3, applied: SI 2008/609 Reg.11, Sch.1 para.1, Sch.1 para.2
Reg.4, applied: SI 2008/609 Reg.11, Reg.13, Reg.15, Sch.1 para.2, SI 2008/614 Reg.4
Reg.4, referred to: SI 2008/1214 Reg.4
Reg.5, applied: SI 2008/609 Reg.6, Reg.12

NO.

2008–cont.

608. Civil Enforcement of Parking Contraventions (Representations and Appeals) (Wales) Regulations 2008–*cont.*
Reg.6, applied: SI 2008/609 Reg.15
Reg.7, applied: SI 2008/609 Reg.13, Reg.15, SI 2008/615 Reg.6
Sch.1, applied: SI 2008/615 Reg.7
Sch.1 Part 1 para.1, referred to: SI 2008/615 Reg.6
Sch.1 Part 1 para.1, varied: SI 2008/615 Reg.6
Sch.1 Part 2 para.2, referred to: SI 2008/615 Reg.6
Sch.1 Part 2 para.2, varied: SI 2008/615 Reg.6
Sch.1 Part 2 para.4, referred to: SI 2008/615 Reg.6

609. Civil Enforcement of Parking Contraventions (Penalty Charge Notices, Enforcement and Adjudication) (Wales) Regulations 2008
applied: SI 2008/608 Reg.8
Reg.5, applied: SI 2008/608 Reg.3, SI 2008/614 Reg.8, SI 2008/615 Reg.3, SI 2008/1214 Reg.8
Reg.6, applied: SI 2008/608 Reg.3, SI 2008/613 Sch.1 para.1
Reg.8, applied: SI 2008/615 Reg.3
Reg.11, applied: SI 2008/608 Reg.3, SI 2008/614 Reg.2, SI 2008/1214 Reg.2
Reg.13, applied: SI 2008/614 Reg.2, SI 2008/1214 Reg.2
Reg.15, applied: SI 2008/608 Sch.1 para.19, SI 2008/614 Reg.2, SI 2008/1214 Reg.2
Sch.1 para.1, amended: SI 2008/913 Reg.2
Sch.1 para.1, referred to: SI 2008/608 Reg.4
Sch.1 para.2, applied: SI 2008/608 Reg.3

614. Civil Enforcement of Parking Contraventions (General Provisions) (Wales) Regulations 2008
revoked: SI 2008/1214 Reg.12
Reg.3, applied: SI 2008/615 Reg.3
Reg.4, applied: SI 2008/609 Reg.3
Reg.9, applied: SI 2008/613 Sch.1 para.3

615. Civil Enforcement of Parking Contraventions (Representations and Appeals) Removed Vehicles (Wales) Regulations 2008
applied: SI 2008/608 Reg.3
Reg.3, applied: SI 2008/608 Reg.8
Reg.6, enabled: SI 2008/608 Sch.1 para.4
Reg.7, applied: SI 2008/608 Reg.8
Reg.8, applied: SI 2008/608 Reg.8
Reg.9, applied: SI 2008/608 Reg.8, Reg.9

620. Civil Enforcement of Parking Contraventions (Approved Devices) (Wales) Order 2008
revoked: SI 2008/1215 Art.3

632. Social Security Benefits Up-rating Order 2008
applied: SI 2008/667 Reg.2, Reg.3

NO.

2008–cont.

632. Social Security Benefits Up-rating Order 2008–*cont.*
Art.24, referred to: SI 2008/698 Reg.1
Sch.14, referred to: SI 2008/698 Reg.1

639. Export Control (Security and Para-military Goods) Order 2008
revoked: SI 2008/3231 Sch.6

640. Fostering Services (Amendment) Regulations 2008
applied: 2008 c.14 s.17

653. National Health Service Pension Scheme Regulations 2008
applied: SSI 2008/224 Reg.2
Reg.1, amended: SI 2008/2263 Reg.25
Reg.1, amended: SI 2008/2263 Reg.30
Reg.1, amended: SI 2008/2263 Reg.54
Reg.1, amended: SI 2008/2263 Reg.60
Reg.1, amended: SI 2008/2263 Reg.85
Reg.2, applied: SSI 2008/224 Reg.2
Reg.2, amended: SI 2008/2263 Reg.26
Reg.2, amended: SI 2008/2263 Reg.31
Reg.2, amended: SI 2008/2263 Reg.32
Reg.2, substituted: SI 2008/2263 Reg.46
Reg.2, substituted: SI 2008/2263 Reg.49
Reg.2, amended: SI 2008/2263 Reg.61
Reg.2, amended: SI 2008/2263 Reg.63
Reg.2, substituted: SI 2008/2263 Reg.78
Reg.2, substituted: SI 2008/2263 Reg.79
Reg.2, amended: SI 2008/2263 Reg.84
Reg.2, substituted: SI 2008/2263 Reg.86
Reg.3, amended: SI 2008/2263 Reg.55
Reg.3, amended: SI 2008/2263 Reg.64
Reg.4, amended: SI 2008/2263 Reg.27
Reg.4, amended: SI 2008/2263 Reg.56
Reg.5, amended: SI 2008/2263 Reg.28
Reg.5, amended: SI 2008/2263 Reg.33
Reg.5, amended: SI 2008/2263 Reg.47
Reg.5, amended: SI 2008/2263 Reg.57
Reg.5, amended: SI 2008/2263 Reg.62
Reg.6, amended: SI 2008/2263 Reg.40
Reg.6, amended: SI 2008/2263 Reg.65
Reg.6, amended: SI 2008/2263 Reg.72
Reg.7, amended: SI 2008/2263 Reg.48
Reg.7, amended: SI 2008/2263 Reg.50
Reg.7, amended: SI 2008/2263 Reg.58
Reg.7, amended: SI 2008/2263 Reg.80
Reg.8, amended: SI 2008/2263 Reg.41
Reg.8, amended: SI 2008/2263 Reg.59
Reg.8, amended: SI 2008/2263 Reg.66
Reg.8, amended: SI 2008/2263 Reg.73
Reg.9, amended: SI 2008/2263 Reg.29
Reg.9, amended: SI 2008/2263 Reg.34
Reg.9, amended: SI 2008/2263 Reg.42
Reg.9, amended: SI 2008/2263 Reg.51
Reg.9, amended: SI 2008/2263 Reg.67
Reg.9, amended: SI 2008/2263 Reg.74
Reg.9, amended: SI 2008/2263 Reg.81
Reg.10, amended: SI 2008/2263 Reg.35
Reg.10, amended: SI 2008/2263 Reg.36
Reg.10, amended: SI 2008/2263 Reg.43

NO.

2008–cont.

653. National Health Service Pension Scheme Regulations 2008–*cont.*
Reg.10, amended: SI 2008/2263 Reg.68
Reg.10, amended: SI 2008/2263 Reg.75
Reg.11, amended: SI 2008/2263 Reg.44
Reg.11, revoked (in part): SI 2008/2263 Reg.44
Reg.11, amended: SI 2008/2263 Reg.52
Reg.11, amended: SI 2008/2263 Reg.76
Reg.11, revoked (in part): SI 2008/2263 Reg.76
Reg.11, amended: SI 2008/2263 Reg.82
Reg.14, amended: SI 2008/2263 Reg.53
Reg.14, amended: SI 2008/2263 Reg.83
Reg.17, added: SI 2008/2263 Reg.45
Reg.17, added: SI 2008/2263 Reg.77
Reg.20A, added: SI 2008/2263 Reg.37
Reg.20A, added: SI 2008/2263 Reg.69
Reg.21, amended: SI 2008/2263 Reg.38
Reg.21, amended: SI 2008/2263 Reg.70
Reg.25, amended: SI 2008/2263 Reg.39
Reg.25, amended: SI 2008/2263 Reg.71

654. National Health Service Pension Scheme (Amendment) Regulations 2008
Reg.1, amended: SI 2008/906 Reg.2
Reg.62, substituted: SI 2008/906 Reg.2
Reg.63, substituted: SI 2008/906 Reg.2
Reg.64, substituted: SI 2008/906 Reg.2
Reg.65, substituted: SI 2008/906 Reg.2
Reg.66, substituted: SI 2008/906 Reg.2

665. Pesticides (Maximum Residue Levels in Crops, Food and Feeding Stuffs) (England and Wales) (Amendment) Regulations 2008
revoked: SI 2008/2570 Sch.2

674. Companies Act 2006 (Commencement No.6, Saving and Commencement Nos 3 and 5 (Amendment)) Order 2008
Sch.3 para.1, revoked: SI 2008/2860 Art.6

686. Wireless Telegraphy (Licence Award) Regulations 2008
applied: SI 2008/687 Art.2

736. Health and Safety (Fees) Regulations 2008
Reg.14, revoked: SI 2008/2852 Sch.10 Part 2
Sch.11, revoked: SI 2008/2852 Sch.10 Part 2

781. Rice Products from the United States of America (Restriction on First Placing on the Market) (Wales) Regulations 2008
Reg.2, amended: SI 2008/1646 Reg.2
Reg.4, amended: SI 2008/1646 Reg.2
Reg.5, amended: SI 2008/1646 Reg.2

794. Employment and Support Allowance Regulations 2008
Part 10, substituted: SI 2008/2428 Reg.20
Part 10, revoked: SI 2008/2428 Reg.20
Reg.2, amended: SI 2008/2428 Reg.3, Reg.20, SI 2008/3157 Reg.11

NO.

2008–cont.

794. Employment and Support Allowance Regulations 2008–*cont.*
Reg.7, amended: SI 2008/3051 Reg.12
Reg.9, amended: SI 2008/2428 Reg.4
Reg.26, amended: SI 2008/2428 Reg.5
Reg.32, amended: SI 2008/2428 Reg.5
Reg.40, amended: SI 2008/2428 Reg.6, SI 2008/2683 Sch.1 para.342
Reg.45, amended: SI 2008/2428 Reg.6
Reg.72A, added: SI 2008/2428 Reg.7
Reg.74, amended: SI 2008/2428 Reg.7
Reg.76, amended: SI 2008/2428 Reg.7
Reg.85, amended: SI 2008/2428 Reg.20
Reg.86, revoked: SI 2008/2428 Reg.20
Reg.94, amended: SI 2008/2428 Reg.8
Reg.95, amended: SI 2008/2428 Reg.8
Reg.99, amended: SI 2008/2428 Reg.8
Reg.103, amended: SI 2008/2428 Reg.8
Reg.104, amended: SI 2008/1599 Reg.7
Reg.107, amended: SI 2008/2428 Reg.8
Reg.109, amended: SI 2008/2428 Reg.8
Reg.111, amended: SI 2008/2428 Reg.8
Reg.112, amended: SI 2008/2428 Reg.8
Reg.115, amended: SI 2008/2428 Reg.8
Reg.118, amended: SI 2008/2428 Reg.20
Reg.119, amended: SI 2008/2428 Reg.20
Reg.120, amended: SI 2008/2428 Reg.20
Reg.123, substituted: SI 2008/2428 Reg.20
Reg.124, amended: SI 2008/2428 Reg.20
Reg.125, amended: SI 2008/2428 Reg.20
Reg.126, revoked: SI 2008/2428 Reg.20
Reg.131, amended: SI 2008/2428 Reg.8
Reg.132, amended: SI 2008/1599 Reg.7
Reg.137, amended: SI 2008/1599 Reg.7
Reg.144, amended: SI 2008/2428 Reg.9
Reg.146, amended: SI 2008/2428 Reg.9
Reg.156, amended: SI 2008/2428 Reg.9
Reg.160, amended: SI 2008/2428 Reg.10
Reg.164, amended: SI 2008/2428 Reg.11
Sch.2 Part 1, amended: SI 2008/2428 Reg.12
Sch.2 Part 1, substituted: SI 2008/2428 Reg.12
Sch.2 Part 2, amended: SI 2008/2428 Reg.12
Sch.3, amended: SI 2008/2428 Reg.13
Sch.4 Part 1 para.1, amended: SI 2008/2428 Reg.14
Sch.4 Part 1 para.1, substituted: SI 2008/2428 Reg.14
Sch.4 Part 3 para.11, amended: SI 2008/2428 Reg.14
Sch.4 Part 4, referred to: SI 2008/2928 Reg.9
Sch.5 Part 1, amended: SI 2008/2428 Reg.15
Sch.6 para.1, amended: SI 2008/2428 Reg.16
Sch.6 para.1, varied: SI 2008/3195 Reg.9
Sch.6 para.2, amended: SI 2008/2428 Reg.16
Sch.6 para.3, amended: SI 2008/2428 Reg.16
Sch.6 para.3, referred to: SI 2008/3195 Reg.8

NO.

2008–cont.

794. Employment and Support Allowance Regulations 2008–*cont.*
Sch.6 para.4, amended: SI 2008/2428 Reg.16
Sch.6 para.5, amended: SI 2008/2428 Reg.16
Sch.6 para.6, amended: SI 2008/2428 Reg.16
Sch.6 para.7, amended: SI 2008/2428 Reg.16
Sch.6 para.8, amended: SI 2008/2428 Reg.16
Sch.6 para.8, applied: SI 2008/3195 Reg.3
Sch.6 para.8, referred to: SI 2008/3195 Reg.3
Sch.6 para.8, varied: SI 2008/3195 Reg.4, Reg.9
Sch.6 para.9, amended: SI 2008/2428 Reg.16
Sch.6 para.9, applied: SI 2008/3195 Reg.3
Sch.6 para.9, referred to: SI 2008/3195 Reg.3
Sch.6 para.9, varied: SI 2008/3195 Reg.4, Reg.9
Sch.6 para.10, amended: SI 2008/2428 Reg.16
Sch.6 para.10, varied: SI 2008/3195 Reg.9
Sch.6 para.11, amended: SI 2008/2428 Reg.16
Sch.6 para.11, varied: SI 2008/3195 Reg.9
Sch.6 para.12, amended: SI 2008/2428 Reg.16
Sch.6 para.12, varied: SI 2008/3195 Reg.4, Reg.9
Sch.6 para.13, amended: SI 2008/2428 Reg.16, SI 2008/3195 Reg.2
Sch.6 para.13, revoked (in part): SI 2008/3195 Reg.2
Sch.6 para.14, amended: SI 2008/2428 Reg.16
Sch.6 para.14, varied: SI 2008/3195 Reg.9
Sch.6 para.15, amended: SI 2008/2428 Reg.16
Sch.6 para.15, varied: SI 2008/3195 Reg.4, Reg.9
Sch.6 para.16, amended: SI 2008/2428 Reg.16
Sch.6 para.16, applied: SI 2008/3195 Reg.12
Sch.6 para.17, amended: SI 2008/2428 Reg.16
Sch.6 para.17, applied: SI 2008/3195 Reg.12
Sch.6 para.18, amended: SI 2008/2428 Reg.16
Sch.6 para.19, amended: SI 2008/2428 Reg.16
Sch.6 para.20, amended: SI 2008/2428 Reg.16
Sch.6 para.20, varied: SI 2008/3195 Reg.9
Sch.7 para.5, amended: SI 2008/2428 Reg.17

NO.

2008–cont.

794. Employment and Support Allowance Regulations 2008–*cont.*
Sch.7 para.6, amended: SI 2008/2428 Reg.17
Sch.7 para.7, amended: SI 2008/2428 Reg.17
Sch.8 para.9, amended: SI 2008/2428 Reg.18
Sch.8 para.17, amended: SI 2008/3157 Reg.11
Sch.8 para.22, amended: SI 2008/2428 Reg.18
Sch.8 para.41, amended: SI 2008/2428 Reg.18
Sch.8 para.50, substituted: SI 2008/3157 Reg.11
Sch.8 para.52, amended: SI 2008/2428 Reg.18
Sch.8 para.60, amended: SI 2008/2428 Reg.20
Sch.9 para.17, amended: SI 2008/2428 Reg.19
Sch.9 para.27, amended: SI 2008/2428 Reg.8, Reg.19
Sch.9 para.31, amended: SI 2008/2428 Reg.19
Sch.9 para.35, amended: SI 2008/2428 Reg.19
Sch.9 para.47, amended: SI 2008/2428 Reg.19
Sch.9 para.54, amended: SI 2008/3157 Reg.11

795. Employment and Support Allowance (Transitional Provisions) Regulations 2008
Reg.1, amended: SI 2008/2428 Reg.42
Reg.2, amended: SI 2008/2783 Reg.2

798. Guardian's Allowance Up-rating Order 2008
applied: SI 2008/840 Reg.3

799. Guardian's Allowance Up-rating (Northern Ireland) Order 2008
applied: SI 2008/840 Reg.3

831. Consumer Credit Act 2006 (Commencement No.4 and Transitional Provisions) Order 2008
Art.3, amended: SI 2008/2444 Art.2
Sch.3, amended: SI 2008/2444 Art.2

915. Local Involvement Networks (Duty of Services-Providers to Allow Entry) Regulations 2008
Reg.3, applied: SI 2008/1185 Sch.1 para.20

916. Plastic Materials and Articles in Contact with Food (England) Regulations 2008
Reg.22, amended: SI 2008/1642 Reg.3
Reg.29, revoked (in part): SI 2008/1642 Reg.4

928. Official Statistics Order 2008
Sch.1, amended: SI 2008/2831 Sch.1 para.17, Sch.2 para.8

NO.

2008–cont.

944. Specified Animal Pathogens Order 2008
disapplied: SI 2008/962 Reg.3

974. Childcare (Early Years Register) Regulations 2008
Sch.2 Part 1 para.6, applied: SI 2008/2261 Sch.2 para.9
Sch.2 Part 1 para.9, applied: SI 2008/2261 Sch.2 para.11, Sch.2 para.12

975. Childcare (General Childcare Register) Regulations 2008
Sch.2 Part 1 para.3, applied: SI 2008/2261 Sch.2 para.10
Sch.2 Part 1 para.6, applied: SI 2008/2261 Sch.2 para.11, Sch.2 para.12
Sch.3 para.11, applied: SI 2008/2261 Sch.2 para.8

976. Childcare (Early Years and General Childcare Registers) (Common Provisions) Regulations 2008
Reg.8, applied: SI 2008/2261 Sch.2 para.24
Reg.12, amended: SI 2008/2683 Sch.1 para.343
Reg.12, applied: SI 2008/2261 Sch.2 para.24

979. Childcare (Exemptions from Registration) Order 2008
applied: SI 2008/2261 Sch.2 para.2, Sch.2 para.5

1038. Motor Vehicles (Driving Licences) (Amendment No.2) Regulations 2008
revoked: SI 2008/1312 Reg.2

1050. Occupational Pension Schemes (Transfer Values) (Amendment) Regulations 2008
applied: SSI 2008/228 Reg.73

1052. Magistrates Courts Fees Order 2008
amended: SI 2008/2855 Art.3
referred to: SI 2008/2855 Art.2
Sch.1, amended: SI 2008/2855 Art.3, Art.4, Art.5, Art.6, Art.7
Sch.2 para.1, amended: SI 2008/2855 Art.8
Sch.2 para.2, amended: SI 2008/2855 Art.9

1053. Civil Proceedings Fees Order 2008
referred to: SI 2008/2853 Art.2
Sch.1, amended: SI 2008/2853 Art.3, Art.4, Art.5, Art.6, Art.7
Sch.2 para.1, amended: SI 2008/2853 Art.8
Sch.2 para.2, amended: SI 2008/2853 Art.9

1054. Family Proceedings Fees Order 2008
referred to: SI 2008/2856 Art.2
Sch.1, amended: SI 2008/2856 Art.3, Art.4, Art.5, Art.6, Art.7, Art.8, Art.9
Sch.1, substituted: SI 2008/2856 Art.5
Sch.2 para.1, amended: SI 2008/2856 Art.10
Sch.2 para.2, amended: SI 2008/2856 Art.11

1082. Employment and Support Allowance (Consequential Provisions) Regulations 2008
Reg.2, amended: SI 2008/2428 Reg.25

NO.

2008–cont.

1082. Employment and Support Allowance (Consequential Provisions) Regulations 2008–*cont.*
Reg.3, substituted: SI 2008/2428 Reg.26
Reg.5, amended: SI 2008/2428 Reg.27
Reg.7A, added: SI 2008/2428 Reg.28
Reg.11, amended: SI 2008/2428 Reg.29
Reg.12, amended: SI 2008/2428 Reg.30
Reg.23, amended: SI 2008/2428 Reg.31
Reg.24, amended: SI 2008/2428 Reg.32
Reg.29, amended: SI 2008/2428 Reg.33
Reg.30, amended: SI 2008/2428 Reg.34
Reg.35, amended: SI 2008/2428 Reg.35
Reg.43, amended: SI 2008/2428 Reg.36
Reg.48, amended: SI 2008/2428 Reg.37
Reg.49, amended: SI 2008/2428 Reg.38
Reg.59, amended: SI 2008/2428 Reg.39
Reg.66, amended: SI 2008/2428 Reg.40

1090. Bluetongue (Wales) Regulations 2008
Reg.17, amended: SI 2008/1583 Reg.2

1160. Teesport Harbour Revision Order 2008
referred to: SI 2008/1238 Art.6

1183. Immigration (Biometric Registration) (Pilot) Regulations 2008
applied: SI 2008/3048 Reg.24
revoked: SI 2008/3048 Reg.24
Reg.3, applied: SI 2008/3048 Reg.24

1184. Mental Health (Hospital, Guardianship and Treatment) (England) Regulations 2008
applied: SI 2008/1210 Art.8
referred to: SI 2008/2560 Reg.1, Reg.2
varied: SI 2008/1210 Art.8
Reg.17, amended: SI 2008/2560 Reg.2
Reg.26, amended: SI 2008/2560 Reg.2
Sch.1, amended: SI 2008/2560 Reg.2

1185. General Ophthalmic Services Contracts Regulations 2008
applied: SI 2008/1209 Reg.2
referred to: SI 2008/1209 Reg.2
Reg.2, amended: SI 2008/1700 Sch.1 para.18
Sch.1 Part 5 para.22, referred to: SI 2008/1700 Reg.5
Sch.1 Part 7 para.46, referred to: SI 2008/1700 Reg.13, Reg.14, Reg.15

1186. Primary Ophthalmic Services Regulations 2008
Reg.2, amended: SI 2008/1700 Sch.1 para.17, SI 2008/2449 Reg.2
Reg.3, amended: SI 2008/2449 Reg.2
Reg.3, referred to: SI 2008/1185 Sch.1 para.1

1187. National Health Service (Performers Lists) Amendment and Transitional Provisions Regulations 2008
applied: SI 2008/1209 Reg.3
referred to: SI 2008/1209 Reg.3
Sch.1, applied: SI 2008/1209 Reg.3

NO.

2008–cont.

1206. Mental Health (Approved Mental Health Professionals) (Approval) (England) Regulations 2008
Reg.5, referred to: SI 2008/1900 Sch.1 para.8
Reg.6, applied: SI 2008/1900 Sch.1 para.9, Sch.1 para.10
Reg.7, applied: SI 2008/1900 Sch.1 para.6
Reg.7, varied: SI 2008/1900 Sch.1 para.7
Reg.8, varied: SI 2008/1900 Sch.1 para.11

1216. Criminal Justice (Northern Ireland) Order 2008
Art.13, applied: 2008 c.28 s.45, s.53
Art.14, applied: 2008 c.28 s.45, s.53
Sch.1 para.31A, added: SI 2008/1769 Sch.1 para.35
Sch.2 Part 2 para.14A, added: SI 2008/1769 Sch.1 para.35

1237. Plastic Materials and Articles in Contact with Food (Wales) Regulations 2008
revoked: SI 2008/1682 Reg.30
Reg.29, revoked (in part): SI 2008/1682 Reg.30

1258. School Admissions (Alteration and Variation of, and Objections to, Arrangements) (England) (Amendment) Regulations 2008
revoked: SI 2008/3089 Sch.1

1273. Assembly Learning Grants and Loans (Higher Education) (Wales) Regulations 2008
applied: SI 2008/3170 Reg.3
revoked: SI 2008/3170 Reg.3
Reg.2, amended: SI 2008/2140 Reg.3, SI 2008/3170 Reg.112
Reg.3, amended: SI 2008/2140 Reg.4
Reg.7, amended: SI 2008/2140 Reg.6
Reg.16, amended: SI 2008/3170 Reg.112
Reg.18, revoked (in part): SI 2008/3170 Reg.112
Reg.21, amended: SI 2008/2140 Reg.7
Reg.23, amended: SI 2008/2140 Reg.8
Reg.27, amended: SI 2008/2140 Reg.9
Reg.30, amended: SI 2008/2140 Reg.10
Reg.33, amended: SI 2008/3170 Reg.112
Reg.38, amended: SI 2008/2140 Reg.12
Reg.40, amended: SI 2008/2140 Reg.13
Reg.54, amended: SI 2008/2140 Reg.14
Reg.56, amended: SI 2008/2140 Reg.15
Reg.59, amended: SI 2008/2140 Reg.16
Reg.67, amended: SI 2008/2140 Reg.17, SI 2008/3170 Reg.112
Reg.79, amended: SI 2008/2140 Reg.18, Reg.19, Reg.20, Reg.21, Reg.22
Reg.82, amended: SI 2008/2140 Reg.23, SI 2008/3170 Reg.112
Reg.83A, added: SI 2008/2140 Reg.24
Reg.83B, added: SI 2008/2140 Reg.24
Reg.83C, added: SI 2008/2140 Reg.24
Reg.83D, added: SI 2008/2140 Reg.24
Reg.83E, added: SI 2008/2140 Reg.24

NO.

2008–cont.

1273. Assembly Learning Grants and Loans (Higher Education) (Wales) Regulations 2008–*cont.*
Reg.83F, added: SI 2008/2140 Reg.24
Reg.83G, added: SI 2008/2140 Reg.24
Reg.83H, added: SI 2008/2140 Reg.24
Reg.83I, added: SI 2008/2140 Reg.24
Reg.83J, added: SI 2008/2140 Reg.24
Reg.84, amended: SI 2008/2140 Reg.25
Reg.87, amended: SI 2008/2140 Reg.26
Reg.88, amended: SI 2008/2140 Reg.27
Reg.89A, added: SI 2008/2140 Reg.28
Reg.91, amended: SI 2008/2140 Reg.29
Sch.1 Part 1 para.1, amended: SI 2008/3170 Reg.112
Sch.1 Part 2 para.8, amended: SI 2008/2140 Reg.30
Sch.6 para.1, added: SI 2008/2140 Reg.31
Sch.6 para.2, added: SI 2008/2140 Reg.31
Sch.6 para.3, added: SI 2008/2140 Reg.31
Sch.6 para.3, amended: SI 2008/3170 Reg.112
Sch.6 para.4, added: SI 2008/2140 Reg.31
Sch.6 para.5, added: SI 2008/2140 Reg.31
Sch.6 para.6, added: SI 2008/2140 Reg.31
Sch.6 para.7, added: SI 2008/2140 Reg.31
Sch.6 para.7, amended: SI 2008/3170 Reg.112

1277. Consumer Protection from Unfair Trading Regulations 2008
Reg.5, applied: SI 2008/1276 Reg.4
Reg.6, applied: SI 2008/1276 Reg.4

1281. Export of Goods, Transfer of Technology and Provision of Technical Assistance (Control) (Amendment) Order 2008
revoked: SI 2008/3231 Sch.6

1284. Cosmetic Products (Safety) Regulations 2008
Reg.2, amended: SI 2008/2173 Reg.2, SI 2008/2566 Reg.2
Reg.9, amended: SI 2008/2173 Reg.2
Sch.2 para.54, added: SI 2008/2173 Reg.2
Sch.2 para.55, added: SI 2008/2566 Reg.2
Sch.3, amended: SI 2008/2173 Reg.2, SI 2008/2566 Reg.2
Sch.4 Part 1, amended: SI 2008/2173 Sch.1, SI 2008/2566 Reg.2, Sch.1 Part 1, Sch.1 Part 2
Sch.6 Part 1, amended: SI 2008/2173 Reg.2

1315. Mental Capacity (Deprivation of Liberty Appointment of Relevant Person's Representative) Regulations 2008
Reg.9, amended: SI 2008/2368 Reg.2

1319. Electoral Administration Act 2006 (Regulation of Loans etc Northern Ireland) Order 2008
Art.6, applied: SI 2008/1737
Art.6, enabled: SI 2008/1737

NO.

2008–cont.

1409. Education (National Curriculum) (Attainment Targets and Programmes of Study) (Wales) Order 2008
Art.4, amended: SI 2008/1787 Art.2
Art.5, amended: SI 2008/1787 Art.2
Art.6, amended: SI 2008/1787 Art.2
Art.7, amended: SI 2008/1787 Art.2
Art.8, amended: SI 2008/1787 Art.2
Art.9, amended: SI 2008/1787 Art.2
Art.10, amended: SI 2008/1787 Art.2
Art.11, amended: SI 2008/1787 Art.2
Art.12, amended: SI 2008/1787 Art.2
Art.13, amended: SI 2008/1787 Art.2
Art.14, amended: SI 2008/1787 Art.2
Art.15, amended: SI 2008/1787 Art.2

1436. Legal Services Act 2007 (Commencement No.2 and Transitory Provisions) Order 2008
Art.2, amended: SI 2008/1591 Art.2

1440. Whole of Government Accounts (Designation of Bodies) Order 2008
revoked: SI 2008/1907 Art.3
Sch.1, varied: 2008 c.14 Sch.10 para.1

1485. Nursing and Midwifery (Amendment) Order 2008
Sch.1 para.1, varied: 2008 c.14 Sch.10 para.1

1488. Naval Medical Compassionate Fund (Amendment) Order 2008
revoked: SI 2008/3129 Sch.1

1497. Protection of Children and Vulnerable Adults and Care Standards Tribunal (Children's and Adults Barred Lists) (Transitional Provisions) Regulations 2008
revoked: SI 2008/2683 Sch.2

1518. Civil Enforcement of Parking Contraventions (The Borough Council of Dudley) Designation Order 2008
revoked: SI 2008/1764 Art.2

1554. Employment and Support Allowance (Consequential Provisions) (No.2) Regulations 2008
Reg.2, amended: SI 2008/2428 Reg.41
Reg.3, amended: SI 2008/2428 Reg.41
Reg.4, amended: SI 2008/2428 Reg.41

1556. Town and Country Planning (Environmental Impact Assessment) (Mineral Permissions and Amendment) (England) Regulations 2008
Reg.3, revoked: SI 2008/2093 Reg.13
Reg.4, revoked: SI 2008/2093 Reg.13

1582. Education (Student Support) (No.2) Regulations 2008
Reg.2, amended: SI 2008/2939 Sch.2 para.1, Sch.2 para.2, Sch.2 para.3
Reg.10, amended: SI 2008/2939 Sch.2 para.4
Reg.13, amended: SI 2008/2094 Sch.2 para.1, SI 2008/2939 Sch.2 para.5
Reg.14, amended: SI 2008/2939 Sch.2 para.6

NO.

2008–cont.

1582. Education (Student Support) (No.2) Regulations 2008–*cont.*
Reg.20, amended: SI 2008/2939 Sch.2 para.7
Reg.57A, added: SI 2008/2939 Sch.2 para.8
Reg.58, amended: SI 2008/2939 Sch.2 para.9, Sch.2 para.10
Reg.60A, added: SI 2008/2939 Sch.2 para.11
Reg.61, amended: SI 2008/2939 Sch.2 para.12, Sch.2 para.13
Reg.64, amended: SI 2008/2094 Sch.2 para.2
Reg.65, amended: SI 2008/2939 Sch.2 para.14
Reg.67, amended: SI 2008/2094 Sch.2 para.3, SI 2008/2939 Sch.2 para.15, Sch.2 para.16
Reg.68, amended: SI 2008/2939 Sch.2 para.17
Reg.68, substituted: SI 2008/2094 Sch.2 para.4
Reg.68A, added: SI 2008/2094 Sch.2 para.5
Reg.68A, amended: SI 2008/2939 Sch.2 para.18
Reg.68B, added: SI 2008/2939 Sch.2 para.19
Reg.68C, added: SI 2008/2939 Sch.2 para.19
Reg.69, amended: SI 2008/2939 Sch.2 para.20, Sch.2 para.21
Reg.70, amended: SI 2008/2939 Sch.2 para.22, Sch.2 para.23
Reg.72, amended: SI 2008/2939 Sch.2 para.24, Sch.2 para.25, Sch.2 para.26, Sch.2 para.27, Sch.2 para.28, Sch.2 para.29
Reg.73, amended: SI 2008/2939 Sch.2 para.30
Reg.79, amended: SI 2008/2939 Sch.2 para.31
Reg.80, amended: SI 2008/2939 Sch.2 para.32
Reg.96, amended: SI 2008/2939 Sch.2 para.33, Sch.2 para.34
Reg.97, amended: SI 2008/2939 Sch.2 para.35, Sch.2 para.36
Reg.99, amended: SI 2008/2939 Sch.2 para.37
Reg.101, amended: SI 2008/2094 Sch.2 para.6, SI 2008/2939 Sch.2 para.38, Sch.2 para.39, Sch.2 para.40, Sch.2 para.41, Sch.2 para.42
Reg.102, amended: SI 2008/2939 Sch.2 para.43
Reg.120, amended: SI 2008/2094 Sch.2 para.7, Sch.2 para.8
Reg.132, amended: SI 2008/2094 Sch.2 para.9, Sch.2 para.10, Sch.2 para.11, Sch.2 para.12, SI 2008/2939 Sch.2 para.44
Reg.137, amended: SI 2008/2094 Sch.2 para.13, Sch.2 para.14

NO.

2008–cont.

1582. Education (Student Support) (No.2) Regulations 2008–*cont.*
Reg.140, amended: SI 2008/2094 Sch.2 para.15
Sch.1 Part 2 para.4, amended: SI 2008/2094 Sch.2 para.16
Sch.4 para.2, amended: SI 2008/2094 Sch.2 para.17
Sch.4 para.5, amended: SI 2008/2939 Sch.2 para.45

1595. Mesothelioma Lump Sum Payments (Claims and Reconsiderations) Regulations 2008
Reg.5, amended: SI 2008/2706 Reg.3
Reg.6, added: SI 2008/2706 Reg.4

1596. Social Security (Recovery of Benefits) (Lump Sum Payments) Regulations 2008
Reg.9, amended: SI 2008/2365 Reg.6
Sch.1 para.5, amended: SI 2008/2683 Sch.1 para.344
Sch.1 para.5, revoked (in part): SI 2008/2683 Sch.1 para.344
Sch.1 para.6, amended: SI 2008/2683 Sch.1 para.344
Sch.1 para.6, substituted: SI 2008/2365 Reg.6
Sch.2 para.1, amended: SI 2008/2365 Reg.6

1641. Financial Services and Markets Act 2000 (Collective Investment Schemes) (Amendment) Order 2008
Art.2, amended: SI 2008/1813 Art.2

1660. Cross-border Railway Services (Working Time) Regulations 2008
Reg.17, referred to: SI 2008/3232 Sch.1 Part 2

1692. Medicines for Human Use (Prescribing by EEA Practitioners) Regulations 2008
Reg.1, amended: SI 2008/3097 Reg.5

1722. Childcare (Provision of Information About Young Children) (England) Regulations 2008
Reg.4, amended: SI 2008/3071 Reg.2

1732. Education (National Curriculum) (Foundation Stage) (Wales) Order 2008
Art.3, amended: SI 2008/2629 Art.2

1774. Health Care and Associated Professions (Miscellaneous Amendments) Order 2008
Art.1, enabled: SI 2008/2556, SI 2008/3150
Art.6, enabled: SI 2008/2556

1797. Trade Marks Rules 2008
applied: SI 2008/2206 Art.3
referred to: SI 2008/1958 r.1, r.2
varied: SI 2008/2206 Art.3
r.5, applied: SI 2008/1958 r.3, Sch.1
r.6, disapplied: SI 2008/2206 Sch.1 Part 2
r.8, applied: SI 2008/1958 Sch.1
r.8, disapplied: SI 2008/2206 Sch.1 Part 2
r.9, disapplied: SI 2008/2206 Sch.1 Part 2

NO.

2008–cont.

1797. Trade Marks Rules 2008–*cont.*
r.12, disapplied: SI 2008/2206 Sch.1 Part 2
r.13, disapplied: SI 2008/2206 Sch.1 Part 2
r.14, applied: SI 2008/1958 Sch.1
r.15, applied: SI 2008/1958 r.3
r.17, applied: SI 2008/1958 Sch.1, SI 2008/2206 Sch.6
r.25, applied: SI 2008/1958 Sch.1
r.26, applied: SI 2008/1958 Sch.1
r.28, applied: SI 2008/1958 Sch.1
r.29, applied: SI 2008/1958 Sch.1, SI 2008/2206 Sch.6
r.30, applied: SI 2008/1958 Sch.1, SI 2008/2206 Sch.6
r.32, applied: SI 2008/1958 Sch.1
r.35, applied: SI 2008/1958 Sch.1
r.36, applied: SI 2008/1958 Sch.1
r.37, applied: SI 2008/1958 Sch.1
r.38, applied: SI 2008/1958 Sch.1, SI 2008/2206 Sch.6
r.39, applied: SI 2008/1958 Sch.1, SI 2008/2206 Sch.6
r.40, amended: SI 2008/2300 r.2
r.41, applied: SI 2008/1958 Sch.1, SI 2008/2206 Sch.6
r.46, disapplied: SI 2008/2206 Sch.1 Part 2
r.47, disapplied: SI 2008/2206 Sch.1 Part 2
r.49, applied: SI 2008/1958 Sch.1
r.51, applied: SI 2008/1958 Sch.1
r.53, applied: SI 2008/1958 Sch.1
r.55, applied: SI 2008/1958 Sch.1
r.56, applied: SI 2008/1958 Sch.1
r.56, disapplied: SI 2008/2206 Sch.1 Part 2
r.66, revoked (in part): SI 2008/2683 Sch.1 para.345
r.69, applied: SI 2008/1958 Sch.1, SI 2008/2206 Sch.6
r.77, applied: SI 2008/1958 Sch.1, SI 2008/2206 Sch.6

1802. Protection of Children and Vulnerable Adults and Care Standards Tribunal (Amendment) Regulations 2008
revoked: SI 2008/2683 Sch.2

1805. Trade in Goods (Categories of Controlled Goods) Order 2008
revoked: SI 2008/3231 Sch.6

1811. Shrimp Fishing Nets (Wales) Order 2008
Art.3, amended: SI 2008/3144 Art.2

1825. Community Emissions Trading Scheme (Allocation of Allowances for Payment) Regulations 2008
Reg.2, amended: SI 2008/1939 Reg.4
Reg.7, amended: SI 2008/1939 Reg.5
Reg.9A, added: SI 2008/1939 Reg.6
Reg.9B, added: SI 2008/1939 Reg.6
Reg.9C, added: SI 2008/1939 Reg.6
Reg.9D, added: SI 2008/1939 Reg.6

1881. Transmissible Spongiform Encephalopathies (England) Regulations 2008
Reg.2, amended: SI 2008/3295 Reg.3

NO.

2008–cont.

1881. Transmissible Spongiform Encephalopathies (England) Regulations 2008–*cont.*

Reg.12, substituted: SI 2008/3295 Reg.4

Reg.20, amended: SI 2008/3295 Reg.5

Sch.2 Part 1 para.1, substituted: SI 2008/3295 Reg.6

Sch.2 Part 1 para.4, amended: SI 2008/2269 Reg.2

Sch.2 Part 1 para.4A, added: SI 2008/3295 Reg.6

Sch.2 Part 2 para.11, amended: SI 2008/3295 Reg.6

Sch.2 Part 2 para.12, amended: SI 2008/3295 Reg.6

Sch.3 para.5, amended: SI 2008/3295 Reg.7

Sch.4 para.9, amended: SI 2008/3295 Reg.8

Sch.8 para.1, substituted: SI 2008/3295 Sch.1

Sch.8 para.1A, substituted: SI 2008/3295 Sch.1

Sch.8 para.1B, substituted: SI 2008/3295 Sch.1

Sch.8 para.2, substituted: SI 2008/3295 Sch.1

Sch.8 para.3, substituted: SI 2008/3295 Sch.1

Sch.8 para.4, substituted: SI 2008/3295 Sch.1

1886. Companies Act 2006 (Commencement No.7, Transitional Provisions and Savings) Order 2008

Art.3, revoked: SI 2008/2860 Art.6

Art.4, revoked: SI 2008/2860 Art.6

Art.5, revoked: SI 2008/2860 Art.6

1892. Value Added Tax (Finance) Order 2008

revoked: SI 2008/2547 Art.2

1907. Whole of Government Accounts (Designation of Bodies) (No.2) Order 2008

Sch.1, varied: 2008 c.14 Sch.10 para.1

1910. Dartmouth-Kingswear Floating Bridge (Vehicle Classifications & Revision of Charges) Order 2008

revoked: SI 2008/2102 Art.4

1911. Limited Liability Partnerships (Accounts and Audit) (Application of Companies Act 2006) Regulations 2008

applied: SI 2008/1912 Reg.1

1921. Land Registration (Proper Office) (Amendment) Order 2008

revoked: SI 2008/3201 Art.4

1938. Health Service Branded Medicines (Control of Prices and Supply of Information) Regulations 2008

revoked: SI 2008/3258 Reg.10

NO.

2008–cont.

1955. Child Support Commissioners (Procedure) (Amendment) Regulations 2008

revoked: SI 2008/2683 Sch.2

1957. Social Security and Child Support (Decisions and Appeals) (Amendment) Regulations 2008

referred to: SI 2008/2683 Art.3

revoked: SI 2008/2683 Sch.2

1963. Mesothelioma Lump Sum Payments (Conditions and Amounts) Regulations 2008

Reg.2, amended: SI 2008/2365 Reg.5

1970. Ecclesiastical Judges, Legal Officers and Others (Fees) Order 2008

applied: SI 2008/1969 Sch.1 Part TABLEa, Sch.2 para.4

2095. Removal, Storage and Disposal of Vehicles (Prescribed Sums and Charges) Regulations 2008

Reg.5, amended: SI 2008/3013 Reg.3

Reg.6, amended: SI 2008/3013 Reg.4

2140. Assembly Learning Grants and Loans (Higher Education) (Wales) (Amendment) Regulations 2008

revoked: SI 2008/3170 Reg.3

2167. Excise Duties (Road Fuel Gas) (Reliefs) Regulations 2008

revoked: SI 2008/3019 Reg.2

2168. Excise Duties (Surcharges or Rebates) (Hydrocarbon Oils etc.) Order 2008

revoked: SI 2008/3018 Art.2

2270. Zoonoses and Animal By-Products (Fees) (England) Regulations 2008

revoked: SI 2008/3196 Reg.4

2297. Veterinary Medicines Regulations 2008

Sch.7 Part 6 para.58A, added: SI 2008/2648 Reg.2

2436. Mental Health (Approval of Persons to be Approved Mental Health Professionals) (Wales) Regulations 2008

applied: SI 2008/2561 Sch.1 para.2

Reg.5, referred to: SI 2008/2561 Sch.1 para.4

Reg.5, varied: SI 2008/2561 Sch.1 para.5

Reg.6, applied: SI 2008/2561 Sch.1 para.7, Sch.1 para.8

Reg.7, referred to: SI 2008/2561 Sch.1 para.6

Reg.9, varied: SI 2008/2561 Sch.1 para.9

2496. National Health Service (Directions by Strategic Health Authorities to Primary Care Trusts Regarding Arrangements for Involvement) Regulations 2008

revoked: SI 2008/2677 Reg.7

2546. Bradford & Bingley plc Transfer of Securities and Property etc Order 2008

Art.4, applied: SI 2008/3249 Sch.1

Art.5, applied: SI 2008/3249 Sch.1

NO.

2008–cont.

2546. Bradford & Bingley plc Transfer of Securities and Property etc Order 2008–*cont.*
Art.6, applied: SI 2008/3249 Sch.1
Art.7, applied: SI 2008/3249 Sch.1
Art.7, referred to: SI 2008/3249 Sch.1

2551. Child Support Information Regulations 2008
Reg.12, amended: SI 2008/2683 Sch.1 para.346

2644. Heritable Bank plc Transfer of Certain Rights and Liabilities Order 2008
applied: SI 2008/2666 Art.9, Art.13, SI 2008/3251 Art.2
Art.3, applied: SI 2008/2666 Art.3
Art.13, amended: SI 2008/2666 Art.10
Art.13, applied: SI 2008/2666 Art.11, Art.12
Art.14, applied: SI 2008/2666 Art.12
Art.15, amended: SI 2008/2666 Art.10
Art.18, varied: SI 2008/2666 Art.15
Art.19, varied: SI 2008/2666 Art.15
Art.20, varied: SI 2008/2666 Art.15
Art.21, varied: SI 2008/2666 Art.15
Art.22, disapplied: SI 2008/2666 Art.15
Art.22, varied: SI 2008/2666 Art.15
Art.23, varied: SI 2008/2666 Art.15
Art.24, varied: SI 2008/2666 Art.15
Art.25, varied: SI 2008/2666 Art.15

2668. Landsbanki Freezing Order 2008
Art.1, amended: SI 2008/2766 Art.3
Art.3, amended: SI 2008/2766 Art.4
Art.5, amended: SI 2008/2766 Art.5
Art.9, amended: SI 2008/2766 Art.6
Art.13, revoked: SI 2008/2766 Art.7
Sch.1 para.2, amended: SI 2008/2766 Art.8
Sch.1 para.3, amended: SI 2008/2766 Art.8
Sch.1 para.3, substituted: SI 2008/2766 Art.8
Sch.1 para.6, amended: SI 2008/2766 Art.8
Sch.1 para.6, substituted: SI 2008/2766 Art.8

2674. Kaupthing Singer & Friedlander Limited Transfer of Certain Rights and Liabilities Order 2008
applied: SI 2008/3250 Art.2

2684. First-tier Tribunal and Upper Tribunal (Chambers) Order 2008
referred to: SI 2008/2686 r.1, SI 2008/2699 r.1

2685. Tribunal Procedure (First-tier Tribunal) (Social Entitlement Chamber) Rules 2008
referred to: SI 2008/2698 r.44

2686. Tribunal Procedure (First-tier Tribunal) (War Pensions and Armed Forces Compensation Chamber) Rules 2008
referred to: SI 2008/2698 r.20

2692. Qualifications for Appointment of Members to the First-tier Tribunal and Upper Tribunal Order 2008
Art.2, applied: SI 2008/794 Reg.40

NO.

2008–cont.

2707. Appeals (Excluded Decisions) Order 2008
Art.2, amended: SI 2008/2780 Art.2

2716. Zoonoses and Animal By-Products (Fees) (Wales) Regulations 2008
Reg.3, amended: SI 2008/3153 Reg.2

2838. Non-Domestic Rating Contributions (Wales) (Amendment) Regulations 2008
revoked: SI 2008/2929 Reg.2

2856. Family Proceedings Fees (Amendment) Order 2008
referred to: SI 2008/3106 Art.2
Art.5, amended: SI 2008/3106 Art.3

2862. Police (Performance) Regulations 2008
applied: SI 2008/2863 r.5, SI 2008/2864 Reg.12, Reg.19, Reg.20
referred to: SI 2008/2863 r.3
Reg.26, applied: SI 2008/2863 r.5
Reg.28, applied: SI 2008/2863 r.5
Reg.37, applied: SI 2008/2863 r.9
Reg.40, applied: SI 2008/2863 r.5

2863. Police Appeals Tribunals Rules 2008
applied: SI 2008/2862 Reg.37

2864. Police (Conduct) Regulations 2008
applied: SI 2008/2863 r.4
referred to: SI 2008/2863 r.3, r.4
Reg.36, applied: SI 2008/2863 r.9
Reg.56, applied: SI 2008/2863 r.9

3026. Alcoholic Liquor Duties (Surcharges) and Tobacco Products Duty Order 2008
Sch.1 para.2, amended: SI 2008/3062 Art.2

3051. Social Security (Lone Parents and Miscellaneous Amendments) Regulations 2008
applied: SI 2008/794 Reg.7, SI 2008/3151 Art.2

3089. School Admissions (Admission Arrangements) (England) Regulations 2008
Reg.12, applied: SI 2008/3091 Reg.16
Reg.12, referred to: SI 2008/3091 Reg.8

3090. School Admissions (Co-ordination of Admission Arrangements) (England) Regulations 2008
Reg.5, applied: SI 2008/3091 Reg.16

3154. Transmissible Spongiform Encephalopathies (Wales) Regulations 2008
Reg.2, amended: SI 2008/3266 Reg.3
Reg.12, amended: SI 2008/3266 Reg.8
Reg.20, amended: SI 2008/3266 Reg.4
Sch.2 Part 1 para.1, substituted: SI 2008/3266 Reg.5
Sch.2 Part 1 para.4A, added: SI 2008/3266 Reg.5
Sch.3 para.5, amended: SI 2008/3266 Reg.6
Sch.8 para.1, substituted: SI 2008/3266 Sch.1

NO.

2008–cont.

3154. Transmissible Spongiform Encephalopathies (Wales) Regulations 2008– *cont.*

Sch.8 para.1A, substituted: SI 2008/3266 Sch.1

Sch.8 para.1B, substituted: SI 2008/3266 Sch.1

Sch.8 para.2, substituted: SI 2008/3266 Sch.1

Sch.8 para.3, substituted: SI 2008/3266 Sch.1

Sch.8 para.4, substituted: SI 2008/3266 Sch.1

3161. Export of Goods, Transfer of Technology and Provision of Technical Assistance (Control) (Amendment) (No.2) Order 2008

revoked: SI 2008/3231 Sch.6

NO.

2008–cont.

3190. Wireless Telegraphy (Licence Award) (Cardiff) Regulations 2008

referred to: SI 2008/3197 Art.2

3191. Wireless Telegraphy (Licence Award) (Manchester) Regulations 2008

referred to: SI 2008/3197 Art.2

2009

37. Safeguarding Vulnerable Groups Act 2006 (Prescribed Criteria and Miscellaneous Provisions) Regulations 2009

applied: SI 2008/473 Art.2